A GEO-BIBLIOGRAPHY OF ANOMALIES

A GEO-BIBLIOGRAPHY OF ANOMALIES

PRIMARY ACCESS TO OBSERVATIONS OF UFOs, GHOSTS, AND OTHER MYSTERIOUS PHENOMENA

Compiled by GEORGE M. EBERHART

GREENWOOD PRESS

WESTPORT, CONNECTICUT • LONDON, ENGLAND

Library of Congress Cataloging in Publication Data

Eberhart, George M
  A geo-bibliography of anomalies.

  Includes indexes.
  1. Curiosities and wonders — Bibliography.
2. Unidentified flying objects — United States — Bibliography.
3. Animal lore — United States — Bibliography.
4. Monsters — United States — Bibliography. 5. Occult sciences —
United States — Bibliography. 6. United States —
Antiquities — Bibliography. I. Title.
Z5705.E23 [AG243] 016.0019′4 79-6183
ISBN 0-313-21337-2 (lib. bdg.)

Library of Congress Catalog Card Number: 79-6183
ISBN: 0-313-21337-2

First published in 1980

Greenwood Press
A division of Congressional Information Service, Inc.
88 Post Road West, Westport, Connecticut 06881

Printed in the United States of America

10 9 8 7 6 5 4 3 2 1

To the late
IVAN T. SANDERSON
a pioneer in the science of anomalies

CONTENTS

ACKNOWLEDGMENTS

Several people were very generous in providing me with sources for this volume. In particular I wish to thank the following individuals for their help: Steve Hicks, Lawrence, Kansas, whose incredible clipping and journal collection increased the size of this volume by at least 10 percent; Lucius Farish, Plumerville, Arkansas; Robert G. Neeley, Jr., Decatur, Illinois; Ron Calais, Lafayette, Louisiana; Robert Warth, Little Silver, New Jersey; Walter H. Andrus, Jr., Seguin, Texas; and my father, Richard C. Eberhart, Columbus, Ohio.

I also wish to thank the following libraries for the use of their facilities: the Society for the Investigation of the Unexplained, Columbia, New Jersey; the Institute for the Study of American Religion, Evanston, Illinois; the Center for UFO Studies, Evanston, Illinois; the Spiritual Frontiers Fellowship, Independence, Missouri; the Ohio State University Library, Columbus, Ohio; and the University of Kansas Library, Lawrence, Kansas, especially the Inter-Library Loan Department.

INTRODUCTION_____

The *Geo-Bibliography of Anomalies* is a comprehensive list of mysterious events, discoveries, people, and places in North America. Over 22,100 separate events are grouped under 10,500 geographic place-names. The types of events listed include: phenomena accepted by 20th-century science but which are incompletely understood (ball lightning, for example); phenomena not accepted by science but still relatively understandable given reality as we know it (lake monsters); phenomena not accepted by science which indicate that the world as we know it occasionally interacts with realities quite alien to it (close encounters with UFOs); and historical and archeological mysteries (European visits to North America in ancient times).

All of these mysterious events are collectively called *anomalies,* and their study is called *anomalistic science.* Anomalies are events, behavior, conditions, or discoveries that do not conform to prevailing world-views. The controversial nature of anomalies requires a close examination of each individual case, which should first be judged on its own merit and then in relation to similar events.

The literature on anomalous events is vast and widely scattered, and it is especially difficult to locate individual cases. Even where relevant articles and books have been listed in standard indexes and bibliographies (such as the *New York Times Index* or *Subject Guide to Books in Print*), specific material is hard to find because there are few terms in universal use. Entries designated in this volume as "humanoids" would be called by other indexers Bigfoot, Yeti, Monsters, or Animals—Mythical. "Unidentified flying object" (UFO) has been a standard term since the mid-1950s, but the Library of Congress used the antiquated and misleading term Flying Saucer as a subject heading until 1979.

In addition, the books and journals that describe anomalous events are often inclusive of a wide range of phenomena. *Fate* magazine, for example, has, for over thirty years, published articles on nearly every type of event listed in this volume, from ice falls and lake monsters to ghosts and archeological sites.

The purpose of the *Geo-Bibliography* is to provide a detailed case index-bibliography for all scientific and some historical anomalies, and to make an attempt at standardization of terms for anomalous events. A geographic arrangement was chosen to underscore the fact that anomalies of many different types may occur in the same area, often in a relatively short period of time. Also, of all six journalistic questions (who, what, why, when, where, and how), *where* is the easiest of all to determine.

The widest possible range of events has been included. Anomalies can turn up in any field of human endeavor, and mysterious astronomical events are related to mysterious psychological events by their very anomalousness. But beyond this basic connection, some anomalies have an even closer relationship. UFO percipients, for example, often experience psychic phenomena before, during, or after their UFO encounter. Humanoids are sometimes reported in areas undergoing intense UFO activity. Many people had precognitions of President Kennedy's assassination, an historical anomaly in itself.

An outline of the types of event included in this volume will be found on pages xxiii-xxiv.

The areas covered by this volume are restricted to the United States, Canada, and Greenland. Arrangement is first by region (Great Plains, Southeast, and so on) and then by specific state or province. Each state or province is further subdivided into: Populated Places; Physical Features; Ethnic Groups; and Unspecified Localities.

An Ethnic Group Index on pages 113-14 provides access to the Indian cultures mentioned in the *Geo-Bibliography*. Unspecified localities contain those events for which a state or province has been determined, but no specific town or physical feature.

All locations have been made as specific as possible, without being obscure. However, for some locations (especially physical features), given the present state of North American atlases and gazetteers, it may be necessary to consult the original sources cited here to pinpoint them on a map.

Military installations are listed under the city or town to which they are adjacent, unless they are remote from any populated place. Unincorporated suburbs of larger cities are listed with the city; separate municipalities in a major metropolitan district are listed under their own name.

Considerable effort has been made to avoid listing the same event twice under two neighboring localities.

Each entry follows the same format:

> *Place*
> -Type-of-event
> >   Date / Observer / Specific Location / Further Information /
> >   Sources

Each event is listed alphabetically below each place name. The Glossary provides definitions for most types of event. All type-of-event entries are indexed in the Subject Index.

Dates have been made as specific as possible. Recurrent events or conditions are given as a range of inclusive dates, for example: 1954, June 10-1955, Nov. 12, *or* 1970s. Cases are arranged chronologically within each event category.

Dates for archeological sites are based either on the literature cited, or on information given in the 1976 National Register of Historic Places published by the U.S. National Park Service. Radiocarbon dates are not necessarily adjusted to tree-ring chronology. Dates for anomalous artifacts and other unusual finds are dates of discovery, rather than estimated age.

Questionable years are introduced by circa (ca.), while questionable months or days are followed by a question mark (?). When the date is unknown it is either omitted entirely, or the notation "n.d." appears in its place.

The name of one observer is given in the Observer section. If more than one person witnessed the event, the name given is either that of the principal observer or the one named first in the account.

In the case of spirit mediums or other people with unusual talents, the name of the medium or talented person is given. In a sense they are observers of their own phenomena.

All observers listed in this volume have had their names appear in print somewhere, usually in the sources given. Many witnesses request anonymity to prevent ridicule, and this privilege is honored by most UFO and psychic investigation organizations. In many cases this is the reason for no name listing in the observer section.

Pseudonyms are not included unless they are those of well-known individuals, such as show business personalities or authors. Titles (Sergeant, Judge, Sheriff, Reverend, Sir, and so on) are not given unless the first name is unknown and a title will help to further identify the person. "Mrs." is used only to distinguish the observer from her husband when her first name is unknown. All observers are listed in the Observer Index.

Ship names are given in quotation marks ("Dynafuel") in a section distinct from the name of the captain or principal observer. All ship names are indexed separately in the Ship Index.

The section called "Specific location" further identifies the site of observation. It may take the form of a street address or intersection (Hollywood x Vine St.) or general direction and distance from town (12 mi. NW).

In the case of spirit mediums or other persons with unusual talents, parapsychology research centers, inner development groups, or others, the street address or Post Office box number is given, if known. Such addresses are not guaranteed to be current.

Any other details serving to identify or elucidate the case are given in one or more additional sections. Most frequently this involves an explanation of the event in question, either possible (= balloon?) or probable (= hoax). Designations of hoax do not necessarily imply fraud on the part of the observer listed, however. Very often the witness is the victim of a hoax perpetrated by another party.

For certain general types-of-event, such as "anomalous fossil," more specific information will be given following an equals sign (= segmented animals in Precambrian rock). Local names for humanoids or monsters are also given here (Jacko, ogopogo).

In "disappearance" cases, this section will sometimes identify the extent of disappearance (= crew only).

No limits have been set on the format, date, origin, or language of the sources used for cases in the Geo-Bibliography. If an event was originally described in a nineteenth-century scientific journal or newspaper, then more modern sources that merely repeat or summarize it are omitted. The most frequently cited sources include newspaper articles; UFO or parapsychology books, journals, and newsletters; and selected literature in the fields of history, archeology, geology, meteorology, ethnology, folklore, and natural history.

The level of treatment depends entirely on the number of details known about each case and this varies widely. Great care has been taken to list original sources when obtainable, as well as the most comprehensive or definitive. Supplementary sources providing new information or a different perspective have also been included. Rambling speculation of a general nature has been omitted, as well as second- or third-hand rewrites.

Page numbers refer to sections of a book or article dealing specifically with the event in question. In the case of journal articles, the page number given first refers to the first page of the article regardless of its relevance to the event (pp. 35, 38-40).

Since some of the literature cited is ephemeral, a few shortcuts have been taken. If no author is specifically credited, only the title of the section in which the case appears is listed—even if the author is known by inference. In some cases the term (Editorial) appears in place of a specific title—this most often refers to the section in Fate magazine written by Curtis Fuller entitled "I See by the Papers" which has appeared in substantially the same form since 1948. The subtitles in this feature have been rather arbitrary, so a general editorial designation was chosen. The same term is sometimes used for newsletter-format sources which usually glean their information from uncredited local newspapers.

Letters to the editor are introduced by the term (Letter), followed by the name of the letter-writer if different from the observer. If observer and letter-writer are identical, the name is not repeated in the source list.

Multiple events from identical sources are listed together, with one source listing beneath to avoid repetition. Multiple sources are generally given in chronological order. In cases where a second or third edition has been used, the date of publication is followed by "ed." (edition) and is placed in the order in which it would have been cited had the first edition been used. This preserves chronology and is a better indication of the development of the event's history.

Many abbreviations have been used for journal titles. A list of commonly-used abbreviations in this volume will be found on pages 00-00.

With newspaper sources the state of origin is omitted if it is the same as the state in which the event occurred. If the source is an out-of-state newspaper, the state is identified—*Los Angeles (Cal.) Times*. The only exceptions to this rule are newspapers incorporating the state's name in their titles, such as the *New York Times*.

Illustrations are indicated by the abbreviation "il." following the source. Usually this indicates a photograph of the event itself or drawings by investigators or eye-witnesses.

Obviously, every case of telepathy or UFO event experienced since the beginning of recorded history cannot be presented in one volume. The vast majority of sources are *published* books, journal articles, newspaper stories, and papers in proceedings. Unpublished papers and personal investigations by ufologists or other researchers have been avoided. The *Geo-Bibliography* is a guide to the literature, rather than a listing of all anomalous events ever witnessed.

Even with the wide range of subject-matter included there has been some selectivity. Inner development organizations are so common that only the more prominent ones have been included. Archeological sites have been limited to sites of great antiquity, sites exhibiting anomalous features, those indicating ancient knowledge of astronomy or Pre-Columbian European contact, and non-anomalous sites of primary importance or interest. Parapsychology research organizations have been included because anomalous events (ESP, psychokinesis, and so on) presumably occur during the course of investigations; but UFO research groups have not been listed because these are generally information clearinghouses, rather than places where UFOs themselves are observed.

Lost mines and hidden treasure sites, while technically qualifying as historical anomalies, have not been included unless they have been associated with other phenomena.

Two features in *Fate* magazine dealing with fairly common psychic phenomena, "True Mystic Experiences" and "My Proof of Survival," have also been omitted. Many sources for anomalous events are so ephemeral and elusive that they were unfindable at the time of compilation, although reference to them is made in the secondary sources cited in this volume.

The *Geo-Bibliography of Anomalies* is only a first step in the process of organizing and consolidating the wealth of literature on anomalies that has blossomed in the past twenty years. Further research will surely uncover many events and sources, both recent and historical, which are not included here.

Not all of the UFO sightings in the U.S. Air Force's Project Blue Book files have been listed—only those which have been reviewed or mentioned in readily available UFO journals or books. Additional information on these and the unlisted reports can be found in the Blue Book case files available on 94 reels of microfilm from the National Archives and Records Service, 8th St. and Pennsylvania Ave. N.W., Washington, D.C. 20408.

Over 60,000 UFO cases have been entered into a computerized data base called UFOCAT. Cases are retrievable by date, place, or characteristics. The Center for UFO Studies, 1609 Sherman Ave., Room 207, Evanston, Ill. 60201, will accept data requests from serious researchers.

Further information on research sources in parapsychology may be found in Rhea A. White & Laura A. Dale, *Parapsychology: Sources of Information* (Metuchen, N.J.: Scarecrow, 1973). Several other author-title and subject bibliographies are also useful: Harry Price, ed., *Short-Title Catalogue of Works on Psychical Research* (London: National Laboratory of Psychical Research, 1929); Thomas C. Clarie, *Occult Bibliography: An Annotated List of Books Published in English, 1971 through 1975* (Metuchen, N.J.: Scarecrow, 1978); and Clyde S. King, *Psychic and Religious Phenomena Limited: A Bibliographical Index* (Westport, Conn.: Greenwood, 1978).

The best guide to "inner development" in America, as well as to more conventional religious groups, is J. Gordon Melton's *Encyclopedia of American Religions,* 2 vols. (Wilmington, N.C.: Consortium, 1978). The Institute for the Study of American Religion, Box 1311, Evanston, Ill. 60201, is directed by Dr. Melton and can handle a limited number of specific requests for information.

Data on lost mines and buried or sunken treasure has not been indexed extensively here, primarily because similar geo-bibliographies have been published for the United States. One of the best is Thomas Probert's *Lost Mines and Buried Treasures of the West* (Berkeley: University of California, 1977).

In general, anomalous events may be unearthed in any body of literature, given enough time and patience. Astronomical, geological, and historical index and abstract services can be very fruitful. The newsclipping services mentioned in the journal list are excellent sources for finding recent cases.

Newspapers and archives available at local historical societies are also helpful. Since anomalous events tend to cluster in time and space, many different types of phenomena may be discovered while one is tracking down a single UFO or humanoid report. The UFO flap of 1897 is a good starting point, for example, since the newspaper reports were voluminous and many states have not yet been researched for local reports. Another technique is to check local newspapers for some of the events listed in this volume, and then search several months before and after. Local town or county histories often list an anomaly or two, and the case files of local UFO or psychic investigators are very helpful for compiling histories of anomalies.

The author would be very interested in receiving information on any additional published sources or events not mentioned, or any errors that may have inadvertently crept into the text.

JOURNAL SOURCES INDEXED

APRO Bulletin, vol. 9, no. 7 (Jan. 1961)-vol. 27, no. 5 (Nov. 1978). First published 1952. Aerial Phenomena Research Organization, 3910 E. Kleindale Rd., Tucson, Ariz. 85712.

American Antiquity, vol. 1 (1935)-vol. 43 (1978). Indexed selectively. Society for American Archaeology, 1703 New Hampshire Ave. NW, Washington, D.C. 20009.

American Society for Psychical Research, Journal, vol. 1 (1907)-vol. 72 (1978). Formerly called *Psychic Research.* American Society for Psychical Research, 5 W. 73d St., New York, N.Y. 10023. Available in microform from UMI.

Anomaly Research Bulletin, no. 2 (Aug.-Sep. 1976)-no. 23 (1978). Ceased with no. 23. P.O. Box 1479, Grand Rapids, Mich. 49501.

Bigfoot/Sasquatch Information Service, vol. 1, no. 1 (Apr. 1977)-vol. 3, no. 3 (Mar. 1979). Newsclipping service. Box 3035, Seattle, Wash. 98114.

Canadian UFO Report, vol. 1, no. 1 (Jan.-Feb. 1969)-vol. 5, no. 1 (winter 1978-79). Most issues indexed. Box 758, Duncan B.C., Canada V9L 3Y1. Available in microform from UMI. Ceased with vol. 5, no. 3.

Chaos, vol. 1, nos. 1-3 (1978-1979). Box 1598, Kingston, Ont., Canada K7L 5C8.

CRIFO Orbit, vol. 1, no. 1 (Apr. 1954)-vol. 3, no. 12 (Mar. 1957). Ceased with vol. 3, no. 12. Formerly *CRIFO Newsletter.* Published in Cincinnati by Civilian Research Interplanetary Flying Objects.

Doubt, no. 1 (Sep. 1937)-no. 61 (1959). Ceased with no. 61. Published in New York City by Tiffany Thayer and the Fortean Society. Formerly *Fortean Society Magazine.*

Epigraphic Society, Occasional Publications, vol. 1 (1974)-vol. 6 (1979). Epigraphic Society, 6 Woodland St., Arlington, Mass. 02174.

Fate, vol. 1, no. 1 (spring 1948)-vol. 32, no. 3 (Mar. 1979). Clark Publishing Co., 500 Hyacinth Pl., Highland Park, Ill. 60035. Available in microform from UMI.

Flying Saucer Review, vol. 10, no. 5 (Sep.-Oct. 1964)-vol. 24, no. 3 (Nov. 1978). First published 1955. Scattered earlier issues indexed. FSR Publications, Ltd., West Malling, Maidstone, Kent, England.

Fortean Times, no. 16 (June 1976)-no. 28 (winter 1979). Formerly called *The News.* 9-12 St. Annes Court, London W1, England.

INFO Journal, vol. 1, no. 1 (spring 1967)-vol. 7, no. 4 (Nov.-Dec. 1978). International Fortean Organization, 7317 Baltimore Ave., College Park, Md. 20740.

International UFO Reporter, vol. 1, no. 1 (Nov. 1976)-vol. 3, no. 10 (Oct. 1978). Center for UFO Studies, 1609 Sherman Ave., Room 207, Evanston, Ill. 60701.

Journal of Parapsychology, vol. 1 (1937)-vol. 42 (1978). Indexed selectively. Parapsychology Press, Box 6847 College Station, Durham, N.C. 27708. Available in microform.

MUFON UFO Journal, no. 1 (Sep. 1967)-no. 132 (Nov.-Dec. 1978). Formerly called *Skylook.* Mutual UFO Network, 103 Oldtowne Rd., Seguin, Tex. 78155.

NEARA Journal, vol. 2, no. 3 (Sep. 1967)-vol. 13, no. 3 (winter 1979). First published 1966. Formerly called *NEARA Newsletter.* New England Antiquities
Research Association, 4 Smith St., Milford, N.H. 03055.

Official UFO, vol. 1, no. 2 (Aug. 1975)-vol. 2, no. 3 (May 1977). Articles no longer
reliable. 257 Park Ave. S., New York, N.Y. 10010.

Probe the Unknown, vol. 1, no. 5 (Oct. 1973)-vol. 5, no. 2 (spring 1977). Ceased with
vol. 5, no. 2.

Pursuit, vol. 1, no. 1 (May 1967)-vol. 12, no. 1 (winter 1979). Society for the Investigation of the Unexplained, RFD 5, Gales Ferry, Conn. 06335. Available in
microform from UMI.

Res Bureaux Bulletin, no. 20 (14 July 1977)-no. 44 (Feb. 1979). Box 1598, Kingston,
Ont., Canada K7L 5C8.

Saga UFO Report, vol. 1, no. 3 (1972)-vol. 7, no. 1 (Feb. 1979). Title varies: currently
called *UFO Report.* 333 Johnson Ave., Brooklyn, N.Y. 11206.

Saucer News, vol. 10, no. 2 (June 1963)-vol. 15, no. 2 (summer 1968). First published
1954; still published irregularly under various titles.

Stigmata, no. 1 (Jan. 1978)-no. 5 (winter 1979). Project Stigma, Box 1094, Paris, Tex.
75460.

UFO Investigator, vol. 1, no. 1 (1957)-vol. 4, no. 6 (May-June 1968). National Invest-
gations Committee on Aerial Phenomena, Washington, D.C. Available in
microform from UMI.

UFO Newsclipping Service, no. 101 (Dec.1977)-no. 116 (Mar. 1979). Route 1,
Box 220, Plumerville, Ark. 72127.

UFO-Quebec, vol. 1 (1975)-vol. 4 (1978). BP 53, Dollard-des-Ormeaux PQ, Canada
H9G 2H5.

OUTLINE OF ANOMALIES

I. PHENOMENA WITHIN ONE REALITY

   A. BORDERLAND SCIENCE—Phenomena partially or totally unacceptable to contemporary science.

     1. *Astronomy*—Anomalies in the structure and behavior of gross bodies (meteorite craters, tektites, intra-Mercurial planets, etc.).

     2. *Geology*—Anomalies in the structure and behavior of the earth (ringing rocks, earthquake luminescence, hollow earth theory, stratigraphic anomalies, etc.).

     3. *Biology*—Anomalies in the structure and behavior of animate entities (plant sensitivity, lake monsters, entombed or erratic animals, giant birds, etc.).

     4. *Chemiphysics*—Anomalies in the structure and behavior of matter and energy (water anomalies, ball lightning, new energy sources, mystery radio transmissions, etc.).

     5. *Fortean Phenomena*—Interdisciplinary anomalies, or anomalies resisting classification (falls, disappearances, animal mutilations, cycle research, spontaneous human combustion, etc.).

   B. PARAPSYCHOLOGY—Anomalies in the structure and behavior of consciousness.

     1. *Extra-Sensory Perception*—Reception of data without using the normal sense channels (animal ESP, clairvoyance, precognition, out-of-body experience, dowsing, etc.).

     2. *Divination*—The use of objects, methods, or events to determine future events or present conditions (astrology, scrying, ornithomancy, etc.).

     3. *Paraphysics*—Phenomena involving mental control of matter and energy (psychokinesis, healing, poltergeists, alchemy, weather control, etc.).

     4. *Altered Consciousness*—Phenomena occurring when the percipient is in one of several different states of heightened awareness (hypnosis, mesmerism, religious ecstasy, etc.).

     5. *Disciplinary Systems*—Methods and theories designed to produce or accentuate parapsychological phenomena (inner development, biofeedback, shamanism, etc.).

II. PHENOMENA DEALING WITH OTHER REALITIES

   A. SURVIVAL—Phenomena relating to communication with, or observation of, persons known to be dead.

1. *Apparitions* — Unsupplicated, visual, paranormal appearances (ghosts, haunts, deathbed apparitions, etc.).
2. *Seance phenomena* — Supplicated observations of apparitions or other paranormal phenomena (spirit medium, automatic writing, paranormal voice recordings, etc.).

B. PHANTOMS — Phenomena relating to communication with, or observation of, non- or quasi-human entities of a paranormal nature not recognizable as dead persons, not directly associated with UFO sightings, and not of the humanoid type.
   1. *Unsupplicated Appearances* of phantoms (phantom panthers, religious apparitions, aerial phantoms, phantom ships, possession, exorcisms, etc.).
   2. *Supplicated Appearances* of phantoms (witchcraft, etc.).

C. UFOLOGY — Phenomena relating to communication with, or observation of, non- or quasi-human entities of a paranormal nature associated with aerial objects (UFOs); or the observation of such objects alone (UFOs, contactees, airship messages, etc.).

III. **BORDERLAND HISTORY** — Anomalies and gaps in the record of human activity.

A. CATACLYSMIC HISTORY — Evidence for vast disasters in ancient times (flood myth, cataclysm myth, etc.)

B. PREHISTORY — Evidence for advanced technology in ancient times (ancient civilization myth, ancient underground city, paleoastronomy, etc.).

C. ARCHEOLOGY — Anomalies and gaps in the record of pre-literate cultures (anomalous artifacts, giant human skeletons, petroglyphs, archeological sites, etc.).

D. HISTORICAL ANOMALIES — Anomalies and gaps in the record of post-literate cultures (ancient sites, Norse discoveries, doubtful responsibility, doubtful geography, lost treasure, doubtful identity, etc.).

GLOSSARY

ACOUSTIC ANOMALY—Mysterious sounds of untraceable origin. These usually take the form of buzzes, beeps, hums, or thumps. This category does not include unexplained aerial booms, which are found under *skyquake*. "Spirit rappings" are included under *poltergeist, haunt,* or *spirit medium.*

ACUPUNCTURE—An ancient Chinese medical technique in which needles are inserted into the body at specific points to stimulate the body's self-*healing* system.

AERIAL PHANTOM—The observation of people, animals, cities, or landscapes in the air which cannot be explained by conventional mirages. Sometimes the figures re-enact historical events.

AEROMANCY—*Divination* by clouds.

AIRPLANE or AIRSHIP INVENTOR—Alleged demonstrations of heavier-than-air flight prior to the Wright brothers' flight in 1903.

AIRSHIP MESSAGE—The discovery of a message allegedly written by the occupants of the 1897 airships (UFOs). If the message was seen to fall from an actual airship, it is listed under *UFO (CE-2)*.

ALCHEMY—The *paraphysical* transformation of chemical elements; in particular, the changing of base metals into gold. Occasionally the term is used symbolically to denote a transformation of the mind into a higher state of awareness (see *Inner development*).

ANCIENT ARTIFACTS and SITES—Evidence for a pre-Norse colonization of North America from Europe, Africa, or the Middle East, circa 4000 B.C.-100 A.D. The most likely candidates are Phoenicians, Libyans, Celt-Iberians, or other seafaring peoples of antiquity. Similarities to the European megalithic culture (the builders of Stonehenge) have often been noted. Frequently reported stone structures include cairns, standing stones, dolmens, slab-roofed chambers, and iron furnaces. The date given usually indicates the date of the artifact's discovery. See also *Norse, Medieval, Chinese,* and *Roman* headings.

ANCIENT INSCRIPTIONS—Stones inscribed with alphanumeric characters identical to, or resembling, the writings of ancient cultures. Middle Eastern and Celtic Ogam scripts are often reported.

ANIMAL ESP—The reception and transmission of information by animals through other than the normal sensory channels. This includes the long-distance migration of individual pets in search of their owners. The name of the animal's owner is given as the observer.

ANOMALIES — Events, behavior, conditions, or discoveries which do not conform to prevailing world views. "Mysteries" in general. Anomalies may occur in any branch of knowledge (genetics, palaeontology, astronomy, history, or architecture), and many kinds of natural phenomena may behave anomalously (lightning, aurorae, whirlwinds, clouds, earthquakes, and so on).

ANOMALOUS ARTIFACTS — Objects found in unusual geological or archeological contexts, such as iron nails embedded in quartz, or Central American pottery in New York.

ANOMALOUS FOSSILS — Fossils inconsistent with conventional geochronology. For example, segmented animal remains in Precambrian rock. See also *Human tracks in stone.*

ANOMALOUS HOLE IN GROUND — Holes or craters not attributable to subsidence or conventional falling objects. When the object causing the crater is seen to fall but no traces are reported, the event is listed as a *Fall* of unknown object. Other mystery holes similar in nature to UFO landing impressions are listed under *UFO (CE-2),* identified as "ground markings only."

ANOMALOUS MOUNDS — Mounds of earth produced by unknown geological processes. For man-made mounds, see *Archeological sites.*

APPARITION — A visual paranormal appearance, usually spontaneous, that suggests the real presence of someone distant or dead.

ARCHEOLOGICAL SITES — Habitation sites, mounds, hearths, artifacts, and other traces left by the prehistoric ancestors of the American Indian and Eskimo. Because of the frequent mention of the subject in the literature of anomalies, a representative sampling of North American archeological sites has been included here. Selection has been limited to sites of great antiquity, sites exhibiting anomalous features, those indicating an ancient knowledge of astronomy or pre-Columbian European contact, and non-anomalous sites of primary importance or interest. The dates given are based on timescales in the literature cited.

ASTROLOGY — *Divination* by the positional and angular relationships of the sun, moon, and planets to themselves, the zodiac, and the horizon at the hour of a person's birth. Modern astrologers often take into account their own ESP abilities and the synchronicity of the universe when explaining the accuracy of their forecasts, although there is much evidence for a direct link between astronomical cycles and influences on the Earth's biosphere.

AUTOMATIC WRITING — Writing not consciously controlled by the writer, who is often in a dissociated state. Usually this phenomenon can be explained as outpourings from the writer's subconscious, but sometimes there are hints that an external agent is influencing the text. See also *Spirit medium* and *Possession.*

AUTOSCOPY—Seeing one's own body, or "double," as if from a point outside the center of consciousness. See also *Out-of-body experience.*

BALL LIGHTNING—A ball- or pear-shaped form of electrical discharge occurring during thunderstorms. Ball lightning has several peculiar characteristics, including the ability to enter houses through small openings, a duration of anywhere up to 10 minutes, and a tendency to explode violently.

BILOCATION—A living person apparently seen in two places at the same time. See also *Out-of-body experience.*

BIOENERGETICS—A particular technique for studying and applying life energies, as developed by Alexander Lowen. See *Orgone energy.*

BIOFEEDBACK—An instrumented technique for the self-monitoring of unconscious or involuntary bodily processes (such as heart rate, brainwaves, and nerve impulses), with the ultimate goal of increasing the conscious control of such functions.

BIORHYTHM—The cycle of an organism's physical, emotional, and intellectual reactions to its environment. The characteristics of these cycles are fairly well-known, but the causes are still uncertain.

BLEEDING ICONS—Religious statues that ooze a bloodlike substance.

BURROWING HOSES—Self-burying garden hoses.

CARTOMANCY—*Divination* by playing cards, especially Tarot cards.

CATACLYSM MYTH—Oral traditions of a major catastrophe in ancient times, usually involving earthquakes, tidal waves, and other vast disasters. See also *Flood myth.*

CHILD PRODIGY—Children gifted with paranormal intellectual or artistic abilities.

CHINESE DISCOVERY—Evidence for a prehistoric discovery of North America by an expedition from China.

CLAIRAUDIENCE—The reception of auditory information through other than the normal sensory channels.

CLAIREMPATHY—The paranormal reception of information from objects and/or the environment. Deduction of past events from the psychic "feel" of things or places connected with them. Sometimes called "psychometry."

CLAIROLFACTION—The reception of olfactory information through other than the normal sensory channels. Psychic smells.

CLAIRVOYANCE—The reception of visual information through other than the normal sensory channels. Psychic "visions" of simultaneous distant events. Clairvoyance is often accompanied by the other clair-senses.

COAL BALLS—Well-preserved and petrified plant tissue appearing in black, rounded lumps of doubtful origin in the upper portions of coal seams.

COFFIN ANOMALY—Oddities associated with coffins, such as coffins that move mysteriously or those that tend to preserve the bodies inside them.

COMBUSTION METAMORPHISM—Oxidative heating of subsurface bituminous sediments causing the formaiton of pseudomagmas. The intensity of the heating may indicate an ancient *cataclysm*.

CONTACTEE—A person who claims to be in contact with extraterrestrial entities. Usually the entities give the contactee the impression that he has been specially chosen for some unique reason—for example, to warn the world about the dangers of nuclear power.

CONTACTEE MYTH—Amerindian or Eskimo traditions of persons akin to modern *contactees*.

CORPSE ANOMALY—Oddities associated with corpses, such as extraordinary preservation from decay, or paranormal petrifactions.

CRISIS APPARITION—A recognized *apparition* perceived within twelve hours of the time when the person represented by the apparition is undergoing a crisis, frequently death.

CROMNIOMANCY—*Divination* by onion sprouts.

DEATHBED APPARITION—A dying person's apparent awareness of the presence of deceased relatives, friends, or other entities.

DEMATERIALIZATION—The paranormal disappearance of an object or person, often instantaneous. See also *Disappearance*.

DERELICT VEHICLES—Cars, ships, or other conveyances which seem to navigate themselves without the aid of human operators.

DISAPPEARANCE—Planes, ships, crews, individuals, and so on, that are never seen again. Often there are very unusual circumstances connected with these cases, which are often associated with (but not confined to) the so-called Bermuda Triangle. In very rare instances, the disappearance is allegedly observed. See *Dematerialization*.

DISEASE ANOMALY—Strange illnesses of unknown origin.

DIVINATION—The use of objects, methods, or events to determine future events or present conditions. A general term covering astrology, palmistry, and so on.

DOUBTFUL GEOGRAPHY—Legendary places which may or may not have existed, or historical events which occurred at indeterminate locations.

DOUBTFUL IDENTITY—The possible identification of persons with people supposedly dead, as in rumors that John Wilkes Booth or George Armstrong Custer survived their "deaths" and lived somewhere under assumed names. Also included are corpses of unidentified persons found in unusual circumstances.

DOUBTFUL RESPONSIBILITY—Murder mysteries, especially in connection with assassination conspiracies. Also, any other historical event for which the agent is unknown, or exploits claimed by persons who cannot provide proof.

DOWSING — A form of *clairempathy* in which underground water, minerals, oil, and so forth is located by means of a forked twig or other device usually called a divining rod.

EARTHQUAKE LUMINESCENCE — Luminous flashes or glows observed in conjunction with earthquakes.

ELECTROMAGNETIC ANOMALY — Oddities associated with the electromagnetic spectrum, such as dental fillings that pick up radio broadcasts, electric lightbulbs of extreme longevity, or mystery power failures.

ELIZABETHAN INSCRIPTIONS — Messages on stone attributable to Sir Walter Raleigh's lost Roanoke colony.

END-OF-THE-WORLD PROPHECY — *Clairvoyant* visions of the cataclysmic destruction of the world.

ENTOMBED ANIMALS — Animals, usually frogs, reptiles, or insects, found partially or completely encased in rock or wood, with very little air penetration. Often the animals revive, usually for a very short time.

ERRATIC ANIMALS — Animals found beyond their normal geographic range and habitat. For erratic panthers, see *Phantom animals.*

EXORCISM — A rite for ridding a person or place of unwanted spirits, phantoms, or other paranormal entities, usually evil.

EYELESS VISION — The ability to perceive color and other visual signals through other parts of the body, usually the fingertips.

FALLS — Objects, animals, and substances alleged to have fallen from the sky.

FERAL PEOPLE — Humans living in the wild, allegedly raised by animals.

FIRE ANOMALY — Mystery fires that recur within a short period of time, or otherwise behave inexplicably.

FIRE IMMUNITY — The ability to come into close or direct contact with fire or red-hot coals without being affected.

FLOOD MYTH — Oral traditions of a widespread flood in ancient times.

FLYING HUMANOID — Flying creatures resembling human or quasi-human beings with wings.

GASOLINE SPRING — Natural wells of petroleum.

GHOST — Post-mortem *apparitions.* Cases in which a recognized apparition is perceived more than twelve hours after the death of the person represented.

GHOST ANIMALS — The ghosts of pets recognized by their owners.

GHOST LIGHT — Strange, moving globes of light that appear periodically at a certain locality.

GIANT HUMAN SKELETONS—Skeletal remains of human beings of much larger-than-average size.

GRAPHOLOGY—The analysis of character by the characteristics of a person's handwriting.

HAUNT—*Apparitions* or other recurrent paranormal phenomena associated with a certain place (houses, streets, woods) rather than a certain person. Haunts are traditionally attributed to the activities of deceased persons.

HEALING—Positive cellular *psychokinesis*. The paranormal transmission of energy from one person to another to improve their physical or mental health.

HERBALISM—The use of the medicinal properties of certain plants to cure and prevent disease.

HEX—Negative cellular *psychokinesis*. The paranormal transmission of energy from one person to another to inflict harm or cause death.

HOLLOW EARTH—The theory that portions of the earth's interior are hollow and inhabitable.

HUMAN ELECTRIFICATION—Cases in which a human being becomes inexplicably charged with electricity for an extended period of time.

HUMANOID—Hairy, quasi-human creatures seen especially in sparsely populated areas. Their size is ordinarily very large, six to ten feet, although smaller ones are reported occasionally. They are generally thought to be pre-Homo sapiens survivals, although some paraphysical theories have been proposed.

HUMANOID TRACKS—The discovery of quasi-human tracks, allegedly those of a *humanoid*.

HUMAN TRACKS IN STONE—The discovery of human footprints in solid, usually sedimentary, rock.

INNER DEVELOPMENT—Organizations or individuals espousing certain techniques for developing and harnessing psychic or life energies and heightening human awareness of the paraphysical realm. They may have either Christian, Eastern, or pagan orientations.

INTRA-MERCURIAL PLANET—Observations of an astronomical body orbiting the Sun within the orbit of Mercury. Some sightings may have been based on either sunspots or UFOs high in the earth's atmosphere.

JINX SHIP—Disaster-prone vessels.

LAKE MONSTER—Large unknown animals, some similar to the Loch Ness monsters, inhabiting lakes. See also *River* and *Sea monster*.

LAND MONSTER—Large unidentified terrestrial animals. *Humanoids* and giant forms of known animals are not included in this category.

LEGEND OF PRE-COLUMBIAN WHITES—Oral traditions of European visits to North America before the arrival of Columbus.

LEMURIAN SAGES—White-robed paranormal *apparitions,* allegedly survivors of the lost Pacific continent of Lemuria.

LOST TREASURE—Legends of mines, caves, chests or other treasure troves yet undiscovered. There are many of these legends in North America—only those which involve other paranormal features have been included here.

LUNAR CYCLE—Specific studies relating the period of the Moon's revolution to physiology, crime, or other events on earth.

MAMMOTHS and MASTODONS—Reports of living elephants in North America in historic times.

MATHEMATICAL PRODIGY—Persons with an incredible ability to mentally calculate complex mathematical problems.

MEDICAL CLAIRVOYANCE—The *clairvoyant* ability to see within another person's body and diagnose illnesses.

MEDIEVAL ARTIFACTS and DISCOVERIES—Evidence for a Medieval discovery of North America, circa 500-1400 A.D., by Europeans other than the Norse.

MEN-IN-BLACK—Strange men, often dressed in black suits, driving black cars with untraceable license plates, having olive skin or a peculiar accent, who visit UFO witnesses or investigators shortly after UFO sightings. Sometimes they flash official credentials, confiscate important evidence, and are never heard from again. All U.S. government agencies have denied any involvement in such cases.

MERMAID—Aquatic, semi-human creatures.

MESMERISM—A mixture of hypnotism and healing common in the early nineteenth century which induced a suggestible state in subjects who then exhibited clairvoyant or mediumistic talents.

METEORITE CRATERS—Geological structures apparently caused by giant meteorites which fell in prehistoric times. Particular sites are rated according to the probability of their origin being astronomical, rather than terrestrial.

MIDDAY DARKNESS—Paranormal darkness in the daytime, often caused by thick cloud cover of doubtful origin.

MONTEZUMA MYTH—Amerindian legends of a white culture-bearing hero in ancient times.

MUSICAL SAND—Sand with peculiar acoustic properties.

MUTILATIONS—Animals, usually cattle, found mutilated in a peculiar manner: eyes, ears, lips, genitals, and tails are often removed, and internal organs are sometimes extracted with surgical, laser-like cuts. The carcasses are often completely bloodless. Usually there are no clues to indicate foul play or predators. Animal mutilations often occur simultaneously with outbreaks of phantom helicopters, UFOs and/or humanoids.

MYSTERY BIRD DEATHS—Falls of dead birds from the sky, cause unknown.

MYSTERY RADIO or TV TRANSMISSIONS—Audio or visual signals of unknown origin.

NEW ENERGY SOURCE—Inventors of machines which allegedly harness subtle energies of an unknown origin. See also *Radionics* and *Orgone energy.*

NORSE ARTIFACTS and SITES—Evidence for penetration and colonization of North America by Norse explorers, 1000-1400 A.D. Although it has been proven that the Norse had at least one settlement along the Eastern seaboard, much controversy still rages about the location of Vinland and their exploration of the interior.

NORSE RUNESTONE—Stones inscribed with alphanumeric characters readily identifiable as the Medieval runic alphabet, and presumably carved by Norse explorers.

NUMEROLOGY—*Divination* by numbers and the numerical values of letters.

ORGONE ENERGY—Omnipresent life energy discovered by Wilhelm Reich in the 1940s.

ORNITHOMANCY—*Divination* by the flight of birds.

OUT-OF-BODY EXPERIENCE—An experience, either spontaneous or induced, in which an individual's consciousness seems to be in a place separate from the physical body. Often the separated center of consciousness is attached to the body by a psychic "cord." Sometimes the individual visits distant persons and places while in this state. Formerly called "astral projecton" or "travelling clairvoyance."

OVOMANCY—*Divination* by eggs.

PALEOASTRONOMY—Oral traditions and other evidence that certain Amerindian groups had relatively advanced knowledge of astronomy in prehistoric times.

PALMISTRY—*Divination* by the lines, mounds, and other characteristics of an individual's hand.

PARANORMAL VOICE RECORDINGS—Tape recordings of sounds alleged to be voices of deceased persons. The voices are usually faint, talking at a rapid speed, and have an unusual rhythm, pitch, or intensity.

PARAPHYSICS—Phenomena involving the mental control of matter and energy. In a broader sense, phenomena and apparitions which appear physical, but do not obey the ordinary laws of physics in some fashion.

PARAPSYCHOLOGY—The study of anomalies in the structure and behavior of the mind.

PATTERNED GROUND—Unusual regularities in geological surface features, such as sorted circles, polygons, steps, or boulder-trains.

PETROGLYPH — Designs pecked or scored into rocks by Amerindians.

PHANTOM — The appearance of non- or quasi-human entities of a paranormal nature, not recognizable as deceased persons, not directly associated with UFO sightings, and not of the *humanoid* type. This category includes many seemingly diverse traditions, including demons, fairies, leprechauns, and others.

PHANTOM ANIMALS — The apparition of nonphysical or paraphysical animals not recognizable as deceased pets. See *Ghost animals.* Phantom panthers are the commonest form, although these merge into observations of *erratic* live panthers. Phantom animals are often characterized by extreme ferocity, a black or other unusual color, bizarre behavior, and a propensity for killing farm animals without eating any or much of them.

PHANTOM IMAGE — The appearance of shapes or pictures on stone, glass, or other materials with no indication of how they were produced. Usually the images appear for a short time, then fade; a few are long-lived. Quite often they are religious in nature.

PHANTOM INSECT — Unidentifiable insects that inflict harsh bites. In the nineteenth century they were called "kissing bugs."

PHANTOM VEHICLES — The apparition of nonphysical or paraphysical airplanes, helicopters, ships, trains, autos, or other vehicles. Their behavior and appearance are distinctly unusual.

PHOTOGRAPHIC ANOMALY — Mysterious images on photographic film. See also *Psychic photography.*

PHRENOLOGY — The study of bumps and other features of the skull as an indication of personality.

PICTOGRAPH — Amerindian rock paintings.

PLAGUE OF ANIMALS — Paranormally large numbers of a particular species infesting a specific locality.

PLANT SENSITIVITY — An undefined sensory system or perception capability existing in plants by which they can respond to human emotions and thought.

POLTERGEIST — Unconscious, recurrent, spontaneous *psychokinesis* centering about one person, usually an adolescent. The phenomena involve the unexplained movement or breakage of objects, paranormal sounds, unexplained fires, and other mischief.

POSSESSION — A state in which an individual appears to be involuntarily controlled by another center of consciousness, usually attributed to a deceased person or *phantom* (demon).

PRECIPITATING TREE — An extremely localized fall of liquid substance around a particular tree, usually attributable to the exudations of certain insects.

PRECOGNITION — The extra-sensory perception of future events which are not predicted or inferred by normal means. Erroneous or unfulfilled predictions are also included in this category.

PSYCHIC PHOTOGRAPHY — The *psychokinetic* projection of mental images on film or photographic plates.

PSYCHOKINESIS — The mental manipulation of objects, particles, or energy from a distance, without the mediation of known physical energies or forces.

PSYCHOLUMINESCENCE — Apparent mental control of photons or visible light.

PYRAMID ENERGY — Unusual energy associated with the unique geometry of pyramids. This energy is supposedly responsible for razor-blade sharpening, food preservation, mummification, and healing.

PYROKINESIS — The mental manipulation of combustion (fire). See also *Fire immunity.*

RADIESTHESIA — *Divination* by means of a pendulum.

RADIONICS — The instrumented use of paranormal radiations to diagnose and treat disease in human beings, animals, and crops.

REINCARNATION — An apparent case of survival in which the mind, or some part of it, of a deceased person is reborn in another body. Such cases may also be attributable to vivid *retrocognition* or *telepathic* reception of the memories of deceased persons. Conflict or confusion between the two centers of consciousness seldom exists. See also *Possession,* where there is a conflict.

RELIGIOUS APPARITION — The appearance of a *phantom* having a decidedly religious nature or message. This includes visions of Jesus, the Virgin Mary, saints, angels, and so on.

RELIGIOUS ECSTASY — Heightened state of awareness induced by religious fervor.

RETROCOGNITION — The extra-sensory perception of past events which are not known or inferred by normal means.

RINGING ROCKS — Rocks with peculiar acoustic properties. See also *Musical sand.*

RIVER MONSTER — Large unknown animals observed in rivers.

ROCK DOUGHNUTS — Shallow depressions on the flat summit of large exposures of granite or other igneous rock.

ROCK PILLARS — Stratigraphically anomalous columnar formations of sedimentary rock.

SCRYING — *Divination* by means of a mirror, glass, or crystal ball.

SEA MONSTER — Large unknown animals observed in the ocean. See also *Lake* and *River monster.*

SEANCE — A sitting with a *spirit medium,* usually for the purpose of obtaining information from deceased persons.

SHAMANISM—Practices of Amerindian or Eskimo medicine men, encompassing spirit communication, healing, hex, herbalism, out-of-body experience, precognition, and other anomalous phenomena.

SHAPE-SHIFTING—The paraphysical transformation of shape or outward appearance, so that an individual appears in another form, usually an animal. Lycanthropy is included in this category.

SKYQUAKE—Unexplained aerial detonations.

SNAKE HANDLING—The practice, espoused by certain fundamentalist Christian sects, of handling poisonous snakes while in a state of *religious ecstasy,* hopefully without being bitten and affected by the venom.

SNOW WORMS—Worms or insect larvae found crawling on the surface of the snow.

SPIRIT MEDIUM—A person capable of receiving communications from deceased persons. The medium may also exhibit other paranormal talents, such as clairvoyance, levitation, psychokinesis, etc., during the *seance.* See also *Automatic writing.*

SPONTANEOUS HUMAN COMBUSTION—Extremely localized, apparently instantaneous, and inexplicable incineration of a human being. See also *Fire anomaly.*

STIGMATA—Paranormal bleeding, generally corresponding to the wounds inflicted on Jesus at his crucifixion.

STRATIGRAPHIC ANOMALY—Geological strata that do not conform to current theories of geochronology and uniformitarianism.

SUBMARINE LIGHT WHEEL—Luminous wheel-like or radial phenomena observed on or below the surface of the ocean.

SURVIVAL—The continuation of consciousness after death.

TASSEOGRAPHY—*Divination* by the forms produced by tea leaves remaining in the cup after the tea has been drunk.

TEKTITES—Rounded, glasslike rocks apparently of extraterrestrial origin.

TELEPATHY—Extra-sensory awareness of another person's thoughts or emotions. Direct mental communication.

TELEPHONE ANOMALY—Mysterious, sometimes metallic, voices of untraceable origin heard on the telephone.

TELEPORTATION—The paraphysical movement of objects or persons over distances or through objects, often instantaneously.

THUNDERSTONE—An ax-shaped stone supposed to have fallen from the sky during a thunderstorm.

UNIDENTIFIED FLYING OBJECT (UFO)—The definitions adopted by the Centr for UFO Studies have been used here. In general, UFOs are any anomalous aerial phenomenon whose appearance and/or behavior cannot be ascribed to conventional objects or effects by the original witnesses as well as by technical analysts who possess qualifications or information that the original observers may lack. Each UFO case has been assigned to one of nine categories, depending on the characteristics described in the literature.

UFO (?) — Objects unclassifiable in any of the categories below due to an incomplete description; or, objects definitely or probably identified as conventional objects or effects (Identified Flying Objects). However, the placing of a UFO sighting in other categories besides this one does not rule out its being an IFO — many cases are insufficiently investigated for assigning a conventional, yet probable, explanation.

UFO (CE-1) — Close Encounter of the First Kind. A UFO in close proximity (usually within 500 feet) to the witness.

UFO (CE-2) — Close Encounter of the Second Kind. A close encounter that influences the environment in some fashion, such as leaving physical evidence of its presence, creating electromagnetic interference, or causing physiological effects. In cases modified by the phrase "ground markings only," physical traces characteristic of CE-2s are reported without a UFO having been seen.

UFO (CE-3) — Close Encounter of the Third Kind. A close encounter with non- or quasi-human "occupants" associated with the object.

UFO (CE-4) — Close Encounter of the Fourth Kind. An abduction case, in which the witness allegedly boards the UFO, voluntarily or involuntarily. See also *Contactee*.

UFO (DD) — Daylight Disc. Distant objects seen in the daytime sky. Often the UFOs are discoidal, but other shapes (spheres, cigars, etc.) are also reported.

UFO (NL) — Nocturnal Light. Any anomalous light seen in the night sky whose description rules out the possibility of aircraft, stars, meteors, and so forth.

UFO (R) — Radar case. UFOs reported on the radar screen only, with no visual confirmation.

UFO (R-V) — Radar-Visual case. UFOs seen both visually and on radar simultaneously, with good agreement between the two accounts.

UNIDENTIFIED SUBMERGED OBJECT — Anomalous underwater objects of varying descriptions, not ascribable to conventional fauna or technology.

WEATHER CONTROL — The paranormal manipulation of clouds, air masses, or precipitation, usually by *psychokinesis,* but also including *orgone energy* devices (Reichian) or unknown chemical methods.

WEEPING ICON — Religious statues that secrete a watery substance from the facial area.

WELSH INDIANS—Amerindian groups rumored to have cultural affinities with the Welsh.

WHITE INDIANS—Amerindian groups rumored to have certain Caucasian features.

WINDSHIELD PITTING—Mysterious holes or dents in windshields, windows, or other glass, caused by unidentifiable or untraceable particles. This category also includes inexplicable shattering of glass.

WITCHCRAFT—A general category used for accusations of persons having unspecified paranormal talents, often including hex, shape-shifting, herbalism, and healing.

WITCH TRIAL—Court cases involving the accusation of persons having paranormal talents and, by inference, having a pact with the Devil. The specific or most prominent accusation is given in parentheses.

KEY TO ABBREVIATIONS

Acad.	Academy	Dep't	Department
Adv.	Advancement	diam.	diameter
AFB	Air Force Base	Doc.	Document
Am.	America, American		
Ann.	Annual	E	east
Anon.	Anonymous	ed.	edition, editor(s)
Anthro.	Anthropological, An-	Ethn.	Ethnology, Ethnological
	thropologist, Anthro-	Eve.	Evening
	pology	Exper.	Experimental
Antiq.	Antiquarian		
AP	Associated Press	FSR	Flying Saucer Review
APRO	Aerial Phenomena		
	Research Organization	Geogr.	Geography,
Arch.	Archeologist(s),		Geographical
	Archeology	Geol.	Geological
ASPR	American Society for	Geophys.	Geophysical
	Psychical Research		
Ass'n	Association	Hist.	History, Historical
Astro.	Astronomical,	hwy.	highway
	Astronomy		
		I., Is.	Island(s)
betw.	between	il.	illustration(s)
Bull.	Bulletin	Ill.	Illinois, Illustrated
Bur.	Bureau	INFO	International Fortean
			Organization
c.	century	Inst.	Institute, Institution
ca.	circa	Int'l	International
Can.	Canadian	Inv.	Investigator
Capt.	Captain		
CFB	Canadian Forces Base	J.	Journal
Coll.	Collections		
Comm'n	Commission	km.	kilometer(s)
Comp.	Comparative		
Cong.	Congress	m.	meter(s)
Contrib.	Contributions	Mag.	Magazine
CRIFO	Civilian Research, Inter-	Mech.	Mechanics
	planetary Flying Objects	Med.	Medical
CUFOS	Center for UFO Studies	Mem.	Memoirs

Meteor.	Meteorological	Rept.	Report
mi.	mile(s)	Rev.	Review
Misc.	Miscellaneous	Rsch.	Research
MUFON	Mutual UFO Network		
Mus.	Museum	S	south
		Sat.	Saturday
N	north	Sci.	Science, Scientific
NAS	Naval Air Station	Seism.	Seismological,
Nat.	Natural		Seismology
Nat'l	National	ser.	series
n.d.	no date	Sess.	Session
NEARA	New England Antiquities Research Association	SITU	Society for the Investigation of the Unexplained
NICAP	National Investigations Committee on Aerial Phenomena	Smith.	Smithsonian
		Soc.	Societe, Social
no.	number	Soc'y	Society
nr.	near	SPR	Society for Psychical Research
Occ.	Occasional	Sta.	Station
		Trans.	Transactions
Pap.	Papers		
Para-	Parapsychology, Para-	UAO	Unexplained Aerial Object
psych.	psychological		
Phil.	Philosophical	UFO	Unidentified Flying Object
Photog.	Photography		
Phys.	Physical	Univ.	University
Pop.	Popular	UPI	United Press International
P.Q.	Province Quebec		
Proc.	Proceedings		
Psych.	Psychology, Psychological	vol.	volume
pt.	part	W	west
Pt.	Point		
Pub.	Publications, Publishing	x	intersection
Quar.	Quarterly	Zool.	Zoological

ALPHABETICAL LIST
OF STATES AND PROVINCES___

UNITED STATES

Alabama	398	Montana	264
Alaska	3	Nebraska	303
Arizona	202	Nevada	187
Arkansas	373	New Hampshire	986
California	88	New Jersey	800
Colorado	239	New Mexico	220
Connecticut	926	New York	827
Delaware	756	North Carolina	454
Florida	407	North Dakota	292
Georgia	434	Ohio	685
Hawaii	178	Oklahoma	328
Idaho	80	Oregon	65
Illinois	521	Pennsylvania	761
Indiana	667	Rhode Island	938
Iowa	590	South Carolina	446
Kansas	313	South Dakota	297
Kentucky	503	Tennessee	491
Louisiana	383	Texas	340
Maine	997	Utah	194
Maryland	741	Vermont	982
Massachusetts	944	Virginia	475
Michigan	641	Washington	43
Minnesota	604	West Virginia	730
Mississippi	391	Wisconsin	621
Missouri	560	Wyoming	257

CANADA

Alberta	274	Northern Canada	12
British Columbia	18	Nova Scotia	1014
Labrador	1028	Ontario	886
Manitoba	286	Prince Edward Island	1022
New Brunswick	1011	Quebec	913
Newfoundland	1023	Saskatchewan	282

GREENLAND   1030

Map of Regional Divisions of States and Provinces

THE PACIFIC

ALASKA

A. Populated Places

Allakaket
-Humanoid myth
  bushman
    John Green, Sasquatch: The Apes Among
    Us (Seattle: Hancock House, 1978),
    pp.301-302.

Anchorage
-Healing
  1960s-   /Mia Lamoureaux
    Hans Holzer, The Witchcraft Report
    (N.Y.: Ace, 1973 ed.), pp.74-75.
-Precognition
  1951, Dec./Rocco Nardelli
    (Editorial), Fate 8 (Jan.1955):13.
-UFO (?)
  1947, July/Fort Richardson
    "What the Air Force Believes About
    Flying Saucers," Fate 2 (Nov.1949):
    69,71.
    Bruce S. Maccabee, "UFO Related In-
    formation from the FBI Files: Part
    3," MUFON UFO J., no.121 (Dec.1977):
    10,13.
  1950, Dec.2/C.G. Kelly/8 mi.SW
    Kenneth Arnold & Ray Palmer, The Com-
    ing of the Saucers (Amherst, Wis.:
    The Authors, 1952), pp.134-35.
  1954, April 21
    Donald E. Keyhoe, The Flying Saucer
    Conspiracy (N.Y.: Holt, 1955), p.133,
    quoting Anchorage Daily News (un-
    dated).
-UFO (DD)
  1947, July 9/Elmendorf Field
    Anchorage Daily Times, 10 July 1947.
  1947, July 12/Elmendorf Field
    Bruce S. Maccabee, "UFO Related In-
    formation from the FBI Files: Part
    3," MUFON UFO J., no.121 (Dec.1977):
    10,13.
  1952, April 14
    Fairbanks News-Miner, 17 Apr.1952.
-UFO (NL)
  1953, Feb.16-17/Elmendorf AFB
    Edward J. Ruppelt, "What Our Air
    Force Found Out About Flying Sau-
    cers," True, May 1954, pp.19-30,124-
    34.
  1965, Jan.27/William C. Langworthy
    Kansas City (Mo.) Times, 29 Jan.1965,
    p.1.
  1974, Oct.15/Don Young
    Ronald Drucker, "Alaska's UFO War,"
    Saga UFO Rept. 2 (winter 1975):15,
    17.
  1974, Oct.22/Edmoana Toews
    Edmoana Toews & Joseph J. Brewer,
    "The UFOs That Led Us Home: Part 2,"
    Fate 30 (July 1977):63,69.
-UFO (R)
  1977, April 23/30 mi.E

Montreal (P.Q.) Star, 16 May 1977.
-UFO (R-V)
  1975, June 17/Andrew R. Chapman/Elmen-
  dorf AFB
    Ronald Drucker, "Alaska's UFO War,"
    Saga UFO Rept. 2 (winter 1975):15-
    17.

Angoon
-Hex
  1957, April
    (Editorial), Fate 10 (Sep.1957):17-
    18.
-UFO (NL)
  1952, Dec.6
    U.S. Air Force, Projects Grudge and
    Blue Book Reports 1-12 (Washington:
    NICAP, 1968), p.185.

Barrow
-UFO (NL)
  1967
    Glenn McWane & David Graham, The New
    UFO Sightings (N.Y.: Warner, 1974),
    p.61.

Bethel
-UFO (DD)
  1947, Aug.4
    Bruce S. Maccabee, "UFO Related In-
    formation from the FBI Files: Part
    3," MUFON UFO J., no.121 (Dec.1977):
    10,14.

College
-Archeological site
  University of Alaska
    N.C. Nelson, "Notes on Cultural Rela-
    tions between Asia and America," Am.
    Antiquity 2 (1937):267-72. il.
    William Irving, "Burins from Central
    Alaska," Am.Antiquity 20 (1955):
    380-83. il.
-Auroral anomaly
    Charles R. Wilson, "Auroral Infra-
    sonic Waves," J.Geophys.Rsch. 74
    (1969):1812-36.

Dillingham
-UFO (CE-1)
  1960, May 19
    J. Allen Hynek, The Hynek UFO Report
    (N.Y.: Dell, 1977), pp.146-49.

Elim
-Land monster myth
  tirichuk
    Charles Lucier, "Buckland Eskimo
    Myths," Anthro.Pap.Univ.Alaska 2
    (May 1954):215-33.

Fairbanks
-Archeological site
  mammoth remains

Frank C. Hibben, "Evidences of Early
Man in Alaska," Am.Antiquity 8
(1943):254-59.
-UFO (?)
1978, Oct.31/=meteor?
Tempe (Ariz.) Daily News, 1 Nov.
1978.
-UFO (NL)
1973, Oct.11/Ken Yates
Ronald Drucker, "Alaska's UFO War,"
Saga UFO Rept. 2 (winter 1975):15,
52.
-UFO (R-V)
1951/Philip Schumann/Ladd AFB
J. Allen Hynek, The Hynek UFO Report
(N.Y.: Dell, 1977), pp.49-50.

Fort Greely
-Mystery caribou deaths
1972, June 21/4 mi.S
New York Times, 31 July 1972, p.3.

Fort Yukon
-Humanoid
n.d.
John Green, Sasquatch: The Apes Among
Us (Seattle: Hancock House, 1978),
p.302.

Galena
-Humanoid
1968, summer/Hazel Strasburg
John Green, The Sasquatch File (Agassiz, B.C.: Cheam, 1973), p.48.

Hawk Inlet
-UFO (CE-1)
1968, Dec.15-16/Ken Marlowe/"Teel"
Juneau Daily Empire, 4 Jan.1969.
"New Info on Alaskan Sighting," APRO
Bull. 18 (July-Aug.1969):7.

Holy Cross
-Humanoid
n.d.
John Green, Sasquatch: The Apes Among
Us (Seattle: Hancock House, 1978),
p.302.

Hoonah
-UFO (DD)
1963, July 22/Mary Luchinette
(Letter), Fate 17 (Apr.1964):116-17.

Huslia
-Humanoid
1960s
John Green, Sasquatch: The Apes Among
Us (Seattle: Hancock House, 1978),
p.301.

Hyder
-UFO (DD)
1965, Aug./John J. Eckhart
Jerome Clark, "The Greatest Flap Yet?
--Part 2," Flying Saucer Rev. 12
(Mar.-Apr.1966):11, quoting Catholic
Northwest Progress (undated).

Kaluka
-Humanoid
ca.1940
John Green, The Sasquatch File (Agassiz, B.C.: Cheam, 1973), p.16.

Ketchikan
-Archeological site
=pyramid and canals
(Letter), Mercedes B. Matter, Fate
15 (July 1962):106-107.
-Humanoid
1960, summer
John Green, Sasquatch: The Apes Among
Us (Seattle: Hancock House, 1978),
pp.430-31.
-UFO (DD)
1974, March 18
Fairbanks News-Miner, 19 Mar.1974.

King Salmon
-UFO (?)
1955, July 30/=meteor
Leonard H. Stringfield, Inside Saucer
Post...3-0 Blue (Cincinnati: CRIFO,
1957), p.58.

Kodiak
-Animal ESP
1964, March 27/Louis Beaty
(Editorial), Fate 17 (Aug.1964):22.
-UFO (CE-2)
1957, Nov.4
Anchorage Daily News, 4 Nov.1957.
-UFO (R-V)
1950, Jan.22-23
Bruce S. Maccabee, "UFO Related Information from the FBI Files: Part
6," MUFON UFO J., no.130 (Sep.1978):
7-9.

Kotzebue
-UFO (NL)
1962, Feb.25
Lloyd Mallan, "Complete Directory of
UFOs: Part II," Sci.& Mech. 38 (Jan.
1967):44,71.

Kulukak
-Humanoid
n.d.
John Green, Sasquatch: The Apes Among
Us (Seattle: Hancock House, 1978),
pp.302,368.

Nenana
-UFO (R)
1952, Jan.22
Edward J. Ruppelt, The Report on Un-
identified Flying Objects (Garden
City: Doubleday, 1956), pp.123-26.
U.S. Air Force, Projects Grudge and
Blue Book Reports 1-12 (Washington:
NICAP, 1968), pp.12-13,128-29.

Nome
-UFO (?)
1952, April 16
New York Times, 18 Apr.1952, p.4.
Nome Nugget, 21 Apr.1952.

-UFO (DD)
  1960, Feb.14/airport
    Anchorage Daily Times, 15 Feb.1960.
    Fairbanks News-Miner, 16 Feb.1960.

Nulato
-Humanoid
  ca.1920/Albert Petka
    John Green, The Sasquatch File (Ag-
      assiz, B.C.: Cheam, 1973), p.17.
  1970, fall/Patty Nollnar
    Jerome Clark & Loren Coleman, Crea-
      tures of the Outer Edge (N.Y.: War-
      ner, 1978), pp.34-35.
-Humanoid tracks
  ca.1940/Mrs. Notti
    John Green, The Sasquatch File (Ag-
      assiz, B.C.: Cheam, 1973), p.16.

Palmer
-UFO (?)
  1962, May 27
    Richard Hall, ed., The UFO Evidence
      (Washington: NICAP, 1964), p.139.

Platinum
-Disappearance
  1954, Sep./E of town/Dakota plane
    Harold T. Wilkins, Flying Saucers
      Uncensored (N.Y.: Pyramid, 1967 ed.)
      p.239.

Portlock
-Humanoid
  1940s
    Anchorage Daily News, 15 Apr.1973.

Ruby
-Humanoid
  1943/John Mire/18 mi.W at DeWilde's
    Camp
    John Green, The Sasquatch File (Ag-
      assiz, B.C.: Cheam, 1973), p.17.
  1949/Robert Kennedy/22 mi.W
  1960, Aug./Paul Peters/10 mi.W
    John Green, The Sasquatch File (Ag-
      assiz, B.C.: Cheam, 1973), p.23.
    Jerome Clark & Loren Coleman, Crea-
      tures of the Outer Edge (N.Y.: War-
      ner, 1978), pp.33-34.

Saint Michael
-Humanoid myth
    Edward William Nelson, "The Eskimo
      about Bering Strait," Ann.Rept.Bur.
      Am.Ethn. 18, pt.1 (1896-97):480-81.
-UFO (CE-2)
  1972, Aug.17/John Cheemuk
    Anchorage Daily Times, 26 Aug.1972.

Sitka
-Haunt
  1867/Baranof Castle
    Charles M. Skinner, Myths and Legends
      Beyond Our Borders (Philadelphia:
      Lippincott, 1899), pp.202-204.

Stebbins
-UFO (?)
  1972, Aug.16/Pius Mike
    Anchorage Daily Times, 26 Aug.1972.

Ughiva
-Giant bird legend
    Edward William Nelson, "The Eskimo
      about Bering Strait," Ann.Rept.Bur.
      Am.Ethn. 18, pt.1 (1896-97):486-87.

Umiat
-UFO (NL)
  1964, Feb.3/Joe Nightingale/nearby
    river
    (Editorial), Fate 17 (June 1964):10.

Unalakleet
-Fall of lemmings
  1952, April?
    Sally Carrighar, Wild Voice of the
      North (N.Y.: Garden City, 1959).
-UFO (DD)
  1960, Feb.14
    Fairbanks News-Miner, 16 Feb.1960.

Valdez
-Healing
  1950s/Jerome Eden
    Jerome Eden, "The Tender Touch," Cre-
      ative Process 1 (Nov.1961):81-86.
-Hex
  ca.1910
    "The Gypsy's Curse," Fate 18 (Jan.
      1965):85.
-Humanoid
  ca.1898/Valdez Glacier
    W.R. Abercrombie, "Copper River Ex-
      ploring Expedition 1898," in A Com-
      pilation of Narratives and Explora-
      tions in Alaska, U.S. Senate Doc.
      1023, 56th Cong., 1st Sess. (Wash-
      ington: U.S. Gov't Print. Office,
      1900), pp.758-59.

Wales
-Humanoid myth
    Edward William Nelson, "The Eskimo
      about Bering Strait," Ann.Rept.Bur.
      Am.Ethn. 18, pt.1 (1896-97):510-11.

Wasilla
-Auroral anomaly
  n.d.
    C.S. Beals, "Audibility of the Aurora
      and Its Appearance at Low Atmospher-
      ic Levels," Quar.J.Royal Meteor.
      Soc'y 59 (1933):71-78.

Yakutat
-Sea monster (carcass)
  1956, May/Earl Flemming/60 mi.SE/=beak-
    ed whale
    Juneau Daily Empire, 22 July 1956.
    San Francisco (Cal.) Chronicle, 22
      July 1956.
    "Mystery of a Monster," Life, 6 Aug.
      1956, p.38. il.

B. Physical Features

Adak I.
-UFO (?)
    1950, Sep.11/George R. Peck/=lens flare
        "And in Groups of 2,3,18, and Infin-
        ity!" in Frank Bowers, ed., The True
        Report on Flying Saucers (Greenwich,
        Ct.: Fawcett, 1967), p.46. il.
-UFO (CE-1)
    1945, March/Robert S. Crawford/"Dela-
    rof"
        "The Question of Submerging UFOs,"
        UFO Inv. 4 (Mar.1968):4-5.
-UFO (R)
    1955, March/Naval station
        Leonard H. Stringfield, Inside Saucer
        Post...3-0 Blue (Cincinnati: CRIFO,
        1957), p.94.

Agattu I.
-Archaeological site
    700 B.C.-900 A.D./Krugloi Pt.
        Albert C. Spaulding, "Archaeological
        Investigations on Agattu, Alaska,"
        Anthro.Pap.Mus.Anthro.Univ.Mich.,
        no.18 (1962).
        A.P. McCartney, "A Proposed Western
        Aleutian Phase in the Near Islands,
        Alaska," Arctic Anthro. 8, no.2
        (1971):92-142.

Aleutian Is.
-Giant human skull
    "Aleutian Islands Skull of Abnormal
    Size," Nature 138 (1936):613.

Alitak, Cape
-Petroglyphs
    Robert F. Heizer, "Petroglyphs from
    Southwestern Kodiak Island, Alaska,"
    Proc.Am.Phil.Soc'y 91 (1947):284-
    93. il.

Amak I.
-Meteorite crater
    64 m.diam. x 15 m.deep/doubtful
        Lincoln LaPaz, "A Possible Meteorite
        Crater in the Aleutians," Pop.Astro.
        55 (1947):156-67.

Anaktuvuk Pass
-Archeological site
    7000-4000 B.C.
        William Irving, "Evidence of Early
        Tundra Cultures in Northern Alaska,"
        Anthro.Pap.Univ.Alaska 1 (May 1953):
        55-85.
        John M. Campbell, "Cultural Succes-
        sion at Anaktuvuk Pass, Alaska,"
        Tech.Pap.Arctic Inst. of N.America,
        no.11 (1962):39-54.

Anangula I.
-Archeological site
    6500-6000 B.C.
        William S. Laughlin & Gordon H.
        Marsh, "The Lamellar Flake Manufac-
        turing Site on Anangula Island in
        the Aleutians," Am.Antiquity 20
        (1954):27-39. il.

Robert F. Black & William S. Laugh-
lin, "Anangula: A Geologic Inter-
pretation of the Oldest Archeologic
Site in the Aleutians," Science 143
(1964):1321-22.
W.S. Laughlin, "Aleuts: Ecosystem,
Holocene, History, and Siberian Or-
igin," Science 189 (1975):507-15.
Jean S. Aigner, "Dating the Early
Holocene Maritime Village of Anan-
gula," Anthro.Pap.Univ.Alaska 18
(Dec.1976):51-62.

Arctic National Wildlife Range
-UFO (?)
    1959, Feb.
        "Report of Saucers Landing in North
        Alaska and North Pole," Flying Sau-
        cer Rev. 5 (May-June 1959):9.

Augustine I.
-Volcano anomaly
    1976, Jan.23/Mt. St. Augustine
        "Volcanic Bomb?" Can.UFO Rept., no.
        23 (spring 1976):15-16, quoting UPI
        release (undated).

Barrow, Pt.
-Anomalous artifact
    1887/John Murdock/=ancient snow goggles
        Alfred R. Wallace, "The Antiquity of
        Man in North America," Nineteenth
        Century 22 (1887):672.
-Archeological site
    500 A.D.-present
        James A. Ford, "Eskimo Prehistory in
        the Vicinity of Point Barrow, Alas-
        ka," Anthro.Pap.Am.Mus.Nat.History
        vol.47, pt.1 (1959).
        Jerry Brown, "Radiocarbon Dating,
        Barrow, Alaska," Arctic 18, no.1
        (1965):37-48.
-Derelict ship
    1931, Nov.-1956, March/"Baychimo"
        Paul Brock, "Floating Ghost of the
        Arctic Sea," Fate 11 (Apr.1958):
        52-58.
-Giant dog myth
    Diamond Jenness, "Stray Notes on the
    Eskimo of Arctic Alaska," Anthro.
    Pap.Univ.Alaska 1 (May 1953):5,9.
-Giant polar bear
    1958
        Chicago (Ill.) Sun-Times, 12 Mar.
        1958.
-Giant polar bear myth
    qoqogaq
        Diamond Jenness, "Stray Notes on the
        Eskimo of Arctic Alaska," Anthro.
        Pap.Univ.Alaska 1 (May 1953):5,9.
-Humanoid myth
    tornait
        Robert F. Spencer, "The North Alas-
        kan Eskimo," Bull.Bur.Am.Ethn., no.
        171 (1959):259-61.

Beluga Pt.
-Archeological site
    ca.8000 B.C.
        Anchorage Daily Times, 25 July 1978.

Big L.
-Lake monster
   1970, Sep.13/Manne Landstrom
      Kodiak Daily Mirror, 29 Oct.1970.

Bogoslof Is.
-Topographic anomaly
   1796-1909
      C. Hart Merriam, "Bogoslof Volcanos,"
      Ann.Rept.Smith.Inst. 51 (1901):367-
      75. il.

Bradfield Canal
-Humanoid
   1969, July/J.W. Huff
      J.W. Huff, "A Possible Sasquatch
      Sighting in Alaska," Bigfoot Bull.,
      Nov.1969, p.303.
      John Green, The Sasquatch File (Ag-
      assiz, B.C.: Cheam, 1973), p.48.

Brooks Range
-UFO (?)
   1952, April 18
      Fairbanks News-Miner, 19 Apr.1952.

Burkett, Mt.
-Chinese discovery
   ca.1000 B.C.
      Henriette Mertz, Gods from the Far
      East (N.Y.:Ballantine, 1975 ed.),
      p.152.

Chandalar L.
-Patterned ground
      A.L. Washburn, "Classification of
      Patterned Ground and Review of Sup-
      posed Origins," Bull.Geol.Soc'y Am.
      67 (1956):823-66. il.

Chichagof I.
-Mystery metal sphere
   1949, April 8/Leo E. Young
      "Found on Ground," Doubt, no.42
      (1953):238,239.

Choris Peninsula
-Archeological sites
   ca.1000 B.C.
      James L. Giddings, Jr., The Archae-
      ology of Cape Denbigh (Providence:
      Brown Univ., 1964).

Chugach Mts.
-UFO (?)
   1957, March 17/=meteor
      Leonard H. Stringfield, Inside Sau-
      cer Post...3-0 Blue (Cincinnati:
      CRIFO, 1957), p.59.
   1967
      Glenn McWane & David Graham, The New
      UFO Sightings (N.Y.: Warner, 1974),
      p.61, quoting Anchorage News (un-
      dated).
-UFO (DD)
   1968, March 27/77 mi.E of Anchorage
      "French General, Scientists, Report
      UFOs," UFO Inv. 4 (May-June 1968):
      3.
-UFO (NL)
   1977, April 23

Montreal (P.Q.) Star, 16 May 1977.

Denbigh, Cape
-Archeological site
   ca.5000 B.C.-800 A.D./Iyatayet
      James L. Giddings, Jr., The Archae-
      ology of Cape Denbigh (Providence:
      Brown Univ., 1964).

Douglas I.
-UFO (NL)
   1973, Aug.14/Wayne Smallwood, Jr.
      Juneau Empire, 15 Aug. 1973.

Dry Creek
-Archeological site
   ca.9000 B.C.
      New York Times, 29 Sep.1976, p.15.
      Christian Science Monitor, 11 Oct.
      1977.

Ester Creek
-Archeological site
      Froelich Rainey, "Archaeological In-
      vestigation in Central Alaska," Am.
      Antiquity 5 (1940):299-308.

Fairweather, Mt.
-Aerial phantom
   1897, Aug./Luigi, Duke of the Abruzzi
      New York Herald, 5 Sep.1897, sec.4,
      p.1.
      "Phénomène de mirage du mont Fair-
      weather," La Nature 29 (1901):303.
-Chinese discovery
   ca.1000 B.C.
      Henriette Mertz, Gods from the Far
      East (N.Y.: Ballantine, 1975 ed.),
      pp.151-52.

Glacier Bay
-Aerial phantom
   1887/Mr. Willoughby/=hoax
      San Francisco (Cal.) Chronicle, 11
      Oct.1889.
      Alexander Badlam, The Wonders of Al-
      aska (San Francisco: The Author,
      1891), pp.130-40. il.
      Miner W. Bruce, Alaska: Its History
      and Resources (Seattle: Lowman &
      Hanford, 1895), pp.86-89. il.
      Victoria (B.C.) Daily Times, 26 Jan.
      1901.
      New York Tribune, 17 Feb.1901.
      "The 'Bristol Mirage,'" Fortean Times,
      no.24 (winter 1978):37-39. il.
   1889, July 2/Lamar B. French
      New York Times, 31 Oct. 1889, p.2.
      Alexander Badlam, The Wonders of Al-
      aska (San Francisco: The Author,
      1891), pp.132-33
   1890/I.W. Taber
      Alexander Badlam, The Wonders of Al-
      aska (San Francisco: The Author,
      1891), pp.134-36, quoting Nevada
      City Daily Transcript (undated). il.

Harvester I.
-Sea monster
   1971/"Totem"
      (Editorial), Pursuit 4 (Oct.1971):

100, quoting Kodiak Daily Mirror
(undated).

Healy L.
-Archeological site
  ca.9000 B.C.-recent
    Robert A. McKennan & John P. Cook,
    "Prehistory of Healy Lake, Alaska,"
    8th Int'l Cong.Anthro. & Ethn.Sci.
    (1968), 3:182-84.
    Albert A. Dekin, Jr., "The Arctic,"
    in James E. Fitting, ed., The De-
    velopment of North American Arch-
    aeology (N.Y.: Anchor, 1973), pp.
    15,38-39.

Hope, Pt.
-Archeological site
  ca.300 A.D./Ipiutak
    Helge Larsen & Froelich Rainey, "Ip-
    iutak and the Arctic Whale Hunting
    Culture," Anthro.Pap.Am.Mus.Nat.
    History, vol.42 (1948). il.

Iliamna L.
-Lake monster
  1929-   /=giant sturgeon?
    Gil Paust, "Alaska's Monster Mystery
    Fish," Sports Afield, Jan.1959, pp.
    54-56,65-67.
    "Alaska's Monster Mystery Fish," Am.
    Legion Mag. 80 (June 1966):52.
    Anchorage News, 23 Oct.1971; and 2
    Apr.1972.
    Anchorage Daily Times, 28 Dec.1971.
-UFO (NL)
  1954/airfield
    (Editorial), Fate 7 (Oct.1954):12-13.

Inside Passage
-Humanoid
  1956, Aug.
    John Green, Sasquatch: The Apes Among
    Us (Seattle; Hancock House, 1978),
    p.303.

Kachemak Bay
-Archeological site
  ca.750 B.C.-800 A.D.
    Frederica de Laguna, The Archaeology
    of Cook Inlet, Alaska (Philadelphia:
    Univ. Pennsylvania, 1934).

Kalooluktuk L.
-Lake monster
  n.d.
    Robert Marshall, Arctic Village
    (N.Y.: Literary Guild, 1933), p.345.

Kenai Peninsula
-Sea monster (carcass)
  1946, Oct./S tip/=Pacific killer whale
    Washington (D.C.) Times-Herald, 27
    Oct.1946.
    (Letters), Don Knudsen & Harold E.
    Anthony, Natural History 58 (Oct.
    1949):338. il.
    "A Straggler from the Age of Great
    Reptiles?" Ill.London News 216 (1
    Apr.1950):513. il.

Kiska I.
-UFO (R)
  1943, July 26/U.S. North Pacific Fleet
  /=radar echo?
    Donald H. Menzel, Flying Saucers
    (Cambridge: Harvard Univ., 1953),
    pp.267-68.
    George W. Harper, "The Battle of the
    Blips," Fate 30 (May 1977):43-50.

Kodiak I.
-Archeological site
    Aleš Hrdlička, The Anthropology of
    Kodiak Island (Philadelphia: Wis-
    tar Inst., 1944).
-Volcano anomaly
  1965/Mrs. William Chisholm
    Salem (Ore.) Statesman, 10 Feb.1971.

Kotzebue Sound
-Humanoid
  n.d.
    John Green, Sasquatch: The Apes Among
    Us (Seattle: Hancock House, 1978),
    p.302.

Kowak R.
-Seance
  1885, Aug.
    O.T. Mason, "Hypnotism and the Eski-
    mo," Am.J.Psychology 1 (1888):553.

Krusenstern, Cape
-Archeological site
  9000 B.C.-recent
    J.L. Giddings, "Cultural Continui-
    ties of Eskimos," Am.Antiquity 27
    (1961):155-73. il.

Kuskokwim R.
-Lake monster myth
  palraiyuk
    Edward William Nelson, "The Eskimo
    about Bering Strait," Ann.Rept.Bur.
    Am.Ethn. 18, pt.1 (1896-97):444-45.

Lynn Canal
-Sea monster tracks
  1931
    (Editorial), Fate 15 (May 1962):12-
    13, quoting Vancouver (B.C.) Daily
    Colonist (undated).

Malaspina Glacier
-Snow worms
  1897, summer/Henry G. Bryant
    J. Percy Moore, "A Snow-Inhabiting
    Enchytraeid," Proc.Acad.Nat.Sci.
    Philadelphia, 1899, pp.125-44.
  1897, Aug./Filippo de Filippi
    E.W. Gudger, "Snow Worms," Natural
    History 23 (1923):451-56.

Martin Pt.
-Mystery deaths
    Diamond Jenness, "Stray Notes on the
    Eskimo of Arctic Alaska," Anthro.
    Pap.Univ.Alaska 1 (May 1953):5-13.

Middleton I.
-Hex
   ca.1790s-1940s
      Robert M. Hyatt, "The Curse of Mid-
      dleton Island," Fate 2 (Sep.1949):
      36-45.

Minivak I.
-UFO (?)
   1950, Sep.6
      "Run of the Mill," Doubt, no.31
      (1950):58.

Muddy R.
-Humanoid
   1925
      Harry D. Colp, The Strangest Story
      Ever Told (N.Y.: Exposition, 1953).

Nelchina Plateau
-Humanoid
   1940s/Russell Annabel
      Roger Patterson, Do Abominable Snow-
      men of America Really Exist? (Yak-
      ima, Wash.: Franklin, 1966), p.118,
      quoting Russell Annabel, "Long Hunt-
      er: Alaskan Style," Sports Afield,
      1963.

Nizki I.
-Giant human skulls
   1943, May/=bottle-nosed whale?
      Harold T. Wilkins, "The Giants in
      the Earth," Fate 5 (Jan.1952):95,
      99-101.
      (Letter), Anon., Fate 5 (July-Aug.
      1952):119-20.
      Ivan T. Sanderson, More Things (N.Y.:
      Pyramid, 1969), pp.80-88.
      "Giant Skulls," Pursuit 7 (Jan.1974):
      12-14.

Nonvianuk L.
-Lake monster
   1954/Bill Hammersley
      Gil Paust, "Alaska's Monster Mystery
      Fish," Sports Afield, Jan.1959, pp.
      54,66.

North Slope
-Oriented lakes
      Robert F. Black & William L. Barks-
      dale, "Oriented Lakes of Northern
      Alaska," J.Geology 57 (1949):105-
      18. il.
      Allan O. Kelly, "The Origin of the
      Carolina Bays and the Oriented
      Lakes of Alaska," Pop.Astro. 59
      (1951):199-205.

Onion Portage
-Archeological site
   8000 B.C.-recent
      J.L. Giddings, "Onion Portage and
      Other Flint Sites of the Kobuk Riv-
      er," Arctic Anthro. 1, no.1 (1962):
      6-27.
      J.L. Giddings, "Cross-Dating the Ar-
      chaeology of Northwestern Alaska,"
      Science 153 (1966):127-35.

Douglas D. Anderson, "A Stone Age
      Campsite at the Gateway to America,"
      Sci.Am. 218 (June 1968):24-33.
      Douglas D. Anderson, "Akmak: An Early
      Archaeological Assemblage from Onion
      Portage," Acta Arctica, vol.16
      (1970).

Pennock I.
-Sea monster
   1947, May 8/Lauri Carlson
      Ketchikan Daily, 10 May 1947.

Prince William Sound
-UFO (NL)
   1969, Jan.16/Charles McCracken
      "US Roundup," APRO Bull. 17 (Mar.-
      Apr.1969):6-7.

Raspberry Strait
-Sea monster
   1969, April 15/"Mylark"
      Kodiak Mirror, 30 Apr.1969.
      Ivan T. Sanderson, Investigating the
      Unexplained (Englewood Cliffs, N.J.:
      Prentice-Hall, 1972), pp.5-16. il.

Russian R.
-UFO (CE-1)
   1965, July 5/Barty Andersson
      Anchorage News, 3 Aug.1965, p.1. il.
      "Attention Scandinavian Members,"
      APRO Bull. 21 (Jan.-Feb.1973):2.
      Adrian Vance, UFOs, the Eye, and the
      Camera (N.Y.: Barlenmir, 1977). il.

Saint Lawrence I.
-Archeological sites
   ca.100 A.D.-recent
      Henry B. Collins, Jr., "Archaeology
      of St. Lawrence Island, Alaska,"
      Smith.Misc.Coll., vol.96, no.1
      (1937).
-Fall of fish
   1940s
      "Polar Geist," Doubt, no.12 (spring-
      summer 1945):175.

Security Bay
-Sea monster
   1947, April/Lou Baggon/"Suntrana"
      Ketchikan Daily, 12 May 1947.

Shemya I.
-Archeological site
      Wesley Hurt, "Artifacts from Shemya,
      Aleutian Is.," Am.Antiquity 16
      (1950):69.

Shuyak I.
-Sea monster
   1951, July/=whale
      Kodiak Mirror, 21 July 1951.

Sithylemenkat L.
-Meteorite crater
   12.4 km.diam. x 500 m.deep/probable
      P. Jan Cannon, "Meteorite Impact
      Crater Discovered in Central Alaska
      with Landsat Imagery," Science 196

(1977):1322-24.

Taku Glacier
-UFO (?)
1948, May/Mikel Conrad/=hoax?
(Review), Variety, 11 Jan.1950, p.6.
Los Angeles (Cal.) Canyon Crier, 29
Apr.1950.
Ray Palmer, "Space Ships, Flying Sau-
cers and Clean Noses," Fate 3 (May
1950):36,43.

Taku R.
-Acoustic anomaly
n.d./Bob Parker
"Music from Somewhere," Fate 5 (Apr.-
May 1952):60.

Talkeetna Mts.
-UFO (CE-4)
1940s/Wasilla
Brad Steiger & Joan Whritenour, The
Allende Letters (N.Y.: Award, 1968),
pp.141-42, quoting Russell Annabel,
"Smart Injun Trick, or UFO?" Sports
Afield, July 1967.

Tanana R.
-Archeological site
Froelich Rainey, "Archaeological In-
vestigation in Central Alaska," Am.
Antiquity 5 (1940):299-308.
F.C. Hibben, "Archaeological Aspects
of the Alaska Muck Deposits," New
Mexico Anthro. 5 (1941):151-57.
Stephen Taber, "Perenially Frozen
Ground in Alaska: Its Origin and
History," Bull.Geol.Soc'y Am. 54
(1943):1433,1482-90.

Thomas Bay
-Humanoid
1900, May/Harry Colp
Harry D. Colp, The Strangest Story
Ever Told (N.Y.: Exposition, 1953).

Trail Creek
-Archeological site
ca.11,000 B.C.-recent
Helge E. Larsen, "Trail Creek: Final
Report on the Excavation of Two
Caves on Seward Peninsula, Alaska,"
Acta Arctica, no.15 (1968). il.

Umnak I.
-Archeological site
1800 B.C.-recent/Chaluka midden
Jean S. Aigner, "Bone Tools and Dec-
orative Motifs from Chaluka, Umnak
Island," Arctic Anthro. 3, no.2
(1966):57-83.
Glenda B. Denniston, "Cultural Change
at Chaluka," Arctic Anthro. 3, no.2
(1966):84-124.

Unalaska I.
-Giant squid
1871, winter/Ilinlik
"Aleutian Cephalopods," Am.Naturalist
7 (1873):484-85.

Ward L.
-UFO (?)
1965, Sep.22
(Editorial), NICAP Reporter, Dec.
1965, pp.4-5.

Wrangell Mts.
-Crustal anomaly
=lost continent?
New York Times, 7 Mar.1978, p.9.

Wrangell Narrows
-Fall of fish
1950, Dec.13
"Some Fish Fall," Doubt, no.32
(1951):75.
-Humanoid
1942, May/Bob Titmus
John Green, The Sasquatch File (Agassiz, B.C.: Cheam, 1973), p.17.

Yakutat Bay
-Aerial phantom
1890/=glacial mirage?
Israel C. Russell, "An Expedition to
Mt. St. Elias, Alaska," Nat'l Geog.
Mag. 3 (29 May 1891):53-204.

Yukon R.
-Mammoth
1887, Dec.
"Mastodon or Buffalo?" Am.Antiquar-
ian 11 (1889):65.
1900, fall/Gregory Hildebrand
Joseph A. Murphy, "Valley of Never
Come Back," Fate 1 (fall 1948):26-
33,

C. Ethnic Groups

Aleut people
-Mummies
W.H. Dall, "Alaskan Mummies," Am.
Naturalist 9 (1875):433-40.
Aleš Hrdlička, "Exploration of Mummy
Caves in the Aleutian Islands," Sci.
Monthly 52 (1941):5-23,113-30. il.
"Mummification in America," Nature
147 (1941):707.
-Shamanism
Ivan Veniaminov, Zapiski ob Ostro-
vakh Unalashkinskago Otdiela, 2 vols.
(St. Petersburg, 1840).
Jay Ellis Ransom, "Aleut Religious
Belief: Veniaminov's Account," J.
Am.Folklore 58 (1945):346-49.

Bering Strait Eskimo
-Contactee myth
Edward William Nelson, "The Eskimo
about Bering Strait," Ann.Rept.Bur.
Am.Ethn. 18, pt.1 (1896-97):494-97.
Clark M. Garber, Stories and Legends
of the Bering Strait Eskimos (Bos-
ton: Christopher, 1940).
-Flood myth
Edward William Nelson, "The Eskimo
about Bering Strait," Ann.Rept.Bur.
Am.Ethn. 18, pt.1 (1896-97):452.

-Shamanism
  Richard H.R. Parkinson, Dreisig Jahre
  in der Südsee (Stuttgart: Strecher
  & Schröder, 1907), p.605.
  E.M. Weyer, The Eskimos (New Haven:
  Yale Univ., 1932).
  Peter Farb, Man's Rise to Civiliza-
  tion (N.Y.: Avon, 1969 ed.), pp.
  73-76.

Kobuk Eskimo
-Flood myth
  Robert Marshall, Arctic Village
  (N.Y.: Literary Guild, 1933), pp.
  340-42.
-Phantom (myth)
  dooneraks
  Robert Marshall, Arctic Village
  (N.Y.: Literary Guild, 1933), pp.
  338-39.

Kutchin Indians
-Shamanism
  Cornelius Osgood, "Contributions to
  the Ethnography of the Kutchin,"
  Pub.Anthro.Yale Univ., no.14 (1936):
  156,158-59,162.

Tanaina Indians
-Humanoid myth
  Cornelius Osgood, "The Ethnography
  of the Tanaina," Pub.Anthro.Yale
  Univ., no.16 (1937):171-73.

Tlingit Indians
-Flood myth
  Hubert Howe Bancroft, Native Races
  of the Pacific States, 5 vols. (N.Y:
  Appleton, 1875), 3:98-104.
  Ella Higginson, Alaska, the Great
  Country (N.Y.: Macmillan, 1917),
  pp.78-79.
-Reincarnation
  A. Pinart, "Notes sur les Koloches,"
  Bull.Soc.d'Anthro.de Paris 7 (1872):
  788-811.
  Ian Stevenson, "Cultural Patterns in
  Cases Suggestive of Reincarnation
  among the Tlingit Indians of South-
  eastern Alaska," J.ASPR 60 (1966):
  229-43.
  Ian Stevenson, "Seven Cases Sugges-
  tive of Reincarnation among the
  Tlingit Indians of Southeastern Al-
  aska," Proc.ASPR 26 (1966):191-240.
  Ian Stevenson, Twenty Cases Sugges-
  tive of Reincarnation (Charlottes-
  ville: Univ. Virginia, 1974), pp.
  216-69.
-Shamanism
  John R. Swanton, "Social Condition,
  Beliefs, and Linguistic Relation-
  ship of the Tlingit Indians," Ann.
  Rept.Bur.Am.Ethn. 26 (1905):391,
  463-71.
  Ella Higginson, Alaska, the Great
  Country (N.Y.: Macmillan, 1917), pp.
  82-83.
  W.Z. Park, Shamanism in Western North
  America (Evanston: Northwestern
  Univ., 1938).

Aurel Krause, The Tlingit Indians
(Seattle: Univ. Washington, 1956).
O.M. Salisbury, The Customs and Legends of the Tlingit Indians of Alaska (N.Y.: Bonanza, 1962), pp.
231-36.
-White Indians
  Peter de Roo, History of America before Columbus, 2 vols. (Philadelphia: Lippincott, 1900), 1:307.

        D. Unspecified Localities

-Ghost
  1952-1954/Ralph W. McInnis
  Ralph W. McInnis, "The Man Who Died
  in My Place," Fate 28 (Apr.1975):
  40-43.

-Humanoid
  1973/Ivan Marx/=hoax?
  William Childress, "The Most Sensa-
  tional Bigfoot Pictures Ever Taken,"
  Saga, Dec.1973, pp.30-33,68-72. il.

-Mammoth
  n.d.
  New York Times, 11 Oct.1887, p.5.
  Portland (Me.) Press, 28 Nov.1896.

-Mystery haze
  "Alaska's Imported Haze," Mosaic 9
  (Sep.-Oct.1978):41.

-Photographic anomaly
  ca.1977/=shutter malfunction
  "SITUations," Pursuit 10 (summer
  1977):92. il.
  "That Wedding Photo," Pursuit 11
  (summer 1978):117-18. il.

-Precognition
  1970s/Jandolin Marks
  Richard De A'Morelli & Rita West,
  "Top Seers Predict Your Future for
  1977," Psychic World, Jan.1977,
  pp.51,55-56.
  "Probe's 1977 Directory of the Psychic World," Probe the Unknown 5
  (spring 1977):33,38,60. il.

NORTHERN CANADA

A. Populated Places

Alert
-Geomagnetic anomaly
  Leroy R. Alldredge & Gerald Van Voor-
  his, "Source of the Great Arctic
  Magnetic Anomaly," J.Geophys.Rsch.
  67 (1962):1573-78.
  Philadelphia (Pa.) Bulletin, 30 Dec.
  1964.
  Toronto (Ont.) Star, 20 Mar.1974.

Carcross
-UFO (?)
  1976, Dec.26
  "Why the Sick or Dead?" Can.UFO Rept.
  no.26 (1976):5.
  Edmonton (Alb.) Journal, 10 Jan.1977.

Dawson
-Contactee
  1904-1925/Richard A. Fox
  Richard A. Fox, The People on Other
  Planets (Benton Harbor, Mich.: Wal-
  ter Southworth, 1925).
-Weather control
  1906, June/Charles Mallory Hatfield/=
  unknown chemical process
  Dawson City News, 1 Mar.1906.
  David R. Morrison, The Politics of
  Yukon Territory 1898-1909 (Toronto:
  Univ. Toronto, 1968), pp.78-79.

Destruction Bay
-UFO (NL)
  1960/Mrs. Pieter van der Veen
  "Light Examines Mountains," Can.UFO
  Rept., no.1 (Jan.-Feb.1969):11.
  1967, March 20/Kenneth Green
  "Mountainside Mystery," Can.UFO Rept.
  no.1 (Jan.-Feb.1969):5-6.

Fort Liard
-Humanoid
  1964, April/John Baptist
  Report on file at SITU.

Fort Norman
-Humanoid
  1973, Nov.
  John Green, Sasquatch: The Apes among
  Us (Seattle: Hancock House, 1978),
  p.242.
-UFO (NL)
  1968, Feb.16
  (Editorial), UFO News (Tasmania), Nov.
  1968, p.2.

Fort Resolution
-Humanoid myth
  Bernard R. Ross, "The Eastern Tinneh,"
  Ann.Rept.Smith.Inst. 16 (1866):304,
  309-10.

Fort Simpson
-Humanoid
  1964, June
  Report on file at SITU.
-UFO (?)
  1967, Nov.15/airport
  "Huge UFOs Reported," UFO Inv. 4
  (Jan.-Feb.1968):1,3.

Fort Smith
-UFO (NL)
  1969, Feb./Gordon Mercredi
  Vancouver (B.C.) Province, 8 Feb.
  1969.
  1979, Jan.10
  Edmonton (Alb.) Journal, 12 Jan.1979.

Igloolik
-Archeological site
  1000 B.C.-1500 A.D.
  Jörgen Meldgaard, "Origin and Evolution of Eskimo Cultures in the Eastern Arctic," Can.Geogr.J. 60 (1960):
  64-75.
-UFO (NL)
  1978, Jan.25
  (Editorial), Res Bureaux Bull., no.
  29 (9 Feb.1978):5.

Jake's Corners
-Humanoid
  1975, Oct.4/Ben Able
  Atlin (B.C.) News-Miner, 17 Dec.1975.

Keno Hill
-Humanoid
  ca.1969
  John Green, The Sasquatch File (Agassiz, B.C.: Cheam, 1973), p.48.

Lake Harbour
-Norse figurine
  1977, July/12 mi.SE
  Betty Lou White, "Vikings Came to
  Baffin Island," Fate 31 (Sep.1978):
  82-85. il.

Lansing
-Humanoid tracks
  1900s
  John Green, Sasquatch: The Apes among
  Us (Seattle: Hancock House, 1978),
  p.242.

Paulatuk
-UFO (NL)
  1977, Dec.30/20 mi.W
  (Editorial), Res Bureaux Bull., no.
  29 (9 Feb.1978):5.

Pelly Crossing
-Ghost
  1970, fall
  Sheila Hervey, Some Canadian Ghosts

(Richmond Hill, Ont.: Pocket Books, 1973), pp.138-41.

Snowdrift
-Humanoid myth
  nakani
    James W. Van Stone, "The Changing Culture of the Snowdrift Chipewyan," Bull.Nat'l Mus.Canada, no.209 (1965), p.105.

Spence Bay
-UFO (NL)
  1978, Jan.25
    (Editorial), Res Bureaux Bull., no. 29 (9 Feb.1978):5.

Swift River
-UFO (NL)
  1965-1968/Mrs. John McCreedy
    "Strange Air Traffic," Can.UFO Rept., no.1 (Jan.-Feb.1969):6-8.

Whitehorse
-Seance
  1960s
    Sheila Hervey, Some Canadian Ghosts (Richmond Hill, Ont.: Pocket Books, 1973), pp.142-46.
-UFO (CE-2)
  1968, Jan.5/Tom Banks/Grey Mt.
    "French General, Scientists, Report UFOs," UFO Inv. 4 (May-June 1968):3.
  1974, Dec./Alcan Hwy.
    Timothy Green Beckley, "Operation Contact," Saga UFO Rept. 3 (Apr. 1976):39,64, quoting Whitehorse Star (undated).
-UFO (NL)
  1968, Dec./Fred Koch/Grey Mt.
    "Another Odd Northern Mountain Light," Can.UFO Rept., no.2 (Mar.-Apr.1969): 18-20, quoting Whitehorse Star (undated).
  1969, March 12
    "The Maritimes: Newest Playground for UFOs?" Flying Saucers, no.69 (June 1970):12,15.

B. Physical Features

Angikuni L.
-Disappearance
  1930, Nov./Joe Labelle/=hoax
    Emmett E. Kelleher, "Tribe Lost in Barrens of North," Halifax (N.S.) Herald, 29 Nov.1930. il.
    Murray T. Pringle, "The Eskimo Village Mystery," Fate 8 (Mar.1955): 103-104.
    "That Disappearing Eskimo 'Village,'" Pursuit 6 (July 1973):58.
    Dwight Whalen, "Vanished Village Revisited," Fate 29 (Nov.1976):67-70.
    (Letter), Betty Hill, Fate 30 (Apr. 1977):113.

Baffin I.
-Norse discovery
  1001/Leif Eriksson/=Helluland?

Arlington H. Mallery, Lost America (Washington: Public Affairs, 1950), pp.56-57.

Bathurst Inlet
-Climatic anomaly
  1958, Sep./W.R. Newman
    (Editorial), Fate 12 (Feb.1959):6-8.

Beaufort Sea
-Underwater mounds
  120 km.NW of Atkinson Pt.
    J.M. Shearer, et al., "Submarine Pingos in the Beaufort Sea," Science 174 (1971):816-18.

Bylot I.
-Humanoid encampment
  =Dorset archeological site?
    Katherine Scherman, Spring on an Arctic Island (Boston: Little, Brown, 1956), pp.157-64.

Camsell Bend
-Ghost
  1860, March 15,18/Roderick Macfarlane/Mackenzie R.
    R.S. Lambert, Exploring the Supernatural (Toronto: McClelland & Stewart, 1955), pp.156-61, quoting The Beaver, 1920.

Canyon Creek
-UFO (CE-1)
  1966, Dec./Bob McKinnon/Indian graveyard
    "Did UFOs Think Small Men Lived in Graveyards?" Can.UFO Rept., no.1 (Jan.-Feb.1969):8-10.
-UFO (NL)
  1968, Jan.31/Pieter van der Veen
    "Second Visit near Graves," Can.UFO Rept., no.1 (Jan.-Feb.1969):10.

Chesterfield Inlet
-Norse discovery
  1005/Thorfinn Karlsefni/=Straumfjord?
    Edward Reman, The Norse Discoveries and Explorations in America (Berkeley: Univ. California, 1949), pp. 138-46.
-UFO (CE-2)
  1960s
    J. Allen Hynek & Jacques Vallee, The Edge of Reality (Chicago: Regnery, 1975), pp.xiii-xv.

Coppermine R.
-Archeological site
  ca.1350 B.C./Bloody Falls
    Robert McGhee, "Excavations at Bloody Falls, N.W.T.," Arctic Anthro. 6 (1970):53-73.
-Shamanism
    John Mason Browne, "Indian Medicine," Atlantic Monthly 18 (July 1866): 113-19.

Cumberland Peninsula
-Norse discovery
  ca.1001/=part of Greenland colony?

Farley Mowat, Westviking (Totowa,
N.J.: Minerva, 1968), pp.62-65,330-
43.

Devon I.
-Meteorite crater
30,000 m.diam./Haughton/probable
J. Classen, "Catalogue of 230...Im-
pact Structures," Meteoritics 12
(1977):61,69.

Dorset, Cape
-Archeological site
ca.600 B.C.-1000 A.D.
Diamond Jenness, "A New Eskimo Cul-
ture in Hudson Bay," Geogr.Rev. 15
(1925):428-37. il.
Hans-Georg Bandi, Eskimo Prehistory
(College: Univ. Alaska, 1969). il.

Dubawnt L.
-Lake monster
angeoa
Farley Mowat, People of the Deer
(Boston: Little, Brown, 1952), pp.
313-16.

Firth R.
-Archeological site
16,000-11,000 B.C./Engigstciak
R.S. MacNeish, "The Engigstciak Site
on the Yukon Arctic Coast," Anthro.
Pap.Univ.Alaska 4 (May 1956):91-111.
il.

Fox L.
-UFO (CE-1)
1975, Nov.16/Arnold Emslie
Vancouver Province, 19 Nov.1975.
Edmonton (Alb.) Journal, 19 Nov.1975.

Frobisher Bay
-Archeological sites
Henry B. Collins, "Excavations at
Frobisher Bay, Baffin Island, North-
west Territories," Bull.Nat'l Mus.
Canada, no.118 (1949):18-43.
-Rock pillars
Silliman's Fossil Mount
Sharat K. Roy, "Columnar Structures
in Limestone," Science 70 (1929):
140-41.

Fullerton, Cape
-Humanoid corpses
1631/Luke Foxe
Luke Foxe, The Voyages of Captain
Luke Foxe of Hull, Hakluyt Soc'y
Works, ser.1, vol.89 (London: Hak-
luyt Soc'y, 1897), pp.319-20.

Grant L.
-Archeological site
6000 B.C.-recent
Bryan H.C. Gordon, "Migod--8,000
Years of Barrenland Prehistory,"
Pap.Arch.Survey Canada, no.56 (1976).
il.

Great Bear L.
-Humanoid myth

nakani
Cornelius B. Osgood, "The Ethnography
of the Great Bear Lake Indians,"
Bull.Nat'l Mus.Canada, no.70 (1931);
31,85-86.
June Helen MacNeish, "Contemporary
Folk Beliefs of a Slave Indian Band,"
J.Am.Folklore 67 (1954):185-88.

King William I.
-Disappearance
1845/Sir John Franklin/=ships icebound
Vilhjalmur Stefansson, Unsolved Mys-
teries of the Arctic (N.Y.: Macmil-
lan, 1939), pp.36-129.
Leslie H. Neatby, The Search for
Franklin (London: Barker, 1970). il.
Roderic Owen, The Fate of Franklin
(London: Hutchinson, 1978). il.

Kluane L.
-UFO (NL)
1969, Feb./Jim Jack/Alaska Hwy.
"Drivers See Giant Object," Can.UFO
Rept., no.1 (Jan.-Feb.1969):3-5.

Lancaster Sound
-Doubtful geography
1818/John Ross/Croker Mts./=visual defect?
L.P. Kirwan, History of Polar Exploration (N.Y.: W.W. Norton, 1960), pp.
83-86.

Loon L.
-Archeological site
Wesley L. Bliss, "Early Man in Western and Northwestern Canada," Science
89 (1939):365-66.

Mackenzie R.
-Seance
1929, July/A.K. Black/White Sands/=
shaking tent
R.S. Lambert, Exploring the Supernatural (Toronto: McClelland & Stewart,
1955), pp.39-41, quoting The Beaver
(undated).

Mansel I.
-Archeological site
1500-1000 B.C./Arnapik site
William E. Taylor, Jr., "The Arnapik
and Tyara Sites: An Archaeological
Study of Dorset Culture Origins,"
Mem.Soc'y Am.Arch., no.22 (1968).

Marble I.
-Ball lightning
1867, July 1/"Orray Taft"
Robert Seyhoth, "An Instance of Ball
Lightning at Sea," Monthly Weather
Rev. 29 (June 1901):249-50.
-Shamanism
Robert Ferguson, "Record of a Case of
Anticoot As Practised Among the Es-
quimaux of the Northern Shores of
Hudson Bay," J.ASPR 3 (1909):54-61.

Meen L.
-Meteorite crater
  4000 m.diam./possible
    J. Classen, "Catalogue of 230...Im-
    pact Structures," Meteoritics 12
    (1977):61,69.

Melville I.
-Meteorite crater
  doubtful
    I.C. Brown, "Circular Structures in
    the Arctic Islands," Am.J.Sci. 249
    (1951):785-94.

Nicholson I.
-Meteorite crater
  12,500 m.diam./certain
    J. Classen, "Catalogue of 230...Im-
    pact Structures," Meteoritics 12
    (1977):61,69.

North Pole
-Doubtful responsibility
  1908-1909/Frederick A. Cook/=first to
  reach pole?
    Frederick A. Cook, My Attainment of
    the Pole (N.Y.: Polar Pub.Co., 1911).
    Marshall B. Gardner, A Journey to the
    Earth's Interior (Aurora, Ill.: The
    Author, 1913).
    Thomas F. Hall, Has the North Pole
    Been Discovered?, 2 vols. (Boston:
    R.G. Badger, 1917-20).
    H.H. Houben, The Call of the North
    (London: E. Mathews & Marrot, 1932).
    J. Gordon Hayes, The Conquest of the
    North Pole (N.Y.: Macmillan, 1934).
    W. Henry Lewin, The Great North Pole
    Fraud (London: C.W. Daniel, 1935).
    Russell W. Gibbons, An Historical
    Evaluation of the Cook-Peary Contro-
    versy (Ada: Ohio Northern Univ.,
    1954).
    Frederick A. Cook, Return from the
    Pole (N.Y.: Pellegrini & Cudahy,
    1951).
    Russell W. Gibbons, "Dr. Frederick A.
    Cook: American Dreyfus?" Doubt, no.
    52 (1956):403-406.
    "Apologies to Leitzell," Doubt, no.
    53 (1956):416.
    Theon Wright, The Big Nail (N.Y.:
    John Day, 1970).
    Dennis Rawlins, Peary at the North
    Pole: Fact or Fiction? (Washington:
    Robert B. Luce, 1973).
    Hugh Eames, Winner Lose All: Dr. Cook
    and the Theft of the North Pole
    (Boston: Little, Brown, 1973).
-Hollow earth entrance
    Adam Seaborn [John Cleves Symmes],
    Symzonia: A Voyage of Discovery
    (N.Y.: J. Seymour, 1820).
    James McBride, Symmes' Theory of Con-
    centric Spheres (Cincinnati: Morgan,
    Lodge & Fisher, 1826).
    M.L. Sherman & William F. Lyon, The
    Hollow Globe (Chicago: Religio-Phil-
    osophical Pub.House, 1871).
    Americus Symmes, The Symmes Theory

of Concentric Spheres (Louisville,
Ky.: Bradley & Gilbert, 1878).
Frederick Culmer, The Inner World
(Salt Lake City: The Author, 1886).
William Reed, The Phantom of the
Poles (N.Y.: Walter S. Rockey, 1906).
John Wells Peck, "Symmes' Theory,"
Ohio Arch.& Hist.Quar. 18 (1909):
28-42.
Marshall B. Gardner, A Journey to the
Earth's Interior (Aurora, Ill.: The
Author, 1913).
Edna Kenton, The Book of Earths
(N.Y.: W. Morrow, 1928).
William Marion Miller, "The Theory
of Concentric Spheres," Isis 33
(Dec.1941):507-14.
Conway Zirkle, "The Theory of Con-
centric Spheres," Isis 37 (July
1947):155-59.
Amadeo Giannini, Worlds Beyond the
Poles (N.Y.: Vantage, 1959).
"'Byrd Did Make North Pole Flight in
Feb., 1947!'--Giannini," Flying Sau-
cers, Feb.1961, pp.4-11.
J.L. Parkhurst, Jr., "The Curious
World of Captain Symmes," Sea Fron-
tiers 7 (Nov.1961):208-10.
Raymond Bernard, The Hollow Earth
(N.Y.: Fieldcrest, 1964).
Joseph H. Cater, "The Hole at the
Pole," Search 84 (Mar.1969):17-25.
Jack Scaparro, "Lost Continents Be-
yond the Poles," Saga, Feb.1970,
pp.22-25,75-81.
"Editorial," Flying Saucers, June
1970, pp.2-6. il.
"More Photos of the North Pole,"
Flying Saucers, Dec.1970, pp.16-20.
il.
Eric Norman Warren Smith, This Hol-
low Earth (N.Y.: Lancer, 1972).
Brinsley Le Poer Trench, Secret of
the Ages (N.Y.: Pinnacle, 1977 ed.).

Old Crow Flats
-Archeological site
  ca.28,000 B.C.
    "Phenomena: Comment and Notes,"
    Smithsonian 4 (Apr.1973):10-11.
    Albert A. Dekin, Jr., "The Arctic,"
    in James E. Fitting, ed., The Devel-
    opment of North American Archaeology
    (N.Y.: Anchor, 1973), p.37.
    Thomas Y. Canby, "The Search for the
    First Americans," Nat'l Geographic
    156 (1979):330-63. il.

Partridge Creek
-Land monster
  1901/Georges Depuy/=hoax?
    Harold T. Wilkins, Secret Cities of
    Old South America (N.Y.: Library
    Publishers, 1952), pp.322-25.

Pelly Bay
-Archeological site
    G. Rousselière, "Palaeo-Eskimo Re-
    mains in the Pelly Bay Region, N.W.
    T.," Contrib.to Anthro., Canada

Nat'l Mus. (1964), pt.1, pp.162-83.

Pilot L.
-Meteorite crater
  6700 m.diam. x 68 m.deep/certain
    J. Classen, "Catalogue of 230...Im-
    pact Structures," Meteoritics 12
    (1977):61,68.

Pointed Mt.
-Archeological site
  ca.10,000-8000 B.C.
    Richard S. MacNeish, "The Pointed
    Mountain Site near Fort Liard, N.W.
    T., Canada," Am.Antiquity 19 (1954):
    234-53. il.

Repulse Bay
-Archeological site
  1000 A.D./Naujan
    Therkel Mathiassen, "Preliminary Re-
    port of the Fifth Thule Expedition:
    Archaeology," 21st Int'l Cong.of
    Americanists, 1925, pp.202-15.

South Nahanni R.
-Giant wolf
  =Dinocyon?
    Ivan T. Sanderson, "The Dire Wolf,"
    Pursuit 7 (Oct.1974):91-94.
-Humanoids and disappearances
  1904-   /Headless Valley/William &
  Frank McLeod
    "Watts Missing," Doubt, no.17 (1947):
    252.
    "Fortean Expedition," Doubt, no.20
    (1948):301-302.
    R.M. Patterson, The Dangerous River
    (London: Allen & Unwin, 1954), pp.
    19-40.
    Pierre Berton, The Mysterious North
    (N.Y.: Knopf, 1956), pp.55-76.
    Winnipeg (Man.) Free Press, 13 Aug.
    1968.
    London (Eng.) Daily Express, 6 Apr.
    1971.
    Ranulph Fiennes, The Headless Valley
    (London: Hodder & Stoughton, 1973),
    pp.78-82.

Takhini R.
-UFO (CE-1)
  1976, Dec.26/Tom Banks/Takhini Bridge
    "Why the Sick or Dead?" Can.UFO Rept.,
    no.26 (1976):4-5.

Teslin L.
-Lake monster
  1977, June 5
    Whitehorse Star, 8 June 1977.

Victoria I.
-Patterned ground
  Holman Island post
    A.L. Washburn, "Classification of Pat-
    terned Ground and Review of Sugges-
    ted Origins," Bull.Geol.Soc'y Am.
    67 (1956):823-66. il.

Wellington Channel
-UFO (DD)
  1850, Sep.15/Elisha Kent Kane
    Elisha Kent Kane, The U.S. Grinnel
    Expedition in Search of Sir John
    Franklin (N.Y.: Harper, 1854), p.190.

Winter I.
-Acoustic anomaly
  1822, Feb.9/W.E. Parry
    Rupert T. Gould, Enigmas (London:
    Geoffrey Blas, 1929), pp.36-39.

            C. Ethnic Groups

Copper Eskimo
-Shamanism
    Knud Rasmussen, "Intellectual Culture
    of the Copper Eskimos," in Report
    of the Fifth Thule Expedition 1921-
    24, 10 vols. (Copenhagen: Gyldendal-
    ske, 1932), 9:27-36.

Eskimo (generally)
-Humanoid myth
  tunit, tornait, toonijuk
    Franz Boas, "Traditions of the Ts'-
    ets'a'ut," J.Am.Folklore 10 (1897):
    35-48.
    Alfred L. Kroeber, "Tales of Smith
    Sound Eskimos," J.Am.Folklore 12
    (1899):166-82.
    Katherine Scherman, Spring on an
    Arctic Island (Boston: Little,
    Brown, 1956), pp.158-59.
    Franz Boas. The Central Eskimo (Lin-
    coln: Univ.of Nebraska, 1964 ed.),
    pp.226-32.
    Hans-Georg Bandi, Eskimo Prehistory
    (College: Univ.of Alaska, 1969),
    pp.148-49.

Kutchin Indians
-Humanoid myth
  weetigo, mahoni, nain
    Michael Mason, The Arctic Forests
    (London: Hodder & Stoughton, 1924),
    pp.60-61.
    Cornelius Osgood, "Contributions to
    the Ethnography of the Kutchin,"
    Pub.Anthro.Yale Univ., no.14 (1936):
    154,157.
    Pierre Berton, The Mysterious North
    (N.Y.: Knopf, 1956), pp.10-11.
    Richard Slobodia, "Some Social Func-
    tions of Kutchin Anxiety," Am.Anthro.
    62 (1960):122,126-29.

          D. Unspecified Localities

-Doubtful geography
  1906/Robert E. Peary/Crocker Land/86°
  N.lat./=looming
    William Herbert Hobbs, Peary (N.Y.:
    Macmillan, 1936), pp.279,289-99.
    Theo Loebsack, Our Atmosphere (N.Y.:
    Mentor, 1961 ed.), pp.39-40.

Theon Wright, The Big Nail (N.Y.:
   John Day, 1970).
1908/Frederick A. Cook/Bradley Land
   Edwin Swift Balch, The North Pole
   and Bradley Land (Philadelphia:
   Campion, 1913).
   Theon Wright, The Big Nail (N.Y.:
   John Day, 1970).

-Haunt
   1961/Alcan Hwy. nr. Indian battlefield
   Sheila Hervey, Some Canadian Ghosts
   (Richmond Hill, Ont.: Pocket Books,
   1973), pp.141-42.

-Humanoid
   1940s/Yukon
   John Green, The Sasquatch File (Agassiz, B.C.: Cheam, 1973), p.17.

-Humanoid tracks
   1924/James Alan Rennie
   James Alan Rennie, Romantic Strath-
   spey (London: Robert Hale, 1956),
   pp.81-82.

-UFO (NL)
   1968, Nov./150 mi.N of Yellowknife
   Jeff Holt, "Rencontre avec un UFO
   dans le grand Nord," UFO-Quebec,
   no.4 (1975):17.

BRITISH COLUMBIA

A. Populated Places

Abbotsford
-UFO (?)
  1973, Sep.9/Robert Dyck
  1973, Sep.10/Mrs. Jake Redekop/29760
  Marshall Extension/=meteor?
    Abbotsford, Samas and Matsqui News,
    19 Sep.1973.

Agassiz
-Archeological site
  McCallum site
    Marian W. Smith, "Archaeology of the
    Columbia-Fraser Region," Mem.Soc'y
    Am.Arch., no.6 (1950).
-Humanoid
  1927, Sep./William Point/Canadian Pacific RR
    J.W. Burns, "Introducing B.C.'s Hairy
    Giants," MacLean's Mag., 1 Apr.1929,
    p.61.
-Humanoid tracks
  1940s
  1961, Apr.19/Mrs. Gerry Stary
  ca.1964/Jean Robertson/Herrling I.
    John Green, The Sasquatch File (Ag-
    assiz, B.C.: Cheam, 1973), pp.14,
    25,27.

Alert Bay
-Humanoid
  1930s/Ellen Neal
    John Green, The Sasquatch File (Ag-
    assiz, B.C.: Cheam, 1973), p.14.

Alexis Creek
-UFO (DD)
  1969/Alexander Robertson
    "New Flap Starts," Can.UFO Rept.,
    no. 6 (Nov.-Dec.1969):17.

Anahim Lake
-Humanoid
  1962, fall/Harry Squiness/Goose Pt.
  1969, Oct.25/Pan Phillips/25 mi.N
    John Green, The Sasquatch File (Ag-
    assiz, B.C.: Cheam, 1973), pp.26,
    41-42.

Bella Bella
-Humanoid
  1963/Jack Wilson
    John Green, The Sasquatch File (Ag-
    assiz, B.C.: Cheam, 1973), p.27.
-UFO (DD)
  1965, Sep./Alex Macdonell
    "Spot News," Can.UFO Rept., no.25
    (fall 1976):21-22.
-UFO (NL)
  1974, winter/Bert Stevens
    "Spot News," Can.UFO Rept., no.25
    (fall 1976):21.

Bella Coola
-Humanoid
  n.d./Qaktlis
    T.F. McIlwraigh, "Certain Beliefs of
    the Bella Coola Indians," Ontario
    Arch.Rept., 1924-25, pp.21-22.
  1962, Apr./Bella Coola R.
    John Green, The Sasquatch File (Ag-
    assiz, B.C.: Cheam, 1973), p.26.
  1965, Nov./Jimmy Nelson/Green Bay
    John Green, On the Track of the Sas-
    quatch (Agassiz, B.C.: Cheam, 1968),
    p.43.
  1975, winter/Tallheo Cannery
    John Green, Sasquatch: The Apes Among
    Us (Seattle: Hancock House, 1978),
    p.365.

Blue River
-UFO (CE-2)
  1966, May/NE of town
    Hamilton (Ont.) Spectator, 19 Oct.
    1973.

Boat Harbor
-UFO (?)
  1968, Dec./Mary A. Kendall/=planet
    (Letter), Can.UFO Rept., no.2 (Mar.-
    Apr.1969):4.

Boundary Bay
-Archeological site
  Great Fraser Midden
    Charles Hill-Tout, "Later Prehistoric
    Man in British Columbia," Proc.Royal
    Soc'y Canada, ser.2, vol.1 (1895):
    103-22.
    Charles Hill-Tout, "The Great Fraser
    Midden," Museum & Art Notes (Vancou-
    ver) 5 (1930):75-83. il.

Bridesville
-Humanoid
  1937/Jane Patterson
    John Green, Sasquatch: The Apes Among
    Us (Seattle: Hancock House, 1978),
    pp.63-64.

Brilliant
-Inner development
  1899-   /Dukhobors
    Frank L. Remington, "They Strip to
    Conquer," Fate 5 (Feb.-Mar.1952):
    79-83. il.
    Doukhobor Research Committee, The
    Doukhobors of British Columbia (Van-
    couver: Univ. of British Columbia,
    1955).
    Marcus Bach, "The Mad, Bad Douks,"
    Fate 15 (Oct.1962):44-51. il.
    (Letter), Beatrice Russell, Fate 16
    (Mar.1963):109-12.
    (Letter), Marcus Bach, Fate 16 (Mar.
    1963):112-14.

Aylmer Maude, A Peculiar People (N.Y.:
AMS, 1970).
John Norris, Strangers Entertained
(Vancouver: Evergreen, 1971), pp.
191-99.
Mark Mealing, "Doukhobor Society and
Folklore: An Introduction," J.Folkl.
Soc'y Greater Washington 4 (spring
1973):6-12.

Burnaby
-Contactee
1969, Apr.-1971, Oct./Robin McPherson
Brad Steiger, The Aquarian Revela-
tions (N.Y.: Dell, 1971).
Brad Steiger, Gods of Aquarius (N.Y.:
Harcourt Brace Jovanovich, 1976),
pp.89-90.
-Inner development
1969-   /Light Affiliates
Brad Steiger, The Aquarian Revela-
tions (N.Y.: Dell, 1971).
Brad Steiger, Revelation: The Divine
Fire (Englewood Cliffs, N.J.: Pren-
tice-Hall, 1973), pp.203-207.
Brad Steiger, Gods of Aquarius (N.Y.:
Harcourt Brace Jovanovich, 1976),
pp.89-97.

Burns Lake
-UFO (NL)
1979, Jan.3
"Recent UFO Reports," Res Bureaux
Bull., no.43 (Jan.1979):3,4.

Butedale
-Humanoid
1965, July/Jack Taylor
John Green, The Sasquatch File (Ag-
assiz, B.C.: Cheam, 1973), p.33.
John Green, Sasquatch: The Apes Among
Us (Seattle: Hancock House, 1978),
p.432.

Campbell River
-Sea monster
1962, Feb.13/Alan Maclean
Vancouver Province, 13 Feb.1962; and
16 Feb.1962.
Seattle (Wash.) Post-Intelligencer,
29 Dec.1962.

Castlegar
-Humanoid
1974/Castlegar-Silverton Hwy.
Peter Byrne, The Search for Bigfoot
(N.Y.: Pocket Books, 1976 ed.), pp.
40-41.
-Humanoid tracks
1972, Dec.24/Gail Davidson
John Green, The Sasquatch File (Agassiz, B.C.: Cheam, 1973), p.52.
-UFO (CE-1)
1966, June 8/Paul Hadikin/S of airport
"World Round-up," Flying Saucer Rev.
12 (Nov.-Dec.1966):iii, quoting Castlegar News (undated).

Chemainus
-Sea monster

1937, June
Vancouver Province, 17 June 1937, p.1.
1938, Dec.6/"Catala Chief"
Vancouver Sun, 8 Dec.1938, p.14.
1939, Mar./Billy Shillito
Vancouver Sun, 17 Mar.1939, p.1.
-UFO (NL)
1969, Mar.22/Mrs. W.R. Bazett
(Letter), Can.UFO Rept., no.4 (July-
Aug.1969):1.

Chetwynd
-Humanoid
1968, Sep.14/Eddie Barnett
John Green, The Sasquatch File (Agassiz, B.C.: Cheam, 1973), p.41.
-Humanoid tracks
1977, Aug.8/Marilyn Wiles/50 mi.S
Seattle (Wash.) Post-Intelligencer,
28 Aug.1977.
"Latest News from the Pacific Northwest," Bigfoot News, no.36 (Sep.
1977):1; no.41 (Feb.1978):1. il.

Chilliwack
-Haunt
1966/Hetty Frederickson/342 Williams
St. N
(Editorial), Fate 19 (Oct.1966):24-
26.
Sheila Hervey, Some Canadian Ghosts
(Richmond Hill, Ont.: Pocket Books,
1973), pp.21-27.
-Poltergeist
1951, Oct.-1952/Anna Duryba
"The Poltergeist of Chilliwack," Fate
5 (July-Aug.1952):91.
R.S. Lambert, Exploring the Supernat-
ural (Toronto: McClelland & Stewart,
1955), pp.147-49.
-UFO (?)
1958, Oct.17
"The Night of September 29," Fate 12
(Feb.1959):31,38.
-UFO (CE-2)
1978, April 6
Chilliwack Progress, 12 Apr.1978.
"Other UFOs," Res Bureaux Bull., no.
35 (15 June 1978):3.
-UFO (NL)
1974, Nov.19
Timothy Green Beckley, "Operation
Contact," Saga UFO Rept. 3 (Apr.
1976):39,62.

Clayoquot
-Sea monster
1791/"Clayoquot"
Harold T. Wilkins, Secret Cities of
Old South America (N.Y.: Library
Publishers, 1952), p.289.

Cobble Hill
-UFO (?)
1977, Jan./Lois Smith
"Spot News," Can.UFO Rept., no.26
(winter 1976-77):19-20.

Colwood
-UFO (CE-2)

1972, Oct.5/Mrs. R. Rennie
  Ted Phillips, Physical Traces Associ-
  ated with UFO Sightings (Evanston:
  Center for UFO Studies, 1975), p.87.

Comox
-Sea monster
  1946, June 23/Winnifred Grist
    Paul H. LeBlond & John Sibert, Obser-
    vations of Large Unidentified Marine
    Animals in British Columbia and Ad-
    jacent Waters (Vancouver: Univ. of
    British Columbia, Inst. of Ocean-
    ography, Manuscript Rept. no.28,
    June 1973), p.32.

Coombes
-Humanoid
  1940s/Alex Oakes
    John Green, The Sasquatch File (Ag-
    assiz, B.C.: Cheam, 1973), p.14.

Courtenay
-Humanoid
  1953, Sep./Jack Twist/20 mi.NW
    John Green, The Sasquatch File (Ag-
    assiz, B.C.: Cheam, 1973), p.18.

Cowichan Bay
-Sea monster
  1945, Feb.
    Mary Moon, Ogopogo (N.Pomfret, Vt.:
    David & Charles, 1977), p.161.
-UFO (NL)
  n.d./Mrs. W.H. Cross
    (Letter), Can.UFO Rept., no.11 (1971):
    33-34.
  1977, March/Denis Hagar
    "CUFOR in Mini-Invasion," Can.UFO
    Rept., no.27 (spring 1977):7.

Cowichan Station
-UFO (CE-3)
  1970, Jan.1/Doreen Kendall/Cowichan
  District Hospital
    Victoria Daily Times, 5 Jan.1970.
    Cowichan Leader, 7 Jan.1970.
    "The Cowichan Occupant Case," APRO
    Bull. 18 (Jan.-Feb.1970):1,3.
    John Magor, Our UFO Visitors (Seat-
    tle: Hancock House, 1977), pp.4-7.

Cranbrook
-UFO (CE-1)
  1969, Oct./Lorraine Goodwin
    "Playground of Gods," Can.UFO Rept.,
    no.11 (1971):2,5.

Crescent Beach
-UFO (NL)
  1974/John R. King
    (Letter), Saga UFO Rept. 4 (July
    1977):79-80.

Crofton
-Sea monster
  1960, March 24/Everett Wilson/Graves
  Pt.
    (Editorial), Fate 13 (Aug.1960):10-11.
-UFO (?)

1959, Oct.3/Mrs. G.B. Barnes
  (Editorial), Fate 13 (Feb.1960):22.

Dawson Creek
-UFO (?)
  1965, March 31/=meteor?
    Richard Hunt, "Canadian Fireballs,"
    Flying Saucer Rev. 12 (Mar.-Apr.
    1966):33.
-UFO (CE-2)
  1972, Feb.16/K.B. Miller
    "Power Project Examined," Can.UFO
    Rept., no.14 (1973):12, 14-15.
    Ted Phillips, Physical Traces Associ-
    ated with UFO Sightings (Evanston:
    Center for UFO Studies, 1975), p.81.

Delta
-UFO (CE-2)
  1974, Aug.28
    Ted R. Phillips, Jr., "Unidentified
    Flying Objects: The Emerging Evi-
    dence," in MUFON 1975 UFO Symposium
    Proc. (Seguin, Tex.: MUFON, 1975),
    p.105.

Duncan
-UFO (?)
  1970, Jan.6/Mrs. G.C. Drinnen
    "Press Reports," APRO Bull. 18 (Jan.-
    Feb.1970):4.
-UFO (CE-1)
  1908, summer/Win Dovey
    (Letter), Can.UFO Rept., no.8 (fall
    1970):36.
  1966, March 25/Albert Kershaw/6 mi.SW
    Victoria Daily Times, 26 Mar.1966.
    "Huge Object Enters Forest," Can.UFO
    Rept., no.4 (July-Aug.1969):9-11.
-UFO (NL)
  1967, Aug./Klaus Muenter
    Klaus Muenter, "UFO Keeps Date with
    Boys," Can.UFO Rept., no.2 (Mar.-
    Apr.1969):9-10.
  1969, March 7/Mrs. William Marshall
    (Letter), Can.UFO Rept., no.3 (May-
    June 1969):4.
  1970, Jan.7/Jim Quaifc
    "Canadian Mayor and Wife See UFO,"
    Skylook, no.30 (May 1970):13.
  1972, Jan./Mel Arenada
    "Power Project Examined," Can.UFO
    Rept., no.14 (1973):12-13.

Edgewater
-UFO (NL)
  1963, spring/Katherine Beamish/S of
  town
    "Playground of Gods," Can.UFO Rept.,
    no.11 (1971):2, 8-9.

Errington
-UFO (CE-1)
  1970, May/Mrs. Jack Graepner
    (Letter), Can.UFO Rept., no.12 (1972):
    31.
-UFO (NL)
  1975, Oct.1/Elin Graepner
    (Letter), Can.UFO Rept., no.23
    (spring 1976):21.

Esquimault
-Sea monster
  1937, Sep.
    Mary Moon, Ogopogo (N.Pomfret, Vt.:
      David & Charles, 1977), p.157.
-UFO (DD)
  1966, Aug.
    Victoria Daily Colonist, 6 Aug.1966.
-UFO (NL)
  1968, Sep.19/Hermanus Voorsluys
    Brian C. Cannon, "Canadian Sighting
      Investigated," Skylook, no.23 (Oct.
      1969):9-12.
    John Magor, Our UFO Visitors (Seat-
      tle: Hancock House, 1977), p.146.
      il.

Fairmont Hot Springs
-UFO (NL)
  1976, Sep./Vern Sattmann
    "Matching Cases," Can.UFO Rept., no.
      33 (winter 1978-79):14.

Flood
-Humanoid
  1956, May 17/Stanley Hunt/Hwy.1
    Toronto (Ont.) Globe, 6 July 1957.

Fort Nelson
-UFO (NL)
  1967, March/Lloyd Arychuk/Steamboat Mt.
    "Canada's Year of 'Invasion': Part
      3," Can.UFO Rept., no.8 (fall 1970):
      17,23, quoting Fort Nelson News (un-
      dated).

Fort Saint James
-UFO (NL)
  1976, Jan.9/Mrs. Inger Larsson
    (Letter), Shelley E. Hallock, Can.
      UFO Rept., no.28 (summer 1977):3.

Fort Saint John
-Crisis apparition
  1934/Gordon Sculthorpe
    Sheila Hervey, Some Canadian Ghosts
      (Richmond Hill, Ont.: Pocket Books,
      1973), pp.149-51.

Gibsons
-UFO (DD)
  1977, April 5/E.R. East
    (Letter), Can.UFO Rept., no.28 (sum-
      mer 1977):[25].
-UFO (NL)
  1966, fall/Mrs. Ewart McMynn
    Bernice Niblett, "I Lived in a Nest
      of UFOs," Can.UFO Rept., no.13
      (1972):2,10.
  1967/E.R. East
    John Magor, Our UFO Visitors (Seat-
      tle: Hancock House, 1977), pp.37-38.

Glenora
-UFO (CE-2)
  1959, Sep.30/Gaynor Wilson
    Vancouver Sun, 5 Oct.1959.

Gold River
-UFO (CE-2)

1968, Dec.1/Bus Stevens
  "UFO Dances over Valley," Can.UFO
    Rept., no.2 (Mar.-Apr.1969):4.
-UFO (DD)
  1967, winter/Ralph R. Hodgson
    (Letter), Can.UFO Rept., no.15
      (1973):31.

Golden
-Humanoid tracks
  1968, March/E of town
    John Green, The Sasquatch File (Ag-
      assiz, B.C.: Cheam, 1973), p.41.

Goldstream
-UFO (DD)
  1897, Aug.1/Mr. Tatum
    Portland Oregonian, 3 Aug.1897.

Grantham's Landing
-UFO (NL)
  1968/Mrs. G.E. Webb
    (Letter), Can.UFO Rept., no.13 (1972).
  1971, summer/Anne Prewer
    Bernice Niblett, "I Lived in a Nest
      of UFOs," Can.UFO Rept., no.13
      (1972):2,10.

Grassy Plains
-UFO (CE-1)
  1959, April 29/Alex Gillis
    "World Roundup," Flying Saucer Rev.
      5 (Nov.-Dec.1959):20, quoting Van-
      couver Sun (undated).

Grindrod
-UFO (DD)
  1968, Nov.22/Mrs. C.M. Karpowich
    "'Dark Mass' with Lights," Can.UFO
      Rept., no.4 (July-Aug.1969):8.

Harrison Hot Springs
-Humanoid
  1970, April 2
    John Green, The Sasquatch File (Ag-
      assiz, B.C.: Cheam, 1973), p.50.

Harrison Mills
-Humanoid
  1935
    R.S. Lambert, Exploring the Supernat-
      ural (Toronto: McClelland & Stewart,
      1955), pp.179-80.
  1965, fall
    John Green, The Sasquatch File (Ag-
      assiz, B.C.: Cheam, 1973), p.33.

Hartley Bay
-Humanoid
  1967, Feb./island
    John Green, The Sasquatch File (Ag-
      assiz, B.C.: Cheam, 1973), p.34.

Hatzic
-Humanoid
  ca.1914/Charley Victor
    J.W. Burns, "Introducing B.C.'s Hairy
      Giants," MacLean's Mag., 1 Apr.1929,
      p.61.

Hazelton
-UFO (DD)
  1897, July 3/Robert Loring
    Portland Oregonian, 12 Aug.1897.

Hixon
-Humanoid
  1962, Aug./Mrs. Calhoun/Caribou Hwy.
    Don Hunter & René Dahinden, Sasquatch
    (Toronto: McClelland & Stewart,
    1973), pp.100-101.

Hope
-Humanoid tracks
  1971, winter/Eileen Yerxa/14 mi.E
    John Green, The Sasquatch File (Ag-
    assiz, B.C.: Cheam, 1973), p.51.
-UFO (NL)
  1973, Aug.25/Mrs. Lorne Nicholson/10
  mi.N
    Abbotsford, Samas and Matsqui News,
    19 Sep.1973.

Horsefly
-UFO (DD)
  1897, Aug./J.B. Hobson/Hydraulic Mining Co.
    "An Interesting Rumor Concerning An-
    drée," Nat'l Geogr.Mag. 9 (March
    1898):102.

Inkaneep Reservation
-Petroglyph
  =depicts UFO?
    John Corner, Pictographs in the In-
    terior of British Columbia (Vernon,
    B.C.: Wayside, 1968), pp.76-79. il.

Invermere
-Humanoid
  n.d.
    John Green, Sasquatch: The Apes Among
    Us (Seattle: Hancock House, 1978),
    p.368.
  1960s
    John Green, The Sasquatch File (Ag-
    assiz, B.C.: Cheam, 1973), p.26.
-UFO (CE-2)
  1969, Nov./S of town
    "Playground of Gods," Can.UFO Rept.,
    no.11 (1971):2,4-5.

Juskatla
-Humanoid
  1970, March
    Vancouver Sun, 24 June 1970.

Kamloops
-Humanoid
  1975, Jan.25-26/Shawn Olszewski/Broc-
  klehurst Reservoir
    Kamloops Daily Sentinel, 28 Jan.1975,
    p.1.
    Vancouver Sun, 28 Jan.1975.
-Psychokinesis
  1896, spring/Matthew F. Crawford/Kam-
  loops L.
    Julie C. Crawford, "The Psychic War-
    ning That Stopped the Train," Fate
    15 (July 1962):61,64-65.

-UFO (?)
  1965, March 31/=meteor?
    Kamloops Daily Sentinel, 1 Apr.1965.
  1965, Aug./=satellite?
    Orin Browning, "Mystery of the Alien
    Satellites," Saga UFO Rept. 2 (sum-
    mer 1975):34,37.

Kaslo
-Humanoid tracks
  1978, Dec./Roy Green
    Lewiston (Id.) Morning Tribune, 8
    Dec.1978.

Katz
-Humanoid
  1942/one mi. from town
    Don Hunter & René Dahinden, Sasquatch
    (Toronto: McClelland & Stewart,
    1973), pp.81-82.

Keating
-UFO (NL)
  1966, April 1/Paula Gammell
    Victoria Daily Colonist, 3 Apr.1966.

Kelowna
-UFO (CE-1)
  1952, Sep./Stewart Sanborn
    "UFO Startles Ferry Crowd," Can.UFO
    Rept., no.4 (July-Aug.1969):5-8.
-UFO (DD)
  1966, March 1/Alfred Quemby
    Vancouver Daily Province, 2 Mar.1966.

Kemano
-Humanoid
  1963, July/Bob Titmus/S of town
    John Green, The Sasquatch File (Ag-
    assiz, B.C.: Cheam, 1973), p.27.

Keremeos
-Petroglyph
  5 mi.NW
    John Corner, Pictographs in the In-
    terior of British Columbia (Vernon,
    B.C.: Wayside, 1968), il.
    Donald M. Viles, "The Rock of Kere-
    meos," NEARA J. 10 (winter-spring
    1976):57-58. il.

Kimberley
-Humanoid
  1976, Sep./Mickey McLelland
    "Latest News," Bigfoot News, no.24
    (Sep.1976):1.
-UFO (NL)
  1958, Feb.21
    (Editorial), Fate 11 (July 1958):17.

Kitchener
-UFO (NL)
  1977, Aug.3/airstrip
    Creston Review, 10 Aug.1977.

Kitimat
-UFO (NL)
  1969, May 7/Glen S. Yearley
    (Letter), Can.UFO Rept., no.4 (July-
    Aug.1969):1-2.

Kitimat Mission
-Humanoid
  1900s
    John Green, The Sasquatch File (Ag-
    assiz, B.C.: Cheam, 1973), pp.9,12.

Klemtu
-Humanoid
  n.d.
    John Green, On the Track of the Sas-
    quatch (Agassiz, B.C.: Cheam, 1968),
    p.41.
  n.d./Tom Brown
    John Green, Sasquatch: The Apes Among
    Us (Seattle: Hancock House, 1978),
    p.429.
  1970, Feb./Andrew Robinson/one mi.S
  1970, April 23/"Bruce I"/one mi.N
    John Green, The Sasquatch File (Ag-
    assiz, B.C.: Cheam, 1973), p.51.

Lac la Hache
-UFO (CE-1)
  1967, Oct?/Herman Sten
    "Looked Like Air Rescue," Can.UFO
    Rept., no.6 (Nov.-Dec.1969):13-14.

Langley
-Moving rocks
    "Erupting Rocks," Pursuit 6 (April
    1973):33-34.
-UFO (NL)
  1961, Jan.18
  1970, Sep.23
  1971, March 9-12
  1971, Nov.11
  1971, Dec.11-12
    (Letter), Anon., Can.UFO Rept., no.
    12 (1972):30-31.

Lantzville
-Sea monster
  1963, Feb?/W.G. Clark
    Victoria Daily Times, 8 Mar.1963.
-UFO (?)
  1972, July/Mrs. G. Lyons
    (Letter), Can.UFO Rept., no.19 (1975):
    23.

Lillooet
-Anomalous artifact
  =carving of humanoid foot?
    John Green, The Sasquatch File (Ag-
    assiz, B.C.: Cheam, 1973), p.66. il.
-Humanoid tracks
  1968, Nov.16
    John Green, The Sasquatch File (Ag-
    assiz, B.C.: Cheam, 1973), p.41.

Lone Butte
-UFO (CE-1)
  1967, July-1968, Feb./Brian Gratton/
  Big G Ranch
    "Canada Flap Continues," APRO Bull.
    16 (July-Aug.1967):6.
    Jon Ruddy, "Look, There's a Flying
    Saucer," Maclean's Mag. 80 (Nov.
    1967):34-36, 92-94.
    "The Year We Were Invaded Without
    Knowing It," Can.UFO Rept., no.6

(Nov.-Dec.1969):3-7.

Lytton
-Humanoid
  1969, Nov.20/Ivan Wally/3 mi.E on Hwy.1
    John Green, Year of the Sasquatch
    (Agassiz, B.C.: Cheam, 1970), p.29.

McBride
-Humanoid tracks
  1951, Nov.
    John Green, The Sasquatch File (Ag-
    assiz, B.C.: Cheam, 1973), p.18.

McLeese Lake
-UFO (DD)
  1967, Aug.2/Lynn Beck
  1967, Nov.25/Lynn Beck
    "Flying Lights, Cigar and Cowboy Hat,"
    Can.UFO Rept., no.6 (Nov.-Dec.1969):
    7,9.
-UFO (NL)
  1967, Aug.26-27/Mrs. Alfred Beck
    "Flying Lights, Cigar and Cowboy Hat,"
    Can.UFO Rept., no.6 (Nov.-Dec.1969):
    7-9.

Maple Ridge
-UFO (NL)
  1977, Aug.23/Tom Michaud
    Graham Conway, "Flying Diamonds," Can.
    UFO Rept., no.29 (fall-winter 1977):
    2-4.
    Graham Conway, "Maple Ridge 'Dia-
    monds,'" Flying Saucer Rev. 23 (Feb.
    1978):19-21.

Massett
-Humanoid
  1969
    John Green, The Sasquatch File (Ag-
    assiz, B.C.: Cheam, 1973), p.41.

Mill Bay
-UFO (NL)
  1970, Jan.1/Jim Drummond
    Cowichan Leader, 7 Jan.1970.
    "Canadian New Years Day Sightings,"
    APRO Bull. 19 (Jan.-Feb.1970):6-7.

Mission City
-Clairvoyance
  1963, June/Mrs. Mathers
    (Editorial), Fate 16 (Dec.1963):18-
    21.
-Humanoid
  1977, May 15/=hoax
    Vancouver Sun, 16 May 1977; and 27
    May 1977.
    Edmonton (Alb.) Journal, 17 May 1977.
    Dennis Gates, "The Mission, B.C., Big-
    foot Hoax," Pursuit 10 (fall 1977):
    127-28.

Moricetown
-Humanoid
  1961/4 mi.S
    John Green, The Sasquatch File (Ag-
    assiz, B.C.: Cheam, 1973), p.26.

Muncho Lake
-Phantom
  1974, Oct.18/Edmoana Toews
    Edmoana Toews, "The UFOs That Led Us
    Home," Fate 30 (June 1977):38-45;
    (July 1977):63-69.

Nanaimo
-Petrogylphs
  Petroglyph Park
    Douglas Leechman, "The Nanaimo Pet-
    roglyph," Can.Geogr.J. 44 (June
    1952):266-67. il.
    Beth & Ray Hill, Indian Petroglyphs
    of the Pacific Northwest (Seattle:
    Univ. of Washington, 1974), pp.101-
    12. il.
-Precognition
  1942, Nov.11/Mrs. Hugh Woodworth
    "Cases," J.ASPR 37 (1943):143-44.
-Sea monster
  1881, summer/Frank J. Stannard
    Mary Moon, Ogopogo (N.Pomfret, Vt.:
    David & Charles, 1977), pp.159-60.
  ca.1950/Evelyn Leighton
    Paul H. LeBlond & John Sibert, Obser-
    vations of Large Unidentified Marine
    Animals in British Columbia and Ad-
    jacent Waters (Vancouver: Univ. of
    British Columbia, Inst. of Ocean-
    ography, Manuscript Rept. no.28,
    June 1973), pp.20-21.
  1954, Feb.24-25/W. Baldwin
    "Monster of Vancouver I.," Fate 8
    (Mar.1955):37.
-UFO (DD)
  1974, Feb./Lance Willet
    (Editorial), Can.UFO Rept., no.20
    (1975):12. il.
-UFO (NL)
  1959, Oct./Lone Mound
    (Editorial), Fate 14 (Jan.1961):26-
    27.
  1970/Wesley Palmer
    (Letter), Can.UFO Rept., no.8 (fall
    1970):[37].
  1974, Dec.21/Robert Gibson
    (Letter), Can.UFO Rept., no.31 (sum-
    mer 1978):[26].
  1977, March/Dena Lane/Strait of Georgia
    "CUFOR in Mini-Invasion," Can.UFO
    Rept., no.27 (spring 1977):7.
-Witchcraft
  1930s/Brother Twelve
    R.H. Grenville, "Deadly Drama, Re-
    run," Fate 22 (Oct.1969):56.

Nelson
-UFO (?)
  1968, Jan.5/Marilyn Horser
    Brad Steiger & Joan Whritenour, Fly-
    ing Saucer Invasion: Target--Earth
    (N.Y.: Award, 1969), pp.95-96.

New Denver
-Humanoid tracks
  1971, summer/Robin Flewin/Silverton Cr.
    John Green, The Sasquatch File (Ag-
    assiz, B.C.: Cheam, 1973), p.51.

New Hazelton
-Humanoid
  1949, Oct./Frank Luxton
    Vancouver Sun, 21 June 1957.
  ca.1958
    John Green, The Sasquatch File (Ag-
    assiz, B.C.: Cheam, 1973), p.18.

New Westminster
-Precognition
  n.d./Peter Gregory
    Eileen Sonin, More Canadian Ghosts
    (Richmond Hill, Ont.: Pocket Books,
    1974 ed.), pp.141-42.
-Sea monster
  1962, Dec.28/Mrs. Robert Guy
    Seattle (Wash.) Post-Intelligencer,
    29 Dec.1962.
-UFO (CE-1)
  1967, April 1
    New Westminster Columbian, 3 Apr.
    1967.

North Vancouver
-Poltergeist
  1973-   /Jason McIntyre
    (Editorial), Fate 30 (May 1977):10-
    15.
-UFO (NL)
  1970/L. Beaulieu
    (Letter), Can.UFO Rept., no.8 (fall
    1970):38.

Oak Bay
-Haunt
  n.d.
    Sheila Hervey, Some Canadian Ghosts
    (Richmond Hill, Ont.: Pocket Books,
    1973), pp.29-32, quoting Victoria
    Daily Colonist (undated).
-UFO (NL)
  1967, Jan.4
    (Letter), Brian C. Cannon, Can.UFO
    Rept., no.3 (May-June 1969):2.

Okanogan Landing
-UFO (NL)
  1918, fall/J.P. Alphonse Dupas/3 mi.SW
    (Letter), Fate 11 (Jan.1958):120-22.

100 Mile House
-UFO (NL)
  1976, Oct.8/3 mi.N
    Glenn R. Duiven, "Object Observed by
    the R.C.M.P.," APRO Bull. 25 (Feb.
    1977):8.

Oyster River
-Sea monster
  1942, March 6/Joe Parkin
    Mary Moon, Ogopogo (N.Pomfret, Vt.:
    David & Charles, 1977), p.161.

Parksville
-UFO (CE-1)
  1968, May/Hans Sorensen
    "One UFO Leaves Another," Can.UFO
    Rept., no.3 (May-June 1969):8-9.
-UFO (NL)
  1967, June/Darwin Bjornson

"Repeated Visits at Dawn," Can.UFO
Rept., no.2 (Mar.-Apr.1969):5-6.
1968, July 1/Bill Hawks
"Pattern of Sky Lights," Can.UFO
Rept., no.2 (Mar.-Apr.1969):6-7.
John Magor, Our UFO Visitors (Seat-
tle: Hancock House, 1977), pp.35-36.

Penticton
-Clairvoyance
1977, Nov.8
E. Jervis Bloomfield, "Dream Pin-
points Crash Site," Fate 31 (Apr.
1978):63.

Port Alice
-UFO (DD)
1969, Oct.3/Gary Godfrey
(Letter), Can.UFO Rept., no.6 (Nov.-
Dec.1969):31-32.

Port Coquitlam
-UFO (CE-2)
1974, Aug.16/David Bates/Coquitlam R.
"Ground Blackened at Landing Site,"
APRO Bull. 23 (July-Aug.1974):1.
Graham Conway, "Close Encounter,"
Can.UFO Rept., no.20 (1975):8-11.
il.

Port Hammond
-UFO (DD)
1952, April 4/Hank Harms
(Editorial), Fate 5 (Oct.1952):7.
-UFO (NL)
1952, March 14/Hank Harms
(Editorial), Fate 5 (Oct.1952):7.
1952, April 4,11
Vancouver Sun, 1 May 1952.

Port MacNeil
-UFO (NL)
1967, March 12/D.L. Siemans
"Sightings Still on Upswing," APRO
Bull. 15 (Mar.-Apr.1967):11-12.

Port Moody
-Out-of-body experience
1939, Aug./A.W. Cameron
(Letter), Fate 10 (Nov.1957):127-28.
-UFO (NL)
1975, Jan.2/Tom Quinlan
Coquitlam Enterprise, 8 Jan.1975.

Port Renfrew
-Sea monster
ca.1961/Rudi Witschi
Paul H. LeBlond & John Sibert, Obser-
vations of Large Unidentified Marine
Animals in British Columbia and Ad-
jacent Waters (Vancouver: Univ. of
British Columbia, Inst. of Ocean-
ography, Manuscript Rept. no.28,
June 1973), pp.36-37.

Port Simpson
-Giant squid
1892
1922, winter/Charles H. Dudoward
Paul H. LeBlond & John Sibert, Obser-

vations of Large Unidentified Marine
Animals in British Columbia and Ad-
jacent Waters (Vancouver: Univ. of
British Columbia, Inst. of Ocean-
ography, Manuscript Rept. no.28,
June 1973), pp.11-12,32. il.

Prince George
-Phantom helicopter
1977, June 19
"UFOs," Res Bureaux Bull., no.22
(25 Aug.1977):3,5.
-Skyquake
1977, Jan.4
Prince George Citizen, 14 Jan.1977.
-UFO (?)
1969, July 15/=balloon?
Prince George Citizen, 15 July 1969.
-UFO (CE-2)
1978, April 6
"Another Menace in the Sky," Res Bur-
eaux Bull., no.35 (15 June 1978):1-
3.
-UFO (CE-4)
1977, Jan.5/Kirk Alore/20 mi.W on Hwy.
16
Michael Sinclair, "Possible Canadian
Abduction," APRO Bull. 25 (Mar.1977)
:1,7.
"Northern Lights and Shakes," Can.UFO
Rept., no.28 (summer 1977):1-3.
"Flying Alligator Skin," Can.UFO
Rept., no.30 (winter-spring 1978):1-
3. il.
W.K. Allen, "The Fort St. James
Sightings," Flying Saucer Rev. 24
(Nov.1978):8-11.
-UFO (NL)
1969, Jan.1/Walter Webster/Fifth St.
Prince George Citizen, 2-3 Jan.1969.
1975, March/Ann Gervais
John Magor, Our UFO Visitors (Seat-
tle: Hancock House, 1977), p.147. il.
1977, May/Mrs. Alore
W.K. Allen, "The Fort St. James
Sightings," Flying Saucer Rev. 24
(Nov.1978):8,11.

Prince Rupert
-Chinese discovery
ca.1000 B.C.
Henriette Mertz, Gods from the Far
East (N.Y.: Ballantine, 1975 ed.),
p.153.
-Mystery bird deaths
1971, Sep.
Toronto (Ont.) Globe and Mail, 28
Sep.1971.
-UFO (NL)
1968, July 27-29/John Olsen/Fulton St.
Hill, Mt.Hays
Prince Rupert Daily News, 29-30 July
1968.

Qualicum Beach
-Sea monster
1951, April/C. Charlton/=hoax
Toronto (Ont.) Sun, 3 Apr.1951.
-UFO (CE-3)
1966, summer/Charlotte A. Horsfall

(Letter), Saga UFO Rept. 3 (Oct.1976)
:76-77.

Radium Hot Springs
-UFO (CE-1)
   1969/Jim Statham
   1969, Jan?/Joanne Hammond
      "Playground of Gods," Can.UFO Rept.,
      no.11 (1971):2,5-7.
   1975, July/Frank Slotta/nr. lodge
      "Time Lost in 'Playground of Gods,'"
      Can.UFO Rept., no.26 (winter 1976-
      77):1-3. il.

Revelstoke
-Psychokinesis
   1904, Jan.21/E of town
      Julie C. Crawford, "The Psychic War-
      ning That Stopped the Train," Fate
      15 (July 1962):61,66-68.
-UFO (?)
   1966, March 31/=meteor?
      Richard Hunt, "Canadian Fireballs,"
      Flying Saucer Rev. 12 (Mar.-Apr.
      1966):33-34.
      (Editorial), Fate 32 (Feb.1979):12.
-UFO (CE-1)
   1968, Aug.7/Harold Howery/W of town
      John Keel, UFOs: Operation Trojan
      Horse (N.Y.: G.P. Putnam, 1970),
      p.156.
-UFO (DD)
   1970, winter/Barry Zettergreen/N of
   town
      (Letter), Arthur N. Zettergreen, Can.
      UFO Rept., no.11 (1971):33.

Richmond
-UFO (DD)
   1975, Sep.24/Elizabeth Montague/Garden
   City Rd.
      (Letter), Can.UFO Rept., no.30 (win-
      ter-spring 1978):23.

Rossland
-UFO (NL)
   1973, Aug./Mrs. A.M. Drumbell
      (Letter), Can.UFO Rept., no.19 (1975)
      :23.

Rosswood
-UFO (NL)
   1968-1969/Steve Tomecek
      Catherine M. Fraser, "Saturn Shaped
      UFO," Can.UFO Rept., no.3 (May-June
      1969):17-18.

Royston
-Sea monster
   1936, June/Mrs. George Tater
      Vancouver Sun, 27 June 1936, p.1.

Ruby Creek
-Humanoid
   1941, Oct./Jeannie Chapman
      Vancouver Province, 21 Oct.1941.
      Ivan T. Sanderson, Abominable Snow-
      men: Legend Come to Life (Philadel-
      phia: Chilton, 1961), pp.65-69.
      John Green, On the Track of the Sas-
      quatch (Agassiz, B.C.: Cheam, 1968),
      pp.4-9.
      John Green, Sasquatch: The Apes Among
      Us (Seattle: Hancock House, 1978),
      pp.51-52,67,351.

Rutland
-UFO (NL)
   1976, July/Richard Cutting
      "Airborne Sasquatch?" Can.UFO Rept.,
      no.32 (fall 1978):1-3.

Saanich
-Fall of unknown object
   1970, July/F.H. Adams/Durrance Rd.
      "UFOs May Be Planting Aerials," Can.
      UFO Rept., no.8 (fall 1970):10-14.
      il.

Salmon Arm
-UFO (DD)
   1973, July
   1974, Sep.11-Oct./Granite Mt.
      (Letter), Mrs. D.M., Can.UFO Rept.,
      no.19 (1975):22-23.

Sechelt
-Disappearance
   1967, Jan.11/"Gulf Master"
      Brad Steiger & Joan Whritenour, All-
      ende Letters: New UFO Breakthrough
      (N.Y.: Tower, 1968), p.111.
-Humanoid
   1971, Oct.
      John Green, The Sasquatch File (Ag-
      assiz, B.C.: Cheam, 1973), p.51.

Sicamous
-UFO (CE-2)
   1970, fall/Barry Zettergreen
      (Letter), Arthur L. Zettergreen, Can.
      UFO Rept., no.11 (1971):33.

Sidney
-Sea monster
   1960, Dec.26
      Victoria Daily Times, 27 Dec.1960.
-UFO (DD)
   1954, Oct.9/Robert I. Knight
      "UFO over Vancouver Island," Flying
      Saucer Rev. 1 (spring 1955):[14].
-UFO (NL)
   1897, July
      Portland Oregonian, 3 Aug.1897.
   1976, Aug.11/Lillias Milne/Bazan Bay
      (Letter), Can.UFO Rept., no.25 (fall
      1976):22.

Skidegate Mission
-Humanoid
   1970, March/Tina Brown/7 mi.N
      Vancouver Sun, 24 June 1970.

Smithers
-UFO (NL)
   1964, Dec.4/Ronald M. Hawkins/E of town
      "Sighting by Canadian Ranger," UFO
      Inv. 3 (Apr.-May 1965):6.

Sooke
-UFO (NL)
  1977, Aug.11
    "UFOs," Res Bureaux Bull., no.22 (25
    Aug.1977):3,4.

Spences Bridge
-UFO (NL) and disappearance
  1863, Aug.5/John Fillmore/disappear-
  ance of mules
    John L. Zeller, "The Phantom of the
    Cariboo Trail," Fate 14 (May 1961):
    38-39.

Spuzzum
-Ancient inscription
  1946
    Bruce A. MacDonald, "The Inscribed
    Rock near Spuzzum, British Colum-
    bia," Occ.Pub.Epigraphic Soc'y 7,
    no.149 (Apr.1979):93-99. il.
-Humanoid
  1977, March 28/Richard Mitchell/N of
  Alexandra Bridge
    Hope Standard, 30 Mar.1977.

Squamish
-Humanoid tracks
  ca.1964/N of town
    John Green, The Sasquatch File (Ag-
    assiz, B.C.: Cheam, 1973), p.27.
  1969, April 6
    John Green, Year of the Sasquatch
    (Agassiz, B.C.: Cheam, 1970), p.44.

Stewart
-Humanoid
  1968, Aug.
    John Green, On the Track of the Sas-
    quatch (Agassiz, B.C.: Cheam, 1968),
    p.1.

Stillwater
-Sea monster
  1946, May 4
    Paul H. LeBlond & John Sibert, Obser-
    vations of Large Unidentified Marine
    Animals in British Columbia and Ad-
    jacent Waters (Vancouver: Univ. of
    British Columbia, Inst. of Ocean-
    ography, Manuscript Rept. no.28,
    June 1973), pp.35-36.

Summerland
-Ghost
  ca.1917
    Sheila Hervey, Some Canadian Ghosts
    (Richmond Hill, Ont.: Pocket Books,
    1973), pp.32-33.
-Sea monster
  ca.1950
    "Sea Monsters of Canada," Res Bureaux
    Bull., no.33 (4 May 1978):5.

Summit Lake
-UFO (NL)
  1967, March 4/Ed Yamitski
    "Canada's 'Year of Invasion': Part
    3," Can.UFO Rept., no.8 (fall 1970):
    17,19-20.

Surrey
-UFO (DD)
  1974, Oct.15/David Knutson/=hoax?
    Vancouver Sun, 26 Oct.1974. il.
    "World Round-up," Flying Saucer Rev.
    20 (Jan.1975):29-30. il.
    (Letter), Barry Greenwood, Flying
    Saucer Rev. 20 (Apr.1975):iii.
    "David Knutson," Can.UFO Rept., no.
    19 (1975):16. il.
    (Letter), G. Conway, Flying Saucer
    Rev. 22 (May 1976):29-30.
    (Letter), Barry Greenwood, Flying
    Saucer Rev. 22 (Oct.1976):28.
  1975, April 8
    (Letter), G. Conway, Flying Saucer
    Rev. 22 (May 1976):29-30.
-UFO (NL)
  1970, June/Peter Borkent
    (Letter), Can.UFO Rept., no.8 (fall
    1970):37-38.

Terrace
-UFO (CE-1)
  1976, April 21/Bill Toffan
    Vancouver Sun, 26 Apr.1976.
-UFO (CE-3)
  1970, Feb.
    John Magor, Our UFO Visitors (Seat-
    tle: Hancock House, 1977), pp.193-
    96.

Trail
-Humanoid tracks
  1970, June/Dennis Merle
    John Green, The Sasquatch File (Ag-
    assiz, B.C.: Cheam, 1973), p.51.

Ucluelet
-Sea monster
  1947, Nov./George W. Saggers
    George W. Saggers, "Sea Serpent off
    Vancouver," Fate 1 (summer 1948):
    124-25.
-UFO (NL)
  1976, Jan./Cliff Mulvey
    "Disc Examines Survey Ship," Can.UFO
    Rept., no.23 (spring 1976):8.

Valemount
-UFO (NL)
  1968, Feb.12/David E. Taylor
    (Letter), Can.UFO Rept., no.2 (Mar.-
    Apr.1969):3-4.

Vancouver
-Animal ESP
  1954, July 17/Edward Rehmus
    E. Edward Rehmus, "Is There Reincar-
    nation among Animals?" Fate 11 (Feb.
    1958):77-80.
-Contactee
  1969, Oct.23-1971/Robin McPherson
    Brad Steiger, The Aquarian Revela-
    tions (N.Y.: Dell, 1971).
  1975, July-   /Dorothy Wilkinson
    Graham Conway, "Another Dimension via
    Film?" Can.UFO Rept., no.32 (fall
    1978):3-6. il.
-Fall of metallic object

1955/Agnes Joyce
  "Falls," Fortean Times, no.25 (spring
  1978):10.
-Ghost
  1930s/west end
  Sheila Hervey, Some Canadian Ghosts
  (Richmond Hill, Ont.: Pocket Books,
  1973), pp.18-20.
-Haunt
  1968, Sep.-Oct./Diane Dunsmore/W.11th
  St.
  Sheila Hervey, Some Canadian Ghosts
  (Richmond Hill, Ont.: Pocket Books,
  1973), pp.27-29.
-Humanoid
  1884/August Jack Khatsalano
  John Green, Sasquatch: The Apes Among
  Us (Seattle: Hancock House, 1978),
  p.368.
-Lightning anomaly
  1918-1934/Maj. Summerford
  Albert A. Brandt, "Lightning to the
  End," Fate 5 (Apr.-May 1952):87.
-Mystery radio transmissions
  1924, Aug./Point Grey Wireless Station
  New York Times, 22 Aug.1924, pp.12,
  13; and 23 Aug.1924, p.1.
-Precognition
  1962, Feb.9/Mary Busch/Bayshore Inn
  (Editorial), Fate 15 (July 1962):20-
  22.
-Sea monster
  1935-1936/C.W. Cates
  Vancouver Sun, 12 Aug.1938, p.1.
  1936, April 6/Harry Twigg
  Vancouver Province, 7 Apr.1936, p.1.
  1937, Feb.16/Robert Urquhart
  Vancouver Province, 18 Feb.1937, p.1.
  1938, Aug.11/Dorothy Burniston
  Vancouver Sun, 12 Aug.1938, p.1.
  1939, May 14/Jeannette Gannonx
  Vancouver Sun, 15 May 1939, p.1.
  1940, March 5
  "Ain't No Such Animal," Fortean Soc'y
  Mag., no.6 (Jan.1942):14.
  1940, June 23/Vivian Knight
  Vancouver Province, 26 June 1940, p.1.
  n.d./Birger Anderson/"Scott Hill"
  "No Such Animal," Doubt, no.16 (1946)
  :237.
  1947, March/Peter Pantages/Siwash Rock
  "Monster of Vancouver Island," Fate
  8 (Mar.1955):37.
  Paul H. LeBlond & John Sibert, Obser-
  vations of Large Unidentified Marine
  Animals in British Columbia and Ad-
  jacent Waters (Vancouver: Univ. of
  British Columbia, Inst. of Ocean-
  ography, Manuscript Rept. no.28,
  June 1973), pp.19-20.
-Sea monster (carcass)
  1936, June 18/Royal Vancouver Yacht
  Club
  Vancouver Sun, 19 June 1936, p.1.
-Spirit medium
  1890s/Charles Hill-Tout
  Charles Hill-Tout, "Some Psychical
  Phenomena Bearing upon the Question
  of Spirit Control," Proc.SPR 11
  (1895):309-16.

-UFO (?)
  1950, April/=airplane?
  Ray Palmer, "New Report on the Flying Saucers," Fate 4 (Jan.1951):
  63,79.
  1952, April 24
  Vancouver Sun, 1 May 1952.
  1957, April 5/Mrs. Frank Sirianni/
  Broughton St.
  "World Roundup," Flying Saucer Rev.
  3 (July-Aug.1957):5.
  1962, May 28/John Lium/=meteor?
  (Editorial), Fate 15 (Nov.1962):14-
  15.
  1973, July
  Ted Phillips, Physical Traces Associated with UFO Sightings (Evanston:
  Center for UFO Studies, 1975), p.
  110.
  1977, April 18/George Thrupp/=meteor?
  Vancouver Sun, 19 Apr.1977.
-UFO (CE-1)
  1967, Dec.23/John S. Martin
  (Letter), Can.UFO Rept., no.2 (Mar.-
  Apr.1969):3.
-UFO (DD)
  1947, May
  John A. Keel, "The Beginning of the
  Saucer Era: June 24th, 1947," Sau-
  cer News 14 (summer 1967):12.
  1947, June 27/William Crodie/1635 Ad-
  anac
  Vancouver Sun, 28 June 1947.
  1966, Aug.2/W.J.H. Bard
  "World Round-up," Flying Saucer Rev.
  12 (Nov.-Dec.1966):iii.
-UFO (NL)
  1952, April 28
  1952, April 30
  Vancouver Sun, 2 May 1952.
  1962, May 28
  Vancouver Sun, 29 May 1962.
  "Giant UFO over Vancouver," Flying
  Saucer Rev. 8 (Sep.-Oct.1962):11.
  1968, Oct.30
  "Around the Globe," APRO Bull. 17
  (Nov.-Dec.1968):6.
  1971, Sep.17
  (Letter), M.V., Can.UFO Rept., no.
  11 (1971):34.
  1974, Nov.
  "Photos by ESP," Can.UFO Rept., no.
  31 (summer 1978):12. il.
  1976, April 21
  "Noteworthy UFO Sightings," Ufology
  2 (fall 1976):60,61.

Vedder Crossing
-Humanoid
  1962, Oct./Joe Gregg
  Don Hunter & René Dahinden, Sasquatch
  (Toronto: McClelland & Stewart,
  1973), pp.66-67.
  John Green, Sasquatch: The Apes Among
  Us (Seattle: Hancock House, 1978),
  pp.396-99.

Victoria
-Contactee
  1957/Marc Norman

(Editorial), <u>Fate</u> 10 (July 1957):13.
-Electromagnetic anomaly
1978, April 4/Mrs. Whyte
  <u>Victoria Times</u>, 5 Apr.1978.
-Fall of radiolarians
1954, April
  (Editorial), <u>Fate</u> 7 (Aug.1954):10-11.
-Haunt
  n.d./park
    Eileen Sonin, <u>More Canadian Ghosts</u>
    (Richmond Hill, Ont.: Pocket Books,
    1974 ed.), pp.92-93.
  1938, Aug./Edith M. Wilson/2668 Uplands
    C.V. Tench, "The Murderous Wraith,"
    <u>Fate</u> 13 (Nov.1960):63-69.
-Psychic photography
1865, Jan.13/B.C. Legislative Council
  (Editorial), <u>Probe the Unknown</u> 1
  (Oct.1973):8-9. il.
-Sea monster
1933, Oct.14/Charles F. Eagles
  Mary Moon, <u>Ogopogo</u> (N.Pomfret, Vt.:
  David & Charles, 1977), p.155.
1933, Nov./James F. Murray
  <u>Vancouver Province</u>, 15 Nov.1933, p.8.
1934, April 15/Audrey Jennings
  Mary Moon, <u>Ogopogo</u> (N.Pomfret, Vt.:
  David & Charles, 1977), pp.156-57.
1934, Oct.8/J.T. Willoughby
  <u>Victoria Colonist</u>, 9 Oct.1934, p.3.
1937, Feb.5/Mrs. Fraser Biscoe
  <u>Victoria Colonist</u>, 6 Feb.1937.
1939, March/Mrs. Roskilly
  <u>Vancouver Sun</u>, 17 March 1939, p.1.
1940, Jan./Cecil Burgess
  <u>Vancouver Sun</u>, 8 Jan.1940, p.1.
1943, spring
  Mary Moon, <u>Ogopogo</u> (N.Pomfret, Vt.:
  David & Charles, 1977), p.157.
1950, Feb.5/James Thomas Brown
  Ray Gardner, "Caddy, King of the
  Coast," <u>Maclean's Mag</u>. 63 (15 June
  1950):24,42-43.
1950, May 27/Patricia Bay
  "No Such Animal," <u>Doubt</u>, no.30 (1950)
  :36.
1950, Dec.
  Mary Moon, <u>Ogopogo</u> (N.Pomfret, Vt.:
  David & Charles, 1977), p.158.
1958, fall/Alison McCord/Dallas Rd.
  Paul H. LeBlond & John Sibert, <u>Obser-</u>
  <u>vations of Large Unidentified Marine</u>
  <u>Animals in British Columbia and Ad-</u>
  <u>jacent Waters</u> (Vancouver: Univ. of
  British Columbia, Inst. of Oceanography, Manuscript Rept. no.28,
  June 1973), p.25.
1969, Sep.-Oct./Mrs. W.S. Foster
1970, Dec./James Bertie
  Mary Moon, <u>Ogopogo</u> (N.Pomfret, Vt.:
  David & Charles, 1977), pp.158-59.
-Seance
1955, Dec.4/Mrs. C. Terry
  (Letter), Rene Harris, <u>Fate</u> 9 (June
  1956):120-21.
-UFO (?)
1962, May 28/Arthur H. Randell/=meteor?
  "Fireball Lights Pacific Northwest,"
  <u>APRO Bull</u>. 11 (July 1962):6.
1967, April 13/=meteor?

"World Round-up," <u>Flying Saucer Rev.</u>
  13 (July-Aug.1967):31.
1968, summer
  J. Allen Hynek, <u>The UFO Experience</u>
  (Chicago: Regnery, 1972), p.6.
1975, May 25/George Stephens/=lens
flare
  (Editorial), <u>Can.UFO Rept.</u>, no.21
  (1975):4. il.
-UFO (CE-1)
1977, March 9/Maria Stratford
  <u>Victoria Times</u>, 11 Mar.1977.
-UFO (CE-2)
1968, Aug.4
  Ted Phillips, <u>Physical Traces Associ-</u>
  <u>ated with UFO Sightings</u> (Evanston:
  Center for UFO Studies, 1975), p.57.
-UFO (NL)
1967, April 14/Ian Squire/Cadboro Bay
Rd.
  "World Round-up," <u>Flying Saucer Rev.</u>
  13 (July-Aug.1967):30-31.
1970/Andrew Birch
  (Letter), <u>Can.UFO Rept.</u>, no.8 (fall
  1970):38.
1970, May/Linda L. Brown
  (Letter), <u>Can.UFO Rept.</u>, no.8 (fall
  1970):35-36.
1970, July/Daryl Brachat
  "UFOs May Be Planting Aerials," <u>Can.</u>
  <u>UFO Rept.</u>, no.8 (fall 1970):10-11.
1978, April 5/Lindsay Gardner
  (Letter), <u>Can.UFO Rept.</u>, no.31 (summer 1978):[26].

Waldo
-Haunt
1957/Eric Henderson
  Sheila Hervey, <u>Some Canadian Ghosts</u>
  (Richmond Hill, Ont.: Pocket Books,
  1973), pp.15-18.

White Rock
-Fall of yellow dust
1972, March
  <u>Vancouver Daily Province</u>, 25 Mar.
  1972.
-Humanoid
1966, July/Mr. Letoul
  John Green, <u>The Sasquatch File</u> (Agassiz, B.C.: Cheam, 1973), p.34.
-UFO (?)
1976, May 20/Leslie Asselstine
  (Letter), <u>Saga UFO Rept.</u> 3 (Dec.1976)
  :6.

Williams Lake
-UFO (NL)
1969/Mrs. Arthur Millard
  "New Flap Starts," <u>Can.UFO Rept.</u>,
  no.6 (Nov.-Dec.1969):16-18.

Windermere
-UFO (CE-1)
1969, Aug./Bud Amy
  "Playground of Gods," <u>Can.UFO Rept.</u>,
  no.11 (1971):2,7.

Woodfibre
-Humanoid

ca.1947/Charles Cates
  Vancouver Daily Province, 9 July
  1947.

Yale
-Archeological sites
  ca.8000 B.C.-recent/Fraser R. canyon
    H.I. Smith, "Remarkable Stone Sculp-
    tures from Yale, British Columbia,"
    19th Int'l Cong.Americanists (1917),
    pp.31-34.
    Charles E. Borden, "DjRi3, an Early
    Site in the Fraser Canyon, British
    Columbia," Bull.Nat'l Mus.Canada,
    no.162 (1960):101-18.
    Thomas H. Ainsworth, "The Stone Car-
    vings of an Unknown People," Beaver,
    no.294 (winter 1963):44-49.
    David Sanger, "7000 Years: Prehis-
    tory in British Columbia," Beaver,
    no.298 (spring 1968):34-40. il.
-Humanoid
  1884, June 30/R.J. Craig/Jacko/=hoax?
    Victoria Daily Colonist, 4 July 1884.
    New Westminster Mainland Guardian,
    9 July 1884.
    New Westminster British Columbian,
    12 July 1884.
    John Green, Year of the Sasquatch
    (Agassiz, B.C.: Cheam, 1970), pp.
    4-5.
    John Green & Sabina W. Sanderson,
    "Alas, Poor Jacko," Pursuit 8 (Jan.
    1975):18-19.
    Russ Kinne, "Jacko Reconsidered,"
    Pursuit 9 (Apr.1976):43.
    John Green, Sasquatch: The Apes Among
    Us (Seattle: Hancock House, 1978),
    pp.83-88.
-UFO (NL) and disappearance
  1863, Aug.8/George Lateau/disappear-
  ance of mules
    John L. Zeller, "The Phantom of the
    Cariboo Trail," Fate 14 (May 1961):
    38-40.

Youbou
-UFO (CE-1)
  1974, May 1/Eric Meuser
    "Return of the Flame-Throwers," Can.
    UFO Rept., no.18 (1974):3,5, quot-
    ing Victoria Colonist (undated).

B. Physical Features

Active Pass
-Mermaid
  1967, June/"Queen of Saanich"/W entrance
    (Editorial), Fate 20 (Nov.1967):22,
    quoting Victoria Daily Colonist (un-
    dated).
-Phantom ship
  1934, July/James Hampson
    James Hampson, "Ghost Ship," Fate 8
    (Jan.1955):31-33.

Adams R.
-Sea monster

ca.1905/Philip Welch
  Paul H. LeBlond & John Sibert, Obser-
  vations of Large Unidentified Marine
  Animals in British Columbia and Ad-
  jacent Waters (Vancouver: Univ. of
  British Columbia, Inst. of Ocean-
  ography, Manuscript Rept. no.28,
  June 1973), p.9.

Anvil I.
-Humanoid
  1900s/smy-a-likh
    John Green, The Sasquatch File (Ag-
    assiz, B.C.: Cheam, 1973), p.9.

Aristazabal I.
-Humanoid
  1959, March/Lawrence Hopkins
    John Green, The Sasquatch File (Ag-
    assiz, B.C.: Cheam, 1973), p.18.
-Humanoid tracks
  1962, summer/Bob Titmus
    John Green, The Sasquatch File (Ag-
    assiz, B.C.: Cheam, 1973), p.26.

Arrow L.
-Precognition
  1932, Nov./Frederick Lindsay
    Frederick William Lindsay, "A Stran-
    ger on the Trail," Fate 18 (July
    1965):83-89.

Atlin L.
-UFO (NL)
  1968, Jan.4
    "UFO Stalks Two Boys," Can.UFO Rept.,
    no.1 (Jan.-Feb.1969):3.

Baldy, Mt.
-Humanoid
  1976, Aug.
    "Airborne Sasquatch?" Can.UFO Rept.,
    no.32 (fall 1978):1-3.
-UFO (CE-2)
  1976, Aug./Richard Cutting
    "Airborne Sasquatch?" Can.UFO Rept.,
    no.32 (fall 1978):1-3.

Barkley Sound
-UFO (NL)
  1975, May/"CSS Parizeau"
    "Disc Examines Survey Ship," Can.UFO
    Rept., no.23 (spring 1976):6-8.

Bella Coola R.
-Humanoid tracks
  1962, Dec./Bob Titmus/Tweedsmuir Prov.
  Park
  1966, Nov./Joshua Moody
    John Green, The Sasquatch File (Ag-
    assiz, B.C.: Cheam, 1973), pp.26,34.

Bishop Cove
-Humanoid
  1907, March?/"Capilano"
    Vancouver Daily Province, 8 Mar.1907.

Black Mt.
-UFO (DD)
  1966, March 1

Vancouver Daily Province, 2 Mar.1966.

Bowron L.
-Humanoid tracks
　1968, Nov./Horst Klein/Bowron Lakes
　　Rd.
　　John Green, The Sasquatch File (Ag-
　　　assiz, B.C.: Cheam, 1973), p.41.

Brewer Creek
-UFO (DD)
　1975, Sep./Roger Richer
　　John Magor, Our UFO Visitors (Seat-
　　　tle: Hancock House, 1977), pp.105-
　　　106.

Broughton I.
-Humanoid
　1968, Feb./Tom Brown
　　Vancouver Daily Province, 22 Feb.
　　　1968.

Burnt Bridge
-Humanoid
　1958, Dec./George Robson
　　John Green, The Sasquatch File (Ag-
　　　assiz, B.C.: Cheam, 1973), p.18.

Bute Inlet
-Humanoid
　1973, March 21/Peter Spika
　　John Green, The Sasquatch File (Ag-
　　　assiz, B.C.: Cheam, 1973), p.73.
-Sea monster
　ca.1930
　　Mary Moon, Ogopogo (N.Pomfret, Vt.:
　　　David & Charles, 1977), p.161.

Cadboro Bay
-Sea monster
　1936, April 17/Arthur B. Dawe
　　Vancouver Sun, 17 Apr.1936, p.1.

Campbell R.
-Humanoid
　ca.1901/Mike King
　　John Green, The Sasquatch File (Ag-
　　　assiz, B.C.: Cheam, 1973), p.9.
　　John Green, Sasquatch: The Apes Among
　　　Us (Seattle: Hancock House, 1978),
　　　p.57.

Cayuse Creek
-Pictograph
　=depicts UFO?
　　John Corner, Pictographs in the In-
　　　terior of British Columbia (Vernon,
　　　B.C.: Wayside, 1968), pp.81-85. il.

Chapman Creek
-Humanoid
　1973, June/nr. Mile Nine
　　John Green, Sasquatch: The Apes Among
　　　Us (Seattle: Hancock House, 1978),
　　　p.420.

Chatham I.
-Sea monster
　1932, Aug.10/F.W. Kemp
　1933, Oct.1/W.H. Langley

1933, Oct.4/R.C. Ross
　Victoria Daily Times, 5 Oct.1933.
　"The Loch Ness Monster Paralleled in
　　Canada: 'Cadborosaurus,'" Ill.Lon-
　　don News 184 (6 Jan.1934):8. il.

Cheakamus R.
-Humanoid
　1970, Jan.7/Bill Taylor/Hwy.99, 6 mi.S
　　of Alta L.
　　John Green, Year of the Sasquatch
　　　(Agassiz, B.C.: Cheam, 1970), pp.31-
　　　33.
　　Peter Byrne, The Search for Bigfoot
　　　(N.Y.: Pocket Books, 1976 ed.), pp.
　　　79-81.

Chehalis R.
-Humanoid
　ca.1909, May/Peter Williams
　　J.W. Burns, "Introducing B.C.'s Hairy
　　　Giants," Maclean's Mag., 1 Apr.1929,
　　　pp.9,61.

Chemainus R.
-Sea monster
　1933, Oct.15/Don Bellamy
　　Vancouver Province, 17 Oct.1933, p.1.

Cherry Point
-UFO (CE-1)
　1968, summer/Mrs. Paul Hillman
　　"Puzzle of Blazing Light," Can.UFO
　　　Rept., no.4 (July-Aug.1969):12.

Chilkat Pass
-Mammoth
　ca.1880
　　Merle Colby, Alaska: Last American
　　　Frontier (N.Y.:Macmillan, 1939), p.
　　　178.

Chilko L.
-Humanoid tracks
　1954/George V.B. Cochran/Sasquatch Pass
　　Peter Byrne, The Search for Bigfoot
　　　(N.Y.: Pocket Books, 1976 ed.), p.
　　　xviii.
　1977, summer/Vince Lee/Franklyn Arm
　　"Two New Footprint Findings," Big-
　　　foot News, no.37 (Oct.1977):2. il.

Chilko R.
-Anomalous artifact
　1961/Daniel Lee/=represents monkey?
　　"What's the Answer?" Can.UFO Rept.,
　　　no.17 (1974):10-11. il.

Christina L.
-Pictograph
　=depicts UFO?
　　John Corner, Pictographs in the In-
　　　terior of British Columbia (Vernon,
　　　B.C.: Wayside, 1968), pp.79-81. il.
　　John Magor, "Strange Strange World:
　　　Part Two," Can.UFO Rept., no.14
　　　(1973):8-11. il.

Clio Bay
-Humanoid

1965, summer
John Green, The Sasquatch File (Agassiz, B.C.: Cheam, 1973), p.33.

Clover Point
-UFO (?)
1977, May 20/Mrs. D.B. Turner
(Letter), Can.UFO Rept., no.28 (summer 1977):24. il.

Collins Bay
-Humanoid
1962, June/=bears?
John Green, The Sasquatch File (Agassiz, B.C.: Cheam, 1973), p.26.

Columbia R.
-UFO (CE-1)
1954, June/Mrs. Dino De Hart
"Playground of Gods," Can.UFO Rept.,
no.11 (1971):2-4.

Conuma R.
-Humanoid
1928/Muchalat Harry/12 mi. upstream
from mouth
Peter Byrne, The Search for Bigfoot
(N.Y.: Pocket Books, 1976 ed.), pp.
1-4.

Copeland Mt.
-UFO (?)
1968/Arthur N. Zettinger
"About Previous Cover Photo," Can.UFO
Rept., no.10 (1971):35. il.

Cowichan L.
-Lake monster
1959, Oct./Abe Johnson/tsinquaw
Fort William (Ont.) Daily Times-Journal, 7 Oct.1959.

Cowichan R.
-UFO (CE-1)
1973, Oct./nr. Quamichan Reservation
"Canada Touched by Flap," Can.UFO
Rept., no.16 (1973-74):7,9-11.

Crane I.
-Sea monster
1968, Feb.13/Jean Scott
Paul H. LeBlond & John Sibert, Obser-
vations of Large Unidentified Marine
Animals in British Columbia and Ad-
jacent Waters (Vancouver: Univ. of
British Columbia, Inst. of Ocean-
ography, Manuscript Rept. no.28,
June 1973), pp.29-30. il.

Cridge Passage
-Sea monster
1926, March 16/C.J. House
Vancouver Province, 28 Mar.1926, p.1.
London (Eng.) Morning Post, 11 Nov.
1934.

Cultus L.
-Humanoid
1964, July 4
John Green, The Sasquatch File (Ag-

assiz, B.C.: Cheam, 1973), p.27.
-UFO (DD)
1947, July 24/Mrs. L. Ker
Vancouver Sun, 25 July 1947.

D'Arcy I.
-Sea monster
1929, April
Mary Moon, Ogopogo (N.Pomfret, Vt.:
David & Charles, 1977), pp.160-61.

Defourse Creek
-Chinese coins
1882, summer
James Deans, "Chinese Coins in British Columbia," Am.Naturalist 18
(1884):98-99.

Denman I.
-Sea monster
1969, Nov./Charles Harper/=mollusk (Nu-
dibranchia)
Paul H. LeBlond & John Sibert, Observations of Large Unidentified Marine
Animals in British Columbia and Adjacent Waters (Vancouver: Univ. of
British Columbia, Inst. of Oceanography, Manuscript Rept. no.28,
June 1973), p.31. il.

Devastation Channel
-Humanoid tracks
1962, Aug./Bob Titmus/unnamed island in
channel
John Green, The Sasquatch File (Agassiz, B.C.: Cheam, 1973), p.26.

Discovery I.
-Sea monster
1933, Nov./Archie Miller
Vancouver Province, 15 Nov.1933, p.8.

Discovery Passage
-Sea monster
1940, Aug./E.H. Luoma
1959, Nov./David J. Miller
Paul H. LeBlond & John Sibert, Observations of Large Unidentified Marine
Animals in British Columbia and Adjacent Waters (Vancouver: Univ. of
British Columbia, Inst. of Oceanography, Manuscript Rept. no.28,
June 1973), pp.16-17,25-27. il.

Dogfish Bay
-Petroglyph
Beth & Ray Hill, Indian Petroglyphs
of the Pacific Northwest (Seattle:
Univ. of Washington, 1974), pp.144-
45.

Effingham I.
-Sea monster (carcass)
1947, Nov.2/Henry Schwarz/=basking
shark
Vancouver Daily Press, 8 Dec.1947.
"Run of the Mill," Doubt, no.20
(1948):303.

Estevan Point
-Sea monster
1942, April
    Ray Gardner, "Caddy, King of the
    Coast," Maclean's Mag. 63 (15 June
    1950):24,42-43.

Finlayson I.
-Sea monster
ca.1944/Fred Dudoward
    Paul H. LeBlond & John Sibert, Obser-
    vations of Large Unidentified Marine
    Animals in British Columbia and Ad-
    jacent Waters (Vancouver: Univ. of
    British Columbia, Inst. of Ocean-
    ography, Manuscript Rept. no.28,
    June 1973), pp.33-35. il.

Fitzwilliam Mt.
-Humanoid tracks
1918
    John Green, The Sasquatch File (Ag-
    assiz, B.C.: Cheam, 1973), p.12.

Flat Top Is.
-Sea monster
1938, Oct./W.A. Roedde
    Vancouver Province, 14 Oct.1938, p.1.

Fly Hill
-UFO (?)
1976, July 8
    "Diary of a Mad Planet," Fortean
    Times, no.18 (Oct.1976):8,17.

Fraser L.
-Pictograph
=depicts UFO?
    John Corner, Pictographs in the In-
    terior of British Columbia (Vernon,
    B.C.: Wayside, 1968), pp.116-18. il.

Fraser R.
-Ghost
1912, Aug./Ed Barney/Mile 81
    Ed Barney, "That's What Happened to
    Rudolf Shipp," Fate 19 (Apr.1966):
    74-77.
-UFO (CE-1)
1977, Dec.12/Metro Zwozdesky
    Prince George Citizen, 13 Dec.1977.

Gabriola I.
-Sea monster
1937, April 30/"Etta Mae"
    Victoria Daily Times, 30 Apr.1937.
1963, Feb./Mrs. R.A. Steward
    Victoria Daily Times, 1 Mar.1963.

Gambier I.
-Sea monster (carcass)
1936, Oct.5/Hector Lawrence
    Vancouver Sun, 7 Oct.1936, p.1.

Gardner Canal
-Humanoid
1905, spring/Billy Hall
    John Green, Sasquatch: The Apes Among
    Us (Seattle: Hancock House, 1978),
    p.368.

Glen L.
-UFO (NL)
1966, March 31/Gordon Young
    Victoria Daily Colonist, 1 Apr.1966.

Graves Point
-Sea monster
ca.1946/Mr. Liston
    Paul H. LeBlond & John Sibert, Obser-
    vations of Large Unidentified Marine
    Animals in British Columbia and Ad-
    jacent Waters (Vancouver: Univ. of
    British Columbia, Inst. of Ocean-
    ography, Manuscript Rept. no.28,
    June 1973), p.35.

Green Drop L.
-Humanoid
1915/Charles Flood
    John Green, The Sasquatch File (Ag-
    assiz, B.C.: Cheam, 1973), p.12.

Green L.
-UFO (NL)
1967, Oct.30/Shirley Hills
    "UFO Big As Building Pays Visit,"
    Can.UFO Rept., no.6 (Nov.-Dec.1969)
    :9-12.
    "That 'Awful Looking Shooting Star,'"
    Can.UFO Rept., no.21 (1975):14.

Grief Point
-Sea monster
1936, Oct./Harold Dixon
    Vancouver Sun, 10 Oct.1936, p.5.

Grouse Mt.
-Humanoid
1947/Nellie Werner
    Don Hunter & René Dahinden, Sasquatch
    (Toronto: McClelland & Stewart,
    1973), pp.101-102.

Harrison L.
-Humanoid
1939, Aug./Burns Yeomans
    John Green, Sasquatch: The Apes Among
    Us (Seattle: Hancock House, 1978),
    pp.60-63.
1974, Aug./Wayne Jones
    Nat'l Observer, 22 Aug.1974.
-Lake monster
1976, Oct.
    Vancouver Daily Province, 18 Oct.1976.

Harrison R.
-Humanoid
1846/Alexander Caulfield Anderson/=
hoax?
    Stephen Franklin, "On the Trail of
    the Sasquatch," Fate 13 (June 1960):
    54,57.
    John Green & Sabina W. Sanderson,
    "Alas, Poor Jacko," Pursuit 8 (Jan.
    1975):18-19.
ca.1871/Seraphine Long
    J.W. Burns & C.V. Tench, "The Hairy
    Giants of British Columbia," Wide
    World Mag., Jan.1940, pp.296-307.

Henry I.
-Sea monster (carcass)
  1934, Nov./=basking shark
    "A Canadian 'Monster,'" Ill.London
    News 185 (15 Dec.1934):1011. il.
    Vancouver Sun, 22-23 Nov.1934; and
    26 Nov.1934.

Heriot Bay
-Sea monster
  1951/George McLean
    Paul H. LeBlond & John Sibert, Obser-
    vations of Large Unidentified Marine
    Animals in British Columbia and Ad-
    jacent Waters (Vancouver: Univ. of
    British Columbia, Inst. of Ocean-
    ography, Manuscript Rept. no.28,
    June 1973), pp.22-23. il.

Heydon L.
-Mystery balls of fiber
  Victoria Daily Colonist, 26 Oct.1969.

Hidden L.
-Humanoid
  1959, Sep./Mrs. Bellvue
    Don Hunter & René Dahinden, Sasquatch
    (Toronto: McClelland & Stewart,
    1973), pp.99-100.

Hornby I.
-UFO (NL)
  1973, April 26/David Holmes
    (Letter), Can.UFO Rept., no.17 (1974)
    :26.

Horne L.
-Humanoid
  1904, Dec./A.R. Crump
    Victoria Daily Colonist, 14 Dec.1904.

Howe Sound
-Sea monster
  1890, July/S.M. Stewart
    Vancouver News-Advertiser, 23 July
    1890.

Jacobsen Bay
-Humanoid
  1940s/Clayton Mack
    John Green, On the Track of the Sas-
    quatch (Agassiz, B.C.: Cheam, 1968),
    pp.41-42.

Jordan R.
-Sea monster
  ca.1948, spring/Rod Kline
    Paul H. LeBlond & John Sibert, Obser-
    vations of Large Unidentified Marine
    Animals in British Columbia and Ad-
    jacent Waters (Vancouver: Univ. of
    British Columbia, Inst. of Ocean-
    ography, Manuscript Rept. no.28,
    June 1973), pp.20-21. il.

Juan de Fuca Strait
-Sea monster
  1934
    Mary Moon, Ogopogo (N.Pomfret, Vt.:
    David & Charles, 1977), p.156.

1936/Alex Stewart
    Vancouver Province, 13 July 1936,
    p.16.
  1955, Jan.2
    Mary Moon, Ogopogo (N.Pomfret, Vt.:
    David & Charles, 1977), p.158.
-Sea monster (carcass)
  1944, May/Ralph Wood/=giant octopus
    "Sea Monsters of Canada," Res Bur-
    eaux Bull., no.33 (4 May 1978):4.

Keats I.
-UFO (CE-1)
  1973, Oct.5/Bernice Niblett
    "Canada Touched by Flap," Can.UFO
    Rept., no.16 (1973-74):7,9.
-UFO (CE-1) and men-in-black
  1968, Jan.27-May 3/Bernice Niblett
    Bernice Niblett, "I Lived in a Nest
    of UFOs," Can.UFO Rept., no.13
    (1972):2-10. il.
    John Magor, Our UFO Visitors (Seat-
    tle: Hancock House, 1977), pp.39-
    58.

Khutze Inlet
-Humanoid
  1969, Feb./Ronnie Nyce
    John Green, The Sasquatch File (Ag-
    assiz, B.C.: Cheam, 1973), p.41.

Klekane Inlet
-Humanoid
  n.d.
    John Green, Sasquatch: The Apes Among
    Us (Seattle: Hancock House, 1978),
    p.368.

Kokanee Glacier Park
-Humanoid
  1961, Oct./John Bringsli
    John Green, The Sasquatch File (Ag-
    assiz, B.C.: Cheam, 1973), p.26.

Kootenay L.
-Ball lightning
  ca.1928, summer/Arthur E. Covington
    Arthur E. Covington, "Ball Light-
    ning," Nature 226 (1970):252-53.
-Pictograph
  =depicts UFO?
    John Corner, Pictographs in the In-
    terior of British Columbia (Vernon,
    B.C.: Wayside, 1968), p.90. il.

Kotcho L.
-UFO (NL)
  1967, March
    "Canada's Year of 'Invasion': Part
    3," Can.UFO Rept., no.8 (fall 1970):
    17,21, quoting Fort Nelson News (un-
    dated).

Kumdis I.
-Humanoid
  1971, Jan./Masset Inlet
    John Green, The Sasquatch File (Ag-
    assiz, B.C.: Cheam, 1973), p.51.

Kwakwa Creek
-Humanoid
  ca.1930
    John Green, The Sasquatch File (Ag-
      assiz, B.C.: Cheam, 1973), p.14.

Kwatna R.
-Humanoid tracks
  1967, Feb./Clayton Mack
    Don Hunter & René Dahinden, Sasquatch
      (Toronto: McClelland & Stewart,
      1973), p.31.
    John Green, Sasquatch: The Apes Among
      Us (Seattle: Hancock House, 1978),
      p.359.

Lama Passage
-Sea monster
  1964, fall/Robert Young/=elephant seal?
    Paul H. LeBlond & John Sibert, Obser-
      vations of Large Unidentified Marine
      Animals in British Columbia and Ad-
      jacent Waters (Vancouver: Univ. of
      British Columbia, Inst. of Ocean-
      ography, Manuscript Rept. no.28-
      June 1973), p.29.

Lemon Creek
-Humanoid
  1960, Aug.7/John Bringsli
    Nelson Daily News, 4 Oct.1960. il.
    John Green, Sasquatch: The Apes Among
      Us (Seattle: Hancock House, 1978),
      pp.416-17.

Lewis L.
-Humanoid tracks
  1969, March
    John Green, The Sasquatch File (Ag-
      assiz, B.C.: Cheam, 1973), p.41.

Lily L.
-Humanoid
  1969, May 18/David Ludlam
    John Green, The Sasquatch File (Ag-
      assiz, B.C.: Cheam, 1973), p.41.

Lookout I.
-UFO (R)
  1972, Aug.22/L.G. Swenson/5 mi.S
    Haydon C. Hewes, "UFO Report," Beyond
      Reality, no.4 (May 1973):48.

Lulu I.
-Humanoid
  1966, July 14-22/Don Gilmore/No.8, 5
  and 2 Rd.
    John Green, The Sasquatch File (Ag-
      assiz, B.C.: Cheam, 1973), p.33.
    John Green, Sasquatch: The Apes Among
      Us (Seattle: Hancock House, 1978),
      pp.449-51.

Malcolm I.
-Sea monster
  1922, May/C.G. Cook
    Paul H. LeBlond & John Sibert, Obser-
      vations of Large Unidentified Marine
      Animals in British Columbia and Ad-
      jacent Waters (Vancouver: Univ. of

British Columbia, Inst. of Oceanography, Manuscript Rept. no.28,
June 1973), pp.10-11. il.

Manning Provincial Park
-Humanoid
  1971, Sep./Allison Pass
    John Green, The Sasquatch File (Ag-
      assiz, B.C.: Cheam, 1973), p.51.

Maple Bay
-UFO (NL)
  1967, fall/Kurt Horn
    "Mystery of Two Lights," Can.UFO
      Rept., no.2 (Mar.-Apr.1969):8.

Mara L.
-Pictograph
  =depicts UFO occupant?
    John Corner, Pictographs in the In-
      terior of British Columbia (Vernon,
      B.C.: Wayside, 1968), pp.109-14. il.

Marble Canyon
-Humanoid
  1975, Sep.
    Lake Windermere Echo, 7 Apr.1977.

Menzies Bay
-Sea monster
  1925/Jack Nord
    R.S. Lambert, Exploring the Supernat-
      ural (Toronto: McClelland & Stewart,
      1955), p.191.

Mica Mt.
-Humanoid
  1955, Oct./William Roe
    John Green, On the Track of the Sas-
      quatch (Agassiz, B.C.: Cheam, 1968),
      pp.10-13.

Mill Bay
-Sea monster
  1940s/Wilfred H. Gibson
    Mary Moon, Ogopogo (N.Pomfret, Vt.:
      David & Charles, 1977), p.160.

Morris Creek
-Humanoid
  1936, July/Frank Dan
    J.W. Burns & C.V. Tench, "The Hairy
      Giants of British Columbia," Wide
      World Mag., Jan.1940, pp.296-307.
  ca.1948/Henry Charlie/Morris Valley Rd.
    John Green, The Sasquatch File (Ag-
      assiz, B.C.: Cheam, 1973), p.14.
-Humanoid tracks
  ca.1900/C.H. Olds
    John Green, The Sasquatch File (Ag-
      assiz, B.C.: Cheam, 1973), p.9.

Morris Mt.
-Humanoid
  1935-1940
    Belle Rendall, Healing Waters: His-
      tory of Harrison Hot Springs and
      Port Douglas Area (Harrison Hot
      Springs, B.C., 1958), pp.30-32.

Mudge, Cape
-Sea monster
    1932, May 26-28/"Adelaide"
        Vancouver Sun, 31 May 1932, p.13.

Murray Ridge
-UFO (NL)
    1976, Feb.11
        (Letter), Shelley E. Hallock, Can.
        UFO Rept., no.28 (summer 1977):3

Nanaimo Lakes
-UFO (NL)
    1973, Aug.26
        "Canada Touched by Flap," Can.UFO
        Rept., no.16 (1973-74):7,8.

Natalkuz L.
-Archeological site
    ca.460 B.C.
        Charles E. Borden, "An Archaeologi-
        cal Reconnaissance of Tweedsmuir
        Park," Museum & Art Notes (Vancou-
        ver), ser.2, vol.2 (1952):9-15.

Nazco R.
-Humanoid
    1960s/Samial Paul/20 mi.S of Nazco
        John Green, The Sasquatch File (Ag-
        assiz, B.C.: Cheam, 1973), p.41.

Nechako R.
-Humanoid myth
    Atnan
        Diamond Jenness, "Myths of the Car-
        rier Indians of B.C.," J.Am.Folklore
        47 (1934):97,247.

Neskain I.
-Giant human skeleton
    1912/=hoax?
        Ivan T. Sanderson, Abominable Snow-
        men: Legend Come to Life (Philadel-
        phia: Chilton, 1961), pp.36-37.

Nicola L.
-Clairvoyance
    1952, Aug./One-Eyed Harry
        (Editorial), Fate 6 (Jan.1953):9.

Nicomen I.
-Humanoid
    1965, May 31/Seraphine Jasper
        John Green, The Sasquatch File (Ag-
        assiz, B.C.: Cheam, 1973), p.33.

Nootka Sound
-Humanoid myth
    matlox
        Jose Mariano Mozino, Noticias de Nut-
        ka (Seattle: Univ. of Washington,
        1970 ed.), p.25.

Okanagan L.
-Lake monster
    1854-   /Ogopogo
        R.P. McLean, Ogopogo: His Story (Ke-
        lowna, B.C.: The Courier, 1952).
        Harold T. Wilkins, Secret Cities of
        Old South America (N.Y.: Library

Publishers, 1952), pp.289-90.
        R.S. Lambert, Exploring the Supernat-
        ural (Toronto: McClelland & Stewart,
        1955), pp.193-97.
        Dorothy Hewlett Gellatly, A Bit of
        Okanagan History (Westbank, B.C.:
        Kelowna Printing Co., 1958).
        "Sea-Cows and Water Horses," Pursuit
        2 (Jan.1969):12-13.
        William Marks, I Saw Ogopogo! (Peach-
        land-Okanagan Review, 1971).
        Mary Moon, "I Saw It This Time As a
        Great, Writhing, Eel-Like Mass,"
        B.C.Motorist, Nov.-Dec.1973, pp.12-
        16,52-62.
        Peter Costello, In Search of Lake
        Monsters (N.Y.: Coward, McCann &
        Geoghegan, 1974), pp.220-27.
        Washington (D.C.) Post, 30 July 1976.
        Mary Moon, Ogopogo (N.Pomfret, Vt.:
        David & Charles, 1977).
        Kelowna Courier, 28-29 Apr.1977; 4
        June 1977; 20 June 1977; 12 July
        1977; and 18 July 1977.
        Vernon Daily News, 26 July 1977; 20
        July 1978; and 16 Aug.1978.
        Penticton Herald, 20 Feb.1978; and
        13 Sep.1978.
        Mary Moon, "Ogopogo: Canada's Loch
        Ness Monster," Fate 31 (Nov.1978):
        34-42. il.
-UFO (?)
    1966, Feb?/Clifford Cole
        Dan Lloyd, "Are They Really Seeing
        Things over Canada?" Flying Saucer
        Rev. 12 (Nov.-Dec.1966):29.

Osborn Bay
-Sea monster
    1937, Jan.8/"Solander"
        Vancouver Sun, 9 Jan.1937, p.16.

Pender I.
-Sea monster
    1933, Dec.3/G.F. Parkyn
    1933, Dec.22/Cyril B. Andrews
        Ray Gardner, "Caddy, King of the
        Coast," Maclean's Mag. 63 (15 June
        1950):24,42-43.
        Mary Moon, Ogopogo (N.Pomfret, Vt.:
        David & Charles, 1977), pp.155-56.

Pinchi L.
-Acoustic anomaly
    1970s
        (Letter), Shelley E. Hallock, Can.
        UFO Rept., no.28 (summer 1977):4.
-UFO (CE-1)
    1976, Nov.
        (Letter), Shelley E. Hallock, Can.
        UFO Rept., no.28 (summer 1977):3.
    1977, Sep./Tom Millard
        "Northern Lights' New Show," Can.UFO
        Rept., no.31 (summer 1978):3-5.
    1977, Oct.10/Irwin Hamilton/Moran Bay
        "Tiny Squadron Flies Fast," Can.UFO
        Rept., no.29 (fall-winter 1977):1-2.

Pitt L.
-Giant lizards

1978, May/Warren Scott
Vancouver Province, 12 May 1978.
-Humanoid
ca.1933/Mr. Cartwright
John Green, Year of the Sasquatch
(Agassiz, B.C.: Cheam, 1970), p.62.
-Humanoid tracks
1965, June/Ron Welch/NW of lake
John Green, Year of the Sasquatch
(Agassiz, B.C.: Cheam, 1970), pp.
29-31. il.
Don Hunter & René Dahinden, Sasquatch
(Toronto: McClelland & Stewart,
1973), pp.43-45.
Peter Byrne, In Search of Bigfoot
(N.Y.: Pocket Books, 1976 ed.), pp.
60-66.

Porlier Pass
-Sea monster
1939, Feb.28/"Wheenamolk"
Vancouver Sun, 1 Mar.1939, p.2.

Powder Mt.
-Humanoid tracks
1969, April/Jack Wilson
John Green, Year of the Sasquatch
(Agassiz, B.C.: Cheam, 1970), pp.
51,53. il.
Don Hunter & René Dahinden, Sasquatch
(Toronto: McClelland & Stewart,
1973), betw.pp.32-33. il.

Price I.
-Archeological site
ca.1000 B.C.-1700 A.D./Great Anchorage
Bjorn O. Simonsen, "Archaeological
Investigations in the Hecate Strait-
Milbanke Sound Area of B.C.," Pap.
Arch.Survey Canada, no.13 (1973).
-Humanoid
1960, Feb./Joe Hopkins/Higgins Passage
John Green, The Sasquatch File (Ag-
assiz, B.C.: Cheam, 1973), p.18.

Purcell Mts.
-UFO (CE-2)
1974, Sep.14/Rene Spocchi
"A Mountain Spectacular," Can.UFO
Rept., no.19 (1975):2-5,7.

Quadra I.
-Ancient glass bottle
ca.1960/Leonard Lakeberg
"What's the Answer?" Can.UFO Rept.,
no.17 (1974):10,11.

Qualicum Bay
-Sea monster
1938
Mary Moon, Ogopogo (N.Pomfret, Vt.:
David & Charles, 1977), p.161.
1953, Feb.13/Frank Waterfall
Bernard Heuvelmans, In the Wake of
the Sea-Serpents (N.Y.: Hill & Wang,
1968), p.506, quoting unidentified
newspaper of 14 Feb.1953.

Quamichan L.
-UFO (?)

1973, Aug.27/Joyce Fox
"Canada Touched by Flap," Can.UFO
Rept., no.16 (1973-74):7,8.

Quatsino Sound
-Ghost
1906, Oct.7/J. Roy Ildstad
J. Roy Ildstad, "Terror in the Night,"
Fate 7 (Nov.1954):47-49.

Queen Charlotte Is.
-Sea monster
1895, June/Mr. Ferguson
Victoria Colonist, 13 Jan.1897, p.5.
1922, Aug.
Vancouver Sun, 22 Aug.1925, p.2.
1925, July-Aug./John J. Van Valkenberg
Vancouver Province, 28 Mar.1926, p.1.
Mary Moon, Ogopogo (N.Pomfret, Vt.:
David & Cahrles, 1977), pp.162-63.
1937, summer
Vancouver Sun, 16 Oct.1937, p.31.

Queen Charlotte Strait
-Sea monster
1937
Vancouver Sun, 28 Apr.1937, p.4.

Race Rocks
-Acoustic anomaly
"Vancouver Island's 'Zone of Silence,'"
Fate 11 (June 1958):42.
-Sea monster
1959, July 19/Jamie Cameron
Vancouver Sun, 24 July 1959.

Relay Creek
-Humanoid
1960s/Chilco Choate
John Green, Year of the Sasquatch
(Agassiz, B.C.: Cheam, 1970), p.5.

Rivers Inlet
-UFO (NL)
1897, July 10/W.S. Fitzgerald
Portland Oregonian, 19 July 1897.

Roberson Point
-Petroglyph
=depicts UFO occupant?
Harlan I. Smith, "The Man Petroglyph
near Prince Rupert, or the Man Who
Fell from Heaven," in R.H. Lewis,
ed., Essays in Anthropology Presented to Alfred Louis Kroeber (Berkeley: Univ. of California, 1936), pp.
309-12.
Beth & Ray Hill, Indian Petroglyphs
of the Pacific Northwest (Seattle:
Univ. of Washington, 1974), pp.192-
93. il.

Roberts Bay
-Sea monster
1943, Aug./Jane Easson
Paul H. LeBlond & John Sibert, Obser-
vations of Large Unidentified Marine
Animals in British Columbia and Ad-
jacent Waters (Vancouver: Univ. of
British Columbia, Inst. of Ocean-

graphy, Manuscript Rept. no.28,
June 1973), pp.17-18. il.

Roderick I.
-Humanoid
  ca.1960, winter/Timothy Robinson/Watson Bay
    John Green, The Sasquatch File (Agassiz, B.C.: Cheam, 1973), p.18.
-Humanoid tracks
  ca.1950/Paul Hopkins/cannery
    John Green, The Sasquatch File (Agassiz, B.C.: Cheam, 1973), p.14.

Rogers Pass
-UFO (CE-1)
  1969/Kern Clement
    "Playground of Gods," Can.UFO Rept.,
    no.11 (1971):2,6.

Roscoe Inlet
-Humanoid
  1973, July
    John Green, "Not All Quiet on the
    Western Front," Pursuit 7 (Oct.1974)
    :98,99.

Ross Bay
-Sea monster
  1956/Mrs. E.F. Spence/Dallas Rd.
    Paul H. LeBlond & John Sibert, Observations of Large Unidentified Marine
    Animals in British Columbia and Adjacent Waters (Vancouver: Univ. of
    British Columbia, Inst. of Oceanography, Manuscript Rept. no.28,
    June 1973), p.23.
-Sea monster (carcass)
  1940, Oct.
    Vancouver Sun, 23 Oct.1940, p.14.

Saanich Inlet
-Sea monster
  1940, July/C.O. Biscaro
    Mary Moon, Ogopogo (N.Pomfret, Vt.:
    David & Charles, 1977), p.160.
-UFO (NL)
  1966, March 25/Mrs. R.H. Chappell
    Saanich Peninsula and Gulf Islands
    Review, 30 Mar.1966.

Saanich Peninsula
-UFO (CE-2)
  1975, March/Kaz Grabanac/ground markings only
    "'Fairy Ring' or UFO?" Can.UFO Rept.,
    no.21 (1975):13. il.

Salmon Inlet
-Humanoid
  1968, May 17/Gordon Baum
    Vancouver Sun, 24 June 1968.

Saltspring I.
-Sea monster
  1944, Jan.
    Mary Moon, Ogopogo (N.Pomfret, Vt.:
    David & Charles, 1977), pp.160-61.
  1946, fall/John Nilsen
    Paul H. LeBlond & John Sibert, Obser-

vations of Large Unidentified Marine
Animals in British Columbia and Adjacent Waters (Vancouver: Univ. of
British Columbia, Inst. of Oceanography, Manuscript Rept. no.28,
June 1973), pp.18-19. il.

Selma Park
-Humanoid
  1973, June
    John Green, "Not All Quiet on the
    Western Front," Pursuit 7 (Oct.
    1974):98.

Seton L.
-Humanoid myth
    W.C. Elliott, "Lake Lillooet Tales,"
    J.Am.Folklore 44 (1931):166,174.
-Lake monster
  1964-1966/=giant sturgeon
    (Editorial), Fate 20 (June 1967):24.
    Ivan T. Sanderson, Invisible Residents (N.Y.: World, 1970), p.63.
-Water anomaly
    "Polyponds," Pursuit 3 (Jan.1970):13.

Shelter Point
-Sea monster
  1963, March/Mrs. J.C. Durrant/klahmahsosaurus
    Victoria Daily Times, 29 Mar.1963.

Shoemaker Bay
-Archeological site
  ca.2000 B.C.-300 A.D.
    Columbus (O.) Dispatch, 15 Aug.1975.

Shuswap L.
-Lake monster
  1904,1948/Ta-Zam-a
    (Editorial), California Native Voice,
    Oct.1948.
-UFO (?)
  1965, March 31/=meteor
    Kamloops Daily Sentinel, 17 Apr 1965.

Sicintine Range
-UFO (CE-1)
  1965, July/John Hembling/Skeena R.
    "Disc Draws Water," Can.UFO Rept.,
    no.3 (May-June 1969):4-6.
    John Magor, Our UFO Visitors (Seattle: Hancock House, 1977), pp.199-200.

Skeena R.
-Humanoid tracks
  1976, July/Eric Gerhardi
    Terrace Northern Times, 20 Aug.1976.
    "Tracks in Northern B.C.," Can.UFO
    Rept., no.28 (summer 1977):22-24. il.
    John Green, Sasquatch: The Apes Among
    Us (Seattle: Hancock House, 1978),
    p.365.

Skidegate Inlet
-Sea monster
  1939, summer
    Vancouver Sun, 17 July 1939, p.1.

South Bentick Arm
-Humanoid
  1928/George Talleo
    John Green, The Sasquatch File (Ag-
    assiz, B.C.: Cheam, 1973), p.14.
    John Green, Sasquatch: The Apes Among
    Us (Seattle: Hancock House, 1978),
    p.377.

Squam Bay
-Fall of stone
  1965, March 31/Elmer Saunders/=meteor-
  ite?
    Kamloops Daily Sentinel, 10 Apr.1965.
    il.

Squamish R.
-Humanoid tracks
  1971, May/G. Conway
    John Green, The Sasquatch File (Ag-
    assiz, B.C.: Cheam, 1973), p.51.

Stanley Park
-UFO (DD)
  1968, July 22/John Narowey
    J.J. Soulières, "Dossier Photo," UFO-
    Québec, no.2 (1975):17. il.

Steamboat Mt.
-UFO (CE-1)
  1974, Oct.18/Edmoana Toews
    Edmoana Toews, "The UFOs That Led Us
    Home: Part One," Fate 30 (June 1977)
    :38-42.

Stein R.
-Petroglyph
  =depicts UFO?
    John Corner, Pictographs in the In-
    terior of British Columbia (Vernon,
    B.C.: Wayside, 1968), pp.42-45. il.

Stokke Creek
-Humanoid
  1974, July/=hoax?
    John Green, "Not All Quiet on the
    Western Front," Pursuit 7 (Oct.1974)
    :98,99.

Stony L.
-Humanoid
  1962, July/Alex Lindstrom
    John Green, The Sasquatch File (Ag-
    assiz, B.C.: Cheam, 1973), p.26.

Stuart Channel
-Sea monster
  1963, Feb./Dave Welham
    Mary Moon, Ogopogo (N.Pomfret, Vt.:
    David & Charles, 1977), pp.161-62.

Stuart L.
-UFO (CE-1)
  1977, Nov.3/Kirk Alore/Parren's Beach
  Rd.
    "Northern Lights' New Show," Can.UFO
    Rept., no.31 (summer 1978):3-5.
    W.K. Allen, "The Fort St. James Sight-
    ings," Flying Saucer Rev. 24 (Nov.
    1978):8,11.

Sunset Beach
-Sea monster
  1937/Mrs. Charles Timeus
  1937/Fred B. Lawrence
    Bernard Heuvelmans, In the Wake of
    the Sea-Serpents (N.Y.: Hill & Wang,
    1968), p.466.

Swansea Mt.
-UFO (NL)
  1968, spring/Cherie Dobbie
    John Magor, Our UFO Visitors (Seat-
    tle: Hancock House, 1978), p.111.

Swartz Bay
-Sea monster
  1939, March
    Mary Moon, Ogopogo (N.Pomfret, Vt.:
    David & Charles, 1977), p.160.

Swindle I.
-Humanoid tracks
  1945, April/Tom Brown/Meyers Pass
  ca.1950, May/Kitasu L.
  1961, July-Dec./Bob Titmus
  1962, fall/Bob Titmus
  ca.1964/Sam Brown
  1968, winter/Paul Hopkins
  1969, June 18/Sam Brown/Kitasu L.
    John Green, The Sasquatch File (Ag-
    assiz, B.C.: Cheam, 1973), pp.14,
    25-26,33-34,41.

Tagai, L.
-Lake monster
  1976, Aug./Phil Streifel
    Prince George Citizen, 13 Aug.1976.

Taylor L.
-UFO (NL)
  1967, July 11/Brian Gratton
    John Magor, Our UFO Visitors (Seat-
    tle: Hancock House, 1977), pp.62-64.

Ten Mile Point
-Sea monster
  1939, summer/Mrs. M. Tildesley
    Paul H. LeBlond & John Sibert, Obser-
    vations of Large Unidentified Marine
    Animals in British Columbia and Ad-
    jacent Waters (Vancouver: Univ. of
    British Columbia, Inst. of Ocean-
    ography, Manuscript Rept. no.28,
    June 1973), pp.14-15. il.

Tezzaron L.
-UFO (CE-1)
  1976, Nov?
    (Letter), Shelley E. Hallock, Can.UFO
    Rept., no.28 (summer 1977):3,4.

Thetis I.
-UFO (NL)
  1971, May 3-6,27/Gwenyth M. Bazett
    (Letter), Can.UFO Rept., no.10 (1971)
    :29-30.

Thetis L.
-Lake monster
  1972, Aug./Gordon Pike

Victoria Daily Times, 22 Aug.1972.

Thompson R.
-Clairvoyance
   1895, spring/Matthew Crawford/Canadian
   Pacific RR
      Julie C. Crawford, "The Psychic War-
      ning That Stopped the Train," *Fate*
      15 (July 1962):61-64.

Thompson Sound
-Humanoid
   1963
      John Green, *The Sasquatch File* (Ag-
      assiz, B.C.: Cheam,1973), pp.26-27.

Toba Inlet
-Humanoid
   1924, summer/Albert Ostman
      Agassiz-Harrison Advance, 22 Aug.
      1957.
      Ivan T. Sanderson, *Abominable Snow-
      men: Legend Come to Life* (Philadel-
      phia : Chilton, 1961), pp.50-61.
      John Green, *On the Track of the Sas-
      quatch* (Agassiz, B.C.: Cheam, 1968),
      pp.13-21.
      John Napier, *Bigfoot* (N.Y.: Dutton,
      1973), pp.76-80.
      John Green, *Sasquatch: The Apes Among
      Us* (Seattle: Hancock House, 1978),
      pp.97-112.

Tree Point Lighthouse
-Sea monster
   1969, Oct./F.M. Leonard/"Mary Foss"
      Paul H. LeBlond & John Sibert, *Obser-
      vations of Large Unidentified Marine
      Animals in British Columbia and Ad-
      jacent Waters* (Vancouver: Univ. of
      British Columbia, Inst. of Ocean-
      ography, Manuscript Rept. no.28,
      June 1973), pp.30-31.

Trial I.
-Sea monster
   1934, Jan.7/Del Marsh
      Vancouver Sun, 8 Jan.1934, p.1.
   1940, Oct./Walter Pratley
      Vancouver Sun, 15 Oct.1940, p.17.

Turnour I.
-Humanoid
   1964, April/=bear?
      John Green, *The Sasquatch File* (Ag-
      assiz, B.C.: Cheam, 1973), p.27.

Tzatus I.
-Sea monster
   1903, April
      Mary Moon, *Ogopogo* (N.Pomfret, Vt.:
      David & Charles, 1977), p.160.

Vancouver I.
-Phantom ship
   1957, Nov.2/"Meitetsu Maru"/30 mi. offshore
      (Editorial), *Fate* 11 (July 1958):6-8.
-Sea monster
   1912, Aug./Hildegarde Forbes

Tim Dinsdale, *The Leviathans* (London:
      Routledge & Kegan Paul, 1966), pp.
      90-91.
   1928, fall/James F. Murray
      Toronto (Ont.) Sun, 6 Jan.1954.
   1943/Ernest Lee
      Ray Gardner, "Caddy, King of the
      Coast," *Maclean's Mag.* 63 (15 June
      1950):24,42-43.
-UFO (NL)
   1897, Aug.
      San Francisco (Cal.) Chronicle, 13
      Aug.1897.

Vedder Mt.
-UFO (NL)
   1973, Aug.24
      Abbotsford, Sumas and Matsqui News,
      19 Sep.1973.

Waddington Mt.
-Chinese discovery
   ca.1000 B.C.
      Henriette Mertz, *Gods from the Far
      East* (N.Y.: Ballantine, 1975 ed.),
      p.153.

Welcome Pass
-Sea monster
   1957, July 7/N. Erickson
      Paul H. LeBlond & John Sibert, *Obser-
      vations of Large Unidentified Marine
      Animals in British Columbia and Ad-
      jacent Waters* (Vancouver: Univ. of
      British Columbia, Inst. of Ocean-
      ography, Manuscript Rept. no.28,
      June 1973), pp.24-25. il.

Wells Gray Provincial Park
-Humanoid tracks
   1970, fall
      John Green, *The Sasquatch File* (Ag-
      assiz, B.C.: Cheam, 1973), p.51.

Windermere, L.
-UFO (NL)
   1972, Aug.10/Mrs. T.N. Weir
      "'Fireball' Below Treetops," *Can.UFO
      Rept.*, no.14 (1973):25-26.
      "More on That 1972 'Meteor,'" *Can.
      UFO Rept.*, no.33 (winter 1978-79):
      7-9.

               C. Ethnic Groups

Bella Coola Indians
-Hex
      H.I. Smith, "Sympathetic Magic and
      Witchcraft among the Bella Coola,"
      Am.Anthro. 27 (1914):116-21.
-Humanoid myth
   snanaik
      Joseph H. Wherry, *Indian Masks and
      Myths of the West* (N.Y.: Funk & Wag-
      nalls, 1969), pp.121-23.

Carrier Indians
-Humanoid myth
      Diamond Jenness, "Myths of the Car-

rier Indians of British Columbia,"
J.Am.Folklore 47 (1934):97,220-22.

Cowichan Indians
-Flood myth
    Martha Harris, History and Folklore
    of the Cowichan Indians (Victoria:
    The Colonist, 1901).

Gitskan Indians
-Shamanism
    Marius Barbeau, "Medicine-Men on the
    North Pacific Coast," Bull.Nat'l
    Mus.Canada, no.152 (1958):29-48,
    74-75. il.

Haida Indians
-Deathbed apparition myth
    Charles Harrison, "Religion and Fam-
    ily among the Haidas," J.Anthro.
    Inst. 21 (1892):14,17-21.
-Flood myth
    James Churchward, The Lost Continent
    of Mu (N.Y.: Paperback Library,
    1968 ed.), pp.57-59.
-Giant bird legend
    James G. Swain, "The Haidah Indians
    of Queen Charlotte's Islands, Brit-
    ish Columbia," Smith.Contrib.Knowl.,
    vol.21, no.267 (1876).
    Garrick Mallery, "On the Pictographs
    of the North American Indians," Ann.
    Rept.Bur.Am.Ethn. 4 (1883):188-90.

Kaska Indians
-Hex
    John J. Honigman, "Witch-Fear in
    Post-Contact Kaska Society," Am.
    Anthro. 49 (1947):222-43.
-Humanoid myth
    James A. Teit, "Kaska Tales," J.Am.
    Folklore 30 (1917):427,438.

Kutenai Indians
-Flood myth
    Franz Boas, "Kutenai Tales," Bull.
    Bur.Am.Ethn., no.59 (1918).
-Shamanism
    Alexander F. Chamberlain, "Kootenay
    Medicine Men," J.Am.Folklore 14
    (1901):95,97.
-Welsh Indians
    Richard Deacon, Madoc and the Discov-
    ery of America (N.Y.: Braziller,
    1966), pp.153-54.
    Olga Johnson, Flathead and Kootenay
    (Glendale, Cal.: A.H. Clark, 1969).

Kwakiutl Indians
-Humanoid myth
    dsonoqua
    Franz Boas, "Kwakiutl Tales, New Ser-
    ies," Contrib.Anthro.Columbia Univ.
    26 (1935):147-56.
    Joseph H. Wherry, Indian Masks and
    Myths of the West (N.Y.: Funk & Wag-
    nalls, 1969), pp.114-21. il.
-Shamanism
    Franz Boas, "Second General Report on
    the Indians of British Columbia,"

Rept.Brit.Ass'n Adv.Sci. 60 (1890):
562,611-13.
J. Adrian Jacobsen,"Geheimbünde der
Küstenbewohner Nordwest-Amerikas,"
Verhandlungen der Berliner Gesell-
schaft für Anthro-, Ethno- und Ur-
geschichte, 1891, pp.384-92.

Lillooet Indians
-Humanoid myth
    haitlo laux
    James A. Teit, "Traditions of the
    Lillooet Indians of British Colum-
    bia," J.Am.Folklore 25 (1912):287,
    346-47.

Nootka Indians
-Shamanism
    Franz Boas, "Second General Report on
    the Indians of British Columbia,"
    Rept.Brit.Ass'n Adv.Sci. 60 (1890):
    562,595-99.

Okanagan Indians
-Flood myth
    Herbert Howe Bancroft, Native Races
    of the Pacific States, 5 vols. (N.Y.:
    Appleton, 1875), 3:153-54.
    James A. Teit, "Tales from the Lower
    Fraser River," in Franz Boas, ed.,
    Folk-Tales of Salishan and Sahaptin
    Tribes (N.Y.: Am.Folklore Soc'y,
    1917), pp.129,132.

Shuswap Indians
-Shamaniam
    Franz Boas, "Second General Report on
    the Indians of British Columbia,"
    Rept.Brit.Ass'n Adv.Sci. 60 (1890):
    562,645-47.

Skagit River Indians
-Humanoid myth
    Emerson N. Matson, Legends of the
    Great Chiefs (N.Y.: Thomas Nelson,
    1972).

Squamish Indians
-Flood myth
    E. Pauline Johnson, Legends of Van-
    couver (Toronto: McClelland & Stew-
    art, 1922), pp.53-58.

Takhelne Indians
-Welsh Indians
    Barry Fell, "Takhelne, a Living Celt-
    iberian Language of North America,"
    Occ.Pub.Epigraphic Soc'y, vol.4, no.
    92 (Nov.1976).
    Barry Fell, "Takhelne, a North Amer-
    ican Celtic Language, Pt.2," Occ.
    Pub.Epigraphic Soc'y 7, no.140 (Apr.
    1979):21-42.

Thompson Indians
-Humanoid myth
    James A. Teit, "Traditions of the
    Thompson River Indians of British
    Columbia," Mem.Am.Folklore Soc'y 6
    (1898):79.

Tsimshian Indians
-Flood myth
Harold T. Wilkins, <u>Mysteries of Ancient South America</u> (N.Y.: Citadel, 1956), p.17.
-Shamanism
Franz Boas, "First General Report on the Indians of British Columbia," <u>Rept.Brit.Ass'n Adv.Sci.</u> 59 (1889): 801,848-55.
Marius Barbeau, "Medicine-Men on the North Pacific Coast," <u>Bull.Nat'l Mus.Canada</u>, no.152 (1958):67-74.

WASHINGTON

A. Populated Places

Almota
-Ancient sword and coat-of-mail
1887/J.H. Hungate
"An Aboriginal Coat of Mail," Am.An-
tiquarian 11 (1889):196-97.

Aloha
-Humanoid
1972, Feb./Don Waugh
1972, Dec.24/Julie Reed
John Green, The Sasquatch File (Agassiz, B.C.: Cheam, 1973), p.54.

Anacortes
-UFO (?)
1967, May 12/Mrs. G.C. Hallett/W of Mt.
Erie
Coral E. Lorenzen, The Shadow of the
Unknown (N.Y.: Signet, 1970), pp.
72-73.

Arden
-Humanoid tracks
1971, March 16
Bigfoot/Sasquatch Clipping Reproduc-
tions Service 1 (June 1977):5.
-UFO (NL)
1908, Feb.2-3
Tacoma News-Tribune, 2 Feb.1950.

Auburn
-UFO (NL)
1975, Nov.3
"UFO Central," CUFOS News Bull., 1
Feb.1976, p.11.

Bellevue
-Haunt
1942/Frank Colacurcio
"The Screaming Ghost," Fate 8 (Aug.
1955):57.

Bellingham
-UFO (DD)
1947, June 24/George Clover
Tacoma News-Tribune, 27 June 1947.
1947, Sep.13/E.L. Lynn/1040 Knox Ave.
Kenneth Arnold & Ray Palmer, The Coming of the Saucers (Boise: The Authors, 1952), p.138.
1956, July 19/J.E. Church
"Case 235," CRIFO Orbit, 7 Dec.1956,
p.1, quoting Bellingham Herald (undated).
1978, Oct.6/Russell Simonsen/1184 E.
Smith Rd.
Bellingham Herald, 8 Oct.1978; and 15
Oct.1978.
-UFO (NL)
1955, Sep.3
Thomas M. Olsen, ed., The Reference
for Outstanding UFO Sighting Reports

(Riderwood, Md.: UFO Information
Retrieval Center, 1966), pp.41-42.
1967, July/Pat Garraghan
(Editorial), Can.UFO Rept., no.30
(winter-spring 1978):3.
-Windshield pitting
1954, April
"A New Look for Windshields," Life,
12 Apr.1954, pp.34-35. il.
"The Windshield Pox-Plague," CRIFO
Newsl., 7 May 1954, p.4.

Bossberg
-Humanoid
1969, April/Williams Lake Rd. x Hwy 25
John Green, Year of the Sasquatch
(Agassiz, B.C.: Cheam, 1970), pp.
74-75.
1970, Oct.6/Ivan Marx/=hoax
Don Hunter & René Dahinden, Sasquatch
(Toronto: McClelland & Stewart,
1973), pp.159-64.
John Green, Sasquatch: The Apes Among
Us (Seattle: Hancock House, 1978),
pp.160-68.
-Humanoid tracks
1969, Nov.24/Joe Rhodes/garbage dump
Don Hunter & René Dahinden, Sasquatch
(Toronto: McClelland & Stewart,
1973), pp.146-47.
1969, Dec.13/René Dahinden/N of town
John Green, Year of the Sasquatch
(Agassiz, B.C.: Cheam, 1970), pp.
45,49,75-76. il.
Don Hunter & René Dahinden, Sasquatch
(Toronto: McClelland & Stewart,
1973), pp.148-52. il.
John Napier, Bigfoot (N.Y.: Dutton,
1973), pp.123-26. il.
New York Times, 30 June 1976, p.39.
1970, July 3/LaVonne Davis/North Gorge
Campground
John Green, The Sasquatch File (Ag-
assiz, B.C.: Cheam, 1973), p.52.

Bothell
-Horse mutilation
1977, Oct.14/Red Henning
Everett Herald, 12 Dec.1977.

Bremerton
-Ball lightning
1951, Nov.6/Robert Burch/YMCA
Gordon W. Hackbarth, "Visit by a
Fireball," Fate 6 (June 1953):49.
-Humanoid
1971, Dec.15/7 mi.NW
1972, Feb./7 mi.NW
John Green, Sasquatch: The Apes Among
Us (Seattle: Hancock House, 1978),
p.14.
-Precognition
1962, Feb./Mrs. Clarence Olson
(Editorial), Fate 15 (June 1962):19-

20.
-UFO (DD)
1947, June 17/H.K. Wheeler
1947, June 24/Emma Shingler
Seattle Post-Intelligencer, 27 June
1947.
1957, Nov.12/Leo Otrin
Bremerton Sun, 16 Nov.1957.
-UFO (NL)
1973, Sep.17/Theresa Deno/Northlake Way
Bremerton Sun, 11 Oct.1973.
1976, April 4
"Noteworthy UFO Sightings," Ufology
2 (fall 1976):61.

Burien
-UFO (?)
1949, July 29
"If It's in the Sky It's a Saucer,"
Doubt, no.27 (1949):416.
-UFO (DD)
1947, July 10/Don Reber
Seattle Post-Intelligencer, 11 July
1947.

Camas
-Dog mutilation
1974, March 30-April 2/animal shelter
B. Ann Slate, "Gods from Inner Space,"
Saga UFO Rept. 3 (Apr.1976):36,38.
-UFO (NL)
1977, Dec.24/SE Everett Rd.
Camas Post-Record, 11 Jan.1978; and
25 Jan.1978.

Carbonado
-UFO (NL)
1959, April 1
Coral E. Lorenzen, Flying Saucers:
The Startling Evidence of the Invasion from Outer Space (N.Y.: Signet, 1966 ed.), p.162.

Carnation
-UFO (DD)
1947, July 10/Mary Jo Burtos
Seattle Post-Intelligencer, 11 July
1947.

Carson
-Humanoid tracks
1969, April/K.L. Cramer/20 mi.NE
John Green, The Sasquatch File (Agassiz, B.C.: Cheam, 1973), p.43.

Centralia
-UFO (DD)
1950, April 29/Mrs. Albert Goelitzer
Los Angeles (Cal.) Times, 30 Apr.
1950.

Chehalis
-Flying humanoid
1948, Jan.6/Bernice Zaikowski
Portland Oregon Journal, 21 Jan.1948.
-Humanoid
1967, fall/Billy Brown/Chehalis R., 4
mi. from town
John Green, The Sasquatch File (Agassiz, B.C.: Cheam, 1973), p.37.

Chewelah
-UFO (DD)
1947, July 9/Buell Throop
Spokane Daily Chronicle, 10 July
1947.

Cinebar
-UFO (?)
1948/nr. Silver Creek
"You Asked for It," Doubt, no.24
(1949):363.

Clark co.
-Humanoid tracks
1974, Oct.7/Cyril Gillette
John Green, Sasquatch: The Apes Among
Us (Seattle: Hancock House, 1978),
pp.364-65, quoting Lewis River News
(undated).

Clipper
-Humanoid
1968, June/Frank Lawrence, Jr./9 mi.E
John Green, The Sasquatch File (Agassiz, B.C.: Cheam, 1973), p.42.

Colville
-Humanoid myth
1840
Peter Byrne, The Search for Bigfoot
(N.Y.: Pocket Books, 1976 ed.), pp.
9-11, quoting letter from Elkanah
Walker to Rev. David Green, April
1840.
-Humanoid tracks
1971/Ray Pickens/=hoax
"Footprints in the..." Pursuit 4
(July 1971):69.
1973, Nov./SW of town
John Green, "Not All Quiet on the
Western Front," Pursuit 7 (Oct.1974)
:99.

Copalis Beach
-Humanoid
1969, July 27/Verlin Herrington/Deekay
Rd.
John Green, Year of the Sasquatch
(Agassiz, B.C.: Cheam, 1970), pp.
27-29.

Copalis Crossing
-Humanoid
1970, May/Rosemary Tucker
Portland Oregonian, 17 June 1970.
1970, May 26/James Figg
John Green, The Sasquatch File (Agassiz, B.C.: Cheam, 1973), p.54.

Coulee City
-UFO (CE-2)
1957, Dec.8
Prairie City (Ore.) Grant County
Journal, 10 Dec.1957.

Custer
-UFO (CE-2)
1965, Jan.12/Mrs. Jubert
J. Allen Hynek, The UFO Experience
(Chicago: Regnery, 1972), pp.132-33.

Ted Phillips, Physical Traces Associated with UFO Sightings (Evanston: Center for UFO Studies, 1975), p.34.
John Magor, Our UFO Visitors (Seattle: Hancock House, 1977), pp.211-12, quoting Spaceview (undated).

Darrington
-UFO (CE-2)
 n.d.
    Ted Phillips, Physical Traces Associated with UFO Sightings (Evanston: Center for UFO Studies, 1975), p.2.

Davenport
-Humanoid tracks
 1978, Feb.10/Sed Englund/8 mi.NW
    Spokane Spokesman-Review, 11 Feb. 1978.
    Aberdeen Daily World, 12 Feb.1978.

Deming
-Humanoid tracks
 1971, Jan.10/Dick Grover
    John Green, The Sasquatch File (Agassiz, B.C.: Cheam, 1973), p.53.

Des Moines
-UFO (NL)
 1973, Nov.
    Des Moines News, 7 Nov.1973.

Eastsound
-UFO (NL)
 1973, Sep.7/Ruth Spignesi
    (Letter), Can.UFO Rept., no.16 (1973-74):32.

Eatonville
-Humanoid
 1977, March 16
    Tacoma News-Tribune, 22-23 Mar.1977.
-Humanoid tracks
 1976, Sep./Don Durden
    Tacoma News-Tribune, 22-23 Mar.1977.
 1977, April
    Seattle Post-Intelligencer, 12 Apr. 1977.

Edmonds
-UFO (NL)
 1931, summer/Lillie M. Wilkison
    Gordon I.R. Lore, Jr. & Harold H. Deneault, Jr., Mysteries of the Skies: UFOs in Perspective (Englewood Cliffs: Prentice-Hall, 1968), pp.108-109.

Ellensburg
-UFO (CE-2)
 1957, Dec.3
    Ellensburg Daily Record, 4 Dec.1957.
-UFO (NL)
 1959, Nov.8
    Richard Hall, ed., The UFO Evidence (Washington: NICAP, 1964), p.156.

Entiat
-Out-of-body experience
 1949, fall/Margaret C. Wilson

Margaret C. Wilson, "I Haunted an Orchard," Fate 12 (Nov.1959):37-40.

Enumclaw
-Ghost
 1959, July 24/Kathleen McNally
    (Letter), Fate 15 (June 1962):120-21.

Ephrata
-UFO (?)
 1965, March 31/=meteor?
    Richard Hunt, "Canadian Fireballs," Flying Saucer Rev. 12 (Mar.-Apr. 1966):33.
-UFO (CE-2)
 1967, April 21/Carey Lee Walt/10 mi.S
    "Car and UAO in Near Collision near Grand Coulee," APRO Bull. 15 (May-June 1967):10.
    Ted Phillips, Physical Traces Associated with UFO Sightings (Evanston: Center for UFO Studies, 1975), p.48.

Evans
-Humanoid
 1968/Mrs. Gruber/Columbia R.
    Peter Byrne, The Search for Bigfoot (N.Y.: Pocket Books, 1976 ed.), p. 83.

Everett
-UFO (?)
 1954, June
    Donald E. Keyhoe, Flying Saucer Conspiracy (N.Y.: Holt, 1955), p.166.
-UFO (NL)
 1975, Sep.12/SE of town
 1975, Sep.21
    "UFO Central," CUFOS News Bull., 15 Nov.1975, pp.18,19.

Fairchild AFB
-UFO (NL)
 1952, Jan.20
    Edward J. Ruppelt, The Report on Unidentified Objects (Garden City: Doubleday, 1956), pp.12-13.
    U.S. Air Force, Projects Grudge and Blue Book Reports 1-12 (Washington: NICAP, 1968), p.90.

Fife
-Humanoid
 1969, Sep.30/Dick Hancock/Fife Hts. Dr.
    John Green, Year of the Sasquatch (Agassiz, B.C.: Cheam, 1970), pp. 23-24. il.

Fort Lewis
-Earthquake anomaly
 1939, Nov./L.M. Button
    Coral E. Lorenzen, The Shadow of the Unknown (N.Y.: Signet, 1970), p.77, quoting letter in Amazing Stories, June 1948.
-UFO (?)
 1976, Nov.10
    Rufus Drake, "Top-Secret Nuclear Plant Besieged by UFOs," Saga UFO Rept. 4 (June 1977):38,60.

Friday Harbor
-UFO (NL)
  1968, April 10
    "U.S. Reports," APRO Bull. 17 (Sep.-
    Oct.1968):8.

Goldendale
-Archeological site
  ca.7000 B.C.
    Claude N. Warren, Alan L. Bryan &
    Donald R. Tuohy, "The Goldendale
    Site and Its Place in Plateau Pre-
    history," Tebiwa 6, no.1 (1963):
    1-21.

Graham
-UFO (?)
  1959, April 1/Sam Snyder
    Coral E. Lorenzen, Flying Saucers:
    The Startling Evidence of the Inva-
    sion from Outer Space (N.Y.: Signet,
    1966 ed.), p.161.

Granite Falls
-Chicken mutilation
  1977, June 1
    "Washington," Phenomena Rsch.Special
    Rept., no.3 (Oct.1977):8-9.

Hanford Works
-UFO (DD)
  1944, March/James E. Emery
    Rufus Drake, "Top-Secret Nuclear
    Plant Besieged by UFOs," Saga UFO
    Rept. 4 (June 1977):38-39.
  1952, July 5/John Baldwin/=balloon?
    New York Times, 6 July 1952, p.51.
    Edward J. Ruppelt, The Report on Un-
    identified Flying Objects (Garden
    City: Doubleday, 1956), p.153.
    Richard Hall, ed., The UFO Evidence
    (Washington: NICAP, 1964), p.38.
-UFO (NL)
  1961, Dec.18
  1975, June 16/Doris Beck
    Rufus Drake, "Top-Secret Nuclear
    Plant Besieged by UFOs," Saga UFO
    Rept. 4 (June 1977):38-40.
-UFO (R-V)
  1949, May 21
    J. Allen Hynek, The Hynek UFO Report
    (N.Y.: Dell, 1977), pp.141-42.

Harrah
-Humanoid
  1976, March/S. Harrah Rd.
    B. Ann Slate, "Saucer Slaughter on
    the Prairies," Saga UFO Rept. 4
    (Sep.1977):37-38.
-UFO (CE-3)
  1975, Dec./Pumphouse Rd.
    B. Ann Slate, "Saucer Slaughter on
    the Prairies," Saga UFO Rept. 4
    (Sep.1977):37-38.
  1977, Jan.19/Mr. Cantu
    Toppenish Review, 26 Jan.1977.
-UFO (NL)
  1975, Aug.-Dec.
  1976, Feb./Pumphouse Rd.
    B. Ann Slate, "Saucer Slaughter on

the Prairies," Saga UFO Rept. 4
(Sep.1977):37-38.

Hobart
-UFO (?)
  1952, May 11/B.C. Carlson/=meteor?
    "Case 50," CRIFO Newsl., 4 Feb.1955,
    p.3.

Hoogdal
-Acoustic anomaly
  1967, April 6-May 14/John Boynton/=saw-
    whet owl?
    "Happening at Hoogdal: An Unidenti-
    fied Beeping Object," Look, 14 Nov.
    1967, pp.42-43.
    Edward U. Condon, ed., Scientific
    Study of Unidentified Flying Objects
    (N.Y.: Bantam, 1969 ed.), pp.306-10.
    Coral E. Lorenzen, The Shadow of the
    Unknown (N.Y.: Signet, 1970), pp.
    72-74.

Hoquiam
-Spontaneous human combustion
  1973, Dec.10/Betty Satlow/Coleman Mor-
    tuary
    Portland Oregonian, 20 Dec.1973.
    (Letter), George Harper, Fate 30
    (Feb.1977):134-36.

Ilwaco
-Ghost
  1919, June/Beard's Hollow
    Portland Oregonian, 20 July 1919.
    Hilda Broughton, "The Ghost That Came
    to Tell," Fate 18 (Nov.1965):62-65.

Irrigon
-UFO (?)
  1945, July 2/Rip Van Discer
    "If It's in the Sky It's a Saucer,"
    Doubt, no.27 (1949):416.

Issaquah
-Fall of magnetic particles
  1957, July
    (Editorial), Fate 10 (Nov.1957):12.

Kalama
-UFO (CE-1)
  1978, fall/Darrel Coffey
    Woodland Lewis River News, 9 Nov.
    1978.

Kapowsin
-Humanoid
  1972, Feb.5/Wanda A. Borton
    (Editorial), Fate 25 (Nov.1972):23-
    24.
    John Green, The Sasquatch File (Ag-
    assiz, B.C.: Cheam, 1973), p.54.

Kelso
-Fall of ashes
  1953, June 12/Charles Lydic/Rose Valley
    (Editorial), Fate 6 (Nov.1953):5.
-UFO (?)
  1947, June 20/Jerry Neels/S of town
    Portland Oregonian, 28 June 1947.

1949, Aug.2
  "If It's in the Sky It's a Saucer,"
  Doubt, no.27 (1949):416.
-UFO (NL)
  1947, June 27
  Portland Oregonian, 28 June 1947.

Kennewick
-Dowsing
  1956/Marston B. Winegar
  John Rieper, "Witching Rod Beats
  Electronic Device," Fate 10 (Feb.
  1957):48.

Kent
-UFO (?)
  1962, May 25/Lake Meridian
  Ivan T. Sanderson, Invisible Resi-
  dents (N.Y.: World, 1970), p.194.
-UFO (CE-1)
  1960, Feb.6/Leon Thompson
  (Letter), Fate 14 (Apr.1961):112-13.
-UFO (CE-2)
  1965, July 2/Mrs. A.W. Brundage
  "Saucer Hovers over Car," Saucer
  News 12 (Dec.1965):27.
-UFO (NL)
  1908, Feb.1-2
  Tacoma Daily Ledger, 4 Feb.1908.
  1959, April 1
  Coral E. Lorenzen, Flying Saucers:
  The Startling Evidence of the Inva-
  sion from Outer Space (N.Y.: Sig-
  net, 1966 ed.), p.162.

Kirkland
-Fall of frogs
  1966, Aug./Mrs. Robert Mitchell
  (Editorial), Fate 20 (June 1967):25.
-Humanoid tracks
  1978, Dec.31/Diana Johnson/Willow Rd.
  x 97th St.
  Bellevue Journal-American, 4 Jan.
  1979; and 10 Jan.1979.

Kittitas
-Electromagnetic anomaly
  1972, Oct.-   /Michael Lamoreaux
  Susy Smith, Voices of the Dead? (N.Y.:
  Signet, 1977), pp.67-75.

Klickitat co.
-Fall of plastic
  1957, Sep.-Oct./George McCredy
  Robert N. Webster, "Things That Fall
  from UFOs," Fate 11 (Oct.1958):25,
  28.

Lake City
-UFO (?)
  1947, July 4/Frank Ryman/12321 22d St.
  NE/=balloon?
  Seattle Post-Intelligencer, 5 July
  1947. il.
  Kenneth Arnold & Ray Palmer, The Com-
  ing of the Saucers (Boise: The Au-
  thors, 1952), p.32.
  Edward J. Ruppelt, The Report on Un-
  identified Flying Objects (Garden
  City: Doubleday, 1956), p.20.

Lake Stevens
-Humanoid
  1964, July/NW of town
  John Green, The Sasquatch File (Agassiz, B.C.: Cheam, 1973), p.28.
-Humanoid tracks
  1977, March/Pilchuk R.
  Jacob A. Davidson & Jerry Phillips,
  "An Examination of Mutilation Phenomena and Attendant Fortean Activity at Machias, Washington State,
  1977," Phenomena Rsch.Special Rept.,
  no.2 (July 1977):1,11.

LaPorte
-Humanoid
  ca.1964, fall/Herb Brown/Johnsonville-
  Quincy Rd.
  John Green, The Sasquatch File (Ag-
  assiz, B.C.: Cheam, 1973), p.34.

Little Falls
-Humanoid
  1977, July 7/Lori Cormany
  Eatonville Dispatch, 13 July 1977.

Longview
-Flying humanoid
  1948, April 9/Viola Johnson
  John A. Keel, Strange Creatures from
  Time and Space (Greenwich, Ct.:
  Fawcett, 1970), p.207.
-UFO (?)
  1975, July 21
  "UFO Central," CUFOS News Bull., 15
  Nov.1975, p.14.
-UFO (DD)
  1949, July 3/M.B. Taylor/fairgrounds
  Richard Hall, ed., The UFO Evidence
  (Washington: NICAP, 1964), p.31.

Lummi Reservation
-Humanoid
  1975, Oct.24/Ken Cooper
  Vancouver (B.C.) Sun, 12-13 Nov.1975.
  W. Ritchie Benedict, "Sasquatch
  Haunts Indian Land," Fate 30 (Sep.
  1977):52.

Lyle
-Archeological site
  T.M. Whitcomb, "Aboriginal Works at
  the Mouth of the Klickitat River,
  Washington Territory," Ann.Rept.
  Smith.Inst. 31 (1881):527.
-Haunt
  1960, fall-1962, Sep./Edithe P. Myers
  Edithe P. Myers, "They Laughed When
  I Cried Ghost!" Fate 29 (June 1976)
  :75-77.

Lynden
-UFO (CE-1)
  1965, Jan.12/Robert E. Kerringer/N of
  town
  Donald E. Keyhoe, Aliens from Space
  (Garden City: Doubleday, 1973), pp.
  13-14.

Lynnwood
-UFO (NL)
1973, Nov.1/Richard Law/Stevens Memorial Hospital
Everett Herald, 2 Nov.1973.

Machias
-Cattle mutilation
1977, March 25/Don Larsen/nr. Pilchuk
R.
Jacob A. Davidson & Jerry Phillips,
"An Examination of Mutilation Phenomena and Attendant Fortean Activity at Machias, Washington State,
1977," Phenomena Rsch.Special Rept.,
no.2 (July 1977):1-5.
-Dog mutilation
1977, March 18/Dubuque Rd.
Jacob A. Davidson & Jerry Phillips,
"An Examination of Mutilation Phenomena and Attendant Fortean Activity at Machais, Washington State,
1977," Phenomena Rsch.Special Rept.,
no.2 (July 1977):1,6.
-Humanoid
1977, April 7-May 16/screams only
Jacob A. Davidson & Jerry Phillips,
"An Examination of Mutilation Phenomena and Attendant Fortean Activity at Machias, Washington State,
1977," Phenomena Rsch.Special Rept.,
no.2 (July 1977):1,9-10.
-UFO (CE-2)
1977, March 24/Mrs. Robert Sharp/Three
Lakes Rd.
Jacob A. Davidson & Jerry Phillips,
"An Examination of Mutilation Phenomena and Attendant Fortean Activity at Machias, Washington State,
1977," Phenomena Rsch.Special Rept.,
no.2 (July 1977):1,6-8.

Maple Valley
-Humanoid
1974, June 9/Tony McClennan
Jerome Clark & Loren Coleman, Crea-
tures of the Outer Edge (N.Y.: War-
ner, 1978), pp.46-47.
-UFO (NL)
1965, Jan.31/William E. Bolson
J. Allen Hynek, The UFO Experience
(Chicago: Regnery, 1972), p.248.

Marietta
-Humanoid
1967, Sep./Joe Brudevold
1967, Dec./Frank Lawrence, Jr./Nook-
sack R.
1969, spring
John Green, Year of the Sasquatch
(Agassiz, B.C.: Cheam, 1970), p.74.
John Green, The Sasquatch File (Agassiz, B.C.: Cheam, 1973), pp.36,37,
43.
1975, fall
John Green, Sasquatch: The Apes Among
Us (Seattle: Hancock House, 1978),
p.430.

Mineral
-UFO (DD)
1947, June 24/Sidney B. Gallagher/10
mi.S
Ted Bloecher, Report on the UFO Wave
of 1947 (Washington: NICAP, 1967),
Appendix, Case 40.

Montesano
-UFO (CE-2)
1971, Jan.3/Keith Brown/Wishkah Rd.
"January Washington Report," APRO
Bull. 19 (May-June 1971):5.

Morton
-UFO (CE-4)
1950, March 28/Samuel Eaton Thompson/
N of town
Isabel Davis & Ted Bloecher, Close
Encounter at Kelly and Others of
1955 (Evanston: Center for UFO Stud-
ies, 1978), p.v.

Moses Lake
-UFO (?)
1953, Aug.8
Harold T. Wilkins, Flying Saucers
Uncensored (N.Y.: Pyramid, 1967 ed.),
p.208.
1964, Aug.21/W.D. Hawes/ground mark-
ings only
"UFO Sighting Wave Persists," UFO
Inv. 2 (Sep.-Oct.1964):5.
Brad Steiger, ed., Project Blue Book
(N.Y.: Ballantine, 1976). betw.pp.
56-57. il.
-UFO (DD)
1953, Jan.8
U.S. Air Force, Projects Grudge and
Blue Book Reports 1-12 (Washington:
NICAP, 1968), p.190.
-UFO (NL)
1947, June 20/Archie Edes/Moses Lake
Hwy.
Seattle Post-Intelligencer, 27 June
1947.
-UFO (R)
1951, Aug.26/Larson AFB
U.S Air Force, Projects Grudge and
Blue Book Reports 1-12 (Washington:
NICAP, 1968), p.12.

Mount Vernon
-Phantom automobile
1975, Oct.23/Edward Kemmerer/Lake Mc-
Murray Rd.
B. Ann Slate, "The Humanoids," Saga
UFO Rept. 6 (Jan.1979):32,48, quot-
ing Skagit Valley Herald, Oct.1975.
-UFO (DD)
1947, July 6/A. Haarval/S of town
Seattle Times, 7 July 1947.

Neah Bay
-Humanoid
ca.1962
John Green, The Sasquatch File (Agassiz, B.C.: Cheam, 1973), p.27.
1964, July 1?/Hwy.112
Port Angeles Evening News, 3 July 1964.

1969, Nov.
  John Green, Year of the Sasquatch
  (Agassiz, B.C.: Cheam, 1970), p.46.
-Humanoid tracks
  1950s
    Ivan T. Sanderson, Abominable Snow-
    men: Legend Come to Life (Philadel-
    phia: Chilton, 1961), pp.143-44.
  1964, Nov.27/George Wright
    John A. Keel, Strange Creatures from
    Time and Space (Greenwich, Ct.:
    Fawcett, 1970), pp.118-19.
-Sea monster
  1918
    Paul H. LeBlond & John Sibert, Obser-
    vations of Large Unidentified Marine
    Animals in British Columbia and Ad-
    jacent Waters (Vancouver: Univ. of
    British Columbia, Inst. of Ocean-
    ography, Manuscript Rept. no.28,
    June 1973), pp.32-33.
-UFO (DD)
  1953, July 6/John H. Leabo/radar station
    (Letter), Fate 7 (Mar.1954):129.

North Bend
-Humanoid
  1970, June 14
    John Green, The Sasquatch File (Ag-
    assiz, B.C.: Cheam, 1973), p.52.
    John Green, Sasquatch: The Apes Among
    Us (Seattle: Hancock House, 1978),
    pp.342-44.
-Humanoid tracks
  1972, winter
    John Green, The Sasquatch File (Ag-
    assiz, B.C.: Cheam, 1973), p.54.

North Bonneville
-Humanoid
  1969, Nov./Louise Baxter/4 mi.W
    John Green, The Sasquatch File (Ag-
    assiz, B.C.: Cheam, 1973), p.43.
  1973, July
    John Green, "Not All Quiet on the
    Western Front," Pursuit 7 (Oct.1974)
    :99.

Northport
-Humanoid
  1975, June/scream only
    "Latest News from the Pacific North-
    west," Bigfoot News, no.8 (June
    1975):1.
-UFO (?)
  1974, Jan./=balloon
    Philip J. Klass, UFOs Explained (N.Y.:
    Random House, 1974), p.292.

Oak Harbor
-Sea monster (carcass)
  1963, Oct./=oarfish
    (Editorial), Fate 17 (Apr.1964):24.
    (Editorial), Saucer News 11 (June
    1964):18.

Oakville
-Humanoid
  1912, fall

1933, spring/Callie Lund/scream only
  John Green, Year of the Sasquatch
  (Agassiz, B.C.: Cheam, 1970), pp.
  23-24.

Odessa
-UFO (R-V)
  1952, Dec.10
    Edward J. Ruppelt, The Report on Un-
    identified Flying Objects (Garden
    City: Doubleday, 1956), p.43.
    Donald H. Menzel & Lyle G. Boyd,
    The World of Flying Saucers (Garden
    City: Doubleday, 1963), pp.62-63.
    U.S. Air Force, Projects Grudge and
    Blue Book Reports 1-12 (Washington:
    NICAP, 1968), p.186.
    Gordon D. Thayer, "Optical and Radar
    Analyses of Field Cases," in Edward
    U. Condon, ed., Scientific Study
    of Unidentified Flying Objects (N.Y.:
    Bantam, 1969 ed.), pp.140-41.

Olympia
-UFO (DD)
  1961, May 8/Melvin Metcalf
    "Burning Silver Object Seen over Olym-
    pia, Washington," APRO Bull. 9 (May
    1961):5.

Orcas
-Inner development
  1948-   /Louis Foundation
    Gordon Keith, "Know Yourself Through
    Astrology," Fate 24 (May 1971):64-
    70.

Orchard
-Humanoid
  1960s/Mr. Lopez
    John Green, The Sasquatch File (Ag-
    assiz, B.C.: Cheam, 1973), p.27.

Orient
-Humanoid
  1969, spring/Betty Peterson/S of Boulder Creek
    John Green, The Sasquatch File (Ag-
    assiz, B.C.: Cheam, 1973), pp.42-43.
-Humanoid tracks
  1968, Dec.21
    John Green, The Sasquatch File (Ag-
    assiz, B.C.: Cheam, 1973), p.42.

Orting
-UFO (NL)
  1959, April 1/Bill Jones
    Coral E. Lorenzen, Flying Saucers:
    The Startling Evidence of the Inva-
    sion from Outer Space (N.Y.: Sig-
    net, 1966 ed.), pp.162-63.

Oysterville
-UFO (?)
  1964, Aug.20/Pat Irwin
    Seattle Post-Intelligencer, 21 Aug.
    1964.

Ozette
-Archeological site

2000 B.C.-1450 A.D./Ozette Indian Village
   (Editorial), Fate 30 (Apr.1977):23-
   24.

Parkland
-Pyrokinesis
   1971, April 19-1974/11015 S. Park Ave.
   George W. Harper, "A Case for Paranormal Pyrotechnics," Fate 29 (May
   1976):74-81.
-UFO (CE-1)
   1957, May 9/Maurice Fletcher/172 E.
   123d St.
      (Editorial), Flying Saucers, Feb.
      1958, p.76.

Pasco
-Electromagnetic anomaly
   1951/Margaret St.
      "Mystery of the Street Lights," Fate
      4 (Nov.-Dec.1951):55.
-UFO (DD)
   1947, July 6/Bill Isaacson
      Spokane Daily Chronicle, 8 July 1947.
   1948, July/Don Newman
      Richard Hall, ed., The UFO Evidence
      (Washington: NICAP, 1964), p.38.
   1950, Nov.21/Perry Torbergson
      Kenneth Arnold & Ray Palmer, The Com-
      ing of the Saucers (Boise: The Au-
      thors, 1952), pp.153-54.

Pe Ell
-Humanoid myth
   P.H. Roundtree, "Autobiography," in
   Told by the Pioneers, 2 vols. (Olym-
   pia: U.S. Works Progress Admin.,
   1937-38), 2:95,115.

Pierce co.
-Horse and dog mutilations
   1976-1978
      Tacoma News-Tribune, 6 Sep.1978; and
      14 Sep.1978.

Pomeroy
-UFO (CE-1)
   1978, Dec.14/Dutch Flat
      Pomeroy East Washingtonian, 21 Dec.
      1978.

Port Angeles
-Sea monster
   1947, July 28
      "Run of the Mill," Doubt, no.20
      (1948):303.
-UFO (NL)
   1975, Sep.9
      "UFO Central," CUFOS News Bull., 15
      Nov.1975, p.18.

Port Madison
-Clairaudience
   1958, Jan./Mrs. John Sparger
      Seattle Post-Intelligencer, 4 Feb.
      1958.

Port Orchard
-UFO (NL)

1968, July 4/Lisa Leurquin
   "UFO's or Hoax?" Skylook, no.11 (July
   1968):1, quoting Bremerton Sun (undated).

Port Townsend
-UFO (?)
   n.d./golf course/=hoax
      Roy Craig, "Direct Physical Evidence,"
      in Edward U. Condon, ed., Scientif-
      ic Study of Unidentified Flying Ob-
      jects (N.Y.: Bantam, 1969 ed.), p.
      89.
-UFO (NL)
   1954, May 1/Peter J. Naughton
      Donald E. Keyhoe, Flying Saucers: Top
      Secret (N.Y.: Putnam, 1960), pp.
      225-26.

Prosser
-Telepathy
   1973/Cristel Weaver
      "Psychic News and Enigmas," Probe the
      Unknown 1 (Aug.1973):9.
-Weather control
   1964, summer
      (Editorial), Saucer News 12 (Mar.
      1965):20.

Puyallup
-Erratic kangaroo
   1967/Willaim A. Shearer
      (Editorial), Fate 20 (June 1967):20-
      22.
-Humanoid
   1972, Aug./Mark Pittinger
   1972-1975/Marlin Ayres/Forest Green/
   screams only
      John Green, Sasquatch: The Apes Among
      Us (Seattle: Hancock House, 1978),
      pp.393-95.
-Humanoid tracks
   1975, Jan./Bob Beckham
      Tacoma News-Tribune, 23 Mar.1977. il.
      Eatonville Dispatch, 30 Mar.1977. il.

Pysht
-Humanoid
   ca.1962/Bob Harrison
      John A. Keel, Strange Creatures from
      Time and Space (Greenwich, Ct.: Faw-
      cett, 1970), p.119.

Quinault
-Humanoid
   1972, June/Allen Ebling
      John Green, The Sasquatch File (Ag-
      assiz, B.C.: Cheam, 1973), p.54.
-Humanoid tracks
   1960s/Len Aiken
   1971, winter/Lyle Ehrdal
      John Green, The Sasquatch File (Ag-
      assiz, B.C.: Cheam, 1973), pp.27,53.

Rainier
-Dowsing
   1972, May/Carl Blunk
      "Doubter Tests Dowser," Fate 25 (Oct.
      1972):95, quoting Longview Daily
      News (undated).

Redmond
-Archeological site
  16,000 B.C.-1900 A.D./Marymoor site/
  6046 W. Lake Sammamish Pkwy.NE
    Robert E. Greengo & Robert Houston,
    "Excavations at the Marymoor Site,"
    Repts.in Arch.Univ.Washington, vol.
    4 (1970).
-UFO (DD)
  1947, Aug.13/Mr. Brummett
    Bruce S. Maccabee, "UFO Related In-
    formation from the FBI Files: Part
    3," MUFON UFO J., no.121 (Dec.1977):
    10,14.
  1949, July 26
    "If It's in the Sky It's a Saucer,"
    Doubt, no.27 (1949):416.
-Windshield pitting
  1954, April/Mary Brown
    (Editorial), Fate 7 (Aug.1954):9-10.

Renton
-UFO (CE-1)
  1968, Nov.30/Scott Sylte
    William Gordon Allen, "The 1968 UFO
    Surveillance of Seattle," in Beyond
    Condon (Flying Saucer Rev. special
    issue no.2, June 1969):31-33. il.
-UFO (CE-3)
  1965, Aug.13/Ellen Grace Ryerson
    Jerome Clark, "The Greatest Flap Yet?
    --Part 2," Flying Saucer Rev. 12
    (Mar.-Apr.1966):8,11, quoting Kent
    News-Journal (undated).
-UFO (DD)
  1947, July 7/Mrs. J.W. Reid
    Seattle Post-Intelligencer, 8 July
    1947.

Republic
-Humanoid tracks
  ca.1964
    John Green, The Sasquatch File (Ag-
    assiz, B.C.: Cheam, 1973), p.28.

Richland
-Fire anomaly
  1953, Oct.19/Glenn Arbuckle
    (Editorial), Fate 7 (Mar.1954):10.
-UFO (CE-2)
  1975, Sep.18
    Rufus Drake, "Top-Secret Nuclear
    Plant Besieged by UFOs," Saga UFO
    Rept. 4 (June 1977):38,40.
-UFO (DD)
  1947, June 24/L.G. Bernier
    Portland (Ore.) Journal, 4 July 1947.

Richland Springs
-UFO (NL)
  1975, Aug.1/Kevin C. Carmichael
    Rufus Drake, "Top-Secret Nuclear
    Plant Besieged by UFOs," Saga UFO
    Rept. 4 (June 1977):38,40-41.

Ringold
-Ghost light
  1930s
    "Phantom Light," Fortean Soc'y Mag.,
    no.8 (Dec.1943):13.

Vincent H. Gaddis, Mysterious Fires
and Lights (N.Y.: Dell, 1968 ed.),
pp.81-82, quoting AP release, 28
Feb.1936.

Riverton Heights
-UFO (NL)
  1948, May 17/Fred Granger/Seattle-Ta-
  coma Airport
    Kenneth Arnold & Ray Palmer, The Com-
    ing of the Saucers (Boise: The Au-
    thors, 1952), p.139.
  1962, July 31/Seattle-Tacoma Airport
    (Editorial), Fate 15 (Nov.1962):15.

Rosalia
-UFO (NL)
  1953, Feb.6/=balloon?
    Donald H. Menzel & Lyle G. Boyd, The
    World of Flying Saucers (Garden
    City: Doubleday, 1963), p.46.

San de Fuca
-UFO (CE-2)
  1967, March 13/Bert James
    Brad Steiger & Joan Whritenour, The
    Allende Letters: New UFO Break-
    through (N.Y.: Award, 1968), p.42.

Sawyer
-Humanoid
  1966, summer
    John Green, The Sasquatch File (Ag-
    assiz, B.C.: Cheam, 1973), p.35.

Seattle
-Ball lightning
  1948, Nov.16/Mrs. Gordon Mitchell
    "You Asked for It," Doubt, no.21
    (1949):363.
-Biofeedback research
  1960s/George Whatmore
    George B. Whatmore & Daniel R. Kohli,
    "Dysponesis: A Neurophysiologic Fac-
    tor in Functional Disorders," Behav-
    ioral Sci. 13 (1968):102-24.
-Clairaudience
  ca.1928/Wallace C. Gaines
    Stuart Whitehouse, "I Heard a Dead
    Man Talk," Fate 6 (Dec.1953):23-25.
-Clairempathy
  1948
    William Perry Bentley, "An Approach
    to a Theory of Survival of Personal-
    ity," J.ASPR 59 (1965):3,11-12.
-Clairvoyance
  1969, Nov.2/Susan Peterson
    Seattle Post-Intelligencer, 12 Dec.
    1969.
  1973, April/Raymond Brown
    "ESP Just in Time," Fate 27 (Nov.
    1974):60.
-Contactee
  1966, Feb./Mr. Ballard
    Seattle Times, 21 Mar.1966.
-Dowsing
  1944, Dec.6/E.J. Peterson
    "Electronic Dowser," Doubt, no.12
    (spring-summer 1945):175.
-Entombed toad

ca.1964/Alice Bott
"The Excavated Toad," Fate 18 (June 1965):72.
-Fall of ice
1950, Dec.28/Firestone Co.
"Ice Falls," Doubt, no.32 (1951):68, 69.
1955, Dec.1
Seattle Daily Times, 2 Dec.1955.
-Ghost
1960, Sep./Miki Gilliland
Miki Gilliland, "A Message from Chicago?" Fate 32 (Mar.1979):75-77.
-Haunt
1960-1965/Jess Cauthorn/905 E. Pine St.
(Editorial), Fate 18 (Oct.1965):24-26.
Susy Smith, Prominent American Ghosts (N.Y.: Dell, 1969 ed.), pp.180-95.
1962, Dec.-1975, Jan./Doris Smith
Bart Ellis, "Tape Recordings Document Seattle Haunting," Probe the Unknown 3 (May 1975):25-27,49.
-Healing
1909/Dr. Livingston
Carol Beery Davis, "Edith's Miracle," Fate 8 (May 1955):97-100.
1962-1963/H. Nye Berkebile
Paul Foght, "The Case of the Acquitted Healer," Fate 17 (Nov.1964):46-52.
-Humanoid
1948, Feb.6
Seattle Times, 6 Feb.1948.
"Critters and Tracks," Doubt, no.21 (1948):321.
-Inner development
1970s/Organization for the Advancement of Knowledge/1406A NE 50th St.
John White & Stanley Krippner, eds., Future Science (Garden City, N.Y.: Anchor, 1977), p.590.
-Men-in-black
1967
John A. Keel, The Mothman Prophecies (N.Y.: Saturday Review, 1975), pp. 178-79.
-Mystery gas
1944, Nov.17
"Seattle Stench," Doubt, no.12 (spring-summer 1945):178.
-Parapsychology research
1965-1969/Helmut Schmidt/Boeing Labs
Helmut Schmidt, "Precognition of a Quantum Process," J.Parapsych. 33 (1969):99-108.
Helmut Schmidt, "Clairvoyance Test with a Machine," J.Parapsych. 33 (1969):300-307.
Helmut Schmidt, "Quantum Processes Predicted," New Scientist, 16 Oct. 1969, pp.114-15.
-Phantom
1911/Raquel de S. Marshall/Boylston St.
Raquel de S. Marshall, "My Family Hears the Banshee Cry," Fate 8 (Nov. 1955):15,16.
-Phantom panther
1947, Nov.20-24/West Seattle
"Run of the Mill," Doubt, no.20

(1948):303,304.
-Precognition
1974, April/Dourth Ave. library
(Editorial), Fate 28 (Feb.1975):28-30, quoting Seattle Post-Intelligencer (undated).
1974-   /Elizabeth Bishop Burrows/
434 72d St. NE
Warren Smith, "Phenomenal Predictions for 1975," Saga, Jan.1975, p. 21.
Warren Smith, "Phenomenal Predictions for 1976," Saga, Jan.1976, p. 16.
"Probe's 1977 Directory of the Psychic World," Probe the Unknown 5 (spring 1977):33-34. il.
-Psychic photography
1920, July 15/Mildred Swanson
Albert A. Brandt, "Jesus of the Flowerbank," Fate 8 (July 1955):36-37.
-Radionics
1919/Alfred M. Hubbard
Seattle Post-Intelligencer, 17 Dec. 1919.
Gaston Burridge, "The Hubbard Energy Transformer," Fate 9 (July 1956): 36-42. il.
-Skyquake
1946, Aug.25,28-29
1946, Sep.12,23
"Seattle Blasts," Doubt, no.17 (1947):260.
1950, March 19
"Bangs," Doubt, no.30 (1950):43.
1952, May 11
"Case 50," CRIFO Newsl., 4 Feb.1955, p.3.
1959, Feb.12
(Editorial), Fate 12 (July 1959):12.
1959, April 1
Coral E. Lorenzen, Flying Saucers: The Startling Evidence of the Invasion from Outer Space (N.Y.: Signet, 1966 ed.), pp.161-62.
-Spirit medium
1954-   /Keith Milton Rhinehart
Agnes F. Reuther, "The Levitated Trumpets," Fate 12 (Feb.1959):73-75. il.
Susy Smith, "Seattle's Psychic Wonder," in Martin Ebon, ed., True Experiences in Communicating with the Dead (N.Y.: Signet, 1968), pp.60-75.
-UFO (?)
1947, June 26/Mrs. I.A. Fay
"The United States of Dreamland," Doubt, no.19 (1947):282,283.
1947, July 16/=hoax
Bruce S. Maccabee, "UFO Related Information from the FBI Files: Part 2," MUFON UFO J., no.120 (Nov.1977):12.
1947, Dec.31
"Disc Dirt," Doubt, no.21 (1948):314, 315.
1950, April 29/S side
Gerald Heard, The Riddle of the Flying Saucers (London: Carroll & Nicholson, 1950), p.77.

1952, May 11/=meteor?
  U.S. Air Force, <u>Projects Grudge and
  Blue Book Reports 1-12</u> (Washington:
  NICAP, 1968), p.124.
1954, June
  Donald E. Keyhoe, <u>Flying Saucer Con-
  spiracy</u> (N.Y.: Holt, 1955), p.164.
1955, Jan.18
  "UFOs over Seattle," <u>Fate</u> 8 (Sep.
  1955):37.
1957, Nov.28/John M. Anderson/1st Ave.
x Pike St.
  (Letter), <u>Fate</u> 11 (July 1958):115-16.
1961, May 19
  (Editorial), <u>APRO Bull.</u> 10 (July
  1961):5.
1961, Aug.4/Tom Stevens, Jr.
  (Letter), Leon Thompson, <u>Fate</u> 14
  (Dec.1961):103.
1965, March 22/Lake Washington
  Ivan T. Sanderson, <u>Invisible Resi-
  dents</u> (N.Y.: World, 1970), pp.196-
  97.
1966, Jan./Jerry Ross/=hoax?
  Frank Bowers, ed., <u>The True Report on
  Flying Saucers</u> (Greenwich, Ct.: Faw-
  cett, 1967), p.39.
-UFO (CE-1)
  1975, Aug.20
  "UFO Central," <u>CUFOS News Bull.</u>, 15
  Nov.1975, p.16.
-UFO (CE-2)
  1968, July 7/Rudy Malaspina/=balloon?
  <u>Seattle Post-Intelligencer</u>, 8-9 July
  1968.
  Brad Steiger & Joan Whritenour, <u>Fly-
  ing Saucer Invasion: Target--Earth</u>
  (N.Y.: Award, 1969), p.98.
  Philip J. Klass, <u>UFOs Explained</u> (N.Y.:
  Random House, 1974), pp.24-25,27-28.
-UFO (CE-3)
  1965, Aug.
  John A. Keel, <u>UFOs: Operation Trojan
  Horse</u> (N.Y.: Putnam, 1970), p.181.
-UFO (DD)
  1947, June 27/Mrs. E.G. Peterson/91 W.
Crockett
  <u>Seattle Times</u>, 9 July 1947.
1947, July 4/Charles Kamp/Univ. of
Washington
  <u>Seattle Post-Intelligencer</u>, 8 July
  1947.
1947, July 5/Florence Frye/538 E. 91st
St.
  <u>Seattle Post-Intelligencer</u>, 6 July
  1947.
1947, July 6/Marie Quinn/655 Yesler Way
  <u>Seattle Times</u>, 7 July 1947.
1947, July 7/Peggy Reyes/661 SW 111th
1947, July 7/Jack Kobalt/843 W.63d St.
  <u>Seattle Post-Intelligencer</u>, 7-8 July
  1947.
  <u>Seattle Times</u>, 7-8 July 1947.
1947, July 8/Chet Proud/Puget Sound
1947, July 8/Earl Klenpke/9004 17th Ave.
  <u>Seattle Post-Intelligencer</u>, 9 July
  1947.
1947, July 10/Armeta Hearst/2433 E.
Valley St.
  <u>Seattle Post-Intelligencer</u>, 11 July

1947.
1947, July 12/John C. Kennedy/Sand
Point NAS
  <u>Seattle Post-Intelligencer</u>, 13 July
  1947.
1947, July 13/Al Rickey/Woodland Park
  <u>Seattle Post-Intelligencer</u>, 14 July
  1947.
1952, Aug./Hazel E. Monte/Ranier Ave.
  (Letter), <u>Fate</u> 7 (Nov.1954):108-109.
1960, June 12
  "News Briefs," <u>Saucer News</u> 11 (Mar.
  1964):24. il.
1961, Oct.4/Bill Clendenon/NE 65th St.
x Roosevelt Way
  W.C. Stevens, "Bell-Shaped UFOs,"
  <u>Official UFO</u> 1 (Nov.1975):36,38.
-UFO (NL)
  1947, June 24/Elvira Forsyth/7018 NE
9th St.
  <u>Seattle Post-Intelligencer</u>, 28 June
  1947.
1947, June 25/M.F. Bly/10909 Linden
  <u>Seattle Post-Intelligencer</u>, 27 June
  1947.
1947, July 3/Mrs. Gordon Lynn/12673
88th Ave.S
  <u>Seattle Times</u>, 8 July 1947.
1947, July 5/Kenneth L. Larson/Green-
wood Park
  Ted Bloecher, <u>Report on the UFO Wave
  of 1947</u> (Washington: NICAP, 1967),
  Appendix, Case 352.
1947, July 5/Mrs. H.B. Fry/3116 Alki
Ave.
  <u>Seattle Post-Intelligencer</u>, 8 July
  1947.
1953, Sep.13
  (Letter), G.K., <u>Fate</u> 7 (Mar.1954):
  124-26.
1975, Sep.9
1975, Sep.19
  "UFO Central," <u>CUFOS News Bull.</u>, 15
  Nov.1975, p.18.
-Windshield pitting
  1954, March-April
  <u>Seattle Times</u>, 15 Apr.1954.
  Donald E. Keyhoe, <u>Flying Saucer Con-
  spiracy</u> (N.Y.: Holt, 1955), p.132.
  Nahum Z. Medalia & Otto N. Larsen,
  "Diffusion and Belief in a Collective Delusion: The Seattle Windshield
  Pitting Epidemic," <u>Am.Sociol.Rev.</u>
  23 (Apr.1958):180-86.

<u>Sedro Woolley</u>
-UFO (NL)
  1976, Feb.9
  "Noteworthy UFO Sightings," <u>Ufology</u>
  2 (summer 1976):63.

<u>Selah</u>
-UFO (CE-3)
  1968, April 28
  Brad Steiger & Joan Whritenour, <u>Fly-
  ing Saucer Invasion: Target--Earth</u>
  (N.Y.: Award, 1969), p.97.

<u>Skagit co.</u>
-Horse mutilation

1978, Feb.
  "A Closer Look," Stigmata, no.4 (summer 1978):3.

Skamania co.
-Humanoid
  1978, Nov.6/Jack Webb
    Stevenson Skamania County Pioneer,
    17 Nov.1978.
-Humanoid protection ordinance
  1969
    Skamania County Ordinance No.69-01
    (1969), in Stevenson Skamania County
    Pioneer, 4 Apr.1969.
    Peter Byrne, The Search for Bigfoot
    (N.Y.: Pocket Books, 1976 ed.), pp.
    84-85.

Skyhomish
-Clairvoyance
  1917/Asa M. Russell/Banning House
    Asa M. Russell, "Our Two-Angel Es-
    cort," Fate 11 (Oct.1958):32,33-35.

Snohomish co.
-Cattle mutilation
  1978, May
    "Animal Reactions," Stigmata, no.5
    (fall-winter 1978):16,18.
-UFO (NL)
  1959, Oct.9
    (Editorial), Fate 13 (June 1960):25.

Snoqualmie
-Precognition
  n.d./Alfred Engelhardt
    (Editorial), Fate 9 (Apr.1956):14.

Spokane
-Ancient inscriptions
  1919-1924/Oluf L. Opsjon
    (Letter), Karl H. Isselstein, Fate
    8 (May 1955):117-20.
    Karl H. Isselstein, Ancient Cata-
    clysms Which Changed Earth's Surface
    (Mokelumne Hill, Cal.: Health Re-
    search, 1965).
-Dowsing
  1957/Willard Taft
    (Editorial), Fate 11 (Mar.1958):13-
    14.
-Fall of ice
  1950, July 4
    "Frogs and Fish," Doubt, no.30 (1950)
    :34.
-Fall of rocks
  1977, Aug.30-Sep.6/Billy Tipton
    Vancouver (B.C.) Daily Province, 6
    Sep.1977.
-Haunt
  1974, Sep.-1975, Feb./Walter F. Leedale
  /Monaghan Hall, Gonzaga Univ.
    Dan Morris, "Jesuit Challenges
    'Force' Haunting Old Mansion," Nat'l
    Observer, 3 May 1975.
    "House with a Split Personality,"
    Probe the Unknown 3 (Sep.1975):46.
    (Editorial), Fate 28 (Dec.1975):22-
    24.
-Humanoid

1962, Oct./Dutch Holler
  John Green, The Sasquatch File (Agassiz, B.C.: Cheam, 1973), p.27.
-Spontaneous human combustion
  1961, Jan./Charles A. McCollough
    (Editorial), Fate 14 (June 1961):19.
-UFO (?)
  1947, Dec.31
    "Disc Dirt," Doubt, no.21 (1948):
    314,315.
  1949
    Harold T. Wilkins, Flying Saucers on
    the Attack (N.Y.: Ace, 1967 ed.),
    p.114.
  1949, May 11
    "If It's in the Sky It's a Saucer,"
    Doubt, no.27 (1949):416.
  1962, May 28/Paul Quam/=meteor?
    "Fireball Lights Pacific Northwest,"
    APRO Bull. 11 (July 1962):6.
  1974, Nov.26/Jack Campbell/=meteor?
    Timothy Green Beckley, "Saucers over
    Our Cities," Saga UFO Rept. 4 (May
    1977):24,74-76.
-UFO (DD)
  1897, April
    Spokane Chronicle, 16 Apr.1897.
  1947, June 21/Guy R. Overman
    Ted Bloecher, Report on the UFO Wave
    of 1947 (Washington: NICAP, 1967),
    p.II-18.
  1947, June 30/John Mourning
    Portland (Ore.) Journal, 2 July 1947.
  1947, July 5/Richard Gregg/2422 Riverside
    Spokane Daily Chronicle, 5 July 1947.
  1947, July 6/Mrs. C.C. Jenkins/N. 2201
  Columbus
  1947, July 7/Mrs. Fred Reehl/S. 3714
  Hatch
    Spokane Daily Chronicle, 7 July 1947.
  1947, July 8/Paul Baenen/Hillyard
    Spokane Daily Chronicle, 8 July 1947.
  1947, July 8/James Davidson/Mt. Spokane
  1947, July 8/J.P. Tracy/E. 365 Third
    Spokane Daily Chronicle, 8-10 July
    1947.
-UFO (NL)
  1950, July 2/Spokane Airport
    Gerald Heard, The Riddle of the Fly-
    ing Saucers (London: Carroll & Nich-
    olson, 1950), p.146.
  1952, April 24
    Spokane Chronicle, 25 Apr.1952.

Steilacoom
-UFO (NL)
  1978, Feb.17/Jesse Powell/46 Queets St.
    Lakewood Center Suburban Times, 22
    Feb.1978.

Stevenson
-Humanoid
  1974, summer/White Salmon Rd.
    Peter Byrne, The Search for Bigfoot
    (N.Y.: Pocket Books, 1976 ed.), p.
    36.
-Humanoid tracks
  1969, March/Ed McLarney
    John Green, The Sasquatch File (Ag-

assiz, B.C.: Cheam, 1973), p.42,
quoting Stevenson Skamania County
Pioneer (undated).
1969, Sep.15/Bill Closner/Stevenson
Ridge
    Stevenson Skamania County Pioneer,
    19 Sep.1969.

Sultan
-UFO (NL)
1976, Jan.25/Skykomish R.
    "Sighting Reports," CUFOS News Bull.,
    June 1976, p.4.

Sumas
-UFO (NL)
1973, Aug.25/Mrs. Alfred Baker
    Abbotsford, Sumas and Matsqui (B.C.)
    News, 19 Sep.1973.

Sumner
-Mystery plane crash
1959, April 1/Robert R. Dimick/C-118/
5 mi.SE nr. Rhodes L.
    (Editorial), Fate 12 (Oct.1959):18-
    20.
    Coral E. Lorenzen, Flying Saucers:
    The Startling Evidence of the Inva-
    sion from Outer Space (N.Y.: Signet,
    1966 ed.), pp.161-63.
    Robert D. Barry, "War of the Planets,"
    Saga UFO Rept. 2 (summer 1975):22-
    23.
-UFO (DD)
1978, July 30/Church of Jesus Christ
    Puyallup Pierce County Herald, 2 Aug.
    1978.

Tacoma
-Animal ESP
1949, April 13/Pt. Defiance Park Zoo
1964, March 27/Pt. Defiance Park Zoo
    (Editorial), Fate 17 (Aug.1964):22.
-Anomalous hole in ground
1920s-   /James Johnson/=bottomless
    Seattle Post-Intelligencer, 16 June
    1974.
-Dog mutilation
1977, Aug./Joe Pavolka
    Tacoma News-Tribune, 27 Aug.1977.
-Entombed toad
1893, Aug.
    Henry Winfred Splitter, "The Impossi-
    ble Fossils," Fate 7 (Jan.1954):65,
    71-72.
-Fall of metallic objects
1952, Jan.13/E of U.S.99/=from airplane?
    "Falls," Doubt, no.37 (1952):149.
-Fall of rocks
1964, Feb.19/Robert S. Saxon/Hwy.99, N
of town
    (Editorial), Fate 27 (June 1974):26,
    quoting Seattle Post-Intelligencer
    (undated).
-Fall of steel ball
1951, Aug.16
    San Francisco (Cal.) Chronicle, 17
    Aug.1951.
-Haunt
1969, Oct.-1970/Francine Pacinda

    (Editorial), Fate 24 (Jan.1971):28-
    30.
-Hex
1947/Jake Bird
    Spokane Spokesman-Review, 27 Nov.
    1948.
    D.R. Linson, "The Bird Hex," Fate 3
    (Sep.1950):32-34.
-Humanoid
1969, Sep.
    John Napier, Bigfoot (N.Y.: Dutton,
    1973), p.211.
-Out-of-body experience
n.d.
    George W. Harper, "The Case of the
    Dangerous Father," Fate 29 (Sep.
    1976):41-45.
-Phantom cat
1954, spring/Darcea Schiesl
    Darcea Schiesl, "The Invisible Cat,"
    Fate 8 (Nov.1955):17.
-UFO (?)
1949, July 25
    "If It's in the Sky It's a Saucer,"
    Doubt, no.27 (1949):416.
1964, April 3
    "News Briefs," Saucer News 11 (Sep.
    1964):18.
-UFO (CE-3)
1947, July 7/Gene Gamachi/Centre x J
St.
    Tacoma News-Tribune, 8 July 1947.
-UFO (DD)
1947, July 5/Lillian Emblem/1115 6th
Ave.
    Tacoma News-Tribune, 8 July 1947.
1947, July 7/Margaret DeMars/105 Longview
    Tacoma News-Tribune, 8 July 1947.
-UFO (NL)
1896, Nov.24/George St. John/Tacoma Ave.
    Loren E. Gross, The UFO Wave of 1896
    (Fremont, Cal.: The Author, 1974),
    pp.26-27.
1908, Feb.1-3
    Tacoma Daily Ledger, 4 Feb.1908.
1947, July 7/Evan Davies/N 33d x Adams
St.
    Tacoma News-Tribune, 7 July 1947.
    Ted Bloecher, Report on the UFO Wave
    of 1947 (Washington: NICAP, 1967),
    p.II-19.
1947, July 7/M.C. Streans/913 S. L St.
    Tacoma News-Tribune, 8 July 1947.
1975, Jan.5
    Robert A. Goerman, "The UFO Modus
    Operandi: January 1975," Official
    UFO 1 (Aug.1976):46,64.
1975, Sep.10
    "UFO Central," CUFOS News Bull., 15
    Nov.1975, p.18.
1975, Oct.9/McChord AFB
    (Letter), American UFO Studies, Saga
    UFO Rept. 3 (Apr.1976):78.
1976/Steven Lund
    (Letter), Saga UFO Rept. 3 (Dec.1976)
    :6.
-UFO (R-V)
1959, Oct.2/McChord AFB/=radar echo?
    Edward U. Condon, ed., Scientific

Study of Unidentified Flying Objects
(N.Y.: Bantam, 1969 ed.), pp145-48.

Taholah
-Humanoid
  1969/Frank Pfau
    Don Hunter & René Dahinden, _Sasquatch_
    (Toronto: McClelland & Stewart,
    1973), pp.136-37.
  1970, June/Allen Ebling
    John Green, _The Sasquatch File_ (Ag-
    assiz, B.C.: Cheam, 1973), p.52.

Tenino
-Humanoid
  1971, March 2/Charles Smith
    Olympia Daily Olympian, 3 Mar.1971.

Tilma
-UFO (NL)
  1975, Nov.5
    "Noteworthy UFO Sightings," _Ufology_
    2 (spring 1976):43.

Toppenish
-Mystery tracks
  1976, May 9/Al Barnes/LaRue Rd. x U.S.
  97
    W.J. Vogel, "Strange Phenomenon in
    Washington," _APRO Bull._ 24 (May
    1976):1,4.
-UFO (NL)
  1975, March 12/SW of town
    "From the Center for UFO Studies,"
    Flying Saucer Rev. 21 (Aug.1975):iii.

Tukwila
-UFO (NL)
  1947, June 24/Mervin Watkins
    "The United States of Dreamland,"
    Doubt, no.19 (1947):283.

Twana
-Midday darkness
  1902, Sep.12/=forest fires?
    M. Eells, "A Dark Day in Washington,"
    Monthly Weather Rev. 30 (Sep.1902):
    440.

Uniontown
-UFO (?)
  1970, Nov.2/=meteor
    "Bang!" _INFO J._, no.4 (Nov.1974):2-3.

Vader
-Humanoid tracks and UFO (CE-2)
  1970, Dec.4,7/Mrs. Wallace Bowers
    Centralia-Chehalis Chronicle, 16 Dec.
    1970.
    Hayden C. Hewes, "International Date-
    line," _Can.UFO Rept._, no.10 (1971):
    18,20.
    Jerome Clark & Loren Coleman, _Crea-
    tures of the Outer Edge_ (N.Y.: War-
    ner, 1978), pp.42-44.

Vancouver
-Intra-mercurial planet
  ca.1860, summer/Richard Covington
    (Letter), _Sci.Am._ 35 (1876):340-41.

-UFO (DD)
  1947, July 4/John Sullivan
    Portland Oregonian, 5 July 1947.

Vashon
-UFO (CE-2)
  1968, Feb.18/Richard Frombach/1 mi.E
    Seattle Post-Intelligencer, 19 Feb.
    1968.
    "The Strange Case of the Frozen Pond,"
    APRO Bull. 16 (Mar.-Apr.1968):1,3.
-UFO (CE-3)
  1974, June 24/Ken Cosby/Sylvan Beach
    Vashon Beachcomber, 3 July 1974.
    George D. Fawcett, "The 'Unreported'
    UFO Wave of 1974," _Saga UFO Rept._
    2 (spring 1975):53.

Waldoboro
-Humanoid
  1955, Jan.2/J.W. McHenri
    Olympia Pioneer and Democrat, 15 May
    1955.

Walla Walla
-UFO (?)
  1947, Dec.
    Harold T. Wilkins, _Flying Saucers on
    the Attack_ (N.Y.: Ace, 1967 ed.),
    p.79.

Washougal
-Fall of ice
  1955, April/Jake Brown
    Portland _Oregon Journal_, 25 Apr.1955.
    "Falls," _Doubt_, no.49 (1955):358,359.

West Richland
-Humanoid
  1966, summer/Greg Pointer/gravel pit
    John Green, _The Sasquatch File_ (Ag-
    assiz, B.C.: Cheam, 1973), p.35.
    Don Hunter & René Dahinden, _Sasquatch_
    (Toronto: McClelland & Stewart,
    1973), pp.106-107.

Willard
-Humanoid
  1974, Aug./Oklahoma Campground
    Peter Byrne, _The Search for Bigfoot_
    (N.Y.: Pocket Books, 1976 ed.), pp.
    39-40.

Winlock
-Humanoid tracks and cattle mutilations
  1972
    Don Worley, "Cattle Mutilations and
    UFOs: Who Are the Mutilators?" _Of-
    ficial UFO_ 1 (Dec.1976):24,48.

Wollochet
-Haunt
  1945, winter-1946/Ann McIntyre
    Ann McIntyre, "What Banished the Cap-
    tain's Restless Spirit?" _Fate_ 20
    (June 1967):45-50.

Woodinville
-Humanoid
  1973, Sep.

John Green, "Not All Quiet on the
Western Front," Pursuit 7 (Oct.1974)
:98-99.
-UFO (CE-1)
  1965, Aug./Mrs. Herb Johnson
  Jerome Clark, "The Greatest Flap Yet?
    --Part 2," Flying Saucer Rev. 12
    (Mar.-Apr.1966):8-9.

Woodland
-Humanoid
  1969, Nov.23/Charles Kent
    Lewis River News, 27 Nov.1969.
-Humanoid tracks
  1966, July/Charlie Erion
    John Green, The Sasquatch File (Ag-
      assiz, B.C.: Cheam, 1973), p.35.
-UFO (DD)
  1947, June 27/Clyde Homen/2 mi.S
    Portland Oregon Journal, 28 June
    1947.

Yakima
-Humanoid
  1960s/Jim Mission/Yakima R.
  1962, winter/River Rd.
  1966, summer
    John Green, The Sasquatch File (Ag-
      assiz, B.C.: Cheam, 1973), pp.27,35.
  1966, Sep.19/Ken Pettijohn/10 mi.W on
    Fisk Rd.
    John Green, On the Track of the Sas-
      quatch (Agassiz, B.C.: Cheam, 1968),
      pp.62-63.
  1966, Oct./Carl Timberbrook/Summer View
    store
  1969, Oct./Ross Hendrick/SW of town at
    Little Cricket
  1970, July 10
    John Green, The Sasquatch File (Ag-
      assiz, B.C.: Cheam, 1973), pp.35,
      44,52.
-Skyquake
  1957, Jan.21
    "Case 295," CRIFO Orbit, 1 Mar.1957,
    p.3, quoting Portland Oregonian (un-
    dated).
  1959, Feb.12
    (Editorial), Fate 12 (July 1959):12.
-UFO (DD)
  1947, June 24/Ethel Wheelhouse
    Tacoma News-Tribune, 27 June 1947.
-UFO (NL)
  1976, Oct.8
    "UFO Central," CUFOS News Bull., 1
    Feb.1976, p.8.

Yakima Reservation
-UFO (NL)
  1976, April 24
    "Sighting Reports," CUFOS News Bull.,
    Sep.1976, p.5.

Yale
-Humanoid
  1963, June/Stan Mattson/Lewis River
    canal
    John Green, The Sasquatch File (Ag-
      assiz, B.C.: Cheam, 1973), p.27.

B. Physical Features

Arcadia Point
-UFO (NL)
  1975, Jan.18/Rick Sheetz
    Robert A. Goerman, "The UFO Modus
      Operandi: January 1975," Official
      UFO 1 (Aug.1976):46,65.

Ash Cave
-Archeological site
  ca.5900 B.C.
    B. Robert Butler, "Ash Cave (45 WW
      61): A Preliminary Report," Wash-
      ington Arch. 2, no.12 (1958):3-10.

Bainbridge I.
-Derelict ship
  n.d./"Sea Lion"
    "Captain Olsen's Wandering Boat,"
      Fate 5 (Sep.1952):41.
-UFO (DD)
  1929, spring/Larry Reynolds
    (Letter), Fate 4 (Oct.1951):116.
    (Letter), Fate 8 (Dec.1955):114.

Baker, Mt.
-Humanoid
  1977, Oct.7/Frank White/=hoax
    Seattle Post-Intelligencer, 17 Oct.
      1977.
    San Francisco (Cal.) Chronicle, 18
      Oct.1977.
    "Latest News from the Pacific North-
      west," Bigfoot News, no.38 (Nov.
      1977):1.
    Dennis Gates, "Another Bigfoot Hoax,"
      Pursuit 11 (spring 1978):78.

Bald Mt.
-Land monster
  1974, Nov.17/Ernest Smith
    Jim Brandon, Weird America (N.Y.:
      Dutton, 1978), p.232.

Beacon Rock State Park
-Humanoid
  1969, March 5/Don Cox
    Don Hunter & René Dahinden, Sasquatch
      (Toronto: McClelland & Stewart,
      1973), pp.132-33, quoting Stevenson
      Skamania County Pioneer (undated).
  1970, July 31
  1970, Aug.19/Louise Baxter
    John Green, The Sasquatch File (Ag-
      assiz, B.C.: Cheam, 1973), pp.52-53.
  1973/Louis Awhile/E of park
    Peter Byrne, The Search for Bigfoot
      (N.Y.: Pocket Books, 1976 ed.), p.
      86.

Bear Creek
-Humanoid
  1969, March 9/John Durrell
    John Green, The Sasquatch File (Ag-
      assiz, B.C.: Cheam, 1973), p.47,
      quoting Stevenson Skamania County
      Pioneer (undated).

Big Quilcene R.
-Humanoid tracks
  1927, Dec?/Jim Atwell
    John Green, Year of the Sasquatch
    (Agassiz, B.C.: Cheam, 1970), pp.
    24-25.

Black Fish Bay
-UFO (CE-2)
  1893, July 2/William Fitzhenry
    Tacoma Daily Ledger, 3 July 1893.

Blewett Pass
-Humanoid
  1977, Jan.23/Dean DeWees
    Wenatchee World, 26 Jan.1977.

Blue Mts.
-Humanoid
  1970, Aug.15/Rich Myers/Mill Creek Rd.
    Walla Walla Union-Bulletin, 30 Aug.
    1970.

Bow L.
-UFO (DD)
  1947, July 4/J.H. Oakley
    Seattle Post-Intelligencer, 5 July
    1947.
  1947, July 7/Mrs. J.A. Ashby
    Seattle Times, 8 July 1947.

Cascade Pass
-Humanoid
  1970, Aug.8/Dick Grover
    John Green, The Sasquatch File (Ag-
    assiz, B.C.: Cheam, 1973), p.53.

Cassidy L.
-Humanoid
  1977, March
    Jacob A. Davidson & Jerry Phillips,
    "An Examination of Mutilation Phe-
    nomena and Attendant Fortean Activ-
    ity at Machias, Washington State,
    1977," Phenomena Rsch.Special Rept.,
    no.2 (July 1977):1,11.

Chehalis Point
-Sea monster
  1930s/Jack Rockwell
    Paul H. LeBlond & John Sibert, Obser-
    vations of Large Unidentified Marine
    Animals in British Columbia and Ad-
    jacent Waters (Vancouver: Univ. of
    British Columbia, Inst. of Ocean-
    ography, Manuscript Rept. no.28
    June 1973), p.33.

Chelan L.
-Lake monster
  19th c.-
    Seattle Times, 21 Dec.1895, p.12.
    Ella E. Clark, Indian Legends of the
    Pacific Northwest (Berkeley: Univ.
    of California, 1958), pp.70-72.
-UFO (CE-1)
  1964, July 28
    Jacques Vallee, Passport to Magonia
    (Chicago: Regnery, 1969), pp.301-302.

Clear L.
-Humanoid
  1977, Aug.27/Vernita Frazier
    Yakima Herald-Republic, 28 Aug.1977.

Clearwater Creek
-Humanoid tracks
  1969, April/Steve Adams
    John Green, Sasquatch: The Apes Among
    Us (Seattle: Hancock House, 1978),
    p.439.

Coleman Ridge
-Humanoid tracks
  1970, Nov.6/Oscar D. Hickerson, Jr.
    John Green, The Sasquatch File (Ag-
    assiz, B.C.: Cheam, 1973), pp.53,
    59. il.
    John Green, Sasquatch: The Apes Among
    Us (Seattle: Hancock House, 1978),
    pp.351-55. il.

Colockum Pass
-Humanoid
  1969, Nov.
    John Green, Year of the Sasquatch
    (Agassiz, B.C.: Cheam, 1970), p.47.

Columbia R.
-Petroglyphs
    Rex Eidson, "Asiatic Rock Carvings
    in America?" Fate 13 (June 1960):
    88-92.
    Beth & Ray Hill, Indian Petroglyphs
    of the Pacific Northwest (Seattle:
    Univ. of Washington, 1974), pp.237-
    63. il.
-Sea monster
  1934/L. Larson/mouth
  1937/Charles E. Graham/mouth
  1950s/mouth
    Portland Oregonian, 24 Sep.1967.

Cowlitz R.
-Humanoid
  1917, fall/Albert M. Fletcher
    John Green, The Sasquatch File (Ag-
    assiz, B.C.: Cheam, 1973), p.12.

Cradle L.
-Humanoid
  1964
    John Green, Year of the Sasquatch
    (Agassiz, B.C.: Cheam, 1970), p.21.

Cub L.
-Humanoid
  1969, Aug.4/Mark Meece
    Seattle Times, 13 Aug.1969.
-Humanoid tracks
  1970, summer
    John Green, The Sasquatch File (Ag-
    assiz, B.C.: Cheam, 1973), p.52.

Dead Man Creek
-UFO (CE-1)
  1897, April/Mr. Thurber
    Spokane Chronicle, 16 Apr.1897.

Deception Pass
-Humanoid
1969, Sep.13
John Green, The Sasquatch File (Agassiz, B.C.: Cheam, 1973), p.43.

Destruction I.
-Sea monster
1939, July?/Paul Sowerby
Paul H. LeBlond & John Sibert, Obser-
vations of Large Unidentified Marine
Animals in British Columbia and Ad-
jacent Waters (Vancouver: Univ. of
British Columbia, Inst. of Ocean-
ography, Manuscript Rept. no.28,
June 1973), pp.15-16. il.

Diamond Gap
-UFO (DD)
1947, June 24/Robert W. Hubach
Portland Oregonian, 29 June 1947.

Dungeness Spit
-Sea monster
1930s/Rusty Beetle
Bernard Heuvelmans, In the Wake of
the Sea-Serpents (N.Y.: Hill & Wang,
1968), p.444n.
ca.1961/Mrs. E. Stout
Paul H. LeBlond & John Sibert, Observations of Large Unidentified Marine
Animals in British Columbia and Adjacent Waters (Vancouver: Univ. of
British Columbia, Inst. of Oceanography, Manuscript Rept.no.28,
June 1973), pp.27-29. il.

Eagle Gorge
-Phantom train
1890-1892/J.M. Pinckney
Jim Brandon, Weird America (N.Y.:
Dutton, 1978), p.234.

Echo L.
-Humanoid
1974, June 9/Tony McLennan
Kent Journal, 14 June 1974.

Entiat R.
-Humanoid tracks
1969, July/Mike Woolfe/N fork
John Green, The Sasquatch File (Agassiz, B.C.: Cheam, 1973), p.43.

Flattery, Cape
-Humanoid tracks
1968, July 4
John Green, The Sasquatch File (Agassiz, B.C.: Cheam, 1973), p.42.
-Jinx ship
1951, summer/"John N. Cobb"
"Unlucky Albatross," Fate 5 (June
1952):43.

Franklin D. Roosevelt L.
-Archeological site
ca.1600-1850
Donald Collier, Alfred E. Hudson &
Arlo Ford, "Archaeology of the Up-
per Columbia Region," Pub.Anthro.

Univ.Wash., vol.9, no.1 (Sep.1942).

Grass Mt.
-Disappearance
1973, July 10/Don Siskar
(Editorial), Fate 27 (May 1974):18-
20.

Green Mt.
-Humanoid tracks
1977, Dec.29/Dan Becker
Everett Herald, 3 Jan.1978.

Hoh R.
-Humanoid
1973/Mike Gilbert
Cliff Crook, "Cover Story--Hoh River,
Washington," Bigfoot Newsl., Jan.
1979, p.3.

Hurricane Ridge
-Humanoid
1974, Dec./Richard Taylor
Peter Byrne, The Search for Bigfoot
(N.Y.: Pocket Books, 1976 ed.), p.
42.

Indian Well
-Archeological site
B. Robert Butler, "The Old Cordiller-
an Culture in the Pacific Northwest," Occ.Pap.Mus.Idaho State Coll.
no.5 (1961).

Jim Creek
-Humanoid
ca.1906/Harry Borden
(Letter), Harriet Clark, Fate 23
(Nov.1970):144.

Lewis R.
-Archeological site
ca.3000 B.C./S fork
Donald R. Tuohy & Alan L. Bryan,
"Southwestern Washington Archaeology: An Appraisal," Tebiwa 2, no.1
(1958):27-58.
-Humanoid
1963, July 24/Martin Hennrich/Ridge-
field RR bridge
Portland Oregon Journal, 30 July
1963.

Lichtenwaash L.
-Humanoid
1941
John Green, Year of the Sasquatch
(Agassiz, B.C.: Cheam, 1970), p.21.

Lind Coulee
-Archeological site
ca.6700 B.C.
Richard D. Daugherty, "Archaeology of
the Lind Coulee Site, Washington,"
Proc.Am.Phil.Soc'y 100 (1956):223-
78.

Logy Creek
-Humanoid
1972/N fork

B. Ann Slate & Alan Berry, Bigfoot
(N.Y.: Bantam, 1976), p.146.
1978, April 30
Yakima Valley Sun, 8 June 1978.

Lost L.
-Humanoid tracks
ca.1964/Joe Barto, Jr.
John Green, The Sasquatch File (Agassiz, B.C.: Cheam, 1973), p.28.

Mad L.
-Humanoid
ca.1948/Clarence M. Foster
John Green, The Sasquatch File (Agassiz, B.C.: Cheam, 1973), p.15.

Margaret Mt.
-Humanoid tracks
1976, Aug.
"Latest News from the Pacific Northwest," Bigfoot News, no.23 (Aug.
1976):1.

Marmes Rockshelter
-Archeological site
10,000-2000 B.C.
New York Times, 30 Apr.1968, p.51;
and 1 Sep.1968, p.44. il.
Ruth Kirk, "The Discovery of Marmes
Man," Nat.History 77 (Dec.1968):56-
59. il.
"The Marmes Year, April 1968-April
1969," Washington Arch. 13, no.2-3
(1969).
Franklin Folsom, America's Ancient
Treasures (N.Y.: Rand McNally, 1974),
p.73. il.

Maury I.
-UFO (CE-2) and men-in-black
1947, June 21/Harold Dahl/=hoax
"The Mystery of the Flying Disks,"
Fate 1 (spring 1948):18,22-27,31-48.
(Editorial), Fate 3 (Jan.1950):5-7.
DeWayne B. Johnson, Flying Saucers:
Fact or Fiction? (M.A. thesis, Univ.
of California at Los Angeles, 1950),
pp.105-15.
Kenneth Arnold & Ray Palmer, The Com-
ing of the Saucers (Boise: The Au-
thors, 1952), pp.25-84,108-11.
Harold T. Wilkins, Flying Saucers on
the Attack (N.Y.: Ace, 1967 ed.),
pp.51-62.
Edward J. Ruppelt, The Report on Un-
identified Flying Objects (Garden
City: Doubleday, 1956), pp.24-27.
Eldon K. Everett, "Saucers over Puget
Sound," Flying Saucers, July-Aug.
1958, pp.52-60.

Mercer I.
-UFO (?)
1973, Oct.19/=searchlight
Seattle Post-Intelligencer, 20 Oct.
1973.

Mica Peak
-UFO (NL)

1970. Nov.22
(Editorial), Fate 24 (Apr.1971):22.

Mima Prairie
-Anomalous mounds
Victor B. Scheffer, "The Mystery of
the Mima Mounds," Sci.Monthly 65
(Oct.1947):283-94.
Allan O. Kelly & Rodney J. Arkley,
"The Mima Mounds," Sci.Monthly 66
(Apr.1948):174-76.
Troy L. Péwé, "Origin of the Mima
Mounds," Sci.Monthly 66 (Oct.1948):
293-96.
(Letter), James Nestor, Fate 8 (Dec.
1955):118-19.
Elton Caton, "The Mima Mounds," INFO
J., no.4 (spring 1969):14-15.
Donald M. Viles, "Pueblo del Valle,"
NEARA J. 10 (winter-spring 1976):
55-56; 11 (winter 1977):41-46. il.
Michael McFaul, "Preliminary Results
of a Field Study of the Mima Mounds
at Their Type Locality in Washington
State," Great Plains & Rocky Mt.
Geogr.J. 6 (Dec.1977):405.

Napeequa R.
-Humanoid tracks
ca.1953/Clarence Fox
John Green, The Sasquatch File (Agassiz, B.C.: Cheam, 1973), p.19.

New Dungeness Bay
-UFO (NL)
1960, March
Seattle Times, 9 Mar.1960.

Olympic National Forest
-Humanoid
1928, summer/Art Reda
Art Reda, "My Experiences with Bigfoot," Fate 23 (Aug.1970):63-67.

Olympus, Mt.
-Chinese discovery
ca.1000 B.C.
Henriette Mertz, Gods from the Far
East (N.Y.: Ballantine, 1975 ed.),
pp.153-54.
-Snow worms
1907/E.W. Gudger
E.W. Gudger, "Snow Worms," Nat.History
23 (Sep.-Oct.1923):451-56. il.

Omak L.
-Humanoid tracks
1976, Jan.
Peter Byrne, The Search for Bigfoot
(N.Y.: Pocket Books, 1976 ed.),
p.233.
-Lake monster myth
Walter Cline, "Religion and World
View," in Leslie Spier, ed., The
Sinkaietk or Southern Okanogon of
Washington (Menasha, Wisc.: George
Banta, 1930), pp.131,171.
-Petroglyph
H. Thomas Cain, Petroglyphs of Cen-
tral Washington (Seattle: Univ. of

Washington, 1950), pp.12-13.

Paddy Go Easy Pass
-Humanoid tracks
  1940, July/Mildred Farris
    John Green, The Sasquatch File (Ag-
    assiz, B.C.: Cheam, 1973), p.15.

Palouse Hills
-Topographic anomaly
    Virgil R.D. Kirkham, et al., "Origin
    of Palouse Hills Topography," Sci-
    ence 73 (1931):207-209.

Pinegrass Ridge
-Humanoid
  1975, Oct.1/Tom V. Gerstmar/Section 3
  Lake
    Yakima Herald-Republic, 3 Oct.1975.
    Jerome Clark & Loren Coleman, Crea-
    tures of the Outer Edge (N.Y.: War-
    ner, 1978), pp.47-48.

Priest Rapids Dam
-Humanoid
  1970, March/Bill Harwood
    John Green, The Sasquatch File (Ag-
    assiz, B.C.: Cheam, 1973), p.52.

Puget Sound
-UFO (DD)
  1920, Aug./C.F. Aus
    C.F. Aus, "What We Saw in the Sky,"
    Fate 5 (Nov.1952):66-67.

Quinault L.
-Lake monster myth
    Albert Reagan & L.V.W. Walters,
    "Tales from the Hoh and Quileute,"
    J.Am.Folklore 46 (1933):297,324-25.

Rainier, Mt.
-Chinese discovery
  ca.1000 B.C.
    Henriette Mertz, Gods from the Far
    East (N.Y.: Ballantine, 1975 ed.),
    p.159.
-Disappearance
  1947, June/C-46 plane/Tahoma Glacier/
  =hoax
    Seattle Post-Intelligencer, 24 Aug.
    1947.
    Harold T. Wilkins, Flying Saucers on
    the Attack (N.Y.: Ace, 1967 ed.),
    pp.59-60.
-Flood myth
    William D. Lyman, "Indian Legends of
    Rainier," Mazama 2 (Dec.1905):203-
    207.
-Humanoid
  1970, July 9/Wayne Thureringer/nr. Sunrise Pt. & Mystic L.
    John Green, Sasquatch: The Apes Among
    Us (Seattle: Hancock House, 1978),
    pp.392-93.
-Snow worms
  n.d./Israel C. Russell
    E.W. Gudger, "Snow Worms," Nat.History
    23 (Sep.-Oct.1923):451-56.
-UFO (DD)

1947, June 24/Kenneth Arnold
    Portland Oregonian, 26 June 1947.
    Kenneth Arnold, "I Did See the Fly-
    ing Disks," Fate 1 (spring 1948):4-
    10.
    John C. Ross, "What Were the Dough-
    nuts?" Fate 1 (spring 1948):12-14.
    Sidney Shalett, "What You Can Be-
    lieve about Flying Saucers," Sat.
    Eve.Post, 20 Apr.1949, p.20.
    Kenneth A. Arnold, The Flying Saucer
    As I Saw It (Boise: The Author,
    1950).
    Kenneth Arnold & Ray Palmer, The Com-
    ing of the Saucers (Boise: The Au-
    thors, 1952), pp.6-16.
    Donald H. Menzel, Flying Saucers
    (Cambridge: Harvard, 1953), pp.7-10.
    Edward J. Ruppelt, The Report on Un-
    identified Flying Objects (Garden
    City: Doubleday, 1956), pp.16-19.
    R.J. Reed, "Flying Saucer over Mount
    Rainier," Weatherwise 11 (1958):43.
    Brad Steiger, ed., Project Blue Book
    (N.Y.: Ballantine, 1976), pp.23-36.
  1949, Sep./Prof. Jekams/Carbon Glacier
    Renato Vesco, Intercept UFO (N.Y.:
    Zebra, 1974 ed.), pp.32-33.
-UFO (NL)
  1959, April 1
    Coral E. Lorenzen, Flying Saucers:
    The Startling Evidence of the Inva-
    sion from Outer Space (N.Y.: Sig-
    net, 1966 ed.), p.162.

Roberts Point
-Clairaudience
  1972, Nov.2/"Bitt"
    "Phantom SOS," Fate 26 (June 1973):
    85, quoting Seattle Post-Intelli-
    gencer (undated).

Rock L.
-Lake monster
  1853
    Charles M. Skinner, Myths and Legends
    of Our Own Land, 2 vols. (Philadel-
    phia: Lippincott, 1896), 2:303.

Rocky Beach Reservoir
-Archeological site
    Richard D. Daugherty, "An Archaeolog-
    ical Survey of Rocky Beach Reser-
    voir," Rsch.Studies Wash.State Coll.
    24 (1956):1-16.
    Alexander Gunkel, "A Comparative Cul-
    tural Analysis of Four Archaeologi-
    cal Sites in the Rocky Beach Reser-
    voir Region, Washington," Theses in
    Anthro., no.1 (1961).

Ross L.
-Humanoid
  1961, Sep.
    John Green, The Sasquatch File (Ag-
    assiz, B.C.: Cheam, 1973), p.27.

Sacajawea L.
-UFO (NL)
  1978, Feb.12/David Mace/Washington Way

Longview News, 13 Feb.1978.

Saint Clair L.
-Humanoid
1969, Nov.1/Lloyd Stringer
John Green, The Sasquatch File (Agassiz, B.C.: Cheam, 1973), p.44.

Saint Helens L.
-Humanoid
ca.1955, summer/Paul McGuire
John Green, The Sasquatch File (Agassiz, B.C.: Cheam, 1973), p.19.

Saint Helens, Mt.
-Disappearance
1950, May/Jim Carter
Don Hunter & René Dahinden, Sasquatch
(Toronto: McClelland & Stewart,
1973), pp.29-30, quoting Portland
Oregon Journal (undated).
-Humanoid
1840s
Paul Kane, Wanderings of an Artist
among the Indians of North America
(Toronto: Rasmussen Soc'y of Canada,
1925), pp.136-37.
1850/Rocque Ducheney
Agnes Eliot, "Some Indian Legends,"
in Told by the Pioneers, 2 vols.
(Olympia: U.S. Works Projects Admin.,
1937-38), 1:111.
1924, July/Fred Beck/Ape Canyon
Portland Oregonian, 13 July 1924.
Fred & R.A. Beck, I Fought the Apeman
of Mt. St. Helens (n.p.: The Authors,
1967). il.
John Green, On the Track of the Sasquatch (Agassiz, B.C.: Cheam, 1968),
p.59.
Don Hunter & René Dahinden, Sasquatch
(Toronto: McClelland & Stewart,
1973), pp.27-29.
John Green, Sasquatch: The Apes Among
Us (Seattle: Hancock House, 1978),
pp.88-97.
1964/Ape Canyon
John Green, The Sasquatch File (Agassiz, B.C.: Cheam, 1973), p.29.
-Humanoid tracks
1965, Aug./Charlie Erion
John Green, The Sasquatch File (Ag-
assiz, B.C.: Cheam, 1973), p.35.
1970, June/Bob Morgan
George H. Harrison, "On the Trail of
Bigfoot," Nat'l Wildlife 8 (Oct.-
Nov.1970):4-9. il.

Saint Lawrence, Mt.
-Humanoid
1918, July
Seattle Times, 16 July 1918.

Samish L.
-Humanoid
1917/Cyrus L. Sachelbottom
Mt. Vernon Skagit Valley Herald, 9
Sep.1971.

San Juan Is.
-Archeological site
Roy L. Carbon, "Chronology and Cul-
ture Change in the San Juan Islands,
Washington," Am.Antiquity 25 (1960)
:562-86.

Satus Pass
-Humanoid
1963, July/Gladys Herrara
John Green, The Sasquatch File (Ag-
assiz, B.C.: Cheam, 1973), p.28.
1963, July 28/Paul Manley
Portland Oregon Journal, 30 July
1963.
-UFO (NL)
1971, Aug./W.J. Vogel/U.S.97
B. Ann Slate & Alan Berry, Bigfoot
(N.Y.: Bantam, 1976), pp.144-45.

Satus Peak
-Acoustic anomaly
n.d./Dorothea Sturm
B. Ann Slate, "Gods from Inner Space,"
Saga UFO Rept. 3 (Apr.1976):36,51.
-UFO (NL)
1974, July 21/Dorothea Sturm/Middle
Fork of Toppenish Creek
B. Ann Slate, "Gods from Inner Space,"
Saga UFO Rept. 3 (Apr.1976):36,51.
1976, Oct.26/Dorothea Sturm
1976, Oct.30/Dorothea Sturm/9 mi.SE
1976, Nov.1/Dorothea Sturm/6 mi.NNW
1976, Nov.3/Dorothea Sturm/16 mi.E
Mel Podell, "Yakima Reports on Increase," APRO Bull. 25 (Dec.1976):
1,5.

Shaw I.
-UFO (NL)
1978, Feb.1,9/Clayton Shaw/Broken Pt.
Seattle Times, 19 Feb.1978.
Friday Harbor Journal, 21 Feb.1978.

Sherman Pass
-Humanoid
1971, winter/George Hildebrand/Repub-
lic R.
Peter Byrne, The Search for Bigfoot
(N.Y.: Pocket Books, 1976 ed.), pp.
83,86.

Si, Mt.
-Humanoid
1969, summer
John Green, The Sasquatch File (Agassiz, B.C.: Cheam, 1973), p.43.
-Humanoid tracks
1973, Jan.17/Robert Parker
John Green, The Sasquatch File (Agassiz, B.C.: Cheam, 1973), p.73.

Smith Springs
-Humanoid
1972
B. Ann Slate & Alan Berry, Bigfoot
(N.Y.: Bantam, 1976), p.146.

Snoqualmie Pass
-UFO (DD)

1947, July 2/H.H. Bowman
    Seattle Post-Intelligencer, 3 July
    1947.
1949, Aug.30/Roger Hamilton
    Kenneth Arnold & Ray Palmer, The Com-
    ing of the Saucers (Boise: The Au-
    thors, 1952), p.144.

Snow L.
-UFO (DD)
1949, Aug.28
    "If It's in the Sky It's a Saucer,"
    Doubt, no.27 (1949):416,417.

Soap Lake Mt.
-UFO (NL)
1971, Feb.16/Neil Yarnell
    "Press Reports," APRO Bull. 19 (Mar,-
    Apr.1971):5.

South Hill
-Humanoid tracks
1976, Jan.
    Renee Dictor LeBlanc, "Peter Byrne
    Stalks the Rarest Game of All--Big-
    foot," Probe the Unknown 4 (Mar.
    1976):24,27.

Spirit L.
-Humanoid
1964, summer
    John Green, The Sasquatch File (Ag-
    assiz, B.C.: Cheam, 1973), p.28.
-Humanoid myth
    Mary Jane Finke, "St. Helens, the
    Haunted Mountain," in Alfred Powers,
    Legends of the Four High Mountains
    (Portland: Junior Historical Jour-
    nal, 1944), pp.30-31.
    Ruth McKee, Mary Richardson Walker:
    Her Book (Caldwell, Id.: Caxton,
    1945), p.207.
-Humanoid tracks
1930, Oct.30
    Portland Oregon Journal, 6 Aug.1963.
    il.
1976, Oct.
    "Latest News," Bigfoot News, no.25
    (Oct.1976):1.

Stevens Pass
-Humanoid tracks
1965, July/Clarence Fox
1967, Sep.17/Clarence Fox
1968, summer/Zarol Johnson
1970, March 20/Greg Lea
    John Green, The Sasquatch File (Ag-
    assiz, B.C.: Cheam, 1973), pp.34-35,
    36,42,52.

Swede's Pass
-Humanoid
ca.1961
    John Green, The Sasquatch File (Ag-
    assiz, B.C.: Cheam, 1973), p.27.

Tannum Valley
-Humanoid
1968, Nov.
    John Green, The Sasquatch File (Ag-

assiz, B.C.: Cheam, 1973), p.42.

Tanwax L.
-UFO (DD)
1952, April 28
    Seattle Post-Intelligencer, 30 Apr.
    1952.

Toppenish Ridge
-UFO (NL)
1960s
    B. Ann Slate & Alan Berry, Bigfoot
    (N.Y.: Bantam, 1976), pp.140-41.
1972, Aug./David Akers
    B. Ann Slate, "Gods from Inner Space,"
    Saga UFO Rept. 3 (Apr.1976):36,51.

Vessey Springs
-Humanoid
n.d.
    B. Ann Slate & Alan Berry, Bigfoot
    (N.Y.: Bantam, 1976), pp.145-46.

Wakemap Mound
-Archeological site
10,000 B.C.-recent
    (Editorial), Fate 10 (Jan.1957):13.
    New York Times, 2 Dec.1957, p.27.
    "Wakemap Mound and Nearby Sites on
    the Long Narrows of the Columbia
    River," Pub.Oregon Arch.Soc'y, no.1
    (1959). il.

Washington, L.
-Erratic crocodilian
ca.1967
    (Editorial), Fate 20 (June 1967):20.
-Fall of stones
1955, Jan./=meteorite fragments?
    "Case 44," CRIFO Newsl., 4 Feb.1955,
    p.2.
-Lake monster
1947, Feb.19/Ivar Haglund
    "No Such Sanderson," Doubt, no.18
    (1947):274.
1964, April 6/Henry B. Joseph/Faben Pt.
    (Editorial), Fate 17 (Aug.1964):18.
-UFO (NL)
1948, Feb.17-18
    "Disc Dirt," Doubt, no.21 (1948):314,
    315.

Wenatchee L.
-Humanoid tracks
1976, Feb.
    Peter Byrne, The Search for Bigfoot
    (N.Y.: Pocket Books, 1976 ed.), p.
    233.

Whidbey I.
-Humanoid myth
see-atco
    Emerson N. Matson, Legends of the
    Great Chiefs (N.Y.: Thomas Nelson,
    1972).
-Sea monster
1958, April 29/John Oosterhoff
    Bernard Heuvelmans, In the Wake of
    the Sea-Serpents (N.Y.: Hill & Wang,
    1968), p.507, quoting AP release,

29 Apr.1958.
-UFO (CE-1)
  1966, April 3/Donald Peterson
    Gordon I.R. Lore, Jr. & Harold H. De-
    neault, Jr., Mysteries of the Skies:
    UFOs in Perspective (Englewood
    Cliffs, N.J.: Prentice-Hall, 1968),
    pp.160-61.
-UFO (CE-3)
  1963, July-Oct.
    "Whidbey Island Contact," Flying
    Saucer Rev. 10 (Nov.-Dec.1964):13-
    14.

Whistle L.
-Humanoid tracks
  1969, Dec./Jack Migs
    John Green, The Sasquatch File (Ag-
    assiz, B.C.: Cheam, 1973), p.44.

White Chuck Mt.
-Humanoid
  1977, Sep./Mildred Quinn
    Portland Oregon Journal, 12 Jan.1978.
    "Latest News from the Pacific North-
    west," Bigfoot News, no.42 (Mar.
    1978):1.

White Pass
-Humanoid tracks
  1966, Nov./Don Harmon
    John Green, The Sasquatch File (Ag-
    assiz, B.C.: Cheam, 1973), p.35.

Woodward Creek
-Humanoid tracks
  1970, June/Leroy Baxter
    John Green, The Sasquatch File (Ag-
    assiz, B.C.: Cheam, 1973), p.52.

Yale Reservoir
-Humanoid
  1971, Oct.2/Elmer Wollenburg
    John Green, Sasquatch: The Apes Among
    Us (Seattle: Hancock House, 1978),
    p.439.

          C. Ethnic Groups

Clallam Indians
-Flood myth
    M. Eells, "Traditions of the 'Deluge'
    among the Tribes of the Northwest,"
    Am.Antiquarian 1 (1878):70.

Makah Indians
-Flood myth
    M. Eells, "Traditions of the 'Deluge'
    among the Tribes of the Northwest,"
    Am.Antiquarian 1 (1878):70,71-72.

Okanagon Indians
-Humanoid myth
    Walter Cline, "Religion and World
    View," in Leslie Spier, ed., The
    Sinkaietk or Southern Okanagon of
    Washington (Menasha, Wisc.: George
    Banta, 1938), pp.131,170-71.
-Shamanism

Walter Cline, "Religion and World
View," in Leslie Spier, ed., The
Sinkaietk or Southern Okanagon of
Washington (Menasha, Wisc.: George
Banta, 1938), pp.131-82.

Puyallup Indians
-Flood myth
    M. Eells, "Traditions of the 'Deluge'
    among the Tribes of the Northwest,"
    Am.Antiquarian 1 (1878):70,71.

Quillayute Indians
-Flood and giant bird myths
    Albert B. Reagan & L.V.W. Waters,
    "Tales from the Hoh and Quillayute,"
    J.Am.Folklore 46 (1933):297,320-21.

Skagit Indians
-Flood myth
    Ella E. Clark, Indian Legends of the
    Pacific Northwest (Berkeley: Univ.
    of California, 1958), pp.138-41.

Snohomish Indians
-Cataclysm myth
    William Shelton, The Story of the
    Totem Pole (Everett: Kane & Harcus,
    1923), pp.11-12.
    Hermann Haeberlin, "Mythology of Pu-
    get Sound," J.Am.Folklore 37 (1924)
    :371,417.

Twana Indians
-Flood myth
    M. Eells, "Traditions of the 'Deluge'
    among the Tribes of the Northwest,"
    Am.Antiquarian 1 (1878):70.

Upper Chehalis Indians
-Flood myth
    Thelma Adamson, "Folk Tales of the
    Coast Salish," Mem.Am.Folklore Soc'y
    27 (1934):1-3.
-Lake monster myth
    Thelma Adamson, "Folk Tales of the
    Coast Salish," Mem.Am.Folklore Soc'y
    27 (1934):1,124-25.

Yakima Indians
-Humanoid myth
  wahteeta
    Ella E. Clark, Indian Legends of the
    Pacific Northwest (Berkeley: Univ.
    of California, 1958), pp.109-10.

OREGON

A. Populated Places

Albany
-UFO (DD)
  1947, July 5/Ted Tannich
    Portland Oregonian, 6 July 1947.

Alder Creek
-Anomalous mound
  1975
    Keith Soesbe, "A Mound of Earth,"
    Bigfoot News, no.8 (June 1975):2.
-Humanoid
  1953, summer
    John Green, The Sasquatch File (Ag-
    assiz, B.C.: Cheam, 1973), p.19.

Aloha
-UFO (DD)
  1947, June/Mrs. A. Krause/E of town
    Ted Bloecher, Report on the UFO Wave
    of 1947 (Washington: NICAP, 1967),
    p. II-14.

Applegate
-UFO (CE-1)
  1975, July 24
    "UFO Central," CUFOS News Bull., 15
    Nov.1975, p.14.

Ashland
-Ghost
  1965, June 12/Earl Ponder/35 S. 2d St.
    Starr Deuel, "Will-o'-the-Wisp Sounds
    Fire Alarm," Fate 26 (Feb.1973):66-
    68.
-Humanoid
  1977, Sep.27/John C. Martin/I-5 x Hwy.
  66
    Ashland Tidings, 28 Sep.1977.
    "Latest News from the Pacific North-
    west," Bigfoot News, no.36 (Sep.
    1977):1.
-Medical clairvoyance
  1950s/Susie Jessel/Idaho St.
    Iris Barry, "The Story of Sleeping
    Lucy," Fate 8 (Dec.1955):103-104.

Astoria
-Fall of sooty pellets
  1954, April 17
    "Fish, Birds Fall," Doubt, no.45
    (1954):294.
    (Editorial), Fate 7 (Aug.1954):9.
-Sea monster
  1939
    Bernard Heuvelmans, In the Wake of
    the Sea-Serpents (N.Y.: Hill & Wang,
    1968), p.469.
-UFO (DD)
  1947, June 30/Jack Hayes/St. Mary's
  Hospital
    Portland Oregonian, 3 July 1947.
  1949, July 6

"If It's in the Sky It's a Saucer,"
    Doubt, no.27 (1949):416.

Azalea
-Psychokinesis
  1945/Nina Lane Faubion
    David Faubion, "Two Watches Stopped
    for Death," Fate 13 (Nov.1960):88-
    90.

Baker
-UFO (NL)
  1964, Dec.5/William Howe
    "News Briefs," Saucer News 12 (Mar.
    1965):25.

Bandon
-Sea monster
  n.d.
    Portland Oregonian, 24 Sep.1967.

Barton
-UFO (CE-1)
  1976/Lee Abbot/Hwy.224
  1978, Dec./Lee Abbot
    Estacada Clackamus County News, 24
    Jan.1979.
-UFO (NL)
  1978, Dec.24/Charles C. Woods/Hwy.224
    Estacada Clackamus County News, 17
    Jan.1979; and 24 Jan.1979.

Beaverton
-Precognition
  1970s/Tenny Hale/Box 125
    Warren Smith, "Phenomenal Predictions
    for 1975," Saga, Jan.1975, p.23.
    Lenny Pinaud, "The Woman Who Lived in
    a Pyramid," Psychic World, May 1976,
    pp.41-43. il.
    Warren Smith, "Phenomenal Predictions
    for 1976," Saga, Jan.1976, pp.16,18.
    "Probe's 1977 Directory of the Psych-
    ic World," Probe the Unknown 5
    (spring 1977):32,36.
-UFO (DD)
  1947, July 4/Harry Hale
    Portland Oregonian, 5 July 1947.

Bend
-Humanoid
  1977, Oct.1/Gary Benson
    San Antonio (Tex.) Express, 4 Oct.
    1977.
    "Latest News from the Pacific North-
    west," Bigfoot News, no.39 (Dec.
    1977):1.
-UFO (DD)
  1949, March 25/Vernon Leverett
    Kenneth Arnold & Ray Palmer, The Com-
    ing of the Saucers (Boise: The Au-
    thors, 1952), p.140.
  1969, July 10
    "Flying Objects Seen in Oregon," Sky-

look, no.22 (Sep.1969):13, quoting
Bend Bulletin (undated).

Blodgett
-Acoustic anomaly
  1967, March 3/Mrs. Lucky Newell/4 mi.N
    Brad Steiger & Joan Whritenour, Al-
    lende Letters: New UFO Breakthrough
    (N.Y.: Award, 1968), p.41.

Boring
-Fall of salamanders
  1911, June/Arlene O. Meyer/Sandy R.
    (Letter), Fate 21 (Dec.1968):131-32.

Central Point
-Contactee
  1958-   /Aleuti Francesca/7700 Ave.
    of the Sun
    Brad Steiger, Revelation: The Divine
    Fire (Englewood Cliffs, N.J.: Pren-
    tice-Hall, 1973), pp.152-53.
    Glenn McWane & David Graham, The New
    UFO Sightings (N.Y.: Warner, 1974),
    pp.120-23.
    Armand Biteaux, The New Consciousness
    (Willits, Cal.: Oliver, 1975), pp.
    129-30.
    Brad Steiger, Gods of Aquarius (N.Y.:
    Harcourt Brace Jovanovich, 1976),
    pp.101-104.

Charleston
-UFO (NL)
  1977, Jan.15
    "UFOs of Limited Merit," Int'l UFO
    Reporter 2 (Mar.1977):5.

Chiloquin
-UFO (NL)
  1953, Sep.11-13/Lew Jones
    Los Angeles (Cal.) Daily News, 15
    Sep.1953.

Clackamus co.
-Haunt
  1941-1957/Lillian A. Ryan/Old Campbell
    Donation Land Claim
    Lillian A. Ryan, "'Old John' Still
    Hunts His Money," Fate 11 (Feb.1958)
    :86-89.
-UFO (?)
  1956, Oct.3/Paul Lowery
    (Editorial), Fate 10 (Mar.1957):16.

Clatsop co.
-Humanoid tracks
  1977, Nov.18/Glenn Lauper
    Astoria Daily Astorian, 16 Dec.1977.
    il.

Clyde
-UFO (CE-2)
  1967, Aug.4/Orrin Anderson
    "Strange Lights, Blast, Seem Connect-
    ed," APRO Bull. 16 (Jan.-Feb.1968):
    3.

Coos Bay
-Fall of seeds

1954, May 3
  "Fish, Birds Fall," Doubt, no.45
    (1954):294.
-Humanoid
  1970, Sep./Edward Flowers/SE of town
    John Green, The Sasquatch File (Ag-
    assiz, B.C.: Cheam, 1973), p.54.
-Sea monster
  n.d./Empire
    Portland Oregonian, 24 Sep.1967.
-UFO (?)
  1969, Jan.16
    Coos Bay World, 18 Jan.1969.
-UFO (CE-2)
  1959, Sep.27/Leo Bartsch/744 S. 4th St.
    Coos Bay World, 28-29 Sep.1959; and
    10 Oct.1959.
-UFO (DD)
  ca.1954/Marvin W. Skipworth
    Richard Hall, ed., The UFO Evidence
    (Washington: NICAP, 1964), p.68.

Copper
-Disappearance
  1974, Sep.1/Richard Cowden/Rogue River
    Campground/=murder
    Portland Oregon Journal, 5 Sep.1974.
    Columbus (O.) Dispatch, 15 Apr.1975.
-Humanoid tracks
  1969, Aug.30/Perry Lovell
    Medford Mail-Tribune, 8 Sep.1969.

Corvallis
-Precognition
  1965, Dec.14/Harry S. Weatherby
    Sally Remaley, "Is Psychically Fore-
    warned Always Forearmed?" Fate 24
    (Sep.1971):81,83-84.
-UFO (CE-1)
  1972, July 14/Sharlene Yocum/34th St.
    Glenn McWane & David Graham, The New
    UFO Sightings (N.Y.: Warner, 1974),
    pp.44-45, quoting Corvallis Herald
    (undated).
-UFO (CE-2)
  1965, March 4
    Jacques Vallee, Passport to Magonia
    (Chicago: Regnery, 1969), p.306.
  1973, Nov.12
    Timothy Green Beckley, "The Strange
    Effects of Flying Saucers," Saga
    UFO Rept. 2 (winter 1974):32,68,
    quoting Corvallis Gazette-Times (un-
    dated).
-UFO (NL)
  1976, May 23
    "Noteworthy UFO Sightings," Ufology
    2 (fall 1976):60.

Dallas
-Humanoid
  1969, June 26/Doris Newton/5 mi.W
    John Green, The Sasquatch File (Ag-
    assiz, B.C.: Cheam, 1973), p.45.
-Humanoid tracks
  1967, fall/Ben Chapman/7 mi.S
    John Green, The Sasquatch File (Ag-
    assiz, B.C.: Cheam, 1973), p.37.

Eagle Creek
-UFO (CE-1)
  1978, summer
    Estacada Clackamus County News, 14
    Feb.1979.
  1978, Dec.30/Mrs. Jim Yoerger
    Estacada Clackamus County News, 24
    Jan.1979.
-UFO (NL)
  1978/H.M. Mason
    Estacada Clackamus County News, 7
    Feb.1979.
  1978, Sep./Ira McBain
    Estacada Clackamus County News, 31
    Jan.1979.
  1979, Feb./Warren Parker/Hwy.224
    Estacada Clackamus County News, 7
    Feb.1979.

Eagle Point
-UFO (DD)
  1958, Feb.
    Coral E. Lorenzen, The Shadow of the
    Unknown (N.Y.: Signet, 1970), p.145.

Elsie
-Humanoid
  1964
    John Green, The Sasquatch File (Ag-
    assiz, B.C.: Cheam, 1973), p.29.

Estacada
-Humanoid
  1964, June
  1968, June
  1968, Oct.
    John Green, The Sasquatch File (Ag-
    assiz, B.C.: Cheam, 1973), pp.29,
    44-45.
  1973, April 5/Don Stratton/12 mi.E
    John Green, The Sasquatch File (Ag-
    assiz, B.C.: Cheam, 1973), p.73.
    John Green, Sasquatch: The Apes Among
    Us (Seattle: Hancock House, 1978),
    pp.408-409.
-Humanoid tracks
  1969, Feb./Glenn Thomas
    John Green, The Sasquatch File (Ag-
    assiz, B.C.: Cheam, 1973), p.45.
-UFO (?)
  1958, May/Marion Fletcher/Rt.2
    (Editorial), Fate 11 (Oct.1958):30.
-UFO (NL)
  1979, Jan./Pam Ledford
    Estacada Clackamus County News, 14
    Feb.1979.

Eugene
-Haunt
  1940-1956/Traver Bornholz
    Traver Bornholz, "We Built a Haunted
    House," Fate 15 (Jan.1962):67-70.
-Humanoid
  1972, June 9/volcano 20 mi.E
    John Green, The Sasquatch File (Ag-
    assiz, B.C.: Cheam, 1973), p.55.
-Humanoid tracks
  1977, Sep.4/SW of town
    "Bigfoot," INFO J., no.26 (Nov.-Dec.
    1977):15.

-Mystery radio transmission
  1976-1978, April/Walter Deposki
    Eugene Register-Guard, 26 Mar.-9 Apr.
    1978.
-UFO (?)
  1947, June 18/E.H. Sprinkle
    Portland Oregonian, 27 June 1947.
-UFO (NL)
  1975, Oct.4
    "UFO Central," CUFOS News Bull., 1
    Feb.1976, p.7.

Falls City
-Acoustic anomaly
  1965, May/Bill Ames/Sample Hill
    Coral E. Lorenzen, The Shadow of the
    Unknown (N.Y.: Signet, 1970), pp.
    71-72, quoting Salem Oregon States-
    man (undated).

Florence
-Humanoid
  1974, March 8/Nick Wells
    Peter Byrne, The Search for Bigfoot
    (N.Y.: Pocket Books, 1976 ed.),
    pp.34-35.
-Humanoid tracks
  1905, April/C.E. Dixon
    Peter Byrne, The Search for Bigfoot
    (N.Y.: Pocket Books, 1976 ed.),
    p.36.

Forest Grove
-UFO (NL)
  1975, Nov.21
    "UFO Central," CUFOS News Bull., 1
    Feb.1976, p.14.

Fort Stevens
-UFO (DD)
  1947, July 1/Mrs. Earl Seado
    Portland Oregon Journal, 2 July 1947.

Galice
-Ancient mining
  =kilns?
    Jim Brandon, Weird America (N.Y.:
    Dutton, 1978), p.188.

Glide
-Humanoid
  1976, Oct.3/Rodney Boder
    "Latest News from the Pacific North-
    west," Bigfoot News, no.26 (Nov.
    1976):1-2. il.

Gold Hill
-Gravity anomaly
  1930-   /House of Mystery/=optical illusion
    Mildred Litster, The Oregon Vortex:
    Notes and Data (Gold Hill: The Au-
    thor, 1944).
    "Hehr on Gold Hill," Doubt, no.14
    (spring 1946):202.
    John P. Bessor, "Oregon's Strange
    Whirlpool of Force," Fate 4 (July
    1951):24-28. il.
    (Editorial), Fate 7 (Jan.1954):6-7.
    (Letter), Rex Eidson, Fate 14 (Apr.

1961):114-17.
Howard E. Jackson, "Solving the Mystery of the 'Oregon Vortex,'" Fate 14 (Jan.1961):52-58. il.
"Vortiginous Vortices," Pursuit 2 (Oct.1969):70-71.
-UFO (NL)
1975, July 28
"UFO Central," CUFOS News Bull., 15 Feb.1975, p.14.

Granite co.
-UFO (CE-2)
1956, fall/Lee A. Finley/ground markings only
Betty Jones, "Mysterious Force Grooves and Twists a Thicket of Trees," Can.UFO Rept., no.17 (1974): 13-15. il.

Grants Pass
-Humanoid
1973, Jan./S of town
John Green, Sasquatch: The Apes Among Us (Seattle: Hancock House, 1978), pp.409-10.
-UFO (DD)
1952, March 26
(Editorial), Fate 5 (Sep.1952):7.
-UFO (NL)
1946, Aug.16
"Damned Reds," Doubt, no.16 (1946): 236, quoting Los Angeles (Cal.) Daily News (undated).

Harney co.
-Cattle mutilation
1975, summer
Ed Sanders, "The Mutilation Mystery," Oui, Sep.1976, pp.51,120.
-Fall of ice
1894, June 3
"Lumps of Ice As Hailstones," Monthly Weather Rev. 22 (July 1894):293.

Heppner
-UFO (DD)
1954, May 6/Albert Lovegren
Donald E. Keyhoe, Flying Saucer Conspiracy (N.Y.: Holt, 1955), p.144.

Hermiston
-Crisis apparition
1955, Aug.11/Phyllis Halstead
Phyllis Halstead, "Grandmother Gave Me a Precious Inheritance," Fate 26 (May 1973):95-98.

Hillsboro
-Humanoid
1978, Nov.13/Baseline Rd.
Portland Oregon Journal, 13 Nov.1978.
-UFO (DD)
1954, Feb.27/Gladie M. Bills
(Letter), Fate 7 (Dec.1954):128-29.
-UFO (NL)
1975, July 6
"UFO Central," CUFOS News Bull., 15 Nov.1975, p.13.

Hood River
-Fall of giant snowflakes
1954, Jan.25
"Fish, Birds Fall," Doubt, no.45 (1954):294.

Hubbard
-UFO (CE-2)
1964, May 19/Michael J. Bizon
"Physical Evidence Landing Reports," UFO Inv. 2 (July-Aug.1964):4,6.

Irrigon
-Cattle mutilation
1977, Sep./Brent Hulse/nr. C & H Market
Hermiston Herald, 22 Sep.1977.

Jacksonville
-Giant human jawbones
1862, May
Oscar T. Schuck, California Scrap-Book (San Francisco: H.H. Bancroft, 1869), p.486.
-UFO (DD)
1947, June 29/Peter Vogel
Ted Bloecher, Report on the UFO Wave of 1947 (Washington: NICAP, 1967), p.II-4.

Jefferson
-UFO (CE-1)
1975, June 23
"Reports from America," Australian UFO Bull., Feb.1976, p.7.

Joseph
-Cattle mutilation
1977, Sep.29/Harold Klages/E of town
Enterprise Wallowa County Chieftain, 13 Oct.1977.
LaGrande Observer, 14 Oct.1977.

Josephine co.
-Mineralogical anomaly
=josephinite
(Editorial), Fate 27 (Sep.1974):30-32.

Keizer
-Fall of ice
1971, May 17/Ernest Davenport
(Editorial), Fate 24 (Oct.1971):35.

Klamath Falls
-Earthquake anomaly
1867, Jan.8
San Francisco (Cal.) Bulletin, 14 Jan.1867.
Edward S. Holden, "Catalogue of Recorded Earthquakes on the Pacific Coast, 1769 to 1897," Smith.Misc. Coll. 37 (1898):71-72.
Warren du Pré Smith, "Earthquakes in Oregon," Bull.Seism.Soc'y Am., no.9 (Sep.1919):59,69.
-UFO (?)
1956, Jan.8/=meteor?
Eugene Register-Guard, 9 Jan.1956.
1969, Dec.5/Noel Cailloutte/=rocket

Klamath Falls Herald & News, 8-9 Dec.
1969.
-UFO (DD)
1949, April 29
1949, July 20
"If It's in the Sky It's a Saucer,"
Doubt, no.27 (1949):416.
1969, Oct.10/Steve Kemp/nr. Stukel Mt.
Klamath Falls Herald & News, 10 Oct.
1969.
-UFO (NL)
1947, July 2
Portland Oregonian, 4 July 1947.
1964, Feb.22/Carl Hoskins
"Leading up to the Big Flap," Fate
17 (Aug.1964):45.
1969, June 30/Gail Bumala
Klamath Falls Herald & News, 13 July
1969.
1970, March 5/Kingsley Field
"Queer Light Seen in Oregon State,"
Skylook, no.30 (May 1970):6, quoting
Klamath Falls Herald & News (undated).

LaGrande
-Cattle mutilation
1977, Aug.15/Nancy Rayburn/1 mi.N of
airport
LaGrande Observer, 17-24 Aug.1977.
"Mutilations," Phenomena Rsch.Special
Rept., no.3 (Oct.1977):2-4.
-Mystery bird deaths
1954, May 3
"Fish, Birds Fall," Doubt, no.45
(1954):294.
-UFO (?)
1963, Oct.
"News Briefs," Saucer News 11 (Mar.
1964):24.
-UFO (DD)
1947, June 28/Leland Jones
Portland Oregonian, 1 July 1947.

Lake Oswego
-UFO (DD)
1947, Sep.3
E.U. Condon, "UFOs: 1947-1968," in
Edward U. Condon, ed., Scientific
Study of Unidentified Flying Objects
(N.Y.: Bantam, 1969 ed.), pp.502,
508.

Lakeview
-Humanoid
1966, Dec.
John Green, The Sasquatch File (Agassiz, B.C.: Cheam, 1973), p.37.

Lebanon
-Humanoid
1885, Dec./Mr. Fitzgerald/nr. Bald
Peter
Carson City (Nev.) Morning Appeal, 31
Dec.1885.
1963, Oct./12 mi.NE
John Green, The Sasquatch File (Ag-
assiz, B.C.: Cheam, 1973), pp.28-29.

Lincoln City
-Sea monster
n.d./Nelscott
Portland Oregonian, 24 Sep.1967.
-Sea monster (carcass)
1950, March 4/Marybell Allum/DeLake/
=shark?
San Francisco (Cal.) Chronicle, 12
Mar.1950.
Portland Oregonian, 24 Sep.1967.
-UFO (CE-1)
1978, Nov.5/Fern Curington/S of town
Lincoln City News Guard, 9 Nov.1978.

McMinnville
-UFO (DD)
1950, May 11/Paul Trent/10 mi.SW nr.
U.S.99W
McMinnville Telephone Register, 8
June 1950. il.
"Farmer Trent's Flying Saucer," Life,
26 June 1950, p.40. il.
Edward U. Condon, ed., Scientific
Study of Unidentified Flying Ob-
jects (N.Y.: Bantam, 1969 ed.), pp.
396-407. il.
Philip J. Klass, UFOs Explained (N.Y.:
Random House, 1974), pp.144-50. il.
Bruce S. Maccabee, "On the Possibil-
ity That the McMinnville Photos
Show a Distant Unidentified Object,"
in Proc.1976 CUFOS Conference (Ev-
anston: Center for UFO Studies,
1976), pp.152-63.
W.H. Spaulding, "Ufology and the Dig-
ital Computer: The Trent Photographs
Revisited," in Proc.1976 CUFOS Con-
ference (Evanston: Center for UFO
Studies, 1976), pp.234-50. il.
Robert Sheaffer, "Is Seeing Always
Believing?" Official UFO 1 (Oct.
1976):26,58-60.

Madras
-UFO (DD)
1947, July 1/Mrs. R.A. Hunt
Portland Oregonian, 3 July 1947.
1964, July 20-21
"UFO Sighting Wave Persists," UFO
Inv. 2 (Sep.-Oct.1964):5.

Malheur co.
-Lava caves
N of Rome
(Editorial), Fate 22 (Jan.1969):15-
18. il.
"The Oregon 'Tunnel' Cave," Pursuit
3 (Oct.1970):75.

Medford
-Spirit medium
1954, May
(Editorial), Fate 8 (Feb.1955):11-12.
-UFO (DD)
1947, July 7/David W. Chase/5 mi.S
Ray Palmer, "New Report on the Flying Saucers," Fate 4 (Jan.1951):63,
73-74.
1949, May 16
"If It's in the Sky It's a Saucer,"

Doubt, no.27 (1949):416.
-UFO (NL)
1975, July 20
1975, Aug.3
"UFO Central," CUFOS News Bull., 15
Nov.1975, pp.14,15.

Mill City
-UFO (NL)
1976, Jan.21
"Noteworthy UFO Sightings," Ufology
2 (summer 1976):62.

Milo
-UFO (DD)
1947, June/Robert Wright/E on Hwy.44
Ted Bloecher, Report on the UFO Wave
of 1947 (Washington: NICAP, 1967),
Appendix, Case 2.

Milton-Freewater
-Fall of burning substance
1967, Dec.28/Arthur J. Wrinkle/=satel-
lite re-entry?
"Strange Lights, Blast, Seem Connected," APRO Bull. 16 (Jan.-Feb.1968):
3.

Milwaukie
-Fall of unknown object
1949, July/Mack Thompson
"If It's in the Sky It's a Saucer,"
Doubt, no.27 (1949):416-17, quoting
Portland Oregonian (undated).
-Humanoid tracks
1977, Sep.25
"Bigfoot," INFO J., no.26 (Nov.-Dec.
1977):15.
-UFO (?)
1957, Nov.5/=Venus
Jacques & Janine Vallee, Challenge to
Science (N.Y.: Ace, 1966), p.131.
-UFO (DD)
1947, July 4/Claude Cross/9200 SE Mc-
Loughlin Blvd.
Portland Oregon Journal, 5 July 1947.

Mollala
-Humanoid
1967, Oct./Glenn Thomas/SE of town nr.
Low Creek
John Green, On the Track of the Sasquatch (Agassiz, B.C.: Cheam, 1968),
pp.63-66.
Don Hunter & René Dahinden, Sasquatch
(Toronto: McClelland & Stewart,
1973), pp.128-29.
John Green, Sasquatch: The Apes Among
Us (Seattle: Hancock House, 1978),
pp.420-25.
1978, June?
"Latest News from the Pacific Northwest," Bigfoot News, no.46 (July
1978):1.

Monroe
-UFO (CE-2)
1966, Dec.25
Ted Phillips, Physical Traces Associated with UFO Sightings (Evanston:

Center for UFO Studies, 1975), p.45.

Myrtle Creek
-UFO (DD)
1947, Aug.6
Bruce S. Maccabee, "UFO Related Information from the FBI Files: Part
3," MUFON UFO J., no.121 (Dec.1977)
:10,14.
-UFO (NL)
1969, Sep.21/Irene Meade
"Oregon Woman and Son See UFO," Skylook, no.25 (Dec.1969):10.

Myrtle Point
-Humanoid
1972, Sep.30/Dewey Strong/Lee Valley
Rd.
Myrtle Point Herald, 12 Oct.1972.

Neahkahnie
-Petroglyphs and lost treasure
ca.1700
Portland Oregonian, 29 May 1890, p.
10; 27 Feb.1906, p.9; 28 Feb.1906,
p.8; 15 Mar.1915, p.5; 1 Aug.1929,
p.1; 21 May 1946, p.10; and 4 Dec.
1961.
Ruby El Hult, Lost Mines and Treas-
ures of the Pacific Northwest (Port-
land: Binfords & Mort, 1957), pp.1-
45.
Joe Beckman, "Treasure on Neah-Kah-
Nie," Golden West 6 (Sep.1970):28-
31,67-68.
Donald M. Viles, "The Northern Mys-
tery," NEARA Newsl. 6 (Dec.1971):
67-69.
"A Correction Regarding the 'Great
Northern Mystery,'" NEARA Newsl. 7
(June 1972):34.
Donald M. Viles, "The Discovery of
English Elizabethan Survey Stones
on the Pacific Coast--and Possible
Parallels on the Atlantic Coast,"
NEARA Newsl. 7 (Dec.1972):69-71.

Newburg
-Humanoid
1978, Jan.15-16/Thomas Martin/Rex Hill
McMinnville News-Register, 18 Jan.
1978.

Newport
-UFO (NL)
1974, March
B. Ann Slate, "Gods from Inner Space,"
Saga UFO Rept. 3 (Apr.1976):36,38.

Nyssa
-UFO (?)
1964, April 29
"Other Recent Sightings," UFO Inv.
2 (July-Aug.1964):7.

Oakridge
-UFO (NL)
1975, Sep.7
"UFO Central," CUFOS News Bull., 15
Nov.1975, p.18.

Oceanlake
-UFO (DD)
1947, Aug.7
Bruce S. Maccabee, "UFO Related Information from the FBI Files: Part
3," MUFON UFO J., no.121 (Dec.1977)
:10,14.

Oregon City
-Animal ESP
1909/John Evans/20 mi. from town
Dora Evans Deck, "Shep Bit the Ped-
dler," Fate 24 (Feb.1971):61-63.
-Skyquake
1959, Feb.12
(Editorial), Fate 12 (July 1959):12.

Pacific City
-UFO (DD)
1950, March 12/Rand Herrmann
Kenneth Arnold & Ray Palmer, The Coming of the Saucers (Boise: The Authors, 1952), p.177. il.

Pendleton
-Fall of ice
1959, Dec.31/Bill Simmons
Coral E. Lorenzen, The Shadow of the
Unknown (N.Y.: Signet, 1970), pp.
120-21.
-Mystery radio transmission
1964, Jan.29/Cessna 1540M/airport
(Editorial), Fate 17 (June 1964):9-
10.
-UFO (?)
1947, June 24/Glen E. Stewart
Chicago (Ill.) Tribune, 26 June 1947.
-UFO (DD)
1947, June 29/Mrs. Morton Elder/7 mi.S
Portland Oregonian, 1 July 1947.
1947, July 1/Mrs. Walter Clark
Portland Oregon Journal, 3 July 1947.

Philomath
-UFO (NL)
1946, Sep.6/N of town
"Balls of Fire," Doubt, no.17 (1947):
255.

Portland
-Acoustic anomaly
1923, Sep./Della Amidon/550 Everett St.
Portland Oregonian, 17 Sep.1923.
"MFS Sheeley Writes," Doubt, no.21
(1948):319.
1962/Newberry Rd.
Coral E. Lorenzen, The Shadow of the
Unknown (N.Y.: Signet, 1970), pp.
68-70.
-Anomalous hole in ground
1947, Dec./Mr. Vink
"Earth Sinking," Doubt, no.20 (1948):
305.
-Crisis apparition
1907, Oct.12/Mrs. James N. Sutton
George A. Thacher, "The Case of Lieut.
James B. Sutton," J.ASPR 5 (1911):
597-664.
Edmond P. Gibson, "The Strange Death
of Lieut. James Sutton, U.S.M.C.,"

Fate 8 (Feb.1955):68-73.
1918, Aug.9/Etna Elliott
Etna Elliott, "Death Wears Johnny's
Face," Fate 13 (Aug.1960):70-74.
-Disappearance
1958, Dec.7/Kenneth Martin/=auto acci-
dent
(Editorial), Fate 12 (June 1959):25-
26.
(Editorial), Fate 12 (Sep.1959):14.
-Erratic crayfish
1954, Sep.10
"Displaced Critters," Doubt, no.49
(1955):358.
-Eyeless vision
1927
Esther Cox Todd, "The Blind Girl Who
Could See," Fate 9 (Mar.1956):84-
89.
-Fall of ice
1947, Jan.1/Leon Thompson/Rocky Butte
"First Prize," Doubt, no.18 (1947):
266, quoting Portland Oregonian
(undated).
1953, Jan.6/Mrs. Charles C. McCoy/3204
NE 26th Ave.
(Editorial), Fate 6 (May 1953):10-11.
-Fall of polished china
1920, July 21/Sellwood
Los Angeles (Cal.) Times, 21 July
1920.
Portland Oregonian, 22 July 1920.
-Fall of rocks
1944, Aug.27-Oct./Andrew E. Mosier
Los Angeles (Cal.) Daily News, 16
Oct.1944.
"Portland in 14 FS," Doubt, no.20
(1948):308.
-Fall of round pellets
1954, April
(Editorial), Fate 7 (Aug.1954):8.
-Ghost
1915-1916/Ruth M. Johnston
Ruth M. Johnston, "The Spirit of Na-
dine," J.ASPR 28 (1934):34-37.
-Haunt
1952/Park Ave.
Hazel E. Monte, "My House of Evil,"
Fate 6 (Feb.1953):42-45.
-Mystery television transmission
1954/1215 NE Broadway
(Editorial), Fate 7 (June 1954):12.
-New energy source (inventor)
1920/John Huston
(Letter), Bert Grater, Fate 9 (Nov.
1956):126-28.
-Poltergeist
1909, Oct.-Dec./Elwin March/546 Mar-
shall St./=trickery?
Portland Oregonian, 29-31 Oct.1909;
and 1 Nov.1909.
J. Allen Gilbert, "The Elwin March
Case of 'Poltergeist,'" J.ASPR 4
(1910):465-524.
George A. Thacher, "The March Polter-
geist Case," J.ASPR 4 (1910):561-
636.
-Precognition
1956/James Gemelli
"Hunch of a Holdup," Fate 9 (July

1956):48.
-Skyquake
  1957, Sep.3
    Salem Capital Journal, 3 Sep.1957.
  1976, Sep.3
    Salem Register-Guard, 3 Sep.1976.
-Spirit medium
  1850s/Mrs. Butler
    Emma Hardinge Britten, Modern Ameri-
    can Spiritualism (N.Y.: The Author,
    1870), p.479.
  1920s/Amelia Bosworth
    Joseph Dunninger, Houdini's Spirit
    World and Dunninger's Psychic Rev-
    elations (N.Y.: Tower, 1968 ed.),
    pp.168-73.
-UFO (?)
  1896, Nov.24/=balloon
    Portland Oregonian, 25 Nov.1896.
  1949, July 30/Vera Sowers
  1949, Aug.16
    "If It's in the Sky It's a Saucer,"
    Doubt, no.27 (1949):416-17.
  1952, Sep.9
    Richard Hall, ed., The UFO Evidence
    (Washington: NICAP, 1964), p.153.
  1972, Aug.11/Terry Bowlby
    Glenn McWane & David Graham, The New
    UFO Sightings (N.Y.: Warner, 1974),
    p.58.
  1975, Sep.10/=meteor?
    Timothy Green Beckley, "Saucers over
    Our Cities," Saga UFO Rept. 4 (Aug.
    1977):27,74, quoting Portland Ore-
    gon Journal (undated).
-UFO (DD)
  1947, July 1/Herbert Balliet/NE 78th x
  Prescott
    Portland Oregon Journal, 2 July 1947.
  1947, July 4/Kenneth A. McDowell/Police
  Precinct no.1
  1947, July 4/Mrs. L.J. Hayward/6124 NE
  21st Ave.
    Portland Oregon Journal, 5 July 1947.
    J. Allen Hynek, The Hynek UFO Report
    (N.Y.: Dell, 1977), pp.100-102.
  1947, July 5/Viva Anderson
    Portland Oregonian, 6 July 1947.
  1947, July 6
    Portland Oregonian, 7 July 1947.
  1947, July 8/Shirley Betts/Hillsdale
  1947, July 8/Mrs. Simon T. Hernandez/
  1830 SE Schiller
  1947, July 8/Bill Gore/NE 33d x Hein-
  cock
    Portland Oregon Journal, 9 July 1947.
  1947, Sep.11
    Bruce S. Maccabee, "UFO Related In-
    formation from the FBI Files: Part
    3," MUFON UFO J., no.121 (Dec.1977)
    :10,14.
  1948, Aug.3/George Jensen
    "You Asked for It," Doubt, no.24
    (1949):363.
  1951, Aug.11/R.O. Dodge
    Richard Hall, ed., The UFO Evidence
    (Washington: NICAP, 1964), p.34.
  1952, Aug./Howard C. Camp
    Curtis Fuller, "Fate's Report on the
    Flying Saucers," Fate 7 (May 1954):

16,20-21.
-UFO (NL)
  1947, June 24/William Kamp/5155 NE 22d
  St.
    Portland Oregon Journal, 27 June
    1947.
  1952, April 7
    Portland Oregonian, 8-9 Apr.1952.
  1955, March 9
    "Green Fireballs in a Squirrel's
    Cage," CRIFO Newsl., 1 Apr.1955,
    p.4.
  1969, Jan.16
    Portland Oregonian, 18 Jan.1969.

Port Orford
-Lost meteorite
  1859/John Evans
    C.T. Jackson, "Remarks on the Speci-
    mens of a Meteorite from Oregon
    Territory," Proc.Boston Soc'y Nat.
    Hist. 7 (1860):161,174-76,279,289.
    Portland Oregonian, 21 July 1938,
    p.4.
    Ruby El Hult, Lost Mines and Treas-
    ures of the Pacific Northwest (Port-
    land: Binford & Mort, 1957), pp.
    94-104.
    Lincoln LaPaz, "Hunting Meteorites:
    Their Recovery, Use, and Abuse from
    Paleolithic to Present," Pub.Meteor-
    itics Univ.New Mexico, no.6 (1969):
    103-38.

Promise
-Whirlwind anomaly
  1969, May 28/Walter J. Wentz
    Walter J. Wentz, "In Relation to
    Charles Fort's The Book of the Damn-
    ed," INFO J., no.6 (spring 1970):
    22-23.

Prospect
-Humanoid
  1960, Aug./Sidney Morse
    John Green, The Sasquatch File (Ag-
    assiz, B.C.: Cheam, 1973), p.20.
-Telephone anomaly
  1961, March 24-25
    Brad Steiger, Mysteries of Time and
    Space (N.Y.: Dell, 1976 ed.), pp.
    143-44.
-UFO (DD)
  1961, Oct.4/Mrs. S. Poole/6 mi.SW
    (Letter), Fate 15 (May 1962):105-106.

Redmond
-UFO (CE-2)
  1976, March 5
    "Sighting Reports," CUFOS News Bull.,
    June 1976, p.5.
-UFO (DD)
  1947, July 4/C.J. Bogne/Mt. Jefferson
    Portland Oregon Journal, 5 July 1947.
-UFO (R-V)
  1959, Sep.24/Robert Dickerson/Prine-
  ville Hwy.
    Richard Hall, ed., The UFO Evidence
    (Washington: NICAP, 1964), pp.44,
    93,113-14.

Donald E. Keyhoe, <u>Aliens from Space</u>
(Garden City: Doubleday, 1973), pp.
40-45.

Remote
-UFO (DD)
1952, May 16/Ellen Beers
(Letter), <u>Fate</u> 5 (Nov.1952):108.

Rogue River
-Humanoid
1968, Aug./Anthony Anable/18 mi.NE
John Green, <u>The Sasquatch File</u> (Agassiz, B.C.: Cheam, 1973), p.44.

Roseburg
-Animal ESP
1975/Tom Worden/Mt. Nebo
(Editorial), <u>Fate</u> 29 (Oct.1976):26-
28.
-UFO (CE-1)
1975, Dec.16
"UFO Central," <u>CUFOS News Bull.</u>, 1
Feb.1976, p.15.
-UFO (DD)
1969, Aug.
<u>Klamath Falls Herald & News</u>, 3 Aug.
1969.
-UFO (NL)
1948, June 28/Pat Schlichtig
(Letter), <u>Fate</u> 1 (fall 1948):123.

Rowena
-Humanoid
1974, Jan./Harry Gilpin/I-80 nr.Rowena
exit
Peter Byrne, <u>The Search for Bigfoot</u>
(N.Y.: Pocket Books, 1976 ed.), p.34.

Saint Helens
-Phantom
1971, Oct.29/Gilbert Crouse
(Editorial), <u>Fate</u> 30 (Apr.1977):24-
27, quoting <u>Salem Capital-Journal</u>
(undated).

Salem
-Photographic anomaly
1953/Marshall W. Hanft
(Editorial), <u>Fate</u> 6 (June 1953):9. il.
-Windshield pitting
1954/Arch Wilson/2375 Lee St.
(Editorial), <u>Fate</u> 8 (Feb.1955):12.
-UFO (CE-1)
1947, June 24/Gertrude Kirkpatrick/1780
Oxford
Salem <u>Oregon Statesman</u>, 29 June 1947.
1967, March 16/Ronald Baker/1893 32d
Ave.
"Photo by Oregon Boy," <u>APRO Bull.</u> 15
(Mar.-Apr.1967):6. il.
Edward U. Condon, <u>Scientific Study
of Unidentified Flying Objects</u> (N.Y.:
Bantam, 1969 ed.), pp.467-69. il.
"Fantastic UFO Photo Flap of 1967,"
<u>Saga UFO Rept.</u> 3 (June 1976):28-29.
il.
Donald H. Menzel & Ernest H. Taves,
<u>The UFO Enigma</u> (Garden City: Double-
day, 1977), p.113.

-UFO (DD)
1947, June 24/Mrs. Dennis Howell
Salem <u>Oregon Statesman</u>, 27 June 1947.
1947, June 25/William A. Bond
Salem <u>Oregon Statesman</u>, 29 June 1947.
1947, July 4/G.R. Graen/3115 D St.
Salem <u>Oregon Statesman</u>, 5 July 1947.

Seaside
-UFO (DD)
1947, June 28/Mrs. Sidney B. Smith
Salem <u>Oregon Statesman</u>, 29 June 1947.

Selma
-Fire immunity and pain control
1970s/Jack Schwarz
David M. Rorvik, "Jack Schwarz Feels
No Pain," <u>Esquire</u>, Dec.1972, pp.
209-11.
Elmer & Alyce Green, "The Ins and
Outs of Mind-Body Energy," in <u>Sci-
ence Year 1974: World Book Science
Annual</u> (Chicago: Field Enterprises,
1973), p.146.
Jack Schwarz, <u>The Path of Action</u>
(N.Y.: Dutton, 1977).
Jack Schwarz, <u>Voluntary Controls</u>
(N.Y.: Dutton, 1978).
Elmer & Alyce Green, <u>Beyond Biofeed-
back</u> (N.Y.: Delta, 1978), pp.225-43.

Silver Lake
-Fall of frogs
1963, July 17/Mrs. R.W. Carpenter
(Editorial), <u>Fate</u> 16 (Nov.1963):13-
14.

Silverton
-Animal ESP
1923-1924/Frank Brazier
Charles Alexander, <u>Bobbie: A Great
Collie of Oregon</u> (N.Y.: Dodd, Mead,
1926).
-Humanoid tracks
1972, summer/10 mi. above Drake's Crossing
<u>Silverton Appeal-Tribune</u>, 24 Aug.
1972.
-UFO (NL)
1978, June 2 7/Joanne Walker/S. Church
St.
<u>Silverton Appeal-Tribune</u>, 6 July 1978.

Sitkum
-Humanoid
1973, May
John Green, "Not All Quiet on the
Western Front," <u>Pursuit</u> 7 (Oct.1974)
:98.

Stayton
-UFO (NL)
1958, Oct.24/E. Norfleet
"Hovering UFO Puzzles South African
Officials," <u>UFO Inv.</u> 1 (Dec.1958):
1,3.

Sweet Home
-Humanoid
1977, March 4/Darlene Emmert

"Latest News," Bigfoot News, no.35 (Aug.1977):1.

Tenmile
-Humanoid
1959, Oct./S of town
John Green, The Sasquatch File (Agassiz, B.C.: Cheam, 1973), pp.19-20.
John Green, Sasquatch: The Apes Among Us (Seattle: Hancock House, 1978), pp.378-79.

The Dalles
-Haunt
1940/Billie McNutt
Billie McNutt, "Our Host the Ghost," Fate 30 (Feb.1977):83-86.
-Humanoid
1965/Dalene Brown/W of town
John Green, The Sasquatch File (Agassiz, B.C.: Cheam, 1973), p.37.
1967, May/Dennis Taylor/N on I-80 nr. cemetery
John Green, Year of the Sasquatch (Agassiz, B.C.: Cheam, 1970), pp. 71-73.
Don Hunter & René Dahinden, Sasquatch (Toronto: McClelland & Stewart, 1973), pp.126-29.
1968, summer
1971, May 27/Joe Medeiros/Pinewood Trailer Court
1971, June 1/Jim Forkan/Pinewood Trailer Court
1971, June 2/Dick Brown/Pinewood Trailer Court
John Green, The Sasquatch File (Agassiz, B.C.: Cheam, 1973), p.55.
Peter Byrne, The Search for Bigfoot (N.Y.: Pocket Books, 1976 ed.), pp. 73-78.
-Petroglyphs
William D. Strong, W. Egbert Schenck, & Julian H. Steward, "Archaeology of the Dalles-Deschutes Region," Univ.California Pub.Am.Arch.& Ethn., 29, no.1 (1930):1-154. il.
Beth & Ray Hill, Indian Petroglyphs of the Pacific Northwest (Seattle: Univ. Washington, 1974), pp.253-59.

Tillamook
-Clairvoyance
1915, spring
C.J. Ragland, "Telepathic Scream," Fate 8 (June 1955):95.
-UFO (?)
1965, Jan.12/Mrs. Paul Zimmerman Gearhart/Tillamook Head
Seaside Signal, 12 Jan.1965.
-UFO (R-V)
1967, March 13-14/=radar echo?
Gordon D. Thayer, "Optical and Radar Analyses of Field Cases," in Edward U. Condon, Scientific Study of Unidentified Flying Objects (N.Y.: Bantam, 1969 ed.), pp.122-23.

Tiller
-UFO (CE-1)
1959, winter/Charles Jackson
Lucius Farish, "The Mini-Saucers," Fate 27 (Dec.1974):59,64.

Toledo
-UFO (CE-1)
1966, March/Kathy Reeves/Pioneer Mt.
Spokane (Wash.) Spokesman-Review, 18 Oct.1966.
Portland Oregon Journal, 20 Oct.1966.
Dan Lloyd, "Crawling Lights--A New Development," Flying Saucer Rev. 13 (May-June 1967):29-30.

Troutdale
-UFO (DD)
1947, July 4/Thomas Berry
Portland Oregonian, 5 July 1947.

Tygh Valley
-Humanoid
1977, Sep.25
"Latest News from the Pacific Northwest," Bigfoot News, no.36-37 (Sep.-Oct.1977):1.
-Humanoid tracks
1975, July/Robert Bellamy, Jr.
Winnipeg (Man.) Free Press, 26 July 1975.
Peter Byrne, The Search for Bigfoot (N.Y.: Pocket Books, 1976 ed.), p. 232.

Umpqua
-Humanoid tracks
1976, Nov.4/Warren Ward/Oak Hill Rd.
Roseburg News-Review, 9 Nov.1976, p. 1.

Union
-UFO (DD)
1947, July 29/Kenneth Arnold
Kenneth Arnold & Ray Palmer, The Coming of the Saucers (Boise: The Authors, 1952), pp.25-27.

Vale
-UFO (NL)
1974, Sep.15/Ed Berry
George D. Fawcett, "The 'Unreported' UFO Wave of 1974," Saga UFO Rept. 2 (spring 1975):50,75.

Waldport
-Contactee
1974-1976/Bonnie Lee Nettles & Marshall Herff Applewhite/=hoax
New York Times, 7 Oct.1975, p.71.
Hayden C. Hewes, "Trips to Eternity," Official UFO 1 (Feb.1976):29-31,51-57.
Leland Joachim, "The Two: A Pair of Prophets or a Couple of 'Space Cadets'?" Probe the Unknown 4 (Mar. 1976):12-15,60. il.
Hayden Hewes & Brad Steiger, UFO Missionaries Extraordinary (N.Y.: Pocket Books, 1976).

-Fall of frogs
  1947, Jan.25/N of town
    "Green Rain Again," Doubt, no.23
    (1948):350.

Wallowa co.
-UFO (CE-2)
  1931/Don Jennings/Floyd Paton ranch
    Win Churchill, "The Fence That Played
    Uncommon Music: A Sighting in Ore-
    gon," Official UFO 1 (Dec.1976):36-
    37.

Wamic
-Humanoid tracks
  1977, Nov.
    "Latest News from the Pacific North-
    west," Bigfoot News, no.38 (Nov.1977)
    :1.

Wilsonville
-Humanoid
  1970, Aug.29
    John Green, Sasquatch: The Apes Among
    Us (Seattle: Hancock House, 1978),
    pp.340-41.

Yachats
-Sea monster
  1937, Jan./2 mi.S
    Paul H. LeBlond & John Sibert, Obser-
    vations of Large Unidentified Marine
    Animals in British Columbia and Ad-
    jacent Waters (Vancouver: Univ. of
    British Columbia, Inst. of Ocean-
    ography, Manuscript Rept. no.28,
    June 1973):12-13. il.
-UFO (?)
  1964, July 20/=satellite?
    Donald H. Menzel, "UFOs: The Modern
    Myth," in Carl Sagan & Thornton
    Page, ed., UFOs--A Scientific Debate
    (Ithaca. N.Y.: Cornell Univ., 1972),
    PP.123,140.

Yankton
-Humanoid
  1926-1928
    Portland Oregon Journal, 12 Aug.1963.

          B. Physical Features

Arbuckle Mt.
-Humanoid tracks
  1976, July
    "Latest News from the Pacific North-
    west," Bigfoot News, no.22 (July
    1976):1.

Arnold Ice Cave
-Ice anomaly
    Lester F. Nieman, "Strange Desert Ice
    Cave," Fate 5 (June 1952):84-85.

Ashland, Mt.
-Humanoid
  1943, Oct./O.R. Edwards
    John Green, On the Track of the Sas-
    quatch (Agassiz, B.C.: Cheam, 1968),

pp.60-61, quoting San Francisco
(Cal.) Chronicle, 1965.
John Green, Sasquatch: The Apes Among
Us (Seattle; Hancock House, 1978),
pp.411-16.

Bachelor Butte
-Chinese discovery
  ca.1000 B.C.
    Henriette Mertz, Gods from the Far
    East (N.Y.: Ballantine, 1975 ed.),
    pp.160-61.
-Humanoid tracks
  1959/Joe Morgan
    John Green, The Sasquatch File (Ag-
    assiz, B.C.: Cheam, 1973), p.20.

Blair L.
-Humanoid tracks
  1970, Nov.14/R.L. Lakey/½ mi.E
    John Green, The Sasquatch File (Ag-
    assiz, B.C.: Cheam, 1973), p.54.

Blue Mts.
-UFO (NL)
  1955, Jan.15-28/Manuel Erickson/Weston-
  Elgin Hwy.
    Portland Oregonian, 29 Jan.1955.

Bonneville Dam
-Archeological site
    Phoenix Arizona Republic, 1 Apr.1978.

Cascade Mts.
-Humanoid
  1976, Aug.
    "Latest News from the Pacific North-
    west," Bigfoot News, no.23 (Aug.
    1976):1.
-Humanoid tracks
  1975, May
    Peter Byrne, The Search for Bigfoot
    (N.Y.: Pocket Books, 1976 ed.), pp.
    231-32.
-UFO (CE-2)
  1947, June 24/Fred Johnson
    Phoenix Arizona Republic, 26 June
    1947.
    Donald H. Menzel, Flying Saucers
    (Cambridge: Harvard Univ., 1953),
    p.24.
-UFO (DD)
  1954/Fred Johnson
    (Letter), Fate 8 (May 1955):114-15.

Catlow Cave
-Archeological site
    L.S. Cressman, et al., "Archaeolog-
    ical Researches in the Northern
    Great Basin," Pub.Carnegie Inst.,
    no.538 (1942):19-20,27-30.
    H.M. Wormington, Ancient Man in North
    America (Denver: Museum of Natural
    History, 1957), pp.182-83.

Catlow Valley
-UFO (DD)
  1956, Aug./Joe Stupfel
    (Letter), Ralph Greenstreet, Flying
    Saucers, Feb.1958, pp.69,77.

Chetco R.
-Humanoid tracks
  ca.1890
    Ivan T. Sanderson, Abominable Snow-
    men: Legend Come to Life (Philadel-
    phia: Chilton, 1961), p.115.

Clackamus R.
-Humanoid
  1968, spring/Glenn Thomas
  1968, Nov./Glenn Thomas
  1968, Dec./Glenn Thomas
    John Green, Sasquatch: The Apes Among
    Us (Seattle: Hancock House, 1978),
    pp.425-26.
  1969, spring
    John Green, The Sasquatch File (Ag-
    assiz, B.C.: Cheam, 1973), p.45.
-Humanoid tracks
  1912, spring/Grover Kiggins
    John Green, The Sasquatch File (Ag-
    assiz, B.C.: Cheam, 1973), p.13.

Clatsop Spit
-Disappearance
  1883, Oct.6/Alonzo Zeiber/"J.C. Cous-
  ins"/crew only
    Walker A. Tompkins, "Was the J.C.
    Cousins Steered to Destruction?"
    Fate 8 (Oct.1955):62-67.

Collawash R.
-Humanoid
  1973, June
    John Green, Sasquatch: The Apes Among
    Us (Seattle: Hancock House, 1978),
    pp.418-20.

Conser L.
-Humanoid
  1960
    Corvallis Benton County Journal, 11
    Aug.1963; and 18 Aug.1963.
    Portland Oregon Journal, 16 Aug.1963.
    Ivan T. Sanderson, Abominable Snow-
    men: Legend Come to Life (Philadel-
    phia: Chilton, 1961), pp.140-41.
-Humanoid tracks
  ca.1974
    Albany Democrat-Herald, 13 Mar.1978.

Coquille R.
-Humanoid
  1969, Aug./Jack Woodruff/E fork
    John Green, The Sasquatch File (Ag-
    assiz, B.C.: Cheam, 1973), p.45.
-Humanoid tracks
  1967, Aug.15/Jack Woodruff/E fork
    John Green, On the Track of the Sas-
    quatch (Agassiz, B.C.: Cheam, 1968),
    p.66. il.
    John Green, Sasquatch: The Apes Among
    Us (Seattle: Hancock House, 1978),
    pp.362-64.
  1969, Feb.
    John Green, Year of the Sasquatch
    (Agassiz, B.C.: Cheam, 1970), p.44.

Cougar Mountain Cave
-Archeological site

ca.6500 B.C.
    John Cowles, Cougar Mountain Cave in
    South Central Oregon (Rainier, Ore.:
    Daily News Press, 1959).

Craggie Mts.
-Humanoid tracks
  1924, Oct.
  1930s, fall/Mr. Frye
    John Green, The Sasquatch File (Ag-
    assiz, B.C.: Cheam, 1973), pp.13,
    15.

Crane Mt.
-Chinese discovery
  ca.1000 B.C.
    Henriette Mertz, Gods from the Far
    East (N.Y.: Ballantine, 1975 ed.),
    p.162.

Crater L.
-Lake monster
    Charles M. Skinner, Myths and Leg-
    ends of Our Own Land, 2 vols. (Phil-
    adelphia: Lippincott, 1896), 2:302-
    303.

Crescent L.
-Lake monster
  n.d./Henry Schwering
    Portland Oregonian, 24 Sep.1967.

Dead Horse Creek
-Humanoid
  1967, fall/Joe Jackson
    John Green, The Sasquatch File (Ag-
    assiz, B.C.: Cheam, 1973), p.37.

Detroit Reservoir
-Humanoid
  ca.1977
    John Green, Sasquatch: The Apes Among
    Us (Seattle: Hancock House, 1978),
    p.434.

Fanny, Mt.
-UFO (NL)
  1978, Sep.29/Diane Willey
    LaGrande Observer, 29 Sep.1978.

Fir Mt.
-Humanoid
  1974, May 12/Jack Cochran
    New York Times, 30 June 1976, p.39.
    Peter Byrne, The Search for Bigfoot
    (N.Y.: Pocket Books, 1976 ed.), pp.
    42-47.

Fivemile Rapids
-Archeological site
  9000-3000 B.C.
    L.S. Cressman, et al., "Cultural Se-
    quences in The Dalles, Oregon,"
    Trans.Am.Phil.Soc'y, n.s.50, pt.10
    (Dec.1960). il.

Fort Rock Cave
-Archeological site
  ca.7100 B.C.
    L.S. Cressman, Howel Williams & Alex

D. Krieger, "Early Man in Oregon: Archaeological Studies in the Northern Great Basin," Studies in Anthro. Univ.Oregon, no.3 (1940).
Stephen F. Bedwell, Fort Rock Basin: Prehistory and Environment (Eugene: Univ. of Oregon, 1973). il.

Freeway L.
-Humanoid tracks
    1978, March 11/Byron Forty
        Albany Democrat-Herald, 13 Mar.1978. il.
        Salem Oregon Statesman, 14 Mar.1978.

Gearhart Mt.
-Chinese discovery
    ca.1000 B.C.
        Henriette Mertz, Gods from the Far East (N.Y.: Ballantine, 1975 ed.), p.161.

Hood, Mt.
-Ancient stone constructions
    1976/Phil Tyler
        "A Strange Stone Formation in Oregon," Bigfoot News, no.24 (Sep.1976):3.
-Chinese discovery
    ca.1000 B.C.
        Henriette Mertz, Gods from the Far East (N.Y.: Ballantine, 1975 ed,), pp.154,160.
-Humanoid
    1975, Nov.1/Leroy Lucas
        Peter Byrne, The Search for Bigfoot (N.Y.: Pocket Books, 1976 ed.), pp.232-33.
-UFO (NL)
    1958, March 10/Jack R. Reef
        Robert N. Webster, "Things That Fall from UFO's," Fate 11 (Oct.1958):25, 29.
    1978, May 6/Roger Wall
        (Letter), Saga UFO Rept. 6 (Aug.1978):4.

Horseshoe L.
-Humanoid
    1959, March 29/Ray McFarland
        Coral E. Lorenzen, The Shadow of the Unknown (N.Y.: Signet, 1970), p.106.

Indigo Creek
-Humanoid tracks
    1968/Jerry Katt
        John Green, The Sasquatch File (Agassiz, B.C.: Cheam, 1973), p.44.

Jefferson, Mt.
-Humanoid
    1972, June/Thomas E. Smith
        B. Ann Slate & Alan Berry, Bigfoot (N.Y.: Bantam, 1976), pp.55-56. il.
-Humanoid tracks
    1974, summer
        Peter Byrne, The Search for Bigfoot (N.Y.: Pocket Books, 1976 ed.), p.47.

John Day R.
-Anomalous artifacts
    =carved humanoid heads
        James Terry, Sculptured Anthropoid Ape Heads Found in or Near the Valley of the John Day River (N.Y.: J.J. Little, 1891). il.
        Alfred R. Wallace, "Remarkable Ancient Sculptures from North-West America," Nature 43 (1891):396.

Johnson Creek
-UFO (DD)
    1946/Lloyd Kenyon
        "The United States of Dreamland," Doubt, no.19 (1947):282,283.

Larch Mt.
-Fall of fish
    1954, Aug./Fred Kuehn/=dumped by hatchery owner
        (Editorial), Fate 8 (Feb.1955):12, quoting Portland Oregon Journal (undated).
        (Letter), M.T. Hoy, Fate 12 (Jan.1959):124-25.

Lewis Peak
-Humanoid
    ca.1969/Wes Sumerlin
        "Bigfoot Is Up There, Folks--Maybe," Bigfoot News, no.39 (Dec.1977):4, quoting LaGrande Observer (undated).

Linton L.
-UFO (NL)
    1973, May 24/Renee Allen
        Spokane (Wash.) Daily Chronicle, 8 June 1973.

Lookout Springs
-Humanoid tracks
    1968, Jan./Millie Kiggins
        John Green, Year of the Sasquatch (Agassiz, B.C.: Cheam, 1970), pp.51-52. il.

McKenzie R.
-Humanoid
    1972, June 27
    1972, July 20
        John Green, Sasquatch: The Apes Among Us (Seattle: Hancock House, 1978), p.418.

McLoughlin, Mt.
-Humanoid tracks
    1962, Aug./Mel Jackson
        John Green, The Sasquatch File (Agassiz, B.C.: Cheam, 1973), p.28.

McNary Reservoir
-Archeological site
        Douglas Osborne, "Excavations in the McNary Reservoir Basin near Umatilla, Oregon," Bull.Bur.Am.Ethn., no.166 (1957). il.
        Joel L. Shiner, "The McNary Reservoir: A Study in Plateau Archeology," Bull.Bur.Am.Ethn., no.179 (1961),

:149-259.

Mosby Creek
-Humanoid
  1930s/Bob Bailey
    Cottage Grove Sentinel, 13 July 1972.

Odell L.
-Archeological site
    L.S. Cressman, "Odell Lake Site: A
    New Paleo-Indian Campsite in Ore-
    gon," Am.Antiquity 14 (1948):57-58.

Paisley Five Mile Point Cave
-Archeological site
  ca.5600 B.C.
    L.S. Cressman, Howel Williams & Alex
    D. Krieger, "Early Man in Oregon:
    Archaeological Studies in the North-
    ern Great Basin," Studies in Anthro.
    Univ.Oregon, no.3 (1940).
    H.M. Wormington, Ancient Man in North
    America (Denver: Museum of Natural
    History, 1957), p.183.

Pamelia L.
-Humanoid tracks
  1971, April/Ronald Corell
    John Green, The Sasquatch File (Ag-
    assiz, B.C.: Cheam, 1973), pp.54-55.

Quartz Creek
-Humanoid
  1963, Aug.
    John Green, The Sasquatch File (Ag-
    assiz, B.C.: Cheam, 1973), p.28.

Rock R.
-UFO (DD)
  1947, July 6/S. Everett
    Portland Oregon Journal, 7 July 1947.

Salmon Creek
-Humanoid tracks
  1972, April 29/Gordon Kliewer
    John Green, The Sasquatch File (Ag-
    assiz, B.C.: Cheam, 1973), p.55,
    quoting Eugene Register-Guard (un-
    dated).

Sandy R.
-Ancient carving
  =stegosaur?
    Harold T. Wilkins, Secret Cities of
    Old South America (N.Y.: Library
    Publishers, 1952), p.271. il.
    "The Hava Supai Canyon 'Dinosaur,'"
    Pursuit 8 (Jan.1975):6. il.
-Humanoid
  1978, June?
    "Latest News from the Pacific North-
    west," Bigfoot News, no.46 (July
    1978):1.

Siskiyou Mts.
-Gravity anomaly
    John P. Bessor, "Oregon's Strange
    Whirlpool of Force," Fate 4 (July
    1951):24,28.

Smith R.
-Humanoid
  1974, Oct.
    Brookings Harbor Pilot, 28 Sep.1978.

South Santiam R.
-Humanoid tracks
  1971, Feb./Hwy.20
    John Green, The Sasquatch File (Ag-
    assiz, B.C.: Cheam, 1973), p.54.

South Sixes R.
-Humanoid
  1899/Mr. Robbins
    John Green, The Sasquatch File (Ag-
    assiz, B.C.: Cheam, 1973), p.5.
  1900/William Page
    Roseburg Daily Review, 24 Dec.1900.
  1904, March/William Ward
    Cottage Grove Lane County Leader, 7
    Apr.1904.
  1969, Aug./Joe Bayless
    John Green, The Sasquatch File (Ag-
    assiz, B.C.: Cheam, 1973), p.45.

Tarzan Spring
-Humanoid
  1972
    Peter Byrne, The Search for Bigfoot
    (N.Y.: Pocket Books, 1976 ed.), p.
    31.

Telephone Ridge
-UFO (NL)
  1959, Oct.
    Lloyd Mallan, "Complete Directory of
    UFOs: Part II," Sci.& Mech. 38 (Jan.
    1967):44,68.

Thomas Creek
-Humanoid
  1978, Sep.25/Barbara Megli
    Brookings Harbor Pilot, 28 Sep.1978.

Three Sisters Wilderness
-Humanoid
  1950s/Zack Hamilton
    San Francisco (Cal.) Chronicle, 7
    Dec.1965.
    John Green, On the Track of the Sas-
    quatch (Agassiz, B.C.: Cheam, 1968),
    pp.51-52. il.
-Humanoid tracks
  1974, summer
    Peter Byrne, The Search for Bigfoot
    (N.Y.: Pocket Books, 1976 ed.), p.
    47.

Timothy L.
-Humanoid
  1970
    Peter Byrne, The Search for Bigfoot
    (N.Y.: Pocket Books, 1976 ed.), p.
    31.
-Humanoid tracks
  1972, March
    John Green, The Sasquatch File (Ag-
    assiz, B.C.: Cheam, 1973), p.55.

Todd L.
-Humanoid
 1942, Sep./Don Hunter
  John Green, On the Track of the Sasquatch (Agassiz, B.C.: Cheam, 1968),
  pp.61-62.

Triangle L.
-Humanoid
 1972, Feb./Jim Kunkle
  John Green, The Sasquatch File (Ag-
  assiz, B.C.: Cheam, 1973), p.55.
  John Green, Sasquatch: The Apes Among
  Us (Seattle: Hancock House, 1978),
  p.375.

Trout L.
-Humanoid tracks
 1967, fall/Clyde Staley
  John Green, The Sasquatch File (Agassiz, B.C.: Cheam, 1973), p.37.

Umpqua National Forest
-Humanoid
 1974/Jean Fitzgerald
  (Editorial), Fate 28 (Feb.1975):20-
  22, quoting Grit, 29 Sep.1974.

Umpqua R.
-Sea monster
 1888, Oct./Edgar Avery/"Estrella"/riv-
 er mouth
  San Francisco (Cal.) Alta, 19 Oct.
  1888.
  New York Times, 28 Oct.1888, p.17.

Upper Klamath L.
-Lake monster myth
  Charles M. Skinner, Myths and Legends
  of Our Own Land, 2 vols. (Philadelphia: Lippincott, 1896), 2:304.
-UFO (?)
 1964, Aug.27
  Klamath Falls Herald News, 27 Aug.
  1964.
 1965, Dec.23/=meteorite?
  Klamath Falls Herald News, 24 Dec.
  1965.

Wallowa L.
-Lake monster
  A.W. Nelson, Those Who Came First
  (LaGrande: The Author, 1934), p.17.
  Enterprise Wallowa County Chieftain,
  28 June 1951.

Wanoga Butte
-Humanoid
 1957, fall/Gary Joanis
  John Green, The Sasquatch File (Agassiz, B.C.: Cheam, 1973), p.19.

White R.
-Humanoid tracks
 1968, Sep./S of Mt. Hood
  John Green, The Sasquatch File (Agassiz, B.C.: Cheam, 1973), p.44.

Willamette Pass
-UFO (CE-1)

 1966, Nov.22/Diamond Park Overlook
  Adrian Vance, "UFOs and 'The Oregon
  Photo,'" Petersen's Photographic
  Mag. 1 (Jan.1973):35-37. il.
  "Postscript on 'The Oregon Photo-
  graph,'" UFO Quar.Rev. 1 (Jan.-Mar.
  1973):18-24. il.
  Adrian Vance, "The Oregon Photo: Us-
  ing Photography to Tackle a Mystery,"
  Flying Saucer Rev. 19 (Mar.-Apr.
  1973):3-6. il.
  (Letter), A. Cramwinckel, Flying Sau-
  cer Rev. 19 (Sep.-Oct.1973):27-28.

C. Ethnic Groups

Kalapuya Indians
-Lake monster myth
 amhúluk
  Albert S. Gatschet, "Water-Monsters
  of American Aborigines," J.Am.Folk-
  lore 12 (1899):255,259-60.

Paiute Indians
-Shamanism
  Beatrice Blyth Whiting, "Paiute Sor-
  cery," Viking Fund Pubs.in Anthro.,
  no.15 (1950).

A. Populated Places

Aberdeen
-UFO (DD)
1947, July 5/Jack Smith
   Salt Lake City (Ut.) Tribune, 7 July
   1947.

Adams co.
-Cattle mutilation
1975, June
   Boise Idaho Statesman, 30 June 1975.

Bayview
-UFO (CE-2)
1973, May 2
   Jerome Eden, "UFOs and Weather Chaos,"
   Official UFO 1 (Aug.1976):31,57.
-Weather control
1973, June 8-25/Jerome Eden/Reichian
method
   Jerome Eden, "UFOs and Weather Chaos,"
   Official UFO 1 (Aug.1976):31,56-58.

Blaine co.
-Phantom
1975
   Roberta Donovan & Keith Wolverton,
   Mystery Stalks the Prairie (Raynes-
   ford, Mont.: THAR, 1976), pp.37-38.

Boise
-Fall of fish
1948, July 12
   "Green Rain Again," Doubt, no.23
   (1948):350.
-Mystery radio transmission
1957, Nov.6
   (Editorial), Fate 11 (Mar.1958):16.
-UFO (DD)
1947, June 24/Donald S. Whitehead/=
planet?
   Boise Idaho Statesman, 3 July 1947.
1947, June 30/Angelo Donefrio/W of town
   Ted Bloecher, Report on the UFO Wave
   of 1947 (Washington: NICAP, 1967),
   p.II-6.
1947, July 4/John Corlett
   Boise Idaho Statesman, 5 July 1947.
1947, July 5/Henry Vanderhoef, Jr./1011
N. 9th St.
   Boise Idaho Statesman, 6 July 1947.
1947, July 6/Lee Eating
   Boise Idaho Statesman, 7 July 1947.
1947, July 9/Dave Johnson/Gowan Field
1947, July 10/Lester Sherill
   Boise Idaho Statesman, 10-11 July
   1947.
1947, July 12/John F. Brown/Main St.
   Boise Idaho Statesman, 13 July 1947.
1947, July 21/James E, Petteway/Idaho
Bldg.
   Boise Idaho Statesman, 22 July 1947.
1947, Aug.13/Charles Shangle

Kenneth Arnold & Ray Palmer, The Coming of the Saucers (Boise: The Authors, 1952), pp.170-71. il.
1948, July 14/Charles Shangle/1402
Colorado St.
   Charles W. Shangle, "True Mystic Experiences," Fate 2 (May 1949):75-76.
1949, summer
   Harold T. Wilkins, Flying Saucers on
   the Attack (N.Y.: Ace, 1967 ed.),
   p.114.
-UFO (NL)
1947, July 8/Oliver Gregerson/Hwy.20
   Boise Idaho Statesman, 9-10 July
   1947.
1947, July 23/E.K. Prestel/1105 Euclid
Ave.
   Boise Idaho Statesman, 24 July 1947.
1947, July 28/Stanley Ewing/Linde Air
Products
   Boise Idaho Statesman, 30 July 1947.

Bonners Ferry
-Out-of-body experience
1954, Feb./Doris M. Meyers
   (Letter), Fate 10 (Sep.1957):115-16.

Bovil
-Humanoid
1973, Aug./E of town
   John Green, Sasquatch: The Apes Among
   Us (Seattle: Hancock House, 1978),
   p.289.

Buhl
-Anomalous hole in ground
1937, Aug.15
   "Farm Sinks in Idaho," Fortean Soc'y
   Mag. 1 (Sep.1937):4.

Burgdorf
-Humanoid tracks
1966, fall
   John Green, Sasquatch: The Apes Among
   Us (Seattle: Hancock House, 1978),
   p.286.

Burley
-UFO (?)
1950/=hoax
   Kenneth Arnold & Ray Palmer, The Coming of the Saucers (Boise: The Authors, 1952), p.173, quoting Burley
   Herald-Bulletin (undated). il.

Butte co.
-UFO (NL)
1954, June 26/Kelly Brooks/AEC station
   Donald E. Keyhoe, Flying Saucer Conspiracy (N.Y.: Holt, 1955), p.168,
   quoting Idaho Falls Post-Register
   (undated).

Cassia co.
-Cattle mutilation
  1975, Oct.
    "To Decompose or Not to Decompose,"
    Stigmata, no.3 (May 1978):3.

Chesterfield
-Humanoid
  1902, Jan.14/John Gooch's ranch
    Wilkesboro (N.C.) Chronicle, 5 Feb.
    1902.

Coeur D'Alene
-UFO (CE-4)
  1977, June 20
    "Idaho Abduction Case," APRO Bull. 26
    (Nov.1977):1-3. il.

Cottonwood
-Archeological site
  ca.6500 B.C.-1800 A.D./Weis Rockshelter
    Franklin Folsom, America's Ancient
    Treasures (N.Y.: Rand McNally,
    1974), p.68.
-UFO (NL)
  1964, May 11/Margaret Neely
    "Other Recent Sightings," UFO Inv.
    4 (May-June 1967):7.

Dixie
-Humanoid
  1972, Sep./Earl Armstrong/NW of town
    John Green, The Sasquatch File (Ag-
    assiz, B.C.: Cheam, 1973), p.57.

Eagle
-UFO (DD)
  1949, July 6/David Frost
    Boise Idaho Statesman, 7 July 1947.

Elmore co.
-UFO (CE-2)
  1972, Aug.5/Michael Boston
    Mountain Home News, 10 Aug.1972.

Emmett
-UFO (DD)
  1947, June 24
    Boise Idaho Statesman, 28 June 1947.
  1947, July 4/Emil J. Smith
    Portland Oregonian, 5-6 July 1947.
    Ted Bloecher, Report on the UFO Wave
    of 1947 (Washington: NICAP, 1967),
    p.III-10.
    J. Allen Hynek, The Hynek UFO Report
    (N.Y.: Dell, 1977), pp.102-103.
  1948, Feb.20/E.G. Hall
    Emmett Messenger, 26 Feb.1948.

Filer
-UFO (?)
  1950, May 1/Walter Mueller/=defect in
  negative
    Kenneth Arnold & Ray Palmer, The Com-
    ing of the Saucers (Boise: The Au-
    thors, 1952), p.182. il.

Fort Hall Reservation
-Contactee
  1969, July/Paul Solem

Boise Idaho State Journal, 13 July
    1969.
    Jerome Clark, "Indian Prophecy and
    the Prescott UFOs," Fate 24 (Apr.
    1971):54,57-58.

Fremont co.
-Cattle mutilation
  1975, Oct.1
    Idaho Falls Post-Register, 2 Oct.
    1975.

Givens Hot Springs
-Petroglyph
    Indian Rock Art
    Richard P. Erwin, Indian Rock Writing
    in Idaho (Boise: Idaho State His-
    torical Soc'y, 1930), pp.77-79. il.
    William Coxon, "Writing on the Rock
    of Ages," Fate 12 (Feb.1959):86.

Golden
-Humanoid
  1968, summer/Fred J. Richardson/S fork
  of Clearwater R.
    Centralia (Wash.) Daily Chronicle,
    10-11 May 1969.

Gooding
-UFO (CE-1)
  1967, April 17/Jack Daines/16 mi.N on
  Hwy.46
    "UAO in Idaho," APRO Bull. 15 (May-
    June 1967):3.

Grace
-UFO (DD)
  1961, March 3
    "Rocket-Shape and Booms over Idaho,"
    APRO Bull. 9 (May 1961):6.

Grangeville
-Humanoid tracks
  1974, Oct.
    John Green, Sasquatch: The Apes Among
    Us (Seattle: Hancock House, 1978),
    p.287.
-UFO (NL)
  1964, May 10-11/James Fuzzell
    Victoria (B.C.) Daily Times, 19 May
    1964.

Greer
-UFO (?)
  1910, Feb.5
    (Editorial), Amazing Stories, Jan.
    1948, back cover.

Hailey
-UFO (CE-1)
  1975, Oct.20/Bob Ellinger/Quigley Summit
    (Editorial), Fate 29 (Apr.1976):30-
    32.
-UFO (DD)
  1947, June 30/Walter Nicholson/Wood R.
    Salt Lake City (Ut.) Deseret News,
    1 July 1947.

Heyburn
-Dowsing
   1967, Dec.14/Howland Croft/Snake R.
      (Editorial), Fate 21 (June 1968):22-
      24.

Howe
-UFO (CE-1)
   1948, June/Paul Solem
      Jerome Clark, "Indian Prophecy and
      the Prescott UFOs," Fate 24 (Apr.
      1971):54,56.

Idaho Falls
-Lake monster
   1900s/Bess Bonar Wagner/former lake in
   Tautphaus Park
      (Letter), Fate 15 (Feb.1962):119-20.
-UFO (CE-3)
   1967, Dec.8/Marilyn Wilding
      Donald E. Keyhoe & Gordon I.R. Lore,
      Jr., eds., UFOs: A New Look (Wash-
      ington: NICAP, 1969), pp.29-30.
-UFO (NL)
   1947, July 20/James Denton
      Boise Idaho Daily Statesman, 21 July
      1947.

Jerome
-UFO (NL)
   1975, July 19
      "UFO Central," CUFOS News Bull., 15
      Nov.1975, p.14.

Kingston
-Humanoid tracks
   1976, Oct.
      "Latest News," Bigfoot News, no.25
      (Oct.1976):1.

Lewiston
-Clairvoyance
   1863, Oct./Hill Beachy
      W.J. McConnell, Early History of Id-
      aho (Caldwell: Caxton, 1913), pp.
      142-60.
      G.H.R. Taylor, "Murders Solved by a
      Dream," Fate 7 (Sep.1954):31-33.
   1966, Nov.
      Grangeville Idaho County Free Press,
      24 Nov.1966.
-UFO (DD)
   1947, July 2/Lloyd Bergh
      Spokane (Wash.) Daily Chronicle, 2
      July 1947.
      Ted Bloecher, Report on the UFO Wave
      of 1947 (Washington: NICAP, 1967),
      Appendix, pp.2-3.
   1947, July 6
      Spokane (Wash.) Daily Chronicle, 7
      July 1947.

Liberty
-Out-of-body experience
   1964, July 16/William Wallace Brown/
   Willowdale Ranch
      Brownie Bernice Brown, "Father's
      Guide Was a Ghost," Fate 25 (Jan.
      1972):89-90.

McCall
-Humanoid
   1968, fall/Roy Fleetwood
      John Green, The Sasquatch File (Ag-
      assiz, B.C.: Cheam, 1973), p.50.
   1970, summer
   1972, fall
      John Green, Sasquatch: The Apes Among
      Us (Seattle: Hancock House, 1978),
      pp.186-87.
   1974, Dec.
      Boise Idaho Statesman, 13 Mar.1977.
   1976, Dec./Mrs. Virgil Donica/2 mi.
   from town
      John Green, Sasquatch: The Apes Among
      Us (Seattle: Hancock House, 1978),
      pp.287-88, quoting Hamilton (Mont.)
      Bitterroot Journal, May 1977.

McCammon
-Mystery auto accidents
   1968-   /betw.Mileposts 47 and 57 on
   I-15
      (Editorial), Fate 30 (Feb.1977):24-
      26.
      "Idaho's 'Devil's Triangle,'" Fate
      31 (May 1978):66.
-Petroglyph
   nr.I-15
      Franklin Folsom, America's Ancient
      Treasures (N.Y.: Rand McNally,
      1974), p.67.

Meridian
-UFO (DD)
   1963, Oct.23/Mrs. Albert Gordon/1231
   W First St.
      (Editorial), Fate 17 (Feb.1964):10-
      12.
-UFO (NL)
   1963, Nov.29/Jim Adamson
      (Editorial), Fate 17 (Feb.1964):15-
      18.

Moscow
-Inner development
   1928-1948/Frank B. Robinson/Psychiana
      Frank B. Robinson, Why I Founded
      "Psychiana" (Moscow: Psychiana,
      1929).
      Frank B. Robisnon, What This War
      Really Means (Moscow: Psychiana,
      1942).
      Frank B. Robinson, Gems of Spiritual
      Truth (Moscow: Psychiana, 1948).
      Frank B. Robinson, The Strange Auto-
      biography of Frank B. Robinson (Mos-
      cow: Psychiana, 1949).
      Marcus Bach, Strange Sects and Cur-
      ious Cults (N.Y.: Dodd, Mead, 1962),
      pp.154-75.
-UFO (DD)
   1947, June 29/Frank Lark
      Spokane (Wash.) Daily Chronicle, 30
      June 1947.
   1947, July 4/Irving C. Allen/E of town
      Chicago (Ill.) Daily News, 5 July
      1947.
-UFO (NL)
   1953, Aug.9/Larry E. Towner

Larry E. Towner, "The Night of August 9th," _Fate_ 7 (May 1954):32-36. il.

Mountain Home
-UFO (CE-1)
  1951, summer/Jim Broede/Mountain Home AFB
    St. Paul (Minn.) Dispatch-East, 11 Jan.1979.
-UFO (DD)
  1947, July 28/Charles F. Gibian
    Boise _Idaho Statesman_, 29 July 1947.

Mud Lake
-UFO (CE-2)
  1978, Aug./Nile Wilding/ground markings only
    Idaho Falls Post-Register, 29 Aug. 1978. il.

Murtaugh
-Cattle mutilation
  1975, Oct./Gunnell farm
    Twin Falls Times-News, 31 Oct.1975.

Nampa
-Anomalous artifact
  1889, Aug.1/M.A. Kurtz/=carved image found at great depth
    G. Frederick Wright, "The Nampa Image," _Proc.Boston Soc'y Natural Hist._ 24 (1890):424-39.
    Albert Allen Wright, "An Examination of the Nampa Image," _Proc.Boston Soc'y Natural Hist._ 24 (1890):439-50.
    G. Frederick Wright, "An Archaeological Discovery in Idaho," _Scribner's Mag._ 7 (Feb.1890):235-38. il.
    G.F. Wright, "Additional News Concerning the Nampa Image," _Proc.Boston Soc'y Natural Hist._ 25 (1891):242-46.
    Annie Laurie Bird, _Boise: The Peace Valley_ (Caldwell: Caxton, 1934), pp. 17-25.
    Guy Archette, "Mystery of the Nampa Image," _Fate_ 7 (Nov.1954):50-53. il.
    Ronald J. Willis, "The Nampa Image," _INFO J._, no.2 (autumn 1967):3-12.
    Gaston Burridge, "The Nampa Image: Artifact or Artifice?" _Fate_ 24 (Nov. 1971):100-104. il.
    (Letter), Theron M. Trombeau, _Fate_ 26 (Aug.1973):130-32.
-UFO (DD)
  1947, July 3/Charles Hughes
    Boise _Idaho Statesman_, 4 July 1947.

New Meadows
-UFO (NL)
  1971, Jan.21/Jack Goforth/nr. Zim's Plunge
    "Press Reports," _APRO Bull._ 19 (Jan.-Feb.1971):7.

Olds Ferry
-River monster
  1868, Aug.22/Snake R./=hoax?

Vardis Fisher, _Idaho Lore_ (Caldwell: Caxton, 1939), pp.104-106.

Olsen
-UFO (NL)
  1947, July 5/Don Baker/Boise R.
    Boise _Idaho Statesman_, 6 July 1947.

Oneida
-UFO (NL)
  1978, July 4/Jim Jones
    Malad City _Idaho Enterprise_, 6 July 1978.

Orofino
-Humanoid
  1969, June/20 mi.N
    Russell Gebhart, "Report from Idaho: Incidents at O Mill," _Bigfoot Bull._, Jan.-Mar.1971.
  1972, fall
  1973, June
  1975, Oct.24
    John Green, _Sasquatch: The Apes Among Us_ (Seattle: Hancock House, 1978), pp.289-90.

Osburn
-UFO (DD)
  1947, July 8/Joe Vandervloedt/Hecla plant
    Spokane (Wash.) _Daily Chronicle_, 8 July 1947.

Parma
-UFO (CE-2)
  1964, April
    "Leading Up to the Big Flap," _Fate_ 17 (Aug.1964):45,47-48.

Payette
-Dowsing
  1950s/Ruth Ritchey
    (Letter), _Fate_ 8 (July 1955):113-14.

Pocatello
-Roman coin
  1903/Albert W. Jones/S. Main St.
    Boise _Idaho Statesman_, 8 May 1932.
-UFO (?)
  1947, July 1/Robert James
    Salt Lake City (Ut.) Tribune, 7 July 1947.
-UFO (CE-1)
  1947, July 6/H.C. McLean
    Seattle (Wash.) Post-Intelligencer, 8 July 1947.
-UFO (DD)
  1947, July 7
    Cheyenne _Wyoming State Tribune_, 7 July 1947.

Rexburg
-UFO (CE-1)
  1966, Jan.29
    Jacques Vallee, _Passport to Magonia_ (Chicago: Regnery, 1969), p.322.
  1967, Nov.26/Blair Sepert
    "More U.S.A. November Reports," _APRO Bull._ 16 (Jan.-Feb.1968):6,7.

Ririe
-UFO (CE-3)
  1967, Nov.2/Will Begay/1 mi.S on U.S.
  26
      Shelly Pioneer, 7 Dec.1967.
      (Editorial), UFO Inv. 5 (Sep.-Oct.
      1969):5-8.
      Donald E. Keyhoe & Gordon I.R. Lore,
      Jr., eds., UFOs: A New Look (Wash-
      ington: NICAP, 1969), pp.31-32.

Saint Maries
-UFO (DD)
  1947, July 3/Mrs. Walter Johnson/But-
  ler's Bay on St. Joe R.
      Spokane (Wash.) Spokesman-Review,
      7 July 1947.

Sandpoint
-Psychokinesis
  1967, summer/Anita Caldwell
      Anita Caldwell, "Has Our Ghost Re-
      tired?" Fate 25 (May 1972):86-88.

Shelley
-UFO (CE-1)
  1967, April 17/Zelma Eaton
  1967, April 28/William P. Carter/5 mi.S
      "Idaho Reports," UFO Inv. 4 (May-
      June 1967):1,3.
  1967, April 28/Shelley High School
      Idaho Falls Post-Register, 12 July
      1967.

Smith's Ferry
-Fall of rock
  1961, Aug.6/Phillip Davis/=lightning?
      Curtis Fuller, "The Boys Who 'Caught'
      a Flying Saucer," Fate 15 (Jan.
      1962):36,39.

Soda Springs
-UFO (CE-1)
  1976, Dec.18/Dennis Abrams/4 mi.NE on
  Wood Canyon Rd.
      "CE-I Seen by Independent Policemen
      in Idaho," Int'l UFO Reporter 2
      (Feb.1977):6-7.

Tamarack
-UFO (CE-2)
  1947, July 30/John E. Ostrom/1 mi.N on
  U.S.95
      Kenneth Arnold, "Are Space Visitors
      Here?" Fate 1 (summer 1948):4,15-
      16. il.
      Kenneth Arnold & Ray Palmer, The Com-
      ing of the Saucers (Boise: The Au-
      thors, 1952), p.168. il.

Twin Falls
-Humanoid
  1969, fall/9 mi.S
      John Green, Sasquatch: The Apes Among
      Us (Seattle: Hancock House, 1978),
      p.290.
-Skyquake
  1964, Feb.
      "Leading Up to the Big Flap," Fate
      17 (Aug.1964):46.

-UFO (?)
  1947, July 11/=hoax
      Bruce S. Maccabee, "UFO Related In-
      formation from the FBI Files: Part
      2," MUFON UFO J., no.120 (Nov.1977):
      12.
-UFO (CE-1)
  1947, Aug.13/A.C. Urie/Snake R. Canyon
      Twin Falls Times-News, 15 Aug.1947.
      J. Allen Hynek, The Hynek UFO Report
      (New York: Dell, 1977), pp.34-38.
-UFO (CE-2)
  1956, Sep.7/E.L. Rayburn/40 mi.S
      New York World Telegram & Sun, 14
      Sep.1956.
-UFO (DD)
  1947, July 4/A.E. Mitchell/Twin Falls
  Park
      Seattle (Wash.) Post-Intelligencer,
      5 July 1947.
  1952, March 8/Guy Ulrich/Snake R. Canyon
      (Editorial), Fate 5 (Sep.1952):6-7.
-UFO (NL)
  1947, Aug.19/Mr. Busby
      J. Allen Hynek, The Hynek UFO Report
      (New York: Dell, 1977), pp.39-40.

Wallace
-Spontaneous human combustion
  1952, June 30
      (Editorial), Fate 5 (Dec.1952):5.

Weippe
-Humanoid tracks
  1974, Jan.
      John Green, Sasquatch: The Apes Among
      Us (Seattle: Hancock House, 1978),
      pp.289-90.

Weiser
-UFO (DD)
  1947, June 12/Mrs. H. Erickson/Rt.2
      Ted Bloecher, Report on the UFO Wave
      of 1947 (Washington: NICAP, 1967),
      p.II-8.

Woodville
-UFO (CE-1)
  1967, April 11
      "Idaho Reports," UFO Inv. 4 (May-
      June 1967):1.

            B. Physical Features

American Falls Reservoir
-Ancient silver coin and box
  n.d.
      Boise Idaho Statesman, 8 May 1932.
-Archeological site
      Donald E. Trimble & Wilfred J. Carr,
      "Late Quaternary History of the
      Snake River in the American Falls
      Region, Idaho," Bull.Geol.Soc'y Am.
      72 (1961):1739-48.

Birch Creek
-Archeological site
  9000 B.C.-1850 A.D.

Earl H. Swanson, Jr. & Alan Lyle
Brown, "Birch Creek Papers No.1: An
Archaeological Reconnaissance in the
Birch Creek Valley of Eastern Idaho,"
Occ.Pap.Idaho State Univ.Museum, no.
13 (1964). il.
B. Robert Butler, A Guide to Under-
standing Idaho Archeology (Pocatel-
lo: Idaho State Univ.Museum, 1966).
il.

Clearwater R.
-UFO (?)
1973, Sep.2/Orval Wyman
Betty Jones, "Cover Picture Story,"
Can.UFO Rept., no.18 (1974):14-16.
il.
Betty Jones, "Blue Energy," Ohio Sky-
watcher, Mar.1975, pp.7-8.
"Bell-Jars and Gargoyles," Can.UFO
Rept., no.20 (1975):1-2. il.

Cove Creek
-Cattle mutilation
1975, Sep.
Ed Sanders, "The Mutilation Mystery,"
Oui, Sep.1976, pp.51,72.

French Creek
-Humanoid
1968, June 16/Frank Bond
Grangeville Idaho County Free Press,
17 June 1968; 4 July 1968; and 22
Aug.1968.
John Green, On the Track of the Sas-
quatch (Agassiz, B.C.: Cheam, 1968),
p.71.
John Green, Sasquatch: The Apes Among
Us (Seattle: Hancock House, 1978),
pp.284-85.

Hatwai Creek
-Archeological site
ca.8500 B.C.
Lewiston Morning Tribune, 23 Sep.1977.

Hauser L.
-UFO (DD)
1947, July 4/George Aster
Spokane (Wash.) Daily Chronicle, 5
July 1947.

Hell's Canyon
-Cattle mutilation
1975
Jim Brandon, Weird America (N.Y.:
Dutton, 1978), p.75.

Jaguar Cave
-Archeological site
ca.8400 B.C.
Alan Lyle Bryan, "Paleo-American Pre-
history," Occ.Pap.Idaho State Univ.
Museum 16 (1965):158-59.

Kelly L.
-Humanoid
1975, Sep.
John Green, Sasquatch: The Apes Among
Us (Seattle: Hancock House, 1978),

p.287.

Kinport Range
-UFO (DD)
1947, July 4/Henry Seymour
Salt Lake City (Ut.) Tribune, 7 July
1947.

Lolo Pass
-Humanoid
n.d.
John Green, The Sasquatch File (Agassiz, B.C.: Cheam, 1973), p.39.

Lost River Sinks
-UFO (CE-3)
1952, fall/Paul Solem
Jerome Clark, "Indian Prophecy and
the Prescott UFOs," Fate 24 (Apr.
1971):54,57.

Mosquito Creek
-Humanoid tracks
ca.1972/Mac Hatcher
John Green, The Sasquatch File (Agassiz, B.C.: Cheam, 1973), pp.56-
57.

Muldoon Canyon
-UFO (NL)
1973, Oct.
"Saucers in the News," Flying Saucers, winter 1974, p.60.

Owyhee Mts.
-Humanoid myth
Granville Stuart, Forty Years on the
Frontier, 2 vols. (Cleveland: Ar-
thur H. Clark, 1925), 2:56-58.
-Spirit medium
1850s/Mr. Wilson
Emma Hardinge Britten, Modern Amer-
ican Spiritualism (N.Y.: The Author,
1870), pp.477-78.

Payette L.
-Lake monster
1930s-
Boise Idaho Statesman, 3 July 1944.
New York World-Telegram, 3 July 1944.
"No Such Animal," Fortean Soc'y Mag.,
no.10 (autumn 1944):144-45.
Peter Costello, In Search of Lake
Monsters (N.Y.: Coward, McCann &
Geoghegan, 1974), p.217, quoting
Boise Idaho Sunday Statesman (un-
dated).
Jim Brandon, Weird America (N.Y.:
Dutton, 1978), pp.74-75.

Pend Oreille L.
-Lake monster
1944/nr. Farragut Naval Training Sta.
Austin E. Fife, "The Bear Lake Mon-
sters," Utah Humanities Rev. 1
(1948):99.
-Petroglyphs
Hope Peninsula
John B. Leiberg, "Petrographs at
Lake Pend d'Oreille, Idaho," Sci-

ence 22 (1893):156.
Richard P. Erwin, Indian Rock Writing
in Idaho (Boise: Idaho State Hist.
Soc'y, 1930), pp.15-18. il.
Robert N. Cheetham, "Bear Paws on the
Feet of Buddha," Fate 17 (Jan.1964)
:64-65.
-UFO (?)
  1972, June 9
    Jerome Eden, "UFOs and Weather Chaos,"
    Official UFO 1 (Aug.1976):31,56.
-Weather control and UFO (NL)
  1971, Dec.23/Jerome Eden/=Reichian
  method
    Jerome Eden, "UFOs and Weather Chaos,"
    Official UFO 1 (Aug.1976):31,56.

Poet Creek
-Humanoid
  1975, July
    John Green, Sasquatch: The Apes Among
    Us (Seattle: Hancock House, 1978),
    p.288.

Priest L.
-Humanoid
  1930s
    John Green, Sasquatch: The Apes Among
    Us (Seattle: Hancock House, 1978),
    p.284.
  1970
    Peter Byrne, The Search for Bigfoot
    (N.Y.: Pocket Books, 1976 ed.),
    pp.31-32.

Reynold's Creek
-Humanoid tracks
  1868/=human giant, Starr Wilkerson
    Adelaide Hawes, The Valley of Tall
    Grass (Bruneau, Id.: The Author,
    1950).
    Humboldt (Cal.) Times, 3 Jan.1959.

Rosebud L.
-Humanoid myth
    James Teit, "The Salishan Tribes of
    the Western Plateaus," Ann.Rept.Bur.
    Am.Ethn. 45 (1927-28):180.

Salmon R.
-Fire anomaly
  1947, July 24/Dewey Bowman/Salmon R.
  bridge
    Kenneth Arnold, "Are Space Visitors
    Here?" Fate 1 (summer 1948):4,17-19,
    21. il.
    Kenneth Arnold & Ray Palmer, The Com-
    ing of the Saucers (Boise: The Au-
    thors, 1952), pp.188-89. il.

Salmon R. Dam
-UFO (DD)
  1947, Aug.13/L.W. Hawkins
    Twin Falls Times-News, 15 Aug.1947.
    Donald E. Keyhoe, Flying Saucers Are
    Real (N.Y.: Fawcett, 1950), p.20.

Sawtooth Range
-Humanoid
  ca.1820s/Mr. Bauman

Theodore Roosevelt, The Wilderness
Hunter, in The Works of Theodore
Roosevelt (N.Y.: Scribner's Sons,
1926 ed.), pp.347-52.

Seigel Creek
-Humanoid
  1976, July
    John Green, Sasquatch: The Apes Among
    Us (Seattle: Hancock House, 1978),
    p.287.

Shafer Butte
-UFO (DD)
  1949, May 13
    "If It's in the Sky It's a Saucer,"
    Doubt, no.27 (1949):416.

Shoup Rockshelters
-Archeological site
  6500-1000 B.C.
    Earl H. Swanson, Jr. & Paul G. Sneed,
    "Birch Creek Papers No.3: The Arch-
    aeology of the Shoup Rockshelters
    in East Central Idaho," Occ.Pap.
    Idaho State Univ.Museum, no.17
    (1966).

Spring Creek Mines
-UFO (DD)
  1960s/Buzz Montague
    "Idaho 'Mining' UFOs," APRO Bull. 22
    (Sep.-Oct.1973):6-7. il.

Wilson Butte Cave
-Archeological site
  13,000 B.C.-1000 A.D.
    Ruth Grulin, "The Archaeology of Wil-
    son Butte Cave, South-Central Idaho,"
    Occ.Pap.Idaho State Univ.Museum, no.
    6 (1961).

        C. Ethnic Groups

Bannock Indians
-Flood myth
    Ella E. Clark, Indian Legends of the
    Northern Rockies (Norman: Univ. of
    Oklahoma, 1966), pp.172-74.

Coeur d'Alene Indians
-Humanoid myth
    James Teit, "The Salishan Tribes of
    the Western Plateaus," Ann.Rept.Bur.
    Am.Ethn. 45 (1927-28):181-83.

Nez Percé Indians
-Flood myth
    Ella E. Clark, Indian Legends of the
    Northern Rockies (Norman: Univ. of
    Oklahoma, 1966), pp.51-52.
-Hex
    Deward F. Walker, Jr., "Nez Percé
    Sorcery," Ethnology 6 (1967):66-96.

        D. Unspecified Localities

-Humanoid

1972, Jan.2/Justin Phelps
  <u>Pocatello Journal</u>, 25 Feb.1972.

CALIFORNIA

A. Populated Places

Acampo
-UFO (?)
  1897, Jan.
    Reno (Nev.) Evening Gazette, 22 Jan.
    1897.
  1947, July 6/Mrs. W.C. Smith
    Los Angeles News, 7 July 1947.

Aetna Springs
-Ghost
  1963/Andrew von Salza/resort
    Hans Holzer, Ghosts of the Golden
    West (N.Y.: Ace, 1968), pp.167-76.
-Psychic photography
  1963, summer/Andrew von Salza
    Hans Holzer, Psychic Photography
    (N.Y.: McGraw-Hill, 1969), pp.20-51,
    86-90. il.

Agoura
-UFO (NL)
  1975, Sep.24
    "UFO Central," CUFOS News Bull., 15
    Nov.1975, p.19.

Alameda
-Haunt
  1965, July/Gertrude Frost
    Hans Holzer, Ghosts of the Golden
    West (N.Y.: Ace, 1968), pp.83-91.
  1966/Ewing D. Dodgson/"USS Garnet County"
    Ewing D. Dodgson, "Haunts That Live
    in Ships," Fate 23 (June 1970):99.
-Precognition
  1972/Harold Michaels/Alameda Hospital
    (Editorial), Fate 26 (July 1973):34-
    36.
-Sea monster
  1885, March 27/J.P. Allen/San Francisco Bay
    San Francisco Chronicle, 28 Mar.1885.
-UFO (?)
  1896, Nov.26/=Venus?
    Sacramento Bee, 28 Nov.1896.
  1950, Feb./J.L. Kraker/Naval Air Sta.
    Los Angeles Herald-Express, 9 Feb.
    1950.
-UFO (NL)
  1896, Nov.24
    Gordon I.R. Lore, Jr. & Harold H.
    Deneault, Jr., Mysteries of the
    Skies: UFOs in Perspective (Engle-
    wood Cliffs, N.J.: Prentice-Hall,
    1968), p.8.

Alhambra
-UFO (NL)
  1947, July 4/Eva Etten/1524½ Argyle Ave.
    Los Angeles Examiner, 6 July 1947.

Alpine
-Humanoid
  1971
    Ken Coon, "Monsters in Our Midst:
    New Clues to the Bigfoot Mystery,"
    Saga, July 1975.

Altadena
-Skyquake
  1948, June 28
    "Explosions, Etc.," Doubt, no.23
    (1948):349.
-UFO (NL)
  1956, Nov.7/W.E. Dickensheetz/Rosemead
x San Gabriel Blvd.
    (Editorial), Fate 10 (Apr.1957):15-
    16.

Anaheim
-Clairvoyance
  1973, April 17/Kebrina Kinkade
    Steve Jacques, "And Along Comes a
    Crime," Probe the Unknown 1 (Oct.
    1973):38-42.
-Fall of ice
  1968, May/Mrs. Tom Brunson/3360 W. Orange Ave.
    Long Beach Independent Press Tele-
    gram, 12 May 1968.
-Inner development
  1962-   /Psynetics Foundation/1212 E.
  Lincoln Ave.
    June & Nicholas Regush, Psi: The Oth-
    er World Catalogue (N.Y.: Putnam,
    1974), p.162.
-Paranormal voice recordings
  1970s/Stewart Robb
    Susy Smith, Voices of the Dead? (N.Y.:
    Signet, 1977), pp.94-98.
-UFO (CE-4)(induced)
  1976-1977/hospital
    Alvin H. Lawson, "What Can We Learn
    from Hypnosis of Imaginary Abduc-
    tees?" in 1977 MUFON UFO Symposium
    Proc. (Seguin, Tex.: MUFON, 1977),
    pp.106-35.
    Alvin H. Lawson, "What Can We Learn
    from Hypnosis of Imaginary Abduc-
    tees?" MUFON UFO J., no.120 (Nov.
    1977):7-9; no.121 (Dec.1977):7-9.
-UFO (DD)
  1970, Feb.23
    "Cigar-Disk Observed over Californ-
    ia," APRO Bull. 18 (Jan.-Feb.1970):
    1,3.
-UFO (NL)
  1957, Nov.6/Edwin G. Leadford
    Garden Grove Daily News, 7 Nov.1957.
    il.
    San Diego Union, 9 Nov.1957.
    Kevin Randle, "The Truth about the
    1957 UFO Flap," Official UFO 2 (Mar.
    1977):24,27-28,46. il.

1975, Nov.5/Peter Guttilla
Peter Guttilla & James Frazier,
"Alien Possession: Strange Saga of
Brian Scott and the UFO Mind Manip-
ulators," Saga UFO Rept. 4 (July
1977):42,75.

Anderson
-Bird attack
1977, May 9/Mrs. Sherlock
Larry E. Arnold, "Birds on the At-
tack," Fate 31 (Aug.1978):54,58.
-Ghost
1919, Dec./Betty Furman
"Footsteps in the Night," Fate 7
(July 1954):66.
-UFO (CE-1)
1972, Nov.13/Les Harris/3 mi.SE on
Shelley Lane
Redding Record-Searchlight, 15 Nov.
1972.
William Murphy, "A Close Encounter
in North California?" FSR Case His-
tories, no.13 (Feb.1973):1-3. il.
-UFO (NL)
1896, Nov.28/E. Center x Ferry St.
Loren E. Gross, The UFO Wave of 1896
(Fremont, Cal.: The Author, 1974),
p.25.

Antioch
-UFO (?)
1896, Nov.23/Pat McGuire
Antioch Ledger, 28 Nov.1896.
1956, July 28
Leonard H. Stringfield, Inside Saucer
Post...3-0 Blue (Cincinnati: CRIFO,
1957), p.58.
-UFO (CE-2)
1975, March 27
Antioch Ledger, 29 Mar.1975.
-UFO (NL)
1978, April 9/James Barrero
Antioch Ledger, 10 Apr.1978.
1978, Dec.6/Ed Martinez
Antioch Ledger, 8 Dec.1978.

Apple Valley
-Poltergeist
1950-1951/John Duval
William H. Gilroy, "Ghosts of Apple
Valley," Fate 4 (May-June 1951):80-
85.

Aptos
-Fall of ice
1965, Feb./John Harward
Ronald J. Willis, "Ice Falls," INFO
J., no.3 (spring 1968):14, quoting
unidentified paper, 19 Feb.1968.
-UFO (NL)
1965, Jan.18/William Nolan
"New UFO Angles," UFO Inv. 3 (Apr.-
May 1965):3.

Arcadia
-Fall of fish
1954, Nov.11
"Snow, Ice and Fish," Doubt, no.48
(1955):341.

"Falls," Doubt, no.53 (1956):417.
-Fall of shrimp
1963, Sep.7/Robert R. Burns/440 N. Old
Ranch Rd.
Los Angeles Times, 8 Sep.1963.
-UFO (DD)
1947, July 4/C.P. Quickel
Los Angeles Examiner, 6 July 1947.
-UFO (NL)
1973, Oct.30/Balboa Dr.
Temple City Times, 4 Nov.1973.

Arcata
-Inner development
1970s/Dancers of the Sacred Circle/
1219 Spear Ave.
Hans Holzer, The Witchcraft Report
(N.Y.: Ace, 1973), pp.134-35.
-UFO (?)
1954, July 2
Donald E. Keyhoe, Flying Saucer Con-
spiracy (N.Y.: Holt, 1955), p.179.
-UFO (R)
1947, summer/Kenneth Ehlers/=radar
echo?
Wesley Price, "The Sky Is Haunted,"
Sat.Eve.Post, 6 Mar.1948, p.12. il.
Kenneth Arnold, "Are Space Visitors
Here?" Fate 1 (summer 1948):4,20-21.
Kenneth Arnold & Ray Palmer, The Com-
ing of the Saucers (Boise: The Au-
thors, 1952), pp.184-85. il.

Aromas
-UFO (NL)
1978, March 22/Lydia Medina/San Juan x
Murphy Rd.
Castroville North County News, 5 Apr.
1978.

Arroyo Grande
-Bird attack
1977, May 12/Santos Saldivar
Kansas City (Mo.) Times, 14 May 1977,
p.6A.

Arvin
-Healing
1967, July/Luis Barreras/Thompson grape
camp
Eddie A. Albalos, "Strange Cure for
Snakebite," Fate 22 (Dec.1969):104-
106.

Atherton
-Fall of ice
1959, spring/Robert von Bernuth/62 Al-
mendral Ave.
(Editorial), Fate 12 (Aug.1959):8.

Auberry
-UFO (CE-2)
ca.1944, spring
"Past Sightings Come to Light," APRO
Bull. 16 (Jan.-Feb.1968):5.

Auburn
-UFO (DD)
1947, July 5/Kjell Qvale
San Francisco Chronicle, 7-8 July 1947.

-UFO (NL)
  1896, Nov.25
    Loren E. Gross, The UFO Wave of 1896
    (Fremont, Cal.: The Author, 1974),
    p.17, quoting Auburn Placer Herald
    (undated).
  1978, Feb.22/Mary Cuneo
    Auburn Journal, 24 Feb.1978; and 1
    Mar.1978.

Avalon
-UFO (CE-3)
  1962, July 28/6 mi.E
    Los Angeles Times, 25 Oct.1962.
-UFO (DD)
  1947, July 8/Bob Jung
    Los Angeles Examiner, 9 July 1947. il.
    Kenneth Arnold & Ray Palmer, The Com-
    ing of the Saucers (Boise: The Au-
    thors, 1952), p.172. il.

Azusa
-Erratic shark
  1954, May 30/Sunset Ave.
    "Displaced Critters," Doubt, no.49
    (1955):358.
-Healing
  1977/Margaret Clement/17067 E. Orkney
    (Letter), Carolyn Johnson, Fate 31
    (Feb.1978):128-29.
-UFO (NL)
  1957, July
    Richard Hall, ed., The UFO Evidence
    (Washington: NICAP, 1964), p.146.

Bagdad
-UFO (NL)
  1978, May 2/David Melton/I-40
    Dave Kenney, "Object over Mojave,"
    APRO Bull. 26 (Apr.1978):6.

Baker
-Ghost
  1966, Feb.13/Wayne Barber
    Hans Holzer, Ghosts of the Golden
    West (N.Y.: Ace, 1968), pp.66-68.
-UFO (CE-1)
  1964, April 30/Gus Biggs/10 mi.W on
  Hwy.91
    Salt Lake City (Utah) Tribune, 1 May
    1964.

Bakersfield
-Erratic rattlesnake
  1955, May 12
    "Displaced Critters," Doubt, no.49
    (1955):358.
-Inner development
  1970s/Church of Wicca of Bakersfield/
  1908 Verde St.
    Hans Holzer, The Witchcraft Report
    (N.Y.: Ace, 1973), pp.133-34.
-UFO (?)
  ca.1941/N on U.S.99
    (Editorial), APRO Bull. 5 (Jan.1957):
    3.
-UFO (CE-2)
  1927, Oct.18/Richard Sweed
    Coral & Jim Lorenzen, UFOs: The Whole
    Story (N.Y.: Signet, 1969), p.18,

quoting Norwalk (Ct.) Hour (undated).
-UFO (DD)
  1947, June 1/Mrs. C.W. Parks
    Harrisburg (Pa.) Patriot, 7 July
    1947.
  1947, June 23/Richard Rankin
    Portland Oregonian, 1 July 1947.
    Kenneth Arnold & Ray Palmer, The Com-
    ing of the Saucers (Boise: The Au-
    thors, 1952), pp.69-71.
  1947, July 4/Norman Culver
    Los Angeles Times, 6 July 1947.
-UFO (NL)
  1896, Nov.26/Mr. Goode
  1896, Nov.27/A. Hughes
    Loren E. Gross, The UFO Wave of 1896
    (Fremont, Cal.: The Author, 1974),
    pp.22-23, quoting Bakersfield Daily
    Californian (undated).
  1965, Dec.29/Leo Marshall
    (Letter), Fate 19 (May 1966):132-33.

Banning
-UFO (CE-1)
  1956, June 6/3 mi.NW on U.S.70
    Thomas M. Olsen, ed., The Reference
    for Outstanding UFO Sighting Reports
    (Riderwood, Md.: UFO Information
    Retrieval Center, 1966), pp.46-48.
-UFO (DD)
  1957, Nov.11/Mrs. Larry Norton
    Riverside Enterprise, 12 Nov.1957.
-UFO (NL)
  1966, Jan.3/Mrs. Gene Knox
    Jerome Clark, "The Greatest Flap Yet?
    --Part IV," Flying Saucer Rev. 12
    (Nov.-Dec.1966):9,13.

Barstow
-UFO (NL)
  1975, July 5
    "UFO Central," CUFOS News Bull., 15
    Nov.1975, p.13.

Baxter
-UFO (CE-1)
  1974, Nov.23/Ronald Messore/I-80
    Ronald Messore, "Possible California
    Landing," APRO Bull. 24 (Sep.1975):
    5-6.

Bayside
-Precognition
  1964/Grace Conrad
    (Letter), Fate 18 (June 1965):107-12.
    (Letter), Barbara A. Hanson, Fate 18
    (Sep.1965):115-16.
    (Letter), Beatrice Collier, Fate 18
    (Dec.1965):123-24.
    (Letter), Dulcie Brown, Fate 18 (Dec.
    1965):124-26.

Bear Creek
-Humanoid tracks
  1978, June
    Madera Tribune, 21 June 1978.

Beaumont
-UFO (DD)
  1955, April 6

J. Allen Hynek, The Hynek UFO Report
(N.Y.: Dell, 1977), p.44.

Benicia
-Fall of muscle tissue
1851, July/U.S. Army station
San Francisco Herald, 24 July 1851.
-Spontaneous human combustion
1956, April 28/Harold J. Hall/141 E.
F St.
(Editorial), Fate 9 (Sep.1956):14-15.

Ben Lomond
-Inner development
1970s/Well-Springs/11667 Alba Rd.
Armand Biteaux, The New Consciousness (Willits, Cal.: Oliver, 1975),
p.146.
-UFO (NL)
1971, June 18/W.C. Thompson/7900 Harvard Dr.
Josephine J. Clark, "UFO Observed
during Californian Blackout," Flying Saucer Rev. 17 (Nov.-Dec.1971):
21-23,29. il.

Berkeley
-Astrology
1970s/Hank Friedman/2006 Cedar St.
Carol & Mary Cocciardi, The Psychic
Yellow Pages (Saratoga: Out of the
Sky, 1977), pp.126-27.
-Bioenergetics research
1973/Malcolm Brown
W. Edward Mann, Orgone, Reich and
Eros (N.Y.: Simon & Schuster, 1973),
p.257.
-Cartomancy
1972/Maggie Anthony
David St. Clair, The Psychic World
of California (N.Y.: Bantam, 1973
ed.), p.92.
-Fall of fish
1950, April 13/city pound
"Frogs and Fish," Doubt, no.30 (1950)
:34.
-Haunt
n.d./Siegal Rock
"Notes and Queries," Calif.Folklore
Quar. 3 (1944):234-35.
1970s/Noriyuki Tokuda/Faculty Club,
Univ. of California
Berkeley Gazette, 19 Mar.1974, p.1.
-Inner development
1970s/Tibetan Nyingmapa Meditation Cen-
ter/1815 Highland Park
David St. Clair, The Psychic World
of California (N.Y.: Bantam, 1973
ed.), p.84.
Armand Biteaux, The New Conscious-
ness (Willits, Cal.: Oliver, 1975),
p.142.
-Precognition
1974, Jan./Berkeley Psychic Institute
David Wallechinsky & Irving Wallace,
The People's Almanac (Garden City,
N.Y.: Doubleday, 1975), p.11.
-UFO (?)
1896, Nov.23/=balloons
San Francisco Chronicle, 24 Nov.1896,

p.10.
Oakland Times, 24 Nov.1896.
n.d.
Jacques Vallee, The Invisible Col-
lege (N.Y.: Dutton, 1975), pp.20-
21.
-UFO (CE-1)
1955, Sep.20/Theodore Walling
Theodore L. Walling, "Saucer Sight-
ing," Fate 9 (Dec.1956):35-37.
-UFO (DD)
1947, July 7/Mrs. Robert Turley/524
Kains Ave.
San Francisco Examiner, 8 July 1947.
1975, Oct.12
"UFO Central," CUFOS News Bull., 1
Feb.1976, p.8.
-UFO (NL)
1953, Feb.13/Roy McLaren
John C. Ross, "Fate's Report on the
Flying Saucers," Fate 6 (Oct.1953)
:6,9.

Beverly Hills
-Cartomancy
1960s/Iolanda Quinn
Neil & Margaret Rau, "Anthony Quinn's
Lovely Witch," Fate 22 (Nov.1969):
36-45.
-Erratic crocodilian
1954, Nov.11/Wilshire Blvd.
San Jose News, 12 Nov.1954.
-Haunt
1946, Aug./2320 Bowman Dr.
"Ghosts," Doubt, no.16 (1946):242.
1964-1968/Elke Sommer/Benedict Canyon
Joe Hyams, "Haunted," Sat.Eve.Post,
2 July 1966, pp.28-31. il.
Joe Hyams, "The Day I Gave Up the
Ghost," Sat.Eve.Post, 3 June 1967,
pp.92-95. il.
James Crenshaw, "Elke Sommer's Haunted House," Fate 21 (Aug.1968):34-
43.
-Inner development
1970s/Arcana Workshops/407 N. Maple Dr.,
no.214
Armand Biteaux, The New Consciousness (Willits, Cal.: Oliver, 1975),
p.10.
-Parapsychology research
1960s-   /Southern California Soc'y
for Psychical Research/170 S. Beverly
Marjorie D. Kern, "The Southern California Branch of the A.S.P.R.,"
J.ASPR 57 (1963):170-71.
June & Nicholas Regush, Psi: The Other World Catalogue (N.Y.: Dutton,
1974), p.21.
Gerald Faris, "The Southern California Society for Psychical Research,"
Psychic 5 (Oct.1974):30-34.
D. Scott Rogo, "Parapsychology Today,"
Probe the Unknown 3 (May 1975):21,
58.
-Precognition
1960s/Monica Peterson
Neil & Margaret Rau, "Monica Peter-
son: Psychic Movie Star," Fate 22
(June 1969):32-39.

ca.1967/Sharon Tate/Benedict Canyon
Dick Kleiner, "Sharon Tate's Tragic
Preview of Murder," Fate 23 (May
1970):40-46.
-Telepathy
1944, Nov.23/Adela Rogers St. Johns
"Warning in the Forest," Fate 11
(Feb.1958):54, quoting American
Weekly (undated).
-UFO (?)
1949, April 29
"If It's in the Sky It's a Saucer,"
Doubt, no.27 (1949):416.
-UFO (DD)
1947, July 7/Jerry McAdams/Coldwater
Canyon
Los Angeles Examiner, 8 July 1947.
-UFO (NL)
1947, July 2/Mrs. Ernest Michel/439 S.
Hamel Rd.
Los Angeles Times, 3-4 July 1947.
1947, July 6/Diane Thompson
Los Angeles Examiner, 8 July 1947.
1947, July 7/Emily Stern/216 S. Hamil-
ton Dr.
Los Angeles Examiner, 9 July 1947.

Big Bear City
-Fall of frogs
1952, July
Los Angeles Times, 26 July 1952.
-Poltergeist
1962, June 15-Nov./Mrs. William M. Lowe
/nr.Rebel Ridge
Los Angeles Times, 10-11 Nov.1962.
Big Bear Lake News-Pictorial, 21 Nov.
1962.
Los Angeles Herald-Examiner, 13 Jan.
1963.
Paul Foght, "Ghost or Poltergeist--
Who Throws the Rocks in San Berdoo?"
Fate 16 (Mar.1963):26-31.
Raymond Bayless, The Enigma of the
Poltergeist (N.Y.: Ace, 1967), pp.
57-67.

Big Pine
-UFO (?)
1952, April 8/H.I. Smith
Richard Hall, ed., The UFO Evidence
(Washington: NICAP, 1964), p.55.

Bishop
-Petroglyphs
Robert F. Heizer & C.W. Clewlow, Jr.,
Prehistoric Rock Art of California,
2 vols. (Ramona, Cal.: Ballena,
1973), 1:23-25.

Blanco
-UFO (?)
1965/Claudette Crashaw/=hoax
"Sex and Saucers in California," Sau-
cer News 13 (Mar.1966):25, quoting
Nat'l Mirror (undated).

Bloomington
-UFO (CE-3)
1951, Sep.
Isabel Davis & Ted Bloecher, Close

Encounter at Kelly and Others of
1955 (Evanston: Center for UFO Studies, 1978), p.v.

Blue Lake
-Humanoid
1956, Aug.1/2 mi.E
Coral E. Lorenzen, The Shadow of the
Unknown (N.Y.: Signet, 1970), pp.
105-106, quoting AP release, 2 Aug.
1956.
1964, Sep.13/Benjamin Wilder
Blue Lake Advocate, 24 Sep.1964.
1965, July/Steve Sanders
John Green, The Sasquatch File (Agassiz, B.C.: Cheam, 1973), pp.37-38.

Blythe
-Archeological site
Mojave Maze/15 mi N
George C. Marshall, "Giant Effigies
of the Southwest," Nat'l Geogr.Mag.
102 (Sep.1952):389. il.
Frank M. Setzler, "Seeking the Sec-
ret of the Giants," Nat'l Geogr.Mag.
102 (Sep.1952):390-404. il.
Henriette Mertz, Gods from the Far
East (N.Y.: Ballantine, 1975 ed.),
pp.73-75.
Richard Smedley, "Blythe, California:
Gigantic Petroglyphs," Probe the Un-
known 3 (May 1975):38-39. il.
-UFO (CE-1)
1973, Nov.8/Patrick Archer/E on I-10
Fontana Herald-News, 9 Nov.1973.
-UFO (NL)
1977, July 15
"UFOs of Limited Merit," Int'l UFO
Reporter 2 (Sep.1977):3.

Bodie
-Ghost mule
ca.1901/John Sturgeon/Standard Mine
Richard Webb, Voices from Another
World (N.Y.: Manor, 1972 ed.), pp.
90-92.
-Haunt
n.d./David V. Cain, Jr.
n.d./Grace Sturgeon/graveyard
Richard Webb, Voices from Another
World (N.Y.: Manor, 1972 ed.), pp.
43-45,259-60.
-Ornithomancy
n.d./Grace Sturgeon
Richard Webb, Voices from Another
World (N.Y.: Manor, 1972 ed.), pp.
48-49.

Bolinas
-Healing
1972/Irving Oyle
Stanley Krippner, Richard Davidson &
Nancy Peterson, "International Re-
port: Soviets Harness Biological
Energy," Fate 26 (Dec.1973):64,68.
-Precognition
1923, Aug./Henrietta Bourne/Audubon
Canyon Ranch
Beatrice Wells, "Mother's Third Eye,"
Fate 26 (Nov.1973):67-71.

Boron
-Fall of fish
  1958, March
    Boron Enterprise, 13 Mar.1958.
-UFO (NL)
  1974, Dec.21/Paula Hayden
    Peter Guttilla, "Bigfoot: Advance
    Guard from Outer Space," Saga UFO
    Rept. 4 (June 1977):22,50.

Borrego Springs
-UFO (NL)
  1957, Nov.4/A.A. Burnard, Jr.
    Long Beach Independent, 6 Nov.1957.

Boulder Creek
-Paraphysics research
  1970s/C-Life Institute/Box 261
    John White & Stanley Krippner, eds.,
    Future Science (Garden City, N.Y.:
    Anchor, 1977), p.585.

Bowman
-UFO (NL)
  1896, Oct.25/C.T. Musse
    San Francisco Call, 23 Nov.1896.

Brawley
-UFO (NL)
  1905, July 29
    Brawley News, 4 Aug.1905.

Brea
-UFO (NL)
  1973, Aug.23/William J. Hornaday/517 S.
  Laurel Ave.
    "Brief Reports," Skylook, no.74 (Jan.
    1974):17.

Brentwood
-Cat mutilations
  1974, June-Oct./nr. UCLA campus
    Kansas City (Mo.) Times, 15 Oct.1974;
    and 18 Oct.1974.
-UFO (CE-2)
  1956, July 28
    "Case 179," CRIFO Orbit, 7 Sep.1956,
    p.2, quoting Oakland Tribune (un-
    dated).
  1975, March 27
    "Reports from America," Australian
    UFO Bull., Feb.1976, p.7.
-UFO (NL)
  1958, Sep.25/Marian Lazar
    (Letter), Fate 12 (Apr.1959):109-10.

Bridgeport
-Crisis apparition
  1968, Aug./Mrs. Roy Higgins
    Richard Webb, Voices from Another
    World (N.Y.: Manor, 1972 ed.), pp.
    218-20.
-Deathbed apparition
  1946/hospital
    Richard Webb, Voices from Another
    World (N.Y.: Manor, 1972 ed.), pp.
    36-38.
-Ghost
  1968, Sep./Clair Brocket/Poor Farm
    Richard Webb, Voices from Another

World (N.Y.: Manor, 1972 ed.), pp.
256-58.
-Haunt
  1920s-1970s/Grace Branden
    Richard Webb, Voices from Another
    World (N.Y.: Manor, 1972 ed.), pp.
    140-42.

Broadmoor
-Fall of monkey
  1956, Oct.26/Faye Swanson/723 Stany-
  ford Dr.
    San Francisco Chronicle, 27 Oct.1956.

Brown's Valley
-UFO (NL)
  1896, Dec.4/Rae D. Swezy/=balloon?
    Marysville Daily Democrat, 5 Dec.
    1896.
    Marysville Semi-Weekly Appeal, 7 Dec.
    1896.

Brush Creek
-UFO (CE-3)
  1953, May 20, June 20/John Q. Black/
  Jordan and Marble Creeks
    San Francisco Chronicle, 24 June
    1953; and 19 July 1953, p.4.
    Wallace Kunkel, "The Little Man Who
    Wasn't There," Fate 7 (May 1954):
    48-52.
    Gray Barker, They Knew Too Much about
    Flying Saucers (N.Y.: Tower, 1967
    ed.), pp.27,32-36.
-UFO (NL)
  1953, Aug.16/J.R. Bowling/Feather R.
    Gray Barker, They Knew Too Much about
    Flying Saucers (N.Y.: Tower, 1967
    ed.), p.37.

Buellton
-UFO (?)
  1953, Jan./Madge Nippert
    (Letter), Fate 6 (July 1953):106.

Buena Park
-UFO (CE-4)
  1973, Oct.25/Brian Scott
    Alvin H. Lawson, "Hypnotic Regression
    of Alleged CE-III Cases: Ambiguities
    on the Road to UFOs," in Proc.1976
    CUFOS Conference (Evanston: Center
    for UFO Studies, 1976), pp.141-51.
    Peter Guttilla & James Frazier, "Ali-
    en Possession: Strange Saga of Brian
    Scott and the UFO Mind Manipulators,"
    Saga UFO Rept. 4 (July 1977):42.

Burbank
-Acoustic anomaly
  1953, spring/Samuel P. Turner
    (Letter), Fate 8 (Apr.1955):112-13.
-Burning rock
  1960, June/Estes Johnson/freeway excavation site
    (Editorial), Fate 13 (Oct.1960):22-
    24.
-Clairempathy
  1963, May 8/Robert Barnes/1130 Olive
    (Editorial), Fate 16 (Sep.1963):22.

-Contactee
  1952, May 23-1953, Dec./Orfeo Angelucci
  /Hyperion Ave. Freeway Bridge
    Orfeo Angelucci, The Secret of the
    Saucers (Amherst, Wisc.: Amherst,
    1955).
    Israel Norkin, Saucer Diary (N.Y.:
    Pageant, 1957).
    Orfeo Angelucci, The Nature of Infin-
    ite Entities (San Diego: Talk of the
    Times, 1958).
    Orfeo Angelucci, Concrete Evidence
    (N.Y.: Flying Saucer News, 1959).
    Orfeo Angelucci, Son of the Sun (Los
    Angeles: DeVorss, 1959).
    Carl Jung, Flying Saucers: A Modern
    Myth of Things Seen in the Skies
    (N.Y.: Signet, 1969 ed.), pp.119-
    24.
-Healing
  1941-   /Mr.A
    Ruth S. Montgomery, Born to Heal
    (N.Y.: Coward, McCann & Geoghegan,
    1973).
-Inner development
  1970s/Church of the Eternal Source/Box
  7091
    Hans Holzer, The Witchcraft Report
    (N.Y.: Ace, 1973), pp.111-14.
-UFO (?)
  1947, July 9/=hoax
    Bruce S. Maccabee, "UFO Related In-
    formation from the FBI Files: Part
    2," MUFON UFO J., no.120 (Nov.1977):
    12.
-UFO (CE-3)
  1973, Oct.16
    Ann Druffel, "The Burbank Landing and
    Occupant Report," Flying Saucer Rev.
    21 (June 1975):3-6. il.
-UFO (DD)
  1947, July 8/John Taylor
    Los Angeles Examiner, 9 July 1947.
-UFO (NL)
  1947, July 2/William H. Sullivan/1115 N.
  Avon St.
    Los Angeles Times, 4 July 1947.
  1957, Feb.13-14/Bob Wells
    "Case 299," CRIFO Orbit, 1 Mar.1957,
    p.4, quoting Los Angeles Times (un-
    dated).
  1977, April 3
    Ann Druffel, "Other Encounters of All
    Different Kinds," MUFON UFO J., no.
    123 (Feb.1978):15,16.

Burlingame
-Ghost
  ca.1965
    Hans Holzer, Ghosts of the Golden
    West (N.Y.: Ace, 1968), pp.64-66.

Burnt Ranch
-UFO (?)
  1975, May
    Peter Guttilla, "Monster Menagerie,"
    Saga UFO Rept. 4 (Sep.1977):32,34.

Butte co.
-Cattle mutilation

  1975, Oct.
    Oroville Mercury-Register, 25 Oct.
    1975.
-Ghost
  n.d./Frank Dean Van Zandt
    Frank Dean Van Zandt, "Nocturnal Vis-
    itor," Fate 5 (Oct.1952):67-69.

Calexico
-UFO (?)
  1950, March 12
    Los Angeles Times, 12 Mar.1950.

Calistoga
-UFO (?)
  1973, Oct.6/Ed Booth/White Cottage Rd.
    Calistoga Calistogan, 25 Oct.1973.
-UFO (DD)
  1957, July 31/William J. Besler
    Richard Hall, ed., The UFO Evidence
    (Washington: NICAP, 1964), p.67.

Camarillo
-Poltergeist
  1962, Oct./State Hospital
    Los Angeles Times, 1 Nov.1962.
-UFO (?)
  1967, Dec.27/Broom Ranch
    Edward U. Condon, ed., Scientific
    Study of Unidentified Flying Objects
    (N.Y.: Bantam, 1969 ed.), pp.475-78.
-UFO (CE-1)
  1976, Aug.31/Somis Rd.
    Dennis Leatart, "1976 California UFO
    Reports," APRO Bull. 25 (Dec.1976):
    1,3.
-UFO (NL)
  1957, Nov.8/Connie Foster
    Camarillo News, 14 Nov.1957.
  1973, Oct.24/Pearl Brown/21 E. Loop Dr.
    Camarillo News, 25 Oct.1973.

Campbell
-Spirit medium
  1974-   /Sylvia Brown/138 W. Campbell
  Ave.
    Carol & Mary Cocciardi, The Psychic
    Yellow Pages (Saratoga: Out of the
    Sky, 1977), pp.81-82.

Camp Pendleton
-Dowsing
  1967/Nelson S. Hardacker
    Elizabeth Read, "In Vietnam Life Can
    Depend on a Dowsing Rod," Fate 21
    (Apr.1968):52-59.

Camptonville
-UFO (CE-3)
  1896, Dec.7/William Bull Meek/Ramm's
  Hill
    San Francisco Examiner, 8 Dec.1896.

Canoga Park
-Haunt
  1971, Feb.-1973, Aug./D. Scott Rogo
    D. Scott Rogo, An Experience of Phan-
    toms (N.Y.: Dell, 1976 ed.), pp.44-
    49.
    D. Scott Rogo, "In Search of Haunted

Houses," Probe the Unknown 4 (Nov.
1976):37-41.
D. Scott Rogo, "Psychic Theft?" Fate
31 (May 1978):61-66.
-UFO (CE-1)
1975, Aug.4
"UFO Central," CUFOS News Bull., 15
Nov.1975, p.15.
-UFO (CE-2)
1971, Nov.28
Ted Phillips, Physical Traces Associ-
ated with UFO Sightings (Evanston:
Center for UFO Studies, 1975), p.79.
-UFO (NL)
1976, Sep.5/Mary Ann Ryman
Ann Druffel & Morrey Allen, "The Sky-
net Log: Circling Ships," MUFON UFO
J.,no.108 (Nov.1976):6-8.

Capay
-Humanoid
1891, May/John W. Clapp/Casey Flat
"A Look Back into History," Bigfoot
News, no.48 (Sep.1978):1.
-UFO (CE-2)
1962, Sep.26/A.T. Gray
"Rancher Sees Hovering Object," APRO
Bull. 12 (July 1963):3, quoting Chi-
co Enterprise-Record (undated).
Ted Phillips, Physical Traces Associ-
ated with UFO Sightings (Evanston:
Center for UFO Studies, 1975), p.27,
quoting Orland Unit-Register (un-
dated).

Capitola
-Mystery bird deaths
1961, Aug./Ed Cunningham
(Editorial), Fate 14 (Dec.1961):18-19.

Carmel
-Cartomancy
1970s/Tarquin
1970s/Clint D. Nix
David St. Clair, The Psychic World
of California (N.Y.: Bantam, 1973
ed.), pp.161-72.
-Healing
1970s/Dorie D'Angelo/San Antonio x 10th
Ave.
David St. Clair, The Psychic World
of California (N.Y.: Bantam, 1973
ed.), pp.172-78.
David St. Clair, Psychic Healers
(N.Y.: Doubleday, 1974), pp.1-25.
-UFO (NL)
1963, Feb.28/John L. Crisan/Carmel Hill
(Editorial), Fate 16 (July 1963):20.

Carmichael
-Skyquake
1952, Jan.4/Clyde Hixon
Marion Kirkpatrick, "California Mystery Blasts," Fate 10 (Apr.1957):86,
88.
-UFO (?)
1977, Dec.22/=hoax
Ted Bloecher, "A Survey of CE3K Reports from 1977," in 1978 MUFON Symposium Proc. (Seguin, Tex.: MUFON,
1978), pp.14,86.

Carrizo
-Phantom stagecoach
n.d.
Philip A. Bailey, Golden Mirages
(N.Y.: Macmillan, 1940), pp.118-23.

Carson
-Giant lizard and UFO (NL)
1975, June/San Diego Freeway
Peter Guttilla, "Monster Menagerie,"
Saga UFO Rept. 4 (Sep.1977):32,66.

Castro Valley
-Inner development
1968-   /Ana Foundation/20204 Catalina
Dr.
Armand Biteaux, The New Conscious-
ness (Willits, Cal.: Oliver, 1975),
p.5.
-Plant sensitivity
1970s/Randy Fontes/21591 Orange Ave.
Carol & Mary Cocciardi, The Psychic
Yellow Pages (Saratoga: Out of the
Sky, 1977), pp.56-59.
-UFO (NL)
1967, May 25/M. Ofinowicz
"Sighting Evidence Grows," UFO Inv.
4 (Nov.-Dec.1967):1,3.

Cedarville
-UFO (CE-1)
1966, Dec.14
"Near Landing in California," Saucer
News 14 (summer 1967):21, quoting
NICAP Reporter (undated).
1976, Jan.28
"Noteworthy UFO Sightings," Ufology
2 (summer 1976):62.

Ceres
-UFO (NL)
1968, Aug.8/Hwy.99
"Around the Globe," APRO Bull. 17
(Nov.-Dec.1968):6.

Chatsworth
-UFO (NL)
1966, March/Charles Forsher/Chatsworth
Park
(Letter), Fate 19 (Oct.1966):145-47.
1976, Nov.20/Doug Betts
Ann Druffel, "SkyNet Log," MUFON UFO
J., no.114 (May 1977):15. i1.

Chester
-Humanoid
1956, Sep./Wilson L.
Paul C. Cerny, "The Wilson Lake Humanoid," MUFON UFO J., no.112 (Mar.
1977):11.

Chico
-Clairvoyance
1948, winter/W.M. Tisher/Calvin Bacca-
la ranch
W.M. Tisher, "How I Found the Lost
Traps," Fate 8 (Dec.1955):43-44.
-Fall of anomalous meteorite
1885, March 5/E of town
Chico Chronicle, 7 Mar.1885.

-Fall of fish
  1878, Aug.20
    Chico Record, 20 Aug.1878.
    New York Times, 2 Sep.1878, p.5.
-Fall of rocks
  1922, Jan.-March/J.W. Charge/6th x Orange St.
    Chico Record, 9 Mar.1922, p.1.
    San Francisco Chronicle, 12-18 Mar.
    1922.
    San Francisco Examiner, 14 Mar.1922.
    San Francisco Call, 16 Mar.1922.
    Charles Fort, The Books of Charles
    Fort (N.Y.: Holt, 1941), pp.533-35.
    Thelma Hall Quest, "Rocks Rain on
    Chico, California," Fate 29 (Jan.
    1976):73-81.
    (Letter), Wade T. Hampton, Fate 29
    (May 1976):112-14.
    (Letter), W. Stewart Windle, Fate 29
    (Sep.1976):111-12.
-UFO (DD)
  1953, July 15/Joyce Battrell
  1953, July 16/Hannah Stone
    Gray Barker, They Knew Too Much about
    Flying Saucers (N.Y.: Tower, 1967
    ed.), pp.36-37.
-UFO (NL)
  1896, Nov.24-25/W.H. Hughes/Normal Bldg.
    Oakland Tribune , 25 Nov.1896.
    San Francisco Chronicle, 25 Nov.1896,
    p.14.
    Chico Enterprise, 25-26 Nov.1896.
  1966, Sep.11/Lina Smith
    (Letter), J.H. Smith, Fate 20 (Feb.
    1967):119-20.
  1973, Oct.17/James Book/Hwy.99 x 149
    San Francisco Chronicle, 18 Oct.1973.

Chino
-Haunt
  1956, Nov.-1959?/Genevieve Siegrist
    Genevieve Siegrist, "Haunted House
    in Chino, California," Fate 14 (Feb.
    1961):77-82.

Chula Vista
-Fall of fish
  1956, April 14
    "Falls," Doubt, no.53 (1956):417.
-UFO (NL)
  1960, Nov.27/Olive Hart/Caravan Trailer Court
    Lloyd Mallan, "The Mysterious 12,"
    Sci. & Mech. 37 (Dec.1966):30,65-67.
  1978, May 28/Ted Simons/4th Ave.
    Imperial Beach Star-News, 1 June 1978.

Cima
-UFO (NL)
  1963, Feb.26/James Brown
    (Editorial), Fate 16 (July 1963):18-
    20.

Cisco
-UFO (CE-3)
  1964, Sep.4/Cisco Grove
    Coral & Jim Lorenzen, Flying Saucer
    Occupants (N.Y.: Signet, 1967 ed.),
    pp.137-40.

Donald E. Keyhoe & Gordon I.R. Lore,
  Jr., UFOs: A New Look (Washington:
  NICAP, 1969), p.31.
J. Allen Hynek, The Hynek UFO Report
  (N.Y.: Dell, 1977), pp.210-12.

Citrus Heights
-UFO (?)
  1956, Aug.20
    Richard Hall, ed., The UFO Evidence
    (Washington: NICAP, 1964), p.145.

Claremont
-Religious apparition
  1971, Sep.27-29/Enrico S. Molnar
    Enrico S. Molnar, "The New Order of
    Agape According to St. Michael,"
    Fate 26 (Apr.1973):36-47. il.

Clarksburg
-UFO (DD)
  1950, March 13/Herbert W. Taylor
    R.B. McLaughlin, "How Scientists
    Tracked Flying Saucers," True, Mar.
    1950, pp.25-27,96-99.

Clayton
-Poltergeist
  1957, July-Aug./Elmer Gomez/nr. town
  hall
    "Some Recent Poltergeist Cases," Para-
    psychology Bull., no.43 (Nov.1957):
    2.
    Coral E. Lorenzen, The Shadow of the
    Unknown (N.Y.: Signet, 1970), pp.39-
    41.

Cleone
-UFO (NL)
  1975, Jan.18/Charles Strong
    Robert A. Goerman, "The UFO Modus
    Operandi: January 1975," Official
    UFO 1 (Aug.1976):46,65.

Coachella
-UFO (CE-1)
  1978, July 29/Frank Garza/Ave. 54
    Riverside Press, 1 Aug.1978.

Coalinga
-UFO (NL)
  1975, Sep.23
    "UFO Central," CUFOS News Bull., 15
    Nov.1975, p.19.

Coarsegold
-UFO (?)
  1967, Aug.15/=aircraft
    Edward U. Condon, ed., Scientific
    Study of Unidentified Flying Ob-
    jects (N.Y.: Bantam, 1969 ed.),
    pp.334-39.

Cold Springs
-Humanoid
  1963, Jan.27/William Huntley/gravel pit
    Sonora Daily Union Democrat, 28-29
    Jan.1963.

Coloma
-Haunt
  1971, Aug./Vinyard House
    (Editorial), Fate 25 (June 1972):34-
    38.

Colusa
-UFO (CE-2)
  1976, Sep.10/Bill Pecha, Jr./Wilson Ave.
    Colusa Sun-Herald, 12 Sep.1976.
    Paul Cerny, "UFO Hovers over Califor-
    nia Farm," MUFON UFO J., no.107
    (Oct.1976):3-8. il.
    Brad Sparks, "Colusa (Calif.) Close
    Encounter," APRO Bull. 25 (Feb.1977)
    :3-6; (Mar.1977):3-6; (Apr.1977):3-
    4. il.
    "Colusa Report Corrections," APRO
    Bull. 26 (July 1977):mailer.

Commerce
-Fall of ice
  1962, March 18/Henry Van Unen/7523 Nee-
    nah St.
    (Editorial), Fate 15 (July 1962):14-
    15.

Compton
-UFO (NL)
  1968, July 9/I. Castano
    Ann Druffel, "Santa Catalina 'Cloud-
    Cigars,'" in Proc.1976 CUFOS Confer-
    ence (Evanston: Center for UFO
    Studies, 1976), pp.62,65-66. il.
  1976, Feb.5/Chico McCall
    Timothy Green Beckley, "Saucers over
    Our Cities," Saga UFO Rept. 4 (Aug.
    1977):24,73.
  1979, Feb.23/B. Neilson/Alondra Blvd.
    Los Angeles Herald-Examiner, 26 Feb.
    1979.

Concord
-Phantom panther
  1972, summer/Naval Weapons Depot
    Loren Coleman, "California Odyssey:
    Observations on Western Para-Pan-
    thers," Anomaly Rsch. Bull., no.23
    (1978):5,7.
-UFO (CE-4)
  1977, Feb.2/Willow Pass Rd.
    Concord Transcript, 2 Feb.1977, p.1.
    Jeffrey Mishlove, "The Wrath of the
    'UFO Prophet,'" Fate 32 (Feb.1979):
    62,69.
-UFO (DD)
  1947, July 15/Frank A. Flynn
    San Francisco News, 18 July 1947.
-UFO (NL)
  1960, Aug.17/Lucille Elmore/Willow Pass
    Rd. x Market St.
    John C. Ross, "State Cops Race 'Fly-
    ing Saucer,'" Fate 13 (Dec.1960):
    44,46-47.
  1964, Feb.28/Mrs. Ted Kvilhaug/Oak
    Grove Rd.
    (Letter), P.C. Cerny, Fate 18 (Jan.
    1965):120-24.
  1975, Aug.14
    "UFO Central," CUFOS News Bull., 15

Nov.1975, p.16
  1976, Dec.19
    "UFOs of Limited Merit," Int'l UFO
    Reporter 2 (Feb.1977):5.

Concordia
-Fall of ice
  1955, Feb.9/Herb Colombo
    Coral E. Lorenzen, The Shadow of the
    Unknown (N.Y.: Signet, 1970), pp.
    121-22.

Conejo
-UFO (DD)
  1973, Feb.8/Richard Coimbra
    Thousand Oaks News-Chronicle, 20 Mar.
    1973. il.
    Adrian Vance, "Conejo Photo: An An-
    alysis," Skylook, no.78 (May 1974):
    7. il.

Contra Costa co.
-Skyquake
  1951, May
    San Francisco Examiner, 23 May 1951.
    Marion Kirkpatrick, "California Mys-
    tery Blasts," Fate 10 (Apr.1957):
    86-87.
-UFO (?)
  1933, fall
    Coral & Jim Lorenzen, UFOs: The Whole
    Story (N.Y.: Signet, 1969), p.19,
    quoting Pittsburg (Cal.) newspaper
    (undated).

Corcoran
-Erratic crocodilian
  1930, summer/Tulare Lake Basin
    Sacramento Union, 17 May 1971.

Corning
-UFO (CE-1)
  1975, Sep.30/Tyrone Philips/7 mi.S nr.
    Hwy.99W
    Corning Daily Observer, 16 Oct.1975.
-UFO (NL)
  1960, Aug.13/Charles A. Carson/Hoag Rd.
    San Francisco Chronicle, 16 Aug.1960.
    Donald H. Menzel & Lyle G. Boyd, The
    World of Flying Saucers (Garden
    City, N.Y.: Doubleday, 1963), pp.
    253-54.
    Richard Hall, ed., The UFO Evidence
    (Washington: NICAP, 1964), pp.61,112.
    Statement of Dr. James A. Harder, in
    U.S., Congress, House, Committee on
    Science & Astronautics, Symposium
    on UFOs, 90th Cong., 2d sess., 1968,
    pp.113-16.
    J. Allen Hynek, The Hynek UFO Report
    (N.Y.: Dell, 1977), pp.92-94.
  1960, Aug.16
    Richard Hall, ed., The UFO Evidence
    (Washington: NICAP, 1964), p.170.
  1967, July 4/Jim Overton/bowling alley
    Reno (Nev.) Evening Gazette, 10 July
    1967.
    "From Dr. McDonald's Files," Can.UFO
    Rept., no.12 (1972):16,23.

Corona
-Humanoid
   1975, Aug.12/Daniel Hinson/E of town
   1975, Aug.14/Irene P. Rambo
      Corona Independent, 15 Aug.1975; and
      19 Aug.1975.
   1975, Aug.17/James Mihalko/Main St.
   Canyon
      Riverside Enterprise, 19 Aug.1975.
      B. Ann Slate & Alan Berry, Bigfoot
      (N.Y.: Bantam, 1976), pp.132-37.
-Humanoid tracks
   1975, Nov./Border Ave.
      Peter Guttilla, "Bigfoot: Advance
      Guard from Outer Space," Saga UFO
      Rept. 4 (June 1977):22,52.
-Men-in-black
   1975, summer
      B. Ann Slate, "The Humanoids," Saga
      UFO Rept. 6 (Jan.1979):32.
-Skyquake
   1956, Sep.12/Dean Strawn
      "Case 218," CRIFO Orbit, 2 Nov.1956,
      p.1.
-UFO (?)
   1947, July 3/S. Basquez
      Los Angeles Times, 6 July 1947.
-UFO (DD)
   1978, Nov.26/Eda Jones
      Riverside Enterprise, 28 Nov.1978.
-UFO (NL)
   1975, Sep./Kathy Rivera
      Peter Guttilla, "Bigfoot: Advance
      Guard from Outer Space," Saga UFO
      Rept. 4 (June 1977):22,52.

Corte Madera
-Horticultural anomaly
   1972/Rose Nickle/=human hair as fertil-
   izer
      Nat'l Enquirer, 29 Oct.1972.
-Spirit medium
   1970s/Rev. Ewald/Holy Innocence Church/
   Redwood Ave. x Tamalpais Dr.
      David St. Clair, The Psychic World
      of California (N.Y.: Bantam, 1973
      ed.), p.96.

Costa Mesa
-Weather control
   1965-1971/Bill Payne/Orange Coast Col-
   lege/=Indian sculpture
      Nat'l Insider, 2 June 1966.
      Durham (N.C.) Morning Herald, 16 Dec.
      1971. il.

Cotati
-Fall of foam
   1964, July 19/Patricia Perry/racetrack
   /=sea foam?
      (Letter), Fate 17 (Dec.1964):130-32.
      (Letter), Maxwell Leland, Fate 18
      (Apr.1965):115-16.

Cottonwood
-UFO (CE-1)
   1953, Oct./Vinna Middleton
      (Letter), Fate 20 (Mar.1967):147-48.

Coulterville
-Clairvoyance
   1964, Jan.23/Carl Plebank
      (Editorial), Fate 17 (May 1964):11-
      13, quoting Fresno Bee (undated).
-Haunt
   1965, Aug.-Dec./Ina Louez Morris/10 mi.
   W on Hwy.32
      Ina Louez Morris, "A Ghost with Mon-
      ey," Fate 21 (Sep.1968):38-43.

Covelo
-Humanoid tracks
   1961, spring/Bob Titmus/NE of town
      John Green, The Sasquatch File (Ag-
      assiz, B.C.: Cheam, 1973), p.29.

Covina
-Inner development
   1942-   /Theosophical Society
      Elsie Benjamin, "Theosophy in Amer-
      ica," Fate 5 (Apr.-May 1952):65-68.

Crestline
-UFO (NL)
   1977, Aug.18/Dennis Leatart
      Dennis Leatart, "Ghost Riders Through
      the Gates of Hercules," APRO Bull.
      26 (Aug.1977):1,3.

Culver City
-Clairaudience
   1938-1970s/Maxine Bell
      "Spirited Music," Fate 27 (Feb.1974):
      63, quoting Nat'l Enquirer (undated).
-Deathbed apparition
   1965, Jan.1/Nancy Wright Lineberger
      Nancy Wright Lineberger, "The Night
      I Died," Fate 19 (Mar.1966):73-75.
-Fall of ice
   1960, Dec.6/Mrs. Robert M. Conlon
      (Editorial), Fate 14 (May 1961):23.
-Healing
   1965, Jan./Nancy Wright Lineberger
      Nancy Wright Lineberger, "Prayer
      Does the Impossible," Fate 19 (July
      1966):81-82.
-Poltergeist
   1976
      Judy Rocha, "Mr. Whose-It: World's
      Most Amazing Poltergeist," Psychic
      World, Mar.1977, pp.61-66,87. il.
-UFO (DD)
   1947, July 7/Evelyn Keel/MGM Studios
      Los Angeles Herald-Express, 8 July
      1947.
   1952, July 23/aircraft plant
      Donald E. Keyhoe, Flying Saucers from
      Outer Space (N.Y.: Holt, 1953), pp.
      156-57.
   1952, Nov.28/MGM Studios
      "Past Sightings Come to Light," APRO
      Bull. 16 (Jan.-Feb.1968):5.

Cupertino
-Animal ESP
   1953-1955/Mas Nijima
      "The Homing Frog," Fate 9 (Oct.1956)
      :24.

Cypress
-Haunt
  1960s-1970s/Jane Cook
    Art Kevin & Jodi Lawrence, "The Paint-
    ing That Comes to Life," Probe the
    Unknown 2 (Feb.1974):32-36.
-UFO (CE-1)
  1977, Feb.25/Cypress College
    "UFOs of Limited Merit," Int'l UFO
    Reporter 2 (Apr.1977):5.

Daggett
-Dowsing
  1950s/Jerry Smith/Coolwater Ranch
    Gaston Burridge, "A Dowser Named
    Smith," Fate 12 (Nov.1959):41-46.
-UFO (DD)
  1950, June 24
    Richard Hall, ed., The UFO Evidence
    (Washington: NICAP, 1964), p.31.

Daly City
-Astrology
  1940s-   /John Mazwek/59 Shoal Dr.
    David St. Clair, The Psychic World
    of California (N.Y.: Bantam, 1973
    ed.), pp.65-68.
    Carol & Mary Cocciardi, The Psychic
    Yellow Pages (Saratoga: Out of the
    Sky, 1977), pp.134-35.
-Poltergeist
  1973, May-Sep.8
    Freda Morris, "Exorcising the Devil
    in California: Part Two," Fate 27
    (Aug.1974):96,103-105.
    Alan Vaughan, "The Devil in Daly
    City," Psychic 5 (Oct.1974):41-43.
-Skyquake
  1971, Oct.22
    Los Angeles Times, 23 Oct.1971.
-UFO (?)
  1974
    "Golden Gate's Golden Lights," Probe
    the Unknown 2 (summer 1974):8.
-UFO (NL)
  1973, Oct.16/Skyline Blvd.
    San Francisco Chronicle, 18 Oct.1973.

Dana
-Fall of green snow
  1953, April 8/Milton S. Mayer/McCloud-
  McArthur Rd.
    San Francisco Chronicle, 11 Apr.1953.
    (Editorial), Fate 6 (Aug.1953):5.

Danby
-UFO (?)
  1958, Oct.2/=reflection
    Donald H. Menzel & Lyle G. Boyd, The
    World of Flying Saucers (Garden
    City, N.Y.: Doubleday, 1963), pp.
    243-44.

Danville
-UFO (?)
  1955, Dec.2/power blackout
    "Lights Out--A Mystery Drama," CRIFO
    Orbit, 6 Jan.1956, pp.1-2.

Davis
-Parapsychology research
  1966-   /Charles T. Tart/Univ. of California at Davis
    Elizabeth Read, "Wanted: Astral Fli-
    ers for Lab Experiment," Fate 21
    (Nov.1968):43-51.
    Charles T. Tart, "Self-Report Scales
    of Hypnotic Depth," Int'l J.Clinical
    & Exper.Hypnosis 18 (1970):105-25.
    Charles T. Tart, "Concerning the
    Scientific Study of the Human Aura,"
    J.SPR 46 (1972):1-21.
    Charles T. Tart, "States of Conscious-
    ness and State-Specific Sciences,"
    Science 176 (1972):1203.
    James Grayson Bolen, "Interview:
    Charles T. Tart, Ph.D," Psychic 4
    (Feb.1973):6-11,27-29.
    Charles T. Tart, States of Conscious-
    ness (N.Y.: Dutton, 1975).
    Charles T. Tart, "Studies of Learn-
    ing Theory Application, 1964-1974,"
    Parapsych.Rev., vol.6, no.4 (1975).
    Charles T. Tart, Learning to Use
    Extra-Sensory Perception (Chicago:
    Univ. of Chicago, 1976).
    Charles T. Tart, "An ESP Card-Guess-
    ing Experiment," in J.D. Morris, et
    al., Research in Parapsychology 1976
    (Metuchen, N.J.: Scarecrow, 1977),
    pp.146-78.
    Charles T. Tart, Psi: Scientific
    Studies of the Psychic Realm (N.Y.:
    Dutton, 1977).
    Charles T. Tart, "Consideration of
    Internal Processes in Using Immed-
    iate Feedback to Teach ESP Ability,"
    in W.G. Roll, ed., Research in Para-
    psychology 1977 (Metuchen, N.J.:
    Scarecrow, 1978), pp.90-122.
    Charles T. Tart, "Space, Time and
    Mind," in W.G. Roll, ed., Research
    in Parapsychology 1977 (Metuchen,
    N.J.: Scarecrow, 1978), pp.197-249.
-UFO (NL)
  1896, Dec.4/George Little
    Marysville Semi-Weekly Appeal, 10
    Dec.1896.
  1975, Sep.5
    "UFO Central," CUFOS News Bull., 15
    Nov.1975, p.17.
  1975, Oct.16
    "UFO Central," CUFOS News Bull., 1
    Feb.1976, p.9.

Delano
-UFO (NL)
  1896, Nov.29
    Loren E. Gross, The UFO Wave of 1896
    (Fremont, Cal.: The Author, 1974),
    p.23.

Del Mar
-Archeological site
  46,000 B.C.
    San Diego Evening Tribune, 14-15 May
    1974; 12 July 1974; and 24 July
    1974.

New York Times, 15 May 1974, p.9; and
16 Aug.1976, p.33. il.
"San Diego's Senior Citizen," Pop.
Arch. 3 (July-Aug.1974):21. il.
-Sea monster
1910, March/Melville Pendleton
(Letter), Fate 18 (Apr.1965):117-18.

Del Rosa
-Fall of fish
1964, Nov.9/Allen Holmes
(Editorial), Fate 18 (Mar.1965):10.

Desert Center
-UFO (CE-3)
1952, Nov.20/George Adamski/10 mi.NE/
=hoax?
Phoenix (Ariz.) Gazette, 24 Nov.1952.
Desmond Leslie & George Adamski,
Flying Saucers Have Landed (N.Y.:
British Book Centre, 1953), pp.185-
215. il.
Leon Davidson, "Why I Believe Adam-
ski," Flying Saucers, Feb.1959, pp.
38-46.
Richard C. Ogden, "The Case for the
R.E. Straith Letter," Flying Sau-
cers, Dec.1959, pp.34-39,47.
Gray Barker, Gray Barker's Book of
Adamski (Clarksburg, W.V.: Saucer-
ian, 1967).
J. Allen Hynek & Jacques Vallee, The
Edge of Reality (Chicago: Regnery,
1975), pp.177-80.
Jerome Clark, "Startling New Evidence
in the Pascagoula and Adamski Ab-
ductions," Saga UFO Rept. 6 (Aug.
1978):36-39,70-78.
David Stupple, "The Man Who Talked
with Venusians," Fate 32 (Jan.1979):
30-39. il.

Desert Hot Springs
-Precognition
1972, fall/Saul Cotton
(Editorial), Fate 26 (May 1973):22-
24, quoting Nat'l Tattler (undated).
-UFO (DD)
1962, June 18/Byron Crawford/Angel
View Crippled Children's Hospital
(Editorial), Fate 15 (Oct.1962):10.

Dixon
-UFO (NL)
1896, Dec.4/Mr. Byrns
Marysville Semi-Weekly Appeal, 10
Dec.1896.
1957, Nov.5
Richard Hall, ed., The UFO Evidence
(Washington: NICAP, 1964), p.165.

Dos Rios
-UFO (DD)
1947, July 7/Mrs. Gus Garner
Sacramento Union, 8 July 1947.

Downey
-Burrowing hose
ca.1955/George DiPeso
Gray Barker, The Saucerian Review

(Clarksburg, W.V.: Saucerian, 1956),
pp.75-77. il.
-UFO (DD)
1951, May 29/Ed J. Sullivan
H.B. Darrach, Jr. & Robert Ginna,
"Have We Visitors from Space?" Life,
7 Apr.1952, pp.80,90.
1978, Jan.1
Ventura County and Harbor News, 20
Jan.1978.
-UFO (NL)
ca.1945/Mrs. J. Watson
(Letter), Can.UFO Rept., no.12 (1972)
:30.
1957, March 23/K.E. Jefferson
Richard Hall, ed., The UFO Evidence
(Washington: NICAP, 1964), p.85.

Dunsmuir
-UFO (NL)
1960, Aug.18
Richard Hall, ed., The UFO Evidence
(Washington: NICAP, 1964), p.170.

East Glendale
-UFO (DD)
1952, Nov.24
U.S. Air Force, Projects Grudge and
Blue Book Reports 1-12 (Washington:
NICAP, 1968), p.168.

East Los Angeles
-UFO (?)
1947, July 2/John Lewis Brown
Los Angeles Herald-Express, 9 July
1947.
-UFO (NL)
1947, July 6/Joseph Harris
Los Angeles News, 7 July 1947.
1973, Nov.12
Sergio Ortiz, "They're Flying over
Los Angeles, Too," Probe the Un-
known 2 (spring 1974):31. il.
Los Angeles Times, 14 Nov.1973.

East Palo Alto
-Phantom image
1973, July/Miracle Revival Fellowship
Church
Jim Brandon, Weird America (N.Y.:
Dutton, 1978), pp.39-40.

Edwards AFB
-Humanoid
1974, March
Peter Guttilla, "Bigfoot: Advance
Guard from Outer Space," Saga UFO
Rept. 4 (June 1977):22,50.
-Precognition
1965-1973/Arlene Adams
Steve Jacques, "Prophet of Disaster,"
Probe the Unknown 1 (Dec.1973):22-
25.
-UFO (?)
1949, Oct.31
"If It's in the Sky It's a Saucer,"
Doubt, no.27 (1949):416,417.
1962, May 1/Joseph Walker/X-15 flight
New York Times, 12 May 1962, p.50;
and 16 May 1962, p.35.

"X-15 Pilot Shows His Film," Flying
Saucer Rev. 8 (July-Aug.1962):3-4,
13.
John C. Ross, "UFOs and the Record
Flight of the X-15," Fate 15 (Aug.
1962):38-44.
1967, Sep.1
Edward U. Condon, ed., Scientific
Study of Unidentified Flying Ob-
jects (N.Y.: Bantam, 1969 ed.), pp.
341-42.
-UFO (CE-3)
1952/crashed UFO
Leonard H. Stringfield, "Retrievals
of the Third Kind," in 1978 MUFON
Symposium Proc. (Seguin, Tex.:
MUFON, 1978), pp.77,82-84.
-UFO (CE-4)
1960, May
Charles Berlitz, Without a Trace
(N.Y.: Ballantine, 1978 ed.), pp.
76-77.
-UFO (DD)
1947, July 8/Joseph C. McHenry
1947, July 8/J.C. Wise
1947, July 8/Richard R. Shoop/Rogers
Dry Lake
Edward J. Ruppelt, The Report on Un-
identified Flying Objects (Garden
City: Doubleday, 1956), pp.21-22.
Ted Bloecher, Report on the UFO Wave
of 1947 (Washington: NICAP, 1967),
p.III-4.
J. Allen Hynek, The Hynek UFO Report
(N.Y.: Dell, 1977), pp.95-98.
1952, Sep.30/Dick Beemer
Richard Hall, ed., The UFO Evidence
(Washington: NICAP, 1964), pp.57-58.
ca.1954/Martin B-57 photo
Ralph Rankow, "The Martin B-57 and
the Changing UFO," Fate 19 (Nov.
1966):36-45. il.
(Letter), Paul K. Stafford, Fate 20
(Mar.1967):140-46.
Robert A. Schmidt, "The Strange Case
of the B-57 Photographs," FSR Case
Histories, no.6 (Aug.1971):1-2. il.
1957, May 3/James Bittick
Los Angeles Times, 9 May 1957.
Brad Steiger, ed., Project Blue Book
(N.Y.: Ballantine, 1976), betw.pp.
360-61. il.
-UFO (NL)
1957, Nov.6
Donald E. Keyhoe, Flying Saucers: Top
Secret (N.Y.: Putnam, 1960), p.124.
-UFO (R-V)
1967, July 30
Gordon D. Thayer, "Optical and Radar
Analyses of Field Cases," in Edward
U. Condon, ed., Scientific Study of
Unidentified Flying Objects (N.Y.:
Bantam, 1969 ed.), p.122.

El Cajon
-Clairaudience
1954, July 28
Laura A. Dale, Rhea White & Gardner
Murphy, "A Selection of Cases from
a Recent Survey of Spontaneous ESP

Phenomena," J.ASPR 56 (1962):3,38-
40.
-Contactee
1954-   /Ruth Norman/145 S. Magnolia
Ernest L. Norman, The Voice of Venus
(Santa Barbara: Unarius-Science of
Life, 1956).
Ernest L. Norman, The Elysium (Glen-
dale: Unarius-Science of Life, 1956).
Ernest L. Norman, Voice of Eros
(Glendale: Unarius-Science of Life,
1958).
Ernest L. Norman, Voice of Hermes
(Glendale: Unarius-Science of Life,
1959).
Ernest L. Norman, Voice of Orion
(Santa Barbara: Unarius-Science of
Life, 1961).
Ernest L. Norman, Tempus Procedium
(Glendale: Unarius-Science of Life,
1965).
Ernest L. Norman, The Story of the
Little Red Box (Glendale: Unarius-
Science of Life, 1968).
Ruth Norman, Bridge to Heaven (Glen-
dale: Unarius, 1969).
Ruth Norman & Vaughn Spaegel, Con-
clave of Light Beings (El Cajon:
Unarius-Science of Life, 1973).
Brad Steiger, Gods of Aquarius (N.Y.:
Harcourt Brace Jovanovich, 1976),
pp.212-17.
Ruth Norman & Thomas Miller, Martian
Underground Cities Discovered! (El
Cajon: Unarius Educational Founda-
tion, 1977).
Ruth Norman, Your Encounter with
Life, Death and Immortality (El Ca-
jon: Unarius Educational Founda-
tion, 1978).
-Parapsychology research
1970s/Academy of Parapsychology, Heal-
ing & Psychic Sciences/Box 1042
(Letter), Dorothy Ellerman, Fate 26
(Aug.1973):129-30.
-UFO (CE-1)
1967, Nov.26/46 air mi.E
"More U.S.A. November Reports," APRO
Bull. 16 (Jan.-Feb.1968):6,7.
-UFO (CE-3)
1957, Dec./Edmund Rucker
Jacques Vallee, Passport to Magonia
(Chicago: Regnery, 1969), p.267,
quoting Flying Saucers, July 1958.

El Centro
-Automatic writing
1960s/Lee Baxter
David St. Clair, The Psychic World
of California (N.Y.: Bantam, 1973
ed.), pp.301-308.
-Phantom
1900s/Del W. Beach
(Letter), Fate 18 (Apr.1965):118,
128-29.
-UFO (?)
1950, April 7
Los Angeles Daily News, 7 Apr.1950.
-UFO (CE-1)
1973, Oct.5/W of town

R. Michael Rasmussen, "Two Interest-
ing California Cases," APRO Bull.
24 (Jan.1976):1,5.
-UFO (DD)
1952, May 13
U.S. Air Force, Projects Grudge and
Blue Book Reports 1-12 (Washington:
NICAP, 1968), p.125.

El Cerrito
-UFO (NL)
1957, May 15/Lou Brubaker
(Letter), Fate 10 (Nov.1957):115-16.

El Monte
-Medical clairvoyance
1950s/William V. King
Leon J. Ricks, "The Riddle of Aging,"
Fate 13 (July 1960):76-83.
-UFO (CE-1)
1975, Oct.5
"UFO Central," CUFOS News Bull., 1
Feb.1976, p.7.

El Segundo
-Earthquake luminescence
1949, July 10
"Quake and Glow," Doubt, no.27 (1949)
:418.

El Sobrante
-UFO (NL)
1963, March 11
Richard Hall, ed., The UFO Evidence
(Washington: NICAP, 1964), p.140.

El Toro
-UFO (?)
1953, Jan.28/Marine Air Station
(Editorial), Fate 6 (June 1953):12.

Emeryville
-Archeological site
Max Uhle, "The Emeryville Shellmound,"
Pub.Am.Arch. & Ethn.Univ.Calif. 7
(1907):1-106.
W. Egbert Schenck, "The Emeryville
Shellmound, Final Report," Pub.Am.
Arch. & Ethn.Univ.Calif. 23 (1926):
147-282. il.
-UFO (NL)
1953, Feb.13/A. Berta
John C. Ross, "Fate's Report on the
Flying Saucers," Fate 6 (Oct.1953):
6,8.

Encinitas
-Humanoid
1975/I-5
Peter Guttilla, "Monster Menagerie,"
Saga UFO Rept. 4 (Sep.1977):32,66.

Encino
-Paranormal voice recordings
1972-1976/William Addams Welch
William Welch, Talks with the Dead
(N.Y.: Pinnacle, 1975).
Susy Smith, Voices of the Dead? (N.Y.:
Signet, 1977), pp.54-66.

Escondido
-Dowsing
1865, fall
W.F. Barrett, "On the So-Called Divining Rod," Proc.SPR 15 (1900):130,
250.
-Inner development
1970s/Harmony Grove Spiritualist Ass'n
/Rt.5, Box 179
Armand Biteaux, The New Consciousness (Willits, Cal.: Oliver, 1975),
pp.56-57.
-Weather control
1951, Aug.26/Elsie Pusl
(Letter), Fate 8 (Nov.1955):124-26.

Eureka
-Dog mutilation
1958, Oct./Curtis Mitchell/Elk Creek
Rd.
Eureka Humboldt Times, 19 Oct.1958.
-Fall of weblike substance
1958, Nov.
"Falls," Doubt, no.60 (1959):58.
-Fall of white substance
1954, Dec./Mrs. John Semenoff/1624
Fourth St.
"Eureka," Doubt, no.48 (1955):341.
-Haunt
1969-   /Gary Brusca
(Editorial), Fate 26 (Apr.1973):32-
35, quoting San Francisco Examiner
and Chronicle (undated).
-UFO (NL)
1955, April 7
"Green Fireball Visits Oakland,"
CRIFO Newsl., 6 May 1955, p.2.
1956, Aug.30
"Case 203," CRIFO Orbit, 5 Oct.1956,
p.3, quoting New Orleans (La.) Times-
Picayune (undated).
1960, Aug.16
Richard Hall, ed., The UFO Evidence
(Washington: NICAP, 1964), p.170.
1976, Sep.16
"UFOs of Limited Merit," Int'l UFO
Reporter 1 (Nov.1976):5.

Exeter
-UFO (DD)
1968, Jan.10/Herbert Coffman
"Late 1967 Sightings," UFO Inv. 4
(Jan.-Feb.1968):6.

Fairfax
-Phantom panther
1975, March/Sir Francis Drake Blvd.
Loren Coleman, "California Odyssey:
Observations on the Western Para-
Panther," Anomaly Rsch.Bull., no.
23 (1978):5,6.

Fairfield
-UFO (?)
1934, Sep.27/John O'Brian/Jamerson Canyon
"Airplane Dodges Shower of 'Meteors,'"
INFO J., no.4 (spring 1969):37, quoting San Francisco newspaper (undated).

1954, Jan.27
  Donald E. Keyhoe, Flying Saucer Con-
    spiracy (N.Y.: Holt, 1955), p.110.
-UFO (CE-1)
  1975, July 16
    "UFO Central," CUFOS News Bull., 15
    Nov.1975, p.13.
-UFO (DD)
  1947, July 6/James H. Burniston/Travis
  AFB
    Ted Bloecher, Report on the UFO Wave
    of 1947 (Washington: NICAP, 1967),
    p.III-3.
-UFO (NL)
  1948, Dec.3/Travis AFB
    Donald E. Keyhoe, Flying Saucers Are
    Real (N.Y.: Fawcett, 1950), pp.79,158.

Fair Oaks
-Spirit medium
  1948-1950s/Benona Dieroff
    Benona Dieroff, "The Ouija Board and
    Mason Tomms," Fate 31 (Nov.1978):
    72-75.

Fallbrook
-Paraphysics research
  1970s/Derald Langham/4702 San Jacinto
  Terr.
    Serge V. King, "Neoenergy and Geomet-
    ric Forms," in John White & Stanley
    Krippner, eds., Future Science (Gar-
    den City, N.Y.: Anchor, 1977), pp.
    191,201,585.

Fall River Mills
-Humanoid
  1947, May 11/Russ Tribble/S of town
    John Green, The Sasquatch File (Ag-
    assiz, B.C.: Cheam, 1973), p.16.

Fallsvale
-UFO (DD)
  1957, July 13/J.A. Mitchek
    (Letter), Kay Sabin, Fate 11 (Feb.
    1958):116-17.

Fern Glade
-Humanoid tracks
  1969, July 3
    John Green, Year of the Sasquatch
    (Agassiz, B.C.: Cheam, 1970), p.45.

Fillmore
-UFO (NL)
  1978, Feb.22/Maria Rangel/Kenny Grove
  Park
    Fillmore Herald, 23 Feb.1978.

Folsom
-UFO (NL)
  1896, Nov.22
    Sacramento Record-Union, 23 Nov.1896.
  1960, Aug.17/Marion Hall
    John C. Ross, "State Cops Race 'Fly-
    ing Saucer,'" Fate 13 (Dec.1960):44,
    46.
    Richard Hall, ed., The UFO Evidence
    (Washington: NICAP, 1964), p.170.

Fontana
-UFO (?)
  1956, June 29-30/June Traugott
    "Report on First International Sau-
    cer Sighting Day," Flying Saucer
    Rev. 2 (July-Aug.1956):14,16.

Forbestown
-UFO (NL)
  1896, Nov.29
    Marysville Daily Democrat, 1 Dec.1896.

Foresthill
-UFO (NL)
  1973, Oct.30/Leonard A. Harris/Big Reservoir Campground
    Truckee Sierra Sun Bonanza, 7 Nov.
    1973.

Fort Bragg
-Clairvoyance
  1974, July 6/Carl Logan
    James Crenshaw, "Carl Logan's Psychic
    Radar," Fate 28 (May 1975):39-44.
-Humanoid
  1962, Feb./Bud Jenkins/Hwy.20
    John Green, Sasquatch: The Apes Among
    Us (Seattle: Hancock House, 1978),
    pp.14-16.
-UFO (DD)
  1947, July 8/Don Wisher
    San Rafael Independent, 10 July 1947.

Fort Irwin
-Seance
  1971, Jan.-June/Joi Smith
    Susy Smith, The Power of the Mind
    (Radnor, Pa.: Chilton, 1975), pp.
    216-20.

Fort Jones
-Weather control
  1959, Dec./Dick Pepper
    "Legend of the Siskiyou Rain Rock,"
    Fate 13 (July 1960):43.

Foster Park
-Spontaneous human combustion
  1965, March 26/Herbert Shinn/Camp Cha-
  fee Rd.
    (Editorial), Fate 18 (Sep.1965):29.

Fremont
-Phantom panther
  1973, Dec.19/Larry Rephahn/Niles Canyon
  Rd.
    Loren Coleman, "California Odyssey:
    Observations on the Western Para-
    Panther," Anomaly Rsch.Bull., no.23
    (1978):5,7-8.
-Poltergeist
  1960, Dec.30-1961, Jan./Richard Odom
    (Editorial), Fate 14 (June 1961):18-
    19.
-UFO (NL)
  1975, Nov.17
    "UFO Central," CUFOS News Bull., 1
    Feb.1976, p.13.
-UFO (R-V)
  1977, Sep.10/Oakland Air Traffic Control

Paul Cerny, "California Airline Sighting and Movie Film," MUFON UFO J., no.119 (Oct.1977):3.

Fresno
-Airship inventor
1896, Dec.6/George Jennings
San Francisco Call, 5 Dec.1896, p.2.
Fresno Semi-Weekly Expositor, 7 Dec. 1896.
-Burrowing hose
n.d./Jennie Betteridge
(Letter), Fate 5 (Sep.1952):128.
-Fall of ice
1956, Aug.7/N side
"Falls," Doubt, no.53 (1956):417, quoting Santa Monica Evening Outlook (undated).
-Ghost
1936, summer/Carmen Chaney/1818 Tyler St.
Joseph Kerska, "The Vanishing Lady," Fate 14 (Jan.1961):62-64.
-Haunt
1890s-1930s/St. John's Cathedral
Betty Lou White, "The Ghosts of Fresno," Fate 20 (Aug.1967):83-85, quoting Fresno Bee (undated).
-Hex
1973, Aug.-1974, June/Antonio Vega
Antonio Vega, "I Fought Off a Witch Attack," Fate 30 (Jan.1977):65-68.
-Inner development
1970s/Blavatsky Foundation/Box 1543
June & Nicholas Regush, Psi: The Other World Catalogue (N.Y.: Putnam, 1974), p.167.
-Poltergeist
n.d./E.H. Burdette
R. DeWitt Miller, Impossible: Yet It Happened (N.Y.: Ace, 1947 ed.), p. 57.
-UFO (?)
1948, Oct.12
"You Asked for It," Doubt, no.24 (1949):363.
-UFO (DD)
1949, May 11
"If It's in the Sky It's a Saucer," Doubt, no.27 (1949):416.
1954, March 24/Harold E. Talbott
"The Thunderhead of Recent Critical Developments," CRIFO Newsl., 4 June 1954, p.1.
(Letter), John P. Bessor, Fate 7 (Nov.1954):115-16.
1956, Aug.21
(Editorial), Fate 9 (Dec.1956):11-12.
-UFO (NL)
1896, Nov.25
Fresno Semi-Weekly Expositor, 30 Nov. 1896.
1977, May 11
"UFOs of Limited Interest," Int'l UFO Reporter 2 (June 1977):8.

Fullerton
-Ghost
1962, April/David Burkman
Hans Holzer, Ghosts of the Golden

West (N.Y.: Ace, 1968), pp.70-71.
-UFO (NL)
1965, Aug.11/Mrs. Jerry Schultz
Jerome Clark, "The Greatest Flap Yet?--Part 2," Flying Saucer Rev. 12 (Mar.-Apr.1966):9.

Galt
-UFO (NL)
1978, June 19/Lower Sacramento Rd.
Galt Herald, 22 June 1978.

Gardena
-Animal ESP
1960s/Fred Kimball
Gardena Valley News, 29 Sep.1963.
Idyllwild Town Crier, 11 Oct.1963.
Gina Cerminara, Many Lives, Many Loves (N.Y.: William Sloan, 1963).
David St. Clair, The Psychic World of California (N.Y.: Bantam, 1973 ed.), pp.284-90.
-Disappearance
1953, Nov.11/Karl Hunrath/airport
Curtis Fuller, "The Men Who Ride in Saucers," Fate 7 (May 1954):44,47, quoting Los Angeles Mirror (undated).

Garden Grove
-Inner development
1960s/Church of Tzaddi/11236 Dale
B. Ann Slate, "Your Daughters Shall Prophesy," Fate 23 (Aug.1970):68-78. il.
-Precognition
1975 /Zalithea de Racan
(Letter), Gayla St. Pierre, Fate 29 (Oct.1976):128.
1970s/Lawrence Ball/13934 Taft St.
Warren Smith, "Phenomenal Predictions for 1975," Saga, Jan.1975, p.20.
Warren Smith, "Phenomenal Predictions for 1976," Saga, Jan.1976, p.16.
-UFO (?)
1975, March 10/Rowine Arenson
(Letter), Saga UFO Rept. 2 (summer 1975):78.
-UFO (CE-1)
1959, Oct.12/Brian Scott
Alvin H. Lawson, "Hypnotic Regression of CE-III Cases: Ambiguities on the Road to UFOs," in Proc.1976 CUFOS Conference (Evanston: Center for UFO Studies, 1976), pp.141-51.
Peter Guttilla & James Frazier, "Alien Possession: Strange Saga of Brian Scott and the UFO Mind Manipulators," Saga UFO Rept. 4 (July 1977):42.
-UFO (CE-3)
1975, Nov.21, Dec.22/Brian Scott
Alvin H. Lawson, "Hypnotic Regression of CE-III Cases: Ambiguities on the Road to UFOs," in Proc.1976 CUFOS Conference (Evanston: Center for UFO Studies, 1976), pp.141-51.
Peter Guttilla & James Frazier, "Alien Possession: Strange Saga of Brian Scott and the UFO Mind Manipulators," Saga UFO Rept. 4 (July

1977):42-45,69-75. il.
-UFO (DD)
  1958/Jack Swaney
    (Letter), Fate 27 (June 1974):160-61.
-UFO(NL)
  1975, Nov.12
    "UFO Central," CUFOS News Bull., 1
    Feb.1976, p.12.

Garlock
-Humanoid tracks
  1976, Feb./Jacques Vallee/Sand Gulch
    B. Ann Slate, "California's Time Tun-
    nel," Saga UFO Rept. 4 (May 1977):
    36,61.
-UFO (NL)
  1975, Feb.17/Ray Evans
    B. Ann Slate, "California's Time Tun-
    nel," Saga UFO Rept. 4 (May 1977):
    36.

Georgetown
-Ghost
  1928, summer/Etna Elliott
    Etna Elliott, "Ghost Soldier in Our
    Attic," Fate 12 (Feb.1959):39-43.
-UFO (NL)
  1972, Sep./Harold J. Whitcomb/SE of
  town
    "Family Reports UFOs," APRO Bull. 21
    (Sep.-Oct.1972):8-9.

Gilroy
-Ball lightning
  1952, March 6/Estelle Martin
    Marian Kirkpatrick, "California Mys-
    tery Blasts," Fate 10 (Apr.1957):
    86,89, quoting AP release, 7 Mar.
    1952.
-UFO (CE-1)
  1975, Aug.18/Tina Garza
    Timothy Beckley & Harold Salkin,
    "UFOs Spotted along California's
    Earthquake Lines," Saga UFO Rept.
    3 (Dec.1976):44,72, quoting Hollis-
    ter Free Lance (undated).
-UFO (CE-2)
  1975, March 13/Ronda Ridge
    Gilroy Dispatch, 21 Mar.1975.
  1975, Aug.10/Terri Smith/El Toro St.
    "Gilroy, CA, Sightings Reported,"
    Skylook, no.94 (Sep.1975):6-7, quot-
    ing Gilroy Dispatch (undated).
-UFO (DD)
  1975, Aug.11/Terri Smith/Las Animas
  Park
    "Gilroy, CA, Sightings Reported,"
    Skylook, no.94 (Sep.1975):6,7, quot-
    ing Gilroy Dispatch (undated).
-UFO (NL)
  1975, Aug.12/Robert Bluemmer/Gavilan
  College
  1975, Aug.12/Glenview School
    "Gilroy, CA, Sightings Reported,"
    Skylook, no.94 (Sep.1975):6,7, quot-
    ing Gilroy Dispatch (undated).
    Timothy Beckley & Harold Salkin,
    "UFOs Spotted along California's
    Earthquake Lines," Saga UFO Rept.
    3 (Dec.1976):44,47,70.

1975, Oct.26
    "UFO Central," CUFOS News Bull., 1
    Feb.1976, p.9.

Glendale
-Contactee
  1967
    John A. Keel, "The Glendale, Califor-
    nia, Contact Claim," in Beyond Con-
    don (Flying Saucer Rev. special
    issue no.2, June 1969):63-65.
-Eyeless vision
  1936-1937/Pat Marquis/=trickery
    Los Angeles Times, 3 May 1936. il.
    "Pat Marquis of California Can See
    Without His Eyes," Life, 19 Apr.
    1937, pp.57-59. il.
    "The 'Paroptic' Illusion," Parapsych.
    Bull., no.66 (Aug.1963):2-4.
-Ghost
  n.d./Mrs. B.E. Weber
    (Letter), Fate 6 (Oct.1953):114-16.
-Haunt
  1959, spring-1961/Louise Hudson
    Alden Campbell, "My Musical Ghost,"
    Fate 24 (Nov.1971):94-99.
-UFO (?)
  1977, Jan.28-Feb.1/Sparr Blvd./=balloon
    Ann Druffel, "Are There Mimicking
    UFOs? Part 2," MUFON UFO J., no.
    113 (Apr.1977):9-10.
-UFO (DD)
  1947, July 5/Donald Dwiggins
    Glendale News-Press, 5 July 1947.
-UFO (NL)
  1973, April 3
    Ann Druffel, "The Los Angeles Basin
    Sightings," FSR Case Histories, no.
    15 (June 1973):7.
  1974, April 12/James F. Clinker/Foot-
  hill Blvd.
    "Strange Light in Sky Drops Orange
    Stream," Skylook, no.78 (May 1974):
    18.
  1975, Dec.31
    "Noteworthy UFO Sightings," Ufology
    2 (spring 1976):42.
  1976, Jan.2
    "Noteworthy UFO Sightings," Ufology
    2 (summer 1976):62.
  1977, Feb.1/Richard Quinn/Glorietta x
  Canada St.
    Ann Druffel, "UFO Sighted from Police
    Helicopter," MUFON UFO J., no.111
    (Feb.1977):13-15. il.
    "UFOs of Limited Merit," Int'l UFO
    Reporter 2 (Mar.1977):8.

Glendora
-Clairempathy
  1960s-   /Dorothy Spence Lauer/Box 637
    Brad Steiger, "Scoring the Seers in
    1969," Fate 23 (Jan.1970):66,69.
    Warren Smith, "Phenomenal Predictions
    for 1975," Saga, Jan.1975, pp.20,50.
    Warren Smith, "Phenomenal Predictions
    for 1976," Saga, Jan.1976, pp.16,19.
    "Probe's 1977 Directory of the Psych-
    ic World," Probe the Unknown 5
    (spring 1977):32,37.

-Fall of ice
  1959, April?/William Bower
    (Editorial), Fate 12 (Aug.1959):6-8.
-UFO (?)
  1957, Jan.27
    Glendora Press, 31 Jan.1957.
-UFO (CE-1)
  1975, Jan.6/Lisa Ramirez
    Robert A. Goerman, "The UFO Modus Op-
    erandi: January 1975," Official UFO
    1 (Aug.1976):46,64.

Glenn
-UFO (CE-1)
  1963, July 25/Margaret Pattison
    (Letter), Fate 30 (Aug.1977):118-19.
-UFO (NL)
  1976, Sep.23/Margaret Pattison
    (Letter), Fate 30 (Aug.1977):118-19.

Goleta
-Precognition
  1960, May/Rena M. Kelley
    (Editorial), Fate 13 (Sep.1960):23-
    24.
-UFO (DD)
  1956, Aug.23/Douglas Horlander
    Torrance Press, 24 Aug.1956.

Grand Terrace
-Fall of ice
  1968, June 14/Mrs. Douglas Bailey/22950
    Terrace Rd.
    (Editorial), Fate 21 (Oct.1968):7-8.

Grass Valley
-Skyquake
  1951, Dec.30
    Marion Kirkpatrick, "California Mys-
    tery Blasts," Fate 10 (Apr.1957):87.

Greenville
-Precognition
  n.d./Mrs. Ralph E. Freeman/district
  hospital
    (Editorial), Fate 16 (June 1963):25.

Hanford
-UFO (?)
  1896, Nov.24/Will Matthewson/=balloon?
    Fresno Semi-Weekly Expositor, 30 Nov.
    1896.

Happy Camp
-Humanoid
  1885/Jack Dover
    L.W. Musick, The Hermit of Siskiyou
    (Crescent City, Cal.: The News,
    1896), pp.79-80, quoting Del Norte
    Record, 2 Jan.1886.
  ca.1959
    Ivan T. Sanderson, Abominable Snow-
    men: Legend Come to Life (Philadel-
    phia: Chilton, 1961), pp.146-47.
-Humanoid (carcass)
  1967
    John Green, Sasquatch: The Apes Among
    Us (Seattle: Hancock House, 1978),
    pp.373-74.
-UFO (CE-3)

  1975, Oct.25-26/Steve Harris/The Saddle
    Alan Berry, "The UFO Creatures of
    Happy Camp," Official UFO 2 (May
    1977):14-16,48-49.
    Paul Cerny, "The Happy Camp, Califor-
    nia Sightings," MUFON UFO J., no.
    121 (Dec.1977):18-20; no.122 (Jan.
    1978):10-13.

Harbor City
-UFO (DD)
  1976, April 21/nr. San Diego Freeway
    "Sighting Reports," CUFOS News Bull.,
    Sep.1976, p.5.

Hawkins Bar
-Humanoid
  1971, Oct.14
    Peter Guttilla, "Monster Menagerie,"
    Saga UFO Rept. 4 (Sep.1977):32-34.

Hawthorne
-Fall of earthworms
  1879, winter
    Henry Winfred Splitter, "Wonders
    from the Sky," Fate 6 (Oct.1953):
    33,35.
-Inner development
  1970s/Martha Adler/4501 W. 141st St.
    Hans Holzer, The Witchcraft Report
    (N.Y.: Ace, 1973), pp.116-19.
-UFO (?)
  1950, March 11/Bette Malles/=lens flare
    Los Angeles Times, 12 Mar.1950.
    Kenneth Arnold & Ray Palmer, The Com-
    ing of the Saucers (Boise: The Au-
    thors, 1952), p.183. il.
-UFO (NL)
  1968, July 9
    Ann Druffel, "Santa Catalina Channel
    'Cloud-Cigars,'" in Proc.1976 CUFOS
    Conference (Evanston: Center for
    UFO Studies, 1976), pp.62-74.

Hayward
-Airship inventor
  1896, Nov./W.H. Warren
    San Francisco Chronicle, 29 Nov.1896,
    p.28.
-Fall of metallic objects
  1957, April
    San Leandro Morning News, 17 Apr.1957.
    "Falls," Doubt, no.57 (1958):4,6.
-Precognition
  1952, Aug.22/Frances P. Moore
    Frances P. Moore, "My Earthquake War-
    ning," Fate 8 (July 1955):38-41.
-UFO (?)
  1966, Jan.1/David Koller/airport
    Jerome Clark, "The Greatest Flap Yet?
    --Part IV," Flying Saucer Rev. 12
    (Nov.-Dec.1966):9,12.
  1970, Jan.10
    "Mysterious Flare Lights California
    Sky," Skylook, no.28 (Mar.1970):10,
    quoting Oakland Tribune (undated).
  1978, Jan.5
    Hayward Daily Review, 10 Jan.1978;
    and 13 Jan.1978.
-UFO (CE-3)

1896, Nov.22/Edward Davis/Cowen Ridge
San Francisco Chronicle, 24 Nov.1896,
p.10.
-UFO (DD)
1971, Feb.28/Michel M. Jaffe/Hwy.17
Michel M. Jaffe, "Personal Observation While Motor Cycling in California," FSR Case Histories, no.5 (June
1971):11-12. il.
-UFO (NL)
1896, Nov.22/B. Taffeimire
San Francisco Chronicle, 24 Nov.1896,
p.10.
1896, Nov.25/Mr. Webb
Hayward Journal, 26 Nov.1896.

Healdsburg
-UFO (CE-2)
1958, March 14
Jacques Vallee, Passport to Magonia
(Chicago: Regnery, 1969), p.270.
1966, Aug.20/Otto Becker
Jacques Vallee, Passport to Magonia
(Chicago: Regnery, 1969), pp.334-
35, quoting NICAP Reporter, Jan.
1967.
-UFO (NL)
1960, Aug.17
Richard Hall, ed., The UFO Evidence
(Washington: NICAP, 1964), p.170.

Hemet
-Precognition
1976/John Manolesco/121 N. Harvard
"Probe's 1977 Directory of the Psychic World," Probe the Unknown 5
(spring 1977):32,37. il.
-UFO (CE-1)
1953, Aug.25/nr. Coyote Pass
Harold T. Wilkins, Flying Saucers on
the Attack (N.Y.: Ace, 1967 ed.),
p.215.

Hermosa Beach
-Entombed crab
1951, Feb.10
"Run of the Mill," Doubt, no.33
(1951):91.
-Inner development
1970s/Gloria Ortega
Hans Holzer, The New Pagans (Garden
City: Doubleday, 1972), pp.42-47.

Hesperia
-Dowsing
1954, Oct./Jerry Smith
Gaston Burridge, "A Dowser Named
Smith," Fate 12 (Nov.1959):41,44.

Hessel
-UFO (CE-1)
1967, April 1/Donald O. Ameral
"Worldwide Sightings Showing Increase," UFO Inv. 4 (Oct.1967):1,3.

Highland
-UFO (NL)
1973, Oct.25
San Bernardino Evening Telegram, 26
Oct.1973.

Highway City
-UFO (NL)
1956, July 22/Mrs. Ray Brown
"Saucer Sightings Mount As Mars
Swings Close," CRIFO Orbit, 7 Sep.
1956, p.1, quoting Los Angeles Evening Herald-Express (undated).

Hillsborough
-Fall of metallic object
1957, Nov.9/Ralph N. Jacobsen
"Metal Object from Skies Rushed to
ATIC for Analysis," UFO Inv. 1 (Jan.
1958):5,6.
"All About Sputs," Doubt, no.56
(1958):460,474, quoting San Mateo
Times (undated).
-Poltergeist
1960, Nov./Mrs. Ernest Schwartz/85
Country Club Dr.
(Editorial), Fate 14 (Apr.1961):16.

Hollister
-Earthquake luminescence
1961/Reese Dooley
John S. Derr, "Earthquake Lights: A
Review of Observations and Present
Theories," Bull.Seism.Soc'y Am. 63
(1973):2177-87.
John S. Derr, "Earthquake Lights,"
Earthquake Information Bull. 9 (May-
June 1977):19.
-Geomagnetic anomaly
1974, Nov.28
B.E. Smith & M.J.S. Johnston, "A Tec-
tomagnetic Effect Observed Before a
Magnitude 5.2 Earthquake near Hol-
lister, California," J. Geophys.
Rsch. 81 (1976):3556-60.
C.E. Mortensen & M.J.S. Johnston,
"Anomalous Tilt Preceding the Hol-
lister Earthquake of November 28,
1974," J.Geophys.Rsch. 81 (1976):
3561-66.
J.C. Savage, M.A. Spieth & W.H. Prescott, "Preseismic and Coseismic Deformation Associated with the Hollister, California, Earthquake of
November 28, 1974," J.Geophys.Rsch.
81 (1976):3567-74.

Hollywood
-Astrology
1939-1970s/Carroll Righter/Hollywood
Hills
John Godwin, Occult America (Garden
City: Doubleday, 1972), pp.6-7.
David St. Clair, The Psychic World
of California (N.Y.: Bantam, 1973
ed.), pp.180-86.
1940s-   /Sidney Omarr
Sidney Omarr, My World of Astrology
(N.Y.: Fleet, 1965).
John Godwin, Occult America (Garden
City: Doubleday, 1972), pp.9-11.
David St. Clair, The Psychic World
of California (N.Y.: Bantam, 1973
ed.), pp.186-87.
Norma Lee Browning, Omarr: Astrology
and the Man (N.Y.: Signet, 1977).

-Automatic writing
   1960s-   /Wanda Sue Parrott
      Wanda Parrott, "Margaret Saw Me,"
      Fate 17 (Aug.1964):59-60. il.
      David St. Clair, The Psychic World
      of California (N.Y.: Bantam, 1973
      ed.), pp.223-28.
      Brad Steiger, Gods of Aquarius (N.Y.:
      Harcourt Brace Jovanovich, 1976),
      pp.78-81.
-Bilocation
   1941, Nov.27/Harry J. Loose/Canterbury
   Apts.
      Harold M. Sherman, You Live After
      Death (N.Y.: Merit, 1949), pp.55-73.
-Cartomancy
   1970s/Diana the Enchantress
      "Probe's 1977 Directory of the Psy-
      chic World," Probe the Unknown 5
      (spring 1977):35-36. il.
-Contactee
   1956, Nov.
      Los Angeles Herald and Express, 8
      Nov.1956.
-Crisis apparition
   1920s/Pola Negri
      Patrick Mahoney, Escape into the Psy-
      chic Kingdom (Hollywood: The Author,
      1975).
   1940/Sara Allgood
      Patrick Mahoney, "A Gift from the
      Grave," Fate 31 (Jan.1978):64-65.
-Electromagnetic anomaly
   1947/MacDonald Carey
      "Radio Teeth," Doubt, no.20 (1948):
      305.
-Fall of ice
   1968, April 25/Bert Martin
      (Editorial), Fate 21 (Oct.1968):7.
-Ghost
   1974, fall/Mae West
      Brenda Shaw, "A Dead Man Shocked Mae
      West," Fate 30 (Apr.1977):38-42.
-Healing
   1953-1960s/Harry Douglas Smith/Church
   of Life
      Harry Douglas Smith, The Secret of
      Instantaneous Healing (W. Nyack,
      N.Y.: Parker, 1965).
   1970s/Holistic Health Center
      Sandra McNeil, "Psychic Medicine: The
      New Frontier," Probe the Unknown 5
      (spring 1977):13-16.
-Inner development
   1955-   /Aetherius Society/6202 Afton
   Pl.
      Anon., The Story of the Aetherius
      Society (Los Angeles: Aetherius
      Soc'y, n.d.).
      Fred Archer, Exploring the Psychic
      World (N.Y.: Paperback Library, 1968
      ed.), pp.119-24.
      John Godwin, Occult America (Garden
      City: Doubleday, 1972), pp.216-21.
      Roy Wallis, "The Aetherius Society:
      A Case Study in the Formation of a
      Mystagogic Congregation," Sociolog-
      ical Rev. 22 (1974):27-44.
   1970s/Int'l New Thought Alliance/6922
   Hollywood Blvd., no.811

Armand Biteaux, The New Conscious-
      ness (Willits, Cal.: Oliver, 1975),
      pp.79-80.
   1970s/National Academy of Applied Awareness
      Ava Gutierrez-O'Neill, "Leagh Caver-
      hill's National Academy for Applied
      Awareness," Occult, Jan.1976, pp.
      62-65,79-82.
-Mystery explosion
   1963, spring/Bertha Fink/1503 Shenandoah St./=whirlwind
      (Editorial), Fate 16 (Aug.1963):13-
      14.
      (Letter), Raymond Bayless, Fate 16
      (Dec.1963):132-34.
-Palmistry
   1930-1936/Cheiro (Count Louis Hamon)/
   Los Feliz Blvd.
      Norman L. Boerman, "Mysterious Chei-
      ro," Fate 11 (Jan.1958):80-85. il.
      (Letter), Paula Andree, Fate 13 (Dec.
      1960):110-14.
      (Letter), Anon., Fate 14 (May 1961):
      121-22.
      Patrick Mahoney, "Cheiro: A Modern
      Prophet," Psychic 4 (Sep.1972):34-
      39. il.
-Paranormal voice recordings and spirit
   medium
   1950s-   /Attila von Szalay
      Raymond Bayless, "Attila von Szalay,
      Investigator of the Invisible,"
      Fate 7 (Jan.1954):92-100. il.
      (Letter), Raymond Bayless, J.ASPR
      53 (1959):35-38.
      D. Scott Rogo, "A Report on Two Con-
      trolled Sittings with Attila von
      Szalay," J.Paraphysics 4 (1970):13.
      Richard Webb, Voices from Another
      World (N.Y.: Manor, 1972 ed.), pp.
      231-41.
      (Letter), Raymond Bayless, Fate 25
      (Oct.1972):142-43.
      D. Scott Rogo, An Experience of Phan-
      toms (N.Y.: Dell, 1976 ed.), pp.
      72-74,87-95.
      Raymond Bayless, "Some Early Experi-
      ments in Tape-Recording Paranormal
      Voices," Fate 27 (June 1974):102-107.
      William Welch, Talks with the Dead
      (N.Y.: Pinnacle, 1975).
      Susy Smith, The Power of the Mind
      (Radnor, Pa.: Chilton, 1975), pp.
      250-55.
      (Letter), Raymond Bayless, Fate 28
      (May 1975):113.
      D. Scott Rogo, In Search of the Un-
      known (N.Y.: Taplinger, 1976).
      D. Scott Rogo, The Haunted Universe
      (N.Y.: Signet, 1977), pp.16-17,70.
      D. Scott Rogo, "Paranormal Tape-Re-
      corded Voices: A Paraphysical Break-
      through," in John White & Stanley
      Krippner, eds., Future Science (Gar-
      den City, N.Y.: Anchor, 1977), pp.
      451-64.
-Precognition
   1940s-   /Jeron King Criswell
      Jeron King Criswell, "Criswell Pre-

dicts for 1949," Fate 1 (winter 1949):85-91.

Jeron King Criswell, "Criswell Predicts," Fate 2 (July 1949):71-77.

Jeron King Criswell, "Criswell Predicts," Fate 4 (Mar.1951):69-73.

J.K. Criswell, Criswell Predicts to the Year Two-Thousand (Anderson, S.C.: Droke House, 1968).

J.K. Criswell, Your Next Ten Years (Anderson, S.C.: Droke House, 1969).

J.K. Criswell, "Criswell Predicts Your Next Ten Years," Saga, Nov. 1969, pp.22-25,72-76.

David Wallechinsky & Irving Wallace, The People's Almanac (Garden City: Doubleday, 1975), pp.2-4.

1947/Dorothy Debiss/Romaine St.
Dorothy Debiss, "Preview of Murder," Fate 9 (May 1956):27.

1954/Mara Corday
(Editorial), Fate 8 (Apr.1955):14.

1957-1960/Mrs. Stanton Pritchard
(Editorial), Fate 14 (Apr.1961):20-21.

1970s/Charo
Timothy Green Beckley, "Charo Keeps in Touch," Fate 29 (Dec.1976):78-80.

1970s/Katharine Kimbrough/Box 1091
Warren Smith, "Phenomenal Predictions for 1975," Saga, Jan.1975, pp.20,48.

Warren Smith, "Phenomenal Predictions for 1976," Saga, Jan.1976, pp.16,19.

1970s/Sandra McNeil/2071 Vista del Mar Ave.
Richard De A'Morelli & Rita West, "Top Seers Predict Your Future for 1977," Psychic World, Jan.1977, pp. 51,53.

"Probe's 1977 Directory of the Psychic World," Probe the Unknown 5 (spring 1977):32,60. il.

-Psychic photography
1964, April 18/Ardmore Blvd.
Hans Holzer, Psychic Photography (N.Y.: McGraw-Hill, 1969), pp.71-74.

-Psychokinesis and contactee
1973-   /Uri Geller
"The Magician and the Think Tank," Time, 12 Mar.1973, p.110.

"Interview: Uri Geller," Psychic 4 (July 1973):1-12.

Alan Vaughan, "The Phenomena of Uri Geller," Psychic 4 (July 1973):13-18. il.

Gordon Creighton, "Uri Geller, the Man Who Bends Science," Flying Saucer Rev. 19 (Sep.-Oct.1973):8-11.

Ray Stanford, "Teleporting a Meteorite," Psychic 5 (Oct.1973):41-43,55.

James Crenshaw, "Uri Geller: Space-Age Magician," Fate 26 (Dec.1973): 38-49; 27 (Jan.1974):78-89; (Feb. 1974):49-59. il.

Andrija Puharich, Uri (Garden City: Doubleday, 1974).

W.E. Cox, "Notes on Some Experiments with Uri Geller," J.Parapsych. 38 (1974):4-8-11.

A.R.G. Owen, "Uri Geller's Mental Phenomena: An Eyewitness Account," New Horizons 1, no.4 (1974):164-71.

Jack Sarfatti, "Geller Performs for Physicists," Science 106 (1974):46.

Andrew Weil, "Andrew Weil's Search for the True Geller," Psych.Today 8 (June 1974):45-50; (July 1974): 74-78,82.

Charles Reynolds, "The Making of a Psychic," Pop.Photog. 75 (June 1974) :74,76,136. il.

Yale Joel, "Uri Through the Lens Cap," Pop.Photog. 75 (June 1974): 75,77,135. il.

Joseph Hanlon, "Uri Geller and Science," New Scientist 64 (1974):170-85. il.

Russell Targ & Harold Puthoff, "Information Transmission Under Conditions of Sensory Shielding," Nature 251 (1974):602-607.

Jeffrey Mishlove, The Roots of Consciousness (N.Y.: Random House, 1974), pp.165-68,200-204. il.

Uri Geller, My Story (N.Y.: Praeger, 1975). il.

John Taylor, Superminds (N.Y.: Viking, 1975).

Martin Ebon, ed., The Amazing Uri Geller (N.Y.: Signet, 1975).

James Randi, The Magic of Uri Geller (N.Y.: Ballantine, 1975).

John L. Wilhelm, The Search for Superman (N.Y.: Pocket, 1976).

Charles Panati, ed., The Geller Papers (N.Y.: Houghton Mifflin, 1976).

Jacques Vallee, "Some Personal Observations of Uri Geller," Flying Saucer Rev. 21 (Feb.1976):12-13,16.

Martin Gardner, "Magic and Paraphysics," Technology Rev. 78 (June 1976) :43-51. il.

J.L. Hickman, "A High-Voltage Photography Experiment with Uri Geller," in J.D. Morris, et al., eds., Research in Parapsychology 1976 (Metuchen, N.J.: Scarecrow, 1977), pp. 15-18.

Howard Smukler, "A Mass Public Experiment in Psychokinesis and Telepathy at a Distance with Uri Geller As Agent," J.Occult Studies 1 (May 1977):3-30.

James Crenshaw, "Uri Geller vs. the Critics," Fate 31 (Feb.1978):74-79; (Mar.1978):67-70.

-Radionics
1918-1963/Ruth B. Drown/La Brae Ave.
Ruth B. Drown, The Theory and Technique of the Drown H.V.R. and Radiovision Instruments (Los Angeles: Artists Press, 1939).

J. Cecil Maby, "The Drown Method of Medical Diagnosis and Therapy," Psychic Science, vol.23, no.4 (Jan. 1945).

"The Drown Technic Fails," J.Am.Med. Ass'n 142 (1950):506-507.

Edward Wriothesley Russell, Report on Radionics (London: Spearman,

1973), pp.76-87.
Trevor James Constable, The Cosmic
Pulse of Life (Santa Ana: Merlin,
1976), pp.236-55.
-Seance
1969, fall/Sal Mineo
"A Spirit's Indelible Signature,"
Fate 24 (Mar.1970):50.
-Spirit medium
1938-1946/Arthur Ford
Allen Spraggett, Arthur Ford: The Man
Who Talked with the Dead (N.Y.: Sig-
net, 1974 ed.), pp.111,198-203.
1940s-   /Mae West
David St. Clair, The Psychic World
of California (N.Y.: Bantam, 1973
ed.), pp.280-83.
Mae West, Mae West on Sex, Health,
and ESP (London: W.H. Allen, 1975).
1955-   /Brenda Crenshaw
James Crenshaw, "I Taped a Dead Man's
Voice," Fate 15 (June 1962):36-41.
David St. Clair, The Psychic World
of California (N.Y.: Bantam, 1973
ed.), pp.198-205.
-Telepathy
1960, Jan.18/Harold Sherman
Harold M. Sherman, "My Hollywood ESP
Tests," Fate 17 (Aug.1964):78-84.
-UFO (DD)
1947, July 5/E.L. Freeman/3138 Shef-
field Ave.
Los Angeles Citizen-News, 5 July 1947.
1947, July 7/Ralph Whitmore
1947, July 8/Sheldon Lowenkopf/603 S.
Charleston Way
Los Angeles Examiner, 8-9 July 1947.
1953, Jan.17/Alson Secor
(Letter), Fate 6 (July 1953):106-109.
-UFO (NL)
1954, March 6/James McNamara/Pan Paci-
fic Auditorium
R. DeWitt Miller, Stranger Than Life
(N.Y.: Ace, 1955 ed.), p.99.
1960, Aug.13
Richard Hall, ed., The UFO Evidence
(Washington: NICAP, 1964), p.170.
1972, Sep.20/Paul T. Collins
(Letter), Fate 27 (June 1974):159.
1973, April 1
Ann Druffel, "The Los Angeles Basin
Sightings," FSR Case Histories, no.
15 (June 1973):7.
1977, Aug.12
Ann Druffel, "Other Encounters of All
Different Kinds," MUFON UFO J., no.
123 (Feb.1978):15,17.

Homewood
-UFO (?)
1947, July 6?/Jay Hall
Sacramento Union, 9 July 1947.

Honeydew
-UFO (NL)
1960, Aug.18
Richard Hall, ed., The UFO Evidence
(Washington: NICAP, 1964), p.170.

Hoopa
-Humanoid
1963, Aug.3
John Green, The Sasquatch File (Agassiz, B.C.: Cheam, 1973), p.30.

Hoopa Valley Indian Reservation
-Humanoid
n.d.
Ivan T. Sanderson, Abominable Snowmen: Legend Come to Life (Philadelphia: Chilton, 1961), p.133.
1960/Leroy Doolittle
John Green, The Sasquatch File (Agassiz, B.C.: Cheam, 1973), p.23.
1963, July/Mr. Peters
Eureka Humboldt Times, 20 July 1963.
1975, May
B. Ann Slate & Alan Berry, Bigfoot
(N.Y.: Bantam, 1976), pp.58-59.

Hornbrook
-Mystery stone spheres
1950/Joseph Wales/=geodes
"Mysterious Monoliths," Fate 3 (May
1950):27. il.
"Stone Spheres--Part 2," Pursuit 1
(30 Sep.1968):13-15.

Huntingdon Beach
-Inner development
1970s/Cassandra Salem
Hans Holzer, The Witchcraft Report
(N.Y.: Ace, 1973), pp.120-23.
-Mystery flotsam
1967, April 16/Louis Duenweg
(Editorial), Fate 21 (Jan.1968):27-
28.
-UFO (NL)
1978, Feb.5/Adams Ave.
Costa Mesa Daily Pilot, 9 Feb.1978.

Huntingdon Park
-UFO (NL)
1947, July 2/Elsie Brooks
Los Angeles Times, 4 July 1947.

Hyampom
-Humanoid
1970, April/Buzz McLaughlin
John Green, The Sasquatch File (Agassiz, B.C.: Cheam, 1973), p.56,
quoting Bigfoot Bull. (undated).
-Humanoid tracks
1963, April/Bob Titmus
John Green, On the Track of the Sasquatch (Agassiz, B.C.: Cheam, 1968),
pp.29,33,34,37. il.
1963, May/Sylvester McCoy
1963, fall
John Green, The Sasquatch File (Agassiz, B.C.: Cheam, 1973), p.30.

Idyllwild
-UFO (DD)
1950, March 22/Bill Elder
Los Angeles Daily News, 23 Mar.1950.
Gerald Heard, The Riddle of the Flying Saucers (London: Carroll & Nicholson, 1950), pp.72-73.

Imperial
-Spanish galleon
1907, summer/Elmer L. Carver/6 mi.E
(Letter), H.S. McCaulley, Adventure,
July 1934.
Harold O. Weight, "A Desert Ship That
Wasn't Lost," Westways 56 (May 1964)
:32-33.
Harold O. Weight, "He Saw the Lost
Desert Ship," Westways 57 (Nov.1965)
:11-13.
-UFO (CE-1)
1905, Aug.2-3/J.A. Jackson
Brawley News, 4 Aug.1905.
-UFO (DD)
1905, Aug./Mr. Reid
Brawley News, 4 Aug.1905.
-UFO (NL)
1905, Aug./Mr. Jones
Brawley News, 4 Aug.1905.

Imperial Beach
-UFO (?)
1952, Nov.16
U.S. Air Force, Projects Grudge and
Blue Book Reports 1-12 (Washington:
NICAP, 1968), p.165.
-UFO (CE-2)
1952, Feb.24/Elmer Kiepert
(Editorial), Fate 5 (Sep.1952):6.
-UFO (DD)
1959, Feb.9/James M. Purdon, Jr.
Richard Hall, ed., The UFO Evidence
(Washington: NICAP, 1964), pp.92-93.

Indio
-Fire anomaly
1966, Jan.4/J.W. Clarke/Southern Pacific RR depot
(Editorial), Fate 20 (Mar.1967):30-
31.
-Healing
ca.1971/Christina Bowlman
David St. Clair, The Psychic World
of California (N.Y.: Bantam, 1973
ed.), pp.308-309.
-Spanish galleon
1882/Tom Brown/40 mi.E
Vincent H. Gaddis, "Ships That Sailed
the Desert," Fate 26 (Jan.1973):63,
65.
-UFO (CE-4)
1896, Dec.3/William Godon/=hoax?
San Francisco Call, 5 Dec.1896, p.2.
-UFO (NL)
1978, Oct.3/Mike Atkins/Nat'l Date Festival Fairgrounds
Indio Daily News, 3 Oct.1978.

Inglenook
-UFO (NL)
1975, Jan.17/Glenn Beck
Robert A. Goerman, "The UFO Modus Operandi: January 1975," Official UFO
1 (Aug.1976):46,65.

Inglewood
-Haunt
n.d.
Barry Taff, "Stalking the Elusive

Spectre," Probe the Unknown 1 (Oct.
1973):30,35-36. il.
1966, July-1967/nr.Hollywood Park Racetrack
Gladys Roberts, "Four Families Share
a Cowboy Ghost," Fate 25 (July 1972)
:53-58.
-Spirit medium
1953-1954/Harold D. Kinney
(Letter), Fate 7 (Aug.1954):114-16.
-UFO (NL)
1956, fall
(Letter), J.N., Fate 12 (Feb.1959):
126.
1972, Jan.12/Paul Whalley
Hayden C. Hewes, "The UFO 'Raid' That
Sparked a White House Alert," Saga's
1973 UFO Special, pp.8,66.
-Yoga
1932, July 25/Roman Ostoja/=buried
alive
Attila von Sealay & Sophia Williams,
"Man of Miracles," Fate 6 (Dec.1953)
:26-31. il.

Irvine
-Humanoid
1974, fall/Trabuco Rd.
Peter Guttilla, "Bigfoot: Advance
Guard from Outer Space," Saga UFO
Rept. 4 (June 1977):22,51.
-Meditation research
1960s/Robert Keith Wallace/UCLA-Irvine
Robert Keith Wallace, "Physiological
Effects of Transcendental Medita-
tion," Science 167 (1970):1751-54.
Robert Keith Wallace & Herbert Ben-
son, "The Physiology of Meditation,"
Sci.Am. 226 (Feb.1972):34-90. il.

Irvine Beach
-Haunt
n.d./Peters Canyon Rd.
Jim Brandon, Weird America (N.Y.:
Dutton, 1978), p.29.

Jackson
-Fall of metal foil
1956, Aug./Carl Balch
(Editorial), Fate 10 (Feb.1957):9.

Juapa
-Fall of blood
1870s, July/John Baldwin
Henry Winfred Splitter, "Wonders from
the Sky," Fate 6 (Oct.1953):33,37,
quoting San Bernardino Guardian
(undated).

Julian
-Dowsing
1969/John Collins
(Editorial), Fate 24 (Mar.1970):34-
36, quoting Escondido Weekly Free
Press (undated).

Kane Springs
-Spanish galleon
1890
Vincent H. Gaddis, "Ships That Sailed

the Desert," Fate 26 (Jan.1973):63, 65.

Kennedy Meadow
-Ghost
  1963, fall/Richard Webb/9-Mile Canyon
    Richard Webb, Voices from Another
    World (N.Y.: Manor, 1972 ed.), pp.
    3-8.
-Humanoid
  1960s
    John Green, Sasquatch: The Apes Among
    Us (Seattle: Hancock House, 1978),
    p.313.
-Humanoid tracks
  1972, Feb./9-Mile Canyon
    John Green, Sasquatch: The Apes Among
    Us (Seattle: Hancock House, 1978),
    pp.312-13.

Kentfield
-Healing
  1970s/House of Man/802 College Ave.
    Carol & Mary Cocciardi, The Psychic
    Yellow Pages (Saratoga: Out of the
    Sky, 1977), pp.151-52.
-UFO (NL)
  1975, Aug.29
    "UFO Central," CUFOS News Bull., 15
    Nov.1975, p.17.

Kenwood
-Fall of frogs
  1940, winter/Virginia Vanderford/E of
  town
    (Letter), Fate 17 (May 1964):112-13.

Kerman
-Mystery deaths
  1894, July
    Brooklyn (N.Y.) Eagle, 1 Aug.1894.
-UFO (CE-2)
  1978, May 13/Manuel Amparano/Del Norte
  x California Ave.
    Fresno Bee, 19 May 1978.
    Los Angeles Herald-Examiner, 5 June
    1978.
    "Officer 'Burned' by UFO," APRO Bull.
    27 (Aug.1978):4-5.
    "California Policeman Burned by UFO,"
    Int'l UFO Reporter 3 (Sep.1978):10-
    11.

Kern co.
-Plague of mice
  1927, fall
    Charles Fort, The Books of Charles
    Fort (N.Y.: Holt, 1941), p.592.

Knights Ferry
-UFO (CE-1)
  1896, Nov.22/John Kirby
    San Francisco Call, 5 Dec.1896, p.1.

La Canada
-UFO (NL)
  1973, April 3/H.F. Penfold
    Ann Druffel, "The Los Angeles Basin
    Sightings," FSR Case Histories, no.
    15 (June 1973):7,8.

La Crescenta
-UFO (NL)
  1973, April 3
    Ann Druffel, "The Los Angeles Basin
    Sightings," FSR Case Histories, no.
    15 (June 1973):7,8.
  1976, Jan.20
    "Noteworthy UFO Sightings," Ufology
    2 (summer 1976):62.
  1977, Nov.26/Mary Watson
    Ann Druffel, "Other Encounters of
    All Different Kinds," MUFON UFO J.,
    no.123 (Feb.1978):15,17.

Lafayette
-Cartomancy
  1970s/Tiffany Martin/950 Mountain View
  Rd.
    Carol & Mary Cocciardi, The Psychic
    Yellow Pages (Saratoga: Out of the
    Sky, 1977), pp.43-45.

Laguna Beach
-Archeological site
  15,000 B.C.
    New York Times, 24 Jan.1969, p.72.
    C.W. Ceram, The First American (N.Y.:
    Mentor, 1972 ed.), pp.339-42.
-Dowsing
  1900s-1950s/H.H. Henshaw
    Gaston Burridge, "The Truth about
    Dowsing," Fate 7 (Dec.1954):17,18.
-Haunt
  1957/Hangover House
    "The Lights in Hangover House," Fate
    10 (Oct.1957):53.
-Psychokinesis
  1960, June/C.C. Craveth
    (Editorial), Fate 13 (Oct.1960):12.
-UFO (DD)
  1943, spring
    (Editorial), APRO Bull. 5 (Jan.1957)
    :3.
  1960, Feb.16/Earl T. Ross
    Richard Hall, ed., The UFO Evidence
    (Washington: NICAP, 1964), pp.67-68.

La Habra
-Precognition
  1970s/Leo Ellis Wagner/2051 Monte Vista
    Warren Smith, "Phenomenal Predictions
    for 1975," Saga, Jan.1975, pp.20,53.
    Warren Smith, "Phenomenal Predictions
    for 1976," Saga, Jan.1976, pp.16,54.
-UFO (DD)
  1975, Aug.8
    "UFO Central," CUFOS News Bull., 15
    Nov.1975, p.15.

Lake Arrowhead
-UFO (?)
  1978, Dec.25/Nemo Anderson/Cedar Glen
    Lake Arrowhead Mountain News and
    Mountaineer, 28 Dec.1978.

Lake Elsinore
-Dowsing
  1920s-1972/Verne L. Cameron
    Verne L. Cameron, "Rev. Cameron and
    His Witching Wand," Fate 8 (Apr.

1955):65-70.

Verne L. Cameron, "Dowser Restores a
Dying Lake," Fate 21 (July 1968):
62-73.

Verne L. Cameron & Bill Cox, Aqua-
video (Elsinore: El Cariso, 1970).

Verne L. Cameron, "Open Letter from
a Dowser," Fate 25 (May 1972):89-93.

"Verne Cameron Dies," Fate 25 (Aug.
1972):45.

Serge V. King, "Neoenergy and Geometric Forms," in John White & Stanley
Krippner, eds., Future Science (Garden City, N.Y.: Anchor, 1977), pp.
199-201.

-Lake monster
1884-1970
Los Angeles Daily Illustrated News,
6 May 1942.
(Editorial), Fate 23 (Nov.1970):32-
36, quoting Riverside Press-Enter-
prise (undated).

-UFO (CE-2)
1967, Nov.8
Edward U. Condon, ed., Scientific
Study of Unidentified Flying Objects (N.Y.: Bantam, 1969 ed.), pp.
380-85.
Donald H. Menzel & Ernest H. Taves,
The UFO Enigma (Garden City: Doubleday, 1977), p.107.

-UFO (DD)
1956, Sep.12/Dwight Lewis
"Case 218," CRIFO Orbit, 2 Nov.1956,
pp.1-2.

-UFO (NL)
1965, Jan.14
Lake Elsinore Valley Sun, 21 Jan.1965.

Lakeport
-UFO (DD)
1961, Oct.9/Melville Phillips
"Snail-Shaped Object in California,"
APRO Bull. 10 (Jan.1962):3.

-UFO (NL)
1961, Feb.16/Victor Sneed/Cow Mt.
"Odds and Ends," APRO Bull. 9 (Jan.
1961):5.

Lakewood
-Precognition
1959, May 14/Florence Williams
(Editorial), Fate 12 (Sep.1959):17.

-UFO (CE-1)
ca.1968/Candlewood Verde Park
Dan Clements, "Space Safari," Official UFO 1 (Nov.1976):35,57.

-UFO (NL)
1960, March 18/Van Wilkinson
(Letter), Fate 13 (Oct.1960):109-10.

La Mesa
-UFO (NL)
1978, Aug.16/Mitch Sosna/9120 Briar Rd.
San Diego Union, 17 Aug.1978.

La Mirada
-UFO (?)
1975, April
Peter Guttilla, "Monster Menagerie,"

Saga UFO Rept. 4 (Sep.1977):32,66.

Lancaster
-Clairvoyance
1950s/Mary Ellen Webb
W.C. Cramp, "The Youngest Clairvoyant," Fate 5 (Apr.-May 1952):32-33.

-Humanoid
1973, June/Bret Baylor/nr.Lovejoy Butte
B. Ann Slate & Alan Berry, Bigfoot
(N.Y.: Bantam, 1976), pp.92-93.

-Telepathy
1964, April 27/Maxine Bell
Maxine Bell, "We Six Foresaw Our
Father's Death," Fate 20 (Apr.1967)
:94.

-UFO (CE-1)
n.d./Stefanie Baylor
B. Ann Slate & Alan Berry, Bigfoot
(N.Y.: Bantam, 1976), pp.93-94.

-UFO (CE-2)
1947, July 7
Los Angeles Times, 8 July 1947.

La Puente
-UFO (CE-1)
1957/E.R. Schultz
(Letter), Fate 12 (Oct.1959):110.

-UFO (CE-2)
1954, Feb.1/Mrs. W.J. Daily
San Fernando Valley Times, 15 Feb.
1954.
James C. McNamara, "Angel's Hair,"
Pageant, Nov.1954, pp.52-56. il.
R. DeWitt Miller, Stranger Than Life
(N.Y.: Ace, 1955 ed.), pp.95-97,99-
100.

La Selva Beach
-UFO (CE-2)
1973, Dec.5
San Jose Mercury, 7 Dec.1973.

Lathrop
-UFO (NL)
1896, Nov.23/Mr. Saguinette
Stockton Daily Independent, 24 Nov.
1896.

Laytonville
-Anomalous crystals
1970/Claud Rose/Boomer's tavern
Donald W. Smoot, "The Mystery of the
Broken Glasses," Fate 28 (June 1975)
:80-83. il.
(Letter), Robert D. Smith, Fate 28
(Dec.1975):128.

Le Grand
-UFO (DD)
1947, June/N.M. De Arman/4 mi.N
Watsonville Register-Pajaronian, 18
July 1947.

Lemon Grove
-UFO (CE-2)
1973, Nov.16/Crane St.
"Boys Encounter Landed Object," APRO
Bull. 22 (Jan.-Feb.1974):7-8. il.
Leonard H. Stringfield, Situation

Red: The UFO Siege (N.Y.: Fawcett
Crest, 1977), pp.141-43.
-UFO (NL)
1966, Dec.19/William H. Gilchrist
(Editorial), Fate 20 (May 1967):27.
Brad Steiger & Joan Whritenour, Fly-
ing Saucer Invasion: Target--Earth
(N.Y.: Award, 1969), p.49.

Lemoore
-UFO (CE-1)
1974, Jan.25/Charlie Kendall
George D. Fawcett, "The 'Unreported'
UFO Wave of 1974," Saga UFO Rept.
2 (spring 1975):51.

Leucadia
-Parapsychology research
1970/Center for Education and Research
/Box 2307
"Psi Counseling Service Available,"
Fate 23 (Nov.1970):91.

Lincoln
-Genetic anomaly
1975/George Magonical
Laredo (Tex.) Times, 15 Jan.1976. il.

Linden
-UFO (CE-1)
1978, June 6/Janet Calle/Baker x Duncan Rd.
Manteca Bulletin, 11 June 1978.

Little River
-Humanoid
1946, Aug./Sylvia B. Snider
(Letter), Fate 9 (Dec.1956):122-24.

Littlerock
-Humanoid
ca.1971/dam
John Green, Sasquatch: The Apes Among
Us (Seattle: Hancock House, 1978),
p.313.
1974/Andrew Stone
B. Ann Slate & Alan Berry, Bigfoot
(N.Y.: Bantam, 1976), pp.59-62.
-UFO (CE-2)
1973, April/Andrew Stone
Peter Guttilla, "Bigfoot: Advance
Guard from Outer Space," Saga UFO
Rept. 4 (June 1977):22,48-50.

Livermore
-Entombed snake
1897, March/Peter Zabella
Green Bay (Wisc.) Gazette, 11 Mar.
1897.
-UFO (DD)
1953, Jan.27/John B. Bean/nr. AEC fa-
cility
Richard Hall, ed., The UFO Evidence
(Washington: NICAP, 1964), pp.39-40.
1966, Oct.21/Robert H. Schultz/Sandia
Corporation
"Major Sighting Wave," UFO Inv. 3
(Jan.-Feb.1967):1,3.
-UFO (NL)
1975, Nov.26

"UFO Central," CUFOS News Bull., 1
Feb.1976, p.14.

Lodi
-UFO (?)
1897, Jan.
Reno (Nev.) Evening Gazette, 22 Jan.
1897.
-UFO (CE-3)
1896, Nov?
Loren Gross, "A New Look at the Lodi
Incident," MUFON UFO J., no.109
(Dec.1976):14-16, quoting Stockton
Evening Mail (undated).

Loma Linda
-Humanoid
1972, Aug./Kenneth Corbin
Peter Guttilla, "Bigfoot: Advance
Guard from Outer Space," Saga UFO
Rept. 4 (June 1977):22,50.
-Humanoid tracks
1976, Sep./Peter Guttilla
Peter Guttilla, "Bigfoot: Advance
Guard from Outer Space," Saga UFO
Rept. 4 (June 1977):22,50.
-UFO (?)
1972, Aug./Santa Ana R. wash
Peter Guttilla, "Bigfoot: Advance
Guard from Outer Space," Saga UFO
Rept. 4 (June 1977):22,50.

Lompoc
-Giant human skeleton
1833
Frank Edwards, Stranger Than Science
(N.Y.: Ace, 1959), pp.96-97.
-UFO (?)
1963, Dec.5/=Venus
Edward U. Condon, ed., Scientific
Study of Unidentified Flying Ob-
jects (N.Y.: Bantam, 1969 ed.), pp.
434-36.
-UFO (R-V)
1967, Oct.6-7/Vandenberg AFB
Gordon D. Thayer, "Optical and Radar
Analyses of Field Cases," in Edward
U. Condon, ed., Scientific Study of
Unidentified Flying Objects (N.Y.:
Bantam, 1969 ed.), pp.171-72,353-65.

Lone Pine
-Ghost
1964
Richard Webb, Voices from Another
World (N.Y.: Manor, 1972 ed.), pp.
221-27.
-Haunt
1946-1961/Earl Richardson
Richard Webb, Voices from Another
World (N.Y.: Manor, 1972 ed.), pp.
200-205.
-Retrocognition
1960s/Portal Rd.
Richard Webb, Voices from Another
World (N.Y.: Manor, 1972 ed.), pp.
197-99.
-UFO (CE-2)
n.d./Fay Clark
Brad Steiger, Mysteries of Time and

Space (N.Y.: Dell, 1976 ed.), pp. 150-52.

Long Barn
-Humanoid
  1937, Jan.25/Emmett R. Ray
    Emmett R. Ray, "The Thing in the Tree," Fate 10 (June 1957):36-39.

Long Beach
-Clairvoyance
  1970s/Certified Psychic Consultants/R. Carl Spurney
    Tim Patterson, "Cops Hesitant to Work with Psychic Colombos," Probe the Unknown 3 (Nov.1975):31-33.
-Erratic crocodilian
  1960/Marion Tucker/2525 Quincy Ave.
    (Editorial), Fate 14 (Feb.1964):8.
-Fall of beans
  1954, April 17/Virginia Hollington
    (Letter), Fate 7 (Nov.1954):116-18.
-Fall of fish
  1951, Jan.2
    "Some Fish Fall," Doubt, no.32 (1951):75.
-Fall of ice
  1953, June 4/L.A. Smith/1480 American Ave.
    Long Beach Tribune, 17 June 1953.
  1965, Nov.19/W.G. Oldham/Bixby Park
    (Editorial), Fate 19 (Mar.1966):14-15.
-Haunt
  1970, Sep.-1971, June/Jody Randall
    Marilyn Estes-Smith, "Haunted Chairs Go Cheap," Fate 26 (July 1973):49-54.
-Healing
  1970s/Stephan Douglas/785 Junitera Ave.
    (Letter), Mrs. S. Tinsley, Fate 25 (Jan.1972):129-30.
-Phantom
  1940s/Sylvia Merritt
    (Letter), Fate 7 (Nov.1954):126-28.
-Precognition
  1963, Jan.29/Mrs. John Walik
    Long Beach Independent, 4 Feb.1963.
-Spontaneous human combustion
  1969, April 7/Grace Walker/5334 Cedar Ave.
    (Editorial), Fate 22 (Aug.1969):24.
-UFO (CE-1)
  1954, April 14/J.M. Schidel
    "Pilot Banks Ship to Avoid Collision with UFO," CRIFO Newsl., 5 Nov.1954, p.2
    Frank Edwards, Flying Saucers: Serious Business (N.Y.: Lyle Stuart, 1966), pp.68-69.
-UFO (CE-2)
  1952, March 26
    Richard Hall, ed., The UFO Evidence (Washington: NICAP, 1964), p.73.
  1954, summer/Alexandri Skolny/=hoax?
    B. Ann Slate, "UFO Kidnappers," Saga, Apr.1975, pp.24,56-57.
-UFO (DD)
  1942, Feb.25/J.H. McClelland/city hall
    Los Angeles Times, 27 Feb.1942.

1947, July 6/Howard Shriver
    Los Angeles Examiner, 7 July 1947.
1951, July
    Coral & Jim Lorenzen, UFOs: The Whole Story (N.Y.: Signet, 1969), pp.39-40.
1951, Sep.23
    Edward J. Ruppelt, The Report on Unidentified Flying Objects (Garden City: Doubleday, 1956), pp.94-95, 113-14.
    U.S. Air Force, Projects Grudge and Blue Book Reports 1-12 (Washington: NICAP, 1968), pp.16,44-47.
1953, Jan.28/airport
    Coral & Jim Lorenzen, UFOs: The Whole Story (N.Y.: Signet, 1969), p.50.
1957, Oct.14-15/Van Wilkinson
    (Letter), Fate 12 (Jan.1959):113.
1957, Nov.5/Joseph Abramavage/airport
    Long Beach Independent, 6 Nov.1957.
1961, May 19/Marsha Howard
    "Youngsters Report UAO," APRO Bull. 9 (May 1961):5.
1962, Aug./Ann Druffel
    Ann Druffel, "Santa Catalina Channel 'Cloud-Cigars,'" in Proc.1976 CUFOS Conference (Evanston: Center for UFO Studies, 1976), pp.62-64.
-UFO (NL)
  1956, fall/A.E. Wilkinson/airport
    (Letter), Fate 10 (July 1957):116-18.
  1960, April 2/Richard Reschka/141 E. 16th St.
    (Letter), C.J. Fortner, Fate 13 (Sep. 1960):110-12.
  1966, Jan.2
    Jerome Clark, "The Greatest Flap Yet? --Part IV," Flying Saucer Rev. 12 (Nov.-Dec.1966):9,12-13.
  1968, July 9/Kevin Allgreen
    Ann Druffel, "Santa Catalina Channel 'Cloud-Cigars,'" in Proc.1976 CUFOS Conference (Evanston: Center for UFO Studies, 1976), pp.62,65.
  1974, July 24/=Jupiter
    Ann Druffel, "Light in Sky Requires Careful Investigation," Skylook, no.95 (Oct.1975):5-7.
-Unidentified submerged object
  1974, Feb./harbor/=mine detector
    "California Object Identified," APRO Bull. 22 (Jan.-Feb.1974):11.

Loomis
-UFO (CE-1)
  1978, Feb.22/Terry Carr-Hall
    Auburn Journal, 1 Mar.1978.

Los Alamitos
-UFO (NL)
  1973, March 23/Karen Harper
    "Press Reports," APRO Bull. 21 (May-June 1973):9.

Los Alamos
-UFO (DD)
  1977, April 11/Fred Svihus
    Paul Cerny, "California Airline Sighting and Movie Film," MUFON UFO

J., no.119 (Oct.1977):3-5. il.

Los Altos
-Parapsychology research
  1970-   /Academy of Parapsychology and
  Medicine/314 Second St.
    June & Nicholas Regush, Psi: The Oth-
    er World Catalogue (N.Y.: Putnam,
    1974), pp.151,210.
    Rhea A. White, "Parapsychology Today,"
    in Edgar Mitchell, ed., Psychic Ex-
    ploration (N.Y.: Capricorn, 1976
    ed.), pp.195,211.
    Leslie Shepard, ed., Occultism Update,
    no.1 (1978):1.
-UFO (CE-1)
  1974, April 6/Christine Ezell Johnson/
  Hwy.280
    "MUFON Reports in Brief," Skylook,
    no.89 (Apr.1975):11.
-UFO (DD)
  1972, Aug.12
    B. Ann Slate, "Scientific Braintrust
    Tackles UFO Mystery," Saga UFO Rept.
    3 (June 1976):43.
-UFO (NL)
  1966, Jan.3/Robert B. Staver
    "National Press Spotlights UFOs," UFO
    Inv. 3 (Jan.-Feb.1966):1,2.

Los Angeles
-Acupuncture
  1970s/Calvin H. Chen/UCLA
    James Crenshaw, "Medical Men Confront
    the New Dimensions in Healing: Part
    1," Fate 26 (June 1973):50,58-59.
-Anomalous hole in ground
  1957, April 15/Manny Blumenfeld/1575 S.
  Ridgeley Dr.
    Los Angeles Herald-Express, 15 Apr.
    1957.
    (Editorial), Fate 10 (Sep.1957):12-
    14. il.
-Archeological site
  ca.8000 B.C./La Brea tar pits
    J.C. Merriam, "The Fauna of Rancho La
    Brea," Mem.Univ.Calif., vol.2 (1911).
    Arthur Woodward, "Atlatl Dart Fore-
    shafts from the La Brea Pits," Bull.
    S.Calif.Acad.Sci. 36, pt.2 (1937):
    41-60.
    A.L. Kroeber, "The Rancho La Brea
    Skull," Am.Antiquity 27 (1962):416-
    17. il.
    "A Real Unpleasantness," Pursuit 2
    (Oct.1969):76-77.
    New York Times, 26 Dec.1969, p.41.
  n.d./Los Angeles R.
    Ivan A. Lopatin, "Fossil Man in the
    Vicinity of Los Angeles, California,"
    Proc.6th Pacific Sci.Cong. 4 (1939):
    177-81.
    Robert F. Heizer & S.F. Cook, "Fluor-
    ine and Other Chemical Lists of Some
    North American Human and Fossil
    Bones," Am.J.Phys.Anthro. 10 (1952):
    289-304.
-Astrology
  1950s/D. Modin
    David St. Clair, The Psychic World

of California (N.Y.: Bantam, 1973
ed.), pp.187-88.
1950s-1970s/Doris Doane
  Doris Doane, Astrology: Thirty Years
  Research (Los Angeles: Professional
  Astrologers, 1956).
  David St. Clair, The Psychic World
  of California (N.Y.: Bantam, 1973
  ed.), pp.192-98.
1970s/Kiyo
  David St. Clair, The Psychic World
  of California (N.Y.: Bantam, 1973
  ed.), pp.188-92.
-Biofeedback research
  1970s/Biofeedback Medical Clinic
    (Editorial), Fate 31 (Oct.1978):12-
    14.
-Clairvoyance
  1954-1966/Pat Michaels
    Paula Michaels, "Pat Michaels, Clair-
    voyant Newsman," Fate 19 (Aug.1966)
    :42-53.
    (Letter), Ulysses G. Kretzmer, Fate
    21 (June 1968):131-32.
    (Letter), Paula Michaels, Fate 21
    (Oct.1968):126-29.
  1960s-   /Laurie Hoffman/W. Los Angeles
    James Crenshaw, "Laurie Hoffman Is a
    Psychic Artist," Fate 22 (Jan.1969):
    34-46. il.
-Contactee
  1950s/Will Miller
    Will & Evelyn Miller, We of the New
    Dimension (Los Angeles: The Authors,
    n.d.).
  1953/Mortimer Bane/Los Angeles Times
  office
    Harold T. Wilkins, Flying Saucers Un-
    censored (N.Y.: Pyramid, 1967 ed.),
    pp.30-33.
    James Crenshaw, "The Great Venusian
    Mystery," Fate 19 (June 1966):32-39.
    (Letter), Gene Dorsey, Fate 19 (Sep.
    1966):121-24.
  1953, Feb.18-1955, April 25/George Adamski
    George Adamski, Inside the Space
    Ships (N.Y.: Abelard-Schuman, 1955).
-Crisis apparition
  1945, March 28
    L.A. Dale, "Spontaneous Cases," J.
    ASPR 46 (1952):31-32.
  1956, Aug./Anna Maria Savino
    Lisa S. Emerson, "Three Dreams and
    You're Dead," Fate 29 (Oct.1976):66,
    70.
  1967
    Thelma Moss, The Probability of the
    Impossible (Los Angeles: Tarcher,
    1974), p.310.
-Disappearance
  1968, Aug.25/Dixie Lee Arensen/Hill-
  crest Church
    Brad Steiger, Strange Disappearances
    (N.Y.: Magnum, 1972), pp.38-41.
  1970, Aug.
    D. Scott Rogo, The Haunted Universe
    (N.Y.: Signet, 1977), pp.9-10.
-Doubtful responsibility

1968, June 5/Sirhan Sirhan/=conspiracy?
Mohammed T. Mehdi, Kennedy and Sir-
han: Why? (N.Y.: New World, 1968).
Peter Noyes, Legacy of Doubt (N.Y.:
Pinnacle, 1973).
John Christian & William Turner, The
Assassination of Robert F. Kennedy
(N.Y.: Random House, 1978).

-Dowsing
1950s-1960s/Alvin B. Kaufman
James Crenshaw, "Science and Industry Look at Dowsing," Fate 18 (Sep.
1965):44-51. il.

-Electromagnetic anomaly
1959, Nov./Marie Shuey/1521½ W. 50th
(Editorial), Fate 13 (Apr.1960):8.
1960, winter/Harold Van Cantford/Kagel
Canyon
(Editorial), Fate 14 (Apr.1961):14-
16, quoting Pacoima Sun (undated).

-Eyeless vision
1955-1960/Margaret Foos/True Sight
Church
(Editorial), Fate 10 (Oct.1957):15,
quoting Richmond (Va.) News-Leader
(undated).
(Editorial), Fate 11 (Jan.1958):16-
17.
(Editorial), Fate 13 (May 1960):10-11.
Stuart Allen, "The Girl Who Sees
without Eyes," Fate 13 (July 1960):
29-35. il.
(Letter), Cecil D. Clayton, Fate 13
(Oct.1960):114.
(Letter), Betty Danko, Fate 14 (Jan.
1961):109-10.
(Letter), Mimi Price, Fate 14 (Jan.
1961):110-12.

-Fall of fish
1960/Howard Wetzel/Int'l Airport
(Editorial), Fate 13 (July 1960):16.

-Fall of ice
1949, Feb./W. 85th St.
Los Angeles Daily News, 12 Feb.1949.
1953, April 9/Edna Lewis/1130 W. 99th
(Editorial), Fate 6 (Aug.1953):6.
1955, Jan./Alton M. Ludvicson/553 W.
Colden Ave.
(Editorial), Fate 8 (June 1955):10.
1956, March 12/9113 Juniper St.
"Falls," Doubt, no.53 (1956):417.
1957, March 18/3667-108th St.
"Ice," Doubt, no.54 (1957):432.
1959, April 22/Ella M. Coleman/3426
Walton St.
(Editorial), Fate 12 (Aug.1959):8.

-Fall of rocks
1874, May/Mr. Valenzuela/San Pedro St.
Henry Winfred Splitter, "Wonders from
the Sky," Fate 6 (Oct.1953):33,34,
quoting Los Angeles Express (undated).

-Fall of yellow wax
1954, Sep./Gertrude Hoffman
Los Angeles Daily News, 24 Sep.1954.

-Ghost
1923, April 11/Harry Houdini
New York American, 11 Feb.1928.
Joseph Dunninger, Houdini's Spirit
World and Dunninger's Psychic Reve-
lations (N.Y.: Tower, n.d.), pp.92-96.

Vincent H. Gaddis, "Mystery of Houdini's Death," Fate 16 (Aug.1963):
66-70. il.

-Ghost dog
1949, March-May/Mrs. W.E. Dickson
L.A. Dale, "Spontaneous Cases," J.
ASPR 46 (1952):154-57.

-Haunt
n.d./Valentino's movie studio
(Letter), Dulcie Brown, Fate 9 (June
1956):118-20.
1944, June 7/Eagle Rock
Raymond Bayless, The Enigma of the
Poltergeist (N.Y.: Ace, 1967 ed.),
pp.144-45.
1947-1958
(Letter), Anon., Fate 12 (May 1959):
120-24.
1947-1960s/96th St.
Hans Holzer, Ghosts of the Golden
West (N.Y.: Ace, 1972), pp.72-75.
1955-1962, July/Raymond Bayless
Raymond Bayless, The Enigma of the
Poltergeist (N.Y.: Ace, 1967 ed.),
pp.88-89,148-57.
1960s
Thelma Moss & Gertrude R. Schmiedler,
"Quantitative Investigation of a
'Haunted House' with Sensitives and
a Control Group," J.ASPR 62 (1968):
399-410.
Thelma Moss, The Probability of the
Impossible (Los Angeles: Tarcher,
1974), pp.323-25.
1960s/Ardmore Blvd.
Hans Holzer, Ghosts I've Met (N.Y.:
Ace, 1965), pp.114-28.
Hans Holzer, Ghosts of the Golden
West (N.Y.: Ace, 1972), pp.150-59.
1965/Benny de Vere/337 S. Main St.
Susy Smith, Prominent American Ghosts
(N.Y.: Dell, 1969 ed.), pp.160-64.
1968-1970/Dick Atwood/Petit St.
Richard Webb, Voices from Another
World (N.Y.: Manor, 1972 ed.), pp.
53-69.
1971, Sep.-1972
Thelma Moss, The Probability of the
Impossible (Los Angeles: Tarcher,
1974), pp.321-23.

-Healing
1960s-   /Franklin Loehr/Religious Re-
search Foundation/510 Franklin Ave.
Franklin Loehr, The Power of Prayer
over Plants (N.Y.: Signet, 1969).
Franklin Loehr, Diary after Death
(N.Y.: Pillar, 1976).
1970s/Ernest Holmes Memorial Rsch.Foun-
dation/3251 W. 6th St.
Sheila Ostrander & Lynn Schroeder,
Handbook of Psi Discoveries (N.Y.:
Berkley, 1974), p.215.
1970s/Doug Johnson/951 Micheltorena
Jess Stearn, The Miracle Workers
(Garden City: Doubleday, 1972).
Janice McDonald, "Doug Johnson: LA's
Psychic Healer," Fate 30 (July 1977)
:74-79. il.
1970s/Maria Papapetro/15109 Camarillo
"Probe's 1977 Directory of the Psy-

chic World," Probe the Unknown 5
(spring 1977):32,65.
1970s/Alberto Aguas/Box 39392
David St. Clair, "Alberto Aguas:
Young Healer from Brazil," Fate 29
(Aug.1976):62-68. il.
1972-   /Charles Cassidy
David St. Clair, Psychic Healers
(Garden City: Doubleday, 1974), pp.
28-55.
-Hex
1863/Doña Petranilla/Rancho Feliz (Grif-
fith Park)
Horace Bell, On the Old West Coast
(N.Y.: William Morrow, 1930), pp.
85-98.
-Inner development
1915-   /Church of Light/659 S. St.
Andrews Pl.
1920s-   /Builders of the Adytum Tem-
ple/5105 N. Figueroa
David St. Clair, The Psychic World
of California (N.Y.: Bantam, 1972
ed.), pp.256-60.
1950s-   /Astara Church/261 S. Mari-
posa Ave.
Peter Ballbusch, "Cross-Country Dem-
onstration of ESP," Fate 13 (Aug.
1960):88-92. il.
David St. Clair, The Psychic World
of California (N.Y.: Bantam, 1973
ed.), pp.253-56.
June & Nicholas Regush, Psi: The Other World Catalogue (N.Y.: Putnam,
1974), pp.154-55.
Robert Chaney, Adventures in ESP
(Los Angeles: Astara, 1975).
1960s-   /Church of Scientology of
California
L. Ron Hubbard, Dianetics Today (Los
Angeles: Church of Scientology,
1975).
1970s/Anderson Research Foundation/3960
Ingraham St.
June & Nicholas Regush, Psi: The Oth-
er World Catalogue (N.Y.: Putnam,
1974), p.155.
-Mystery gas
1944, Sep.8/=pollution?
"Los Angeles Too," Doubt, no.11 (win-
ter 1944-45):156.
1963, May 1
"Fortean Items," Saucer News 10 (Sep.
1963):17.
-New energy source (inventor)
1976, March/Samuel Leach
(Editorial), Fate 29 (Nov.1976):36.
-Out-of-body experience
ca.1961/R.W. Findlater
(Letter), Fate 15 (July 1962):105-106.
1965, Aug./D. Scott Rogo
D. Scott Rogo, The Welcoming Silence
(New Hyde Park, N.Y.: University,
1973).
-Parapsychology research
1960s-   /Higher Sense Perception Re-
search Foundation/9581 W. Pico Blvd./
Shafica Karagulla
Shafica Karagulla, Breakthrough to
Creativity (Santa Monica: DeVorss,

1967).
James Grayson Bolen, "Interview: Sha-
fica Karagulla," Psychic 4 (July-
Aug.1973):6-11,29-31.
John White & Stanley Krippner, eds.,
Future Science (Garden City, N.Y.:
Anchor, 1977), p.586.
1966-   /Al G. Manning/ESP Laboratory
/7559 Santa Monica Blvd.
David St. Clair, The Psychic World
of California (N.Y.: Bantam, 1973
ed.), pp.260-61.
John Godwin, Occult America (Garden
City: Doubleday, 1972), pp.214-16.
Brad Steiger, Revelation: The Divine
Fire (Englewood Cliffs, N.J.: Pren-
tice-Hall, 1973), pp.77-78.
Warren Smith, "Phenomenal Predictions
for 1975," Saga, Jan.1975, pp.20,50.
Warren Smith, "Phenomenal Predictions
for 1976," Saga, Jan.1976, pp.16,19.
1966-   /Thelma Moss/Neuropsychiatric
Institute, UCLA
James Crenshaw, "UCLA Experiment
Proves Emotions Affect ESP," Fate
20 (Feb.1967):61-70.
Thelma Moss & J.A. Gengerelli, "ESP
Effects Generated by Affective
States," J.Parapsych. 32 (1968):90-
100.
Thelma Moss, et al., "Hypnosis and
ESP: A Controlled Experiment," Am
J.Clinical Hypnosis 13 (1970):46-56.
James Bolen, "Interview: Thelma S.
Moss," Psychic 2 (Aug.1970):4-7,32-
37. il.
David St. Clair, The Psychic World
of California (N.Y.: Bantam, 1973
ed.), pp.261-68.
Thelma Moss & Kendall Johnson, "Rad-
iation Field Photography," Psychic
3 (July 1972):50-54. il.
Thelma Moss, The Probability of the
Impossible (Los Angeles: Tarcher,
1974), pp.30-62,98-101,103-13,133-
36,179-87,218-21,248-49,355-56.
Sheila Ostrander & Lynn Schroeder,
Handbook of Psi Discoveries (N.Y.:
Berkley, 1974), pp.83-87,98-99. il.
James Crenshaw, "Science Proves Psy-
chic Healing," Fate 29 (Feb.1976):
67-74.
-Phantom image
1971, Aug.27/Mable Davis/Faith Baptist
Church
David Techter, "A Flap of Glowing
Crosses," Fate 25 (June 1972):52,
quoting Nat'l Enquirer (undated).
-Plague of bees
1959, April 9/Marsha Melcombe/Toluca L.
(Editorial), Fate 12 (Aug.1959):8.
-Poltergeist
1939, July/Harry Park/nr. City Hall
Los Angeles Herald-Express, 12 July
1939.
1942, Dec.-1943, Jan./Norma Moore
Los Angeles Times, 5-6 Jan.1943.
1950s/Dulcie Brown
(Letter), Fate 16 (July 1963):110-12.
-Precognition

n.d./A.R. Thompson/Cahengua Pass
A.R. Thompson, "My Unseen Savior,"
   Fate 8 (May 1955):60-63.
1892/George Herbert Wyman
   "The Draftsman and the Planchette,"
   Fate 17 (June 1964):49.
1959, March/Charles E. Bogardus/3843 S.
Cimarron St.
   (Editorial), Fate 12 (Aug.1959):12-
   14.
1960s/Jacqueline Eastlund
   James Crenshaw, "Jacqueline Eastlund:
   Seeress on TV," Fate 20 (Sep.1967):
   64-74. il.
ca.1963/Dennis Benetatos/108 W. 7th St.
   (Editorial), Fate 16 (June 1963):23.
1963, Oct.-Nov./Helen Greenwood
   Los Angeles Herald-Examiner, 22 Nov.
   1963.
1966/Evelyn Allinger/1719 W. 50th St.
   Redlands Daily Facts, 29 Jan.1966.
   James Crenshaw, "California Court Up-
   holds the Right to Prophesy," Fate
   19 (Aug.1966):33-41.
1969-   /Ernesto A. Montgomery/1800
W. Adams Blvd.
   (Editorial), Fate 23 (Nov.1970):22-
   25.
   Warren Smith, "How Did the Seers in
   1970?" Fate 24 (Feb.1971):87,89. il.
   Warren Smith, "Phenomenal Predictions
   for 1975," Saga, Jan.1975, pp.20,50.
   Warren Smith, "Phenomenal Predictions
   for 1976," Saga, Jan.1976, pp.16,50.
1970s/Alice Lane/Box 49007
   "Probe's 1977 Directory of the Psy-
   chic World," Probe the Unknown 5
   (spring 1977):35,37. il.
-Psychic photography
1886-1911/Edward Wyllie/507-13 S. Spring
St.
   H.A. Reid, Unseen Faces Photographed
   (Los Angeles: The Author, 1901).
   Isaac K. Funk, The Widow's Mite (N.Y.:
   Funk & Wagnalls, 1904), pp.454-84.
   James Coates, Photographing the In-
   visible (Chicago: Advanced Thought,
   1911), pp.155-79,188-288. il.
   Charles H. Cook, "Experiments in
   Photography," J.ASPR 10 (1916):1-114.
   Nandor Fodor, Encyclopaedia of Psy-
   chic Science (London: Arthurs,
   1933), pp. 409-10.
1932, Jan./Edison Pettit/Los Angeles
Times office
   Los Angeles Times, 3 Feb.1932. il.
-Psychokinesis
1958-1961/Roy A. Crain
   Max B. Miller, "Mind over Matter: A
   New Breakthrough?" Fate 15 (Jan.
   1962):71-84. il.
1960s-   /Louise Huebner
   Kansas City (Mo.) Star, 25 May 1970.
   Louise Huebner, Never Strike a Happy
   Medium (Los Angeles: Nash, 1970).
   (Editorial), Fate 24 (May 1971):28-
   30.
   John Godwin, Occult America (Garden
   City: Doubleday, 1972), pp.60-62.
   David St. Clair, The Psychic World

of California (N.Y.: Bantam, 1973
   ed.), pp.228-36.
   Louise Huebner, regular column; see
   issues of Coronet.
-Seance
1930, July 16/Arthur Ford/People's
Spiritualist Church
   Upton Sinclair, "Is This Jack London?" in Bernhardt J. Hurwood, ed.,
   The First Occult Review Reader (N.Y.:
   Award, 1968), pp.13-26.
1955/Bertie Candler
   Dana Howard, Diane: She Came from
   Venus (London: Regency, 1955).
-Skyquake
1952, Jan.5/Int'l Airport
   Marion Kirkpatrick, "California Mys-
   tery Blasts," Fate 10 (Apr.1957):
   86,88.
1954, Oct.25/Dulcie Brown
   "First Prize," Doubt, no.47 (1955):
   316,318.
1957, May 21/Mrs. Edward P. James
   "Flying Saucer Roundup," Flying Sau-
   cer Rev. 11 (Feb.1958):31.
   Coral E. Lorenzen, The Shadow of the
   Unknown (N.Y.: Signet, 1970), p.80.
1972, Jan.6
   Los Angeles Times, 7 Jan.1972.
1974, June 20-21
   San Francisco Examiner, 22 June 1974.
-Spirit medium
1919/Mrs. Carl H. Wickland/6027 Hayes
   Mary H. Jacobs, "A Mediumistic Ex-
   periment," J.ASPR 18 (1924):479-82.
1930s-1950s/Richard Zenor/460 N. West-
ern
   James Crenshaw, Telephone Between
   Worlds (Los Angeles: DeVorss, 1950).
   il.
   James Crenshaw, "Telephone Between
   Worlds," Fate 7 (Mar.1954):34-40.
   (Letter), Philip Hastings, Fate 13
   (Feb.1960):122-24.
1930s-1960s/Sophia Williams
   Hamlin Garland, The Mystery of the
   Buried Crosses (N.Y.: Dutton, 1939).
   Sophia Williams, You Are Psychic
   (Hollywood: Murray & Gee, 1946).
   Attila von Sealay, "The Mediumship
   of Sophia Williams," Fate 5 (Apr.-
   May 1952):76-86.
   Danton Walker, Spooks Deluxe (N.Y.:
   Franklin Watts, 1956), pp.106-108.
   Leslie M. LeCron, "Sophia Williams
   and Her Whispering Voices," Fate
   25 (Apr.1972):94-101. il.
   (Letter), Verna Arvey, Fate 25 (July
   1972):140-41.
1950s-   /Joe Koperski/Topanga Canyon
   David St. Clair, The Psychic World
   of California (N.Y.: Bantam, 1973
   ed.), pp.293-96.
1960s-   /Bill Corrado
   Jess Stearn, The Miracle Workers
   (Garden City: Doubleday, 1972).
1960s-   /Clara Schuff/7023 La Tijera
Blvd.
   David St. Clair, The Psychic World
   of California (N.Y.: Bantam, 1973

ed.), pp. 212-16.
"Probe's 1977 Directory of the Psy-
chic World," Probe the Unknown 5
(spring 1977):65.
-Spontaneous human combustion
1953, May/Esther Dulin/210 W. 110th St.
(Editorial), Fate 6 (Dec.1953):5.
-Telepathy
1951, July 1/Frances Wall/McArthur Park
Los Angeles Daily Mirror, 2 July 1951.
William H. Gilroy, "Voice from the
Lake," Fate 4 (Nov.-Dec.1951):77-78.
1960/E.A. Chitwood
(Editorial), Fate 14 (Apr.1961):23.
1973, July 8/Doris Collins/Los Angeles
Spiritualist Church
James Crenshaw, "Case of the Trans-
atlantic Messages," Fate 29 (Nov.
1976):82-91.
-UFO (?)
1954, July
Donald E. Keyhoe, Flying Saucer Con-
spiracy (N.Y.: Holt, 1955), p.190.
1954, Oct.8/=aircraft refueling
Edward J. Ruppelt, The Report on Un-
identified Flying Objects (Garden
City: Doubleday, 1956), p.8.
1955, May 19/=pelicans?
Los Angeles Times, 21 May 1955.
"A Classical Case of Contradictory
Claptrap," CRIFO Newsl., 3 June
1955, pp.5-6.
1966, April 3/Int'l Airport
"Typical Reports," UFO Inv. 3 (Mar.-
Apr.1966):8.
1967, July 18/Wilmington/=hoax
Edward U. Condon, ed., Scientific
Study of Unidentified Flying Objects
(N.Y.: Bantam, 1969 ed.), pp.331-32.
1967, Oct.6/Griffith Park/=balloon
Philip J. Klass, UFOs Explained (N.Y.:
Random House, 1974), p.29.
-UFO (CE-1)
1944/J.S. Taylor/Slauson Ave.
Gordon I.R. Lore, Jr. & Harold H. Den-
eault, Jr., Mysteries of the Skies:
UFOs in Perspective (Englewood
Cliffs, N.J.: Prentice-Hall, 1968),
p.144.
1973, Oct.24/Griffith Park
Santa Ana Register, 8 Nov.1973.
1974, May 23/Ethel Bergman
Ann Druffel, "Close-in Lighted Globe
Reported," Skylook, no.86 (Jan.
1975):5-7. il.
-UFO (CE-3)
1956, July 20/Panorama City
Arthur Constance, The Inexplicable
Sky (N.Y.: Citadel, 1957), p.282.
Donald B. Hanlon, "Questions on the
Occupants," in The Humanoids (FSR
special issue no.1, 1967), p.64.
1957, Nov.6/Richard Kehoe/Vista del
Mar/=hoax?
Los Angeles Mirror-News, 6 Nov.1957.
Aimé Michel, Flying Saucers and the
Straight-Line Mystery (N.Y.: Cri-
terion, 1958), p.272.
-UFO (DD)
1896, Nov.30/Mr. Woods

San Francisco Call, 1 Dec.1896, p.7.
1945, July/Raymond Bayless/Firestone
Bldg.
Raymond Bayless, Experiences of a
Psychical Investigator (New Hyde
Park, N.Y.: University, 1972).
1947, March/Mary Schwarzkopf/Woodland
Hills
(Letter), Fate 5 (Oct.1952):114-19.
1947, June 28/Tony Shaputis
Portland Oregonian, 29 June 1947.
1947, July 4/Verna Edwards/Highland
Park
Los Angeles Examiner, 6 July 1947.
1947, July 5/Donald Levine/Eagle Rock
Los Angeles Times, 6 July 1947.
1949, April 8/Griffith Park
Los Angeles Times, 8 Apr.1949.
Bruce S. Maccabee, "UFO Related In-
formation from the FBI Files: Part
5," MUFON UFO J., no.124 (Mar.1978):
7,10.
1949, May 6
"If It's in the Sky It's a Saucer,"
Doubt, no.27 (1949):416.
1949, July/J.S. Stankavage
Denver (Colo.) Post, 9 Apr.1950.
1952, Sep.22/Alan K. Stazer
"Saucer Sightings by IFSB Members,"
Space Rev. 2 (Jan.1953):10.
1952, Nov.24/Paul T. Collins/Sperry St.
x San Fernando Rd.
(Editorial), Fate 10 (June 1957):13.
1954, Sep.16/Cherie May
(Letter), Fate 8 (Mar.1955):109.
1955, March/Norman F. Schulte/Baldwin
Hills
Santa Ana Register, 25 Oct.1972; and
1 Nov.1972.
1955, Oct.6/Marie Lindquist/Wilshire
Blvd. x Bonnie Brae St.
(Letter), Fate 9 (Feb.1956):128.
1956, Dec.27/Jack Telaneus
Richard Hall, ed., The UFO Evidence
(Washington: NICAP, 1964), p.71.
1957, Dec.1/Ralph Benn
Richard Hall, ed., The UFO Evidence
(Washington: NICAP, 1964), p.90,
quoting Saucers, spring 1958.
1968, Oct.16/Harriet Dzik
Ann Druffel, "The Dzik Report: Los
Angeles UFO," FSR Case Histories,
no.9 (Feb.1972):11-12. il.
1975, Sep.26
"From the Center for UFO Studies,"
Flying Saucer Rev. 21 (Apr.1976):25.
-UFO (NL)
1896, Nov.27/Frank B. Taylor/N. Key
West St.
Los Angeles Times, 1 Dec.1896.
1896, Nov.29
San Francisco Call, 1 Dec.1896, p.7.
1896, Nov.30/W.A. Ryan/Nadeau Hotel
San Francisco Call, 3 Dec.1896, p.9.
1930, Dec.24/Frank Thomas/S. Hauser Ave.
Los Angeles Examiner, 26 Dec.1930.
1942, Feb.25/Raymond Angier
Washington (D.C.) Post, 26-27 Feb.
1942.
Los Angeles Times, 26-28 Feb.1942;

and 5-6 Mar.1942. il.
W.F. Craven & J.L. Cate, eds., The
Army Air Forces in World War II, 7
vols. (Chicago: Univ. of Chicago,
1948), 1:283-86.
Gordon I.R. Lore, Jr. & Harold H.
Deneault, Jr., Mysteries of the
Skies: UFOs in Perspective (Englewood Cliffs, N.J.: Prentice-Hall,
1968), pp.74-87.
1947, July 4/Herman V. Friede/nr. Elysian Park
Los Angeles Times, 6 July 1947.
1951, July 7/J. Eddie Olson
(Letter), Fate 4 (Nov.-Dec.1951):124-
25.
1952, April 20
People Today Mag., 18 June 1952.
Desmond Leslie & George Adamski, Flying Saucers Have Landed (N.Y.: British Book Centre, 1953), pp.59-60.
1952, July/Int'l Airport
Harold T. Wilkins, Flying Saucers on
the Attack (N.Y.: Ace, 1967 ed.),
p.276, quoting Los Angeles Examiner,
July 1952.
1954, Feb.18/Roy Safire/629 S. Woods
Harold T. Wilkins, Flying Saucers Uncensored (N.Y.: Pyramid, 1967 ed.),
p.129.
1956, July 16/Int'l Airport
Los Angeles Examiner, 17 July 1956.
1956, Aug.21/Viviane Machu
Los Angeles Times, 22 Aug.1956.
"Case 196," CRIFO Orbit, 5 Oct.1956,
p.1.
1956, Sep.21/Robert Short/5132 Lincoln
Brad Steiger, Gods of Aquarius (N.Y.:
Harcourt Brace Jovanovich, 1976),
p.111. il.
1958, April 20/Thelma Robertson
(Letter), Fate 11 (Sep.1958):114-16.
1964, Sep.24/George Cabrera
(Letter), Fate 18 (Apr.1965):108.
1973, April 3/Lake View Terrace
1973, April 3/1 mi.W of Civic Center
Ann Druffel, "The Los Angeles Basin
Sightings," FSR Case Histories, no.
15 (June 1973):7-8.
1973, Oct.19/Bill Morgan/Lucille Ave.
x Sunset Blvd.
(Editorial), Probe the Unknown 2
(spring 1974):62.
1973, Nov.12/C.C. Smith/Whittier x Euclid Ave.
Los Angeles Times, 14 Nov.1973.
Sergio Ortiz, "They're Flying over
Los Angeles Too," Probe the Unknown
2 (spring 1974):31. il.
1975, Sep.17
"UFO Central," CUFOS News Bull., 15
Nov.1975, p.18.
1976, Jan.20
"Noteworthy UFO Sightings," Ufology
2 (summer 1976):62.
1977, Aug.23
Ann Druffel, "Other Encounters of All
Different Kinds," MUFON UFO J., no.
123 (Feb.1978):15,17.
-UFO (R)

1952, June 1
Edward J. Ruppelt, The Report on Un-
identified Flying Objects (Garden
City: Doubleday, 1956), pp.141-43.
-UFO (R-V)
1957, March 23/CAA radar post
New York Times, 12 July 1957, p.6.
Richard Hall, ed., The UFO Evidence
(Washington: NICAP, 1964), pp.84-86.
-Weather control
1971, Sep.12-16/Trevor James Constable
/neo-Reichian method
Trevor James Constable, "Operation
'Kooler': Conquest of a Southern
California Heat Wave," J.Orgonomy,
vol.6 (May 1972), reprinted in John
White & Stanley Krippner, eds., Fu-
ture Science (Garden City, N.Y.:
Anchor, 1977), pp.556-71.
-Weeping icon
1960, May 17-1964, Dec./Holy Transfig-
uration Russian Church
Los Angeles Times, 28 Nov.1964. il.
Raymond Bayless, "Investigating a
Weeping Icon," Fate 19 (Mar.1966):
59-64. il.

Los Banos
-UFO (CE-3)
1975, Oct./Jack Edleson/I-5 x Hwy.152
Peter Guttilla, "Monster Menagerie,"
Saga UFO Rept. 4 (Sep.1977):32,64-
65.

Los Gatos
-Bird attack
1977, May
Los Gatos Evening News, 11 May 1977.
-Chinese discovery
ca.1000 B.C.
Henriette Mertz, Gods from the Far
East (N.Y.: Ballantine, 1975 ed.),
p.156.
-Precognition
1977/Clarissa Bernhardt
(Editorial), Fate 30 (Jan.1977):26.

Los Nietos
-Fall of flesh and blood
1869, Aug.1/J. Hudson
Los Angeles News, 3 Aug.1869.
San Francisco Evening Bulletin, 9
Aug.1869.

Los Osos
-UFO (NL)
1966, March 16/J.R. Kingham
(Letter), Fate 19 (Sep.1966):134,135.

Lynwood
-Haunt
1953/Lago Ave.
Hans Holzer, Gothic Ghosts (N.Y.:
Pocket Books, 1972), pp.146-57.
-Poltergeist
1960, Sep.9-11/Harry W. Moore
(Editorial), Fate 14 (Jan.1961):19-22.
Raymond Bayless, The Enigma of the
Poltergeist (N.Y.: Ace, 1967 ed.),
pp.68-75.

McKinleyville
-Fall of weblike substance
    1958, Nov.9
        Eureka Humboldt Times, 11-12 Nov.1958.

Madera
-UFO (NL)
    1973, Oct.17
        Madera Tribune, 17 Oct.1973.

Malibu
-Sea monster (carcass)
    1963, Sep.25/C. Richards/=oarfish
        Los Angeles Times, 26 Sep.1963.
-UFO (?)
    1949, Jan.9
        "You Asked for It," Doubt, no.24
        (1949):363.
-UFO (DD)
    1947, July 7/Jerry Chase
        Los Angeles Examiner, 8 July 1947.
    1953, Jan.29/Rex Hardy, Jr.
        (Editorial), Fate 6 (June 1953):12,
        quoting Los Angeles Examiner (unda-
        ted).
-UFO (NL)
    1956, Nov.
        Richard Hall, ed., The UFO Evidence
        (Washington: NICAP, 1964), p.146.
    1975, Sep.17
        "UFO Central," CUFOS News Bull., 15
        Nov.1975, p.18.
    1976, Jan.21/Gary W. Humecke
        D. Scott Rogo, The Haunted Universe
        (N.Y.: Signet, 1977), pp.120-21.
    1978, March/Bruce Buffer
        Malibu Times, 31 Mar.1978.

Mammoth
-Humanoid
    1971, Sep.1/SE of town
        John Green, The Sasquatch File (Ag-
        assiz, B.C.: Cheam, 1973), p.56.
-Humanoid tracks
    1970, July 15/8 mi.N
        John Green, The Sasquatch File (Ag-
        assiz, B.C.: Cheam, 1973), p.56.

Manhattan Beach
-UFO (?)
    1957, Feb.5/=radar chaff
        Roy Craig, "Direct Physical Evidence,"
        in Edward U. Condon, ed., Scientific
        Study of Unidentified Flying Objects
        (N.Y.: Bantam, 1969 ed.), p.90.
-UFO (DD)
    1952, July 27
        Donald H. Menzel & Lyle G. Boyd, The
        World of Flying Saucers (Garden
        City: Doubleday, 1963), pp.49-50.
        Thomas M. Olsen, ed., The Reference
        for Outstanding UFO Sighting Reports
        (Riderwood, Md.: UFO Information Re-
        trieval Center, 1966), p.12.

Manteca
-UFO (NL)
    1975, Aug.15
        "UFO Central," CUFOS News Bull., 15
        Nov.1975, p.16.

Maple Creek
-UFO (NL)
    1964, Sep.21/Eddie Williams
        Curtis Fuller, "Collected UFO Sight-
        ings for August and September,"
        Fate 18 (Jan.1965):40, quoting Eu-
        reka Humboldt Standard (undated).

Marina
-UFO (?)
    1971, March 22/Ted Baldwin/Monterey Bay
        Monterey Peninsula-Herald, 23 Mar.
        1971.

Martin's Ferry
-Humanoid tracks
    1961, Aug.
        John Green, The Sasquatch File (Ag-
        assiz, B.C.: Cheam, 1973), p.29.

Marysville
-Skyquake
    1952, Feb.25
        Marion Kirkpatrick, "California Mys-
        tery Blasts," Fate 10 (Apr.1957):
        88-89.
-UFO (?)
    1947, July 8/Marie A. Seward
        Sacramento Union, 9 July 1947.
-UFO (CE-1)
    1953, Dec.28/Richard Brandt/Yuba Coun-
    ty Airport
        "Reports from Everywhere," Fate 7
        (May 1954):29, quoting San Francis-
        co Examiner (undated).
-UFO (NL)
    1896, Nov.28/Mrs. E.B. Gray
    1896, Nov.30/Robert Boyd
    1896, Dec.2/Will J. Greely
        Marysville Daily Democrat, 3 Dec.1896.

Mendocino
-Inner development
    1971-   /Church of the One/Box 875
        Armand Biteaux, The New Conscious-
        ness (Willits, Cal.: Oliver, 1975),
        p.23.
-Paraphysics research
    1970s/Thaumaturgical Engineering Asso-
    ciates/Box 875
        Armand Biteaux, The New Conscious-
        ness (Willits, Cal.: Oliver, 1975),
        pp.141-42.

Mendota
-UFO (CE-1)
    1967, Oct.14
        J. Allen Hynek, The UFO Experience
        (Chicago: Regnery, 1972), p.238.

Menlo Park
-Parapsychology research
    1970s/Stanford Research Institute/333
    Ravenswood Ave.
        Russell Targ & D. Hurt, "Learning
        Clairvoyance and Precognition with
        an ESP Testing Machine," Parapsych.
        Rev., July-Aug.1972, pp.9-11.
        Russell Targ & Harold Puthoff, "In-
        formation Transmission under Condi-

tions of Sensory Shielding," Nature 251 (1974):602-607.

"Investigating the Paranormal," Nature 251 (1974):559-60.

Russell Targ & Harold Puthoff, "Remote Viewing of Natural Targets," in Laura Oteri, ed., Quantum Physics and Parapsychology (N.Y.: Parapsychology Foundation, 1975).

Ingo Swann, To Kiss Earth Good-Bye (N.Y.: Hawthorn, 1975).

Harold Puthoff & Russell Targ, "Psychic Research and Modern Physics," in Edgar Mitchell, ed., Psychic Exploration (N.Y.: Capricorn, 1976 ed.), pp.524-42.

Harold E. Puthoff & Russell Targ, "A Perceptual Channel for Information Transfer över Kilometer Distances: Historical Perspective and Recent Research," Proc.Inst.Electrical & Electronic Engineers 64 (1976):329-54. il.

Russell Targ & Harold E. Puthoff, Mind-Reach (N.Y.: Delacorte, 1977).

Jeffrey Goodman, Psychic Archeology (N.Y.: Berkley, 1978 ed.), pp.177-80.

1973-   /Institute of Noetic Science/ 530 Oak Grove Ave.

Edgar D. Mitchell, "Noetics: The Emerging Science of Consciousness," Psychic 4 (Apr.1973):18-20.

June & Nicholas Regush, Psi: The Other World Catalogue (N.Y.: Putnam, 1974), p.21.

-UFO (CE-1)
1972, Feb./W of town nr. linear accelerator
Jacques Vallee, "UFOs: The Psychic Component," Psychic 5 (Jan.-Feb. 1974):12-14.

-UFO (NL)
1896, Nov.22/Henry Smith/nr. Flood's Pond
Redwood City Times-Gazette, 28 Nov. 1896.

Merced
-UFO (NL)
1896, Nov.30/T.M. Edmunds
San Francisco Call, 2 Dec.1896, p.14.
Merced Express, 4 Dec.1896.
1949, April 4/1 mi.W
Bruce S. Maccabee, "UFO Related Information from the FBI Files: Part 5," MUFON UFO J., no.124 (Mar.1978):7,10-11.

Meridian
-UFO (?)
1896, Nov./=Venus?
Marysville Semi-Weekly Appeal, 3 Dec. 1896.

Millbrae
-Poltergeist
1966-1967/Jean Grasso
Hans Holzer, Ghosts of the Golden West (N.Y.: Ace, 1972), pp.139-50.

Mill Valley
-Haunt
1910s/Miriam Allen de Ford
Miriam Allen de Ford, "California Haunted House," Tomorrow 4 (summer 1956):94-100.
1973-1977/Christine Woodbury
(Editorial), Fate 30 (July 1977):30-33.
-Precognition
1967, March 30/Paul Cohen
(Editorial), Fate 20 (Oct.1967):16.
-Skyquake
1952, Feb.5/Lee Sells
Marion Kirkpatrick, "California Mystery Blasts," Fate 10 (Apr.1957):86,88.
-UFO (DD)
1947, July 6/Charles W. Butler
San Francisco Chronicle, 7-8 July 1947.
-UFO (R)
n.d./George W. Monk, Jr.
"AF Intimidates Witnesses," UFO Inv. 3 (Mar.-Apr.1965):2.

Milton
-Retrocognition
1938, spring/Marguerite A. Vassar
Marguerite A. Vassar, "I Saw the Reenactment of a Farm Tragedy," Fate 18 (Mar.1965):49-52.
Gracia Fay Ellwood, Psychic Visits to the Past (N.Y.: Signet, 1971), pp.143-49.

Mineral
-UFO (NL)
1960, Aug.16/Bill Gonzales
John C. Ross, "State Cops Race 'Flying Saucer,'" Fate 13 (Dec.1960):44,46.

Modesto
-Skyquake
1950, Oct.3
Brad Steiger, Strange Disappearances (N.Y.: Magnum, 1972), p.105.
-UFO (?)
1945, Nov.29/=meteor?
"Fire-Ball in Reverse," Doubt, no.14 (spring 1946):210, quoting Turlock Daily Journal (undated).
-UFO (CE-1)
1942, Sep./Lillie Brown
(Letter), Fate 7 (June 1954):109-10.
1975, Aug.15/Leonard Murray
Timothy Beckley & Harold Salkin, "UFOs Spotted Along California's Earthquake Lines," Saga UFO Rept. 3 (Dec.1976):44,70-72.
-UFO (CE-2)
1962, April 13/Ustick Rd.
"Glow Seen, Numbness Follows," APRO Bull. 10 (May 1962):1.
-UFO (NL)
1896, Nov.26/J.E. Ward
San Francisco Call, 28 Nov.1896.
1953, Sep.3/Charles Rogers
"Saucers on the Hot Line," in Frank

Bowers, ed., The True Report on
Flying Saucers (Greenwich, Ct.: Fawcett, 1967), p.34. il.
1953, Sep.9/Walker L.
Donald E. Keyhoe, Flying Saucer Conspiracy (N.Y.: Holt, 1955), p.49.
1963, Feb.28
Modesto Bee, 28 Feb.1963.
1976, Feb.14
Timothy Green Beckley, "Saucers over
Our Cities," Saga UFO Rept. 4 (Aug.
1977):24,73.
1976, Sep.16
"UFOs of Limited Merit," Int'l UFO
Reporter 1 (Nov.1976):5.

Mokelumne Hill
-UFO (?)
1896, Dec.3
Mokelumne Hill Calaveras Chronicle,
5 Dec.1896.

Monoville
-Ghost
1873
Richard Webb, Voices from Another
World (N.Y.: Manor, 1972 ed.), pp.
39-42.

Monrovia
-UFO (NL)
1961, March 31
"Floating Fire Ball," Fate 15 (Feb.
1962):66.

Montague
-UFO (DD)
ca.1952/Leo Purinton
William Murphy, "UFOs Reliably Repor-
ted," Flying Saucer Rev. 18 (Jan.-
Feb.1972):18.

Monta Vista
-Healing
1970s/Harold Kupel/20760 Stevens Creek
Blvd.
Carol & Mary Cocciardi, The Psychic
Yellow Pages (Saratoga: Out of the
Sky, 1977), pp.155-56.
-UFO (DD)
1963, Sep.26/George W. Scott/Permanente
cement plant
Richard Hall, ed., The UFO Evidence
(Washington: NICAP, 1964), p.63.

Monterey
-Haunt
1970/Barbara Burdick/Robert Louis Ste-
venson house/Houston St.
(Editorial), Fate 24 (Jan.1971):25-28.
-UFO (CE-1)
1967, Nov.4/Mrs. James C. Cross/S of
town on Hwy.101
"New Close-Ups, Pacings," UFO Inv. 4
(Mar.1968):3.
-UFO (CE-2)
1971, Oct.4
"Webs," INFO J., no.9 (fall 1972):25-
26.
-UFO (DD)

1947, July 3/Mrs. Louis Goldstein
San Francisco News, 3 July 1947.
1950, April 10
Los Angeles Times, 11 Apr.1950.
-UFO (NL)
1965, Jan.29/George Clemens
Monterey Peninsula-Herald, 30 Jan.
1965.
1973/Christopher P. Aune/316 Van Buren
(Editorial), Skylook, no.74 (Jan.
1974):11, quoting Monterey Peninsula-
Herald (undated).

Monterey Park
-Poltergeist
1973/Salvitor Delgados
Barry Taff, "Stalking the Elusive
Spectre," Probe the Unknown 1 (Oct.
1973):30,33-35. il.
-Precognition
1958, fall/Richard Brammer
(Editorial), Fate 12 (Apr.1959):8.

Monticello
-Mystery plane crash
1954, Aug.25/Peter D. McArthur/B-25
bomber
Harold T. Wilkins, Strange Mysteries
of Time and Space (N.Y.: Ace, 1958),
p.139.

Montrose
-UFO (?)
1955, May 19/=pelicans?
"A Classical Case of Contradictory
Claptrap," CRIFO Newsl., 3 June
1955, p.5.
1955, Nov.7
Richard Hall, ed., The UFO Evidence
(Washington: NICAP, 1964), p.155.
-UFO (NL)
1947, July 2
Los Angeles Times, 4 July 1947.

Morgan Hill
-UFO (?)
1896, Nov.26/=hoax
San Jose Daily Herald, 27 Nov.1896.
-UFO (NL)
1975, Sep.10
"UFO Central," CUFOS News Bull., 15
Nov.1975, p.18.

Morningside
-UFO (?)
1953, Oct.10/Alfred J. Fitzgerald/3505
W. 79th St./=meteorite?
Morningside Post, 15 Oct.1953.

Morongo Valley
-UFO (CE-1)
1943, summer/Mrs. L. Chapman
B. Ann Slate & Stanton Friedman, "UFO
Battles the Air Force Couldn't Cover
Up," Saga UFO Rept. 2 (winter 1974):
29,60-61.

Morro Bay
-UFO (DD)
1946, Dec.30/Ella Young

Harold T. Wilkins, Flying Saucers on
the Attack (N.Y.: Ace, 1967 ed.),
p.41.

Mountain View
-Fall of weblike substance
  1963, June 17
    Palo Alto Times, 17 June 1963.
-UFO (DD)
  1947, July 5/Charles R. Sigala/nr.
  Black Mt.
    San Francisco Examiner, 6 July 1947.
-UFO (NL)
  1975, Aug.18
    "UFO Central," CUFOS News Bull., 15
    Nov.1975, p.16.

Mount Baldy
-UFO (DD)
  1947, July 8/A.E. Morman
    Edward J. Ruppelt, The Report on Un-
    identified Flying Objects (Garden
    City: Doubleday, 1956), p.22.
    Ted Bloecher, Report on the UFO Wave
    of 1947 (Washington: NICAP, 1967),
    p.III-12.
    Bruce S. Maccabee, "UFO Related In-
    formation from the FBI Files: Part
    3," MUFON UFO J., no.121 (Dec.1977)
    :10,13.

Mount Hamilton
-UFO (?)
  1950, Feb.16/C.D. Shane/Lick Observatory
    Harold T. Wilkins, Flying Saucers on
    the Attack (N.Y.: Ace, 1967 ed.),
    p.130.
-UFO (NL)
  1921, Aug.7/W.W. Campbell/Lick Observatory
    "'Planets' at Large," Can.UFO Rept.,
    no.12 (1972):9-10.

Mount Hermon
-Spirit medium
  1941, summer
    David C. Reed, "A Spirit Saves a
    Skeptic," Fate 25 (Oct.1972):92-95.

Mount Wilson
-Paraphysics research
  1917-1946/Gustaf Strömberg/Observatory
    Gustaf Strömberg, The Soul of the
    Universe (Philadelphia: David McKay,
    1940).
    Gustaf Strömberg, "The Autonomous
    Field," J. Franklin Inst. 239 (1945)
    :27-40.
    Gustaf Strömberg, "Emergent Energy,"
    J.Franklin Inst. 241 (1946):323-39.
    Gustaf Strömberg, "An Astronomer
    Looks at Psychic Phenomena," Tomor-
    row 5 (winter 1957):27-35.
    James Crenshaw, "Dr. Gustaf Ström-
    berg's Nonphysical World," Fate 24
    (May 1971):98-107; (June 1971):89-
    95.
-UFO (DD)
  1961, April 28/Trevor James Constable

Trevor James Constable, The Cosmic
Pulse of Life (Santa Ana: Merlin,
1976), p.99. il.

Murphys
-Ancient mine
  1849
    "Extraordinary Discovery in Califor-
    nia," Sci.Am. 5 (1 Dec.1849):82.

Myers Flat
-Humanoid
  1976, July
    "Latest News from the Pacific North-
    west," Bigfoot News, no.22 (July
    1976):1.

Napa
-Eyeless vision
  1971/Napa State Hospital
    Larry Ashby, "Perils Involved in Fin-
    gertip Vision," Fate 29 (July 1976)
    :70-75. il.
    (Letter), Hazel Hartley, Fate 29
    (Nov.1976):125.
-Fall of ice
  1958, April/Leo J. Kozlowski/560 Hoover St.
    (Editorial), Fate 11 (Aug.1958):8-
    10, quoting Napa Register (undated).
-Spirit medium
  1970s/Marceil Moore
    David St. Clair, The Psychic World
    of California (N.Y.: Bantam, 1973
    ed.), p.96.
-UFO (DD)
  1959, Oct.23-Nov./Joan Capps
    (Letter), Fate 13 (Aug.1960):109-10.
-UFO (NL)
  1896, Nov.25/Samuel Clark
    San Francisco Chronicle, 6 Dec.1896,
    p.20.
  1965, March 8,15,18/William Bishop
    "Deputy Sheriffs Ridiculed," UFO Inv.
    3 (Apr.-May 1965):4, quoting San
    Francisco Examiner (undated).

National City
-Clairvoyance
  1967, Nov./Mrs. Ralph C. Foree
    "I Just Had a Feeling," Fate 21
    (June 1968):39.
-UFO (NL)
  1952, May 12/Donald R. Carr
    "Issue 6) Saucer Cases on Official
    Record Belie U.S. Weapon Theory,"
    CRIFO Newsl., 4 Mar.1955, p.6.

Newbury Park
-Haunt
  1965-1966/Gwen Hinzie
    Hans Holzer, Ghosts of the Golden
    West (N.Y.: Ace, 1968), pp.107-27.

Newman
-Fire anomaly
  n.d./Truman Stenseth
    "Burning Earth," Fate 5 (Sep.1952):
    41.
    "Flaming Earth," Fate 6 (Sep.1953):

62.

Newport Beach
-Gasoline spring
  1947, Oct./William Tallman
    "Gasoline Springs," Doubt, no.20
    (1948):305.
-Sea monster
  1954, Oct./Barney Armstrong/"Sea-Fern"
  /=hoax?
    (Editorial), Fate 8 (May 1955):10.
-Sea monster (carcass)
  1901, Feb.22/Horatio J. Forgy/=oarfish
    J. Charles Davis II, "The San Clem-
    ente Monster," Animal Life, July
    1954, p.36. il.
    Bernard Heuvelmans, In the Wake of
    the Sea-Serpents (N.Y.: Hill & Wang,
    1968), pp.85-86. il.
-UFO (CE-1)
  1955, July 11
    "World Roundup," Flying Saucer Rev.
    1 (Sep.-Oct.1955):29-30.
-UFO (DD)
  1959, Jan.1/Fred Gunzelman
    Coral & Jim Lorenzen, UFOs: The Whole
    Story (N.Y.: Signet, 1969), p.95.
-UFO (NL)
  1957, Nov.5/Corona del Mar
  1958, April 9/R. Gordon
    Richard Hall, ed., The UFO Evidence
    (Washington: NICAP, 1964), pp.64,
    147,165.

Nicasio
-Mystery plane crash
  1952, July
    Harold T. Wilkins, Flying Saucers on
    the Attack (N.Y.: Ace, 1967 ed.),
    p.267.
-UFO (CE-3)
  1963, March 31/Angelo Mosteccioli
    Petaluma Argus-Courier, 1 Apr.1963.

Niland
-Fall of metallic object
  1950, May 27/5 mi.N
    "Found on Ground," Doubt, no.42
    (1953):238,239.

Norco
-Fall of ice
  1951, Feb.12/Arvin C. Sorenson/540
  Hillside
    "Ice Is Still Falling," Fate 4 (Aug.-
    Sep.1951):106.
-UFO (CE-3)
  1954, Sep.
    Donald B. Hanlon, "Occupants Obser-
    ved at Norco," Flying Saucer Rev. 14
    (May-June 1968):15-16.

North Bloomfield
-UFO (NL)
  1896, Dec.4
    Marysville Semi-Weekly Appeal, 10
    Dec.1896.

North Hollywood
-Clairempathy

1965-1970s/Peter Hurkos/12214 View-
crest Rd.
    Peter Hurkos, Psychic: The Story of
    Peter Hurkos (Indianapolis: Bobbs-
    Merrill, 1961).
    James Grayson Bolen, "Interview:
    Peter Hurkos," Psychic 1 (Mar.-Apr.
    1970):5.
    (Editorial), Fate 23 (Aug.1970):12-
    14.
    Wanda Sue Parrott, "Peter Hurkos
    Speaks," Fate 27 (Mar.1974):36-43.
    Melbourne Christopher, Mediums, Mys-
    tics and the Occult (N.Y.: Crowell,
    1975), pp.66-76.
    B. Ann Slate, "The Amazing UFO Dis-
    coveries of Peter Hurkos," Saga UFO
    Rept. 2 (winter 1975):27-30,51-52.
    il.
    Norma L. Browning, Peter Hurkos: I
    Have Many Lives (Garden City: Dou-
    bleday, 1976).
-Haunt
  1951-1970s/Evelyn Garrett/Riverside Dr.
    Richard Webb, Voices from Another
    World (N.Y.: Manor, 1972 ed.), pp.
    70-73.
-Psychic photography
  1954, Oct.-1960s/Raymond Welsh
    Margaret E.W. Fleming, "The Man in
    the Polka Dot Tie and Other Stran-
    gers," Fate 29 (June 1976):36-44.
    il.
-UFO (DD)
  1950, March 25/Daniel Swinton
    Los Angeles Mirror, 25 Mar.1950.
-UFO (NL)
  1947, July 6/Mrs. William A. Becker/
  6240 Sunset Ave.
    Los Angeles Herald-Express, 8 July
    1947.
  1973, April 5,8
    Ann Druffel, "The Los Angeles Basin
    Sightings," FSR Case Histories, no.
    16 (Aug.1973):7-9.

Northridge
-Haunt
  1960s/Jack Meyers
    Richard Webb, Voices from Another
    World (N.Y.: Manor, 1972 ed.), pp.
    265-78.
-Spirit medium
  1970/Pauline Byrne
    Richard Webb, Voices from Another
    World (N.Y.: Manor, 1972 ed.), pp.
    125-35.
-Telepathy research
  1960, Dec.2/Riker Laboratories
    Andrija Puharich, Beyond Telepathy
    (Garden City, N.Y.: Anchor, 1973),
    pp.6-9.
-UFO (NL)
  1977, Aug.12
  1977, Sep.3
    Ann Druffel, "Other Encounters of All
    Different Kinds," MUFON UFO J., no.
    123 (Feb.1978):15,16-17.

North San Juan
-UFO (?)
1967, June 2/Tony Spurill/=hoax
"Landed UAO Photographed," APRO Bull.
15 (May-June 1967):8.
"Follow-Up," APRO Bull. 24 (Mar.
1976):6.

Norwalk
-Bird attack
1963, April/Claude Hollicot/14525 Horst
Ave.
(Editorial), Fate 16 (Aug.1963):18.
-Precognition
1964, April 6/Lucille Homer
Mary Margaret Fuller, "Dreams of the
Lost," Fate 17 (Aug.1964):85,86-87.

Novato
-Spirit medium
1970s/Betty Bethards/Box 761
David St. Clair, The Psychic World
of California (N.Y.: Bantam, 1973
ed.), pp.96-99.
David St. Clair, Psychic Healers
(Garden City: Doubleday, 1974), pp.
175-202.
Armand Biteaux, The New Conscious-
ness (Willits, Cal.: Oliver, 1975),
p.70.
Carol & Mary Cocciardi, The Psychic
Yellow Pages (Saratoga: Out of the
Sky, 1977), pp.11-12.
-UFO (?)
n.d./Hamilton AFB/=radar echo
Philip J. Klass, UFOs Explained (N.Y.:
Random House, 1974), pp.179-80.
-UFO (DD)
1947, July 6/Robert O'Hara/Hamilton AFB
San Francisco News, 7 July 1947.
1947, July 29/William H. Ryherd/nr.
Hamilton AFB
Ted Bloecher, Report on the UFO Wave
of 1947 (Washington: NICAP, 1967),
p.III-5.
-UFO (NL)
1950, June 21/Garland L. Pryor/Hamil-
ton AFB
Ray Palmer, "New Report on the Fly-
ing Saucers," Fate 4 (Jan.1951):63,
80.
Richard Hall, ed., The UFO Evidence
(Washington: NICAP, 1964), p.20,
quoting AP release, 21 June 1950.
-UFO (R-V)
1952, Aug.3/Duane Swimley/Hamilton AFB
Donald H. Menzel & Lyle G. Boyd, The
World of Flying Saucers (Garden City:
Doubleday, 1963), pp.46-47.
Richard Hall, ed., The UFO Evidence
(Washington: NICAP, 1964), pp.21,78.

Oakdale
-UFO (CE-1)
1959, Dec.22/Kenneth Lindsley/Claribel
Rd. x Mettenry Ave.
Stockton Record, 24 Dec.1959.
"World Roundup," Flying Saucer Rev.
6 (May-June 1960):21.

Oakland
-Crisis apparition
1893, Feb.25/Isabel Maury/Mills College
Isabel McLane Maury, "My Father Said
Goodbye," Fate 5 (Feb.-Mar.1952):
104-106.
-Fall of ice
1949, Dec./Frank Trunkey/633 Douglas
Oakland Tribune, 8 Dec.1949.
-Fall of metallic object
1949, Oct.21
"If It's in the Sky It's a Saucer,"
Doubt, no.27 (1949):416,417.
-Fall of steel cable
1945, June 5/347 Hale St.
"A Sky Anchor Of Course," Doubt, no.
14 (spring 1946):208.
-Haunt
1942/Hazel Leggio
(Letter), Fate 17 (Oct.1964):119.
-Healing
1960s-1970s/Bob Hoffman/1305 Franklin
David St. Clair, Psychic Healers
(Garden City: Doubleday, 1974), pp.
205-24.
-Inner development
1960s-   /Nemeton/Box 13037
Hans Holzer, The Witchcraft Report
(N.Y.: Ace, 1973), pp.135-49.
-Mystery light beam
1973/Harriet Powers
(Letter), Fate 27 (Mar.1974):131-32.
-Poltergeist
1874, April 23-25/Thomas Brownell
Clarke
J.H. Hyslop, "A Case of Poltergeist,"
Proc.ASPR 7 (1913):193-425.
1964, June 15-29/George Wheeler/1904
Franklin St.
Jim Hazelwood, "Poltergeist Wrecks
Business Office," Fate 17 (Nov.
1964):38-45. il.
Arthur C. Hastings, "The Oakland Pol-
tergeist," J.ASPR 72 (1978):233-56.
il.
-Precognition
1954, April 25/Bob Barr
"The Seismographic Stomach," Fate 7
(Dec.1954):43.
1955, Jan./Jennie Terrell
(Editorial), Fate 8 (June 1955):13.
1963, April 7/Diane Patmont
(Editorial), Fate 16 (Sep.1963):24-
25.
-Sea monster
1922, Feb.14/Long Wharf
"No Such Sanderson," Doubt, no.18
(1947):274, quoting Oakland Tribune
(undated).
-Skyquake
1952, Jan.4
Marion Kirkpatrick, "California Mystery Blasts," Fate 10 (Apr.1957):86,
88.
-Stigmata
1972, March 19-April 7/Cloretta Robertson
(Editorial), Fate 25 (July 1972):19.
Susy Smith, The Power of the Mind
(Radnor, Pa.: Chilton, 1975), pp.

57-58.
John Michell & Robert J.M. Rickard,
Phenomena: A Book of Wonders (Lon-
don: Thames & Hudson, 1977), p.43,
quoting General Psychiatry, May
1974. il.
-Telepathy
1970s/Jim Donahoe/Box 24635
Jim Donahoe, "Exploring Mutual Dream-
ing," Psychic 6 (Dec.1975):23-25.
Jim Donahoe, Dream Reality (Oakland:
Bench, 1976).
Carol & Mary Cocciardi, The Psychic
Yellow Pages (Saratoga: Out of the
Sky, 1977), pp.52-54.
-UFO (?)
1896, Nov.26/=kite
San Francisco Chronicle, 27 Nov.1896,
p.7.
1949, May 7/Benjamin F. Smith
Ray Arnold & Kenneth Palmer, The Com-
ing of the Saucers (Boise: The Au-
thors, 1952), p.141.
1954, July
Donald E. Keyhoe, Flying Saucer Con-
spiracy (N.Y.: Holt, 1955), p.190.
1954, Sep.18/Charles Embree
"Case 52," CRIFO Newsl., 4 Feb.1955,
p.4.
-UFO (DD)
1896, Nov.21/Selby Yost/24th St. x New
Broadway
San Francisco Call, 22 Nov.1896.
San Francisco Chronicle, 22 Nov.1896,
p.36.
ca.1951/D. Bruce Berry
(Letter), Fate 18 (Jan.1965):124,126.
1952, March 10/Clarence K. Greenwood
Richard Hall, ed., The UFO Evidence
(Washington: NICAP, 1964), pp.56-57.
il.
-UFO (NL)
1896, Oct?/26th St. x Telegraph Ave.
San Francisco Chronicle, 22 Nov.1896,
p.36.
1896, Nov./D.P. Mitchell
San Francisco Chronicle, 25 Nov.1896,
p.14.
1896, Nov.22/Ms.Wilson
Oakland Tribune, 23 Nov.1896.
1896, Nov.23
San Francisco Call, 24 Nov.1896.
1896, Nov.24/George Hatton/6th St.
Gordon I.R. Lore, Jr. & Harold H. Deneault, Jr., Mysteries of the Skies:
UFOs in Perspective (Englewood
Cliffs, N.J.: Prentice-Hall, 1968),
p.8.
1896, Nov.24/Case Gilson
Oakland Tribune, 1 Dec.1896.
San Francisco Call, 2 Dec.1896, p.14.
1896, Nov.25/Dr. Paulin/19th St.
Gordon I.R. Lore, Jr. & Harold H. Deneault, Jr., Mysteries of the Skies:
UFOs in Perspective (Englewood
Cliffs, N.J.: Prentice-Hall, 1968),
p.9.
1896, Nov.29/Percy Drew
San Francisco Call, 2 Dec.1896, p.14.
1897, March/Kate N. Bassett/522 10th

Beloit (Wisc.) Daily News, 3 Apr.
1897, p.1, quoting San Francisco
Examiner (undated).
ca.1932, summer/Fred W. Van Sant
Gordon I.R. Lore, Jr. & Harold H.
Deneault, Jr., Mysteries of the
Skies: UFOs in Perspective (Engle-
wood Cliffs, N.J.: Prentice-Hall,
1968), pp.110-11.
1947, July 3/Estelle DeVaughn/1212
Oakland Ave.
San Francisco Chronicle, 6 July 1947.
1947, July 5/Mrs. Donald Nelson/9942
Birch St.
San Francisco Examiner, 6 July 1947.
1953, June 13/Joseph J. Weger/5623
Amy Dr.
Oakland Tribune, 16 June 1953.
1955, April 7
"Green Fireball Visits Oakland,"
CRIFO Newsl., 6 May 1955, p.2.
1958, March 11
(Editorial), Fate 11 (July 1958):17.
1967, Dec.28/Richard A. Steeg
"Observer's Notebook," Sky & Telescope 35 (May 1968):331. il.
1973, Oct.16/golf course
San Diego Evening Tribune, 17 Oct.
1973.

Oak Run
-UFO (NL)
1973, Oct.25/M.H. Strom
Redding Record-Searchlight, 26 Oct.
1973.

Oceano
-Spontaneous human combustion
1966, Aug.19/Doris Lee Jacobs/1342
23d St.
Mary Margaret Fuller, "Three Cases
of Spontaneous Combustion," Fate
20 (June 1967):93-95, quoting Santa
Maria Times (undated).

Oceanside
-Inner development
1909-   /Rosicrucian Fellowship/2222
Mission Ave.
Max Heindel, The Rosicrucian Cosmo-
Conception (Oceanside: Rosicrucian
Fellowship, 1909).
Mrs. Max Heindel, The Birth of the
Rosicrucian Fellowship (Oceanside:
Rosicrucian Fellowship, n.d.).

Ojai
-Astrology and reincarnation research
1960s-   /Marcia Moore
Marcia Moore & Douglas Mark, Yoga:
Science of the Self (York Harbor,
Me.: Arcane, 1967).
Marcia Moore & Douglas Mark, Reincar-
nation: Key to Immortality (York
Harbor, Me.: Arcane, 1968).
Marcia Moore & Douglas Mark, Diet,
Sex and Yoga (York Harbor, Me.:
Arcane, 1970 ed.).
Marcia Moore & Douglas Mark, Astrol-
ogy in Action (York Harbor, Me.:

Arcane, 1970).
Marcia Moore & Douglas Mark, Astrology: The Divine Science (York Harbor, Me.: Arcane, 1975).
Marcia Moore, Hypersentience (N.Y.:
Crown, 1976).
-Inner development
1970s/Meditation Group for the New Age
/Box 566
Armand Biteaux, The New Consciousness (Willits, Cal.: Oliver, 1975),
p.103.
-Spirit medium
1977-   /Belita Adair
James Crenshaw, "Belita Adair's Musical Mediumship," Fate 31 (May 1978)
:68-74. il.

Ontario
-Contactee
1967
David R. Saunders & R. Roger Harkins,
UFOs? Yes! (N.Y.: Signet, 1968), pp.
151-52.
-Electromagnetic anomaly
1964, March 4-7/Lola L. Surbur
(Letter), Evelyn Sisneros, Fate 18
(June 1965):128-29.
-Haunt
n.d.
Hans Holzer, Ghosts of the Golden
West (N.Y.: Ace, 1968), p.183.
-UFO (?)
1947, July 7/B.A. Runner
Los Angeles Times, 8 July 1947.
-UFO (NL)
1973, Oct.25
Ontario-Upland Daily Report, 26 Oct.
1973.
1977, Feb.26/=balloon?
"UFOs of Limited Merit," Int'l UFO
Reporter 2 (Apr.1977):6.

Orange
-Precognition
ca.1950/Marion Wayne
Bee Wood, "The Missing Tile," Fate 5
(Feb.-Mar.1952):53.
-UFO (CE-2)
1978, Feb.4/Claire Semaza
Costa Mesa Daily Pilot, 7 Feb.1978.
Idabel Epperson, "Canine Mother Hides
Puppies from UFO," MUFON UFO J., no.
122 (Jan.1978):7.
"Unusual Animal Reaction in Califor-
nia NL Case," Int'l UFO Reporter 3
(Apr.1978):newsfront sec.

Orange co.
-Out-of-body experience
1951-1958/Frances Shaw
Frances Shaw, "Scenes from an Astral
Journey," Fate 18 (Sep.1965):64-68.

Orland
-UFO (NL)
1972, April 14/Robert McGarr
"Two See UFO near Orland, California,"
Skylook, no.66 (May 1973):14.
1976, Jan.28

"Noteworthy UFO Sightings," Ufology
2 (summer 1976):62.

Orleans
-Humanoid
1952/Bear Valley Rd.
1960s/Benjamin Wilder/E of town
John Green, The Sasquatch File (Agassiz, B.C.: Cheam, 1973), pp.20-21,
29.
-Humanoid tracks
1960, April/John Green/Cedar Camp Rd.
John Green, Sasquatch: The Apes Among
Us (Seattle: Hancock House, 1978),
pp.71-72.
1968, Dec./S.C. Buttram/4 mi.N
John Green, The Sasquatch File (Agassiz, B.C.: Cheam, 1973), p.46.

Oro Grande
-Contactee
1955-1962/Gloria Lee/Cosmon Research
Gloria Lee, Why We Are Here (Palos
Verdes Estates: Cosmon Research
Foundation, 1959).
J.W. of Jupiter [Gloria Lee], The
Changing Condition of Your World
(Palos Verdes Estates: Cosmon Re-
search, 1962).
Verity [Gloria Lee], The Going and
the Glory (Auckland, N.Z.: Heralds
of the New Age, 1966 ed.).
Gray Barker, Book of Saucers (Clarks-
burg, W.V.: Saucerian, 1965), pp.
51-52.
Peter Kor, "The Strange Case of Glor-
ia Lee," Search 52 (June 1963):30-
31.

Oroville
-Airship inventor
1896, Nov./E.H. Benjamin
San Francisco Chronicle, 22 Nov.1896,
p.36; 23 Nov.1896, p.12; 24 Nov.
1896, p.9; 25 Nov.1896, p.16; and
26 Nov.1896, p.14.
San Francisco Call, 23-29 Nov.1896.
Sacramento Daily Record-Union, 23-24
Nov.1896.
Sacramento Bee, 23-24 Nov.1896.
Oakland Tribune, 24 Nov.1896.
Gordon I.R. Lore, Jr. & Harold H. De-
neault, Jr., Mysteries of the Skies:
UFOs in Perspective (Englewood
Cliffs, N.J.: Prentice-Hall, 1968),
pp.26-40.
-Humanoid
1960/Leonard Mack
1969, April/Ed Saville
John Green, The Sasquatch File (Ag-
assiz, B.C.: Cheam, 1973), pp.23,46.
1969, summer/Charles Jackson/Cherokee
Rd.
1969, July/Homer Stickley/Cherokee Rd.
John Green, Year of the Sasquatch
(Agassiz, B.C.: Cheam, 1970), pp.
77-78.
Don Hunter & René Dahinden, Sasquatch
(Toronto: McClelland & Stewart,
1973), pp.137-39.

1969, fall/French Creek
1969, Oct./Charles Mauldin/Feather R.
1969, Oct.31/Wes Strang
  John Green, The Sasquatch File (Agassiz, B.C.: Cheam, 1973), p.47.
1975, Sep.3/Mark Karr/Cherokee Rd.
  Chico Enterprise-Record, 3 Sep.1975.
-Humanoid tracks
1970, Jan./Ken Coon
1970, April 16/Homer Stickley
  John Green, The Sasquatch File (Ag-
  assiz, B.C.: Cheam, 1973), p.56.
-UFO (?)
1887, Jan.2/=meteor
  "Meteors," Monthly Weather Rev. 15
  (Jan.1887):24.
1947, July 8/A.L. Watson
  Sacramento Union, 9 July 1947.
1953, Aug.10/Susan Perdue
  Gray Barker, They Knew Too Much about
  Flying Saucers (N.Y.: Tower, 1967
  ed.), p.37.
-UFO (CE-1)
1956, Nov.19/Leo McInturf/Hwy.70
  (Editorial), Fate 10 (Mar.1957):16-
  17.
1975, Aug.13
  "UFO Central," CUFOS News Bull., 15
  Nov.1975, p.16.
-UFO (DD)
1953, June 30/Robert L. Wright
  (Letter), Fate 6 (Dec.1953):103-104.
1953, July 21/Joe Carlos/Feather R.
  Gray Barker, They Knew Too Much about
  Flying Saucers (N.Y.: Tower, 1967
  ed.), p.37.
1955, May 27/Robert L. Wright
1955, June 4/Robert L. Wright
  (Letter), Fate 8 (Dec.1955):113-14.
-UFO (NL)
1896, Nov.23/S.B. Onyett
  San Francisco Chronicle, 24 Nov.1896,
  p.10.
1970
1973, Oct.
  George H. Gallup, Jr. & Tom Reinken,
  "Who Believes in UFOs?" Fate 27
  (Aug.1974):54.

Oxnard
-Precognition
1963, Nov.22/General Telephone Co.
  John C. Ross, "Premonitions of Ken-
  nedy's Death," Fate 17 (May 1964):
  30.
-UFO (CE-1)
1976, Oct.16/Sturgis Rd.
  Dennis Leatart, "1976 California UFO
  Reports," APRO Bull. 25 (Dec.1976):
  3.
-UFO (NL)
1957, March 23/Dick McKendry/Oxnard AFB
  Donald E. Keyhoe, Flying Saucers: Top
  Secret (N.Y.: Putnam, 1960), pp.58-
  63.
  J. Allen Hynek, The Hynek UFO Report
  (N.Y.: Dell, 1977), pp.53-54.
1977, Aug.23-25, Sep.1/Dennis Leatart/
1301 Dahlia/=satellite?
  Dennis Leatart, "Ghost Riders Through

the Gates of Hercules," APRO Bull.
  26 (Aug.1977):1,3.
Dennis Leatart, "Update: Ghost Rid-
  ers," APRO Bull. 26 (Oct.1977):4.
(Letter), D. Herbison-Evans, APRO
  Bull. 26 (Dec.1977):mailer.

Pacifica
-UFO (DD)
1963, July/Cliff Robertson
  Timothy Green Beckley, "Saucers and
  Celebrities," Saga UFO Rept. 4
  (July 1977):40-41.
-UFO (NL)
1974
  "Golden Gate's Glowing Lights,"
  Probe the Unknown 2 (summer 1974):8.

Pacific Grove
-Skyquake
1953, Dec.5/300 block, Laurel Ave./
=meteor
  Harland Wilson, "There Are Meteors,
  After All," Fate 7 (May 1954):40,43.
-UFO (CE-3)
1896, Dec.2/Giuseppe Valinziano
  San Francisco Call, 3 Dec.1896, p.1.

Pacific Palisades
-Derelict automobile
1967, summer/Antioch x Via de la Paz
  Coral E. Lorenzen, The Shadow of the
  Unknown (N.Y.: Signet, 1970), pp.
  197-98.
-Haunt
1970s/Mr. Trafton
  Barry Taff, "Stalking the Elusive
  Spectre," Probe the Unknown 1 (Oct.
  1973):30-32. il.
-UFO (DD)
1947, July 4/Frank E. Chester
  Hollywood Citizen-News, 5 July 1947.
-UFO (NL)
1973, Dec.20/Robert B. Klinn
  Santa Ana Register, 26 Dec.1973. il.
Ann Druffel, "Santa Catalina Channel
  'Cloud-Cigars,'" Proc.1976 CUFOS
  Conference (Evanston: Center for
  UFO Studies, 1976), pp.62,67-68. il.
1978, June 22
  "UFOs of Limited Morit," Int'l UFO
  Reporter 3 (Aug.1978):3.

Palermo
-UFO (CE-1)
1958, July 1/Emma Porter/Esparanza Ave.
  (Editorial), Fate 11 (Dec.1958):20.

Palmdale
-Humanoid
1972/Ron Bailey
1973/Ron Bailey
1973/Kent Lacy
  B. Ann Slate & Alan Berry, Bigfoot
  (N.Y.: Bantam, 1976), pp.89-91,96-
  97,99-100.
1973, March 14/Ave.J, E of 110th St.E
  Antelope Valley Ledger-Gazette, 24
  Mar.1973.
  Jerome Clark & Loren Coleman, Crea-

tures of the Outer Edge (N.Y.: Warner, 1978), pp.30-32.
1973, March 24/Kim Allyn McDonald
Antelope Valley Ledger-Gazette, 30
Mar.1973.
John Green, Sasquatch: The Apes Among
Us (Seattle: Hancock House, 1978),
pp.314-15.
1973, April 14/John Parkhurst/Ave.J x
180th St.
1973, summer/Mike Pense
1973, Aug./Ron Bailey
B. Ann Slate & Alan Berry, Bigfoot
(N.Y.: Bantam, 1976), pp.68-70,91-
92,97-99.
1973, Dec.27
John Green, Sasquatch: The Apes Among
Us (Seattle: Hancock House, 1978),
p.315.
1974, Sep./Neil Forn/E end of Ave.J
B. Ann Slate & Alan Berry, Bigfoot
(N.Y.: Bantam, 1976), pp.78-79.
-UFO (DD)
1953, Jan.24
Donald E. Keyhoe, Flying Saucers from
Outer Space (N.Y.: Holt, 1953), p.
219.
-UFO (NL)
1947, July 6/Amy Herdliska/Four Corners
Los Angeles Times, 7 July 1947.

Palm Springs
-Fall of wheel
1969, April 16/Ruth Stevens
Jim Brandon, Weird America (N.Y.:
Dutton, 1978), p.31.
-Hex
1940
New York Herald-Tribune, 20 Feb.1940.
-UFO (?)
1957, Nov.7
Richard Hall, ed., The UFO Evidence
(Washington: NICAP, 1964), p.166.
1970, May/Kaye Ballard
Timothy Green Beckley, "Saucers and
Celebrities," Saga UFO Rept. 3 (Oct.
1976):40.
-UFO (CE-2)
1970, Dec.28/Lee Levin
"Landing Trace Case: Circle Found
near Palm Springs," Skylook, no.53
(Apr.1972):17-18.
-UFO (CE-4)
1978, July 29
Palm Springs Desert Sun, 4 Aug.1978.
-UFO (DD)
1978, March 18/15 mi.W
"UFOs of Limited Merit," Int'l UFO
Reporter 3 (May 1978):3.
"Case Update: Number 3-5-18," Int'l
UFO Reporter 3 (Aug.1978):8. il.
-UFO (NL)
1956, Feb.13/D. Dyer
(Letter), Dana Howard, Fate 10 (June
1957):113.

Palo Alto
-Automatic writing
1947-1951/Catharine Adair Robinson
Catharine Adair Robinson, "Scroll

Writing of Atlantis," Fate 4 (Aug.-
Sep.1951):107-13.
-Ghost
1928/Ralph Madison/500 block, Emerson
St.
Hans Holzer, Ghosts of the Golden
West (N.Y.: Ace, 1968), pp.63-64.
-Inner development
1970s/Spectrum Research Institute/231
Emerson St.
Carol & Mary Cocciardi, The Psychic
Yellow Pages (Saratoga: Out of the
Sky, 1977), pp.96-97.
-UFO (DD)
1963, July 18/Joseph Cappels
"Recent Sightings Confirm Admissions,"
UFO Inv. 2 (June-Sep.1963):3-4.
-UFO (NL)
1952, Oct.12/Harry C. Potter
Richard Hall, ed., The UFO Evidence
(Washington: NICAP, 1964), p.45.
1976, Oct.22/Jack Hickling/Alma St.
Mike Mills, "UFO Sighting over Palo
Alto," MUFON UFO J., no.109 (Dec.
1976):6. il.

Palos Verdes
-UFO (CE-3)
1971, Aug.17/Dapple Gray Lane
Ann Druffel, "Encounter on Dapple
Gray Lane," Flying Saucer Rev. 23
(June 1977):19-23,26; (Aug.1977):20-
21,27. il.
-UFO (NL)
1975, Nov.12
"UFO Central," CUFOS News Bull., 1
Feb.1976, p.12.

Paradise
-Humanoid
1969, April/Mrs. Robert Behme/N of town
John Green, The Sasquatch File (Agassiz, B.C.: Cheam, 1973), p.46.
-UFO (CE-2)
1950, Oct.11/W.H. Hutchinson
Chico Enterprise-Record, 12 Oct.1950.
W.H. Hutchinson, "Those Things in
the Sky," Natural History 60 (Jan.
1951):1-2.

Pasadena
-Dowsing
1890s/Capt. Godfrey
W.F. Barrett, "On the So-Called Div-
ining Rod," Proc.SPR 15 (1900):130,
250-52.
-Inner development
1915-1950s/Ordo Templi Orientis/1003
and 1071 S. Orange Grove Ave.
Ellic Howe, The Magicians of the Gol-
den Dawn (London: Routledge & Kegan
Paul, 1972).
Kenneth Grant, The Magical Revival
(N.Y.: Weiser, 1973).
Kenneth Grant, Aleister Crowley and
the Hidden God (N.Y.: Weiser, 1975).
Francis King, The Secret Rituals of
the O.T.O. (N.Y.: Weiser, 1975).
Armand Biteaux, The New Conscious-
ness (Willits, Cal.: Oliver, 1975),

pp.107-108.
Jim Brandon, <u>Weird America</u> (N.Y.:
Dutton, 1978), p.27.
1960s-   /Ordo Templi Ashtart/Box 3125
1960s-   /Fera-feria
1960s-   /Sara Cunningham/170 S. Oak-
land St.
Hans Holzer, <u>The New Pagans</u> (Garden
City: Doubleday, 1972), pp.84-123,
141-48.
Hans Holzer, <u>The Witchcraft Report</u>
(N.Y.: Ace, 1973), pp.107-11,123-33.
-Seance
1930, July 18/Arthur Ford
Upton Sinclair, <u>The Autobiography of</u>
<u>Upton Sinclair</u> (N.Y.: Harcourt,
Brace & World, 1962), pp.245-47.
Upton Sinclair, "'Spirits,' or Tele-
pathy?" in Bernhardt J. Hurwood, ed.,
<u>The Second Occult Review Reader</u>
(N.Y.: Award, 1969), pp.9-23.
Allen Spraggett, <u>Arthur Ford: The</u>
<u>Man Who Talked with the Dead</u> (N.Y.:
Signet, 1973), pp.227-29.
-Skyquake
1952, Jan.26
Marion Kirkpatrick, "California Mys-
tery Blasts," <u>Fate</u> 10 (Apr.1957):
86,88.
-Telepathy
1928/Upton Sinclair
Upton Sinclair, <u>Mental Radio</u> (Pasa-
dena: The Author, 1930).
-UFO (CE-3)
1976, Aug.30/Francis de John
Ann Druffel, "Entities and Their
Carriages," <u>MUFON UFO J.</u>, no.129
(Aug.1978):15-16.
-UFO (DD)
1956, Jan.3/Daniel L. Cramer
<u>Ontario-Upland Daily Report</u>, 1 Mar.
1956.
-UFO (NL)
1896, Nov.25/George Smith
<u>Los Angeles Record</u>, 26 Nov.1896.
1947, July 2/Frank Newcomb
<u>Los Angeles Times</u>, 4 July 1947.
1954, May 22-23/Jean Miller
(Letter), <u>Fate</u> 8 (Mar.1955):106-107.
1956, July 29/Homer Clem
<u>San Bernardino Telegram</u>, 30 July 1956.
1956, Sep.6/Mark Matlock
"Case 210," <u>CRIFO Orbit</u>, 5 Oct.1956,
p.4, quoting <u>Los Angeles Times</u> (undated).
1957, March 23/Dewey Crow/Filter Center
Richard Hall, ed., <u>The UFO Evidence</u>
(Washington: NICAP, 1964), p.85.
1958, Nov.20/Earl Poe
(Letter), Salvatore Alfieri, <u>Fate</u> 12
(Apr.1959):111.
1966, March 28
<u>Columbus (O.) Dispatch</u>, 29 Mar.1966.

Paso Robles
-Haunt
1957, Dec.-1966/Mr. Adams
Hans Holzer, <u>Ghosts of the Golden</u>
<u>West</u> (N.Y.: Ace, 1968), pp.61-63.
-UFO (CE-3)

1973, Dec.14/Lance Mathias/36 mi.N on
Hwy.101
Ted Phillips, <u>Physical Traces Asso-</u>
<u>ciated with UFO Sightings</u> (Evans-
ton: Center for UFO Studies, 1975),
p.98.
-UFO (DD)
1957, Aug.29
J. Allen Hynek, <u>The Hynek UFO Report</u>
(N.Y.: Dell, 1977), p.44.

Pearblossom
-Weather control
1920s-1958/Charles Mallory Hatfield/=
unknown chemical method
<u>New York Times</u>, 15 Apr.1958, p.40.
Brad Williams & Choral Pepper, <u>Lost</u>
<u>Legends of the West</u> (N.Y.: Holt,
Rinehart & Winston, 1970), pp.147-
56.

Pescadero
-UFO (?)
1896, Dec./=balloon
<u>Redwood City Times-Gazette</u>, 5 Dec.
1896.

Petaluma
-Poltergeist
1970, Nov.-1973, March/Patricia Ever-
son
Patricia Everson, "Our Racketing
Ghost," <u>Fate</u> 29 (Apr.1976):45-48.
-UFO (NL)
1896, Nov.25
Gordon I.R. Lore, Jr. & Harold H.
Deneault, Jr., <u>Mysteries of the</u>
<u>Skies: UFOs in Perspective</u> (Engle-
wood Cliffs. N.J.: Prentice-Hall,
1968), p.9.
1949, June 3
"If It's in the Sky It's a Saucer,"
<u>Doubt</u>, no.27 (1949):416.

Pico Rivera
-Retrocognition
1933, Dec.22/Edith Elden Robinson
"Case-Record of Vision of a Vanished
Civilization in the Californian
Area," <u>J.ASPR</u> 28 (1934):292.

Piercy
-Gravity anomaly
Arthur Shuttlewood, <u>UFOs: Key to the</u>
<u>New Age</u> (London: Regency, 1971), p.
82.

Pinecrest
-Humanoid
1964, Jan.
(Editorial), <u>Fate</u> 17 (May 1964):20-
21.
(Editorial), <u>Fate</u> 17 (July 1964):14-
15.
-UFO (?)
1963, June 26
Richard Hall, ed., <u>The UFO Evidence</u>
(Washington: NICAP, 1964), p.140.

Pine Grove
-Dowsing
  1965/Jack Livingston
    Christopher Bird, "Applications of
    Dowsing: An Ancient Biopsychophys-
    ical Art," in John White & Stanley
    Krippner, Future Science (Garden
    City, N.Y.: Anchor, 1977), pp.346,
    351-52.

Pinole
-Clairvoyance
  1976, Aug./Jeanne Borgen
    (Editorial), Fate 30 (Feb.1977):34-
    38.
-UFO (NL)
  1975, Oct.1
    "UFO Central," CUFOS News Bull., 1
    Feb.1976, p.7.

Pittsburg
-UFO (CE-1)
  1947, July 7/Mrs. Edward Puckhaber
    San Francisco Examiner, 8 July 1947.
-UFO (DD)
  1947, July 6/Frank Tylman/2 mi.W
    San Francisco Call-Bulletin, 7 July
    1947.

Pixley
-Mystery plane crash
  1956, July 22/Merwin M. Stenvers/C131D
  Convair
    San Francisco Chronicle, 22 July
    1956; and 24 July 1956.
-UFO (?)
  1956, July 22/Kenneth McMullins
    Coral & Jim Lorenzen, UFOs: The Whole
    Story (N.Y.: Signet, 1969), p.72.

Placentia
-UFO (NL)
  1976, June 22
    "Noteworthy UFO Sightings," Ufology
    2 (fall 1976):60.
  1977, Oct.31
    "UFOs of Limited Merit," Int'l UFO
    Reporter 2 (Dec.1977):9. il.

Placerville
-Disappearance
  1962/R.W. Balcom/restaurant E of town
  on U.S.50/=destroyed by fire
    (Letter), Fate 21 (Sep.1968):130-31.
    (Letter), Mrs. Cecil B. Hay, Fate 22
    (Aug.1969):127.
-Ghost
  1968, Nov./Joiy Robbins
    Joiy Robbins, "The Lady in Grandfath-
    er's Chair," Fate 24 (Dec.1971):92-
    95.
-UFO (?)
  1874, Sep.30/James Blake
    James Blake, "Curious Electrical Light
    Observed during the Storm of Septem-
    ber 30th," Proc.Calif.Academy Sci.
    5 (1873-74):406.
  1947, July 8/Maud Lawyer
    Sacramento Union, 9 July 1947.
-UFO (DD)

1947, Aug.14
  Bruce S. Maccabee, "UFO Related Information from the FBI Flies: Part
  3," MUFON UFO J., no.121 (Dec.1977)
  :10,14.
-UFO (NL)
  1957, Feb.13/Steve Papina
    Coral & Jim Lorenzen, UFOs: The Whole
    Story (N.Y.: Signet, 1969), pp.76-
    77.

Platina
-Humanoid tracks
  1966, winter/Mr. Hampton/2 mi.W
    John Green, The Sasquatch File (Ag-
    assiz, B.C.: Cheam, 1973), p.38.

Pleasant Hill
-Fall of weblike substance
  1977, Oct.11/=spider web
    Dallas (Tex.) Times-Herald, 12 Oct.
    1977.
-UFO (CE-2)
  1953, Oct.13/Mrs. Edwin E. Meyer/Cort-
  sen Rd.
    "Reports from Everywhere," Fate 7
    (May 1954):26.
-UFO (NL)
  1960, Aug.17
    Richard Hall, ed., The UFO Evidence
    (Washington: NICAP, 1964), p.170.
  1975, Nov.8
    "UFO Central," CUFOS News Bull., 1
    Feb.1976, p.12.

Pleasanton
-UFO (CE-1)
  1976, June 25/Ellen Roberts/I-680
    Dave Reeve, "California Flyover Case
    Revealed," MUFON UFO J., no.112
    (Mar.1977):8-9. il.

Pleasant Valley
-UFO (NL)
  1953, July 13/Ethel G. Carson
    Gray Barker, They Knew Too Much about
    Flying Saucers (N.Y.: Tower, 1967
    ed.), p.36.

Point Arena
-UFO (CE-2)
  1973, Oct.19/S on Hwy.1
    "Teacher and Students See UFO As
    Large As a Small House," Skylook,
    no.94 (Jan.1974):10-11.

Pomona
-Haunt
  1967/Jo Ann Leimbach/Casa Alvarado
    Hans Holzer, Gothic Ghosts (N.Y.:
    Pocket Books, 1972), pp.126-36.
-UFO (?)
  1950, Oct.3/J.D. Laudermilk
    Richard Hall, ed., The UFO Evidence
    (Washington: NICAP, 1964), p.49.
  1953, Jan.23
    Donald E. Keyhoe, Flying Saucers from
    Outer Space (N.Y.: Holt, 1955), p.
    219.

Port Costa
-Giant human skeleton
  1973/Wonders of the World Museum/=hoax
    "Beware an Alleged 'Bigfoot' Skele-
    ton," Pursuit 6 (Apr.1973):37.

Porterville
-UFO (?)
  1956, Jan.30/Baker Ranch/=test missile
    Los Angeles Times, 31 Jan.1956.
    (Letter), Thomas M. Olsen, CRIFO
    Orbit, 4 May 1956, pp.3-4.

Port Hueneme
-Chinese discovery
  ca.490 A.D./Hwui Shan
    Henriette Mertz, Gods from the Far
    East (N.Y.: Ballantine, 1975 ed.),
    pp.23-34,91,97.
-Fall of unknown object
  1968, Aug.12/"Pacific Seal"/Pt. Mugu
    Kansas City (Mo.) Star, 13 Aug.1968.
-UFO (DD)
  1954, June/Pt. Mugu
    Donald E. Keyhoe, Flying Saucer Con-
    spiracy (N.Y.: Holt, 1955), p.164.
-UFO (NL)
  1976, Nov.7/Bob Johnson/Willowbrook Dr.
    Dennis Leatart, "1976 California UFO
    Reports," APRO Bull. 25 (Dec.1976):
    1,4, quoting Port Hueneme Press-Cou-
    rier (undated).

Potter Valley
-UFO (CE-1)
  1896, Nov.28/E.G. Case
    Loren E. Gross, The UFO Wave of 1896
    (Fremont, Cal.: The Author, 1974),
    p.25.

Quartz Hill
-Humanoid
  1966
  1973, Sep.17
    John Green, Sasquatch: The Apes Among
    Us (Seattle: Hancock House, 1978),
    pp.309,315.

Ramona
-UFO (CE-2)
  1974, Nov.15?/Jennie Overfelt
    George D. Fawcett, "What We Can Ex-
    pect of UFOs in 1975," Official UFO
    1 (Aug.1975):12,51.
    R. Michael Rasmussen, "The UFO Chal-
    lenge--Science on Trial," Official
    UFO 1 (Aug.1975):44.

Rancho Cordova
-UFO (DD)
  1976, Feb.18
    "Sighting Reports," CUFOS News Bull.,
    June 1976, p.5.

Randsburg
-Haunt
  n.d./painting
    Richard Webb, Voices from Another
    World (N.Y.: Manor, 1972 ed.), pp.
    253-55.

-Weather control
  n.d./Charles Mallory Hatfield/=unknown
  chemical process
    Frank Edwards, Strange People (N.Y.:
    Popular Library, 1961), p.125.
    Richard Dillon, Humbugs and Heroes
    (Garden City: Doubleday, 1970), pp.
    134-40.

Red Bluff
-UFO (NL)
  1896, Nov.24/J.A. Owen/Walnut x Washington St.
    Oakland Tribune, 25 Nov.1896.
    San Francisco Bulletin, 25 Nov.1896.
    San Francisco Chronicle, 26 Nov.
    1896, p.14.
  1960, Aug.17/Clarence Fry/prison
    John C. Ross, "State Cops Race 'Fly-
    ing Saucer,'" Fate 13 (Dec.1960):
    44-45.

Redding
-UFO (CE-2)
  1969, Oct.30/Jane Chapin/Mary Hazel
  Mine
    "Redding Couple's Episodes," APRO
    Bull. 26 (Oct.1977):5.
    "The Redding, California CEII Case,"
    Int'l UFO Reporter 3 (Mar.1978):
    newsfront sec.
    Paul Cerny, "The Redding, California,
    Mining Case," MUFON UFO J., no.125
    (Apr.1978):6-8. il.
  1976, Dec.29/Jane Chapin/Mary Hazel
  Mine
    San Francisco Examiner-Chronicle, 5
    Feb.1978.
    "The Redding, California CEII Case,"
    Int'l UFO Reporter 3 (Mar.1978):
    newsfront sec.
    Paul Cerny, "The Redding,California,
    Mining Case," MUFON UFO J., no.125
    (Apr.1978):6,8-10. il.
-UFO (DD)
  1967, June 10/William M. Murphy/Hwy.99
  x Cypress St.
    "World Round-up," Flying Saucer Rev.
    13 (Nov.-Dec.1967):32.
  1967, Nov.19
    "U.S.A.," APRO Bull.16 (Mar.-Apr.
    1968):8.

Redlands
-Spirit medium
  1914-1918/Violet Parent
    Hamlin Garland, The Mystery of the
    Buried Crosses (N.Y.: Dutton, 1939).
    il.
-UFO (CE-2)
  1968, Feb.4
    "Disc over Redlands, Calif.," APRO
    Bull. 16 (Jan.-Feb.1968):6.
    Coral Lorenzen, "UFO in California,"
    Fate 22 (Mar.1969):74-79. il.
-UFO (DD)
  1947, July 7/H.J. Stell
    Los Angeles Times, 8 July 1947.
  1958, Dec.13/John D. Penney
    Jacques Vallee, "A New Look at Sau-

cer Mysteries," in Frank Bowers, ed.,
The True Report on Flying Saucers
(Greenwich, Ct.: Fawcett, 1967), p.
18. il.
-UFO (NL)
1896, Nov.30
Loren E. Gross, The UFO Wave of 1896
(Fremont, Cal.: The Author, 1974),
pp.24-25.
1960, Aug.18/Corrine Bay/917 Washington
John C. Ross, "State Cops Race 'Flying Saucer,'" Fate 13 (Dec.1960):
44,47.

Redondo Beach
-Fall of fish
1954, Jan.26
"Falls(?)," Doubt, no.44 (1954):275.
-UFO (DD)
1947, July 4/T.W. Peters
Los Angeles Examiner, 6 July 1947.
-UFO (NL)
1956, Jan.18/Bill Stidham
"Sea-Saucer or Searchlight?" CRIFO
Orbit, 2 Mar.1956, p.4.
Coral & Jim Lorenzen, UFOs: The Whole
Story (N.Y.: Signet, 1969), pp.69-
70.

Redway
-Ghost
1963, Feb.1/Thomas P. Meehan/Forty
Winks Motel/=disorientation and acci-
dental death by LSD?
(Editorial), Fate 16 (June 1963):16-
18.
(Editorial), Fate 17 (July 1964):27-
28.

Redwood City
-Healing
1970s/Harold Plume/878 Main St.
David St. Clair, Psychic Healers
(Garden City: Doubleday, 1974), pp.
90-115.
Fay C. Oliver, "Harold Plume and His
Team of Spirit Doctors," Fate 27
(May 1974):71-78. il.
-Precognition
1951, July/Edythe Hanson
"Weird Prophecy," Fate 5 (Feb.-Mar.
1952):114.
-Sea monster
1955, July/Joseph Korhummel/=oarfish
(Editorial), Fate 9 (May 1956):6.
-UFO (DD)
1947, July 5/Augustine Fernandez/S of
town
San Francisco Examiner, 6 July 1947.
-UFO (NL)
1947, July 9/Benjamin Ballard
San Francisco Chronicle, 11 July
1947.
1978, May 16
Redwood City Tribune, 17 May 1978.

Reseda
-UFO (CE-2)
1953, Nov.16/Mrs. Louis Dangelo
San Fernando Valley Times, 15 Feb.

1954.
James C. McNamara, "Angel's Hair,"
Pageant, Nov.1954, pp.52-56. il.
-UFO (DD)
1947, May/Guy W. Grant
(Letter), Fate 19 (Dec.1966):148-49.
1957, March 28
Jacques & Janine Vallee, Challenge
to Science (N.Y.: Ace, 1966), p.
199.
-UFO (NL)
1976, Sep.5
Ann Druffel & Morrey Allen, "The Sky-
net Log: Circling Ships," MUFON UFO
J., no.108 (Nov.1976):6-8. il.
1976, Sep.25/Shirley Johnson/Kittridge
Ave.
Mike Mills, "California Sighting,"
MUFON UFO J., no.109 (Dec.1976):10.

Richmond
-Archeological site
11th St./Harborgate Tract
N.C. Nelson, "The Ellis Landing Shell-
mound," Pub.Am.Arch. & Ethn.Univ.
Calif. 7 (1910):357-426. il.
Llewellyn L. Loud, "The Stege Mounds
at Richmond, California," Pub.Am.
Arch. & Ethn.Univ.Calif. 17 (1924):
355-72. il.
-Fall of metallic object
1957, July 31/Albert T. Haynes/600
Key Blvd.
Jim Brandon, Weird America (N.Y.:
Dutton, 1978), p.43.
-UFO (?)
1953, Jan.22
Donald E. Keyhoe, Flying Saucers from
Outer Space (N.Y.: Holt, 1953), p.
219.
-UFO (NL)
1952, Feb.25/Jack Fickes
(Editorial), Fate 5 (Sep.1952):6.

Ridgecrest
-UFO (NL)
1959, July 12/Albert Guerrero/SW of
China L.
Richard Hall, ed., The UFO Evidence
(Washington: NICAP, 1964), p.31.
1960, Sep.10
Lloyd Mallan, "Complete Directory of
UFOs: Part II," Sci.& Mech. 38 (Jan.
1967):44,76.

Rio Bonita
-UFO (NL)
1896, Dec.2/Hatch & Rock Co. orchard
Marysville Semi-Weekly Appeal, 10
Dec.1896.

Rio Dell
-Fall of weblike substance
1958, Nov.9
Eureka Humboldt Times, 11-12 Nov.
1958.
-UFO (NL)
1964, Sep.20/Donald H. Martin
Curtis Fuller, "Collected UFO Sightings for August and September," Fate

18 (Jan.1965):35,39-40, quoting Eureka Humboldt Times (undated).

Rio Linda
-UFO (NL)
1967, July 11/Leon L. Oeming
(Letter), Fate 27 (Nov.1974):144-45.

Rio Vista
-UFO (CE-1)
1965, Sep.21/Danny Bland/Riverview Rd.
San Diego Union, 1 Oct.1965.
-UFO (CE-2)
1964, May 13/Mrs. M. Walter McKarley
"Physical Evidence Landing Reports,"
UFO Inv. 2 (July-Aug.1964):6.
"Two Saucer Landings in California,"
Saucer News 11 (Sep.1964):15.
-UFO (CE-3)
1965, Oct.4/Betty Valine
Jerome Clark, "The Greatest Flap Yet?
--Part III," Flying Saucer Rev. 12
(May-June 1966):13-14.

Ripon
-UFO (CE-1)
1968, summer/Jack Thompson/Hwy.99
Ann Druffel, "California Report: Police and UFOs," Skylook, no.97 (Dec.
1975):8-9.

Riverside
-Bird attack
1964, May 1/Marcus Yerkes/7290 Grey-
locks St.
(Editorial), Fate 17 (Oct.1964):18-
20, quoting Los Angeles Times (un-
dated).
-Fall of foam
1957, Dec.18
"All About Sputs," Doubt, no.56
(1958):460,479.
-Fall of ice
1972, May 23
Los Angeles Times, 24 May 1972.
-Fall of plastic
1962, Dec.2/Jack Brazil/6324 Neva St.
(Editorial), Fate 16 (Apr.1963):9.
-Haunt
1956, June/R. Eveline Blank
R. Eveline Blank, "Tragedies Live
After," Fate 24 (Dec.1971):74-77.
-Humanoid
1958, Nov.8/Charles Wetzel/N. Main St.
nr. Santa Ana R.
Los Angeles Examiner, 9 Nov.1958.
(Editorial), Fate 12 (Mar.1959):21-
22.
1976, July/Santa Ana R.
John Green, Sasquatch: The Apes Among
Us (Seattle: Hancock House, 1978),
p.321.
-Paraphysics research
1960s/Joseph Molitorisz
Peter Tompkins & Christopher Bird,
The Secret Life of Plants (N.Y.:
Harper & Row, 1973), pp.178-79.
-Skyquake
1952, April 24
Riverside Daily Press, 25 Apr.1952.

-UFO (?)
1951, Nov.11/Guy B. Marquand, Jr./=
hoax
(Editorial), Fate 5 (Apr.-May 1952):
9. il.
Harold T. Wilkins, Flying Saucers on
the Attack (N.Y.: Ace, 1967 ed.),
p.143.
Frank Bowers, ed., The True Report
on Flying Saucers (Greenwich, Ct.:
Fawcett, 1967), p.59. il.
-UFO (CE-1)
1965, Jan.12
"News Briefs," Saucer News 12 (Mar.
1965):26.
-UFO (CE-3)
1955, Aug.29/Kermit Douglas/Casa Blanca
Riverside Daily Press, 30 Aug.1955,
p.17.
Riverside Enterprise, 30 Aug.1955.
Gordon Creighton, "The Extraordinary
Happenings at Casa Blanca," Flying
Saucer Rev. 13 (Sep.-Oct.1967):16-
18. il.
Isabel Davis & Ted Bloecher, Close
Encounter at Kelly and Others of
1955 (Evanston: Center for UFO
Studies, 1978), pp.186-89.
-UFO (DD)
1947, July 7/R.V. Allen
Los Angeles Times, 8 July 1947.
-UFO (NL)
1947, July 10/L.W. Face/4 mi.NE
Ted Bloecher, Report on the UFO Wave
of 1947 (Washington: NICAP, 1967),
Appendix, Case 822.
1975, Aug.2
"UFO Central," CUFOS News Bull.,15
Nov.1975, p.15.
1977, March 22/March AFB
Kansas City (Mo.) Star, 23 Mar.1977.

Riverside co.
-UFO (DD)
1978, March 18/Leo Giampietro/I-10
John DeHerrera, "Disc Photographed
in California," APRO Bull. 26 (June
1978):1,3. il.

Rosemead
-Inner development
1974/Movement of Spiritual Inner Aware-
ness/Box 676
June & Nicholas Regush, Psi: The Other World Catalogue (N.Y.: Putnam,
1974), p.157.
-UFO (NL)
1952, Aug.25/Thomas H. Houldridge
(Letter), Fate 6 (Jan.1953):106-107.

Roseville
-UFO (CE-1)
1968, summer/Jack Thompson/N of town
Ann Druffel, "California Report: Police and UFOs," Skylook, no.97 (Dec.
1975):8-9.
-UFO (NL)
1947, June 24/Viola Wendt
Sacramento Union, 2 July 1947.
1960, Aug.17/Hugh McGuigan/Base Line

Rd.
John C. Ross, "State Cops Race 'Flying Saucer,'" Fate 13 (Dec.1960):
44,46.

Round Mountain
-Humanoid tracks
1971, Jan.6/Fenders Ferry Rd.
Redding Record-Searchlight, 8 Jan.
1971.
1975, Feb./John Russak
Renee Dictor LeBlanc, "Peter Byrne
Stalks the Rarest Game of All--Big-
foot," Probe the Unknown 4 (Mar.
1976):24,27.

Rubidoux
-UFO (CE-1)
1963, June 19/A.W. Creech/De la Vista
Rd.
Arlington Times, 26 June 1963.
Gray Barker, Book of Saucers (Clarks-
burg, W.V.: Saucerian, 1965), p.
19.

Sacramento
-Animal ESP
1966/Earl W. Chester
(Editorial), Fate 19 (Aug.1966):20.
-Archeological site
500 A.D./Kadema site/nr. Watt Ave.
(Editorial), Fate 13 (July 1960):18-
19.
-Contactee
1978/Sue McMahon
Toronto (Ont.) Sun, 7 June 1978.
-Disappearance
1955, Nov.13/AF jet fighter/McClelland
AFB
M.K. Jessup, The Expanding Case for
the UFO (N.Y.: Citadel, 1957), p.63.
-Fall of fish
1951, March 5/Robla
"Run of the Mill," Doubt, no.33
(1951):91.
-Fall of salamanders
1870, Aug./Judge Spicer/Colorado St.
Henry Winfred Splitter, "Wonders from
the Sky," Fate 6 (Oct.1953):33,36,
quoting Sacramento Reporter (un-
dated).
-Fall of stones
1946, July 15/Hagginwood
"Stone Shower," Doubt, no.16 (1946):
244.
-Fall of weblike substance
1955, July 29
Leonard H. Stringfield, Inside Saucer
Post...3-0 Blue (Cincinnati: CRIFO,
1957), p.50.
-Haunt
1964, June/Dorothy Lunsford/5848 14th
Ave.
(Editorial), Fate 17 (Nov.1964):10,
quoting Sacramento Bee (undated).
1970s/Lillian Martinez
(Editorial), Fate 26 (Mar.1973):16-
18, quoting San Francisco Chronicle
(undated).
-UFO (CE-1)

1896, Nov.17/Mr. Johnson
San Francisco Call, 18 Nov.1896.
1972, Aug./H.J. Whitcombe
Sacramento Bee, 16 Aug.1972.
-UFO (CE-3)
1896, Nov.17/R.L. Lowry/East Park
Sacramento Record-Union, 18-20 Nov.
1896.
Sacramento Bee, 18 Nov.1896.
San Francisco Chronicle, 19 Nov.1896,
p.5.
San Francisco Call, 19 Nov.1896.
-UFO (DD)
1896, Nov.18/Oak Park
San Francisco Call, 19 Nov.1896.
1947, July 5/Municipal Airport
Sacramento Union, 6 July 1947.
1947, July 5/A.K. Carr
1947, July 7/L.L. Ransom
Sacramento Union, 8 July 1947.
1947, July 8/Savina Rosette/518½ V St.
1947, July 8/Jerry Grayham/4639 Buck-
ingham Way
Sacramento Union, 9 July 1947.
1957, Nov. 9
Richard Hall, ed., The UFO Evidence
(Washington: NICAP, 1964), p.167.
1963, Jan.20/McClellan AFB
Gray Barker, Book of Saucers (Clarks-
burg, W.V.: Saucerian, 1965), p.18.
1966, Jan.1/Mather AFB
Jerome Clark, "The Greatest Flap Yet?
--Part IV," Flying Saucer Rev. 12
(Nov.-Dec.1966):9,12.
1978, April 9/Jacob Davidson
Antioch Ledger, 10 Apr.1978.
-UFO (NL)
1896, Nov.17/Frank Ross/18th St.
Sacramento Bee, 18-19 Nov.1896.
Sacramento Union, 19-20 Nov.1896.
San Francisco Chronicle, 19 Nov.1896,
p.5.
1896, Nov.22/Jacob Zemansky
1896, Nov.22/Nick White/3d x K St.
Sacramento Record-Union, 23 Nov.1896.
San Francisco Chronicle, 23 Nov.1896,
p.12.
1896, Nov.25/3d x J St.
Sacramento Record-Union, 25 Nov.1896.
1896, Nov.26/N.A. Bunce/Oak Park
Sacramento Bee, 27 Nov.1896.
1955, July-1957, Dec./William D. Leet/
McClellan AFB
1957, Nov.5
1961, July 1
Richard Hall, ed., The UFO Evidence
(Washington: NICAP, 1964), pp.24,
156,165.
1970, Feb.6/F.E. Burchardt
"Object over Sacramento," APRO Bull.
18 (Jan.-Feb.1970):5.

Saint Helena
-Haunt
1950s/Jeanne Owen/Spring Hill Farm
Danton Walker, Spooks Deluxe (N.Y.:
Franklin Watts, 1956), pp.86-92.

Salinas
-Gravity anomaly

Wonder Hill
  Catherine Christopher, "Another Vortex?" Fate 5 (Jan.1952):21.
-UFO (CE-1)
  1950, March 11/Mrs. Sam Raguindin/S of town
    Los Angeles Times, 12 Mar.1950.
    Kenneth Arnold & Ray Palmer, The Coming of the Saucers (Boise: The Authors, 1952), p.146.
-UFO (DD)
  1973, Oct.26/David Gonyea/933 Garden Way
    Salinas Californian, 27 Oct.1973.
-UFO (NL)
  1896, Nov.28/Fred R. Howe
    Salinas Democrat, 5 Dec.1896.
  1973, Oct.27/Santos Martinez/1042 Fifth St.
    Salinas Californian, 27 Oct.1973.
  1978, Feb.26/Richard Lockwood
    Monterey Peninsula Herald, 27 Feb. 1978.

Salyer
-Humanoid
  1968, July 11/Trinity R.
    John Green, The Sasquatch File (Agassiz, B.C.: Cheam, 1973), p.46.

San Andreas
-UFO (NL)
  1896, Nov.15/Hannah Harney
    San Andreas Calaveras Prospect, 21 Nov.1896; and 28 Nov.1896.

San Anselmo
-UFO (DD)
  1952, July
    Harold T. Wilkins, Flying Saucers on the Attack (N.Y.: Ace, 1967 ed.), p.267.
-UFO (NL)
  1975, Sep.5
    "UFO Central," CUFOS News Bull., 15 Nov.1975, p.18.

San Ardo
-UFO (CE-3)
  1973, Dec.14
    David Webb, 1973--Year of the Humanoids (Evanston: Center for UFO Studies, 1976 ed.), p.21.

San Bernardino
-Clairvoyance
  1949, Jan./Denice Tobin
    Denice Tobin, "I Shared a Dream," Fate 13 (Mar.1960):53-54.
-Haunt
  1948-1952/Leina Murphy
    M.G. Murphy, "The Ghost That Moved to Our House," Fate 16 (May 1963):36, 43-44.
  1957-1966, Oct./Verna Kunze/G St.
    Hans Holzer, Ghosts of the Golden West (N.Y.: Ace, 1968), pp.41-50.
-Skyquake
  1946, Dec.28/Genevieve x 29th St.
    "Explosions," Doubt, no.18 (1947):271.

-UFO (?)
  1956, July 19/Michael Savage
    "UFO Picture of 1956," Flying Saucer Rev. 2 (July-Aug.1956):2-3. il.
    "Case 174," CRIFO Orbit, 7 Sep.1956, p.1, quoting San Bernardino Daily Sun (undated).
    Richard Hall, ed., The UFO Evidence (Washington: NICAP, 1964), p.89.
-UFO (NL)
  1970, Feb.15
    "Many See 'Thing' in Sky," Skylook, no.29 (Apr.1970):19, quoting San Bernardino Sun-Telegram (undated).

San Bruno
-UFO (?)
  1950, April 28/=Venus?
    Los Angeles Times, 29 Apr.1950.
-UFO (NL)
  1973, Oct.19/Josephine Day/nr. airport
    San Mateo Times, 20 Oct.1973.

San Carlos
-Fall of metallic object
  1978, Nov.7/Tim Bollinger/Dallard Elementary School
    San Diego Daily Union, 8 Nov.1978.
-Haunt
  n.d.
    (Editorial), Fate 25 (Sep.1972):32.
-UFO (CE-3)
  1966, Dec.3/Vern Morse/Bayshore Hwy.
    John A. Keel, Strange Creatures from Time and Space (Greenwich, Ct.: Fawcett, 1970), p.211.
-UFO (DD)
  1947, July 7/Marie Maranta
    San Francisco Call-Bulletin, 8 July 1947.

San Clemente
-UFO (NL)
  1960, Aug.16/Roman Maykowski
    Santa Ana Register, 17 Aug.1960.
    (Letter), Fate 13 (Dec.1960):116-17.

San Diego
-Animal ESP
  1940s/Lewis Thompson
    Morton Thompson, "The Man Who Talked to Horses," Am.Mercury 59 (Nov.1944):603-609.
    Morton Thompson, Joe, the Wounded Tennis Player (N.Y.: Doubleday, 1945).
-Anomalous hole in ground
  n.d./Henry Matill
    (Editorial), Fate 22 (Jan.1969):14.
-Anomalous mounds
    G.W. Barnes, "The Hillocks or Mound-Formations of San Diego, California," Am.Naturalist 13 (1879):565-71. il.
    Victor B. Scheffer, "The Mystery of the Mima Mounds," Sci.Monthly 65 (Oct.1947):283-94.
-Archeological site
  100,000 B.C./nr. Mission San Diego de Alcala
    Baltimore (Md.) Sun, 11 Aug.1973, p.3.

Phoenix <u>Arizona Republic</u>, 23 Apr.1977.
Texas St.

G.F. Carter, "Interglacial Artifacts
from the San Diego Area," <u>Southwest-</u>
<u>ern J.Anthro.</u> 8 (1952):444-56. il.

George F. Carter, "An Interglacial
Site at San Diego, California," <u>Mas-</u>
<u>terkey</u> 28 (1954):165-74.

John Witthoft, "Texas Street Artifacts," <u>New World Antiquity</u> 2, no.9
(1955):132-33.

George F. Carter, <u>Pleistocene Man at</u>
<u>San Diego</u> (Baltimore: Johns Hopkins,
1957), pp.304-45. il.

L.W. Patterson, "Comments on Texas
Street Lithic Artifacts," <u>Anthro.J.</u>
<u>Canada</u> 15, no.4 (1977):15-25. il.

Buchanan Canyon

James Robert Moriarty III & Herbert
Minshall, "A New Pre-Desert Site
Discovered near Texas Street," <u>An-</u>
<u>thro.J.Canada</u> 10, no.3 (1972):10-13.

-Bioenergetics research

1970s/Western Institute for Bioenergetics Analysis/7522 Clairemont Mesa

Stanley Keleman, "Bio-energetic Concepts of Grounding," <u>Energy & Char-</u>
<u>acter</u> 1 (Sep.1970):10-19.

W. Edward Mann, <u>Orgone, Reich and</u>
<u>Eros</u> (N.Y.: Simon & Schuster, 1973),
p.256.

-Cartomancy and precognition

1960s-   /Katharine Cover Sabin

Elizabeth Read, "Everyone Can Be a
Prophet," <u>Fate</u> 22 (Nov.1969):84-95.
il.

Herbert B. Greenhouse, <u>Premonitions:</u>
<u>A Leap into the Future</u> (N.Y.: War-
ner, 1973 ed.), p.28.

Katharine Cover Sabin, "Noted Psychic
Tells How to Program Your Dreams,"
<u>Fate</u> 28 (Apr.1975):44-51.

-Child prodigy

1950s/Alphydesie Omega

(Editorial), <u>Fate</u> 12 (May 1959):14-
17.

-Clairvoyance

1921, April 3/Blanche DeVere/Ocean
Beach

Hereward Carrington, "A Spirit Sends
a Wire," <u>Fate</u> 28 (Mar.1975):90-92.

-Crisis apparition

1975, July/Anna Maria Savino

Lisa S. Emerson, "Three Dreams and
You're Dead," <u>Fate</u> 29 (Oct.1976):
66,70-71.

-Erratic boulders

1958, Sep.24/Frank Luckel

Allan O. Kelley, "Erratic Boulders on
Point Loma," <u>Scientists Forum</u> 1
(Jan.1973):80-81.

-Fall of fish

1958, Sep.24/Frank Luckel

"Falls," <u>Doubt</u>, no.59 (1959):37.

-Fall of localized rain

1959, July 19/Charles Coval/6611 Bur-
gundy St./=leafhopper excretions

(Editorial), <u>Fate</u> 12 (Nov.1959):14-
17.

-Fall of rocks

1962, Aug./Kenneth Snyder/5673 Barclay

San Diego Union, 10 Sep.1962.
1963, Sep./=prankster

Raymond Bayless, "The Great Catapult
Mystery," <u>Fate</u> 19 (Sep.1966):63,65.

-Haunt

1894

Charles M. Skinner, <u>American Myths</u>
<u>and Legends</u>, 2 vols. (Philadelphia:
Lippincott, 1903), 2:320.

1945/Earle Burney/Navy Electronics Lab,
Loma Portal

Hans Holzer, <u>Ghosts of the Golden</u>
<u>West</u> (N.Y.: Ace, 1968), pp.81-83.

1950s-1960s/Whaley House

"The Ghost of Whaley House," <u>Fate</u> 15
(Sep.1962):48.

Hans Holzer, <u>Ghosts of the Golden</u>
<u>West</u> (N.Y.: Ace, 1968), pp.11-41.

Susy Smith, <u>Prominent American Ghosts</u>
(N.Y.: Dell, 1969 ed.), pp.36-45.

-Healing

1925/Helen B. Walters

Helen B. Walters, "I Would Not Let
Ben Die," <u>Fate</u> 24 (Sep.1971):68-70.

-Hex

1972

(Editorial), <u>Fate</u> 25 (Oct.1972):22-
30.

-Humanoid

1966, July/nearby forest

John A. Keel, <u>Strange Creatures from</u>
<u>Time and Space</u> (Greenwich, Ct.: Faw-
cett, 1970), p.101.

-Inner development

1897-1942/Theosophical Society/Point
Loma

Omaha (Neb.) Bee, 15 Mar.1897, p.6.

Ray Stannard Baker, "An Extraordinary
Experiment in Brotherhood," <u>Ameri-</u>
<u>can Mag.</u> 63 (1907):227-40.

Katherine Tingley, <u>The Life at Point</u>
<u>Loma</u> (Pt. Loma: Theosophical Soc'y,
1908).

William Alfred Hinds, <u>American Com-</u>
<u>munities and Co-Operative Colonies</u>
(Chicago: Charles H. Kerr, 1908),
pp.464-70.

Elsie Benjamin, "Theosophy in America," <u>Fate</u> 5 (Apr.-May 1952):65-68.

Robert V. Hine, <u>California's Utopian</u>
<u>Colonies</u> (New Haven: Yale Univ.,
1966), pp.33-54.

1970s/Mandala Society/Box 23231

June & Nicholas Regush, <u>Psi: The Oth-</u>
<u>er World Catalogue</u> (N.Y.: Putnam,
1974), p.183.

-Mystery plane crash

1939, summer/military transport/North
Island NAS

Jerome Clark, "Why UFOs Are Hostile,"
<u>Flying Saucer Rev.</u> 13 (Nov.-Dec.
1967):18.

Leonard H. Stringfield, <u>Situation</u>
<u>Red: The UFO Siege</u> (N.Y.: Fawcett,
1977), pp.167-68.

-Out-of-body experience

1930s/Eileen Garrett

Eileen Garrett, <u>My Life As a Search</u>
<u>for the Meaning of Mediumship</u> (Lon-
don: Rider, 1939).

Eileen Garrett, Many Voices (N.Y.: Dell, 1969).

Allan Angoff, Eileen Garrett and the World Beyond the Senses (N.Y.: Morrow, 1974).

-Parapsychology research
1960s-   /California Parapsychology Foundation/3580 Adams Ave.
(Review), David Techter, Fate 23 (Dec.1970):121.

-Phantom
n.d.
Brad Steiger, Gods of Aquarius (N.Y.: Harcourt Brace Jovanovich, 1976), p.84.

-Phantom ship
1943, April/Howard H. Brisbane/150 mi. W/"USS Kennison"
Howard H. Brisbane, "U.S. Navy Meets a Phantom Ship," Fate 15 (Apr.1962): 41-44.

-Plant sensitivity
1970s/Backster Associates/645 Ash St.
John White & Stanley Krippner, Future Science (Garden City, N.Y.: Anchor, 1977), p.584.

-Psychokinesis
n.d./Jessop Clock/1041 Fifth Ave.
(Editorial), Probe the Unknown 2 (summer 1974):5,8. il.
1944, Feb.19/Elizabeth Rutan
Elizabeth Rutan, "The Prophetic Day the Mirror Fell," Fate 23 (May 1970) :93-94.

-Sea monster
1954, Oct?/Phil Parker/La Jolla
(Editorial), Fate 8 (May 1955):10.

-Seance
1942, May 21-26/H. Robert Moore/Beech x 2d Ave.
A.V. Bragg, "Rain of Jewels," Fate 2 (Nov.1949):84-85.

-Skyquake
1952, Jan.5/Mission Hill
Marion Kirkpatrick, "California Mystery Blasts," Fate 10 (Apr.1957):86, 88.
1952, April 19
San Diego Union, 20 Apr.1952.
1957, April 2
San Diego Evening Tribune, 2 Apr. 1957, p.1.
1978, Aug.23
Kansas City (Mo.) Star, 24 Aug.1978.

-Spirit medium
1867-1920s/Francis Grierson (Jesse Shepard)/Villa Montezuma
Francis Grierson, Psycho-Phone Messages (Los Angeles: Austin, 1921).
Nandor Fodor, Between Two Worlds (W. Nyack, N.Y.: Parker, 1964), pp.12-18.
Harold P. Simonson, Francis Grierson (N.Y.: Twayne, 1966), pp.34-38,131-34.
Vincent Gaddis, "Jesse Shepard the Musical Medium," Fate 25 (June 1972) :60-71. il.
1920s-1940s/H. Robert Moore
N. Meade Layne, "Seance Phenomena in

San Diego," Psychic Rsch. 25 (1931): 261-62.
A.V. Bragg, "Rain of Jewels," Fate 2 (Nov.1949):84-85.
1946-1969/Mark Probert
Meade Layne, "Mark Probert, Baffling San Diego Medium," Fate 2 (May 1949) :16-21. il.
Gray Barker, They Knew Too Much about Flying Saucers (N.Y.: Tower, 1967 ed.), pp.137-47.
Mark Probert, The Magic Bag (San Diego: Inner Circle Kethra E'Da Foundation, 1963).
Meade Layne, The Coming of the Guardians (Vista, Cal.: Borderland Sciences Rsch. Associates Foundation, 1964).
Lehmann Hisey, Keys to Inner Space (N.Y.: Julian, 1974).
Trevor James Constable, The Cosmic Pulse of Life (Santa Ana: Merlin, 1976), pp.196-211.

-Tasseography
1928, May 4/Myrtle Hoffman/Marlborough Ave.
Walter J. Macy & Edward A. Dieckman, "Tempest from a Tea Cup," Tomorrow 6 (winter 1958):17-23.

-Telepathy
1918, Dec./J.H. Shaw
J.H. Shaw, "Of Psychics and Sunken Subs," Fate 24 (Nov.1971):52-56.

-UFO (?)
1947, Sep.20
Harold T. Wilkins, Flying Saucers on the Attack (N.Y.: Ace, 1967 ed.), p.72.
1949, April 25
"If It's in the Sky It's a Saucer," Doubt, no.27 (1949):416.
1955, Feb./Annabell Culverwell/Ocean Beach
(Letter), Fate 11 (Apr.1958):114.
1976, Feb.27/Curtis Fuller/Vacation Village/=missile
(Editorial), Fate 29 (July 1976):30.

-UFO (DD)
1947, July 3/Robert Jackson/North Island NAS
San Francisco Examiner, 5 July 1947.
1968, May 20/Linda Stine/Kettner Blvd.
Allen Benz, "Unusual Object Seen over San Diego," Skylook, no.43 (June 1971):7-8.

-UFO (NL)
1946, Oct.9/Mark Probert
"Sizzling Zinner," Doubt, no.17 (1947):251-52.
Harold T. Wilkins, Flying Saucers on the Attack (N.Y.: Ace, 1967 ed.), pp.38-40.
(Letter), Mark Probert, Flying Saucers, Feb.1958, p.66.
Harold T. Wilkins, "Light on Flying Saucers," in Bernhardt J. Hurwood, ed., The First Occult Review Reader (N.Y.: Award, 1968), pp.65,74-75.
ca.1958
J. Allen Hynek, The Hynek UFO Report

(N.Y.: Dell, 1977), pp.78-79.
1961, March 13/William Friel/311 First
St.
Lloyd Mallan, "The Mysterious 12,"
Sci.& Mech. 37 (Dec.1966):30,67.
1966, Dec.16/John Schmitt/Ream Field
Brad Steiger & Joan Whritenour, Fly-
ing Saucer Invasion: Target--Earth
(N.Y.: Award, 1969), pp.53-54.
1966, Dec.19/Allied Gardens
(Editorial), Fate 20 (May 1967):27.
-Weather control
1916, Jan./Charles Mallory Hatfield/=
unknown chemical process
Ford Ashman Carpenter, "Alleged Man-
ufacture of Rain in Southern Cali-
fornia," Monthly Weather Rev. 46
(Aug.1918):376-77.
San Diego Union, 2 Jan.1961.
Richard F. Pourade, Gold in the Sun
(San Diego: Union-Tribune, 1965),
pp.203-18. il.
Richard Dillon, Humbugs and Heroes
(Garden City: Doubleday, 1970), pp.
134-40.
Brad Williams & Choral Pepper, Lost
Legends of the West (N.Y.: Holt,
Rinehart & Winston, 1970), pp.147-
56.

San Felipe Station
-Haunt
1850s
Philip A. Bailey, Golden Mirages
(N.Y.: Macmillan, 1940), pp.128-29.

San Fernando
-Fall of white beans
1964, Jan.22/Maclay x Library St.
Raymond Bayless, "Beanfall in San
Fernando," Fate 17 (May 1964):27-29.
-UFO (CE-1)
1950, Oct.5/Cecil Hardin
San Francisco Chronicle, 7 Oct.1950.

San Francisco
-Animal ESP
1942, Nov.
Chester S. Geier, "How Our Dogs Pro-
tect Us," Fate 7 (Oct.1954):29.
1955/Welcome Lewis/Lafayette Park
(Editorial), Fate 9 (May 1956):10,
quoting San Francisco Call-Bulletin
(undated).
-Astrology
1870s/William Henry Cheney
William H. Cheney, Primer of Astrology and Urania (St. Louis: The Author, 1870).
William Wingfield, "Jack London and
the Occult," Fate 28 (July 1975):
70-75.
1919/Albert Porta
Alson J. Smith, "Doom Days That Never
Cracked," Fate 15 (Nov.1962):36,46.
1931-   /Gavin Arthur
Gavin Arthur, The Circle of Sex (San
Francisco: Pangraphic, 1962).
David St. Clair, The Psychic World
of California (N.Y.: Bantam, 1973

ed.), p.62.
1960s-   /Solunar/1805 Polk St.
1970s/Sue Christeen Handley
1970s/Daisy Jamison
David St. Clair, The Psychic World
of California (N.Y.: Bantam, 1973
ed.), pp.58-65,69-71,328.
-Automatic writing
1874/Charles H. Foster
Nandor Fodor, Encyclopaedia of Psychic Science (London: Arthurs,
1933), pp.143,181.
-Biofeedback research
1958-1970s/Joe Kamiya/Langley Porter
Neuropsychiatric Institute
Johann Stoyva & Joseph Kamiya, "El-
ectrophysiological Studies of Dreaming As the Prototype of a New Strat-
egy in the Study of Consciousness,"
Psych.Rev. 75 (1968):192-205.
Joseph Kamiya, "Conscious Control of
Brain Waves," Psych.Today 1 (1968):
56-60.
Joseph Kamiya, "A Fourth Dimension
of Consciousness," J.Experimental
Medicine & Surgery 27 (1969):13-18.
Joseph Kamiya, "Operant Control of
the EEG Alpha Rhythm and Some of
Its Reported Effects on Conscious-
ness," in Charles Tart, ed., Alter-
ed States of Consciousness (N.Y.:
Wiley, 1969), pp.507-17.
John White, "The Yogi in the Lab:
Part One," Fate 24 (June 1971):43,
46-47.
-Cartomancy
1970s/Judy Mar
David St. Clair, The Psychic World
of California (N.Y.: Bantam, 1973
ed.), pp.71-73.
-Clairvoyance
1960, May 20
Hans Holzer, Ghosts of the Golden
West (N.Y.: Ace, 1968), pp.183-84.
-Cloud anomaly
1950, Aug.23
"Fortean Cloud," Doubt, no.30 (1950):
36.
-Disappearance
1942, Aug.16/Ernest D. Cody/L-8 blimp/
crew only
San Francisco Chronicle, 17 Aug.1942.
William O. Foss, "The Missing Crew
of the Airship L-8," Fate 12 (Nov.
1959):74-78. il.
1956, June 26/Gordon Bennett/9F-6F Con-
ger/N of Oakland Bridge
Harold T. Wilkins, Strange Mysteries
of Time and Space (N.Y.: Ace, 1958),
p.148.
-Doubtful responsibility
1769, Nov.1/José Francisco Ortega
Raymund F. Wood, "The Discovery of
the Golden Gate: Legend and Reality,"
Southern Calif.Quar. 58 (1976):205-
25.
-Electromagnetic anomaly
1963, Nov.26/Alene Davis/1445 Eddy St.
(Editorial), Fate 17 (Apr.1964):18-
20, quoting San Francisco Examiner

(undated).
-Erratic monkey
  1945, May 30/Mary Murray
    "More Animals," Doubt, no.14 (spring
    1946):203,204.
-Erratic octopus
  1978, April 21/Hyatt Regency Hotel
    Washington (D.C.) Post, 23 Apr.1978.
-Fall of crabs
  1890, Feb./Morton St.
    Lima (O.) Daily Republican, 21 Feb.
    1890.
-Fall of explosive metal balls
  1967, June/Golden Gate Park/=Naval ordnance
    New York Daily News, 25 June 1967.
-Fall of fish
  1957, July/golf course
    Los Angeles Herald-Express, 31 July
    1957.
-Fall of weblike substance
  1977, Oct.11/=spider web
    Lawrence (Kan.) Journal-World, 12
    Oct.1977.
-Fire immunity
  n.d./Jeffrey Mishlove
    Jeffrey Mishlove, The Roots of Con-
    sciousness (N.Y.: Random House,
    1975), p.157. il.
-Ghost
  1907, Aug.5/George Hall Hyslop
    "Apparitions," J.ASPR 1 (1907):530-33.
  1951, Dec./Angelo Biondini/Bank of America
    (Editorial), Fate 5 (July-Aug.1952):
    7, quoting San Francisco Chronicle
    (undated).
  1961, Sep.24-29/James Clarke/Sutro's
  Baths
    (Editorial), Fate 15 (Feb.1962):19-
    22, quoting San Francisco Chronicle
    (undated).
-Haunt
  1856, Sep.19/Russian Hill
    Robert O'Brien, This Is San Francis-
    co (San Carlos: Nourse, 1948), pp.
    126-28.
  1893-1897/John Santine/2544 Clement Ave.
    Canton (O.) Repository, 8 Apr.1897,
    quoting San Francisco Chronicle (un-
    dated).
  1893-1920s/Bush x Octavia St.
    Robert O'Brien, This Is San Francis-
    co (San Carlos: Nourse, 1948), pp.
    101-107.
  1920s-1962/California St. nr. Fairmont
  Hall
    James Reynolds, Ghosts in American
    Houses (N.Y.: Paperback Library,
    1967 ed.), pp.78-85.
    Hans Holzer, Ghosts of the Golden
    West (N.Y.: Ace, 1968), pp.97-98.
    Hans Holzer, Haunted Houses (N.Y.:
    Crown, 1971), pp.25-27.
  1946/2221 Washington St.
    Robert O'Brien, This Is San Francis-
    co (San Carlos: Nourse, 1948), pp.
    155-57.
  1959-1960/Toravel St.
    Hans Holzer, Ghosts of the Golden

West (N.Y.: Ace, 1968), pp.80-81.
  1967-1970/Pat Montandon/Lombard St.
    Pat Montandon, The Intruders (N.Y.:
    Coward, McCann & Geoghegan, 1975).
    Kansas City (Mo.) Times, 1 Nov.1975.
  1976, Sep.-Nov./Joseph Harker
    (Editorial), Fate 30 (Apr.1977):32-
    34, quoting San Francisco Chronicle
    (undated).
-Hex
  1880, July 17/Adelaide Neilson/black
  pearl curse
    Robert O'Brien, This Is San Francis-
    co (San Carlos: Nourse, 1948), pp.
    307-308.
    Pauline Saltzman, Ghosts and Other
    Strangers (N.Y.: Lancer, 1970 ed.),
    pp.71-73.
-Inner development
  1960s/Psychedelic Venus Church
    Los Angeles Free Press, 13 Mar.1970.
  1965-   /Anton LaVey/Church of Satan/
  6114 California St.
    Paul R. Jeschke, "Speak of the Devil,"
    Fate 20 (Sep.1967):76-79. il.
    Anton Szandor LaVey, The Satanic Bi-
    ble (N.Y.: Avon, 1969).
    Edward J. Moody, "Urban Witches," in
    James P. Sradly & David W. McCurdy,
    eds., Conformity and Conflict (Bos-
    ton: Little, Brown, 1971), pp.280-
    90.
    Anton LaVey, The Compleat Witch (N.Y.:
    Dodd, 1971).
    John Godwin, Occult America (Garden
    City: Doubleday, 1972), pp.242-49.
    Anton LaVey, Satanic Rituals (N.Y.:
    Avon, 1972).
    "The Occult: A Substitute Faith,"
    Time, 19 June 1972, pp.62,65-66. il.
    David St. Clair, The Psychic World
    of California (N.Y.: Bantam, 1973
    ed.), pp.88-92.
    Hans Holzer, The Witchcraft Report
    (N.Y.: Ace, 1973), pp.151-52.
    Daniel Logan, America Bewitched
    (N.Y.: Manor, 1975), pp.58-60.
  1970s/Order of the Illuminati/1437 Polk
    Armand Biteaux, The New Conscious-
    ness (Willits, Cal.: Oliver, 1975),
    pp.106-107.
  1974-   /Starseed (Carl Spann)
    Terri Riley, "Starseed Claims You
    Don't Have to Die," Fate 29 (Apr.
    1976):49-57.
-Mystery plane crash
  1957, Nov.8/Boeing Stratocruiser
    Robert Serling, The Probable Cause
    (Garden City: Doubleday, 1960), pp.
    86-99.
-Mystery radio transmission
  1977, July/"Greenpeace"
    "Matching Cases," Can.UFO Rept., no.
    29 (fall-winter 1977):4-5, quoting
    Vancouver Sun, July 1977.
-Mystery stench
  1948, Oct.15
    Harold T. Wilkins, Flying Saucers Un-
    censored (N.Y.: Pyramid, 1967 ed.),
    p.116.

-Palmistry
  1970s/Joy Kapur/314 Columbus Ave.
    David St. Clair, The Psychic World
    of California (N.Y.: Bantam, 1973
    ed.), pp.73-76.
-Parapsychology research
  1970s/Humanistic Psychology Institute
    Carol & Mary Cocciardi, The Psychic
    Yellow Pages (Saratoga: Out of the
    Sky, 1977), pp.64-66.
-Phantom image
  1870s/Mason St., North Beach
    Henry Winfred Splitter, "Nature's
    Strange Photographs," Fate 8 (Jan.
    1955):21,23, quoting Los Angeles
    Express (undated).
-Plague of butterflies
  1945, Sep.28
    "Stretter Selections," Doubt, no.14
    (spring 1946):205.
-Poltergeist
  1933
    R. DeWitt Miller, Impossible: Yet It
    Happened (N.Y.: Ace, 1947 ed.), pp.
    54-56.
  1974, Jan.
    Fontana Herald-News, 19 Jan.1974.
-Possession
  1956, June
    Beatrice Russell, "Two Against a
    Demon," Fate 17 (June 1964):64-67.
-Precognition
  1906, April 16/Leonard R. Ingham
    San Francisco Chronicle, 23 Apr.1965.
    Gordon Thomas & Max Morgan Witts, The
    San Francisco Earthquake (N.Y.:
    Stein & Day, 1971), pp.22-23.
  1906, April 18/Sarah Toner Steenson
    Pat Tyler, "San Francisco Earthquake:
    A Night to Remember," Fate 31 (Mar.
    1978):78-83.
  1930s/Margaret Foley
    Harold H.V. Cross, "The Metagnomy of
    Margaret Foley," J.ASPR 31 (1937):
    355-64.
  1952, July/Eugene Maffei
    (Editorial), Fate 6 (Jan.1953):10-11.
  1955, Jan./Norman Thomas, Jr.
    (Editorial), Fate 8 (July 1955):9.
  1960s/Gaye Spiegelman
    Hans Holzer, Ghosts of the Golden
    West (N.Y.: Ace, 1968), pp.185-87.
-Seance
  1853, Aug.20-21/Ferdinand Cartwright
    Ewer/=hoax
    F.C. Ewer, "The Eventful Nights of
    August 20th and 21st," Pioneer, or
    Calif.Monthly Mag. 2 (Sep.1854):
    129-39; (Oct.1854):193-205.
    Gwen Gaines, "When Fiction Fooled a
    Spiritualist," Fate 26 (Feb.1973):
    83-87.
  1865-1866/Ada Hoyt Foye
    San Francisco Golden Era, 4 Feb.1866;
    and 11 Mar.1866.
  1913,Sep.-1914, May 9
    John E. Coover, "Investigation with
    a 'Trumpet' Medium," Proc.ASPR 8
    (1914):201-52. il.
-Skyquake

1948, Feb.8/=earthquake?
  "Booms--No Clues," Doubt, no.21
  (1948):317.
1950, April 26
  "Bangs," Doubt, no.30 (1950):43.
1955, Sep.29, Oct.7
  (Editorial), Fate 9 (Feb.1956):8.
  "Bangs," Doubt, no.51 (1956):382.
1957, July 22/Montgomery St.
  San Francisco Chronicle, 22 July
  1957.
1959, March 11
  (Editorial), Fate 12 (July 1959):14.
1962, Aug.18
  (Editorial), Fate 15 (Dec.1962):10-
  12.
1974, March 20
  San Francisco Examiner, 20 Mar.1974.
  San Francisco Chronicle, 21 Mar.
  1974.
-Spirit medium
  1850s
  1856, Sep.-Oct./Russian Hill
    Emma Hardinge Britten, Modern Amer-
    ican Spiritualism (N.Y.: The Au-
    thor, 1870), pp.444-56.
  1870s/Flora Wellman
    William Wingfield, "Jack London and
    the Occult," Fate 28 (July 1975):
    70-75. il.
  1880s/Fred P. Evans
    James J. Owen, Psychography (San Fran-
    cisco: Hicks-Judd, 1893).
    Alfred Russell Wallace, My Life: A
    Record of Events and Opinions, 2
    vols. (N.Y.: Dodd, Mead, 1905), 2:
    363-65.
  1890s/Sarah Seal
    Gertrude O. Tubby, "A Case of Spirit
    Identity," J.ASPR 17 (1923):552-55.
  1903-1908/C.V. Miller
    Willy Reichel, Occult Experiences
    (London: Office of Light, 1906).
    Nandor Fodor, Encyclopaedia of Psy-
    chic Science (London: Arthurs, 1933),
    pp.116,242-43.
    Nandor Fodor, "Mind over Space: The
    Mystery of Teleportation," Fate 10
    (Mar.1957):82-84.
  1910s
    John E. Coover, "Investigation with
    a 'Trumpet' Medium," Proc.ASPR 8
    (1914):201-52. il.
  1920s/Madame Lowe/Mission St./=fraud
    Joseph Dunninger, Houdini's Spirit
    World and Dunninger's Psychic Rev-
    elations (N.Y.: Tower, 1968 ed.),
    pp.150-53.
  1930s/Philip S. Haley/4030 Cabrillo St.
    Earl Gilmore, "Psychical Manifesta-
    tions Exhibited by Dr. P.S. Haley,
    a Psychic," J.ASPR 27 (1933):292-95.
    Philip S. Haley, "Experiments with
    Ectoplasm," J.ASPR 27 (1933):295-99.
  1930-1931/M.J. Williams
    Philip S. Haley, "A Study of Ecto-
    plasm," Psychic Rsch. 25 (1931):
    326-33. il.
    Philip S. Haley, "Studies of Ecto-
    plasm by Daylight," Psychic Rsch.

25 (1931):414-16. il.
1970s/Harold White
David St. Clair, The Psychic World
of California (N.Y.: Bantam, 1973
ed.), pp.52-57.
-Spirit medium and clairempathy
1930s/Chester Grady
"The Pre-Vision of a Fatal Accident,"
J.ASPR 30 (1940):345-50.
L.A. Dale, "An Informal Experiment
with Mr. Chester Grady," J.ASPR 38
(1944):202-21.
-Spontaneous human combustion
1959, Jan.31/Jack Larber/Laguna Honda
Home
(Editorial), Fate 12 (June 1959):18-
19.
-Stigmata
1873
(Letter), M.H. Biggs, J.SPR 3 (1887):
100-103.
-UFO (?)
1896, Nov.1/=meteor?
Portland Oregonian, 2 Nov.1896.
1896, Nov.24/=Venus?
San Francisco Chronicle, 25 Nov.1896,
p.16.
1896, Dec.4/=hoax
San Francisco Chronicle, 4 Dec.1896,
p.5.
San Francisco Call, 4 Dec.1896, p.1;
and 5 Dec.1896, p.2.
1950, Aug.2
Gerald Heard, The Riddle of the Flying Saucers (London: Carroll & Nicholson, 1950), p.147.
1953, Dec?
(Editorial), Fate 7 (Mar.1954):9.
1954, March 10
Richard Hall, ed., The UFO Evidence
(Washington: NICAP, 1964), p.14.
1957, Jan.2/Int'l Airport/=meteor?
"Case 292," CRIFO Orbit, 1 Mar.1957,
p.3, quoting San Francisco Chronicle
(undated).
1960, Aug.9/Jay Rees/=balloon
Richard Hall, ed., The UFO Evidence
(Washington: NICAP, 1964), pp.94-95.
1963, Nov.8/=meteor
"Fireballs," UFO Inv. 2 (Dec.-Jan.
1963-64):3.
1967, Nov.1/Joo Claridge/-balloon
Eminence Reynolds County Times, 2
Nov.1967.
-UFO (CE-1)
1956/Jerry Teeguarden/California Tennis
Club
(Editorial), Fate 9 (June 1956):14.
1964, Nov.21/"SS President Wilson"
(Letter), Johan Eichelberger, Fate
18 (Mar.1965):112-14.
-UFO (CE-2)
1963, Nov.7
San Francisco Examiner, 8 Nov.1963.
-UFO (CE-3)
1896, Nov.22/A.T. Cooper/Market x 5th
St.
San Francisco Chronicle, 24 Nov.1896,
p.10.
1966, March 31

Jacques Vallee, Passport to Magonia
(Chicago: Regnery, 1969), p.326,
quoting NICAP Reporter, June 1966.
-UFO (DD)
1947, July 2/David Menary/Golden Gate
Bridge
San Francisco Chronicle, 3 July 1947.
1947, July 6/Amy Shearer/14th Ave. x
Irving St.
1947, July 6/Albert Schlegel/Golden
Gate Bridge
San Francisco Chronicle, 7 July 1947.
1947, July 7/Gerald Lewis/1479 San
Bruno Ave.
San Francisco Examiner, 8 July 1947.
1952, April 5
Brad Steiger, Project Blue Book
(N.Y.: Ballantine, 1976), betw. pp.
360-61. il.
1956, Oct.10/Joe Kerska/Twin Peaks/=
hoax?
Richard Hall, ed., The UFO Evidence
(Washington: NICAP, 1964), p.89,
quoting Saucers, vol.5, no.1.
Otto Binder, What We Really Know
about Flying Saucers (Greenwich, Ct.:
Fawcett, 1967), p.131. il.
1957, March/Ardell Langford/Golden
Gate Bridge
(Letter), Fate 11 (May 1958):126-27.
-UFO (NL)
1896, Nov.18/Mr. McGovern/Mills Bldg.
1896, Nov.20/16th x Valencia St.
San Francisco Chronicle, 22 Nov.1896,
p.36.
1896, Nov.20/Colvin Brown/7th x K St.
Gordon I.R. Lore, Jr. & Harold H. Deneault, Jr., Mysteries of the Skies:
UFOs in Perspective (Englewood
Cliffs, N.J.: Prentice-Hall, 1968),
pp.5-6.
1896, Nov.22/John Bagley/nr. City Hall
San Francisco Chronicle, 23 Nov.1896,
p.12; and 24 Nov.1896, p.9.
1896, Nov.22/Cliff House
Sacramento Bee, 23 Nov.1896.
San Francisco Chronicle, 24 Nov.1896,
p.10.
1896, Nov.23/Clarence Coogan/Golden
Gate Park
San Francisco Chronicle, 24 Nov.1896,
p.9.
1948, Sep.11/D. Bruce Berry
D. Bruce Berry, "Flying Saucer over
the Golden Gate," Fate 11 (Feb.1958)
:52-54.
1953, Feb.13/Al Turner/Bay Bridge
John C. Ross, "Fate's Report on the
Flying Saucers," Fate 6 (Oct.1953):
6,8.
1957, Aug.12/E.O. Moore/Shell Oil Bldg.
(Letter), Fate 11 (Feb.1958):118-20.
1973, Oct.16
San Francisco Examiner, 17 Oct.1973.
1975, Sep.23
"UFO Central," CUFOS News Bull., 15
Nov.1975, p.19.
1975, Nov.10,27
"Noteworthy UFO Sightings," Ufology
2 (spring 1976):42.

1976, Jan.12
"Noteworthy UFO Sightings," Ufology
2 (summer 1976):62.
-Weather control
1959, Dec.12/1145 Market St./Pueblo
Indians
(Editorial), Fate 13 (Apr.1960):24.

San Gabriel
-Fall of ice
1957, March 19/6856 N. Ruthlee Ave.
Pasadena Independent, 20 Mar.1957.
-Fall of unknown object
1957, April 9/Oscar Murphy/8831 Greenwood Ave.
(Editorial), Fate 10 (Aug.1957):13-
14.
"Falls," Doubt, no.54 (1957):435,436.
-Poltergeist
1854, winter/Mr. Hildreth
Emma Hardinge Britten, Modern American Spiritualism (N.Y.: The Author,
1870), pp.439-41.

San Jose
-Airship inventor
1896, Nov./John A. Horen
Oakland Tribune, 1 Dec.1896.
San Jose Daily Herald, 2 Dec.1896.
Honolulu Hawaiian Gazette, 15 Dec.
1896, p.6.
-Ball lightning
1952, March 6/Walter Bagar
Marion Kirkpatrick, "California Mys-
tery Blasts," Fate 10 (Apr.1957):
86,88, quoting AP Release, 7 Mar.
1952.
-Bilocation
n.d.
Richard Webb, Voices from Another
World (N.Y.: Manor, 1972 ed.), pp.
81-85.
-Deathbed apparition
1864, Oct./Daisy Dryden
James H. Hyslop, "Death Visions,"
J.ASPR 12 (1918):375.
-Doubtful identity
1976, June 13-1977, Nov./David Grubbs
San Jose Mercury, 15-17 Nov.1977;
and 24 Nov.1977.
-Electromagnetic anomaly
1966/Ralph Morgan
(Editorial), Fate 20 (July 1967):30.
-Fall of oily substance
1954, April 5/=pollution?
"Colored Rain--Snow," Doubt, no.45
(1954):289.
-Fall of weblike substance
1977, Oct.11/airport
Kirkland (Wash.) Journal-American,
12 Oct.1977.
-Haunt
1884-1922/Sarah Winchester/Winchester
Mystery House/Winchester Blvd.
Vincent H. Gaddis, "The House That
Spirits Built," Fate 3 (May 1950):
55-61.
New York Times, 31 May 1970, sec.X,
p.9.
Alvin T. Guthertz, "How a Publicity

Stunt Turned Up a Ghost," Psychic
World, Sep.1976, pp.52-55,84-85.
James Dale Davidson, An Eccentric
Guide to the United States (N.Y.:
Berkley, 1977), pp.423-26. il.
-Hex
1939, Nov./Mary Botelho
San Jose Mercury-Herald, 15 Nov.1939.
-Inner development
1927-   /AMORC Rosicrucian Order/1342
Naglee Ave.
R. Swinburne Clymer, The Rosicrucian
Fraternity in America, 2 vols. (Qua-
kertown, Pa.: Rosicrucian Fratern-
ity, 1935).
David St. Clair, The Psychic World
of California (N.Y.: Bantam, 1973
ed.), pp.110-11.
Jim Brandon, Weird America (N.Y.:
Dutton, 1978), p.44.
1968-   /Universal Receivers Prayer
Group/Box 5535
David St. Clair, The Psychic World
of California (N.Y.: Bantam, 1973
ed.), pp.99-110.
-Numerology
1970s/Rita Brown
David St. Clair, The Psychic World
of California (N.Y.: Bantam, 1973
ed.), pp.117-21.
Carol & Mary Cocciardi, The Psychic
Yellow Pages (Saratoga: Out of the
Sky, 1977), pp.33-34.
-Palmistry
1970s/Bob Ellis/498 Patton Ave.
Carol & Mary Cocciardi, The Psychic
Yellow Pages (Saratoga: Out of the
Sky, 1977), pp.25-26.
-Paraphysics research
1970s/Richard Szumski/San Jose State
University
Richard Szumski, "A New Hard Look at
Kirlian Photography: Has It Lost Its
Halo?" Fate 29 (Jan.1976):30-38;
(Feb.1976):78-85. il.
-Phantom panther
1973, Dec./Thomas Mantei
Loren Coleman, "California Odyssey:
Observations on California's Para-
Panther," Anomaly Rsch.Bull., no.23
(1978):5,6-7.
-Plant sensitivity
1969-   /Marcel Vogel/819 Morse
Warren Meyer, "Man-and-Plant Communi-
cation: Interview with Marcel Vogel,"
Unity 153 (Jan.1973):9-12.
Peter Tompkins & Christopher Bird,
The Secret Life of Plants (N.Y.: Har-
per & Row, 1974), pp.17-32.
Marcel Vogel, "Man-Plant Communica-
tion," in Edgar D. Mitchell, ed.,
Psychic Exploration (N.Y.: Capricorn,
1976 ed.), pp.289-312. il.
Carol & Mary Cocciardi, The Psychic
Yellow Pages (Saratoga: Out of the
Sky, 1977), pp.104-105.
-Precognition
1974, Jan.-Aug./Brandon Gates
Wadyne B. Lindberg, "The Nightmare
Animal," Fate 30 (Dec.1977):72-75.

-Spirit medium
    1960s-1970s/Doris Heather Buckley/4018
    Rincon Ave.
        Doris Heather Buckley, Science of
        Mind (Los Angeles: Sherbourne, 1970).
        Doris Heather Buckley, Conversations
        with the Beyond (Los Angeles: Sher-
        bourne, 1971).
        Doris Heather Buckley, Spirit Commu-
        nications (N.Y.: Award, 1971 ed.).
        David St. Clair, The Psychic World
        of California (N.Y.: Bantam, 1973
        ed.), pp.122-24.
    1960s-1970s/Neva Johnston Avery
        David St. Clair, The Psychic World
        of California (N.Y.: Bantam, 1973
        ed.), pp.126-30.
    1960s-1970s/Dorothy Vurnovas/2150 S.
    First St.
        David St. Clair, The Psychic World
        of California (N.Y.: Bantam, 1973
        ed.), pp.124-26.
        David St. Clair, Psychic Healers
        (Garden City: Doubleday, 1974), pp.
        227-52.
-Spirit medium and healing
    1887-1905/Mary Hayes Chynoweth/Eden
    Vale
        Louisa Johnson Clay, The Spirit Dom-
        inant (San Jose: Mercury-Herald,
        n.d.).
        Stanwood Cobb & David Techter, "The
        Woman Who Dowsed a Fortune," Fate
        26 (Oct.1973):38-47; (Nov.1973):96-
        104; (Dec.1973):88-96. il.
-UFO (?)
    1896, Nov.26/H.B. Worcester/=balloon?
        San Jose Daily Herald, 27 Nov.1896.
        San Francisco Call, 29 Nov.1896.
    1978, April 3/Carol Sanford/Hwy.280/=
    ad plane
        Gilroy Dispatch, 5 Apr.1978; and 14
        Apr.1978.
-UFO (CE-1)
    1973, Oct.16/Sig McGill
        San Jose News, 17 Oct.1973.
    1973, Oct.16/Ann Rodriguez
        San Francisco Examiner, 17 Oct.1973.
    1975, April 15/Ed Handley
        Slava Mach & Ross Redeker, "A Close
        Encounter of the First Kind," MUFON
        UFO J., no.124 (Mar.1978):14-15.
-UFO (DD)
    1947, July 6/George Mayberry/15 mi.S
        Sacramento Union, 7 July 1947.
-UFO (NL)
    1896, Oct?/SW of town
        San Jose Daily Herald, 25 Nov.1896.
    1896, Nov.22
        Sacramento Record-Union, 23 Nov.1896.
    1896, Nov.24/Eugene Barre
        Gordon I.R. Lore, Jr. & Harold H. Den-
        eault, Jr., Mysteries of the Skies:
        UFOs in Perspective (Englewood
        Cliffs, N.J.: Prentice-Hall, 1968),
        p.9.
    1951, Aug.16/Mrs. Claude Bayle
        (Letter), Fate 5 (Jan.1952):114.
    1952, April 16
        San Jose Mercury-News, 24 Apr.1952.

1952, April 28
    San Jose Mercury-News, 30 Apr.1952.

San Juan Capistrano
-Fall of conglomerate
    1973, March 15/Jack Scurlock
        Santa Ana Register, 18 Apr.1973.
-UFO (DD)
    1947, July 5/John K. Street
        Los Angeles Examiner, 6 July 1947.

San Leandro
-Fall of soot
    1953, Nov.2
        "Falls(?)," Doubt, no.44 (1954):275.
-UFO (DD)
    1947, July 5/S.D. Capitola
        San Francisco News, 7 July 1947.
    1947, July 8
        San Francisco Chronicle, 9 July 1947.
-UFO (NL)
    1896, Nov.22
        San Francisco Chronicle, 24 Nov.1896,
        p.10.
    1947,June 29/Frank M. King/430 Breed
    Ave.
        San Francisco Chronicle, 30 June
        1947.

San Lorenzo
-Ball lightning
    1954, Dec.23/Hazel Leggio/Washington
    St.
        (Letter), Fate 11 (Mar.1958):118-20.
-UFO (NL)
    1896, Nov.25/Fred Hoyt/Liedel Place
        Loren E. Gross, The UFO Wave of 1896
        (Fremont, Cal.: The Author, 1974),
        p.17.

San Luis Obispo
-Archeological site
    ca.1579/Sir Francis Drake
        Donald M. Vilas, "The Discovery of
        Elizabethan Survey Stones on the
        Pacific Coast and Possible Parallels
        on the Atlantic Coast," NEARA Newsl.
        7 (Dec.1972):69-71.
-Meditation research
    1970s/Michael L. Emmons/California
    State Polytechnical
        Michael L. Emmons, Inner Source (San
        Luis Obispo: Impact, 1978).
-Mystery bird deaths
    1976, Nov.24-25
        Kansas City (Mo.) Star, 25 Nov.1976.
        Kansas City (Mo.) Times, 26 Nov.1976.
-UFO (NL)
    1956, Dec.2
        "Case 278," CRIFO Orbit, 1 Feb.1957,
        p.4, quoting San Diego Union (un-
        dated).
    1962, Aug.7/Albert E. Redstone
        (Letter), Fate 15 (June 1962):108-10.
    1973, Oct.16/Joe Lewis/1801 Garnette
    Dr.
        San Luis Obispo Telegram-Tribune, 18
        Oct.1973.

San Mateo
-Clairvoyance
  1960, May 9/Judi Wegley
    (Letter), Fate 29 (Sep.1976):115.
-Fall of ice
  1966, March 25/Lorraine Nuckels
    (Editorial), Fate 19 (Aug.1966):13.
-Giant rat
  1975/San Mateo Canyon
    Peter Guttilla, "Monster Menagerie,"
    Saga UFO Rept. 4 (Sep.1977):32,66.
-Telepathy
  1946, Feb./Mary Dunham
    Hereward Carrington, "Apologetic
    Dream," Fate 28 (Mar.1975):52.
-UFO (?)
  1967, Jan?/Donald Bennett
    (Editorial), Fate 20 (May 1967):29.
-UFO (CE-1)
  1952/Leonard L. Musel/Hillsdale Blvd.
    Richard Hall, ed., The UFO Evidence
    (Washington: NICAP, 1964), p.45.
-UFO (DD)
  1973, Oct.20/Wayne Hall/College
    San Mateo Times, 20 Oct.1973.
-UFO (NL)
  1965, March 27
    Orin Browning, "Mystery of the Alien
    Satellites," Saga UFO Rept. 2 (sum-
    mer 1975):34,37.
  1970, Feb.10/Laurie Diane Walther
    "Sights Flying Saucer on Birthday!"
    Skylook, no.29 (Apr.1970):19, quot-
    ing San Mateo Times and News Leader
    (undated).

San Miguel
-Psychokinesis
  1959, Dec.10/Southern Pacific train/
    16th St.
    (Editorial), Fate 13 (Apr.1960):14.

San Pablo
-Archeological site
  2000 B.C.-500 A.D.
    (Editorial), Fate 22 (Dec.1969):24,
    28.
-Hex
  1960, Dec./George Baca
    (Editorial), Fate 14 (Apr.1961):16-
    17.

San Pedro
-Derelict ship
  1935, Aug.8/"Humboldt"
    Claire Spofford, "The Last Voyage,"
    Fate 5 (Dec.1952):63-64.
-Earthquake luminescence
  1952, July 21
    "Very Quakey," Doubt, no.38 (1952):
    163.
-Oceanographic anomaly
  1966/dead sea offshore
    St. Louis (Mo.) Post-Dispatch, 6
    Dec.1966.
-Psychokinesis research
  1959/Mrs. C. Ross/Consciousness Research Foundation
    Andrija Puharich, Beyond Telepathy
    (Garden City: Anchor, 1973), pp.

54-59.
-UFO (DD)
  1947, July 4/Edward Mutchler
    Los Angeles Examiner, 6 July 1947.
-UFO (NL)
  1947, July 5/Clifton A. Hix
    Los Angeles Examiner, 6 July 1947.
  1965, Dec.2/Mrs. Irwin Cohen
    San Pedro News Pilot, 3 Dec.1965.
-Weather control
  1968-   /Trevor James Constable/Mer-
  lin Weather Engineering/=neo-Reichian
    Trevor James Constable, The Cosmic
    Pulse of Life (Santa Ana: Merlin,
    1976).
    Trevor James Constable, "Orgone Wea-
    ther Engineering Through the Cloud-
    buster," in John White & Stanley
    Krippner, eds., Future Science (Gar-
    den City, N.Y.: Anchor, 1977), pp.
    404-19.

San Rafael
-Fall of ice
  1958, Jan.25/James Carmine/2154 Fourth
    St.
    (Editorial), Fate 11 (May 1958):22.
    (Editorial), Fate 11 (June 1958):23.
-Fall of sulphurous rock
  1964, May 23/Edward Vrabel
    (Editorial), Saucer News 11 (Sep.
    1964):19.
-Haunt
  n.d.
    (Editorial), Fate 30 (Mar.1977):36.
-UFO (DD)
  1947, July 6/Arthur H. Fellows
    San Francisco Examiner, 8 July 1947.
  1947, July 8/John Cockcroft
    San Francisco Chronicle, 11 July
    1947.

San Simeon
-Haunt
  1963, March/Hearst Castle/=exaggeration
    Fresno Bee, 10 Mar.1963.
    (Letter), Raymond Bayless, Fate 16
    (Nov.1963):113-14.

Santa Ana
-Fall of clams
  1877, March/Dr. Jones
    Santa Ana News, 13 Mar.1877.
-Phantom image
  1878, July/Dr. Elfiendorf
    Henry Winfred Splitter, "Nature's
    Strange Photographs," Fate 8 (Jan.
    1955):21,23, quoting Los Angeles
    Express (undated).
-Talking cat
  1970/Jesse Yowell
    (Editorial), Fate 23 (Sep.1970):17-
    18, quoting Los Angeles Times (un-
    dated).
-UFO (?)
  1958, April 7
    Richard Hall, ed., The UFO Evidence
    (Washington: NICAP, 1964), p.147.
  1973, Jan.2/=blimp?
    "Brilliantly-Lit UFO Sighted in San-

ta Ana, California, Probably a
Blimp," Skylook, no.64 (Mar.1973):
4-6.
Ann Druffel, "Are There Mimicking
UFOs? Part 1," MUFON UFO J., no.112
(Mar.1977):15. il.
-UFO (CE-1)
1973, Oct.17/Michael A. Thomas
"Saucers in the News," Flying Sau-
cers, winter 1974, pp.44,60.
-UFO (CE-2)
1954, Jan.29
Richard Hall, ed., The UFO Evidence
(Washington: NICAP, 1964), p.73.
1965, Aug.3/Rex Heflin/Myford Rd.
Santa Ana Register, 20 Sep.1965. il.
"Photo 'Hoax' Label Questioned," UFO
Inv. 3 (Nov.-Dec.1965):8. il.
"The Heflin Story," UFO Inv. 3 (Jan.-
Feb.1966):7-8. il.
Ralph Rankow, "The Disc with the
Domed Top," Fate 19 (Aug.1966):54-
61. il.
(Letter), Charles H. Gibbs-Smith,
Flying Saucer Rev. 13 (July-Aug.
1967):19-20.
(Letter), A. Lloyd-Taylor, Flying
Saucer Rev. 14 (May-June 1967):20.
(Letter), Ralph Rankow, Flying Sau-
cer Rev. 14 (May-June 1968):20-21.
(Letter), Charles H. Gibbs-Smith,
Flying Saucer Rev. 14 (May-June
1968):21.
(Letter), Stuart Ackley, Flying Sau-
cer Rev. 14 (Sep.-Oct.1968):20.
Edward U. Condon, ed., Scientific
Study of Unidentified Flying Objects
(N.Y.: Bantam, 1969 ed.), pp.437-
55. il.
John R. Gray, "More Light on the Hef-
lin Case," Flying Saucer Rev. 15
(Mar.-Apr.1969):24-28. il.
Idabel Epperson, "The Heflin Contro-
versy," MUFON UFO J., no.111 (Feb.
1977):7-8. il.
Richard Hall, "Recapping and Comment-
ing," MUFON UFO J., no.112 (Mar.
1977):20.
Donald H. Menzel & Ernest H. Taves,
The UFO Enigma (Garden City: Double-
day, 1977), pp.111-12.
(Letter), Ann Druffel, Fate 31 (Jan.
1978):113.
1966, Dec.28/Billy Waldman
Santa Ana Register, 30 Dec.1966.
-UFO (CE-3)
1974, summer
Peter Guttilla, "Bigfoot: Advance
Guard from Outer Space," Saga UFO
Rept. 4 (June 1977):22,51.
-UFO (NL)
1953, Jan.9
Richard Hall, ed., The UFO Evidence
(Washington: NICAP, 1964), p.21.
1960, Aug.17
(Editorial), Fate 13 (Dec.1960):117,
120.
1965, Aug.10
Columbus (O.) Dispatch, 11 Aug.1965.

Santa Barbara
-Ancient underground city and mummies
ca.1890
Ron Anjard, "Ancient American Under-
ground Cities?" Pursuit 11 (summer
1978):90, quoting New Atlantean J.
(undated).
-Archeological site
ca.4500 B.C.
D.B. Rogers, Prehistoric Men of the
Santa Barbara Coast (Santa Barbara:
Museum of Natural History, 1929).
(Editorial), Nature 112 (1923):699.
-Chinese discovery
ca.1000 B.C.
Henriette Mertz, Gods from the Far
East (N.Y.: Ballantine, 1975 ed.),
pp.156-58.
-Healing
1920s-   /Helen Van Cleve
Helen Van Cleve, "The Healing Power
of Prayer," Fate 28 (July 1975):
76-78. il.
-Sea monster
1962, Feb./Forrest Adrian/2 mi.off-
shore/=oarfish?
(Editorial), Fate 16 (Mar.1963):9-10.
(Editorial), Fate 16 (Apr.1963):10.
(Editorial), Fate 16 (May 1963):16.
-Stigmata
1879
(Letter), M.H. Biggs, J.SPR 3 (1887):
100-103.
-Telepathy
1962, Oct.28/Alfred Johansen/"Horn Cru-
sader"/20 mi.offshore
(Editorial), Fate 16 (Apr.1963):10-
11.
-UFO (CE-1)
1943, Oct./Wilberta M. Finley
(Letter), Fate 11 (Nov.1958):116-18.
-UFO (DD)
1957, Oct.1/H.F. Hoag/La Mesa Park
"Flying Saucer Roundup," Fate 11
(Feb.1958):29,35, quoting Santa Bar-
bara News Press (undated).
-UFO (NL)
1968, Aug.14
Brad Steiger & Joan Whritenour, Fly-
ing Saucer Invasion: Target--Earth
(N.Y.: Award, 1969), p.99.
-Weather control
1977, July 26/Trevor James Constable/
=neo-Reichian
Trevor Constable, The Sycamore Fire
and Primary Energy Weather Engineering (unpublished manuscript,
1977, available from Merlin Weather
Engineering, Santa Ana, Cal.).

Santa Clara
-UFO (CE-1)
1975, Oct.6
"UFO Central," CUFOS News Bull., 1
Feb.1976, p.8.
-UFO (NL)
1896, Nov.22/Frank Everette
Loren E. Gross, The UFO Wave of 1896
(Fremont, Cal.: The Author, 1974),
p.10.

1963, Sep.25/Glen J. Davis
(Editorial), Fate 17 (Feb.1964):9.

Santa Clara co.
-Fall of flesh and blood
1869, June
San Francisco Evening Bulletin, 9
Aug.1869.

Santa Cruz
-Astrology
1970s/Robert Cole/127 Ocean St.
Carol & Mary Cocciardi, The Psychic
Yellow Pages (Saratoga: Out of the
Sky, 1977), pp.118-20.
-Gravity anomaly
Mystery Spot/1953 Branciforte Dr.
"Steady, Boys," Doubt, no.13 (winter
1945):193.
(Letter), C.R. Marks, Fate 6 (Feb.
1953):114-16.
-Mystery fish
1874, July/Moss Landing
Santa Cruz Sentinel, 14 July 1874.
-Sea monster (carcass)
1925, May/=beaked whale?
M.E. McLellan Davidson, "Baird's
Beaked Whale at Santa Cruz, Calif.,"
Am.J.Mammalogy 10 (Nov.1929):356-58.
Rupert T. Gould, The Loch Ness Mon-
ster (London: Geoffrey Bles, 1934),
pp.196-200. il.
"A Definitely Unclassified Marine
Animal," Pursuit 5 (July 1972):60-
62. il.
"The Improperly Classified Marine
Animal," Pursuit 5 (Oct.1972):83.
-Seance
1886/Georgiana Kirby
Thelma Moss, The Probability of the
Impossible (Los Angeles: J.P. Tar-
cher, 1974), pp.231-32.
-Skyquake
1952, April 24
"Jest Planes Again," Doubt, no.37
(1952):148,149.
-UFO (?)
1955, Dec.2/Frank Lazarotti/Cave Gulch
Coast Rd.
(Editorial), Fate 9 (July 1956):17.
-UFO (CE-1)
1975, Jan.2
Robert A. Goerman, "The UFO Modus Op-
erandi: January 1975," Official UFO
1 (Aug.1976):47.
-UFO (CE-2)
1956/Muriel McDowell
George D. Fawcett, "The Dangers of
Close UFO Encounters," Official UFO
1 (Oct.1975):34,59.
1973, Dec.6/S of town
Madison Wisconsin State Journal, 8
Dec.1973.
James A. Harder, "Santa Cruz E-M
Case," APRO Bull. 22 (Nov.-Dec.1973)
:1,3.
-UFO (DD)
1961, Nov.2/Mark Simpson
"Boy Reports Disc," APRO Bull. 10
(Jan.1962):3.

-UFO (NL)
1896, Nov.20?
San Francisco Chronicle, 24 Nov.1896,
p.10.
1957, Oct.21/Jeanita C. Morse/203
Swift St.
"Saucers in the News," Flying Saucers, Feb.1958, p.75.
1957, Dec.5/Judy Fitch
(Letter), Fate 11 (July 1958):114-15.
1964, Dec.28/Tom Goold/nearby mt. park
"New Sightings Put AF on Spot," UFO
Inv. 3 (Mar.-Apr.1965):4.

Santa Maria
-Dowsing
1950s/Ray D. Carse
Gaston Burridge, "The Truth about
Dowsing," Fate 7 (Dec.1954):17,20.
-Mystery death
1968, Jan.10/Patricia Rush
Coral E. Lorenzen, The Shadow of the
Unknown (N.Y.: Signet, 1970), p.198.
-UFO (?)
1955, Jan.1/Rita N. Barnhart/=balloon?
(Letter), Fate 13 (July 1960):109-11.
-UFO (DD)
1955, July 22
"The Question of Submerging UFO's,"
UFO Inv. 4 (Mar.1968):5.

Santa Monica
-Fall of fish
1877, March
Henry Winfred Splitter, "Wonders
from the Sky," Fate 6 (Oct.1953):33,
37, quoting Santa Monica Outlook
(undated).
-Inner development
1970s/Huna Enterprises/2617 Lincoln
Blvd.
John White & Stanley Krippner, eds.,
Future Science (Garden City, N.Y.:
Anchor, 1977), p.586.
-Phantom
ca.1960/Paul M. Vest
Paul M. Vest, "What Healed Gringo?"
Fate 17 (Feb.1964):63-64.
-Pyramid energy research
1970s/Paris Garefis/1304-15th St.
Russ Idler, "Practical Uses of Pyra-
mid Energy Extend Beyond Prolonging
Razor Blades," Probe the Unknown 4
(Jan.1976):31-34. il.
1973-   /Huna Enterprises/2617 Lin-
coln Blvd.
Serge V. King, Pyramid Energy Hand-
book (N.Y.: Warner, 1977). il.
-Reincarnation
1960s/Glenn Ford
Neil & Margaret Rau, "Glenn Ford:
The Timeless Horseman," Fate 22
(Feb.1969):34-43.
-Telepathy
1950s/Jack Kelly/Mae West's beach home
Danton Walker, Spooks Deluxe (N.Y.:
Franklin Watts, 1956), pp.100-104.
Jess Stearn, The Door to the Future
(N.Y.: Macfadden, 1964), pp.178-80.
Brenda Shaw, "A Dead Man Shocked Mae

West," Fate 30 (Apr.1977):38-42.
-UFO (DD)
  1953, June/Frederick G. Hehr
    Harold T. Wilkins, Flying Saucers on
    the Attack (N.Y.: Ace, 1967 ed.),
    p.284.
  1976, Jan.28/Lacuion Johnson
    William F. Hassel, "Santa Monica UFO
    Sighting," MUFON UFO J., no.103
    (June 1976):16.
  1978, Jan.1/Floyd Hallstrom
    Ventura County and Harbor News, 13
    Jan.1978; and 20 Jan.1978.
    Richard Hall, "Veteran Pilot Spots
    Daylight Disc," MUFON UFO J., no.
    122 (Jan.1978):3-5.
    "An Air-Visual Sighting of a Daylight
    Disc in California," Int'l UFO Re-
    porter 3 (Apr.1978):newsfront sec.
    Dennis Leatart, "UFO over LAX," APRO
    Bull. 26 (Apr.1978):3-4.
    Robert J. Kirkpatrick, "Pilot's-Eye
    View: IFO over California," Fate 31
    (June 1978):66-72. il.
-UFO (NL)
  1955, March 8/F.P. Cooper
    (Letter), Fate 9 (Jan.1956):116-17.
  1956, Aug.16
    "Case 195," CRIFO Orbit, 5 Oct.1956,
    p.2, quoting Los Angeles Examiner
    (undated).
  1958, April 4
    Richard Hall, ed., The UFO Evidence
    (Washington: NICAP, 1964), p.147.
  1964, Oct./airport
    (Letter), Anon., Sci.& Mech. 38 (May
    1967):71.
  1968, Dec.31/Sipke Kuiper
    (Letter), Fate 23 (Jan.1970):132.
  1975, Sep.9
    "UFO Central," CUFOS News Bull., 15
    Nov.1975, p.18.

Santa Paula
-UFO (DD)
  1978, July 4/Floyd Hallstrom
    "UFOs of Limited Merit," Int'l UFO
    Reporter 3 (Aug.1978):4.

Santa Rosa
-Derelict automobile
  1938, Aug.3
    "Car Crash Driver Gone," Fortean
    Soc'y Mag., no.3 (Jan.1940):4.
-Earthquake luminescence
  1969, Oct.1
    John S. Derr, "Earthquake Lights: A
    Review of Observations and Recent
    Theories," Bull.Seism.Soc'y Am. 63
    (1973):2177-87.
    John S. Derr, "Earthquake Lights,"
    Earthquake Information Bull. 9 (May-
    June 1977):18-20.
-Gravity anomaly
  1955, July 2/W.A. Thomson
    (Editorial), Fate 9 (May 1956):10.
-Inner development
  1875-1900/Thomas Lake Harris/Fountain
  Grove
    William P. Swainson, Thomas Lake Har-

ris and His Occult Teaching (London: Rider, 1922).
Herbert W. Schneider & George Lawton,
A Prophet and a Pilgrim (N.Y.: Columbia Univ., 1942).
Robert V. Hine, California's Utopian
Colonies (New Haven: Yale Univ.,
1966), pp.12-32.
-Parapsychology research
  1970s/Psychotronics Research Institute
  /720 Beaver St.
    John White & Stanley Krippner, eds.,
    Future Science (Garden City, N.Y.:
    Anchor, 1977), pp.591-92.
-UFO (?)
  1951
    Ted Phillips, Physical Traces Asso-
    ciated with UFO Sightings (Evanston:
    Center for UFO Studies, 1975), p.
    108.
-UFO (DD)
  1947, July 3
    Santa Rosa Press-Democrat, 8 July
    1947, p.1.
  1947, July 5/Calvin McEntire
    San Francisco Chronicle, 6 July 1947;
    and 8 July 1947.
  1947, July 7
    San Francisco Examiner, 8 July 1947.
-UFO (NL)
  1896, Nov.21,23
    Loren E. Gross, The UFO Wave of 1896
    (Fremont, Cal.: The Author, 1974),
    p.15.
  1896, Dec.
    Antioch Ledger, 12 Dec.1896.
  1978, April 9
    Santa Rosa Press-Democrat, 11 Apr.
    1978.

Santa Susana
-Ghost
  1958
    Hans Holzer, Ghosts of the Golden
    West (N.Y.: Ace, 1968), pp.60-61.

Santa Ysabel
-Doubtful identity
  1934-1936/Lucky Blackie Blackiet/=
  Judge Crater?
    Leland Lovelace, Lost Mines and Hid-
    den Treasure (N.Y.: Ace, 1956), pp.
    44-50.

Saugus
-Humanoid
  1974, Oct./Mr. McBride/Santa Clarita
  Valley
  1974, Nov./Texas Canyon
    Peter Guttilla, "Bigfoot: Advance
    Guard from Outer Space," Saga UFO
    Rept. 4 (June 1977):22-24, quoting
    Saugus-Newhall Signal (undated).
  1974, Dec./S of town
  1974, Dec.31
    John Green, Sasquatch: The Apes Among
    Us (Seattle: Hancock House, 1978),
    pp.319-21.
-UFO (CE-3)
  1975, spring/Patrick Macey/Texas Canyon

Peter Guttilla, "Bigfoot: Advance
Guard from Outer Space," Saga UFO
Rept. 4 (June 1977):22,48.

Sausalito
-Precognition
n.d./Ellen Erhard
"She Dreamed of Baby Falling," Fate
20 (Feb.1967):91, quoting San Francisco Examiner (undated).
-UFO (DD)
1927/Ella Young/Casa Madrona Hotel/156
Bulkley Ave.
Harold T. Wilkins, Flying Saucers on
the Attack (N.Y.: Ace, 1967 ed.),
p.40.
-Weeping icon
1957, Jan./Marin Art Gallery
(Editorial), Fate 10 (June 1957):12.

Seal Beach
-Mystery flotsam
1967, April
(Editorial), Fate 21 (Jan.1968):28.

Seeley
-UFO (NL)
1905, Aug.3/J.A. Jackson
Brawley News, 4 Aug.1905.

Selma
-UFO (NL)
1896, Dec.3/N.W. Stewart
San Francisco Call, 5 Dec.1896, p.2.

Sepulveda
-Biofeedback research
1960s-   /Barbara Brown/Veteran's Ad-
ministration Hospital
David M. Rorvik, "Brain Waves," Look,
6 Oct.1970, pp.88-97.
Barbara Brown, "Recognition of As-
pects of Consciousness through Asso-
ciation with EEG Alpha Activity
Represented by a Light Signal,"
Psychophysiology 6 (1970):442-52.
Barbara Brown, "Awareness of EEG-
Subjective Activity Relationships
Detected within a Closed Feedback
System," Psychophysiology 7 (1971):
4-1-64.
Barbara Brown, New Mind, New Body
(N.Y.: Harper & Row, 1974).
1970s/Maurice B. Sterman/Veteran's Ad-
ministration Hospital
Maurice B. Sterman, "Neurophysiolog-
ic and Clinical Studies of Sensori-
motor Cortex EEG Feedback Training:
Some Effects on Epilepsy," Seminars
in Psychiatry 5 (1974):507-25.
-Ghost
n.d./Mrs. Kay
Richard Webb, Voices from Another
World (N.Y.: Manor, 1972 ed.), pp.
262-64.

Sheridan
-Exploding bird
1972, June/Mrs. Al Stewart
(Editorial), Fate 26 (Feb.1973):34.

Shingle Springs
-UFO (DD)
1947, July 8/Donald Barter
Sacramento Union, 9 July 1947.

Shingletown
-Precognition
1970s/Vicki Amesquita/Rt.2, Box 901
"Probe's 1977 Directory of the Psychic World," Probe the Unknown 5
(spring 1977):33.
1970s/Richard De A'Morelli/Rt.2, Box
904
Richard De A'Morelli, Psychic Power
(Chatsworth: Books for Better Living, 1973).
Warren Smith, "Phenomenal Predictions
for 1975," Saga, Jan.1975, p.20.
Richard De A'Morelli & Rita West,
"Top Seers Predict Your Future for
1977," Psychic World, Jan.1977, pp.
51,57.

Sierra Madre
-UFO (NL)
1896, Sep.20/Lewis Swift/Lowe Observatory
"Note from Dr. L. Swift," Astron.J.
17 (1896):8.
(Letter), W.J. Hussey, Astron.J. 17
(1896):103.

Siskiyou co.
-Humanoid
1962, Aug.10/Joseph Wattenbarger/30 mi.
E of McLeod
John Green, The Sasquatch File (Ag-
assiz, B.C.: Cheam, 1973), p.29.

Sonoma
-Reincarnation
1964, spring/Dorothy Ann Richards/So-
noma State College
Dorothy Ann Richards, "Doorway to a
Previous Life," Fate 31 (Dec.1978):
86-88.
-Seance
1850s/Vallejo Estate
Emma Hardinge Britten, Modern Ameri-
can Spiritualism (N.Y.: The Author,
1870), pp.441-43.
-UFO (?)
1966, Jan.1/Julie Herrick/8 mi.N
Jerome Clark, "The Greatest Flap Yet?
--Part IV," Flying Saucer Rev. 12
(Nov.-Dec.1966):9,12.
-UFO (DD)
1953, Jan.10/8 mi.NW
U.S. Air Force, Projects Grudge and
Blue Book Reports 1-12 (Washington:
NICAP, 1968), p.190.
1976, Dec.8/Steven Poleskie
Berkeley Gazette, 10 Dec.1976.
Jeffrey Mishlove, "The Wrath of the
'UFO Prophet,'" Fate 32 (Feb.1979):
62,68-69.

Sonoma co.
-Skyquake
1951, Nov.17/William D. Lund/Mangles

Ranch
    Marion Kirkpatrick, "California Mys-
    tery Blasts," Fate 10 (Apr.1957):
    87.
-UFO (?)
  1960, Sep.5
    Richard Hall, ed., The UFO Evidence
    (Washington: NICAP, 1964), p.15.

Sonora
-Airship inventor
  1850s/C.A.A. Dellschau
    Jerome Clark & Loren Coleman, "Mys-
    tery Airships of the 1800's," Fate
    26 (May 1973):84,88-91.
-Humanoid
  1963, Feb.28/Lennart Strand
    Toronto (Ont.) Daily Star, 4 Mar.
    1963.
    (Editorial), Fate 16 (July 1963):22-
    23.
-UFO (?)
  1967, Nov.1
    Edward U. Condon, ed., Scientific
    Study of Unidentified Flying Objects
    (N.Y.: Bantam, 1969 ed.), pp.475-78.
    il.
-UFO (CE-2)
  1976, Oct.12/Mrs. Parker/=spider web
    "Angel Hair...Under Analysis: A Pre-
    liminary Report," Int'l UFO Report-
    er 2 (Aug.1977):4,8.
    "Angel-Hair Analysis Complete," Int'l
    UFO Reporter 3 (Mar.1978):newsfront
    sec.
-UFO (NL)
  1973, Sep.14/Jean Cleveland
    "UFO Seen over Football Game in Cal-
    ifornia," Skylook, no.74 (Jan.1974):
    11.
  1977, Dec.6/Cherokee Rd.
    Sonora Union-Democrat, 7 Dec.1977.

South Gate
-UFO (NL)
  1953, Oct.9
    Donald E. Keyhoe, Flying Saucer Con-
    spiracy (N.Y.: Holt, 1955), p.63.
  1977, March 22/Firestone
    Kansas City (Mo.) Star, 23 Mar.1977.

South Lake Tahoe
-UFO (CE-1)
  1956, June 14/M. Stevens/Al Tahoe
    (Letter), Fate 19 (Sep.1966):134.
-UFO (NL)
  1973, Oct.
    Glenn McWane & David Graham, The New
    UFO Sightings (N.Y.: Warner, 1974),
    p.23.

South San Francisco
-Astrology
  1970s/Macielle Oriana Brown/719 Southwood Dr.
    David St. Clair, The Psychic World of
    California (N.Y.: Bantam, 1973 ed.),
    pp.68-69,329.
-Poltergeist
  1972, May-Aug.

Freda Morris, "Exorcising the Devil
    in California," Fate 27 (July 1974)
    :36-46; (Aug.1974):96-105.
    Alan Vaughan, "The Devil in Daly
    City," Psychic 5 (Oct.1974):41-43.
    Susy Smith, The Power of the Mind
    (Radnor, Pa.: Chilton, 1975), pp.
    190-94.
-Suicide epidemic
  1964, Nov.28-1965, May
    (Editorial), Fate 19 (Oct.1966):26-
    30.
-UFO (NL)
  1973, Oct./Edward Cottman
    San Francisco Chronicle, 18 Oct.1973.

South San Gabriel
-UFO (NL)
  1973, April 5
    Ann Druffel, "The Los Angeles Basin
    Sightings," FSR Case Histories, no.
    16 (Aug.1973):7.

Spring Valley
-UFO (NL)
  1974, Nov.25
    R. Michael Rasmussen, "Two Interest-
    ing California Cases," APRO Bull.
    24 (Jan.1976):1,5-6.

Stanford
-Animal ESP
  1976, June/outdoor primate facility
    (Editorial), Fate 30 (Mar.1977):34.
-Archeological site
    Robert F. Heizer, "The Stanford
    Skull: A Probable Early Man from
    Santa Clara County, California,"
    Rept.Univ.Calif.Arch.Survey, no.6
    (1950):1-9.
    Theodore D. McCown, "The Stanford
    Skull: The Physical Characteristics,"
    Rept.Univ.Calif.Arch.Survey, no.6
    (1950):10-17.
-Out-of-body experience
  1965/Stanford University
    Charles T. Tart, "A Psychophysiologi-
    cal Study of Out-of-the-Body Exper-
    iences in a Selected Subject," J.
    ASPR 62 (1968):3-27.
    Larry Ashby, "Astral Witness to Girl's
    Murder," Fate 26 (Nov.1973):78-81.
-Paraphysics research
  1970s/William A. Tiller/Material Science Dep't, Stanford University
    William A. Tiller, "Radionics, Radi-
    esthesia, and Physics," in Proc.of
    the Varieties of Healing Experience
    Symposium (Los Altos: Academy of
    Parapsychology and Medicine, 1972).
    W.A. Tiller, D.G. Boyers & H.S. Dakin,
    Towards a Kirlian Device for Moni-
    toring Physiological States--Part I
    (Stanford: Dep't of Materials Sci.,
    1974).
    William A. Tiller, "Devices for Moni-
    toring Nonphysical Energies," in
    Edgar D. Mitchell, ed., Psychic Ex-
    ploration (N.Y.: Capricorn, 1976 ed.)
    pp.488-521. il.

Carolyn Dobervich, "Kirlian Photography Revealed?" Psychic 6 (Nov.-Dec.1974):34-39. il.
William A. Tiller, "The Positive and Negative Space/Time Frames as Conjugate Systems," in John White & Stanley Krippner, eds., Future Science (Garden City, N.Y.: Anchor, 1977), pp.256-79.
-Precognition
1959, May 5/Dick Zimmerman
(Editorial), Fate 12 (Sep.1959):20.
-Radionics
1915-1924/Albert Abrams/Stanford Medical School
Albert Abrams, New Concepts in Diagnosis and Treatment (San Francisco: Philopolis, 1916).
Jean Du Plessis, The Electronic Reactions of Abrams (Chicago: Blanche & Jeanne R. Abrams Memorial Foundation, 1922).
Albert Abrams, Iconography: Electronic Reactions of Abrams (San Francisco: The Author, 1923).
William F. Hudgings, Dr. Abrams and the Electron Theory (N.Y.: Century, 1923).
"Our Abrams Investigation," Sci.Am. 129 (1923):230,306-307,392; 130 (1924):16-17,87,159,240-41,313; 131 (1924):16,96,159-60. il.
New York Times, 18 Jan.1925.
"Electronic Reactions," Lancet, 24 Jan.1925, pp.177-81,192.
(Letter), J.Douglas Webster, Lancet, 24 Jan.1925, pp.206-207.
(Letter), F.G. Crookshank, Lancet, 31 Jan.1925, p.255.
(Letter), Stanley Melville, Lancet, 7 Feb.1925, p.310.
"The Electronic Reactions of Abrams," Nature 115 (1925):789-90.
Sir James Barr, ed., Abrams' Methods of Diagnosis and Treatment (London: W. Heineman, 1925).
Eric Perkins, The Original Concepts of the Late Dr. Albert Abrams (Burford, Eng.: Radionic Association, 1956).
Edward Wriothesley Russell, Report on Radionics (London: Spearman, 1973), pp.15-50. il.
-Telepathy research
1916/John E. Coover/Stanford University
John Edgar Coover, Experiments in Psychical Research at Leland Stanford Junior University (Palo Alto: Stanford, 1917).
Frederick C. Dommeyer & Rhea White, "Psychical Research in Colleges and Universities," J.ASPR 57 (1963):3, 16-22.
-UFO (DD)
1967, Feb.2/Seth Morrell
"Boys Snap Photos near Stanford University," APRO Bull. 15 (May-June 1967):7. il.
-UFO (NL)
1896, Nov.30/R.S. Garfield

San Francisco Call, 2 Dec.1896, p.14.

Stateline
-UFO (CE-2)
1957, July 22/Karen Zunino
Leonard H. Stringfield, Inside Saucer Post...3-0 Blue (Cincinnati: CRIFO, 1957), p.55, quoting APRG Reporter, Aug.1957.

Stockton
-Archeological site
Phillip Mills Jones, "Mound Excavation near Stockton," Pub.Am.Arch.& Ethn.Univ.Calif. 20 (1923):113-24.
-Poltergeist
1953, Feb./Miriam Grinstead/Rose St.
Miriam Grinstead, "Unruly Poltergeist," Fate 9 (June 1956):61-66.
-UFO (NL)
1896, Nov.24
Loren E. Gross, The UFO Wave of 1896 (Fremont, Cal.: The Author, 1974), p.13, quoting Stockton Daily Independent (undated).
1896, Nov.26/W. Bruce Harrison
Sacramento Bee, 28 Nov.1896.
Loren E. Gross, The UFO Wave of 1896 (Fremont, Cal.: The Author, 1974), pp.13-14, quoting Stockton Daily Independent (undated).
1968, April 2/Robert T. Hays
"Engineer Saw UFO," Skylook, no.11 (July 1968):3.
1975, Aug.14/Joe Savage/airport
"Gilroy, CA, Sightings Reported," Skylook, no.94 (Sep.1975):8,8.
"California Pilot Encounters UFO," Skylook, no.99 (Feb.1976):16. il.
Timothy Beckley & Harold Salkin, "UFOs Spotted Along California's Earthquake Lines," Saga UFO Rept. 3 (Dec.1976):44-46.

Strawberry
-Humanoid
1963, March/Linda Campbell/nr. Jack and Jill Ski Lodge
John Green, The Sasquatch File (Agassiz, B.C.: Cheam, 1973), p.30.
1971, July-1976/Warren Johnson/voice recordings
The Star, 9 Nov.1976, p.13.
B. Ann Slate & Alan Berry, Bigfoot (N.Y.: Bantam, 1976), pp.1-2,11-54, 166-71.
Univ. of Wyoming Branding Iron, 7 Mar.1978.
Eugene (Ore.) Register-Guard, 5 Apr. 1978, p.12B.
-Humanoid tracks
1963, Dec./Elbert Miller
John Green, The Sasquatch File (Agassiz, B.C.: Cheam, 1973), p.30.
B. Ann Slate & Alan Berry, Bigfoot (N.Y.: Bantam, 1976), pp.7-9.

Suisun City
-UFO (NL)
1896, Nov.15

Loren E. Gross, The UFO Wave of 1896
(Fremont, Cal.: The Author, 1974),
p.3, quoting San Francisco Call (undated).

Summerland
-Sea monster
  1950, Dec./Opal Lambert
    Bernard Heuvelmans, In the Wake of
    the Sea-Serpents (N.Y.: Hill & Wang,
    1968), p.480, quoting UP release,
    23 Dec.1950.

Sunland
-Fall of metallic object
  1961, Aug.24/Sunland Blvd. x Olinda St.
    Curtis Fuller, "The Boys Who 'Caught'
    a Flying Saucer," Fate 15 (Jan.1962)
    :36,39.

Sun Valley
-UFO (?)
  1957, Oct./Chet Kennedy
    "Flying Saucer Roundup," Fate 11
    (Feb.1958):29,36.

Sunnyvale
-Archeological site
  63,000 B.C.
    New York Times, 3 Sep.1975, p.34.
    "'Sunnyvale Girl' Discovery and Dat-
    ing," Newsl.Soc'y Calif.Arch. 9, no.
    5-6 (1975):15.
-Telepathy
  1959, April 14/Wanda Ping
    (Editorial), Fate 12 (Sep.1959):17.
-UFO (?)
  1963, May 23
    Richard Hall, ed., The UFO Evidence
    (Washington: NICAP, 1964), p.140.
-UFO (CE-1)
  1964, June 2/Mrs. Bruce A. Holmes/Mc-
  Kinley Ave.
    "Other Recent Sightings," UFO Inv. 2
    (July-Aug.1964):8.
    Donald E. Keyhoe & Gordon I.R. Lore,
    Jr., UFOs: A New Look (Washington:
    NICAP, 1969), p.14.
  1974, June 20/Carlo Ciravlo
    (Letter), Saga UFO Rept. 2 (fall
    1974):76.
-UFO (DD)
  1963, July 18
    Richard Hall, ed., The UFO Evidence
    (Washington: NICAP, 1964), pp.140-
    41.
-UFO (NL)
  1960, Dec.1
    "Odds and Ends," APRO Bull. 9 (Jan.
    1961):5.
  1963, Sep.26/Galen Anderson
    San Jose Mercury-News, 26 Sep.1963.
    Richard Hall, ed., The UFO Evidence
    (Washington: NICAP, 1964), p.63. il.

Susanville
-UFO (?)
  1963, Sep.14
    Richard Hall, ed., The UFO Evidence
    (Washington: NICAP, 1964), p.141.

Sutter
-UFO (NL)
  1896, Dec.2/E.T. Schellinger/3 mi.E
    Marysville Daily Democrat, 3 Dec.
    1896.
    Marysville Semi-Weekly Appeal, 7 Dec.
    1896.

Sutter co.
-Mystery bird deaths
  1946, Jan.30/O'Bannion's Corner
    "More Birds," Doubt, no.15 (summer
    1946):226.

Sylmar
-Dowsing
  1956, April/Emmuel Carroll
    Gaston Burridge, "Miracles of Map
    Dowsing," Fate 11 (June 1958):71-
    80.
-Precognition
  1970s/Jacquelinn Twiford/13637 Eldridge
    "Probe's 1977 Directory of the Psy-
    chic World," Probe the Unknown 5
    (spring 1977):22,65.
-UFO (CE-2)
  1977, March 6/Douglas Kriese
    Ann Druffel, "California Report,"
    MUFON UFO J., no.124 (Mar.1978):12-
    14. il.
-UFO (NL)
  1976, Oct.9/Rick Lannard
    Ann Druffel, "SkyNet Log," MUFON UFO
    J., no.113 (Apr.1977):15-16.

Tagus
-UFO (DD)
  1896, Nov.20/D.H. Risdon
    Sacramento Record-Union, 23 Nov.1896.

Tarzana
-Poltergeist
  1960s/Fred Maguire/Hatteras St.
    Richard Webb, Voices from Another
    World (N.Y.: Manor, 1972 ed.), pp.
    171-82.
-UFO (?)
  1973, April 10/=blimp?
    Ann Druffel, "Are There Mimicking
    UFOs?--Part 1," MUFON UFO J., no.
    112 (Mar.1977):15.

Tecate
-Spanish galleon
  n.d./10 mi.NE
    Vincent H. Gaddis, "Ships That Sailed
    the Desert," Fate 26 (Jan.1973):63,
    66.

Temple City
-Fall of unknown object
  1957, April 9
    Leonard H. Stringfield, Inside Sau-
    cer Post...3-0 Blue (Cincinnati:
    CRIFO, 1957), p.59.
-UFO (CE-1)
  1966, May 24
    Ann Druffel, "Oddities among the Er-
    ratics," MUFON UFO J., no.103 (June
    1976):10-11. il.

-UFO (NL)
  1964, July 29
    Curtis Fuller, "Collected UFO Sight-
    ings for August and September," Fate
    18 (Jan.1965):35.

Thermal
-Giant human skeletons
  1902/=hoax?
    (Letter), William Hoggatt, Fate 22
    (Dec.1969):150.

Thermalito
-UFO (NL)
  1967, July 18/Mrs. Tony Mackelprange/
  Alma Ave.
    "Campers Disturbed by Cigar-Shaped
    Object," APRO Bull. 16 (July-Aug.
    1967):8.

Thousand Oaks
-Haunt
  1960s/Stagecoach Inn
  1960s/Missionary Baptist Church
    Hans Holzer, Ghosts of the Golden
    West (N.Y.: Ace, 1968), pp.127-39.
-UFO (?)
  1966, Jan.1
    Jerome Clark, "The Greatest Flap Yet?
    --Part IV," Flying Saucer Rev. 12
    (Nov.-Dec.1966):9,12.

Thousand Palms
-Weather control and UFO (DD)
  1968, May 11/James O. Woods/=neo-Reich-
  ian method
    Trevor James Constable, The Cosmic
    Pulse of Life (Santa Ana: Merlin,
    1976), betw. pp.206-207. il.

Tiburon
-UFO (DD)
  1956, Aug.26/James Geer
    "Case 201," CRIFO Orbit, 5 Oct.1956,
    p.3.

Torrance
-Inner development
  1968-   /Foundation of Scientific
  Spiritual Understanding/328 Calle Mayor
    David St. Clair, The Psychic World
    of California (N.Y.: Bantam, 1973
    ed.), pp.291-92.
-Out-of-body experience
  1951, Feb./Charles C. Lacy/1540 W. 224th
  St.
    Minnie Clough, "Experiment in Astral
    Projection," Fate 4 (Nov.-Dec.1951):
    44-47.
-Precognition
  1960/Mary Jane Kent
    (Editorial), Fate 14 (Apr.1961):22-
    23.
-Talking dog
  1965/Mrs. Genova
    Clare Adele Lambert, "Pepe, the Talk-
    ing Dog of Torrance, California,"
    Fate 19 (July 1966):68-73. il.

Tracy
-Fall of unknown object
  1958, June/Joe Kudo
    Coral E. Lorenzen, The Shadow of the
    Unknown (N.Y.: Signet, 1970), p.62.
-UFO (CE-1)
  1955, Sep./Wanda Lockwood
    (Letter), Fate 17 (May 1964):117-18.

Train
-Humanoid
  1969, July/Lester Orlinger
    Oroville Mercury-Register, 15 July
    1969.

Tranquillity
-Archeological site
    Gordon W. Hewes, "Early Man in Cali-
    fornia and the Tranquillity Site,"
    Am.Antiquity 11 (1946):209-15.

Trinidad
-Fall of weblike substance
  1958, Nov.9
    Eureka Humboldt Times, 11-12 Nov.
    1958.

Trinity Center
-Humanoid
  1969, June?/Don Ballard
    John Green, The Sasquatch File (Ag-
    assiz, B.C.: Cheam, 1973), pp.46-
    47.

Truckee
-Psychokinesis
  1960, Aug./A.W. Riedel
    Sacramento Bee, 22 Aug.1960.
-UFO (CE-1)
  1972, Aug.4/Tom Garret
    Glenn McWane & David Graham, The New
    UFO Sightings (N.Y.: Warner, 1974),
    p.56, quoting Truckee Sierra Sun-
    Bonanza (undated).
-UFO (NL)
  1973, Oct.16/Pete Werbel/Bridge St.
    Glenn McWane & David Graham, The New
    UFO Sightings (N.Y.: Warner, 1974),
    p.23.

Tujunga
-Clairempathy
  1939-   /Maris De Long/Box 25
    Richard De A'Morelli & Rita West,
    "Top Seers Predict Your Future for
    1977," Psychic World, Jan.1977, pp.
    51,56-57.
    "Probe's 1977 Directory of the Psy-
    chic World," Probe the Unknown 5
    (spring 1977):32,35. il.
-Contactee
  1967, July 26/Maris De Long
    John A. Keel, The Mothman Prophecies
    (N.Y.: Saturday Review, 1975), pp.
    158-59.
-Fall of beans
  1964, Jan.22/Dudley Williams/6816 Val-
  mont Ave.
    Raymond Bayless, "Beanfall in San
    Fernando," Fate 17 (May 1964):27-29.

-Inner development
  1970s/Fellowship of Kouretes
    Armand Biteaux, The New Conscious-
    ness (Willits, Cal.: Oliver, 1975),
    pp.42-43.
-Phantom helicopter
  1975, Sep.3
    Ann Druffel, "California Report: The
    Mystery Helicopters," MUFON UFO J.,
    no.99 (Feb.1976):8-9.
-UFO (CE-4)
  1953, March 22/Tujunga Canyon
    David Webb, "Analysis of Humanoid
    Abduction Reports," in Proc.1976
    CUFOS Conference (Evanston: Center
    for UFO Studies, 1976), pp.266,268-
    69.
-UFO (NL)
  1947, July 2/C.T. Grove
    Los Angeles Times, 4 July 1947.

Tulare
-UFO (NL)
  1896, Nov.29/E.T. Cooper
    Loren E. Gross, The UFO Wave of 1896
    (Fremont, Cal.: The Author, 1974),
    p.23.

Tulare co.
-Anomalous mounds
    Victor B. Sheffer, "The Mystery of
    the Mima Mounds," Sci.Monthly 65
    (Oct.1947):283-94.

Tuolumne
-UFO (NL)
  1977, Nov.29/Belleview Rd.
    Sonora Union-Democrat, 30 Nov.1977.

Tuolumne co.
-UFO (NL)
  1949, June 21
    "If It's in the Sky It's a Saucer,"
    Doubt, no.27 (1949):416.

Turlock
-Poltergeist
  1886, Oct./Willie Brough
    New York Herald, 16 Oct.1886.
    Los Angeles Daily News, 25 Aug.1948.

Tustin
-Haunt
  1917/Pat Murphy/Pacific St.
    M.G. Murphy, "The Ghost That Moved to
    Our House," Fate 16 (May 1963):36-
    42.

Twain Harte
-UFO (DD)
  1973, Sep.12/Donald Hardin/2 mi.E on
    Hwy.108
    Paul Cerny, "Daytime Silver Disc Seen
    at Sonora, California," Skylook, no.
    74 (Jan.1974):10.
-UFO (NL)
  1977, June/Sherwood Forest
    Sonora Union-Democrat, 30 Nov.1977.

Twentynine Palms
-Contactee
  1954, Dec./Orfeo Angelucci
    Orfeo Angelucci, Son of the Sun (Los
    Angeles: DeVorss, 1959).
  1950s-1960s/Lisa Henderson
    David St. Clair, The Psychic World
    of California (N.Y.: Bantam, 1973
    ed.), pp.317-26.
-UFO (?)
  1949, April 27
    "If It's in the Sky It's a Saucer,"
    Doubt, no.27 (1949):416.
-UFO (CE-1)
  1954
    "C-4," CRIFO Newsl., 6 Aug.1954, p.4.

Upland
-Fire anomaly
  1944, Nov.6/Mabel Duncanson
    "Add Pyrotics," Doubt, no.13 (winter
    1945):191.

Vacaville
-Humanoid
  1976, June
    "Latest News from the Pacific North-
    west," Bigfoot News, no.22 (July
    1976):1.
-UFO (CE-1)
  1975, Nov.2/Robert Perry/water treat-
    ment plant
    Timothy Green Beckley, "Saucers over
    Our Cities," Saga UFO Rept. 4 (Aug.
    1977):24,73.
-UFO (CE-2)
  1968, Sep.2/Marion Boykin
    Vacaville Reporter, 3 Sep.1968.
-UFO (DD)
  1947, July 6
    San Francisco Examiner, 7 July 1947.
-UFO (NL)
  1967, April 25/James Coats
    "Strange Lights over Mts.," APRO
    Bull. 15 (May-June 1967):3.
  1975, Oct.16
    "UFO Central," CUFOS News Bull., 1
    Feb.1976, p.9.

Vallecito
-Fall of weblike substance
  1887-1891
    George Marx, "On Spiders' Web," Proc.
    Entomological Soc'y of Washington 2
    (1892):385-86.
-Phantom horse
  n.d.
    Philip A. Bailey, Golden Mirages
    (N.Y.: Macmillan, 1940), pp.126-27.

Vallejo
-Skyquake
  1951, May
    San Francisco Examiner, 23 May 1951.
-UFO (NL)
  1896, Dec.4-5/M.H. Denio
    San Francisco Chronicle, 6 Dec.1896,
    p.20.

Van Nuys
-Fall of beans
  1958, March 6/Teto Emerson
    Detroit (Mich.) Free Press, 11 Mar.
      1958.
    "Falls," Doubt, no.57 (1958):4.
-Mystery plane crash
  1957, Jan.31/airliner
    "An Orgy of Crashes," CRIFO Orbit, 1
      Mar.1957, p.1.
-Poltergeist
  1973/Jim Wiseman
    Barry Taff, "Stalking the Elusive
      Spectre," Probe the Unknown 1 (Oct.
      1973):30,31-32. il.
-UFO (DD)
  1950, March 9
    Donald E. Keyhoe, Flying Saucers Are
      Real (N.Y.: Fawcett, 1950), pp.167-
      68.
-UFO (NL)
  1972, July 27/Russell Shuffert
    Glenn McWane & David Graham, The New
      UFO Sightings (N.Y.: Warner, 1974),
      p.49, quoting Van Nuys Valley News
      (undated).
  1975, Aug.22
    "UFO Central," CUFOS News Bull., 15
      Nov.1975, p.16.
  1977, June 26
  1977, Aug.20, 23
    Ann Druffel, "Other Encounters of All
      Different Kinds," MUFON UFO J., no.
      123 (Feb.1978):15,16-17.

Venice
-Cartomancy
  1975, April/Zsuzsanna Budapest
    David St. Clair, "Los Angeles Witch-
      Hunt 1975," Fate 28 (Sep.1975):77-
      83.
    Jack Murray, "Selective Enforcement
      Strikes Again," Probe the Unknown
      4 (Jan.1976):12-15.
    (Letter), Gavin Frost, Fate 29 (Feb.
      1976):111.
    (Letter), David St. Clair, Fate 29
      (May 1976):115-16.
-Fall of chicks
  1956, April/Elsie Moore/Clune Ave.
    Santa Monica Outlook, 1 May 1956.
-Paranormal voice recordings
  1976, Feb.15/Bart Ellis/Marina del Rey
    Susy Smith, Voices of the Dead? (N.Y.:
      Signet, 1977), pp.64-66.
-Sea monster (carcass)
  1955, Dec./=oarfish?
    (Editorial), Fate 9 (May 1956):6.
-UFO (NL)
  1976, Jan.2/Marina del Rey
    "Noteworthy UFO Sightings," Ufology
      2 (summer 1976):62.

Ventura
-Cloud anomaly
  1954, Dec.25/9 mi.E
    (Letter), L.B., Fate 8 (May 1955):
      115-16.
-Haunt
  1959/Mildred Powers/Meta St.

Mildred Powers, "Friendly Ghosts of
  Meta St.," Fate 19 (July 1966):45-
  49.
-Phantom panther
  1967, Dec.12/Henry Madrid/sewer plant
  1968, Jan./Kenneth French
    Loren Coleman, "California Odyssey:
      Observations on the Western Para-
      Panther," Anomaly Rsch.Bull., no.23
      (1978):5-6.
-UFO (DD)
  1978, July 22
    "UFOs of Limited Merit," Int'l UFO
      Reporter 3 (Sep.1978):6.
  1978, Sep.19/Dave Williams/Police Dep't
    Oxnard Press-Courier, 19 Sep.1978.
-UFO (NL)
  1973, Oct.23/Sal Sanchez/3101 Porter
    Lane
    Oxnard Press-Courier, 24 Oct.1973.

Verona
-Land monster and poultry killings
  1936, Feb.13
    "How to Prevent Panic," Fortean Soc'y
      Mag., no.3 (Jan.1940):13, quoting
      Los Angeles Herald-Examiner (undated).

Victorville
-Dowsing
  1950s/Della Truax
    Gaston Burridge, "The Truth about
      Dowsing," Fate 7 (Dec.1954):17,18.
-UFO (CE-2)
  1959, Feb.24
    J. Allen Hynek, The Hynek UFO Report
      (N.Y.: Dell, 1977), pp.167-70.
-UFO (DD)
  1952, May 1-20/George AFB
    U.S. Air Force, Projects Grudge and
      Blue Book Reports 1-12 (Washington:
      1968), pp.126-27.
    J. Allen Hynek, The Hynek UFO Report
      (N.Y.: Dell, 1977), pp.107-109.
  1958, Sep.13/Trevor James Constable
    Trevor James Constable, The Cosmic
      Pulse of Life (Santa Ana: Merlin,
      1976), betw. pp.206-207.
-UFO (NL)
  1972, June 19/Gary Corley/George AFB
    San Bernardino Sun-Telegram, 20 June
      1972.
  1977, Feb.20
    "UFOs of Limited Merit," Int'l UFO
      Reporter 2 (Apr.1977):5.

Vina
-UFO (CE-1)
  1978, Oct.-Nov./Mike Farmer/E of town
    Chico Enterprise-Record, 11 Jan.1979.
-UFO (NL)
  1969, May 24/Tom Kitchen/Woodson Bridge
    "Police, Farmers Watch UFO in Calif.,"
      APRO Bull. 17 (May-June 1969):1,4.
    "Mystery in California Sky," Skylook,
      no.23 (Oct.1969):14.

Visalia
-Bird attack
  1977, May 13/Connie Spain/449 S. Church

Kansas City (Mo.) Times, 14 May 1977,
p.6A.
-Phantom image
1968/William Wingfield
(Letter), Fate 25 (Oct.1972):146.
-UFO (DD)
1896, April 18
Visalia Weekly Delta, 19 Apr.1896.
-UFO (NL)
1896, Nov.25/E.O. Larkin
Visalia Weekly Delta, 26 Nov.1896.

Vista
-UFO (?)
1958, Jan.11
Richard Hall, ed., The UFO Evidence
(Washington: NICAP, 1964), p.17.

Walnut Creek
-Phantom panther
1972, spring
Loren Coleman, "California Odyssey:
Observations on Western Para-Pan-
thers," Anomaly Rsch.Bull., no.23
(1978):5,7.
-Precognition
1968, June 4/Felicia Dominguez
"'Don't Vote for Him,'" Fate 22
(Jan.1969):52, quoting Oakland Trib-
une (undated).
-Reincarnation research
1977/Helen Wambach/20 Wayne Ct.
James Crenshaw, "Clinical Psycholo-
gist Researches Hang-Ups from Past
Lives," Fate 31 (Apr.1978):55-63.
-UFO (NL)
1978, Feb.28/Sonia Hofioni/29 Park Ter-
race Ct.
Walnut Creek Contra Costa Times, 2
Mar.1978.

Walnut Grove
-UFO (?)
1947, July 5
San Francisco Chronicle, 8 July 1947.

Warner Springs
-Humanoid and mystery deaths
1858-1889/Deadman Hole/=hoax
San Diego Union, 1-2 Apr.1888.
Philip A. Bailey, Golden Mirages
(N.Y.: Macmillan, 1940), pp.278-80.
"The Monster of Deadman's Hole," Fate
17 (Mar.1964):46, quoting San Diego
Evening Tribune (undated).
John Green, The Sasquatch File (Ag-
assiz, B.C.: Cheam, 1973), p.6.
Jim Brandon, Weird America (N.Y.:
Dutton, 1978), pp.36-37.
John Green, Sasquatch: The Apes Among
Us (Seattle: Hancock House, 1978),
p.371.

Warner's Ranch
-Humanoid
1876, Feb.25/Turner Helm/10 mi.E
San Diego Union, 9 Mar.1876.

Watertown
-UFO (CE-3)

1896, Nov.20/Robert McQuarrie
San Francisco Call, 3 Dec.1896, p.9.

Watsonville
-UFO (NL)
1952, Jan.5/Al Bolman
(Editorial), Fate 5 (Sep.1952):6.
1966, Jan.29/George M. Clemins
San Francisco News Call Bulletin, 12
Feb.1966.
1973, Nov.20/Teresa Montoya
San Jose Mercury-News, 22 Nov.1973.

Weitchpec
-Humanoid tracks
1960, Aug.7/Bob Titmus/9 mi.S
1968, Jan./Martin's Ferry Hill
John Green, The Sasquatch File (Agassiz, B.C.: Cheam, 1973), pp.23,
45.

West Covina
-Clairempathy
1960s/Joyce Partise
Wanda Sue Parrott, "Will ESP Tests
Revolutionize Psychology?" Fate 22
(Jan.1969):59-65. il.
-Paranormal strength
1965, Nov./Clint Collins
(Editorial), Fate 19 (Sep.1966):20.
-UFO (NL)
1975, Sep.26
"UFO Central," CUFOS News Bull., 15
Nov.1975, p.19.

West Hollywood
-Inner development
1966-1968/Mental Investigations of New
Dimensions
Fritz Kron & B. Ann Slate, "The Great
UFO 'Ride,'" Fate 24 (May 1971):38-
50. il.
-Poltergeist
1960s/Beverly Rostoker
Richard Webb, Voices from Another
World (N.Y.: Manor, 1972 ed.), pp.
163-70.
-Precognition
1970s/Ralph Campo/6716 Drexel Ave.
Warren Smith, "Phenomenal Predictions
for 1976," Saga, Jan.1976, p.16.
"Probe's 1977 Directory of the Psy-
chic World," Probe the Unknown 5
(spring 1977):32,34.

West Pittsburg
-UFO (CE-3)
1977, May 20/Lennie Young/Bayview Ave.
x Willow Pass Rd./=hoax?
Pittsburg Post-Dispatch, 23 May 1977.
Richmond Independent, 24 May 1977.
"UFO with 'Dark Figures' in Califor-
nia," Int'l UFO Reporter 2 (July
1977):4-5.
"CE II in California," Int'l UFO Re-
porter 2 (Oct.1977):7.
Oakland Tribune, 2 Apr.1978, p.5.

Westwood
-Bird attack

1970, April 27/Larry Benson
(Editorial), Fate 23 (Sep.1970):18-
22, quoting Los Angeles Times (un-
dated).
"Bird Attacks on Houses," Fortean
Times, no.17 (Aug.1976):4, quoting
Nat'l Enquirer (undated).
-Clairempathy
1960s-   /Lotte von Strahl/437 Gayley
(Editorial), Fate 16 (Dec.1963):21-
22.
D. Scott Rogo, "Tripping over the
Ectoplasm," Fate 23 (Nov.1970):67,
70.
David St. Clair, The Psychic World
of California (N.Y.: Bantam, 1973
ed.), pp.205-11.
Tim Patterson, "Cops Hesitant to Work
with Psychic Colombos," Probe the
Unknown 3 (Nov.1975):31-32.

Wheatland
-UFO (NL)
1896, Oct.23
Portland Oregonian, 24 Oct.1896.

Whittier
-Fall of ice
1953, Jan.16/Catherine Martin/134 West
Rd.
(Editorial), Fate 6 (Aug.1953):6.
-UFO (CE-1)
1975, Aug.16
"UFO Central," CUFOS News Bull., 15
Nov.1975, p.16.
-UFO (NL)
1966, Dec.17
J. Allen Hynek, The UFO Experience
(Chicago: Regnery, 1972), pp.38,236.

Wildwood
-Humanoid
1969, June/Bob Kelley/Wildwood Inn
1969, July 4/Eldon Brackett/N of town
John Green, The Sasquatch File (Agassiz, B.C.: Cheam, 1973), pp.46,47.
-Humanoid tracks
1970, May 14/Archie Buckley/Basin Gulch
campground
John Green, The Sasquatch File (Agassiz, B.C.: Cheam, 1973), p.56.

Willits
-UFO (CE-2)
1976, Oct.7/Jean Gibson/Brookside
School
Willits News, 13 Oct.1976.

Willow Brook
-UFO (?)
1956, Oct.21/2410 E. 113th St.
"Case 243," CRIFO Orbit, 7 Dec.1956,
p.3, quoting Los Angeles Examiner
(undated).

Willow Creek
-Humanoid
1967, summer?/Russel Summerville/½ mi.W
John Green, The Sasquatch File (Agassiz, B.C.: Cheam, 1973), p.38.

-UFO (CE-2)
1976, Jan./Wendy Allen
Peter Guttilla, "Monster Menagerie,"
Saga UFO Rept. 4 (Sep.1977):32,34.
-UFO (NL)
1960, Aug.13
Richard Hall, ed., The UFO Evidence
(Washington: MUFON, 1964), p.170.
1971, Oct.11/Mary Ann Wegner
"Hat-Shaped Object Reported," Sky-
look, no.51 (Feb.1972):8, quoting
Willow Creek Klam-ity Courier (un-
dated).

Wilton
-Fall of plastic
1955, July-Aug.4
Sacramento Union, 29 July 1955; and
4 Aug.1955.
-UFO (DD)
1947, July 6/Mrs. K. Spotts/River Rd.
Sacramento Union, 7 July 1947.

Woodland
-UFO (DD)
1947, July 5/Katie Cavalli
Sacramento Union, 6 July 1947.
-UFO (NL)
1896, Nov.27
Woodland Daily Democrat, 28 Nov.1896.
1976, Feb./Vicki Richter
Timothy Green Beckley, "Saucers over
Our Cities," Saga UFO Rept. 4 (Aug.
1977):24,73.

Woodland Hills
-Haunt
1969, April-June/Terri Lee Robbe
Terri Lee Robbe, "The Insistent
Ghost," Fate 23 (June 1970):49-56.
-UFO (DD)
1957, Aug.15/Eugene S. Allison
Richard Hall, ed., The UFO Evidence
(Washington: NICAP, 1964), p.32.

Woodside
-Fall of metal pellets
1954, Aug.27/Portola Rd.
San Jose Mercury-News, 29 Aug.1954.
"Mystery Metal Ignites Road," CRIFO
Newsl., 1 Oct.1954, p.6, quoting
San Francisco Call-Bulletin (undat-
ed).
(Editorial), Fate 8 (Apr.1955):13-14.
Donald E. Keyhoe, Flying Saucer Con-
spiracy (N.Y.: Holt, 1955), pp.196-
97.
Thomas M. Comella, "Why the Real Sau-
cer Is Interplanetary," Fate 8 (Dec.
1955):17,18-19.

Wrightwood
-UFO (NL)
1973, Oct.25
"Woman Is Frightened by Large, Bright
Object," Skylook, no.74 (Jan.1974):
11-12.

Yorba Linda
-UFO (CE-1)

1975, May 5/Mary Nystul
Ann Druffel, "Semi-Transparent UFO
Reported," Skylook, no.94 (Sep.1975)
:10.
-UFO (DD)
1967, Jan.24
Santa Ana Register, 7 June 1967, p.
A14.
Ann Druffel, "The Yorba Linda Photo-
graph," in UFO Encounters (Flying
Saucer Rev. special issue no.5, Nov.
1973), pp.26-35. il.

Yreka
-Humanoid tracks
1960s
John Green, The Sasquatch File (Agassiz, B.C.: Cheam, 1973), p.38.

Yuba City
-UFO (?)
1947, July 8/Leona McKean
Sacramento Union, 9 July 1947.
-UFO (NL)
n.d./airport
Harold T. Wilkins, Flying Saucers Uncensored (N.Y.: Pyramid, 1967 ed.),
p.63.
1978, March 11/Peggy Lenderman/Colusa
x Walton Ave.
Yuba City Independent-Herald, 13 Mar.
1978.

Yucaipa
-Haunt
1966, Apr.-Sep./Ward Roy
Ward A. Roy, "Our Smelly Ghost," Fate
23 (May 1970):74-77.
-Poltergeist
1965, Dec./Billie Cannon/33843 Fair-
view Rd.
Los Angeles Times, 10 Dec.1965; 15
Dec.1965; 10 Jan.1966; and 19 Jan.
1966.
Raymond Bayless & Henry Gilroy,
"Thumping, Bumping Poltergeist in
California," Fate 19 (May 1966):32-
38. il.
-UFO (CE-1)
1968, Jan.3/Highland Blvd.
Coral E. Lorenzen, The Shadow of the
Unknown (N.Y.: Signet, 1970), pp.
161-63.

Yucca Valley
-Contactee
1950s-   /George Van Tassel/Box 458
George Van Tassel, I Rode a Flying
Saucer (Los Angeles: New Age, 1952).
George Van Tassel, Proceedings of the
Ministry of Universal Wisdom (n.p.:
The Author, 1 Dec.1953).
George Van Tassel, Into This World
and Out Again (Los Angeles: DeVorss,
1957).
George Van Tassel, The Council of
Seven Lights (Los Angeles: DeVorss,
1958).
(Editorial), Saucer News 8 (Dec.1961)
:15.

Long John Nebel, The Way Out World
(N.Y.: Lancer, 1962 ed.), pp.43-47.
Trevor James Constable, The Cosmic
Pulse of Life (Santa Ana: Merlin,
1976), pp.44-47.
-Contactee conventions
1954-   /George Van Tassel/Giant Rock
Max B. Miller, "The Spaceniks of
Giant Rock," Argosy, July 1963, pp.
34-37.
Jacob Konrath, "The Wonderful World
of Giant Rock," Real, Dec.1966, pp.
20-21,52-54.
Gabriel Green, Let's Face the Facts
about Flying Saucers (N.Y.: Popular
Library, 1967), pp.107-109.
"Believers, Unite!" in Flying Saucers
(N.Y.: Look Magazine special issue,
1967), pp.54-55. il.
James Moseley, "Giant Rock," Saucers,
Space & Sci. 60 (1971):7-9.
Paris Flammonde, The Age of Flying
Saucers (N.Y.: Hawthorn, 1971), pp.
63,75,91-93,143,156,167.
David Michael Jacobs, The UFO Contro-
versy in America (Bloomington: Univ.
of Indiana, 1975), pp.121,203,222-
23.
Gray Barker, Gray Barker at Giant
Rock (Clarksburg, W.V.: Saucerian,
1975).
-Inner development
1941-   /Institute of Mentalphysics/
Box 640
John Godwin, Occult America (Garden
City: Doubleday, 1972), pp.221-23.
June & Nicholas Regush, Psi: The Oth-
er World Catalogue (N.Y.: Putnam,
1974), p.160.
Armand Biteaux, The New Consciousness (Willits, Cal.: Oliver, 1975),
pp.73-74.
-UFO (CE-1)
1955, March 12/Giant Rock
Michel X. Barton, Flying Saucer Rev-
elations (Los Angeles: Futura, 1957).
1958, May 3/Trevor James Constable
Trevor James Constable, The Cosmic
Pulse of Life (Santa Ana: Merlin,
1976), p.91. il.
1960, Oct./Allen Noonan/Giant Rock
Allen Noonan, "I Went to Venus--and
Beyond," in True Magazine, ed., New
Report on Flying Saucers (Greenwich,
Ct.: Fawcett, 1967), pp.50-52,76-77.
1967, June 14/Richard T. Sandburg/Gi-
ant Rock
Wendelle C. Stevens, "Fantastic UFO
Photo Flap of 1967: Part II," Saga
UFO Rept. 3 (Aug.1976):24,29.
-UFO (NL)
1969, May 11
Santa Ana Register, 23 Aug.1972.

B. Physical Features

Alabama Hills
-Ghost
    1950s
        Richard Webb, Voices from Another
        World (N.Y.: Manor, 1972 ed.), pp.
        194-95,249-52.

Amargosa Mts.
-Ancient underground city
    =hoax?
        Jim Brandon, Weird America (N.Y.:
        Dutton, 1978), p.30.

Andreas Hills
-UFO (CE-2)
    1976, June 9/Nancy Shuken
        "June Report," APRO Bull. 24 (Oct.
        1976):6.

Angeles National Forest
-Humanoid
    1974, Nov.16/Jim Mangano
        B. Ann Slate & Alan Berry, Bigfoot
        (N.Y.: Bantam, 1976), pp.105-107.
-Humanoid tracks
    1974, Oct./Jim Mangano
        B. Ann Slate & Alan Berry, Bigfoot
        (N.Y.: Bantam, 1976), pp.102-103.

Anza Borrego Desert
-Ancient ship
    1933/Myrtle Botts/Agua Caliente Hot
    Springs
        Brad Williams & Choral Pepper, The
        Mysterious West (Cleveland: World,
        1966), pp.30-32.
-Archeological sites
    9000-6500 B.C.
        Malcolm J. Rogers, Ancient Hunters
        of the Far West (San Diego: Union-
        Tribune, 1966). il.
-Humanoid
    1930/Ken Coon
        John Green, Sasquatch: The Apes Among
        Us (Seattle: Hancock House, 1978),
        p.306.
-Phantom
    n.d./Charley Arizona
        Philip A. Bailey, Golden Mirages
        (N.Y.: Macmillan, 1940), pp.123-26.
-UFO (CE-3)
    1968, spring/Ed Sampson
        Peter Guttilla, "Bigfoot: Advance
        Guard from Outer Space," Saga UFO
        Rept. 4 (June 1977):22,50.

Arguello Pt.
-Mystery shipwrecks
    1848-1955/Devil's Jaw
        Richard Winer, From the Devil's Tri-
        angle to the Devil's Jaw (N.Y.: Ban-
        tam, 1977), pp.222-34.

Bailey Ridge
-Humanoid tracks
    1970, June/Wes Chormicle
        B. Ann Slate & Alan Berry, Bigfoot
        (N.Y.: Bantam, 1976), pp.9-10.

Bald Hill
-Archeological site
        J.D. Whitney, "Notice of a Human
        Skull Recently Taken from a Shaft
        near Angels, Calaveras Co.," Proc.
        Calif.Acad.Sci. 3 (1868):277-78.
        J.D. Whitney, "The Auriferous Grav-
        els of the Sierra Nevada of Calif-
        ornia," Mem.Mus.Comp.Zool.Harvard
        College, vol.6 (1880).
        William H. Holmes, "Review of the
        Evidence Relating to Auriferous
        Gravel Man in California," Ann.Rept.
        Smith.Inst., 1899, pp.419-72.
        Tuolumne Independent, 14 Sep.1901.
        William J. Sinclair, "Recent Inves-
        tigations Bearing on the Question
        of the Occurrence of Neocene Man
        in the Auriferous Gravels of the
        Sierra Nevada," Pub.Am.Arch.& Ethn.
        Univ.Calif. 7 (1908):107,123-29.
        John C. Merriam, "The True Story of
        the Calaveras Skull," Sunset 24
        (Feb.1910):153-58.

Baldwin Hills Reservoir
-UFO (R)
    1955, March/Ralph Bock
        "Unusual Radar Tracking Reported,"
        Skylook, no.39 (Feb.1971):8.

Baldy, Mt.
-UFO (DD)
    1953, Jan.25/Pierre L. Tissot
        (Letter), Fate 6 (June 1953):108.

Battle Creek
-UFO (CE-3)
    1972, Jan.19/Darrell Rich/bridge
        Redding Record-Searchlight, 21 Jan.
        1972.
        "Multiple Witness Case in California,"
        APRO Bull. 20 (Mar.-Apr.1972):1,5.

Benson Creek
-UFO (DD)
    1964, Aug.15/Edward J. Haug
        Thomas M. Olsen, ed., The Reference
        for Outstanding UFO Sighting Reports
        (Riderwood, Md.: UFO Information
        Retrieval Center, 1966), p.102.

Berkeley Hills
-Ancient walls
        Oakland Tribune, 15 Oct.1916.
        Sibley S. Morrill, "The Mysterious
        Walls of the Berkeley and Oakland
        Hills," Pursuit 5 (Oct.1974):90-92.
        il.

Bicycle L.
-Erratic shrimp
    1955, Aug.23
        "Mystery of the Desert Shrimp," Fate
        9 (Mar.1956):57.

Big Sur State Park
-UFO (DD)
    1954, July 29/E. Long/S on San Simeon
    Hwy.

(Letter), Fate 9 (Apr.1956):112-13.

Blue Creek Mt.
-Humanoid tracks
  1967, Aug./Bud Ryerson
    John Green, On the Track of the Sas-
    quatch (Agassiz, B.C.: Cheam, 1968),
    pp.30,38-39,44-49. il.
    John Green, Year of the Sasquatch
    (Agassiz, B.C.: Cheam, 1970), pp.
    6,60. il.
    Don Hunter & René Dahinden, Sasquatch
    (Toronto: McClelland & Stewart,
    1973), pp.109-12. il.
    John Green, Sasquatch: The Apes Among
    Us (Seattle: Hancock House, 1978),
    pp.74-82. il.

Bluff Creek
-Humanoid
  1958, Oct.12/Ray Kerr
    Ivan T. Sanderson, Abominable Snow-
    men: Legend Come to Life (Philadel-
    phia: Chilton, 1961), pp.131-33.
  1958, Oct.17/George Smith
    John Green, The Sasquatch File (Ag-
    assiz, B.C.: Cheam, 1973), p.22.
  1959, April
    Ivan T. Sanderson, Abominable Snow-
    men: Legend Come to Life (Philadel-
    phia: Chilton, 1961), p.133.
  1966/Richard Sides
    John Green, The Sasquatch File (Ag-
    assiz, B.C.: Cheam, 1973), p.38.
  1967, Oct.20/Roger Patterson/movie
    Ivan T. Sanderson, "First Photos of
    'Bigfoot,' California's Legendary
    'Abominable Snowman,'" Argosy, Feb.
    1968, pp.23-31,127. il.
    Ivan T. Sanderson, "The Patterson
    Affair," Pursuit 1 (June 1968):8-10.
    John Green, On the Track of the Sas-
    quatch (Agassiz, B.C.: Cheam, 1968),
    pp.51-57. il.
    Dick Kirkpatrick, "Search for Big-
    foot," Nat'l Wildlife, Apr.-May 1968,
    pp.43-47. il.
    Don Hunter & René Dahinden, Sasquatch
    (Toronto: McClelland & Stewart,
    1973), pp.113-25,173-78,189-92. il.
    John Napier, Bigfoot (N.Y.: Dutton,
    1973), pp.89-95.
    Yakima (Wash.) Herald-Republic, 5
    Feb.1976.
    Peter Byrne, The Search for Bigfoot
    (N.Y.: Pocket Books, 1976 ed.), pp.
    118-55. il.
    Vancouver (B.C.) Sun, 15 May 1978.
    John Green, Sasquatch: The Apes Among
    Us (Seattle: Hancock House, 1978),
    pp.113-31. il.
  1968, June/Steve Martin
    John Green, The Sasquatch File (Ag-
    assiz, B.C.: Cheam, 1973), pp.45-46.
  1973, fall
    Peter Guttilla, "Monster Menagerie,"
    Saga UFO Rept. 4 (Sep.1977):32,34.
  1976, May 22/Sherie Darvell/=hoax
    New York Herald Tribune, 26-27 May
    1976.

Redding Record-Searchlight, 21 June
1977.
Eureka Times-Standard, 4 Oct.1977.
-Humanoid tracks
  1958, Aug.27/Jerry Crew
    Ivan T. Sanderson, Abominable Snow-
    men: Legend Come to Life (Philadel-
    phia: Chilton, 1961), pp.124-27.
  1958, Oct.2/Jerry Crew
    Eureka Humboldt Times, 5 Oct.1958;
    and 9 Oct.1958. il.
    Vancouver (B.C.) Province, 6 Oct.
    1958. il.
    Ivan T. Sanderson, Abominable Snow-
    men: Legend Come to Life (Philadel-
    phia: Chilton, 1961), pp.128-31.
    John Green, On the Track of the Sas-
    quatch (Agassiz, B.C.: Cheam, 1968),
    pp.25-26. il.
    John Green, Sasquatch: The Apes Among
    Us (Seattle: Hancock House, 1978),
    pp.65-67. il.
  1958, Oct.23-30
    John Green, The Sasquatch File (Ag-
    assiz, B.C.: Cheam, 1973), p.22.
  1958, Nov.2/Bob Titmus/sandbar
    John Green, On the Track of the Sas-
    quatch (Agassiz, B.C.: Cheam, 1968),
    p.26. il.
  1958, Dec.18/Betty Allen
  1959, Nov.1/Bob Titmus/sandbar
    John Green, The Sasquatch File (Ag-
    assiz, B.C.: Cheam, 1973), p.22.
  1960, Jan.30/Betty Allen/Humboldt Fir
  Rd.
    Betty Allen, Bigfoot Diary (Eureka:
    The Author, 1963).
  1962, Aug. /Skip Clark/sandbar
    Eureka Humboldt Times, 10 Aug.1962.
  1962, Aug.21/Betty Allen/Lonesome Ridge
  1962, Sep.26/Bob Titmus
  1963, June 13/Betty White/Notice Creek
  Rd.
  1963, June 22/Skip Clark/sandbar
  1963, June 30/Betty Allen
    John Green, The Sasquatch File (Ag-
    assiz, B.C.: Cheam, 1973), pp.29-30.
  1963, Aug./Notice Creek bridge
    Eureka Humboldt Times, 1 Sep.1963.
  1963, Oct./Al Hodgson/sandbar
    John Green, On the Track of the Sas-
    quatch (Agassiz, B.C.: Cheam, 1968),
    p.32. il.
  1964, Sep./Samuel A. Brewer, Jr.
    John Green, The Sasquatch File (Ag-
    assiz, B.C.: Cheam, 1973), p.31.
  1968, Dec.2
    Willow Creek Klam-ity Courier, 11
    Dec.1968.
  1969, Jan./Pat Graves
  1969, May/Dick Frey/Cedar Camp Rd.
  1969, May/Bernard Northrup
    John Green, The Sasquatch File (Ag-
    assiz, B.C.: Cheam, 1973), p.46.

Bodega Bay
-Unidentified submerged object
  1958, March 13
    Ivan T. Sanderson, Invisible Resi-
    dents (N.Y.: World, 1970), p.42,

quoting AP release, 18 Mar.1958.

Bolsa Chica State Park
-Archeological site
  7000 B.C.
    Hal Eberhart, "Cogged Stones of
    Southern California," Am.Antiquity
    26 (1961):361-70. il.
    New York Post, 19 Aug.1970.

Borax L.
-Archeological site
  5000-2500 B.C.
    Mark R. Harrington, "An Ancient Site
    at Borax Lake, California," South-
    west Mus.Pap., no.16 (1948).
    Clement W. Meighan & C. Vance Haynes,
    "New Studies on the Age of the Bor-
    ax Lake Site," Masterkey 42 (1968):
    4-9.
    Clement W. Meighan & C. Vance Haynes,
    "The Borax Lake Site Revisited,"
    Science 167 (1970):1213-21. il.
    Clement W. Meighan & C. Vance Haynes,
    "Further Investigations of Borax
    Lake," Masterkey 44 (1970):112-13.

Borrego Sink
-Humanoid
  1968, July/Harold Lancaster
    John A. Keel, Strange Creatures from
    Time and Space (Greenwich, Ct.: Faw-
    cett, 1970), p.102,quoting Saga,
    July 1969.

Breckenridge Mt.
-Ghost
  1900s
    Richard Webb, Voices from Another
    World (N.Y.: Manor, 1972 ed.), pp.
    13-17.

Buena Vista L.
-Archeological site
    Waldo R. Wedel, "Archaeological In-
    vestigations at Buena Vista Lake,
    Kern County, California," Bull.Bur.
    Am.Ethn., no.130 (1941). il.

Bull Creek
-Acoustic anomaly
  1905, April 20/Rose W. Bushnell
    Rose W. Bushnell, "Screams from the
    Sky," Fate 6 (Dec.1953):57-58.
-Humanoid tracks
  1969, Sep.
    John Green, The Sasquatch File (Ag-
    assiz, B.C.: Cheam, 1973), p.47.

Butano Creek
-UFO (CE-1)
  1964, Nov.2/Rudolph H. Huizen/Butano
  Girl Scout Camp
    "Saucer Signals to California Sight-
    er," Saucer News 12 (Mar.1965):20.
    (Editorial), Fate 18 (Apr.1965):26-
    27.
    Coral & Jim Lorenzen, UFOs: The Whole
    Story (N.Y.: Signet, 1969), p.242.

Buttes National Monument
-UFO (?)
  1971, winter
    Peter Guttilla, "Bigfoot: Advance
    Guard from Outer Space," Saga UFO
    Rept. 4 (June 1977):22,48.

Buzzard Creek
-Humanoid tracks
  1962, summer/Bud Ryerson
    John Green, The Sasquatch File (Ag-
    assiz, B.C.: Cheam, 1973), p.29.

Cache Creek
-UFO (CE-3)
  ca.1971, Nov./Judy Kendall/I-505
    Davis Enterprise, 31 Jan.1977.
    Beatrice M. Zimmer, "Report & Ana-
    lysis of Kendall Case," Can.UFO
    Rept., no.28 (summer 1977):12-15.

Calico Mts.
-Archeological site
  40,000 B.C.?
    L.S.B. Leakey, et al., "Archaeolog-
    ical Excavations in the Calico
    Mountains, California," Science 160
    (1968):1022-23.
    New York Times, 1 June 1968, p.15.
    Los Angeles Times, 27 Oct.1970.
    Letha Curtis Musgrave, "Big Dig at
    Calico," Westways, June 1971, pp.
    28-32.
    Thomas E. Lee, "Calico Mountains Con-
    ference," Anthro.J.Canada 9, no.4
    (1971):11-12.
    Vance Haynes, "The Calico Site: Art-
    ifacts or Geofacts?" Science 181
    (1973):305-10. il.

Camp Creek
-Humanoid tracks
  1971, Dec.7/Mike Burke
    Willow Creek Klam-ity Courier, 15
    Dec.1971.

Carlsbad Beach
-UFO (?)
  1970, Nov.5/Ronald Hemingway/=barium
  cloud?
    Bob Smulling, "New Photograph of Sky
    Phenomenon," Skylook, no.43 (June
    1971):4.

Carmel R.
-Sea monster
  1948, April/John Cunningham/nr. mouth
    "A Definitely Unclassified Marine
    Animal," Pursuit 5 (July 1972):60-
    61, quoting What's Doing, May 1948.

Cascade Mts.
-Giant human skeletons
  1904/J.C. Brown/cave/=hoax?
    Leland Lovelace, Lost Mines and Hid-
    den Treasure (N.Y.: Ace, 1956), pp.
    57-67.

Casitas Dam
-UFO (CE-1)

ca.1964/Frank S. Kinsey
"Witness Says UFO Came Out of Water,"
Skylook, no.82 (Sep.1974):8. il.

Castle Crags
-Humanoid
1973, July
John Green, "Not All Quiet on the
Western Front," Pursuit 7 (Oct.
1974):99.

China L.
-Petroglyphs
Franklin Folsom, America's Ancient
Treasures (N.Y.: Rand McNally,
1974), p.46.
-UFO (CE-1)
1966/Naval Weapons Center
B. Ann Slate & Stanton T. Friedman,
"UFO Battles the Air Force Couldn't
Cover Up," Saga UFO Rept. 2 (winter
1974):29,31,60.

Cima Dome
-Petroglyph
San Francisco Call, 18-19 Mar.1898;
and 27 Mar.1898.
Frank & A.J. Bock, "Eisen's Enigma:
In Quest of a Mojave Desert Mystery,"
Masterkey 48 (1974):44-58. il.

Clear Creek
-Humanoid
1972, Oct.8/Randy Norton/Placer Street
Bridge
Redding Record-Searchlight, 10 Oct.
1972.

Clear L.
-Archeological site
Franklin Folsom, America's Ancient
Treasures (N.Y.: Rand McNally, 1974),
pp.46-48.
-Fall of sugary syrup
1857, fall/J.R. Hale
Henry Winfred Splitter, "Wonders
from the Sky," Fate 6 (Oct.1953):33,
35, quoting Napa Republican (undat-
ed).
-Haunt
1850
"The Ghost of Clear Lake," Fate 8
(July 1955):22.

Cobblestone Mt.
-Ghost
ca.1887
Calgary (Alb.) Tribune, 8 Apr.1887.

Confidence Ridge
-Humanoid
1968, Jan.6/Robert James, Jr.
(Editorial), Fate 21 (July 1968):24-
26.
John Green, The Sasquatch File (Agassiz, B.C.: Cheam, 1973), p.45.

Coso Mts.
-Anomalous artifact
1961, Feb.13/Mike Mikesell/nr. Owens

Lake/=ancient spark plug?
Ronald J. Willis, "The Coso Arti-
fact," INFO J., no.4 (spring 1969):
4-11, quoting (Letter), Virginia
Maxey, Desert Mag., 1961. il.
-Petroglyphs
Campbell Grant, James W. Baird & J.
Kenneth Pringle, Rock Drawings of
the Coso Range (China Lake: Matur-
ango Museum, Pub.no.4, 1968). il.

Crow Canyon
-Humanoid
1869, fall
San Joaquin Republican, 19 Sep.1870.
Oroville Butte Record, 5 Nov.1870.

Dead Mts.
-UFO (NL)
1943, Oct?/Thomas J. Duzynski/Camp
Ibis, E of U.S.95
Coral & Jim Lorenzen, UFOs: The Whole
Story (N.Y.: Signet, 1969), pp.22-
23.

Deadwood Creek
-Humanoid
ca.1952
John Green, The Sasquatch File (Agassiz, B.C.: Cheam, 1973), p.21.

Death Valley
-Archeological sites
7000 B.C.-recent
Thomas & Lydia Clements, "Evidence
of Pleistocene Man in Death Valley,
California," Bull.Geol.Soc'y Am. 64
(1953):1189-1204. il.
Lydia Clements, "Pictographs Discov-
ered in Death Valley, California,"
Masterkey 32 (1958):108-10.
Alice Hunt, "Archaeology of the Death
Valley Salt Pan, California," Anthro.
Pap.Univ.Utah, no.47 (1960).
William J. Wallace, "A Half Century
of Death Valley Archeology," J.
Calif.Arch. 4 (1977):249-58.
Philip J. Wilke, "Cairn Burials of
the California Deserts," Am.Anti-
quity 43 (1978):444-48.
William J. Wallace, "Death Valley
Indian Use of Caves and Rockshel-
ters," Masterkey 52 (1978):125-31.
il.
William J. & Edith Wallace, Ancient
Peoples and Cultures of Death Val-
ley National Monument (Ramona:
Acoma, 1978). il.
-Clairaudience
1889/Borax works
Richard Webb, Voices from Another
World (N.Y.: Manor, 1972 ed.), pp.
50-52.
-Phantom image
1878
Henry Winfred Splitter, "Nature's
Strange Photographs," Fate 8 (Jan.
1955):21,24, quoting Independence
Inyo Independent, 1878.
-Phantom wagon train

1901/Col. Parker
Vincent H. Gaddis, "Caravan of the Lost," Fate 2 (May 1949):36,38.
-UFO (CE-2)
1966, Nov.27/ground markings only
Ted Phillips, Physical Traces Associated with UFO Sightings (Evanston: Center for UFO Studies, 1975), p.45.
-UFO (CE-3)
1949, Aug.19/Buck Fitzgerald
Bakersfield Californian, 20 Aug.1949, p.13.
(Editorial), Fate 3 (Jan.1950):4.

Deep Creek
-Humanoid
1965, Sep./Jim Gorrell/Bowen's Ranch
John Green, Sasquatch: The Apes Among Us (Seattle: Hancock House, 1978), pp.307-308.

Desolation Valley
-UFO (CE-2)
1947, Sep.3/Dale Edwards
"True Mystic Experiences," Fate 2 (Sep.1949):76-77.

Devil's Gate Reservoir
-Disappearance
1956, Aug.5/Donald Lee Baker
1957, March 23/Tommy Bowman
1960, July 13/Bruce Kiemen
Stuart S. Allen, "Forest of Disappearing Children," Fate 14 (July 1961): 36-41.
(Letter), Paul T. Collins, Fate 14 (Nov.1961):115-18.
(Letter), Charles Nickum, Fate 15 (Nov.1962):110-11.

Diablo, Mt.
-Entombed frog
1873/Black Diamond Coal Co. Mine
Henry Winfred Splitter, "The Impossible Fossils," Fate 7 (Jan.1954): 65,70.
-Phantom
1806
Jim Brandon, Weird America (N.Y.: Dutton, 1978), p.43.
-Phantom panther
1972, fall
Loren Coleman, "California Odyssey: Observations on the Western Para-Panther," Anomaly Rsch.Bull., no.23 (1978):5,7.
-UFO (NL)
1945, Feb.9
"Light on Diablo," Doubt, no.12 (spring-summer 1945):178.

Doctor Rock
-Humanoid
1973, Oct.1/Rick Blagden
Brookings (Ore.) Harbor Pilot, 4 Oct. 1973.

Drake's Bay
-Doubtful geography
1579, June 17/Sir Francis Drake/lost

plate of brass/=Drake's anchorage?
George C. Davidson, "Francis Drake on the Northwest Coast of California in the Year 1579," Trans.& Proc. Geogr.Soc'y Pacific, vol.5 (1908).
Henry R. Wagner, Sir Francis Drake's Voyage Round the World (San Francisco: John Howell, 1926).
Herbert Eugene Bolton, "Francis Drake's Plate of Brass," Calif.Hist. Soc'y Quar. 16 (1937):1-16.
R.B. Haselden, "Is the Drake Plate of Brass Genuine?" Calif.Hist.Soc'y Quar. 16 (1937):271-74.
Allen L. Chickering, "Some Notes with Regard to Drake's Plate of Brass," Calif.Hist.Soc'y Quar. 16 (1937): 275-81.
Colin Garfield Fink, Drake's Plate of Brass Authenticated (San Francisco: The Author, 1938).
Allen L. Chickering, "Further Notes on the Drake Plate," Calif.Hist. Soc'y Quar. 18 (1939):251-53.
Robert F. Heizer, "Francis Drake and the California Indians, 1579," Pub. Am.Arch.& Ethn.Univ.Calif. 42 (1947) :251-92. il.
Sir Francis Drake, The World Encompassed, in Hakluyt Soc'y Works, ser. 1, vol.16 (N.Y.: Burt Franklin, 1963 ed.), pp.115-33.
Robert H. Power, "Drake's Landing in California: A Case for San Francisco Bay," Calif.Hist.Quar. 52 (1973): 101-30. il.
Marilyn Ziebarth, "The Francis Drake Controversy: His California Anchorage, June 17-July 23, 1579," Calif. Hist.Quar. 53 (1974):196-292. il.
New York Times, 11 Nov.1974.
Edward Von der Porten, "Drake's Cup: A Study of..." Popular Arch. 15, no. 2 (1976):10-12. il.

Dume Pt.
-UFO (NL)
1973, March 23/Scott Aalund
Los Angeles Times, 25 Mar.1973.

Eagle Mts.
-Ancient jade mine
1500 B.C./Barry Storm
"Mayan Jade Mine in California," Fate 14 (Oct.1961):41.

Eagle Rock
-UFO (NL)
1973, Oct.23/Clifford McLaughlin
Felton Valley Press, 24 Oct.1973.

Eel R.
-Humanoid
ca.1950
Ivan T. Sanderson, Abominable Snowmen: Legend Come to Life (Philadelphia: Chilton, 1961), pp.144-45.

Elizabeth L.
-Lake monster

1830s-1880s
  Horace Bell, On the Old West Coast
  (N.Y.: William Morrow, 1930), pp.
  198-206.

Emma Mt.
-Humanoid tracks
  1973, April
    Peter Guttilla, "Bigfoot: Advance
    Guard from Outer Space," Saga UFO
    Rept. 4 (June 1977):22,50.
-UFO (CE-1)
  1973, April/Andrew Stone
    Peter Guttilla, "Bigfoot: Advance
    Guard from Outer Space," Saga UFO
    Rept. 4 (June 1977):22,48-50.

Fairmont Reservoir
-Humanoid tracks
  ca.1970,Dec./Kim Polumbo
    John Green, The Sasquatch File (Ag-
    assiz, B.C.: Cheam, 1973), p.56.

Farallon Is.
-Giant sponge
  1976, Sep./Robert S. Dyer/nr. radioactive waste dump
    Oakland Tribune, 12 Sep.1976; and 31
    Oct.1977.
-Phantom ship
  1942, fall/Howard H. Brisbane/"USS Kennison"
    Howard H. Brisbane, "U.S. Navy Meets
    a Phantom Ship," Fate 15 (Apr.1962):
    41-42.

Fern Cave
-Petroglyphs
    John C. Brandt, et al., "Possible
    Rock Art Records of the Crab Nebula
    Supernova in the Western United
    States," in Anthony F. Aveni, ed.,
    Archaeoastronomy in Pre-Columbian
    America (Austin: Univ. of Texas,
    1975), pp.45,49-53. il.

Folsom L.
-Erratic crocodilian
  1957, Sep.-1958, June
    Sacramento Union, 17 May 1971.

Funeral Mts.
-Phantom wagon train
  1922, spring/G.W. MacNurlen
    Vincent H. Gaddis, "Caravan of the
    Lost," Fate 2 (May 1949):36,38-40.

Giant Rock
-SEE Yucca Valley, p.160.

Green L.
-Haunt
  1960s
    Richard Webb, Voices from Another
    World (N.Y.: Manor, 1972 ed.), pp.
    18-20.

Grimes Valley
-Combustion metamorphism
  =evidence for cataclysm?

Y.K. Bentor & M. Kastner, "Combustion
Metamorphism in Southern California,"
Science 193 (1976):486-87. il.

Hayfork Creek
-Humanoid
  1966, Jan./Bob Kelley/nr. Wildwood
    John Green, The Sasquatch File (Ag-
    assiz, B.C.: Cheam, 1973), p.38,
    quoting Redding Record-Searchlight
    (undated).

Hecker Mts.
-UFO (?)
  1964, Dec.28
    Jerome Clark & Loren Coleman, The Un-
    identified (N.Y.: Warner, 1975), p.
    230.

Homer L.
-Lake monster
  n.d.
    Charles M. Skinner, American Myths
    and Legends, 2 vols. (Philadelphia:
    Lippincott, 1903), 2:275-76.

Imperial Valley
-Archeological site
  ca.1400
    Kansas City (Mo.), Times, 27 Dec.1974.
-Doubtful geography
  17th c./=inland sea?
    Juan Mateo Manje, Luz de Tierra Incóg-
    nita, trans. Harry J. Karns (Tucson:
    Arizona Silhouettes, 1954), pp.227-
    34.
    Henry R. Wagner, "Some Imaginary Cal-
    ifornia Geography," Proc.Am.Antiq.
    Soc'y, n.s., 36 (1926):83-129.
    Henry R. Wagner, The Cartography of
    the Northwest Coast of America to
    the Year 1800, 2 vols. (Berkeley:
    Univ. of California, 1937), 1:114,
    144-47,152. il.
    Ernest J. Burrus, Kino and the Carto-
    graphy of Northwestern New Spain
    (Tucson: Arizona Pioneers' Histori-
    cal Soc'y, 1965), pp.17,27-28,46-48.
    il.
    Donald M. Viles, "California Is an
    Island--And Always Has Been!" NEARA
    Newsl. 8 (summer 1973):26-29.
    Raymond H. Ramsay, No Longer on the
    Map (N.Y.: Ballantine, 1973 ed.),
    pp.191-95.

Inyo Mts.
-Earthquake luminescence
  1872, March 26/Eclipse Mines
    (Editorial), Nature 6 (1872):89-90,
    quoting Inyo Independent (undated).

Iron Gate Reservoir
-Archeological site
  1400-1600
    Frank C. Leonhardy, "The Archeology of
    a Late Prehistoric Village in North-
    western California," Bull.Mus.Nat.
    Hist.Univ.Oregon, no.4 (1967). il.
-UFO (NL)

1979, Jan.17/Stan Krute
    Yreka Siskiyou News, 18 Jan.1979.

Isabella Reservoir
-Humanoid
    1972, Feb.
        John Green, Sasquatch: The Apes Among
        Us (Seattle: Hancock House, 1978),
        p.313.
-UFO (CE-3)
    1957, May 10/Shirley McBride
        Ann Druffel, "Entities and Their Car-
        riages," MUFON UFO J., no.129 (Aug.
        1978):15,16.

Jacoby Creek
-Humanoid tracks
    ca.1960
        (Editorial), Fate 13 (Nov.1960):8,
        quoting Eureka Humboldt Standard
        (undated).

Kelso Valley
-Phantom deer
    n.d./Sheep Springs
        Richard Webb, Voices from Another
        World (N.Y.: Manor, 1972 ed.), pp.
        86-89.

Kern R.
-Giant human skeleton
    1871
        New York Times, 22 May 1871, p.5.

Kingsley Cave
-Archeological site
        Martin A. Baumhoff, "Excavation of
        Teh-1 (Kingsley Cave)," Calif.Arch.
        Pap. 33 (1955):40-73.

Klamath R.
-Humanoid tracks
    1960, June 19/Charles Johnson/W of
    Bluff Creek
        Eureka Humboldt Standard, 23 June
        1960.
        John Green, The Sasquatch File (Ag-
        assiz, B.C.: Cheam, 1973), p.23.
    1969, June/Bob Hardesty
        Walnut Creek Contra Costa Times, 11
        July 1969.

Laird Meadow
-Humanoid tracks
    1964, summer/Dave Blake
        John Green, The Sasquatch File (Ag-
        assiz, B.C.: Cheam, 1973), p.31.

Lassen Peak
-Humanoid
    1974, May
        John Green, "Not All Quiet on the
        Western Front," Pursuit 7 (Oct.1974)
        :98-99.

Las Trampas Regional Park
-Phantom panther
    1973, winter
        Loren Coleman, "California Odyssey:
        Observations on the Western Para-

Panther," Anomaly Rsch.Bull., no.23
        (1978):5,7.

Little L.
-Ghost
    1968, Oct./Luisa Armendariz/motel
        Richard Webb, Voices from Another
        World (N.Y.: Manor, 1972 ed.), pp.
        190-92.
-Haunt
    1960s
        Richard Webb, Voices from Another
        World (N.Y.: Manor, 1972 ed.), pp.
        186-89.

Live Oak Springs
-UFO (?)
    1942, Jan.25/Tracey Henderson/=meteor?
        Tracey Henderson, Imperial Valley
        (San Diego: Neyenesch, 1968), p.226.

Lobos, Pt.
-Psychokinesis
    1963, June 3/Lawrence Farrell/Carmel-
    ite Monastery
        Monterey Peninsula Herald, 18 June
        1963.

Los Angeles L.
-UFO (?)
    1975, Feb./Mrs. John Baylor
        Peter Guttilla, "Bigfoot: Advance
        Guard from Outer Space," Saga UFO
        Rept. 4 (June 1977):22,50.
-UFO (NL)
    1975, Jan.5
        Peter Guttilla, "Bigfoot: Advance
        Guard from Outer Space," Saga UFO
        Rept. 4 (June 1977):22,50.

Los Padres National Forest
-Humanoid tracks
    1969, Dec.
        San Jose Mercury-News, 4 Jan.1970.

Low Gap
-Humanoid tracks
    1964, Aug.
        John Green, The Sasquatch File (Ag-
        assiz, B.C.: Cheam, 1973), p.31.

Lucerne Valley
-Dowsing
    1950s/Fred Tomlinson
        Gaston Burridge, "The Truth about
        Dowsing," Fate 7 (Dec.1954):17-18.
-UFO (CE-1)
    1957, summer-1958, Sep./Trevor James
    Constable/betw. Yucca Valley and Old
    Woman Springs
        Trevor James [Constable], They Live
        in the Sky (Los Angeles: New Age,
        1958). il.
        Trevor James Constable, The Cosmic
        Pulse of Life (Santa Ana: Merlin,
        1976), pp.70-131. il.
-UFO (CE-2)
    1971, Nov.13
        Santa Ana Register, 12 Dec.1971.

Lytle Creek
-Humanoid
   1966, Aug.27/Geri Lou Mendenhall
      Philadelphia (Pa.) Inquirer, 2 Sep.
      1966.
      Robert & Frances Guenette, Bigfoot:
      The Mysterious Monster (Los Angeles:
      Sun Classic, 1975).
      John Green, Sasquatch: The Apes Among
      Us (Seattle: Hancock House, 1978),
      pp.308-309.

Mad R.
-Humanoid tracks
   ca.1950
      Ivan T. Sanderson, Abominable Snow-
      men: Legend Come to Life (Philadel-
      phia: Chilton, 1961), p.121.

Madonna Mt.
   UFO (DD)
   1960s
      Timothy Beckley & Harold Salkin,
      "UFOs Spotted Along California's
      Earthquake Lines," Saga UFO Rept.
      3 (Dec.1976):44,72.

Manresa Beach
-UFO (CE-3)
   1965, Jan.30/Sid Padrick
      Jerome Clark, "Two New Contact
      Claims," Flying Saucer Rev. 11 (May-
      June 1965):20-23.
      Jerome Clark & Loren Coleman, The Un-
      identified (N.Y.: Warner, 1975), pp.
      228-30, quoting Sid Padrick, "The
      Padrick 'Space Contact,'" Little
      Listening Post, fall 1965.

Maple Springs
-Humanoid
   1969, summer
      John Green, The Sasquatch File (Ag-
      assiz, B.C.: Cheam, 1973), p.47.

Mare I.
-Haunt
   ca.1900/Naval Reserve
      Charles M. Skinner, American Myths
      and Legends, 2 vols. (Philadelphia:
      Lippincott, 1903), 2:186-89.
-UFO (DD)
   1978, Feb.22/Hwy.37
      Vallejo Times-Herald, 23 Feb.1978.
-UFO (NL)
   1896, Dec.3/W.I. Sargent
      San Francisco Chronicle, 6 Dec.1896,
      p.20.

Mary L.
-UFO (NL)
   1956, July 22/Ms. Okes
      "Case 176," CRIFO Orbit, 7 Sep.1956,
      p.1.

Mendocino, Cape
-Ancient Chinese anchor
   1973, May/Roland von Huene/"Bartlett"
      San Diego Evening Tribune, 26 Feb.
      1975; and 16 Nov.1975.

-Unidentified submerged object
   1964, Feb.5/R.W. Rutherford/"Hattie D'
      Coral E. Lorenzen, The Shadow of the
      Unknown (N.Y.: Signet, 1970), pp.
      84-85.

Minaret Mts.
-Humanoid skull
   1965, July/Robert W. Denton
      B. Ann Slate & Alan Berry, Bigfoot
      (N.Y.: Bantam, 1976), pp.160-65.

Misery Hill
-Ghost
   n.d./Jim Brandon
      Charles M. Skinner, Myths and Legends
      of Our Own Land, 2 vols. (Philadel-
      phia: Lippincott, 1896), 2:255-57.

Mitchell Caverns
-UFO (CE-4)
   1974, May 26/Mr. Susedik
      Ted Bloecher, "A Catalog of Humanoid
      Reports for 1974," in MUFON 1975
      UFO Symposium Proc. (Seguin, Tex.:
      MUFON, 1975), pp.51,57-58.

Mojave Desert
-Ancient inscription
      Barry Fell, America B.C. (N.Y.: Quad-
      rangle, 1976), p.182. il.
-Ancient pyramid
      Auburn Placer Herald, 20 Aug.1853.
-Archeological site
   ca.5000 B.C./Pleistocene Lake Mojave
      Elizabeth W. & William H. Campbell,
      "The Lake Mohave Site in the Arch-
      aeology of Pleistocene Lake Mohave:
      A Symposium," Southwest Mus.Pap. 11
      (1937):9-43.
      Charles Avery Amsden, "The Lake Mo-
      have Artifacts," Southwest Mus.Pap.
      11 (1937):51-97.
      George W. Brainerd, "A Re-Examination
      of the Dating Evidence for the Lake
      Mohave Artifact Assemblage," Am.
      Antiquity 18 (1953):270-71.
      Robert F. Heizer, "Problems in Dating
      Lake Mojave Artifacts," Masterkey
      39 (1965):125-34. il.
      George F. Carter, "Cross Check on the
      Dating of Lake Mojave Artifacts,"
      Masterkey 41 (1967):26-33.
-Fall of steel meteorite
   1878
      (Editorial), Nature 19 (1878):61,
      quoting Yuma (Ariz.) Sentinel (un-
      dated).
-Humanoid
   1973, July 24
      Peter Guttilla, "Bigfoot: 3 Tales of
      Terror," Saga UFO Rept. 3 (Oct.1976)
      :46,64-66.
-UFO (CE-1)
   1954, April 4/Carl Anderson
      Carl Anderson, Two Nights to Remem-
      ber (Los Angeles: New Age, 1956).
-UFO (CE-3)
   1973, July 17
      Peter Guttilla, "Bigfoot: 3 Tales of

Terror," Saga UFO Report 3 (Oct.
1976):46,49,63-64.
-UFO (DD)
1955, Nov.1/Frank Halstead
1957, Nov.11/Robert D. Hahn
Richard Hall, ed., The UFO Evidence
(Washington: NICAP, 1964), pp.52-
53,67.

Mojave Maze
-Archeological sites
George C. Marshall, "Giant Effigies
of the Southwest," Nat'l Geogr.Mag.
102 (Sep.1952):389. il.
Frank M. Setzler, "Seeking the Secret
of the Giants," Nat'l Geogr.Mag. 102
(Sep.1952):390-404. il.
Henriette Mertz, Gods from the Far
East (N.Y.: Ballantine, 1975 ed.),
pp.73-75.
Richard Smedley, "Blythe, California:
Gigantic Petroglyphs," Probe the
Unknown 3 (May 1975):38-39. il.

Mojave R.
-Archeological site
ca.2000 B.C./fossil footprints
Christian Science Monitor, 16 Aug.
1978.

Monterey Bay
-Sea monster
1930s-1940s
(Letter), Jim Martin, Sat.Eve.Post,
12 Apr.1947, p.4.

Moro Rock
-UFO (NL)
1953, July/E.T. Scoyen
Coral E. Lorenzen, Flying Saucers:
The Startling Evidence of the Invasion from Outer Space (N.Y.: Signet,
1966 ed.), pp.161-63.

Mule Mts.
-Mystery tracks and tank treads
1966/Emma Lou Davis/=Army maneuvers?
Houston (Tex.) Chronicle, 14 Dec.1966.

New R.
-UFO (NL)
1971, Oct.8/Nelson E. Divine
Willow Creek Klam-ity Courier, 27
Oct.1971.

Nikowitz Creek
-Humanoid tracks
1960s/Jay Roland
John Green, The Sasquatch File (Agassiz, B.C.: Cheam, 1973), p.29.

Notice Creek
-Humanoid tracks
1967, Sep.25/Dan Mullins
John Green, The Sasquatch File (Agassiz, B.C.: Cheam, 1973), p.39.

O'Brien Mt.
-UFO (DD)
1968, June/Jack Humphrey

William Murphy, "UFOs Reliably Reported," Flying Saucer Rev. 18 (Jan.
-Feb.1972):28.

Offield Mt.
-Humanoid tracks
1960, March/Ivan Marx
John Green, On the Track of the Sasquatch (Agassiz, B.C.: Cheam, 1968),
p.27. il.
John Green, The Sasquatch File (Agassiz, B.C.: Cheam, 1973), p.23.

Onion Mt.
-Humanoid tracks
1967, Aug.
John Green, The Sasquatch File (Agassiz, B.C.: Cheam, 1973), p.38.

Orias Timbers Creek
-Humanoid tracks
1870, Sep./F.J. Hildreth
Oakland Daily Transcript, 27 Sep.
1870.

Oriflamme Mts.
-Ghost light
n.d.
Russ Leadabrand, "Let's Explore a
Byway: Along the Butterfield Trail,"
Westways 53 (Apr.1961):4-6.

Owens L.
-Retrocognition
n.d.
Richard Webb, Voices from Another
World (N.Y.: Manor, 1972 ed.), p.
199.

Owens Valley
-Archeological site
George R. Mead & Jason Smith, "Micro-
tools from Owens Valley, California," Masterkey 42 (1968):148-51.

Pacheco Pass
-UFO (CE-1)
1967, July 28/Randy Higgins
"Worldwide Sightings Showing Increase," UFO Inv. 4 (Oct.1967):1,3.

Palomar, Mt.
-UFO (?)
1949/George Adamski
San Diego Tribune-Sun, 4 Apr.1950.
Maurice Weekley & George Adamski,
"Flying Saucers As Astronomers See
Them," Fate 3 (Sep.1950):56-59. il.
George Adamski, "I Photographed
Space Ships," Fate 4 (July 1951):
64-74.
Desmond Leslie & George Adamski, Fly-
ing Saucers Have Landed (N.Y.: Brit-
ish Book Centre, 1953), pp.175-77.
1950, May/George Adamski
George Adamski, "I Photographed
Space Ships," Fate 4 (July 1951):
64-74. il.
(Letter), Lorenzo Dove, Fate 4 (Oct.
1951):117-19.

(Letter), Richard McMahon, Fate 4
(Oct.1951):119.
1950, June 6/George Adamski
    Desmond Leslie & George Adamski, Fly-
    ing Saucers Have Landed (N.Y.: Brit-
    ish Book Centre, 1953), p.48. il.
1951, March 5/George Adamski
    Desmond Leslie & George Adamski, Fly-
    ing Saucers Have Landed (N.Y.: Brit-
    ish Book Centre, 1953), p.179. il.
    George Adamski, Inside the Space
    Ships (N.Y.: Abelard-Schuman, 1955),
    betw. pp.80-81. il.
    David Stupple, "The Man Who Talked
    to Venusians," Fate 32 (Jan.1979):
    30-39. il.
1951, March 9/George Adamski
1951, May 16/George Adamski
    George Adamski, Inside the Space
    Ships (N.Y.: Abelard-Schuman, 1955),
    pp.49,144 45.
1952, May 1/George Adamski
    Desmond Leslie & George Adamski, Fly-
    ing Saucers Have Landed (N.Y.: Brit-
    ish Book Centre, 1953), p.179. il.
1952, Dec.13/George Adamski
    Oceanside Blade-Tribune, 4-6 Feb.
    1953.
    Desmond Leslie & George Adamski, Fly-
    ing Saucers Have Landed (N.Y.: Brit-
    ish Book Centre, 1953), pp.217-21.
    il.
    Waveney Girvan, Flying Saucers and
    Common Sense (N.Y.: Citadel, 1956),
    pp.82-92. il.
-UFO (DD)
1963, summer/Michael G. Mann/Observa-
tory
    Gray Barker, Book of Saucers (Clarks-
    burg, W.V.: Saucerian, 1965), pp.
    63-65. il.
-UFO (NL)
1946, Oct.9/George Adamski
1947, Aug./George Adamski
    Desmond Leslie & George Adamski, Fly-
    ing Saucers Have Landed (N.Y.: Brit-
    ish Book Centre, 1953), pp.172-74.

Panamint Mts.
-Ancient civilization myth
    Hav-musuvs
    Oge-Make, "Tribal Memories of Flying
    Saucers," Fate 2 (Sep.1949):17-21.

Panamint Valley
-Meteorite crater
    76 m.diam. x 13 m.deep/=terrestrial
    Robert S. Dietz & Edwin C. Buffing-
    ton, "Panamint Crater, California:
    Not Meteorite," Meteoritics 2 (1964)
    :179-81. il.
-Out-of-body experience
    n.d./Richard Webb/Surprise Canyon
    Richard Webb, Voices from Another
    World (N.Y.: Manor, 1972 ed.), pp.
    78-80.

Pechanga Reservation
-Plant sensitivity
    1971, Oct.29/L. George Lawrence

L. George Lawrence, "Interstellar
Communications Signals," Ecola Inst.
Info.Bull., no.72-6 (1972).
L. George Lawrence, "Biological Sig-
nals from Outer Space," Human Di-
mensions, summer 1973.
Joseph F. Goodavage, "Contact with
Extraterrestrial Life!" Saga's UFO
Special, 1973, pp.28-30,68-74.
Peter Tompkins & Christopher Bird,
The Secret Life of Plants (N.Y.:
Harper & Row, 1973), pp.46-51.

Pecwan Mt.
-Humanoid tracks
    1960/Bud Ryerson
    1961, spring/Bud Ryerson
    John Green, The Sasquatch File (Ag-
    assiz, B.C.: Cheam, 1973), pp.23,
    29.

Piedmont Reservoir
-Skyquake
    1952, Aug.8
    San Francisco Chronicle, 9 Aug.1952.

Pigeon Pt.
-Haunt
    n.d./Coast Guard lighthouse
    (Editorial), Fate 30 (Mar.1977):36.

Pine Canyon
-UFO (DD)
    1978, June 10/Don Ogawa
    Salinas Californian, 12 June 1978.

Pisgah Crater
-Plant sensitivity
    1972, April 10/L. George Lawrence
    L. George Lawrence, "Interstellar
    Communications--What Are the Pros-
    pects?" Electronics World 86 (Oct.
    1971):34-35,56.
    Joseph F. Goodavage, "Contact with
    Extraterrestrial Life!" Saga's UFO
    Special, 1973, pp.28-30,70-72. il.
    Peter Tompkins & Christopher Bird,
    The Secret Life of Plants (N.Y.:
    Harper & Row, 1973), pp.48-51.
    Ecola Institute, "Hello Out There!"
    Beyond Reality, no.18 (Jan.1976):
    46-49. il.
    L. George Lawrence, "Magnetometers
    for Investigating UFOs and Other
    Magnetic Phenomena," Pop.Electronics,
    May 1978, pp.41-46. il.

Potter Creek
-Archeological site
    William J. Sinclair, "The Explora-
    tion of Potter Creek Cave," Pub.Am.
    Arch.& Ethn.Univ.Calif. 2 (1904):1-
    27.
    F.W. Putnam, "Evidence of the Work
    of Man in Objects from Quaternary
    Caves in California," Am.Anthro.,
    n.s., 8 (1906):229-35.
    Alex D. Krieger, "New World Culture
    History: Anglo America," in A.L.
    Kroeber, ed., Anthropology Today

(Chicago: Univ. of Chicago, 1953).
Louis A. Payen & R.E. Taylor, "Man
and Pleistocene Fauna at Potter
Cave, California," J.Calif.Anthro.
3 (1976):50-58. il.

Puddingstone Reservoir
-UFO (DD)
1954, March 14/J.W. Wagner
R. DeWitt Miller, Stranger Than Life
(N.Y.: Ace, 1955 ed.), pp.101-103.

Racetrack Playa
-Moving rocks
J.F. McAllister & A.F. Agnew, "Playa
Scrapers and Furrows on the Race-
track Playa, Inyo County, Califor-
nia," Bull.Geol.Soc'y Am. 59 (1948):
1377.
"The Case of the Skating Stones,"
Life, 10 Mar.1952, pp.53-54. il.
L.G. Kirk, "The Racetrack Mystery,"
Westways 44 (1952):24-25.
Kirtley F. Mather, The Earth Beneath
Us (N.Y.: Random House, 1964), opp.
p.208. il.
(Editorial), Fate 24 (May 1971):8-
12, quoting Los Angeles Times (un-
dated).
Robert P. Sharp & Dwight L. Carey,
"Sliding Stones, Racetrack Playa,
California," Bull.Geol.Soc'y Am. 87
(1976):1704-17.
Malcolm Balfour, "Secret of Myster-
ious Moving Stones," Nat'l Enquirer,
20 Nov.1977.

Robinson's Ferry
-UFO (?)
1896, Nov.25/P.F. Perryman/=distant
candle?
San Francisco Call, 2 Dec.1896, p.14.
San Francisco Examiner, 8 Dec.1896.

Rock Creek
-UFO (DD)
1947, Aug.9/Aubrey V. Brooks
Kenneth Arnold & Ray Palmer, The Coming of the Saucers (Boise: The Authors, 1952), p.138.

Saddleback Butte
-UFO (?)
1972
Peter Guttilla, "Bigfoot: Advance
Guard from Outer Space," Saga UFO
Rept. 4 (June 1977):22,48.

Salton Sea
-Ancient ship
1870, Nov./Charley Clusker
San Bernardino Guardian, 10 Sep.1870;
15 Oct.1870; 26 Nov.1870; 31 Dec.
1870; and 14 Jan.1871.
Los Angeles Star, 12 Nov.1870; 15
Nov.1870; and 1 Dec.1870.
Philip A. Bayley, Golden Mirages
(N.Y.: Macmillan, 1940), pp.142-44.
Harold O. Weight, "Charley Clusker
and the Lost Ship," Desert Mag.,

Mar.1977, pp.32-37. il.
-Petroglyphs
7100 B.C.
"Dating Salton Sea Petroglyphs," Sci.
News 111 (26 Feb.1977):138.
-UFO (NL)
1968, June
Peter Guttilla, "Bigfoot: Advance
Guard from Outer Space," Saga UFO
Rept. 4 (June 1977):22,50.

San Bernardino Mts.
-Spanish galleon
1870s-1880s
San Diego Union, 17 Nov.1889.
Vincent H. Gaddis, "Ships That Sail-
ed the Desert," Fate 26 (Jan.1973):
63,65.
-UFO (CE-2)
1954, Feb./A.P. Wheeler
B. Ann Slate, "The Case of the Crip-
pled Flying Saucer," Saga's UFO
Special, 1972, pp.40-43,51.
-UFO (NL)
1955, Nov.14/Gene Miller
Los Angeles Times, 26 Nov.1955.

San Clemente I.
-Acoustic anomaly
1935, July-Sep.
"Ghost Spot in Pacific," Fortean
Soc'y Mag., no.8 (Dec.1943):13.
-Sea monster
1914-1919/Percy Neal
Ralph Bandini, Tight Lines (Los An-
geles: Tight Lines, 1932).
Ralph Bandini, "I Saw a Sea Monster,"
Esquire 2 (June 1934):90-92.
J. Charles Davis II, "The San Clem-
ente Monster," Animal Life, July
1954.
1920, Sep./Ralph Bandini/1 mi.W of
Mosquito Harbor
Ralph Bandini, Tight Lines (Los An-
geles: Tight Lines, 1932).
1953, June 8/Sam Randazzo
Los Angeles Examiner, 8 June 1953.

San Dieguito Canyon
-Archeological site
7000 B.C.
Malcolm J. Rogers, "Archaeological
and Geological Investigations of
the Cultural Levels in an Old Chan-
nel of San Dieguito Valley," Year-
book Carnegie Inst. 37 (1938):344-
45.
George F. Foster, Pleistocene Man at
San Diego (Baltimore: Johns Hopkins,
1957), pp.199-201.
Claude N. Warren, "The San Dieguito
Complex: A Review and Hypothesis,"
Am.Antiquity 32 (1967):168-85.
James Robert Moriarty III, "The San
Dieguito Complex: Suggested Envir-
onmental and Cultural Relationships," Anthro.J.Canada 7, no.3
(1969):2-18. il.
Claude N. Warren, "The San Dieguito
Type Site," San Diego Mus.Pap.,

vol.5 (1970).

San Felipe Creek
-Ghost light
  1930s/E.P. Barclay
    N. Meade Layne, "A 'Spirit Light'
    Phenomenon," J.ASPR 34 (1940):51-
    54.
-UFO (NL)
  ca.1968/Fritz Webber
    Peter Guttilla, "Bigfoot: Advance
    Guard from Outer Space," Saga UFO
    Rept. 4 (June 1977):22,50.

San Fernando Valley
-Clairvoyance and healing
  1966, Aug.2/Shirley Brett
    Alex H. Brett, "'Death Go Back!'"
    Fate 25 (Oct.1972):87-90.
-Disappearance
  1946, Nov./house
    "Lost Houses," Doubt, no.18 (1947):
    268.
-Poltergeist
  1972-1973
    D. Scott Rogo, An Experience of Phan-
    toms (N.Y.: Dell, 1976 ed.), pp.
    119-23.
-UFO (DD)
  1957, Nov.11/Harold R. Lamb, Jr.
    Donald E. Keyhoe, Flying Saucers: Top
    Secret (N.Y.: Putnam, 1960), pp.
    186-87. il.

San Gabriel Mts.
-Acoustic anomaly
  1973, summer
    B. Ann Slate, "Gods from Inner Space,"
    Saga UFO Rept. 3 (Apr.1976):36,52.
-Humanoid
  1973, April 22/Willie Roemermann/Syc-
  amore Flats
    B. Ann Slate, "Gods from Inner Space,"
    Saga UFO Rept. 3 (Apr.1976):36,52.
    B. Ann Slate & Alan Berry, Bigfoot
    (N.Y.: Bantam, 1976), pp.71-73.
  1973, Nov./Margaret Bailey
    John Green, Sasquatch: The Apes Among
    Us (Seattle: Hancock House, 1978),
    p.317.
  1974/Bruce Morgan/Big Rock campground
  1975, Feb.14/Willie Roemermann/Big Rock
  campground
    B. Ann Slate & Alan Berry, Bigfoot
    (N.Y.: Bantam, 1976), pp.73-82,85-
    87.
  1976, Jan./Willie Roemermann/Sycamore
  Flats
    John Green, Sasquatch: The Apes Among
    Us (Seattle: Hancock House, 1978),
    p.319.
-Humanoid tracks
  1973, Oct./South Fork campground
    John Green, Sasquatch: The Apes Among
    Us (Seattle: Hancock House, 1978),
    p.317.

San Gabriel R.
-UFO (?)
  1958, May 26/=planet?

Robert N. Webster, "Things That Fall
from UFOs," Fate 11 (Oct.1958):25,
30.
  1966, March/=balloon
    Philip J. Klass, UFOs Explained
    (N.Y.: Random House, 1974), pp.26-
    27.

San Gorgonio Mts.
-Fall of bracelet
  1952, summer/Robert V. Fagan
    Robert V. Fagan, "The Night-Flying
    Bracelet," Fate 20 (May 1967):77-
    80.

San Jacinto Mt.
-UFO (DD)
  1963, May
    "Odd-Shaped UFO Seen in California,"
    Skylook, no.47 (Oct.1971):12.

San Joaquin Valley
-Animal ESP
  1956/Ina L. Morris
    Ina L. Morris, "Mr. Blue's Call for
    Help," Fate 23 (Sep.1970):76-80.
-Anomalous mounds
    J.C. Branner, "Natural Mounds or
    'Hog Wallows,'" Science 21 (1905):
    514-16.
-Phantom image
  1854, summer
    Henry Winfred Splitter, "Nature's
    Strange Photographs," Fate 8 (Jan.
    1955):21,24, quoting Tuolumne City
    News (undated).

San Martin, Cape
-Sea monster
  1946, Nov.7
    "No Such Animal," Doubt, no.17
    (1947):260.

San Nicolas I.
-Archeological site
    Hector Alliot, "Burial Methods of
    the Southern California Islanders,"
    Masterkey 43 (1969):125-31. il.
-Feral woman
  n.d.
    George Nidever, Life and Adventures
    of George Nidever (Berkeley: Univ.
    of California, 1937), p.81.
    "Notes and Queries," Calif.Folklore
    Quar. 2 (1942):149-50; 3 (1943):59-
    60,148-49.
    Robert Heizer & Albert Elsasser, "Or-
    iginal Accounts of the Lone Woman
    of San Nicolas Island," Arch.Survey
    Rept.Univ.Calif., no.55 (1961).
    Travis Hudson, "Some J.P. Harrington
    Notes on the 'Lone Woman' of San
    Nicolas," Masterkey 52 (1978):23-28.
    Travis Hudson, "An Additional Har-
    rington Note on the 'Lone Woman' of
    San Nicolas," Masterkey 52 (1978):
    151-54.
-UFO (CE-2)
  1954, April 22
    Jacques Vallee, Passport to Magonia

(Chicago: Regnery, 1969), p.206.

Santa Ana R.
-Humanoid tracks
1976, Aug.
    John Green, Sasquatch: The Apes Among Us (Seattle: Hancock House, 1978), p.321.

Santa Barbara I.
-Land monster myth
    Charles M. Skinner, Myths and Legends of Our Own Land, 2 vols. (Philadelphia: Lippincott, 1896), 2:300.

Santa Catalina I.
-UFO (?)
1955, July 9/channel
    Richard Hall, ed., The UFO Evidence (Washington: NICAP, 1964), p.150.
1974, Sep./Isthmus Harbor
    Dan Clements, "Saucer Safari," Official UFO 1 (Nov.1976):35,57.
-UFO (CE-1)
1968, Oct./George Hiner/off E end
    Coral E. Lorenzen, The Shadow of the Unknown (N.Y.: Signet, 1970), p.87.
-UFO (DD)
1966, April 15/S of island
    R. Michael Rasmussen, "Santa Catalina Filmclip," APRO Bull. 23 (Nov.-Dec.1974):1,9.
    "An Authentic Film," Ohio Skywatcher, Mar.1975, p.4. il.
-UFO (NL)
1968, Jan.22/Richard Callen/NW of island
    Long Beach Press-Telegram, 23 Jan. 1968.
    Coral E. Lorenzen, The Shadow of the Unknown (N.Y.: Signet, 1970), p.86.

Santa Cruz Mts.
-Poltergeist
1955, Dec.-1956/Nadine Banducea
    (Editorial), Fate 9 (June 1956):12, quoting San Jose Mercury-News (undated).

Santa Rosa I.
-Archeological site
40,000 B.C.
    New York Times, 17 Mar.1977, p.20.
    Phoenix Arizona Republic, 2 Mar.1978.
8000-1000 B.C./Arlington Springs
    Chester Stock & E.L. Furlong, "The Pleistocene Elephants of Santa Rosa Island, California," Science 68 (1928):140-41.
    Phil C. Orr, "Radiocarbon Dates from Santa Rosa Island," Anthro.Bull. Santa Barbara Mus.Nat.Hist., no.2 (1956).
    Phil C. Orr, "Arlington Springs Man," Science 135 (1962):219.
    Phil C. Orr, "The Arlington Springs Site, Santa Rosa Island, California," Am.Antiquity 27 (1962):417-19.
    Phil C. Orr, Prehistory of Santa Rosa Island (Santa Barbara: Museum of

Natural History, 1968). il.
-Giant human skeleton
    Frank Edwards, Stranger Than Science (N.Y.: Ace, 1959 ed.), p.97.

Scorpion Creek
-Humanoid tracks
1966, fall/Jay Roland
    John Green, The Sasquatch File (Agassiz, B.C.: Cheam, 1973), p.38.

Sequoia National Park
-UFO (CE-3)
1955, July 1/Oscar F. Knight
    Oscar F. Knight, Wolverton Trail Event: A Visitor from Venus (Strathmore, Cal.: The Author, 1963).
-UFO (NL)
1953, Aug.1
    Donald E. Keyhoe, Aliens from Space (Garden City: Doubleday, 1973), p.49.

Shasta, Mt.
-Anomalous mounds
    Oakland Tribune, 22 Nov.1946.
    "Stade Sums Up," Doubt, no.18 (1947):270.
    Johnny Noble, "The Mysterious Circles of Shasta," Fate 4 (Nov.-Dec.1951):96-100. il.
-Humanoid
1850s
    John Green, Year of the Sasquatch (Agassiz, B.C.: Cheam, 1970), p.10, quoting True (undated).
1897, summer
    Tawani Wakawa, "Encounters with the Matah Kagmi," Many Smokes, fall 1968, reprinted in INFO J., no.6 (spring 1970):39-40.
1956, Aug./Mrs. J. Pomray/N of mt.
ca.1963
    John Green, The Sasquatch File (Agassiz, B.C.: Cheam, 1973), pp.21,31.
1976, Sep./Virgil Larsen
    "Latest News," Bigfoot News, no.25 (Oct.1976):1.
-Humanoid myth
    Joaquin Miller, Unwritten History: Life Amongst the Modocs (Hartford, Ct.: American, 1874), pp.272-76.
-Lemurian sages
    Frederick Spencer Oliver, A Dweller on Two Planets, by Phylos the Tibetan (Los Angeles: Baumgardt, 1905).
    Wishar S. Cervé [Harve Spencer Lewis], Lemuria, the Lost Continent of the Pacific (San Jose: Rosicrucian Press, 1931), pp.209-63.
    Lewis Spence, The Problem of Lemuria (London: Rider, 1932).
    Godfré Ray King [Guy Warren Ballard], Unveiled Mysteries (Chicago: Saint Germain, 1939).
    "Notes and Queries," Calif.Folklore Quar. 1 (1942):291-92; 2 (1943):47.
    Eugene E. Thomas, Brotherhood of Mt. Shasta (Los Angeles: DeVorss, 1946).
    "Stade Sums Up," Doubt, no.18 (1947):

270.
A.F. Eichorn, Sr., The Mt. Shasta Story (Mt.Shasta: The Herald, 1957).
Jules B. St. Germain, "Count St. Germain and the 'I Am's,'" Fate 16 (Oct.1963):48-54.
(Editorial), Fate 21 (Feb.1968):26-32.
(Letter), John J. Sanz, Fate 21 (June 1968):126.
(Editorial), Fate 25 (Feb.1972):36-37.
John Godwin, Occult America (Garden City: Doubleday, 1972), pp.181-83.
David St. Clair, The Psychic World of California (N.Y.: Bantam, 1973 ed.), pp.145-51.
"The Magic Mountain," Newsweek, 30 July 1973, p.40.
Richard R. Andrews, The Truth Behind the Legends of Mt. Shasta (N.Y.: Carleton, 1976).
-UFO (DD)
1967, Feb.
Wendelle C. Stevens, "Spherical UFOs," Saga UFO Rept. 4 (May 1977):44. il.

Sierra Madre Mts.
-Out-of-body experience
1928, April/William Dudley Pelley
William Dudley Pelley, "Seven Minutes in Eternity," American Mag. 107 (Mar.1929):7-9,139-44.
-UFO (DD)
1929, Dec.15/J.E. Goodhue
(Letter), "Skjellerup Comet Discovered Anew," Pop.Astron. 36 (1928): 135.

Sierra Paloma Mts.
-UFO (CE-1)
1975, April 11/Diana Coolins
Peter Guttilla, "Monster Menagerie," Saga UFO Rept. 4 (Sep.1977):32,66.

Simi Valley
-UFO (CE-3)
1973, Oct.4/Gary J. Chopic/Simi Valley Freeway
Santa Ana Register, 10 Oct.1973.
Simi Valley Enterprise Sun and News, 12 Oct.1973.
(Editorial), Skylook, no.73 (Dec. 1973):4.
-UFO (NL)
1976, June 17
"Noteworthy UFO Sightings," Ufology 2 (fall 1976):60.
1976, Sep.6/W. Simi Valley
1976, Oct.7/Central Simi Valley
1976, Nov.2/NE Simi Valley
Dennis Leatart, "1976 California UFO Reports," APRO Bull. 25 (Dec.1976): 1,3-4.
1977, Aug.13
B. Ann Slate, "UFOs in Trouble," Saga UFO Rept. 6 (Sep.1978):49,53.
1978, April 14/Billy Pontbriand
Simi Valley Enterprise Sun and News, 16 April 1978.

Siskiyou Mts.
-Disappearance
1964, Oct.11/Charles F. Holden/27 mi. E of Crescent City
(Editorial), Fate 18 (Mar.1965):10-12.
-UFO (NL)
1955, Jan.27/Mrs. Lou Brubaker
(Letter), Fate 8 (Mar.1955):114.

Smith Valley
-Haunt
1890s
Richard Webb, Voices from Another World (N.Y.: Manor, 1972 ed.), pp. 151-54.

Stanislaus R.
-UFO (CE-2)
1972/Tom McCully
Modesto Bee, 13 Sep.1976; and 30 Sep. 1976.
Jerome Clark, "Saucer Central, USA," Saga UFO Rept. 4 (June 1977):8.

Stuart Gap
-Humanoid
1970, June 17/Archie Buckley
John Green, The Sasquatch File (Agassiz, B.C.: Cheam, 1973), p.56.

Table Mt.
-Archeological site
J.D. Whitney, "The Auriferous Gravels of the Sierra Nevada of California," Mem.Mus.Comp.Zool.Harvard College, vol.6 (1880).
William J. Sinclair, "Recent Investigations Bearing on the Question of the Occurrence of Neocene Man in the Auriferous Gravels of the Sierra Nevada," Pub.Am.Arch.& Ethn.Univ. Calif. 7 (1908):107,114-17.

Tahoe, L.
-Ghost
ca.1956
Richard Webb, Voices from Another World (N.Y.: Manor, 1972 ed.), pp. 245-48.
-Haunt
n.d.
Richard Webb, Voices from Another World (N.Y.: Manor, 1972 ed.), pp. 155-61.
-Humanoid
1973, July 29/Donald Cowdell/Kingsbury Grade
Reno (Nev.) Evening Gazette, 11 Aug. 1973.
B. Ann Slate & Alan Berry, Bigfoot (N.Y.: Bantam, 1976), pp.149-51,154-55.
1978, April/Marion Schubert
1978, Sep./Marion Schubert
Walnut Creek Contra Costa Times, 14 Nov.1978.
-Humanoid tracks
ca.1940/Mrs. Carl M. Warner
Eugene (Ore.) Register-Guard, 13 May

1959.
-Lake monster
  1898, Nov./=hoax?
    Charles M. Skinner, American Myths
    and Legends, 2 vols. (Philadelphia:
    Lippincott, 1903), 2:283-84.

Tamalpais Mt.
-Humanoid
  1976, April 16/Caroline Morris
    Washington (D.C.) Star, 23 Apr.1976.
    Leonard H. Stringfield, Situation
    Red: The UFO Siege (N.Y.: Fawcett,
    1977 ed.), p.89.
-Phantom panther
  1964, July/Paul Conant
    (Editorial), Fate 17 (Dec.1964):27.
-UFO (CE-3)
  1896, Aug./William Jordan
    San Francisco Call, 23 Nov.1896.
-UFO (NL)
  1953, Feb.13
    John C. Ross, "Fate's Report on the
    Flying Saucers," Fate 6 (Oct.1953):
    6,9.

Tehachapi Mts.
-Haunt
  1968, Aug.-   /Frances Little/Piute
  House
    Frances Little, "I Keep House for a
    Ghost," Fate 31 (Oct.1978):46-50.

Temblor Range
-Humanoid
  1868, Nov./E. Wright
    Ukiah City Mendocino Herald, 25 Dec.
    1868.

Thunder Mt.
-UFO (DD)
  1952, Feb./Pierre L. Tissot
    (Letter), Fate 23 (July 1970):132-
    34,144.

Trinity Alps
-Giant salamander
  1960, Jan./Vern Harden
    San Francisco Examiner, 18 Jan.1960.
    Eureka Humboldt Times, 24 Jan.1960;
    and 1 Sep.1960.
-Humanoid
  1966, April 3-4/Nick Campbell
  1968, April 6-8/Larry Browning
    John Green, The Sasquatch File (Ag-
    assiz, B.C.: Cheam, 1973), pp.38,45.
-Humanoid tracks
  1947
    John Green, On the Track of the Sas-
    quatch (Agassiz, B.C.: Cheam, 1968),
    p.31. il.

Tulare Lake Bed
-Archeological site
  4500 B.C.
    Frances A. Riddell & William H. Olsen,
    "An Early Man Site in the San Joa-
    quin Valley, California," Am.Antiq-
    uity 34 (1969):121-30. il.

Underwood Mt.
-Humanoid tracks
  1976, Feb./Jason Ownbey
    Peter Guttilla, "Monster Menagerie,"
    Saga UFO Rept. 4 (Sep.1977):32,34.

Vallecito Mts.
-Ghost light
  1858-1892
    Philip A. Bailey, Golden Mirages
    (N.Y.: Macmillan, 1940), pp.159-61.

Warner Mts.
-UFO (?)
  1947, July/Charles Leaderer/N of Al-
  turas
    Los Angeles Herald Express, 4 July
    1947.

Weaver Bally Mt.
-Humanoid tracks
  1934, winter/Dave Zebo
    Eureka Humboldt Times, 18 Nov.1960.
    il.

West Low Gap
-Humanoid tracks
  1969, July 14/George Haas
    John Green, The Sasquatch File (Ag-
    assiz, B.C.: Cheam, 1973), p.47.

Whitney, Mt.
-UFO (CE-2)
  1977, July
    (Letter), W.S., Saga UFO Rept. 5
    (Nov.1977):6.

Wildcat Creek
-Humanoid tracks
  1964/Pat Graves
    John Green, The Sasquatch File (Ag-
    assiz, B.C.: Cheam, 1973), p.31.

Wolf Mt.
-Clairvoyance
  1965, Jan./James P. Stewart
    (Letter), Fate 20 (Aug.1967):125-28.

Yerba Buena I.
-Ghost
  ca.1952/lighthouse
    (Editorial), Fate 30 (Mar.1977):36.

Yosemite National Park
-Animal ESP
  1879/Priest's Hotel
    W.D. Gunning, "Intellect in Brutes,"
    Nature 20 (1879):30.
-Entombed frog
  n.d./D.L. Albasio
    Sabina W. Sanderson, "Entombed Toads,"
    Pursuit 6 (July 1973):61.
-Giant mummy
  1895, July/G.F. Martindale
    Richard Smedley, "Sasquatch: Myth and
    Legend," Probe the Unknown 3 (Mar.
    1975):23-25,52. il.
-Phantom (myth)
    W.Y. Evans-Wentz, The Fairy-Faith in
    Celtic Countries (London: H. Frowde,

1911), pp.47-48.
-Telepathy
    1887, July/John Muir
        Walter F. Prince, "Peculiar Exper-
        iences Connected with Noted Persons,"
        J.ASPR 15 (1921):378,394-96.
-UFO (CE-1)
    1955, Aug./Carl Anderson
        Carl Anderson, Two Nights to Remem-
        ber (Los Angeles: New Age, 1956).

Yuha Desert
-Archeological site
    20,000 B.C.
        New York Long Island Press, 9 Oct.
        1972.
        W.M. Childers, "Preliminary Report
        on the Yuha Burial, California,"
        Anthro.J.Canada 12, no.1 (1974):2-9.
        James L. Bischoff, et al., "Antiquity
        of Man in America Indicated by Rad-
        iometric Dates on the Yuha Burial
        Site," Nature 261 (1976):129-30.
        Louis A. Payen, et al., "Comments on
        the Pleistocene Age Assignment and
        Associations of a Human Burial from
        the Yuha Desert, California," Am.
        Antiquity 43 (1978):448-53.
        James L. Bischoff, et al., "Comments
        on the Pleistocene Age Assignment
        and Associations of a Human Burial
        from the Yuha Desert, California:
        A Rebuttal," Am.Antiquity 43 (1978):
        747-49.

                C. Ethnic Groups

Cahuilla Indians
-Legend of Precolumbian Whites
        Vincent H. Gaddis, "Ships That Sail-
        ed the Desert," Fate 26 (Jan.1973):
        63,68.
-Shamanism
        Lucile Hooper, "The Cahuilla Indians,"
        Pub.Am.Arch.& Ethn.Univ.Calif. 16
        (1920):315,333-42.
        John Hilton, "Black Magic of the Ca-
        huilla," Desert Mag., May 1949.

Chumash Indians
-Shamanism
        Campbell Grant, The Rock Paintings
        of the Chumash (Berkeley: Univ. of
        California, 1965), pp.63-68.

Juaneño Indians
-Flood myth
        A.L. Kroeber, Handbook of the Indi-
        ans of California (Berkeley: Cali-
        fornia, 1953), pp.638-39.

Maidu Indians
-Shamanism
        Roland B. Dixon, "The Northern Maidu,"
        Bull.Am.Mus.Nat.Hist. 17 (1905):119,
        267.
        A.L. Kroeber, Handbook of the Indi-
        ans of California (Berkeley: Cali-
        fornia, 1965), pp.422-41.

Mattole Indians
-Flood myth
        Hubert Howe Bancroft, Native Races
        of the Pacific States, 5 vols.
        (N.Y.: Appleton, 1875), 3:86.

Miwok Indians
-Flood myth
        Jaime de Angulo & L.S. Freeland,
        "Miwok and Pomo Myths," J.Am.Folk-
        lore 41 (1928):232-34.
-Humanoid myth
        C. Hart Merriam, The Dawn of the
        World (Cleveland: Arthur H. Clark,
        1910), pp.231-36.
        Edward Winslow Gifford, "Miwok
        Myths," Pub.Am.Arch.& Ethn.Univ.
        Calif. 12 (1917):283,292-302.
        S.A. Barrett, "Myths of the Southern
        Sierra Miwok," Pub.Am.Arch.& Ethn.
        Univ.Calif. 16 (1919):1-28.

Mojave Indians
-Humanoid myth
        Kenneth M. Stewart, "The Amatpathen-
        ya--Mohave Leprechauns?" Affword 3,
        no.1 (spring 1973):40-41.
-Shamanism
        George Devereux, "Mohave Dreams of
        Omen and Power," Tomorrow 4 (spring
        1956):17-24.
        Kenneth M. Stewart, "Mojave Indian
        Shamanism," Masterkey 44 (1970):
        15-24.
        Kenneth M. Stewart, "Mojave Indian
        Ghosts and the Land of the Dead,"
        Masterkey 51 (1977):14-21. il.

Seri Indians
-Legend of Precolumbian Whites
        Dane & Mary Roberts Coolidge, Last
        of the Seris (N.Y.: Dutton, 1939).

Shasta Indians
-Shamanism
        A.L. Kroeber, Handbook of the Indi-
        ans of California (Berkeley: Cali-
        fornia, 1953), pp.301-304.

Washo Indians
-Flood myth
        Harold T. Wilkins, Mysteries of An-
        cient South America (Secaucus, N.J.:
        Citadel, 1956), p.16.
-Humanoid myth
        Robert H. Lowie, "Ethnographic Notes
        on the Washo," Pub.Am.Arch.& Ethn.
        Univ.Calif. 36 (1935):301,322-23,
        347-48.
-Shamanism
        Robert H. Lowie, "Ethnographic Notes
        on the Washo," Pub.Am.Arch.& Ethn.
        Univ.Calif. 36 (1935):301,318-21.
        Don Handelman, "The Development of a
        Washo Shaman," Ethnology 6 (1967):
        444-64.

Wintu Indians
-Flood and humanoid myth
        Cora du Bois & Dorothy Demetracopoulu,

"Wintu Myths," Pub.Am.Arch.& Ethn.
Univ.Calif. 28 (1931):281-86,372-74.

Yurok Indians
-Flood myth
   A.L. Kroeber, Yurok Myths (Berkeley:
   Univ. of California, 1976).

          D. Unspecified Localities

-Anomalous artifact
 1851/Hiram de Witt/=nail embedded in
 quartz
   London (Eng.) Times, 24 Dec.1851,
   p.5.

-UFO (?)
   1975, Mar./northern sector
     Lee Frey, "Close Encounters Type II:
     The UFO Fragments," Official UFO
     2 (Mar.1977):14-15. il.
     Howard Smukler, "In Search of the
     First Extraterrestrial Fragment: A
     Political and Journalistic Narra-
     tive," J.Occult Studies 1 (Aug.
     1977):171-85. il.

HAWAII

A. Populated Places

Aina Haina
-Clairvoyance
  1960, May 25/Thomas Powers
    (Editorial), Fate 13 (Oct.1960):12.

Anahole
-Ghost
  n.d./Joseph Kauanui
    Susy Smith, Prominent American Ghosts
    (N.Y.: Dell, 1969 ed.), pp.78-79.

Ewa
-Poltergeist
  1972, May/Tokiko Sasaki/91-1668 Pahiki
  St.
    Honolulu Advertiser, 9 May 1972.

Hakalau
-UFO (?)
  1957, Nov.28
    Honolulu Star-Bulletin, 29 Nov.1957.

Hilo
-UFO (CE-1)
  1967, April 21
    "Sightings over Hawaii," APRO Bull.
    15 (May-June 1967):8.
-UFO (NL)
  1967, Jan.22/T. Walker Hashimoto
    Honolulu Advertiser, 26 Jan.1967.
  1967, April 26/Ed Shirley
    "Sightings over Hawaii," APRO Bull.
    15 (May-June 1967):8.
  1973, Oct.25
    Ontario-Upland (Cal.) Daily Report,
    26 Oct.1973.

Honolulu
-Cartomancy
  1960s-   /Ron Warmoth/Box 22610
    Brad Steiger, "Ron Warmoth Reads the
    Tarot," Fate 22 (Apr.1969):62-72.
    (Letter), Barbara Smith, Fate 22
    (July 1969):126-27.
    John Godwin, Occult America (Garden
    City: Doubleday, 1972), pp.123-27.
    Brad Steiger & Ron Warmoth, Tarot
    (N.Y.: Award, 1973 ed.).
-Crisis apparition
  1945, Aug.19/Mary McGowan Slappey
    Mary McGowan Slappey, "Christmas Let-
    ter from Heaven," Fate 8 (Jan.1955):
    77-79.
-Disappearance
  1978, March 26/Carla Iris Bodmer/=
  jumped overboard?
    Kansas City (Mo.) Star, 5 Apr.1978,
    p.12A.
-Exorcism
  1971, Sep./Emma de Fries/Contessa Apart-
  ment House
    Yao Shen, "Hawaiian Kahuna Saved My

Sanity," Fate 29 (July 1976):63-68.
-Fire immunity
  1901, Jan.19/Papa Ita
    Frank Davey, "The Fire Walker," Cur-
    rent Literature 32 (1901):98-99.
    Frederick O'Brien, The Mystic Isles
    of the South Seas (Garden City,
    N.Y.: Garden City Pub., 1921).
  1949, Jan.-Feb./Tunui Ariipeu/Univ. of
  Hawaii ampitheater
    Hereward Carrington & D.C. McGowan,
    "Walking on Fire," Fate 2 (Sep.
    1949):46,54-58.
    Vincent H. Gaddis, Mysterious Fires
    and Lights (N.Y.: Dell, 1968 ed.),
    pp.129-31, quoting J.Borderland
    Rsch. (June-July 1949).
-Ghost
  1959, Aug./Hawaiian Village Hilton
    Honolulu Sunday Advertiser, 16 Aug.
    1959.
-Hex
  1948
    "Aloha," Doubt, no.23 (1948):350.
    Erle Stanley Gardner, "Nightmare
    Deaths of Honolulu," Tomorrow 7
    (winter 1959):9-21.
  1973, Nov./Violet Pelio/Halawa Stadium
    "Curse Halts Construction," Fate 28
    (Feb.1975):92.
-Precognition
  1941, Dec.6/Dorothy Flynn
    Dorothy Flynn, "And the Japs Came,"
    Fate 11 (June 1958):81-83.
  1960s/Mary Ann Glenn
    Leona Elliott, "Mary Ann Glenn--Ha-
    waii's Woman Prophet," Fate 14 (May
    1961):61-65. il.
-Religious apparition
  1971, Dec./Andrea Peters
    Brad Steiger, Revelation: The Divine
    Fire (Englewood Cliffs, N.J.: Pren-
    tice-Hall, 1973), pp.74-75.
-Skyquake
  1978, Feb./=sonic boom?
    Houston (Tex.) Chronicle, 23 Feb.1978.
-Spontaneous human combustion
  1956, Dec./Young Sik Kim/1130 Maunakea
  St.
    (Editorial), Fate 10 (May 1957):13-
    14.
-Telepathy research
  1970/William MacBain/University of Hawaii
    William N. MacBain, et al., "Quasi-
    Sensory Communication," J.Personal-
    ity & Social Psych. 14 (1970):281-
    91.
-UFO (?)
  1970, Aug.
    Buffalo (N.Y.) Courier-Express, 17
    Aug.1970.
    "That Mysterious Green Flash," Sky-
    look, no.35 (Oct.1970):10.

-UFO (DD)
1956, Jan.7
"Case 125," CRIFO Orbit, 3 Feb.1956,
p.1.
1958, Jan.3/Clifford DeLacy/Harding
Ave. x 6th St.
Vallejo (Cal.) Times-Herald, 19 Jan.
1958.
R.M.L. Baker, Jr., "Motion Pictures
of UFOs," in Carl Sagan & Thornton
Page, eds., UFOs: A Scientific Debate (Ithaca, N.Y.: Cornell Univ.,
1972), pp.203-206. il.
1974, April 25/Tsutomu Nakayama/=hoax?
Colman Von Keviczky, "UFO over Hawaii," Official UFO 1 (Nov.1976):
32-33. il.
-UFO (NL)
1956, March 5/William J. Wannall/10th
Ave.
1963, Aug.13/Richard Turse
Richard Hall, ed., The UFO Evidence
(Washington: NICAP, 1964), pp.89,
141.

Kahului
-UFO (DD)
1962, March 9/Jeanne Booth Johnson
Honolulu Advertiser, 13 Mar.1962. il.
Frank Edwards, "Mystery Blast over
Nevada," Fate 15 (Aug.1962):69. il.
Jeanne Booth Johnson, "A Photograph
from Hawaii," Flying Saucer Rev. 9
(July-Aug.1963):16-17. il.
Richard Hall, ed., The UFO Evidence
(Washington: NICAP, 1964), p.96.

Kailua
-Poltergeist
1964, Jan.-Feb.
(Editorial), Fate 17 (June 1964):12,
quoting Honolulu Advertiser (undated).

Kailua (Kona)
-Out-of-body experience
1892/Kalima
Thomas G. Thrum, Hawaiian Folk Tales
(Chicago: A.C. McClurg, 1917), pp.
58-62.
Leona Elliott, "Visit with the Dead,"
Fate 15 (Nov.1962):66-69, quoting
Hawaiian Almanac & Annual (1892).

Kaneohe
-UFO (CE-2)
1944/Naval Air Station/captured UFO/
=hoax?
Don Worley, "UFO Occupants: The Heart
of the Enigma," Official UFO 1 (Nov.
1976):15,46.

Kapaa
-UFO (DD)
1975, Jan.2/Mike Lindstrom/Coco Palms
Lodge
Mike Lindstrom, "The Lindstrom Photos," Official UFO 1 (July 1976):28-
30,59-60. il.

Kapahi
-Ghost
1951, May 18-23/Shirley Teves
Hitoshi Kinoshita, "The Whistling
Angel," Fate 5 (Oct.1952):35-38.

Milolii
-UFO (NL)
1967, April 21
"Sightings over Hawaii," APRO Bull.
15 (May-June 1967):8.

Old Waimea
-Haunt
1946, April 1-May 3/William Carreira/
firehouse
Catherine Christopher, "The Waimea
Firehouse Ghost," Fate 5 (Nov.1952)
:56-58.

Panaluu
-Tidal wave anomaly
1975, Nov.30/restaurant
(Editorial), Fate 29 (Sep.1976):22-
24.

Parker Ranch
-Ghost light
n.d.
Vincent H. Gaddis, Mysterious Fires
and Lights (N.Y.: Dell, 1968 ed.),
p.77.

Waialua
-UFO (NL)
1978, March 16/Daisy Nakatsu
Honolulu Star-Bulletin, 16 Mar.1978.

Waianae
-Phantom
1964, Oct.22/Mark Choo/85-904 Imipono
St.
(Editorial), Fate 18 (Feb.1965):18-
20, quoting Honolulu Advertiser
(undated).

Waikiki
-Hex
1972/Paul Yamanaka/Kapiolani Park
Joseph Backus, "Kahuna Stones on
Guard," Fate 29 (Aug.1976):41.
1976, March 15/Wendel Simpson/Waikiki
Shopping Plaza
Chet Novicki, "The World's First
'Curse-In,'" Fate 30 (May 1977):76.
-UFO (DD)
1959, June 18/Joseph Sigel
Frank Bowers, ed., The True Report
on Flying Saucers (Greenwich, Ct.:
Fawcett, 1967), p.14. il.
Wendelle C. Stevens, "UFOs: Seeing
Is Believing," Saga UFO Rept. 2
(fall 1974):51. il.
-UFO (NL)
1967, Jan.22
Honolulu Advertiser, 23 Jan.1967.

Waimanalo Beach
-Mystery flotsam
1972/=phosphorus

(Editorial), Fate 26 (Jan.1973):34-
36.

Waipahu
-Mystery flotsam
1955/Jackson McBride
(Editorial), Fate 8 (Oct.1955):12.

B. Physical Features

Barbers Point
-UFO (CE-1)
1952, March/James Kuenzle/Naval Air
Station
"Former Navy Man Reports 1952 Sighting," Skylook, no.28 (Mar.1970):4.
1953, Aug.6
Donald E. Keyhoe, Flying Saucer Conspiracy (N.Y.: Holt, 1955), pp.63-
64,182.

Barking Sands
-Musical sand
H.C. Bolton & A.A. Julien, "The Sing-
ing Beach of Manchester, Mass.,"
Proc.Am.Ass'n Adv.Sci. 32 (1883):
251-52.
H. Carrington Bolton, "The 'Barking
Sands' of the Hawaiian Islands,"
Nature 42 (1890):389-90.

Hadeakala National Park
-UFO (NL)
1966, Feb.12/observatory
1967, Sep.11/observatory
Frederick Ayer II, "Instrumentation
for UFO Searches," in Edward U. Condon, Scientific Study of Unidentified Flying Objects (N.Y.: Bantam,
1969 ed.), pp.761,777-85.

Kahoolawe
-Archeological site
J. Gilbert McAllister, "Archaeology
of Kahoolawe," B.P.Bishop Mus.Bull.,
no.116 (1933). il.

"Kane's Hidden Island"
-Doubtful geography
Martha Warren Beckwith, "Kepelino's
Traditions of Hawaii," B.P.Bishop
Mus.Bull., no.95 (1932), p.189.
Martha Beckwith, Hawaiian Mythology
(New Haven: Yale Univ., 1940), pp.
67-80.

Kauai
-Musical sand
H.C. Bolton & A.A. Julien, "The Sing-
ing Beach of Manchester, Mass.,"
Proc.Am.Ass'n Adv.Sci. 32 (1883):
251-52.
H. Carrington Bolton, "The 'Barking
Sands' of the Hawaiian Islands,"
Proc.Am.Ass'n Adv.Sci. 39 (1890):
257-59.
H. Carrington Bolton, "Researches on
Musical Sand in the Hawaiian Islands
and in California," N.Y.Acad.Sci.

Inst. 10 (1890):28-35.
-UFO (NL)
1975, Oct.2
"Noteworthy UFO Sightings," Ufology
2 (spring 1976):43.
-UFO (R-V)
1965, Aug.3/Barking Sand Station
Los Angeles (Cal.) Herald-Examiner,
4 Aug.1965.

Kawela Bay
-Ghost
1920s/John Dominis Holt
Susy Smith, Prominent American Ghosts
(N.Y.: Dell, 1969 ed.), pp.79-80.

Kilauea Crater
-Fire immunity
1860s/William Tufts Brigham
Max Freedom Long, The Secret Science
Behind Miracles (Los Angeles: Kos-
mon, 1948), pp.31-39.
-Hex
1972
"Hawaiian Hex," Fate 29 (Sep.1976):
73.
-Suspended animation (natural)
1929, Oct.
G.R. Wieland, "A Sacrifice to Pele,"
Science 71 (1930):386.

Kohala Mts.
-Haunt
n.d./Napua Stevens Poire
"Saved from the 'Night Marchers,'"
Fate 25 (May 1972):88, quoting Honolulu Star-Bulletin and Advertiser
(undated).

Koko Head
-UFO (NL)
1967, Jan.22
Honolulu Advertiser, 23 Jan.1967.

Kuki'i
-Archeological site
Abraham Fornander & Thomas G. Thrum,
"Fornander Collection of Hawaiian
Antiquities and Folk-lore," Mem.
B.P.Bishop Mus. 5 (1918-19):200.

Luahiwa
-Petroglyph
Ruth K. Hanner, "Egyptian Influence
in Hawaiian Petroglyphs," Occas.Pub.
Epigraphic Soc'y 2, no.37 (Mar.1975).
il.

Manoa Valley
-UFO (NL)
1975, Sep.29
Honolulu Star-Bulletin, 29 Sep.1975.

Maui
-Precognition
1972, May/Barbara Schwartz
(Editorial), Fate 25 (Sep.1972):12.

Mauna Kea
-Ice anomaly

New York Times, 23 Mar.1970, p.43.
-UFO (NL)
   n.d./observatory
      J. Allen Hynek & Jacques Vallee, The
      Edge of Reality (Chicago: Regnery,
      1975), p.27.

Mauna Loa
-Hex
   1977, summer/Ralph Loffert
      Columbus (O.) Dispatch, 31 Oct.1978.
      London (Eng.) Sunday Express, 3 Dec.
      1978.
-Phantom dog
   1959-1960, Oct./Ka-upe
      "Kaupe's Warning," Newsweek, 5 June
      1961, p.34.
      (Editorial), Fate 14 (Sep.1961):20.
      (Editorial), Fate 14 (Dec.1961):24.
      (Letter), Theodore Kelsey, Fate 15
      (Jan.1962):106-108.
   1961, May-1964
      (Editorial), Fate 17 (Aug.1964):22-
      24.
      (Editorial), Fate 18 (Mar.1965):15,
      18.

Moanalua Valley
-Petroglyph
   Pohaku ka Luahine
      Honolulu Star-Bulletin, 10 Dec.1974,
      p.A1.

Mokepu Peninsula
-Archeological site
   recent
      Charles E. Snow, Early Hawaiians
      (Lexington: Univ. Kentucky, 1974).
      il.

Molokai
-Archeological site
      Barry Fell, America B.C. (N.Y.: Quad-
      rangle, 1976), p.223.
-Oceanographic anomaly
   1925/Penguin Bank
      "A New Pacific Continent Forming?"
      Literary Digest 86 (5 Sep.1925):25-
      26.

Necker I.
-Archeological site
      Kenneth P. Emory, "Archaeology of
      Nihoa and Necker Islands," B.P. Bis-
      hop Mus.Bull., no.53 (1928). il.
      L. Sprague & Catherine C. de Camp,
      Citadels of Mystery (N.Y.: Ballan-
      tine, 1973 ed.), p.257.

Nuuanu Valley
-Phantom dog
   Ka-upe
      W.D. Westervelt, Legends of Old Hon-
      olulu (Boston: George Ellis, 1915),
      pp.82-89.
      Martha Beckwith, Hawaiian Mythology
      (New Haven: Yale Univ., 1940), pp.
      345-46.
      George T. Armitage & Henry P. Judd,
      Ghost Dog and Other Hawaiian Legends

(Honolulu: The Advertiser, 1944).

Oahu
-Electromagnetic anomaly
   1973, April 26
      "Pre-Earthquake Phenomena," Pursuit
      6 (Oct.1973):83-84.
      (Editorial), Fate 26 (Dec.1973):24-
      26, quoting AP release, 18 Aug.1973.
-UFO (NL)
   1963, March 11-12/George Joy
      "Hawaiian UFO Still Unexplained,"
      UFO Inv. 2 (Jan.-Feb.1963):4.
      Honolulu Advertiser, 13 Mar.1962.
      (Editorial), Fate 16 (July 1963):20-
      21.

Pearl Harbor
-Telepathy
   1944/Mrs. Raymond Lee/Hickam AFB
      Mrs. Raymond Lee, "A Call of Danger,"
      Fate 4 (July 1951):47.
-UFO (DD)
   1947, July 8/Ted Perdue
      Honolulu Star-Bulletin, 9 July 1947.

Saddle Road
-Gravity anomaly and ghost light
   1955, Jan.-Feb./Melvin B. Summerfield
      (Editorial), Fate 8 (June 1955):8-
      10.
      Susy Smith, Prominent American Ghosts
      (N.Y.: Dell, 1969 ed.), p.76.
-UFO (NL)
   1955, winter/Ernest B. de Silva
      (Editorial), Fate 8 (June 1955):10.

Ulupau
-Archeological site
      J. Gilbert McAllister, "Archaeology
      of Oahu," B.P.Bishop Mus.Bull., no.
      104 (1933).

Waolani Valley
-Phantom (myth)
      W.D. Westervelt, Legends of Old Hon-
      olulu (Boston: George Ellis, 1915),
      pp.5-6.

                  C. Ethnic Groups

Hawaiian native people
-Flood myth
      Abraham Fornander & Thomas G. Thrum,
      "Fornander Collection of Hawaiian
      Antiquities and Folk-lore," Mem.
      B.P.Bishop Mus. 5 (1918-19):522-27.
      Padraic Colum, At the Gateways of
      the Day (New Haven: Yale Univ.,
      1924), pp.193-98.
      David Malo, Hawaiian Antiquities
      (Mooleo Hawaii) (Honolulu: B.P.
      Bishop Museum, 1951), pp.234-38.
      David Kalakaua, The Legends and Myths
      of Hawaii (Rutland, Vt.: C.E. Tut-
      tle, 1972).
-Flying humanoid myth
      W.D. Westervelt, Legends of Old Hon-
      olulu (Boston: George Ellis, 1915),

pp.121-26.
Samuel Kamakau, Ka Po'e Kahiko: The
People of Old (Honolulu: B.P.Bishop
Museum, 1964), pp.47-53.
-Ghost legends
W.D. Westervelt, Legends of Gods and
Ghosts (Boston: George H. Ellis,
1915), pp.84-107,241-55.
-Healing and ESP
Huna magic
Thomas G. Thrum, Hawaiian Folk Tales
(Chicago: A.C. McClurg, 1917), pp.
51-57.
Antoinette Withington, "Ghostly Pro-
cessions in Hawaii," Harper's Month-
ly Mag. 174 (May 1937):605-10.
Armine von Tempski, Born in Paradise
(N.Y.: Literary Guild, 1940), pp.
125-45.
Martha Beckwith, Hawaiian Mythology
(New Haven: Yale Univ., 1940), pp.
105-21.
Max Freedom Long, The Secret Science
Behind Miracles (Los Angeles: Kos-
mon, 1948).
David Malo, Hawaiian Antiquities
(Moolelo Hawaii) (Honolulu: B.P.
Bishop Museum, 1951), pp.112-18.
Catherine Christopher, "Curse of the
Ka'ahapehau," Fate 5 (July-Aug.1952)
:69-72.
Max Freedom Long, The Secret Science
at Work (Los Angeles: DeVorss, 1953).
Samuel Kamakau, Ka Po'e Kahiko: The
People of Old (Honolulu: B.P.Bishop
Museum, 1964).
Harold M. Johnson, "The Kahuna Hawa-
iian Sorcerer: Its Dermatological
Implications," Archives of Dermatol-
ogy 90 (1964):530-51. il.
Max Freedom Long, The Huna Code in
Religions (Los Angeles: DeVorss,
1965).
Sibley S. Morill, Kahunas: The Black
and White Magicians of Hawaii (San
Francisco: The Author, 1968).
Brad Steiger, Secrets of Kahuna Magic
(N.Y.: Award, 1971).
B. Ann Slate, "Stalked by a Giant
Cat," Fate 27 (Aug.1974):75-78.
Samuel Manaiakalani Kamakau, The
Works of the People of Old (Honolu-
lu: B.P.Bishop Museum, 1976), pp.
129-47.
-Jewish origins
Christine Christopher, "Hawaiians
and the Bible," Fate 6 (Mar.1953):
98-101.
-Lake monster myth
W.D. Westervelt, Legends of Gods and
Ghosts (Boston: George H. Ellis,
1915), pp.255-58.
-Lost continent myth
Leinani Melville, Children of the
Rainbow (Wheaton, Ill.: Theosophic-
al Pub.House, 1969).
Nikolai Zhirov, Atlantis (Moscow:
Progress, 1970).
-Phantom (myth)
menehune

S. Percy Smith, Hawaiki: The Origin-
al Home of the Maori (Christchurch,
N.Z.: Whitcombe & Tombs, 1910).
W.D. Westervelt, Hawaiian Legends
of Volcanoes (Boston: George Ellis,
1916), pp.96-103.
Thomas G. Thrum, Hawaiian Folk Tales
(Chicago: A.C. McClurg, 1917), pp.
107-17.
William Hyde Rice, "Hawaiian Legends,"
B.P.Bishop Mus.Bull., no.3 (1923):
33-46.
Padraic Colum, At the Gateways of
the Day (New Haven: Yale Univ.,
1924), pp.149-64.
Martha Beckwith, Hawaiian Mythology
(New Haven: Yale Univ., 1940), pp.
321-36.
Otto Degener, Naturalists' South
Pacific Expedition: Fiji (Honolulu:
Paradise of the Pacific, 1949), pp.
193-94.
Katharine Luomala, "The Menehune of
Polynesia and Other Mythical Little
People of Oceana," B.P.Bishop Mus.
Bull., no.203 (1951):3-51.
Leinani Melville, Children of the
Rainbow (Wheaton, Ill.: Theosophi-
cal Pub.House, 1969).
J. Halley Cox, Hawaiian Petroglyphs
(Honolulu: B.P.Bishop Museum, spec.
pub.no.60, 1970). il.
William Hyde Rice, Hawaiian Legends
(Honolulu: B.P.Bishop Museum, spec.
pub.no.63, 1977), pp.36-56.
-Shape-shifting myth
Martha Beckwith, Hawaiian Mythology
(New Haven: Yale Univ., 1940), pp.
140-43.

D. Unspecified Localities

-Ancient roads
Wendell Clark Bennett, "Archaeology
of Kauai," B.P.Bishop Mus.Bull., no.
80 (1931):16.
J. Gilbert McAllister, "Archaeology
of Oahu," B.P.Bishop Mus.Bull., no.
104 (1933):34. il.

-Archeological sites
Francis A. Allen, Polynesian Antiquities: A Link Between the Ancient
Civilizations of Asia and America
(Copenhagen: Thiele, 1884).
Gerrard Fowke, "Archaeological Investigations," Bull.Bur.Am.Ethn., no.
76 (1922):174-95.
J. Gilbert McAllister, "Archaeology
of Oahu," B.P.Bishop Mus.Bull., no.
104 (1933). il.
Robert Suggs, The Island Civilizations of Polynesia (N.Y.: Mentor,
1960), pp.149-68.
Richard Pearson, ed., Archaeology on
the Island of Hawaii (Honolulu: Univ.
Hawaii Social Sci.Rsch.Inst., 1969).

-Contactee

1968/hospital
   Brad Steiger, Mysteries of Time and
   Space (N.Y.: Dell, 1976 ed.), pp.
   169-72.

-Disappearance
 1928, March 22/"Asiatic Prince"
   Raymond Lamont Brown, "The Reappear-
   ance of the Asiatic Prince," Fate
   30 (Mar.1977):78-81. il,

-Discovery, pre-Cook
   (Editorial), Fate 31 (Nov.1978):12-
   16.

-Petroglyphs
   Wendell Clark Bennett, "Archaeology
   of Kauai," B.P.Bishop Mus.Bull., no.
   80 (1931):90-94. il.
   J. Halley Cox, Hawaiian Petroglyphs
   (Honolulu: B.P.Bishop Museum, spec.
   pub.60, 1970). il.
   B. Ch. Chhabra, "Remains of Indo-
   Aryan Culture on Hawaiian Islands,"
   Occas.Pub.Epigraphic Soc'y 3, no.
   71 (Sep.1976).

THE SOUTHWEST

NEVADA

A. Populated Places

Austin
-Entombed toad
  1866/Metacom Mine
    Henry Winfred Splitter, "The Impossible Fossils," Fate 7 (Jan.1954): 65,72.
-UFO (?)
  1962, Feb.1/Dick Magee/Hwy.30
    "Mysterious Flash in Nevada, U.S.A.," APRO Bull. 10 (Mar.1962):6.

Baker
-UFO (DD)
  1950, June 26
    Gerald Heard, The Riddle of the Flying Saucers (London: Carroll & Nicholson, 1950), p.145.

Beatty
-Cartomancy
  1960s
    Richard Webb, Voices from Another World (N.Y.: Manor, 1972 ed.), p. 188.
-Petroglyph
  Gold Gulch
    James Churchward, The Lost Continent of Mu (N.Y.: Paperback Library, 1968 ed.), p.177.
-UFO (CE-1)
  1949, Jan./Sarah Elizabeth Lampe/Old Burns Ranch
    Sarah Elizabeth Lampe, "A Stream of Liquid Light," Fate 4 (Mar.1951):86-87.

Belmont
-Hex
  1870s
    "Belmont's Curse of Blood," Fate 4 (Mar.1951):47-48.

Blue Diamond
-UFO (CE-3)
  1976, Jan.29/Johnny Sands/Blue Diamond Rd.
    Las Vegas Sun, 31 Jan.1976.
    "The Johnny Sands Case," APRO Bull. 24 (Mar.1976):1,3-4.
    "In All Fairness," APRO Bull. 24 (June 1976):2,4-5.

Boulder City
-UFO (NL)
  1956, Aug./Edison F. Carpenter
    Richard Hall, ed., The UFO Evidence (Washington: NICAP, 1964), p.58.

Carson City
-Ghost
  1880s
    James Reynolds, Ghosts in American

Houses (N.Y.: Paperback Library, 1967 ed.), pp.40-45.
-Human tracks in sandstone
  1882/State Penitentiary/=Mylodon tracks?
    San Francisco (Cal.) Call, 4 Aug. 1882.
    (Letter), Argyll, Nature 27 (1883): 578.
    (Letter), Joseph Le Conte, Nature 28 (1883):101-102.
    E.D. Cope, "The Nevada Biped Tracks," Am.Naturalist 17 (1883):69-71.
    San Francisco (Cal.) Bulletin, 23 July 1883.
    O.C. Marsh, "On the Supposed Human Foot-prints Recently Found in Nevada," Am.J.Sci., ser.3, 26 (1883): 139-40. il.
    Sacramento (Cal.) Daily Record-Union, 25 Mar.1885.
-UFO (CE-2)
  1963, Nov.14/Blanche Pritchett
    Carson City Nevada Appeal, 14 Nov. 1963.

Denio
-Cattle mutilation
  1975, Oct.
    Don Worley, "Cattle Mutilations & UFOs: Who Are the Mutilators? Part 2," Official UFO 1 (Dec.1976):25.

Duckwater
-Meteorite crater
  68 m.diam. x 5 m.deep/doubtful
    Tonopah Daily Times, 5 Aug.1936.
    John S. Rinehart & C.T. Elvery, "A Possible Meteorite Crater near Duckwater, Nye County, Nevada," Pop. Astro. 59 (1951):209-11.

Elko
-Ball lightning
  1960
    M.A. Uman, "Some Comments on Ball Lightning," J.Atmospheric & Terrestrial Physics 30 (1968):1245-46.
-Skyquake
  1952, Jan.1
    Marion Kirkpatrick, "California Mystery Blasts," Fate 10 (Apr.1957): 86,87.
-UFO (?)
  1959, Oct.12/Virgil L. Welch/=hoax
    Frank Bowers, ed., The True Report on Flying Saucers (Greenwich, Ct.: Fawcett, 1967), p.62. il.

Ely
-UFO (?)
  1973, Oct.23/Mike Francone/=balloon
    Ely Record, 27 Oct.1973.
-UFO (DD)

1950, May 7/14 mi.S
Jacques Vallee, Passport to Magonia
(Chicago: Regnery, 1969), p.195.

Eureka
-Burning soil
1937, Oct.-Nov./John Heggerson
"Earth Flames," Fortean Soc'y Mag.,
no.3 (Jan.1940):13, quoting Los Angeles (Cal.) Times (undated).
-Entombed wasp nest
1877
Henry Winfred Splitter, "The Impossible Fossils," Fate 7 (Jan.1954):
65,68.
-Spirit medium
1887/Otelia Anderson
James H. Hyslop, "Mediumistic Phenomena," J.ASPR 2 (1908):456-63.

Fallon
-UFO (NL)
1967, Feb.28/Fallon AFB
"UAO near AFB in Nevada," APRO Bull.
15 (Mar.-Apr.1967):9.

Henderson
-UFO (DD)
1959, June 11/Ed D. Arnold
Richard Hall, ed., The UFO Evidence
(Washington: NICAP, 1964), p.71.

Johntown
-Scrying
1858, winter/Eilley Orrum Bowers
B. Palmer Sullivan, "She Divined the
Comstock Lode," Fate 6 (Dec.1953):
17-20. il.

Las Vegas
-Anomalous mounds
(Letter), Verne L. Cameron, Fate 8
(Dec.1955):120-23.
-Haunt
1964, Aug.-1965, June/Mrs. Reid
Hans Holzer, Ghosts of the Golden
West (N.Y.: Ace, 1968), pp.161-64.
-Inner development
1950s-   /Eck, Inc.
Paul Twitchell, An Introduction to
Eckankar (Las Vegas: Illuminated
Way, 1966).
John Godwin, Occult America (Garden
City: Doubleday, 1972), pp.112-22.
-Precognition
1955/Aileen Smithwich
Laura A. Dale, Rhea White & Gardner
Murphy, "A Selection of Cases from
a Recent Survey of Spontaneous ESP
Phenomena," J.ASPR 56 (1962):3,32-
34.
-Skyquake
1951, Sep.24
Marion Kirkpatrick, "California Mys-
tery Blasts," Fate 10 (Apr.1957):
86-87.
-UFO (?)
1977, Jan.19/=balloon
Allan Hendry, "UFO's vs. IFO's,"
Int'l UFO Reporter 2 (Apr.1977):8.

-UFO (CE-1)
1963, May/Danny Columbo
Timothy Green Beckley, "Saucers and
Celebrities," Saga UFO Rept. 3
(Apr.1976):34.
1968, Oct.28/Tropicana Blvd.
"Around the Globe," APRO Bull. 17
(Nov.-Dec.1968):6.
-UFO (CE-2)
1954, May 24/jet destroyed
Christian Vogt, "Non dramatique in-
cident," Phénomènes Spatiaux, Feb.
1965, pp.5-6.
1956, summer/nr. Nellis AFB
Coral & Jim Lorenzen, Flying Saucer
Occupants (N.Y.: Signet, 1967), pp.
28-29.
1961, July 17/one mi.N of Bonny Spring
Ranch
Jacques Vallee, Passport to Magonia
(Chicago: Regnery, 1969), p.282.
1971, June 26
"E-M Case in Nevada," APRO Bull. 19
(May-June 1971):7.
Kevin D. Randle, "UFOs and the Mys-
terious EM Effect," Official UFO 2
(May 1977):22,66.
-UFO (CE-3)
1968/Nellis AFB
Leonard H. Stringfield, "Retrievals
of the Third Kind--Part 2," MUFON
UFO J., no.129 (Aug.1978):8,11.
-UFO (DD)
1947, July 8/W.S. Erwin/139 St. Louis
Las Vegas Review-Journal, 9 July
1947.
1950, June 26/airport
Aimé Michel, The Truth about Flying
Saucers (N.Y.: Pyramid, 1967 ed.),
p.64.
1952, April 17/Orville Lawson/Nellis
AFB
Philadelphia (Pa.) Bulletin, 18 Apr.
1952.
-UFO (NL)
1947, July 8/Lee Crenshaw/McCarran
Field restaurant
Las Vegas Review-Journal, 9 July
1947.
1947, Oct.8?
J. Allen Hynek, The Hynek UFO Report
(N.Y.: Dell, 1977), p.16.
1947, Dec.8
Aimé Michel, The Truth about Flying
Saucers (N.Y.: Pyramid, 1967 ed.),
pp.34-35.
1957, Jan.14/Art Johnson/Decatur Blvd.
"Case 294," CRIFO Orbit, 1 Mar.1957,
p.3, quoting Las Vegas Sun (undated).
1966, March 28/Ralph Salvory
Toledo (O.) Blade, 29 Mar.1966, p.6.
1968, Sep.17/Nellis AFB
J. Allen Hynek, The UFO Experience
(Chicago: Regnery, 1972), pp.38,236.
1976, Jan.29/Mt. Charleston
Las Vegas Sun, 31 Jan.1976.
"UFO News," Official UFO 1 (Dec.1976)
:12,63.
1978, Dec.16/McCarran Int'l Airport
Las Vegas Sun, 17 Dec.1978.

-Weather control
  1949, May 14
    Eugene Grossenheider, "Does Man Make
    the Weather?" Fate 9 (Feb.1956):80-
    81, quoting AP release, 20 May 1949.

Lovelock
-Scrying
  1930s/Max Freedom Long
    Max Freedom Long, The Secret Science
    Behind Miracles (Los Angeles: Kos-
    mon, 1948), pp.157-58,181-83.

McDermitt
-Ghost light
  1922-1948/Oregon Canyon Ranch
    Kenneth Arnold, "Phantom Lights in
    Nevada," Fate 1 (fall 1948):96-98.
    (Letter), H.N. Cranmer, Fate 3 (July
    1950):88.

Mesquite
-UFO (?)
  1962, April 18/=meteor?
    Frank Edwards, "Mystery Blast over
    Nevada," Fate 15 (Aug.1962):68,70.

North Las Vegas
-Inner development
  1963/Nadina K. Grove
    Nadina K. Grove, A Personal Explora-
    tion of Expansion of Consciousness
    (North Las Vegas: The Author, 1968).
-Precognition
  1957, Dec./Mrs. Arthur Mann
    (Editorial), Fate 11 (Apr.1958):20.

Overton
-Paranormal amnesia
  1927, May/Richard "Dave" Jacobi
    (Editorial), Fate 15 (Sep.1962):16-
    18.

Perth
-Archeological site
    Jim Brandon, Weird America (N.Y.:
    Dutton, 1978), p.133.

Reno
-Inner development
  1973-   /Pansophic Institute/Box 2971
    Leslie Shepard, ed., Occultism Up-
    date, no.1 (1978):33.
-UFO (?)
  1947, July 6
    Reno Nevada State Journal, 8 July
    1947.
-UFO (CE-3)
  1973, Oct.28/Imogene Proctor
    "Nevada Sighting," UFO Inv., Oct.
    1974, pp.3-4.
-UFO (DD)
  1947, July 7/John Brackett
    Reno Nevada State Journal, 8 July
    1947.
  1953, June 3/E 9th x Lake St.
    U.S. Air Force, Projects Grudge and
    Blue Book Reports 1-12 (Washington:
    NICAP, 1968), pp.224-25.
-UFO (NL)

1950, March 26/Marie H. Matthews/Hub-
bard Field
  Reno Evening Gazette, 27 Mar.1950.
1952, April 23
  Reno Evening Gazette, 24 Apr.1952.
1973, Nov.1/Bud Loomis/Court St.
  Reno Gazette, 2 Nov.1973.
1976, Jan.28
  "Noteworthy UFO Sightings," Ufology
  2 (summer 1976):62.

Sloan
-UFO (?)
  1965, March 20/=lenticular cloud?
    Frank Bowers, ed., The True Report
    on Flying Saucers (Greenwich, Ct.:
    Fawcett, 1967), p.1. il.

Sparks
-UFO (CE-2)
  1973, Oct.
    Reno Gazette, 2 Nov.1973.

Stonehouse
-Fall of mud
  1879, March
    Henry Winfred Splitter, "Wonders
    from the Sky," Fate 6 (Oct.1953):34,
    quoting Winnemucca Silver State (un-
    dated).

Sun Valley
-UFO (NL)
  1973, Oct.31/Monte Clothier
    Reno Gazette, 2 Nov.1973.

Sweetwater
-UFO (DD)
  1953, April 12
    U.S. Air Force, Projects Grudge and
    Blue Book Reports 1-12 (Washington:
    NICAP, 1968), p.206.

Tonopah
-UFO (CE-2)
  1957, Nov.23/30 mi.W
    J. Allen Hynek, The Hynek UFO Report
    (N.Y.: Dell, 1977), pp.182-86.

Treasure City
-Anomalous artifact
  1869, winter/Abbey mine/=metal screw
    embedded in feldspar
    Henry Winfred Splitter, "The Impos-
    sible Fossils," Fate 7 (Jan.1954):
    65,67.

Tuscarora
-Entombed frog
  1879/Grand Prize mine
    Henry Winfred Splitter, "The Impos-
    sible Fossils," Fate 7 (Jan.1954):
    65,70-71, quoting Tuscarora paper
    (undated).

Verdi
-UFO (DD)
  1947, July 7/Harry Rose/Sierra Pacific
    Power Co.
    Reno Nevada State Journal, 8 July

1947.

Virginia City
-Fall of earthworms
   1879, April
      Henry Winfred Splitter, "Wonders
      from the Sky," Fate 6 (Oct.1953):
      33,35, quoting Virginia City Dis-
      patch (undated).
-Giant human skull
   1860s/Judge Baldwin
      Decatur (Ill.) Republican, 23 Sep.
      1873, quoting Virginia Bulletin
      (undated).
-Haunt
   1964, April-1968/St. Mary Louise Hospital
      Dolores K. O'Brien, "The White Nun
      Haunting," Fate 23 (Aug.1970):84-88.
-Telepathy
   1874/William H. Wright
      Mark Twain, "Mental Telegraphy: A
      Manuscript with a History," Harper's
      Monthly Mag. 84 (Dec.1891):95-104.

Wells
-UFO (DD)
   1967, Nov.2/40 mi.S
      "UFOs--November--U.S.A.," APRO Bull.
      16 (Nov.-Dec.1967):8.

              B. Physical Features

Black Rock Range
-Haunt
   1965, Dec./Richard E. York
      Jim Brandon, Weird America (N.Y.:
      Dutton, 1978), p.130.

Capitol Peak
-Chinese discovery
   ca.1000 B.C.
      Henriette Mertz, Gods from the Far
      East (N.Y.: Ballantine, 1975 ed.),
      pp.163-64.

Carson Sink
-UFO (DD)
   1952, July 24
      Edward J. Ruppelt, The Report on Un-
      identified Flying Objects (Garden
      City: Doubleday, 1956), pp.10-12.

Cherry Creek Mt.
-UFO (CE-2)
   1974, Feb.14/55 mi.N of Ely on U.S.93
      Santa Ana (Cal.) Register, 27 Mar.
      1974.
      "Brothers Report Chase by Flying
      Lights," Skylook, no.78 (May 1974):
      19.
      "Car Disabled by UFO?" APRO Bull. 22
      (May-June 1974):4-5.
      J. Allen Hynek & Jacques Vallee, The
      Edge of Reality (Chicago: Regnery,
      1975), pp.10-15,34-42.

Dead Mt.
-Giant mountain sheep horns

1957/Oran C. Buck
   San Francisco (Cal.) Chronicle, 29
   Dec.1969.

Deer Creek
-Archeological site
   8000 B.C.-1250 A.D.
      Mary Elizabeth & Richard Shutler, Jr.,
      "Deer Creek Cave, Elko County, Nev-
      ada," Anthro.Pap.Nevada State Mus.,
      no.11 (1963). il.

Diamond Mts.
-Humanoid
   1960s/Dion Pollard
      John Green, The Sasquatch File (Ag-
      assiz, B.C.: Cheam, 1973), p.31.
-Humanoid tracks
   1960, Nov./Dean Pollard
      John Green, The Sasquatch File (Ag-
      assiz, B.C.: Cheam, 1973), p.23.

Etna Cave
-Archeological site
   ca.1500 B.C.
      S.M. Wheeler, Archaeology of Etna
      Cave, Lincoln County, Nevada (Car-
      son City: Nevada State Park Comm'n,
      1942). il.

Fisher Canyon
-Fossil human shoeprint
   1927, Jan./Albert E. Knapp
      Brad Steiger, Mysteries of Time and
      Space (N.Y.: Dell, 1976), p.31.

Flat Mesa
-UFO (CE-1)
   1925/Don Wood, Jr.
      Trevor James Constable, The Cosmic
      Pulse of Life (Santa Ana: Merlin,
      1976), pp.110-12, quoting letter in
      Flying Saucers, Oct.1959.

Grapevine Canyon
-Petroglyph
      Alexander M'Allen, Ancient Chinese
      Account of the Grand Canyon, or
      Course of the Colorado (College
      Corner, O.: F.T. Snyder, 1913).
      Julian H. Steward, "Petroglyphs of
      California and Adjoining States,"
      Pub.Am.Arch.& Ethn.Univ.Calif. 24
      (1929):47,148-50. il.
      James Churchward, The Lost Continent
      of Mu (N.Y.: Paperback Library,
      1968 ed.), pp.175-77. il.
      Robert F. Heizer & Martin A. Baumhoff,
      Rock Paintings of Nevada and Eastern
      California (Berkeley: Univ. of Cal-
      ifornia, 1962), pp.28-29. il.

Gypsum Cave
-Archeological site
   8500-6500 B.C.
      Chester Stock, "Problems of Antiquity
      Presented in Gypsum Cave, Nevada,"
      Sci.Monthly 32 (Jan.1931):22-32. il.
      Mark R. Harrington, "Gypsum Cave,
      Nevada," Southwest Mus.Pap., no.8

(1933).

Hoover Dam
-UFO (NL)
1973, Nov.1/Ken Martin
Reno Gazette, 2 Nov.1973.

Kettle Creek
-Ghost light
1940s
(Letter), H.N. Cranmer, Fate 3 (July
1950):88.

Leonard Rockshelter
-Archeological site
9200 B.C.
Robert F. Heizer, "Preliminary Report on Leonard Rock Shelter, Persh-
ing County, Nevada," Am.Antiquity
17 (1951):89-98.

Lovelock Cave
-Archeological site
2500 B.C.-1850 A.D.
Sarah Winnemucca Hopkins, Life Among
the Paiutes (N.Y.: Putnam, 1883),
pp.73-75.
Llewellyn L. Loud & M.R. Harrington,
"Lovelock Cave," Pap.Am.Arch.& Ethn.
Univ.Calif. 25 (1929):vii-183. il.
Lovelock Review-Miner, 19 June 1931;
and 29 Sep.1939.
Gordon L. Grosscup, "The Culture His-
tory of Lovelock Cave, Nevada," Rept.
Univ.Calif.Arch.Survey, no.52 (1960).
St. Paul (Minn.) Sunday Pioneer Press,
27 Sep.1970.
Dorothy P. Dansie, "John T. Reid's
Case for the Redheaded Giants,"
Nevada Hist.Soc'y Quar. 18 (1975):
152-67. il.

Mahogany Peak
-Chinese discovery
ca.1000 B.C.
Henriette Mertz, Gods from the Far
East (N.Y.: Ballantine, 1975 ed.),
pp.162-63.

Mead, L.
-Phantom wagon train
1886
Vincent H. Gaddis, "Caravan of the
Lost," Fate 2 (May 1949):36,37.
-UFO (DD)
1947, June 28/Eric B. Armstrong/30 mi.
NW
Ted Bloecher, Report on the UFO Wave
of 1947 (Washington: NICAP, 1967),
p.III-10.

Moapa Valley
-Archeological site
500-700 A.D./Lost city
M.R. Harrington, "The 'Lost City' of
Nevada," Sci.Am. 133 (July 1925):14-
16. il.
Richard Shutler, Jr., "Lost City:
Pueblo Grande de Nevada," Anthro.
Pap.Nevada State Mus., no.5 (1961).

il.
"Indian Relics in Peril," Fate 26
(May 1973):57.
Edwin C. Soule, "Lost City Revisit-
ed," Masterkey 49 (1975):4-19. il.
Edwin C. Soule, "Lost City II," Mas-
terkey 50 (1976):10-18. il.
Edwin C. Soule, "A Desert Mystery--
Or, It's Greek to Me," Masterkey 51
(1977):101-108. il.

Monitor Valley
-UFO (NL)
1961, Sep.24/Hwy.82 nr. Pine Creek
Ranch
Lloyd Mallan, "Complete Directory of
UFOs: Part III," Sci.& Mech. 38
(Feb.1967):56,92.

Mormon Mesa
-UFO (CE-4)
1952, July 27-Nov./Truman Bethurum
Truman Bethurum, Aboard a Flying Sau-
cer (Los Angeles: DeVorss, 1954).
Truman Bethurum, The Voice of the
Planet Clarion (Prescott, Ariz.:
The Author, 1957).

Muddy Mts.
-Stratigraphic anomaly
=inverted strata
William G. Brock & Terry Engelder,
"Deformation Associated with the
Movement of the Muddy Mountain Over-
thrust," Bull.Geol.Soc'y Am. 88
(1977):1667-77.

Newark Valley
-Fall of frogs
n.d./George C. Stoker
Charles Fort, The Books of Charles
Fort (N.Y.: Holt, 1941), p.544.

New York Canyon
-Ancient pyramid
Jim Brandon, Weird America (N.Y.:
Dutton, 1978), p.132.
-Human tracks in sandstone
1879/Joseph Walker
Eureka Daily Leader, 14 Feb.1879.

Peavine Foothills
-UFO (DD)
1947, July 7/Pete Giusti
Reno Nevada State Journal, 8 July
1947.

Pegrand L.
-Lake monster
Harold T. Wilkins, Secret Cities of
Old South America (N.Y.: Library,
1952), p.308n.

Pyramid L.
-Cartomancy
1948, June/Judith Childs Speer/Pyramid
Lake Ranch
Judith Childs Speer, "Command Per-
formance: 'I Must Read Your Cards,'"
Fate 16 (July 1963):85-88.

-Lake monster
   (Editorial), Fate 12 (July 1959):8-
   10.
   Catherine S. Fowler, et al., "Miscellaneous Papers on Nevada Archaeology
   1-8," Anthro.Pap.Nevada State Mus.,
   no.14 (1969).
   "Worms: Sea, Lake, River," INFO J.,
   no.10 (spring 1973):8,11.

Ruby Hill
-Entombed worms
   1881/Joe Molino/Wide West mine
   Henry Winfred Splitter, "The Impossible Fossils," Fate 7 (Jan.1954):
   65,68.

Sand Mt.
-Musical sand
   off U.S.50 SE of Fallon
   "Musical Sands," Am.Meteorological
   J. 1 (1885):509.
   John F. Lindsay, et al., "Sound Pro-
   ducing Dune and Beach Sands," Bull.
   Geol.Soc'y Am. 87 (1976):463-73. il.
   Milwaukee (Wisc.) Journal, 25 Dec.
   1977.
   Harrisburg (Pa.) Patriot, 23 Mar.
   1978.

Sheep Range
-UFO (?) and Men-in-black
   1978, May 21/Ray Thomas/=hoax
   Allan Hendry, "IUR Takes on Its
   First 'Men in Black' Case, and
   'Wins' One," Int'l UFO Reporter 3
   (July 1978):10-15.

Spring Mts.
-Mystery plane crashes
   1978/USAF O-2 Skymaster Spotter
   Star Magazine, 27 Feb.1978.

Spring Valley
-Giant human skeleton
   1877, summer/=femur embedded in quartzite
   Henry Winfred Splitter, "The Impossible Fossils," Fate 7 (Jan.1954):
   65-66.
-UFO (CE-1)
   1964, June 25/George W. Rogers
   Ely Record, 1 July 1964.
   Lloyd Mallan, "Complete Directory of
   UFOs: Part II," Sci.& Mech. 38 (Jan.
   1967):44,45-46.

Trident Peak
-Chinese discovery
   ca.1000 B.C.
   Henriette Mertz, Gods from the Far
   East (N.Y.: Ballantine, 1975 ed.),
   p.163.

Tule Springs
-Archeological site
   11,000 B.C.
   M.R. Harrington, "A Camel Hunter's
   Camp in Nevada," Masterkey 8 (1934)
   :22-24.

M.R. Harrington, "The Oldest Camp-
fires," Masterkey 28 (1954):233-34.
M.R. Harrington, "A New Tule Springs
Expedition," Masterkey 29 (1955):
112-13.
Mark R. Harrington & Ruth DeEtte
Simpson, "Tule Springs, Nevada,"
Southwest Mus.Pap., no.18 (1961).
Margaret L. Susia, "Tule Springs
Archaeological Surface Survey," An-
thro.Pap.Nevada State Mus., no.12
(1964). il.
Richard Shutler, "Tule Springs Exped-
ition," Current Anthro. 6 (1965):
110-11.
Richard Shutler, Jr., et al., "Pleis-
tocene Studies in Southern Nevada,"
Anthro.Pap.Nevada State Mus., no.13
(1967). il.
Bruce Bryan, "Tule Springs Site Re-
evaluated," Masterkey 42 (1968):112.

Valley of Fire
-Archeological site
   300 B.C.-1150 A.D.
   Robert F. Heizer & Martin A. Baumhoff,
   Prehistoric Rock Art of Nevada and
   Eastern California (Berkeley: Univ.
   of California, 1962), p.28.
   Richard & Mary Elizabeth Shutler,
   "Archaeological Survey in Southern
   Nevada," Anthro.Pap.Nevada State
   Mus., no.7 (1962):3-16. il.
   Franklin Folsom, America's Ancient
   Treasures (N.Y.: Rand McNally, 1974),
   p.54.

Walker L.
-Anomalous artifact
   =Indian spindle whorl
   (Editorial), Fate 18 (July 1965):25-
   26.
-Lake monster
   Hawthorne Mineral County Independent-
   News, 3 Feb.1965.
   J.K. Parrish, "Our Country's Myster-
   ious Monsters," Old West, fall 1969,
   p.25.

Walker R.
-Anomalous artifact
   1882/=obsidian spear head
   O.T. Mason, "Archaeological Enigmas,"
   Science 8 (1886):528-29.
   W.J. McGee, "An Obsidian Implement
   from Pleistocene Deposits in Nevada,"
   Am.Anthro. 2 (1889):301-12.

Washoe L.
-UFO (NL)
   1967, Oct.4
   "UFOs--October--U.S.A.," APRO Bull.
   16 (Nov.-Dec.1967):8.

Yellow Rock Canyon
-Petroglyph
   =depicts elephant?
   Thomas N. Layton, "Stalking Elephants
   in Nevada," Western Folklore 35
   (1976):250-57. il.

C. Ethnic Groups

Paiute Indians
-Shamanism
    Omer C. Stewart, "Three Gods for
    Joe," Tomorrow 4 (spring 1956):71-
    76.
    Francis A. Riddell, "Honey Lake Pai-
    ute Ethnography," Anthro.Pap.Nevada
    State Mus., no.4 (1960):61-72.

D. Unspecified Localities

-Fossil human shoeprint
  opal mine/=similarity only
    "Footprints in the...," Pursuit 3
    (Oct.1970):77-79. il.

-Humanoid
  1870, summer/northern sector
    Lansing (Mich.) Republican, 4 Aug.
    1870.

A. Populated Places

Alta
-Fall of brown snow
  1955, April 19
  "Falls," Doubt, no.49 (1955):358,359,
  quoting Boston (Mass.) American
  (undated).

American Fork
-UFO (NL)
  1956, July 25/Mt. Timpanogos
  "Case 191," CRIFO Orbit, 5 Oct.1956,
  p.1, quoting Salt Lake City Deseret
  News Telegram (undated).

Arcadia
-UFO (CE-1)
  1965, summer/Carlos Reed
  Frank B. Salisbury, The Utah UFO Dis-
  play (Old Greenwich, Ct.: Devin-
  Adair, 1974), Appendix B.

Ballard
-UFO (DD)
  1978, Aug.19/Telintha Rasmussen
  Salt Lake City Deseret News, 4 Sep.
  1978.
  Andrea Granum, "The Dale Wood Sight-
  ing: UFOs of the High Uintas," Saga
  UFO Rept. 7 (Feb.1979):28,31.

Beaver
-UFO (NL)
  1947, July 5/Lucy Osborne
  Salt Lake City Tribune, 6 July 1947.

Boneta
-UFO (CE-1)
  1967, Feb.23/Roy Marchant
  Frank B. Salisbury, The Utah UFO Dis-
  play (Old Greenwich, Ct.: Devin-
  Adair, 1974), p.39.

Bountiful
-UFO (?)
  1967, March/=balloon
  Gabriel Green, Let's Face the Facts
  about Flying Saucers (N.Y.: Popular
  Library, 1967), p.100.
-UFO (NL)
  1969, May 2/nr. North Canyon
  "Around the Globe," APRO Bull. 18
  (July-Aug.1969):8.

Bridgeland
-UFO (CE-1)
  1956, summer/Sandy Richman/E of town
  Frank B. Salisbury, The Utah UFO Dis-
  play (Old Greenwich, Ct.: Devin-
  Adair, 1974), Appendix B.

Carbon co.
-Cattle mutilation
  1975, Oct.
  Twin Falls (Ida.) Times-News, 21 Oct.
  1975.

Castle Gate
-Anomalous fossil
  William Peterson, "Dinosaur Tracks
  in the Roofs of Coal Mines," Natural History 24 (1924):388-91. il.

Cedar City
-UFO (CE-2)
  1959, Feb.28/Bernard "Gerry" Irwin/SE
  on Hwy.14
  Jim Lorenzen, "Where Is Private Irwin?" Flying Saucers, Nov.1962, pp.
  17-26.
  Coral & Jim Lorenzen, Encounters
  with UFO Occupants (N.Y.: Berkley,
  1976), pp.347-56.
-UFO (DD)
  1947, June 26/Roy Walter/municipal airport
  Salt Lake City Tribune, 28 June 1947.

Duchesne
-UFO (?)
  1967, fall/Douglas Horrocks/=Venus
  Frank B. Salisbury, The Utah UFO Dis-
  play (Old Greenwich, Ct.: Devin-
  Adair, 1974), pp.12-13.

Emory
-Cattle mutilation
  1975, Sep.30/Robert Hedelius
  Ed Sanders, "The Mutilation Mystery,"
  Oui, Sep.1976, pp.51,120-21.

Eureka
-UFO (CE-2)
  1962, April 18
  Las Vegas (Nev.) Sun, 19 Apr.1962,
  p.1.
  "Three Bright Fireballs in Spring
  Skies," Sky & Telescope 23 (June
  1962):323.
  Frank Edwards, "Mystery Blast over
  Nevada," Fate 15 (Aug.1962):68,70.

Fort Duchesne
-UFO (CE-1)
  1966, Sep.28/Joe Ann Harris/½ mi.S
  Frank B. Salisbury, The Utah UFO Dis-
  play (Old Greenwich, Ct.: Devin-
  Adair, 1974), pp.28-36.
-UFO (NL)
  1966, Sep.28/Kent Denver/Agency Hill
  1966, Oct.9/Susan Denver
  1972, Nov.1/Jessie Pickup/S of town
  Frank B. Salisbury, The Utah UFO Dis-
  play (Old Greenwich, Ct.: Devin-
  Adair, 1974), pp.24-25,37,95, and
  Appendix B.

Greenwood
-Clairaudience
    1924, Dec.26/Velma Dorrity Cloward
    Velma Dorrity Cloward, "Call in the
    Night," Tomorrow 6 (winter 1958):
    47-50.

Hanna
-UFO (DD)
    1966, June/Dean Powell/post office
    Frank B. Salisbury, The Utah UFO Dis-
    play (Old Greenwich, Ct.: Devin-
    Adair, 1974), pp.13-17.

Kanab
-UFO (CE-1)
    1968, March 21/Fritz Van Nest/8 mi.S
    W.C. Stevens, "Bell-Shaped UFOs,"
    Official UFO 1 (Nov.1975):34,38-39.
    il.

Lapoint
-UFO (NL)
    1967, April 22/Cliff Hackford
    1967, Oct.11/Weston Justice
    1968, March 4/William Taylor
    Frank B. Salisbury, The Utah UFO Dis-
    play (Old Greenwich, Ct.: Devin-
    Adair, 1974), pp.48,56,61, and Ap-
    pendix B.
    1978, Aug.10/David Murray/Hwy.40
    Andrea Granum, "The Dale Wood Sight-
    ing: UFOs of the High Uintas," Saga
    UFO Rept. 7 (Feb.1979):28,30-31.

La Sal
-UFO (?)
    1957, May 12/Samuel E. Craig
    Richard Hall, ed., The UFO Evidence
    (Washington: NICAP, 1964), p.30.

Lehi
-UFO (CE-4)
    1973, Oct.17
    David Webb, 1973: Year of the Human-
    oids (Evanston: Center for UFO Stud-
    ies, 1976 ed.), p.13.
    Coral & Jim Lorenzen, Encounters with
    UFO Occupants (N.Y.: Berkley, 1976),
    pp.340-42.

Little Mountain
-UFO (CE-1)
    1973, Oct.16/Diane G. Sessions
    (Letter), Fate 31 (Jan.1978):117-18.

Logan
-UFO (?)
    1949, April 5/=aircraft
    Bruce S. Maccabee, "UFO Related In-
    formation from the FBI Files: Part
    5," MUFON UFO J., no.124 (Mar.1978):
    7,11.
-UFO (CE-2)
    1954, May 1/James Fuller
    Salt Lake City Tribune, 5 May 1954;
    and 7 May 1954.
    "Logan, Utah Jolted by Violent Explo-
    sion and Gaping Crater Following
    Mysterious 'Streak of Light' in Sky,"

CRIFO Newsl., 1 Oct.1954, p.4.
    Curtis Fuller, "Unsolved Saucer Mys-
    teries," Fate 8 (Mar.1955):6.
-UFO (DD)
    1947, June 26/Glen Bunting
    Salt Lake City Deseret News, 30 June
    1947.
-UFO (NL)
    1947, Sep.8
    Bruce S. Maccabee, "UFO Related In-
    formation from the FBI Files: Part
    3," MUFON UFO J., no.121 (Dec.1977)
    :10,14.

Maeser
-UFO (NL)
    1967, April 21/David B. Hall
    Frank B. Salisbury, The Utah UFO Dis-
    play (Old Greenwich, Ct.: Devin-
    Adair, 1974), p.48, and Appendix B.

Midvale
-Animal ESP
    1953/Mrs. J.T. Davis
    Salt Lake City Deseret News, 3 Apr.
    1953.
    (Editorial), Fate 7 (Mar.1954):9.

Moab
-Anomalous fossil
    =human bones in Cretaceous rock
    F.A. Barnes, "The Case of the Bones
    in Stone," Desert Mag. 38 (Feb.1975)
    :36-39. il.

Mount Olympus
-UFO (DD)
    1964, Oct.24/Thomas McLelland
    Salt Lake City Deseret News Telegram,
    24 Oct.1964.

Murray
-Astrology
    1975/Sharon Naccarato/5263 Gravenstein
    Warren Smith, "Phenomenal Predictions
    for 1976," Saga, Jan.1976, pp.16,50.
-Fire anomaly
    1949, Jan.4/James E. Reid
    "First Prize," Doubt, no.24 (1949):
    362.
-Haunt
    1960s
    Susy Smith, Ghosts Around the House
    (N.Y.: World, 1970).
-UFO (DD)
    1978, Feb.4/Kent Peterson/E of Fashion
    Place Mall
    Utah Technical College Points West,
    14 Feb.1978.

Myton
-UFO (?)
    1957, Oct.10/W.F. Norris/=meteorite
    "Flying Saucer Roundup," Fate 11
    (Feb.1958):29,36.
    H.H. Nininger, "Identification of
    Meteorites, or What on Earth Is a
    Meteorite?" Meteoritics 3 (1967):
    239,241-42.

Naples
-UFO (DD)
1961, Oct.5/Marian Southam
"More Discs in Utah," APRO Bull. 10
(Mar.1962):2.

Neola
-UFO (DD)
1967, May 12/Richard Faucett/5 mi.S
Frank B. Salisbury, The Utah UFO Display (Old Greenwich, Ct.: Devin-
Adair, 1974), pp.69-70, and Appendix B.

Nephi
-UFO (NL)
1962, April 18
Frank Edwards, "Mystery Blast over
Nevada," Fate 15 (Aug.1962):68,70.

North Ogden
-Skyquake
1977, Aug.29-Sep.1
Ogden Standard-Examiner, 30 Aug.1977;
and 2 Sep.1977.

Ogden
-Fall of unknown object
1957, Dec./Van E. Heninger
Kansas City (Mo.) Times, 18 Dec.1957.
-UFO (?)
1949, April 4/=aircraft
Bruce S. Maccabee, "UFO Related In-
formation from the FBI Files: Part
5," MUFON UFO J., no.124 (Mar.1978):
7,11.
1952, Nov.28/=aircraft?
U.S. Air Force, Projects Grudge and
Blue Book Reports 1-12 (Washington:
NICAP, 1968), p.172.
-UFO (NL)
1978, Nov.16/Randy Dalton
Ogden Standard-Examiner, 17 Nov.1978.

Park City
-Humanoids and ghosts
1880s
Wayland D. Hand, "Folklore from Utah's
Silver Mining Camps," J.Am.Folklore
54 (1941):132,142-46.

Price
-UFO (NL)
1966, Oct.8?
Brad Steiger, ed., Project Blue Book
(N.Y.: Ballantine, 1975), betw. pp.
56-57. il.

Provo
-UFO (DD)
1947, June 30/G.W. Eades/12 mi.N
Salt Lake City Deseret News, 1 July
1947.
1966, July/H. Williams/25 mi.SW
Edward U. Condon, ed., Scientific
Study of Unidentified Flying Objects
(N.Y.: Bantam, 1969 ed.), pp.270-73.
Hayden C. Hewes, "International Dead-
line," Can.UFO Rept., no.10 (1971):
18,19. il.

1978, Aug.12/nr. Sundance resort
Mildred Biesele, "Utah Notes," MUFON
UFO J., no.131 (Oct.1978):19.

Randlett
-UFO (CE-1)
1966, Aug.20/Gladys Cuch
Frank B. Salisbury, The Utah UFO Dis-
play (Old Greenwich, Ct.: Devin-
Adair, 1974), pp.18-19, and Appen-
dix B.
-UFO (CE-2)
1966, Sep.20/Priscilla Sireech
Frank B. Salisbury, The Utah UFO Dis-
play (Old Greenwich, Ct.: Devin-
Adair, 1974), p.23, and Appendix B.

Roosevelt
-UFO (CE-1)
1966, Sep.30/Kevin Ercanbrack/NE of
airport
1966, Oct.15/Freddie Gruenwald
1970, Dec./David Martin/Crescent Rd.
Frank B. Salisbury, The Utah UFO Dis-
play (Old Greenwich, Ct.: Devin-
Adair, 1974), pp.36-37,88-93, and
Appendix B.
-UFO (CE-2)
1978, Aug.10/Dale Wood/7 mi.NE
Salt Lake City Deseret News, 4 Sep.
1978.
Andrea Granum, "The Dale Wood Sighting: UFOs of the High Uintas," Saga
UFO Rept. 7 (Feb.1979):28-31.
-UFO (CE-3)
1963, spring/Sam Brough/3 mi.E
Frank B. Salisbury, The Utah UFO Display (Old Greenwich, Ct.: Devin-
Adair, 1974), p.17, and Appendix B.
-UFO (DD)
1965, July 20/Bill Locke/½ mi.W
1968, May 21/Carma Winterton/Union High
School
1973, March 16/David Hunt/N of town
Frank B. Salisbury, The Utah UFO Display (Old Greenwich, Ct.: Devin-
Adair, 1974), pp.61,95-96, and Appendix B.
-UFO (NL)
1966, March 2/Norma Denver/2 mi.E
1966, Sep./Verl Haslem/E of town
1967, Feb.23/Mrs. Clyde McDonald
1968, June 19
1970, Sep.4/Leland Mecham/2 mi.W
Frank B. Salisbury, The Utah UFO Display (Old Greenwich, Ct.: Devin
Adair, 1974), pp.25-28,38-39,61-62,
76-87, and Appendix B.
1978, Aug.21/Jimmy Justice/23 mi.SE
Salt Lake City Deseret News, 4 Sep.
1978.
Andrea Granum, "The Dale Wood Sighting: UFOs of the High Uintas," Saga
UFO Rept. 7 (Feb.1979):28,31.

Saint George
-Giant mummies
1947/F. Bruce Russell
L. Sprague de Camp, Lost Continents
(N.Y.: Dover, 1970 ed.), p.50.

William Peterson, "Dinosaur Tracks in the Roofs of Coal Mines," Natural History 24 (1924):388-91.

Tooele
-UFO (NL)
1977, Sep.7
"UFOs of Limited Merit," Int'l UFO Reporter 2 (Oct.1977):3.

Torrey
-UFO (NL)
1978, June 22/Martin Jones
Salt Lake City Deseret News, 23 June 1978.

Tremonton
-UFO (DD)
1952, July 2/Delbert C. Newhouse/7 mi. N on U.S.30
"An Open Letter, from Scientist, Exposes Truth in Detail of Famous Tremonton Film," CRIFO Newsl., 3 Sep. 1954, pp.3-4.
Edward J. Ruppelt, The Report on Unidentified Flying Objects (Garden City: Doubleday, 1956), pp.220-24, 228.
R.M.L. Baker, Jr., "Photogrammetric Analysis of the 'Utah' Film," Saucers, winter 1956-57.
Donald H. Menzel & Lyle G. Boyd, The World of Flying Saucers (Garden City: Doubleday, 1963), pp.130-32.
Richard Hall, ed., The UFO Evidence (Washington: NICAP, 1964), pp.88, 112.
Edward U. Condon, ed., Scientific Study of Unidentified Flying Objects (N.Y.: Bantam, 1969 ed.), pp.418-26, 905,911-13. il.
R.M.L. Baker, Jr., "Motion Pictures of UFO's," in Carl Sagan & Thornton Page, eds., UFO's: A Scientific Debate (Ithaca: Cornell Univ., 1972), pp.190,198-201. il.
William H. Spaulding, "Modern Image Processing Revisits the Great Falls, Montana and Tremonton, Utah Movies," in 1977 MUFON UFO Symposium Proc. (Seguin, Tex.: MUFON, 1977), pp.79-105. il.
J. Allen Hynek, The Hynek UFO Report (N.Y.: Dell, 1977), pp.235-39.
"Turner on Tremonton," Int'l UFO Reporter 3 (May 1978):6.

Vernal
-UFO (CE-1)
1967, Feb.27/Thyrena Daniels/W on Hwy. 40
Frank B. Salisbury, The Utah UFO Display (Old Greenwich, Ct.: Devin-Adair, 1974), pp.39-46.
-UFO (NL)
1966, Sep.7,10/Valda Massey
1966, Sep.26/Mrs. Ronald Batty/½ mi.NE
ca.1967/Richard Faucett/15 mi.N
Frank B. Salisbury, The Utah UFO Display (Old Greenwich, Ct.: Devin-

Adair, 1974), pp.19-22,24,71-72, and Appendix B.

Wasatch co.
-UFO (CE-2)
ca.1942, Oct./James P. Sharp/Hwy.40 x 30
Lucius Farish, "Before," Skylook, no.32 (July 1970):14.

Wattis
-Ancient coal mines
1953/Lion Coal Mine
"Utah Mystery: Prehistoric Mining?" Coal Age 59 (Feb.1954):111.

Whiterocks
-UFO (CE-1)
1966, Sep.15/James Cuch
Frank B. Salisbury, The Utah UFO Display (Old Greenwich, Ct.: Devin-Adair, 1974), pp.22-23.
-UFO (NL)
1968, June 19/Mr. Hackford
Frank B. Salisbury, The Utah UFO Display (Old Greenwich, Ct.: Devin-Adair, 1974), p.62.

Woods Cross
-Fall of ice
1965, Feb./Phillips Petroleum Plant
(Editorial), Fate 18 (June 1965):14.

B. Physical Features

Alkali Ridge
-Archeological site
ca.900-1400
John O. Brew, "Archaeology of Alkali Ridge, Southeastern Utah," Pap.Peabody Mus.Am.Arch.& Ethn., no.21 (1946).

Antelope Springs
-Human tracks in stone
1968/William J. Meister/=associated with trilobite fossils
Trenton (N.J.) Times, 14 July 1968.
William J. Meister, "Discovery of Trilobite Fossils in Shod Footprint of Human in 'Trilobite Beds,'" Creation Rsch.Soc'y Quar., Dec.1968.
Melvin Cook, "William J. Meister's Discovery of Human Footprint with Trilobites in a Cambrian Formation of Western Utah," Creation Rsch. Soc'y Quar., Dec.1968.

Bear L.
-Lake monster
1830-1876
Salt Lake City Deseret News, 27 July 1868; 3 Aug.1868; 25 Sep.1868; and 30 Oct.1868.
Phil Robinson, "Saunterings in Utah," Harper's New Monthly Mag. 67 (Oct. 1883):705-14.
Dale L. Morgan, The Great Salt Lake (Indianapolis: Bobbs-Merrill, 1947),

pp.380-84.
Austin E. Fife, "The Bear Lake Mon-
sters," Utah Humanities Rev. 1
(June 1948):99-106.
Peter Costello, In Search of Lake
Monsters (N.Y.: Coward, McCann &
Geoghegan, 1974), pp.212-16,281.

Black Rock Cave
-Archeological site
Julian H. Steward, "Ancient Caves of
the Great Salt Lake Region," Bull.
Bur.Am.Ethn. 116 (1937):106-23. il.

Buck Canyon
-UFO (NL)
1967, Sep.1/Lee Albertson
Frank B. Salisbury, The Utah UFO Dis-
play (Old Greenwich, Ct.: Devin-
Adair, 1974), pp.49-53.

Capitol Reef National Monument
-Petroglyphs
"Rock Art Documented by Utah Student,"
Pop.Arch. 3 (Nov.-Dec.1974):38-42.
il.
Franklin Folsom, America's Ancient
Treasures (N.Y.: Rand McNally,
1974), p.40.

Cedar Mts.
-Mystery horse deaths
1976, July/=nerve gas from proving
grounds?
Kansas City (Mo.) Star, 8 July 1976.
Washington (D.C.) Post, 3 Sep.1976.
"Horses Die at Dugway," Fortean Times,
no.23 (autumn 1977):3.

Clear Creek Canyon
-UFO (DD)
1965, Oct./V. Lee Oertle
Trevor James Constable, The Cosmic
Pulse of Life (Santa Ana: Merlin,
1976), betw. pp.206-207. il.

Colorado R.
-Petroglyph
=depicts rhinoceros or mastodon?
A. Hyatt Verrill, Strange Prehistoric
Animals and Their Stories (Boston:
I.C. Page, 1948). il.
John Guerrasio, "Dinosaur Graffiti--
Hava Supai Style," Pursuit 10
(spring 1977):62-63. il.
-Phantom wagon train
1865/Andy MacDonald/Upper Forks
Vincent H. Gaddis, "Caravan of the
Lost," Fate 2 (May 1949):36,37.

Confusion Range
-UFO (CE-2)
1968, Aug.29/Larry Sorenson/U.S.6
Frank B. Salisbury, The Utah UFO Dis-
play (Old Greenwich, Ct.: Devin-
Adair, 1974), pp.207-11.

Cuberant Basin
-Humanoid
1977, Aug./Jay Barker

Ogden Standard-Examiner, 25 Aug.1977.
Seattle (Wash.) Post-Intelligencer,
28 Aug.1977.

Danger Cave
-Archeological site
9500 B.C.-500 A.D.
Jesse D. Jennings, "Danger Cave," El
Palacio 60 (May 1953):179-213. il.
Jesse D. Jennings, "Danger Cave,"
Mem.Soc'y Am.Arch., vol.14 (1957).
Jesse D. Jennings, "Danger Cave,"
Anthro.Pap.Univ.Utah, vol.27 (1957).

Diamond Fork Canyon
-UFO (DD)
1947, June 26/Roy Freshwater
Salt Lake City Tribune, 6 July 1947.

Dry Fork Canyon
-Petroglyphs
=resemble Phoenicians?
Campbell Grant, Rock Art of the American Indian (N.Y.: Crowell, 1967),
pp.115-16. il.
Hugh Fox, Gods of the Cataclysm
(N.Y.: Harper's, 1976), pp.218-20.
il.

Elizabeth L.
-Humanoid
1977, July 10/Robert Melka
Bountiful Davis County Clipper, 2
Sep.1977.

Farm Creek
-UFO (NL)
1967, Oct.11/Dick Hackford
Frank B. Salisbury, The Utah UFO Dis-
play (Old Greenwich, Ct.: Devin-
Adair, 1974), p.56.

Farmington Bay
-UFO (DD)
1962, Oct.23/Farmington Bay Refuge
Thomas M. Olsen, ed., The Reference
for Outstanding UFO Sighting Reports
(Riderwood, Md.: UFO Information
Retrieval Center, 1966), p.82.

Grand Gulch
-Archeological site
Frank McNitt, Richard Wetherill: Ana-
sazi (Albuquerque: Univ. of New
Mexico, 1966), pp.61-72,153-63. il.
Franklin Folsom, America's Ancient
Treasures (N.Y.: Rand McNally, 1974),
pp.40-41.

Great Salt L.
-Lake monster
1877, July 8/J.H. McNeil
Corinne Record, 11 July 1877.
Salt Lake City Semi-Weekly Herald,
14 July 1877.
-Petroglyphs
"Pre-Egyptian Civilization?" Fate 6
(Aug.1953):86.

Halfway Hollow
-UFO (CE-1)
  1967, March 12/Tony Zufelt
  1973, March 23/Max Burdick
    Frank B. Salisbury, The Utah UFO Dis-
    play (Old Greenwich, Ct.: Devin-
    Adair, 1974), pp.46-48,96-97.
-UFO (NL)
  1967, Aug.24/Richard Faucett/=Venus?
  1967, Oct.14/Orvil Rudy
    Frank B. Salisbury, The Utah UFO Dis-
    play (Old Greenwich, Ct.: Devin-
    Adair, 1974), pp.53-55,70-71,75.

Hill Creek
-UFO (CE-1)
  1972, Oct./Frank Myore
    Frank B. Salisbury, The Utah UFO Dis-
    play (Old Greenwich, Ct.: Devin-
    Adair, 1974), p.94.

Hogup Cave
-Archeological site
    New York Times, 9 July 1968, p.12.
    C. Melvin Aikens, "Hogup Cave,"
    Anthro.Pap.Univ.Utah, no.93 (1970).
    Joel Gunn, "An Envirotechnological
    System for Hogup Cave," Am.Antiquity
    40 (1975):3-21.

Hovenweep
-Archeological site
  ca.400-1300 A.D.
    J. Walter Fewkes, "The Hovenweep
    National Monument," Ann.Rept.Smith.
    Inst., 1923, pp.465-80. il.
    Franklin Folsom, America's Ancient
    Treasures (N.Y.: Rand McNally, 1974),
    p.41.
    Ray A. Williamson, "Anasazi Solar
    Observatories," in Anthony F. Aveni,
    ed., Native American Astronomy (Aus-
    tin: Univ. of Texas, 1971), pp.213-
    14.

Indian Creek
-Petroglyph
  ca.900-1200 A.D.
    Franklin Folsom, America's Ancient
    Treasures (N.Y.: Rand McNally, 1974),
    p.41.

Kaiparowits Plateau
-Mystery rock markings
    J.E. Talmage, "Notes Concerning a
    Peculiarly Marked Sedimentary Rock,"
    J.Geology 4 (1896):653-54.

Nine Mile Canyon
-Archeological site and petroglyphs
  ca.500-1100 A.D.
    Noel Morss, "The Ancient Culture of
    the Fremont River in Utah," Pap.
    Peabody Mus.Am.Arch.& Ethn. 12, no.
    3 (1931). il.
    James H. Gunnerson, "An Archeologi-
    cal Survey of the Fremont Area,"
    Anthro.Pap.Univ.Utah, no.28 (1957).
    Wilfred M. Husted & Oscar L. Mallory,
    "The Fremont Culture: Its Derivation

and Ultimate Fate," Plains Anthro.
12 (1967):222-32.
Brad Steiger, Gods of Aquarius (N.Y.:
Harcourt Brace Jovanovich, 1976),
pp.21-22.

Pelican L.
-UFO (DD)
  1968, Nov.14/Morlin Buchanan
    Frank B. Salisbury, The Utah UFO Dis-
    play (Old Greenwich, Ct.: Devin-
    Adair, 1974), pp.63-69,72-76.

Provo Canyon
-Ringing rocks
    (Letter), Ruth Louise Partridge,
    Natural History 80 (Feb.1971):100.

Sevier L.
-Lake monster
  1873
    Decatur (Ill.) Republican, 10 June
    1873, quoting Salt Lake City Trib-
    une (undated).

Skull Valley
-Mystery sheep deaths
  1968, March/=Army nerve gas?
    David R. Saunders & R. Roger Harkins,
    UFOs? Yes! (N.Y.: Signet, 1968),
    p.169.
    (Editorial), Fate 23 (May 1969):12-
    15.

South Myton Bench
-UFO (CE-1)
  1965, Aug.9/Kent Denver
    Frank B. Salisbury, The Utah UFO Dis-
    play (Old Greenwich, Ct.: Devin-
    Adair, 1974), pp.17-18.

Tavaputs Plateau
-Petroglyph
  =depicts humanoid?
    Salt Lake City Tribune, 31 Jan.1971.

Totum Knob
-UFO (DD)
  1956, May 10/Harvey Mecham
    Salt Lake City Deseret News Telegram,
    12 May 1956.

Upheaval Dome
-Meteorite crater
  4800 m.diam./possible/=collapsed salt
  dome?
    T.S. Harrison, "Colorado-Utah Salt
    Domes," Bull.Am.Ass'n Petroleum
    Geologists, no.11 (1927):111-33.

Utah L.
-Lake monster
  1880s
    Phil Robinson, "Saunterings in Utah,"
    Harper's New Monthly Mag. 67 (Oct.
    1883):705-14.
-UFO (DD)
  1947, July 12/Earl Page
    "1947 Pilot Sighting Revealed," APRO
    Bull. 10 (May 1962):5.

Frank B. Salisbury, The Utah UFO Display (Old Greenwich, Ct.: Devin-
Adair, 1974), p. xvii.

Weber R.
-UFO (DD)
  1947, Sep./Frank J. Falkner
    (Letter), Fate 6 (July 1953):109-12.

        D. Unspecified Localities

-Ancient ceremonial shields
  1937/E.P. Pectol
    "Pre-Egyptian Civilization," Fate 6
    (Aug.1953):86.

-Ghost light
  ca.1910
    (Letter), Hazel Johnson, Fate 19
    (Oct.1966):160-61.

-Phantoms (myth)
    Austin E. Fife, "The Legend of the
    Three Nephites Among the Mormons,"
    J.Am.Folklore 53 (1940):1-49.
    W.D. Hand, "The Three Nephites," Am.
    Notes & Queries 2 (1942):56-57.
    Hector Lee, The Three Nephites (Al-
    buquerque: Univ. of New Mexico,
    Pub.in Language & Literature, no.2,
    1949).
    Austin & Alta Fife, Saints of Sage
    and Saddle (Bloomington: Indiana
    Univ., 1956), pp.233-49.

ARIZONA

A. Populated Places

Alto
-Ghost light
  1940s
    Union High School, Patagonia, "Folk
    Tales from the Patagonia Area, San-
    ta Cruz Co., Arizona," General Bull.
    Univ.Arizona, no.13 (1949):13.

Amado
-Weather control
  ca.1974/L.A. Farrar/rain rock
    (Letter), Fate 27 (Sep.1974):130-31.

Apache co.
-Cattle mutilation
  1975/Art Lee
    Ed Sanders, "The Mutilation Mystery,"
    Oui, Sep.1976, pp.51,120.

Apache Junction
-UFO (CE-1)
  1970, June 2/Lulu Luebben/Lu-Roy Lane
    Apache Sentinel, 10 June 1970.
-UFO (CE-2)
  1965/=hoax?
    "New Physical Evidence Case," APRO
    Bull. 18 (Jan.-Feb.1970):1,3.
    Walter W. Walker, "The Apache Junct-
    ion Physical Evidence Case," APRO
    Bull. 18 (May-June 1970):1,4.
-UFO (CE-4)
  1971, March 14/Brian Scott
  1973, March 21/Brian Scott
    Alvin H. Lawson, "Hypnotic Regression
    of Alleged CE-III Cases: Ambiguities
    on the Road to UFOs," in Proc.1976
    CUFOS Conference (Evanston: Center
    for UFO Studies, 1976), pp.141-51.
    Peter Guttilla & James Frazier, "Al-
    ien Possession: Strange Saga of
    Brian Scott and the UFO Mind Manipu-
    lators," Saga UFO Rept. 4 (July
    1977):42-45.
    John de Herrera, The Etherian Inva-
    sion (Los Alamitos: Hwong, 1978).

Ash Fork
-Human tracks in stone
    Clifford Burdick, The Challenge of
    Creation (Caldwell, Id.: Bible-Sci-
    ence Ass'n, 1965).

Aztec
-UFO (CE-4)
  1977, Nov.14
    Ted Bloecher, "A Survey of CE3K Re-
    ports for 1977," in 1978 MUFON Sym-
    posium Proc. (Seguin, Tex.: MUFON,
    1978), pp.14,36.

Bisbee
-UFO (DD)

Black Canyon
1947, June 27/George B. Wilcox
1947, June 27/John A. Petsche/Denn
Shaft, Phelps-Dodge mines
    Coral E. Lorenzen, Flying Saucers:
    The Startling Evidence of the Inva-
    sion from Outer Space (N.Y.: Sig-
    net, 1966 ed.), pp.17-18.

Black Canyon
-UFO (NL)
  1965, June 3/Black Canyon Hwy.
    Coral E. Lorenzen, Flying Saucers:
    The Startling Evidence of the Inva-
    sion from Outer Space (N.Y.: Sig-
    net, 1966 ed.), p.236.
  1971, Dec.14/S on I-17
    (Letter), M.V., Can.UFO Rept., no.12
    (1972):32.

Buckeye
-Fall of phosphorus
  1965, Dec.20/George Hamner
    (Editorial), Fate 19 (May 1966):30-
    31, quoting Phoenix Sun (undated).
-Precognition
  1962, April 1/Clement Kelly, Jr.
    (Editorial), Fate 15 (Aug.1962):10.
-UFO (?)
  1969, Dec.17/Larry Rankin/30 mi.SW
    "Bright Red Flash Observed in Ari-
    zona," Skylook, no.26 (Jan.1970):17,
    quoting Phoenix Gazette (undated).

Bylas
-UFO (CE-2)
  1974, July 24/Paul Anderson
    "Flap in Arizona," APRO Bull. 23
    (July-Aug.1974):1,3.

Catalina
-UFO (DD)
  1967, March 24/Observatory
    "Astronomers and UFO's: A Survey,"
    Int'l UFO Reporter 2 (Apr.1977):3-4.

Chandler
-UFO (CE-1)
  1975, July 20/William B. Royce/Williams
  AFB
    Rufus Drake, "Air Force Base Besieged
    by Saucers," Saga UFO Rept. 4 (July
    1977):37-38.
-UFO (CE-2)
  n.d./Williams AFB (Flat Rock)
    Lawrence J. Fenwick, "UFO Fragments
    Said To Be Recovered after Collis-
    ion," Can.UFO Rept., no.28 (summer
    1977):5-6.
-UFO (CE-3)
  1976, Jan./James B. Pitrelli/Baseline
  Rd.
    Rufus Drake, "Air Force Base Besieged
    by Saucers," Saga UFO Rept. 4 (July
    1977):37,57-58.

-UFO (DD)
  1947, July 1/Robert E. Johnson/E of
  town
    Tucson Daily Citizen, 7 July 1947.
  1976, May 13/Williams AFB
    Rufus Drake, "Air Force Base Besieged
    by Saucers," Saga UFO Rept. 4 (July
    1977):37,57.
-UFO (R-V)
  1970, April 4/Williams AFB
    Rufus Drake, "Air Force Base Besieged
    by Saucers," Saga UFO Rept. 4 (July
    1977):37,39,56-57.

Childs
-UFO (CE-1)
  1975, Jan.13, 25/Mrs. Jack Soulages
    Raymond Jordan, "1975 UFO Wave in
    Arizona," APRO Bull. 24 (Apr.1976):
    5.

Chino Valley
-Clairvoyance
  1964, March 8/Virgil Maxwell
    Mary Margaret Fuller, "Dreams of the
    Lost," Fate 17 (Aug.1964):85-86.

Clarkdale
-Archeological site
  1000-1400/Tuzigoot/2 mi.E
    Edward H. Spicer & Louis R. Caywood,
    "Two Pueblo Ruins in West Central
    Arizona," Soc.Sci.Bull.Univ.Arizona,
    no.10 (1936).
-Ghost cat
  1920, July/Charles C. Stemmer
    Charles C. Stemmer, "Animals Live in
    Spirit Too," Fate 13 (Dec.1960):87,
    89-90.

Cleator
-UFO (NL)
  1962, Feb./Al Hubbard/Zeno mine
    Frank Edwards, "Mystery Blast over
    Nevada," Fate 15 (Aug.1962):68,72-
    73.

Clifton
-Entombed beetle
  1892/Z.T. White/Longfellow mine
    Henry Winfred Splitter, "The Impos-
    sible Fossils," Fate 7 (Jan.1954):
    65,68-69, quoting El Paso (Tex.)
    Bulletin (undated).

Cochise
-UFO (?)
  1955
    Jacques Vallee, Anatomy of a Phenom-
    enon (N.Y.: Ace, 1965 ed.), p.114.

Cochise co.
-Cattle mutilation
  1977, Jan.
    "Recent Mutes 1977," Cattle Report,
    no.1 (Mar.1977):3, quoting Bisbee
    Daily Review (undated).

Cochran
-Ancient mining

=probable date 1880s
  Ronald L. Ives, "The Cochran Coke
  Ovens," J.Arizona History 13 (sum-
  mer 1972):73-81. il.

Colorado City
-Dowsing
  1973, Oct./Sam Barlow
    "Divining Rod Solves Thefts," Fate
    27 (Nov.1974):57.

Coolidge
-Archeological site
  ca.900-1450/Casa Grande
    A.F. Bandelier, "Contributions to
    the History of the Southwestern Por-
    tion of the United States," Pap.
    Arch.Inst.Am., vol.5 (1890).
    Cosmos Mindeleff, "Casa Grande Ruin,"
    Ann.Rept.Bur.Am.Ethn. 13 (1896):
    289-319.
    Jesse Walter Fewkes, "Archaeological
    Expedition to Arizona in 1895," Ann.
    Rept.Bur.Am.Ethn. 17 (1898):527-741.
    Freda Holloran, "Mystery Indians and
    Their Skyscraper," Fate 6 (Oct.1953)
    :54-59. il.
    Harold Sterling Gladwin, A History
    of the Ancient Southwest (Portland,
    Me.: Bond Wheelright, 1957), pp.
    252-68. il.
    Frank Midvale, "Prehistoric Irriga-
    tion of the Casa Grande Ruins Area,"
    Kiva 30 (Feb.1965):82-86.
    Paul S. Martin & Fred Plog, Archaeol-
    ogy of Arizona (Garden City: Doub-
    leday, 1973), pp.313-17.
    Robert D. Hicks III, "Astronomy in
    the Ancient Americas," Sky & Tele-
    scope 51 (June 1976):372-78.
    Jim Brandon, Weird America (N.Y.:
    Dutton, 1978), pp.4-5.
    Scottsdale Daily Progress, 17 Aug.
    1978.
-Electromagnetic anomaly
  1952, April 10
    Los Angeles (Cal.) Times, 11 Apr.
    1952.

Copper Mines
-UFO (NL)
  1965, June 3/Edward Coyle
    Coral E. Lorenzen, Flying Saucers:
    The Startling Evidence of the Inva-
    sion from Outer Space (N.Y.: Sig-
    net, 1966 ed.), p.236.

Cottonwood
-Ghost dog
  1917, June/Charles C. Stemmer
    Charles C. Stemmer, "Animals Live in
    Spirit Too," Fate 13 (Dec.1960):87,
    89.
-Phantom image
  1925, April/Charles C. Stemmer
    Charles C. Stemmer, "Blood on My
    Hands?" Fate 9 (Sep.1956):69-75.

Crittenden
-Giant sarcophagus

1891
   Salt Lake City (Utah) Deseret Weekly,
   14 Mar.1891.

Douglas
-UFO (DD)
   1947, July 8/Mrs. Ray Wilder
   1947, July 10/Mrs. L.B. Ogle
      Coral E. Lorenzen, Flying Saucers:
      The Startling Evidence of the Inva-
      sion from Outer Space (N.Y.: Sig-
      net, 1966 ed.), pp.19-20, quoting
      Douglas Dispatch (undated).
-UFO (NL)
   1947, June 10/Coral E. Lorenzen
   1947, July 11/Mrs. W.P. Hopkins/15th
   St. Park
   1947, Aug./B.L. Fields
      Coral E. Lorenzen, Flying Saucers:
      The Startling Evidence of the Inva-
      sion from Outer Space (N.Y.: Sig-
      net, 1966 ed.), pp.16-17,20.

Fairbank
-Archeological site
   George S. Cattanack, Jr., "A San Pedro Stage Site near Fairbank, Arizona," Kiva 32, no.1 (1966):1-24.

Flagstaff
-Cloud anomaly
   1963, Feb.28
      "Rainbow of Moonbeams...and a High
      Cloud Ring of Mystery," Life, 17
      May 1963, pp.111-12. il.
-Humanoid
   1971, Jan.23
      Flagstaff Daily Sun, 23 Jan.1971.
-Skyquake
   1959, Feb.12/Bill Hoyt
      (Editorial), Fate 12 (July 1959):12-
      14, quoting Flagstaff Arizona Daily
      Sun (undated).
-UFO (CE-2)
   1975, Nov.7
      "UFO Central," CUFOS News Bull., 1
      Feb.1976, p.12.
-UFO (DD)
   1950, May 20/Seymour L. Hess/Lowell Observatory
      Richard Hall, ed., The UFO Evidence
      (Washington: NICAP, 1964), p.3.
   1953, Dec.2/Calvin B. Decker
      "Reports from Everywhere," Fate 7
      (May 1954):29, quoting Flagstaff
      Arizona Daily Sun (undated).
-UFO (NL)
   1960, Oct./Henry L. Giglas/Lowell Observatory
      Harlan Wilson, "Strange Case of the
      Mystery Satellite," Fate 14 (June
      1961):25,28-29.
   1975, Oct.16
   1975, Dec.28/White R.
      "UFO Central," CUFOS News Bull., 1
      Feb.1976, pp.9,15.

Florence
-Anomalous artifact
   1883/SE of town/=china teacups at great

depth
   Tombstone Epitaph, 18 Oct.1903.
-UFO (DD)
   1978, March 6/Jerry Ysaguerre
      "'Garbage Can Lid' over Arizona,"
      APRO Bull. 26 (Mar.1978):1,3.

Fort Huachuca
-UFO (?)
   1950s
      Coral E. Lorenzen, Flying Saucers:
      The Startling Evidence of the Inva-
      sion from Outer Space (N.Y.: Sig-
      net, 1966 ed.), p.40.
-UFO (NL)
   1974, Aug.1
      "Flap in Arizona," APRO Bull. 23
      (July-Aug.1974):1,3.

Gila Bend
-Archeological site
   1000-1500/Gatlin site
      William W. Wasley, "A Hohokam Plat-
      form Mound at the Gatlin Site, Gila
      Bend, Arizona," Am.Antiquity 26
      (1960):244-62.
-Paranormal strength
   1929, Aug.30/John V. Haggard/W of town
      John V. Haggard, "A Surge of Super-
      human Strength," Fate 31 (Oct.1978)
      :73-74.

Glendale
-UFO (DD)
   1953, March 3/Roderick D. Thompson/W
   of Luke AFB
      Edward J. Ruppelt, The Report on Un-
      identified Flying Objects (Garden
      City: Doubleday, 1956), pp.229-31.
      Frank Bowers, ed., The True Report
      on Flying Saucers (Greenwich, Ct.:
      Fawcett, 1967), p.82. il.
      U.S. Air Force, Projects Grudge and
      Blue Book Reports 1-12 (Washington:
      NICAP, 1968), pp.208-209.

Globe
-Phantom dogs
   1930/Jean W. Floyd
      Jean W. Floyd, "Dogs of Death," Fate
      8 (Oct.1955):75.
-UFO (CE-3)
   1960, June 9/15 mi.E
      Coral & Jim Lorenzen, UFO Occupants
      (N.Y.: Signet, 1967), pp.128-29.

Heber
-UFO (CE-4)
   1975, Nov.5/Travis Walton/10½ mi.S
      Phoenix Arizona Republic, 11-12 Nov.
      1975; and 12 July 1976.
      Phoenix Gazette, 12 Nov.1975; and 23
      Mar.1976.
      "The Travis Walton Case," APRO Bull.
      24 (Nov.1975):1-5. il.
      Jim & Coral Lorenzen, "Walton Takes
      Polygraph Test," APRO Bull. 24 (Dec.
      1975):1,3.
      "Alleged Arizona Abduction Case Stud-
      ied," Skylook, no.97 (Dec.1975):3-6.

"Follow-Up," APRO Bull. 24 (Feb. 1976):1,4.

"APRO, NICAP, GSW Reports Disagree," Skylook, no.99 (Feb.1976):5-7.

"More Walton Verification," APRO Bull. 24 (Mar.1976):1,4-5.

Travis Walton, "Walton Explains Controversies," Skylook, no.101 (Apr. 1976):7-8.

Michael Rogers, "Painting Depicts Experience," Skylook, no.101 (Apr. 1976):9.

"The Walton-Klass Controversy," APRO Bull. 25 (July 1976):1,4-5; (Aug. 1976):1,3-5.

Philip J. Klass, "The Travis Walton Abduction," MUFON UFO J., no.104 (July 1976):8-12; no.105 (Aug.1976) :8-14.

James E. Oberg, "The Travis Walton Controversy: Philip Klass," Official UFO 2 (Feb.1977):18,42-47.

James E. Oberg, "The Travis Walton Controversy: Jim Lorenzen," Official UFO 2 (Mar.1977):32-33,52-56.

Coral and Jim Lorenzen, Abducted! (N.Y.: Berkley, 1977), pp.80-113, 161-90.

Travis Walton, The Walton Experience (N.Y.: Berkley, 1978). il.

Bill Barry, The Ultimate Encounter (N.Y.: Pocket, 1978). il.

Jerome Clark, "UFO Abductee Tells the Truth," Fate 31 (Oct.1978):54-62.

Hayden C. Hewes, "Through a Glass Darkly," Saga UFO Rept. 7 (May 1979) :26-27,70-72.

Holbrook
-Earthquake anomaly
1912, Aug.18
    C.F. Tolman, Jr., "An Arizona Earthquake," Bull.Seism.Soc'y Am. 2 (1912):209.
-Fall of anomalous meteorite
1912, July 19
    Warren M. Foote, "Preliminary Note on the Shower of Meteoric Stones near Holbrook," Am.J.Sci., ser.4, 34 (1912):437-56.
    George P. Merrill, "A Recent Meteorite Fall near Holbrook, Navajo County, Arizona," Smith.Misc.Coll., vol.60, no.9 (1912).
    Brian Mason & H.B. Wiik, "The Holbrook, Arizona, Chondrite," Geochimica et Cosmochimica Acta 21 (1961): 276-83.

Hotevilla
-UFO (CE-3)
1969/Titus Lamson
    Jerome Clark & Loren Coleman, The Unidentified (N.Y.: Warner, 1975), p. 215.

Joseph City
-UFO (DD)
1955, March 28/Glenn Blansett

"The Undisciplined Formation over Arizona," CRIFO Newsl., 6 May 1955, p.6.

Keams Canyon
-UFO (CE-2)
1975, Aug.17
    William H. Spaulding, "Arizona Patrol Officer Reports EM Effects," Skylook, no.97 (Dec.1975):6-7.

Kearny
-UFO (?)
1958/=Venus
    Coral & Jim Lorenzen, UFOs: The Whole Story (N.Y.: Signet, 1969), pp.140-44.

Kingman
-UFO (?)
1945, Nov./Edward W. Joyce, Jr.
    Letter from Edward W. Joyce, Jr., to Civilian Saucer Investigation, 4 Mar.1952, in Lucius Farish's files.
-UFO (CE-1)
1974, March 27
    "UFO-Car Encounters Continue," APRO Bull. 23 (June 1975):1.
-UFO (CE-3)
1953, May/crashed UFO
    Raymond E. Fowler, "What About Crashed UFOs?" Official UFO 1 (Apr. 1976):24,55-58.
    Leonard H. Stringfield, Situation Red: The UFO Siege (N.Y.: Fawcett, 1977), pp.208-14.
    Leonard H. Stringfield, "Retrievals of the Third Kind," in 1978 MUFON Symposium Proc. (Seguin, Tex.: MUFON, 1978), pp.77,87-89.
1968, Oct.15
    David Webb & Ted Bloecher, "MUFON's Humanoid Study Group Very Active," Skylook, no.93 (Aug.1975):10.
-UFO (NL)
1967, Feb.16/Max Recod/S on U.S.66
    "Sighting Evidence Grows," UFO Inv. 4 (Nov.-Dec.1967):1,3.
1975, Dec.15
    "UFO Central," CUFOS News Bull., 1 Feb.1976, p.15.

Kinishba
-Archeological site
1100-1350
    Gordon C. Baldwin, "The Excavation at Kinishba," Am.Antiquity 4 (1938) :11-21. il.

Lake Havasu City
-UFO (DD)
1969, March 17/Herman Slater/12 mi. from town
    Phoenix Gazette, 21 Mar.1969.
    "Large UFO Formation over Arizona," APRO Bull. 17 (Mar.-Apr.1969):1,4.

Laveen
-Petroglyphs
    Elizabeth L. Coombs, "The Leveen

Petroglyphs, Arizona," <u>NEARA J.</u> 13
(fall 1978):37-40. il.

Lukachukai
-Archeological site
  Lost City of Lukachukai
    Ann Axtell Morris, <u>Digging in the
    Southwest</u> (Garden City: Doubleday,
    1933), pp.290-301.
    C.W. Ceram, <u>The First American</u> (N.Y.:
    Mentor, 1972 ed.), pp.197-99.

Marana
-UFO (DD)
  1952, April 3/airport
    Bisbee Daily Review, 4 Apr.1952.
    U.S. Air Force, <u>Projects Grudge and
    Blue Book Reports 1-12</u> (Washington:
    NICAP, 1968), pp.102,107,112.
-UFO (NL)
  1974, Aug.21/Chamma tewa Buck
    "Flap in Arizona," <u>APRO Bull.</u> 23
    (July-Aug.1974):1,4-5.

Mesa
-Hex
  1942-1952, Sep./Maria Miranda
    "No Other Cure," <u>Fate</u> 6 (Feb.1953):
    38.
-Psychokinesis
  1969, Oct.25/Richard Webb/Velda Rose
  Motel
    Richard Webb, <u>Voices from Another
    World</u> (N.Y.: Manor, 1972 ed.), pp.
    148-50.
-UFO (DD)
  1965, Aug.9/Mrs. Charles Biggs
    Jerome Clark, "The Greatest Flap Yet?
    --Part 2," <u>Flying Saucer Rev.</u> 12
    (Mar.-Apr.1966):9.
  1972, Nov.11/Lee Elders
    Wendelle C. Stevens, "Domed Cone
    UFOs," <u>APRO Bull.</u> 26 (July 1977):
    1,3-4. il.
-UFO (NL)
  1960, Aug.26/Clete L. Miller
    Richard Hall, ed., <u>The UFO Evidence</u>
    (Washington: NICAP, 1964), pp.68-69.
  1975, July 20/Gerald Taylor/I-10
    Rufus Drake, "Air Force Base Besieged
    by Saucers," <u>Saga UFO Rept.</u> 4 (July
    1977):37.
  1975, Nov.10
    "UFO Central," <u>CUFOS News Bull.</u>, 1
    Feb.1976, p.12.

Mishongnovi
-Petroglyph
  =depicts UFOs?
    Brad Steiger, "American Indians and
    the Star People," <u>Saga UFO Rept.</u> 3
    (June 1976):33-34.
-Weather control
  1935, Aug.23/Hopi Indians
    Eugene Grossenheider, "Does Man Make
    the Weather?" <u>Fate</u> 9 (Feb.1956):80,
    81.

Montezuma Castle
-Archeological site

600-1450
  Victor Mindeleff, "A Study of Pueblo
  Archaeology: Tusayan and Cibola,"
  Ann.Rept.Bur.Am.Ethn. 8 (1886):3-
  228.
  Harold S. Colton, "The Sinagua: A
  Summary of the Archaeology of the
  Region of Flagstaff, Arizona," <u>Bull.
  Mus.N.Arizona</u>, no.22 (1946).
  Earl Jackson & Sallie Pierce Van Val-
  kenbrugh, <u>Montezuma Castle Archeol-
  ogy</u> (Globe, Ariz.: Southwestern
  Monuments Ass'n, Tech.Ser., vol.3,
  no.1, 1954). il.
  Harold S. Colton, <u>Black Sand: Pre-
  history in Northern Arizona</u> (Albu-
  querque: Univ. of New Mexico, 1960).
  David A. Breternitz, "Excavations at
  Three Sites in the Verde Valley,
  Arizona," <u>Bull.Mus.N.Arizona</u>, no.
  34 (1960).
  George Hunt Williamson, <u>Secret Places of the Lion</u> (N.Y.: Warner,
  1977 ed.), pp.228-31.

Naco
-Archeological site
  ca.10,000 B.C.
    Emil Haury, "Artifacts with Mammoth
    Remains, Naco, Arizona," <u>Am.Antiq-
    uity</u> 19 (1953):1-14.

Nogales
-UFO (DD)
  1947, July 9/Guy Fuller
    Coral E. Lorenzen, <u>Flying Saucers:
    The Startling Evidence of the Inva-
    sion from Outer Space</u> (N.Y.: Sig-
    net, 1966 ed.), p.20.
-UFO (NL)
  1972, Aug.20/Helen Sutherlin
    "Incident at Nogales, Arizona," <u>APRO
    Bull.</u> 21 (Nov.-Dec.1972):1,3-4. il.
    "Follow-Ups," <u>APRO Bull.</u> 21 (Jan.-
    Feb.1973):4. il.

Oracle
-UFO (NL)
  1962, Aug.7/Titan missile site
    Coral & Jim Lorenzen, <u>UFOs: The Whole
    Story</u> (N.Y.: Signet, 1969), pp.235-
    36.

Oraibi
-Archeological site
  1100-present
    Franklin Folsom, <u>America's Ancient
    Treasures</u> (N.Y.: Rand McNally, 1974),
    p.19.

Paradise Valley
-UFO (NL)
  1974, July 22/Dorothy Tessmer
    Phoenix Gazette, 26 July 1974.
    W.J. Hart, "'Cluster' UFO over Ari-
    zona," <u>APRO Bull.</u> 23 (May 1975):2,4.

Parker
-Erratic crocodilian
  1943, June/Tommy Kinder/Colorado R.

Raymond S. Hock, "The Alligator in
Arizona," Copeia, 1954, pp.222-23.
-UFO (CE-2)
1953, April 9/Lucille Revels/15 mi.W
(Letter), Fate 7 (Nov.1952):112-14.

Payson
-Archeological site
9000 B.C.-1600 A.D.
Phoenix Arizona Republic, 28 May
1978.

Phoenix
-Acoustic anomaly
1964/Sunland School
(Editorial), Fate 18 (May 1965):26.
-Aerial phantom
1971, Dec./Estelle Holfinger
(Letter), Fate 25 (Oct.1972):145.
-Animal ESP
1955-1960/William Esenwein
William Esenwein, "Telepathy with
Rattlesnakes," Fate 14 (Feb.1961):
45-54.
-Archeological site
300 B.C.-1450 A.D./Pueblo Grande/4619
E. Washington St./Park of the Four
Waters
F.W. Hodge, "Prehistoric Irrigation
in Arizona," Am.Anthro. 6 (1893):
323-30.
O.A. Turney, Prehistoric Irrigation
in Arizona (Phoenix: Arizona State
Historian, 1929).
Richard B. Woodbury, "The Hohokam
Canals at Pueblo Grande, Arizona,"
Am.Antiquity 26 (1960):267-70.
Frank Midvale, "Prehistoric Irriga-
tion in the Salt River Valley, Ari-
zona," Kiva 34, no.1 (1968):28-32.
Paul S. Martin & Fred Plog, The Arch-
eology of Arizona (Garden City:
Doubleday, 1973), pp.175,269-70.
Phoenix Arizona Republic, 19 Mar.
1976; and 4 Feb.1977.
Phoenix Gazette, 7 Jan.1977.
-Contactee
1966, Oct.1-1970s
Brad Steiger, Revelation: The Divine
Fire (Englewood Cliffs, N.J.: Pren-
tice-Hall, 1973), pp.143-51,161-62.
-Dowsing
1958/Landon C. Himes
"The Modern Divining Rod," Fate 11
(Sep.1958):36.
-Fire immunity
1975, March/Komar (Vernon Craig)/Phoe-
nix Psychic Seminar
Wanda Sue Parrott, "Gift from the
Hindu Fakir Cheesemaker," Fate 29
(Dec.1976):74-76.
(Letter), William J. Finch, Fate 30
(Apr.1977):115-16.
-Haunt
1932, Nov./Florence Emick
Florence Emick, "Mama Buried the
Haunted Bone," Fate 32 (Mar.1979):
66-69.
1961-1962/Bob Young
(Editorial), Fate 16 (Feb.1963):15-

16, quoting Phoenix Arizona Repub-
lic (undated).
-Healing
1970-   /A.R.E. Clinic/4018 N. 40th
Robert Neubert, "Healing by the Cay-
ce Readings: The A.R.E. Clinic,"
Psychic 5 (Jan.-Feb.1974):21-25. il.
David St. Clair, Psychic Healers
(Garden City: Doubleday, 1974), pp.
289-307.
Kansas City (Mo.) Star, 9 Oct.1974.
-Hex
1962
Bill D. Schul, "The Link," Probe the
Unknown 1 (Dec.1973):34,38.
-Inner development
1952-1955/L. Ron Hubbard
L. Ron Hubbard, Dianetics (N.Y.: Her-
mitage, 1950).
John Godwin, Occult America (Garden
City: Doubleday, 1972), pp.86-88.
-Mystery plane crash
1957, April 21/DC-3
Leonard H. Stringfield, Inside Sau-
cer Post...3-0 Blue (Cincinnati:
CRIFO, 1957), p.32n, quoting Cincin-
nati Post (undated).
-Parapsychology research
1966-1971/James Kidd's will
Mary Margaret Fuller, "$233,000...
for a Soul Search," Fate 21 (Apr.
1968):76-89. il.
John G. Fuller, The Great Soul Trial
(N.Y.: Macmillan, 1968).
(Editorial), Fate 24 (Aug.1971):26-
32.
(Editorial), Fate 28 (Oct.1975):22.
-Phantom
1957, March 18/Llewelyn Jarman/E. In-
dian School Rd.
(Editorial), Fate 10 (Aug.1957):15.
1968, Feb.26
John A. Keel, Strange Creatures from
Time and Space (Greenwich, Ct.:
Fawcett, 1970), p.191.
-Possession
n.d./Brother Paul (exorcist)
Jerome Wilson Lloyd, "Giving the Devil His Due," Probe the Unknown 2
(summer 1974):12,16-17,60.
-Precognition
1970s/Gil E. Gilly/4822 N. 27th Ave.
1970s/Louis Anthony Russo/Box 5888
Warren Smith, "Phenomenal Predictions
for 1975," Saga, Jan.1975, pp.20,23,
52.
Warren Smith, "Phenomenal Predictions
for 1976," Saga, Jan.1976, pp.16,18,
52.
-Retrocognition
1970, Dec.28-1971, Jan.1/Mervin Hock-
enberry/Van Buren St.
Phoenix Arizona Republic, 10 Jan.
1971.
William G. Allen, "Arizona's Psychic
Detective," Fate 24 (Aug.1971):88-
92.
-Skyquake
1978, Nov.21
Phoenix Gazette, 21 Nov.1978.

-UFO (?)
  1896, Dec./G. Purdy/=meteor?
    Los Angeles (Cal.) Record, 9 Dec.
    1896.
  1956, July 19
    Richard Hall, ed., The UFO Evidence
    (Washington: NICAP, 1964), p.150.
  1958, March
    Robert N. Webster, "Things That Fall
    from UFO's," Fate 11 (Oct.1958):25,
    29.
  1978, Oct.29/Hal Starr/=meteor
    "Bright Fireball over Arizona," APRO
    Bull. 27 (Nov.1978):4.
-UFO (CE-1)
  1978, Feb.2/11th Place
    "CE I Case in Phoenix, Arizona,"
    APRO Bull. 26 (Mar.1978):1-3.
-UFO (CE-2)
  1963, May?/E. Portland x 12th St.
    "CE-II Encounter in Phoenix, Arizona,"
    APRO Bull. 26 (Apr.1978):1-3.
-UFO (CE-4)
  1973, June 23
    David Webb, "Analysis of Humanoid/Ab-
    duction Reports," in Proc.1976 CUFOS
    Conference (Evanston: Center for
    UFO Studies, 1976), pp.270-71.
-UFO (DD)
  1947, July 7/William A. Rhoades/4333 N.
  14th St.
    Phoenix Arizona Republic, 9 July
    1947, p.1. il.
    (Letter), Fate 1 (fall 1948):121.
    Kenneth Arnold & Ray Palmer, The Com-
    ing of the Saucers (Boise: The Auth-
    ors, 1952), pp.164-65. il.
    Ted Bloecher, Report on the UFO Wave
    of 1947 (Washington: NICAP, 1967),
    p.IV-4. il.
    E.U. Condon, "UFOs: 1947-1968," in
    Edward U. Condon, ed., Scientific
    Study of Unidentified Flying Objects
    (N.Y.: Bantam, 1969 ed.), pp.502,
    508.
    Hayden C. Hewes, "The Rhoades UFO,"
    Saga UFO Rept. 6 (Oct.1978):40-43.
    il.
  1947, July 7/Heard Bldg.
    Phoenix Arizona Republic, 8 July
    1947.
  1948, Aug.15/Walter H. Andrus, Jr.
    Report on file at MUFON.
  1951, Nov.4/Cassian Brenner
    Philip J. Klass, UFOs: Identified
    (N.Y.: Random House, 1968), pp.178-
    80.
  1971, March 11/William J. Finch
    "Double Sphere Watched over Phoenix,"
    Skylook, no.41 (Apr.1971):11.
  1972, Sep.12/Dale Faut/N of town
    Hayden C. Hewes, "The Phoenix Day-
    light Disc," Saga UFO Rept. 6 (Sep.
    1978):28-31. il.
-UFO (NL)
  1920s/James T. Kirk/nr. Barber's Pro-
  duce Market
    Jerome Clark & Lucius Farish, "UFOs
    of the Roaring 20s," Saga UFO Rept.
    2 (fall 1975):48,60.

1947, July/Frank Nunn
  San Francisco (Cal.) Chronicle, 3
  July 1947.
1951, Sep.9-10/South Mt.
  Robert N. Webster, "Let's Get Up to
  Date on the Flying Saucers," Fate
  5 (Jan.1952):7, quoting Phoenix
  Gazette (undated).
1952, April 15
  Phoenix Arizona Republic, 17 Apr.
  1952.
1964, Aug.29/South Mt.
  Phoenix Arizona Republic, 30 Aug.
  1969.
1969, Jan.11
  Phoenix Arizona Republic, 13 Jan.
  1969.
1977, Sep.21/Jim Ray, Jr.
  "Eight Objects over Phoenix," APRO
  Bull. 26 (Aug.1977):4. il.
  "UFOs of Limited Merit," Int'l UFO
  Reporter 2 (Nov.1977):3.
-UFO (R-V)
  1950, June 29
    Bruce S. Maccabee, "UFO Related In-
    formation from the FBI Files: Part
    7," MUFON UFO J., no.132 (Nov.-Dec.
    1978):11,14.
-Weather control
  1959, Dec./Westward Ho Motel
    (Editorial), Fate 14 (Jan.1961):24-
    26, quoting Albuquerque (N.M.) Tri-
    bune (undated).

Pima
-Archeological site
  Donald A. Johnson, "Rocky Mountain
  Medicine Wheels: Part II," INFO J.,
  no.24 (July-Aug.1977):12.

Polacca
-Humanoid
  1979, Feb./Polacca Wash
    Phoenix Arizona Republic, 10 Feb.
    1979.

Portal
-UFO (NL)
  1957, Oct.6/Carson Morrow
    "Saucers in the News," Flying Saucers,
    Feb.1958, p.75.

Prescott
-Animal ESP
  1962/Dora Sessions Lee
    (Editorial), Fate 15 (Oct.1962):12-
    13, quoting Phoenix Arizona Repub-
    lic (undated).
-Precognition
  1924, Jan.17/Isabel Cyra
    William Crocker, "A Vision and Its
    Subsequent Fulfilment," J.ASPR 19
    (1925):248-58.
    Edmond P. Gibson, "Murder Foreseen,"
    Fate 5 (July-Aug.1952):44-47.
-UFO (?)
  1899, March 8/W.E. Day/=Venus?
    "Clearness of the Atmsophere in Ari-
    zona," Monthly Weather Rev. 27 (Mar.
    1899):110.

1952, Nov.27/SE of town
   U.S. Air Force, Projects Grudge and
   Blue Book Reports 1-12 (Washington:
   NICAP, 1968), p.171.
-UFO (DD)
  1974, July 13
   "Color Movie Film of UFO," APRO Bull.
   23 (July-Aug.1974):9.
-UFO (NL)
  1970, July 31-Aug.3
   "Press Reports," APRO Bull. 19 (July-
   Aug.1970):9.
  1970, Aug.7-17/Paul Solem/741 6th St.
   Prescott Arizona Courier, 9 Aug.
   1970, p.1; and 18 Aug.1970, p.1.
   Jerome Clark, "Indian Prophecy and
   the Prescott UFOs," Fate 24 (Apr.
   1971):54-61.
   (Letter), Red Cloud Mason, Fate 24
   (Sep.1971):142-44.
   Jerome Clark & Loren Coleman, The Un-
   identified (N.Y.: Warner, 1975),
   pp.216-23.

Rimrock
-UFO (NL)
  1967, May
   "Sightings Continue in Arizona,"
   APRO Bull. 16 (July-Aug.1967):2.

Safford
-UFO (NL)
  1959, Dec.20/A.W. Rogers/7 mi.E on U.S.
  70
   (Letter), Fate 13 (Sep.1960):109-10.

San Luis
-UFO (DD)
  1955, Aug./A.P. Wheeler
   B. Ann Slate, "The Case of the Crip-
   pled Flying Saucer," Saga's UFO
   Special, 1972, pp.40,51-52.

San Manuel
-UFO (DD)
  1974, Aug.3/Larry Lanthorn/mine
   "Flap in Arizona," APRO Bull. 23
   (July-Aug.1974):1,3.
-UFO (NL)
  1968, Dec.2/Joe Bertoldo
   "U.S. Roundup," APRO Bull. 17 (Mar.-
   Apr.1969):6.

Scottsdale
-Precognition
  1972, Nov.12/Leticia Shindo
   (Editorial), Fate 26 (May 1973):18-
   22, quoting Los Angeles (Cal.)
   Times (undated).
  1975/Kingdom Brown/6508 E. Cactus Rd.
   Warren Smith, "Phenomenal Predictions
   for 1975," Saga, Jan.1975, pp.20-21.
-UFO (NL)
  1968, June 17/=meteor?
   Scottsdale Daily Progress, 18 June
   1968; and 25 June 1968.
   Philip J. Klass, UFOs Explained
   (N.Y.: Random House, 1974), pp.50-
   51.

Sedona
-UFO (?)
  1975, May 5/Esther Beardsley/=Venus
   Raymond Jordan, "1975 UFO Wave in
   Arizona," APRO Bull. 24 (Apr.1976):
   5-6.
   "UFO Identified," APRO Bull. 24
   (June 1976):2.
-UFO (CE-1)
  1975, May 13, 15/Esther Beardsley/Air-
  port Rd.
   Raymond Jordan, "1975 UFO Wave in
   Arizona," APRO Bull. 24 (Apr.1976):
   5-6; (May 1976):5.
-UFO (DD)
  1967, Sep.23/C. Dwight Ghormley/1 mi.
  from town/=lens reflection?
   James A. Harder, "The Sedona 'UFO
   Track' Photo," APRO Bull. 21 (Mar.-
   Apr.1973):5-6. il.
   B.C. Sparks, "Technical Comments,"
   APRO Bull. 22 (Sep.-Oct.1973):7.
   W.H. Spaulding, "The Sedona, Arizona
   Photograph and Evaluation," MUFON
   UFO J., no.105 (Aug.1976):3-6. il.
   Eric Herr, "The MUFON Analysis of
   the Sedona Photograph: A Rebuttal,"
   MUFON UFO J., no.115 (June 1977):
   5-7.
   W.H. Spaulding, "Photographic Anal-
   ysis Utilizing Computer Image Pro-
   cessing," APRO Bull. 26 (Aug.1977):
   mailer.
-UFO (NL)
  1975, May 6/Bill Norman
  1975, May 23/Evelyn Thompson/Gray Back
  Mt.
   Raymond Jordan, "1975 UFO Wave in
   Arizona," APRO Bull. 24 (May 1976):
   5.

Shongopovi
-Archeological site
  ca.1 A.D.
   Henriette Mertz, Gods from the Far
   East (N.Y.: Ballantine, 1975 ed.),
   p.42.

Silver Bell
-UFO (CE-2)
  1974, Aug.10/Avra Valley Rd.
   "Flap in Arizona," APRO Bull. 23
   (July-Aug.1974):1,4.
-UFO (DD)
  1957, June 14
   Coral E. Lorenzen, The Shadow of the
   Unknown (N.Y.: Signet, 1970), pp.
   146-47.

Sun City
-UFO (CE-2)
  1973, Oct.22
   Sun City News-Sun, 26 Oct.1973.

Tempe
-Astrology
  1938-   /American Federation of As-
  trologers/Box 22040
   Leslie Shepard, ed., Occultism Update, no.1 (1978):2.

-UFO (DD)
    1947, July 6/Francis Howell/317 Ash St.
        Phoenix Arizona Reoublic, 7 July
        1947.
-UFO (NL)
    1959, Sep.13/Frank C. Haglin
        (Letter), Fate 13 (Apr.1960):110-11.
    1961, May 8/Frank C. Haglin
        (Letter), Fate 14 (Sep.1961):105-106.
    1975, Oct.4
        "UFO Central," CUFOS News Bull., 1
        Feb.1976, p.7.

Temporal
-UFO (NL)
    1920s/Bob Bergier
        Union High School, Patagonia, "Folk
        Tales from the Patagonia Area, San-
        ta Cruz Co., Arizona," Gen.Bull.
        Univ.Arizona, no.13 (1949):12-13.

Tombstone
-Giant bird
    ca.1886
        (Letter), H.M. Cranmer, Fate 16 (Sep.
        1963):116.
        (Letter), H.M. Cranmer, Fate 19 (Mar.
        1966):131-32.
        (Letter), Wayne Winters, Fate 19
        (Aug.1966):128-29.
        "Thunderbirds Again--and Again," Pur-
        suit 5 (Apr.1972):40-41.
        "Department of Loose Ends," Pursuit
        5 (Oct.1972):93.
        David R. Weidl, "That Thunderbird
        Photo," Pursuit 8 (Apr.1975):37-38.
    1890, April
        Tombstone Epitaph, 26 Apr.1890, p.3.
        J.K. Parrish, "Our Country's Myster-
        ious Monsters," Old West, fall 1969,
        p.25.
        "Letter Rip!" Old West, summer 1970.
-Precognition
    1887-1890/John Slaughter
        Herman Stowell King, "The Sheriff Who
        Was Not Wyatt Earp," Fate 14 (Jan.
        1961):48-51. il.
-UFO (?)
    1897, Feb.24
        "Fall of an Aerolite in Arizona,"
        Monthly Weather Rev. 25 (Feb.1897):
        56.
-UFO (DD)
    1952, June/John D. Williams
        Richard Hall, ed., The UFO Evidence
        (Washington: NICAP, 1964), p.31.
    1968
        "Here Is a Choice Photographic Sel-
        ection of Spherical UFOs," Saga UFO
        Rept. 4 (May 1977):40. il.
-UFO (NL)
    1969, Jan.11/W on U.S.80
        Phoenix Arizona Republic, 13 Jan.
        1969.

Tonopah
-UFO (NL)
    1976, April 24
        "Noteworthy UFO Sightings," Ufology
        2 (fall 1976):60.

Tonto Basin
-UFO (?)
    1899, March 7/G.O. Scott/=Venus?
        "Clearness of the Atmosphere in Ari-
        zona," Monthly Weather Rev. 27
        (Mar.1899):110.

Tuba City
-UFO (NL)
    1975, Aug.17
        William H. Spaulding, "Arizona Pat-
        rol Officer Reports EM Effects,"
        Skylook, no.97 (Dec.1975):6-7.

Tucson
-Cloud anomaly
    1976, Jan.25/Aden B. Meinel
        Aden B. Meinel, Marjorie P. Meinel
        & Glenn E. Shaw, "Trajectory of the
        Mt. St. Augustine 1976 Eruption Ash
        Cloud," Science 193 (1976):420-22.
        il.
-Crisis apparition
    1971, May/Bonnie MacConnell
        Susy Smith, The Power of the Mind
        (Radnor, Pa.: Chilton, 1975), pp.
        171-73.
-Erratic crocodilian
    1949, fall/irrigation ditch
    1950, spring/tourist court
        Raymond J. Hock, "The Alligator in
        Arizona," Copeia, 1954, pp.222-23.
-Fall of fish
    1933, Aug.21
        "Falls," Doubt, no.51 (1956):383.
-Fall of lava-like object and men-in-
    black
    1979, Feb.17/Warren Weisman/Winstel
    Blvd.
        Tucson Arizona Daily Star, 21 Feb.
        1979.
-Ghost cat
    1975/Noelle Fojut
        Martin Ebon, The Evidence for Life
        after Death (N.Y.: Signet, 1977),
        pp.97-98.
-Hex
    1970s
        Londell F. Snow, "I Was Born Just
        Exactly with the Gift," J.Am.Folk-
        lore 86 (1973):272-81.
-Mystery radio transmission
    1978, May 15/Dallas Payton
        Tucson Arizona Daily Star, 16 May
        1978.
-Phantom panther
    1976, Sep.-Oct.
        Tucson Arizona Daily Star, 15 Oct.
        1976.
-Precognition and astrology
    1951-   /Carl Payne Tobey/10901 E.
    Speedway Blvd.
        Tucson Daily Citizen, 9 July 1953;
        and 1 Nov.1967.
        Carl Payne Tobey, An Astrology Primer
        for the Millions (Los Angeles: Sher-
        bourne, 1965).
        Coral E. Lorenzen, The Shadow of the
        Unknown (N.Y.: Signet, 1970), pp.
        25-26.

Carl Payne Tobey, The Astrology of
Inner Space (Tucson: Omen, 1972).
-Radionics
1950-1951/Curtis P. Upton/Cortaro-Mar-
ana tract
Edward Wriothesley Russell, Report
on Radionics (London: Spearman,
1973), pp.55-56.
Peter Tompkins & Christopher Bird,
The Secret Life of Plants (N.Y.:
Harper & Row, 1973), pp.323,325.
-Reincarnation
1960/Jannene Farnum
(Editorial), Fate 13 (May 1960):6.
-Roman crosses
1924/Charles E. Manier/Silverbell Rd./
date approx. 800 A.D./=hoax?
Tucson Arizona Daily Star, 21 Sep.
1924; 13-17 Dec.1925; 21 Dec.1925;
23 Dec.1925; 16 Dec.1925; 5 Jan.
1926; 15 Jan.1926; 19 Jan.1926; 1
Mar.1926; 4 Mar.1926; and 7 Mar.
1926.
New York Times, 13-14 Dec.1925, p.1;
15-16 Dec.1925, p.4; and 20 Jan.
1926, p.7.
Thomas W. Bent, The Tucson Artifacts
(Los Angeles: The Author, 1964). il.
E.B. Sayles, Fantasies of Gold (Tuc-
son: Univ. of Arizona, 1968), pp.
103-12. il.
Gaston Burridge, "Riddle of the Lead
Crosses," Fate 24 (Feb.1971):48-54.
il.
Bill Mack, "An Ancient Roman Settle-
ment in America?" Argosy, Mar.1972,
pp.42-43. il.
-Skyquake
1950, May 6
"Bangs," Doubt, no.30 (1950):43.
1960, Aug.23/Davis-Monthan AFB
Tucson Daily Citizen, 24 Aug.1960.
-Spirit medium
1960s-   /Susy Smith
Susy Smith, Confessions of a Psychic
(N.Y.: Macmillan, 1971).
Susy Smith, The Book of James (N.Y.:
Putnam, 1974).
-Survival research
1970s/Survival Research Foundation
Susy Smith, "A Research Foundation
Studies Survival after Death," Psy-
chic World, May 1976, pp.22-25,84-
86.
Susy Smith, Voices of the Dead? (N.Y.:
Signet, 1977), pp.82-88.
Martin Ebon, The Evidence for Life
after Death (N.Y.: Signet, 1977),
pp.48-56.
-UFO (?)
1952, Aug.13/Stanley W. Thompson
1955, March 2
1958, April 9
Richard Hall, ed., The UFO Evidence
(Washington: NICAP, 1964), pp.15,
21,153.
-UFO (CE-1)
1962, June 25/John Westmoreland/Pantano
Wash
Tucson Daily Citizen, 26 June 1962.

Coral E. Lorenzen, "Saucers Shoot
Rockets over Tucson, Arizona," APRO
Bull. 11 (July 1962):1,3-4.
Jim & Coral Lorenzen, UFOs over the
Americas (N.Y.: Signet, 1968), pp.
114-18.
1975, May 7/Ruby Lopez/Sunrock Dr.
"Tucson Area Has Mini Flap," APRO
Bull. 23 (May 1975):1,3.
1977, Feb.21/Dorothy Sanders/733 E.
Lester St.
"Occupant Case in Tucson," APRO Bull.
25 (Feb.1977):1,7.
1978, Feb.19/Sharon Moon/4201 W. Bilby
1978, Feb.20/Harold Stevens/755 W.
Grant
"Extended UFO Flap over Tucson,"
APRO Bull. 26 (Feb.1978):1.
-UFO (CE-2)
1954, Nov.
Leonard H. Stringfield, Inside Sau-
cer Post...3-0 Blue (Cincinnati:
CRIFO, 1957), p.50.
1955, March 30/Andy Florio/E on Hwy.80
Ted Phillips, Physical Traces Asso-
ciated with UFO Sightings (Evans-
ton: Center for UFO Studies, 1975),
p.18, quoting Modern People, 27 Oct.
1974.
1967, Oct.9/nr. Speedway & Harrison Rd.
Jim & Coral Lorenzen, UFOs over the
Americas (N.Y.: Signet, 1968), pp.
118-20.
Coral & Jim Lorenzen, Encounters with
UFO Occupants (N.Y.: Berkley, 1976),
pp.15-16.
-UFO (CE-3)
1977, Feb.10/Lois Stovall/2150 Poquita
Vista
"Occupant Case in Tucson," APRO Bull.
25 (Feb.1977):1-2,7.
-UFO (CE-4)
1977, April 4
Ted Bloecher, "A Survey of CE3K Reports for 1977," in 1978 MUFON UFO
Symposium Proc. (Seguin, Tex.:
MUFON, 1978), pp.14,32.
-UFO (DD)
1947, April 29/Mrs. H.C. Olavick/2101
E. Hawthorne St.
Ted Bloecher, Report on the UFO Wave
of 1947 (Washington: NICAP, 1967),
pp. ix-x.
1947, June 22/Walter Laos
Tucson Daily Citizen, 7 July 1947.
1947, June 29/Charles Weaver/708 E. 1st
Tucson Daily Citizen, 4 July 1947.
Ted Bloecher, Report on the UFO Wave
of 1947 (Washington: NICAP, 1967),
Appendix, p.2.
1947, July 6/Wallace B. Magness/1132 E.
Blacklidge
1947, July 6/Walter Laos/723 E. 1st St.
Tucson Daily Citizen, 7 July 1947.
Ted Bloecher, Report on the UFO Wave
of 1947 (Washington: NICAP, 1967),
pp.II-7,18.
1947, July 8/William Holland/mts. to E
Coral E. Lorenzen, Flying Saucers:
The Startling Evidence of the Inva-

sion from Outer Space (N.Y.: Signet, 1966 ed.), p.20.
1952/Davis-Monthan AFB
  Coral & Jim Lorenzen, Encounters with
  UFO Occupants (N.Y.: Berkley, 1976),
  p.245.
1952, May 1/Maj. Pestalozzi/Davis-Mon-
than AFB
  J. Allen Hynek, The Hynek UFO Report
  (N.Y.: Dell, 1977), pp.109-12,292-94.
1957, Oct.6/Earl E. Sydow
  "Large, Small UAOs over Tucson in
  1957," APRO Bull. 10 (Mar.1962):4.
1965, Sep.17/M.L. Nelson/247 S. Cherry
  W.C. Stevens, "Bell-Shaped UFOs,"
  Official UFO 1 (Nov.1975):35-36.
1967, spring
  "Sighting at Tucson," Skylook, no.1
  (Sep.1967):3.
1972, Feb.2/Carol Kerstetter
  "UFO Air Chase over Tucson," APRO
  Bull. 20 (Jan.-Feb.1972):7.
1972, June 10/Ervin R. Cooper
  "Tucson UFOs Sighted," APRO Bull. 20
  (May-June 1972):4.
1973, Sep.12-13/Mrs. Jack Miller/nr.
Pima St. x Columbus Blvd.
  "Repeat Cases in Arizona," APRO Bull.
  22 (May-June 1974):1,3.
1978, Feb.27/Dale Mazur/2336 S. Hemlock
  "Extended UFO Flap over Tucson," APRO
  Bull. 26 (Feb.1978):1,4.
-UFO (NL)
  1949, April 9
  Richard Hall, ed., The UFO Evidence
  (Washington: NICAP, 1964), p.155.
1950, Feb.2/Roy L. Jones/Davis-Monthan
AFB
  Tucson Daily Citizen, 2-3 Feb.1950.
1966, Dec.13/John T. Hopf
  Wendelle C. Stevens, "UFO Tracks in
  the Sky," Saga UFO Rept. 2 (fall
  1975):23.
1967, April 21
  "Yellow Disc in Tucson," APRO Bull.
  15 (May-June 1967):7.
1967, July 25
  "Sightings Continue in Arizona,"
  APRO Bull. 16 (July-Aug.1967):2.
1968, Dec.4/Jim Lorenzen/3910 E. Kleindale Rd.
  "Staff Members See UFO," APRO Bull.
  17 (Nov.-Dec.1968):2.
1969, June 14/Don Reasor
  "UFO Filmed over Tucson," APRO Bull.
  17 (May-June 1969):1.
1974, Aug.3
  "Flap in Arizona," APRO Bull. 23
  (July-Aug.1974):3.
1975, May 11/Donna Robbins/Mission Rd.
  "Tucson Area Has Mini Flap," APRO
  Bull. 23 (May 1975):1,3.
1975, Sep.3/Mike Cooper/Pinal Dr.
  Timothy Green Beckley, "Saucers over
  Our Cities," Saga UFO Rept. 4 (Aug.
  1977):24,74.
1977, Dec.23/Pat Till
1978, Jan.19/Kenneth Kmac/Craycroft
  W.C. Stevens, "UFO Low over Tucson,"
  APRO Bull. 26 (Jan.1978):1-3.

1978, Feb.21/Reita Lipsitz/Campbell x
Silver St.
  "Extended UFO Flap over Tucson,"
  APRO Bull. 26 (Feb.1978):1,3-4.

Winslow
-Contactee
  1952, Aug.-1953, summer/George Hunt
  Williamson
    George Hunt Williamson & Alfred C.
    Bailey, The Saucers Speak (Los An-
    geles, New Age, 1954).
    George Hunt Williamson & John McCoy,
    UFOs Confidential (Corpus Christi:
    Essene, 1958).
-Giant human skull
  n.d./30 mi.S
    Jesse James Benton, Cow by the Tail
    (Boston: Houghton Mifflin, 1943),
    p.170.
-Humanoid
  1965, fall/N of town
    John Green, Sasquatch: The Apes Among
    Us (Seattle: Hancock House, 1978),
    p.176.
-UFO (R-V)
  1967, Jan.13
    J. Allen Hynek, The UFO Experience
    (Chicago: Regnery, 1972), pp.72,237.

Yarnell
-Humanoid
  1975
    John Green, Sasquatch: The Apes Among
    Us (Seattle: Hancock House, 1978),
    p.176.
-Skyquake
  1898, Sep.12/Leopold Walloth/=meteor-
  ite?
    "Notes from the September Reports of
    the Climate and Crop Sections,"
    Monthly Weather Rev. 26 (Oct.1898):
    463.

Yuma
-Disappearance
  1951, July 15/Klaus W. Martens/SE of
  town
    B. Ann Slate, "The UFO Kidnappers,"
    Saga, Apr.1975, pp.24,52-54, quot-
    ing Pasadena (Cal.) Star-News (un-
    dated).
-Earthquake anomaly
  1867, June 17/Earl Chipley
    (Editorial), Fate 20 (Dec.1967):20-
    24.
-Fall of clam
  1941, Aug.
    New York Post, 20 Aug.1941.
-Hex
  1957-1958
    Wick Evans, "Witchcraft (1958)," Fate
    11 (Dec.1958):75-78.
-UFO (?)
  1960, Jan.11/=oil explosion?
    (Letter), Mera Gaskill, Fate 13 (June
    1960):111-13.
-UFO (DD)
  1947, July 9/Henry Vardela
    Coral E. Lorenzen, Flying Saucers:

The Startling Evidence of the Invasion from Outer Space (N.Y.: Signet, 1966 ed.), p.20.
1953, Feb.4
U.S. Air Force, Projects Grudge and
Blue Book Reports 1-12 (Washington:
NICAP, 1968), p.194.
1953, March 7/Yuma AFB
Richard Hall, ed., The UFO Evidence
(Washington: NICAP, 1964), p.22,
quoting AP release, 9 Mar.1953.
1953, May 5/Wells Alan Webb/Vacuum
Cooling Co. plant
Wells Alan Webb, Mars, the New Fron-
tier (San Francisco: Fearon, 1956),
p.127.
Charles A. Maney, "Scientific Meas-
urement of UFOs," Fate 18 (June
1965):31,37.
Philip J. Klass, UFOs: Identified
(N.Y.: Random House, 1968), pp.99-
100.
-UFO (NL)
1952, April 16/Sally Ann Diggs/nr.
Yuma AFB
"Saturn-Shaped UFO," UFO Inv. 3 (May-
June 1966):4-5.
1953, Jan.30/Wells Alan Webb/7 mi.E on
Hwy.80
Wells Alan Webb, Mars, the New Fron-
tier (San Francisco: Fearon, 1956),
p.125.
1973, Oct?/Thomas Stilde/Yuma Proving
Grounds
(Editorial), Probe the Unknown 2
(spring 1974):63.

B. Physical Features

Agua Fria R.
-UFO (CE-2)
1943/Pierre Perry
Trevor James [Constable], They Live
in the Sky (Los Angeles: New Age,
1958), pp.139-41.

Alamo L.
-UFO (CE-1)
1975, March 9/Stuart Hill
Raymond Jordan, "1975 UFO Wave in
Arizona," APRO Bull. 24 (Apr.1976):
5.

Camelback Mt.
-Archeological site
(Editorial), Fate 12 (Oct.1959):15-
16.

Canyon de Chelly
-Archeological site
350-1300 A.D.
J.H. Simpson, Journal of a Military
Reconnaissance from Santa Fe, New
Mexico, to the Navajo Country, in
Rept. of Secretary of War, U.S. Sen-
ate Doc.no.64, 31st Cong., 1st Sess.
(14 July 1850), pp.56-139.
Cosmos Mindeleff, "Cliff Ruins of
Canyon de Chelly, Arizona," Am.An-

thro. 8 (1895):153-74.
Cosmos Mindeleff, "Cliff Ruins of
Canyon de Chelly, Arizona," Ann.
Rept.Bur.Am.Ethn. 16 (1897):73-198.
Anna Morris, Digging in the South-
west (Garden City: Doubleday, Dor-
an, 1933). il.
Charlie R. Steen, Excavations at Tse-
ta'a (Washington: U.S. Nat'l Park
Service, 1966). il.
Franklin Folsom, America's Ancient
Treasures (N.Y.: Rand McNally,
1974), pp.14-15.
Claude Britt, "Early Navajo Astronom-
ical Pictographs in Canyon de Chel-
ly, Northeastern Arizona, U.S.A.,"
in Anthony F. Aveni, ed., Archaeo-
astronomy in Pre-Columbian America
(Austin: Univ. of Texas, 1975), pp.
89-107. il.
Mahmoud Y. El-Najjar, et al., "An
Unusual Pathology with High Inci-
dence among the Ancient Cliff-Dwell-
ers of Canyon de Chelly," Plateau
48 (1975):13-22.
Campbell Grant, Canyon de Chelly:
Its People and Rock Art (Tucson:
Univ. of Arizona, 1978). il.
-Donkey mutilation
1972, Aug.13/Mrs. Eric Bluhm
"Could This Be Another 'Snippy?'"
Skylook, no.59 (Oct.1972):3.

Carrizo R.
-Archeological site
14th c./Grasshopper site
P. Bion Griffin, "A High Status Bur-
ial from Grasshopper Ruin, Arizona,"
Kiva 33, no.2 (1967):37-53.
Geoffrey A. Clark, "A Preliminary
Analysis of Burial Clusters at the
Grasshopper Site, East Central Ari-
zona," Kiva 35, no.2 (1969):57-86.

Cerbat Mts.
-Electromagnetic anomaly
1883-1895
Leland Lovelace, Lost Mines and Hidden Treasure (N.Y.: Ace, 1956), pp.
233-38.

Charleston R.
-UFO (NL)
1974, Aug.9/Nina Hipsley/bridge
"Flap in Arizona," APRO Bull. 23
(July-Aug.1974):1,4.

Chuska Mts.
-Humanoid
ca.1967/Mrs. C.A. Cheeseman
John Green, The Sasquatch File (Agassiz, B.C.: Cheam, 1973), p.40.

Del Rio Springs Creek
-UFO (DD)
1953, May 21/Bill Beers
Prescott Evening Courier, 22 May 1953.

Flowing Springs
-Petroglyph

ca.100 A.D./=calendar
    Ralph S. Fisher, Sr., "Our Hidden
    13th Month Calendar," Pop.Arch. 4
    (Mar.-Apr.1975):49. il.

Forestdale Valley
-Archeological site
    350 A.D./=Chinese discovery?
        Emil W. Haury & E.B. Sayles, "An
        Early Pit House of the Mogollon Cul-
        ture," Univ.Arizona Social Sci.Bull.
        no.16 (Oct.1947). il.
        Henriette Mertz, Gods from the Far
        East (N.Y.: Ballantine, 1975 ed.),
        pp.39-41.

Gates' Pass
-UFO (CE-2)
    1967, Dec.24
        "EM Case at Tucson," APRO Bull. 16
        (Nov.-Dec.1967):1.

Gila R.
-Phantom wagon train
    1867
        Vincent H. Gaddis, "Caravan of the
        Lost," Fate 2 (May 1949):36,37.

Grand Canyon
-Archeological site
    1500 B.C.
        Douglas W. Schwartz, Arthur L. Lange
        & Raymond deSaussure, "Split-Twig
        Figurines in the Grand Canyon," Am.
        Antiquity 23 (1958):264-74.
        Robert C. Euler & Alan P. Olson,
        "Split-Twig Figurines from Northern
        Arizona: New Radiocarbon Dates,"
        Science 148 (1965):368-69.
        Alan R. Schroedl, "The Grand Canyon
        Figurine Complex," Am.Antiquity 42
        (1977):254-65. il.
    ca.750-1250 A.D./Tusayan and others
        Douglas W. Schwartz, "Prehistoric
        Man in the Grand Canyon," Sci.Am.
        198 (Feb.1958):97-102. il.
        P.T. Reilly, "Isolated Rim Sites of
        Grand Canyon," Masterkey 44 (1970):
        103-107.
-Chinese discovery
    ca.1000 B.C.
        Alexander M'Allan, Ancient Chinese
        Account of the Grand Canyon (College
        Corner, O.: F.T. Snyder, 1913).
        Henriette Mertz, Gods from the Far
        East (N.Y.: Ballantine, 1975 ed.),
        pp.174,182-85.
-Healing
    1933, Nov./Jerry Palmer
        Hoyt Palmer, "When a Cowboy Prayed,"
        Fate 30 (Nov.1977):68-71.
-Out-of-body experience
    1948/Charles W. Ingersoll
        Brad Steiger, Mysteries of Time and
        Space (N.Y.: Dell, 1976 ed.), pp.
        182-84.
-Precognition
    1956, Sep.4/Mrs. Paul H. McCahen
        Laura A. Dale, Rhea White & Gardner
        Murphy, "A Selection of Cases from

a Recent Survey of Spontaneous ESP
        Phenomena," J.ASPR 56 (1962):3,37.
-UFO (DD)
    1947, June 30/William G. McGinty
        Ted Bloecher, Report on the UFO Wave
        of 1947 (Washington: NICAP, 1967),
        p.II-12.

Havasu Canyon
-Petroglyph
    1924/Doheny expedition/=depicts dino-
    saur?
        A. Hyatt Verrill, Strange Prehistor-
        ic Animals and Their Stories (Bos-
        ton: I.C. Page, 1948). il.
        "The Hava Supai Canyon 'Dinosaur,'"
        Pursuit 8 (Jan.1975):6.
        John Guerrasio, "Dinosaur Graffiti--
        Hava Supai Style," Pursuit 10
        (spring 1977):62-63. il.
-UFO (NL)
    1954, April 16/Elbert Edwards
        Las Vegas (Nev.) Sun, 22 Apr.1954.

Hay Hollow
-Archeological site
    450 B.C.-300 A.D.
        Paul S. Martin & Fred Plog, The Arch-
        eology of Arizona (Garden City:
        Doubleday, 1973), pp.77-79.

Hell Canyon
-UFO (CE-1)
    1975, March 11/U.S.89
    1975, March 28/U.S.89
        Raymond Jordan, "1975 UFO Wave in
        Arizona," APRO Bull. 24 (Apr.1976):
        5-6.

Hohokam Pima National Monument
-Archeological site
    400 B.C.-1200 A.D./Snaketown
        Harold S. Gladwin, et al., Excava-
        tions at Snaketown: Material Cul-
        ture (Globe, Ariz.: Gila Pueblo
        Medallion Pap.no.25, 1937).
        Harold S. Gladwin, Excavations at
        Snaketown IV (Globe, Ariz.: Gila
        Pueblo Medallion Pap.no.38, 1948).
        Emil W. Haury, "Snaketown, 1964-1965,"
        Kiva 31, no.1 (1965):1-13.
        Emil W. Haury, "First Masters of the
        American Desert: The Hohokam," Nat'l
        Geogr.Mag. 131 (May 1967):670-95. il.
        Vorsilia L. Bohrer, "Paleoecology of
        Snaketown," Kiva 36, no.3 (1971).
        11-19.
        Maggie Wilson, "How the Hohokam Came
        and Never Left," Phoenix Arizona
        Republic, 17 Mar.1976.
        Emil W. Haury, Hohokam: Desert Farm-
        ers and Craftsmen (Tucson: Univ. of
        Arizona, 1976). il.

Kitt Peak
-UFO (NL)
    1971, Jan.22/C. Roger Lynds/observatory
        "'Planets' at Large," Can.UFO Rept.,
        no.12 (1972):9.

Little Jedito Wash
-Humanoid
  1965, fall/Roger Heath
    Jerome Clark & Loren Coleman, Crea-
    tures of the Outer Edge (N.Y.: War-
    ner, 1978), pp.109-10.

Lynx Creek
-UFO (CE-3)
  1936, June 9-Nov.21/Charles C. Stemmer
    Charles C. Stemmer, "Strange Events
    at Poltergeist Canyon," Fate 7
    (Apr.1954):65-72.

Meteor Crater
-Meteorite crater
  1295 m.diam. x 174 m.deep/certain
    A.E. Foote, "A New Locality for Met-
    eoric Iron with a Preliminary Notice
    of the Discovery of Diamonds in the
    Iron," Proc.Am.Ass'n Adv.Sci. 40
    (1891):279-83.
    Daniel Moreau Barringer, "Coon Moun-
    tain and Its Crater," Proc.Acad.
    Nat.Sci.Philadelphia 57 (1905):861-
    86.
    J.W. Mallet, "A Stony Meteorite from
    Coon Butte, Arizona," Am.J.Sci.,
    ser.4, 21 (1906):353.
    George P. Merrill, "The Meteor Crat-
    er of Canyon Diablo, Arizona,"
    Smith.Misc.Coll. 50 (1908):461-98.
    il.
    J.J. Jakosky, "Geophysical Methods
    Locate Meteorite," Engineering &
    Mining J. 133 (1932):392.
    H.H. Nininger, "A Résumé of Research-
    es at the Arizona Meteorite Crater,"
    Sci.Monthly 72 (Feb.1951):75-86.
    H.H. Nininger, "Symmetries and Asym-
    metries in Barringer Crater," Earth
    Sci. 7 (July 1953):17-19.
    H.H. Nininger, "Impactite Slag at
    Barringer Crater," Am.J.Sci. 252
    (1954):277-90. il.
    H.H. Nininger, Arizona's Meteorite
    Crater (Sedona, Ariz.: American
    Meteorite Museum, 1956). il.
    Otto Struve, "The Making of the Bar-
    ringer Meteorite Crater," Sky &
    Telescope 18 (Feb.1959):187-89. il.
    Eugene M. Shoemaker, "Penetration
    Mechanics of High Velocity Meteor-
    ites, Illustrated by Meteor Crater,
    Arizona," Proc.21st Int'l Geol.Cong.
    (1960), sec.18, pp.418-34.
    Michael E. Lipschutz & Edward Anders,
    "On the Mechanism of Diamond Form-
    ation," Science 134 (1961):2095-99.
    George Foster, The Meteor Crater
    Story (Winslow: Meteor Crater, 1964).
    E.L. Krinov, Giant Meteorites (Ox-
    ford: Pergamon, 1966), pp.78-124.
    il.
    George Seddon, "Meteor Crater: A Geo-
    logical Debate," J.Geol.Soc'y Aus-
    tralia 17 (1970):1-12. il.
    "Where Does the Iron Go?" Pursuit 5
    (July 1972):57-58.
    Gennady P. Vdovykin, "The Canyon Di-

    ablo Meteorite," Space Science Rev.
    14 (1973):758-72.
    "Moon, Earth Impact Similarities
    Studied," Aviation Week, 17 June
    1974, p.44.
    H.D. Ackerman, et al., "A Seismic
    Refraction Technique Used for Sub-
    surface Investigations at Meteor
    Crater, Arizona," J.Geophys.Rsch.
    805 (1975):765-75.
    Diana J. Briley & Carleton B. Moore,
    A Checklist of Published References
    to Barringer Meteorite Crater, Ari-
    zona, 1891-1970 (Tempe: Arizona
    State Univ., Center for Meteorite
    Studies, Pub.no.15, 1976).

Murray Springs
-Archeological site
  ca.9000 B.C.
    C. Vance Haynes & E. Thomas Hemmings,
    "Mammoth-Bone Shaft Wrench from
    Murray Springs, Arizona," Science
    159 (1968):186-87. il.

Nakai Canyon
-Clairvoyance
  n.d./Bela Arquot
    "Psychic Navajo Finds Lost Boys,"
    Fate 6 (Oct.1953):17.

Navaho Canyon
-Petroglyph
    William C. Miller, "Two Prehistoric
    Drawings of Possible Astronomical
    Significance," Astron.Soc'y Pacific,
    Leaflet, no.314 (1955):1-8. il.
    Dorothy Mayer, "An Examination of
    Miller's Hypothesis," in Anthony F.
    Aveni, ed., Native American Astron-
    omy (Austin: Univ. of Texas, 1977),
    pp.179-201.

Navajo National Monument
-Archeological site
  200-1300 A.D.
    Alfred Vincent Kidder & Samuel J.
    Guernsey, "Archaeological Explora-
    tions in Northeastern Arizona,"
    Bull.Bur.Am.Ethn., vol.65 (1919).
    il.
    Samuel James Guernsey & Alfred Vin-
    cent Kidder, "Basket-Maker Caves of
    Northeastern Arizona," Pap.Peabody
    Mus.Am.Arch.& Ethn., vol.8, no.2
    (1921). il.
    Samuel James Guernsey, "Explorations
    in Northeastern Arizona," Pap.Pea-
    body Mus.Am.Arch.& Ethn., vol.12,
    no.1 (1931). il.
    Frank McNitt, Richard Wetherill: An-
    asazi (Albuquerque: Univ. of New
    Mexico, 1966), pp.78-84.

Oak Creek
-UFO (NL)
  1975, May 6/John Spencer
    Raymond Jordan, "1975 UFO Wave in
    Arizona," APRO Bull. 24 (May 1976):
    5.

Painted Desert
-Phantom wagon train
  1872
    Vincent H. Gaddis, "Caravan of the
    Lost," Fate 2 (May 1949):36,37.

Painted Rock Reservoir
-Archeological site
    "Arizona's Amazing Pyramid-Mound,"
    Fate 12 (Aug.1959):90.

Plomora Mts.
-UFO (CE-1)
  1951, July 4
    (Letter), Edna A. Ward, Fate 7 (July
    1954):107.

Point of Pines
-Archeological site
  2000 B.C.-1450 A.D.
    Fred Wendorf, "A Report on the Excav-
    ation of a Small Ruin near Point of
    Pines, East Central Arizona," Univ.
    Arizona Soc.Sci.Bull., no.19 (July
    1950). il.
    Terah L. Smiley, "Four Late Prehis-
    toric Kivas at Point of Pines, Ari-
    zona," Univ.Arizona Soc.Sci.Bull.,
    no.21 (July 1952). il.
    Joe Ben Wheat, "Mogollon Culture
    Prior to A.D.1000," Mem.Soc'y Am.
    Arch., vol.10 (1955).
    Emil W. Haury, "Evidence at Point of
    Pines for a Prehistoric Migration
    from Northern Arizona," Univ.Arizona
    Soc.Sci.Bull., no.27 (July 1958):
    1-6.
    David A. Breternitz, "Excavations at
    Nantack Village, Point of Pines,
    Arizona," Anthro.Pap.Univ.Arizona,
    no.1 (1959). il.
    Richard B. Woodbury, "Prehistoric
    Agriculture at Point of Pines, Ari-
    zona," Mem.Soc'y Am.Arch., vol.17
    (1961).

Salt R.
-UFO (NL)
  1970, Sep.8/=meteor?
    Phoenix Arizona Republic, 9-10 Sep.
    1970.

San Francisco Mts.
-Archeological site and clairempathy
  ca.23,000 B.C./Aron Abrahamsen
    Jeffrey Goodman, "Psychic Archeology:
    Methodology and Empirical Evidence
    from Flagstaff, Arizona," in Joseph
    K. Long, ed., Extrasensory Ecology:
    Parapsychology and Anthropology
    (Metuchen, N.J.: Scarecrow, 1977),
    pp.313-29.
    Jeffrey Goodman, Psychic Archeology
    (N.Y.: Berkley, 1978), pp.85-135.
    il.
-Humanoid
  1924, summer/Mabel Fulcher
    (Letter), Fate 25 (Nov.1972):146,
    159-60.
    John Green, Sasquatch: The Apes Among

Us (Seattle: Hancock House, 1978),
p.176.

San Pedro R.
-Archeological site
  ca.11,000 B.C./Lehner site/SW of Hereford
    Emil W. Haury, "The Lehner Mammoth
    Site," Kiva 21 (1956):23-24. il.
    Emil W. Haury, et al., "The Lehner
    Mammoth Site," Am.Antiquity 25
    (1959):2-30. il.
    Ernst Antevs, "Geological Age of
    the Lehner Mammoth Site," Am.An-
    tiquity 25 (1959):31-34.

Santa Catalina Mts.
-Fire anomaly
  1955, Feb.7
    Tucson Arizona Daily Star, 7-10 Feb.
    1955.
    "Rich Run of the Mill," Doubt, no.
    48 (1955):338-39.
    "The Santa Catalina Mystery Fire,"
    Fate 9 (Nov.1956):62.
-UFO (NL)
  1948, Nov.19/Hugh Downs
    "You Asked for It," Doubt, no.24
    (1949):363.

Santa Rita Mts.
-Abundant meteoritic iron
    John L. Leconte, "Notice of Meteoric
    Iron in the Mexican Province of
    Sonora," Am.J.Sci., ser.2, 13
    (1852):290.
-UFO (DD)
  1970, Jan.27/Hwy.83
    "UFO Trio over Tucson Area," APRO
    Bull. 18 (Jan.-Feb.1970):4.

Sierra Ancha Mts.
-Anomalous fossil
  1972/=segmented animals in Precambrian
  sandstone
    (Editorial), Fate 26 (June 1973):19.
    il.

Sonoita R.
-UFO (NL)
  1940s/Angel Laguna
    Union High School, Patagonia, "Folk
    Tales from the Patagonia Area, San-
    ta Cruz Co., Arizona," Gen.Bull.
    Univ.Arizona, no.13 (1949):12.

Squaw Peak Range
-Humanoid
  1870s
    Charles M. Skinner, Myths and Legends
    of Our Own Land, 2 vols. (Philadel-
    phia: Lippincott, 1896), 2:221-22.

Sulphur Spring Valley
-Archeological site
  8000-3000 B.C./Double Adobe site
    E.B. Sayles & Ernst Antevs, "The
    Cochise Culture," Medallion Papers,
    no.29 (1941).
    Paul S. Martin & Fred Plog, The Arch-

eology of Arizona (Garden City: Doubleday, 1973), p.65.

Sunset Crater
-Lava anomaly
Harold S. Cotton & Charles F. Park, Jr., "Anosma or 'Squeeze-ups,'" Science 72 (1930):579.

Superstition Mts.
-Humanoid myth
Gary Jennings, Treasure of the Superstition Mountains (N.Y.: Norton, 1973), p.106.
-UFO (DD)
1968, March/Marie Arnold "UFO Photographed over Superstition Mountains," APRO Bull. 19 (Nov.-Dec.1970):8. il.
-UFO (NL)
1955/Otto W. Davidson (Letter), Fate 24 (Feb.1971):159.

Tinajas Altas Spring
-Disappearance
n.d./Laguna Prieta and Mission of the Four Evangelists
Jim Brandon, Weird America (N.Y.: Dutton, 1978), p.14.

Tonto National Monument
-Archeological site
1350-1425
Charles R. Steen, et al., Archeological Studies at Tonto National Monument (Globe, Ariz.: Southwestern Monuments Ass'n, 1962). il.
Bucky King, "Egyptian Sprang Technique in a Medieval Textile from Tonto, Arizona," Occ.Pub.Epigraphic Soc'y, vol.2, no.33 (Feb.1975).

Tonto Rim
-UFO (DD)
ca.1913/Gene Holder
Coral E. Lorenzen, Flying Saucers: The Startling Evidence of the Invasion from Outer Space (N.Y.: Signet, 1966 ed.), p.20, quoting Bisbee Review (undated).

Tucson Mts.
-UFO (NL)
1974, Aug.17/William Wilkins "Flap in Arizona," APRO Bull. 23 (July-Aug.1974):1,4.

Ventana Cave
-Archeological site
11,000 B.C.-recent
Emil W. Haury, The Stratigraphy and Archeology of Ventana Cave, Arizona (Albuquerque: Univ. of New Mexico, 1950).

Verde R.
-UFO (CE-1)
1900, June/Charles C. Stemmer
Charles C. Stemmer, "Saved by a Coffin," Fate 8 (June 1955):73-75.

White Mesa
-Pictograph
William C. Miller, "Two Prehistoric Drawings of Possible Astronomical Significance," Astron.Soc'y Pacific, Leaflet, no.314 (1955):1-8. il.
Dorothy Mayer, "An Examination of Miller's Hypothesis," in Anthony F. Aveni, ed., Native American Astronomy (Austin: Univ. of Texas, 1977), pp.179-201.

C. Ethnic Groups

Apache Indians
-Flood myth
Hubert Henry Bancroft, Native Races of the Pacific States, 5 vols. (N.Y.: Appleton, 1874), 3:149.
Morris Edward Opler, "Myths and Tales of the Jicarilla Apache Indians," Mem.Am.Folklore Soc'y 31 (1938):111-13.
Morris Edward Opler, "Myths and Tales of the Chiricahua Apache Indians," Mem.Am.Folklore Soc'y 37 (1942):1-2.
-Lake monster myth
Morris Edward Opler, "Myths and Legends of the Lipan Apache Indians," Mem.Am.Folklore Soc'y 36 (1940): 62-65.
Morris Edward Opler, "Myths and Tales of the Chiricahua Apache Indians," Mem.Am.Folklore Soc'y 37 (1942):79-81.
-Shamanism
J.G. Bourke, "The Medicine Men of the Apache," Ann.Rept.Bur.Am.Ethn. 9 (1892):451-595.
Keith H. Basso, "Western Apache Witchcraft," Anthro.Pap.Univ.Arizona, no.15 (1969).
Marc Simmons, Witchcraft in the Southwest (Flagstaff: Northland, 1974), pp.144-46.

Hopi Indians
-Cataclysm myth
Frank Waters, Book of the Hopi (N.Y.: Viking, 1963), pp.12-22.
-Contactee myth
Kachina clan
Jesse Walter Fewkes, "Hopi Kachinas Drawn by Native Artists," Ann.Rept. Bur.Am.Ethn., vol.21 (1903). il.
Frederick Dockstader, "The Hopi Kachina Cult," Tomorrow 4 (spring 1956):57-63.
George Hunt Williamson, Road in the Sky (London: Spearman, 1959).
Frank Waters, Book of the Hopi (N.Y.: Viking, 1963).
Edwin Earle, Hopi Kachinas (N.Y.: Museum of the American Indian, 1971).
Jack Stoneley & A.T. Lawton, Is Anyone Out There? (N.Y.:Warner, 1974), pp.235-39. il.
-Hex

Frank Waters, <u>Book of the Hopi</u> (N.Y.:
Viking, 1963), pp.246-47.
-Paleoastronomy
C. Daryll Forde, <u>Habitat, Economy and
Society</u> (London: Methuen, 1934), p.
227.
Colin Renfrew, <u>Before Civilization</u>
(N.Y.: Knopf, 1973), pp.238-40.
Stephen C. McCluskey, "The Astronomy
of the Hopi Indians," <u>J. for the
History of Astron.</u> 8 (1977):174-95.
-Petroglyphs
J. Walter Fewkes, "A Few Tusayan
Pictographs," <u>Am.Anthro.</u> 5 (1892):
9-26. il.
-Shamanism
Mischa Titiev, "Shamans, Witches and
Chiefs among the Hopi," <u>Tomorrow</u>
4 (spring 1956):51-56.
John A. Keel, "America's Unrecognized
UFO Experts," <u>Saga</u>, Apr.1973, pp.
35-37,68-71.
Brad Steiger, <u>Medicine Power</u> (Garden
City: Doubleday, 1974).
-Similarity to Balkan copper age culture
Colin Renfrew, <u>Before Civilization</u>
(N.Y.: Knopf, 1973), pp.183-84.
-Similarity to Cretan culture
Hugh Fox, <u>Gods of the Cataclysm</u>
(N.Y.: Harper's, 1976), pp.210-12,
233-34. il.
-Use of ancient Libyan symbols
Barry Fell, <u>America B.C.</u> (N.Y.: Quad-
rangle, 1976), pp.190-91.
-Weather control
J.H. McGibbeny, "Children of the
Sun," <u>Arizona Highways</u> 23 (1947):
16-27.
O.E. Singer, "Rain from the Hopi
Snake Dance," <u>Fate</u> 4 (Nov.-Dec.
1951):24-35.

Navajo Indians
-Hex
Dane & Mary Roberts Coolidge, <u>The
Navajo Indians</u> (Boston: Houghton
Mifflin, 1930), pp.142-65.
Gladys A. Reichard, <u>Navajo Medicine
Man: Sandpaintings and Legends of
Miguelito</u> (N.Y.: J.J. Augustin,
1939).
Gladys A. Reichard, "The Navaho and
Christianity," <u>Am.Anthro.</u> 51 (1949)
:66-71.
Gladys A. Reichard, <u>Navajo Religion</u>,
2 vols. (N.Y.: Pantheon, 1950), 1:
82-88.
Clyde Kluckhohn, <u>Navaho Witchcraft</u>
(Boston: Beacon, 1962).
Marc Simmons, <u>Witchcraft in the
Southwest</u> (Flagstaff: Northland,
1974), pp.135-44.
-Humanoid myth
Patrick Walsh, "The Skinwalker," <u>Aff-
word</u> 4, no.1 (spring 1974):20-22.
-Lake monster myth
Gladys A. Reichard, <u>Navaho Religion</u>,
2 vols. (N.Y.: Pantheon, 1950), 2:
490-91.
-Shamanism

Washington Matthews, "The Prayer of
a Navajo Shaman," <u>Am.Anthro.</u> 1
(1888):149-71.
Dane & Mary Roberts Coolidge, <u>The
Navajo Indians</u> (Boston: Houghton
Mifflin, 1930), pp.150-65.
Leland C. Wyman, "Navaho Diagnosti-
cians," <u>Am.Anthro.</u> 38 (1936):236-
46.
Gladys A. Reichard, <u>Navajo Religion</u>,
2 vols. (N.Y.: Pantheon, 1950).
Leland C. Wyman, "Psychotherapy of
the Navaho," <u>Tomorrow</u> 4 (spring
1956):77-84.
Richard Reichbart, "The Navajo Hand
Trembler: Multiple Roles of the
Psychic in Traditional Navajo So-
ciety," <u>J.ASPR</u> 70 (1976):381-96.
-Shape-shifting myth
William Morgan, "Human-Wolves Among
the Navaho," <u>Yale Pubs.in Anthro.</u>,
no.11 (1936).

Papago Indians
-Legend of Precolumbian whites and lost
treasure
John D. Mitchell, <u>Lost Mines of the
Great Southwest</u> (Phoenix: Journal,
1933), pp.89-90.
Leland Lovelace, <u>Lost Mines and Hid-
den Treasure</u> (N.Y.: Ace, 1956), pp.
124-27.
-Montezuma myth
J. Alden Mason, "The Papago Migration
Legend," <u>J.Am.Folklore</u> 34 (1921):
254-68.
Ross Calvin, ed., <u>Lieutenant Emory
Reports: A Reprint of Lieutenant
W.H. Emory's Notes of a Military
Reconnaissance</u> (Albuquerque: Univ.
of New Mexico, 1951), pp.106,132.
-Precognition
Ben Townsend, "My Stay with the Pap-
agos," <u>Fate</u> 25 (Nov.1972):48-52.
-Shamanism
Ruth Murray Underhill, <u>Singing for
Power</u> (Berkeley: Univ. of Californ-
ia, 1968).

Pima Indians
-Flood myth
Frank Russell, "The Pima Indians,"
<u>Ann.Rept.Bur.Am.Ethn.</u> 26 (1905):3,
206-30.
Anna Shaw, <u>Pima Indians Legends</u> (Tem-
pe: Indian Education Center, 1963),
pp.1-4.
Dean & Lucille Saxon, <u>Legends and
Lore of the Papago and Pima Indians</u>
(Tucson: Univ. of Arizona, 1973),
pp.45-61.
-Giant bird legend
Juan Mateo Manje, <u>Luz de Tierra In-
cógnita</u>, trans. Harry J. Karns
(Tucson: Arizona Silhouettes, 1954),
pp.105-106.
-Shamanism
Frank Russell, "The Pima Indians,"
<u>Ann.Rept.Bur.Am.Ethn.</u> 26 (1905):3,
250-68.

Donald M. Bahr, et al., <u>Piman Sha-
manism and Staying Sickness</u> (Tucson:
Univ. of Arizona, 1974).
-Use of Semitic language
    Frank Russell, "The Pima Indians,"
    <u>Ann.Rept.Bur.Am.Ethn.</u> 26 (1905):3,
    269-389.
    Barry Fell, <u>America B.C.</u> (N.Y.: Quad-
    rangle, 1976), pp.169-73.
    Barry Fell, "The Pima Myth of Per-
    sephone," <u>Occ.Pub.Epigraphic Soc'y</u>,
    vol.3, no.74 (Sep.1976).
-Weather control
    Juan Mateo Manje, <u>Luz de Tierra In-
    cógnita</u>, trans. Harry J. Karns
    (Tucson: Arizona Silhouettes, 1954),
    pp.244-45.

<u>Yuma Indians</u>
-Out-of-body experience legend
    1620-1623/La Señorita Azul (María de
    Jesús de Ágreda)
        Juan Mateo Manje, <u>Luz de Tierra In-
        cógnita</u>, trans. Harry J. Karns
        (Tucson: Arizona Silhouettes, 1954),
        pp.115-17.
        Cleve Hallenbeck & Juanita H. Will-
        iams, <u>Legends of the Spanish South-
        west</u> (Glendale, Cal.: Arthur H.
        Clark, 1938), pp.117,305-14.
        T.D. Kendrick, <u>Mary of Ágreda: The
        Life and Legend of a Spanish Nun</u>
        (London: Routledge & Kegan Paul,
        1967), pp.28-55.

                D. Unspecified Localities

-Haunt
    La Llorona
        Betty Leddy, "La Llorona in Southern
        Arizona," <u>Western Folklore</u> 7 (1948):
        272-77.
-White Indians
    Rufus Sage, <u>Scenes in the Rocky Moun-
    tains</u> (Philadelphia: Carey & Hart,
    1846), pp.250-54.

NEW MEXICO

A. Populated Places

Abiquiu
-Witch trial (hex)
  1766
    Marc Simmons, Witchcraft in the
    Southwest (Flagstaff: Northland,
    1974), p.32.

Abo
-Archeological site
  ca.1300-1674
    Franklin Folsom, America's Ancient
    Treasures (N.Y.: Rand McNally,
    1974), p.28.
-Petroglyph
  =depicts humanoid tracks?
    Michael Grumley, There Are Giants in
    the Earth (Garden City: Doubleday,
    1974), p.140. il.

Acoma
-Archeological site
  1200-present
    New York City Long Island Press, 10
    Oct.1971.
    Ward Alan Minge, Acoma: Pueblo in
    the Sky (Albuquerque: Univ. of New
    Mexico, 1976). il.
-Fall of tadpoles
  n.d.
    "Tadpoles from the Sky," Fate 11
    (Jan.1958):32.
-Flood myth
    Matthew W. Stirling, "Origin Myth of
    Acoma and Other Records," Bull.Bur.
    Am.Ethn., no.135 (1942):77-78.
-Hex
    Leslie A. White, "The Acoma Indians,"
    Ann.Rept.Bur.Am.Ethn. 47 (1929-30):
    23,108,120-24.

Alamogordo
-Phantom
  1958, summer/Coral E. Lorenzen/1712
  Van Court
    Coral E. Lorenzen, The Shadow of the
    Unknown (N.Y.: Signet, 1970), pp.
    36-37.
-UFO (?)
  1952, July 14/Holloman AFB
    Brad Steiger, ed., Project Blue Book
    (N.Y.: Ballantine, 1976), betw. pp.
    360-61. il.
  1957, Oct.16/Ella Louise Fortune/nr.
  Holloman AFB/=lenticular cloud
    William H. Spaulding, "The Computer
    Tackles UFO Photographs," Official
    UFO 2 (Mar.1977):16-18,46. il.
  1958, Oct.11/Jim Lorenzen/1712 Van
  Court/=jet
    Alamogordo Daily News, 12 Oct.1958.
    Coral & Jim Lorenzen, UFOs: The Whole
    Story (N.Y.: Signet, 1969), pp.136-

40.
  1961, July/U.S.54/=tumbleweed
    Donald H. Menzel & Lyle G. Boyd, The
    World of Flying Saucers (Garden
    City: Doubleday, 1963), p.57.
-UFO (CE-1)
  1958, summer/Holloman AFB
    Santa Ana (Cal.) Register, 15 Nov.
    1972.
    "White Sands Sightings Kept Secret,
    Now Told," Skylook, no.64 (Mar.1973)
    :3.
-UFO (CE-2)
  1956, Sep./12 mi.W on U.S.70
    Santa Ana (Cal.) Register, 23 Nov.
    1972.
    "UFO Landing in Proximity of Hollo-
    man Air Force Base Told," Skylook,
    no.64 (Mar.1973):5.
-UFO (CE-4)
  1975, Aug.13/Charles L. Moody
    National Enquirer, 11 May 1976.
    L.J. Lorenzen, "The Moody Case," APRO
    Bull. 24 (June 1976):6; (July 1976):
    2,5-6.
    Coral & Jim Lorenzen, Abducted! (N.Y.:
    Berkley, 1977), pp.38-51.
-UFO (DD)
  1948, April 5/Holloman AFB
    R.B. McLaughlin, "How Scientists
    Tracked Flying Saucers," True, Mar.
    1950, pp.25-28,96-99.
  1950, July/Holloman AFB
    Coral E. Lorenzen, Flying Saucers:
    The Startling Evidence of the Inva-
    sion from Outer Space (N.Y.: Signet,
    1966 ed.), pp.27-29.
  1951, Feb.14/J.E. Cocker
    Daniel Lang, "A Reporter at Large:
    Something in the Sky," New Yorker,
    6 Sep.1952, pp.68,83-84.
-UFO (NL)
  1953, Feb./John Proctor
    John G. Ross, "Fate's Report on the
    Flying Saucers," Fate 6 (Oct.1953):
    6,9, quoting El Paso (Tex.) Times
    (undated).
  1957, Nov.5/Don Clarke/E of town
  1957, Nov.5/Lyman Brown, Jr./N of town
  1957, Nov.7/Bradford Rickets/Holloman
  AFB
    Coral E. Lorenzen, Flying Saucers:
    The Startling Evidence of the Inva-
    sion from Outer Space (N.Y.: Signet,
    1966 ed.), pp.98,100-101.
  1958, Aug.8/Sally Car
    "Sighting Round-Up," UFO Inv. 1 (Aug.-
    Sep.1958):6.
    (Editorial), Fate 11 (Dec.1958):21.

Albuquerque
-Animal ESP
  1960, Sep./Roy Apodaca/343 Isleta Blvd.
    (Editorial), Fate 14 (Jan.1961):11.

-Disappearance
  1976, May 26
    Leonard H. Stringfield, Situation
    Red: The UFO Siege (N.Y.: Fawcett,
    1977 ed.), p.177.
-Fire anomaly
  1962, March 4/M.A. Salazar/1439 Saunders
    (Editorial), Fate 15 (Aug.1962):16.
-Healing
  1895, summer/Francis Schlatter
    Estella DeFord Graham, "Francis
    Schlatter: A Fool for God," Fate 8
    (Oct.1955):56-61. il.
-Humanoid
  1966, Sep.-Oct./Clifford McGuire/415
  Wilshire
    Albuquerque Journal, 15-20 Oct. 1966;
    23 Oct. 1966; and 26 Oct.1966.
    (Editorial), Fate 20 (Feb.1967):21-
    23.
-UFO (?)
  1949, Jan./Kirtland AFB
    Bruce S. Maccabee, "UFO Related In-
    formation from the FBI Files: Part
    5," MUFON UFO J., no.124 (Mar.1978):
    7,10.
  1963, June 16/Paul A. Villa, Jr./=hoax
    Frank Bowers, ed., The True Report
    on Flying Saucers (Greenwich, Ct.:
    Fawcett, 1967), p.52. il.
    Lloyd Mallan, "UFO Hoaxes and Hallu-
    cinations: Part II," Sci.& Mech. 38
    (Apr.1967):44,83. il.
  1975, summer/=hoax
    Rudi Beardman, "UFOs Kidnapped My
    Daughter," Official UFO 2 (Feb.
    1977):29.
-UFO (CE-1)
  1973, Nov.6/Manzano Laboratory
    R.C. Hecker, "New Mexico Reports,"
    APRO Bull. 23 (Sep.-Oct.1974):5.
  1975, Aug.7
    "UFO Central," CUFOS News Bull., 15
    Nov.1975, p.15.
-UFO (CE-2)
  1959, Aug.13/SE of town
    "AF Secretly Warns Pilot of Danger,"
    UFO Inv. 2 (Mar.-Apr.1965):5.
  1964, April 28/Sharon Stull
    Albuquerque Journal, 28 Apr.1964.
    "The Stull Case," APRO Bull. 12 (May
    1964):1-2.
    "Girl Burned by Strange Rays While
    Watching UFO," Saucer News 11 (Sep.
    1964):11-12.
    Timothy Green Beckley, "The Strange
    Effects of Flying Saucers," Saga
    UFO Rept. 2 (winter 1974):32,69.
  1967, May 26/Bobby Grant/Atrisco Ave.
    "Car Buzzing Incidents on Increase,"
    APRO Bull. 15 (May-June 1967):5,6.
  1973, May 25/Michael Paulikonis/4938
  Palo Alto SE
    R.C. Hecker, "New Mexico Reports,"
    APRO Bull. 23 (Sep.-Oct.1974):5.
  1974, May 28
    George D. Fawcett, "A Review of Some
    of the Thousands of UFO Sightings
    in 1974 to Date," Flying Saucers,

Dec.1974, p.38.
-UFO (DD)
  1947, July 5/Jess Satahite
  1947, July 5/John Goyng
    Albuquerque Journal, 6 July 1947.
  1948, July 27
    Jacques Vallee, Anatomy of a Phenom-
    enon (N.Y.: Ace, 1965 ed.), p.94.
  1952, Feb.18/Tijeras Canyon
    H.B. Darrach, Jr. & Robert Ginna,
    "Have We Visitors from Space?"
    Life, 7 Apr.1952, pp.80,91-92.
    Donald H. Menzel, Flying Saucers
    (Cambridge: Harvard Univ., 1953),
    pp.30-31.
  1952, April 23/Carl Hawk/Kirtland AFB
    "Flying Wing over Albuquerque," Fate
    11 (Apr.1958):51.
    Coral E. Lorenzen, Flying Saucers:
    The Startling Evidence of the Inva-
    sion from Outer Space (N.Y.: Signet,
    1966 ed.), p.37.
  1952, June 28/Kirtland AFB
    J. Allen Hynek, The UFO Experience
    (Chicago: Regnery, 1972), pp.60-61.
  1974, April 15/George Torres/Tijeras
  Canyon
    R.C. Hecker, "New Mexico Reports,"
    APRO Bull. 23 (Sep.-Oct.1974):5-6.
-UFO (NL)
  1917, Nov./Arthur L. Campa/N. 4th St.
  1930, fall/Arthur L. Campa/N. Albuquerque St.
    Arthur L. Campa, Treasure of the San-
    gre de Cristos (Norman: Univ. of
    Oklahoma, 1963), pp.157-59.
  1947, July 1/Max Hood/Candelaria Rd.
    Albuquerque Journal, 2 July 1947.
  1948, Nov./Kirtland AFB
    Edward J. Ruppelt, The Report on Un-
    identified Flying Object (Garden
    City: Doubleday, 1956), p.47.
  1949, Feb.17
    Bruce S. Maccabee, "UFO Related In-
    formation from the FBI Files: Part
    6," MUFON UFO J., no.130 (Sep.1978)
    :8,11-12.
  1951, Aug.25/Central Ave.
    Edward J. Ruppelt, The Report on Un-
    identified Flying Objects (Garden
    City: Doubleday, 1956), pp.96-97.
    Jacques Vallee, Anatomy of a Phenom-
    enon (N.Y.: Ace, 1965 ed.), p.99.
    U.S. Air Force, Project Grudge and
    Blue Book Reports 1-12 (Washington:
    NICAP, 1968), pp.11,41-42.
  1951, Nov.10
    Richard Hall, ed., The UFO Evidence
    (Washington: NICAP, 1964), p.131.
  1952, April 29/Tijeras Canyon
    Albuquerque Journal, 30 Apr.1952.
  1952, July 29
    U.S. Air Force, Project Grudge and
    Blue Book Reports 1-12 (Washington:
    NICAP, 1968), p.148.
  1952, Aug.2/Doyle Kline
    Albuquerque Journal, 2 Aug.1952.
  1952, Dec.28
    U.S. Air Force, Project Grudge and
    Blue Book Reports 1-12 (Washington:

NICAP, 1968), p.188.
1956, Sep./J.F. Ramseier
    (Editorial), Fate 10 (Feb.1957):9.
1957, Nov.4/Dale Van Fleet
1957, Nov.5/Delbert Boyd/5 mi.SW
    Coral E. Lorenzen, Flying Saucers:
    The Startling Evidence of the Inva-
    sion from Outer Space (N.Y.: Signet,
    1966 ed.), pp.98-99.
1958, April 14/Oliver Dean
    Richard Hall, ed., The UFO Evidence
    (Washington: NICAP, 1964), p.22.
1961, Sep.2
    Jacques Vallee, Anatomy of a Phenom-
    enon (N.Y.: Ace, 1965 ed.), p.218.
1972, Jan.13
    Hayden C. Hewes, "The UFO 'Raid' That
    Sparked a White House Alert," Saga's
    1973 UFO Special, pp.8,66.
1975, Dec.11
    "Noteworthy UFO Sightings," Ufology
    2 (spring 1976):43.
1978, Nov.30/Mabe Elliot/S on Hwy.47
    Raton Daily Range, 14 Dec.1978.
-UFO (R)
1959, Sep.13/Kirtland AFB
1959, Oct.1/Kirtland AFB
    Coral & Jim Lorenzen, UFOs: The Whole
    Story (N.Y.: Signet, 1969), pp.103-
    104.
-UFO (R-V)
1953, Jan.26
    Edward J. Ruppelt, "What Our Air
    Force Found Out about Flying Sau-
    cers," True, May 1954, pp.19-30,
    124-34.
1954, July 3/20 mi.N
    "Saucer Files Reviewed," CRIFO Newsl.,
    6 Aug.1954, p.4.
1957, Nov.4/R.M. Kaser/Kirtland AFB
    Gordon D. Thayer, "Optical and Radar
    Analyses of Field Cases," in Edward
    U. Condon, ed., Scientific Study of
    Unidentified Flying Objects (N.Y.:
    Bantam, 1969 ed.), pp.141-43.
    James E. McDonald, "The Kirtland Air-
    field UFO," Flying Saucer Rev. 16
    (Sep.-Oct.1970):6-8.
    J. Allen Hynek, The UFO Experience
    (Chicago: Regnery, 1972), pp.76-79.
1975, Jan.16/Kirtland AFB
    (Letter), Randall C. Hecker, Fate 28
    (Nov.1975):117-18.

Alcalde
-UFO (CE-2)
1958, Feb.20/Mrs. Leroy Evans/NE on
U.S.64
    Santa Fe New Mexican, 20 Feb.1958;
    and 23 Feb.1958.
    (Editorial), Fate 11 (July 1958):18-
    19.

Anthony
-Humanoid
1968, summer/Cosette Willoughby/6 mi.N
1971/Mildred Sanders
    (Letter), Cosette Willoughby, Fate
    24 (June 1971):132,145.
-UFO (DD)

1964, April 28
    "Other Recent Sightings," UFO Inv.
    2 (July-Aug.1964):7.

Arrey
-UFO (DD)
1949, April 24/Charles B. Moore, Jr./
3 mi.N
    H.B. Darrach, Jr. & Robert Ginna,
    "Have We Visitors from Space?" Life,
    7 Apr.1952, pp.80,89.
    J. Gordon Vaeth, 200 Miles Up: The
    Conquest of the Upper Air (N.Y.:
    Ronald, 1956), pp.113-16.
    J. Allen Hynek, The UFO Experience
    (Chicago: Regnery, 1972), pp.63-64.
    J. Allen Hynek, The Hynek UFO Report
    (N.Y.: Dell, 1977), pp.104-105.

Artesia
-Entombed frog and lizard
1946, Oct.13
    "Fight! Fight!" Doubt, no.17 (1947):
    258.
-UFO (DD)
1952, Jan.16/Alvin H. Hazel/airport
    Thomas M. Olsen, ed., The Reference
    for Outstanding UFO Sighting Re-
    ports (Riderwood, Md.: UFO Informa-
    tion Retrieval Center, 1966), pp.
    5-6.
    Jacques & Janine Vallee, Challenge
    to Science (N.Y.: Ace, 1966 ed.),
    pp.19-21.
    U.S. Air Force, Project Grudge and
    Blue Book Reports 1-12 (Washington:
    NICAP, 1968), p.104.
    J. Allen Hynek, The UFO Experience
    (Chicago: Regnery, 1972), pp.61-62.
-UFO (NL)
1965, Aug.1
    Coral E. Lorenzen, "Western UFO Flap,"
    Fate 18 (Nov.1965):42,47.

Aztec
-Archeological site
1100-1150, 1225-1285/1 mi.N
    Earl H. Morris, "The Aztec Ruin,"
    Anthro.Pap.Am.Mus.Nat.History, vol.
    26 (1928).
    John M. Corbett, Aztec Ruins Nation-
    al Monument, New Mexico (Washing-
    ton: National Park Service, 1963).
    Roland Richert, Excavation of a Por-
    tion of the East Ruin, Aztec Ruins
    National Monument, New Mexico
    (Globe, Ariz.: Southwestern Monument
    Ass'n, Tech.ser., vol.4, 1964). il.
-UFO (?)
1948, spring/Silas Newton/crashed UFO/
=hoax?
    Kansas City (Kan.) Wyandotte Echo,
    16 Jan.1950.
    Denver (Colo.) Post, 12 Mar.1950; 9
    Oct.1950; 14 Oct.1950; and 19 Oct.
    1950.
    Denver (Colo.) Rocky Mountain News,
    9 Sep.1950.
    Frank Scully, Behind the Flying Sau-
    cers (N.Y.: Holt, 1950), pp.19-26,

28-30,127-40.
J.P. Cahn, "Flying Saucers and the
Mysterious Little Men," True, Sep.
1952, pp.17-19,102-12.
Roland Gelatt, "Flying Saucer Hoax,"
Saturday Review, 6 Dec.1952, p.31.
Donald H. Menzel, Flying Saucers
(Cambridge: Harvard Univ., 1953),
pp.149-66.
Mike McClellan, "The UFO Crash of
1948 Is a Hoax," Official UFO 1
(Oct.1975):36-37,60-64.
(Letter), Robert Spencer Carr, Of-
ficial UFO 1 (Feb.1976):8.
Leonard H. Stringfield, "Retrievals
of the Third Kind," in 1978 MUFON
UFO Symposium Proc. (Seguin, Tex.:
MUFON, 1978), pp.77-79,100-101.

Bandelier National Monument
-Archeological site
1200-1550
Alfred V. Kidder, "An Introduction to
the Study of Southwestern Archaeology," Pap.Phillips Acad.Southwestern
Expedition, no.1 (1924).

Belen
-Haunt
1976/Gordon Snidow
(Editorial), Fate 29 (June 1976):24-
26.
-Phantom image
1927-1951/Ramon Baca/511 Dalies Ave.
O.E. Singer, "The Vision in the Window," Fate 4 (Oct.1951):49-51.

Bernalillo
-Hex
n.d.
Wesley R. Hurt, Jr., "Witchcraft in
New Mexico," El Palacio 47 (Apr.
1940):73-83.

Bingham
-UFO (NL)
1933, summer/Holm O. Bursum, Jr./nr.
Bursum Ranch
Socorro El Defensor Chieftain, 31
Sep.1965.

Blanco
-Human tracks in sandstone
1900/Dennis Chavez
Albuquerque Daily Times, 22 Nov.1974.

Capitan
-UFO (DD)
1947, June 27/Mrs. Cummins
Albuquerque Journal, 2 July 1947.

Carlsbad
-UFO (CE-1)
1969, March 1
(Editorial), Fate 22 (Oct.1969):32.
-UFO (DD)
1953, Sep.24/Wayne Evrage
"Reports from Everywhere," Fate 7
(May 1954):23,26, quoting AP re-
lease, 25 Sep.1953.

-UFO (NL)
1944, March
Richard Hall, ed., The UFO Evidence
(Washington: NICAP, 1964), p.19.
1958, Aug./Arnold Crabb
(Editorial), Fate 11 (Dec.1958):22.
1965, Aug.1
Coral E. Lorenzen, "Western UFO Flap,"
Fate 18 (Nov.1965):42,47.

Carrizozo
-UFO (NL)
1957, Nov.9/Coral E. Lorenzen/10 mi.E
on U.S.380
Coral E. Lorenzen, Flying Saucers:
The Startling Evidence of the Inva-
sion from Outer Space (N.Y.: Signet,
1966 ed.), p.102.
1972, Jan.12/10 mi.N
Hayden C. Hewes, "The UFO 'Raid'
That Sparked a White House Alert,"
Saga's 1973 UFO Special, pp.8,66.

Central
-UFO (DD)
1951, Aug./Alford Roos
Richard Hall, ed., The UFO Evidence
(Washington: NICAP, 1964), p.56.

Chama
-UFO (NL)
n.d.
Juan B. Rael, ed., Cuentos Españoles
de Colorado y de Nuevo Méjico, 2
vols. (Philadelphia: American Folklore Society, 1939-42), 2:595.

Chamberino
-Haunt
1970s
L.C. Hayden, "A Haunting in Chamberino," New Mexico Folklore Record
13 (1973):19-21.

Chilili
-UFO (?)
1974, May 17/Manzano Laboratory
R.C. Hecker, "New Mexico Reports,"
APRO Bull. 23 (Sep.-Oct.1974):6.

Chimayo
-Cattle mutilation
1978, Nov.26/Ramon Medina
Santa Fe New Mexican, 28 Nov.1978.
Espanola Rio Grande Sun, 30 Nov.1978.
-Healing
1975/Shrine of Our Lord of Esquipulas
"Miracle Clay?" Fate 28 (Sep.1975):
45, quoting Chicago (Ill.) Daily
News (undated).
"The American Lourdes," Newsweek, 19
Apr.1976, pp.89-90. il.
(Editorial), Fate 29 (Dec.1976):26-
28.

Cimarron
-UFO (NL)
1961, Jan.17
"New Mexico Sightings Continue," APRO
Bull. 9 (Jan.1961):1,4.

Coral & Jim Lorenzen, UFOs: The Whole Story (N.Y.: Signet, 1969), pp.226-27.

Clayton
-Fire anomaly
1960, Oct.22-23/Allen Polling/40 mi.SW
(Editorial), Fate 14 (Feb.1961):8-10.

Cliff
-Archeological site
ca.1420-1575/Kwilleylekia
Franklin Folsom, America's Ancient Treasures (N.Y.: Rand McNally, 1974), p.34.
-UFO (CE-2)
1947, June 29/Arthur Howard
Albuquerque Journal, 30 June 1947.

Cloudcroft
-UFO (DD)
1974, Oct.11
"Astronomers and UFO's: A Survey, Part 2--Sightings," Int'l UFO Reporter 2 (Apr.1977):4.

Clovis
-Aeromancy
1956, June 12
H. Addington Bruce, "Have You Tried Scrying?" Fate 10 (Apr.1957):75,78.
-Clairvoyance
1964, Feb.16/Rose Smith
(Editorial), Fate 17 (June 1964):6.
-UFO (?)
1976, Jan.23/Scott Price/=Saturn
Chicago (Ill.) Sun-Times, 26 Jan. 1976.
Columbus (O.) Dispatch, 27 Jan.1976.
Joe Brill, "Clovis, NM, Sightings," Skylook, no.99 (Feb.1976):14.
Eugene W. Cross, "The Clovis Affair," APRO Bull. 24 (May 1976):2-3.
Ray Stanford, "Clovis, NM, 'UFO' Was Unfocussed Saturn," Skylook, no.102 (May 1976):8-9. il.
-UFO (CE-2)
1954, May 18/Frederick J. Brown/nr. Cannon AFB
Otto D. Binder, "'Oddball' Saucers... That Fit No Pattern," Fate 21 (Feb. 1968):54,57.
-UFO (NL)
1952, April 21/Norman G. Markham/501 Pile St.
"The Picture Shown Here..." Doubt, no.37 (1952):153-54. il.
1957, Nov.2/Odis Echols
Donald E. Keyhoe, Flying Saucers: Top Secret (N.Y.: Putnam, 1960), p. 114.

Cochiti Pueblo
-Humanoid myth
pinini
John Peabody Harrington, "The Ethnogeography of the Tewa Indians," Ann. Rept.Bur.Am.Ethn. 29 (1907-1908): 29,418,435,500-501,549.

Columbus
-Inner development
1970s/City of Sun Foundation
Jim Brandon, Weird America (N.Y.: Dutton, 1978), p.144.

Continental Divide
-UFO (?)
1953, Jan.26/=balloon
Gordon D. Thayer, "Optical and Radar Analyses of Field Cases," in Edward U. Condon, ed., Scientific Study of Unidentified Flying Objects (N.Y.: Bantam, 1969 ed.), pp.143-45.
U.S. Air Force, Project Grudge and Blue Book Reports 1-12 (Washington: NICAP, 1968), pp.192-93.

Corrales
-UFO (CE-2)
1972, Nov./Charles Coulter/I-25 frontage rd.
Cliff Booth, "UFO-Cycle Encounter," APRO Bull. 26 (May 1978):1-3.
-UFO (NL)
1966, June 23/Julian Sandoval/U.S.85 nr. Sandia Crest
Christian Science Monitor, 11 July 1966.
"New Reports by Space Experts Add to UFO Proof," UFO Inv. 3 (Aug.-Sep.1966):3.

Coyote
-Cattle mutilation
1978, May/Julius Ferran
"A Weekend in April," Stigmata, no. 4 (summer 1978):6,11.

Datil
-Healing
1896, Jan.-March/Francis Schlatter
Harry Byron Magill, Biography of Francis Schlatter, the Healer (Denver: Schlatter, 1896).
Francis Schlatter, The Life of the Harp in the Hand of the Harper (Denver: Smith-Brooks, 1897).
Francis Schlatter, Modern Miracles of Healing (Kalamazoo, Mich.: The Author, 1903).
Francis Schlatter, The Secret of Schlatter's Healing Revealed (Kalamazoo, Mich.: The Author, 1903).
Agnes Morley Cleaveland, No Life for a Lady (Boston: Houghton Mifflin, 1941).
-UFO (CE-1)
1961, Oct.23/Rhonda DuBois/W on U.S.60
"Young Couple Terrified by Pursuing Light," APRO Bull. 10 (Jan.1962):1.
-UFO (NL)
1950, Feb.24
Bruce S. Maccabee, "UFO Related Information from the FBI Files: Part 6," MUFON UFO J., no.130 (Sep.1978) :8,12.

Deming
-UFO (?)

1957, Nov.3/Robert Toby
Donald E. Keyhoe, Flying Saucers:
Top Secret (N.Y.: Putnam, 1960), p.
116.
-UFO (CE-3)
1972, June?/Hilda McAfee/23 mi.E on
I-10
"New Mexico Occupant Case," APRO
Bull. 24 (Dec.1975):1,3.

Dulce
-Cattle mutilation
1976, June/Manuel Gomez/13 mi.E
Newhall (Cal.) Signal and Saugus En-
terprise, 19 July 1976.
Ray Nelson, "Night Mutilators of the
Southwest," Saga UFO Rept. 6 (Nov.
1978):24,52.
Jim Brandon, Weird America (N.Y.:
Dutton, 1978), p.149.
1978, April 24/Manuel Gomez/13 mi.E
Albuquerque Journal, 25 Apr.1978.
"A Weekend in April," Stigmata, no.
4 (summer 1978):6,9-10.
Ray Nelson, "Night Mutilators of the
Southwest," Saga UFO Rept. 6 (Nov.
1978):24-26. il.
1978, May 29/Howard Vigil/S of town
Ray Nelson, "Night Mutilators of the
Southwest," Saga UFO Rept. 6 (Nov.
1978):24,26.
1978,June 12/Manuel Gomez/13 mi.E
Albuquerque Journal, 16 June 1978;
and 13 Dec.1978.
"A Weekend in April," Stigmata, no.
4 (summer 1978):6,11-12.
1978, Oct.4/18 mi.SW
Espanola Rio Grande Sun, 14 Dec.1978.
-UFO (NL)
1978, Dec./Joe Lucero
Espanola Rio Grande Sun, 14 Dec.1978.

Duran
-Cattle mutilation
1979, Jan.29
Estancia Torrance County Citizen, 1
Feb.1979.

Edgewood
-UFO (CE-2)
1964, April 28/Don Adams
Coral Lorenzen, "Southwestern UFO's
and the Straight-Line Mystery,"
Fate 17 (Aug.1964):39,41-42.
"Green Object at Edgewood," APRO
Bull. 13 (Sep.1964):3.

El Morro
-Petroglyphs
Franklin Folsom, America's Ancient
Treasures (N.Y.: Rand McNally,
1974), p.33.

El Vado
-UFO (R)
1952, Nov.9/=radar echo?
U.S. Air Force, Project Grudge and
Blue Book Reports 1-12 (Washington:
NICAP, 1968), p.161.

Engle
-Cattle mutilation
1976, Feb./Rhea Howe Ranch
Ed Sanders, "On the Trail of the
Night Surgeons," Oui, May 1977, pp.
79,121.
-UFO (DD)
1947, June 27/Robert Dwan
Albuquerque Journal, 29 June 1947.
Ted Bloecher, Report on the UFO Wave
of 1947 (Washington: NICAP, 1967),
p.III-10.

Espanola
-UFO (NL)
1966, Nov.8/Nick Naranjo
"Light Clusters over N.M.," APRO Bull.
15 (Jan.-Feb.1967):8.

Estancia
-UFO (NL)
1961, Jan.1/Mary Salazar/Hwy.41
"New Mexico Sightings Continue," APRO
Bull. 9 (Jan.1961):1,4.

Fairacres
-Phantom
1976/Cosette Willoughby
(Letter), Probe the Unknown 4 (Nov.
1976):8.

Farmington
-UFO (?)
1966, April 22/=flare experiment?
Edward U. Condon, ed., Scientific
Study of Unidentified Flying Objects
(N.Y.: Bantam, 1969 ed.), pp.463-
67. il.
1972, Jan.13
Hayden C. Hewes, "The UFO 'Raid' That
Sparked a White House Alert," Saga's
1973 UFO Special, pp.8,66.
-UFO (DD)
1950, March 17/Clayton J. Boddy/=bal-
loon?
Farmington Daily Times, 18 Mar.1950.
Edward J. Ruppelt, The Report on Un-
identified Flying Objects (Garden
City: Doubleday, 1956), pp.75-76.

Fence Lake
-Dowsing
1933
E.Z. Vogt, "Water Witching: An Inter-
pretation of a Ritual Pattern in a
Rural American Community," Sci.
Monthly 75 (Sep.1952):175-86.

Flora Vista
-Ancient inscription
1910/Earl Halstead Morris
E.B. Sayles, Fantasies of Gold (Tucson: Univ. of Arizona, 1968), pp.
87-102. il.
Neill J. Harris, "The Riddle of America's Elephant Slabs," Sci.Digest
69 (Mar.1971):74-77. il.

Folsom
-Archeological site

ca.9000 B.C./8 mi.W
    J.D. Figgins, "The Antiquity of Man
    in America," Nat.History 27 (1927):
    229-39. il.
    Harold J. Cook, "New Geological and
    Palaeontological Evidence Bearing
    on the Antiquity of Mankind in A-
    merica," Nat.History 27 (1927):
    240-47. il.
    C.W. Ceram, The First American (N.Y.:
    Mentor, 1972 ed.), pp.290-94,305-12.

Fort Bayard
-UFO (CE-1)
    1967, Oct.9/Macario Borrego/golf
    course
        Jim & Coral Lorenzen, UFOs over the
        Americas (N.Y.: Signet, 1968), p.
        169.

Fort Sumner
-UFO (DD)
    1947, July 10/Lincoln LaPaz
        H.B. Darrach, Jr. & Robert Ginna,
        "Have We Visitors from Space?"
        Life, 7 Apr.1952, pp.80,84-89.

Fort Union
-Ghost
    n.d.
        Charles M. Skinner, Myths and Legends
        of Our Own Land, 2 vols. (Philadel-
        phia: Lippincott, 1896), 2:208-10.

Fort Wingate
-Fire immunity
    1884/Washington Matthews/20 mi.NW
        Washington Matthews, "The Mountain
        Chant: A Navajo Ceremony," Ann.Rept.
        Bur.Am.Ethn. 5 (1883-84):385,441-
        43. il.

Gallup
-UFO (DD)
    1952, Jan.
        Harold T. Wilkins, Flying Saucers on
        the Attack (N.Y.: Ace, 1967 ed.),
        p.265.
-UFO (NL)
    1947, June 27/Art Roberts
        Santa Fe New Mexican, 30 June 1947.

Gran Quivira
-Archeological site
    800-1675
        Elisha Jones, "Prehistoric Ruins in
        New Mexico," Am.Antiquarian 15
        (1893):150-51.
        Gordon Vivian, Excavations in Sev-
        enteenth Century Jumano Pueblo--
        Gran Quivira (Washington: National
        Park Service, 1964). il.

Grants
-Out-of-body experience
    1935, fall/William W. Bathlot
        William W. Bathlot, "Miraculous
        Cure," Fate 4 (May-June 1951):51-53.

Groveton
-UFO (NL)
    1978, Nov.16/Bob Hart
        Berlin Reporter, 29 Nov.1978.

Hermanas
-UFO (DD)
    1952, Aug.24/Carl Sanderson
        Donald E. Keyhoe, Flying Saucers from
        Outer Space (N.Y.: Holt, 1953), p.
        121.
        Donald H. Menzel & Lyle G. Boyd, The
        World of Flying Saucers (Garden
        City: Doubleday, 1963), pp.47-48.

Hernandez
-Cattle mutilation
    1978, Nov.26/Joe Morfin
        Santa Fe New Mexican, 28 Nov.1978.

Hobbs
-UFO (CE-2)
    1957, Nov.5
        El Paso (Tex.) Times, 7 Nov.1957.
    1959, Feb.25/Jim Dobbs, Jr./S on Hwy.18
        Coral & Jim Lorenzen, UFOs: The Whole
        Story (N.Y.: Signet, 1969), pp.93-
        94.
    1964, June 2/Charles Davis
        Houston (Tex.) Chronicle, 4 June
        1964.
        Coral E. Lorenzen, Flying Saucers:
        The Startling Evidence of the Inva-
        sion from Outer Space (N.Y.: Signet,
        1966 ed.), pp.226-27.
-UFO (CE-4)
    1974, Sep.
        Leonard H. Stringfield, Situation
        Red: The UFO Siege (N.Y.: Fawcett,
        1977 ed.), p.177.
-UFO (DD)
    1955, April 6/Bill Watson/S of U.S.62
        "The Hobbs Incident," CRIFO Newsl.,
        6 May 1955, p.1.
    1964, April 28
        "Other Recent Sightings," UFO Inv.
        2 (July-Aug.1964):7.
-UFO (NL)
    1954, Sep.24/Fred H. Talbot
        "New Mexico's Haunted Skies," CRIFO
        Newsl., 5 Nov.1954, p.4.
    1954, Oct.14/R.S. Fleming
        "Five Neo-Type Saucers Shuttle over
        Hobbs," CRIFO Newsl., 5 Nov.1954,
        p.5, quoting Hobbs Daily News (un-
        dated).
    1965, Aug.1
        Coral E. Lorenzen, "Western UFO Flap,"
        Fate 18 (Nov.1965):42,47.
    1973, Oct.29/Jerry Doughty/airport
        Hobbs Daily News-Sun, 30 Oct.1973.

Holman
-Phantom image
    1975, May 18-   /Immaculate Heart of
    Mary Church
        Kansas City (Mo.) Star, 8 June 1975.
        National Enquirer, 19 Aug.1975. il.

Hope
-UFO (DD)
  1947, June 27/W.C. Dodds
    Albuquerque Journal, 2 July 1947.
    Ted Bloecher, Report on the UFO Wave
    of 1947 (Washington: NICAP, 1967),
    p.III-9.

Isleta
-Coffin anomaly
  1775-   /Juan José de Padilla/Church
  of St. Augustine
    Edmond P. Gibson, "Father Padilla:
    The Monk Who Rose from the Grave,"
    Fate 8 (Sep.1955):32-37.
-Ghost
  ca.1911/Juan Pancho
    Winifred Hawkridge Dixon, "Isleta:
    Why the Church Has a Wooden Floor,"
    Scribner's 70 (Aug.1921):193-99.
-Hex
    Elsie Clews Parsons, "Isleta, New
    Mexico," Ann.Rept.Bur.Am.Ethn. 47
    (1929-30):201,204-205,242-43,278,
    340,425-43.
-Witch trial (hex)
  1733/Melchor Trujillo
    Tibo J. Chávez, "Early Witchcraft in
    New Mexico," El Palacio 77 (1970):
    7-9.
    Marc Simmons, Witchcraft in the
    Southwest (Flagstaff: Northland,
    1974), pp.30-32.

Jemez Springs
-Archeological site
  prehistoric-1658
    Elsie Clews Parsons, "The Pueblo of
    Jemez," Pap.Phillips Acad.Southwes-
    tern Expedition, no.3 (1925). il.
    Franklin Folsom, America's Ancient
    Treasures (N.Y.: Rand McNally,
    1974), p.34.

Jicarilla Apache Reservation
-Cattle mutilation
  1978, April 30/Rawleigh Tafoya
    "A Weekend in April," Stigmata, no.
    4 (summer 1978):6,10-11.
    Ray Nelson, "Night Mutilators of the
    Southwest," Saga UFO Rept. 6 (Nov.
    1978):24,26-27. il.
  1978, Oct.6/Anna Baltazar
    Albuquerque Journal, 8 Oct.1978.

Laguna
-Rock pillars
    J.S. Schlee, "Sandstone Pipes of the
    Laguna Area, New Mexico," J.Sedi-
    mentary Petrology 33 (1963):112-23.

La Madera
-Hex
  1930s
    Marc Simmons, Witchcraft in the
    Southwest (Flagstaff: Northland,
    1974), p.49.
-UFO (CE-2)
  1964, April 26/Orlando Gallegos
    Albuquerque Journal, 28 Apr.1964.

"Incident at La Madera," APRO Bull.
    13 (July 1964):4,6.
"Physical Evidence Landing Reports,"
    UFO Inv. 2 (July-Aug.1964):5.
Coral Lorenzen, "Southwestern UFO's
    and the Straight-Line Mystery," Fate
    17 (Aug.1964):39-40.
Reading (Pa.) Eagle, 14 Jan.1970.

Lamy
-Cattle mutilation
  1978, Nov.12
    Espanola Rio Grande Sun, 30 Nov.1978.
-UFO (CE-3)
  1880, March 26
    Santa Fe Daily New Mexican, 27-28
    Mar.1880.

Las Cruces
-Hex
  1955, spring
    Albuquerque Journal, 8 June 1955.
-UFO (?)
  1957, Nov.2?
    Houston (Tex.) Chronicle, 7 Nov.1957.
-UFO (DD)
  1947, June 29/C.J. Zohn/15 mi.NE on
  Hwy.17
    Washington (D.C.) Times-Herald, 8
    July 1947.
    Ted Bloecher, Report on the UFO Wave
    of 1947 (Washington: NICAP, 1967),
    p.III-18.
-UFO (NL)
  1949, Aug.20/Clyde W. Tombaugh
    H.B. Darrach, Jr. & Robert Ginna,
    Life, 7 Apr.1952, pp.80,89.
    Donald H. Menzel, Flying Saucers
    (Cambridge: Harvard Univ., 1953),
    pp.36-38.
    "World-Renowned Astronomer Describes
    Sighting," CRIFO Orbit, 4 May 1956,
    p.3.
    Richard Hall, ed., The UFO Evidence
    (Washington: NICAP, 1964), p.53.
    Donald H. Menzel & Lyle G. Boyd, The
    World of Flying Saucers (Garden
    City: Doubleday, 1963), pp.266-70.
  1957, May 1/Cosette Weiss
    (Letter), Fate 10 (Dec.1957):116-17.
  1962, Jan.15/Dan Garcia
    El Paso (Tex.) Herald-Post, 16 Jan.
    1962.
  1967, March 3,9,11,13/New Mexico State
  University
    "The White Sands Incidents," APRO
    Bull. 15 (Mar.-Apr.1967):1,3-4.
  1968, Aug.12/Willy Barela, Jr.
    "Around the World," APRO Bull. 17
    (Sep.-Oct.1968):6.

Las Vegas
-Cattle mutilation
  1978, June 16?/nr. Camp Luna
    Albuquerque Journal, 22 June 1978.
-Haunt
    La Llorona
    Elsa & Omar Barker, "La Llorona,"
    True West, Sep.-Oct.1972, p.39.
-Horse mutilation

1978, June 9/Albert Padilla
  Las Vegas Optic, 12 June 1978.
  Alamogordo Daily News, 15 June 1978,
  p.11.
-UFO (?)
  1950, June 26/E.L. Remlin
    Ray Palmer, "New Report on the Fly-
    ing Saucers," Fate 4 (Jan.1951):63,
    80.
    Kenneth Arnold & Ray Palmer, The Com-
    ing of the Saucers (Boise: The Au-
    thors, 1952), p.152.
-UFO (DD)
  1950, March 17/Robert Hilgers
    Las Vegas Optic, 18 Mar.1950.
-UFO (NL)
  1948, Dec.5, 8
    Edward J. Ruppelt, The Report on Un-
    identified Flying Objects (Garden
    City: Doubleday, 1956), pp.48-50.

Lindreth
-Cattle mutilation
  1978, July 10
    Ray Nelson, "Night Mutilators of the
    Southwest," Saga UFO Rept. 6 (Nov.
    1978):24,52.

Llano
-Poltergeist
  1966, July/Jane Quintana
    Santa Fe New Mexican, 25-29 July
    1966.
    V.M. Windes, "Flying Rocks and Boun-
    cing Lights in Llano, New Mexico,"
    Fate 20 (Nov.1967):96-99.
-Shape-shifting and witchcraft
  n.d.
    Cleofas M. Jaramillo, Shadows of the
    Past (Santa Fe: Ancient City, 1972),
    pp.101-103.

Lordsburg
-Haunt
  1950s/Frank Hill/2½ mi.S
    "The Sulphurous Spook," Fate 11 (Feb.
    1958):80.
-UFO (?)
  1955, April 6/Paul Mallott/Burro Mts.
    "Green Fireballs Strike--Target New
    Mexico!" CRIFO Newsl., 6 May 1955,
    p.1.
-UFO (CE-1)
  1964, April 22/Marie Morrow/20 mi.E
    "Huge Light Buzzed Car in New Mexi-
    co," APRO Bull. 12 (May 1964):10.
-UFO (CE-2)
  1975, Jan.6/Lady Mary Mine Rd.
    "UFO-Car Encounters Continue," APRO
    Bull. 23 (June 1975):3-4.
-UFO (NL)
  1975, June 14-15/Rick Campbell/5 mi.W
    Patti Morris, "Apparent Landing in
    New Mexico," APRO Bull. 24 (July
    1975):5-6.
  1979, Feb.22/Bill Tufts/nr. I-10
    Lordsburg Liberal, 2 Mar.1979.

Los Alamos
-Ghost

1975, July 4/Golda David
  Golda David, "Bubi Warned Me," Fate
  32 (Jan.1979):65-67.
-UFO (?)
  1945, Aug./Enrico Fermi/=Venus
    Donald H. Menzel, Flying Saucers
    (Cambridge: Harvard Univ., 1953),
    p.28.
    (Letter), George L. Weil, Washington
    (D.C.) Post, 8 Nov.1973.
-UFO (CE-3)
  1949/Nicholas E. von Poppen/crashed
  UFO
    Gray Barker, "America's Captured
    Flying Saucers: Cover-Up of the
    Century," Saga UFO Rept. 4 (May
    1977):32,66-73.
-UFO (DD)
  1952, July 29/Los Alamos Canyon
    J. Allen Hynek, The Hynek UFO Report
    (N.Y.: Dell, 1977), pp.61-64.
  1967, March 24
    J. Allen Hynek, The UFO Experience
    (Chicago: Regnery, 1972), p.56.
-UFO (NL)
  1948, Dec.5-1949, Jan.6/AEC installa-
  tion
    Bruce S. Maccabee, "UFO Related In-
    formation from the FBI Files: Part
    5," MUFON UFO J., no.124 (Mar.1978)
    :7-8.
  1952, July 29
    Donald E. Keyhoe, Flying Saucers
    from Outer Space (N.Y.: Holt, 1953),
    p.97.
    U.S. Air Force, Project Grudge and
    Blue Book Reports 1-12 (Washington:
    NICAP, 1968), p.147.

Los Cerrillos
-UFO (NL)
  1977, Oct.24
    "UFOs of Limited Merit," Int'l UFO
    Reporter 2 (Dec.1977):3.

Los Lunas
-Ancient inscription
  Inscription Rock
    Bill Mack, "An Ancient Roman Settle-
    ment in America?" Argosy, Mar.1972,
    pp.42-43. il.
    Jack Kutz, "New Mexico's Mystery
    Stone," Desert Mag., Aug.1973, pp.
    12-41.
    Jim Brandon, Weird America (N.Y.:
    Dutton, 1978), pp.145-46. il.
-Fall of weblike substance
  1958, Feb.21/Mrs. Joe Tondre/1 mi.S
    (Editorial), Fate 11 (July 1958):16.
    "Falls," Doubt, no.57 (1958):4,6-7,
    quoting Santa Fe New Mexican (un-
    dated).

Lovington
-Mystery plane crash
  1955, Oct./B-47
    John A. Keel, Our Haunted Planet
    (Greenwich, Ct.: Fawcett, 1971), p.
    207.
-UFO (NL)

1976, Sep.30/Mrs. Merle Arledge
Bobbie Wolf, "UFO over New Mexico,"
APRO Bull. 26 (Aug.1977):5-6.

Lucy
-Archeological site
   William B. Roosa, "The Lucy Site in
   Central New Mexico," Am.Antiquity
   21 (1956):310.

Magdalena
-Cave anomaly
   1963/R.L. Dobbins
      "Recent News Stories," Saucer News
      10 (June 1963):19; (Sep.1963):13.
-UFO (NL)
   1963, June
      "Recent News Stories," Saucer News
      10 (Sep.1963):13.

Malaga
-Horse mutilation
   1979, Jan./Clarence McDonald
      Las Cruces Sun-News, 28 Jan.1979.
      Carlsbad Current Argus, 29 Jan.1979.

Manzano
-Hex
   n.d.
      Wesley R. Hurt, Jr., "Witchcraft in
      New Mexico," El Palacio 47 (Apr.
      1940):73-83.

Maxwell
-UFO (DD)
   1953, June 13/Walter L. Vance
      (Letter), Fate 6 (Oct.1953):104-106.

Mora
-Hex
   1939, Dec.25/Evelion Espinosa
      New York Times, 1 Jan.1940.

Mora co.
-Meteorite crater
   10 m.diam. x 1 m.deep/terrestrial
      Lincoln LaPaz, "A Possible Meteorite
      Crater in Northeastern New Mexico,"
      Pop.Astron. 57 (1949):136-37. il.

Moriarty
-UFO (DD)
   1952, April 13/E of town
      U.S. Air Force, Projects Grudge and
      Blue Book Reports 1-12 (Washington:
      NICAP, 1968), p.109.

Nambé
-Hex
   1822/Juan Inocencio
      Marc Simmons, Witchcraft in the
      Southwest (FLagstaff: Northland,
      1974), p.100.
-Witch trial (cannibalism)
   1854, March/Luis Romero
      W.W.H. Davis, El Gringo (N.Y.: Har-
      per, 1857).
      Marc Simmons, Witchcraft in the
      Southwest (Flagstaff: Northland,
      1974), pp.96-98.

-Witchcraft
   1850s-1880s
      Marc Simmons, Witchcraft in the
      Southwest (Flagstaff: Northland,
      1974), pp.102-105.

Nara Visa
-UFO (NL)
   1975
      "A Non-Encounter," Stigmata, no.4
      (summer 1978):16.

Newcomb
-UFO (DD)
   1947, June 25/B.A. Tillery
      Santa Fe New Mexican, 30 June 1947.

Newman
-UFO (DD)
   1952, April
      Coral & Jim Lorenzen, UFOs: The Whole
      Story (N.Y.: Signet, 1969), p.43.

Ojo Caliente
-UFO (NL)
   1978, Nov.17/Comanche Canyon
      Espanola Rio Grande Sun, 23 Nov.1978.

Orogrande
-UFO (CE-2)
   1957, Nov.4/James Stokes/U.S.54
      Alamogordo Daily News, 5 Nov.1957.
      Terry Clarke, "The Day All Roads
      Led to Alamogordo," Writer's Digest
      38 (Dec.1957):24-31.
      Coral E. Lorenzen, Flying Saucers:
      The Startling Evidence of the Inva-
      sion from Outer Space (N.Y.: Signet,
      1966 ed.), pp.94-98.
   1957, Nov.7/Trent Lindsey/U.S.54
      Coral E. Lorenzen, Flying Saucers:
      The Startling Evidence of the Inva-
      sion from Outer Space (N.Y.: Signet,
      1966 ed.), pp.99-100.

Oscura
-UFO (NL)
   1967, Feb.10/Richard Martinez/U.S.54
      "UFOs Reported in Tularosa Basin,"
      APRO Bull. 15 (Jan.-Feb.1967):8.

Pecos
-Archeological site
   ca.1450-1838
      "The Last of the Montezumas," Sci.Am.
      2 (1847):205.
      A.F. Bandelier, "Report on the Ruins
      of the Pueblo of Pecos," Pap.Arch.
      Inst.Am. (Am.ser., vol.1, 1883),
      pp.35-133.
      Alfred Vincent Kidder & Charles Avery
      Amsden, "The Pottery of Pecos, Vol.
      I," Pap.Phillips Acad.Southwestern
      Expedition, no.5 (1931).
      Alfred Vincent Kidder, "The Artifacts
      of Pecos," Pap.Phillips Acad.South-
      western Expedition, no.6 (1932). il.
      Alfred Vincent Kidder & Anna O. Shep-
      ard, "The Pottery of Pecos, Vol.II,"
      Pap.Phillips Acad.Southwestern Ex-

pedition, no.7 (1936).
Alfred V. Kidder, "Pecos, New Mexico:
Archeological Notes," Pap.Peabody
Found.for Arch., no.5 (1958).
-Montezuma myth
A.F. Bandelier, "Report on the Ruins
of the Pueblo of Pecos," Pap.Arch.
Inst.Am. (Am.ser., vol.1, 1883),
pp.35,111-12.
Frank G. Applegate, Indian Stories
from the Pueblos (Philadelphia:
Lippincott, 1929), pp.171-78.
Josiah Gregg, Commerce of the Prair-
ies (Norman: Univ. of Oklahoma,
1954), p.189.
Marc Simmons, Witchcraft in the
Southwest (Flagstaff: Northland,
1974), pp.130-34.

Picurís
-Archeological site
ca.1275-recent
Franklin Folsom, America's Ancient
Treasures (N.Y.: Rand McNally,
1974), p.37.
-Hex
1800
Marc Simmons, Witchcraft in the
Southwest (Flagstaff: Northland,
1974), pp.34-35.

Pintada
-UFO (DD)
1952, April 9
Albuquerque Journal, 10 Apr.1952.

Portales
-Fall of weblike substance
1957, Oct.23-24
Portales News-Tribune, 24-25 Oct.
1957; and 27 Oct.1957.
1958, Oct.9
"Falls," Doubt, no.59 (1959):37.
Richard Hall, ed., The UFO Evidence
(Washington: NICAP, 1964), p.101,
quoting AP release, 10 Oct.1958.

Prewitt
-Archeological site and haunt
L.A.6383/9 mi.E
Rick Lane, "Apache Warrior Finds
Peace," Fate 20 (Feb.1967):72-79.

Puyé
-Archeological site
ca.1250-1550
Edgar Lee Hewett, "The Excavation at
Puye, New Mexico," Pap.Arch.Inst.
Am., no.4 (1909).

Quay co.
-Phantom helicopter
1975, Nov.
Denver (Colo.) Record Stockman, 13
Nov.1975.

Questa
-Stigmata and healing
1972-1975/Sr. Lucy Rael
Kansas City (Mo.) Star, 10 Apr.1975.

Bill Starr, "Texas Stigmatist: Sister Lucy Heals for Christ," Fate
28 (Aug.1975):34-40. il.
Raymond Bayless, "Stigmata," Probe
the Unknown 3 (Sep.1975):14-17. il.

Raton
-UFO (NL)
1978, Nov.-Dec.
Raton Daily Range, 14 Dec.1978.

Rodarte
-Cattle mutilation
1978, Sep.17/George Maestas
Taos News, 21 Sep.1978.

Roswell
-UFO (?)
1967, Oct.
"After You, Alphonse!" Fate 22 (Apr.
1969):97.
-UFO (CE-1)
1968, June 20/Larry Ferney
Donald E. Keyhoe & Gordon I.R. Lore,
Jr., UFOs: A New Look (Washington:
NICAP, 1969), p.6.
-UFO (CE-2)
1947, July 8/crashed UFO
Harold T. Wilkins, Flying Saucers on
the Attack (N.Y.: Ace, 1967 ed.),
pp.66-67.
Bruce S. Maccabee, "UFO Related In-
formation from the FBI Files," APRO
Bull. 26 (Nov.1977):6.
Leonard H. Stringfield, "Retrievals
of the Third Kind: Part 2," MUFON
UFO J., no.129 (Aug.1978):8,10-11.
-UFO (DD)
1952, July 29/Walker AFB
J. Allen Hynek, The Hynek UFO Report
(N.Y.: Dell, 1977), pp.114-15.
-UFO (NL)
1948, summer
Donald H. Menzel, Flying Saucers
(Cambridge: Harvard Univ., 1953),
pp.33-34.
1963, July 11/Joe A. Nieto
(Editorial), Fate 16 (Nov.1963):18.
1974, Nov.30/NE of town
"UFO-Car Encounters Continue," APRO
Bull. 23 (June 1975):1,3.

Ruidoso Downs
-Gravity anomaly
Arthur Shuttlewood, UFOs: Key to the
New Age (London: Regency, 1971),
p.82.

San Acacia
-UFO (?)
1948, July 17
Donald E. Keyhoe, Flying Saucers: Top
Secret (N.Y.: Putnam, 1960), p.90.

San Cristobal
-Inner development
1970s/Lama Foundation
Armand Biteaux, The New Consciousness (Willits, Cal.: Oliver, 1975),
p.89.

-Petroglyph
   John C. Brandt & Ray A. Williamson,
   "Rock Art Representations of the
   A.D.1054 Supernova: A Progress Re-
   port," in Anthony F. Aveni, ed.,
   Archaeoastronomy in Pre-Columbian
   America (Austin: Univ. of Texas,
   1975), pp.171-77. il.

Sandia Pueblo
-Witch trial (hex)
   1797/Sr. Cristóbal
   Marc Simmons, Witchcraft in the
   Southwest (Flagstaff: Northland,
   1974), pp.32-33.

San Ildefonso
-Hex
   1799/Juan Domingo Caracho
   Marc Simmons, Witchcraft in the
   Southwest (Flagstaff: Northland,
   1974), pp.33-34.

San Juan Pueblo
-Hex
   1708
   Marc Simmons, Witchcraft in the
   Southwest (Flagstaff: Northland,
   1974), pp.28-30.

San Mateo
-Shape-shifting
   1887-1888/Juan Perea
   Charles F. Lummis, Some Strange Cor-
   ners of Our Country (N.Y.: Century,
   1892), p.71.
   Charles F. Lummis, Mesa, Cañon and
   Pueblo (N.Y.: Century, 1925), p.351.
-UFO (?)
   n.d./Nicolás Mariño
   Charles F. Lummis, A New Mexico David
   (N.Y.: Scribner, 1905), p.129.

San Miguel
-UFO (DD)
   1947, June 27/Mrs. David Appelzoller
   Santa Fe New Mexican, 3 July 1947.

San Rafael
-Shape-shifting
   1880s/Antonia Morales
   Charles F. Lummis, A New Mexico David
   (N.Y.: Scribner, 1905), p.125.

Santa Clara Pueblo
-Cattle mutilation
   1978, Nov.11-13/Star Gutierrez, Sr.
   Santa Fe New Mexican, 15 Nov.1978.
   Espanola Rio Grande Sun, 16 Nov.1978;
   and 30 Nov.1978.

Santa Fe
-Hex
   1630s/Beatriz de los Angeles
   France V. Scholes, "The First Decade
   of the Inquisition in New Mexico,"
   New Mexico Hist.Rev. 10 (1935):195,
   220-22.
   Angélico Chávez, Origins of New Mexico Families in the Spanish Colonial

Period (Santa Fe: Historical .Soc'y
   of New Mexico, 1954), p.69.
-Poltergeist
   1930, Nov./Charles M. Cree
   Charles M. Cree, "Piano-Playing Pol-
   tergeist," Fate 8 (June 1955):46-48.
-UFO (?)
   1949, Dec.4
   Santa Fe New Mexican, 5 Dec.1949.
   1977, Sep.24/airport/=clouds
   "Strange Cloud over New Mexico,"
   APRO Bull. 26 (Oct.1977):5.
-UFO (CE-1)
   1953, Oct.25/Jim Milligan/Bishop Lodge
   Rd. x Ball Park Rd.
   Albuquerque Tribune, 3 Nov.1953.
-UFO (CE-2)
   1957, Nov.6/Joe Martinez
   Santa Fe New Mexican, 6 Nov.1957.
   1962, Jan.16
   "Aerial Phenomena--Radio Failure,"
   APRO Bull. 10 (Mar.1962):3.
-UFO (NL)
   1949, Dec.4/Howard Atkins
   Santa Fe New Mexican, 5 Dec.1949.
   1952, Jan./airport
   Harold T. Wilkins, Flying Saucers
   on the Attack (N.Y.: Ace, 1967 ed.),
   p.265.
   1954, Aug.6
   Harold T. Wilkins, Flying Saucers
   Uncensored (N.Y.: Pyramid, 1967 ed.),
   p.237.
   1954, Sep.18
   "Giant Fireball Terrifies New Mexi-
   cans," CRIFO Newsl., 5 Nov.1954,
   p.4.
   Edward J. Ruppelt, The Report on Unidentified Flying Objects (Garden
   City: Doubleday, 1956), p.47.
   1964, April 27/Dorothy Tinkham/Arroyo
   Mascaras
   Coral Lorenzen, "Southwestern UFO's
   and the Straight-Line Mystery," Fate
   17 (Aug.1964):39,41.
   1975, Dec.19
   "UFO Central," CUFOS News Bull., 1
   Feb.1976, p.15.
-Weather control
   n.d./Church of Our Lady of Guadelupe/
   417 Agua Fria
   Charles M. Skinner, Myths and Legends
   of Our Own Land, 2 vols. (Philadelphia: Lippincott, 1896), 2:210-12.
-Witch trial (hex)
   1628/Luís de Rivera
   France V. Scholes, "The First Decade
   of the Inquisition in New Mexico,"
   New Mexico Hist.Rev. 10 (1935):195,
   208-14.
   1668/Bernardo Gruber
   Marc Simmons, Witchcraft in the
   Southwest (Flagstaff: Northland,
   1974), pp.23-25.

Santa Rosa
-UFO (DD)
   1972, Aug.10/Henry Baros
   Santa Rosa News, 10 Aug.1972.

Scholle
-Petroglyph
John C. Brandt & Ray A. Williamson,
"Rock Art Representations of the
A.D.1054 Supernova: A Progress Re-
port," in Anthony F. Aveni, ed.,
Archaeoastronomy in Pre-Columbian
America (Austin: Univ. of Texas,
1975), pp.171-77. il.

Shiprock
-UFO (DD)
1947, June 27/R.L. Hopkins/25 mi.S
Denver (Colo.) Post, 28 June 1947.

Silver City
-UFO (NL)
1947, June 25/R.F. Sensenbaugher
Santa Fe New Mexican, 27 June 1947.
1958/R.V. Shoemaker/E St.
(Letter), Fate 21 (Dec.1968):132-34.

Socorro
-Geomagnetic anomaly
"Magma Body Beneath El Paso," Sci.
News 110 (1976):394.
-UFO (CE-3)
1964, April 24/Lonnie Zamora/W of Old
Rodeo St.
"UAO Landing in New Mexico," APRO
Bull. 12 (May 1964):1,3-10. il.
"Physical Landing Evidence Reports,"
UFO Inv. 2 (July-Aug.1964):4-5. il.
Coral Lorenzen, "UFO Lands in New
Mexico," Fate 17 (Aug.1964):27-38.
il.
"Socorro Analysis," UFO Inv. 2 (Sep.-
Oct.1964):4.
Coral Lorenzen, "Do You Recognize
This Symbol?" Fate 17 (Oct.1964):47.
(Letter), Frank Keel, Fate 18 (Feb.
1965):119-20.
El Paso (Tex.) Times, 24 Apr.1965.
Coral E. Lorenzen, Flying Saucers:
The Startling Evidence of the Inva-
sion from Outer Space (N.Y.: Signet,
1966 ed.), pp.218-22.
W.T. Powers, "The Landing at Socorro,"
in The Humanoids (FSR special issue
no.1, Aug.1967), pp.47-51. il.
Philip J. Klass, UFOs: Identified
(N.Y.: Random House, 1968), pp.194-
225. il.
Philip J. Klass, UFOs Explained (N.Y.:
Random House, 1974), pp.105-14. il.
Brad Steiger, ed., Project Blue Book
(N.Y.: Ballantine, 1976), pp.106-37.
il.
Ray Stanford, Socorro "Saucer" in a
Pentagon Pantry (Austin: Blueapple,
1976). il.
Richard Hall, "Pentagon Pantry: Is
the Cupboard Bare?" MUFON UFO J.,
no.108 (Nov.1976):15-18.
J. Allen Hynek, The Hynek UFO Report
(N.Y.: Dell, 1977), pp.223-29. il.
"The Socorro, New Mexico Landing--
Additional Witnesses?" Int'l UFO
Reporter 3 (Sep.1978):15.
Ralph C. DeGraw, "Socorro Witness

Interviews," MUFON UFO J., no.131
(Oct.1978):14-15.
Robert Barrow, "An Incredible Admis-
sion: What Did the Air Force Mean?"
Pursuit 12 (winter 1979):10-12.
-UFO (NL)
1883, Oct.5/Socorro Park
Decatur (Ill.) Daily Republican, 6
Oct.1883, p.2.
1977, Oct.10
"Airline Crew Spots UFO," APRO Bull.
26 (Sep.1977):1,3.

Taos
-Cattle mutilation
1979, Jan.12/Frank Suazo/2 mi.W
Albuquerque Journal, 15 Jan.1979.
Taos News, 18 Jan.1979.
-Giant frog legend
J. Mooney, "Jicarilla Genesis," Am.
Anthro. 11 (1898):197,201-202.
-Haunt
1970-   /Dennis Hopper's hacienda
(Editorial), Probe the Unknown 4
(Mar.1976):10.
-Montezuma myth
John E. Sunder, Matt Field on the
Santa Fe Trail (Norman: Univ. of
Oklahoma, 1960), pp.184-86.
-Phantom image
1896-   /Henri Ault/Mission of St.
Francis Assisi
Toby Harnett, "Mystery Cross of Taos,"
Fate 12 (Dec.1959):56-58. il.
-UFO (CE-2)
1975, Nov.10/David Rivera/Kit Carson
Rd.
"Huge Object over New Mexico," APRO
Bull. 24 (Jan.1976):3-4.
1978, July 1/Mrs. Elias Vargas/3 mi.NW
Albuquerque Journal, 13 Dec.1978.
Taos News, 21 Dec.1978.
-UFO (NL)
1952, Jan./U.S. Hill
(Editorial), Fate 5 (Apr.-May 1952):
9-10.
-Witchcraft
1675-1680/Popé
Fray Angelico Chávez, "Pohé-yemo's
Representative and the Pueblo Re-
volt of 1680," New Mexico Hist.Rev.
42 (1967):85-126.

Tapia Azul
-Hex
Floy Padilla, "Witch Stories from
Tapia Azul and Tres Fulgores," New
Mexico Folklore Record 6 (1951-52):
11-19.

Texico
-UFO (NL)
1976, Jan.23/Willie Ronquillo
Ray Stanford, "Clovis, NM, 'UFO' Was
Unfocused Saturn," Skylook, no.102
(May 1976):8-9.

Tierra Amarilla
-Cattle mutilation
1978, July 3/Robert Rodela

Ray Nelson, "Night Mutilators of the
Southwest," Saga UFO Rept. 6 (Nov.
1978):24,54.
-Hex
  1882
  Santa Fe New Mexican, 2 Oct.1882.

Truth or Consequences
-UFO (DD)
  1947, June 20/Annabel Mobley
  Albuquerque Journal, 2 July 1947.
  1952, Aug.3
  U.S. Air Force, Projects Grudge and
  Blue Book Reports 1-12 (Washington:
  NICAP, 1968), p.150.

Tucumcari
-UFO (CE-2)
  1951, Dec.13/Lorenzo Gutierrez
  Cleveland (O.) Plain Dealer, 14 Dec.
  1951.
  (Editorial), Fate 5 (June 1952):4-5.
  Coral & Jim Lorenzen, UFOs: The Whole
  Story (N.Y.: Signet, 1969), pp.40-
  41.
-UFO (CE-3)
  ca.1956/Bill Browder/N of town/=hoax?
  (Letter), Mrs. H.R. Dickson, Fate 10
  (May 1957):116-19.
-UFO (DD)
  1950, Jan.10
  Los Angeles (Cal.) Times, 11 Jan.
  1950.

Tularosa
-UFO (?)
  1947, June 27
  Albuquerque Journal, 29 June 1947.
-UFO (DD)
  1967, March 2
  "The White Sands Incidents," APRO
  Bull. 15 (Mar.-Apr.1967):1,3.

Vaughn
-UFO (?)
  1957, Nov.7/Erwin de Oliviera
  Coral E. Lorenzen, Flying Saucers:
  The Startling Evidence of the Invasion from Outer Space (N.Y.: Signet,
  1966 ed.), p.99.

Wagon Mound
-UFO (DD)
  1933, April 14/17 mi.SE
  1941, April 11
  1975, March 28
  "Pre-1947 Reports," APRO Bull. 24
  (Feb.1976):4.

Waterflow
-Ancient inscription
  Don Rickey, "Two Southwestern Petro-
  glyph Sites," Occ.Pub.Epigraphic
  Soc'y 6, no.138 (Jan.1979):200-208.
  il.
  Barry Fell, "Report on a Rupestral
  Inscription from Waterflow, New Mex-
  ico," Occ.Pub.Epigraphic Soc'y 6,
  no.139 (Jan.1979):209-10.

Weed
-UFO (?)
  1955, April 6
  "Green Fireballs Strike--Target New
  Mexico!" CRIFO Newsl., 6 May 1955,
  p.1.

White Oaks
-UFO (CE-2)
  1957, Nov.9
  Richard Hall, ed., The UFO Evidence
  (Washington: NICAP, 1964), p.75,
  quoting APRO Bull., Nov.1957.

Whitewater
-Humanoid
  1970, Jan./Clifford Heronemus
  Gallup Independent, 21 Jan.1970.

Zuñi
-Archeological site
  J. Walter Fewkes, "Reconnaissance of
  Ruins in or near the Zuñi Reserva-
  tion," J.Am.Ethn.& Arch. 1 (1891):
  93-132.
  F.W. Hodge, "The First Discovered
  City of Cibola," Am.Anthro. 8 (1895)
  :142-52.
  A.L. Kroeber, "Zuñi Potsherds," An-
  thro.Pap.Am.Mus.Nat.Hist., vol.18,
  no.1 (1916).
  Leslie Spier, "An Outline for a
  Chronology of Zuñi Ruins," Anthro.
  Pap.Am.Mus.Nat.Hist., vol.18, no.3
  (1917).
  F.H.H. Roberts, Jr., "The Village of
  the Great Kivas on the Zuñi Reser-
  vation, New Mexico," Bull.Bur.Am.
  Ethn., no.111 (1932). il.
  Frederick Webb Hodge, History of Ha-
  wikuh, New Mexico (Los Angeles:
  Ward Ritchie, 1937). il.
  Carl C. Seltzer, "Racial Prehistory
  in the Southwest and the Hawikuh
  Zunis," Pap.Peabody Mus., vol.23,
  no.1 (1944).
-Flood myth
  George Wharton James, New Mexico: The
  Land of the Delight Makers (Boston:
  Page, 1920), pp.72-74.
-Hex
  Matilda Coxe Stevenson, "The Zuñi
  Indians," Ann.Rept.Bur.Am.Ethn. 23
  (1901-1902):392-406.
  George Wharton James, New Mexico: The
  Land of the Delight Makers (Boston:
  Page, 1920), pp.80-97.
  Elsie Clews Parsons, "Witchcraft
  among the Pueblos: Indian or Span-
  ish?" Man 27 (1927):106-12,125-28.
  Ruth L. Bunzel, "Introduction to
  Zuñi Ceremonialism," Ann.Rept.Bur.
  Am.Ethn. 47 (1929):467,479,482.
  Florence Hawley, "The Mechanics of
  Perpetuation in Pueblo Witchcraft,"
  in Erik K. Reed & Dale S. King, eds.,
  For the Dean (Tucson: Hohokam Muse-
  ums Ass'n, 1950), pp.143-58.
  Arthur Woodward, "Concerning Witch-
  es," Masterkey 24 (1950):187-88.

Frank Cushing, My Adventures in Zuñi
(Palo Alto, Cal.: American West,
1970 ed.).
Marc Simmons, Witchcraft in the
Southwest (Flagstaff: Northland,
1974), pp.106-26.
-Paleoastronomy
Frank H. Cushing, "My Adventures in
Zuñi," Century Mag. 26 (May 1883):
28-47.
Matilda Coxe Stevenson, "The Zuñi In-
dians," Ann.Rept.Bur.Am.Ethn. 23
(1901-1902):108-62.
John C. Brandt & Ray A. Williamson,
"Rock Art Representations of the
A.D.1054 Supernova: A Progress Re-
port," in Anthony F. Aveni, ed.,
Archaeoastronomy in Pre-Columbian
America (Austin: Univ. of Texas,
1975), pp.171-77. il.
-Use of ancient Libyan symbols
Ignatius Donnelly, Atlantis: The An-
tediluvian World, ed. Egerton Sykes
(N.Y.: Gramercy, 1949), p.144, quot-
ing U.S. Explorations for a Rail-
road Route to the Pacific Ocean.
Barry Fell, America B.C. (N.Y.: Quad-
rangle, 1976), pp.174-91. il.
Barry Fell, "The Structure of the
Zuni Language," Occ.Pub.Epigraphic
Soc'y, vol.3, no.64 (Sep.1976).
George F. Carter, "Some Notes on
Zuni," Occ.Pub.Epigraphic Soc'y,
vol.4, no.94 (Sep.1977).
-Weather control
Matilda Coxe Stevenson, "The Zuñi In-
dians," Ann.Rept.Bur.Am.Ethn. 23
(1901-1902):163-204. il.

B. Physical Features

Animas Peak
-Chinese discovery
ca.1000 B.C.
Henriette Mertz, Gods from the Far
East (N.Y.: Ballantine, 1975 ed.),
p.148.

Animas Valley
-Patterned ground
Walter B. Lang, "Gigantic Drying
Cracks in Animas Valley, New Mexico,"
Science 98 (1943):583-84.
A.L. Washburn, "Classification of
Patterned Ground and Review of Sug-
gested Origins," Bull.Geol.Soc'y
Am. 67 (1956):823-66.

Bat Cave
-Archeological site
3600 B.C.
Herbert W. Dick, "Evidences of Early
Man in Bat Cave and on the Plains
of San Augustin, New Mexico," in
Selected Pap. 29th Int'l Congress
of Americanists (1952), pp.158-63.
Paul S. Mangelsdorf, "Ancestor of
Corn," Science 128 (1958):1313-20.
il.

Blackwater Draw
-Archeological site
ca.9220-7840 B.C.
Edgar B. Howard, "The Occurrence of
Flints and Extinct Animals in Plu-
vial Deposits near Clovis, New Mex-
ico," Proc.Acad.Nat.Sci.Philadelphia
87 (1935):299-303.
John L. Cotter, "The Occurrence of
Flints and Extinct Animals in Plu-
vial Deposits near Clovis, New Mex-
ico," Proc.Acad.Nat.Sci.Philadelphia
89 (1937):2-16; 90 (1938):113-17.
H.M. Wormington, Ancient Man in Am-
erica, 4th ed. (Denver: Museum of
Natural History, 1957), pp.47-51.
il.
F.E. Green, "Additional Notes on Pre-
historic Wells at the Clovis Site,"
Am.Antiquity 28 (1962):230-34.
F.E. Green, "The Clovis Blades: An
Important Addition to the Llano
Complex," Am.Antiquity 29 (1963):
145-65.
James M. Warnica, "New Discoveries at
the Clovis Site," Am.Antiquity 31
(1966):345-57. il.
C. Vance Haynes, Jr., "Elephant Hunt-
ing in North America," Sci.Am. 14
(June 1966):104-12. il.
-Fall of fish
1952, May 3/Fred H. Koch
Fred H. Koch, "Storms and Little
Fishes," Fate 19 (Aug.1966):62-64.

Burnet Cave
-Archeological site
ca.6000 B.C.
Edgar B. Howard, "Evidence of Early
Man in North America," Mus.J.Univ.
Pennsylvania, vol.24, no.2-3 (1935).
Alan Lyle Bryan, "Paleo-American Pre-
history," Occ.Pap.Idaho State Univ.
Mus., no.16 (1965), p.142.

Caballo Reservoir
-UFO (CE-1)
1964, April 26/George Mitropoulis/U.S.
85
Columbus (O.) Dispatch, 28 Apr.1964.
Coral Lorenzen, "Southwestern UFO's
and Straight-Line Mystery," Fate 17
(Aug.1964):39,41.

Carlsbad Caverns
-Mummies
Coral E. Lorenzen, The Shadow of the
Unknown (N.Y.: Signet, 1970), p.58.

Chaco Canyon
-Archeological site
ca.600-1200 A.D./Pueblo Bonito
George H. Pepper, "Pueblo Bonito,"
Anthro.Pap.Am.Mus.Nat.Hist., vol.27
(1920). il.
Andrew Elliott Douglass, "Dating Pueb-
lo Bonito and Other Ruins of the
Southwest," Contrib.Tech.Pap.Nat'l
Geogr.Soc'y, no.1 (1935).
Kirk Bryan, "The Geology of Chaco Can-

yon, New Mexico, in Relation to the
Life and Remains of the Prehistoric
Peoples of Pueblo Bonito," Smith.
Misc.Coll., vol.122, no.7 (1954).
Neil M. Judd, "The Material Culture
of Pueblo Bonito," Smith.Misc.Coll.,
vol.124 (1954). il.
Neil M. Judd, "The Architecture of
Pueblo Bonito," Smith.Misc.Coll.,
vol.147, no.1 (1964). il.
R. Gwinn Vivian, "An Inquiry into
Prehistoric Social Organization in
Chaco Canyon, New Mexico," in Wil-
liam A. Longacre, ed., Reconstruct-
ing Prehistoric Pueblo Societies
(Albuquerque: Univ. of New Mexico,
1970), pp.59-83.
Las Cruces Bulletin, 22 July 1971.
Houston (Tex.) Chronicle, 1 Oct.1974.
Ray A. Williamson, et al., "The As-
tronomical Record in Chaco Canyon,
New Mexico," in Anthony F. Aveni,
ed., Archaeoastronomy in Pre-Colum-
bian America (Austin: Univ. of Texas,
1975), pp.33-43. il.
John C. Brandt, et al., "Possible
Rock Art Records of the Crab Nebula
Supernova in the Western United
States," in Anthony F. Aveni, ed.,
Archaeoastronomy in Pre-Columbian
America (Austin: Univ. of Texas,
1975), pp.45,53-56. il.
Florence Hawley Ellis, "A Thousand
Years of the Pueblo Sun-Moon-Star
Calendar," in Anthony F. Aveni, ed.,
Archaeoastronomy in Pre-Columbian
America (Austin: Univ. of Texas,
1975), pp.59-87.
James I. Ebert & Robert K. Hitchcock,
"Chaco Canyon's Mysterious Highways,"
Horizon 17 (autumn 1975):48-53. il.
Ray A. Williamson, Howard J. Fisher
& Donnel O'Flynn, "Anasazi Solar
Observatories," in Anthony F. Aveni,
ed., Native American Astronomy (Aus-
tin: Univ. of Texas, 1977), pp.203-
13. il.
Jeffrey Goodman, Psychic Archeology
(N.Y.: Berkley, 1978), pp.188-89.
Barry Fell, "Additional Lirian Com-
pass Dial Inscriptions from Spain
and New Mexico," Occ.Pub.Epigraphic
Soc'y 7, no.142 (Apr.1979):51-53.

Chuska Mts.
-Humanoid
  1960s
  1971
    John Green, The Sasquatch File (Ag-
    assiz, B.C.: Cheam, 1973), pp.50,57.

Comanche Spring
-Archaeological site
  5000 B.C.
    New York Times, 17 Dec.1972, p.43.

Cook Mts.
-Roman coins
  n.d.
    Bill Mack, "An Ancient Roman Settle-

ment in America?" Argosy, Mar.1972,
pp.42-43.

Cooks Peak
-Chinese discovery
  ca.1000 B.C.
    Henriette Mertz, Gods from the Far
    East (N.Y.: Ballantine, 1975 ed.),
    pp.147-48.

Florida Mts.
-UFO (NL)
  1968, April/Georgia Hill
    "UFO Blinks Off-On, As Car Lights
    Do," Skylook, no.23 (Oct.1969):6.

Gallinas R.
-Archeological site
  ca.1150
    Frank C. Hibben, "The Mystery of the
    Stone Towers," Sat.Eve.Post, 9 Dec.
    1944, pp.14-15,68-70.
    C.W. Ceram, The First American (N.Y.:
    Mentor, 1972 ed.), pp.327-34.

Gila Cliff
-Archeological site
  ca.100-1400 A.D.
    Elizabeth McFarland, Forever Fron-
    tier: The Gila Cliff Dwellings (San-
    ta Fe: Univ. of New Mexico, 1967).
-Mummy
  1884/James A. McKenna
    James A. McKenna, Black Range Tales
    (N.Y.: Wilson-Erickson, 1936), pp.
    48-49.

Kilbourne Hole
-Mystery tracks
  1954, Jan., 1955/Cosette Weiss
    (Letter), Fate 7 (June 1954):110. il.
    (Editorial), Fate 8 (Mar.1955):8.
    (Letter), Fate 9 (Mar.1956):116-17.

Manzano Peak
-Chinese discovery
  ca.1000 B.C.
    Henriette Mertz, Gods from the Far
    East (N.Y.: Ballantine, 1975 ed.),
    p.136.

Organ Mts.
-UFO (DD)
  1957, July 24/Nathan Wagner
    Coral & Jim Lorenzen, UFOs: The Whole
    Story (N.Y.: Signet, 1969), p.79,
    quoting El Paso (Tex.) Times (un-
    dated).

Picacho Peak
-UFO (DD)
  1967, March 12
    "Student Snaps Disc in N.M.," APRO
    Bull. 15 (Mar.-Apr.1967):1. il.

Pigeon Cliffs
-Archeological site
  6000 B.C.
    Charlie R. Steen, "The Pigeon Cliffs
    Site: A Preliminary Report," El Pal-

acio 62 (1955):174-80. il.
Alan Lyle Bryan, "Paleo-American Pre-
history," Occ.Pap.Idaho State Univ.
Mus., no.16 (1965), p.118.

Pine Lawn Valley
-Archeological site
    Paul S. Martin, John B. Rinaldo &
    Ernst Antevs, "Cochise and Mogollon
    Sites, Pine Lawn Valley, Western
    New Mexico," Fieldiana: Anthropology,
    vol.38, no.1 (1949). il.
    Paul S. Martin, Digging into History
    (Chicago: Natural History Museum,
    Pop.Ser.: Anthro., no.38, 1959). il.
    Elaine A. Bluhm, "Mogollon Settlement
    Patterns in Pine Lawn Valley, New
    Mexico," Am.Antiquity 25 (1960):
    538-46.

Red R.
-Precognition
    1933/Roscoe Netz
        William W. Bathlot, "Roscoe's Three
        Dreams," Fate 8 (Oct.1955):17.

Round Mt.
-UFO (DD)
    1964, April 25/J.D. Hatch
        Coral Lorenzen, "Southwestern UFO's
        and the Straight-Line Mystery," Fate
        17 (Aug.1964):39,40-41.

Sacramento Mts.
-UFO (?)
    1947
        Coral E. Lorenzen, Flying Saucers:
        The Startling Evidence of the Inva-
        sion from Outer Space (N.Y.: Signet,
        1966 ed.), p.21.
    1955, April 6/Camilla Saenz
        "Green Fireballs Strike--Target New
        Mexico!" CRIFO Newsl., 6 May 1955,
        p.1.
-UFO (R-V)
    1967, March 2
        "The White Sands Incidents," APRO
        Bull. 15 (Mar.-Apr.1967):1,3.
        Edward U. Condon, ed., Scientific
        Study of Unidentified Flying Objects
        (N.Y.: Bantam, 1969 ed.), pp.150-51,
        291-95. il.

Saint Augustine Pass
-UFO (DD)
    1947, June 27/E.B. Detchmendy
        Albuquerque Journal, 29 June 1947.
        Ted Bloecher, Report on the UFO Wave
        of 1947 (Washington: NICAP, 1967),
        p.III-9.

Salt L.
-Weather control
    Jim Brandon, Weird America (N.Y.:
    Dutton, 1978), p.143.

San Andres Mts.
-UFO (?)
    1947
        Coral E. Lorenzen, Flying Saucers:

The Startling Evidence of the Invasion from Outer Space (N.Y.: Signet,
1966 ed.), pp.20-21.

Sandia Cave
-Archeological site
    10,000-8000 B.C.
        Frank C. Hibben, "Evidences of Early
        Occupation in Sandia Cave, New Mex-
        ico and Other Sites in the Sandia-
        Manzano Region," Smith.Misc.Coll.,
        vol.99, no.23 (1941).
        Frank C. Hibben, "We Found the Home
        of the First American," Sat.Eve.
        Post, 7 Apr.1945, pp.11-12. il.
        Alan Lyle Bryan, "Paleo-American Pre-
        history," Occ.Pap.Idaho State Univ.
        Mus., no.16 (1965), pp.142-45.

Sandia Mts.
-Ghost light
    n.d.
        Arthur L. Campa, Treasure of the San-
        gre de Cristos (Norman: Univ. of
        Oklahoma, 1963), pp.155-56.
-UFO (NL)
    1948, Dec.5/Capt. Goede
        Edward J. Ruppelt, The Report on Un-
        identified Flying Objects (Garden
        City: Doubleday, 1956), pp.48-49.
    1957, Nov.1
        Richard Hall, ed., The UFO Evidence
        (Washington: NICAP, 1964), p.163.

Sangre de Cristo Mts.
-Out-of-body experience
    n.d./Frank M. Chapman
        Frank M. Chapman, "Operation 'Impos-
        sible,'" Fate 5 (July-Aug.1952):
        104-106.

Sierra Blanca
-Chinese discovery
    ca.1000 B.C.
        Henriette Mertz, Gods from the Far
        East (N.Y.: Ballantine, 1975 ed.),
        pp.136-37.

South Baldy
-Chinese discovery
    ca.1000 B.C.
        Henriette Mertz, Gods from the Far
        East (N.Y.: Ballantine, 1975 ed.),
        p.147.

Truchas Peak
-Chinese discovery
    ca.1000 B.C.
        Henriette Mertz, Gods from the Far
        East (N.Y.: Ballantine, 1975 ed.),
        pp.135-36.

Tschicoma Peak
-Chinese discovery
    ca.1000 B.C.
        Henriette Mertz, Gods from the Far
        East (N.Y.: Ballantine, 1975 ed.),
        pp.146-47.

Twin Buttes
-UFO (CE-1)
  1962, summer
    Santa Ana (Cal.) Register, 23 Nov.
    1972.

White Sands
-Human tracks in stone
  1932/Ellis Wright
    Brad Steiger, Mysteries of Time and
    Space (N.Y.: Dell, 1976 ed.), p.31,
    quoting The Story of the Great White
    Sands.
-UFO (?)
  1957, Oct./John Romero
    "The Night of September 29," Fate 12
    (Feb.1959):31,38.
-UFO (CE-4)
  ca.1949, July 4/Daniel Fry/nr. Organ
  Mts.
    Daniel Fry, The White Sands Incident
    (Los Angeles: New Age, 1954). il.
    Daniel W. Fry, Steps to the Stars
    (Lakemont, Ga.: CSA, 1956).
    Daniel W. Fry, The Curve of Develop-
    ment (Lakemont, Ga.: CSA, 1965).
    Philip J. Klass, UFOs Explained (N.Y.:
    Random House, 1974), pp.248-49.
-UFO (DD)
  1949, June 10/Missile Test Center
    R.B. McLaughlin, "How Scientists
    Tracked Flying Saucers," True, Mar.
    1950, pp.25-28,96-99.
  1949, Aug.29/Missile Test Center
    Los Angeles (Cal.) Times, 29 Aug.1949.
  1950, April 27/Missile Test Center
  1950, May 29/Missile Test Center
    Edward J. Ruppelt, The Report on Un-
    identified Flying Objects (Garden
    City: Doubleday, 1956), pp.88-89.
  1964, April 30/Stallion Site
    "UFO Landing at Air Force Base," APRO
    Bull. 13 (July 1964):1,3-4.
    Coral Lorenzen, "UFO Lands at Air
    Force Base," Fate 17 (Oct.1964):45-
    52.
  1966, Sep.1/Hwy.70
    "The White Sands Incidents," APRO
    Bull. 15 (Mar.-Apr.1967):1.
  1975, Aug.23
    "UFO Central," CUFOS News Bull., 15
    Nov.1975, p.16.
-UFO (NL)
  1952, Nov.25
    U.S. Air Force, Projects Grudge and
    Blue Book Reports 1-12 (Washington:
    NICAP, 1968), p.169.
  1957, Nov.3/Glenn H. Toy/Stallion Site
  1957, Nov.3/Forest R. Oakes/Stallion
  Site
    Albuquerque Journal, 6 Nov.1957.
    Donald E. Keyhoe, Flying Saucers: Top
    Secret (N.Y.: Putnam, 1960), pp.115-
    16.
  1966, Sep.2/Missile Test Center
    "The White Sands Incidents," APRO
    Bull. 15 (Mar.-Apr.1967):1,3.
-UFO (R)
  1964, May 22/Stallion Site
    Coral Lorenzen, "UFO Lands at Air

Force Base," Fate 17 (Oct.1964):45,
48-49.
-UFO (R-V)
  1951, July 14/Missile Test Center
    Donald E. Keyhoe, Flying Saucers
    from Outer Space (N.Y.: Holt, 1953),
    p.48.
  1956, April 30-May 4/Missile Test Center
    Richard Hall, "The UFO Sightings You
    Haven't Heard About," Official UFO
    1 (Apr.1976):36,64.
  1964, May 15/Stallion Site
    Coral Lorenzen, "UFO Lands at Air
    Force Base," Fate 17 (Oct.1964):45,
    48.

            C. Ethnic Groups

Tewa Indians
-Thunderstone legend
    John Peabody Harrington, "The Ethno-
    geography of the Tewa Indians," Ann.
    Rept.Bur.Am.Ethn. 29 (1907-1908):
    29,59.

        D. Unspecified Localities

-Cattle mutilation
  ca.1977
    San Diego (Cal.) Evening Tribune, 7
    Jan.1978.

-Doubtful geography
  1500s/Cibola/=Zuñi Pueblo communities
    Lewis H. Morgan, "The 'Seven Cities
    of Cibola,'" North Am.Rev. 108
    (1869):457-98. il.
    George Parker Winship, "The Coronado
    Expedition, 1540-1542," Ann.Rept.
    Bur.Am.Ethn. 14 (1892-93):329-613.
    Frederick Webb Hodge, History of Ha-
    wikuh, New Mexico (Los Angeles:
    Ward Ritchie, 1937). il.
    Cleve Hallenbeck & Juanita H. Will-
    iams, Legends of the Spanish South-
    west (Glendale, Cal.: Arthur H.
    Clark, 1938), pp.62-73,315-21.
    A. Grove Day, Coronado's Quest (Ber-
    keley: Univ. of California, 1940).
    Stephen Clissold, The Seven Cities of
    Cibola (London: Eyre & Spottiswoode,
    1961). il.
    Paul Horgan, Conquistadors in North
    American History (N.Y.: Farrar,
    Straus, 1963), pp.154-79.
    John L. Sinclair, "Hawikuh--City of
    Cibola," Westways 56 (Jan.1964):23-
    25.
    C.W. Ceram, The First American (N.Y.:
    Mentor, 1972), pp.59-85.

-Fall of limestone
  1933/northern sector
    Frank C. Cross, "Hypothetical Meteor-
    ites of Sedimentary Origin," Pop.
    Astron. 55 (1947):96-102.

-Entombed lizard

ca.1850/Judge Houghton
"Imprisoned Reptiles," Sci.Am. 8
(1853):366.

-Inner development
ca.1830s-   /Los Hermanos Penitentes
Alexander M. Darley, The Passionists
of the Southwest (Pueblo, Colo.:
The Author, 1893). il.
Alice Corbin Henderson, Brothers of
Light (N.Y.: Harcourt, Brace, 1937).
Kessel Schwartz & James Chaplin, Los
Hermanos Penitentes (Lexington:
Univ. of Kentucky Library, 1958).
Cosette Chavez Lowe, "A Lash for the
Grace of God," New Mexico Folklore
Record 11 (1963):18-20.
George Mills & Richard Grove, Lucifer
and the Crucifer (Colorado Springs:
Fine Arts Center, 1966).
Lorayne Ann Horka-Follick, Los Her-
manos Penitentes (Los Angeles: West-
ernlore, 1969). il.
Louisa R. Stark, "The Origin of the
Penitente 'Death Cart,'" J.Am.Folk-
lore 84 (1971):304-10.
Angelico Chavez, My Penitente Land
(Albuquerque: Univ. of New Mexico,
1975).
Marta Weigle, Brothers of Light,
Brothers of Blood (Albuquerque:
Univ. of New Mexico, 1976). il.
Marta Weigle, A Penitente Bibliography
(Albuquerque: Univ. of New Mexico,
1976).
T.H. Watkins, "The Brotherhood of the
Mountains," Am.Heritage 30 (Apr.-
May 1979):58-67. il.

-UFO (CE-2)
1953, summer/Peggy Hight/northern sector
Peggy Hight, "Health Restoring Light,"
Fate 9 (June 1956):26.

-UFO (CE-3)
1962
Leonard H. Stringfield, "Retrievals
of the Third Kind," in 1978 MUFON
UFO Symposium Proc. (Seguin, Tex.:
MUFON, 1978), pp.77,96-98.

-Witchcraft
Marc Simmons, Witchcraft in the
Southwest (Flagstaff: Northland,
1974), pp.69-95.

COLORADO

A. Populated Places

Adams co.
-Cattle mutilation
  n.d.
    Scott Dial, "The Mystery of the Cat-
    tle Mutilations," Westerner, spring
    1976, pp.34,37.

Aguilar
-UFO (CE-1)
  1946, Oct.
    Denver Post, 20 Oct.1968.
    Philip J. Klass, UFOs Explained (N.Y.:
    Random House, 1974), pp.96-97.

Akron
-Cattle mutilation
  1975/NW of town
    Kansas City (Mo.) Times, 11 Sep.1975,
    p.6C.

Alamosa
-UFO (?)
  1967, Sep.28/Brown Hills
    David R. Saunders & R. Roger Harkins,
    UFOs? Yes! (N.Y.: Signet, 1968), p.
    157.
-UFO (DD)
  1964, April 30
    Coral Lorenzen, "Southwestern UFO's
    and the Straight-Line Mystery," Fate
    17 (Aug.1964):39,43-44.
  1978, Dec.19/Bob Trower
    Alamosa Valley Courier, 20 Dec.1978.

Alamosa co.
-Cattle mutilation
  n.d./H.V. Holmes ranch
    Don Worley, "Cattle Mutilations and
    UFOs: Who Are the Mutilators?" Of-
    ficial UFO 1 (Dec.1976):25.
-Horse mutilation
  1967, Sep.9/Berle Lewis/King Ranch
    Alamosa Valley Courier, 6-9 Oct.1967.
    Alamosa Pueblo Chieftain, 5 Oct.1967;
    and 18 Nov.1967.
    Denver Post, 6-12 Oct.1967; and 17
    Nov.1967.
    Denver Rocky Mountain News, 16 Oct.
    1967.
    "Colorado Horse Death Ruled No UFO
    Case," UFO Inv. 4 (Oct.1967):4.
    (Editorial), APRO Bull. 16 (Sep.-
    Oct.1967):1-6.
    "'Snippy' Still Not Dead Issue," APRO
    Bull. 16 (Nov.-Dec.1967):1.
    Coral Lorenzen, "The Great UFO Con-
    troversy: The Appaloosa from Alamo-
    sa," Fate 21 (Mar.1968):34,36-44.
    il.
    Donald Merker, "The Great UFO Con-
    troversy: The Appaloosa from Alamo-
    sa," Fate 21 (Mar.1968):35,45-52.

David R. Saunders & R. Roger Harkins,
    UFOs? Yes! (N.Y.: Signet, 1968),
    pp.155-69.
    (Letter), C.J. Fortner, Fate 22 (Mar.
    1969):125-28.
    Edward U. Condon, ed., Scientific
    Study of Unidentified Flying Objects
    (N.Y.: Bantam, 1969 ed.), pp.344-
    45.
    Jim Brandon, Weird America (N.Y.:
    Dutton, 1978), pp.51-52.
-UFO (?)
  1967, Sep.7/Agnes King/King Ranch
    David R. Saunders & R. Roger Harkins,
    UFOs? Yes! (N.Y.: Signet, 1968),
    p.155.
-UFO (CE-1)
  ca.1962
    Edward U. Condon, ed., Scientific
    Study of Unidentified Flying Objects
    (N.Y.: Bantam, 1969 ed.), pp.345-
    46.
  1967, May 12/Harry King/Sand Dunes Rd.
    Coral Lorenzen, "The Great UFO Con-
    troversy: The Appaloosa from Alamo-
    sa," Fate 21 (Mar.1968):34,39.
  1968, Feb.26/K.P. Wilson/Sand Dunes
    Rd.
    "More from Colorado," APRO Bull. 17
    (Sep.-Oct.1968):7.
-UFO (CE-2)
  1967, May 17/Steve Hardwick/River Rd.
    Coral Lorenzen, "The Great UFO Con-
    troversy: The Appaloosa from Alamo-
    sa," Fate 21 (Mar.1968):34,39.
-UFO (NL)
  1962, Oct.26
    Coral & Jim Lorenzen, UFOs: The Whole
    Story (N.Y.: Signet, 1969), pp.236-
    37.
  1968, Feb.1/K.P. Wilson/NE of King
    Ranch
  1968, Feb.24/K.P. Wilson/nr. King Ranch
    "More from Colorado," APRO Bull. 17
    (Sep.-Oct.1968):7.
-UFOs and other anomalies
  1967-1971/Berle Lewis
    Edward U. Condon, ed., Scientific
    Study of Unidentified Flying Objects
    (N.Y.: Bantam, 1969 ed.), pp.346-47.
    "More UFOs in the Alamosa, Colorado
    Area," Skylook, no.52 (Mar.1972):9.
    Janet Bord, "After Snippy--What Next?"
    Flying Saucer Rev. 18 (Nov.-Dec.
    1972):19-22.

Appleton
-UFO (CE-1)
  1947, June 28/H.E. Soule
    Salt Lake City (Utah) Deseret News,
    5 July 1947.

Arvada
-Animal ESP

1978, Feb./Denny Crites
Sterling Journal-Advocate, 9 Mar.
1978.
"Now Raccoons Are Doing It," Fate 32
(Mar.1979):92.
-Fall of ice
1978, May
Kingston (Ont.) Whig-Standard, 5 May
1978, p.30.

Aspen
-UFO (DD)
1961, June 27/Dave Joranson
"Colorado Campers Sight Oval Object,"
APRO Bull. 10 (July 1961):4.
1977, Jan.21
"UFOs of Limited Merit," Int'l UFO
Reporter 2 (Mar.1977):5.

Atwood
-Humanoid and cattle mutilation
1976, Aug.5/Lebsack Feed Yard
Ed Sanders, "On the Trail of the
Night Surgeons," Oui, May 1977, pp.
79,129.

Aurora
-UFO (DD)
1947, July 7/Ernest Westfall
Denver Rocky Mountain News, 8 July
1947.
1947, July 10
Denver Rocky Mountain News, 11 July
1947.

Bachelor
-Retrocognition
1975, Aug.16/R.G. Williams/=hoax?
R.G. Williams, "Tragedy of the Bachelor Ghosts," Fate 31 (Feb.1978):
47-50.
(Letter), N. Nelson, Fate 31 (July
1978):118-19.
(Letter), Dale Allen, Fate 31 (Oct.
1978):115.
(Letter), Jim Fruth, Fate 31 (Nov.
1978):115-16.

Bellvue
-UFO (?)
1967, Feb.24/=Venus
Edward U. Condon, ed., Scientific
Study of Unidentified Flying Objects
(N.Y.: Bantam, 1969 ed.), pp.290-
91.

Beulah
-Gravity anomaly
Camp Burch/=hoax?
John P. Bessor, "Oregon's Strange
Whirlpool of Force," Fate 4 (July
1951):24,28.
(Letter), J.W. Allen, Fate 5 (Jan.
1952):124-25.

Boulder
-Biofeedback research
1970s/University of Colorado
Thomas H. Budzynski & Johann Stoyva,
"An Instrument for Producing Deep

Muscle Relaxation by Means of Ana-
log Information Feedback," J.Applied
Behavior Analysis 2 (1969):231-37.
Thomas H. Budzynski, et al., "Feed-
back-Induced Muscle Relaxation: Ap-
plication to Tension Headache," J.
Behavior Therapy & Experimental
Psychiatry 1 (1970):205-11.
Gay Luce & Erik Peper, "Biofeedback:
Mind over Body, Mind over Mind,"
New York Times Mag., 12 Sep.1971,
p.132.
Thomas H. Budzynski, et al., "EMG
Biofeedback and Tension Headache:
A Controlled Outcome Study," Psy-
chosomatic Med. 35 (1973):484-96.
-Contactee
1967, Oct./Mr. Dixsun/=hoax
David R. Saunders & R. Roger Harkins,
UFOs? Yes! (N.Y.: Signet, 1968),
pp.152-53,160-61.
-Parapsychology research
1937-1939/Dorothy R. Martin/University
of Colorado
Dorothy R. Martin, "Chance and Extra-
Chance Results in Card Matching,"
J.Parapsych. 1 (1937):185-90.
Dorothy R. Martin & Frances P. Strib-
ic, "Studies in Extra-Sensory Per-
ception," J.Parapsych. 2 (1938):23-
30,287-95; 4 (1940):159-248.
J.G. Pratt, "Change of Call in ESP
Tests," J.Parapsych. 13 (1949):
225-46.
J.G. Pratt & E.B. Foster, "Displace-
ment in ESP Card Test in Relation
to Hits and Misses," J.Parapsych.
14 (1950):37-52,95-115.
J.G. Pratt, Dorothy R. Martin & Fran-
ces P. Stribic, "Computer Studies
of the ESP Process in Card Guessing:
III. Displacement Effects in the
C.J. Records from the Colorado Ser-
ies," J.ASPR 68 (1974):357-84.
-UFO (?)
1951/Leo Sprinkle
1957/Leo Sprinkle/Flatirons
Springdale (Ark.) News, 24 July 1978.
1967, April 1/=balloon?
Edward U. Condon, ed., Scientific
Study of Unidentified Flying Objects
(N.Y.: Bantam, 1969 ed.), pp.300-
305.
-UFO (DD)
1959, Feb.6/Craig L. Johnson/Flagstaff
Mt.
Donald H. Menzel & Lyle G. Boyd, The
World of Flying Saucers (Garden
City: Doubleday, 1963), p.249. il.
Frank Bowers, ed., The True Report
on Flying Saucers (Greenwich, Ct.:
Fawcett, 1967), p.48. il.
-UFO (NL)
1973, Oct.11/Allen Robbins
"1973 Reports Correlate," APRO Bull.
24 (May 1976):1,3-4.

Broomfield
-UFO (NL)
1973, Oct.11/Judy Ruth/SE on U.S.36

"1973 Reports Correlate," APRO Bull.
24 (May 1976):1,4.

Burlington
-UFO (CE-1)
1972, Sep.13/Ronald Ludwig/5 mi.S
"Trio Observe Object in Colorado,"
APRO Bull. 21 (Sep.-Oct.1972):4.
"UFO Passes over Car and Lands in
Corn Field, Burlington, Colo.,"
Skylook, no.60 (Nov.1972):3.

Cañon City
-Archeological sites
E.B. Renaud, "Indian Stone Enclosures
of Colorado and New Mexico," Arch.
Ser.Univ.Denver Dep't of Anthro.,
no.2 (1942):6-9. il.
-Clairvoyance
1884/José Sancho
"A Dream," Light 4 (1884):347, quot-
ing Denver Tribune (undated).
-Poltergeist
1954, Nov.
(Editorial), Fate 8 (June 1955):6.
-UFO (DD)
1967, Nov.3/Eldon W. Arthur/8 mi.W
"UFOs--Nov.--USA," APRO Bull. 16
(Nov.-Dec.1967):8.
-UFO (NL)
1965, Aug.1/Don Stites/Colorado State
Penitentiary
Coral E. Lorenzen, "Western UFO Flap,"
Fate 18 (Nov.1965):42,48, quoting
Denver Rocky Mountain News (undated).

Castle Rock
-UFO (?)
1968, Jan.2/Howard Ellis/=balloon
Owensboro (Ky.) Messenger, 4 Jan.
1968.
Edward U. Condon, ed., Scientific
Study of Unidentified Flying Objects
(N.Y.: Bantam, 1969 ed.), pp.18,
395-96.

Cedaredge
-UFO (NL)
1962, Oct.25/Ed Marah
Kansas City (Mo.) Star, 26 Oct.1962,
p.17.
Richard Hall, ed., The UFO Evidence
(Washington: NICAP, 1964), p.63.

Clifton
-UFO (DD)
1947, July 4/Cora Burks
Denver Post, 6 July 1947.

Colorado Springs
-Bison mutilation
1975, Oct.22/Rodney Walker/Cheyenne
Mountain Zoo
Colorado Springs Gazette-Telegraph,
23 Oct.1975.
Ed Sanders, "The Mutilation Mystery,"
Oui, Sep.1976, pp.51,116-17.
-Clairvoyance and precognition
1930s-1970s/Oilve Wehr/20 mi.NW
Olive C. Wehr, "My Dreams Prophesy,"

Fate 27 (Oct.1974):81-83.
-Electromagnetic anomaly (experiments)
1899, summer/Nikola Tesla
Nikola Tesla, Experiments with Al-
ternating Current of High Potential
and High Frequency (N.Y.: McGraw-
Hill, 1904). il.
John J. O'Neill, Prodigal Genius:
The Life of Nikola Tesla (N.Y.:
Ives Washburn, 1944), pp.175-94.
Kenneth M. Swazey, "Nikola Tesla,"
Science 127 (1958):1147,1154-58.
Inez Hunt & Wanetta W. Draper,
Lightning in His Hand: The Life
Story of Nikola Tesla (Denver:
Sage, 1964). il.
Vojislav M. Popović, Nikola Tesla
(Belgrade: Tehnička Kujiga, 1967),
pp.138-43.
Harry L. Goldman, "Nikola Tesla's
Bold Adventure," American West 8
(Mar.1971):4-9. il.
Gaston Burridge, "Nikola Tesla,"
Pursuit 4 (Apr.1971):36-38.
-Humanoid
1975
John Green, Sasquatch: The Apes Among
Us (Seattle: Hancock House, 1978),
p.173.
-Mystery radio transmission
1899, summer/Nikola Tesla
Leadville Herald-Democrat, 27 Jan.
1901.
Nikola Tesla, "Talking with the Plan-
ets," Collier's Weekly 26 (9 Feb.
1901):4-5.
Leland I. Anderson, "Extra-Terres-
trial Radio Transmissions," Nature
190 (1961):374.
-UFO (?)
1961, Jan.29/=meteor?
"Fireball over Colorado and Kansas,"
APRO Bull. 9 (Jan.1961):6.
-UFO (DD)
1947, July 4/Colorado Springs Air Base
Colorado Springs Gazette-Telegraph,
6 July 1947.
-UFO (NL)
1955, Dec.13
"Latest Saucer Sightings," Fate 9
(Apr.1956):43,47.
-UFO (R)
1967, May 13/airport
Gordon D. Thayer, "Optical and Radar
Analyses of Field Cases," in Edward
U. Condon, ed., Scientific Study of
Unidentified Flying Objects (N.Y.:
Bantam, 1969 ed.), pp.170-71.
Edward U. Condon, ed., Scientific
Study of Unidentified Flying Objects
(N.Y.: Bantam, 1969 ed.), pp.310-16.
Donald H. Menzel, "UFOs--The Modern
Myth," in Carl Sagan & Thornton
Page, eds., UFOs: A Scientific De-
bate (Ithaca, N.Y.: Cornell Univ.,
1972), pp.123,161-63.
Donald H. Menzel & Ernest H. Taves,
The UFO Enigma (Garden City: Double-
day, 1977), pp.103-104,124-25.

Commerce City
-UFO (DD)
1967, Oct.26/Dan Kiscaden
Jim & Coral Lorenzen, UFOs over the
Americas (N.Y.: Signet, 1968), p.
177.

Conejos
-UFO (NL)
19th c./Simeon
Lavette J. Davidson & Forrester Blake,
Rocky Mountain Tales (Norman: Univ.
of Oklahoma, 1947), p.57.

Cortez
-UFO (CE-1)
1970, Oct.13/Dale Kell/5 mi.S
"UFOs in Colorado," Skylook, no.37
(Dec.1970):6.
(Editorial), Fate 24 (Apr.1971):22-
24.

Cripple Creek
-Airship message
1897, April 19/James Graham
Columbus (O.) Evening Press, 20 Apr.
1897.
-Ancient inscription
"The Cripple Creek Inscription in
Greek," NEARA Newsl. 3 (Sep.1968):
54-55. il.
-UFO (DD)
1897, April 19
Columbus (O.) Evening Press, 20 Apr.
1897.

Crook
-UFO (CE-2)
1976, July 15
Ed Sanders, "On the Trail of the
Night Surgeons," Oui, May 1977, pp.
79,126.

Crowley co.
-Cattle mutilation
1975, Sep.
"Animal Reactions," Stigmata, no.5
(fall-winter 1978):16,18.

Cuchara
-Archeological site
E.B. Renaud, "Indian Stone Enclos-
ures of Colorado and New Mexico,"
Arch.Ser.Univ.Denver Dep't of An-
thro., no.2 (1942):11-13.

Del Camino
-UFO (CE-1)
1972, Nov.5/2 mi.S on I-25
Longmont Daily Times-Call, 5 Nov.
1972.

Del Norte
-Archeological site
3½ mi. from town
E.T. Elliott, "The Age of Cave-Dwell-
ers in America," Pop.Sci.Monthly 15
(Aug.1879):488-91.

Delta
-UFO (NL)
1962, Oct.25/Helen G. Mitchell
Kansas City (Mo.) Star, 26 Oct.1962,
p.17.
Richard Hall, ed., The UFO Evidence
(Washington: NICAP, 1964), p.63.

Dent
-Archeological site
ca.9200 B.C.
J.D. Figgins, "A Further Contribution
to the Antiquity of Man in America,"
Proc.Colorado Mus.Nat.Hist. 12
(1933):4-8. il.

Denver
-Animal ESP
1964-1966/Mildred B. Probert
(Editorial), Fate 18 (Mar.1965):12-
14, quoting Denver Rocky Mountain
News (undated).
(Editorial), Fate 18 (July 1965):31.
(Letter), Fate 19 (Dec.1966):147.
(Editorial), Fate 20 (Oct.1967):14-
16.
-Astrology
1930s-1970s/Lucile Wilson
Gordon Keith, "Know Yourself Through
Astrology," Fate 24 (May 1971):64-
70.
1970s/Cora Sitrusis/Box 10295
Warren Smith, "Phenomenal Predictions
for 1975," Saga, Jan.1975, pp.20,52.
Warren Smith, "Phenomenal Predictions
for 1976," Saga, Jan.1976, pp.16,52.
-Clairaudience
1973/Leila Howe
Leila Paulson Howe, "Help Me Mom!
Please Help Me!" Beyond Reality,
no.32 (May-June 1978):22,25.
-Clairvoyance
1959
J. Eisenbud, et al., "A Further Study
of Teacher-Pupil Attitudes and Re-
sults on Clairvoyance Tests in the
Fifth and Sixth Grades," J.ASPR 54
(1960):72-80.
-Disappearance
1931, April 6/Meyer Harrison/house only
"Houses Missing," Fortean Soc'y Mag.
no.9 (spring 1944):3.
-Electromagnetic anomaly
1963, Feb.14/Cherokee Electric Plant
(Editorial), Fate 16 (July 1963):10.
-Fall of ice
1978, July 23/Windsor Gardens
Denver Post, 25 July 1978.
-Fall of unknown substance
1951, Oct.
Harold T. Wilkins, Flying Saucers on
the Attack (N.Y.: Ace, 1967 ed.),
pp.280-81.
-Haunt
1875-   /2334 Lawrence St.
Dennis Bardens, Ghosts and Hauntings
(N.Y.: Ace, 1965), pp.172-74.
1960s/Bradmar House
Susy Smith, Ghosts Around the House
(N.Y.: World, 1970).

1962, Oct.-1964, Feb.
  Hans Holzer, Ghosts of the Golden
  West (N.Y.: Ace, 1968), pp.164-67.
1966, Nov.-   /Arlene Zimmerman
Arlene Zimmerman, "Ghost Money,"
  Fate 22 (June 1969):84-87.
-Healing
  1895, Sep.16-Nov.13/Francis Schlatter
  Henry Byron Magill, Biography of
  Francis Schlatter, the Healer (Den-
  ver: Schlatter, 1896).
  Estella DeFord Graham, "Francis
  Schlatter: A Fool for God," Fate
  8 (Oct.1955):56-61. il.
  (Letter), Elizabeth Tischler, Fate
  9 (Mar.1956):123-24.
  1963-   /Laurel Elizabeth Keyes/2168
  S. Lafayette St.
  Bill D. Schul, "Keeping in 'Tone'
  with Your Body," Probe the Unknown
  2 (summer 1974):28-33. il.
  Armand Biteaux, The New Conscious-
  ness (Willits, Cal.: Oliver, 1975),
  p.49.
-Hex
  1901, Nov./Mr. Maguire/hexed opal
  T.C. Bridges, "Unlucky Possessions,"
  in Bernhardt J. Hurwood, ed., The
  First Occult Review Reader (N.Y.:
  Award, 1968), pp.37,40.
  1961
  "Witchcraft in Denver," Newsweek, 13
  Nov.1961, p.60.
  James A.V. Galvin & Arnold M. Ludwig,
  "A Case of Witchcraft," J.Nervous
  & Mental Disease 133 (1961):161-68.
-Inner development
  1960s-   /Holy Order of Briget
  J. Gordon Melton, The Encyclopedia
  of American Religions, 2 vols.
  (Wilmington, N.C.: Consortium,
  1978), 2:284.
  1974-   /Astro Consciousness Insti-
  tute/1627 S. Emerson St.
  June & Nicholas Regush, Psi: The Oth-
  er World Catalogue (N.Y.: Putnam,
  1974), p.152.
-Intra-mercurial planet
  1878, July 29/Lewis Swift
  Lewis Swift, "Discovery of Vulcan,"
  Nature 18 (1878):539.
  Lewis Swift, "Supposed Discovery of
  Vulcan," Observatory 2 (1878):161-
  62.
  "The Intra-Mercurial Planet," Nature
  18 (1878):569-70.
  (Letter), Lewis Swift, Am.J.Sci.,
  ser.3, 16 (1878):313.
  Lewis Swift, "Planète intra-mercuri-
  elle vue aux États-Unis, pendant
  l'éclipse totale du Soleil du 29
  juillet 1878," Comptes rendus 87
  (1878):427.
  Lewis Swift, "Schreiben des Herrn L.
  Swift an den Herausgeber," Astronom-
  ische Nachrichten 95 (1879):319-24.
-Out-of-body experience
  1926/Edyth Jonze
  Edyth Elizabeth Jonze, "I Saved My
  Son's Life in a Dream," Fate 16

  (Jan.1963):79-83.
-Phantom image
  1976, April/Episcopal church
  Milwaukee (Wisc.) Journal, 24 Apr.
  1976.
-Plant sensitivity
  1968-1971/Dorothy Retallack/Temple
  Buell College
  Denver Post, 21 June 1970, mag.supp.
  New York Times, 21 Feb.1971, p.64.
  Dorothy Retallack, The Sound of Mu-
  sic and Plants (Santa Monica, Cal.:
  DeVorss, 1973).
  Peter Tompkins & Christopher Bird,
  The Secret Life of Plants (N.Y.:
  Harper & Row, 1973), pp.153-61.
-Poltergeist
  1962-1969/Robert A. Bradley/4100 S.
  University Ave.
  (Editorial), Fate 18 (Oct.1965):22-
  24.
  Dennis Bardens, Ghosts and Hauntings
  (N.Y.: Ace, 1965 ed.), pp.176-77.
  Robert A. & Dorothy Bomar Bradley,
  "Our Pregnant Angels," Fate 22
  (Dec.1969):76-83. il.
-Precognition
  1896/John R.M. Taylor
  John R.M. Taylor, "Two Case Records,"
  Psychic Rsch. 25 (1931):513-14.
  1930, March 5/R.G. Gruber
  "Prevision of a Tragedy," Psychic
  Rsch. 24 (1930):239.
-Psychic photography
  1900s-1910s/Alex Martin/Lincoln Hall
  James H. Hyslop, "Experiments with
  Phantasmographs," J.ASPR 14 (1920):
  284-306. il.
  Tom Patterson, 100 Years of Spirit
  Photography (London: Regency, 1965),
  p.30.
-Psychokinesis
  1909-1957/Helen Verba
  Dennis Bardens, Ghosts and Hauntings
  (N.Y.: Ace, 1965 ed.), pp.233-34.
-Religious apparition
  1973, May/Carmen Prieto/Larimer St.
  (Editorial), Fate 27 (Jan.1974):20-
  22, quoting Denver Post (undated).
  il.
-Spirit medium
  1932/Dolly Graves/Delaware St.
  Mary Sue Bissell, "The Medium's Message: Go Tonight, Tomorrow Will Be
  Too Late," Fate 18 (Oct.1965):78-82.
-UFO (?)
  1897, March 30
  New York Herald, 12 Apr.1897, p.5.
  1947, July 3/A.L. Cochran
  Denver Post, 5 July 1947.
  1950, June 29/=balloon
  Donald H. Menzel, Flying Saucers (Cambridge: Harvard Univ., 1953), pp.26-
  27. il.
  1961, Jan.27
  "Green Light at Denver," APRO Bull.
  9 (May 1961):6, quoting Denver Post
  (undated).
  1963, March/Bela Scheiber/Lake Junior
  High School

(Letter), Fate 18 (Mar.1965):114-15.
-UFO (CE-2)
1934/Fort Logan
   Gordon I.R. Lore, Jr. & Harold H.
   Deneault, Jr., Mysteries of the
   Skies: UFOs in Perspective (Engle-
   wood Cliffs, N.J.: Prentice-Hall,
   1968), pp.111-12.
1974, Oct.16/Stapleton Airport
   Ted Phillips, Physical Traces Associated with UFO Sightings (Evanston:
   Center for UFO Studies, 1975), p.
   105, quoting National Enquirer (undated).
   B.R. Strong, "Mysterious Bleeps on
   Radar Screens," Official UFO 1 (Aug.
   1976):28,54-55.
-UFO (DD)
1947, July 3/William F. LeFevre/River
Dr. x W. 8th St.
   Denver Post, 5 July 1947.
1947, July 5/Ed Zimmerman/1354 Elati
   Denver Post, 6-7 July 1947.
1947, July 6/LeRoy Krieger/Buckley NAS
   Denver Rocky Mountain News, 7 July
   1947.
1947, July 6/George Kuger/2385 Ash St.
   Denver Post, 7 July 1947.
1947, July 7/Harry N. Gurley/1644 Lincoln St.
1947, July 7/Mike Miller/2843 Race St.
   Denver Rocky Mountain News, 8 July
   1947.
1947, July 7/John Todd/Lowry Field
   Denver Post, 7 July 1947.
1947, July 8/Fred Cullins/233 Inca St.
   Denver Post, 8 July 1947.
   Denver Rocky Mountain News, 9 July
   1947.
1947, July 8/Richard McNulty/Fitzsim-
mons Hospital
   Denver Rocky Mountain News, 9 July
   1947.
1947, July 9/country club
   Denver Rocky Mountain News, 10 July
   1947.
1950, April 6
   Denver Rocky Mountain News, 6 Apr.
   1950.
1967, May 25/Norman G. Markham
   (Letter), INFO J., no.3 (spring 1968)
   :45-46.
-UFO (NL)
1947, July 2/Henry Martin/700 block
Monroe St.
   Denver Post, 3 July 1947.
1947, July 4/L.A. Walgren/1574 Eliot
   Denver Rocky Mountain News, 6 July
   1947.
1947, July 4/Mrs. John N. Perrin/nr.
Union Station
   Denver Post, 6 July 1947.
1947, July 6/Harold Wallace
   Denver Rocky Mountain News, 7 July
   1947.
1952, spring
   (Editorial), Fate 6 (Feb.1953):11,
   quoting Denver Post (undated).
1952, July 18/Paul L. Carpenter
   Richard Hall, ed., The UFO Evidence

(Washington: NICAP, 1964), p.158,
   quoting UP release, 18 July 1952.
1952, Dec.29/Helen Berglund
   (Editorial), Fate 6 (May 1953):9.
1954, Sep.18
   Edward J. Ruppelt, The Report on Unidentified Flying Objects (Garden
   City: Doubleday, 1956), p.47.
1955, Oct.3-21/C.H. Marck
   "Denver's Devilish Disc," CRIFO Orbit, 2 Dec.1955, p.3.
1956, Aug.12/Mary McCaffrey
   "Case 185," CRIFO Orbit, 7 Sep.1956,
   p.3, quoting Denver Rocky Mountain
   News (undated).
1956, Oct.12/Tom Nalty
   "Case 232," CRIFO Orbit, 2 Nov.1956,
   p.4, quoting Denver Post (undated).
1967, Sep.30-Oct.1/Dan Svoboda
   David R. Saunders & R. Roger Harkins,
   UFOs? Yes! (N.Y.: Signet, 1968),
   p.157.
1967, Oct.5/Charles Bennett
   Jim & Coral Lorenzen, UFOs over the
   Americas (N.Y.: Signet, 1968), p.
   165.
1975, Nov.5
   "UFO Central," CUFOS News Bull., 1
   Feb.1976, p.12.
1976, Feb.13
   "Noteworthy UFO Sightings," Ufology
   2 (summer 1976):62.
1977, Oct.10
   Dave Kenney, "Airline Crew Spots
   UFO," APRO Bull. 26 (Sep.1977):1,3.

Dillon
-UFO (CE-1)
1978, Aug.4
   (Letter), R.D., Saga UFO Rept. 6
   (Jan.1979):4-6.

Dolores
-UFO (CE-2)
1975, Oct.
   D. Ann Slate, "Saucer Slaughter on
   the Prairies," Saga UFO Rept. 4
   (Sep.1977):37,39.

Durango
-Cattle mutilation
1978, Sep.8
   Espanola (N.M.) Rio Grande Sun, 14
   Dec.1978.
-Clairempathy
1970s/Jack Gurian
   (Editorial), Fate 28 (Sep.1975):26-
   28.
-UFO (?)
1952, Aug./=jets
   Donald H. Menzel & Lyle G. Boyd, The
   World of Flying Saucers (Garden
   City: Doubleday, 1963), p.50.
1956, Aug.8/Malcolm Dayton
   "Case 184," CRIFO Orbit, 7 Sep.1956,
   p.3, quoting Denver Rocky Mountain
   News (undated).
-UFO (CE-2)
1960, Dec.24/Wade Folsom
   Durango Herald, 28 Dec.1960.

-UFO (DD)
  1958, July 26/Mrs. Elton Highland
    Richard Hall, ed., The UFO Evidence
    (Washington: NICAP, 1964), p.66,
    quoting UPI release, 26 July 1958.
-UFO (NL)
  1957, Nov.5/Richard Schaeffer
    Coral E. Lorenzen, Flying Saucers:
    The Startling Evidence of the Inva-
    sion from Outer Space (N.Y.: Signet,
    1966 ed.), p.99.
-Weather control
  1934, Aug.1/Navaho Indians
    Eugene Grossenheider, "Does Man Make
    the Weather?" Fate 9 (Feb.1956):
    80,81.

Eaton
-Fall of brass meteorite
  1931, May
    H.H. Nininger, "The Eaton, Colorado,
    Meteorite: Introducing a New Type,"
    Pop.Astron. 51 (1943):273-80. il.
    H.H. Nininger, Out of the Sky (Den-
    ver: Univ. of Denver, 1952), pp.
    82-83.
    Donald H. Menzel, Flying Saucers
    (Cambridge: Harvard Univ., 1953),
    p.250.

Echo Lake
-UFO (CE-3)
  1976, June 9/Michael Lusignan
    Georgetown Clear Creek Courant, 18
    June 1976.

Elbert co.
-Cattle mutilation
  1975, June-Oct.
    Kansas City (Mo.) Times, 11 Sep.
    1975, p.6C.
    Ed Sanders, "The Mutilation Mystery,"
    Oui, Sep.1976, pp.51,114-15.
    Jerome Eden, "Cattle Mutilations and
    UFOs: A Look at the Facts," Offi-
    cial UFO 1 (Dec.1976):22-23.

Englewood
-Inner development
  1915-   /Order of the Lily and the
  Eagle
    J. Gordon Melton, The Encyclopedia
    of American Religions, 2 vols.
    (Wilmington, N.C.: Consortium,
    1978), 2:264.
-Precognition
  1920s-1960s/Elma Hays Sunderlin
    Henry W. Hough, "The Blind Seer Who
    Could 'See,'" Fate 24 (Apr.1971):
    62-68.

Estrella
-UFO (NL)
  1968, April 10/Rickey Bahr/1½ mi.S on
  Hwy.285
    "More from Colorado," APRO Bull. 17
    (Sep.-Oct.1968):7, quoting Alamosa
    Valley Courier (undated).

Fort Collins
-Fall of unknown substance
  1965, April?/=slime mold?
    Coral E. Lorenzen, The Shadow of the
    Unknown (N.Y.: Signet, 1970), pp.
    139-40.
-UFO (DD)
  1947, July 5/Mrs. J.S. Mason
    Denver Post, 6 July 1947.
  1950, June 29/Hubert Hutt
    Kenneth Arnold & Ray Palmer, The Com-
    ing of the Saucers (Boise: The Au-
    thors, 1952), p.152.
-UFO (NL)
  1956, Aug.24-29/Jeanette Frantz
    "Case 200," CRIFO Orbit, 5 Oct.1956,
    pp.2-3, quoting Denver Post (undated).

Fort Lyon
-Fall of ice
  1877, June 24
    (Editorial), Monthly Weather Rev.,
    June 1877, p.7.

Fort Morgan
-UFO (DD)
  1969, Aug.28/Norman Vedaa/I-805
    William H. Spaulding, "Observational
    Data of an Anomalistic Aerial Phe-
    nomenon," Flying Saucer Rev. 22
    (May 1976):12-17. il.
-UFO (NL)
  1957, April 27/Myrtle Longacre
    (Letter), Fate 10 (Nov.1957):117-20.

Franktown
-Phantom helicopter
  1975, Aug.
    Denver Post, 24 Aug.1975.

Gardner
-UFO (NL)
  1920s
    John DeHerrara, "The Ball-of-Light
    Phenomenon," APRO Bull. 25 (Feb.
    1977):8.

Garfield co.
-Cattle mutilation
  1976, April
    Grand Junction Daily Sentinel, 20
    Apr.1976.

Georgetown
-Fall of worms
  1880, Oct./W.E. Sisty
    Aledo (Ill.) Democrat, 5 Nov.1880,
    p.4, quoting Georgetown Colorado
    Miner (undated).

Gilman
-Anomalous fossil
  n.d./Rocky Point Mine/=human bone in
  silver vein
    Iowa City (Ia.) Saturday Herald, 10
    Apr.1867.

Gilpin co.
-Poltergeist

1861, Dec./Julia Hull Dory/Dory Hill
James Crenshaw, "The Colorado Poltergeist," Tomorrow 7 (autumn 1959)
:46-54.

Gleeson
-UFO (CE-2)
1968, Aug.26/Pearl Christiansen
Ted Phillips, Physical Traces Associated with UFO Sightings (Evanston: Center for UFO Studies, 1975),
p.58.

Glenwood Springs
-Cattle mutilation
1974
Denver Rocky Mountain News, 16 Dec.
1974.
(Editorial), Fate 28 (Apr.1975):20-
22.
1976, May 4/5 mi.S
(Editorial), Fate 29 (Sep.1976):12-
14, quoting Denver Post (undated).

Golden
-Erratic kangaroo
1976, Aug.17/Donald Douglas/Clear
Creek Canyon
Tulsa (Okla.) World, 18 Aug.1976.
-UFO (?)
1961, Jan.1/Mr. Bellett/=lens defect
Richard Hall, ed., The UFO Evidence
(Washington: NICAP, 1964), p.95.
-UFO (CE-1)
1965, Sep./Lookout Mt. School for Boys
"Strange Object near Denver in 1965,"
APRO Bull. 15 (Mar.-Apr.1967):6.
-UFO (DD)
1956, Oct.12/Ralph Churches
"Case 232," CRIFO Orbit, 2 Nov.1956,
p.4, quoting Denver Post (undated).
-UFO (NL)
1966, April 10/Dave Courtney
"Typical Reports," UFO Inv. 3 (Mar.-
Apr.1966):8.

Goodpasture
-Archeological site
E.B. Renaud, "Indian Stone Enclos-
ures of Colorado and New Mexico,"
Arch.Ser.Univ.Denver Dep't Anthro.,
no.2 (1942):10-11.

Granby
-Anomalous artifact
1924/Mr. Jordan/=stone figure with car-
ving of mammoth
Harold T. Wilkins, Secret Cities of
Old South America (N.Y.: Library
Publishers, 1952), pp.269-70.
Bernice & Jack McGee, "Granby Idol,"
True West 19 (Nov.-Dec.1971):12-14,
57-58. il.

Grand Junction
-UFO (DD)
1968, April 14/SE of town
"More from Colorado," APRO Bull. 17
(Sep.-Oct.1968):7, quoting Alamosa
Valley Courier (undated).

-UFO (NL)
1964, May 15
"News Briefs," Saucer News 11 (Sep.
1964):19.

Greeley
-Haunt
1970s/Poudre R.
Louise Russell, "Llorona Legends
Collected from Junior High School
Students in Greeley, Colorado," Aff-
word 4, no.2 (1974):1-4.

Gunnison co.
-Fall of toads
n.d./A.P. Hawxhurst
(Letter), Fate 6 (Oct.1953):116.

Idaho Springs
-UFO (DD)
1947, July 6/Pat Price
Denver Post, 7 July 1947.

Jamestown
-Haunt
1904/quartz mine
(Letter), D.W. Beach, Fate 27 (Feb.
1974):132,144.

Kersey
-Archeological site
Jurgens site
Sally Thompson Greiser, "Micro-Anal-
ysis of Wear Patterns on Projectile
Points and Knives from the Jurgens
Site, Kersey, Colorado," Plains
Anthro. 22 (1977):107-16. il.
Joe Ben Wheat, "Olsen-Chubbuck and
Jurgens Sites: Four Aspects of the
Paleo-Indian Bison Economy," Plains
Anthro. 23 (1978):84-89. il.

Kiowa
-Cattle mutilation
1975, June/Jim Russell/3 mi.W
Kansas City (Mo.) Times, 11 Sep.1975,
p.6C.
-Haunt
1894/J. Earl Stone
Dennis Bardens, Ghosts and Hauntings
(N.Y.: Ace, 1965 ed.), pp.150-52.
-Phantom helicopter
1975/16 mi.NE
Kansas City (Mo.) Times, 11 Sep.1975,
p.6C.

Lafayette
-UFO (?)
1950, June 4
Donald H. Menzel & Lyle G. Boyd, The
World of Flying Saucers (Garden
City: Doubleday, 1963), p.95.

La Junta
-Haunt
1967/Christina Westerberg
Christina Westerberg, "Thad Chris-
tian: The La Junta Haunt," Fate 23
(July 1970):44-49.
-UFO (DD)

1965, Aug.2/Mrs. Henry Rawlings
Coral E. Lorenzen, "Western UFO Flap,"
Fate 18 (Nov.1965):42,50.

Lakewood
-UFO (NL)
1967, Sep.30-Oct.1
Jim & Coral Lorenzen, UFOs over the
Americas (N.Y.: Signet, 1968), pp.
164-65.

Las Animas
-Archeological site
E.B. Renaud, "Indian Stone Enclos-
ures of Colorado and New Mexico,"
Arch.Ser.Univ.Denver Dep't Anthro.,
no.2 (1942):21-23.

Lasauses
-UFO (NL)
1968, March 29/Tom Martinez/2 mi.W
"More from Colorado," APRO Bull. 17
(Sep.-Oct.1968):7, quoting Alamosa
Valley Courier (undated).

Leadville
-Dowsing
n.d./W.P. Jones
Don L. & Jean Hauley Griswold, The
Carbonate Camp Called Leadville
(Denver: Univ. of Denver, 1951).
Henry Winfred Splitter, "Electrically
Charged People," Fate 8 (Mar.1955):
83,86.
-Precognition
1881/Maude Lord-Drake
Maude Lord-Drake, Psychic Light: The
Continuity of Law and Life (Kansas
City: F.T. Riley, 1904).
W.D. Chesney, "That Great Medium:
Maude Lord-Drake," Fate 14 (Apr.
1961):82,88.

Littleton
-UFO (NL)
1969, Jan.7-9/Randall J. Pocius/W.
Shepperd Ave.
Denver Rocky Mountain News, 10 Oct.
1969.
1975, July 4
"UFO Central," CUFOS News Bull., 15
Nov.1975, p.12.

Logan co.
-Cattle mutilation
1975-1976
1976, Feb./radar chaff in mouth
Ed Sanders, "On the Trail of the
Night Surgeons," Oui, May 1977, pp.
79,122-26.
R. Martin Wolf & Steven N. Mayne,
"More on Mutilations," Pursuit 10
(summer 1977):95. il.
1976, June-Sep.
Sterling Journal-Advocate, 8 June
1976; 14 Sep.1976; and 18 Sep.1976.
Ed Sanders, "On the Trail of the
Night Surgeons," Oui, May 1977, pp.
79,134.
1976, Nov.-Dec.

Sterling Journal-Advocate, 22-23
Nov.1976; and 17 Dec.1976.
1978, Oct.
"A Closer Look," Stigmata, no.5
(fall-winter 1978):3.
-Phantom helicopter
1975, Aug.21/Larry Graves
Greeley Tribune, 22 Aug.1975.
"The Air Force and the Great Chase
of Northern Colorado," Cattle Re-
port, no.1 (Mar.1977):6-7.
-UFO (CE-2)
n.d./Larry Graves
Ed Sanders, "On the Trail of the
Night Surgeons," Oui, May 1977, pp.
79,126.
-UFO (NL)
1975, fall/Larry Graves
Ed Sanders, "On the Trail of the
Night Surgeons," Oui, May 1977, pp.
79,125.

Longmont
-UFO (DD)
1948, July 4
Richard Hall, ed., The UFO Evidence
(Washington: NICAP, 1964), p.149.

Loveland
-Poltergeist
n.d./Marguerite Miller
Dennis Bardens, Ghosts and Hauntings
(N.Y.: Ace, 1965 ed.), pp.149-50.
-UFO (NL)
1964, Aug.12/Marvin E. Watson
Brad Steiger, Mysteries of Time and
Space (N.Y.: Dell, 1976 ed.), p.145.

Manassa
-UFO (NL)
1967, Oct.11
Jim & Coral Lorenzen, UFOs over the
Americas (N.Y.: Signet, 1968), p.
165.

Mancos
-Cattle mutilation
1978, Aug.31/Roland Bartel/5 mi.NE of
U.S.160
Durango Herald, 1 Sep.1978.

Manitou Springs
-UFO (DD)
1947, May 19/Dean A. Hauser
Denver Post, 28-29 June 1947.
Ted Bloecher, Report on the UFO Wave
of 1947 (Washington: NICAP, 1967),
p.I-1.

Mesa co.
-Fall of toads
n.d./A.P. Hawxhurst
(Letter), Fate 6 (Oct.1953):116.

Monarch
-Archeological site
4 mi.W
"Ancient Stone Remains on Summit of
Rocky Mountains," Sci.Am. 46 (1882)
:3.

Monte Vista
-UFO (?)
    1967, Sep.28/Frank Malouff/Brown Hills
    Jim & Coral Lorenzen, UFOs over the
    Americas (N.Y.: Signet, 1968), p.
    164.

Montrose
-Fall of red snow
    1935, July
    Buffalo (N.Y.) Times, 23 July 1935.
-UFO (?)
    1949, April 7
    "Unidentifieds," INFO J., no.7 (fall
    1970):41, quoting San Francisco
    (Cal.) News (undated).
    1967, March 18/Moraine Rd/ground mark-
    ings only
    Jim & Coral Lorenzen, UFOs over the
    Americas (N.Y.: Signet, 1968), pp.
    162-63.
-UFO (DD)
    1950, May 24/Mrs. Clyde Seevers
    Kenneth Arnold & Ray Palmer, The Com-
    ing of the Saucers (Boise: The Au-
    thors, 1952), p.151.

Monument
-UFO (NL)
    1978, April 17/Sally Beck
    B.V. Wilson, "Object near Monument,
    Colorado," APRO Bull. 26 (May 1978)
    :5-6.

Mosca
-Mystery horse deaths
    1967, Oct.
    David R. Saunders & R. Roger Harkins,
    UFOs? Yes! (N.Y.: Signet, 1968),
    p.160.

Niwot
-UFO (DD)
    1947, July 10
    Denver Rocky Mountain News, 11 July
    1947.

Ouray
-Humanoid
    1976, July 4/Heinz Fritz Goedde
    Ouray Plain Dealer, 3 Feb.1977.

Palmer Lake
-UFO (NL)
    1966, April 1/Warren Heckman
    Columbus (O.) Dispatch, 2 Apr.1966.

Pueblo
-Fall of weblike substance
    1960/James R. Little/=spider web?
    (Letter), Fate 13 (Dec.1960):121.
-Reincarnation
    1952, Nov.29/Virginia Tighe
    William J. Barker, "The Strange
    Search for Bridey Murphy," Denver
    Post, 12 Sep.1954; 29 Sep.1954; and
    26 Sep.1954.
    Morey Bernstein, The Search for Bri-
    dey Murphy (Garden City: Doubleday,
    1956).

Eric J. Dingwall, "The Woman Who Nev-
    er Was," Tomorrow 4 (summer 1956):
    9-14.
George Devereux, "Bridey Murphy: A
    Psychoanalytic View," Tomorrow 4
    (summer 1956):15-23.
Milton V. Kline, ed., A Scientific
    Report on "The Search for Bridey
    Murphy" (N.Y.: Julian, 1956).
    (Editorial), Fate 9 (Aug.1956):6-8.
William J. Barker, "Bridey Murphy in
    Ireland," Fate 9 (Nov.1956):17-43.
    il.
    (Editorial), Fate 10 (Feb.1957):13-
    14.
C.J. Ducasse, A Critical Examination
    of the Belief in a Life After Death
    (Springfield, Ill.: Charles C.
    Thomas, 1961), pp.276-99.
Harlan Wilson, "Bridey Murphy Revis-
    ited," Fate 13 (July 1960):59-62.
    (Editorial), Fate 14 (Apr.1961):11-
    12.
-UFO (?)
    1953, Oct.30/Cirullo O. Ortiz
    Harlan Wilson, "There Are Meteors,
    After All," Fate 7 (May 1954):40,43.
    1972, June 9/ground markings only
    Ted Phillips, Physical Traces Associ-
    ated with UFO Sightings (Evanston:
    Center for UFO Studies, 1975), p.83.
-UFO (CE-1)
    1947, June 25/Lloyd M. Lowry
    New Orleans (La.) Times-Picayune, 7
    July 1947.
-UFO (DD)
    1947, July 8
    Denver Post, 9 July 1947.
    1956, Dec.4
    (Editorial), Fate 10 (Apr.1957):16.
    1958, June 14
    Lloyd Mallan, "Complete Directory of
    UFOs: Part I," Sci.& Mech. 37 (Dec.
    1966):36,73.
-UFO (NL)
    1956, May 6-11/Gilbert Nelson
    Denver Rocky Mountain News, 11 May
    1956.
    1978, July 14/Diego DeGadoi/25th Lane
    x Everett Rd.
    Pueblo Star-Journal, 14 July 1978.

Rangely
-UFO (NL)
    1950, April 27/A.W. Jay
    Rangely Driller, 28 Apr.1950.

Rio Grande co.
-UFO (NL)
    1967, April 24/Sam Grazier
    Coral Lorenzen, "The Great UFO Con-
    troversy: The Appaloosa from Alamo-
    sa," Fate 21 (Mar.1968):34,39.

Rollinsville
-UFO (DD)
    1947, July 9
    Denver Rocky Mountain News, 10 July
    1947.

Saguache
-Archeological site
    E.B. Renaud, "Indian Stone Enclos-
    ures of Colorado and New Mexico,"
    Arch.Ser.Univ.Denver Dep't Anthro.,
    no.2 (1942):23-27. il.
    Donald A. Johnson, "Rocky Mountain
    Medicine Wheels," INFO J., no.24
    (July-Aug.1977):12.

Salida
-Fall of red snow
    1935, July
        Buffalo (N.Y.) Times, 23 July 1935.

Sanford
-UFO (NL)
    1968, May 7/Felix Gallegos
        "New Mystery in Colorado," APRO Bull.
        17 (July-Aug.1968):8.

Sedalia
-Inner development
    1930-   /Brotherhood of the White
    Temple
        J. Gordon Melton, The Encyclopedia
        of American Religions, 2 vols.
        (Wilmington, N.C.: Consortium,
        1978), 2:185.

Shaffer's Crossing
-UFO (NL)
    1974, Feb.3/Ken Fitzpatrick/U.S.285
        George D. Fawcett, "The 'Unreported'
        UFO Wave of 1974," Saga UFO Rept.
        2 (spring 1975):51.

Silver Cliff
-Cattle mutilation
    1976, Aug./thorium mine
        Jim Brandon, Weird America (N.Y.:
        Dutton, 1978), p.53.
-Ghost light
    1880-   /Ray DeWall/graveyard
        (Editorial), Fate 9 (Aug.1956):12,
        quoting Wet Mountain Tribune (un-
        dated).
        Olive Peabody, "Lights of the Ghost-
        ly Miners," Fate 10 (July 1957):
        87-88.
        (Editorial), Fate 18 (Jan.1965):13-
        14.
        New York Times, 20 Aug.1967, sec.10,
        p.19.
        Edward J. Linehan, "The Rockies' Pot
        of Gold," Nat'l Geogr. 136 (Aug.
        1969):157,201.

Sterling
-Cattle mutilation
    1976, March
        Ed Sanders, "The Mutilation Mystery,"
        Oui, Sep.1976, pp.51,119.
    1976, July
        Ed Sanders, "On the Trail of the
        Night Surgeons," Oui, May 1977, pp.
        79,122.
-UFO (DD)
    1897, Aug./G.A. Nenstein
        Portland Oregonian, 1 Sep.1897.

-UFO (NL)
    1976, July/Ed Sanders/7 mi.NE
        Ed Sanders, "On the Trail of the
        Night Surgeons," Oui, May 1977, pp.
        79,126-29.

Stratton
-UFO (NL)
    1972, Sep.18
        "Trio Observe Object in Colorado,"
        APRO Bull. 21 (Sep.-Oct.1972):4.

Teller co.
-Phantom helicopter
    1975, Sep.
        James Butler Bonham, "Cattle Mutila-
        tions and UFOs: Satanic Rite or Al-
        ien Abduction," Official UFO 1 (Dec.
        1976):26,55.

Telluride
-Mystery elk deaths
    ca.1976
        Telluride Times, 30 June 1977.

Texas Creek
-UFO (CE-2)
    1967, Aug.26/Kenneth Flack/½ mi.W
        Coral E. Lorenzen, The Shadow of the
        Unknown (N.Y.: Signet, 1970), pp.
        158-60.

Thornton
-Skyquake
    1955, Sep.8
        Coral E. Lorenzen, The Shadow of the
        Unknown (N.Y.: Signet, 1970), p.80.

Trinidad
-UFO (DD)
    1966, March 23/Eulah Mae Hoch
        Coral & Jim Lorenzen, UFOs: The Whole
        Story (N.Y.: Signet, 1969), pp.253-
        54.

Troutdale
-UFO (DD)
    1947, July 10
        Denver Rocky Mountain News, 11 July
        1947.

Vail
-Weather control
    1963, Dec.7-8/Ute Indians
        (Editorial), Fate 17 (Apr.1964):20-
        21.

Walsenburg
-Cattle mutilation
    ca.1975
        Ed Sanders, "The Mutilation Mystery,"
        Oui, Sep.1976, pp.51,117.
-UFO (CE-2)
    1964, May 1/Ross Quintana
        "News Briefs," Saucer News 11 (Sep.
        1964):19.
-UFO (NL)
    1955, Dec.13/William Thach
        "Latest Saucer Sightings," Fate 9
        (Apr.1956):43,47.

Westminster
-Haunt
  1921-1922/Audrey Morse Andrews
    Agnes M. Pharo, "House with a Curse,"
    Fate 16 (Jan.1963):62-66.
-UFO (DD)
  1947, July 10
    Denver Rocky Mountain News, 10 July
    1947.

Wheatridge
-UFO (NL)
  1962, June 26/Philip Nichols/W. 48th
  Ave.
    "Flashing Lights Seen in Colorado,"
    APRO Bull. 11 (July 1962):6.

Wild Horse
-Fall of fish
  1914/Mary Katherine Spencer/Wild Horse
  Creek
    Mary Katherine Spencer, "Mystery of
    the Swimming Bass," Fate 18 (Jan.
    1965):62.

Woodrow
-Cattle mutilation
  n.d./John Kalous
    Scott Dial, "The Mystery of the Cat-
    tle Mutilations," Westerner, spring
    1976, pp.34,37.
-UFO (NL)
  1975, Oct./ Mr. Bohannon/Hwy.71
    Ed Sanders, "On the Trail of the
    Night Surgeons," Oui, May 1977, pp.
    79,125.

Wray
-Archeological site
    Dennis J. Stanford, "The Jones-Miller
    Site: An Example of Hell Gap Bison
    Procurement Strategy," Plains Anthro.
    23 (1978):90-97. il.
-Cattle mutilation
  1974, Nov./Marvin Dickson ranch
    (Editorial), Fate 28 (Apr.1975):20,
    quoting Yuma (Ariz.) Pioneer (un-
    dated).

Yuma
-UFO (DD)
  1950, Aug.12/William Schocke/Main St.
    Kenneth Arnold & Ray Palmer, The Com-
    ing of the Saucers (Boise: The Au-
    thors, 1952), p.153.

  B. Physical Features

Apishapa R.
-Archeological sites
    E.B. Renaud, "Indian Stone Enclos-
    ures of Colorado and New Mexico,"
    Arch.Ser.Univ.Denver Dep't Anthro.,
    no.2 (1942):13-20. il.

Arena Creek
-Disappearance
  n.d.
    Harry Hansen, Colorado: A Guide to

the Highest State (N.Y.: Hastings
House, 1970), p.348.

Arkansas R.
-Precognition
  1830s/John Brown
    Bill Wallrich, "John Brown--Prophet
    of the Rockies," Fate 3 (Nov.1950):
    16-18.

Battle Mt.
-Precognition
  1891, July 3/Winfield Scott Stratton
    Frank Waters, Midas of the Rockies
    (N.Y.: Sage, 1937), pp.122-24.
    Shawn Dawson, "The Dream That Made
    Colorado History," Fate 12 (Dec.
    1959):67-70.

Blanca, Mt.
-Chinese discovery
  ca.1000 B.C.
    Henriette Mertz, Gods from the Far
    East (N.Y.: Ballantine, 1975 ed.),
    p.135.
-UFO (CE-2)
  ca.1969/Berle Lewis
    Janet Bord, "After Snippy--What Next?"
    Flying Saucer Rev. 18 (Nov.-Dec.
    1972):19-20.
-UFO (CE-3)
  1971, June/Charles Cranston
    "Mountain Climbers See Strange Light
    and Are Followed by 'Thing,'" Sky-
    look, no.52 (Mar.1972):7-8.
-UFO (NL)
  1967, Sep.28/Berle Lewis/U.S.60 x Sand
  Dunes Rd.
    Jim & Coral Lorenzen, UFOs over the
    Americas (N.Y.: Signet, 1968), pp.
    163-64.
    Edward U. Condon, ed., Scientific
    Study of Unidentified Flying Objects
    (N.Y.: Bantam, 1969 ed.), p.346.
  1967, Oct.13/Bill McFedries
    Coral Lorenzen, "The Great UFO Con-
    troversy: The Appaloosa from Alamo-
    sa," Fate 21 (Mar.1968):34,42-43.
    Edward U. Condon, ed., Scientific
    Study of Unidentified Flying Objects
    (N.Y.: Bantam, 1969 ed.), pp.385-89.

Bush Creek
-Rock pillars
    J.W. Gabelman, "Cylindrical Structures
    in Permian(?) Siltstone, Eagle Coun-
    ty, Colorado," J.Geology 63 (1955):
    214-27.

Chalk Mt.
-UFO (?)
  1967, March/Robert Rinker
    (Editorial), Fate 21 (June 1968):16.
    il.

Cheyenne Mt.
-Cattle mutilation
  1976, Aug.22/Flying Horse Ranch
    Ed Sanders, "On the Trail of the
    Night Surgeons," Oui, May 1977, pp.

79,134.

Chimney Canyon
-Cattle mutilation
1975
Ed Sanders, "The Mutilation Mystery,"
Oui. Sep.1976, pp.51,118.

Claypool Site
-Archeological site
6000 B.C.
Herbert W. Dick & Bert Mountain,
"The Claypool Site: A Cody Complex
Site in Northeastern Colorado,"
Am.Antiquity 26 (1960):223-35. il.

Conejos Canyon
-UFO (NL)
1967, Oct.11-12/Curtis Smith
David R. Saunders & R. Roger Harkins,
UFOs? Yes! (N.Y.: Signet, 1968), p.
163.

Crater L.
-Erratic platypus
n.d./Leonard Calkins
Janet Bord, "After Snippy--What Next?"
Flying Saucer Rev. 18 (Nov.-Dec.
1972):19.

Crow Creek
-Archeological site
E.L. Berthoud, "On Prehistoric Human
Art from Wyoming and Colorado,"
Proc.Acad.Nat.Sci.Philadelphia,
1872, pp.46-49.

Daniels Park
-UFO (CE-3)
1966, April 7/Mary Zolar
Gabriel Green, Let's Face the Facts
About Flying Saucers (N.Y.: Popular
Library, 1967), pp.8-10.

Deadman Creek
-Ghost
1867, Sep./Marshall P. Felch
Lee Beecher, "Canyon of Ghosts,"
Fate 4 (Mar.1951):49-55.

Dry Creek Basin
-UFO (CE-2)
1967, March
Edward U. Condon, ed., Scientific
Study of Unidentified Flying Objects
(N.Y.: Bantam, 1969 ed.), pp.295-
300.
Donald H. Menzel & Ernest H. Taves,
The UFO Enigma (Garden City: Double-
day, 1977), p.103.

Elbert Mt.
-Humanoid
1960s
John Green, Sasquatch: The Apes Among
Us (Seattle: Hancock House, 1978),
p.173.

Evans Mt.
-Lightning anomaly

n.d./Wilson M. Powell
B. Vonnegut, "Lightning," Weather 27
(1972):213.

Gray's Peak
-Chinese discovery
ca.1000 B.C.
Henriette Mertz, Gods from the Far
East (N.Y.: Ballantine, 1975 ed.),
p.134.

Great Sand Dunes National Monument
-Men-in-black
1967, June/Mrs. Charles Blundell
Alamosa Valley Courier, 6 Oct.1967,
p.1.
-UFO (?)
1967, spring/Mrs. Charles Blundell
Alamosa Valley Courier, 6 Oct.1967,
p.1.
-UFO (CE-1)
1968, Feb.2/Harvey Smalley/Great Sand
Dunes Rd.
"More from Colorado," APRO Bull. 17
(Sep.-Oct.1968):7.
-Web-footed horses
n.d.
Harry Hansen, Colorado: A Guide to
the Highest State (N.Y.: Hastings
House, 1970), p.347.
"Mystery Sand Dunes," Pursuit 5
(July 1972):58-59.

Gulch L.
-Mystery radioactive disc
1955, April/Morris Steen/=U.S. Army
marker
Curtis Fuller, "The Saucers Are Flying," Fate 8 (Aug.1955):10,13.
"Mystery of Tiny Disc Found in 1955
Now Solved," UFO Inv. 1 (Jan.1958):
8.

Hackberry Spring
-Petroglyph
Don Rickey, "Two Southwestern Petro-
glyph Sites," Occ.Pub.Epigraphic
Soc'y 6, no.138 (Jan.1979):200-208.

Hall Valley
-Phantom
1976, May 26/Earl Mortimeyer
Earl Mortimeyer, "Four Solid Hiking
Ghosts: A Strange Encounter," Fate
30 (Oct.1977):80-84.

Harvard Mt.
-Chinese discovery
ca.1000 B.C.
Henriette Mertz, Gods from the Far
East (N.Y.: Ballantine, 1975 ed.),
pp.145-46.

Holy Cross, Mt. of the
-Fall of red snow
1881, July
New York Times, 10 July 1881, p.10.

Horsetooth Reservoir
-UFO (DD)

Kenosha Pass
-UFO (DD)
    1967, April 1
        J. Allen Hynek, The UFO Experience
        (Chicago: Regnery, 1972), p.235.

Left Hand Canyon
-UFO (CE-2)
    1960, Aug.11/Ray Hawks
        Coral E. Lorenzen, Flying Saucers:
        The Startling Evidence of the Inva-
        sion from Outer Space (N.Y.: Sig-
        net, 1966 ed.), pp.182-83.

Lincoln, Mt.
-Lightning anomaly
    1863, summer/Wilbur F. Stone
        New York Times, 21 Nov.1875, p.5.

Lindenmeier Site
-Archeological site
    ca.8800 B.C.
        Frank H.H. Roberts, Jr., "A Folsom
        Complex: Preliminary Report on In-
        vestigations at the Lindenmeier
        Site in Northern Colorado," Smith.
        Misc.Coll., vol.94 (1935). il.
        Frank H.H. Roberts, Jr., "Additional
        Information on the Folsom Complex,"
        Smith.Misc.Coll., vol.95, no.10
        (1936). il.
        Vance Haynes & George Agogino, "Geo-
        logical Significance of a New Radio-
        carbon Date from the Lindenmeier
        Site," Proc.Denver Mus.Nat.Hist.,
        no.9 (1960). il.
        Edward Wilmsen, Lindenmeier: A
        Pleistocene Hunting Society (N.Y.:
        Harper & Row, 1974). il.

Lone Cone Mt.
-UFO (NL)
    1967, Oct.28/David Barnard
        Jim & Coral Lorenzen, UFOs over the
        Americas (N.Y.: Signet, 1968), pp.
        177-78, quoting Denver Post (un-
        dated).

Long's Peak
-Chinese discovery
    ca.1000 B.C.
        Henriette Mertz, Gods from the Far
        East (N.Y.: Ballantine, 1975 ed.),
        pp.133-34,145.

Loveland Pass
-UFO (CE-2)
    1971
        Ted Phillips, Physical Traces Associ-
        ated with UFO Sightings (Evanston:
        Center for UFO Studies, 1975), p.74.

Lowry Site
-Archeological site
    ca.1100
        Paul S. Martin, "Lowry Ruin in South-
        western Colorado," Anthro.Ser.Field
        Mus., vol.23, no.1 (1936). il.

Magic Mt.
-Archeological site
    3000 B.C.-1000 A.D.
        Cynthia Irwin-Williams & Henry J.
        Irwin, "Excavations at Magic Moun-
        tain," Proc.Denver Mus.Nat.Hist.,
        no.12 (1966). il.

Marshall Pass
-Phantom train
    n.d./Nelson Edwards
        Charles M. Skinner, Myths and Legends
        of Our Own Land, 2 vols. (Philadel-
        phia: Lippincott, 1896), 2:192.
        Albert Parry, "When Trains Go Ghost-
        ly," Fate 8 (July 1955):93-96.

Mesa Verde
-Archeological site
    ca.400-1300 A.D.
        Gustav Nordenskïold, The Cliffdwell-
        ers of the Mesa Verde, Southwestern
        Colorado, D.L. Morgan trans. (Stock-
        holm: P.A. Norstedt, 1895). il.
        T. Mitchell Prudden, "An Elder Broth-
        er to the Cliff Dwellers," Harper's
        Monthly Mag. 95 (June 1897):56-62.
        William Henry Jackson, Time Exposure
        (N.Y.: Putnam, 1940), pp.228-37. il.
        James A. Lancaster, Archeological
        Excavations in Mesa Verde National
        Park, Colorado, 1950 (Washington:
        U.S. Nat'l Park Service, 1954). il.
        J.B. Priestly & Jacquetta Hawkes,
        Journey Down a Rainbow (N.Y.: Har-
        per, 1955), pp.101-22.
        Alden C. Hayes, Archeological Survey
        of Wetherill Mesa, Mesa Verde Na-
        tional Park, Colorado (Washington:
        U.S. Nat'l Park Service, 1964). il.
        Douglas Osborne, ed., "Contributions
        of the Wetherill Mesa Archeological
        Project," Am.Antiquity 31 (1965):
        1-230. il.
        Frank McNitt, Richard Wetherill: Ana-
        sazi (Albuquerque: Univ. of New Mex-
        ico, 1966). il.
        Robert H. Lister, "Archeology for
        Layman and Scientist at Mesa Verde,"
        Science 160 (1968):489-96. il.
        Franklin Folsom, America's Ancient
        Treasures (N.Y.: Rand McNally, 1974),
        pp.23-28. il.
        Kenneth A. Bennett, Skeletal Remains
        from Mesa Verde National Park, Colo-
        rado (Washington: U.S. Nat'l Park
        Service, 1975). il.
-Weather control
    1934, Aug.1-2/Navaho Indians
        Ivan T. Sanderson, Investigating the
        Unexplained (Englewood Cliffs, N.J.:
        Prentice-Hall, 1972), p.216, quoting
        AP release, 2 Aug.1934.

Mestas, Mt.
-UFO (DD)
    1955, Nov.25/Samuel T. Taylor
        Thomas M. Olsen, The Reference for
        Outstanding UFO Sighting Reports
        (Riderwood, Md.: UFO Information

Retrieval Center, 1966), p.43.

Mosca Pass
-Disappearance
n.d./Peter Hansen
Harry Hansen, Colorado: A Guide to
the Highest State (N.Y.: Hastings
House, 1970), pp.347-48.

Olsen-Chubbuck Site
-Archeological site
ca.5000 B.C.
Jerry Chubbuck, "The Discovery and
Exploration of the Olsen-Chubbuck
Site (CH-3)," Southwestern Lore 25
(1959):4-10.
Joe Ben Wheat, "A Paleo-Indian Bison
Kill," Sci.Am. 216 (Jan.1967):44-
52. il.
Joe Ben Wheat, "Olsen-Chubbuck and
Jurgens Sites: Four Aspects of the
Paleo-Indian Bison Economy," Plains
Anthro. 23 (1978):84-89. il.

Pike's Peak
-Erratic cow
1949, Sep.
"Run of the Mill," Doubt, no.27
(1949):420.
-Lightning anomalies
1874-1888
"Meteorological Observations Made on
the Summit of Pike's Peak, Colorado," Annals Astron.Observatory Harvard College 22 (1889):459-75.
-Phantom
1877, summer
"A Collective Apparition," J.ASPR
7 (1913):395-400.

Plateau Valley
-Ancient pavement
1936/Tom Kenny
W.L. Vallette, "Is America the Birth-
place of Man?" Fate 6 (Mar.1953):
82,85.

Plum Creek
-Humanoid
1954, spring/=hoax
(Editorial), Fate 8 (Jan.1955):14-
15, quoting Littleton Independent
(undated).

Princeton Mt.
-Chinese discovery
ca.1000 B.C.
Henriette Mertz, Gods from the Far
East (N.Y.: Ballantine, 1975 ed.),
pp.134-35.

Purgatoire R.
-Petroglyph
Henry Winfred Splitter, "Nature's
Strange Photographs," Fate 8 (Jan.
1955):21-22.

Rainbow Lakes
-Archeological site
Wilfred H. Husted, "A Rock Alignment

in the Colorado Front Range," Plains
Anthro. 8 (1963):221-24.

Red Creek
-UFO (CE-2)
1973, May 15
Jim Brandon, Weird America (N.Y.:
Dutton, 1978), pp.49-50.

Rocky Mountain National Park
-Archeological site
nr. Trail Ridge Rd.
John A. Eddy, "Medicine Wheels and
Plains Indian Astronomy," in An-
thony F. Aveni, ed., Native American
Astronomy (Austin: Univ. of Texas,
1977), pp.147-53. il.

Rocky Mts.
-Skyquake
1810
David H. Coyner, The Lost Trappers
(Albuquerque: Univ. of New Mexico,
1970), pp.109-10.

South Table Mt.
-UFO (CE-2)
1950, Jan.29/C. Frank Quintana
Kenneth Arnold & Ray Palmer, The Coming of the Saucers (Boise: The Authors, 1952), pp.145-46.

Summit Peak
-Chinese discovery
ca.1000 B.C.
Henriette Mertz, Gods from the Far
East (N.Y.: Ballantine, 1975 ed.),
p.146.

Turkey Creek
-Archeological site
E.B. Renaud, "Indian Stone Enclos-
ures of Colorado and New Mexico,"
Arch.Ser.Univ.Denver Dep't Anthro.,
no.2 (1942):4-6. il.

Upper Hunter Creek
-UFO (CE-1)
1975, Aug.25
Aspen Times, 25 Sep.1975.

West Plum Creek
-UFO (NL)
1967, May 30/Mr. Martin
1967, June 5/Helen Esquibel
"Colorado Sightings," APRO Bull. 15
(May-June 1967):10.

D. Unspecified Localities

-Ghost pony
n.d.
James Reynolds, Ghosts in American
Houses (N.Y.: Paperback Library,
1967 ed.), p.185.

-UFO (CE-3), humanoids and mutilations
1975, Oct.-1977
John S. Derr & R. Leo Sprinkle, "Mul-

tiple Phenomena on Colorado Ranch,"
APRO Bull. 27 (July 1978):5-8; (Aug.
1978):7-8; (Sep.1978):6-8; (Oct.
1978):5-8; (Nov.1978):5-8; (Dec.
1978):7-8.

THE GREAT PLAINS————————

WYOMING

A. Populated Places

Beryl Springs
-UFO (?)
  1950, Oct./Louis Mandrich/=mirage?
    Denver (Colo.) Post, 19 Oct.1950.
    Donald H. Menzel, Flying Saucers
    (Cambridge: Harvard Univ., 1953),
    pp.212-13.

Big Horn
-UFO (NL)
  1971, Sep.6/Robert Connell
    Ken Steinmetz, "UFOs in Formation
    over Wyoming," Skylook, no.50 (Jan.
    1972):6-7.

Buffalo
-UFO (NL)
  1963, Sep.26/Al Bailey
    Sheridan Press, 27 Sep.1963.

Burlington
-UFO (CE-1)
  1964, June 7-8/Gary Brown
    Sheridan Press, 10 June 1964.

Casper
-Archeological site
  8000-7500 B.C.
    George Frison, ed., The Casper Site
    (N.Y.: Academic, 1974). il.
-Phantom ship
  1887, fall/Gene Wilson/10 mi.E on
  Platte R.
    Vincent H. Gaddis, "Wyoming's Ship
    of Death," Fate 1 (spring 1948):112,
    114-15.
-Precognition
  1955, July 16/Barbara Taylor
    L.A. Dale, "Spontaneous Cases," J.
    ASPR 50 (1956):158-61.
  1975
    (Editorial), Fate 29 (Mar.1976):26-
    27, quoting Casper Star-Tribune (un-
    dated).
-UFO (CE-2)
  1957, Oct.30/Shirley Moyer/10 mi.N
    Casper Tribune-Herald, 5 Nov.1957.
-UFO (DD)
  1947, July 6/G.W. Gibson/2007 Oakcrest
    Casper Tribune-Herald, 7 July 1947.
-UFO (NL)
  1947, July 4/Margaret McLeod/818 W.
  11th St.
    Casper Tribune-Herald, 6 July 1947.
  1976, Dec.4
    "UFO Central," CUFOS News Bull., 1
    Feb.1976, p.14.

Cheyenne
-Fall of toads
  n.d./A.P. Hawxhurst
    (Letter), Fate 6 (Oct.1953):116.

-Ghost
  ca.1900
    Levette J. Davidson & Forrester Blake,
    eds., Rocky Mountain Tales (Norman:
    Univ. of Oklahoma, 1947), pp.101-
    103.
-Poltergeist
  1945, Nov./Harold Hickman
    Cheyenne Wyoming State Tribune, 21
    Nov.1945.
-UFO (DD)
  1950, Dec./J.E. Broyles
    Richard Hall, ed., The UFO Evidence
    (Washington: NICAP, 1964), p.20.
  1957, Nov./R.V. Walker/Warren AFB
    (Letter), Fate 12 (Nov.1959):109-10.
-UFO (NL)
  1947, July 7
    Cheyenne Wyoming State Tribune, 7
    July 1947.
  1964, April 28
    Coral Lorenzen, "Southwestern UFOs
    and the Straight-Line Mystery," Fate
    17 (Aug.1964):39,42.
  1965, Aug.1/Gary Harvey
    Coral E. Lorenzen, "Western UFO Flap,"
    Fate 18 (Nov.1965):42,48-49.
-Weather control
  1892-1894/Frank Melbourne/chemical
  method/=hoax
    Alvin T. Steinel & D.W. Working, His-
    tory of Agriculture in Colorado...
    1858 to 1926 (Fort Collins, Colo.:
    State Agricultural College, 1926),
    pp.260-62.
    Martha B. Caldwell, "Some Kansas
    Rainmakers," Kansas Hist.Quar. 7
    (Aug.1938):306,308-15.

Clay
-UFO (NL)
  1975, Oct.19
    "Noteworthy UFO Sightings," Ufology
    2 (spring 1976):43.

Cody
-Archeological site
  5000 B.C./Horner site/4 mi.NE
    Glenn L. Jepsen, "Ancient Buffalo
    Hunters of Northwestern Wyoming,"
    Southwestern Lore 19 (1953):19-25.
    il.
    H.M. Wormington, Ancient Man in North
    America, 4th ed. (Denver: Museum of
    Natural History, Pop.ser., no.4,
    1957), pp.127-28.
-Phantom airplane
  1936, Feb.14
    Portland Oregonian, 15 Feb.1936; and
    18 Feb.1936.
-UFO (DD)
  1947, July 6/Mrs. Frank Walters
    Casper Tribune-Herald, 7 July 1947.

Converse co.
-UFO (?)
  1950, April 20/Everett Fletcher/=U.S.
  Navy device
    Ray Palmer, "New Report on the Fly-
    ing Saucers," Fate 4 (Jan.1951):63,
    79.

East Thermopolis
-UFO (CE-1)
  1957, Aug.30/Molly Wertz
    "Flying Saucer Roundup," Fate 11
    (Feb.1958):29,34.

Eden
-Archeological site
  ca.6000 B.C./Finley site
    Edgar B. Howard, "The Finley Site,"
    Am.Antiquity 8 (1943):224-34. il.
    John T. Hack, "Antiquity of the Fin-
    ley Site," Am.Antiquity 8 (1943):
    235-41. il.
    John H. Moss, Early Man in the Eden
    Valley (Philadelphia: Univ. of Penn-
    sylvania Museum, 1951). il.
    Linton Satterthwaite, Stone Artifacts
    at and near the Finley Site, near
    Eden, Wyoming (Philadelphia: Univ.
    of Pennsylvania Museum, 1957). il.

Encampment
-UFO (DD)
  1947, July 6/David A. Kenney
    Ted Bloecher, Report on the UFO Wave
    of 1947 (Washington: NICAP, 1967),
    p.III-17.

Evanston
-UFO (NL)
  1978, Sep.23/Eugene Mallory/NW on Hwy.
  89
  1978, Sep.24
    Rock Springs Rocket, 28 Sep.1978.

Fort Bridger
-Disappearance
  1851, June 17/wagon train
    Vincent H. Gaddis, "Caravan of the
    Lost," Fate 2 (May 1949):36-37.

Gillette
-Precognition
  1909, June/Francis J. Keller
    Raymond C. Otto, "Answer to a Dying
    Man's Prayer," Fate 16 (June 1963):
    71.

Glenrock
-UFO (DD)
  1947, July 6/Jim Drury/1 mi.E on Hwy.87
    Casper Tribune-Herald, 7 July 1947.

Green River
-Archeological site
    Donald A. Johnson, "Rocky Mountain
    Medicine Wheels: Part 2," INFO J.,
    no.24 (July-Aug.1977):12.
-UFO (NL)
  1964, April 29-30/Mrs. James Pace/115
  Keith Dr.

Salt Lake City (Utah) Deseret News,
    2 May 1964.
  1978, May 18/Alan Trudel
    Green River Star, 24 May 1978.

Hanna
-UFO (NL)
  1951, Oct.27/W. Barton Williams/U.S.30
    (Letter), Fate 5 (June 1952):124-26.

Jackson
-Animal ESP
  1954/Mr. Hunter
    "Canny Canine," Fate 7 (Aug.1954):66.
-Humanoid
  1972, summer/20 mi.S
    John Green, Sasquatch: The Apes Among
    Us (Seattle: Hancock House, 1978),
    pp.177-78.
-UFO (NL)
  1975, Sep.22/Clara Tappan
    Jackson Hole News, 25 Sep.1975.

Johnson co.
-UFO (NL) and cattle mutilations
  1975, Nov.-Dec./Charlie Firnekas/Fir-
  nekas Ranch
    R. Leo Sprinkle, "Mysterious Lights
    Seen on Wyoming Ranch," Skylook, no.
    102 (May 1976):16-17.

Lander
-Humanoid
  1920s
    Casper Tribune-Herald, 11 Mar.1962.
-UFO (NL)
  1967, Jan.30/Joe C. Kenney
    "Major Sighting Wave," UFO Inv. 3
    (Jan.-Feb.1967):1,4.

Laramie
-Archeological site
  ca.6000 B.C./Jimmy Allen site/16 mi.S
    H.M. Wormington, Ancient Man in North
    America, 4th ed. (Denver: Museum of
    Natural History, Pop.ser., no.4,
    1957), pp.144-46. il.
-Humanoid
  1968, Feb./S of town
    Coral E. Lorenzen, The Shadow of the
    Unknown (N.Y.: Signet, 1970), p.108.
-Telepathy research
  1890s/E.E. Slosson/Univ. of Wyoming
    "Experiments in Telepathy," J.ASPR
    12 (1918):134-40.
-UFO (?)
  1954, Sep.18
    Donald H. Menzel & Lyle G. Boyd, The
    World of Flying Saucers (Garden
    City: Doubleday, 1963), p.93.
-UFO (CE-4)
  1968
    B. Ann Slate, "Is Earth an Extrater-
    restrial Laboratory?" Saga UFO Rept.
    2 (fall 1974):13,69-70.
-UFO (NL)
  1965, March 12
    Coral E. Lorenzen, Flying Saucers:
    The Startling Evidence of the Inva-
    sion from Outer Space (N.Y.: Signet,

1966 ed.), p.256.
1975, Aug.6
"UFO Central," CUFOS News Bull., 15
Nov.1975, p.15.
1975, Oct.20
"Noteworthy UFO Sightings," Ufology
2 (spring 1976):43.

Leefe
-UFO (DD)
1960, July 1/slag dump
Coral & Jim Lorenzen, UFOs: The Whole
Story (N.Y.: Signet, 1969), p.221.

Lusk
-UFO (NL)
1975, Oct.18
"Noteworthy UFO Sightings," Ufology
2 (spring 1976):43.

Natrona co.
-Cattle mutilation
1978, April 22/Vern Robinett
Casper Star-Tribune, 27 Apr.1978.
"A Weekend in April," Stigmata, no.4
(summer 1978):6-8.
"Mute Testimony from the Victims,"
Stigmata, no.5 (fall-winter 1978):
8-9. il.

Newcastle
-Cattle mutilation
1975, Oct.3/Raymond Jones
Jerome Clark, "Saucer Central U.S.A.,"
Saga UFO Rept. 3 (Apr.1976):8,67.
-Ghost light
Wyoming Writers' Program, Wyoming: A
Guide to Its History, Highways, and
People (N.Y.: Oxford Univ., 1941),
pp.123,221.
-Phantom helicopter
1975, Oct.7/Willis Larson
Jerome Clark, "Saucer Central U.S.A.,"
Saga UFO Rept. 3 (Apr.1976):8,67,
quoting Laramie Branding Iron (un-
dated).

Osage
-UFO (DD)
1948, Oct.9/Leroy Griffin
Kenneth Arnold & Ray Palmer, The Coming of the Saucers (Boise: The Authors, 1952), p.140.

Rawhide Village
-UFO (NL)
1978, July 14/Mrs. Robert Starr
Gillette News-Record, 17 July 1978.

Rawlins
-Intra-mercurial planet
1878, July 29/James C. Watson
"The Eclipse of the Sun," Nature 18
(1878):353.
New York Times, 8 Aug.1878, p.5; and
16 Aug.1878, p.5.
G.B. Airy, "An Intra-Mercurial Planet," Nature 18 (1878):380-81.
"The Reported Observation of 'Vulcan,'" Nature 18 (1878):385.

E. Mouchez, "Nouvelle observation
probable de la planète Vulcain par
M. le professeur Watson," Comptes
Rendus 87 (1878):229-30.
"The Planet Vulcan," Sci.Am. 39
(1878):128.
"The Intra-Mercurial Planet," Nature
18 (1878):495-96.
Lewis Swift, "Discovery of Vulcan,"
Nature 18 (1878):539.
James C. Watson, "Intra-Mercurial
Planets," Nature 18 (1878):616.
C.H.F. Peters, "Some Critical Remarks
on So-Called Intra-Mercurial Planet
Observations," Astronomische Nach-
richten 94 (1879):321-36.
James C. Watson, "Schreiben des Herrn
Prof. Watson an den Herausgeber,"
Astronomische Nachrichten 95 (1879)
:102-106.
Th. von Oppolzer, "Sur l'existence
de la planète intra-mercurielle ru-
diquée par Le Verrier," Comptes
Rendus 88 (1879):26-27.
-UFO (NL)
1978, Aug.23/Jess Bartlett
Rawlins Times, 25 Aug.1978.

Rock Springs
-UFO (DD)
1964, April 29/Richard Surline
Coral Lorenzen, "Southwestern UFOs
and the Straight-Line Mystery,"
Fate 17 (Aug.1964):39,43.
1967, July 25/Ed McAuslan
"Wyoming Hosts Objects Again," APRO
Bull. 16 (July-Aug.1967):2.
-UFO (NL)
1967, July 24/Joe Mann
"Wyoming Hosts Objects Again," APRO
Bull. 16 (July-Aug.1967):2.

Torrington
-Archeological site
W.W.Howells, "Crania from Wyoming
Resembling 'Minnesota Man,'" Am.An-
tiquity 7 (1941):70-74.

Upton
-Cattle mutilation
1975, Sep.29/Bill Barton
Jerome Clark, "Saucer Central U.S.A.,"
Saga UFO Rept. 3 (Apr.1976):8.
-UFO (NL)
1947, Aug.8/Mrs. Jay Engle
Kenneth Arnold & Ray Palmer, The Com-
ing of the Saucers (Boise: The Au-
thors, 1952), pp.137-38.

Weston
-UFO (CE-1)
1952, Jan./Little Powder R.
Jacques Vallee, Passport to Magonia
(Chicago: Regnery, 1969), p.197.

Wind River Reservation
-Humanoid
1972, Aug./Tom Hernandez/10 mi.W of
Lander
Casper Star-Tribune, 23 Aug.1972.

Salt Lake City (Utah) Tribune, 14
Jan.1973.

Yoder
-Bird attack
1974, Nov./Terry Hauf
   Larry E. Arnold, "Birds on the Attack," Fate 31 (Aug.1978):54,57.

B. Physical Features

Absaroka Mts.
-Archeological site
   Waldo R. Wedel, Wilfred M. Husted &
   John H. Moss, "Mummy Cave: Prehistoric Record from Rocky Mountains
   of Wyoming," Science 160 (1968):
   184-85.

Agate Basin
-Archeological site
   ca.8000 B.C.
   Frank Roberts, "The Agate Basin Complex," in Homenaje a Pablo Mertinéz
   del Río (Mexico City: Instituto Na-
   cional de Antro. e Historia, 1961),
   pp.125-32. il.

Alcova Reservoir
-UFO (NL)
   1972, Sep.16
   "UFOs over Reservoir," APRO Bull. 21
   (Sep.-Oct.1972):8.

Belle Fourche R.
-Archeological site
   3500-1450 B.C./McKean site
   William B. Mulloy, "The McKean Site,"
   Southwestern J.Anthro. 10 (1954):
   432-60. il.

Bessemer Bend
-Phantom ship
   1903, Nov.20/Victor Heibe
   Vincent H. Gaddis, "Wyoming's Ship
   of Death," Fate 1 (spring 1948):112,
   115,128.

Bighorn Mts.
-Healing
   1890s-   /Emile Pascal/nr. Worland
   Keith Ayling, "The Mud That Heals,"
   Probe the Unknown 2 (Feb.1974):46-
   51. il.
-UFO (NL)
   1965, Aug.1/George Broussard
   Coral E. Lorenzen, "Western UFO Flap,"
   Fate 18 (Nov.1965):42,48.

Blacks Fork R.
-Archeological site
   Etienne B. Renaud, Archaeology of the
   High Western Plains (Denver: Univ.
   of Denver, 1947).
   Floyd W. Sharrock, "Prehistoric Occu-
   pation Patterns in Southwest Wyoming
   and Cultural Relationships with the
   Great Basin and Plains Culture
   Areas," Anthro.Pap.Univ.Utah, no.

77 (1966).

Castle Gardens
-Petroglyphs
   Arthur Randall, "Pictographs and
   Petroglyphs of the Castle Gardens
   Area, Fremont County, Wyoming,"
   Wyoming Arch. 7 (fall 1964):21-25.
   il.

Dead Indian Campsite
-Archeological site
   ca.2500 B.C.-1800 A.D.
   Sharon K. Smith, "A Preliminary Report on the Dead Indian Site,"
   Trowel & Screen 11, no.6 (1970):2-
   4.

DeSmet L.
-Lake monster
   1890s
   Edward Gillette, Locating the Iron
   Trail (Boston: Christopher, 1925),
   pp.164-66.
   Ella E. Clark, Indian Legends from
   the Northern Rockies (Norman: Univ.
   of Oklahoma, 1966), pp.302-303.
   Sheridan Press, 1-4 Dec.1970.

Dinwoody Canyon
-Petroglyphs
   David S. Gebhard & Harold A. Cahn,
   "The Petroglyphs of Dinwoody, Wyo-
   ming," Am.Antiquity 3 (1950):219-
   28. il.
   Grant Willson, "Portfolio of Petro-
   glyphs from Dinwoody," Wyoming Arch.
   8, no.3-4 (1965):28-50. il.
   David Gebhard, The Rock Art of Din-
   woody, Wyoming (Santa Barbara:
   Univ. of California, 1969). il.

Eagle Creek
-Phantom bear
   1923, July/Tom Rousseau
   Tom Rousseau, "I Saw the Spirit of
   All Animal Life," Fate 14 (Sep.1961)
   :84-85.

Heart Mt.
-Stratigraphic anomaly
   W.H. Bucher, "Problem of the Heart
   Mountain Thrust," Proc.Geol.Soc'y
   Am., 1933, p.57.
   William G. Pierce, "Heart Mountain
   and South Fork Detachment Thrusts
   of Wyoming," Bull.Am.Ass'n Petroleum
   Geologists 41 (1957):591-626.
   Clifford L. Burdick, "Heart Mountain
   Revisited," Creation Rsch.Soc'y
   Quar. 13 (Mar.1977):207-10.

Hell Gap Valley
-Archeological site
   ca.8800 B.C.
   George A. Agogino, "A New Point Type
   from Hell Gap Valley, Eastern Wyoming," Am.Antiquity 26 (1961):558-
   60. il.
   C. Vance Haynes, "The Hell Gap Site,

Wyoming," <u>Wyoming Arch.</u> 8, no.2
(1965):35-39.
Henry V. Irwin, et al., "Resumé of
Cultural Complexes at the Hell Gap
Site, Guernsey, Wyoming," <u>Wyoming
Arch.</u> 9, no.2 (1966):11-13.

Horse Creek
-Ghost cat
  1905/Charles Smith
    Charles C. Stemmer, "Animals Live in
    Spirit, Too," <u>Fate</u> 13 (Dec.1960):
    87,88-89.
-UFO (NL)
  1947, July 5/N of oil fields
    Cheyenne <u>Wyoming State Tribune</u>, 7
    July 1947.

Hutton L.
-Lake monster
    Charles M. Skinner, <u>Myths and Legends
    of Our Own Land</u>, 2 vols. (Philadel-
    phia: Lippincott, 1896), 2:304-305.

Jackson Hole
-Phantom horse
  1950s/Stuart Cloete
    Danton Walker, <u>Spooks Deluxe</u> (N.Y.:
    Franklin Watts, 1956), pp.57-58.

Medicine Bow National Forest
-UFO (CE-4)
  1974, Oct.25/Carl Higdon
    <u>Rawlins Daily Times</u>, 29 Oct.1974.
    <u>National Star</u>, 22 Mar.1975.
    "Two New 'Kidnapping Cases,'" APRO
    <u>Bull.</u> 23 (Mar.1975):1,3.
    Timothy Green Beckley, "Kidnapped by
    Aliens!" <u>Saga UFO Rept.</u> 2 (fall
    1975):41-43,71-79.
    Coral & Jim Lorenzen, <u>Abducted!</u> (N.Y.:
    Berkley, 1977), pp.25-37.

Medicine Bow Peak
-Anomalous fossils
  =Precambrian worms
    "Ancient 'Dubiofossils' of Wyoming,"
    <u>Science News</u> 110 (1976):346.
-Chinese discovery
  ca.1000 B.C.
    Henriette Mertz, <u>Gods from the Far
    East</u> (N.Y.: Ballantine, 1975 ed.),
    pp.133,144-45.
-Mystery plane crash
  1955, Oct.6/DC-4
    "The Mystery at Medicine Bow Peak,"
    <u>CRIFO Orbit</u>, 4 Nov.1955, p.3.

Medicine Mt.
-Archeological site
  Medicine Wheel site
    S.C. Simms, "A Wheel-Shaped Stone
    Monument in Wyoming," <u>Am.Anthro.</u> 5
    (1903):107-10. il.
    G.B. Grinnell, "The Medicine Wheel,"
    <u>Am.Anthro.</u> 24 (1922):299-310. il.
    <u>Sheridan Post</u>, 11 Mar.1923.
    <u>Casper Herald-Tribune</u>, 16 Mar.1941.
    Ulric S. Vance, "Mystery Medicine
    Wheel of the Big Horns," <u>Fate</u> 4

(Aug.-Sep.1951):9-12.
    <u>New York Times</u>, 31 May 1959, sec.II,
    p.15.
    Don Grey, "Big Horn Medicine Wheel
    Site, 48BH302," <u>Plains Anthro.</u> 8
    (1963):27-40. il.
    Ella E. Clark, <u>Indian Legends of the
    Northern Rockies</u> (Norman: Univ. of
    Oklahoma, 1966), pp.303-305.
    John A. Eddy, "Astronomical Align-
    ments of the Big Horn Medicine
    Wheel," <u>Science</u> 184 (1974):1035-43.
    il.
    <u>Houston (Tex.) Chronicle</u>, 8 Oct.1975.
    John A. Eddy, "Medicine Wheels and
    Plains Indian Astronomy," in Anthony
    F. Aveni, ed., <u>Native American As-
    tronomy</u> (Austin: Univ. of Texas,
    1977), pp.147-53. il.
    John A. Eddy, "Probing the Mystery
    of the Medicine Wheels," <u>Nat'l
    Geogr.</u> 151 (Jan.1977):140-46. il.
    Donald A. Johnson, "Rocky Mountain
    Medicine Wheels: Part I," <u>INFO J.</u>,
    no.23 (May 1977):2-5. il.

Pathfinder Dam
-UFO (DD)
  1947, July 6/Dan Browder
    <u>Casper Tribune-Herald</u>, 7 July 1947.

Pedro Mts.
-Mummy
  1932, Oct.
    "Wyoming 'Mummy' Mystery Solved,"
    <u>Bull.Chicago Nat.Hist.Mus.</u> 21, no.4
    (1950):5.
    Ray Palmer, "Mystery of the Midget
    Mummy," <u>Fate</u> 3 (Sep.1950):74-76. il.
    (Letter), Elvina Colburn, <u>Fate</u> 4
    (Apr.1951):96-97.
    "Members' Forum," <u>Pursuit</u> 6 (July
    1973):73.
    Duane Valentry, "Mystery of the Mis-
    sing Mummy," <u>Pop.Arch.</u> 4 (Mar.-Apr.
    1975):57-58.
    Jim Brandon, <u>Weird America</u> (N.Y.:
    Dutton, 1978), pp.247-48.

Pine Spring
-Archeological site
  6000 B.C.-1400 A.D.
    Floyd W. Sharrock, "Prehistoric Occu-
    pation Patterns in Southwest Wyoming
    and Cultural Relationships with the
    Great Basin and Plains Culture
    Areas," <u>Anthro.Pap.Univ.Utah</u>, no.
    77 (1966).

Piney Creek
-Healing
  1866/Creeping
    Frederick J. Goshe, "Could the Sioux
    Control the Weather?" <u>Fate</u> 10 (Apr.
    1957):57,58.

Pole Creek
-Erratic starfish
  1968, July/Bob Nayler
    (Editorial), <u>Fate</u> 21 (Dec.1968):8,

quoting Casper Star-Tribune (undated).

Powder R.
-Crisis apparition
  1905, Aug./Laura Christine Moore/50 mi.
  from Gillette
    Norma Trout, "The Powder River Ghost,"
    Fate 22 (Feb.1969):79-81.

Ralph White L.
-UFO (NL)
  1978, May 9/James Wehunt
    Baggs Snake River Press, 11 May 1978.

Ring Mt.
-Archeological site
    Donald A. Johnson, "Rocky Mountain
    Medicine Wheels: Part II," INFO J.,
    no.24 (July-Aug.1977):12.

Rock L.
-UFO (DD)
  1974, Sep.24/Ralph McConahy
    "UFO Fleet over Wyoming," APRO Bull.,
    24 (Dec.1975):6.
    Cheyenne Eagle, 10 Dec.1978, Sunday
    mag.

Spanish Diggings
-Archeological site
  16th c.
    Robert F. Gilder, "The 'Spanish Dig-
    gings,'" Putnam's Monthly 2 (June
    1907):277-84. il.
    James Duguid & Gabriel Bedish, "An
    Analysis of the Spanish Diggings
    Region of Wyoming during Paleolith-
    ic Inhabitance," Wyoming Arch. 11,
    no.1 (1968):20-38. il.
    Donald M. Viles, "Archaeological
    Treasure with a Hidden History: The
    Great Stone Cross of Wyoming," NEARA
    J. 11 (summer 1976):7-10.

Sweetwater R.
-Chinese discovery
  ca.1000 B.C.
    Henriette Mertz, Gods from the Far
    East (N.Y.: Ballantine, 1975 ed.),
    pp.132-33.

Telephone Canyon
-Phantom
  1946, April/Gordon Barrows
    Danton Walker, Spooks Deluxe (N.Y.:
    Franklin Watts, 1956), pp.64-69.

Teton Forest
-Humanoid
  1967, Dec./nr. Jackson Hole
    John Green, The Sasquatch File (Ag-
    assiz, B.C.: Cheam, 1973), p.39.
    John Green, Sasquatch: The Apes Among
    Us (Seattle: Hancock House, 1978),
    p.178.

Union Pacific Mammoth Kill
-Archeological site
  9300 B.C.

Cynthia Irwin, Henry Irwin & George
Agogino, "Wyoming Muck Tells of
Battle: Ice Age Man vs. Mammoth,"
Nat'l Geogr. 121 (June 1962):829-
37. il.

Whalen Dam
-Phantom ship
  1862, Sep.12/Leon Webber
    Vincent H. Gaddis, "Wyoming's Ship
    of Death," Fate 1 (spring 1948):
    112-14.

Wolf Mt.
-Chinese discovery
  ca.1000 B.C.
    Henriette Mertz, Gods from the Far
    East (N.Y.: Ballantine, 1975 ed.),
    pp.143-44.

Yellowstone National Park
-Acoustic anomaly
  1890-   /Yellowstone L.
    Edwin Linton, "Overhead Sounds in
    the Vicinity of Yellowstone Lake,"
    Science 22 (1893):244-46.
    Hiram Martin Chittenden, The Yellow-
    stone National Park (Cincinnati:
    Stewart & Kidd, 1917), pp.288-89.
    S.A. Forbes, "A Preliminary Report
    on the Aquatic Invertebrate Fauna
    of the Yellowstone National Park,
    Wyoming, and of the Flathead Region
    of Montana," Bull.U.S.Fish Comm'n
    11 (1891):207,215.
    (Editorial), Fate 19 (Mar.1966):31.
    William A. Corliss, ed., Strange
    Phenomena (Glen Arm, Md.: The Au-
    thor, 1974), p.G1-235.
-Humanoid
  1959, summer
    John Green, Sasquatch: The Apes Among
    Us (Seattle: Hancock House, 1978),
    p.177.
-UFO (?)
  1962, Aug.15/L.A. Peebler/Old Faithful/
  =lens defect?
    "Can the Camera See What the Eye Does
    Not?" Fate 17 (Oct.1964):53. il.
    (Letter), Zelma P. Cordwell, Fate 18
    (Jan.1965):131.
  1972, Aug.27/Robert J. Ewald/Old Faith-
  ful/=lens defect?
    (Letter), Saga UFO Rept. 2 (summer
    1975):78. il.

                C. Ethnic Groups

Arapaho Indians
-Flood myth
    George A. Dorsey & Alfred L. Kroeber,
    Traditions of the Arapaho (Chicago:
    Field Museum, Pub.no.81, 1903), pp.
    8-19.
    Wyoming Writers' Program, Wyoming: A
    Guide to Its History, Highways, and
    People (N.Y.: Oxford Univ., 1941),
    pp.55-56.
    Ella E. Clark, Indian Legends of the

Northern Rockies (Norman: Univ. of
Oklahoma, 1966), pp.225-31.
-Humanoid myth
  George A. Dorsey & Alfred L. Kroeber,
  Traditions of the Arapaho (Chicago:
  Field Museum, Pub.no.81, 1903), pp.
  122-36.
  Sarah E. Olden, Shoshone Folklore
  (Milwaukee: Milwaukee Pub. Co.,
  1923), pp.8-12.
-Lake monster myth
  George A. Dorsey & Alfred L. Kroeber,
  Traditions of the Arapaho (Chicago:
  Field Museum, Pub.no.81, 1903), pp.
  136-46.

Kiowa Indians
-Lake monster myth
  Albert S. Gatschet, "Water-Monsters
  of the American Aborigines," J.Am.
  Folklore 12 (1899):255,259.

Shoshoni Indians
-Cataclysm myth
  Robert H. Lowie, "Shoshonean Tales,"
  J.Am.Folklore 37 (1924):1,59-62.
-Flood myth
  Wyoming Writers' Program, Wyoming: A
  Guide to Its History, Highways, and
  People (N.Y.: Oxford Univ., 1941),
  pp.53-54.
-Humanoid myth
  ninnimbe
  Sarah E. Olden, Shoshone Folklore
  (Milwaukee: Milwaukee Pub. Co.,
  1923), pp.8,33-34.
  Åke Hultkrantz, "An Ideological Di-
  chotomy: Myths and Folk Beliefs
  among the Shoshoni Indians of Wyo-
  ming," History of Religions 11
  (1972):339-53.

        D. Unspecified Localities

-Mystery haze
  ca.1970
  Gordon Creighton, "More on Teleportations," Flying Saucer Rev. 18
  (Sep.-Oct.1972):31.

MONTANA

A. Populated Places

Arlee
-UFO (NL)
  1964, Aug.14-15/Earl Johnston
    Curtis Fuller, "Collected UFO Sight-
    ings for August and September,"
    Fate 18 (Jan.1965):36.

Armington
-Cattle mutilation
  1976
    (Editorial), Fate 29 (Nov.1976):26-
    28, quoting Great Falls Tribune
    (undated).

Augusta
-Phantom automobile
  1976, Feb.6/S of town
    Roberta Donovan & Keith Wolverton,
    Mystery Stalks the Prairie (Raynes-
    ford, Mont.: THAR, 1976), p.86.
-UFO (NL)
  1976, Jan.17
    Roberta Donovan & Keith Wolverton,
    Mystery Stalks the Prairie (Raynes-
    ford, Mont.: THAR, 1976), pp.75-76.

Babb
-Humanoid
  1975, summer
    Roberta Donovan & Keith Wolverton,
    Mystery Stalks the Prairie (Raynes-
    ford, Mont.: THAR, 1976), p.90.

Bearcreek
-Giant fossil human teeth
  1926, Nov./J.C.F. Siegfriedt/Bearcreek
  Mutual Coal Mine
    Red Lodge Carbon County News, 11 Nov.
    1926, p.5.

Beaverhead co.
-Fall of metallic object
  1950, July 4/Floyd Kennison
    "Found on Ground," Doubt, no.42
    (1953):238,239.

Belgrade
-UFO (CE-2)
  1963, Feb.21
    Jacques Vallee, Passport to Magonia
    (Chicago: Regnery, 1969), p.291.

Belt
-Cattle mutilation
  1975, Aug.14
  1975, Sep.22
  1976, Oct.16
    Roberta Donovan & Keith Wolverton,
    Mystery Stalks the Prairie (Raynes-
    ford, Mont.: THAR, 1976), pp.1-5,
    14-15.
-UFO (CE-1)

  1976, Jan.10
  1976, March/NW on U.S.87
    Roberta Donovan & Keith Wolverton,
    Mystery Stalks the Prairie (Raynes-
    ford, Mont.: THAR, 1976), pp.74-75,
    84-85.
-UFO (NL)
  1967, March 24/Ken Williams
    "UAO near Great Falls," APRO Bull.
    15 (May-June 1967):6.

Big Arm
-UFO (NL)
  1976, May 13
    "Noteworthy UFO Sightings," Ufology
    2 (fall 1976):60.

Big Fork
-UFO (CE-2)
  1967, Feb.13/Mrs. James Thompson
    Brad Steiger & Joan Whritenour, Al-
    lende Letters: New UFO Breakthrough
    (N.Y.: Award, 1968), p.40.

Billings
-Humanoid
  1968, Sep.11/Harold E. Nelson/hwy.out-
  side town
    John A. Keel, Strange Creatures from
    Time and Space (Greenwich, Ct.:
    Fawcett, 1970), p.111, quoting Saga,
    July 1969.
-UFO (?)
  1972, Aug.10/W.T. Rogers/=meteor
    (Editorial), Fate 28 (Apr.1975):30.
-UFO (NL)
  1956, Aug.21/J. Gordon Campbell/S of
  town
    Minneapolis (Minn.) Star, 15 Nov.
    1956.

Boulder
-Clairvoyance
  1912-1913/Training School for Backward
  Children
    "Apparent Clairvoyance," J.ASPR 9
    (1915):289-305.

Bowman's Corner
UFO (NL)
  1975, Oct.15
    Roberta Donovan & Keith Wolverton,
    Mystery Stalks the Prairie (Raynes-
    ford, Mont.: THAR, 1976), p.63.

Bozeman
-Fire anomaly
  1953, Aug.3/Harold Minder
    (Editorial), Fate 7 (Mar.1954):10.
-Ghost
  1895, April 2/E. Broox Martin
    "Apparent Materialization," J.ASPR
    12 (1918):184-88.
-UFO (CE-2)

1963, Feb.21/Bill DeHaan
"News Briefs," Saucer News 10 (June
1963):22.
-UFO (NL)
1956, Sep.4
(Editorial), Fate 10 (Feb.1957):9.

Butte
-Haunt
1965, Sep./Orphan Girl Mine
Kansas City (Mo.) Times, 6 Sep.1965.
-Precognition
1958, April/Gordon Carl Brown
(Editorial), Fate 11 (Aug.1958):10.
-UFO (?)
1954, June
Donald E. Keyhoe, Flying Saucer Con-
spiracy (N.Y.: Holt, 1955), p.166.
1973, summer/=kite
Philip J. Klass, UFOs Explained (N.Y.:
Random House, 1974), pp.269-70.
-UFO (NL)
1918, summer/Maurice McKenney
Gordon I.R. Lore, Jr. & Harold H.
Deneault, Jr., Mysteries of the
Skies: UFOs in Perspective (Engle-
wood Cliffs, N.J.: Prentice-Hall,
1968), pp.105-106.
1947, July 5/Shirley Hefferson
Casper (Wyo.) Tribune-Herald, 7 July
1947.

Canyon Ferry
-UFO (CE-2)
1964, April 30/Linda Davis
Jim & Coral Lorenzen, UFOs over the
Americas (N.Y.: Signet, 1968), pp.
104-106.
Brad Steiger, ed., Project Blue Book
(N.Y.: Ballantine, 1976), betw. pp.
56-57. il.
-UFO (DD)
1947, July 29
Bruce S. Maccabee, "UFO Related Information from the FBI Files: Part
3," MUFON UFO J., no.121 (Dec.1977)
:10,13.

Carter
-Phantom helicopter
1975, Dec.2/5 mi.NE
Roberta Donovan & Keith Wolverton,
Mystery Stalks the Prairie (Raynes-
ford, Mont.: THAR, 1976), p.50.

Cascade
-Cattle mutilation
1976, Feb.20/NW of town
Roberta Donovan & Keith Wolverton,
Mystery Stalks the Prairie (Raynes-
ford, Mont.: THAR, 1976), pp.31-32.
-Giant snake
1978, Oct./Eileen Blackburn/2½ mi.S on
I-15
Great Falls Tribune, 28 Oct.1978.

Cascade co.
-Phantom helicopter
1975
Roberta Donovan & Keith Wolverton,

Mystery Stalks the Prairie (Raynes-
ford, Mont.: THAR, 1976), pp.43-44.

Castner Falls
-Cattle mutilation
1976, April 29
Roberta Donovan & Keith Wolverton,
Mystery Stalks the Prairie (Raynes-
ford, Mont.: THAR, 1976), pp.103-
105.

Choteau
-Phantom helicopter
1975, Sep.15
1975, Dec.8/Fox 10 missile site
Roberta Donovan & Keith Wolverton,
Mystery Stalks the Prairie (Raynes-
ford, Mont.: THAR, 1976), pp.45,57.
-UFO (DD)
n.d.
(Letter), Sandra Lavell Gollehon,
Fate 18 (Apr.1965):107-108.
1976, Feb.22/W of town
Roberta Donovan & Keith Wolverton,
Mystery Stalks the Prairie (Raynes-
ford, Mont.: THAR, 1976), pp.83-84.

Chouteau co.
-Cattle mutilation
1975, March 24
Roberta Donovan & Keith Wolverton,
Mystery Stalks the Prairie (Raynes-
ford, Mont.: THAR, 1976), pp.16-17.

Clinton
-Fall of metallic object
1952, Dec./Weideman Ranch
Missoula Daily Missoulian, 31 Dec.
1952.

Columbia Falls
-Humanoid
1960s/Tom Tiede
John Green, Sasquatch: The Apes Among
Us (Seattle: Hancock House, 1978),
pp.291-92.

Columbus
-UFO (CE-1)
1967/9 mi. from town
Dan Clements, "Saucer Safari," Official UFO 1 (Nov.1976):35,44.

Conrad
-Phantom helicopter
1975, Dec.2/missile site
Roberta Donovan & Keith Wolverton,
Mystery Stalks the Prairie (Raynes-
ford, Mont.: THAR, 1976), p.51.
-UFO (DD)
1950
"Montana Sighting Reported by Former
Air Force Captain," Skylook, no.35
(Oct.1970):7.
-UFO (NL)
1975, Oct.19/Allan S. Michals
(Editorial), Fate 29 (Apr.1976):30.
Roberta Donovan & Keith Wolverton,
Mystery Stalks the Prairie (Raynes-
ford, Mont.: THAR, 1976), pp.65-66.

Coram
-UFO (CE-3)
1970, Feb./Leona Nielson/Flat Head R.
    (Letter), Can.UFO Rept., no.17 (1974)
    :25-26.

Craig
-UFO (DD)
1947, July 4/Curt Dennis/N of town on
Missouri R.
    Cheyenne Wyoming State Tribune, 6
        July 1947.
    Ted Bloecher, Report on the UFO Wave
        of 1947 (Washington: NICAP, 1967),
        p.II-2.
-UFO (NL)
1953, Jan.3
    U.S. Air Force, Projects Grudge and
        Blue Book Reports 1-12 (Washington:
        NICAP, 1968), p.189.

Cut Bank
-UFO (?)
1956, Sep.9/Don LeGrande
    "Case 215," CRIFO Orbit, 5 Oct.1956,
        p.4, quoting Great Falls Tribune
        (undated).

Deer Lodge
-UFO (DD)
1949, Aug.15/Edgar Thompson
1949, Aug.22/Peter Mohan
    Kenneth Arnold & Ray Palmer, The Com-
        ing of the Saucers (Boise: The Au-
        thors, 1952), p.144.

Dutton
-Phantom helicopter
1975, Dec.3/S of town
    Roberta Donovan & Keith Wolverton,
        Mystery Stalks the Prairie (Raynes-
        ford, Mont.: THAR, 1976), pp.53-55.
-UFO (CE-3)
1953, fall/Cecil Tenney/crashed UFO
    Leonard H. Stringfield, "Retrievals
        of the Third Kind," in 1978 MUFON
        UFO Symposium Proc. (Seguin, Tex.:
        MUFON, 1978), pp.77,93-94.

Fairfield
-Phantom helicopter
1975, Dec.2
    Roberta Donovan & Keith Wolverton,
        Mystery Stalks the Prairie (Raynes-
        ford, Mont.: THAR, 1976), p.50.
-UFO (CE-1)
1976, Jan.21
    Roberta Donovan & Keith Wolverton,
        Mystery Stalks the Prairie (Raynes-
        ford, Mont.: THAR, 1976), pp.78-82.
-UFO (R-V)
1975, Dec.
    Roberta Donovan & Keith Wolverton,
        Mystery Stalks the Prairie (Raynes-
        ford, Mont.: THAR, 1976), pp.72-73.

Fife
-UFO (NL)
1976, April 30
    Roberta Donovan & Keith Wolverton,

Mystery Stalks the Prairie (Raynes-
    ford, Mont.: THAR, 1976), p.105.

Fort Benton
-Phantom helicopter
1975, Dec.2-3/Juliet 5 missile site
    Roberta Donovan & Keith Wolverton,
        Mystery Stalks the Prairie (Raynes-
        ford, Mont.: THAR, 1976), pp.51-54.

Fort Keogh
-Fall of giant snowflakes
1887, Jan.28/Matthew Coleman
    (Letter), New York World, 14 Feb.
        1887.
    "Gigantic Snowflakes," Monthly Weath-
        er Rev. 43 (Feb.1915):73.

Fort Shaw
-Phantom helicopter
1975, Sep.15/Arne Sand
    Roberta Donovan & Keith Wolverton,
        Mystery Stalks the Prairie (Raynes-
        ford, Mont.: THAR, 1976), pp.44-45.

Fort Smith
-Archeological site
    L.A. Brown, "The Fort Smith Medicine
        Wheel," Plains Anthro. 8 (1963):
        225-30. il.
    John A. Eddy, "Medicine Wheels and
        Plains Indian Astronomy," in Anthony
        F. Aveni, ed., Native American As-
        tronomy (Austin: Univ. of Texas,
        1977), pp.147,156-58. il.

Geyser
-Cattle mutilation
1975, Sep.
    Roberta Donovan & Keith Wolverton,
        Mystery Stalks the Prairie (Raynes-
        ford, Mont.: THAR, 1976), pp.45-46.
-UFO (CE-1)
1975, Aug.26
    Roberta Donovan & Keith Wolverton,
        Mystery Stalks the Prairie (Raynes-
        ford, Mont.: THAR, 1976), pp.62-63.
    Tim Church, "Funny Doin's in Montana
        1975-1976," in Bigfoot: Tales of
        Unexplained Creatures (Rome, O.:
        Page Research, 1978), pp.19-20.

Glasgow
-UFO (NL)
1952, Nov.13
    U.S. Air Force, Projects Grudge and
        Blue Book Reports 1-12 (Washington:
        NICAP, 1968), p.163.

Glendive
-Archeological site
1600 A.D./Hagen site/5 mi.SE
    William Mulloy, "The Hagen Site,"
        Pub.in Soc.Sci.Univ.Montana, no.1
        (1942). il.
-Fire anomaly
1958, Jan.10/Mrs. Charles King
    (Editorial), Fate 11 (May 1958):6-8.
-Precognition
1963, Nov.22/Donna Radin

John C. Ross, "Premonitions of Kennedy's Death," Fate 17 (May 1964):
31-32.

Great Falls
-Humanoid
1974, Dec./Bootlegger Trail
Roberta Donovan & Keith Wolverton,
Mystery Stalks the Prairie (Raynes-
ford, Mont.: THAR, 1976), p.90.
1976, March/Dempsey Rd.
John Green, Sasquatch: The Apes Among
Us (Seattle: Hancock House, 1978),
p.299.
1976, July 28/I-15
Great Falls Tribune, 31 July 1976.
-Phantom helicopter
1975, fall
1975, Dec.2-4
Roberta Donovan & Keith Wolverton,
Mystery Stalks the Prairie (Raynes-
ford, Mont.: THAR, 1976), pp.47-50,
53-56.
-Skyquake
1805, July 4/Meriwether Lewis
Meriwether Lewis & William Clark,
Travels to the Source of the Missou-
ri River, 3 vols. (London: Longmans,
Hurst, 1815), 1:398-99.
-UFO (CE-1)
1975, Nov.7/Thomas W. O'Brien/Malm-
strom AFB
Little Rock Arkansas Democrat, 19
Jan.1979.
1975, Dec.23/airport
Roberta Donovan & Keith Wolverton,
Mystery Stalks the Prairie (Raynes-
ford, Mont.: THAR, 1976), pp.77-78.
-UFO (DD)
1950, Aug.15/Nick Mariana/ball park
Great Falls Leader, 15 Aug.1950, p.1.
Edward J. Ruppelt, The Report on Un-
identified Flying Objects (Garden
City: Doubleday, 1956), pp.219-20.
Robert M.L. Baker, Jr., "Observation-
al Evidence of Anomalistic Phenom-
ena," J.Astronautical Sci. 15 (Jan.-
Feb.1968):31.
David R. Saunders & R. Roger Harkins,
UFOs? Yes! (N.Y.: Signet, 1968),
pp.81-108.
Edward U. Condon, ed., Scientific
Study of Unidentified Flying Objects
(N.Y.: Bantam, 1969 ed.), pp.51-54,
407-15. il.
R.M.L. Baker, Jr., "Motion Pictures
of UFO's," in Carl Sagan & Thornton
Page, eds., UFO's: A Scientific De-
bate (Ithaca, N.Y.: Cornell Univ.,
1972), pp.190-98. il.
Philip J. Klass, UFOs Explained (N.Y.:
Random House, 1974), pp.152-66. il.
Donald H. Menzel & Ernest H. Taves,
The UFO Enigma (Garden City: Double-
day, 1977), pp.110-11.
William H. Spaulding, "Modern Image
Processing Revisits the Great Falls,
Montana and Tremonton, Utah Movies,"
in 1977 MUFON UFO Symposium Proc.
(Seguin, Tex.: MUFON, 1977), pp.

78-105. il.
-UFO (NL)
1948, Dec.18/George Doakes
"You Asked for It," Doubt, no.24
(1949):363.
1975, Oct.17-19
Roberta Donovan & Keith Wolverton,
Mystery Stalks the Prairie (Raynes-
ford, Mont.: THAR, 1976), pp.63-67.
1975, Dec.2
Great Falls Tribune, 5 Dec.1975.
1975, Dec.9
"UFO Central," CUFOS News Bull., 1
Feb.1976, p.14.
1976, Jan.17/Keith Wolverton
1976, May 1
Roberta Donovan & Keith Wolverton,
Mystery Stalks the Prairie (Raynes-
ford, Mont.: THAR, 1976), pp.74,
105-106.
-UFO (R-V)
1951
Stanton T. Friedman, "UFOs on Radar,"
Can.UFO Rept., no.11 (1971):13.

Havre
-UFO (NL)
1976, June 20
"Noteworthy UFO Sightings," Ufology
2 (fall 1976):60.

Helena
-Archeological site
MacHaffie site
Richard G. Forbis & J.D. Sperry, "An
Early Man Site in Montana," Am.An-
tiquity 18 (1952):127-32. il.
-Humanoid
1976, March 23
1976, April 4
1976, April 23
Roberta Donovan & Keith Wolverton,
Mystery Stalks the Prairie (Raynes-
ford, Mont.: THAR, 1976), pp.91-94.
il.
John Green, Sasquatch: The Apes Among
Us (Seattle: Hancock House, 1978),
p.300.
-UFO (NL)
1958, July 7/A.M. Jasmin
(Editorial), Fate 11 (Dec.1958):20.
1963, Oct.17
"UFO Sightings Centered in Western
U.S.," UFO Inv. 11 (Dec.1963-Jan.
1964):3.
1975, Oct.20
"Noteworthy UFO Sightings," Ufology
2 (spring 1976):43.
1976, March
Roberta Donovan & Keith Wolverton,
Mystery Stalks the Prairie (Raynes-
ford, Mont.: THAR, 1976), p.84.

Jackson
-Humanoid tracks
1960, Oct./Dean Staton/15 mi.S
John Green, The Sasquatch File (Agassiz, B.C.: Cheam, 1973), p.23.

Kalispell
-Humanoid
  1973, Sep.2/20 mi.W on U.S.2
    (Letter), Betty Jones, Can.UFO Rept.,
    no.16 (1973-74):31-32, quoting Kal-
    ispell Daily Inter Lake (undated),
-UFO (CE-2)
  1964, June 24/Douglas C. Duncan
    "Other Recent Sightings," UFO Inv.
    2 (July-Aug.1964):8.
    "Correction," UFO Inv. 2 (Sep.-Oct.
    1964):7.
-UFO (DD)
  1975, April 21/Betty Jones
    (Letter), Can.UFO Rept., no.21
    (1975):22-23.
-UFO (NL)
  1956, Sep.4/Eddy Geddes
    "Case 209," CRIFO Orbit, 5 Oct.1956,
    p.4.
    (Editorial), Fate 10 (Feb.1957):9.
  1959, Feb.8
    (Editorial), Fate 12 (July 1959):17.
  1972, June 29-30/Betty Jones
    (Letter), Can.UFO Rept., no.19
    (1975):24.
  1973, Jan.2/Betty Jones
    (Letter), Can.UFO Rept., no.19
    (1975):24.
  1973, May 19-21/Betty Jones
    (Letter), Can.UFO Rept., no.15
    (1973):32-33.
  1974, Dec.20/Betty Jones
    (Letter), Can.UFO Rept., no.20
    (1975):23.

Lewistown
-Aerial phantom
  1892, Jan.17
    Brooklyn (N.Y.) Eagle , 18 Jan.1892.
-Phantom helicopter
  1975, Sep.25
  1975, Nov.8/missile site
    Roberta Donovan & Keith Wolverton,
    Mystery Stalks the Prairie (Raynes-
    ford, Mont.: THAR, 1976), pp.45,49.
-UFO (CE-1)
  1964, May 15/Pat Minette
    "Other Recent Sightings," UFO Inv. 2
    (July-Aug.1964):7.

Libby
-UFO (CE-1)
  1909, Aug./Grace A. Kenelty
    "Before--Pre-1947 Sightings from the
    Files of Lucius Farish," Skylook,
    no.55 (June 1972):20.

Madison co.
-Cattle mutilation
  1976, summer
    Anaconda Leader, 19 Jan.1977.

Malta
-UFO (NL)
  1967, Jan./Wilfred Tremblay
    "Landed Object in Montana," APRO Bull.
    15 (Jan.-Feb.1967):8.

Miles City
-UFO (CE-2)
  1923, Jan./N of town
    Glasgow Courier, 12 Jan.1923.
-UFO (NL)
  1956, Nov.16/Otis Miller
    "Case 249," CRIFO Orbit, 4 Jan.1957,
    p.1, quoting Great Falls Tribune
    (undated).

Millegan
-Phantom helicopter
  1975, fall
    Roberta Donovan & Keith Wolverton,
    Mystery Stalks the Prairie (Raynes-
    ford, Mont.: THAR, 1976), p.47.

Missoula
-Bird attack
  1952, Oct.
    "First Prize," Doubt, no.39 (1952):
    178,180.
-Electromagnetic anomaly
  1963, Nov./county attorney's office
    (Editorial), Fate 17 (Apr.1964):20.
-Fall of fish
  1958, July 11/Mr. Pike
    "Falls," Doubt, no.59 (1959):37.
-Haunt
  1934-1956/Eleanor Zakos/S. Fifth St.
    Henriette Lambros, "Our Ghost Was a
    Scream," Fate 28 (Aug.1975):76-80.
-Pollution anomaly
  1961, Nov.29/Laurence Parker/4002 S.
    Seventh St.
    (Editorial), Fate 15 (Apr.1962):22-
    23.
-UFO (?)
  1956, Nov.20/Earl T. Latta/Grass Val-
    ley/=meteor?
    (Editorial), Fate 10 (Mar.1957):17.
  1972, Aug.10/=meteor
    (Editorial), Fate 26 (Jan.1973):28.
-UFO (CE-2)
  1956, Sep.
    (Letter), Alferd Anderson, Fate 10
    (May 1957):113-14.
  1964, April-Aug./Allen Lund
    Defiance (O.) Crescent-News, 13 Aug.
    1964.
    "More Saucer Landings in Montana,"
    Saucer News 11 (Dec.1964):22-23.
-UFO (NL)
  1964, July 12-Aug.14/Reuben Dittert
    Missoulian Sentinel, 31 July 1964.
    "New York and Montana Flurries," UFO
    Inv. 2 (Sep.-Oct.1964):6.
    Curtis Fuller, "Collected UFO Sight-
    ings for August and September," Fate
    18 (Jan.1965):36-37.
  1973, Oct.23/Mullan Rd.
    Missoula Daily Missoulian, 24 Oct.
    1973.

Ovando
-UFO (?)
  1956, Feb.15
    "Montana's Phantom Plane," CRIFO Or-
    bit, 6 Apr.1956, pp.2-3.

Portage
-Phantom helicopter
  1975, Dec.
    Roberta Donovan & Keith Wolverton,
    Mystery Stalks the Prairie (Raynes-
    ford, Mont.: THAR, 1976), p.57.

Red Lodge
-Sheep mutilation
  1975, Aug.
    Roberta Donovan & Keith Wolverton,
    Mystery Stalks the Prairie (Raynes-
    ford, Mont.: THAR, 1976), p.27.

Roy
-UFO (NL)
  1975, Oct.10
    "Noteworthy UFO Sightings," Ufology
    2 (spring 1976):43.
  1975, Dec.20/W of town
    Roberta Donovan & Keith Wolverton,
    Mystery Stalks the Prairie (Raynes-
    ford, Mont.: THAR, 1976), p.72.

Saint Regis
-UFO (NL)
  1964, Aug.23-24/Mrs. W.A. Chisholm
    Curtis Fuller, "Collected UFO Sight-
    ings for August and September,"
    Fate 18 (Jan.1965):35,37.

Sand Coulee
-Phantom helicopter
  1975, fall
    Roberta Donovan & Keith Wolverton,
    Mystery Stalks the Prairie (Raynes-
    ford, Mont.: THAR, 1976), p.47.

Scobey
-Psychokinesis
  1908-1960s/Burley Bowler/Main St.
    (Editorial), Fate 17 (Aug.1964):9-10,
    quoting Billings Gazette (undated).

Shelby
-UFO (NL)
  1957, Oct.-1960, April 25
    Lloyd Mallan, "Complete Directory of
    UFOs: Part I," Sci.& Mech. 37 (Dec.
    1966):38.
  1975, Oct.18
    Roberta Donovan & Keith Wolverton,
    Mystery Stalks the Prairie (Raynes-
    ford, Mont.: THAR, 1976), pp.64-65.

Silver City
-Humanoid
  1977, June 14/Arthur Roy
    Helena Independent-Record, 16 June
    1977.

Simms
-Cattle mutilation
  1975, Dec.8-9/Sun R.
    Jerome Clark, "Saucer Central U.S.A.,"
    Saga UFO Rept. 3 (Apr.1976):8,67-68.
    Roberta Donovan & Keith Wolverton,
    Mystery Stalks the Prairie (Raynes-
    ford, Mont.: THAR, 1976), pp.70-72.
-UFO (CE-2)

  1975, Dec.8/Sun R.
    Roberta Donovan & Keith Wolverton,
    Mystery Stalks the Prairie (Raynes-
    ford, Mont.: THAR, 1976), pp.70-72.
-UFO (NL)
  1976, Feb.5
    Roberta Donovan & Keith Wolverton,
    Mystery Stalks the Prairie (Raynes-
    ford, Mont.: THAR, 1976), pp.82-83.

Square Butte
-Cattle mutilation
  1975, Aug.
    Roberta Donovan & Keith Wolverton,
    Mystery Stalks the Prairie (Raynes-
    ford, Mont.: THAR, 1976), pp.13-14.
    il.

Stanford
-Cattle mutilation
  1975, Sep./SE of town
    Roberta Donovan & Keith Wolverton,
    Mystery Stalks the Prairie (Raynes-
    ford, Mont.: THAR, 1976), p.45.

Stevensville
-UFO (NL)
  1975, July 28
    "UFO Central," CUFOS News Bull., 15
    Nov.1975, p.14.

Stockett
-Cattle mutilation
  1975/Mundt ranch
    Roberta Donovan & Keith Wolverton,
    Mystery Stalks the Prairie (Raynes-
    ford, Mont.: THAR, 1976), p.31. il.
    Don Worley, "Cattle Mutilations and
    UFOs: Who Are the Mutilators?" Of-
    ficial UFO 1 (Dec.1976):24-25.

Teton co.
-Archeological site
    Thomas P. Newcomb, "Some Fact and
    Much Conjecture Concerning the Sun
    River Medicine Wheel, Teton County,
    Montana," Arch. in Montana 8, no.1
    (1967):17-23.
-Cattle mutilations
  1975, Aug.
    Roberta Donovan & Keith Wolverton,
    Mystery Stalks the Prairie (Raynes-
    ford, Mont.: THAR, 1976), pp.10-13.
-Horse mutilation
  n.d.
    Roberta Donovan & Keith Wolverton,
    Mystery Stalks the Prairie (Raynes-
    ford, Mont.: THAR, 1976), pp.6-8. il.
-Phantom helicopter
  1975, fall
    Roberta Donovan & Keith Wolverton,
    Mystery Stalks the Prairie (Raynes-
    ford, Mont.: THAR, 1976), p.47.

Three Forks
-Paranormal strength
  n.d./Gary Allen
    (Editorial), Fate 19 (Jan.1966):15-
    18.

Ulm
-Humanoid
  1976, Feb.21/Missouri R.
    Jerome Clark, "Saucer Central U.S.A.,"
    Saga UFO Rept. 3 (June 1976):8.
-Phantom helicopter
  1975, Dec.22/SW of town
    Roberta Donovan & Keith Wolverton,
    Mystery Stalks the Prairie (Raynes-
    ford, Mont.: THAR, 1976), p.59.
-UFO (CE-3)
  1976, Feb.22/Leonard Hegele/N on I-15
    Great Falls Tribune, 23 Feb.1976.

Utica
-Cattle mutilation
  1975, Oct.9
    Roberta Donovan & Keith Wolverton,
    Mystery Stalks the Prairie (Raynes-
    ford, Mont.: THAR, 1976), pp.5-6.
    il.

Valier
-Fall of lizards
  1930s, Aug./Basil Hritsco/5 mi.NE
    Coral E. Lorenzen, The Shadow of the
    Unknown (N.Y.: Signet, 1970), pp.
    130-32.

Vaughn
-Humanoid
  1975, Dec.25-26
    Roberta Donovan & Keith Wolverton,
    Mystery Stalks the Prairie (Raynes-
    ford, Mont.: THAR, 1976), pp.87-89.
    Jerome Clark, "Saucer Central U.S.A.,"
    Saga UFO Rept. 3 (June 1976):8.
  1976, Jan.
    Roberta Donovan & Keith Wolverton,
    Mystery Stalks the Prairie (Raynes-
    ford, Mont.: THAR, 1976), p.90.
  1976, March 7/N of town
    John Green, Sasquatch: The Apes Among
    Us (Seattle: Hancock House, 1978),
    p.299.
-Phantom helicopter
  1975, Dec.8/Bootlegger Trail
    Roberta Donovan & Keith Wolverton,
    Mystery Stalks the Prairie (Raynes-
    ford, Mont.: THAR, 1976), p.57.
-UFO (?)
  1970, Feb.8/Mrs. Roy Curtis
    Great Falls Tribune, 9 Feb.1970.
-UFO (DD)
  1975/I-15
    Roberta Donovan & Keith Wolverton,
    Mystery Stalks the Prairie (Raynes-
    ford, Mont.: THAR, 1976), p.62. il.
-UFO (NL)
  1975, Dec.3/Arne Sand/missile site
    Roberta Donovan & Keith Wolverton,
    Mystery Stalks the Prairie (Raynes-
    ford, Mont.: THAR, 1976), p.55.

West Yellowstone
-Precognition
  1959, Aug.17/Dorothy Graeber
    Dorothy Graeber, "What Powered My
    Tongue?" Fate 22 (Dec.1969):62-64.

Whitefish
-UFO (NL)
  1975, Nov.17
    Don Worley, "Cattle Mutilations and
    UFOs: Who Are the Mutilators?" Of-
    ficial UFO 1 (Dec.1976):24.

Willard
-UFO (NL)
  1967, March/Stanley Ketchum
    Baker Fallon County Times, 9 Mar.
    1967.

Williams
-Ancient pyramids
  10 mi.N
    (Letter), E.D. Bufmeyer, Fate 20
    (June 1967):127-28.

Yaak
-UFO (R-V)
  1952, Aug.1/USAF radar site
    Edward J. Ruppelt, The Report on Un-
    identified Flying Objects (Garden
    City: Doubleday, 1956), p.194.
  1953, summer/William Kelly/USAF radar
  site
    Richard Hall, ed., The UFO Evidence
    (Washington: NICAP, 1964), p.85.

B. Physical Features

Ash Coulee
-Archeological site
    William T. Mulloy, "The Ash Coulee
    Site," Am.Antiquity 19 (1953):73-
    75. il.

Ashlot Bench
-Cattle mutilation and UFO (NL)
  1975, July
    Roberta Donovan & Keith Wolverton,
    Mystery Stalks the Prairie (Raynes-
    ford, Mont.: THAR, 1976), pp.60-61.
    il.

Bass Creek
-Humanoid tracks
  1964/Gary Hall
    John Green, Sasquatch: The Apes Among
    Us (Seattle: Hancock House, 1978),
    p.296.

Beaver Creek
-Humanoid tracks
  1976, Feb.11
    Roberta Donovan & Keith Wolverton,
    Mystery Stalks the Prairie (Raynes-
    Ford, Mont.: THAR, 1976), p.91.

Belt Creek Canyon
-Humanoid
  1977, Aug.20/Fred C. Wilson
    Missoula Daily Missoulian, 27 Aug.
    1977, p.20.
    John Green, Sasquatch: The Apes Among
    Us (Seattle: Hancock House, 1978),
    pp.300-301.

Bighorn Canyon
-Archeological site
  6700 B.C.-recent/Mangus site
    Wilfred M. Husted, "Bighorn Canyon
    Archeology," Pub.Salvage Arch.Smith.
    Inst., no.12 (1969). il.

Big Snowy Mts.
-Humanoid
  1900s
    John Green, Sasquatch: The Apes Among
    Us (Seattle: Hancock House, 1978),
    pp.283-84.

Bitterroot Range
-Humanoid
  ca.1930s
    John Green, The Year of the Sasquatch
    (Agassiz, B.C.: Cheam, 1970), p.24.

Bridger Mts.
-UFO (DD)
  1947, May 5
    "At the Same Time," Doubt, no.19
    (1947):290,291.

Brown's Gulch
-Humanoid
  1964, May 17/Gary Simons
    John Green, Sasquatch: The Apes Among
    Us (Seattle: Hancock House, 1978),
    pp.293-94.

Crystal Creek
-UFO (NL)
  1964, Aug./Mrs. Bill Crismore
    Curtis Fuller, "Collected UFO Sight-
    ings for August and September,"
    Fate 18 (Jan.1965):35,37.

Crystal L.
-UFO (CE-1)
  1963, March 9/Amos Biggs
    "Saucer Landing in Montana," Saucer
    News 10 (Sep.1963):13-14.

Flathead L.
-Lake monster
  1885-
    Polson Flathead Courier, 27 May 1937.
    New York Times, 13 June 1965, sec.X,
    p.48.
    Tim Church, "The Flathead Lake Mon-
    ster," Pursuit 8 (Oct.1975):89-92.
    Tim Church, "Flathead Lake Monster
    Update," Pursuit 9 (summer 1976):62.

Ford Creek
-UFO (NL)
  1975, Dec./Barry Michelotti
    Roberta Donovan & Keith Wolverton,
    Mystery Stalks the Prairie (Raynes-
    ford, Mont.: THAR, 1976), pp.73-74.

Freezeout L.
-UFO (?)
  1975, Oct.
    Roberta Donovan & Keith Wolverton,
    Mystery Stalks the Prairie (Raynes-
    ford, Mont.: THAR, 1976), p.69.

Gallatin R.
-Archeological site
  ca.300-1750/Antonsen site
    Leslie B. Davis & Charles D. Zeier,
    "Multi-Phase Late Period Bison Pro-
    curement at the Antonsen Site,
    Southwestern Montana," Plains An-
    thro. 23 (1978):222-35.
-Telepathy
  ca.1940/Lincoln Sartwell
    "The Floating Baby," Fate 3 (Dec.
    1950):40.

Gird Creek
-Humanoid
  1964, Aug./Lou Bigley
    Eric Norman, The Abominable Snowman
    (N.Y.: Award, 1969), pp.87-88.

Glacier National Park
-UFO (NL)
  1966, July
    John A. Keel, UFOs: Operation Trojan
    Horse (N.Y.: Putnam, 1970), p.155.

Gold Peak
-Lightning anomaly
  1927, July 2/Stanley Lukens
    H.F. Gisborne, "Lightning from a
    Clear Sky," Monthly Weather Rev. 56
    (Mar.1928):108.

Gore Hill
-Humanoid
  1976, May 7
    Roberta Donovan & Keith Wolverton,
    Mystery Stalks the Prairie (Raynes-
    ford, Mont.: THAR, 1976), p.106.

Hebgen L.
-Animal ESP
  1956, Aug.17
    Victor Wilson, "Montana's Birds
    Sensed Disaster," Tomorrow 8 (win-
    ter 1960):21-23.
-Earthquake luminescence
  1956, Aug.17
    John S. Derr, "Earthquake Lights: A
    Review of Observations and Present
    Theories," Bull.Seism.Soc'y Am. 63
    (1973):2177-87.

Highwood Mts.
-Cattle mutilation
  1975
    Roberta Donovan & Keith Wolverton,
    Mystery Stalks the Prairie (Raynes-
    ford, Mont.: THAR, 1976), p.30. il.
-UFO (CE-1)
  1975, Oct.17
    Roberta Donovan & Keith Wolverton,
    Mystery Stalks the Prairie (Raynes-
    ford, Mont.: THAR, 1976), pp.66-67.
-UFO (NL)
  1975, Dec.3
    Roberta Donovan & Keith Wolverton,
    Mystery Stalks the Prairie (Raynes-
    ford, Mont.: THAR, 1976), pp.51-52.

Little Bighorn R.
-Doubtful identity
   1930s/=George Armstrong Custer?
      Sheridan (Wyo.) News, 8 Dec.1937.
      "Is General Custer Alive Today?"
      Annals of Wyoming 48 (1976):129-31.

Logan Pass
-Humanoid
   1975, summer
      Roberta Donovan & Keith Wolverton,
      Mystery Stalks the Prairie (Raynes-
      ford, Mont.: THAR, 1976), pp.90-91.

Lone Pine State Park
-UFO (NL)
   1977, March/Betty Jones
      "Mystery in Montana Park," Can.UFO
      Rept., no.29 (fall-winter 1977):9-
      10. il.

Lost Trail Pass
-Humanoid
   1962, Nov./Reed Christenson
   1969, Sep.
      John Green, Sasquatch: The Apes Among
      Us (Seattle: Hancock House, 1978),
      p.296.

Mission Mts.
-Humanoid
   1959/R.W. Rye
      Missoula Daily Missoulian, 2 Dec.
      1960.
      Billings Gazette, 4 Dec.1960.
      John Green, Sasquatch: The Apes Among
      Us (Seattle: Hancock House, 1978),
      pp.292-93, quoting "Snowman or Snow-
      job?" Montana Sports Outdoors, Dec.
      1960.

Missouri R.
-River monster
   1970, summer/Ronald J. Haller/betw.
   Fort Benton & Lewistown/=giant fish?
      Ella E. Clark, Indian Legends of the
      Northern Rockies (Norman: Univ. of
      Oklahoma, 1966), pp.295-97.
      Missoula Daily Missoulian, 27 Jan.
      1971.

Moose Creek
-Phantom helicopter
   1975, fall
      Roberta Donovan & Keith Wolverton,
      Mystery Stalks the Prairie (Raynes-
      ford, Mont.: THAR, 1976), p.47.

Pfeiling Gulch
-Humanoid
   1976, July
      John Green, Sasquatch: The Apes Among
      Us (Seattle: Hancock House, 1978),
      pp.296-97.

Pictograph Cave
-Archeological site
   ca.2000 B.C.
      William B. Mulloy, "A Preliminary
      Historical Outline for the Northwes-

tern Plains," Pub.Univ.Wyoming, vol.
22, no.1 (1958).
Dan Stockton, "History of Pictograph
Cave Excavations," Arch. in Montana
4, no.3 (1962):2-7. il.
Stuart W. Connor, "Pictograph Cave
Pictorial," Arch. in Montana 8, no.
3 (1967):1-15. il.

Piquett Creek
-Humanoid tracks
   1965, fall/Bob Shook
      John Green, Sasquatch: The Apes Among
      Us (Seattle: Hancock House, 1978),
      p.296.

Prickly Pear Canyon
-Phantom helicopter
   1976, Feb.18
      Roberta Donovan & Keith Wolverton,
      Mystery Stalks the Prairie (Raynes-
      ford, Mont.: THAR, 1976), p.59.

Rainbow Dam
-Humanoid
   1976, July 21/E of dam
      Great Falls Tribune, 31 July 1976.

Rocky Mts.
-Humanoid
   1892/nr. Wyoming line
      New Haven (Ct.) Evening Register,
      11 Nov.1892.

Smith R.
-Pictograph
      James D. Keyser, "Audrey's Overhang:
      A Pictographic Maze in Central Mon-
      tana," Plains Anthro. 22 (1977):
      183-87.

Stanton L.
-Photographic anomaly
   1977, June/Betty Jones
      (Letter), Can.UFO Rept., no. 33
      (winter 1978-79):22-23. il.

Waterton L.
-Lake monster
   1944-1956, Aug.5
      Ivan T. Sanderson, Things (N.Y.:
      Pyramid, 1967), pp.36-37.
      Jim Brandon, Weird America (N.Y.:
      Dutton, 1978), p.127.

                  C. Ethnic Groups

Flathead Indians
-Flood myth
      Ella E. Clark, Indian Legends of the
      Northern Rockies (Norman: Univ. of
      Oklahoma, 1966), p.90.
-Humanoid myth
      H.H. Turney-High, "The Flathead In-
      dians of Montana," Mem.Am.Anthro.
      Ass'n, no.48 (1937):13.
-UFO (CE-3) legend
      Ella E. Clark, Indian Legends of the
      Northern Rockies (Norman: Univ. of

Oklahoma, 1966), pp.125-28.

Gros Ventre Indians
-Flood myth
    H.S. Bellamy, Moons, Myths and Man
    (London: Faber and Faber, 1936), p.
    96.

      D. Unspecified Localities

-Archeological sites
  tipi rings
    Thomas F. Kehoe, "Stone 'Medicine
    Wheels' in Southern Alberta and the
    Adjacent Portion of Montana," J.
    Wash.Acad.Sci. 44 (May 1954):133-37.
    il.
    Thomas F. Kehoe, "Stone Tipi Rings
    in North-Central Montana and the
    Adjacent Portion of Alberta, Can-
    ada," Bull.Bur.Am.Ethn., no.173
    (1960):421-73. il.

-Clairvoyance
  1878, Oct./Piks-ah-ki
    Paul A. Hout, "The Crow Woman Who
    Died for Love," Fate 23 (Aug.1970):
    46-50.

-Fall of fish
  1946/western sector
    Seattle (Wash.) Star, 26 Aug.1946.

-Mystery stone spheres
  eastern sector
    (Letter), K. Bodenhamer, Fate 5
    (Oct.1952):128-29.

ALBERTA

A. Populated Places

Abee
-Humanoid tracks
  1977, Dec.9/Andy Zachary
    Edmonton Journal, 10 Dec.1977.
-UFO (CE-2)
  1969, July 16/Sylvia Annola
    Ashley Pachal, "When a UFO Came to
    Abee," FSR Case Histories, no.15
    (June 1973):15-16.

Aldersyde
-UFO (CE-2)
  1967, Oct.11/Nora Tibbs/Hwy.2
    Jim & Coral Lorenzen, UFOs over the
    Americas (N.Y.: Signet, 1968), p.33.
  1967, Nov.28/Harold Lee/S on Hwy.1A
    "On the Canadian Scene," APRO Bull.
    16 (Jan.-Feb.1968):4,5.

Banff
-Humanoid
  1971, July/E of town
    John Green, Sasquatch: The Apes Among
    Us (Seattle: Hancock House, 1978),
    p.239.
-UFO (CE-1)
  1977, Aug.4/nr. Glen Ave.
    (Editorial), Res Bureaux Bull., no.
    22 (25 Aug.1977):4-5.
-UFO (NL)
  1967, May/Lloyd Mewburn/Stony Squaw
    "Light Examines Mountains," Can.UFO
    Rept., no.1 (Jan.-Feb.1969):11.
    John Magor, Our UFO Visitors (Seat-
    tle: Hancock House, 1977), pp.153-
    54.
  1968, Oct./Jean Watts/Mt. Rundle
  1969, Dec./Dan Bittorf
  1970, Aug./Jean Watts/Mt. Norquay
    John Magor, Our UFO Visitors (Seat-
    tle: Hancock House, 1977), pp.120-
    26, 155-56.
-Weather control
  1974, Feb./Bruno Engler
    Kansas City (Mo.) Star, 6 Mar.1974.

Barrhead
-UFO (NL)
  1979, Jan.16
    "Recent UFO Reports," Res Bureaux
    Bull., no.44 (Feb.1979):4.

Bashaw
-UFO (CE-2)
  1968, Aug./Glenn Hunter/ground markings
  only
    Bashaw Star, 7 Aug.1968.

Beaverlodge
-UFO (NL)
  1969, Feb.3
    Vancouver (B.C.) Province, 4 Feb.1969.

Bluesky
-UFO (DD)
  1952, Nov./Fred Clarke/W of town
    Edmonton Journal, 28 Nov.1952.

Bowden
-UFO (CE-2)
  1967, Sep./Grant Field/James R./ground
  markings only
    Gene Duplantier, "The Mystery of the
    Burned Circles," in Brad Steiger &
    Joan Whritenour, Flying Saucer In-
    vasion: Target--Earth (N.Y.: Award,
    1969), p.23.

Bowness
-Phantom
  n.d./Dorothy Nielson
    Eileen Sonin, More Canadian Ghosts
    (Richmond Hill, Ont.: Pocket Books,
    1974 ed.), p.67.

Bragg Creek
-UFO (?)
  1968/Harold Norton
    "UFO Beeps on Record," Australian
    UFO Bull., Nov.1968, p.6, quoting
    Saucers Space & Sci. (undated).

Calgary
-Mystery bird deaths
  1968, June 1/William Holmberg/=strych-
  nine poisoning
    Vancouver (B.C.) Province, 26 Oct.
    1968.
    (Editorial), Fate 21 (Oct.1968):10-
    14.
    (Editorial), Fate 22 (May 1969):33.
-UFO (?)
  1973, April/Mike Dudley
    (Letter), Can.UFO Rept., no.15
    (1973):33.
-UFO (CE-2)
  1957, Nov.3
    Winnipeg (Man.) Tribune, 7 Nov.1957.
  1974, Oct.13/David Gundy/10 mi.W
    Timothy Green Beckley, "Operation
    Contact," Saga UFO Rept. 3 (Apr.
    1976):39,62.
-UFO (CE-4)
  1967, Nov.14/David Seewalt
    "Similar Incident at Calgary," Can.
    UFO Rept., no.16 (1973-74):6-7.
    W.K. Allan, "Crocodile-Skinned Enti-
    ties at Calgary," Flying Saucer Rev.
    20 (Apr.1975):25-26.
    B. Ann Slate, "Contactee Supplies
    New Clues to UFO Mystery," Saga UFO
    Rept. 3 (Apr.1976):26-30.
    John Magor, Our UFO Visitors (Seat-
    tle: Hancock House, 1977), pp.165-
    70.
-UFO (DD)
  1928

James H. Gray, The Roar of the Twen-
ties (Toronto: Macmillan, 1975),
betw. pp.309-10. il.
(Letter), W. Ritchie Benedict, Can.
UFO Rept., no.26 (winter 1976-77):
23.
1952, June 8
Marc Leduc, "Notes sur le projet
'Magnet,'" UFO-Québec, no.4 (1975):
12,15.
1958, Feb.10/Dick Clark/617 Elizabeth
Ave.
(Editorial), Fate 11 (July 1958):16.
1972, Aug.10/Charles Harwood
(Editorial), Fate 26 (Jan.1973):28.
1978, April 2/Warren Smith/8 mi.NW
"Foreign Forum," Int'l UFO Reporter
3 (May 1978):2.
-UFO (NL)
1950, April 19
"Fortean Cloud," Doubt, no.30 (1950)
:36.
1966, April 4
Calgary Herald, 5 Apr.1966.
1967, Oct.19/N of town
"On the Canadian Scene," APRO Bull.
16 (Jan.-Feb.1968):4.
1970, Oct./Paul Chemerys/foothills W
of town
John Magor, Our UFO Visitors (Seattle: Hancock House, 1977), pp.163-
64.
1975, Aug./Bessie O'Connor/2 mi.S
W.K. Allan, "UFO with Base and One
That Heard," Can.UFO Rept., no.25
(fall 1976):5.

Camrose
-UFO (CE-2)
1967, July/Edgar Shielke/ground markings only
Jim & Coral Lorenzen, UFOs over the
Americas (N.Y.: Signet, 1968), pp.
30-32, quoting Calgary Herald (undated).
Gene Duplantier, "The Mystery of the
Burned Circles," in Brad Steiger &
Joan Whritenour, Flying Saucer Invasion: Target--Earth (N.Y.: Award,
1969), pp.22-23.

Caroline
-Humanoid
1976, Sep.1/W of town
John Green, Sasquatch: The Apes Among
Us (Seattle: Hancock House, 1978),
p.241.

Clairmont
-UFO (NL)
1979, Jan.25
"Recent UFO Reports," Res Bureaux
Bull., no.44 (Feb.1979):4.

Cluny
-UFO (?)
1961, Jan.22/Mrs. Fred Bertscky/S of
town/=meteor?
"UAO Sighted by Many over Calgary,
Alberta," APRO Bull. 9 (Jan.1961):5.

Cochrane
-UFO (CE-1)
1965, Oct./Bill Hertzke/Circle Jay
Ranch
Jim & Coral Lorenzen, UFOs over the
Americas (N.Y.: Signet, 1968), pp.
87-102.

Consort
-Archeological site
H.M. Wormington & Richard G. Forbis,
"An Introduction to the Archeology
of Alberta, Canada," Proc.Denver
Mus.Nat.Hist., no.11 (1965), pp.
97-100. il.

Craigmyle
-UFO (CE-2)
1969, Feb.18/Barbara Smyth
W.K. Allan, "A UFO and the Car Which
'Floated Along,'" FSR Case Histor-
ies, no.6 (Aug.1971):8,iii.

Dapp
-UFO (NL)
1968, Nov.7
"Around the Globe," APRO Bull. 17
(Nov.-Dec.1968):6.

Daysland
-Poltergeist
1935
Hereward Carrington & Nandor Fodor,
Haunted People (N.Y.: Signet, 1968
ed.), p.65, quoting Light, 21 Mar.
1935.

Didsbury
-UFO (CE-2)
1969, summer
Ted Phillips, Physical Traces Associated with UFO Sightings (Evanston:
Center for UFO Studies, 1975), p.
67, quoting Saucers Space & Sci.
(undated).

Drayton Valley
-UFO (NL)
1975, Oct.25/Hwy.57
Drayton Valley Western Review, 30
Oct.1975.

Drumheller
-UFO (CE-1)
1967, summer/Ruth Pears
"Highway Snoop," Can.UFO Rept., no.
12 (1972):5.
-UFO (CE-2)
1971, Sep.23/Joe Klimek
"Badland Rovers," Can.UFO Rept., no.
12 (1972):7-9.

Eaglesham
-UFO (NL)
1977, Aug.6
(Editorial), Res Bureaux Bull., no.
22 (25 Aug.1977):4.

Edmonton
-Dowsing

1900-1950s/Don Belknap
  (Editorial), Fate 10 (July 1957):16.
-Mystery explosion
  1971, April 8/M.A. Woodworth/10819
  122d St.
    Brad Steiger, Strange Disappearances
    (N.Y.: Lancer, 1972), pp.114-15.
-Poltergeist
  1963, Jan./Harold Sydora
    (Editorial), Fate 17 (May 1964): 9-10.
    Sheila Hervey, Some Canadian Ghosts
    (Richmond Hill, Ont.: Pocket Books,
    1973), pp.198-201, quoting Edmonton
    Journal (undated).
-UFO (CE-1)
  1969, Sep./Sharon Radomski/Lansdown
  School
  1969, Oct./Leo LeBlanc
    "Action over the Prairies," Can.UFO
    Rept., no.10 (1971):13,15-16.
-UFO (CE-2)
  1967, May 7/Ricky Banyard/Allendale
    Edmonton Journal, 8 May 1967.
    "Eerie Object in Graveyard," APRO
    Bull. 15 (May-June 1967):7.
-UFO (DD)
  1959, June 18
    Lloyd Mallan, "Complete Directory of
    UFOs: Part III," Sci.& Mech. 38
    (Feb.1967):56,58.
  1970, April/Ashley Pachal
    "Action over the Prairies," Can.UFO
    Rept., no.10 (1971):13,14.
  1979, Jan.12-15/=balloon?
    Edmonton Journal, 17 Jan.1979.
-UFO (NL)
  1968, summer/John Pearce/3 mi.N
  1969, Aug.2/Geraldine Scott
  1970, Aug.2/Gerry Malaniuk
    "Action over the Prairies," Can.UFO
    Rept., no.10 (1971):13-15.
  1977, March 11
  1977, April 23/Charles R. Elliott
    Edmonton Report, 2 May 1977.
    John Brent Musgrave, "Red Lights and
    Other UFOs over Canada," MUFON UFO
    J., no.118 (Sep.1977):14-15. il.
  1979, Jan.15/SW of town
    "Recent UFO Reports," Res Bureaux
    Bull., no.44 (Feb.1979):4.
-UFO (R-V)
  1967, April 6/airport
    "Sightings Still on Upswing," APRO
    Bull. 15 (Mar.-Apr.1967):11,12,
    quoting Edmonton Journal (undated).
    Gordon D. Thayer, "Optical and Radar
    Analyses of Field Reports," in Ed-
    ward U. Condon, ed., Scientific
    Study of Unidentified Flying Objects
    (N.Y.: Bantam, 1969 ed.), pp.130-31.

Fitzgerald
-Clairvoyance
  1921, fall/John James Daniels
    Jean W. Godsell, "Moccasin Telegraph,"
    Fate 7 (Sep.1954):95-99.

Fort MacLeod
-Phantom bear
  n.d./Chief Heavy Collar

Charles M. Skinner, Myths and Legends
  Beyond Our Borders (Philadelphia:
  Lippincott, 1899), pp.178-80.
-UFO (DD)
  1956, Aug.29/Robert J. Childerhose
    Montreal (P.Q.) Star, 13 Nov.1966.
    Philip J. Klass, UFOs: Identified
    (N.Y.: Random House, 1968), pp.146-
    48.

Frog Lake
-Aerial phantom
  1885, May/Theresa Gowanlock
    Francis Dickie, "The Vision That
    Stopped an Indian Rebellion," Fate
    14 (Apr.1961):58-64. il.

Gleichen
-UFO (CE-2)
  1971, May 14/Wilton Raw Eater/Black-
  foot Reservation
    "Strange Case of 'Flying Cars,'"
    Can.UFO Rept., no.12 (1972):3-5.
    W.K. Allan, "Car Levitation on the
    Blackfoot Reserve," FSR Case His-
    tories, no.11 (Aug.1972):8.

Grande Prairie
-UFO (?)
  1969, July 16
    Prince George (B.C.) Citizen, 16
    July 1969.
-UFO (CE-1)
  1979, Jan.31
    "Recent UFO Reports," Res Bureaux
    Bull., no.44 (Feb.1979):4.
-UFO (CE-2)
  1970, Nov.4/Jack Hickey
    (Editorial), Fate 24 (Apr.1971):24-
    26.

High Prairie
-UFO (CE-1)
  1978, Dec.7/Eastern Prairie Metis
  Colony
    "Recent UFO Reports," Res Bureaux
    Bull., no.43 (Jan.1979):3,4.

Highwood Ranger Station
-UFO (CE-2)
  1967, Sep.18/Russell Hill
  1967, Oct.7/Russell Hill
    Jim & Coral Lorenzen, UFOs over the
    Americas (N.Y.: Signet, 1968), p.34.
-UFO (DD)
  1967, July 3/Warren Smith/3 mi.SSW
    Edward U. Condon, ed., Scientific
    Study of Unidentified Flying Objects
    (N.Y.: Bantam, 1969 ed.), pp.469-
    75.il.
    J. Allen Hynek, The UFO Experience
    (Chicago: Regnery, 1972), pp.58-60.
    il.
    Donald H. Menzel & Ernest H. Taves,
    The UFO Enigma (Garden City:
    Doubleday, 1977), pp.113-114.
    Hayden C. Hewes, "The Calgary Day-
    light Disc," Saga UFO Rept. 6 (July
    1978):24-27. il.

Hinton
-UFO (NL)
  1976, April 9
    "Noteworthy UFO Sightings," Ufology
    2 (fall 1976):61.

Horse Lake Reservation
-Clairvoyance
  1948, July
    Jean W. Godsell, "Moccasin Telegraph,"
    Fate 7 (Sep.1954):95,98-99, quoting
    Edmonton Journal (undated).

Joussard
-UFO (NL)
  1978, Dec.13/Lesser Slave L.
    "Recent UFO Reports," Res Bureaux
    Bull., no.43 (Jan.1979):3,4.

Lac la Biche
-UFO (CE-1)
  1970, Jan./Mugler Cardinal/Reserve
    "Close Encounter," Can.UFO Rept.,
    no.15 (1972):13-15.

Lake Louise
-UFO (NL)
  1968, Oct.
    John Magor, Our UFO Visitors (Seat-
    tle: Hancock House, 1977), p.122,
    quoting Calgary Herald (undated).

Lethbridge
-Archeological site
    H.M. Wormington & Richard G. Forbis,
    "An Introduction to the Archeology
    of Alberta, Canada," Proc.Denver
    Mus.Nat.Hist., no.11 (1965), p.135.
    il.
-Clairvoyance
  1974, June 17/Mrs. Joachim Huemer
    "Dream Depicts Death," Fate 28 (Oct.
    1975):41.
-UFO (CE-1)
  1975, Jan.23/Ouida McAdams
    Timothy Green Beckley, "Operation
    Contact," Saga UFO Rept. 3 (Apr.
    1976):38,64, quoting Lethbridge
    Herald (undated).

Linaria
-UFO (CE-2)
  1977, June 21/Sunniebend Bridge/ground
  markings only
    Westlock News, 27 July 1977.
    John Brent Musgrave, "Strange Mark-
    ings," Can.UFO Rept., no.29 (fall-
    winter 1977):5-6. il.

Majorville
-Archeological site
  2500 B.C.
    R.G. Forbis & J.M. Calder, Archeo-
    logical Investigations of the Major-
    ville Cairn, Alberta (Calgary:
    Univ. of Calgary, 1971). il.
    James M. Calder, "The Majorville
    Cairn and Medicine Wheel Site, Al-
    berta," Pap.Arch.Survey Canada, no.
    62 (1977). il.

John A. Eddy, "Medicine Wheels and
    Plains Indian Astronomy," in
    Anthony F. Aveni, ed., Native Amer-
    ican Astronomy (Austin: Univ. of
    Texas, 1977), pp.147,159-62.

Mannville
-Clairempathy
  1928, July/Maximilian Langsner
    Michael Gier & Kurt Singer, "Brain
    Waves Don't Lie," Tomorrow 5 (au-
    tumn 1957):9-21.
    Alan Hynd, "Mind-Reader Who Trapped
    Alberta's Mad Murderer," Fate 11
    (Mar.1958):49-54.

Manyberries
-Humanoid tracks
  1977, Dec.1 /Thelma Dunlop
    Medicine Hat News, 2 Dec.1977.
    Calgary Herald, 2 Dec.1977.
    Lethbridge Herald, 3 Dec.1977.

Mayerthorpe
-Out-of-body experience
  1938/Frank M. Mitchell Adams
    Frank M. Mitchell Adams, "The Girl I
    Found Waiting," Fate 9 (Aug.1956):
    87-88.

Medicine Hat
-UFO (NL)
  1968, April 18/Nick Didack
    Brad Steiger & Joan Whritenour, Fly-
    ing Saucer Invasion: Target--Earth
    (N.Y.: Award, 1968), p.97.

Midnapore
-Acoustic anomaly
  1968/Mrs. G.C. Marshall
    "UFO Beeps on Record," Australian
    UFO Bull., Nov.1968, p.6, quoting
    Saucers Space & Sci. (undated).
-Ball lightning
  1968, July 27/John Ehrmantraut
    "Lightning Hits UFO," Can.UFO Rept.,
    no.14 (1973):25.

Millet
-UFO (NL)
  1969, Aug./Monka Swanson/9 mi. W
    "1969 Canadian Sighting Reported,"
    Skylook, no.61 (Dec.1972):8.

Minburn
-UFO (NL)
  1973, Oct.25/Percy Davies
    Vermillion Standard, 7 Nov.1973.
    "Canada Touched by Flap," Can.UFO
    Rept., no.16 (1973-74):7,8.

Mirror
-UFO (CE-1)
  1967, Oct.13/Larry Mazure/Canadian
  Nat'l Railroad
    "Object Trails Train," APRO Bull. 16
    (Jan.-Feb.1968):3.
    Donald E. Keyhoe & Gordon I.R. Lore,
    Jr., UFOs: A New Look (Washington:
    NICAP, 1969), pp.10-11.

Mountain View
-Clairvoyance
    1919, Dec./Lila L. Smith/7 mi. from
    town
        Lila L. Smith, "My Dream Saved Our
        Starving Sheep," Fate 21 (July
        1968):57-60.

Olds
-UFO (CE-2)
    1969, July 1/Fred Yoos
        Ted Phillips, Physical Traces Asso-
        ciated with UFO Sightings (Evanston:
        Center for UFO Studies, 1975), p.
        66, quoting Saucers Space & Sci.
        (undated).

Paddle Prairie
-UFO (CE-1)
    1972, May 26/Joe Anderson/5 mi. S
        "Visitors Play Tag," Can.UFO Rept.,
        no.14 (1973):104-105.

Peace River
-UFO (?)
    1978, Jan.25/1 mi. from town
        (Editorial), Res Bureaux Bull., no.
        29 (9 Feb.1978):5.

Peers
-UFO (CE-3)
    1975, Oct.14/Judy Powers
        Edson Leader, 15 Oct.1975.

Penhold
-UFO (R-V)
    1971, Aug.15
        W. Ritchie Benedict, "Canadian UFO
        Still a Puzzle," Fate 25 (Sep.1972)
        :89.

Pincher Creek
-Archeological site
    ca.600 A.D.
        H.M. Wormington & Richard G. Forbis,
        "An Introduction to the Archeology
        of Alberta, Canada," Proc.Denver
        Mus.Nat.Hist., no.11 (1965), pp.
        136-38. il.

Priddis
-UFO (NL)
    1974, Oct.13,18
        Edmonton Journal, 21 Oct.1974.

Red Deer
-Ancient tin utensils
        Red Deer Advocate, 25 June 1909.
-UFO (NL)
    1971, Aug.15
        W. Ritchie Benedict, "Canadian UFO
        Still a Puzzle," Fate 25 (Sep.1972)
        :89.

Rochester
-Humanoid
    1976, Oct.31/Daryl Lange/10 mi. E
        Athabaska Echo, 3 Nov.1976.

Rocky Mountain House

-Humanoid
    1972, summer/12 mi. from town
        John Green, The Sasquatch File (Ag-
        assiz, B.C.: Cheam, 1973), p.56.
-Seance
    1806, summer/David Thompson/shaking
    tent
        J.B. Tyrrell, ed., David Thompson's
        Narrative of His Explorations in
        Western America 1784-1812 (Toronto:
        Champlain Soc'y, Pub.no.12, 1916),
        pp.90-92.

Rosedale
-UFO (CE-3)
    1971, June 9/Esther A. Clappison
        "Roadside Visitors," Can.UFO Rept.,
        no.12 (1972):5-7.
        W.K. Allan, "Humanoids and Craft Seen
        at Rosedale," FSR Case Histories,
        no.10 (June 1972):4-5.
        Brian James, "The Rosedale Humanoids:
        Further Details," FSR Case Histor-
        ies, no.16 (Aug.1973):6-7. il.

Saint Michael
-Fall of fish
    1959, Dec./John Bryks
        (Editorial), Fate 13 (June 1960):20.

Saint Paul
-UFO (NL)
    1974, Dec.16/Kevin Bradshaw/N of town
        (Letter), Can.UFO Rept., no.20
        (1975):23.

Sarcee Indian Reservation
-UFO (CE-2)
    1970, Aug.
        John Magor, "Horse Ill after UFO In-
        cident," FSR Case Histories, no.6
        (Aug.1971):3-4. il.

Sentinel
-Crisis apparition
    1941, March 9/Mrs. Dawson
        Eileen Sonin, More Canadian Ghosts
        (Richmond Hill, Ont.: Pocket Books,
        1974 ed.), pp.104-105.

Seven Persons
-Humanoid
    1972, fall-1973, Dec./Seven Persons
    Creek
        John Green, Sasquatch: The Apes
        Among Us (Seattle: Hancock House,
        1978), p.240.

Sexsmith
-Humanoid
    1975, Oct.2/Bob Moody/11 mi. N on Hwy.2
        John Green, Sasquatch: The Apes Among
        Us (Seattle: Hancock House, 1978),
        pp.240-241, quoting Grande Prairie
        Daily Herald (undated).

Sibbald
-UFO (CE-2)
    1957, Nov.3/Edna Ireland
        Calgary Herald, 6 Nov.1957.

Standoff
-UFO (CE-2)
   1968, May/Mrs. Hoeffer
      Ted Phillips, Physical Traces Asso-
      ciated with UFO Sightings (Evanston:
      Center for UFO Studies, 1975), p.56.
   n.d./Standoff Church Colony
      (Letter), Mrs. E. Stahl, Saga UFO
      Rept. 2 (fall 1975):6. il.

Strathmore
-UFO (CE-2)
   1976, spring/Grace Thomson
      W.K. Allan, "UFO with Base and One
      That Heard," Can.UFO Rept., no.25
      (fall 1976):3-5.

Taber
-Archeological site
   ca.37,000-9000 B.C./Bayrock and Stalker
   sites
      Wann Langston & Lawrence Oschinsky,
      "Notes on Taber 'Early Man' Site,"
      Anthropoligica, new ser., vol.5, no.
      2 (1963).
      H.M. Wormington & Richard G. Forbis,
      "An Introduction to the Archeology
      of Alberta, Canada," Proc.Denver
      Mus.Nat.Hist., no.11 (1965), pp.
      116-22. il.
-UFO (CE-1)
   1974, Dec.2/Marvin Marose
      Taber Times, 4 Dec.1974.
-UFO (CE-2)
   1967, Sep./Evan Evanson/Hwy.36, 1 mi.
   S of Hwy.3
      Jim & Coral Lorenzen, UFOs over the
      Americas (N.Y.: Signet, 1968), p.32.

Three Hills
-UFO (CE-2)
   1972, June 3/Florian Nottell/Ghost
   Pine Mine
      W.K. Allan, "The Sighting at Ghost
      Pine Mine," FSR Case Histories, no.
      12 (Dec.1972):16.
-UFO (DD)
   1968, Jan.15
      J.Allen Hynek, The UFO Experience
      (Chicago: Regnery, 1972), pp.53-55.

Valleyview
-UFO (NL)
   1969, Jan.21
      "RCMP Observe UFO in Canada," APRO
      Bull. 17 (Mar.-Apr.1969):5.

Wetaskiwin
-UFO (CE-3)
   1961, Aug.8
      John Brent Musgrave, "Cosmic Voyeurs:
      19th and 20th Century Style," Can.
      UFO Rept., no.27 (spring 1977):21-
      22.
      John Brent Musgrave, "The Behavior
      and Origins of Canadian UFO Occu-
      pants and Critters: Part 2," Can.
      UFO Rept., no.31 (summer 1978):20,
      21.

Wildwood
-Horse mutilation
   1976, spring
      "Inquiries," Stigmata, no.3 (May
      1978):1.

            B. Physical Features

Abraham L.
-Humanoid
   1974, May 11/Ron Gummell/David Thompson Hwy.
      John Green, Sasquatch: The Apes
      Among Us (Seattle: Hancock House,
      1978), p.240, quoting CP release,
      12 Aug. 1974.

Athabasca R.
-Crisis apparition
   1918, July 4/Luelia Evelyn Potts
      Luelia Evelyn Potts, "Uncle Allan
      and the Handcar," Fate 25 (June
      1972):89-91.

Banff National Park
-Fall of midges
   1952, Feb.
      "Falls--Maybe," Doubt, no.38 (1952):
      170.
-UFO (?)
   1959, summer/Allan Laing
      "Psychic Sightings," Can.UFO Rept.,
      no.10 (1971):2-4. il.
      John Magor, Our UFO Visitors (Seat-
      tle: Hancock House, 1977), pp.159-
      62. il.
-UFO (CE-2)
   1974, Aug.18/Brent Herbert
      (Letter), Can.UFO Rept., no.20
      (1975):23-24.
-UFO (DD)
   1967, fall/Lloyd Mewburn
      "Peek-A-Boo Material," Can.UFO Rept.,
      no.1 (Jan.-Feb.1969):11-12.
      John Magor, Our UFO Visitors (Seat-
      tle: Hancock House, 1977), pp.154-
      55.

Bellvue L.
-Humanoid tracks
   1977, July 2
      Lloydminster Meridian Booster, 14
      July 1977.

Big Horn Dam
-Humanoid
   1969, Aug.24/Harley Peterson
      Edmonton Journal, 30 Aug.1969, p.2.
      John Green, Year of the Sasquatch
      (Agassiz, B.C.: Cheam, 1970), pp.
      47,68-70.
      Don Hunter & René Dahinden, Sasquatch
      (Toronto: McClelland & Stewart,
      1973), pp.142-44.

British Block Cairn
-Archeological site
   ca.1000 A.D.
      H.M. Wormington & Richard G. Forbis,

"An Introduction to the Archeology
of Alberta, Canada," Proc.Denver
Mus.Nat.Hist., no.11 (1965), pp.
122-25. il.

Castor Creek
-Archeological site
   ca.2500 B.C.
      H.M. Wormington & Richard G. Forbis,
      "An Introduction to the Archeology
      of Alberta, Canada," Proc.Denver
      Mus.Nat.Hist., no.11 (1965), pp.
      113-16. il.

Chappice L.
-Weather control
   1921, April-Aug./Charles Mallory Hat-
   field/=unknown chemical method
      Robert E. Gard, Johnny Chinook (Lon-
      don: Longmans, Green, 1945), pp.
      91-97, quoting Edmonton Journal
      (undated).

Chin Coulee L.
-Archeological site
   ca.7000 B.C./Fletcher site
      H.M. Wormington & Richard G. Forbis,
      "An Introduction to the Archeology
      of Alberta, Canada," Proc.Denver
      Mus.Nat.Hist., no.11 (1965), pp.
      120-21. il.

Cold L.
-Humanoid
   1976, summer
      John Green, Sasquatch: The Apes Among
      Us (Seattle: Hancock House, 1978),
      p.241.

Columbia Icefields
-Humanoid
   1968, Aug./Gerald Martin
      John Green, The Sasquatch File (Ag-
      assiz, B.C.: Cheam, 1973), p.48.

Cooking L.
-UFO (DD)
   1957/Allan Laing
      "Psychic Sightings," Can.UFO Rept.,
      no.10 (1971):2,4.

Crowsnest Forest
-Humanoid tracks
   1972, spring/Stan Fisher/30 mi.N of
   Lundbreck
      John Green, The Sasquatch File (Ag-
      assiz, B.C.: Cheam, 1973), p.56.

Daisy Creek
-UFO (NL)
   1974, Aug.17/Gordon Parker
      High River Times, 22 Aug.1974.

Head-Smashed-In Buffalo Jump
-Archeological site
   2500 B.C.-recent
      H.M. Wormington & Richard G. Forbis,
      "An Introduction to the Archeology
      of Alberta, Canada," Proc.Denver
      Mus.Nat.Hist., no.11 (1965).

Brian O.K. Reeves, "Head-Smashed-In:
5500 Years of Bison Jumping on the
Alberta Plains," Plains Anthro. 23
(1978):151-74. il.

Heart R.
-UFO (DD)
   1970, April 13/Michael Ursulak
      "Action over the Prairies," Can.UFO
      Rept., no.10 (1971):13,16-17. il.

Kananaskis Lakes
-Humanoid
   1969, Sep.
      John Green, The Sasquatch File (Ag-
      assiz, B.C.: Cheam, 1973), p.49.

Kananaskis R.
-Weather control
   1959, Feb./Johnny Bearspaw/Stony Indians
      "The Amazing Snow Dance of the
      Stonys," Fate 14 (Oct.1961):33.

Lesser Slave L.
-Clairvoyance
   1904, Sep./George Hayward
      Philip H. Godsell, "The Dream That
      Solved a Murder," Fate 13 (Apr.
      1960):62-70.
-UFO (NL)
   1977, March-April/=planets?
      Slave Lake Scope, 16 Mar.1977; 23
      Mar.1977; 30 Mar.1977; 6 Apr.1977;
      20 Apr.1977; and 11 May 1977.
      "Spot News," Can.UFO Rept., no.27
      (spring 1977):17, quoting Edmonton
      Journal (undated).

North Saskatchewan R.
-River monster
   1939/Walking Eagle/nr. Rocky Mountain
   House
      Robert E. Gard, Johnny Chinook (Lon-
      don: Longmans, Green, 1945), pp.
      212-13.

Oldman R.
-Archeological site
   450-600 A.D./Ross site
      Richard G. Forbis, "Some Late Sites
      in the Oldman River Region, Alberta,"
      Bull.Nat'l Mus.Canada, no.162
      (1960):119-64. il.
-Retrocognition
   1875/Cecil Edward Denny/40 mi.E of
   Fort Walsh
      Cecil Edward Denny, The Riders of the
      Plains (Calgary: The Herald, 1905).
      Andrew Ballentine, "The Indians from
      Out of Time," Fate 13 (Dec.1960):
      39-43.

Red Deer R.
-Seance
   1879, summer/Cecil Edward Denny/shak-
   ing tent
      R.S. Lambert, Exploring the Super-
      natural (Toronto: McClelland &
      Stewart, 1955), pp.38-39.

Francis Dickie, "Mystery of the Shaking Tents," Real West 7 (Sep.1964): 18-19.

Rocky Mts.
-UFO (NL)
1870, Dec.16/William Francis Butler/SW of Edmonton
William Francis Butler, The Great Lone Land (London: Low, Marston, Low & Searle, 1872), p.292.

Slave Lake Forest
-Humanoid
1976
John Green, Sasquatch: The Apes Among Us (Seattle: Hancock House, 1978), p.241.

South Saskatchewan R.
-Erratic crocodilian
1950, June
"No Such Animal," Doubt, no.30 (1950):36,37, quoting New York Herald-Tribune (undated).

Squaw Coulee
-Archeological site
ca.10-1500 A.D./Old Woman's Buffalo Jump
Richard G. Forbis, "The Old Woman's Buffalo Jump, Alberta," Bull.Nat'l Mus.Canada, no.180 (1962):56-123. il.

Steen R.
-Meteorite crater
25,000 m.diam/certain
J. Classen, "Catalogue of 230 Certain, Probable, Possible, and Doubtful Impact Structures," Meteoritics 12 (1977):61,68.

Stutfield Glacier
-UFO (?)
1971, Sep.6/Jack Bryant
W.K. Allan, "Light Phenomenon at Stutfield Glacier," Flying Saucer Rev. 18 (July-Aug.1972):20,30. il.

Whirlpool R.
-Humanoid tracks
1811, Jan.7/David Thompson/=bear?
J.B. Tyrrell, ed., David Thompson's Narrative of His Explorations in Western America (Toronto: Champlain Soc'y, Pub.no.12, 1916), p.445.

Windy Point
-Humanoid
1969, March/Mark Yellowbird
1969, June/Edith Yellowbird
1969, summer/Alec Shortneck
Edmonton Journal, 30 Aug.1969, p.2.
-Humanoid tracks
1968, Sep./George Harris
John Green, Year of the Sasquatch (Agassiz, B.C.: Cheam, 1970), p.69. il.
John Green, The Sasquatch File (Agassiz, B.C.: Cheam, 1973), p.49.

Writing-on-Stone Provincial Park
-Pictographs
ca.1600-1750
Selwyn Dewdney, "Writings on Stone along the Milk River," Beaver, no. 295 (winter 1964):22-29. il.
H.M. Wormington & Richard G. Forbis, "An Introduction to the Archeology of Alberta, Canada," Proc.Denver Mus.Nat.Hist., no.11 (1965), pp. 125-28. il.
Henriette Mertz, Gods from the Far East (N.Y.: Ballantine, 1975 ed.), pp.142-43. il.

C. Ethnic Groups

Blackfoot Indians
-Shamanism
George Bird Grinnell, Blackfoot Lodge Tales (Lincoln: Univ. of Nebraska, 1962), pp.276-86.
-Weather control
George Bird Grinnell, Blackfoot Lodge Tales (Lincoln: Univ. of Nebraska, 1962), p.262.

Blood Indians
-Flood myth
Robert E. Gard, Johnny Chinook (London: Longmans, Green, 1945), pp. 56-60.

Cree Indians
-Flood myth
J.B. Tyrrell, ed., David Thompson's Narrative of His Explorations in Western Canada (Toronto: Champlain Soc'y, Pub.no.12, 1916), pp.88-89.

Peace River Indians
-Mammoth legend
Harold T. Wilkins, Secret Cities of Old South America (N.Y.: Library Publishers, 1952), p.280.

SASKATCHEWAN

A. Populated Places

Beechy
-Clairempathy
  1932, Dec.10-11/Prof. Gladstone
    Philip H. Godsell, "How a Mentalist
    Solved a Murder," Fate 12 (Jan.
    1959):36-43. il.

Bengough
-UFO (CE-2)
  1968, Feb.19/Martha Heggs
    "French General, Scientists, Report
    UFOs," UFO Inv. 4 (May-June 1968):3.
    Donald E. Keyhoe & Gordon I.R. Lore,
    Jr., UFOs: A New Look (Washington:
    NICAP, 1968), pp.11-12.

Bladworth
-UFO (CE-2)
  1969, May 20/Bill Turanich
    Ted Phillips, Physical Traces Associ-
    ated with UFO Sightings (Evanston:
    Center for UFO Studies, 1975), p.
    65, quoting Saucers Space & Sci.
    (undated).

Blaine Lake
-UFO (?)
  1957/Lawrence Cheveldayoff
    Gray Barker, "Chasing the Flying
    Saucers," Flying Saucers, Feb.1958,
    p.47.

Central Butte
-Disease anomaly
  1977, fall-   /Fred Bradford
    Regina Leader-Post, 1 June 1978; 8
    June 1978; and 14 June 1978.
    Lethbridge (Alb.) Herald, 8 June
    1978.
    Fort McMurray To-Day, 26 July 1978.
    "That 'Force' in Saskatchewan," Res
    Bureaux Bull., no.37 (17 Aug.1978):
    4-5.

Crystal Springs
-UFO (CE-1)
  1967, Dec.3/Mrs. Gary Kostiuk/Hwy.20
    "On the Canadian Scene," APRO Bull.
    16 (Jan.-Feb.1968):4,5.

Dinsmore
-UFO (CE-2)
  1974, Oct./ground markings only
    Ted Phillips, Physical Traces Associ-
    ated with UFO Sightings (Evanston:
    Center for UFO Studies, 1975), p.104.

Duval
-UFO (CE-1)
  1968, June 29/Martin Keulen
    "Like 'Car in Sky,'" Can.UFO Rept.,
    no.2 (Mar.-Apr.1969):8-9.

Eldorado
-UFO (NL)
  1969, Feb./Merle Marshall
    "The Maritimes: Newest Playground
    for UFOs?" Flying Saucers, June
    1970, pp.12,15.

Esterhazy
-UFO (NL)
  1965, July 22
    Marc Leduc, "Le Triangle du 14.7.74,"
    UFO-Québec, no.2 (1975):9,11. il.

Flaxcombe
-UFO (CE-2)
  1978, Feb.20/Hwy.7
    "Other UFOs," Res Bureaux Bull., no.
    35 (15 June 1978):4.

Glentworth
-UFO (CE-2)
  ca.1976
    "That 'Force' in Saskatchewan," Res
    Bureaux Bull., no.37 (17 Aug.1978):
    5.

Gravelbourg
-Human tracks in granite
  1910/Curtis McCammack
    Paul Bonneau, "Footprint in Granite,"
    True West 18 (Jan.-Feb.1971):35. il.
    "Footprints in the..." Pursuit 4
    (July 1971):69-70. il.

Gull Lake
-Archeological site
  ca.50-800 A.D.
    Thomas F. Kehoe, The Gull Lake Site:
    A Prehistoric Bison Drive Site in
    Southwestern Saskatchewan (Milwau-
    kee: Public Museum, Pub.in Anthro.
    & History, no.1, 1973). il.
-UFO (NL)
  1969, Feb.10
    "The Maritimes: Newest Playground
    for UFOs?" Flying Saucers, June
    1970, pp.12,15.

Humboldt
-UFO (?)
  1978, Aug.30/=balloon
    Humboldt Journal, 7 Sep.1978.

Kelstern
-UFO (NL)
  ca.1944/William C. McCargar/20 mi.E
    Gordon I.R. Lore, Jr. & Harold H. Den-
    eault, Jr., Mysteries of the Skies:
    UFOs in Perspective (Englewood
    Cliffs, N.J.: Prentice-Hall, 1968),
    pp.144-45.

Kindersley
-Haunt

1968-1969
  Sheila Hervey, Some Canadian Ghosts
  (Richmond Hill, Ont.: Pocket Books,
  1973), pp.187-89.

Lake Lenore
-UFO (CE-2)
  1974, Oct./ground markings only
    Ted Phillips, Physical Traces Associ-
    ated with UFO Sightings (Evanston:
    Center for UFO Studies, 1975), p.
    104.

Langenburg
-Ghost light
  1938, Nov.-Dec./Tabor cemetery
    Eric Frank Russell, "British Corres-
    pondence," Fortean Soc'y Mag., no.
    3 (Jan.1940):8.
-UFO (CE-2)
  1974, Sep.1/Edwin Fuhr/5½ mi.NE
    Edmonton (Alb.) Journal, 4 Sep.1974.
    J. Allen Hynek & Jacques Vallee, The
    Edge of Reality (Chicago: Regnery,
    1975), pp.265-79. il.

Lumsden
-UFO (NL)
  1967, Oct.24/2 mi.SE
    "Huge Disc Seen by Teenagers," APRO
    Bull. 16 (Jan.-Feb.1968):1,3.

Melfort
-UFO (CE-2)
  1968, Sep.
    "Family Flees Heat from UFO," Sky-
    look, no.17 (Apr.1969):9.

Melville
-UFO (NL)
  1977, Aug.22
    Melville Advance, 31 Aug.1977.

Moose Jaw
-UFO (NL)
  1966, Oct.20
    J. Allen Hynek, The UFO Experience
    (Chicago: Regnery, 1972), pp.39,236.
  1978, Dec.15/CFB Moose Jaw
    "Recent UFO Reports," Res Bureaux
    Bull., no.43 (Jan.1979):3,4.

Mortlach
-Archeological site
  1450 B.C.-1800 A.D.
    Boyd Wettlaufer, "The Mortlach Site
    in the Besant Valley of Saskatch-
    ewan," Anthro.Ser.Saskatchewan Mus.
    Nat.Hist., no.1 (1956). il.
-UFO (?)
  1913, Feb.9/Jno. R. Smith/=meteor pro-
    cession/most westerly observation
    C.A. Chant, "An Extraordinary Meteor-
    ic Display," J.Roy.Astron.Soc'y Can-
    ada 7 (1913):145,189.

Nipawin
-UFO (CE-3)
  1933, summer
    John Brent Musgrave, "Saskatchewan,

1933: UFO Stops for 'Repairs,'"
    Flying Saucer Rev. 22 (Apr.1977):
    16-17. il.

North Battleford
-UFO (NL)
  1975, Nov.18/Ken Sheppard
    Saskatoon Star-Phoenix, 19 Nov.1975.

Peebles
-UFO (CE-2)
  1974, Oct./Evan Richards/ground mark-
    ings only
    Ted Phillips, Physical Traces Associ-
    ated with UFO Sightings (Evanston:
    Center for UFO Studies, 1975), p.
    104.

Peesane
-UFO (CE-2)
  1975, May 12/Lyle Carson/2½ mi.E
    Ted Phillips, Physical Traces Associ-
    ated with UFO Sightings (Evanston:
    Center for UFO Studies, 1975), p.
    107.

Perdue
-UFO (CE-1)
  1979, Jan.4
    "Recent UFO Reports," Res Bureaux
    Bull., no.43 (Jan.1979):3,4.

Pierceland
-UFO (NL)
  1979, Jan.7
    "Recent UFO Reports," Res Bureaux
    Bull., no.44 (Feb.1979):4.

Qu'Appelle
-UFO (CE-2)
  1968, Aug.4
    Ted Phillips, Physical Traces Associ-
    ated with UFO Sightings (Evanston:
    Center for UFO Studies, 1975), p.57.

Regina
-UFO (?)
  1961, May/Wayne Stevenson
    (Editorial), APRO Bull. 10 (July
    1961):3.
-UFO (NL)
  1952, April 24
    Toronto (Ont.) Daily Star, 26 Apr.
    1952.
  1952, Dec.27, 31/airport
    Marc Leduc, "Notes sur le projet
    'Magnet,'" UFO-Québec, no.4 (1975):
    12,15.
  1964, April?/1 mi.SE
    "Prairie Foo-Fighter," Can.UFO Rept.,
    no.3 (May-June 1969):10.

Robsart
-UFO (CE-1)
  1929, July/Mrs. Einar Rostwold/15-20
    mi. from town
    (Letter), Fate 11 (Jan.1958):122-23.

Roche Percée
-UFO (NL)

1897, April 13
Minneapolis (Minn.) Times, 15 Apr.
1897.

Saskatoon
-UFO (CE-3)
1963, Sep.19/Brian Whitehead
Jerome Clark, "Return of the 'Mon-
ster,'" in Beyond Condon (Flying
Saucer Rev. special issue no.2,
June 1969), pp.55-56.
-UFO (DD)
1975, Nov./Louis Dekker
Edmonton (Alb.) Journal, 18 Nov.1975.

Shaunavon
-UFO (CE-1)
1967, June 1/Evelyn Brown
"French General, Scientists, Report
UFOs," UFO Inv. 4 (May-June 1968):3.

Theodore
-Humanoid tracks
1977, June/John Besborotko
Medicine Hat (Alb.) News, 11 June
1977.

Viewfield
-Meteorite crater
probable
H.B. Sawatzky, "Viewfield--A Produc-
ing Fossil Crater?" J.Can.Soc'y Ex-
ploration Geophysicists 18 (1972):
22-40.
H.B. Sawatzky, "Buried Impact Craters
in the Williston Basin and Adjacent
Area," in D.J. Roddy, et al., eds.,
Impact and Explosion Cratering (N.Y.:
Pergamon, 1977), pp.461-80.

Webb
-UFO (NL)
1969, April 1
"The Maritimes: Newest Playground
for UFOs?" Flying Saucers, June
1970, pp.12,15.

Weyburn
-Lightning anomaly
n.d./F.C. Paisey
A. Steadworthy, "Black Lightning,"
J.Roy.Astron.Soc'y Canada 9 (1915):
173-75. il.
-UFO (CE-2)
1948/Mrs. T.C. Orsted
Ted Phillips, Physical Traces Associ-
ated with UFO Sightings (Evanston:
Center for UFO Studies, 1975), p.5.
-UFO (NL)
1971, Jan.13
"Press Reports," APRO Bull. 19 (Jan.-
Feb.1971):7.

Yellow Grass
-UFO (CE-2)
1978, July 31/ground markings only
"UFOs," Res Bureaux Bull., no.38 (7
Sep.1978):3.

Yorkton
-Fall of molten substance
1974, June
Decatur (Ill.) Herald, 9 June 1974.
-Haunt
n.d./Elinor Telsky
Sheila Hervey, Some Canadian Ghosts
(Richmond Hill, Ont.: Pocket Books,
1973), pp.192-95.
-UFO (NL)
1969, Feb.3
"The Maritimes: Newest Playground
for UFOs?" Flying Saucers, June
1970, pp.12,14-15.

Young
-UFO (CE-2)
1974, Sep./Ken Teneyke/ground markings
only
"Another Mystery Circle," APRO Bull.
23 (Jan.-Feb.1975):9.

B. Physical Features

Amisk L.
-Humanoid
n.d./George Custer
Ivan T. Sanderson, Things (N.Y.: Pyramid, 1967), p.104.

Birch L.
-Humanoid tracks
1963, July
John Green, The Sasquatch File (Agassiz, B.C.: Cheam, 1973), p.31.

Buffalo Basin
-Ghost light
1912-1925
Minneapolis (Minn.) Journal, 16 Dec.
1925.

Carswell L.
-Meteorite crater
32,000 m.diam. x 60 m.deep/certain
C.S. Beals, M.J.S. Innes & J.A. Rot-
tenberg, "The Search for Fossil
Meteorite Craters," Current Sci. 29
(1960):205-18,249-62.
F.A. Fahrig, "General Geology of the
Carswell Formation," Bull.Geol.Sur-
vey Canada 68 (1961):18-21.

Deep Bay
-Meteorite crater
13,600 m.diam. x 1314 m.deep/certain
M.J.S. Innes, "A Possible Meteorite
Structure at Deep Bay, Saskatchewan,"
J.Roy.Astron.Soc'y Canada 51 (1957)
:235-40. il.

Gow L.
-Meteorite crater
certain
M.D. Thomas & M.J.S. Innes, "The Gow
Lake Impact Structure, Northern
Saskatchewan," Can.J.Earth Sci. 14
(1977):1788-95.

Keeley L.
-Meteorite crater
  13,000 m.diam./doubtful
    C.S. Beals, M.J.S. Innes & J.A. Rot-
    tenberg, "The Search for Fossil
    Meteorite Craters," Current Sci. 29
    (1960):205-18,249-62.

Last Mountain L.
-UFO (NL)
  1967, Oct.24
    Jim & Coral Lorenzen, UFOs over the
    Americas (N.Y.: Signet, 1968), p.
    176.

Long Creek
-Archeological site
  ca.3000 B.C.-1600 A.D.
    Boyd Wettlaufer, et al., "The Long
    Creek Site," Anthro.Ser.Saskatche-
    wan Mus.Nat.Hist., no.2 (1960). il.

Moose Mountain Provincial Park
-Archeological site
  ca.1 A.D.
    Milwaukee (Wisc.) Journal, 13 Nov.
    1975; and 24 Feb.1977.
    Thomas F. & Alice B. Kehoe, "Stones,
    Solstices and Sun Dance Cultures,"
    Plains Anthro. 22 (1977):85-95. il.
-Chinese discovery
  ca.1000 B.C.
    Henriette Mertz, Gods from the Far
    East (N.Y.: Ballantine, 1975 ed.),
    pp.140-41.

Oxbow Dam
-Archeological site
  3250 B.C.
    Robert W. Nero & Bruce A. McCorgus-
    dale, "Report of an Excavation at
    the Oxbow Dam Site," Blue Jay, vol.
    16, no.2 (1958).

Swiftcurrent Creek
-UFO (CE-2)
  1967, Nov.19/Cedric Cunningham
    Gene Duplantier, "The Mystery of the
    Burned Circles," in Brad Steiger &
    Joan Whritenour, Flying Saucer In-
    vasion: Target--Earth (N.Y.: Award,
    1969), p.24.

        D. Unspecified Localities

-Auroral anomaly
  1928/northern sector
    C.M. Botley, Polar Lights (Tunbridge
    Wells, Eng.: The Author, 1947).

-UFO (NL)
  1923/T.W. Soper
    Jerome Clark & Lucius Farish, "UFOs
    of the Roaring Twenties," Saga UFO
    Rept. 2 (fall 1975):49.

MANITOBA

A. Populated Places

Altona
-UFO (NL)
1967, March 26/John Dick/2 mi.S
   Altona Red River Valley Echo, 19 Apr.
   1967.

Arden
-UFO (NL)
1969, May/Frank Harder
   "Canadian Couple Watch UFO," Skylook,
   no.20 (July 1969):15, quoting Neep-
   awa Press (undated).

Beausejour
-Humanoid
1975, June
   John Green, Sasquatch: The Apes Among
   Us (Seattle: Hancock House, 1978),
   p.246.
-UFO (CE-1)
1972, Sep./William McFarland
   "Visitors Play Tag," Can.UFO Rept.,
   no.14 (1973):23-24.
-UFO (CE-2)
1967, May 31
   "Second Landing in Canada," APRO
   Bull. 15 (May-June 1967):2.
   Coral & Jim Lorenzen, Encounters with
   UFO Occupants (N.Y.: Berkley, 1976),
   p.13, quoting Saucers Space & Sci.
   (undated).

Berens River
-Norse mooring stone
n.d./Evald Hansen/1½ mi.N
   Hjalmar R. Holand, A Pre-Columbian
   Crusade to America (N.Y.: Twayne,
   1962), pp.126-27, il.
-Seance
1848, July 28/Paul Kane/shaking tent
   Paul Kane, Wanderings of an Artist
   Among the Indians of North America
   (Toronto: Radisson Soc'y of Canada,
   1925), pp.311-12.
1930/Irving Hollowell/shaking tent
   R.S. Lambert, Exploring the Supernat-
   ural (Toronto: McClelland & Stewart,
   1955), p.41.

Brandon
-Clairvoyance
1940-1941/Indian Residential School
   A.A. Foster, "ESP Tests with American
   Indian Children," J.Parapsych. 7
   (1943):94-103.
-UFO (CE-2)
n.d./Marjorie Brignall
   (Letter), Can.UFO Rept., no.10
   (1971):29.
1967, Sep.28/Jim Wall
   Gene Duplantier, "The Mystery of the
   Burned Circles," in Brad Steiger &

Joan Whritenour, Flying Saucer Invasion: Target--Earth (N.Y.: Award,
   1969), pp.23-24.
-UFO (NL)
1969, Oct.1/Jack Warkentin
   "Press Reports," APRO Bull. 18 (Nov.-
   Dec.1969):8.

Brokenhead
-UFO (NL)
1969, Feb.10/Ray Kryschuk
   "The Maritimes: Newest Playground
   for UFOs?" Flying Saucers, June
   1970, pp.12,15.

Carman
-UFO (CE-1)
1975, April 10/Bob Diemert
   Gregory M. Kanon, "Strange Visitors
   in Manitoba Skies," Can.UFO Rept.,
   no.25 (fall 1976):16.
-UFO (CE-2)
1975, May 13
   Gregory M. Kanon, "Strange Visitors
   in Manitoba Skies," Can.UFO Rept.,
   no.25 (fall 1976):16-17.
-UFO (NL)
1967, Oct.22
   "On the Canadian Scene," APRO Bull.
   16 (Jan.-Feb.1968):4.
1968, Dec.16/Ed Weiler/Hwy.3 x 13
   "The Maritimes: Newest Playground
   for UFOs?" Flying Saucers, June
   1970, pp.12,14.
1975, May 7-9/Ian Nicholson
   Gregory M. Kanon, "Strange Visitors
   in Manitoba Skies," Can.UFO Rept.,
   no.25 (fall 1976):16-17.

Dauphin
-UFO (?)
1947, Oct.13/=meteor
   J. Allen Hynek, The Hynek UFO Report
   (N.Y.: Dell, 1977), p.15.
-UFO (CE-1)
1968, March/Marjorie Brignall
   (Letter), Can.UFO Rept., no.10
   (1971):29.
-UFO (DD)
1957, Nov.5
   Richard Hall, ed., The UFO Evidence
   (Washington: NICAP, 1964), p.165.

Easterville
-Humanoid
1968, Aug.23
1969, summer
1970, Nov.
1973, April
1976, April
   John Green, Sasquatch: The Apes Among
   Us (Seattle: Hancock House, 1978),
   pp.243,245-46, quoting Winnipeg Free
   Press (undated).

Flin Flon
-Retrocognition
1951, June/Donald McLeod/15 mi.S
"Dream Locates Lost Couple," Fate
26 (Nov.1973):95.

Glenboro
-UFO (NL)
1897, April 13
Minneapolis (Minn.) Times, 15 Apr.
1897.

Grand Rapids
-Humanoid
n.d./Saskatchewan R.
John Green, Sasquatch: The Apes Among
Us (Seattle: Hancock House, 1978),
p.246.

Halbstadt
-UFO (CE-2)
1975, June 25/ground markings only
Ted Phillips, Physical Traces Associated with UFO Sightings (Evanston:
Center for UFO Studies, 1975), pp.
16-17.

Hartney
-Meteorite crater
6000 m.diam./possible
J. Classen, "Catalogue of 230 Certain, Probable, Possible, and Doubtful Impact Structures," Meteoritics
12 (1977):61,69.

Lac du Bonnet
-Humanoid
1975, Dec./S of town
John Green, Sasquatch: The Apes Among
Us (Seattle: Hancock Jouse, 1978),
pp.246-47.

Libau
-UFO (NL)
1977, Oct.1/Leo Girardeau/3 mi.W
"Foreign Forum," Int'l UFO Reporter
2 (Dec.1977):2.

MacDonald
-UFO (DD)
1952, Aug.27/airport
Marc Leduc, "Notes sur le projet
'Magnet,'" UFO-Québec, no.4 (1975):
12,15.

Melita
-UFO (NL)
1897, April 13
Minneapolis (Minn.) Times, 15 Apr.
1897.
1969, Oct./G.R. Gratton
1969, Oct.28/Frank Warsaba
Brandon Sun, 24 Dec.1976.

Menzie
-UFO (CE-2)
1977, summer/ground markings only
Brandon Sun, 4 Feb.1978.

Miniota
-UFO (?)
1978, Jan.15
Brandon Sun, 4 Feb.1978.

Molson
-UFO (NL)
1952, April 21
Toronto (Ont.) Daily Star, 23 Apr.
1952.

Morden
-UFO (CE-1)
1975, May/Abe Hildebrand
Gregory M. Kanon, "Strange Visitors
in Manitoba Skies," Can.UFO Rept.,
no.25 (fall 1976):16-17.
-UFO (CE-2)
1967, Aug./Ben Weibe/ground markings
only
Ted Phillips, Physical Traces Associated with UFO Sightings (Evanston:
Center for UFO Studies, 1975), p.
50, quoting Saucers Space & Sci.
(undated).

Oakburn
-UFO (CE-2)
1977, summer/ground markings only
Brandon Sun, 4 Feb.1978.

Pine Falls
-UFO (CE-1)
1974, Oct.19
Gary Lanham, "'Meteor' Again?" Can.
UFO Rept., no.26 (winter 1976-77):
5. il.

Pointe du Bois
-Humanoid
1974, July/W of town
John Green, Sasquatch: The Apes Among
Us (Seattle: Hancock House, 1978),
p.246, quoting Beausejour Manitoba
Beaver (undated).

Portage-la-Prairie
-UFO (?)
1976, July 14
"Diary of a Mad Planet," Fortean
Times, no.18 (Oct.1976):8,17.
-UFO (CE-1)
ca.1922/Russell M. Woodard/Island Park
(Letter), Can.UFO Rept., no.11
(1971):34.
-UFO (NL)
1969, Jan.6
Portage Leader, 9 Jan.1969.
1969, April 27/George Whitehurst
"The Maritimes: Newest Playground
for UFOs?" Flying Saucers, June
1970, pp.12,15.

Reynolds
-Humanoid
1970, summer
John Green, Sasquatch: The Apes Among
Us (Seattle: Hancock House, 1978),
pp.245-46.

Rossburn
-UFO (CE-2)
  1977, Sep./Pomechychuk farm/ground
  markings only
    Brandon Sun, 10 Sep.1977.
-UFO (NL)
  1978, Jan.19/Angelo Ryshytylo
    Brandon Sun, 4 Feb.1978.

Sainte Anne
-UFO (CE-2)
  1968, Sep.18
    "Hairy Material Defies Analysis,"
    Can.UFO Rept., no.2 (Mar.-Apr.1969)
    :12-14. il.
    Tommy Roy Blann, "What UFOs Can Do
    to Us: Part 2," Official UFO 1 (July
    1976):31,63.

Sainte Rose du Lac
-UFO (DD)
  1969, Feb.2/Gordon Bishop
    "Five Canadians Watch UFO," Skylook,
    no.17 (Apr.1969):9, quoting Winnipeg
    Free Press (undated).

Saint Martin
-Meteorite crater
  24,000 m.diam./probable
    J. Classen, "Catalogue of 230 Cer-
    tain, Probable, Possible, and Doubt-
    ful Impact Structures," Meteoritics
    12 (1977):61,69.

Selkirk
-UFO (NL)
  1978, Oct.22/Fort Garry
    Winnipeg Tribune, 23-24 Oct.1978.

Shilo
-UFO (NL)
  1977, April 20
    Brandon Sun, 16 May 1977.
  1978, April 6/CFB Shilo
    "Other UFOs," Res Bureaux Bull.,no.
    35 (15 June 1978):4.

Stephenfield
-UFO (NL)
  1975, March 27
    Gregory M. Kanon, "Strange Visitors
    in Manitoba Skies," Can.UFO Rept.,
    no.25 (fall 1976):16.

The Pas
-Amphibious moose
  n.d.
    "Paradoxes," Fortean Soc'y Mag., no.
    3 (Jan.1940):10.

Thompson
-UFO (CE-2)
  1967, June/Mrs. D.F. LeMarquands
    Joe Brill, "Possible Kidnapping by
    UFO Averted by Youth," Skylook, no.
    98 (Jan.1976):15, quoting Saucers
    Space & Sci. (undated).

Tuxedo
-UFO (NL)

1952, April 21
  Winnipeg Free Press, 23 Apr.1952.

Vivian
-UFO (CE-2)
  1954/ground markings only
    Ted Phillips, Physical Traces Associ-
    ated with UFO Sightings (Evanston:
    Center for UFO Studies, 1975), p.
    11.

Whitemouth
-UFO (DD)
  1897, July 29/Mr. Henderson
    Portland Oregonian, 2 Aug.1897, quot-
    ing Winnipeg Free Press (undated).

Winnipeg
-Acoustic anomaly
  1953, Dec./H.J. Skynner/St. John's
  Cathedral
    Sioux City (Iowa) Journal, 15 Dec.
    1953.
    "The Invisible Organist," Fate 7
    (June 1954):45.
-Clairvoyance
  1912, April 14/Charles Morgan/Rosedale
  Methodist Church
    R. DeWitt Miller, Stranger Than Life
    (N.Y.: Ace, 1955 ed.), p.50.
-Dowsing
  1960s/Michael Huska
    (Editorial), Fate 14 (Jan.1961):22-
    24.
-Eyeless vision
  1960/Ronald Coyne
    (Editorial), Fate 13 (Nov.1960):19-
    20.
-Fall of ants
  1895, May 1
    Winnipeg Free Press, 3 May 1895, p.6.
    "A Shower of Black Ants," Sci.Am.
    72 (1895):385.
-Fall of metallic object
  1947, April 24
    "At the Same Time," Doubt, no.19
    (1947):290,291.
-Haunt
  n.d./Carol Skippir
    Eileen Sonin, More Canadian Ghosts
    (Richmond Hill, Ont.: Pocket Books,
    1974 ed.), pp.23-24.
-Lunar cycle and birth
  1970/Michael A. Persinger/University
  of Manitoba
    Michael A. Persinger, "Prenatal Ex-
    posure to an ELF Rotating Magnetic
    Field, Ambulatory Behavior, and Lu-
    nar Distance at Birth: A Correla-
    tion," Psych.Reports 28 (1971):435-
    38.
-Lunar cycle and injuries
  1971
    K.P. & Margitta D. Ossenkopp, "Self
    Inflicted Injuries and the Lunar
    Cycle: A Preliminary Report," J.
    Interdisciplinary Cycle Rsch. 4
    (1973):337-48.
-Poltergeist
  1877-1879/George H. Ham/Main St., S of

Grace Church
George H. Ham, Reminiscences of a
Raconteur (Toronto: Musson, 1921).
-Precognition
n.d./Eveline Farler
Eileen Sonin, More Canadian Ghosts
(Richmond Hill, Ont.: Pocket Books,
1974 ed.), pp.162-63.
-Psychic photography
n.d./Mary MacPherson
Tom Patterson, 100 Years of Spirit
Photography (London: Regency, 1965),
p.31. il.
-Spirit mediums and psychic photography
1918-1935/Glen Hamilton circle/Mary
Marshall
T. Glen Hamilton, "The Teleplasms of
Mary M.," Psychic Rsch. 25 (1931):
5-9. il.
T. Glen Hamilton, "Some Physical
Phenomena Observed with the Medium
Elizabeth M.," Psychic Rsch. 25
(1931):378-86. il.
Nandor Fodor, Encyclopaedia of Psy-
chic Science (London: Arthurs, 1933),
pp. xxv,xxviii,xxx,xxxiii,xxxiv,157,
191,192,216,256. il.
T. Glen Hamilton, "A Study of the
Winnipeg Group-Mediumship in Its
Relation to the Dawn Teleplasms,"
J.ASPR 28 (1934):117-30. il.
T. Glen Hamilton, Intention and Sur-
vival (Toronto: Macmillan, 1942).
C.A.L. Brownlow, "A History of Sur-
vival after Death," Fate 12 (Aug.
1959):41,44-45.
Tom Patterson, 100 Years of Spirit
Photography (London: Regency, 1965),
pp.31-33.
-Telepathy
1956, Dec./Portage x Main St.
"Coincidence or Telepathy?" Fate 10
(Apr.1957):70, quoting Winnipeg
Tribune (undated).
-UFO (CE-1)
1967, Oct.22-23/Charleswood
"On the Canadian Scene," APRO Bull.
17 (Jan.-Feb.1969):4-5.
(Letter), Brian C. Cannon, Can.UFO
Rept., no.3 (May-June 1969):2.
-UFO (DD)
1957, Nov.5
Richard Hall, ed., The UFO Evidence
(Washington: NICAP, 1964), p.165.
1968, April 24/Hudson's Bay store
"Rectangular UFO," Skylook, no.11
(July 1968):6.
-UFO (NL)
1897, April/Lt.Gov. Patterson
St. Paul (Minn.) Pioneer Press, 2
May 1897.
1897, July 1
Portland Oregonian, 2 July 1897.
1952, April 21
Winnipeg Free Press, 23 Apr.1952.
1967, June 27/Arbuthnotte St. x Cory-
don Ave.
1967, July 18
"Canada Flap Continues," APRO Bull.
16 (July-Aug.1967):6.

1967, Oct.22/Westdale
"On the Canadian Scene," APRO Bull.
16 (Jan.-Feb.1968):4.
1969, April 15/10 mi.NE
"The Maritimes: Newest Playground
for UFOs?" Flying Saucers, June
1970, pp.12,15.
1969, Aug./Janice Kormilo/20 mi.N
(Letter), Can.UFO Rept., no.6 (Nov.-
Dec.1969):30.
1973, Oct.23
Winnipeg Free Press, 24 Oct.1973.
1978, Oct.22/Belle Ede
"Matching Cases," Can.UFO Rept., no.
33 (winter 1978-79):5.

Woodridge
-Ghost light
ca.1950-1970/Donna Freeman
Winnipeg Free Press, 7 Dec.1970.

B. Physical Features

Agassiz Provincial Forest
-Humanoid
1975, Oct.
John Green, Sasquatch: The Apes Among
Us (Seattle: Hancock House, 1978),
p.247.

Assiniboine R.
-Clairvoyance
1950s/Louis Prince
Winnipeg Tribune, 26 July 1954.

Blood Vein R.
-Seance
1862/W. Cornwallis King/shaking tent
R.S. Lambert, Exploring the Supernatural (Toronto: McClelland & Stewart,
1955), pp.37-38.

Cedar L.
-Lake monster
1909, Sep./Valentine McKay
Winnipeg Free Press, 15 Aug.1962.

Dirty Water L.
-Lake monster
1935/C.F. Ross
Winnipeg Free Press, 15 Aug.1962.

Falcon L.
-UFO (CE-2)
1967, May 20/Steve Michalak
"Man Burned in Canada Landing," APRO
Bull. 15 (May-June 1967):1,3.
Steve Michalak, My Encounter with
the UFO (Winnipeg: Osnova, 1967).
Toronto (Ont.) Daily Star, 7 Nov.
1967.
Jim & Coral Lorenzen, UFOs over the
Americas (N.Y.: Signet, 1968), pp.
38-41.
"Michalak Illness Recurring," APRO
Bull. 16 (Mar.-Apr.1968):4.
Edward U. Condon, ed., Scientific
Study of Unidentified Flying Objects
(N.Y.: Bantam, 1969 ed.), pp.316-24.

Brian Cannon, "Strange Case of Falcon Lake," Can.UFO Rept., no.2 (Mar.-
Apr.1969):10-12; no.3 (May-June
1969):11-12; no.4 (July-Aug.1969):
24-26. il.
Donald H. Menzel & Ernest H. Taves,
The UFO Enigma (Garden City: Doubleday, 1977), p.104.
1967, June 18
Ted Phillips, Physical Traces Associated with UFO Sightings (Evanston:
Center for UFO Studies, 1975), p.
49.

Hart Mt.
-Chinese discovery
ca.1000 B.C.
Henriette Mertz, Gods from the Far
East (N.Y.: Ballantine, 1975 ed.),
p.140.

Landing L.
-UFO (CE-1)
1792, Nov./David Thompson
J.B. Tyrrell, ed., David Thompson's
Narrative of His Explorations in
Western America 1784-1812 (Toronto:
Champlain Soc'y, Pub.no.12, 1916),
pp.118-19.

Landry L.
-Humanoid tracks
1973, Sep.29/Bob Uchtmann
John Green, Sasquatch: The Apes Among
Us (Seattle: Hancock House, 1978),
pp.243-44. il.

Little Grand Rapids
-Seance
1936/Allan Nelson/shaking tent
R.S. Lambert, Exploring the Supernatural (Toronto: McClelland & Stewart,
1955), p.41.

Long Plains Reserve
-Humanoid
1975, July
John Green, Sasquatch: The Apes Among
Us (Seattle: Hancock House, 1978),
p.246.

Manitoba, L.
-Lake monster
1948-   /manipogo
Winnipeg Free Press, 21 Aug.1961;
and 15 Aug.1962. il.
Peter Costello, In Search of Lake
Monsters (N.Y.: Coward, McCann &
Geoghegan, 1974), pp.229-32.
-Precognition
1870s
Frederick J. Goshe, "Could the
Sioux Control Weather?" Fate 10
(Apr.1957):57,60-61.

Nelson R.
-Norse discovery
1009/Thorfinn Karlsefni/=Hóp?
Edward Reman, The Norse Discoveries
and Explorations in America (Berkeley: Univ. of California, 1949),
pp.147-61.

Poplar R.
-Humanoid
1976, July
John Green, Sasquatch: The Apes Among
Us (Seattle: Hancock House, 1978),
p.247.

Red R.
-Seance
ca.1848/G.J. Mountain/shaking tent
R.S. Lambert, Exploring the Supernatural (Toronto: McClelland & Stewart,
1955), p.34.

Rock L.
-Archeological site
R.S. MacNeish & K.H. Capes, "The
United Church Site near Rock Lake
in Manitoba," Anthropologica 6
(1958):119-55.

Swan L.
-UFO (NL)
1969, July/Roy Crawford
"Ballet at Swan Lake," Can.UFO Rept.,
no.21 (1975):9-11.

Swan R.
-Archeological site
Eugene M. Gryba, "A Possible Paleo-
Indian and Archaic Site in the Swan
Valley, Manitoba," Plains Anthro.
13 (1968):218-27.

West Hawk L.
-Meteorite crater
3200 m.diam. x 75 m.deep/certain
J.F. Davies, Geology of the West Hawk
Lake-Falcon Lake Area (Winnipeg:
Manitoba Dep't of Mines & Natural
Resources, 1954).
Ian Halliday & A.A. Griffin, "Appli-
cation of the Scientific Method to
Problems of Crater Recognition,"
Meteoritics 2 (1964):79-84. il.
Ian Halliday & A. Griffin, "Summary
of Drilling at the West Hawk Lake
Crater," J.Roy.Astron.Soc'y Canada
61 (1967):1-18.
N.M. Short, "Anatomy of a Meteorite
Impact Crater," Bull.Geol.Soc'y Am.
81 (1970):609-48.

Whiteshell Provincial Park
-Archeological site
Franklin Folsom, America's Ancient
Treasures (N.Y.: Rand McNally,
1974), pp.87-88.

Winnipegosis, L.
-Lake monster
1918-
Winnipeg Free Press, 5 Aug.1961; and
15 Aug.1962.
Peter Costello, In Search of Lake
Monsters (N.Y.: Coward, McCann &
Geoghegan, 1974), pp.229-32.

C. Ethnic Groups

Saulteaux Indians
-Humanoid myth
  windigo
    Winnipeg Free Press, 26 Jan.1974.
-Shamanism
    A. Irving Hallowell, The Role of Con-
    juring in Saulteaux Society (Phila-
    delphia: Univ. of Pennsylvania,
    1942).

D. Unspecified Localities

-Aerial phantom
  1890s/William Parker
    Hugh A. Dempsey, ed., William Parker:
    Mounted Policeman (Calgary: Glenbow-
    Alberta Institute, 1973), pp.29-30.

-Seance
  1920/shaking tent/northern barrens
    Winifred G. Barton, ed., Canada's
    Psi-Century (Ottawa: Bartonian Meta-
    physical Society, 1967).

-UFO (NL)
  1968, March/Sally Remaley/northern
  barrens
    Sally Remaley, "Luminous Objects on
    Arctic Ice," Fate 22 (June 1969):
    66-72.
  1972, Oct.23/Daryle Brown/northern
  barrens
    Jeff Holt, "Rencontre avec un UFO
    dans le grand Nord Canadien," UFO-
    Quebec, no.9 (1977):13-14.

NORTH DAKOTA

A. Populated Places

Benedict
-UFO (CE-1)
1964, June 10/R.D. Rued
"New UFO Angles," UFO Inv. 3 (Apr.-
May 1965):3.

Bismarck
-Fall of flint
1884, May 22-23
"Miscellaneous Phenomena," Monthly
Weather Rev. 12 (May 1884):134.
-Haunt
1952
(Letter), Mrs. William Nelson, Fate
11 (Feb.1958):128.
-UFO (?)
1953, Aug.5/Bismarck Filter Center/=
stars and planets
Gordon D. Thayer, "Optical and Radar
Analyses of Field Cases," in Edward
U. Condon, ed., Scientific Study of
Unidentified Flying Objects (N.Y.:
Bantam, 1969 ed.), pp.132-36.
1956, Nov.16/Eldon Ray/=meteor?
"Case 250," CRIFO Orbit, 4 Jan.1957,
p.1, quoting UP release (undated).
1956, Nov.29
"Case 261," CRIFO Orbit, 4 Jan.1957,
p.3.
-UFO (NL)
1968, Nov.26/Jack Wilhelm/airport
"Airport Tower Personnel Observe
UFO," APRO Bull. 17 (Nov.-Dec.1968)
:5.
J. Allen Hynek, The UFO Experience
(Chicago: Regnery, 1972), pp.38,45.

Buffalo
-UFO (CE-4)
1975, Aug.26/Sandy Larson
"Woman Reports Abduction, Examina-
tion," Skylook, no.100 (Mar.1976):
10-11.
Jerome Clark, "The Bizarre Sandy Lar-
son Contact: UFO Abduction in North
Dakota," Saga UFO Rept. 3 (Aug.1976)
:21-23,46-53.
Coral & Jim Lorenzen, Abducted! (N.Y.:
Berkley, 1977), pp.52-69.
Jerome Clark, "Kidnapped! The North
Dakota Contact," Saga UFO Rept. 6
(Oct.1978):20-23,50-51.

Cannon Ball
-Mystery stone spheres
North Dakota Writers' Program, North
Dakota: A Guide to the Northern
Prairie State (N.Y.: Oxford Univ.,
1950), p.297.
(Letter), A.C. Nelson, Fate 5 (Apr.-
May 1952):122.

Crosby
-UFO (DD)
1967, Jan.30
J. Allen Hynek, The UFO Experience
(Chicago: Regnery, 1972), p.65.

Deapolis
-Norse runestone
1894, summer
North Dakota Writers' Program, North
Dakota: A Guide to the Northern
Prairie State (N.Y.: Oxford Univ.,
1950), p.317.

De Lamere
-UFO (DD)
1947, July 8/Leslie Miller/2 mi.N
Fargo Forum, 9 July 1947.

Des Lacs
-UFO (NL)
1956, Nov./Bernard Hall
(Editorial), Fate 10 (Mar.1957):15.

Dickinson
-UFO (?)
1956, Nov.8/Laudie Dvorak
(Editorial), Fate 10 (Mar.1957):15.

Donnybrook
-UFO (CE-2)
1966, Aug.19
Edward U. Condon, ed., Scientific
Study of Unidentified Flying Objects
(N.Y.: Bantam, 1969 ed.), pp.273-74.
Ted Phillips, Physical Traces Associ-
ated with UFO Sightings (Evanston:
Center for UFO Studies, 1975), p.43.
Donald H. Menzel & Ernest H. Taves,
The UFO Enigma (Garden City: Double-
day, 1977), pp.98-99.

Elliott
-UFO (CE-1)
1947, July 4/Virgil Been
Fargo Forum, 6 July 1947.

Fargo
-UFO (?)
1952, April 25, 28/=ducks?
U.S. Air Force, Projects Grudge and
Blue Book Reports 1-12 (Washington:
NICAP, 1968), p.122.
1954, Sep.25/=meteor?
"North Central States Alarmed by Soar-
ing Blue-White 'Ball,'" CRIFO Newsl.,
5 Nov.1954, p.3.
1957, Nov.9/Alf Olsen
Fargo Forum, 10 Nov.1957. il.
-UFO (CE-1)
1948, Oct.1/George F. Gorman
Fargo Forum, 3-4 Oct.1948.
"Flying Saucers Definitely Proved,"
Fate 1 (winter 1949):47-51.

Sidney Shalett, "What You Can Believe About Flying Saucers: Conclusion," Sat.Eve.Post, 7 May 1949, pp.36, 184-85.

Edward J. Ruppelt, The Report on Unidentified Flying Objects (Garden City: Doubleday, 1956), pp.41-43.

Aimé Michel, The Truth About Flying Saucers (N.Y.: Pyramid, 1967 ed.), pp.69-76.

Donald H. Menzel & Lyle G. Boyd, The World of Flying Saucers (Garden City: Doubleday, 1963), pp.77-85.

Brad Steiger, ed., Project Blue Book (N.Y.: Ballantine, 1976), pp.65-78.

-UFO (NL)
1967, Feb.26
J. Allen Hynek, The UFO Experience (Chicago: Regnery, 1972), pp.49, 236. il.

J. Allen Hynek & Jacques Vallee, The Edge of Reality (Chicago: Regnery, 1975), p.122. il.

Fordville
-Archeological site
Walter M. Hlady, "Mound C, Fordville Mound Group, Walsh County, North Dakota," N.Dakota History 17 (1950) :253-60.

Fort Ransom
-Petroglyph
T.H. Lewis, "Cupstones near Old Fort Ransom, N.D.," Am.Naturalist 25 (1891):455-61. il.

Garrison
-UFO (NL)
1967, July 25/LaVern Affeldt
"Worldwide Sightings Showing Increase," UFO Inv. 4 (Oct.1967):1,4.

Gascoyne
-UFO (NL)
1956, Nov.26/Mrs. Donald Hedman/W of town
(Editorial), Fate 10 (Apr.1957):14, quoting Twin Butte Bowman County Pioneer (undated).

Grafton
-UFO (CE-1)
1965, Nov.3/Diane Dymowski/Hwy.17
Jerome Clark, "The Greatest Flap Yet? Part 4," Flying Saucer Rev. 12 (Nov.-Dec.1966):10.
-UFO (DD)
1979, Jan.5/Terry Henriksen
Grafton Record, 6 Jan.1979.
-UFO (NL)
1961, Sep.25/Bill Janousek/nr. airport
Curtis Fuller, "The Boys Who 'Caught' a Flying Saucer," Fate 15 (Jan.1962) :36,40-41.

1961, Nov.22/Melvin C. Vagle, Jr./S on U.S.81
Richard Hall, ed., The UFO Evidence (Washington: NICAP, 1964), p.54, quoting Honeywell World, 1 Jan.1962.

1979, Jan.4/Isadore Kasprick
Grafton Record, 6 Jan.1979.

Grand Forks
-Anomalous artifact
1936/Red River Valley, N of town/= ancient telescope?
New York Times, 24 May 1936, sec.IV, p.11.
-UFO (CE-3)
1965, Aug.9/Becky Evanson/Lincoln Park golf course
Jerome Clark, "The Greatest Flap Yet? Part 2," Flying Saucer Rev. 12 (Mar.-Apr.1966):8-9.

Hankinson
-Norse harpoon
n.d.
"New Discoveries Supporting Medieval Norse Presence in the Upper Midwest," NEARA Newsl. 9 (spring 1974) :15-16. il.

Huff
-Archeological site
1400-1600
Raymond W. Wood, "An Interpretation of Mandan Culture History," Bull. Bur.Am.Ethn., no.198 (1967). il.

Hurdsfield
-UFO (CE-1)
1951, Aug./Florence Newsom
(Letter), Fate 5 (June 1952):127-28.

Inkster
-UFO (CE-2)
1973, Nov.4/Robert Johnson
Ted Phillips, Physical Traces Associated with UFO Sightings (Evanston: Center for UFO Studies, 1975), p.96.

Kindred
-Phantom
1976, Aug.
(Editorial), Fate 30 (Feb.1977):39-40.
1976, Sep.11/nr. Millsite Park
(Editorial), Fate 30 (Feb.1977):40, quoting Fargo Forum (undated).
Ed Sanders, "On the Trail of the Night Surgeons," Oui, May 1977, pp. 79,134.
-UFO (CE-3)
1968, May 5/Jerome Clark
Jerome Clark, "Experiences and Observations," Flying Saucer Rev. 15 (Nov.-Dec.1969):19.
Jerome Clark, "Paranormal Terror," Saga UFO Rept. 4 (July 1977):8,75.

Lakota
-UFO (CE-2)
1960, Jan.18
Grand Forks Herald, 21 Jan.1960.

Langdon
-Fall of metallic object
1957, Dec.14/Ed Waslashi

St. Paul (Minn.) Pioneer Press, 16
Dec.1957.
(Editorial), Fate 11 (Apr.1958):17.
il.
Coral & Jim Lorenzen, UFOs: The Whole
Story (N.Y.: Signet, 1969), p.87.

Litchville
-Fall of metallic object
    1971, April/=satellite re-entry
        Fargo Forum, 9 May 1971; and 14 May
        1971. il.

McClusky
-UFO (NL)
    1969, March 14/Roger Motschenbacher
        "Strange Blue Lighted Object in North
        Dakota," Skylook, no.19 (June 1969)
        :19, quoting McClusky Gazette (un-
        dated).

Mandan
-Mystery stone spheres
    (Letter), A.C. Nelson, Fate 5 (Apr.-
    May 1952):122.
-Norse runestones
    1905
        G.F. Will & H.F. Spinden, "The Man-
        dans: A Study of Their Culture,
        Archaeology and Language," Pap.Pea-
        body Mus. 3 (1906):165-66,172-73.
        il.
        O.G. Landsverk, Runic Records of the
        Norsemen in America (N.Y.: Friis,
        1974), pp.234-38. il.

Max
-UFO (CE-1)
    1967, Oct.27/Chris Helgesen
        "New Close-Ups, Pacings," UFO Inv. 4
        (Mar.1968):1,3.

Milton
-UFO (CE-1)
    1928, Nov./Norman H. Sabie/4 mi.NE
        Orvil R. Hartle, A Carbon Experiment?
        (LaPorte, Ind.: The Author, 1963),
        p.146.
        Gordon I.R. Lore, Jr. & Harold H.
        Deneault, Jr., Mysteries of the
        Skies: UFOs in Perspective (Engle-
        wood Cliffs, N.J.: Prentice-Hall,
        1968), pp.107-108.

Minot
-UFO (CE-1)
    1975, Sep.11
        "UFO Central," CUFOS News Bull., 15
        Nov.1975, p.18.
-UFO (CE-2)
    1965, Oct.13/Marg Gudajtes
        Jerome Clark, "The Greatest Flap Yet?
        --Part 3," Flying Saucer Rev. 12
        (May-June 1966):13,14.
-UFO (CE-3)
    1961, Nov.
        J. Allen Hynek, The UFO Experience
        (Chicago: Regnery, 1972), pp.143-
        44.
-UFO (NL)

1897, April 13/Charles Herms
    Minneapolis (Minn.) Times, 15 Apr.
    1897.
-UFO (R-V)
    1966, Aug.25/Minot AFB
        Jacques Vallee, Passport to Magonia
        (Chicago: Regnery, 1969), p.335.
        Raymond E. Fowler, UFOs: Interplan-
        etary Visitors (N.Y.: Exposition,
        1974), pp.295-96.
    1967, March 5/Minot AFB
        Donald E. Keyhoe, Aliens from Space
        (Garden City: Doubleday, 1973),
        pp.10-11.
    1968, Oct.24/Minot AFB
        J. Allen Hynek, The Hynek UFO Report
        (N.Y.: Dell, 1977), pp.125,137-39.

Moorhead
-UFO (CE-2)
    1978, May 2/Carol Sannes
        Fargo Forum, 4 May 1978.

Neche
-UFO (CE-1)
    1963, Nov.20/Nita Kain/E on Hwy.55
        "UFO Sightings Centered in Western
        U.S.," UFO Inv. 2 (Dec.1963-Jan.
        1964):3.

Oakes
-Fall of metallic object
    1971, April/=satellite re-entry
        Fargo Forum, 30 Apr.1971; 9 May
        1971; and 14 May 1971.

Parshall
-UFO (CE-1)
    1967, Oct.27/Glen D. Brunsell
        Donald E. Keyhoe & Gordon I.R. Lore,
        Jr., UFOs: A New Look (Washington:
        NICAP, 1969), p.6.
        J. Allen Hynek, The UFO Experience
        (Chicago: Regnery, 1972), p.89.

Penn
-Ghost
    1912, summer/Miriam Grinstead
        Miriam Grinstead, "The Hanging Spec-
        tre," Fate 9 (Mar.1956):22-24.

Portal
-Fall of salamanders
    ca.1941
        "Nelson Bond Writes," Doubt, no.11
        (winter 1944-1945):164.
        Gus Mager, "Game Gimmicks," Outdoor
        Life, Oct.1949, p.86.
-UFO (NL)
    1897, April 13
        Minneapolis (Minn.) Times, 15 Apr.
        1897.

Powers Lake
-Disappearance
    1956, Oct.28/LaVern Enget
        Harold T. Wilkins, Strange Mysteries
        of Time and Space (N.Y.: Ace, 1958
        ed.), p.140.

Richardton
-Poltergeist
  1944, spring/Pauline Rebel/Wild Plum
  School
    "Witchery in North Dakota," Time, 24
    Apr.1944, pp.75-76.
    "Wild Plum Speaks," Fortean Soc'y
    Mag., no.10 (autumn 1944):137-38.
    "Nelson Bond Writes," Doubt, no.11
    (winter 1944-1945):164.

Sawyer
-UFO (CE-1)
  1967, Aug.5/Ronald Sherven/N of town
    "Worldwide Sightings Showing In-
    crease," UFO Inv. 4 (Oct.1967):1,3.

Solen
-Humanoid
  1977, Sep.11/Chris Howiatow/4 mi.W
    Bonnie Lake, "Bigfoot on the Buttes:
    The Invasion of Little Eagle," Saga
    UFO Rept. 5 (June 1978):28-29.
  1977, Nov./droppings only
    Bismarck Tribune, 26 Nov.1977.
    Worthington (Minn.) Globe, 31 Jan.
    1978.

Stirum
-UFO (CE-2)
  1966, Sep.13/Randy Rotenberger
    Coral & Jim Lorenzen, Flying Saucer
    Occupants (N.Y.: Signet, 1967), pp.
    29-30.
    Ted Phillips, Physical Traces Associ-
    ated with UFO Sightings (Evanston:
    Center for UFO Studies, 1975), p.43.

Upham
-UFO (CE-2)
  1965, Oct.28
    Jerome Clark, "The Greatest Flap Yet?
    Part 4," Flying Saucer Rev. 12
    (Nov.-Dec.1966):9.

Valley City
-Phantoms and livestock mutilations
  1976, summer
    (Editorial), Fate 30 (Feb.1977):39.
-UFO (NL)
  1948, July 26-27/L.S. Eberly
    Kenneth Arnold & Ray Palmer, The Com-
    ing of the Saucers (Boise: The Au-
    thors, 1952), p.139.

Watford City
-UFO (NL)
  1978, Nov.9/Barb Johnsrud/Hwy.85
    Watford Guide, 10 Nov.1978.

West Fargo
-UFO (NL)
  1967, March 25/Wilson Ferrgut
    Wendelle C. Stevens, "Fantastic UFO
    Photo Flap of 1967," Saga UFO Rept.
    3 (June 1976):24. il.

Westhope
-UFO (CE-2)
  1969, March 10/Lavern Janzen

"Police Car Radio Affected by UFO,"
  Skylook, no.20 (July 1969):15-16.
Donald E. Keyhoe, Aliens from Space
  (Garden City: Doubleday, 1973), pp.
  272-73.
  1969, April 1/Rosemary Lee
    Ted Phillips, Physical Traces Associ-
    ated with UFO Sightings (Evanston:
    Center for UFO Studies, 1975), p.64.

Williston
-UFO (?)
  1957, Jan.5/Larry Wagenman
    "Case 293," CRIFO Orbit, 1 Mar.1957,
    p.3, quoting Williston Herald (un-
    dated).
-UFO (NL)
  1956, Sep.22/Reuben Borrud
    "Case 222," CRIFO Orbit, 2 Nov.1956,
    p.3, quoting Williston Plains Reg-
    ister (undated).

Woodworth
-Windshield pitting
  1961, Oct.31/Lyla Martin
    (Letter), Fate 15 (May 1962):118-19.

York
-UFO (CE-2)
  1972, Aug.27/James Deplazes
    Ted Phillips, Physical Traces Associ-
    ated with UFO Sightings (Evanston:
    Center for UFO Studies, 1975), p.85.

            B. Physical Features

Bald Hill
-Archeological site
  ca.125 A.D.
    Gordon W. Hewes, "Burial Mounds in
    the Baldhill Area, North Dakota,"
    Am.Antiquity 14 (1949):322-28. il.

Cannonball R.
-Humanoid
  1977, Sep.16/Paul Monzelowsky
    Bonnie Lake, "Bigfoot on the Buttes:
    The Invasion of Little Eagle," Saga
    UFO Rept. 5 (June 1978):28-29.

Devil's L.
-Lake monster
    Charles M. Skinner, American Myths
    and Legends, 2 vols. (Philadelphia:
    Lippincott, 1903), 2:281-83.

Fort Lincoln State Park
-Archeological site
  ca.1000-1800/Slant Indian Village
    Franklin Folsom, America's Ancient
    Treasures (N.Y.: Rand McNally,
    1974), pp.91-92.

Kildeer Mts.
-Humanoid
  1900s/Myrtle Paschen
    John Green, Sasquatch: The Apes Among
    Us (Seattle: Hancock House, 1978),
    p.172.

Missouri R.
-Norse runestone
  1738/Pierre Gaultier de Varennes (La
  Vérendrye)
    Peter Kalm, Travels into North Amer-
    ica, 2 vols., J.H. Forster trans.
    (London: T. Lowndes, 1772), 2:278-
    81.
    Hjalmar R. Holand, The Kensington
    Stone (Ephraim, Wisc.: The Author,
    1932), pp.182-200.
    Hjalmar R. Holand, Westward to Vin-
    land (N.Y.: Duell, Sloan & Pearce,
    1940), pp.263-86.
    Hjalmar R. Holand, A Pre-Columbian
    Crusade to America (N.Y.: Twayne,
    1962), pp.180-84.

Red Wing Creek
-Meteorite crater
  probable
    R.L. Brenan, B.L. Peterson & H.J.
    Smith, "The Origin of Red Wing
    Creek Structure: McKenzie County,
    North Dakota," Earth Sci.Bull.Wyo-
    ming Geol.Ass'n 8 (1975):1-41.

Sheyanne R.
-Archeological site
    George F. Will, "The Cheyenne Indi-
    ans in North Dakota," Proc.Miss.
    Valley Hist.Ass'n 7 (1914):67-78.
    George Bird Grinnell, "Early Chey-
    enne Villages," Am.Anthro. 20
    (1918):359-80.
    William Duncan Strong, "From History
    to Prehistory in the Northern Great
    Plains," Smith.Misc.Coll. 100
    (1940):353,370-76. il.

Writing Rock Historic Site
-Petroglyph
    Henriette Mertz, Gods from the Far
    East (N.Y.: Ballantine, 1975 ed.),
    p.142. il.
    Franklin Folsom, America's Ancient
    Treasures (N.Y.: Rand McNally,
    1974), p.92.

C. Ethnic Groups

Mandan Indians
-Flood myth
    George Catlin, Letters and Notes on
    the...North American Indians, 2 vols.
    (London: D. Bogue, 1844), 1:88,158.
    Ignatius Donnelly, Atlantis: The
    Antediluvian World, Egerton Sykes
    ed. (N.Y.: Gramercy, 1949), pp.
    92-96.
-Weather control
    George Catlin, Letters and Notes on
    the...North American Indians, 2 vols.
    (London: D. Bogue, 1844), 1:134-40.
-White Indians and similarity to Welsh
    George Burder, The Welch Indians
    (London: T. Chapman, 1787).
    Amos Stoddard, Sketches Historical
    and Descriptive of Louisiana (Phil-

adelphia: Mathew Carey, 1812), pp.
465-88.
Prince Maximilian of Wied-Neuwied,
Travels in the Interior of North
America (London: Ackermans, 1843).
George Catlin, Letters and Notes on
the...North American Indians, 2 vols.
(London: D. Bogue, 1844), 1:93-95,
104,205-207; 2:257-61.
Reuben T. Durrett, Traditions of the
Earliest Visits of Foreigners to
North America (Louisville, Ky.: Fil-
son Club, Pub.no.23, 1908).
Laurence J. Burpee, Journals and Let-
ters of Pierre Gaultier de Varennes
de la Vérendrye and His Sons (Tor-
onto: Champlain Soc'y, Pub.no.16,
1927), p.340.
Hjalmar R. Holand, The Kensington
Stone (Ephraim, Wisc.: The Author,
1932), pp.201-23.
David Williams, "John Evans' Strange
Journey," Am.Hist.Rev. 54 (1949):
277-95,508-29.
Marshal T. Newman, "The Blond Mandan:
A Critical Review of an Old Problem,"
Southwestern J.Anthro. 6 (1950):
255-72. il.
David Williams, John Evans and the
Legend of Madoc (Cardiff: Univ. of
Wales, 1963).
Richard Deacon, Madoc and the Discov-
ery of America (N.Y.: George Braz-
iller, 1966), pp.114-23,137-50,207-
39. il.

D. Unspecified Localities

-Archeological sites
    Thomas F. & Alice B. Kehoe, "Boulder
    Effigy Monuments in the Northern
    Plains," J.Am.Folklore 72 (1959):
    115-27.

-UFO (DD)
  1958, Nov./Michael Moore
    Dr. & Mrs. Michael Moore, "The Mys-
    tery of the Purple Clouds," Flying
    Saucer Rev. 9 (July-Aug.1963):5-7.

-UFO (NL)
  1970, July 14/William J. Finch
    William J. Finch, "Red Light Follows
    Satellite over North Dakota," Sky-
    look, no.34 (Sep.1970):26.

SOUTH DAKOTA

A. Populated Places

Aberdeen
-Electromagnetic anomaly
1964/Mrs. Robert Eby
(Editorial), Fate 17 (Aug.1964):12.
-Fall of fish
1886/S,W. Narregang
E.W. Gudger, "More Rains of Fishes,"
Annals & Mag.of Nat.Hist., ser.10,
3 (Jan.1929):1,21-22.
-UFO (?)
1897, April 9
Aberdeen Daily News, 12 Apr.1897, p.3.
1897, April 13
Aberdeen Daily News, 14 Apr.1897, p.3.
1897, April 14/=Venus
Aberdeen Daily News, 15 Apr.1897, p.3.

Alexandria
-UFO (NL)
1897, April
Alexandria Herald, 15 Apr.1897, p.5.

Betts
-Disappearance
1971, March/rural school
"The Vanishing One-Room Schoolhouse,"
Fate 26 (July 1973):85.

Black Hawk
-UFO (NL)
1953, Aug.12
Gordon D. Thayer, "Optical and Radar
Analyses of Field Cases," in Edward
U. Condon, ed., Scientific Study of
Unidentified Flying Objects (N.Y.:
Bantam, 1969 ed.), p.133.

Bowdle
-Whirlwind anomaly
1955, July 1/Sharon Weron
(Editorial), Fate 9 (May 1956):9-10.

Buffalo
-UFO (NL)
1972, June 29
Glenn McWane & David Graham, The New
UFO Sightings (N.Y.: Warner, 1974),
quoting Buffalo Times-Herald (undated).

Canova
-Fall of toads
1930, summer/Bob Jacobson
(Letter), Mrs. Charles Jacobson, Fate
11 (Nov.1958):118-20.

Canton
-UFO (NL)
1897, April 13/Mayor Seely
Omaha (Nebr.) Daily Bee, 15 Apr.1897,
p.1.

Carthage
-Anomalous hole in ground
1955, April/Ernest Hall
"Hot Coals and the Curious Hole from
Nowhere," CRIFO Newsl., 6 May 1955,
p.2.

Davis
-Humanoid
1978, Jan.12
Hurley Leader, 19 Jan.1978.

Deadwood
-Fall of ice
1881, June 6/=hailstone
"Hailstorms," Monthly Weather Rev.
9 (June 1881):17.
-Ghost
1883/Martha Jane Canary (Calamity Jane)
Glenn Clairmonte, "A Ghost Won for
Calamity Jane," Fate 26 (June 1973)
:62-64.
-UFO (NL)
1897, April 12/Albert Sawre
Omaha (Nebr.) Daily Bee, 14 Apr.1897,
p.3.
1966, Sep.22
"Selected UFO Cases," in Carl Sagan
& Thornton Page, eds., UFO's: A
Scientific Debate (Ithaca, N.Y.:
Cornell Univ., 1972), pp. xxii-xxiii.

Dell Rapids
-UFO (DD)
1947, July 5/Anna Dahl/S of town
Sioux Falls Daily Argus-Leader, 7
July 1947.

Faulkton
-UFO (?)
1956, Nov./Adams Rauhs
(Editorial), Fate 10 (Mar.1957):15.

Flandreau
-UFO (NL)
1966, Aug.16/Mrs. Ray Allen/=barium
cloud?
John A. Keel, "The Night the Sky
Turned On," Fate 20 (Sep.1967):30.

Fort Pierre
-UFO (NL)
1897, April 15/J.R. McLoud
Sioux City (Iowa) Journal, 17 Apr.
1897.

Hayes
-UFO (CE-2)
1967, March 5/Russell Carter/10 mi.E
"Sightings Still on Upswing," APRO
Bull. 15 (Mar.-Apr.1967):11.
Brad Steiger & Joan Whritenour, The
Allende Letters: New UFO Breakthrough
(N.Y.: Award, 1968), pp.41-42.

Hermosa
-UFO (NL)
    1956, Nov.16/Willis Mountain/5 mi.S
    "Case 251," CRIFO Orbit, 4 Jan.1957,
    p.1, quoting St. Paul (Minn.) Pio-
    neer Press (undated).

Hot Springs
-UFO (R-V)
    1956, Nov.25/Allen Coates
    Pierre Daily Capitol-Journal, 25
    Nov.1956.

Howard
-UFO (NL)
    1897, April 15/Joe Wright
    Jerome Clark, "The Strange Case of
    the 1897 Airship," Flying Saucer
    Rev. 12 (July-Aug.1966):10,12,
    quoting Madison Sentinel (undated).

Huron
-UFO (NL)
    1950, Nov.27/Gene Fowler
    Richard Hall, ed., The UFO Evidence
    (Washington: NICAP, 1964), p.45.

Igloo
-UFO (DD)
    1964, Sep./August Powell
    "Two UFOs Photographed," Interplane-
    tary Intelligence Rept. 1 (July
    1965):20. il.

Jefferson
-Humanoid
    1974, Sep.6/Jim Douglas/3½ mi.N on Hwy.
    77
    Jerome Clark, "Are 'Manimals' Space
    Beings?" Saga UFO Rept. 2 (summer
    1975):49,58-59.

Keystone
-UFO (NL)
    1978, Jan.29
    Rapid City Journal, 1 Feb.1978.

Lake Norden
-Precognition
    1970s/Kathy Sotka/Box 211
    Richard De A'Morelli & Rita West,
    "Top Seers Predict Your Future for
    1977," Psychic World, Jan.1977, pp.
    51,53.
    "Probe's 1977 Directory of the Psy-
    chic World," Probe the Unknown 5
    (spring 1977):32,65.

Little Eagle
-Humanoids
    1977, Sep.-Nov.23/Lemar Bear Rib and
    others
    McIntosh News, 3 Nov.1977, p.1.
    Bismarck (N.D.) Tribune, 10 Nov.
    1977, p.1; and 26 Nov.1977.
    Sam Dart, "A Bigfoot Sighting in
    South Dakota," Argosy, Mar.1978, pp.
    47-49,67-69.
    Bonnie Lake, "Bigfoot on the Buttes:
    The Invasion of Little Eagle," Saga

UFO Rept. 5 (June 1978):28-31,67-
    74.
-Humanoid tracks
    1977, Oct.2/Verdell Veo
    Sioux Falls Argus-Leader, 3 Oct.1977.
    McIntosh News, 6 Oct.1977. il.
    Sam Dart, "A Bigfoot Sighting in
    South Dakota," Argosy, Mar.1978,
    pp.47-49,67. il.
-UFO (?)
    1977, April?/Sherman Red Legs
    Bonnie Lake, "Bigfoot on the Buttes:
    The Invasion of Little Eagle," Saga
    UFO Rept. 5 (June 1978):28,30.
-UFO (NL)
    1977, Aug./Verdell Veo
    Bonnie Lake, "Bigfoot on the Buttes:
    The Invasion of Little Eagle," Saga
    UFO Rept. 5 (June 1978):28,30.

McIntosh
-UFO (CE-1)
    ca.1974/Gary Alexander/E on U.S.12
    Bonnie Lake, "Bigfoot on the Buttes:
    The Invasion of Little Eagle," Saga
    UFO Rept. 5 (June 1978):28,30.
-UFO (CE-2)
    1967, March 12/Larry Burke/1 mi.W
    "Car Buzzing Incidents on Increase,"
    APRO Bull. 15 (May-June 1967):5.

Madison
-UFO (?)
    1897, April 9
    Burlington (Iowa) Hawk-Eye, 10 Apr.
    1897.

Milbank
-UFO (CE-1)
    1976, Nov.27-Dec.11/Mike Foss/SW of
    town
    William M. Moore, "Repeat Sightings
    in S.D., U.S.," APRO Bull. 25 (Nov.
    1976):1,3-5.
    1977, March 1/Mike Foss/SW of town
    "Foss Episode Reoccurs," APRO Bull.
    25 (Apr.1977):2,6.

Mitchell
-Archeological site
    ca.1000 A.D./Firesteel Creek golf course
    E.E. Meleen, "A Preliminary Report on
    the Mitchell Indian Village Site and
    Burial Mounds," Arch.Studies S.Da-
    kota Arch.Comm'n, no.2 (1938).
-UFO (CE-3)
    1906/Herbert DeMott
    Jerome Clark & Lucius Farish, "The
    Phantom Airships of 1913," Saga UFO
    Rept. 1 (summer 1974):36,58.
-UFO (DD)
    1947, July 8/Mrs. Ed Anderson/airport
    Fargo (N.D.) Forum, 9 July 1947.

Mobridge
-Norse runestones
    Ariskara site
    O.G. Landsverk, Runic Records of the
    Norsemen in America (N.Y.: Friis,
    1974), pp.237-38. il.

Morristown
-UFO (NL)
  1967, March 12/Terry Nelson
    Jim & Coral Lorenzen, UFOs over the
    Americas (N.Y.: Signet, 1968), p.26.

Mount Vernon
-Norse halberd
  1946, Sep./Richard D. Knox
    Hjalmar R. Holand, A Pre-Columbian
    Crusade to America (N.Y.: Twayne,
    1962), pp.177-78. il.

Nemo
-Humanoid
  1974, March
    John Green, Sasquatch: The Apes Among
    Us (Seattle: Hancock House, 1978),
    p.172.

Onida
-Dowsing
  1950s/Carol Terbush
    (Editorial), Fate 8 (May 1955):11.

Piedmont
-UFO (NL)
  ca.1969
    Rapid City Journal, 13 Dec.1977.
  1977, Nov.1/Duane Holsworth/Big Elk
  burn
    Rapid City Journal, 13 Dec.1977; and
    20 Dec.1977.

Pierre
-Archeological site
  ca.1400-1550/Arzberger site/7 mi.E
    Albert C. Spaulding, "The Arzberger
    Site, Hughes County, South Dakota,"
    Occ.Contrib.Mus.Anthro.Univ.Michi-
    gan, no.16 (1956). il.
-UFO (CE-1)
  1956, Nov.25/Don Kelm
    Minneapolis (Minn.) Star, 28 Nov.
    1956.
    "Case 257," CRIFO Orbit, 4 Jan.1957,
    p.2, quoting Williston (N.D.) Her-
    ald (undated).
-UFO (NL)
  1897, April 15/Mr. Monkhouse
    Minneapolis (Minn.) Journal, 16 Apr.
    1897.
    Omaha (Nebr.) Daily Bee, 17 Apr.1897,
    p.2.

Pine Ridge
-Precognition
  1903/Tall Holy
    Frederick J. Goshe, "Could the Sioux
    Control Weather?" Fate 10 (Apr.1957)
    :57,61-62.

Porcupine
-Humanoid
  1977, Nov.5/David Dunn/E of town
    Bismarck (N.D.) Tribune, 10 Nov.1977,
    p.1.

Rapid City
-UFO (?)

1956, Oct.9
  Arthur Constance, The Inexplicable
  Sky (N.Y.: Citadel, 1956), p.285.
-UFO (CE-2)
  ca.1957/Ellsworth AFB
    Ann Druffel, "The Importance of the
    Past," MUFON UFO J., no.126 (May
    1978):14-15.
-UFO (NL)
  1947, Aug./Ellsworth AFB
    J. Allen Hynek, The Hynek UFO Report
    (N.Y.: Dell, 1977), pp.40-42.
  1956, Nov.24/Glenn Best
    "Case 256," CRIFO Orbit, 4 Jan.1957,
    pp.1-2, quoting Williston (N.D.) Her-
    ald (undated).
  1967, June 30/Dennis Eisnach
    Brad Steiger & Joan Whritenour, Al-
    lende Letters: New UFO Breakthrough
    (N.Y.: Award, 1968), pp.48-49.
  1968, Aug.10, 12/Ellsworth AFB
    Coral E. Lorenzen, The Shadow of the
    Unknown (N.Y.: Signet, 1970), pp.
    165-66.
  1972, July 4/Robert D. Stapelberg
  1974/Robert D. Stapelberg
    (Letter), Saga UFO Rept. 2 (fall
    1975):4.
  1977, July 4
    "UFO Analysis," Int'l UFO Reporter 2
    (Sep.1977):[9].
-UFO (R-V)
  1953, Aug.12/Ellsworth AFB
    Edward J. Ruppelt, "What Our Air
    Force Found Out about Flying Sau-
    cers," True, May 1954, pp.19-30,124-
    34.
    Edward J. Ruppelt, The Report on Un-
    identified Flying Objects (Garden
    City: Doubleday, 1956), pp.232-35.
    Donald H. Menzel & Lyle G. Boyd, The
    World of Flying Saucers (Garden
    City: Doubleday, 1963), pp.167-71.
    U.S. Air Force, Projects Grudge and
    Blue Book Reports 1-12 (Washington:
    NICAP, 1968), pp.226-29.
    Gordon D. Thayer, "Optical and Radar
    Analyses of Field Cases," in Edward
    U. Condon, ed., Scientific Study of
    Unidentified Flying Objects (N.Y.:
    Bantam, 1969 ed.), pp.132-36.

Roberts co.
-Petroglyphs
    T.H. Lewis, "Incised Boulders in the
    Upper Minnesota Valley," Am.Natural-
    ist 21 (1887):639-42. il.

Scenic
-UFO (?)
  1967, May 27/=airplane
    Edward U. Condon, ed., Scientific
    Study of Unidentified Flying Objects
    (N.Y.: Bantam, 1969 ed.), pp.324-26.

Sioux Falls
-Archeological site
  ca.400 A.D./Sherman Park
    Franklin Folsom, America's Ancient
    Treasures (N.Y.: Rand McNally, 1974),

p.96.
-Cattle mutilations
  1974, Sep.
    Roberta Donovan & Keith Wolverton,
    Mystery Stalks the Prairie (Raynes-
    ford, Mont.: THAR, 1976), pp.27-29.
-UFO (?)
  1954, Sep.25/=meteor?
    "North Central States Alarmed by
    Soaring Blue-White 'Ball,'" CRIFO
    Newsl., 5 Nov.1954, p.3.
-UFO (CE-1)
  1976, Aug.
    "Diary of a Mad Planet," Fortean
    Times, no.18 (Oct.1976):8,20.
-UFO (DD)
  1947, July 6/Gregory Zimmer/1328 W.
  Sioux St.
    Sioux Falls Daily Argus-Leader, 7
    July 1947.
-UFO (NL)
  1947, July 4/Ronald C. Jordon/807 W.
  13th St.
    Sioux Falls Daily Argus-Leader, 7
    July 1947.

Spearfish
-Dowsing
  ca.1900/George Glover
    M. Marsh, "Our Water-Witched Well,"
    Fate 11 (Feb.1958):76.
-Precognition
  1975/Larry Headrick/Box 683
    Warren Smith, "Phenomenal Predictions
    for 1976," Saga, Jan.1976, pp.16,18.

Sturgis
-Fall of unknown object
  1946, May
    "Hole in Back Yard," Doubt, no.15
    (summer 1946):225.
    "Follow Ups," Doubt, no.16 (1946):
    243.

Timber Lake
-Humanoid
  1977, Oct.29/Albert Kougl/NW of town
    Timber Lakes Topic, 3 Nov.1977.

Vermillion
-UFO (?)
  1897, April 15/=kite
    Sioux City (Iowa) Journal, 17 Apr.
    1897.
-UFO (CE-1)
  1968, Jan.20/Robert Ballard
    "New Close-Ups, Pacings," UFO Inv. 4
    (Mar.1968):1,3.
-UFO (NL)
  1956, Dec.4/James Kavanagh
    "Case 263," CRIFO Orbit, 4 Jan.1957,
    p.3.

Wanblee
-UFO (?)
  1977, Jan.
    Omaha (Nebr.) World-Herald, 7 Jan.
    1977.

Webster
-UFO (NL)
  1956, Nov.27/Otto Premus/Hwy.25, nr.
  airport
    "Case 259," CRIFO Orbit, 4 Jan.1957,
    pp.2-3, quoting Webster Reporter &
    Farmer (undated).

Wessington Springs
-UFO (NL)
  1947, July 7/Emmitt Barta
    Fargo (N.D.) Forum, 9 July 1947.

Wilmot
-UFO (DD)
  1961, Oct.2/Leon Jurgens
    "Balloon-Shaped Object in South Da-
    kota, USA," APRO Bull. 10 (Mar.
    1962):2.

Winfred
-UFO (NL)
  1956, Nov.23/Mrs. Robert Wassanaar
    "Case 255," CRIFO Orbit, 4 Jan.1957,
    p.1, quoting St. Paul (Minn.) Pio-
    neer Press (undated).

Woonsocket
-UFO (NL)
  1897, April 13
    Omaha (Nebr.) Daily Bee, 15 Apr.1897,
    p.1.

        B. Physical Features

Big Bend Reservoir
-Archeological site
  ca.1450-1500/Black Partizan site
    Warren W. Caldwell, "The Black Par-
    tizan Site (39LM218), Big Ben Res-
    ervoir," Plains Anthro. 5, no.10
    (1960):53-57.
    Warren W. Caldwell, "The Black Par-
    tizan Site," Pub.Salvage Arch.Smith.
    Inst., no.2 (1966). 11.

Black Hills
-Skyquakes
  18th-19th c.
    Washington Irving, Astoria (Boston:
    Twayne, 1976 ed.), pp.166-67.
    Abbe Em. Domenech, The Deserts of
    North America (London: Longmans,
    Green, 1860), pp.299-301.
    Peter Rosen, Pa-ha-sa-ah, or the
    Black Hills of South Dakota (St. Lou-
    is: Nixon Jones, 1895), p.264.
    Ella E. Clark, Indian Legends of the
    Northern Rockies (Norman: Univ. of
    Oklahoma, 1966), pp.307-308.

Campbell L.
-Lake monster
  ca.1934
    "More Monsters," Doubt, no.16 (1946):
    236-37.

Crow Creek
-Archeological site

ca.1090
    Carlyle S. Smith, "The Temporal Re-
    lationships of Coalescent Village
    Sites in Fort Randall Reservoir,
    South Dakota," Trans.Int'l Cong.
    Americanists 33, pt.2 (1958):111-
    23.
-Retrocognition
    1957, summer/John B. Johnson
        J.B. Johnson, "The Girl with the
        Green Eyes," Fate 30 (Apr.1977):60-
        65.

Elk Butte
-Humanoid
    1977, Oct.29/Verdell Veo
        McIntosh News, 3 Nov.1977.
        Bonnie Lake, "Bigfoot on the Buttes:
        The Invasion of Little Eagle," Saga
        UFO Rept. 5 (June 1978):28,69.

Fort Randall Reservoir
-Archeological sites
    ca.500-1750/Hitchell site
        Carlyle S. Smith, "The Temporal Re-
        lationships of Coalescent Village
        Sites in Fort Randall Reservoir,
        South Dakota," Trans.Int'l Cong.
        Americanists 33, pt.2 (1958):111-
        23.
        Richard B. Johnston, "The Hitchell
        Site," Pub.Salvage Arch.Smith.Inst.,
        no.3 (1967). il.

Grand R.
-Humanoid tracks
    1977, Sep.6/Windy Village Thunder
        Sam Dart, "A Bigfoot Sighting in
        South Dakota!" Argosy, Mar.1978, pp.
        47,48.
        Bonnie Lake, "Bigfoot on the Buttes:
        The Invasion of Little Eagle," Saga
        UFO Rept. 5 (June 1978):28,29.

Johnson Siding
-Humanoid
    1973, Nov.
        John Green, Sasquatch: The Apes Among
        Us (Seattle: Hancock House, 1978),
        p.172.

Little Oil Creek
-UFO (?)
    1957, summer/W. Clinton Giles/Canyon
    Branch/=meteor?
        Gray Barker, "Chasing the Flying Sau-
        cers," Flying Saucers, Feb.1958,
        pp.46,47.

Ludlow Cave
-Archeological site
        W.H. Over, "The Archeology of Ludlow
        Cave and Its Significance," Am.An-
        tiquity 2 (1936):126-29.
        William Duncan Strong, "Unanswered
        Questions on Ludlow Cave," Am.An-
        tiquity 2 (1937):205-207.

Medicine Knoll
-Archeological site

E.A. Allen, "Stone Snakes in Minne-
    sota," Am.Antiquarian 6 (1884):349.
M.E. Reisinger, "The Serpent Effigy
    on Medicine Butte," Wisconsin Arch.
    14 (1934):23-24.

Pickerel L.
-Humanoid
    ca.1974
        Jerome Clark, "Unidentified Furry Ob-
        jects," Saga UFO Rept. 5 (Mar.1978):
        12.

Punished Woman's L.
-Archeological site
    3 mi.S
        Jim Brandon, Weird America (N.Y.:
        Dutton, 1978), pp.201-202.

Ray Long site
-Archeological site
    7000 B.C.
        Jack T. Hughes, "Investigations in
        Western South Dakota and Northeast-
        ern Wyoming," Am.Antiquity 14
        (1949):266-77.

Traverse L.
-Petroglyphs
    13 mi.NW
        T.H. Lewis, "Ancient Rock Inscriptions
        in Eastern Dakota," Am.Naturalist
        20 (1886):423-24. il.

              C. Ethnic Groups

Crow Indians
-Contactee myth
        George P. Belden, Belden, the White
        Chief (Cincinnati: C.F. Vent, 1871),
        pp.212-16.

Sioux Indians (Dakota)
-Flood myth
        James W. Lynd, "History of the Dako-
        tas," Coll.Minn.Hist.Soc'y 2 (1865):
        57-84.
-Humanoid myth
        Mary Eastman, Dacotah (N.Y.: J.A.
        Wiley, 1849), pp.208-11.
        Henry Rowe Schoolcraft, History and
        Statistical Information...of the In-
        dian Tribes of the United States, 6
        vols. (Philadelphia: Lippincott,
        1851-60), 3:232.
        J. Owen Dorsey, "Teton Folk-lore,"
        Am.Anthro. 2 (1889):143,155.
-Thunderstone legend
        William H. Keating, Narrative of an
        Expedition to the Source of St. Pet-
        er's River, 2 vols. (Philadelphia:
        H.C. Carey & I. Lea, 1824), 1:407.
        Isaac M'Coy, History of Baptist Indi-
        an Missions (Washington: William A.
        Morrison, 1840), p.363.
        Mary Eastman, Dacotah (N.Y.: J.A.
        Wiley, 1849), p.71.
-Weather control
        Frederick J. Goshe, "Could the Sioux

Control Weather?" <u>Fate</u> 10 (Apr.
1957):57-63.

D. Unspecified Localities

-Archeological sites
   T.H. Lewis, "Stone Monuments in
   Southern Dakota," <u>Am.Anthro.</u> 2
   (1889):159-64.
   T.H. Lewis, "Bowlder Outline Figures
   in the Dakotas, Surveyed in the
   Summer of 1890," <u>Am.Anthro.</u> 4
   (1891):19-24.

-Ghost
   1943
   James Reynolds, <u>Ghosts in American
   Houses</u> (N.Y.: Paperback Library,
   1967 ed.), pp.179-80.

-Reincarnation
   1892/Nellie Foster
   <u>St. Louis (Mo.) Globe-Democrat</u>, 14
   Sep.1892.

NEBRASKA

A. Populated Places

Ainsworth
-Mystery radio transmission
1958, Dec.5/KBR Rural Power radio
Coral & Jim Lorenzen, UFOs: The Whole
Story (N.Y.: Signet, 1969), p.94,
quoting Ainsworth Star-Journal (un-
dated).
-UFO (NL)
1965, Aug.2
Coral E. Lorenzen, "Western UFO Flap,"
Fate 18 (Nov.1965):42,49.

Albion
-UFO (?)
1897, April/Bert Disher/=hoax
Rudolph Umland, "Phantom Airships of
the Nineties," Prairie Schooner 12
(1938):247,255, quoting Albion Weekly News (undated).

Angus
-Archeological site
=hoax?
J.D. Figgins, "An Additional Discov-
ery of the Association of a 'Folsom'
Artifact and Fossil Mammal Remains,"
Proc.Colorado Mus.Nat.Hist., vol.10,
no.2 (1931).
George Agogino & Bobbie Ferguson,
"The Angus Mammoth: Was It a Valid
Kill Site?" Anthro.J.Canada 16, no.
3 (1978):7-9.

Arago
-Phantom panther
1964
Jerome Clark & Loren Coleman, "On the
Trail of Pumas, Panthers and ULAs:
Part 2," Fate 25 (July 1972):92,97.

Arcadia
-UFO (?)
1966, July 13
John A. Keel, UFOs: Operation Trojan
Horse (N.Y.: Putnam, 1970), p.155.

Arthur
-UFO (NL)
1977, Aug.17/Janet Magnuson
1977, Oct.31/Norm Kramer
Hyannis Grant County Tribune, 3 Nov.
1977.

Ashland
-UFO (CE-4)
1967, Dec.3/Herbert L. Schirmer/Hwy.6
x 63
"Landed UAO Reported in Nebraska,"
APRO Bull. 16 (Nov.-Dec.1967):3-4.
National Enquirer, 19 May 1968, pp.
1,3,4.
Edward U. Condon, ed., Scientific
Study of Unidentified Flying Objects
(N.Y.: Bantam, 1969 ed.), pp.389-91.
Eric Norman [Warren Smith], Gods,
Demons and UFOs (N.Y.: Lancer, 1970),
pp.169-93.
Roy Norton, "World's Most Incredible
UFO Contact Case," Saga, Apr.1970,
pp.22-25,54-57.
Donald H. Menzel & Ernest H. Taves,
The UFO Enigma (Garden City: Double-
day, 1977), pp.107-108.
-UFO (NL)
1897, April 11
Ashland Gazette, 16 Apr.1897.
1967, Dec.25
Edward U. Condon, ed., Scientific
Study of Unidentified Flying Objects
(N.Y.: Bantam, 1969 ed.), pp.394-95.
Donald H. Menzel & Ernest H. Taves,
The UFO Enigma (Garden City: Double-
day, 1977), pp.108-109.

Aurora
-UFO (?)
1977, Dec.28
"Family Has Repeat Sightings," APRO
Bull. 26 (May 1978):4,5.

Bassett
-UFO (NL)
1973, Sep.20
Bassett Rock County Leader, 20 Sep.
1973.

Beatrice
-Airship inventor
1897, Feb./Anton Pallardy
Beatrice Daily Express, 6 Mar.1897.
-UFO (?)
1967/Tom Shuffs
(Letter), FSR Case Histories, no.18
(Feb.1974):18.
-UFO (NL)
1897, March
Mt. Morris (Ill.) News, 7 Apr.1897,
p.8.
1978, June 10/Doug Klevemann
1978, June 15/Charles Chapp/nr. airport
Beatrice Sun, 28 June 1978.

Big Springs
-UFO (CE-2)
1973, Oct.17
Ted Phillips, Physical Traces Associ-
ated with UFO Sightings (Evanston:
Center for UFO Studies, 1975), p.94.

Blue Hill
-UFO (NL)
1897, Feb.26/Tom Delahoyde
Omaha Daily Bee, 28 Feb.1897, p.2.

Brewster
-UFO (?)

1966, July 13
    John A. Keel, UFOs: Operation Trojan
    Horse (N.Y.: Putnam, 1970), p.154.

Broken Bow
-UFO (NL)
    1965, July 31
        Coral E. Lorenzen, "Western UFO Flap,"
        Fate 18 (Nov.1965):42,50.

Burr
-Phantom panther
    1965, March/Orlin Moss
        Jerome Clark & Loren Coleman, "On the
        Trail of Pumas, Panthers and ULAs:
        Part 2," Fate 25 (July 1972):92,97.

Bushnell
-Phantom helicopter and cattle mutilation
    1975, Aug.21/Mr. Hillman
        Kimball Western Nebraska Observer,
        28 Aug.1975.
        Curt Sutherly & David Fideler, "The
        Phantom Starships," Saga UFO Rept.
        5 (May 1978):16,19.

Callaway
-Cattle mutilation
    1974, March 31/Norman Robertson
        Omaha World-Herald, 9 Apr.1974.

Campbell
-Cattle mutilation
    1976, Nov.22/Norman Scheibel/W of town
        Hastings Daily Tribune, 26 Nov.1976.

Cedar Creek
-UFO (NL)
    1968, Nov.1, 3/Mrs. Gerald McGill
        "Multi-Witness Sighting in Nebraska,"
        APRO Bull. 17 (Mar.-Apr.1969):8.

Central City
-UFO (NL)
    1897, April 8/C. Jacobson
        York Daily Times, 10 Apr.1897.

Chadron
-UFO (CE-2)
    1961, Nov.8/Theodore Goff
        Chadron Record, 30 Nov.1961.
        "Angel's Hair Fall in Nebraska, USA,"
        APRO Bull. 10 (Jan.1962):3.

Chase co.
-Archeological site
    ca.1700/Lovitt site
        A.T. Hill & George Metcalf, "A Site
        of the Dismal River Aspect in Chase
        County, Nebraska," Nebraska History
        22 (1941):155-215. il.

Clarks
-UFO (NL)
    1897, March 3/Viola Daniels
        Omaha Daily Bee, 5 Mar.1897, p.2.

Clay Center
-UFO (NL)
    1897, April 15

Omaha Daily Bee, 17 Apr.1897, p.2.

Columbus
-Skyquake
    1978, Nov.7/Hugh Riley/23d St.
        Columbus Telegram, 10 Nov.1978.
-UFO (NL)
    1897, April 15/James Breedlove
        Omaha Daily Bee, 17 Apr.1897, p.2.

Cozad
-UFO (?)
    1966, July 13/Muny Park
        John A. Keel, UFOs: Operation Trojan
        Horse (N.Y.: Putnam, 1970), p.152.

Crete
-UFO (?)
    1974, Sep.
        Jerome Clark, "Are 'Manimals' Space
        Beings?" Saga UFO Rept. 2 (summer
        1975):49,62.

Culbertson
-UFO (DD)
    1965, Aug.2/Mr. Friehe
        Coral E. Lorenzen, "Western UFO Flap,"
        Fate 18 (Nov.1965):42,49.
-UFO (R-V)
    1970, Feb.28/Dale Nowka/5 mi.N
        McCook Gazette, 28 Feb.1970.
        Dick Henry, "1970 UFO over Nebraska,"
        Fate 23 (Sep.1970):82-87.

Cuming co.
-UFO (CE-1)
    1968, July 28/William C. Rogers/=
    meteor?
        Philip J. Klass, UFOs Explained (N.Y.:
        Random House, 1974), pp.167-74.

Davey
-UFO (NL)
    1978, Feb.19
        Lincoln Star, 21 Feb.1978.

Dawson
-Dowsing
    1950-1960/Carl Windrum
        Frank Edwards, Strange People (N.Y.:
        Popular Library, 1961 ed.), p.120.

Decatur
-UFO (NL)
    1897, April 6
        Omaha Daily Bee, 9 Apr.1897, p.2.
    1897, April 10
        Omaha Daily Bee, 14 Apr.1897, p.3.

Dodge
-Lightning anomaly
    1935, June 24
        J.C. Jensen, "The Dodge, Nebraska,
        'Fireball,'" Science 83 (1936):574-
        75.

Dunbar
-Phantom panther
    1965, March/David Wirth
    1965, March 13/Tom Easter

Jerome Clark & Loren Coleman, "On the Trail of Pumas, Panthers and ULAs: Part 2," Fate 25 (July 1972):92,97.

Fairmont
-Phantom panther
1897, Feb.16/A.W. Loomis
Omaha Daily Bee, 18 Feb.1897, p.2.

Franklin
-UFO (NL)
1897, April
Hastings Daily Republican, 22 Apr. 1897.

Fremont
-UFO (?)
1974, Sep.
Jerome Clark, "Are 'Manimals' Space Beings?" Saga UFO Rept. 2 (summer 1975):47,51.
-UFO (NL)
1897, March 14
Omaha Daily Bee, 17 Mar.1897, p.2.

Furnas co.
-Cattle mutilation
1975, Oct./Mr. Hays
Hastings Daily Tribune, 8 Nov.1975.
"To Decompose or Not to Decompose," Stigmata, no.3 (May 1978):3.

Geneva
-Weather control
1894, July 23-26
Lincoln Nebraska State Journal, 27 July 1894, p.3.

Gering
-Humanoid
1972, July 16
Lincoln Journal and Star, 16 July 1972.
-UFO (DD)
1947, June 15/Mrs. H. Ackley
Sacramento (Cal.) Union, 8 July 1947.
-UFO (NL)
1950, March 7/E.L. Ekberg/W of town
Denver (Colo.) Post, 7 Mar.1950.
Kenneth Arnold & Ray Palmer, The Coming of the Saucers (Boise: The Authors, 1952), p.146.

Grafton
-Cattle mutilation
1974, May 15/Dean Stuckey
(Editorial), Fate 27 (Nov.1974):12-14.

Grand Island
-Archeological site
ca.6500 B.C./Meserve site
C. Bertrand Schultz, "Association of Artifacts and Extinct Mammals in Nebraska," Bull.Nebraska Mus., no. 33 (1932):171-83.
-UFO (?)
1897, April/=hoax
Rudolph Umland, "Phantom Airships of the Nineties," Prairie Schooner 12

(1938):247,258.
1965, July 31
Coral E. Lorenzen, Flying Saucers: The Startling Evidence of the Invasion from Outer Space (N.Y.: Signet, 1966 ed.), p.238.
-UFO (NL)
1897, Feb.25
Grand Island Independent, 26 Feb. 1897.
1957, May 18/J.D. Hoeft
"Flying Saucer Roundup," Fate 11 (Feb.1958):29,31.
1967, April 9/nr. Cornhusker Ordnance Plant
"1967 Nebraska Sighting Told," Skylook, no.57 (Aug.1972):12.

Grant
-UFO (NL)
1975, Oct.3, 16
"Noteworthy UFO Sightings," Ufology 2 (spring 1976):43.

Gretna
-UFO (DD)
1947, July 6/E of town
1947, July 7/S of town
Omaha World-Herald, 7 July 1947.
1975, Nov.6
"Noteworthy UFO Sightings," Ufology 2 (spring 1976):43.

Haigler
-UFO (NL)
1897, Feb./Edna Campbell
Jerry Mathers, "The 1890s 'Flap,'" APRO Bull. 25 (Dec.1976):5.

Hamburg
-Ghost light
1894-   /Mrs. Jesse Duckworth
James Melvin Reinhardt, "Ghost Fireball of Hamburg," Fate 8 (Jan.1955) :60-62.

Harrison
-UFO (CE-3)
1897, April 13/=hoax?
Rudolph Umland, "Phantom Airships of the Nineties," Prairie Schooner 12 (1938):247,256, quoting Omaha World-Herald (undated).

Hartington
-Petroglyph
1869/S of town
Lincoln Nebraska State Journal, 6 Nov.1961, p.8. il.
Wilbert Rusch, "Human Footprints in Rock," Creation Rsch.Soc'y Quar., March 1971, pp.204,206-207. il.

Hastings
-UFO (?)
1973, July 19/James Shriver/physical trace only
Ted Phillips, Physical Traces Associated with UFO Sightings (Evanston: Center for UFO Studies, 1975), p.91.

-UFO (NL)
  1897, Jan.31/W of town
    Omaha Daily Bee, 2 Feb.1897, p.2.
    Juniata Herald, 10-17 Feb.1897.
-Weather control
  1894, July/chemical method
    Lincoln Nebraska State Journal, 29
    July 1894, p.3.

Hubbell
-UFO (CE-3)
  1922, Feb.22/William C. Lamb
    Jacques Vallee, Anatomy of a Phenom-
    enon (N.Y.: Ace, 1965 ed.), p.175.

Inavale
-UFO (CE-1)
  1897, Feb.4
    Omaha Daily Bee, 6 Feb.1897, p.6.
    Hastings Tribune, 12 Feb.1897.

Juniata
-Hog mutilation
  1977, Nov.24/6 mi.N on Alda Rd.
    Des Moines (Iowa) Register, 25 Nov.
    1977.
-UFO (NL)
  1897, April 18
    Omaha Daily Bee, 20 Apr.1897, p.5.

Kearney
-Clairvoyance
  1880s/Lucy Darling
    Grace Darling Ludwick, "My Mother's
    Miracles," Fate 9 (Apr.1956):72-73.
-Inner development
  1970s/Order of Osirus/Box 654
    Samuel R. Graves, Witchcraft: The
    Osirian Order (Kearney: Osirus,
    1971).
    Hans Holzer, The Witchcraft Report
    (N.Y.: Ace, 1973 ed.), pp.114-15.
-UFO (?)
  1897, Feb.18-21/M.A. Brown
    Omaha Daily Bee, 23 Feb.1897, p.2.
-UFO (CE-3)
  1957, Nov.5/Reinhold Schmidt/SE of town
  nr. Platte R./=hoax?
    Chicago (Ill.) Sun-Times, 8 Nov.1957.
    Alameda (Cal.) Times-Star, 8 Nov.
    1957.
    Reinhold Schmidt, The Kearney Inci-
    dent and to the Arctic Circle in a
    Spacecraft (Hollywood, Cal.: The
    Author, 1958).
    Gray Barker, "Chasing the Flying Sau-
    cers," Flying Saucers, May 1958, pp.
    20-35,80.
    Reinhold O. Schmidt, "The Kearney
    Incident," Flying Saucers, Oct.1959,
    pp.31-45.
    Reinhold Schmidt, The Reinhold Schmidt
    Story (Los Angeles: Amalgamated Fly-
    ing Saucer Clubs of America, 1960).
    (Editorial), Fate 15 (Feb.1962):24.
    (Editorial), Fate 15 (Apr.1962):22.

Kenesaw
-UFO (?)
  1897, April/5 mi.W/=hoax

Rudolph Umland, "Phantom Airships of
the Nineties," Prairie Schooner 12
(1938):247,259.

Knox co.
-Cattle mutilations and phantom helicopters
  1974, Sep.
    Washington (D.C.) Post, 8 Sep.1974.

Lancaster co.
-Cattle mutilation
  1974, June-July
    Washington (D.C.) Post, 8 Sep.1974.
    (Editorial), Fate 27 (Nov.1974):14.

Lexington
-UFO (NL)
  1897, Feb.
    North Platte Semi-Weekly Tribune, 9
    Mar.1897.

Lincoln
-Ball lightning
  1930, Aug.30/J.C. Jensen
    C.M. Botley, The Air and Its Mys-
    teries (London: G. Bell, 1938). il.
-Erratic galago
  1931, Oct./E.R. Mathers
    Lincoln Nebraska State Journal, 23-
    25 Oct.1931. il.
    New York Sun, 12 Nov.1931.
    Charles Fort, The Books of Charles
    Fort (N.Y.: Holt, 1941), pp.900-901.
-Fall of unknown substance
  1952, July 22/Mrs. Leo L. Baruch
    Harold T. Wilkins, Flying Saucers on
    the Attack (N.Y.: Ace, 1967 ed.),
    pp.278-79.
-Ghost
  1963, Oct.3/Coleen Buterbaugh/C.C.
  White bldg., Nebraska Wesleyan Univ.
    (Editorial), Fate 17 (Mar.1964):10-
    14, quoting Lincoln Nebraska State
    Journal (undated).
    Gardner Murphy & Herbert L. Klemme,
    "Unfinished Business," J.ASPR 60
    (1966):306-20.
    Brad Steiger, Irene Hughes on Psychic
    Safari (N.Y.: Warner, 1972), pp.
    126-40.
    D. Scott Rogo, An Experience of Phan-
    toms (N.Y.: Dell, 1976), pp.145-54.
-Haunt
  1970
    Brad Steiger, Irene Hughes on Psychic
    Safari (N.Y.: Warner, 1972), pp.107-
    24,141-55.
-UFO (?)
  1897, March
    Mt. Morris (Ill.) News, 7 Apr.1897,
    p.8.
-UFO (CE-1)
  1965, Aug.12/Don Huff/Missouri-Pacific
  train
    "Record Year for New UFO Evidence,"
    UFO Inv. 3 (Nov.-Dec.1965):2.
-UFO (CE-3)
  1922
    Gray Barker, Book of Saucers (Clarks-

burg, W.V.: Saucerian, 1965), p.41,
quoting Lincoln Daily Star (undated).
-UFO (NL)
1958, April 16
Richard Hall, ed., The UFO Evidence
(Washington: NICAP, 1964), p.156.
1959, Oct.6
Thomas M. Olson, ed., The Reference
for Outstanding UFO Sighting Reports
(Riderwood, Md.: UFO Information
Retrieval Center, 1966), p.68.
-UFO (R-V)
1957, Feb.13/Lincoln AFB
J. Allen Hynek, The UFO Experience
(Chicago: Regnery, 1972), p.84.
-Weather control
1890s/William F. Wright/chemical method
1890s/William B. Swisher/chemical meth-
od
Lincoln Nebraska State Journal, 4
Aug.1901.
Addison Erwin Sheldon, Nebraska Old
and New (Lincoln: University, 1937),
p.359.
Martha B. Caldwell, "Some Kansas
Rainmakers," Kansas Hist.Quar. 7
(Aug.1938):306,318-19.
Louise Pound, Nebraska Folklore
(Lincoln: Univ. of Nebraska, 1959),
pp.55-58.

Long Pine
-UFO (?)
1957, Sep.15/Clarence E. Potter/Hwy.7
x 20
(Letter), Fate 11 (June 1958):116-18.

Lyons
-Humanoid
1974, Aug./Irwin Wiese
Jerome Clark, "Are 'Manimals' Space
Beings?" Saga UFO Rept. 2 (summer
1975):49,51.
-UFO (NL)
1897, April 18
Omaha Daily Bee, 20 Apr.1897, p.5.

McPherson co.
-UFO (DD)
1916, April/Elizabeth Reams
1917, Aug./Elizabeth Reams
(Letter), Flying Saucers, Feb.1958,
p.62.

Madison
-Cattle mutilation
1974, June 10/John Sunderman
"The Midnight Marauders," Newsweek,
30 Sep.1974, p.32.
1974, July 6/Vern Stringfield
(Editorial), Fate 27 (Nov.1974):14-
16.

Minatare
-UFO (CE-3)
1967, March 26/Robert Lore
Ted Phillips, Physical Traces Associ-
ated with UFO Sightings (Evanston:
Center for UFO Studies, 1975), p.47.

Mitchell
-UFO (DD)
1949, July 26/H.G. LauBach
Kenneth Arnold & Ray Palmer, The Coming of the Saucers (Boise: The Author, 1952), p.143.
-UFO (NL)
1978, May 4
Scottsbluff Star-Herald, 6 May 1978.

Nebraska City
-UFO (DD)
1860, Sep.24/Joel Draper
Atlanta (Ga.) Constitution, 30 Sep.
1860.
-UFO (NL)
1897, April 8
Chicago (Ill.) Tribune, 10 Apr.1897,
p.1.
1976, Jan.5
"Noteworthy UFO Sightings," Ufology
2 (summer 1976):62.

Neligh
-Dowsing
1978/Merritt DeCamp
Kansas City (Mo.) Star, 29 Sep.1978.

Norfolk
-UFO (CE-1)
1897, April 15/W.H. Dexter
Norfolk News, 16 Apr.1897.
-UFO (NL)
1966, July 5/3 mi.NW
John A. Keel, UFOs: Operation Trojan
Horse (N.Y.: Putnam, 1970), p.152.

North Loup
-UFO (NL)
1897, March 13
Omaha Daily Bee, 16 Mar.1897, p.2.

North Platte
-UFO (?)
1897, April 18/William Smallwood
North Platte Daily Telegraph, 20
Apr.1897.
-UFO (CE-3)
1955, Aug.23-24/Elizabeth Reams
(Letter), Flying Saucers, Feb.1958,
p.63.
-UFO (NL)
1952, Sep./Elizabeth Reams
(Letter), Flying Saucers, Feb.1958,
p.63.
1965, Aug.2
Coral E. Lorenzen, "Western UFO Flap,"
Fate 18 (Nov.1965):42,49.
1978, June 17
Haverhill (Mass.) Gazette, 20 June
1978.

Oak
-UFO (NL)
1897, April 12/L.R. Young
Omaha Daily Bee, 14 Apr.1897, p.5.

Oakland
-Acoustic anomaly
1974, Aug.9/Gary Parker

Jerome Clark, "Are 'Manimals' Space Beings?" Saga UFO Rept. 2 (summer 1975):49,51.
-Humanoid
1974, July 4/Emory Wickstrom
1974, July 5/Dale Jones/2 mi.S
1974, Aug./Connie Johnson
Jerome Clark, "Are 'Manimals' Space Beings?" Saga UFO Rept. 2 (summer 1975):49,51.

Ogallala
-UFO (R-V)
1975, Oct.18
"Noteworthy UFO Sightings," Ufology 2 (spring 1976):43.

Omaha
-Airship inventor
1897, April/John O. Preast
Omaha Globe-Democrat, 10 Apr.1897.
1897, April/Clinton A. Case (A.C. Clinton)
Chicago (Ill.) Tribune, 12 Apr.1897, p.5; and 26 Apr.1897, p.3.
-Archeological site
Florence
Omaha World-Herald, 21 Oct.1906. il.
E.H. Barbour & H.B. Ward, "Discovery of an Early Type of Man in Nebraska," Science 24 (1906):628-29.
Henry Fairfield Osborn, "Discovery of a Supposed Primitive Race of Men in Nebraska," Century Mag. 51 (Jan. 1907):371-75. il.
Erwin Hinckley Barbour, "Evidence of Loess Man in Nebraska," Nebraska Geol.Survey 2, pt.6 (1907):331-48.
Robert F. Gilder, "Nebraska Loess," Am.Antiquarian 29 (1907):378-81.
-Erratic pelicans .
1978, May
St. Louis (Mo.) Globe-Democrat, 17 May 1978.
-Fall of ashes
1947, July 7/Fred R. Reibold/Himebaugh Ave.
Omaha World-Herald, 8 July 1947.
Ted Bloecher, Report on the UFO Wave of 1947 (Washington: NICAP, 1967), p.IV-2.
-Fall of iron ball
1957, Dec.13/Anton Timmerman
Coral E. Lorenzen, The Shadow of the Unknown (N.Y.: Signet, 1970), pp. 136-37.
-Haunt
1913, Jan./Court House/=hoax?
"Another Ghost Story," J.ASPR 7 (1913):392-94.
-Hex
1939, Aug.-Sep./Grazia Trino
William Seabrook, Witchcraft: Its Power in the World Today (N.Y.: Lancer, 1968 ed.), pp.21-22, quoting Omaha World-Herald (undated).
-Precognition
1957, March/D.A. Campbell
(Editorial), Fate 10 (Aug.1957):6.
-Reincarnation

1970
Hans Holzer, The New Pagans (Garden City: Doubleday, 1972), pp.47-56.
-Skyquake
1897, April 18
Omaha Daily Bee, 19 Apr.1897, p.6.
-UFO (?)
1957, June 13
Donald E. Keyhoe, Flying Saucers: Top Secret (N.Y.: Putnam, 1960), p.93.
1966, July 13
John A. Keel, UFOs: Operation Trojan Horse (N.Y.: Putnam, 1970), p.153.
1968, July 28/=meteor?
Philip J. Klass, UFOs Explained (N.Y.: Random House, 1974), pp.170-74.
1972, Aug.10/James Baker/=meteor (Editorial), Fate 28 (Apr.1975):30.
-UFO (CE-1)
1897, Feb.15
Omaha Daily Bee, 16 Feb.1897.
1967, Jan.18/Judy Bradley
"UFO with Ports at Omaha," APRO Bull. 15 (Jan.-Feb.1967):4.
-UFO (CE-3)
1976, Jan.2
"Sighting Reports," CUFOS News Bull., June 1976, p.4.
-UFO (DD)
1958, Sep.8/Paul A. Duich/Offutt AFB
Richard Hall, ed., The UFO Evidence (Washington: NICAP, 1964), pp.25,27.
-UFO (NL)
1897, March 14/I.J. Copenharve
Omaha Daily Bee, 14 Mar.1897, p.7.
1897, March 28/24th x Lake St.
Topeka (Kan.) State Journal, 29 Mar. 1897.
Omaha Daily Bee, 30 Mar.1897, p.8.
1897, April 5/O.D. Kiplinger/=hoax?
Omaha Daily Bee, 6 Apr.1897, p.2.
Omaha Morning World-Herald, 6 Apr. 1897, p.5; and 8 Apr.1897.
Chicago (Ill.) Tribune, 7 Apr.1897, p.1.
Cincinnati (O.) Enquirer, 13 Apr. 1897.
St. Louis (Mo.) Post-Dispatch, 14 Apr.1897.
Akron (O.) Times-Democrat, 14 Apr. 1897.
1947, July 3/Mrs. Fred Nelson/5530 Mayberry Ave.
Omaha World-Herald, 4 July 1947.
Ted Bloecher, Report on the UFO Wave of 1947 (Washington: NICAP, 1967), Appendix, p.4.
1947, July 5/Katherine Bauer/5525 S. 28th Ave.
Omaha World-Herald, 6 July 1947.
1947, July 6/N. 59th St.
Omaha World-Herald, 7 July 1947.
1953, Nov.9
Harold T. Wilkins, Flying Saucers Uncensored (N.Y.: Pyramid, 1967 ed.), pp.136-37.
1955, Nov.7-1956, Feb.2/Waldo B. Richards
(Letter), Fate 9 (June 1956):111-12.

1967, Jan.17/Jerry Swan
"Major Sighting Wave," UFO Inv. 3
(Jan.-Feb.1967):1,4.
1968, May 11/Brandeis Crossings Shop-
ping Center
Brad Steiger & Joan Whritenour, Fly-
ing Saucer Invasion: Target--Earth
(N.Y.: Award, 1969), pp.97-98.

O'Neill
-Weather control
1894, July-Aug./chemical method
Valentine Republican, 3-4 Aug.1894.

Ord
-UFO (?)
1966, July 13/George Bremer
John A. Keel, UFOs: Operation Trojan
Horse (N.Y.: Putnam, 1970), p.155.
-UFO (CE-3)
1978, Oct.8 /Deanne Kearns/2 mi.N of
North Loup R. bridge
Ord Quiz, 12 Oct.1978.
Grand Island Independent, 18 Oct.
1978.

Palmer
-UFO (CE-2)
1967, April?/George Szatko/5 mi.N
"Nebraska Sighting Recalled," Skylook, no.59 (Oct.1972):13.

Pender
-UFO (CE-4)
1977, Aug.12
1977, Sep.12, 27
Ted Bloecher, "A Survey of CE3K Re-
ports for 1977," in 1978 MUFON UFO
Symposium Proc. (Seguin, Tex.:
MUFON, 1978), pp.14,25,34,36.

Peru
-UFO (CE-1)
1951, Dec./NW of town
Jacques Vallee, Passport to Magonia
(Chicago: Regnery, 1969), p.197.
-UFO (CE-3)
1897, April 5/James Southard/N of town
Auburn Granger, 9 Apr.1897.

Pierce
-UFO (CE-2)
1973, Nov.
Pierce Pierce County Leader, 22 Nov.
1973.

Pierce co.
-Cattle mutilation
1974, Sep./Eugene Scott
Washington (D.C.) Post, 8 Sep.1974.

Plainview
-UFO (NL)
1897, April 13/Mr. Murphy
Chicago (Ill.) Times-Herald, 15 Apr.
1897, p.7.

Pleas nton
-UFO (?)
1966, July 13

John A. Keel, UFOs: Operation Trojan
Horse (N.Y.: Putnam, 1970), p.154.

Ponca
-UFO (?)
1897, April/=hoax
Ponca Northern Nebraska Journal, 22
Apr.1897.
Lincoln Evening Post, 22 Apr.1897.

Portal
-UFO (NL)
1897, April/Mrs. John McCarthy
Omaha Daily Bee, 20 Apr.1897, p.8.

Potter
-Fall of ice
ca.1875/Union Pacific RR
M.K. Jessup, The Case for the UFO
(N.Y.: Bantam, 1955 ed.), pp.43-44,
quoting Science Record, 1876.
1928, July 6/J.J. Norcross
Potter Review, 13 July 1928.
Thomas A. Blair, "Hailstones of Great
Size at Potter, Nebr.," Monthly
Weather Rev. 56 (Aug.1928):313. il.

Ravenna
-Humanoid
1959, Dec./Billy Hauschild/E of town
Omaha World-Herald, 24 Dec.1959.

Red Cloud
-UFO (NL)
1897, April 12/Dick Ferris
Omaha Daily Bee, 15 Apr.1897, p.1.

Sarpy co.
-Cattle mutilations and phantom helicopters
1974, March/Ernest Peterson
Washington (D.C.) Post, 8 Sep.1974.

Scotia
-UFO (?)
1966, July 13
John A. Keel, UFOs: Operation Trojan
Horse (N.Y.: Putnam, 1970), pp.152,
154.
-UFO (CE-2)
1957, Nov.3/Roger Groetzinger
Richard Hall, ed., The UFO Evidence
(Washington: NICAP, 1964), p.98.

Scottsbluff
-Animal ESP
1961-1964, March/Joe Martinez
(Editorial), Fate 17 (Oct.1964):18.
-Archeological site
Edwin Hinckley Barbour & C. Bertrand
Schultz, "The Scottsbluff Bison
Quarry and Its Artifacts," Bull.
Nebraska State Mus. 1 (1932):283-86.
il.
C. Bertrand Schultz & Loren C. Eise-
ley, "Paleontological Evidence of
the Antiquity of the Scottsbluff
Bison Quarry and Its Associated Ar-
tifacts," Am.Anthro. 37 (1935):306-
18.

C. Bertrand Schultz & Loren C. Eiseley, "An Added Note on the Scottsbluff Quarry," Am.Anthro. 38 (1936):521-24.
Don Antisdal, "The Scottsbluff Site," Newsl.Northwest Chapter Iowa Arch. Soc'y 8, no.6 (1960):7-8.
-UFO (NL)
  1965, Aug.2
    Coral E. Lorenzen, "Western UFO Flap," Fate 18 (Nov.1965):42,49.

Scribner
-UFO (NL)
  1967, Nov.19/nr. Maple Creek
    "More U.S.A. November Reports," APRO Bull. 16 (Jan.-Feb.1968):6.

Sidney
-UFO (NL)
  1965, July 31-Aug.1/Lee Beekin/Sioux Ordnance Depot
    Coral E. Lorenzen, "Western UFO Flap," Fate 18 (Nov.1965):42,50, quoting Omaha World-Herald (undated).
    J. Allen Hynek, The UFO Experience (Chicago: Regnery, 1972), p.185.
-Weather control
  1890s/chemical method
    Mari Sandoz, Old Jules (Boston: Little, Brown, 1935), pp.149-52.

Silver Creek
-UFO (NL)
  1897, April 15/Charles Dee
    Omaha Daily Bee, 17 Apr.1897, p.2.

South Sioux City
-UFO (CE-1)
  1976, Dec.1/Dale Spath/Roundhouse Rd. x I-29
    Laurence Lacey, "Red Object Hovers behind Highway Overpass in Nebraska," MUFON UFO J., no.109 (Dec.1976):3-4. il.
    Bill Slaughter, "Reddish-Orange UFO Spotted," MUFON UFO J., no.109 (Dec.1976):11.
-UFO (CE-2)
  1972, Jan./Dave Snyder
    Laurence Lacey, "Red Object Hovers behind Highway Overpass in Nebraska," MUFON UFO J., no.109 (Dec.1976):3-4.
-UFO (NL)
  1976, Nov./Dave Snyder
    Laurence Lacey, "Red Object Hovers behind Highway Overpass in Nebraska," MUFON UFO J., no.109 (Dec.1976):3-4.

Stanton
-UFO (CE-1)
  1975, March 2/Dave Dolezal (Letter), Saga UFO Rept. 2 (summer 1975):77.

Sweetwater
-Archeological site
  1100-1450

John L. Champe, "The Sweetwater Culture Complex," in E.H. Bell, Chapters in Nebraska Archeology (Lincoln: Univ. of Nebraska, 1936), 1:249-99. il.

Table Rock
-UFO (NL)
  1897, April 13
    Table Rock Argus, 16 Apr.1897.

Tekamah
-UFO (?)
  1897, April 9/=balloon
    Omaha Daily Bee, 14 Apr.1897, p.5.

Utica
-Mystery television transmission
  1968
    Eric Norman [Warren Smith], Gods, Demons and UFOs (N.Y.: Lancer, 1970), pp.83-84.

Valentine
-UFO (NL)
  1965, Aug.2/Judi Hatcher
    Coral E. Lorenzen, "Western UFO Flap," Fate 18 (Nov.1965):42,50, quoting Lincoln Nebraska State Journal (undated).
    J. Allen Hynek, The UFO Experience (Chicago: Regnery, 1972), betw. pp. 52-53. il.

Valparaiso
-Mystery bird deaths
  1975, Nov.9/Ermin Bennes
    Harrisburg (Pa.) Patriot, 13 Nov. 1975.

Verdigre
-Clairvoyance
  1902, winter/Lucy Darling
    Grace Darling Ludwick, "My Mother's Miracles," Fate 9 (Apr.1956):72, 74-75.

Wahoo
-UFO (NL)
  1968, April 25/Kenneth Dailey
    "U.S. Reports," APRO Bull. 17 (Sep.-Oct.1968):6.

Waterloo
-Weather control
  1976, June/Sioux Indians
    Omaha World-Herald, 18 June 1976. il.

Wayne co.
-Telepathy
  1897, Feb.
    Omaha Daily Bee, 8 Feb.1897, p.2.

Wilsonville
-UFO (?)
  1897, April 5/=hoax
    Wilsonville Review, 6 Apr.1897.

Wymore
-UFO (NL)

1897, Feb.25/Joe Litty
Wymore Arbor State, 5 Mar.1897.

York
-UFO (?)
1966, July 13
John A. Keel, UFOs: Operation Trojan
Horse (N.Y.: Putnam, 1970), p.154.
-UFO (NL)
1897, Feb.7/George S. Cook
Omaha Daily Bee, 9 Feb.1897, p.2.
1947, July 8
Fargo (N.D.) Forum, 9 July 1947.

B. Physical Features

Ash Hollow Cave
-Archeological site
ca.2000 B.C.-1700 A.D.
John L. Champe, "Ash Hollow Cave,"
Univ.Nebraska Studies, ser.2, no.1
(1946). il.

Big Bear Hollow
-Humanoid myth
Lincoln Journal and Star, 9 Dec.1934.
Nebraska Writers' Program, Nebraska:
A Guide to the Cornhusker State
(N.Y.: Viking, 1939), p.261.
Roger L. Welsch, A Treasury of Ne-
braska Pioneer Folklore (Lincoln:
Univ. of Nebraska, 1966), pp.182-
85.

Blackbird Hill
-Haunt
n.d.
Roger L. Welsch, A Treasury of Nebraska Pioneer Folklore (Lincoln:
Univ. of Nebraska, 1966), pp.181-
82.

Dismal R.
-Archeological site
John L. Champe, "White Cat Village,"
Am.Antiquity 14 (1949):285-92. il.
James H. Gunnerson, "An Introduction
to Plains Apache Archeology--the
Dismal River Aspect," Bull.Bur.Am.
Ethn., no.173 (1960):131-260.

Lime Creek
-Archeological site
ca.8000 B.C.
Preston Holder & Joyce Wike, "The
Frontier Culture Complex: A Prelim-
inary Report on a Prehistoric Hunt-
er's Camp in Southwestern Nebraska,"
Am.Antiquity 14 (1949):260-66. il.
E. Mott Davis, "Recent Data from Two
Paleo-Indian Sites on Medicine
Creek, Nebraska," Am.Antiquity 18
(1953):380-86. il.
E. Mott Davis, Archeology of the Lime
Creek Site in Southwestern Nebraska
(Lincoln: Univ. of Nebraska State
Museum, Spec.Pub.no.3, 1962). il.

Logan Creek
-Archeological site
6000-4000 B.C.
Waldo R. Wedel, Prehistoric Man on
the Great Plains (Norman: Univ. of
Oklahoma, 1961), pp.87,283.

Missouri R.
-River monster
1857-1858
Jerome Clark & Loren Coleman, "Serpents and UFOs," Flying Saucer Rev.
18 (May-June 1972):18,20.

Mowry Bluff
-Archeological site
ca.1150-1200
W.R. Wood, ed., "Two House Sites in
the Central Plains: An Experiment
in Archeology," Plains Anthro., Mem.
6, vol.14, no.44, pt.2 (1969). il.
Waldo R. Wedel, "Some Observations
on Two House Sites in the Central
Plains: An Experiment in Archeology," Nebraska History 51 (1970):
225-52.

Nehawka Flint Quarry
-Archeological site
ca.3000 B.C.-1500 A.D.
William D. Strong, "An Introduction
to Nebraska Archaeology," Smith.
Misc.Coll. 39, no.10 (1935):43-44,
203-205.

Nemaha R.
-Archeological site
1500-1600/Leary site
A.T. Hill & Waldo R. Wedel, "Excavations at the Leary Indian Village
and Burial Site, Richardson County,
Nebraska," Nebraska History Mag. 17
(1936):2-73. il.
William M. Bass, "1960 Excavations
at the Leary Site, 25RH1, Richardson County, Nebraska," Plains Anthro. 6 (1961):201-202.

Pine Ridge
-Archeological site
ca.7000 B.C.
Larry D. Agenbroad, "The Hudson-Meng
Site: An Alberta Bison Kill on the
High Plains," Plains Anthro. 23
(1978):128-31.

Pony Creek
-Phantom panther tracks
1965, March/Roy Pardee
Jerome Clark & Loren Coleman, "On
the Trail of Pumas, Panthers and
ULAs: Part 2," Fate 75 (July 1972):
92,97.

Signal Butte
-Archeological site
2500 B.C.-1700 A.D.
"Excavations on Signal Butte," El
Palacio 33 (1932):151.

William D. Strong, "An Introduction
Nebraska Archeology," Smith.Misc.
Coll. 93, no.10 (1935):224-39.

Walgren L.
-Lake monster
1880s-1920s
    Minneapolis (Minn.) Journal, 25-27
    July 1922.
    Hay Springs News, 23 Mar.1923; and
    6 July 1925.
    Omaha World-Herald, 20 Nov.1925.
    Rushville Recorder, 2 Sep.1937.
    Louise Pound, Nebraska Folklore (Lin-
    coln: Univ. of Nebraska, 1959), pp.
    114-16.

Winnebago Creek
-Phantom panther
1964
    Jerome Clark & Loren Coleman, "On the
    Trail of Pumas, Panthers and ULAs:
    Part 2," Fate 25 (July 1972):92,97.

                C. Ethnic Groups

Omaha Indians
-Humanoid myth
  pa-snu-ta
    Eric Norman [Brad Steiger], The Abom-
    inable Snowman (N.Y.: Award, 1969),
    p.70.
-Lake monster myth
  wakandagi
    R.F. Fortune, Omaha Secret Societies
    (N.Y.: AMS, 1969), pp.90-97.
-Shamanism
    Alice C. Fletcher, "The Supernatural
    among the Omaha Tribe of Indians,"
    Proc.ASPR 1 (1887):135-50.
    Alice C. Fletcher & Francis la
    Flesche, "The Omaha Tribe," Ann.
    Rept.Bur.Am.Ethn. 27 (1905-1906):17,
    459-602.
    R.F. Fortune, Omaha Secret Societies
    (N.Y.: AMS, 1969).
-Weather control
    J. Owen Dorsey, "Omaha Sociology,"
    Ann.Rept.Bur.Am.Ethn. 3 (1881):211,
    241,347.

Oto Indians
-Humanoid myth
    Meriwether Lewis, History of the Ex-
    pedition under the Command of Cap-
    tains Lewis and Clark, 2 vols.
    (Philadelphia: Bradford & Inskeep,
    1814), 1:52-53.

Pawnee Indians
-Contactee myth
    George A. Dorsey, The Pawnee Myth-
    ology (Part 1) (Washington: Carnegie
    Institute, Pub.no.59, 1906), pp.
    56-58,61-62.
-Paleoastronomy
    Waldo R. Wedel, "Native Astronomy and
    the Plains Caddoans," in Anthony F.
    Aveni, ed., Native American Astron-

omy (Austin: Univ. of Texas, 1977),
    pp.131-45.
-Weather control
    Ralph Linton, The Thunder Ceremony
    of the Pawnee (Chicago: Field Mus.,
    Antho.leaflet no.5, 1922). il.

Winnebago Indians
-Lake monster myth
  waktchexi
    Albert S. Gatschet, "Water-Monsters
    of the American Aborigines," J.Am.
    Folklore 12 (1899):255-60.

            D. Unspecified Localities

-Cattle mutilation
1978, Jan./western sector
    "A Rancher's Report," Stigmata, no.3
    (May 1978):2.

KANSAS

A. Populated Places

Abilene
-Electromagnetic anomaly
  1965, Aug.4/Girl Scout camp
    Abilene Reflector-Chronicle, 7 Aug.
    1965, p.1.
-Erratic kangaroo
  1965, July 26/Bert Radar/E on I-70
    Kansas City (Mo.) Star, 19 Aug.1965.
  1971, Nov.1/Mrs. Edward Johnson
    "UFO Knocks Down Tree," Skylook, no.
    50 (Jan.1972):2,3, quoting Wichita
    Eagle (undated).
-UFO (?)
  1965, Aug./country club golf course/=
  golf cart tracks
    Abilene Reflector-Chronicle, 6 Aug.
    1965, p.1.
-UFO (CE-2)
  1965, Aug.4/Don Tennopir/25 mi.S on
  Hwy.15
    Wichita Beacon, 4 Aug.1965, p.5A.
    Abilene Reflector-Chronicle, 5 Aug.
    1965, p.1.

Agra
-UFO (CE-1)
  1965, Nov.17/Rita Goracke
    Phillipsburg Phillips County Review,
    2 Dec.1965, p.1.

Arkansas City
-UFO (?)
  1897, April/=hoax
    Arkansas City Gate City Journal, 23
    Apr.1897, p.2.
-UFO (NL)
  1956, July 19/Brian Coyne
    Arkansas City Daily Traveler, 19
    July 1956, p.1.
    Topeka Daily Capital, 20 July 1956,
    p.3.
  1972, Aug.24-25/Beth Lilley/=Venus?
    Kansas City (Mo.) Star, 27 Aug.1972,
    p.4.
    (Editorial), Fate 26 (Jan.1973):30,
    quoting AP release, 25 Aug.1972;
    and 27 Aug.1972.
    Philip J. Klass, UFOs Explained (N.Y.:
    Random House, 1974), pp.85-86.

Ashland
-Bird attack
  1978, Aug.
    Kansas City (Mo.) Star, 18 Aug.1978.

Atchison
-Cattle mutilation
  1979, March 14/Leonard Penning
    Atchison Globe, 15 Mar.1979.
-Erratic crocodilian
  1869, Aug./Missouri R.
    St. Louis (Mo.) Democrat, 3 Sep.1869,
    p.1.
-UFO (?)
  1897, March 28/wild geese singed
    Atchison Daily Champion, 29 Mar.
    1897, p.4.
-UFO (NL)
  1897, April 2
    Atchison Daily Champion, 2 Apr.1897,
    p.1; and 3 Apr.1897, p.4.
  1897, April 16/Mrs. J.A. Harouff
    Atchison Daily Champion, 17 Apr.1897,
    p.4.
  1897, April 19/Charley Garside
    Atchison Daily Champion, 19 Apr.1897,
    p.4.
  1957, Aug.15/Violet Cleveland/Profes-
  sional Bldg.
    Atchison Daily Globe, 16 Aug.1957.

Attica
-Anomalous hole in ground
  1963, Feb.7-March/nr. Bluff Creek/=
  gas geyser
    (Editorial), Fate 16 (Aug.1963):22.

Atwood
-UFO (NL)
  1967, March 12
    Norton Daily Telegram, 14 Mar.1967,
    p.5.

Baxter Springs
-Human track in sandstone
  1963
    Seattle (Wash.) Post-Intelligencer,
    15 Apr.1963.

Belle Plaine
-UFO (?)
  1965, Aug.2
    Jacques & Janine Vallee, Challenge
    to Science (N.Y.: Ace, 1966 ed.),
    p.66.

Belleville
-UFO (NL)
  1897, March 26/J.A. Rhea
    Topeka Daily Capital, 28 Mar.1897,
    p.1.
    Chicago (Ill.) Tribune, 29 Mar.1897.
    p.4.
    Salina Weekly Republican-Journal, 2
    Apr.1897.

Bonner Springs
-Cattle mutilation
  1975, Nov.15/Jim Kreider/122d St.
    Bonner Springs Chieftain, 20 Nov.
    1975.
-Erratic peccary
  1937, Dec./Roy Jons
    Bonner Springs Chieftain, 26 Dec.
    1937.
-Humanoid

1978, Sep.28/E on I-70
Topeka Capital-Journal, 30 Sep.1978,
p.6.
-Phantom panther
1938, April 5/Mrs. C.B. South/Jaggard
Station
Bonner Springs Chieftain, 7 Apr.1938;
and 14 Apr.1938.
-UFO (NL)
1977, May 11
"UFO Analysis," Int'l UFO Reporter
2 (June 1977):9.

Burdett
-Cattle mutilation
1976, Sep.29/Adam Hummel/5 mi.SW
Larned Tiller and Toiler, 29 Sep.
1976.
-UFO (NL)
1972, Feb./Alice Coe
Larned Tiller and Toiler, 8 Feb.
1972.

Caldwell
-UFO (CE-1)
1965, Aug.2/Edwin Roberts/airport
Wichita Beacon, 2 Aug.1965, p.1.
Kansas City (Mo.) Star, 2 Aug.1965.

Cawker City
-UFO (?)
1978, Dec.31/Viola Kincheloe/=flare?
Belleville Telescope, 11 Jan.1979.

Chanute
-Crisis apparition
1926, June/Rosalind John
Rosalind John, "Olga Keeps Her Pro-
mise," Fate 8 (Apr.1955):71-73.
-Dog mutilation
1978, April
Kansas City (Mo.) Times, 10 Apr.
1978, p.4A.
-Healing
1933, Aug.30/Helen Donaldson/201 S.
Santa Fe
Chanute Tribune, 31 Aug.1933, p.1;
1 Sep.1933, p.1; and 5 Sep.1933, p.1.
Rosalind John, "It Was Jesus," Fate
15 (Mar.1962):37-39.

Chapman
-UFO (NL)
1897, April 12/NW of town
Salina Weekly Republican-Journal, 16
April 1897.

Chetopa
-Humanoid tracks
1978, Feb./=hoax
Kansas City (Mo.) Times, 20 Feb.1978.

Clay Center
-Mystery auto accidents
1978, Jan.-Oct./W on U.S.24
Clay Center Dispatch, 19 Oct.1978.
-UFO (DD)
1947, July 6/Archie B. Browning
Ted Bloecher, Report on the UFO Wave
of 1947 (Washington: NICAP, 1967),

p.III-11.

Coffeyville
-Fall of ashes
1953, July 2/New x Maple St.
Coffeyville Daily Journal, 3 July
1953, p.1.
-Horse mutilation
1977, Nov./Roy K. Hartwig
Kansas City (Mo.) Star, 20 Nov.1977.
-Mystery radio transmission
1967, Jan./C.V. Robinson
John A. Keel, "Mysterious Voices
from Outer Space," Saga UFO Rept. 2
(winter 1975):36,38.
-UFO (?)
1967, Jan.16/=rocket
Edward U. Condon, ed., Scientific
Study of Unidentified Flying Objects
(N.Y.: Bantam, 1969 ed.), p.288.
-UFO (CE-1)
1956, April 2/R.H. Smith/3 mi.E
Coffeyville Daily Journal, 3 Apr.
1956, p.1.
Luis Schönherr, "Time Travel, UFOs,
and the Fourth Dimension," Flying
Saucer Rev. 22 (Oct.1976):11,12.
-UFO (NL)
1973, Nov.2/Kim Lofts
Chanute Tribune, 3 Nov.1973.

Colby
-UFO (CE-2)
1972, Aug.19/Paul Carter/2 mi.S
Kansas City (Mo.) Star, 20 Aug.1972,
p.5A; and 21 Aug.1972, p.3.
"Spectacular Report from Kansas,"
APRO Bull. 21 (July-Aug.1972):1,4.
Salina Journal, 12 Sep.1972.
Hayden C. Hewes, "UFOs over Kansas,"
Fate 26 (Mar.1973):84-87. il.
-UFO (NL)
1967, March 8
Norton Daily Telegram, 14 Mar.1967,
p.1.

Coldwater
-UFO (CE-3)
1954, Sep./John J. Swaim
Wichita Evening Eagle, 8 Sep.1954,
pp.1A,1C.
Pratt Daily Tribune, 14 Sep.1954.
Coral Lorenzen, "UFO Occupants in
United States Reports," in The Hu-
manoids (Flying Saucer Rev. special
issue no.1, 1967), pp.53-54.

Columbus
-UFO (NL)
1967, Jan.13
Pittsburg Headlight-Sun, 14 Jan.1967,
p.1.

Concordia
-Cattle mutilation
1973, Dec.20/Ross Doyen/2 mi.E
Kansas City (Mo.) Times, 22 Dec.1973,
p.1A. il.
Jerome Clark, "Strange Case of the
Cattle Killings," Fate 27 (Aug.1974)

:79,84,87.
-UFO (?)
  1967, Dec.5
    Edward U. Condon, ed., Scientific
    Study of Unidentified Flying Objects
    (N.Y.: Bantam, 1969 ed.), pp.391-94.
    Donald H. Menzel & Ernest H. Taves,
    The UFO Enigma (Garden City: Double-
    day, 1977), p.108.
-UFO (NL)
  1897, March
    Chicago (Ill.) Tribune, 29 Mar.1897,
    p.4.
  1978, July 31/Curtis Sullivan
    Concordia Blade-Empire, 31 July 1978.

Conway Springs
-Cattle mutilation
  1977, June 11/Clem Baldwin/SW of town
    Kansas City (Mo.) Times, 15 June
    1977.

Cunningham
-UFO (NL)
  1961, Aug.4
    Curtis Fuller, "The Boys Who 'Caught'
    a Flying Saucer," Fate 15 (Jan.
    1962):36,40.

Delia
-Fall of unknown object
  1971, Feb.1/Fred Lundin/=aerial flare
    "Fall of Burning Material in Kansas,"
    APRO Bull. 19 (Jan.-Feb.1971):1,3.
    "Follow-Up," APRO Bull. 19 (Mar.-
    Apr.1971):2,4.
-Humanoid and hog killings
  1964, July 20/Roy McKinsey
    Topeka Daily Capital, 21 July 1964,
    p.1.

Delphos
-Fall of ice
  1879, May 29/Peter Bock
    J.P. Finley, "Report of the Tornadoes
    of May 29 and 30, 1879, in Kansas,
    Nebraska, Missouri, and Iowa," Prof.
    Pap.Signal Service, no.4 (1881):67.
-Feral child
  1974, July 22-29/Mrs. Joe Stout
    Kansas City (Mo.) Times, 29 July
    1974.
    Wichita Morning Eagle, 31 July 1974.
-Phantom panther
  1974, July 16/Larry Kline
    Delphos Republican, 18 July 1974.
-UFO (CE-2)
  1971, Nov.2/Ronald Johnson
    Delphos Republican, 4 Nov.1971, p.1.
    "Landing Case in Kansas," APRO Bull.
    20 (Nov.-Dec.1971):1,3. il.
    Valley Falls Vindicator, 23 Dec.1971.
    Kietha M. Fish, "Kansas UFO Landing,"
    Kansas-Oklahoma Newsl., Feb.1972,
    pp.6-8.
    Ted Phillips, "Landing Report from
    Delphos," FSR Case Histories, no.9
    (Feb.1972):4-10. il.
    "More on Kansas Case," APRO Bull. 20
    (Mar.-Apr.1972):8-9.

Ted Phillips, "Delphos, Kansas--An
Interim Report," Skylook, no.58
(Sep.1972):2-4.
"'National Enquirer' Awards $5,000,"
APRO Bull. 21 (Mar.-Apr.1973):1,4.
B. Ann Slate, "Kansas UFO Leaves
Hard Evidence," Fate 26 (Apr.1973):
88-96. il.
Philip J. Klass, UFOs Explained (N.Y.:
Random House, 1974), pp.312-32. il.
Ted Phillips, Physical Traces Associ-
ated with UFO Sightings (Evanston:
Center for UFO Studies, 1975), pp.
79,137-38.
B. Ann Slate, "The Amazing UFO Dis-
coveries of Peter Hurkos," Saga UFO
Rept. 2 (winter 1975):27,29-30.
(Letter), Donald F. Weitzel, Fate
28 (Aug.1975):115-16.
Hayden Hewes, "The Delphos Landing
Case: Part 2," Official UFO 1 (Jan.
1976):39,63-66.

Dighton
-UFO (CE-2)
  1972, July/Pam Krehbiel/ground markings
  only
    Ted Phillips, Physical Traces Associ-
    ated with UFO Sightings (Evanston:
    Center for UFO Studies, 1975), p.
    84, quoting Garden City Telegram
    (undated).
-UFO (NL)
  1972, Feb.-May/M.R. Shelton/10 mi.W
  1972, March 22-24/John Banninger
  1972, July 5-9/John Banninger
  1972, Aug.15-16/John Banninger
    "Kansas UFO Reports," APRO Bull. 21
    (July-Aug.1972):5.
    "Were Kansas Sightings Weather Bal-
    loons?" Skylook, no.59 (Oct.1972):
    18.
    Hayden C. Hewes, "UFOs over Kansas,"
    Fate 26 (Mar.1973):84,87-89.

Dodge City
-Airship inventor
  1897, April/Charles Clinton
    Chicago (Ill.) Journal, 12 Apr.1897,
    p.8.
    Dodge City Globe-Republican, 15 Apr.
    1897, p.1.
-UFO (NL)
  1951, May 22/W.R. Hunt
    Harold T. Wilkins, Flying Saucers on
    the Attack (N.Y.: Ace, 1967 ed.),
    p.139.
    Richard Hall, ed., The UFO Evidence
    (Washington: NICAP, 1964), p.34,
    quoting UP release, 23 May 1951.
  1964, Sep.12/Martin Caidin/5 mi.N
    "Martin Caidin Observes UFO," APRO
    Bull. 13 (Nov.1964):3.

Doniphan
-Phantom
  1921, Aug./Doniphan L.
    Atchison Daily Globe, 12 Aug.1921,
    p.5; and 19 Aug.1921, p.4.

Douglass
-UFO (NL)
  1897, April
    Wichita Daily Eagle, 4 Apr.1897, p.9.

DuQuoin
-UFO (NL)
  1966, July 13/Elmer Spain/3 mi.N
    Kingman Leader-Courier, 15 July 1966,
    p.1; and 16 July 1966, p.1.

Edwardsville
-UFO (DD)
  1878, July 29/J.F. Timmons
    Atchison Globe, 7 Aug.1878.

El Dorado
-Fall of frogs
  1957, July
    El Dorado Times, 3 July 1957; and
    26 July 1957.
-Phantom
  1891, Aug./William Allen White
    William Allen White, Autobiography
    (N.Y.: Macmillan, 1966 ed.), p.200.
-UFO (?)
  1956, July 19
    Denver (Colo.) Post, 19 July 1956.
    Topeka Daily Capital, 20 July 1956,
    p.3.
-UFO (CE-2)
  1969, March 24/Steve Gladfelter/4 mi.
    SE
    "Strange Lights Deflect Car's Steer-
    ing," Skylook, no.19 (June 1969):7.

Ellinwood
-Poltergeist
  1927, summer/Fred Koett
    New York Herald-Tribune, 12 Aug.1927.
-UFO (?)
  1972, Aug.
    Hayden C. Hewes, "UFOs over Kansas,"
    Fate 26 (Mar.1973):84,89.

Ellis
-UFO (?)
  1944, June?/S of town
    "Family Has Repeat Sightings," APRO
    Bull. 26 (May 1978):4.
-UFO (CE-1)
  1960, summer/3 mi.E
    "Family Has Repeat Sightings," APRO
    Bull. 26 (May 1978):4.
-UFO (NL)
  1972, Aug.16
    Kansas City (Mo.) Times, 17 Aug.1972,
    p.6A.
    Hayden C. Hewes, "UFOs over Kansas,"
    Fate 26 (Mar.1973):84,88-89.

Ellsworth
-UFO (NL)
  1972, Aug.17
    Kansas City (Mo.) Times, 18 Aug.1972,
    p.26.

El Quartelejo
-Archeological site
  1660-1720

S.W. Williston & H.T. Martin, "Some
  Pueblo Ruins in Scott County, Kan-
  sas," Kansas Hist.Coll. 6 (1897-
  1900):124-30.
H.T. Martin, "Further Notes on the
  Pueblo Ruins of Scott County," Sci.
  Bull.Univ.Kansas, vol.5, no.2 (1910).
  Scott City News-Chronicle, 24 June
  1937, p.26.
Thomas A. Witty, "Reconstruction of
  the Scott County Pueblo Ruins,"
  Newsl.Kansas Anthro.Ass'n 16 (Apr.
  1971):1-3.
"El Cuartelejo," Kansas!, 1st issue,
  1972, pp.7-8. il.

Emporia
-Lightning anomaly
  1891, April 29/Redmond P. Dwyer
    St. Louis (Mo.) Republic, 29 Apr.
    1891.
-Spirit medium
  1890s/David Lewis
    William Allen White, In Our Town
    (N.Y.: McClure, Phillips, 1906), pp.
    40-71.
-Telepathy
  n.d./James King
    "The Bond between Twins," Fate 10
    (Aug.1957):88.
-UFO (?)
  1897, April 4/=Venus
    Atchison Daily Champion, 5 Apr.1897,
    p.1.
-UFO (NL)
  1897, April 10/Willie Puffer
    Emporia Daily Gazette, 11 Apr.1897,
    p.1.
  1956, July 19/Merle Hayes
    Arkansas City Daily Traveler, 19
    July 1956, p.1.

Erie
-Precognition
  1962/Judy Beeney/=inaccurate
    (Editorial), Fate 15 (Sep.1962):14.

Eureka
-UFO (NL)
  1897, April 16/S.N. Warner
    Eureka Democratic Messenger, 22 Apr.
    1897, p.3.
  1897, May 3/Mrs. J.J. Durkee/White
    Bldg.
    Eureka Herald, 7 May 1897, p.1.
  1956, July 19
    Topeka Daily Capital, 20 July 1956,
    p.3.

Everest
-UFO (NL)
  1897, April 1/J.E. Gun
    Topeka State Journal, 2 Apr.1897, p.3.
    Wichita Daily Eagle, 2 Apr.1897, p.2.
    Kansas City (Mo.) Times, 2 Apr.1897,
    p.1.

Fairview
-Dowsing
  1872/S.D. Storrs

Bliss Isely, Sunbonnet Days (Caldwell,
Ida.: Caxton, 1935), pp.176-79.

Fort Riley
-Haunt
1952/William A. Gibbons/Custer house
"Custer's Last Stand?" Fate 5 (Nov.
1952):35.
-UFO (CE-2)
1964, Dec.10/crashed UFO
Leonard H. Stringfield, "Retrievals
of the Third Kind--Part 2," MUFON
UFO J., no.129 (Aug.1978):8,11-12.
-UFO (NL)
1967, Nov.4/U.S.77 x Hwy.82
"Ft. Riley Unit Watches UFOs," Sky-
look, no.3 (Nov.1967):5.

Fort Scott
-UFO (?)
1873, June 26
Fort Scott Daily Monitor, 27 June
1873, p.1.
New York Times, 7 July 1873, p.4.

Frontenac
-UFO (CE-2)
1952, Aug.25/William V. Squyres/Yale
Rd. x U.S.160
Pittsburg Headlight, 25 Aug.1952, p.
1.
Neosho (Mo.) Daily Democrat, 26 Aug.
1952.
Thomas M. Olsen, ed., The Reference
for Outstanding UFO Sighting Reports
(Riderwood, Md.: UFO Information Re-
trieval Center, 1966), pp.16-18.
Gray Barker, They Knew Too Much About
Flying Saucers (N.Y.: University,
1956), pp.76-78.
J. Allen Hynek, The Hynek UFO Report
(N.Y.: Dell, 1977), pp.200-203.

Gardner
-UFO (DD)
1975, Oct.7
"Noteworthy UFO Sightings," Ufology
2 (spring 1976):42.

Gaylord
-Haunt
1887, Nov./3 mi. from town
Voltaire Sherman County News, 2 Dec.
1887.

Gem
-UFO (CE-1)
1972, Aug.19/John Calkins
Kansas City (Mo.) Star, 20 Aug.1972,
p.5A; and 21 Aug.1972, p.3.

Girard
-UFO (NL)
1897, April 1
Girard Press, 8 Apr.1897.

Goddard
-UFO (CE-2)
1967, Feb.9/Wes Herbert
"UFO, Barn Fire Connected," APRO Bull.

15 (Jan.-Feb.1967):7.

Goodland
-UFO (CE-4)
1976, June 20/E on I-70
"Abduction in Western Kansas," Int'l
UFO Reporter 2 (Oct.1977):4-7. il.
(Letter), Richard Sigismond, Int'l
UFO Reporter 2 (Nov.1977):2.
-UFO (NL)
1967, March 8/Ron Weehunt
Norton Daily Telegram, 14 Mar.1967,
p.1.
-Weather control
1892-1893/Clayton B. Jewell/chemical
method
Mark W. Harrington, "Weather Making
Ancient and Modern," Ann.Rept.Smith.
Inst., 1894, pp.260-67.
Walter Prescott Webb, The Great Plains
(Boston: Ginn, 1931), pp.382-83.
Martha B. Caldwell, "Some Kansas
Rainmakers," Kansas Hist.Quar. 7
(1938):306,320-24.

Gorham
-Phantom airplane
1978, July 22
Russell Daily News, 24 July 1978.

Greensburg
-Tornado anomaly
1928, June 22/Will Keller/3 mi.SE
Alonzo A. Justice, "Seeing the Inside
of a Tornado," Monthly Weather Rev.
58 (May 1930):205-206.

Haddam
-UFO (?)
1897, March
Mt. Morris (Ill.) News, 7 Apr.1897,
p.8.

Harper
-Cattle mutilation
1979, Feb./Glenn Hall/4 mi.N on Mur-
dock Rd.
Harper Advocate, 22 Feb.1979.

Haviland
-Meteorite crater
15 m.diam. x 3 m.deep/certain
H.H. Nininger & J.D. Figgins, "Notes
on the Excavation of the Haviland,
Kiowa County, Kansas, Meteorite Cra-
ter," Proc.Colorado Mus.Nat.Hist. 12,
no.3 (1933):9-15.
H.H. Nininger, "Further Notes on the
Excavation of the Haviland, Kiowa
County, Kansas, Meteorite Crater,"
Pop.Astron. 46 (1938):110.

Hays
-UFO (NL)
1957, Oct.24
"All about Sputs," Doubt, no. 56
(1958):460,469.
1966, spring/NW of town
"Family Has Repeat Sightings," APRO
Bull. 16 (May 1978):4-5.

1972, Aug.15-16/Glen Windholz
Kansas City (Mo.) Times, 17 Aug.1972,
p.6C; and 19 Aug.1972, p.5A.
Kansas City (Mo.) Star, 20 Aug.1972,
p.5A.
Hayden C. Hewes, "UFOs over Kansas,"
Fate 26 (Mar.1973):84,88.

Helena
-Archeological site
140 B.C.-330 A.D.
James A. Ford, "Hopewell Culture
Burial Mounds near Helena, Kansas,"
Anthro.Pap.Am.Mus.Nat.Hist., no.50
(1963):3-55. il.

Hiawatha
-UFO (NL)
1897, March 27
Chicago (Ill.) Tribune, 29 Mar.1897,
p.4.
Hiawatha Kansas Democrat, 1 Apr.1897,
p.7.

Hill City
-UFO (?)
1969, April 14/Edwin H. Bohl, Jr./5 mi.
E on Hwy.24
"Kansas Man Goes UFO Hunting--Finds
One!" Skylook, no.20 (July 1969):4.
"UFO Hunt Was Too Easy," Skylook, no.
21 (Aug.1969):17.

Hillsboro
-UFO (CE-2)
1967, March 21/Mary Beth Neufeld/1 mi.
W on U.S.56
"Car Buzzing Incidents on Increase,"
APRO Bull. 15 (May-June 1967):5.
-UFO (CE-4)
1971, Nov.
Wichita Beacon, 2 June 1978.

Holton
-UFO (CE-2)
1972, June/ground markings only
Ted Phillips, Physical Traces Associ-
ated with UFO Sightings (Evanston:
Center for UFO Studies, 1975), p.69.
-UFO (NL)
1897, March 27
Chicago (Ill.) Tribune, 29 Mar.1897,
p.4.

Holyrood
-UFO (?)
1972, Aug.18
"Press Reports," APRO Bull. 21 (July-
Aug.1972):8.

Humboldt
-Electromagnetic anomaly
1970, June 26/Humboldt Hill on U.S.169
Humboldt Union, 2 July 1970, p.1.
Topeka Daily Capital, 2 July 1970,
p.30.
-Phantom panther tracks
n.d.
Topeka Daily Capital, 2 July 1970,
p.30.

-UFO (CE-2)
ca.1967/Humboldt Hill
Topeka Daily Capital, 2 July 1970,
p.30.

Hutchinson
-Inner development
1970s/School of Metaphysics/1006 N.
Main
Hutchinson News, 13 Oct.1978.
-UFO (?)
1956, July 20/=Mars
Topeka Daily Capital, 21 July 1956,
p.11.
-UFO (R-V)
1956, July 19
Denver (Colo.) Post, 19 July 1956.
Topeka Daily Capital, 20 July 1956,
p.3.
-Witch trial (civil liberty)
1973-1974/Robert J. Williams/Kansas
State Industrial Reformatory
Kansas City (Mo.) Times, 1 Mar.1974,
p.14A; 21 Mar.1974, p.24C; and 5
Aug.1974, p.1.
Kansas City (Mo.) Star, 18 Nov.1973,
p.22A; 9 Jan.1974; and 20 Mar.1974.

Iola
-UFO (?)
1955, Dec.17/=meteor?
Topeka Daily Capital, 18 Dec.1955,
p.1.
-UFO (CE-3)
1967, Jan.13
Ted Phillips, Physical Traces Associ-
ated with UFO Sightings (Evanston:
Center for UFO Studies, 1975), p.46.

Iowa Point
-Ghost
1885/Henry Swanzey/SW of town
Topeka Commonwealth, 7 Aug.1885, p.
3, quoting White Cloud Review (undated).

Irving
-UFO (NL)
1897, April 20/J.F. Rogers/M.E. church
Atchison Daily Champion, 22 Apr.1897,
p.1.

Iuka
-Fall of metallic object
1970, Aug.28/N of town/=Soviet cosmos
satellite
Pratt Tribune, 29 Aug.1970, p.1; and
30 Aug.1970, p.1.

Junction City
-UFO (?)
1967, Nov.5
"November Sightings in Kansas," Skylook, no.4 (Dec.1967):3.
-UFO (CE-1)
1977, Dec./10 mi.E on I-70
Junction City Daily Union, 16 Dec.
1977.
-UFO (DD)
1965, Aug.1/George Goodson/airport

Junction City Daily Union, 2 Aug.
1965, p.1. il.

Kansas City
-Anomalous hole in ice
1978, Feb.17/C.A. Preussner/13751 State
St.
Kansas City Kansan, 27 Feb. 1978; 28
Feb.1978; 2 Mar.1978; and 9 Mar.
1978. il.
Kansas City (Mo.) Times, 11 Mar.1978.
1978, March 20/Wyandotte County Lake
Kansas City Kansan, 21 Mar.1978, p.2.
-Clairvoyance
1908, Sep./Mr. Stege
"Dream Dooms Culprit," Fate 28 (July
1975):78.
-UFO (?)
1972, March 22/=helicopter
Kansas City Kansan, 23 Mar.1972.
-UFO (DD)
1947, July 6/Barbara Mehner/nr. U.S.24
Kansas City (Mo.) Star, 7 July 1947.
1958, Aug.17
Richard Hall, ed., The UFO Evidence
(Washington: NICAP, 1964), p.147.
1976, Oct.7
"UFO Central," CUFOS News Bull., 1
Feb.1976, p.8.
-UFO (NL)
1897, March 26
Kansas City (Mo.) Star, 28 Mar.1897,
p.2.
1897, April 1
Topeka State Journal, 2 Apr.1897, p.3.
1897, April 15/Mr. Kincaid
Salina Weekly Republican-Journal, 16
Apr.1897.
1947, July 4/Mrs. Arthur Gustafson/
Rosedale
Kansas City (Mo.) Star, 6 July 1947.
1961, Aug.12/Tom Phipps
Lloyd Mallan, "The Mysterious 12,"
Sci.& Mech. 37 (Dec.1966):30,63-64.
"From Dr. McDonald's Files," Can.UFO
Rept., no.12 (1972):16,23-24.

Kingman
-Cattle mutilation
1967, Oct.23/Gene Walker/SE of town
Kingman Leader-Courier, 27 Oct.1967,
p.1.
-UFO (CE-1)
1950, June 30/Ross Vermilion/9 mi.W on
U.S.54
Harold T. Wilkins, Flying Saucers on
the Attack (N.Y.: Ace, 1967 ed.),
pp.225-26.
Richard Hall, ed., The UFO Evidence
(Washington: NICAP, 1964), p.149.

Kirwin
-UFO (CE-1)
1976, Jan./Jimmy DeBey
Hayden C. Hewes, "Travis Walton: Abduction Case Studied," Can.UFO Rept.
no.23 (spring 1976):9.

La Crosse
-UFO (NL)

1972, Aug.16
Kansas City (Mo.) Times, 17 Aug.
1972, p.6A.

Lane
-Phantom helicopter
1975, Dec./Sharon Kotouc
1975, Dec.18/Bob Wilson
1976, Jan.16/Dorothy Detwiler
Ottawa Herald, 4 Feb.1976.

Lansing
-Archeological site
ca.3800 B.C.
William Henry Holmes, "Fossil Human
Remains Found near Lansing, Kansas,"
Am.Anthro. 4 (1902):743-52. il.
Warren Upham, "Man in the Ice Age,
at Lansing, Kans.," Am.Geologist
30 (Sep.1902):136-50.
Thromas Chrowder Chamberlin, "The
Geologic Relations of the Human
Relics in Lansing, Kansas," J.Geol-
ogy 10 (1902):745-93. il.
Ales Hrdickla, "The Lansing Skele-
ton," Am.Anthro. 5 (1903):323-30.
il.
G.F. Wright, "The Age of the Lansing
Skeleton," Records of the Past 2
(1903):119-24. il.

Larned
-Fall of paper
1963, Aug.28/W of town
"Fortean Items," Saucer News 10
(Dec.1963):20.
-UFO (CE-2)
1972, Feb.25/Johnnie Beer
Larned Tiller and Toiler, 28 Feb.
1972.
-UFO (NL)
1970, Aug.5/Phil Atteberry/State Hos-
pital
"Press Reports," APRO Bull. 19 (July-
Aug.1970):9, quoting Hutchinson
News (undated).

Lawrence
-Animal ESP
n.d.
Dorothy Pope, "Science Searches for
ESP in Animals," Fate 7 (Oct.1954):
16-17.
-Fall of fish
1918, spring/Rose B. McCalmont/800
block Kentucky Ave.
Rose B. McCalmont, "Catfish from
Heaven," Fate 12 (Mar.1959):64-65.
-Humanoid
1978, Oct.15/Jim Swager/=local man
Lawrence Journal-World, 17 Oct.1978;
and 24 Oct.1978.
-UFO (NL)
1975, Oct.27/Richard Ross
Timothy Green Beckley, "Saucers over
Our Cities," Saga UFO Rept. 4 (Aug.
1977):24,74.
1976, Dec.27/8th x Connecticut Ave.
Lawrence Journal-World, 27 Dec.1976.
1979, March 6/John Pozdro/Louisiana St.

Lawrence Journal-World, 7 Mar.1979,
p.1.

Leavenworth
-Humanoid
   1968, summer
      John Green, The Sasquatch File (Ag-
      assiz, B.C.: Cheam, 1973), p.50.
-Precognition and archeological site
   1907, April/G.B. LaRue
      Leavenworth Times, 28 Apr.1907.
-Psychokinesis
   1930s/Hadad/Fort Leavenworth prison
      Donald Powell Wilson, My Six Con-
      victs (N.Y.: Rinehart, 1951), pp.
      310-24.
-UFO (NL)
   1897, April 1/ Fort Leavenworth prison
      Kansas City (Mo.) Times, 3 Apr.1897,
      p.1.
   1968, Aug.7/Robert Hrabak
      St. Louis (Mo.) Globe-Democrat, 9
      Aug.1968.

Lenexa
-Dowsing
   1970s/Phil Kline
      Kansas City (Mo.) Star, 23 Feb.1975,
      mag.sec., pp.22-23. il.

Le Roy
-UFO (?)
   1897, April 19/Alexander Hamilton/=
   hoax
      Yates Center Farmer's Advocate, 23
      Apr.1897; and 7 May 1897.
      St. Louis (Mo.) Globe-Democrat, 28
      Apr.1897.
      (Letter), Ed F. Hudson, Buffalo En-
      terprise, 28 Jan.1943.
      Jerome Clark, "The Strange Case of
      the 1897 Airship," Flying Saucer
      Rev. 12 (July-Aug.1966):10,12-14.
      Jerome Clark, "The Great Airship
      Hoax," Fate 30 (Feb.1977):94-97.

Liberal
-Fall of frog
   n.d./E.E. Stoddard
      "Mystery Bullfrog," Fate 6 (Dec.1953)
      :44.
      (Letter), Alfred L. Smith, Fate 7
      (Mar.1954):120.
-UFO (NL)
   1962, Aug.2/Jack Metzker/airport
      (Editorial), Fate 15 (Nov.1962):15.
      Richard Hall, ed., The UFO Evidence
      (Washington: NICAP, 1964), p.38.

Lindsborg
-UFO (DD)
   1950, April 5/P.E. Patchin
      Salina Sun, 10 Apr.1950.

Little River
-Cattle mutilation
   1978, May 8/Norman Crandall/6 mi.N
      Little River Rice County Monitor-
      Journal, 11 May 1978.

Logan
-Mystery bird deaths
   1978, Aug.14/Harold Brooks
      Norton Daily Telegram, 21 Aug.1978,
      p.1.

Lyons
-UFO (NL)
   1972, Aug.17/Bill Walsh
      Kansas City (Mo.) Times, 18 Aug.1972,
      p.26.

McLouth
-Dowsing
   1950s-   /J.E. Bradford
      Lawrence Journal-World, 24 Dec.1976.

McPherson
-UFO (?)
   1946, Dec.10/=meteor
      "Balls of Fire," Doubt, no.17 (1947):
      255.

McPherson co.
-Cattle mutilation
   1973, Nov.30
   1974, Jan.8
      Jerome Clark, "Strange Case of the
      Cattle Killings," Fate 27 (Aug.
      1974):79,86-87.
      Curt Sutherly, "Mutilations: Who--or
      What--Really Is Killing the Cattle?"
      Pursuit 9 (fall 1976):91-92.

Manhattan
-Haunt
   n.d./Manhattan Ave.
      S.J. Sackett & William E. Koch, Kan-
      sas Folklore (Lincoln: Univ. of
      Nebraska, 1961), p.45.
-UFO (NL)
   1972, April
      "Graduate Engineer Sees UFO in Kan-
      sas," Skylook, no.58 (Sep.1972):13.

Marion
-UFO (NL)
   1967, March 8/Sterling Frame
      Marion County Record, 9 Mar.1967.

Marysville
-UFO (?)
   1897, March
      Mt. Morris (Ill.) News, 7 Apr.1897,
      p.8.

Medicine Lodge
-UFO (?)
   1965, Aug.1
      Coral E. Lorenzen, Flying Saucers:
      The Startling Evidence of the Inva-
      sion from Outer Space (N.Y.: Signet,
      1966 ed.), p.238.

Milford
-Healing
   1918-1932/John R. Brinkley/=quackery
      Clement Wood, The Life of a Man (Kan-
      sas City: Goshorn, 1934). il.
      Jack D. Walker, "The Goat Gland Sur-

geon," J.Kansas Med.Soc'y 57 (1956)
:749-55. il.
Gerald Carson, The Roguish World of
Doctor Brinkley (N.Y.: Holt, Rine-
hart & Winston, 1960). il.
Long John Nebel, The Way Out World
(N.Y.: Lancer, 1962 ed.), pp.106-
10.

Minneapolis
-Archeological site
  ca.1200
    Waldo R. Wedel, "Minneapolis 1: A
    Prehistoric Village Site in Ottawa
    County, Kansas," Nebraska History
    Mag. 15 (1934):210-37. il.
-Cattle mutilation
  1973, Nov.-Dec./Almond Baker
    Kansas City (Mo.) Times, 22 Dec.
    1973, p.16A.
-Mystery stone spheres
  Rock City concretions
    Topeka Daily Capital, 31 Aug.1965.
    "Rock City," Kansas!, 3d issue, 1970,
    pp.29-30. il.
    Jim Brandon, Weird America (N.Y.:
    Dutton, 1978), pp.88-89.
-UFO (NL)
  1972, July 14/Mrs. Nathan Pierce/north
  launderette
    Minneapolis Messenger, 20 July 1972,
    p.10.

Mission
-UFO (DD)
  1958, Sep.7/Hayes Walker, Jr.
    Richard Hall, ed., The UFO Evidence
    (Washington: NICAP, 1964), p.67.

Mulvane
-UFO (?)
  1965, Aug.2
    Jacques & Janine Vallee, Challenge
    to Science (N.Y.: Ace, 1966 ed.),
    p.66.

Munjor
-UFO (CE-3)
  1966, spring
    "Family Has Repeat Sightings," APRO
    Bull. 26 (May 1978):4,5.

Natoma
-Anomalous hole in ground
  1978/Eldon Chrisler/SW of town
    Plainsville Times, 29 June 1978. il.
    Hutchison News, 30 June 1978.
    Kansas City (Mo.) Star, 12 July 1978,
    p.4A.

New Albany
-Cattle mutilation
  1978, Sep./Carl Worrell
    Fredonia Wilson County Citizen, 25
    Sep.1978.

Newton
-Erratic crocodilian
  1970, July/Mrs. Pete Becker/419 N. Duncan St.

Newton Kansan, 16 July 1970, p.1.
-UFO (?)
  1967, June 9/Jerry Killfoil/=meteor?
    Kansas City (Mo.) Times, 10 June
    1967.

Norton
-UFO (?)
  1948, Feb.18/=meteorite
    Kansas City (Mo.) Times, 19 Feb.1948.
    Kenneth Arnold, "Are Space Visitors
    Here?" Fate 1 (summer 1948):4-9. il.
    H.H. Nininger, "Tracing the Norton,
    Kansas, Meteorite Fall," Sky & Tel-
    escope 7 (1948):293-95. il.
    Lincoln LaPaz, "The Achondritic
    Shower of February 18, 1948," Pub.
    Astron.Soc'y Pacific 61 (1949):63-
    73. il.
-UFO (CE-1)
  ca.1971/Raymond Rojas
  1978, Aug.27/John Rojas/504 E. Lincoln
    Norton Daily Telegram, 31 Aug.1978.
-UFO (NL)
  1966, Dec./Harold Holste
    Norton Daily Telegram, 15 Mar.1967,
    p.1.
  1967, Feb./Mrs. Glenn Brinkman/N of
  Townsman Motel
    Norton Daily Telegram, 15 Mar.1967,
    p.7.
  1978, Aug.27/Abbie Davenport/501 E.
  Lincoln
    Norton Daily Telegram, 30-31 Aug.
    1978.

Olathe
-UFO (NL)
  1975, Sep.1
    "UFO Central," CUFOS News Bull., 15
    Nov.1975, p.17.

Olpe
-UFO (NL)
  1967, March 6/Delbert Stevenson
    Norton Daily Telegram, 9 Mar.1967,
    p.2.

Osborne
-UFO (DD)
  1949, Nov.7/Delmar Remick
    Kenneth Arnold & Ray Palmer, The Com-
    ing of the Saucers (Boise: The Au-
    thors, 1952), p.145.

Oskaloosa
-Precognition
  1930, May 1/Edward Vance
    Edward Vance, "Limitless Reach of the
    Mind," Fate 21 (Oct.1968):51,53-54.
-UFO (?)
  1976, Aug.17/7 mi.SW/ground markings
  only/=hoax?
    Lawrence Journal-World, 18 Aug.1976.

Ottawa
-UFO (?)
  1955, Dec.17/=meteor?
    Topeka Daily Capital, 18 Dec.1955,
    p.1.

-UFO (CE-2)
    1976, summer
        (Editorial), Int'l UFO Reporter 1
        (Dec.1976):13.

Ottawa co.
-Cattle mutilations
    1973, fall
        Kansas City (Mo.) Times, 22 Dec.
        1973, p.16A.
        Jerome Clark, "Strange Case of the
        Cattle Killings," Fate 27 (Aug.1974)
        :79,84-87.
        Ed Sanders, "The Mutilation Mystery,"
        Oui, Sep.1976, p.51.

Overland Park
-Bird attack
    1978, June 4/Richard Lees/Nall x 107th
    St.
        Kansas City (Mo.) Star, 7 June 1978.
        "Birds and the Bees," Res Bureaux
        Bull., no.38 (7 Sep.1978):4.
        Steve Hicks, "Big Bird Interviews,"
        INFO J., no.31 (Sep.-Oct.1978):6-8,
        11-14; no.32 (Nov.-Dec.1978):2-4.
-UFO (NL)
    1972, Aug.12/Robert Mount/7000 Mackey
        Kansas City (Mo.) Star, 20 Aug.
        1972, p.5A.

Oxford
-UFO (NL)
    1965, Aug.2/Paul Rader
        Kansas City (Mo.) Star, 2 Aug.1965.

Palco
-Mystery bird deaths
    1978, Aug.14/Terry Kortan
        Plainville Times, 17 Aug.1978, p.1.
        il.

Parsons
-Clairempathy
    1974, Sep.-   /Ben Townsend
        Ben Townsend, "Treasure Hunting with
        ESP," Fate 31 (Feb.1978):57-58.
-UFO (CE-1)
    1977, Jan.25/Clyde V. Basey/W on U.S.
    160
        Parsons News, 15 Dec.1977.

Peabody
-UFO (?)
    1971, Jan.22
        Ted Phillips, Physical Traces Associ-
        ated with UFO Sightings (Evanston:
        Center for UFO Studies, 1975), p.110.

Peru
-UFO (NL)
    1978, Aug.24
        Norton Daily Telegram, 28 Aug.1978,
        p.1.

Phillipsburg
-UFO (NL)
    1972, Aug.16
        Kansas City (Mo.) Times, 17 Aug.1972,
        p.6A.

Pittsburg
-Humanoid
    1978, Dec.16/Hwy.126
        Pittsburg Morning Sun, 17 Dec.1978.
-UFO (?)
    1954, Feb.4
        Paris Flammonde, The Age of Flying
        Saucers (N.Y.: Hawthorn, 1971), p.
        63.
-UFO (CE-2)
    1967, Jan.13/Jim Cunningham
        Pittsburg Headlight-Sun, 14 Jan.1967,
        p.1.
        Robert Loftin, Identified Flying Sau-
        cers (N.Y.: David McKay, 1968), p.
        139.
        Edward U. Condon, ed., Scientific
        Study of Unidentified Flying Objects
        (N.Y.: Bantam, 1969 ed.), p.288.
        Donald H. Menzel & Ernest H. Taves,
        The UFO Enigma (Garden City: Double-
        day, 1977), pp.102-103.
-UFO (DD)
    1947, summer/L.H. Witherspoon
        Richard Hall, ed., The UFO Evidence
        (Washington: NICAP, 1964), p.30.

Pottawatomie Indian Reservation
-Humanoid
    ca.1959/Nadine Goslin
        John Green, The Sasquatch File (Ag-
        assiz, B.C.: Cheam, 1973), p.23.

Prairie View
-UFO (NL)
    1967, March 8/Jake Jansonius
        Phillipsburg Review, 16 Mar.1967.

Prairie Village
-UFO (NL)
    1976, May 26
        "Noteworthy UFO Sightings," Ufology
        2 (fall 1976):60.
    1978, June 29/183d St. x U.S.69
        Olathe Daily News, 1 July 1978.

Pratt
-Electromagnetic anomaly
    1977, May 3/Karen Detwiler
        Pratt Tribune, 4 May 1977.

Pratt co.
-Cattle mutilation
    1976, Aug./Arthur Beck
        (Editorial), Fate 30 (Feb.1977):39.

Princeton
-Skyquake
    1977, Dec.3
        U.S. Naval Rsch.Laboratory, NRL In-
        vestigations of East Coast Acoustic
        Events (Washington: Naval Rsch. Lab-
        oratory, 10 Mar.1978), p.138.
        "Aerial Detonations," Res Bureaux
        Bull., no.40 (9 Nov.1978):6.

Rantoul
-Phantom helicopter
    1975, Dec.18/Virginia Burkdoll
    1976, Jan.16, 26/Virginia Burkdoll

Ottawa Herald, 4 Feb.1976.

Reading
-UFO (?)
 1970/ground markings only
  Ted Phillips, Physical Traces Associ-
  ated with UFO Sightings (Evanston:
  Center for UFO Studies, 1975), p.69.

Rice co.
-Archeological site
 ca.17th c.
  Waldo R. Wedel, "The Council Circles
  of Central Kansas: Were They Sol-
  stice Registers?" Am.Antiquity 32
  (1967):54-63. il.
  Waldo R. Wedel, "After Coronado in
  Quivira," Kansas Hist.Quar. 34
  (1968):369-85.
  Waldo R. Wedel, "Native Astronomy and
  the Plains Caddoans," in Anthony F.
  Aveni, ed., Native American Astronomy (Austin: Univ. of Texas, 1977),
  pp.131-45.

Rossville
-UFO (NL)
 1967, Feb.8/Tommy Mansfield/2 mi.E
  "UFO Returns Spotlight," Flying Saucers, June 1970, p.48.

Russell
-Animal ESP
 1961/Ray Hainke
  (Editorial), Fate 14 (July 1961):23.
-Dog mutilation
 1978, June 2/NE of town
  Russell Daily News, 12 June 1978, p.
  6.
-UFO (NL)
 1972, Aug.16/Ralph Augustine/NE of air-
 port
  Kansas City (Mo.) Times, 17 Aug.1972,
  p.6C.
  Hayden C. Hewes, "UFOs over Kansas,"
  Fate 26 (Mar.1973):84,88.
 1978, Jan.27/N on U.S.281
  Russell Daily News, 28 Jan.1978.

Saint John
-Animal ESP
 1954, April/George Hilton
  (Editorial), Fate 7 (Nov.1954):6-8.

Salina
-Archeological site
 ca.900 A.D.
  Richard L. Stauffer, "A Salina County
  Site," Newsl.Kansas Anthro.Ass'n 2
  no.9 (1957):197-202. il.
  Franklin Folsom, America's Ancient
  Treasures (N.Y.: Rand McNally,
  1974), p.86.
-Ball lightning
 1919, Oct.8/Santa Fe x Iron Ave.
  "Ball Lightning at Salina, Kans.,"
  Monthly Weather Rev. 47 (Oct.1919):
  728.
-Cattle mutilations
 1973

Kansas City (Mo.) Times, 22 Dec.1973,
 p.1A.
-Fall of ice
 1882, July 11/Martin Ellwood/6 mi.W
  Salina Saline County Journal, 13
  July 1882; and 20 July 1882.
  "An Eighty Pound Hailstone," Sci.Am.
  47 (1882):119.
-Humanoid
 1977, July 18/W. Elm St.
  Salina Journal, 20 July 1977.
-Mystery bird deaths
 1954, Oct.7/Smokey Hill AFB
  Salina Journal, 7 Oct.1954, p.1; and
  8 Oct.1954, p.1. il.
-Snow worms
 1886/Warren Knaus
  E.W. Gudger, "Snow Worms," Nat.Hist.
  Mag. 23 (1923):451-56.
-UFO (?)
 1897, April 15/Sam Samuelson/=balloon
  Salina Weekly Republican-Journal, 23
  Apr.1897.
 1967, Nov.4
  "November Sightings in Kansas," Sky-
  look, no.4 (Dec.1967):3.
-UFO (NL)
 1970, June 24/Jim Swindler/U.S.40
  R.F. Sibol, "Ballet in the Sky,"
  Fate 24 (June 1971):68-70.
-UFO (R)
 1956, Sep.10/Schilling AFB/=radar echo
  David Atlas, "Sub-Horizon Radar
  Echoes by Scatter Propagation," J.
  Geophysical Rsch. 64 (1959):1205-
  18. il.

Scott City
-UFO (NL)
 1972, July 7/Reginald Ford
  Hayden C. Hewes, "UFOs over Kansas,"
  Fate 26 (Mar.1973):84,88.

Sedan
-UFO (NL)
 1978, Aug.24/Juanita Thomas
  Sedan Times-Star, 30 Aug.1978.

Sharon Springs
-UFO (NL)
 1967, March 8/G.L. Sullivan/15 mi.N
  Los Angeles (Cal.) Times, 10 Mar.
  1967.
  Norton Daily Telegram, 14 Mar.1967,
  p.1.

Shawnee
-UFO (NL)
 1975, Nov.10
  "UFO Central," CUFOS News Bull., 1
  Feb.1976, p.12.

Skiddy
-Out-of-body experience
 1889, July/A.S. Wiltse
  A.S. Wiltse, "A Case of Typhoid Fever
  with Subnormal Temperature and
  Pulse," St. Louis Med.& Surgical J.
  57 (1889):281-88.
  A.S. Wiltse, "Astonishing Psycho-

logical Phenomena," Mid-Continental
Rev. 1 (Feb.1890):43-51.
Frederic W.H. Myers, "On Indications
of Continued Terrene Knowledge on
the Part of Phantasms of the Dead,"
Proc.SPR 8 (1892):170,180-94.

Smith Center
-UFO (CE-1)
1969, Sep.12/Mrs. Gary Lare
"Light Frightens Kansas Residents,"
Skylook, no.25 (Dec.1969):6, quot-
ing Topeka Daily Capital (undated).

Spring Hill
-Spirit medium
1888-1910/William W. Aber
J.H. Nixon, ed., Rending the Vail
(Kansas City: Hudson-Kimberly,
1899). il.
Nandor Fodor, Encyclopaedia of Psychic Science (London: Arthurs,
1933), p.137.

Stafford
-Cattle mutilation
1976, summer
Ed Sanders, "On the Trail of the
Night Surgeons," Oui, May 1977, pp.
79,125.
-Ghost
1919, March 8/Fred Andrews
Jessica Downs, "The Reach of a Mother's Concern," Fate 24 (Apr.1971):
101-104.

Sterling
-Haunt
1970-   /Wade Russell/Broadway Station
Sterling Bulletin, 11 Jan.1979, p.1.

Stillwell
-Erratic crocodilian
1979, March/Dan LeStourgeon
Hutchinson News, 10 Mar.1979, p.1.
il.

Stockton
-Cattle mutilation
1978, Sep./Bob Becker
Stockton Rooks County Record, 21 Sep.
1978.
-UFO (?)
1948, Feb.18/=meteorite?
Omaha (Neb.) Herald, 18 Feb.1948.
1972, Aug.16
Kansas City (Mo.) Times, 17 Aug.1972,
p.6A.
Hayden C. Hewes, "UFOs over Kansas,"
Fate 26 (Mar.1973):84,89.
-UFO (DD)
1952, April 1
Stockton Rooks County Record, 3 Apr.
1952.
Salina Journal, 5 Apr.1952.

Topeka
-Biofeedback research
1960s-1970s/Elmer Green/Menninger Foundation

Elmer E. Green & E. Dale Walters,
"Feedback Technique for Deep Relax-
ation," Psychophysiology 6 (1969):
371-77.
Elmer & Alyce Green, "Conference on
Voluntary Control of Internal States,"
Psychologia 12 (1969):107-108.
Elmer Green, Alyce Green & E. Dale
Walters, "Voluntary Control of In-
ternal States: Psychological and
Physiological," J.Transpersonal
Psych. 1 (1970):1-26.
Elmer & Alyce Green, "On the Meaning
of Transpersonal: Some Metaphysical
Perspectives," J.Transpersonal Psych.
3 (1971):27-46.
John White, "The Yogi in the Lab:
Part One," Fate 24 (June 1971):43,
50-52.
Brad Steiger, "An Interview with
Swami Rama," Fate 25 (Jan.1972):66-
73.
Joseph D. Sargent, Elmer E. Green &
E. Dale Waters, "Psychosomatic Self-
Regulation of Migraine and Tension
Headaches," Seminars in Psychiatry
5 (1973):415-42.
James Crenshaw, "New Dimensions in
Healing: Part One," Fate 26 (June
1973):50,53-54.
Elmer & Alyce Green, "The Dangers of
Mind Control," Fate 27 (Nov.1974):
98-108. 11.
David Hammond, The Search for Psychic
Power (N.Y.: Bantam, 1975), pp.62-
77,165-77,224-35.
Elmer & Alyce Green, Beyond Biofeed-
back (N.Y.: Delacorte, 1977).
-Fall of mud
1959, Dec.19/Mrs. O.W. Marney/410 Bur-
gess
Topeka Sunday Capital-Journal, 20
Dec.1959. il.
-Parapsychology research
1952-1968/Gardner Murphy/Menninger
Foundation
Gardner Murphy, "Psychology and Psy-
chical Research," Proc.SPR 50 (1953)
:26-49.
Gardner Murphy, "Triumphs and Defeats
in the Study of Mediumship," J.ASPR
51 (1957):125-35.
Gardner Murphy, The Challenge of
Psychical Research (N.Y.: Harper &
Row, 1961).
Gardner Murphy, "A Qualitative Study
of Telepathic Phenomena," J.ASPR 56
(1962):63-79.
Gardner Murphy, "Lawfulness Versus
Caprice: Is There a Law of Psychic
Phenomena?" J.ASPR 58 (1964):239.
Gardner Murphy, "Research in Crea-
tiveness: What Can It Tell Us About
Extra-Sensory Perception?" J.ASPR
60 (1966):8-22.
Alice E. Moriarty & Gardner Murphy,
"Some Thoughts about Prerequisite
Conditions or States in Creativity
and Paranormal Experience," J.ASPR
61 (1967):203-18.

Gardner Murphy, "Direct Contacts
with Past and Future: Retrocognition
and Precognition," J.ASPR 61 (1967)
:3-23.
Alice E. Moriarty & Gardner Murphy,
"An Experimental Study of ESP Po-
tential and Its Relationship to
Creativity in a Group of Normal
Children," J.ASPR 61 (1967):326-38.
-Precognition
1957, June/Patrick Williams/321 Chand-
ler St.
(Editorial), Fate 10 (Nov.1957):14-
15.
-Psychokinesis
1919, Oct.1/Charles J. Jones
Olive Jones Whitmer, "Mediumistic
Communications and Physical Pheno-
mena," J.ASPR 18 (1924):568-81.
-Seances
1880s-1890s/W.D. Chesney/1916 Lincoln
W.D. Chesney, "How to Run a Home
Seance," Fate 11 (July 1958):63-68.
-UFO (?)
1955, Dec.17/=meteor?
Topeka Daily Capital, 18 Dec.1955,
p.1.
-UFO (CE-2)
1969
Ted Phillips, Physical Traces Associ-
ated with UFO Sightings (Evanston:
Center for UFO Studies, 1975), p.60.
-UFO (DD)
1947, July 8/Mrs. Leonard Sheafor/114
Boswell
Oklahoma City Daily Oklahoman, 8 July
1947.
-UFO (NL)
1897, March 27/John W. Leedy
Topeka Daily Capital, 28 Mar.1897,
p.1; and 30 Mar.1897, p.3.
Topeka State Journal, 29 Mar.1897,
p.3.
Omaha (Neb.) Daily Bee, 29 Mar.1897.
1897, April 12/G.C. Clemens
Kansas City (Mo.) Times, 14 Apr.1897.
1961, Aug.14/S of town
Curtis Fuller, "The Boys Who 'Caught'
a Flying Saucer," Fate 15 (Jan.1962)
:36,40.
1967, June
George H. Gallup III & John O. Davies III, "Five Million Americans
Have Seen 'Flying Saucers,'" Fate
20 (Oct.1967):41,43.

Toronto
-UFO (CE-2)
1978, Oct./Jim Smith/Walnut R./ground
markings only/=blast holes
Fredonia Daily Herald, 19 Oct.1978.
Yates Center News, 26 Oct.1978.
Eureka Herald, 9 Nov.1978.

Towanda
-UFO (NL)
1967, March 8/Virgil Osborne/Wilson
Field
Whitewater Independent, 9 Mar.1967.

Troy
-UFO (NL)
1897, April 4/Sol Miller
Kansas City (Mo.) Times, 9 Apr.1897.

Ulysses
-UFO (CE-1)
1964, Sep.11/Karen Campbell/1 mi.W
Wichita Eagle, 17 Sep.1964, p.1.
Hayden Hewes, "The Oklahoma Humanoid,"
True Flying Saucers & UFOs Quar.,
no.1 (spring 1976):12-13,16-17.

Victoria
-UFO (NL)
1972, Aug.16
Kansas City (Mo.) Times, 17 Aug.1972,
p.6A.

Wakefield
-Erratic kangaroo
1965, Aug.15/Jerry L. Condray/NE of
town
Abilene Reflector-Chronicle, 18 Aug.
1965.
Kansas City (Mo.) Star, 19 Aug.1965.

Washington
-UFO (?)
1897, March
Mt. Morris (Ill.) News, 7 Apr.1897,
p.3.

Welda
-UFO (DD)
1971, Nov.4/Dean H. Stewart/1½ mi.E
"UFO Knocks Down Tree," Skylook, no.
50 (Jan.1972):2,3, quoting Wichita
Eagle (undated).
"Kansas Sighting," Kansas-Oklahoma
Newsl., Feb.1972, p.8.

Wellington
-UFO (DD)
1965, Aug.2/Charles Schreck
Kansas City (Mo.) Star, 2 Aug.1965.
-UFO (NL)
1956, July 19
Denver (Colo.) Post, 19 July 1956.
Topeka Daily Capital, 20 July 1956,
p.3.
1965, Aug.2/Everett Tucker
Wichita Beacon, 2 Aug.1965, p.1A.

Wichita
-Dowsing
1960/Nathan J. Kelly
(Letter), Fate 14 (Aug.1961):117,120.
-Erratic crocodilian
1978, June 30/Vernon Bennett/Little Ar-
kansas R.
Wichita Eagle & Beacon, 6-8 July
1978.
Kansas City (Mo.) Times, 6-8 July
1978.
Atchison News, 8 July 1978.
-Fall of knife
1925/Mabel Kronke
Mabel Kronke, "Knife of Destiny,"
Fate 5 (Nov.1952):59-60.

-Ghost
  n.d./Sandra Stover
    Hans Holzer, Ghosts I've Met (N.Y.:
    Ace, 1965), p.55.
-Ghost dog
  n.d./Lowanda Cady
    Martin Ebon, The Evidence for Life
    After Death (N.Y.: Signet, 1977),
    p.99.
-Lunar cycle and blood
  1974/Wichita State University
    Harry D. Rounds, "A Lunar Rhythm in
    the Occurrence of Blood-Borne Fac-
    tors in Cockroaches, Mice and Men,"
    Comparative Biochem.& Physiol., pt.
    C: Comparative Pharmacology 50 (1975)
    :193-98. il.
-Precognition
  1970s/Allene Cunningham/1602 E. Central
  1970s/Darhla McCord/3011 E. Funston
    Warren Smith, "Phenomenal Predictions
    for 1976," Saga, Jan.1976, pp.16,17,
    50.
-Spontaneous human combustion
  1955/Eva Ola Godfrey
    (Editorial), Fate 9 (Apr.1956):12.
-UFO (?)
  1952, Nov.15
    U.S. Air Force, Projects Grudge and
    Blue Book Reports 1-12 (Washington:
    NICAP, 1968), p.164.
  1965, Nov.16/David Faidley/=meteors
    Jerome Clark, "The Greatest Flap Yet?
    Part IV," Flying Saucer Rev. 12
    (Nov.-Dec.1966):9,10-11.
    (Letter), T.A. Williamson, Flying
    Saucer Rev. 13 (Mar.-Apr.1967):18.
  1974/Hugo E. Schmidt/ground markings
  only/=fungus
    (Letter), Fate 27 (Nov.1974):160.
-UFO (DD)
  1947, July 7/James Miller
    Wichita Eagle, 8 July 1947.
  1967, June 27/Jefferson Villar
    "Power Play," in The New Report on
    Flying Saucers (Greenwich, Ct.: Faw-
    cett, 1967), p.43. il.
-UFO (NL)
  1897, March 29/Judge Hatton
    Topeka State Journal, 30 Mar.1897, p.
    7.
  1897, June 20/J.F. Costello/=meteor?
    Wichita Daily Eagle, 22 June 1897,
    p.5.
  1897, June 22/G.L. Miller/N of town/=
  meteor?
    Wichita Daily Eagle, 23 June 1897,
    p.5.
  1947, July 7/S.B. Keefer/236 N. Athen-
  ian
    Wichita Eagle, 8 July 1947.
  1956, July 19/Jimmy Walker
    (Editorial), Fate 9 (Dec.1956):10.
  1960, Aug.23
    Lloyd Mallan, "Complete Directory of
    UFOs: Part 1," Sci.& Mech. 37 (Dec.
    1966):36,70-71.
  1961, Aug.4/Mrs. M.S. Buck
    Curtis Fuller, "The Boys Who 'Caught'
    a Flying Saucer," Fate 15 (Jan.1962)

:36,40.
  1965, July 29-31/Scott Nelson/1421 El
  Monte
    Wichita Beacon, 2 Aug.1965, p.2A.
  1975, April 8/Danny Walker
    (Letter), Saga UFO Rept. 2 (fall
    1975):6.
  1975, Dec.11
    "Noteworthy UFO Sightings," Ufology
    2 (spring 1976):42.
  1978, July 24
    Burlington Daily Republic, 25 July
    1978.
-UFO (R)
  1965, Aug.2/John Shockley
    Wichita Beacon, 2 Aug.1965, p.1A.
    Jerome Clark, "The Greatest Flap
    Yet?" Flying Saucer Rev. 12 (Jan.-
    Feb.1966):27.
    Gordon D. Thayer, "Optical and Radar
    Analyses of Field Cases," in Edward
    U. Condon, ed., Scientific Study of
    Unidentified Flying Objects (N.Y.:
    Bantam, 1969 ed.), pp.158-60.

Winfield
-UFO (?)
  1965, Aug.2
    Jacques & Janine Vallee, Challenge
    to Science (N.Y.: Ace, 1966), p.66.
-UFO (NL)
  1913/W.L. Shelley
    Harold T. Wilkins, Flying Saucers Un-
    censored (N.Y.: Pyramid, 1967 ed.),
    p.130.
  1956, July 19
    Topeka Daily Capital, 20 July 1956,
    p.3.
  1976, May 20
    "Noteworthy UFO Sightings," Ufology
    2 (fall 1976):60.

Yates Center
-UFO (?)
  1955, Dec.17/=meteor?
    Topeka Daily Capital, 18 Dec.1955,
    p.1.

Yocemento
-UFO (NL)
  1972, Aug.16
    Kansas City (Mo.) Times, 17 Aug.1972,
    p.6A.

           B. Physical Features

Arcadia Valley
-Humanoid
  1869, Aug.
    Junction City Weekly Union, 11 Sep.
    1869.
    Girard Press, 15 Oct.1869, p.1.
    Osage City Journal-Free Press, 6 Aug.
    1969.

Kanapolis L.
-Petroglyph
    Franklin Folsom, America's Ancient
    Treasures (N.Y.: Rand McNally,

1974), p.86.

Kingman County L.
-Lake monster
   1969, July-Aug.
      Kingman Leader-Courier, 8 Aug.1969;
      and 15 Aug.1969, p.1.

Labette Creek
-Archeological site
   ca.500 A.D.
      Lawrence Journal-World, 16 Aug.1978,
      p.24.

McDowell Creek
-Archeological site
   ca.300-500 A.D.
      Patricia J. O'Brien, et al., "The
      Ashland Bottoms Site (14RY603): A
      Kansas City Hopewell Site in North-
      Central Kansas," Plains Anthro. 23
      (1979):1-20.

Neosho R.
-Ancient ax marks
   1868, Nov.
      Fort Scott Press, 27 Nov.1868.

Norton Reservoir
-UFO (NL)
   1978, Aug.28/Sylvia Rojas
      Norton Daily Telegram, 31 Aug.1978.

Paint Creek
-Archeological site
   16th c.
      J.A. Udden, "An Old Indian Village,"
      Pub.Augustana Library, no.2 (1900).
      Waldo R. Wedel, "An Introduction to
      Kansas Archeology," Bull.Bur.Am.
      Ethn., no.174 (1959).

Saline R.
-Ghost
   1879, Jan.23/nr. Oak Canyon
      Floyd Benjamin Streeter, "Tokaluma,
      the Phantom Indian," The Aerend 4
      (winter 1933):157-59.

           C. Ethnic Groups

Kansa Indians
-Flood myth
      Lawrence Journal-World, 8 Nov.1976,
      p.1.

OKLAHOMA

A. Populated Places

Ada
-Ghost light
  1962/Ronnie Black/Busby Ranch
    (Editorial), Fate 15 (Nov.1962):16-
    18, quoting Ada Evening News (un-
    dated).
-UFO (?)
  1957, Nov.9
    Hayden C. Hewes, "Flying Saucer Mys-
    tery Still Unsolved," Oklahoma City
    Sunday Oklahoman, 18 Apr.1965.
-UFO (DD)
  1956, May 17/Kent Meyer/Washington
  School
    "World Roundup," Flying Saucer Rev.
    2 (July-Aug.1956):27.

Afton
-Archeological site
    William Henry Holmes, "Flint Imple-
    ments and Fossil Remains from a
    Sulphur Spring at Afton, Indian
    Territory," Ann.Rept.U.S.Nat'l Mus.,
    1901, pp.237-52. il.

Allen
-UFO (NL)
  1967, Sep.22/Simon Williams
    Jim & Coral Lorenzen, UFOs over the
    Americas (N.Y.: Signet, 1968), p.
    168.

Altus
-UFO (?)
  1957, Nov.9
    Hayden C. Hewes, "Flying Saucer Mys-
    tery Still Unsolved," Oklahoma City
    Sunday Oklahoman, 18 Apr.1965.
-UFO (CE-2)
  1973, Nov.21/Hurbert Young
    Altus Times-Democrat, 21 Nov.1973.

Anadarko
-Fall of metal foil
  1951, Nov.10
    "Found on Ground," Doubt, no.42
    (1953):238,239.
-UFO (CE-1)
  1906, Nov./Roy Russell
    Coral & Jim Lorenzen, UFOs: The Whole
    Story (N.Y.: Signet, 1969), p.16.
-UFO (DD)
  1947, July 6-7
    Oklahoma City Daily Oklahoman, 8
    July 1947.
-UFO (NL)
  1954, April 1
    (Letter), H.C. Randells, Fate 7 (Aug.
    1954):118-20.
-Weather control
  1952, Aug.18/Jemez Apache Indians
    (Editorial), Fate 6 (Jan.1953):11,

quoting UP release, 20 Aug.1952.

Apache
-UFO (?)
  1944, Oct./Robert L. Spearman
    (Letter), Fate 21 (July 1968):130-
    31.
    Jerome Clark & Lucius Farish, "The
    Mysterious 'Foo Fighters' of WWII,"
    Saga UFO Rept. 2 (spring 1975):44,
    47.

Ardmore
-Ancient inscription
  1977/Barbara Jean Woodward
    Gloria Farley, "The Ardmore Inscrip-
    tion," Occ.Pub.Epigraphic Soc'y 5,
    no.101 (Sep.1977):22-23.
-Ghost
  n.d./Louise Riotte
    Louise Riotte, "A Gift of Roses,"
    Fate 22 (Aug.1969):47-54.
-UFO (CE-1)
  1964, April 9
    Jacques & Janine Vallee, Challenge
    to Science (N.Y.: Ace, 1966 ed.),
    p.56.
-UFO (NL)
  1977, Sep.22
    "UFOs of Limited Merit," Int'l UFO
    Reporter 2 (Nov.1977):3.
  1978, Oct.17/Mike Bracken
    Tulsa World, 18 Oct.1978.

Arnett
-UFO (CE-1)
  1967, May 7/Jerry Luck
    "Car Buzzing Incidents on Increase,"
    APRO Bull. 15 (May-June 1967):5.

Atoka
-Cattle mutilation
  1975, Feb./Robert Brown/12 mi.SE
    Ponca City News, 19 Feb.1975.

Bache
-Ancient inscription
  1943/J.W. Hawkins
    Barry Fell, America B.C. (N.Y.: Quad-
    rangle, 1976), p.160. il.
    Gloria Farley, "The Bache Gravestone,"
    Occ.Pub.Epigraphic Soc'y, vol.5, no.
    109 (Oct.1977). il.

Beaver
-Fall of metallic object
  1970, Aug.28/Kenneth Long/=Soviet Cosmos satellite
    Louisville (Ky.) Courier-Journal, 31
    Aug.1970.
    San Francisco (Cal.) Chronicle, 31
    Aug.1970.

Beaver co.
-Ghost light
   ca.1905, June/William W. Bathlot
   William Bathlot, "Phantom Lights in
   Oklahoma," Fate 5 (Jan.1952):48-50.

Big Cabin
-Phantom panther
   1961, Jan.-March
   "Lion at Large?" Newsweek, 27 Mar.
   1961, pp.31-34.
-UFO (CE-1)
   1975, Jan.19
   Robert A. Goerman, "The UFO Modus
   Operandi: January 1975," Official
   UFO 1 (Aug.1976):46,65.

Blackwell
-Tornado anomaly
   1955, May 25
   Floyd C. Montgomery, "Tornadoes at
   Blackwell, Okla., May 25, 1955,"
   Monthly Weather Rev. 83 (May 1955):
   109.
   B. Vonnegut & C.B. Moore, "Electrical
   Activity Associated with the Black-
   well-Udall Tornado," J.Meteorology
   14 (June 1957):284-85.
   B. Vonnegut & James Weyer, "Luminous
   Phenomena in Nocturnal Tornadoes,"
   Science 153 (1966):1213-20.
-UFO (NL)
   1967, May
   Blackwell Journal-Tribune, 12 Apr.
   1978.

Bristow
-Phantom
   1960/Thad Wilson/jailhouse
   (Editorial), Fate 14 (Apr.1961):18-
   19.

Calera
-UFO (CE-2)
   1974, June 13/ground markings only
   Ted Phillips, Physical Traces Associated with UFO Sightings (Evanston:
   Center for UFO Studies, 1975), p.
   102.

Calumet
-Humanoid
   1970/Howard Dreeson
   Oklahoma City Oklahoma Journal, 28
   Feb.1971.
   Jerome Clark, "'Manimals' Make Tracks
   in Oklahoma," Fate 24 (Sep.1971):60,
   63-64.
-Phantom panther
   1949/Mrs. Laurence Laub
   1951/Mrs. Laurence Laub
   1969/Howard Dreeson/9 mi.N on Okarche
   Rd.
   Jerome Clark, "'Manimals' Make Tracks
   in Oklahoma," Fate 24 (Sep.1971):60,
   64-65.

Cardin
-UFO (NL)
   1973, Nov.1/Irene Powell

Miami News-Record, 1 Nov.1973, p.1.

Carnegie
-Humanoid
   1973, Dec.5/2 mi.W/=hoax
   Tulsa World, 6 Dec.1973.
   Kansas City (Mo.) Times, 7 Dec.1973.

Chandler
-UFO (?)
   1928, Aug./Aaron C. Stern
   (Letter), Fate 26 (Oct.1973):127-28.
-UFO (NL)
   1965, Aug.1/Mrs. Bill Tipton
   Coral E. Lorenzen, Flying Saucers:
   The Startling Evidence of the Inva-
   sion from Outer Space (N.Y.: Signet,
   1966 ed.), p.237.

Chickasha
-UFO (NL)
   ca.1951/Jim Bush
   (Letter), Fate 11 (Oct.1958):114.
   1965, Aug.1
   Coral E. Lorenzen, Flying Saucers:
   The Startling Evidence of the Invasion from Outer Space (N.Y.: Signet,
   1966 ed.), p.237.

Claremore
-UFO (NL)
   1979, Jan.1/John Fahey/Hwy.44
   Milford (Mass.) Daily News, 3 Jan.
   1979.

Clinton
-Skyquake
   1943, Nov.27
   "Aerial Explosion," Doubt, no.12
   (spring-summer 1945):173.
-UFO (?)
   1958
   Hayden C. Hewes, "Flying Saucer Mys-
   tery Still Unsolved," Oklahoma City
   Sunday Oklahoman, 18 Apr.1965.
-UFO (CE-1)
   n.d./Albert Harris
   "Recent News," Saucer News 15 (sum-
   mer 1968):20.

Colony
-Archeological site
   ca.1300/McLemore site
   Alice M. Brues, "Skeletal Material
   from the McLemore Site," Bull.Okla-
   homa Anthro.Soc'y 10 (1962):69-78.
   il.
   David R. Lopez, "The McLemore Cemetery Complex: An Analysis of Prehistoric Burial Customs," Bull.Okla-
   homa Anthro.Soc'y 19 (1970):137-50.
   il.

Coweta
-Ghost light
   n.d./Charley Parkerson farm
   (Letter), Fate 27 (Sep.1974):129-30.

Crescent
-Fall of carbonaceous meteorite

1936, Aug.17
Oscar E. Monning & Robert Brown, "The
Meteorite Fall in Oklahoma," Pop.
Astron. 44 (1936):568-69.

Cushing
-UFO (NL)
1965, Aug.1/C.V. Barnhill
Coral E. Lorenzen, "Western UFO Flap,"
Fate 18 (Nov.1965):42,46.

Delaware co.
-Archeological site
Rhoades Mound
Paul Foght, "Mayan Treasure from an
Oklahoma Grave," Fate 14 (Nov.1961)
:84-86. il.

Dibble
-UFO (?)
1956, Warner Hayhurst
(Editorial), Fate 9 (Dec.1956):13.

Duke
-Archeological site
ca.5000 B.C.
Roger S. Saunders & John T. Penman,
"Perry Ranch: A Plainview Bison
Kill on the Southern Plains," Plains
Anthro. 23 (1979):51-65. il.

Duncan
-Humanoid
1967, Oct.21/Ivan Ritter/E on Hwy.7
Jim & Coral Lorenzen, UFOs over the
Americas (N.Y.: Signet, 1968), pp.
84-85.
-UFO (NL)
1973, Oct.27
Duncan Daily Banner, 29 Oct.1973.

Durant
-UFO (?)
1952, April 2/=meteor?
Desmond Leslie & George Adamski, Fly-
ing Saucers Have Landed (N,Y,: Brit-
ish Book Centre, 1953), p.52.
1957, Nov.9
Hayden C. Hewes, "Flying Saucer Mys-
tery Still Unsolved," Oklahoma City
Sunday Oklahoman, 18 Apr.1965.
-UFO (NL)
1965, Aug.2/Bill Quires
Coral E. Lorenzen, "Western UFO Flap,"
Fate 18 (Nov.1965):42,44.

Eagletown
-Erratic crocodilian
1949, July/E.M. Wagnon/7 mi.E in Rich
Creek
Albert P. Blair, "The Alligator in
Oklahoma," Copeia, 1950, no.1, p.57.
-Humanoid
1849, May 13/One-Eye Bascomb/SW of town
McCurtain Sunday Gazette, 9 July 1978.

Edmond
-Anomalous artifact
1969, June 27/122d St. on Broadway Ex-
tension/=mosaic tile floor

Tulsa World, 29 June 1969.
Edmond Booster, 3 July 1969. il.
-UFO (NL)
1950
Hayden C. Hewes, "Flying Saucer Mys-
tery Still Unsolved," Oklahoma City
Sunday Oklahoman, 18 Apr.1965.

Elk City
-Moving rocks
1972, Nov.-1973, Feb./James Walter/=
propane gas leak
Oklahoma City Daily Oklahoman, 1
Mar.1973.
"Erupting Rocks," Pursuit 6 (Apr.
1973):33-35.
-Skyquake
1943, Nov.27
"Aerial Explosion," Doubt, no.12
(spring-summer 1945):173.

El Reno
-Humanoid tracks
1970, Dec.
Oklahoma City Oklahoma Journal, 28
Feb.1971.
Midnight, 31 May 1971, p.9.
Jerome Clark, "'Manimals' Make Tracks
in Oklahoma," Fate 24 (Sep.1971):
60,63, quoting AP release, 27 Feb.
1971.
-Phantom panther
1956/Melvin Harmon
Jerome Clark, "'Manimals' Make Tracks
in Oklahoma," Fate 24 (Sep.1971):
60,64-65.
-UFO (DD)
1964, Oct.24
Hayden C. Hewes, "Flying Saucer Mys-
tery Still Unsolved," Oklahoma City
Sunday Oklahoman, 18 Apr.1965.

Enid
-Doubtful identity
1903/David E. George/=John Wilkes
Booth?
R.H. Crozier, The Bloody Junto (Lit-
tle Rock: Woodruff & Blocker, 1869).
Finis L. Bates, The Escape and Sui-
cide of John Wilkes Booth (Atlanta:
J.L. Nichols, 1908).
Francis Wilson, John Wilkes Booth:
Fact and Fiction of Lincoln's Ass-
assination (Boston: Houghton Mif-
flin, 1929).
Fred Allsopp, Folklore of Romantic
Arkansas (N.Y.: Grolier Soc'y, 1931),
pp.264-69.
-UFO (DD)
1947, July 7/Ed Herbig
Oklahoma City Daily Oklahoman, 8
July 1947.

Fittstown
-UFO (NL)
1967, Sep.22
Jim & Coral Lorenzen, UFOs over the
Americas (N.Y.: Signet, 1968), p.
168.

Floris
-Fall of toads
  1912, Oct./William W. Bathlot/1 mi.
  from town
    William W. Bathlot, "Does It Rain
    Toads?" Fate 6 (June 1953):90-92.

Fort Sill
-Precognition
  1964, June
    Paul Foght, "The Search for Big Bow's
    Grave," Fate 18 (May 1965):72-77.
    il.
-UFO (DD)
  1965, Sep.
    J. Allen Hynek, The UFO Experience
    (Chicago: Regnery, 1972), p.235.

Frederick
-Entombed frogs
  ca.1918/Andy Holloman
    (Letter), B.L. Dillingham, Fate 7
    (May 1954):110-11, quoting Frederick
    Leader (undated).
    Dallas (Tex.) Morning News, 9 Aug.
    1960.

Gage
-Animal ESP
  1951/Stacy Woods
    (Editorial), Fate 21 (Nov.1968):30.

Goodwater
-Humanoid
  1926, spring
    McCurtain Sunday Gazette, 9 July
    1978.

Gowen
-Ancient inscription
    Gloria Farley, "The Gowen Bluff Shel-
    ter," Occ.Pub.Epigraphic Soc'y, vol.
    3, no.68 (Sep.1976).

Guthrie
-UFO (NL)
  1897, April 8
    Dallas (Tex.) Morning News, 8 Apr.
    1897, p.3.

Guymon
-UFO (?)
  1966, Oct.30/E.M. Thomason
    (Letter), Fate 20 (Mar.1967):136-38.
    il.

Harrah
-UFO (NL)
  1947, July 7/J.P. Barnes
    Oklahoma City Daily Oklahoman, 8
    July 1947.

Hartshorne
-UFO (NL)
  1965, July 26-Sep./Altaclair Morgan
    Robert Loftin, Identified Flying Sau-
    cers (N.Y.: David McKay, 1968), pp.
    87-90.
    Donald E. Keyhoe & Gordon I.R. Lore,
    Jr., UFOs: A New Look (Washington:

NICAP, 1969), p.45.

Haskell co.
-Anomalous mounds
    Maxwell M. Knechtel, "Pimpled Plains
    of Eastern Oklahoma," Bull.Geol.
    Soc'y Am. 63 (1952):689-700.

Heavener
-Carthaginian coin
  1976, Sep.24/Wilbert Stewart
    Gloria Farley, "Ancient Coins Found,"
    Oklahoma Today 27 (spring 1977):
    31. il.
-Norse runestones
  2 mi.NE on Poteau Mt.
    Lorren Williams, "Did the Norsemen
    Reach Oklahoma?" Fate 8 (Feb.1955)
    :56-60. il.
    George H. Shirk, "Report on the
    Heavener 'Rune Stone,'" Chronicles
    of Oklahoma 37 (autumn 1959):363-
    68.
    Frederick J. Pohl, Atlantic Crossings
    Before Columbus (N.Y.: Norton,
    1961), pp.45-54.
    Leslie A. McRill, "The Heavener Enig-
    ma: A Rune Stone," Chronicles of
    Oklahoma 44 (summer 1966):122-29.
    Alf Mongé & O.G. Landsverk, Norse
    Medieval Cryptography in Runic Car-
    vings (Glendale, Cal.: Norseman,
    1967), pp.103-17,139-41. il.
    "The Problem of the Heavener Rune-
    stone," NEARA Newsl. 3 (Sep.1968):
    50-54.
    O.G. Landsverk, Ancient Norse Mess-
    ages on American Stones (Glendale,
    Cal.: Norseman, 1969), pp.52-74. il.
    Gloria Farley, The Vikings Were Here
    (Poteau: The Independent, 1970).
    Gloria Farley, "The Oklahoma Rune-
    stones Are Authentic," Pop.Arch. 2
    (Aug.1973):4-15. il.
    Don G. Wyckoff, "No Stones Unturned,"
    Pop.Arch. 2 (Aug.1973): 17-31. il.
    Gloria Farley, "The Runestones Are
    Still Authentic: A Challenge," Pop.
    Arch. 4 (May-June 1975):9-14.
    Gloria Farley, "The Stones Speak,"
    Oklahoma Today 26 (winter 1975-76):
    23-27.
    (Editorial), Oklahoma Today 26
    (spring 1976):20. il.

Henryetta
-UFO (NL)
  1967, March 8/Mrs. Homer Smith/9th St.
    Henryetta Daily Free Lance, 9 Mar.
    1967.

Hobart
-Humanoid
  1973
    Allen V. Noe, "ABSMal Affairs in
    Pennsylvania and Elsewhere," Pursuit
    6 (Oct.1973):84.
-Weather control
  1955, May 7/J.R. Bledsoe
    (Editorial), Fate 8 (Nov.1955):13.

Eugene Grossenheider, "Does Man Make
the Weather?" Fate 9 (Feb.1956):
80,83.

Hooker
-UFO (?)
1969, Oct.15/=balloon?
"Oklahoma Residents See Large, Floating Object," Skylook, no.26 (Jan.
1970):11, quoting Hooker Advance
(undated).

Hugo
-UFO (NL)
1964, Aug.3
Hayden C. Hewes, "Flying Saucer Mys-
tery Still Unsolved," Oklahoma City
Sunday Oklahoman, 18 Apr.1965.
-Water anomaly
1979, Feb.14/municipal water pressure
Hugo Daily News, 14 Feb.1979, p.1;
and 16 Feb.1979, p.1.

Hulbert
-UFO (NL)
1973, Oct.24/Gaylon Head
Muskogee Phoenix & Times-Democrat,
26 Oct.1973.

Hydro
-UFO (NL)
1973, Nov.29/George Meacham
Clinton Daily News, 30 Nov.1973.

Idabel
-Religious apparition
1927, Aug.2/SW of town
Idabel McCurtain Gazette, 14 Aug.
1976.

Indianola
-Humanoid
1975, Sep.
John Green, Sasquatch: The Apes Among
Us (Seattle: Hancock House, 1978),
p.182.

Kendrick
-Ball lightning
1908/Verne L. Cameron
(Letter), Fate 20 (Mar.1967):138-40.

Kenton
-Ghost light
n.d./8 mi.E and 15 mi.SW
Minneapolis (Minn.) Journal, 26 June
1923.

Kiowa
-UFO (?)
1952, April 2
McAlester News-Capital, 2 April
1952; and 10-11 April 1952.

Lamar
-UFO (NL)
1956, Jan./Sherman J. McDonald
McAlester News-Capital, 30 Jan.1956.

Latimer co.
-UFO (R-V)
1973, Feb.14
Raymond E. Fowler, "UFO Watergate?"
Official UFO 1 (May 1976):18-19.

Laverne
-UFO (?)
1955, Aug./M.M. Bulla/S on U.S.270
Hayden C. Hewes, "Flying Saucer Mys-
tery Still Unsolved," Oklahoma City
Sunday Oklahoman, 18 Apr.1965.

Lawton
-Cattle mutilations
1970-1971/3 mi.S
Jerome Clark, "'Manimals' Make Tracks
in Oklahoma," Fate 24 (Sep.1971):
60,62.
-Humanoid
1971, Feb.26-March 1/C. Edward Green/
Lake Ave.
Lawton Morning Press,2-3 Mar.1971.
Jerome Clark, "'Manimals' Make Tracks
in Oklahoma," Fate 24 (Sep.1971):
60-63.
-Inner development
1970s/Joe Ferrante/Box 364
Hans Holzer, The Witchcraft Report
(N.Y.: Ace, 1973), pp.80-81.
-UFO (NL)
1958
Hayden C. Hewes, "Flying Saucer Mys-
tery Still Unsolved," Oklahoma City
Sunday Oklahoman, 18 Apr.1965.
1975, Jan.9/Frances Elix/W of town
Robert A. Goerman, "The UFO Modus
Operandi: January 1975," Official
UFO 1 (Aug.1976):46,64-65.
-UFO (R-V)
n.d./Court House
Timothy Green Beckley, "Saucers over
Our Cities," Saga UFO Rept. 4 (Aug.
1977):24,74.

Le Flore co.
-Ancient inscription
Gloria Farley/6 mi. from San Bois R.
Barry Fell, America B.C. (N.Y.: Quad-
rangle, 1976), p.181. il.
-Anomalous mounds
Maxwell M. Knechtel, "Pimpled Plains
of Eastern Oklahoma," Bull.Geol.
Soc'y Am. 63 (1952):689-700.

Lincoln co.
-Chinese figurine
1940s/Alleyne K. Ecker
"Chinese God in Oklahoma?" Fate 5
(Sep.1952):81.
Frank Volkmann, "Oklahoma's Chinese
Idol," Fate 8 (Dec.1955):82-84. il.
Cyclone Covey & Bill Burchardt, "What
Is a Chinese God Doing in Oklahoma?"
Catholic Digest, Dec.1973, pp.67-69.

McAlester
-Ghost
1909, May 24/C. Schadow
C. Schadow, "Colonel Reed's Return,"

Fate 4 (Jan.1951):41-43.
-UFO (?)
    1897, April 12
        Peoria (Ill.) Journal, 15 Apr.1897,
        p.2.
-UFO (DD)
    1947, July 7/Mrs. John Alexander
        Oklahoma City Daily Oklahoman, 8
        July 1947.
-UFO (NL)
    1973, Oct.
        McAlester News-Capital, 24 Oct.1973.

McLoud
-UFO (CE-1)
    1978, Jan.1/Cindy Arteberry/Wynnewood
    Rd.
        McLoud News, 12 Jan.1978.

Madill
-UFO (?)
    1957, Nov.9
        Hayden C. Hewes, "Flying Saucer Mys-
        tery Still Unsolved," Oklahoma City
        Sunday Oklahoman, 18 Apr.1965.

Mangum
-UFO (CE-1)
    1967, April 28/E.A. Griffith
        "Car Buzzing Incidents on Increase,"
        APRO Bull. 15 (May-June 1967):5.

May
-UFO (?)
    1978/Mrs. Leo Long/ground markings=
    fairy ring fungus
        "UFO Impact: Natural Sciences," Int'l
        UFO Reporter 3 (July 1978):9.

Medford
-Dowsing
    1978/Lawrence Schneider
        Caldwell (Kan.) Messenger, 2 Oct.
        1978, p.1.

Meeker
-UFO (NL)
    1947, July 5/Bert Hall
        Oklahoma City Daily Oklahoman, 8
        July 1947.

Miami
-UFO (NL)
    1967, Oct.21/18 mi.W
        "UFOs--October--U.S.A.," APRO Bull.
        16 (Nov.-Dec.1967):8.
    1973, Oct.31/Gary Garton/W on Hwy.10
        Miami News-Record, 1 Nov.1973, p.1.

Midwest City
-UFO (?)
    1952/Mrs. Hugh Ellis
        Hayden C. Hewes, "Flying Saucer Mys-
        tery Still Unsolved," Oklahoma City
        Sunday Oklahoman, 18 Apr.1965.

Moore
-UFO (NL)
    1965, Aug.2/Ray C. Hall
        Robert Loftin, Identified Flying Sau-

cers (N.Y.: David McKay, 1968),
        pp.26-27.
        Hayden C. Hewes, "The Tulsa, Okla-
        homa Photo & Analysis," Official
        UFO 1 (Apr.1976):16,49-50.

Muldrow
-UFO (NL)
    1969, Sep.12-13/Jean Lamb
        "Red Ball Hovers 20 Minutes in Okla-
        homa Sky," Skylook, no.24 (Nov.
        1969):7.
    1970, Aug.19/Jean Lamb
        "SKYLOOK Reader and Family Watch UFO
        in Oklahoma," Skylook, no.35 (Oct.
        1970):17.

Muskogee
-UFO (?)
    1969, Oct.9/=balloon?
        "More on the Meteor of Oct.9, 1969,"
        Skylook, no.25 (Dec.1969):2,3,
        quoting Muskogee Daily Phoenix (un-
        dated).
-UFO (NL)
    1973, Oct.31
        Tulsa Daily World, 1 Nov.1973, p.1A.

Nelagoney
-Humanoid
    1967/George Burns
        "The Road to Noxie," Probe the Un-
        known 4 (Mar.1976):44.
        John Green, Sasquatch: The Apes Among
        Us (Seattle: Hancock House, 1978),
        p.180.
-UFO (NL)
    1978, Feb./Virginia Craun
    1978, May/Billy Mitchell
    1978, June/Mary Powers/5 mi.N
        Oklahoma City Daily Oklahoman, 7
        Aug.1978.

Norman
-Erratic crocodilian
    1901, Nov./S. Canadian R.
        H.H. Lane, "Alligator mississippien-
        sis in Oklahoma," Science 30 (1909)
        :923-24.
-UFO (NL)
    1973, Sep.24/Denise Prieve/nr. Blue
    Creek
        Norman Oklahoma Daily, 26 Sep.1973.

Noxie
-Humanoid
    1975, Sep.1-Oct.11/Kenneth Tosh
        Coffeyville (Kan.) Journal, 2 Sep.
        1975.
        Little Rock Arkansas Gazette, 5 Sep.
        1975.
        Kansas City (Mo.) Star, 9 Sep.1975.
        Kansas City (Mo.) Times, 11 Sep.1975.
        Hayden C. Hewes, "The Creature Takes
        a Holiday," Probe the Unknown 4
        (Mar.1976):43-45.
        Jerome Clark, "Oklahoma Monsters
        Come in Pairs," Fate 29 (Dec.1976):
        70-73.

Oklahoma City Daily Oklahoman, 8
July 1947.
1958, March 3/L. Hefner
1958, Nov.12
1959, Feb.20
   Hayden C. Hewes, "Flying Saucer Mystery Still Unsolved," Oklahoma City
   Sunday Oklahoman, 18 Apr.1965.
1971, April 2/Morris Heflin/Crosstown
Expy. x May Ave.
   Brad Steiger, Mysteries of Time and
   Space (N.Y.: Dell, 1976 ed.), pp.
   145-46.
-UFO (R-V)
   1954, Aug.28/Tinker AFB
   Donald E. Keyhoe, Flying Saucer Conspiracy (N.Y.: Holt, 1955), pp.25-
   26.
   1965, Aug.1-2/Tinker AFB
   Wichita (Kan.) Beacon, 2 Aug.1965,
   p.1.
   Coral E. Lorenzen, "Western UFO Flap,"
   Fate 18 (Nov.1965):42,44,46-47.

Okmulgee
-UFO (?)
   1920, June 8/=meteor?
   St. Joseph (Mo.) News Press, 9 June
   1920.
   Atchison (Kan.) Daily Globe, 9 June
   1920.

Ottawa co.
-UFO (NL)
   1967, March 27/Hwy.10C
   "Red Discs in Oklahoma," APRO Bull.
   15 (May-June 1967):1.

Pawhuska
-UFO (?)
   1978, June 15/Tom Gillette
   Little Rock Arkansas Gazette, 17
   June 1978.
-UFO (CE-1)
   1978, June 13/Paul Kendricks
   Oklahoma City Daily Oklahoman, 16
   June 1978.

Peggs
-UFO (NL)
   1957, Sep.16/C.M. Welch
   (Letter), Fate 11 (Mar.1958):114-16.

Perry
-UFO (NL)
   1897, April 12/Col. Yates
   St. Louis (Mo.) Post-Dispatch, 14
   Apr.1897, p.2.
   Peoria (Ill.) Journal, 15 Apr.1897,
   p.2.
   1969, March 10/Johnny Robbins/Perry
   Lanes
   Perry Journal, 11 Mar.1969.

Ponca City
-UFO (CE-1)
   1964, Sep.11
   Hayden C. Hewes, "Flying Saucer Mys-
   tery Still Unsolved," Oklahoma City
   Sunday Oklahoman, 18 Apr.1965.

Pontotoc co.
-Ancient inscription
   n.d./Elmer Ellis/nr. S. Canadian R.
   Barry Fell, America B.C. (N.Y.: Quad-
   rangle, 1976), p.159. il.
   Gloria Farley, "The Pontotoc Stone,"
   Oklahoma Today 26 (spring 1976):36.
   Gloria Farley, "The Pontotoc Stone,"
   Occ.Pub.Epigraphic Soc'y, vol.4,
   no.109 (Oct.1977). il.

Poteau
-Norse runestone
   1967/Mike Griffeth
   O.G. Landsverk, Ancient Norse Mess-
   ages on American Stones (Glendale,
   Cal.: Norseman, 1969), pp.52-74. il.
   Gloria Farley, "The Oklahoma Rune-
   stones Are Authentic," Pop.Arch. 2
   (Aug.1973):4,6,12. il.
   Don G. Wyckoff, "No Stones Upturned,"
   Pop.Arch. 2 (Aug.1973):17-31. il.
   Gloria Farley, "The Runestones Are
   Still Authentic: A Challenge," Pop.
   Arch. 4 (May-June 1975):9,11.

Quapaw
-UFO (NL)
   n.d./Louise Graham
   Robert Loftin, Spookville's Ghost
   Lights (Tulsa: The Author, 1967).
   1972, Sep.19/George McWatters/Devil's
   Promenade
   Miami News-Record, 19 Sep.1972.

Raiford
-Human handprints in rock
   Handprint Hollow
   Grit, 15 June 1975.

Rocky
-UFO (CE-1)
   1965, June 19
   J. Allen Hynek, The UFO Experience
   (Chicago: Regnery, 1972), pp.91-93.

Roger Mills co.
-Pollution anomaly
   1963, Jan.22-1965/Daniel Allen
   (Editorial), Fate 19 (Sep.1966):20-
   25, quoting Amarillo (Tex.) Daily
   News (undated).
   Jack Porter & Tex Lowell, "The Dead-
   ly 'Stuff' of Roger Mills County,
   Oklahoma," Fate 19 (Dec.1966):92-
   95. il.
   (Letter), J.W. Thompson, Fate 20
   (Feb.1967):122.
   (Letter), R.H. Johns, Fate 20 (Feb.
   1967):122-24.
   (Letter), D. Bruce Berry, Fate 20
   (Apr.1967):146-47.

Rush Springs
-Cattle mutilation
   1975, Feb./Lloyd Wright
   Annie Rosenbloom, "Cow Deaths," Ohio
   Sky Watcher, Mar.1975, pp.17,18.

Sallisaw
-Phantom panther
    n.d.
        Vance Randolph, We Always Lie to
        Strangers (N.Y.: Columbia Univ.,
        1951), p.57.
-UFO (CE-1)
    1977, June 1
        Tulsa Tribune, 1 June 1977.

Sand Springs
-Humanoid hand
    1973, Jan./C.L. Hufford
        Dallas (Tex.) Morning News, 17 Jan.
        1973.
-UFO (NL)
    1954, Sep./2 mi.W
        Vincent H. Gaddis, Mysterious Fires
        and Lights (N.Y.: Dell, 1967 ed.),
        p.82, quoting AP release, 27 Sep.
        1954.

Sapulpa
-UFO (CE-2)
    1956, Nov.22
        Oklahoma City Times, 7 Nov.1957.

Savanna
-UFO (CE-1)
    1976, July 12-13
        McAlester Democrat, 15 July 1976.

Seiling
-UFO (CE-2)
    1957, Dec.8/7 mi.NW
        Jacques Vallee, Passport to Magonia
        (Chicago: Regnery, 1969), pp.267-68.

Seminole co.
-Dowsing
    1911
        (Review), Burton Rascoe, New York
        Sun, 30 Oct.1931.

Shawnee
-Norse runestone
    1969/Jim Estep
        Gloria Farley, "The Oklahoma Rune-
        stones Are Authentic," Pop.Arch. 2
        (Aug.1973):4,8,14. il.
        Don G. Wyckoff, "No Stones Unturned,"
        Pop.Arch. 2 (Aug.1973):16-31. il.
        Gloria Farley, "The Runestones Are
        Still Authentic: A Challenge," Pop.
        Arch. 4 (May-June 1975):9,11.
-UFO (R-V)
    1965, Aug.1
        Coral E. Lorenzen, "Western UFO Flap,"
        Fate 18 (Nov.1965):42,46.

Spiro
-Archeological site
    ca.1150-1450
        Sarah White, "Human Effigy Pipes from
        Spiro Mound, Leflore County, Okla-
        homa," Oklahoma Prehistorian 3, no.
        1 (1940):10-11. il.
        Forrest E. Clements, "Historical
        Sketch of the Spiro Mound," Contrib.
        Mus.Am.Indian 14 (1945):48-68. il.

        Henry W. Hamilton, "The Spiro Mound,"
        Missouri Arch. 14 (Oct.1952):17-
        88. il.
        J. Joseph Bauxar, "Evidence of a Sub-
        surface Chamber under the Brown
        Mound at Spiro," Am.Antiquity 19
        (1953):169-70. il.
        David A. Baerreis, "The Southern Cult
        and the Spiro Ceremonial Complex,"
        Bull.Oklahoma Anthro.Soc'y 5 (Mar.
        1957):23-38.
        Don G. Wyckoff, The Prehistoric Site
        of Spiro, Leflore County, Oklahoma
        (Norman: Oklahoma Arch. Survey,
        1968). il.
        C.W. Ceram, The First American (N.Y.:
        Mentor, 1974 ed.), pp.243-45.
        Barry Fell, America B.C. (N.Y.: Quad-
        rangle, 1976), pp.140-41. il.

Stillwater
-Fall of localized rain
    1892, Oct./Robert Copper
        New York Sun, 30 Oct.1892, p.4.
        "Another 'Weeping Tree,'" Insect
        Life 5 (Jan.1893):204.
-Humanoid tracks
    1971
        Jerome Clark, "'Manimals' Make Tracks
        in Oklahoma," Fate 24 (Sep.1971):
        60,63.
-Telepathy research
    1972/Oklahoma State University
        Gary A. France & Robert A. Hogan,
        "Thought Concordance in Twins and
        Siblings and Associated Personality
        Variables," Psych.Reports 32 (1973)
        :707-10.
-UFO (NL)
    1955, Sep.13/Felix Schwartz
        Hayden C. Hewes, "Flying Saucer Mys-
        tery Still Unsolved," Oklahoma City
        Sunday Oklahoman, 18 Apr.1965.
    1973, Nov.5/Gary Gallagher/W of town
        Stillwater Daily O'Collegian, 6 Nov.
        1973.

Stilwell
-Goat mutilations
    1977, Aug.
        Kansas City (Mo.) Star, 24 Aug.1977.
-Humanoid
    1977, Aug.5/Brian Jones/=hoax
        Oklahoma City Daily Oklahoman, 10
        Aug.1977.
        Tulsa Tribune, 26 Aug.1977.

Stonewall
-Hex
    1897, March/Lucy Factor
        Omaha (Neb.) Daily Bee, 11 Mar.1897,
        p.3.

Tahlequah
-Clairvoyance
    1965, May/Nancy Lawhead
        Rosemary Clark, "Modern Indian Medi-
        cine Woman Rescues a Marriage," Fate
        24 (Jan.1971):80-86.
-Skyquake

1979, Jan.2-3
  Oklahoma City <u>Daily Oklahoman</u>, 3-4
  Jan.1979.
-UFO (DD)
  1973, Oct.31/5 mi.S
  <u>Tulsa Daily World</u>, 1 Nov.1973, p.A1.

Talihina
-Humanoid
  1970/Dusty Rhoades
  "The Road to Noxie," <u>Probe the Un-</u>
  <u>known</u> 4 (Mar.1976):44.
-Phantom panther
  1976-1977/Herman Coussen
  <u>Talihina American</u>, 20 Jan.1977.
-UFO (CE-1) and cattle mutilation
  1971, Sep.1/R.J. Rankin
  Tommy Roy Blann, "The Mysterious
  Link Between UFOs and Animal Mutilations," <u>Saga UFO Rept.</u> 3 (Apr.
  1976):18,21,69.

Taloga
-UFO (CE-3)
  1954, Aug.
  <u>Clinton Daily News</u>, 17 Sep.1954; and
  19 Sep.1954.
  Oklahoma City <u>Daily Oklahoman</u>, 20
  Sep.1954.

Tangier
-UFO (CE-2)
  1966, April 1/6 mi.S
  Jacques Vallee, <u>Passport to Magonia</u>
  (Chicago: Regnery, 1969), p.326.

Temple
-UFO (CE-3)
  1966, March 23/Eddie Laxson/S on U.S.
  70
  <u>Lawton Morning Press</u>, 24 Mar.1966.
  <u>Dallas (Tex.) Times-Herald</u>, 27 Mar.
  1966.
  Robert Loftin, <u>Identified Flying Sau-</u>
  <u>cers</u> (N.Y.: David McKay, 1968), pp.
  91-94.

Texhoma
-UFO (CE-2)
  1966, March 26
  Jacques Vallee, <u>Passport to Magonia</u>
  (Chicago: Regnery, 1969), p.325.

Thackerville
-Hex
  1977, Sep./Red River Cemetery
  Idabel <u>McCurtain Gazette</u>, 30 Sep.
  1977.

Tishomingo
-Acoustic anomaly
  1892, May/John Willis
  Charles M. Skinner, <u>Myths and Legends</u>
  <u>of Our Own Land</u>, 2 vols. (Philadelphia: Lippincott, 1896), 2:237-38.

Tulsa
-Animal ESP
  n.d./Freda Aston
  Freda Aston, "Fife's New Body," <u>Fate</u>

6 (Apr.1953):79-80.
-Clairempathy
  1953, March/Leontine Bryant
  William Earle, "Dowsing for Murder,"
  <u>Fate</u> 9 (Sep.1956):30-31.
-Clairvoyance
  1937, Jan./John W. Campbell
  John W. Campbell, "I Was the Last to
  See Dickey Alive," <u>Fate</u> 24 (Mar.
  1970):47-50.
-Haunt
  1972, Mar.-Dec./Craig Roberts
  (Editorial), <u>Fate</u> 26 (June 1973):32-
  35, quoting <u>Tulsa Daily World</u> (undated).
-Human tracks in sandstone
  1969/Troy Johnson/E of town
  <u>Tulsa Sunday World</u>, 25 May 1969.
-Norse runestone
  1965/Jim Shipley/Bull Dog Hill
  <u>Tulsa Tribune</u>, 14 Oct.1965.
  O.G. Landsverk, <u>Ancient Norse Mess-</u>
  <u>ages on American Stones</u> (Glendale,
  Cal.: Norseman, 1969), pp.52-74. il.
  Gloria Farley, "The Oklahoma Runestones Are Authentic," <u>Pop.Arch.</u> 2
  (Aug.1973):4,6,12-14. il.
  Don G. Wyckoff, "No Stones Unturned,"
  <u>Pop.Arch.</u> 2 (Aug.1973):16-31.
-Plague of ticks
  1978, Aug.5/Ray Hubbard
  <u>Dallas (Tex.) Times-Herald</u>, 7 Aug.
  1978.
-Poltergeist
  1957, July-Aug./C.A. Wilkinson/3951 S.
  61st Ave.
  Curtis Fuller, "'Haunted House' on
  Berryhill," <u>Fate</u> 11 (Jan.1958):68-
  72.
-UFO (DD)
  1947, July 7/Marvin LeBow
  Oklahoma City <u>Daily Oklahoman</u>, 8
  July 1947.
  1971, Nov.30/Todd Kyle
  "Round, White Object Seen over Tulsa," <u>Skylook</u>, no.50 (Jan.1972):7.
-UFO (NL)
  1950, March 27/C.W. Hughes/1228 N.
  Boston Pl.
  Kenneth Arnold & Ray Palmer, <u>The Com-</u>
  <u>ing of the Saucers</u> (Boise: The Authors, 1952), p.148.
  1965, Aug.3/Alan Smith
  <u>Oklahoma City Journal</u>, 5 Oct.1965,
  p.1.
  "Luminous Pulsating Shapes That Hover
  in the Night," <u>Life</u>, 1 Apr.1966, p.
  27. il.
  Robert Loftin, <u>Identified Flying Sau-</u>
  <u>cers</u> (N.Y.: David McKay, 1968), pp.
  22-26.
  Hayden Hewes, "The Tulsa, Oklahoma
  Photo & Analysis," <u>Official UFO</u> 1
  (Apr.1976):16-17,49-51. il.
  Hayden Hewes, James Maney & William
  Spaulding, "Investigation of the
  1965 Tulsa, Oklahoma UFO Sighting
  with Computer Photographic Analysis,"
  <u>J.Occult Studies</u> 1 (Aug.1977):186-
  203. il.

1966, Feb.28/Al Newport
"News Briefs," Saucer News 13 (June
1966):30, quoting Tulsa newspaper,
1 Mar.1966. il.
1967, Aug.12/Gordon Smith
Tulsa World, 13 Aug.1967.
1973, Oct.31/Jim Tinkler/Broken Arrow
Expy.
Tulsa World, 1 Nov.1973, p.A1.
1978, May 30
"UFOs of Limited Merit," Int'l UFO
Reporter 3 (July 1978):3-4.
-Weather control
1963
(Editorial), Fate 17 (Apr.1964):21,
quoting Tulsa World (undated).

Tuttle
-Fall of metal foil
1951, Nov.13/Alvin Poage
"Found on Ground," Doubt, no.42
(1953):238,239.

Vinita
-Phantom
1880-1881/McMichael Bean/Circle J Ranch
McMichael Bean & A.L. Lloyd, "The
Little Man Who Was Sometimes There,"
Fate 15 (Mar.1962):76-79.
-UFO (CE-1)
1974, Feb.18/Clay Knight
"Oklahoma Dairy Farmer Reports Object
Landed in His Pasture," Skylook, no.
76 (Mar.1974):15.
-UFO (NL)
1975, Jan.19/Harold Willingham/7½ mi.
SE
Robert A. Goerman, "The UFO Modus
Operandi: January 1975," Official
UFO 1 (Aug.1976):46,65.

Walters
-UFO (NL)
1947, June 25/C.E. Holman
Oklahoma City Daily Oklahoman, 6
July 1947.

Wann
-Humanoid
ca.1915/Crum King
Jerome Clark & Loren Coleman, Creatures of the Outer Edge (N.Y.: Warner, 1978), p.65.

Warner
-Ancient inscription
1972/Brent Gorman
Gloria Farley, "The Stones Speak,"
Oklahoma Today 26 (winter 1975-76):
23-27.
(Editorial), Oklahoma Today 26
(spring 1976):20. il.
Gloria Farley, "Inscriptions from
Mid-America," Occ.Pub.Epigraphic
Soc'y 3, no.69 (Sep.1976):9.

Watonga
-UFO (NL)
1969, March 7/Milton Banta
Watonga Republican, 13 Mar.1969.

Watova
-Humanoid
1974, July-Aug./Margie Lee
Jerome Clark, "Oklahoma Monsters
Come in Pairs," Fate 29 (Dec.1976):
70-71.

Waukomis
-UFO (CE-2)
1952, July 29/Sid Eubank/S on U.S.81
Harold T. Wilkins, Flying Saucers on
the Attack (N.Y.: Ace, 1967 ed.),
p.280.

Weatherford
-UFO (CE-1)
1973, Nov.29/Darrel Nickels/Dead Woman's Crossing
Weatherford News, 30 Nov.1973.

Whitefield
-Precognition
1900, summer/Rev. Collier
Hereward Carrington, "Fateful Premonition," Fate 28 (Apr.1975):39.

Wilburton
-Anomalous artifact
1912/Frank J. Kenwood/=iron pot encased
in coal
Wilbert H. Rusch, Sr., "Human Foot-
prints in Rocks," Creation Rsch.
Soc'y Quar., Mar.1971, p.201. il.
-Humanoid
ca.1956/13 mi. from town
John Green, Sasquatch: The Apes Among
Us (Seattle: Hancock House, 1978),
p.182.

Willis
-UFO (NL)
1957, Nov./Glenn Northcutt
"All About Sputs," Doubt, no.56
(1958):460,471.

Wynnewood
-UFO (R-V)
1965, July 31/Lewis Sikes
Coral E. Lorenzen, Flying Saucers:
The Startling Evidence of the Invasion from Outer Space (N.Y.: Signet, 1966 ed.), p.237.

B. Physical Features

Black Mesa
-Human tracks in sandstone
1975/R. Truman Tucker
Kansas City (Mo.) Star, 10 Aug.1975.
R. Truman Tucker, "Human Footprints
in Stone," Oklahoma Today 25 (spring
1975):2-4. il.

Cimarron R.
-Ancient inscriptions
Barry Fell, America B.C. (N.Y.: Quad-
rangle, 1976), pp.182-83,186,243-
44. il.
Gloria Farley, "The Stones Speak,"

Oklahoma Today 26 (winter 1975-76):
23-27.
(Editorial), Oklahoma Today 26
(spring 1976):20. il.
Gloria Farley, "Inscriptions from
Mid-America," Occ.Pub.Epigraphic
Soc'y 3, no.69 (Sep.1976):4-8. il.
Gloria Farley, "Five-Foot Ogam from
Cimarron," Occ.Pub.Epigraphic Soc'y
5, no.101 (Sep.1977):31-32.

Domebo Canyon
-Archeological site
Adrian D. Anderson & Franklin L.
Chappabitty, "A Bison Kill from
Domebo Canyon," Great Plains J. 8
(1968):48-52.

Keystone Dam
-UFO (CE-2)
1973, Oct.16/Donna Hatchett/4 mi.away
on Coyote Trail
Tulsa World, 19 Oct.1973.
Fort Smith (Ark.) Southwest Times-
Record, 19 Oct.1973.
"Close Encounter in Oklahoma," APRO
Bull. 22 (Sep.-Oct.1973):8-9.

Kiamichi Mts.
-Ghost dog
1879, March 1/Edouard Jacques
Edouard Jacques & A.L. Lloyd, "Ghost
Dog of the Kiamichi Mts.," Fate 14
(Aug.1961):78-84.

Little R.
-Humanoid
n.d.
1975, June
Idabel McCurtain Sunday Gazette, 9
July 1978.

Mountain Fork R.
-Humanoid
1926, spring
Idabel McCurtain Sunday Gazette, 9
July 1978.

Texhoma L.
-Phantom panther
ca.1959/Ray Sutterfield/E shore
Jerome Clark, "'Manimals' Make Tracks
in Oklahoma," Fate 24 (Sep.1971):
60,66.

Turkey Mt.
-Ancient inscription
1968/Randall Walls
Barry Fell, America B.C. (N.Y.: Quad-
rangle, 1976), pp.49,299.
Gloria Farley, "Inscriptions from
Mid-America," Occ.Pub.Epigraphic
Soc'y 3, no.69 (Sep.1976):4.

Washita R.
-Unicorn legends
Letter from James Mackay to John
Evans, 28 Jan.1796, in A.P. Nasatir,
ed., Before Lewis and Clark, 2 vols.
(St. Louis: Historical Documents

Foundation, 1952), 2:412.
Harold T. Wilkins, Secret Cities of
Old South America (N.Y.: Library,
1952), p.282.

Wichita Mts.
-Pictographs
S. Weidman, "Indian Pictographs in
the Wichita Mountains," Oklahoma
Acad.Sci., n.s., no.271 (1923):125-
27.

C. Ethnic Groups

Delaware Indians
-Shamanism and herbalism
C.A. Weslager, Magic Medicines of the
Indians (N.Y.: Signet, 1973 ed.).

Wichita Indians
-Contactee myth
George A. Dorsey, The Mythology of
the Wichita (Washington: Carnegie
Inst., 1904), pp.298-99.
-Flood myth
George A. Dorsey, The Mythology of
the Wichita (Washington: Carnegie
Inst., 1904), pp.290-97.
-Lake monster myth
George A. Dorsey, The Mythology of
the Wichita (Washington: Carnegie
Inst., 1904), pp.102-106.
-Paleoastronomy
Waldo R. Wedel, "Native Astronomy
and the Plains Caddoans," in Anthony
F. Aveni, ed., Native American As-
tronomy (Austin: Univ. of Texas,
1977), pp.131-45.

Yuchi Indians
-Similarity to Indus Valley and Minoan
cultures
Cyrus Gordon, "The Metcalf Stone,"
Manuscripts 21 (1969):158-68.
Joseph Mahan, Identification of the
Tsoyaha Waeno, Builders of Temple
Mounds (Ph.D dissertation, Univ. of
North Carolina at Chapel Hill, 1970).
William D. Connor, "Archeologists
Link Georgia Indians to Crete," Fate
24 (Jan.1971):36-44. il.
Joseph B. Mahan, "They Actually Were
Indians," Oklahoma Today 27 (autumn
1977):2-6.
Lawrence (Kan.) Journal-World, 17
Oct.1977.

D. Unspecified Localities

-Fall of fish, frogs, snakes and rocks
1909-1914/Eula B. Yoder
Eula B. Yoder, "God's Special Frogs,"
Fate 24 (Oct.1971):74.

A. Populated Places

Abilene
-Genetic anomaly
1945, Sep./J.S. Moses/Oaks Tourist
Court
Jack Hampton, "Where Was Moses?"
Fate 8 (Apr.1955):56-58.
-Out-of-body experience
1943, Dec.20-24/George Ritchie/Camp
Barkeley
[George Ritchie], "I Found Life Be-
yond Death," Fate 23 (Dec.1970):40-
50.
Herbert B. Greenhouse, The Astral
Journey (N.Y.: Avon, 1976 ed.), pp.
144-46.
-UFO (NL)
1948, Jan.1
Edward J. Ruppelt, The Report on Un-
identified Flying Objects (Garden
City: Doubleday, 1956), pp.29-30.
1951, Nov.2
Donald E. Keyhoe, Aliens from Space
(Garden City: Doubleday, 1973), pp.
204-205.
1957, Nov.9/James Morrow
Los Angeles (Cal.) Examiner, 10 Nov.
1957.

Adrian
-Fall of metallic object
1970, Aug.30/George Gruhl/=Soviet Cos-
mos satellite
Louisville (Ky.) Courier-Journal, 31
Aug.1970.
San Francisco (Cal.) Chronicle, 31
Aug.1970.

Alice
-UFO (DD)
1948, July 27/William G. Delahan
Alice Daily Echo, 27 July 1948.
(Letter), Fate 2 (May 1949):93-94.

Alvarado
-UFO (DD)
1947, June 25
Dallas Morning News, 1 July 1947.

Amarillo
-Telephone anomaly
n.d./Carolyn Jones
"Carolyn Jones' Weird Experience,"
Fate 19 (Apr.1966):77.
-UFO (CE-1)
1957, July 22/G.M. Schemel
Kansas City (Mo.) Star, 23 July 1957,
p.1.
Donald E. Keyhoe, Flying Saucers: Top
Secret (N.Y.: Putnam, 1960), pp.
98-99.
1957, Nov.3
Donald E. Keyhoe, Flying Saucers: Top

Secret (N.Y.: Putnam, 1960), pp.
116-17.
-UFO (CE-2)
1950, April 8/David Lightfoot/nr. Con-
valescent Home, 10 mi.NW
Amarillo Sunday News-Globe, 9 Apr.
1950.
1957, Nov.2/S of town
Amarillo Daily News, 4 Nov.1957.
1965, Aug.4/Harvey Burgman
Abilene (Kan.) Reflector-Chronicle,
6 Aug.1965, p.1.
-UFO (NL)
1956, Aug.2/J.G. Kirby
"Air Force Denies UFO Witnesses Muz-
zled Despite Order at Dallas," UFO
Inv. 1 (Jan.1958):21. il.
"All About Sputs," Doubt, no.56
(1958):460,472, quoting Dallas
Morning News (undated).
1957, Nov.2/Calvin Harris/airport
Donald E. Keyhoe, Flying Saucers:
Top Secret (N.Y.: Putnam, 1960), p.
114.
1965, Aug.1/SW of airport
Coral E. Lorenzen, "Western UFO Flap,"
Fate 18 (Nov.1965):42,47.

Angleton
-Ghost light
1830s-1960/Bailey's Prairie, 5 mi.W
Gloria Swanson, "Bailey's Light," in
Mody C. Boatright & Donald Day, eds.,
Backwoods to Border (Austin: Texas
Folklore Soc'y, Pub.no.18, 1943),
pp.144-45.
"The Ghost of Brazoria County," Fate
9 (Dec.1956):34.
"Trail of a Texas Ghost," Fate 17
(Apr.1964):74.

Aquilla
-UFO (CE-1)
1897, April/3 mi.N
Dallas News, 28 Apr.1897.

Aransas Pass
-Mystery plane crash
1930, July 10/5 mi. from town
Vincent Gaddis, Invisible Horizons
(Philadelphia: Chilton, 1965), pp.
201-202, quoting AP release, 11
July 1930.

Arlington
-UFO (NL)
1960, Sep.29/J. Rodriguez, Jr.
Richard Hall, ed., The UFO Evidence
(Washington: NICAP, 1964), p.45.

Atlanta
-UFO (NL)
1897, April 19/Jim Nelson
Houston Post, 22 Apr.1897.

Aurora
-UFO (?)
1897, April 17/J.T. Weems/Proctor's
windmill/=hoax
Dallas Morning News, 19 Apr.1897,
p.5.
Frank Masquelette, "Claims Made of
UFO Evidence," Houston Post, 13
June 1966.
(Letter), D.B. Hanlon & J.F. Vallee,
Flying Saucer Rev. 13 (Jan.-Feb.
1967):27.
"The Aurora, Texas Case," APRO Bull.
21 (May-June 1973):1,3-4.
"More on Aurora," APRO Bull. 22
(July-Aug.1973):5.
"The Mystery Airship," Pursuit 6
(July 1973):55.
Hayden C. Hewes, "Search for the Au-
rora Astronaut," Probe the Unknown
1 (Dec.1973):46-51. il.
(Letter), Edward E. Dickey, Probe
the Unknown 2 (spring 1974):4-5.
Hayden C. Hewes, "The UFO Crash of
1897: Aurora Astronaut Update," Of-
ficial UFO 1 (Jan.1976):29-31. il.

Austin
-Acoustic anomaly
1975, Nov.9/Ray Stanford/20 mi.NW
1976, Feb.27/Max Wilson/15 mi.NW
Jerold R. Johnson, "Reports of Fly-
ing, Pulsating Sound in Texas,"
MUFON UFO J., no.103 (June 1976):
17.
-Archeological site
A.T. Jackson, "A Deep Archaeological
Site in Travis County, Texas," Bull.
Texas Arch.& Paleont.Soc'y 11 (1939)
:203-25.
-Clairvoyance
1833, Aug./Mrs. Reuben Hornsby
Josiah W. Wilbarger, Indian Depred-
ations in Texas (Austin: Hutchings,
1889), pp.7-14.
-Erratic jellyfish
1954, Oct./Mrs. W.M. Reynolds
(Editorial), Fate 8 (Apr.1955):11.
-Fall of ice
1946, May 16
"Hail Grapefruit Size," Doubt, no.15
(summer 1946):226.
-Ghost
1913/Mr. Joyce/School for the Blind
Mrs. Fritz Weber & Molly Anstiss,
"Emmy Lou's Mother Came Too," Fate
10 (Feb.1957):84-86.
-Haunt
1972, June 24-1976/A. Guerrero
(Letter), Fate 30 (Jan.1977):117-18.
-Humanoid
1875, Sep.
Helena (Mont.) Daily Independent, 19
Sep.1875.
-Inner development
1971-   /Ass'n for the Understanding
of Man/3724 Jefferson
Ray Stanford, Fatima Prophecy/Days
of Darkness/Promise of Light (Aus-
tin: AUM, 1972).

"Interview: Ray Stanford," Psychic 5
(Mar.-Apr.1974):6-11,36-38. il.
Ray Stanford, The Spirit unto the
Churches (Austin: AUM, 1977).
-Parapsychology research
1960s, 1976-   /Rex G. Stanford/Cen-
ter for Parapsychological Research
Rex G. Stanford, "Differential Posi-
tion Effects for Above-Chance Scoring Sheep and Goats," J.Parapsych.
28 (1964):155-65.
Rex G. Stanford, "A Further Study of
High-Versus Low-Scoring Sheep," J.
Parapsych. 29 (1965):141-58.
Rex G. Stanford, "The Effect of Re-
striction of Calling upon Run-Score
Variance," J.Parapsych. 30 (1966):
160-71.
Rex G. Stanford, "Response Bias and
the Correctness of ESP Test Responses," J.Parapsych. 31 (1967):280-89.
Rex G. Stanford, "'Associative Acti-
vation of the Unconscious' and 'Vis-
ualization' as Methods for Influen-
cing the PK Target," J.ASPR 63
(1969):338-51.
Rex G. Stanford & A. Stio, "A Study
of Associative Mediation in Psi-Med-
iated Instrumental Response," J.ASPR
70 (1976):55-64.
Rex G. Stanford, et al., "A Study of
Motivational Arousal and Self-Con-
cept in Psi-Mediated Instrumental
Response," J.ASPR 70 (1976):167-78.
Rex G. Stanford & Angelo Costello,
"Cognitive Mode and Extrasensory
Function in a Timing-Based PMIR
Task," in J.D. Morris, et al., eds.,
Research in Parapsych. 1976 (Metu-
chen, N.J.: Scarecrow, 1977), pp.
142-46.
-Precognition
1977, May/Ruben Diaz
(Editorial), Fate 30 (Oct.1977):22-
24.
-Stratigraphic anomaly
Robert T. Hill, "Two Limestone Forma-
tions of the Cretaceous of Texas
Which Transgress Time Diagonally,"
Science 53 (1921):190-91.
-UFO (?)
1952, April 2/=meteor?
Austin Statesman, 3 Apr.1952 .
-UFO (CE-3)
1971, Nov.3/Trudy Van Riper
(Letter), Fate 25 (Dec.1972):142-43.
-UFO (DD)
1968, April 16/Henry Ford II
Donald E. Keyhoe, Aliens from Space
(Garden City: Doubleday, 1973), p.
177.
-UFO (NL)
1952, April 23
Oklahoma City Times, 25 Apr.1952.
1952, April 24
Austin American, 25 Apr.1952.
1957, Nov.14
Richard Hall, ed., The UFO Evidence
(Washington: NICAP, 1964), p.167.
1972, May/Project Starlight/15 mi.NW

"UFO Research Facility Constructed,"
Skylook, no.86 (Jan.1975):17.
1973, Oct.22/Ray Stanford/Project Starlight International/15 mi.NW
Columbus (O.) Dispatch, 15 Oct.1974,
p.48.
1974, Oct.4/Project Starlight Inter-
national/15 mi.NW
Columbus (O.) Dispatch, 15 Oct.1974,
p.48. il.
"PSI Releases Photo of UFO Passage,"
Skylook, no.85 (Dec.1974):16. il.
1974, Oct.12/Ray Stanford/Project Starlight International/15 mi.NW
"The Charles Hickson--P.S.I. Sighting," J.Instrumented UFO Rsch. 1
(Oct.1975):13-15.
Jerome Clark, "Startling New Evidence
in the Pascagoula and Adamski Ab-
ductions," Saga UFO Rept. 6 (Aug.
1978):36,76-78.
1974, Nov.11/Project Starlight Inter-
national/15 mi.NW
1975, Dec.10/Project Starlight Inter-
national/15 mi.NW
Bruce A. Schaffenberger, "Prepared
for the Unknown: Project Starlight
International," Official UFO 2 (May
1977):42-44. il.
-Ufology project
1973-   /Ray Stanford/Project Star-
light International/15 mi.NW
Austin American, 19 Oct.1973.
"Interview: Ray Stanford," Psychic 5
(Mar.-Apr.1974):6-11,36-38. il.
Ray Stanford, "The Operation Argus
Concept: A New Look at UFO Events
Sharing and Data Sharing," in 1976
MUFON UFO Symposium Proc. (Seguin,
Tex.: MUFON, 1976), pp.20-28. il.
Franco Cernero, "Project Starlight:
An Invitation to UFOs," Saga UFO
Rept. 3 (June 1976):46-49. il.
Ray Stanford, "A Technological Ap-
proach to UFOs," Int'l UFO Reporter
2 (Aug.1977):5-7. il.
Jerome Clark, "Startling New Evidence
in the Pascagoula and Adamski Ab-
ductions," Saga UFO Rept. 6 (Aug.
1978):36-39,70-78.

Bandera
-UFO (CE-1)
1974, Dec.1/Van Smith/N on Hwy.173
Van Smith, "Report a UFO at Your Own
Risk," Fate 31 (Jan.1978):59-63.

Baytown
-Psychokinesis
1959, June/Walter C. Thompson/Lakewood
"Mystery of the Toppled Tree," Fate
13 (Apr.1960):52.
-UFO (CE-1)
1966, July 18/W.T. Jackson
Houston Post, 9 Sep.1966.
-UFO (CE-2)
1966, March 30
Lubbock Advance-Journal, 31 Mar.1966,
p.A8.

Beaumont
-Fall of white substance
1978, May 16
Dallas Times-Herald, 17 May 1978.
-UFO (?)
1957, Nov.5/Clyde C. Rush
Donald E. Keyhoe, Flying Saucers:
Top Secret (N.Y.: Putnam, 1960), p.
122.
1970s/Thomas B. Combs
(Letter), Saga UFO Rept. 5 (June
1978):4.
1972, April 29-30/=balloon?
Beaumont Journal, 1 May 1972.
-UFO (CE-3)
1897, April 19/J.B. Ligon
Houston Post, 21 Apr.1897, p.2.
Pittsfield (Ill.) Pike County Demo-
crat, 7 May 1897, p.1, quoting New
Orleans (La.) Picayune (undated).
-UFO (DD)
1967, Sep.20/Lyle Gaulding/Cardinal Dr.
x Galveston Hwy.
(Letter), INFO J., no.3 (spring 1968)
:46.
-UFO (NL)
1967, Oct.21
"UFOs--October--U.S.A.," APRO Bull.
16 (Nov.-Dec.1967):8.
1975, July 4/Judy James
(Letter), Saga UFO Rept. 3 (Apr.
1976):6.

Beeville
-Archeological site
E.H. Sellards, T.N. Campbell & Glen
L. Evans, "Pleistocene Artifacts
and Associated Fossils from Bee
County, Texas," Bull.Geol.Soc'y Am.
51 (1940):1627-58.

Bells
-Fall of carbonaceous meteorite
1961, Sep.9
Oscar E. Monning, "The Bells, Texas,
Meteorite," Meteoritics 2 (1963):67.

Belton
-UFO (CE-1)
1897, April 19/Peay Hotel
Houston Post, 22 Apr.1897, p.9.

Benbrook
-Humanoid
1973, March 19/Mark Fricke
"The Road to Noxie," Probe the Unknown 4 (Mar.1976):44-45.

Benchley
-UFO (DD)
1974
Timothy Green Beckley, "Calvert, Texas: Flying Saucer Way Station," Saga
UFO Rept. 2 (spring 1975):18,22,68.
il.

Benjamin
-UFO (NL)
1961, Jan.10/W.K. Rutledge
Richard Hall, ed., The UFO Evidence

(Washington: NICAP, 1964), p.43.

Bethel
-Giant bird
1976, Dec.18/Mrs. O.M. Moore
Palestine Herald-Press, 22 Dec.1976.

Bexar co.
-Haunt
1960, July/southern sector
(Editorial), Fate 13 (Dec.1960):20-
22.
-Skyquake
1964, March 25
"Leading Up to the Big Flap," Fate
17 (Aug.1964):45,46.

Big Spring
-Cattle mutilation
1975, March/N of town
Ed Sanders, "The Mutilation Mystery,"
Oui, Sep.1976, pp.51,113.

Blanco
-Haunt
1952-1954/Mr. Mackford
Peggy Pearson, "Is My House Haunted?"
Fate 11 (Apr.1958):90-93.

Boerne
-UFO (CE-1)
1957, Nov.6
Jacques Vallee, Passport to Magonia
(Chicago: Regnery, 1969), p.264.

Bonham
-UFO (?)
1873, June/Mr. Harden/5 mi.E
Fort Scott (Kan.) Monitor, 24 June
1873, p.4.
New York Times, 6 July 1873, p.1.
1897, April 17
Dallas Morning News, 18 Apr.1897.
1973, Oct.
"Saucers in the News," Flying Saucers,
no.83 (winter 1974):44,59.

Borger
-UFO (DD)
1947, July 4
Houston Post, 6 July 1947.
-UFO (NL)
1956, May 13/Helen Turner
(Letter), Fate 9 (Oct.1956):113.
1965, Aug.1
Coral E. Lorenzen, "Western UFO Flap,"
Fate 18 (Nov.1965):42,47.

Brady
-Anomalous artifact
1900s/Mrs. Frank Kidd/=secret society
medallion?
Steve Yankee, "The Mystery of the
Medallions," Probe the Unknown 3
(Sep.1975):22-23,54-55. il.
(Letter), Orval E. Brown, Probe the
Unknown 4 (Jan.1976):8.
(Letter), Anon., Probe the Unknown
4 (Jan.1976):8-9.

Brazos
-UFO (CE-2)
1975, Oct.16
"UFO Central," CUFOS News Bull., 1
Feb.1976, p.9.

Bremond
-UFO (CE-1)
1973, Nov.18/Faye Seeley
Tommy R. Blann, "Bright Lights over
Them Purple Plains," Probe the Un-
known 2 (summer 1974):56,58-59.

Brenham
-UFO (DD)
1957, April 5/Wilhelmina Kaechele
(Letter), Fate 10 (Aug.1957):116-20.

Brownsville
-Erratic crocidilian
1970, Sep.21/Max Cody
Brownsville Herald, 21 Sep.1970.
-Giant bird
1976, Jan./Libby Ford/NE of town
1976, Jan.7/Alverico Guajardo/2 mi.N
on Hwy.77
Brownsville Herald, 18 Jan.1976.
Jerome Clark & Loren Coleman, Creatures of the Outer Edge (N.Y.: Warner, 1978), pp.173-74,179.
-UFO (CE-1)
1973, Nov.14/Eddie Gonzalez/N of town
Columbus (O.) Dispatch, 15 Nov.1973,
p.17A.
Leonard H. Stringfield, Situation
Red: The UFO Siege (N.Y.: Fawcett,
1977 ed.), pp.139-41.
-UFO (CE-2)
1956, Oct.21/Ray Stanford/10 mi.NE
Jerome Clark, "Startling New Evidence
in the Pascagoula and Adamski Ab-
ductions," Saga UFO Rept. 6 (Aug.
1978):36,38.

Brownwood
-Cattle mutilation
1975, Jan.
Ed Sanders, "The Mutilation Mystery,"
Oui, Sep.1976, pp.51,113, quoting
Fort Worth Star-Telegram (undated).
-Erratic spotted rail
1977, Aug.
Paris News, 11 Aug.1977.
-UFO (?)
1973, Oct.23
Brownwood Bulletin, 24 Oct.1973.
-UFO (CE-1)
1949, July 17/Hazel Armstrong/1507
Durham
Kenneth Arnold & Ray Palmer, The Com-
ing of the Saucers (Boise: The Au-
thor, 1952), p.143.

Bryan
-UFO (?)
1966, March 28
New York Herald-Tribune, 29 Mar.1966,
p.2.
1968, July 4/John West/=meteor?
"Some Recent Fireballs," Sky & Tele-

scope 36 (Sep.1968):195.
-UFO (NL)
    1897, April 17
        Houston Post, 20 Apr.1897.

Buffalo
-Mystery plane crash
    1959, Sep.29/Electra, Braniff Flight
    542
        Donald E. Keyhoe, Aliens from Space
        (Garden City: Doubleday, 1973), pp.
        193-95.

Calvert
-Acoustic anomaly
    ca.1974/5 mi. from town
        Timothy Green Beckley, "Calvert, Tex-
        as: Flying Saucer Way Station," Saga
        UFO Rept. 2 (spring 1975):18,71.
-Humanoid
    1973, Dec?
        Timothy Green Beckley, "Calvert, Tex-
        as: Flying Saucer Way Station," Saga
        UFO Rept. 2 (spring 1975):18,66.
-Mystery radio transmission
    1973, Nov./Virgil Chappell
        Timothy Green Beckley, "Calvert, Tex-
        as: Flying Saucer Way Station," Saga
        UFO Rept. 2 (spring 1975):18,20.
-Phantom automobile
    1973, Dec?/Alfred Conitz
        Timothy Green Beckley, "Calvert, Tex-
        as: Flying Saucer Way Station," Saga
        UFO Rept. 2 (spring 1975):18,69.
-UFO (?)
    1973, Nov.-Dec.
        Timothy Green Beckley, "Calvert, Tex-
        as: Flying Saucer Way Station," Saga
        UFO Rept. 2 (spring 1975):18,69.
-UFO (CE-1)
    1956/Gracia Unger/E on Hwy.6
    1973, Nov./Lillian Juarez/Farm Rd. 1644
    1973, Dec.19
    1974, June 27/Alice Tribble
        Timothy Green Beckley, "Calvert, Tex-
        as: Flying Saucer Way Station," Saga
        UFO Rept. 2 (spring 1975):18,20,66,
        68,70.
-UFO (CE-2)
    1973, Oct.28/Gracia Unger/S of town
        Tommy R. Blann, "Bright Lights over
        Them Purple Plains," Probe the Un-
        known 2 (summer 1974):56,59.
    1973, Nov./Felix R. Luna/Brazos R.
    1973, Nov.-Dec./Steve Abraham/ground
    markings only
    1973, Dec.11/Cleo Smitherman/Old Hearne
    Rd.
        Timothy Green Beckley, "Calvert, Tex-
        as: Flying Saucer Way Station," Saga
        UFO Rept. 2 (spring 1975):18,66-69.
    1974, Aug.2/Hwy.979
        George D. Fawcett, "A Review of Some
        of the Thousands of UFO Sightings
        in 1974 to Date," Flying Saucers,
        no.86 (Dec.1974):39.
-UFO (NL)
    1973, Nov./Duncan Mack/Brazos R. Bridge
    1973, Nov.15/Virgil Chappell
    1973, Nov.21/Tommy R. Blann/Brazos R.

1974, Feb.4/Charles Juarez
    Timothy Green Beckley, "Calvert, Tex-
    as: Flying Saucer Way Station," Saga
    UFO Rept. 2 (spring 1975):18,20-23,
    66,70.

Cameron
-UFO (CE-1)
    1897, April/Tom Peoples
        Dallas Morning News, 19 Apr.1897, p.
        5.

Canadian
-UFO (CE-3)
    1957, Nov.2/3 mi.W
        Jacques Vallee, Passport to Magonia
        (Chicago: Regnery, 1969), pp.261-
        62.

Canutillo
-UFO (DD)
    1957, Nov.22/Mrs. G.A. Baker
        Richard Hall, ed., The UFO Evidence
        (Washington: NICAP, 1964), p.66.

Canyon
-UFO (NL)
    1965, Aug.3/Dan Carter
        Abilene (Kan.) Reflector-Chronicle,
        3 Aug.1965, p.1.

Castroville
-Ghost
    n.d./August Gauchemain
        Charles M. Skinner, American Myths
        and Legends, 2 vols. (Philadelphia:
        Lippincott, 1903), 2:129-34.

Cedar Hill
-Phantom image
    1972, May 25/Everett Foster
        Dorris Wainscott, "Phantom Pictures
        on the Wall," Fate 26 (Apr.1973):58.

Cedar Park
-UFO (NL)
    1974, Oct.2/Dan Harris
        Wendelle C. Stevens, "UFO Tracks in
        the Sky," Saga UFO Rept. 2 (fall
        1975):23,25.

Celeste
-UFO (NL)
    1915/Silbie Latham
        Alex Evans, "Encounters with Little
        Men," Fate 31 (Nov.1978):83,84.

Childress
-UFO (DD)
    1950, April 18/Carl Gray
        Donald E. Keyhoe, "Flight 117 and
        the Flying Saucer," True 27 (Aug.
        1950):24,75.
-UFO (NL)
    1897, April 17/J.W. Smith
        Houston Post, 22 Apr.1897.

Chilton
-UFO (NL)
    1973, Dec.19/Tommy R. Blann

Timothy Green Beckley, "Calvert, Texas: Flying Saucer Way Station," Saga UFO Rept. 2 (spring 1975):18,22,68. il.

China Spring
-UFO (CE-1)
 1975, Jan.16
    "From the Center for UFO Studies,"
    Flying Saucer Rev. 21 (Aug.1975):32.

Cisco
-Poltergeist
 1881/R.T. Woodson/5 mi.S
    O.G. Lawson & Kenneth W. Porter,
    "Texas Poltergeist, 1881," J.Am.
    Folklore 64 (1951):371-82.

Cleburne
-UFO (?)
 1897, April 17
    Dallas Morning News, 18 Apr.1897, p.
    5.

Clifton
-Mystery bird deaths
 1976, April 13/Cy Landau/10 mi.W/=
 pelicans
    (Editorial), Fate 29 (Oct.1976):19,
    22.

Coleman
-UFO (NL)
 1957, Nov.1
    Richard Hall, ed., The UFO Evidence
    (Washington: NICAP, 1964), p.163.

Columbus
-Fall of ice
 1967, March 11/Wayne Knappick
    (Editorial), Fate 20 (Sep.1967):9-10.

Comanche
-Fall of frogs
 1912/Ruby L. Mitchell
    (Letter), Fate 16 (Aug.1963):129.
-Healing
 1910
    Anne Hubbard, "The Healing String,"
    Fate 9 (Sep.1956):96.

Commerce
-Phantom airplane
 1968, spring/Gary Massey/5 mi.E on Hwy.
 11
    "A 'Mystery Airplane' Sighting in
    Hopkins County, Texas, Spring,
    1968," Skylook, no.29 (Apr.1970):13.

Conroe
-UFO (?)
 1897, April 22/G.L. Witherspoon
    Jerome Clark & Loren Coleman, "Mystery Airships of the 1800s," Fate
    26 (June 1973):96,100.

Copperas Cove
-Cattle mutilation and UFO (NL)
 1975/Sheppard Farm
    Tommy Roy Blann, "The Mysterious

Link Between UFOs and Animal Mutilations," Saga UFO Rept. 3 (Apr.
    1976):18,70-72.
-UFO (DD)
 1969, May/Dennis D. Bradford/Meadow x
 Post Oak Rd.
    "Copperas Cove, Texas, Sighting,"
    Skylook, no.22 (Sep.1969):13.

Corpus Christi
-Fall of metallic objects
 1954, Oct./O.L. Breitkreutz/3117
 Churchill Dr./=hoax
    (Editorial), Fate 8 (Aug.1955):10-11.
    (Letter), John R. Leslie, Fate 8
    (Dec.1955):123-24.
-UFO (DD)
 1959, July 28/Ray Stanford
    Richard Hall, ed., The UFO Evidence
    (Washington: NICAP, 1964), pp.91-
    92.
-UFO (NL)
 1944, March 2/Kevin Phillips
    (Letter), Saga UFO Rept. 2 (summer
    1975):4.
 1961, Jan.10-16/W.J. Mobley/Tule L.
 bridge
    "Bright Object Puzzles Texans," APRO
    Bull. 9 (Jan.1961):5.

Corsicana
-Humanoid
 1977, Sep.2/E on Hwy.31
    John Green, Sasquatch: The Apes Among
    Us (Seattle: Hancock House, 1978),
    p.188, quoting Corsicana Daily Sun
    (undated).
-UFO (NL)
 1897, April 14
    Dallas Morning News, 16 Apr.1897.

Cranfills Gap
-Mystery bird deaths
 1974, April 13/=pelicans
    Los Angeles (Cal.) Times, 27 Apr.
    1974.

Crowell
-Entombed toad
 n.d./W.H. McGonagle
    W.E. Farbstein, "Strange Finds,"
    Fate 4 (Mar.1951):15.

Dalhart
-UFO (CE-4)
 1958, summer/John Alter/15 mi. from
 town
    B. Ann Slate, "UFOs in Trouble," Saga
    UFO Rept. 6 (Sep.1978):49-50.
-UFO (NL)
 1965, Aug.1
    Coral E. Lorenzen, "Western UFO Flap,"
    Fate 18 (Nov.1965):42,47.

Dallas
-Animal ESP
 1954, March/Raiberto Comini/J.N. Holt
 Animal Clinic
    (Editorial), Fate 7 (Oct.1954):6.
-Clairempathy and precognition

1930s-   /Ann Jensen
    Charles E. Stuart, "An Analysis to
    Determine a Test Predictive of Ex-
    tra-Chance Scoring in Card-Calling
    Tests," J.Parapsych. 5 (June 1941):
    99-137.
    Helen Reagan, "Ann Jensen: Texas
    Psychic," Fate 23 (Sep.1970):36-
    44. il.
    Herbert B. Greenhouse, Premonitions:
    A Leap into the Future (N.Y.: War-
    ner, 1973 ed.), pp.207-209.
    David Wallechinsky & Irving Wallace,
    The People's Almanac (Garden City:
    Doubleday, 1975), pp.6-7.
    Martin Ebon, The Evidence for Life
    After Death (N.Y.: Signet, 1977),
    pp.81-82.
-Clairvoyance and palmistry
1962-   /Carl Logan
    James Crenshaw, "Psychic Locates
    Missing Plane," Fate 25 (Nov.1972):
    59-64. il.
    James Crenshaw, "Carl Logan's Psy-
    chic Radar," Fate 28 (May 1975):
    39-44. il.
    Jack Murray, "Selective Enforcement
    Strikes Again," Probe the Unknown
    4 (Jan.1976):12.
-Crisis apparition
1934, April 20
    "Case," J.ASPR 39 (1945):113-25.
-Deathbed apparition
1956, 1971/Helen Hadsell
    Brad Steiger, Revelation: The Divine
    Fire (Englewood Cliffs, N.J.: Pren-
    tice-Hall, 1973), pp.126-27.
-Disappearance
1937/Keshaven Vijayadev/Parkland Hospital
    Don Aronoff & Mitzi Molina, "The
    Vanished Seer," Fate 20 (Mar.1967):
    86-93.
-Doubtful responsibility
1963, Nov.22/Lee Harvey Oswald/Kennedy
assassination/=conspiracy?
    U.S. President's Comm'n on the Ass-
    assination of President Kennedy,
    Investigation of the Assassination
    of President Kennedy, 26 vols.
    (Washington: U.S. Gov't Printing
    Office, 1964).
    Thomas G. Buchanan, Who Killed Ken-
    nedy? (London: Secker & Warburg,
    1964).
    Joachim Joesten, Oswald: Assassin or
    Fall Guy? (N.Y.: Marzani & Munsell,
    1964).
    Gerald R. Ford & John R. Stiles, Por-
    trait of the Assassin (N.Y.: Simon
    & Schuster, 1965).
    Mark Lane, Rush to Judgment (N.Y.:
    Holt, 1966).
    Edward J. Epstein, Inquest (N.Y.:
    Viking, 1966).
    Léo Sauvage, The Oswald Affair (Cleve-
    land: World, 1966).
    Rosemary James & Jack Wardlaw, Plot
    or Politics? The Garrison Case and
    Its Cast (New Orleans: Pelican,

1967).
Lincoln Lawrence, Were We Controlled?
(N.Y.: University, 1967).
Jim Garrison, Heritage of Stone
(N.Y.: Putnam, 1970).
James Kirkwood, American Grotesque
(N.Y.: Simon & Schuster, 1970).
David Belin, November Twenty-Second,
1963: You Are the Jury (N.Y.: Quad-
rangle, 1973).
David R. Drone, Assassination of
John Fitzgerald Kennedy: An Annota-
ted Bibliography (Madison: Wiscon-
sin State Historical Soc'y, 1973).
Donald Freed & Mark Lane, Executive
Action (N.Y.: Dell, 1973).
Peter F. Model, JFK: The Case for
Conspiracy (N.Y.: Manor, 1975).
Michael Canfield & Alan J. Weberman,
Coup d'Etat in America (N.Y.: Third
Press, 1975).
George O'Toole, The Assassination
Tapes (N.Y.: Penthouse, 1975).
Sylvia Meagher, Accessories After
the Fact (N.Y.: Random House, 1976).
Peter Dale Scott, et al., The Ass-
assinations: Dallas and Beyond
(N.Y.: Random House, 1976).
Joe Manguno, "Was Jim Garrison Right
After All?" New Orleans 10 (June
1976):26-31.
Michael Eddowes, The Oswald File
(N.Y.: Crown, 1977).
Priscilla Johnson McMillan, Marina
and Lee (N.Y.: Harper & Row, 1977).
Robert Anton Wilson, Cosmic Trigger:
Final Secret of the Illuminati (Ber-
keley: And/Or, 1977), pp.31-33,61-
63,149-56.
Edward Jay Epstein, Legend: The Se-
cret World of Lee Harvey Oswald
(N.Y.: McGraw-Hill, 1978).
U.S. Congress, House, Select Comm.
on Assassinations, Investigation of
the Assassination of President John
F. Kennedy, 5 vols. Hearings, 95th
Cong., 2d sess., 1978.
David W. Belin, "The Second-Gunman
Syndrome," Nat'l Review 31 (1979):
553-55.
-Dowsing
1953/6936 Holloway St.
    (Editorial), Fate 6 (Oct.1953):44-45,
    quoting Dallas Morning News (un-
    dated).
-Entombed scorpion
1935
    Ottawa (Ont.) Journal, 16 Oct.1939,
    p.29.
-Exploding tree
1951
    "First Prize," Doubt, no.36 (1952):
    130.
-Fall of fish
1958, June 18/Martha Brumley/Pentagon
Parkway
    Dallas Morning News, 18 June 1958.
    (Editorial), Fate 11 (Oct.1958):17-
    18.
-Fall of unknown object

1972, Aug.11/W.R. Draper/5700 block of
Forney St.
  Dallas Morning News, 13 Aug.1972.
-Haunt
  1962-1964/Dale Berry/White Rock L.
    (Editorial), Fate 15 (Dec.1962):24-
    25, quoting Dallas Times-Herald (un-
    dated).
    "The Ghost of White Rock Lake," Fate
    17 (Nov.1964):110, quoting Dallas
    Morning News (undated).
  1971-1973/Leo Furrh/Prairie Ave.
    (Editorial), Fate 26 (Mar.1973):20-
    21, quoting Dallas Times-Herald (un-
    dated).
  1973/Weldon Maxey/haunted table
    Dallas Morning News, 4 Nov.1973.
-Inner development
  1960s-   /Mark Roberts/Dianic Wicca/
  Box 116
    Hans Holzer, The Witchcraft Report
    (N.Y.: Ace, 1973 ed.), pp.56-57.
    J. Gordon Melton, Encyclopedia of
    American Religions (Wilmington, N.C.:
    Consortium, 1978), 2:276.
-Poltergeist
  1943, July 6
    "Ghosts Active," Fortean Soc'y Mag.,
    no.10 (autumn 1944):142.
-Precognition
  1963, Nov.22
    San Francisco (Cal.) Chronicle, 27
    Nov.1963.
  1969-   /Bertie Catchings/5731 Harvest
  Hill Rd.
    Warren Smith, "How Did the Seers in
    1970?" Fate 24 (Feb.1971):84,86-87.
    il.
    Otto O. Binder, "Are UFOs Here to
    Save the Earth?" Saga UFO Rept. 1
    (summer 1974):14,68.
    Warren Smith, "Phenomenal Predictions
    for 1975," Saga, Jan.1975, pp.21-22.
    Warren Smith, "Phenomenal Predictions
    for 1976," Saga, Jan.1976, pp.16-17.
-Scrying
  1890s/Mary Meriwether
    "Experiments in Crystal Vision, and
    Other Experiences," J.ASPR 12 (1918)
    :209-12.
-Skyquake
  1951, Dec.12
    Coral E. Lorenzen, The Shadow of the
    Unknown (N.Y.: Signet, 1970), pp.
    67-68.
-Spontaneous human combustion
  1964, Oct./Olga Worth Stephens/E. Grand
  Ave.
    (Editorial), Fate 18 (Feb.1965):15.
-UFO (?)
  1897, April/M.E. Griffin/court house
    Dallas Morning News, 17 Apr.1897, p.
    8.
  1950, April 19
    Jacques & Janine Vallee, Challenge
    to Science (N.Y.: Ace, 1966 ed.),
    p.199.
  1952, April 2/=meteor?
    Fort Worth Star-Telegram, 3-4 Apr.
    1952.

1956, Nov.24/J.J. Jobe/Love Field/=
meteor
  "Case 272," CRIFO Orbit, 1 Feb.1957,
  p.3, quoting Dallas Morning News
  (undated).
1964, Feb.26/=meteor
  "Leading Up to the Big Flap," Fate
  17 (Aug.1964):45.
-UFO (CE-1)
  1965, Aug.4
    Jacques Vallee, Passport to Magonia
    (Chicago: Regnery, 1969), p.312.
  1966, Sep.28/Fred Lovern
    "Close UFO Sighting in Dallas," Sau-
    cer News 14 (spring 1967):29.
  1973, Oct./nr. Texas Stadium
    Irving News, 28 Oct.1973.
-UFO (CE-3)
  1974, Nov./Dora Ellen Afelbaum
    (Letter), Fate 30 (Feb.1977):133-34.
-UFO (DD)
  1947, June 28/Mrs. Ramsey C. Johnson/
  929 S. Oak Cliff Blvd.
    Dallas Morning News, 1 July 1947.
  1947, July 5/J.A. Reeder
    Dallas Morning News, 7 July 1947.
  1950, March 7/C.E. Edmundson/Naval Air
  Station
    Donald E. Keyhoe, Flying Saucers Are
    Real (N.Y.: Fawcett, 1950), pp.168-
    69.
  1950, March 16/Charles Lewis/Naval Air
  Station
    Kenneth Arnold & Ray Palmer, The Com-
    ing of the Saucers (Boise: The Au-
    thors, 1952), pp.146-47.
    Edward J. Ruppelt, The Report on Un-
    identified Flying Objects (Garden
    City: Doubleday, 1956), p.75.
  1952, April 5/Hensley Naval Air Station
    Dallas Morning News, 6-7 Apr.1952.
  1954, May 14/Charles Scarborough/6 mi.W
    Dallas Times-Herald, 17 May 1954.
    Richard Hall, ed., The UFO Evidence
    (Washington: NICAP, 1964), p.32.
  1973
    "Prize Selections from a Researcher's
    Photo Collection," Saga UFO Rept.
    6 (Nov.1978):38,42. il.
-UFO (NL)
  1947, July 1/Tom Dean/W on Hwy.183
    Dallas Morning News, 3 July 1947.
  1947, July 5/Dexter McEwen
  1947, July 6/Joe Lovelace/1504 Melbourne
    Dallas Morning News, 7 July 1947.
  1952, Aug.13/Max M. Jacoby
    Richard Hall, ed., The UFO Evidence
    (Washington: NICAP, 1964), pp.40-
    41, quoting UP release, 15 Aug.1952.
  1956, Sep.25/Mrs. M.A. Ferrano
    "Case 224," CRIFO Orbit, 2 Nov.1956,
    p.3.
  1965, Aug.2/Mr. Achzeheuer
    Coral E. Lorenzen, "Western UFO Flap,"
    Fate 18 (Nov.1965):42,50-51.
  1972, Aug.24/S.H. Lane/Dallas-Fort
  Worth Airport
    "Domed Object over Texas," APRO Bull.
    21 (July-Aug.1972):9.

1972, Oct.12
"Texas Women Frightened by Bright
Sky Objects," Skylook, no.62 (Jan.
1973):10.
1975, Feb.
Tommy Roy Blann, "The Mysterious
Link Between UFOs and Animal Muti-
lations," Saga UFO Rept. 3 (Apr.
1976):18,70.
-UFO (R-V)
1953, Jan.6/M.F. Fetchenbach/Love
Field
(Editorial), Fate 6 (May 1953):18.
Donald E. Keyhoe, Flying Saucers
from Outer Space (N.Y.: Holt, 1953),
p.218.
1957, Sep.19
Edward U. Condon, ed., Scientific
Study of Unidentified Flying Objects
(N.Y.: Bantam, 1969 ed.), pp.56-58,
260-66.

Damon
-UFO (CE-2)
1965, Sep.3/Robert W. Goode/S on Hwy.
35
Freeport Brazo-Sport Facts, 6-9 Sep.
1965.
"UFOs Panic Police, Motorists," UFO
Inv. 3 (Aug.-Sep.1965):1,3.
Donald E. Keyhoe & Gordon I.R. Lore,
Jr., UFOs: A New Look (Washington:
NICAP, 1969), pp.7-8.
Coral & Jim Lorenzen, UFOs: The Whole
Story (N.Y.: Signet, 1969), pp.248-
51.

Danforth
-UFO (NL)
1897, April 14
Washington Court House (O.) Cyclone
& Fayette Republican, 22 Apr.1897.

Deadwood
-UFO (CE-2)
1897, April 23/H.L. Lagrame/airship
message
Shreveport (La.) Times, 29 Apr.1897.
Houston Post, 30 Apr.1897, p.7.

Deaf Smith co.
-Cattle mutilations and UFO (NL)
1978, June-July
San Antonio News, 11 July 1978.

DeKalb
-UFO (CE-1)
1947, July 2/Wendell L. Carson
Dallas Morning News, 4 July 1947.

Del Rio
-Healing
1932-1942/John R. Brinkley/=quackery
Clement Wood, The Life of a Man (Kan-
sas City" Goshorn, 1934). il.
Jack D. Walker, "The Goat Gland Sur-
geon," J.Kansas Med.Soc'y 57 (1956)
:749-55. il.
Gerald Carson, The Roguish World of
Doctor Brinkley (N.Y.: Holt, Rine-

hart & Winston, 1960). il.

Denison
-UFO (DD)
1878, Jan.22/John Martin/6 mi.S
Denison Daily News, 25 Jan.1878.

Denton
-Out-of-body experience
1917, summer/Mai Whiteside
Mai Whiteside, "Almost Buried Alive,"
Fate 26 (Oct.1973):69-71.
-UFO (?)
1897, April 13
Dallas Morning News, 15 Apr.1897.

Denton Community
-UFO (CE-1)
1959, Nov./Mills Grantham/Hwy.36
"That Well-Made Look--Plus Occupants,"
Can.UFO Rept., no.12 (1972):10-11.

Diana
-Humanoid tracks
1977, April 1/Delores Waggoner/S of
town
Longview Morning Journal, 2 Apr.1977.

Direct
-Humanoid
1965, June
Paris News, 26 July 1965.
John Green, Sasquatch: The Apes Among
Us (Seattle: Hancock House, 1978),
pp.183-84.

Duncanville
-UFO (?)
1953, Jan.6/airport
Donald E. Keyhoe, Flying Saucers
from Outer Space (N.Y.: Holt, 1953),
p.255.
1971, Jan.31/Earl F. Watts
"Two More Reports on Sighting of Jan.
31, 1971," Skylook, no.41 (Apr.1971)
:9-10.
-UFO (R-V)
1957, July 17/USAF radar station
"UFO Encounter I: Sample Case Select-
ed by the UFO Subcommittee of the
AIAA," Astronautics & Aeronautics 9
(July 1971):66-70.
Philip J. Klass, UFOs Explained (N.Y.:
Random House, 1974), p.193.
William L. Moore, "The Puzzling Flight
of the Lacy 17," Saga UFO Rept. 6
(Aug.1978):40-43,62-66.

Eagle Pass
-Giant bird
1976, Jan.21/=hoax
Jerome Clark & Loren Coleman, Creatures of the Outer Edge (N.Y.: Warner, 1978), pp.176-78.

Eastland
-Entombed toad
1928, Feb.28/Edward S. Pritchard/East-
land County Courthouse
E.B. Sayles, Fantasies of Gold (Tuc-

son: Univ. of Arizona, 1968), pp.
113-14.

East Mountain
-Humanoid tracks
  1977, June 20/Tony McCullough/2 mi.S
  Longview Journal, 23 June 1977.

Edgewood
-UFO (NL)
  1947, July 6/E.C. Sneed
  Dallas Morning News, 7 July 1947.

Edna
-UFO (NL)
  1897, April/Frank Dickson
  Galveston Daily News, 24 Apr.1897,
  p.3.
  1949, Nov.25/A.A. Prurok/W of town
  Kenneth Arnold & Ray Palmer, The Coming of the Saucers (Boise: The Authors, 1952), p.145.

El Campo
-UFO (CE-1)
  1966, Nov.2/Mrs. Mark deFriend
  1966, Nov.28/Bryan Fritz/nr. Farm Rd.
  1300
  1966, Dec./Janis Bodungen/Farm Rd.1300
  Houston Tribune, 19 Jan.1967.
-UFO (CE-2)
  1966, Sep./Ed Korenek/Hwy.71
  Houston Tribune, 19 Jan.1967.
  "The Texas Flap," APRO Bull. 15 (Jan.
  -Feb.1967):3,5.

El Lago
-UFO (CE-1)
  1975, Oct.9/Eileen Cahill
  Len Stringfield, "The Stringfield Report," Skylook, no.100 (Mar.1976):
  15.

El Paso
-Disease anomaly
  1929, June 19
  New York Sun, 6 Dec.1930.
-Fall of metallic object
  1956, March 7/J.W. Thompson
  "Reports from Texas," CRIFO Orbit, 6
  Apr.1956, p.2, quoting El Paso
  Times (undated).
-Religious apparition
  1955, April 7/Lawrence E. Gaynor/1007
  Geronimo Dr.
  Betty Pierce, "Apparition of Saint
  Pius X," Fate 9 (Feb.1956):73-77.
-UFO (?)
  1899, March 2/=Venus?
  "A Remarkable Daylight Appearance of
  Venus," Observatory 22 (1899):247.
  1947, June 27/Mrs. W.B. Cummings
  Dallas Morning News, 1 July 1947.
  1947, Oct.10
  Harold T. Wilkins, Flying Saucers on
  the Attack (N.Y.: Ace, 1967 ed.),
  p.72.
  1952, Feb.25
  U.S. Air Force, Projects Grudge and
  Blue Book Reports 1-12 (Washington:

NICAP, 1968), p.94.
-UFO (CE-1)
  1897, April 19
  El Paso Herald, 20 Apr.1897.
-UFO (CE-2)
  1957, Nov.4/3 mi.SE of airport
  J. Allen Hynek, The Hynek UFO Report
  (N.Y.: Dell, 1977), p.181.
-UFO (DD)
  1947, June 22/G. Oliver Dickson
  Albuquerque (N.M.) Journal, 29 June
  1947.
  1964, April 30/Mrs. R.R. Reyes
  Coral Lorenzen, "Southwestern UFOs
  and the Straight Line Mystery,"
  Fate 17 (Aug.1964):39,42-43.
  1967, Dec.7/William C. Collins
  "New Close-Ups, Pacings," UFO Inv.
  4 (Mar.1968):1,3.
-UFO (NL)
  1967, Jan.16/Teresa G. Trittipoe
  "Major Sighting Wave," UFO Inv. 3
  (Jan.-Feb.1967):1,3.
  1977, Sep.22/George Didlake
  Dave Kenney, "Airline Crew Spots
  UFO," APRO Bull. 26 (Sep.1977):1,3.

Farmersville
-Fall of gray powder
  ca.1918/Silbie Latham
  Alex Evans, "Encounters with Little
  Men," Fate 31 (Nov.1978):83,84.
-Phantom
  1913, May/Silbie Latham/2½ mi.W
  Alex Evans, "Encounters with Little
  Men," Fate 31 (Nov.1978):83-85.
-UFO (CE-3)
  1897, April 15/Mr. Brown
  Dallas Morning News, 18 Apr.1897,
  p.4.

Floydada
-Anomalous holes in ground
  1964, May/Doodle Milton
  "More News Briefs," Saucer News 11
  (Sep.1964):23.
  (Editorial), Fate 17 (Oct.1964):10-
  12.

Forney
-UFO (?)
  1897, April 17
  Dallas Morning News, 18 Apr.1897,
  p.5.

Fort Hood
-UFO (?)
  1949, March
  Bruce S. Maccabee, "UFO Related Information from the FBI Files: Part
  5," MUFON UFO J., no.124 (Mar.1978)
  :7,8,10.

Fort Stockton
-Stratigraphic anomaly
  Robert T. Hill, "Two Limestone Form-
  ations of the Cretaceous of Texas
  Which Transgress Time Diagonally,"
  Science 53 (1921):190-91.
-UFO (R)

1952, March 26
    Brad Steiger, Project Blue Book (N.Y.:
    Ballantine, 1976), betw. pp.360-61.
    il.

Fort Worth
-Cloud anomaly
  1913, April 8
    Howard H. Martin, "Cloud-Shadow Pro-
    jection," Monthly Weather Rev. 41
    (Apr.1913):599.
-Electromagnetic anomaly
  1908, Sep.21-   /Barry Burke/Palace
  Theater
    "Bulbsnatcher's Dream," INFO J., no.
    8 (winter-spring 1972):9.
    London (Eng.) Daily Mail, 26 Nov.
    1974.
    James Dale Davidson, An Eccentric
    Guide to the United States (N.Y.:
    Berkley, 1977), p.488.
-Entombed turtle
  1975, Aug.20/7137 Meadowhook Dr.
    Fort Worth Star-Telegram, 21 Aug.
    1975. il.
    Gary S. Mangiacopra, "The Entombed
    Turtle," Pursuit 9 (Apr.1976):41.
    il.
-Meditation research
  1970s/Carl & Stephanie Simonton/Cancer
  Counseling & Research Center, 1300 Sum-
  mit Ave./Oncology Associates, 1413 8th
  Ave.
    Jean Shinoda Bolen, "Meditation and
    Psychotherapy in the Treatment of
    Cancer," Psychic 4 (July-Aug.1973):
    19.
    O. Carl & Stephanie Simonton, "Belief
    Systems and Management of the Emo-
    tional Aspects of Malignancy," J.
    Transpersonal Psych. 7 (1975):29-47.
    Elmer & Alyce Green, Beyond Biofeed-
    back (N.Y.: Delta, 1978 ed.), pp.
    169-71,175-76,189.
    O. Carl & Stephanie Simonton, & James
    Creighton, Getting Well Again (Los
    Angeles: J.P. Tarcher, 1978).
    (Editorial), Fate 31 (Oct.1978):28-
    30.
-Precognition
  1944, Dec.30/H.F. Horstmann
    "Giles Grist," Doubt, no.12 (spring-
    summer 1945):173.
-UFO (?)
  1950, April 9/Ira E. Maxey/=defect in
  negative?
    Los Angeles (Cal.) Daily News, 19
    Apr.1950.
    Kenneth Arnold & Ray Palmer, The Com-
    ing of the Saucers (Boise: The Au-
    thors, 1952), p.175. il.
  1952, April 2/=meteor?
    Fort Worth Star-Telegram, 3-4 Apr.
    1952.
  1953, Jan.25
    (Editorial), Fate 6 (June 1953):12.
  1973, Oct.24/Lawrence Brown/Texas
  Christian Univ.
    Tommy R. Blann, "Bright Lights over
    Them Purple Plains," Probe the Un-

known 2 (summer 1974):56,58.
  1974, Oct.
    Brad Steiger, Gods of Aquarius (N.Y.:
    Harcourt Brace Jovanovich, 1976),
    p.108. il.
  1977, July 22
    Fort Worth Star-Telegram, 4 Dec.1977.
-UFO (CE-3)
  ca.1947
    Brinsley Le Poer Trench, The Flying
    Saucer Story (N.Y.: Ace, 1966 ed.),
    pp.91-92.
-UFO (DD)
  1952, April 23
    San Antonio Evening News, 24 Apr.
    1952.
-UFO (NL)
  1897, April 14
    Dallas Morning News, 16 Apr.1897,
    p.5.
  1967, Oct.19
    "UFOs--October--U.S.A.," APRO Bull.
    16 (Nov.-Dec.1967):8.
  1971, Feb./Robert Rozelle/nr. Quarter-
  master's Depot
    "Huge Cigar-Shaped Object in Texas,"
    Skylook, no.44 (July 1971):9-10,
    quoting Cross-Country News, 22 Apr.
    1971.
-UFO (R)
  1965, July 31
    Coral E. Lorenzen, Flying Saucers:
    The Startling Evidence for the Inva-
    sion from Outer Space (N.Y.: Signet,
    1966 ed.), p.237.
-UFO (R-V)
  1953, Feb.13/Carswell AFB
    Gordon D. Thayer, "Optical and Radar
    Analyses of Field Cases," in Edward
    U. Condon, ed., Scientific Study of
    Unidentified Flying Objects (N.Y.:
    Bantam, 1969 ed.), p.123.

Freeport
-Mystery shipwreck
  1972, Feb.1/"V.A. Fogg"/50 mi.E
    Galveston Daily News, 14-20 Feb.1972.
    Richard Winer, The Devil's Triangle
    (N.Y.: Bantam, 1974), pp.136-38. il.
    Lawrence David Kusche, The Bermuda
    Triangle Mystery--Solved (N.Y.:
    Harper & Row, 1975), pp.240-45.
-UFO (CE-2)
  1959, Aug.13
    Jacques Vallee, Passport to Magonia
    (Chicago: Regnery, 1969), p.277,
    quoting APRO Bull., Sep.1959.
  1966, March 20/John R. Weitlich/Coast
  Guard cutter "Legare"
    Houston Post, 25 Mar.1966.
    Philip J. Klass, UFOs Explained (N.Y.:
    Random House, 1974), pp.92-96.

Gainesville
-UFO (NL)
  1954, Aug.3/Bob Farmer
    (Letter), Fate 8 (Feb.1955):105.

Galveston
-Derelict coffin

1900, Sep.8-1908, Oct./Charles Coghlan/
=hoax
 Johnston Forbes-Robertson, A Player
 Under Three Reigns (London: T. Fish-
 er Unwin, 1925), p.166.
 Charlottetown (P.E.I.) Guardian, 5
 Oct.1950; and 10 June 1965.
 Albert A. Brandt, "The Man Who Came
 Home," Fate 5 (June 1952):102-103.
 Dwight Whalen, "Charles Coghlan Never
 Came Home," Fate 32 (Mar.1979):88-
 92.
-UFO (?)
 1950, March/=hoax
 Edward J. Ruppelt, The Report on Un-
 identified Flying Objects (Garden
 City: Doubleday, 1956), p.76.
 Renato Vesco, Intercept UFO (N.Y.:
 Zebra, 1974 ed.), p.39.
 1955, Aug.14/W.L. Hughes/=meteor?
 Arthur Constance, The Inexplicable
 Sky (N.Y.: Citadel, 1957), p.225.
-UFO (NL)
 1920, fall/C.B. Alves
 (Letter), Fate 8 (Feb.1955):120-23.

Garland
-Fall of gelatinous substance
 1973, May/Marie Harris/=slime mold
 Columbus (O.) Dispatch, 30 May 1973.
 il.
 "Blobs," INFO J., no.10 (spring 1973)
 :29-30. il.
 "The Blob," Pursuit 6 (July 1973):67-
 68.
-UFO (?)
 1897, April 17
 Dallas Morning News, 18 Apr.1897.

Glen Rose
-Human tracks in limestone
 Paluxy R.
 Roland T. Bird, "Thunder in His Foot-
 steps," Natural History 43 (May
 1939):255-61,302. il.
 Clifford Burdick, The Challenge of
 Creation (Caldwell, Ida.: Bible-
 Science Ass'n, 1965), pp.35-38.
 A.E. Wilder Smith, Man's Origin Man's
 Destiny (Wheaton, Ill.: Harold
 Shaw, 1968), pp.135-41,293-98. il.
 Dallas Morning News, 7 Sep.1968; 16
 Aug.1969; 29 Aug.1969; and 14 Aug.
 1975.
 Brad Steiger, Mysteries of Time and
 Space (N.Y.: Dell, 1976 ed.), pp.22-
 24.
 John Green, "Fossil Tracks at Glen
 Rose," Pursuit 9 (fall 1976):83-85.
 il.
 John Green, Sasquatch: The Apes Among
 Us (Seattle: Hancock House, 1978),
 pp.323-31. il.

Goliad
-Haunt
 1936/A.W. Shaw/La Bahia mission
 "The Ghost of Goliad," Fate 9 (May
 1956):55, quoting Houston Chronicle
 (undated).

Gonzales
-Telepathy
 1950/Jim Walker/=hoax
 Jimmy Walker, "Everyone Is a Mind-
 reader," Fate 3 (Dec.1950):20-27.
 Robert N. Webster, "The Amazing Jim
 Walker and the Imaginary Dr. McClen-
 ahan," Fate 4 (Mar.1951):4-5.

Graham
-Poltergeist
 1972/Hollis W. Proffit
 (Editorial), Fate 25 (Sep.1972):18-
 20.

Granbury
-UFO (?)
 1897, April 17/Newt Gresham
 Dallas Morning News, 19 Apr.1897,
 p.5.

Gray Hill
-Fall of ice
 1892, Dec.6
 "Dangerous Hailstones," Sci.Am. 68
 (1893):58, quoting Dallas Morning
 News (undated).

Greenville
-UFO (CE-3)
 1897, April 17/C.G. Williams
 Dallas Morning News, 19 Apr.1897,
 p.5.

Grimes co.
-Tektite field
 Henry Faul, "Tektites Are Terrestri-
 al," Science 152 (1966):1341-45.

Groesbeck
-UFO (NL)
 1897, April 19/B.F. Johnson
 Houston Post, 22 Apr.1897, p.9.

Groves
-UFO (?)
 1965/Judy James
 (Letter), Saga UFO Rept. 3 (Apr.
 1976):6.

Hallsville
-Humanoid
 1976, summer
 Longview Journal, 28 Nov.1976.

Hamilton
-Sheep mutilation
 1975, June-Sep./Leon Broughton
 Jerome Clark, "Saucer Central U.S.A.,"
 Saga UFO Rept. 3 (Apr.1976):8.

Hardin co.
-Phantom panther
 n.d.
 Archer Fullingim, "Folklore in the
 Big Thicket," in Francis E. Aber-
 nethy, Tales from the Big Thicket
 (Austin: Univ. of Texas, 1966), pp.
 24-25.

Harlingen
-Animal ESP
  1964-1966/Cecil Stephens
    (Editorial), Fate 19 (May 1966):22-
    24.
-Doubtful identity
  1969, Feb.21/John Rollins/=mystery mummies
    (Editorial), Fate 23 (Aug.1970):17,
    quoting UPI release (undated). il.
-Giant bird
  1976, Jan.1/Jackie Davis/Ed Carey Rd.
    Jack Murray, "The 'Big Bird' You'll
    Never See on Sesame Street," Probe
    the Unknown 4 (Nov.1976):44,46.
    Jerome Clark & Loren Coleman, Crea-
    tures of the Outer Edge (N.Y.: War-
    ner, 1978), pp.171-73.
-Healing
  1970s/Mother Tina/7 mi.W on U.S.83
    Bill Starr, "Witchcraft Pays Off
    Along the Rio Grande," Fate 24
    (Dec.1971):78,83-84. il.
-Hex
  1960s
    Bill Starr, "Red Carpet for a Texas
    Witch," Fate 20 (Aug.1967):29-31.
-UFO (NL)
  1957, June/Manuel Chavez
    (Editorial), Fate 10 (Nov.1957):9-
    10, quoting Harlingen Valley Morning
    Star (undated).

Harris co.
-Cattle mutilations and panther tracks
  1977, Jan.1
    Sherman Democrat, 5 Jan.1977.

Hawley
-Humanoid
  1977, July 6/Tom Roberts
    Abilene Reporter-News, 7 July 1977.

Hearne
-UFO (NL)
  1975, Dec.2
    "Noteworthy UFO Sightings," Ufology
    2 (spring 1976):43.

Hedley
-UFO (CE-2)
  1957, Nov.5
    Amarillo News, 7 Nov.1957.

Helotes
-Dog mutilation
  1975, Feb./Sam V. Snell
    "Now It's Dogs," Ohio Sky Watcher,
    Mar.1975, p.13.

Hereford
-Horse mutilation
  1978, July 28/Jau Don McCathern/12 mi.
  N
    Amarillo Daily News, 3 Aug.1978.

Hillsboro
-Fall of metallic object
  1947, July 4/Bob Scott/2 mi.E
    San Antonio Express, 7 July 1947.

-UFO (CE-1)
  1897, April/J. Spence Bounds
    Dallas Morning News, 17 Apr.1897, p.
    8.

Hondo
-Cattle mutilation
  1975, Feb./Albert Wilson
    Annie Rosenbloom, "Cow Deaths," Ohio
    Sky Watcher, Mar.1975, pp.17-18.
    Tommy Roy Blann, "The Mysterious
    Link Between UFOs and Animal Muti-
    lations," Saga UFO Rept. 3 (Apr.
    1976):18,70.
-UFO (DD)
  1964, Aug.27/Hondo AFB
    Frank Bowers, ed., The True Report
    on Flying Saucers (Greenwich, Ct.:
    Fawcett, 1967), p.23. il.

Houston
-Airship inventor
  1900-1924/C.A.A. Dellschau
    Jerome Clark & Loren Coleman, "Mys-
    tery Airships of the 1800s," Fate
    26 (May 1973):84,88-91.
-Animal ESP
  1954, April/Billie Smith
    (Editorial), Fate 7 (Oct.1954):6-8.
  1966
    Houston Post, 15 May 1966.
-Electromagnetic anomaly
  1955/Kyle Chapman/LaPorte Rd.
    (Editorial), Fate 9 (Apr.1956):12.
-Exploding fishbowl
  1954, Feb.6/Mrs. Henry Dressler
    (Editorial), Fate 8 (Jan.1955):10.
    Harold T. Wilkins, Flying Saucers Un-
    censored (N.Y.: Pyramid, 1967 ed.),
    p.232.
-Fall of crabs
  1973, April 17/Gilbert Ramirez/8700
  block Covent Gardens
    (Editorial), Fate 26 (Nov.1973):24-
    26.
-Fall of turtle
  1957, Feb./Becky Adamson/=hoax?
    Houston Chronicle, 9 Feb.1957.
    "Falls," Doubt, no.54 (1957):435,436.
-Flying humanoid
  1953, June 18/Hilda Walker/118 E. 3d
  St.
    William C. Thompson, "Houston Bat
    Man," Fate 6 (Oct.1953):26-27,
    quoting Houston Chronicle (undated).
-Ghost
  n.d./Rudolph Klimp
    "I Could Not Run Her Down," Fate 5
    (June 1952):57.
-Haunt
  1961/Houston Public Library
    (Editorial), Fate 14 (Nov.1961):19-
    21, quoting Houston Post (undated).
  1971/Joe Bob Westerfield
    (Editorial), Fate 24 (Oct.1971):23-
    30, quoting Houston Post (undated).
-Healing
  1965-   /Norbu Chen/Chakpori Ling
  Foundation/8303 Gulf Freeway, Suite 108
    Tom Valentine, "America's Tibetan

Lama: Norbu Chen, Healer," Fate 27
(Aug.1974):38-46. il.
(Editorial), Fate 28 (June 1975):26-
30, quoting Houston Chronicle (un-
dated).
(Letter), John Bell, Fate 28 (June
1975):131-32.
(Letter), Kenneth S. Gusé, Fate 28
(June 1975):132-33.
(Letter), Norbu Chen, Fate 28 (Oct.
1975):115-18.
"Norbu Chen Heals Singer," Fate 28
(Nov.1975):85.
(Letter), Roy C. Alexander, Fate 28
(Nov.1975):113-14.
William A. Nolen, Healing: A Doctor
in Search of a Miracle (N.Y.: Ran-
dom House, 1975).
-Inner development
  1971-   /Foundation
  J. Gordon Melton, Encyclopedia of
  American Religions, 2 vols. (Wil-
  mington, N.C.: Consortium, 1978),
  2:263.
-Lunar cycle, homicide and insanity
  1960s/Alex D. Pokorny
  Alex D. Pokorny, "Moon Phases and
  Mental Hospital Admissions," J.
  Psychiatric Nursing 6 (1962):325-27.
  Alex D. Pokorny & Fred Davis, "Homi-
  cide and Weather," Am.J.Psychiatry
  120 (1964):806-808.
  Alex D. Pokorny, "Moon Phases, Sui-
  cide and Homicide," Am.J.Psychiatry
  121 (1964):66-67.
-Mystery animal
  1955, May/Mrs. Leo Eaves/3600 Rural
  (Editorial), Fate 8 (Oct.1955):12.
-Mystery gas
  1961, Dec./Baptist Church
  Jerome Clark & Loren Coleman, "The
  Mad Gasser of Mattoon," Fate 25
  (Feb.1972):38,46.
  1969, Feb.6/south side
  John A. Keel, UFOs: Operation Trojan
  Horse (N.Y.: Putnam, 1970), p.165.
-Mystery television transmission
  1953, Sep.-1954, Jan./KLEE-TV/=hoax?
  (Editorial), Fate 10 (Jan.1957):14-
  15.
  Houston Post, 14 Feb.1960.
  Curtis Fuller, "KLEE: Still Calling,"
  Fate 17 (Apr.1964):37-41.
  Joseph E. Risius, "KLEE: Outlaw or
  Amateur?" Fate 18 (Jan.1965):41-43.
  "The KLEE-TV Case Again," Pursuit 5
  (Oct.1972):77-78.
  Frank D. Drake, "On the Abilities
  and Limitations of Witnesses of UFOs
  and Similar Phenomena," in Carl Sagan
  & Thornton Page, eds., UFOs: A Sci-
  entific Debate (Ithaca, N.Y.: Cor-
  nell Univ., 1972), pp.247-53.
-Parapsychology research
  1970s/William G. Braud/Univ. of Houston
  W.G. & L.W. Braud, "Preliminary Ex-
  ploration of Psi-Conducive States:
  Progressive Muscular Relaxation,"
  J.ASPR 67 (1973):26-46.
  L.W. & W.G. Braud, "Further Studies

of Relaxation As a Psi-Conducive
State," J.ASPR 68 (1974):229-45.
K. Andrew, "Psychokinetic Influences
on an Electromechanical Random Number Generator During Evocation of
'Left-Hemispheric' vs. 'Right-Hem-
ispheric' Functioning," in J.D.
Morris, ed., Research in Parapsy-
chology 1974 (Metuchen, N.J.: Scare-
crow, 1975), pp.58-61.
W.G. Braud, et al., "Psychokinetic
Influences on an Electromechanical
Random Number Generator During Evo-
cation of 'Analytic' vs. 'Nonanal-
ytic' Modes of Information Process-
ing," in J.D. Morris, ed., Research
in Parapsychology 1974 (Metuchen,
N.J.: Scarecrow, 1975), pp.85-88.
W.G. Braud, "Psi-Conducive States,"
J.Communication 25 (1975):142-52.
William G. Braud, Robert Wood & Len-
dell W. Braud, "Free-Response GESP
Performance During an Experimental
Hypnagogic State Induced by Visual
and Acoustic Ganzfeld Techniques,"
J.ASPR 69 (1975):105-13.
William G. Braud, "Conscious vs. Un-
conscious Clairvoyance in the Con-
text of an Academic Examination,"
J.Parapsych. 39 (1975):277-78.
William G. Braud, "Psychokinesis in
Aggressive and Nonaggressive Fish
with Mirror Presentation Feedback
for Hits," J.Parapsych. 40 (1976):
296-307.
William Braud, "Allobiofeedback," in
William G. Roll, ed., Research in
Parapsychology 1977 (Metuchen, N.J.:
Scarecrow, 1978), pp.123-34.
Lendell & William Braud, "Psychokin-
etic Effects upon a Random Event
Generator under Conditions of Lim-
ited Feedback to Volunteers and Ex-
perimenter," in William G. Roll, ed.,
Research in Parapsychology 1977
(Metuchen, N.J.: Scarecrow, 1978),
pp.135-43.
-Phantom
  1971, May 8/nr. NASA Space Center
  "Possible Occupants in Texas," APRO
  Bull. 19 (May-June 1971):4-5.
-Poltergeist
  1946
  Hereward Carrington & Nandor Fodor,
  Haunted People (N.Y.: Signet, 1968
  ed.), p.68, quoting Digest and Re-
  view, Oct.1946.
  1954, Feb./Mrs. W.E. Murray/7224 Ker-
  nel St.
  (Editorial), Fate 7 (July 1954):12.
  1961, June 26-July/Doris King/106 E.
  John Alber St.
  (Editorial), Fate 14 (Oct.1961):18-
  19, quoting Houston Press (undated).
  Curtis Fuller & David Wuliger, "Hous-
  ton's Mysterious Blood Spots," Fate
  14 (Nov.1961):34-40. il.
  (Letter), Guiula Mahaffey, Fate 15
  (Feb.1962):136.
  Brad Steiger, Irene Hughes on Psychic

Safari (N.Y.: Warner, 1972), pp.74-78.

1961-1964/Joe Flores/1110 Edwards St.
Houston Post, 25 Apr.1964.
(Editorial), *Fate* 17 (Sep.1964):18-20.
-Precognition
n.d./Letitia Olridge/7619 Elm St., Harrisburg
  Sigman Byrd, "Aunt Tishy and the Witches of Ellum Street," *Fate* 6 (Apr.1953):21-23.
-Spirit medium
1920s/Mary McKenzie
  George H. Breaker, "A Series of Mediumistic Experiments, and Their Correlation with the Facts," *J.ASPR* 21 (1927):584-600,642-64,7-8-17.
-Teleportation
1951, Oct./Adolph Flores/1425 W. Gray
Houston Press, 1 Nov.1951.
-UFO (?)
1947, July 6/Mrs. Bernard Shelansky
Houston Post, 7 July 1947.
1952, April 2/=meteor?
Houston Post, 3 Apr.1952.
1957, Feb.27/J.R. Poole/radar site
  Richard Hall, ed., *The UFO Evidence* (Washington: NICAP, 1964), p.22, quoting AP release, 28 Feb.1957.
1957, March 8/Victor Hancock
  (Editorial), *Fate* 10 (July 1957):12.
  Donald E. Keyhoe, *Flying Saucers: Top Secret* (N.Y.: Putnam, 1960), pp.55-56, quoting UP release, 10 Mar.1957.
-UFO (CE-2)
1957, Nov.6
Houston Chronicle, 6 Nov.1957.
1966, March 28/Donella Banning
  "Nation-Wide Saucer Flap Continues," *Saucer News* 13 (June 1966):31.
1968, Nov.6/Robert Hubbard
Houston Post, 20 Dec.1968.
-UFO (CE-3)
1947, July 8/Acres Home area/=hoax?
Houston Post, 9 July 1947, p.1.
1977, Aug.30
  Ted Bloecher, "A Survey of CE3K Reports for 1977," in *1978 MUFON UFO Symposium Proc.* (Seguin, Tex.: MUFON, 1978), pp.14,34.
-UFO (DD)
1947, July 6/John Cooley
1947, July 6/Arthur Reid
Houston Post, 7 July 1947.
-UFO (NL)
1947, June 27/Laveta Davidson/604 Peden
Houston Post, 28 June 1947.
1952, July 24/Arrowhead Park
  Curtis Fuller, "Let's Get Straight About the Saucers," *Fate* 5 (Dec. 1952):20,27.
1957, Nov.5
  Richard Hall, ed., *The UFO Evidence* (Washington: NICAP, 1964), p.165.
1958, May 8
  Robert N. Webster, "Things That Fall from UFOs," *Fate* 11 (Oct.1958):25, 30.

1967, Jan.21/Alfred Kuntz
  (Editorial), *Fate* 20 (May 1967):28.
1977, Sep.22
  Dave Kenney, "Airline Crew Spots UFO," *APRO Bull.* 26 (Sep.1977):1,3.

Humble
-UFO (NL)
1965, Nov.18/Mrs. R. Kennedy/NE of town
  (Letter), *Fate* 19 (May 1966):130-32.

Iraan
-Rainbow anomaly
1973, Sep.1/Paul A. Roales
  Paul A. Roales, "A Meteorological Puzzle," *INFO J.*, no.15 (May 1975):14.

Irving
-Clairaudience
1977, March 6/Ryue Yoshida
  Ryue Yoshida, "A Japanese Flute's Sad Song," *Fate* 30 (Nov.1977):72-73.

Jewett
-UFO (NL)
1910, summer/Elizabeth Hamilton
  Coral & Jim Lorenzen, *UFOs: The Whole Story* (N.Y.: Signet, 1969), p.18.

Johnson co.
-Phantom panther
1977, Sep./=bobcat?
Dallas Morning News, 9 Oct.1977.

Jones co.
-Cattle mutilation
1974, Dec.
Fort Worth Star-Telegram, 25 Jan. 1975.

Josserand
-UFO (CE-3)
1897, April 22/Frank Nichols/2 mi.E
Houston Post, 26 Apr.1897.

Katemcy
-Rock doughnuts
  Horace R. Blank, "'Rock Doughnuts,' a Product of Granite Weathering," *Am.J.Sci.* 249 (1951):822-29.

Kaufman
-Cattle mutilation
1975, Feb./Caggie Evans
  Tommy Roy Blann, "The Mysterious Link Between UFOs and Animal Mutilations," *Saga UFO Rept.* 3 (Apr. 1976):18,20.
-Phantom helicopters
1975, Jan.
  Ed Sanders, "The Mutilation Mystery," *Oui*, Sep.1976, pp.51,113.

Kemah
-UFO (DD)
1958, spring/Nellie M. Herren/800 Bradford
  John F. Schuessler, "'Silver and

Beautiful' Object Observed by Texas
Woman," Skylook, no.87 (Feb.1975):
21.

Kerrville
-UFO (CE-2)
   1953, Jan.9
      Donald E. Keyhoe, Flying Saucers from
      Outer Space (N.Y.: Holt, 1953), pp.
      218-29.
      Richard Hall, ed., The UFO Evidence
      (Washington: NICAP, 1964), p.73.

Kingsville
-UFO (?)
   1961, April 9
      Richard Hall, ed., The UFO Evidence
      (Washington: NICAP, 1964), p.151.

Kountze
-UFO (CE-3)
   1897, April 23
      Houston Post, 25 Apr.1897, p.5.

La Feria
-Hex
   1960s/Madame Azteca
      Bill Starr, "Red Carpet for a Texas
      Witch," Fate 20 (Aug.1967):29,31-33.
-Precipitating tree
   1966, July-Dec./Samuel F. Morse
      St. Louis (Mo.) Post-Dispatch, 21
      Aug.1966.
      Bill Starr, "The Crying Tree," Fate
      20 (May 1967):66-71. il.
      Bill Starr, "Crying Tree Weeps No
      More," Fate 21 (Feb.1968):73.

La Grange
-Archeological site
   13,000 B.C.-1000 A.D.
      Houston Chronicle, 30 Apr.1978.

Lamar co.
-Lightning anomaly
   1894, Aug./Mrs. Griggs
      St. Louis (Mo.) Globe-Democrat, 8
      Aug.1894.

La Marque
-Precognition
   1958, July/Mrs. Allen Luker
      (Editorial), Fate 11 (Dec.1958):12-
      13.

Lampasas
-Ghost light
   1958, Dec.20-1959, Jan.24/Franklin
   Richardson/10 mi.N on Spivey-Tapp Rd.
      (Editorial), Fate 12 (June 1959):19-
      20.

La Porte
-UFO (DD)
   1947, July 4/Mrs. W.F. Parchman/Sylvan
   Beach
      Houston Post, 6 July 1947.

La Pryor
-Clairempathy

1900-1960s/Guy Finley
   "The Boy with the 'X-Ray Eyes,'"
   Fate 19 (Jan.1966):36, quoting Dal-
   las Morning News (undated).

Laredo
-Biofeedback research
   1944-   /Silva Mind Control Inter-
   national/1110 Cedar
      Harry McKnight, Silva Mind Control
      Through Psychorientology (Laredo:
      Institute of Psychorientology,
      1972).
      June & Nicholas Regush, Psi: The
      Other World Catalogue (N.Y.: Putnam,
      1974), pp.146-47.
      Elmer & Alyce Green, "The Dangers of
      Mind Control," Fate 27 (Nov.1974):
      98-108.
      (Letter), Paul Solomon, Fate 28
      (Apr.1975):111-15.
      Bob Brier, Gertrude Schmiedler &
      Barry Savits, "Three Experiments in
      Clairvoyant Diagnosis with Silva
      Mind Control Graduates," J.ASPR 69
      (1975):263-71.
      José Silva & Philip Miele, The Silva
      Mind Control Method (N.Y.: Simon &
      Schuster, 1977).
      Richard N. Barraclough, "Silva Mind
      Control," Club, Aug.1977, pp.75-
      76,90.
-Cattle mutilation
   1978, April/Eloy Garcia
      Houston Chronicle, 28 Apr.1978.
-Giant bird
   1976, Jan.14/Arturo Rodriguez/=great
   blue heron?
      Jerome Clark & Loren Coleman, Crea-
      tures of the Outer Edge (N.Y.: War-
      ner, 1978), p.176.
-UFO (CE-1)
   1952, Dec.4
      Donald E. Keyhoe, Flying Saucers from
      Outer Space (N.Y.: Holt, 1953), pp.
      3-4,17-19.
-UFO (DD)
   1953, April/Edward B. Wilford III
      Richard Hall, ed., The UFO Evidence
      (Washington: NICAP, 1964), p.25.
   1954, March 8/Laredo AFB
      Donald E. Keyhoe, Flying Saucer Con-
      spiracy (N.Y.: Holt, 1955), p.110.

La Salle co.
-Cattle mutilations
   1975, Feb.
      Longview Morning Journal, 26 Feb.1975.

Levelland
-UFO (CE-1)
   1957, Nov.3/Weir Clem/Oklahoma Flat Rd.
      Richard Hall, ed., The UFO Evidence
      (Washington: NICAP, 1964), pp.168-
      69.
      J. Allen Hynek, The UFO Experience
      (Chicago: Regnery, 1972), pp.126-27.
-UFO (CE-2)
   1957, Nov.2/Pedro Saucedo/4 mi.W
   1957, Nov.2/Jim Wheeler/4 mi.E

1957, Nov.3/Newell Wright/10 mi.E
1957, Nov.3/Ronald Martin/11 mi.W
1957, Nov.3/James Long/Oklahoma Flat Rd.
1957, Nov.3/Ray Jones/13 mi.N
 Fort Worth Star-Telegram, 4 Nov.1957.
 Levelland Sun-News, 5-6 Nov.1957.
 Denver (Colo.) Post, 6 Nov.1957.
 Donald H. Menzel & Lyle G. Boyd, The
 World of Flying Saucers (Garden
 City: Doubleday, 1963), pp.172-90.
 Richard Hall, ed., The UFO Evidence
 (Washington: NICAP, 1964), pp.168-
 69.
 J. Allen Hynek, The UFO Experience
 (Chicago: Regnery, 1972), pp.123-26.
 Don Berliner, "The Levelland Sight-
 ings," Official UFO 1 (Jan.1976):
 22-23,46-49.
-UFO (NL)
 1957, Nov.7
 Midland Reporter-Telegram, 8 Nov.1957.

Lewalla
-UFO (NL)
 1897, April 16/Virgil Brown
 New York Sun, 18 Apr.1897, p.3.

Lewisville
-Archeological site
 ca.36,000 B.C.
 Wilson W. Crook, Jr. & R.K. Harris,
 "Hearths and Artifacts of Early Man
 near Lewisville, Texas," Bull.Texas
 Arch.Soc'y 28 (1957):7-97. il.
 Wilson W. Crook & R.K. Harris, "A
 Pleistocene Campsite near Lewis-
 ville, Texas," Am.Antiquity 23
 (1958):233-46.
 Bob H. Slaughter, et al., "The Hill-
 Shuler Local Faunas of the Upper
 Trinity River, Dallas and Denton
 Counties, Texas," Rept.of Investi-
 gations Univ.Texas Bur.Econ.Geol.,
 no.48 (1962).
 Robert F. Heizer & R.A. Brooks, "Lew-
 isville: Ancient Campsite or Wood
 Rat Houses?" Southwestern J.Anthro.
 21 (1965):155-65. il.
-UFO (CE-2)
 1973, Oct.31/Norman Hearn
 George D. Fawcett, "What We Can Ex-
 pect of UFOs in 1975," Official UFO
 1 (Aug.1975):12,48.
-UFO (NL)
 1965, Aug.2/Lewisville Dam
 Coral E. Lorenzen, Flying Saucers:
 The Startling Evidence of the Invasion from Outer Space (N.Y.: Signet,
 1966 ed.), p.248.

Lindale
-UFO (DD)
 1949, Aug./Jarrell M. Oliver
 "The Search for Hidden Reports," UFO
 Inv. 4 (Mar.1968):7.

Livingston
-UFO (?)
 1973, Oct./J.F. Chesson/L. Livingston
 "Saucers in the News," Flying Saucers,

winter 1974, pp.44,59-60.

Loco
-UFO (CE-1)
 1967, March 24/Johnny Ferguson
 "Car Buzzing Incidents on Increase,"
 APRO Bull. 15 (May-June 1967):5.
 Coral & Jim Lorenzen, Encounters
 with UFO Occupants (N.Y.: Berkley,
 1976), pp.45-46.
-UFO (CE-3)
 1967, March 31/Carroll Wayne Watts
 Seattle (Wash.) Post-Intelligencer,
 2 Apr.1967.

Lone Star
-Skyquake
 1957, Oct.30
 Kansas City (Mo.) Times, 31 Oct.1957.

Longview
-Clairvoyance
 1964, Oct.7/Rex Dale, Jr.
 (Editorial), Fate 18 (Feb.1965):20-
 22.
 (Editorial), Fate 19 (Feb.1966):33.
-UFO (?)
 1973, Oct./airport/=snow geese
 Little Rock Arkansas Gazette, 18
 Oct.1973, p.10A.
 Philip J. Klass, UFOs Explained (N.Y.:
 Random House, 1974), p.281.
-UFO (CE-1)
 1948, Aug./Doris Delburt Gregg
 Doris Delburt Gregg, "I Am Being
 Watched by a UFO!" Fate 14 (Nov.
 1961):27-33.
 1961, April 15/Doris Delburt Gregg
 1961, May 30/Doris Delburt Gregg
 Doris Delburt Gregg, "I Am Being
 Watched by a UFO!" Fate 14 (Nov.
 1961):27,33.
-UFO (DD)
 1977, Oct.29/Aaron M. Sawyer
 Longview Journal, 3 Nov.1977.
-UFO (NL)
 1897, April 19
 Houston Post, 22 Apr.1897.
 1947, Aug./Doris Delburt Gregg
 Doris Delburt Gregg, "True Mystic
 Experiences," Fate 1 (fall 1948):
 106-108.

Lovelady
-UFO (CE-3)
 1897, April
 Galveston Daily News, 22 Apr.1897,
 p.4.

Lubbock
-Archeological site
 10,650-250 B.C./Clovis Hwy.x Loop 289
 Joe Ben Wheat, "Two Archeological
 Sites near Lubbock, Texas," Panhan-
 dle-Plains Hist.Rev. 28 (1955):71-
 77.
-UFO (?)
 1963, July 11/J.W. Page/=meteor?
 (Editorial), Fate 16 (Nov.1963):18.
 1969, Aug.10/=meteor?

"Texans Report Great, Glowing Ball,"
Skylook, no.22 (Sep.1969):7.
-UFO (CE-1)
1977, June 24
Lubbock Advance-Journal, 25 June 1977.
-UFO (CE-2)
n.d./Fr. Murphy
1957, Jan.16/Howard T. Wright/E of town
Richard Hall, "The UFO Sightings You
Haven't Heard About," Official UFO
1 (Apr.1976):36-37.
-UFO (NL)
1951, Aug.25, 30/Carl Hart, Jr.
Lubbock Evening Avalanche, 26 Aug.
1951.
H.B. Darrach, Jr. & Robert Ginna,
"Have We Visitors from Space?" Life,
7 Apr.1952, pp.80,82. il.
Edward J. Ruppelt, "What Our Air
Force Found Out about Flying Sau-
cers," True, May 1954, pp.19-30,
124-34/ il.
Edward J. Ruppelt, The Report on Un-
identified Flying Objects (Garden
City: Doubleday, 1956), pp.96-110.
Donald H. Menzel & Lyle G. Boyd, The
World of Flying Saucers (Garden
City: Doubleday, 1963), pp.123-29.
U.S. Air Force, Projects Grudge and
Blue Book Reports 1-12 (Washington:
NICAP, 1968), pp.8-10,37-40.
Brad Steiger, Project Blue Book (N.Y.:
Ballantine, 1976), pp.78-100. il.
Kevin Randle, "The Lubbock Lights,"
Official UFO 1 (Nov.1976):28-29,
42-44. il.

Lufkin
-Ghost light
n.d.
Sue Henderson, "Sam's Lantern," in
Mody C. Boatright & Donald Day, eds.,
Backwoods to Border (Austin: Texas
Folklore Soc'y, Pub.no.18, 1943),
p.144.
-UFO (?)
1955, Feb.13/John Fontaine
"Case 67," CRIFO Newsl., 1 Apr.1955,
pp.5-6.
-UFO (CE-2)
1950, April 20/Jack Robertson/9 mi.W
on Hwy.94
Kenneth Arnold & Ray Palmer, The Com-
ing of the Saucers (Boise: The Au-
thors, 1952), pp.149-50.

McAllen
-UFO (NL)
1977, Feb.18/Jimmy Boyd
"Amateur Astronomer Observes UFO,"
APRO Bull. 26 (Sep.1977):4.

McGregor
-UFO (CE-2)
1977, Oct.
Timothy Green Beckley, "Calvert, Tex-
as: Flying Saucer Way Station," Saga
UFO Rept. 2 (spring 1975):18,68.

McKinney
-UFO (CE-1)
1956, April 4/5 mi.E
Jacques Vallee, Passport to Magonia
(Chicago: Regnery, 1969), pp.252-
53.

Madisonville
-Gravity anomaly
1963, April 19/Louis A. Johnson/N on
U.S.75
(Editorial), Fate 16 (Oct.1963):10-
13.

Malakoff
-Archeological site
carved stone heads/5 mi.W
E.H. Sellards, "Stone Images from
Henderson County, Texas," Am.Antiq-
uity 7 (1941):29-38. il.

Manassa
-Fire anomaly
1976, Sep.22
"Diary of a Mad Planet," Fortean
Times, no.18 (Oct.1976):8,22.

Mansfield
-UFO (NL)
1897, April 17
Dallas Morning News, 18 Apr.1897, p.
5.

Marble Falls
-UFO (?)
1973, July 25
Paris Flammonde, UFO Exist! (N.Y.:
Putnam, 1976), p.314.

Marfa
-Ghost light
1883-   /abandoned airport
Riley Aiken, "More Chisos Ghosts,"
in Mody C. Boatright, et al., Mad-
stones and Twisters (Dallas: South-
ern Methodist Univ., Texas Folklore
Soc'y Pub.no.28, 1958), pp.123-27.
"Texas Mystery Lights," Fate 11 (Apr.
1958):76.
San Angelo Standard-Times, 14 Jan.
1965, p.B1.
Marge Crumbaker, "The Unsolved Mys-
tery of the Ghost Lights," Houston
Post, 7 Jan.1968, Sunday magazine.
Elton Miles, Tales of the Big Bend
(College Station: Texas A & M, 1976),
pp.129,149-67. il.
Hayden C. Hewes, "The Mysterious
Marfa Lights," Saga UFO Rept. 6
(Aug.1978):24-27. il.
-Poltergeist
1966/Margaret Everett/Marfa Elementary
School
(Editorial), Fate 20 (Apr.1967):14-
16.

Marion co.
-Humanoid
1965, Sep.
Cincinnati (O.) Post & Times-Star,

20 Sep.1965.

Marlin
-Fall of fossil bone
  1973/Ina Blann
    (Editorial), Fate 26 (Nov.1973):26-
    28.
-UFO (CE-1)
  1970, Oct.20/Tommy Roy Blann/1½ mi.N
  on Hwy.6
    Tommy Roy Blann, "Personal Report of
    Texas UFO Sighting," Skylook, no.
    46 (Sep.1971):9.

Marquez
-UFO (DD)
  1973, Sep./Mrs. Dewitt Donaldson
    Tommy R. Blann, "Bright Lights over
    Them Purple Plains," Probe the Un-
    known 2 (summer 1974):56-57.

Marshall
-Fall of rock
  1961, July 11/Troy Peterson
    Curtis Fuller, "The Boys Who 'Caught'
    a Flying Saucer," Fate 15 (Jan.
    1962):36,38-39.
-Humanoid
  1978, Jan.11/8 mi.W
    Marshall News-Messenger, 16 Jan.1978.
  1978, Feb.7/Sand Hill
    Longview News, 9 Feb.1978.
-UFO (?)
  1958, March 3
    Richard Hall, ed., The UFO Evidence
    (Washington: NICAP, 1964), p.17.

Mart
-UFO (?)
  1972, Feb.27/Les Roll/217 N. Emerson/
  =hoax
    Waco News-Tribune, 28 Feb.1972.
    Mart Herald, 2 Mar.1972.
    "Cover Story Outstanding Photo," Can.
    UFO Rept., no.12 (1972):12-14. il.
    Jerry Johnson, "Hoax Suspected in
    UFO Photos," Skylook, no.58 (Sep.
    1972):8-9.

Martin co.
-UFO (CE-1)
  1952, summer/Flora Rogers/18 mi. from
  Garden City
    Gray Barker, They Knew Too Much About
    Flying Saucers (N.Y.: University,
    1956), pp.78-80, quoting Big Spring
    Weekly News (undated).

Mason
-Fall of ice
  1877, May 3
    "Large Hail-stones," Monthly Weather
    Rev. 1 (May 1877):5.

Matador
-UFO (DD)
  1951, Aug.31
    Edward J. Ruppelt, The Report on Un-
    identified Flying Objects (Garden
    City: Doubleday, 1956), pp.102-103.

U.S. Air Force, Projects Grudge and
Blue Book Reports 1-12 (Washington:
NICAP, 1968), pp.14,43.

Matagorda
-Cattle mutilation
  1975
    Tommy Roy Blann, "The Mysterious
    Link Between UFOs and Cattle Mutila-
    tions," Saga UFO Rept. 3 (Apr.1976)
    :18,72.

Merkel
-UFO (CE-3)
  1897, April 25/=hoax?
    Houston Post, 28 Apr.1897.
    Frank Masquelette, "Claims Made of
    UFO Evidence," Houston Post, 13
    June 1966.

Mexia
-Electromagnetic anomaly
  1945, July/Wallace Welsh
    Vincent H. Gaddis, Mysterious Fires
    and Lights (N.Y.: Dell, 1968 ed.),
    p.47, quoting UP release, 5 Sep.
    1945.

Midland
-Animal ESP
  1972, July/Mrs. Max T. Brown
    Samuel Gordon, "Mourning Dogs," Fate
    27 (May 1974):106.
-Archeological site
  ca.7000 B.C./Scharbauer site
    Fred Wendorf, et al., The Midland
    Discovery (Austin: Univ. of Texas,
    1955). il.
    H.M. Wormington, Ancient Man in Am-
    erica, 4th ed. (Denver: Museum of
    Natural History, 1957), pp.241-47.
    il.
    Fred Wendorf & Alex D. Krieger, "New
    Light on the Midland Discovery,"
    Am.Antiquity 25 (1959):66-78.
-Electromagnetic anomaly
  1960, Nov./Virginia Kimmey
    "Music in the Bath," Fate 14 (July
    1961):35.
-UFO (NL)
  1957, Nov.2
    Donald E. Keyhoe, Flying Saucers: Top
    Secret (N.Y.: Putnam, 1960), p.114.
  1957, Nov.5
    "All About Sputs," Doubt, no.56
    (1958):460,471.

Milano
-Ancient wall
    Rapid City (S.D.) Black Hills Weekly,
    1 Jan.1896, p.3.

Millersville
-UFO (CE-1)
  1966, April 17
    Jacques Vallee, Passport to Magonia
    (Chicago: Regnery, 1969), p.329.

Mission
-Cattle mutilations

1975, Nov.-1976
   Don Worley, "Cattle Mutilations &
   UFOs: Who Are the Mutilators?" Of-
   ficial UFO 1 (Dec.1976):25.
-Healing and precognition
   1940s-1972/Dan. A. Laning/St. Paul's
   Church
   Bill Starr, "How Texas Priest Uses
   ESP," Fate 12 (Sep.1968):78-82. il.
   (Letter), Fate 26 (Feb.1973):142.
-Hex
   n.d.
   Bill Starr, "Witchcraft Pays Off
   Along the Rio Grande," Fate 24
   (Dec.1971):78,83.

Montalba
-Giant bird
   1976, Dec.8/John S. Carroll, Jr./3 mi.
   E
   Palestine Herald-Press, 16 Dec.1976;
   and 19 Dec.1976.

Monticello
-UFO (CE-2)
   1973, Dec.
   Timothy Green Beckley, "Calvert, Tex-
   as: Flying Saucer Way Station," Saga
   UFO Rept. 2 (spring 1975):18,68.

Nederland
-UFO (CE-2)
   1966, Feb.6
   J. Allen Hynek, The UFO Experience
   (Chicago: Regnery, 1972), pp.90-91.
   J. Allen Hynek, The Hynek UFO Report
   (N.Y.: Dell, 1977), pp.186-89.

New Braunfels
-UFO (?)
   1978, March 18/=film flaw
   "Is a UFO Buzzing the President's
   Helicopter?" Int'l UFO Reporter 3
   (Aug.1978):10. il.

Newcastle
-Coal ball
   A.C. Noe, "Coal Balls," Science 57
   (1923):385.

Odessa
-Archeological site
   Houston Post, 6 Jan.1977.
-Meteorite crater
   168 m.diam. x 6 m.deep/7 mi.W/certain
   A.B. Bibbins, "A Small Meteor Crater
   in Texas," Engineering & Mining J.
   121 (1926):932.
   E.H. Sellards, "Unusual Structural
   Feature in the Plains Region of
   Texas," Bull.Geol.Soc'y Am. 38
   (1927):149.
   D.M. Barringer, Jr., "A New Meteor
   Crater," Proc.Acad.Nat.Sci.Philadel-
   phia 80 (1929):307-11.
   Oscar E. Monnig & Robert Brown, "The
   Odessa, Rexas, Meteorite Crater,"
   Pop.Astron. 43 (1935):34-38.
   E.H. Sellards & G. Evans, "Odessa
   Meteor Craters," Museum Notes, Views

in Texas Memorial Museum 6 (July
1944):13.
   Carl W. Beck & Lincoln LaPaz, "The
   Odessa, Texas, Siderite," Pop.Astron.
   59 (1951):145-51.
   Ralph B. Baldwin, The Measure of the
   Moon (Chicago: Univ. of Chicago,
   1963), pp.18-22,123-25,148-51,181-
   83. il.

Olmito
-Giant bird
   1976, Jan.
   Jack Murray, "The 'Big Bird' You'll
   Never See on Sesame Street," Probe
   the Unknown 4 (Nov.1976):44,46.

Olney
-Cattle mutilation
   1974, Nov.13/J.R. Allison/5 mi.S
   Tommy Roy Blann, "The Mysterious
   Link Between UFOs and Animal Mutilations," Saga UFO Rept. 3 (Apr.
   1976):18,20.

Orange
-UFO (NL)
   1952, Oct.17/E.G. Sparks
   (Editorial), Fate 6 (Apr.1953):10-11.

Palestine
-Ball lightning
   n.d.
   M.K. Jessup, The Case for the UFO
   (N.Y.: Bantam, 1955 ed.), p.150.
-Fall of pebbles
   1888, July 6/Mr. Lacy
   (Letter), W.H. Perry, Monthly Weather
   Rev. 16 (July 1888):173.
-Giant bird
   1976, Dec./Donnie Simmons
   Palestine Herald-Press, 16 Dec.1976;
   19 Dec.1976.
-UFO (NL)
   1947, July 8/Horace Valentine
   San Antonio Express, 10 July 1947.

Palo Pinto co.
-Clairvoyance
   1890s/Belle and Jim Schrum
   Dallas Morning News, 8 Nov.1894.
   Edley W. Cox, "The Children Who Saw
   Everywhere," Fate 2 (Nov.1949):8-15.

Pampa
-UFO (NL)
   1957, Oct.23/Emerson E. Goff
   "Commercial Pilots Report 1957 UFO,"
   UFO Inv. 3 (Oct.-Nov.1966):7-8.

Paris
-Humanoid and cattle mutilation
   1970, April/Bob Allison/E of town
   Big Spring Herald, 27 Apr.1970.
-UFO (?)
   1967, March 7
   Gordon D. Thayer, "Optical and Radar
   Analyses of Field Cases," in Edward
   U. Condon, ed., Scientific Study of
   Unidentified Flying Objects (N.Y.:

Bantam, 1969 ed.), pp.131-32.
-UFO (CE-1)
  1897, April 15/J.A. Black
    Dallas Morning News, 17 Apr.1897,
    p.8.

Pearsall
-Cattle mutilation
  1975, Feb./Ray Goad/14 mi.NW
    Annie Rosenbloom, "Cow Deaths," Ohio
    Sky Watcher, Mar.1975, p.17.

Pecos
-UFO (?)
  1956, Feb.10/25 mi.NW/=meteor?
    "Fiery Object Explodes near Pecos,"
    CRIFO Orbit, 6 Apr.1956, p.2, quot-
    ing El Paso Herald-Post (undated).
-UFO (CE-1)
  1966, March 30
    Lubbock Avalanche-Journal, 31 Mar.
    1966, p.A8.
-UFO (DD)
  1952, April 10/6 mi.W
    J. Allen Hynek, The Hynek UFO Report
    (N.Y.: Dell, 1977), p.43.

Pettit
-UFO (CE-2)
  1957, Nov.2
    Richard Hall, ed., The UFO Evidence
    (Washington: NICAP, 1964), p.168.

Pharr
-Healing
  1962-1970s/Sister Rosa/2 mi.N on U.S.
  281
    Bill Starr, "Witchcraft Pays Off along
    the Rio Grande," Fate 24 (Dec.1971)
    :78,80-82.

Pine Valley
-UFO (?)
  1897, April 25
    Houston Post, 28 Apr.1897.

Plainview
-Archeological site
  ca.7000 B.C.
    E.H. Sellards, Glen L. Evans & Gray-
    son E. Meade, "Fossil Bison and As-
    sociated Artifacts from Plainview,
    Texas," Bull.Geol.Soc'y Am. 58
    (1947):927-54. il.

Plano
-Animal ESP
  1973, April/Jerry Reid
    (Editorial), Fate 26 (Sep.1973):28-
    31.
-UFO (?)
  1897, April 17/Harris Wyatt/=hoax
    Dallas Morning News, 19 Apr.1897, p.
    5.

Port Aransas
-Disappearance
  1968, March 10/Mrs. Joe Sanchez
    Brad Steiger, Strange Disappearances
    (N.Y.: Magnum, 1972), pp.9-10.

-Unidentified submerged object
  1961, July/Ira Pete/"Ruby E."
    (Editorial), Fate 14 (Dec.1961):27.

Port Arthur
-Fall of white dust
  1978, May 16
    Dallas Times-Herald, 17 May 1978.
-UFO (R-V)
  1961, July 20/A.V. Beatherd/nr. Jefferson County Airport
    Lloyd Mallan, "The Mysterious 12,"
    Sci.& Mech. 37 (Dec.1966):30,64-65.

Porter
-UFO (NL)
  1977, July 21
    San Antonio Evening News, 21 July
    1977.

Port Isabel
-Disappearance
  1966, Oct.29/Grady A. Reynolds/"Southern Cities"/95 mi.SE
    John Wallace Spencer, Limbo of the
    Lost (N.Y.: Bantam, 1973), pp.75-
    79.
-Fall of nails
  1888, Oct./Mrs. Schreiber/lighthouse
    St. Louis (Mo.) Globe-Democrat, 16
    Oct.1888.

Port Lavaca
-Skyquake
  1978, Feb.
    Kansas City (Mo.) Star, 9 Feb.1978.

Port Neches
-Phantom image
  1969, June 10/Lela Bass/816 Ave.C
    Port Neches Chronicle, 18 June 1969.

Poteet
-Giant bird
  1976, Jan.11/Jesse Garcia/N of town
    Jerome Clark & Loren Coleman, Crea-
    tures of the Outer Edge (N.Y.: War-
    ner, 1978), p.179.
-UFO (CE-3)
  1973, Nov.13/2 mi.E on Hwy.1470
    Austin Evening Statesman, 14 Nov.
    1973.
    David Webb, 1973: Year of the Human-
    oids (Evanston: Center for UFO
    Studies, 1976 ed.), p.20.

Randolph AFB
-UFO (?)
  1952, May 25
    Edward J. Ruppelt, The Report on Un-
    identified Flying Objects (Garden
    City: Doubleday, 1956), p.140.

Ranger
-Fall of fish
  1924/Velma T. Hickey
    (Letter), Fate 14 (Dec.1961):129.

Raymondville
-Giant bird

1976, Jan.14/Armando Grimaldo
  Jerome Clark & Loren Coleman, Creatures of the Outer Edge (N.Y.: Warner, 1978), pp.167-69.

Red River co.
-Archeological site
  ca.1000-1700/Sam Kaufman site
  R.K. Harris, "The Sam Kaufman Site,
  Red River County, Texas," Bull.Texas
  Arch.Soc'y 24 (1953):43-68. il.

Richardson
-Telepathy
  1970s/John Gary
  Sally Remaley, "John Gary's Power of
  Positive Thought," Fate 31 (Oct.
  1978):51-53.
-UFO (CE-1)
  1972, Sep.24/Billy Erwin
  "Press Reports," APRO Bull. 21 (Sep.-
  Oct.1972):11.

Rio Grande City
-Giant bird
  1975, Nov.-1976
  Jack Murray, "The 'Big Bird' You'll
  Never See on Sesame Street," Probe
  the Unknown 4 (Nov.1976):44,46.
  Jerome Clark & Loren Coleman, Crea-
  tures of the Outer Edge (N.Y.: War-
  ner, 1978), p.170.
-Hex
  1890s
  John G. Bourke, "Superstitions of the
  Rio Grande," J.Am.Folklore 7 (1894):
  122,143.

Robert Lee
-UFO (NL)
  1947, Aug.6/Jim Reid
  Kenneth Arnold & Ray Palmer, The Coming of the Saucers (Boise: The Authors, 1952), p.137.

Robstown
-Giant bird
  1975, Nov.
  Houston Chronicle, 14 Jan.1976; and
  26 Feb.1976.

Rockland
-UFO (CE-3)
  1897, April 22/John M. Barclay
  Houston Post, 25 Apr.1897, p.13.

Rockwall
-Ancient walls
  "Mystery Walls in Texas," Fate 17
  (Feb.1964):35, quoting San Antonio
  News (undated).
  Dallas Morning News, 5 Nov.1967.

Rosenberg
-UFO (NL)
  1976, Jan.26
  "Noteworthy UFO Sightings," Ufology
  2 (summer 1976):63.

Round Rock
-Roman coin
  1963/Walter L. Horton, Jr./Indian
  mound
  Dallas Morning News, 26 Dec.1976.

Rusk
-UFO (CE-3)
  1897, April/G.E. Long
  Houston Daily Post, 28 Apr.1897, p.
  8.

Salt Flat
-UFO (CE-1)
  1957, July 17/Ed Bachner/=aircraft?
  (Editorial), Fate 10 (Nov.1957):9.
  Coral & Jim Lorenzen, UFOs: The Whole
  Story (N.Y.: Signet, 1969), p.79.
  James E. McDonald, "Science in De-
  fault: Twenty-two Years of Inade-
  quate UFO Investigations," in Carl
  Sagan & Thornton Page, eds., UFOs:
  A Scientific Debate (Ithaca, N.Y.:
  Cornell Univ., 1972), pp.52,69.

San Angelo
-Fire anomaly
  1959, March/G.T. Trussler
  (Editorial), Fate 12 (Sep.1959):8-10.
-UFO (?)
  1952, Aug./E.M. Thomason/=meteor?
  (Letter), Fate 20 (Mar.1967):136-38.
-UFO (DD)
  1968, June 15/Anton Fitzgerald/NE of
  town
  Anton Fitzgerald, "Repeat Perform-
  ance," Flying Saucer Rev. 15 (May-
  June 1969):6-8.

San Antonio
-Ball lightning
  1953, Aug.21
  "Falls and Balls," Doubt, no.43
  (1954):256.
-Cave anomaly
  Alexander Bradford, American Antiquities and Researches into the Or-
  igin and History of the Red Race
  (N.Y.: Dayton & Saxton, 1841).
-Fall of poisonous hailstones
  1953, April 23
  "Falls," Doubt, no.41 (1953):221,
  222, quoting Dallas News (undated).
-Giant bird
  1976, Feb.24/Patricia Bryant/SW of
  town/=hoax?
  Cedar Rapids (Ia.) Gazette, 26 Feb.
  1976.
  Jerome Clark & Loren Coleman, Crea-
  tures of the Outer Edge (N.Y.: War-
  ner, 1978), pp.178-79.
-Haunt
  1960s/Brooks House
  Susy Smith, Ghosts around the House
  (N.Y.: World, 1970).
-Healing
  1960s
  Ari Kiev, Curanderismo (N.Y.: Free
  Press, 1968).
-Hex

1974, July/Juanita Vasquez Garcia
  "Judge Defies Hex," Fate 27 (Dec.
  1974):95, quoting UPI release (undated).
1976, Sep.-1977, Jan.
  San Antonio Light, 10 Sep.1976; and
  30 Jan.1977.
-Humanoid
  n.d.
    Adina de Zavala, History and Legends
    of the Alamo (San Antonio: The Au-
    thor, 1917), pp.58-65.
  1957, fall/35 mi.N
    John Green, The Sasquatch File (Ag-
    assiz, B.C.: Cheam, 1973), p.24.
    John Green, Sasquatch: The Apes Among
    Us (Seattle: Hancock House, 1978),
    pp.182-83.
  1976, Aug./Ed Olivarri/1370 W. Fenfield
    San Antonio Light, 1 Sep.1976.
  1976, Aug.29/Rosa Medina/1362 W. Fenfield
    "Forteana," Anomaly Rsch.Bull., no.
    3 (Oct.-Nov.1976):7-8, quoting San
    Antonio Light (undated).
-Parapsychology research
  1970s/Helmut Schmidt/Mind Science Foun-
  dation/102 W. Rector
    Helmut Schmidt, "Observation of Sub-
    conscious PK Effects with and with-
    out Time Displacement," in J.D. Mor-
    ris, et al., eds., Research in Para-
    psychology 1974 (Metuchen, N.J.:
    Scarecrow, 1975), pp.116-21.
    Helmut Schmidt, "Toward a Mathemati-
    cal Theory of Psi," J.ASPR 69 (1975)
    :301-19.
    D. Scott Rogo, "Meditation and Mind
    over Matter," Saga UFO Rept. 5
    (Mar.1978):20,50-51.
-Phantoms
  ca.1900
    Arthur Conan Doyle, The Coming of
    the Fairies (N.Y.: Samuel Weiser,
    1975 ed.), p.154.
-Poltergeist
  1965, summer-1968/Vi Strand
    Vi Strand, "Our House Pest the Pol-
    tergeist," Fate 21 (May 1968):65-
    71.
-Precognition
  1958/Spencer Thornton
    (Editorial), Fate 11 (Aug.1958):14-
    15.
-Seance
  1855, Jan.
    Emma Hardinge Britten, Modern Ameri-
    can Spiritualism (N.Y.: The Author,
    1870), pp.405-406.
-Spontaneous human combustion
  1880, Nov.11/Fred Bader
    Shreveport (La.) Times, 18 Nov.1880.
-UFO (CE-1)
  1946, July/Ruby L. Mitchell
    (Letter), Fate 14 (June 1961):110-13.
-UFO (CE-2)
  1957, Nov.5
    San Antonio Light, 6 Nov.1957.
-UFO (CE-3)
  1975, May 3/Alois Olenick/Mogford Rd.

San Antonio Light, 5 May 1975.
Gary Graber, "Two Occupants in Craft,"
  Skylook, no.99 (Feb.1976):3-4. il.
-UFO (DD)
  1952, July 7/Ruby L. Mitchell
    (Letter), Fate 14 (June 1961):110-13.
  1953, June 16/Kelly AFB
    U.S. Air Force, Projects Grudge and
    Blue Book Reports 1-12 (Washington:
    NICAP, 1968), p.222.
-UFO (DD) and Men-in-black
  1970, Sep./Lackland AFB
    Rufus Drake, "Return of the 'Men in
    Black,'" Saga UFO Rept. 3 (Oct.
    1976):37-39.
-UFO (NL)
  1953, Sep./Vic Damone/Fort Sam Houston
    Timothy Green Beckley, "Saucers and
    Celebrities," Saga UFO Rept. 3
    (Apr.1976):35.
  1972, July 25
    Glenn McWane & David Graham, The New
    UFO Sightings (N.Y.: Paperback Li-
    brary, 1974), p.45.
-UFO (R-V)
  1973, Oct.23/James Stevens/airport
    "San Antonio Airline Case," APRO
    Bull. 23 (Sep.-Oct.1974):1,4.

San Benito
-Giant bird
  1940s-1970s
    Jerome Clark & Loren Coleman, Crea-
    tures of the Outer Edge (N.Y.: War-
    ner, 1978), pp.182-87.
  1975, Dec.28/Arturo Padilla
    Jack Murray, "The 'Big Bird' You'll
    Never See on Sesame Street," Probe
    the Unknown 4 (Nov.1976):44-46.
    Jerome Clark & Loren Coleman, Crea-
    tures of the Outer Edge (N.Y.: War-
    ner, 1978), pp.170-71.
  1975, Dec.31
    "Diary of a Mad Planet," Fortean
    Times, no.18 (Oct.1976):8,11.
  1976, April/Guadalupe Cantu III
    Jerome Clark & Loren Coleman, Crea-
    tures of the Outer Edge (N.Y.: War-
    ner, 1978), p.187.
-Giant bird droppings
  1975, May-1976/Guadalupe Cantu III
    Jerome Clark & Loren Coleman, Crea-
    tures of the Outer Edge (N.Y.: War-
    ner, 1978), pp.180-82.
-UFO (CE-1)
  1973, Nov.14
    Columbus (O.) Dispatch, 15 Nov.1973,
    p.17A.
-UFO (CE-3)
  1973, June/Guadalupe Cantu III
    Jerome Clark, "Saucer Central U.S.A.,"
    Saga UFO Rept. 3 (June 1976):8,58.

Sand Hill
-Humanoid
  1978, Jan.11
    Marshall News-Messenger, 16 Jan.1978.

Sanger
-Precognition

1917, June 11/J.W. Koons
"Possible Premonition," J.ASPR 18
(1924):30-35.

San Juan
-Hex
  n.d.
    Bill Starr, "Witchcraft Pays Off
    Along the Rio Grande," Fate 24
    (Dec.1971):78,80.

San Marcos
-Entombed salamander
  1899, April/=found in underground
  stream
    Charles M. Blackford, "A Curious
    Salamander," Nature 60 (1899):389-
    90.
-Haunt
  1960s/bridge
    Susy Smith, Ghosts Around the House
    (N.Y.: World, 1970).
-Humanoid
  1875, July
    Austin Statesman, 21 July 1875.
-UFO (NL)
  1968, Sep.18/Arthur H. Byrd/I-35
    Coral & Jim Lorenzen, UFOs: The Whole
    Story (N.Y.: Signet, 1969), p.297.
  1976, March 15/Scott Smith/NW of town
    Jerold R. Johnson, "Reports of Fly-
    ing, Pulsating Sound in Texas,"
    MUFON UFO J., no.103 (June 1976):
    17-18.

Santa Rosa
-UFO (?)
  1957, Nov.25/=Venus
    Jacques & Janine Vallee, Challenge
    to Science (N.Y.: Ace, 1966 ed.),
    p.132.

Saratoga
-Ghost light
  1960-   /Bragg Rd.
    (Editorial), Fate 14 (May 1961):22-
    23.
    (Editorial), Fate 19 (Jan.1966):29.
    Francis E. Abernethy, Tales from the
    Big Thicket (Austin: Univ. of Texas,
    1966), pp.227-33.
    Don Moser, "Big Thicket of Texas,"
    Nat'l Geographic 146 (Oct.1974):504,
    524-28. il.
    Hutchinson (Kan.) News, 14 Sep.1978.

Seminole
-UFO (?)
  1963, July/E.M. Thomason
    (Letter), Fate 20 (Mar.1967):136-38.
-UFO (CE-2)
  1957, Nov.2
    Hobbs (N.M.) News-Sun, 5 Nov.1957.

Sherman
-UFO (CE-1)
  1978, Oct.30/Macky Parson/nr. E. Lamar
  St.
    Denison Herald, 31 Oct.1978.
-UFO (NL)

1897, April 15/W.S. Hellier/public
square
    Dallas Morning News, 17 Apr.1897.

Smithville
-Haunt
  ca.1923/Lorna Farrar
    Lorna Farrar, "Our Ghost Came Knock-
    ing," Fate 17 (Mar.1964):49-53.

Smyer
-UFO (DD)
  1947, June 29
    Dallas Morning News, 1 July 1947.

Stafford
-Haunt
  1955/Hwy.59 nr. Harris co. line
    (Editorial), Fate 9 (Apr.1956):9.

Stephens co.
-Fall of ice
  1949, Sep.11/Robert Botts/Eugene Tipton ranch
    Lewis W. Mathews, "The Great Hail,"
    Fate 3 (Aug.1950):86.

Stephenville
-UFO (CE-3)
  1897, April 17/C.L. McIllhaney
    Dallas Morning News, 19 Apr.1897, p.
    5.

Sulphur Springs
-Fall of blood
  1870s
    Henry Winfred Splitter, "Wonders
    from the Sky," Fate 6 (Oct.1953):
    33,37, quoting Sacramento (Cal.)
    Reporter (undated).
-Haunt
  1945, summer
    Haldeen Braddy, Mexico and the Old
    Southwest (Port Washington, N.Y.:
    Kennikat, 1971), pp.185-89, quoting
    Sulphur Springs News-Telegram (un-
    dated).

Sundown
-UFO (NL)
  1957, Nov.4/J.B. Cogburn/7 mi.N on
  Farm Rd.300
    Don Berliner, "The Levelland Sight-
    ings," Official UFO 1 (Jan.1976):
    22,48-49.

Temple
-UFO (CE-2)
  1973, Oct.21/Bruce Holleman/Adams Ave.
    Tommy R. Blann, "Bright Lights over
    Them Purple Plains," Probe the Un-
    known 2 (summer 1974):56-57.
-UFO (NL)
  1973, Oct.24/Roscoe Harrison
    Tommy R. Blann, "Bright Lights over
    Them Purple Plains," Probe the Un-
    known 2 (summer 1974):56-57.

Terlingua
-UFO (NL)

1971, Dec.10/Earl F. Watts
Earl F. Watts, "Sighting at Terlingua
Ranch, Texas," Skylook, no.51 (Feb.
1972):11.

Texarkana
-Skyquake
1977, Nov.12
Texarkana Gazette, 14 Nov.1977.
-UFO (?)
1897, April 17
Dallas Morning News, 18 Apr.1897.
1952, April
Coral & Jim Lorenzen, UFOs: The Whole
Story (N.Y.: Signet, 1969), p.43.
-UFO (NL)
1947, July 2/W.O. Robertson
Dallas Morning News, 4 July 1947.
1964, June 5
Jacques & Janine Vallee, Challenge
to Science (N.Y.: Ace, 1966 ed.),
pp.58-59.

Texas City
-Precognition
1952, June/Jimmy Key
(Editorial), Fate 6 (Nov.1953):9.
-UFO (?)
1947, July 6
Houston Post, 7 July 1947.
1951, Nov./E.M. Thomason
(Letter), Fate 20 (Mar.1967):136-38.

Tioga
-UFO (?)
1897, April 17/James Daugherty
Dallas Morning News, 18 Apr.1897, p.
5.

Trinidad
-Humanoid
1977, Aug.22/N on Hwy.274
John Green, Sasquatch: The Apes Among
Us (Seattle: Hancock House, 1978),
p.188, quoting Corsicana Daily Sun
(undated).

Tyler
-UFO (?)
1955, Feb.13/J.N. Aber/Pound's Field
"Case 67," CRIFO Newsl., 1 Apr.1955,
p.5.
Donald E. Keyhoe, Flying Saucer Con-
spiracy (N.Y.: Holt, 1955), p.260.
-UFO (CE-1)
1972, July 27/Joe Carter
Tyler Courier-Times, 27 July 1972.

Uvalde
-Dowsing
1890s-1900s/Guy Fenley
Alpine Avalanche, 30 Nov.1900.
-UFO (CE-3)
1897, April 20/H.W. Baylor
Galveston Daily News, 24 Apr.1897,
p.3; and 28 Apr.1897, p.6.
-UFO (DD)
1952, July 22
Edward J. Ruppelt, The Report on Un-
identified Flying Objects (Garden

City: Doubleday, 1956), p.163.

Vernon
-UFO (?)
1954, July
Donald E. Keyhoe, Flying Saucer Conspiracy (N.Y.: Holt, 1955), p.190.

Victoria
-Spirit mediums
1850s
Emma Hardinge Britten, Modern American Spiritualism (N.Y.: The Author,
1870), pp.404-405.

Vidor
-Humanoid
1978, June 19/Bobby Bussinger/3925 N.
Tram Rd.
Orange Leader, 20-21 June 1978.
"Bigfoot," APRO Bull. 27 (Oct.1978):
4-5.

Waco
-Child prodigy
1880s/Oscar Moore
S.V. Clevenger, "An Infant Prodigy,"
Alienist & Neurologist 11 (1890):
359-65.
"Notes and News," Science 17 (1891):
353.
-Haunt
1966, summer/William Cameron home
"Ghosts A-go-go," Fate 21 (Jan.1968)
:98.
-UFO (?)
1973, Oct.23/Ben Collins/WACO radio
Tommy R. Blann, "Bright Lights over
Them Purple Plains," Probe the Un-
known 2 (summer 1974):56-57.
-UFO (CE-2)
1967, Aug.
Timothy Green Beckley, "Mind Manip-
ulation: The New UFO Terror Tactic,"
Saga UFO Rept. 2 (winter 1975):31,
33,56-58.
1973, Dec.
Timothy Green Beckley, "Calvert, Tex-
as: Flying Saucer Way Station," Saga
UFO Rept. 2 (spring 1975):18,68.
-UFO (DD)
1918/Edwin T. Bauhan/Rich Field
Gordon I.R. Lore, Jr. & Harold H. Den-
eault, Jr., Mysteries of the Skies:
UFOs in Perspective (Englewood
Cliffs, N.J.: Prentice-Hall, 1968),
p.105, quoting CSI Quar.Bull., win-
ter 1954.
-UFO (NL)
1951, Aug.
Coral & Jim Lorenzen, UFOs: The Whole
Story (N.Y.: Signet, 1969), pp.41-
42.

Waller
-Precognition
n.d./A.D. Purvis
V.B. Shay, "He Dreamed Up His Busi-
ness," Fate 2 (Sep.1949):21.
(Letter), Otto E. Krohn, Fate 3 (May

1950):91-93.

Waxahachie
-UFO (CE-3)
1897, April 17/Judge Love
Dallas Morning News, 17 Apr.1897, p.
5.

Weatherford
-UFO (NL)
1897, April 14
Dallas Morning News, 16 Apr.1897.
1945, Dec.18/George McKinney
"Light in Sky," Doubt, no.16 (1946):
241.

Wellington
-UFO (CE-1)
1967, Nov.3/Hazel McKinney/U.S.83
"U.S.A.," APRO Bull. 16 (Mar.-Apr.
1968):8.
-UFO (CE-4)
1967, April 11/Carroll Wayne Watts
"Recent News," Saucer News 15 (sum-
mer 1968):18.
Robert B. Loftin, Identified Flying
Saucers (N.Y.: David McKay, 1968).
John A. Keel, Strange Creatures from
Time and Space (Greenwich, Ct.:
Fawcett, 1970), pp.155-57.
-UFO (NL)
1968, March 2/Alvis Maddox/2 mi.S
"Texas Lawman Pursues UAO," APRO
Bull. 16 (Mar.-Apr.1968):7.

Wharton
-Hex
1930s/Moe Green
Archie Steagall, "The Voodoo Man of
the Brazos," Pub.Texas Folklore
Soc'y 17 (1941):113-14.

Whiteface
-Cattle mutilation and UFOs
1975, March 10/Darwood Marshall/6 mi.S
Tommy Roy Blann, "The Mysterious
Link Between UFOs and Animal Muti-
lations," Saga UFO Rept. 3 (Apr.
1976):18,20.
Ed Sanders, "The Mutilation Mystery,"
Oui, Sep.1976, pp.51,113.

Whitharral
-UFO (CE-2)
1957, Nov.2/Jose Alvarez/S on Hwy.51
1957, Nov.3/Frank Williams/S on Hwy.51
Richard Hall, ed., The UFO Evidence
(Washington: NICAP, 1964), pp.168-
69.

Whitney
-UFO (NL)
1897, April 17/O.H. Young
Dallas Morning News, 18 Apr.1897, p.
5.

Wichita Falls
-Animal ESP
1961/airport
(Editorial), Fate 14 (May 1961):18.

-Erratic ostrich
1977, July 4/Allendale x Old Seymour
Rd.
Wichita Falls Record-News, 5-6 July
1977.
-Fall of metallic object
1961, Nov.13/7th x Indiana St./=hoax
Wichita Falls Record-News, 14 Nov.
1961.
-Healing
1955, May/Anna Williams
(Editorial), Fate 8 (Oct.1955):13.
-UFO (?)
1952, April 2/=meteor?
Wichita Falls News, 3 Apr.1952.
-UFO (DD)
1957, Nov.5
Amarillo Daily News, 7 Nov.1957.

Wilbarger co.
-Meteorite crater
=terrestrial
Oscar E. Monnig, "A Probable Small
Astrobleme in North Texas," Meteor-
itics 2 (1964):71.

Yellow Falls
-UFO (CE-3)
1957, Sep.26
Jacques Vallee, Passport to Magonia
(Chicago: Regnery, 1969), p.258.

B. Physical Features

Addicks Dam
-Archeological site
Doering site
Joe Ben Wheat, "An Archeological Sur-
vey of the Addicks Dam Basin, South-
east Texas," Bull.Bur.Am.Ethn. 154
(1953):143-252. il.
Marshall T. Newman, "Indian Skeletal
Remains from the Doering and Kobs
Sites, Addicks Reservoir, Texas,"
Bull.Bur.Am.Ethn. 154 (1953):253-
66.

Alibates Flint Quarry
-Archeological site
ca.9000 B.C.-1450 A.D.
J.B. Shaeffer, "The Alibates Flint
Quarry, Texas," Am.Antiquity 24
(1958):189-91.
Sam Ed Spence, "Alibates: The Prehistoric Treasure," Desert Mag. 27, no.
8 (1964):30-31.

Baker Cave
-Archeological site
7000 B.C.-1400 A.D.
Houston Chronicle, 11 Sep.1976.

Bald Peak
-Chinese discovery
ca.1000 B.C.
Henriette Mertz, Gods from the Far
East (N.Y.: Ballantine, 1975 ed.),
pp.137-38.

Big Bend National Park
-Dowsing
    Elton Miles, Tales of the Big Bend
    (College Station, Tex.: Texas A &
    M, 1976), pp.72-89.
-Ghost calf
  n.d.
    (Editorial), Fate 31 (June 1978):14.

Blue Creek
-Humanoid
  1960s
    John Green, Sasquatch: The Apes Among
    Us (Seattle: Hancock House, 1978),
    p.184.

Boquillas Canyon
-Rainbow anomaly
  1973, Sep.2/Paul A. Roales
    Paul A. Roales, "A Meteorological
    Puzzle," INFO J., no.15 (May 1975):
    14-15. il.

Brazos R.
-Acoustic anomaly
    Charles D. Hudgins, The Maid of San
    Jacinto (N.Y.: J.S. Ogilvie, 1900),
    pp.12-13.
    Bertha McKee Dobie, "The Death Bell
    of the Brazos," in J. Frank Dobie,
    Legends of Texas (Austin: Texas
    Folklore Soc'y, Pub.no.3, 1924),
    pp.141-42.
-River monster
  n.d.
    Galveston Weekly Journal, 12 May 1853.

Bush Creek
-UFO (NL)
  1947, July 8
    San Antonio Express, 10 July 1947.

Catfish Creek
-Giant bird
  1976, Dec.22
    Palestine Herald-Press, 22 Dec.1976.

Chinati Peak
-Chinese discovery
  ca.1000 B.C.
    Henriette Mertz, Gods from the Far
    East (N.Y.: Ballantine, 1975 ed.),
    pp.138-39.

Chisholm Hollow
-Haunt
  1840-1941
    Harold Preece, "Devil Rider of Chis-
    holm Hollow," Fate 5 (Oct.1952):46-
    50.

Chisos Mts.
-Ghost light and haunt
    Elton Miles, Tales of the Big Bend
    (College Station, Tex.: Texas A &
    M, 1976), pp.37-48.

Eagle Mountain L.
-UFO (NL)
  1965, Aug.2/Bennie G. Barton

Coral E. Lorenzen, "Western UFO Flap,"
    Fate 18 (Nov.1965):42,49.

East Mt.
-Humanoid tracks
  1977, July/2 mi.S
    Longview Journal, 20 July 1977.

Edwards Plateau
-Archeological site
  8000 B.C.-1000 A.D./Bonfire Shelter
    David S. Dibble & Dessamae Lorrain,
    "Bonfire Shelter: A Stratified Bi-
    son Kill Site, Val Verde County,
    Texas," Misc.Pap.Texas Memorial
    Mus., no.1 (1968).
    David S. Dibble, "On the Significance
    of Additional Radiocarbon Dates
    from Bonfire Shelter, Texas," Plains
    Anthro. 15 (1970):251-54.

Enchanted Rock
-Ringing rocks
    W.B. Dewees, Letters from an Early
    Settler of Texas (Louisville, Ky.:
    The Author, 1852), p.152.
-Rock doughnuts
    Horace R. Blank, "'Rock Doughnuts,'
    A Product of Granite Weathering,"
    Am.J.Sci. 249 (1951):822-29. il.

Esperanza Creek
-Ghost light
    John William Blackwell, "Will-o-the-
    Wisp of the Esperanza," in J.Frank
    Dobie, ed., Texian Stamping Grounds
    (Austin: Texas Folklore Soc'y, Pub.
    no.17, 1941), pp.118-19.

Ferrell's Bridge Reservoir
-Archeological site
  Jake Martin Site
    W.A. & E. Mott Davis, "The Jake Mar-
    tin Site," Arch.Ser.Anthro.Dep't
    Univ.Texas, no.3 (1960).

Fish Creek
-UFO (CE-1)
  1974/Steve Abraham/Hwy.6
    Timothy Green Beckley, "Calvert, Tex-
    as: Flying Saucer Way Station," Saga
    UFO Rept. 2 (spring 1975):18,68-69.

Foggy Hill
-UFO (CE-1)
  1965, summer/William Howell
    Brad Steiger & Joan Whritenour, Fly-
    ing Saucers Are Hostile (N.Y.:
    Award, 1967).

Friesenhahn Cavern
-Archeological site
    Glen L. Evans, "The Friesenhahn
    Cave," Bull.Texas Memorial Mus.,
    no.2, pt.1 (1961):3-22. il.

Guadalupe Peak
-Chinese discovery
  ca.1000 B.C.
    Henriette Mertz, Gods from the Far

East (N.Y.: Ballantine, 1975 ed.),
p.137.

Hollywood Bottom
-UFO (DD)
1967, Feb.15
Donald E. Keyhoe & Gordon I.R. Lore,
Jr., UFOs: A New Look (Washington:
NICAP, 1969), p.45.

Jackson L.
-UFO (DD)
1947, July 4/Louise Jacobs
Houston Post, 7 July 1947.

Kiowa Peak
-Humanoid
1960s
John Green, Sasquatch: The Apes Among
Us (Seattle: Hancock House, 1978),
pp.184-85.

Kyle Shelter
-Archeological site
500-1550 A.D.
Edward B. Jelks, "The Kyle Site,"
Arch.Ser.Dep't Anthro.Univ.Texas,
no.5 (1962). il.

Leon R.
-Ghost light
Helen Newton, "The Farmer's Lantern,"
in Mody C. Boatright & Donald Day,
eds., Backwoods to Border (Austin:
Texas Folklore Soc'y, Pub.no.18,
1943), pp.145-46.

Levi Rock Shelter
-Archeological site
8000-5000 B.C.
Herbert L. Alexander, Jr., "The Levi
Site: A Paleo-Indian Campsite in
Central Texas," Am.Antiquity 28
(1963):510-28.

Little R.
-Humanoid
1978, July 27/Jeffrey Gelner/=hoax?
Bryan-College Station Eagle, 28 July
1978; and 31 July 1978.
Cameron Herald, 30 July 1978.

Long Wolf Creek
-Archeological site
Harold J. Cook, "The Antiquity of
Man in America," Sci.Am. 135 (1926)
:334-36.

Matagorda I.
-Animal ESP
1969, June 19/E.J. Lemaire/5 mi. offshore
"Friendly Porpoises," Fate 23 (Aug.
1970):83.

Nueces R.
-Giant bird
1950s/nr. Swinney Switch
Jerome Clark & Loren Coleman, Creatures of the Outer Edge (N.Y.: War-

ner, 1978), pp.169-70.
-UFO (CE-3)
1955, Aug./Dan Martin
D.M. Martin, Seven Hours Aboard a
Space Ship (Detroit: The Author,
1959).
Dan Martin, The Watcher (Clarksburg,
W.V.: Saucerian, 1961).

Padre I.
-UFO (NL)
1954, Nov.6/Ray Stanford
Ray Stanford, "Contact with a Flying
Saucer," Fate 9 (May 1956):12-18.

Panther Springs
-Fall of insects
1867, May/Charles W. Libby
"A Shower of Insects," Sci.Am. 24
(1871):227.

Pedernales R.
-UFO (CE-1)
1966, April 24/Tom M. Lasseter/30 mi.
from LBJ Ranch
"Bulletin," UFO Inv. 3 (May-June
1966):8.

Possum Kingdom Dam
-Giant bird
1944, Dec.28
"Texas Bird," Doubt, no.12 (spring-
summer 1945):175.

Rattlesnake Canyon
-Archeological site
prehistoric-1650 A.D.
Aaron D. Riggs, "Rattlesnake Shelter:
41CX29," Bull.Texas Arch.Soc'y 40
(1969):107-17. il.

Red R.
-UFO (CE-3)
1966, April 22/Eula Page
"UFO Seminar Held in Oklahoma City--
Stanton Friedman Main Speaker,"
Skylook, no.41 (Apr.1971):4.
"A Correction--And More Information
on Oklahoma Sighting," Skylook, no.
42 (May 1971):12.

Rio Grande R.
-Ancient inscription
Barry Fell, America B.C. (N.Y.: Quad-
rangle, 1976), p.185. il.

San Bernard R.
-Acoustic anomaly
Bertha McKee Dobie, "Mysterious Mu-
sic in the San Bernard River," in
J. Frank Dobie, ed., Legends of Tex-
as (Austin: Texas Folklore Soc'y,
Pub.no.3, 1924), pp.137-41.

Sierra Madera
-Meteorite crater
13,000 m.diam. x 2400 m. deep/certain
E. Eggleton & E.M. Shoemaker, "Brec-
cia at Sierra Madera, Texas," Spec.
Pap.U.S.Geol.Survey, no.68 (1962):

169-70.
Jack R. Van Lopik & Richard A. Geyer, "Gravity and Magnetic Anomalies of the Sierra Madera, Texas, 'Dome,'" Science 142 (1963):45-47.
Ralph B. Baldwin, The Measure of the Moon (Chicago: Univ. of Chicago, 1963), pp.92-93.
H.G. Wilshire, et al., "Geology of the Sierra Madera Cryptoexplosion Structure, Pecos County, Texas," Prof.Pap.U.S.Geol.Survey, no.599-H (1972), pp. H 1-42.

Smith Rockshelter
-Archeological site
    "The Smith Rockshelter, Travis County: A Preliminary Report," Student Pap.in Anthro., Dep't Anthro.Univ. Texas 1, no.2 (1954):25-27. il.

South Sulphur R.
-Humanoid
    1973, Sep.
    John Green, Sasquatch: The Apes Among Us (Seattle: Hancock House, 1978), p.187.

Steele Creek
-UFO (CE-1)
    1973, Dec.7
    Timothy Green Beckley, "Calvert, Texas: Flying Saucer Way Station," Saga UFO Rept. 2 (spring 1975):18,69.

Tornillo Creek
-Ancient inscription
    1962
    Bernice & Jack McGee, "Mystery Tablet of the Big Bend," True West 19 (July-Aug.1972):10-15,42-47,50. il.

Travis L.
-Humanoid
    n.d./Judy Adamek
    John Green, The Sasquatch File (Agassiz, B.C.: Cheam, 1973), p.39.

Waco L.
-Mystery bird deaths
    1974, April 13/Leo Lyons/pelicans
    Los Angeles (Cal.) Times, 27 Apr. 1974.

Worth, L.
-Humanoid
    1967/Mosque Pt.
    John A. Keel, Strange Creatures from Space and Time (Greenwich, Ct.: Fawcett, 1970), p.118.
    1969, July 10-11/John Reichart
    Fort Worth Star-Telegram, 10 July 1969, p.2A; and 11 July 1969, p.1A.
    Sallie Ann Clarke, The Lake Worth Monster (Fort Worth: The Author, 1969).
    John Green, Sasquatch: The Apes Among Us (Seattle: Hancock House, 1978), pp.185-87.
    1969, Nov.7/Charles Buchanan

Jerome Clark & Loren Coleman, Creatures of the Outer Edge (N.Y.: Warner, 1978), p.53.

C. Ethnic Groups

Alabama-Coushatta Indians
-Flood myth
    Howard H. Martin, "Tales of the Alabama-Coushatta Indians," in Francis E. Abernethy, Tales from the Big Thicket (Austin: Univ. of Texas, 1966), pp.33,49.

Comanche Indians
-Weather control
    H.H. Bancroft, Native Races of the Pacific States, 5 vols. (N.Y.: Appleton, 1875), 1:520.

Jumano Indians
-Out-of-body experience legend
    1620-1623/La Senorita Azul (Maria de Jesus de Agreda)
    Edmond J.P. Schmitt, "Ven. Maria Jesus de Agreda: A Correction," Texas State Hist.Ass'n Quar. 1 (1897):121-22.
    Lilia M. Casas, ed., "Letter of Don Damian Manzanet to Don Carlos de Siguenza Relative to the Discovery of the Bay of Espiritu Santo," Texas State Hist.Ass'n Quar. 2 (1898):281,282-83.
    Charles H. Heimsath, "The Mysterious Woman in Blue," in J. Frank Dobie, ed., Legends of Texas (Austin: Texas Folklore Soc'y, Pub.no.3, 1924), pp.132-35.
    P.J. Rasch, "New Mexico's Strangest Story," Fate 2 (July 1949):58-62.
    William H. Donahue, "Mary of Agreda and the Southwest United States," The Americas 9 (1953):291-314.
    T.D. Kendrick, Mary of Agreda: The Life and Legend of a Spanish Nun (London: Routledge & Kegan Paul, 1967), pp.28-55.

Paducah Indians
-Welsh Indians
    1764/Isaac Stewart
    Richard Deacon, Madoc and the Discovery of America (N.Y.: George Braziller, 1966), pp.120-21, quoting American Museum, 1797.

D. Unspecified Localities

-Ancient roads
    western sector/=ley lines?
    Toronto (Ont.) Star, 6 July 1922.

-Crisis apparition
    1874, Aug.25/V. de Kerkhove
    Camille Flammarion, The Unknown (N.Y.: Harper, 1900), p.53.

-Healing
     William Madsden, <u>The Mexican-Ameri-</u>
     <u>cans of South Texas</u> (N.Y.: Holt,
     Rinehart & Winston, 1964), pp.68-
     79,87-105.

-Hex
     William Madsden, <u>The Mexican-Ameri-</u>
     <u>cans of South Texas</u> (N.Y.: Holt,
     Rinehart & Winston, 1964), pp.80-
     86.
     Arthur J. Rubel, <u>Across the Tracks</u>
     (Austin: Univ. of Texas, 1966), pp.
     93-97,157-61.

-Patterned ground
  western sector
     Walter B. Lank, "Ten O'Clock Marks,"
     <u>Science</u> 100 (1944):288.

THE SOUTHEAST

ARKANSAS

A. Populated Places

Alma
-Ghost dog
 n.d.
  Vance Randolph, Ozark Superstitions
   (N.Y.: Columbia Univ., 1947), p.225.
-UFO (CE-1)
 1978, Feb.1
  Van Buren Press-Argus, 2 Feb.1978.

Altus
-Ghost
 1897, Nov.18/Mike Metz
  C. Schadow, "The Stopped Watch,"
   Fate 5 (Sep.1952):25-27.

Antioch
-UFO (CE-1)
 1978, Nov.11/Mike Simpfenderfer/U.S.67
  Searcy Daily Citizen, 12 Nov.1978.

Arkadelphia
-Haunt
 n.d./Barkman House/Caddo R.
  Fred W. Allsopp, Folklore of Romantic
   Arkansas, 2 vols. (N.Y.: Grolier
   Soc'y, 1931), 2:252.
-UFO (DD)
 1947, July 1?
  Little Rock Arkansas Gazette, 8 July
   1947.

Arkansas co.
-UFO (DD)
 1963, Oct.1
  (Editorial), Fate 17 (Feb.1964):10.

Ashdown
-UFO (?)
 1947, July 4/J.L. Stinson
  Little Rock Arkansas Gazette, 8 July
   1947.
-UFO (DD)
 1952, Oct.28
  (Editorial), Fate 6 (Mar.1953):10.

Atkins
-UFO (DD)
 1947, Aug.15/Corry Burnett
  Atkins Chronicle, 15 Aug.1947.

Avoca
-Cattle mutilation
 1978, Oct.8/Johnny Smith
  Rogers Daily News, 9 Oct.1978.

Baring Cross
-UFO (DD)
 1897, April 26/C.D. Lawrence
  Jerome Clark, "More on 1897," Flying
   Saucer Rev. 13 (July-Aug.1967):22.

Bear Creek Springs
-UFO (NL)
 1974, March 26/Nina Coffey/1 mi.E
  Harrison Daily Times, 27 Mar.1974.

Benton
-Humanoid
 1978, Aug.29/Mildred Wilton/Walnut St.
  Benton Courier, 31 Aug.1978.

Benton co.
-Cattle and dog mutilations
 1978, April 3-May 1/China Grove Ceme-
  tery
  Kansas City (Mo.) Star, 5 May 1978.
  Little Rock Arkansas Gazette, 5 May
   1978; and 7 May 1978.
  "A Closer Look," Stigmata, no.4
   (summer 1978):5.
 1978, Nov.12/Don Rystrom
  Rogers Daily News, 13 Nov.1978.
  Springdale News, 26 Nov.1978.
-Ghost
 1900s-1940
  Vance Randolph, Ozark Superstitions
   (N.Y.: Columbia Univ., 1947), p.220.
-Inner development
 1850s/Harmonial Society
  Nandor Fodor, Encyclopaedia of Psy-
   chic Science (London: Arthurs,
   1934), p.158.

Bentonville
-UFO (?)
 1969, Oct.9/Marion Foster/=balloon?
  "More on the Meteor of Oct.9, 1969,"
   Skylook, no.25 (Dec.1969):2-3,
   quoting Rogers Sun (undated).

Berryville
-Archeological site
 miniature doorway in rock/8 mi.SW
  Jim Brandon, Weird America (N.Y.:
   Dutton, 1978), p.15.
-UFO (CE-2)
 1977, Dec.15/Mrs. Arlie Long
  Berryville Star Progress, 22 Dec.
   1977; and 1 Jan.1978.
-UFO (NL)
 1977, Dec.18/Marietta Edens/2 mi.E on
  Hwy.62
  Berryville Star Progress, 22 Dec.
   1977.
 1977, Dec.27/Mrs. Arlie Long
  Berryville Star Progress, 1 Jan.
   1978.

Black Rock
-Time anomaly
 1958, Nov./R.D. Smalldridge
  R.D. Smalldridge, "The Night My Truck
   Flew," Fate 22 (Mar.1969):59-60.

Bluffton
-Archeological site
  Aikman Mounds
    Jim Brandon, Weird America (N.Y.:
    Dutton, 1978), p.20.

Blytheville
-Giant bird
  1958/Mrs. Gene Sutton
    (Editorial), Fate 11 (Nov.1958):22.
-UFO (DD)
  1967, Oct.21/Blytheville AFB
    J. Allen Hynek, The UFO Experience
    (Chicago: Regnery, 1972), pp.53,
    54-55,65-66.
-UFO (NL)
  1973, Sep.30-Oct.1/S. Lake St.
    Blytheville Courier-News, 2 Oct.
    1973.

Bono
-UFO (?)
  1973, Oct.21/U.S.63/=hoax
    Little Rock Arkansas Gazette, 23 Oct.
    1973.

Boxley
-UFO (NL)
  1974, March 17
    Harrison Boone County Headlight, 21
    Mar.1974.

Bradley
-Phantom image
  1956
    (Letter), Leon Thompson, Fate 10
    (Sep.1957):120.

Brinkley
-UFO (NL)
  1967, March 8/Mrs. Ned Warnock
    Clarendon Monroe County Sun, 16 Mar.
    1967.

Brush Creek
-Cattle mutilation
  1978, Nov.5
    Rogers Northwest Arkansas Morning
    News, 10 Nov.1978.

Burdette
-UFO (CE-1)
  1970, April 22
    Little Rock Arkansas Gazette, 29 Apr.
    1970.
    "Two Women See UFO near Blytheville,
    Ark.," Skylook, no.31 (June 1970):3.

Cabot
-UFO (CE-3)
  1976, Sep.6/Mrs. William H. Doyal
    (Letter), Little Rock Arkansas Demo-
    crat, 15 Jan.1978.

Camden
-Fall of frogs
  1972, Dec.
    Camden News, 2 Jan.1973.
-Ghost light
  1960s/Confederate Cemetery

    John Hicks, "Foolish Fire," Little
    Rock Arkansas Democrat Magazine, 16
    Oct.1969.
-Humanoid
  1975, March
    John Green, Sasquatch: The Apes Among
    Us (Seattle: Hancock House, 1978),
    p.192, quoting Camden News (undated).
-UFO (NL)
  1973, Oct.17-18/C.L. Bryant/105 Riverside Ct.
    Camden News, 18 Oct.1973.

Cauthron
-Carthaginian coin
  1973/Jesse Ray Kelley/Hwy.28
    Gloria Farley, "Ancient Coins Found,"
    Oklahoma Today 27 (spring 1977):31.
    Norman Totten, "Carthaginian Coins
    Found in Arkansas and Alabama," Occ.
    Pub.Epigraphic Soc'y vol.4, no.88
    (1977). il.

Cave Springs
-Cattle mutilation
  1978, Aug.16/Bill Philpot/W of town
    Rogers Northwest Arkansas Morning
    News, 18 Aug.1978.
  1978, Nov.6/NW of town
    Rogers Northwest Arkansas Morning
    News, 10 Nov.1978.

Center Point
-Cattle mutilation
  1978, Feb.
    Nashville News, 3 Mar.1978.

Center Ridge
-Hog mutilation
  1978, March/Ed Andrews
    Morrilton Petit Jean Country Headlight,
    8 Mar.1978.
-Humanoid tracks
  1978, March 5/Weldon Flowers/Hwy.124
    Morrilton Petit Jean Country Headlight,
    8 Mar.1978. il.

Centerton
-Cattle mutilation
  1978, Aug.17/W of town
    Pea Ridge Graphic, 24 Aug.1978.

Cincinnati
-UFO (NL)
  1972, Aug.26/Oscar Nichols/S of town
    Fayetteville Northwest Arkansas
    Times, 28 Aug.1972.

Clarksville
-Fall of unknown object
  1969, Oct.2/Doris Richardson/Horsehead
  Lake
    "Did Meteor Cause Fire?" Skylook, no.
    25 (Dec.1969):8, quoting Fort Smith
    Southwest Times-Record (undated).
    "Cause of Fire Still Mystery," Sky-
    look, no.28 (Mar.1970):10, quoting
    Clarksville Johnson County Graphic
    (undated).
-Haunt

1973, Sep.-Oct./Gilbert Parks/College
of the Ozarks
   Dayton (O.) Journal-Herald, 17 Oct.
   1973.
-Human tracks in rock
1832/Billy Fritz/5 mi.W
   S.H. Logan, "Mysterious Footprints
   in a Rock near Clarksville," Arkansas Hist.Quar. 1 (1942):355-57.

Conway
-Disease anomaly
1970/J.W. Hart
   (Editorial), Fate 23 (Aug.1970):14-
   17, quoting AP release (undated).
-Fall of metallic object
1967, Nov./Richard Cummings/=military
target sphere?
   Kansas City (Mo.) Times, 24 Nov.1967.
   "Mystery Object," Saucer News 14
   (winter 1967):18. il.
   (Editorial), Fate 21 (June 1968):16,
   quoting AP release (undated).

Crossett
-Ghost light
1951, Sep.
   Jack Henderson, "Arkansas Mystery
   Light," Fate 8 (Aug.1955):68-72.
   (Letter), W. Parks Grant, Fate 9
   (Jan.1956):122-24.

DeQueen
-Phantom panther
1960s/DeQueen Wood Products Co.
   Jim Brandon, Weird America (N.Y.:
   Dutton, 1978), pp.15-16.

Dermott
-Ball lightning
ca.1902/J.W. Bernard
   W.J. Humphries, "Ball Lightning,"
   Proc.Am.Phil.Soc'y 76 (1936):613-26.

DeWitt
-Fall of frogs
1942, Oct.18
   Buffalo (N.Y.) Evening News, 31 Oct.
   1942.

Dover
-Phantom panther
1977, May
   Memphis (Tenn.) Press-Scimitar, 17
   May 1977.

Dutch Mills
-Humanoid tracks
1977, Aug.12/Ed Bailey/=hoax?
   Stilwell (Okla.) Democrat-Journal,
   18 Aug.1977.
   Kansas City (Mo.) Star, 24 Aug.1977.

El Dorado
-UFO (DD)
1947, July 5/E.E. Boyland
   Little Rock Arkansas Democrat, 7
   July 1947.

Elkins
-UFO (CE-2)
1955/Frank Hudson/ground markings only
   Ted Phillips, Physical Traces Associated with UFO Sightings (Evanston:
   Center for UFO Studies, 1975), p.
   18.

England
-UFO (DD)
1947, July 3/J.L. Hampton/6 mi.E
   Little Rock Arkansas Democrat, 5
   July 1947.

Eureka Springs
-Haunt
n.d./Lida Pyles
   Lida Wilson Pyles, "Haunted Honey-
   moon," Fate 5 (July-Aug.1952):11-
   14.

Farmington
-UFO (NL)
1956, July/Janet Shreve
   (Letter), Fate 10 (Jan.1957):113.

Fayetteville
-Fall of metal foil
1970, May 23/Mildred Higgins/E of town
   Lucius Farish, "'Space Grass' in Arkansas (Again)," Skylook, no.32
   (July 1970):6.
-Hex
1970, Feb./Sheila Garmon/=misattribu-
tion
   (Editorial), Fate 23 (July 1970):22-
   24.
-Skyquake
1970, Sep.18
   "Bang!" INFO J., no.14 (Nov.1974):2,
   quoting Ohio UFO Reporter (Nov.
   1970-Feb.1971).
-UFO (CE-2)
1947, July 4-5/Henry Seay
   Little Rock Arkansas Gazette, 7 July
   1947.
   Ted Bloecher, Report on the UFO Wave
   of 1947 (Washington: NICAP, 1967),
   p.IV-1.
-UFO (NL)
1971, July 15/Mrs. Dick Dyer
   Fayetteville Northwest Arkansas
   Times, 16 July 1971.
1973, Oct.19/Ravena Murphy
   Fayetteville Northwest Arkansas
   Times, 20 Oct.1973.
1974, March
   Fayetteville Northwest Arkansas
   Times, 18 Mar.1974.

Flippin
-UFO (?)
1969, July 16/Vivian Kocher/airport
   "Object Photographed in Arkansas,"
   APRO Bull. 18 (Sep.-Oct.1969):6. il.
-UFO (CE-2)
1969, March/L.J. Treat
   Ted Phillips, Physical Traces Associ-
   ated with UFO Sightings (Evanston:
   Center for UFO Studies, 1975), p.63.

-UFO (DD)
1970, June 24/Herman Hazel
  Lucius Farish, "UFO at Flippin, Arkansas," Skylook, no.34 (Sep.1970):
  13.

Fordyce
-Humanoid
1974, Oct.31/Myzell Thompson/Bunn Rd.
  Fordyce News-Advocate, 6 Nov.1974.
-UFO (DD)
1956, Dec.12/J.Willard Clary
  (Editorial), Fate 10 (Apr.1957):16,
  quoting Little Rock Arkansas Gazette (undated).

Forrest City
-UFO (NL)
1959, Oct.7/E.L. Barksdale
  Memphis (Tenn.) Press-Scimitar, 8
  Oct.1959.
1966, Aug.16
  John A. Keel, "The Night the Sky
  Turned On," Fate 20 (Sep.1967):30,
  35.

Fort Smith
-Haunt
n.d./Rector Heights
1890s/jail
  Fred W. Allsopp, Folklore of Romantic
  Arkansas, 2 vols. (N.Y.: Grolier
  Soc'y, 1931), 1:332, 2:253-54.
-UFO (?)
1949, April 16
  Bruce S. Maccabee, "UFO Related Information from the FBI Files: Part
  5," MUFON UFO J., no.124 (Mar.1978):
  7,11.
-UFO (CE-1)
ca.1967/Bill Pitts
  (Letter), APRO Bull. 23 (Jan.-Feb.
  1975):6.
-UFO (NL)
1966, Aug.16/J.W. Gilbreth, Jr./KFSA-
  radio
  Fort Smith Times-Record, 17 Aug.1966,
  p.1.
  Robert Loftin, Identified Flying Saucers (N.Y.: David McKay, 1968), pp.
  132-36.
1972
  "UFO Reported in Arkansas," Skylook,
  no.59 (Oct.1972):19.
1975, June 19/Bill Pitts
  "Police Officers Continue to Sight
  UFOs," UFO Inv., Aug.1975, pp.1,2.

Fouke
-Humanoid
1955/Willie Smith
  "The Road to Noxie," Probe the Unknown 4 (Mar.1976):45.
1971, May 2/Bobby Ford
1971, May 23/D.C. Woods, Jr./U.S.71
  Hope Star, 8 May 1971; and 25 May
  1971.
  "Arkansas Has a Problem," Pursuit 4
  (Oct.1971):89-90.
1971, July 31/U.S.71 x Hwy.134

Washington (D.C.) Post, 31 July 1971.
1972, Oct.
  Allen V. Noe, "ABSMal Affairs in
  Pennsylvania and Elsewhere," Pur-
  suit 6 (Oct.1973):84.
1973, Nov./Orville Scoggins
  Little Rock Arkansas Gazette, 27
  Nov.1973.
-Humanoid tracks
1971, June 14/W.M. Smith/3 mi.SE
  Washington (D.C.) Post, 31 July 1971.
  "Arkansas Has a Problem," Pursuit 4
  (Oct.1971):89,90.
  Smokey Crabtree, Smokey and the
  Fouke Monster (Fouke: Days Creek
  Production, 1974).

Gentry
-Mystery train accidents
1972
  Fayetteville Northwest Arkansas
  Times, 22 Dec.1972.

Grannis
-End-of-the-world prophecy
1976-1977/Elizabeth Nance Bard
  "Psychic Happenings," Probe the Unknown 5 (spring 1977):6.

Greene co.
-Humanoid
1851, March/Mr. Hamilton
  Memphis (Tenn.) Enquirer, 9 May 1851.
  New Orleans (La.) Times-Picayune, 16
  May 1851.

Hamburg
-Humanoid
1968, Sep.
  Little Rock Arkansas Gazette, 26
  Sep.1968.

Hardy
-UFO (DD)
1959, April 2/Marie Mahan
  (Letter), Fate 12 (Dec.1959):109.

Harrisburg
-UFO (CE-3)
1897, April 21/Ex-Senator Harris
  Harrisburg Modern News, 23 Apr.1897.

Harrison
-UFO (NL)
1965, Aug.3/Shelby Crain
  Coral E. Lorenzen, "Western UFO Flap,"
  Fate 18 (Nov.1965):42,52.

Hartman
-Fire anomaly
1958, April/Mrs. Hardy Morris
  (Editorial), Fate 11 (Oct.1958):8.

Helena
-Ghost
1919/Peggy Gregson/404 College St.
  Peggy Maurine Gregson, "Aunt Caro-
  line's Tryst with Death," Fate 13
  (Oct.1960):33-35.

Hiwassee
-UFO (NL)
   1966, Aug.16/Paul Seymore
      John A. Keel, "The Night the Sky
      Turned On," Fate 20 (Sep.1967):30,
      35.

Homan
-UFO (CE-3)
   1897, April/James Hooton
      Little Rock Arkansas Gazette, 22 Apr.
      1897.

Hot Springs
-UFO (CE-3)
   1897, May 6/John L. Sumpter, Jr./NW of
   town
      Fort Smith Daily News-Record, 13 May
      1897.
-UFO (DD)
   1947, July 2
      Little Rock Arkansas Gazette, 4 July
      1947.
   1958, April 14
      Richard Hall, ed., The UFO Evidence
      (Washington: NICAP, 1964), p.156.

Huntsville
-UFO (?)
   1963, Sep.20
      Richard Hall, ed., The UFO Evidence
      (Washington: NICAP, 1964), p.141.

Imboden
-UFO (NL)
   1973, Sep.27/Irene Hinshaw
      Imboden Ozark Journal, 4 Oct.1973.

Jenny Lind
-UFO (CE-3)
   1897, May 4/James Davis
      St. Louis (Mo.) Post-Dispatch, 5 May
      1897, p.7.

Jerusalem
-Humanoid tracks
   1978, March/Joe D. Cook
      Russellville Courier-Democrat, 12
      Mar.1978. il.

Jonesboro
-UFO (CE-2)
   1973, Oct.1
      Ted Phillips, Physical Traces Associ-
      ated with UFO Sightings (Evanston:
      Center for UFO Studies, 1975), p.92,
      quoting Pulaski (Tenn.) Citizen
      (undated).
-UFO (NL)
   1973, Sep.26-27
      Jonesboro Evening Sun, 27-28 Sep.
      1973.
      Little Rock Arkansas Gazette, 27
      Sep.1973.
   1973, Oct.17
      Jonesboro Evening Sun, 18 Oct.1973.

Jonesville
-Humanoid
   1965/James Lynn Crabtree

John Green, Sasquatch: The Apes Among
      Us (Seattle: Hancock House, 1978),
      pp.189-90.
-UFO (?)
   1979, March 3/Halbert Jones/Carter L.
   Conway Log Cabin Democrat, 5 Mar.
   1979.

Judsonia
-UFO (NL)
   1977, Dec.9/Herbert Robbins/Searcy-
   Judsonia Rd.
      Judsonia White County Record, 15
      Dec.1977.

Lavaca
-Clairempathy
   1959, Aug./Paul P. Sprowl/8 mi.NE
      Paul P. Sprowl, "Oil Detective Uses
      Maps," Fate 20 (Aug.1967):86-88.
-Humanoid
   1977, Aug.
      Fort Smith Southwest Times-Record,
      14 Aug.1977.

Lawrenceville
-Hex
   n.d.
      Fred W. Allsopp, Folklore of Romantic
      Arkansas, 2 vols. (N.Y.: Grolier
      Soc'y, 1931), 1:160.

Little River co.
-Cattle mutilation
   1977, Aug./Ezekiel Green
      Texarkana Gazette, 21 Aug.1977.

Little Rock
-Electromagnetic anomaly
   1973/Floyd Crotchett
      Lucius Farish, "Ma Bell's Channel,"
      Fate 26 (Sep.1973):72.
-Haunt
   1899-1949/Mrs. Arthur Alexander
      Pauline Saltzman, Ghosts and Other
      Strangers (N.Y.: Lancer, 1970 ed.),
      pp.93-94, quoting AP release, 28
      Mar.1949.
-Inner development
   1970s/Institute of Psychic Science/
   2015 S. Broadway
      June & Nicholas Regush, Psi: The Oth-
      er World Catalogue (N.Y.: Putnam,
      1974), p.159.
-Parapsychology research
   1970s/ESP Research Associates Founda-
   tion/1660 Union Nat'l Plaza
      John White & Stanley Krippner, eds.,
      Future Science (Garden City, N.Y.:
      Anchor, 1977), p.585.
-UFO (DD)
   1947, July 4/A.J. Parsel
      Little Rock Arkansas Democrat, 5-6
      July 1947.
-UFO (NL)
   1909, Dec.20
      Little Rock Arkansas Gazette, 20
      Dec.1909.
   1947, July 4/J. Vance Clayton
      Little Rock Arkansas Democrat, 6 July

1947.
1964, Jan.28/John M. Brannen
1964, Feb.12/John M. Brannen
"Splitting Disc Seen in Arkansas,"
   APRO Bull. 13 (July 1964):1,4.
1973, Oct.4
   West Helena Twin City Tribune, 4
   Oct.1973.

Lockesburg
-Haunt
   n.d./Locke House
      Fred W. Allsopp, Folklore of Romantic
      Arkansas, 2 vols. (N.Y.: Grolier
      Soc'y, 1931), 2:252-55.

Lonoke
-UFO (CE-1)
   1973, Oct.27/Charles Hamm/Jackson Pit
      Lonoke Democrat, 1 Nov.1973.

Mabelvale
-UFO (NL)
   1909, Dec.13/A.W. Norris
      Little Rock Arkansas Gazette, 15
      Dec.1909.

Magnolia
-UFO (NL)
   1952, Sep./E.E. Graham
      (Editorial), Fate 6 (Mar.1953):10.

Malvern
-Humanoid
   1966, Aug.22/Fabar Mills
      Malvern Daily Record, 23 Aug.1966.
-UFO (DD)
   1968, Feb.29/Winston Rogers
      "UFO Sighted in Arkansas," Skylook,
      no.8 (Apr.1968):6, quoting Little
      Rock Arkansas Democrat (undated).

Marshall
-UFO (NL)
   1978, April 24/Lisa Breckenridge
      Marshall Mountain Wave, 11 May 1978.
   1978, Oct.16
   1978, Nov.2
   1978, Dec.13
      Marshall Mountain Wave, 15 Feb.1979.

Mena
-Poltergeist
   1960, Dec.-1961, Dec./C.E. Shinn
      John C. Ross, "In Mena, Arkansas:
      Poltergeist or Prankster?" Fate 15
      (Apr.1962):37-40.

Midland
-Fire anomaly
   1945, Sep.9-14/Annie Bryan
      "30 Fires in One Week," Doubt, no.14
      (spring 1946):204.

Mineral Springs
-Cattle mutilation
   1977, fall
      Nashville News, 3 Mar.1978.

Morrilton
-UFO (NL)
   1972, Jan.6/Allen Love
      "Bright Light over Morrilton, Ark.,"
      Skylook, no.51 (Feb.1972):10.

Mountain Home
-UFO (DD)
   1947, June 27
      Little Rock Arkansas Democrat, 2
      July 1947.
-UFO (NL)
   1965, Aug.1
      Coral E. Lorenzen, Flying Saucers:
      The Startling Evidence of the Inva-
      sion from Outer Space (N.Y.: Sig-
      net, 1966 ed.), p.238.
   1973, Sep.30
      Mountain Home Baxter Bulletin, 4
      Oct.1973.

Mountain View
-Precognition and clairvoyance
   1947-   /Harold Sherman
      Harold Sherman, You Live After Death
      (N.Y.: Anthony, 1949).
      Harold Sherman, "Did I Hear from the
      Beyond?" Tomorrow 7 (summer 1959):
      43-50.
      Harold Sherman, How to Make ESP Work
      for You (Santa Monica: DeVorss,
      1964).
      James Crenshaw, "Harold Sherman Lo-
      cates Missing Plane Through ESP,"
      Fate 19 (Jan.1966):30-36.
      Harold Sherman, "Harold Sherman Pre-
      vents Cat-Astrophe," Fate 21 (Aug.
      1968):73-78.
      James Grayson Bolen, "Interview: Har-
      old Sherman," Psychic 5 (Jan.-Feb.
      1974):6-11,36-39.
      Harold Sherman, How to Communicate
      with the Unseen World (N.Y.: Faw-
      cett, 1974).
-UFO (NL)
   1971, July 21/Alfred Kiessig
      (Letter), Fate 25 (Sep.1972):159.

Murfreesboro
-Archeological site
      Franklin Folsom, America's Ancient
      Treasures (N.Y.: Rand McNally,
      1974), p.109.

Myrtle
-Land monster
   n.d./E.J. Rhodes/Devil's Hole Cave, 3
   mi.NW
      Vance Randolph, We Always Lie to
      Strangers (N.Y.: Columbia Univ.,
      1951), pp.44-45, quoting Arcadian
      Life, June 1935, pp.18-19.

Nashville
-Cattle mutilation
   1977, fall/N of town
      Nashville News, 3 Mar.1978.
-UFO (CE-1)
   1897, April
      Jerome Clark, "More on 1897," Flying

Saucer Rev. 13 (July-Aug.1967):22,
23.

New Hope
-Cattle mutilation
1978, May/Jerry Hunton
1978, July 7/F.J. Mathias
Springdale News, 11 July 1978.
Lincoln Leader, 12 July 1978.

Newport
-Clairvoyance
1930s/Carolyn Dye
Bernie Babcock, "Carolyn Dye Had
Second Sight," Fate 10 (Feb.1957):
36-40.
-Mystery tracks
1971, June/Towhead I.
Little Rock Arkansas Gazette, 7 July
1971.
"Arkansas Has a Problem," Pursuit 4
(Oct.1971):89,91-95. il.
-Phantom image
1976, Aug.1/Irene Rogers
National Enquirer, 26 Oct.1976.
-Plague of crickets
1972, Sep.27
Lucius Farish, "Crickets, by Jiminy!"
Fate 26 (Aug.1973):93.
-River monster
1937, July 1-Sep./Bramblett Bateman/
White R.
Little Rock Commercial Appeal, 11
July 1937.
"Fresh-Water Monster Dropped," Fort-
ean Soc'y Mag. 1 (Sep.1937):5.
Curtis MacDougall, Hoaxes (N.Y.:
Dover, 1958 ed.), pp.256-57.
1971, June-Aug.24/Cloyce Warren/White
River
1972, June 5/R.C. McClaughlin
"Arkansas Has a Problem," Pursuit 4
(Oct.1971):89,91-95. il.
Jerome Clark & Lucius Farish, "Amer-
ica's Mysterious 'Loch Ness' Mon-
ster," Saga, Nov.1974, pp.44-45,60.
-UFO (NL)
1897, April 20
Cincinnati (O.) Commercial Tribune,
21 Apr.1897.
1966, Aug.16/Velma Dunavin
John A. Keel, "The Night the Sky
Turned On," Fate 20 (Sep.1967):30,
36.
1972, Feb.13/Don Shelton
"Weird Glowing Sphere Seen in Arkansas," Skylook, no.53 (Apr.1972):7-8.

North Little Rock
-UFO (?)
1973, Oct.18/James M. Henry/5124 Glen-
mere Rd./=Saturn
Little Rock Arkansas Gazette, 19 Oct.
1973.

Oil Trough
-UFO (NL)
1972, Jan.5/James H. Shaw
Newport Independent, 6 Jan.1972.

Okolona
-Haunt
n.d.
Fred W. Allsopp, Folklore of Romantic
Arkansas, 2 vols. (N.Y.: Grolier
Soc'y, 1931), 2:255-57.

Osceola
-UFO (R-V)
1950, July 11/J.W. Martin/10 mi.NE
New York Post, 12 July 1950.

Ozark
-Fall of pebbles
1880, Nov.
Henry Winfred Splitter, "Wonders
from the Sky," Fate 6 (Oct.1953):
33,34, quoting Little Rock Dispatch
(undated).

Paragould
-UFO (CE-1)
1967, March/Joy Brackman
Paragould Daily Press, 12 Mar.1967;
and 16 Mar.1967.
-UFO (NL)
1966, Aug.16/Ken Bock
John A. Keel, "The Night the Sky
Turned On," Fate 20 (Sep.1967):30,
35.

Pea Ridge
-Horse mutilation
1978, Aug.19/Utah Smith
Pea Ridge Graphic, 24 Aug.1978.

Piggott
-Fall of metal foil
1967, Sep.
Lucius Farish, "'Space Grass' in Ar-
kansas (Again)," Skylook, no.32
(July 1970):6.

Pine Bluff
-Haunt
n.d./Sawdust Bridge
Fred W. Allsopp, Folklore of Romantic
Arkansas, 2 vols. (N.Y.: Grolier
Soc'y, 1931), 1:176-78.
-Humanoid
1973, Sep.
Allen V. Noe, "ABSMal Affairs in
Pennsylvania and Elsewhere," Pursuit
6 (Oct.1973):84.
-UFO (?)
1947, July 4/T.L. Huckaby
Little Rock Arkansas Gazette, 8 July
1947.
1973, Oct.17/=balloon
Little Rock Arkansas Gazette, 18
Oct.1973, p.3A.
-UFO (NL)
1967, April 27/Ken Kesterson
"UAO in Arkansas," APRO Bull. 15
(May-June 1967):4.

Pleasant Grove
-Humanoid
1970, Feb.
Harrisburg Modern News, 5 Feb.1970.

Plumerville
-UFO (NL)
   1970, May 10/Lucius Farish
      Lucius Farish, "Red Lights Seen in
      Arkansas," Skylook, no.32 (July
      1970):15.

Pulaski co.
-Humanoid
   1875, Dec.
      Jerome Clark & Loren Coleman, Crea-
      tures of the Outer Edge (N.Y.: War-
      ner, 1978), p.61, quoting Little
      Rock Arkansas Gazette (undated).

Reyno
-Retrocognition
   1933, summer/Effreda S. Kibiger
      Effreda S. Kibiger, "Time Played Us
      a Trick," Fate 9 (June 1956):15-21.

Rogers
-UFO (?)
   1973, Oct.4/Mrs. Lester Subbert/=star
      Rogers Daily News, 4 Oct.1973.
-UFO (NL)
   1947, June 30/J.P. Crumpler
      Little Rock Arkansas Democrat, 6
      July 1947.
   1973, Sep.30/Pearl Keene/901 S. Second
      Rogers Daily News, 1 Oct.1973.

Royal
-UFO (NL)
   1978, April 10/Trudy Vawter/Bear Rd.
      Hot Springs Sentinel-Record, 12 Apr.
      1978; and 19 Apr.1978.
   1978, April 17/Don Joyce/Brady Mt.
      Hot Springs Sentinel-Record, 19 Apr.
      1978.

Russellville
-UFO (NL)
   1897, April 12/C.W. Nugent
      Little Rock Arkansas Gazette, 15
      Apr.1897.

Saline co.
-Humanoid
   1870s
      Otto Ernest Rayburn, Ozark Country
      (N.Y.: Duell, Sloan & Pearce, 1941),
      pp.313-14.

Searcy
-Erratic rock
   1977, July/Harley Harris
      Searcy Daily Citizen, 14 July 1977.
-UFO (NL)
   1958, April 23/William Kirk Floyd
      (Letter), Fate 11 (Sep.1958):113-14.

Searcy co.
-Land monster
   1897/William Miller/gowrow/=hoax
      Vance Randolph, We Always Lie to
      Strangers (N.Y.: Columbia Univ.,
      1951), pp.43-44, quoting Arcadian
      Life, June 1935, pp.18-19.

Shady Grove
-UFO (NL)
   1973, Oct.4
      Mountain Home Baxter Bulletin, 4
      Oct.1973.

South Crossett
-Humanoid
   1978, June 26/Mike Lofton
      Crossett News-Observer, 29 June 1978.

Springdale
-Humanoid
   1969, Sep.6/Barbara Robinson/612 W.
   Allen Ave.
      Fayetteville Northwest Arkansas
      Times, 8 Sep.1969.
   1972, Jan./Mrs. C.W. Humphrey
   1972, July/Pete Ragland
   1972, July 20/Mrs. C.W. Humphrey
      Jerome Clark & Loren Coleman, "An-
      thropoids, Monsters and UFOs," Fly-
      ing Saucer Rev. 19 (Jan.-Feb.1973):
      18,23, quoting Fayetteville North-
      west Arkansas Times (undated).
-UFO (NL)
   1969, Feb.9/Leslie Tom Walker/1819
   Taylor Ave.
      Springdale News, 11 Feb.1969.

Stuttgart
-Hex
   1973, Oct.-1974, Feb./Sadie May Maze
      (Editorial), Fate 27 (July 1974):
      32-34.
-Mystery bird deaths
   1973, Nov.30
      Denver (Colo.) Post, 5 Dec.1973.
-UFO (CE-1)
   1950, March 21/Jack Adams/15 mi.N
      Memphis (Tenn.) Commercial Appeal,
      22 Mar.1950.
      Curtis Fuller, "The Flying Saucers:
      Fact or Fiction?" Flying 47 (July
      1950):16-17,59.

Texarkana
-UFO (DD)
   1947, July 3
      Little Rock Arkansas Gazette, 4 July
      1947.
   1952, Oct.28
      (Editorial), Fate 6 (Mar.1953):10.
-UFO (NL)
   1947, July 4/Charley Pappas
      Little Rock Arkansas Gazette, 6 July
      1947.

Trumann
-Humanoid
   1970, Jan.30/Nathan Russell
      Harrisburg Modern News, 5 Feb.1970.
      Midnight, 19 Oct.1970.
-UFO (?)
   1973, Oct.5/Carla Whitlatch
      Trumann Democrat, 11 Oct.1973.
-UFO (NL)
   1973, Sep.26
      Little Rock Arkansas Gazette, 27 Sep.
      1973.

Tucker
-Haunt
  1969/Prison Farm
    Little Rock Arkansas Gazette, 25 Feb.
    1969.

Tupelo
-UFO (DD)
  1947, June 30/T.A. Morris
    Little Rock Arkansas Gazette, 3 July
    1947.

Van Buren
-UFO (CE-1)
  1978, Feb.1
    Van Buren Press-Argus, 2 Feb.1978.

Vineygrove
-UFO (CE-1)
  1965, Aug.4/Bill Estep/8 mi.from town
    Jerome Clark, "The Greatest Flap Yet?
    --Part 2," Flying Saucer Rev. 12
    (Mar.-Apr.1966):9.

Walnut Ridge
-Weather control
  1894, Aug.1/Rev. Robinson
    St. Louis (Mo.) Globe-Democrat, 2
    Aug.1894.

Walton Heights
-Phantom panther
  1976, Nov.16/Odell Davis, Jr./11233
    Bainbridge Dr.
    Little Rock Arkansas Gazette, 17
    Nov.1976.

Washington co.
-Fire anomaly
  1920s
    "House of the Phantom Flames," Fate
    11 (Apr.1958):65, quoting Little
    Rock Arkansas Democrat Mag. (undat-
    ed).

Wedington
-River monster
  1973, May 27/Illinois R.
    Fayetteville Northwest Arkansas
    Times, 28 May 1973.

West Helena
-UFO (NL)
  1973, Oct.4
    West Helena Twin City Tribune, 4
    Oct.1973.

West Memphis
-Fall of frogs
  1949, Sep.23/Mr. Rains
    "Run of the Mill," Doubt, no.27
    (1950):27.
-UFO (NL)
  1973, Sep.26/Lena Henry/513 N. 15th St.
    West Memphis Evening Times, 27 Sep.
    1973.

White co.
-Ghost
  1880s/Annie Pate Watson

J.R. Butler, "The Bloodstained Ghost:
  Witness for the Prosecution," Fate
  27 (May 1974):54-57.

Wilson
-Archeological site
  Nodena Mound
    Franklin Folsom, America's Ancient
    Treasures (N.Y.: Rand McNally,
    1974), pp.109-10.

Woodson
-Anomalous mound
  Jim Brandon, Weird America (N.Y.:
    Dutton, 1978), p.20.

            B. Physical Features

Big Danger Mt.
-UFO (NL)
  1971, Sep.4/Tessie Lemley
    Clarksville Herald-Democrat, 4 Nov.
    1971.
    Tommy Roy Blann, "The Mysterious
    Link Between UFOs and Animal Muti-
    lations," Saga UFO Rept. 3 (Apr.
    1976):18,69.

Brant L.
-Humanoid
  1856
    Shreveport (La.) Caddo Gazette, 28
    Mar.1856.
    Little Rock Arkansas Gazette, 27
    June 1971.

Cave Hollow
-Archeological site
  Horace Miner, "Cave Hollow, an Ozark
    Bluff-Dweller Site," Anthro.Pap.
    Univ.Michigan, no.3 (1950). il.

Crooked Creek
-Mystery gas
  1973-1975/Albert J. Trahant, Jr.
    (Editorial), Fate 28 (Apr.1975):23-
    25, quoting Little Rock Arkansas
    Gazette (undated).

Crowley's Ridge
-Clairvoyance and anomalous artifact
  1921/D. Rowlans/King Crowley/=hoax?
    Fred W. Allsopp, Folklore of Romantic
    Arkansas, 2 vols. (N.Y.: Grolier
    Soc'y, 1931), 1:14. il.
    Jim Brandon, Weird America (N.Y.:
    Dutton, 1978), p.18.

Current R.
-Retrocognition
  1941, Aug./Leonard Hall
    Eric Norman [Brad Steiger], Weird
    Unsolved Mysteries (N.Y.: Award,
    1969), pp.87-88, quoting St. Louis
    (Mo.) Post-Dispatch (undated).

McKinney Bayou
-UFO (CE-3)
  1897, April 23/Lawrence A. Byrne

Texarkana Daily Texarkanan, 25 Apr.
1897.

Melody Mt.
-UFO (NL)
1974, May 27-1975, Sep.30/Lisa E. Breckenridge
Lisa E. Breckenridge, "UFOLOG," Ufology 2 (spring 1976):35-37.
(Letter), Lisa Breckenridge, Ufology
2 (summer 1976):64.
1976, Feb.12-26
"Noteworthy UFO Sightings," Ufology
2 (summer 1976):62.

Menard Mounds
-Archeological site
James A. Ford, "Menard Site: The Qua-
paw Village of Osotouy on the Arkan-
sas River," Anthro.Pap.Am.Mus.Nat.
Hist., vol.48, no.2 (1961).

Mud L.
-Lake monster
1897, May/=hoax?
Forrest City Times, 28 May 1897.

Mulberry R.
-Ancient inscription
Gloria Farley, "Inscriptions from
Mid-America," Occ.Pub.Epigraphic
Soc'y 3, no.69 (Sep.1976):2-3.

Ozark Mts.
-Archeological sites
ca.8000-1000 B.C.
M.R. Harrington, "The Ozark Bluff-
Dwellers," Am.Anthro. 26 (1924):1-
21. il.
M.R. Gilmore, "Vegetal Remains of the
Ozark Bluff-Dweller Culture," Pap.
Michigan Acad.Sci.Arts & Letters 14
(1930):83-102. il.
Don R. Dickson, "Bluffs of the South
Central Ozarks," Central States
Arch.J. 6 (1959):56-58.
M.R. Harrington, "The Ozark Bluff-
Dwellers," Indian Notes & Mono-
graphs, no.12 (1960). il.
-Haunt
n.d.
James Reynolds, Ghosts in American
Houses (N.Y.: Paperback Library,
1967 ed.), pp.186-91.
-Precognition
1950s/Ted Richmond
Hartzell Spence, "Modern Shepherd of
the Hills," Sat.Eve.Post, 8 Nov.
1952, pp.26-27,130-33. il.
-UFO (CE-3)
1963
Ted Phillips, Physical Traces Associ-
ated with UFO Sightings (Evanston:
Center for UFO Studies, 1975), p.27.

Skylight Mt.
-UFO (DD)
1952, Aug.
J. Allen Hynek, The Hynek UFO Report
(N.Y.: Dell, 1977), pp.106-107.

Winona L.
-Fall of unknown object
1968, April/O.A. Hughes
Little Rock Arkansas Gazette, 14
Apr.1968.

D. Unspecified Localities

-Archeological sites
Clarence B. Moore, "Antiquities of
the St. Francis, White, and Black
Rivers, Arkansas," J.Acad.Nat.Sci.
Philadelphia 14 (1910):253-364. il.
Clarence B. Moore, "Some Aboriginal
Sites on Mississippi River," J.
Acad.Nat.Sci.Philadelphia 14 (1911)
:365-480. il.
Clarence B. Moore, "Some Aboriginal
Sites on Red River," J.Acad.Nat.
Sci.Philadelphia 14 (1912):481-644.
il.
Clarence B. Moore, "Some Aboriginal
Sites in Louisiana and in Arkansas,"
J.Acad.Nat.Sci.Philadelphia 16
(1916):5-93. il.

-UFO (CE-3)
ca.1976
"Ordeal in Arkansas," Stigmata, no.
4 (summer 1978):13-15.

LOUISIANA

A. Populated Places

Alexandria
-Fall of localized rain
  1958, Nov.11/Mrs. R. Babington
    Alexandria Daily Town Talk, 11 Nov.
    1958.
    William C. Bailey, Jr., "The Backyard
    Rainstorm of Alexandria, La.," Fate
    12 (May 1959):76-78.
-Spontaneous human combustion
  1869, Dec./A.B. Flowers
    (Letter), Sci.Am. 22 (1870):72.
    (Letter), Anon., Sci.Am. 22 (1870):
    108.
-UFO (DD)
  1973, Oct.18/Pamela Jackson
    Alexandria Daily Town Talk, 18 Oct.
    1973.
-UFO (NL)
  1958, June 23/England AFB
    Richard Hall, ed., The UFO Evidence
    (Washington: NICAP, 1964), p.91,
    quoting Alexandria Daily Town Talk
    (undated).
  1964, Sep.15
    Curtis Fuller, "Collected UFO Sight-
    ings for August and September,"
    Fate 18 (Jan.1965):35,38.

Allen parish
-Anomalous artifact
  n.d./=medallion
    (Letter), N.S., Fate 28 (Feb.1975):
    127-28.

Amite
-UFO (NL)
  1973, Oct.15/Jeff Easley/court house
    Amite Tangi Talk, 17 Oct.1973.

Baton Rouge
-Clairvoyance
  ca.1890-1964/Carrie May King
    "Woman with the 'Radio Mind,'" Fate
    17 (Nov.1964):98.
-Fall of unknown object
  1964, April 6/Floyd L. Marston
    "Leading Up to the Big Flap," Fate
    17 (Aug.1964):45,46.
-Haunt
  n.d./The Cottage
  n.d./Skolfield House
    Lyle Saxon, Gumbo Ya-Ya (N.Y.: Hough-
    ton-Mifflin, 1945), pp.271-73.
-Mystery bird deaths
  1896/National Ave.
    San Jose (Cal.) Gazette, 4 Nov.1896.
    Marysville (Cal.) Daily Democrat, 2
    Dec.1896, quoting Philadelphia (Pa.)
    Times (undated).
-UFO (?)
  1800, April 5/=meteor?
    William Dunbar, "Description of a

Singular Phenomenon Seen at Baton
    Rouge," Trans.Am.Phil.Soc'y 6
    (1804):25. il.
    Mrs. Dunbar Rowland, ed., Life, Let-
    ters and Papers of William Dunbar
    (Jackson: Miss.Hist.Soc'y, 1930),
    pp.104-105.
  1973, Oct.20/LSU football stadium/=
    balloon
    Little Rock Arkansas Gazette, 22
    Oct.1973.
-UFO (CE-1)
  1964, Sep.15/James Warren/Core Lane
    Curtis Fuller, "Collected UFO Sight-
    ings for August and September,"
    Fate 18 (Jan.1965):35,38.
  1973, Oct.10
    Baton Rouge State Times, 12 Oct.1973.
-UFO (DD)
  1957, Nov.26
    Richard Hall, ed., The UFO Evidence
    (Washington: NICAP, 1964), p.167.
-UFO (NL)
  1977, July 16
    "UFOs of Limited Merit," Int'l UFO
    Reporter 2 (Sep.1977):3.

Belle Chasse
-Phantom automobile
  1968, May/Mrs. Don Dodd
    (Letter), Fate 30 (Mar.1977):117.

Bellevue
-Disease anomaly
  1939/high school
    "The Weird Epidemic at School," Fate
    11 (Nov.1958):48.

Belville
-Humanoid
  1977, Oct?/Leonce Boudreaux
    Chattanooga (Tenn.) News-Free Press,
    5 June 1978.

Berwick
-UFO (NL)
  1975, Aug.24
    "UFO Central," CUFOS News Bull., 15
    Nov.1975, p.16.

Bossier City
-Precognition
  1949, Jan.22/Leo J. Hopcroft
    Margaret Ruth McDonald, "Hopcroft
    Predicted His Own Death--Five Years
    Ago," Fate 7 (Nov.1954):44-46, quo-
    ting Shreveport Times (undated).

Brusly
-Clairaudience
  1926, Feb./Glenn C. Gunn
    Glenn C. Gunn, "Notified in Advance
    by the Sound of Music," Fate 24
    (Apr.1971):105-106.

Chalmette
-UFO (?)
    1955, Aug.21
        Richard Hall, ed., The UFO Evidence
        (Washington: NICAP, 1964), p.143.
-UFO (NL)
    1977, Jan.15/Peter Degangi/Judge Perez
    Hwy.
        Ted Peters, "Low Lights in Louisiana,"
        APRO Bull. 25 (Mar.1977):1.
    1977, Jan.22/Jean Lafitte Parkway
        Ted Peters, "Near Landing in Louisi-
        ana," MUFON UFO J., no.112 (Mar.
        1977):10-11.
    1977, Feb.8/Gayle Rodriguez/St. Ber-
    nard Hwy.
        Ted Peters, "Maneuvering UFO Seen
        from Car," MUFON UFO J., no.112
        (Mar.1977):6-7.

Chestnut
-UFO (CE-2)
    1957, Dec.11/Mary Louise Tobin/Hwy.1
        Jacques Vallee, Passport to Magonia
        (Chicago: Regnery, 1969), p.268,
        quoting Flying Saucers, July 1958.

Claiborne parish
-UFO (NL)
    1973, Oct./Earl Hancock
        Tommy R. Blann, "Bright Lights over
        Them Purple Plains," Probe the Un-
        known 2 (summer 1974):56,58.

Clifton
-UFO (NL)
    1973, Oct.15/Jerry Brumfield/W on Hwy.
    38
        Bogalusa Daily News, 16 Oct.1973.

Converse
-Humanoid tracks
    1977, Nov.23
        Many Sabine Index, 1 Dec.1977. il.

Crowley
-Humanoid
    1978, Jan.16/Martin Francis
        Lafayette Advertiser, 17 Jan.1978.

DeQuincy
-Crisis apparition
    1937, March/Nina Ramey
    1939, April 12/Nina Ramey
    1943/Nina Ramey
        Nina Ramey, "My Best Friend Is a
        Ghost," Fate 8 (Sep.1955):72-85.

DeRidder
-UFO (CE-1)
    1965, Dec.4
        Gabriel Green, Let's Face the Facts
        About Flying Saucers (N.Y.: Popular
        Library, 1967), p.30.

East Baton Rouge parish
-Humanoid
    1977, summer/Chris Denaro
        John Green, Sasquatch: The Apes Among
        Us (Seattle: Hancock House, 1978),
        pp.192-93.

Elm Grove
-UFO (?)
    1978, Aug.6/=electrical explosion
        "Identified 'IFO' Highlights," Int'l
        UFO Reporter 3 (Sep.1978):9-10.

Estopinal
-Haunt
    n.d./Kenilworth Plantation
        Lyle Saxon, Gumbo Ya-Ya (N.Y.: Hough-
        ton-Mifflin, 1945), p.273.

Farmerville
-UFO (NL)
    1973, Oct.16-17/George Cothrau/Lake
    D'Arbonne
        Farmerville Gazette, 18 Oct.1973.
        Shreveport Times, 18 Oct.1973.

Franklin
-Ovomancy
    ca.1900-1955/Wawa
        Tracey Peterson, "Find the Answer in
        an Egg," Fate 23 (Apr.1970):90-91.

Franklinton
-UFO (NL)
    1973, Oct.13/Riverside Hospital
        Hammond Daily Star, 17 Oct.1973.

Golden Meadow
-UFO (NL)
    1973, Oct.14/=helicopter?
        New Orleans Daily Record, 17 Oct.
        1973.

Gonzales
-Ghost light
    1951, April/Hickley Waguespack
        V.B. Shay, "Lights Without Flame,"
        Fate 4 (Aug.-Sep.1951):96-97.

Hahnville
-Haunt
    n.d./Vie Fortune Plantation
        James Reynolds, Ghosts in American
        Houses (N.Y.: Paperback Library,
        1967 ed.), pp.109-19.

Hammond
-UFO (NL)
    1973, Oct.15/Carl Enna
        Hammond Daily Star, 16 Oct.1973.

Harrisonburg
-Fall of ice
    1978, May 15/Otis Boothe
        Lafayette Advertiser, 19 May 1978.

Haynesville
-UFO (CE-2)
    1966, Dec.30/N on U.S.79
        Edward U. Condon, ed., Scientific
        Study of Unidentified Flying Objects
        (N.Y.: Bantam, 1968 ed.), pp.277-80.
        Jacques Vallee, Passport to Magonia
        (Chicago: Regnery, 1969), pp.45,338.
        Donald H. Menzel & Ernest H. Taves,

The UFO Enigma (Garden City: Doubleday, 1977), pp.99-100.

Houma
-UFO (DD)
  1973, Oct.13/Whitney Armond/Mike St.
    Houma Daily Courier, 16 Oct.1973.
-UFO (NL)
  1973, Oct.15/Jackie Hebert/Richmond St.
    Houma Daily Courier, 16 Oct.1973.

Innis
-UFO (CE-2)
  1967, Jan.12-13/Old R., S of town
    "Three Photos in Louisiana," APRO
    Bull. 15 (Mar.-Apr.1967):8. il.
    "Fisherman's Photos 'Authentic,'"
    UFO Inv. 3 (Mar.-Apr.1967):6.
    Wendelle C. Stevens, "Fantastic UFO
    Photo Flap of 1967," Saga UFO Rept.
    3 (June 1976):24,29. il.

Jonesville
-Archeological site
    E.G. Squier & E.H. Davis, Ancient
    Monuments of the Mississippi Valley
    (Washington: Smithsonian Institution,
    Contrib. to Knowledge, no.1, 1848),
    pp.109-10. il.
-Spirit medium
  1930s/Alice Belle Kirby
    Eric E. Montgomery, "An Account of
    Some Extraordinary Psychic Experi-
    ences with Alice Belle Kirby,"
    J.ASPR 34 (1940):275-84. il.

Kenner
-UFO (NL)
  1976, Nov.23/nr. Moisant Airport
    "UFOs of Limited Merit," Int'l UFO
    Reporter 2 (Jan.1977):5.

Krotz Springs
-Humanoid
  1978, June 4/Leonce Boudreaux
    Chattanooga (Tenn.) News-Free Press,
    5 June 1978.
    New Orleans Times-Picayune, 7 June
    1978.

Lacamp
-UFO (CE-2)
  1960, April 18/Monroe Arnold
    Lloyd Mallan, "The Mysterious 12,"
    Sci.& Mech. 37 (Dec.1966):30,67.

Lafayette
-UFO (DD)
  1957, Nov.9/Truman Gile/airport
    New Orleans Item, 10 Nov.1957.
    New Orleans Times-Picayune, 10 Nov.
    1957.

Lake Charles
-UFO (CE-2)
  1957, Nov.7/Mrs. Frank Lain
    Aimé Michel, Flying Saucers and the
    Straight-Line Mystery (N.Y.: Criter-
    ion, 1958), p.263, quoting Saucer
    News (Feb.-March 1958).

Lake Providence
-Fall of fish scales
  1873
    S.F. Baird, "Alleged Showers of Fish
    Scales," Ann.Record of Sci.& Indus-
    try, 1873, pp.350-51.

Marksville
-Archeological site
  ca.1500 B.C.-1200 A.D.
    G.S. Vescelins, "Mound 2 at Marks-
    ville," Am.Antiquity 22 (1957):
    416-20. il.
    Alan Toth, "Archeology and Ceramics
    at the Marksville Site," Anthro.Pap.
    Univ.Michigan Mus.Anthro., no.56
    (1974). il.
-Fall of fish
  1947, Oct.23/J.M. Barham
    (Letter), A.J. Bajkov, Science 109
    (1949):402.
-Haunt
  n.d./forest
    Lyle Saxon, Gumbo Ya-Ya (N.Y.: Hough-
    ton-Mifflin, 1945), pp.272-73.

Melville
-Humanoid
  1978, June/Don Hardy/=hoax
    Baton Rouge Advocate, 8 June 1978.

Metairie
-Erratic crocodilian
  1970, Sep./Green Acres
    Lucius Farish, "Has the Alligator
    Invasion Begun?" Fate 24 (Mar.1971)
    :71.

Minden
-UFO (CE-2)
  1976, June 22
    "Noteworthy UFO Sightings," Ufology
    2 (fall 1976):60.
-UFO (NL)
  1976, June 28
    "Noteworthy UFO Sightings," Ufology
    2 (fall 1976):60.

Monroe
-Corpse anomaly
  1955, Feb.
    (Editorial), Fate 8 (June 1955):14.
-Haunt
  n.d./Limerick Plantation
    Lyle Saxon, Gumbo Ya-Ya (N.Y.: Hough-
    ton-Mifflin, 1945), p.273.

Morehouse parish
-Archeological site
  Prairie Jefferson
    E.G. Squier & E.H. Davis, Ancient
    Monuments of the Mississippi Valley
    (Washington: Smithsonian Institut
    Contrib. to Knowlegde, no.1, 1848),
    pp.113-14.

Myrtle Grove
-Haunt
  n.d./Myrtle Grove Plantation
    Lyle Saxon, Gumbo Ya-Ya (N.Y.: Hough-

ton-Mifflin, 1945), p.273.

Natchitoches
-Haunt
  n.d./Lacey Branch
  n.d./Simmons House
    Lyle Saxon, Gumbo Ya-Ya (N.Y.: Hough-
    ton-Mifflin, 1945), p.272.
-UFO (NL)
  1897, April 20
    New Orleans Times-Picayune, 21 Apr.
    1897.

New Iberia
-UFO (DD)
  1962, July 10
    Richard Hall, ed., The UFO Evidence
    (Washington: NICAP, 1964), p.32.

New Orleans
-Ancient ax marks
  before 1853/Rampart St.
    (Editorial), Fate 12 (Aug.1959):8.
-Crisis apparition
  n.d./Mary Wood/Valence St.
    Danton Walker, Spooks Deluxe (N.Y.:
    Franklin Watts, 1956), pp.70-72.
-Fall of yellow rain
  1879, March
    "Pollen," Monthly Weather Rev. 7
    (Mar.1879):16.
-Fire immunity
  1850s/Tom Jenkins
    Emma Hardinge Britten, Modern Ameri-
    can Spiritualism (N.Y.: The Author,
    1870), p.205.
-Ghost
  n.d./St. Louis Cemetery No.1
    Lyle Saxon, Gumbo Ya-Ya (N.Y.: Hough-
    ton-Mifflin, 1945), p.287.
  1882/prison at Tulane x Saratoga St.
    New Orleans Daily Picayune, 23 Jan.
    1882.
  1907/St. Ann St. nr Royal St.
    New Orleans Daily News, 4 July 1907.
  1955, March/Ann Jensen/Governor Nichols
  St.
    Ann Jensen, "The Little Children Who
    Weren't There," Fate 18 (Dec.1965):
    77-79.
-Haunt
  n.d./Devil's Mansion, St. Charles St.
  n.d./1447 Constance St.
  n.d./Saratoga St.
  n.d./Seaman's Bethel, St. Thomas St.
    Lyle Saxon, Gumbo Ya-Ya (N.Y.: Hough-
    ton-Mifflin, 1945), pp.280-84.
  n.d./1140 Royal St.
    Lyle Saxon, Fabulous New Orleans
    (N.Y.: Appleton-Century, 1935), pp.
    202-17. il.
    Herbert Asbury, The French Quarter
    (N.Y.: Garden City, 1938), pp.247-
    52.
  n.d./Beauregard House/1113 Chartres St.
    Jeanne de Lavigne, Ghost Stories of
    Old New Orleans (N.Y.: Rinehart,
    1946).
    Susy Smith, Prominent American Ghosts
    (N.Y.: Dell, 1969 ed.), p.174.

n.d./Gardette-Le Prêtre Mansion/Dau-
phine x Orleans St.
  Susy Smith, Prominent American Ghosts
  (N.Y.: Dell, 1969 ed.), pp.174-79.
n.d./Fourth St.
  New Orleans Times-Picayune, 17 Sep.
  1933.
1874, April/Tremé St. Bridge
  Lyle Saxon, Gumbo Ya-Ya (N.Y.: Hough-
  ton-Mifflin, 1945), p.282.
1899/Carrollton Jail
  Lyle Saxon, Gumbo Ya-Ya (N.Y.: Hough-
  ton-Mifflin, 1945), pp.287-88.
-Healing
  1920/John Cudney
    John M. Fletcher, "The Miracle Man
    of New Orleans," Am.J.Psych. 33
    (1922):113-20.
  1935/Sr. Gertrude Korzendorfer
    (Editorial), Fate 16 (Aug.1963):21.
-Hex (voodoo)
  18th c.-   /Marie Laveau, etc.
    Lafcadio Hearn, "New Orleans Super-
    stitions," Harper's Weekly 30
    (1886):843.
    Alcée Fortier, "Customs and Super-
    stitions in Louisiana," J.Am.Folk-
    lore 1 (1888):136-40.
    William W. Newell, "Reports of Voodoo
    Worship in Hayti and Louisiana," J.
    Am.Folklore 2 (1889):41-47.
    Henry C. Castellanos, New Orleans As
    It Was (N.Y.: L. Graham, 1895), pp.
    90-101.
    Lyle Saxon, "Voodoo," New Republic
    50 (23 Mar.1927):135-39.
    Herbert Asbury, The French Quarter
    (N.Y.: Garden City, 1938), pp.254-
    83.
    Robert Tallant, Voodoo in New Orleans
    (N.Y.: Macmillan, 1946).
    Raymond J. Martinez, Mysterious Mar-
    ie Laveau: Voodoo Queen (New Orleans:
    Harmonson, 1956).
    George M. Kelley, "New Orleans Devil
    Worship," Fate 9 (Aug.1956):16-20.
    Samuel Gibbs, Jr., "Voodoo Practices
    in Modern New Orleans," Louisiana
    Folklore Miscellany 3 (Apr.1971):
    12-14.
    Blake Touchstone, "Voodoo in New Or-
    leans," Louisiana History 13 (fall
    1972):371-86. il.
    Jim Brandon, Weird America (N.Y.:
    Dutton, 1978), pp.96-97.
-Inner development
  1971-   /Mary Oneida Toups/521 St.
  Philip St.
    Chicago (Ill.) Sun-Times, 22 Apr.
    1973.
    Hans Holzer, The Witchcraft Report
    (N.Y.: Ace, 1973 ed.), pp.54-56.
-Palmistry
  1961/Alfred R. Hale/New Orleans Charity
  Hospital
    (Editorial), Fate 14 (Aug.1961):12.
-Phantom
  1905/Mrs. R.H. Adams
    Raquel de S. Marshall, "My Family
    Hears the Banshee Cry," Fate 8 (Nov.

1955):15,16.
1969, Nov.18/Ronald R. Sherman
Brian Marsden, "The Spirits of Old
New Orleans," *Fate* 23 (May 1970):46.
-Poltergeist
n.d./200 block Cherokee St.
1930s/1813 St. Anthony St.
Lyle Saxon, *Gumbo Ya-Ya* (N.Y.: Hough-
ton-Mifflin, 1945), p.285.
-Precognition
1958, Sep./Mrs. Roger H. Fellom/82 N.
Wren St.
Ian Stevenson, "An Example Illustra-
ting the Criteria and Characteristics of Precognitive Dreams," *J.ASPR*
55 (1961):98-103.
-Spirit medium
1850s/James Wingard
1854-1855
Emma Hardinge Britten, *Modern American Spiritualism* (N.Y.: The Author,
1870), pp.420-27.
-Spontaneous human combustion
1952, Sep.18/Glen B. Denney/Algiers
New Orleans Item, 18 Sep.1952; and
21 Sep.1952.
New Orleans Times-Picayune, 19 Sep.
1952.
Otto Burma, "Cremation in New Orleans," *Fate* 6 (May 1953):12-15. il.
-UFO (?)
1949, May 18-19
1949, May 23
Bruce S. Maccabee, "UFO-Related Information from the FBI Files: Part
5," *MUFON UFO J.*, no.124 (Mar.1978)
:7,11.
1950, June 23/H.J. Patterson/=meteor?
New Orleans Times-Picayune, 24 June
1950. il.
"Lights in the Sky," *Flying Saucers*,
winter 1974, p.7.
1955, Oct.14/=meteor?
"Space Fireball Blows Up, Sets Off
Louisiana Fires," *CRIFO Orbit*, 4
Nov.1955, p.4.
1957, June 1
New Orleans Times-Picayune, 2 June
1957.
-UFO (CE-1)
1977, Jan.18/Jackson Blvd.
Ted Peters, "Low Lights in Louisiana,"
APRO Bull. 25 (Mar.1977):1.
-UFO (DD)
1947, July 4/Lillian Lawless
New Orleans Item, 5 July 1947.
1947, July 5
Columbus (O.) Citizen, 6 July 1947.
1947, July 6/Robert G. Hellman/Canal
St.
New Orleans Item, 7 July 1947.
1963, May 7/E.L. Hill
Gray Barker, *Book of Saucers* (Clarks-
burg, W.Va.: Saucerian, 1965), p.18,
quoting *Saucer Researcher*, July-Aug.
1963.
1967, Dec.29/Leonard Evans
Wendelle C. Stevens, "Fantastic UFO
Photo Flap of 1967: Part II," *Saga
UFO Rept.* 3 (Aug.1976):24,26-27. il.

-UFO (NL)
1946, Sep.6/Mystery St. x Grand Route
St. John
"Greenleaf Writes," *Doubt*, no.17
(1947):253.
1954, July 18/Paul F. Serpas/Wisner
Blvd.
Paul F. Serpas, "The Saucer That Got
Away," *Fate* 8 (Aug.1955):34-37.
1956, Jan.22/Robert Mueller/offshore
"Cigar-Shaped UFO Seen by Pan American Crew," *CRIFO Orbit*, 2 Mar.1956,
p.3.
1956, Feb.1
"Case 135," *CRIFO Orbit*, 2 Mar.1956,
p.3, quoting *New Orleans States* (undated).
1956, Aug.23/Richard Hall
"Case 198," *CRIFO Orbit*, 5 Oct.1956,
p.2.
1956, Sep.12/Jesse Rodriguez
"Case 217," *CRIFO Orbit*, 2 Nov.1956,
p.1, quoting *New Orleans Times-Picayune* (undated).
1959, Jan.10
Richard Hall, ed., *The UFO Evidence*
(Washington: NICAP, 1964), p.156.
1966, March 24
"Typical Reports," *UFO Inv.* 3 (Mar.-
Apr.1966):8.
1977, Jan.22/Mark Boudreaux/Milan St.
1977, Jan.25/Claire Wetta/nr. City Park
Ted Peters, "Low Lights in Louisiana,"
APRO Bull. 25 (Mar.1977):1-2.
1977, Sep.8
"UFOs of Limited Merit," *Int'l UFO
Reporter* 2 (Oct.1977):3.
-Unidentified submerged object
1954/"Dynafuel"
(Editorial), *Fate* 8 (Feb.1955):11.
-Weeping icon
1972, July/Elmo L. Romagosa/Ramada Inn
New Orleans Clarion-Herald, 20 July
1972. il.
David Techter, "The Virgin Weeps in
New Orleans," *Fate* 25 (Dec.1972):
92-95. il.

Oak Grove
-UFO (CE-1)
1951, Jan.1/Katie Sowell
Huntsville (Ala.) Times, 5 Feb.1974.

Opelousas
-UFO (NL)
1973, Oct.17-18
Lafayette Advertiser, 18 Oct.1973.

Pine
-UFO (NL)
1973, Oct.15/Ralph Cotten
Bogalusa Daily News, 16 Oct.1973.

Ponchatoula
-Precipitating tree
n.d.
Lyle Saxon, *Gumbo Ya-Ya* (N.Y.: Hough-
ton-Mifflin, 1945), p.273.

Port Eads
-UFO (NL)
  1952, Oct.11/S.E. Hays/Associated Bar
  Pilots Station
    (Letter), Fate 6 (Apr.1953):109-10.

Port Hudson
-Ancient ax marks in coal
  1838/Mississippi R.
    W.M. Carpenter, "Miscellaneous No-
    tices in Opelousas, Attakapas, &c.,"
    Am.J.Sci., ser.1, 35 (1839):344-46.
    William Carpenter, "Account of the
    Bituminization of Wood in the Human
    Era," Am.J.Sci., ser.1, 36 (1839):
    118-24.

Provencal
-UFO (CE-2)
  1957, Nov.20/Haskell Raper, Jr./Hwy.117
    (Editorial), Fate 11 (Apr.1958):20-
    21.
    Lucius Farish & Dale M. Titler, "UFO
    Symbols: Message or Mystery," Offi-
    cial UFO 1 (July 1976):16-17.

Redland
-Corpse anomaly
  1885/A.H. Herring
    "The Photographs in the Tomb," Fate
    7 (Aug.1954):108.

Riceville
-Humanoid tracks
  1978, Jan.1/Rhonda Duval/nr.Bayou Queue
  de Tortue
    Crowley Post-Signal, 7 Jan.1978. il.

Ruston
-UFO (CE-2)
  1973, Oct.18
    New Orleans Times-Picayune, 19 Oct.
    1973.

Saint Bernard
-Haunt
  n.d./Mercier Plantation
    Lyle Saxon, Gumbo Ya-Ya (N.Y.: Hough-
    ton-Mifflin, 1945), p.274.

Saint Joseph
-Crisis apparition
  1918, Nov.4/Alice Davidson Baxter
    "Apparition Coinciding with Death,"
    J.ASPR 18 (1924):482-84.

Shreveport
-Ball lightning
  1866, summer
    "Meteoric Explosion," Eclectic Mag.,
    n.s., 4 (1866):253, quoting Shreve-
    port Southwestern (undated).
-Fall of peaches
  1961, July 12/C.K. Carter, Jr./2065
  Lovers Lane
    (Editorial), Fate 14 (Nov.1961):13-
    14.
-Hex
  1960, Oct.-Nov.
    Eva Martin Moutray, "Haitian Voodoo

in Louisiana," Fate 23 (Apr.1970):
85-88.
-Mystery bird deaths
  1940, March 20/Barksdale Field
    Eric Frank Russell, "British Corres-
    pondence," Fortean Soc'y Mag., no.5
    (Oct.1941):4.
-UFO (?)
  1947, June 2/Carl Achee, Jr.
    New Orleans Times-Picayune, 7 July
    1947.
  1947, July 7/=hoax
    "Speaking of Pictures...A Rash of
    Flying Disks Breaks Out over the
    U.S.," Life, 21 July 1947, p.14. il.
    Bruce S. Maccabee, "UFO Related In-
    formation from the FBI Files: Part
    2," MUFON UFO J., no.120 (Nov.1977)
    :12.
-UFO (CE-2)
  1973, Oct.18
    New Orleans Times-Picayune, 19 Oct.
    1973.
-UFO (DD)
  1947, July 5/Henry Herbert
    New Orleans Times-Picayune, 7 July
    1947.
  1952, April 9
    U.S. Air Force, Projects Grudge and
    Blue Book Reports 1-12 (Washington:
    NICAP, 1968), p.108.
-UFO (NL)
  1947, July 4/G.E. Baird/Centenary College
    New Orleans Times-Picayune, 7 July
    1947.
  1952, Feb.
    Dallas (Tex.) Morning News, 2 Feb.
    1952.
  1976, June 21
    "Noteworthy UFO Sightings," Ufology
    2 (fall 1976):60.
-UFO (R-V)
  1957, June 3/airport
    J. Allen Hynek, The UFO Experience
    (Chicago: Regnery, 1972), pp.82-83.

Slidell
-UFO (CE-2)
  1973, Oct.8/Robert A. Lonardo/Avery Estates
    Slidell St. Tammany Times, 9 Oct.1973.
    Thibodaux Daily Comet, 10 Oct.1973.
    Hammond Daily Star, 10 Oct.1973.
    David Techter, "Terror Aboard a UFO,"
    Fate 27 (Feb.1974):36,39.
    Ralph & Judy Blum, Beyond Earth: Man's
    Contact with UFOs (N.Y.: Bantam,
    1974), pp.128-30.
    Earl Robertson, "Pascagoula Update,"
    Ufology 2 (spring 1976):33.

Sorrento
-UFO (NL)
  1947, Aug.18/Joseph Hofard
    "The Mystery of the Flying Disks,"
    Fate 1 (spring 1948):18,33. il.
    Harold T. Wilkins, Flying Saucers on
    the Attack (N.Y.: Ace, 1967 ed.),
    p.73.

Springhill
-UFO (CE-2)
1973, Oct.18
New Orleans Times-Picayune, 19 Oct.
1973.

Tangipahoa
-UFO (DD)
1967, Oct.
Wendelle C. Stevens, "Fantastic UFO
Photo Flap of 1967: Part II," Saga
UFO Rept. 3 (Aug.1976):24,26-27. il.

Tensas parish
-Humanoid
1830s/=amnesiac? fiction?
Frederick Marryat, Monsieur Violet,
in R. Brimley Johnson, ed., The
Novels of Captain Marryat (London:
J.M. Dent, 1896), 15:308-309, ch.
33.

Thibodaux
-UFO (NL)
1973, Oct.15/Bernel Tolbert/Lafargue
School
Thibodaux Daily Comet, 16 Oct.1973.

Tickfaw
-UFO (NL)
1973, Oct.12/Sandra Anthony
Hammond Daily Star, 16 Oct.1973.

Tioga
-UFO (DD)
1947, July 6
New Orleans Item, 7 July 1947.

Vidalia
-Haunt
n.d./jailhouse
James Reynolds, Ghosts in American
Houses (N.Y.: Paperback Library,
1967 ed.), pp.109-19.

Vivian
-Haunt
1936/Joan Briscoe
Joan Briscoe, "My Friend, the Black
Ghost Child," Fate 28 (Feb.1975):
65-68.

Winnfield
-UFO (CE-3)
1973, Nov.7/NE of town, nr. Beech Creek
Bridge
Winnfield Winn Parish Enterprise, 14
Nov.1973.

Yscloskey
-UFO (CE-2)
1977, Jan.21/Robert Melerine/Dike Canal
Ted Peters, "Warm Light Stops Every-
thing!" MUFON UFO J., no.111 (Feb.
1977):3-6. il.

Zachary
-UFO (CE-2)
1973, Oct.18
Baton Rouge State-Times, 19 Oct.1973.

B. Physical Features

Bayou Grand Sara
-Haunt
n.d./Moonrise Plantation
James Reynolds, Ghosts in American
Houses (N.Y.: Paperback Library,
1967 ed.), pp.200-11.

Bayou LaFourche
-UFO (?)
1956, Jan.26/Gilbert Duet/=balloon?
New Orleans Item, 26 Jan.1956.
New Orleans Picayune, 27 Jan.1956.

Bayou Queue de Tortue
-Humanoid
1978, Jan./Mike Richard
Crowley Post-Signal, 7 Jan.1978.
Lafayette Advertiser, 17 Jan.1978.

Carrion Crow Creek
-Mastodon
n.d.
Harold T. Wilkins, Secret Cities of
Old South America (N.Y.: Library
Publishers, 1952), p.280.

Chandeleur Is.
-Underwater pyramid
1978
(Editorial), Fate 31 (July 1978):26-
27.
Eddy Allman & Bill Elder, "The Re-
discovery of Atlantis," Saga UFO
Rept. 6 (Nov.1978):44-47.
-UFO (CE-1)
1968, Nov./Preston L. Mallette, Sr./
"Gulf Central"
"Shrimper Crew Sight UFO," APRO Bull.
17 (Nov.-Dec.1968):7.
A.E. Chambers, "Saucer Scans Shrimp
Boat," in Brad Steiger & Joan Whri-
tenour, Flying Saucer Invasion: Tar-
get--Earth (N.Y.: Award, 1969), pp.
134-36.

Gombi, J. de
-Haunt
n.d.
Lyle Saxon, Gumbo Ya-Ya (N.Y.: Hough-
ton-Mifflin, 1945), pp.275-76.

Honey Island Swamp
-Humanoid
1973
John Green, Sasquatch: The Apes Among
Us (Seattle: Hancock House, 1978),
p.192.

Le Bourgeois Mound
-Anomalous mounds
M.H. Simons, "'Mud Lumps' and Mounds
near New Orleans," Am.Naturalist 16
(1882):418-20.

Long L.
-Acoustic anomaly
1962, May/F.O. Didier/=locusts
(Editorial), Fate 15 (Sep.1962):16.

Marsh I.
-UFO (?)
  1957, March 15/=meteor
    Leonard H. Stringfield, Inside Saucer
    Post...3-0 Blue (Cincinnati: CRIFO,
    1957), p.59.

Pearl R.
-Acoustic anomaly
  n.d.
    Lyle Saxon, Gumbo Ya-Ya (N.Y.: Hough-
    ton-Mifflin, 1945), pp.274-75.

Petit Anse I.
-Archeological site
    J.P. MacLean, Mastodon, Mammoth, and
    Man (Cincinnati: Williamson & Cant-
    well, 1878).

Pontchartrain, L.
-Haunt
  1953, fall/Torben Angus Rogers/N shore
    William E. Sorensen, "The Haunted
    Orchard," Fate 10 (Feb.1957):71-73.
-Mystery plane crash
  1971, Jan.8/USAF FB-111A plane
    "Disappearing Plane--Well! Not Quite,"
    Pursuit 4 (Apr.1971):35-36.
-UFO (DD)
  1947, July 6/H. Lee Brady
    New Orleans Item, 7 July 1947.
  1964, Sep.14/Charles G. Smither
    Curtis Fuller, "Collected UFO Sight-
    ings for August and September,"
    Fate 18 (Jan.1965):35,39, quoting
    New Orleans Times-Picayune (undated).

Poverty Point
-Archeological site
  1000-600 B.C.
    E.G. Squier & E.H. Davis, Ancient
    Monuments of the Mississippi Valley
    (Washington: Smithsonian Institution,
    Contributions to Knowledge, no.1,
    1848), pp.115-16.
    Clarence B. Moore, "Some Aboriginal
    Sites in Louisiana and in Arkansas,"
    J.Acad.Nat.Sci.Philadelphia 16
    (1916):5,66-76. il.
    Clarence H. Webb, "Evidence of Pre-
    Pottery Cultures in Louisiana," Am.
    Antiquity 13 (1948):227-31.
    James A. Ford, "The Puzzle of Poverty
    Point," Nat.History 64 (1955):466-
    72. il.
    James A. Ford & Clarence H. Webb,
    "Poverty Point: A Late Archaic Site
    in Louisiana," Anthro.Pap.Am.Mus.
    Nat.Hist., vol.46, no.1 (1956).
    John Lear, "Ancient America's Geo-
    meters," Sat.Review, 3 Oct.1964, pp.
    53-56. il.
    Clarence H. Webb, "The Extent and
    Content of Poverty Point Culture,"
    Am.Antiquity 33 (1968):297-321.
    Gerald Hawkins, Beyond Stonehenge
    (N.Y.: Harper & Row, 1973), pp.177-
    79.

Raccourci I.
-Phantom ship
  n.d.
    Lyle Saxon, Gumbo Ya-Ya (N.Y.: Hough-
    ton-Mifflin, 1945), p.275.

Red R.
-Fall of salt
  1867, March/mouth
    Frank Edwards, Strange World (N.Y.:
    Lyle Stuart, 1964), p.230, quoting
    New Orleans Times (undated).

Vermillion Bay
-Fall of fish
  1921, June 11/E.A. McIlhenny/=water-
  spout
    E.W. Gudger, "More Rains of Fishes,"
    Annals & Mag.of Nat.Hist., ser.10,
    3 (1929):1,22-23.

        D. Unspecified Localities

-Anomalous mounds
  sand mounds/southwestern sector
    F.W. Hilgard, "The Prairie Mounds
    of Louisiana," Science 21 (1905):
    551-52.
    Frederick C. Coons, "The Sand Mounds
    of Louisiana and Texas," Scientific
    Monthly 66 (Apr.1948):297-300.

-Dowsing
    Lyle Saxon, Gumbo Ya-Ya (N.Y.: Hough-
    ton-Mifflin, 1945), pp.266-67.

-Land monster myth
    Henry C. Mercer, The Lenape Stone:
    or, the Indian and the Mammoth (N.Y.:
    Putnam, 1885).

-Phantom dog
  n.d./Paul F. Serpas
    Paul F. Serpas, "Noisy Phantom of the
    Louisiana Swamp," Fate 9 (Oct.1956):
    73-75.

-Shape-shifting
    Lyle Saxon, Gumbo Ya-Ya (N.Y.: Hough-
    ton-Mifflin, 1945), pp.190-91.

-UFO (CE-1)
  1973
    "Underwater UFOs," APRO Bull. 26
    (June 1978):8.

MISSISSIPPI

A. Populated Places

Aberdeen
-Fall of lava
  1856, July 8/John Fortson/10 mi.W
    Aberdeen Sunny South, 17 Sep.1857.
    "Supposed Meteorite," Am.J.Sci., ser.
    2, 24 (1857):449.

Ashland
-UFO (NL)
  1973, Oct.2/J.D. Green
    Tupelo Daily Journal, 3 Oct.1973.

Bay Springs
-Hog mutilations and phantom wolf
  1977, Jan.6-March 10/Joe McCullough
    Jacksonville (Fla.) Times-Union, 21
    Mar.1977.
    "Notes," Anomaly Rsch.Bull., no.6
    (spring 1977):9-10, quoting Bay
    Springs Jasper County News (undated).

Beaumont
-UFO (CE-1)
  1974, May 12/Charles Hickson
    "Second Meeting with Aliens," Flying
    Saucers, Dec.1974, pp.57-59.

Beauregard
-Haunt
  1926/E.A. Rowan house
    Federal Writers' Program, Mississippi:
    A Guide to the Magnolia State (N.Y.:
    Hastings House, 1949), p.395.

Biloxi
-UFO (DD)
  1959, Nov.8
    Richard Hall, ed., The UFO Evidence
    (Washington: NICAP, 1964), p.153.
  1977, Jan.10
    "UFOs of Limited Merit," Int'l UFO
    Reporter 2 (Jan.1977):5.
-UFO (NL)
  1957, Nov.5/William J. Mey/Keesler AFB
    Richard Hall, ed., The UFO Evidence
    (Washington: NICAP, 1964), p.86.
  1965, April 4/Keesler AFB
    Lloyd Mallan, "Complete Directory of
    UFOs: Part III," Sci.& Mech. 38
    (Feb.1967):56-57.

Blue Mountain
-Poltergeist
  1959, July 26/Willis Booth
    Doctor X, "Mississippi's Blue Moun-
    tain Poltergeist," Fate 13 (Jan.
    1960):59-61.

Bovina
-Fall of turtle
  1894, May 11
    "Remarkable Hail," Monthly Weather

Rev. 22 (May 1894):215.

Brewer
-UFO (CE-2)
  1967, March 17/K.O. Walley
    Brad Steiger & Joan Whritenour, Al-
    lende Letters: New UFO Breakthrough
    (N.Y.: Award, 1968), p.43.

Brookhaven
-Humanoid tracks
  1977, Feb.14/Dewayne Case/Blue Mill Rd.
    Brookhaven Leader, 16 Feb.1977.

Canton
-UFO (NL)
  1977, Feb.16
    "UFOs of Limited Merit," Int'l UFO
    Reporter 2 (Apr.1977):5.

Clarksdale
-UFO (?)
  1973, Oct.5/Thomas Davis/Russell St./
    =star?
    Clarksdale Press-Register, 6 Oct.
    1973.

Coldspring
-Lightning anomaly
  n.d./Coldspring Plantation
    Federal Writers' Program, Mississippi:
    A Guide to the Magnolia State (N.Y.:
    Hastings House, 1949), p.359.

Collins
-Precognition
  1940s-1950s/Jane Berry Owen
    Ruby Moore Huff, "Aunt Jane: 'The
    Fortune Woman,'" Fate 5 (July-Aug.
    1952):54-56.

Columbia
-UFO (NL)
  1969, Jan.20
    Columbia Columbian Progress, 23 Jan.
    1969.
-UFO (R)
  1973, Oct.14/James Thornhill
    Jackson Daily News, 15 Oct.1973.
    Raymond E. Fowler, UFOs: Interplane-
    tary Visitors (N.Y.: Exposition,
    1974), p.319.

Columbus
-UFO (?)
  1942, Aug.29/Michael Solomon/Army Air
  Corps Flying School
    Richard Hall, ed., The UFO Evidence
    (Washington: NICAP, 1964), p.19.

Copiah co.
-Cattle mutilations
  1978, summer
    Brookhaven Daily Leader, 19 June 1978.

Corinth
-Cloud anomaly
   1883, Nov.24/T.E. Whitfield
      "Miscellaneous Phenomena," Monthly
      Weather Rev. 11 (Nov.1883):264.
-Humanoid tracks
   1976, March 14/Smith Bridge Rd.
      Corinth Daily Corinthian, 16 Mar.
      1976.
-Precognition
   1947, Nov.21/Lotta McIntyre
      Laura A. Dale, Rhea White & Gardner
      Murphy, "A Selection of Cases from
      a Recent Survey of Spontaneous ESP
      Phenomena," J.ASPR 56 (1962):3,25-
      27.
-UFO (CE-1)
   1973, Oct.4/Arlin Mohundro/WKCU
      Jackson Clarion-Ledger, 5 Oct.1973.

Cruger
-Coffin anomaly
   1969/Egypt Plantation
      (Editorial), Fate 22 (Nov.1969):32.

Eupora
-UFO (CE-3)
   1973, Oct.17/Hwy.82
      Columbus Triangle-Advertiser, 24
      Oct.1973.
      David Webb, 1973: Year of the Human-
      oids (Evanston: Center for UFO
      Studies, 1976 ed.), p.14.
-UFO (NL)
   1955, Nov.21/Glen Naramore
      (Letter), Fate 10 (Jan.1957):113-14.

Farmington
-UFO (NL)
   1973, Oct.4
      Corinth Daily Corinthian, 5 Oct.1973.

Flora
-UFO (CE-1)
   1977, Feb.9/Ken Creel/4 mi.W on Cox-
   ferry Rd.
      Canton Madison County Herald, 17 Feb.
      1977.
      "Close Encounter in Mississippi,"
      Int'l UFO Reporter 2 (Apr.1977):7.

Gautier
-UFO (NL)
   1973, Oct.11/Judson Kirke
      David Techter, "Terror Aboard a UFO,"
      Fate 27 (Feb.1974):36,38.

Greenville
-Archeological site
   ca.1000 A.D./Winterville Mounds/10 mi.N
      Franklin Folsom, America's Ancient
      Treasures (N.Y.: Rand McNally,
      1974), p.120.
-Haunt
   1924/Lela R. Holt
      Lela R. Holt, "The Signora Finds
      Peace," Fate 25 (Jan.1972):45-51.
-Humanoid
   1971, June/Mae Pearl Young
      Greenville Delta Democrat-Times, 22

June 1971.

Grenada
-UFO (?)
   1944, summer
      Richard Hall, ed., The UFO Evidence
      (Washington: NICAP, 1964), p.16.
   1973, Oct.3/Clint Holley
      Grenada Sentinel-Star, 4 Oct.1973.
-UFO (CE-1)
   ca.1935/Mrs. Latra Lane
      Grenada Sentinel-Star, 4 Oct.1973.

Gulfport
-Haunt
   1970, July-Sep./Cahill House
      (Editorial), Fate 25 (Aug.1972):32.
-Skyquake
   1977, Dec.18/I-10 x Lorraine Rd.
      Biloxi-Gulfport Daily Herald, 19
      Dec.1977.
-UFO (?)
   1967, April 7, 11
   1967, July 10
      (Editorial), Fate 23 (Dec.1970):25.
   1970, July/John P. Bessor
      (Editorial), Fate 23 (Dec.1970):24-
      25, quoting Biloxi-Gulfport Daily
      Herald (undated).
   1973, Oct.16/John Lane/U.S.90/=hoax
      Pascagoula Mississippi Press-Regis-
      ter, 16 Oct.1973.
      New Orleans (La.) States-Item, 17
      Oct.1973, and 19 Oct.1973.
      Philip J. Klass, UFOs Explained (N.Y.:
      Random House, 1974), pp.283,306.
-UFO (CE-1)
   1973, Oct./B.W. Kirkwood
      Victoria (Tex.) Advocate, 5 Nov.1973.
-UFO (DD)
   1954, Dec.3/Hwy.49
      Thomas M. Olsen, ed., The Reference
      for Outstanding UFO Sighting Reports
      (Riderwood, Md.: UFO Information
      Retrieval Center, 1966), p.39.
-UFO (NL)
   1973, Oct.5
      Biloxi-Gulfport Daily Herald, 7 Oct.
      1973.
-UFO (R-V)
   1957, July 17/Lewis D. Chase/RB-47 aircraft
      Edward U. Condon, ed., Scientific
      Study of Unidentified Flying Objects
      (N.Y.: Bantam, 1969 ed.), pp.136-
      37,260-66.
      James E. McDonald, "The 1957 Gulf
      Coast RB-47 Incident," Flying Sau-
      cer Rev. 16 (May-June 1970):2-6.
      James E. McDonald, "Science in De-
      fault: Twenty-Two Years of Inade-
      quate UFO Investigations," in Carl
      Sagan & Thornton Page, eds., UFO's:
      A Scientific Debate (Ithaca, N.Y.:
      Cornell Univ., 1972), pp.52,56-70.
      Philip J. Klass, UFOs Explained (N.Y.:
      Random House, 1974), pp.186-215.
      Donald H. Menzel & Ernest H. Taves,
      The UFO Enigma (Garden City: Double-
      day, 1977), pp.93-96.

William L. Moore, "The Puzzling
Flight of the Lacy 17," Saga UFO
Rept. 6 (Aug.1978):40-43,62-66.

Hancock co.
-UFO (CE-2)
1973, Oct.16/Frances Necaise/Hwy.43
David Techter, "Terror Aboard a UFO,"
Fate 27 (Feb.1974):36,41-42.
-UFO (CE-3)
1977, June/I-10
Palm Springs (Cal.) Desert Sun, 4
Aug.1977.

Hattiesburg
-Phantom
1943, Nov./J. Russel Virden
J. Russell Virden, "The Alien," Fate
23 (Feb.1970):69-70.
1973, Aug./Ann Whitton
Ann Whitton, "The Devil and the 12-
Year-Old," Fate 27 (Sep.1974):82-86.
-UFO (NL)
1974, Feb.19/Harold Stanton
George D. Fawcett, "The 'Unreported'
UFO Wave of 1974," Saga UFO Rept. 2
(spring 1975):51.

Henryville
-UFO (CE-2)
1973, Oct.15
Starkville Daily News, 18 Oct.1973.

House
-UFO (CE-3)
1957, Nov.6/Malvan Stevens
Meridian Star, 7 Nov.1957.
Jackson State Times, 8 Nov.1957.

Improve
-UFO (CE-1)
1978, April 17/Glen McKenzie
Tylertown Times, 20 Apr.1978.

Indianola
-UFO (NL)
1973, Sep.30/Wallace Dabbs
Jackson Clarion-Ledger, 5 Oct.1973.

Itta Bena
-Clairvoyance
1898/Annie H. Hunter
W.H. Rucker, "Incident of the Ear-
Ring," J.ASPR 16 (1922):269-75.
-Precognition
1896/J.L. Haley
Walter F. Prince, "Premonition of
Deaths on the Same Day," J.ASPR 18
(1924):26-30.

Jackson
-Clairvoyance
1964, April 11/Mrs. James F. Runnels
A. Karl Austin, "The Body at River
Bend," Fate 17 (Sep.1964):79-80.
-Fall of fish
1962, April 5/Walter Miller/police sta-
tion
(Editorial), Fate 15 (Aug.1962):19.
-Fall of money

1952, Jan.11/Mrs. S.W. Valentine
Eugene Burr, "Birds Fall on the Em-
pire State," Fate 24 (Apr.1971):
75,78-79, quoting Jackson Daily
News (undated).
-Humanoid
1977, Aug., Dec.20-21/Donald Bracey
Jackson News, 22-23 Dec.1977.
-Psychokinesis
1894, Feb.7/Will Purvis
Frank Edwards, Strange People (N.Y.:
Popular Library, 1961 ed.), pp.
162-63.
-Telepathy
1961/Terry and Sherry Young
(Editorial), Fate 15 (Feb.1962):16-
18.
-UFO (?)
1947, July 8/Mrs. E.B. Brown
Jackson Clarion-Ledger, 9 July 1947.
-UFO (CE-1)
1949, Jan.1/Tom Rush/Dixie Airport
Donald H. Menzel, Flying Saucers
(Cambridge: Harvard Univ., 1953),
p.15.
-UFO (DD)
1957, Oct.25/Frank Noone
(Editorial), Fate 10 (Mar.1957):16.
-UFO (NL)
1947, July 7/Leslie Everett/605 Burns
St.
Jackson Clarion-Ledger, 8 July 1947.
1957, June 18/Henry Carlock
Donald E. Keyhoe, Flying Saucers: Top
Secret (N.Y.: Putnam, 1960), p.93.
1957, Nov.9
"All About Sputs," Doubt, no.56
(!958):460,474.
1972, Aug.8
"Good View of UFO in Mississippi,"
Skylook, no.61 (Dec.1972):10.

Kilmichael
-Meteorite crater
13,000 m.diam./possible
R.R. Priddy & T.E. McCutcheon, "Mont-
gomery County Mineral Resources,"
Bull.Mississippi Geol.Survey, no.
51 (1943). il.
Mark D. Butler, "The Meteor Crater
in Mississippi," J.Mississippi Acad.
Sci. 8 (1962):51-52.

Laurel
-UFO (CE-1)
1974, Aug.12
George D. Fawcett, "A Review of Some
of the Thousands of UFO Sightings
in 1974 to Date," Flying Saucers,
Dec.1974, pp.37,39.

Linden
-Haunt
n.d./Everhope
Federal Writers' Program, Mississippi:
A Guide to the Magnolia State (N.Y.:
Hastings House, 1949), p.356.

Long Beach
-Hex

n.d./Pitcher's Point
Federal Writers' Program, Mississippi:
A Guide to the Magnolia State (N.Y.:
Hastings House, 1949), p.296.
-UFO (CE-3)
1965, Jan.20
Donald B. Hanlon, "Virginia 1965
Flap," Flying Saucer Rev. 12 (Mar.-
Apr.1966):15.

Lumberton
-Precognition
1966, Dec./Frances Ladner
Marion Boe, "A Nightmare and Its
Startling Aftermath," Fate 26 (Feb.
1973):51-57.

Lyman
-UFO (NL)
1979, March 7/Mrs. O.M. Patton
Biloxi-Gulfport Daily Herald, 7 Mar.
1979.

Maben
-UFO (DD)
1973, Feb.6/Mrs. E. McMullen
"Glowing Circle Seen in Mississippi,"
Skylook, no.64 (Mar.1973):9.

McClain
-Fall of unknown object
1971, April 12/Willie Hamilton
Jackson Clarion-Ledger, 13 Apr.1971.
"Press Reports," APRO Bull. 19 (Mar.-
Apr.1971):5.

McComb
-UFO (NL)
1978, July 12/Jim Russ/Ren Drive-In
Theater
McComb Enterprise-Journal, 13 July
1978.

Magnolia
-UFO (DD)
1973, Oct.17
Jackson Clarion-Ledger, 18 Oct.1973.

Mendenhall
-UFO (?)
1973, Oct.2/=Mars?
Jackson Clarion-Ledger, 4-5 Oct.1973.

Meridian
-Animal ESP
1954/Rosa Daigle
(Editorial), Fate 8 (Jan.1955):13.
-Clairvoyance
1960/Mrs. John Holcomb
(Editorial), Fate 14 (Jan.1961):22.
-Fall of tree limb
1956, Sep.5/P.F. Watkins/Route 4
(Editorial), Fate 10 (Jan.1957):9.
-UFO (DD)
1947, July 6/Marty Fleming
Meridian Star, 7 July 1947.
-UFO (NL)
1973, Oct.5/Oakland Heights
Meridian Star, 5 Oct.1973.
1973, Oct.6/E of town

Meridian Star, 7 Oct.1973.

Mississippi City
-Haunt
n.d.
Federal Writers' Program, Mississippi:
A Guide to the Magnolia State (N.Y.:
Hastings House, 1949), p.295.

Natchez
-Archeological site
Charles Lyell, A Second Visit to the
United States of North America, 2
vols. (N.Y.: Harper, 1849), 2:151-
52.
Thomas Wilson, "On the Presence of
Fluorine As a Test for the Fossil-
ization of Animal Bones," Am.Nat-
uralist 29 (1895):301,725.
Horace G. Richards, "The Vindication
of Natchez Man," Frontiers 15, no.
5 (1951):139-40.
George I. Quimby, "The Locus of the
Natchez Pelvis Find," Am.Antiquity
22 (1956):77-78.
-Haunt
n.d./Cottage Gardens
Marion Lowndes, Ghosts That Still
Walk (N.Y.: Knopf, 1941), pp.74-78.
-Humanoid
1977, Jan.17/Dorothy Abraham/Irving
Lane
Natchez Democrat, 19-20 Jan.1977, p.
1A.
Jackson Daily News, 19 Jan.1977.
-UFO (?)
1724, fall/Le Page du Pratz/=meteor?
Le Page du Pratz, The History of
Louisiana, 2 vols. (London: T. Bec-
ket & P.A. de Hondt, 1763), 1:66-68.

New Albany
-UFO (NL)
1959, July 5
Jacques Vallee, Anatomy of a Phenomenon (N.Y.: Ace, 1965 ed.), pp.208-
209.

Ocean Springs
-UFO (NL)
1962, July 30
Thomas M. Olsen, ed., The Reference
for Outstanding UFO Sighting Reports
(Riderwood, Md.: UFO Information
Retrieval Center, 1966), pp.81-82.
1976, Feb.18
"Noteworthy UFO Sightings," Ufology
2 (summer 1976):62.

Okolona
-UFO (?)
1973, Oct.3/=helicopter?
Tupelo Daily Journal, 4 Oct.1973.

Osyka
-UFO (DD)
1973, Oct.
McComb Enterprise-Journal, 16 Oct.
1973.

Oxford
-UFO (NL)
1973, Oct.1-2/Bobby Laney/Old Sardis
Rd.
Oxford Eagle, 4 Oct.1973.

Pascagoula
-UFO (CE-4)
1973, Oct.11/Charles Hickson/Shaupeter
Shipyard
Pascagoula Mississippi Press-Regis-
ter, 19 Oct.1973; and 12 Apr.1974.
"The Pascagoula Affair," APRO Bull.
22 (Sep.-Oct.1973):1,3-4.
"Follow-Up," APRO Bull. 22 (Nov.-Dec.
1973):6. il.
National Tattler, 2 Dec.1973.
Joe Eszterhas, "Claw Men from Outer
Space," Rolling Stone, 17 Jan.1974,
pp.26-27,38-47.
Hayden C. Hewes, "Kidnapped," Probe
the Unknown 2 (spring 1974):10-14.
Stanton T. Friedman & B. Ann Slate,
"The Truth Behind the Amazing Pas-
cagoula Contact," Saga UFO Rept. 1
(spring 1974):18-21,51-54.
Philip J. Klass, UFOs Explained (N.Y.:
Random House, 1974), pp.293-311.
Ralph & Judy Blum, Beyond Earth:
Man's Contact with UFOs (N.Y.: Ban-
tam, 1974), pp.9-36,124-40,195-205.
Biloxi-Gulfport Daily Herald, 6 June
1974.
J. Allen Hynek & Jacques Vallee, The
Edge of Reality (Chicago: Regnery,
1975), pp.101-10.
Ted Peters, "Pascagoula Update,"
MUFON UFO J., no.107 (Oct.1976):15.
Hayden C. Hewes, "Pascagoula Abduc-
tion Confirmed!" Saga UFO Rept. 6
(Nov.1978):36-37.

Pass Christian
-UFO (NL)
1963, June 4/Michael Webb
(Letter), Fate 17 (Jan.1964):129.
1973, Oct.13/Mrs. Richard Harper
Hammond (La.) Daily Star, 17 Oct.
1973.

Petal
-UFO (CE-2)
1973, Oct./Charles Delk
Mobile (Ala.) Register, 9 Oct.1973.

Pine Flat
-UFO (NL)
1973, Oct.4/M.E. Burke/Old Paris Rd. x
Hwy.9
Oxford Eagle, 4 Oct.1974.

Raleigh
-Haunt
n.d./cemetery
Federal Writers' Program, Mississippi:
A Guide to the Magnolia State (N.Y.:
Hastings House, 1949), p.497.

Sandersville
-UFO (NL)

1978, Sep.12/Stella Hodge
Laurel Leader-Call, 13 Sep.1978.

Scott
-Flying humanoid
1966, Sep.1/Mrs. James Ikart/Pine Land
Plantation
Greenville Delta Democrat-Times, 2
Sep.1966.

Shannon
-UFO (NL)
1973, Oct.4
Tupelo Daily Journal, 5 Oct.1973,
p.14.

Shaw
-Fall of fish
n.d./J.L. Bole/nr. Porter Bayou
1888/George Prentiss
George Prentiss, The Ages of Ice and
Creation (Chicago: Common Good,
1915), pp.107-14.

Stanton
-Archeological site
1300-1600/Emerald Mound
John L. Cotter, "Archeological Sur-
vey of Emerald Mound," J.Missis-
ippi History, Jan.1949.
John L. Cotter, "Stratigraphic and
Area Tests at the Emerald and Anna
Mound Sites," Am.Antiquity 17
(1951):18-32.

Sumner
-Haunt
n.d./Boone Jenkins House
Federal Writers' Program, Mississippi:
A Guide to the Magnolia State (N.Y.:
Hastings House, 1949), p.421.

Tippah co.
-Abduction of child by eagle
1868, fall/Jemmie Kenney
F.A. Pouchet, The Universe (London:
Blackie, 1870).

Tunica
-Genetic anomaly
1958, Oct./J.I. McClurkin/12 mi.SW
(Editorial), Fate 12 (Feb.1959):11-
12.

Tupelo
-UFO (NL)
1973, Sep.30/Kim Foreman/President St.
1973, Oct.3/Thomas E. Westmoreland
1973, Oct.3-4
Tupelo Daily Journal, 4-5 Oct.1973.
Grenada Sentinel-Star, 4 Oct.1973.
Jackson Clarion-Ledger, 5 Oct.1973.

Verona
-UFO (NL)
1973, Oct.4
Tupelo Daily Journal, 5 Oct.1973.

Vicksburg
-Disappearance

ca.1885, June/"Iron Mountain"/N on Miss-
issippi R./=hoax?
    "The Missing Steamboat," Fate 4 (Nov.-
    Dec.1951):23.
-Fall of alabaster
    1894, May 11
    "Remarkable Hail," Monthly Weather
    Rev. 22 (May 1894):215.
-UFO (?)
    1976, May 3
    "Noteworthy UFO Sightings," Ufology
    2 (fall 1976):60.

Waynesboro
-Hex
    1935, Oct./Voodoo Gray
    London (Eng.) Sunday Express, 27
    Oct.1935.

West Point
-UFO (DD)
    1900s/C.W. Paisley
    Leonard H. Stringfield, Inside Sau-
    cer Post...3-0 Blue (Cincinnati:
    CRIFO, 1957), pp.83-84.
-UFO (NL)
    1973, Oct.2/E of town
    Clarksdale Press-Register, 3 Oct.
    1973.

Wiggins
-UFO (NL)
    1954, Oct./Belle M. Ingersoll
    (Letter), Fate 8 (Mar.1955):118-19.

Winona
-Humanoid
    1966, Nov.8/James Cagle/E of town
    Eric Norman [Brad Steiger], The Abom-
    inable Snowmen (N.Y.: Award, 1969),
    pp.83-86.
    Jerome Clark & Loren Coleman, Crea-
    tures of the Outer Edge (N.Y.: War-
    ner, 1978), pp.89-91.

                B. Physical Features

Black R.
-Precognition
    1863, Aug./John R. Davis/Messenger's
    Fort
    F.W.H. Myers, "The Subliminal Self,"
    Proc.SPR 11 (1895):334,582-85.

Bynum Mounds
-Archeological site
    ca.700 A.D.
    John L. Cotter & John M. Corbett,
    "Archeology of the Bynum Mounds,
    Mississippi, Arch.Rsch.Ser.Nat'l
    Park Service, no.1 (1951). il.

Clear Creek
-Archeological site
    E.G. Squier & E.H. Davis, Ancient
    Monuments of the Mississippi Valley
    (Washington: Smithsonian Institution,
    Contrib.to Knowledge, no.1, 1848),
    pp.111-12.

Robert M. Thorne & Samuel O. McGahey,
"Archeological Excavation of the
Clear Creek Mound," Anthro.Pap.Mus.
Anthro.Univ.Mississippi, vol.1, no.
1-4, pp.24-39.

Hell Creek Bottom
-UFO (NL)
    1973, Sep.30/Ollie Berry/Harmony Rd.
    New Albany Gazette, 4 Oct.1973.

Island No. 95
-River monster
    1877, Dec.9/John Caughlin
    New York Times, 27 Dec.1877, p.2,
    quoting Natchez Democrat (undated).

Lafayette Bayou
-Ancient inscription
    1870
    John P. MacLean, The Mound Builders
    (Cincinnati: Robert Clarke, 1904),
    p.110.

Lost Gap
-Humanoid
    1962, Nov.
    Great Falls (Mont.) Tribune, 15 Nov.
    1962.

Magee's Creek
-Humanoid tracks
    1977, April
    Tylertown Times, 17 Apr.1977.

Mud Creek
-UFO (CE-2)
    1973, Oct.6/ground markings only
    Ted Phillips, Physical Traces Associ-
    ated with UFO Sightings (Evanston:
    Center for UFO Studies, 1975), p.
    93.

Owl Creek
-Archeological site
    Franklin Folsom, America's Ancient
    Treasures (N.Y.: Rand McNally,
    1974), p.119.

Pascagoula R.
-Acoustic anomaly
    Federal Writers' Program, Mississippi:
    A Guide to the Magnolia State (N.Y.:
    Hastings House, 1949), pp.287-88.
    "Singing River," Fate 6 (July 1953):
    37.
-Unidentified submerged object
    1973, Nov.6/Raymond Ryan
    Santa Ana (Cal.) Register, 14 Nov.
    1973.
    "USO Update," INFO J., no.13 (May
    1974):30-33.
    Robert Klinn, "Pascagoula II: Phan-
    tom Submerged Object Sighted Maneu-
    vering by Sites of UFO Kidnap, Navy
    Shipbuilding Facility," Probe the
    Unknown 4 (Jan.1976):27-30.
    Leonard H. Stringfield, Situation
    Red: The UFO Siege (N.Y.: Fawcett
    Crest, 1977 ed.), pp.131-35.

Tallahatchie R.
-Archeological site
    E.G. Squier & E.H. Davis, Ancient
    Monuments of the Mississippi Valley
    (Washington: Smithsonian Institution,
    Contrib.to Knowledge, no.1, 1848),
    pp.110-11.

Williams' Bayou
-Archeological site
    E.G. Squier & E.H. Davis, Ancient
    Monuments of the Mississippi Valley
    (Washington: Smithsonian Institution,
    Contrib.to Knowledge, no.1, 1848),
    pp.116-17.

C. Ethnic Groups

Chickasaw Indians
-Flood myth
    James William Lynd, History of the
    Dakotas, in Minnesota Hist.Coll. 2
    (1865):57-84.

Choctaw Indians
-Flood myth
    George Catlin, Letters and Notes on
    the...North American Indians, 2
    vols. (London: D. Bogue, 1844), 2:
    127.
    "A Choctaw Account of the Flood,"
    Nature 129 (1932):619.
-Welsh Indians
    Guy Soulliard Klett, Journals of
    Charles Beatty, 1762-1769 (Univer-
    sity Park: Univ. of Pennsylvania,
    1962), pp.52-53.
    Amos Stoddard, Sketches Historical
    and Descriptive of Louisiana (Phila-
    delphia: Mathew Carey, 1812), p.477.

ALABAMA

A. Populated Places

Albertville
-Humanoid
  n.d.
    Birmingham News, 29 Dec.1974.

Anderson
-UFO (?)
  1973, March
    Glenn O. Rutherford, "UFO-Gazing in the Land of Blue Grass," Probe the Unknown 2 (spring 1974):20.

Anniston
-UFO (?)
  1947, July 6/Fain Cole
    Anniston Star, 8 July 1947.

Arab
-Precognition
  1954, Oct.
    (Editorial), Fate 8 (Apr.1955):14.

Athens
-Humanoid
  1978, Aug.6/David Conley/Blue Hole
    Athens News-Courier, 8 Aug.1978. il.
-Medical clairvoyance
  1854-1876/Rev. C.B. Saunders
    G.W. Mitchell, X + Y = Z, or the Sleeping Preacher of North Alabama (N.Y.: W.C. Smith, 1877).
    Walter Franklin Prince, "Two Old Cases Reviewed," Bull.Boston SPR, no.11 (1930).
    Edmond P. Gibson, "Alabama's 'Sleeping Preacher,'" Tomorrow 7 (autumn 1959):78-86.

Auburn
-UFO (?)
  1973, Sep.17
    Ted Phillips, Physical Traces Associated with UFO Sightings (Evanston: Center for UFO Studies, 1975), p. 110.
-UFO (NL)
  1973, Sep.9/Keith Broach
    Columbus (Ga.) Enquirer, 10 Sep.1973.
    Leonard H. Stringfield, Situation Red: The UFO Siege (N.Y.: Fawcett Crest, 1977 ed.), p.22.

Barbour co.
-Dowsing
    Ray B. Browne, "Popular Beliefs and Practices from Alabama," Univ.California Folklore Studies, no.9 (1958):201.

Battles Wharf
-Haunt
    Federal Writers' Program, Alabama: A Guide to the Deep South (N.Y.: Hastings House, 1941), p.398.

Bessemer
-Poltergeist
  1953, July/Nathan Irvin
    (Editorial), Fate 6 (Dec.1953):8.
    Gray Barker, They Knew Too Much About Flying Saucers (N.Y.: University, 1956), p.41.
-UFO (NL)
  1947, July 6/Gordon Miz
    Birmingham News & Age-Herald, 7 July 1947.

Bethel
-UFO (NL)
  1947, Aug.
    "What the Air Force Believes About Flying Saucers," Fate 2 (Nov.1949): 69,71.
    Donald E. Keyhoe, Flying Saucers Are Real (N.Y.: Fawcett, 1950), pp.71-72.

Birmingham
-Animal ESP
  n.d.
    "Dog Takes 2000-Mile Junket," Fate 32 (Mar.1979):77.
-Anomalous hole in ground
  1971, May/Aaron Brasher/=excavation
    Midnight, 31 May 1971.
    "On Trashpapers," Pursuit 4 (July 1971):58.
-Crisis apparition
  1952, Nov./Mrs. R.B. Storrs
    Laura A. Dale, Rhea White & Gardner Murphy, "A Selection of Cases from a Recent Survey of Spontaneous ESP Phenomena," J.ASPR 56 (1962):3,12-14.
-Doubtful responsibility
  1888, Nov./murder mystery
    St. Louis (Mo.) Globe-Democrat, 20 Dec.1888.
-Fall of black snow
  1949, Jan.9
    "Black Snow," Doubt, no.24 (1949): 366.
-Fall of fish
  1944, March 28/I.J. Williams
    "More Animals," Doubt, no.14 (spring 1946):203.
-Fall of unknown object
  1957, June/Locust Park
    Birmingham News, 13 June 1957.
-Flying humanoid
  1956, April 5/steel plant
    (Editorial), Fate 9 (Dec.1956):12.
-Mystery glass etchings
  1960/G.R. Lawrence
    (Editorial), Fate 13 (Aug.1960):16.
-UFO (?)

1951, fall
  Richard Hall, ed., The UFO Evidence
  (Washington: NICAP, 1964), p.16.
1954, spring
  Harold T. Wilkins, Flying Saucers
  Uncensored (N.Y.: Pyramid, 1967 ed.),
  p.82.
1958, Sep.25/W.B. George/Zion City/=
meteor?
  "The Night of September 29," Fate
  12 (Feb.1959):31,36.
-UFO (DD)
1947, June 18/Mrs. H. Akins/Green
Springs
  Birmingham News & Age-Herald, 9 July
  1947.
-UFO (NL)
1947, July 6/Ira L. Livingston/1354
Meadow Lane
  Birmingham News & Age-Herald, 7 July
  1947.
  Ted Bloecher, Report on the UFO Wave
  of 1947 (Washington: NICAP, 1967),
  pp.III-3, IV-4.
1947, July 6/J.A. Hafner/Ensley
  Birmingham News & Age-Herald, 7 July
  1947.
1947, July 7/Horace Guttery/1131 N.
29th St.
  Birmingham News & Age-Herald, 8 July
  1947.

Cahaba Heights
-UFO (CE-3)
1975, Oct.26
  Ted Bloecher, "Close Encounters of
  the Third Kind," Fate 31 (Jan.1978):
  34-36.

Carrollton
-Lightning anomaly
1878/Henry Wells/court house
  Alabama Writers' Program, Alabama: A
  Guide to the Deep South (N.Y.: Rich-
  ard A. Smith, 1941), pp.394-95.
  Mildred Barnett Mitcham, "A Tale in
  the Making: The Face in the Window,"
  Southern Folklore Quar. 12 (1948):
  241-57.

Chickasaw
-Fall of soap flakes
1974/=residue from water treatment
plant
  (Editorial), Fate 28 (Apr.1975):28-
  30.

Citronelle
-UFO (DD)
1967, Dec.9/Marion Boe
  Marion Boe, "A Nightmare and Its
  Startling Aftermath," Fate 26 (Feb.
  1973):51,53-54.

Clanton
-Humanoid
1960, fall/E.C. Hand/Walnut Creek
  Clanton Union-Banner, 30 Aug.1965.
  John A. Keel, Strange Creatures from
  Time and Space (Greenwich, Ct.: Faw-

cett, 1970), pp.98-99.

Clay
-UFO (CE-1)
1962, summer/Dean Self/Clay-Palmerdale
Rd.
  Mildred Higgins, "Prepare to Meet a
  UFO," Fate 30 (May 1977):73,75-76.

Coalburg
-Fall of fish
1892, May
  New York Sun, 29 May 1892, p.5.

Coaling
-Humanoid tracks
1978, July 11/=hoax
  Tuscaloosa News, 13 July 1978.

Columbiana
-UFO (NL)
1947, July 12
  Birmingham News & Age-Herald, 13
  July 1947.

Cook Springs
-UFO (DD)
1947, July 8
  Birmingham News & Age-Herald, 8 July
  1947.
  Ted Bloecher, Report on the UFO Wave
  of 1947 (Washington: NICAP, 1967),
  p.III-12.

Courtland
-Haunt
1950s/Rocky Hill Castle
  "The Rocky Hill Castle Ghosts," Fate
  10 (Nov.1957):34, quoting Birmingham News (undated).

Dawes
-UFO (CE-1)
1973, Oct.17
  Mobile Register, 19 Oct.1973.
-UFO (CE-2)
1973, Oct.
  "Alabama UFO Group Summarizes 1975,"
  Skylook, no.102 (May 1976):7.
-UFO (NL)
1973, Oct.18
  Mobile Register, 19 Oct.1973.

Decatur
-Archeological site
Quad site
  Frank J. Soday, "The Quad Site, a
  Paleo-Indian Village in Northern
  Alabama," Tennessee Arch. 10, no.1
  (1954):1-20.
  James W. Cambron & David C. Hulse,
  "An Excavation on the Quad Site,"
  Tennessee Arch. 16, no.1 (1960):14-
  26.
-UFO (NL)
1966, Sep./Dennis Billings
1970, Oct.6/Dennis Billings
  "Object Photographed in Alabama,"
  APRO Bull. 19 (Nov.-Dec.1970):5-6.
  il.

Dora
-Ghost
    1975, April 18/Chunda Micklow
        (Editorial), Probe the Unknown 3
        (Sep.1975):47.

Dothan
-Humanoid
    1976, May 23/Old Taylor Rd.
        John Green, Sasquatch: The Apes Among
        Us (Seattle: Hancock House, 1978),
        pp.214-15.

Eastaboga
-Derelict automobile
    1975-   /Hubert East
        (Editorial), Fate 29 (June 1976):
        23-24.

East Brewton
-Humanoid
    1978, March 7/Luke McDaniels/Conecuh R.
        Mobile Press-Register, 12 Mar.1978.
        Fort Walton Beach (Fla.) Playground
        News, 26 Nov.1978.

Etowah co.
-UFO (NL)
    1976, Feb.26
        Gadsden Times, 27 Feb.1976.

Evergreen
-UFO (?)
    1973, Oct.17
        Colman Von Keviczky, "The 1973 UFO
        Invasion: Part 1," Official UFO 1
        (Aug.1975):16,18.

Falkville
-UFO (?)
    1973, Oct.17/Jeff Greenhaw/W of town/
        =hoax
        Birmingham News, 19 Oct.1973; and
            4-5 Sep.1974.
        Christian Science Monitor, 24 Oct.
            1973.
        Colman Von Keviczky, "The 1973 UFO
        Invasion--Part 2: Incident at Falk-
        ville," Official UFO 1 (Aug.1975):
        20-23,52. il.
        Colman Von Keviczky, "Invasion '73
        Aftermath: The Terror Begins," Of-
        ficial UFO 1 (Aug.1975):24-25. il.
        Colman Von Keviczky, "The 1973 UFO
        Invasion--Part 3: The Space Crea-
        ture Photos Are Not a Hoax," Offi-
        cial UFO 1 (Aug.1975):26-27,52-54.
        il.
        Bernard O'Connor, "The Greenhaw Case:
        A Possible Explanation," Official
        UFO 1 (Nov.1975):6-7.
        William Spaulding, "Falkville Crea-
        ture Photographs Analyzed," MUFON
        UFO J., no.108 (Nov.1976):3-5. il.

Florence
-Animal ESP
    n.d.
        Dorothy H. Pope, "Science Searches
        for ESP in Animals," Fate 7 (Oct.

1954):16,19-20.
-Archeological site
    E.G. Squier & E.H. Davis, Ancient
    Monuments of the Mississippi Valley
    (Washington: Smithsonian Institution,
    Contrib.to Knowledge, no.1, 1848),
    pp.109-10. il.
-UFO (NL)
    1972, Dec.27-29/Hwy.72
        "Press Reports," APRO Bull. 21 (Jan.-
        Feb.1973):13.

Foley
-UFO (NL)
    1953, Jan.28/E.H. Haines/Barin Field
        (Editorial), Fate 6 (June 1953):12-
        13.

Fort Mims
-Retrocognition
    1966, March 27/Floyd Boone
        Sally Remaley, "The Uneasy Dead at
        Fort Mims," Fate 21 (Dec.1968):46-
        51.

Fort Payne
-Snake handling
    1950s-1960s/Charles H. Hall
        M.E. Counselman, "I Saw Them Take Up
        Serpents," Fate 15 (Sep.1962):85-
        90.
-UFO (?)
    1966, Aug.26/B.J. Funk
        "New Reports by Space Experts Add to
        UFO Proof," UFO Inv. 3 (Aug.-Sep.
        1966):3.

Fort Rucker
-UFO (?) and plane crash
    1972
        Rufus Drake, "Return of the 'Men in
        Black,'" Saga UFO Rept. 3 (Oct.1976)
        :36,54.

Gadsden
-Dowsing
    1960s/Almon Bailey
        George Butler, "Gadsden's Official
        Dowser," Fate 23 (Apr.1970):92-93.
-Healing
    1960s/Mama Louise Cain/2403 James St.
        George Butler, "Mama Louise 'Talks
        Out Fire,'" Fate 20 (Nov.1967):100-
        102.
-Mystery explosion
    1954, Jan.30/Mrs. Robert Arledge
        "The Exploding House," Fate 8 (Feb.
        1955):45.
-Telepathy
    1960s/Frank N. Rains
        George Butler, "First Report on 'Si-
        multaneous Speaking,'" Fate 20 (July
        1967):93-95.
-UFO (?)
    1956, Sep.20/O.C. Smith/Ivalee Community
        (Editorial), Fate 10 (Feb.1957):9.
-UFO (NL)
    1973, Oct.16/Republic Steel Plant
        (Editorial), Fate 27 (Feb.1974):34-
        35.

Georgetown
-UFO (DD)
    1966, Jan.7/3 mi.SW on Hwy.63
        Mobile Register, 13 Jan.1966.
        J. Allen Hynek, The Hynek UFO Report
        (N.Y.: Dell, 1977), p.42.

Greensboro
-UFO (NL)
    1975, Nov.14
        "Noteworthy UFO Sightings," Ufology
        2 (spring 1976):42.

Gulf Shores
-UFO (CE-2)
    1975, Oct.
        "Alabama UFO Group Summarizes 1975,"
        Skylook, no.102 (May 1976):6.

Guntersville
-Doubtful identity
    1953, June 21/Tennessee R. bridge/=
    man from future?
        (Editorial), Fate 6 (Nov.1953):4,
        quoting UP release (undated).

Hackneyville
-UFO (CE-1)
    1974, Feb.12/Kenneth Sherrer
        Vincent Gaddis, "UFO Theories: Space
        Animals--Fish of the Atmospheric
        Sea," Official UFO 1 (Oct.1975):31,
        50.

Hammondville
-UFO (NL)
    1976, May 9/Larry Smith/Hwy.40 x 117
        Clifford Collier, "UFOlog," Ufology
        2 (fall 1976):53,56.

Hanceville
-Haunt
    n.d.
        Brad Steiger, "1972: A Bumper Year
        for Hauntings," Beyond Reality, no.
        4 (May 1973):15,17.

Hayden
-UFO (NL)
    1977, Aug.11
        "Case Analysis," Int'l UFO Reporter
        2 (Oct.1977):newsfront sec.
    1977, Aug.28
        "UFOs of Limited Merit," Int'l UFO
        Reporter 2 (Oct.1977):3.

Hazel Green
-UFO (NL)
    1947, June 23/E.B. Parks
        Huntsville Times, 7 July 1947.

Huntsville
-Humanoid
    1976, April 17-27
        Clifford Collier, "UFOlog," Ufology
        2 (fall 1976):53.
-Mystery explosion
    1957, Nov.2
        "All About Sputs," Doubt, no.56
        (1958):460,471.

-UFO (CE-1)
    1976, April 25-26
        Clifford Collier, "UFOlog," Ufology
        2 (fall 1976):53.
-UFO (DD)
    1962, Feb./U.S.72
        Frank Edwards, "Mystery Blast over
        Nevada," Fate 15 (Aug.1962):68,73.
    1966, March 11/Gulfstream Aircraft
        Edward U. Condon, ed., Scientific
        Study of Unidentified Flying Objects
        (N.Y.: Bantam, 1969 ed.), pp.457-
        63. il.
-UFO (NL)
    1910, Jan.12
        New York Tribune, 13 Jan.1910.

Ironaton
-Anomalous hole in ground
        Paul Jasper, "The Ironaton, Alabama,
        Pit," Meteoritics 2 (1964):175-76.

Jackson
-UFO (NL)
    1956, Nov.14/W.J. Hull
        Richard Hall, ed., The UFO Evidence
        (Washington: NICAP, 1964), pp.4-5.
        Edward U. Condon, ed., Scientific
        Study of Unidentified Flying Objects
        (N.Y.: Bantam, 1969 ed.), pp.127-
        28.

Kimberly
-UFO (CE-1)
    1976, Jan.9
        "Noteworthy UFO Sightings," Ufology
        2 (summer 1976):62.

Lanett
-UFO (NL)
    1973, Sep./Dave Maddux
        Columbus (Ga.) Enquirer, 10 Sep.
        1973.
        Leonard H. Stringfield, Situation
        Red. The UFO Siege (N.Y.: Fawcett
        Crest, 1977 ed.), p.22, quoting
        Nat'l Enquirer (undated).

Lawrence co.
-Petroglyphs
        Spencer & Betty Ann Waters, "Petro-
        glyphs in Lawrence County, Alabama,"
        Tennessee Arch. 12 (1956):16-21. il.

Leeds
-Ball lightning
    1894, June 25/Bud Simpson
        St. Louis (Mo.) Republic, 26 June
        1894.
-UFO (?)
    1972, June 16
        Ted Phillips, Physical Traces Associ-
        ated with UFO Sightings (Evanston:
        Center for UFO Studies, 1975), p.
        110.

Lexington
-UFO (CE-1)
    1973, Feb.2/Philip Nix/Hwy.64
        "Flap in Alabama," APRO Bull. 21

Dr.
Birmingham News, 30 Oct.1969.
"Landing Claimed at Mobile," APRO
Bull. 18 (Sep.-Oct.1969):1.
Nat'l Enquirer, 22 Feb.1970.
-UFO (NL)
1964, April 17
Mobile Register, 2 May 1964.
1971, Aug.13/Holcombe Ave.
Mobile Press-Register, 15 Aug.1971.
1975, July/Kushla
1975, July 24
1975, Oct.29/nr. airport
1975, Nov.30/betw. Cottage Hill and
Hillcrest
"Alabama UFO Group Summarizes 1975,"
Skylook, no.102 (May 1976):6-7.
-UFO (R-V)
1952, Sep./Brookley AFB
Edward J. Ruppelt, The Report on Un-
identified Flying Objects (Garden
City: Doubleday, 1956), pp.193-94.
1954, June 30/Brookley AFB
"Air Force and News Wires Clam Up As
Science Ponders Life on Mars," CRIFO
Newsl., 6 Aug.1954,p.3.
Coral and Jim Lorenzen, UFOs: The
Whole Story (N.Y.: Signet, 1969),
pp.57-58, quoting UP release, 2
July 1954.

Molloy
-Ghost light
1950s/Gardner Lampkin/S of Hwy.18
(Editorial), Fate 12 (July 1959):17.

Montevallo
-Anomalous hole in ground
1972, Dec.2/Hershel Byrd/=giant sink-
hole
(Editorial), Probe the Unknown 1
(Oct.1973):65.
-Telepathy
1940, summer/Justus Joiner
Mrs. L.D. Gilbert, "I Sent a Mental
Message," Fate 10 (July 1957):17.

Montgomery
-Clairvoyance research
1930s/C. Hilton Rice
J.G. Pratt, "The Work of Dr. C. Hil-
ton Rice in Extra-Sensory Percep-
tion," J.Parapsych. 1 (1937):239-59.
-Fall of weblike substance
1898, Nov.21
"Floating Spider Webs," Monthly Weath-
er Rev. 26 (Dec.1898):566, quoting
Montgomery Advertiser (undated).
-Precognition
1811/Tecumseh/Tuckabatchee Town
James Mooney, "The Ghost-Dance Relig-
ion and the Sioux Outbreak of 1890,"
Ann.Rept.Bur.Am.Ethn. 14 (1892-93):
687.
Virginia Stumbough, "Tecumseh's
Earthquake," Fate 6 (Aug.1953):91-
95.
Allan W. Eckert, The Frontiersmen
(N.Y.: Bantam, 1970 ed.), pp.632-37.
James Penick, Jr., The New Madrid

Earthquakes of 1811-1812 (Columbia:
Univ. of Missouri, 1976), pp.126-29.
1860, Jan./Emma Hardinge/State House
Emma Hardinge Britten, Modern American Spiritualism (N.Y.: The Author,
1870), pp.416-19.
-UFO (DD)
1947, July 7/Tommy Estes/Lanier
Montgomery Advertiser, 8 July 1947.
-UFO (NL)
1947, June 28/William H. Kayko/Max-
well AFB
Edward J. Ruppelt, The Report on Un-
identified Flying Objects (Garden
City: Doubleday, 1956), p.19.
Ted Bloecher, Report on the UFO Wave
of 1947 (Washington: NICAP, 1967),
p.III-3.
1948, July 24/Clarence S. Chiles/20
mi.SW/=meteor?
L. Taylor Hansen, "The Mystery Ship,"
Fate 1 (winter 1949):30-33.
Sidney Shallett, "What You Can Be-
lieve About Flying Saucers: Part
Two," Sat.Eve.Post, 7 May 1949, pp.
36,189.
Curtis Fuller, "The Flying Saucers--
Fact or Fiction," Flying 47 (July
1950):16,59-60.
Donald Keyhoe, Flying Saucers Are
Real (N.Y: Fawcett, 1950), pp.67-
71.
Edward J. Ruppelt, The Report on Un-
identified Flying Objects (Garden
City: Doubleday, 1956), pp.40-41.
Donald H. Menzel & Lyle G. Boyd, The
World of Flying Saucers (Garden
City: Doubleday, 1963), pp.108-13.
David Michael Jacobs, The UFO Con-
troversy in America (Bloomington:
Univ. of Indiana, 1975), pp.46,309.
1973, Sep.20/Mrs. Charles Rogers/4614
Sunshine Dr.
Montgomery Advertiser, 21 Sep.1973.

Morgan co.
-UFO (?)
1976, Feb.26/=plane?
Gadsden Times, 27 Feb.1976.

Morris
-UFO (CE-1)
1976, Jan.5
"Noteworthy UFO Sightings," Ufology
2 (summer 1976):62.

Moundville
-Archeological site
1000-1500
Clarence B. Moore, "Moundville Re-
visited," J.Acad.Nat.Sci.Philadel-
phia 13 (1907):337-405.
W.B. Jones, "Recent Work at Mound-
ville," Arrow Points 16 (1930):2-
4. il.
Charles E. Snow, "Anthropological
Studies at Moundville," Mus.Pap.
Alabama Mus.Nat.Hist., no.15 (1941).
il.
Mound State Monument, Moundville,

Alabama (Alabama Mus.Nat.Hist., Pap.
no.20, 1942). il.
Christopher Spalding Peebles, "Moundville and Surrounding Sites," Mem.
Soc'y Am.Arch., no.25 (1971):68-91.
il.
Franklin Folsom, America's Ancient
Treasures (N.Y.: Rand McNally,
1974), pp.107-108.

Newton
-Anomalous hole in ground
1860s-   /west bank of Choctawatchee
River
"Mystery of Alabama's 'Hanging Hole,'"
Fate 20 (Dec.1967):65.

Ohatchee
-UFO (CE-2)
1976, Feb.18/Charlotte Staples/Hwy.77
Talladega-Sylacauga Daily Home, 20
Feb.1976. il.
Jerry Harris, "We Were Chased by
UFOs!" Fate 29 (Oct.1976):52-56. il.

Painter
-Fall of ice
1973, Sep.2/Lonnie West
(Editorial), Fate 27 (May 1974):20,
24.

Parrish
-UFO (NL)
1973, Oct.11/Mrs. Norman Blanton
"World Round-Up," Flying Saucer Rev.
20 (Oct.1974):30-31, quoting News-
Extra, 16 Dec.1973.

Peeks Corner
-UFO (NL)
1976, May 9/James Hester
Clifford Collier, "UFOlog," Ufology
2 (fall 1976):53-55.

Pell City
-UFO (CE-2)
1957, Nov.6/James Moore/7 mi.E
Birmingham News, 6 Nov.1957.
Aimé Michel, Flying Saucers and the
Straight-Line Mystery (N.Y.: Cri-
terion, 1958), p.247.

Phenix City
-Carthaginian coin
1957
Joseph B. Mahan & Douglas C. Braith-
waite, "Discovery of Ancient Coins
in the United States," Anthro.J.
Canada 13, no.2 (1975):15-17. il.
Norman Totten, "Carthaginian Coins
Found in Arkansas and Alabama,"
Occ.Pub.Epigraphic Soc'y 4, no.88
(Oct.1977):5-6. il.

Pike co.
-UFO (?)
1973, Oct.17
Colman Von Keviczky, "The 1973 UFO
Invasion: Part I," Official UFO 1
(Aug.1975):16,18.

Prichard
-Haunt
1958/Bliunt High School
Mai Kampitt, "The Ghost Who Gradua-
ted," Fate 22 (Apr.1969):79-81.
-UFO (CE-1)
1968, March 2
Mobile Press, 5 Mar.1968.

Rainsville
-UFO (NL)
1976, May 9/Jerrold Bethune/4 mi.NE
Clifford Collier, "UFOlog," Ufology
2 (fall 1976):53,55.

Ramer
-UFO (DD)
1953, Feb.16
U.S. Air Force, Projects Grudge and
Bluebook Reports 1-12 (Washington:
NICAP, 1968), p.196.

Red Bay
-Fall of unknown object
1957, Dec./William Blackburn/12 mi.NE
(Editorial), Fate 11 (Apr.1958):19-
20.
Coral E. Lorenzen, The Shadow of the
Unknown (N.Y.: Signet, 1970), p.61.

Renfroe
-UFO (?)
1973, Oct.15/=balloon
Columbia (S.C.) Record, 17 Oct.1973.

Rock City
-Precipitating tree
1950s/E.C. Aldridge
(Editorial), Fate 12 (July 1959):20-
21.

Saint Clair co.
-UFO (NL)
1976, Feb.26
Gadsden Times, 27 Feb.1976.

Saraland
-UFO (NL)
1966, Jan.7
Mobile Register, 13 Jan.1966.

Satsuma
-UFO (NL)
1966, Jan.11
Mobile Register, 13 Jan.1966.

Selma
-UFO (?)
1950, March 30
Richard Hall, ed., The UFO Evidence
(Washington: NICAP, 1964), p.14.

Semmes
-Weather control
1948, Nov./Lulubelle Turner
Lulubelle Turner & Anna E. Gilbert,
"Power of Prayer," Fate 9 (June 1956)
:66.

Spanish Fort
-UFO (?)
  1973, Aug.16/=meteor
    Mobile Register, 16 Aug.1973.

Sylacauga
-Fall of anomalous meteorite
  1954, Nov.30/Mrs. E. Hulitt Hodges/Oak
  Grove/caused injury
    George W. Swindel & Walter B. Jones,
    "The Sylacauga, Talladega County,
    Alabama, Aerolite: A Recent Meteor-
    ite Fall That Injured a Human
    Being," Meteoritics 1 (1954):125-32.
    "Meteorites--The Sylacauga Incident,"
    CRIFO Newsl., 4 Feb.1955, p.1.
    Gray Barker, ed., The Saucerian Re-
    view (Clarksburg, W.V.: Saucerian,
    1956), p.84. il.

Talladega
-Fire anomaly
  1958, Aug.25-Sep./Calvin Tuck
    R.E. Hogan, "Fire Poltergeist in Ala-
    bama?" Fate 12 (Jan.1959):44-52. il.
    (Letter), Malcolm Claire, Fate 12
    (Apr.1959):117,120.
-UFO (?)
  1957, Nov.6
    Aimé Michel, Flying Saucers and the
    Straight-Line Mystery (N.Y.: Cri-
    terion, 1958), p.256.
-UFO (CE-1)
  1976, March 27/Fariah Parker
    Jerry Harris, "We Were Chased by
    UFOs!" Fate 29 (Oct.1976):52,56.
-UFO (DD)
  1947, July 12
    Birmingham News & Age-Herald, 13
    July 1947.
-UFO (NL)
  1976, March 28
    Jerry Harris, "We Were Chased by
    UFOs!" Fate 29 (Oct.1976):52,56.

Tanner Williams
-Phantom
  1973, Oct.11
    Pottstown (Pa.) Mercury, 19 Oct.1973.
-UFO (CE-2)
  1973, Oct.16/Ira Lundy
    Mobile Press-Register, 17 Oct.1973.

Tillmans Corner
-UFO (NL)
  1975, March 20/U.S.90
    "Alabama UFO Group Summarizes 1975,"
    Skylook, no.102 (May 1976):6,7.

Town Creek
-Humanoid
  1969, summer/Mrs. Floyd Milligan
    Asheville (N.C.) Times, 4 June 1969;
    and 4 Aug.1969.

Troy
-Hex
  n.d.
    Alabama Writers' Program, Alabama: A
    Guide to the Deep South (N.Y.: Rich-

ard R. Smith, 1941), p.380.

Trussville
-UFO (NL)
  1975, Oct.25
    "Noteworthy UFO Sightings," Ufology
    2 (spring 1976):42.

Tuscaloosa
-Haunt
  1950s-   /Smith Hall Museum, Univ. of
  Alabama
    (Editorial), Fate 25 (Aug.1972):28-31,
    quoting The Crimson White (undated).

Tuskegee
-Corpse anomaly
  1894, Aug.28/J.S. Webb/1 mi.S
    J.M. Stedman & J.T. Anderson, "Ob-
    servations on a So-Called Petrified
    Man," Am.Naturalist 29 (1895):326-
    29.

Wetumpka
-Hex
  1959/Mrs. Francis Webb Smith
    Bill D. Schul, "The Link," Probe the
    Unknown 1 (Dec.1973):34,38.
-Meteorite crater
  6.5 k.diam./probable
    Thornton L. Neathery, Robert D. Bent-
    ley & Gregory C. Lines, "Cryptoex-
    plosive Structure near Wetumpka,
    Alabama," Bull.Geol.Soc'y Am. 87
    (1976):567-73. il.

Wilmer
-UFO (CE-2)
  1966, Jan.7/Gary Finch
    "Past Sightings Come to Light," APRO
    Bull. 16 (Jan.-Feb.1968):5-6.

Wilsonville
-Fall of frogs
  1888, summer
    (Letter), Mrs. E. Williamson, Fate
    11 (July 1958):126.

Winfield
-Phantom image
  1960-   /Robert L. Musgrove/tombstone/
  3 mi.S on Hwy.43
    (Editorial), Fate 16 (Feb.1963):16.

        B. Physical Features

Alabama R.
-Archeological site
    Frank Volkmann, "Stone Riddle in
    Georgia," Fate 30 (Jan.1977):70,75.

Bear Creek
-Humanoid
  1880s/Jade Davis/Horseshoe Bend
    Red Bay News, 6 May 1976.

Choccolocco Creek
-Humanoid
  1969, May-June/Johnny Ray Teague

Anniston Star, 30 May 1969; and 8
June 1969.

Colbert Creek
-Archeological site
     William S. Webb & David L. DeJarnette,
     "An Archeological Survey of Pick-
     wick Basin," Bull.Bur.Am.Ethn., no.
     129 (1942):92-93. il.

Flint Creek
-Archeological site
     ca.7000-5000 B.C.
     James W. Cambron & Spencer A. Waters,
     "Flint Creek Rock Shelter (Part 1),"
     Tennessee Arch. 15 (1959):72-87. il.

Joe Wheeler Dam
-UFO (NL)
     1973, Feb.4/Bill Rogers
     "Flap in Alabama," APRO Bull. 21
     (Jan.-Feb.1973):12.

Mobile Bay
-UFO (CE-3)
     1973, Nov.17/west shore
     "Alabama UFO Group Summarizes 1975,"
     Skylook, no.102 (May 1976):7.
-UFO (NL)
     1973, Nov.9/west shore
     "Alabama UFO Group Summarizes 1975,"
     Skylook, no.102 (May 1976):7.

Purdy L.
-UFO (?)
     1957, Nov.6
     Aimé Michel, Flying Saucers and the
     Straight-Line Mystery (N.Y.: Criter-
     ion, 1958), p.256.

Russell Cave
-Archeological site
     ca.7000 B.C.-1000 A.D.
     Carl F. Miller, "Life Eight Thousand
     Years Ago Uncovered in an Alabama
     Cave," Nat'l Geographic 110 (Oct.
     1956):542 58. il.
     Carl F. Miller, "Radiocarbon Dates
     from an Early Archaic Deposit in
     Russell Cave, Alabama," Am.Antiquity
     23 (1957):84.
     Carl F. Miller, "Russell Cave: New
     Light on Stone Age Life," Nat'l Geo-
     graphic 113 (1958):426-37. il.
     John W. Griffin, "Preliminary Report
     on Excavations in Russell Cave Na-
     tional Monument," Proc.Southeastern
     Arch.Conference 19 (1962):33-35.
     Carl F. Miller, "Paleo-Indian and
     Early Archaic Projectile Point Forms
     from Russell Cave, Northern Ala-
     bama," Anthro.J.Canada 3, no.2
     (1965):2-5.

Ryan Mt.
-UFO (CE-4)
     1975, April/John Womack
     John Womack & Hugh Helms, "I Was
     Picked Up by a UFO," Official UFO
     2 (May 1977):27,56-59.

Tombigbee R.
-Phantom ship
     n.d.
     Brad Steiger, "1972: A Bumper Year
     for Hauntings," Beyond Reality, no.
     4 (May 1973):15,17.

C. Ethnic Groups

Creek Indians
-Flood myth
     John R. Swanton, "Religious Beliefs
     and Medical Practices of the Creek
     Indians," Ann.Rept.Bur.Am.Ethn. 42
     (1924-25):473,487-88.
-Phantom (myth)
     isti luputski
     John R. Swanton, "Religious Beliefs
     and Medical Practices of the Creek
     Indians," Ann.Rept.Bur.Am.Ethn. 42
     (1924-25):473,496-97.
-Shamanism
     John R. Swanton, "Religious Beliefs
     and Medical Practices of the Creek
     Indians," Ann.Rept.Bur.Am.Ethn. 42
     (1924-25):473,631-36.
-Similarity to European Bronze Age cul-
ture
     Colin Renfrew, Before Civilization
     (N.Y.: Knopf, 1973), pp.231-37.
-Weather control
     John R. Swanton, "Religious Beliefs
     and Medical Practices of the Creek
     Indians," Ann.Rept.Bur.Am.Ethn. 42
     (1924-25):473,629-31.

D. Unspecified Localities

-Archeological sites
     pebble-tool complex
     Matthew Lively, The Lively Complex
     (Birmingham: Alabama Archeological
     Society, 1965).
     Matthew Lively, "The Lively Complex,"
     J.Alabama Arch. 11, pt.2 (1965):
     103-22. il.
     Daniel W. Josselyn, "Announcing Ac-
     cepted American Pebble Tools," An-
     thro.J.Canada 4, no.1 (1966):24-31.
     Daniel W. Josselyn, "Pebble Tools:
     An Open Letter from Alabama," INFO
     J., no.1 (spring 1967):35-37.
     A.B. Hooper, "Pebble Tools: Lively
     Complex Duplicated in Bear Creek
     Watershed," J.Alabama Arch. 14, pt.
     1 (1968):1-16. il.
     Alice M. Burns, et al., "Lively Com-
     plex Tools on Other Than Pebbles,"
     J.Alabama Arch. 14, no.2 (1968):51-
     61. il.

-Men-in-black
     1932, May/Stanley Spears/north sector
     (Letter), Fate 6 (Mar.1953):120-22.

-Petroglyphs
     B. Bart Henson, "Stone Markings by
     Aborigines of North Alabama," J.
     Alabama Arch. 10, pt.1 (1964):61-65.

FLORIDA

A. Populated Places

Alafia
-Fall of unknown object
  1955, Nov./W.R. Wacaser
    Ft. Lauderdale Sunday News, 1 Apr.
    1956.

Apalachicola
-Archeological site
  Francis Harper, ed., The Travels of
    William Bartram (New Haven: Yale
    Univ., 1958), Part 3, ch. v, pp.246-
    51.
-Phantom image
  1971, Sep./First Born Holiness Church
    David Techter, "A Flap of Glowing
    Crosses," Fate 25 (June 1972):52-
    54, quoting Tallahassee Democrat
    (undated).

Apopka
-Humanoid
  1977, Oct.3/Donnie Hall/John's Nursery
    Apopka Chief, 7 Oct.1977.
-UFO (CE-2)
  1970, June 29/Lester-Schopke Rd.
    "Car Chase Incident in Florida,"
    APRO Bull. 19 (July-Aug.1970):1,5.

Arcadia
-Fall of fish
  1940s/Paul Henderson/Carlstrom Field
    (Letter), Fate 15 (July 1962):120-21.

Ashton
-UFO (CE-1)
  1963, Aug.21/J. Manson Valentine
    Charles Berlitz, The Bermuda Triangle
    (Garden City: Doubleday, 1974), p.
    111.

Auburndale
-UFO (NL)
  1969, Jan.6
    Winter Haven News-Chief, 7 Jan.1969.

Avalon Beach
-Poltergeist
  1967-1968/Mickey Childers
    (Editorial), Fate 21 (June 1968):30-
    32, quoting Pensacola News-Journal
    (undated).

Avon Park
-Clairaudience
  1942, Dec./Paul F. Try/bombing range
    Paul F. Try, "My Guardian Voice,"
    Fate 23 (July 1970):71-73.

Bartow
-Phantom automobile
  1934/Lois B. Tracy/S of town
    Lois B. Tracy, "Vanishing Car," Fate

17 (June 1964):60-61.
-Phantom train
  n.d./Oak Ave.
    "They Forgot a Train," Fate 25 (May
    1972):93.
-UFO (NL)
  1975, Nov.4
    "UFO Central," CUFOS News Bull., 1
    Feb.1976, p.11.

Belle Glade
-UFO (CE-2)
  1952, Sep.14/Fred J. Brown/Everglades
    Experimental Station
    Miami Daily News, 16 Sep.1952.

Belleview
-Humanoid
  1977, Oct.2
    Orlando Sentinel, 5 Oct.1977.

Big Cypress Indian Reservation
-UFO (CE-2)
  1965, March 15/James W. Flynn/18 mi.E
    "Man Reported Injured by UFO," UFO
    Inv. 3 (Mar.-Apr.1965):6.
    Coral E. Lorenzen, "UFO Mystery Ray
    Blinds Florida Man," Fate 18 (Sep.
    1965):30-36.

Boca Raton
-UFO (NL)
  1973, Sep.24/W of town
    Pompano Beach Sun-Sentinel, 10 Oct.
    1973.
  1973, Oct.17/U.S.441 nr. Watergate
    Mobile Home Park
    Boca Raton News, 18 Oct.1973.
  1975, Oct.9
    "Noteworthy UFO Sightings," Ufology
    2 (spring 1976):42.
  1976, Jan.26, 29/Peter C. Petraccoro
    "Noteworthy UFO Sightings," Ufology
    2 (summer 1976):62.
    (Letter), Saga UFO Rept. 3 (Oct.1976)
    :6.
  1978, March 1/Edgar Norman/Boca Lago
    Palm Beach Times, 1 Mar.1978.

Bradenton
-Auroral anomaly
  1901, May 30/H.H. Broeck
    "Electrical Phenomena: Incandescent
    Cloud," Monthly Weather Rev. 29
    (Oct.1901):466.
-Precognition
  ca.1970/Geneva Sharp
    Sally Remaley, "Is Psychically Fore-
    warned Always Forearmed?" Fate 24
    (Sep.1971):81,84-85.
-Psychokinesis
  n.d./Gladys Pitman
    Sally Remaley, "A Question of Accu-
    racy," Fate 23 (July 1970):70.

-UFO (CE-2)
  1973, Dec.13/Patrick Thrush/Braden R.
    St. Petersburg Times, 23 Dec.1973.
    Florida Pinellas Times, 31 Dec.1973.
    "Photos, Rocks Offered in Florida
    Sighting," Skylook, no.79 (June
    1974):4-5.
    B. Ann Slate, "Alien Prospectors Are
    Here," Probe the Unknown 3 (Sep.
    1975):40-42,56-57.
-UFO (NL)
  1975, Dec.21
    "UFO Central," CUFOS News Bull., 1
    Feb.1976, p.15.

Bradenton Beach
-Poltergeist
  1967-1969/Glenn P. Thomasson/Romaine's
  Unusuals
    Sally Remaley, "The Perfumed Ghost,"
    Fate 22 (Sep.1969):44-54. il.
    Eileen Sonin, More Canadian Ghosts
    (Richmond Hill, Ont.: Pocket Books,
    1974 ed.), pp.21-22.

Bronson
-UFO (CE-2)
  1964, March 31/4 mi.W on U.S.Alt.27
    "Leading Up to the Big Flap," Fate
    17 (Aug.1964):45,46-47.

Brooksville
-Humanoid
  1964/ Eulah Lewis
  1966, April/Eulah Lewis
  1966, Nov.30
  1967, Jan.
  1967, Sep.11
    Brad Steiger & John Whritenour, The
    Allende Letters: New UFO Breakthrough
    (N.Y.: Award, 1968), pp.79-84,90-91.
    John Green, Sasquatch: The Apes Among
    Us (Seattle: Hancock House, 1978),
    p.272.
  1973, Dec.
    Allen V. Noe, "And Still the Reports
    Roll In..." Pursuit 7 (Jan.1974):17.
  1974, Feb./Ramona Hibner
    B. Ann Slate, "Man-Ape's Reign of
    Terror," Saga UFO Rept. 4 (Aug.1977)
    :20,54.
-UFO (CE-1)
  1974, Jan./nr. Lucky K Ranch
    B. Ann Slate, "Man-Ape's Reign of
    Terror," Saga UFO Rept. 4 (Aug.1977)
    :20,54.
-UFO (NL)
  1962, Nov.17/F.L. Swindal/SE of town
    Thomas M. Olsen, ed., The Reference
    for Outstanding UFO Sighting Reports
    (Riderwood, Md.: UFO Information Re-
    trieval Center, 1966), pp.82-83.
  1966, Aug.4/Marcile Ganley
  1966, Aug.17/Barbara Mason
  1966, Aug.31/Norman Hill
    Robert Loftin, Identified Flying Sau-
    cers (N.Y.: David McKay, 1968), p.
    80.

Bunnell
-UFO (CE-3)
  1960, Sep.2
    David Webb & Ted Bloecher, "MUFON's
    Humanoid Study Group Very Active,"
    Skylook, no.93 (Aug.1975):9.
-UFO (NL)
  1975, Dec.12/Charlotte Shearer/NW of
  town
    Jim Jones, "Repeating Reports in
    Florida," APRO Bull. 24 (Jan.1976):
    1,3.

Cape Coral
-Humanoid
  1975, Feb.2/Richard Davis
    Marty Wolf, "An Interview with Bob
    Morgan," Pursuit 8 (July 1975):70-
    71.

Carrabelle
-Sea monster
  1896, Aug./"Crescent City"/=unknown
  shark?
    Bernard Heuvelmans, In the Wake of
    the Sea-Serpents (N.Y.: Hill & Wang,
    1968), p.140, quoting Shipping Ga-
    zette, 21 Aug.1896.

Cassadaga
-Inner development
  1893-   /National Spiritualist Association of Churches/Box 128
    Nandor Fodor, Encyclopaedia of Psy-
    chic Science (London: Arthurs,
    1933), p.262.
    Nancy Beth Jackson, "Cassadaga: The
    Spiritualist Spa," Psychic 2 (Feb.
    1971):40-44.
    R. Laurence Moore, In Search of White
    Crows (N.Y.: Oxford Univ., 1977),
    pp.67-68.
    J. Gordon Melton, Encyclopedia of
    American Religions, 2 vols. (Wil-
    mington, N.C.: Consortium, 1978),
    2:96-98.
-Spirit mediums
  1875-   /Eloise Page, etc.
    George L. Traffarn, "Experiences
    with Two Mediums," J.ASPR 15 (1921):
    576-612.
    (Letter), Maxwell S. Dunn, Fate 8
    (Nov.1955):126-28.
    New York Times, 15 Mar.1970, sec.X,
    p.3.
    Kansas City (Mo.) Times, 7 Mar.1974.
    Jim Brandon, Weird America (N.Y.:
    Dutton, 1978), p.59.

Cassia
-UFO (CE-1)
  1970, Jan.29/James K. Pendarvis/U.S.44
    George D. Fawcett, Quarter Century
    of Studies of UFOs in Florida, North
    Carolina and Tennessee (Mount Airy:
    Pioneer, 1975), p.15.

Charlotte Harbor
-UFO (CE-1)

1972, July 10/Scott McCormick
Punta Gorda Herald-News, 15 July
1972.

Chester
-Hex
1936/Brundas Hartwell
Federal Writers' Program, Florida: A
Guide to the Southernmost State
(N.Y.: Oxford Univ., 1939), p.131.

Citrus co.
-Humanoid
1975/John Sohl/Rock Crusher Quarry
St. Petersburg Times, 1 Jan.1976.
B. Ann Slate, "Man-Ape's Reign of
Terror," Saga UFO Rept. 4 (Aug.1977)
:20,22-23.

Clearwater
-Giant bird tracks
1948, Feb.-March 6
Tampa Sun-Tribune, 14 Nov.1948.
Ivan T. Sanderson, More Things (N.Y.:
Pyramid, 1969), pp.34-55.
-UFO (?)
1964, July 4/R.H. Henry/=flares
Clearwater Sun, 6 July 1964; and 9
July 1964.
-UFO (DD)
1947, July 7/Imogene Richards/609 High-
land Ave.
Tampa Morning Tribune, 8 July 1947.
-UFO (NL)
1975, Nov.5
"UFO Central," CUFOS News Bull., 1
Feb.1976, p.12.

Cooper City
-UFO (NL)
1973, Oct.7, 10/Neal Riley
Pompano Beach Sun-Sentinel, 10 Oct.
1973.

Coral Gables
-UFO (?)
1952, Aug.14
Richard Hall, ed., The UFO Evidence
(Washington: NICAP, 1964), p.153.

Coral Springs
-UFO (NL)
1973, Sep.27
Pompano Beach Sun-Sentinel, 10 Oct.
1973.

Cortez
-Phantom ship
1970, Aug.8/Glenn P. Thomasson/sea to
SW
Glenn P. Thomasson, "Message from a
Phantom Ship," Fate 24 (June 1971):
63-67.

Crawfordville
-UFO (NL)
1976, Jan.1
"Noteworthy UFO Sightings," Ufology
2 (summer 1976):62.

Crescent City
-UFO (CE-1)
1968, Feb.28/Robert F. Reilman
Donald E. Keyhoe & Gordon I.R. Lore,
Jr., UFOs: A New Look (Washington:
NICAP, 1969), pp.5-6.

Crystal River
-Humanoid
1976, Feb.
B. Ann Slate, "Man-Ape's Reign of
Terror," Saga UFO Rept. 4 (Aug.1977)
:20,55-56.

Dade co.
-Humanoid
1975, March 24/Michael Bennett/Black
Pt.
John Green, Sasquatch: The Apes Among
Us (Seattle: Hancock House, 1978),
p.279.

Dade City
-Fall of anomalous meteorite
n.d./I.T. Cumbie
(Editorial), Fate 14 (Sep.1961):10,
quoting Tampa Tribune (undated).

Davie
-UFO (NL)
1976, March 14
"Noteworthy UFO Sightings," Ufology
2 (summer 1976):62.

Daytona Beach
-Clairvoyance
1950s/Carol Hunn
George F. Brietz, "Everyone Has Psy-
chic Powers," Fate 9 (May 1956):44-
48.
-Electromagnetic anomaly
1970, March 15-April
Washington (D.C.) Post, 28 Mar.1970,
p.C2.
(Editorial), Fate 23 (Aug.1970):30-
34.
-Phantom airplane
1935, Feb.27/Forrest Additon/Hotel Day-
tona Beach
Richard Winer, The Devil's Triangle
(N.Y.: Bantam, 1974), pp.155-57.
-Poltergeist
1967, May-June/Mary Alice Cord
(Editorial), Fate 20 (Oct.1967):7-9.
Susy Smith, The Power of the Mind
(Radnor, Pa.: Chilton, 1975), pp.
205-208.

Defuniak Springs
-Haunt
1895-   /William H. Wesley/Eden State
Garden
William H. Wesley, "The Trouble with
Eden," Fate 32 (Jan.1979):86-90. il.

DeLand
-UFO (CE-2)
1968, Nov.
George D. Fawcett, "Florida Report,"
Flying Saucers, June 1970, p.31.

-UFO (DD)
   1969, Aug./Billy Anderson
      George D. Fawcett, Quarter Century
      of Studies of UFOs in Florida, North
      Carolina and Tennessee (Mount Airy:
      Pioneer, 1975), p.79. il.
      DeLand Sun News, 16 Jan.1978.
   1978, Jan.15/Bruce Dahlstrand/Stetson
   Univ.
      DeLand Sun News, 16 Jan.1978. il.
-UFO (NL)
   1957, Oct.23/Gladys Mraz
      (Letter), Fate 11 (July 1958):114.
   1968, July 21
      Brad Steiger & Joan Whritenour, Fly-
      ing Saucer Invasion: Target--Earth
      (N.Y.: Award, 1969), pp.98-99.

DeLeon Springs
-UFO (NL)
   1968, July 21/trailer court
      Brad Steiger & Joan Whritenour, Fly-
      ing Saucer Invasion: Target--Earth
      (N.Y.: Award, 1969), pp.98-99.

Delray Beach
-Astrology
   1968-   /Herb Stanton
      Warren Smith, "How Did the Seers in
      1970?" Fate 24 (Feb.1971):84,90.
      Herb Stanton, "Voodoo Worked at Mid-
      night," Fate 27 (Dec.1974):74-76.
      "Checking the Prophets," Fate 29
      (May 1976):73.
-Humanoid
   1977, Feb./golf course
      Miami News, 18 Feb.1977.
   1977, March 25/David Smith/W of town
      Boynton Beach News-Journal, 31 Mar.
      1977.

Destin
-UFO (NL)
   1973, Oct.14/Philip M. Lynch/15 mi.E
      Ft. Walton Beach Playground News, 16
      Oct.1973.

Dunedin
-Fall of frogs
   1949, Sep.
      St. Petersburg Times, 18 Sep.1949.
-River monster
   1948, Nov.14/Suwanee R.
      Ivan T. Sanderson, More Things (N.Y.:
      Pyramid, 1969), p.38.

Dunnellon
-Ball lightning
   1965, Aug.25/Robert B. Greenlee
      Frederick B. Mohr, "A Truly Remark-
      able Fly," Science 151 (1966):634.
-Humanoid
   1976, May/Donald Duncan
   1976, July 17/Chris Duncan
      B. Ann Slate, "Florida's Rampaging
      Man-Ape," Saga UFO Rept. 4 (July
      1977):32,34.
      B. Ann Slate, "Man-Ape's Reign of
      Terror," Saga UFO Rept. 4 (Aug.1977)
      :20,56-57.

Eau Gallie
-UFO (NL)
   1953, Jan.4
      U.S. Air Force, Projects Grudge and
      Bluebook Reports 1-12 (Washington:
      NICAP, 1968), p.189.

Eglin AFB
-UFO (DD)
   1961, Jan.22/Harry Caslar/beach
      Richard Hall, ed., The UFO Evidence
      (Washington: NICAP, 1964), p.95.

Elfers
-Humanoid
   1967, Jan.
   1967, summer/Ralph Chambers
      Brad Steiger & Joan Whritenour, Al-
      lende Letters: New UFO Breakthrough
      (N.Y.: Award, 1968), pp.78-79,89.

Englewood
-Humanoid
   1976, June/Roberts St., Grove City/=
   bear?
      Punta Gorda Herald-News, 18 June
      1976.
-UFO (?)
   1956, April 4/=meteor?
      Sarasota Herald-Tribune, 5 Apr.1956.
      "Case 155," CRIFO Orbit, 4 May 1956,
      p.1.
-UFO (NL)
   1968, Dec.2/Howard Schmidt/"Vagabond"/
   15 mi.W
      George D. Fawcett, "Florida Report,"
      Flying Saucers, June 1970, p.31.

Estero
-Inner development
   1894-1940s/Cyrus R. Teed/Koreshan cult
      Koresh [Cyrus Reed Teed], The Cellu-
      lar Cosmogony (Chicago: Guiding
      Star, 1899).
      Koresh [Cyrus Reed Teed], The Immor-
      tal Manhood (Chicago: Guiding Star,
      1902).
      Koresh [Cyrus Reed Teed], Fundamen-
      tals of Koreshan Universology (Es-
      tero: Guiding Star, 1922).
      Koresh [Cyrus Reed Teed], The Mys-
      tery of the Gentiles (Estero: Guid-
      ing Star, 1926).
      "This Hollow World," Newsweek, 6 Dec.
      1948, p.26.
      Karl H. Grismer, The Story of Fort
      Myers (St.Petersburg: St.Petersburg
      Print Co., 1949).
      Marjorie F. Thole, "They Live Inside
      the Earth," Fate 9 (Aug.1956):74-79.
      New York Times, 5 Mar.1967.

Everglades
-UFO (NL)
   1968, April 18/George M. Blair/15 mi.
   away on U.S.41
      George M. Blair, "1968 Florida Sight-
      ing," Skylook, no.53 (Apr.1972):20-
      21.

Fernandina Beach
-Skyquake
 1974, Jan.20
  Miami Herald, 22 Jan.1974.
-UFO (NL)
 1973, Sep.30
  Jacksonville Journal, 1 Oct.1973.

Flagler co.
-UFO (NL)
 1975, Dec.14/Tedra Middleton/Flagler
 Estates
  Gray Barker, "America's Captured Flying Saucers: Cover-Up of the Century," *Saga UFO Rept.* 4 (May 1977):
  32,64-66.

Fort Lauderdale
-Contactee
 1970s/Dave W. Bent
  J. Gordon Melton, *Encyclopedia of
  American Religions*, 2 vols. (Wil-
  mington, N.C.: Consortium, 1978),
  2:211.
-Disappearance
 1945, Dec.5/Charles C. Taylor/Flight
 19/ocean to N or NE
  Miami Herald, 6-10 Dec.1945, p.1.
  New York Times, 9 Mar.1946, p.9.
  *Board of Investigation into Five Mis-
  sing TBM Airplanes* (Washington: U.S.
  Navy, 1946).
  Allen W. Eckert, "The Mystery of the
  Lost Patrol," *Am.Legion Mag.*, Apr.
  1962.
  Edward Vance, "Limitless Reach of the
  Mind," *Fate* 21 (Oct.1968):51,54.
  Michael McDonell, "Lost Patrol,"
  Naval Aviation News, June 1973, p.8.
  Charles Berlitz, *The Bermuda Triangle*
  (Garden City: Doubleday, 1974), pp.
  12-21.
  Richard Winer, *The Devil's Triangle*
  (N.Y.: Bantam, 1974), pp.1-24.
  Lawrence David Kusche, *The Bermuda
  Triangle Mystery--Solved* (N.Y.:
  Harper & Row, 1975), pp.97-122. il.
  Stuart W. Greenwood, "Disorientation
  on Flight 19," *Can.UFO Rept.*, no.
  20 (1975):16-18.
  X, "Navy to Investigate Sunken Air-
  craft," *Pursuit* 10 (summer 1977):
  70-72.
 1972, March 19/David La France
  Charles Berlitz, *Without a Trace*
  (N.Y.: Ballantine, 1978 ed.), pp.
  34,36.
 1972, June 19/Tom Robinson/dinghy/off-
 shore
 1973, Aug.10/Robert N. Fischer/Beech-
 craft Bonanza/ocean to SE
  Richard Winer, *The Devil's Triangle*
  (N.Y.: Bantam, 1974), pp.58-62,149-
  51.
 1976, Dec.20/Herb Rippe/sloop/ocean to
 SE
  Richard Winer, *From the Devil's Triangle to the Devil's Jaw* (N.Y.: Bantam, 1977), pp.8-9.
-Healing

 1950s/Clifton M. Stone/447 SW Third
  John Goldstein, "Florida's Psychic
  Healer," *Fate* 7 (Oct.1954):57-61.
  Guy Archette, "New Cures by Florida's
  Psychic Healer," *Fate* 11 (Apr.1958)
  :73-76.
-Humanoid
 1974, Jan.
  Allen V. Noe, "And Still the Reports
  Roll In..." *Pursuit* 7 (Jan.1974):
  16,18.
-Mystery plane crash
 1960/Mooney 4-seater/3 mi.offshore
  Richard Winer, *From the Devil's Tri-
  angle to the Devil's Jaw* (N.Y.:
  Bantam, 1977), pp.11-12.
 1967, Jan.11/Charles Lundgren/Chase
 YC-122
  Miami Herald, 12 Jan.1967, p.B1.
  Richard Winer, *The Devil's Triangle*
  (N.Y.: Bantam, 1974), pp.47-48.
-Sea monster
 1920, July/"Craigsmere"
  Bernard Heuvelmans, *In the Wake of
  the Sea-Serpents* (N.Y.: Hill & Wang,
  1968), pp.463-64.
-Sea monster (carcass)
 1885, spring/Rev.Mr. Gordon/New River
 Inlet/=whale-shark?
  J.B. Holder, "The Great Unknown,"
  Century Mag. 44 (June 1892):247,
  252-53. il.
-UFO (?)
 1975, Nov./Priscilla Gessler
  Robert Shapiro, "Florida Flurries,"
  Ufology 2 (spring 1976):28.
-UFO (CE-1)
 1952, March/Lillian Roth/N on U.S.1
  Timothy Green Beckley, "Saucers and
  Celebrities," *Saga UFO Rept.* 2 (sum-
  mer 1975):39.
-UFO (DD)
 1975, Nov.5/Deborah Geis/Atlantic Vo-
 cational School
  Gray Barker, "America's Captured Fly-
  ing Saucers: Cover-Up of the Cen-
  tury," *Saga UFO Rept.* 4 (May 1977):
  32,34-35.
-UFO (NL)
 n.d./John Carpenter/offshore
  Richard Winer, *The Devil's Triangle*
  (N.Y.: Bantam, 1974), pp.204-205.
 1956, Aug.21
  "Case 197," *CRIFO Orbit*, 5 Oct.1956,
  pp.1-2.
 1958, May 17
  Richard Hall, ed., *The UFO Evidence*
  (Washington: NICAP, 1964), p.12.
 1963, March 18
  "UFO Seen As Rocket Veers Offcourse,"
  UFO Inv. 2 (Jan.-Feb.1963):4.
 1973, Sep.24/W of Victoria Park
  Pompano Beach Sun-Sentinel, 10 Oct.
  1973.
 1975, Nov.20/Arthur Attridge
  Robert Shapiro, "Florida Flurries,"
  Ufology 2 (spring 1976):28.
 1976, Jan.2
 1976, March 14
  "Noteworthy UFO Sightings," *Ufology*

2 (summer 1976):62.
1976, April 5
1976, May 10
"Noteworthy UFO Sightings," Ufology
2 (fall 1976):60.

Fort Myers
-Humanoid
1975/Jim Spink/SW of town
B. Ann Slate, "Florida's Rampaging
Monster," Saga UFO Rept. 4 (July
1977):32,34.
-Inner development
1950s-   /Ordo Templi Orientis
J. Gordon Melton, Encyclopedia of
American Religions, 2 vols. (Wilmington, N.C.: Consortium, 1978),
2:260.
-Radionics
1971-1972/George W. Meek
Edward Wriothesley Russell, Report
on Radionics (London: Neville Spearman, 1973), pp.189-94.
-UFO (NL)
1976, June 26/nr. Page Field
"Florida Report," APRO Bull. 24 (Oct.
1976):6.

Fort Myers Beach
-Humanoid
1975, Aug.11/nearby island
B. Ann Slate, "Man-Ape's Reign of
Terror," Saga UFO Rept. 4 (Aug.1977)
:20,56.

Fort Pierce
-UFO (?)
1955, Feb.7/Capt. Black/=meteor?
"February, Fireballs, and the Facts,"
CRIFO Newsl., 1 Apr.1955, pp.4-5.
1961, March 23/=aircraft
"UFOs Continue Earth Observation,"
UFO Inv. 1 (Apr.-May 1961):5.
Donald H. Menzel & Lyle G. Boyd, The
World of Flying Saucers (Garden
City: Doubleday, 1963), pp.250-52.
1966, March 23
Jacques Vallee, Passport to Magonia
(Chicago: Regnery, 1969), p.324.
1969, June 25/8 mi. offshore
"Unexplained Lights Dubbed 'Cosmic
Phenomena,'" Skylook, no.23 (Oct.
1969):13.
-UFO (CE-1)
1975, Feb.6
"From the Center for UFO Studies,"
Flying Saucer Rev. 21 (Aug.1975):32.
-UFO (NL)
1949, July 14/Joe Snyder/606 S. 5th St.
Kenneth Arnold & Ray Palmer, The Com-
ing of the Saucers (Boise: The Au-
thors, 1952), p.142.
1974, Jan.18/Danny Prezkop/Indian R.
Fort Pierce News-Tribune, 20 Jan.1974.
1975, Oct.7
"UFO Central," CUFOS News Bull., 1
Feb.1976, p.8.
-Unidentified submerged object
1965, July 5/Dmitri Rebikoff/offshore
Los Angeles (Cal.) Times, 6 July 1965.

(Editorial), Fate 18 (Nov.1965):12-
13.
1975, summer/Charles Pitts/offshore
Timothy Green Beckley, "Saucers and
Celebrities," Saga UFO Rept. 2
(fall 1975):39.

Fort Walton Beach
-UFO (NL)
1973, Oct.15/Greg E. Havard/U.S.10
Ft. Walton Beach Playground News, 16
Oct.1973.

Frostproof
-Weather control
1939, March 27/Lillie Stoate
"Shower of Pebbles," Fortean Soc'y
Mag., no.3 (Jan.1940):12.

Gainesville
-Fall of weblike substance
1892, Sep.20/J.O. Andrews
George Marx, "On Spiders' Web," Proc.
Entomological Soc'y of Washington
2 (1892):385-88.
-UFO (?)
1955, Oct.31/J.H. Bruening/=bombers
refueling?
"Behind Scenes of a Saucer Sighting,"
CRIFO Orbit, 2 Mar.1956, pp.5-6.

Gibsonton
-Humanoid
1977, March 15/Fern Hill Dr./=hoax?
Tampa Times, 18 Mar.1977.
-Humanoid tracks
1977, March/Linda St. x Gibsonton Dr.
Tampa Times, 18 Mar.1977.

Golden Beach
-UFO (?)
1953, March 31/N. Bean
Harold T. Wilkins, Flying Saucers on
the Attack (N.Y.: Ace, 1967 ed.),
p.262.

Greenville
-UFO (NL)
1977, Oct./Jake Sullivan/E on U.S.90
Madison County Carrier, 16 Feb.1978.

Hague
-UFO (CE-1)
1966, April 4
Jacques Vallee, Passport to Magonia
(Chicago: Regnery, 1969), p.327.

Hastings
-UFO (DD)
1975, Dec.26
"Noteworthy UFO Sightings," Ufology
2 (spring 1976):42.
-UFO (NL)
1975, Dec.12/Patricia Beck Goodwin/2
mi.S on Hwy.13
1975, Dec.12/Richard Beck/nr. 10,000
acre block
1975, Dec.12-13/Marcus Barnes/S on Hwy.
13
1975, Dec.14/Larry Masters/Hwy.13

Jim Jones, "Repeating Reports in
Florida," APRO Bull. 24 (Jan.1976):
1,3.
Columbus (O.) Dispatch, 15 Dec.1975,
p.A10.

Hialeah
-Clairvoyance
1978, winter/Henry Sims
"Dead Boy Sounds Fire Alarm," Fate
32 (Jan.1979):90.
-UFO (CE-4)
1979, Jan.3/Filiberto Cardenes/Okee-
chobee Rd.
Miami Herald, 5 Jan.1979.
-UFO (NL)
1975, Nov.11
"UFO Central," CUFOS News Bull., 1
Feb.1976, p.12.

Hobe Sound
-UFO (NL)
1976, Oct.8/George Lauricella/U.S.1
(Letter), Saga UFO Rept. 3 (Mar.
1977):4.

Hollywood
-Animal ESP
1964/J. Fenn Smith
"Wags Tail, Reads Lips," Fate 17
(June 1964):67.
-Inner development
1967-   /Hollywood Coven
J. Gordon Melton, Encyclopedia of
American Religions, 2 vols. (Wil-
mington, N.C.: Consortium, 1978),
2:273.
-UFO (NL)
1973, Aug.22/Frank Burke
Hollywood Sun-Tattler, 22 Aug.1973.
1976, June 30
"Noteworthy UFO Sightings," Ufology
2 (fall 1976):60.

Holmes Beach
-UFO (NL)
1975, Sep.11/Carol Lancaster
Robert Shapiro, "Florida Flurries,"
Ufology 2 (spring 1976):28, quoting
Tampa Islander (undated).

Holopaw
-Humanoid
1963
1966-1967
John A. Keel, Strange Creatures from
Time and Space (Greenwich, Ct.: Fawcett, 1970), p.102.

Holt
-UFO (?)
1955, June 26
J. Allen Hynek, The Hynek UFO Report
(N.Y.: Dell, 1977), p.45.

Homestead
-Architectural anomaly
1920/Ed Leedskalnin/Coral Castle
James W. Moseley, "Florida's Coral
Castle," Saucer News 10 (Sep.1963):

6-8. il.
Vincent H. Gaddis, "Florida's Coral
Castle Mystery," Fate 24 (Mar.1970)
:84-91. il.
(Letter), Otto W. Davidson, Fate 24
(June 1970):145-46.
Marston C. Leonard, "Coral Castle:
Mystical Key to the Great Pyra-
mids?" Psychic World, Jan.1977, pp.
66-70,84. il.
James Dale Davidson, An Eccentric
Guide to the United States (N.Y.:
Berkley, 1977), pp.185-89.
-UFO (CE-2)
1968, April 24
Brad Steiger & Joan Whritenour, Fly-
ing Saucer Invasion: Target--Earth
(N.Y.: Award, 1969), p.97.
-UFO (DD)
1978, Dec.31/Mike Betancourt/8990 SW
112th St.
Homestead Dade News-Leader, 3 Jan.
1979.
-UFO (R-V)
1975, June 17/Joseph Walters/Homestead
AFB
(Letter), R. Drake, Saga UFO Rept.
3 (Apr.1976):77.
Timothy Green Beckley, "Saucers over
Our Cities," Saga UFO Rept. 4 (Aug.
1977):24,74, quoting Miami News
(undated).
-Unidentified submerged object
1966, Sep./offshore/=part of rocket
Hartford (Ct.) Times, 27 Sep.1966.
"News Briefs," Saucer News 14
(spring 1967):16.

Immokalee
-Ancient pyramids
Jim Brandon, Weird America (N.Y.:
Dutton, 1978), p.59.
-UFO (?)
1956, April 4/Mr. Denham/N of town/=
meteor?
Sarasota Herald-Tribune, 5 Apr.1956.
"Case 155," CRIFO Orbit, 4 May 1956,
p.1.

Interlachen
-Ivory-billed woodpecker
1969, April 4, 15/Frank Shields
"An Ivory-Billed Woodpecker," Pur-
suit 2 (July 1969):49.
-UFO (NL)
1960, Nov.28/Josephine Mitchell
(Letter), Fate 14 (Apr.1961):110-12.

Islamorada
-Disappearance
1969, Oct.27/"Keela"/in Florida Bay
to N
Richard Winer, The Devil's Triangle
(N.Y.: Bantam, 1974), pp.84-85.

Jacksonville
-Clairvoyance
1964, March 9/Ira Berry/Sibbald Rd.
Mary Margaret Fuller, "Dreams of the
Lost," Fate 17 (Aug.1964):85,87-88.

-Disappearance
  1964/"Crystal"/150 mi.E/crew only
    Fort Lauderdale News, 15 July 1968.
    Richard Winer, The Devil's Triangle
    (N.Y.: Bantam, 1974), pp.69-70.
-Healing
  1960s-   /Willard Fuller/7500 Powers
  Ave., no.146
    Jacksonville Times-Union, 2 Oct.1971.
    Brad Steiger, Revelation: The Divine
    Fire (Englewood Cliffs, N.J.: Pren-
    tice-Hall, 1973), pp.68-72.
    David St. Clair, Psychic Healers
    (Garden City: Doubleday, 1974), pp.
    147-73.
    James Crenshaw, "Reverend Fuller's
    Ministry of Dental Healing," Fate
    28 (Mar.1975):78-89; (Apr.1975):
    68-79. il.
-Mystery holes in clothing
  1954, April
    (Editorial), Fate 7 (Sep.1954):12.
-Mystery plane crash
  1955, Dec.21/Eastern Air Lines Con-
  stellation/airport
    Miami Daily News, 26-27 Jan.1956.
-Paranormal flotation
  1920s-1931/Angelo Faticoni
    New York Herald Tribune, 13 Aug.1931.
    "Human Corks," Fortean Soc'y Mag.,
    no.9 (spring 1944):11.
-Phantom image
  1971, Sep./Paxon Revival Center
  1971, Sep./10th St. Baptist Church
  1971, Sep./Church of Christ Written in
  Heaven
    David Techter, "A Flap of Glowing
    Crosses," Fate 25 (June 1972):52,
    54, quoting Jacksonville Times-
    Union (undated). il.
-Precognition
  1942, Dec.28/Ted Smiley
    Ted Smiley, "I Saw a Fire Before It
    Happened!" Fate 1 (winter 1949):
    44-46.
-Seance
  1940s/Maurice D. Strickland
    Roy Clyde Weidler, "Voices from Some-
    where," Fate 4 (Oct.1951):73-75.
-Time anomaly
  1970, June/Navy P-2 plane
    Charles Berlitz, Without a Trace
    (N.Y.: Ballantine, 1978 ed.), pp.
    135-36.
-UFO (?)
  1952, July 30
  1954/Mrs. V.B. Lamoureux
    George D. Fawcett, Quarter Century of
    Studies of UFOs in Florida, North
    Carolina and Tennessee (Mount Airy:
    Pioneer, 1975), p.20.
-UFO (CE-1)
  1956, May 9/Joan Frost
    "Saucer Descends on Dark Street,
    Scares Youth," CRIFO Orbit, 6 July
    1956, p.3.
  1957, March 9/Matthew Van Winkle/off-
  shore/=meteor?
    Donald H. Menzel & Lyle G. Boyd, The
    World of Flying Saucers (Garden

City: Doubleday, 1963), pp.104-105.
    Robert Charles Cornett, "Stapleton,
    This Is Flight 239: We're Being
    Followed," Official UFO 1 (Apr.
    1976):35,61-62.
-UFO (CE-2)
  1957, Aug.22/Cecil Naval Air Station
    Jacques Vallee, Passport to Magonia
    (Chicago: Regnery, 1969), p.257.
  1962, Oct.10/Spring Park Rd.
    George D. Fawcett, Quarter Century of
    Studies of UFOs in Florida, North
    Carolina and Tennessee (Mount Airy:
    Pioneer, 1975), p.16.
-UFO (NL)
  1897, April 20
    Cincinnati (O.) Commercial Tribune,
    21 Apr.1897.
  1949, July 12/Toni Ververka
    Kenneth Arnold & Ray Palmer, The Com-
    ing of the Saucers (Boise: The Au-
    thors, 1952), p.142.
  1958, May 16
    Robert N. Webster, "Things That Fall
    from UFOs," Fate 11 (Oct.1958):25,
    30.
  1964, Dec.28/Naval Air Station
    "New Sightings Put AF on Spot," UFO
    Inv. 3 (Mar.-Apr.1965):1,4.
  1969, Jan.5
    George D. Fawcett, "Florida Report,"
    Flying Saucers, June 1970, p.31.
  1973, Sep.29/Mrs. H.W. Steffen/5332
  Penn Circle
    Jacksonville Journal, 1 Oct.1973.
-UFO (R-V)
  1955, Dec.11/Naval Air Station
    Donald E. Keyhoe, Flying Saucers: Top
    Secret (N.Y.: Putnam, 1960), p.195.
-Unidentified submerged object
  1957/"Franklin D. Roosevelt"
    (Editorial), Fate 10 (Sep.1957):6-8.

Jacksonville Beach
-Cloud anomaly
  1969, Feb.3/James Alford
    "Noisy Clouds," Pursuit 2 (Apr.1969)
    :32, quoting AP release, 3 Feb.1969.

Jensen Beach
-UFO (NL)
  1973, Oct.3/Mrs. Glen Evans/Starlight
  Trailer Park
    Stuart News, 4 Oct.1973.

Jupiter
-UFO (?)
  1961, May 19
    "Help Asked in Tracking 'Suspected
    and Unpredicted Satellite,'" APRO
    Bull. 9 (May 1961):6.

Key Biscayne
-Fall of weblike substance
  1957, summer/Craig Phillips/3 mi. offshore
    Richard Hall, ed., The UFO Evidence
    (Washington: NICAP, 1964), pp.99-
    100.
-Men-in-black

1971, Oct./Shirley Cromartie/nr.
Florida White House
Washington (D.C.) Post, 23 Oct.1971.

Key Largo
-Disappearance
1967, Jan.14/Robert Van Westerborg/
Beechcraft Bonanza
Miami Herald, 18 Jan.1967, p.B2; 21
Jan.1967, p.B2; and 22 Jan.1967,
p.B1.
-Underwater ruins
Charles Berlitz, Mysteries from For-
gotten Worlds (Garden City: Double-
day, 1972), p.93.

Keystone Heights
-UFO (NL)
1952, July 22/Corbit Terrel
Gainesville Sun, 23 July 1952.
(Letter), Robert Dodd, Fate 6 (Jan.
1953):107.

Key West
-Auroral anomaly
1897, Nov.8/H.B. Boyer
"Anomalous and Sporadic Auroras,"
Monthly Weather Rev. 26 (June 1898)
:260-61.
-Clairempathy
1974, June 18/Olof Jonsson/towards
Quick Sands
David Techter, "Sunken Treasure!"
Fate 28 (June 1975):36-43. il.
-Fog anomaly
1948, April/Joe Talley/"Wild Goose"
Charles Berlitz, Without a Trace
(N.Y.: Ballantine, 1978 ed.), pp.
29,117-18.
-Haunt
1960s/Audobon House
Susy Smith, Ghosts Around the House
(N.Y.: World, 1970).
-UFO (?)
1966, March 22
"Close-Range Sightings Increase,"
UFO Inv. 3 (Mar.-Apr.1966):3.
-UFO (CE-2)
1969, Jan.1
Joseph Ule, "The Key West Incident,"
in Beyond Condon (Flying Saucer Rev.
special issue no.2, June 1969), pp.
71-72.
-UFO (NL)
1952, July 26/Naval Air Station
Donald E. Keyhoe, Flying Saucers
from Outer Space (N.Y.: Holt, 1953),
p.68.
1953, July 24
U.S. Air Force, Projects Grudge and
Bluebook Reports 1-12 (Washington:
NICAP, 1968), p.223.
1959, Oct.20/Naval Air Station
Richard Hall, ed., The UFO Evidence
(Washington: NICAP, 1964), p.31.
1973, Oct.22/Holiday Inn
"Interesting 1973 Case," APRO Bull.
24 (July 1975):1,5. il.
1973, Oct.24/Pat Hart/Simonton St.
Key West Citizen, 25 Oct.1973.

1978, Jan.27
"UFOs of Limited Merit," Int'l UFO
Reporter 3 (Mar.1978):3.
-UFO (R-V)
1950, Feb.22/Naval Air Station
Donald E. Keyhoe, Flying Saucers Are
Real (N.Y.: Fawcett, 1950), p.12.
-Windshield pitting
1954
Harold T. Wilkins, Flying Saucers Un-
censored (N.Y.: Pyramid, 1967 ed.),
p.153.

Kissimmee
-Skyquake
1895, Feb.8
"The Noise Made by a Meteor," Monthly
Weather Rev. 23 (Feb.1895):57.

LaBelle
-Humanoid
1977, May 23/10 mi.S on Hwy.29
Belle Glade Herald, 26 May 1977.

La Grange
-UFO (DD)
1946, May/Andrew A. Titcomb
Richard Hall, ed., The UFO Evidence
(Washington: NICAP, 1964), p.6.

Lake City
-UFO (CE-3)
1976, Feb.10
"Sighting Reports," CUFOS News Bull.,
June 1976, p.4.

Lake Hamilton
-Talking cat
1964/James Deem
Tampa Tribune, 16 Aug.1964.
Susy Smith, "The Search for the Talking Cat," Fate 18 (Nov.1965):32-41.
il.

Lakeland
-Fall of unknown object
1968, Oct.13/George Wimberly/Watkins
Motor Lines
Lee Butcher, "Florida Reports UFO
Swarm," Fate 23 (May 1969):44-47,
quoting Lakeland Ledger (undated).
-Fall of weblike substance
1962, Nov.11
Lakeland Ledger, 12 Nov.1962.
-Humanoid
1947
John Green, Sasquatch: The Apes Among
Us (Seattle: Hancock House, 1978),
p.271.
1972/=hoax
(Editorial), Fate 25 (Nov.1972):23.
-Precognition
1918-1960s/Jane Savage
George Butler, "Woman Who 'Sees' To-
morrow," Fate 14 (Nov.1961):41-45.
-UFO (?)
1955, Jan.26/=missile?
Jacques Vallee, Anatomy of a Phenom-
enon (N.Y.: Ace, 1965 ed.), p.143.
-UFO (CE-3)

1968, Nov.9
Brad Steiger & Joan Whritenour, Flying Saucer Invasion: Target--Earth (N.Y.: Award, 1969), p.100.
-UFO (NL)
1975, Dec.16
"UFO Central," CUFOS News Bull., 1 Feb.1976, p.15.
1978, Jan.3/Charles Loveland
Lakeland Ledger, 5 Jan.1978.

Lake Placid
-Precognition and spirit medium
1960s-   /Joseph Donnelly/Route 3
Joseph W. Donnelly, Diary of a Psychic (Hollywood, Fla: The Author, 1966).
Brad Steiger, "Scoring the Seers in 1969," Fate 23 (Jan.1970):66,69.
Warren Smith, "Phenomenal Predictions for 1976," Saga, Jan.1976, pp.16,17.

Lakeport
-Humanoid and cattle mutilation
1974
B. Ann Slate, "Florida's Rampaging Man-Ape," Saga UFO Rept. 4 (July 1977):32,35.

Lake Wales
-Gravity anomaly
Spook Hill
James Dale Davidson, An Eccentric Guide to the United States (N.Y.: Berkley, 1977), pp.177-78.
Jim Brandon, Weird America (N.Y.: Dutton, 1978), p.65.
-UFO (NL)
1965, Feb.9
Otto Binder, "'Oddball' Saucers That Fit No Pattern," Fate 21 (Feb.1968):54,60.

Lake Worth
-Fall of ice
1978, Sep./Helen Goddard/711 N. Lakeside Dr.
Palm Beach Post, 12 Sep.1978.

Lantana
-UFO (CE-3)
1952, Aug.19/Sonny Desvergers/nr. Lantana Rd. x Military Trail
Edward J. Ruppelt, The Report on Unidentified Flying Objects (Garden City: Doubleday, 1956), pp.176-86.
Thomas M. Olsen, ed., The Reference for Outstanding UFO Sighting Reports (Riderwood, Md.: UFO Information Retrieval Center, 1966), pp.13-16. il.
John A. Keel, The Mothman Prophecies (N.Y.: Saturday Review, 1975), pp.110-11.

Largo
-Fall of crayfish
n.d./Nada Domay
(Letter), Fate 7 (June 1954):122-24.
-Fall of fish
n.d./Nada Domay

(Letter), Fate 7 (June 1954):122,124.
-Fall of toads
1910/Nada Domay
(Letter), Fate 7 (June 1954):122-24.

Leesburg
-Ghost
1972, Feb./Frank Fields
(Editorial), Fate 25 (Sep.1972):22-28, quoting Lake Sentinel (undated).
-Inner development
1970s/Frontier Community Church/Box 1589
Armand Biteaux, The New Consciousness (Willits, Cal.: Oliver, 1975), pp.51-53.

Live Oak
-UFO (NL)
1975, July/S on Hwy.129
1976, Oct.
Live Oak Independent-Post, 11 Jan.1978.

Loxahatchee
-Phantom panther
1978, Jan.3
Palm Beach Post, 24 Jan.1978.

Madeira Beach
-UFO (CE-3)
1968, Aug.
David Webb & Ted Bloecher, "MUFON's Humanoid Study Group Very Active," Skylook, no.93 (Aug.1975):9.

Malabar
-Possession
1968, Sep./Pam Johnson/Malabar Teen Center
(Editorial), Fate 22 (Apr.1969):26-30.

Marathon
-UFO (NL)
1978, March 15/Jennie Walterson/Seven Mile Bridge
Key West Citizen, 15 Mar.1978.

Marianna
-Mystery stain
n.d./N of town
Dale M. Titler, "The Bleeding Grave," Fate 9 (Sep.1956):97-98.
-UFO (DD)
ca.1954/William Coleman
"Air Force UFO Spokesman Describes Personal Sighting," MUFON UFO J., no.123 (Feb.1978):3-4.

Martin co.
-Humanoid
1975, March 6/Steve Humphreys/nr. Lake Okeechobee
Marty Wolf, "An Interview with Bob Morgan," Pursuit 8 (July 1975):70,71.

Mayport
-Archeological site
ca.1-300 A.D.

Rex L. Wilson, "Excavations at the Mayport Mound, Florida," Contrib. Florida State Mus.Soc.Sci., no.13 (1965). il.

Medulla
-UFO (CE-3)
  1968, Oct.18/Grace McMullen
    Lee Butcher, "Florida Reports UFO Swarm," Fate 23 (May 1969):44,47-50.

Melbourne
-Archeological site
    J.W. Gidley & F.B. Loomis, "Fossil Man in Florida," Am.J.Sci., ser.5, 12 (1926):254-64.
    James W. Gidley, "Ancient Man in Florida: Further Investigations," Bull.Geol.Soc'y Am. 40 (1929):491-501. il.
    T.D. Stewart, "A Reexamination of the Fossil Human Skeletal Remains from Melbourne, Florida," Smith. Misc.Coll. vol.106, no.10 (1946). il.
    Irving Rouse, "Vero and Melbourne Man: A Cultural and Chronological Interpretation," Trans.N.Y.Acad. Sci., ser.2, 12 (1950):220-24.
    Irving Rouse, "The Age of the Melbourne Interval," Bull.Texas Arch. & Palaeont.Soc'y 23 (1952):293-99.
    H.M. Wormington, Ancient Man in America (Denver: Mus.of Natural History, pop. ser., no.4, 1957), pp.227-30.
-UFO (CE-1)
  1955, Feb.21/William R. Reece
    (Letter), Fate 8 (Mar.1955):116-18.
-UFO (DD)
  1968, Nov.27/L.P. Duplantis/20 mi.W
    "Planes Paced by UFOs over Florida," APRO Bull. 17 (Nov.-Dec.1968):1.
-UFO (NL)
  1956, Sep.4/Mary Mann
    Mary Mann & Amey Hoag, "We Saw a Flying Saucer," Fate 10 (Apr.1957):54-56.
  1959, May 14/Dana Franklin
    (Editorial), Fate 12 (Nov.1959):12, quoting Orlando Sentinel (undated).
  1968, Dec.11/Florida Institute of Technology
    George D. Fawcett, "Florida Reports," Flying Saucers, June 1970, p.31.

Melbourne Beach
-Clairempathy, precognition, spirit medium, and astrology
  1964-   /Sybil Leek/Box 158
    S.K. Oberbeck, "Bell, Book, and TV," Newsweek, 9 Jan.1967, p.67A.
    Sybil Leek, Diary of a Witch (Englewood Cliffs, N.J.: Prentice-Hall, 1968).
    "Interview: Sybil Leek," Psychic 1 (Nov.1969):4-7,26-32. il.
    Sybil Leek, The Complete Art of Witchcraft (N.Y.: World, 1971).
    Sybil Leek, ESP: The Magic Within

You (London: Abelard-Schuman, 1972).
    Sybil Leek, My Life in Astrology (Englewood Cliffs, N.J.: Prentice-Hall, 1972).
    Sybil Leek, Tomorrow's Headlines Today (Englewood Cliffs, N.J.: Prentice-Hall, 1974).
    Sybil Leek, Herbs: Medicine and Mysticism (Chicago: Regnery, 1975).
    Sybil Leek, Stars Speak (N.Y.: Arbor House, 1975).
    "People," Time, 26 Jan.1976, p.43.
    "Probe's 1977 Directory of the Psychic World," Probe the Unknown 5 (spring 1977):32,37. il.

Merritt Island
-UFO (NL)
  1975, Nov.6
    "UFO Central," CUFOS News Bull., 1 Feb.1976, p.12.

Mexico Beach
-Phantom image
  1971, Sep.22/United Methodist Church
    David Techter, "A Flap of Glowing Crosses," Fate 25 (June 1972):52, 54.

Miami
-Ancient harbor
  nr. Dupont Plaza
    Charles Berlitz, Mysteries from Forgotten Worlds (Garden City: Doubleday, 1972), p.93.
-Autoscopy
  1960, July
    Edward Podolsky, "Have You Seen Your Double?" Fate 19 (Apr.1966):79.
-Clairaudience
  1964, May 19/Florence Gutierrez
    (Editorial), Fate 17 (Sep.1964):10-12.
-Clairempathy
  1957-1961/Peter Hurkos
    Gilbert N. Holloway, "Hurkos Reads the Future on Channel 10," Fate 13 (Feb.1960):76-83.
    Peter Hurkos, Psychic: The Story of Peter Hurkos (Indianapolis: Bobbs-Merrill, 1961).
    Jess Stearn, The Door to the Future (N.Y.: Macfadden, 1964), pp.199-200.
    Andrija Puharich, Beyond Telepathy (Garden City: Anchor, 1973), pp. 38-59.
  1971-   /Rien Dykshoorn
    M.B. Dykshoorn & Russell H. Felton, My Passport Says Clairvoyant (N.Y.: Jove, 1978 ed.), pp.172-202.
-Clairvoyance
  1962, May 7/Mrs. James A. Young/200 E. Flagler St.
    (Editorial), Fate 15 (Sep.1962):18.
-Cloud anomaly
  1969, Feb.9/William Ward
    Chicago (Ill.) Daily News, 10 Feb. 1969.
-Contactee
  1958-   /Nada-Yolanda/Mark-Age Meta Center/327 NE 20th Terr.

Mark-Age, Mark-Age Period and Program (Miami: Mark-Age, 1970).
Brad Steiger, Gods of Aquarius (N.Y.: Harcourt Brace Jovanovich, 1976), pp.104-107.
1960s/Ufology Research Institute
"News Briefs," Saucer News 14 (spring 1967):17.
"Saucer Flight by Earthlings Delayed Indefinitely," Saucer News 14 (summer 1967):24.

-Disappearance
1944, Oct.22/"Rubicon"/crew only
New York Times, 23 Oct.1944, p.21.
Richard Winer, The Devil's Triangle (N.Y.: Bantam, 1974), pp.179-80.
1945, July 18/William C. Bailey/PB-4YW
John Wallace Spencer, Limbo of the Lost (N.Y.: Bantam, 1973 ed.), p.19.
1948, Dec.28/Robert Linquist/DC-3/ ocean to S
Miami Herald, 29-31 Dec.1948, p.1; 1 Jan.1949, p.2; and 19 July 1949, p.7.
George X. Sand, "Sea Mystery at Our Back Door," Fate 5 (Oct.1952):11, 15-16.
John Wallace Spencer, Limbo of the Lost (N.Y.: Bantam, 1973 ed.), pp. 30-34.
Richard Winer, The Devil's Triangle (N.Y.: Bantam, 1974), pp.139-42.
Lawrence David Kusche, The Bermuda Triangle Mystery--Solved (N.Y.: Harper & Row, 1975), pp.142-50.
1958, Jan.6/Harvey Conover/"Revonoc"/ ocean to S
New York Times, 7 Jan.1958, p.24.
Edward Rowe Snow, Unsolved Mysteries of Sea and Shore (N.Y.: Dodd, Mead, 1963), pp.219-23.

-Dog mutilations
1976/Coconut Grove
Hunter S. Thompson, "Third-Rate Romance, Low-Rent Rendezvous," Rolling Stone, 3 June 1976, pp.54-55.

-Erratic African snails
1969, Sep./Miami Shores
New York Times, 28 Sep.1969.
"Giant Snails in Florida," Pursuit 2 (Oct.1969):73-74.

-Fall of gelatinous substance
1958, Feb.28/Faustin Gallegos/1151 NW 116th St.
Miami Herald, 1 Mar.1958.
Faustin Gallegos, "The Pulsing Honeycomb from Space," Fate 11 (Sep.1958) :40-43.

-Fall of oily substance
1962
(Editorial), Fate 15 (Aug.1962):16.

-Fall of unknown object
1968, June 11/Phoebe Klein
(Editorial), Fate 21 (Oct.1968):9-10, quoting Miami Herald (undated).

-Fire anomaly
1959, Feb./Evelyn Byrnes/2111 NW 28th St.
(Editorial), Fate 12 (July 1959):22.

-Ghost cat

n.d./Chérie Hughes
1965, July-   /James Merrick
Susy Smith, More ESP for the Millions (Los Angeles: Sherbourne, 1969).

-Haunt
1969/Tommy Thompson/22d Ave. x 28th St.
Susy Smith, The Power of the Mind (Radnor, Pa.: Chilton, 1975), pp. 167-68.

-Healing
1969, fall/Lola
Raquel Garcia, "Healed by a Santera," Fate 27 (Apr.1974):77-79.

-Inner development
1960s-   /Awareness Research Foundation
Brad Steiger, Revelation: The Divine Fire (Englewood Cliffs, N.J.: Prentice-Hall, 1973), pp.119-23,209.
1970s/Prince Van Dercar/Royal Order of Warlocks and Witches
John Godwin, Occult America (Garden City: Doubleday, 1972), pp.72-73.
1971-   /Lotus Ashram
Noel Street, Kundalini, Sex and Magnetism (Miami: Lotus Ashram, 1972).

-Lunar cycle and homicides
1956-1970/Carolyn Sherin/University of Miami
A.L. Lieber & C.R. Sherin, "Homicides and the Lunar Cycle," Am.J.Psychiatry 129 (1972):69-74.
Pat Rogers, "Moon Myths and Madness," Probe the Unknown 5 (spring 1977): 28,30-31.

-Mystery plane crash and haunts
1972, Dec.29/Robert Loft/18 mi.W
Miami News, 1 Jan.1973.
Jack Murray, "Crash Victim's Ghost Haunts Eastern Airlines," Probe the Unknown 3 (Nov.1975):12-16. il.
John G. Fuller, The Ghost of Flight 401 (N.Y.: Berkley, 1976).
Elizabeth Fuller, My Search for the Ghost of Flight 401 (N.Y.: Berkley, 1978).

-Mystery shipwreck
1976, Jan.16/Jackson R. Baldwin/Fowey Rock Light
Richard Winer, From the Devil's Triangle to the Devil's Jaw (N.Y.: Bantam, 1977), p.1.

-Poltergeist
1967, Jan.11-Feb./Alvin Laubheim/Tropication Arts, 117 NE 54th St.
Susy Smith, Prominent American Ghosts (N.Y.: Dell, 1969 ed.), pp.196-218.
Susy Smith, Ghosts Around the House (N.Y.: World, 1970).
W.G. Roll & J.G. Pratt, "The Miami Disturbances," J.ASPR 65 (1971):409-54.
W.G. Roll, Donald S. Burdick & William T. Joines, "Radial and Tangential Forces in the Miami Poltergeist," J.ASPR 67 (1973):267-81.
William G. Roll, The Poltergeist (N.Y.: Signet, 1974), pp.104-33.
Susy Smith, The Power of the Mind (Radnor, Pa.: Chilton, 1975), pp.

195-205.
-Precognition
n.d./S.O. Cohee
"They Dreamed of Disaster," _Fate_ 9
(Aug.1956):46.
1957, July 8/Bill Bergens/525 NW 62d
St.
(Editorial), _Fate_ 10 (Nov.1957):17-
18.
1963, July/Royce Atwood Wight
(Editorial), _Fate_ 16 (Dec.1963):18.
1964, Feb.2/Mrs. John Pisarik/2120 NW
13th St.
(Editorial), _Fate_ 17 (June 1964):6-
8, quoting _Miami Herald_ (undated).
1972, June 17/James W. Cox/7th Ave. x
54th St.
Lorraine J. Carbary, "Fatal Premoni-
tion Fulfilled," _Fate_ 26 (Mar.1973)
:104.
-Skyquake
1951, Dec.26-27
"Jest Planes Again," _Doubt_, no.37
(1952):148,149.
1958, Nov.13
(Editorial), _Fate_ 12 (May 1959):19.
-Spirit medium
1946-1949/Arthur Ford/38th St. x 2d
Ave. NE
Allen Spraggett, _Arthur Ford: The
Man Who Talked with the Dead_ (N.Y.:
Signet, 1974), pp.203-205.
-Spontaneous human combustion
1975, Jan.12/Esther Cooks
Miami Herald, 13 Jan.1975.
R. Martin Wolf, "Another Case of
SHC?" _Pursuit_ 9 (Jan.1976):16-17.
-Tornado anomaly
1959, June 17
B. Vonnegut & James Weyer, "Luminous
Phenomena in Nocturnal Tornadoes,"
Science 153 (1966):1213-20.
-UFO (?)
1954, July
Donald E. Keyhoe, _Flying Saucer Con-
spiracy_ (N.Y.: Holt, 1955), p.190.
-UFO (DD)
1959, Dec.4/Anna T. Ochipa/N. Miami
Ave.
(Letter), _Fate_ 13 (Oct.1960):109.
1974, June/S.A. Davidson/Coconut Grove
S.A. Davidson, "Multicolored UFOs,"
Fate 28 (Jan.1975):49.
1975, Dec.12
"UFO Central," _CUFOS News Bull._, 1
Feb.1976, p.14.
-UFO (NL)
1952, July 29/Ralph Mayher
Leonard H. Stringfield, _Inside Sau-
cer Post...3-0 Blue_ (Cincinnati:
CRIFO, 1957), pp.70-71.
Hayden C. Hewes, "The Mayher-Miami
Movie," _Saga UFO Rept._ 4 (July 1977)
:28-29,60. il.
1954, May 6
Harold T. Wilkins, _Flying Saucers Un-
censored_ (N.Y.: Pyramid, 1967 ed.),
p.217.
1959, Nov.29/J.J. Rehill
Miami Herald, 6 Dec.1959. il.

Richard Hall, ed., _The UFO Evidence_
(Washington: NICAP, 1964), p.93.
1968, Oct.20
George D. Fawcett, "Florida Report,"
Flying Saucers, June 1970, p.30.
1971, Feb.6/Rod McDonald
(Letter), _FSR Case Histories_, no.5
(June 1971):16.
1975, Nov.5/Thomas Leis/Midway Mall
Gray Barker, "America's Captured Fly-
ing Saucers: Cover-Up of the Cen-
tury," _Saga UFO Rept._ 4 (May 1977):
32,34.
1975, Nov.13
"UFO Central," _CUFOS News Bull._, 1
Feb.1976, p.13.
1976, Dec.18
"UFOs of Limited Merit," _Int'l UFO
Reporter_ 2 (Feb.1977):5.
-UFO (R)
1956, Nov.8/Donald Freestone
Miami Daily News, 8 Nov.1956.
"Case 269," _CRIFO Orbit_, 4 Jan.1957,
p.4.
-UFO (R-V)
1957, March 29/Kenneth G. Brosdal
Richard Hall, ed., _The UFO Evidence_
(Washington: NICAP, 1964), p.42.
-Unidentified submerged object
1966, Sep.27/Martin Meylach/4 mi. off-
shore
Miami Herald, 27 Sep.1966.
-Water anomaly
1947, July 17
"More Squirts," _Doubt_, no.20 (1948):
307, quoting _Columbus (O.) Citizen_
(undated).
-Weather control
1946, July 5/Jack Parsons
J. Gordon Melton, _Encyclopedia of
American Religions_, 2 vols. (Wil-
mington, N.C.: Consortium, 1978),
2:257-58.
1960/Rolf Alexander
Rolf Alexander, _The Power of the Mind_
(London: Laurie, 1956). il.

Miami Beach
-Disappearance
1967, Dec.22/Dan Burack/"Witchcraft"
Miami Herald, 24-29 Dec.1967.
Richard Winer, _The Devil's Triangle_
(N.Y.: Bantam, 1974), pp.142-44.
Lawrence David Kusche, _The Bermuda
Triangle Mystery--Solved_ (N.Y.:
Harper & Row, 1975), pp.216-18.
-Precognition
1975, March 2/Richard Trado
Lorraine J. Carbary, "Policeman's
Premonition Was No Dream," _Fate_ 28
(Aug.1975):62-63.
-Sea monster
1959/Bob Wall/"Comrade II"/2 mi.offshore
(Editorial), _Fate_ 12 (July 1959):10-
11.
-UFO (DD)
1948, Feb./Mr. Bohland
"Disc Dirt," _Doubt_, no.21 (1948):314,
315.
-UFO (NL)

1976, April 13
"Noteworthy UFO Sightings," Ufology
2 (fall 1976):60.

Miami Lakes
-UFO (DD)
1975, June 16/R. Drake
(Letter), Saga UFO Rept. 3 (Apr.1976)
:76-77.

Miami Springs
-UFO (DD)
1947, July 6/Fred Walsh/N of Hialeah
Bridge
Miami Herald, 7 July 1947.

Middleburg
-Fall of limonite
ca.1888
George F. Kunz, "A Pseudo-Meteorite,"
Science 11 (1888):119.

Monticello
-UFO (NL)
1978, Oct.
Monticello News, 2 Nov.1978.

Naples
-Archeological site
Andrew E. Douglass, "Ancient Canals
on the South-West Coast of Florida,"
Am.Antiquarian 7 (1885):277-85.
-UFO (CE-1)
1966, May 6/Bill Keralas
Miami Herald, 7 May 1966.
-UFO (NL)
1976, April 4
"Noteworthy UFO Sightings," Ufology
2 (fall 1976):60.

New Port Richey
-Fall of fish
1971, Sep.7/Jason Bennett
New Port Richey Press, 7 Sep.1971.
-Giant bird tracks and cattle disappear-
ance
1967, May
Brad Steiger & Joan Whritenour, Al-
lende Letters: New UFO Breakthrough
(N.Y.: Award, 1968), pp.84-85.
-UFO (?)
1967
George D. Fawcett, Quarter Century of
Studies of UFOs in Florida, North
Carolina and Tennessee (Mount Airy:
Pioneer, 1975), p.18.
-UFO (NL)
1969, May 21
"'Cigar-Shaped' UFO's Reported All
Over the Globe," Skylook, no.20
(July 1969):9,10.

New Smyrna Beach
-UFO (DD)
1952, July 22
Richard Hall, ed., The UFO Evidence
(Washington: NICAP, 1964), p.160.

Niceville
-UFO (CE-1)

1978, Aug.12
"UFOs of Limited Merit," Int'l UFO
Reporter 3 (Sep.1978):6,9.

Nobleton
-Humanoid
1977, May
John Green, Sasquatch: The Apes Among
Us (Seattle: Hancock House, 1978),
p.280.

North Fort Myers
-Humanoid
1975, summer
John Green, Sasquatch: The Apes Among
Us (Seattle: Hancock House, 1978),
p.278.
1976, June
Atlanta (Ga.) Constitution, 11 June
1976.

North Miami
-Contactee
1960s-   /Helen I. Hoag/Box 610143
Helen I. Hoag, My Visits to Other
Planets, the Sun, Moon and the Star
Capella (Miami: Awareness Research
Foundation, 1970).
Helen I. Hoag, "Aboard a Saturn
Spacecraft," Awareness Rsch.Founda-
tion Newsl., Sep.1973.
Glenn McWane & David Graham, The New
UFO Sightings (N.Y.: Warner, 1974),
pp.116-19.

North Miami Beach
-UFO (NL)
1956, Oct.3/Stephen Grisillo/Dixie Hwy.
(Letter), Fate 10 (Aug.1957):113-15.

Ocala
-Phantom image
1972, Jan./Belle Williams/Ocala Theo-
logical Seminary
David Techter, "A Flap of Glowing
Crosses," Fate 25 (June 1972):52,
56-57, quoting Orlando Sentinel
(undated).
-UFO (DD)
1950, July 13/C.L. Quixley/Greenville
Terrace
Ray Palmer, "New Report on the Fly-
ing Saucers," Fate 4 (Jan.1951):63,
79-80.
-UFO (NL)
1955, Oct.30-31/A.H. Perkins
"Latest Saucer Sightings," Fate 9
(Apr.1956):43,46.
1966, April 28/Haydon Burns/S of town
"Florida Governor Sights UFO," UFO
Inv. 3 (May-June 1966):3, quoting
Tampa Tribune (undated).

Ocoee
-UFO (NL)
1959, April 3/John F. Wilmeth
Richard Hall, ed., The UFO Evidence
(Washington: NICAP, 1964), p.64.

Oklawaha
-Haunt
1935-   /Mrs. James S. Ternent/Brad-
ford House
Susy Smith, The Power of the Mind
(Radnor, Pa.: Chilton, 1975), pp.
160-65.

Old Town
-UFO (CE-1)
1961, Nov.21/7 mi.NE
Lloyd Mallan, "Complete Directory of
UFOs: Part III," Sci.& Mech. 38
(Feb.1967):56,92.

Ona
-UFO (CE-1)
1979, Jan.2/Joe Guerrero/Hwy.64
Wauchula Herald-Advocate, 4 Jan.1979.

Opa-Locka
-UFO (DD)
1967, April 6-7/Robert Apfal/Crestview
Elementary School
1967, April 8/John Wolf/Crestview Ele-
mentary School
Miami Herald, 8 April 1967; and 11
April 1967.
"The North Dade Affair," APRO Bull.
15 (Mar.-Apr.1967):10.
"More on the North Dade Incident,"
APRO Bull. 15 (May-June 1967):8-9.

Orange Heights
-Erratic fish
1888/Charles B. Palmer
(Editorial), Nature 39 (1888):208.

Orlando
-Fall of egg
1959, May 19/Mrs. William J. Houliston/
421 Buckminster Circle
(Editorial), Fate 12 (Sep.1959):8.
-Fall of frogs
1953, Sep.26/J.S. Russell
(Letter), Fate 7 (Feb.1954):117-18.
-Poltergeist
1950s/Mary Jane Knisely
(Letter), Fate 6 (Mar.1953):117-18.
(Letter), Fate 9 (Feb.1956):113-14.
-Precognition
1955/J.R. Spence
(Editorial), Fate 8 (Oct.1955):12.
-Skyquake
1895, Feb.7/=meteor?
"The Noise Made by a Meteor," Month-
ly Weather Rev. 23 (Feb.1895):57.
-UFO (?)
1958, March 17
(Editorial), Fate 11 (July 1958):17.
-UFO (NL)
1949, July 14/Lawrence McDonald/air-
port
Kenneth Arnold & Ray Palmer, The Com-
ing of the Saucers (Boise: The Au-
thors, 1952), pp.142-43.
1975, Nov.13
"UFO Central," CUFOS News Bull., 1
Feb.1976, p.13.
1976, June 25/Colonial Plaza Shopping

Mall
Orlando Sentinel-Star, 26 June 1976.
"Late June Reports in Florida," APRO
Bull. 24 (June 1976):1,3.
1976, June 30/Summerlin Ave.
"Late June Reports in Florida," APRO
Bull. 24 (June 1976):1,3.
-Weather control
1961, June 9/Hawaiian dancers
(Editorial), Fate 14 (Oct.1961):20-
22.
-Windshield pitting
1954/H.A. Brasfield
(Editorial), Fate 8 (Feb.1955):12.

Osceola co.
-UFO (CE-1)
1964, June 23/Harry Taylor/Hwy.60, nr.
20-Mile Bend
Fort Pierce News-Tribune, 24 June
1964.

Oviedo
-Ghost light
1971/Big Econ R. bridge/Hwy.13
"Back Track," Skylook, no.53 (Apr.
1972):13.

Palatka
-Archeological site
Francis Harper, ed., The Travels of
William Bartram (New Haven: Yale
Univ., 1958), Part 2, ch. xi, pp.
192-93.
-Humanoid
1977, Oct.3/Listene Maxwell/Booker
Field
Palatka News, 4 Oct.1977.
-UFO (NL)
1961, July 25
Jacques Vallee, Anatomy of a Phenom-
enon (N.Y.: Ace, 1965 ed.), pp.211-
12.
1975, Dec.12/Ted Gaunz
Gray Barker, "America's Captured Fly-
ing Saucers: Cover-Up of the Cen-
tury," Saga UFO Rept. 4 (May 1977):
32,35,64.

Palm Beach
-Mystery plane crash
1976, May 29/Fritz Hensel/Cessna 210/
40 mi.SE
Richard Winer, From the Devil's Triangle to the Devil's Jaw (N.Y.:
Bantam, 1977), pp.14-15.

Panama City
-Phantom image
1971, Sep./Jackson Jones/St. John's
Baptist Church
1971, Sep./Greater Bethel Church
1971, Sep./Nazarene Church
David Techter, "A Flap of Glowing
Crosses," Fate 25 (June 1972):52,54.

Patrick AFB
-UFO (DD)
1956, Dec.11
"Case 280," CRIFO Orbit, 1 Feb.1957,

p.4.
-UFO (NL)
　1952, July 18
　　Edward J. Ruppelt, The Report on Un-
　　identified Flying Objects (Garden
　　City: Doubleday, 1956), pp.155-56.
　　U.S. Air Force, Projects Grudge and
　　Bluebook Reports 1-12 (Washington:
　　NICAP, 1968), p.145.
　1957, Oct.7
　　Coral & Jim Lorenzen, UFOs: The Whole
　　Story (N.Y.: Signet, 1969), p.81.

Pensacola
-Dowsing
　ca.1972/John Shelley, Jr./Naval Air
　Station
　　Christopher Bird, "Applications of
　　Dowsing: An Ancient Biopsychophys-
　　ical Art," in John White & Stanley
　　Krippner, eds., Future Science
　　(Garden City, N.Y.: Anchor, 1977),
　　pp.346-48.
-Fall of metallic object
　1952, April 9/Naval Air Station
　　"First Prize," Doubt, no.37 (1952):
　　146,147.
-Haunt
　1963-1964, May/George Glines
　　John A. Keel, Strange Creatures from
　　Time and Space (Greenwich, Ct.: Faw-
　　cett, 1970), pp.182-83.
-Paranormal hypnosis
　1960, March 27
　　Harry Arons, "How Hypnosis Cleared
　　Two Murder Suspects," Fate 16 (Aug.
　　1963):82-91.
-Precognition
　1917
　　Garrett Manker, "Thoroughly Psychic
　　Millie," Fate 24 (Mar.1970):80-83.
-Sea monster
　1962, March 24/Edward McCleary
　　Edward Brian McCleary, "My Escape
　　from a Sea Monster," Fate 18 (May
　　1965):52-60.
　　Tim Dinsdale, The Leviathans (London:
　　Routledge & Kegan Paul, 1966), pp.
　　91-94.
-UFO (?)
　1952, April 9/=meteor?
　　Pensacola News, 10-12 Apr.1952.
　　Pensacola Journal, 11 Apr.1952.
-UFO (NL)
　ca.1975/Ed Gillotte/yacht club
　　Timothy Green Beckley, "Saucers over
　　Our Cities," Saga UFO Rept. 4 (Aug.
　　1977):74.
　1975, Nov.11/Howard Davis/Cordova Park
　　fire station
　1975, Nov.18/Karl Bohl
　　Robert Shapiro, "Florida Flurries,"
　　Ufology 2 (spring 1976):28. il.

Perrine
-UFO (DD)
　1956, Nov.14/Keith A. Morrison/S on
　　U.S.1
　　(Letter), Fate 10 (Apr.1957):113-14.

Placida
-Humanoid
　1975/20 mi. offshore
　　B. Ann Slate, "Florida's Rampaging
　　Man-Ape," Saga UFO Rept. 4 (July
　　1977):32,65.

Plantation
-UFO (NL)
　1976, March 14
　　"Noteworthy UFO Sightings," Ufology
　　2 (summer 1976):62.
　1977, Jan.13
　　"UFO Analysis," Int'l UFO Reporter
　　2 (Feb.1977):newsfront sec.

Plant City
-UFO (CE-1)
　1974, Oct.2/Frank Smith
　　George D. Fawcett, "The 'Unreported'
　　UFO Wave of 1974," Saga UFO Rept.
　　2 (spring 1975):50,75.

Polk City
-Humanoid
　1975, March/Green Swamp
　　Orlando Sentinel-Star, 23 Mar.1975.
-UFO (CE-1)
　1975, Dec.12/Marcum Rd., SW of town
　　Gray Barker, "America's Captured Fly-
　　ing Saucers: Cover-Up of the Cen-
　　tury," Saga UFO Rept. 4 (May 1977):
　　32,35.

Pompano Beach
-Disappearance
　1969, Dec.29/Peggy Rahn/seashore
　　Richard Winer, The Devil's Triangle
　　(N.Y.: Bantam, 1974), pp.151-52.
-UFO (NL)
　1962, May 18/Elizabeth Scott
　　Richard Hall, ed., The UFO Evidence
　　(Washington: NICAP, 1964), p.71.
　1968, Oct.8/Robert Manning
　　George D. Fawcett, "Florida Report,"
　　Flying Saucers, June 1970, p.30.
　1976, March 14
　　"Noteworthy UFO Sightings," Ufology
　　2 (summer 1976):62.

Ponce de Leon
-UFO (NL)
　1975, April 21/James Townsend
　　Bradenton Herald, 23 Apr.1975.

Port Charlotte
-UFO (NL)
　1975, Oct.20
　　Robert Shapiro, "Florida Flurries,"
　　Ufology 2 (spring 1976):28.
　1978, Aug.28/Stanley Gomiela/Midway
　　Blvd. x Hwy.41
　　Sarasota Herald-Tribune, 30 Aug.1978.

Punta Gorda
-Disease anomaly
　1968, Aug.11
　　Jim Brandon, Weird America (N.Y.:
　　Dutton, 1978), p.63.
-Fall of golf balls

1969, Sep.3
"Rain of Golf Balls," INFO J., no.7
(fall-winter 1970):40.
-Humanoid
1974
B. Ann Slate, "Man-Ape's Reign of
Terror," Saga UFO Rept. 4 (Aug.1977)
:20.

Riverview
-Lightning anomaly
1949/Charles Sappal
1950, June 22/ Charles Sappal
John Michell & Robert J.M. Rickard,
Phenomena: A Book of Wonders (London: Thomas & Hudson, 1977), p.88.

Riviera Beach
-Fire immunity and paraphysics
1950s-   /Mayne Reid Coe, Jr.
(Editorial), Fate 10 (Dec.1957):9-10.
Mayne Reid Coe, Jr., "Fire-Walking
and Related Behaviors," J.ASPR 52
(1958):85,93-97.
Mayne R. Coe, Jr., "Does Science Ex-
plain Poltergeists?" Fate 12 (July
1959):79-90.
Mayne R. Coe, Jr., "Discovering the
Yogis' Secret," Fate 22 (Sep.1969):
77-84.
Mayne R. Coe, Jr., "Safely Across the
Fiery Pit," Fate 31 (June 1978):84-
86. il.

Safety Harbor
-Archeological site
John W. Griffin & Ripley P. Bullen,
"The Safety Harbor Site, Pinellas
County, Florida," Pub.Florida Arch.
Soc'y, no.2 (1950). il.
Franklin Folsom, America's Ancient
Treasures (N.Y.: Rand McNally,
1974), pp.111-12.

Saint Augustine
-Disappearance
1843, March 3/"Grampus"/ocean to N
Richard Winer, The Devil's Triangle
(N.Y.: Bantam, 1974), pp.67-68.
-Medieval Irish discovery
ca.550 A.D./St. Brendan
Charles Michael Boland, They All Dis-
covered America (N.Y.: Pocket Books,
1963 ed.), pp.121-24.
-Oceanographic anomaly
1971/30 mi.E/=hole in ocean floor
"What's New in the Navy," All Hands,
Apr.1971, p.50.
-Sea monster (carcass)
1896, Nov.30/Herbert Colee/Anastasia
Beach
Jacksonville Florida Times-Union, 1
Dec.1896.
New York Herald, 2 Dec.1896; 3 Jan.
1897; 14 Feb.1897; and 7 Mar.1897.
A.E. Verrill, "A Gigantic Cephalopod
on the Florida Coast," Am.J.Sci.,
ser.4, 3 (1897):79.
A.E. Verrill, "Additional Information
Concerning the Giant Cephalopod of

Florida," Am.J.Sci., ser.4, 3 (1897)
:162-63.
New Haven (Ct.) Register, 14 Feb.
1897.
Omaha (Neb.) Daily Bee, 20 Mar.1897.
A. Hyatt Verrill, "The Florida Mon-
ster," Science 5 (1897):392.
Frederic Augustus Lucas, "The Flor-
ida Monster," Science 5 (1897):467.
A.E. Verrill, "The Supposed Great
Octopus of Florida: Certainly Not
a Cephalopod," Am.J.Sci., ser.4, 3
(1897):355-56.
A.E. Verrill, "The Florida Sea-Mon-
ster," Am.Naturalist 31 (1897):304-
307. il.
Forrest G. Wood & Joseph G. Gennaro,
Jr., "An Octopus Trilogy," Natural
History 80 (Mar.1971):15-24,84-87.
il.
Gary S. Mangiacopra, "Monster on the
Florida Beach," INFO J., no.17 (May
1976):2-6; no.18 (July 1976):2-6.
il.
-Skyquake
1974, Jan.20/=bombing?
Miami Herald, 22 Jan.1974.

Saint Lucie co.
-UFO (CE-2)
1978, May 18/Helen Knapp/Hwy.70
Okeechobee News, 25 May 1978.

Saint Petersburg
-Animal ESP
1949-1952/Charles D. Smith
"That's Our Tom," Fate 5 (Nov.1952):
19.
-Archeological site
900-600 B.C./Canton St.
Ripley P. Bullen, et al., "The Can-
ton Street Site, St. Petersburg,
Florida," Pub.Florida Anthro.Soc'y,
no.9 (June 1978). il.
ca.900-1200 A.D.
William H. Sears, "The Bayshore Homes
Site, St. Petersburg, Florida,"
Contrib.Florida State Mus.Soc.Sci.,
no.6 (1960). il.
Charles E. Snow, "Indian Burials from
St. Petersburg, Florida," Contrib.
Florida State Mus.Soc.Sci., no.8
(1962). il.
-Astrology
1970s/Michael Helens
Peter Tompkins, Mysteries of the Mex-
ican Pyramids (N.Y.: Harper & Row,
1976), p.275.
-Clairvoyance
1955/Mrs. Burt White
(Editorial), Fate 8 (July 1955):8-9.
-Fall of fish
1950, July 10
St. Petersburg Times, 12 July 1950.
-Radiesthesia
1940s/Emil Nordstrom
M.P. Rea, "Wizard with a String,"
Fate 1 (winter 1949):42-43.
-Skyquake
1970, Jan.9

"Bang!" INFO J., no.14 (Nov.1974):2,
quoting unidentified paper, 10 Jan.
1970.
-Spontaneous human combustion
1951, July 1/Mary Reeser/1200 Cherry
St. NE
    Tampa Tribune, 4 July 1951.
    Mary Fuller, "Another Mysterious Cre-
    mation," Fate 4 (Nov.-Dec.1951):56-
    62.
    (Letter), Basil Hritsco, Fate 5
    (Apr.-May 1952):116-17.
    Vincent H. Gaddis, Mysterious Fires
    and Lights (N.Y.: Dell, 1968), pp.
    208-19.
    (Editorial), Fate 28 (Oct.1975):22-
    24.
-UFO (CE-1)
1968, Aug.15/Leonard B. Bartlett
    Brad Steiger & Joan Whritenour, Fly-
    ing Saucer Invasion: Target--Earth
    (N.Y.: Award, 1969), p.99.
-UFO (DD)
1957, Sep.19/Albert Whitted Airport
    "Flying Saucer Roundup," Fate 11
    (Feb.1958):29,34.
1957, Nov.5/Paul Hayes
    Donald E. Keyhoe, Flying Saucers: Top
    Secret (N.Y.: Putnam, 1960), p.124.
1958, Dec.12/Leonard L. Minthorne
    "UFO Press Story Censorship Report-
    ed," UFO Inv. 1 (Feb.-Mar.1959):6.
-UFO (NL)
1947, July 10/Mrs. William Krahenbuehl
    St. Petersburg Times, 14 July 1947.
1947, July 11/Robert Downs/520 25th
Ave. N
    St. Petersburg Times, 12 July 1947.
1956, Oct.2/Griff Richcreek
    (Editorial), Fate 10 (Mar.1957):16.
1964, July 8/Vernon C. Fields
    "UFO Sighting Wave Persists," UFO
    Inv. 2 (Sep.-Oct.1964):5.
1965, Sep.21/Robert W. Elliot
    "Theodolite Tracking of UFO," UFO
    Inv. 3 (Oct.-Nov.1966):8.
1976, June 18
    "Noteworthy UFO Sightings," Ufology
    2 (fall 1976):60.

Saint Petersburg Beach
-UFO (?)
1977, April 10/Judith Luckwell/Pass-a-
grille/=lens defect?
    (Letter), Fate 30 (Dec.1977):116-17.
    il.

Salt Springs
-UFO (CE-2)
1975, Dec.14/Eugene Bell/1 mi.NE
    Jim Jones, "Possible E-M Case in
    Florida," APRO Bull. 24 (Jan.1976):
    2,5. il.

Sanford
-UFO (NL)
1963, Aug.6/Orvil Hartle
    Richard Hall, ed., The UFO Evidence
    (Washington: NICAP, 1964), p.141.
1978, March 31/Vicki Bryant/W. 25th St.

Sanford Herald, 7 Apr.1978.
Sarasota
-Animal ESP
1973, Oct./Margaret Armstrong
    Margaret Armstrong, "Telepathic Fish
    Story," Fate 28 (Aug.1975):61.
-Astrology
1974/Russell Tingley/Box 5424
    Warren Smith, "Phenomenal Predictions
    for 1975," Saga, Jan.1975, pp.20,53.
-Fall of yellow rain
1970, March
    San Jose (Cal.) Mercury, 11 Mar.1970.
-Healing
1959-1970s/Celia Conkey/St. Boniface
Episcopal Church/Siesta Key
    Lee Butcher, "The Faith Healers of
    Florida," Fate 28 (Jan.1975):81-85.
-Paraphysics research
1960s/Wallace Minto/Sarasota Research
& Development Corp./1121 Lewis Ave.
    Rexford Daniels, "The Possibility of
    a New Force in Nature," in John
    White & Stanley Krippner, eds., Fu-
    ture Science (Garden City, N.Y.:
    Anchor, 1977), pp.35,39,592.
-Skyquake
1956, April 4
    "Case 155," CRIFO Orbit, 4 May 1956,
    pp.1-2, quoting Sarasota Herald-
    Tribune (undated).
-Telepathy research
1930s/Esther Bond
    J.B. Rhine, New Frontiers of the
    Mind (N.Y.: Farrar & Rinehart, 1937),
    pp.148-50.
-UFO (CE-1)
1960, May 4/S.D. Parker, Jr.
    "Recent UFO Sightings," NICAP Spec.
    Bull., May 1960, p.4.
    Richard Hall, ed., The UFO Evidence
    (Washington: NICAP, 1964), p.147.
    il.
-UFO (CE-2)
1957, Dec.18
    Richard Hall, ed., The UFO Evidence
    (Washington: NICAP, 1964), p.75.
-UFO (DD)
1969, May 21
    "'Cigar-Shaped' UFO's Reported All
    Over the Globe," Skylook, no.20
    (July 1969):9,10.
1975, Nov.30
    "Noteworthy UFO Sightings," Ufology
    2 (spring 1976):42.
-UFO (NL)
1954, Jan.4/MacKinlay Kantor
    MacKinlay Kantor, "Why I Believe in
    Flying Saucers," Pop.Sci.Monthly 188
    (Jan.1966):72-74,198-200.
1958, Jan.14
    Richard Hall, ed., The UFO Evidence
    (Washington: NICAP, 1964), p.146.
1976, March 30
    "Noteworthy UFO Sightings," Ufology
    2 (summer 1976):62.
1976, April 7
    "Noteworthy UFO Sightings," Ufology
    2 (fall 1976):60.

Sebastian
-Fall of weblike substance
  1967, Feb.1/U.S.1
    "'Angel Hair' in Florida," APRO Bull.
    15 (Jan.-Feb.1967):6.

Sebring
-UFO (CE-1)
  1966, Sep.20/James J. O'Connor
    "Plane Paced over Florida," UFO Inv.
    3 (Oct.-Nov.1966):4.
    Donald E. Keyhoe & Gordon I.R. Lore,
    Jr., UFOs: A New Look (Washington:
    NICAP, 1969), p.7.
-UFO (DD)
  1957, March/Evelyn Hogan/N of town
    (Letter), Fate 10 (Oct.1957):119-20.
-UFO (NL)
  1976, June 25
    "Sighting Reports," CUFOS News Bull.,
    Sep.1976, p.6.

Siesta Key
-UFO (NL)
  1969, June
    "Florida Resident Reports Sightings,"
    Skylook, no.47 (Oct.1971):10.

Silver Glen Springs
-UFO (CE-1)
  1978, May 14
    Ocala Star-Banner, 16 May 1978.

South Miami
-Phantom image
  1957/South Miami Lutheran Church
    William H. Leach, "The Phantom
    Cross," Fate 10 (Nov.1957):42-43.
-UFO (CE-3)
  1961, March 6
    Gabriel Green, Let's Face the Facts
    About Flying Saucers (N.Y.: Popular
    Library, 1967), pp.70-71.
    B. Ann Slate, "The Humanoids," Saga
    UFO Report 6 (Jan.1979):32,34, quot-
    ing SPACE Bull., no.52 (Apr.1961).

Stuart
-Animal ESP
  1977, Sep.30/Vi Brodka
    (Editorial), Fate 31 (May 1978):22-
    24, quoting Stuart News (undated).

Surfside
-UFO (NL)
  1956, March/Anne R. Cardona
    (Letter), Fate 10 (Feb.1957):113-16.

Tallahassee
-Lunar cycle and blood
  1956-1958
    Edson J. Andrews, "Moon Talk: The
    Cyclic Periodicity of Postoperative
    Hemorrhage," J.Florida State Med.
    Ass'n 46 (1961):1362-66.
-Snake handling
  1947-1948/Beauregard Barefoot
    Weston La Barre, They Shall Take Up
    Serpents (Minneapolis: Univ. of
    Minnesota, 1962), pp.113-75.

-UFO (?)
  1973, Oct.5/=Venus
    Tallahassee Democrat, 6 Oct.1973.
-UFO (NL)
  1972, Sep.16/Robert C. Burgun/S on Sunshine Turnpike
    "Flap in Florida," APRO Bull. 21
    (Sep.-Oct.1972):7.
  1973, Sep.24/Doug Barkley/3309 Robin
  Hood Rd.
    Tallahassee Democrat, 25 Sep.1973.
  1973, Nov.12/R.C. Cook
    "Flight Crew Sighting in Florida,"
    APRO Bull. 22 (Jan.-Feb.1974):10,
    quoting Southernaire, Dec.1973.

Tamarac
-UFO (NL)
  1973, Oct.7
    Pompano Beach Sun-Sentinel, 10 Oct.
    1973.

Tampa
-Clairvoyance
  1954, March/I. Moore/Tampa Hospital
    "The Nurse Dreamed of Death," Fate
    7 (Oct.1954):38.
-Doubtful responsibility
  1957, July 23/Mrs. Neil Keen/mystery
  skull fracture
  1957, Aug.18/Hope Leverne Brown/mys-
  tery skull fracture
    (Editorial), Fate 10 (Dec.1957):19.
-Fall of soot
  1961, June 19/Eloise Cozens/=pollution
    (Editorial), Fate 14 (Oct.1961):25.
  1961, Sep./Mrs. Harrison Thompson, Jr./
  Davis I./=pollution
    Tampa Tribune, 9 Sep.1961.
    (Editorial), Fate 15 (Jan.1962):22-
    24.
    (Letter), Olive R. Imhof, Fate 15
    (July 1962):116.
    (Letter), George Butler, Fate 16
    (Sep.1963):128-29.
  1961, Oct.25/=pollution
    (Editorial), Fate 15 (Feb.1962):19.
-Haunt
  1959, May/Garry Johnson
    Dolores Beaudry & Rosalie Kollett,
    "Ghosts of the Playful Kind," Fate
    22 (Oct.1969):72-75.
-Paranormal strength
  1960/Charles Rogers
    (Editorial), Fate 13 (Sep.1960):25.
-Precognition
  1975/Robert E. Hill/Rt.6, Box 349
    Warren Smith, "Phenomenal Predictions
    for 1976," Saga, Jan.1976, pp.16,18.
-Telepathy research
  1960s-   /David B. Cohen/St. Leo College
    E. Zotti & D.B. Cohen, "Effect of an
    ESP Transmitter Vs. a Non-ESP Trans-
    mitter in Telepathy," J.Parapsych.
    34 (1970):232-33.
    (Editorial), Fate 29 (Nov.1976):20-
    22.
-UFO (DD)
  1946, Aug.1/Jack E. Puckett/30 mi.NE

Donald E. Keyhoe, Flying Saucers: Top Secret (N.Y.: Putnam, 1960), pp. 102-103.
1947, July 6/E.H. Kleiser/Twiggs St.
Tampa Tribune, 7 July 1947.
1947, July 7/Jeanine Eason/shipyard
1947, July 7/John Garcia/Davis Causeway
1947, July 7/Russell Pollar/Causeway x 22d St.
1947, July 7/George Gortez/2506 21st St.
Tampa Tribune, 8 July 1947.
-UFO (NL)
1897, April/Scott St.
Jacksonville Florida Times-Union, 16 Apr.1897.
1957, July 17/Tom Candileri/Zambito Rd.
1957, July 18/Geraldine Sammons/Temple Terrace Hwy.
(Editorial), Fate 10 (Nov.1957):10-11.
1958, March 2/airfield
Jacques Vallee, Passport to Magonia (Chicago: Regnery, 1969), p.270.
1975, Nov.19
"UFO Central," CUFOS News Bull., 1 Feb.1976, p.13.
-UFO (R-V)
1952, summer/Don Widener/MacDill AFB
Richard Hall, ed., The UFO Evidence (Washington: NICAP, 1964), p.25.

Tarpon Springs
-Sea monster
1948, Aug./coast to N
Ivan T. Sanderson, More Things (N.Y.: Pyramid, 1969), pp.36-37.
-Weeping icon
1969, Dec.4-1972/Elias Kalariotes/Greek Orthodox Church
(Editorial), Fate 23 (Apr.1970):34-36.
(Editorial), Fate 26 (June 1973):24-26.

Terra Ceia
-Archeological site
1000 B.C.-1600 A.D./Madira Bickel Mound
Ripley P. Bullen, "The Terra Ceia Site, Manatee County, Florida," Pub. Florida Anthro.Soc'y, no.3 (1951).
W.J. Armistead, "An Unusual Shell Gorget from Terra Ceia Island, Manatee County, Florida," Florida Anthro. 12 (1959):105-107. il.
Franklin Folsom, America's Ancient Treasures (N.Y.: Rand McNally, 1974), p.111.

Tice
-UFO (NL)
1970, Oct.5/Richard V. Stebbins
(Editorial), Fate 24 (Apr.1971):18-19.

Titusville
-UFO (?)
1961, March 25/=aircraft
Donald H. Menzel & Lyle G. Boyd, The

World of Flying Saucers (Garden City: Doubleday, 1963), pp.250-52.

Trenton
-Precognition
1935-   /Frances Mathis Williams
Frances Williams, "The Missing Mathis Kids," Fate 31 (July 1978):44-47. il.

Tyndall AFB
-UFO (DD)
1961, May 22
Richard Hall, ed., The UFO Evidence (Washington: NICAP, 1964), p.22.
Lloyd Mallan, "Complete Directory of UFOs: Part I," Sci.& Mech. 37 (Dec. 1966):36,74.
-UFO (NL)
1973, Oct./Earl Colvin
Panama City News-Herald, 7 Oct.1973.

Valrico
-UFO (CE-1)
1976, March 10
"Noteworthy UFO Sightings," Ufology 2 (summer 1976):62.

Venice
-Humanoid
1975, June 7/Ronnie Steves/Jackson Rd.
Venice Sun Coast Times, 17 Jan.1976.
B. Ann Slate, "Florida's Rampaging Man-Ape," Saga UFO Rept. 4 (July 1977):32,65.
1977
Fayetteville Northwest Arkansas Times, 9 Mar.1978.
-Rabbit and raccoon mutilations
1975, June/Mrs. Donald Madison/Venice Farms Rd.
B. Ann Slate, "Florida's Rampaging Man-Ape," Saga UFO Rept. 4 (July 1977):32,65-67.
-UFO (CE-1)
1978, July 25/Joe Nigro
Venice Sun Coast Gondolier, 27 July 1978.
-UFO (NL)
1975, March/Louis Sinclair
Venice Sun Coast Gondolier, 10 Mar. 1975.

Vero Beach
-Archeological site
E.H. Sellards, et al., "Symposium on the Age and Relations of the Fossil Human Remains Found at Vero, Florida," J.Geology 25 (1917):1-62. il.
Rollin T. Chamberlin, "Further Studies at Vero, Florida," J.Geology 25 (1917):667-83. il.
T.D. Stewart, "A Reexamination of the Fossil Human Skeletal Remains from Melbourne, Florida," Smith.Misc.Coll. vol.106, no.10 (1946). il.
Irving Rouse, "Vero and Melbourne Man: A Cultural and Chronological Interpretation," Trans.N.Y.Acad. Sci., ser.2, 12 (1950):220-24.

H.M. Wormington, <u>Ancient Man in Amer-</u>
<u>ica</u> (Denver: Mus.Nat.Hist., Pop.
Ser., no.4, 1957), pp.226-30.
Robert D. Weigel, "Fossil Vertebrates
of Vero, Florida," <u>Spec.Pub.Florida</u>
<u>Geol.Survey</u>, no.10 (1962). il.
-UFO (?)
 1955, Feb.7/=meteor?
 "February, Fireballs & the Facts,"
 <u>CRIFO Newsl.</u>, 1 Apr.1955, pp.4-5.
-UFO (DD)
 1978, Dec?/Frank Cox/King's Hwy.
 <u>Vero Beach Press-Journal</u>, 31 Jan.
 1979.
 1979, Jan.13/Mary Deans/Hwy.713
 <u>Vero Beach Press-Journal</u>, 17 Jan.
 1979.
 1979, Jan.15/Vivian Slimak/43d Ave. x
 Hwy.60
 <u>Vero Beach Press-Journal</u>, 31 Jan.
 1979.
-UFO (NL)
 1977, summer
 <u>Vero Beach Press-Journal</u>, 4 Feb.1979.

<u>Volusia co.</u>
-Hex
 1971/graveyard
 (Editorial), <u>Fate</u> 25 (Dec.1972):36.

<u>Wahneta</u>
-UFO (NL)
 1973, Oct.23
 Bartow <u>Polk County Democrat</u>, 25 Oct.
 1973.

<u>Walton co.</u>
-UFO (CE-1)
 1978, Aug.5/Kevin Davison/Hwy.20
 <u>Fort Walton Beach Playground News</u>,
 6 Aug.1978.

<u>Weeki-Wachee</u>
-Humanoid tracks
 1965, Oct.21/John F. Reeves/=hoax
 William J. Dunn, Jr., "An Analysis
 of the 1965 Brooksville Landing
 Case," <u>Saucer News</u> 13 (June 1966):
 6-8,19. il.
-UFO (?)
 1966, Aug.2/Eulah Lewis
 Robert Loftin, <u>Identified Flying Sau-</u>
 <u>cers</u> (N.Y.: David McKay, 1968), p.
 80.
-UFO (CE-2)
 1966, Dec.4/John F. Reeves
 <u>Largo Sentinel</u>, 8 Dec.1966.
 "Another UFO Landing at Brooksville,
 Florida," <u>Saucer News</u> 14 (summer
 1967):25-26.
 Brad Steiger & Joan Whritenour, <u>Fly-</u>
 <u>ing Saucers Are Hostile</u> (N.Y.:
 Award, 1967).
 Robert Loftin, <u>Identified Flying Sau-</u>
 <u>cers</u> (N.Y.: David McKay, 1968), pp.
 80-81, quoting <u>Saucer Scoop</u>, Jan.
 1967.
-UFO (CE-3)
 1965, March 2/John F. Reeves
 "The Florida 'Landing' Incident,"

<u>APRO Bull.</u> 13 (Mar.-Apr.1965):1.
"Reeves Story," <u>UFO Inv.</u> 3 (Apr.-May
 1965):8.
Coral E. Lorenzen, "Did a UFO Land
 in Florida?" <u>Fate</u> 18 (Oct.1965):
 32-39. il.
William J. Dunn, Jr., "An Analysis
 of the 1965 Brooksville Landing
 Case," <u>Saucer News</u> 13 (June 1966):
 6-8,19. il.
Robert Loftin, <u>Identified Flying Sau-</u>
 <u>cers</u> (N.Y.: David McKay, 1968), pp.
 71-79.
 1974, Aug.27
 Ted Bloecher, "A Catalog of Humanoid
 Reports for 1974," <u>Proc.MUFON 1975</u>
 <u>UFO Symposium</u> (Seguin, Tex.: MUFON,
 1975), pp.51,60.
-UFO (CE-4)
 1968, Aug.6/John F. Reeves
 David Webb, "Analysis of Humanoid/
 Abduction Reports," in <u>Proc.1976</u>
 <u>CUFOS Conference</u> (Evanston: Center
 for UFO Studies, 1976), pp.266,268-
 69.
-UFO (NL)
 1965, June/Barbara I.W. Falk/a few mi.S
 (Letter), <u>Fate</u> 19 (June 1966):119-21.

<u>Wellborn</u>
-UFO (NL)
 1978, Jan.4, 9/Elaine Beasley
 <u>Live Oak Independent Post</u>, 11 Jan.
 1978.

<u>West Hollywood</u>
-Humanoid
 1974, Jan.9/Richard Lee Smith/W on Hwy.
 820
 <u>Miami Herald</u>, 10 Jan.1974.

<u>West Palm Beach</u>
-Disappearance
 1924, March/Ed Ashley/ocean to SE
 1931, June/Herbie Pond/Curtiss Robin
 monoplane/ocean to SE
 Richard Winer, <u>The Devil's Triangle</u>
 (N.Y.: Bantam, 1974), pp.32-33,74-
 75.
 1970, Nov.23/Piper Comanche plane/
 ocean to S
 <u>Miami Herald</u>, 26 Nov.1970, p.22D.
 Lawrence David Kusche, <u>The Bermuda</u>
 <u>Triangle Mystery--Solved</u> (N.Y.: Harper & Row, 1975), pp.232-34.
 1973, May 25/Robert Corner/Navion 16
 plane/ocean to SE
 Richard Winer, <u>The Devil's Triangle</u>
 (N.Y.: Bantam, 1974), pp.55-56.
-Humanoid
 1974, Sep.24/Cary Kanter/Hwy.441 nr.
 Wellington
 <u>Palm Beach Post</u>, 26 Sep.1974.
-Precognition
 1965, May 13/Helen Westmoreland
 <u>Palm Beach Post-Times</u>, 13 June 1965.
-UFO (NL)
 1948, Feb.20/Charles Francis Coe
 <u>Miami Herald</u>, 21 Feb.1948.
 1972, Sep.12-13/Holiday Plaza Mobile

Park
1972, Sep.14/Katherine Gould
"Flap in Florida," APRO Bull. 21
(Sep.-Oct.1972):7, quoting Palm
Beach Post (undated).
-UFO (R-V)
1972, Sep.14/James Moon, Jr./airport
"Flap in Florida," APRO Bull. 21
(Sep.-Oct.1972):7, quoting Ft. Lau-
derdale Sun (undated).
Donald E. Keyhoe, Aliens from Space
(Garden City: Doubleday, 1973), pp.
3-4.
Philip J. Klass, UFOs Explained (N.Y.:
Random House, 1974), pp.182-85.

Williston
-UFO (CE-2)
1955, Nov.2/C.F. Bell
"Saucer Numbs Policeman," CRIFO Or-
bit, 2 Mar.1956, p.6, quoting
Gainesville Daily Sun (undated).
-UFO (NL)
1955, Nov.3/Sam Verones
"Saucer Numbs Policeman," CRIFO Or-
bit, 2 Mar.1956, p.6.

Winter Haven
-UFO (NL)
1979, Jan.3/Jeannette Bagley/Lake Mar-
tha Dr.
Winter Haven News-Chief, 7 Jan.1979.
1979, Jan.4/Ron Perdue/Polk Community
College
Palm Beach Post-Times, 6 Jan.1979.

Winter Park
-Animal ESP
1970, Feb./Elizabeth S. Wilson
Elizabeth S. Wilson, "Middy (And All
Cats) Go to Heaven," Fate 25 (Apr.
1972):63-65.
-Fall of fish
1893
Thomas R. Baker, "A Rain of Fishes,"
Science 21 (1893):335.
-Out-of-body experience
n.d./Henry Hoffbower
Henry Hoffbower, "My Doppelgänger
and I," Fate 21 (June 1968):70-75.
-Plant sensitivity
1977/Robbins College
Hoyt L. Edge, "Plant PK on an RNG
and the Experimenter Effect," in
William G. Roll, ed., Research in
Parapsychology 1977 (Metuchen, N.J.:
Scarecrow, 1978), pp.169-74.
-Poltergeist
1968, Jan./Hilda Blazey/La Petite
Poodle
(Editorial), Fate 21 (Sep.1968):28-
29.
-Skyquake
1895, Feb.7/=meteor?
"The Noise Made by a Meteor," Month-
ly Weather Rev. 23 (Feb.1895):57.

B. Physical Features

Alexander Spring Creek
-Disappearance
1966, Oct.1/Nancy Liechner
Eric Norman [Brad Steiger], Weird Unsolved Mysteries (N.Y.: Award,
1969), pp.18-20.

Amelia I.
-Archeological site
ca.2000 B.C.-1600 A.D.
E. Thomas Hemmings, Kathleen A. Dea-
gan & Adelaide K. Bullen, "Excavations on Amelia Island in Northeast
Florida," Contrib.Univ.Florida State
Mus.Anthro.& History, no.18 (1973).
il.

Anclote Keys
-Archeological site
Jim Brandon, Weird America (N.Y.:
Dutton, 1978), p.67, quoting ETM
Log, autumn 1969.

Anclote R.
-Anomalous hole in ground
1968, Dec.17/U.S.19 bridge/=sinkhole
Otto O. Binder, "The Mystery of Underground UFO Bases," Saga UFO Rept. 1
(spring 1974):22,44.
-Humanoid
1966, summer/Ralph Chambers
Brad Steiger & Joan Whritenour, Allende Letters: New UFO Breakthrough
(N.Y.: Award, 1968), p.88.
1966, Dec.
John Green, The Sasquatch File (Agassiz, B.C.: Cheam, 1973), p.40.
1967/Ralph Chambers
Brad Steiger & Joan Whritenour, Allende Letters: New UFO Breakthrough
(N.Y.: Award, 1968), pp.88-89.

Angelfish Creek
-Teleportation
man-of-war fish
Craig Phillips, "Nomeus: A Fish That
Disappears," Pursuit 6 (Apr.1973):
38-40.

Apalachicola National Forest
-Smoke anomaly
1880s
Barton D. Jones, "On the Gulf Coast,"
Lippincott's Mag., Mar.1882.
Charles Ledyard Norton, A Handbook of
Florida (N.Y.: Longmans, Green, 1892),
p.346. il.
Roland M. Harper, "Geography and Vege-
tation of Northern Florida," Ann.Rept.
Florida Geol.Survey 6 (1914):163,303.
"Anybody Remember 'The Great Florida
Mystery'?" INFO J., no.7 (fall 1970)
:33-34, quoting (Letter), William C.
Wood, Adventure, July 1934.

Apalachicola R.
-UFO (CE-1)
1978, May 15/"Lisa C"/nr. mile 51 marker

Panama City News-Herald, 18 May 1978.
"UFOs of Limited Merit," *Int'l UFO
Reporter* 3 (July 1978):3.

Big Cypress Swamp
-Ancient pyramid
    Charles Berlitz, *Mysteries from For-
    gotten Worlds* (Garden City: Double-
    day, 1972), p.145.
    "Florida Ancient Ruins," *Search &
    Discovery*, May 1976, p.5.
-Humanoid
    1957
        John Green, *Sasquatch: The Apes Among
        Us* (Seattle: Hancock House, 1978),
        pp.271-72.
    1971, spring/H.C. Osborn
        Washington (D.C.) Star, 9 Aug.1971.
        New York Times, 18 Aug.1971.
        National Enquirer, 7 Nov.1971.
        John Green, *Sasquatch: The Apes Among
        Us* (Seattle: Hancock House, 1978),
        pp.272-73.
    n.d./Gordon Prescott
        B. Ann Slate, "Florida's Rampaging
        Man-Ape," *Saga UFO Rept.* 4 (July
        1977):32,64-65, quoting *St. Peters-
        burg Times*, 26 Aug.1975.

Big Pass
-Sea monster
    1948, Feb.
        Ivan T. Sanderson, *More Things* (N.Y.:
        Pyramid, 1969), p.36.

Biscayne Bay
-UFO (?)
    1955, Feb.7/Charles Elmore/=meteor?
        "February, Fireballs & the Facts,"
        CRIFO Newsl., 1 Apr.1955, pp.4-5.
-UFO (NL)
    1956, Oct./Harry Emerson
        "Case 266," *CRIFO Orbit*, 4 Jan.1957,
        p.3.

Blount I.
-UFO (CE-3)
    1972, Jan./Norman Chastain
        Jacksonville Journal, 28 Jan.1974.
        B. Ann Slate, "The Alien of Blount
        Island," *Saga UFO Rept.* 1 (summer
        1974):32-35,77-78.

Burtine I.
-Archeological site
    ca.700 B.C.-1700 A.D.
        Ripley P. Bullen, "Burtine Island,
        Citrus County, Florida," *Contrib.
        Florida State Mus.Soc.Sci.*, no.14
        (1966). il.

Caloosahatchee R.
-Humanoid
    ca.1970/8 mi.NE of Fort Myers
        (Letter), Zack T. Barnard, *Fate* 28
        (June 1975):144.

Cape Haze Peninsula
-Archeological sites
    ca.850 B.C.-recent
        Ripley P. & Adelaide K. Bullen, "Ex-

cavations on Cape Haze Peninsula,
Florida," *Contrib.Florida State Mus.
Soc.Sci.*, no.1 (1956). il.

Canaveral, Cape
-Electromagnetic anomaly
    1945, March 25/Marcus Billson/PBM
        Charles Berlitz, *Without a Trace*
        (N.Y.: Ballantine, 1978 ed.), pp.
        45-46.
-Fall of weblike substance
    1969, Oct.20
        George D. Fawcett, "Florida Report,"
        Flying Saucers, June 1970, p.30.
-Mystery radio transmission
    1958, Oct./Cape Kennedy Missile Test
    Center
        "'Runaway' Sputnik Tracked Past Moon,"
        Missiles & Rockets 4 (15 Dec.1958):
        17.
        Max B. Miller, "Scientists Track
        Space Radio Signals," *Fate* 12 (June
        1959):57-58.
-UFO (CE-3)
    1966, June/James Harkins
        Lucius Farish & Dale Titler, "Mys-
        teries of the Deep: Underwater
        UFOs," *Official UFO* 2 (May 1977):
        38,54.
-UFO (DD)
    1965, Aug.21/James R. Peek/=film de-
    fect?
        Orlando Sentinel, 21 Sep.1965.
        "Gemini 5 Launching Observed by UFOs?"
        UFO Inv. 3 (Aug.-Sep.1965):6.
        (Letter), Sara B. Hunt, *Saucer News*
        12 (Dec.1965):5.
-UFO (NL)
    1957, Oct.7/Al Leonard/Cape Kennedy
    Missile Test Center
        "Flying Saucer Roundup," *Fate* 11
        (Feb.1958):29,35.
    1964, Dec.5
        "News Briefs," *Saucer News* 12 (Mar.
        1965):24-25.
    1965, Feb.-April/John R. Frick
        John R. Frick, "The Saga of the Alien
        Spacecraft," *Official UFO* 2 (Feb.
        1977):25,50-51.
-UFO (R)
    1961, Jan.10
        Frank Edwards, *Flying Saucers: Ser-
        ious Business* (N.Y.: Lyle Stuart,
        1966), pp. 205-206, quoting *True*,
        Jan.1965.

Cayo Pelau
-Haunt
    n.d.
        B. Ann Slate, "Florida's Rampaging
        Man-Ape," *Saga UFO Rept.* 4 (July
        1977):32,34, quoting Herb Goldberger,
        "The Ghost of Cayo Pelau," *Gold*,
        winter 1974.

Cedar Keys
-Archeological site
        S.T. Walker, "The Aborigines of Flor-
        ida," *Ann.Rept.Smith.Inst.*, 1881,
        pp.677-80.
-Skyquake

1885, Dec.28/W.S. Cooper/20 mi.SE
   W.S. Cooper, "Barisal Guns," Sci.Am.
   75 (1896):123.
-UFO (NL)
   n.d./R.B. Davis
      (Editorial), Fate 7 (Apr.1954):5,
      quoting St. Petersburg Times (un-
      dated).

Crystal R.
-Archeological site
   540 B.C.-1000 A.D.
      Clarence B. Moore, "Crystal River
      Revisited," J.Acad.Nat.Sci.Phila-
      delphia 13 (1907):406-25.
      Ripley P. Bullen, "The Enigmatic
      Crystal River Site," Am.Antiquity
      17 (1951):142-43.
      Ripley P. Bullen, "The Famous Crys-
      tal River Site," Florida Anthro. 6
      (1953):9-37. il.
      Adelaide K. Bullen, "Wash Island in
      Crystal River," Florida Anthro. 14,
      no.3-4 (1962):69-73. il.
      Adelaide K. & Ripley P. Bullen, "The
      Wash Island Site, Crystal River,
      Florida," Florida Anthro. 16, no.3
      (1963):81-92. il.
      Ripley P. Bullen, "Stelae at the
      Crystal River Site, Florida," Am.
      Antiquity 31 (1966):861-65. il.
      Clark Hardman, "The Primitive Solar
      Observatory at Crystal River and
      Its Implications," Florida Anthro.
      24, no.4 (1971):135-68. il.
      Franklin Folsom, America's Ancient
      Treasures (N.Y.: Rand McNally,
      1974), p.111.

Cypress L.
-UFO (CE-1)
   1968, Nov.26
      Donald E. Keyhoe, Aliens from Space
      (Garden City: Doubleday, 1973),
      p.266.

Dan's I.
-Giant bird tracks
   1948, March 20
      Ivan T. Sanderson, More Things (N.Y.:
      Pyramid, 1969), p.34.

Dora L.
-Archeological site
   "Ancient Works in Florida," Knowledge
   2 (1882):271, quoting Travers Herald (undated).

Dry Tortugas
-Mystery shipwreck
   1963, Feb.4/"Marine Sulphur Queen"
      New York Times, 11 Feb.1963, p.11.
      John Wallace Spencer, Limbo of the
      Lost (N.Y.: Bantam, 1973 ed.), pp.
      66-74.
      Lawrence David Kusche, The Bermuda
      Triangle Mystery--Solved (N.Y.: Har-
      per & Row, 1975)--pp.185-96.

Estero Bay
-Archeological site
   Jim Brandon, Weird America (N.Y.:
   Dutton, 1978), pp.60-61, quoting
   ETM Log, autumn 1969.

Everglades
-Humanoid
   1973, Nov./Bill Allen
      B. Ann Slate, "Man-Ape's Reign of
      Terror," Saga UFO Rept. 4 (Aug.1977)
      :20,22.
   ca.1975
      Marty Wolf, "An Interview with Bob
      Morgan," Pursuit 8 (July 1975):70,
      71.

Fort George I.
-Mystery metal sphere
   1974, March 27/Antoine Betz
      "Florida's Mystery Sphere," APRO Bull.
      22 (Mar.-Apr.1974):1,4. il.
      (Editorial), Fate 27 (Aug.1974):20,
      30-32. il.
      (Editorial), Fate 28 (Mar.1975):18-
      20.
      Bill Baker, "The Mysterious Betz
      'Space Sphere,'" Saga UFO Rept. 2
      (spring 1975):28-31,60. il.

George, L.
-UFO (NL)
   1897, April 30
      Jacksonville Florida Times-Union, 2
      May 1897.

Gordon's Pass
-Archeological site
   3 mi.N/ancient canal
      Andrew E. Douglass, "Ancient Canals
      on the South-West Coast of Florida,"
      Am.Antiquarian 7 (1885):277-85.

Grassy Key
-Animal ESP
   1977, Oct.24-Nov./Patricia Hayes/Flip-
   per's Sea School
      Fred P. Graham, "The Telepathic Dol-
      phins," Fate 31 (July 1978):36-43.
      il.

Hog I.
-Sea monster
   1948, July 25/George Orfanides
      Clearwater Sun, 26 July 1948.
      St. Petersburg Times, 26 July 1948.

Indian R.
-UFO (NL)
   1979, Jan.24/James Oliver/U.S.1
      Vero Beach Press-Journal, 2 Feb.1979.

Indian Rocks
-Giant bird tracks
   1948, April 3
      Ivan T. Sanderson, More Things (N.Y.:
      Pyramid, 1969), p.34.

Itchtucknee R.
-Archeological site

Albert Ernest Jenks & Mrs. H.H. Simpson, Sr., "Bevelled Artifacts in
Florida," Am.Antiquity 6 (1941):314-
19.

Jackson L.
-Archeological site
1300-1600
Gordon R. Willey, "Archeology of the
Florida Gulf Coast," Smith.Misc.
Coll., vol.113 (1949). il.
John W. Griffin, "Test Excavations
at the Lake Jackson Site," Am.An-
tiquity 16 (1950):99-112. il.

Jewfish Creek
-UFO (CE-2)
1967, July 21/Barbara Fawcett
"Landing in Florida," APRO Bull. 16
(July-Aug.1967):7.
"Worldwide Sightings Showing In-
crease," UFO Inv. 4 (Oct.1967):1,4.

Jupiter Inlet
-UFO (?)
1978, Jan.20/John Johnson/offshore
Little Rock Arkansas Gazette, 22 Jan.
1978.

Key Largo
-Humanoid
1977, July 14/Charles Stoeckman
1977, July 22/Mrs. Charles Stoeckman
Marathon Florida Keys Keynoter, 28
July 1977.

Key Marco
-Archeological site
ca.100-1500 A.D.
Frank H. Cushing, "Exploration of An-
cient Key Dwellers' Remains on the
Gulf Coast of Florida," Proc.Am.
Phil.Soc'y 25 (1897):329-432.
H. Newell Wardle, "The Pile Dwellers
of Key Marco," Archaeology 4 (1951):
181-86. il.
Marion Spjut Gilliland, The Material
Culture of Key Marco, Florida
(Gainesville: Univ. of Florida,
1975). il.
Jim Brandon, Weird America (N.Y.:
Dutton, 1978), pp.59-60.
-Disappearance
1973, April 7/William Forshee/motor-
boat
Richard Winer, The Devil's Triangle
(N.Y.: Bantam, 1974), pp.91-92.

Little Salt Springs
-Archeological site
ca.10,000-5000 B.C.
"Florida's Pool of the Dead," Fate
13 (May 1960):54.
William Royal & Eugenie Clark, "Nat-
ural Preservation of Human Brain,
Warm Mineral Springs, Florida," Am.
Antiquity 26 (1960):285-87.
New York Times, 17 June 1973, p.42.
Carl J. Clausen, H.K. Brooks & A.B.
Wesolowsky, "Florida Spring Con-

firmed As 10,000 Year Old Early Man
Site," Pub.Florida Anthro.Soc'y, no.
7 (1975). il.
Jacksonville Florida Times-Union, 24
July 1977.
"Florida Burial Site: Brains to Boom-
erangs," Science News 112 (1977):90.

Long Key
-Oceanographic anomaly
1965, May/Irwin Brown/25 mi.SE
Charles Berlitz, Without a Trace
(N.Y.: Ballantine, 1978 ed.), pp.
114-15.

Matheson Hammock Park
-Giant bird
1961, winter/Eric Harnew
(Editorial), Fate 14 (May 1961):16.

Miami Canal
-UFO (NL)
1947, Oct.7/Frances Mathis Williams/
Devil's Garden
Frances Mathis Williams, "UFOs in
the Florida Swamp," Fate 26 (Aug.
1973):74-76.

Moon L.
-Humanoid
1977, Feb.-April
John Green, Sasquatch: The Apes Among
Us (Seattle: Hancock House, 1978),
p.280.

Mount Royal
-Archeological site
Clarence B. Moore, Certain Sand
Mounds of the St. John's River,
Florida (Philadelphia: Levytype,
1894), pp.16-17. il.
Francis Harper, ed., The Travels of
William Bartram (New Haven: Yale
Univ., 1958), pt.2, ch. iv, pp.64-
65.

Ocala Caverns
-Polynesian idol
Jim Brandon, Weird America (N.Y.:
Dutton, 1978), p.66.

Ocala National Forest
-Humanoid
1977, Oct.24/S.L. Whatley
New York Times, 10 Nov.1977.
Ocala Star-Banner, 16 Nov.1977.
1977, Nov.
Ocala Star-Banner, 19 Nov.1977.
-UFO (R-V)
1978, May 14/Robert J. Clark/Pinecastle
Electronic Warfare Range
Ocala Star-Banner, 16 May 1978; and
18 May 1978.
"Navy Radar-Visual in Florida," Int'l
UFO Reporter 3 (June 1978):4-5.
Marsha Lane, "Close Encounter of the
Radar/Visual Kind," Saga UFO Rept.
6 (Sep.1978):16-19.

Okeechobee, L.
-UFO (?)
    1974, July 8/Katherine Andrew/=space
    debris?
        Columbus (O.) Dispatch, 9-10 July
        1974.
-UFO (NL)
    1975, Jan.
        B. Ann Slate, "Florida's Rampaging
        Man-Ape," Saga UFO Rept. 4 (July
        1977):32,35, quoting Palm Beach
        Evening Times (undated).

Old Rhodes Key
-Archeological site
    S shore
        Jim Brandon, Weird America (N.Y.:
        Dutton, 1978), p.65.

Paynes Prairie
-Archeological site
    ca.8000 B.C.-1600 A.D.
        Ripley P. Bullen, "The Bolen Bluff
        Site on Paynes Prairie, Florida,"
        Contrib.Florida State Mus.Soc.Sci.,
        no.4 (1958). il.
        Houston (Tex.) Chronicle, 5 Feb.1978.

Philip's Hammock
-Giant bird tracks
    1948, April
        Ivan T. Sanderson, More Things (N.Y.:
        Pyramid, 1969), p.34.

Pine I.
-Archeological site
    ancient canal
        Andrew E. Douglass, "Ancient Canals
        on the South-West Coast of Florida,"
        Am.Antiquarian 7 (1885):277-85.

Sable, Cape
-Sea monster
    1892
        Karl Bickel, The Mangrove Coast (N.Y.:
        Coward-McCann, 1942).

Saga Bay
-Humanoid
    ca.1975
        Marty Wolf, "An Interview with Bob
        Morgan," Pursuit 8 (July 1975):70,
        71.

Saint Andrew's Bay
-Sea monster
    1943, March/Thomas Helm
        Thomas Helm, Monsters of the Deep
        (N.Y.: Dodd, Mead, 1963), pp.162-65.

Saint George I.
-Ghost light
    1953/Walter Yearty
        (Editorial), Fate 6 (Dec.1953):8-9.

Saint John's R.
-Archeological sites
        Francis Harper, ed., The Travels of
        William Bartram (New Haven: Yale
        Univ., 1958), pt.2, ch. iii-v, pp.

61-101.
        Daniel G. Brinton, "Artificial Shell
        Deposits of the United States," Ann.
        Rept.Smith.Inst., 1866, pp.356-58.
        Jeffries Wyman, "Fresh-Water Shell
        Mounds of the St. John's River,
        Florida," Mem.Peabody Acad.Sci.,
        vol.1, no.4 (1875).
        Clarence B. Moore, "Certain Shell
        Mounds of the St. John's River,
        Florida, Hitherto Unexplored," Am.
        Naturalist 26 (1892):912-22; 28
        (1894):15-26.
        J.B. Griffin, "The Significance of
        the Fiber-Tempered Pottery of the
        St. Johns," J.Washington Acad.Sci.
        35 (1945):218-23.
        John M. Goggin, "Space and Time Per-
        spective in Northern St. Johns Ar-
        cheology, Florida," Pub.Anthro.Yale
        Univ., no.47 (1952).
        William H. Sears, "Excavations on the
        Lower St. Johns River, Florida,"
        Contrib.Florida State Mus.Soc.Sci.,
        no.2 (1957). il.
        Otto L. Jahn & Ripley P. Bullen,
        "The Tick Island Site, St. Johns
        River, Florida," Pub.Florida Anthro.
        Soc'y, no.10 (Dec.1978). il.
-Cave anomaly
    1968
        "The Florida Underground," Pursuit 2
        (Jan.1969):9-10.
-Medieval Irish discovery
    ca.550 A.D./St. Brendan
        George A. Little, Brendan the Navi-
        gator (Dublin: M.H. Gill, 1946), pp.
        148-51.
-Out-of-body experience
    ca.1905
        Hornell Hart, "ESP Projection: Spon-
        taneous Cases and the Experimental
        Method," J.ASPR 48 (1954):121,133.
-Sea monster
    1975, June 7/Charles Abrams/mouth
        Richard Winer, From the Devil's Tri-
        angle to the Devil's Jaw (N.Y.: Ban-
        tam, 1977), pp.131-32.

Sand Key
-Giant bird
    1961
        (Editorial), Fate 14 (May 1961):16.

Sandy Key
-Disappearance
    1948, March 5/Al Snider/"Evelyn K"
        Miami Herald, 7-20 Mar.1948.
        George X. Sand, "Sea Mystery at Our
        Back Door," Fate 5 (Oct.1952):11,14-
        15.
        Lawrence David Kusche, The Bermuda
        Triangle Mystery--Solved (N.Y.: Har-
        per & Row, 1975), pp.139-41.

Sanibel I.
-UFO (NL)
    1976, June 26/Les Kessler
        "Florida Report," APRO Bull. 24 (Oct.
        1976):6.

Silver Springs
-Archeological site
Wilfred T. Neill, "A Stratified Early
Site at Silver Springs, Florida,"
Florida Anthro. 11, no.2 (1958):
33-52. il.
E. Thomas Hemmings, "The Silver
Springs Site: Prehistory in the
Silver Springs Valley, Florida,"
Florida Anthro. 28 (Dec.1975):141-
58. il.
-Erratic monkeys
1930s-   /=descended from Tarzan mov-
ie imports
"Florida's Wild Wildlife," Pursuit 6
(Apr.1973):37-38.
W.R. Maples, A.B. Brown & P.M. Hutch-
ens, "Introduced Monkey Populations
at Silver Springs, Florida," Flor-
ida Anthro. 29 (Dec.1976):133-36.
il.

Stock I.
-UFO (NL)
1976, Jan.27
"Noteworthy UFO Sightings," Ufology
2 (summer 1976):62.

Sunday Bluff
-Archeological site
Ripley P. Bullen, "Excavations at
Sunday Bluff, Florida," Contrib.
Florida State Mus.Soc.Sci., no.15
(1969). il.

Suwanee Gables
-Giant bird tracks
1948, Oct.21
Ivan T. Sanderson, More Things (N.Y.:
Pyramid, 1969), pp.34,38-55.
-River monster
1948, Oct./Martin Sharpe
Ivan T. Sanderson, More Things (N.Y.:
Pyramid, 1969), pp.37-38.

Suwanee R.
-River monster
1948, Oct.19/Mr. Hayes/nr. Cheflin
1948, Oct.20/Mary Belle Smith/Hwy.19
overpass
1948, Nov./Ivan T. Sanderson
Ivan T. Sanderson, More Things (N.Y.:
Pyramid, 1969), pp.37-38.

Turtle Mound
-Archeological site
800-1400 A.D.
Franklin Folsom, America's Ancient
Treasures (N.Y.: Rand McNally,
1974), pp.112-14.

Upper Matecumbe Key
-Archeological site
John M. Goggin & Frank H. Sommer III,
"Excavations on Upper Matecumbe Key,
Florida," Pub.Anthro.Yale Univ., no.
41 (1949). il.

Wakulla Springs
-Phantom (myth)

Federal Writers' Program, Florida: A
Guide to the Southernmost State
(N.Y.: Oxford Univ., 1956), p.486.

Weeden I.
-Archeological site
ca.500-1000 A.D.
J.W. Fewkes, "Preliminary Archeolog-
ical Explorations at Weeden Island,
Florida," Smith.Misc.Coll., vol.76,
no.13 (1924). il.
Gordon R. Willey, "The Weeden Island
Culture: A Preliminary Definition,"
Am.Antiquity 10 (1945):225-54. il.
Gordon R. Willey, "Archeology of the
Florida Gulf Coast," Smith.Misc.
Coll., vol.113 (1949). il.
William H. Sears, "The Weeden Island
Site, St. Petersburg," Florida An-
thro. 24, no.2 (1971):51-60. il.

Whitehurst L.
-Humanoid
1974
B. Ann Slate, "Man-Ape's Reign of
Terror," Saga UFO Rept. 4 (Aug.1977)
:20,55.

Withlacoochee R.
-Humanoid tracks
1976, Feb./Ramona Hibner
B. Ann Slate, "Man-Ape's Reign of
Terror," Saga UFO Rept. 4 (Aug.1977)
:20,56.

D. Unspecified Localities

-Giant human skeletons
1936, June/island off southern coast
New York Times, 9 June 1936, p.25.

A. Populated Places

Acworth
-Flying humanoid
1897, June/Litchfield Hotel
Atlanta Journal, 14 June 1897, quoting Acworth Post (undated).

Adairsville
-Seance
1939/Alice B. Howard
Jim Miles, "110 Years Later: Two Unknown Soldiers Identified," Fate
29 (Jan.1976):40-44.

Aiken
-UFO (NL)
1957, Nov.5
Richard Hall, ed., The UFO Evidence
(Washington: NICAP, 1964), p.164.

Albany
-UFO (CE-2)
1968, Nov.
"Spate of Reports in Georgia," APRO
Bull. 17 (Nov.-Dec.1968):7.
Brad Steiger & Joan Whritenour, Fly-
ing Saucer Invasion: Target--Earth
(N.Y.: Award, 1969), p.100.
-UFO (DD)
1963, March 12
"The Above Photo," Saucer News 10
(June 1963):1. il.
"Editor's Note," Saucer News 10 (Sep.
1963):4.
-UFO (NL)
1956/Don D. Emerson/20 mi.NW
"The Search for Hidden Reports," UFO
Inv. 4 (Mar.1968):7.
1973, Aug.31/Susan Shingler
Macon News, 31 Aug.1973.
1973, Sep.5/5 mi.S on U.S.19
Albany Herald, 5 Sep.1973.
1973, Nov.20
Jacksonville (Fla.) Times-Union, 21
Nov.1973.
-UFO (R-V)
1953, Jan.28
Edward J. Ruppelt, The Report on Un-
identified Flying Objects (Garden
City: Doubleday, 1956), pp.226-27.

Americus
-Lightning anomaly
1880s
Henry Winfred Splitter, "Nature's
Strange Photographs," Fate 8 (Jan.
1955):21,28, quoting San Francisco
(Cal.) Bulletin, 1886.
-Tornado anomaly
1881, July 18
"Local Storms," Monthly Weather Rev.
9 (July 1881):19.
-UFO (NL)

1973, Aug.31
Allen H. Greenfield, "Aerial Pheno-
mena 1970-1974," Flying Saucers,
Dec.1974, pp.5,11.

Ashburn
-UFO (?)
1973, Oct.19/I-75/=hoax?
Huntsville (Ala.) Times, 30 Oct.1973.
"Possible Hoax in Georgia," APRO
Bull. 22 (May-June 1974):5-6.

Athens
-Petroglyphs
Lustrat House
Margaret Perryman, "Sculptured Mono-
liths of Georgia: Part 2," Tennes-
see Arch. 13 (1962):14-22. il.
-UFO (CE-3)
1973, Oct.20/Mars Walker
Athens Banner-Herald, 21 Oct.1973.

Atlanta
-Clairvoyance
1959, June/Albert Robinson
"Dream of a Burglary," Fate 13 (Jan.
1960):32.
-Ghost
1957, Jan.17/Truman W. Powell
Truman W. Powell, "My Birthday Gift
from Ben Franklin," Fate 25 (Feb.
1972):80-83.
-Haunt
n.d./St. Michael's Church
Charles M. Skinner, Myths and Legends
of Our Own Land, 2 vols. (Philadelphia: Lippincott, 1896), 2:88-89.
1933/E.H. Bentley/Oakland Cemetery
John Philip Bessor, "Restless Spirits," Fate 6 (Mar.1953):27,28-29,
quoting Am.Weekly Mag., fall 1933.
1962-1968/nr. Fort McPherson
Hans Holzer, Gothic Ghosts (N.Y.:
Pocket Books, 1972), pp.19-27.
-Healing research
1965-   /Robert N. Miller/Agnes Scott
College
Robert N. Miller, "The Positive Effect of Prayer on Plants," Psychic
3 (Mar.-Apr.1972):24-25.
Robert N. Miller, Phillip B. Reinhart & Anita Kern, "Research Report:
Ernest Holmes Research Foundation,"
Science of Mind, July 1974, pp.12-
16.
Robert N. Miller & Phillip B. Rein-
hart, "Measuring Psychic Energy,"
Psychic 6 (Mar.-Apr.1975):46-47.
James Crenshaw, "Science Proves Psy-
chic Healing, Part One," Fate 29
(Jan.1976):47-54.
Robert N. Miller, "Methods of Detect-
ing and Measuring Healing Energies,"
in John White & Stanley Krippner,

eds., Future Science (Garden City: Anchor, 1977), pp.431-44.

-Hex
1948, Jan./James Ford
"Faith Its Wonderful," Doubt, no.21 (1948):323.

-Mystery bird deaths
1978, March 20/Northside Dr.
San Antonio (Tex.) News, 21 Mar.1978.
1978, May 7/=hoax?
San Antonio (Tex.) News, 8 May 1978.
"Pranksters Blamed for Killing Crows," Pursuit 11 (fall 1978):170, quoting S.U.News, 8 May 1978.

-Phantom panther
1958, April/J.F. Porter
Jerome Clark & Loren Coleman, Creatures of the Outer Edge (N.Y.: Warner, 1978), pp.122-23.

-Plague of snakes
1972, April/Claudine Jackson
(Editorial), Fate 25 (Nov.1972):34-36.

-UFO (?)
1955, July 30
"Rationalizing the Little Green Men," CRIFO Orbit, 7 Oct.1955, pp.3-4.
1966, March 28
"Typical Reports," UFO Inv. 3 (Mar.-Apr.1966):8.
1967, Oct.6-8
Jim & Coral Lorenzen, UFOs over the Americas (N.Y.: Signet, 1968), p.177.
1973, Oct.
Allen H. Greenfield, "Aerial Phenomena 1970-1974," Flying Saucers, Dec. 1974, pp.5,14.

-UFO (CE-3)
1969, Dec.27/Dairy Castle shop
Ted Phillips, "School Teacher Reports UFO and Occupants," Skylook, no.43 (June 1971):3.

-UFO (DD)
1954, June 11/H. Percy Wilkins
H. Percy Wilkins, Mysteries of Space and Time (London: Muller, 1955), p.41.

-UFO (NL)
1897, June 7
Atlanta Journal, 7 June 1897.
1918, April 15/Flora M. Shaw
Flora M. Shaw, "The Angel of Death," Fate 21 (Sep.1968):58-59.
1952, Aug.28/M.J. Spears
Richard Hall, ed., The UFO Evidence (Washington: NICAP, 1964), p.64, quoting INS release, 28 Aug.1952.
1954/Buddy Rich
Timothy Green Beckley, "Saucers and Celebrities," Saga UFO Rept. 2 (winter 1975):34-35.
1957, Nov.6/Mary Joyce Rudder
Jackson (Miss.) State Times, 7 Nov. 1957.
1966, July 26/Robert A. Bennett/airport
Orlando (Fla.) Sentinel, 27 July 1966.
1967, Sep.8/Sandra Ford
"Non-Believer Sights UFO," Saucer News 14 (winter 1967-68):19.
1971, July 27/B.G. Hodnett

Chicago (Ill.) Daily News, 29 July 1971.
1973, Sep.9/James R. Wyatt
Harry L. Helms, Jr., "Pres. Jimmy Carter and Georgia's UFO Wave," Saga UFO Rept. 4 (May 1977):17-18.
1976, May 10
"Noteworthy UFO Sightings," Ufology 2 (fall 1976):60.

Augusta
-Deathbed apparition
ca.1898/Margaret Sargent
"Incidents," J.ASPR 9 (1915):392-93.
-UFO (CE-1)
1951, summer/George Kinman
Richard Hall, ed., The UFO Evidence (Washington: NICAP, 1964), p.23, quoting Cleveland (O.) Press, 30 July 1952.
ca.1970/Darlene Sevier/1905 Castleton Ct.
Ralph & Judy Blum, Beyond Earth: Man's Contact with UFOs (N.Y.: Bantam, 1974), p.133.

Ball Ground
-Mineralogical anomaly
"Fairy Crosses," Pursuit 4 (Apr.1971):41.

Barnesville
-UFO (NL)
1973, Sep.18-19/Richard Wilson/Go Kart Race Track
Barnesville News-Gazette, 26 Sep. 1973.

Blairsville
-UFO (?)
1973, Sep.24/Carlton Shaw
1973, Sep.26/=Skylab
Blairsville North Georgia News, 26 Sep.1973.

Bloomingdale
-Fall of seeds
1958, Feb./Douglas Turner
(Letter), Fate 11 (Aug.1958):118-19.

Boston
-Humanoid
ca.1951
John Green, Sasquatch: The Apes Among Us (Seattle: Hancock House, 1978), p.215.

Bronwood
-Humanoid
1955, Aug.1/Joseph Whaley/NE on Hwy.118
Americus Times-Recorder, 3 Aug.1955, p.1.
Atlanta Constitution, 4 Aug.1955, p. 1; 5 Aug.1955, p.37; and 6 Aug.1955, p.1.
"Rationalizing the Little Green Men," CRIFO Orbit, 7 Oct.1955, pp.3-4.
Isabel Davis & Ted Bloecher, Close Encounter at Kelly and Others of 1955 (Evanston: Center for UFO Stud-

ies, 1978), pp.170-77.

Brooks
-UFO (CE-2)
  1973, Sep.14/Roy Lawhorn
    Atlanta Constitution, 18 Sep.1973.

Brunswick
-Phantom image
  1971, Oct./Glynn-Brunswick Memorial
  Hospital
  1971, Oct./Mt. Olive Baptist Church
  1971, Oct./St. Andrews Methodist
  Church
    David Techter, "A Flap of Glowing
    Crosses," Fate 25 (June 1972):52,
    54-55, quoting Savannah News-Press
    (undated).
-Psychic photography
  1970s/Jules Hamilton
    B.J. Baronitis, "The Psychic Photo-
    graphs of Jules Hamilton," Beyond
    Reality, no.32 (May-June 1978):40-
    43. il.
    (Letter), Harold A. Youtz, Beyond
    Reality, no.34 (Nov.-Dec.1978):6-7.
-UFO (NL)
  1973, Sep.28-30
    Jacksonville (Fla.) Journal, 1 Oct.
    1973.

Buford
-Precognition
  1970s/Ellen Evans/3837 Sudderth Rd.
    Warren Smith, "Phenomenal Predictions
    for 1976," Saga, Jan.1976, pp.17-18.
-UFO (NL)
  1973, Sep.21/Lanier Cantrell/shopping
  center
    Gwinnett Daily News, 23 Sep.1973.

Camilla
-UFO (NL)
  1973, Aug.31/Robert Welch
    Americus Times-Recorder, 31 Aug.1973.
  1973, Sep.1/Chester A. Tatum
    Atlanta Journal, 5 Sep.1973.
    Glenn McWane & David Graham, The New
    UFO Sightings (N.Y.: Paperback Li-
    brary, 1974), pp.90-91. il.

Canton
-Archeological site
  W of town
    William H. Sears, "The Wilbanks Site
    (9CK-5), Georgia," Bull.Bur.Am.Ethn.
    no.169 (1958):129-94.

Cedartown
-Psychokinesis
  1883, Aug.-1885/Lulu Hurst
    Chicago (Ill.) Tribune, 20 Jan.1884.
    Lulu Hurst [Mrs. Paul Atkinson], Lu-
    lu Hurst (The Georgia Wonder) Writes
    Her Autobiography (Rome, Ga.: Lulu
    Hurst, 1897).
    A. Campbell Holms, The Facts of Psy-
    chic Science and Philosophy Collated
    and Discussed (London: Kegan Paul,
    1925).

Dorothy Hampson Pope, "Lulu Hurst:
The Georgia Wonder," Fate 7 (Mar.
1954):100-10. il.
(Letter), William W. Bathlot, Fate
7 (Sep.1954):102-103.
E. Merton Coulter, "Lulu Hurst,
'Georgia Wonder,'" Georgia Hist.
Quar. 55 (1971):26-61.

Centerville
-Fall of weblike substance
  1959, Nov.3
    Atlanta Journal, 5 Nov.1959.

Cherokee co.
-Psychic photography
  1971-1975/Chester H. Heath
    Chester H. Heath, Spirit Photographs
    at Treasure Sites (N.Y.: Vantage,
    1976). il.

Clarkston
-UFO (NL)
  1975, Dec.5
    "UFO Central," CUFOS News Bull., 1
    Feb.1976, p.14.

Clayton co.
-UFO (NL)
  1973, Sep.24-25
    Allen Greenfield, "Aerial Phenomena
    1970-1974," Flying Saucers, Dec.
    1974, pp.5,13.

Columbus
-Fall of flesh
  1876
    Henry Winfred Splitter, "Wonders from
    the Sky," Fate 6 (Oct.1953):33,38,
    quoting Columbus Enquirer (undated).
-Haunt
  1967-1969
    Hans Holzer, Gothic Ghosts (N.Y.:
    Pocket Books, 1972), pp.42-51.
-Hex
  1952, Dec./Emma Smith
    Eleanor Dayhoof, "Voodoo: Death Be-
    side the Hearth," Fate 21 (Oct.1968)
    :61-65.
-Humanoid
  ca.1956
    John Green, The Sasquatch File (Ag-
    assiz, B.C.: Cheam, 1973), p.24.
-Roman coin
  1945/Mrs. H. Billy Arenowitch/Cedar Ave.
    Joseph B. Mahan & Douglas C. Braith-
    waite, "Discovery of Ancient Coins
    in the United States," Anthro.J.Can-
    ada, vol.13, 2 (1975):15-16. il.
-UFO (NL)
  1973, Sep.8/Leonard Waller/Beallwood
  Ave. x 41st St.
    Columbus Enquirer, 10 Sep.1973.
  1973, Sep.19/Jeff Brawer
    Columbus Enquirer, 20 Sep.1973.
-UFO (R-V)
  1966, March 28
    "Typical Reports," UFO Inv. 3 (Mar.-
    Apr.1966):8.

Conyers
-UFO (CE-1)
 1968, Nov.17/Jim Beecham
  "Spate of Reports in Georgia," APRO
  Bull. 17 (Nov.-Dec.1968):7, quoting
  Atlanta Journal (undated).
-UFO (DD)
 ca.1950/Jack R. Aiken/1 mi.W
  (Letter), Fate 5 (Dec.1952):111-17.

Coosawattee Old Town
-Archeological site
  Charles C. Jones, "Silver Crosses
  from an Indian Grave-Mound at Coosawattee Old Town, Murray County,
  Georgia," Ann.Rept.Smith.Inst.,
  1881, pp.619-24. il.
  George Irving Quimby, Indian Culture
  and European Trade Goods (Madison:
  Univ. of Wisconsin, 1966), pp.94-
  99. il.

Cordele
-UFO (NL)
 1973, Aug.31
  Macon News, 31 Aug.1973.

Covington
-UFO (NL)
 ca.1949, Aug.
  Harold T. Wilkins, Flying Saucers on
  the Attack (N.Y.: Ace, 1967 ed.),
  p.98.

Crawfordville
-Fall of weblike substance
 1959, Oct.12/M.B. Moore/=silver halide
 from cloud seeding?
  (Editorial), Fate 13 (Apr.1960):22-
  24.
  Donald H. Menzel & Lyle G. Boyd, The
  World of Flying Saucers (Garden
  City: Doubleday, 1963), pp.225-26.

Cuthbert
-Crisis apparition
 1865/Charles Murphy
  Charles M. Skinner, Myths and Legends
  of Our Own Land, 2 vols. (Philadelphia: Lippincott, 1896), 2:86-88.

Dale
-Poltergeist
 1911, Jan./Mr. Bright/telegraph tower
  W.F. Barrett, "Poltergeists Old and
  New," Proc.SPR 24 (1911):404-406.

Danielsville
-UFO (CE-3)
 1973, Oct.17/Paul H. Brown/U.S.29
  Athens Banner-Herald, 18 Oct.1973.
  Atlanta Constitution, 19 Oct.1973.
-UFO (NL)
 1973, Sep.12/Allen Gurley/5 mi.S on
 Piedmont Rd.
  Athens Banner-Herald, 14 Sep.1973.

Darien
-Phantom image
 1971, Oct./George C. Hall

David Techter, "A Flap of Glowing
 Crosses," Fate 25 (June 1972):52,56.

Dawson
-Fall of localized rain
 1886, Sep.
  Charles Fort, The Books of Charles
  Fort (N.Y.: Holt, 1941), p.562.
-UFO (NL)
 1973, Aug.30/A.L. Cahill
  Atlanta Journal & Constitution, 21
  Oct.1973.
  Americus Times-Recorder, 31 Aug.1973.

Decatur
-UFO (CE-1)
 1975, Sep.4
  "UFO Central," CUFOS News Bull., 15
  Nov.1975, p.17.

Doraville
-UFO (NL)
 1973, Sep.9/Mary Alice Rodes
  Harry L. Helms, Jr., "Pres. Jimmy
  Carter and Georgia's UFO Wave," Saga
  UFO Rept. 3 (May 1977):16,18.

Douglas
-Anomalous hole in ground
 1956/Earl Meeks/7 mi. from town
  Atlanta Journal, 19 Aug.1956.
-UFO (NL)
 1952, Dec.6/J. Manson Valentine
  Charles Berlitz, The Bermuda Triangle
  (Garden City: Doubleday, 1974), p.
  112.

Douglas co.
-Psychic photography
 1971-1975/Chester H. Heath
  Chester H. Heath, Spirit Photographs
  at Treasure Sites (N.Y.: Vantage,
  1976). il.

Douglasville
-UFO (CE-1)
 1974, March 2/Raymond R. Michaels
  Ronald Drucker, "The Southern U.S.--
  Target for Flying Saucers," Saga UFO
  Rept. 2 (fall 1975):15,68-70.

Dublin
-Fall of localized rain
 1920, Oct.16
  "Water from Nowhere," Doubt, no.14
  (spring 1946):208, quoting Oakland
  (Cal.) Tribune (undated).

East Point
-Ball lightning
 n.d.
  T.C. Mendenhall, "On Globular Lightning," Am.Meteor.J., Feb.1890, pp.
  437-47, quoting Macon Telegraph (undated).

Eatonton
-Archeological site
  Rock Eagle Effigy Mound/8 mi.N
   Charles C. Jones, Jr., "Aboriginal

Structures in Georgia," Ann.Rept.
Smith.Inst., 1877, pp.278-82. il.
Charles C. Jones, Jr., "Bird-Shaped
Mounds in Putnam County, Georgia,
U.S.A.," J.Royal Anthro.Inst. 8
(1879):92-96.
Franklin Folsom, America's Ancient
Treasures (N.Y.: Rand McNally,
1974), p.117.
"Giant Rock Eagle Holds Secret of An-
cient Origin," Grit, 13 Mar.1977.
-UFO (?)
1897, June 16/=meteor?
Atlanta Journal, 21 June 1897.

Edison
-Humanoid
1955, July 20-25/Tant King
Atlanta Constitution, 28 July 1955;
and 3-6 Aug.1955.
Atlanta Journal, 29 July 1955; and
2 Aug.1955.
Isabel Davis & Ted Bloecher, Close
Encounter at Kelly and Others of
1955 (Evanston: Center for UFO
Studies, 1978), pp.161-69.

Elbert co.
-Archeological site
Rembert's Mounds/Savannah R.
Charles C. Jones, Jr., "Aboriginal
Structures in Georgia," Ann.Rept.
Smith.Inst., 1877, pp.278,283-86.
Joseph R. Caldwell, "The Rembert
Mounds, Elbert County, Georgia," Pap.
U.S.River Basin Surveys, no.6 (1953)
:303-20.
Francis Harper, ed., The Travels of
William Bartram (New Haven: Yale
Univ., 1958), pt.3, ch. ii, pp.206-
207.

Elberton
-Fall of crayfish
1949, April 5
"Frog-Falls, Etc.," Doubt, no.27
(1949):411.
-Fall of string
1972, June/Hut Wallace
Atlanta Journal & Constitution, 11
June 1972.
"More Sky-Lines," Pursuit 5 (July
1972):53-54.

Fannin co.
-Shape-shifting
Charles M. Skinner, American Myths
and Legends, 2 vols. (Philadelphia:
Lippincott, 1903), 1:327-28.

Fayetteville
-UFO (CE-2)
1952, Oct.31/Charles Smith, Jr./4 mi.
away on Hwy.85
J. Allen Hynek, The Hynek UFO Report
(N.Y.: Dell, 1977), pp.191-92.

Forsyth co.
-Petroglyphs
Charles Rau, "Observations on Cup-

Shaped and Other Lapidarian Sculptures in the Old World and America,"
in Contrib.N.Am.Ethn., vol.5, pt.1
(1881). il.
Margaret Perryman, "Sculptured Monoliths of Georgia," Tennessee Arch.
17 (1961):1-9. il.
Margaret Perryman, "Georgia Petroglyphs," Archaeology 17 (spring
1964):54-56. il.

Fort Benning
-Ancient inscription
1966/Manfred Metcalf/Underwood Mill
Cyrus Gordon, "The Metcalf Stone,"
Manuscripts 21 (1969):158-68. il.
Andrew E. Rothovius, "An Aegean
Script Stone from Georgia?" NEARA
Newsl. 5, no.2 (1970):27-28. il.
William D. Connor, "Archaeologists
Link Georgia Indians to Crete,"
Fate 24 (Jan.1971):36-44. il.
Cyrus H. Gordon, Before Columbus
(N.Y.: Crown, 1971), pp.89-92. il.
-Haunt
1916, Nov./Karl Dayhoof
Eleanor Dayhoof, "Ghost Still Guards
Buried Treasure at Fort Benning,"
Fate 20 (Apr.1967):54-61.
(Letter), Eleanor Dayhoof, Fate 20
(July 1967):123.

Fort Oglethorpe
-UFO (CE-2)
1957, Nov.5
Richard Hall, ed., The UFO Evidence
(Washington: NICAP, 1964), pp.74,
164.
-UFO (NL)
1973, Oct.15/Frank Frills
(Editorial), Fate 27 (Feb.1974):32.

Franklin co.
-Fall of ice
1960, Oct.2/Ted Overman
(Editorial), Fate 14 (Feb.1961):20-
22.

Fulton co.
-Archeological site
Owl Rock
Margaret Perryman, "Sculptured Mono-
liths of Georgia," Tennessee Arch.
17 (1961):1-9. il.

Gainesville
-UFO (NL)
1964, July 14/Tom Winfield
Atlanta Constitution, 15 July 1964.

Garden City
-UFO (DD)
1975, Jan.3
Robert A. Goermann, "The UFO Modus
Operandi: January 1975," Official
UFO 1 (Aug.1976):47.

Griffin
-UFO (NL)
1973, Sep.9/Mrs. Hugh D. Beall

Leonard H. Stringfield, Situation Red: The UFO Siege (N.Y.: Fawcett, 1977 ed.), p.21, quoting UPI release, 9 Sep.1973.

Grovetown
-Healing
    Roland Steiner, "Observations on the Practice of Conjuring in Georgia," J.Am.Folklore 14 (1901):173-80.

Hartwell
-UFO (?)
    1897, June 16/=meteor?
        Atlanta Journal, 22 June 1897.

Hollywood
-Archeological site
    Cyrus Thomas, "Report on the Mound Explorations of the Bureau of Ethnology," Ann.Rept.Bur.Am.Ethn. 12 (1890-91):3,317-26. il.
    Clemens de Baillou, "A Test Excavation of the Hollywood Mound (9Ri 1), Georgia," Southern Indian Stud. 17 (1965):3-11. il.

Jesup
-UFO (NL)
    1973, Sep.23
        Jesup Wayne County Press, 25 Sep. 1973.

Kingsland
-Phantom image
    1971, Oct./First African Baptist Church
        David Techter, "A Flap of Glowing Crosses," Fate 25 (June 1972):52, 56.

LaGrange
-Ancient inscription
    1963/Mrs. Joe Hearn
        Y. Lynn Holmes, "The Mysterious Hearn Tablet," Anthro.J.Canada 13, no.1 (1975):11-13. il.

Lakemont
-Inner development
    1962-   /Center for Spiritual Awareness/Box 7
        Eugene R. Davis, This Is Reality (Lakemont: CSA, 1962).
        Armand Biteaux, The New Consciousness (Willits, Cal.: Oliver, 1975), p.17.
        D.R. Butler, "My Experience with 'Shaktipat': Instant Cosmic Consciousness?" Fate 28 (July 1975): 40-44.
-Parapsychology research
    1940s-   /Advanced Sciences Research & Development Corp./Box 109
        Rexford Daniels, "The Possibility of a New Force in Nature," in John White & Stanley Krippner, eds., Future Science (Garden City, N.Y.: Anchor, 1977), pp.35,38-39,582.

Lavonia
-UFO (CE-2)
    1964, June 29/Beauford E. Parham/SW on Hwy.59
        Anderson (S.C.) Independent, 1 July 1964.
        Charlotte (N.C.) News, 3 July 1964.
        Ted Phillips, Physical Traces Associated with UFO Sightings (Evanston: Center for UFO Studies, 1975), p.31.

Lawrenceville
-Mystery plane crash
    1953, Dec.6/four Thunderjets
        "Case 61," CRIFO Newsl., 4 Mar.1955, p.3.
-UFO (NL)
    1973, Sep.1
        Allen H. Greenfield, "Aerial Phenomena 1970-1974," Flying Saucers, Dec.1974, pp.5,11.

Leary
-UFO (CE-2)
    1975, Nov.20/James Spivey
        Jacksonville (Fla.) Times-Union, 21 Nov.1975.
        Memphis (Tenn.) Press-Scimitar, 14 Feb.1978.
-UFO (NL)
    1970, Jan./Jimmy Carter/Lions Club Hall
        Atlanta Journal, 12 Sep.1973.
        "The Carter Sighting," APRO Bull. 25 (Nov.1976):1,4-5.
        Harry L. Helms, Jr., "Pres. Jimmy Carter and Georgia's UFO Wave," Saga UFO Rept. 4 (May 1977):16-19.
        Memphis (Tenn.) Press-Scimitar, 14 Feb.1978.

Leesburg
-UFO (NL)
    1973, Aug.31/Albert Smith
        Macon News, 31 Aug.1973.

Lenox
-UFO (CE-1)
    1966, Nov.28/Charlotte Nipper/I-75
        Mona Darden, "One UFO for the Road," Fate 20 (June 1967):66-70.

Little River
-UFO (CE-2)
    ca.1903/Dick Smith
        E.A. Smith, "Death of an Engineer," Fate 21 (Nov.1968):72-74.

Mableton
-Fall of ice
    1960, Oct./Mrs. James A. West (Editorial), Fate 14 (Feb.1961):22.
-UFO (?)
    1953, July 7/Edward Waters/U.S.78/=hoax
        U.S. Air Force, Projects Grudge and Bluebook Reports 1-12 (Washington: NICAP, 1968), p.224.
-UFO (NL)
    1967, Oct.8/C.L. Curry
        Jim & Coral Lorenzen, UFOs over the Americas (N.Y.: Signet, 1968), p.177.

Macon
-Archeological site
  ca.1000 B.C.-1200 A.D./Ocmulgee Nat'l
  Monument
    Francis Harper, ed., The Travels of
    William Bartram (New Haven: Yale
    Univ., 1958), pt.1, ch. v, pp.34-35.
    A.R. Kelley, "A Preliminary Report
    on Archaeological Explorations at
    Macon, Georgia," Bull.Bur.Am.Ethn.,
    no.119 (1938):1-69.
    Jesse D. Jennings, "Ocmulgee Arch-
    aeology," Monthly Rept.Southwestern
    Monuments U.S.Nat'l Park Service,
    June 1938, pp.551-55.
    Franklin Folsom, America's Ancient
    Treasures (N.Y.: Rand McNally,
    1974), pp.115-17.
-Disappearance
  1955, summer/Carl M. Jones
    Brad Steiger, "People Are Disappear-
    ing," Probe the Unknown 3 (May
    1975):29,58.
-Fire immunity
  1850s
    Emma Hardinge Britten, Modern Ameri-
    can Spiritualism (N.Y.: The Author,
    1870), p.205.
-UFO (NL)
  1957, May 28
    Brad Steiger, Project Blue Book (N.Y.:
    Ballantine, 1976), betw.pp.56-57. il.
  1973, Aug.31/R.M. Barreth/Clisby Pt.
    Macon News, 31 Aug.1973.

Madison
-Animal ESP
  1955/Gladys Carter
    Gladys Carter, "Bobby Sox Knew," Fate
    9 (Feb.1956):61-62.

Manchester
-UFO (CE-1)
  1973, Sep.9/Sam Taylor/Pine Mt.
    Columbus Enquirer, 10 Sep.1973.
    J. Allen Hynek & Jacques Vallee, The
    Edge of Reality (Chicago: Regnery,
    1975), p.21.
    Leonard H. Stringfield, Situation
    Red: The UFO Siege (N.Y.: Fawcett,
    1977 ed.), p.22, quoting Nat'l En-
    quirer (undated).
-UFO (NL)
  1973, Sep.8/Joanne Cornwell/Pine Mt.
    Columbus Enquirer, 10 Sep.1973.

Marietta
-Aerial phantom
  1882, Feb.
    Aledo (Ill.) Democrat, 17 Feb.1882,
    quoting Atlanta Constitution (un-
    dated).
-Haunt
  1943, Dec.-1944, Sep./Mathilda Childers
  /15 mi. from town
    Mathilda A. Childers, "Who Opened
    the Door?" Fate 9 (Jan.1956):79.
-UFO (NL)
  1973, Sep.10/Mark Headrick/110 Lanier
  Rd.

Marietta Journal, 11 Sep.1973.
-UFO (R)
  1952, July 21/Dobbins AFB
    Richard Hall, ed., The UFO Evidence
    (Washington: NICAP, 1964), pp.77,
    160, quoting INS release, 24 July
    1952.

Martin
-Fall of ice
  1959, Oct.29/Claude LeCroy
    Paul Foght, "The Ice-Falls Continu-
    eth," Fate 13 (Feb.1960):27-31. il.
    (Editorial), Fate 13 (Apr.1960):20-
    21.
    (Letter), Everett L. Gayhart, Fate
    13 (July 1960):124,128.
    (Editorial), Fate 13 (Sep.1960):10-
    11.

Metter
-UFO (?)
  1972, Dec.12
    Savannah News, 24 Sep.1973.

Milledgeville
-UFO (DD)
  1967, Oct.22/David William Vitalli
    Wendelle C. Stevens, "Fantastic UFO
    Photo Flap of 1967," Saga UFO Rept.
    3 (Aug.1976):24,26-27. il.
-UFO (NL)
  1967, Oct.20, 22-23/Charles Mixon/E on
  Hwy.22
    Jim & Coral Lorenzen, UFOs over the
    Americas (N.Y.: Signet, 1968), pp.
    170-71.
    Edward U. Condon, Scientific Study
    of Unidentified Flying Objects
    (N.Y.: Bantam, 1969 ed.), pp.368-
    75.
    Philip J. Klass, UFOs Explained (N.Y.:
    Random House, 1974), pp.78-81.

Millen
-UFO (NL)
  1965, May 20/Larry G. Johnson/10 mi.SW
    (Letter), Fate 19 (Apr.1966):128-31.

Montezuma
-UFO (?)
  1978, Dec.31/Bubba Thompson
    Macon News, 5 Jan.1979.

Moultrie
-Clairempathy
  1930, Oct.17/C.H. Posey
    George L. Mock, Jr., "The Murder at
    the Old Ches Mullis Place," Fate 4
    (Nov.-Dec.1951):89-94.
-Fall of waterbugs
  1952, Sep.20
    "Falls," Doubt, no.41 (1953):221.

Nacoochee
-Archeological site
    George G. Heye, Frederick W. Hodge &
    George H. Pepper, "The Nacoochee
    Mound in Georgia," Contrib.Mus.Am.
    Indian, vol.2, no.1 (1918).

Newnan
-UFO (CE-1)
 1967, Oct.22/Dale Spradlin
   Boston (Mass.) Record-American, 23
   Oct.1967.
   Jim & Coral Lorenzen, UFOs over the
   Americas (N.Y.: Signet, 1968), pp.
   171-72.
   Edward U. Condon, Scientific Study
   of Unidentified Flying Objects
   (N.Y.: Bantam, 1969 ed.), pp.371-
   72.

Newton
-UFO (CE-2)
 1968, Nov.22/Conway Jones/10 mi.W on
 Hwy.91
   "New Rush of 'Buzzing' Incidents,"
   APRO Bull. 17 (Nov.-Dec.1968):5.
   J. Allen Hynek, The Hynek UFO Report
   (N.Y.: Dell, 1977), pp.189-91.

Orchard Hill
-UFO (CE-2)
 1973, Sep.10/Rast Clayton
   Atlanta Constitution, 11 Sep.1973.
   Athens Banner-Herald, 14 Sep.1973.
   Little Rock (Ark.) Gazette, 15 Sep.
   1973.

Oxford
-UFO (NL)
 1973, Oct.17/Elmo Shupe
   Harry L. Helms, Jr., "Pres. Jimmy
   Carter and Georgia's UFO Wave," Saga
   UFO Rept. 3 (May 1977):16,19.

Pearson
-UFO (CE-1)
 n.d./J. Manson Valentine/S on U.S.441
   Charles Berlitz, The Bermuda Triangle
   (Garden City: Doubleday, 1974), p.
   111.
 1973, Feb.18
   "Old Sighting Department," APRO Bull.
   27 (Sep.1978):5.

Pelham
-UFO (CE-4)
 1977, Aug.6/Mr. Dawson
   Camilla Enterprise, 10 Aug.1977.
   Pelham Journal, 11 Aug.1977, p.1.
   Jerome Clark, "The Most Bizarre UFO
   Encounter of the Year," Saga UFO
   Rept. 5 (Jan.1978):12-13.
-UFO (NL)
 1973, Aug.31
   "Golden Egg UFO over Georgia," Fly-
   ing Saucers, winter 1974, p.20. il.

Plains
-Haunt
 1919-   /Rosalynn Carter
   (Editorial), Probe the Unknown 4
   (Mar.1976):10.
-Healing
 1958-   /Ruth Carter Stapleton
   (Editorial), Fate 29 (Sep.1976):26-
   28, quoting Los Angeles (Cal.) Her-
   ald-Examiner (undated).

Ruth Carter Stapleton, Experiencing
   Inner Healing (Waco, Tex.: Word,
   1977).
 Ruth Carter Stapleton, The Gift of
   Inner Healing (N.Y.: Bantam, 1977).
   New York Times, 27 Jan.1978, p.15.
   "Sister Ruth," Newsweek, 17 July
   1978, pp.58-66. il.

Rome
-Hex
 1929, May
   William Seabrook, Witchcraft: Its
   Power in the World Today (N.Y.:
   Lancer, 1968 ed.), p.271.
-UFO (NL)
 1897, May
   Atlanta Journal, 15 May 1897.
 1973, Oct.16/John Ronner/Booger Hollow
 Rd.
   "Saucers in the News," Flying Saucers,
   winter 1974, pp.44,49, quoting Rome
   News-Tribune (undated).

Rossville
-Precognition
 1918, Nov.-   /R.C. "Doc" Anderson/
 302 W. Gordon Ave.
   Marguerite Steedman, "Prophecies of
   the Georgia Seer," Fate 17 (Aug.
   1964):49-56. il.
   Brad Steiger & Warren Smith, "How
   the Seers Scored in 1968," Fate 22
   (Jan.1969):72,74-75. il.
   Robert E. Smith, The Man Who Sees
   Tomorrow (N.Y.: Paperback Library,
   1970).
   Warren Smith, "How Did the Seers in
   1970?" Fate 24 (Feb.1971):84-86. il.
   Eric Norman [Warren Smith], This Hol-
   low Earth (N.Y.: Lancer, 1972), pp.
   63-84.
   A.L. Gary, The Psychic World of Doc
   Anderson (Anderson, S.C.: Droke
   House, 1973).
   Warren Smith, "Phenomenal Predictions
   for 1975," Saga, Jan.1975, p.20.
   (Letter), Donald Williamson, Fate 28
   (Mar.1975):117-18.
   (Letter), Loyd Foutz, Fate 28 (Oct.
   1975):118,128.
   James Bolen, "Interview: 'Doc' Ander-
   son," Psychic 7 (Apr.1976):48-53.

Roswell
-River monster
 1897, April/Mrs. Farmer/Chattahoochie
 River
   Cincinnati (O.) Enquirer, 10 Apr.1897,
   quoting Roswell Banner (undated).

Royston
-Roman coin
 1965, July/Billy Norris
   Kansas City (Mo.) Star, 27 July 1965.

Rydal
-UFO (DD)
 1957, Nov.11
   Cartersville Tribune-News, 13 Nov.1957.

Sandersville
-Archeological site
    2 mi.W
        Eleanor Rawlings & Clyde Keeler, "An
        Executed Amerindian?" NEARA J. 6
        (fall 1976):30-32. il.
-UFO (NL)
    1973, Aug.31/Ray Smith
        Jacksonville (Fla.) Journal, 1 Sep.
        1973.

Savannah
-Disappearance
    1950, April 5/"Sandra"
        Savannah Morning News, 20 Apr.1950,
        p.20.
        George X. Sand, "Sea Mystery at Our
        Back Door," Fate 5 (Oct.1952):11-12.
        Lawrence David Kusche, The Bermuda
        Triangle Mystery--Solved (N.Y.:
        Harper & Row, 1975), pp.161-63.
-Earthquake luminescence
    1811, Dec.16
        Samuel Latham Mitchill, "A Detailed
        Narrative of the Earthquakes,"
        Trans.Lit.& Phil.Soc'y N.Y. 1
        (1814):281,299.
-Fall of soot
    1951, July 6
        "Sooty Down in Ga.," Doubt, no.34
        (1951):106.
-Fall of weblike substance
    1959, Oct.26-27
        Savannah Morning News, 1 Nov.1959.
-Phantom image
    1971, Oct./Union Baptist Church
        David Techter, "A Flap of Glowing
        Crosses," Fate 25 (June 1972):52,56.
-UFO (CE-1)
    1973, Sep.
        News of Screven, 27 Sep.1973.
    1973, Sep.8/Bart J. Burns/Hunter Army
    Airfield
        Augusta Chronicle-Herald, 9 Sep.1973.
-UFO (CE-3)
    1973, Sep.9/Laurel Grove Cemetery
        Savannah News, 10 Sep.1973.
    1973, Oct.18/U.S.17
        Savannah News, 20 Oct.1973.
-UFO (DD)
    1975, Jan.3
        Timothy Green Beckley, "Saucers over
        Our Cities," Saga UFO Rept. 4 (Aug.
        1977):25,74.
-UFO (NL)
    1973, Sep.24/Larchmont Estates
        Savannah Press, 25 Sep.1973.

Screven
-UFO (NL)
    1973, Sep.20/Mrs. Conrad Mosley
        News of Screven, 27 Sep.1973.

Smyrna
-Inner development
    1973-   /Cymry Wicca
        J. Gordon Melton, Encyclopedia of
        American Religions, 2 vols. (Wil-
        mington, N.C.: Consortium, 1978),
        2:273-74.

-UFO (CE-2)
    1972/Mrs. Charles Roberts/ground mark-
    ings only
        (Letter), Fate 27 (June 1974):145.
-UFO (NL)
    1977, Nov.24
        "UFOs of Limited Merit," Int'l UFO
        Reporter 3 (Jan.1978):3.

Stockbridge
-Phantom panther and cattle killings
    1975, Sep.
        (Letter), Jim Miles, Fate 31 (Dec.
        1978):128-29.

Stockton
-UFO (CE-3)
    1955, July 3/Mrs. Wesley Symmonds
        Cincinnati (O.) Post, 23 Aug.1955.
        "The Controversial Little Green Men
        and the Tingling Facts," CRIFO Orbit,
        2 Sep.1955, p.4.
        Leonard H. Stringfield, Inside Saucer
        Post...3-0 Blue (Cincinnati: CRIFO,
        1957), pp.63-65. il.
        Isabel Davis & Ted Bloecher, Close
        Encounter at Kelly and Others of
        1955 (Evanston: Center for UFO
        Studies, 1978), pp.149-60.

Stone Mountain
-Clairvoyance
    1958, Nov./Josephine Pittman
        Jess Stearn, The Door to the Future
        (N.Y.: MacFadden, 1964), pp.195-96.

Surrency
-Haunt
    1870s/Clem Surrency
        Allie M. Doster, "The Surrency Ghost,"
        Psychic Rsch. 25 (1931):64-69.

Sylvester
-Clairvoyance
    1955, spring/Ella Mae Weston
        "A Dream Solved the Crime," Fate 8
        (Oct.1955):61.

Talbotton
-UFO (CE-1)
    1973, Sep.8/Charles Pope/2 mi.E
        Columbus Enquirer, 10 Sep.1973.

Tallulah Falls
-UFO (CE-1)
    1964, July 14/Patty Upton
        Jeffrey Liss, "UFO's That Look Like
        Tops," Fate 17 (Nov.1964):66,71,
        quoting Atlanta Constitution (un-
        dated).
-UFO (CE-2)
    1964, July 7/Jimmy Ivester
        Jeffrey Liss, "UFO's That Look Like
        Tops," Fate 17 (Nov.1964):66,70-71,
        quoting Atlanta Constitution (un-
        dated).
        "Near Landing in Georgia," Saucer
        News 11 (Dec.1964):22.

Tarrytown
-Humanoid
  ca.1965
    John Green, Sasquatch: The Apes Among
    Us (Seattle: Hancock House, 1978),
    p.217.

Ticknor
-Precognition
  1904, Dec./Dick Smith
    E.A. Smith, "Death of an Engineer,"
    Fate 21 (Nov.1968):72-74.

Tifton
-UFO (NL)
  1973, Aug.31
    Jacksonville (Fla.) Journal, 1 Sep.
    1973.

Toccoa
-Healing
  1960s/William C. Brown
    Vivian Buchan, "Miracles Happen
    Every Day," Fate 24 (Feb.1971):64-72.
    (Letter), Mary Glowacki, Fate 25
    (Aug.1972):144-45.
-Petroglyphs
  Jarrett Manor
    Margaret Perryman, "Sculptured Mono-
    liths of Georgia: Part 2," Tennes-
    see Arch. 18 (1962):14-22. il.
-Skyquake
  1959, June 22
    Coral E. Lorenzen, The Shadow of the
    Unknown (N.Y.: Signet, 1970), pp.
    118-19.

Valdosta
-Ball lightning
  '1952/Moody AFB
    Martin D. Altschuler, "Atmospheric
    Electricity and Plasma Interpreta-
    tion of UFOs," in Edward U. Condon,
    ed., Scientific Study of Unidenti-
    fied Flying Objects (N.Y.: Bantam,
    1969 ed.), pp.723,733.

Wadley
-Ghost
  1942, Jan./Mary Smith
    "Dream That Solved a Murder," Fate
    6 (July 1953):21.

Waleska
-Petroglyphs
    Margaret Perryman, "Sculptured Mono-
    liths of Georgia: Part 3," Tennes-
    see Arch. 18 (1962):75-84. il.

Warner Robins
-UFO (NL)
  1948, July 23/Robins AFB
    Donald E. Keyhoe, Flying Saucers Are
    Real (N.Y.: Fawcett, 1950), p.69.
  1959, Oct.6/Robins AFB
    (Editorial), Fate 13 (Feb.1960):22-
    24.
-UFO (R-V)
  1967, Oct.23/Robins AFB
    Philip J. Klass, UFOs Explained (N.Y.:

Random House: 1974), pp.79-80.

Washington
-Fall of weblike substance
  1959, Oct.12/J.R. Rider/=silver halide
  from cloud seeding
    (Editorial), Fate 13 (Apr.1960):22-
    24.
    (Letter), Anatolij Bojko, Fate 13
    (July 1960):120-22.
    Donald H. Menzel & Lyle G. Boyd, The
    World of Flying Saucers (Garden
    City: Doubleday, 1963), pp.225-26.

Waycross
-Humanoid
  n.d.
    John Green, Sasquatch: The Apes Among
    Us (Seattle: Hancock House, 1978),
    p.217.
-UFO (NL)
  1973, Aug.31
    Macon News, 31 Aug.1973.

            B. Physical Features

Blackburn State Park
-Humanoid
  1974, Sep.2/Les Alexander
    John Green, Sasquatch: The Apes Among
    Us (Seattle: Hancock House, 1978),
    p.217.

Blood Mt.
-Humanoid myth
  Yunwee chuns dee
    Federal Writers' Program, Georgia: A
    Guide to Its Towns and Countryside
    (Atlanta: Tupper & Love, 1954), pp.
    384-85.

Chattahoochee National Forest
-Petroglyphs
    Franklin Folsom, America's Ancient
    Treasures (N.Y.: Rand McNally,
    1974), p.117.

Chattahoochee R.
-Elizabethan inscriptions
  1939/William Eberhart/=hoax?
    Brenau College, The Dare Stones
    (Gainesville, Ga.: Brenau College,
    1940). il.
    Boyden Sparkes, "Writ on Rocke," Sat.
    Eve.Post, 26 Apr.1941, pp.9-11,118-
    28.
    Charles Whedbee, The Flaming Ship of
    Okracoke (Winston-Salem: John F.
    Blair, 1971), pp.104-14.

Cumberland I.
-Sea monster
  1849, Feb.18/Capt. Adams/"Lucy and
  Nancy"
    "The Great Sea-Serpent," Zoologist 7
    (1849):2459, quoting Boston (Mass.)
    Atlas (undated).

Duke's Creek
-Ancient mining
    "New Findings of Pre-Columbian Con-
    tacts with North America," NEARA
    Newsl. 9 (spring 1974):9.

Etowah R.
-Archeological site
  ca.1100-1400
    E.G. Squier & E.H. Davis, Ancient
    Monuments of the Mississippi Valley
    (Washington: Smithsonian Institution,
    Contrib.to Knowledge, no.1, 1848),
    pp.108-10.
    M.F. Stephenson, "Account of Ancient
    Mounds in Georgia," Ann.Rept.Smith.
    Inst., 1870, pp.380-81.
    Charles Whittlesey, "The Great Mound
    on the Etawah River, near Carters-
    ville, Georgia," Am.Naturalist 5
    (1871):542-44.
    Charles C. Jones, Antiquities of the
    Southern Indians (N.Y.: Appleton,
    1873)m pp.136-43. il.
    Cyrus Thomas, "The Story of a Mound,"
    Am.Anthro. 4 (1891):109-59,237-73.
    Cyrus Thomas, "Report on the Mound
    Explorations of the Bureau of Eth-
    nology," Ann.Rept.Bur.Am.Ethn. 12
    (1894):3,292-311. il.
    Warren K. Moorehead, Etowah Papers
    (New Haven: Yale Univ., 1932). il.
    A.R. Kelley & Lewis H. Larson, "Ex-
    plorations at Etowah, Georgia 1954-
    1956," Archaeology 10 (1957):39-48.
    Vernon J. Hurst, "On the Source of
    Copper at the Etowah Site, Georgia,"
    Am.Antiquity 24 (1958):177-81. il.

Fort Mt.
-Archeological site
    Robert Shackleton, Jr., "Fort Moun-
    tain," Am.Antiquarian 15 (1893):
    295-304.
    Federal Writers' Program, Georgia: A
    Guide to Its Towns and Countryside
    (Atlanta: Tupper & Love, 1954), p.
    206.
    Richard Deacon, Madoc and the Discov-
    ery of America (N.Y.: George Braz-
    iller, 1966), pp.204-206.
    John Fleming, "The Mystery of the
    Mountain Wall," Southern Living,
    Dec.1969.
    Frank Volkmann, "Stone Riddle in
    Georgia," Fate 30 (Jan.1977):70-75.
    il.

Glynn I.
-Disappearance
  1927, Aug.25/Paul Redfern/Stinson De-
  troiter biplane
    Richard Winer, From the Devil's Tri-
    angle to the Devil's Jaw (N.Y.:
    Bantam, 1977), p.9.

Kinchafoonee Creek
-Haunt
    Charles M. Skinner, American Myths
    and Legends, 2 vols. (Philadelphia:

Lippincott, 1903), 1:326-27.

Little Kolomoki Creek
-Archeological site
  600-1400
    Charles C. Jones, Monumental Remains
    of Georgia (Savannah: John M. Coop-
    er, 1861).
    Charles H. Fairbanks, "The Kolomoki
    Mound Group, Early County, Georgia,"
    Am.Antiquity 11 (1946):258-60.
    William H. Sears, Excavations at
    Kolomoki, 4 vols. (Athens: Univ. of
    Georgia, 1956). il.

Oconee R.
-Archeological site
  eagle effigy
    Charles C. Jones, Jr., "Aboriginal
    Structures in Georgia," Ann.Rept.
    Smith.Inst., 1877, pp.278-82.
    Charles C. Jones, Jr., "Bird-Shaped
    Mounds in Putnam County, Georgia,
    U.S.A.," J.Royal Anthro.Inst. 8
    (1879):92-96.

Okefenokee Swamp
-Ancient brass armor
  1920s
    A.S. McQueen & Hamp Mizell, History
    of Okefenokee Swamp (Folkston: The
    Authors, 1949), p.157.
-Ancient coin
  1920s
    A.S. McQueen & Hamp Mizell, History
    of Okefenokee Swamp (Folkston: The
    Authors, 1949), p.157.
-Doubtful geography
  =Creek Indian "paradise"
    Francis Harper, ed., The Travels of
    William Bartram (New Haven: Yale
    Univ., 1958), pt.1, ch. iii, pp.17-
    18.

Ossabaw I.
-Mystery metallic object
  1955, Sep.
    "Navy Investigates Grounded Metal
    Object," CRIFO Orbit, 2 Mar.1956,
    p.4.

Saint Simon's I.
-Archeological sites
  2500 B.C.-1650 A.D.
    Charles Lyell, A Second Visit to the
    United States of North America, 2
    vols. (London: John Murray, 1850),
    1:338.
    Clarence B. Moore, Certain Aborigin-
    al Mounds of the Georgia Coast (Phil-
    adelphia: P.C. Stockhausen, 1897).
    Preston Holder, "Excavations on Saint
    Simons Island and Vicinity," Proc.
    Soc'y Georgia Arch. 1 (1938):8-9.
    Jerald I. Milanich, "A Chronology for
    the Aboriginal Cultures of Northern
    St. Simon's Island, Georgia," Flor-
    ida Anthro. 30 (1977):134-42.
-Haunt
  n.d./Christ Church

Betsy Fancher, *The Lost Legacy of Georgia's Golden Isles* (Garden City: Doubleday, 1971), pp.155-56.
n.d./Ebo Landing
Federal Writers' Program, *Georgia: A Guide to Its Towns and Countryside* (Atlanta: Tupper & Love, 1954), p. 298.
-Skyquake
1977, Nov.14
U.S. Naval Rsch. Laboratory, *NRL Investigations of East Coast Acoustic Events* (Washington: Naval Rsch. Laboratory, 10 Mar.1978), p.134.

Savannah R.
-River monster
1854, spring/Capt. Peat/"William Seabrook"
1854, spring/Capt. Rollins/"Isabel"
Amelia Matilda Murray, *Letters from the United States, Cuba and Canada* (N.Y.: Putnam, 1856), p.235.
-UFO (R-V)
1953, March 5
U.S. Air Force, *Projects Grudge and Bluebook Reports 1-12* (Washington: NICAP, 1968), p.207.

Stalling's I.
-Archeological site
ca.3000-1700 B.C.
Charles C. Jones, *Antiquities of the Southern Indians* (N.Y.: Appleton, 1873), pp.197-98.
W.H. Claflin, Jr., "The Stalling's Island Mound, Columbia County, Georgia," *Pap.Peabody Mus.*, vol.14, no.1 (1931). il.
Charles H. Fairbanks, "The Taxonomic Position of Stalling's Island, Georgia," *Am.Antiquity* 7 (1942): 223-31,311-18. il.
Bert W. Bierer, *Discovering South Carolina* (Columbia: The Author, 1969).

Thunderbolt Bluff
-UFO (NL)
1973, Sep.24/William H. Whitten
Savannah Press, 25 Sep.1973.

Track Rock Gap
-Petroglyphs
Margaret Perryman, "Sculptured Monoliths of Georgia: Part 2," *Tennessee Arch.* 18 (1962):14-22. il.

Tybee I.
-UFO (?)
1973, Sep.6/Allen Hendrix
Savannah Morning News, 7 Sep.1973.

Whitmire Hill
-Haunt
Charles M. Skinner, *Myths and Legends in Our Own Land*, 2 vols. (Philadelphia: Lippincott, 1896), 2:308.

Withlacoochee R.
-UFO (CE-1)
1979, Jan.28/Butch Thompson
Valdosta Daily Times, 1 Feb.1979.

D. Unspecified Localities

-Humanoid
ca.1943
1974, July 29
John Green, *Sasquatch: The Apes Among Us* (Seattle: Hancock House, 1978), pp.217,370.

-UFO (CE-1)
1954, Sep./Neil Deane/offshore
Lucius Farish & Dale Titler, "Mysteries of the Deep: Underwater UFOs," *Official UFO* 2 (May 1977): 38,54-55.

SOUTH CAROLINA

A. Populated Places

Aiken
-Deathbed apparition
  1975, Oct./Danion Brinkley
    Washington (D.C.) Post, 27 Mar.1977,
    p.B3.
-Fall of localized rain
  1886, Oct.
    Charles Fort, The Books of Charles
    Fort (N.Y.: Holt, 1941), p.562,
    quoting Charleston News & Courier,
    Oct.1886.
-UFO (?)
  1957, Nov.5/=Venus
    Richard Hall, ed., The UFO Evidence
    (Washington: NICAP, 1964), p.164.
    Jacques Vallee, Anatomy of a Pheno-
    menon (N.Y.: Ace, 1965), pp.131-32.

Anderson
-UFO (CE-1)
  n.d./Hartwell L.
    Otto O. Binder, "'Oddball' Saucers
    That Fit No Pattern," Fate 21 (Feb.
    1968):54,57-58.
-UFO (NL)
  1956, Feb.17
    Anderson Independent, 21 Feb.1956.

Bamberg
-Poltergeist
  1958, April 25-May/Hector de Rienzo/
  4 mi.S on U.S.301
    St. Paul (Minn.) Pioneer Press, 27
    Apr.1958.
    (Editorial), Fate 11 (Aug.1958):8.

Barnwell
-UFO (?)
  1969, Jan.6
    Barnwell People-Sentinel, 15 Jan.1969.

Bath
-UFO (NL)
  1947, June 28/Jack Reams
    Raleigh (N.C.) News and Observer, 4
    July 1947.

Beaufort
-UFO (CE-1)
  1974, Jan.1/Bennie D. Morris
    Ronald Drucker, "The Southern U.S.--
    Target for Flying Saucers," Saga
    UFO Rept. 2 (fall 1975):15,17,66-68.

Berea
-UFO (?)
  1969, July 25/Mrs. T.W. Burden/122
  Cherrylane Dr./=meteor?
    "Huge Ball of Fire Seen in South
    Carolina," Skylook, no.23 (Oct.
    1969):4, quoting Greenville News
    (undated).

Bishopville
-Anomalous gas fissure
  1963, Jan.5/Henry Radcliffe
    (Editorial), Fate 16 (Aug.1963):22-
    24.
=Ghost
  1826/William Bateman
    Emma Hardinge Britten, Modern Ameri-
    can Spiritualism (N.Y.: The Author,
    1870), p.434.

Bluffton
-UFO (DD)
  1956, Nov.13/R.A. Smith/Bluffton-Ridge-
  land Hwy.
    (Editorial), Fate 10 (Apr.1957):16.

Camden
-Archeological sites
  Wateree R.
    E.G. Squier & E.H. Davis, Ancient
    Monuments of the Mississippi Valley
    (Washington: Smithsonian Institution,
    Contrib.to Knowledge, no.1, 1848),
    pp.105-108.
-Haunt
  1820s-1970s/116 Mill St.
    Lee R. Gandee, "Haunted House in South
    Carolina," Fate 14 (Apr.1961):32-39.
    (Letter), Lee R. Gandee, Fate 24 (Nov.
    1971):148,159-60.
  n.d./Court Inn
    C.D. Kershaw, The Gray Lady: A Legend
    of Old Camden (Charleston: Walker,
    Evans & Coggsweil, n.d.).
    South Carolina Writers' Program,
    "South Carolina Folk Tales," Univ.
    S.C.Bull., Oct.1941, pp.64-65.
-UFO (?)
  1973, Oct.13-14/=balloon
    Edmonton (Alb.) Journal, 15 Oct.1973.

Central
-UFO (NL)
  1976, Jan.7
    "Noteworthy UFO Sightings," Ufology
    2 (summer 1976):63.

Charleston
-Auroral anomaly
  1895, Aug.26/Lewis N. Jesunofsky
    "An Aurora in South Carolina and Ken-
    tucky," Monthly Weather Rev. 23 (Aug.
    1895):297.
-Ball lightning
  1857, Nov.16/Sparkman R. Scriven/Morris
  St.
    Charles Upham Shepard, "On a Shooting
    Meteor, Seen to Fall at Charleston,
    South Carolina," Am.J.Sci., ser.2,
    28 (1859):270-74.
-Cloud anomaly
  1886, Sep.8
    Charleston News & Courier, 10 Sep.1886.

-Crisis apparition
1805, Jan./Maria Heyward/31 Legare St.
Margaret Rhett Martin, Charleston
Ghosts (Columbia: Univ. of South
Carolina, 1963), pp.92-95.
-Disappearance
1925, Nov.29/"Cotopaxi"/ocean to SE
Lawrence David Kusche, The Bermuda
Triangle Mystery--Solved (N.Y.: Har-
per & Row, 1975), pp.76-77.
1954, Dec.7/"Southern Districts"/ocean
to S
New York Times, 14 Dec.1954, p.26;
15 Dec.1954, p.63; 1 Jan.1955, p.25;
3 Jan.1955, p.39; and 4 Jan.1955,
p.91.
Alan Villiers, Posted Missing (N.Y.:
Scribner's, 1956), pp.286-95.
Lawrence David Kusche, The Bermuda
Triangle Mystery--Solved (N.Y.: Har-
Harper & Row, 1975), pp.168-71.
-Fall of alligator
1843, July 2/Anson St.
Charleston Evening Post, 11 Aug.1971.
-Fall of localized rain
1886, Oct.
New York Sun, 24 Oct.1886, p.1.
Charleston News & Courier, 5 Nov.1886.
-Fall of pebbles
1886, Sep.4
Charleston News & Courier, 6 Sep.1886.
Richmond (Va.) Whig, 7 Sep.1886.
T.C. Mendenhall, "Report on the Char-
leston Earthquake," Monthly Weather
Rev. 14 (Sep.1886):233-35.
Carl McKinley, A Descriptive Narra-
tive of the Earthquake of August 31,
1886 (Charleston: Walker, Evans &
Cogswell, 1887).
-Haunt
1796-   /Belvidere Mansion/Cooper R.
Margaret Rhett Martin, Charleston
Ghosts (Columbia: Univ. of South
Carolina, 1963), pp.5-10.
n.d./59 Church St.
Nancy & Bruce Roberts, Ghosts of the
Carolinas (Charlotte: McNally &
Loftin, 1962), pp.47-49.
n.d./nr. St. Philip's
n.d./Medway
Margaret Rhett Martin, Charleston
Ghosts (Columbia: Univ. of South
Carolina, 1963), pp.51-55,83-86.
n.d./Ann Fenwick/Fenwick Hall
Fairfax Harrison, The John's Island
Stud (Richmond, Va.: Old Dominion
Press, 1931).
South Carolina Writers' Program,
"South Carolina Folk Tales," Univ.
S.C.Bull., Oct.1941, pp.63-64.
Margaret Rhett Martin, Charleston
Ghosts (Columbia: Univ. of South
Carolina, 1963), pp.56-62.
n.d./Old Goose Creek Plantation
Octogenarian Lady [Elizabeth Anne
Poyas], The Olden Time of Carolina
(Charleston: S.G. Courtenay, 1855).
Margaret Rhett Martin, Charleston
Ghosts (Columbia: Univ. of South
Carolina, 1963), pp.66-70.

-Hex research
1971/Ramsey R. Mellette/Medical Univ.
of South Carolina
(Editorial), Fate 24 (Aug.1971):16.
-Inner development
1801-   /Ancient and Accepted (Scottish) Rite/Church x Broad St.
Albert Pike, Morals and Dogma of the
Ancient and Accepted Scottish Rite
of Freemasonry (Charleston: A.M.
5632, 1871).
Albert Gallatin Mackey, An Ecyclope-
dia of Freemasonry (Philadelphia:
Moss, 1874).
Albert Gallatin Mackey, The History
of Freemasonry (N.Y.: Masonic His-
tory Co., 1898-1906).
Lady Queensborough [Edith Starr Mil-
ler], Occult Theocracy, 2 vols.
(Abbeville, Fr.: Paillart, 1932),
1:194-99,207-40,286-301,357-64.
Susan B. Riley, The Life and Works
of Albert Pike to 1860 (Nashville:
George Peabody College, 1934).
Henry C. Clausen, Masons Who Helped
Shape Our Nation (Charleston: Su-
preme Council, Ancient and Accepted
Scottish Rite, 1976).
Henry C. Clausen, Messages for a Mis-
sion (Charleston: Supreme Council,
Ancient and Accepted Scottish Rite,
1977).
-Meteor and earthquake
1886, Aug.31
Carl McKinley, A Descriptive Narra-
tive of the Earthquake of August 31,
1886 (Charleston: Walker, Evans &
Cogswell, 1887).
1886, Sep.5
Charleston News & Courier, 6 Sep.1886.
London (Eng.) Times, 7 Sep.1886.
1886, Oct.22, 24, 28
Charleston News & Courier, 28 Oct.
1886.
"Meteors," Monthly Weather Rev. 14
(Oct.1886):296.
New York Sun, 1 Nov.1886.
-Skyquake
1977, Jan.3-6
U.S.Naval Rsch.Laboratory, NRL Investigations of East Coast Acoustic
Events (Washington: Naval Rsch. Laboratory, 10 Mar.1978), pp.14-15,121-
27.
1977, Dec.2
Dallas (Tex.) Times-Herald, 17 Dec.
1977.
U.S.Naval Rsch.Laboratory, NRL Investigations of East Coast Acoustic
Events (Washington: Naval Rsch. Laboratory, 10 Mar.1978), pp.12,18,121-
27.
1977, Dec.15
Washington (D.C.) Post, 17 Dec.1977,
p.A6.
U.S.Naval Rsch. Laboratory, NRL Investigations of East Coast Acoustic
Events (Washington: Naval Rsch. Laboratory, 10 Mar.1978), pp.12,121-27.
1977, Dec.20-22, 25

Huntsville (Ala.) Times, 22 Dec.1977.
Atlanta (Ga.) Constitution, 23 Dec.
1977.
New York Times, 23 Dec.1977, pp.A1,
B5; and 24 Dec.1977, pp.1,33.
U.S.Naval Rsch.Laboratory, NRL In-
vestigations of East Coast Acoustic
Events (Washington: Naval Rsch.Lab-
oratory, 10 Mar.1978), pp.12-13,
121-27.
Jon Douglas Singer, "Skyquakes--
Things That Go Bump in the Night,"
Pursuit 11 (spring 1978):45-47,50.
David Rind, "'Skyquakes'--and Sep-
arate Realities," Pursuit 11 (spring
1978):51-54.
1978, Jan.12
Kansas City (Mo.) Star, 13 Jan.1978.
Washington (D.C.) Post, 14 Jan.1978,
p.A9.
New York Times, 19 Jan.1978.
U.S.Naval Rsch.Laboratory, NRL In-
vestigations of East Coast Acoustic
Events (Washington: Naval Rsch.Lab-
oratory, 10 Mar.1978), pp.71,121-27,
1978, Feb.21
Washington (D.C.) Star, 22 Feb.1978,
p.A5.
Little Rock Arkansas Gazette, 22 Feb.
1978.
-UFO (?)
1973, Oct.17/Randolph M. Eldredge/=
balloon
Charleston News & Courier, 19 Oct.
1973.
1975, Jan.14/Jerry Lambrakos/Cooper R.
Robert A. Goerman, "The UFO Modus
Operandi: January 1975," Official
UFO 1 (Aug.1976):46,65.
-UFO (DD)
1947, July 5/Samuel A. Cothran
Charleston News & Courier, 6 July
1947.
1947, July 6/J.G. O'Brien/Lee x Meeting St.
Charleston News & Courier, 7 July
1947.
1947, July 7/Stewart Oltman/Byrnes
Downes
1947, July 7/Mary Strickland
Charleston News & Courier, 8 July
1947.
1966, March 30/C. Philip Lambert/Meet-
ing Street Rd.
John A. Keel, UFOs: Operation Trojan
Horse (N.Y.: Putnam, 1970), p.15.
-UFO (NL)
1880, Dec.9
New York Times, 13 Dec.1880.
1947, July 1/Mrs. Fred J. Bischoff/
Sullivan's I.
Charleston News & Courier, 6 July
1947.
1959, Feb.11
"UFO Sightings Rapidly Increase,"
UFO Inv. 1 (Feb.-Mar.1959):5.
1973, Sep.26/Bill Bardsley
Charleston Evening Post, 26 Sep.1973.
Greenville (N.C.) News, 27 Sep.1973,
p.25.

1973, Sep.26/Alice Dr.
Charleston Evening Post, 28 Sep.1973.
-UFO (R-V)
1967, Jan.16
Gordon D. Thayer, "Optical and Radar
Analyses of Field Cases," in Edward
U. Condon, ed., Scientific Study of
Unidentified Flying Objects (N.Y.:
Bantam, 1969 ed.), pp.129-30.
-Witchcraft
1703-1709
Samuel Drake, Annals of Witchcraft
in New England (Boston: W.E. Wood-
ward, 1869), pp.215-16.
Rossell Hope Robbins, Encyclopedia of
Witchcraft and Demonology (N.Y.:
Crown, 1959), pp.519-20.

Cheraw
-Fall of localized rain
1886, Oct.
Charles Fort, The Books of Charles
Fort (N.Y.: Holt, 1941), p.562,
quoting Charleston News & Courier,
Oct.1886.

Cherokee co.
-Humanoid tracks
1948, winter
"Critters and Tracks," Doubt, no.21
(1948):321.

Chesterfield co.
-Fall of localized rain
1886, Oct.
New York Sun, 24 Oct.1886, p.1.

Columbia
-Earthquake anomaly
1812, Feb.7
Edward Darrell Smith, "On the Changes
Which Have Taken Place in the Wells
Situated in Columbia, S.C., Since the
Earthquakes of 1811-12," Am.J.Sci.,
ser 1, 1 (1818):93 06.
Myron L. Fuller, "The New Madrid
Earthquake," Bull.U.S.Geol.Survey,
no.494 (1912).
-Ghost
n.d.
Nancy Roberts, Ghosts of the Carolinas
(Charlotte: McNally & Loftin, 1962).
Cecil de Vada, "The Phantom Hitch-
hiker," Fate 21 (Aug.1968):86-88.
-Meteor and earthquake
1886, Sep.5
New York Sun, 7 Sep.1886, p.1.
-Precognition
1967, June 30/M.K. Phillips, Jr./Blue
Cross office bldg.
John W. Higgins, "A One-in-a-Million
Chance," Fate 21 (July 1968):44.
-UFO (DD)
1954, Aug.14/A.H. Joyner/Main St.
"C-17," CRIFO Newsl., 3 Sep.1954, p.6.
-UFO (NL)
1957, March 9
Baltimore (Md.) Sun, 9 Mar.1957.

Congaree
-UFO (R)
1952, Aug.20/Congaree AFB
Donald E. Keyhoe, Flying Saucers from
Outer Space (N.Y.: Holt, 1953), p.
96.

Conway
-Precognition
1963, Feb./Andrew Washington Stackhouse
(Editorial), Fate 16 (Aug.1963):14.
-UFO (CE-1)
1953, Jan.29/Lloyd C. Booth
Frank Edwards, Flying Saucers: Serious Business (N.Y.: Lyle Stuart,
1966), p.52.

Cordova
-UFO (NL)
1972, July 27
Glenn McWane & David Graham, The New
UFO Sightings (N.Y.: Warner, 1974),
pp.48-49, quoting Orangeburg Times
& Democrat (undated).

Darlington
-UFO (DD)
1947, July 6/J.V. Watts, Jr./Black
Creek
Charleston News & Courier, 7 July
1947.
Bruce S. Maccabee, "UFO Related Information from the FBI Files: Part
2," MUFON UFO J., no.120 (Nov.1977)
:12.
-UFO (NL)
1947, July 6/Mrs. James Howle
Charleston News & Courier, 8 July
1947.

Darlington co.
-UFO (?)
1888, May 27/Ida Davis
New York Times, 30 May 1888, p.3.

Dillon
-Anomalous hole in ground
1953, July 31/Mrs. John C. Allen
(Editorial), Fate 6 (Dec.1953):5-6.

Draytonville
-UFO (?)
1973, Jan.-Feb.
Paris Flammonde, UFO Exist! (N.Y.:
Putnam, 1976), p.313.
-UFO (NL)
1979, Jan.3/Kelly Love
Gaffney Ledger, 5 Jan.1979.

Easley
-UFO (CE-1)
1973, Oct.17/Mrs. Paul Gillespie/Hwy.
123
Greenville Piedmont, 19 Oct.1973.
-UFO (NL)
1973, Sep.21/Sherry Smith/U.S.123
Easley Progress, 26 Sep.1973.

Elloree
-UFO (NL)
1959, Feb.11
"UFO Sightings Rapidly Increase," UFO
Inv. 1 (Feb.-Mar.1959):5.

Fairfield co.
-Witch trial (hex, levitation)
1792/Mary Ingleman
Philip Edward Pearson, History of
Fairfield District of South Carolina (ser.VV, vol.24, Lyman C. Draper
manuscripts, Univ.of Wisconsin).
Lee R. Gandee, "The Witches of Fairfield, S.C.," Fate 23 (Jan.1970):
36-44.

Florence
-Poltergeist
1960, March 25-31/Edward Morris
(Editorial), Fate 13 (Aug.1960):14-
15.
-UFO (DD)
1952, Nov.17
Richard Hall, ed., The UFO Evidence
(Washington: NICAP, 1964), p.89.
U.S. Air Force, Projects Grudge and
Bluebook Reports 1-12 (Washington:
NICAP, 1968), p.167.
-UFO (NL)
1975, Jan.14/Larry Huggins/Hwy.52
Robert A. Goerman, "The UFO Modus
Operandi: January 1975," Official
UFO 1 (Aug.1976):46,65.

Fort Mill
-Humanoid tracks
1977, Feb.12/Helen Gromoske/221 Grier
St.
Rock Hill Herald, 14 Feb.1977; and
17-18 Feb.1977. il.

Fort Watson
-Archeological site
Bert W. Bierer, Discovering South
Carolina (Columbia: The Author,
1969).

Gaffney
-Electromagnetic anomaly
1960, spring/Brian Eppley
(Editorial), Fate 14 (Apr.1961):14.
1967
John A. Keel, "The Little Man of
Gaffney," Flying Saucer Rev. 14
(Mar.-Apr.1968):17,19.
-UFO (CE-3)
1966, Nov.17/A.G. Huskey
Gaffney Ledger, 17 Nov.1966.
John A. Keel, "The Little Man of
Gaffney," Flying Saucer Rev. 14
(Mar.-Apr.1968):17-19.
1973, Jan.19/13 mi.S on Hwy.18
Gaffney Ledger, 26 Jan.1973.

Gaston
-Haunt
1860s-1960s/Poor Hope Plantation
Lee R. Gandee, "A House Called 'Poor
Hope,'" Fate 25 (Feb.1972):48-61.

Georgetown
-Anomalous hole in ground
  1953, July 30/6 mi.S
    (Editorial), Fate 6 (Dec.1953):5-6.
-Haunt
  n.d./Litchfield Plantation
    Nancy & Bruce Roberts, Ghosts of the
    Carolinas (Charlotte: McNally &
    Loftin, 1962), pp.24-25.
-Mystery explosion
  1951, April 17/Mrs. Ernest Harrelson/
  S of town
    Charleston News & Courier, 24 Apr.
    1951.
-UFO (DD)
  1964, Nov.22/Mr. Lissauer
    Jacques Vallee, Anatomy of a Pheno-
    menon (N.Y.: Ace, 1965), pp.209,214.

Goshen
-Phantom dog
  1855-   /Buncombe Rd.
    Nancy & Bruce Roberts, Ghosts of the
    Carolinas (Charlotte: McNally &
    Loftin, 1962), pp.4-6.

Greenville
-Electromagnetic anomaly
  ca.1960/Pam Alex
    (Editorial), Fate 14 (June 1961):13-
    14.
-Plant sensitivity
  1960s/James Lee Scribner
    Peter Tompkins & Christopher Bird,
    The Secret Life of Plants (N.Y.:
    Harper & Row, 1973), pp.180-81.
-Spontaneous human combustion
  1953, March 1/Waymon Price Wood/Bypass
  Hwy.291
    (Editorial), Fate 6 (July 1953):6.
-UFO (?)
  1973, Oct.4/Nanette Long
  1973, Oct.6/hospital
    Greenville Piedmont, 4 Oct.1973; and
    8 Oct.1973.
-UFO (CE-1)
  1977, Jan.1/Sarah Christopher/White
  Horse Rd.
    Greenville Piedmont, 7 Jan.1977.
-UFO (CE-3)
  1973, Nov.11
    David Webb, 1973: Year of the Human-
    oids (Evanston: Center for UFO
    Studies, 1976 ed.), p.19.
-UFO (NL)
  1952, May 13
    Donald E. Keyhoe, Flying Saucers from
    Outer Space (N.Y.: Holt, 1953), pp.
    148-49.
    U.S. Air Force, Projects Grudge and
    Bluebook Reports 1-12 (Washington:
    NICAP, 1968), p.144.
  1973, Sep.29/Harrison McLauren
    Greenville News, 1 Oct.1973.
  1973, Oct.3/Fletcher W. Ross/Stone Ave.
  x I-385
    Greenville News, 4 Oct.1973.
  1973, Oct.4/Billy Jordan/513 Perry Ave.
    Greenville News, 5 Oct.1973.
  1973, Oct.8/Bell Tower Mall

Greenville Piedmont, 8 Oct.1973.

Greenwood
-UFO (NL)
  1969, Jan.6
    Greenwood Index-Journal, 7 Jan.1969.

Hagley
-Ghost
  1918, summer/Eugene F. LaBruce
    South Carolina Writers' Program,
    "South Carolina Folk Tales," Univ.
    of South Carolina Bull., Oct.1941,
    pp.66-71.
    Nancy & Bruce Roberts, Ghosts of the
    Carolinas (Charlotte: McNally &
    Loftin, 1962), pp.39-42.

Jasper co.
-Paranormal strength
  1965, Oct.1/Mrs. Gene Perryman
    (Editorial), Fate 19 (June 1966):20.

Jefferson
-Phantom image
  1971, Feb./Jasper Barrett
    (Editorial), Fate 24 (June 1971):28-
    30, quoting Charlotte (N.C.) Obser-
    ver (undated).

Lake View
-UFO (CE-3)
  1976, Oct.28/Richie Britt
    Florence Morning News, 14 Nov.1976.

Lancaster
-UFO (NL)
  1973, Oct.3/Lora Minerd/Sherwood Circle
    Lancaster News, 8 Oct.1973.

Landrum
-UFO (DD)
  1952, Nov.16/David S. Bunch
    Richard Hall, ed., The UFO Evidence
    (Washington: NICAP, 1964), p.89.

Lyman
-UFO (DD)
  1978, May 19/Ed Bischoffberger
    Greer Citizen, 31 May 1978.

Mauldin
-UFO (CE-2)
  1973, Sep.28/Mrs. Ernie Craig/108
  Devon
    Greenville Piedmont, 29 Sep.1973.
    Fountain Inn Tribune Times, 3 Oct.
    1973.

North Charleston
-UFO (CE-2)
  1977, Dec.2/William J. Herrmann/Dor-
  chester Rd.
    North Charleston Banner, 7 Dec.1977.
    Charleston Evening Post, 31 May 1978.
    "Object Photographed over Charleston,
    S.C.," APRO Bull. 27 (July 1978):
    1,2-3. il.
-UFO (DD)

1977, Nov.12, 27/William J. Herrmann/
Dorchester Rd.
North Charleston Banner, 7 Dec.1977.
Charleston Evening Post, 31 May 1978.
"Object Photographed over Charleston,
S.C.," APRO Bull. 27 (July 1978):
1-2.
1978, Jan.22/William J. Herrmann/Dor-
chester Rd.
"Object Photographed over Charleston,
S.C.," APRO Bull. 27 (July 1978):
1,3. il.
-UFO (NL)
1977, Dec.24/William J. Herrmann
"Object Photographed over Charleston,
S.C.," APRO Bull. 27 (July 1978):
1,3.

Norway
-UFO (CE-2)
1978, Dec.6
Orangeburg Times-Democrat, 1 Feb.
1979.

Orangeburg
-UFO (DD)
1950, March 10/J.L. Sims
Kenneth Arnold & Ray Palmer, The Com-
ing of the Saucers (Boise: The Au-
thors, 1952), p.146.
-UFO (NL)
1959, Feb.11/Mrs. James Hutto
"UFO Sightings Rapidly Increase,"
UFO Inv. 1 (Feb.-Mar.1959):5.

Pawley's Island
-Haunt
1893-
"The Ghost That Heralds Storms,"
Fate 9 (Mar.1956):55, quoting Char-
lotte (N.C.) Observer (undated).

Pendleton
-UFO (NL)
1976, Jan.1
"Noteworthy UFO Sightings," Ufology
2 (summer 1976):63.

Pierpont
-UFO (DD)
1947, July 8/Johnny Crowe
Charleston News & Courier, 9 July
1947.

Pontiac
-Phantom image
1977/Frank Harley
(Editorial), Fate 30 (June 1977):18.

Richland
-Fall of brick
1846, summer
"Prof. C.U. Shepard, on Meteorites,"
Am.J.Sci., ser.2, 10 (1850):127.
"So-Called Meteoric Stone from Rich-
land," Am.J.Sci., ser.2, 34 (1862):
298.

Ridgeland
-UFO (NL)

1973, Oct.1/Hwy.17
Ridgeland News, 4 Oct.1973.

Saint Matthews
-UFO (?)
1950, March
Harold T. Wilkins, Flying Saucers on
the Attack (N.Y.: Ace, 1967 ed.),
pp.57,119,210.

Saluda co.
-Humanoid tracks
1977, Feb.6
Rock Hill Herald, 18 Feb.1977, p.1.
il.

Savannah River Plant
-UFO (NL)
1957, Nov.5
"All About Sputs," Doubt, no.56
(1958):460,471.

Seneca
-UFO (CE-2)
1964, July 20/ground markings only
"News Briefs," Saucer News 11 (Dec.
1964):25.

Sheldon
-Hex and inner development
1970-   /Oseijeman Adefumi Efuntola/
Oyo-Tunji Village
New York Times, 31 Dec.1973, p.4.
Ron Sympson, "There's Something
Strange in Them Thar Hills," Probe
the Unknown 2 (winter 1974):28-35.
Daniel St. Albin Greene, "Voodoo?
Yes, a Few Do," Nat'l Observer, 29
Nov.1975.
Carlos Canet, Oyotunji (Miami: Edi-
torial AIP, n.d.).

Silverton twp.
-Fall of alligator
1877, Dec./J.L. Smith
New York Times, 26 Dec.1877, p.1,
quoting Aiken Journal (undated).

Spartanburg
-Crisis apparition
1931, May/Benita Rivers
Benita Rivers, "I Dreamt My Husband's
Death," Tomorrow 5 (winter 1957):
51-52.
-Disease anomaly
1952, spring/Mrs. Joe Rubin
(Editorial), Fate 5 (Oct.1952):10.
-Haunt
1936-1960s/James Ruff/Foster's Tavern
Spartanburg Herald, 24 Aug.1964.
-UFO (CE-1)
1975, Feb.25/Willie Campbell/Byrnes
Blvd.
"UFO-Car Encounters Continue," APRO
Bull. 23 (June 1975):1,4.
-UFO (NL)
1969, Jan.6/Louis Beliste/SW of town
"Large Object Spotted by Many in South
Carolina," APRO Bull. 17 (Mar.-Apr.
1969):4.

Springfield
-Poltergeist
1970, July/Ida Mae Johnson
Anderson Independent, 12 July 1970.

Summerville
-Ghost light
1961, Dec.-1962, March/Sheep Island Rd.
(Editorial), Fate 15 (July 1962):16-
18, quoting Charlotte (N.C.) News,
Mar.1962.
-UFO (NL)
1973, Oct.1/Leonard Lang/Pine Hill
Acres
Summerville Scene, 3 Oct.1973.

Swansea
-Fall of fish
1971, March 4/Rick Bailey
(Editorial), Fate 24 (July 1971):24-
26, quoting Columbia State (undated).

Tillers Ferry
-Fall of fish
1901, June 27/J.W. Gardner
J.W. Gardner, "A Rain of Small Fish,"
Monthly Weather Rev. 29 (June 1901)
:263.

Timmonsville
-UFO (NL)
1893, Dec.30/H.K. Corbett
Charleston News & Courier, 31 Dec.
1893.

Walterboro
-Fall of lead pellets
1886, Nov.
Charleston News & Courier, 12 Nov.
1886.
-UFO (DD)
1975, Nov.22/Frank Auman, Jr./15 mi.N
Arlan Keith Andrews, "Bright UFO
Seen from Private Plane," Skylook,
no.98 (Jan.1976):19.

Wando Woods
-UFO (CE-4)
1978, March 18/William J. Herrmann
Summerville Journal, 31 Jan.1979.

Wattsville
-UFO (CE-2)
1978, Dec.29/Roger Sheahy/Hwy.308
Laurens Advertiser, 2 Jan.1979.

Wellford
-Animal ESP
1975, April/James Daves
(Editorial), Fate 29 (Feb.1976):26-
27.

Williamston
-Phantom image
1901/James W. Huff/cemetery
"Ghost on the Tombstone," Fate 7
(Mar.1954):81.

Woodruff
-Mystery animal

1965, Jan./Clarence Lemuell/=hoax
(Editorial), Fate 18 (June 1965):10-
12.
(Letter), J.C. Fluhart, Fate 18
(Sep.1965):116-17.
(Letter), Cecil D. Clayton, Fate 19
(Jan.1966):132-33.

Yemassee
-Phantom panther
1957, Sep.
(Editorial), Fate 11 (Jan.1958):18.

York
-UFO (DD)
1973, Sep.29
George D. Fawcett, "What We Can Ex-
pect of UFOs in 1975," Official
UFO 1 (Aug.1975):12,50.

B. Physical Features

Bush R.
-Ghost
1770s
Nancy & Bruce Roberts, Ghosts of the
Carolinas (Charlotte: McNally &
Loftin, 1962), pp.10-12.

Dutch Fork
-Healing
1760-
Lee R. Gandee, "'Using' to Heal in
South Carolina," Fate 14 (Mar.1961)
:34-39.
(Letter), Lee R. Gandee, Fate 14
(June 1961):120.

Edisto I.
-Haunt
n.d./Margaret Rhett Martin/Old House
Margaret Rhett Martin, Charleston
Ghosts (Columbia: Univ.of South Car-
olina, 1963), pp.1-4.
n.d./Legere mausoleum
Eileen Sonin, More Canadian Ghosts
(Richmond Hill, Ont.: Pocket Books,
1974 ed.), pp.22-23.

Fowey Rock
-Unidentified submerged object
1975, March-May/Robert Kuhne/7 mi.SE
Charles Berlitz, Without a Trace
(N.Y.: Ballantine, 1978 ed.), p.120.

Goose Creek Lagoon
-Lake monster
1920s/Herbert Ravenal Sass
"The Pink What-Is-It?" Sat.Eve.Post,
4 Dec.1948, p.10.
-UFO (DD)
1947, July 7/J.J. Kornahrens
Charleston News & Courier, 8 July
1947.

Moultrie, L.
-UFO (DD)
1947, July 5/H.L. Babson
Charleston News & Courier, 8 July

1947.

Saluda R.
-Elizabethan inscriptions
  1931/William Eberhart/=hoax?
    Brenau College, The Dare Stones
    (Gainesville, Ga.: Brenau College,
    1940). il.
    Boyden Sparkes, "Writ on Rocke," Sat.
    Eve.Post, 26 Apr.1941, pp.9-11,118-
    28.
    Charles Whedbee, The Flaming Ship of
    Okracoke (Winston-Salem: John F.
    Blair, 1971), pp.104-14.

Sewee Mound
-Archeological site
  ca.2000 B.C.
    Franklin Folsom, America's Ancient
    Treasures (N.Y.: Rand McNally,
    1974), pp.121-22.

Simon's Bay
-Sea monster
  1830, March 23/Capt. Deland/"Eagle"
    (Editorial), Notizbl.Gebiete Nat.
    Heilk., bd.27, nr.589, June 1830.

Skull Creek
-Sea monster
  1850, March 15
    "The Great Sea-Serpent," Ill.London
    News, 20 Apr.1850.
    (Editorial), Zoologist 1 (1850):2308.

Wateree R.
-Anomalous artifacts
  =discoidal stones
    Samuel G. Morton, "Some Observations
    on the Ethnography and Archaeology
    of the American Aborigines," Am.J.
    Sci., ser.2, 2 (1846):1-15. il.
    E.G. Squier, "On the Discoidal
    Stones of the Indian Mounds," Am.J.
    Sci., ser.2, 2 (1846):216-18.

White Oak Swamp
-Phantom panther
  1948, fall/Sam Lee
    Jerome Clark & Loren Coleman, Crea-
    tures of the Outer Edge (N.Y.: War-
    ner, 1978), p.136.

C. Ethnic Groups

Tuscarora Indians
-Welsh Indians
  1666/Morgan Jones/"Doeg" tribe
    Theophilus Evans, "The Crown of Eng-
    land's Title to America Prior to
    That of Spain," Gentleman's Mag. 10
    (1740):103-105.
    Amos Stoddard, Sketches Historical
    and Descriptive of Louisiana (Phil-
    adelphia: Mathew Carey, 1812), pp.
    482-83.
    David Williams, John Evans and the
    Legend of Madoc 1770-1799 (Cardiff:
    Univ. of Wales, 1963).

Richard Deacon, Madoc and the Discovery of America (N.Y.: George Braz-
iller, 1966), pp.110-13.

D. Unspecified Localities

-Hex
  1960s
    (Editorial), Fate 24 (Aug.1971):16.

-Humanoid tracks
  n.d./Dean Poucher
    St. Petersburg (Fla.) Times, 8 July
    1974.

-UFO (NL)
  1959, Feb.7/Emmet West/U.S.601
    "TV Engineer's UFO Sighting Brings
    Harried AF Check-Up," UFO Inv. 1
    (Feb.-Mar.1959):7.

A. Populated Places

Albemarle
-Fall of toads
  1961/Cecil Moose/Norwood Rd.
    (Editorial), Fate 14 (Nov.1961):14,
    quoting Stanley News & Press (un-
    dated).
-UFO (CE-3)
  1973, Nov.
    David Webb, 1973: Year of the Human-
    oids (Evanston: Center for UFO Stud-
    ies, 1976 ed.), p.21.
-UFO (NL)
  1974, Aug.1
    George D. Fawcett, "The 'Unreported'
    UFO Wave of 1974," Saga UFO Rept. 2
    (spring 1975):50,53.
  1975, Jan.14/Bernice Thompson/U.S.1
    George D. Fawcett, "The 1975 UFO
    Wave in North Carolina," Official
    UFO 1 (Nov.1975):13.

Apex
-UFO (NL)
  1976, Jan.21
    "Noteworthy UFO Sightings," Ufology
    2 (summer 1976):62.

Asheboro
-UFO (?)
  1962, July 19
    (Editorial), Saucer News 9 (Sep.1962)
    :24.
-UFO (CE-2)
  1953, Aug.18/Ralph Dixon/ground markings only
    Ted Phillips, Physical Traces Associ-
    ated with UFO Sightings (Evanston:
    Center for UFO Studies, 1975), p.10.
-UFO (NL)
  1975, April 1
    George D. Fawcett, "The 1975 UFO
    Wave in North Carolina," Official
    UFO 1 (Nov.1975):12,45-46.

Asheville
-Clairvoyance
  1953/Mrs. Paul Boatwright
    "They Dreamed of Disaster," Fate 9
    (Aug.1956):46.
-Haunt
  n.d./Stella Metchling/Starnes Ave.
    Dennis Bardens, Ghosts and Hauntings
    (N.Y.: Ace, 1965 ed.), pp.237-38.
  1933-1953/Grady Hamby
    (Editorial), Fate 7 (Feb.1954):8,
    quoting Asheville Citizen (undated).
  1974-1976/Jesse Fonda
    Jesse Fonda, "I Met the Real Phantom
    Hitchhiker," Fate 30 (Jan.1977):55-
    57.
-UFO (DD)
  1947, July 3/Mrs. J.D. Norwood
  1947, July 7/Carroll Emery/141 Ashland

    Asheville Citizen, 8 July 1947.
-UFO (NL)
  1947, July 7/Bob Rumbough/Forks of Ivy
    Asheville Citizen, 8 July 1947.
-UFO (R-V)
  1974, Sep.23/Tony Weatherville/Bitt-
more
    George D. Fawcett, "The 'Unreported'
    UFO Wave of 1974," Saga UFO Rept. 2
    (spring 1975):50,75.

Balsam Grove
-Healing
  1909/Addie Welch
    Sarah Tylor, "Our Friendly Neighbor-
    hood Witch," Fate 17 (Nov.1964):86-
    89.

Banner Elk
-UFO (CE-2)
  1967, April 8
    Ted Phillips, Physical Traces Associ-
    ated with UFO Sightings (Evanston:
    Center for UFO Studies, 1975), p.47.

Bath
-Ghost light
  n.d.
    Raleigh News & Observer, 10 Sep.1933.
-Mystery tracks
  1813-   /Camp Leech Rd./Devil's Hoof-
marks
    John Harden, The Devil's Tramping
    Ground (Chapel Hill: Univ. of North
    Carolina, 1949), pp.69-77.
    (Letter), Tommy Inge, Fate 6 (Nov.
    1953):118-20.
    Nancy Roberts, An Illustrated Guide
    to Ghosts and Mysterious Occurrences
    in the Old North State (Charlotte:
    Heritage House, 1959), pp.50-51. il.
    Charles Whedbee, Legends of the Outer
    Banks (Winston-Salem: John F. Blair,
    1966).

Belmont
-UFO (CE-2)
  1975/Harold F. Spencer
    George D. Fawcett, "The 1975 UFO Wave
    in North Carolina," Official UFO 1
    (Nov.1975):12,49.

Bentonville
-Retrocognition
  ca.1905/Jim Weaver/Harper House
    Nancy Roberts, An Illustrated Guide
    to Ghosts and Mysterious Occurrences
    in the Old North State (Charlotte:
    Heritage House, 1959), pp.47-49.

Bertie co.
-Healing
  1920s/Lorenza Smallwood/Indian Woods
    F. Roy Johnson, Witches and Demons in

History and Folklore (Murfreesboro:
Johnson, 1969), pp.148-52.
-Humanoid
n.d./Uncle Ned/Butterton Plantation
F. Roy Johnson, Witches and Demons in
History and Folklore (Murfreesboro:
Johnson, 1969), pp.9-11.

Big Laurel
-Ghost light
n.d.
N.I. White, ed., Frank C. Brown Collection of North Carolina Folklore
(Durham: Duke Univ., 1952), 1:684-
85.

Big Lick
-Hex
1880s/Lynn Bird
Nancy Roberts, An Illustrated Guide
to Ghosts and Mysterious Occurrences
in the Old North State (Charlotte:
Heritage House, 1959), pp.1-4.

Black Mountain
-Fall of anomalous meteorite
1955, Dec./Mrs. J.A. Padgett/Montreal
Rd.
Asheville Citizen, 28 Dec.1955.
-Healing
1971/David Pelletier
(Editorial), Fate 25 (Feb.1972):19.

Bladenboro
-Fire anomaly
1932, Jan.-Feb./Charles H. Williamson
New York Sun, 2 Feb.1932.
Charles Fort, The Books of Charles
Fort (N.Y.: Holt, 1941), pp.925,
1050.
Vincent H. Gaddis, Mysterious Fires
and Lights (N.Y.: Dell, 1968 ed.),
pp.159-60, quoting M.E. Counselman,
in True Strange, Mar.1957.

Boone
-Animal ESP
1959/Mrs. Lawrence H. Owsley
(Editorial), Fate 13 (Jan.1960):18.

Buck Shoals
-UFO (NL)
1973, Oct.24-25/Jim Taylor
Mount Airy Times, 26 Oct.1973.
Atlanta (Ga.) Constitution, 26 Oct.
1973.

Burlington
-UFO (NL)
1956, March 4-5,8-9/George Newcomer
(Editorial), Fate 9 (July 1956):17.

Buttons
-Medieval coin
1954, Oct.
"Puzzle for Coin Collectors," Fate 9
(Feb.1956):64.
(Letter), Thomas O. Mabbott, Fate 9
(May 1956):126-28.

Caldwell co.
-Poltergeist
1888, Jan./P.C. Martin
St. Louis (Mo.) Globe-Democrat, 27
Jan.1888.

Calypso
-UFO (NL)
1973, Oct.26/Nelson Bland
Mount Olive Tribune, 30 Oct.1973.

Carolina Beach
-UFO (NL)
1947, July 1/Mrs. Elmo Fountain
Raleigh News & Observer, 8 July 1947.

Cartaret co.
-Lightning anomaly
1806, Aug.10/Samuel Leffers
Denison Olmsted, "Case of a Paralytic
Affection, Cured by a Stroke of
Lightning," Am.J.Sci., ser.1, 3
(1821):100-102.

Casar
-Humanoid
1979, Jan.15/Kay Price/Hwy.10, nr.
Cedar Park
Charlotte News, 18 Jan.1979.

Caswell Beach
-Fall of stone
1810, April 30
R.P. Greg, "A Catalogue of Meteorites
and Fireballs, from A.D. 2 to A.D.
1860," Rept.Brit.Ass'n Adv.Sci. 30
(1860):48,64.
R.P. Greg, "Catalogue of Luminous
Meteors and Aerolites: Supp.No.II,"
Rept.Brit.Ass'n Adv.Sci. 37 (1867):
415.

Chapel Hill
-Disappearance
1831/Peter Dromgoole/Univ. of North
Carolina campus
Kemp P. Battle, History of the Univer-
sity of North Carolina, 2 vols.
(Raleigh: Edwards & Broughton, 1907),
1:343-44.
Greensboro Daily News, 25 Mar.1945.
John Harden, The Devil's Tramping
Ground (Chapel Hill: Univ. of North
Carolina, 1949), pp.33-40.
-Parapsychology research
1962-1963/Charles T. Tart/Univ. of
North Carolina
Charles T. Tart, "Physiological Cor-
relates of Psi Cognition," Int'l J.
Parapsych. 5 (1963):375-86.

Charlotte
-Animal ESP
1962-   /John Marver
(Editorial), Fate 22 (Aug.1969):10-
14, quoting Charlotte News (undated).
-Clairempathy
1970, July-1971/Rien Dykshoorn
M.B. Dykshoorn & Russell H. Felton,
My Passport Says Clairvoyant (N.Y.:

Jove, 1978 ed.), pp.162-71.
-Fall of flint
1876, May?
Decatur (Ill.) Republican, 15 May
1876, p.1, quoting Charlotte Obser-
ver (undated).
-Fall of foam
1957, March 20/W.B. Brown
St. Louis (Mo.) Post-Dispatch, 21
Mar.1957, p.1.
-Fall of localized rain
1886, Oct./9th x D St.
Charlotte Chronicle, 21 Oct.1886.
"Rain from Cloudless Sky," Monthly
Weather Rev. 14 (Oct.1886):287.
-Haunt
1967, Aug.-1970, Aug./Joey St. Clair
Joey St. Clair, "Ghosts of 'The
Great Gray Barn,'" Fate 26 (Mar.
1973):76-83.
1973-1974/Ivey's Dep't Store/South
Park Shopping Center
(Editorial), Fate 27 (Oct.1974):28-
32.
-Mystery animal
1963, April/=former circus fake?
"Fortean Items," Saucer News 11 (Mar.
1964):21.
-Mystery bird deaths
1955, Sep.27/Douglas Airport
Columbia (S.C.) State, 28 Sep.1955.
-UFO (CE-2)
1972, Feb.8/Providence Rd.
George D. Fawcett, Quarter Century of
Studies of UFOs in Florida, North
Carolina and Tennessee (Mount Airy:
Pioneer, 1975), p.31.
Ted Phillips, Physical Traces Associ-
ated with UFO Sightings (Evanston:
Center for UFO Studies, 1975), p.81.
1978, March 5
George D. Fawcett, "MUFON-NC Train-
ing Conference," MUFON UFO J., no.
127 (June 1978):14-15.
-UFO (DD)
1944, July/Joanne Broome
George D. Fawcett, Quarter Century of
Studies of UFOs in Florida, North
Carolina and Tennessee (Mount Airy:
Pioneer, 1975), p.24.
-UFO (NL)
1973, Oct.26/Cynthia White
"North Carolinian Reports Light in
Sky," Skylook, no.78 (May 1974):13.
(Letter), Fate 27 (June 1974):139-40.
1974, Oct.9/Barbara B. Jones
George D. Fawcett, "The 'Unreported'
UFO Wave of 1974," Saga UFO Rept. 2
(spring 1975):50,75.
1975/Harold F. Spencer/Westinghouse
Bldg.
George D. Fawcett, "The 1975 UFO Wave
in North Carolina," Official UFO 1
(Nov.1975):12,48-49.
1977, Dec.17/Wayne Laporte
Wanda L. June & Wayne Laporte, "A
Helicopter/UFO Encounter," Saga UFO
Rept. 6 (Aug.1978):18,68-70.
1979, March 5/Hwy.29
Charlotte News, 12 Mar.1979.

-UFO (R-V)
1977, Dec.27/Ronald Arey/nr. Coliseum
Charlotte Observer, 31 Dec.1977.
Walt Andrus, et al., "Radar-Visual
Case Involving Police Helicopter,"
MUFON UFO J., no.121 (Dec.1977):3-6.
Maiden Times, 16 Feb.1978.
"A Radar-Visual in Charlotte: UFO or
Prank Balloon?" Int'l UFO Reporter
3 (Mar.1978):7-8.
Wanda L. June & Wayne Laporte, "A
Helicopter/UFO Encounter," Saga UFO
Rept. 6 (Aug.1978):18-20,66-70.

Chatham co.
-Humanoid
1976, spring/Brody Parker
Chapel Hill Regional News, 14 Sep.
1976.
-Humanoid tracks
1975, Sep.10/Brody Parker
Greensboro Daily News, 19 Sep.1975.

Cherokee
-UFO (NL)
1957, Nov.10
"Skillie from the Sky," Newsweek, 25
Nov.1957, p.38.

Clayton
-Poltergeist
1962, June-Aug./Pearl Howell
William G. Roll, The Poltergeist
(N.Y.: Signet, 1974), pp.64-79.

Clemmons
-UFO (NL)
1957, Nov.2
Richard Hall, ed., The UFO Evidence
(Washington: NICAP, 1964), p.163.

Cleveland
-Doubtful identity
1820-1846/Peter Stuart Ney/=Marshal
Ney?
John Harden, The Devil's Tramping
Ground (Chapel Hill: Univ. of North
Carolina, 1949), pp.97-108.

Cleveland co.
-Haunt
ca.1919/Kadesh Church
Nancy Roberts, An Illustrated Guide
to Ghosts and Mysterious Occurrences
in the Old North State (Charlotte:
Heritage House, 1959), pp.17-19.

Clinton
-UFO (NL)
1948, Jan.9
Jacques Vallee, Anatomy of a Phenomenon (N.Y.: Ace, 1965 ed.), p.92.

Concord
-Fall of metallic object
1962, Aug.28/Grady Honeycutt/Twin L.
Augusta (Ga.) Chronicle, 30 Aug.1962.
-UFO (NL)
1973, Jan.17/Gerald Summey/I-85
Charlotte News, 23 Jan.1973.

Greenville (S.C.) News, 26 Feb.1973.
1978, Aug.25/Lisa Potter/court house
Charlotte Observer, 29 Aug.1978.

Copeland
-UFO (CE-3)
1973, Oct.19/David A. Doby
Mt. Airy News, 30 Nov.1973.
George D. Fawcett, Quarter Century of
Studies of UFOs in Florida, North
Carolina and Tennessee (Mount Airy:
Pioneer, 1975), pp.43-44.

Currituck co.
-Witch trial (hex)
1697/Susannah Evans
Francis L. Hawks, History of North
Carolina, 2 vols. (Fayetteville:
E.J. Hale, 1858), 2:116-17.
ca.1700/Martha Richardson
William L. Saunders, ed., North Car-
olina Colonial Records, 10 vols.
(Raleigh: P.M. Hale, 1886-1890), 2:
588,590,819.

Dare co.
-Elizabethan coffin
n.d./Beechland
Charles Whedbee, Legends of the Outer
Banks (Winston-Salem: John F. Blair,
1966), pp.31-33.

Davie co.
-Ghost
1925, June/James Pinkney Chaffin
"Case of the Will of Mr. James L.
Chaffin," Proc.SPR 36 (1927):517-24.
Alson J. Smith, "The Strange Case of
the Chaffin Will," Fate 5 (June
1952):10-13.
J.B. Rhine & J.G. Pratt, Parapsych-
ology: Frontier Science of the Mind
(Springfield, Ill.: Thomas, 1957).

Dobson
-UFO (CE-3)
1973, Oct.24/David Simpson/U.S.601
George D. Fawcett, "Many North Caro-
lina UFO Sightings Remain Unsolved,"
Skylook, no.74 (Jan.1974):14.
-UFO (NL)
1974, Nov.28
George D. Fawcett, "The 'Unreported'
UFO Wave of 1974," Saga UFO Rept. 2
(spring 1975):50,77-78.

Drexel
-Humanoid
1972, Jan.14
John Green, Sasquatch: The Apes Among
Us (Seattle: Hancock House, 1978),
pp.220-21.

Dublin
-UFO (NL)
1975, April 5/Gordon Hester
Jennie Zeidman, The Lumberton Report
(Evanston: Center for UFO Studies,
1976), p.20.

Dudley
-UFO (CE-1)
1975, April 21/Dale Parks/Smith Brother's Store
George D. Fawcett, "The 1975 UFO Wave
in North Carolina," Official UFO 1
(Nov.1975):12,48.

Dunn
-Phantom
1976, Oct.12/Tonnlie Barefoot
1976, Oct.25/Shirley McCrimmon/809 E.
Harnett
Fred H. Bost, "A Few Small Steps on
the Earth: A Tiny Leap for Mankind?"
Pursuit 10 (spring 1977):50-53. il.
-Mystery bird deaths
1954, April 17
"Fish, Birds Fall," Doubt, no.45
(1954):294.
-UFO (DD)
1957, Nov.6/Lester Lee
Dunn Dispatch, 7 Nov.1957.
-UFO (NL)
1970, Feb./John E. Norris, Jr./Broad
St.
Dunn Record, 10 Feb.1970.
1970, June 18/Mrs. Jerry Smith/S on
U.S.421
Angelo Capparella III, "Residents of
Dunn, N.C., Report Bright, Moving
Light," Skylook, no.33 (Aug.1970):5.

Duplin co.
-UFO (NL)
1975, April 21/S.C. Dempsey/U.S.117
George D. Fawcett, "The 1975 UFO Wave
in North Carolina," Official UFO 1
(Nov.1975):12,48.

Durham
-Parapsychology research
1930-1965/J.B. Rhine/Parapsychology
Lab, Duke University
J.B. Rhine, Extra-Sensory Perception
(Boston: Bruce Humphries, 1934).
Robert H. Thouless, "Dr. Rhine's Re-
cent Experiments on Telepathy and
Clairvoyance," Proc.SPR 43 (1935):
24-37.
J.B. Rhine, "Some Selected Experiments
in Extra-Sensory Perception," J.Ab-
normal & Social Psych. 31 (1936):
216-28.
J.B. Rhine, New Frontiers of the Mind
(N.Y.: Farrar & Rinehart, 1937).
Christian Paul & Julia Heil Heinland,
"Critique of the Premises and Sta-
tistical Methodology of Parapsych-
ology," J.Psych. 5 (1938):135-48.
Eileen Garrett, My Life As a Search
for the Meaning of Mediumship (Lon-
don: Rider, 1939).
J.G. Pratt & J.L. Woodruff, "Size of
Stimulus Symbols in Extra-Sensory
Perception," J.Parapsych. 3 (1939):
121-58.
J.B. Rhine, et al., Extra-Sensory
Perception After Sixty Years (Bos-
ton: Bruce Humphries, 1940).

J.B. Rhine, "Experiments Bearing on the Precognition Hypothesis," J. Parapsych. 2 (1938):38-54,119-31; 5 (1941):1-58.

J.B. Rhine, "Evidence of Precognition in the Covariation of Salience Ratios," J.Parapsych. 6 (1942):111-43.

Margaret Pegram Reeves & J.B. Rhine, "Exceptional Scores in ESP Tests and the Conditions," J.Parapsych. 6 (1942):164-73.

J.G. Pratt & Dorothy H. Pope, "The ESP Controversy," J.Parapsych. 6 (1942):186.

Hugh Woodworth, "Report on Investigations into an Obscure Function of the Subconscious Mind," J.ASPR 36 (1942):185-230.

J.B. & L.E. Rhine, "The Psychokinetic Effect," J.Parapsych. 7 (1943):20-43.

Hugh Woodworth, "Further Consideration of Multiple-Blocking and Unblocking in Normal Subjects," J.ASPR 37 (1943):117-37.

"Editorial: The PK Research at the Point of Decision," J.Parapsych. 8 (1944):1-2.

J.B. Rhine & Betty Humphrey, "The PK Effect: Special Evidence from Hit Patterns," J.Parapsych. 8 (1944):18-60.

Betty M. Humphrey, Handbook of Tests in Parapsychology (Durham: Parapsychology Lab, 1948).

J.B. Rhine, "The Value of Reports of Spontaneous Psi Experiences," J. Parapsych. 12 (1948):231-35.

J.G. Pratt & William R. Birge, "Appraising Verbal Test Material in Parapsychology," J.Parapsych. 12 (1948):236-56.

D.J. West, "The Parapsychology Laboratory at Duke University, and the American Society for Psychical Research. Some Impressions," J.SPR 35 (1950):165-74.

W.E. Cox, "The Effect of PK on the Placement of Falling Objects," J. Parapsych. 15 (1951):40-48.

J.B. Rhine, "The Forwald Experiments with Placement PK," J.Parapsych. 15 (1951):49-56.

J.G. Pratt, "The Cormack Placement PK Experiments," J.Parapsych. 15 (1951):57-73.

J.B.Rhine, "The Present Outlook on the Question of Psi in Animals," J. Parapsych. 15 (1951):230-51.

Louisa E. Rhine, "Subjective Forms of Spontaneous Psi Experiences," J. Parapsych. 17 (1953):77-114.

J. Fraser Nicol & Betty M. Humphrey, "The Exploration of ESP and Human Personality," J.ASPR 47 (1953):133-78.

Louisa E. Rhine, "Frequency of Types of Experience in Spontaneous Precognition," J.Parapsych. 18 (1954):93-123.

J.B. Rhine & J.G. Pratt, "A Review of the Pearce-Pratt Distance Series of ESP Tests," J.Parapsych. 18 (1954):165-77.

Betty M. Humphrey & J. Fraser Nicol, "The Feeling of Success in ESP," J. ASPR 49 (1955):3-37.

Robert H. Thouless, "An Examination of the Humphrey-Nicol Experiments on the Feeling of Success in ESP," J.ASPR 50 (1956):34-39.

Betty Humphrey & J. Fraser Nicol, "An Answer to the 'Examination,'" J.ASPR 50 (1956):39-44.

Hornell Hart, "Six Theories About Apparitions," Proc.SPR 50 (1956):153-239.

Louisa E. Rhine, "The Relationship of Agent and Percipient in Spontaneous Telepathy," J.Parapsych. 20 (1956):1-32.

J.G. Van Busschbach, "An Investigation of ESP between Teacher and Pupils in American Schools," J.Parapsych. 20 (1956):71-80.

Louisa E. Rhine, "Hallucinatory Psi Experiences," J.Parapsych. 20 (1956):233-56; 21 (1957):13-46, 186-226.

J.B. Rhine & J.G. Pratt, Parapsychology: Frontier Science of the Mind (Springfield, Ill.: Thomas, 1957).

R.L. Van de Castle, "Differential Patterns of ESP Scoring As a Function of Differential Attitudes Toward ESP," J.ASPR 51 (1957):43-61.

J.G. Pratt & Haakon Forwald, "Confirmation of the PK Placement Effect," J.Parapsych. 22 (1958):1-19.

R.L. Van de Castle, "An Exploratory Study of Some Personality Correlates Associated with PK Performance," J. ASPR 52 (1958):134-50.

D.H. Rawcliffe, Illusions and Delusions of the Supernatural and the Occult (N.Y.: Dover, 1959), pp.426-55.

Jarl Fahler, "Exploratory 'Sealed' PK Placement Tests with Nine College Students with and without Distance," J.ASPR 53 (1959):106-13.

Karlis Osis, "Some Explorations with Dowsing Techniques," J.ASPR 54 (1960):141-52.

Louisa E. Rhine, Hidden Channels of the Mind (N.Y.: William Sloan, 1961).

J.B. Rhine & S.R. Feather, "The Study of Cases of 'Psi-Trailing' in Animals," J.Parapsych. 26 (1962):1-22.

Louisa E. Rhine, "Psychological Processes in ESP Experiences," J.Parapsych. 26 (1962):88-111,172-99.

Louisa E. Rhine, "Spontaneous Physical Effects and the Psi Process," J. Parapsych. 27 (1963):84-122.

J.B. Rhine, et al., Parapsychology from Duke to FRNM (Durham: Parapsychology Press, 1965).

C.E.M. Hansel, ESP: A Scientific Evaluation (N.Y.: Scribner, 1966).

Louisa Rhine, ESP in Life and Lab

(N.Y.: Macmillan, 1967).

Hornell Hart, "Scientific Survival Research," Int'l J.Parapsych. 9 (1967):43-52.

J.B. Rhine & R. Brier, eds., Parapsychology Today (N.Y.: Citadel, 1968).

Louisa Rhine, Mind over Matter: Psychokinesis (N.Y.: Macmillan, 1970).

R. Laurence Moore, In Search of White Crows (N.Y.: Oxford Univ., 1977), pp.185-203.

J.G. Pratt, "New Evidence Supporting the ESP Interpretation of the Pratt-Woodruff Experiment," J.Parapsych. 40 (1976):217-27.

Martin Ebon, The Evidence for Life after Death (N.Y.: Signet, 1977), pp.77-85.

1960-   /Psychical Research Foundation /2015 Erwin Rd.

W.G. Roll & Charles T. Tart, "Exploratory Token Objects Tests with a 'Sensitive,'" J.ASPR 59 (1965):226-36.

W.G. Roll, "Further Token Object Tests with a 'Sensitive,'" J.ASPR 60 (1966):270-80.

W.G. Roll, "Token Object Matching Tests: A Third Series," J.ASPR 60 (1966):363-79.

Robert Morris, "Survival Research at the Psychical Research Foundation," Newsl.ASPR, no.18 (summer 1973).

William G. Roll, The Poltergeist (N.Y.: Signet, 1974 ed.), pp. xiii-xvi.

June & Nicholas Regush, Psi: The Other World Catalogue (N.Y.: Putnam, 1974), p.11.

D. Scott Rogo, "Parapsychology Today," Probe the Unknown 3 (May 1975):21, 23,52.

Judith L. Taddonio, "The Relationship of Experimenter Expectancy to Performance on ESP Tasks," J.Parapsych. 40 (1976):107-14.

Stuart Blue Harary & Gerald Solfvin, "A Study of Out-of-Body Experiences Using Auditory Targets," in J.D. Morris, et al., eds., Research in Parapsychology 1976 (Metuchen, N.J.: Scarecrow, 1977), pp.57-59.

Martin Ebon, The Evidence for Life after Death (N.Y.: Signet, 1977), pp.86-94.

G.F. Solfvin, et al., "A Psychphysiological Study of Mediumistic Communicators," Parapsych.Rev. 8 (May-June 1977):21-22.

Edward F. Kelly, "Physiological Correlates of Psi Processes," Parapsych. Rev. 8 (July-Aug.1977):1-9.

D. Scott Rogo, ed., Mind Beyond the Body: The Mystery of ESP Projection (N.Y.: Penguin, 1978), pp.17-34,43-51,170-92.

Robert L. Morris, et al., "Studies of Communication during Out-of-Body Experience," J.ASPR 72 (1978):1-21.

1962-   /Foundation for Research on the Nature of Man/402 Buchanan Blvd.

J.B. Rhine, Parapsychology from Duke to FRNM (Durham: Parapsychology Press, 1965).

Charles Honorton, "A Combination of Techniques for the Separation of High- and Low-Scoring ESP Subjects," J.ASPR 63 (1969):69-82.

Charles Honorton & John P. Stump, "A Preliminary Study of Hypnotically-Induced Clairvoyant Dreams," J.ASPR 63 (1969):175-84.

Helmut Schmidt, "A PK Test with Electronic Equipment," J.Parapsych. 34 (1970):175-81.

Helmut Schmidt, "A Quantum Mechanical Random Number Generator for Psi Tests," J.Parapsych. 34 (1970):219-24.

Helmut Schmidt, "PK Experiments with Animals As Subjects," J.Parapsych. 34 (1970):255-61.

Helmut Schmidt & L. Pantas, "Psi Tests with Psychologically Equivalent Conditions and Internally Different Machines," Proc.Parapsych. Ass'n 8 (1971):49-51.

Helmut Schmidt, "Mental Influence on Random Events," New Scientist, 24 June 1971, pp.757-58.

W.J. Levy, "The Effect of the Test Situation on Precognition in Mice and Birds," J.Parapsych. 36 (1972): 46-55.

Helmut Schmidt & Lee Pantas, "Psi Tests with Internally Different Machines," J.Parapsych. 36 (1972):222-32.

Jean Shinoda Bolen, "Interview: Dr. J.B. Rhine," Psychic 3 (July 1972): 7-11,30-34. il.

Helmut Schmidt, "PK Tests with a High-Speed Random Number Generator," J. Parapsych. 37 (1973):105-18.

June & Nicholas Regush, Psi: The Other World Catalogue (N.Y.: Putnam, 1974), pp.12-13.

Helmut Schmidt, "PK Effect on Random Time Intervals," in W.G. Roll, et al., eds., Research in Parapsychology 1973 (Metuchen, N.J.: Scarecrow, 1974), pp.46-48.

New York Times, 20 Aug.1974.

J.B. Rhine, "A New Case of Experimenter Unreliability," J.Parapsych. 38 (1974):215-25.

Helmut Schmidt, "Comparison of PK Action on Two Different Random Number Generators," J.Parapsych. 38 (1974):47-55.

H. Kanthamani & E.F. Kelly, "Awareness of Success in an Exceptional Subject," J.Parapsych. 38 (1974): 355-82.

D. Scott Rogo, "Parapsychology Today," Probe the Unknown 3 (May 1975):21-23.

J.B. Rhine, "Second Report on a Case of Experimenter Fraud," J.Parapsych.

39 (1975):306-25.
K. Ramakrishna Rao, et al., "Paired
Associates Recall and ESP," in Wil-
liam G. Roll, ed., Research in
Parapsychology 1977 (Metuchen, N.J.:
Scarecrow, 1978), pp.65-84.
M.B. Dykshoorn & Russell H. Felton,
My Passport Says Clairvoyant (N.Y.:
Jove, 1978 ed.), pp.153-61.
-Precognition
1977, March 21/Lee Fried
(Editorial), Fate 30 (Aug.1977):18-
20.
-Snake handling
1930s-   /Zion Tabernacle
Weston La Barre, They Shall Take Up
Serpents (Minneapolis: Univ. of
Minnesota, 1962), pp.34-38.
William Sargent, The Mind Possessed
(N.Y.: Penguin, 1975), pp.182-91.
-UFO (?)
1946, Aug.24
"Balls of Fire," Doubt, no.17 (1947)
:255.
-UFO (NL)
1974, Nov.
1975, Jan./N.J. Lemmons
1975, Feb.26
George D. Fawcett, "The 1975 UFO Wave
in North Carolina," Official UFO 1
(Nov.1975):12,13,48.
"From the Center for UFO Studies,"
Flying Saucer Rev. 21 (Aug.1975):
32-iii.
1978, May 25
Durham Sun, 26 May 1978.

East Laport
-Petroglyph
Caney Fork Creek
John Harden, "North Carolina's Mys-
tery Rock Writing," Fate 8 (June
1955):87-90. il.

Eden
-UFO (NL)
1951, summer
George D. Fawcett, Quarter Century of
Studies of UFOs in Florida, North
Carolina and Tennessee (Mount Airy:
Pioneer, 1975), p.25.
1972, Feb.3/Henry H. Harris, Jr.
1972, Feb.7/Carolyn Redford
Eden News, 8 Feb.1972.
1975, March 13/Robert James Wilson/Vir-
ginia St.
George D. Fawcett, "The 1975 UFO Wave
in North Carolina," Official UFO 1
(Nov.1975):12,45.

Edenton
-UFO (DD)
1963, Oct.15
"UFO Sightings Centered in Western
U.S.," UFO Inv. 2 (Dec.-Jan.1963-
64):3.

Elizabethtown
-UFO (NL)
1975, April 3-4/Phillip Little

Raleigh News & Observer, 6 Apr.1975.
Dwight Connelly, "Landing Reported
in N.Carolina," Skylook, no.90 (May
1975):3.
Jennie Zeidman, The Lumberton Report
(Evanston: Center for UFO Studies,
1976), pp.7,16.

Elkin
-Phantom panther
1897, June
Wilkesboro Chronicle, 9 June 1897.
-UFO (CE-1)
1965, Sep.21/Mabel Absher
Winston-Salem Journal, 25 Sep.1965.

Ellenboro
-UFO (CE-2)
1973, Jan.8/Billy Gowan
"Motorists in North and South Caro-
lina Frightened by UFOs in January,"
Skylook, no.64 (Mar.1973):8.

Elm City
-UFO (NL)
1977, Dec.1
"UFOs of Limited Merit," Int'l UFO
Reporter 3 (Jan.1978):3.

Fayetteville
-Fire anomaly
1945, Dec.25
George D. Fawcett, Quarter Century of
Studies of UFOs in Florida, North
Carolina and Tennessee (Mount Airy:
Pioneer, 1975), p.24.
-Ghost
ca.1910/A.S. Slocumb house
Nancy Roberts, An Illustrated Guide
to Ghosts and Mysterious Occurrences
in the Old North State (Charlotte:
Heritage House, 1959), pp.52-53.
-UFO (?)
1949, Dec.
Hollywood (Cal.) Citizen-News, 29
Dec.1949.

Fort Bragg
-Lightning anomaly
1951, July 15/Floyd Stump
South Bend (Ind.) Tribune, 3 Aug.1951.
-UFO (DD)
1960, Aug.
"Helicopter Pilot Reveals 1960 Sighting," UFO Inv. 3 (May-June 1966):3.
-UFO (NL)
1958, June 20/1 mi.N of hospital
Thomas M. Olsen, ed., The Reference
for Outstanding UFO Sighting Reports
(Riderwood, Md.: UFO Information Retrieval Center, 1966), pp.57-58.
1978, March 22/Steve Molnar/82d Air-
borne Museum
Fayetteville Times, 3 Apr.1978. il.

Franklinville
-UFO (NL)
1975, Jan.18/Eric Allred
George D. Fawcett, "The 1975 UFO Wave
in North Carolina," Official UFO 1

(Nov.1975):12,13.

Fuquay-Varina
-UFO (NL)
   1947, July 7/Albert Duke
      Raleigh News & Observer, 8 July 1947.

Gastonia
-Fall of coin
   1958, Oct./Basil McGee/1005 Woodland
   Dr.
      (Editorial), Fate 12 (Apr.1959):18-
      19, quoting Gastonia Gazette (un-
      dated).
-Fall of flesh
   1876, Oct.28/James M. Hanna
      Charlotte Observer, 31 Oct.1876.
-Fall of foam
   1950s/Avery R. Jenkins
      (Letter), Fate 13 (Jan.1960):116-17.
-UFO (CE-1)
   1976, Sep.10/H.L. Amor
      "Matching Cases," Can.UFO Rept., no.
      26 (winter 1976-77):18-19.
-UFO (CE-2)
   1966
      John A. Keel, UFOs: Operation Trojan
      Horse (N.Y.: Putnam, 1970), p.175.
   1966, Sep.25
      Gastonia Gazette, 26 Sep.1966.
-UFO (NL)
   1967, Nov.15/Delores Jamison/Hollywood
   Cemetery
      Gastonia Gazette, 16 Nov.1967.
   1973, Oct.25
      Gastonia Gazette, 26 Oct.1973.
   1975, April 3/Diane Glenn/Meek Rd.
      George D. Fawcett, "The 1975 UFO Wave
      in North Carolina," Official UFO 1
      (Nov.1975):12,46.
   1976, Nov.11/Maria Bingham/Eastridge
   Mall
      Gastonia Gazette, 13 Nov.1976.

Goldsboro
-UFO (CE-1)
   1973, Oct.27
      Goldsboro News Argus, 28 Oct.1973.
-UFO (NL)
   1976, April 22
      "Noteworthy UFO Sightings," Ufology
      2 (fall 1976):60.

Grantham
-UFO (CE-1)
   1974, June 12/Joyce Henderson
      Frank R. Harrison, "N.C. UFO Moves
      Erratically," Skylook, no.80 (July
      1974):20.

Greensboro
-Fall of ice
   1954, Dec.1/Benny Lewis
      "Snow, Ice and Fish," Doubt, no.48
      (1955):341.
-Fall of unknown object
   1969, Aug.26/George Wright
      "Unidentifieds," INFO J., no.7 (fall
      1970):43, quoting Danville (Va.)
      News (undated).

-Plant sensitivity
   1970s/Gaylord T. Hageseth/Univ. of
   North Carolina at Greensboro
      Peter Tompkins & Christopher Bird,
      The Secret Life of Plants (N.Y.:
      Harper & Row, 1973), p.152.
-Poltergeist
   1954, July 29-31/J.A. McCarn
      Greensboro Record, 31 July 1954.
-Skyquake
   1955, April 21
      "Blue Flash and Thunderous Explosion
      Rocks North Carolina," CRIFO Newsl.,
      6 May 1955, p.5.
-UFO (CE-1)
   1947, July 7/Albert Riggs/nr. Greens-
   boro-High Point Airport
      Raleigh News & Observer, 8 July 1947.
   1948, spring/Jerry A. Manual, Sr./Cone
   Mills Plant
      George D. Fawcett, Quarter Century of
      Studies of UFOs in Florida, North
      Carolina and Tennessee (Mount Airy:
      Pioneer, 1975), pp.24-25.
-UFO (CE-2)
   1975, June 16
      Greensboro Record, 20 June 1975.
      Timothy Green Beckley, "Saucers over
      Our Cities," Saga UFO Rept. 4 (Aug.
      1977):24,74.
-UFO (CE-3)
   1930s, May/J.T. Rankin
      George D. Fawcett, "The 1975 UFO Wave
      in North Carolina," Official UFO 1
      (Nov.1975):12,49.
-UFO (NL)
   1974, Sep.9/Linda B. Scheff
      George D. Fawcett, "The 'Unreported'
      UFO Wave of 1974," Saga UFO Rept. 2
      (spring 1975):50,74-75.
   1975, March 20/Karen Hartle
   1975, April 5/WCOG station
      George D. Fawcett, "The 1975 UFO Wave
      in North Carolina," Official UFO 1
      (Nov.1975):12,45,46.
-UFO (R-V)
   1966, July 27/Greensboro-High Point
   Airport
      John A. Keel, UFOs: Operation Trojan
      Horse (N.Y.: Putnam, 1970), p.14.

Grover
-Haunt
   n.d./Elizabeth Carnes
      Winston-Salem Journal & Sentinel, 31
      Oct.1954.

Halifax co.
-Possession and phantoms
   1785-1790/William Glendenning
      William Glendenning, The Life of Wil-
      liam Glendenning, Preacher of the
      Gospel (Philadelphia: W.W. Woodward,
      1795), pp.1-35.

Hamlet
-UFO (?)
   1949, Dec.28/=balloon?
      Los Angeles (Cal.) Times, 29 Dec.1949.
-UFO (CE-3)

1975, March 27
George D. Fawcett, "The 1975 UFO Wave
in North Carolina," Official UFO 1
(Nov.1975):12,45.

Harrellsville
-Ghost
ca.1915/Cecil Wiggins
F. Roy Johnson, Witches and Demons
in History and Folklore (Murfreesboro: Johnson, 1969), p.184.

Havelock
-Haunt
n.d./S.A. Long plantation/Slocum Village
John Harden, Tar Heel Ghosts (Chapel
Hill: Univ. of North Carolina,
1954), pp.116-20.

Henderson
-Skyquake
1959
"'Mystery Blasts' Across the U.S.A.,"
Fate 12 (Oct.1959):78.
-UFO (CE-1)
1956, April 16/Hwy.1
Jacques Vallee, Passport to Magonia
(Chicago: Regnery, 1969), p.253.

Hertford co.
-UFO (NL)
ca.1910/Walter Vinson
F. Roy Johnson, Witches and Demons
in History and Folklore (Murfreesboro: Johnson, 1969), pp.120-21.

Hickory
-UFO (NL)
1972, March 16
Memphis (Tenn.) Commercial Appeal,
16 Mar.1972.
1978, March 17/Connie Miller/Hunting
Park Apt.
Hickory Record, 20 Mar.1978.

Highlands
-Ghost
1904/Mrs. M.A. Pierson
"Aunt Ella's Ghost," Fate 7 (July
1954):20.
-UFO (NL)
1937, June 11/Dorothy Morrison
(Editorial), UFO Reporter, no.2
(1956):1-2.

High Point
-Ghost
1923/Burke Hardison
Nancy Roberts, An Illustrated Guide
to Ghosts and Mysterious Occurrences
in the Old North State (Charlotte:
Heritage House, 1959), pp.9-10.
1960/Edward Bell
John Macklin, The Enigma of the Unknown (N.Y.: Ace, 1967).
-UFO (CE-2)
1966, April 19
High Point Enterprise, 20 Apr.1966.
1974, March 24/Randall Hall/May Rd. x

Hwy.109
Ted Phillips, Physical Traces Associ-
ated with UFO Sightings (Evanston:
Center for UFO Studies, 1975), p.99.
-UFO (NL)
1966, July 27/Art Richardson
High Point Enterprise, 27 July 1966.
il.

Hillsborough
-Haunt
18th c.-   /Haw Place
Winston-Salem Journal & Sentinel, 31
Oct.1954.
1960s/Robert Murphy/157 E. King St.
Sarah Kenan, "Ghosts at Seven
Hearths," North Carolina Folklore 19
(1971):123-30.

Hudson
-UFO (NL)
1979, Jan.15/Ronnie Simmons/U.S.321
Charlotte Observer, 16 Jan.1979.

Iredell co.
-Fall of pebbles
1864, Oct./William Knox
Salisbury Carolina Watchman, 23 Dec.
1864.
-Phantom panther
1890, Aug.-Sep./=hoax?
Statesville Landmark, 28 Aug.1890.
Salisbury Carolina Watchman, 11 Sep.
1890.
Angelo Capparella III, "The Santer:
North Carolina's Own Mystery Cat?"
Shadows, no.4 (Jan.1977):1-2.

Jacksonville
-UFO (DD)
1975, April 4
Jennie Zeidman, The Lumberton Report
(Evanston: Center for UFO Studies,
1976), pp.12-13.

Kernersville
-UFO (CE-1)
1974, Aug.27/Joseph Kent Needham/E on
U.S.421
"Object Reported on Road," Skylook,
no.86 (Jan.1975):19.

King
-UFO (NL)
1975, Feb.
George D. Fawcett, "The 1975 UFO Wave
in North Carolina," Official UFO 1
(Nov.1975):12,13.

King's Mountain
-UFO (?)
1973, Oct.25/=searchlight
Gastonia Gazette, 26 Oct.1973.
-UFO (DD)
1968, Aug.1/Daniel Shuttles
George D. Fawcett, Quarter Century of
Studies of UFOs in Florida, North
Carolina and Tennessee (Mount Airy:
Pioneer, 1975), p.27.

Laurinburg
-UFO (NL)
  1897, April 18
    Rockingham Rocket, 29 Apr.1897.
  1975, April 7/St. Andrews College
    George D. Fawcett, "The 1975 UFO Wave
    in North Carolina," Official UFO 1
    (Nov.1975):12,48.

Lenoir
-Anatomical anomaly
  1978, Jan./Doug Pritchard/=tooth grow-
    ing from foot
    Dallas (Tex.) Morning News, 22 Jan.
    1978.
-UFO (CE-2)
  1919, Nov./Mr. Franklin
    Lenoir News-Topic, 27 Nov.1919.

Lexington
-UFO (CE-1)
  1973, Oct.25/Lee Phillips/nr. Friend-
    ship Methodist Church
    Lexington Dispatch, 26 Oct.1973.
-UFO (DD)
  1955, Nov.6/Jack Swain
    "Latest Saucer Sightings," Fate 9
    (Apr.1956):43,46-47.

Lincoln co.
-Haunt
  18th c.-   /Engleside Mansion
    Winston-Salem Journal & Sentinel, 31
    Oct.1954.

Lincolnton
-UFO (CE-2)
  1978, Oct.10/Horace Abee
    Maiden Times, 13 Dec.1978.
-UFO (NL)
  1977, April 5
    "UFO Analysis," Int'l UFO Reporter 2
    (June 1977):newsfront sec.

Lumberton
-Gravity anomaly
  1955, April 15/Ed Glover
    Curtis Fuller, "The Saucers Are Fly-
    ing," Fate 8 (Aug.1955):10,16.
-Mystery radio transmission
  1975, April 12/James E. Floyd
    Jennie Zeidman, The Lumberton Report
    (Evanston: Center for UFO Studies,
    1976), pp.36-37.
-UFO (?)
  1970, Jan.27/Billy Lewis/=meteor
    "Fireball Seen over Robeson County,
    N.C.," Skylook, no.29 (Apr.1970):20,
    quoting Lumberton Robesonian (un-
    dated).
  1975, April 7/police dep't
    George D. Fawcett, "The 1975 UFO Wave
    in North Carolina," Official UFO 1
    (Nov.1975):12,48.
-UFO (CE-1)
  1975, April 3/Phil Stanton/Hwy.30T N.
    Raleigh News & Observer, 8 Apr.1975.
    Dwight Connelly, "Landing Reported
    in N. Carolina," Skylook, no.90
    (May 1975):3.

Jennie Zeidman, The Lumberton Report
  (Evanston: Center for UFO Studies,
  1976), pp.3-4.
1975, April 4-9/James E. Floyd/Alamac
Knitting Mill
  Jennie Zeidman, The Lumberton Report
  (Evanston: Center for UFO Studies,
  1976), pp.35-36.
-UFO (CE-2)
  1952, Aug.27/Gabriel Durocher
    Ted Phillips, Physical Traces Associ-
    ated with UFO Sightings (Evanston:
    Center for UFO Studies, 1975), p.9,
    quoting Lumberton Robesonian (un-
    dated).
  1957, Oct.31
    Charlotte Observer, 4 Nov.1957.
-UFO (CE-3)
  1952, Aug.6/James J. Allen
    Lumberton Robesonian, 7 Aug.1952.
  1974, Dec.29/Forest Rd. x Barker Ten
    Mile Rd.
    George D. Fawcett, "What We Can Ex-
    pect of UFOs in 1975," Official UFO
    1 (Aug.1975):12,50.

McAdenville
-Haunt
  n.d.
    Nancy Roberts, An Illustrated Guide
    to Ghosts and Mysterious Occurrences
    in the Old North State (Charlotte:
    Heritage House, 1959), pp.15-16.

Maco
-Ghost light
  1867-   /nr. Hood's Creek
    John Harden, Tar Heel Ghosts (Chapel
    Hill: Univ. of North Carolina,
    1954), pp.44-51.
    Nina Leen, "Ghostly American Legends,"
    Life, 28 Oct.1957, pp.86,88. il.
    Wilmington Star-News, 8-26 Apr.1964.
    Hans Holzer, Ghosts I've Met (N.Y.:
    Ace, 1965), pp.93-107.
    David B. Stansel, Jr., "Unique Exper-
    iences at the Maco Light," North
    Carolina Folklore 21 (1973):18-22.

Maiden
-UFO (CE-2)
  1978, Aug.5/Terry Mayo/Buffalo Shoals
    Rd.
    Maiden Times, 16 Aug.1978; and 30
    Aug.1978.
  1978, Oct.16/Betty Morrow/Spooky Hollow
    Rd.
    Newton Observer-News-Enterprise, 24
    Oct.1978.
-UFO (DD)
  1963, Feb.18/Floyd Hester
    "News Briefs," Saucer News 10 (June
    1963):22.
  1963, May 4/Robert D. Null
    Gray Barker, Book of Saucers (Clarks-
    burg, W.V.: Saucerian, 1965), p.19.
-UFO (NL)
  1972, March 16
    Memphis (Tenn.) Commercial Appeal, 16
    Mar.1972.

Maney's Neck twp.
-Healing
1900s/Jim Jordan
F. Roy Johnson, The Fabled Doctor
Jim Jordan (Murfreesboro: Johnson,
1963).

Matthews
-Erratic bison
ca.1974
Wayne Laporte & David Fideler, "Mystery Baboon Invades North Carolina,"
Anomaly Rsch.Bull., no.23 (1978):
12,13.
-Phantom baboon
1977, Aug.8/Mike Jones
Wayne Laporte & David Fideler, "Mystery Baboon Invades North Carolina,"
Anomaly Rsch.Bull., no.23 (1978):
12-13.

Maxton
-UFO (CE-1)
1974, May 12
George D. Fawcett, "A Review of Some
of the Thousands of UFO Sightings
in 1974 to Date," Flying Saucers,
Dec.1974, pp.37,38.

Monroe
-UFO (CE-1)
1967, April 28/Dennis Whitley
"Car Buzzing Incidents on Increase,"
APRO Bull. 15 (May-June 1967):5-6.
-UFO (NL)
1979, March/Steve Morton/Corinth Church
Rd.
Charlotte News, 12 Mar.1979.

Mooresville
-UFO (NL)
1966, Nov.16
Brad Steiger, Project Blue Book (N.Y.:
Ballantine, 1976), betw.pp.56-57. il.

Morehead City
-UFO (NL)
1973, Nov.1/Crab Point Rd.
Morehead City Carteret County News-
Times, 8 Nov.1973.

Morganton
-Acoustic anomaly
1950-1952/Pap Caldwell
Greensboro Daily News, 18 Aug.1950.
(Editorial), Fate 5 (Dec.1952):5,
quoting Charlotte Observer (undated).
-Spirit medium
1976/Joann Denton/Lenoir St.
"A Real-Life Ghost Story," Newsweek,
3 May 1976, p.29.
-UFO (DD)
1945, June 1
"'Rocket' in N. Carol.," Doubt, no.
14 (spring 1946):209.

Mountain Park
-Plague of mold
1961, summer/Grady Norman
Lee R. Gandee, "A Pestilence of Mold,"
Fate 15 (Jan.1962):27-35.

Mount Airy
-UFO (?)
1952, Sep.12/Lawrence Phillips
G.D. Fawcett, "Mount Airy's Own UFO
Enigma Puzzles Many," Australian
Flying Saucer Rev. 3 (Dec.1972):13,
14.
-UFO (CE-1)
1967, Dec.24/Teresa Ann Dobson
1971, March 13/Jim Barber/Lowgap Wild-
life Club
George D. Fawcett, Quarter Century of
Studies of UFOs in Florida, North
Carolina and Tennessee (Mount Airy:
Pioneer, 1975), pp.39,41.
1975, July 16
"UFO Central," CUFOS News Bull., 15
Nov.1975, p.13.
-UFO (CE-2)
1962/Buford King
George D. Fawcett, Quarter Century of
Studies of UFOs in Florida, North
Carolina and Tennessee (Mount Airy:
Pioneer, 1975), p.38.
1965, Aug.19/Thelma Schumaker/Piper's
Gap Rd.
Jerome Clark, "The Greatest Flap Yet?
--Part 2," Flying Saucer Rev. 12
(Mar.-Apr.1966):8,11, quoting Win-
ston-Salem Journal (undated).
George D. Fawcett, Quarter Century of
Studies of UFOs in Florida, North
Carolina and Tennessee (Mount Airy:
Pioneer, 1975), pp.32,38-39.
1972, Feb.25/Danny Lee Forest/Lewis Dr.
George D. Fawcett, Quarter Century of
Studies of UFOs in Florida, North
Carolina and Tennessee (Mount Airy:
Pioneer, 1975), pp.41-42.
-UFO (CE-3)
1962, Jan.19/Harry Epperson
1968, July?/Mrs. Harold B. Eggers/Buck
Shoals Rd.
George D. Fawcett, Quarter Century of
Studies of UFOs in Florida, North
Carolina and Tennessee (Mount Airy:
Pioneer, 1975), pp.26-27,38,40,43.
-UFO (DD)
1952, Oct.13/Wallace Shelton
G.D. Fawcett, "Mount Airy's Own UFO
Enigma Puzzles Many," Australian
Flying Saucer Rev. 3 (Dec.1972):13,
14.
-UFO (NL)
1954, summer/H.A. Hair/Blue Ridge Pkwy.
1965, July 31/Johnny Parries/Granite
Quarry
1965, Sep.6/K.T. Campbell
1967, March 3/Francis E. Andrews/nr.
Pilot Mt.
1967, May-June/R.J. Berrier
1968, Jan.18/Otis B. Fleming/North
Surry Hospital
1968, Aug.4/Don Hiatt/Sheltontown
1972, Jan.16/Robert Ferguson/Jones Elementary School
1972, April 3/Mrs. Rufus W. Walters
George D. Fawcett, Quarter Century of

Studies of UFOs in Florida, North
Carolina and Tennessee (Mount Airy:
Pioneer, 1975), pp.27,37-42.
1973, Feb.3/Bobby Williams/507 Lovill
St.
  Mt. Airy Times, 16 Feb.1973.
1975, Feb.
  George D. Fawcett, "The 1975 UFO Wave
  in North Carolina," Official UFO 1
  (Nov.1975):12-13.

Mount Holly
-Humanoid
1976, July 30/Roger Hoffman
  Durham Morning Herald, 6 Aug.1976.

Mount Olive
-Lightning anomaly
1890/J.H. Smith
  Henry Winfred Splitter, "Nature's
  Strange Photographs," Fate 8 (Jan.
  1955):21,25.
-UFO (CE-1)
1973, Oct.27/Dwight Hudson/E. William-
son St.
  Mount Olive Tribune, 30 Oct.1973.
1974, April 1/Nelson Bland/Hwy.117
  Mount Olive Tribune, 5 Apr.1974. il.
1975, Feb.4/Bessie Holmes
  "MUFON Reports in Brief," Skylook,
  no.89 (Apr.1975):11.
  "From the Center for UFO Studies,"
  Flying Saucer Rev. 21 (Aug.1975):32.
1975, April 11
  George D. Fawcett, "The 1975 UFO Wave
  in North Carolina," Official UFO 1
  (Nov.1975):12,48.
-UFO (NL)
1973, Oct.28/Billy Daniels/S. Johnson
St.
  Mount Olive Tribune, 30 Oct.1973.
1975, April 21/Bass Mitchell
  George D. Fawcett, "The 1975 UFO Wave
  in North America," Official UFO 1
  (Nov.1975):12,48.
1975, Dec.16
  "UFO Central," CUFOS News Bull., 1
  Feb.1976, p.15.

Murphy
-River monster myth
tlanusi/Valley R.
  Albert S. Gatschet, "Water-Monsters
  of the American Aborigines," J.Am.
  Folklore 12 (1899):255-60.

Nags Head
-Disappearance
1812, Dec.31/Theodosia Burr Alston/
"Patriot"
  John Harden, The Devil's Tramping
  Ground (Chapel Hill: Univ. of North
  Carolina, 1949).
  Charles Whedbee, Legends of the Outer
  Banks (Winston-Salem: John F. Blair,
  1966), p.77.
-Sea monster
1888, May 14/John Beauchamp/"Alice
Hodges"
  Baltimore (Md.) Sun, 21 May 1888.

New York Times, 22 May 1888, p.9.

Nashville
-UFO (CE-2)
1964, July 8/Mrs. D.P. McCain
  Coral E. Lorenzen, The Shadow of the
  Unknown (N.Y.: Signet, 1970), p.152.

New Bern
-Inner development
1970s/Church of Wicca
  Gavin & Yvonne Frost, The Witch's
  Bible (Los Angeles: Nash, 1972).
  J. Gordon Melton, Encyclopedia of
  American Religions, 2 vols. (Wil-
  mington, N.C.: Co   ium, 1978),
  2:283-84.
-UFO (?)
1975, Jan.15/=high altitude rocket?
  George D. Fawcett, "The 1975 UFO Wave
  in North Carolina," Official UFO 1
  (Nov.1975):12,13.
-UFO (NL)
1973, Oct.27
  New Bern Sun-Journal, 27 Oct.1973.

Newton
-UFO (CE-2)
1968, Sep.6/Samuel H. Boyer/Hwy.10
  Samuel H. Boyer, "UFO Encounter
  Brings Elation," Fate 23 (May 1969)
  :40-43.
-UFO (NL)
1966, March 27
  "Nation-Wide Saucer Flap Continues,"
  Saucer News 13 (June 1966):31.
1972, March 16/Paul Burgess
  Memphis (Tenn.) Commercial Appeal,
  16 Mar.1972.
1973, Oct.25/George Wilkerson
  Hickory Record, 26 Oct.1973.

Newton Grove
-UFO (CE-1)
1975, April 4/Evander Parnell
  Dwight Connelly, "Landing Reported in
  N. Carolina," Skylook, no.90 (May
  1975):3,4.

North Belmont
-UFO (NL)
1976, Nov.8
  "UFOs of Limited Merit," Int'l UFO
  Reporter 1 (Dec.1976):11, quoting
  Gastonia Gazette (undated).

Oakdale
-Phantom panther
1953, Feb./V.S. Hynes
  Jim Brandon, Weird America (N.Y.:
  Dutton, 1978), p.175.

Ocracoke
-Ghost light
n.d.
  Charles Whedbee, Legends of the Outer
  Banks (Winston-Salem: John F. Blair,
  1966), pp.31-33.
-Phantom ship
n.d.

Carolina Watchman, 23 Sep.1842.
"The Pirates and the Palatines,"
North Carolina Folklore 7 (1957):
23-26.
Charles Whedbee, The Flaming Ship of
Ocracoke (Winston-Salem: John F.
Blair, 1971), pp.14-20.

Orange co.
-Hex and shape-shifting
  19th c.
    Raleigh News & Observer, 11 July
    1948.

Oriental
-UFO (?)
  1967, July 21/Ronnie Hill/=hoax?
    John A. Keel, "The 'Little Man' of
    North Carolina," Flying Saucer Rev.
    15 (Jan.-Feb.1969):15-16.

Parkton
-UFO (NL)
  1975, April 4/Steven Murray/Hwy.1726 x
  U.S.301
    Raleigh News & Observer, 6 Apr.1975.

Pasquotank co.
-Vampire legend
    Raleigh News & Observer, 1 June 1950.
    F. Roy Johnson, Witches and Demons
    in History and Folklore (Murfrees-
    boro: Johnson, 1969), pp.60-62.

Patterson
-Archeological sites
    Cyrus Thomas, "Report on the Mound
    Explorations of the Bureau of Eth-
    nology," Ann.Rept.Bur.Am.Ethn. 12
    (1890-91):333-42. il.

Pembroke
-UFO (CE-2)
  1975, April 6/Ray Strickland/Philadel-
  phus Rd.
    Raleigh News & Observer, 8 Apr.1975.
    Dwight Connelly, "Landing Reported
    in N. Carolina," Skylook, no.90 (May
    1975):3,4-5. il.
    Jennie Zeidman, The Lumberton Report
    (Evanston: Center for UFO Studies,
    1976), pp.20-35,44-45,51.

Perquimans co.
-Witch trial (?)
  1680, Oct.
    Mattie Erma Edwards Parker, ed., North
    Carolina Higher Court Records 1670-
    1696 (Raleigh: N.C. Dep't of Arch-
    ives & History, 1968), p.420.

Pilot Mountain
-UFO (CE-1)
  1973, Oct.1/Bruce Snow/7 mi.NW
    Mount Airy Times, 5 Oct.1973.
  1975, Feb.
    George D. Fawcett, "The 1975 UFO Wave
    in North Carolina," Official UFO 1
    (Nov.1975):12,13.

Piney Grove
-Phantom panther
  1897, Oct./Charlie Smoot
    Wilkesboro Chronicle, 20 Oct.1897.

Plumtree
-Child prodigy
  1966-   /Joe Hall
    (Editorial), Fate 29 (July 1976):24-
    26, quoting Nat'l Enquirer (undated).

Plymouth
-UFO (CE-1)
  1977/Bob Brannigan
    George D. Fawcett, "MUFON-NC Train-
    ing Conference," MUFON UFO J., no.
    127 (June 1978):14.

Poplar Branch
-UFO (CE-1)
  1978, Aug.24/Colon Grandy, Jr.
    Charlotte Observer, 29 Aug.1978.

Poplar Springs
-UFO (NL)
  1975, Oct.27
    "Noteworthy UFO Sightings," Ufology
    2 (spring 1976):43.

Purlear
-Telepathy
  1930-1961/Bobby Jean & Betty Jo Eller
    Tom Allen, "The Twins Who Willed
    Their Death," Fate 17 (Nov.1964):53-
    58.

Raleigh
-Haunt
  n.d./Holman House/209 E. Morgan St.
  1890s/Poole's Woods/5 mi.SE
    John Harden, Tar Heel Ghosts (Chapel
    Hill: Univ. of North Carolina, 1954),
    59-62,108-15.
  1960s/Robert W. Scott/Governor's Mansion
    Robert W. Scott, "The Governor Fowle
    Ghost at the Executive Mansion,"
    North Carolina Folklore 18 (1970):
    115-16.
-UFO (?)
  1947, July 7/Fayette Cloud/=hoax
    Raleigh News & Observer, 8 July 1947.
    Ted Bloecher, Report on the UFO Wave
    of 1947 (Washington: NICAP, 1967),
    p.I-14.
-UFO (NL)
  1881, Feb.22/Jack Beasley
    Raleigh Times, 22 Feb.1950.
  1975, March 1
    George D. Fawcett, "The 1975 UFO Wave
    in North Carolina," Official UFO 1
    (Nov.1975):12,13.

Red Springs
-UFO (CE-3)
  1951, Dec./Sam Coley
    Lumberton Robesonian, 7 Aug.1952.
    Coral Lorenzen, "UFO Occupants in
    United States Reports," in The Hu-
    manoids (Flying Saucer Rev. special

no.1, Aug.1967), p.52, quoting CSI
Public Meeting Digest, 24 May 1965.
George D. Fawcett, Quarter Century of
Studies of UFOs in Florida, North
Carolina and Tennessee (Mount Airy:
Pioneer, 1975), pp.25-26.
George D. Fawcett, "MUFON-NC Train-
ing Conference," MUFON UFO J., no.
127 (June 1978):14,15.
-UFO (NL)
1975, April 4-5/Lee Speigel
Jennie Zeidman, The Lumberton Report
(Evanston: Center for UFO Studies,
1976), pp.17-20.

Rockford
-Haunt
n.d./Burris House
Winston-Salem Journal & Sentinel, 31
Oct.1954.

Rockingham
-Ball lightning
1883, winter/Mrs. Gay
Decatur (Ill.) Daily Republican, 2
Mar.1883, p.4.

Roseboro
-UFO (CE-1)
1975, April 3/Jim Driver
Dwight Connelly, "Landing Reported
in N. Carolina," Skylook, no.90 (May
1975):3.
Jennie Zeidman, The Lumberton Report
(Evanston: Center for UFO Studies,
1976), pp.5-7.

Rowland
-UFO (CE-1)
1975, April 4/Ronn Thompson/Hwy.130
Raleigh News & Observer, 16 Apr.1975.
Jennie Zeidman, The Lumberton Report
(Evanston: Center for UFO Studies,
1976), pp.16-17.

Rutherfordton
-Fall of forged iron
1850s/Mr. Pinner
Charles Upham Shepard, "Examination
of a Supposed Meteoric Iron, Found
near Rutherfordton, North Carolina,"
Am.J.Sci., ser.2, 28 (1859):259-70.
-Fall of frozen bubbles
1955, May?
"Falls," Doubt, no.53 (1956):417.
-Haunt
1880-1949/jailhouse
Nancy Roberts, An Illustrated Guide
to Ghosts and Mysterious Occurrences
in the Old North State (Charlotte:
Heritage House, 1959), pp.5-7.

Saddletree
-UFO (NL)
1975, April 5
Dwight Connelly, "Landing Reported in
N. Carolina," Skylook, no.90 (May
1975):3,5.

Salisbury
-Skyquake
1970, Oct.6
Atlanta (Ga.) Journal, 7 Oct.1970.
"Bang!" INFO J., no.14 (Nov.1974):2.
-UFO (CE-1)
1966, Feb.2
Lloyd Mallan, "The Mysterious 12,"
Sci.& Mech. 37 (Dec.1966):30,33-34.
-UFO (CE-2)
1959, July 14
Richard Hall, ed., The UFO Evidence
(Washington: NICAP, 1964), p.75.
1971, Aug./Samuel G. Martin/ground
markings only
George D. Fawcett, Quarter Century of
Studies of UFOs in Florida, North
Carolina and Tennessee (Mount Airy:
Pioneer, 1975), p.33.
Ted Phillips, Physical Traces Associ-
ated with UFO Sightings (Evanston:
Center for UFO Studies, 1975), p.78.
-UFO (NL)
1970, Feb.18/Roy Barrow, Jr./Hwy.601
Salisbury Evening Post, 19 Feb.1970.

Sampson co.
-Fall of flesh
1850, Feb.15/Thomas F. Clarkson
Fayetteville North Carolinian, 9 Mar.
1850.

Shelby
-UFO (CE-1)
1975, April/Hwy.74
1975, May 20/Spring Valley Terrace
George D. Fawcett, "The 1975 UFO Wave
in North Carolina," Official UFO 1
(Nov.1975):12,46,48.
-UFO (DD)
1950, April 9
Richard Hall, ed., The UFO Evidence
(Washington: NICAP, 1964), pp.149,
152.

Sherwood
-UFO (CE-1)
1978, March 1/U.S.421
Boone Watauga Democrat, 6 Mar.1978.

Shinnville
-Phantom panther
1934, May
Statesville Landmark, 28 May 1934.

Siler City
-Mystery ground markings
Devil's Tramping Ground/10 mi.W nr.
Harper Cross Rds.
John Harden, The Devil's Tramping
Ground (Chapel Hill: Univ. of North
Carolina, 1949), pp.53-60.
Durham Morning Herald, 26 July 1959.
Nancy Roberts, An Illustrated Guide
to Ghosts and Mysterious Occurrences
in the Old North State (Charlotte:
Heritage House, 1959), pp.32-35. il.
Greensboro Daily News, 1 Oct.1964.
Jimmy Stevens, "A Night at the Devil's
Tramping Ground," North Carolina

Folklore 15 (May 1967):28-29.
James M. Donahue, "A New Theory on
the Devil's Tramping Ground," North
Carolina Folklore 20 (Feb.1972):47-
53.

Southern Pines
-Precognition
1944, Dec./Wade Stevick
W.E. Cox, "Precognition: An Analysis,
II," J.ASPR 50 (1956):99,106-107.

South Mills
-Hex
18th c.
F. Roy Johnson, Witches and Demons in
History and Folklore (Murfreesboro:
Johnson, 1969), pp.49-51.

Southport
-Lightning anomaly
1952, July 30/Cora Norris
(Editorial), Fate 6 (Jan.1953):9.

Spring Hope
-UFO (DD)
1943, Nov./Julian H. Warren
Raleigh News & Observer, 9 July 1947.

Statesville
-UFO (CE-1)
1959, Nov.3/R.L. James
Donald E. Keyhoe, Flying Saucers: Top
Secret (N.Y.: Putnam, 1960), p.256.

Swanquarter
-Flood anomaly
1876, Sep.16/Methodist church/Oyster
Creek Rd.
"The Church That Moved," Fate 9 (Oct.
1956):43.
Raymond J. Ross, "The Church God
Moved," Fate 29 (Sep.1976):46-49.

Sylva
-UFO (CE-1)
1978, March 10
Sylva Herald, 16 Mar.1978.

Tabor City
-UFO (CE-3)
1973, Sep./Rose Williamson/4 mi.N
Tabor City Tribune, 26 Sep.1973.
Lumberton Robesonian, 30 Sep.1973.

Thomasville
-UFO (CE-1)
1965, Aug.19
Jerome Clark, "The Greatest Flap Yet?
--Part 2," Flying Saucer Rev. 12
(Mar.-Apr.1966):8,11.

Tobaccoville
-UFO (CE-2)
1974, Sep.
George D. Fawcett, "The 'Unreported'
UFO Wave of 1974," Saga UFO Rept. 2
(spring 1975):50,75.

Toluca
-Humanoid
1978, Dec.21-1979, Jan.14/Minnie Cook/
Hwy.10
Shelby Star, 15 Jan.1979.
Charlotte News, 15 Jan.1979.
Gastonia Gazette, 17 Jan.1979; 19
Jan.1979; and 21 Jan.1979.

Troy
-Fall of snakes
1950, April 16
"Frogs and Fish," Doubt, no.30
(1950):34.
-Haunt
1953, Feb./Floyd Allen/Sut Creek Bridge
(Editorial), Fate 6 (July 1953):7-8.
-Mystery bird deaths
1955, Sep.26
Columbia (S.C.) State, 28 Sep.1955.
-UFO (CE-1)
1953, March 2/D.D. Lemons/Sut Creek
Bridge
George D. Fawcett, Quarter Century of
Studies of UFOs in Florida, North
Carolina and Tennessee (Mount Airy:
Pioneer, 1975), p.33.

Tryon
-UFO (NL)
1960/John P. Uptegrove
(Letter), Fate 14 (May 1961):112.

Unionville
-UFO (CE-2)
1978, Sep.7/Dillard Sizemore
Monroe Enquirer-Journal, 11 Sep.1978.

Valdese
-UFO (?)
1966, March 27
New York Herald-Tribune, 29 Mar.1966,
p.2.

Vale
-UFO (NL)
1978, Oct.24
Gastonia Gazette, 28 Oct.1978.

Valle Crucis
-UFO (NL)
1978, March 1
Boone Watauga Democrat, 6 Mar.1978.

Vanceboro
-UFO (CE-1)
1966, July 25/NW of town
Jacques Vallee, Passport to Magonia
(Chicago: Regnery, 1969), p.333.

Wadesboro
-Humanoid
1956, May 11/Henry Morton/nr. Pee Dee
R./=hoax
(Editorial), Fate 9 (Sep.1956):10.
(Letter), John Zeller, Fate 10 (Feb.
1957):129.
-Phantom images
1860s-1918
John Harden, Tar Heel Ghosts (Chapel

Hill: Univ. of North Carolina, 1954),
pp.86-91.

Wakulla
-Seance
1965/Freida Ann Oxendine
(Editorial), Fate 18 (Sep.1965):15,
18, quoting Greensboro Daily News
(undated).

Warren co.
-Human track in stone
Anne J. Weathersbee, "The Devil's
Rock," North Carolina Folklore 16
(1968):35.

Warsaw
-Phantom train
1906, Nov./Henry McCauley
Nancy Roberts, An Illustrated Guide
to Ghosts and Mysterious Occurrences
in the Old North State (Charlotte:
Heritage House, 1959), pp.11-13.

Washington
-UFO (NL)
1953, Feb.3/Ed Balocco
John C. Ross, "Fate's Report on the
Flying Saucers," Fate 6 (Oct.1953):
6-8.
Richard Hall, ed., The UFO Evidence
(Washington: NICAP, 1964), pp.31-32.
Coral & Jim Lorenzen, UFOs: The Whole
Story (N.Y.: Signet, 1969), pp.50-
51, quoting UP release, 11 Feb.1953.

Weddington
-Inner development
1977/satanic church
David Fideler, "Cemetery Weirdness,
Toppling Tombstones, and Things
Best Left Alone," Anomaly Rsch.Bull.
no.8 (spring 1978):16,18.

White Lake
-UFO (CE-1)
1975, April 4/Gary Moore/Hwy.53
Raleigh News & Observer, 6 Apr.1975.
Dwight Connelly, "Landing Reported
in N. Carolina," Skylook, no.90
(May 1975):3,4-5.
Jennie Zeidman, The Lumberton Report
(Evanston: Center for UFO Studies,
1976), pp.14-16.

White Oak
-Haunt
n.d./Old Roberson Place
Winston-Salem Journal & Sentinel, 31
Oct.1954.

Whitsett
-UFO (CE-2)
1955, Oct.27/H.D. Lambeth, Jr./Whit-
sett School
"Latest Saucer Sightings," Fate 9
(Apr.1956):43-44, quoting Greens-
boro Daily News (undated).
(Editorial), Fate 9 (Dec.1956):8.
George D. Fawcett, Quarter Century of

Studies of UFOs in Florida, North
Carolina and Tennessee (Mount Airy:
Pioneer, 1975), pp.33-34.

Wilkesboro
-Phantom panther
1899, May 27/Mr. Smoak
Wilkesboro Chronicle, 31 May 1899.

Williamston
-UFO (NL)
1976, Jan.26
"Noteworthy UFO Sightings," Ufology
2 (summer 1976):62.
1978, Jan.26
"UFOs of Limited Merit," Int'l UFO
Reporter 3 (Mar.1978):3.

Wilmington
-Ghost
ca.1810/Alex Hostler
John Harden, Tar Heel Ghosts (Chapel
Hill: Univ. of North Carolina,
1954), pp.10-16.
W.E. Cox, "But I Wasn't Dead!" Fate
8 (May 1955):38-40.
Nancy & Bruce Roberts, Ghosts of the
Carolinas (Charlotte: McNally &
Loftin, 1962), pp.43-46.
-Haunt
1840s-   /Price-Gause House/514 Mar-
ket St.
Richard Devon, "The Staircase Ghost,"
Fate 23 (Dec.1970):58-66. il.
(Letter), H.A. Graham, Fate 24 (Oct.
1971):128-29.
-Spirit medium
1900-1910s/Emma Caton
Henry A. Burr, "Experiments with Mrs.
Caton," Proc.ASPR 8 (1914):1-151.
-UFO (?)
1946, Aug.24/=meteor?
"Balls of Fire," Doubt, no.17 (1947)
:255.
-UFO (DD)
1954, Dec.3/Luther O'Banian/sirport
Richard Hall, ed., The UFO Evidence
(Washington: NICAP, 1964), p.45,
quoting AP release, 3 Dec.1954.
-UFO (NL)
1897, April 5/Market St.
Wilmington Messenger, 6 Apr.1897.
1947, July 1/Mrs. W.H. Pemberton/715
Dock St.
Raleigh News & Observer, 8 July 1947.

Wilson
-Fall of fish
1913, spring/James R. Daniels
E.W. Gudger, "More Rains of Fishes,"
Annals & Mag.of Nat.Hist., ser.10,
3 (1929):1,22.
-UFO (NL)
1976, May 20
"Noteworthy UFO Sightings," Ufology
2 (fall 1976):60.

Windsor
-UFO (NL)
1976, Feb.28

"Noteworthy UFO Sightings," Ufology 2 (summer 1976):62.

Winston-Salem
-Crisis apparition
  n.d./Salem Tavern
    Nancy & Bruce Roberts, Ghosts of the Carolinas (Charlotte: McNally & Loftin, 1962), pp.1-3.
-Erratic rattlesnake
  1954
    Air Force Daily, 6 May 1954.
-Fall of plastic
  1960, May 25/Fred H. Laughter
    George D. Fawcett, Quarter Century of Studies of UFOs in Florida, North Carolina and Tennessee (Mount Airy: Pioneer, 1975), p.31.
-Haunt
  1786-   /Brothers House
    John Harden, Tar Heel Ghosts (Chapel Hill: Univ. of North Carolina, 1954), pp.36-43.
    Nancy Roberts, An Illustrated Guide to Ghosts and Mysterious Occurrences in the Old North State (Charlotte: Heritage House, 1959), pp.25-27.
-UFO (?)
  1970, June 28
    Ted Phillips, Physical Traces Associated with UFO Sightings (Evanston: Center for UFO Studies, 1975), p.109.
-UFO (CE-1)
  1972, Jan.
    Brad Steiger, Mysteries of Time and Space (N.Y.: Dell, 1976 ed.), p.149.
  1975, March
    George D. Fawcett, "The 1975 UFO Wave in North Carolina," Official UFO 1 (Nov.1975):12,45.
-UFO (CE-2)
  1973, Jan.16/nr. Country Club Rd.
    Winston-Salem City Sentinel, 17 Jan. 1973.
-UFO (NL)
  1966, July 27
    Winston-Salem Twin City Sentinel, 27 July 1966.
  1972, April 3
    George D. Fawcett, Quarter Century of Studies of UFOs in Florida, North Carolina and Tennessee (Mount Airy: Pioneer, 1975), p.42.
  1975, Jan.10/Ray Shutt
    George D. Fawcett, "The 1975 UFO Wave in North Carolina," Official UFO 1 (Nov.1975):12,13.
Worthville
-Fall of metallic object
  1968, Sep.4/Lawrence Holland
    George D. Fawcett, Quarter Century of Studies of UFOs in Florida, North Carolina and Tennessee (Mount Airy: Pioneer, 1975), p.31.

B. Physical Features

Acorn Hill
-Ancient ship

ca.1900/Hugh Rice
    "The Mystery of the Great Dismal Swamp," Beyond Reality, no.32 (May-June 1978):66.

Albemarle Sound
-Norse discovery
  1009/Thorfinn Karlsefni/=Hóp?
    Charles Michael Boland, They All Discovered America (N.Y.: Pocket Books, 1963 ed.), pp.257-59.
-Phantom ship
  17th-19th c.
    John Lawson, Lawson's History of North Carolina (London: W. Tayler & F. Baker, 1714), p.62.
    F. Roy Johnson, Witches and Demons in History and Folklore (Murfrees-boro: Johnson, 1969), p.62.

Alum Cave
-Lightning anomaly
  1939, July/Hosea Campbell
    Harrison M. Reed, "The Hand That Lightning Carved," Fate 6 (Oct.1953):99-103.

Balsam Mts.
-Haunt
  n.d.
    Charles M. Skinner, Myths and Legends of Our Own Land, 2 vols. (Phila-delphia: Lippincott, 1896), 2:313-15.

Black Mt.
-Roman coin
  1967
    Joseph B. Mahan & Douglas C. Braith-waite, "Discovery of Ancient Coins in the United States," Anthro.J. Canada 13, no.2 (1975):15.
-Skyquake
  1876/=rock settling
    C.F. Marvin, "Report upon the Earth-quake of October 31, 1895," Monthly Weather Rev. 23 (Oct.1895):374-75.

Bogue Inlet
-UFO (NL)
  1974, June 29-30/Ward Sullivan
    George D. Fawcett, "The 'Unreported' UFO Wave of 1974," Saga UFO Rept. 2 (spring 1975):50,53.

Brown Mt.
-Ghost light
  1771-
    Charlotte Daily Observer, 23 Sep.1913.
    "The Queer Lights on Brown Mountain," Lit.Digest 87 (1925):44,49.
    Asheville Citizen-Times, 5 June 1938; 10 Nov.1940; and 5 June 1952.
    J.T. Fulton, "The Lights of Brown Mountain," North Carolina Folklore 1 (1948):6-7.
    John Harden, The Devil's Tramping Ground (Chapel Hill: Univ. of North Carolina, 1949), pp.127-37.
    John P. Bessor, "Mystery of Brown

Mountain," Fate 4 (Mar.1951):13-15.
Raleigh News & Observer, 18 Sep.1952;
31 July 1962; 3 Aug.1962; and 6 Aug.
1962.
Morganton News-Herald, 5 Feb.1959.
Ralph I. Lael, The Brown Mountain
Lights (Morganton: The Author, 1965).
Herbert Bailey, "Come See the Flying
Saucers!" Argosy, Dec.1968, pp.21-
25. il.
George Rogers Mansfield, Origin of
the "Brown Mountain Light" in North
Carolina (Washington: U.S. Geologi-
cal Survey, Circular no.646, 1971).
Dennis Stamey, "The Brown Mountain
Lights," Caveat Emptor, no.4 (sum-
mer 1972):11-13,23.
Malcolm Bessent, "The Lights of
Brown Mountain," New Horizons 1, no.
1 (summer 1972):3-5.
Philip J. Klass, UFOs Explained (N.Y.:
Random House, 1974), pp.63-71.
"Orion's Brown Mountain Light Exped-
ition," Int'l UFO Reporter 2 (July
1977):newsfront sec.

Buck Creek Gap
-Precognition
    1879
        John Harden, Tar Heel Ghosts (Chapel
        Hill: Univ. of North Carolina,
        1954), pp.63-68.

Cane Creek
-Humanoid
    1910s
        Bigfoot/Sasquatch Information Ser-
        vice 11 (Dec.1978):6, quoting Win-
        ston-Salem Journal (undated).

Cape Fear R.
-Haunt
    1970s/Alice Arrington
        (Editorial), Fate 25 (Sep.1972):30-
        32.
-Humanoid
    1976
        John Green, Sasquatch: The Apes Among
        Us (Seattle: Hancock House, 1978),
        p.219.

Carolina Bays
-Meteorite craters
    doubtful
        L.C. Glenn, "Some Notes on the Dar-
        lington (S.C.) 'Bays,'" Science 2
        (1895):472-75.
        F.A. Melton & William Schriever, "The
        Carolina 'Bays'--Are They Meteoric
        Scars?" J.Geology 41 (1933):52-66.
        il.
        C. Wythe Cooke, "Discussion of the
        Origin of the Supposed Meteorite
        Scars of South Carolina," J.Geology
        42 (1934):88-104. il.
        Douglas Johnson, The Origin of the
        Carolina Bays (N.Y.: Columbia Univ.,
        1942). il.
        Herbert Ravenel Sass, "When the Comet
        Struck," Sat.Eve.Post, 9 Sep.1944,

pp.12-13.
        Brandon Barringer, "Observations on
        the Carolina 'Craters' or 'Bays,'"
        Pop.Astron. 55 (1947):215-17.
        William F. Prouty, "A Reply to an Ar-
        ticle by Mr. Brandon Barringer on
        the Origin of the 'Carolina Bays,'"
        Pop.Astron. 56 (1948):499-501.
        Chapman Grant, "Meteoric Origin of
        the 'Carolina Bays' Questioned,"
        Pop.Astron. 56 (1948):511-27. il.
        F.A. Melton & William Schriever,
        "The Carolina 'Bays,'" J.Geology
        58 (1950):128-34.
        Allan O. Kelly, "The Origin of the
        Carolina Bays and the Oriented
        Lakes of Alaska," Pop.Astron. 59
        (1951):199-205.
        H.H. Nininger, Out of the Sky (Den-
        ver: University Press, 1952), pp.
        226-28.
        W.F. Prouty, "Carolina Bays and Their
        Origin," Bull.Geol.Soc'y Am. 63
        (1952):167-224. il.
        Howard T. Odum, "The Carolina Bays
        and a Pleistocene Weather Map," Am.
        J.Sci. 250 (1952):263-70.
        Allen O. Kelly & Frank Dachille, Tar-
        get: Earth (Pensacola, Fla.: Pensa-
        cola Engraving, 1953).

Catawba R.
-UFO (?)
    1957, Sep.7
        "Flying Saucer Roundup," Fate 11
        (Feb.1958):29,34.

Chimney Rock
-Aerial phantoms
    1806, July 31/Patsy Reaves
        Raleigh Register & State Gazette, 23
        Sep.1806.
        Edmond P. Gibson, "Phantoms of Chim-
        ney Rock Pass," Fate 4 (Oct.1951):
        14-17.
    1811
        Wilber G. Zeigler & Ben S. Grosscup,
        The Heart of the Alleghenies (Ra-
        leigh: Williams, 1883).
-Humanoid myth
        Blackwell P. Robinson, ed., The North
        Carolina Guide (Chapel Hill: Univ.
        of North Carolina, 1955), p.544.

Chowan R.
-Elizabethan inscription
    1937, Sep./L.E. Hammond
        Brenau College, The Dare Stones
        (Gainesville, Ga.: Brenau College,
        1940). il.
        Boyden Sparkes, "Writ on Rocke," Sat.
        Eve.Post, 26 Apr.1941, pp.9-11,118-
        28.
        Charles Whedbee, The Flaming Ship of
        Ocracoke (Winston-Salem: John F.
        Blair, 1971), pp.104-14.

Diamond Shoals
-Disappearance
    1921, Jan.30/Willis B. Wormwell/"Car-

roll A. Deering"/crew only
  Norfolk Virginian-Pilot, 1 Feb.1921,
  p.3; 2 Feb.1921, p.3; 3 Feb.1921,
  p.3; 4 Feb.1921, p.2; and 5 Feb.
  1921, p.4.
  New York Times, 21 June 1921, p.1;
  22 June 1921, p.1; 23 June 1921, p.
  1; 24 June 1921, p.2; 25 June 1921,
  p.2; 27 June 1921, p.12; 4 July
  1921, p.8; 8 July 1921, p.2; 9 July
  1921, p.7; 11 July 1921, p.10; and
  26 Aug.1921, p.2.
  Edward Rowe Snow, Mysteries and Adventures Along the Atlantic Coast
  (N.Y.: Dodd, Mead, 1948), pp.288-
  304.
  John Harden, The Devil's Tramping
  Ground (Chapel Hill: Univ. of North
  Carolina, 1949).
  Lawrence David Kusche, The Bermuda
  Triangle Mystery--Solved (N.Y.:
  Harper & Row, 1975), pp.65-73.

Fear, Cape
-Skyquakes
  1966-1976
  "Audible Microquakes off Cape Fear,"
  Sci.News 110 (1976):346.

French Broad R.
-Phantom (myth)
  Charles M. Skinner, Myths and Legends
  of Our Own Land, 2 vols. (Philadelphia: Lippincott, 1896), 2:77-78.

Grandfather Mt.
-Glacial anomaly
  James O. Berkland & Loren A. Raymond,
  "Pleistocene Glaciation in the Blue
  Ridge Province," Science 181 (1973)
  :651-53.
-Haunt
  n.d./Dave Kinder/sawmill
  John Harden, Tar Heel Ghosts (Chapel
  Hill: Univ. of North Carolina,
  1954), pp.22-26.

Great Smoky Mts.
-Phantom horse
  Charles M. Skinner, American Myths
  and Legends, 2 vols. (Philadelphia:
  Lippincott, 1903), 1:324.

Green Hill
-Humanoid
  n.d./Haunted Hollow
  F. Hampton Porter, "Folk-Lore of the
  Mountain Whites of the Alleghenies,"
  J.Am.Folklore 7 (1894):110.

Hatteras, Cape
-Animal ESP
  1790s/Hatteras Jack the Pilot Porpoise
  Charles Whedbee, Legends of the Outer
  Banks (Winston-Salem: John F. Blair,
  1966), pp.69-76.
-Gravity anomaly
  1936, Jan.31/Anthony Restivo/"Superior"
  (Editorial), Fate 30 (Aug.1977):20-
  22, quoting Charleston (S.C.) Eve-

ning Post (undated).
-Mystery shipwreck
  1975, Dec.11/"Drosia"
  Charles Berlitz, Without a Trace
  (N.Y.: Ballantine, 1978 ed.), p.116.
-Phantom ship
  1973, Feb.1
  (Editorial), Fate 26 (Sep.1973):22.
-UFO (?)
  1890, Aug.29/"Doris"
  Gordon I.R. Lore, Jr. & Harold H.
  Deneault, Jr., Mysteries of the
  Skies: UFOs in Perspective (Engle-
  wood Cliffs, N.J.: Prentice-Hall,
  1968), p.43.

Haw Creek
-UFO (DD)
  1947, July 7/Fred C. Meekins
  Asheville Citizen, 8 July 1947.

Knotts I.
-Haunt and buried treasure
  Henry B. Ansell, "Recollections of a
  Knotts Island Boyhood," North Caro-
  lina Folklore 7 (1957):12.

Little Green Swamp
-Humanoid tracks
  1977, Dec./=hoax
  Wilmington Star, 4 Apr.1978.

Little Tennessee R.
-River monster myth
  dakwa/nr. Toccoa Creek
  Albert S. Gatschet, "Water-Monsters
  of the American Aborigines," J.Am.
  Folklore 12 (1899):255-60.

Max Patch
-Contactee myth
  Blackwell P. Robinson, ed., The North
  Carolina Guide (Chapel Hill: Univ.
  of North Carolina, 1955), p.565.

Mitchell, Mt.
-UFO (CE-2)
  1966, June 19/Bruce Sterett
  Ted Phillips, Physical Traces Associ-
  ated with UFO Sightings (Evanston:
  Center for UFO Studies, 1975), p.42.

Nags Head Woods
-Weather control
  ca.1920/Miss Mabe
  Charles Whedbee, Legends of the Outer
  Banks (Winston-Salem: John F. Blair,
  1966), pp.106-10.

Neuse R.
-UFO (NL)
  1978, Oct.24/David Waller/Falls of the
  Neuse Rd.
  Raleigh Times, 31 Oct.1978.

Pisgah Mt.
-Ancient figurines
  "Pre-Indian Relics from Virginia,"
  Sci.Am. 47 (1882):56.

Roan Mt.
-Witchcraft
  n.d.
    Wilmington Messenger, 30 July 1901.

Roanoke I.
-Disappearance
  1587/Virginia Dare/Raleigh's Colony
    David Beers Quinn, ed., The Roanoke
      Voyages 1584-1590, 2 vols. (London:
      Hakluyt Soc'y Works, ser.2, vols.
      104-105, 1955).
    John Lawson, A New Voyage to Carolina,
      Hugh Talmage Lefler ed. (Chapel
      Hill: Univ. of North Carolina, 1967),
      pp.68-70.
    Hamilton McMillan, Sir Walter Ra-
      leigh's Lost Colony (Wilson, N.C.:
      Advance, 1888).
    Stephen B. Weeks, "The Lost Colony
      of Roanoke: Its Fate and Survival,"
      Pap.Am.Hist.Ass'n 5 (1891):441-80.
    Samuel A'Court Ashe, History of
      North Carolina, 2 vols. (Greensboro:
      C.L. Van Noppen, 1908-25), 1:39-49.
    Melvin Robinson, Riddle of the Lost
      Colony (New Bern, N.C.: Owen G.
      Dunn, 1946).
    C.K. Howe, Solving the Riddle of the
      Lost Colony (Beaufort, N.C.: M.P.
      Skarren, 1947).
    Charles Whedbee, Legends of the Outer
      Banks (Winston-Salem: John F. Blair,
      1966), pp.7-33.
    Charles A. Huguenin & Robert M. Dell,
      "The Lumbee (or Lumber) Indians of
      North Carolina," NEARA Newsl. 7
      (June 1972):25-31; (Sep.1972):53-55.
    Houston (Tex.) Chronicle, 21 Dec.
      1977.
-Sea monster
  1884, Feb.14/William Page/"Edward Waite"
    Philadelphia (Pa.) Record, 18 Feb.
      1884.
    New York Times, 19 Feb.1884, p.2.

Roaring R.
-Phantom panther
  1897, March-May
    Wilkesboro Chronicle, 17 Mar.1897;
      and 5 May 1897.

Royal Mt.
-Haunt
  1964
    (Editorial), Fate 18 (Jan.1965):12-
      13.

Rumbling Bald Mt.
-Skyquakes
  n.d.
    "Moodus and Others," Doubt, no.17
      (1947):253.

Salola Mt.
-Haunt
  n.d./John Drew
    John Harden, Tar Heel Ghosts (Chapel
      Hill: Univ. of North Carolina,
      1954), pp.92-99.

Second Creek
-Phantom panther
  1890, Sep.-Oct./Abe Harbin
    Salisbury Carolina Watchman, 9 Oct.
      1890.

Shalotte Inlet
-Healing
    Atlanta (Ga.) Journal & Constitution,
      29 Mar.1964.
    Charles Whedbee, Legends of the Outer
      Banks (Winston-Salem: John F. Blair,
      1966), pp.3-6.

South Mt.
-Humanoid
  1974
    John Green, Sasquatch: The Apes Among
      Us (Seattle: Hancock House, 1978),
      pp.219-20.

Town Creek
-Archeological site
  ca.1550-1650
    J. Jefferson Reid, "A Comparative
      Statement on Ceramics from the Hol-
      lywood and the Town Creek Mounds,"
      Southern Indian Studies 17 (1965):
      12-25. il.
    Franklin Folsom, America's Ancient
      Treasures (N.Y.: Rand McNally,
      1974), pp.120-21.

Turkey Hollow
-Phantom panther
  1944, Nov./Slim Davis
    John Harden, The Devil's Tramping
      Ground (Chapel Hill: Univ. of North
      Carolina, 1949), pp.147-54.

Willow Creek
-Haunt
  n.d./Jones Mill
    John Harden, Tar Heel Ghosts (Chapel
      Hill: Univ. of North Carolina,
      1954), pp.27-35.

Woodstock Pt.
-Witch trial (?)
  17th c.
    F. Roy Johnson, Witches and Demons
      in History and Folklore (Murfrees-
      boro: Johnson, 1969), p.51.

Yadkin R.
-Archeological site
  ca.5000 B.C.-recent/Doerschuk site
    Herbert M. Doerschuk, "A Site on the
      Yadkin River in North Carolina,"
      Notebook Soc'y for Am.Arch. 2 (1941)
      :18-20. il.
    Charles D. Howell & Donald C. Dear-
      born, "The Excavation of an Indian
      Village on the Yadkin River near
      Trading Ford," Southern Indian Stud-
      ies 5 (1953):3-20. il.
    Douglas L. Rights, "Copper Specimens
      from Yadkin River in Piedmont, North
      Carolina," Am.Antiquity 18 (1953):
      389. il.

John Witthoft, "Notes on the Archaic
of the Appalachian Region," Am.An-
tiquity 25 (1959):79-85. il.

C. Ethnic Groups

Lumbee Indians
-White Indians
    Charles A. Huguenin & Robert M. Dell,
    "The Lumbee (or Lumber) Indians of
    North Carolina," NEARA Newsl. 7
    (June 1972):25-31; (Sep.1972):53-55.
    Los Angeles (Cal.) Times, 12 May
    1977.

D. Unspecified Localities

-Hex
    Tom Pete Cross, "Witchcraft in North
    Carolina," Studies in Philology 16
    (1919):217-87.
    Columbia (S.C.) State, 1 Apr.1961.
    Patricia S. McLean, "Conjure Doctors
    in Eastern North Carolina," North
    Carolina Folklore 20 (1972):21-29.

VIRGINIA

A. Populated Places

Abingdon
-UFO (?)
  1869, Aug.7/Albert J. Meyer/=meteors
    M.K. Jessup, The Expanding Case for
    the UFO (N.Y.: Citadel, 1957), p.44.

Alexandria
-Fall of fish
  1955, Dec.22/William Shannon
    Pittsburgh (Pa.) Press, 23 Dec.1955.
    (Editorial), Fate 9 (May 1956):8.
-Haunt
  1962, June-   /Henry Koch/Robert E.
  Lee mansion
    Susy Smith, Prominent American Ghosts
    (N.Y.: Dell, 1969 ed.), pp.27-35.
-Humanoid
  1965, July/Marsha A. Capra/nr. Hwy.630
  1965, Sep./Marsha A. Capra/Hollin Hills
    Marsha A. Capra, "A Snuffly, Smelly,
    Seven-Foot What?" Fate 31 (July
    1978):68-70.
-Mathematical prodigy
  1780s/Thomas Cullen
    Elizabethtown New Jersey Journal &
    Political Intelligencer, 21 Jan.
    1789.
    "An Old Case of Mathematical Prodigy,"
    J.ASPR 12 (1918):446-50.
-UFO (DD)
  1949, July 9/C.S. Dupree
    Kenneth Arnold & Ray Palmer, The Com-
    ing of the Saucers (Boise: The Au-
    thors, 1952), pp.141-42.
-UFO (NL)
  1947, July 4/Mrs. Martin Kole/3202 Valley Dr.
    Washington (D.C.) Evening Star, 5
    July 1947.
  1952, May
    Edward J. Ruppelt, The Report on Un-
    identified Flying Objects (Garden
    City: Doubleday, 1956), pp.135-36.
  1967, May 12/Richard J. Butler/Hwy.7
    "Sparks and Explosion," UFO Inv. 4
    (May-June 1967):3.
  1975, Aug.28
    "UFO Central," CUFOS News Bull., 15
    Nov.1975, p.17.
  1975, Nov.2, 23
    "UFO Central," CUFOS News Bull., 1
    Feb.1976, pp.11,14.

Alma
-UFO (NL)
  1966, Aug.18
    "New Reports by Space Experts Add to
    UFO Proof," UFO Inv. 3 (Aug.-Sep.
    1966):3,4.

Alton
-UFO (CE-2)
  1966, Nov.4/Mrs. W.J. Long

"Major Sighting Wave," UFO Inv. 3
(Jan.-Feb.1967):1,3.

Annandale
-Whirlwind anomaly
  1974, July 19/7401 E. Maryland Rd.
    Arlington Northern Virginia Sun, 20
    July 1974.
    Washington (D.C.) Star-News, 20 July
    1974.
    "Falls," INFO J., no.14 (Nov.1974):
    22,24.

Apple Grove
-Disappearance and clairempathy
  1959, Jan.11/Carroll V. Jackson, Jr./
  Peter Hurkos/=murder
    (Editorial), Fate 12 (June 1959):24-
    25.
    (Editorial), Fate 12 (July 1959):18.
    Curtis Fuller, "Peter Hurkos and the
    Jackson Family Murders," Fate 13
    (Oct.1960):49-54.
    Jess Stearn, The Door to the Future
    (N.Y.: Macfadden, 1964), pp.200-208.

Appomattox
-UFO (CE-2)
  1963, April 20/Harry W. Ranson
    "Fortean Items," Saucer News 10
    (Sep.1963):17.

Arlington
-Acoustic anomaly
  1959-1960/Lucille C. Hieber
    (Letter), Fate 14 (Mar.1961):122,128.
-Ball lightning
  1968, Dec.14/4633 S. 2d St.
    Washington (D.C.) Daily News, 14
    Dec.1968.
-Gasoline spring
  1947, Jan.15
    "Free Gasoline," Doubt, no.18 (1947)
    :268.
-Phantom panther
  1974, June/Four Mile Run
    Columbus (O.) Dispatch, 21 June 1974.
    (Editorial), Fate 28 (May 1975):22-
    23.
-UFO (?)
  1958, Aug.7/Fairlington
    Richard Hall, ed., The UFO Evidence
    (Washington: NICAP, 1964), p.15.
-UFO (DD)
  1966, Oct.11
    "Capital Area Sightings," UFO Inv. 3
    (Oct.-Nov.1966):7.
-UFO (NL)
  1947, July 7
    Bruce S. Maccabee, "UFO Related In-
    formation from the FBI Files: Part
    3," MUFON UFO J., no.121 (Dec.1977)
    :10,13.
  1956, July 14
    Richard Hall, ed., The UFO Evidence

(Washington: NICAP, 1964), p.153.

Augusta co.
-Ghost light
  1967, May-June
    Richmond Times-Dispatch, 23 June
    1967.
-Poltergeist
  n.d.
    William Oliver Stevens, Psychics and
    Common Sense (N.Y.: Dutton, 1953),
    p.158.

Austinville
-Ghost light
  1970s/Olive Branch Methodist Church
    Washington (D.C.) Star, 21 May 1977,
    p.D3.
    "Eerie Glow in Church," Fate 30 (Oct.
    1977):48.
    "Luminous Appearances," Res Bureaux
    Bull., no.24 (6 Oct.1977):4.

Bealeton
-Precognition
  1970s/Carson Weaver/Box 104
    Warren Smith, "Phenomenal Predictions
    for 1975," Saga, Jan.1975, pp.20,53.
    Warren Smith, "Phenomenal Predictions
    for 1976," Saga, Jan.1976, pp.16,54.
    Richard De A'Morelli & Rita West,
    "Top Seers Predict Your Future for
    1977," Psychic World, Jan.1977, pp.
    51,54.
    "Probe's 1977 Directory of the Psy-
    chic World," Probe the Unknown 5
    (spring 1977):32,37,65. il.

Bedford
-UFO (DD)
  1965, Jan.25/3 mi.N
    Donald B. Hanlon, "Virginia 1965
    Flap," Flying Saucer Rev. 12 (Mar.-
    Apr.1966):14,15.

Delle Haven
-Haunt
  n.d.
    George Carey, A Faraway Time and
    Place (Washington: Robert B. Luce,
    1971), p.175.

Bethel Academy
-Out-of-body experience
  1894-1897
    "Hypnotic Experiments," J.ASPR 9
    (1915):330-34.

Blacksburg
-Skyquake
  1973, Oct.12/Virginia Polytechnic State
  Univ.
    Washington (D.C.) Post, 13 Oct.1973.

Blackstone
-Fall of beans
  1962, Aug./Mrs. H.C. Gamble
    (Editorial), Fate 15 (Dec.1962):12,
    quoting Blackstone Courier-Record
    (undated).

Boykins
-Healing
  1902-1970s/Lewis Lee Jones
    Patricia S. McLean, "Conjure Doctors
    in Eastern North Carolina," North
    Carolina Folklore 20 (1972):21,24-
    27.

Bristol
-UFO (NL)
  1978, Oct.25/Charlie Cross/Bob Morrison Blvd.
    Bristol Virginia-Tennessean, 26 Oct.
    1978.

Buchanan
-Poltergeist
  1870, Nov.-1871, Feb./G.C. Thrasher
    New York Times, 18 Jan.1871, p.4.
    Eugene Crowell, The Identity of Prim-
    itive Christianity and Modern Spir-
    itualism, 2 vols. (N.Y.: G.W.
    Carleton, 1874-75), 1:183-86.
    Herbert Thurston, Ghosts and Polter-
    geists (Chicago: Regnery, 1954),
    pp.216-20, quoting Lexington Ga-
    zette (undated).

Cape Charles
-Contactee, psychokinesis and weather
  control
  1964-   /Ted Owens
    Ted Owens, Flying Saucer Intelli-
    gences Speak (New Brunswick, N.J.:
    Interplanetary News Service, 1966).
    (Letter), Fate 19 (Dec.1966):146-47.
    (Letter), Saucer News 14 (summer
    1967):9.
    Ted Owens, "The SI's Want to Help,"
    Saucer News 14 (winter 1967-68):8-
    9.
    Ted Owens, How to Contact Space
    People (Clarksburg, W.V.: Saucerian,
    1969).
    Ted Owens, The Incredible Truth Be-
    hind the UFOs Mission to Earth
    (Clarksburg, W.V.: Saucerian, 1970).
    Norfolk Virginian-Pilot, 23 July
    1970.
    Otto O. Binder, "Ted Owens--Flying
    Saucer Missionary," Saga's Special
    UFO Rept. 3 (1972):52-55,68-72.
    John Godwin, Occult America (Garden
    City: Doubleday, 1972), pp.155-56.
    Brad Steiger, Revelation: The Divine
    Fire (Englewood Cliffs, N.J.: Pren-
    tice-Hall, 1973), pp.154-56.
    Ted Owens, "How You Can Communicate
    with UFO Space Intelligences," Saga's
    Special UFO Rept. 4 (1973):24-27,
    52-58.
    Glenn McWane & David Graham, The New
    UFO Sightings (N.Y.: Warner, 1974),
    pp.111-16.
    Warren Smith, "Phenomenal Predictions
    for 1975," Saga, Jan.1975, pp.20,50-
    52.
    Warren Smith, "Phenomenal Predictions
    for 1976," Saga, Jan.1976, pp.16,50-
    52.

Jeffrey Mishlove, "The Wrath of the 'UFO Prophet,'" Fate 32 (Feb.1979): 62-70.

Cedar Creek
-Haunt
1860s
Clifton Johnson, Battleground Adventures (Boston: Houghton Mifflin, 1915), pp.416-22.

Centreville
-UFO (?)
1952
Harold T. Wilkins, Flying Saucers on the Attack (N.Y.: Ace, 1967 ed.), p.144.

Charles City
-Haunt
n.d./Westover Mansion
Marion Lowndes, Ghosts That Still Walk (N.Y.: Knopf, 1941), pp.44-49.
1858- /Shirley Plantation
(Editorial), Fate 29 (Feb.1976):23-26.
-Precognition
1862/Julia Gardiner Tyler/Sherwood Forest
William Oliver Stevens, The Mystery of Dreams (N.Y.: Dodd, Mead, 1949).

Charlottesville
-Archeological site
Jefferson's mound/nr. Monticello
Thomas Jefferson, Notes on the State of Virginia (Chapel Hill: Univ. of North Carolina, 1955 ed.), pp.98-100.
Karl Lehmann-Hartleben, "Thomas Jefferson, Archaeologist," Am.J.Arch., ser.2, 47 (1943):161-63.
-Doubtful identity
1920- /Anna Anderson/=Anastasia Romanov?
Pierre Gilliard, La fausse Anastasie (Paris: Payot, 1929).
Roland Krug von Nidda, ed., I, Anastasia (London: Michael Joseph, 1959).
Anthony Summers & Tom Mangold, The File on the Tsar (N.Y.: Harper & Row, 1976). il.
-Haunt
n.d./Castle Hill
Hans Holzer, Ghosts I've Met (N.Y.: Ace, 1965), pp.75-78.
Hans Holzer, Haunted Houses (N.Y.: Crown, 1971), pp.94-96. il.
1951-1960s/Virginia Cloud
Hans Holzer, Ghosts I've Met (N.Y.: Ace, 1965), pp.85-87.
1956/Horace Burr/Carrsgrove
Hans Holzer, Ghosts I've Met (N.Y.: Ace, 1965), pp.78-79.
-Out-of-body experience
1958- /Robert A. Monroe
Charles T. Tart, "A Second Psychophysiological Study of Out-of-the-Body Experiences in a Gifted Subject," Int'l J.Parapsych. 9 (1967):

251-58.
Robert A. Monroe, Journeys Out of the Body (Garden City: Doubleday, 1971).
D. Scott Rogo, "Introduction: Autobiographical Accounts," in Mind Beyond the Body (N.Y.: Penguin, 1978), pp.231,254-57.
-Parapsychology research
1967- /Ian Stevenson/Parapsychology Division, Univ. of Virginia School of Medicine
"New Division of Parapsychology at University of Virginia," Fate 22 (Feb.1969):59.
Rex G. Stanford, "Associative Activation of the Unconscious' and 'Visualization' As Methods for Influencing the PK Target," J.ASPR 63 (1969):338-51.
Ian Stevenson, Telepathic Impressions: A Review and Report of Thirty-Five New Cases (Charlottesville: Univ. of Virginia, 1970).
Rex G. Stanford, "Extrasensory Effects upon 'Memory,'" J.ASPR 64 (1970):161-86.
Ian Stevenson, "Precognition of Disasters," J.ASPR 64 (1970):187-210.
Rex G. Stanford & Carole Ann Lovin, "EEG Alpha Activity and ESP Performance," J.ASPR 64 (1970):375-84.
Rex G. Stanford, "EEG Alpha Activity and ESP Performance: A Replicative Study," J.ASPR 65 (1971):144-54.
Rex G. Stanford, "Suggestibility and Success at Augury--Divination from Chance Outcomes," J.ASPR 66 (1972):42-62.
Rex G. Stanford & Ian Stevenson, "EEG Correlates of Free-Response GESP in an Individual Subject," J.ASPR 66 (1972):357-68.
Rex G. Stanford & J. Palmer, "Meditation Prior to the ESP Task: An EEG Study with an Outstanding ESP Subject," in W.G. Roll, et al., eds., Research in Parapsychology 1972 (Metuchen, N.J.: Scarecrow, 1973), pp.34-36.
Rex G. Stanford, "Extrasensory Effects upon Associative Processes in a Directed Free-Response Test," J.ASPR 67 (1973):147-90.
John Palmer & Carol Vassar, "ESP and Out-of-the-Body Experiences: An Exploratory Study," J.ASPR 68 (1974):257-80.
D. Scott Rogo, "Parapsychology Today," Probe the Unknown 3 (May 1975):21, 53,56.
John Palmer & Ronald Lieberman, "The Influence of Psychological Set on ESP and Out-of-Body Experiences," J.ASPR 69 (1975):193-213.
Rex G. Stanford & John Palmer, "Free-Response ESP Performance and Occipital Alpha Rhythms," J.ASPR 69 (1975):235-43.
Ian Stevenson, "Research into the Evidence of Man's Survival after

Death," J.Nervous & Mental Disease
165, no.3 (1977):152-70.
Ian Stevenson, "The Explanatory Value
of the Idea of Reincarnation," J.
Nervous & Mental Disease 164, no.5
(1977):305-26.
John Palmer, "ESP and Out-of-Body
Experiences: An Experimental Approach," in D. Scott Rogo, ed.,
Mind Beyond the Body (N.Y.: Penguin,
1978), pp.193-217.
-Retrocognition
  1961, Nov.9
    Ian Stevenson, "A Postcognitive
    Dream Illustrating Some Aspects of
    the Pictographic Process," J.ASPR
    57 (1963):182-202.
-Telepathy research
  1977/Univ. of Virginia Hospital
    Bruce Greyson, "Telepathy in Mental
    Illness: Deluge or Delusion?" J.
    Nervous & Mental Disease 165, no.3
    (1977):184-200.
-UFO (?)
  1970, Nov.22
    "Unidentifieds," INFO J., no.7 (fall
    1970):43.
-UFO (DD)
  1952, Dec.14/Roy Franke/Univ. of Virginia Airport
    (Editorial), Fate 6 (May 1953):9-10.
-UFO (NL)
  1963, Feb.7/Carl Chambers
    Richard Hall, ed., The UFO Evidence
    (Washington: NICAP, 1964), p.43.

Chesapeake
-UFO (NL)
  1975, Oct.21
    "UFO Central," CUFOS News Bull., 1
    Feb.1976, p.9.
  1975, Nov.20/Robert Hitt
    Timothy Green Beckley, "The UFO Base
    40 Miles from the White House,"
    Saga UFO Rept. 5 (May 1978):44.

Chesterfield co.
-UFO (NL)
  1967, Jan.11
    (Editorial), Saucer News 14 (summer
    1967):29. il.

Cockburn
-UFO (CE-2)
  1959, March-April/Sheep Rock Mt./=radar
  chaff?
    Donald H. Menzel & Lyle G. Boyd, The
    World of Flying Saucers (Garden City:
    Doubleday, 1963), pp.224-25.

Cold Harbor
-Lightning anomaly
  1900, Aug.7/W.R. White
    "Lightning from a Cloudless Sky,"
    Monthly Weather Rev. 28 (July 1900):
    293.

Covington
-UFO (NL)
  1973, Oct.4

Covington Virginian, 5 Oct.1973.

Crittenden
-UFO (CE-2)
  1969, Jan.17
    Robert Emenegger, UFOs: Past, Pres-
    ent and Future (N.Y.: Ballantine,
    1974), pp.92-99.

Crozier
-Cattle mutilations and UFOs (NL)
  1978, March-April/Virginia State Farm
    Manakin Gazette, 25 May 1978.
    Charlottesville Daily Progress, 3
    July 1978.
    "A Closer Look," Stigmata, no.4
    (summer 1978):3-4.
-UFO (NL)
  1978, April 10-11/Ben Eldridge/Virgin-
  ia State Farm
    Charlottesville Daily Progress, 3
    July 1978.

Danville
-Fall of mud
  1929, March 29
    "Run of the Mill," Doubt, no.29
    (1950):27.
-UFO (DD)
  1959, June 27
    Jacques Vallee, Anatomy of a Phenom-
    enon (N.Y.: Ace, 1965 ed.), p.208.

Dinwiddie
-UFO (NL)
  1977, July 13
    "UFOs of Limited Merit," Int'l UFO
    Reporter 2 (Aug.1977):inside cover.

Dinwiddie co.
-Humanoid tracks
  1977, May/Rupert Williamson
    Roanoke World-News, 3 May 1977.

Dixie
-Fall of shredded lead
  ca.1963/H.J.T. Mead
    (Letter), Fate 19 (Aug.1966):133.

Dolphin
-Ancient inscription
  1950
    Richmond Times-Dispatch, 28 May 1950.
    Charles Michael Boland, They All Dis-
    covered America (N.Y.: Pocket Books,
    1963 ed.), pp.66-67,74-77. il.

Dooms
-Lightning anomaly
  1942, April-1977/Roy Cleveland Sullivan
    "Sub-Section 'K'," Pursuit 5 (July
    1972):54-55, quoting Washington
    (D.C.) Post (undated).
    Washington (D.C.) Post, 27 Aug.1973.
    Harrisonburg Daily News-Record, 3
    July 1976; and 28 June 1977.
-UFO (NL)
  1965, Jan.14
    Harold H. Deneault, Jr., "UFOs Return
    to Washington," Fate 18 (July 1965):

46,49.

Dumfries
-UFO (NL)
 1978, April 8/Lydia Thomas/Colder Dr.
  Dumfries Potomac News, 18 Apr.1978.

Eagle Rock
-UFO (DD)
 1978, May
  "Prize Selections from a Researcher's
  Photo Collection," Saga UFO Rept.
  6 (Nov.1978):38,43. il.

Elkton
-Phantom image
 1956, May/Elk Run cemetery
  (Editorial), Fate 10 (Oct.1957):14.
-Reincarnation and possession
 1970-   /Dolores Jay
  Columbus (O.) Dispatch, 26 Jan.1975,
  p.F-7. il.
  Ian Stevenson, "A Preliminary Report
  of a New Case of Responsive Xeno-
  glossy: The Case of Gretchen," J.
  ASPR 70 (1976):65-77.
  Carroll E. Jay, Gretchen, I Am (N.Y.:
  Avon, 1979 ed.).

Emory
-UFO (NL)
 1976, Jan.18/Mrs. Roy Barrett
  Bristol Herald-Courier, 19-22 Jan.
  1976.
  Ken Childress, "Ball of Light, Landing, Explosion," APRO Bull. 24 (Jan.
  1976):1,4-5.

Emporia
-UFO (NL)
 1975, Nov.19/C.S. Wilson
  Washington (D.C.) Post, 21 Nov.1975.
  Washington (D.C.) Star, 22 Nov.1975.
  "Mystery Rockets over Eastern U.S.,"
  APRO Bull. 24 (Dec.1975):1.

Fairfax
-Fall of bugs
 1855, Dec.
  Henry Winfred Splitter, "Wonders from
  the Sky," Fate 6 (Oct.1953):33,35,
  quoting Alexandria Gazette (undated).
-UFO (NL)
 1975, July 6
  "UFO Central," CUFOS News Bull., 15
  Nov.1975, p.13.

Fairfax co.
-Phantom panther
 1971, Feb./George Correll
  Washington (D.C.) Daily News, 8 Feb.
  1971.
-UFO (DD)
 1950, March 26/Bertram A. Totten
  Los Angeles (Cal.) Daily News, 27
  Mar.1950.
  Kenneth Arnold & Ray Palmer, The Com-
  ing of the Saucers (Boise: The Au-
  thors, 1952), pp.147-48.

Falls Church
-UFO (NL)
 1952, Aug.
  Donald E. Keyhoe, Flying Saucers from
  Outer Space (N.Y.: Holt, 1953), p.
  258.

Farmville
-Hog mutilation
 1976, July 1/Sam Dunevants
  Farmville Herald, 2 July 1976.
-UFO (NL)
 1966, July 24/Clinton Childress/W of
 town
  Richmond Times-Dispatch, 28 July
  1966.

Floyd
-Exploding grave
 1952, Feb.2/George Via/Topeco Church
  (Editorial), Fate 5 (July-Aug.1952):
  6.

Fluvanna co.
-Spirit medium
 1871/Hunter's Lodge
  New York Herald, 7 Sep.1871, pp.4,7.

Fork Union
-Haunt
 1960s/Careby Hall
  Susy Smith, Ghosts Around the House
  (N.Y.: World, 1970).

Fort Belvoir
-UFO (?)
 1957, Sep./=atomic bomb simulation de-
 vice
  Edward U. Condon, ed., Scientific
  Study of Unidentified Flying Objects
  (N.Y.: Bantam, 1969 ed.), pp.427-
  34. il.

Franklin
-UFO (CE-1)
 1953, Feb.9
  Desmond Leslie & George Adamski, Flying Saucers Have Landed (N.Y.: British Book Centre, 1953), p.222n.

Frederick co.
-Ancient stone chambers
  William Pidgeon, Traditions of Dee-
  coo-dah (N.Y.: Horace Thayer, 1858),
  pp.22-25.

Fredericksburg
-Aerial phantom
 1881, Oct.
  Richmond Dispatch, 7 Oct.1881.
-UFO (NL)
 1965, Jan.25/Rappahannock R.
  Fredericksburg Free Lance Star, 26
  Jan.1965.

Front Royal
-UFO (?)
 1973, Oct./=balloon
  Philip J. Klass, UFOs Identified
  (N.Y.: Random House, 1974), p.291.

Arlington H. Mallery, Lost America
(Washington: Public Affairs, 1950),
pp.194-96,200-202,213-14.
J.V. Howe, "The Howe Iron Sites of
Mecklenburg County," Bull.Eastern
States Arch.Federation, no.9 (1950)
:8.
J.V. Howe, "The Pre-Columbian Iron
Age of Virginia," Bull.Eastern
States Arch.Federation, no.10 (1951)
:6.
Charles Michael Boland, They All
Discovered America (N.Y.: Paperback
Library, 1963 ed.), pp.64-74.

Jonesville
-Poltergeist
1938, Dec./Bertha Marie Sybert
"Bouncing Bed," Fortean Soc'y Mag.,
no.3 (Jan.1940):10.
-UFO (CE-3)
1957, Nov.6/Buford Seabolt
Ted Phillips, Physical Traces Associ-
ated with UFO Sightings (Evanston:
Center for UFO Studies, 1975), p.22.

Lebanon
-UFO (NL)
1976, June 15
"Noteworthy UFO Sightings," Ufology
2 (fall 1976):61.

Lexington
-Fall of explosive hail
ca.1895/W.G. Brown
W.G. Brown, "Explosive Hail," Nature
88 (1912):350.

Limeton
-Archeological site
9500-2000 B.C.
Washington (D.C.) Post, 6 Dec.1976.

Linden
-Haunt
19th c./Pecatone
Federal Writers' Program, Virginia:
A Guide to the Old Dominion (N.Y.:
Oxford Univ., 1941), p.142.

Lorton
-Dowsing
1960s-   /Zaboj V. Harvalik
Z.V. Harvalik, "A Biophysical Magnet-
ometer-Gradiometer," Virginia J.Sci.
21 (1970):59-60.
Peter Tompkins & Christopher Bird,
The Secret Life of Plants (N.Y.:
Harper & Row, 1973), pp.297,302,
351-52.

Loudoun co.
-Haunt
n.d./Noland House
James Reynolds, Ghosts in American
Houses (N.Y.: Paperback Library,
1967 ed.), pp.96-98.

Lunenburg co.
-UFO (CE-2)

1967, June 21/Doris Simon/ground markings only
Richmond Times-Dispatch, 23 June
1967.
"Saucer Briefs," Saucer News 14
(fall 1967):36.

Luray
-Haunt
n.d./Corry House/Mary Ann Creek
James Reynolds, Ghosts in American
Houses (N.Y.: Paperback Library.
1967 ed.), pp.192-99.

Lynchburg
-Fall of unknown substance
1963, April 20/Shirley Dunn
"Fortean Items," Saucer News 10
(Sep.1963):17.
-Fall of yellow rain
1879, March 20
"Pollen," Monthly Weather Rev. 7
(Mar.1879):16.
-UFO (?)
1968
Ted Phillips, Physical Traces Associ-
ated with UFO Sightings (Evanston:
Center for UFO Studies, 1975), p.
109.
-UFO (CE-3)
1964, Jan.23
"Saucer Landing in Virginia," Saucer
News 12 (Mar.1965):18.
-UFO (DD)
1951, July 6/George D. Fawcett
"Saucer Sightings by IFSB Members,"
Space Rev. 1 (Oct.1952):10.
Albert K. Bender, Flying Saucers and
the Three Men (N.Y.: Paperback Li-
brary, 1968 ed.), p.38.

Manassas
-Elizabethan inscription
1969, Dec./Nicky Cornish/=hoax?
(Editorial), Fate 23 (Sep.1970):28-
32.
-Fall of ice
1897, Aug.10/Charles H. Winston
(Letter), Science, n.s., 6 (1897):
448-49. i1.
-Fall of powder
1974, July 18
"Atmospherics, Falls (?), Fish Kill,"
INFO J., no.14 (Nov.1974):24.

Manassas Park
-UFO (NL)
1973, Dec.28/Joseph Scalici
Culpeper Star-Exponent, 29 Dec.1973.

Marion
-UFO (CE-2)
1954, Sep.16/Sam Peavler
Lancaster (Pa.) Intelligencer-Jour-
nal, 17 Sep.1954.
1965, Jan.25/Woody Darnell
Harold H. Deneault, Jr., "UFOs Return to Washington," Fate 18 (July
1965):46,52.
-UFO (NL)

1965, Jan.26/H. Preston Robinson
"Opposition Flap 1965," Flying Saucer Rev. 11 (May-June 1965):3,5.
Harold H. Deneault, Jr., "UFOs Return to Washington," Fate 18 (July
1965):46,52.

Marshall
-UFO (NL)
1973, Dec.28/John Payne/Hwy.55
Timothy Green Beckley, "The UFO Base
40 Miles from the White House,"
Saga UFO Rept. 5 (May 1978):44,63,
quoting Fauquier Democrat (undated).

Mathews
-Haunt and lost treasure
n.d./Old House Woods
Howard M. Duffy, "The Haunted Treasure of Old House Woods," Beyond
Reality, no.34 (Nov.-Dec.1978):32-
33.

Mechanicsville
-UFO (CE-2)
1967, June 21
Ted Phillips, Physical Traces Associ-
ated with UFO Sightings (Evanston:
Center for UFO Studies, 1975), p.49.

Middlebrook
-Humanoid
1978, March 30/=poacher
Staunton Leader, 4 Apr.1978.
Richmond Times-Dispatch, 5 Apr.1978.
(Letter), Linda M. Suto, Saga UFO
Rept. 6 (Oct.1978):4.

Moneta
-UFO (DD)
1965, Jan.25
Donald B. Hanlon, "Virginia 1965
Flap," Flying Saucer Rev. 12 (Mar.-
Apr.1966):14,15.

Mount Vernon
-UFO (NL)
1950, May 29/Willis T. Sperry/7 mi.W
(Letter), Flying 47 (Sep.1950):64.
Ray Palmer, "New Report on the Fly-
ing Saucers," Fate 4 (Jan.1951):63,
71-72.
Edward J. Ruppelt, The Report on Un-
identified Flying Objects (Garden
City: Doubleday, 1956), pp.85-86.

Nelson co.
-Fall of gelatinous substance
1833, Nov.13/H.H. Garland
Denison Olmsted, "Observations on the
Meteors of November 13th, 1833," Am.
J.Sci., ser.1, 25 (1834):363,396,
quoting Richmond Enquirer (undated).

New Baltimore
-Aerial phantom
1881, Sep.
"Visions in the Clouds," Sci.Am. 45
(1881):291, quoting Warrenton Solid
South (undated).

New Canton
-Skyquake
1921, Aug.7
Richmond Times-Dispatch, 10 Aug.1921;
and 15 Aug.1921.

Newport News
-Biofeedback research
1970s/James Howerton
Elmer & Alyce Green, Beyond Biofeed-
back (N.Y.: Delta, 1978 ed.), pp.
90-91.
-UFO (?)
1952, Oct.11
Richard Hall, ed., The UFO Evidence
(Washington: NICAP, 1964), pp.11,
150.
-UFO (NL)
1952, July 14/William B. Nash
William B. Nash & W.H. Fortenberry,
"We Flew Above Flying Saucers,"
True, Oct.1952.
Donald H. Menzel & Lyle G. Boyd, The
World of Flying Saucers (Garden
City: Doubleday, 1963), pp.256-65.
Richard Hall, ed., The UFO Evidence
(Washington: NICAP, 1964), pp.38-39.
Charles A. Maney, "Donald Menzel and
the Newport News UFO: A Critical
Report," Fate 18 (Apr.1965):64-75.
Thomas M. Olsen, ed., The Reference
for Outstanding UFO Sighting Reports
(Riderwood, Md.: UFO Information Re-
trieval Center, 1966), pp.11-12.
1952, July 26/William Patterson
Edward J. Ruppelt, The Report on Un-
identified Flying Objects (Garden
City: Doubleday, 1956), pp.165-66,
168.
1977, March 17/Denbigh
"UFOs of Limited Merit," Int'l UFO
Reporter 2 (May 1977):5.

Norfolk
-Crisis apparition
n.d./Roger Rageot/Norfolk Museum
Roger Rageot, "Locket from the Dead,"
Fate 16 (Nov.1963):48-51.
-Disappearance
1973, March 23/"Norse Variant"/ocean to
NE
1973, March 23/"Anita"/ocean to NE
New York Times, 23 Mar.1973, p.1; 24
Mar.1973, p.66; 25 Mar.1973, p.47;
26 Mar.1973, p.1; 27 Mar.1973, p.
32; 28 Mar.1973, p.1; and 29 Mar.
1973, p.93.
Lawrence David Kusche, The Bermuda
Triangle Mystery--Solved (N.Y.: Har-
per & Row, 1975), pp.246-47.
-Fall of fish
1853
Charles Fort, The Books of Charles
Fort (N.Y.: Holt, 1941), p.183, quo-
ting Cosmos, vol.13, p.120.
1961, April 15/Emma Bright
(Editorial), Fate 14 (Oct.1961):23,
quoting Norfolk Ledger-Dispatch &
Star (undated). il.
-Fall of metal foil

1956/Capitola Paxton
(Letter), Fate 10 (May 1957):114-16.
-Fall of yellow dust
1794, April 2/=pollen?
Kenneth & Anna M. Roberts, ed., Mor-
eau de St. Mary's American Journey
(Garden City: Doubleday, 1947), p.
56.
-Haunt
1908, Sep.-1909/Eddie Harrell/nr. City
Park
Eddie Harrell, "The Ghost with the
Rose in Her Hair," Fate 13 (Jan.
1960):33-37.
-Hex
1679/Alice Cartwright
Philip Alexander Bruce, Institution-
al History of Virginia, 2 vols.
(N.Y.: Putnam, 1910), 1:282.
-Midday darkness
1831, Aug.13
William S. Forrest, Historical and
Descriptive Sketches of Norfolk and
Vicinity (Philadelphia: Lindsay &
Blakiston, 1853), pp.192-93.
-Musical sand
H. Carrington Bolton & Alexis A. Ju-
lien, "Musical Sand, Its Wide Dis-
tribution and Properties," Proc.Am.
Ass'n Adv.Sci. 33 (1884):408-13.
-Phantom
1952/Yevonna Fox
Brad Steiger, Sex and the Supernat-
ural (N.Y.: Lancer, 1968), pp.168-
70, quoting Pat Fox, "The Demon
That Stole My Wife," Forum, Nov.
1967.
-Poltergeist
1967, Sep.-Nov./Woodrow Wilson Franks/
Robin Hood Apts.
(Editorial), Fate 21 (June 1968):26-
30.
D. Scott Rogo, An Experience of Phan-
toms (N.Y.: Dell, 1974 ed.), pp.
154-55.
-Roman coin
1833, Sep.
William S. Forrest, Historical and
Descriptive Sketches of Norfolk and
Vicinity (Philadelphia: Lindsay &
Blakiston, 1853), pp.35-36.
-Sea monster
1935/W.C. Hogan/"Electra"
Bernard Heuvelmans, In the Wake of
the Sea-Serpents (N.Y.: Hill &
Wang, 1968), p.464.
-Seance
1958, June/Keith Milton Rhinehart
Agnes F. Reuther, "The Levitated
Trumpets," Fate 12 (Feb.1959):73-
75. il.
-UFO (?)
1860, Aug.
Baltimore (Md.) Sun, 6 Aug.1860.
-UFO (DD)
1947, July 8/William Turrentine
R. DeWitt Miller, Stranger Than Life
(N.Y.: Ace, 1955 ed.), p.103.
Bruce S. Maccabee, "UFO Related In-
formation from the FBI Files: Part

3," MUFON UFO J., no.121 (Dec.1977)
:10,13.
1957, Nov.5
Richard Hall, ed., The UFO Evidence
(Washington: NICAP, 1964), p.164.
-UFO (NL)
1965, Jan.14/James Myers
Harold H. Deneault, Jr., "UFOs Re-
turn to Washington," Fate 18 (July
1965):46,49, quoting Norfolk Virginian-Pilot (undated).
-UFO (R-V)
1957, Aug.30
Gordon D. Thayer, "Optical and Radar
Analyses of Field Cases," in Edward
U. Condon, ed., Scientific Study of
Unidentified Flying Objects (N.Y.:
Bantam, 1969 ed.), pp.115,128.
-Witchcraft
1641/Mrs. George Busher
1655-1656
1698/Anne Byrd
1698/Jane Jennings
Philip Alexander Bruce, Institution-
al History of Virginia, 2 vols.
(N.Y.: Putnam, 1910), 1:279-81,287-
88.
F. Roy Johnson, Witches and Demons
in History and Folklore (Murfreesboro: Johnson, 1969), pp.28-32.

Northumberland co.
-Hex
1671/Mrs. Neal
Philip Alexander Bruce, Institution-
al History of Virginia, 2 vols.
(N.Y.: Putnam, 1910), 1:282.

Norton
-Ancient inscription
Vernon J. Calhoun, "Libyan Evidence
in Southeast Kentucky," Occ.Pub.
Epigraphic Soc'y 6, no.127 (Jan.
1979):109,113. il.

Paces
-UFO (DD)
1926, fall/R.A. Marshall, Jr.
(Letter), Fate 5 (Oct.1952):114.

Pearisburg
-Poltergeist
1976, Dec.19-24/Beulah Wilson
Washington (D.C.) Post, 31 Dec.1976;
and 5 Jan.1977, p.1.
Nat'l Enquirer, 14 Feb.1978.
J.G. Pratt, "The Pearisburg Poltergeist," in William G. Roll, ed., Research in Parapsychology 1977 (Metuchen, N.J.: Scarecrow, 1978), pp.
174-82.

Petersburg
-Clairvoyance
1959, Sep.16/Allyson Brady
(Editorial), Fate 13 (Jan.1960):18,
quoting Richmond Times-Dispatch (undated).
-Fall of frogs
1877, June

Petersburg Index-Appeal, 22 June
1877.
New York Times, 25 June 1877, p.8.
-Poltergeist
1950/William Walker Roberts
Ellaine Elmore, "The Flying Milk Bot-
tles of Petersburg, Va.," Fate 4
(Mar.1951):26-28.

Pittsylvania co.
-Humanoid
1977, May
Danville Bee, 17 May 1977.

Portsmouth
-Ghost
1871, Dec./London St. x Canal St.
Decatur (Ill.) Republican, 7 Dec.
1871.
-Haunt
1950s/Chickahominy R.
(Editorial), Fate 16 (Jan.1963):16,
quoting Richmond News-Leader (un-
dated).
-Poltergeist
1962, Sep.6-11/Mrs. Charles Daughtrey/
949 Florida Ave.
Norfolk Virginian-Pilot, 9 Sep.1962.
Richmond News-Leader, 11 Sep.1962.
Mary Margaret Fuller, "The House-
breaking Ghost in Portsmouth, Vir-
ginia," Fate 15 (Dec.1962):26-31.
il.
(Editorial), Fate 16 (Jan.1963):14-
16.
William G. Roll, The Poltergeist
(N.Y.: Signet, 1974 ed.), pp.102-103.
-UFO (CE-2)
1965, Aug.16/Steve L. Anderson/U.S.58
"News Briefs," Saucer News 12 (Dec.
1965):25-26.
Jerome Clark, "The Greatest Flap Yet?
--Part 2," Flying Saucer Rev. 12
(Mar.-Apr.1966):8,10.
1975, July 2
"UFO Central," CUFOS News Bull., 15
Nov.1975, p.12.
-UFO (DD)
1947, July 6/Mrs. A.H. Whittaker
Richmond Times-Dispatch, 7 July 1947.
1965, Aug.15/James Gilman
Jerome Clark, "The Greatest Flap Yet?
--Part 2," Flying Saucer Rev. 12
(Mar.-Apr.1966):8,10.

Pounding Mill
-UFO (DD)
1978, May 17/Troy Proffit/Hwy.637
Richlands News-Press, 17 May 1978.

Quantico
-Acoustic anomaly
1977, Feb./Krin N. Stolpa/Marine Base
Washington (D.C.) Star, 13 Feb.1977.
-Dowsing
1970s/Louis Matacia/Marine Base
Christopher Bird, "Applications of
Dowsing: An Ancient Biopsychophysi-
cal Art," in John White & Stanley
Krippner, eds., Future Science (Gar-

den City: Anchor, 1977), pp.346,348-
49.
-Humanoid
1977, Jan./Marine Base
Dumfries Potomac News, 17 Jan.1977.
-UFO (NL)
1952, July 10
Edward J. Ruppelt, The Report on Un-
identified Flying Objects (Garden
City: Doubleday, 1956), p.157.
1953, Dec.30-1954, Jan.4/Norman Viets/
Tank Park Marine Base
Washington (D.C.) Daily News, 4 Jan.
1954.
John C. Ross, "The Lights That Fail-
ed," Fate 7 (May 1954):37-39.
1959, July 8/Mary A. Cook/Potomac R.
(Letter), Fate 12 (Nov.1959):109.

Radford
-UFO (?)
1949, May 12
Bruce S. Maccabee, "UFO Related Information from the FBI Files: Part
5," MUFON UFO J., no.124 (Mar.1978)
:7,11.
-UFO (DD)
1964, Sep.9/Albert Tolley/New R.
Roanoke Times, 10 Sep.1964; and 12
Sep.1964.

Reston
-UFO (CE-1)
1973, May 2/Hwy.602
Rufus Drake, "Return of the 'Men in
Black,'" Saga UFO Rept. 3 (Oct.1976)
:36-37.

Richmond
-Animal ESP
1925-1957/Claudia Fonda
New York Times, 28 May 1928, p.24.
J.B. & Louisa Rhine, "An Investiga-
tion of a 'Mind-Reading' Horse,"
J.Abnormal & Social Psych. 23 (1929)
:449-66.
Mary Judith Hyde, "The Talking Horse
of Virginia," Fate 3 (May 1950):28-
30.
"Lady, a Clairvoyant Mare, Solves
Problems," Life, 22 Dec.1952, pp.
20,21. il.
(Editorial), Fate 6 (Jan.1953):5.
(Editorial), Fate 6 (Apr.1953):7-8.
il.
(Letter), Lillian Patterson, Fate 6
(Nov.1953):110-11.
(Editorial), Fate 10 (Aug.1957):12.
Jack Woodford, "Lady Was a Wonder,"
Fate 16 (Feb.1963):66-73. il.
(Letter), George Massinger, Fate 16
(May 1963):117-18.
-Contactee
1969, summer-1970, April 1
Brad Steiger, Revelation: The Divine
Fire (Englewood Cliffs, N.J.: Pren-
tice-Hall, 1973), pp.224-28.
-Poltergeist
1869, April 27-June 1/W.R. Chiles/9th
St.

Richmond Enquirer, 1 Sep.1869.
-Precognition
1880s-1945/Charlotte Roubio Pollock
Nathan Oppleman, "Charlotte Roubio
Pollock: The Medium of Richmond,"
Fate 6 (May 1953):97-105. il.
1884/Pearl Tyler
William Oliver Stevens, _The Mystery_
of Dreams (N.Y.: Dodd, Mead, 1949).
-Spirit medium
1930s/Margaret Sizer
Austin Hart Burr, "Evidences of Iden-
tity Received Through the Medium-
ship of Mrs. Margaret Sizer," _J._
ASPR 34 (1940):375-81.
-UFO (?)
1952, Oct.29/Francisco Rivas
New York Journal-American, 30 Oct.
1952.
1962, June 30
Richard Hall, ed., _The UFO Evidence_
(Washington: NICAP, 1964), p.139.
1965, Jan.24
Donald B. Hanlon, "Virginia 1965
Flap," _Flying Saucer Rev._ 12 (Mar.-
Apr.1966):14,15.
-UFO (CE-1)
1966, June 24/William L. Stevens, Jr./
Meadow Bridge Rd.
"New Reports by Space Experts Add to
UFO Proof," _UFO Inv._ 3 (Aug.-Sep.
1966):3. il.
Donald E. Keyhoe & Gordon I.R. Lore,
Jr., _UFOs: A New Look_ (Washington:
NICAP, 1969), p.9.
1967, April 26/Beverly Brussells
Richmond News-Leader, 19 May 1967.
-UFO (CE-2)
1958, May
Richard Hall, ed., _The UFO Evidence_
(Washington: NICAP, 1964), p.75.
1967, June 1/John Norton/Tuckahoe
"Startling Cases Investigated," _UFO_
Inv. 4 (May-June 1967):7.
-UFO (DD)
1947, April
Donald E. Keyhoe, _The Flying Saucers_
Are Real (N.Y.: Fawcett, 1950), pp.
65-66.
1947, July 6/Walter Broadwell/NW of
town
Richmond Times-Dispatch, 7 July 1947.
1952, June 15/NW of town
Edward J. Ruppelt, _The Report on Un-_
identified Flying Objects (Garden
City: Doubleday, 1956), p.144.
-UFO (NL)
1956, Nov.29
(Editorial), _Fate_ 10 (Apr.1957):16.
1966, July 27
Richmond Times-Dispatch, 28 July
1966.
1969, Dec.6/W.W. Tanner/Boulevard x
Grove Ave.
Richmond Times-Dispatch, 6 Dec.1969.
1977, Nov.18
"UFOs of Limited Merit," _Int'l UFO_
Reporter 3 (Jan.1978):3.

Roanoke
-Entombed frogs
n.d./John J. Kealey
"Out of the Concrete," _Fate_ 8 (July
1955):32.
-Healing
1951/Oral Roberts/American Legion Aud-
itorium
Lee R. Gandee, "Oral Roberts' Heal-
ing of Willie Phelps," _Fate_ 13
(Mar.1960):36-43.
-Inner development
1950s-   /Ordo Templi Orientis
J. Gordon Melton, _Encyclopedia of_
American Religions, 2 vols. (Wil-
mington, N.C.: Consortium, 1978),
2:260-61.
-Lunar cycle and birth hour
1940s
A.G. Schnurman, "The Effect of the
Moon on Childbirth," _Virginia Med._
Monthly 76 (1949):78.
-Precognition
ca.1860s/Julia Tyler
William Oliver Stevens, _The Mystery_
of Dreams (N.Y.: Dodd, Mead, 1949).
-UFO (NL)
1955, Sep.11/David Brugh
(Letter), _Fate_ 9 (Sep.1956):114.

Rockville
-UFO (CE-3)
1969, May 11/Michael Luczkowich/Hwy.
622
Ted Bloecher, "A Typical Humanoid
Encounter," _Skylook_, no.93 (Aug.
1975):5,7-8. il.

Salem
-Disappearance
1885, April 22/Isaac Martin
New York Sun, 25 Apr.1885, p.3.
-UFO (CE-1)
1965, Jan.24
Donald B. Hanlon, "Virginia 1965
Flap," _Flying Saucer Rev._ 12 (Mar.-
Apr.1966):15, quoting Arlington
Northern Virginia Sun (undated).

Scott co.
-Clairvoyance
n.d./Marv Austin
"The Prospector's Dream," _Fate_ 6
(Nov.1953):37.

South Hill
-UFO (CE-2) and Men-in-black
1967, April 21/Clifton N. Crowder/Hwy.
747
Richmond News-Leader, 22 Apr.1967;
and 3 May 1967.
South Hill Enterprise, 27 Apr.1967.
"UFO Scorches Highway," _UFO Inv._ 3
(Mar.-Apr.1967):1,5. il.
Richmond Times-Dispatch, 10 May 1967.
"Physical Evidence Analyzed," _UFO_
Inv. 3 (May-June 1967):7.
"Saucer Landing in Virginia Investi-
gated by Saucer News Editor," _Sau-_
cer News 14 (fall 1967):32-33. il.

Jim & Coral Lorenzen, UFOs over the Americas (N.Y.: Signet, 1968), pp. 47-48.
Philip J. Klass, UFOs Explained (N.Y.: Random House, 1974), pp.115-33. il.
Stanton T. Friedman, "Klass Book Unscientific," Skylook, no.94 (Sep. 1965):14.

Spring Hill
-Precognition
1870, Sep.22/Samuel Frame
F. Beatrice Macintyre, "Monument to a Miracle," Fate 19 (Sep.1966):54-56.

Staunton
-Clairvoyance
1774, Oct.10/John Frogg's daughter
Frank Ball, "The Bright Red Jacket," Fate 31 (July 1978):81.
-Erratic crocodilian
1939, Aug.7/Honeoye Creek
New York Times, 7 Aug.1939, p.17.
-Ghost
1892/Grandma Moses/Dudley place
Grandma Moses, "Grandma Moses and the Spirit," Fate 6 (Jan.1953):18-20.
-Phantom train
1856
Decatur Illinois State Chronicle, 7 Aug.1856, p.1, quoting Staunton Spectator (undated).
-UFO (CE-2)
1964, Dec.21/Horace Burns/4 mi.E on Hwy.250
Richmond Times-Dispatch, 14-15 Jan. 1965; 17 Jan.1965; and 27 Jan.1965.
"Opposition Flap 1965," Flying Saucer Rev. 11 (May-June 1965):3-4.
Harold H. Deneault, Jr., "Anatomy of a UFO Cover-up," Fate 19 (May 1966): 84-91. il.
Donald E. Keyhoe & Gordon I.R. Lore, Jr., UFOs: A New Look (Washington: NICAP, 1969), pp.21-22.
-UFO (DD)
1965, Jan.14/Jody Smith
Harold H. Deneault, Jr., "UFOs Return to Washington," Fate 18 (July 1965):46,49.

Stuart
-UFO (NL)
1966, Aug.18
"New Reports by Space Experts Add to UFO Proof," UFO Inv. 3 (Aug.-Sep. 1966):3,4.

Suffolk
-Ghost light
1870s-1951/Jackson Rd.
"It Looks Like a Train on the Track," Fate 4 (Aug.-Sep.1951):97, quoting UP release, 13 Apr.1951.
(Letter), George Wetzel, Fate 6 (May 1953):109.

Sussex co.
-UFO (NL)
1973, Oct./William Rodgester, Jr.
Little Rock Arkansas Gazette, 18 Oct. 1973.

Timberville
-Fall of ice
1976, March 7-8/Wilbert W. Cullers
Harrisonburg Daily News-Record, 8-10 Mar.1976.
P.J. Willis, "The Timberville, Virginia, Ice Fall," INFO J., no.19 (Sep.1976):14-17; no.21 (Jan.1977): 13. il.

Toano
-UFO (CE-2)
1965, Jan.23/U.S.60
Harold H. Deneault, Jr., "UFOs Return to Washington," Fate 18 (July 1965):46,51.
J. Allen Hynek, The Hynek UFO Report (N.Y.: Dell, 1977), pp.177-78.

Toms Creek
-Fall of metallic sodium
1953, July 19/Harold Adams
(Editorial), Fate 7 (Jan.1954):11-12.

Unionville
-UFO (DD)
1952, June 15/=balloon?
Edward J. Ruppelt, The Report on Unidentified Flying Objects (Garden City: Doubleday, 1956), p.144.

Verona
-UFO (NL)
1965, Jan.24
Donald B. Hanlon, "Virginia 1965 Flap," Flying Saucer Rev. 12 (Mar.-Apr.1966):14,15.

Vesta
-UFO (CE-3)
1974, March 1/Bill Wayne Plasters
Stuart Enterprise, 20 Mar.1974.
"Near Landing, Humanoid Reported," Skylook, no.81 (Aug.1974):10-11.

Vesuvius
-UFO (NL)
1965, Sep.21/J.M. Westbrook
(Letter), Fate 19 (May 1966):126-27.

Vienna
-UFO (?)
1935, Jan.22
C.G. Abbot, "Unusual Sky Appearance," Science 81 (1935):294.

Virginia Beach
-Electromagnetic anomaly
1961/Mark Cordrey/Diamond Springs
(Editorial), Fate 14 (Sep.1961):10.
-Medical clairvoyance
1974-   /Paul Solomon/Fellowship of the Inner Light/1353 Laskin Rd.
William Beidler, "Paul Solomon...

Another Cayce?" Fate 30 (Feb.1977):
56–61.
-Medical clairvoyance, healing, and ret-
rocognition
1925-   /Edgar Cayce/Association for
Research and Enlightenment/67th St. x
Atlantic Ave.
   Thomas Sugrue, There Is a River (N.Y.:
   Holt, Rinehart & Winston, 1942).
   Edgar Cayce, Auras (Virginia Beach:
   A.R.E., 1945).
   Edgar Cayce, "I Can See the Human
   Aura!" Fate 1 (summer 1948):91–100.
   Sherwood Eddy, You Will Survive After
   Death (N.Y.: Rinehart, 1950).
   Vaughn Shelton, "Edgar Cayce's Mail
   Order Miracle," Fate 8 (June 1955):
   34–41.
   Vaughn Shelton, "Edgar Cayce's Win-
   dow to Eternity," Fate 8 (Dec.1955):
   68–75.
   John E. Malloy, "Lapis Lingua--Psy-
   chic Stone?" Fate 9 (July 1956):58–
   62. il.
   Jeffrey Furst, Edgar Cayce on Jesus
   (N.Y.: Paperback Library, 1960).
   Edgar Evans Cayce, "Miracles Were My
   Father's Business," Fate 13 (May
   1960):35–41.
   Long John Nebel, The Way Out World
   (N.Y.: Lancer, 1962 ed.), pp.103–
   106.
   Jess Stearn, The Door to the Future
   (N.Y.: Macfadden, 1964), pp.49–78.
   Jess Stearn, Edgar Cayce: The Sleep-
   ing Prophet (Garden City: Doubleday,
   1967).
   Harmon Hartzell Bro, "My Experiences
   with Edgar Cayce," Fate 20 (Mar.
   1967):94–103.
   Edgar Evans Cayce, Edgar Cayce on
   Atlantis (N.Y.: Paperback Library,
   1968).
   "A.R.E.: Edgar Cayce's Expanding Leg-
   acy," Psychic 1 (Sep.1969):18–23.
   David Kahn & Will Oursler, My Life
   with Edgar Cayce (Garden City: Doub-
   leday, 1970).
   Mary Ellen Carter, My Years with Ed-
   gar Cayce (N.Y.: Harper & Row, 1972).
   John Godwin, Occult America (Garden
   City: Doubleday, 1972), pp.100–11.
   June & Nicholas Regush, Psi: The Oth-
   er World Catalogue (N.Y.: Dutton,
   1974), pp.118–19. il.
   Harold J. Reilly & Ruth Hagy Brod,
   The Edgar Cayce Handbook for Health
   Through Drugless Therapy (N.Y.: Mac-
   millan, 1975).
   Reba Ann Karp, "Edgar Cayce Cures
   Still Baffle Science," Fate 29 (Feb.
   1976):34–41.
   Lytle Robinson, Edgar Cayce's Story
   of the Origin and Destiny of Man
   (N.Y.: Berkley, 1973).
   Cleveland (O.) Plain Dealer, 15 Jan.
   1978.
   Jeffrey Goodman, Psychic Archeology
   (N.Y.: Berkley, 1978), pp.53–82.
-Poltergeist

1890s–1906/Eugene Y. Burroughs/Sigma
Eugene Y. Burroughs & Mary Ellen
Carter, "I Live with a Poltergeist,"
Fate 8 (Nov.1955):90–97.

Warminster
-Acoustic anomaly
1934, March/E. Emma Robinson
E. Emma Robinson, "Music in the
Storm," Fate 10 (Apr.1957):64–67.

Warrenton
-UFO (CE-1)
1953, summer/Martha Long
   Timothy Green Beckley, "The UFO Base
   40 Miles from the White House,"
   Saga UFO Rept. 5 (May 1978):44,46–
   47.
1967, winter/Martha Long
   Timothy Green Beckley, "The UFO Base
   40 Miles from the White House,"
   Saga UFO Rept. 5 (May 1978):44,58–
   60.
-UFO (CE-3)
1957/Martha Long/20 mi. from town
   Timothy Green Beckley, "The UFO Base
   40 Miles from the White House,"
   Saga UFO Rept. 5 (May 1978):44,47.
-UFO (DD)
1961, Sep.29/Harvey B. Savage, Jr.
   Richard Hall, ed., The UFO Evidence
   (Washington: NICAP, 1964), p.96.
1973, April/Martha Long
   Timothy Green Beckley, "The UFO Base
   40 Miles from the White House,"
   Saga UFO Rept. 5 (May 1978):44,64.
-UFO (NL)
1954, Jan.8/Edgar S. Payne
   (Letter), Fate 7 (June 1954):122.
   Harold T. Wilkins, Flying Saucers Un-
   censored (N.Y.: Ballantine, 1967
   ed.), pp.136,211.

Waynesboro
-UFO (CE-3)
1965, Jan.26/U.S.250
   Jerome Clark, "Two New Contact
   Claims," Flying Saucer Rev. 11 (May-
   June 1965):20–21.
   Jerome Clark, "Postscript to Contact,"
   Flying Saucer Rev. 11 (July-Aug.
   1965):5.
-UFO (CE-3) and men-in-black
1965, Jan.19, 25/William Blackburn/Au-
gusta Archery Range, nr.U.S.250
   Waynesboro News-Virginian, 23 Jan.
   1965.
   Donald E. Keyhoe & Gordon I.R. Lore,
   Jr., UFOs: A New Look (Washington:
   NICAP, 1969), p.30.
   Richard H. Hall, "The CIA, UFOs and
   Spacemen," Official UFO 1 (Oct.1975)
   :22–23,45–48.
-UFO (NL)
1965, Jan.14/Bruce Hogshead
   Harold H. Deneault, Jr., "UFOs Re-
   turn to Washington," Fate 18 (July
   1965):46,49.

Westmoreland co.
-Hex
  1694/Phyllis Money
    Philip Alexander Bruce, Institution-
    al History of Virginia, 2 vols.
    (N.Y.: Putnam, 1910), 1:284.

Williamsburg
-Anomalous hole in ground
  1975/Henry D. Pillow
    "Enigmas," Probe the Unknown 3 (May
    1975):45.
-Mystery vault
  1676/Bruton Parish Church
    Marie Bauer Hall, Foundations Un-
    earthed (Los Angeles: Veritas, 1974).
-Paraphysics research
  1950s-1960s/Leonard J. Ravitz/William
  and Mary College
    Leonard J. Ravitz, "Electrodynamic
    Field Theory in Psychiatry," South-
    ern Med.J. 46 (1953):650-60.
    Leonard J. Ravitz, "Comparative Clin-
    ical and Electrocyclic Observations
    on Twin Brothers," J.Nervous & Men-
    tal Disease 121 (1955):72-87.
    Leonard J. Ravitz, "Application of
    the Electrodynamic Field Theory in
    Biology, Psychiatry, Medicine and
    Hypnosis," Am.J.Clinical Hypnosis
    1 (1959):135-50.
    Leonard J. Ravitz, "History, Meas-
    urement and Applicability of Period-
    ic Changes in the Electromagnetic
    Field in Health and Disease," Annals
    N.Y.Acad.Sci. 98 (1962):1144-1201.

Winchester
-Archeological site
    William Pidgeon, Traditions of De-
    coo-dah (N.Y.: Horace Thayer, 1858),
    pp.25-26.
-UFO (NL)
  1952, April 12
    Winchester Evening Star, 14 Apr.1952.

Yorktown
-Lightning anomaly
  1736, summer
    William Byrd, A Journey to the Land
    of Eden and Other Papers (N.Y.:
    Macy-Masius, 1928 ed.), p.189.

          B. Physical Features

Bradford, L.
-Erratic crocodilian
  1949, Aug.9-16/Fred L. Lunsford
    "Alligator Escapees in Southeastern
    Virginia," Herpetologia 9 (1953):
    71-72.

Buck Hill
-Acoustic anomaly
  1889, Oct./Henry Parsons
    J.P. Folinsbee, "The Phantom of Buck
    Hill Caves," Coronet 30 (June 1951):
    58-60.

Burke L.
-UFO (CE-2)
  1976, Aug.13/Ted Nelson
    Midnight, 8 Nov.1976.

Chesapeake Bay
-Ball lightning
  1855, May 23/B.A. Colonna
    T.C. Mendenhall, "On Globular Light-
    ning," Am.Meteor.J., Feb.1890, pp.
    437-47.
-Sea monster
  1978, July 25/Donald Kyker
    Kansas City (Mo.) Star, 18 Aug.1978;
    and 12 Oct.1978, p.16C.

Coggins Point
-Norse discovery
  1009/Thorfinn Karlsefni/=Hóp?
    Frederick J. Pohl, The Viking Settle-
    ments of North America (N.Y.: Clark-
    son N. Potter, 1972), pp.104-15.

Dismal Swamp
-Humanoid
  n.d.
    Isaac Weld, Jr., Travels Through the
    States of North America (London: J.
    Stockdale, 1800), p.180.
-Phantom ship
    Charles M. Skinner, American Myths
    and Legends, 2 vols. (Philadelphia:
    Lippincott, 1903), 1:295-96.

Drummond, L.
-Phantom canoe
    Charles M. Skinner, Myths and Legends
    of Our Own Land, 2 vols. (Philadel-
    phia: Lippincott, 1896), 2:69-70.

Fairy Stone State Park
-Mineralogical anomaly
    Powhatan Bouldin, "Patrick County,
    Va., and Its Curious 'Fairy Stones,'"
    79 (1898):394-95.
    G.O. Stovall, "The Fairy Stones of
    Virginia," Harper's Weekly 50 (1906)
    :715.
    John P. Bessor, "Mystery of the Fairy
    Crosses," Fate 5 (June 1952):72-73.
    "'Fairy Crosses,'" Pursuit 4 (Apr.
    1971):41.

Henry, Cape
-Mystery explosion
  1945, Oct.31/J. Arthur Addenbrook
    "Going Up," Doubt, no.14 (spring
    1946):204.
-Sea monster
  1818, June/"Wilson"/=hoax?
    Boston (Mass.) Commercial Advertiser,
    9 June 1818.
    "American Sea-Serpent," Quar.J.Sci.
    Lit.& Arts Royal Inst. 6 (1818):163,
    165.
  1846, Feb./Capt. Lawson
    Charles Lyell, A Second Visit to the
    United States of North America, 2
    vols. (London: John Murray, 1849),
    1:134.

Hunting Creek
-Hex
   n.d.
      George Carey, A Faraway Time and
      Place (Washington: Robert B. Luce,
      1971), pp.159-60.

Little Cattail Creek
-Archeological site
   ca.9000 B.C./Williamson site
      Ben C. McCary, "A Workshop Site of
      Early Man in Dinwiddie County, Vir-
      ginia," Am.Antiquity 17 (1951):9-
      17. il.
      Ben C. McCary, "Survey of Virginia
      Fluted Points Nos.232-263," Quar.
      Bull.Arch.Soc'y Virginia 10, no.3
      (1956):10-16.
      Charles Edgar Gilliam, "Type Early
      Man Graver, Williamson Site, Din-
      widdie County, Virginia," Quar.Bull.
      Arch.Soc'y Virginia 13, no.1 (1958)
      :8-9.
      Floyd Painter, "The Cattail Creek
      Fluting Tradition and Its Complex-
      Determining Lithic Debris," Am.Arch.
      1 (summer 1974):20-32. il.
      Ben C. McCary, "The Williamson Paleo-
      Indian Site, Dinwiddie County, Vir-
      ginia," Chesopeian 13 (1975):48-131.

Lynnhaven Bay
-Skyquakes
   n.d.
      Federal Writers' Program, Virginia:
      A Guide to the Old Dominion (N.Y.:
      Oxford Univ., 1941), pp.141-42.

Lynnhaven R.
-Witch trial (hex)
   1698-1706/Grace Sherwood/Witch Duck
   Farm
      "Record of Grace Sherwood's Trial for
      Witchcraft," Coll.Virginia Hist.Soc'y
      1 (1833):69-78.
      William S. Forrest, Historical and
      Descriptive Sketches of Norfolk and
      Vicinity (Philadelphia: Lindsay &
      Blakiston, 1853), pp.464-65.
      Samuel G. Drake, Annals of Witchcraft
      in New England (Boston: W.E. Wood-
      ward, 1869), pp.210-15.
      Tom Pete Cross, "Witchcraft in North
      Carolina," Studies in Philology 16
      (1919):217,220-21.
      George Lincoln Burr, Narratives of
      the Witchcraft Cases 1648-1706 (N.Y.:
      Barnes & Noble, 1946), pp.438-42.
      Betty Oliver, "Grace Sherwood of
      Princess Anne," North Carolina Folk-
      lore 10 (July 1962):36-39.
      F. Roy Johnson, Witches and Demons in
      History and Folklore (Murfreesboro:
      Johnson, 1969), pp.33-42.

Marcey Creek
-Archeological site
      Carl Manson, "Marcey Creek Site: An
      Early Manifestation in the Potomac
      Valley," Am.Antiquity 13 (1948):223-

27. il.

Moccasin Creek
-Phantom dog
   1859, Jan./Robert J. Fugate
      Robert J. Fugate, "The Devil Is a
      Black Dog," Fate 9 (Jan.1956):22-
      24.

Nottoway R.
-UFO (NL)
   1964, June 29
      "Wave of Close-Range Sightings Re-
      ported," UFO Inv. 2 (July-Aug.1964)
      :1,3.

Old Rag Mt.
-Haunt
   n.d./Pheasant Hill
      James Reynolds, Gallery of Ghosts
      (N.Y.: Paperback Library, 1970 ed.),
      pp.223-37.

Rappahannock R.
-Phantom ship
   1870s-1886
      Charles M. Skinner, Myths and Legends
      of Our Own Land, 2 vols. (Philadel-
      phia: Lippincott, 1896), 2:71-72.

Tangier I.
-Hex
   n.d.
      George Carey, A Faraway Time and
      Place (Washington: Robert B. Luce,
      1971), pp.160-61.

Wallop's I.
-UFO (?)
   1960, April 1/=balloon
      "Recent UFO Sightings," NICAP Spec.
      Bull., May 1960, p.4.
      "Sightings Increase As Mars Approach-
      es Earth," UFO Inv. 1 (July-Aug.
      1960):5.
      Donald H. Menzel & Lyle G. Boyd, The
      World of Flying Saucers (Garden
      City: Doubleday, 1963), pp.44-45.
   1964, Oct./NASA station
      Harold H. Deneault, Jr., "UFOs Re-
      turn to Washington," Fate 18 (July
      1965):46,48-49, quoting Norfolk
      Virginian-Pilot (undated).
-UFO (DD)
   1965, Jan.5/Dempsey Bruton/NASA station
      "New Sightings Put AF on Spot," UFO
      Inv. 3 (Mar.-Apr.1965):1, quoting
      Norfolk Virginian-Pilot (undated).
   1965, Jan.12/Mr. Milliner/NASA station
      Harold H. Deneault, Jr., "UFOs Re-
      turn to Washington," Fate 18 (July
      1965):46,48.
-UFO (R)
   1962/NASA station
      Vincent H. Gaddis, Mysterious Fires
      and Lights (N.Y.: Dell, 1968 ed.),
      p.36, quoting U.S. Air Force Cam-
      bridge Rsch.Laboratories, Report
      63-434 (1963).

White Oak Mt.
-UFO (CE-3)
   1973, Oct.18/Bill Hines
      Danville Bee, 19 Oct.1973.

            D. Unspecified Localities

-Humanoid
   1972, June 29
      John Green, Sasquatch: The Apes Among
      Us (Seattle: Hancock House, 1978),
      p.225.

-UFO (NL)
   1952, July 13/W. Bruen/60 mi.SW of
   Washington
      Richard Hall, ed., The UFO Evidence
      (Washington: NICAP, 1964), pp.35,
      158.
      J. Allen Hynek, The Hynek UFO Report
      (N.Y.: Dell, 1977), pp.90-91.

TENNESSEE

A. Populated Places

Adams
-Poltergeist
  1817-1821/John Bell
    M.V. Ingram, An Authenticated History
    of the Famous Bell Witch (Clarks-
    ville, Tenn.: William P. Titus,
    1894).
    Harriet Parks Miller, The Bell Witch
    of Tennessee (Clarksville, Tenn.:
    Leaf-Chronicle, 1930).
    Charles Bailey Bell, The Bell Witch:
    A Mysterious Spirit (Nashville:
    Lark Bindery, 1934).
    Arthur Palmer Hudson & Pete Kyle
    McCarter, "The Bell Witch of Ten-
    nessee and Mississippi: A Folk Leg-
    end," J.Am.Folklore 47 (1934):45-63.
    Hereward Carrington & Nandor Fodor,
    Haunted People (N.Y.: Signet, 1968
    ed.), pp.121-46.
    Susy Smith, Prominent American Ghosts
    (N.Y.: Dell, 1969 ed.), pp.129-53.
    Jack Welsh, "The Bell Witch," Ken-
    tucky Folklore Record 19 (Oct.-Dec.
    1973):112-16.

Alcoa
-UFO (NL)
  1969, May 10/Ray L. Hupp/McGhee-Tyson
  airport
    "Another Metallic Cylinder," Skylook,
    no.21 (Aug.1969):17.

Allisona
-Magnetic ion motor (inventor)
  1959/Herman P. Anderson
    (Editorial), Fate 13 (May 1960):18-
    19.

Alto
-UFO (NL)
  1966, April 5
    Jacques Vallee, Passport to Magonia
    (Chicago: Regnery, 1969), p.328.

Anthony Hill
-UFO (CE-3)
  1973, Oct.1
    Pulaski Citizen, 3 Oct.1973.

Athens
-UFO (NL)
  1968, Nov.26/Larry Green
    George D. Fawcett, Quarter Century of
    Studies of UFOs in Florida, North
    Carolina and Tennessee (Mount Airy:
    Pioneer, 1975), p.49.

Bairds Mill
-Fall of flesh and blood
  1841, Aug.17/=hoax?
    "Shower of Red Matter Like Blood and
    Muscle," Am.J.Sci., ser.1, 41 (1841)
    :403-404.
    "Correction," Am.J.Sci., ser.1, 44
    (1842):216.
    Decatur (Ill.) Republican, 21 Mar.
    1876, p.2.

Bakerville
-UFO (DD)
  1977, June/Helen Fuller
    (Letter), Saga UFO Rept. 5 (Nov.1977)
    :6-8. il.

Bedford co.
-Ancient ax mark
  1812/Samuel Pearse/Garrison Fork
    John Haywood, Natural and Aboriginal
    History of Tennessee (Nashville:
    George Wilson, 1823), pp.181-82.

Berea
-UFO (CE-3)
  1973, Oct.15/Earl Fralix
    Pulaski Citizen, 24 Oct.1973.

Big Sandy
-UFO (NL)
  1977, Dec.6
    "UFOs of Limited Merit," Int'l UFO
    Reporter 3 (Jan.1978):9.

Blue Creek
-UFO (CE-2)
  1973, Jan./K.O. Wilkes
    Pulaski Citizen, 24 Oct.1973.

Braytown
-Human track in stone
  2 mi.S
    Thomas Dobson, American Encyclopedia
    (Philadelphia: Budd & Bartram, 1778-
    1803), Suppl., 3:344.
    Jedediah Morse, American Universal
    Geography, 3 vols. (Boston: J.T.
    Buckingham, 1805), 1:693-94.
    John Haywood, Natural and Aboriginal
    History of Tennessee (Nashville:
    George Wilson, 1823), pp.160-62.
    Josiah Priest, American Antiquities
    and Discoveries in the West (Albany:
    Hoffman & White, 1834), pp.151-52.

Brentwood
-Archeological site
  ca.1200-1700/Arnold Village
    Joseph Jones, "The Aboriginal Mound
    Builders of Tennessee," Am.Natural-
    ist 3 (1869):57.
    Robert Ferguson, "The Arnold Village
    Site Excavations of 1965-1966," in
    The Middle Cumberland Culture (Nash-
    ville: Vanderbilt Univ., Pubs. in
    Anthro., no.3, 1972), pp.1-49. il.

Briceville
-Crisis apparition
  1900, Nov.12/A.J. Howard
    "The Collective Experience of the
      Howards," J.ASPR 17 (1923):669-76.
    (Letter), Florence L. Bodge, J.ASPR
      18 (1924):193-94.
    (Letter), W.F. Prince, J.ASPR 18
      (1924):194-97.
-UFO (?)
  1958, Sep.22/radar station
    Oak Ridger, 23 Sep.1958.

Bristol
-UFO (?)
  1956, Nov.11
    Leonard H. Stringfield, Inside Sau-
      cer Post...3-0 Blue (Cincinnati:
      CRIFO, 1957), p.58.

Carthage
-Phantom panther
  1946, Nov.
    "More Critters," Doubt, no.18 (1947):
      273.

Charleston
-UFO (CE-1)
  1973, Oct./Annette Tinker
    Leonard H. Stringfield, Situation
      Red: The UFO Siege (N.Y.: Fawcett
      Crest, 1977 ed.), pp.128-29.

Chatata
-Ancient inscription
  1891/J.H. Hooper
    New York Sun, 7 June 1891.
    A.L. Rawson, "The Ancient Inscription
      on a Wall at Chatata, Tennessee,"
      Trans.N.Y.Acad.Sci. 11 (1891):26-29.
    A.L. Rawson, "The Ancient Inscription
      at Chatata, Tennessee," Am.Antiquar-
      ian 14 (1892):221-23.

Chattanooga
-Clairvoyance
  1970s/Kenneth Pennington
    Nat'l Enquirer, 15 Apr.1973.
    Jeffrey Goodman, Psychic Archaeology
      (N.Y.: Berkley, 1978), pp.176-77.
-Thermal anomaly
  1963, Sep.24/George Bozeman
    (Editorial), Fate 17 (May 1964):14-
      15.
-UFO (CE-2)
  1973, Oct.15/Loraine Evans
    Chattanooga News-Free Press, 17 Oct.
      1973.
  1973, Oct.17/Lester Shell/Charles A.
    Bell Elementary School
    "Tennessee Report," APRO Bull. 22
      (Jan.-Feb.1974):10.
    Leonard H. Stringfield, Situation
      Red: The UFO Siege (N.Y.: Fawcett
      Crest, 1977 ed.), pp.126-28.
-UFO (CE-3)
  1897, April 23/=hoax?
    St. Louis (Mo.) Post-Dispatch, 25
      Apr.1897, p.9.
-UFO (DD)

1910, Jan.12-14
  Chattanooga Daily Times, 13-15 Jan.
    1910; and 17 Jan.1910.
  New York Tribune, 13-15 Jan.1910.
1947, July 7/Walter Henderson
  Chattanooga Daily Times, 8 July 1947.
1966, July 27/Randy Vincent
  Otto Binder, What We Really Know
    About Flying Saucers (Greenwich, Ct.:
    Fawcett, 1967), p.44, quoting Saucer
    Scoop, Sep.1966.
-UFO (NL)
  1957, Nov.6
    Richard Hall, ed., The UFO Evidence
      (Washington: NICAP, 1964), p.166.
  1960, Dec.16
    "Odds and Ends," APRO Bull. 9 (Jan.
      1961):6.

Clarksville
-UFO (CE-3)
  1977, Jan.27
    Leonard H. Stringfield, "New Close
      Encounter Cases Under Investigation,"
      MUFON UFO J., no.110 (Jan.1977):16.
-UFO (DD)
  1977, May 15
    "UFOs of Limited Merit," Int'l UFO
      Reporter 2 (July 1977):3.
-UFO (NL)
  1897, April 15
    Columbus (O.) Evening Press, 17 Apr.
      1897.

Cleveland
-UFO (NL)
  1956, Aug.27/Geneva Branam
    (Letter), Fate 10 (Nov.1957):116-17.

Clifton
-Fire anomaly
  1969, July/W.J. Baker
    Sacramento (Cal.) Union, 28 July 1969.

Cocke co.
-UFO (CE-1)
  1973, Oct.25/Mrs. Billy Pat Cureton/
    Old Cave Church Rd.
    "Saucers in the News," Flying Saucers,
      winter 1974, pp.53-54.

Collierville
-UFO (NL)
  1973, Sep.30/Flanning Glover
    Memphis Press-Scimitar, 1 Oct.1973.

Columbia
-Ancient iron sword and bricks
    John Haywood, The Natural and Aborig-
      inal History of Tennessee (Nashville:
      George Wilson, 1823), p.189.
-Earthquake anomaly
  1812, Feb.7
    Samuel Latham Mitchill, "A Detailed
      Narrative of the Earthquakes," Trans.
      Lit.& Phil.Soc'y N.Y. 1 (1814):285,
      287.
    Myron L. Fuller, "The New Madrid
      Earthquake," Bull.U.S.Geol.Survey,
      no.494 (1912):45.

Cookeville
-Haunt
  1967/Herman Carr
    (Editorial), Fate 20 (Nov.1967):18-
    19, quoting Cookeville Putnam Coun-
    ty Herald (undated).
-UFO (CE-4)
  1977, Jan.27/Mr. Fender
    Clarksville Leaf-Chronicle, 2 Feb.
    1977.

Dante
-UFO (CE-3)
  1957, Nov.6/Everett Clark
    Knoxville News-Sentinel, 6 Nov.1957.

Dayton
-Genetic anomaly
  1978, Feb./John Sneed/=zebra-donkey
  hybrid
    Chattanooga Times, 23 Feb.1978.

Dixie Lee Junction
-UFO (CE-1)
  1957, May 7
    "Flying Saucer Roundup," Fate 11
    (Feb.1958):29,30, quoting Knoxville
    Journal (undated).

Donelson
-UFO (CE-2)
  1956, summer/Eugene Wright/2526 Hib-
  bits Dr.
    (Editorial), Fate 9 (Dec.1956):12.
-UFO (NL)
  1953, Nov./Paul Norman/Central Hill
  powerhouse
    George D. Fawcett, Quarter Century of
    Studies of UFOs in Florida, North
    Carolina and Tennessee (Mount Airy:
    Pioneer, 1975), p.46.

Dukedom
-Lightning anomaly
  1932, June/Tom Young
    H.M. Cantrell, "Cured by Lightning,"
    Fate 8 (Feb.1955):64-65.

Dyersburg
-Disappearance
  1910, Sep./building
    "Calling Tennessee," Doubt, no.38
    (1952):170, quoting Tit-Bits, 13
    Oct.1951.
-Fall of fish
  1952, May 12/Tom Fowlkes
    "Calling Tennessee," Doubt, no.38
    (1952):170.

Elkton
-Mystery vibrations
  1955-1960/Lester B. Cole/Elkton Rd.
    (Editorial), Fate 14 (May 1961):12-
    13, quoting Nashville Tennessean
    (undated).

Emert's Cove
-UFO (NL)
  1973, Oct.18/Dan Sanders/Proffitt's
  Trailer Park

"UFOs over Sevier County, Tennessee,"
    Flying Saucers, winter 1974, pp.33,
    36.

Estill Springs
-UFO (CE-1)
  1973, Oct.15/James Parks
    "Saucers in the News," Flying Sau-
    cers, winter 1974, pp.47-48.

Ethridge
-Fall of unknown substance
  1962, May/Rufus Nix/Rte.1
    (Editorial), Fate 15 (Sep.1962):19-
    20.

Eva
-Archeological site
  6000-1000 B.C.
    Thomas M.N. & Madeline Kneberg Lewis,
    Eva: An Archaic Site (Knoxville:
    Univ. of Tennessee, 1961). il.

Fayetteville
-Ancient silver buttons
  1819, spring/Oliver Williams
    John Haywood, Natural and Aboriginal
    History of Tennessee (Nashville:
    George Wilson, 1823), pp.180-81.
-Roman coins
  ca.1819/Elk R.
  1823/Mr. Colter
    John Haywood, Natural and Aboriginal
    History of Tennessee (Nashville:
    George Wilson, 1823), pp.173-79,
    xlv-li.
-UFO (CE-1)
  1976, April 26
    "Noteworthy UFO Sightings," Ufology
    2 (fall 1976):61.
-UFO (CE-2)
  1966, March 28
    Jacques Vallee, Passport to Magonia
    (Chicago: Regnery, 1969), p.325.
    George D. Fawcett, Quarter Century of
    Studies of UFOs in Florida, North
    Carolina and Tennessee (Mount Airy:
    Pioneer, 1975), p.47.

Flintville
-Humanoid
  1976, April 23/Jennie Robertson
    The Star, 18 May 1976.
    Nat'l Enquirer, 29 June 1976.

Franklin
-Archeological sites
  Big Harpeth R.
    Joseph Jones, "The Aboriginal Mound
    Builders of Tennessee," Am.Natural-
    ist 3 (1869):57-72.

Gallatin
-Disappearance
  1880, Sep.23/David Lang/=hoax
    Stuart Palmer, "How Lost Was My Fath-
    er?" Fate 6 (July 1953):75-85.
    George Wagner, "What Ever Happened to
    Davey Lang?" Probe the Unknown 4
    (Jan.1976):17-21.

"The Disappearance of David Lang,"
Fortean Times, no.18 (Oct.1976):6-7.
Robert Schadewald, "David Lang Van-
ishes...Forever," Fate 30 (Dec.1977)
:54-60.
(Letter), Curtis L. Gibson, Fate 31
(Aug.1978):120,129.

Giles co.
-Humanoid
1975, Oct.
Don Worley, "UFO Anthropoids in the
U.S.A.," Argosy UFO, July 1977.
-UFO (CE-2)
1973, Oct.31
Pulaski Citizen, 31 Oct.1973.

Graysville
-Mystery stone spheres
(Letter), J.S. Russell, Fate 5 (Sep.
1952):116-18.

Greeneville
-UFO (CE-1)
1973, Oct.16/8 mi.E
Johnson City Press-Chronicle, 17
Oct.1973, p.2.
-UFO (CE-2)
1964, July/H.F. Ramsey/13 mi.N
George D. Fawcett, Quarter Century of
Studies of UFOs in Florida, North
Carolina and Tennessee (Mount Airy:
Pioneer, 1975), p.47.
Wendelle C. Stevens, "UFO Calling
Card: Angel's Hair," Saga, Jan.1976,
pp.24,60, quoting Saucers, Space &
Sci. (undated).
-UFO (DD)
1966, March/Goldene Fillers Burgner/10
mi.S on Old Asheville Hwy.
George D. Fawcett, Quarter Century of
Studies of UFOs in Florida, North
Carolina and Tennessee (Mount Airy:
Pioneer, 1975), p.47.
-UFO (NL)
1969, Oct./Don Craft/nr. Viking Mt.
1970, March 11/Pajan Cox
1970, Oct./Gary Graham
George D. Fawcett, Quarter Century of
Studies of UFOs in Florida, North
Carolina and Tennessee (Mount Airy:
Pioneer, 1975), pp.50-51.

Hamburg
-Erratic kangaroo
1934, Jan.13/W.J. Hancock
New York Times, 17 Jan.1934.

Hardin co.
-Burning soil
1969, summer/E.E. Willis
"Burning Dirt," INFO J., no.5 (fall
1969):39.

Harriman
-UFO (?)
1954, June
Donald E. Keyhoe, Flying Saucer Conspiracy (N.Y.: Holt, 1955), p.164.

Hixson
-UFO (DD)
1947, July 7/Irving Johnson
Chattanooga Daily Times, 8 July 1947.

Hopson
-UFO (CE-3)
1978, July 19/Hank Knowll
(Letter), Saga UFO Rept. 6 (Jan.1979)
:8.

Howell
-Meteorite crater
2400 m.diam./possible
Kendall E. Born & Charles W. Wilson,
Jr., "The Howell Structure, Lincoln
County, Tennessee," J.Geology 47
(1939):371-88.

Humboldt
-UFO (NL)
1975, Oct.12
"UFO Central," CUFOS News Bull., 1
Feb.1976, p.8.

Jackson
-Humanoid
1957/James M. Meacham
Ivan T. Sanderson, Abominable Snow-
men: Legend Come to Life (Philadel-
phia: Chilton, 1961), pp.93-94.
-Precognition
1900, April 30/Mrs. Casey Jones
David Ragan, "Casey Jones Could Be
Alive Today," Fate 8 (July 1955):26-
32.
-UFO (NL)
1977, March 20/Gloria Dewhurst/Hwy.40
(Letter), Fate 30 (Sep.1977):129.

Jamestown
-UFO (CE-1)
1976, May 20
"Noteworthy UFO Sightings," Ufology
2 (fall 1976):61.

Johnson City
-UFO (CE-2)
1973/John Maddox
Ted Phillips, Physical Traces Associ-
ated with UFO Sightings (Evanston:
Center for UFO Studies, 1975), p.88.
-UFO (DD)
1973, Oct.17/Anita Byrd/W of town
Johnson City Press-Chronicle, 18 Oct.
1973.
-UFO (NL)
1966, Oct.7
George D. Fawcett, Quarter Century of
Studies of UFOs in Florida, North
Carolina and Tennessee (Mount Airy:
Pioneer, 1975), p.48.
1973, Oct.16/Harold Barnett
Johnson City Press-Chronicle, 16 Oct.
1973.
1973, Oct.17/Betty Berry/1415 Orleans
St.
Johnson City Press-Chronicle, 18 Oct.
1973.

Jonesboro
-UFO (CE-2)
  1966, Oct.12/Burnette S. Fox
    Johnson City Press-Chronicle, 13 Oct.
    1966.
    "FAA Investigates in Tennessee," UFO
    Inv. 3 (Oct.-Nov.1966):5-6.
-UFO (NL)
  1966, Oct.11/Maxie J. Fox
    "FAA Investigates in Tennessee," UFO
    Inv. 3 (Oct.-Nov.1966):5.

Kingsport
-UFO (?)
  1945/Charles Hamlet
    Jacques Vallee, Anatomy of a Phenom-
    enon (N.Y.: Ace, 1965 ed.), p.51.
-UFO (NL)
  1976, Jan.2
    "Noteworthy UFO Sightings," Ufology
    2 (summer 1976):63.

Knoxville
-Animal ESP
  1930-1943/Herbert Neff
    Eldon Roark, Just a Mutt (N.Y.:
    McGraw-Hill, 1947), pp.18-22.
-Ball lightning
  1957, July 27
    Leonard H. Stringfield, Inside Sau-
    cer Post...3-0 Blue (Cincinnati:
    CRIFO, 1957), p.54.
-Clairvoyance
  1976-1977/Bernadine Villanueva/=fraud?
    Jane Bandy, "Bernadine Villanueva:
    Misunderstood Mystic or Clever Con
    Artist?" Fate 31 (Nov.1978):43-49;
    (Dec.1978):54-58.
-Earthquake anomaly
  1811, Dec.16
    Samuel Latham Mitchill, "A Detailed
    Narrative of the Earthquakes," Trans.
    Lit.& Phil.Soc'y N.Y. 1 (1814):285,
    287.
-Fall of frogs
  1958, Sep.20/H.R. Reedy/Emory Rd.
    Knoxville News-Sentinel, 26 Sep.1958.
-Humanoid
  1959, Sep.23/Earl Taylor/Clapps Chapel
  Rd.
    Knoxville Journal, 24 Sep.1959.
-Precognition
  n.d./Martha Miller
    "Death As Denied," Fate 8 (Nov.1955)
    :39.
-UFO (?)
  1954, June
    Donald E. Keyhoe, Flying Saucer Con-
    spiracy (N.Y.: Holt, 1955), p.93.
  1956, Nov.16/Jim McAshan III
    "Case 253," CRIFO Orbit, 4 Jan.1957,
    p.1.
-UFO (CE-2)
  1957, Jan.21/Addis Williams
    "Case 296," CRIFO Orbit, 1 Mar.1957,
    p.3, quoting Knoxville Journal (un-
    dated).
  1957, Jan.25/Sharp's Ridge
    Leonard H. Stringfield, Inside Sau-
    cer Post...3-0 Blue (Cincinnati:

    CRIFO, 1957), p.93.
-UFO (DD)
  1947, June 30/Park City
    Knoxville Journal, 7 July 1947.
  1957, June 13/Jack L. Fincannon/River
  Breeze Drive-In
    (Letter), Fate 10 (Nov.1957):114-15.
-UFO (NL)
  1910, Jan.15
    Chattanooga Daily Times, 15 Jan.1910.
  1947, June 30/C.E. Brehm/1721 White
  Ave.
    Knoxville Journal, 8 July 1947.
  1963, Nov.30
    "News Briefs," Saucer News 11 (Mar.
    1964):24.
  1966, Nov.3/Fred Fields
    "Professor Views UAO in Tennessee,"
    APRO Bull. 15 (Jan.-Feb.1967):5.
  1968, Jan.27
    "New Close-Ups, Pacings," UFO Inv. 4
    (Mar.1968):1,3.
  1968, Sep.10-11
    George D. Fawcett, Quarter Century of
    Studies of UFOs in Florida, North
    Carolina and Tennessee (Mount Airy:
    Pioneer, 1975), p.49.
  1973, Oct.15/Mrs. Charles Seymour/Crest-
  wood Hills
    "Saucers in the News," Flying Saucers,
    winter 1974, pp.44,47.

Lake City
-UFO (NL)
  1958, Sep.22/Hazel Bunch/Rte.2
    "The Night of September 29," Fate 12
    (Feb.1959):31,35.

Lascassas
-Humanoid
  1965, Aug./Roy Hudson/Brown's Mill Rd.
    Nashville Tennessean, 24 Aug.1965.

Lebanon
-UFO (NL)
  1973, Sep.14/5 mi.W on U.S.66
    Springfield (Mo.) Leader & Press, 14
    Sep.1973.
  1973, Oct.15/Mrs. Fred Singleton
    "Saucers in the News," Flying Saucers,
    winter 1974, pp.44,47.

Lewisburg
-Cattle mutilation
  1975
    Don Worley, "Cattle Mutilations and
    UFOs: Who Are the Mutilators?" Offi-
    cial UFO 1 (Dec.1976):24-27,48. il.

McMinnville
-UFO (CE-1)
  1957, Nov.20
    Richard Hall, ed., The UFO Evidence
    (Washington: NICAP, 1964), p.167.

Macon co.
-Hex
    Lewis David Bandy, "Witchcraft and
    Divination in Macon County," Bull.
    Tennessee Folklore Soc'y 9, no.2

(1943):1-13.

Manchester
-Archeological site
    ca.30-400 A.D./Old Stone Fort
        John Haywood, Natural and Aboriginal
        History of Tennessee (Nashville:
        George Wilson, 1823), pp.169-72.
        Charles H. Faulkner, The Old Stone
        Fort (Knoxville: Univ. of Tennessee,
        1968). il.
        Charles H. Faulkner, "The Age and
        Probable Purpose of the Old Stone
        Fort, Manchester, Tenn.," NEARA
        Newsl. 3 (Sep.1968):56-59.
        Clyde Keeler, "A 'Bog Iron Furnace'
        That Isn't!" NEARA Newsl. 8 (fall
        1973):53-55. il.

Martin
-UFO (CE-2)
    1960, July 22/Shirley Sisk
        George D. Fawcett, Quarter Century of
        Studies of UFOs in Florida, North
        Carolina and Tennessee (Mount Airy:
        Pioneer, 1975), pp.46-47.
        Ted Phillips, Physical Traces Associ-
        ated with UFO Sightings (Evanston:
        Center for UFO Studies, 1975), p.24.

Memphis
-Archeological site
    900-1600 A.D./Chucalissa Indian Town
        Charles H. Nash & Rodney Gates, Jr.,
        "Chucalissa Indian Town," Tennessee
        Hist.Quar. 21 (1962):103-21. il.
-Clairaudience
    ca.1900/Glenn C. Gunn
        Glenn C. Gunn, "Notified in Advance
        by the Sound of Music," Fate 24
        (Apr.1971):105.
-Clairvoyance and precognition
    1969-   /David N. Bubar/Spiritual Out-
    reach Society/2151 Young Ave.
        Rene Noorbergen, You Are Psychic
        (N.Y.: William Morrow, 1971).
        David Wallechinsky & Irving Wallace,
        The People's Almanac (Garden City:
        Doubleday, 1975), pp.1-2.
-Disappearance
    1873, April 17/"Mississippi Queen"
        "The Steamboat That Vanished," Fate
        10 (Apr.1959):64.
        (Letter), A.B. Pierson, Fate 12 (Oct.
        1959):111-14.
        Frank Edwards, Strangest of All (N.Y.:
        Ace, 1962), pp.68-69.
        (Letter), M.I. Hensley, Fate 16 (July
        1963):120.
-Doubtful responsibility
    1968, April 4/James Earl Ray/King ass-
    assination/=conspiracy?
        Harold Weisberg, Frame-Up (N.Y.: Out-
        erbridge & Dienstfrey, 1971).
        William B. Huie, Did the FBI Kill
        Martin Luther King? (Nashville:
        Nelson, 1977).
        Mark Lane & Dick Gregory, Code Name
        "Zorro" (Englewood Cliffs, N.J.:
        Prentice-Hall, 1977).

Jacob Cohen, Conspiracy Fever (N.Y.:
        Macmillan, 1978).
        U.S. Congress, House, Select Comm.
        on Assassinations, Investigation of
        the Assassination of Martin Luther
        King, Jr., 12 vols. Hearings, 95th
        Cong., 2d sess., 1978.
-Fall of fish
    1952, May 12/Louise Durham
        Coral E. Lorenzen, The Shadow of the
        Unknown (N.Y.: Signet, 1970), p.133.
-Fall of frogs
    ca.1949/C.J. Denkman
        "Frog-Falls, Etc.," Doubt, no.27
        (1949):411.
-Fall of ice
    1975, March 12
        Columbus (O.) Dispatch, 13 Mar.1975,
        p.A4.
-Fall of snakes
    1877, Jan.15/Vance St.
        (Editorial), Monthly Weather Rev. 1
        (Jan.1877):8.
        "A Snake Rain," Sci.Am. 36 (1877):86.
-Ghost
    1963/Earl Johnson
        (Editorial), Fate 16 (June 1963):12-
        13.
-Midday darkness
    1904, Dec.2
        "Darkness at Memphis," Monthly Weath-
        er Rev. 32 (Nov.1904):522.
-Mystery plane crash
    1966, Sep.1/F-89 jet
        Ronald Drucker, "The Southern U.S.--
        Target for Flying Saucers," Saga
        UFO Rept. 2 (fall 1975):15,17.
-Pyrokinesis
    1927, July
        New York Sun, 9 July 1927.
-Spirit medium
    1850s/Mrs. Winchester
        Emma Hardinge Britten, Modern Ameri-
        can Spiritualism (N.Y.: The Author,
        1870), p 413.
-UFO (?)
    1968, March 17/John Ray/=balloon?
        Memphis Commercial Appeal, 18 Mar.
        1968.
        "Another Hoax?" Skylook, no.8 (Apr.
        1968):6.
    1973, Sep.
        Memphis Commercial Appeal, 5 Oct.1973.
-UFO (CE-1)
    1969, May 31/Jimmy Baird/Forest Hill
    Rd.
        Memphis Commercial Appeal, 1 June
        1969.
-UFO (DD)
    1947, July 6/J.A. Conrow/3541 Watauga
    St.
        Memphis Commercial Appeal, 7 July
        1947.
-UFO (NL)
    1968, Sep.27/Carrie Wimberly/Lausanne
    School
        George D. Fawcett, Quarter Century of
        Studies of UFOs in Florida, North
        Carolina and Tennessee (Mount Airy:
        Pioneer, 1975), p.49.

1973, Oct.1/Joyce Alexander
  Memphis Commercial Appeal, 2 Oct.
  1973.
1973, Oct.2
  Memphis Commercial Appeal, 5 Oct.
  1973.
-Weeping deer head
  ca.1958/Herschel Selph/Whitehaven
  (Editorial), Fate 11 (Dec.1958):13-
  14.

Milan
-Flying humanoid
  1887, July 16
    Milan Exchange, 23 July 1887.
    Beulah M. D'Olive Price, "Angels
    over Milan, Tennessee: A Legend?"
    Mississippi Folklore Register 5
    (1971):122-23.

Millington
-UFO (NL)
  1973, Sep.30/R.L. Beam
    Memphis Press-Scimitar, 1 Oct.1973.

Morgan co.
-Clairvoyance
  1878, spring/A.S. Wiltse
    Mrs. Henry Sidgwick, "On the Evidence
    for Clairvoyance," Proc.SPR 7
    (1891-92):30,72-81.
    F.W.H. Myers, Human Personality and
    Its Survival of Bodily Death, 2
    vols. (London: Longmans, Green,
    1903), 1:668-69.

Mosheim
-UFO (CE-1)
  1971, Oct.
    George D. Fawcett, "UFOs Show Dram-
    atic Worldwide Increase," Fate 25
    (June 1972):59.
-UFO (DD)
  1970, June/Karen Sapp
    George D. Fawcett, Quarter Century of
    Studies of UFOs in Florida, North
    Carolina and Tennessee (Mount Airy:
    Pioneer, 1975), p.51.
-UFO (NL)
  1970, Feb./Patricia Long/Hwy.2
    George D. Fawcett, Quarter Century of
    Studies of UFOs in Florida, North
    Carolina and Tennessee (Mount Airy:
    Pioneer, 1975), p.50.

Mount Pleasant
-UFO (NL)
  1976, Sep.
    Nashville Banner, 30 Dec.1976.

Murfreesboro
-Ball lightning
  1880, July/Chattanooga Railroad
    Nashville American, 15 July 1880.
-Roman coin
  1823/2½ mi.E
    John Haywood, Natural and Aboriginal
    History of Tennessee (Nashville:
    George Wilson, 1823), pp.182-84.

Nashville
-Ancient inscription
  1890s
    James P. Whittall II, "An Inscribed
    Libyan Token from a Necropolis in
    Tennessee," Bull.Early Sites Rsch.
    Soc'y 6 (1978):37-38.
-Animal ESP
  1951-1958, Nov./Harold King
    "Mac Goes Home," Fate 5 (Nov.1952):
    80.
    (Editorial), Fate 13 (Jan.1960):17-
    18.
-Archeological sites
    Joseph Jones, "The Aboriginal Mound
    Builders of Tennessee," Am.Natural-
    ist 3 (1869):57-72.
    R.S. Robertson, "Antiquities of Nash-
    ville, Tenn.," Ann.Rept.Smith.Inst.
    27 (1877):276-78.
    F.W. Putnam, "Archaeological Explor-
    ations in Tennessee," Ann.Rept.Pea-
    body Museum, no.10 (1878):305-60.
    Joseph Jones, "Explorations of the
    Aboriginal Remains of Tennessee,"
    Smith.Contrib.Knowl., vol.22 (1880).
    Gates P. Thruston, The Antiquities
    of Tennessee (Cincinnati: Robert
    Clarke, 1890).
    Jesse D. Jennings, "Hopewell-Copena
    Sites near Nashville," Am.Antiquity
    12 (1946):126. il.
-Clairvoyance
  1963/Buryl Townsend
    (Editorial), Fate 16 (Dec.1963):18.
-Fall of giant snowflakes
  1891, Jan.24
    "Snow," Monthly Weather Rev. 19 (Jan.
    1891):11.
-Poltergeist
  1962, Oct./John Hawkins/1627 9th Ave.
    (Editorial), Fate 16 (Feb.1963):14-
    15, quoting Nashville Tennessean
    (undated).
    Raymond Bayless, The Enigma of the
    Poltergeist (N.Y.: Ace, 1967 ed.),
    pp.77-78.
-Precognition
  1959/Spencer Thornton
    Jess Stearn, The Door to the Future
    (N.Y.: Macfadden, 1964), pp.95-101.
-Spirit medium
  1850s/Mrs. Jesse Babcock Ferguson
    Jesse Babcock Ferguson, Spirit Com-
    munion (Nashville: Union & American,
    1854).
    T.L. Nichols, Supramundane Facts in
    the Life of Rev. Jesse Babcock Fer-
    guson (London: F. Pitman, 1865).
    Emma Hardinge Britten, Modern Ameri-
    can Spiritualism (N.Y.: The Author,
    1870), pp.411-13.
-Spontaneous human combustion
  1835, Jan.5/James Hamilton/nr. Univ. of
  Nashville
    "Case of Spontaneous Combustion,"
    Transylvania J.Med. 8 (1835):445-48,
    quoting John Overton, Trans.Med.
    Soc'y Tennessee, 1835.
-UFO (?)

1956, Nov.16/J.A. Gheen/=meteor
"Case 253," CRIFO Orbit, 4 Jan.1957,
p.1, quoting Knoxville Journal
(undated).
1961, May 27/=balloon
Richard Hall, ed., The UFO Evidence
(Washington: NICAP, 1964), p.95.
George D. Fawcett, Quarter Century of
Studies of UFOs in Florida, North
Carolina and Tennessee (Mount Airy:
Pioneer, 1975), p.47.
-UFO (NL)
1979, Jan.4/Mike Smith
Little Rock Arkansas Gazette, 5 Jan.
1979.

Oak Ridge
-Precognition
1900s/John Hendrix/nr. Pine Ridge
Richard B. Gehman, "The Amazing
Prophet of Oak Ridge," Fate 1 (fall
1948):114-20. il.
-UFO (?)
1947, July/Mr. Presley/=flaw in nega-
tive?
Bruce S. Maccabee, "UFO Related In-
formation from the FBI Files: Part
III," APRO Bull. 26 (Jan.1978):7.
-UFO (DD)
1940, June
Coral & Jim Lorenzen, UFOs: The Whole
Story (N.Y.: Signet, 1969), p.21.
1950, Dec.18/AEC Laboratory
Bruce S. Maccabee, "UFO Related In-
formation from the FBI Files: Part
7," MUFON UFO J., no.132 (Nov.-Dec.
1978):11,15.
-UFO (NL)
1973, July-Aug./Mrs. James R. Guyton,
Jr.
Knoxville News-Sentinel, 5 Aug.1973.
1973, Nov.-Dec./C.R. Clough
C.R. Clough & Howard Whetsel, "NICAP
Uncovers Photos from 1973 Wave,"
UFO Inv., June 1975, pp.1-3. il.
Kevin D. Randle, "Where Are the UFO
Movies?" Saga UFO Rept. 3 (Dec.
1976):24,52-54.
-UFO (R)
1950, Oct.12
1950, Dec.
Bruce S. Maccabee, "UFO Related In-
formation from the FBI Files: Part
7," MUFON UFO J., no.132 (Nov.-Dec.
1978):11,14-15.
-UFO (R-V)
1952, June 21/AEC Laboratory
Edward J. Ruppelt, The Report on Un-
identified Flying Objects (Garden
City: Doubleday, 1956), p.43.
Donald H. Menzel & Lyle G. Boyd, The
World of Flying Saucers (Garden
City: Doubleday, 1963), p.76.

Oliver Springs
-UFO (CE-1)
1944, Sep./Mr. Nelson/2 mi.SE
Coral & Jim Lorenzen, UFOs: The Whole
Story (N.Y.: Signet, 1969), pp.23-
24.

Ooltewah
-Lightning anomaly
1887/Mrs. Osborne
Henry Winfred Splitter, "Nature's
Strange Photographs," Fate 8 (Jan.
1955):21,29-30.

Petersburg
-Fall of anomalous meteorite
1855, Aug.5
J. Lawrence Smith, "Description of
Three New Meteorites," Am.J.Sci.,
ser.2, 31 (1861):264-65.

Pigeon Forge
-UFO (CE-2)
1973, Oct.17-18/Patricia Ramsey/Pine
Mountain Rd.
"UFOs over Sevier County, Tennessee,"
Flying Saucers, winter 1974, pp.
33,35.
-UFO (NL)
1973, Oct.19/Van McCarter
1973, Oct.20/R.L. Chance
"UFOs over Sevier County, Tennessee,"
Flying Saucers, winter 1974, pp.
33,36-37.

Pinson
-Archeological site
550-850 A.D.
John B. Nuckolls, "The Pinson Mounds,"
Tennessee Arch. 14 (1958):1-8. il.
Fred W. Fischer & C.H. McNutt, "Test
Excavations at Pinson Mounds, 1961,"
Tennessee Arch. 18 (1962):1-13. il.

Pittman Center
-Fall of unknown object
1957, Oct.6/Melvin D. Carr/Turkey Pen
Branch
(Editorial), Fate 11 (Feb.1958):16.

Pleasantville
-Weather-forecasting rock
1910- /Olin Murray
"Limestone Weather Prophet," Fate 5
(July-Aug.1952):72.

Red Bank
-UFO (NL)
1957, Nov.5
Richard Hall, ed., The UFO Evidence
(Washington: NICAP, 1964), p.165.

Richwood
-Precognition
n.d./James Kirby
"They Dreamed of Disaster," Fate 9
(Aug.1956):46.

Ripley
-Fall of ice
1978, April 23/Ashport School
Chattanooga News-Free Press, 25 Apr.
1978.
-UFO (NL)
1973, Sep./City Hall
Memphis Commercial Appeal, 5 Oct.1973.

Roane
-UFO (NL)
  1957, Oct.8/James Myers
    George D. Fawcett, Quarter Century of
    Studies of UFOs in Florida, North
    Carolina and Tennessee (Mount Airy:
    Pioneer, 1975), p.46.

Rockbridge
-Erratic monkey
  1969, May/Mable Rippy
    "Do You Believe Wild Monkeys in
    Tennessee?" Fate 23 (Jan.1970):84.

Saint Elmo
-UFO (CE-1)
  1973, Oct.17/Oscar Eaves
    Leonard H. Stringfield, Situation
    Red: The UFO Siege (N.Y.: Fawcett
    Crest, 1977 ed.), p.128.

Sevier co.
-Fall of carbonaceous meteorite
  1840
    Walter Flight, "Meteorites and the
    Origin of Life," Eclectic Mag., n.s.,
    26 (Dec.1877):711-18.

Sevierville
-UFO (NL)
  1973, Sep./Mrs. Ray Reagan
  1973, Oct.16/Steve Whaley/Allensville
  Rd.
  1973, Oct.16/Harry Montgomery/Sevier
  County High School
  1973, Oct.18/Nadine Oakley/Love Addition
  1973, Oct.19/Robbie Rainwater/Pittman
  Center Rd.
  1973, Oct.19/Nancy Mannis/Glades Rd.
    "UFOs over Sevier County, Tennessee,"
    Flying Saucers, winter 1974, pp.33-
    37.

Shelby co.
-UFO (CE-1)
  1973, Sep.23/T.L. Pilalas/Hwy.70
    Memphis Commercial Appeal, 24 Sep.
    1973.
    Memphis Press Scimitar, 24 Sep.1973.

Shiloh
-Archeological site
  ca.1300-1700
    J. Parish Stelle, "Account of Aborig-
    inal Ruins at Savannah, Tennessee,"
    Ann.Rept.Smith.Inst., 1870, pp.408-
    15. il.
    Clarence B. Moore, "Aboriginal Sites
    on the Tennessee River," J.Acad.Nat.
    Sci.Philadelphia 16 (1916):169,
    224-27. il.
    Frank Harold Hanna Roberts, Jr., "In-
    dian Mounds on Shiloh Battlefield,"
    Smith.Inst.Explorations & Field-
    work, 1934, pp.56-68. il.
    Thomas M.N. Lewis & Madeline Kneburg,
    Tribes That Slumber (Knoxville:
    Univ. of Tennessee, 1958), pp.78-79.

Shores
-UFO (CE-2)
  1973, Sep.30/David Swanner
    Pulaski Citizen, 10 Oct.1973.
    Lawrenceburg Democrat-Union, 18 Oct.
    1973.
    David Webb, 1973: Year of the Human-
    oids (Evanston: Center for UFO
    Studies, 1976 ed.), p.18.
-UFO (CE-3)
  1974, Jan.17/David Swanner
  1974, Feb.4/David Swanner
    Ted Bloecher, "A Catalog of Humanoid
    Reports for 1974," in MUFON 1975
    UFO Symposium Proc. (Seguin, Tex.:
    MUFON, 1975), pp.51,54.
-UFO (CE-4)
  1974, Feb.9/David Swanner
    Ted Bloecher, "A Catalog of Humanoid
    Reports for 1974," in MUFON 1975
    UFO Symposium Proc. (Seguin, Tex.:
    MUFON, 1975), pp.51,54.

Shouns
-UFO (?)
  1947, Sep.6
    Bruce S. Maccabee, "UFO Related In-
    formation from the FBI Files: Part
    3," MUFON UFO J., no.121 (Dec.1977)
    :10,14.

Smyrna
-UFO (?)
  1948, March 7
    J. Allen Hynek, The Hynek UFO Report
    (N.Y.: Dell, 1977), p.16.

South Pittsburgh
-UFO (CE-1)
  1973, Oct./Carolyn Terrell
    Leonard H. Stringfield, Situation
    Red: The UFO Siege (N.Y.: Fawcett
    Crest, 1977 ed.), p.128.

Sparta
-Archeological site
    John Haywood, Natural and Aboriginal
    History of Tennessee (Nashville:
    George Wilson, 1823), pp.153,193-94,
    196-209.
    Charles W. Webber, Romance of Natural
    History (Philadelphia: Lippincott,
    1852).
    William A. Seaver, "Giants and
    Dwarfs," Harper's Monthly Mag. 39
    (July 1869):202,208.
    Joseph Jones, "The Aboriginal Mound
    Builders of Tennessee," Am.Natural-
    ist 3 (1869):57-72.
    Joseph Jones, "Explorations of the
    Aboriginal Remains of Tennessee,"
    Smith.Contrib.Knowl. 22 (1880):2-13.

Springfield
-UFO (NL)
  1897, April
    Louisville (Ky.) Courier-Journal, 15
    Apr.1897, p.5.

Stewart co.
-Erratic crocodilian
1877/William Todd/Tennessee R.
   New York Times, 29 July 1877, p.8,
   quoting Evensville Courier (undated).

Sycamore
-Archeological site
   Joseph Jones, "The Aboriginal Mound
   Builders of Tennessee," Am.Natural-
   ist 3 (1869):57.

Tennessee Ridge
-UFO (NL)
1971, Sep.8-10/Dewey Carroll
   (Letter), Fate 25 (Sep.1972):146,159.

Tullahoma
-Healing
1921, July 13/George Evans
   Elma Mayes, "Cured by a Magical Mad-
   stone," Fate 23 (Nov.1970):45-49.

Tusculum
-UFO (CE-1)
1971, Oct.
   George D. Fawcett, "UFOs Show Dram-
   atic Worldwide Increase," Fate 25
   (June 1972):59.

Union City
-UFO (?)
1973, Oct./=balloon
   Memphis Commercial Appeal, 5 Oct.1973.

Victoria
-UFO (CE-2)
1967, Jan.20/4 mi. from town
   "Saucer Briefs," Saucer News 14 (summer 1967):27, quoting unidentified
   paper, 21 Jan.1967.

Watauga
-UFO (CE-3)
1973, Oct.17/Linda Greene
   Johnson City Press-Chronicle, 18 Oct.
   1973.

White Oak Flat
-Fall of plastic film
1961, Nov.25/R.A. Finney/=balloon?
   (Editorial), Fate 15 (May 1962):20-
   21.

                B. Physical Features

Bat Creek
-Ancient inscription
1885
   Cyrus Thomas, "Report on the Mound
   Explorations of the Bureau of Eth-
   nology," Ann.Rept.Bur.Am.Ethn. 12
   (1890-91):1,391-94. il.
   Henriette Mertz, The Wine Dark Sea
   (Chicago: The Author, 1964), p.130.
   Cyrus H. Gordon, Before Columbus
   (N.Y.: Crown, 1971), pp.179-87. il.
   Joseph B. Mahan, Jr., "The Bat Creek
   Stone," Tennessee Arch. 27 (1971):

38-45.
   Robert R. Stieglitz, "An Ancient Ju-
   dean Inscription from Tennessee,"
   Occ.Pub.Epigraphic Soc'y, vol.3, no.
   65 (Sep.1976).

Bledsoe Creek
-Ancient inscription
1874
   G.P. Thruston, The Antiquities of
   Tennessee (Cincinnati: Robert Clarke,
   1890), p.91.
   W.H. Holmes, "The Thruston Tablet,"
   Am.Anthro. 4 (1891):161-65.
   Malcolm Parker, "A Study of the Rocky
   Creek Pictograph," Tennessee Arch.
   5 (1949):13-17. il.
   "Counterfeiting of Indian Artifacts,"
   Tennessee Arch. 5 (1949):33-34. il.
   Ruth Verrill & Clyde E. Keeler, "A
   Viking Saga in Tennessee?" Bull.
   Georgia Acad.Sci. 19 (1961):78-82.
   il.
   Clyde E. Keeler & Ruth Verrill, "The
   Viking Boat Finale," Bull.Georgia
   Acad.Sci. 19 (1962):29-37. il.
   Clyde Keeler, "Viking Saga in Tennes-
   see," Fate 26 (Sep.1973):36-42. il.
   (Letter), Fate 26 (Dec.1973):145-46.
   Frederick J. Pohl, The Viking Settle-
   ments of North America (N.Y.: Clark-
   son N. Potter, 1974), pp.318-24. il.

Chickamauga L.
-Archeological site
   LeCroy site
   Le Baron Pahmeyer, "A Lake Chicka-
   mauga Burial," Tennessee Arch. 9
   (1953):9-10. il.
   Thomas M.N. Lewis & Madeline Kneberg,
   "The Paleo-Indian Complex on the
   LeCroy Site," Tennessee Arch. 12
   (1956):5-11. il.

Clinch Mt.
-UFO (?)
1958, Sep.29/George Emory/Shipe Addi-
   tion Rd.
   "The Night of September 29," Fate 12
   (Feb.1959):31,35.

Cross Mt.
-UFO (CE-3)
1974, Nov.11/Billy Joe Lodnar
   Ronald Drucker, "The Southern U.S.--
   Target for Flying Saucers," Saga UFO
   Rept. 2 (fall 1975):15-16.

Duck R.
-Ancient sculpture
1896, April 28/Billy Hensley
   Carl S. Compton, "Duck River and Sim-
   ilar Artifacts," Tennessee Arch. 14
   (1958):54-59. il.
   "Sculptured Images in State Memorial
   Museum," Tennessee Arch. 16 (1960):
   40. il.
-Archeological site
1200-1400
   E.G. Squier & E.H. Davis, Ancient

Monuments of the Mississippi Valley
(Washington: Smithsonian Institution,
Contrib.to Knowl., no.1, 1848), pp.
31-32.

Dycus Structure
-Meteorite crater
　43 m.deep/possible
　　R.M. Mitchum, Jr., The Dycus Disturb-
　　ance, Jackson County, Tennessee
　　(Master's thesis, Vanderbilt Univ.,
　　1951).

Flynn Creek
-Meteorite crater
　3600 m.diam./certain
　　C.W. Wilson, Jr. & K.E. Born, "The
　　Flynn Creek Disturbance, Jackson
　　County, Tennessee," J.Geology 44
　　(1936):815-36. il.
　　David J. Roddy, "Geologic Section
　　Across the Flynn Creek Structure,"
　　Ann.Rept.Astrogeologic Studies, Aug.
　　25,1962 to July 1,1963, Part B:
　　Crater Investigations, May 1964,
　　pp.53-73.
　　David J. Roddy, "Tabular Comparisons
　　of the Flynn Creek Impact Crater,
　　United States, Steinheim Impact Cra-
　　ter, Germany and Snowball Explosion
　　Crater, Canada," in D.J. Roddy, et
　　al., eds., Impact and Explosion Cra-
　　tering (N.Y.: Pergamon, 1977), pp.
　　125-62.
　　David J. Roddy, "Pre-Impact Condi-
　　tions and Cratering Processes at the
　　Flynn Creek Crater, Tennessee," in
　　D.J. Roddy, et al., eds., Impact
　　and Explosion Cratering (N.Y.: Per-
　　gamon, 1977), pp.277-308.

Great Smoky Mts.
-Disappearance
　1969, summer/Dennis Martin
　　John A. Keel, Our Haunted Planet
　　(Greenwich, Ct.: Fawcett, 1971),
　　p.203.
-Mystery plane crashes
　1928-
　　The Star, 14 Feb.1978.

Hiwassee I.
-Ancient inscription
　　"Unusual Stone Gorget," Tennessee
　　Arch. 18 (1962):58. il.
　　Barry Fell, "Ancient Iberian Magnetic
　　Compass Dials from Liria, Spain,"
　　Occ.Pub.Epigraphic Soc'y 3, no.57
　　(Sep.1976):4. il.
　　Gloria Farley, "The Tennessee Disk,"
　　Occ.Pub.Epigraphic Soc'y 5, no.101
　　(Sep.1977):23-24.
　　James E. Kelley, Jr., "The Tennessee
　　Disk," Occ.Pub.Epigraphic Soc'y 5,
　　no.101 (Sep.1977):25-30. il.
　　Rollin W. Gillespie, "Analysis of
　　Markings on the Tennessee Disk,"
　　Occ.Pub.Epigraphic Soc'y 5, no.101
　　(Sep.1977):32-35.
-Archeological site

ca.1100-1300
　　Clarence B. Moore, "Aboriginal Sites
　　on the Tennessee River," J.Acad.Nat.
　　Sci.Philadelphia 16 (1916):169,394-
　　96. il.
　　Thomas M.N. Lewis & Madeline Kneberg,
　　Hiwassee Island (Knoxville: Univ.
　　of Tennessee, 1946). il.
　　J.P. Brown, "'Hiwassee Island,' an
　　Appreciation," Tennessee Arch. 2
　　(1946):81-84.

Holston Mt.
-UFO (DD)
　1956, Nov.11
　　Arthur Constance, The Inexplicable
　　Sky (N.Y.: Citadel, 1956), p.286,
　　quoting UP release, 11 Nov.1956.
-UFO (NL)
　1959, Jan.9/Ed Allen/U.S.421, E of
　South Holston L.
　　Phil Calhoun, "Guided by the Lord's
　　Beacon?" Fate 12 (May 1959):25-29.

Icehouse Bottom
-Archeological site
　7500 B.C.-1300 A.D.
　　New York Long Island Press, 5 Mar.
　　1976.
　　New York Times, 3 Jan.1977.

Island 35
-Archeological site
　　Stephen Williams, "The Island 35 Mas-
　　todon: Its Bearing on the Age of
　　Archaic Cultures in the East," Am.
　　Antiquity 22 (1957):359-71. il.

Little Spring Creek
-UFO (CE-3)
　1952, June
　　W.A. Darbro & Stanley L. Ingram, Un-
　　identified Flying Objects over the
　　Tennessee Valley (Huntsville, Ala.:
　　South, 1974), p.65.

Lookout Mt.
-Archeological site
　　Horace F. Silliman, "Madoc and the
　　Pre-Columbian Stone Forts in South-
　　ern Illinois: A Possible Connection,"
　　NEARA Newsl. 6 (June 1971):33.

Manscoe's Creek
-Ancient iron furnace
　1794/Mr. Caffrey
　　John Haywood, Natural and Aboriginal
　　History of Tennessee (Nashville:
　　George Wilson, 1823), p.181.
　　"New Findings of Pre-Columbian Con-
　　tacts with North America," NEARA
　　Newsl. 9 (spring 1974):9.

Monteagle Mt.
-Humanoid
　1968, spring/Brenda Ann Adkins
　　Eric Norman [Brad Steiger], The Abom-
　　inable Snowmen (N.Y.: Award, 1969),
　　pp.139-40, quoting Saga, July 1969.

Norris Dam State Park
-Acoustic anomaly
   n.d.
      "On Bells," Pursuit 4 (Oct.1971):80.

Sharp's Ridge
-UFO (DD)
   1947, July 5/Bill Anderson
      Knoxville Journal, 8 July 1947.

Snow Creek
-Phantom horse
   1968-1970/Leo Miller
      Leo Miller, "The Ghost of Crazy Horse
      Hollow," Fate 31 (June 1978):87-92.

Tennessee R.
-Archeological sites
      Clarence B. Moore, "Aboriginal Sites
      on the Tennessee River," J.Acad.Nat.
      Philadelphia 16 (1916):169-428. il.

Webb Mt.
-UFO (NL)
   1973, Oct.16/Bernard Quinn/Pine Top
   Lodge
      "UFOs over Sevier County, Tennessee,"
      Flying Saucers, winter 1974, p.34.

Wells Creek
-Meteorite crater
   14,000 m.diam./certain
      Charles W. Wilson, Jr., "Wilcox De-
      posits in Explosion Craters, Stew-
      art County, Tennessee, and Their
      Relations to Origin and Age of Wells
      Creek Basin Structure," Bull.Geol.
      Soc'y Am. 64 (1953):753-68. il.
      Robert S. Dietz, "Shatter Cones in
      Cryptoexplosion Structures (Meteor-
      ite Impact?)" J.Geology 67 (1959):
      496-505. il.
      Walter H. Bucher, "Are Cryptovolcan-
      ic Structures Due to Meteorite Im-
      pact?" Nature 197 (1963):1241-45.
      Charles W. Wilson, Jr. & R.G. Stearns,
      "Geology of the Wells Creek Struc-
      ture, Tennessee," Bull.Tennessee
      Div.Geol., no.68 (1968).

            C. Ethnic Groups

Cherokee Indians
-Cataclysm myth
      Hartley Burr Alexander, North Ameri-
      can Mythology (Boston: Marshall
      Jones, 1916; Mythology of All the
      Races, vol.10), pp.60-61.
-Shamanism
      James Mooney, "Sacred Formulas of
      the Cherokees," Ann.Rept.Bur.Am.
      Ethn. 7 (1885-86):307-97.
-Similarity to European Bronze Age cul-
   ture
      Colin Renfrew, Before Civilization
      (N.Y.: Knopf, 1973), pp.233-42.
-Weather control
      James Mooney, "Sacred Formulas of
      the Cherokees," Ann.Rept.Bur.Am.

   7 (1885-86):307,387-88.
-Welsh Indians
      Amos Stoddard, Sketches Historical
      and Descriptive of Louisiana (Phil-
      adelphia: Mathew Carey, 1812), pp.
      483-85.
      Eliza C. Campbell, Tales About Wales
      (Edinburgh: Robert Cadell, 1837).
      Richard Deacon, Madoc and the Dis-
      covery of America (N.Y.: George
      Braziller, 1966), pp.130,154-55,
      185-88,191-92.
-White Indians
      Benjamin Smith Barton, New Views of
      the Origins of the Tribes and Na-
      tions of America (Philadelphia:
      John Bioren, 1797), pp. xliv-xlv.

Melungeons
-Doubtful origin
      Swan M. Burnett, "A Note on the Me-
      lungeons," Am.Anthro. 2 (1889):347-
      49.
      Will Allen Dromgoole, "The Malunge-
      ons," Arena 3 (1891):470-79.
      William Allen Dromgoole, "The Melun-
      geon Tree and Its Four Branches,"
      Arena 3 (1891):749-51.
      Knoxville Journal, 20 Oct.1970, p.3.
      New York Times, 10 Aug.1971, p.33.
      Charles A. Huguenin, "The Mystery of
      the Origins of the Melungeons,"
      NEARA Newsl. 6 (Sep.1971):47-52.
      Saundra Keyes Ivey, Oral, Printed
      and Popular Culture Traditions Re-
      lated to the Melungeons of Hancock
      County, Tennessee (PhD. diss.,
      Indiana Univ., 1976).
      Jim Brandon, Weird America (N.Y.:
      Dutton, 1978), pp.210-11.

            D. Unspecified Localities

-Humanoid
   1878
      Louisville (Ky.) Courier-Journal, 24
      Oct.1878.
   1888/Mr. Wyatt/Humboldt Line
      Brad Steiger, Mysteries of Time and
      Space (N.Y.: Dell, 1976 ed.), pp.
      117-19.

-Snake handling
      Weston La Barre, They Shall Take Up
      Serpents (Minneapolis: Univ. of
      Minnesota, 1962).
      Ken Mink, "Tennessee Snake Cult,"
      Argosy, Aug.1973, pp.44-45,86-87.
      William Sargent, The Mind Possessed
      (N.Y.: Penguin, 1975), pp.185-86.

KENTUCKY

A. Populated Places

Albany
-Humanoid
    1973, fall/Gary Pierce
        Jerome Clark & Loren Coleman, Crea-
        tures of the Outer Edge (N.Y.: War-
        ner, 1978), pp.114-16.

Allen co.
-Giant human skeletons
        Lewis Collins, Historical Sketches
        of Kentucky (Maysville: The Author,
        1848), p.168.
-Humanoid
    1870s/Monkey Cave Hollow
        John Green, Sasquatch: The Apes Among
        Us (Seattle: Hancock House, 1978),
        pp.222-23.

Allensville
-UFO (NL)
    1897, April 15
        St. Louis (Mo.) Post-Dispatch, 16
        Apr.1897, p.2.

Anchorage
-UFO (NL)
    1966, Aug.18/Rudolph V. Thompson
        "New Reports by Space Experts Add to
        UFO Proof," UFO Inv. 3 (Aug.-Sep.
        1966):4.

Ashland
-Archeological site
    8000 B.C.-800 A.D./Central Park
        W.D. Funkhouser & W.S. Webb, "Arch-
        aeological Survey of Kentucky,"
        Pub.Anthro.Univ.Kentucky 2 (1932):
        41-42.
        Franklin Folsom, America's Ancient
        Treasures (N.Y.: Rand McNally,
        1974), p.140.
-UFO (?)
    1974, Aug.5/Les Johnson
        (Letter), Saga UFO Rept. 3 (Apr.1976)
        :6.
-UFO (CE-2)
    1967, May/ground markings only
        Ted Phillips, Physical Traces Associ-
        ated with UFO Sightings (Evanston:
        Center for UFO Studies, 1975), p.48.
-UFO (NL)
    1972, March 4
        "UFO over Ashland, Kentucky," Skylook,
        no.59 (Oct.1972):13.

Barbourville
-UFO (DD)
    1954, Nov.12
        "Louisville Stops Work to Watch Sau-
        cer," CRIFO Newsl., 3 Dec.1954, p.3.

Bardstown
-Haunt
    1897/Nelson County Jail
        Cleveland (O.) Plain Dealer, 8 May
        1897.

Beattyville
-Clairvoyance
    1956/Rowland Chrisman
        (Editorial), Fate 10 (May 1957):15.

Bedford
-Phantom hogs
    1975, Oct.
        Peter Guttilla, "Monster Menagerie,"
        Saga UFO Rept. 4 (Sep.1977):32,65.

Bellevue
-UFO (CE-2)
    1977, July 15
        Leonard H. Stringfield, "The UFO
        Status Quo: Incidents in Kentucky,"
        MUFON UFO J., no.122 (Jan.1978):9.

Boone co.
-UFO (CE-1)
    1949/Greater Cincinnati Airport
        "Ball of Light Circles Control Tower,"
        CRIFO Newsl., 4 Mar.1955, p.7.
-UFO (NL)
    1956, July 2/Jack Pease/nr. Greater
    Cincinnati Airport
        "Case 164," CRIFO Orbit, 3 Aug.1956,
        p.1.

Bourbon co.
-UFO (?)
    1947, July 7/Joe Bell
        Louisville Times, 8 July 1947.

Bowling Green
-UFO (CE-1)
    1913, summer/Mrs. Robert Bailey
        "Amazing Indifference," Doubt, no.
        33 (1951):83,84.
-UFO (NL)
    1973, Oct.3
        Glenn O. Rutherford, "UFO-Gazing in
        the Land of Blue Grass," Probe the
        Unknown 2 (spring 1974):20,21.

Bracken co.
-Ancient iron bracelets
    1820
        "New Findings of Pre-Columbian Con-
        tacts with North America," NEARA
        Newsl. 9 (spring 1974):9.

Brandenburg
-UFO (DD)
    1947, July 7/E.L. Ornstein
        Louisville Times, 8 July 1947.

Bromley
-UFO (NL)
  1956, July 2/Harlan Grimes
    "Case 163," CRIFO Orbit, 3 Aug.1956,
    p.1.
-Windshield pitting
  1954
    (Editorial), Fate 7 (Aug.1954):8.

Bullitt co.
-UFO (CE-1)
  1978, July 13/Elisabeth Stephenson/5
  mi.S of Glass House on I-65
    Glasgow Times, 9 Aug.1978.
-UFO (DD)
  1973, Oct.3
    Glenn O. Rutherford, "UFO-Gazing in
    the Land of Blue Grass," Probe the
    Unknown 2 (spring 1974):20,22-23,
    quoting Louisville Courier-Journal
    (undated). il.

Burnaugh
-UFO (?)
  1973, Oct.24/=balloon
    Grayson Journal-Enquirer, 1 Nov.1973.

Butler co.
-Archeological site
  ca.2000 B.C./Carlson Annis site
    William S. Webb, "The Carlson Annis
    Mound," Rept.in Anthro.Univ.Ken-
    tucky 7 (1950):265-354. il.

Calhoun
-Fall of fish
  1964/Gordon McLaughlin
    (Editorial), Fate 18 (Mar.1965):10.

California
-Phantom panther
  1977, Feb.-March/Ted Brookbank
    Ron Schaffner, "A Report on Ohio An-
    thropoids and Other Strange Crea-
    tures," in Bigfoot: Tales of Unex-
    plained Creatures (Rome, O.: Page
    Research, 1978), pp.40,48.

Campbell co.
-Humanoid
  1964, June/John Adank/Pools Creek Rd.
    Cincinnati (O.) Enquirer, 16 June
    1964.
-UFO (NL)
  1975, Oct.28
    Len Stringfield, "Cincinnati Area Has
    Variety of Sightings," Skylook, no.
    98 (Jan.1976):5.
    "UFO Central," CUFOS News Bull., 1
    Feb.1976, p.10.

Campbellsville
-UFO (DD)
  1957, Nov.1
    Richard Hall, ed., The UFO Evidence
    (Washington: NICAP, 1964), p.163.
-UFO (NL)
  1973, Oct.19-20/Sam Richerson/Rte.1-2
    Campbellsville News-Journal, 25 Oct.
    1973.

Carroll co.
-Giant human skeleton and silver snuff
box
  1837
    Lewis Collins, Historical Sketches
    of Kentucky (Maysville: The Author,
    1848), p.229.

Carrollton
-Ancient limestone effigy
    Lewis Collins, Historical Sketches
    of Kentucky (Maysville: The Author,
    1848), p.229.

Christian co.
-Giant human skeletons
    William Henry Perrin, County of
    Christian, Kentucky: Historical and
    Biographical (Chicago: F.A. Battey,
    1884).

Clay co.
-Religious ecstasy
  1960s
    William Sargent, The Mind Possessed
    (N.Y.: Penguin, 1975), pp.191-92.

Clay City
-Ancient coins
  1952/Robert Cox
    Louisville Courier-Journal, 12 July
    1953.

Cold Spring
-UFO (DD)
  1956, Aug.15
    "Case 189," CRIFO Orbit, 7 Sep.1956,
    p.4.
-UFO (NL)
  1955, Aug.5
    "Case 97," CRIFO Orbit, 2 Sep.1955,
    p.1.

Columbia
-UFO (DD)
  1977, Nov.13/Ruby Keltner/Bethany Chapel
    Columbia Statesman, 16 Nov.1977.

Concord
-Fall of rock
  1971, May/Robert Donal
    Falmouth Outlook, 28 May 1971.

Conoloway
-Cattle mutilations
  1977, Jan.4, 6/Don White
    Leitchfield Grayson County News, 13
    Jan.1977.

Corbin
-Precognition
  1934, March/Kitty Ward
    Kitty Ward, "Visions of a Mountain
    Girl," Fate 22 (Sep.1969):74-76.

Covington
-Clairempathy research
  1830s-1890s/J. Rodes Buchanan
    J. Rodes Buchanan, A Practical Test

of the Value of Psychometry (Chicago: The Author, 1878).
J. Rodes Buchanan, Manual of Psycho-
metry: The Dawn of a New Civiliza-
tion (Boston: Holman Bros., 1885).
J. Rodes Buchanan, Periodicity: The
Absolute Law of the Entire Universe
(San Jose: E.S. Buchanan, 1897).
J. Rodes Buchanan, Primitive Christ-
ianity (San Jose: The Author, 1897-
98).
Nandor Fodor, Encyclopaedia of Psy-
chic Science (London: Arthurs, 1934),
pp.39-40.
-Gasoline spring
1946, Dec.12-14
"Free Gasoline," Doubt, no.18 (1947):
268.
-Ghost
n.d./Dan Beard
Dan Beard, Hardly a Man Is Now Alive
(Garden City: Doubleday, 1939).
-Haunt
n.d.
James Reynolds, Ghosts in American
Houses (N.Y.: Paperback Library,
1967 ed.), pp.163-66.
-Mystery explosion
1953, April/John Gulick/1811 Greenup
St.
(Editorial), Fate 6 (Oct.1953):42-43.
-Phantom panther
1959, Jan.30/Licking R. bridge
George Wagner, "Cincinnati's 'What-
Was-It?' Monster," Beyond Reality,
no.21 (July-Aug.1976):62.
-UFO (DD)
1956, Oct.14/Harlan Grimes
"Case 242," CRIFO Orbit, 7 Dec.1956,
p.3.
1956, Nov.12/Harlan Grimes
"Case 246," CRIFO Orbit, 7 Dec.1956,
p.4.
-UFO (NL)
1975, Oct.22/Municipal Bldg.
Len Stringfield, "Cincinnati Area
Has Variety of Sightings," Skylook,
no.98 (Jan.1976):5.

Crab Orchard
-Human tracks in limestone
New York Times, 16 Aug.1888, p.8.

Cynthiana
-Precognition
1865
"Premonitory Dream," J.ASPR 3 (1909):
124-29.

Danville
-Phantom panther
1966/Glenn Lucas/2 mi.E
(Editorial), Fate 20 (June 1967):12-
13.
-UFO (CE-1)
1977, Dec.
Leonard H. Stringfield, "The UFO
Status Quo: Incidents in Kentucky,"
MUFON UFO J., no.122 (Jan.1978):9.

Demossville
-Phantom image
1865, spring/Jesse Smith/6 mi.W
Henry Winfred Splitter, "Nature's
Strange Photographs," Fate 8 (Jan.
1955):21,22-23, quoting Cincinnati
(O.) Enquirer, summer 1882.

Dunnville
-Haunt
1897, April/Old Bailey House/2 mi.N
Cincinnati (O.) Enquirer, 2 May 1897.

Eddyville
-Anomalous artifact
=iron fork in Indian mound
Bennett H. Young, The Prehistoric
Men of Kentucky (Louisville: Filson
Club, Pub.no.25, 1910).
(Editorial), Fate 13 (Mar.1960):22.

Elizabethtown
-UFO (?)
1948, Jan.7/=balloon
Aimé Michel, The Truth About Flying
Saucers (N.Y.: Pyramid, 1967 ed.),
pp.41-43.

Erlanger
-Disappearance
1977, Dec.21/Keith Holliday
Leonard H. Stringfield, "The UFO
Status Quo: Incidents in Kentucky,"
MUFON UFO J., no.122 (Jan.1978):9.
-UFO (NL)
1978, Jan.18/Ron Jones
Leonard H. Stringfield, "The UFO
Status Quo: Incidents in Kentucky,"
MUFON UFO J., no.122 (Jan.1978):8.

Falmouth
-UFO (?)
1869, Aug.7/Mrs. Murphy/=meteors
"Meteors Observed During a Total
Eclipse of the Sun," Pop.Astron. 2
(1895):332-33.
Dorrit Hoffleit, "Daytime Meteors of
August 7, 1869," Pop.Astron. 58
(1950):407-409.

Fayette co.
-UFO (NL)
1954, Nov.11/Wheeler Boone
"Louisville Stops Work to Watch Saucer," CRIFO Newsl., 3 Dec.1954, p.3.

Fern Creek
-UFO (CE-3)
1963, July 18
David Webb & Ted Bloecher, "MUFON's
Humanoid Study Group Very Active,"
Skylook, no.93 (Aug.1975):9.

Fisherville
-UFO (NL)
1945, April 4/James L. Hendry
"Another Sky-Light," Doubt, no.13
(winter 1945):195, quoting Louisville Courier-Journal (undated).

Flatwoods
-UFO (NL)
  1976, Jan.22
    "Noteworthy UFO Sightings," Ufology
    2 (summer 1976):62.

Fleming co.
-Haunt
  1961-1973/Juliet Overstreet
    Juliet Overstreet, "The Future Came
    Courting," Fate 30 (Aug.1977):85-
    87.

Flemingsburg
-UFO (DD)
  1977, Oct.3/Erma Bryant/512 Woodlawn
  Ave.
    Flemingsburg Fleming County Gazette,
    3 Nov.1977.

Florence
-UFO (CE-2)
  1975, May 10/Chuck Doyle
    Leonard H. Stringfield, Situation
    Red: The UFO Siege (N.Y.: Fawcett
    Crest, 1977 ed.), pp.63-69.
-UFO (NL)
  1956, Sep.9/Jack Juelg
    "Case 216," CRIFO Orbit, 5 Oct.1956,
    p.4.
  1978, Jan.18/Melody Harrison
    Cincinnati Post & Times-Star, 6 Feb.
    1978.
    Leonard H. Stringfield, "The UFO
    Status Quo: Incidents in Kentucky,"
    MUFON UFO J., no.122 (Jan.1978):8.

Floyd co.
-Phantom dog
  1978, May 24/Curtis Blackburn
    Kansas City (Mo.) Times, 6 June 1978.

Fort Knox
-UFO (?)
  1948, Jan.7/Thomas Mantell/=balloon?
    Louisville Courier Journal, 7 Jan.
    1948.
    Sidney Shalett, "What You Can Believe
    about Flying Saucers," Sat.Eve.Post,
    30 Apr.1949, pp.20-21,136-37.
    Donald E. Keyhoe, Flying Saucers Are
    Real (N.Y.: Fawcett, 1950), pp.15-
    17,27 40.
    Donald H. Menzel, Flying Saucers (Cam-
    bridge: Harvard Univ., 1953), pp.
    22,198.
    "Captain Tom Mantell's Last Words,"
    CRIFO Newsl., 3 Dec.1954, p.4.
    Desmond Leslie, "Captain Mantell: No
    Further Doubts About Interception,"
    Flying Saucer Rev. 1 (Nov.-Dec.1955)
    :7,30.
    Edward J. Ruppelt, The Report on Un-
    identified Flying Objects (Garden
    City: Doubleday, 1956), pp.31-39.
    Aimé Michel, The Truth About Flying
    Saucers (N.Y.: Pyramid, 1967 ed.),
    pp.38-51.
    "More on Mantell," APRO Bull. 10
    (May 1962):6.

Donald H. Menzel & Lyle G. Boyd, The
    World of Flying Saucers (Garden
    City: Doubleday, 1963), pp.33-39.
Coral & Jim Lorenzen, UFOs: The Whole
    Story (N.Y.: Signet, 1969), pp.31-
    34.
B.R. Strong, "The Truth About the
    Mantell Crash," Official UFO 1 (Feb.
    1975):20-21,45-47. il.
Brad Steiger, Project Blue Book (N.Y.:
    Ballantine, 1976), pp.43-62. il.
Leonard H. Stringfield, Situation
    Red: The UFO Siege (N.Y.: Fawcett
    Crest, 1977 ed.), p.165.
"New Information on the Mantell
    Case," APRO Bull. 25 (June 1977):8;
    (July 1977):5-8.
-UFO (NL)
  1973, Oct.18/Ralph E. Green
    Elizabethtown News, 25 Oct.1973.

Fort Mitchell
-UFO (CE-1)
  1977, Dec.
    Leonard H. Stringfield, "The UFO
    Status Quo: Incidents in Kentucky,"
    MUFON UFO J., no.122 (Jan.1978):9.

Fort Thomas
-River monster
  1959, Jan.30/Ohio R.
    George Wagner, "Cincinnati's 'What-
    Was-It?' Monster," Beyond Reality,
    no.21 (July-Aug.1976):62.
-UFO (NL)
  1962, May 25
    "Noises, Lights over Cincinnati,"
    APRO Bull. 10 (May 1962):6.

Fort Wright
-UFO (NL)
  1978, Jan./Rick Gibson
    Cincinnati (O.) Post & Times Star, 6
    Feb.1978.

Frankfort
-Haunt
  19th c.-   /Liberty Hall
    "The Gray Lady of Liberty Hall," Fate
    19 (Oct.1966):50, quoting Frankfort
    State Journal (undated).
    "Liberty Hall," Scenic South 23 (Dec.
    1966):4-7.
-UFO (CE-2)
  1968, April 1
    J. Allen Hynek, The UFO Experience
    (Chicago: Regnery, 1972), p.239.
-UFO (NL)
  1967, Jan.15-18
    "Flurry in Kentucky," APRO Bull. 15
    (May-June 1967):12.

Franklin
-UFO (CE-1)
  1973, Oct.3/Sara Thompson
    Glenn O. Rutherford, "UFO-Gazing in
    the Land of Blue Grass," Probe the
    Unknown 2 (spring 1974):20-21.

Glasgow
-Fall of weblike substance
  1970, Oct.
    Glasgow Daily Times, 9 Oct.1970.

Goody
-UFO (NL)
  1978, Jan.4-Feb.6/Joe Slone/Pond Creek
    Ashland Independent, 8 Feb.1978.

Grahn
-Airplane inventor
  1901-1902/Matthew Sellers/=date too
    early
    Paul Lewis Atkinson, Kentucky: Land
      of Legend and Lore (Fort Thomas:
      Northern Kentucky Hist.Soc'y, 1962).
    George Wagner, "The First Airplane,"
      Fate 28 (Oct.1975):79.
    (Letter), Gordon Codding, Fate 29
      (Feb.1976):116-17.
    (Letter), Gary S. Mangiacopra, Fate
      29 (Aug.1976):115-17.

Gravel Switch
-UFO (CE-2)
  1976, July 18/Charles Gilpin
    Leonard H. Stringfield, Situation
      Red: The UFO Siege (N.Y.: Fawcett
      Crest, 1977 ed.), pp.242-43.

Grayson Springs
-Cattle mutilation
  1977, Jan.6/Clifford Large/Hwy.88
    Leitchfield Grayson County News, 13
    Jan.1977.

Harlan
-Ghost
  1959, June/Sim Swain/=hoax
    (Editorial), Fate 12 (Oct.1959):26-
    27.

Harlan co.
-Snake handling
  1950s-1960s
    Ellen Stekert, "The Snake-Handling
      Sect of Harlan County, Kentucky:
      Its Influences on Folk Tradition,"
      Southern Folklore Quar. 27 (1963):
      316-22.

Harrison co.
-UFO (NL)
  1977, Dec.16/Mitchell Bruce Walters/
    Coppage Pike x Dividing Ridge Pike
    Cynthiana Democrat, 22 Dec.1977.

Harrodsburg
-Fall of knitting needles
  ca.1845/F.W. Curry
    Decatur (Ill.) Republican, 6 Apr.
      1876, p.2.
    Harold T. Wilkins, Flying Saucers
      Uncensored (N.Y.: Pyramid, 1967
      ed.), p.111, quoting Louisville
      Courier-Journal (undated).
-Ghost light
  n.d./Shakertown Rd.
    Ethel Owens, "Ghost Tales from Ken-

tucky," Midwest Folklore 8 (spring
1958):29,31-32.

Hazel
-Giant snake
  1962, June
    John A. Keel, Strange Creatures from
      Time and Space (Greenwich, Ct.:
      Fawcett, 1970), p.107.

Highland Heights
-UFO (DD)
  1956, Oct.14/Donald Schneider
    "Case 242," CRIFO Orbit, 7 Dec.1956,
    p.3.

Hodgenville
-UFO (NL)
  1976, Jan.7
    "Noteworthy UFO Sightings," Ufology
    2 (summer 1976):62.

Hopkins co.
-Archeological site
  3000-2000 B.C./Parrish Village
    William S. Webb, "The Parrish Village
      Site: Site 45, Hopkins County, Ken-
      tucky," Rept.Anthro.Univ.Kentucky,
      vol.7, no.6 (1951). il.
    Martha Ann Rolingson, Late Paleo-In-
      dian and Early Archaic Manifesta-
      tions in Western Kentucky (Lexing-
      ton: Univ. of Kentucky, 1966), pp.
      127-44. il.
-Phantom panther
  ca.1918/eastern sector/=timber wolf
  1950-1951/western sector/=wolf?
    (Letter), Cecil D. Clayton, Fate 25
      (Nov.1972):144.

Hopkinsville
-Ancient coin
  1967, Feb.
    Louisville Courier-Journal, 14 Mar.
      1967; and 20 Mar.1967.
-Medical clairvoyance
  1901-1925/Edgar Cayce
    New York Times, 9 Oct.1910, pt.5, p.
      11.
    Thomas Sugrue, There Is a River (N.Y.:
      Holt, Rinehart & Winston, 1942).
    Gina Cerminara, Many Mansions (N.Y.:
      William Sloane, 1950).
    Paul M. Vest, "Edgar Cayce: Modern
      Man of Miracles," Fate 6 (Feb.1953):
      98-107.
    Jess Stearn, Edgar Cayce: The Sleep-
      ing Prophet (Garden City: Doubleday,
      1967).
    Noel Langley, Edgar Cayce on Reincar-
      nation (N.Y.: Hawthorn, 1968).
    Edgar Evans Cayce, Edgar Cayce on
      Atlantis (N.Y.: Paperback Library,
      1968).
    David E. Kahn, My Life with Edgar
      Cayce (Garden City: Doubleday, 1970).
    Lytle Robinson, Edgar Cayce's Story
      of the Origin and Destiny of Man
      (N.Y.: Coward, McCann & Geoghegan,
      1972).

Mary Ellen Carter, <u>My Years with Edgar Cayce</u> (N.Y.: Harper & Row, 1972).
Jess Stearn, <u>A Prophet in His Own Country</u> (N.Y.: William Morrow, 1974).
Harold J. Reilly & Ruth Hagy Brod, <u>The Edgar Cayce Handbook for Health Through Drugless Therapy</u> (N.Y.: Macmillan, 1975).
-UFO (DD)
  1947, July 9/William Sherill
    <u>Louisville Times</u>, 9 July 1947.

Irvine
-Ghost light
  1972-1977/Ronald Aldridge
    <u>Lexington Leader</u>, 14 Dec.1977.
-UFO (NL)
  1978, Feb.19/Jim Whittaker/3 mi.S on Hwy.89
    <u>Irvine Citizens Voice & Times</u>, 2 Mar.1978.

Irvington
-UFO (?)
  1948, Jan.7/=balloon
    Edward J. Ruppelt, <u>The Report on Unidentified Flying Objects</u> (Garden City: Doubleday, 1956), p.31.
    Brad Steiger, <u>Project Blue Book</u> (N.Y.: Ballantine, 1976), pp.47-48.

Jefferson co.
-Ancient iron hatchet
  1808
    "New Findings of Pre-Columbian Contacts with North America," <u>NEARA Newsl.</u> 9 (spting 1974):9.

Jeffersontown
-UFO (DD)
  1947, July 8/Mary Wheeler
    <u>Louisville Times</u>, 8 July 1947.
-UFO (NL)
  1046, April
    Vincent H. Gaddis, "Visitors from the Void," <u>Amazing Stories</u> 21 (June 1947):159,161.

Jeffersonville
-Ancient armor
  1755/Jonathan Taylor
    (Letter), Thomas S. Hinde, <u>Am.Pioneer</u> 1 (1842):373-75.
-Giant human skeleton
  ca.1871
    <u>New York Times</u>, 22 May 1871, p.5, quoting <u>Louisville Courier-Journal</u> (undated).

Jessamine co.
-Humanoid
  1830, Dec./Patrick C. Flourney/Kentucky R.
    <u>Cambridge (Md.) Chronicle</u>, 12 Feb. 1831, quoting <u>Lexington Gazette</u> (undated).
-UFO (NL)
  1947, July 7/Frances Maxedon

<u>Louisville Times</u>, 8 July 1947.
  1954, Nov.11/Richard Hood
    "Louisville Stops Work to Watch Saucer," <u>CRIFO Newsl.</u>, 3 Dec.1954, p. 3.

Kelly
-UFO (CE-3)
  1955, Aug.22/J. Cecil Sutton
    <u>Chicago (Ill.) Sun-Times</u>, 23 Aug. 1955.
    J. Allen Hynek, <u>The UFO Experience</u> (Chicago: Regnery, 1972), pp.150-55.
    J. Allen Hynek, <u>The Hynek UFO Report</u> (N.Y.: Dell, 1977), pp.212-16.
    Isabel Davis & Ted Bloecher, <u>Close Encounter at Kelly and Others of 1955</u> (Evanston: Center for UFO Studies, 1955), pp.1-120. il.

Kenton co.
-UFO (CE-2)
  1978, Jan.21-22
    <u>Cincinnati (O.) Post & Times Star</u>, 14 Feb.1978.

LaGrange
-Lake monster
  1965/Reynolds L.
    (Editorial), <u>Fate</u> 18 (Dec.1965):22.

Lexington
-Ancient coins
    John Haywood, <u>Natural and Aboriginal History of Tennessee</u> (Nashville: George Wilson, 1823), pp.319-20.
-Ancient mines
    J.S. Newberry, "Ancient Mining in North America," <u>Am.Antiquarian</u> 11 (1889):164-67.
-Ancient wall
  1881/Frankfort Pike
    "A Fossil Stone Wall," <u>Sci.Am.</u> 46 (1882):16, quoting <u>Lexington Press</u> (undated).
-Archeological sites
    Thomas Ashe, <u>Travels in America Performed in 1806</u> (London: William Sawyer, 1808), pp.196-200.
    Josiah Priest, <u>American Antiquities and Discoveries in the West</u> (Albany: Hoffman & White, 1834), pp.110-16.
    Lewis Collins, <u>Historical Sketches of Kentucky</u> (Maysville: The Author, 1848), pp.294-95.
    E.G. Squier & E.H. Davis, <u>Ancient Monuments of the Mississippi Valley</u> (Washington: Smithsonian Institution, Contrib.to Knowl., no.1, 1848), pp. 26,36.
    John Filson, <u>The Discovery, Settlement and Present State of Kentucky</u> (N.Y.: Corinth, 1962 ed.), pp.97-98.
    Robert Peter, "Ancient Mound, near Lexington, Kentucky," <u>Ann.Rept. Smith.Inst.</u>, 1871, pp.420-23.
    George W. Ranck, <u>History of Lexington, Kentucky</u> (Cincinnati: R. Clarke, 1872).

W.D. Funkhouser & W.S. Webb, "Arche-
olcgical Survey of Kentucky," Rept.
in Arch.& Anthro.Univ.Kentucky, vol.
2 (1932), p.119.
-Medieval coin
1928/L.B. Redding
Brad Steiger, Mysteries of Time and
Space (N.Y.: Dell, 1976 ed.), pp.
77-78, quoting Newsl.& Proc.Soc'y
for Early Hist.Arch., 16 Feb.1966.
-Precognition
1964, April/Charles Holland
Maxine Bell, "We Six Foresaw Our
Father's Death," Fate 20 (Apr.1967)
:94,96.
-UFO (?)
1963, Jan.24
Richard Hall, ed., The UFO Evidence
(Washington: NICAP, 1964), p.140.
-UFO (CE-1)
1960, summer/Milan Rafayko/Brian Sta-
tion High School
(Letter), Fate 14 (Aug.1961):123.
-UFO (CE-3)
1897, April 17/George Alverson/Manches-
ter St.
Cincinnati (O.) Enquirer, 19 Apr.
1897.
-UFO (DD)
1959/Milan Rafayko
(Letter), Fate 13 (Jan.1960):109-10.
1960, Oct.27/B.L. Kissinger, Jr.
Richard Hall, ed., The UFO Evidence
(Washington: NICAP, 1964), p.68.
-UFO (NL)
1952, July 30/Mrs. Glenn C. Fuller
Albert K. Bender, Flying Saucers and
the Three Men (N.Y.: Paperback Li-
brary, 1968 ed.), p.39, quoting
Lexington Herald (undated).
1959/Milan Rafayko
(Letter), Fate 13 (Jan.1960):109-10.
1960, Sep.4/John R. Cooke
Richard Hall, ed., The UFO Evidence
(Washington: NICAP, 1964), p.59.
1977, April 8
"UFO Analysis," Int'l UFO Reporter
2 (June 1977):9.

Lincoln
-UFO (NL)
1978, Aug.7/Kelly Meredith/Gap Hill Rd.
Brownsville Edmonson County News, 10
Aug.1978.

Livingston co.
-Hollow earth entrance
John Uri Lloyd, Etidorhpa, or The
End of the Earth (Cincinnati: The
Author, 1895).

Logan co.
-Religious ecstasy and hysterical jerking
1790s-1800s/James McGready/Cane Ridge
Richard M'Nemar, The Kentucky Revival
(N.Y.: Edward O. Jenkins, 1846).
David W. Yandell, "Epidemic Convul-
sions," Pop.Sci.Monthly 20 (1882):
498-507.
J.P. MacLean, Shakers of Ohio (Co-

lumbus: F.J. Heer, 1907), pp.21-58.

Louisville
-Airship inventor
1897, April/Harry Tibbs
Louisville Courier-Journal, 19 Apr.
1897, p.1.
-Ancient coin
1932/Joseph Bray/1522 Anderson Ave.
Louisville Courier-Journal, 12 July
1953.
-Archeological sites
Reuben T. Durrett, The Centenary of
Louisville (Louisville: Filson Club,
Pub.no.8, 1893), pp.9-11.
Donald E. Janzen, "Archeological In-
vestigations in Louisville and Vi-
cinity: A Historical Sketch," Fil-
son Club Hist.Quar. 46 (1972):305-
11.
-Fall of cookies
1965, May/Stanley Morris
"Fortean Items," Saucer News 12 (Sep.
1965):28.
St. Louis (Mo.) Post-Dispatch, 10
Nov.1965.
(Editorial), Fate 19 (July 1966):25.
-Fall of fish
1837, July 21/Dr. Wood
"A Fish Storm," Niles' Weekly Regis-
ter 52 (5 Aug.1837):356.
-Fall of frost
1897, Feb?
Aurora (Ill.) Beacon, 6 Mar.1897.
-Fall of unknown objects
1898/Bud Hawkins
"Bud Hawkins' Invisible Nemesis,"
Fate 8 (May 1955):40.
-Flying humanoid
1880, July 28/C.A. Youngman
Louisville Courier-Journal, 29 July
1880.
-Giant human skeletons
1876
New York Times, 8 Feb.1876, p.4.
-Glacial anomaly
John Bryson, "The Terminal Moraine
near Louisville," Am.Geologist 4
(1889):125-26.
-Haunt
1967, July-1969
(Letter), L.S., Fate 22 (Sep.1969):
127-28.
-Hex
1956, March
(Editorial), Fate 9 (July 1956):15-
16, quoting Louisville Courier-Jour-
nal (undated).
-Midday darkness
1911, March 7
Ferdinand J. Walz, "A Pall of Dark-
ness, at Louisville, Ky., and Sur-
rounding Districts," Monthly Weather
Rev. 39 (Mar.1911):345.
-Mystery explosion
1967, July 11/Donald R. Fell
"Mystery Blast in Kentucky," APRO
Bull. 16 (July-Aug.1967):7.
-Poltergeist
1951, Dec.-1952, Jan./Henry Thacker/

Fern Creek
  Los Angeles (Cal.) Herald-Express,
  4-5 Jan.1952.
  (Editorial), Fate 5 (Apr.-May 1952):
  4-6, quoting Chicago (Ill.) Daily
  News (undated). il.
  1971/Camp Taylor
  (Editorial), Fate 25 (Mar.1972):32-
  34, quoting Louisville Times (undated).
-Precognition
  n.d./J.B. Stoll
  (Letter), Fate 15 (May 1962):114.
  1957, May 3/Ralph Lowe
  Alson J. Smith, "Dream Winners at
  the Track," Fate 14 (Dec.1961):33-
  34.
  1964, April/Margurite Hemingway
  Maxine Bell, "We Six Foresaw Our
  Father's Death," Fate 20 (Apr.1967)
  :94-96.
-Skyquake
  1945, Jan.22, 29, Feb.6
  "Saturday Blasts," Doubt, no.12
  (spring-summer 1945):172.
  1968, Dec.11/Mrs. Earl Johnson
  Kansas City (Mo.) Star, 12 Dec.1968.
-Tornado anomaly
  1890, March
  "Weird Phantoms of the Air," Pop.
  Mechanics 48 (1927):979-82.
-UFO (CE-1)
  1977, Jan.26/Neil Belmont
  Burton Monroe, "Another Kentucky Abduction," APRO Bull. 25 (Jan.1977):
  4-5.
-UFO (CE-2)
  1977, Feb.2/Neil Belmont
  Burton Monroe, "Another Kentucky Abduction," APRO Bull. 25 (Jan.1977):
  4-5.
-UFO (DD)
  1950, June 27/Al Hixenbaugh
  Otto Binder, What We Really Know
  About Flying Saucers (Greenwich,
  Ct.: Fawcett, 1967), p.163. il.
-UFO (NL)
  1897, April 20/Ed Farrell
  Louisville Courier-Journal, 22 Apr.
  1897.
  1947, July 1/J.L. Laemmle
  1947, July 1/E.E. Unger/Highlands
  Louisville Courier-Journal, 3 July
  1947.
  1947, July 7/W.B. Robinson
  1947, July 7/Al Hixenbaugh/Preston St.
  Rd. x Bickels Lane
  Louisville Courier-Journal, 8 July
  1947.
  Louisville Times, 8 July 1947. il.
  "The Mystery of the Flying Disks,"
  Fate 1 (spring 1948):18. il.
-UFO (R-V)
  1954, Nov.11-12/Lee Merkel/=balloon?
  "Louisville Stops Work to Watch Sau-
  cer," CRIFO Newsl., 3 Dec.1954, p.
  3.
  J. Allen Hynek, The Hynek UFO Report
  (N.Y.: Dell, 1977), pp.51-52.
-White Indians

Sand I.
  (Letter), William Owen, "Discovery
  of the Madawgwys," Gentleman's Mag.
  61 (1791):329,396-97,534-36.
  Frankfort Palladium, 12 Dec.1804.
  Louisville Public Advertiser, 15 May
  1818.
  Henry McMurtrie, Sketches of Louis-
  ville (Louisville: P. Senn, 1819),
  pp.104-106.
  Albert James Pickett, History of Ala-
  bama (Charleston: Walker & James,
  1851).
  Benjamin F. Bowen, America Discovered
  by the Welsh in 1170 A.D. (Philadel-
  phia: Lippincott, 1876).
  Reuben Durrett, The Centenary of
  Louisville (Louisville: Filson Club,
  Pub.no.8, 1893).
  Reuben F. Durrett, Traditions of the
  Earliest Visits of Foreigners to
  North America (Louisville: Filson
  Club, Pub.no.23, 1908), pp.46-52.
  Bennett H. Young, The Prehistoric
  Men of Kentucky (Louisville: Filson
  Club, Pub.no.25, 1910).
  William S. Webb & William Funkhouser,
  "Ancient Life in Kentucky," Kentucky
  Geol.Survey, ser.6, vol.34 (1928).
  W.D. Funkhouser & W.S. Webb, "Archeo-
  logical Survey of Kentucky," Rept.in
  Arch.& Anthro.Univ.Kentucky, vol.2
  (1932), pp.197-200.
  Jeffersonville Evening News, 17 Sep.
  1957.
  Donald E. Janzen, "Archeological In-
  vestigations in Louisville and Vi-
  cinity: A Historical Sketch," Fil-
  son Club Hist.Quar. 46 (1972):305-
  11.

Lyndon
-Child prodigy
  1957-1961/Bobby/Kentucky Children's
  Home
  (Editorial), Fate 15 (July 1962):10-
  12.

McKinney
-UFO (CE-1)
  1978, March 1/Curt Folger/1 mi. from
  town
  Stanford Interior Journal, 2 Mar.
  1978.

Madisonville
-UFO (?)
  1948, Jan.7/=balloon
  Aimé Michel, The Truth About Flying
  Saucers (N.Y.: Paperback Library,
  1967 ed.), pp.38,44.
-UFO (CE-1)
  1973, Oct.11
  Madisonville Messenger, 17 Oct.1973.
-UFO (NL)
  1880, July 28/Mr. Royster
  Louisville Courier-Journal, 6 Aug.
  1880.

Mayfield
-UFO (DD)
  1978, Feb.2/Wayne Carr
    Mayfield Messenger, 3 Feb.1978.

Maysville
-Flying humanoid
  1966, Dec.6
    John A. Keel, "West Virginia's Enig-
    matic 'Bird,'" Flying Saucer Rev.
    14 (July-Aug.1968):7,13.
-UFO (?)
  1948, Jan.7/=balloon
    Edward J. Ruppelt, The Report on Un-
    identified Flying Objects (Garden
    City: Doubleday, 1956), p.31.
    Brad Steiger, Project Blue Book (N.Y.:
    Ballantine, 1975), pp.47-48.
-UFO (DD)
  1975, May 11
    Leonard H. Stringfield, Situation
    Red: The UFO Siege (N.Y.: Fawcett
    Crest, 1977 ed.), p.68.

Middlesboro
-Meteorite crater
  7000 m.diam./certain
    Max H. Hey, Catalogue of Meteorites
    (London: British Museum, 1966), p.
    553.

Middletown
-Ancient coin
  ca.1805/Mr. Spear/Big Grass Creek
    John Haywood, Natural and Aboriginal
    History of Tennessee (Nashville:
    George Wilson, 1823), p.179.

Milton
-Giant lizard
  1975, Oct./Clarence Cable
    Peter Guttilla, "Monster Menagerie,"
    Saga UFO Rept. 4 (Sep.1977):32,65,
    quoting Trimble County Democrat
    (undated).

Monroe co.
-Phantom panther
  ca.1900
    William Lynwood Montell, Ghosts Along
    the Cumberland (Knoxville: Univ. of
    Tennessee, 1975), pp.47-48.

Moodyville
-UFO (NL)
  1978, July 25/Beulah Moody
    Brownsville Edmonson County News, 10
    Aug.1978.

Morehead
-UFO (CE-1)
  1973, Oct.26/Dale Mabry/U.S.60
    Grayson Journal-Enquirer, 1 Nov.1973.
    Olive Hill Times, 1 Nov.1973.

Morgantown
-Lightning anomaly
  1872
    Henry Winfred Splitter, "Nature's
    Strange Photographs," Fate 8 (Jan.

1955):21,28.

Mount Sterling
-Archeological site
    E.G. Squier & E.H. Davis, Ancient
    Monuments of the Mississippi Valley
    (Washington: Smithsonian Institu-
    tion, Contrib.to Knowl., no.1,
    1848), p.93.
-Haunt
  n.d./Tandy Chenault
    "The Ghost in Gray," Fate 10 (Mar.
    1957):26.

Mulberry Hill
-Ghost
  1961
    (Editorial), Fate 14 (Nov.1961):18-
    19, quoting Lexington Leader (un-
    dated).

Munfordville
-UFO (CE-2)
  1973, Oct.14/Kenny Sims
    Glenn O. Rutherford, "UFO-Gazing in
    the Land of Blue Grass," Probe the
    Unknown 2 (spring 1974):20,21-22.

Murray
-Fall of carbonaceous meteorite
  1950, Sep.20/9 mi.E nr. Wildcat Creek
    John R. Horan, "The Murray, Calloway
    County, Kentucky, Aerolite," Meteor-
    itics 1 (1953):115-21. il.
    Melvin Calvin & Susan K. Vaughn,
    "Extraterrestrial Life: Some Organic
    Constituents of Meteorites and Their
    Significance for Possible Extrater-
    restrial Biological Evolution," in
    Hilde Kallmann, ed., Space Research:
    Proc.First Int'l Space Sci.Sympos-
    ium (Amsterdam: North-Holland, 1960),
    pp.1171-91.
    David Bergamini, "Wax and Wigglers:
    Life in Space?" Life, 5 May 1961,
    pp.57-62. il.
    (Discussion), F.D. Sisler, Proc.Lu-
    nar & Planetary Exploration Collo-
    quium, 15 Nov.1961, vol.2, no.4,
    pp.67-73. il.
    George Claus & B. Nagy, "A Microbio-
    logical Examination of Some Carbon-
    aceous Chondrites," Nature 192
    (1961):594-96.
    Donald P. Elston, "Accretion of Mur-
    ray Carbonaceous Chondrite and Im-
    plications Regarding Chondrule and
    Chondrite Formation," Pub.Center
    for Meteorite Studies, no.8 (1969).
    il.
-Humanoid
  1968/Richard Young
    Nashville (Tenn.) Banner, 11 July
    1977.
-UFO (DD)
  1951, Aug.
    Richard Hall, ed., The UFO Evidence
    (Washington: NICAP, 1964), p.149.
-Wireless inventor
  1885-1902/Nathan Stubblefield

Washington (D.C.) Evening Star, 21
May 1902.
Frank Edwards, "Stubblefield's Voices
in the Wind," Fate 10 (June 1957):
79-85.

Newport
-Airship message
1897, April 23
    Cincinnati (O.) Commercial Tribune,
    25 Apr.1897, p.10.
-UFO (DD)
1978, Jan./Dave Pruitt/66 Broadway
    Cincinnati (O.) Post & Times-Star, 6
    Feb.1978.
-UFO (NL)
1897, April 23/Ezra Van Duzen
    Cincinnati (O.) Commercial Tribune,
    25 Apr.1897, p.10.
1897, May 8
    Cincinnati (O.) Commercial Tribune,
    9 May 1897.

Olive Hill
-Poltergeist
1968, Nov.15-Dec./Roger Callihan
    Ashland Daily Independent, 20 Nov.
    1968; and 11 Dec.1968.
    William G. Roll, The Poltergeist
    (N.Y.: Signet, 1974), pp.134-42.

Olympia Springs
-Fall of flesh
1876, March 3/Mrs. Allen Crouch
    Owingsville Bath County News, 9 Mar.
    1876.
    New York Times, 10-12 Mar.1876.
    "A Shower of Meat," Sci.Am. 34
    (1876):197.
    "The Kentucky Shower of Flesh," Sci.
    Am.Suppl. 2 (1876):426.
    (Letter), A. Mead Edwards, Sci.Am.
    Suppl. 2 (1876):473.

Owensboro
-Animal ESP
1959, Oct.-1960, March 10/Allen W. Neal
    (Editorial), Fate 13 (Aug.1960):6-8,
    quoting Los Angeles (Cal.) Herald-
    Express (undated).
-Eyeless vision
1939-1960s/Patricia Ainsworth Stanley
    Hale Sparks, "Seeing with the Finger-
    tips," in Borderline Magazine, ed.,
    Strange, Stranger, Strangest (N.Y.:
    Paperback Library, 1966), pp.24-26.
-Humanoid
1978, Aug./Larry Nelson/Fairview St.
    Keith Lawrence, "The Fairview Horror,"
    Saga UFO Rept. 7 (May 1979):29-31,
    70.
-Phantom
1945, Oct.31/Frank Bollinger/Wilson's
Ferry
    Pauline Saltzman, "Spectre of Wil-
    son's Ferry," Fate 6 (June 1953):
    62-63.
-UFO (?)
1948, Jan.7/=balloon
    Edward J. Ruppelt, The Report on Un-

identified Flying Objects (Garden
City: Doubleday, 1956), p.31.
Brad Steiger, ed., Project Blue Book
(N.Y.: Ballantine, 1977), pp.47-48.

Paducah
-Ball lightning
1905, July 6/Mrs. A.E. Russell
    "Ball Lightning," Monthly Weather
    Rev. 33 (Nov.1905):409.
-Precognition
1970s/David Hoy/Box 57
    John Godwin, Super-Psychic: The In-
    credible Dr. Hoy (N.Y.: Pocket
    Books, 1974).
    Warren Smith, "Phenomenal Predictions
    for 1975," Saga, Jan.1975, pp.20,48.
    Warren Smith, "Phenomenal Predictions
    for 1976," Saga, Jan.1976, pp.16,18.
    "Checking the Prophets," Fate 29
    (May 1976):73.
-UFO (NL)
1897, April 17/George Langstaff, Jr.
    Cincinnati (O.) Enquirer, 19 Apr.
    1897.

Paris
-Dowsing
1803
    John Haywood, Natural and Aboriginal
    History of Tennessee (Nashville:
    George Wilson, 1823), p.18.
-Fire anomaly
1958, Dec./Charles Johnson
    (Editorial), Fate 12 (July 1959):22-
    23.
-UFO (?)
1949, Jan.16/Mrs. Paul Brannon
    Kenneth Arnold & Ray Palmer, The Com-
    ing of the Saucers (Boise: The Au-
    thors, 1952), p.176, quoting Carlisle
    Nicholas County Star (undated). il.
-UFO (NL)
1947, July 7/George Wyatt/N of town
    Louisville Times, 8 July 1947

Park Hills
-UFO (NL)
1954, Aug.
    "Astronomers and UFO's: A Survey,"
    Int'l UFO Reporter 2 (Apr.1977):3.

Parksville
-Dowsing
n.d./J.J. Isham
    (Letter), J. Marshall Isham, Fate 23
    (Nov.1970):142.
-Precognition
1913/Ruby Carroll
    Vincent H. Gaddis, "When the Paranor-
    mal Played Cupid," Beyond Reality,
    no.14 (Mar.-Apr.1975):35-37, quoting
    Coronet, Apr.1942.

Pikeville
-Disappearance
1949, Sep./Marvin Johnson/Chloe Creek
    "Mystery at the Mine," Fate 11 (Nov.
    1958):71.
-Spontaneous human combustion

1960, Nov.13/Buddy Hopkins/Greasy Creek
Rd.
  Syracuse (N.Y.) Herald-Journal, 21
  Nov.1960.
  Coral E. Lorenzen, The Shadow of the
  Unknown (N.Y.: Signet, 1970), p.203,
  quoting AP release, 24 Nov.1960.
-UFO (NL)
1976, Jan.22
  "Noteworthy UFO Sightings," Ufology
  2 (summer 1976):62.

Pine Mountain
-Snake handling
1930s/Church of God
  Keith Kerman, "Rattlesnake Religion,"
  in Lealon N. Jones, ed., Eve's
  Stepchildren (Caldwell, Id.: Caxton,
  1942), pp.93-102.
  E. Baird, "They Shall Take Up Ser-
  pents," Woman 17, no.2 (1946):36-39.
  Weston La Barre, They Shall Take Up
  Serpents (Minneapolis: Univ. of
  Minnesota, 1962), pp.11-33.

Pinhook
-UFO (DD)
1973, Oct.23/Mrs. Robert Walton/Pinhook
Pike
  Mt. Olivet Robertson County Review,
  1 Nov.1973.
-UFO (NL)
1973, Oct./Frank Berry/Pinhook Pike
  Mt. Olivet Robertson County Review,
  1 Nov.1973.

Plum Springs
-Archeological site
ca.4000 B.C.
  Lawrence (Kans.) Journal-World, 6
  Jan.1977. il.

Powell co.
-UFO (NL)
1973, Oct.25
  Olive Hill Times, 1 Nov.1973.

Prospect
-UFO (CE-4)
1977, Jan.27/Lee Parrish/Hwy.329
  Carla Rueckert, "Another Kentucky Abduction," APRO Bull. 25 (Jan.1977):
  1,3-4.
  "Single Witness Abduction in Kentucky," Int'l UFO Reporter 2 (Apr.
  1977):6-7.

Rabbit Hash
-Giant bird
1977, May 16/=eagle?
  Lima (O.) News, 18 May 1977.

Reedyville
-Petroglyphs
  Fred E. Coy, Jr. & Thomas C. Fuller,
  "Reedyville Petroglyphs, Butler
  County, Kentucky," Central States
  Arch.J. 17 (1970):100-109.

Richmond
-UFO (CE-2)
1978, Nov.28/Vickie Allen/Log Cabin Rd.
  Richmond Register, 30 Nov.1978.

River
-Fall of toads
n.d./H. Hollister
  (Letter), Fate 13 (Aug.1960):116.

Rockcastle co.
-Humanoid
1962, June 30
  Report in SITU files.

Rogers
-Phantom
1961, Aug.
  Leonard H. Stringfield, Situation
  Red: The UFO Siege (N.Y.: Fawcett
  Crest, 1977), pp.78-79.

Russell Springs
-UFO (CE-3)
1973, Oct. 23
  Russell Springs Times-Journal, 25
  Oct.1973.

Russellville
-Phantom panther
1823
  Boston (Mass.) New England Farmer,
  3 Aug.1823.
-UFO (NL)
1897, April 15/B.B. Andrews
  Columbus (O.) Evening Press, 17 Apr.
  1897.

Saint Matthews
-Fall of ice
1963, Feb.6/Charles Rader/528 Harris
Pl.
  (Editorial), Fate 16 (June 1963):22-
  23.

Sebree
-Fall of weblike substance
1962, Sep.11/=spider web
  Donald H. Menzel & Lyle G. Boyd, The
  World of Flying Saucers (Garden
  City: Doubleday, 1963), pp.223-24.
-Flying humanoid
ca.1950
  Coral E. Lorenzen, The Shadow of the
  Unknown (N.Y.: Signet, 1970), pp.
  144-45.

Shelbyville
-Fall of rocks
1971, July 16/U.S.60
  Shelbyville Shelby News, 22 July 1971.
-Ghost
ca.1918/Mrs. J.M. Benton
  "The Ghost Wore Red," Fate 18 (Aug.
  1965):35, quoting Louisville Cour-
  ier-Journal (undated).
  (Letter), Ivan T. Sanderson, Fate 18
  (Oct.1965):145.
  (Letter), Raymond W. Hill, Fate 18
  (Nov.1965):121.

(Letter), Mrs. L. Johnson, Fate 19 (Sep.1966):126-27.

-UFO (?)
1869, Aug.7/Alvan G. Clark, Jr./=meteors
"Meteors Observed During a Total Eclipse of the Sun," Pop.Astron. 2 (1895):332-33.
Dorrit Haffleit, "Daytime Meteors of August 7, 1869," Pop.Astron. 58 (1950):407-409.

-UFO (CE-2)
1967, Jan.15
(Editorial), Fate 20 (May 1967):29.
"Flurry in Kentucky," APRO Bull. 15 (May-June 1967):12.

Simpson co.
-Humanoid
1977, Jan.
John Green, Sasquatch: The Apes Among Us (Seattle: Hancock House, 1978), p.223.

Somerset
-Phantom panther tracks
1971, May/Clement Bolton/Pitman Creek
Somerset Commonwealth-Journal, 5 May 1971.

South Union
-Fall of yellow rain
1867, March 12/H.L. Eades
"Yellow Rain," Sci.Am. 16 (1867):233.

Spottsville
-Humanoid
1975
Owensburg Messenger-Inquirer, 9 Feb. 1977.

Springlake
-UFO (NL)
1942, April/R.M. Danner
Gordon I.R. Lore, Jr. & Harold H. Deneault, Jr., Mysteries of the Skies: UFOs In Perspective (Englewood Cliffs, N.J.: Prentice-Hall, 1968), pp.141-42.

Stanford
-UFO (CE-4)
1976, Jan.6/Mona Stafford/1 mi.SW
Danville Kentucky Advocate, 1 Feb. 1976.
Liberty Casey County News, 12 Feb. 1976.
Nat'l Enquirer, 19 Oct.1976.
"The Kentucky Abduction," APRO Bull. 24 (Oct.1976):1,3-6.
Jim Miller, "The Kentucky Abduction," Ohio Sky Watcher, Oct.-Dec.1976, pp. 1-9. il.
Leonard H. Stringfield, "The Stanford, Kentucky, Abduction," MUFON UFO J., no.110 (Jan.1977):5-15. il.
"The Kentucky Abduction," Int'l UFO Reporter 2 (Mar.1977):6-7.
Leonard H. Stringfield, Situation Red: The UFO Siege (N.Y.: Fawcett Crest, 1977 ed.), pp.228-42,246-51.

Coral & Jim Lorenzen, Abducted! (N.Y.: Berkley, 1977), pp.114-31.

-UFO (NL)
1977, Nov.19/Larry Caldwell/Lancaster Rd.
Stanford Interior Journal, 24 Nov. 1977.

Stephensburg
-UFO (CE-1)
1958, Oct.3/Mrs. Harvey DeVore
"New Wave of UFO Sightings Cracks Censorship Wall," NICAP Spec.Bull., Nov.1958, pp.1,3.

-UFO (NL)
1973, Oct.16/Jim Coghill
"Saucers in the News," Flying Saucers, winter 1974, pp.44,48.

Trimble co.
-Humanoid and cattle mutilations
1962, June/Owen Powell
John A. Keel, Strange Creatures from Time and Space (Greenwich, Ct.: Fawcett, 1970), pp.106-107, quoting Louisville Courier-Journal (undated).

Verona
-UFO (NL)
1978, Feb.2/Luther Barton
Cincinnati (O.) Post & Times-Star, 6 Feb.1978.

Versailles
-Meteorite crater
1500 m.diam./possible
Douglas F.B. Slack, "Cryptoexplosive Structure near Versailles, Kentucky," Prof.Pap.U.S.Geol.Survey, no.501 (1964):B9-B12. il.

Wallingford
-UFO (CE-2)
1959, Sep.7
"Kentucky Near-Landing Analysis," UFO Inv. 1 (Mar.1960):5.

Weeksbury
-Out-of-body experience
1927, Feb.14/Beeda Brown
Beeda Brown, "Did My Soul Leave My Body?" Fate 5 (Dec.1952):78-82.

Whitesville
-Fall of weblike substance
1964, Sep.19/Robert Millburn
(Letter), Fate 18 (Jan.1965):120.

Wickliffe
-Archeological site
Ancient Buried City
Lorine Letcher Butler, "The Ancient Buried City of Kentucky," Natural History 36 (1935):398-404. il.
Blanche Busey King, "Recent Excavations at the King Mounds, Wickliffe, Kentucky," Trans.Illinois Acad.Sci. 30 (1937):83-90. il.
Mate Graye Hunt, "Ancient Buried City: Wickliffe, Kentucky," Dallas

Arch.Soc'y Record 3 (1942):25-27.
Franklin Folsom, America's Ancient
Treasures (N.Y.: Rand McNally,
1974), p.140.

Williamstown
-UFO (?)
 1956, Aug.30
 "Case 204," CRIFO Orbit, 5 Oct.1956,
 p.3.
-UFO (DD)
 1974, Oct.18/Steven Hisel
 1975, June 23/Steven Hisel
 (Letter), Saga UFO Rept. 4 (July
 1977):80.
-UFO (NL)
 1974, Oct.19/Steven Hisel
 (Letter), Saga UFO Rept. 4 (July
 1977):80.

Willow Shade
-Dowsing
 1970s/Clarence Hollett
 Frederic Golden, "In Vermont: Is
 Dowsing Going to the Dogs?" Time,
 9 Oct.1978, pp.11-12.

Wilmore
-Animal ESP
 1900-1910/Volney G. Mullikan
 Vincent & Margaret Gaddis, The Strange
 World of Animals and Pets (N.Y.:
 Pocket Books, 1971), pp.47-51, quot-
 ing True, Mar.1957.

Wolfe co.
-UFO (DD)
 1927, summer/Reece A. Lacey
 (Letter), Fate 11 (Dec.1958):111-12.

Woodstock
-Clairvoyance
 1955/Jim Denney
 (Editorial), Fate 8 (July 1955):9,
 quoting Louisville Courier-Journal
 (undated).
-Giant human skeletons
 ca.1951/Jim Denney
 Quentin R. Howard, "Bones in the
 Shed," Fate 9 (May 1956):65-67.

      B. Physical Features

Big Bone Lick
-Mastodon bones
 Lewis Collins, Historical Sketches
 of Kentucky (Maysville: The Author,
 1848), pp.180-81.
 W.D. Funkhouser & W.S. Webb, "Arche-
 ological Survey of Kentucky," Rept.
 Arch.& Anthro.Univ. of Kentucky, vol.
 2 (1932), pp.29-32.
 Willard Jillson, Big Bone Lick (Lou-
 isville: Standard, 1936). il.
 Richard Carrington, Elephants (N.Y.:
 Basic Books, 1959), pp.236-37.

Big Hill
-Human tracks in sandstone

E.A. Allen, "Footmarks in Stone in
Kentucky," Am.Antiquarian 7 (1885):
39.

Blue Lick Springs
-Ancient pavement and mastodon bones
 W.D. Funkhouser & W.S. Webb, "Arche-
 ological Survey of Kentucky," Rept.
 Arch.& Anthro.Univ. of Kentucky,
 vol.2 (1932), pp.321-22.
 Willard Rouse Jillson, Big Bones at
 Lower Blue Licks (Louisville: Stan-
 dard, 1946).
 Willard Rouse Jillson, "Pleistocene
 Fossil Excavations at Blue Lick
 Springs, Kentucky," Science 103
 (1946):58-59.
 W.L. Vallette, "Is America the Birth-
 place of Man?" Fate 6 (Mar.1953):
 82,85-86.
 Franklin Folsom, America's Ancient
 Treasures (N.Y.: Rand McNally,
 1974), pp.140-41.

Blue Mts.
-Haunt
 1930s
 Harold T. Wilkins, "Buried Treasure
 and the Occult," in Bernhardt J.
 Hurwood, ed., The First Occult Review Reader (N.Y.: Award, 1968),
 pp.172,178.

Clear Creek
-Archeological site
 ca.6000 B.C.-1650 A.D./Morris site
 Martha Ann Rolingson & Douglas W.
 Schwartz, Late Paleo-Indian and
 Early Archaic Manifestations in
 Western Kentucky (Lexington: Univ.
 Kentucky, Studies in Anthro., no.3,
 1966), pp.64-126. il.

Cumberland Falls
-Fall of anomalous meteorite
 1919, April 9
 "An Interesting Meteorite," Nature
 105 (1920):759.

Drake Mound
-Archeological site
 William S. Webb, "Mt. Horeb Earth-
 works and the Drake Mound," Pub.
 Anthro.& Arch.Univ.Kentucky, vol.5,
 no.2 (1941). il.
 William S. Webb & Raymond S. Baby,
 The Adena People, No.2 (Columbus:
 Ohio State Univ., 1957).

Eagle Creek
-Archeological site
 Ayres Mound
 Richard T. Crowe, "Wolfmen of the
 Ohio Valley," Fate 25 (Jan.1972):
 52-56. il.

Eddy Creek
-Archeological site
 ca.6000 B.C./Henderson site
 Martha Ann Rolingson & Douglas W.

Schwartz, Late Paleo-Indian and
Early Archaic Manifestations in
Western Kentucky (Lexington: Univ.
Kentucky, Studies in Anthro., no.3,
1966), pp.17-27. il.

Ewes Branch
-Archeological site
ca.6000 B.C.-1550 A.D./Roach site
    Martha Ann Rolingson & Douglas W.
    Schwartz, Late Paleo-Indian and
    Early Archaic Manifestations in
    Western Kentucky (Lexington: Univ.
    Kentucky, Studies in Anthro., no.3,
    1966), pp.28-63. il.

Green R.
-Archeological sites
    Clarence Moore, "Some Aboriginal
    Sites on Green River, Kentucky," J.
    Acad.Nat.Sci.Philadelphia 16 (1916):
    432-511. il.
    William S. Webb & William G. Haag,
    "Cypress Creek Villages," Rept.Arch.
    & Anthro.Univ.Kentucky, vol.4, no.
    2 (1939). il.
    Martha Ann Rolingson & Douglas W.
    Schwartz, Late Paleo-Indian and
    Early Archaic Manifestations in
    Western Kentucky (Lexington: Univ.
    Kentucky, Studies in Anthro., no.3,
    1966).

Herrington L.
-Lake monster
    1972, summer/Lawrence S. Thompson
    Louisville Courier-Journal, 7 Aug.
    1972.

Indian Knoll
-Archeological site
4000-1500 B.C.
    Clarence Moore, "Some Aboriginal
    Sites on Green River, Kentucky," J.
    Acad.Nat.Sci.Philadelphia 16 (1916);
    432,444-80. il.
    H.N. Wardle, "The Indian Knoll," Am.
    Indian Mag. 7 (1919):31-38. il.
    William S. Webb, Indian Knoll (Knox-
    ville: Univ. of Tennessee, 1974).

Jeptha Knob
-Meteorite crater
3200 m.diam./possible
    Walter H. Bucher, "Geology of Jeptha
    Knob," Kentucky Geol.Survey, ser.6,
    21 (1925):193-237.
    R.S. Dietz, "Meteorite Impact Sug-
    gested by Shatter Cones in Rock,"
    Science 131 (1960):1781-84.
    Ralph B. Baldwin, The Measure of the
    Moon (Chicago: Univ. of Chicago,
    1963), pp.98-99.

Loman Hill
-Human tracks in sandstone
1931/Ott Finnell
    New York Times, 20 Jan.1938, p.25.
    "Human-Like Tracks in Stone Are Rid-
    dle to Scientists," Science News

Letter 34 (1938):278-79.
    "Geology and Ethnology Disagree About
    Rock Prints," Science News Letter
    34 (1938):372.
    Albert G. Ingalls, "The Carbonifer-
    ous Mystery," Sci.Am. 162 (1940):
    14. il.
    Louisville Courier-Journal, 24 May
    1953.
    Wilbert Rusch, "Human Footprints in
    Rock," Creation Rsch.Soc'y Quar.,
    Mar.1971, pp.204,207-12. il.
    Jack Bowman, Jr., "Footprints of
    Adam?" Fate 28 (Feb.1975):54-58. il.

Mammoth Cave
-Archeological site
ca.400 B.C.
    N.C. Nelson, "Contributions to the
    Archeology of Mammoth Cave and Vi-
    cinity, Kentucky," Anthro.Pap.Am.
    Mus.Nat.Hist., vol.22, pt.1 (1917),
    pp.1-73.
    Douglas W. Schwartz, Conceptions of
    Kentucky Prehistory (Lexington:
    Univ. of Kentucky, 1967).
    Patty Jo Watson, ed., Archeology of
    the Mammoth Cave Area (N.Y.: Aca-
    demic, 1974). il.
-Giant human skeletons
    [Alexander Bullitt], Rambles in Mam-
    moth Cave During the Year 1844
    (Louisville: Morton & Griswold,
    1845).
-Mummy
1935/Lost John
    Alonzo W. Pond, "Lost John of Mummy
    Ledge," Nat.History 39 (Mar.1937):
    176-84. il.
    Georg K. Neumann, "The Human Remains
    from Mammoth Cave, Kentucky," Am.
    Antiquity 3 (1938):339-53.
    Harold Meloy, Mummies of Mammoth Cave
    (Shelbyville, Ind.: Micron, 1973),
    pp.14 20. il.
    Louise M. Robbins, "Prehistoric Peo-
    ple of the Mammoth Cave Area," in
    Patty Jo Watson, ed., Archeology of
    the Mammoth Cave Area (N.Y.: Acad-
    emic, 1974), pp.137-62. il.

Mitchellsburg Knob
-Phantom panther
1966/Miles Penn
    (Editorial), Fate 20 (June 1967):12.

North Elkhorn Creek
-Archeological site
Adena Park
    Franklin Folsom, America's Ancient
    Treasures (N.Y.: Rand McNally,
    1974), p.140.

Ohio R.
-Phantom panther
1972
    Peter Guttilla, "Monster Menagerie,"
    Saga UFO Rept. 4 (Sep.1977):32,65.

Redbird R.
-Petroglyph
Vernon J. Calhoun, "Redbird River Inscription," Occ.Pub.Epigraphic Soc'y
7, no.148 (Apr.1979):90-91. il.

Salts Cave
-Mummy
1875/Little Alice
Horace Carter Hovey & Richard Ells-
worth Call, Mammoth Cave of Kentucky
(Louisville: John P. Morton, 1897),
p.28.
Patty Jo Watson, "Prehistoric Miners
of Salts Cave, Kentucky," Archaeol-
ogy 19 (Oct.1966):242.
Robert L. Hall, "Archeology by Lamp-
light: An Exploration of Salts
Cave, Kentucky," Central States
Arch.J., vol.15, no.1 (1968):7-12.
Patty Jo Watson, "The Prehistory of
Salts Cave, Kentucky," Rept.Invests.
Illinois State Mus., no.16 (1969).
il.
Louise M. Robbins, "A Woodland 'Mum-
my' from Salts Cave, Kentucky," Am.
Antiquity 36 (1971):200-206. il.
Harold Meloy, Mummies in Mammoth Cave
(Shelbyville, Ind.: Micron, 1973),
pp.7-13. il.

Scott's Fork
-UFO (NL)
1955, Oct./Oakie Montgomery
(Editorial), Fate 9 (Feb.1956):7-8.

Short Cave
-Mummies
1811-1814
(Editorial), Medical Repository 17
(Mar.1815):391.
(Letter), Samuel L. Mitchill, Analec-
teck Mag., Sep.1815, pp.260-61.
Worcester Massachusetts Spy, 17 July
1816, p.4.
(Letter), Charles Wilkins, Trans.&
Coll.Am.Antiquarian Soc'y 1 (1820):
361-64.
C.S. Rafinesque, "The Caves of Ken-
tucky," Atlantic J. 1 (1832):29.
Ebenezer Meriam, "Mammoth Cave," N.Y.
Municipal Gazette 1 (21 Feb.1844):
317-18.
N. Parker Willis, Health Trip to the
Tropics (N.Y.: Scribner, 1853), pp.
203-204.
Charles W. Wright, Guide Manual to
Mammoth Cave (Louisville: Bradley &
Gilbert, 1860), p.49.
Charles H. Rogers, Incidents of Trav-
el in the Southern States (N.Y.: R.
Craigherd, 1862), p.282.
W. Stump Forwood, Mammoth Cave of
Kentucky (Philadelphia: Lippincott,
1870), p.170.
Frederick W. Putnam, "Archaeological
Researches in Kentucky and Indiana
1874," Proc.Boston Soc'y Nat.Hist.
17 (1875):319-31.
Harold Meloy, Mummies in Mammoth Cave

(Shelbyville, Ind.: Micron, 1973),
pp.5-7,22-38. il.
Louise M. Robbins, "Prehistoric People of the Mammoth Cave Area," in
Patty Jo Watson, ed., Archeology of
the Mammoth Cave Area (N.Y.: Academic, 1974), pp.137-62.

Stonor's Creek
-Archeological site
E.G. Squier & E.H. Davis, Ancient
Monuments of the Mississippi Valley
(Washington: Smithsonian Institution,
Contrib.to Knowl., no.1, 1848), p.
35.

Tar Springs
-Petroglyphs
Fred E. Coy, Jr. & Thomas C. Fuller,
"Tar Springs Petroglyphs, Brecken-
ridge County, Kentucky," Tennessee
Arch. 24 (1968):29-35. il.

Troublesome Creek
-Genetic anomaly
=hereditary blue coloring
(Editorial), Fate 28 (Mar.1975):20-
23, quoting Los Angeles (Cal.) Times
(undated).

Turkey Foot Gap
-UFO (DD)
1977, Nov.12/Linda Russell
Stanford Interior Journal, 24 Nov.
1977.

Turkey Rock
-Petroglyphs
Fred E. Coy, Jr. & Thomas C. Fuller,
"Turkey Rock Petroglyphs, Green
River, Kentucky," Tennessee Arch.
23 (1967):58-79. il.

U.S. 60
-Fall of mud balls
1973, Aug./William Franklin Leviness
(Editorial), Fate 27 (Jan.1974):34.
(Letter), Jerry Noble, Fate 27 (May
1974):160.
(Letter), Gary Parrish, Fate 27 (May
1974):160.

Wright Mounds
-Archeological site
William S. Webb, "The Wright Mounds,"
Pub.Anthro.& Arch.Univ.Kentucky,
vol.5, no.1 (1940). il.

D. Unspecified Localities

-Ancient sculptures
Virginia border
Vernon J. Calhoun, "Libyan Evidence
in Southeast Kentucky," Occ.Pub.
Epigraphic Soc'y 6, no.127 (Jan.
1979):109-14. il.
Barry Fell, "Inscriptions on Kentucky
Sculptures," Occ.Pub. Epigraphic
Soc'y 6, no.128 (Jan.1979):115-16.

-Fall of stone
  ca.1810
    Vance Randolph, Ozark Superstitions
    (N.Y.: Columbia Univ., 1947), p.72.

-Glacial anomaly
    "High Level Gravels of Kentucky,"
    Science 3 (1896):276.
    Willard R. Jillson, "Glacial Pebbles
    in Eastern Kentucky," Science 60
    (1924):101-102.

-Phantom
  1784, May 24/John Chesselden/Kenfry?
  Kentontown?
    John Chesselden & James Arkins, A
    Surprising Account of the Devil's
    Appearing to John Chesselden and
    James Arkins (Norwich: John Trum-
    bull, 1785).
    Henry Wysham Lanier, "When the Devil
    Appeared in the Mississippi Valley,"
    Golden Book Mag. 3 (1926):355-58.
    Fred W. Allsopp, Folklore of Romantic
    Arkansas, 2 vols. (N.Y.: Grolier
    Soc'y, 1931), 1:234-38.

THE NORTH CENTRAL

ILLINOIS

A. Populated Places

Adams co.
-Archeological site
  serpent effigy
    Stephen D. Peet, "The Great Serpent
    and Other Effigies," Am.Antiquarian
    12 (1890):211-28.
    "Were the Druids in America?" Am.
    Antiquarian 12 (1890):294-302.
-Ball lightning and UFO (NL)
  n.d.
    Harry Middleton Hyatt, Folk-lore from
    Adams County, Illinois (Hannibal,
    Mo.: Alma Egan Hyatt Foundation,
    1965), pp.762-65.
-Poltergeists
  n.d.
    Harry Middleton Hyatt, Folk-lore from
    Adams County, Illinois (Hannibal,
    Mo.: Alma Egan Hyatt Foundation,
    1965), pp.726-30.

Alden
-Fall of dolomite
  1960, July/Charley Wissell
    (Editorial), Fate 13 (Dec.1960):12-
    16, quoting Chicago Sun-Times (un-
    dated).

Algonquin
-Seance
  1930s/W.D. Chesney
    W.D. Chesney, "A Trick-Proof Spirit
    Cabinet," Fate 22 (Aug.1969):92-96.
-UFO (NL)
  1969, Jan.9/Russell Hickman
    Chicago Tribune, 10 Jan.1969.
    "More on January Sightings in Illi-
    nois," Skylook, no.16 (Mar.1969):
    14-15.
    "U.S. Roundup," APRO Bull. 17 (Mar.-
    Apr.1969):6.

Alma
-UFO (NL)
  1910, May 19/Myron Craig
    Myron Craig, "An Enigma of the Heav-
    ens," Skylook, no.29 (Apr.1970):4-8.

Alton
-Giant bird
  1948, April 4/Walter Siegmund
  1948, April 24/E.M. Coleman
    Jerome Clark & Loren Coleman, "Winged
    Wierdies," Fate 25 (Mar.1972):80,
    85-86.
-Skyquake
  1951, Nov.20
    "Jest Planes Again," Doubt, no.37
    (1952):148,149.
-UFO (CE-3)
  1971, June 15/Tony Wilkens/1009 W. 9th
    Alton Evening Telegraph, 16 June 1971.

"More on Tony Wilkens," Skylook, no.
    46 (Sep.1971):5.
  1975, Oct.13/Ms. Hicks
    David Schroth, "Woman Sees Possible
    Humanoids," Skylook, no.98 (Jan.
    1976):3-5.
-UFO (NL)
  1897, April 14/Peter Demuth/Apple St.
    Alton Evening Telegraph, 14 Apr.1897,
    p.3.
  1897, April 14/Elmus Clapp
    Alton Evening Telegraph, 15 Apr.1897,
    p.3.
  1952, July 12/William H. Scott
    (Letter), Fate 5 (Dec.1952):117-18.

Amboy
-Precognition
  1918-1920/Edgar B. Smith
    Ruby Smith, "Father's 'Spell of Know-
    ing,'" Fate 23 (Dec.1970):92-97.

Andalusia
-UFO (NL)
  1897, April 14/Jim Dinkerson
    Washington Court House (O.) Cyclone
    & Fayette Republican, 22 Apr.1897.

Arcola
-UFO (NL)
  1897, April 11/Count Ferguson
    Tuscola Journal, 17 Apr.1897, p.1.

Armington
-Giant bird
  1977, July/James Major/W of town
    Gilbert J. Ziemba, "Mysterious 'Giant
    Bird'--Invades Central Illinois,"
    Page Rsch.Library Newsl., no.20
    (18 Sep.1977):14.

Arrowsmith
-UFO (NL)
  1897, April 16
    Bloomington Pantagraph, 17 Apr.1897,
    p.5.

Astoria
-Airship message
  1897, April 17/Bert Swearengen
    Astoria Searchlight, 22 Apr.1897, p.
    4.

Auburn
-Fall of worms
  1878, Jan.11
    Auburn Advertiser, 11 Jan.1878.

Aurora
-Clairvoyance
  1949, Nov.23/Herbert Hopkins
    Berthold Eric Schwarz, "The Man-in-
    Black Syndrome: 2," Flying Saucer
    Rev. 23 (Feb.1978):22,23.

-Haunt
  n.d./Bill Freitag
    Brad Steiger, Mysteries of Time and
      Space (N.Y.: Dell, 1976 ed.), p.222.
  1970s/Herbert Hopkins
    Berthold Eric Schwarz, "The Man-in-
      Black Syndrome: 2," Flying Saucer
      Rev. 23 (Feb.1978):22,24.
-Humanoid and dog mutilations
  1974, Jan.
    Elgin Daily News-Courier, 26 Jan.
      1974.
-Precognition
  1957/Herbert Hopkins
    Berthold Eric Schwarz, "The Man-in-
      Black Syndrome: 2," Flying Saucer
      Rev. 23 (Feb.1978):22,23-24.
-UFO (?)
  1978, April 29/=advertising plane
    Allan Hendry, "The Case for IFO
      Study: A Recent Example," Int'l UFO
      Reporter 3 (June 1978):6-7.
-UFO (DD)
  1967, March 8/Lonnie Davis
    Aurora Beacon-News, 9 Mar.1967.
-UFO (NL)
  1897, April 9
    Aurora Beacon, 10 Apr.1897, p.1.
  1897, April 11
    Aurora Beacon, 12 Apr.1897, p.8.
  1958, Oct.12/William Hornyan
    Chicago Daily News, 13 Oct.1958.
  1958, Oct.14
    "New Wave of UFO Sightings Cracks
      Censorship Wall," NICAP Spec.Bull.,
      Nov.1958, pp.1,2.
  1967, Jan.-Feb./Ronald Kolberg
    Aurora Beacon-News, 9 Mar.1967.

Aviston
-UFO (NL)
  1970, Nov.26/Bob Crow/W on Hwy.50
    "Ball of Light over Aviston, Ill.,"
      Skylook, no.38 (Jan.1971):4.
  1971, Jan.26/Arnold T. Wessel
    "Illinois Man Watches Bell-Shaped
      Object," Skylook, no.40 (Mar.1971):
      16.

Barrington
-UFO (CE-1)
  1975, Aug.18
    "UFO Central," CUFOS News Bull., 15
      Nov.1975, p.16.
-UFO (NL)
  1969, Jan.9
    Chicago Tribune, 10 Jan.1969.
    "U.S. Roundup," APRO Bull. 17 (Mar.-
      Apr.1969):6.
  1975, Sep.26
    "UFO Central," CUFOS News Bull., 15
      Nov.1975, p.19.
  1975, Nov.19
    "UFO Central," CUFOS News Bull., 1
      Feb.1976, p.13.

Bartelso
-UFO (CE-1)
  1972, Jan./Donna Wilken
    East St. Louis Journal, 31 May 1972.

"Triangular Object Follows Car," Skylook, no.55 (June 1972):9.

Bartlett
-UFO (CE-1)
  1967, March 7/Lucille Drzonek
    "Sightings Still on Upswing," APRO
      Bull. 15 (Mar.-Apr.1967):11.

Bartonville
-Haunt
  1915, June-   /cemetery at State Hospital
    James Anderson, "Haunted Cemetery,"
      Fate 28 (June 1975):68, quoting In-
      stitute Quar., 1916.

Beardstown
-Archeological site
  J.F. Snyder, "Deposits of Flint Im-
    plements," Ann.Rept.Smith.Inst.,
    1876, pp.433,437.

Beckemeyer
-UFO (?)
  1972, Aug.2/Edward Albat
    "Beckemeyer Couple See Fireball,"
      Skylook, no.59 (Oct.1972):13.
-UFO (DD)
  1970, Aug./Debbie Tallman
    "High School Girls Watch Objects,"
      Skylook, no.38 (Jan.1971):4.
-UFO (NL)
  1967, Sep./Mae Jannett
    "UFO Reports Made at the Carlyle Sky-
      watch and Picnic," Skylook, no.34
      (Sep.1970):6.
  1970, Nov.16/Jacqueline Lanter/public
school
    Breese Journal, 19 Nov.1970.
  1971, spring
    "Men Believe They Saw UFO Take Off,"
      Skylook, no.55 (June 1972):8.
  1971, April 13
    "Moving Bright Light Observed," Sky-
      look, no.45 (Aug.1971):13.
  1971, June 16/Gerald Skiver
  1971, June 18/Terry S. Turner
  1971, Aug.25/Gerald Skiver
    "UFO Reports from Illinois," Skylook,
      no.47 (Oct.1971):13.
  1971, Nov.1/George Jannett
    "Flashing Light Crosses Illinois Sky,"
      Skylook, no.49 (Dec.1971):18.
  1972, Jan.8/Gerald Skiver
    "Student Studies Stars--Sees UFO,"
      Skylook, no.55 (June 1972):9.
  1972, Feb.18/George Jannett/Hwy.50
    "Bright Light at Beckemeyer, Ill.,"
      Skylook, no.53 (Apr.1972):7.
  1972, Sep.23/Steve Garner
    "Two See Bright Light over Beckemeyer,
      Ill.," Skylook, no.62 (Jan.1973):10.
  1975, Jan.3/Olive Kohrs
    "MUFON Reports in Brief," Skylook, no.
      89 (Apr.1975):10.

Beecher
-UFO (NL)
  1976, Nov.25

"UFOs of Limited Merit," Int'l UFO
Reporter 2 (Jan.1977):5.

Belleville
-Coffin anomaly
1968, July 18/=Fisk Metallic Burial
Case
Ruth Duy, "This 100-Year-Old Beauty,"
Fate 22 (Feb.1969):60-63. il.
-Haunt
1962-1967/Dollie Walta/Main x 17th St.
Hans Holzer, Gothic Ghosts (N.Y.:
Pocket Books, 1972), pp.136-45.
-Precognition
1941, spring/Victor Werner/Scott AFB
Victor Werner, "The Making of a Be-
liever," Fate 27 (Jan.1974):90-92.
-UFO (?)
1897, April/=kite
Sterling Evening Gazette, 10 Apr.1897,
p.4.
Edwardsville Intelligencer, 29 Apr.
1897, p.4.
-UFO (NL)
1968, Jan.18/Kenneth A. Klamm
"Six UFO's over Missouri and Illi-
nois," Skylook, no.6-7 (Feb.-Mar.
1968):9.
1970, Sep./Maxine Frantz/112 N. Vine
"Was This a Blimp?" Skylook, no.36
(Niv.1970):6.
1971, Jan.21/Mrs. Don Rogier
(Letter), Can.UFO Rept., no.10 (1971)
:30.
1971, June 6
"Illinois Housewife Sights Bright
Object," Skylook, no.44 (July 1971)
:10.
1972, June 11/Paul Dorn/59th St.
"Lights Moving in Circle Sighted in
Illinois," Skylook, no.56 (July
1972):7.
1972, July 31/John Rosenkranz
Belleville News-Democrat, 1 Aug.1972.
1975, Jan.1/James Williams
Robert A. Goerman, "The UFO Modus
Operandi: January 1975," Official
UFO 1 (Aug.1976):46.

Belvidere
-Phantom panther
1970-1971/Floyd C. Palhill/nr.Green
Giant Plant
(Letter), Patricia Ann Moeller, Fate
24 (Sep.1971):159-60.

Bensenville
-UFO (CE-1)
1972, Aug.11/Hwy.83
"Orange UFO Sighted in Chicago Sub-
urbs," Skylook, no.59 (Oct.1972):11.
-UFO (NL)
1975, July 1
"UFO Central," CUFOS News Bull., 15
Nov.1975, p.12.

Bismarck
-UFO (NL)
1897, April 12/Hardy H. Whitlock
Danville Daily News, 17 Apr.1897, p.2.

Bloomingdale
-UFO (NL)
1976, June 24
"Noteworthy UFO Sightings," Ufology
2 (fall 1976):60.

Bloomington
-Dowsing
n.d./Mrs. J.M. Curry
(Editorial), Fate 9 (Nov.1956):6.
-Giant bird
1977, July 31/Mrs. Albert Dunham
Bloomington Pantagraph, 1 Aug.1977.
-Humanoid
1970, Aug./Vicki Otto/3 mi.SE on Ire-
land Grove Rd.
Loren E. Coleman, "Mystery Animals
in Illinois," Fate 24 (Mar.1971):
48,53.
-Spontaneous human combustion
n.d./Aura Troyer
"Pyrotics," Doubt, no.29 (1950):26.
-UFO (DD)
1897, April 11
Bloomington Pantagraph, 12 Apr.1897,
p.5.

Bonnie
-Humanoid
1942, March
Carbondale Free Press, 26 Mar.1942.
Jesse Harris, "Myths and Legends
from Southern Illinois," Hoosier
Folklore 5 (Mar.1946):14,19.

Boulder
-UFO (CE-1)
1967, Jan./Randy Hutchin/3 mi.N
"Illinois Pre-Law Student Sees UFO,"
Skylook, no.23 (Oct.1969):22.
-UFO (NL)
1969, Aug./Duane Bright/SE of town
"Carlyle Business Man Reports 1969
Sighting," Skylook, no.44 (July
1971):11.
1971, July 6/Duane Bright/3 mi.E
"UFO Reports from Illinois," Skylook,
no.47 (Oct.1971):13.

Bradford
-UFO (DD)
1950, March 18/Robert Fisher/5 mi.NE
Robert Fisher, "Confidentially," Air
Facts 13 (1 May 1950):29-30.
-UFO (NL)
1950, Dec.27/Art Shutts
William A. Dixon, "Saucers or Illu-
sions?" Air Facts 14 (1 Sep.1951):37-
43.

Breese
-UFO (CE-2)
1967, Dec.29/Charles Grapperhaus
"Illinois Boys See UFO," Skylook, no.
17 (Apr.1969):11.
-UFO (NL)
1971, March 30/Harold Meyer
Breese Journal, 1 Apr.1971.
"UFO Sighted at Breese, Ill.," Sky-
look, no.42 (May 1971):9.

1971, May 20/nr. Beaver Creek Bridge
"Cone-Shaped Object Hovers near Coal
Mine," Skylook, no.45 (Aug.1971):13.

Brimfield
-UFO (NL)
1976, Jan.8
"Noteworthy UFO Sightings," Ufology
2 (summer 1976):62.

Broadview
-UFO (NL)
1976, June 21
"Noteworthy UFO Sightings," Ufology
2 (fall 1976):60.

Brookfield
-UFO (NL)
1975, Nov.16
"UFO Central," CUFOS News Bull., 1
Feb.1976, p.13.

Brownstown
-UFO (CE-4)
1975, Jan.5/David Mahon
Vandalia Leader-Union, 4 Feb.1975.
il.

Brussels
-Rock pillars
R.V. Dietrich, "Conical and Cylindri-
cal Structures in the Potsdam Sandstone, Redwood, New York," N.Y.
State Mus.Circular, no.34 (1953):
8-9.

Burnt Prairie
-UFO (CE-2)
1975, Aug.31, Sep.3/Ivan Phillips/
ground markings only
Fairfield Wayne County Press, 8 Sep.
1975.

Bushnell
-UFO (NL)
1970, Sep.3/Allen Robinson/McDonough
F-S grain bins
Macomb Journal, 5 Sep.1970.

Cairo
-Fall of frogs
1883, Aug.2/"Success"
Decatun Daily Republican, 3 Aug.1883,
p.2.
-Humanoid
1972, July 25/Leroy Summers/Ohio River
levee
Cairo Evening Citizen, 26 July 1972.
-UFO (?)
1897, April 16/Evelyn Baldwin/=Venus
Chicago Times-Herald, 17 Apr.1897,
p.6.
1967, Jan.
St. Louis (Mo.) Post-Dispatch, 21
Jan.1967.
-UFO (CE-1)
1973, Oct.11
Cairo Evening Citizen, 17 Oct.1973.

Caledonia
-Giant bird
1948, April 9/Robert Price
Jerome Clark & Loren Coleman, "Winged
Wierdies," Fate 25 (Mar.1972):80,84.

Cambridge
-UFO (NL)
1973, Oct.15/Gilbert Phillis, Jr.
Glenn McWane & David Graham, The New
UFO Sightings (N.Y.: Warner, 1974),
pp.16-17.

Canton
-Precognition
1974/Don Davis/Box 587
Warren Smith, "Phenomenal Predictions
for 1975," Saga, Jan.1975, pp.20,22.
-UFO (CE-1)
1965, Aug.1
Lucius Farish, "The Mini-Saucers,"
Fate 27 (Dec.1974):59,64.
-UFO (NL)
1897, April 13
Canton Register, 15 Apr.1897, p.1.
1971, Jan.24/Edward L. Sale
"Object Seen over Canton, Ill.,"
Skylook, no.40 (Mar.1971):15.
1971, July 21/Mike Hinds
Canton Daily Ledger, 22 July 1971.

Carbondale
-Giant lizard
1973, June 22/Jack Downs/Crab Orchard
Wildlife Refuge
Carbondale Southern Illinoisan, 27
June 1973, p.3; and 28 June 1973,
p.3.
-UFO (DD)
1950, April 23/Don Holt/N on U.S.51
Dean Margen, "The Red Bud, Illinois
Photo," Flying Saucers, no.36 (Oct.
1959):5-7.

Carlyle
-Archeological site
ca.100 B.C.-1000 A.D./Hatchery West
Lewis R. Binford, et al., "Archeology at Hatchery West," Mem.Soc'y Am.
Arch., no.24 (1970). il.
-Mystery fog
1956, Sep.23, 25/=pollution
June E. Weidemann, "Mystery of the
Charred Paint," Fate 10 (May 1957):
60-61.
-UFO (NL)
1897, April 14
Chicago Times-Herald, 16 Apr.1897,
p.1.
1970, Jan.8/Carol Johnson/5 mi.S
"Unusual Incident Reported in Illinois," Skylook, no.28 (Mar.1970):3.
1971, April 30/Herb Williams/2090 Washington
"Illinois Man Follows Sky Object,"
Skylook, no.43 (June 1971):6.
1971, May 4/Herb Alexander/E on Hwy.77
"Carlyle Men Observe Light," Skylook,
no.45 (Aug.1971):18.
1971, May 11/Jerell Garner/Carlyle L.

"Huge UFO Sighted near Carlyle Lake,"
Skylook, no.44 (July 1971):9, quoting Breese Journal (undated).
1971, June 17
1971, July 10
"UFO Reports from Illinois," Skylook,
no.47 (Oct.1971):13.
1972, April 19/S on U.S.50
"Carlyle Woman Reports UFO," Skylook,
no.55 (June 1972):8.

Carmi
-UFO (NL)
1978, Aug.16-17/Dee Heil
Indianapolis (Ind.) Star, 18 Aug.
1978.

Carol Stream
-Humanoid
1974, Aug.27/Bob Calusinsky
Chicago Tribune, 6 Oct.1974.
"Report from Illinois," Sasquatch
News 1 (Oct.1974):3-4.
B. Ann Slate, "Man-Ape's Reign of
Terror," Saga UFO Rept. 4 (Aug.1977)
:20-22.
-UFO (CE-2)
1968, March 4/Don Ryon
"Use of Detectors in Spotting UFO,"
APRO Bull. 16 (Mar.-Apr.1968):7.

Carpentersville
-UFO (NL)
1975, Aug.8
"UFO Central," CUFOS News Bull., 15
Nov.1975, p.15.

Carroll co.
-UFO (NL)
1897, April 8/Mrs. W.H. Stiteley
Dixon Telegraph, 12 Apr.1897, p.8.

Carrollton
-Cattle mutilation
1975/Chester Gourley
(Editorial), Fate 28 (Sep.1975):10.
-UFO (NL)
1897, April 14
Carrollton Gazette, 16 Apr.1897, p.6.
Carrollton Patriot, 16 Apr.1897, p.4.

Carthage
-UFO (CE-1)
n.d.
Harry Middleton Hyatt, Folk-lore from
Adams County, Illinois (Hannibal,
Mo.: Alma Egan Hyatt Foundation,
1965), p.771.
-UFO (NL)
1970, Oct.14/Mrs. Raymond Todd/W on
U.S.136
Robert Smulling, "A Midwest Flap?"
Skylook, no.36 (Nov.1970):1.
1971, Feb.2/Ruby Simmons/N on Hwy.96
Robert Smulling, "More UFO Reports,"
Skylook, no.40 (Mar.1971):13.
1976, April 21
Raymond E. Fowler, "MUFON Quarterly
UFO Activity Report," MUFON UFO J.,
no.104 (July 1976):3.

Cary
-UFO (NL)
1969, Jan.9/Vera Matter
Chicago Tribune, 10 Jan.1969.
"More on January Sightings in Illi-
nois," Skylook, no.16 (Mar.1969):
14-15.
"U.S. Roundup," APRO Bull. 17 (Mar.-
Apr.1969):6.

Cass co.
-Roman coin
1882
"An Ancient Roman Coin Found in Illinois," Sci.Am. 46 (1882):382.

Cedar Point
-Mystery stone spheres
"Stone Spheres: Part 2," Pursuit 1
(30 Sep.1968):13,14.

Centralia
-Phantom panther
1971, Feb./E of town
Centralia Sentinel, 1 Mar.1971.
-UFO (CE-2)
1968, May-June
"Illinois Family Reports Strange Ex-
perience in 1968," Skylook, no.58
(Sep.1972):11.
-UFO (NL)
1963, Aug.7
Jacques Vallee, Passport to Magonia
(Chicago: Regnery, 1969), p.293.
1970, Sep.9/Mrs. Arnold Gluck/615 W.
Kell St.
Centralia Sentinel, 11 Sep.1970.
1970, Nov.24/Sam Alli
"Two Observers Watch Round Object
Move Across Illinois Sky," Skylook,
no.38 (Jan.1971):1.
1978, Aug.17/N. Cherry St.
Centralia Sentinel, 18 Aug.1978.

Centreville
-Humanoid
1963, May/James McKinney
Chicago Daily News, 24 May 1963.

Champaign
-Tornado anomaly
1942, summer
B. Vonnegut & James Weyer, "Luminous
Phenomena in Nocturnal Tornadoes,"
Science 153 (1966):1213-20.
-UFO (DD)
1977, Oct.13
"UFOs of Limited Merit," Int'l UFO
Reporter 2 (Nov.1977):newsfront sec.
-UFO (NL)
1970, Aug.31/Robert Peterson/Mattis x
Kirby Ave.
Champaign-Urbana Courier, 1 Sep.1970.
1971, Oct.6/David R. James/S on I-57
"Several See UFOs near Champaign,
Ill.," Skylook, no.48 (Nov.1971):4.

Chenoa
-Erratic crocodilian
1972, Sep.22/U.S.66

Champaign-Urbana Courier, 22 Sep.
1972, p.6.

Cherry Valley
-UFO (CE-2)
1956, Sep.30/Mrs. L.L. Leonard
"Case 234," CRIFO Orbit, 7 Dec.1956,
p.1.

Chester
-UFO (?)
1977, Aug.2/=hoax
Luke Grisholm, "The Night an American
Town Died of Fright," Official UFO
3 (Jan.1978):24-27,53-56.
Ann Druffel, "Magazine Hoax Exposed,"
MUFON UFO J., no.120 (Nov.1977):20.
Allan Hendry, "Sleep Well, Chester,
Illinois...It's UFOlogy That's Hurt-
ing," Int'l UFO Reporter 3 (Jan.
1978):Newsfront sec.
Barbara Jordison, "The Town That
Wasn't Zapped by UFOs," Pursuit 13
(winter 1979):20-21.

Chicago
-Acoustic anomaly
1952/George Mueller/near N side/=TV
tube?
(Letter), Fate 8 (Oct.1955):111-12.
-Animal ESP
1974, June/E.P. Ladd/Clark St.
(Letter), Fate 27 (Dec.1974):130-31.
-Astrology
1960s/Katherine de Jersey
Katherine de Jersey & Isabella Taves,
Destiny Times Six: An Astrologer's
Casebook (Philadelphia: M. Evans,
1970).
1960s/Mrs. Merle Meyer
Brad Steiger, "The Seers Speak for
1970," Fate 23 (May 1970):78,83-84.
Warren Smith, "How Did the Seers in
1970?" Fate 24 (Feb.1971):84,89.
-Autoscopy
1958, March
Edward Podolsky, "Have You Seen Your
Double?" Fate 19 (Apr.1966):79.
-Ball lightning
1894, Sep.9/Mr. Austin
St. Louis (Mo.) Globe-Democrat, 10
Sep.1894.
Bleeding icon
1970, spring/L.S. McNamara/St. Adrian
Catholic Church
Worcester (Mass.) Telegram, 10 May
1970.
(Editorial), Fate 23 (Oct.1970):17.
il.
-Clairvoyance
n.d./Ms. Loganson
Nandor Fodor, Encyclopaedia of Psy-
chic Science (London: Arthurs,
1933), p.108.
1860s/Abraham James
Emma Hardinge Britten, Modern Ameri-
can Spiritualism (N.Y.: The Author,
1870), pp.528-30.
1934, fall/Miriam Golding
Miriam Golding, "I Was Lost in the

Fourth Dimension," Fate 9 (Sep.
1956):61-64.
1953-   /Olof Jonsson
Brad Steiger, "The Seers Speak for
1970," Fate 23 (May 1970):78,80.
Warren Smith, "How Did the Seers in
1970?" Fate 24 (Feb.1971):84,88.
Edgar D. Mitchell, "An ESP Test from
Apollo 14," J.Parapsych. 35 (1971):
89-107.
Brad Steiger, The Psychic Feats of
Olof Jonsson (Englewood Cliffs,
N.J.: Prentice-Hall, 1972).
David Wallechinsky & Irving Wallace,
The People's Almanac (Garden City:
Doubleday, 1975), p.7.
Warren Smith, "Phenomenal Predictions
for 1975," Saga, Jan.1975, pp.20,48.
Brad Steiger, Psychic City: Chicago
(Garden City: Doubleday, 1976), pp.
114-23. il.
-Contactee
1938-1962/William Ferguson/Cosmic Cir-
cle of Fellowship
William Ferguson, My Trip to Mars
(Chicago: Cosmic Circle of Fellow-
ship, 1954).
William Ferguson, A Message from
Outer Space (Oak Park, Ill.: Golden
Age, 1955).
1954, Nov.28-   /John Otto
Gray Barker, "Chasing the Flying Sau-
cers," Flying Saucers, July-Aug.
1958, pp.20-35.
1969/Salvatore/=hoax?
Brad Steiger, Mysteries of Time and
Space (N.Y.: Dell, 1976 ed.), pp.
174-80.
1970s/Sheila Schultz
Brad Steiger, Gods of Aquarius (N.Y.:
Harcourt Brace Jovanovich, 1976),
pp.126-29.
-Crisis apparition
1918, April/K Ave.
"Apparition and Veridical Auditory
Experience," J.ASPR 16 (1922):213-
14.
-Dematerialization
1898/Jean Durant
Nandor Fodor, "Falling into the
Fourth Dimension," Fate 9 (Dec.1956)
:04,05, quoting Guide and Ideas, 14
Nov.1936.
-Disappearance
1960, Nov.29/Meigs Field/Piper PA-23
Jay Gourley, The Great Lakes Triangle
(Greenwich, Ct.: Fawcett, 1977), p.
60.
1965, March 20/Joan Williams/Wings Air-
port
Chicago Daily News, 29 Mar.1965.
Jay Gourley, The Great Lakes Triangle
(Greenwich, Ct.: Fawcett, 1977), pp.
164-65.
-Divination
1903-1904/Lilliace M. Mitchell/40th St.
x Grand Ave.
Lilliace M. Mitchell, "Pictures on
the Bank Wall," Fate 21 (Dec.1968):
86-89.

-Erratic deer
  1945, Nov.2
    "More Animals," Doubt, no.14 (spring
    1946):203.
-Erratic kangaroo
  1974, Oct.18/Michael Byrne/Jefferson
  Park
  1974, Oct.19/Kenneth Griesheimer/Sunny-
  side x Mulligan St.
  1974, Oct.23/Schiller Woods
  1974, Oct.25/Cathy Battaglia/5600 block
  S. New England Ave.
  1974, Nov.3/Frank Kocherver/NW side
  1974, Nov.15/Joe Bernotus/Damon Ave.
  x Montrose St.
    Chicago Sun-Times, 19-21 Oct.1974.
    Wall Street Journal, 11 Dec.1974, p.
    1.
    David Fideler & Loren Coleman, "Kan-
    garoos from Nowhere," Fate 31 (Apr.
    1978):68-74.
-Fall of brown snow
  1947, Jan.27
    New York Herald-Tribune, 9 Mar.1947.
    "Color Falls," Doubt, no.18 (1947):
    267.
-Fall of fish
  1937, June 7/train "City of Denver"
    "Train Catches Fish," Fortean Soc'y
    Mag. 1 (Oct.1937):6.
-Fall of ice
  1973, Feb.15/4026 Bobby Lane
    (Editorial), Fate 26 (Nov.1973):28.
-Fall of money
  1975, Dec./Allen Davidson/LaSalle St.
    (Editorial), Fate 29 (Sep.1976):26.
-Fall of slag
  1879, April 9
    Chicago Tribune, 10 Apr.1879; and 11
    Apr.1879.
    New York Times, 14 Apr.1879, p.3.
    E.S. Bastin, "The Supposed Meteorite
    of Chicago," Am.J.Sci., ser.3, 18
    (1879):78.
-Fall of soot
  1958, Nov.23/T.E. Maroney/S side/=pol-
  lution
    "Falls," Doubt, no.59 (1959):37.
-Fire anomaly
  1871, Oct.8
    James W. Sheahan & George P. Upson,
    History of the Great Conflagration
    (Chicago: Union, 1872), pp.85-87,
    119-21,160-64,416-18.
    Ignatius Donnelly, Ragnarok: The Age
    of Fire and Gravel (Chicago: R.S.
    Peale, 1887), pp.413-23.
    Edgar Lee Masters, The Tale of Chi-
    cago (N.Y.: Putnam, 1933), pp.168-
    83.
    Paul M. Angle, ed., The Great Chicago
    Fire (Chicago: Chicago Historical
    Soc'y, 1946), pp.67-69.
  1953, Dec.
    Chicago Daily News, 9 Dec.1953.
-Ghost
  1971, March/kidney transplant patients
    Sheila Hervey, Some Canadian Ghosts
    (Richmond Hill, Ont.: Pocket Books,
    1973), p.129.

-Haunt
  n.d./Anthony Klimas
    Hans Holzer, Ghosts I've Met (N.Y.:
    Ace, 1965), p.55.
  1931-1936/Ernest Schroeter/Kedzie Ave.
    Ernest Schroeter, "My Five Years
    with a Ghost," Fate 15 (May 1962):
    72-74.
  1941/E. de Solminihac/Clark St. nr.
  Lincoln Park
    (Letter), Fate 6 (Apr.1953):124-26.
  1960-   /St. Rita's Church/6243 S.
  Fairfield Ave.
    Brad Steiger, Psychic City: Chicago
    (Garden City: Doubleday, 1976), p.
    94.
  1967/Alexandria Stewart/Hyde Park
    Henry Cole, "Chicago's WBBM-TV Hunts
    a Ghost," Fate 21 (June 1968):40-
    43.
    Hans Holzer, Psychic Investigator
    (N.Y.: Hawthorn, 1968).
  1970s/Holy Family Church/542 W. Hobbie
    Brad Steiger, Psychic City: Chicago
    (Garden City: Doubleday, 1976), pp.
    92-93.
  1970s/near N side
    "Enigmas," Probe the Unknown 1 (Oct.
    1973):10.
-Healing
  1960-1975/George Ivan Carter
    Thomas Millstead, "Healing Through
    Bone Symmetry," Fate 31 (Jan.1978):
    79-86.
  1970-   /Incol Foundation/2127 N.
  Seminary Dr.
    Thomas Millstead, "Healing Through
    Bone Symmetry," Fate 31 (Jan.1978):
    79,81-82.
  1973/Henry Rucker
    Brad Steiger, "How Much of Medicine
    Is Really Faith Healing?" Probe the
    Unknown 3 (Nov.1975):16-17.
    Brad Steiger, Psychic City: Chicago
    (Garden City: Doubleday, 1976), pp.
    78-86. il.
  1976/Theron Randolph/505 N. Lake Shore
  Dr.
    Paul Martin, "Fasting for Mental,
    Physical, Spiritual Health," Fate
    29 (Oct.1976):36,40.
-Hex
  1937/Frances Martin/Monroe St. nr.
  Damen Ave.
    Frances Louise Martin, "I Practiced
    Black Magic," Fate 9 (Oct.1956):15-
    18.
  1960s
    Chicago Daily News, 14 Jan.1966.
    Henry Cole, "Voodoo in Chicago," Fate
    19 (Oct.1966):84-95.
-Inner development
  1940s-   /Stelle Group
    Eklal Kueshana [Richard Kieninger],
    The Ultimate Frontier (Chicago:
    Stelle Group, 1963).
    Stelle Group, Stelle: A City for To-
    morrow (Chicago: Stelle Group, 1970).
    J. Gordon Melton, Encyclopedia of
    American Religions, 2 vols. (Wil-

mington, N.C.: Consortium, 1978),
2:189-90.
1940s-   /Neo-Pythagorean Gnostic
Church
    J. Gordon Melton, Encyclopedia of
    American Religions, 2 vols. (Wil-
    mington, N.C.: Consortium, 1978),
    2:264-65.
1950-   /Urantia Foundation
    Urantia Foundation, The Urantia Book
    (Chicago: Urantia, 1955).
    J. Gordon Melton, Encyclopedia of
    American Religions, 2 vols. (Wil-
    mington, N.C.: Consortium, 1978),
    2:119.
1960s-   /Sabaeans/2553 N. Halstead
    Hans Holzer, The New Pagans (Garden
    City: Doubleday, 1972), pp.124-37.
    Hans Holzer, The Witchcraft Report
    (N.Y.: Ace, 1973), pp.93-106.
    J. Gordon Melton, Encyclopedia of
    American Religions, 2 vols. (Wil-
    mington, N.C.: Consortium, 1978),
    2:298.
1963-   /Pristine Egyptian Orthodox
Church/2551 N. Halstead
    Hans Holzer, The Witchcraft Report
    (N.Y.: Ace, 1973), pp.115-16.
    Patrick Butler, "Ancient Egyptian
    Gods Come to Chicago," Fate 27 (Mar.
    1974):84-92. il.
    J. Gordon Melton, Encyclopedia of
    American Religions, 2 vols. (Wil-
    mington, N.C.: Consortium, 1978),
    2:295.
1966-   /Uranus Temple
    J. Gordon Melton, Encyclopedia of
    American Religions, 2 vols. (Wil-
    mington, N.C.: Consortium, 1978),
    2:290-91.
1970s/House of Occult/3109 N. Central
Ave.
    Brad Steiger, Psychic City: Chicago
    (Garden City: Doubleday, 1976), pp.
    71-74.
1970s/Ordo Templi Orientis Antiqua/30
E. Division St.
    Jim Brandon, Weird America (N.Y.:
    Dutton, 1978), p.77.
1971-   /Thee Satanic Orthodox Church
    J. Gordon Melton, Encyclopedia of
    American Religions, 2 vols. (Wil-
    mington, N.C.. Consortium, 1978),
    2:304-305.
-Lake monster
1867, Aug.6/Joseph Muhlke/L. Michigan,
off Hyde Park
    Chicago Tribune, 7 Aug.1867.
1892/Capt. McKee/L. Michigan/=hoax?
    Chicago Tribune, 24 July 1892.
-Mystery plane crash
1961, Feb.6/Peter Dekeita/nr. Meigs
Field/PA-22
1964, Feb.14/Robert Ryan Ferris/L.
Michigan/Cessna 150
1968, March 8/James Edmund Looker/De-
Haviland Dove/L. Michigan
    Jay Gourley, The Great Lakes Triangle
    (Greenwich, Ct.: Fawcett, 1977), pp.
    35-37,102-104,134.

1969, Nov.10/Dennis Head/PA-32
    Chicago Tribune, 11 Nov.1969.
    Jay Gourley, The Great Lakes Triangle
    (Greenwich, Ct.: Fawcett, 1977), pp.
    111-12.
1973, Oct.3/John J. Fair/L. Michigan/
Aerostar 601
    Chicago Daily News, 3 Oct.1973.
    Jay Gourley, The Great Lakes Triangle
    (Greenwich, Ct.: Fawcett, 1977), p.
    130.
-Norse mooring stone
1804/Waubansee stone/Chicago R.
    W.R. Anderson, "Norse Mooring Stone
    in Chicago?" Anthro.J.Canada 13,
    no.1 (1975):22. il.
    Chicago Tribune, 25 June 1975. il.
    "Vikings in Chicago? The Waubansee
    Stone," NEARA Newsl. 10 (summer-
    fall 1975):18.
-Out-of-body experience
1862, April 16/Henry Stanley/Camp
Douglas
    Henry Morton Stanley, The Autobiog-
    raphy of Henry Morton Stanley (Bos-
    ton: Houghton Mifflin, 1909), pp.
    207-208.
n.d.
    Herbert B. Greenhouse, The Astral
    Journey (N.Y.: Avon, 1976), pp.151-
    52, quoting R.B. Hout, Prediction,
    June 1936.
-Phantom
n.d./Dyan Cannon
    Brad Steiger, Revelation: The Divine
    Fire (Englewood Cliffs, N.J.: Pren-
    tice-Hall, 1973), p.125, quoting On
    View (undated).
-Poltergeist
1892, March
    Brooklyn (N.Y.) Eagle, 19 Apr.1892.
1900, Jan./Hyde Park
    New York Tribune, 7 Jan.1900.
1950s/Francis Filas
    (Editorial), Fate 11 (June 1958):12-
    13.
-Precognition
1870, summer/William Bates/26 Cottage
Grove Ave.
    Vaughn Shelton, "The Nightmare That
    Caught a Thief," Fate 9 (Apr.1956):
    55-57
1898, March 16/Mrs. A.P. Hill-Forsythe
    Chicago Inter-Ocean, 15 May 1898.
    "Premonition," J.ASPR 8 (1914):592-
    95.
1930s/Irene Kuhn/Michigan Ave.
    Irene Kuhn, Assigned to Adventure
    (Philadelphia: Lippincott, 1938).
ca.1930; 1940, July 10/Bob Farnham
    Bob Farnham, "My Grandmother's Spirit
    Guides Me," Fate 8 (July 1955):33-
    35.
1933, Jan.; 1962, Jan./Madam Bathsheba
    Jess Stearn, The Door to the Future
    (N.Y.: Macfadden, 1963), p.276.
1942, fall/Richard Szumski
    Richard Szumski, "An Unreliable Vis-
    ion: We're Living in the Wrong
    House," Fate 31 (Sep.1978):44-48.

1947/Ted Serios
  Ted Serios, "My Father's Promise,"
  Fate 17 (May 1964):66-70.
1957, June 3/Lee Geldhof
  (Letter), Fate 11 (Feb.1958):120-24.
1961-   /Irene Hughes/500 N. Michigan
  Ave., Suite 1039-40
  Chicago Sun-Times, 9 Feb.1967.
  David Techter, "One of Our Aircraft
  Is Missing: Can a Psychic Help?"
  Fate 21 (Nov.1968):37-42.
  Brad Steiger & Warren Smith, "How
  the Seers Scored in 1968," Fate 22
  (Jan.1969):72,77-78. il.
  Brad Steiger, "Scoring the Seers in
  1969," Fate 23 (Jan.1970):66,67. il.
  Brad Steiger, "Irene Hughes's Person-
  al Predictions for 1970," Saga, Jan.
  1970, pp.22-25,78-80.
  Brad Steiger, Know the Future Today
  (N.Y.: Paperback Library, 1970).
  Brad Steiger, "The Seers Speak for
  1970," Fate 23 (May 1970):78,84. il.
  Warren Smith, "How Did the Seers in
  1970?" Fate 24 (Feb.1971):84,88.
  Jerome Clark, "Fate Readers Predict
  for 1971," Fate 24 (June 1971):53,
  55-56.
  Brad Steiger, "Irene Hughes and the
  Canadian Kidnappings," Fate 24
  (July 1971):36-44.
  Alan Vaughan, "Interview: Irene
  Hughes," Psychic 3 (Dec.1971):4-7,
  32-35.
  Brad Steiger, Irene Hughes on Psychic
  Safari (N.Y.: Warner, 1972).
  Irene Hughes, ESPecially Irene (Blau-
  velt, N.Y.: Rudolf Steiner, 1972).
  David Wallechinsky & Irving Wallace,
  The People's Almanac (Garden City:
  Doubleday, 1975), pp.5-6.
  Warren Smith, "Phenomenal Predictions
  for 1976," Saga, Jan.1976, pp.16,19.
  Brad Steiger, Psychic City: Chicago
  (Garden City: Doubleday, 1976), pp.
  31-46.
  "Probe's 1977 Directory of the Psy-
  chic World," Probe the Unknown 5
  (spring 1977):32,36. il.
1967-   /Joseph DeLouise/6 E. Munro St.
  Chicago Sun-Times, 29 Dec.1967.
  David Techter, "Prediction of the
  Year," Fate 21 (June 1968):43.
  Brad Steiger & Warren Smith, "How
  the Seers Scored in 1968," Fate 22
  (Jan.1969):72,79.
  Brad Steiger, "Scoring the Seers in
  1969," Fate 23 (Jan.1970):66,70. il.
  Brad Steiger, "The Seers Speak for
  1970," Fate 23 (May 1970):78,81. il.
  Joseph DeLouise & Tom Valentine, Psy-
  chic Mission (Chicago: Regnery,
  1971).
  Warren Smith, "How Did the Seers in
  1970?" Fate 24 (Feb.1971):84,87-88.
  (Letter), Mrs. A.E. Boe, Fate 24
  (June 1971):128-30.
  John Godwin, Occult America (Garden
  City: Doubleday, 1972), pp.45-48.
  "Boom, Then Bust," Fate 26 (Feb.1973)

  :65, quoting Chicago Sun-Times (un-
  dated).
  Wall Street Journal, 23 Mar.1973.
  Herbert B. Greenhouse, Premonitions:
  A Leap into the Future (N.Y.: War-
  ner, 1973), pp.71-72.
  Kurt Saxon, Keeping Score on Our
  Modern Prophets (Eureka, Cal.: At-
  lan Foundation, 1974).
  David Wallechinsky & Irving Wallace,
  The People's Almanac (Garden City:
  Doubleday, 1975), p.4.
  Brad Steiger, Psychic City: Chicago
  (Garden City: Doubleday, 1976), pp.
  61-70.
  "Probe's 1977 Directory of the Psy-
  chic World," Probe the Unknown 5
  (spring 1977):32,35. il.
1967-1974/Clifford Matthew Royse/1961
  W. Farragut Ave.
  Brad Steiger & Warren Smith, "How
  the Seers Scored in 1968," Fate 22
  (Jan.1969):72,75.
  John Godwin, Occult America (Garden
  City: Doubleday, 1972), pp.33-35.
  Brad Steiger, Psychic City: Chicago
  (Garden City: Doubleday, 1976), pp.
  109-13.
1968/Teddy O'Hearn
  Brad Steiger & Warren Smith, "How
  the Seers Scored in 1968," Fate 22
  (Jan.1969):72,80.
  Brad Steiger, "Scoring the Seers in
  1969," Fate 23 (Jan.1970):66,71.
1969/Mae Darling
  Brad Steiger, "The Seers Speak for
  1970," Fate 23 (May 1970):78,81.
  Warren Smith, "How Did the Seers in
  1970?" Fate 24 (Feb.1971):84,87.
1974-   /Joseph East/4533 N. Whipple
  Warren Smith, "Phenomenal Predictions
  for 1975," Saga, Jan.1975, pp.20,22.
  Warren Smith, "Phenomenal Predictions
  for 1976," Saga, Jan.1976, pp.16,17.
1975/Mundelein College
  J.P. Bisaha & B.J. Dunne, "Precognitive Remote Viewing in the Chicago
  Area," in J.D. Morris, et al., eds.,
  Research in Parapsychology 1976 (Metuchen, N.J.: Scarecrow, 1977), pp.
  84-86.
1975/Joseph Pinkston/625 Arlington Pl.
  Warren Smith, "Phenomenal Predictions
  for 1976," Saga, Jan.1976, pp.16,52.
1976, Aug.6/Emmett Stovall/Midway Airport
  (Editorial), Fate 30 (Jan.1977):25.
1977/Laurie Brady/505 N. Lake Shore Dr.
  "Probe's 1977 Directory of the Psychic World," Probe the Unknown 5
  (spring 1977):32,34. il.
-Psychic photography
  1954-   /Ted Serios
  Pauline Oehler, "The Psychic Photography of Ted Serios," Fate 15 (Dec.
  1962):67-82. il.
  (Editorial), Fate 16 (Apr.1963):6.
  Allen Spraggett, "Toronto Test of Ted
  Serios' Paranormal Photographs,"
  Fate 18 (July 1965):38-45. il.

Jule Eisenbud, et al., "Some Unusual Data from a Session with Ted Serios," J.ASPR 61 (1967):241-53. il. (Editorial), Fate 20 (Aug.1967):7-28.

Charles Reynolds & David B. Eisendrath, Jr., "An Amazing Weekend with the Amazing Ted Serios," Pop.Photography 61 (Oct.1967):81-87,131-40, 158. il.

Jule Eisenbud, "The Cruel, Cruel World of Ted Serios," Pop.Photography 61 (Nov.1967):31-34,134-36-il.

Jule Eisenbud, The World of Ted Serios (N.Y.: William Morrow, 1967). il.

Ian Stevenson & J.G. Pratt, "Exploratory Investigations of the Psychic Photography of Ted Serios," J.ASPR 62 (1968):103-29. il.

W.A.H. Ruston, "Serios-Photos: If Contrary to Natural Law, Which Law?" J.SPR 44 (1968):289-93. il.

Jule Eisenbud, et al., "Two Experiments with Ted Serios," J.ASPR 62 (1968):309-20. il.

Jule Eisenbud, "Serios-Photos," J. SPR 44 (1968):424-25.

Ian Stevenson & J.G. Pratt, "Further Investigations of the Psychic Photography of Ted Serios," J.ASPR 63 (1969):352-64. il.

John F. Luttmer, "We Told Ted Serios ..." Fate 23 (Mar.1970):64-69. il.

Jule Eisenbud, "Light and the Serios Images," J.SPR 45 (1970):424-27.

Jule Eisenbud, et al., "An Archaeological Tour de Force with Ted Serios," J.ASPR 64 (1970):40-52. il.

Jule Eisenbud, et al., "Two Camera and Television Experiments with Ted Serios," J.ASPR 64 (1970):261-76. il.

Jule Eisenbud, "The Serios 'Blackies' and Related Phenomena," J.ASPR 66 (1972):180-92. il.

Curtis Fuller. "Dr. Jule Eisenbud vs. the Amazing Randi," Fate 27 (Aug. 1974):65-74.

Curtis Fuller, "Is This Patricia Hearst?" Fate 28 (Oct.1975):34-41. il.

(Letter), Hazel M. MacDonald, Fate 29 (Sep.1976):129.

1070   /Willi Schwanholz
Curtis Fuller, "Psychic Pictures of Willi Schwanholz," Fate 29 (Dec. 1976):36-42. il.

(Letter), Charles E. Lyle, Fate 30 (May 1977):114-15.

-Radionics
1930s/Pathometric Association
Peter Tompkins & Christopher Bird, The Secret Life of Plants (N.Y.: Harper & Row, 1973), pp.333-34.

Edward Wriothesley Russell, Report on Radionics (London: Spearman, 1973), p.87.

-Seance
1870s/Jesse Shepard (Francis Grierson)
Vincent Gaddis, "Jesse Shepard: The Musical Medium," Fate 25 (June 1972)

:60,66.

1912, Dec./Margaret Eastlund
King Hamilton Grayson, "When Spirits Guided Me," Fate 7 (Sep.1954):76-84.

1920, April 24
Irving Hamlin, "A Questionnaire Based upon a Materialization Séance, with an Introductory Description of the Séance," J.ASPR 17 (1923):121-57.

-Spirit medium
1871-1880/Mary J. Hollis
N.B. Wolfe, Startling Facts in Modern Spiritualism (Cincinnati: The Author, 1874).

1880-1911/Lizzie & Mary Bangs
Almon B. Richmond, What I Saw at Cassadaga Lake (Boston: Colby & Rich, 1888).

(Letter), Lyman C. Howe, Light of Truth Weekly, 23 Jan.1898.

James Coates, Photographing the Invisible (Chicago: Advanced Thought, 1911), pp.292-313.

W. Usborne Moore, Glimpses of the Next State (London: Watts, 1911), pp.235-75,309-46.

Nandor Fodor, Encyclopaedia of Psychic Science (London: Arthurs, 1933), pp.27-28,91.

Betty Jean Johnson, "Artists Without Brushes," Fate 31 (May 1978):48-54. il.

1920s/Mrs. Brockman
Joseph Dunninger, Houdini's Spirit World and Dunninger's Psychic Revelations (N.Y.: Tower, 1968 ed.), pp.140-44.

1950-   /Deon Frey/4346 N. Clarendon
Brad Steiger, "Deon Frey: Medium," Fate 24 (Aug.1971):96-106. il.

Brad Steiger, Psychic City: Chicago (Garden City: Doubleday, 1976), pp. 47-60. il.

Brad Steiger, Gods of Aquarius (N.Y.: Harcourt Brace Jovanovich, 1976), pp.75-78.

-Tide anomaly
seiche/Belmont & Montrose Harbors
(Editorial), Fate 15 (Nov.1962):8.
Chicago Tribune, 23 May 1974.

-UFO (?)
1897, April 11/Walter McCann/Rogers Park/=hoax
Chicago Evening Post, 12 Apr.1897, p.3.

Chicago Times-Herald, 12 Apr.1897, p.1.

Chicago Tribune, 12 Apr.1897, p.5.

1897, April 17/Daniel J. Schroeder/Lincoln Park/airship message
Sioux Falls (S.D.) Argus-Leader, 21 Apr.1897.

1954, April 8/yacht club
Larry W. Bryant, "The FBI's Secret Role in the Flying Saucer Mystery," Saga UFO Rept. 3 (Mar.1977):16,66.

1954, June
Donald E. Keyhoe, Flying Saucer Conspiracy (N.Y.: Holt, 1955), p.166.

1954, Aug.22
  Richard Hall, ed., The UFO Evidence
  (Washington: NICAP, 1964), p.155.
1955, July 25/=meteorite?
  Leonard H. Stringfield, Inside Sau-
  cer Post...3-0 Blue (Cincinnati:
  CRIFO, 1957), p.58.
1963, April 22/L. Michigan/=bolide?
  Chicago Tribune, 22 Apr.1963.
1963, June 21
  Richard Hall, ed., The UFO Evidence
  (Washington: NICAP, 1964), p.140.
1966, March 14/L. Michigan/=bolide?
  Detroit (Mich.) News, 14 Mar.1966.
1967, Jan.26/O'Hare Airport/=bolide?
  John A. Keel, UFOs: Operation Trojan
  Horse (N.Y.: Putnam, 1970), p.163.
1971, June 17/=meteor
  Chicago Tribune, 18 June 1971.
  Chicago Today, 18 June 1971.
1975, Oct.3/=balloon
  "UFO Central," CUFOS News Bull., 1
  Feb.1976, p.7.
-UFO (CE-1)
1952, Dec.8/Ernie Thorpe
  Chicago Sun-Times, 10 Dec.1952.
-UFO (CE-2)
1957, Nov.8
  Coral & Jim Lorenzen, UFOs: The Whole
  Story (N.Y.: Signet, 1969), p.85.
-UFO (CE-3)
1950s/UFO and occupants stored at Mu-
  seum of Science and Industry?
  Leonard H. Stringfield, Situation
  Red: The UFO Siege (N.Y.: Fawcett
  Crest, 1977 ed.), pp.207-208.
1954, April 8/Lelah H. Stoker
  Isabel Davis & Ted Bloecher, Close
  Encounter at Kelly and Others of
  1955 (Evanston: Center for UFO Stud-
  ies, 1978), pp. vii-viii.
-UFO (DD)
1897, April 12/F.L. Bullard/Western Ave.
  St. Louis (Mo.) Globe-Democrat, 13
  Apr.1897.
1947, June 25/Mrs. Nels Thor/10436 S.
  Forest Ave.
  Chicago Tribune, 6 July 1947.
1947, July 7/George Jones/Western x
  Archer Ave.
  Chicago Times, 8 July 1947.
1947, July 7/Nina Warner/3332 S. 84th
  St.
  Chicago Tribune, 8 July 1947.
1947, July 8/Mabel Vinterum/Martha
  Washington Hospital
  Chicago Times, 8 July 1947.
1947, July 8/Donald Klipstein/1545 W.
  50th St.
  Chicago Herald-American, 8 July 1947.
1949, July 11
  "If It's in the Sky It's a Saucer,"
  Doubt, no.27 (1949):416.
-UFO (NL)
1897, April 9/South Chicago
  Chicago Tribune, 10 Apr.1897, p.1.
1897, April 9/Oakley x Milwaukee Ave.
  Chicago Tribune, 10 Apr.1897, p.1.
  Chicago Times-Herald, 10 Apr.1897, p.
  1.

Chicago Journal, 10 Apr.1897, p.5.
St. Louis Post-Dispatch, 11 Apr.
  1897, p.2.
1897, April 10/R.W. Allen/W. Chicago x
Hamlin Ave.
  Chicago Times-Herald, 11 Apr.1897,
  p.2.
1897, April 11/Herman Fry/North Ave. x
Larabee St.
  Chicago Times-Herald, 12 Apr.1897,
  p.1.
1897, April 17/Samuel Roeder
  Bloomington Pantagraph, 22 Apr.1897,
  p.5.
1947, June 26/Mrs. W.M. Harrison/4639
Oakenwald
  Chicago Tribune, 6 July 1947.
1947, July 4/Ida Bauer/4414 N. Clark
1947, July 5/Jean Dorsett/10406 Wentworth
1947, July 6/George Wilkinson/Broadway
x Lawrence Ave.
  Chicago Times, 7 July 1947.
1947, July 7/Charles Allen/6406 S.
Winchester Ave.
  Chicago Herald-American, 7 July 1947.
1947, July 7/Thomas W. Gorman/7427 S.
Park St.
  Chicago Tribune, 8 July 1947.
1947, July 8/Marvin Goldberg/Foster Ave.
1947, July 9/Thomas O'Brien/500 W. 42d
Pl.
  Chicago Tribune, 9 July 1947.
1950, July 1/N. Chicago
1950, July 4
  Bruce S. Maccabee, "UFO Related Information in the FBI Files: Part
  7," MUFON UFO J., no.132 (Nov.-Dec.
  1978):11,14.
1952, April 26/Victor Root
  Albert K. Bender, Flying Saucers and
  the Three Men (N.Y.: Paperback Library, 1968 ed.), p.38.
1952, July 12/Montrose Beach
  Edward J. Ruppelt, The Report on Unidentified Flying Objects (Garden
  City: Doubleday, 1956), p.153.
1953, July 16/Hazel McCombs
  (Letter), Fate 6 (Dec.1953):103.
1957, July/Nick Sciurba
  (Letter), Fate 10 (Dec.1957):117-20.
  (Letter), Fate 11 (Mar.1958):124-26.
1960, Aug.26/Robert I. Johnson/Adler
Planetarium
  Harlan Wilson, "Strange Case of the
  Mystery Satellite," Fate 14 (June
  1961):25-26.
1961, Feb.6
  Chicago Tribune, 7 Feb.1961.
1962, Oct.3/Patrick McAley
  Richard Hall, ed., The UFO Evidence
  (Washington: NICAP, 1964), p.68.
1970/Taka Boom
  Timothy Green Beckley, "Saucers and
  Celebrities," Saga UFO Rept. 4 (July
  1977):40.
1972, July 19/Peter Reich/L. Michigan
  Chicago Today, 20 July 1972.
  "Newsman Sights UFO," APRO Bull. 21
  (July-Aug.1972):5-6.

1973, Jan.23/Lee Shapiro
  Chicago Sun-Times, 24 Jan.1973.
1974, Jan.23
  Brad Steiger, Psychic City: Chicago
  (Garden City: Doubleday, 1976), pp.
  99-100.
1975, May/Brian Crumpler
  (Letter), Saga UFO Rept. 3 (Dec.1976)
  :6.
1975, July 23
  "UFO Central," CUFOS News Bull., 15
  Nov.1975, p.14.
1975, Aug.
1975, Oct.8/Cynthia Zusel/O'Hare Airport
  Timothy Green Beckley, "Saucers over
  Our Cities," Saga UFO Rept. 4 (Aug.
  1977):24,72.
1975, Oct.10
1975, Nov.26
  "Noteworthy UFO Sightings," Ufology
  2 (spring 1976):42.
1978, Jan.10/S side
  "UFOs of Limited Merit," Int'l UFO
  Reporter 3 (Feb.1978):3.
-UFO (R)
1952, Sep.2/William Maitland/=radar
echo?
  Harold T. Wilkins, Flying Saucers Uncensored (N.Y.: Pyramid, 1967 ed.),
  p.117.
-Windshield pitting
1955, June/Curtis Fuller/Grand x Rush
St.
  (Editorial), Fate 8 (Oct.1955):6-8.

Chicago Heights
-UFO (NL)
1967, March 3/Eugene LaBelle
  Brad Steiger & Joan Whritenour, The
  Allende Letters: New UFO Breakthrough
  (N.Y.: Tower, 1968), p.41.
1975, Sep.4
  "UFO Central," CUFOS News Bull., 15
  Nov.1975, p.17.

Chittyville
-Humanoid
1968, Aug.11/Tim Bullock
  Carbondale Southern Illinoisan, 19
  Aug.1968, p.3.
  Southern Illinois Univ, Daily Egypt-
  ian, 11 Dec.1968.

Chrisman
-Clairvoyance
1963, May 13
  (Editorial), Fate 16 (Sep.1963):22.

Cicero
-UFO (DD)
1947, July 7/Richard Allen
  Chicago Times, 8 July 1947.

Cisne
-Time anomaly
1971, June 28/Alice M. Hearle
  "Car and Occupants Move 'Backward' in
  Time and Space," Skylook, no.45
  (Aug.1971):4-5.

-UFO (NL)
1966, July/Alice M. Hearle
  "Back Track," Skylook, no.53 (Apr.
  1972):12,14.

Clay co.
-Phantom panther and chicken killings
1950, Nov./Dollie Hobbs
  Jerome Clark & Loren Coleman, "On
  the Trail of Pumas, Panthers and
  ULAs: Part 2," Fate 25 (July 1972):
  92,93.

Clinton
-UFO (NL)
1897, April 12
  Rock Island Argus, 13 Apr.1897, p.3.
1968, Aug.15/Ralph Mollet/W on U.S.54
  "College Student Reports 1968 Sight-
  ing in Illinois," Skylook, no.34
  (Sep.1970):10.
1973, Oct.17/Charles Williams
  Bloomington Pantagraph, 18 Oct.1973.

Coatsburg
-UFO (NL)
1970, July 7/N on Hwy.1
  "Illinois Mother and Children Watch
  Orange-Colored Object," Skylook, no.
  34 (Sep.1970):8.

Coffeen
-UFO (CE-1)
1967, Jan.26/Hwy.185
  Jacques Vallee, Passport to Magonia
  (Chicago: Regnery, 1969), p.339.

Collinsville
-Mystery fog
1956, Sep.23/=pollution
  June E. Weidemann, "Mystery of the
  Charred Paint," Fate 10 (May 1957):
  60-61.

Covington
-UFO (NL)
1971, May 4/Herb Williams/Hwy.177
  "Carlyle Man Sights Three UFO's,"
  Skylook, no.44 (July 1971):13,14.

Crestwood
-Haunt
n.d./Bachelor Grove Cemetery/Rubio
Woods Forest Preserve/143d St. nr. Mid-
lothian
  Brad Steiger, Psychic City: Chicago
  (Garden City: Doubleday, 1976), pp.
  88-89.
  Jim Brandon, Weird America (N.Y.:
  Dutton, 1978), pp.77-78.
-UFO (NL)
1975, Dec.10
  "UFO Central," CUFOS News Bull., 1
  Feb.1976, p.14.

Crete
-UFO (CE-1)
n.d./Virginia Miller
  (Letter), Fate 10 (Aug.1957):120-22.
-UFO (DD)

1960, Aug.29/Mr. Schneeweis/Hwy.1
Lloyd Mallan, "Complete Directory of
UFOs: Part III," Sci.& Mech. 38
(Feb.1967):56.

Creve Coeur
-Humanoid
1972, July 25-27/Illinois R.
Pekin Daily Times, 27 July 1972.

Crossville
-Animal ESP
1960/Ed Stout
(Editorial), Fate 13 (July 1960):16.

Crystal Lake
-UFO (CE-3)
1977, June 12/Mr. Bosga
Ted Bloecher, "A Survey of CE3K Re-
ports for 1977," in 1978 MUFON UFO
Symposium Proc. (Seguin, Tex.:
MUFON, 1978), pp.14,21,34. il.

Cuba
-UFO (NL)
1897, April 14
Cuba Journal, 15 Apr.1897, p.3.

Dalton City
-Erratic kangaroo
1975, July 14/Rosemary Hapwood/S on
Hwy.128
David Fideler & Loren Coleman, "Kangaroos from Nowhere," Fate 31 (Apr.
1978):68,73.

Danvers
-UFO (CE-1)
1970, July 1
"Incident in Illinois," APRO Bull. 19
(July-Aug.1970):4,6.
-UFO (CE-3)
1897, April 16
Bloomington Pantagraph, 17 Apr.1897,
p.5.

Danville
-UFO (CE-2)
1957, Nov.6/Calvin Showers
Chicago Sun-Times, 8 Nov.1957.

Darmstadt
-UFO (CE-2)
1974, Dec.21-22/Kim Lloyd/4 mi.W
W.J. Mills, "Illinois Youths Report
Strange UFO Effects," Skylook, no.
90 (May 1975):12-14.

Darwin
-Animal ESP
1850/Fey Ellen
LaVenia Jones, "Fey Ellen Routed the
Armyworms," Fate 28 (June 1975):76-
79.

Davis Junction
-UFO (NL)
1973, Nov.3/Hwy.51
Glenn McWane & David Graham, The New
UFO Sightings (N.Y.: Warner, 1974),

p.18.

Decatur
-Clairvoyance
1918, July 26/Frank Hampton Fox/436 W.
Eldorado St.
"A Vision of a Submarine Battle,"
J.ASPR 14 (1920):49-52.
-Erratic crocodilian
1937, Aug.30/L. Decatur
Decatur Herald, 1 Sep.1937, p.3.
1966, Oct.24/L. Decatur
Decatur Review, 26 Oct.1966.
1967, June 26/895 W. Eldorado St.
Decatur Review, 27 June 1967, p.22.
-Fall of fish
1876, June 28
Decatur Republican, 28 June 1876.
-Fall of ice
1978, Aug.29/Stephen High School
Decatur Herald-Review, 30 Aug.1978.
-Humanoid
ca.1962/Steven Collins/E. William St.
John A. Keel, Strange Creatures from
Time and Space (Greenwich, Ct.:
Fawcett, 1970), p.105.
1965, Sep.
Decatur Review, 22 Sep.1965.
-Phantom panther
1917, July 17/Earl Cavanaugh/Allen's
Bend
Decatur Herald, 18-20 July 1917.
1917, July 29/Earl Hill/Springfield Rd.
Decatur Herald, 30 July 1917, p.1.
1917, July 31/James Rutherford
Decatur Herald, 1 Aug.1917.
1955, Sep.13-14/Rea's Bridge
Decatur Review, 15 Sep.1955.
1955, Oct.25/Paul G. Meyers
Decatur Review, 27 Oct.1955; and 1
Nov.1955.
1965, June 25/Mrs. Rogers
1965, June 27/Anthony Viccone/S of town
1965, June 28/Lincoln Park
Jerome Clark & Loren Coleman, "On the
Trail of Pumas, Panthers and ULAs:
Part 2," Fate 25 (July 1972):92,98-
99.
-Phantom panther tracks
1917, July 17
Decatur Herald, 18 July 1917.
-Sheep mutilation
1967, June/Burton Stollard
Jerome Clark & Loren Coleman, "On the
Trail of Pumas, Panthers and ULAs:
Part 2," Fate 25 (July 1972):92,99.
-Skyquake
1970, Oct.7
Decatur Review, 8 Oct.1970.
-UFO (?)
1897, April 14/=balloon
Decatur Republican, 15 Apr.1897, p.8.
1971, Feb.2/=meteor
Decatur Review, 2 Feb.1971.
-UFO (CE-1)
1970, July 1/Ralph Kramer/Hwy.24 nr.
Rea's Bridge
"Colored Lights in Geometric Pattern
Cross Illinois Sky," Skylook, no.33
(Aug.1970):2.

-UFO (DD)
  1930, Aug./Jack Huffman
    "We Correct an Error," Skylook, no.
    66 (May 1973):15.
  1973, Feb.11/Mrs. Jack Huffman/Tolly's
  Supermarket
    "Decatur Residents Watch Oval Shaped
    Object," Skylook, no.64 (Mar.1973):
    11.
    "We Correct an Error," Skylook, no.
    66 (May 1973):15.
-UFO (NL)
  1897, April 11
    Decatur Republican, 12 Apr.1897.
  1947, July 3/Claude Price/Hwy.36
    Springfield Illinois State Journal,
    5 July 1947.
  1970, July 22/Leon Worley/Grove Rd.
  1970, July 30/John Garren/W of town
    "Two UFO Reports from Decatur, Ill.,"
    Skylook, no.34 (Sep.1970):7.
  1971, June 22/David Krause/116 Point
  Bluff Dr.
    "Boy Sees UFO Near Home in Decatur,
    Ill.," Skylook, no.46 (Sep.1971):4.
  1971, Sep.7/Robert T. Dillow
    "Chop Chop," Skylook, no.47 (Oct.
    1971):4.
  1971, Sep.7-18
    Leonard Sturm, "UFO Flap, Decatur,
    Ill. Area," Skylook, no.49 (Dec.
    1971):7-8.
  1972, July 11/Ralph Donovan/1801 S.
  Fairview Ave.
    "Teachers Report UFO over Decatur,
    Ill.," Skylook, no.57 (Aug.1972):13.

Deerfield
-UFO (DD)
  1977, April 5/I-94
    "UFOs of Limited Merit," Int'l UFO
    Reporter 2 (May 1977):5.
-UFO (NL)
  1977, June 10
    "UFO Analysis," Int'l UFO Reporter
    2 (July 1977):Newsfront sec.

De Kalb
-UFO (NL)
  1897, April 16
    De Kalb Evening Chronicle, 17 Apr.
    1897, p.1.
  1978, Oct.30/Clinton Jessel
    De Kalb Chronicle, 30 Oct.1978.

De Kalb co.
-UFO (NL)
  1973, Nov.3/Hwy.64
    Glenn McWane & David Graham, The New
    UFO Sightings (N.Y.: Warner, 1974),
    p.18.

Delavan
-Mystery plane crash
  1938, June 10
    Chicago Daily News, 11 June 1938.
    New York Times, 11 June 1938, p.1;
    and 12 June 1938, p.38.
-Precognition
  1975/Gretna Alexander

Warren Smith, "Phenomenal Predictions
    for 1976," Saga, Jan.1976, p.16.
-UFO (NL)
  1897, April 16/Emma Tibbetts
    Harvard Herald, 23 Apr.1897, p.2.

Des Plaines
-Meteorite crater
  10,000 m.diam./possible
    H.M. Bannister, "Geology of Cook
    County," Econ.Geol.Illinois 2 (1882)
    :192.
    G.H. Emrich & R.E. Bergstrom, "In-
    tense Faulting at Des Plaines,
    Northeastern Illinois," Bull.Geol.
    Soc'y Am. 70, pt.2 (1959):1596-97.
-Precognition
  1960s-   /Milton Kramer/9029 N. Columbus Dr.
    Brad Steiger, "The Seers Speak for
    1970," Fate 23 (May 1970):78,82. il.
-UFO (DD)
  1978, Nov.5/Howard Ave.
    Des Plaines Suburban Times, 9 Nov.
    1978.
-UFO (NL)
  1975, Oct.10
    "Noteworthy UFO Sightings," Ufology
    2 (spring 1976):42.

Dixon
-Healing
  1850s/Mrs. Briggs
    Emma Hardinge Britten, Modern Ameri-
    can Spiritualism (N.Y.: The Author,
    1870), p.388.
  n.d./Peter Hurkos
    Marguerite Harmon Bro, "Healing:
    Peter Hurkos' 7th Sense," Fate 25
    (Oct.1972):96-102. il.
-Humanoid tracks
  1976, July/Rock R.
    "Illinois Sasquatches 1974-1976,"
    Shadows, no.3 (Dec.1976):1.
-UFO (NL)
  1897, April 8/James H. Clark
    Dixon Telegraph, 10 Apr.1897, p.1.
  1897, April 13
    Sterling Evening Gazette, 14 Apr.
    1897, p.5.

Dolton
-UFO (NL)
  1947, July 4/Andrew Wolfe
    Chicago Herald-American, 7 July 1947.

Downs
-Giant bird
  1977, July 30
    "Big Bird 1977," Fortean Times, no.
    24 (winter 1978):10.
-UFO (CE-3)
  1897, April/Haney Savage
    Bloomington Pantagraph, 17 Apr.1897,
    p.5.

Dunleith twp.
-Ancient stone chamber
    Cyrus Thomas, "Report on the Mound
    Explorations of the Bureau of Eth-

nology," Ann.Rept.Bur.Am.Ethn. 12
(1890-91):1,114.

Dupo
-UFO (CE-2)
  1969, Aug.21
    Ted Phillips, Physical Traces Associ-
    ated with UFO Sightings (Evanston:
    Center for UFO Studies, 1975), p.67.
-UFO (NL)
  1970, Oct.4/Russell Griffin
    Cahokia Herald, 15 Oct.1970.

DuQuoin
-Lake monster
  1879, summer/Mr. Paquette/L. DuQuoin
    Jerome Clark & Loren Coleman, "Ameri-
    ca's Lake Monsters," Beyond Reality,
    no.14 (Mar.-Apr.1975):28,33.
  1964/Allyn Dunmyer/Stump Pond/=catfish
    (Editorial), Fate 18 (Jan.1965):24-
    25.
    (Editorial), Fate 18 (Feb.1965):24.
-Poltergeist
  ca.1860
    Emma Hardinge Britten, Modern Ameri-
    can Spiritualism (N.Y.: The Author,
    1870), pp.435-36.

East Dundee
-UFO (NL)
  1975, Aug.9
    "UFO Central," CUFOS News Bull., 15
    Nov.1975, p.15.

East Peoria
-Humanoid
  1972, June-July/Randy Emert/Cole Hollow
  Rd.
    Peoria Journal-Star, 26 July 1972.
    Pekin Daily Times, 27 July 1972.
-UFO (CE-1)
  1966, Sep.24/Ray Watts
    "Peoria Group Investigates Strange
    Sky Sightings," Skylook, no.16 (Mar.
    1969):12.
-UFO (DD)
  1947, July 7/Forrest L. Higginbotham
    Springfield Illinois State Journal,
    8 July 1947.
-UFO (NL)
  1971, April 12/Ray Watts
    "Like a Boomerang," Skylook, no.43
    (June 1971):5.

East Saint Louis
-Giant human skeletons
  1930/Edgemont/=normal size
    "Story of Giant Skeletons Disproved,"
    El Palacio 31 (1931):93-94.
-UFO (DD)
  1957, Nov.5
    Richard Hall, ed., The UFO Evidence
    (Washington: NICAP, 1964), p.165.
-UFO (NL)
  1897, April 10
    East St. Louis Journal, 12 Apr.1897,
    p.3.

Edgewood
-Haunt
  1894
    "True Mystic Experiences," Fate 2
    (May 1949):77-79.

Edwardsville
-Humanoid
  1973, June
    Jerome Clark & Loren Coleman, "Swamp
    Slobs Invade Illinois," Fate 27
    (July 1974):84,89-90.
-Phantom panther
  1977, April 21?
    Alton Telegraph, 23 Apr.1977.
-Poltergeist
  1974/R.C. Scheffel & Co.
    "Enigmas," Probe the Unknown 3 (Mar.
    1975):50-51.
-UFO (NL)
  1897, April 10
    Edwardsville Intelligencer, 13 Apr.
    1897, p.1.
  1976, Jan.14
    "Noteworthy UFO Sightings," Ufology
    2 (summer 1976):62.

Effingham
-Humanoid
  1910s/S of town
    (Letter), Beulah Schroat, Decatur
    Review, 2 Aug.1972.
-UFO (NL)
  1970, Dec.6/Mae Jannett/E on I-70
    Mae Jannett, "Illinois Family Watch
    Bright Object," Skylook, no.38
    (Jan.1971):3.

Elburn
-UFO (CE-3)
  1897, April 11
    Rockford Republic, 12 Apr.1897, p.1.
-UFO (NL)
  1897, April 9
    De Kalb Evening Chronicle, 10 Apr.
    1897, p.1.
  1959, Aug.19
    Jacques & Janine Vallee, Challenge
    to Science (N.Y.: Ace, 1966 ed.),
    p.201.

Elco
-Phantom panther
  1966, April 13/Joseph Moad
    Cairo Evening Citizen, 20 Apr.1966.
    Jerome Clark & Loren Coleman, "On the
    Trail of Pumas, Panthers and ULAs:
    Part 2," Fate 25 (July 1972):92,98.

Elgin
-UFO (NL)
  1897, April 9/Mr. Younger
    Chicago Tribune, 11 Apr.1897, p.4.
  1897, April 11
    Chicago Post, 12 Apr.1897, p.3.
  1952, Aug.22/D.C. Scott
    Richard Hall, ed., The UFO Evidence
    (Washington: NICAP, 1964), p.66.

Elk Grove Village
-UFO (CE-2)
  1973, May 10/Mr. Schmidt/Ned Brown Forest Preserve
    Chicago Tribune, 11 May 1973.
-UFO (NL)
  1975, July 23
    "UFO Central," CUFOS News Bull., 15
    Nov.1975.

Elmhurst
-UFO (NL)
  1947, July 8/Peter Monte
    Chicago Tribune, 9 July 1947.
  1975, Nov.16
    "UFO Central," CUFOS News Bull., 1
    Feb.1976, p.13.

Elmwood Park
-UFO (CE-2)
  1957, Nov.4/Joseph Lukasek/Elmwood Cemetery
    Chicago Sun-Times, 5 Nov.1957.
    Chicago Tribune, 5 Nov.1957.
    J. Allen Hynek, The Hynek UFO Report
    (N.Y.: Dell, 1977), pp.172-76.

El Paso
-UFO (NL)
  1897, April 15/Robert Hitch
    Bloomington Pantagraph, 17 Apr.1897,
    p.5.

Elvaston
-UFO (NL)
  1970, Dec.31/L.H. McGinnis/W on Hwy.96
    "A 'Flying Flame' Seen in Illinois,"
    Skylook, no.39 (Feb.1971):18.

Elwin
-UFO (DD)
  1971, Feb.13/Leonard Sturm/3 mi.S on
  Hwy.51
    Leonard Sturm, "UFO Flap, Decatur,
    Ill., Area," Skylook, no.49 (Dec.
    1971):7,8.

Enfield
-Humanoid
  1973, April 25/Henry McDaniel
  1973, May 6/Henry McDaniel
    Columbus (O.) Dispatch, 7-8 May 1973.
    Jerome Clark & Loren Coleman, "Swamp
    Slobs Invade Illinois," Fate 27
    (July 1974):84,88-89.
  1973, May 8
    Jerome Clark & Loren Coleman, "Swamp
    Slobs Invade Illinois," Fate 27
    (July 1974):84,89.

Evanston
-Astrology research
  1950s/Vernon Clark
    John C. Ross, "Astrology: New Evidence
    to Support an Ancient Science," Fate
    14 (July 1961):25-32.
    Paul Foght, "Astrology: New Support
    for an Ancient Science: II," Fate
    18 (Feb.1965):70-76.
    John Anthony West & Jan Gerhard Toon-

der, The Case for Astrology (Balti-
    more: Penguin, 1973), pp.204-209.
-Ball lightning
  1924, April/Harriet Allyn/Northwestern
  University
    Charles Fitzhugh Talman, "Nature's
    Bag of Tricks," Reader's Digest 26
    (June 1935):89,91.
-Biorhythm research
  1950s-   /Frank A. Brown, Jr./North-
  western University
    Frank A. Brown, Jr., "Persistent Act-
    ivity Rhythms in the Oyster," Am.J.
    Physiology 178 (1954):510-14.
    F.A. Brown, H.M. Webb & M.K. Bennett,
    "Proof for an Endogeneous Component
    in Persistent Solar and Lunar Rhyth-
    micity in Organisms," Proc.Nat'l
    Acad.Sci. 41 (1955):93-100.
    F.A. Brown, J. Shriner & C.L. Ralph,
    "Solar and Lunar Rhythmicity in the
    Rat in Constant Conditions and the
    Mechanism of Physiological Time
    Measurement," Am.J.Physiology 184
    (1956):491-96.
    Frank A. Brown, Jr., "The Rhythmic
    Nature of Animals and Plants," Am.
    Scientist 47 (June 1959):147.
    Frank A. Brown, Jr. & Erma D. Terra-
    cini, "Exogenous Timing of Rat Spon-
    taneous Activity Periods," Proc.
    Soc'y for Experimental Biol.& Med.
    101 (1959):457-60.
    Frank A. Brown, Jr., et al., "Magnet-
    ic Response of an Organism and Its
    Solar Relationships," Biol.Bull. 118
    (1960):367-81.
    Frank A. Brown, Jr., H.M. Webb & W.J.
    Brett, "Magnetic Response of an Or-
    ganism and its Lunar Relationships,"
    Biol.Bull. 118 (1960):389-92.
    Frank A. Brown, Jr., "Endogenous Bio-
    rhythmicity Reviewed with New Evi-
    dence," Scientia 103 (1962):1-6.
    Frank A. Brown, Jr., Biological Clocks
    (Boston: American Institute of Bio-
    logical Sciences, 1962).
    Frank A. Brown, Jr., "Extrinsic Rhyth-
    micity," Annals N.Y. Acad.Sci. 98
    (1962):775-87.
    Frank Brown, "How Animals Respond to
    Magnetism," Discovery 01 (Nov.1963):
    18-22.
    Frank A. Brown, Jr., "Propensity for
    Lunar Periodicity in Hamsters and
    Its Significance for Biological
    Clock Theories," Proc.Soc'y for Ex-
    perimental Biol.& Med. 120 (1965):
    792-97.
    Frank A. Brown, Jr., Young H. Park &
    Joseph R. Zeno, "Diurnal Variation
    in Organismic Response to Very Weak
    Gamma Radiation," Nature 211 (1966):
    830-33.
    Frank A. Brown & Young H. Park, "Syn-
    odic Monthly Modulation of the Di-
    urnal Rhythm of Hamsters," Proc.
    Soc'y for Experimental Biol.& Med.
    125 (1967):712-13.
    F.A. Brown & C.S. Chow, "Lunar-Corre-

lated Variations in Water Uptake by Bean Seeds," Biol.Bull. 145 (1973): 265-78.

Frank A. Brown, Jr. & Carol S. Chow, "Phase Shifting an Exogenous Variation in Hamster Activity by Uniform Daily Rotation," Proc.Soc'y for Experimental Biol.& Med. 145 (1974): 7-11.

Frank A. Brown, Jr., "Biological Clocks: Endogenous Cycles Synchronized by Subtle Geophysical Rhythms," Biosystems 8 (1976):67-81.

F.A. Brown, Jr. & C.S. Chow, "Uniform Daily Rotation and Biological Rhythms and Clocks in Hamsters," Physiol. Zoology 49 (1976):263-85.

-Erratic kangaroo
1971/Northwestern University
David Fideler & Loren Coleman, "Kangaroos from Nowhere," Fate 31 (Apr. 1978):68.

-Fall of weblike substance
1922, Oct.15/Northwestern University
Charles Fort, The Books of Charles Fort (N.Y.: Holt, 1940), pp.536-37.

-Humanoid
1946, Oct.11
"Land Beasties," Doubt, no.17 (1947): 260.

-Lake monster
1867, Aug.5/"George W. Wood"
Chicago Tribune, 6-7 Aug.1867.

-Parapsychology research
1956-1976/Spiritual Frontiers Fellowship/800 Custer Ave.
Armand Biteaux, The New Consciousness (Willits, Cal.: Oliver, 1975), pp.130-31.
Brad Steiger, Psychic City: Chicago (Garden City: Doubleday, 1976), pp. 137-51.
1972-   /Academy of Religion and Psychical Research/Box 1311
June & Nicholas Regush, Psi: The Other World Catalogue (N.Y.: Putnam, 1974), p.179.

-Possession
1977, July-Aug./Remibias Chua
Chicago Tribune, 5 Mar.1978, p.1.
Lesley Sussman, "Did Voice from Grave Name Killer?" Fate 31 (July 1978): 61-67.

-UFO (DD)
1942, spring/Robert H. Moore
Gordon I.R. Lore, Jr. & Harold H. Deneault, Jr., Mysteries of the Skies: UFOs in Perspective (Englewood Cliffs, N.J.: Prentice-Hall, 1968), p.142.

-UFO (NL)
1897, April 3
Chicago Times-Herald, 4 Apr.1897, p.1.
1897, April 9/Robert Lowen
Chicago Post, 10 Apr.1897, p.3.
Chicago Times-Herald, 10 Apr.1897, p. 1.
Evanston Index, 10 Apr.1897.

Evergreen Park
-UFO (NL)
1972, Jan.9/C.H. Van Welzen
"Three Planes Circle UFO," Skylook, no.52 (Mar.1972):14.

Fairfield
-UFO (NL)
1897, April 16/John Gaddis
Fairfield Wayne County Record, 22 Apr.1897, p.4.
1963, Aug.5/Mr. Gidcumb
1963, Aug.5/Dick Cochran
1963, Aug.7/Raymond L. Owen
1963, Aug.8/Leslie Mason
Jeffrey G. Liss, "The Light That Chased a Car," Fate 16 (Nov.1963): 26,32-33, quoting Fairfield Wayne County Press (undated).
1963, Aug.15/W. Scott Lawrence
Chicago American, 17 Aug.1963.

Fall Creek
-UFO (DD)
1969, Feb.11/Vi Gregory/nr. Hwy.57
"Hannibal, Mo. Women See UFO," Skylook, no.16 (Mar.1969):10.

Farmer City
-Humanoid
1970, July 9-15/Don Ennis/nr. Salt Creek
Loren Coleman, "Mystery Animals in Illinois," Fate 24 (Mar.1971):48, 52-53.
-Sheep mutilation
1970, spring
Loren Coleman, "Mystery Animals in Illinois," Fate 24 (Mar.1971):48, 52.

Farmington
-UFO (NL)
1969, Aug.10/Mrs. John Belagna/S of town
"Peoria Club Meets--Reports Recent Sighting," Skylook, no.23 (Oct. 1969):17.

Flanagan
-UFO (NL)
1967, March 8/Mr. Kennedy/U.S.51
Bloomington Pantagraph, 10 Mar.1967.

Flossmoor
-Deathbed apparition research
1960s-   /Elisabeth Kubler-Ross
Elisabeth Kubler-Ross, Of Death and Dying (N.Y.: Macmillan, 1969).
Elisabeth Kubler-Ross, Questions and Answers on Death and Dying (N.Y.: Macmillan, 1974).
Elisabeth Kubler-Ross, Death: The Final Stage of Growth (Englewood Cliffs, N.J.: Prentice-Hall, 1975).
James Crenshaw, "An Interview with Elisabeth Kubler-Ross," Fate 30 (Apr.1977):45-52.
Martin Ebon, The Evidence for Life After Death (N.Y.: Signet, 1977),

pp.37-47.

Fox Lake
-Mystery television transmission
   n.d./Mrs. Roy Stallsmith/Ingleside
      Vincent H. Gaddis, "When TV Tunes to
      Another Dimension," Probe the Un-
      known 3 (May 1975):32.

Fox River Grove
-UFO (NL)
   1969, Jan.9
      Chicago Tribune, 10 Jan.1969.
      "More on January Sighting in Illi-
      nois," Skylook, no.16 (Mar.1969):14.
      "U.S. Roundup," APRO Bull. 17 (Mar.-
      Apr.1969):6.

Franklin
-Phantom panther
   ca.1959/W of town
      Jacksonville Courier, 2 June 1961,
      p.1.

Frederickville
-Archeological site
   Illinois R.
      J.F. Snyder, "Deposits of Flint Im-
      plements," Ann.Rept.Smith.Inst.,
      1876, pp.433,437.

Freeburg
-UFO (NL)
   1968, Jan.19/Phil Nichols
      "Six UFO's over Missouri and Illi-
      nois," Skylook, no.6-7 (Feb.-Mar.
      1968):9.
   1971, Aug.13/Beulah Wilderman
      "Chop Chop," Skylook, no.47 (Oct.
      1971):4.

Freeport
-Giant bird
   1948, April 9/Veryl Babb
      Jerome Clark & Loren Coleman, "Winged
      Wiordics," Fate 25 (Mar.1972):80,84.
-UFO (DD)
   1947, July 6/Elmer H. Schmirmer
      Chicago Sun, 8 July 1947.
-UFO (NL)
   1967, Nov.8/Harvey Toepfer
      St. Louis (Mo.) Globe-Democrat, 9
      Nov.1967.

Galena
-UFO (?)
   1897, April 14/=balloon
      Galena Gazette, 15 Apr.1897, p.5.
   1977, Aug.7/ground markings only/=slime
mold
      Allan Hendry, "A Physical Trace Doth
      Not a CEII Make," Int'l UFO Reporter
      2 (Sep.1977):4. il.
      "The Galena & Chesterton Fungus
      Rings," Int'l UFO Reporter 3 (Mar.
      1978):Newsfront sec.
-UFO (NL)
   1969, Feb.13
      "U.S. Roundup," APRO Bull. 17 (Mar.-
      Apr.1969):7.

Galesburg
-UFO (?)
   1967, Jan.11-15/Samuel S. Westfall
      "Man Reported Struck by Falling Ob-
      ject," APRO Bull. 15 (Jan.-Feb.
      1967):1.
      Brent Raynes, "UFO Witness Gets the
      Point," Skylook, no.18 (May 1969):
      13.
      "More on 'UFO Witness Gets the
      Point,'" Skylook, no.23 (Oct.1969):
      4.

Gallatin co.
-Haunt
   1966, April/Old Slave House
      Ridgway News, 28 Apr.1966.
      (Letter), Harriet B. Vaught, Fate
      20 (Apr.1967):148-50.

Galton
-UFO (CE-3)
   1897, April 19/Aaron Watson
      Chicago Inter-Ocean, 26 Apr.1897.

Galva
-UFO (CE-2)
   1972, Aug./R.E. Royce
      Glenn McWane & David Graham, The New
      UFO Sightings (N.Y.: Warner, 1974),
      pp.62-63, quoting Galva News (un-
      dated).

Germantown
-UFO (DD)
   1972, May 14/Janice Schwaegel
      "Three Sisters Watch Half-Moon Shaped
      Object," Skylook, no.56 (July 1972):
      8.

Girard
-UFO (CE-3)
   1897, April 12/Paul McCramer/2 mi.S/
=hoax?
      Chicago Record, 14 Apr.1897.
      Chicago Tribune, 14 Apr.1897.
      St. Louis (Mo.) Post-Dispatch, 14
      Apr.1897, p.2.
      Carlinville Democrat, 29 Apr.1897,
      p.1.

Glasford
-Meteorite crater
   5000 m.diam./possible
      T.C. Buschbach & Robert Ryan, "Glas-
      ford (Illinois) Cryptoexplosion
      Structure," Spec.Pap.Geol.Soc'y Am.,
      no.73 (1962):126.

Glasgow
-Phantom panther
   1947, July 28
      "Run of the Mill," Doubt, no.20
      (1948):303,304.
-UFO (DD)
   1947, July 7/J.C. Star
      St. Louis (Mo.) Post-Dispatch, 8 July
      1947.

Glendale
-Giant bird
  1948, Jan./James Trares
    Jerome Clark & Loren Coleman, "Winged
    Wierdies," Fate 25 (Mar.1972):80,85.

Glenview
-Biorhythm research
  1970s/Cyclomatic Engineering
    Brad Steiger, Psychic City: Chicago
    (Garden City: Doubleday, 1976), pp.
    156-59.
-UFO (CE-1)
  1975, July 4
    "UFO Central," CUFOS News Bull., 15
    Nov.1975, p.12.
-UFO (NL)
  1977, July 21
    "UFOs of Limited Merit," Int'l UFO
    Reporter 2 (Sep.1977):3.

Godfrey
-UFO (NL)
  1965, Nov./Bob Hewitt
    (Letter), Sci.& Mech. 38 (May 1967):
    34-35.
  1970, Aug.9/Duane Springman
    Jacksonville Courier, 11 Aug.1970.

Goodrich
-UFO (NL)
  1897, April 9
    Streator Free Press, 10 Apr.1897, p.
    3.

Goreville
-Haunt
  1952/Tom Lannon/haunted chair
    (Editorial), Fate 6 (Nov.1953):11.

Grafton
-Fall of metallic slivers
  1968, July 20
    "More Metal from the Sky," Skylook,
    no.12-13 (Aug.-Sep.1968):9.

Grand Tower
-UFO (?)
  1973, April 16
    Jerome Clark, "The Brushy Creek UFO
    Scare," Fate 27 (May 1974):96,103.
-UFO (CE-1)
  1973, March 22/Oscar Wills
    "Public Service Company Employee
    Sees UFO over Illinois Power Sta-
    tion," Skylook, no.66 (May 1973):
    7-8.
    "Engineer Observes UFO," APRO Bull.
    21 (May-June 1973):4-5.
    "Strange Survey of Power Plant," Can.
    UFO Rept., no.15 (1973):17-19.
    Jerome Clark, "The Brushy Creek UFO
    Scare," Fate 27 (May 1974):96,102-
    103.
-UFO (NL)
  1956, March/C.B. Clark
    "Farmer Watches Red Light," Skylook,
    no.44 (July 1971):10.

Grayslake
-Mystery plane crash
  1969, June 17/Piper PA-28
    Jay Gourley, The Great Lakes Triangle
    (Greenwich, Ct.: Fawcett, 1970),
    pp.78-79.

Greenfield
-UFO (CE-3)
  1897, April 19/M.G. Sisson
    Carrollton Patriot, 23 Apr.1897, p.1.

Greenup
-UFO (CE-1)
  1973, Aug.4/Bud Sedgwick/E of town
    "Flying Object 'Big As Boxcar' Seen
    in Greenup, Ill. Area," Skylook,
    no.71 (Oct.1973):5-6.

Greenville
-Fall of metallic object
  1971, June 10/Armintta Raypole/Millers-
    burg Rd.
    Greenville Advocate, 14 June 1971.
-UFO (NL)
  1897, April 17
    Greenville Advocate, 22 Apr.1897,
    p.1.

Hamilton
-UFO (?)
  1969, Dec.2/Mrs. M.G. Sterne, Jr./Hwy.
    96/=airplane?
    Robert Smulling, "Plane? UFO?" Sky-
    look, no.27 (Feb.1970):10.
-UFO (CE-2)
  1969, Aug.29/Ken Thomas
    "Two Boys Report Strange Lights,"
    Skylook, no.23 (Oct.1969):5.
-UFO (DD)
  1969, Sep.27/Toby Sterne
    "Bright Object Seen in Illinois,"
    Skylook, no.24 (Nov.1969):6.
-UFO (NL)
  1968, Dec.31/Gary Hanson
    "UFO Sightings in Iowa and Illinois,"
    Skylook, no.15 (Feb.1969):1.
    Robert Smulling, "More UFO Reports,"
    Skylook, no.40 (Mar.1971):13.
  1970, Sep.4/Mrs. Otto Dennison
    Robert Smulling, "A Midwest Flap?"
    Skylook, no.36 (Nov.1970):1.
  1971, Jan.21/Raymond Todd
    Robert Smulling, "More UFO Reports,"
    Skylook, no.40 (Mar.1971):13.

Harrisburg
-Coal balls
  1920s/O'Gara Mine No.9
    A.C. Noe, "Coal Balls," Science 57
    (1923):385.
-Erratic giant anteater
  1963, Aug.
    Jeffrey G. Liss, "The Light That
    Chased a Car," Fate 16 (Nov.1963):
    26,34.

Harvard
-UFO (NL)
  1897, April 11/W.D. Hall

Harvard Herald, 18 Apr.1897, p.8.

Havana
-Archeological site
    Robert M. Grogan, "Beads of Meteoric
    Iron from an Indian Mound near Ha-
    vana, Illinois," Am.Antiquity 13
    (1948):302-305. il.
    John C. McGregor, "The Havana Site,"
    in Thorne Duel, ed., Hopewellian
    Communities in Illinois (Spring-
    field: Illinois State Museum, Sci.
    Pap., vol.5, 1952), pp.43-91. il.
-UFO (NL)
    1897, April 20/Mr. Everhart
    Virginia Enquirer, 22 Apr.1897, p.1.
    1946, March 14/Paul Cummings, Jr./10
    mi.E on U.S.136
    Coral & Jim Lorenxen, UFOs: The Whole
    Story (N.Y.: Signet, 1969), pp.26-
    27.

Hazel Crest
-Contactee
    1966, spring-1970s/Shirley Marlowe
    B. Ann Slate, "Is Earth an Extrater-
    restrial Laboratory?" Saga UFO Rept.
    2 (fall 1974):13,66.
-UFO (DD)
    1966, Oct./Shirley Marlowe
    Shirley Marlowe, "Second UFO Sighting
    Changes Scoffing to Deep Interest,"
    Skylook, no.40 (Mar.1971):8.
-UFO (NL)
    1967, Jan.31/Shirley Marlowe
    Shirley Marlowe, "Second UFO Sighting
    Changes Scoffing to Deep Interest,"
    Skylook, no.40 (Mar.1971):8-9.
    1971, Jan.26/Ronald G. Pearson
    "Sky Phenomenon," Skylook, no.45
    (Aug.1971):14.
    1971, Feb.8/Shirley Marlowe
    "Another Report from Hazelcrest,
    Ill.," Skylook, no.41 (Apr.1971):8.
    1973, Nov.7
    Chicago Tribune, 8 Nov.1973.

Henry
-UFO (NL)
    1897, April 12/Ed Sterrett
    Henry Republican, 15 Apr.1897, p.3.

Herald
-UFO (NL)
    1960, Aug./Nella-Jo Newcomb
    (Letter), Fate 14 (Apr.1961):112.

Herrin
-UFO (NL)
    1967, Oct.12
    "U.S.A.," APRO Bull. 16 (Mar.-Apr.
    1968):8.

Highland
-UFO (CE-2)
    1973, Oct.28/Don Taylor
    East St. Louis Metro East Journal,
    30 Oct.1973.

Hillsboro
-Fall of stones
    1883, May 18
    "Local Storms," Monthly Weather Rev.
    11 (May 1883):115.
-UFO (?)
    1897, April 14
    Hillsboro Montgomery News, 16 Apr.
    1897, p.1.

Hillside
-UFO (CE-2)
    1963, June 21/Janice McKay/=ad plane?
    (Letter), Fate 16 (Nov.1963):109-10.
    1968, Jan.24-March 24/Tom Hall
    "Use of Detectors in Spotting UFO,"
    APRO Bull. 16 (Mar.-Apr.1968):7.

Hoffman
-UFO (NL)
    1971, March 13
    "Bright Object Moves West," Skylook,
    no.45 (Aug.1971):14.

Homewood
-Healing
    1970s/John Scudder
    "Healing: Mind over Matter?" News-
    week, 29 Apr.1974, pp.67-68. il.
    Beverly Siegel, "Healer John Scudder
    of Illinois," Fate 28 (Sep.1975):
    32-41. il.
    Jerome Clark, "Irene Gubrud's Pursuit
    of a Miracle," Fate 31 (May 1978):
    34-42. il.
    (Letter), Clinton J. Young, Fate 31
    (Dec.1978):113-14.
-UFO (NL)
    1967, March 3
    Brad Steiger & Joan Whritenour, Allen-
    de Letters: New UFO Breakthrough
    (N.Y.: Award, 1968), p.41.

Hoopeston
-UFO (NL)
    1975, Nov.14
    "UFO Central," CUFOS News Bull., 1
    Feb.1976, p.13.

Hoyleton
-UFO (NL)
    1975, Dec.17
    "UFO Central," CUFOS News Bull., 1
    Feb.1976, p.15.

Huey
-UFO (CE-2)
    1967, Aug.15/1 mi.S
    "Burned Circle in Illinois," Skylook,
    no.33 (Aug.1970):11.

Huntley
-UFO (CE-1)
    1955, March 2
    Jacques Vallee, Passport to Magonia
    (Chicago: Regnery, 1969), p.249.

Huntsville
-UFO (NL)
    1975, Oct.15

"Noteworthy UFO Sightings," Ufology
2 (spring 1976):42.

Hutsonville
-UFO (CE-2)
n.d.
Charles A. Maney, "Scientific Meas-
urement of UFO's," Fate 18 (June
1965):31,32-34.

Indianola
-Plant sensitivity
1940s/Edward W. Block
"Can the Mind Make Plants Grow?"
Fate 2 (Nov.1949):24.

Itasca
-UFO (NL)
1969, March 8/Raymond Richards/Hwy.53
x Thorndale Rd.
Chicago Daily News, 11 Mar.1969.

Jackson co.
-Phantom panther tracks
1970, March
Loren Coleman, "Mystery Animals in
Illinois," Fate 24 (Mar.1971):48.

Jacksonville
-UFO (?)
1971, Feb.2/Howard W. Killebrew/=meteor
"Another Report on the Feb.2nd Light
in Sky," Skylook, no.40 (Mar.1971):
26.
-UFO (NL)
1897, April 10
Quincy Whig, 11 Apr.1897, p.8.
1971, Oct.5/John Irlam
Springfield Illinois State Register,
6 Oct.1971.

Jasper co.
-Phantom panther
1970, Feb./Mrs. Donald Miller
Loren Coleman, "Mystery Animals in
Illinois," Fate 24 (Mar.1971):48,50.

Jersey co.
-Phantom panther
1970, Feb./James Warford
Loren Coleman, "Mystery Animals in
Illinois," Fate 24 (Mar.1971):48,50.

Jerseyville
-UFO (?)
1897, April 14/=balloon
Jerseyville Daily Democrat, 15 Apr.
1897, p.1.

Joliet
-Ball lightning
1946, March 11
"Blue Balls of Joliet," Doubt, no.15
(summer 1946):224.
-Mystery radio transmission
1957, Nov.8/Richard Gerdes
Coral & Jim Lorenzen, UFOs: The Whole
Story (N.Y.: Signet, 1969), p.85.
-Phantom panther
1963, April/Emmett McKaney/gravel pit

Joliet Herald-News, 24 Apr.1963.
1964, July/J.J. Smith
Joliet Herald-News, 30 July 1964.
Jerome Clark & Loren Coleman, "On
the Trail of Pumas, Panthers and
ULAs: Part 2," Fate 25 (July 1972):
92,96-97.
-UFO (DD)
1947, June 24/Charles Kastl/10 mi.E
Chicago Times, 27 June 1947.
1954, May 17
Joliet Herald-News, 17 May 1954.
1977, Aug.5
"UFOs of Limited Merit," Int'l UFO
Reporter 2 (June 1977):8.
-UFO (NL)
1897, April 9
Ottawa Republican-Times, 15 Apr.
1897, p.2.

Joppa
-UFO (NL)
1966, March 23
"Typical Reports," UFO Inv. 3 (Mar.-
Apr.1966):8.

Junction City
-Haunt
1970s
Grit, 29 July 1973.

Justice
-Haunt
1931-   /Resurrection Cemetery/7200
S. Archer Rd.
Chicago Sun-Times, 9 Aug.1975.
Brad Steiger, Psychic City: Chicago
(Garden City: Doubleday, 1976), pp.
95-97.
"Ghosts and Visions," Fortean Times,
no.24 (winter 1978):13.

Kampsville
-UFO (DD)
1974, Nov./Janice Ewen
"MUFON Reports in Brief," Skylook,
no.89 (Apr.1975):10.

Kankakee
-Phantom image
1897, May
Bucyrus (O.) Evening Telegraph, 27
May 1897.
-UFO (CE-1)
1964, Jan.27/Earl Applegate/Peotone
Blacktop
(Editorial), Fate 17 (June 1964):22-
24, quoting Kankakee Daily Journal
(undated).
1970, Oct.12/Ronald Scrogham/480 S.
Harrison Ave.
Kankakee Journal, 13 Oct.1970.
-UFO (CE-2)
1954, Nov.
Leonard H. Stringfield, Inside Saucer
Post...3-0 Blue (Cincinnati: CRIFO,
1957), p.50.
-UFO (NL)
1897, April 9/R.D. Sherman
Chicago Times-Herald, 10 Apr.1897, p.1.

Kankakee Gazette, 15 Apr.1897, p.1.
1947, July 6/Jesse L. Hendrickson
Chicago Times, 7 July 1947.
Chicago Sun, 8 July 1947.
1975, Jan.1/William Caldwell/Kankakee
R.
Robert A. Goerman, "The UFO Modus Op-
erandi: January 1975," *Official UFO*
1 (Aug.1976):46.
1975, Sep.1
"UFO Central," *CUFOS News Bull.*, 15
Nov.1975, p.17.

Kaskaskia
-Hex
n.d.
Grit, 24 Feb.1963.
"Did a Curse Destroy Kaskaskia?"
Fate 16 (Oct.1963):85.
-Welsh Indians
1770s/Abraham Chaplain
John Filson, *The Discovery, Settle-
ment and Present State of Kentucke*
(N.Y.: Corinth, 1962 ed.), pp.
96-97.

Kewanee
-UFO (NL)
1897, April 10
Galesburg Evening Mail, 10 Apr.1897,
p.1.
1897, April 21
Princeton *Bureau County Republican*,
22 Apr.1897, p.2.

Keyesport
-UFO (CE-2)
1975, Jan.1/Debbie Jannett/Tomalco x
Mulberry-Keyesport Rd.
"MUFON Reports in Brief," *Skylook*,
no.89 (Apr.1975):10.
Robert A. Goerman, "The UFO Modus Op-
erandi" January 1975," *Official UFO*
1 (Aug.1976):46, quoting *Carlyle
Union-Banner* (undated).

Kincaid
-Archeological site
ca.1200-1300
John Bennett, "Excavations at Kin-
caid," *Southeastern Arch.Conference
Newsl.* 2, no.4 (1940):13-17
"Pyramids in Illinois," *El Palacio*
48 (1941):260-61.
Fay-Cooper Cole, et al., *Kincaid: A
Prehistoric Metropolis* (Chicago:
Univ. of Chicago, 1951). il.

Kinderhook
-Ancient inscription
1842/W.P. Harris/=hoax
Garrick Mallery, "Pictographs of the
North American Indians," *Ann.Rept.
Bur.Am.Ethn.* 4 (1882-83):3,247.
Stuart Martin, *The Mystery of Mormon-
ism* (London: Odhams, 1920), p.69.
Joseph Smith, *History of the Church
of Jesus Christ of Latter-Day Saints*,
7 vols. (Salt Lake City: Deseret
News, 1950), 5:372-77.

William Alexander Linn, *The Story of
the Mormons* (N.Y.: Russell & Russell,
1963), pp.86-87. il.
-UFO (NL)
1972, Feb.19/Mrs. Michael Murphy
"UFO Seen at Kinderhook, Ill.," *Skylook*, no.53 (Apr.1972):10.

Kinmundy
-UFO (NL)
1897, April 10
Moline Dispatch, 12 Apr.1897, p.5.
1972, April 14/William Allen
"Senior Citizens Report Bright Light,"
Skylook, no.55 (June 1972):8.

LaHarpe
-UFO (CE-3)
1966, Jan.5/2 mi.N on Hwy.94
Robert Smulling, "Report on Craft and
Occupant Seen near LaHarpe, Illinois,
1966," *Skylook*, no.33 (Aug.1970):19.
-UFO (NL)
1897, April 10
Burlington (Ia.) Hawk-Eye, 15 Apr.
1897.

Lake Forest
-UFO (NL)
1897, April 11/F.W. Alex
Chicago Times-Herald, 13 Apr.1897,
p.2.

Lake Zurich
-UFO (CE-1)
1969, May 12/Greg Lucht/Hwy.53 x Dundee
Rd.
Chicago Tribune, 25 May 1969; and 28
May 1969.
"Saucer-Shaped UFO Seen in Northeast
Illinois," *Skylook*, no.20 (July
1969):3-4.
Philip J. Klass, *UFOs Explained* (N.Y.:
Random House, 1974), pp.16-18,21.

Lansing
-Erratic kangaroo
1974, Nov.6
Wall Street Journal, 11 Dec.1974, p.1.

Lawndale
-Giant bird
1977, July 25/Marlan Lowe
Chicago Daily News, 27 July 1977, p.
18.
Jerome Clark & Loren Coleman, *Creatures of the Outer Edge* (N.Y.: Warner, 1978), pp.225-27.

Lawn Ridge
-Ancient coin
1871, July/Jacob W. Moffit
William E. Dubois, "On a Quasi Coin
Reported Found in a Boring in Ill-
inois," *Proc.Am.Phil.Soc'y* 12 (1871)
:224-28. il.
Alexander Winchell, *Sparks from a
Geologist's Hammer* (Chicago: S.C.
Griggs, 1881), p.170.

Lawrence co.
-Phantom panther
  1963, May
    Loren Coleman, "Mystery Animals in
    Illinois," Fate 24 (Mar.1971):48.

Lawrenceville
-Ghost
  1975, Oct.31/Rick McDonald/high school
    Rabern Herrin, "The Old School Spir-
    it," Fate 30 (Aug.1977):41-44.
-UFO (CE-1)
  1964, June 8/Helen Reed/2½ mi.W on
  U.S.50
    Thomas M. Olsen, ed., The Reference
    for Outstanding UFO Sighting Reports
    (Riderwood, Md.: UFO Information
    Retrieval Center, 1966), p.98.
    Donald E. Keyhoe & Gordon I.R. Lore,
    Jr., UFOs: A New Look (Washington:
    NICAP, 1969), p.14.

Leland
-Lightning anomaly
  1959, April 2
    "Lightning," INFO J., no.6 (spring
    1970):42, quoting Weatherwise, June
    1959, p.133.

Le Roy
-UFO (NL)
  1897, April 14/James Hammond
    Bloomington Pantagraph, 16 Apr.1897,
    p.6.

Lewistown
-UFO (NL)
  1971, July 19/Robert Feger
    Canton Daily Ledger, 20 July 1971.

Liberty
-UFO (NL)
  1971, Oct.5/Lyle Ferguson
    "More on Springfield, Illinois, Sight-
    ing," Skylook, no.49 (Dec.1971):20.

Lincoln
-Giant bird
  1977, July 27/Frank Jackson
  1977, July 28/Stan Thompson
    Chicago Daily News, 30-31 July 1977.
    Gilbert J. Ziemba, "Mysterious 'Giant
    Bird' Invades Central Illinois,"
    Page Rsch.Library Newsl., no.20
    (18 Sep.1977):14.
    "Big Bird 1977," Fortean Times, no.
    24 (winter 1978):10,12.
-UFO (NL)
  1897, April 12/John Fitzgerald/Pulaski
  St.
    Lincoln Courier, 13 Apr.1897, p.3.
    Lincoln News, 13 Apr.1897, p.5.
  1964, April/Clarence A. Snyder/Hwy.66
  1971, Aug.12/Clarence A. Snyder
    (Letter), Fate 27 (Apr.1974):132.

Lincolnshire
-UFO (CE-1)
  1975, June 30
    "From the Center for UFO Studies,"

Flying Saucer Rev. 21 (Apr.1976):24.

Lindendale Park
-UFO (NL)
  1975, Jan.4
    Robert A. Goerman, "The UFO Modus Op-
    erandi: January 1975," Official UFO
    1 (Aug.1976):46,47.

Lisle
-Lake monster
  1970, Oct./Robert Seeger/Four Lakes
  Village Quarry
    Chicago Today, 10 Nov.1970.

Litchfield
-UFO (NL)
  1970, April/Jerrel Carner/drive-in
    "Illinois Man Watches Bright Object,"
    Skylook, no.35 (Oct.1970):4.

Littleton
-UFO (NL)
  1964, July 20/Joseph J. Winkel/2 mi.W
  on Hwy.101
    Thomas M. Olsen, ed., The Reference
    for Outstanding UFO Sighting Reports
    (Riderwood, Md.: UFO Information Re-
    trieval Center, 1966), pp.100-101.

Lockport
-UFO (NL)
  1912, May/Carl Howe
    Gordon I.R. Lore, Jr. & Harold H.
    Deneault, Jr., Mysteries of the
    Skies: UFOs in Perspective (Engle-
    wood Cliffs, N.J.: Prentice-Hall,
    1968), p.101.

Lombard
-Erratic crocodilian
  1970, July 30
    Chicago Tribune, 31 July 1970, p.3.
-UFO (CE-1)
  1972, Aug.11
    "Press Reports," APRO Bull. 21 (July-
    Aug.1972):8.

London Mills
-UFO (NL)
  1978, Dec.14/Ralph Brashear/Hwy.116
    London Mills Times, 21 Dec.1978.

Long Grove
-UFO (NL)
  1977, March 9
    "UFO Analysis," Int'l UFO Reporter
    2 (May 1977):Newsfront sec.

Long Point
-UFO (DD)
  1960, Oct.9/Jack L. Sanford
    Richard Hall, ed., The UFO Evidence
    (Washington: NICAP, 1964), p.69.

Loraine
-UFO (NL)
  1972, Oct.14/Edward Hagerbaumer
    "Illinois Farmer Reports Object Out-
    lined in Blue Light," Skylook, no.

62 (Jan.1973):10.

Loves Park
-Ghost dog
 n.d./Mrs. L. Justice
  Martin Ebon, The Evidence for Life
  After Death (N.Y.: Signet, 1977),
  pp.96-97, quoting The Star (undated).

McHenry
-UFO (NL)
 1975, Oct.12
  "UFO Central," CUFOS News Bull., 1
  Feb.1976, p.8.

McLeansboro
-Haunt
 n.d./Lakey's Creek
  John W. Allen, Legends and Lore of
  Southern Illinois (Carbondale:
  Southern Illinois Univ., 1963), pp.
  58-59.

Macomb
-Fire anomaly
 1948, Aug.7-20/Charles Willey/12 mi.S
  Kansas City (Mo.) Star, 18 Aug.1948,
  p.1; and 20 Aug.1948, p.1.
  Richmond (Ind.) Palladium-Item & Sun-
  Telegram, 20 Aug.1948, p.2; 21 Aug.
  1948, p.2; 22 Aug.1948, p.14; 31
  Aug.1948, p.2; and 1 Sep.1948, p.2.
  "We Break Down," Doubt, no.23 (1948):
  348.
  "Hi-Spots in Mail," Doubt, no.24
  (1949):370,372.
  Vincent H. Gaddis, Mysterious Fires
  and Lights (N.Y.: Dell, 1968 ed.),
  pp.165-67.

Mahomet
-Phantom panther
 1963, Jan./Everett J. Hedrick
  Jerome Clark & Loren Coleman, "On the
  Trail of Pumas, Panthers and ULAs:
  Part 2," Fate 25 (July 1972):92,95.
-UFO (CE-2)
 1967, Dec.19/Maryellen Kelly/U.S.150
  Maryellen Kelly, "UFO Made Me Sick,
  Says Housewife," Fate 23 (May 1969):
  34-39.

Maquon
-Spirit medium
 1855-1856
  Emma Hardinge Britten, Modern American Spiritualism (N.Y.: The Author,
  1870), p.389.

Marblehead
-Ghost light
 n.d.
  Harry Middleton Hyatt, Folklore from
  Adams County, Illinois (Hannibal,
  Mo.: Alma Egan Hyatt Foundation,
  1965), pp.740-41.

Marion
-UFO (?)
 1958, Jan.9

Richard Hall, ed., The UFO Evidence
(Washington: NICAP, 1964), p.15.

Markham
-Mystery plane crash
 1964, Sep.6/Piper PA-23
  Jay Gourley, The Great Lakes Triangle
  (Greenwich, Ct.: Fawcett, 1977), pp.
  74-75.
-UFO (DD)
 1971, Jan.26/Helen Swanson
  "Pink and Yellow Circle Seen near
  Markham, Ill.," Skylook, no.40
  (Mar.1971):16.

Marshall
-Ghost
 1907, April/LaVenia Jones/5 mi.SE
  LaVenia Jones, "An Apparition Warns
  the Baby-Sitter," Fate 26 (Dec.
  1973):61-63.

Martinsville
-Phantom image
 1868, April/William Henry Randall/Mill
 Creek
  Louise Cork, "Warning from a Golden
  Cross," Fate 19 (Jan.1966):37-41.
-UFO (NL)
 1968, July/James Lee
  (Letter), Fate 27 (Feb.1974):144-45.

Mascoutah
-UFO (?)
 1970, Oct.4, 13/Paulette Rodenberg
  Belleville News-Democrat, 13 Oct.
  1970.
-UFO (NL)
 1971, May 3/Herb Williams/Hwy.177
  "Carlyle Man Sights Three UFO's,"
  Skylook, no.44 (July 1971):13-14.

Mason
-Haunt
 1890/William W. Bathlot/Little Wabash
 R. Bridge
  William W. Bathlot, "The Haunted
  Bridge," Fate 9 (Apr.1956):98-101.

Mason City
-UFO (NL)
 1897, April 16
  Bloomington Pantagraph, 17 Apr.1897,
  p.5.

Mattoon
-Mystery gas
 1944, Aug.31-Sep.14
  "First Prize," Doubt, no.11 (winter
  1944-45):154.
  Donald M. Johnson, "The Phantom Anes-
  thetist of Mattoon: A Field Study of
  Mass Hysteria," J.Abnormal & Social
  Psych. 40 (1945):175-86.
  Jerome Clark & Loren Coleman, "The
  Mad Gasser of Mattoon," Fate 25 (Feb.
  1972):38-47.
  (Letter), E.J. Ramaley, Fate 27 (Mar.
  1974):132,143.
-UFO (?)

1869, Aug.7/Lewis Swift/=meteors?
   Lewis Swift, "Meteors Seen During a
   Total Eclipse," Pop.Astron. 3
   (1895):159.
-UFO (CE-1)
   1970, Sep.7/Mrs. James Turner/1100 Rudy
   Mattoon Journal-Gazette, 9 Sep.1970.
-UFO (NL)
   1966, June 26/Jim Waltrip
   (Letter), Sci.& Mech. 38 (May 1967):
   72.
   1969, July 14/Fred McKibben/712 Edgar
   St./=planet?
   "Bright Object Sighted over Mattoon,
   Ill.," Skylook, no.21 (Aug.1969):2.
   "More on Mattoon, Ill. Sighting,"
   Skylook, no.22 (Sep.1969):6.

Maywood
-Hypnosis research
   1960s/Society for Hypnotic Research/
   206 Oak St.
   (Letter), Gerald M. Loe, Fate 18
   (Oct.1965):133.
-UFO (CE-1)
   1975, Oct.30
   "UFO Central," CUFOS News Bull., 1
   Feb.1976, p.10.

Meredosia
-UFO (NL)
   1971, Nov.7/William Cole, Jr./E on Hwy.
   104
   "Glowing Object Shaped Like Hub Cap
   Seen by Two Witnesses," Skylook, no.
   49 (Dec.1971):18.

Metropolis
-Aerial phantom
   1874, Feb.18/=city of Paducah?
   Decatur Local Review, 19 Feb.1874,
   p.4.
-UFO (NL)
   1897, April 17/Mr. Starks
   Cincinnati (O.) Enquirer, 19 Apr.1897.

Milan
-UFO (NL)
   1956/Quad City airport
   (Editorial), Fate 10 (May 1957):13.

Minonk
-UFO (NL)
   1897, April 16/William Walmsley/S of
   town
   Bloomington Pantagraph, 17 Apr.1897,
   p.5.

Mitchell
-Archeological site
   ca.900 A.D.
   Coral E. Lorenzen, The Shadow of the
   Unknown (N.Y.: Signet, 1970), p.51,
   quoting St. Louis (Mo.) Post-Dispatch (undated).

Mokena
-UFO (CE-4)
   1951, Sep.24/Harrison E. Bailey
   Ann Druffel, "Harrison Bailey and the

'Flying Saucer Disease,'" Fate 31
   (Apr.1978):38-44; (May 1978):75-82.
   il.

Moline
-Fall of radioactive blue rain
   1954, April 8
   "Colored Rain--Snow," Doubt, no.45
   (1954):289.
-Haunt
   1971
   Brad Steiger, Irene Hughes on Psychic
   Safari (N.Y.: Warner, 1972), pp.58-
   73.
-Skyquake
   1948, March 27
   "Booms--No Clues," Doubt, no.21
   (1948):317.
-UFO (DD)
   1967, March 9/William Fisher/14th St.
   x 16th Ave.
   New York Post, 10 Mar.1967.
   "The Moline Sighting and Film," APRO
   Bull. 15 (Mar.-Apr.1967):7. il.
   "Skylook Editor Gets Expert Views on
   UFO Film at Moline, Ill.," Skylook,
   no.10 (June 1968):1,3.
   R.M.L. Baker, Jr., "Motion Pictures
   of UFOs," in Carl Sagan & Thornton
   Page, eds., UFOs: A Scientific De-
   bate (Ithaca: Cornell Univ., 1972),
   pp.190,201-203. il.
   Kevin D. Randle, "UFOs Caught by the
   Movie Camera," Official UFO 1 (Oct.
   1975):27,29,49-50. il.
-UFO (NL)
   1897, April 10
   Moline Mail, 12 Apr.1897, p.1.
   1897, April 11
   Moline Dispatch, 12 Apr.1897, p.5.
   1897, April 12/C.E. Battles/=Venus?
   Moline Mail, 13 Apr.1897, p.1.

Momence
-Phantom panther
   1946, Sep.24
   "Land Beasties," Doubt, no.17 (1947):
   260.

Monmouth
-UFO (?)
   1897, April 13/=kite
   Monmouth Review, 14 Apr.1897, p.1.
-UFO (NL)
   1897, April 10/J. Doner Diffenbaugh
   Monmouth Review, 12 Apr.1897, p.1.
   1966, July 13
   John A. Keel, UFOs: Operation Trojan
   Horse (N.Y.: Putnam, 1970), p.153.

Monee
-Precognition
   1960s-1970s/Ruth Zimmerman
   Brad Steiger, "Scoring the Seers in
   1969," Fate 23 (Jan.1970):66,69-70.
   Warren Smith, "How Did the Seers in
   1970?" Fate 24 (Feb.1971):84,90-91.
   Herbert B. Greenhouse, Premonitions:
   A Leap into the Future (N.Y.: War-
   ner, 1973 ed.), pp.76-77.

Monticello
-Phantom panther
   1917, July 13/Thomas Gullett/SW of town
      Decatur Herald, 14 July 1917; and 16
      July 1917.

Moro
-Phantom
   1869, April/=hoax?
      Decatur Republican, 15 Apr.1897, p.1.

Morris
-UFO (NL)
   1897, April 9
      Morris Herald, 10 Apr.1897, p.10.

Morrison
-Phantom panther
   1937, Nov.1
      "How to Prevent Panic," Fortean Soc'y
      Mag., no.3 (Jan.1940):13.

Morrisonville
-Anomalous artifact
   1891, June 9/Mrs. S.W. Culp/=gold chain
   in coal lump
      Morrisonville Times, 11 June 1891.
      "A Necklace of a Prehistoric God,"
      INFO J., no.3 (spring 1968):47-48.

Mount Carmel
-Airship inventor
   1890s/Edward J. Pennington
      "Did Pennington Build the 1897 U.S.A.
      Airship?" Flying Saucers, June 1970,
      pp.26-28.
-Fall of tadpole
   1977, Sep.5
      Mt. Carmel Daily Republican-Register,
      7 Sep.1977.

Mount Carroll
-Archeological site
   4 mi.W
      William Pidgeon, Traditions of De-Coo-
      Dah (N.Y.: Horace Thayer, 1858), pp.
      175-77.
-UFO (NL)
   1897, April 9/Owen McGinnis
      Sterling Evening Gazette, 10 Apr.
      1897, p.4.
      Chicago Times-Herald, 10 Apr.1897,
      p.1.

Mount Morris
-UFO (NL)
   1973, Nov.3
      Glenn McWane & David Graham, The New
      UFO Sightings (N.Y.: Warner, 1974),
      p.19.

Mount Olive
-UFO (NL)
   1970, Dec.20/John F. Schuessler/1 mi.N
   on U.S.66
      "Staff Member Spots Green Lights in
      Sky--Has No Explanation," Skylook,
      no.39 (Feb.1971):1.

Mount Prospect
-Mystery television transmission
   1978, April/Joachim Kaupe
      Chicago Sun-Times, 9 Apr.1978.

Mount Vernon
-UFO (?)
   ca.1961/Lucy Hampton/N of town
      "Older UFO Report from Illinois,"
      Skylook, no.61 (Dec.1972):10.
-UFO (CE-1)
   1963, Aug.9/Harry Bishop/Centralia Rd.
      Jeffrey G. Liss, "The Light That
      Chased a Car," Fate 16 (Nov.1963):
      26,35.
      Jacques Vallee, Passport to Magonia
      (Chicago: Regnery, 1969), p.293,
      quoting UPI release, 10 Aug.1963.
-UFO (CE-2)
   1963, Aug.4/Ronnie Austin/E on Hwy.15
      Fairfield Wayne County Press, 5 Aug.
      1963, p.1.
      Jeffrey G. Liss, "The Light That
      Chased a Car," Fate 16 (Nov.1963):
      26-35.
-UFO (NL)
   1897, April 14/B.C. Wells
      Mt. Vernon Daily Register, 15 Apr.
      1897, p.4.
      Chicago Tribune, 16 Apr.1897, p.4.
   1968, April 30/Jay DeWitt
      "UFO in Illinois," Skylook, no.10
      (June 1968):4.
   1969, April 23/SE of town
      "UFO over Mt. Vernon, Ill.," Skylook,
      no.19 (June 1969):7, quoting Mt.
      Vernon Register-News (undated).
   1971, May 3/6 mi.N
      "Illinois Housewife Sees UFO," Sky-
      look, no.44 (July 1971):11.

Mount Zion
-Fall of worm
   1877, March 20/John Scott
      Decatur Republican, 26 Mar.1877, p.3.

Murphysboro
-Humanoid
   1973, June 25/Randy Creath/Big Muddy R.
   1973, June 26/Westwood Hills
      Carbondale Southern Illinoisan, 26
      June 1070, p.5, 27 June 1973, p.3;
      and 28 June 1973, p.3.
      New York Times, 1 Nov.1973, p.45. il.
      Kansas City (Mo.) Star, 2 Dec.1973,
      p.1.
      Jerome Clark & Loren Coleman, "Swamp
      Slobs Invade Illinois," Fate 27
      (July 1974):84-88.
   1973, July 7/Nedra Green/scream only
      Jerome Clark & Loren Coleman, "Swamp
      Slobs Invade Illinois," Fate 27
      (July 1974):84,88.
   1973, July 7/city park
   1973, Nov.26/Harlan Lee Sorkin/scream
   only
      Kansas City (Mo.) Star, 2 Dec.1973,
      p.4.
   1974, July
   1975, July

Centralia Sentinel, 9 July 1975.
-Humanoid tracks
  1973, Nov./Jim Nash/10 mi.SW
    Kansas City (Mo.) Star, 2 Dec.1973,
    p.4.
-UFO (DD)
  1957, Nov.30
    Richard Hall, ed., The UFO Evidence
    (Washington: NICAP, 1964), p.167.

Murrayville
-Phantom panther
  1961, June/E of town
    Jacksonville Courier, 2 June 1961,
    p.1.

Naperville
-UFO (NL)
  1962, March 26
    Lloyd Mallan, "Complete Directory of
    UFOs: Part I," Sci.& Mech. 37 (Dec.
    1966):36,76.

Naples
-Entombed toad
  1853
    A.H. Worthen, "How Living Toads May
    Occur in Limestone," Am.Naturalist
    5 (1871):786-87.

Nashville
-UFO (CE-3)
  1976, Feb.25/NW of town
    "Sighting Reports," CUFOS News Bull.,
    June 1976, p.5.
-UFO (NL)
  1897, April 5
    Chicago Times-Herald, 6 Apr.1897, p.
    1.
  1975, Jan.3/Mrs. Ralph Kleine
    Robert A. Goerman, "The UFO Modus Op-
    erandi: January 1975," Official UFO
    1 (Aug.1976):46,47.

Nauvoo
-UFO (CE-2)
  1970, Nov.29
    Robert Smulling, "More UFO Reports,"
    Skylook, no.40 (Mar.1971):13, quot-
    ing Nauvoo Independent (undated).

New Athens
-Clairvoyance
  1954/June E. Weidemann
    (Letter), Fate 7 (Aug.1954):110-11.
-UFO (NL)
  1973, June 16-17
    New Athens Journal-Press, 21 June
    1973.

New Baden
-UFO (CE-1)
  1969, Aug.5?/Charles J. Brandmeyer/E
  on Hwy.161
    "UFO Paces Car in Illinois," Skylook,
    no.23 (Oct.1969):5.
    "Marine Colonel Reports UFO in Illi-
    nois," Skylook, no.33 (Aug.1970):4.
-UFO (CE-2)
  1967, March 21/nr. Hwy.161

"1967 Landing Site Reported," Sky-
    look, no.46 (Sep.1971):4.
Ted Phillips, Physical Traces Associ-
    ated with UFO Sightings (Evanston:
    Center for UFO Studies, 1975), p.
    46.

New Delhi
-UFO (NL)
  1956, July 2/Mrs. Horace Ash
    "Cigar-Shaped Object Seen near Alton,
    Ill.," Skylook, no.45 (Aug.1971):13.

New Haven
-Entombed toad
  1872-1879/Chapel St.
    Decatur Republican, 18 Nov.1879, p.4.

New Lenox
-Phantom panther
  1949, Aug.
    Jerome Clark & Loren Coleman, "On the
    Trail of Pumas, Panthers and ULAs:
    Part 2," Fate 25 (July 1972):92,93.
  1964, Aug.
    Joliet Spectator, 20 Aug.1964.
    Jerome Clark & Loren Coleman, "On the
    Trail of Pumas, Panthers and ULAs:
    Part 2," Fate 25 (July 1972):92,97.

Newton
-Phantom panther
  1949, Aug.
    Jerome Clark & Loren Coleman, "On the
    Trail of Pumas, Panthers and ULAs:
    Part 2," Fate 25 (July 1972):92,93.
-UFO (CE-1)
  1966, Oct.10
    Carl Sagan & Thornton Page, eds.,
    UFOs: A Scientific Debate (Ithaca:
    Cornell Univ., 1972), pp. xxix-xxx.
-UFO (CE-2)
  1966, Oct.14
    Jacques Vallee, Passport to Magonia
    (Chicago: Regnery, 1969), p.337.

Niles
-Windshield pitting
  1960, July/Gertrude A. Lederer
    (Letter), Fate 15 (June 1962):119-20.

Nilwood
-UFO (DD)
  1897, April 12/William Street/1 mi.N
    Decatur Republican, 14 Apr.1897, p.1.
    Chicago Times-Herald, 14 Apr.1897,
    p.2.

Nora
-UFO (NL)
  1897, April 10/Charles Lutter
    Warren Sentinel, 14 Apr.1897, p.1.

Normal
-Disappearance
  1965/Bruce Cottingham
    Brad Steiger, Strange Disappearances
    (N.Y.: Magnum, 1972), p.18.
-Plant sensitivity
  1961-1962/George E. Smith

Peter Tompkins & Christopher Bird,
The Secret Life of Plants (N.Y.:
Harper & Row, 1973), pp.148-51.
-UFO (DD)
1977, July 31
"UFOs of Limited Merit," Int'l UFO
Reporter 3 (Sep.1977):3.
-UFO (NL)
1975, Oct.27
"UFO Central," CUFOS News Bull., 1
Feb.1976, p.10.

Northbrook
-UFO (?)
1949, Feb.28/Ben Cole, Jr./=meteor?
Kenneth Arnold & Ray Palmer, The Coming of the Saucers (Boise: The Authors, 1952), p.140.

North Henderson
-Telepathy
1880/Mrs. Harvey C. Pitman
Florence Freeman, "Psychic Message,"
Fate 9 (Mar.1956):77.

Nutwood
-UFO (NL)
1969, Jan.17/Edward Clark/S of town
Jersey County Democrat News, 23 Jan.
1969.
"'Flying Wheel' in Illinois," APRO
Bull. 17 (Mar.-Apr.1969):7.

Oak Brook
-UFO (NL)
1972, Aug.11
Glenn McWane & David Graham, The New
UFO Sightings (N.Y.: Warner, 1974),
p.58, quoting Chicago Today (un-
dated).
1975, Nov.19
"UFO Central," CUFOS News Bull., 1
Feb.1976, p.13.

Oak Forest
-UFO (DD)
1960, Aug.18/Harry J. Deerwester
Richard Hall, ed., The UFO Evidence
(Washington: NICAP, 1964), p.37.

Oak Lawn
-Haunt
1000s   /Holy Sepulchre Cemetery/S of
111th St.
Brad Steiger, Psychic City: Chicago
(Garden City: Doubleday, 1976), pp.
93-94.
Jim Brandon, Weird America (N.Y.:
Dutton, 1978), p.78.

Oakley
-Erratic crocodilian
1971, Aug./Sangamon R.
Decatur Herald, 9 Aug.1971.

Oak Park
-Fall of metal foil
1957, Nov.4
"All About Sputs," Doubt, no.56
(1958):460,471.

1960, summer/=radar chaff?
(Letter), Mrs. Martin Roseberry, Fate
19 (June 1966):125.
(Letter), Lewis F. Garber, Fate 19
(Oct.1966):144.
-Fall of unknown object
1969, Jan.26/Dominick Garifo/Oak Park
Ave. x Roosevelt Rd./=satellite?
Chicago Tribune, 27 Jan.1969.
-Healing
1970s/Rosita Rodriguez/714 S. Scoville
David St. Clair, Psychic Healers
(Garden City: Doubleday, 1974), pp.
58-88.
-Inner development
1970s/Satanic Church/208 S. Taylor
June & Nicholas Regush, Psi: The Oth-
er World Catalogue (N.Y.: Putnam,
1974), p.307.
-Precognition
1960s-   /Harold Schroeppel/719 S.
Clarence Ave.
"Predictions for 1967," Fate 20
(June 1967):34,44.
Brad Steiger, "The Seers Speak for
1970," Fate 23 (May 1970):78-80. il.
Warren Smith, "How Did the Seers in
1970?" Fate 24 (Feb.1971):84,89-90.
Warren Smith, "Phenomenal Predictions
for 1975," Saga, Jan.1975, pp.20,52.
Warren Smith, "Phenomenal Predictions
for 1976," Saga, Jan.1976, pp.16,52.

Odin
-Giant bird
1977, Aug.11/John Chappell
Gilbert J. Ziemba, "Mysterious 'Giant
Bird'--Invades Central Illinois,"
Page Rsch.Library Newsl., no.20
(18 Sep.1977):14,15-16.
-UFO (NL)
1968/Ira Prahl
"Retired Farmer Reports 1968 Sight-
ing," Skylook, no.43 (June 1971):6.

O'Fallon
-UFO (CE-2)
1973, Oct.18
Ted Phillips, Physical Traces Associ-
ated with UFO Sightings (Evanston:
Center for UFO Studies, 1975), p.95.
-UFO (DD)
1950, Aug./Clarence O. Dargie
"UFO Reports Made at the Carlyle Sky-
watch and Picnic," Skylook, no.34
(Sep.1970):6.

Okawville
-Humanoid
1942
Jesse Harris, "Myths and Legends from
Southern Illinois," Hoosier Folklore
5 (Mar.1946):14,20.

Olive Branch
-Erratic baboon
1950
"Run of the Mill," Doubt, no.31
(1950):58.
-Phantom panther

1970, April 10/Mike Busby/S on Hwy.3
Cairo Evening Citizen, 20 Apr.1970.
Loren Coleman, "Mystery Animals in
Illinois," Fate 24 (Mar.1971):48,
50-51.

Oquawka
-Phantom panther
1946, Sep.19
"Land Beasties," Doubt, no.17 (1947):
260.

Orangeville
-UFO (NL)
1897, Feb.13/=hoax?
Orangeville Courier, 19 Apr.1897, p.
8.

Oregon
-UFO (NL)
1971, Sep./Myrnie Worsley
(Letter), Fate 27 (June 1974):159-60.

Orion
-UFO (NL)
1897, April 12
Orion Times, 15 Apr.1897, p.1.

Ottawa
-Archeological site
ca.1300/Gentleman Farm site/2 mi.E
James A. Brown, et al., "The Gentle-
man Farm Site," Rept.Investigations
Illinois State Mus., no.12 (1969).
il.
-Fall of scoria
1857, June 17/L.H. Bradley
"Supposed Meteorite," Am.J.Sci., ser.
2, 24 (1857):447.
-Fire anomaly
1952, July 16/William Lambert
(Editorial), Fate 5 (Dec.1952):5.
-UFO (NL)
1897, April 10/William Trabing, Sr.
Ottawa Republican-Times, 15 Apr.1897,
p.2.

Palestine
-Archeological site
1500-1000 B.C./Riverton site
Howard D. Winters, "The Riverton Cul-
ture," Rept.Investigations Illinois
State Mus., no.13 (1969). il.
-Ball lightning
ca.1939, summer
C. Maxwell Cade & Delphine Davis, The
Taming of the Thunderbolts (London:
Abelard-Schuman, 1969), p.89, quot-
ing Edmond M. Dewan, Eyewitness Ac-
counts of Kugelblitz.

Pana
-Phantom panther
1970, Sep.19/A.V. Hamm
Jerome Clark & Loren Coleman, "On the
Trail of Pumas, Panthers and ULAs:
Part 1," Fate 25 (June 1972):72.
-UFO (NL)
1973, Feb.8/Robert Woidt
"Orange Ball Seen in Illinois," Sky-

look, no.66 (May 1973):16.

Paris
-UFO (CE-2)
1955, March 9/Eugene Metcalf
Brent Raynes, "Flying Saucer Landings
and UFO Kidnapping Reports," Flying
Saucers, June 1970, p.32.
-UFO (DD)
1951, Oct.9/Charles Warren/E of town
Edward J. Ruppelt, The Report on Un-
identified Flying Objects (Garden
City: Doubleday, 1956), pp.112-13.
U.S. Air Force, Projects Grudge and
Blue Book Reports 1-12 (Washington:
NICAP, 1968), pp.18,49.
J. Allen Hynek, The Hynek UFO Report
(N.Y.: Dell, 1977), p.118.
1957, July 18/Harold Mathes
Frank Edwards, Strangest of All
(N.Y.: Ace, 1962), pp.185-86.

Parker
-Ghost cat
1926, Jan./O'Helen Sullivan
O'Helen Sullivan, "The Phantom Cat,"
Fate 5 (Sep.1952):59-60.

Park Ridge
-UFO (CE-1)
1978, Dec.9/Patty Kelly/339 Cuttriss
Park Ridge Herald, 21 Dec.1978.
-UFO (NL)
1975, July 17
"UFO Central," CUFOS News Bull., 15
Nov.1975, p.3.
1978, Dec.14/Collette Loll/West Park
Park Ridge Advocate, 21 Dec.1978.

Patoka
-UFO (DD)
1972, Nov.24/Rosemary A. Bricker/2 mi.
NW
"Several Report Silver Disc in Illi-
nois," Skylook, no.62 (Jan.1973):11.

Pekin
-Humanoid
1972, July 25/Illinois R.
Peoria Journal-Star, 26 July 1972.
-Phantom image
1890s
Gentry (Ark.) Journal-Advance, 30
Apr.1897.
-Precognition
1918, July 5/Warren M. Cohenour
Warren M. Cohenour, "The Sinking of
the Columbia," Fate 30 (Nov.1977):
74-75. il.
-UFO (NL)
1969, Feb.19/Ray Watts/SW on Hwy.24
"Peoria Group Investigates Strange
Sky Sightings," Skylook, no.16 (Mar.
1969):12.

Peoria
-Archeological site
Cyrus Thomas, "Report on the Mound
Explorations of the Bureau of Eth-
nology," Ann.Rept.Bur.Am.Ethn. 12

(1890-91):1,308.
-Ball lightning
 1929, Aug.28/George Winchester
  George Winchester, "A Peculiar Light-
  ning Phenomenon," Science 70 (1929)
  :501-502.
-Out-of-body experience
 1890s/Alice Gifford Bowman
  Alice Gifford Bowman & Josephine
  Wetzler, "The Mallard in the Woods,"
  Fate 18 (Apr.1965):43-46.
-Poltergeist
 1873, Dec.-1874, Feb./Lydia Bradley
  Peoria Transcript, 10 Feb.1874.
  New York Times, 28 Feb.1874, p.9.
-UFO (?)
 1897, April 14/M.E. Wilson/=balloon
  Peoria Transcript, 15 Apr.1897, p.1.
 1947, July 7/Harry L. Spooner
  Springfield Illinois State Journal,
  8 July 1947.
 1950, Dec.
  "The Cloth Speaks," Doubt, no.32
  (1951):67.
 1969, June 5/Alan Harkrader, Jr./=
 meteor
  (Letter), Raymond M. Watts, Skylook,
  no.43 (June 1971):21.
  Philip J. Klass, UFOs Explained (N.Y.:
  Random House, 1974), pp.45-49. il.
-UFO (CE-2)
 1952, May 21/Rose Murphy/10 mi. from
 town
  Harold T. Wilkins, Flying Saucers Uncensored (N.Y.: Pyramid, 1967 ed.),
  pp.60-61.
 1966, Sep.24
  "Peoria Group Investigates Strange
  Sky Sightings," Skylook, no.16 (Mar.
  1969):12-13.
-UFO (CE-3)
 1897, April 17/Mr. Hardenburg/nr. Insane Asylum/=hoax?
  Peoria Herald, 18 Apr.1897, p.5.
  Peoria Times, 19 Apr.1897, p.6.
-UFO (DD)
 1947, July 7/Michael Boyer
  Springfield Illinois State Journal,
  8 July 1947.
-UFO (NL)
 1968/Laird S. Carter
 1968, Aug./Northmoor Hills
  "Peoria Group Investigates Strange
  Sky Sightings," Skylook, no.16 (Mar.
  1969):12,13.
 1973, Oct.22/Lois Hartig/University St.
  Glenn McWane & David Graham, The New
  UFO Sightings (N.Y.: Warner, 1974),
  pp.25-26.
 1978, Feb.5/Bradley University
  "UFOs of Limited Merit," Int'l UFO
  Reporter 3 (Mar.1978):Newsfront sec.
 1978, Aug.7/War Memorial Dr.
  "UFOs of Limited Merit," Int'l UFO
  Reporter 3 (Sep.1978):6,9.

Peoria co.
-Phantom panther and livestock killings
 1950, Nov./Fred Perdelwitz
  Jerome Clark & Loren Coleman, "On the

Trail of Pumas, Panthers and ULAs:
Part 2," Fate 25 (July 1972):92,93.

Perry
-UFO (NL)
 1897, April 12/Charles P. Malley
  Quincy Herald, 13 Apr.1897, p.3.
 1897, April 15/Charles P. Malley
  Quincy Herald, 16 Apr.1897, p.8.

Perry co.
-UFO (NL)
 1968, fall
  "Illinois Woman Reports Strange Object," Skylook, no.31 (June 1970):3.

Peru
-UFO (CE-1)
 1969, June 17/Thomas J. Reed/I-80
  "Flying Instructor Reports UFOs in
  Illinois Sky," Skylook, no.41 (Apr.
  1971):7-8.
-UFO (NL)
 1975, Oct.12
  "UFO Central," CUFOS News Bull., 1
  Feb.1976, p.9.

Plainfield
-Phantom panther
 1978, March 6, 8/Mrs. William Hughes/
 =black bull mastiff?
  Joliet Metro East Herald-News, 10
  Mar.1978; and 28-29 Apr.1978.

Plainville
-UFO (CE-2)
 1969, Nov.30/Russell Ator/Hwy.96
  Walt Andrus, Jr., "Car Rises from
  Highway As UFO Passes Overhead,"
  Skylook, no.26 (Jan.1970):7-8.

Plano
-Erratic kangaroo
 1974, Oct.25/John Orr/Riverview Rd.
 1974, Nov.2/Jerry Wagner/Shafer Rd.
 1974, Nov.4
  Kansas City (Mo.) Times, 4-5 Nov.
  1974.
  David Fideler & Loren Coleman, "Kangaroos from Nowhere," Fate 31 (Apr.
  1978):68,69-70.

Pleasant Ridge
-Paranormal longevity
  (Editorial), Fate 29 (Dec.1976):32.

Pontiac
-UFO (NL)
 1967, March 8
  Pontiac Leader, 10 Mar.1967.

Prospect Heights
-UFO (CE-3)
 1953, spring
  David Webb & Ted Bloecher, "MUFON's
  Humanoid Study Group Very Active,"
  Skylook, no.93 (Aug.1975):9.
-UFO (NL)
 1975, Sep./Greg Poch
  (Letter), Saga UFO Rept. 3 (Apr.1976):6.

Quincy
-Disappearance
  1878, Nov.9/Charles Ashmore/=fiction
    Ambrose Bierce, "Charles Ashmore's
    Trail," in E.F. Bleiler, ed., Ghost
    and Horror Stories of Ambrose Bierce
    (N.Y.: Dover, 1964 ed.), pp.88-90.
-Haunt
  n.d.
    Harry Middleton Hyatt, Folk-lore from
    Adams County, Illinois (Hannibal,
    Mo.: Alma Egan Hyatt Foundation,
    1965), pp.743-44.
-Healing
  1870s/Maude Lord-Drake
    W.D. Chesney, "That Great Medium:
    Maude Lord-Drake," Fate 14 (Apr.
    1961):82,86-87.
-Hex
  ca.1898/7 mi.NE
    Harry Middleton Hyatt, Folk-lore from
    Adams County, Illinois (Hannibal,
    Mo.: Alma Egan Hyatt Foundation,
    1965), pp.847-49.
-UFO (?)
  1972, Feb.17/Marilyn Holtman/=airplane?
    "UFO or Plane," Skylook, no.53 (Apr.
    1972):9-10.
-UFO (CE-1)
  1971, Jan.18/Mrs. James Weertz/Spring
  St.
    "Mother, Daughter and Grandchild See
    Domed Object with Light Beam," Sky-
    look, no.45 (Aug.1971):15.
-UFO (CE-2)
  1969, Dec.19/Marvin Mixer/Ellington Rd.
    "Unknown Force Lifts Vehicle from
    Highway," Skylook, no.42 (May 1971)
    :7-8.
  1972, Feb.
    Quincy Herald-Whig, 20 Feb.1972.
-UFO (DD)
  1970, May 20/Craig Triplett/Summit Dr.
    "Quincy Lads Watch UFO--Father of
    One Boy Catches Glimpse," Skylook,
    no.34 (Sep.1970):8.
-UFO (NL)
  1897, April 10
    Quincy Whig, 11 Apr.1897, p.8.
  1897, April 15/George Lane/Main St.
    Quincy Herald, 16 Apr.1897, p.1.
  1971, April 9/Victor M. Hubbard/2020
  Broadway
    "Object with Lights in Triangle For-
    mation Flies over Country," Skylook,
    no.42 (May 1971):4.
  1972, June 15/Earl F. Watts
    "Plan to Photograph Meteor Shower--
    Get UFO," Skylook, no.57 (Aug.1972):
    13.
  1972, Aug.29/Hilda Christison/Motorola
  plant
    "Two Watch Fast Moving Light," Sky-
    look, no.60 (Nov.1972):10.
  1972, Oct.3/Richard H. Baldwin
    Quincy Whig-Herald, 8 Oct.1972.
  1973, Sep.28
    Quincy Whig-Herald, 30 Sep.1973.
  1975, Oct.12
    "Noteworthy UFO Sightings," Ufology

2 (spring 1976):42.

Ramsey
-Phantom panther tracks
  1969-1971/Merle C. Corrington
  1972, April/Merle C. Corrington
    (Letter), Fate 25 (Nov.1972):145-46.

Randolph
-UFO (CE-2)
  1974, May/ground markings only
    Ted Phillips, Physical Traces Associ-
    ated with UFO Sightings (Evanston:
    Center for UFO Studies, 1975), p.
    100.

Rankin
-UFO (NL)
  1897, April 16
    Bloomington Pantagraph, 17 Apr.1897,
    p.5.

Rantoul
-Precognition
  1951, March-April/Jesse M. Caldwell/
  Chanute AFB
    "Predicts Air Crashes," Fate 4 (Aug.-
    Sep.1951):47.
    Vincent H. Gaddis, Invisible Hori-
    zons (Philadelphia: Chilton, 1965),
    pp.221-22.
-UFO (NL)
  1956, Jan.9/20 mi.SW
    Jacques Vallee, Passport to Magonia
    (Chicago: Regnery, 1969), pp.143-
    44.

Rapids City
-Haunt
  1900/Vincent Hellstern
    "A Haunted House," J.ASPR 12 (1918):
    392-94.

Red Bud
-UFO (CE-2)
  1973, Oct.15/Robert Eicholz
    "New Twist to Fish Story," Skylook,
    no.76 (Mar.1974):4.
-UFO (DD)
  1950, April 23/Dean Margen
    Dean Margen, "The Red Bud, Illinois
    Photo," Flying Saucers, Oct.1959,
    pp.5-7. il.
    Wendelle Stevens, "UFO Scrapbook,"
    Official UFO 1 (Feb.1976):27-28. il.

Reed City
-UFO (NL)
  1923/Veral P. Lager
    "School Teacher Reports UFO," Skylook,
    no.57 (Aug.1972):12.

Ridgway
-Moving tree stump
  1976, Jan.-Feb.
    Lebanon (Pa.) Daily News, 9 Feb.1976.

Ringwood
-UFO (CE-2)
  1957, Nov.5

Aurora Beacon-News, 7 Nov.1957.

Robinson
-UFO (NL)
 1897, April 9/Ike Cunningham/depot
  Robinson Argus, 14 Apr.1897, p.1.

Rochelle
-UFO (NL)
 1897, April 3
  Aurora Beacon, 6 Apr.1897, p.1.
 1897, April 11
  Rochelle Register, 16 Apr.1897, p.1.

Rockdale
-Humanoid
 1957/Gerald E. Wilda/Larkin Ave. x Hwy.
 80
  (Letter), *Fate* 26 (Jan.1973):142-43.

Rock Falls
-UFO (CE-1)
 1968, June 15/Mary Kathleen Knowles/
 Hwy.88
  "Young Women Observe Apparent UFO
  Landing," *Skylook*, no.21 (Aug.1969)
  :4.

Rockford
-Phantom dog tracks
 1970, June/Lyle Imig
  Loren Coleman, "Mystery Animals in
  Illinois," *Fate* 24 (Mar.1971):48,52.
-Precognition
 1918/Arthur Ford/Camp Grant
  Allen Spraggett & William Rauscher,
  *Arthur Ford: The Man Who Talked
  with the Dead* (N.Y.: Signet, 1974),
  pp.30-31.
-Seance
 1856, Aug.
  Emma Hardinge Britten, *Modern Ameri-
  can Spiritualism* (N.Y.: The Author,
  1870), p.388.
-Spontaneous human combustion
 1959, Feb?/Ricky Paul Pruitt
  (Editorial), *Fate* 12 (June 1959):19.
-UFO (?)
 1952, Aug./Roy Munson
  "Multiple Object Sightings by Credit-
  able Observers Continue," *CRIFO
  Newsl.*, 2 July 1954, p.3.
-UFO (NN)
 1947, July 7/Wilbur Luckey
  Chicago Times, 7 July 1947.
 1955, April 8/John C. Gregory
  Rockford Register-Republic, 8 Apr.
  1955.
  "Official Postscript to the Rockford
  Incident," *CRIFO Orbit*, 5 Aug.1955,
  p.2.
 1967, Oct.1
  "Good Sighting in Illinois," *Skylook*,
  no.2 (Oct.1967):6.
-UFO (NL)
 1897, April 9/Elisha Thayer
  Rockford Gazette, 10 Apr.1897, p.2.
  Rockford Republic, 10 Apr.1897, p.1.
-UFO (R-V)
 1956, Nov.27/John C. Gregory

Rockford Morning Star, 28 Nov.1956.

Rock Island
-Animal ESP
 1924-1936/St. Anthony's Hospital
  Eldon Roark, *Just a Mutt* (N.Y.: Whittlesey House, 1947), pp.123-25.
-Erratic kangaroo
 1976, April 7/Harry Masterton
  Montreal (P.Q.) Star, 8 Apr.1976.
  David Fideler & Loren Coleman, "Kan-
  garoos from Nowhere," *Fate* 31 (Apr.
  1978):68,73-74.
-UFO (?)
 1953, Oct.9
  Donald E. Keyhoe, *Flying Saucer Con-
  spiracy* (N.Y.: Holt, 1955), pp.62-
  63.
-UFO (NL)
 1897, April 8
  Rock Island Argus, 9 Apr.1897, p.5.
 1897, April 12/Second Ave.
  Rock Island Argus, 13 Apr.1897, p.3.
 1897, April 13/Robert Solomon
  Rock Island Argus, 14 Apr.1897, p.5.
  Rock Island Union, 14 Apr.1897, p.4.

Roselle
-UFO (CE-1)
 1963, Sep.20/Richard Abel
  Chicago American, 20 Sep.1963.

Rossville
-UFO (NL)
 1897, April 25/George Smith
  Chicago Inter-Ocean, 26 Apr.1897.

Rushville
-UFO (NL)
 1897, April 12/L. Warren Clarke/Hotel
 Schuyler
  Rushville Times, 15 Apr.1897, p.2.

Saint Charles
-UFO (?)
 1897, April 10/=balloon
  St. Charles Valley Chronicle, 16 Apr.
  1897, p.1.
-UFO (CE-2)
 1972/ground markings only
  Ted Phillips, *Physical Traces Associ-
  ated with UFO Sightings* (Evanston:
  Center for UFO Studies, 1975), p.80.

Saint Francisville
-Phantom panther
 1963, May 4-5/Maurice Ivers
 1963, May 24/John King
  Jacksonville Courier, 22 May 1963, p.
  1.
  Jerome Clark & Loren Coleman, "On the
  Trail of Pumas, Panthers and ULAs:
  Part 2," *Fate* 25 (July 1972):92,95-
  96, quoting *Lawrenceville Daily Record* (undated).

Saint Jacob
-UFO (NL)
 1975, Jan.1/Charles Green/Old Hwy.40
  "MUFON Reports in Brief," *Skylook*,

no.89 (Apr.1975):10.

Saint Joseph
-Humanoid
  1973, Oct.16/Bill Duncan/Salt Fork
  Bridge
    Champaign-Urbana Courier, 17 Oct.
    1973.
-UFO (NL)
  1897, April 23/Ollie Kellogg
    St. Joseph Record, 24 Apr.1897, p.1.

Saint Mary's twp.
-Phantom snowballs
  1849/Mr. Groves
    Charles M. Skinner, Myths and Legends
    of Our Own Land, 2 vols. (Philadel-
    phia: Lippincott, 1896), 2:308-309.

Salem
-Disappearance
  1970, Feb.-April/hogs
    Loren Coleman, "Mystery Animals in
    Illinois," Fate 24 (Mar.1971):48,52.

Saline co.
-Phantom panther
  1963, summer
    Loren Coleman, "Mystery Animals in
    Illinois," Fate 24 (Mar.1971):48.

Schaumburg
-UFO (?)
  1970, June 6
    Elk Grove Herald, 10 June 1970.
-UFO (CE-2)
  1973, May 10/Fred Schmidt/Schaumburg
  Rd. x I-90
    Brad Steiger, Psychic City: Chicago
    (Garden City: Doubleday, 1976), p.
    100.
-UFO (DD)
  1978, July 4
    "UFOs of Limited Merit," Int'l UFO
    Reporter 3 (Aug.1978):4.

Seneca
-Spontaneous human combustion
  1885, Dec.25/Mrs. Patrick Rooney
    Ottawa Daily Republican-Times, 28
    Dec.1885.
    Ottawa Free Trader, 9 Jan.1886.
    Nora Bell, "The Seneca Cremation,"
    Fate 9 (Dec.1956):78-81.

Shabbona
-UFO (CE-2)
  1974, Nov.28/Hugo W. Feugen
    "Pilot Says Compass Affected," Sky-
    look, no.89 (Apr.1975):5.

Sherman
-UFO (NL)
  1897, April 12
    Peoria Journal, 15 Apr.1897, p.2.

Skokie
-UFO (NL)
  1897, April 9/George Clem
    Chicago Times-Herald, 10 Apr.1897.

1957, Nov.26/James Chapman/Skokie Hwy.
    (Letter), Fate 11 (June 1958):114.

South Chicago Heights
-UFO (NL)
  1975, July 17
    "UFO Central," CUFOS News Bull., 15
    Nov.1975, p.13.

South Elgin
-Animal ESP
  1977, Dec./Jack Millikan
    Omaha (Neb.) World-Herald, 13 Dec.
    1977.

South Moline twp.
-UFO (DD)
  1897, April 12/Ben Carr/Hennepin Canal
    Moline Mail, 12 Apr.1897, p.1.
    Rock Island Argus, 12 Apr.1897, p.5.

Sparta
-UFO (NL)
  1978, Feb.13/Steve Patton
    Sparta News-Plaindealer, 16 Feb.1978.

Springfield
-Haunt
  1973/Shirlee Laughlin/Lincoln Home
    (Editorial), Fate 29 (June 1976):26-
    30.
-Precognition
  1860, Nov./Abraham Lincoln/Lincoln Home
    New York Herald, 17 July 1882.
-Seances
  1923, Dec.29-1925, April 8
    Kennan D. Herman, "Experiments in
    Automatism," J.ASPR 20 (1926):93-
    102.
    (Letter), Kennan D. Herman, J.ASPR
    20 (1926):249-50.
-Skyquake
  1954, Oct.7/Mrs. H. Baggerly
    "Case 53," CRIFO Newsl., 4 Feb.1955,
    p.4.
  1970, Oct.9/Mrs. John Worth
    "Mysterious Boom Is Unexplained,"
    Skylook, no.36 (Nov.1970):2.
-UFO (?)
  1869, Aug.7/C.N. Fay/=meteors
    Dorrit Hoffleit, "Daytime Meteors of
    August 7, 1869," Pop.Astron. 58
    (1950):407-409.
  1950, Dec.
    "The Cloth Speaks," Doubt, no.32
    (1951):67.
-UFO (CE-3)
  1897, April 15/Adolph Winkle/2 mi.N
    Springfield News, 15 Apr.1897.
-UFO (DD)
  1947, July 8/William Bender/6th x Washington St.
    Springfield Illinois State Journal,
    9 July 1947.
  1963, July 20
    Richard Hall, ed., The UFO Evidence
    (Washington: NICAP, 1964), p.141.
-UFO (NL)
  1897, April 15/5th x Monroe St.
    Springfield Illinois State Register,

16 Apr.1897, p.2.
Springfield Illinois State Journal,
16 Apr.1897, p.5.
1947, July 3/George Mayfield/W of town
Springfield Illinois State Register,
5 July 1947.
1947, July 8/John C. Burs
1947, July 9/Marvin Wright/S. McArthur
Blvd. x Outer Park Dr.
Springfield Illinois State Register,
9 July 1947.
1950, July 29/Jim Graham
    Gerald Heard, The Riddle of the Fly-
    ing Saucers (London: Carroll &
    Nicholson, 1950), p.148.
    Ray Palmer, "New Report on the Fly-
    ing Saucers," Fate 4 (Jan.1951):63,
    80.
1971, Oct.5/John Wells
    Springfield Illinois State Register,
    6 Oct.1971.
    Springfield College Spectrum, 12 Oct.
    1971.

State Park Place
-Archeological site
ca.700-1500/Cahokia Mounds
    Henry M. Brackenridge, Views of Lou-
    isiana (Pittsburgh: Cramer, Spear &
    Eichbaum, 1814), pp.186-89.
    E.G. Squier & E.H. Davis, Ancient
    Monuments of the Mississippi Valley
    (Washington: Smithsonian Institution,
    Contrib.to Knowl., no.1, 1848), pp.
    174-75.
    Cyrus Thomas, "Report on the Mound
    Explorations of the Bureau of Eth-
    nology," Ann.Rept.Bur.Am.Ethn. 12
    (1890-91):1,131-34. il.
    "Cahokia Tablet," Am.Antiquarian 13
    (18-1):58.
    Donald I. Bushnell, Jr., "Archaeolog-
    ical Reconnaissance of the Cahokia
    and Related Mound Groups," Smith.
    Misc.Coll. 72 (1922):92-105.
    Warren K. Moorehead & Morris M. Leigh-
    ton, "The Cahokia Mounds," Bull.
    Univ.Illinois, vol.21, no.6 (1923).
    il.
    Warren K. Moorehead, "The Cahokia
    Mounds," Bull.Univ.Illinois, vol.26,
    no.4 (1928).
    P.F. Titterington, "The Cahokia Mound
    Group and Its Surface Material,"
    Wisconsin Arch. 13 (1933):7-14. il.
    A.R. Kelly, "Some Problems of Recent
    Cahokia Archaeology," Trans.Illinois
    State Acad.Sci. 25 (1933):101-103.
    Greater St. Louis Archeological Soc'y,
    Cahokia Brought to Life (St. Louis:
    Wellington, 1950). il.
    Gregory Perino, "Cahokia," Central
    States Arch.J. 3 (1957):84-87. il.
    W. Wittry, "An American Woodhenge,"
    Newsl.Cranbrook Inst.Sci. 33 (1964):
    102-107.
    Gregory Perino, "Additional Discover-
    ies of Filed Teeth in the Cahokia
    Area," Am.Antiquity 32 (1967):538-
    42.

    Melvin L. Fowler, ed., "Explorations
    into Cahokia Archeology," Bull.
    Illinois Arch.Survey, no.7 (1970).
    il.
    Gerald Hawkins, Beyond Stonehenge
    (N.Y.: Harper & Row, 1973), pp.176-
    77.
    Franklin Folsom, America's Ancient
    Treasures (N.Y.: Rand McNally,
    1974), pp.130-32.
    William R. Iseminger, "Cahokia: A
    Mississippian Metropolis," Central
    States Arch.J. 24 (1977):116-29. il.
    Melvin L. Fowler, "Aerial Archeology
    at the Cahokia Site," Rept.Charo
    Center, no.2 (1977):65-80. il.
    Kansas City (Mo.) Star, 17 Sep.1977.
    St. Louis (Mo.) Post-Dispatch, 20
    Mar.1978.
    Dick Norrish, "This Priest Astrono-
    mer, This Genius!" Central States
    Arch.J. 26 (1979):12-23. il.

Sterling
-Ancient inscription
    Albert D. Hager, "Inscribed Tablet
    Found at Sterling, Ill.," Am.Anti-
    quarian 2 (1879):65-66.
-Haunt
1943, Nov.6-13
    "Ghosts Active," Fortean Soc'y Mag.,
    no.10 (autumn 1944):142.
-Lake monster
1937, Oct.
    Curtis D. MacDougall, Hoaxes (N.Y.:
    Dover, 1958 ed.), p.14.
-UFO (NL)
1897, April 8-9
    Sterling Gazette, 10 Apr.1897, p.4.
1897, April 12/W.C. Brown
    Rock Island Argus, 13 Apr.1897, p.3.
1897, April 14/F.H. Geyer
    Sterling Gazette, 15 Apr.1897, p.1.

Stockton
-UFO (NL)
1978, Aug.22/Dennis Jagodzinski/Hwy.78
    x U.S.20
    Rockford Morning Star, 24 Aug.1978.

Stonefort
-Archeological site
    Loren Coleman, "Pre-Columbian Stone
    Structures in Southern Illinois,"
    NEARA Newsl. 5 (Sep.1970):68.

Streator
-UFO (NL)
1976, April 25
    "Noteworthy UFO Sightings," Ufology
    2 (fall 1976):60.

Sycamore
-UFO (NL)
1897, April 9/Jack Connell
    Sycamore True Republican, 14 Apr.
    1897, p.1.
    Sycamore City Weekly, 15 Apr.1897,
    p.1.
1897, April 18/Vernon Allen

Sycamore City Weekly, 22 Apr.1897, p.
6.

Tamaroa
-UFO (CE-2)
1957, Nov.14/Mrs. John Riead/U.S.1
Chicago American, 15 Nov.1957.
Mt. Vernon Register-News, 15 Nov.1957.

Taylorville
-Roman coin
1883
Decatur Daily Republican, 20 Apr.
1883, p.1.
-UFO (NL)
1897, April 9/Mrs. W.E. Andrews
Taylorsville Breeze, 13 Apr.1897, p.
1.

Trenton
-Humanoid tracks
ca.1965/Brian Schwaz
John Green, The Sasquatch File (Agassiz, B.C.: Cheam, 1973), p.40.

Trivoli
-UFO (CE-2)
1966, Feb.26
Jacques Vallee, Passport to Magonia
(Chicago: Regnery, 1969), p.323.

Urbana
-UFO (NL)
1957, Nov.6
"All About Sputs," Doubt, no.56
(1958):460,471.

Ursa
-Haunt
n.d./old covered bridge
Harry Middleton Hyatt, Folk-lore from
Adams County, Illinois (Hannibal,
Mo.: Alma Egan Hyatt Foundation,
1965), pp.722-23.

Vandalia
-Airship inventor
1897, April/C. Devonbaugh
Decatur Evening Republican, 15 Apr.
1897, p.8.
-UFO (DD)
1953, June?/airport
"Back Track," Skylook, no.53 (Apr.
1972):13.
-UFO (NL)
1897, April 16
Chicago Times-Herald, 17 Apr.1897,
p.6.
1951, Aug.27/Ray Williams
Vandalia Leader, 30 Aug.1951.

Villa Park
-UFO (CE-1)
1976, March 28
"Sighting Reports," CUFOS News Bull.,
June 1976, p.5.
-UFO (CE-2)
1968, Jan.15/Lori Achzehner
"Use of Detectors in Spotting UFO,"
APRO Bull. 16 (Mar.-Apr.1968):7.

Walsh
-UFO (CE-1)
1970, Oct.5
"Illinois Farmer Watches Red UFO with
Beams of Bright Light," Skylook, no.
36 (Nov.1970):7-8.
"Object over Illinois Farm," APRO
Bull. 19 (Nov.-Dec.1970):1,3.

Warsaw
-Clairvoyance and spirit medium
1860s-1870s/Maude Lord-Drake
Maude Lord-Drake, Psychic Light: The
Continuity of Law and Life (Kansas
City, Mo.: F.T. Riley, 1904).
W.D. Chesney, "That Great Medium,
Maude Lord Drake," Fate 14 (Apr.
1961):82,85-87.
-UFO (NL)
1897, April 13-14/Jake Breitenstein
Warsaw Bulletin, 16 Apr.1897, p.3.
1971, July 19
Canton Daily Ledger, 20 July 1971.

Watseka
-Spirit medium
1878, Feb.1-May 21/Lurancy Vennum
E. Winchester Stevens, The Watseka
Wonder (Chicago: Religio-Philosoph-
ical Pub.House, 1878).
William James, The Principles of Psy-
chology, 2 vols. (N.Y.: Holt, 1890),
1:397-99.
John Philip Bessor, "The Return of
Mary Roff," Fate 8 (Mar.1955):70-80.
Susy Smith, "The One White Crow?"
Tomorrow 8 (winter 1960):47-57.
David St. Clair, Watseka (Chicago:
Playboy, 1977).

Waukegan
-Ghost
1881/Belle Milner
Walter F. Prince, "Peculiar Exper-
iences Connected with Noted Persons,"
J.ASPR 15 (1921):378,389-93.
-Spirit medium
1850s-1860s/Mrs. Seymour
Emma Hardinge Britten, Modern Ameri-
can Spiritualism (N.Y.: The Author,
1870), pp.108-109.
London Dialectical Soc'y, Report on
Spiritualism (London: Longmans,
Green, Reader & Dyer, 1871).
Nandor Fodor, Encyclopaedia of Psy-
chic Science (London: Arthurs,
1933), p.87.
-UFO (CE-1)
1963, May 19/R. Dean Johnson/Green Bay
Rd.
R. Dean Johnson, "The Priest and the
Saucer," Fate 17 (Jan.1964):26-31.
-UFO (CE-2)
1955, July 6/Ron Castator/Illinois
Beach State Park
(Letter), Fate 9 (Feb.1956):112-13.
-UFO (NL)
1897, April 11/Harry Defweller
Chicago Times-Herald, 13 Apr.1897, p.
2.

1967, Jan.3/Frank Waters
(Letter), <u>Fate</u> 20 (June 1967):122.
1976, April 7
"Noteworthy UFO Sightings," <u>Ufology</u>
2 (fall 1976):60.

Waverly
-UFO (NL)
1973, Oct.17
Springfield <u>Illinois State Register</u>,
17 Oct.1973.

Wayne City
-UFO (CE-1)
1971, Sep.21/Kimmy Gammon/Starvation
Corner
Fairfield <u>Wayne County Press</u>, 23
Sep.1971.
"Strange Object Seen in Sky South of
Wayne City, Illinois," <u>Skylook</u>, no.
49 (Dec.1971):4.

Waynesville
-Giant bird
1977, July 30
"Big Bird 1977," <u>Fortean Times</u>, no.
24 (winter 1978):11.
-Humanoid
1970, Aug.11/Steve Rich/2 mi.NE
<u>Bloomington Pantagraph</u>, 12 Aug.1970.
Loren Coleman, "Mystery Animals in
Illinois," <u>Fate</u> 24 (Mar.1971):48,
53-54.

Western Springs
-UFO (NL)
1957, Nov.6
Richard Hall, ed., <u>The UFO Evidence</u>
(Washington: NICAP, 1964), p.166.

West Frankfort
-Precognition
1924/Roscoe Harris
"Prevision That Saved 29 Lives," <u>Fate</u>
19 (Sep.1966):81, quoting <u>West Frank-
fort Daily American</u> (undated).
-Telephone anomaly
1967, Feb.17
John A. Keel, <u>The Mothman Prophecies</u>
(N.Y.: Saturday Review, 1975), pp.
239-40.
-UFO (CE-2)
1927, March?
"Child Spanked for Reporting Strange
Object, Repeats Story 42 Years
Later," <u>Skylook</u>, no.27 (Feb.1970):9.

Westmont
-UFO (DD)
1926, Aug./Frank Tezky
Jerome Clark & Lucius Farish, "UFOs
of the Roaring '20s," <u>Saga UFO Rept.</u>
2 (fall 1975):48,60.

Wheaton
-Mystery radio transmission
1939/Grote Reber
Ray Palmer, "The Mystery of Sugar
Grove," <u>Flying Saucers</u>, Dec.1975,
pp.26,28-29, quoting <u>Chicago Tribune</u>

(undated).
-UFO (CE-1)
1958, Sep.29
"The Night of September 29," <u>Fate</u>
12 (Feb.1959):31,37, quoting <u>Wheat-
on Daily Journal</u> (undated).
-UFO (DD)
1972, Aug.29/Ted Vratry/court house
<u>Du Page Press</u>, 31 Aug.1972.
1977, Aug.9
"UFOs of Limited Merit," <u>Int'l UFO
Reporter</u> 2 (Sep.1977):8.

Wheeling
-UFO (CE-1)
1975, June 30/Patricia Parhad/Deer-
field x River Rd.
Patricia Parhad, "UFO over Chicago,"
<u>Fate</u> 29 (Mar.1976):34-37.

White Oak twp.
-UFO (NL)
1975, Jan.1/Frank M. Brown
"MUFON Reports in Brief," <u>Skylook</u>,
no.89 (Apr.1975):10.

Whiteside co.
-Ancient boat hook and copper ring
1851
Frank Edwards, <u>Strangest of All</u> (N.Y.:
Ace, 1962), p.101.

Williamsville
-UFO (NL)
1897, April 12
<u>Peoria Journal</u>, 15 Apr.1897, p.2.

Willow Springs
-Clairempathy
1978, April/Evelyn Paglini
<u>North Du Page County Suburban Trib-
une</u>, 12 Apr.1978, p.1.
-UFO (DD)
1947, July 7/Robert Meegan
<u>Chicago Times</u>, 7 July 1947.

Wilmington
-Poltergeist
1957, Aug./James Mikulecky/4 mi.S
(Editorial), <u>Fate</u> 10 (Dec.1957):13-
15, quoting <u>Joliet Herald-News</u> (undated).

Winfield
-UFO (NL)
1961, June 9/Barry Stark/Sunnyside St.
Curtis Fuller, "The Boys Who 'Caught'
a Flying Saucer," <u>Fate</u> 15 (Jan.1962)
:36,38, quoting <u>Wheaton Daily Jour-
nal</u> (undated).

Winnebago co.
-Phantom panther
1970, May/I-90
Loren Coleman, "Mystery Animals in
Illinois," <u>Fate</u> 24 (Mar.1971):48,
51-52.

Winnetka
-Norse drinking horn

1952/Ronald E. Mason
   O.G. Landsverk, Runic Records of the
   Norsemen in America (N.Y.: E.J.
   Friis, 1974), pp.239-41. il.

Wood Dale
-UFO (NL)
   1971, May 13/Irene Rogozinski
   (Letter), Thomas E. Miller, Skylook,
   no.44 (July 1971):12.

Woodstock
-Haunt
   n.d./Opera House
   "The Ghost in Seat DD113," Beyond
   Reality, no.32 (May-June 1978):83.
-UFO (NL)
   1975, Aug.8
   "UFO Central," CUFOS News Bull., 15
   Nov.1975, p.15.

Zeigler
-UFO (CE-2)
   1973, Oct.5/Agnes Wehrle/604 S. Pine
   St.
   Carbondale Southern Illinoisan, 9
   Oct.1973.

        B. Physical Features

Big Muddy R.
-Humanoid
   1942
   Jesse Harris, "Myths and Legends from
   Southern Illinois," Hoosier Folklore
   5 (Mar.1946):14,20.

Carlyle L.
-UFO (?)
   1972, Oct.1/Hazlet's Park
   "Was It a Weather Balloon?" Skylook,
   no.62 (Jan.1973):11.
-UFO (NL)
   1971, July 1/Terry S. Turner
   "UFOs Along Carlyle Lake, Ill.," Skylook, no.46 (Sep.1971):6.

Cave-in-Rock
-Petroglyphs
   Thomas Ashe, Travels in America Per-
   formed in 1806 (London: William Saw-
   yer, 1808), pp.256-62.
   Josiah Priest, American Antiquities
   and Discoveries in the West (Albany:
   Hoffman & White, 1834), pp.139-45.

Diamond I.
-UFO (CE-3)
   1888, Sep.
   Herman Stowell King, "The Ghost of
   Diamond Island," Fate 3 (July 1950)
   :59.

Dickson Mounds
-Archeological site
   ca.100-1200
   T.T. Brown, "The Dickson Mound Builders' Tomb," Wisconsin Arch. 8 (1928)
   :29-32. il.

Don F. Dickson, "Dickson Mounds, A
   Mississippi Cemetery Site," J.Illi-
   nois State Arch.Soc'y 5, no.2
   (1947):9-10. il.
Winslow M. Walker, "The Dickson
   Mound Group, Peoria County," in
   Thorne Duel, ed., Hopewellian Com-
   munities in Illinois (Springfield:
   Illinois State Mus., Sci.Pap., vol.
   5, 1952), pp.13-41.
Alan D. Harn, The Prehistory of Dick-
   son Mounds: A Preliminary Report
   (Springfield: Illinois State Mus.,
   1971). il.
Franklin Folsom, America's Ancient
   Treasures (N.Y.: Rand McNally,
   1974), pp.132-33.

Duck L.
-Clairvoyance
   1937, April 5/Florence Thomas
   "The Spiritualists and the Lost Body,"
   Fate 8 (Aug.1955):74.

Embarrass R.
-Poltergeist
   1895/Elisha Elliot
   William Bathlot, "Cumberland County
   Poltergeist," Fate 5 (June 1952):
   29-35.

Giant City State Park
-Archeological site
   Loren Coleman, "Pre-Columbian Stone
   Structures in Southern Illinois,"
   NEARA Newsl. 5 (Sep.1970):68.

Gun Creek
-Humanoid
   1941, Oct./Lepton Harpole
   Carbondale Free Press, 26 Mar.1942,
   p.1; and 30 Mar.1942, p.3.
   Jesse Harris, "Myths and Legends from
   Southern Illinois," Hoosier Folklore
   5 (Mar.1946):14,19.

Hicks Dome
-Meteorite crater
   9 mi.diam.
   Walter H. Bucher, "Cryptoexplosion
   Structures Caused from Without or
   from Within the Earth," Am.J.Sci.
   261 (1963):597,622-25.

Kickapoo Creek
-Humanoid
   1970, Aug.
   Champaign-Urbana News-Gazette, 10
   Aug.1970.
-Phantom panther
   1970, Aug.16/Don Lindsey/Hwy.136 bridge
   Loren Coleman, "Mystery Animals in
   Illinois," Fate 24 (Mar.1971):48,54.

Koster Site
-Archeological site
   6500 B.C.-1200 A.D.
   Gail L. Houart, "Koster: A Stratified
   Archaic Site in the Illinois Valley,"
   Rept.Investigations Illinois State

Mus., no.22. il.
Nancy B. Asch, Richard I. Ford & David L. Asch, "Paleoethnobotany of
the Koster Site," Rept.Investiga-
tions Illinois State Mus., no.24
(1972).
(Editorial), Fate 25 (July 1972):10-
12.
New York Times, 15 July 1973, sec. X,
p.1.
Manfred E.W. Jaehnig, "Koster 1973,"
Central States Arch.J. 21, no.2
(1974):51-58. il.
Franklin Folsom, America's Ancient
Treasures (N.Y.: Rand McNally,
1974), pp.134-35.
Columbus (O.) Dispatch, 3 Aug.1975,
p.B4. il.
Stuart Streuver, "New Developments
at the Koster Site," Central States
Arch.J. 24 (1977):59-64. il.
Karl W. Butzer, "Changing Holocene
Environments at the Koster Site: A
Geo-Archaeological Perspective,"
Am.Antiquity 43 (1978):408-13.
Stuart Streuver & Felicia Antonelli
Holton, Koster: Americans in Search
of Their Prehistoric Past (Garden
City: Doubleday, 1979). il.

Mazon Creek
-Anomalous fossil
Tullimonstrum gregarium
Eugene S. Richardson, Jr., "Wormlike
Fossil from the Pennsylvanian of
Illinois," Science 151 (1966):75-76.
Ralph Gordon Johnson & Eugene S. Rich-
ardson, Jr., "A Remarkable Pennsyl-
vanian Fauna from the Mazon Creek
Area, Illinois," J.Geology 74
(1966):626-31.
F.W. Holiday, The Great Orm of Loch
Ness (N.Y.: Avon, 1970 ed.), pp.149-
54,197-202. il.

Mill Creek
-Ghost light
n.d.
Harry Middleton Hyatt, Folk-lore from
Adams County, Illinois (Hannibal,
Mo.: Alma Egan Hyatt Foundation,
1965), p.741.

Modoc Rockshelter
-Archeological site
ca.8000 B.C.-1500 A.D.
Thorne Deuel, "The Modoc Shelter,"
Natural History 66 (1957):401-405.
Melvin L. Fowler, "Summary Report of
Modoc Rock Shelter, 1952, 1953, 1955,
1956," Rept.Investigations Illinois
State Mus., no.8 (1959). il.
Melvin L. Fowler, "Modoc Rock Shel-
ter: An Early Archaic Site in South-
ern Illinois," Am.Antiquity 24
(1959):257-70. il.
Holm Wolfram Neumann, "The Paleopath-
ology of the Archaic Modoc Rock
Shelter Inhabitants," Rept.Investi-
gations Illinois State Mus., no.11

(1967). il.

Père Marquette State Park
-Phantom panther
1970, Feb.
Loren Coleman, "Mystery Animals in
Illinois," Fate 24 (Mar.1971):48,50.

Piasa Rock
-Pictograph
=depicts giant bird
Alton Evening Telegraph, 28 Sep.1836.
Cairo Delta, 13 June 1848.
Francis Parkman, LaSalle and the Dis-
covery of the Great West (N.Y.:
Signet, 1963 ed.), pp.72-73.
Père Marquette, "Voyage and Discov-
ery of Father Marquette and Sieur
Joliet in North America," in Sidney
Breese, The Early History of Illi-
nois(Chicago: E.B. Myers, 1884),
pp.235,258-59.
Stephen D. Peet, "A Map of the Em-
blematic Mounds, Showing the Origin
and Object of Effigies," Am.Anti-
quarian 11 (1889):73,76-77.
T.H. English, "The Piasa Petroglyph:
The Devourer from the Bluffs," Art
& Arch. 14 (1922):151-56. il.
Ruth Means, The Piasa (Alton: Alton-
Godfrey Rotary Club, n.d.).
Norbert Hildebrand, "The Monster on
the Rock," Fate 7 (Mar.1954):13-19.
il.
(Letter), Dale Kaye Mead, Fate 7
(June 1954):115.
John W. Allen, Legends and Lore of
Southern Illinois (Carbondale:
Southern Illinois Univ., 1963), pp.
106-108.
Henry Lewis, The Valley of the Miss-
issippi Illustrated (St. Paul:
Minnesota Hist.Soc'y, 1967 ed.),
pp.281-83,303.

Prairie du Long Creek
-Humanoid
1921
Jesse Harris, "Myths and Legends from
Southern Illinois," Hoosier Folklore
5 (Mar.1946):14,19.

Sangamon R.
-Archeological site
1000-1200/Hood site
R. Barry Lewis, "The Hood Site,"
Rept.Investigations Illinois State
Mus., no.31 (1975). il.

Shawnee Forest
-Phantom panther
1920s-1966, April
Cairo Evening Citizen, 20 Apr.1966.
Jerome Clark & Loren Coleman, "On the
Trail of Pumas, Panthers and ULAs:
Part 2," Fate 25 (July 1972):92,98-
99.

Shelbyville L.
-Giant bird

1977, July 30/John Huffer/=California condor?
> Gilbert J. Ziemba, "Mysterious 'Giant Bird'--Invades Central Illinois," Page Rsch.Library Newsl., no.20 (18 Sep.1977):14-16.
> Don Berliner, "Big Bird," INFO J., no.25 (Sep.-Oct.1977):15-16.

Starved Rock
-Archeological site
ca.3000-500 B.C.
> William J. Mayer-Oakes, "Starved Rock Archaic: A Pre-Pottery Horizon from Northern Illinois," Am.Antiquity 16 (1951):313-24.
> Gail Schroeder Schnell, "Hotel Plaza," Rept.Investigations Illinois State Mus., no.29 (1974). il.
> Franklin Folsom, America's Ancient Treasures (N.Y.: Rand McNally, 1974), pp.135-36.

Thompson's L.
-Lake monster
> Charles M. Skinner, American Myths and Legends, 2 vols. (Philadelphia: Lippincott, 1903), 2:281.

Vermilion R.
-UFO (DD)
1971, May 9/Paul Doss/observatory
> "Black, Cone-Shaped Object Is Photographed over Illinois Observatory," Skylook, no.52 (Mar.1972):5-6.

Weldon Springs State Park
-Phantom panther
1966, June/Bernard Harrold/S of Park
> Jerome Clark & Loren Coleman, "On the Trail of Pumas, Panthers and ULAs: Part 2," Fate 25 (July 1972):92,99.
1970, July 24/nr. Willis Bridge
> Loren Coleman, "Mystery Animals in Illinois," Fate 24 (Mar.1971):48,53.

C. Ethnic Groups

Illinois Indians
-Giant bird legend
> Norbert Hildebrand, "The Monster on the Rock," Fate 7 (Mar.1954):13,15-19.
-Hex
> Pierre François Xavier de Charlevoix, Journal of a Voyage to North America, 2 vols. Louise Phelps Kellogg, trans. (Chicago: Caxton Club, 1923), 2:154-55.

Peoria Indians
-Lake monster myth
lenapizha
> Albert S. Gatschet, "Water-Monsters of the American Aborigines," J.Am. Folklore 12 (1899):255-60.

D. Unspecified Localities

-Hex
> Jesse W. Harris, "Some Southern Illinois Witch Lore," Southern Folklore Quar. 10 (1946):183-90.

MISSOURI

A. Populated Places

Abesville
-Phantom panther
  1945, June/Mr. Warren
    Jerome Clark & Loren Coleman, _Creatures of the Outer Edge_ (N.Y.: Warner, 1978), pp.135-36.

Alton
-Humanoid
  1925, summer
    Mountain View Standard, 26 June 1925; and 13 Aug.1925.

Anderson
-Magnetic spring water
    Vance Randolph, _Ozark Superstitions_ (N.Y.: Columbia Univ., 1947), p.332.
-UFO (NL)
  1979, Jan.8/John Andrews
    Springfield News & Leader, 14 Jan. 1979.

Arnold
-UFO (NL)
  1969, March 19-20/Carol Lindwedel/nr. Hwy.67 x VV
    "Arnold, Mo., Family Watches UFO," _Skylook_, no.18 (May 1969):3.
  1970, Sep.15/Mrs. Kurt Koenig/I-55
    "Six Watch Bright Light over Power Plant," _Skylook_, no.35 (Oct.1970):2.

Ash Grove
-UFO (NL)
  1967, June 30/Bob Stanton
    "Strange Light at Ash Grove," _Skylook_, no.2 (Oct.1967):2.

Atlanta
-UFO (CE-2)
  1969, March 4/William Overstreet/4 mi. W on Hwy.J
    Macon Chronicle-Herald, 5 Mar.1969.
    "Missouri Has Flurry of UFO Reports," _Skylook_, no.17 (Apr.1969):1-2.
    "Missouri Sightings--More!--More!" _Skylook_, no.17 (Apr.1969):4.
    "E-M Effect on Truck in Missouri," _APRO Bull._ 17 (May-June 1969):4.

Aurora
-Humanoid
  1977, Aug.27/Mark Cryer/2 mi.S of Hwy.K
    Monett Missouri-Times, 29 Aug.1977.
-UFO (NL)
  1978, April 29/Robert Scholls/Redwood Dr. x Illinois Ave.
    Milan Standard, 8 June 1978.

Ballwin
-Clairempathy and precognition
  1971-   /Beverly C. Jaegers/United States PSI Squad/Box 483
    A.F. Leber, "Psychic Rescue Squads: Extraordinary Talents of Ordinary People," _Fate_ 28 (Sep.1975):46-52.
    (Letter), _Fate_ 28 (Dec.1975):112.
    Warren Smith, "Phenomenal Predictions for 1976," _Saga_, Jan.1976, pp.16,19.
    L. Lee Kyro, "Beverly Jaegers: Pioneer in the Field of Palmistry and the Planets," _Psychic World_, May 1977, pp.52-57. il.
    Laura L. Kyro, "Bevy Jaegers, Psychic Sleuth," _Fate_ 32 (Mar.1979): 39-43.
    Jeffrey Goodman, _Psychic Archaeology_ (N.Y.: Berkley, 1978), pp.119,172.

Barnett
-UFO (CE-2)
  1967
    Ted Phillips, "UFOs Leave Their Mark in Missouri," _Skylook_, no.43 (June 1971):10.
    Ted Phillips, _Physical Traces Associated with UFO Sightings_ (Evanston: Center for UFO Studies, 1975), p.45.

Bates co.
-UFO (CE-2)
  1972
    Ted Phillips, _Physical Traces Associated with UFO Sightings_ (Evanston: Center for UFO Studies, 1975), p.80.

Belleville
-UFO (?)
  1968, Nov.20
    "A Whatzit over Marion County, Missouri," _Skylook_, no.14 (Jan.1969):5.

Belton
-UFO (R-V)
  1978, Aug.8/Joseph Staudinger, Jr.
    "Heavily-Witnessed Radar-Visual Case near Kansas City," _Int'l UFO Reporter_ 3 (Sep.1978):3-6.

Benton
-Precognition
  1929/Tom Chewning
    Mary Stiehm Fuller, "Tom Chewning's Treasure," _Fate_ 6 (Aug.1953):75-77.
-UFO (CE-1)
  1966, spring/Sadie Hagar/Hwy.77
    Lou Farish, "1966 Close-Range Sighting in Southeastern Missouri," _Skylook_, no.42 (May 1971):11.
    Mildred Higgins, "Prepare to Meet a UFO," _Fate_ 30 (May 1977):73.
-UFO (NL)
  1971, Dec.19/Mildred Higgins
    "Orange-Colored Object Seen at Benton, Mo.," _Skylook_, no.51 (Feb.1972):9.

Berkeley
-UFO (?)
1971, Jan.31/Merlin Checkett/=Apollo 13
"Two More Reports on Sighting of Jan.
31, 1971," Skylook, no.41 (Apr.1971)
:9,10.

Bernie
-UFO (NL)
1973, April/Norman Swafford
Sikeston Daily Standard, 11 Apr.1973.

Bismarck
-UFO (NL)
1897, April 15/George Clarkson
St. Louis Post-Dispatch, 16 Apr.1897,
p.2.

Bixby
-UFO (NL)
1973, July 25/John E. Girresch/5 mi.SE
"Brief Reports," Skylook, no.74 (Jan.
1974):16-17.

Black Jack
-Ghost light
1959, March/Duane Witt
(Editorial), Fate 12 (July 1959):16-
17.
-UFO (NL)
1973, Sep.28/Mary E. Carr
"Spinning Disc Reported in Missouri,"
Skylook, no.79 (June 1974):2.

Blue Springs
-Cattle mutilation
1977, Dec./Paul Collier
Independence Examiner, 21 Dec.1977,
Blue Springs ed.

Bolivar
-Phantom horseman
n.d./Hwy.13
Earl A. Collins, Folk Tales of Missouri (Boston: Christopher, 1935),
pp.123-25.
Vance Randolph, Ozark Superstitions
(N.Y.: Columbia Univ., 1947), pp.
232-33.

Boonville
-Haunt
n.d./Muir Mansion
Earl A. Collins, Folk Tales of Missouri (Boston: Christopher, 1935),
pp.125-28.
-UFO (CE-1)
1969, Sep.26/I-70
"Missouri Sightings," APRO Bull. 18
(Nov.-Dec.1969):1,5.
-UFO (NL)
1970, Nov.17/Don P. Kabler
Ted Phillips, "Two Witnesses to Boonville, Mo., Sighting," Skylook, no.
38 (Jan.1971):3.
1975, Oct.29
"Noteworthy UFO Sightings," Ufology
2 (spring 1976):43.

Bowling Green
-UFO (CE-1)
1972, July 21
Brad Steiger, Mysteries of Time and
Space (N.Y.: Dell, 1976 ed.), p.
116.

Braggadocio
-Phantom dog
n.d.
Vance Randolph, Ozark Superstitions
(N.Y.: Columbia Univ., 1947), pp.
225-26.

Branson
-Clairvoyance
n.d./Rube Meadows
Vance Randolph, Ozark Superstitions
(N.Y.: Columbia Univ., 1947), pp.
316-17.

Bridgeton
-UFO (DD)
1947, July 4/Nova Hart/Old St. Charles
Rd.
St. Louis Post-Dispatch, 5-6 July
1947.
Ted Bloecher, Report on the UFO Wave
of 1947 (Washington: NICAP, 1967),
p. II-14.
1960, May 26/nr. Lambert Airport
"Older Missouri Sighting Reported,"
Skylook, no.25 (Dec.1969):4.

Brockfield
-UFO (NL)
1969, March 10
Macon Chronicle-Herald, 11 Mar.1969.

Brunswick
-UFO (CE-2)
1972
Ted Phillips, Physical Traces Associ-
ated with UFO Sightings (Evanston:
Center for UFO Studies, 1975), p.80.

Bunceton
-UFO (NL)
1967, March 8/Phyllis Rowles
Boonville Daily News, 9 Mar.1967.

Bunker
-Phantom dog
n.d./J. Gordon/Bay Cemetery
Vance Randolph, Ozark Superstitions
(N.Y.: Columbia Univ., 1947), p.224.

Burlington Junction
-Retrocognition
n.d./Gussie Ross Jobe
Gussie Ross Jobe, "I Saw a Murder by
Psychometry," Fate 8 (May 1955):29-
31.

Butler
-Dowsing
1930s/Water Surveyors' Club
Springfield News, 28 Apr.1938.
Vance Randolph, Ozark Superstitions
(N.Y.: Columbia Univ., 1947), p.86.

-UFO (DD)
  1952, March 29/Carl J. Henry
    Richard Hall, ed., The UFO Evidence
    (Washington: NICAP, 1964), p.68.

Caledonia
-UFO (NL)
  1967, March 15/J. Sloan Muir
    Bardstown (Ky.) Kentucky Standard,
    16 Mar.1967.

California
-UFO (CE-1)
  1967, March/3 mi.E on Hwy.50
    "Older Sighting from California, Mo.,"
    Skylook, no.45 (Aug.1971):16.
-UFO (NL)
  1967, Jan.31/11 mi.S on Hwy.87
    "A 'Box' in the Sky," Skylook, no.43
    (June 1971):8.

Camdenton
-UFO (?)
  1967, March 16
    "UFO Seen near Lake of the Ozarks,"
    Skylook, no.1 (Sep.1967):5.
-UFO (NL)
  1969, Aug.2
    "Child Alerts Mother to Sky Object,"
    Skylook, no.22 (Sep.1969):5.

Cape Girardeau
-Haunt
  Lorimer Cemetery
    Vance Randolph, Ozark Ghost Stories
    (Girard, Kan.: Haldeman-Julius,
    1944), p.7.
    Earl A. Collins, Legends and Lore of
    Missouri (San Antonio: Naylor, 1951),
    pp.57-59.
    John T. Richards, "Search for the
    Strange and Unexplained," Beyond
    Reality, no.32 (May-June 1978):26.
-Photographic anomaly
  1976, summer/Gene Moore/Hobb's Chapel
  Cemetery
    Gene Moore, "Reaping the Whirlwind,"
    Fate 31 (Dec.1978):85. il.
-Pyrokinesis
  1969/Katherine Parrish/Themis St.
    John T. Richards, "Search for the
    Strange and Unexplained," Beyond
    Reality, no.32 (May-June 1978):26-
    28. il.
    John Thomas Richards, "Katherine, the
    Flame Thrower," Fate 32 (Feb.1979):
    71-74. il.
-UFO (CE-1)
  1975, Jan.21/Saundra Peterman
    Robert A. Goerman, "The UFO Modus Op-
    erandi: January 1975," Official UFO
    1 (Aug.1976):46,65-66.
-UFO (CE-2)
  1973, Oct.3/Eddie Webb/I-55 nr. Jackson
  exit
    Cape Girardeau Southeast Missourian,
    4 Oct.1973; and 9 Oct.1973.
    Madison Wisconsin State Journal, 6
    Oct.1973, p.3.
    Atlanta (Ga.) Constitution, 6 Oct.1973.

Leonard H. Stringfield, Situation
    Red: The UFO Siege (N.Y.: Fawcett
    Crest, 1977 ed.), pp.220-23.
-UFO (NL)
  1967, Jan.18
    "Major Sighting Wave," UFO Inv. 3
    (Jan.-Feb.1967):1,4.

Carter co.
-Crisis apparition
  1926, fall/S.J. Chenowith
    Shannon C. Graham, "The Doctor Meets
    a Ghost," Fate 18 (Oct.1965):90-93.
-Dowsing
  n.d./Mr. Patterson
    Vance Randolph, Ozark Superstitions
    (N.Y.: Columbia Univ., 1947), p.84.

Carterville
-UFO (?)
  1969, Jan.2/=Venus?
    "UFO or Venus?" Skylook, no.15 (Feb.
    1969):1.

Carthage
-Mystery bird deaths
  1977, May
    Kansas City Times, 25 May 1977, p.4A.
-UFO (NL)
  1977, Feb.1
    "UFOs of Limited Merit," Int'l UFO
    Reporter 2 (Mar.1977):8.

Cassville
-Haunt
  1860s-   /Moaning Mt.
    Ona Lacy Hunter, "The Ghosts on Moan-
    ing Mountain," Fate 29 (Mar.1976):
    71-74.
-UFO (CE-1)
  1967, May/Hwy.76
    "Strange Object on Road," Skylook,
    no.15 (Feb.1969):6.
    Ted Phillips, Physical Traces Associ-
    ated with UFO Sightings (Evanston:
    Center for UFO Studies, 1975), pp.9,
    10.

Chadwick
-Plague of snakes
  1965, July/Frank Farmer/Pine Ridge
  Church
    (Editorial), Fate 18 (Nov.1965):26-
    28, quoting Springfield Daily News
    (undated).

Chaffee
-UFO (NL)
  1976, Jan.3
    "Noteworthy UFO Sightings," Ufology
    2 (summer 1976):62.

Chillicothe
-Phantom panther
  1957, July/Walter Bigelow/Mound Creek
    Kansas City Times, 23 July 1957, p.
    5, Business Sec.
-UFO (NL)
  1897, April 11
    St. Louis Post-Dispatch, 12 Apr.1897,

p.2.
Albany Ledger, 23 Apr.1897, p.4.

Christian co.
-Dowsing
n.d.
    Vance Randolph, Ozark Superstitions
    (N.Y.: Columbia Univ., 1947), pp.87-
    88.

Clark co.
-Clairvoyance
ca.1852
    "Saw Murder in a Dream," J.ASPR 8
    (1914):129-33.

Clarksburg
-UFO (NL)
1969, Nov.22
    "Old Year Goes Out with Many Missouri
    Reports Coming In," Skylook, no.26
    (Jan.1970):2-3.

Clifton Hill
-UFO (NL)
1972, Aug.27/W on Hwy.24
    "Another Report from Moberly, Mo.,"
    Skylook, no.59 (Oct.1972):12.

Clinton
-Precognition
1957, April/Mrs. John Eversole
    (Letter), Fate 10 (Sep.1957):128-29.

Coldwater
-UFO (NL)
1966, Sep.24/Richard Melson
    "Missouri Man Reports 1966 Sighting,"
    Skylook, no.48 (Nov.1971):19.

Cole Camp
-UFO (CE-2)
1978, June 15/Elaine Rost/SE of town
    Stover Morgan County Press, 21 June
    1978.
-UFO (NL)
1970, April 4/Ed Brummitt
    Ted Phillips, Jr., "Object Seen in
    Missouri Sky, April 4th," Skylook,
    no.30 (May 1970):3.

Columbia
-Fall of explosive hail
1911, Nov.11
    W.G. Brown, "Explosive Hail," Nature
    88 (1912):350.
-Parapsychology research
1961-   /Society for Research in Rap-
port and Telekinesis
    John Thomas Richards, "Personal Ven-
    ture with a 'Spirit-Flying' Psychic,"
    Psychic World, Sep.1976, pp.50-51.
    John Thomas Richards, "What Happens
    When You Experiment with Psi Energy,"
    Psychic World, Nov.1976, pp.42-47.
    il.
    John Thomas Richards, "In Search of
    the 'Myra' Apparition," ESP, Mar.
    1977, p.18.
    Michael K. Brown, PK (N.Y.: Multi-

media, 1977).
    John Thomas Richards, "Target-Object
    Movements in Control Test Boxes of
    the SORRAT Psychokinesis Experi-
    ments," J.Occult Studies 1 (winter-
    spring 1977-78):229-41. il.
-UFO (?)
1970, Aug.17/Alice M. Thompson/6 mi.N
on Wagon Trail Rd./=parachute flare?
    Columbia Daily Tribune, 18-19 Aug.
    1970.
    "Columbia Light Probably a Parachute
    Flare," Skylook, no.36 (Nov.1970):
    8.
-UFO (CE-2)
1973, June 28/James G. Richards/nr.
State Rd.WW
    Ted Phillips, "Landing at Columbia,
    Missouri," Flying Saucer Rev. 19
    (Nov.-Dec.1973):18-26. il.
    Ted Phillips, "UFO Trace-Landing
    Cases," in 1974 MUFON UFO Symposium
    Proc. (Seguin, Tex.: MUFON, 1974),
    pp.46,54-68.
    Ted Phillips, Physical Traces Associ-
    ated with UFO Sightings (Evanston:
    Center for UFO Studies, 1975), pp.
    xii-xiv,90. il.
    Leonard H. Stringfield, Situation
    Red: The UFO Siege (N.Y.: Fawcett
    Crest, 1977 ed.), pp.135-39.
    Kansas City Star, 29 Jan.1978.
-UFO (NL)
1947, July 7/Ray Taylor
    Kansas City Star, 7 July 1947.
1975, Sep.2
    "UFO Central," CUFOS News Bull., 15
    Nov.1975, p.17.

Columbus
-UFO (NL)
n.d./Mr. Davidson
    Earl A. Collins, Folk Tales of Mis-
    souri (Boston: Christopher, 1935),
    pp.114-17.

Crane
-Archeological site
6000 B.C.
    Kansas City Star, 23 Dec.1977.

Crestwood
-UFO (NL)
1965, July 4/A. Benach/Crestwood Shopping Center
    "Old Year Goes Out with Many Missouri
    Reports Coming In," Skylook, no.26
    (Jan.1970):2,5-6.

Creve Coeur
-Clairempathy and precognition
1970s/Beverly C. Jaegers/652 Emerson
Ct.
    Warren Smith, "Phenomenal Predictions
    for 1975," Saga, Jan.1975, pp.20,48.
    "Probe's 1977 Directory of the Psychic
    World," Probe the Unknown 5 (spring
    1977):32,36.

Cuba
-Seance
  1890, Aug.29
    Edmond P. Gibson, "The Table Told
    the Story," Fate 8 (Mar.1955):94-98,
    quoting Religio-Philosophical J., 1
    Nov.1890.

Daviess co.
-Archeological site
  ca.13,000-8000 B.C./Shriver site
    Michael J. Reagan, et al., "Flake
    Tools Stratified Below Paleo-Indian
    Artifacts," Science 200 (1978):
    1272-75. il.

Decaturville
-Meteorite crater
  6000 m.diam./certain
    E.M. Shepard, "Spring System of the
    Decaturville Dome, Camden County,
    Missouri," Water Supply Pap.U.S.
    Geol.Survey, no.110 (1905), p.113.
    D.S. Krishnaswamy & G.C. Amstutz,
    "Geology of the Decaturville Dis-
    turbance in Missouri," Bull.Geol.
    Soc'y Am. 71 (1960):1910.
    F.G. Snyder, et al., "Cryptoexplosive
    Structures in Missouri," Rept.Inves-
    tigations Missouri Geol.Survey &
    Water Resources, no.35 (1965), pp.
    45-46.
    Terry W. Offield & Howard A. Pohn,
    "Deformation of the Decaturville
    Impact Structure, Missouri," in D.J.
    Roddy, et al., eds., Impact and Ex-
    plosion Cratering (N.Y.: Pergamon,
    1977), pp.321-41.

Dexter
-UFO (NL)
  1973, Sep./Joe Marcus/NW of town
    Dexter Daily Statesman Messenger, 17
    Sep.1973.

Dixon
-Cattle mutilation
  1978, Aug.4/Kenneth Warnol
  1978, Oct.12/Jim Cox/Hwy.HH
    Dixon Pilot, 19 Oct.1978, p.1.

Edina
-Disappearance
  1886, Nov.23
    Charleston (S.C.) News and Courier,
    25 Nov.1886.
-UFO (CE-3)
  1969, Jan./Adeline Davis
    "Occupant Sighting in Missouri," APRO
    Bull. 19 (Jan.-Feb.1971):1,3. il.
    "Corrections," APRO Bull. 20 (Nov.-
    Dec.1971):6-7.

Eldon
-UFO (CE-1)
  1967, Aug.25
    Ted Phillips, "UFO Events in Missouri
    1857-1971," FSR Case Histories, no.8
    (Dec.1971):9-10.
-UFO (CE-2)

1967/Mrs. Bob Baily
    Ted Phillips, "UFOs Leave Their Mark
    in Missouri," Skylook, no.43 (June
    1971):10.
    Ted Phillips, Physical Traces Associ-
    ated with UFO Sightings (Evanston:
    Center for UFO Studies, 1975), p.45.

Ellisville
-UFO (DD)
  1971, Sep.30/Jack W. Jareo, Jr./Zayres
  Dep't Store
    "Husband Expresses Doubt re UFOs--
    Then Wife Points at One!" Skylook,
    no.50 (Jan.1972):8.

Ellsinore
-UFO (CE-2)
  1973, April 3/Mrs. Raymond Stucker/Hwy.
  60
    Jerome Clark, "The Brushy Creek UFO
    Scare," Fate 27 (May 1974):96,104-
    105.
    (Letter), Hayden C. Hewes, Fate 27
    (July 1974):129.

Elmer
-UFO (CE-1)
  1969, March 11?/Mrs. Jim Taylor/Hwy.3
    "Missouri Sightings--More!--More!"
    Skylook, no.17 (Apr.1969):4.
    "A Missouri Sighting, 1969," Skylook,
    no.37 (Dec.1970):2.

Elmira
-UFO (NL)
  1947, July 4/Mrs. W.T. Bisbee
    Kansas City Star, 6 July 1947.

Elsberry
-Cattle mutilation
  1978, April 26/John Mayes/1 mi.W
  1978, June 8/Forrest Gladney/12 mi.SW
  1978, June 17/Gary Hagemeier
  1978, June 17/Sam Mayes
    Elsberry Democrat, 15 June 1978; and
    22 June 1978.
    St. Louis Post-Dispatch, 20 June 1978.
    St. Louis Globe-Democrat, 21 June
    1978.
    "Background on the Elsberry Events,"
    Int'l UFO Reporter 3 (Aug.1978):5-6.
    R. Martin Wolf & S.N. Mayne, "Muti-
    lations: The Elsberry Enigma," Pur-
    suit 13 (winter 1979):26-35.
  1978, Aug.4, 8/Joe Vitro/SW of town
    Elsberry Democrat, 10 Aug.1978. il.
    St. Louis Post-Dispatch, 13 Aug.1978.
    R. Martin Wolf & S.N. Mayne, "Muti-
    lations: The Elsberry Enigma," Pur-
    suit 13 (winter 1979):26-35. il.
-Mystery stench
  1978, July 19-20
  1978, Aug.12-13
  1978, Sep.3
    R. Martin Wolf & S.N. Mayne, "Muti-
    lations: The Elsberry Enigma," Pur-
    suit 13 (winter 1979):26,30-31.
-UFO (CE-2)
  1978, Aug.4

R. Martin Wolf & S.N. Mayne, "Mutilations: The Elsberry Enigma," Pursuit 13 (winter 1979):26,30-31.
-UFO (NL)
1978, June 9-12/Forrest Gladney
R. Martin Wolf & S.N. Mayne, "Mutilations: The Elsberry Enigma," Pursuit 13 (winter 1979):26,28.
1978, June 16/Forrest Gladney
St. Louis Globe-Democrat, 21 June
1978.
Nat'l Enquirer, 29 Aug.1978.
1978, June 18/Manford Hammond
St. Louis Post-Dispatch, 20 June
1978.
Nat'l Enquirer, 29 Aug.1978.
"UFOs of Limited Merit," Int'l UFO
Reporter 3 (Aug.1978):3.
1978, June 19/Gary Hagemeier
St. Louis Globe-Democrat, 25 June
1978.
1978, June 20/Margaret Watts
St. Louis Globe-Democrat, 25 June
1978.
1978, June 24-Aug.7
St. Louis Post-Dispatch, 13 Aug.1978.

Everton
-Dowsing
1930s/Fred Goudy
Kansas City Times, 13 Oct.1936.
-Ghost
n.d./Old Payne Orchard
Vance Randolph, Ozark Superstitions
(N.Y.: Columbia Univ., 1947), pp.
231-32.
-Ghost light
1945, July
Kansas City Times, 11 July 1945.

Excelsior Springs
-Doubtful identity
1882-1951/Jesse Frank Dalton/=Jesse
James?
Frank O. Hall & Lindsey H. Whitten,
Jesse James Rides Again (Lawton,
Okla.: LaHoma, 1948).
Homer Croy, Jesse James Was My Neigh-
bor (N.Y.: Duell, Sloan & Pearce,
1949).
Carl W. Breihan, The Complete and Au-
thentic Life of Jesse James (N.Y.:
Frederick Fell, 1953). il.
William A. Settle, Jr., Jesse James
Was His Name (Columbia: Univ. of
Missouri, 1966), pp.168-71.
W.D. Chesney, "Psychic Warnings Kept
Jesse James Alive!" Fate 25 (Sep.
1972):56-61. il.
(Letter), Tonna Lusareta, Fate 25
(Dec.1972):144.
(Letter), W.D. Chesney, Fate 26 (Mar.
1973):139.
(Letter), Glenn Clairmonte, Fate 26
(Mar.1973):139-40.
(Letter), Charles S. Robison, Fate
26 (June 1973):147-48.
(Letter), Iola B. (Ford) Parker, Fate
26 (June 1973):148.
(Letter), W.D. Chesney, Fate 26 (June

1973):148,159.
(Letter), Marian Titus Ellis, Fate
27 (Feb.1974):128-30.

Fair Grove
-Phantom image
1895, Dec.19-20/Methodist Church
Springfield Republican, 5 Jan.1896.

Farmington
-UFO (NL)
1973, April 12/Kenneth Pingel
Steve Erdmann, "The Distortion Factor," Probe the Unknown 2 (spring
1974):42,46.

Fayette
-Haunt
1974-1977/Joe Davis/Lilac Hill
(Editorial), Fate 30 (July 1977):24-
30.

Ferguson
-UFO (DD)
1947, July 6/William A. Good/20 Miller
Pl.
St. Louis Globe-Democrat, 7 July
1947.
-UFO (NL)
1897, April 12
Lincoln (Ill.) Courier, 13 Apr.1897,
p.3.

Festus
-Fall of graphite
1970, May 26/Elida Kent/Hwy.CC
St. Louis Globe-Democrat, 26 May 1970.
"Aerial Artifact Retrieved in Mis-
souri," APRO Bull. 18 (May-June
1970):5.
"Report on Unidentified Fallen Ob-
ject," Skylook, no.32 (July 1970):5.
"Falls," INFO J., no.7 (fall 1970):40.

Flat River
-Haunt
n.d./Red Onion Cave
Vance Randolph, Ozark Ghost Stories
(Girard, Kan.: Haldeman-Julius,
1944), p.7.
-UFO (?)
1973, April 19/Henry Hagger/U.S.67
Steve Erdmann, "The Distortion Fac-
tor," Probe the Unknown 2 (spring
1974):42,46, quoting St. Francis
County Daily Journal (undated).

Florissant
-UFO (NL)
1967, July 11/David Brazie
"Missouri Object Is Watched by Police," APRO Bull. 16 (July-Aug.
1967):8.
1973, Oct.19/Ron Hanson
"Brief Reports," Skylook, no.74 (Jan.
1974):17.

Foley
-Cattle mutilations and UFO (?)
1975

St. Louis Post-Dispatch, 20 June
1978.
-Humanoid
1972, July
Brad Steiger, Mysteries of Time and
Space (N.Y.: Dell, 1976 ed.), p.111.

Fort Leonard Wood
-UFO (CE-1)
1973, Sep.14
Ted Phillips, "Summary of UFO Reports
in Missouri During 1973," Skylook,
no.74 (Jan.1974):13.
-UFO (DD)
1966, Dec./Larry Hill
"UFO Near Army Base," Skylook, no.2
(Oct.1967):3.
-UFO (NL)
1978, July 25-27/Gary Love
St. Louis Globe-Democrat, 29-30 July
1978.
Waynesville Fort Gateway Guide, 1
Aug.1978.

Franklin co.
-Ancient mines
Henry C. Shetrone, The Moundbuilders
(N.Y.: Appleton, 1930).

Fredericktown
-UFO (NL)
1973, May 24-25/Harley D. Rutledge
Kansas City Times, 8 Dec.1973, p.1A.
il.
Steve Erdmann, "The Distortion Factor," Probe the Unknown 2 (spring
1974):42,47.
"Strange Lights in Missouri," Flying
Saucers, winter 1974, pp.38,41-42.
Wendelle C. Stevens, "UFO Tracks in
the Sky," Saga UFO Rept. 2 (fall
1975):23,25,52-53.
(Editorial), Fate 31 (Aug.1978):14-
15.

Freeman
-Cattle mutilation
1976, fall/Bob Hocker
Jane McMahon, "Who Are the Cattle
Mutilators?" Kansas City Star Mag.,
12 June 1977, pp.8-15. il.

Gainesville
-Healing
n.d.
Vance Randolph, Ozark Superstitions
(N.Y.: Columbia Univ., 1947), p.122.

Galena
-Ghost
n.d.
Tom Moore, Mysterious Tales and Leg-
ends of the Ozarks (Philadelphia:
Dorrance, 1938), pp.142-48.
-Haunt
n.d./Fred McCord farm
Vance Randolph, Ozark Superstitions
(N.Y.: Columbia Univ., 1947), p.233.
-Precognition
1901-1903/Billy Carmain

W.D. Chesney, "Hunches of Billy Carmain," Fate 6 (Sep.1953):36-41.

Gallatin
-UFO (NL)
1972, Aug.12/Anna May Cummings
Glenn McWane & David Graham, The New
UFO Sightings (N.Y.: Warner, 1974),
p.51, quoting Grant City Times-
Tribune (undated).

Gerald
-UFO (CE-2)
1965/Margaret H. Boyer
(Letter), Fate 30 (Aug.1977):127.

Gladden
-UFO (NL)
1967, Aug.21/Dorothy Rummel/Hwy.19
"Strange Light over Gladden," Sky-
look, no.1 (Sep.1967):1, quoting
Eminence Times (undated).

Gordonville
-Ghost light
n.d.
Earl A. Collins, Legends and Lore of
Missouri (San Antonio: Naylor,
1951), pp.52-57.

Gower
-UFO (?)
1968, Feb.9
"UFO at Gower, Mo.," Skylook, no.9
(May 1968):1, quoting Kansas City
Times (undated).

Granby
-Fall of unknown object
1976, Sep./Allen Schnakenberg/N on Hwy.
E
(Editorial), Fate 30 (Feb.1977):26-
28.

Grand Falls
-Humanoid
1975, Sep.27/Steve McFall/nr. Shoal
Creek
Kansas City Star, 28 Sep.1975.

Grandview
-UFO (NL)
1960, April 17/Richards-Gebaur AFB
Lloyd Mallan, "Complete Directory of
UFOs: Part III," Sci.& Mech. 38
(Feb.1967):56,92-93.

Gravois Mills
-UFO (NL)
1967, May 22
"Gravois Mills Sighting," Skylook,
no.2 (Oct.1967):6.
1967, Sep.22/3 mi. from town
"Priest Observes UFO," Skylook, no.5
(Jan.1968):1,3-4.

Greene co.
-UFO (NL)
1969, Jan.12
John A. Keel, UFOs: Operation Trojan

Horse (N.Y.: Putnam, 1970), pp.162-
63.

Green Ridge
-UFO (DD)
  1948, summer
    "UFO Observed near Greenridge, Mo.,"
    Skylook, no.61 (Dec.1972):4.

Greentop
-UFO (NL)
  1969, March 4/Art Buchanan
    "Missouri Has Flurry of UFO Reports,"
    Skylook, no.17 (Apr.1969):1,2.

Greenwood
-UFO (DD)
  1947, July 6/Helen Chiddix/1 mi.E
    Kansas City Star, 7 July 1947.

Groveton
-UFO (CE-2)
  1968, Feb.9
    J. Allen Hynek, The Hynek UFO Report
    (N.Y.: Dell, 1977), pp.193-95.

Hannibal
-Haunt
  1964, summer/Bear Creek Cemetery
    Kansas City Star, 12 Sep.1964.
-UFO (DD)
  1969, Feb.11
    Otto O. Binder, "The Mystery of Under-
    ground UFO Bases," Saga UFO Rept. 1
    (spring 1974):22,45.
-UFO (NL)
  1975, Oct.10
    "UFO Central," CUFOS News Bull., 1
    Feb.1976, p.8.

Harrisonville
-Disappearances
  1978, summer-Oct./dogs
    Kansas City Star, 29 Oct.1978.
-Fire anomaly
  1959/Hotel Harrisonville
    (Editorial), Fate 12 (June 1959):18.
-Precognition
  1905, Aug.
    "Premonitory Dream," J.ASPR 5 (1911):
    373-76.
-Rotating tombstone
  1898
    (Editorial), Fate 9 (Aug.1956):13. il.

Hartville
-Fall of iron particles
  1966, May 10/Roy Dowden
    (Editorial), Fate 19 (Sep.1966):14.
-Ghost light
  1925, Dec.23, 26/Little Creek Cemetery
    Vance Randolph, Ozark Superstitions
    (N.Y.: Columbia Univ., 1947), p.235.
-Poltergeist
  1957, June-Aug./Clinton Ward
    (Editorial), Fate 10 (Oct.1957):17.
    "Some Recent Poltergeist Cases," Para-
    psych.Bull., no.43 (Nov.1957):1,
    quoting Lebanon Daily Record (undat-
    ed).

W.E. Cox, "Hartville Poltergeist,"
Fate 11 (Aug.1958):64-70. il.

Harvester
-Animal ESP
  1976, May 8/Bruce R. Morris
    (Editorial), Fate 29 (Oct.1976):24-
    26.
-UFO (NL)
  1978, June 19
    Elsberry Democrat, 22 June 1978.

Hazelwood
-UFO (NL)
  1973, Sep.12/Pearlee Whyman/Olive
    Street Rd. x Hwy.244
    "Brief Reports," Skylook, no.74 (Jan.
    1974):17.

Henrietta
-UFO (?)
  1958, March 20
    Richard Hall, ed., The UFO Evidence
    (Washington: NICAP, 1964), p.145.

Herculaneum
-Human tracks in limestone
  1817
    Henry R. Schoolcraft, "Remarks on the
    Prints of Human Feet," Am.J.Sci.,
    ser.1, 5 (1822):223-30.
-Midday darkness and earthquake
  1812, Feb.7
    Samuel Latham Mitchill, "A Detailed
    Narrative of the Earthquakes," Trans.
    Literary & Phil.Soc'y N.Y. 1 (1814):
    281,285,291.

Hickory co.
-Dowsing
  n.d.
    Vance Randolph, Ozark Superstitions
    (N.Y.: Columbia Univ., 1947), p.84.

Hornet
-Ghost light
  ca.1900-   /Spooklight Rd./=headlight
    refraction?
    Jay L.B. Taylor, "Luminous Spectre
    Hunted to Its Lair," Missouri Mag.,
    Oct.1934, pp.11-12.
    Neosho (Okla.) Daily News, 9 Sep.
    1935.
    Vance Randolph, Ozark Superstitions
    (N.Y.: Columbia Univ., 1947), pp.
    233-35.
    Carl Junction Standard, 22 Sep.1955.
    Kansas City Star, 2 Oct.1955.
    (Editorial), Fate 9 (Feb.1956):7. il.
    (Letter), Myrtle Collins Masmer, Fate
    9 (Mar.1956):128.
    Chester S. Geier, "Ghost Light of
    Hornet," Fate 9 (Apr.1956):58-61. il.
    (Letter), G.R., Fate 9 (July 1956):
    118-19.
    "A 'Spook Light' Mystery Solved?"
    Fate 13 (Sep.1960):85.
    (Letter), Edna W. Billings, Fate 14
    (Aug.1961):108-109.
    (Editorial), Fate 16 (Sep.1963):6-8.

(Letter), Fern L. Magee, Fate 17 (Mar.1964):120,129.
Raymond Bayless, "Ozark Spook Light: A Scientific Report," Fate 17 (Sep. 1964):27-33; (Oct.1964):81-87.
(Editorial), Fate 17 (Nov.1964):28.
Robert Gannon, "Balls o' Fire!" Pop. Mechanics, Sep.1965, pp.116-19,207-11. il.
Bob Loftin, Spookville's Ghost Lights (Tulsa: The Author, 1967). il.
Robert Loftin, Identified Flying Saucers (N.Y.: David McKay, 1968), pp. 99-104.
Springfield Daily News, 15 May 1969.
J.A. Hynek & W.T. Powers, "The Tri-State Spook Light," New Horizons 1, no.1 (summer 1972):6-8.
J. Allen Hynek & W.T. Powers, "The Tri-State Spooklight Explained," Fate 26 (Nov.1973):92-95.
Jim Brandon, Weird America (N.Y.: Dutton, 1978), pp.120-22.

Houston
-UFO (CE-2)
1972, Sep.14
Ted Phillips, "UFO Landing Case in Missouri," Skylook, no.66 (May 1973):10-11.

Howell co.
-Anomalous mounds
J.W. Blankinship, "Peculiar Earth-Heaps in Missouri," Am.Antiquarian 11 (1889):117.

Iatan
-Archeological site
1000 A.D.
Lawrence (Kan.) Daily Journal-World, 12 Jan.1978. il.

Iberia
-Cattle mutilation
1978, Aug.
Dixon Pilot, 19 Oct.1978, p.1.

Illmo
-UFO (CE-1)
1968, fall/S on Hwy.61
Mildred Higgins, "Prepare to Meet a UFO," Fate 30 (May 1977):73,74.

Imperial
-UFO (NL)
1969, July 30-Aug.1/Mark Wallace
"Bright Object Sighted near Imperial, Mo.," Skylook, no.22 (Sep.1969), inside cover.

Independence
-Ghost light and lost treasure
1860s
Charles M. Skinner, American Myths and Legends, 2 vols. (Philadelphia: Lippincott, 1903), 2:299-300.
-Humanoid
1966, Sep./Brookside Dr. x Truman Rd.
R.A. Johnson, "Fact or Fantasy?"

Sasquatch News 1 (Aug.1974):3.
-Parapsychology research
1970s/Academy of Religion and Psychical Research/10715 Winner Rd.
John White & Stanley Krippner, eds., Future Science (Garden City: Anchor, 1977), p.582.
-Seances
n.d./Donna Johnson
Hans Holzer, Ghosts I've Met (N.Y.: Ace, 1965), pp.57-58.
-UFO (CE-1)
1968, Aug.21/Hwy.M-78
"Around the World," APRO Bull. 17 (Sep.-Oct.1968):6.
-UFO (NL)
1975, July 19
"UFO Central," CUFOS News Bull., 15 Nov.1975, p.14.

Ironton
-UFO (CE-2)
1967
Ted Phillips, Physical Traces Associated with UFO Sightings (Evanston: Center for UFO Studies, 1975), p.46.

Jadwin
-UFO (NL)
1959, Dec.25/Frank Andres/Lester Connell farm
Salem News, 31 Dec.1959.

Jefferson co.
-UFO (NL)
1949, May 3
"If It's in the Sky It's a Saucer," Doubt, no.27 (1949):416.

Jefferson City
-UFO (CE-1)
1967, April 17
J. Allen Hynek, The UFO Experience (Chicago: Regnery, 1972), pp.96-97.
-UFO (DD)
1973, Oct.15
Ted Phillips, "Summary of UFO Reports in Missouri During 1973," Skylook, no.74 (Jan.1974):13.
-UFO (NL)
1897, April 16/Al Miller
St. Louis Globe-Democrat, 17 Apr. 1897.
1967, June/Jack Kuntz
"Object Trails Sparks," Skylook, no. 2 (Oct.1967):4.
1970, Nov.22/Betty Kehoe/5 mi. away on Hwy.40
"Revolving Light Seen near Jefferson City, Mo.," Skylook, no.38 (Jan. 1971):4.
1972, Aug.26
"State Highway Employees Report UFOs," Skylook, no.59 (Oct.1972):7.

Jenkins
-UFO (CE-2)
1978, Oct.8/Marlett Sturgell
Joplin Globe, 24 Oct.1978.

Jennings
-UFO (NL)
1967, Jan./Mrs. Meyer
St. Louis Globe-Democrat, 31 Jan.
1967.
1967, March 1
Art Epstein, "A Sky 'Submarine' with
'Strange Lightning,'" Skylook, no.
39 (Feb.1971):9-10.

Joplin
-Dowsing
n.d./A.M. Haswell
Vance Randolph, Ozark Superstitions
(N.Y.: Columbia Univ., 1947), p.85.
-Ghost
1961, Feb./Jack Reitz
Buel B. Buzzard, "The Object of Spir-
it Affection," Fate 31 (July 1978):
71-73.
-Human electrification
1889/Frank McKinstry
Henry Winfred Splitter, "Electrically
Charged People," Fate 8 (Mar.1955):
83,85-86, quoting St. Louis Globe-
Democrat (undated).
-Precognition
1938, Nov.30/Dollie Board
James Bartholomew, "Dollie Board's
Premonition," Fate 3 (Mar.1950):62-
63.
-Telephone anomaly
n.d./Elizabeth Molly
(Editorial), Fate 13 (Mar.1960):18,
quoting Joplin Globe (undated).
-UFO (?)
1969, Jan.2/=Venus?
"UFO or Venus?" Skylook, no.15 (Feb.
1969):1.
-UFO (NL)
1967, Jan.13/Charles Hickman
Pittsburg (Kan.) Headlight-Sun, 14
Jan.1967, p.1.
Robert Loftin, Identified Flying Sau-
cers (N.Y.: David McKay, 1968), pp.
139-41.
Edward U. Condon, ed., Scientific
Study of Unidentified Flying Objects
(N.Y.: Bantam, 1969 ed.), pp.287-88,
290.
Donald H. Menzel & Ernest H. Taves,
The UFO Enigma (Garden City: Double-
day, 1977), pp.102-103.
1967, Jan.17
Edward U. Condon, ed., Scientific
Study of Unidentified Flying Objects
(N.Y.: Bantam, 1969 ed.), pp.288-89.
Donald H. Menzel & Ernest H. Taves,
The UFO Enigma (Garden City: Double-
day, 1977), pp.102-103.

Kahoka
-UFO (NL)
1969, Dec.13
"Kahoka, Mo. UFO Seen," Skylook, no.
30 (May 1970):2.
1970, Oct.5/Robert Benjamin
Robert Smulling, "A Midwest Flap?"
Skylook, no.36 (Nov.1970):1.

Kansas City
-Archeological sites
ca.500 B.C.-700 A.D.
W.H.R. Lykins, "Antiquities of Kan-
sas City, Missouri," Ann.Rept.Smith.
Inst., 1877, pp.251-53.
Waldo R. Wedel, "Hopewellian Remains
near Kansas City, Missouri," Proc.
U.S.Nat'l Mus. 86 (1938):99-106. il.
Leo J. Roedl & James H. Howard,
"Archeological Investigations at
the Renner Site," Missouri Arch. 19
(1957):53-96. il.
J.M. Shippee, Archeological Remains
in the Area of Kansas City: Paleo-
Indians and the Archaic Period (Co-
lumbia: Missouri Arch.Soc'y, Rsch.
Ser., no.2, 1964). il.
J.M. Shippee, Archeological Remains
in the Area of Kansas City: The
Woodland Period (Columbia: Missouri
Arch.Soc'y, Rsch.Ser., no.5, 1967).
il.
J.M. Shippee, Archeological Remains
in the Area of Kansas City: The
Mississippean Occupation (Columbia:
Missouri Arch.Soc'y, Rsch.Ser., no.
9, 1972). il.
-Autoscopy
1961, Aug.-Sep.
Edward Podolsky, "Have You Seen Your
Double?" Fate 19 (Apr.1966):78,79.
-Clairaudience
n.d./Timothy Adams
(Editorial), Fate 22 (Aug.1969):7,
quoting undated AP release.
-Disappearance
1931/H.R. Ennis/house
1934, April 1/Charles M. Bush/411 Park
Ave./house
"Houses Missing," Fortean Soc'y Mag.,
no.9 (spring 1944):3.
-Electromagnetic anomaly
1970, July 1-Aug./Mrs. Kevin Eisen-
brandt/Waddell & Reed, Inc./20 W. 9th
St.
Kansas City Star, 5 Aug.1970, p.1B.
-Fall of frogs
1873, June?
(Editorial), Sci.Am. 29 (1873):17.
-Fall of ice
1955, Feb.21/Byron Beaty/=fell from
airplane?
Kansas City Star, 21 Feb.1955, p.3.
-Fall of metal foil
1953, Dec.10
Sioux City (Ia.) Journal-Tribune, 11
Dec.1953.
-Fall of metal stampings
1965, Nov.1/Dale McCollum/Forest Ave.
x 12th St.
Kansas City Star, 2 Nov.1965, p.4A.
il.
-Haunt
1958-
1964
Hans Holzer, Gothic Ghosts (N.Y.:
Pocket Books, 1972), pp.117-26.
1970s/Emerson House/UMKC campus
Kansas City Star, 27 May 1979, p.46A.

-Healing
  1888/J.M. Dickson
    "Madstone Cures Hydrophobia," Fate
    26 (Feb.1973):104, quoting Kansas
    City Journal, May 1888.
  1890s/Charles Fillmore/Hall Bldg.
    Marcus Bach, "Unity: A New Religion
    and How It Grew," Fate 16 (Jan.1963)
    :28-36.
    W.D. Chesney, "I Remember the Man
    Who Founded Unity," Fate 16 (Jan.
    1963):37-40. il.
-Hex
  1908/Adam God/Engine Company No.25
    "The Curse of Adam God," Fate 18
    (June 1965):66.
-Precognition
  1970s/Psychical Research Soc'y of Kan-
    sas City
    Kansas City Times, 24 Jan.1975.
-Radionics
  1930s-   /T. Galen Hieronymus
    T. Galen Hieronymus, The Truth About
    Radionics and Some of the Criticism
    Made About It by Its Enemies (Spring-
    field, Mo.: Int'l Radionic Ass'n,
    1947).
    John W. Campbell, Jr., "Psionic Ma-
    chine--Type One," Astounding Science
    Fiction 57 (June 1956):97-108. il.
    John W. Campbell, Jr., "Unprovable
    Speculation," Astounding Science
    Fiction 58 (Feb.1957):54-70. il.
    John W. Campbell, Jr., "Addendum on
    the Symbolic Psionic Machine," As-
    tounding Science Fiction 59 (June
    1957):125-27.
    (Letter), Anon., Astounding Science
    Fiction 62 (Feb.1959):150-54.
    David M. Dressler, "The Phenomenal
    Psionic Machine," Fate 15 (Nov.
    1962):72-81; (Dec.1962):46-53. il.
    T. Galen Hieronymus, Tracking the
    Astronauts in Apollo "8" (Kansas
    City: The Author, 1968).
    Louise & T. Galen Hieronymus, Track-
    ing the Astronauts in Apollo "11"
    with Data from Apollo "8" Included
    (Kansas City: The Authors, 1969).
    Peter Tompkins & Christopher Bird,
    The Secret Life of Plants (N.Y.:
    Harper & Row, 1973), pp.333-42,355-
    56.
    Edward Wriothesley Russell, Report
    on Radionics (London: Spearman,
    1973), pp.97-102.
    Joseph F. Goodavage, "The Incredible
    Hieronymus Machine," in John White
    & Stanley Krippner, eds., Future
    Science (Garden City: Anchor, 1977),
    pp.386-403.
-Reincarnation
  1969
    Dell Leonardi, The Reincarnation of
    John Wilkes Booth (Old Greenwich,
    Ct.: Devin-Adair, 1975).
-Seance
  1910, Jan.25/Judge Dill
    John S. King, Dawn of the Awakened
    Mind (N.Y.: James A. McCann, 1920).

-Spirit medium
  1880s-1928/Arthur Stilwell
    Arthur Edward Stilwell, To All the
    World (Except Germany) (London: G.
    Allen & Unwin, 1915).
    Arthur E. Stilwell, The Empire of
    the Soul (N.Y.: Youth, 1921).
    Arthur E. Stilwell, Live and Grow
    Young (N.Y.: Youth, 1921), pp.2-5.
    Darrell Garwood, Crossroads of Amer-
    ica (N.Y.: W.W. Norton, 1948), pp.
    132-45.
    Stuart Palmer, "Arthur Stilwell: Psy-
    chic Empire Builder," Fate 6 (Mar.
    1953):40-46. il.
    Keith L. Bryant, Jr., Arthur E. Stil-
    well: Promoter with a Hunch (Nash-
    ville: Vanderbilt Univ., 1971), pp.
    224-44.
  1886-1892/Maude Lord-Drake
    Maude Lord-Drake, Psychic Light: The
    Continuity of Law and Life (Kansas
    City: F.T. Riley, 1904).
    W.D. Chesney, "That Great Medium:
    Maude Lord Drake," Fate 14 (Apr.
    1961):82,89.
  1900s
    James H. Hyslop, "An Experiment for
    Raps," J.ASPR 14 (1920):252-56.
  1964
    Hans Holzer, Gothic Ghosts (N.Y.:
    Pocket Books, 1972), pp.117-26.
-UFO (?)
  1954, June 2/Henry Hurst/=balloon
    Kansas City Times, 3 June 1954, p.1.
  1978, Jan.28/=meteor
    Kansas City Star, 6 Feb.1978.
-UFO (CE-2)
  1973, Nov.4
    Ted Phillips, Physical Traces Associ-
    ated with UFO Sightings (Evanston:
    Center for UFO Studies, 1975), p.96.
-UFO (CE-4)
  1958, Dec./George Adamski/=hoax?
    George Adamski, Behind the Flying
    Saucer Mystery (N.Y.: Paperback Li-
    brary, 1967 ed.), pp.59-60.
-UFO (DD)
  1947, June 25/W.I. Davenport/82d x
    Holmes St.
    Kansas City Star, 26 June 1947.
  1947, July 7/Stanley Schniderman
    Kansas City Star, 7 July 1947.
  1951, Dec.7/Frank Gibson, Jr.
    (Editorial), Fate 5 (July-Aug.1952):
    5.
  1952, Feb.11/=balloon?
    U.S. Air Force, Projects Grudge and
    Blue Book Reports (Washington: NICAP,
    1968), pp.91-92.
  1953/Richard Marquis
    (Letter), Fate 8 (Mar.1955):107-109.
  1953, June
    Harold T. Wilkins, Flying Saucers Un-
    censored (N.Y.: Pyramid, 1967 ed.),
    p.226.
-UFO (NL)
  1897, April 1
    Kansas City Times, 2 Apr.1897, p.1.
  1897, April 24/Jeff Brennan/15th x

Olive St.
  Kansas City Times, 25 Apr.1897.
1957, Nov.5
  Richard Hall, ed., The UFO Evidence
  (Washington: NICAP, 1964), p.165.
1961, Aug.12
  Jacques Vallee, Passport to Magonia
  (Chicago: Regnery, 1969), p.282.
1968, Dec.9/Plaza
  "Many See UFO over Kansas City," Sky-
  look, no.14 (Jan.1969):4.
1971, March 27/Robert B. Parsons/Blue
Ridge Blvd. x 104th St.
  "Naval Reserve Pilot Reports UFO,"
  Skylook, no.46 (Sep.1971):5.
1972, Aug.19/=balloon?
  Kansas City Star, 20 Aug.1972, p.5A.
-Windshield pitting
  1965, Nov.1/=vandalism?
  Kansas City Star, 2 Nov.1965, p.1.

Kinloch
-Humanoid
  1968, July
  Southern Illinois University Daily
  Egyptian, 11 Dec.1968.

Kirksville
-Phantom cat
  1920/W.E. Farbstein/College of Osteo-
  pathy
  W.E. Farbstein, "Black Visitor," Fate
  7 (Oct.1954):70-71.
-UFO (CE-1)
  1972, Nov.22/Mrs. Ray Myers/U.S.63 x
  Hwy.11
  Kirksville Daily Express, 22 Nov.1972.
  "Kirksville, Mo. Woman Gets Good Look
  at Large UFO," Skylook, no.62 (Jan.
  1973):5.
-UFO (DD)
  1952, March
  Edward J. Ruppelt, The Report on Un-
  identified Flying Objects (Garden
  City: Doubleday, 1956), pp.80-81.
  1967, Aug.20/Janice Shipley/State Park
  Lake
  "Teacher and Friends Watch UFO's,"
  Skylook, no.4 (Dec.1967):5.
  1972, Sep.6/Mrs. Howard E. Gross/8 mi.
  NW on Hwy.149
  "Kirksville, Mo. Woman Reports Bright
  Silver UFO," Skylook, no.59 (Oct.
  1972):7.
-UFO (NL)
  1969, March 2/Ed Metzer
  "Missouri Has Flurry of UFO Sight-
  ings," Skylook, no.17 (Apr.1969):
  1,3.
  1972, July 24
  Kirksville Daily Express, 25 July
  1972.
  1977, Sep.27/David Burden/3 mi.W
  Kansas City Times, 28 Sep.1977.
  "UFOs of Limited Merit," Int'l UFO
  Reporter 2 (Nov.1977):3.
  1978, Oct.
  Kirksville Daily Express, 24 Oct.1978.
-UFO (R)
  1952, July 12

Donald E. Keyhoe, Flying Saucers from
Outer Space (N.Y.: Holt, 1953), p.
57.

Kirkwood
-Men-in-black
  1973, Dec.13/Robert E. Baez/605 E. Fil-
  more St.
  Steve Erdmann, "The Curious Case of
  Robert Baez," Beyond Reality, no.18
  (Jan.1976):25-27,50.
-UFO (CE-4)
  1973, Nov.14/Robert E. Baez/S. Filmore
  x Rosehill St.
  Steve Erdmann, "The Curious Case of
  Robert Baez," Beyond Reality, no.18
  (Jan.1976):25-27,50.

Knob Lick
-Stratigraphic anomaly
  St. Francois R.
  Erasmus Haworth, "Prismatic Sand-
  stone from Missouri," Science
  19 (1892):34.

Knob Noster
-Ghost light
  n.d.
  Earl A. Collins, Folk Tales of Missouri (Boston: Christopher, 1935),
  pp.117-21.
-UFO (NL)
  1970, Oct.5/R.L. McCown/600 Summit Rd./
  =barium cloud?
  "Yellow-Orange Object Seen at Warrensburg and Knob Noster, Mo.," Skylook,
  no.36 (Nov.1970):7.

Knox City
-UFO (CE-1)
  1972, April 19/Lena Miller/W on Hwy.6
  "Missouri Woman Reports Glowing Ob-
  ject," Skylook, no.57 (Aug.1972):12.
  "Missouri Woman and Son Watch Sky
  Object," Skylook, no.60 (Nov.1972):
  8.
-UFO (CE-3)
  1967, Jan.29/Enid Campbell/4 mi.SW
  Ted Phillips, "Woman and Teen Age
  Sons Report Space Ship with Occu-
  pants," Skylook, no.41 (Apr.1971):
  13-14.

Laddonia
-Haunt
  1934/Jim Harbison
  Oliver Bigler, "The Dairy Farm Ghost,"
  Fate 24 (Apr.1971):84-87.
-UFO (NL)
  1972, July 29
  "UFOs Seen at Laddonia, Mo.," Sky-
  look, no.60 (Nov.1972):10.

Ladue
-UFO (DD)
  1947, July 6/Walter Hoefer/23 Black
  Creek Lane
  St. Louis Globe-Democrat, 7 July
  1947.
  St. Louis Post-Dispatch, 7 July 1947.

-UFO (NL)
1969, Sep.26/I-70
St. Louis Globe-Democrat, 13 Nov.1969.
1970, Jan.29/Price x Ladue Rd.
"UFO's with Pink Lights Reported, St.
Louis, Mo.," Skylook, no.28 (Mar.
1970):3.

LaGrange
-UFO (?)
1973, Jan.24/Mrs. Wilfred Shumate/=
planes refueling
"Missouri UFO Probably Planes Refueling," Skylook, no.64 (Mar.1973):14.

Lake City
-UFO (CE-2)
1957, Nov.9
Jacques Vallee, Passport to Magonia
(Chicago: Regnery, 1969), p.266.

Lake Spring
-UFO (NL)
1962/Larry Yoder
"Moberly Resident Reports on UFO's,"
Skylook, no.19 (June 1969):3.

Lamar
-Haunt
n.d./Mathilda Alter
Hans Holzer, Ghosts I've Met (N.Y.:
Ace, 1965), pp.55-57.
-UFO (?)
1972, Sep.20/=balloon
"Lamar, Mo., UFO Was Weather Balloon,"
Skylook, no.63 (Feb.1973):16.
-UFO (NL)
1974, Jan.2
George D. Fawcett, "A Review of Some
of the Thousands of UFO Sightings
in 1974 to Date," Flying Saucers,
Dec.1974, p.37.

Lamine
-UFO (NL)
1969, Sep.26/I-70
"Missouri Sightings," APRO Bull. 18
(Nov.-Dec.1969):1,6.
"Old Year Goes Out with Many Missouri
Reports Coming In," Skylook, no.26
(Jan.1970):2.

La Monte
-UFO (CE-2)
1952/ground markings only
Ted Phillips, Physical Traces Associated with UFO Sightings (Evanston:
Center for UFO Studies, 1975), p.8.
-UFO (NL)
1973, Sep.15
Ted Phillips, "Summary of UFO Reports
in Missouri during 1973," Skylook,
no.74 (Jan.1974):13.

Lancaster
-UFO (CE-2)
1969, March 6/Hwy.202
"UFO Slows Car," Skylook, no.18 (May
1969):4.
"Car Buzzing Incidents Continue,"

APRO Bull. 17 (May-June 1969):6-7.
Ted Phillips, "UFO Events in Missouri
1857-1971," FSR Case Histories, no.
8 (Dec.1971):9,11.

La Plata
-UFO (?)
1954, June
Donald E. Keyhoe, Flying Saucer Conspiracy (N.Y.: Holt, 1955), p.166.

Laurie
-UFO (CE-1)
1978, Aug.5/2 mi.SE on Hwy.5
"UFOs of Limited Merit," Int'l UFO
Reporter 3 (Sep.1978):6,8-9.

Lawrence co.
-Anomalous mounds
W.J. Spillman, "Natural Mounds,"
Science 21 (1905):632.

Lebanon
-Ghost
1860/Rev. Cummings
Charles M. Skinner, Myths and Legends
of Our Own Land, 2 vols. (Philadel-
phia: Lippincott, 1896), 2:182-83.
Pauline Saltzman, Ghosts and Other
Strangers (N.Y.: Lancer, 1970), pp.
89-91.
-Healing
1972/Stella Reed Gallagher/12 mi.E on
I-44
"This Is God's Well," Fate 26 (Jan.
1973):88.
(Letter), John R. Murphy, Fate 27
(July 1974):130.

Lemay
-Stigmata
1951/Joan Rosso/St. Andrews Church
"Stigmata for a High School Girl,"
Fate 4 (May-June 1951):11.
-UFO (NL)
1972, Aug.6/Karen Buck/Monsanto Plant
"Couple Follows Glowing Object," Sky-
look, no.59 (Oct.1972):13.
1974, March 24/Marlies Dombroska
"Around the Network," Skylook, no.79
(June 1974):17.

Levasy
-Ghost light
n.d./Bone Hill
Earl A. Collins, Folk Tales of Missouri (Boston: Christopher, 1935),
pp.130-33.

Lewis co.
-UFO (DD)
1971, March 19/Walter Davis/County Rd.
2
Quincy (Ill.) Herald-Whig, 24 Apr.
1971.

Lexington
-UFO (NL)
1974, July 22/Waneta Burris
George D. Fawcett, "The 'Unreported'

UFO Wave of 1974," Saga UFO Rept. 2
(spring 1975):50,53.

Liberty
-UFO (CE-2)
1972, Aug.7/ground markings only
"Missouri Sightings in August Report-
ed to Ted Phillips," Skylook, no.59
(Oct.1972):12.
Ted Phillips, Physical Traces Associ-
ated with UFO Sightings (Evanston:
Center for UFO Studies, 1975), p.84.
-UFO (CE-3)
1966, April 1/Darlene Underwood
Jacques Vallee, Passport to Magonia
(Chicago: Regnery, 1969), pp.326-
27, quoting Interplanetary Intelli-
gence Rept., May 1966.
-UFO (NL)
1975, Nov.10
"UFO Central," CUFOS News Bull., 1
Feb.1976, p.12.

Linn Creek
-UFO (NL)
1967, March/Lee Case
Versailles Leader-Statesman, 16 Mar.
1967.
"Newsman Sights UFO, Osage Beach,
Mo.," Skylook, no.1 (Sep.1967):3.

Livingston co.
-Earthquake luminescence
1812, Feb.7
Samuel Latham Mitchill, "A Detailed
Narrative of the Earthquakes,"
Trans.Lit.& Phil.Soc'y N.Y. 1 (1814)
:281,298.

Lone Jack
-UFO (DD)
1947, June 24/Lester Swingleson/2 mi.N
Kansas City Times, 28 June 1947.

Louisiana
-Archeological site
E.G. Squier & E.H. Davis, Ancient
Monuments of the Mississippi Valley
(Washington: Smithsonian Institution,
Contrib.to Knowl., no.1, 1848), p.
136.
-Humanoid
1971, July/Joan Mills/Hwy.79
1972, July 11/Terry Harrison/Allen St.
1972, July 14/Edgar Harrison/Marzolf
Hill
1972, July 15/Pat Howard/Third St.
1972, July 21/Ellis Minor/River Rd.
Centralia (Ill.) Sentinel, 24 July
1972.
Richard Crowe, "Missouri Monster,"
Fate 25 (Dec.1972):58-60,62.
Jerome Clark & Loren Coleman, "Anthro-
poids, Monsters and UFOs," Flying
Saucer Rev. 19 (Jan.-Feb.1973):18,
19-21.
Glenn McWane & David Graham, The New
UFO Sightings (N.Y.: Warner, 1974),
pp.137-40.
-Humanoid tracks

1972, July/Freddie Robbins/8 mi.S
1972, July 20/Edgar Harrison/Marzolf
Hill
1972, Aug.3/Betty Suddarth/NW of town
Richard Crowe, "Missouri Monster,"
Fate 25 (Dec.1972):58,61,63-64. il.
Brad Steiger, Mysteries of Time and
Space (N.Y.: Dell, 1976 ed.), pp.
112-13.
-Mystery death
1954, winter
Jerome Clark & Loren Coleman, "Anthro-
poids, Monsters and UFOs," Flying
Saucer Rev. 19 (Jan.-Feb.1973):18,
19.
-Mystery voices
1972, July 29/Edgar Harrison
1972, Aug.5/Pat Howard
Richard Crowe, "Missouri Monster,"
Fate 25 (Dec.1972):58,64.
-Phantom
1940s/River Rd.
Jerome Clark & Loren Coleman, "Anthro-
poids, Monsters and UFOs," Flying
Saucer Rev. 19 (Jan.-Feb.1973):18,
19.
-UFO (NL)
1972, July 14/Edgar Harrison/Marzolf
Hill
Jerome Clark & Loren Coleman, "Anthro-
poids, Monsters and UFOs," Flying
Saucer Rev. 19 (Jan.-Feb.1973):18,
20-21.
1972, July 26-29/Lois Shade/River Rd.
1972, July 30-31/Ernest Shade
Richard Crowe, "Missouri Monster,"
Fate 25 (Dec.1972):58,65-66.
1972, Aug.12/Ernest Shade
Glenn McWane & David Graham, The New
UFO Sightings (N.Y.: Warner, 1974),
p.140.
Brad Steiger, Mysteries of Time and
Space (N.Y.: Dell, 1976 ed.), pp.
115-16.

Lutesville
-UFO (CE-2)
1969, Feb./F.X. Peters
Ted Phillips, Physical Traces Associ-
ated with UFO Sightings (Evanston:
Center for UFO Studies, 1975), p.61.

McDonald co.
-Haunt
n.d.
Vance Randolph, Ozark Ghost Stories
(Girard, Kan.: Haldeman-Julius,
1944), p.8.
-Phantom wolf
n.d.
Vance Randolph, Ozark Ghost Stories
(Girard, Kan.: Haldeman-Julius,
1944), p.14.

McNatt
-UFO (CE-3)
1977, March 5/Lonnie Stites
St. Louis Post-Dispatch, 1 May 1977.
Bob Pratt, "Close Encounter with a
Terrifying UFO," Nat'l Enquirer, 10

Jan.1978.

Madison
-UFO (CE-2)
  1969, April 16/N on Hwy.151
    "Moberly Resident Reports on UFO's,"
    Skylook, no.19 (June 1969):3,4.

Malden
-UFO (DD)
  1950, Sep.19
    Ray Palmer, "New Report on the Fly-
    ing Saucers," Fate 4 (Jan.1951):63,
    80-81.

Malta Bend
-UFO (CE-2)
  1973, Oct.3
    Ted Phillips, Physical Traces Associ-
    ated with UFO Sightings (Evanston:
    Center for UFO Studies, 1975), p.93.

Manchester
-UFO (NL)
  1969, Oct.1/Michele Lee/Weidmann Rd.
    "Old Year Goes Out with Many Missouri
    Reports Coming In," Skylook, no.26
    (Jan.1970):2,4-5.

Marceline
-UFO (NL)
  1969, March
    "Missouri Has Flurry of UFO Sight-
    ings," Skylook, no.17 (Apr.1969):3,
    5.

Marion co.
-UFO (NL)
  1968, Nov.21
    "A Whatzit over Marion County, Mis-
    souri," Skylook, no.14 (Jan.1969):5.

Marionville
-Healing
  1940s/Mrs. M.R. Smith
    Vance Randolph, Ozark Superstitions
    (N.Y.: Columbia Univ., 1947), p.124.

Marshall
-UFO (CE-2)
  1974, April
    Ted Phillips, Physical Traces Associ-
    ated with UFO Sightings (Evanston:
    Center for UFO Studies, 1975), p.99.

Marshfield
-UFO (CE-2)
  1954, Sep.22/Jack Williams/Scout Camp
    Rd.
    Ted Phillips, Physical Traces Associ-
    ated with UFO Sightings (Evanston:
    Center for UFO Studies, 1975), p.13.
    J. Allen Hynek, The Hynek UFO Report
    (N.Y.: Dell, 1977), pp.178-81.

Maryville
-UFO (?)
  1897, April 13/=hoax?
    St. Joseph News, 14 Apr.1897.
-UFO (NL)

1978, July 28/Sheri Harbison
  Maryville Forum, 30 July 1978.

Mexico
-UFO (NL)
  1897, April 11
    Columbus (O.) Evening Press, 13 Apr.
    1897.
  1944, May 10
    Washington (D.C.) Times-Herald, 23
    May 1944.
    Vincent H. Gaddis, "Visitors from
    the Void," Amazing Stories 21 (June
    1947):159,161.
-White blackberries
  1943, Aug./F.L. Calkin
    New York News, 29 Aug.1943.

Miller co.
-UFO (CE-1)
  1967, Feb.19
    "Dog Alerts Master to UFO," Skylook,
    no.15 (Feb.1969):6.
    Ted Phillips, "Farmer Sees Object,
    Humanoids on Ground," Skylook, no.
    93 (Aug.1975):15.
-UFO (CE-3)
  1967, Feb.14
    Ted Phillips, Jr., "UFO Observed at
    Close Range in Mo.," Skylook, no.8
    (Apr.1968):1,3.
    "Outstanding 1967 Report," APRO Bull.
    18 (Sep.-Oct.1969):5-6.
    Ted Phillips, "Farmer Sees Object,
    Humanoids on Ground," Skylook, no.
    93 (Aug.1975):15.

Mill Spring
-UFO (NL)
  1973, Feb.21/Edith Boatwright
    Jerome Clark, "The Brushy Creek UFO
    Scare," Fate 27 (May 1974):96,98-99.

Milton
-Ancient silver and iron mask
  1879/Hannibal Fox
    "A Silver and Iron Mask Found in Mis-
    souri," Am.Antiquarian 3 (1881):336.

Mincy
-Phantom cabin
  n.d./Mrs. C.P. Mahnkey
    Vance Randolph, Ozark Ghost Stories
    (Girard, Kan.: Haldeman-Julius,
    1944), p.7.

Mine La Motte
-Archeological site
    E.G. Squier & E.H. Davis, Ancient
    Monuments of the Mississippi Valley
    (Washington: Smithsonian Institution,
    Contrib.to Knowl., no.1, 1848), pp.
    136-37.
-UFO (NL)
  1973, April/Eva Jane Simms
    "Brief Reports," Skylook, no.74 (Jan.
    1974):16.

Missouri City
-Archeological site

ca.500 B.C.-700 A.D.
  J.M. Shippee, "Nebo Hill: A Lithic
  Complex in Western Missouri," Am.
  Antiquity 14 (1948):29-32.
  J.M. Shippee, "The Diagnostic Point
  Type of the Nebo Hill Complex,"
  Missouri Arch. 19, no.3 (1957):42-
  46. il.

Moberly
-UFO (?)
  1897, April/crashed airship
    Rockford (Ill.) Republic, 12 Apr.
    1897, p.1.
-UFO (NL)
  1948/Virgil Humphrey/900 W. Rollins St.
    "UFO Seen over Moberly, Mo., in 1948,"
    Skylook, no.28 (Mar.1970):13.
  1970, Sep.29/Larry Yoder/Rothwell Park
    Larry Yoder, "Moberly, Mo., Residents
    Watch Moving Objects," Skylook, no.
    36 (Nov.1970):20.
  1971, Jan.31/W.E. Shewmon/518 Monroe
  Rd.
    "Press Reports," APRO Bull. 19 (Jan.-
    Feb.1971):7.
    "Amateur Astronomer Reports Unidenti-
    fied Object," Skylook, no.40 (Mar.
    1971):12.
  1971, April 21/Larry Yoder
    "Was It a UFO?" Skylook, no.43 (June
    1971):8.
  1972, Aug.28
    "Missouri Sightings in August Report-
    ed to Ted Phillips," Skylook, no.59
    (Oct.1972):12.

Monett
-UFO (NL)
  1954, Aug.26/Mrs. George Faris
    (Letter), Fate 8 (Mar.1955):109-10.

Morgan co.
-Haunt
  1850-   /John A. Hannay
    Vance Randolph, Ozark Superstitions
    (N.Y.: Columbia Univ., 1947), pp.
    228-29.

Morley
-Animal ESP
  1959, Feb./Ruby Parker/Forest Hills
  Cemetery
    Ruby Parker, "The Telling of the
    Bees," Fate 17 (Mar.1964):36-38.

Mountain View
-Contactee
  1954, July 30-1955, April 24/Buck Nelson
    Buck Nelson, My Trip to Mars, the
    Moon, and Venus (Grand Rapids, Mich.:
    Grand Rapids Flying Saucer Club,
    1956).
    Kansas City Times, 4 Nov.1957.
    (Letter), Anna B. Kness, Fate 12
    (Jan.1959):125,129.
    Long John Nebel, The Way Out World
    (N.Y.: Lancer, 1961 ed.), pp.52-53.
    "All Sizes and Shapes..." in Frank

Bowers, ed., The True Report on Flying Saucers (Greenwich, Ct.: Fawcett, 1967), p.43. il.

Neosho
-Ancient sculpture
  1975/Marcele J. Mitchell
    Kansas City Star, 14 Feb.1978; and
    26 Feb.1978. il.
-Mummy
  1923, March/Cowskin Bluffs
    New York Times, 14 Mar.1923, p.21.

Nevada
-Mystery bird deaths
  1909, Dec.
    Grand Rapids (Mich.) Herald, 10 Dec.
    1909.
-UFO (DD)
  1948, Nov.30/C.D. Fife
    (Editorial), Fate 2 (May 1949):3.

Newark
-UFO (CE-2)
  1970
    "Two Feel Heat from Red Light," Sky-
    look, no.50 (Jan.1972):13.

New Halls Ferry
-UFO (?)
  1973, July 11/Herman J. Musing/Hwy.140
  /=Skylab?
    "Brief Reports," Skylook, no.74 (Jan.
    1974):16.

New Haven
-Humanoid
  1972, July 20/Hwy.C
    Brad Steiger, Mysteries of Time and
    Space (N.Y.: Dell, 1976 ed.), pp.
    116-17.
-UFO (?)
  1901/Mr. Welter
    (Letter), Edd Koch, Tulsa (Okla.)
    Daily World, 10 Apr.1966.

New Madrid
-Archeological sites
    Henry M. Brackenridge, "On the Popu-
    lation and Tumuli of the Aborigines
    of North America," Trans.Am.Phil.
    Soc'y 1 (1818):151-59.
    Frederic W. Putnam, "The Swallow
    Collection," Ann.Rept.Peabody Mus.,
    vol.8 (1875). il.
-Earthquake luminescence
  1811, Dec.16-1812, Feb.7
    New York Evening Post, 22 Feb.1812.
    Samuel Latham Mitchill, "A Detailed
    Narrative of the Earthquakes," Trans.
    Lit.& Phil.Soc'y N.Y. 1 (1814):281,
    299-300.
    L. Bringier, "Notices of the Geology
    ...of the Regions Around the Miss-
    issippi and Its Confluent Waters,"
    Am.J.Sci., ser.1, 3 (1821):15,20n.
    Myron L. Fuller, "The New Madrid
    Earthquake," Bull.U.S.Geol.Survey,
    no.494 (1912):46-47.
-Ghost light

n.d.
    John T. Richards, "Search for the
    Strange and Unexplained," Beyond
    Reality, no.32 (May-June 1978):26.

Nixa
-Phantom automobile
    1932, spring/Frank Jones
    Vance Randolph, Ozark Superstitions
    (N.Y.: Columbia Univ., 1947), p.232.

Novelty
-UFO (NL)
    1969, March 3-5/Harold Forman
    "Missouri Has Flurry of UFO Sight-
    ings," Skylook, no.17 (Apr.1969):1,
    2-3.
    "Missouri Sightings--More!--More!"
    Skylook, no.17 (Apr.1969):4-5.

O'Fallon
-Humanoid
    1972, July 24, 26
    Brad Steiger, Mysteries of Time and
    Space (N.Y.: Dell, 1976 ed.), p.112.
-UFO (DD)
    1974, April 30/Mike Haney
    "Missouri Man Reports Three Objects
    in Sky," Skylook, no.79 (June 1974)
    :7.
-UFO (NL)
    1968, Aug.23/Cool Springs Rd.
    "UFO over O'Fallon," Skylook, no.12/
    13 (Aug.-Sep.1968):6-7.

Olivette
-UFO (NL)
    1957, Nov.
    "All About Sputs," Doubt, no.56
    (1958):460,471, quoting St. Louis
    Globe-Democrat (undated).

Osage Beach
-UFO (?)
    1969, Aug.12/=balloon?
    Ted Phillips, Jr., "UFO or Balloon?"
    Skylook, no.22 (Sep.1969):4.

Otterville
-UFO (CE-1)
    1975, Nov.13
    Ted Phillips, "Other Sightings Re-
    ported in Sedalia, MO," Skylook, no.
    98 (Jan.1976):8.

Overland
-Giant bird
    1948, April 10/Clyde C. Smith
    Jerome Clark & Loren Coleman, "Winged
    Wierdies," Fate 25 (Mar.1972):80,85.

Pacific
-Humanoid
    1975, Oct./Brush Creek
    1977, May 18/Denton Rd.
    Union Franklin County Tribune, 25
    May 1977.
-UFO (?)
    1971/Mrs. Samuel Prichard, Jr./502 N.
    First St.

"Slow Moving Object Changes Colors,"
    Skylook, no.45 (Aug.1971):13.
-UFO (CE-2)
    1975, Nov.15/Betty Prichard
    David Schroth, "St. Louis Group Re-
    views 156 Reports from 1975," Sky-
    look, no.99 (Feb.1976):11.

Palmyra
-UFO (?)
    1969, Oct.17/Wayne Beever/=balloon?
    "Silvery Object Floats over Palmyra,
    Mo.," Skylook, no.24 (Nov.1969):17.

Paris
-Haunt
    ca.1863-1934
    Vance Randolph, Ozark Superstitions
    (N.Y.: Columbia Univ., 1947), p.221,
    quoting AP release, Nov.1934.

Patterson
-Acoustic anomaly
    1973, April
    Jerome Clark, "The Brushy Creek UFO
    Scare," Fate 27 (May 1974):96,104.
-UFO (DD)
    1973, March 22/Joe King/E on Hwy.34
    Jerome Clark, "The Brushy Creek UFO
    Scare," Fate 27 (May 1974):96,103.

Peculiar
-Cattle mutilation
    1977, Sep.25/Raymond R. Welch/1½ mi.NW
    1977, Oct.4/Harold Cowger/1 mi.S
    1977, Oct.9/John D. Rice/2½ mi.SW
    Kansas City Times, 14 Oct.1977.

Pemiscot co.
-Phantom dog
    n.d.
    Vance Randolph, Ozark Superstitions
    (N.Y.: Columbia Univ., 1947), pp.
    225-26.

Perryville
-Ghost light
    n.d.
    Vance Randolph, Ozark Ghost Stories
    (Girard, Kan.: Haldeman-Julius,
    1944), p.22.
-Stratigraphic anomaly
    Avon Diatremes
    Albert L. Kidwell, "Post-Devonian
    Igneous Activity in Southeastern
    Missouri," Rept.Investigations Mis-
    souri Geol.Survey, no.4 (1947).
    F.G. Snyder, et al., "Cryptoexplo-
    sive Structures in Missouri," Rept.
    Investigations Missouri Geol.Survey
    & Water Resources, no.30 (1965), p.
    24.

Peveley
-Mystery gas
    1978, Sep.17-27/Bonnie Boyer/Blackberry
    Hills
    St. Louis Post-Dispatch, 20-22 Sep.
    1978; and 24 Sep.1978.
    St. Louis Globe-Democrat, 27 Sep.1978;

29 Sep.1978; and 7-8 Oct.1978.
William Zeiser, "The Peveley Mystery
Toxin," _Pursuit_ 13 (winter 1979):21-
26. il.

Piedmont
-UFO (?)
1973, March/=stars
   Philip J. Klass, _UFOs Explained_ (N.Y.:
   Random House, 1974), pp.87-89.
1973, March 14/Maude Jefferies/=lens
flare
   Walt Andrus, "My Personal Evaluation
   of the Piedmont UFO Sightings," _Sky-
   look_, no.66 (May 1973):3-4.
   Jerome Clark, "The Brushy Creek UFO
   Scare," _Fate_ 27 (May 1974):96,101.
   Steve Erdmann, "The Distortion Factor," _Probe the Unknown_ 2 (spring
   1974):42,45.
1973, April 7/Ben Baron/Pyle's Hill/=
barium flare?
   Steve Erdmann, "The Distortion Factor," _Probe the Unknown_ 2 (spring
   1974):42,45-46.
-UFO (NL)
1973, March 22/Dennis Kenney
   Hayden C. Hewes, "International Dead-
   line," _Can.UFO Rept._, no.15 (1973):
   18-19.
   Jerome Clark, "The Brushy Creek UFO
   Scare," _Fate_ 27 (May 1974):96,103.
1973, March 23/Leonard Adams
   Jerome Clark, "The Brushy Creek UFO
   Scare," _Fate_ 27 (May 1974):96,103-
   104.
1973, May 11/Harley D. Rutledge
   "Press Reports," _APRO Bull._ 22 (July-
   Aug.1973):9.
   "Strange Lights in Missouri," _Flying
   Saucers_, winter 1974, pp.38-41.
   Steve Erdmann, "The Distortion Fac-
   tor," _Probe the Unknown_ 2 (spring
   1974):42,47.
1973, May 25/James Sage
   Steve Erdmann, "The Distortion Fac-
   tor," _Probe the Unknown_ 2 (spring
   1974):42,47.
1973, June 23/W.L. Harrington/Rothwell
Ranch
   "Brief Reports," _Skylook_, no.74 (Jan.
   1974):16.

Pineville
-Dowsing
1910s/Oakley St. John
   Vance Randolph, _Ozark Superstitions_
   (N.Y.: Columbia Univ., 1947), pp.82-
   84.
-Ghost
n.d.
   Vance Randolph, _Ozark Ghost Stories_
   (Girard, Kan.: Haldeman-Julius,
   1944), p.8.
-UFO (CE-2)
1977, Feb./Lawrence McCool
   Bentonville (Ark.) Vista, 6 Apr.1978.
-UFO (NL)
1977, March-April
   Kansas City Star, 19 Apr.1977, p.3;

and 29 Jan.1978, p.C1.
   "Comment," _Int'l UFO Reporter_ 2
   (July 1977):Newsfront sec.

Platte co.
-Humanoid
1973, fall
   J.A. Lloyd, "Sasquatch Seen in Platte
   County Missouri," _Sasquatch News_ 1
   (June 1974):2.

Platte City
-UFO (NL)
1897, April 10
   Columbus (O.) Evening Press, 12 Apr.
   1897.

Pleasant Hill
-UFO (CE-1)
1965, Dec.7/Joe Troutman
   "1965 Missouri Sighting Reported,"
   Skylook, no.40 (Mar.1971):15.

Poplar Bluff
-Precognition
1923, Nov.-1940/Grace Jaco
   Grace Jaco, "My 17 Year Dream," _Fate_
   19 (Apr.1966):82-85.
-UFO (DD)
1950, Sep.19/Harwood Inman
   Ray Palmer, "New Report on the Flying Saucers," _Fate_ 4 (Jan.1951):63,
   80-81.

Portageville
-UFO (NL)
1978, June
   Elsberry Democrat, 15 June 1978.

Potosi
-Human tracks in limestone
   Wilbert Rusch, "Human Footprints in
   Rock," _Creation Rsch.Soc'y Quar._,
   Mar.1971, pp.204,206. il.

Princeton
-UFO (NL)
1896, summer/C.N. Crotsenburg
   "Ball Lightning," _Monthly Weather
   Rev._ 26 (Aug.1898):358.
   "Ball Lightning," _Monthly Weather
   Rev._ 26 (Dec.1898):565.

Purcell
-UFO (?)
1971, Jan.5/James Henderson/=Venus
   Joplin Globe, 6 Jan.1971.
   "Much Ado About Venus," _Skylook_, no.
   39 (Feb.1971):7-8.

Purdy
-UFO (CE-2)
1978, Oct.12/Mrs. Everett Smith
   Joplin Globe, 24 Oct.1978.

Reeds Spring
-Dowsing
n.d./Truman Powell
   Vance Randolph, _Ozark Superstitions_
   (N.Y.: Columbia Univ., 1947), p.84.

-Haunt
  n.d./Ghost Pond/3 mi.W nr.Hwy.43
    Earl A. Collins, Folk Tales of Mis-
    souri (Boston: Christopher, 1935),
    pp.111-13.
    Vance Randolph, Ozark Superstitions
    (N.Y.: Columbia Univ., 1947), pp.
    221-22.
-Weather control
  1929
    Vance Randolph, Ozark Superstitions
    (N.Y.: Columbia Univ., 1947), pp.31-
    32.

Richmond Heights
-Giant bird
  1948, April 18/Chet Burke
    Jerome Clark & Loren Coleman, "Winged
    Wierdies," Fate 25 (Mar.1972):80,85.

Rock Hill
-Fall of metal chain
  1959, May 14/Wallace Baker/Crestvale
    Sioux City (Ia.) Journal, 15 May
    1959.

Rogersville
-Haunt
  n.d.
    Vance Randolph, Ozark Ghost Stories
    (Girard, Kan.: Haldeman-Julius,
    1944), p.5.

Rolla
-UFO (NL)
  1968, summer/SE on Hwy.72
    "UFO over Salem, Mo.," Skylook, no.
    14 (Jan.1969):4.
  1970, Sep.30/Esther Brockelmeyer/W on
  U.S.66
    "Object Watched from Highway 66, West
    of Rolla, Mo.," Skylook, no.37 (Dec.
    1970):9.
  1970, Oct.6/Garth Morris/12 mi.N on
  U.S.63
    Kansas City Times, 6 Oct.1970.

Roscoe
-UFO (NL)
  1960-1972
    "Series of UFO Sightings near Small
    Missouri Town," Skylook, no.54
    (May 1972):7.

Russellville
-UFO (NL)
  1973, Oct.-Nov./James Hasty/Route 1
    St. Louis Globe-Democrat, 1-2 Dec.
    1973.

Saint Ann
-UFO (DD)
  1967, Aug./Lee Poor
    "Missouri Couple Report UFO's Seen
    in 1967," Skylook, no.34 (Sep.1970):
    11,12.
-UFO (NL)
  1967, March 30/Mary Lou Poor
    "Missouri Couple Report UFO's Seen
    in 1967," Skylook, no.34 (Sep.1970):

11-12.

Saint Charles
-Inner development
  1970s/Gavin Frost/School of Wicca
    Hans Holzer, The Witchcraft Report
    (N.Y.: Ace, 1973), pp.82-92,189-94.
    Gavin & Yvonne Frost, The Witches'
    Bible (Los Angeles: Nash, 1973).
    Gavin Frost, Witchcraft: The Way to
    Serenity (Cottonwood, Ariz.: Eso-
    teric, n.d.).
    Warren Smith, "Phenomenal Predictions
    for 1975," Saga, Jan.1975, pp.20,
    22-23.
    Gavin & Yvonne Frost, The Magic Power
    of Witchcraft (W. Nyack, N.Y.:
    Parker, 1976).
    Gavin & Yvonne Frost, Meta Psycho-
    metry (Englewood Cliffs, N.J.: Pren-
    tice-Hall, 1977).
    J. Gordon Melton, Encyclopedia of
    American Religions, 2 vols. (Wil-
    mington, N.C.: Consortium, 1978),
    2:283-84.
-UFO (?)
  1957, Nov.12/=Venus
    Jacques & Janine Vallee, Challenge
    to Science (N.Y.: Ace, 1966 ed.),
    p.132.
-UFO (CE-2)
  1973, May 2/William Wright
    "Brief Reports," Skylook, no.74 (Jan.
    1974):16.
-UFO (CE-3)
  1971, Feb.18/J.W. Mueller
    "Cone-Shaped Object in Missouri,"
    Skylook, no.45 (Aug.1971):13.
-UFO (NL)
  1973, June 12/Robert Baumbach/Charann
  St.
    St. Louis Post-Dispatch, 14 June
    1973.
    Steve Erdmann, "Lightning UFOs over
    Missouri," Official UFO 1 (Nov.1976)
    :25-26,51-52.
  1974, Jan.5/Reuben Abbington
    George D. Fawcett, "The 'Unreported'
    UFO Wave of 1974," Saga UFO Rept. 2
    (spring 1975):50.

Saint Clair
-UFO (DD)
  1967, March 6/Webb Briddell
    "Three at St. Clair See Object," Sky-
    look, no.3 (Nov.1967):1.

Sainte Genevieve
-Haunt
  n.d./Jules Valle/1 North St.
    Susy Smith, Prominent American Ghosts
    (N.Y.: Dell, 1969 ed.), pp.87-91.
-River monster
  1877, Aug.29/Jacob Erst/10 mi.NW, in
  Mississippi R.
    St. Louis Globe-Democrat, 2 Sep.1877.

Saint George
-UFO (NL)
  1972, July 22/I-55 x Union Rd.

"Large UFO 'Launches' Smaller Ones over St. Louis County," <u>Skylook</u>, no. 58 (Sep.1972):10.

Saint James
-Precognition
1975/Joseph Jeffers/Box 492
Warren Smith, "Phenomenal Predictions for 1976," <u>Saga</u>, Jan.1976, pp.16,19.

Saint Joseph
-Ghost
1876/Pacific House
F.W.H. Myers, "On Recognized Apparitions Occurring More Than a Year After Death," <u>Proc.SPR</u> 6 (8 July 1889):13,17-20.
-Phantom
1943, Aug./Jack Clements/S of town
Lida Wilson Pyles, "The Phantom Hitch-hiker," <u>Fate</u> 8 (Apr.1955):41-43.
-UFO (?)
1897, April 21/=balloon
<u>Ashland (O.) Press</u>, 6 May 1897.
-UFO (CE-1)
1973, Oct.
<u>St. Joseph Gazette</u>, 9 Oct.1973.
-UFO (CE-2)
1973, Aug.22/Mr. Duckworth
Ted Phillips, <u>Physical Traces Associ-ated with UFO Sightings</u> (Evanston: Center for UFO Studies, 1975), p.91.
-UFO (NL)
1881, Nov.
<u>Lamoni (Ia.) Saints Herald</u>, 1 Dec. 1881, quoting <u>St. Joseph Evening News</u> (undated).

Saint Louis
-Archeological site
Big Mound
H.H. Brackenridge, "On the Population and Tumuli of the Aborigines of North America," <u>Trans.Am.Phil.Soc'y</u> 1 (1818):151-59.
T.R. Peale, "Ancient Mounds at St. Louis, Missouri, in 1819," <u>Ann.Rept. Smith.Inst.</u>, 1861, pp.386-91. il.
T.T. Richards, "Relics from the Great Mound (St. Louis)," <u>Am.Naturalist</u> 4 (1870):62.
-Ball lightning
1956, Sep./Ronald L. Stelzleni/4574 N. 79th St.
1957, Apr./Ronald L. Stelzleni/4574 N. 79th St.
(Letter), <u>Flying Saucers</u>, Feb.1957, p.67.
1970, May 15/Murray Felsher
Murray Felsher, "Ball Lightning," <u>Nature</u> 227 (1970):982.
-Cartomancy
1930s-1960s/Grace Cassidy
Grace Cassidy, "The Death Card Fell for Me," <u>Fate</u> 22 (Feb.1969):74-78.
-Contactee
1900s/Sara Weiss
Sara Weiss, <u>Journeys to the Planet Mars</u> (N.Y.: Bradford, 1903).

Sara Weiss, <u>Decimon Huÿdas: A Romance of Mars</u> (Rochester, N.Y.: Austin, 1906).
James H. Hyslop, "Journeys to the Planet Mars," <u>J.ASPR</u> 7 (1913):272-83.
1950s-1960s/George Marlo
Long John Nebel, <u>The Way Out World</u> (N.Y.: Lancer, 1961 ed.), pp.63-64.
-Earthquake luminescence
1812, Feb.7
Samuel Latham Mitchill, "A Detailed Narrative of the Earthquakes," <u>Trans. Lit.& Phil.Soc'y N.Y.</u> 1 (1814):281, 288.
-Erratic deer
1978, March 26/Mansion House
<u>St. Louis Globe-Democrat</u>, 27 Mar. 1978.
-Fall of anomalous meteorite
1862, July 9/Chestnut St.
"Supposed Fall of Meteoric Iron at St. Louis, Mo.," <u>Am.J.Sci.</u>, ser.2, 34 (1862):443-44.
-Fall of beans
1945, Sep.22
"Rain of Beans," <u>Doubt</u>, no.14 (spring 1946):212.
-Fall of foam
1956, Aug.20/Mrs. William Jenkins/1961 E. Adlade St.
June E. Weidemann, "Mysterious Foam in St. Louis," <u>Fate</u> 9 (Dec.1956): 20-21, quoting <u>St. Louis Post-Dis-patch</u> (undated). il.
-Fall of ice
1957, March 28/1929 Crown Point Dr.
"Ice," <u>Doubt</u>, no.54 (1957):432,433.
-Fall of steel container
1966, May 24/1738 Biddle St.
(Editorial), <u>Fate</u> 19 (Sep.1966):8-9.
-Fall of weblike substance
1969, Oct./Donald Pecsok/nr. McDonnell Douglas plant/=spider web
<u>Washington (D.C.) Post</u>, 28 Mar.1970.
"A Classic Case of 'Angel-Hair,'" <u>Pursuit</u> 3 (Oct.1970):72-73.
1970, Oct.16/Joe Gurney/nr. McDonnell Douglas plant/=spider web
"'Angel Hair' Falls in St. Louis County," <u>Skylook</u>, no.36 (Nov.1970): 8.
"More on October Angel Hair Report," <u>Skylook</u>, no.40 (Mar.1971):10.
"Back Track," <u>Skylook</u>, no.53 (Apr. 1972):13,14.
-Flying humanoid
1948, April 26/Kristine Dolezal
1948, April 27/Harry Bradford/Red Feath-er Express Hwy. x Kings Hwy. Blvd.
1948, May 1/Charles Dunn
1948, May 2/Albert T. Bertram, Jr.
<u>Kansas City Star</u>, 29 Apr.1948, p.13; and 30 Apr.1948, p.22
<u>St. Louis Post-Dispatch</u>, 2 May 1948, magazine sec.
-Ghost
n.d./Mrs. Charles E. Wofford
Hans Holzer, <u>Ghosts I've Met</u> (N.Y.: Ace, 1965), p.59.

-Healing
  1850s/Dr. Hotchkiss
    Emma Hardinge Britten, Modern Ameri-
    can Spiritualism (N.Y.: The Author,
    1870), pp.371-75.
-Human tracks in limestone
    Henry R. Schoolcraft, "Remarks on the
    Prints of Human Feet, Observed in
    the Secondary Limestone of the Miss-
    issippi Valley," Am.J.Sci., ser.1,
    5 (1822):223-31. il.
    Josiah Priest, American Antiquities
    and Discoveries in the West (Albany:
    Hoffman & White, 1834 ed.), pp.153-
    54.
    David Dale Owen, "Regarding Human
    Foot-Prints in Solid Limestone," Am.
    J.Sci., ser.1, 43 (1842):14-32. il.
    A. McA., "The Pre-Adamite Track," Am.
    Antiquarian 7 (1885):364-67.
-Humanoid
  1963, May/Ninth St.
    Chicago (Ill.) Daily News, 24 May
    1963.
-Inner development
  1967-   /Church of All Worlds/Box 2953
    Hans Holzer, The Witchcraft Report
    (N.Y.: Ace, 1973), pp.92-93,177-82.
    June & Nicholas Regush, Psi: The Oth-
    er World Catalogue (N.Y.: Dutton,
    1974), pp.202-203.
    J. Gordon Melton, Encyclopedia of Am-
    erican Religions, 2 vols. (Wilming-
    ton, N.C.: Consortium, 1978), 2:288-
    89.
-Mystery fog
  1951, Dec.30-31
    "St. Louis Fog," Doubt, no.36 (1952):
    139.
-Mystery stench
  1978, July 25/River des Peres
    St. Louis Globe-Democrat, 25 July
    1978.
-Out-of-body experience
  n.d./Emily Grant Hutchings
    Emily Grant Hutchings, Where Do We
    Go from Here? (N.Y.: Putnam, 1933).
-Paranormal strength
  1950, Nov./Earl E. Times
    W.E. Farbstein, "The Man Who Fools
    Gravity," Fate 6 (May 1953):68-70.
    il.
-Parapsychology research
  1960s/Psychical Research Society
    St. Louis Post-Dispatch, 27 Mar.1966.
-Phantom airplane
  1969, Dec.12, 17/Gateway Arch
    John A. Keel, "Mystery Aeroplanes of
    the 1930s: Part 1," Flying Saucer
    Rev. 16 (May-June 1970):10,11, quot-
    ing AP release, 22 Dec.1969.
-Phantom image
  1932, March/Cell 8, Central Police
  Station
    H.N. Ferguson, "Mystery Painting in
    St. Louis Jail," Fate 12 (Mar.1959):
    66-68. il.
-Possession
  1976, winter
    Steve Erdmann, "Devils, Demons, and a

Case of Possession," Beyond Reality,
    no.34 (Nov.-Dec.1978):20,62-64.
-Precognition
  1933, spring/Geneva Abbott
    "The Prophetic Drawing," Fate 21
    (Dec.1968):54, quoting St. Louis
    Globe-Democrat (undated).
  1957, Nov.1
    Laura A. Dale, Rhea White & Gardner
    Murphy, "A Selection of Cases from
    a Recent Survey of Spontaneous ESP
    Phenomena," J.ASPR 56 (1962):3,17.
  1962/Skinner & Kennedy Co.
    "Precognition in Print," Fate 22
    (Oct.1969):84. il.
-Psychokinesis
  1851/Harriet Hosmer
    Sylvan Muldoon, Psychic Experiences
    of Famous People (Chicago: Aries,
    1947), pp.8-9.
    Eugene Grossenheider, "Harriet Hos-
    mer, Sculptor and Psychic," Fate 11
    (Aug.1958):84,86.
  1976, June 25/Uri Geller
    Walter H. Uphoff, "The Watch That
    Could Not Run," Fate 30 (Mar.1977):
    60.
-Psycholuminescence
  1960-   /Edward Gansner
    Steve Erdmann, "The Curious Case of
    Robert Baez," Beyond Reality, no.18
    (Jan.1976):25,27.
-Retrocognition
  1912-1942/Armand LeClerc Golay
    Armand LeClerc Golay, "Does Ancestral
    Memory Explain My Dream?" Fate 21
    (Aug.1968):68-72.
-River monster
  1877, Aug./Mr. Eagan/Quarantine Station
  on Mississippi R.
    St. Louis Globe-Democrat, 2 Sep.1877.
-Roman coin
  1821/River des Peres
    Josiah Priest, American Antiquities
    and Discoveries in the West (Albany:
    Hoffman & White, 1834 ed.), p.49.
-Skyquake
  1972, July 8
    "Was It a Sonic Boom?" Skylook, no.58
    (Sep.1972):13.
-Skyquakes and earthquake luminescence
  1857, Oct.5-8
    St. Louis Intelligencer, 8 Oct.1857.
    New York Times, 12 Oct.1857, p.5.
    Mungo Ponton, Earthquakes (London:
    T. Nelson, 1888), p.118.
    F.A. Sampson, "The New Madrid and
    Other Earthquakes of Missouri," Bull.
    Seismological Soc'y Am. 3 (1913):57,
    68-69.
-Spirit medium
  1850s/Amanda Britt
  1850s/Thomas Gales Forster
    Emma Hardinge Britten, Modern Ameri-
    can Spiritualism (N.Y.: The Author,
    1870), pp.354,356.
  1910s/Mrs. Hays
    James H. Hyslop, "The Return of Mark
    Twain," J.ASPR 12 (1918):4-38.
    "Dream Coincidences," J.ASPR 13 (1919)

:361-65.
1913, spring-1937/Pearl Lenore Curran
St. Louis Globe-Democrat, 7 Feb.
1915, magazine sec.
William Marion Reedy, "My Flirtation
with Patience Worth," Reedy's Mir-
ror, 1 Oct.1915.
Casper S. Yost, Patience Worth: A
Psychic Mystery (N.Y.: Holt, 1916).
(Review), James H. Hyslop, J.ASPR 10
(1916):189-94.
Patience Worth, The Sorry Tale (N.Y.:
Holt, 1917).
C.E. Cory, "Patience Worth," Psych.
Rev. 26 (1919):397-406.
Pearl L. Curran, "A Nut for Psychol-
ogists," Unpartizan Rev. 13 (1920):
357-72.
Patience Worth, Light from Beyond
(Brooklyn: Patience Worth Pub. Co.,
1923).
Walter Franklin Prince, "The Riddle
of Patience Worth," Sci.Am. 135
(1926):20-22. il.
Walter Franklin Prince, The Case of
Patience Worth (Boston: Boston SPR,
1927).
(Review), F.C.S. Schiller, Proc.SPR
36 (1927):573-76.
"Editorial Note on 'Patience Worth,'"
J.ASPR 32 (1938):111-13.
Hettie Rhoda Meade, "The Songs of
Patience Worth," J.ASPR 42 (1948):
15-27.
Vincent Gaddis, "America's Most Fam-
ous Ghost Story," Fate 1 (fall 1948)
:70-77.
Charles Waldron Clowe, "The Case of
Patience Worth: A Theory," J.ASPR
43 (1949):70-81.
(Letter), Edmund P. Gibson, J.ASPR
43 (1949):166-68.
Bert Groth, "Reviewing the Classic
Case of Patience Worth," Fate 18
(Apr.1965):80-86.
Irving Litvag, Singer in the Shadows:
The Strange Story of Patience Worth
(N.Y.: Macmillan, 1972).
-Spontaneous human combustion
1966, May/Ethel Woodward
St. Louis Post-Dispatch, 1 June 1966.
-Tornado anomaly
1959, Feb.10/Martin Maurer
Bernard Vonnegut, "Luminosity Accom-
panying St. Louis Tornado--February
10, 1959," Monthly Weather Rev. 87
(Feb.1959):64.
-UFO (?)
1949, May 7
"If It's in the Sky It's a Saucer,"
Doubt, no.27 (1949):416.
1953, Feb.1
Donald E. Keyhoe, Flying Saucers from
Outer Space (N.Y.: Holt, 1953), p.
240.
1969, June 5/James V. Beardsley/=
meteor
"FAA Controller Recounts '69 Sight-
ing," UFO Inv., Feb.1972, p.2.
Philip J. Klass, UFOs Explained (N.Y.:

Random House, 1974), pp.42-51.
1969, Oct.9
Ted Phillips, Physical Traces Associ-
ated with UFO Sightings (Evanston:
Center for UFO Studies, 1975), p.
109.
1972, Oct.1/=balloon
St. Louis Globe-Democrat, 2 Oct.1972.
1973, March/Edward Gansner
Steve Erdmann, "The Curious Case of
Robert Baez," Beyond Reality, no.
18 (Jan.1976):25,27.
-UFO (CE-1)
1954, July 14/McDonnell Aircraft Corp.
J. Allen Hynek, The Hynek UFO Report
(N.Y.: Dell, 1977), pp.149-51.
1971, July 14/Edward J. Hicks/10633
Lavinia Dr.
"Observer Signals UFO--Lights Flash,"
Skylook, no.42 (May 1971):10.
-UFO (CE-4)
1967, Feb.16/Raymond Wettling/I-70
Chicago (Ill.) American, 17 Feb.1967.
-UFO (DD)
1947, June 29/Mrs. H.J. Beckmeyer/5531
Cabanne Ave.
St. Louis Post-Dispatch, 8 July 1947.
1947, July 4/Thomas Rose
St. Louis Post-Dispatch, 6 July 1947.
1947, July 6/Mrs. N.P. McDonald/5941
Scanlon Ave.
St. Louis Globe-Democrat, 7 July
1947.
St. Louis Post-Dispatch, 7 July 1947.
1947, July 7/Ed Hooley
1947, July 8/Oliver Obenhaus
St. Louis Post-Dispatch, 8 July 1947.
1947, July 8/Thiemo Wolf/3515 Hartford
St.
St. Louis Globe-Democrat, 9 July
1947.
1947, Aug.11
(Letter), C.W., Sci.& Mech. 38 (May
1967):34.
1950, Nov./Paul Seligsohn/Washington
Univ.
"UFOs Cross Football Field," Skylook,
no.56 (June 1972):8.
1954, June 14/Leo F. Wicklinski/Benton
x Ballwin St.
"UFOs Fly in Formation," Skylook, no.
45 (Aug.1971):17.
1960/Mrs. Edward S. Madigan/2842 Iowa
"Lady Recalls Older Sighting," Skylook, no.59 (Oct.1972):19.
1967, July 14/Edward J. Hicks
"Observer Signals UFO--Lights Flash,"
Skylook, no.42 (May 1971):10.
1969, March 3/Cliff Hasamear/Potomac x
Dekalb St.
"St. Louis Workman Sees UFO," Skylook, no.18 (May 1969):3.
1971, May 4/Marvin H. Whyman
"Oblong Object over St. Louis," Skylook, no.44 (June 1971):10.
1972, July 25/5000 Oleatha
"Several See Lighted, Silent Object
over St. Louis," Skylook, no.61
(Dec.1972):12.
1974, April 9/SW of town

"Around the Network," Skylook, no.79
(June 1974):17.
-UFO (NL)
1897, April 10/William Mulhall/Kings-
hwy. x Easton Ave.
St. Louis Post-Dispatch, 12 Apr.1897,
p.1.
1897, April 12/Planters' Hotel
St. Louis Post-Dispatch, 13 Apr.1897,
p.1.
1897, April 15/Leo Caplan
St. Louis Post-Dispatch, 16 Apr.1897,
p.1.
1947, July 4/Nelson Vickrey/Francis
Field
St. Louis Post-Dispatch, 6 July 1947.
1947, July 7/Allen Tanner
St. Louis Post-Dispatch, 8 July 1947.
1952, Jan.3/Larry Touzinsky
Albert K. Bender, Flying Saucers and
the Three Men (N.Y.: Paperback Library, 1968 ed.), p.38.
1954, Aug.26/Mr. Faris
Harold T. Wilkins, Flying Saucers Uncensored (N.Y.: Pyramid, 1967 ed.),
p.238.
1956, Aug.14/Ed Oldendorph
(Letter), Fate 10 (Sep.1957):113-15.
1957, Sep.23/Dennis Todaro
(Letter), Flying Saucers, Feb.1958,
pp.63-64.
1960, July 19-20
Lloyd Mallan, "Complete Directory of
UFOs: Part I," Sci.& Mech. 37 (Dec.
1966):36,39.
1963, May/Monty G. Bowenschulte/5213
Hilda Ave.
"Five Objects over St. Louis," Skylook, no.2 (Oct.1967):4.
1966, March 25
"Nation-wide Saucer Flap Continues,"
Saucer News 13 (June 1966):30,31.
1967, Feb?/Doris Schneider/Hampton x
Gravois Ave.
"'Seeing Is Believing' for St. Louis
Woman," Skylook, no.21 (Aug.1969):3.
1970, Jan.31/South St. Louis
"UFOs with Pink Lights Reported, St.
Louis, Mo.," Skylook, no.28 (Mar.
1970):3.
"More on St. Louis Lights," Skylook,
no.28 (Mar.1970):4.
1972, Jan.4/Diane Giamauno/nr. Lind-
bergh Blvd.
"St. Louis House Wife Watches Rectangular UFO," Skylook, no.54 (May
1972):7.
1972, Aug.11/Mildred Craft/8620 Gravois
"St. Louis Women See Lighted Object,"
Skylook, no.59 (Oct.1972):19.
1973, Sep.11/Ronald Allen/4304 Wabash
"Brief Reports," Skylook, no.74 (Jan.
1974):17.
1975, Aug.7
1975, Aug.31
1975, Sep.4
"UFO Central," CUFOS News Bull., 15
Nov.1975, pp.15,17.
1977, April 8
"UFO Analysis," Int'l UFO Reporter 2

(June 1977):Newsfront sec.
1977, May 21
"UFOs of Limited Merit," Int'l UFO
Reporter 2 (July 1977):3.

Saint Patrick
-Retrocognition
1935/Frances E. Peterson
Frances E. Peterson, "Where Is This
Valley?" Fate 12 (Apr.1959):54-55.

Salem
-UFO (DD)
1970, May
Salem Ozark New Era, 4 June 1970.
-UFO (NL)
1967, Nov.8/Dee Headrick
Salem News, 13 Nov.1967; and 16 Nov.
1967.
1968, Sep.
"UFO over Salem, Mo.," Skylook, no.
14 (Jan.1969):4.
1973, Nov.16/Lawrence Green/Brandon
Heights
Salem News, 19 Nov.1973.
1975, Jan.3
Robert A. Goerman, "The UFO Modus Operandi: January 1975," Official UFO
1 (Aug.1976):46,47.

Salisbury
-UFO (CE-1)
1969, Feb.26/Carl William Eberlein
Salisbury Press-Spectator, 14 Mar.
1969.
-UFO (NL)
1897, April 12
St. Louis Post-Dispatch, 13 Apr.1897,
p.2.

Sarcoxie
-UFO (NL)
1967, July 9
"Girls See Object," Skylook, no.3
(Nov.1967):5.

Sedalia
-Animal ESP
1929-1936/Sam Van Arsdale
Vincent & Margaret Gaddis, The Strange
World of Animals and Pets (N.Y.:
Pocket Books, 1971 ed.), pp.152-53,
quoting Coronet, Nov.1954.
"Missouri's Canine Wizard," Fate 8
(Mar.1955):93.
-Haunt
1860s
Earl A. Collins, Folk Tales of Mis-
souri (Boston: Christopher, 1935),
pp.128-30.
-Human electrification
1895/Jennie Moran
Henry Winfred Splitter, "Electrically
Charged People," Fate 8 (Mar.1955):
83.
-Mystery bird deaths
1978, Jan./nr. cemetery
Kansas City Star, 6 Jan.1978; and 10
Jan.1978.
-UFO (?)

1969, Jan.26/Ted Phillips, Jr./=meteor
Ted Phillips, Jr., "A UFO Sighting,
Almost!" Skylook, no.16 (Mar.1969):
1.
1970, July 3/NW on Hwy.H/=Venus?
"Bright Object May Have Been Venus,"
Skylook, no.33 (Aug.1970):11.
1971, Oct.15/=meteor?
"Brilliant Flash of Light," Skylook,
no.50 (Jan.1972):13.
-UFO (CE-1)
1973, Sep.22/1½ mi.N
Ted Phillips, "Summary of UFO Reports
in Missouri During 1973," Skylook,
no.74 (Jan.1974):13.
1975, Nov.28
Ted Phillips, "Missouri Woman Reports
Close Sighting," Skylook, no.98
(Jan.1976):6-8. il.
1975, Dec.7/16th St.
Ted Phillips, "Other Sightings Re-
ported in Sedalia, Mo.," Skylook,
no.98 (Jan.1976):8.
-UFO (CE-2)
1966, May/Whiteman AFB
Ted Phillips, Physical Traces Associ-
ated with UFO Sightings (Evanston:
Center for UFO Studies, 1975), p.41.
1969/Whiteman AFB
"Reported UFO Landing at Air Base,"
Skylook, no.22 (Sep.1969):7.
Ted Phillips, Physical Traces Associated with UFO Sightings (Evanston:
Center for UFO Studies, 1975), p.60.
1974
Ted Phillips, Physical Traces Associated with UFO Sightings (Evanston:
Center for UFO Studies, 1975), p.99.
-UFO (DD)
1947, July 9
"Older Sighting in '25 Years Ago'
Column," Skylook, no.57 (Aug.1972):
11, quoting Sedalia Democrat (un-
dated).
1952, summer/Ohio St.
"Sedalia Woman Recalls 1952 Sighting," Skylook, no.21 (Aug.1969):1.
1967, April 5/W on Hwy.50
"Truck Driver Sees Disc," Skylook,
no.6-7 (Feb.-Mar.1968):2.
1967, July 15/1 mi.S
"Domed Object Seen over Sedalia, Mo.,"
Skylook, no.37 (Dec.1970):8.
1967, Oct.2
"What Was It?" Skylook, no.3 (Nov.
1967):3.
-UFO (NL)
1967, June/Joe Husky
"Couple Watch Object," Skylook, no.
2 (Oct.1967):2.
1967, Sep.24/William C. Rayl/2342 W.
Second St.
"Sedalia Men See Object," Skylook,
no.2 (Oct.1967):1.
1969, March 22
Ted Phillips, Jr., "Bright Light
Moves over Sedalia, Mo.," Skylook,
no.18 (May 1969):5.
1969, July 19/Leroy's Steak House
"Several Watch Bright Object over

Sedalia, Mo.," Skylook, no.22 (Sep.
1969):7.
1971, Oct.11
"Couple Report Bright Light," Skylook, no.50 (Jan.1972):13.
1971, Nov.28
"Bright Red Light Seen Through Falling Snow," Skylook, no.50 (Jan.
1972):13.
1972, Aug.27
"Missouri Sightings in August Reported to Ted Phillips," Skylook, no.
59 (Oct.1972):12.
1972, Sep.13
"State Highway Employees Report
UFOs," Skylook, no.59 (Oct.1972):7.

Seymour
-Healing
1940/Callie Brake
Springfield News, 29 July 1940.

Shannon co.
-Fall of ice
1873, Oct.5/William Elmwood/nr. Pine
Hollow
Decatur (Ill.) Republican, 27 Nov.
1873, p.2.
-UFO (CE-1)
1967, March 28/Darrell Broadfoot
"Farmer and Son See Lights," Skylook,
no.2 (Oct.1967):6, quoting Eminence
Reynolds County Times (undated).

Shelbina
-UFO (NL)
1978, June
Elsberry Democrat, 15 June 1978.

Shirley
-Phantom panther
1955, May 13/Les Brown/Floyd Tower Rd.
Dunbar Robb, "Cougar in Missouri,"
Missouri Conservationist 16 (July
1955):14.

Shrewsbury
-UFO (DD)
1947, July 6/G.W. Willson/5125 Michael
Ave.
St. Louis Globe-Democrat, 7 July 1947.

Simmons
-Self-replenishing barrel
1950, May 15-1951, Feb.13/Johnnie Orr/
=trick barrel?
Mrs. Von Craft, "Mystery Barrel of
the Ozarks," Fate 4 (May-June 1951):
12-16.
(Letter), Mrs. Von Craft, Fate 4
(July 1951):96-97.
(Letter), J.W. Mooney, Fate 4 (Oct.
1951):116; 5 (Feb.-Mar.1952):120-21.
(Letter), Mrs. Von Hutchcraft, Fate
5 (Apr.-May 1952):117.

Slater
-Spontaneous human combustion
1957/William H. Peel/G,M & O Railroad
(Editorial), Fate 10 (July 1957):16.

Smithton
-UFO (CE-1)
  1970, July 25/Stanley Dillon
    "Strange Lights Glow Among Trees on
    Missouri Farm--and England," Sky-
    look, no.34 (Sep.1970):9.
-UFO (DD)
  1973, Oct.31
    Ted Phillips, "Summary of UFO Reports
    in Missouri During 1973," Skylook,
    no.74 (Jan.1974):13.

South Campbell
-UFO (NL)
  1967, Oct.21/Jerry Immon/Hwy.M
    Springfield Leader & Press, 22 Oct.
    1967.

Spanish Lake
-Precognition
  1963, Aug./Jeaneane M. Rigoni/Criter-
  ion Ave.
    Jeaneane M. Rigoni, "Beth Was Drown-
    ing," Fate 21 (July 1968):39-44.

Spokane
-Ghost light
  n.d./Hwy.123
    Vance Randolph, Ozark Superstitions
    (N.Y.: Columbia Univ., 1947), p.235.

Springfield
-Dowsing
  n.d./J.O. Jackson
    Vance Randolph, Ozark Superstitions
    (N.Y.: Columbia Univ., 1947), pp.
    84-85,87.
-Fall of rocks
  1954, June 25-July/Victor Bunch/812 N.
  Wheeler
    (Editorial), Fate 7 (Nov.1954):11-12.
    (Editorial), Fate 7 (Dec.1954):10.
-UFO (?)
  1969, Jan.14/Charles Carter/Southwest-
  ern Rendering Plant
    Ted Phillips, Jr., "UFO Reports from
    Greene County, Missouri," Skylook,
    no.17 (Apr.1969):6.
-UFO (CE-1)
  1969, Jan.2/Frank Gilmore
    Ted Phillips, Jr., "UFO Reports from
    Greene County, Missouri," Skylook,
    no.17 (Apr.1969):6.
    Ted Phillips, "UFO Events in Missouri
    1857-1971," FSR Case Histories, no.
    8 (Dec.1971):9,11.
-UFO (CE-2)
  1966, Aug.1
    Ted Phillips, Physical Traces Associ-
    ated with UFO Sightings (Evanston:
    Center for UFO Studies, 1975), p.43.
  1973, Oct.12/ground markings only
    Ted Phillips, "Summary of UFO Reports
    in Missouri During 1973," Skylook,
    no.74 (Jan.1974):13.
    Ted Phillips, Physical Traces Associ-
    ated with UFO Sightings (Evanston:
    Center for UFO Studies, 1975), p.94.
-UFO (CE-3)
  1897, April 16/W.H. Hopkins/E of town

St. Louis Post-Dispatch, 19 Apr.1897.
-UFO (DD)
  1967, Oct.21
    "UFOs--October--U.S.A.," APRO Bull.
    16 (Nov.-Dec.1967):8.
-UFO (NL)
  1967, Sep.2/Mrs. Ted Phillips, Jr.
    "Sees First UFO," Skylook, no.3
    (Nov.1967):2.
  1969, Jan.12/Ken Nobles
    "Flying Object near Springfield, Mo.
    Jan.12," Skylook, no.15 (Feb.1969):
    1.
    "More on Springfield, Mo. Sighting,"
    Skylook, no.16 (Mar.1969):1.
  1971, March 26/8 mi.E
    "Springfield, Mo., Couple See High
    Speed UFO," Skylook, no.42 (May
    1971):9.

Steele
-Healing
  1937, Feb./Mr. Howell
    Irene Douglas, "Missouri 'Witch Doc-
    tor,'" Fate 12 (June 1959):71-74.
-Humanoid
  1971, May
    Kansas City Times, 21 May 1971, p.13.

Stoddard co.
-Dowsing
  1890s/Mr. Dillard
    Vance Randolph, Ozark Ghost Stories
    (Girard, Kan.: Haldeman-Julius,
    1944), p.9.

Stover
-UFO (?)
  1968, fall/Mrs. Dennis Sousley/=meteor?
    "Old Year Goes Out with Many Missouri
    Reports Coming In," Skylook, no.26
    (Jan.1970):2,6.
  1969, Aug.12/Norma Short
    Ted Phillips, Jr., "UFO or Balloon?"
    Skylook, no.22 (Sep.1969):4.
-UFO (CE-1)
  ca.1961, Aug./Reed Blackman
    "Sighting near Stover, Mo.," Skylook,
    no.18 (May 1969):4.
  1969, March 6/Bill Anderson/SW on County Rd.FF
    "Missouri Has Flurry of UFO Reports,"
    Skylook, no.17 (Apr.1969):1,3.
-UFO (CE-2)
  1956
    Ted Phillips, Physical Traces Associ-
    ated with UFO Sightings (Evanston:
    Center for UFO Studies, 1975), p.19.
-UFO (NL)
  1967, July/L.A. Boeschen
    "Red Object Seen at Stover," Skylook,
    no.3 (Nov.1967):3.
  1969, Aug.31/Hwy.135
    "UFO Scares Turkeys," Skylook, no.
    23 (Oct.1969):5.
  1969, Oct.18/Victor Smith/Hwy.52 x 135
    "Strange Object Seen in Stover, Mo.,"
    Skylook, no.24 (Nov.1969):6.
  1972, Dec.2/Dorothy Ingersoll/1 mi.S
    "Bar-Shaped Object Seen over Stover,

Mo.," Skylook, no.62 (Jan.1973):11.

Strafford
-UFO (NL)
  1939, Oct.15/Paul Murrell/=balloon?
    Springfield News & Leader, 22 Oct.
    1939.

Sullivan
-UFO (?)
  1974, Feb./Gordon Matlock
    John Magor, Our UFO Visitors (Seat-
    tle: Hancock House, 1977), p.24.

Sweet Springs
-UFO (DD)
  1971, July 12
    "Saucer with Streamers Observed in
    Missouri," Skylook, no.46 (Sep.
    1971):5.

Taney co.
-Ghost
  n.d./Lou Beardon
    Tom Moore, Mysterious Tales and Leg-
    ends of the Ozarks (Philadelphia:
    Dorrance, 1938), pp.116-21.
    Vance Randolph, Ozark Superstitions
    (N.Y.: Columbia Univ., 1947), pp.
    215-16.
-Phantom dog
  ca.1900/Lewis Blair
    Vance Randolph, Ozark Superstitions
    (N.Y.: Columbia Univ., 1947), p.225.

Taskee
-Haunt
  n.d.
    Vance Randolph, Ozark Ghost Stories
    (Girard, Kan.: Haldeman-Julius,
    1944), pp.9-10.

Thayer
-UFO (?)
  1967, Oct.20
    "Objects Seen at Thayer," Skylook,
    no.3 (Nov.1967):4.

Tipton
-UFO (CE-1)
  1967, spring
    "Two See Beam of Green Light," Sky-
    look, no.50 (Jan.1972):13.

Troy
-UFO (NL)
  1965, Nov./Mrs. G.C. Henry/N of town
    "Moving Object Seen over Wheat Field,"
    Skylook, no.45 (Aug.1971):14.
  1972, Oct.17/Erna Stiner/Hwy.1
    "Troy Woman Reports Sighting to Study
    Group Director," Skylook, no.61
    (Dec.1972):5.

Tuscumbia
-UFO (DD)
  1967, Nov.24
    Ted Phillips, "UFO Events in Missouri
    1857-1971," FSR Case Histories, no.
    8 (Dec.1971):9-10.

Union
-UFO (CE-2)
  1972/ground markings only
    Ted Phillips, Physical Traces Associ-
    ated with UFO Sightings (Evanston:
    Center for UFO Studies, 1975), p.80.
  1978, July 27/Clora Winscher/E on Hwy.
  50
    St. Louis Globe-Democrat, 28-29 July
    1978.
    Washington Citizen, 29 July 1978.
    "UFOs of Limited Merit," Int'l UFO
    Reporter 3 (Sep.1978):7. il.
-UFO (NL)
  1978, July 26/Jeannie Carter
  1978, July 27/Velma Clines
    St. Louis Globe-Democrat, 28-29 July
    1978.

University City
-UFO (NL)
  1947, July 7/Floyd Emert
    St. Louis Post-Dispatch, 8 July 1947.

Versailles
-UFO (CE-1)
  1967, Oct.14
    "UFO over Wheat Field," Skylook, no.
    5 (Jan.1968):7.
-UFO (NL)
  1971, Feb.6
    "Moving Object Observed over Ver-
    sailles, Mo., Feb.6, 1971," Skylook,
    no.40 (Mar.1971):15.

Wallace
-UFO (NL)
  1947, July 6/C.D. Frank/E of town
    Kansas City Times, 7 July 1947.

Warrensburg
-Mathematical prodigy
  1880s-1890s/Reub Field
    N.T. Allison, "Another Mathematical
    Prodigy," Sci.Am. 66 (1892):276.
    Walter F. Prince, "Reub. Field, Math-
    ematical Prodigy," J.ASPR 14 (1920)
    :232-41.
-UFO (CE-2)
  1957, June
    J. Allen Hynek, The UFO Experience
    (Chicago: Regnery, 1972), p.240.
-UFO (NL)
  1970, Oct.5/Mrs. Hubert Paul/323 Chris-
  topher/=barium cloud?
    "Yellow-Orange Object Seen at War-
    rensburg and Knob Noster, Mo.," Sky-
    look, no.36 (Nov.1970):7.
    "Missouri Sightings of Oct.14 Be-
    lieved to Be Barium Cloud," Skylook,
    no.37 (Dec.1970):8.

Warrenton
-UFO (NL)
  1969, Nov./Leonard Rifkin/nr. I-70
    "Another Deer Hunter Sights UFO,"
    Skylook, no.45 (Aug.1971):17.

Warsaw
-UFO (?)

1973, Jan./=balloon
"UFO Hoax in Missouri," Skylook, no.
63 (Feb.1973):12.

Washington
-UFO (NL)
1978, July 27/Second x Stafford St.
Washington Citizen, 29 July 1978.

Webb City
-UFO (?)
1969, Jan.2/=Venus?
"UFO or Venus?" Skylook, no.15 (Feb.
1969):1.
-UFO (NL)
1968, Aug.4/W nr. U.S.171
"Cops Spot Crescent in Mo.," APRO
Bull. 17 (July-Aug.1968):8.

Webster Groves
-Haunt
1955-1966/Mrs. S.L. Furry
Hans Holzer, Gothic Ghosts (N.Y.:
Pocket Books, 1972), pp.65-76.
-UFO (NL)
1965, July 4/W.J. Treme
"More on an Earlier Report," Skylook,
no.37 (Dec.1970):9.

Weldon Springs
-UFO (NL)
1959
J. Allen Hynek, The Hynek UFO Report
(N.Y.: Dell, 1977), pp.80-82.

Wellston
-Phantom image
1972, May/France Roques
(Letter), Fate 25 (Oct.1972):145.

Wellsville
-Lightning anomaly
1886, Aug./Rev. Moore
St. Louis Chronicle, 24 Nov.1894.
-UFO (NL)
1897, April 15/S.S. Kettle
Columbus (O.) Evening Press, 17 Apr.
1897.

Wentzville
-Cattle mutilation
1978, June/Clete Parr
St. Louis Post-Dispatch, 24 June 1978.
St. Louis Globe-Democrat, 25 June
1978.

Weston
-UFO (CE-1)
1967, Feb.16/E on Hwy.P
Ted Phillips, Jr., "Missouri Man Re-
ports 1967 Sighting," Skylook, no.
33 (Aug.1970):3.
-UFO (NL)
1961, summer
"It Happened in 1961," Skylook, no.31
(June 1970):10.

West Plains
-Healing
n.d.

Vance Randolph, Ozark Superstitions
(N.Y.: Columbia Univ., 1947), pp.
122-23.
-Water anomaly
1953, Dec.26-1954, April/Aids Dep't
Store
(Editorial), Fate 7 (Oct.1954):11-12.

Wilder
-Flying child
1956/R.E. Lee
(Editorial), Fate 9 (Sep.1956):10.

Willard
-Ancient inscription
Gloria Farley, "The Willard Stone,"
Occ.Pub.Epigraphic Soc'y 5, no.101
(Sep.1977):20. il.

Willow Springs
-Flying horses
1913/=meteor procession?
(Letter), Kenneth O. Baldwin, Fate
22 (Jan.1969):133-34.

Winona
-Gravity anomaly
1950s/Thomas O'Bannon/1½ mi.E
(Letter), June E. Weidemann, Fate
11 (Mar.1958):126-27.
-UFO (?)
1957, June 28/Thomas O'Bannon/1½ mi.E
(Editorial), Fate 11 (May 1958):17.
il.

Winston
-UFO (NL)
1976, July 22
"Sighting Reports," CUFOS News Bull.,
Sep.1976, p.6.

B. Physical Features

Adam-Ondi-Ahman
-Ghost light
n.d./nr. Mill Port
Earl A. Collins, Folk Tales of Missouri (Boston: Christopher, 1935),
pp.97-99.

Back Creek
-Haunt
n.d./nr. Hwy.61
Vance Randolph, Ozark Superstitions
(N.Y.: Columbia Univ., 1947), p.229.

Big Moniteau Bluff
-Pictographs
Richard S. Brownlee, "The Big Moni-
teau Bluff Pictographs in Boone
County, Missouri," Missouri Arch.
18, no.4 (1956):49-54. il.

Black R.
-UFO (NL)
1973, April 13/Harley D. Rutledge
Jerome Clark, "The Brushy Creek UFO
Scare," Fate 27 (May 1974):96,105.
Steve Erdmann, "The Distortion Fac-

tor," <u>Probe the Unknown</u> 2 (spring 1974):4̄2,47.

Wendelle C. Stevens, "UFO Tracks in the Sky," <u>Saga UFO Rept.</u> 2 (fall 1975):23,2̄5,52.

Boeuf Creek
-UFO (CE-1)
1971, April 15/Joel J. Hassler/3 mi.E on Hwy.100
"'Camera' on Boom Extends from UFO," <u>Skylook</u>, no.45 (Aug.1971):6.

Breadtray Mt.
-Haunt
Branson <u>White River Leader</u>, 11 Jan. 1934.
Earl A. Collins, <u>Folk Tales of Missouri</u> (Boston: Christopher, 1935), pp.99-101.
Tom Moore, <u>Mysterious Tales and Legends of the Ozarks</u> (Philadelphia: Dorrance, 1938), pp.8-13.
Otto Rayburn, <u>Ozark Country</u> (N.Y.: Duell, Sloan & Pearce, 1941), pp. 304-305.
Vance Randolph, <u>Ozark Ghost Stories</u> (Girard, Kan.: Haldeman-Julius, 1944), pp.7-8.

Brushy Creek
-Humanoid
1971, Dec./Reggie Bone
Jerome Clark, "The Brushy Creek UFO Scare," <u>Fate</u> 27 (May 1974):96,105-106.
-UFO (NL)
1973, Feb.21/Reggie Bone
1973, Feb.22/Roy Burch
1973, March 1, 14/Earl Turnbough
"The Piedmont, Missouri, Mess," <u>APRO Bull.</u> 21 (Mar.-Apr.1973):1,3.
Jerome Clark, "The Brushy Creek UFO Scare," <u>Fate</u> 27 (May 1974):96-98, 100-101.
Steve Erdmann, "The Distortion Factor," <u>Probe the Unknown</u> 2 (spring 1974):4̄2-44.

Clearwater Dam
-UFO (CE-2)
1973, March 28?/Margorie Cundiff
"The Piedmont, Missouri, Mess," <u>APRO Bull.</u> 21 (Mar.-Apr.1973):1,3.
-UFO (DD)
1973, March 25/Margorie Cundiff
"The Piedmont, Missouri, Mess," <u>APRO Bull.</u> 21 (Mar.-Apr.1973):1,3.
-UFO (NL)
1973, March 21/Jean Coleman
Jerome Clark, "The Brushy Creek UFO Scare," <u>Fate</u> 27 (May 1974):96,101-102.
Steve Erdmann, "The Distortion Factor," <u>Probe the Unknown</u> 2 (spring 1974):4̄2,45.

Creve Coeur, L.
-Lake monster
n.d.

Charles M. Skinner, <u>Myths and Legends of Our Own Land</u>, 2 vols. (Philadelphia: Lippincott, 1896), 1:180-82.
Earl A. Collins, <u>Folk Tales of Missouri</u> (Boston: Christopher, 1935), pp.1̄13-14.

Crooked Creek
-Meteorite crater
5000 m.diam./certain
V.H. Hughes, "Reconnaissance Work," <u>Biennial Rept.Missouri Bur.Geol.& Mines</u>, 1909-10, 1911.
E.E. Hendricks, "The Geology of the Steelville Quadrangle, Missouri," <u>Missouri Geol.Survey & Water Resources</u>, ser.2, vol.36 (1954).
F.G. Snyder, et al., "Cryptoexplosive Structures in Missouri," <u>Rept. Investigations Missouri Geol.Survey & Water Resources</u>, no.30 (1965), pp. 35-37,68-71.

Cuivre R.
-Humanoid
1972, June 30
Brad Steiger, <u>Mysteries of Time and Space</u> (N.Y.: Dell, 1976 ed.), pp. 111-12.

Current R.
-Retrocognition
1941, fall/Leonard Hall
Leonard Hall, "Glimpses of the Past on Current River," <u>Fate</u> 10 (Sep. 1957):95-98.

Delbridge Ridge
-UFO (NL)
1969, Oct.19/John Chaklos
"Old Year Goes Out with Many Missouri UFO Reports Coming In," <u>Skylook</u>, no.26 (Jan.1970):2,4.

Gasconade R.
-Ancient iron axes and hammers
"New Findings of Pre-Columbian Contacts with North America," <u>NEARA Newsl.</u> 9 (spring 1974):9.

Graham Cave
-Archeological site
8000-4000 B.C.
Wilfred D. Logan, "Graham Cave: An Archaic Site in Montgomery County, Missouri," <u>Mem.Missouri Arch.Soc'y</u>, no.2 (1952). il.
Walter E. Klippel, "Graham Cave Revisited: A Re-Evaluation of Its Cultural Position During the Archaic Period," <u>Mem.Missouri Arch.Soc'y</u>, no.9 (1971).
Franklin Folsom, <u>America's Ancient Treasures</u> (N.Y.: Rand McNally, 1974), p.146.

Grand R.
-Archeological site
ca.13,000 B.C.-1100 A.D./Shriver site
Michael J. Reagan, "Flake Tools

Stratified Below Paleo-Indian Artifacts," Science 200 (1978):1272-75.
il.

Jacob's Cavern
-Archeological site
Charles Peabody & W.K. Moorehead,
"The Exploration of Jacobs Cavern,
McDonald County, Missouri," Bull.
Phillips Acad.Dep't Arch., no.1
(1904).
J.L.B. Taylor, "Did the Indian Know
the Mastodon?" Nat.History 21 (1921)
:591-97. il.
Vernon C. Allison, "The Antiquity of
the Deposits in Jacob's Cavern,"
Anthro.Pap.Am.Mus.Nat.Hist. 19
(1926):292-335. il.
N.C. Nelson, "The Jacobs Cavern Mas-
todon Again," Science 66 (1927):
258-59.
Jay L.B. Taylor, "Again: The 'Masto-
don Bone,'" Am.Anthro. 49 (1947):
689-95.

Lake of the Ozarks
-Ancient sculpture
1932/=stone head
New York Times, 2 Oct.1932, sec.2,
p.6.
-Haunt
n.d./Glaize Park
Vance Randolph, Ozark Superstitions
(N.Y.: Columbia Univ., 1947), p.219.
-Lake monster
1935
Vance Randolph, Ozark Superstitions
(N.Y.: Columbia Univ., 1947), p.219.
Jim Brandon, Weird America (N.Y.:
Dutton, 1978), p.120.
-UFO (?)
1970, April 26/=comet
"Oval Shaped Object Seen in Missouri
Sky," Skylook, no.31 (June 1970):4.
"UFO Becomes IFI," Skylook, no.32
(July 1970):15.
-UFO (NL)
1952
Ted Phillips, "UFO Events in Missouri
1857-1971," FSR Case Histories, no.
8 (Dec.1971):9.
1965, Dec./Lowell Reed
"Dogs Refuse to Hunt after Bright
Light in Sky," Skylook, no.39 (Feb.
1971):8.
1970, April 26
"Oval Shaped Object Seen in Missouri
Sky," Skylook, no.31 (June 1970):4.
1973, Oct.16
Ted Phillips, "Summary of UFO Reports
in Missouri During 1973," Skylook,
no.74 (Jan.1974):13.

Little Creek
-UFO (NL)
1925, Dec.23, 26/A.J. Graves/cemetery
Vance Randolph, Ozark Ghost Stories
(Girard, Kan.: Haldeman-Julius,
1944), p.21.

Lotawana L.
-UFO (DD)
1947, July 6/David S. Long, Jr.
Kansas City Star, 7 July 1947.

Missouri R.
-Giant human skeletons
1875
Phyla Phillips, "Giants in Ancient
America," Fate 1 (spring 1948):126,
128.

Nigger Wool Swamps
-Humanoid and cattle mutilations
1940s
John A. Keel, Strange Creatures from
Time and Space (Greenwich, Ct.: Faw-
cett, 1970), p.111.

Osage R.
-UFO (CE-1)
1902
"They Were Around in 1902!" Skylook,
no.63 (Feb.1973):8.

Ozark Mts.
-Hex
n.d.
(Letter), Vance Randolph, Life, 19
June 1939, pp.82-83. il.
-UFO (CE-1)
1968, Nov.11
"Large UFO Seen in Missouri Ozarks,"
Skylook, no.14 (Jan.1969):3.

Piney Ridge
-Humanoid and sheep killings
1947, Oct./Glenn Payne
John Green, The Sasquatch File (Agassiz, B.C.: Cheam, 1973), p.17.

Roaring River State Park
-UFO (CE-2)
1966, Nov.22
Ted Phillips, Physical Traces Associ-
ated with UFO Sightings (Evanston:
Center for UFO Studies, 1975), p.44.

Sandy Creek
-Ancient inscription
ca.1955/Frank Magre
Gloria Farley, "Inscriptions from
Mid-America," Occ.Pub.Epigraphic
Soc'y 3, no.69 (Sep.1976):10. il.
-Cattle mutilation
1975, Jan.25
Elsberry Democrat, 22 June 1978.

Swan L.
-UFO (?)
1971, Oct.31/Raymond Huffman
"Triangular Objects over Swan Lake,
Mo.," Skylook, no.50 (Jan.1972):13.

Tip Top Mts.
-UFO (NL)
1973, Feb.26/Pat Toney
Jerome Clark, "The Brushy Creek UFO
Scare," Fate 27 (May 1974):96,100.

Towosahgy State Park
-Archeological site
  ca.900 A.D.
    Franklin Folsom, America's Ancient
    Treasures (N.Y.: Rand McNally,
    1974), p.147.
    Michael D. Southard, "A Cache of Ag-
    ricultural Implements from Towosah-
    gy State Archaeological Site," Newsl.
    Missouri Arch.Soc'y, no.300 (1976):
    1-4. il.

Van Meter State Park
-Archeological site
  Utz site
    Federal Writers Program, Missouri: A
    Guide to the "Show Me" State (N.Y.:
    Hastings House, 1959), p.30.
    Phil P. Betancourt, "A Description
    of Certain Engraved Artifacts from
    Utz Oneota Site," Plains Anthro. 10
    (1965):256-70. il.
    Franklin Folsom, America's Ancient
    Treasures (N.Y.: Rand McNally,
    1974), p.147.

Washington State Park
-Petroglyphs
  1000-1600
    Eugene H. Diesing, "Archaeological
    Features in and around Washington
    State Park in Washington and Jeffer-
    son Counties, Missouri," Missouri
    Arch. 17 (1955):2-23. il.
    Franklin Folsom, America's Ancient
    Treasures (N.Y.: Rand McNally,
    1974), p.148.

Weaubleau Creek
-Stratigraphic anomaly
    T.R. Beveridge, "The Geology of the
    Weaubleau Creek Area, Missouri,"
    Missouri Geol.Survey & Water Re-
    sources, ser.2, vol.32 (1951).
    F.G. Snyder, et al., "Cryptoexplo-
    sive Structures in Missouri," Rept.
    Investigations Missouri Geol.Survey
    & Water Resources, no.30 (1965),
    pp.54-57.

White R.
-Ghost
  1915/Tomp Turner/Hwy.13
    Vance Randolph, Ozark Superstitions
    (N.Y.: Columbia Univ., 1947), p.228.

D. Unspecified Localities

-Giant bird
  1882, March/Thomas Campbell
  New York Times, 29 Mar.1882, p.4.

-Phantom panthers
  n.d./SW sector
    Earl A. Collins, Folk Tales of Mis-
    souri (Boston: Christopher, 1935),
    pp.121-23.

-UFO (DD)

1977, Oct.3
  "Old Sighting Department," APRO Bull.
  27 (Sep.1978):5-6.

IOWA

A. Populated Places

Ackworth
-UFO (CE-2)
    1973, June 27/Duane Woodruff/E of town
        Des Moines Register, 28 June 1973.
        il.
        "'Chopped Off' Corn," Pursuit 6 (July
        1973):59-60. il.

Albia
-UFO (NL)
    1897, April 3
        Chicago (Ill.) Tribune, 4 Apr.1897,
        p.4.
    1897, April 10
        Chicago (Ill.) Tribune, 11 Apr.1897.

Algona
-Fall of nails
    n.d./Hans Swenson
        (Letter), W.H. Cronkhite, Fate 10
        (Nov.1957):124.
-UFO (CE-1)
    1975, Dec.24
        "Noteworthy UFO Sightings," Ufology
        2 (spring 1976):42.

Alta
-Auroral anomaly
    1902, March 29/David E. Hadden
        David E. Hadden, "Auroral Phenomena
        at Alta, Iowa," Pop.Astron. 10
        (1902):249-51.

Ames
-Dog mutilation
    1978, winter
        Kansas City (Mo.) Times, 10 Apr.1978,
        p.4A.
-UFO (NL)
    1897, April 10-11
        Ames Intelligencer, 15 Apr.1897.

Anita
-UFO (NL)
    1955, June 15
        Jacques Vallee, Anatomy of a Phenom-
        enon (N.Y.: Ace, 1965 ed.), p.144.

Asbury
-UFO (NL)
    1972, Aug.23/Leslie Avery
        Ralph DeGraw, "Iowa Report," Skylook,
        no.62 (Jan.1973):12, quoting Du-
        buque Telegraph-Herald (undated).

Balltown
-UFO (NL)
    1970, March 22/Lavern Duehr
        "Iowa Family Reports UFO," Skylook,
        no.30 (May 1970):2, quoting Capper's
        Weekly, 31 Mar.1970.

Bayard
-UFO (NL)
    1897, April 10
        Marshalltown Times-Republican, 13
        Apr.1897.

Belle Plaine
-UFO (CE-3)
    1897, April 15
        Chicago (Ill.) Times-Herald, 16 Apr.
        1897, p.1.

Bellevue
-Coffin anomaly
    1975
        (Editorial), Fate 29 (Feb.1976):32-
        33.

Bennett
-UFO (CE-2)
    1964, Aug.30/Connie Thies/Hwy.150
        Curtis Fuller, "Collected UFO Sight-
        ings for August and September,"
        Fate 18 (Jan.1965):35,37-38.

Birmingham
-UFO (CE-3)
    1897, April 16
        New York Herald, 17 Apr.1897.

Boone
-UFO (CE-2)
    1972, July 15?/Lesley Poling
        "Those Iowa Craters," APRO Bull. 21
        (July-Aug.1972):1,4-5.
        Kevin D. Randle, "The Iowa UFO Land-
        ings," Official UFO 1 (Aug.1975):40-
        43. il.
-UFO (DD)
    1947, July 3/Mr. Otis
        "You Asked for It," Doubt, no.24
        (1949):363.
-UFO (NL)
    1967, March 8/Mrs. L.E. Koppenhaver
        Boone News-Republican, 10 Mar.1967.

Bradgate
-Humanoid
    1978, Sep.24/=farm implement
        Des Moines Register, 1 Oct.1978.

Britt
-UFO (NL)
    1897, April 9
        Marshalltown Times-Republican, 13
        Apr.1897.

Brooklyn
-UFO (CE-2)
    1973, Feb.23/Mrs. Frank Benesh
        Des Moines Register, 25 Feb.1973.
-UFO (NL)
    1897, April 10
        Marshalltown Times-Republican, 13

Apr.1897.

Burlington
-Phantom insect
  1899, July 17/William F. Schneelock
    Chicago (Ill.) Tribune, 18 July 1899,
    p.2.
-UFO (?)
  1897, April 10/James Dunn/=balloon
    Burlington Hawk-Eye, 11 Apr.1897.
    Des Moines Leader, 11 Apr.1897, p.3.
-UFO (DD)
  1977, Sep.28
    "UFOs of Limited Merit," Int'l UFO
    Reporter 2 (Nov.1977):3.
-UFO (NL)
  1967, March 8/Homer Dickson/Dam 18
    John A. Keel, UFOs: Operation Trojan
    Horse (N.Y.: Putnam, 1970), p.25,
    quoting Burlington newspaper, 9 Mar.
    1967.

Burroak
-UFO (DD)
  1972, June 17/U.S.52/=blimp?
    "Dome-Shaped Object Follows Car,"
    Skylook, no.58 (Sep.1972):14.
    "Dome-Shaped Object May Have Been
    Blimp," Skylook, no.59 (Oct.1972):4.

Calmar
-Ghost
  1868, fall/J.A. Weaver
    "A Collective Apparition," J.ASPR 12
    (1918):450-53.
-UFO (NL)
  1978, Feb.7/Gary Linnevold
    "Policeman Loses Job over UFO Chase,"
    Int'l UFO Reporter 3 (July 1978):8-
    9.

Carson
-Precognition
  1969, March/Lynn Frank/Graybill Creek
    "ESP at Work," Fate 26 (Sep.1973):58.

Cascade
-UFO (NL)
  1953, Oct.24
    Donald E. Keyhoe, Flying Saucer Con-
    spiracy (N.Y.: Holt, 1955), p.79.

Cedar Falls
-UFO (CE-1)
  1969, Hune 4/George Mazenska
    Rufus Drake, "Return of the 'Men in
    Black,'" Saga UFO Rept. 3 (Oct.1976)
    :36,54.
  1973, Oct.22/Goldie Fox/4 mi.E on Hwy.
    57
    "Two Reports of Strange Lights Sent
    from Fayette County, Iowa," Skylook,
    no.78 (May 1974):20.
-UFO (NL)
  1897, April 5
  1897, April 12
    Minneapolis (Minn.) Journal, 13 Apr.
    1897.

Cedar Rapids
-Mystery radio transmission and UFO (NL)
  1956
    Brad Steiger, Revelation: The Divine
    Fire (Englewood Cliffs, N.J.: Pren-
    tice-Hall, 1973), pp.140-41.
-UFO (?)
  1969, June 5/=meteor
    Philip J. Klass, UFOs Explained (N.Y.:
    Random House, 1974), pp.46-47.
-UFO (DD)
  1947, June 19/R.D. Taylor
    Des Moines Register, 8 July 1947.
  1947, June 23
    Richard Hall, ed., The UFO Evidence
    (Washington: NICAP, 1964), pp.14,
    152.
-UFO (NL)
  1897, April 8
    Chicago (Ill.) Times-Herald, 9 Apr.
    1897.
    Burlington Hawk-Eye, 10 Apr.1897.
  1897, April 10
    Omaha (Nebr.) Bee, 11 Apr.1897, p.6.
  1976, Nov.15
    "UFOs of Limited Merit," Int'l UFO
    Reporter 2 (Jan.1977):5.

Centerville
-UFO (NL)
  1897, April 8
    Marshalltown Statesman-Press, 13
    Apr.1897.

Charles City
-Clairvoyance
  1963, winter/Sherman Lee Pompey/N of
  town
    (Letter), Fate 20 (June 1967):122-25.
-UFO (NL)
  1979, Jan.21/Bethel Osier/N. Jackson
  St.
    Charles City Press, 24 Jan.1979.

Cherokee
-Archeological site
  4000-2000 B.C.
    Duane C. Anderson & Richard Shutler,
    Jr., "The Cherokee Sewer Site (13
    CK 405): A Summary and Assessment,"
    Plains Anthro. 23 (1978):132-39. il.

Clarence
-Fall of pebbles
  1962, Aug.16-17/Henry Hasenbank
    (Editorial), Fate 16 (Jan.1963):6-8.
    (Letter), Milton H. Nothdurft, Fate
    16 (Nov.1963):116-18.
    Raymond Bayless, The Enigma of the
    Poltergeist (N.Y.: Ace, 1967 ed.),
    pp.52-56.
-UFO (CE-3)
  1897, April 11/I. Nelson/=hoax?
    Cumberland (Wisc.) Advocate, 15 Apr.
    1897, quoting Chicago (Ill.) Record
    (undated).

Clarinda
-UFO (CE-2)
  1966, April 23

Ted Phillips, Physical Traces Associated with UFO Sightings (Evanston:
Center for UFO Studies, 1975), p.41.

Clarion
-Humanoid
1978, Oct.3/Le Ann Tonderum/=hoax?
Fort Dodge Messenger, 28 Oct.1978.
Des Moines Register, 12 Nov.1978.
Mark A. Hall, "Stories of 'Bigfoot'
in Iowa During 1978 As Drawn from
Newspaper Sources," Minnesota Arch.
38, no.1 (1979):3-17.
-UFO (CE-2)
1973, July 10, 18/Howard Groves/ground
markings only
Ted Phillips, Physical Traces Associated with UFO Sightings (Evanston:
Center for UFO Studies, 1975), p.91,
quoting Des Moines Register (undated).
Kevin D. Randle, "The Iowa UFO Landings," Official UFO 1 (Aug.1975):
40,43,62-63. il.
-UFO (DD)
1947, June 29/Dale Bays
Jacques Vallee, Anatomy of a Phenomenon (N.Y.: Ace, 1965 ed.), p.91.
Ted Bloecher, Report on the UFO Wave
of 1947 (Washington: NICAP, 1967),
Appendix, Case 112.

Clayton co.
-UFO (CE-3)
1969, spring
Ted Phillips, Physical Traces Associated with UFO Sightings (Evanston:
Center for UFO Studies, 1975), p.64,
quoting Saucers Space & Sci., no.
61 (1971).
Brad Steiger, Mysteries of Time and
Space (N.Y.: Dell, 1976 ed.), pp.
129-31.

Cleona twp.
-Ancient inscriptions
1877
Jacob Gass, "Description of Some Inscribed Stones Found in Cleona Township, Scott County, Iowa," Proc.
Davenport Acad.Nat.Sci. 2 (1877):
142.
Jacob Gass, "Inscribed Rocks in Cleona Township," Proc.Davenport Acad.
Nat.Sci. 2 (1877):172-73.

Clinton
-Haunt
1971
Brad Steiger, Irene Hughes on Psychic
Safari (N.Y.: Warner, 1972), pp.79-
84.
-Phantom airplane
1956, Dec.20
Davenport Morning Democrat, 21 Dec.
1956.
(Editorial), Fate 10 (May 1957):13.
-UFO (CE-1)
1975, July 2
"UFO Central," CUFOS News Bull., 15

Nov.1975, p.12.
-UFO (NL)
1897, April 9
Marshalltown Statesman-Press, 13
Apr.1897.
1964, July 20/7 mi.W on U.S.30
Thomas M. Olsen, ed., The Reference
for Outstanding UFO Sighting Reports
(Riderwood, Md.: UFO Information Retrieval Center, 1966), p.101.
n.d./Mrs. Harold Cox
(Letter), Saga UFO Rept. 6 (Oct.
1978):8.

Coggon
-UFO (DD)
1951, summer
Harold T. Wilkins, Flying Saucers on
the Attack (N.Y.: Ace, 1967 ed.),
p.140.

Columbus Junction
-Haunt
1970
Brad Steiger, Irene Hughes on Psychic
Safari (N.Y.: Warner, 1972), pp.85-
95.
-Phantom panther tracks
1947, Jan.3
"More Critters," Doubt, no.18 (1947)
:273,274.

Council Bluffs
-Fall of metallic object
1977, Dec.17/nr. Big Lake Park
Council Bluffs Nonpareil, 18 Dec.
1977.
Omaha (Nebr.) World-Herald, 21 Dec.
1977.
Sebi Breci, "Something Fell Out of
the Sky," Fate 32 (Mar.1979):70-74.
il.
1978, July 5/McGee Ave. x Harrison St.
1978, July 10/3d St. x High School Ave.
Omaha (Nebr.) World-Herald, 11 July
1978.
-Phantom panther tracks
1978, June/Lou Keister/trailer park
Hutchinson (Kan.) News, 3 July 1978.
-Skyquake
1894, Nov.27/=meteorite?
New York Times, 29 Nov.1894, p.16.
-UFO (CE-2)
1976, July 31/Debbie Focken/Eldon's
Standard Service Station
"Gas Station Damaged by UFO?" Int'l
UFO Reporter 1 (Dec.1976):13.
"Council Bluffs CEII," Int'l UFO Re-
porter 2 (Mar.1977):7.

Creston
-UFO (NL)
1969, March 9/Ada Vanderpluijm/Lone
Star Corner
Creston News-Advertiser, 10 Mar.1969.

Crystal Lake
-UFO (NL)
1975, Sep.9
"UFO Central," CUFOS News Bull., 15

Nov.1975, p.18.

Danville
-UFO (CE-1)
  1966, fall/T.W. Van Winkel
    "UFO Reports from Iowa," Skylook, no.
    31 (June 1970):11.

Davenport
-Ancient inscription and elephant carvings
  1874-1878/Jacob Gass/=hoax?
    Jacob Gass, "A Connected Account of
    the Explorations of Mound No.3,
    Cook's Farm Group," Proc.Davenport
    Acad.Nat.Sci. 2 (1877):92-98. il.
    R.J. Farquharson, "On the Inscribed
    Tablets, Found by Rev. J. Gass in
    a Mound near Davenport, Iowa," Proc.
    Davenport Acad.Nat.Sci. 2 (1877):
    103-15.
    Charles E. Harrison, "Exploration of
    Mound No.11 Cook's Farm Group, and
    Discovery of an Inscribed Tablet of
    Limestone," Proc.Davenport Acad.Nat.
    Sci. 2 (1878):221-24. il.
    "Elephant and Bear Pipes Exhibited,"
    Proc.Davenport Acad.Nat.Sci. 2
    (1878):348-49. il.
    G. Seyffarth, "The Indian Inhabitants
    of Davenport, Iowa," Proc.Davenport
    Acad.Nat.Sci. 3 (1879):72-80. il.
    John T. Short, North Americans of
    Antiquity (N.Y.: Harper, 1880), pp.
    37-40. il.
    Henry W. Henshaw, "Animal Carvings
    from Mounds of the Mississippi Val-
    ley," Ann.Rept.Bur.Am.Ethn. 2 (1882)
    :117-66.
    Charles E. Putnam, "Elephant Pipes
    and Inscribed Tablets," Proc.Daven-
    port Acad.Nat.Sci. 4 (1885):253-
    347. il.
    Stephen D. Peet, "The Mound-Builders
    and the Mastodon," Am.Antiquarian
    14 (1892):72-74. il.
    Marshall McKusick, The Davenport Con-
    spiracy (Iowa City: Univ. of Iowa,
    1970). il.
    Marjorie Kling, "The Davenport For-
    geries Problem," NEARA Newsl. 5
    (June 1970):29-33. il.
    Barry Fell, America B.C. (N.Y.: Quad-
    rangle, 1976), pp.162,180,188,261-
    69,272-74. il.
-Animal ESP
  1957/Jane Duggan
    (Editorial), Fate 10 (Dec.1957):18-
    19.
    Rhea A. White, "The Investigation of
    Behavior Suggestive of ESP in Dogs,"
    J.ASPR 58 (1964):250,265-77.
-Fall of radioactive blue rain
  1954, April 8
    "Colored Rain--Snow," Doubt, no.45
    (1954):289.
    (Editorial), Fate 7 (Oct.1954):14.
-Haunt
  1972, May/Pi Kappa Chi Fraternity
    Brad Steiger, "1972: A Bumper Year

for Hauntings," Beyond Reality, no.
4 (May 1973):15-16, quoting Davenport Times-Democrat (Undated).
-UFO (?)
  1954, June
    Donald E. Keyhoe, Flying Saucer Con-
    spiracy (N.Y.: Holt, 1955), p.166.
-UFO (NL)
  1897, April 12
    Davenport Sunday Democrat, 13 Apr.
    1897.
  1976, April 29
    "Noteworthy UFO Sightings," Ufology
    2 (fall 1976):60.

Dean
-Humanoid
  1978, Aug.28/Dean Bottoms
    Des Moines Register, 12 Nov.1978.

Decorah
-Cave anomaly
    N.M. Lowe, "Paradoxical Phenomena in
    Ice-Caves," J.Science 16 (1879):
    524-26. il.
-Contactee
  1960s-   /W. John Weilgart/100 Elm
  Court
    W. John Weilgart, aUI: The Language
    of Space (Decorah: Cosmic Communi-
    cations, 1962).
    Glenn McWane & David Graham, The New
    UFO Sightings (N.Y.: Warner, 1974),
    pp.149-57.
    W. John Weilgart, Cosmic Elements of
    Meaning (Decorah: Cosmic Communica-
    tions, 1975).
    W. John Weilgart, Cosmic Logo-Therapy
    (Decorah: Cosmic Commuincations,
    1977).
-UFO (NL)
  1968, May/Marilyn Olson
    Brad Steiger, Mysteries of Time and
    Space (N.Y.: Dell, 1976 ed.), pp.
    202-203.

Deloit
-UFO (CE-2)
  1969, July/Eldridge Winey/ground markings only
    Denison Review, 3 July 1969.

Denison
-Humanoid
  1960s/Barry Bergamo/Midwestern College
    John Green, The Sasquatch File (Ag-
    assiz, B.C.: Cheam, 1973), p.32.

Des Moines
-Fall of pebbles
  1955, April 23/Barbara Kephart/Roose-
  velt Shopping Center
    Des Moines Register, 24 Apr.1955. il.
-Reincarnation
  n.d./George Emery/Spiritual Consultants
    Eileen Sonin, More Canadian Ghosts
    (Richmond Hill, Ont.: Pocket Books,
    1974 ed.), p.124.
-UFO (?)
  1959, May 14

Richard Hall, ed., The UFO Evidence
(Washington: NICAP, 1964), p.151,
quoting AP release, 15 May 1959.
-UFO (DD)
1947, July 7/Merle Steffenson/F.M. Hubbell Ave.
Des Moines Register, 8 July 1947.
-UFO (NL)
1897, April 9
Marshalltown Statesman-Press, 13
Apr.1897.
1949, April 7/Mr. Ahern
Harold T. Wilkins, Flying Saucers on
the Attack (N.Y.: Ace, 1967 ed.),
pp.109-10.
1961, Jan.6/airport
"Odds and Ends," APRO Bull. 9 (Jan.
1961):5,6.

Dows
-UFO (NL)
1970, March 7/golf course
Clarion Wright County Monitor, 12
Mar.1970.

Dubuque
-Fall of frogs
1882, June 16/Novelty Iron Works
"Hail," Monthly Weather Rev. 10
(June 1882):14.
-UFO (CE-1)
1967, Oct.12
"The States," APRO Bull. 16 (Sep.-
Oct.1967):10.
-UFO (DD)
1960, March 4/Charles R. Morris
Richard Hall, ed., The UFO Evidence
(Washington: NICAP, 1964), p.40.
Lloyd Mallan, "Complete Directory of
UFOs: Part I," Sci.& Mech. 37 (Dec.
1966):36,38.
ca.1965, Feb./Fred Kammiller/Fairmont
Farms
"Bubbles, Bubbling, Et Cetera," INFO
J., no.9 (fall 1972):31,32.
-UFO (NL)
1897, April 10
Chicago (Ill.) Times-Herald, 12 Apr.
1897, p.1.
1969, Feb.13
"U.S. Roundup," APRO Bull. 17 (Mar.-
Apr.1969):7.
1972, Aug.22/Brian Downey
Ralph DeGraw, "Iowa Report," Skylook,
no.62 (Jan.1973):12, quoting Dubuque
Telegraph-Herald (undated).
1975, Nov.8
"UFO Central," CUFOS News Bull., 1
Feb.1976, p.12.

Dumont
-Humanoid tracks
1976, Aug.10/nr. West Fork R.
John Green, Sasquatch: The Apes Among
Us (Seattle: Hancock House, 1978),
p.196.

Earling
-Possession
1928, Sep./Anna Ecklund/Franciscan Sis-

ters Convent
Carl Vogl, Begone Satan! (College-
ville, Minn.: Rev. Celestine Kaps-
ner, 1935).
Reginald Rhodes, "Nemesis of Evil
Spirits," True Mystics Mag., Apr.
1939, reprinted in Martin Ebon, ed.,
Exorcism: Fact Not Fiction (N.Y.:
Signet, 1974), pp.246-50.
"Satan in Iowa," Doubt, no.15 (sum-
mer 1946):224.
James L. Waring, "The Exorcism of
the Five Devils of Anna Ecklund,"
Fate 12 (June 1959):36-47; (July
1959):40-46. il.
"Noted Exorcist Dies," Fate 16 (Apr.
1963):50.

Eldon
-Clairvoyance
ca.1880/Mrs. Gage
Mildred Goff, "Mrs. Gage's Profit-
able Dream," Fate 8 (July 1955):23-
25.
-UFO (NL)
1897, April 10
Minneapolis (Minn.) Tribune, 11 Apr.
1897.

Eldora
-UFO (DD)
1897, April 9
Chicago (Ill.) Tribune, 11 Apr.1897,
p.4.
-UFO (NL)
1967, March 8-10/W.G. Tietz
Eldora Herald-Ledger, 14 Mar.1967.

Elkader
-Ghost
n.d.
Hans Holzer, Ghosts I've Met (N.Y.:
Ace, 1965), p.57.
-UFO (CE-1)
1969, Aug.6/Don Wilke/2 mi.E
Elkader Clayton County Register, 27
Aug.1969.
-UFO (CE-2)
1969, Aug.7-Sep.22/ground markings only
Ted Phillips, Physical Traces Associ-
ated with UFO Sightings (Evanston:
Center for UFO Studies, 1975), pp.
67-68,109, quoting Elkader Clayton
County Register (undated).

Emerson
-UFO (NL)
1897, April 15/Mr. Parmelee
Sioux City Journal, 17 Apr.1897.

Emmetsburg
-UFO (NL)
1897, April 8
Chicago (Ill.) Times-Herald, 10 Apr.
1897, p.1.

Evans
-UFO (NL)
1897, April 10
Burlington Hawk-Eye, 11 Apr.1897.

Fairfield
-Ancient inscription
1896, Sep.9
Ionia (Mich.) Daily Standard, 24 Apr.
1897, p.3.
-UFO (NL)
1897, April 8/Stanley DuBois
Burlington Hawk-Eye, 10 Apr.1897.

Fayette co.
-Spirit medium
1850s/Oliver T. Fox
Emma Hardinge Britten, Modern American Spiritualism (N.Y.: The Author,
1870), pp.389-90.

Floyd
-Archeological site
Clement L. Webster, "Indian Graves
in Floyd and Chickasaw Counties,
Iowa," Ann.Rept.Smith.Inst., 1887,
pp.590-92.
Clement L. Webster, "Ancient Mounds
at Floyd, Iowa," Nature 43 (1891):
213-14.

Fonda
-UFO (NL)
1973, July 8/Chester Wolter
Fort Dodge Messenger, 9 July 1973.

Fontanelle
-UFO (NL)
1897, April 12/J.H. Hulbert
Des Moines Leader, 13 Apr.1897, p.3.

Fort Dodge
-Fall of anomalous meteorite
1977, Nov.12/Willis Moeller/407 Loomis
Ave.
Fort Dodge Messenger, 17 Nov.1977.
-UFO (NL)
1897, April 8
Marshalltown Statesman-Press, 13
Apr.1897.

Fort Madison
-UFO (NL)
1975, Oct.4
"Noteworthy UFO Sightings," Ufology
2 (spring 1976):42.
-Weather control
n.d./R.D. Fahey
"The Rain Dance Worked," Fate 24
(June 1971):52.

Four Corners
-Humanoid
1975, Oct.3/Herbert Peiffer/Turkey
Creek
Fairfield Ledger, 17 Oct.1975.
Des Moines Register, 25 Oct.1975; and
15 Dec.1975.
Cedar Rapids Gazette, 13 Dec.1975.

Fredericksburg
-UFO (NL)
1972, Oct.22/W on Hwy.18
Ralph DeGraw, "Iowa Report," Skylook,
no.63 (Feb.1973):12.

Garrison
-UFO (CE-2)
1969, July 13/Patti Barr/7 mi.S
Cedar Rapids Gazette, 6 Aug.1969.
"UFO over Iowa Bean Field," APRO
Bull. 18 (July-Aug.1969):1,4.
"Saucer Near Landing in Iowa," Sky-
look, no.23 (Oct.1969), inside
front cover.
J. Allen Hynek, The UFO Experience
(Chicago: Regnery, 1972), pp.129-
30. il.
Kevin D. Randle, "The Iowa UFO Land-
ings," Official UFO 1 (Aug.1975):
40-41.
Brad Steiger, Mysteries of Time and
Space (N.Y.: Dell, 1976 ed.), pp.
126-29.

Gifford
-Anomalous hole in ground
1897
Omaha (Nebr.) Daily Bee, 29 Apr.
1897, p.3.

Goldfield
-UFO (CE-2)
1972, June 27/Donald Slaikeu/ground
markings only
Des Moines Register, 11-12 July 1972.
Fort Dodge Messenger, 19 July 1972.
"'Mysterious' Field Damage in Iowa
Caused by Lightning," Skylook, no.
57 (Aug.1972):4.
Vivian Buchan, "UFO Damages Iowa
Soybeans," Fate 26 (Feb.1973):88-
92. il.
(Letter), C.J. Fortner, Fate 26 (Oct.
1973):144-45.
(Letter), John Vitomski, Fate 26
(Oct.1973):145.

Green Island
-UFO (NL)
1897, April
Rockford (Ill.) Republic, 12 Apr.
1897, p.2.

Grinnell
-UFO (NL)
1897, April/J.W. Lansing
Cincinnati (O.) Enquirer, 25 Apr.
1897.

Grundy Center
-UFO (CE-3)
1897, April 10
Marshalltown Times-Republican, 13
Apr.1897.

Harlan
-UFO (NL)
1976, May 5
"Noteworthy UFO Sightings," Ufology
2 (fall 1976):60.

Harvey
-Humanoid
1978, Feb.20
Des Moines Register, 12 Nov.1978.

Hazleton
-UFO (NL)
1972, Oct.2-17/Jack Stolfus
"Law Officer Keeps Eye on Sky," Skylook, no.61 (Dec.1972):11.

Hiawatha
-Psychic photography
1964, March 29/Fay Clark
Brad Steiger, Mysteries of Time and
Space (N.Y.: Dell, 1976 ed.), p.139.
-UFO (DD)
1955, Sep.3/Sam Stochl
Brad Steiger, Mysteries of Time and
Space (N.Y.: Dell, 1976 ed.), betw.
pp.128-29. il.

Hinton
-Humanoid tracks
1970s
Jerome Clark, "Are 'Manimals' Space
Beings?" Saga UFO Rept. 2 (summer
1975):49,59.

Honey Creek
-Phantom helicopter
1974, July 15/Robert Smith, Jr.
Curt Sutherly, "Mutilations: Who--or
What--Really Is Killing the Cattle?
Part 2," Pursuit 10 (winter 1977):
15,16.

Howard co.
-Humanoid tracks
1965, winter
Eric Norman [Brad Steiger], The Abominable Snowmen (N.Y.: Award, 1969),
p.89.

Humboldt
-Humanoid
1978, Sep./3 mi.NE
Des Moines Register, 12 Nov.1978.

Humboldt co.
-Humanoid
1965, winter
Eric Norman [Brad Steiger], The Abominable Snowmen (N.Y.: Award, 1969),
p.89.

Iowa City
-Haunt
1971/Sumter House
Brad Steiger, Irene Hughes on Psychic
Safari (B.Y.: Warner, 1972), pp.32-
42.
-UFO (?)
1968, July 28/=meteor
Philip J. Klass, UFOs Explained (N.Y.:
Random House, 1974), p.170.
-UFO (CE-3)
1971, summer
Brad Steiger, Gods of Aquarius (N.Y.:
Harcourt, Brace, Jovanovich, 1976),
pp.19-20.
-UFO (NL)
1966, April 6, 10
Columbus (O.) Dispatch, 11 Apr.1966.
"Typical Reports," UFO Inv. 3 (Mar.-

Apr.1966):8.

Iowa Falls
-Lightning anomaly
1966/James Lindsay/Siloam Rd.
(Editorial), Fate 19 (Dec.1966):18-
20.
-Norse ax
"More Viking Evidence?" Fate 5 (June
1952):40.

Jefferson
-UFO (?)
1897, April 14
Chicago (Ill.) Times-Herald, 17 Apr.
1897, p.6.

Keokuk
-Fall of fish
1869, Aug./Dr. Sanderson
San Francisco (Cal.) Evening Bulletin,
23 Aug.1869.
-UFO (DD)
1947, July 3/S.M. Barker
Sioux City Sunday Journal, 6 July
1947.
-UFO (NL)
1969, Jan.9
Keokuk Daily Gate City, 11 Jan.1969.
1970, Dec.31/Mrs. J.O. Hoerner
"A 'Flying Flame' Seen in Illinois,"
Skylook, no.39 (Feb.1971):18.

Kossuth co.
-Psychokinesis
1892, July/Cecil de Vada
Cecil de Vada, "The Clock Tolled
Twice," Fate 5 (Apr.-May 1952):29-
31.

Lake City
-UFO (CE-2)
1973, Aug.20/Mrs. Darryl Crandall/N of
town
Glenn McWane & David Graham, The New
UFO Sightings (N.Y.: Warner, 1974),
pp.12-13.

Lake Mills
-Humanoid tracks
1978, Oct./nr. Hogsback
Lake Mills Graphic, 18 Oct.1978. il.

Laurens
-UFO (CE-2)
1972, July 6/Jerry Dean/ground markings
only
"Those Iowa Craters," APRO Bull. 21
(July-Aug.1972):1,4-5.
"'Mysterious' Field Damage in Iowa
Caused by Lightning," Skylook, no.
57 (Aug.1972):4.
Vivian Buchan, "UFO Damages Iowa
Soybeans," Fate 26 (Feb.1973):88,
90-91.

LeMars
-UFO (?)
1957, Sep.1
Richard Hall, ed., The UFO Evidence

(Washington: NICAP, 1964), p.75,
quoting Saucers, winter 1957-58.

Linn Grove
-UFO (CE-3)
1897, April 15/James Evans/=hoax?
Chicago Times-Herald, 16 Apr.1897.
Jerome Clark & Lucius Farish, "The
1897 Story: Part 2," Flying Saucer
Rev. 14 (Nov.-Dec.1968):6.
(Letter), John F. Lundt, Fate 26
(Dec.1973):143.

Lockridge
-Humanoid
1975, July/Gloria Olson
Des Moines Register, 25 Oct.1975.

Lyon co.
-Archeological sites
Frederick Starr, "Mounds and Lodge
Circles in Iowa," Am.Antiquarian 9
(1887):361-63.
T.H. Lewis, "Stone Monuments in North-
western Iowa and Southwestern Min-
nesota," Am.Anthro. 3 (1890):269-74.

McGregor
-UFO (CE-2)
1967, Jan./Mrs. C.J. Ferguson/ground
markings only
Ted Phillips, Physical Traces Associated with UFO Sightings (Evanston:
Center for UFO Studies, 1975), p.45.

Madison co.
-Cattle mutilation
1975, Oct.15/Orville Henry
Des Moines Register, 17 Oct.1975.

Malvern
-UFO (NL)
1897, April 10/G.L. Cleaver
Omaha (Nebr.) Daily Bee, 12 Apr.
1897, p.3.

Manson
-Meteorite crater
32,000 m.diam./certain
R.A. Hoppin & J.E. Dryden, "An Un-
usual Occurrence of Pre-Cambrian
Crystalline Rocks Beneath Glacial
Drift near Manson, Iowa," J.Geology
66 (1958):694-99.

Maquoketa
-UFO (NL)
1951, summer
Harold T. Wilkins, Flying Saucers on
the Attack (N.Y.: Ace, 1967 ed.),
p.140.

Marathon
-UFO (CE-2)
1974, July 23/Ned Holmberg/ground markings only
Ted Phillips, Physical Traces Associated with UFO Sightings (Evanston:
Center for UFO Studies, 1975), p.103.

Marion
-UFO (NL)
1897, April 9
Chicago (Ill.) Times-Herald, 10 Apr.
1897, p.1.

Marquette
-Archeological site
ca.100 B.C.-1400 A.D./Effigy Mounds
National Monument
Paul L. Beaubien, "Some Hopewellian
Mounds at the Effigy Mounds Nation-
al Monument," Wisconsin Arch. 34
(1953):125-38. il.
Marshall McKusick, Men of Ancient
Iowa (Ames: Iowa State Univ., 1964),
pp.120,127-29.
Wilfred D. Logan & John Earl Ingman-
son, "Effigy Mounds National Mon-
ument," Palimpsest 50 (1969):273-
304. il.
Franklin Folsom, America's Ancient
Treasures (N.Y.: Rand McNally,
1974), p.139.
Thaddeus M. Cowan, "Effigy Mounds
and Stellar Representation: A Com-
parison of Old World and New World
Alignment Schemes," in Anthony F.
Aveni, ed., Archaeoastronomy in Pre-
columbian America (Austin: Univ. of
Texas, 1975), pp.217-34.
R. Clark Mallam, The Iowa Effigy
Mound Manifestation (Iowa City: Office of the State Archaeologist,
1976). il.

Marshalltown
-UFO (CE-3)
1897, April 11/Charles Dixon/Linn St.
x 8th Ave.
Marshalltown Statesman-Press, 13
Apr.1897.

Mason City
-Child prodigy
1922, Sep./Mrs. Peter Zoutes/Mercy Hos-
pital
Vincent H. Gaddis, "From the Mouths
of Babes," Fate 4 (Mar.1951):12.
Margaret Gaddis, "We Remember Other
Lives," Fate 7 (Jan.1954):86,89.
-Healing
1970s/David Pederson
(Letter), James H. Neal, Fate 27
(Jan.1974):129.
(Letter), Alice Lundberg, Fate 27
(Sep.1974):131.
-UFO (NL)
1897, April 8
Marshalltown Statesman-Press, 13 Apr.
1897.
1977, Oct.17/15th St.
Mason City Globe-Gazette, 18 Oct.1977.

Maynard
-UFO (?)
1971, April 14/Michael Potratz/=hoax
Philip J. Klass, UFOs Explained (N.Y.:
Random House, 1974), pp.72-76.

Milan
-UFO (CE-2)
  1957, Jan.21
    Leonard H. Stringfield, Inside Sau-
    cer Post...3-0 Blue (Cincinnati:
    CRIFO, 1957), p.59.

Mills co.
-Cattle mutilation
  1974, May
    (Editorial), Fate 27 (Nov.1974):14.

Millville
-Poltergeist
  1959, Nov.-1960, Jan./William Meyer/
  nr. Split-Level Rd.
    United Press International, "Polter-
    geist Evicts Couple in Millville,
    Iowa," Fate 13 (May 1960):42-49. il.
    Jack Magarrell, "I Don't Believe It,
    But It Happened," Tomorrow 8 (spring
    1960):17-23.
    Coral E. Lorenzen, The Shadow of the
    Unknown (N.Y.: Signet, 1970), pp.
    41-42.

Mitchellville
-Clairvoyance
  1860s/Maude Lord-Drake
    W.D. Chesney, "That Great Medium:
    Maude Lord Drake," Fate 14 (Apr.
    1961):82,85.

Monona
-UFO (NL)
  1969, Dec.7/Donald Hurlbut
    "Press Reports," APRO Bull. 18 (Jan.-
    Feb.1970):4, quoting Elkader Clayton
    County Register (undated).

Monroe
-UFO (NL)
  1897, April 9
    Marshalltown Times-Republican, 13
    Apr.1897.

Montezuma
-UFO (NL)
  1967, May 2/Dennis Latcham
    "Hovering Object in Iowa," APRO Bull.
    15 (May-June 1967):8.

Mount Joy
-UFO (DD)
  1950, April 30/Louis Wedemeyer
    Kenneth Arnold & Ray Palmer, The Com-
    ing of the Saucers (Boise: The Au-
    thors, 1952), pp.150-51.

Mount Pleasant
-Haunt
  1970
    Brad Steiger, Irene Hughes on Psychic
    Safari (N.Y.: Warner, 1972), pp.100-
    106.
-UFO (CE-2)
  1920, June 3/Clark Linch/NE of town
    Jerome Clark & Lucius Farish, "UFOs
    of the Roaring '20s," Saga UFO Rept.
    2 (fall 1975):48.

-UFO (NL)
  1897, April 8/W.J. Martin/Jefferson x
  Henry St.
    Burlington Hawk-Eye, 10 Apr.1897.
  1897, April 10
    Burlington Hawk-Eye, 11 Apr.1897.
  1973, Aug.15/John Haynes/W on Hwy.34
    "Brief Reports," Skylook, no.74 (Jan.
    1974):17.

Moville
-UFO (NL)
  1897, April 15/W.L. Sanborn
    Sioux City Journal, 17 Apr.1897.

Muscatine
-Haunt
  1950/Floyd Holladay/rocking chair
    W.E. Farbstein, "Answer This One,"
    Fate 5 (Feb.-Mar.1952):28-29.
    Marcus Bach, "Of Life and Death: The
    Case for Spirit Communication: Part
    One," Fate 22 (Sep.1969):61,63.
    Pauline Saltzman, Ghosts and Other
    Strangers (N.Y.: Lancer, 1970), pp.
    94-95.
-UFO (NL)
  1946, July/Orrie Miller/SW of town
    Dubuque Telegraph-Herald, 7 July
    1947, p.1.

New Albin
-Archeological site and ancient stone
chamber
    Cyrus Thomas, "Report on the Mound
    Explorations of the Bureau of Eth-
    nology," Ann.Rept.Bur.Am.Ethn. 12
    (1890-91):1,99-108.
    Franklin Folsom, America's Ancient
    Treasures (N.Y.: Rand McNally,
    1974), p.139.

Newell
-Fall of ice
  1961/Everett Nelson
    (Editorial), Fate 14 (June 1961):22.

New London
-Animal ESP
  1955
    (Editorial), Fate 9 (May 1956):7,
    quoting New London Journal (undated).

Newton
-UFO (NL)
  1897, April 10
    Chicago (Ill.) Tribune, 11 Apr.1897,
    p.4.

Northwood
-UFO (NL)
  1897, April 8
    Minneapolis (Minn.) Tribune, 9 Apr.
    1897.
    Burlington Hawk-Eye, 10 Apr.1897.

Oakley
-UFO (NL)
  1897, April 10
    Rock Island (Ill.) Union, 11 Apr.1897.

Ocheyedan
-Humanoid
1976, Aug.22/Dan Radunz/Ocheyedan R.
Sibley Osceola County Tribune, 26
Aug.1976.
Sioux City Journal, 28 Aug.1976.

Oelwein
-Fall of metallic object
1947, summer/Lloyd Bennet
Harold T. Wilkins, Flying Saucers on
the Attack (N.Y.: Ace, 1967 ed.),
pp.65-66.
-Skyquake
1967, Oct.9
Jim & Coral Lorenzen, UFOs over the
Americas (N.Y.: Signet, 1968), p.
170.
-UFO (NL)
1967, Oct.10/Jack Stolfus/city park
Jim & Coral Lorenzen, UFOs over the
Americas (N.Y.: Signet, 1968), p.
169.
1973, Oct.15/Mrs. Hibbens
"Two Reports of Strange Lights Sent
from Fayette County, Iowa," Skylook,
no.78 (May 1974):20.
1977, Oct.18/E of town
Oelwein Daily Register, 18 Oct.1977.

Onawa
-UFO (NL)
1967, March 9
J. Allen Hynek, The UFO Experience
(Chicago: Regnery, 1972), p.236.

Osborne
-UFO (CE-1)
1969, Sep.28/Hwy.13
Elkader Register, 1 Oct.1969.

Oskaloosa
-Humanoid
1977, Dec.19/Theresa McGee/3 mi.NE
Oskaloosa Herald, 20 Dec.1977.
-UFO (CE-2)
1880s
Ted Phillips, Physical Traces Associ-
ated with UFO Sightings (Evanston:
Center for UFO Studies, 1975), p.3.

Ottosen
-Humanoid
1978, July 27-31/Donnette Henkins
1978, Sep.11/Anna Dodrill
1978, Sep.12/Robert B. Newell
Fort Dodge Messenger, 1 Aug.1978; 3
Aug.1978; and 14 Sep.1978.
Des Moines Register, 2 Aug.1978; and
24 Sep.1978.
Algona Upper Des Moines, 3 Aug.1978.
Algona Kossuth County Advance, 7 Aug.
1978; and 18 Sep.1978.
Humboldt Independent, 16 Sep.1978.
Mark A. Hall, "Stories of 'Bigfoot'
in Iowa During 1978 As Drawn from
Newspaper Sources," Minnesota Arch.
38, no.1 (1979):3-17.

Ottumwa
-UFO (?)
1869, Aug.7/Mr. Zentmeyer/=meteors?
Philadelphia Photographic Expedition,
"Solar Eclipse--August 7, 1869," J.
Franklin Inst., ser.3, 58 (1869):
214.
-UFO (NL)
1897, April 9
Burlington Hawk-Eye, 10 Apr.1897.
1897, April 10
Omaha (Nebr.) Bee, 11 Apr.1897, p.6.

Oxford Junction
-Fall of pebbles
1962, Aug.16/Henry Hasenbank
Cedar Rapids Gazette, 16 Aug.1962.
(Letter), Milton H. Nothdurft, Fate
16 (Nov.1963):116-18.
Raymond Bayless, The Enigma of the
Poltergeist (N.Y.: Ace, 1967 ed.),
pp.52-56.

Pella
-Humanoid
1978, Feb.25/Pella Bridge
Des Moines Register, 12 Nov.1978.
-UFO (NL)
1897, April 9
Marshalltown Times-Republican, 13
Apr.1897.

Red Oak
-UFO (NL)
1897, April 14/John Brinkley
Washington Court House (O.) Cyclone
& Fayette Republican, 22 Apr.1897.

Reinbeck
-UFO (NL)
1897, April 10
Minneapolis (Minn.) Tribune, 11 Apr.
1897.

Renwick
-Humanoid
1978, Sep.27/S of town
1978, Sep.27/Mark Thompson/4 mi.NW
1978, Sep.30?/2 mi.S
Fort Dodge Messenger, 29-30 Sep.1978.
Des Moines Register, 1 Oct.1978.
Eagle Grove Eagle, 4 Oct.1978.
Mark A. Hall, "Stories of 'Bigfoot'
in Iowa During 1978 As Drawn from
Newspaper Sources," Minnesota Arch.
38, no.1 (1979):3-17.

Rhodes
-UFO (?)
1897, April 9/reservoir
Burlington Hawk-Eye, 14 Apr.1897.

Rippey
-Anomalous hole in ground
1959, Aug.5/Berthal Devilbiss
Coral E. Lorenzen, The Shadow of the
Unknown (N.Y.: Signet, 1970), p.64.

Riverton
-Phantom panther

1897, March/Nishna Botna R.
Omaha (Nebr.) Daily Bee, 9 Mar.1897,
p.3.

Rock Rapids
-Tornado anomaly
1932, July 9/George Raveling
J.C. Jensen, "Ball Lightning," Sci.
Monthly 37 (Aug.1933):190-92.
-UFO (CE-2)
1978, June 8/Harlan Berg/3 mi.W/ground
markings only
Des Moines Register, 13 June 1978.

Rolfe
-Norse mooring stone
"New Discoveries Supporting Medieval
Norse Presence in the Upper Mid-
west," NEARA Newsl. 9 (spring 1974):
15-16. il.

Saint Lucas
-UFO (NL)
1973, Jan.5/SE of town
Ralph DeGraw, "Iowa Reports," Skylook,
no.63 (Feb.1973):12.

Saint Mary's
-Ghost light
1874-1947
"The St. Mary's Ghost," Annals of
Iowa 37 (spring 1965):610-14.

Saint Paul
-UFO (?)
1869, Aug.7/W.S. Gilman, Jr./=meteors?
Des Moines Register, 8 Aug.1869.
J.R. Hind, "Stellar Objects Seen during the Eclipse of 1869," Nature 18
(1878):663-64.

Salem
-UFO (NL)
1967, spring/Steve Heise
"UFO Reports from Iowa," Skylook, no.
31 (June 1970):11.

Sanborn
-Dowsing
1920s-   /LeRoy Getting
Vivian Buchan, "LeRoy Getting: Iowa's
Dowser," Fate 25 (July 1972):75-82.
il.

Sergeant Bluff
-UFO (NL)
1974, Nov.
Jerome Clark, "Are 'Manimals' Space
Beings?" Saga UFO Rept. 2 (summer
1975):49,60-62.

Sioux City
-Acoustic anomaly
1945/Carl J. Barnes
Carl J. Barnes, "Music in the Sky,"
Fate 4 (July 1951):84.
1952/Marian Cox/Sioux City Air Base
(Letter), Fate 5 (Nov.1952):112-15.
-Cattle mutilation and UFO (NL)
1975, Dec.

James Butler Bonham, "Cattle Mutilations and UFOs: Satanic Rite or Alien Abduction?" Official UFO 1
(Dec.1976):26,54.
-Fire anomaly
n.d./Paul V. Weekly
"3 Human Tinders," Fortean Soc'y Mag.,
no.7 (June 1943):5.
-Humanoid
1971, summer/Gary Parker/Stone Park
1974, Jan./Jim Britton
1974, Aug./Riverside Blvd.
1974, Aug.30
Sioux City Journal, 31 Aug.1974.
Jerome Clark, "Are 'Manimals' Space
Beings?" Saga UFO Rept. 2 (summer
1975):49,50-51,58.
-UFO (?)
1897, March/Robert Hibbard/15 mi.N
Topeka (Kan.) State Journal, 29 Mar.
1897.
Saginaw (Mich.) Evening News, 5 Apr.
1897.
-UFO (CE-1)
1897, April/R.H. Butler
Augusta (Me.) Daily Kennebec Journal,
12 Apr.1897.
1974, Sep.7/Mrs. Merlin Mosier
Jerome Clark, "Are 'Manimals' Space
Beings?" Saga UFO Rept. 2 (summer
1975):49,59.
-UFO (CE-2)
1974, Sep.4/George Hoffman
Ted Phillips, Physical Traces Associ-
ated with UFO Sightings (Evanston:
Center for UFO Studies, 1975), p.104.
1975, summer/Tim Kellog
(Letter), Saga UFO Rept. 2 (winter
1975):4-6.
-UFO (CE-3)
1974, Sep.9
Jerome Clark, "Are 'Manimals' Space
Beings?" Saga UFO Rept. 2 (summer
1975):49,59-60.
-UFO (DD)
1947, June 29/H.F. Angus/NW on Hwy.141
Des Moines Register, 6 July 1947.
1947, July 6/W.A. Verzani
Sioux City Journal, 7 July 1947.
1947, July 8/J.V. Gibbons/Willis x Isa-
bella
Sioux City Journal, 9 July 1947.
-UFO (NL)
1947, July 2/Mrs. E.B. Morrison/1724
W. 2d St.
Sioux City Journal, 6 July 1947.
1947, July 3/Jacob Kriv/1310 W. 15th St.
Sioux City Journal, 8 July 1947.
1947, July 7/Warren Bowen
Sioux City Journal, 9 July 1947.
1951, Jan.20/Lawrence W. Vinther
Lawrence W. Vinther, "Another Saucer
Mystery," Flying 48 (June 1951):23,
56.
Edward J. Ruppelt, The Report on Un-
identified Flying Objects (Garden
City: Doubleday, 1956), pp.84-85.
(Letter), Herbert S. Taylor, Saucer
News 11 (Mar.1964):5.
1965, Aug.3

Coral E. Lorenzen, "Western UFO Flap,"
Fate 18 (Nov.1965):42,52.
1974, Sep.4-5/Mrs. Merlin Mosier
1974, Sep.5/Jim Corran
Jerome Clark, "Are 'Manimals' Space
Beings?" Saga UFO Rept. 2 (summer
1975):49,59.

Sny-Magill
-Archeological site
Paul L. Beaubien, "Cultural Variation
within Two Woodland Mound Groups in
Northeastern Iowa," Am.Antiquity 19
(1953):56-66.

Solon
-UFO (NL)
1897, April 8
Minneapolis (Minn.) Journal, 9 Apr.
1897.

Spirit Lake
-UFO (DD)
1955, Nov.23/Earl Rose/1 mi.W
Des Moines Register, 24 Nov.1955.

Storm Lake
-UFO (NL)
1897, April 9
Dixon (Ill.) Telegraph, 10 Apr.1897,
p.1.

Story City
-UFO (CE-2)
1972, June 27/Mervin Teig/ground mark-
ings only
Des Moines Register, 11-12 July 1972.
"Those Iowa Craters," APRO Bull. 21
(July-Aug.1972):1,5.
"'Mysterious' Field Damage in Iowa
Caused by Lightning," Skylook, no.
57 (Aug.1972):4.
Vivian Buchan, "UFO Damages Iowa
Soybeans," Fate 26 (Feb.1973):88,90.

Sumner
-UFO (?)
1897, April/=hoax
Fort Dodge Messenger & Chronicle, 9
Apr. 1897, p.9.

Sutherland
-Norse habitation site
"New Discoveries Supporting Medieval
Norse Presence in the Upper Mid-
west," NEARA Newsl. 9 (spring 1974):
15.

Tiffin
-Anomalous hole in ground
1930s
C.C. Wylie, "A Peculiar Hole near
Tiffin, Iowa," Pop.Astron. 45 (1937)
:445-49.
C.C. Wylie, "A Peculiar Hole near
Tiffin, Iowa," Pop.Astron. 46 (1938)
:221-22.

Toolesboro
-Archeological site

W.H. Pratt, "Report of Explorations
of the Ancient Mounds at Toolesboro,
Louisa County, Iowa," Proc.Daven-
port Acad.Nat.Sci. 1 (1876):106-11.
J. Gass, "Ancient Fortification in
Louisa County, Iowa," Proc.Daven-
port Acad.Nat.Sci. 3 (1879):173-84.
E.F. Lynch, et al., "Mound Explorations at Toolesboro, Iowa," Proc.
Davenport Acad.Nat.Sci. 5 (1884):
29-32.

Underwood
-UFO (NL)
1897, April 14
Omaha (Nebr.) Daily Bee, 16 Apr.
1897, p.1.

Valley
-Automatic writing
1855-1856
Emma Hardinge Britten, Modern American Spiritualism (N.Y.: The Author,
1870), pp.400-401.

Villisca
-UFO (NL)
1897, April 14-15/F.J. Taylor
Omaha (Nebr.) Daily Bee, 17 Apr.
1897, p.2.

Vinton
-UFO (NL)
1897, April 3/Lot Thomas
Marshalltown Times-Republican, 13
Apr.1897.
1897, April 6
Chicago (Ill.) Times-Herald, 8 Apr.
1897, p.1.
1897, April 8-9
Burlington Hawk-Eye, 10 Apr.1897.

Walcott
-UFO (CE-2)
1977, Oct.9/Holly Prunchak/Freach &
Hecht plant
"CEII in Iowa," Int'l UFO Reporter
2 (Dec.1977):4,8.
Moline (Ill.) Daily Dispatch, 7 Jan.
1978.

Walker
-Mystery bird deaths
1978, April 7/Clarence Williams
Cedar Rapids Gazette, 9 Apr.1978.

Wapello
-Phantom panther
1946, Dec.25
"More Critters," Doubt, no.18 (1947):
273-74.
-UFO (CE-1)
1967, March 22/Douglas Eutsler
Ann Druffel, "Oddities Among the Er-
ratics," MUFON UFO J., no.103 (June
1976):10, quoting True Report on
Flying Saucers, no.2 (Dec.1967):68.
il.

Washington
-UFO (NL)
  1897, April 16
    New York Herald, 17 Apr.1897.

Waterloo
-Cattle mutilation
  1977, Oct.26/Mrs. Polly Mills/5714 N.
    Elk Run Rd.
    Waterloo Courier, 27 Oct.1977.
-Phantom insect
  1899, July/Mary Vaughan
    Chicago (Ill.) Tribune, 15 July 1899,
    p.3.
-UFO (?)
  1897, April 16/=hoax
    Chicago (Ill.) Times-Herald, 17 Apr.
    1897, p.6.
    Freeport (Ill.) Journal, 20 Apr.1897,
    p.8.
-UFO (CE-1)
  1947, July 5/J.E. Johnston
    Sioux City Journal, 6 July 1947.
-UFO (NL)
  1897, April 10
    Minneapolis (Minn.) Tribune, 11 Apr.
    1897.
  1957, Nov.8/Paul Rutledge
    Aimé Michel, Flying Saucers and the
    Straight-Line Mystery (N.Y.: Cri-
    terion, 1958), p.265.

Waucoma
-UFO (NL)
  1897, April 10
    Minneapolis (Minn.) Journal, 13 Apr.
    1897.

Waverly
-UFO (CE-3)
  1965, Aug.13?
    "1965 Occupant Report," APRO Bull.
    23 (Jan.-Feb.1975):9.
-UFO (NL)
  1972, July 14/Eugene Hudson
    Ralph DeGraw, "Iowa Report," Skylook,
    no.63 (Feb.1973):12.

Webster City
-Anomalous artifact
  1897, April 2/Lehigh coal mine/=carved
    rock in coal shaft
    Chicago (Ill.) Times-Herald, 3 Apr.
    1897, p.2.
-Poltergeist
  n.d./McKinlay Kantor
    Brad Steiger, Mysteries of Time and
    Space (N.Y.: Dell, 1976 ed.), p.93.

West Bend
-Humanoid tracks
  1978, Sep.7/Ellis Shellmeyer/W. Des
    Moines R.
    Emmetsburg Democrat, 21 Sep.1978.
    Algona Kossuth County Advance, 25
    Sep.1978.
    Mark A. Hall, "Stories of 'Bigfoot'
    in Iowa During 1978 As Drawn from
    Newspaper Reports," Minnesota Arch.
    38, no.1 (1979):3-17. il.

West Branch
-UFO (NL)
  1897, April 12
    Burlington Hawk-Eye, 14 Apr.1897.

Westgate
-UFO (?)
  1967/=hoax
    Donald H. Menzel & Ernest H. Taves,
    The UFO Enigma (Garden City: Doub-
    leday, 1977), pp.181-84.
-UFO (CE-2)
  1971, April 25/ground markings only
    Ted Phillips, Physical Traces Associ-
    ated with UFO Sightings (Evanston:
    Center for UFO Studies, 1975), p.76.

West Liberty
-UFO (NL)
  1897, April 8
    Quincy (Ill.) Whig, 10 Apr.1897, p.1.

Williamstown
-UFO (NL)
  1972, Dec.14?/Mike Braun/1 mi.E
    Ralph DeGraw, "Iowa Report," Skylook,
    no.64 (Mar.1973):13.

Wilton
-Phantom
  1970, Jan.29/Tom Myers/I-80
    Eric Norman [Warren Smith], Gods,
    Demons and UFOs (N.Y.: Lancer,
    1970), pp.81-82.

Winthrop
-Clairvoyance
  1961, March/Peter Hurkos
    Marcus Bach, "ESP and the Missing
    Farm Boy," Fate 15 (Feb.1962):36-40.

Wolf Creek twp.
-UFO (CE-1)
  1897, April 4/Dick Butler
    Springfield Illinois State Register,
    11 Apr.1897.
    Marshalltown Times-Republican, 13
    Apr.1897.

Yorktown
-UFO (CE-2)
  1966, April 23/Ronald E. Johnson/Hwy.2
    Donald E. Keyhoe & Gordon I.R. Lore,
    Jr., UFOs: A New Look (Washington:
    NICAP, 1969), p.22.

          B. Physical Features

Big Cedar Creek
-Humanoid tracks
  1946, Dec./Duane Hibner
    B. Ann Slate, "Man-Ape's Reign of
    Terror," Saga UFO Rept. 4 (Aug.1977)
    :20,23.

Big Sioux R.
-Land monster myth
  Spirit Canyon
    Charles M. Skinner, Myths and Legends

of Our Own Land, 2 vols. (Philadelphia: Lippincott, 1896), 2:300.

Coralville Reservoir
-UFO (NL)
   1965, Aug.4
      Coral E. Lorenzen, Flying Saucers:
      The Startling Evidence of the Inva-
      sion from Outer Space (N.Y.: Sig-
      net, 1966 ed.), p.248.

Little Sioux R.
-Archeological site
   ca.6000 B.C./Simonsen site
      George A. Agogino & W.D. Frankforter,
      "A Paleo-Indian Bison-Kill in North-
      western Iowa," Am.Antiquity 25
      (1960):414-15.
      W.D. Frankforter & George A. Agogino,
      "The Simonsen Site: Report for the
      Summer of 1959," Plains Anthro. 5,
      no.10 (1960):65-70.
      Marshall McKusick, Men of Ancient
      Iowa (Ames: Ioaw State Univ., 1964),
      pp.59-64. il.

Maquoketa R.
-Humanoid
   n.d./Gary Koontz
      John Green, Sasquatch: The Apes Among
      Us (Seattle: Hancock House, 1978),
      pp.195-96.

Red Rock Reservoir
-UFO (NL)
   1976, Sep.24
      "UFOs of Limited Merit," Int'l UFO
      Reporter 1 (Nov.1976):5.

Skunk R.
-Humanoid
   1978, Jan.1
      Des Moines Register, 12 Nov.1978.

Stephens State Forest
-Humanoid
   1978
      Des Moines Register, 12 Nov.1978.

-UFO (CE-3)
   1969
      Brad Steiger, Mysteries of Time and
      Space (N.Y.: Dell, 1976 ed.), pp.
      131-32.

           C. Ethnic Groups

Iowa Indians
-Contactee myth
      Brad Steiger, "American Indians and
      the Star People," Saga UFO Rept. 3
      (June 1976):33,62.
-Flood myth
      Ignatius Donnelly, Atlantis: The An-
      tediluvian World (N.Y.: Gramercy,
      1949 ed.), p.95.

        D. Unspecified Localities

-Acoustic anomaly
   1971, Oct.
      Brad Steiger, Mysteries of Time and
      Space (N.Y.: Dell, 1976 ed.), pp.
      147-49.

MINNESOTA

A. Populated Places

Aitken
-Fall of fish
  n.d./Fergus Olafson
    (Letter), David W. Nystuen, Fate 10
    (Nov.1957):122-24.
-Midday darkness and fall of black snow
  1889, April 2
    New York Times, 4 Apr.1889, p.1.
    (Editorial), Science 13 (1889):300.
-UFO (NL)
  1960, Dec.5/Oliver Bakken/S of town
    "Odds and Ends," APRO Bull. 9 (Jan.
    1961):5.

Alberta
-Norse spearhead
  1947
    Alf Mongé & Ole G. Landsverk, Norse
    Medieval Cryptography in Runic Carv-
    ings (Glendale, Cal.: Norseman,
    1967), p.195.

Albert Lea
-Crisis apparition
  1942, Nov./Maureen Hayter/312 Grove Ave.
    Dennis Bardens, Ghosts and Hauntings
    (N.Y.: Ace, 1965 ed.), pp.67-68.
-UFO (?)
  1947, July 8?/William Schultz
    Minneapolis Star, 9 July 1947.
-UFO (NL)
  1897, April 8-10
    Minneapolis Tribune, 9 Apr.1897; and
    11 Apr.1897.
    St. Paul Pioneer-Press, 12 Apr.1897.

Alexandria
-Norse boathook
  1938
    Alf Mongé & Ole G. Landsverk, Norse
    Medieval Cryptography in Runic Carv-
    ings (Glendale, Cal.: Norseman,
    1967), p.195.
-Norse halberd
  1923
    Alf Mongé & Ole G. Landsverk, Norse
    Medieval Cryptography in Runic Carv-
    ings (Glendale, Cal.: Norseman,
    1967), p.195.

Anoka
-Erratic kangaroo
  1967, April 24/Hazel Hays/nr. Fairgrounds
    David Fideler & Loren Coleman, "Kan-
    garoos from Nowhere," Fate 31 (Apr.
    1978):68,72.
-Mystery plane crash
  1972, Aug.24/Joseph Kavanaugh/Skylane
    Jay Gourley, The Great Lakes Triangle
    (Greenwich, Ct.: Fawcett, 1977),
    pp.89-93.

-UFO (?)
  1897, April 10-11,13
    Anoka Herald, 16 Apr.1897.
-UFO (CE-1)
  1976, Jan.6
    "Woman Reports Possible UFO Effects,"
    Skylook, no.101 (Apr.1976):4,7.

Austin
-UFO (NL)
  1963, June 4
    Gray Barker, Book of Saucers (Clarks-
    burg, W.V.: Saucerian, 1965), pp.
    19-20.
  1976, Jan.1
    "Noteworthy UFO Sightings," Ufology
    2 (summer 1976):62.

Bagley
-UFO (CE-3)
  1966, April 22
    Timothy Green Beckley, "On the Trail
    of the Flying Saucers," Flying Sau-
    cers, Mar.1967, pp.22,24.

Baudette
-Phantom train
  1914/Mabel W. Stevens
    Mabel W. Stevens, "The Phantom Train,"
    Fate 2 (May 1949):21.

Bemidji
-Humanoid
  n.d.
    Eric Norman [Brad Steiger], The Abom-
    inable Snowman (N.Y.: Award, 1969),
    p.81.
  n.d./Helen Westring/=hoax
    Nat'l Bulletin, 30 June 1969.

Bigelow
-UFO (NL)
  1897, April 13
    Chicago (Ill.) Times-Herald, 15 Apr.
    1897, p.7.

Biwabik
-UFO (NL)
  1978, July
    Two Harbors Lake City News-Chronicle,
    2 Aug.1978.

Blaine
-UFO (NL)
  1965, Aug.3
    Coral E. Lorenzen, "Western UFO Flap,"
    Fate 18 (Nov.1965):42,51.
  1975, Aug.24
    "From the Center for UFO Studies,"
    Flying Saucer Rev. 21 (Apr.1976):
    24,25.

Brandon
-Norse ax

1915/John Nelson
   Hjalmar R. Holand, The Kensington
   Stone (Ephraim, Wisc.: The Author,
   1932), pp.159-61,172-73. il.
   Hjalmar R. Holand, Westward from
   Vinland (N.Y.: Duell, Sloan & Pearce,
   1940), pp.225-26. il.

Breckenridge
-UFO (NL)
   1897, April 13
   Minneapolis Times, 15 Apr.1897.

Brookston
-UFO (?)
   1954, Nov.20/=meteor?
   "Mystery Fireball Crashes in Woods,"
   CRIFO Newsl., 3 Dec.1954, p.6.

Brooten
-Norse sword
   ca.1925/Andrew Stene/2 mi.W
   Hjalmar R. Holand, A Pre-Columbian
   Crusade to America (N.Y.: Twayne,
   1962), p.177. il.

Browns Valley
-Archeological site
   Albert Ernest Jenks, "Minnesota's
   Browns Valley Man and Associated
   Burial Artifacts," Mem.Am.Anthro.
   Ass'n, no.49 (1937). il.
   Louis H. Powell, "Browns Valley and
   Milnesand Similarities," Am.Anti-
   quity 22 (1957):298-300.
   Eldon Johnson, "The Prehistory of
   the Red River Valley," Minnesota
   History 38 (1962):157-65.
-Norse mooring stone
   "New Discoveries Supporting Medieval
   Norse Presence in the Upper Mid-
   west," NEARA Newsl. 9 (spring 1974):
   15.

Burnsville
-UFO (NL)
   1978, Oct./Ruth M. Dutton
   Dodge Center Star-Record, 2 Nov.1978.

Canby
-Acoustic anomaly
   1968, June/Jerome Clark
   Jerome Clark, "Paranormal Terror,"
   Saga UFO Rept. 4 (July 1977):8.
-Cattle mutilation
   1973, Nov.5/Leonard Van Hyfte
   Jerome Clark, "Strange Case of the
   Cattle Killings," Fate 27 (Aug.1974)
   :79-82. il.
   1976, Nov.6/NE of town
   Canby News, 17 Nov.1976.
-Phantom
   1960s
   John A. Keel, Strange Creatures from
   Time and Space (Greenwich, Ct.: Faw-
   cett, 1970), pp.185-86.

Carver co.
-UFO (NL)
   1973, Oct.18

(Editorial), Fate 27 (Feb.1974):35.

Cass Lake
-UFO (?)
   1966, Aug.16/=barium cloud
   John A. Keel, "The Night the Sky
   Turned On," Fate 20 (Sep.1967):30,
   32.

Cedar
-UFO (CE-2)
   1976, Jan.6/Janet Stewart/County Rd.15
   "Woman Reports Possible UFO Effects,"
   Skylook, no.101 (Apr.1976):4-7.

Chatfield
-Giant human skeletons
   n.d./7 mi.SW on Jordan Creek
   N.H. Winchell, The Aborigines of
   Minnesota (St. Paul: Minnesota Hist.
   Soc'y, 1911), p.94, quoting Chat-
   field Democrat (undated).

Chisago City
-UFO (NL)
   1974, Sep.11/Dale Olson/2 mi.S
   Chisago County Press, 18 Sep.1974.

Chokio
-Norse runestone
   "New Discoveries Supporting Medieval
   Norse Presence in the Upper Mid-
   west," NEARA Newsl. 9 (spring 1974)
   :15-16. il.
-Norse spearhead and fish-hook
   1961-1962
   Alf Mongé & Ole G. Landsverk, Norse
   Medieval Cryptography in Runic Carv-
   ings (Glendale, Cal.: Norseman,
   1967), p.195.

Clearwater
-Giant human skeletons
   1888, June/Charles W. Pinkerton/12 mi.
   from town
   St. Paul Pioneer-Press, 29 June 1888;
   and 1 July 1888.

Climax
-Norse firesteel
   1871/Ole Jevning/4 mi.N
   Hjalmar R. Holand, The Kensington
   Stone (Ephraim, Wisc.: The Author,
   1932), pp.167-68. il.

Cloquet
-UFO (CE-2)
   1976, June 20/I-35W
   "Sighting Reports," CUFOS News Bull.,
   Sep.1976, p.5.

Collegeville
-Haunt
   1960s/St. John's Abbey/=hoax
   Helen Gilbert, "The Crack in the Ab-
   bey Floor: A Laboratory Analysis of
   a Legend," Indiana Folklore 8, no.
   1-2 (1975):61-78.

Comstock
-UFO (CE-2)
 1964, May 5/Alfred Ernst
 "Physical Evidence Landing Reports,"
 UFO Inv. 2 (July-Aug.1964):4,5.

Cook
-UFO (CE-2)
 1966, March 24
 "Typical Reports," UFO Inv. 3 (Mar.-
 Apr.1966):8.

Coon Rapids
-Erratic kangaroo
 1957/Barbara Battmer
 1958/Linda Brodie
 David Fideler & Loren Coleman, "Kangaroos from Nowhere," Fate 31 (Apr.
 1978):68,72.
-UFO (NL)
 1978, April 10/Bessie Wilson/Hwy.10
 Coon Rapids Herald, 21 Apr.1978.

Cottonwood
-UFO (CE-1)
 1956, Nov.29/Harold Thompson
 "Case 260," CRIFO Orbit, 4 Jan.1957,
 p.3.
-UFO (NL)
 1960, Dec.25/Roger J. Birner
 "1960 Sighting of UAO Carrier," APRO
 Bull. 11 (Nov.1962):2.
 (Letter), Flying Saucer Rev. 8 (Nov.-
 Dec.1962):iii.
 Richard Hall, ed., The UFO Evidence
 (Washington: NICAP, 1964), p.147.

Crookston
-Haunt
 1943, Dec.17
 "Ghosts Active," Fortean Soc'y Mag.,
 no.10 (autumn 1944):142.

Crystal
-Fall of corn kernels
 1967, April 30/Herman Jedneak
 (Editorial), Fate 20 (Sep.1967):12.
-UFO (NL)
 1978, Jan.16/Jon Spizale/4733 Maryland
 Ave.N
 Minneapolis Star, 16 Jan.1978.

Cyrus
-UFO (CE-2)
 1965, Nov.16/Tom Untiedt/Hwy.28
 Jerome Clark, "The Greatest Flap Yet?
 Part IV," Flying Saucer Rev. 12
 (Nov.-Dec.1966):9,11.

Dilworth
-UFO (?)
 1954, Sep.25/=meteor?
 "North Central States Alarmed by
 Soaring Blue-White 'Ball,'" CRIFO
 Newsl., 5 Nov.1954, p.3.

Dresbach
-Giant human skeletons
 n.d.
 N.H. Winchell, The Aborigines of

Minnesota (St. Paul: Minnesota Hist.
 Soc'y, 1911), pp.89-90.

Duluth
-UFO (?)
 1959, March 13/=Venus?
 Donald H. Menzel & Lyle G. Boyd, The
 World of Flying Saucers (Garden
 City: Doubleday, 1963), pp.72-73.
-UFO (CE-2)
 1966, Aug.16/James Luhm/Hwy.8
 Duluth News-Tribune, 18 Aug.1966.
 John A. Keel, "The Night the Sky
 Turned On," Fate 20 (Sep.1967):30,
 33-34.
 J. Allen Hynek & Jacques Vallee, The
 Edge of Reality (Chicago: Regnery,
 1975), pp.172-74.
 1973, Oct.7
 "Cloud Hides UFO," APRO Bull. 22
 (Nov.-Dec.1973):1,4.
-UFO (NL)
 1897, April 12
 Eau Claire (Wisc.) Telegram, 13 Apr.
 1897.
 1966, Aug.17/Dennis Tyo/West Tischer
 Rd.
 Duluth News-Tribune, 18 Aug.1966.
 John A. Keel, "The Night the Sky
 Turned On," Fate 20 (Sep.1967):30,
 37.
-UFO (R-V)
 1965, Aug.4
 Rochester Bulletin, 5 Aug.1965.
 Flint (Mich.) Journal, 5 Aug.1965.
 Alameda (Cal.) Times-Star, 10 Aug.
 1965.

Eagle Bend
-UFO (CE-2)
 1961, May 10/Richard Vogt/S of town
 Eagle Bend News, 25 May 1961.

Eagle Lake
-Fall of unknown object
 1962, Jan.28/Charles Jude
 Frank Edwards, "Mystery Blast over
 Nevada," Fate 15 (Aug.1962):68,72.
-Phantom
 1976, Sep.
 Fargo (N.D.) Forum, 4 Sep.1976.
-UFO (?)
 1966, Aug.16/Lawrence Frenzel/=barium
 cloud
 John A. Keel, "The Night the Sky
 Turned On," Fate 20 (Sep.1967):30,
 31.

East Grand Forks
-UFO (NL)
 1897, April 15/Mr. McGraw
 East Grand Forks Courier, 16 Apr.1897.

Eden Prairie
-UFO (CE-1)
 1978, April 26/Sally Stoddart/Baker Rd.
 Eden Prairie News, 4 May 1978.
 1978, May 1/Rhoda Haas/Pioneer Trail
 1978, May 3/Tracy Kowalczyk/The Preserve

Eden Prairie News, 11 May 1978.
-UFO (NL)
  1965, Nov.9/LeRoy Hattery/airport
  Jerome Clark, "The Greatest Flap Yet?
  Part IV," Flying Saucer Rev. 12
  (Nov.-Dec.1966):9,10.

Elbow Lake
-UFO (NL)
  1897, April 18
  Elbow Lake Grant County Herald, 22
  Apr.1897.

Elysian
-UFO (CE-3)
  1897, April 19
  Mankato Review, 20 Apr.1897.

Erdahl
-Norse ax
  1893/Julius Davidson/3 mi.SE/=French
  weapon
    Hjalmar R. Holand, The Kensington
    Stone (Ephraim, Wisc.: The Author,
    1932), pp.156-59,171-72. il.
    Hjalmar R. Holand, A Pre-Columbian
    Crusade to America (N.Y.: Twayne,
    1962), pp.167-69. il.
    Alf Mongé & Ole G. Landsverk, Norse
    Medieval Cryptography in Runic Carv-
    ings (Glendale, Cal.: Norseman,
    1967), pp.203-204.

Erskine
-UFO (NL)
  1965, Nov.16
  Jerome Clark, "The Greatest Flap Yet?
  Part IV," Flying Saucer Rev. 12
  (Nov.-Dec.1966):9,11.

Essig
-UFO (NL)
  1897, April 15/Dr. James
  Sleepy Eye Dispatch, 22 Apr.1897.

Excelsior
-UFO (NL)
  1897, April 11/Mr. Newell
  Minneapolis Journal, 12 Apr.1897.

Fairfax
-Telepathy
  1946, June 20/Arthur A. Strauch/12 mi.
  SE on Minnesota R.
    Arthur A. Strauch, "Telepathy Saved
    My Wife," Fate 18 (June 1965):73-74.

Fairmont
-UFO (?)
  1967, Oct.19
  "UFOs--October--U.S.A.," APRO Bull.
  16 (Nov.-Dec.1967):8.

Faribault
-UFO (NL)
  1977, Oct.
  Waseca Daily Journal, 14 Oct.1967.

Farwell
-UFO (CE-2)

1967, Jan./Robert Blaine/2 mi.E on
Hwy.55
  "Car Buzzing Incidents on Increase,"
  APRO Bull. 15 (May-June 1967):5.
  Jim & Coral Lorenzen, UFOs over the
  Americas (N.Y.: Signet, 1968), pp.
  25-26.

Fergus Falls
-UFO (NL)
  1897, April 21
  Elbow Lake Grant County Herald, 22
  Apr.1897.
  1975, Sep.1
  "UFO Central," CUFOS News Bull., 15
  Nov.1975, p.17.

Finland
-UFO (NL)
  1978, July
  Two Harbors Lake City News-Chronicle,
  2 Aug.1978.
-UFO (R)
  1966, Sep.5/Finland AFB/=radar echo
  Gordon D. Thayer, "Radar and Optical
  Analyses of Field Cases," in Edward
  U. Condon, ed., Scientific Study of
  Unidentified Flying Objects (N.Y.:
  Bantam, 1969 ed.), pp.115,119-22.

Floodwood
-Humanoid
  1968, Nov.12/Uno Heikkila/10 mi.N
  John Green, The Sasquatch File (Ag-
  assiz, B.C.: Cheam, 1973), p.50.
-UFO (NL)
  1967, March
  Floodwood Rural Forum, 9 Mar.1967.

Forest Lake
-UFO (NL)
  1956, Dec.2/Mr. Moffett
  "Case 286," CRIFO Orbit, 1 Mar.1957,
  p.2, quoting Forest Lake Times (undated).
  1975, Oct.28
  "UFO Central," CUFOS News Bull., 1
  Feb.1976, p.10.

Fort Ripley
-UFO (NL)
  1965, Nov.16/Russell Nelson
  Jerome Clark, "The Greatest Flap Yet?
  Part IV," Flying Saucer Rev. 12
  (Nov.-Dec.1966):9,11.

Fountain
-UFO (NL)
  1897, April 13/Hugo Heck
  Winona Daily Herald, 14 Apr.1897.

Garvin
-UFO (CE-1)
  1966, Nov.26/John Nelson/nr. L. Sarah
  Marshall Messenger, 26 Nov.1966.
  Lamberton News, 8 Dec.1966.

Gibbon
-Ghost
  1926, June/Mrs. Strauch

Art Strauch, "Hometown Witch,"
Fate 17 (Sep.1964):43,47-48.
1948, July 10/Katherine Strauch
Arthur A. Strauch, "Telepathy Saved
My Wife," Fate 18 (June 1965):73,76.
-Ghost light
1930, Aug./Arthur A. Strauch/cemetery
Art Strauch, "Hometown Witch," Fate
17 (Sep.1964):43,48-49.
-Hex
1916-1918
Art Strauch, "Hometown Witch," Fate
17 (Sep.1964):43-47.
-Telepathy
1948, April 25/Katherine Strauch
Arthur A. Strauch, "Telepathy Saved
My Wife," Fate 18 (June 1965):73,75.

Glenwood
-UFO (?)
1954, Sep.25/Mrs. Harlan Iverson/
=meteor?
"North Central States Alarmed by
Soaring Blue-White 'Ball,'" CRIFO
Newsl., 5 Nov.1954, p.3.

Golden Valley
-UFO (NL)
1965, Aug.3
Coral E. Lorenzen, "Western UFO Flap,"
Fate 18 (Nov.1965):42,51.
1975, Oct.8
"UFO Central," CUFOS News Bull., 1
Feb.1976, p.8.

Graceville
-UFO (?)
1954, Sep.25/=meteor?
"North Central States Alarmed by
Soaring Blue-White 'Ball,'" CRIFO
Newsl., 5 Nov.1954, p.3.
-UFO (NL)
1956, Nov.14/Marlen Hewitt/U.S.75
"Case 247," CRIFO Orbit, 7 Dec.1956,
p.4, quoting Duluth News-Tribune
(undated).
(Editorial), Fate 10 (Mar.1957):14-
15.

Grand Marais
-UFO (?)
1966, Sep.5-6/=star
Gordon D. Thayer, "Optical and Radar
Analyses of Field Cases," in Edward
U. Condon, ed., Scientific Study of
Unidentified Flying Objects (N.Y.:
Bantam, 1969 ed.), pp.115,119-22.

Grand Portage
-Seance
1767, July/Jonathan Carver/shaking tent
Jonathan Carver, Travels Through the
Interior Parts of North America
(London: J. Walter & S. Crowder,
1778), pp.123-28.

Hallock
-Reincarnation
1968/Natalie Merle
Shirley A. Merle, "Four-Year-Old Nat-

alie Remembers," Fate 29 (June
1976):53-55.

Hastings
-Haunt
1860s
St. Louis Missouri Democrat, 5 Sep.
1869, p.3.
-UFO (?)
1878, March 13/=meteor
Hastings Gazette, 16 Mar.1878.
-UFO (NL)
1897, April 13/Vermillion St.
Hastings Democrat, 15 Apr.1897.

Hawley
-Norse mooring stone
n.d./O.N. Bjorndal/7 mi.S
n.d./2 mi.E
Hjalmar R. Holand, A Pre-Columbian
Crusade to America (N.Y.: Twayne,
1962), pp.128,145.

Hector
-UFO (NL)
1897, April 13
Minneapolis Times, 15 Apr.1897.

Herman
-UFO (CE-1)
1965, Nov.16/Ray Schuman
Jerome Clark, "The Greatest Flap Yet?
Part IV," Flying Saucer Rev. 12
(Nov.-Dec.1966):9,11.
-UFO (CE-2)
1965, Dec.20/Edward Bruns
Herman Review, 23 Dec.1965.

Hibbing
-Norse sword hilt
1942, June 3/Mike Pribich
Hjalmar R. Holand, America: 1355-
1364 (N.Y.: Duell, Sloan & Pearce,
1946), pp.178-83. il.
-UFO (?)
1966, Aug.16/Patrick McKenzie/=barium
cloud
John A. Keel, "The Night the Sky
Turned On," Fate 20 (Sep.1967):30,
32, quoting Hibbing Tribune (undated).
-UFO (NL)
1975, Aug.14
"UFO Central," CUFOS News Bull., 15
Nov.1975, p.16.

Hopkins
-UFO (?)
1957, Nov.11/=Venus
Jacques & Janine Vallee, Challenge
to Science (N.Y.: Ace, 1966 ed.),
p.132.

Hutchinson
-Cloud anomaly
ca.1899/John Zeleny
John Zeleny, "Rumbling Clouds and
Luminous Clouds," Science 75 (1932)
:80-81.

International Falls
-Lightning anomaly
  1955, July/Mrs. Cline
    (Editorial), Fate 8 (Nov.1955):6.
-UFO (?)
  1951, summer
    Harold T. Wilkins, Flying Saucers on
    the Attack (N.Y.: Ace, 1967 ed.),
    p.140.
-UFO (DD)
  1975, Oct.19
    "Noteworthy UFO Sightings," Ufology
    2 (spring 1976):42.
  1976, June 28
    "Noteworthy UFO Sightings," Ufology
    2 (fall 1976):60.

Isabella
-Mystery plane crash
  1960, March 13
    Jay Gourley, The Great Lakes Triangle
    (Greenwich, Ct.: Fawcett, 1977), pp.
    73-74.

Ivanhoe
-Cattle mutilation
  1973, May/Paul Rolling
    Jerome Clark, "Strange Case of the
    Cattle Killings," Fate 27 (Aug.1974)
    :79,82-83.

Johnson
-Norse ax
  1917
    Alf Mongé & Ole G. Landsverk, Norse
    Medieval Cryptography in Runic Carv-
    ings (Glendale, Cal.: Norseman,
    1967), p.195.

Jonesville
-UFO (NL)
  1897, April 12/J.A. Henry
    Minneapolis Journal, 14 Apr.1897.

Kensington
-Norse runestone
  1898, Nov.8/Olaf Ohman
    Chicago (Ill.) Tribune, 21 Feb.1899,
    p.7; 23 Feb.1899, p.9; and 24 Feb.
    1899, p.3.
    Minneapolis Journal, 22 Feb.1899, p.1.
    Chicago (Ill.) Skandinaven, 22 Feb.
    1899, p.4.
    Alexandria Post-News, 2 Mar.1899, p.
    1. il.
    Oslo (Norway) Morgenbladet, 12 Mar.
    1899.
    Minneapolis Svenska Amerikanska Post-
    en, 23 May 1899.
    Knut O. Hoegh, "Kensington og Elbow
    Lake stenene," Symra 5 (1909):178-
    79.
    George T. Flom, "The Kensington Rune-
    Stone," Trans.Illinois Hist.Soc'y,
    10 May 1910, pp.105-25.
    Warren Upham, "The Rune Stone of Ken-
    sington, Minnesota," Mag.of History
    13 (Feb.1911):67-73.
    "The Kensington Rune Stone," Minne-
    sota Hist.Coll. 15 (1915):221-86. il.

Constant Larson, History of Douglas
and Grant Counties, Minnesota (Indianapolis: B.F. Bowen, 1916), 1:
72-122.
Charles C. Willson, "A Lawyer's View
of the Kensington Rune Stone," Minnesota History Bull. 2 (1917):13-
19.
H.R. Holand, "The Kensington Rune
Stone," Wisconsin Mag.History 3
(Dec.1919):153-83. il.
Rasmus B. Anderson, "Another View
of the Kensington Rune Stone," Wis-
consin Mag.History 3 (June 1920):
413-19.
Laurence M. Larson, "The Kensington
Rune Stone," Wisconsin Mag.History
4 (June 1921):382-87.
Hjalmar R. Holand, The Kensington
Stone (Ephraim, Wisc.: The Author,
1932). il.
Laurence M. Larson, "The Kensington
Rune Stone," Minnesota History 17
(1936):20-37.
Hjalmar R. Holand, Westward from
Vinland (N.Y.: Duell, Sloan &
Pearce, 1940), pp.97-197. il.
C. Stewart Peterson, America's Rune
Stone of AD 1362 Gains Favor (N.Y.:
Hobson, 1946).
Johannes N. Brøndsted, "Problemet om
nordboer i Nordamerika for Cölum-
bus," Aarboger før Nordisk Oldkyn-
dighed og Historie, 1950, pp.1-152.
Arlington H. Mallery, Lost America
(Washington: Public Affairs, 1950),
pp.176-81.
S.N. Hagen, "The Kensington Runic
Inscription," Speculum 25 (July
1950):321-56.
Eric Moltke, "The Kensington Stone,"
Antiquity 25 (June 1951):87-93.
William Thalbitzer, "Two Runic Stones,
from Greenland and Minnesota," Smith.
Misc.Coll., vol.116, no.3 (1951).
il.
Johannes Brøndsted, "Norsemen in
North America Before Columbus," Ann.
Rept.Smith.Inst. 103 (1953):367-
405. il.
Erik Moltke, "The Ghost of the Ken-
sington Stone," Scandinavian Stud-
ies 25 (1953):1-14.
Minneapolis Star, 18-19 May 1955.
Hjalmar R. Holand, Explorations in
America Before Columbus (N.Y.:
Twayne, 1956), pp.161-76,313-50.
Erik Wahlgren, The Kensington Stone:
A Mystery Solved (Madison: Univ. of
Wisconsin, 1958). il.
O.G. Landsverk, The Discovery of the
Kensington Runestone: A Reappraisal
(Glendale, Cal.: Church Press, 1961).
Hjalmar R. Holand, A Pre-Columbian
Crusade to America (N.Y.: Twayne,
1962), pp.28-102. il.
Alf Mongé & Ole G. Landsverk, Norse
Medieval Cryptography in Runic Carv-
ings (Glendale, Cal.: Norseman,
1967), pp.77-97,178-89. il.

Theodore C. Blegen, The Kensington
Rune Stone: New Light on an Old
Riddle (St. Paul: Minnesota Hist.
Soc'y, 1968). il.
O.G. Landsverk, Ancient Norse Mes-
sages on American Stones (Glendale,
Cal.: Norseman, 1969). il.
Rochester Post-Bulletin, 6 Aug.1974.
Alexandria Lake Region Echo, 23 Oct.
1974; and 20 July 1976.
Hoffman Tribune, 7 Nov.1974.
Minneapolis Star, 7 Jan.1977; and 10
Jan.1977.
Morris Tribune, 9 May 1978; and 13
July 1978.

Kimball
-Cattle mutilation
 1974, Dec./Frank Schifelbein/=predators
   Farmington Tribune, 2 Jan.1975.
   James Butler Bonham, "The Truth About
   the Cattle Mutilations," Official
   UFO 1 (Feb.1976):38,62-66.
   Ed Sanders, "The Mutilation Mystery,"
   Oui, Sep.1976, pp.51,52.
   Jerome Eden, "Cattle Mutilations and
   UFOs: A Look at the Facts," Official
   UFO 1 (Dec.1976):22-23.
   Jerome Clark, "A Rejoinder to Jacob
   Davidson," Pursuit 11 (summer 1978)
   :88.

Kinbrae
-UFO (CE-2)
 1965, April 8
   Jacques Vallee, Passport to Magonia
   (Chicago: Regnery, 1969), p.307.

Kingston
-UFO (CE-2)
 1978, July 3/Kim Cates/=lightning?
   St. Cloud Daily Times, 9 Aug.1978.
-UFO (NL)
 1977, Dec.31/Kim Cates
   St. Cloud Daily Times, 9 Aug.1978.

LaCrescent
-Giant human skeletons
 n.d.
   N.H. Winchell, The Aborigines of
   Minnesota (St. Paul: Minnesota Hist.
   Soc'y, 1911), p.80.
-Humanoid
 1968, fall
   Eric Norman [Brad Steiger], The Abom-
   inable Snowmen (N.Y.: Award, 1969),
   pp.81-82.

Lake Crystal
-UFO (NL)
 1897, April 10/Henry LeClair
   Lake Crystal Union, 21 Apr.1897.

Lake Elmo
-Precognition
 n.d./Bradley Earl Ayers
   Bradley Earl Ayers, "Terror Rode in
   a Red Car," Fate 28 (Dec.1975):57-
   61.
-UFO (CE-3)

1897, April 13/Frederick Chamberlain
   St. Paul Pioneer-Press, 15 Apr.1897.

Lakefield
-Erratic crocodilian
 1941, June
   Minneapolis Sunday Tribune & Star-
   Tribune, 22 June 1941, p.12.

Lake Lillian
-UFO (NL)
 1897, April 13/Thomas Marshall
   Minneapolis Times, 14 Apr.1897.

Lake Park
-Phantom
 1976, Aug.
   Ed Sanders, "On the Trail of the
   Night Surgeons," Oui, May 1977, pp.
   79,134.

LaSalle
-UFO (NL)
 1969, Nov.12/Ernest Tande
   "Minnesota Deputy Sheriff Trails Low
   Flying Object," Skylook, no.26
   (Jan.1970):18, quoting Sleepy Eye
   Herald-Dispatch (undated).

Lengby
-UFO (NL)
 1975, Oct.14
   "Noteworthy UFO Sightings," Ufology
   2 (spring 1976):42.

LeRoy
-UFO (NL)
 1976, Jan.1
   "Noteworthy UFO Sightings," Ufology
   2 (summer 1976):62.

Lindstrom
-UFO (NL)
 1978, March 22/Greg Darr/=helicopters?
   Lindstrom Chisago County Press, 29
   Mar.1978.

Litchfield
-Midday darkness
 1880, April 18
   New York Times, 25 Apr.1880, p.5,
   quoting St. Paul Pioneer-Press (undated).

Little Falls
-Fall of metal foil
 1957, Aug.1
   St. Paul Pioneer-Press, 2 Aug.1957.
   (Editorial), Fate 10 (Dec.1957):12-
   13.
-UFO (CE-1)
 1976, March 23
   "Noteworthy UFO Sightings," Ufology
   2 (summer 1976):62.

Littlefork
-UFO (CE-1)
 1976, Feb.10
   "Noteworthy UFO Sightings," Ufology
   2 (summer 1976):62.

Long Prairie
-UFO (CE-3)
　　1965, Oct.23/James Townsend/Hwy.27
　　　St. Paul Pioneer-Press, 25 Oct.1965.
　　　Minneapolis Star, 25 Oct.1965.
　　　Clare John Jansen, "Little Tin Men
　　　in Minnesota," Fate 19 (Feb.1966):
　　　36-40.
　　　Jerome Clark, "The Greatest Flap Yet?
　　　Part III," Flying Saucer Rev. 12
　　　(May-June 1966):13,14-15.
-UFO (DD)
　　1952, April 20/Louie Masonick, Jr.
　　　"Saucer Sightings by IFSB Members,"
　　　Space Rev. 2 (Jan.1953):10.

Luverne
-UFO (?)
　　1965, Nov.15
　　　Jerome Clark, "The Greatest Flap Yet?
　　　Part IV," Flying Saucer Rev. 12
　　　(Nov.-Dec.1966):9,11.

Lyle
-UFO (NL)
　　1963, June 4/Zearl Leinen
　　　"News Briefs," Saucer News 10 (Dec.
　　　1963):22.
　　　Jacques Vallee, Passport to Magonia
　　　(Chicago: Regnery, 1969), p.292.

McGregor
-UFO (NL)
　　1975, Oct.21
　　　"Noteworthy UFO Sightings," Ufology
　　　2 (spring 1976):42.

Madison Lake
-UFO (NL)
　　1897, April 13/A.M. Haynes
　　　Mankato Daily Free Press, 14 Apr.
　　　1897.

Mankato
-Out-of-body experience
　　1890s/W.A. Laufman
　　　John Philip Bessor, "A 'Dead' Man
　　　Returned to Life," Fate 8 (July
　　　1955):42-43, quoting Boston (Mass.)
　　　Post (undated).
-UFO (NL)
　　1897, April 13
　　　Mankato Daily Free Press, 14 Apr.1897.
　　1897, April 14
　　　Mankato Weekly Ledger, 19 Apr.1897.
　　1897, April 19
　　　Mankato Review, 20 Apr.1897.

Medford
-UFO (CE-2)
　　1975, Nov.2
　　　"From the Center for UFO Studies,"
　　　Flying Saucer Rev. 21 (Apr.1976):
　　　24,26.
　　　Edward J. Zeller, "The Use of Thermo-
　　　luminescence for the Evaluation of
　　　UFO Landing Site Effects," in Proc.
　　　1976 CUFOS Conference (Evanston:
　　　Center for UFO Studies, 1976), pp.
　　　301-308.

Medina
-UFO (CE-2)
　　1948, Aug.11
　　　Harold T. Wilkins, Flying Saucers on
　　　the Attack (N.Y.: Ace, 1967 ed.),
　　　p.98.
　　　Donald E. Keyhoe, Flying Saucers: Top
　　　Secret (N.Y.: Putnam, 1960), p.90.

Meeker co.
-Cattle and hog mutilations
　　1975, Aug.
　　　Roberta Donovan & Keith Wolverton,
　　　Mystery Stalks the Prairie (Raynes-
　　　ford, Mont.: THAR, 1976), pp.26-27.

Mendota
-Fall of unknown object
　　1956, Sep.22/George White
　　　"Case 221," CRIFO Orbit, 2 Nov.1956,
　　　pp.2-3, quoting St. Paul Dispatch
　　　(undated).

Middle River
-UFO (CE-2)
　　1966, Dec./Lorraine Mayone/2 mi.E
　　　(Letter), Ufology 2 (spring 1976):48.

Minneapolis
-Ball lightning
　　1971, Aug.
　　　F.J. Anderson, "A Report on Ball
　　　Lightning," J.Geophys.Rsch. 77
　　　(1972):3928-30.
-Clairvoyance
　　1898, Dec.-1899, May/Louise Spink
　　　Hereward Carrington, "Apparent Hal-
　　　lucination," J.ASPR 2 (1908):448-55.
-Fall of bubbles
　　1971, July 26
　　　St. Paul Dispatch, 28 July 1971.
-Fall of red snow
　　1954, March 13
　　　(Editorial), Fate 8 (Jan.1955):9-10.
-Inner development
　　1960s-　　　/Mental Science Institute
　　　J. Gordon Melton, Encyclopedia of
　　　American Religions, 2 vols. (Wil-
　　　mington, N.C.: Consortium, 1978),
　　　2:285.
　　1970s/Gnostic Aquarian Society/1414
　　Laurel Ave.
　　　Armand Biteaux, The New Conscious-
　　　ness (Willits, Cal.: Oliver, 1975),
　　　p.55.
-Moving lamp fixture
　　1952/vacant building
　　　(Editorial), Fate 6 (Apr.1953):8.
　　　(Letter), Paul Brandt, Fate 6 (Aug.
　　　1953):115-16.
-Phantom
　　1974, Nov.26/Mike Gribovski
　　　Kevin D. Randle, "The UFO Pictures
　　　That Nobody Wanted," Official·UFO 2
　　　(Feb.1977):20,21-22.
-Precognition
　　1956, Aug./Evelyn Melberg
　　　Laura A. Dale, Rhea White & Gardner
　　　Murphy, "A Selection of Cases from
　　　a Recent Survey of Spontaneous ESP

Phenomena," J.ASPR 56 (1962):3,23-
25.
-Reincarnation
1945, Aug./Univ. of Minnesota
Juan H. McBroom, "Can Ancestral Memories Be Inherited?" Fate 2 (July
1949):86-90.
-Seance
1921, Fall/O.A. Ostby
O.A. Ostby, "He Murdered Me!" Fate
7 (Dec.1954):36-39.
-Skyquake
1946, Dec.16
"Explosions," Doubt, no.18 (1947):
271.
-UFO (?)
1897, April 13/=star?
Minneapolis Times, 14 Apr.1897.
1897, April 16/William Cranik/8th St.
x Hennepin Ave./=hoax?
Minneapolis Tribune, 19 Apr.1897.
1954, May 5
Richard Hall,ed., The UFO Evidence
(Washington: NICAP, 1964), p.14.
1954, June 30/Marvin Tjornhom
(Editorial), Fate 8 (May 1955):13.
il.
1957, Jan.1/R.H. Scrimshaw/=meteor?
"Case 291," CRIFO Orbit, 1 Mar.1957,
p.3.
-UFO (CE-1)
1947, July 6/Mrs. Clarence Lasseson/
606 W. 31st St.
Minneapolis Star, 7 July 1947.
1975, Oct.5
"UFO Central," CUFOS News Bull., 1
Feb.1976, pp.7-8.
1977, Feb.5/Rose Strand
Minneapolis Star, 16 Feb.1977.
-UFO (DD)
1938/Harvey L. Sperry
Gordon I.R. Lore, Jr. & Harold H. Den-
eault, Jr., Mysteries of the Skies:
UFOs in Perspective (Englewood
Cliffs, N.J.: Prentice-Hall, 1968),
p.136.
1947, July 7/Dean Ireton/Omaha Railroad
Yards
St. Paul Pioneer-Press, 8 July 1947.
1951, Oct.11/J.J. Kaliszewski/N of
town
Richard Hall, ed., The UFO Evidence
(Washington: NICAP, 1964), p.56.
U.S. Air Force, Projects Grudge and
Blue Book Reports 1-12 (Washington:
NICAP, 1968), pp.19,50-51.
1953, Oct.15/General Mills Laboratory
J. Allen Hynek, The UFO Experience
(Chicago: Regnery, 1972), p.62.
J. Allen Hynek, The Hynek UFO Report
(N.Y.: Dell, 1977), pp.113-14.
-UFO (NL)
1897, April 10/J.J. Barrett/Guaranty
Loan Restaurant/=balloon?
Minneapolis Tribune, 11 Apr.1897.
Minneapolis Journal, 14 Apr.1897.
1897, April 11/R.G. Adams/3128 Fourth
Ave. S/=balloon?
Minneapolis Journal, 12 Apr.1897;
and 14 Apr.1897.

St. Paul Pioneer-Press, 12 Apr.1897.
1954, May 5/Univ. of Minnesota Physics
Bldg.
"C-3," CRIFO Newsl., 6 Aug.1954, p.
4.
1954, Sep.25
"North Central States Alarmed by
Soaring Blue-White 'Ball,'" CRIFO
Newsl., 5 Nov.1954, p.3.
1956, Nov.30/Fred Ewing
"Case 262," CRIFO Orbit, 4 Jan.1957,
p.3.
1956, Dec.11/John Talley
"Case 287," CRIFO Orbit, 1 Mar.1957,
p.2.
1965, Aug.3
Minneapolis Tribune, 4 Aug.1965.
1965, Oct.23/Ray Blessing
Clare John Jansen, "Little Tin Men
in Minnesota," Fate 19 (Feb.1966):
36,40.
Jerome Clark, "The Greatest Flap Yet?
Part III," Flying Saucer Rev. 12
(May-June 1966):13,14-15.
1966, Aug.16/Flying Cloud Airport
Duluth News-Tribune, 18 Aug.1966.
John A. Keel, "The Night the Sky
Turned On," Fate 20 (Sep.1967):30,
34-35.
J. Allen Hynek & Jacques Vallee, The
Edge of Reality (Chicago: Regnery,
1975), pp.172-74.
1967, Feb.25/Joseph E. Sullivan/1st
Ave. x 25th St.
"News Camera Man Sees UFO," APRO
Bull. 15 (Mar.-Apr.1967):6.
1974, Nov.26/Mike Gribovski
Kevin D. Randle, "The UFO Pictures
That Nobody Wanted," Official UFO
2 (Feb.1977):20-22,48-50. il.
1976, Oct.19/L. Harriet
"UFOs of Limited Merit," Int'l UFO
Reporter 1 (Dec.1976):11.

Minnetonka
-UFO (NL)
1897, April 11/Stuart Mackroth
Minneapolis Tribune, 13 Apr.1897.

Montgomery
-UFO (?)
1897, April 11
Minneapolis Times, 14 Apr.1897.

Moorhead
-Phantom
1968, May
Jerome Clark, "Paranormal Terror,"
Saga UFO Rept. 4 (July 1977):8.
-UFO (NL)
1952, April 26/=ducks?
Minneapolis Tribune, 29 Apr.1952.
Edward J. Ruppelt, The Report on Un-
identified Flying Objects (Garden
City: Doubleday, 1956), p.140.

Mora
-Norse ax
1933/William H. Williams/8 mi.S
Hjalmar H. Holand, A Pre-Columbian

Crusade to America (N.Y.: Twayne, 1962), pp.178-79. il.

Motley
-UFO (CE-1)
1969, Sep./Sean Blackburn
Jerome Clark & Loren Coleman, The Unidentified (N.Y.: Warner, 1975), pp.21-22.

Mound
-UFO (NL)
1973, Oct.18/Bradford Roy
Reno Nevada State Journal, 24 Oct. 1973.
(Editorial), Fate 27 (Feb.1974):35.

Murray co.
-Archeological site
T.H. Lewis, "Stone Monuments in Northwestern Iowa and Southwestern Minnesota," Am.Anthro. 3 (1890):269-74.

New Brighton
-UFO (NL)
1978, March 22/Fritz Werdonschegg/Long Lake Rd.
St. Paul Dispatch-North, 25 Apr.1978.

Newfolden
-UFO (NL)
1976, Dec.18
"UFOs of Limited Merit," Int'l UFO Reporter 2 (Feb.1977):5.

New London
-UFO (CE-1)
1965, April 26/Gary Green
"Near-Landing in Minnesota," Saucer News 12 (Sep.1965):26-27.

Newport
-UFO (NL)
1954, Oct.22/J.J. Mealy
(Letter), Fate 8 (May 1955):112.

New Scandia twp.
-UFO (NL)
1978, March 22/Cathy Hawkinson/=helicopters?
St. Paul Pioneer Press-Dispatch, 25 Mar.1978, p.28.
St. Paul Dispatch, 31 Mar.1978; and 20 June 1978.
Brad Ayers, "A Mini-Flap in Minnesota: UFO or Helicopters?" Int'l UFO Reporter 3 (May 1978):Newsfront sec.
"Huge UFO over Minnesota," APRO Bull. 26 (June 1978):1-3.
"Follow-Up," APRO Bull. 27 (Nov.1978):1.

New Ulm
-Spirit medium
1850s-1874/Mrs. Albert Blanchard
Frederick Bligh Bond, "Some Rare Forms of Mediumship," Psychic Rsch. 24 (1930):437-39. il.
-UFO (?)

1897, April 13/=Venus
New Ulm News, 17 Apr.1897.
-UFO (DD)
1963, June/Carl Pfaender
Arthur A. Strauch, "I Photographed a UFO," Fate 19 (June 1966):67,70-72.
-UFO (NL)
1897, April 19
Mankato Review, 20 Apr.1897.
St. Paul Pioneer Press, 20 Apr.1897.

Northfield
-Inner development
1963-   /Reformed Druids of North America
Isaac Bonewits, Druid Chronicles (Evolved) (Berkeley, Cal.: The Author, 1977).
J. Gordon Melton, Encyclopedia of American Religions, 2 vols. (Wilmington, N.C.: Consortium, 1978), 2:292-93.

Norwood
-UFO (NL)
1897, April 13/Leopold Henkleman
Norwood Times, 16 Apr.1897.

Owatonna
-Clairvoyance and precognition
1959/David Symons/10 mi.S
(Editorial), Fate 12 (Sep.1959):12.
-Men-in-black
1967, May/Mrs. Ralph Butler
John A. Keel, UFOs: Operation Trojan Horse (N.Y.: Putnam, 1970), p.185.
-Poltergeist
1880/Mr. Dimant
Charles Fort, The Books of Charles Fort (N.Y.: Holt, 1941), p.943, quoting Religio-Philosophical J., 25 Dec.1880.
1966-1968/Mrs. Ralph Butler
John A. Keel, UFOs: Operation Trojan Horse (N.Y.: Putnam, 1970), p.186.
-UFO (CE-3)
1966, Nov./Mrs. Ralph Butler
John A. Keel, UFOs: Operation Trojan Horse (N.Y.: Putnam, 1970), pp.184-85.

Palo
-UFO (CE-3)
1967, March 12
Ted Phillips, Physical Traces Associated with UFO Sightings (Evanston: Center for UFO Studies, 1975), p.46.

Pelican Rapids
-Archeological site
Minnesota "Man"/3 mi.N
Minneapolis Journal, 18 Dec.1932, p.6.
Albert E. Jenks, Pleistocene Man in Minnesota: A Fossil Homo Sapiens (Minneapolis: Univ. of Minnesota, 1936). il.
Aleš Hrdička, "The 'Minnesota Man,'" Am.J.Physical Anthro. 22 (1937):175-99.

Ernst Antevs, "The Age of 'Minnesota Man,'" Yearbook Carnegie Inst. Washington, no.36 (1937):335-38.

George F. Kay & Morris M. Leighton, "Geological Notes on the Occurrence of Minnesota Man," J.Geology 46 (1938):266-78.

Kirk Bryan & Paul MacClintock, "What Is Implied by 'Disturbance' at the Site of Minnesota Man," J.Geology 46 (1938):279-92.

Ernst Antevs, "Was Minnesota Girl Buried in a Gully?" J.Geology 46 (1938):293-95.

Albert E. Jenks, "A Reply to a Review by Dr. Aleš Hrdička," Am. Anthro. 40 (1938):328-36.

Lloyd A. Wilford, "A Revised Classification of the Prehistoric Cultures of Minnesota," Am.Antiquity 21 (1955):130-42.

Irwin Rovner & G.A. Agogino, "Minnesota Man: Archaeology's Fickle Female," Anthro.J.Canada 7, no.1 (1969):2-12.

Franklin Folsom, America's Ancient Treasures (N.Y.: Rand McNally, 1974), p.145.

New York Times, 19 Mar.1976, p.35.

Pine City
-Giant human skeleton
n.d.
N.H. Winchell, The Aborigines of Minnesota (St.Paul: Minnesota Hist. Soc'y, 1911), p.341.

Pine River
-UFO (CE-3)
1968, Jan?
Coral E. Lorenzen, The Shadow of the Unknown (N.Y.: Signet, 1970), pp. 160-61.

Preston
-UFO (NL)
1897, April 11/Thomas Quinn
Minneapolis Times, 14 Apr.1897.

Ranier
-UFO (?)
1966, Aug.16/=barium cloud
John A. Keel, "The Night the Sky Turned On," Fate 20 (Sep.1967): 30,32.

Regal
-UFO (CE-3)
1976, Sep.22
"UFOs of Limited Merit," Int'l UFO Reporter 1 (Nov.1976):5.

Remer
-Erratic snake
1953, Oct.25
"Follow Up," Doubt, no.45 (1954):284, 286.

Rochester
-Healing and contactee

1970s/Lorraine Darr
Brad Steiger, Gods of Aquarius (N.Y.: Harcourt Brace Jovanovich, 1976), pp.159-64.
-Humanoid
1968/Larry Hawkins/S on Hwy.52
Brad Steiger & Joan Whritenour, Allende Letters: New UFO Breakthrough (N.Y.: Award, 1968), pp.86-88, quoting Saga, June 1969.
-UFO (?)
1966, Aug.16/=barium cloud
J. Allen Hynek & Jacques Vallee, The Edge of Reality (Chicago: Regnery, 1975), pp.172-73.
-UFO (CE-1)
1967, March 12
Jacques Vallee, Passport to Magonia (Chicago: Regnery, 1969), p.341.
-UFO (CE-2)
1975, Aug.6
Ted Phillips, "Several Possible Traces Reported in 1975," Skylook, no.97 (Dec.1975):16.
-UFO (DD)
1973, Oct./Leroy Martell
"Saucers in the News," Flying Saucers, winter 1974, pp.44,60.

Rock co.
-Cattle mutilation
1974, Oct.4/Charles Metzger
Ed Sanders, "The Mutilation Mystery," Oui, Sep.1976, pp.51-52.

Rock Creek
-UFO (DD)
1947, July 6/Carl Dion/5 mi.E
St. Paul Dispatch, 7 July 1947.

Roseau
-UFO (?)
1954, July
Donald E. Keyhoe, Flying Saucer Conspiracy (N.Y.: Holt, 1955), p.190.

Roseville
-UFO (NL)
1965, Nov.16
Jerome Clark, "The Greatest Flap Yet? Part IV," Flying Saucer Rev. 12 (Nov.-Dec.1966):9,11.

Royalton
-UFO (NL)
1897, April 13
Minneapolis Times, 14 Apr.1897.

Russell
-Ghost
1957, Aug.10/William P. Schramm/5 mi.NW
William P. Schramm, "Time Marched Backwards," Fate 15 (Oct.1962):81, 83-84.

Sacred Heart
-UFO (CE-1)
1958, Jan.15/Richard Hoberg/Hwy.212
Arthur A. Strauch, "I Photographed a UFO," Fate 19 (June 1966):67,70.

Saint Anthony
-UFO (NL)
  1965, Aug.3
    Coral E. Lorenzen, "Western UFO Flap,"
    Fate 18 (Nov.1965):42,51.

Saint Cloud
-Clairvoyance
  1929, May/Mr. Halleckson
    Corette Halleckson, "The Missing
    Boys," Fate 9 (Mar.1956):52.

Saint George
-UFO (NL)
  1965, Oct.21/Arthur A. Strauch/NW of
  town
    "Deputy Snaps UFO Color Photo," APRO
    Bull. 14 (Nov.-Dec.1965):1,3. il.
    Arthur A. Strauch, "I Photographed a
    UFO," Fate 19 (June 1966):67-70.
    (Letter), Ralph Rankow, Fate 19 (Sep.
    1966):145.
    Jerome Clark, "The Greatest Flap Yet?
    Part IV," Flying Saucer Rev. 12
    (Nov.-Dec.1966):9.
    Robert Loftin, Identified Flying Sau-
    cers (N.Y.: David McKay, 1968), pp.
    94-99.
    "On Our Cover," Official UFO 1 (Feb.
    1976):4. il.
    Hayden C. Hewes, "The Arthur Strauch
    UFO Photo," Saga UFO Rept. 5 (Mar.
    1978):36-39. il.

Saint Louis Park
-UFO (NL)
  1968, April 28
    "U.S. Reports," APRO Bull. 17 (Sep.-
    Oct.1968):8.

Saint Paul
-Archeological site
    Edward Duffield Neill, The History
    of Minnesota (Philadelphia: Lippin-
    cott, 1858).
    T.H. Lewis, "Prehistoric Remains at
    St. Paul, Minnesota," Am.Antiquarian
    18 (1896):207-10.
    T.H. Lewis, "Mounds and Stone Cists
    at St. Paul, Minnesota," Am.Antiquar-
    ian 18 (1896):314-20.
    N.H. Winchell, The Aborigines of
    Minnesota (St. Paul: Minnesota Hist.
    Soc'y, 1911).
    T.H. Lewis, "Prehistoric Fire-place
    and Human Bones Found at St. Paul,"
    Minnesota Arch. 3 (1937):82-86.
-Fall of unknown substance
  1956, Sep.22/Mendota x Euclid St.
    "Falls," Doubt, no.53 (1956):417,
    quoting St. Paul Dispatch (undated).
-Inner development
  1970s/Council of American Witches/476
  Summit Ave.
    Lady Sheba, The Book of Shadows (St.
    Paul: Llewellyn, 1973).
    Armand Biteaux, The New Conscious-
    ness (Willits, Cal.: Oliver, 1975),
    pp.25-26.
    J. Gordon Melton, Encyclopedia of

American Religions, 2 vols. (Wil-
    mington, N.C.: Consortium, 1978),
    2:277-78.
-Precognition
  1886/E.P.P.
    Jack Greb, "An Old Editor's Prophe-
    cies," Fate 29 (Apr.1976):81.
-Skyquake
  1959, May 15
    (Letter), Elmer O. Dahl, Fate 12
    (Sep.1959):110-11.
-Spirit medium
  1978-   /Jerry Gross
    Midnight Globe, 8 Aug.1978. il.
-UFO (?)
  1957, Nov.11/=Venus
    Jacques & Janine Vallee, Challenge
    to Science (N.Y.: Ace, 1966 ed.),
    p.132.
-UFO (CE-1)
  1944, Oct./Nellie Carlin/400 block
  Marshall Ave.
    (Letter), Fate 10 (Mar.1957):113-16.
  1951/Deke Slayton
    J. Allen Hynek, The Hynek UFO Report
    (N.Y.: Dell, 1977), pp.290-91.
-UFO (CE-2)
  1965, Nov.26/Nick DeVara/Maryland x
  Supornick Lane
    St. Paul Pioneer Press, 27 Nov.1965.
    Coral E. Lorenzen, Flying Saucers:
    The Startling Evidence of the Inva-
    sion from Outer Space (N.Y.: Signet,
    1966 ed.), pp.256-57.
-UFO (DD)
  1966, Dec.27
    Brad Steiger, Project Blue Book (N.Y.:
    Ballantine, 1976), betw.pp.360-61.
    il.
  1978, April 28/E. George St. x Livingston Ave.
    St. Paul Dispatch, 29 Apr.1978.
-UFO (NL)
  1897, April 11/Frank Leavitt
    Minneapolis Journal, 12 Apr.1897.
  1897, April 13/James Feeley/Selby Ave.
  x Victoria St.
    St. Paul Globe, 14 Apr.1897.
  1947, July 4/Laura Behrens/625 Grand
  Ave.
    St. Paul Dispatch, 8 July 1947.
  1956, Nov.14/Mrs. William O'Keefe
    "Case 248," CRIFO Orbit, 7 Dec.1956,
    p.4, quoting St. Paul Dispatch (un-
    dated).
  1963, June 4
    Gray Barker, Book of Saucers (Clarks-
    burg, W.V.: Saucerian, 1965), p.19.
  1975, July 2
    "UFO Central," CUFOS News Bull., 15
    Nov.1975, p.12.
-UFO (R-V)
  1952, July 28
    Donald E. Keyhoe, Flying Saucers from
    Outer Space (N.Y.: Holt, 1953), p.
    98.

Saint Peter
-UFO (NL)
  1976, Nov.19

"UFOs of Limited Merit," Int'l UFO
Reporter 2 (Jan.1977):5.

Sartell
-Fire anomaly
  1978, March/Steve Curtis
    R. Thomas Holden, "Bought at a Fire
    Sale?" Fate 32 (Mar.1979):69.

Sauk Rapids
-Giant human skeleton
  1868, Dec.16
    Sauk Rapids Sentinel, 18 Dec.1868.
    New York Times, 25 Dec.1868, p.7.

Scandia
-UFO (CE-1)
  1978, March 22/Carol Anderson/Olinda
  Trail
    St. Croix Falls (Wisc.) Dalles Vis-
    itor, no.10 (May 1978):23.

Shafer
-UFO (NL)
  1978, March 22/Kari Driver
    St. Croix Falls (Wisc.) Dalles Vis-
    itor, no.10 (May 1978):23.

Shevlin
-UFO (NL)
  1978, May 15/Gladys Swanson
    Grand Forks (N.D.) Herald, 21 May
    1978.

Shorewood
-UFO (NL)
  1965, Aug.3
    Coral E. Lorenzen, "Western UFO Flap,"
    Fate 18 (Nov.1965):42,51.

Silver Lake
-Disappearance
  1958, Dec.29/Earl Zrust/=debt evasion
    (Editorial), Fate 12 (June 1959):25.
    (Editorial), Fate 12 (Sep.1959):14.

Sleepy Eye
-UFO (?)
  1966, Aug.16/Herb Geiger/=barium cloud
    John A. Keel, "The Night the Sky
    Turned On," Fate 20 (Sep.1967):30,
    35.
-UFO (NL)
  1897, April 15/C. Salkowske
  1897, April 16/F. Meilke
  1897, April 17/Tennessee Jubilee Sing-
  ers/Auditorium
    Sleepy Eye Dispatch, 22 Apr.1897.

Starbuck
-Norse habitation site
    "New Discoveries Supporting Medieval
    Norse Presence in the Upper Mid-
    west," NEARA Newsl. 9 (spring 1974)
    :15.
-UFO (CE-2)
  1975, Sep.10/ground markings only
    Starbuck Times, 17 Sep.1975.

Stewart
-UFO (CE-2)
  1971, June 24/Arnold Windschitl
    Stewart Tribune, 1 July 1971.
    Coral & Jim Lorenzen, Encounters
    with UFO Occupants (N.Y.: Berkley,
    1976), pp.20-22.

Stewartville
-UFO (CE-1)
  1968, Oct.24/Warren Anding
    Brad Steiger & Joan Whritenour, Fly-
    ing Saucer Invasion: Target--Earth
    (N.Y.: Award, 1969), p.100.

Stillwater
-Precognition
  1950s-1960s/Arthur R. Strand
    Paul Light, "Proving Dreams Come
    True," Fate 15 (May 1962):62-65.
    (Letter), Fate 17 (Apr.1964):110-11.
-UFO (?)
  1871, Dec.11/=lightning rod?
    Stillwater Gazette, 12 Dec.1871.
  1890, Jan.20/N.A. Nelson/=meteor
    Stillwater Gazette, 22 Jan.1890.
  1961, Aug.17
    Richard Hall, ed., The UFO Evidence
    (Washington: NICAP, 1964), p.15.
-UFO (CE-1)
  1978, March 22/Dean Andrie/N on Hwy.95
    St. Croix Falls (Wisc.) Dalles Vis-
    itor, no.10 (May 1978):23.
-UFO (NL)
  1897, April 13/Omaha Railroad
    Minneapolis Times, 14 Apr.1897.
  1975, July 18
    "UFO Central," CUFOS News Bull., 15
    Nov.1975, p.13.

Sunrise
-Aerial phantom
  1857
    St. Croix Falls (Wisc.) Dalles Vis-
    itor, no.10 (May 1978):2, quoting
    William H.C. Folsom papers, Minne-
    sota Historical Soc'y.
-UFO (NL)
  1975, Dec.2
    Rush City East Central Post Review,
    4 Dec.1975.

Taylors Falls
-Fall of sulphur
  1861, June 27
    St. Croix Falls (Wisc.) Dalles Vis-
    itor, no.10 (May 1978):2, quoting
    Taylors Falls Reporter (undated).
-UFO (?)
  1897, April 8/=hoax
    Minneapolis Journal, 9 Apr.1897.
    Chicago (Ill.) Chronicle, 11 Apr.1897.
  1899, Feb.6/=meteor?
    Taylors Falls Journal, 9 Feb.1899.

Thief River Falls
-Norse hatchet
  1919, June/Sam S. Brandvold/3½ mi.S
    Hjalmar R. Holand, The Kensington
    Stone (Ephraim, Wisc.: The Author,

1932), pp.166-67. il.
Hjalmar R. Holand, Westward from Vin-
land (N.Y.: Duell, Sloan & Pearce,
1940), pp.239-40. il.
-UFO (CE-2)
1972, Aug./N on U.S.59
"Object Emits Three Discs," APRO
Bull. 25 (Aug.1976):1,3.

Togo
-UFO (NL)
1969, Jan.3
Togo Cook News-Herald, 9 Jan.1969.

Two Harbors
-UFO (CE-1)
1975, April 1
"From the Center for UFO Studies,"
Flying Saucer Rev. 21 (Aug.1975):
32.
-UFO (DD)
1961, Oct.14/L. Superior
(Editorial), APRO Bull. 10 (Nov.
1961):3.
Coral & Jim Lorenzen, UFOs: The Whole
Story (N.Y.: Signet, 1969), pp.230-
31.
-UFO (NL)
1975, Sep.25
"UFO Central," CUFOS News Bull., 15
Nov.1975, p.19.

Ulen
-Norse habitation site
"New Discoveries Supporting Medieval
Norse Presence in the Upper Mid-
west," NEARA Newsl. 9 (spring 1974)
:15-16.
-Norse sword
1911, spring/Hans O. Hanson/3 mi.W
Hjalmar R. Holand, America: 1355-
1364 (N.Y.: Duell, Sloan & Pearce,
1946), pp.179-83. il.
Hjalmar R. Holand, A Pre-Columbian
Crusade to America (N.Y.: Twayne,
1962), pp.169-71. il.

Villard
-UFO (CE-1)
1976, Sep.29/Mrs. Donald Robideaux
(Letter), Saga UFO Rept. 3 (Mar.1977)
:4-6.

Virginia
-UFO (NL)
1897, April 12
Minneapolis Times, 14 Apr.1897.

Vondell Brook
-Haunt
1923/Linnea E. Reed
Linnea E. Reed & Pauline Saltzman,
"Boots That Walked Alone," Fate 16
(Mar.1963):78-83.

Walker
-UFO (NL)
1966, Aug.5/Hwy.34
1966, Aug.16/Jack Miller/Hwy.71
John A. Keel, "The Night the Sky

Turned On," Fate 20 (Sep.1967):30,
32-33.

Warren
-Giant human skeletons
1882
N.H. Winchell, The Aborigines of
Minnesota (St. Paul: Minnesota Hist.
Soc'y, 1911).

Warroad
-UFO (?)
1966, Aug.16/=barium cloud
John A. Keel, "The Night the Sky
Turned On," Fate 20 (Sep.1967):30,
32.

Waseca
-UFO (DD)
1978, Jan.22/Janet Roeglin
Mankato Free Press, 18 Feb.1978.
-UFO (NL)
1897, April 9
Burlington (Ia.) Hawk-Eye, 10 Apr.
1897.
1977, Oct.13
Waseca Daily Journal, 14 Oct.1977.

West Union
-Archeological site
Kirk Bryan, Henry Retzek & Franklin
T. McCann, "Discovery of the Sauk
Valley Man of Minnesota," Bull.Texas
Arch.& Paleon.Soc'y 10 (1938):112-
35. il.
Albert E. Jenks & Lloyd A. Wilford,
"The Sauk Valley Skeleton," Bull.
Texas Arch.& Paleon.Soc'y 10 (1938)
:136-39.

White Bear Lake
-UFO (DD)
1958, Oct.17/Edward Stevens
"Hovering UFO Puzzles South African
Officials," UFO Inv. 1 (Dec.1958):1,
3.

Windom
-UFO (?)
1965, Nov.15
Jerome Clark, "The Greatest Flap Yet?
Part IV," Flying Saucer Rev. 12
(Nov.-Dec.1966):9,11.
-UFO (NL)
1897, April 14/W.A. Peterson
Windom Reporter, 22 Apr.1897.
1959, June 2/Mrs. Henry X. Buller/NE
of town
(Letter), Fate 12 (Oct.1959):109-10.

Winona
-UFO (DD)
1967, Nov.17/Kenneth Malenke
"UFOs--November--U.S.A.," APRO Bull.
16 (Nov.-Dec.1967):8.
-UFO (NL)
1897, April 11/Harry Friday/=star?
Winona Daily Herald, 12 Apr.1897.
1965, Nov.9/William Bohn
Jerome Clark, "The Greatest Flap Yet?

Part IV," Flying Saucer Rev. 12
(Nov.-Dec.1966):9,10.
1970, Nov.3/L. Winona
(Editorial), Fate 24 (Apr.1971):19.

Winsted
-UFO (CE-3)
1967, Jan.25
Jacques Vallee, Passport to Magonia
(Chicago: Regnery, 1969), p.339.

Woodside twp.
-UFO (CE-2)
1965, Nov.16?
Jerome Clark, "The Greatest Flap Yet?
Part IV," Flying Saucer Rev. 12
(Nov.-Dec.1966):9,11.

Young America
-UFO (NL)
1897, April 13
Minneapolis Times, 15 Apr.1897.

B. Physical Features

Beaver L.
-UFO (CE-1)
1978, March 22/Jeane Pluff
"Huge UFO over Minnesota," APRO Bull.
26 (June 1978):1,2.

Big Marine L.
-UFO (DD)
1977, Sep.30
St. Paul Dispatch, 13 Oct.1977.

Big Sandy L.
-Lake monster
1886, Aug./Christopher Engstein
New York Sun, 19 Aug.1886.
Charles Fort, The Books of Charles
Fort (N.Y.: Holt, 1941), p.615,
quoting London (Ont.) Advertiser
(undated).

Carlos Avery Game Preserve
-Livestock mutilations, UFOs and humanoid
1971-1977, April
Bradley Earl Ayers, "The Thing That
Stalks the Game Preserve," Fate 30
(Dec.1977):38-46.

Cormorant L.
-Norse mooring stone and firesteel
1870/E.O. Estenson
Hjalmar R. Holand, A Pre-Columbian
Crusade to America (N.Y.: Twayne,
1962), pp.121-25. il.

Darling L.
-Norse ax
1923/Mrs. C.I. Mansur
Hjalmar R. Holand, America: 1355-
1364 (N.Y.: Duell, Sloan & Pearce,
1946), pp.190-91. il.

Detroit L.
-Norse mooring stone
Hjalmar R. Holand, America: 1355-

1364 (N.Y.: Duell, Sloan & Pearce,
1946), pp.153-55. il.

Grant's L.
-Norse boat
ca.1910
Hjalmar R. Holand, Westward from Vinland (N.Y.: Duell, Sloan & Pearce,
1940), p.211.

Height-of-Land L.
-Norse firesteel
1940/Otto F. Zeck/NE side
Hjalmar R. Holand, America: 1355-
1364 (N.Y.: Duell, Sloan & Pearce,
1946), pp.188-89. il.

Island L.
-Humanoid
1972, Jan.26/Donald McGregor/Abbott Rd.
(Editorial), Fate 25 (Nov.1972):25,
quoting Duluth News-Tribune (undated).

Jessie L.
-Norse mooring stone
Hjalmar R. Holand, A Pre-Columbian
Crusade to America (N.Y.: Twayne,
1962), p.148.

Koronis L.
-Giant human skeleton
n.d.
St. Paul Globe, 12 Aug.1896.

Lac qui Parle L.
-UFO (NL)
1897, April 13/I.J. Monnie
Minneapolis Times, 14 Apr.1897.

Latoka L.
-Norse boathook
1939/Fred W. Krafthefer/E side
Hjalmar R. Holand, A Pre-Columbian
Crusade to America (N.Y.: Twayne,
1962), pp.173-76. il.
-Norse mooring stone
n.d.
Hjalmar R. Holand, A Pre-Columbian
Crusade to America (N.Y.: Twayne,
1962), p.148.

Mantrap L.
-Humanoid
n.d.
Eric Norman [Brad Steiger], The Abominable Snowmen (N.Y.: Award, 1969),
pp.80-81.

Mille Lacs L.
-UFO (NL)
1960, Jan.16-17/John Hogan
(Editorial), Fate 13 (Nov.1960):24-
25.

Minnetonka, L.
-UFO (NL)
1963, June 4
Gray Barker, Book of Saucers (Clarksburg, W.V.: Saucerian, 1965), p.19.

1965, Aug.3
    Coral E. Lorenzen, "Western UFO Flap,"
    Fate 18 (Nov.1965):42,51.

Moose Island L.
-Giant human skeletons
    1861, Sep.
    N.H. Winchell, The Aborigines of
    Minnesota (St. Paul: Minnesota Hist.
    Soc'y, 1911), p.301.

Movil L.
-UFO (CE-3)
    1962, Aug./Mildred Anderson
    "The 1962 Occupants Case," APRO Bull.
    21 (Sep.-Oct.1972):6.

Mud L.
-UFO (CE-3)
    n.d./Glen Miller
    Brad Steiger & Joan Whritenour, Fly-
    ing Saucer Invasion: Target--Earth
    (N.Y.: Award, 1969), pp.13-14.

Nelson L.
-Norse mooring stone
    Hjalmar R. Holand, A Pre-Columbian
    Crusade to America (N.Y.: Twayne,
    1962), p.146.

Nicollet Creek
-Archeological site
    7700 B.C.-100 A.D.
    Albert E. Jenks, "A Minnesota Kitchen
    Midden with Fossil Bison," Science
    86 (1937):243-44.
    Creighton T. Shay, The Itasca Bison
    Kill Site (St. Paul: Minnesota Hist.
    Soc'y, 1971). il.
    C. Thomas Shay, "Bison Procurement
    on the Eastern Margin of the Plains:
    The Itasca Site," Plains Anthro. 23
    (1978):140-50.

Norway L.
-Norse ax
    1908/Ole Skaalerud
    Hjalmar R. Holand, The Kensington
    Stone (Ephraim, Wisc.: The Author,
    1932), pp.161-66. il.
    Hjalmar R. Holand, A Pre-Columbian
    Crusade to America (N.Y.: Twayne,
    1962), pp.166-67. il.
    1962
    Alf Mongé & Ole G. Landsverk, Norse
    Medieval Cryptography in Runic Carv-
    ings (Glendale, Cal.: Norseman,
    1967), p.195.

Osakis L.
-Norse mooring stone
    1944, April/Harold Holand
    Hjalmar R. Holand, America: 1355-
    1364 (N.Y.: Duell, Sloan & Pearce,
    1946), pp.151-53.

Pelican L.
-Norse mooring stone
    Hjalmar R. Holand, A Pre-Columbian
    Crusade to America (N.Y.: Twayne,

1962), p.146.

Petaga Point
-Archeological site
    Peter Bleed, The Archeology of Pet-
    aga Point (St. Paul: Minnesota
    Hist.Soc'y, 1969). il.

Rainy L.
-UFO (DD)
    1951, May 22
    "Monthly Report on the Saucers,"
    Fate 4 (Oct.1951):13.

Rainy R.
-Giant human skeleton
    1884/McKinstry Mounds
    St. Paul Globe, 14 Feb.1897; and 18
    Dec.1898.
    N.H. Winchell, The Aborigines of
    Minnesota (St. Paul: Minnesota Hist.
    Soc'y, 1911), pp.372-73.

Sauk L.
-Norse altar
    1892
    Hjalmar R. Holand, A Pre-Columbian
    Crusade to America (N.Y.: Twayne,
    1962), pp.150-57. il.
    Sauk Centre Herald, 29 Aug.1974. il.

Stinking L.
-Norse mooring stones
    Hjalmar R. Holand, A Pre-Columbian
    Crusade to America (N.Y.: Twayne,
    1962), pp.149-51. il.

Ten Mile L.
-Norse mooring stone
    Hjalmar R. Holand, A Pre-Columbian
    Crusade to America (N.Y.: Twayne,
    1962), p.147.

Tofte L.
-Neanderthaloid skulls
    1968/Norman Saari
    Minneapolis Star, 12 July 1972.
    "Skullduggery, Scientific Style,"
    Pursuit 5 (Oct.1972):89.

Traverse L.
-Norse spearhead
    1944
    Alf Mongé & Ole G. Landsverk, Norse
    Medieval Cryptography in Runic Carv-
    ings (Glendale, Cal.: Norseman,
    1967), p.195.

Tub L.
-Norse mooring stone
    1940/Alfred Johnson
    Hjalmar R. Holand, America: 1355-
    1364 (N.Y.: Duell, Sloan & Pearce,
    1946), pp.148-49. il.

Venus L.
-Norse mooring stone
    Hjalmar R. Holand, A Pre-Columbian
    Crusade to America (N.Y.: Twayne,
    1962), pp.147-48.

West Battle L.
-UFO (?)
  1966, Aug.16/Harold Pikal/=barium cloud
    John A. Keel, "The Night the Sky
    Turned On," Fate 20 (Sep.1967):30,
    31.

Whiteface Reservoir
-Humanoid
  1960/Frank Hansen/=hoax
    Bernard Heuvelmans, "Note prélimin-
    aire sur un specimen conservé dans
    la glace, d'une forme encore incon-
    nue d'hominide vivant: Homo pongoid-
    es," Bull.Inst.Roy.Sci.Nat.Belg. 45
    (1969):1-24.
    Detroit (Mich.) News, 28 Mar.1969.
    Rochester Post-Bulletin, 21 Apr.1969.
    Ivan T. Sanderson, "The Missing
    Link," Argosy, May 1969, pp.23-31.
    il.
    "Ends 'Bozo'--We Think," Pursuit 2
    (July 1969):54-55.
    Ivan T. Sanderson, "Preliminary De-
    scription of the External Morphology
    of What Appeared to Be the Fresh
    Corpse of an Hitherto Unknown Form
    of Living Hominid," Genus 25 (1969)
    :249-78, reprinted in Pursuit 8
    (Apr.1975):41-47; (July 1975):62-
    66. il.
    Frank Hansen, "I Killed the Ape-Man
    Creature of Whiteface," Saga, July
    1970, pp.8-11,55-60. il.
    "'Bozo': The 'Iceman,'" Pursuit 3
    (Oct.1970):89.
    John Napier, Bigfoot (N.Y.: Dutton,
    1973), pp.98-114. il.
    Bernard Heuvelmans & B.F. Porchnev,
    L'Homme de Neanderthal est toujours
    vivant (Paris: Plon, 1974). il.
    Robert J. Durant, "Epilogue on Bozo,"
    Pursuit 8 (July 1975):66-67.

Winnibigoshish L.
-UFO (?)
  1857, April 11/=meteor
    B.F. Odell, "Notice of a Brilliant
    Meteor Seen near Lake Winnibigosh-
    ish, Minnesota," Am.J.Sci., ser.2,
    24 (1857):158.

        C. Ethnic Groups

Ojibwa Indians
-Flood myth
    Johan G. Kohl, Kitchi-Gami: Wander-
    ings Round Lake Superior (London:
    Chapman & Hall, 1860), pp.386-91.
-Humanoid myth
    Johan G. Kohl, Kitchi-Gami: Wander-
    ings Round Lake Superior (London:
    Chapman & Hall, 1860), pp.358-66.
    Sr. Bernard Coleman, "The Religion
    of the Ojibwa of Northern Minnesota,"
    Primitive Man 10 (1937):33-57.
-Phantom (myth)
    George Copway, Indian Life and Indian
    History (Boston: A. Colby, 1858).

-Shamanism
    Johan G. Kohl, Kitchi-Gami: Wander-
    ings Round Lake Superior (London:
    Chapman & Hall, 1860).
    W.J. Hoffman, "Pictography and Sha-
    manistic Rites of the Ojibwa," Am.
    Anthro. 1 (1888):209-30.
    Sr. M. Bernard, "Religion and Magic
    Among Cass Lake Ojibwa," Primitive
    Man 2 (1929):52-55.
    John Tanner, A Narrative of the Cap-
    tivity and Adventures of John Tan-
    ner, ed. Edwin James (Minneapolis:
    Ross & Haines, 1956).
    Joseph B. Casagrande, "The Ojibwa's
    Psychic Universe," Tomorrow 4
    (spring 1956):33-40.
    Ruth Landes, Ojibwa Religion and the
    Midewiwin (Madison: Univ. of Wis-
    consin, 1968).
    Ralph Christian Albertsen, "Ojibwa
    Vision-Quest: The Search for a
    Guardian Spirit," Fate 30 (May 1977)
    :57-62.

Sioux Indians
-Humanoid myth
  Tallegwi
    Gerard Fowke, "Some Popular Errors
    in Regard to Mound Builders and
    Indians," Ohio Hist.& Arch.Soc'y
    Quar. 2 (1888):380,395-97.

        D. Unspecified Localities

-Contactee
  1950s
    Leon Festinger, Henry W. Riecken &
    Stanley Schachter, When Prophecy
    Fails (Minneapolis: Univ. of Minne-
    sota, 1956).

-Humanoid
  1911
    Ivan T. Sanderson, Things (N.Y.: Pyr-
    amid, 1967), pp.103-104.

WISCONSIN

A. Populated Places

Adams co.
-Telepathy
1902, March/Frank Bisbee
Ruth B. Allen, "God Sent Three Bags
of Flour," Fate 22 (July 1969):63-
65.

Algoma
-UFO (NL)
1951, Oct./John Schopf
Coral E. Lorenzen, Flying Saucers:
The Startling Evidence of the Invasion from Outer Space (N.Y.: Signet,
1966 ed.), p.26.
1976, June 1/Mark Kopecky
Algoma Record-Herald, 2 June 1976.

Antigo
-UFO (CE-3)
1974, Nov.17
Ted Bloecher, "A Catalog of Humanoid
Reports for 1974," in MUFON 1975 UFO
Symposium Proc. (Seguin, Tex.:
MUFON, 1975), pp.51,63.

Appleton
-Electromagnetic anomaly
1941/Dick Williams
Los Angeles (Cal.) Daily Mirror, 23
Jan.1950.
-UFO (?)
1897, April 11/N.B. Clark/airship mes-
sage
Chicago (Ill.) Times-Herald, 15 Apr.
1897, p.7.
Fort Atkinson Jefferson County Union,
16 Apr.1897, p.6.
1897, April 12/Arthur C. Lunn/=star
Ottawa (Ill.) Journal, 14 Apr.1897,
p.4.
-UFO (CE-1)
1972, Sep.26/4 mi.W
Milwaukee Sentinel, 28 Sep.1972.
1975, Aug.2
"From the Center for UFO Studies,"
Flying Saucer Rev. 21 (Apr.1976):24.
-UFO (CE-2)
1969, Jan.26/=meteor?
"Skylight Flashes in Mid-West Night,"
Skylook, no.16 (Mar.1969):2.
-UFO (NL)
1967, March 22/Frank Goddard
"Sightings Still on Upswing," APRO
Bull. 15 (Mar.-Apr.1967):11,12.

Ashland
-Fall of fish
n.d./Richard Hagstrom
"Dear Abby" column, 1 Jan.1973.
-Spirit medium
1882-1887/Mary Hayes Chynoweth
Louisa Johnson Clay, The Spirit Dom-

inant (San Jose: Mercury-Herald,
n.d.).
Stanwood Cobb & David Techter, "The
Woman Who Dowsed a Fortune," Fate
26 (Oct.1973):38-47; (Nov.1973):96-
104; (Dec.1973):88-96. il.
-UFO (NL)
1975, March 13
"Landing in Wisconsin," APRO Bull.
23 (Apr.1975):1.
-White Indians
1891/Johan G.R. Baner
"Vikings in Michigan?" Fate 9 (Feb.
1956):77.

Baraboo
-Phantom elephant
1930, Jan.1-15/Rose Holiday/8th St.
Chicago (Ill.) Tribune, 22 Jan.1930.
Stuart Palmer, "Baraboo's 10 Ton
Ghosts," Fate 6 (Dec.1953):76-83.
-UFO (NL)
1897, April 11
Chicago (Ill.) Times-Herald, 14 Apr.
1897, p.2.
1897, April 13/M.B. Marshall
Baraboo Evening News, 14 Apr.1897,
p.2.

Barron
-Phantom
1919, summer/Harry Anderson/E of town
Alex Evans, "Encounters with Little
Men," Fate 31 (Nov.1978):83,85-86.
-UFO (DD)
1934, summer/Coral E. Lorenzen
Coral E. Lorenzen, Flying Saucers:
The Startling Evidence of the Inva-
sion from Outer Space (N.Y.: Signet,
1966 ed.), pp.15-16.

Bayfield
-UFO (DD)
1975, Sep.15/Garner Hadland
Eugene T. Lundholm, "Man Reports Daylight Disc," Skylook, no.97 (Dec.
1975):15.

Beaver Brook
-UFO (?)
1978, Aug./Charles Larson/ground markings only/=fungus?
Spooner Advocate, 31 Aug.1978.

Beloit
-UFO (?)
1954, June
Donald E. Keyhoe, Flying Saucer Con-
spiracy (N.Y.: Holt, 1955), p.164.
-UFO (NL)
1960, Nov.23/Dougan farm/Colley Rd.
Curtis Fuller, "The Nov.23 UFO,"
Fate 14 (Mar.1961):46,50.
1962, June 26/Jack Reiley/1700 block

Arlington Ave.
  (Editorial), Fate 15 (Oct.1962):10.
  1969, Feb.13/Gene Bradzon
  "U.S. Roundup," APRO Bull. 17 (Mar.-
    Apr.1969):7.

Benton
-Humanoid
  1970, Aug.
    Everett (Wash.) Herald, 5 Sep.1970.
    Nashville Tennessean, 23 Sep.1970.

Black River Falls
-Fall of metallic object
  1947, summer/=hoax
    Donald H. Menzel, Flying Saucers
      (Cambridge: Harvard Univ., 1953),
      p.43.
    Bruce S. Maccabee, "UFO Related In-
      formation from the FBI Files: Part
      2," MUFON UFO J., no.120 (Nov.1977):
      12.
-UFO (NL)
  1966, March 14
    "Report on the Michigan Flap," Saucer
    News 13 (June 1966):23.

Boscobel
-UFO (?)
  1897, April/Smalley House
    Boscobel Dial, 7 Apr.1897, p.4.

Brodhead
-UFO (?)
  1897, April 13/=kite
    Brodhead Independent, 15 Apr.1897, p.
    5.

Brookfield
-Erratic kangaroo
  1978, April 23-24/Lance Nero
    Green Bay Press-Gazette, 25 Apr.1978.
    il.
-UFO (NL)
  1978, Aug.13/N. Brookfield Rd.
    Brookfield News, 17 Aug.1978.

Browntown
-UFO (CE-1)
  1969, April 20/Robert Phillips/1 mi.W
    on Hwy.11
    "Car Buzzing Incidents Continue,"
    APRO Bull. 17 (May-June 1969):6,8.

Bruce
-Hex
  1928, Sep./John Wierzba
    New York Evening World, 14 Sep.1928.

Brule
-Airship inventor
  1897, April/Volney Stewart
    New York Herald, 26 Apr.1897.

Burlington
-Archeological site
  serpent effigy/Fox R.
    Stephen D. Peet, "The Great Serpent
    and Other Effigies," Am.Antiquarian
    12 (1890):211-28. il.

-UFO (DD)
  1956, Sep.7
    "Case 211," CRIFO Orbit, 5 Oct.1956,
    p.4.
-UFO (NL)
  1947, July 6/Gordon Nielson/SW of town
    Milwaukee Sentinel, 8 July 1947.
  1948, Aug./M.L. Amoreaux
    (Letter), Fate 4 (Nov.-Dec.1951):
    122-24.
  1978, Aug.8/Pat Nelson/Henry St.
    Burlington Standard-Press, 9 Aug.
    1978.

Cameron
-UFO (CE-2)
  1966, Aug.16/E of town
    John A. Keel, "The Night the Sky
    Turned On," Fate 20 (Sep.1967):30,
    34.

Cashton
-Humanoid
  1976, Sep.1
    Cashton Record, 27 Oct.1976.

Cecil
-UFO (NL)
  1972, Sep.29/R.W. Pedersen
    "Press Reports," APRO Bull. 21 (Jan.-
    Feb.1973):12-13, quoting Milwaukee
    Journal (undated).

Chilton
-UFO (NL)
  1897, April 10/Art Hipke
    Chilton Times, 17 Apr.1897, p.5.

Chippewa Falls
-Phantom panther
  1977, Oct.31/Bill Bergeman/Tower Hill
    Chippewa Falls Herald-Telegram, 16
    Nov.1977.
-UFO (CE-2)
  1954, Dec.28
    Harold T. Wilkins, Flying Saucers Un-
    censored (N.Y.: Pyramid, 1967 ed.),
    p.259.
  1965
    Ted Phillips, Physical Traces Associ-
    ated with UFO Sightings (Evanston:
    Center for UFO Studies, 1975), p.33.
-UFO (DD)
  1954, summer/Leon L. Oeming
    (Letter), Fate 27 (Nov.1974):144-45.
-UFO (NL)
  1968, Aug.11/Jean Perry
    "Object Is Photographed over Wiscon-
    sin," APRO Bull. 17 (May-June 1969):
    5.
  1975, Jan.26/Kevin Guibord
    "MUFON Reports in Brief," Skylook,
    no.89 (Apr.1975):10.

Clam Falls twp.
-UFO (CE-2)
  1976/Bruce Don/ground markings only
    Ruth Christiansen, "More Mystery in
    Wisconsin," Can.UFO Rept., no.25
    (fall 1976):1-2. il.

Clayton
-UFO (NL)
    1897, April 13
    St. Paul (Minn.) Pioneer Press, 14
    Apr.1897.

Clintonville
-UFO (NL)
    1972, Sep.26
    Milwaukee Sentinel, 28 Sep.1972.

Cochrane
-UFO (CE-2)
    1968, April 4/Hwy.35
    "U.S. Reports," APRO Bull. 17 (Sep.-
    Oct.1968):8.
    J. Allen Hynek, The UFO Experience
    (Chicago: Regnery, 1972), pp.116-18.

Colby
-Fall of anomalous meteorite
    1917, July 4
    Henry L. Ward, "A New Meteorite,"
    Science 46 (1917):262.

Cudahy
-UFO (NL)
    1947, July 8
    Madison Capital-Times, 9 July 1947.

Cumberland
-UFO (?)
    1897, April 13
    Cumberland Advocate, 15 Apr.1897, p.
    8.
-UFO (NL)
    1897, April 11
    St. Paul (Minn.) Pioneer Press, 12
    Apr.1897.
    1978, March 22/Jim Nystrom/5 mi.W on
    Hwy.48
    "Huge UFO over Minnesota," APRO Bull.
    26 (June 1978):1,2.
    "Follow Up," APRO Bull. 27 (Nov.1978)
    :1,3.

Dane co.
-Archeological sites
    E.G. Squier & E.H. Davis, Ancient
    Monuments of the Mississippi Valley
    (Washington: Smithsonian Institution,
    Contrib.to Knowl., no.1, 1848), pp.
    126-28.

Darien
-UFO (?)
    1897, April 14/=balloon
    Elkhorn Independent, 22 Apr.1897, p.
    2.

Darlington
-Out-of-body experiences
    1915-1971/Sylvan Muldoon
    Sylvan Muldoon & Hereward Carrington,
    The Projection of the Astral Body
    (London: Rider, 1929).
    Sylvan Muldoon, The Case for Astral
    Projection (Chicago: Aries, 1936).
    Sylvan Muldoon & Hereward Carrington,
    The Phenomena of Astral Projection

(London: Rider, 1951).
    D. Scott Rogo, ed., Mind Beyond the
    Body (New York: Penguin, 1978), pp.
    233-46.
-UFO (NL)
    1897, April 4
    Elkhorn Independent, 15 Apr.1897, p.
    2.
    1953, June 1/Glen Winslow
    John C. Ross, "Fate's Report on the
    Flying Saucers," Fate 6 (Oct.1953)
    :6,10.

Delafield
-Ghost
    1905, Nov./Mrs. Sidney Thomas Smythe/
    Rosslynne Manse
    W.F. Prince, "The Ghost of Rosslynne
    Manse," J.ASPR 18 (1924):715-22.
-UFO (NL)
    1967, March 22/Carl Rohde/Lapham Peak
    "Sightings Still on Upswing," APRO
    Bull. 15 (Mar.-Apr.1967):11,12.

Delaven
-Humanoid
    1964, July/Dennis Fewless/Hwy.89 x U.S.
    14
    John Green, The Sasquatch File (Ag-
    assiz, B.C.: Cheam, 1973), p.32.
-UFO (NL)
    1897, April 11
    Delaven Enterprise, 15 Apr.1897, p.
    5.
    1978, Jan.14
    "UFOs of Limited Merit," Int'l UFO
    Reporter 3 (Feb.1978):3.

Dotyville
-UFO (NL)
    1976, Aug.7/Mike Thompson/S on County
    Rd.W
    Fond du Lac Reporter, 10 Aug.1976.

Dresser
-Humanoid
    1976, Jan./Jerry Strese/nr. Sullivan's
    Corner
    "What's Happening in Wisconsin?" Can.
    UFO Rept., no.23 (spring 1976):9,10.
-UFO (NL)
    1978, March 22/Dave Bierman
    St. Croix Falls Dalles Visitor, no.
    10 (May 1978):23.

Durand
-UFO (CE-1)
    1966, Sep.7/Mrs. E. Bruns/10 mi.E
    "Wisconsin Officers Watch UAO," APRO
    Bull. 15 (Sep.-Oct.1966):4.
    1975, Jan.21/Scott Fedie/4 mi.SW
    "MUFON Reports in Brief," Skylook,
    no.89 (Apr.1975):10.
-UFO (NL)
    1897, April 13
    Eau Claire Telegram, 14 Apr.1897, p.
    3.
    1975, Jan.22/Mitchell Doverspike/5 mi.
    SE
    1975, Jan.29/Mrs. Al Gund

1975, Jan.31/Mrs. Al Gund
"MUFON Reports in Brief," Skylook,
no.89 (Apr.1975):10-11.

Eagle
-UFO (DD)
1947, July 7/R.J. Southey/SE of town
Milwaukee Journal, 8 July 1947.

Eagle Point twp.
-Cattle and horse mutilations
1977, Oct.
Chippewa Falls Herald-Telegraph, 16
Nov.1977.

Eagle River
-UFO (CE-3)
1961, April 18/Joe Simonton
Milwaukee Journal, 23-24 Apr.1961.
"The Case of the Interplanetary Cook-
ies," APRO Bull. 9 (May 1961):1-3.
"The Eagle River Incident," Flying
Saucer Rev. 7 (July-Aug.1961):7-8;
(Nov.-Dec.1961):20; 8 (May-June
1962):9-10.
Paul Foght, "Inside the Flying Sau-
cers...Pancakes," Fate 14 (Aug.1961)
:32-36. il.
Ray Palmer, "NICAP: National Non-In-
vestigations Committee on Aerial
Phenomena," Flying Saucers, Sep.
1961, p.4.
Gray Barker, "Chasing the Flying Sau-
cers," Flying Saucers, Sep.1961, pp.
33,39-44.
Ray Palmer, "Editorial," Flying Saucers, Mar.1962, pp.2,8-10.
Lloyd Mallan, "UFO Hoaxes and Hallucinations," Sci.& Mech. 38 (Mar.
1967):48-51.
J. Allen Hynek & Jacques Vallee, The
Edge of Reality (Chicago: Regnery,
1975), pp.152-55.
-UFO (NL)
1976, May 28
"Noteworthy UFO Sightings," Ufology
2 (fall 1976):61.

Eastman
-Cattle mutilation
1975, Oct./Richard Boom
Milwaukee Journal, 12 Oct.1975.

Eau Claire
-UFO (NL)
1897, April 11/depot
Eau Claire Telegram, 13 Apr.1897, p.
3.
1971, Nov.5/T. Frank/W. Clairement Ave.
"Kidney-Shape Light Seen in Wisconsin," Skylook, no.52 (Mar.1972):9.
1975, Nov.13
"UFO Central," CUFOS News Bull., 1
Feb.1976, p.13.

Edgerton
-UFO (NL)
1947, July 4/Mrs. Melvin Voigt
Madison Capital-Times, 7 July 1947.

Elkhorn
-UFO (DD)
1947, July 7/Kenneth Jones/10 mi.from
town
Madison Wisconsin State Journal, 8
July 1947.

Ellsworth
-UFO (CE-1)
1957, Dec.11
Jacques Vallee, Passport to Magonia
(Chicago: Regnery, 1969), p.268,
quoting Flying Saucers, July 1958.

Elmwood
-UFO (CE-2)
1976, April 22/George Wheeler/Tuttle
Hill
Eau Claire Leader-Telegram, 14 May
1976, p.1.
"Officer Has Repeat Sighting," APRO
Bull. 24 (Apr.1976):1-4.
Jack M. Bostrack, "Wisconsin Police-
man Hospitalized after UFO Encoun-
ter," MUFON UFO J., no.103 (June
1976):4-5.

Evansville
-UFO (?)
1950, Nov.27/Bill Blair
Richard Hall, ed., The UFO Evidence
(Washington: NICAP, 1964), p.34.
-UFO (NL)
1897, April 9/Charles Fuller
Janesville Gazette, 14 Apr.1897, p.5.

Fennimore
-UFO (NL)
1975, Nov.5
"Wisconsin Sighting Reported," Skylook, no.97 (Dec.1975):7. il.

Fond du Lac
-Clairempathy
1930s/Arthur Price Roberts/Windsor
House
Vincent H. Gaddis, "Psychic Detect-
ive," Fate 6 (Sep.1953):51,54.
-Crisis apparition
ca.1858/N.P. Tallmadge
Emma Hardinge Britten, Modern Ameri-
can Spiritualism (N.Y.: The Author,
1870), p.263.
-Fall of weblike substance
1956, Oct.16
Leonard H. Stringfield, Inside Sau-
cer Post...3-0 Blue (Cincinnati:
CRIFO, 1957), p.50.
-UFO (NL)
1897, April 13/=balloon
Fond du Lac Commonwealth, 14 Apr.
1897, p.3.
-UFO (NL)
1897, April 10-11
Fond du Lac Commonwealth, 12 Apr.
1897, p.3.
1978, Sep.10/Harland Olsen/Timber
Trails Rd.
Fond du Lac Reporter, 12 Sep.1978.

Footville
-UFO (DD)
   1978, April 16/County Rd.B
     Janesville Gazette, 17 Apr.1978.

Fort Atkinson
-Archeological site
   panther intaglio/W on Hwy.106
     H. Wheaton & C.E. Brown, "The Dedi-
     cation of Fort Atkinson Intaglio,"
     Wisconsin Arch. 19 (1920):197-208.
     il.
     Franklin Folsom, America's Ancient
     Treasures (N.Y.: Rand McNally,
     1974), p.160.
-UFO (CE-3)
   1972, Aug.25/Steve Cleveland
     "Who and Where Is Steve Cleveland?"
     APRO Bull. 21 (Sep.-Oct.1972):2.
-UFO (NL)
   1897, April 9
     Milwaukee Sentinel, 11 Apr.1897, p.
     11.
   1897, April 13
     Fort Atkinson Jefferson County Union,
     16 Apr.1897, p.7.
   1975, Nov.13
     "UFO Central," CUFOS News Bull., 1
     Feb.1976, p.13.

Frederic
-Humanoid
   1975, Dec./Olander Jensen
     "What's Happening in Wisconsin?" Can.
     UFO Rept., no.23 (spring 1976):9-10.
-Humanoid tracks
   1975, Jan.3?/Ruth Christiansen
     "Woman Photographs Strange Tracks,"
     APRO Bull. 23 (June 1975):1,4. il.
     Ruth Christiansen, "Mystery of Tracks
     and Lights," Can.UFO Rept., no.22
     (1975):5-10. il.
-UFO (CE-3)
   1974, Dec.2/William Bosak/SE on County
   Rd.W
     St. Paul (Minn.) Pioneer Press, 19
     Jan.1975, p.1.
     Centuria Inter County Leader, 22 Jan.
     1975.
     "Occupant Case in Wisconsin," APRO
     Bull. 23 (Jan.-Feb.1975):1,4.
     "Another Gargoyle and Bell-Jar," Can.
     UFO Rept., no.21 (1975):1-7.
     Jerome Clark, "The Frightened Crea-
     ture on County Road W," Flying Sau-
     cer Rev. 21 (June 1975):20-21.
-UFO (NL)
   1974, Dec./Gunnard Linder
     Centuria Inter County Leader, 29 Jan.
     1975.
   1975, Feb.24/Ray Kurkowski/Slush Pump
   Bar
     Centuria Inter County Leader, 26 Feb.
     1975.

Genesee
-UFO (NL)
   1977, June 27
     "UFOs of Limited Merit," Int'l UFO
     Reporter 2 (Aug.1977):3.

Germantown
-UFO (NL)
   1976, July 22
     "Sighting Reports," CUFOS News Bull.,
     Sep.1976, p.6.

Gillett twp.
-UFO (NL)
   1978, March 3/Edward Erickson
     Marinette Eagle-Star, 4 Mar.1978.

Gills Rock
-UFO (NL)
   1959, Sep.13/Roland H. Daubner/1½ mi.SE
     Lloyd Mallan, "Complete Directory of
     UFOs: Part I," Sci.& Mech. 37 (Dec.
     1966):36,75-76.
     Thomas M. Olsen, ed., The Reference
     for Outstanding UFO Sighting Reports
     (Riderwood, Md.: UFO Information Re-
     trieval Center, 1966), pp.66-68.

Grafton
-Fall of metallic object
   1947, summer/=circular saw blade
     Harold T. Wilkins, Flying Saucers on
     the Attack (N.Y.: Ace, 1967 ed.),
     p.65.
     Ted Bloecher, Report on the UFO Wave
     of 1947 (Washington: NICAP, 1967),
     p. I-14.

Grantsburg
-UFO (NL)
   1897, April 13/St. Croix R.
     Minneapolis (Minn.) Times, 14 Apr.
     1897.

Green Bay
-Fall of weblike substance
   1881, Oct.
     "A Rain of Spider Web," Sci.Am. 45
     (1881):337.
-UFO (?)
   1958, Oct.5/Milford Vickman
     "Pulsating Fireball," APRO Bull. 10
     (Jan.1962):4.
-UFO (CE-1)
   1967, Dec.21/Ed Batz
     "UFO near Green Bay," Skylook, no.11,
     (July 1968):6.
-UFO (DD)
   1947, July 2/Eugene LaPlant
     Madison Capital-Times, 7 July 1947.
-UFO (NL)
   1965, Aug.1-3/Mrs. Jack Lackman
     Green Bay Press-Gazette, 4 Aug.1965.
   1967, Nov.4
     Green Bay Press-Gazette, 4 Nov.1967.

Greenfield
-UFO (CE-1)
   1975, Aug.9
     "From the Center for UFO Studies,"
     Flying Saucer Rev. 21 (Apr.1976):24.

Green Lake
-UFO (NL)
   1967, April 27
     Jacques Vallee, Passport to Magonia

(Chicago: Regnery, 1969), p.344.

Gresham
-UFO (CE-2)
1972, Aug.30
"Eyes Swell and Ears Ache After UFO
Sighting," Skylook, no.60 (Nov.
1972):11.
-UFO (NL)
1972, June 22-25/Colin Lawe/Hwy.45
"Unidentified Object Seen in Illinois," Skylook, no.57 (Aug.1972):
11.
"More Reports from Wisconsin," Skylook, no.59 (Oct.1972):8-9.
Glenn McWane & David Graham, The New
UFO Sightings (N.Y.: Warner, 1974),
p.42.
(Letter), R.E.K., Saga UFO Rept. 2
(winter 1975):6,76.
1972, July 29/Hwy.29
1972, Nov.24/S on Hwy.U
(Letter), R.E.K., Saga UFO Rept. 2
(winter 1975):6,76-78.

Hayward
-UFO (NL)
1897, April 12/Al Carey
Hayward Republican, 15 Apr.1897, p.1.
1975, Aug.14
"UFO Central," CUFOS News Bull., 15
Nov.1975, p.17.

Hazel Green
-UFO (?)
1960, April 11/Mary Jo Curwen
Richard Hall, ed., The UFO Evidence
(Washington: NICAP, 1964), p.94.

Hillsboro
-UFO (NL)
1897, April 24/William Clark
Hillsboro Sentry, 29 Apr.1897, p.3.

Hortonville
-UFO (NL)
1972, Sep.26
Milwaukee Sentinel, 28 Sep.1972.

Hudson
-UFO (?)
1897, April 13/=hoax
Hudson Stars and Times, 16 Apr.1897,
p.4.

Hurley
-Mystery plane crash
1961, Feb.24/B-47
1961, May 2/B-47
"Plane Crashes in Northern Wisconsin
Unexplained," APRO Bull. 9 (May
1961):1,4.
-UFO (DD)
1961, Oct.15
Coral & Jim Lorenzen, UFOs: The Whole
Story (N.Y.: Signet, 1969), p.231.

Independence
-Haunt
1951, Aug./Lawrence Hoff

"A Treasure-Seeking Spirit,"·Fate 5
(Feb.-Mar.1952):108.

Iron Mountain
-Mystery plane crash
1967, Oct.29/Guy R. Cordell/Beech C-
45H
Jay Gourley, The Great Lakes Triangle
(Greenwich, Ct.: Fawcett, 1977),
pp.116-17.

Iron Ridge
-UFO (DD)
1959, Jan.8/Mrs. Earl Becker
"UFO Sightings Rapidly Increase,"
UFO Inv. 1 (Feb.-Mar.1959):5.

Janesville
-Disappearance
1972, Dec.7/James Rose
Jay Gourley, The Great Lakes Triangle
(Greenwich, Ct.: Fawcett, 1977),
pp.162-63.
-Erratic crocodilian
1892, Feb./Rock R.
Chicago (Ill.) Citizen, 27 Feb.1892.
-Hex
1930, Oct./Henry Dorn
New York Times, 9 Oct.1930, p.12.
-UFO (NL)
1897, April 10/Frank C. Haselton
Janesville Gazette, 14 Apr.1897, p.5.
1947, July 5/Al Sievert
Madison Capital-Times, 7 July 1947.
1969, Feb.13/Bill Leitz/5 mi.S
"U.S. Roundup," APRO Bull. 17 (Mar.-
Apr.1969):7.

Juda
-UFO (NL)
1978, April 24/Jake Kaderly/Hwy.11-81
Monroe Times, 25 Apr.1978.

Kenosha
-Animal ESP
1960s/Chet Petersen
Rhea A. White, "The Investigation of
Behavior Suggestive of ESP in Dogs,"
J.ASPR 58 (1964):250,260-62.
-Ghost light
1930s-   /County Rd.NN
Jon Ziomek, "Those Mysterious Kenosha
Lights," Probe the Unknown 3 (Mar.
1975):36-38,56-59.
-UFO (NL)
1897, April 11/R.H. Slosson
Chicago (Ill.) Times-Herald, 13 Apr.
1897, p.2.
1973, Jan.24/Francis J. Reich/Hwy.32
"Lights Seen over Lake Michigan,"
Skylook, no.65 (Apr.1973):13.
1978, July 6
"UFOs of Limited Merit," Int'l UFO
Reporter 3 (Aug.1978):4.

Kewaunee
-Disappearance
1913, Nov.26/Herman Schunemann/"Rouse
Simmons"
Chicago (Ill.) American, 21 Dec.1917;

and 20 Aug.1919.
Dwight Boyer, Ghost Ships of the
Great Lakes (N.Y.: Dodd, Mead, 1968),
pp.97-109.

Kiel
-Inner development
1967-   /Mu-ne-dowk Foundation/Box 268
June & Nicholas Regush, Psi: The Other World Catalogue (N.Y.: Dutton,
1974), p.183.
Brad Steiger, Gods of Aquarius (N.Y.:
Harcourt Brace Jovanovich, 1976),
pp.107-12.

Kronenwetter twp.
-UFO (NL)
1978, Dec.26/Happy Hollow Rd.
Wausau Daily Herald, 27 Dec.1978.

LaCrosse
-Electromagnetic anomaly
1931/Fay Clark/Northern State Power Co.
Brad Steiger, Mysteries of Time and
Space (N.Y.: Dell, 1976 ed.), pp.
136-37.
-Meditation research
1973, July/Komar (Vernon Craig)/St.
Francis Hospital
Brad Steiger, Mysteries of Time and
Space (N.Y.: Dell, 1976 ed.), pp.
230-31. il.
-Phantom wolf
ca.1922/D.R. Clark
Jerome Clark & Loren Coleman, Crea-
tures of the Outer Edge (N.Y.: War-
ner, 1978), pp.156-57.
-UFO (CE-1)
1976, June 5
"Noteworthy UFO Sightings," Ufology
2 (fall 1976):61.

Ladysmith
-UFO (NL)
1957, June 14/A.W. Daniels
(Letter), Fate 10 (Dec.1957):113-16.

Lafayette
-Phantom panther
1977, Nov.4/Ken Wheeler/County Rd.O
Chippewa Falls Herald-Telegraph, 16
Nov.1977.

LaGrange
-UFO (DD)
1972, Dec.31/nr. Kettle Moraine State
Forest
1973, Jan.20
Richard Heiden, "UFOs in Southern
Wisconsin," APRO Bull. 22 (July-Aug.
1973):1,4.
-UFO (NL)
1973, March 20
Richard Heiden, "UFOs in Southern
Wisconsin," APRO Bull. 22 (July-Aug.
1973):1,4.

Lake co.
-UFO (DD)
1971, Sep.29/James Rogers/U.S.27 x Hwy.

474
"Flying Saucer Visits Disneyland,"
Skylook, no.52 (Mar.1972):14.

Lake Geneva
-Lake monster
1892, July 22/=hoax
Chicago (Ill.) Tribune, 24 July 1892.
-Teleportation
1958, Sep.27/Sonette Taggart
Barbara Taggart, "My Daughter Was
Teleported," Fate 13 (Nov.1960):59-
60.

Lake Mills
-UFO (NL)
1897, April
Elkhorn Independent, 15 Apr.1897, p.
2.
1897, April 22
Fort Atkinson Jefferson County Union,
30 Apr.1897.

Lamont
-UFO (NL)
1897, April 16
Darlington Democrat, 22 Apr.1897, p.
1.

Lancaster
-UFO (CE-1)
1975, Nov.4
"UFO Central," CUFOS News Bull., 1
Feb.1976, p.11.

Lincoln co.
-Cattle mutilation
1978, Aug.
"Late News," Stigmata, no.5 (fall-
winter 1978):23.

Lodi
-UFO (NL)
1897, April 12/James Wilson
Milwaukee Sentinel, 13 Apr.1897, p.2.

Lomira
-UFO (CE-1)
1974, Oct.18/Bob Kuehn
(Letter), Flying Saucers, Mar.1975,
p.54.

Lone Rock
-UFO (DD)
1976, Sep.28
"UFOs of Limited Merit," Int'l UFO
Reporter 1 (Nov.1976):5.

Madison
-Archeological sites
University of Wisconsin campus
Stephen D. Peet, "The Great Serpent
and Other Effigies," Am.Antiquarian
12 (1890):211-28.
Clark S. Matteson, The History of
Wisconsin (Milwaukee: Wisconsin Hist.
Pub.Co., 1893).
"Indian Mound Groups and Village
Sites about Madison," Am.Antiquarian
33 (1911):240-41.

Franklin Folsom, America's Ancient
Treasures (N.Y.: Rand McNally,
1974), p.161.
-Derelict automobile
1954, March 6/Herman Thomas/University
Ave.
(Editorial), Fate 7 (June 1954):6.
-Disappearance
1955, May 22/F-80
"Case 91," CRIFO Orbit, 1 July 1955,
pp.1-2.
-Inner development
1970s/Church of the Wyccan Rede
J. Gordon Melton, Encyclopedia of Am-
erican Religions, 2 vols. (Wilming-
ton, N.C.: Consortium, 1978), 2:274.
-UFO (?)
1966, Aug.16/Truax Field/=barium cloud
J. Allen Hynek & Jacques Vallee, The
Edge of Reality (Chicago: Regnery,
1975), pp.172-75.
-UFO (CE-1)
1970, Sep.8/Denise Fritz/L. Monona
"Wisconsin Sightings," APRO Bull. 19
(May-June 1971):8-9.
-UFO (CE-2)
1973, Oct?/campgrounds
David Michael Jacobs, The UFO Contro-
versy in America (Bloomington: In-
diana Univ., 1975), p.272.
-UFO (CE-4)
1970, April/20 mi. from town on Inter-
state Hwy.
Warren Smith, "Contact with a UFO
Crew," Saga UFO Rept. 1 (summer
1974):28-31,76-77.
-UFO (DD)
1947, July 7/Richard Y. Schulkin
Madison Capital-Times, 8 July 1947.
1970, Sep.8/Ann Georgeson
1970, Sep.11/Ann Georgeson/Beltline x
Nakoma Rd.
"Sept.8 Wisconsin Reports," APRO
Bull. 19 (Mar.-Apr.1971):8,9.
-UFO (NL)
1947, June 17/E.B. McGilvery/Middleton
Ave.
Madison Wisconsin State Journal, 7
July 1947.
1947, July 4/William Ecker/2071 Winne-
bago St.
Madison Wisconsin State Journal, 8
July 1947.
1947, July 7/Nancy Goff
Madison Capital-Times, 8 July 1947.
1947, July 8/Collins Reese/Glenway
Golf Links
Madison Wisconsin State Journal, 9
July 1947.
1952, April 16
U.S. Air Force, Projects Grudge and
Blue Book Reports 1-12 (Washington:
NICAP, 1968), p.110.
1970, Sep.8/Martin Verhoven/Hwy.14 x
Beltline
1970, Sep.8/5700 Pheasant Hill Dr.
"Sept.8 Wisconsin Reports," APRO
Bull. 19 (Mat.-Apr.1971):8-9.
1970, Sep.11/David Joranson/L. Monona
1970, Sep.16/Mrs. G.C. Klingbeil

"Wisconsin Sightings," APRO Bull. 19
(May-June 1971):8-9.
1975, Sep.25
"UFO Central," CUFOS News Bull., 15
Nov.1975, p.19.
1976, May 4
"Noteworthy UFO Sightings," Ufology
2 (fall 1976):61.
-UFO (R-V)
1978, June 24/Joan Mahr/airport
"Radar Visual in Wisconsin," Int'l
UFO Reporter 3 (Aug.1978):11-15.

Malone
-UFO (CE-3)
1976, Aug.7/Mark Ziegelbauer/Route 1
Fond du Lac Reporter, 10 Aug.1976.

Manawa
-Haunt
1963, Sep.-1965/Nora A. Miller/N of
town
Nora A. Miller, "The Ghosts We Dug
Up," Fate 22 (July 1969):82-85. il.

Manitowoc
-Erratic crocodilian
1978, Nov./Manitowoc R.
San Francisco (Cal.) Chronicle, 6
Nov.1978.
-Fall of metallic object
1962, Sep./=satellite re-entry
(Editorial), Fate 16 (Jan.1963):10.
Frank Edwards, Strange World (N.Y.:
Lyle Stuart, 1964), p.369.
-UFO (NL)
1897, April 10
Berlin Journal, 12 Apr.1897, p.4.

Marion
-UFO (NL)
1973, Jan.13/Hwy.G x 110
"Press Reports," APRO Bull. 21 (Jan.-
Feb.1973):13.

Marshfield
-UFO (NL)
1897, April 10
Minneapolis (Minn.) Tribune, 11 Apr.
1897.
1976, April 28
"Noteworthy UFO Sightings," Ufology
2 (fall 1976):61.

Mattoon
-UFO (NL)
1975, March 2/Jim Zahn
Leonard J. Bongle, "Ball of Fire
Viewed by Many," APRO Bull. 23
(Apr.1975):1,6.

Mayhew
-UFO (NL)
1897, May
Fort Atkinson Jefferson County Union,
7 May 1897, p.5.

Mayville
-Pictographs
Edgar G. Bruder, "The Mayville Indian

Rock Paintings," <u>Wisconsin Arch.</u> 30 (1949):73-78. il.

Medford
-Humanoid
1977, Sep./Hwy.64/=horse?
<u>Madison Capital-Times</u>, 6 Oct.1977.

Mellen
-UFO (CE-2)
1975, March 13-14/Jane Baker
"Landing in Wisconsin," <u>APRO Bull.</u>
23 (Apr.1975):1,3.
"Family Reports UFO Landing on Road near Mellen, WI," <u>Skylook</u>, no.93 (Aug.1975):11.

Menasha
-Archeological site
ca.900 A.D.
Franklin Folsom, <u>America's Ancient Treasures</u> (N.Y.: Rand McNally, 1974), p.159.
-UFO (NL)
1978, June 26/Virginia Adrian/833 Broad St.
<u>Oshkosh Daily Northwestern</u>, 27 June 1978.

Menominee co.
-UFO (NL)
1972, July 30
(Letter), R.E.K., <u>Saga UFO Rept.</u> 2 (winter 1975):6,77.

Menomonie
-Rock pillar
Sharat K. Roy, "Columnar Structure in Limestone," <u>Science</u> 70 (1929): 140-41.

Merrillan
-UFO (NL)
1897, April 11
<u>St. Paul (Minn.) Pioneer Press</u>, 12 Apr.1897.

Merton twp.
-Erratic kangaroo
1978, April 24/Tom Frank
<u>Green Bay Press-Gazette</u>, 25 Apr.1978.

Middleton
-UFO (NL)
1978, Sep.29/Joel Ward/8048 Mineral Point Rd.
<u>Dane County News-Sickle-Arrow</u>, 5 Oct. 1978.

Milton
-Roman coin
ca.1881
James D. Butler, "Early Historic Relics of the Northwest," <u>Wisconsin Hist.Coll.</u> 9 (1880-82):97,120-21.
-UFO (DD)
1947, July 7/Paul Schroeder
Madison <u>Wisconsin State Journal</u>, 8 July 1947.

Milwaukee
-Acoustic anomaly
1961/Henry H. Wohrer
(Letter), <u>Fate</u> 14 (Aug.1961):114-16.
-Clairempathy and precognition
ca.1900-1940/Arthur Price Roberts
Milwaukee <u>Wisconsin News</u>, 6 Nov.1935.
Vincent H. Gaddis, "Psychic Detective," <u>Fate</u> 6 (Sep.1953):51-55.
1961-1965/Peter Hurkos
Jess Stearn, <u>The Door to the Future</u> (N.Y.: Macfadden, 1964), pp.210-23.
(Editorial), <u>Fate</u> 18 (Mar.1965):9-10.
Norma L. Browning, <u>Peter Hurkos: I Have Many Lives</u> (Garden City: Doubleday, 1976).
-Clairvoyance
1950/Jesse James/Colored New Jerusalem Spiritual Church/418 W. Cherry St.
"Milwaukee's Boy Genius," <u>Fate</u> 3 (Aug.1950):44.
-Disappearance
1972, July 21/Anderson Duggar, Jr./ Piper PA-31
Jay Gourley, <u>The Great Lakes Triangle</u> (Greenwich, Ct.: Fawcett, 1977), pp. 20-22,162.
-Fall of coin
1976, Sep./Mr. Kiolbasse
<u>Milwaukee Journal</u>, 16 Sep.1976.
-Fall of metallic object
1974, Aug.22/William Murray
"Fall of Metal Chunk," <u>INFO J.</u>, no. 14 (Nov.1974):23.
-Fall of weblike substance
1881, Oct.
"A Rain of Spider Webs," <u>Sci.Am.</u> 45 (1881):337.
-Healing
1954/George Eharoshe/5010 W. Wisconsin Ave.
Florence H. Sutter, "Prayer Cured My Cancer," <u>Fate</u> 13 (June 1960):35-40.
-Mystery plane crash
1969, May 19/Donald E. DeMott/Piper PA-20
Jay Gourley, <u>The Great Lakes Triangle</u> (Greenwich, Ct.: Fawcett, 1977), pp.132-33.
-Mystery television transmission
1962, Feb./Rosella Rose/KLEE-TV
Curtis Fuller, "KLEE...Still Calling," <u>Fate</u> 17 (Apr.1964):37,39-40.
-Poltergeist
1874/Mary Spiegel
Herbert Thurston, <u>Ghosts and Poltergeists</u> (Chicago: Regnery, 1954), pp.213-16, quoting <u>Religio-Philosophical J.</u>, 29 Aug.1874, and <u>Milwaukee Sentinel</u> (undated).
-Precognition
1950, Aug./Jay Meader
<u>New York Herald-Tribune</u>, 3 Sep.1950.
1952/Irene Pike/2136 N. 40th St.
(Editorial), <u>Fate</u> 6 (Jan.1953):9-10.
1960/Karl Ratzsch
(Editorial), <u>Fate</u> 14 (Apr.1961):21-22.
1970s/Bright Star/3118 N. 13th St.
Warren Smith, "Phenomenal Predictions

for 1975," Saga, Jan.1975, p.20.
Warren Smith, "Phenomenal Predictions
for 1976," Saga, Jan.1976, pp.16,
52-54.
Brad Steiger, Gods of Aquarius (N.Y.:
Harcourt Brace Jovanovich, 1976),
pp.97-100.
-Seance
ca.1925/Madam Beiderman/=fraudulent
Joseph Dunninger, Houdini's Spirit
World and Dunninger's Psychic Revelations (N.Y.: Tower, 1968), pp.
158-62.
-Skyquake
1956, Oct.13
"Case 233," CRIFO Orbit, 2 Nov.1956,
p.4, quoting Milwaukee Journal (un-
dated).
1969, March 22
Milwaukee Journal, 23 Mar.1969.
(Letter), Leo D. Eledge, Fate 23
(July 1970):128-29.
-Spirit medium
1852
Emma Hardinge Britten, Modern Ameri-
can Spiritualism (N.Y.: The Author,
1870), pp.80-81.
-UFO (?)
1952, April 26
Desmond Leslie & George Adamski, Fly-
ing Saucers Have Landed (N.Y.: British Book Centre, 1953), p.62.
-UFO (CE-1)
1975/George Koleas
(Letter), Saga UFO Rept. 2 (fall
1975):4.
-UFO (CE-3)
1897, April 11/Mr. Mayer
Milwaukee Sentinel, 11 Apr.1897, p.11.
Chicago (Ill.) Tribune, 12 Apr.1897,
p.5.
-UFO (DD)
1947, July 6/John Bosch
Milwaukee Sentinel, 7 July 1947.
1947, July 6/Erwin Rottman
Milwaukee Journal, 7 July 1947.
-UFO (NL)
1947, July 6/Frank Phifer
Madison Capital-Times, 7 July 1947.
1947, July 6/Anthony Hoffman/3410 W.
Layton Ave.
1947, July 6/William Humphrey/3148 S.
20th St.
1947, July 6/Glen Bowden/Billy Mitchell
Field
Milwaukee Journal, 7 July 1947.
1947, July 8
Madison Capital-Times, 9 July 1947.
1962, Jan.16/Mrs. Norbert J. Schoeneman
/S. 43d St. x W. Oklahoma Ave.
(Letter), Fate 15 (May 1962):115,118.
1975, Jan.29
"From the Center for UFO Studies,"
Flying Saucer Rev. 21 (Aug.1975):iii.
1975, July 10
1975, Aug.17
"UFO Central," CUFOS News Bull., 15
Nov.1975, pp.13,16.

Mineral Point
-Disappearance
1878, May 23/barn and horse/during
tornado
"Winds," Monthly Weather Rev. 6 (May
1878):8-9.

Monona
-UFO (NL)
1970, Sep.8/Mrs. Richard Hodges/2 mi.E
"Sept.8 Wisconsin Reports," APRO
Bull. 19 (Mar.-Apr.1971):8.

Monroe
-Erratic crocodilian
1977/Tom Neumann
"Wisconsin Farm Pond Site of the
Great 'Gator Hunt," Anomaly Rsch.
Bull., no.5 (Mar.1977):19-20, quot-
ing UPI release (undated).
-UFO (NL)
1953, Feb.3
John C. Ross, "Fate's Report on the
Flying Saucers," Fate 6 (Oct.1953):
6,9.
1978, April 11/2 mi.NW on Hwy.81
Monroe Evening Times, 12 Apr.1978.
1979, Feb.25
Madison Wisconsin State Journal, 26
Feb.1979.

Montello
-Precognition
1850s
"Premonition Stops Trip," J.ASPR 8
(1914):191-92.
-UFO (NL)
1972, May 18/George Snow/Vinci's L.
Montello Tribune, 18 May 1972.

Monticello
-UFO (CE-1)
1964, April 3/1 mi.W on Hwy.C
Thomas M. Olsen, ed., The Reference
for Outstanding UFO Sighting Reports
(Riderwood, Md.: UFO Information Retrieval Center, 1966), p.89.
Jacques & Janine Vallee, Challenge
to Science (N.Y.: Ace, 1966 ed.),
pp.53-55.

Morgan Sidings
-UFO (CE-2)
1972, July 30
(Letter), R.E.K., Saga UFO Rept. 2
(winter 1975):6,77.

Morrisonville
-UFO (DD)
1947, July 1
Madison Capital-Times, 8 July 1947.

Mosinee
-UFO (CE-2)
1968, May 29
J. Allen Hynek, The UFO Experience
(Chicago: Regnery, 1972), p.239.

Mount Pleasant twp.
-UFO (NL)

1976, Sep.9/Joann Sawicki/Hwy.20 x
West Rd.
    Racine Journal-Times, 10 Sep.1976.
    Oak Creek Pictorial, 15 Sep.1976.

Muscoda
-Archeological site
    E.G. Squier & E.H. Davis, Ancient
    Monuments of the Mississippi Valley
    (Washington: Smithsonian Institution,
    Contrib.to Knowl., no.1, 1848), pp.
    129-31,133.

Muskego
-Mystery plane crash
    1960, Sep.23/Cessna 140
    Jay Gourley, The Great Lakes Triangle
    (Greenwich, Ct.: Fawcett, 1977),
    p.79.

Necedah
-Healing
    1950s
    "Berta Was Cured at Necedah," Fate
    8 (Sep.1955):97-101, quoting Nece-
    dah Marquee (undated).
-Religious apparition
    1949, Nov.12-1950, Oct.7/Mary Anna van
    Hoof
    John C. Ross, "Vision at Necedah,"
    Fate 4 (Mar.1951):6-12.
    Kansas City (Mo.) Times, 5 May 1975.
    Kansas City (Mo.) Star, 17 Aug.1975.

Neillsville
-UFO (NL)
    1976, April 23
    "Noteworthy UFO Sightings," Ufology
    2 (fall 1976):61.

New Berlin
-UFO (NL)
    1975, July 28
    "UFO Central," CUFOS News Bull., 15
    Nov.1975, p.14.

New Richmond
-Erratic kangaroo
    1899, June 12/Mrs. Glover
    Robert H. Gollmar, My Father Owned a
    Circus (Caldwell, Id.: Caxton,
    1965), p.137.

North Hudson
-UFO (NL)
    1976, March 1
    "Noteworthy UFO Sightings," Ufology
    2 (summer 1976):63.

Oak Grove
-Corpse anomaly
    1851, April 11/Abner P. Phelps
    Marshall (Mich.) Statesman, 7 May
    1851.
    J.W. Bancroft, "Petrifactions," Sci.
    Am. 10 (1855):211.

Ogema
-UFO (CE-1)
    1967, Aug.12/Robert Miedtke/12 mi.W on

County Trunk One
    "Possible Landing in Wisconsin,"
    APRO Bull. 16 (Sep.-Oct.1967):11.
    Jim & Coral Lorenzen, UFOs over the
    Americas (N.Y.: Signet, 1968), pp.
    27-29.
-UFO (CE-2)
    1975, summer
    Len Stringfield, "The Stringfield
    Report," Skylook, no.100 (Mar.1976)
    :14,15.

Okauchee
-UFO (DD)
    1947, July 7/Charles Pettit
    Milwaukee Sentinel, 9 July 1947.

Omro
-UFO (CE-1)
    1897, April 13
    Omro Herald, 17 Apr.1897, p.5.
-UFO (CE-4)
    1973, Oct.15/George Willis
    David Webb, 1973: Year of the Human-
    oids (Evanston: Center for UFO
    Studies, 1976 ed.), p.12.
    Leonard H. Stringfield, Situation
    Red: The UFO Siege (N.Y.: Fawcett
    Crest, 1977 ed.), pp.77-78.

Orfordville
-UFO (CE-1)
    1976, May 4
    "Sighting Reports," CUFOS News Bull.,
    Sep.1976, p.5.

Osceola
-UFO (NL)
    1978, March 22/Neil Johnson/4 mi.S
    "Follow Up," APRO Bull. 27 (Nov.
    1978):1,3-4.
-UFO (R)
    1952, July 25, 29
    Brad Steiger, Project Blue Book (N.Y.:
    Ballantine, 1975), betw.pp.360-61.
    il.

Oshkosh
-Midday darkness
    1886, March 19
    LaCrosse Daily Republican, 20 Mar.
    1886.
    "Atmospheric Phenomenon," Monthly
    Weather Rev. 14 (Mar.1886):79.
-Precognition
    1890, Jan./Nick Becker
    "Premonitory Dream," J.ASPR 9 (1915):
    642-43.
-Roman coin
    1883/A.M. Brainerd/=campaign medal?
    New York Times, 4 Aug.1883, p.4.
    J.D. Butler, "Roman Coins Found in
    Oshkosh," Am.Antiquarian 8 (1886):
    372.
-UFO (?)
    1964, Jan.27/L. Winnebago
    Oshkosh Northwestern, 28 Jan.1964.
-UFO (DD)
    n.d./Mort Taylor
    "Ex-Navy Man Reports UFO near Osh-
    kosh, Wisconsin," Skylook, no.51

(Feb.1972):7-8, quoting Cross Country News, 28 Oct.1971.
-UFO (NL)
  1897, April 11
    Omro Herald, 12 Apr.1897, p.1.

Ozaukee co.
-Fall of weblike substance
  1881, Oct.
    "A Rain of Spider Web," Sci.Am. 45
    (1881):337.

Palmyra
-Fall of worms
  1897, April 23
    Palmyra Enterprise, 29 Apr.1897, p.1.
-UFO (DD)
  ca.1943
    Richard Heiden, "UFOs in Southern
    Wisconsin," APRO Bull. 22 (July-
    Aug.1973):1,5.
-UFO (NL)
  1897, April
    Chicago (Ill.) Times-Herald, 14 Apr.
    1897, p.2.

Park Falls
-UFO (CE-1)
  1978, May 25/Stephen M. Vuchetich/But-
    ternut L.
    Park Falls Herald, 1 June 1978.
-UFO (NL)
  1977, July 17/Ken JuVette
    (Letter), Park Falls Herald, 15 June
    1978.

Patch Grove
-UFO (NL)
  1975, Nov.6/Harold Posten
    "Wisconsin Sighting Reported," Sky-
    look, no.97 (Dec.1975):7.

Pepin
-UFO (CE-3)
  1945, Nov.
    Peter Guttilla, "UFO Nights of Ter-
    ror," Saga UFO Rept. 6 (July 1978):
    52-54.

Peshtigo
-Fire anomaly
  1871, Oct.8
    James W. Sheahan & George P. Upson,
    History of the Great Conflagration
    (Chicago: Union, 1872), pp.371-86,
    393-98.
    Ignatius Donnelly, Ragnarok: The Age
    of Fire and Gravel (N.Y.: Appleton,
    1883), pp.413-23.
    Ben Kartman & Leonard Brown, ed.,
    Disaster! (N.Y.: Pellegrini & Cud-
    ahy, 1948).
    Robert W. Wells, Fire at Peshtigo
    (Englewood Cliffs, N.J.: Prentice-
    Hall, 1968), pp.201-13.

Pewaukee
-Erratic kangaroo
  1978, April
    (Editorial), Fate 31 (Sep.1978):22.

Phillips
-UFO (CE-1)
  1975, March 2
    "From the Center for UFO Studies,"
    Flying Saucer Rev. 21 (Aug.1975):32.

Pierce co.
-UFO (NL)
  1975, March-April/George Wheeler
    Eau Claire Leader-Telegram, 8 Apr.
    1975.
    Ellsworth Pierce County Herald, 10
    Apr.1975.

Plain
-UFO (NL)
  1975, July 14
    "UFO Central," CUFOS News Bull., 15
    Nov.1975, p.13.

Platteville
-Haunt
  n.d./Nigger Head
    Charles M. Skinner, American Myths
    and Legends, 2 vols. (Philadelphia:
    Lippincott, 1903), 2:257.
-UFO (NL)
  1977, Jan.28
    "UFOs of Limited Merit," Int'l UFO
    Reporter 2 (Mar.1977):5.

Plover
-UFO (NL)
  1972, Aug.21/Jack West/Hwy.51 Beltline
    Glenn McWane & David Graham, The New
    UFO Sightings (N.Y.: Warner, 1974),
    p.55, quoting Stevens Point Journal
    (undated).

Potosi
-Archeological site
  serpent effigy
    Stephen D. Peet, "The Great Serpent
    and Other Effigies," Am.Antiquarian
    12 (1890):211-28. il.
-Giant human skeletons
  1869, Dec./Mr. Patterson
    Dubuque (Ia.) Times, 5 Jan.1870.

Poy Sippi
-Haunt
  1955-1963/William Monroe/1 mi.W
    Mary Margaret Fuller, "The Haunted
    Quilt of Poy Sippi," Fate 17 (Apr.
    1964):32-36. il.

Prairie du Chien
-Archeological site
    William Pidgeon, Traditions of De-
    coo-dah (N.Y.: Horace Thayer, 1858),
    pp.180-82.
    Stephen D. Peet, "Emblematic Mounds
    in Wisconsin," Wisconsin Hist.Soc'y
    Coll. 9 (1880-82):40-74.
    T.H. Lewis, "The Camel and Elephant
    Mounds at Prairie du Chien," Am.
    Antiquarian 6 (1884):348-49. il.
-Cattle mutilation
  1975, Oct.
    James Butler Bonham, "Cattle Mutila-

tions and UFOs: Satanic Rite or Alien Abduction," Official UFO 1 (Dec. 1976):26,54,55.
-UFO (CE-1)
1967, Oct.19/Michael Layh
Jim & Coral Lorenzen, UFOs over the Americas (N.Y.: Signet, 1968), p. 170.
-UFO (NL)
1788, Oct.12/Jean Baptiste Perrault
Jean Baptiste Perrault, "Narrative of the Travels and Adventures of a Merchant Voyageur in the Savage Territories of Northern America," in Michigan Pioneer & Hist.Colls. 37 (1909-10):508,547.

Price co.
-UFO (CE-2)
1960, Nov.3/Douglas Fox
"Small Boys See Warm, Landed UAO," APRO Bull. 9 (Jan.1961):1,4.

Racine
-Disappearance
1880, Oct.16/"Alpena"
Jesse Watkins, Jr., "The Alpena Mystery," Chicago (Ill.) Tribune Mag., 15 Oct.1950.
Dwight Boyer, Ghost Ships of the Great Lakes (N.Y.: Dodd, Mead, 1968), pp.176-88.
1969, Nov.6/James R. Simmons/Lear jet
Chicago (Ill.) Tribune, 7 Nov.1969.
Jay Gourley, The Great Lakes Triangle (Greenwich, Ct.: Fawcett, 1977), pp.160-62.
-Fall of lignite
1946, April 25
"Ball of Fire," Doubt, no.15 (summer 1946):223.
-Men-in-black
1953, Dec.6/=hoax?
Harold T. Wilkins, Flying Saucers on the Attack (N.Y.: Ace, 1967 ed.), pp.299-300.
-UFO (?)
1966, Aug.16/=ad plane
John A. Keel, "The Night the Sky Turned On," Fate 20 (Sep.1967):30, 34.
(Letter), O.L. Maves, Fate 21 (Jan. 1968):127.
-UFO (NL)
1947, July 7
Milwaukee Sentinel, 9 July 1947.
1952, April 7
Racine Journal-Times, 7-8 Apr.1952.
1965, Nov.27
Racine Journal-Times, 28 Nov.1965.

Reedsburg
-Norse mooring stone
7 mi.NE
W.R. Anderson, "Evidence of Norse Exploration in Illinois and Wisconsin," Anthro.J.Canada 12, no.3 (1974):29.

Rhinelander
-UFO (NL)

1978, Feb./Shirley Peters
York (Pa.) Daily Record, 10 Mar.1978.

Rice Lake
-UFO (?)
1897, April 9/J.P. Valby
Minneapolis (Minn.) Tribune, 13 Apr. 1897.

Richland co.
-Archeological sites
E.G. Squier & E.H. Davis, Ancient Monuments of the Mississippi Valley (Washington: Smithsonian Institution, Contrib.to Knowl., no.1, 1848), pp. 128-29.
Barbara Mead & David E. Berwick, "The Blake Site (47-RI-49): A Late Paleo-Indian Site in Richland County, Wisconsin," Wisconsin Arch. 58 (1977):24-32. il.

Rio
-Clairaudience
1953, May 15/Ralph Scott
Laura A. Dale, Rhea White & Gardner Murphy, "A Selection of Cases from a Recent Survey of Spontaneous ESP Phenomena," J.ASPR 56 (1962):3, 40-43.
-UFO (NL)
1897, April 11
Baraboo Evening News, 14 Apr.1897, p.2.

Ripon
-UFO (?)
1897, April 11/Jerre Dobbs/=balloon
Chicago (Ill.) Times-Herald, 13 Apr. 1897, p.2.
Peoria (Ill.) Journal, 15 Apr.1897, p.2.
-UFO (NL)
1965, April 19/drive-in theater
"News Briefs," Saucer News 10 (Sep. 1963):19.

Rock co.
-Archeological site
"Ancient Earthworks in Rock County, Wisconsin," Am.Antiquarian 6 (1884): 317-22.

Rockfield
-UFO (DD)
1947, June 28/Marion Beuschler
Ted Bloecher, Report on the UFO Wave of 1947 (Washington: NICAP, 1967), Appendix, Case 96.

Saint Croix co.
-Poltergeist
1873, Sep.-Oct./Mr. Lynch
Decatur (Ill.) Local Review, 30 Oct. 1873, p.3, quoting St. Paul (Minn.) Pioneer Press (undated).
Charles Fort, The Books of Charles Fort (N.Y.: Holt, 1941), pp.873-74, quoting Religio-Philosophical J., 4 Oct.1873.

Saint Croix Falls
-Humanoid tracks
  1976, Oct./=hoax
    St. Croix Falls Standard-Press, 14
    Oct.1976; 21 Oct.1976; and 28 Oct.
    1976. il.
-UFO (?)
  1952, April 12/J.J. Kaliszewski
    (Editorial), Fate 5 (Sep.1952):7.
-UFO (DD)
  1951, Oct.10/J.J. Kaliszewski/10 mi.E
    Richard Hall, ed., The UFO Evidence
    (Washington: NICAP, 1964), p.56.
-UFO (NL)
  1976, July/St. Croix R.
  1978, March 22/Lorena McClain/State Rd.
    St. Croix Falls Dalles Visitor, no.
    10 (May 1978):1,23.

Sawyer co.
-Norse ax
  n.d./George M. Huss
    "A Remarkable Stone Ax," Am.Anthro.,
    n.s. 8 (1906):220.

Sheboygan
-Archeological site
  500-1000 A.D./Sheboygan Mound Park
    M.S. Thomson, "Two Bone Implements
    from Sheboygan," Wisconsin Arch.,
    n.s. 10 (1931):121-22. il.
    Franklin Folsom, America's Ancient
    Treasures (N.Y.: Rand McNally,
    1974), pp.160-61.
-Fall of weblike substance
  1881, Oct.
    "A Rain of Spider Web," Sci.Am. 45
    (1881):337.
-UFO (CE-1)
  1966, March 24
    Jacques Vallee, Passport to Magonia
    (Chicago: Regnery, 1969), p.324.
-UFO (NL)
  1897, April 11/Jacob Schlicht
    Chicago (Ill.) Times-Herald, 12 Apr.
    1897, p.1.
  1960, Nov.23
    Curtis Fuller, "The Nov.23 UFO," Fate
    14 (Mar.1961):46,50.

Shawano co.
-UFO (NL)
  1972, July 29
    Milwaukee Journal, 29 July 1972.
    Glenn McWane & David Graham, The New
    UFO Sightings (N.Y.: Warner, 1974),
    pp.53-54, quoting Wittenberg Enter-
    prise & News (undated).

Somerset
-UFO (NL)
  1978, May 2
    River Falls Journal, 11 May 1978.

South Byron
-UFO (NL)
  1897, April
    Fond du Lac Commonwealth, 12 Apr.
    1897, p.3.

Sparta
-UFO (NL)
  1972, Aug./Ray Harris/County Rd.Q
    Glenn McWane & David Graham, The New
    UFO Sightings (N.Y.: Warner, 1974),
    p.54, quoting Sparta Herald (undat-
    ed).

Spooner
-UFO (CE-2)
  1978, Aug./ground markings only
    "Late News," Stigmata, no.5 (fall-
    winter 1978):23.
-UFO (DD)
  1957, Nov.4
    Spooner Advocate, 7 Nov.1957.
-UFO (NL)
  1897, April 13/James G. Macpherson
    Saginaw (Mich.) Globe, 19 Apr.1897.

Stanley
-UFO (DD)
  1962, July 18/Florence Cummins
    "Twin Dumbells Seen in Wisconsin,"
    APRO Bull. 11 (May 1963):4.

Stevens Point
-UFO (CE-1)
  1971, Nov.
    "Mental Impressions from UFO's?" APRO
    Bull. 22 (July-Aug.1973):9.
-UFO (DD)
  1947, July 8
    Madison Capital-Times, 9 July 1947.

Stinnet twp.
-UFO (DD)
  1957, Nov.4
    Richard Hall, ed., The UFO Evidence
    (Washington: NICAP, 1964), p.164.

Stoughton
-UFO (CE-1)
  1968, Jan.21/Ida Knifer/I-90 x Hwy.N
    Eric Norman [Warren Smith], Gods, De-
    mons and UFOs (N.Y.: Lancer, 1970),
    pp.195-97.
  1974, Dec.23/Marcia Knipfer
    "Flaming UFO Frightens Wisconsin
    Pair," APRO Bull. 24 (July 1975):6.
-UFO (NL)
  1967/Richard Dvorak/W on Hwy.57
  1967-1968
    Eric Norman [Warren Smith], Gods, De-
    mons and UFOs (N.Y.: Lancer, 1970),
    pp.197-200.

Strum
-UFO (DD)
  1957, Nov.11
    Richard Hall, ed., The UFO Evidence
    (Washington: NICAP, 1964), p.167.

Sturgeon Bay
-UFO (?)
  1967, Nov.4/Green Bay
    "UFOs--November--U.S.A.," APRO Bull.
    16 (Nov.-Dec.1967):8.
-UFO (CE-2)
  1970, Sep.6/ground markings only

Ted Phillips, Physical Traces Associated with UFO Sightings (Evanston: Center for UFO Studies, 1975), p.72.
-UFO (DD)
1952, May 21/Coral E. Lorenzen/3d Ave.
Coral E. Lorenzen, Flying Saucers: The Startling Evidence of the Invasion from Outer Space (N.Y.: Signet, 1966 ed.), pp.32-35.
-UFO (NL)
1947, summer/Ronald Larsen
Coral E. Lorenzen, Flying Saucers: The Startling Evidence of the Invasion from Outer Space (N.Y.: Signet, 1966 ed.), pp.21-22.
1953, Feb.21, 23
John C. Ross, "Fate's Report on the Flying Saucers," Fate 6 (Oct.1953): 6,9.
1975, Aug.6
"UFO Central," CUFOS News Bull., 15 Nov.1975, p.15.

Sugar Camp twp.
-UFO (DD)
1961, April 27/Brent Lorbetski
Paul Foght, "Inside the Flying Saucers: Pancakes," Fate 14 (Aug.1961): 32,36.

Sun Prairie
-UFO (NL)
1970, Dec.1/Jan Peterson
"UFO Sighting in Sun Prairie, Wisconsin," APRO Bull. 19 (Mar.-Apr.1971): 9.

Superior
-Haunt
1909-   /Hildur Lundholm
Hans Holzer, Ghosts I've Met (N.Y.: Ace, 1965 ed.), pp.58-59.
-Phantom
1968, May 25/Mr. Clark
John A. Keel, Strange Creatures from Time and Space (Greenwich, Ct.: Fawcett, 1970), p.191.
Jerome Clark, "Paranormal Terror," Saga UFO Report 4 (July 1977):8.
-UFO (NL)
1897, April 12
Milwaukee Sentinel, 13 Apr.1897.

Tigerton
-UFO (NL)
1972, July 29/Dennis Kussman/Hwy.45 x County Rd.M
"More Reports from Wisconsin," Skylook, no.59 (Oct.1972):8,9.

Tilden
-Phantom panther
1977, Oct.25/Mrs. Charlie Kern/U.S.53
Chippewa Falls Herald-Telegraph, 16 Nov.1977.

Trade Lake
-UFO (CE-2)
ca.1973, fall/Art Baker/County Rd.M
"What's Happening in Wisconsin?" Can.

UFO Rept., no.23 (spring 1976):9-10.

Turtle Lake
-UFO (NL)
1897, April 14/Dr. Brown
Minneapolis (Minn.) Times, 15 Apr. 1897.

Twin Lakes
-UFO (NL)
1975, Aug.14
"UFO Central," CUFOS News Bull., 15 Nov.1975, p.16.

Two Rivers
-UFO (NL)
1978, July 27/Gary Randall/Coast Guard station
Muskegon (Mich.) Chronicle, 30 July 1978.
1978, Aug.9/Tom Gordon/nr. Coast Guard station
Manitowoc-Two Rivers Herald-Times-Reporter, 11 Aug.1978.

Vernon co.
-Petroglyphs
A. Dewey Buck & William H. Wilson, "The Hanson Petroglyphs," Wisconsin Arch. 41, no.4 (1960):98-101. il.

Verona
-Haunt
1950/William Grabrandt, Jr./Route 1
"Laying a Wisconsin Ghost," Fate 4 (Jan.1951):48-49, quoting Madison Capital-Times (undated).

Vilas co.
-Fall of metallic object
1966, Oct.14/=space debris
"Saucer Briefs," Saucer News 14 (spring 1967):35, quoting AP releases, 15 Oct.1966, and 24 Oct. 1966.

Viroqua
-UFO (CE-1)
1975, Oct.28
"UFO Central," CUFOS News Bull., 1 Feb.1976, p.10.

Walworth
-UFO (DD)
1959, Jan.8/Gordon Higgins/U.S.14
Richard Hall, ed., The UFO Evidence (Washington: NICAP, 1964), pp.45-46.

Washburn
-UFO (DD)
1975, July 8
"UFO Central," CUFOS News Bull., 15 Nov.1975, p.13.
-UFO (NL)
1975, Nov.2
"UFO Central," CUFOS News Bull., 1 Feb.1976, p.11.
1977, April 22
"UFOs of Limited Merit," Int'l UFO Reporter 2 (June 1977):3.

Waterloo
-Spirit medium and healing
  1850-1882/Mary Hayes Chynoweth
    Louisa Johnson Clay, The Spirit Dom-
    inant (San Jose: Mercury Herald,
    n.d.).
    Stanwood Cobb & David Techter, "The
    Woman Who Dowsed a Fortune," Fate
    26 (Oct.1973):38-47; (Nov.1973):96-
    104; (Dec.1973):88-96. il.

Watertown
-Healing
  1853/Healy Ackley
    Emma Hardinge Britten, Modern Ameri-
    can Spiritualism (N.Y.: The Author,
    1870), p.391.
-Norse runestone
    W.R. Anderson, "Evidence of Norse
    Exploration in Illinois and Wiscon-
    sin," Anthro.J.Canada 12, no.3
    (1974):29.

Waukesha
-Erratic kangaroo
  1978, April 12/Jill Haeselich
    Lawrence (Kan.) Journal-World, 14
    Apr.1978.
-UFO (DD)
  1947, July 3/Ted Boyle
    Madison Capital-Times, 7 July 1947.

Waukesha co.
-Erratic kangaroo
  1978, April 16/Greg Napientek
    Little Rock Arkansas Democrat, 18
    Apr.1978.
    (Editorial), Fate 31 (Sep.1978):24.
-Haunt
  1966-1973
    (Editorial), Fate 26 (Apr.1973):30-
    32.
-UFO (CE-2)
  1966/Patricia Blake/County Rd.J-F
    Glenn McWane & David Graham, The New
    UFO Sightings (N.Y.: Warner, 1974),
    p.55.
  1972, Aug.21/Greg V. Faltersack/County
  Rd.J-F
    Milwaukee Journal, 21 Aug.1972.
    "Car Failure Case in Wisconsin," APRO
    Bull. 21 (Sep.-Oct.1972):7-8.
    "The Faltersack Case," APRO Bull. 21
    (Nov.-Dec.1972):1,5.

Waunakee
-Mystery plane crash
  1961, March 26/Wittman Tailwind
    Jay Gourley, The Great Lakes Triangle
    (Greenwich, Ct.: Fawcett, 1977), p.
    131.

Waupaca
-UFO (NL)
  1972, Aug.
    Glenn McWane & David Graham, The New
    UFO Sightings (N.Y.: Warner, 1974),
    p.54.

Wausau
-Mystery plane crash
  1970, Nov.18/Robert A. Rufflo/Piper
  PA-24-180
    Jay Gourley, The Great Lakes Triangle
    (Greenwich, Ct.: Fawcett, 1977),
    pp.115-16.
-UFO (?)
  1965, Aug.22
    Jerome Clark, "The Greatest Flap Yet?
    Part 2," Flying Saucer Rev. 12
    (Mar.-Apr.1966):8,10.
-UFO (NL)
  1897, April 8
    Chicago (Ill.) Times-Herald, 10 Apr.
    1897, p.1.
  1975, March 3
    "From the Center for UFO Studies,"
    Flying Saucer Rev. 21 (Aug.1975):iii.
  1978, Dec.28/Bernice Rainville/1409 S.
  26th St.
    Wausau Daily Herald, 29 Dec.1978.

Wautoma
-UFO (CE-1)
  1979, Jan.6/Richard Singles
    Wautoma Waushara Argus, 10 Jan.1979.

Wauwatosa
-Plant sensitivity
  1950s/Arthur Locker
    Peter Tompkins & Christopher Bird,
    The Secret Life of Plants (N.Y.:
    Harper & Row, 1973), p.148.
-UFO (CE-3)
  1975, Nov.10/Peter Eilbes
    West Allis Post, 8 Mar.1976.
    Nat'l Star, 11 May 1976.
    "World Round-up," Flying Saucer Rev.
    22 (Feb.1977):iii.

West Allis
-UFO (DD)
  1967, Jan.12/Art Hoerres
    Wendelle C. Stevens, "Fantastic UFO
    Photo Flap of 1967," Saga UFO Rept.
    3 (June 1976):24,28-29. il.

Westboro
-UFO (DD)
  1953, May 13/Mrs. Lloyd Surprise
    (Letter), Fate 6 (Oct.1953):108-109.

Westby
-Precognition
  1957/Mabel Peterson
    (Editorial), Fate 10 (Aug.1957):6-8.

West Jacksonport
-UFO (CE-3)
  1977, March 15/Mr. LeClair
    Sturgeon Bay Advocate, 17 Mar.1977.

Whitefish Bay
-UFO (NL)
  1950, June 24/SE of town
    Chicago (Ill.) Tribune, 25 June 1950.

Whitewater
-Inner development

1920s/Morris Pratt Institute
Nandor Fodor, Encyclopaedia of Psy-
chic Science (London: Arthurs,
1933), p.248.
-UFO (NL)
1975, Nov.13
"UFO Central," CUFOS News Bull., 1
Feb.1976, p.13.

Wisconsin Rapids
-Fall of ice
1973, Jan.29/Herb Klug
Columbus (O.) Dispatch, 30 Jan.1973.
Chicago (Ill.) Daily News, 31 Jan.
1973.

B. Physical Features

Amalgamation Mound
-Archeological site
William Pidgeon, Traditions of De-
coo-dah (N.Y.: Horace Thayer, 1858),
pp.61-67.

Aztalan State Park
-Archeological site
ca.1000-1200
E.G. Squier & E.H. Davis, Ancient
Monuments of the Mississippi Valley
(Washington: Smithsonian Institution,
Contrib.to Knowl., no.1, 1848), pp.
131-32.
Clark S. Matteson, The History of
Wisconsin (Milwaukee: Wisconsin
Hist.Pub.Co., 1893).
T.H. Lewis, "The Aztalan Enclosure
Newly Described," Am.Antiquarian 16
(1894):205-208.
"The Pilgrimage to Aztalan," Wiscon-
sin Arch. 18 (1919):152-56.
William T. Sterling, "A Visit to Az-
talan in 1838," Wisconsin Arch. 19
(1920):18-19.
R.P. Perry, "Present Condition of
Aztalan," Wisconsin Arch., n.s. 11
(1932):108-10.
Samuel A. Barrett, "Ancient Aztalan,"
Bull.Milwaukee Pub.Mus., no.13
(1933). il.
Samuel A. Barrett, "Recent Excava-
tions at Aztalan," Wisconsin Arch.,
n.s. 12 (1933):74-86. il.
Moreau S. Maxwell, "Clay Ear Spools
from the Aztalan Site, Wisconsin,"
Am.Antiquity 18 (1952):61-63. il.
Robert F. Maher & David R. Baerreis,
"The Aztalan Lithic Complex," Wis-
consin Arch. 39 (1958):5-25. il.
James N. Porter, "Petrographic Anal-
ysis of Eight Aztalan Celts," Wis-
consin Arch. 39 (1958):26-35.
Warren L. Wittry & David R. Baerreis,
"Domestic Houses at Aztalan," Wis-
consin Arch. 39 (1958):62-76. il.
Robert F. Maher, "The Excavation and
Reconstruction of the Southwest Pyr-
amidal Mound at Aztalan," Wisconsin
Arch. 39 (1958):77-100. il.
Chandler W. Rowe, "A Crematorium at

Aztalan," Wisconsin Arch. 39 (1958)
:101-10. il.
Lee A. Parsons, "Aztalan State Park,
Wisconsin," Lore 10 (1960):104-108.
Paul W. Parmalee, "Animal Remains
from the Aztalan Site, Jefferson
County, Wisconsin," Wisconsin Arch.
41 (1960):1-10.
Robert Ritzenthaler, "Radiocarbon
Dates for Aztalan," Wisconsin Arch.
42 (1961):139.
Robert E. Ritzenthaler, "Another
Radiocarbon Date for Aztalan," Wis-
consin Arch. 44 (1963):180.
William M. Hurley, "The Recent Az-
talan Date," Wisconsin Arch. 45
(1964):139-42. il.
Helen A. Schultz, ed., The Ancient
Aztalan Story (Lake Mills: Lake
Mills-Aztalan Hist.Soc'y, 1969). il.
Franklin Folsom, America's Ancient
Treasures (N.Y.: Rand McNally,
1974), pp.154-55.
Gordon R. Peters, "A Reevaluation
of Aztalan: Some Temporal and Caus-
al Factors," Wisconsin Arch. 57
(1976):2-11.
Fred K. Steube, "Site Survey and
Test Excavations in the Aztalan
Area," Wisconsin Arch. 57 (1976):
198-259. il.

Brown's L.
-Lake monster
1876, Aug.4
Burlington Standard-Press, 10 Aug.
1876.

Brule R.
-Mystery stone sphere
n.d./Sandra Koskie/nr. mouth
"Stone Spheres--Part 2," Pursuit 1
(30 Sep.1968):13,15.

Buffalo L.
-Archeological site
T.H. Lewis, "The Effigy Mounds at
Buffalo Lake, Marquette County,
Wisconsin," Am.Antiquarian 13
(1891):115-17.
W.C. McKern, "The Neale and McClaugh-
ry Mound Groups," Bull.Milwaukee
Pub.Mus., no.3 (1927):213-416. il.

Chippewa R.
-Meteorite crater
"Moon, Earth Impact Similarities
Studied," Aviation Week, 17 June
1974, pp.44,47.

Comfort, Pt.
-Archeological site
ca.6000 B.C./Renier site
Ronald J. Mason & Carol Irwin, "An
Eden-Scottsbluff Burial in Northeastern Wisconsin," Am.Antiquity 26
(1960):43-57. il.

Deltox Marsh
-Humanoid

1968, Oct./Bob Parry
  Ivan T. Sanderson, "Wisconsin's 'Abominable Snowman,'" Argosy, Apr.1969,
  pp.27-29,70.
1968, Nov.19, 30-31/Bob Parry/=hoax?
  Milwaukee Journal, 28 Dec.1968.
  Ivan T. Sanderson, "Wisconsin's 'Abominable Snowman,'" Argosy, Apr.1969,
  pp.27-29,70.
  Waukesha Freeman, 28 Feb.1977.
-Humanoid tracks
  1968, Dec./=hoax?
    Ivan T. Sanderson, "Wisconsin's 'Abom-
    inable Snowman,'" Argosy, Apr.1969,
    pp.27-29,70. il.

Devil's L.
-Lake monster
  1889, Aug./B.C. Deane
    Chicago (Ill.) Tribune, 24 July 1892.
-Phantom canoe
    Charles M. Skinner, American Myths
    and Legends, 2 vols. (Philadelphia:
    Lippincott, 1903), 2:257-58.

Durst Rockshelter
-Archeological site
    Paul W. Parmelee, "Animal Remains
    from the Durst Rockshelter, Sauk
    County, Wisconsin," Wisconsin Arch.
    41 (1960):11-17.
    Franklin Folsom, America's Ancient
    Treasures (N.Y.: Rand McNally,
    1974), p.158.

Elephant Mound
-Archeological site
    Jared Warner, "The Big Elephant Mound
    in Grant County, Wisconsin," Ann.
    Rept.Smith.Inst., 1872, p.416.
    Henry W. Henshaw, "Animal Carvings
    from Mounds in the Mississippi Val-
    ley," Ann.Rept.Bur.Am.Ethn. 2 (1882)
    :123,152-58.

Elkhart L.
-Lake monster
    Peter Costello, In Search of Lake
    Monsters (N.Y.: Coward, McCann &
    Geoghegan, 1974), p.209.
-UFO (DD)
  1970, Oct.15
    (Letter), Anon., Saga UFO Rept. 2
    (summer 1975):78.

Fowler L.
-Lake monster
  1886, June/C.I. Peck/=giant fish?
    Madison Wisconsin State Journal, 28
    June 1883.
    Chicago (Ill.) Tribune, 24 July 1892.

Glover Bluff
-Meteorite crater
  430 m.diam./possible
    W.C. Allen, "Quaternary Geology of
    Southeastern Wisconsin," Prof.Pap.
    U.S.Geol.Survey, no.106 (1918):207-
    208.
    George L. Ekern & F.T. Thwaites, "The

Glovers Bluff Structure: A Disturbed
    Area in the Paleozoics of Wiscon-
    sin," Trans.Wisconsin Acad.Sci. 25
    (1930):89-97.

Grand R.
-Archeological site
    John A. Jeske, "The Grand River Mound
    Group and Camp Site," Bull.Milwau-
    kee Pub.Mus., no.3 (1927):139-212.
    il.

Gullickson's Glen
-Petroglyphs
    Franklin Folsom, America's Ancient
    Treasures (N.Y.: Rand McNally,
    1974), p.158.

High Cliff State Park
-Archeological site
    William F. Read, "The High Cliff
    Mounds," Wisconsin Arch. 28 (1947):
    1-5.
    Franklin Folsom, America's Ancient
    Treasures (N.Y.: Rand McNally,
    1974), p.158.

Horseshoe L.
-UFO (NL)
  1975, Aug./Donald Peterson
    Lindstrom (Minn.)/Donald Peterson
    Press, 20 Aug.1975.

Koshkonong L.
-UFO (?)
  1971, spring
    Richard Heiden, "UFOs in Southern
    Wisconsin," APRO Bull. 22 (July-
    Aug.1973):1,5.

Kratz Creek
-Archeological site
    S.A. Barrett & E.W. Hawkes, "The
    Kratz Creek Mound Focus," Bull.Mil-
    waukee Pub.Mus., no.3 (1919):1-138.
    il.

Lizard Mound State Park
-Archeological site
  ca.500-1000
    Lee A. Parsons, "Unique Display of
    Skeleton at Lizard State Park," Wis-
    consin Arch. 41 (1960):53-65.
    Franklin Folsom, America's Ancient
    Treasures (N.Y.: Rand McNally,
    1974), pp.158-59.

Man Mound
-Archeological site
    C.E. Brown, "The Preservation of the
    Man Mound," Wisconsin Arch. 7 (1908)
    :139-54.
    Franklin Folsom, America's Ancient
    Treasures (N.Y.: Rand McNally,
    1974), p.159.

Mason L.
-UFO (CE-4)
  1965, May 30
    David Webb, "Analysis of Humanoid/

Abduction Reports," in Proc.1976
CUFOS Conference (Evanston: Center
for UFO Studies, 1976), pp.268-69.

Mendota L.
-Lake monster
  1883, June 27/Billy Dunn/=hoax?
    Madison Wisconsin State Journal, 28
    June 1883.
    Chicago (Ill.) Tribune, 24 July 1892.

Mirrow L.
-Humanoid
  1910
    John Green, Sasquatch: The Apes Among
    Us (Seattle: Hancock House, 1978),
    pp.197-98.

Monona L.
-Lake monster
  1897, June 11/Eugene Heath
    Madison Wisconsin State Journal, 12
    June 1897.
-Mystery plane crash
  1967, Dec.10/Richard P. Fraser/Beech
  H-18
    Jay Gourley, The Great Lakes Triangle
    (Greenwich, Ct.: Fawcett, 1977), pp.
    68-70.

Muskellunge L.
-UFO (NL)
  1970, Aug.2/Barney W. Nashold
    (Letter), Fate 24 (Feb.1971):161.

Nelson Dewey State Park
-Archeological site
    Franklin Folsom, America's Ancient
    Treasures (N.Y.: Rand McNally,
    1974), p.159.

North Point
-Lake monster
  1875, Feb./William Crosston/=hoax?
    Decatur (Ill.) Local Review, 2 Mar.
    1875, p.3.

Pewaukee L.
-Erratic crocodilian
  1971, July 9
    Milwaukee Journal, 10 July 1971, p.1.
-Lake monster
    Peter Costello, In Search of Lake
    Monsters (N.Y.: Coward, McCann &
    Geoghegan, 1974), p.209.

Pigeon Creek
-Norse spearhead
  1899, fall/Nils Windjue
    Hjalmar R. Holand, The Kensington
    Stone (Ephraim, Wisc.: The Author,
    1932), pp.168-70,177.
    Hjalmar R. Holand, Westward from Vin-
    land (N.Y.: Duell, Sloan & Pearce,
    1940), pp.229-31. il.

Red Cedar L.
-Lake monster
  1891
    Peter Costello, In Search of Lake

Monsters (N.Y.: Coward, McCann &
Geoghegan, 1974), p.209.

Rice Creek
-Land monster
  n.d./Eugene S. Shepard/hodag/=hoax
    Lake Shore [Luke Sylvester] Kearney,
    The Hodag (Wausau: The Author,
    1928).
    Curtis D. MacDougall, Hoaxes (N.Y.:
    Dover, 1958 ed.), pp.17-18.

Rock L.
-Archeological site
    C.E. Brown, "Rock Lake," Wisconsin
    Arch., n.s. 5 (1926):107-29. il.
-Lake monster
  1867-1882
    Lake Mills Spike, 31 Aug.1882.
-Underwater pyramids
    Lon Mericle, "The Underwater Search
    for Pyramids in Rock Lake, Jeffer-
    son County, Wisconsin," Wisconsin
    Arch. 43 (1962):70-75.
    Ben Whitcomb, "The Lost Pyramids of
    Rock Lake," Skin Diver, Jan.1970,
    pp.24-25,84.

Shawano L.
-UFO (NL)
  1978, Aug.20
    Shawano Evening Leader, 21 Aug.1978.

Sherwood L.
-UFO (NL)
  1978, March 4/Chris Marceau
    Friendship Reporter, 16 Mar.1978.

Sinsinawa Mound
-Humanoid myth
    Charles M. Skinner, Myths and Legends
    of Our Own Land, 2 vols. (Philadel-
    phia: Lippincott, 1896), 2:330.

Spencer L.
-Archeological site
  ca.490 A.D./horse skull
    W.C. McKern, "Wisconsin Archaeology
    in Light of Recent Finds in Other
    Areas," Wisconsin Arch. 20 (1929):
    1-5.
    "Notes and News," Am.Antiquity 2
    (1936):147-48.
    Robert Ritzenthaler, "The Riddle of
    the Spencer Lake Horse Skull," Wis-
    consin Arch. 45 (1964):115-23.
    Robert Ritzenthaler, "Radiocarbon
    Dates for Clam River Focus," Wiscon-
    sin Arch. 47 (1966):219-20.

Winnebago L.
-Mystery plane crash
  1972, June 29/Convair 580 and DeHavil-
  land DHC-6
    Chicago (Ill.) Tribune, 30 June 1972.
    Jay Gourley, The Great Lakes Triangle
    (Greenwich, Ct.: Fawcett, 1977), p.
    63.
-UFO (NL)
  1897, April

<u>Berlin Daily Journal</u>, 10 Apr.1897,
p.4.

C. Ethnic Groups

<u>Menominee Indians</u>
-Lake monster myth
W.J. Hoffman, "Mythology of the Men-
omoni Indians," <u>Am.Anthro.</u> 3 (1890):
243,247-49.
-White Indians
John T. Short, <u>North Americans of</u>
<u>Antiquity</u> (N.Y.: Harper, 1880), p.
189.

D. Unspecified Localities

-Archeological sites
William Pidgeon, <u>Traditions of De-</u>
<u>coo-dah</u> (N.Y.: Horace Thayer, 1858).
il.

MICHIGAN

A. Populated Places

Adrian
-UFO (NL)
1897, April 13/William Peckmann
Adrian Evening Telegram, 14 Apr.1897.

Albion
-UFO (NL)
1973, Aug.28
Grand Rapids Press, 29 Aug.1973.

Allegan
-UFO (DD)
1947, July 5/Dan Conroy/Lake Allegan
Country Club
Grand Rapids Herald, 7 July 1947.

Allen Park
-Healing
1966, Jan.-May/Russell E. Smith
Russell E. Smith, "I Watched God
Heal," Fate 25 (Aug.1972):62-66.
-UFO (CE-3)
1957, Oct.
David Webb & Ted Bloecher, "MUFON's
Humanoid Study Group Very Active,"
Skylook, no.93 (Aug.1975):9.

Alpena
-Ball lightning
1907, Aug.1
"Ball Lightning at Alpena, Michigan,"
Nature 126 (1930):153.
-Lake monster
1888, June 18/Thunder Bay
Delphos (Kan.) Carrier, 22 June 1888.

Ann Arbor
-Burrowing hose
n.d.
W.E. Farbstein, "Answer This One,"
Fate 5 (Feb.-Mar.1952):28.
-Medieval bronze plate
1886
F.C. Clark, "Bronze Plate of Charle-
magne Found near Ann Arbor," Am.An-
tiquarian 8 (1886):175-76.
-Mystery plane crash
1973, May 23/Cessna 310G
Jay Gourley, The Great Lakes Triangle
(Greenwich, Ct.: Fawcett, 1977), p.
116.
-Out-of-body experience death
1975, June 7/Robert Antoszcyk
"Death or Just Astral Projection?"
Probe the Unknown 3 (Nov.1975):44-
45.
-UFO (?)
1952, April 29/=vapor trails
Ann Arbor News, 30 Apr.1952.
1959, March 22/=rotating radio telescope
Donald H. Menzel & Lyle G. Boyd, The
World of Flying Saucers (Garden City:

Doubleday, 1963), pp.241-42.
-UFO (CE-2)
1957, Dec.1/=aurora?
Ann Arbor News, 2 Dec.1957.
-UFO (DD)
1952, July 27/Charles H. Otis/3724
Dexter Rd.
Richard Hall, ed., The UFO Evidence
(Washington: NICAP, 1964), pp.50-
51.
1966, May 4/Sara Huff
Otto O. Binder, "'Oddball' Saucers
...That Fit No Pattern," Fate 21
(Feb.1968):54,56.
-UFO (NL)
1897, April 16
Chicago (Ill.) Times-Herald, 17 Apr.
1897, p.6.
1952, April 27
Ann Arbor News, 29 Apr.1952.
1966, March 14/Charles Mason
Detroit News, 14 Mar.1966.
1966, March 24/4 mi.W
Mark Carpenter, "The Great UFO Flap
at Ann Arbor," Fate 19 (July 1966):
50,56.

Avon twp.
-UFO (NL)
1978, March 6/Crooks x Auburn Rd.
Port Huron Times-Herald, 8 Mar.1978.

Bad Axe
-UFO (?)
1958/Jerry Sprague/=hoax
(Editorial), Fate 11 (Sep.1958):20.
-UFO (NL)
1956, July 28/Calvin Glassford
"Case 177," CRIFO Orbit, 7 Sep.1956,
p.2, quoting Port Huron Times-Herald (undated).
1956, July 30/Fred Cubernuss/N of town
"Case 178," CRIFO Orbit, 7 Sep.1956,
p.2.
1966, March 26
"Typical Reports," UFO Inv. 3 (Mar.-
Apr.1966):8.

Bailey
-UFO (NL)
1897, April 17/Grant Station
Muskegon Daily Chronicle, 20 Apr.1897.

Bark River
-UFO (NL)
1961, Feb.28/Mrs. Alex Lapalm/Escanaba
Route 1
Lloyd Mallan, "The Mysterious 12,"
Sci.& Mech. 37 (Dec.1966):30,65.

Barryton
-Humanoid tracks
1977, Sep.3/Bob Kurtz/nr. Martiny L.
Traverse City Record-Eagle, 8 Sep.

1977.
Bay City Times, 17 Sep.1977. il.
Jackson Citizen-Patriot, 18 Sep.1977.

Battle Creek
-Disappearance
  1900, Jan./Sherman Church/Augusta Mills
    Chicago (Ill.) Tribune, 5 Jan.1900.
-Dowsing
  1950s/Larry Crandall
    "Battle Creek's 'Official Dowser,'"
    Fate 14 (Oct.1961):49.
-Possession
  1851
    New York Mercury, 13 Sep.1851.
    Mrinal Kanti Ghosh, Life Beyond Death
    (Calcutta: Sri Gouranga, 1934).
    (Letter), C.T.K. Chari, J.ASPR 57
    (1963):163-67.
-UFO (CE-1)
  1966, April 18
    Jacques Vallee, Passport to Magonia
    (Chicago: Regnery, 1969), p.329.
-UFO (DD)
  1949, June 17/Lloyd Sanders/Route 1
    Kenneth Arnold & Ray Palmer, The Com-
    ing of the Saucers (Boise: The Au-
    thors, 1952), p.172. il.
-UFO (NL)
  1897, April 12/L.E. Clawson/sanitarium
    Grand Rapids Evening Press, 13 Apr.
    1897.
    Detroit Evening News, 13 Apr.1897.
  1897, April 15
    Jerome Clark & Lucius Farish, "The
    1897 Story: Part 2," Flying Saucer
    Rev. 14 (Nov.-Dec.1968):6, quoting
    Battle Creek Daily Moon (undated).

Bay co.
-Archeological site
  ca.600 B.C.-1000 A.D./Butterfield site
    Martin H. Wobst, "The Butterfield
    Site, 20 BY 29, Bay County, Michi-
    gan," Anthro.Pap.Mus.Anthro.Univ.
    Michigan, no.32 (1968):173-275. il.

Bay City
-Animal ESP
  1949, Sep.24/Frederick Howey
    "The Saga of Two Bits," Fate 3 (Mar.
    1950):55.
-Humanoid
  1973, summer
    John Green, Sasquatch: The Apes Among
    Us (Seattle: Hancock House, 1978),
    p.201.
-Mystery plane crash
  1969, Aug.15/Cessna 182
    Jay Gourley, The Great Lakes Triangle
    (Greenwich, Ct.: Fawcett, 1977), p.
    133.
-UFO (CE-1)
  1970, Oct.11/Roger G. Jayo/N on Hwy.15
    "Two Low Flying Saucers Seen in Mich-
    igan," Skylook, no.37 (Dec.1970):1-
    2.
-UFO (NL)
  1897, April 15
    Bay City Free Press, 17 Apr.1897.

1969, March 13/Jane Barnard/301 N.
Catherine
    "More on the Michigan Lights," Sky-
    look, no.19 (June 1969):5, quoting
    Bay City Times (undated).

Bear Lake
-Phantom image
  1977, Oct.22/Laila Cooley/United Methodist Church
    Nat'l Enquirer, 7 Mar.1978. il.

Benton Harbor
-Mystery plane crash
  1950, June 23/Robert C. Lind/DC-4
    Chicago (Ill.) Tribune, 25-27 June
    1950.
    Donald E. Keyhoe, Flying Saucers from
    Outer Space (N.Y.: Holt, 1953), pp.
    18-19.
    Jay Gourley, The Great Lakes Triangle
    (Greenwich, Ct.: Fawcett, 1977),
    pp.8-10.
-UFO (?)
  1966, March
    Lloyd Mallan, "Complete Directory of
    UFOs: Part I," Sci.& Mech. 37 (Dec.
    1966):36,76.
-UFO (CE-1)
  1966, April 17/Merle McCarroll
    New York Times, 18 Apr.1966, p.30.
    "Another Saucer 'Flap' in the Mid-
    West," Saucer News 13 (fall 1966):
    24,25.
-UFO (DD)
  1977, July 2
    "UFOs of Limited Merit," Int'l UFO
    Reporter 2 (Aug.1977):3.
-UFO (NL)
  1897, April 13
    Detroit Free Press, 14 Apr.1897.

Benzie co.
-Humanoid
  1974
    Billings (Mont.) Gazette, 29 May
    1977, p.5A.
-Humanoid tracks
  1976
  1977/Abe Roorda
    Billings (Mont.) Gazette, 29 May
    1977, p.5A. il.

Berkley
-UFO (NL)
  1955, Sep.20/Theodore L. Walling/12
  Mile Rd.
    Theodore L. Walling, "Walling Saucer
    Sighting," Fate 9 (Dec.1956):35-37.

Beulah
-UFO (NL)
  1961, July 8/Terry Gregory/Zimmerman
  Rd.
    Lloyd Mallan, "The Mysterious 12,"
    Sci.& Mech. 37 (Dec.1966):30,64.

Big Rapids
-UFO (CE-1)
  1966, March 19

Donald E. Keyhoe & Gordon I.R. Lore,
Jr., UFOs: A New Look (Washington:
NICAP, 1969), p.46.

Birmingham
-UFO (NL)
1952, April 27/15 Mile Rd.
J. Allen Hynek, The Hynek UFO Report
(N.Y.: Dell, 1977), pp.70-73.
-Windshield pitting
1954, spring
"'Blue Dart' Phenomena," CRIFO Newsl.,
4 Feb.1955, p.3.

Blissfield
-Mystery plane crash
1965, April 1/Cessna 310
Jay Gourley, The Great Lakes Triangle
(Greenwich, Ct.: Fawcett, 1977),
pp.79-81.

Bloomfield Hills
-Skyquake
1959, Jan.19
(Editorial), Fate 12 (July 1959):12.

Branch co.
-UFO (?)
1949, April 14/Clifford Cline
Kenneth Arnold & Ray Palmer, The Coming of the Saucers (Boise: The Authors, 1952), p.140.

Bridgeport
-UFO (NL)
1956, July 30
(Editorial), Fate 9 (Dec.1956):11.

Bruce Crossing
-UFO (DD)
1978, May 2/Gail Brady/2 Mile Rd.
Ironwood Daily Globe, 2 May 1978.

Burt
-UFO (NL)
1956, July 30/GOC station
"Case 178," CRIFO Orbit, 7 Sep.1956,
p.2, quoting Saginaw News (undated).
(Editorial), Fate 9 (Dec.1956):11.

Burton
-UFO (CE-2)
1897, April 23/Daniel Gray
Saginaw Globe, 26 Apr.1897.

Byron
-Humanoid
1978, Aug.30/Chester Johnson/102½ E.
Saginaw/=hoax
Flint Journal, 31 Aug.1978; and 1
Sep.1978.

Cadillac
-UFO (NL)
1956, July 28/Willard Wood
"Case 177," CRIFO Orbit, 7 Sep.1956,
p.2, quoting Detroit Free Press (undated).

Cadmus
-UFO (NL)
1897, April 16
Adrian Evening Telegram, 17 Apr.
1897.

Caledonia
-UFO (NL)
1954, Sep.20
"Astronomers Track Three Mysterious
Lights over Michigan," CRIFO Newsl.,
5 Nov.1954, p.6.

California
-Erratic shark
1978, June/Edward Stowe/=hoax
Topeka (Kan.) Daily Capital, 6 July
1978.

Calumet
-Gravity anomaly
1901/Tamarack Mines
Raymond A. Palmer, "Earth's Center
of Gravity: Up or Down?" Flying
Saucers, Dec.1959.
-UFO (NL)
1969, March
"More on the Michigan Lights," Sky-
look, no.19 (June 1969):5, quoting
Houghton Daily Mining Gazette (un-
dated).
-UFO (R-V)
1965, summer/USAF radar post
B. Ann Slate & Stanton T. Friedman,
"UFO Battles the Air Force Couldn't
Cover Up," Saga UFO Rept. 2 (winter
1974):29,31.

Canton twp.
-Phantom panther and livestock killings
1971, Aug./Glenn Brothers
Jerome Clark & Loren Coleman, "On
the Trail of Pumas, Panthers and
ULAs," Fate 25 (June 1972):72,75.

Caro
-Humanoid
1977, Sep.5/Karl Traster/2918 E. Bevens
Saginaw News, 13 Nov.1978.

Caseville
-UFO (NL)
1897, March
Benton Harbor Evening News, 1 Apr.
1897.

Cassopolis
-UFO (?)
1952, April 17
Richard Hall, ed., The UFO Evidence
(Washington: NICAP, 1964), p.153.

Cedar Springs
-UFO (NL)
1977, April 8
"UFO Analysis," Int'l UFO Reporter
2 (May 1977):Newsfront sec.

Cedarville
-Phantom panther tracks

1959, Feb.25/Ed La May
    (Editorial), Fate 12 (July 1959):8½

Center Line
-Precognition
    1964, June-Dec./Miles Jerome Anderson
        (Editorial), Fate 18 (Apr.1965):12-
        14.

Charleston twp.
-UFO (CE-1)
    1897, March 31/Mrs. Wyngate
        Detroit Evening News, 1 Apr.1897.

Charlevoix
-UFO (CE-1)
    1973, Sep.7/U.S.31
        Charlevoix Courier, 13 Sep.1973.
-UFO (NL)
    1973, Aug./Robert Young
        Grand Rapids Press, 26 Aug.1973.

Charlotte
-Humanoid
    1950, July 14
        "Land Beasties," Doubt, no.30 (1950):
        43.
    1951, fall/W of town
        John Green, Sasquatch: The Apes Among
        Us (Seattle: Hancock House, 1978),
        p.200.
-UFO (?)
    1957, Nov.6
        Aimé Michel, Flying Saucers and the
        Straight-Line Mystery (N.Y.: Criter-
        ion, 1958), p.256.
-UFO (NL)
    1897, April 15
        Detroit Evening News, 16 Apr.1897.

Cheboygan
-Fall of worms
    ca.1891/Rev. Manion
        Richard M. Dorson, Bloodstoppers and
        Bearwalkers (Cambridge: Harvard
        Univ., 1952), p.161.
-Healing
    1890s/Rose Sweeney
        Richard M. Dorson, Bloodstoppers and
        Bearwalkers (Cambridge: Harvard
        Univ., 1952), p.161.
-Lake monster
    1976, June 21-22/Stanley McKervey
        Grand Rapids Press, 25 June 1976.
-Precognition
    1955, Oct.2/Lawrence Monk
        "The Airman Sensed Death," Fate 9
        (May 1956):11.
-UFO (?)
    1947, July 9
        Detroit Free Press, 10 July 1947.

Clare
-Ghost light
    1971, April-May/Herrick Rd./=hoax
        "Eerie 'Ghost Light' Turns Out to Be
        a Hoax," Skylook, no.44 (July 1971)
        :11.

Clare co.
-Humanoid
    1977, June 4/U.S.27
        John Green, Sasquatch: The Apes Among
        Us (Seattle: Hancock House, 1978),
        p.201.

Clayton
-UFO (?)
    1957, Nov.6
        Aimé Michel, Flying Saucers and the
        Straight-Line Mystery (N.Y.: Criter-
        ion, 1958), p.256.
-UFO (NL)
    1897, April 16/J.B. Kessler
        Adrian Evening Telegram, 17 Apr.1897.

Clinton
-UFO (CE-1)
    1967, Dec.14/Kenneth Kennedy/Hwy.12
        "Late 1967 Sightings," UFO Inv. 4
        (Jan.-Feb.1968):6.
    1975, Nov.25/Warren Klofkorn/U.S.12 x
    Moon Rd.
        (Letter), Saga UFO Rept. 3 (June
        1976):6.

Clio
-Precognition
    1958, Feb./Eugene Bovee
        (Editorial), Fate 11 (Aug.1958):20-
        21.

Coldwater
-Precognition
    ca.1955/Zulah Larkin
        (Editorial), Fate 10 (May 1957):14-
        15.
        (Editorial), Fate 12 (Dec.1959):28-
        29, quoting Detroit Free Press (un-
        dated).
-UFO (NL)
    1954, June
        Donald E. Keyhoe, Flying Saucer Con-
        spiracy (N.Y.: Holt, 1955), p.164.
    1965, Oct.4/Larry Fraser/County jail
        Columbus (O.) Dispatch, 8 Oct.1965,
        p.1.

Comstock twp.
-UFO (?)
    1897, April 11
        Chicago (Ill.) Times-Herald, 14 Apr.
        1897, p.2.

Concord
-Fall of metallic object
    1965, Dec.9/Roy Root
        Jerome Clark, "The Greatest Flap Yet?
        Part IV," Flying Saucer Rev. 12
        (Nov.-Dec.1966):9,12.

Constantine
-UFO (NL)
    1897, April 14
        Kalamazoo Gazette, 16 Apr.1897.

Copemish
-UFO (NL)
    1961, July 7

Lloyd Mallan, "Complete Directory of
UFOs: Part II," Sci.& Mech. 38
(Jan.1967):44,71,76.

Crystal
-UFO (?)
1975, Aug.17/Mrs. Harvey Waldron/Tow
Rd. x County Rd.522/=rocket
Grand Rapids Press, 18 Aug.1975.
"What Really Happened," Michigan
Anomaly Rsch.Bull., no.2 (Aug.-
Sep.1976):5.

Cutlerville
-UFO (NL)
1955, Aug.22/Earl Kirkpatrick
"Case 99," CRIFO Orbit, 2 Sep.1955,
p.3.

Dansville
-Humanoid
1978, July 13/Francis Jones/Hwy.36
Lansing State Journal, 18 Aug.1978.

Dayton
-UFO (CE-3)
1897, April 29
Saginaw Globe, 1 May 1897.

Dearborn
-Derelict automobile
1962, Jan./Wanda Stanley
(Editorial), Fate 15 (May 1962):15-
16.
-Eyeless vision
1965-1968/Fred and David Hagelthorn
Joyce Hagelthorn, "Blindfolded, My
Son 'Sees,'" Fate 22 (June 1969):88,
90-95. il.
Pauline Saltzman, "I Was a Witness,"
Fate 22 (June 1969):89,95-98.
-UFO (CE-3)
1954, Sep.30/Lawrence Cardenas
Detroit Free Press, 28 Nov.1954.
-UFO (NL)
1975, Oct.25
"UFO Central," CUFOS News Bull., 1
Feb.1976, p.9.

Dearborn Heights
-Fall of rocks
1972, Oct.2-3/Glengary St.
(Editorial), Fate 26 (July 1973):31-
32, quoting Detroit Free Press (undated).

Decatur
-UFO (?)
1957, Nov.5/Waldron Stewart
Donald E. Keyhoe, Flying Saucers: Top
Secret (N.Y.: Putnam, 1960), p.124,
quoting Adrian Telegram (undated).

Delta twp.
-UFO (NL)
1964, May 25/Dexter Reuckert/fire house
"Other Recent Sightings," UFO Inv. 2
(July-Aug.1964):7.

De Tour Village
-Contactee
1970s/Warren H. Goetz
Warren H. Goetz, The Intelligence
of the Universe Speaks (De Tour
Village: The Author, 1974).

Detroit
-Acoustic anomaly
1959, Jan.18-25/Beverly Gnam/Aster St.
(Editorial), Fate 12 (July 1959):15-
16.
-Automatic writing
1950s/DeWitt B. Lucas
DeWitt B. Lucas, "My Invisible Wife,"
Fate 9 (Sep.1956):40-46.
-Contactee
1950s-   /Baird Wallace
Baird Wallace, The Space Story and
the Inner Light (Grosse Ile: The
Author, 1972).
-Disappearance
1972, Nov.30/Lawrence Nelms/Beech Ex-
peditor 3TM
Jay Gourley, The Great Lakes Triangle
(Greenwich, Ct.: Fawcett, 1977), p.
164.
-Dowsing
1884/Cyrus Fuller
"The Divining Rod," Light 4 (1884):
358-59.
-Erratic crocodilian
1960, Nov.18/Hines Park
Detroit News, 20 Nov.1960.
-Erratic shark
1978, March 6/Detroit R., Edison's
Trenton Channel Power Plant
Washington (D.C.) Post, 9 Mar.1978.
-Fall of black rain
1762, Oct.
Marie Caroline Watson Hamlin, Legends
of Le Détroit (Detroit: Nourse,
1884), pp.99-100.
Jonathan Carver, Travels Through the
Interior Parts of North America
(London: J. Walter & S. Crowder,
1778), p.153.
-Fall of fish
1954, April
Edwardsville (Ill.) Intelligencer,
29 Apr.1954.
-Fall of radioactive blue rain
1954, April 8
"Colored Rain--Snow," Doubt, no.45
(1954):289.
(Editorial), Fate 7 (Oct.1954):14.
-Haunt
1710/Ste. Anne's Shrine/Howard St. x
19th St.
Marie Caroline Watson Hamlin, Legends
of Le Détroit (Detroit: Nourse,
1884), pp.40-47.
1962-1963/Lillian Adams/5508 Martin St.
Detroit Free Press, 4 Nov.1962.
Cornelius Sheehan, "There's a Ghost
in Detroit," Fate 16 (Feb.1963):26-
33. il.
"Fortean Items," Saucer News 10 (June
1963):23.

1972
   (Editorial), Fate 25 (Sep.1972):20.
-Hex
   1700s/Mde. Felix Robert/Connor's Creek
   Marie Caroline Watson Hamlin, Legends
   of Le Détroit (Detroit: Nourse,
   1884), pp.71-76.
   1939, March/Jacqueline Thomas
   Detroit Free Press, 9 Mar.1939.
-Lightning anomaly
   1900, Oct.4/B.S. Pague/Woodward Ave.
   B.S. Pague, "Lightning from a Cloud-
   less Sky," Monthly Weather Rev. 28
   (Oct.1900):429-30.
-Mystery air turbulence
   1968, Nov.16/Boeing 727
   R.J. Durant, "On Time Anomalies,"
   Pursuit 4 (Oct.1971):82-85.
-Mystery escape
   1906, Nov.27/Harry Houdini/Belle Island
   Bridge
   Milbourne Christopher, Houdini: The
   Untold Story (N.Y.: Pocket Books,
   1970 ed.), pp.100-102.
-Mystery plane crash
   1963, Jan.12
   1964, Feb.29
   1964, Dec.30/Alfred Oliver Fallon/Cur-
   tis Wright C-46A
   1972, Dec.15/Daniel K. Green/Lear jet
   Jay Gourley, The Great Lakes Triangle
   (Greenwich, Ct.: Fawcett, 1977),
   pp.22-23,72-73,112-13,118-19.
-Phantom
   1707, May 1/Antoine de la Mothe Cadil-
   lac/Nain Rouge
   1763, July 30
   1805, June 5
   1812, Aug./Nain Rouge
   Marie Caroline Watson Hamlin, Legends
   of Le Détroit (Detroit: Nourse,
   1884), pp.22-39.
-Phantom image
   1959, Dec./Leonard Page
   Detroit Times, 31 Dec.1959.
-Poltergeist
   1965, Aug.-Oct.
   Detroit Free Press, 8 Aug.1965.
   William G. Roll, The Poltergeist
   (N.Y.: Signet, 1974 ed.), pp.97-101.
   1972, Aug./Louise Reardon
   (Editorial), Fate 26 (May 1973):31-
   34, quoting Detroit News, Aug.1972.
-Precognition
   1755, spring/Miami chief
   Marie Caroline Watson Hamlin, Legends
   of Le Détroit (Detroit: Nourse,
   1884), pp.91-96.
-Skyquake
   1956, Sep.28
   "Case 228," CRIFO Orbit, 2 Nov.1956,
   pp.3-4, quoting Detroit Times (undated).
-Spirit medium
   1900s/J.B. Jonson
   Nandor Fodor, Encyclopaedia of Psychic Science (London: Arthurs,
   1933), p.224.
   1900s-1910s/Etta Wriedt
   W. Usborne Moore, Glimpses of the

Next State (London: Watts, 1911),
   pp.276-308,355-94,400-18.
   W. Usborne Moore, The Voices (London: Watts, 1913).
   Nandor Fodor, Encyclopaedia of Psychic Science (London: Arthurs,
   1933), pp.92,227-28,250,409, quoting Light, 11 Nov.1911, and 3 Aug.
   1912.
   1910s/A.W. Kaiser/297 Cass Ave.
   W. Usborne Moore, Glimpses of the
   Next State (London: Watts, 1911),
   pp.295-307,394-400.
   Nandor Fodor, Encyclopaedia of Psychic Science (London: Arthurs,
   1933), p.188.
   1930/John Slater
   Nandor Fodor, Encyclopaedia of Psychic Science (London: Arthurs,
   1933), p.346.
-UFO (?)
   1947, July 17
   1947, Aug.18
   1947, Oct.19
   "The Mystery of the Flying Disks,"
   Fate 1 (spring 1948):18,36.
   1957, Nov.1/=Venus
   Jacques & Janine Vallee, Challenge
   to Science (N.Y.: Ace, 1966 ed.),
   p.131.
   1966, Sep./J.R. Tafel
   "Objects Cross Moon Disc," APRO Bull.
   15 (Jan.-Feb.1967):5.
   1973, Oct.23
   Ted Phillips, Physical Traces Associated with UFO Sightings (Evanston:
   Center for UFO Studies, 1975), p.110.
-UFO (CE-1)
   1978, Feb.10/Marc Avery
   Detroit News, 28 Feb.1978.
-UFO (CE-4)
   1956, June 11/Dan Martin
   D.M. Martin, Seven Hours Aboard a
   Space Ship (Detroit: The Author,
   1959).
   Dan Martin, The Watcher (Clarksburg,
   W.V.: Saucerian, 1961).
-UFO (DD)
   1947, June 28/Robert Ward/2427 Edsel
   Ave.
   Detroit News, 6 July 1947.
   1947, July 1/Rose Holson
   Detroit Times, 6 July 1947.
   1952, April 20
   Toronto (Ont.) Globe & Mail, 21 Apr.
   1952.
   1977, May 26
   "UFOs of Limited Merit," Int'l UFO
   Reporter 2 (July 1977):3.
-UFO (NL)
   1947, July 4/Edward V. Jeffers/Eastwood
   Park
   Detroit Times, 6 July 1947.
   1947, July 5
   Detroit Times, 7 July 1947.
   1947, July 7/Elizabeth Mason/1179 Wel-
   lington
   Detroit Times, 8 July 1947.
   1952, April 15
   Toronto (Ont.) Star, 17 Apr.1952.

1953, June 10/Wayne University
    U.S. Air Force, Projects Grudge and
    Blue Book Reports 1-12 (Washington:
    NICAP, 1968), p.222.
1953, Nov.10/Louis Kozma
    Detroit Times, 11 Nov.1953.
1955, May 8/Dominic Sondy
1956, Sep.8/Dominic Sondy
    Dominic Sondy, "Space Ship over De-
    troit," Fate 10 (June 1957):86-87,
    89.
1958, July 12/William Berg/=sputnik?
    (Editorial), Fate 11 (Dec.1958):20-
    21.
1958, Aug.9/Wayne County Airport
    (Editorial), Fate 11 (Dec.1958):22.
    Richard Hall, ed., The UFO Evidence
    (Washington: NICAP, 1964), p.156.
1964, July 29/Herbert Marz
    "UFO Sighting Wave Persists," UFO
    Inv. 2 (Sep.-Oct.1964):5.
1978, Nov.9/John Wingett/1149 Crickle-
wood St.
    Grand Rapids Press, 11 Nov.1978.
-UFO (R-V)
1953, March/Howard C. Strand/30 mi.NW/
    =mirage?
    Gordon D. Thayer, "Optical and Radar
    Analyses of Field Cases," in Edward
    U. Condon, ed., Scientific Studies
    of Unidentified Flying Objects (N.Y.:
    Bantam, 1969 ed.), pp.115,151-53.
    Brad Steiger & Joan Whritenour, Fly-
    ing Saucer Invasion: Target--Earth
    (N.Y.: Award, 1969), pp.51-53.
    Trevor James Constable, The Cosmic
    Pulse of Life (Santa Ana, Cal.:
    Merlin, 1976), pp.16-18.

Dexter
-UFO (NL)
1966, March 20/Frank Mannor
1966, March 20/Robert R. Taylor/Island
    Lake x Wylie Rd.
1966, March 20/Buford Bushroe
    Detroit News, 21-22 Mar.1966.
    Columbus (O.) Dispatch, 23 Mar.1966.
    Paul O'Neil, "It Wasn't No Hullabil-
    lusion," Life, 1 Apr.1966, p.29. il.
    "Recent UFO Sightings," Saucer News
    13 (June 1966):23.
    Mark Carpenter, "The Great UFO Flap
    at Ann Arbor," Fate 19 (July 1966):
    50-58.
    Allen R. Utke, "Swamp Gas, Will-o'-
    the-Wisp, or UFOs?" Fate 20 (Oct.
    1967):32-40.
    J. Allen Hynek & Jacques Vallee, The
    Edge of Reality (Chicago: Regnery,
    1975), pp.199-202.

Dixboro
-Phantom
1840s
    Eli Curtis, Wonderful Phenomena (N.Y.:
    The Author, 1850).
-UFO (NL)
1904/W.M. Covest
    Gordon I.R. Lore, Jr. & Harold H. Den-
    eault, Jr., Mysteries of the Skies:

UFOs in Perspective (Englewood
    Cliffs, N.J.: Prentice-Hall, 1968),
    pp.92-93.

Dowagiac
-UFO (DD)
1977, May 26
    "UFOs of Limited Merit," Int'l UFO
    Reporter 2 (July 1977):3-4.
-UFO (NL)
1897, April 14
    Washington Court House (O.) Cyclone
    & Fayette Republican, 22 Apr.1897.
1978, April 1/George Florian/715 Alma
    Edwardsburg Argus, 6 Apr.1978.

Drummond Island
-Healing
1888
    Richard M. Dorson, Bloodstoppers and
    Bearwalkers (Cambridge: Harvard
    Univ., 1952), pp.153-54.

East Lansing
-Erratic kangaroo
1968, Aug.3/=escapee from MSU Veter-
    inary School?
    "Wallaby Keeps Jump Ahead of MSU
    Police," INFO J., no.5 (fall 1969):
    15, quoting unidentified paper, 4
    Aug.1969.
-Skyquake
1954, Dec.11
    "Case 55," CRIFO Newsl., 4 Feb.1955,
    p.5.
-UFO (NL)
1945, Aug.4
    "Stetter Selections," Doubt, no.14
    (spring 1946):205.

East Leroy
-UFO (CE-1)
1978, Aug.4
    "UFOs of Limited Merit," Int'l UFO
    Reporter 3 (Sep.1978):6,8.

Eaton Rapids
-Telepathy
1958, April 13/Austin Wallace/Spiritual
    Episcopal Church
    Peter Ballbusch, "Cross-Country Dem-
    onstration of ESP," Fate 13 (Aug.
    1960):88-92. il.

Edmore
-UFO (CE-2)
1955, Sep.1
    Edmore Times, 9 Sep.1955.

Elmwood twp.
-UFO (CE-1)
1973, Sep.16/Ethel Peacock
    Leland Leelanau Enterprise-Tribune,
    20 Sep.1973.
-UFO (NL)
1973, Sep.30/Mrs. Leroy Hunt/614 Fouch
    Rd.
    Traverse City Record-Eagle, 1 Oct.
    1973.

Escanaba
-Clairvoyance
    1963, Sep.20/Arthur Baznar
        (Editorial), Fate 17 (Feb.1964):21.
-Fall of fish
    1958, April
        "Falls," Doubt,no.59 (1959):37.
-UFO (DD)
    1957, Nov.16/Joseph Guay
        (Letter), Fate 12 (June 1959):109-10.

Estral Beach
-UFO (NL)
    1978, May 1/Mavis McBride
        Monroe Evening News, 3 May 1978.

Fenton
-Precognition
    1905, summer/Jed Morrison/Hartland Rd.
        Mary Jane Roberts, "Death in the
        Barn," Fate 28 (Jan.1975):60-62.

Flat Rock
-UFO (CE-1)
    1977, July 9/Telegraph Rd.
        "UFOs of Limited Merit," Int'l UFO
        Reporter 2 (Aug.1977):3.
-UFO legend
    chasse galerie
        Richard M. Dorson, Bloodstoppers and
        Bearwalkers (Cambridge: Harvard
        Univ., 1952), pp.80-81.

Flint
-Clairvoyance
    1957, April 13/Burrell Autry
        (Editorial), Fate 10 (Sep.1957):14.
-Eyeless vision
    1956-1960s/Patricia Stanley
        Flint Journal, 5 Dec.1963.
        New York Times, 8 Jan.1964, p.23; 2
        Feb.1964, p.77; 6 Feb.1964, p.28; 5
        Apr.1964, sec.6, p.68; and 26 Apr.
        1964, sec.6, p.80.
        Pauline Saltzman, "Testing the Fin-
        gertip Vision of Pat Stanley," Fate
        17 (May 1964):38-45.
        "'Eyeless Vision' Unmasked," Sci.Am.
        212 (Mar.1965):57.
        (Letter), Richard P. Youtz, Sci.Am.
        212 (June 1965):8-10.
        Martin Gardner, "Dermo-Optical Per-
        ception: A Peek Down the Nose,"
        Science 151 (1966):654-57.
        Richard P. Youtz, et al., "Dermo-Op-
        tical Perception," Science 152
        (1966):1108-10.
-UFO (NL)
    1947, July 6/Homer Thompson
        Detroit Times, 6 July 1947.
    1973, Oct.15/John J. Gilligan/S on U.S.
        23
        Columbus (O.) Dispatch, 17 Oct.1973.
        Dayton (O.) Journal-Herald, 18-19
        Oct.1973.
        Philip J. Klass, UFOs Explained (N.Y.:
        Random House, 1974), pp.287-88.

Fowlerville
-Humanoid

1978, July 30-31
1978, Aug.12
1978, Aug.16/Gary Browning/4748 Deal
Rd.
    Lansing State Journal, 18 Aug.1978;
    and 27 Aug.1978.
-Paranormal somnambulism
    1890-1892/Stephen Haven
        Brooklyn (N.Y.) Eagle, 18 Nov.1892.

Fraser
-Haunt
    1970, May
        Detroit Free Press, 24 May 1970.
-UFO (NL)
    1978, March 6/Edward Oakie/14 Mile Rd.
        nr. Van Dyke Rd.
        Port Huron Times-Herald, 8 Mar.1978.

Freeland
-UFO (NL)
    1897, April 25/Leonard Krause
        Saginaw Courier-Herald, 30 Apr.1897.

Galesburg
-UFO (NL)
    1897, March 31
        Chicago (Ill.) Tribune, 2 Apr.1897.

Garfield twp., Kalkaska co.
-Clairvoyance
    1978
        Kansas City (Mo.) Star, 9 May 1978,
        p.5A.

Genoa twp.
-UFO (NL)
    1978, Feb.10
        Brighton Argus, 15 Feb.1978.

Gilbert Siding
-Precognition
    1900-1914/Harriet Terpenning
        Edmond P. Gibson, "Mrs. Harriet Ter-
        penning Dreams the Future," Fate 7
        (Oct.1954):62-66.

Gorden
-Medical clairvoyance
    1970s/Ross Peterson
        Allen Spraggett, Ross Peterson: The
        New Edgar Cayce (Garden City: Doub-
        leday, 1977).

Grand Blanc
-UFO (?) and Men-in-black
    1960, Feb.13/Joe Perry/=film defect
        Detroit Times, 9 Mar.1960.
        "FBI Disowns UFO Photo," NICAP Spec.
        Bull., May 1960, p.3.
        Richard Hall, ed., The UFO Evidence
        (Washington: NICAP, 1964), pp.93-94.
        Orlando (Fla.) Sentinel, 3 Feb.1967.
        "The 'Silencers' at Work," Flying
        Saucer Rev. 13 (Mar.-Apr.1967):10.

Grand Haven
-Skyquake
    1919, Nov.27/15 mi.S/=meteor?
        New York Times, 28 Nov.1919, p.1.

-UFO (NL)
  1976, Feb.11
    "Noteworthy UFO Sightings," Ufology
    2 (summer 1976):62.
  1978, Nov.10/Amy Christiansen/1025
  Sheldon
    Grand Haven Tribune, 13 Nov.1978.

Grand Junction
-UFO (CE-1)
  1978, March 6/Arthur Collins
    Benton Harbor Herald-Palladium, 7
    Mar.1978.

Grand Ledge
-UFO (NL)
  1964, May 22/Robert Nourse
    "Other Recent Sightings," UFO Inv. 2
    (July-Aug.1964):7.

Grand Rapids
-Archeological site
  10 B.C.-400 A.D./Norton Mounds
    W.L. Coffinberry & E.A. Strong,
    "Notes upon Some Explorations of
    Ancient Mounds in the Vicinity of
    Grand Rapids, Michigan," Proc.Am.
    Ass'n Adv.Sci. 24 (1875):293-97.
    Wilbert B. Hinsdale, Primitive Man
    in Michigan (Ann Arbor: Univ. of
    Michigan, 1925).
    Edmond P. Gibson, "The Norton Mounds
    in Wyoming Township, Kent County,
    Michigan," Michigan Arch. 5, no.2
    (1959):19-38. il.
    Richard E. Flanders, "Engraved Turtle
    Shells from the Norton Mounds near
    Grand Rapids, Michigan," Pap.Michi-
    gan Acad.Sci. 50 (1965):361-64. il.
    Robert Smith, "Excavating the Hope-
    well Burial Mounds at Grand Rapids,"
    Rsch.News, Office of Rsch.Admin.,
    Univ. of Michigan, vol.16, no.8
    (1966).
    James E. Fitting, The Archeology of
    Michigan (Garden City: Natural His-
    tory Press, 1970), pp.107-12. il.
-Haunt
  1940, June-1941, Jan./Katherine Fred-
  erick/Prospect Ave. SE
    Katherine Frederick, "Our Apartment
    Had to Be Exorcised," Fate 11 (Sep.
    1958):65-67.
    (Letter), L.J., Fate 11 (Nov.1958):
    122-24.
-Healing
  1840s/Wright L. Coffinberry
    Edmond P. Gibson, "Hypnotic Healings
    of W.L. Coffinberry," Fate 13 (Dec.
    1960):79-86.
-Inner development
  1924-   /Independent Spiritualist
  Ass'n/855 Butterworth Ave.
    Nandor Fodor, Encyclopaedia of Psy-
    chic Science (London: Arthurs,
    1933), p.183.
    J. Gordon Melton, Encyclopedia of Am-
    erican Religions, 2 vols. (Wilming-
    ton, N.C.: Consortium, 1978), 2:99.
-Mystery plane crash

  1967, Dec.6/Lee Norman Sanborn/Piper
  PA-30
    Jay Gourley, The Great Lakes Triangle
    (Greenwich, Ct.: Fawcett, 1977),
    pp.104-109.
-Poltergeist
  1934, May 9-July/Edmond P. Gibson
    Edmond P. Gibson, "The Case of the
    Noisy Intruder," Tomorrow 8 (spring
    1960):29-36.
-Precognition
  1930s-1950s/Harriet Terpenning
    Edmond P. Gibson, "Mrs. Harriet Ter-
    penning Dreams the Future," Fate 7
    (Oct.1954):62-66.
-Psychic photography
  1870s-1900s/Frank Foster
    James Coates, Photographing the In-
    visible (Chicago: Advanced Thought,
    1911), pp.151-55.
-Psychokinesis
  1946, Aug.18/Edmond P. Gibson
    Edmond P. Gibson, "Note on an Impromp-
    tu Experiment in Psychokinesis,"
    J.ASPR 41 (1947):22-28.
-Skyquake
  1976, Dec.27/Dick Wheaton
    Grand Rapids Press, 28 Dec.1976.
-Spirit medium
  1930s-1940s/Mrs. Clifford A. Paige
    Edmond P. Gibson, "A Study of Com-
    parative Performance in Several ESP
    Procedures," J.Parapsych. 1 (1937):
    264-75.
    "Cases," J.ASPR 36 (1942):29,31-35.
    "Cases," J.ASPR 37 (1943):86-90.
    Edmond P. Gibson, "Voice from the
    Past," Fate 5 (Sep.1952):64-67.
  1940s/William H. Thatcher
    Edmond P. Gibson, "'The World Turned
    Upside Down': Incident from a Series
    of Mediumistic Sittings," J.ASPR 44
    (1950):113-17.
    Edmond P. Gibson, "Slate Writing in
    a Box," Fate 5 (Feb.-Mar.1952):86-
    90.
    Edmond P. Gibson, "Strange Return of
    Dave Dean," Fate 10 (Aug.1957):73-
    82.
-Spontaneous human combustion
  1959, summer/Lemoyne Unkefer
    (Editorial), Fate 13 (Mar.1960):22.
-Teleportation
  1952/James Hanenburg/Calvin College
  cafeteria
    (Editorial), Fate 5 (Sep.1952):9-10.
    il.
-UFO (?)
  1958, Oct.17
    J. Allen Hynek, The Hynek UFO Report
    (N.Y.: Dell, 1977), p.44.
-UFO (CE-2)
  1897, April 17/C.T. Smith/S. Division
  x Williams St./airship message
    Grand Rapids Evening Press, 17 Apr.
    1897.
-UFO (DD)
  1963, Dec.2/Mrs. Wayne Elliott
    "UFO Sightings Centered in Western
    U.S.," UFO Inv. 2 (Dec.1963-Jan.

1964):3.
1978, Nov.5/Jack Smith/2100 Burlingame
Ave. SW
　Grand Rapids Press, 7 Nov.1978.
-UFO (NL)
1897, April 11
　Chicago (Ill.) Times-Herald, 13 Apr.
　1897, p.2.
1897, April 16
　Grand Rapids Evening Press, 17 Apr.
　1897.
1947, June 1/Inez Nostrant
　Grand Rapids Herald, 7 July 1947.
1951, Nov.24
　U.S. Air Force, Projects Grudge and
　Blue Book Reports 1-12 (Washington:
　NICAP, 1968), pp.52-53.
1953, Jan.25-26
　(Editorial), Fate 6 (June 1953):12.
1954, Sep.20
　"Astronomers Track Three Mysterious
　Lights over Michigan," CRIFO Newsl.,
　5 Nov.1954, p.6.
1970, Sep.10/Michael Kooistra
　Jerome S. Gardeski, "Grand Rapids
　Spherical UFO," FSR Case Histories,
　no.3 (Feb.1971):13.
1975, Aug.24
　"UFO Central," CUFOS News Bull., 15
　Nov.1975, p.16.

Grattan
-UFO (NL)
1978, Nov.8
　Grand Rapids Press, 9 Nov.1978.

Green Oak twp.
-UFO (NL)
1978, Feb.11
　Howell Livingston County Press, 15
　Feb.1978.

Greenville
-UFO (NL)
1973, Sep.30
　Greenville Daily News, 1 Oct.1973.
1973, Oct.1/Mildred Schulte
　Greenville Daily News, 2 Oct.1973.

Grosse Pointe Park
-Phantom
1746/Jacques L'Esperance
　Marie Caroline Watson Hamlin, Legends
　of Le Détroit (Detroit: Nourse,
　1884), pp.77-84.
-Shape-shifting
1770s/Jacques Morand
　Charles M. Skinner, Myths and Legends
　of Our Own Land, 2 vols. (Philadel-
　phia: Lippincott, 1896), 2:138-40.
1770s/Archange Simonet
　Marie Caroline Watson Hamlin, Legends
　of Le Détroit (Detroit: Nourse,
　1884), pp.113-21.

Grosse Pointe Woods
-Telepathy
1959-1960/Donald M. Sabel
　(Editorial), Fate 13 (Nov.1960):15-
　16.

-UFO (NL)
1967, March 8/Liggett School
　Detroit Free Press, 11 Mar.1967.

Hale
-UFO (NL)
1969, March 13/Larry Johnson/Esmond Rd.
　Bay City Times, 15 Mar.1969.
　"Car Buzzing Incidents Continue,"
　APRO Bull. 17 (May-June 1969):6,7-8.
　"More on the Michigan Lights," Sky-
　look, no.19 (June 1969):5-6.

Hamtramck
-Poltergeist
1945, Jan.28-Feb./John Czarnik/9485
Mitchell
　Edmond P. Gibson, "The Ghost of Ham-
　tramck," Fate 3 (May 1950):20-22,
　quoting Detroit Times (undated).

Hemlock
-UFO (NL)
1897, April 22
　Saginaw Courier-Herald, 28 Apr.1897.

Highland Park
-Healing
1933/Louis Arbogast
　H.L. Lawson, "We Called a Healer,"
　Fate 31 (June 1978):94-96.

Hillsdale
-Fall of fish
1944, June 24/Clyde Parshall
　"Fish After Rain," Doubt, no.10
　(spring-summer 1945):175.
-Lightning anomaly
1887, summer/Amos J. Biggs
　Henry Winfred Splitter, "Nature's
　Strange Photographs," Fate 8 (Jan.
　1955):21,25-26.
-UFO (?)
1966, July/William Van Horn/=lens flare
　Curtis Fuller, "Air Force Grants
　$313,000 to Study UFOs," Fate 20
　(Feb.1967):32,35. il.
　William B. Mead, "Four Nights of
　UFO's Rock Michigan," in Flying Sau-
　cers (Look Magazine spec.issue,
　1967), p.22. il.
　Colman S. Von Kevicsky, "A Re-Anal-
　ysis," Can.UFO Rept., no.24 (summer
　1976):19,22-23. il.
-UFO (NL)
1966, March 21/William Van Horn/Hills-
dale College
　Duluth (Minn.) News-Tribune, 23 Mar.
　1966.
　New York Times, 23 Mar.1966, pp.22,46.
　Christian Science Monitor, 28-30 Mar.
　1966.
　Columbus (O.) Dispatch, 16 May 1966,
　p.1.
　J. Allen Hynek, "Statement on the
　Dexter and Hillsdale UFO Sightings,"
　Flying Saucer Rev. 12 (May-June
　1966):7-8.
　"Recent News," Saucer News 13 (fall
　1966):14.

"An Account of the Michigan Incident Through the Experts and Witnesses," Flying Saucers, June 1967, pp.9-11.
John C. Sherwood, Flying Saucers Are Watching You (Clarksburg, W.V.: Saucerian, 1967).
William B. Mead, "Four Nights of UFO's Rock Michigan," in Flying Saucers (Look Magazine spec.issue, 1967), pp.22-23.
E.U. Condon, "UFOs: 1947-1968," in Scientific Study of Unidentified Flying Objects (N.Y.: Bantam, 1969 ed.), pp.502,539-41.
1966, March 24/William Van Horn
New York Journal-American, 26-29 Mar.1966.

Holland
-Haunt
1954, Feb./GOC post
Grand Rapids Herald, 7 Feb.1954.
-Lightning anomaly
1948-1954/Harvey Breuker
(Editorial), Fate 7 (Nov.1954):8.
-Mystery plane crash
1964, April 29/James Taylor/Cessna 172
Jay Gourley, The Great Lakes Triangle (Greenwich, Ct.: Fawcett, 1977), pp.127-29.
-UFO (NL)
1897, March 30
Grand Traverse Herald, 1 Apr.1897.
1897, April
Benton Harbor Evening News, 19 Apr. 1897.
1966, March 24
"Typical Reports," UFO Inv. 3 (Mar.-Apr.1966):8.
1969, March 13
"More on the Michigan Lights," Skylook, no.19 (June 1969):5, quoting Holland Evening Sentinel (undated).

Holly
-Ghost
n.d./Carol Robinson
Carol Robinson, "The Portrait in the Attic," Fate 27 (Oct.1974):84-86.

Holton
-UFO (?)
1897, April 29/=hoax?
Muskegon Daily Chronicle, 30 Apr.1897.

Homer
-Passenger pigeon
1965, March/Irene Llewellyn/=mourning dove?
(Letter), Fate 18 (Sep.1965):129.
-UFO (DD)
1949, April 29
"If It's In the Sky It's a Saucer," Doubt, no.27 (1949):416.

Houghton
-Precognition
1951, May 15
"Prophecy Fulfilled," Fate 5 (June 1952):57.

Houghton Lake
-UFO (CE-1)
1964, July 16/Kenneth Jannereth/15 mi. S
Thomas M. Olsen, ed., The Reference for Outstanding UFO Sighting Reports (Riderwood, Md.: UFO Information Retrieval Center, 1966), p.99.

Howard City
-UFO (CE-1)
1966, Dec.6/Diane Brown
Niles Daily Star, 7 Dec.1966.

Hudson
-UFO (?)
1897, April 15/Gene Knapp/=hoax
Hudson Gazette, 16 Apr.1897.
Adrian Weekly Times & Expositor, 17 Apr.1897.

Huntington Woods
-Deathbed apparition
1977/Diana Prowse
(Editorial), Fate 30 (July 1977):21, quoting Royal Oak Daily Tribune (undated).

Imlay City
-UFO (CE-2)
1967, Feb./Earl Anspaugh/ground markings only
Coral E. Lorenzen, The Shadow of the Unknown (N.Y.: Signet, 1970), pp. 64-65, quoting Detroit Free Press (undated).

Indian Lake
-UFO (CE-2)
1966, Oct.7
J. Allen Hynek, The UFO Experience (Chicago: Regnery, 1972), p.240.

Ingham co.
-UFO (CE-2)
1965, Dec.9/Donald Hilton
Jerome Clark, "The Greatest Flap Yet? Part IV," Flying Saucer Rev. 12 (Nov.-Dec.1966):9,12.

Ionia
-UFO (NL)
1954, Sep.20/William R. McLaughlin
"Astronomers Track Three Mysterious Lights over Michigan," CRIFO Newsl., 5 Nov.1954, p.6.

Iron Mountain
-UFO (NL)
1974, Feb.12/Brian Rowell/Mille Hill
(Letter), Fate 28 (Aug.1975):128-29.

Ironton
-UFO (DD)
1950, March 17/Robert Gregory
Kenneth Arnold & Ray Palmer, The Coming of the Saucers (Boise: The Authors, 1952), p.147.

Ironwood
-UFO (CE-1)
  1967, Dec.14/Randall Baribeau/E on U.S.
  2
    "Late 1967 Sightings," UFO Inv. 3
    (Jan.-Feb.1968):6.
-UFO (DD)
  1950, March 29/Tom Christensen/airport
    Ironwood Daily Globe, 30 Mar.1950.
-UFO (NL)
  1967, Dec.18/Gordon Holemo/airport
    "Late 1967 Sightings," UFO Inv. 3
    (Jan.-Feb.1968):6.

Jackson
-Haunt
  1960s/Joyce Soule
    Hans Holzer, Ghosts I've Met (N.Y.:
    Ace, 1965), p.54.
-Mystery plane crash
  1965, Oct.21/Glen E. David/Lear 23
  1972, Feb.16/Beech 18
    Jay Gourley, The Great Lakes Triangle
    (Greenwich, Ct.: Fawcett, 1977),
    pp.78,94-98.
-Poltergeist
  1959-1962/Victor Lincoln
    Raymond V. Meagher, "Two Midwest Pol-
    tergeists," Fate 15 (July 1962):24,
    33-38.
-UFO (?)
  1973, fall/James Thulke/=balloon
    Philip J. Klass, UFOs Explained (N.Y.:
    Random House, 1974), pp.40-41.
-UFO (NL)
  1897, April 21/George Mitchell
    Detroit Evening News, 22 Apr.1897.
  1978, Jan.29/Denise Reule/736 Edgewood
    Jackson Citizen Patriot, 1 Feb.1978.
  1978, Nov.1/Tom Williams/1012 W. High
    Jackson Citizen Patriot, 2 Nov.1978.

Jefferson
-UFO (NL)
  1897, March 26
    Hudson Post, 27 Mar.1897.

Kalamazoo
-Inner development
  1930s/Independent Spiritualist Churches
  of America
    Nandor Fodor, Encyclopaedia of Psy-
    chic Science (London: Arthurs,
    1933), p.183.
-UFO (?)
  1957, Nov.6
    Aimé Michel, Flying Saucers and the
    Straight-Line Mystery (N.Y.: Criter-
    ion, 1958), p.256.
-UFO (CE-2)
  1897, April 11/NE of town
    Freeport (Ill.) Bulletin, 15 Apr.
    1897, p.4.

Kalkaska
-UFO (NL)
  1978, Nov.2-3/Mike Maxwell
    Traverse City Record-Eagle, 3 Nov.
    1978.

Kingsley
-Precognition
  1915-1930s/Harriet Terpenning
    Edmond P. Gibson, "Mrs. Harriet Ter-
    penning Dreams the Future," Fate 7
    (Oct.1954):62-66.

Lake co.
-Healing
  n.d./George MacDonald
    Richard M. Dorson, Bloodstoppers and
    Bearwalkers (Cambridge: Harvard
    Univ., 1952), p.153.

Lansing
-Coffin anomaly
  1963, July 14/St. Joseph Cemetery
    (Editorial), Fate 16 (Dec.1963):15,
    18.
-Contactee
  1954/Charles A. Laughead
    Lillian Laughead, "A Message from
    the Flying Saucers?" Mystic 8 (Feb.
    1955):63-69.
    Alson J. Smith, "Doom Days That
    Never Cracked," Fate 15 (Nov.1962)
    :36,48-47.
-Erratic crocodilian
  1968, June 6/Capitol Bldg.
    Lansing State Journal, 7 June 1968.
-Erratic kangaroo
  1968, Aug.3/College x Jolly Rd.
    David Fideler & Loren Coleman, "Kan-
    garoos from Nowhere," Fate 31
    (Apr.1978):68,73.
-Fall of ice
  1974/Erma Schuon
    (Editorial), Fate 28 (Mar.1975):26.
-Humanoid
  1978, Dec.2/Morse Easterling
    Bay City Times, 16 Feb.1979.
-Psychokinesis
  1932, May/Margaret Holly
    Joan C. Holly, "Grandfather's
    Clocks," Fate 7 (Sep.1954):25-30.
-UFO (?)
  1897, April 16/Bid Osborne
    Lansing State Republican, 17 Apr.
    1897.
-UFO (CE-1)
  1976, April 19
    "Noteworthy UFO Sightings," Ufology
    2 (fall 1976):60.
-UFO (DD)
  1913, summer/Lloyd L. Arnold
    Jerome Clark & Lucius Farish, "The
    Phantom Airships of 1913," Saga UFO
    Rept. 1 (summer 1974):36,57-58.
  1913, June 29/Arthur Goodnoe
    Lansing Evening Press, 30 June 1913.
  1964, May 27/John C. Gallagher
    "More News Briefs," Saucer News 11
    (Sep.1964):23.
-UFO (NL)
  1964, May 21/Mrs. Edward Cole
    "Other Recent Sightings," UFO Inv. 2
    (July-Aug.1964):7.
    Jeffrey Liss, "UFO's That Look Like
    Tops," Fate 17 (Nov.1964):66,68.
  1978, Oct.12/nr. Pleasant Grove Rd.

Lansing State Journal, 13 Oct.1978.

Lapeer
-Fall of lead
1965, Dec.9
Columbus (O.) Dispatch, 10 Dec.1965.
-Haunt
1963, Jan.-1964/Margaret Hall/Calhoun St.
L. Berger Copeman, "A Slap in the Face for Margaret," Fate 18 (Apr. 1965):76-79.

Lathrop
-UFO (CE-1)
1978, Nov.28/Mike Nelson/Hwy.35
Menominee Herald-Leader, 15 Dec.1978.

Lawton
-Mystery plane crash
1970, Sep.2/Waco ZGC-7
Jay Gourley, The Great Lakes Triangle (Greenwich, Ct.: Fawcett, 1977), p.133.

Lincoln Park
-UFO (NL)
1976, Sep.7/Gene Mierzejewski
Allen Parker, 15 Sep.1976.

Livonia
-Fall of metallic object
1965, Dec.9/Brian Parent
Jerome Clark, "The Greatest Flap Yet? Part IV," Flying Saucer Rev. 12 (Nov.-Dec.1966):9,12.
-UFO (CE-2)
n.d./nr. Bryant Junior High School/ ground markings only
(Letter), Paul B. McIntyre, Fate 18 (Jan.1965):133-34.

Lowell
-UFO (DD)
1947, July 5
Grand Rapids Herald, 7 July 1947.

Ludington
-Disappearance
1910/"Pere Marquette"
Michigan Writers' Program, Michigan: A Guide to the Wolverine State (N.Y.: Oxford Univ., 1956), p.121.
1964, March 19/Lawrence Kolarik
"Michigan's 'Port of Disappearing People,'" Fate 17 (Aug.1964):77.
-UFO (NL)
1978, July 27/Don Clark/Consumers Power project
Muskegon Chronicle, 30 July 1978.
Traverse City Record-Eagle, 4 Aug. 1978.
1978, Oct.1/Dave Waller
Colorado Springs (Colo.) Gazette-Telegraph, 13 Oct.1978.

Lulu
-Fall of ice
1966, March 14/Mrs. Chester Kolakowski/ 13950 Lulu Rd.

(Editorial), Fate 19 (July 1966):24-25, quoting Monroe Evening News (undated).

McBain
-Haunt
1899, winter/Jim Hill/McBain House
James S. Starr, "The Door That Opened Itself," Fate 4 (July 1951):18.

Manchester
-UFO (NL)
1952, April 27
Ann Arbor News, 28 Apr.1952.

Manistee co.
-Mystery flotsam
1956, Aug./Margaret A. Florman/shore of L. Michigan
(Letter), Fate 18 (Apr.1965):116-17.

Manistique
-UFO (NL)
1897, April 19/C.R. Orr
Sault Ste. Marie News, 24 Apr.1897.

Manton
-UFO (NL)
1976, Aug.31/Robert Truesdale
Grand Rapids Press, 3 Sep.1976.

Marion
-Electromagnetic anomaly
1960, June/Mrs. James Dunn
(Letter), Fate 14 (Feb.1961):116-17.

Marquette
-Fall of brown snow
1951, March 3
"Run on the Mill," Doubt, no.34 (1951):108.
-Humanoid
1977, Oct.
David Fideler, "1977: Year of the Creature," Anomaly Rsch.Bull., no.8 (spring 1978):8,13.
-UFO (?)
1965, Sep.5
Seattle (Wash.) Post-Intelligencer, 7 Sep.1965.
-UFO (CE-2)
1971, June/Brad Peterson/L. Superior
(Letter), Saga UFO Rept. 5 (Mar.1978) :6.
-UFO (NL)
1967, Sep.2-7
Milwaukee (Wisc.) Sentinel, 9 Sep. 1967.
Green Bay (Wisc.) Press-Gazette, 10 Sep.1967.

Marshall
-Humanoid
1956, May/Otto Collins
John A. Keel, Strange Creatures from Time and Space (Greenwich, Ct.: Fawcett, 1970), p.107, quoting Marshall Evening Chronicle (undated).
Gray Barker, "UFO Creatures on the Prowl," Saga UFO Rept. 3 (Mar.1977)

:20,48-49.
-UFO (DD)
1978, July 27
"UFOs of Limited Merit," Int'l UFO
Reporter 3 (Sep.1978):6,8.

Mason
-Humanoid
1978, April 30/Raynor Park
Lansing State Journal, 2 May 1978.
1978, May 31/James Jenks/768 Howell St.
Lansing State Journal, 2 July 1978.

Menomonee
-Disappearance
1969, May 21/Richard B. Dotson/Beech
35
Jay Gourley, The Great Lakes Triangle
(Greenwich, Ct.: Fawcett, 1977),
pp.165-66.
-UFO (?)
1947, July 9
Detroit Free Press, 10 July 1947.

Middleville
-UFO (NL)
1897, April 15
Detroit Free Press, 16 Apr.1897, p.3.

Midland
-UFO (CE-2)
1947, July 9/Raymond Edward Lane
Ted Bloecher, Report on the UFO Wave
of 1947 (Washington: NICAP, 1967),
p. IV-2.

Milan
-UFO (?)
1967, April-July/=aircraft
Philip J. Klass, UFOs Explained (N.Y.:
Random House, 1974), pp.15-23.
-UFO (CE-1)
1966, June 13
Jacques Vallee, Passport to Magonia
(Chicago: Regnery, 1969), p.332.
-UFO (CE-2)
1966, March 17/Nuel Schneider/photo=
time exposure of Moon and Venus
New York Times, 25 Mar.1966, p.43;
and 26 Mar.1966, p.31.
"Swamp Gas," UFO Inv. 3 (Mar.-Apr.
1966):5,6.
Lloyd Mallan, "UFO Hoaxes and Hallu-
cinations," Sci.& Mech. 38 (Apr.
1967):44,84-85. il.
"Recent UFO Sightings," Saucer News
13 (June 1966):19,23. il.
Jacques Vallee, Passport to Magonia
(Chicago: Regnery, 1969), p.323.

Milford
-UFO (?)
1949, summer
Harold T. Wilkins, Flying Saucers on
the Attack (N.Y.: Ace, 1967 ed.),
p.114.
-UFO (NL)
1966, March 23
Mark Carpenter, "The Great UFO Flap
at Ann Arbor," Fate 19 (July 1966):

50,56.

Millington
-Humanoid
1978, Oct.21/George A. Proctor/5275 W.
Millington Rd.
Detroit Free Press, 13 Nov.1978.
Saginaw News, 13 Nov.1978.
1978, Dec.13/Diane Meharg/Barnes Rd.
Millington Herald, 2 Jan.1979.

Mohawk
-Healing
n.d./John Buddo
Richard M. Dorson, Bloodstoppers and
Bearwalkers (Cambridge: Harvard
Univ., 1952), pp.156-57.

Monroe
-Humanoid
1965, Aug.11/David Thomas
John A. Keel, Strange Creatures of
Space and Time (Greenwich, Ct.: Faw-
cett, 1970), p.109.
1965, Aug.13/Ruth Owens/Mentel Rd.
Detroit Free Press, 20 Aug.1965, p.12.
"Monster Season," Newsweek, 30 Aug.
1965, p.22.
Gene Ceasar, "The Hellzapoppin' Hunt
for the Michigan Monster," True,
June 1966, pp.59,84-85.
Curtis K. Sutherly, "Case History of
a UFO Flap," Official UFO 1 (Dec.
1976):40,59-60.
-Humanoid tracks
1965, Aug.18/Johnny Mayes/3245 Mentel
Detroit Free Press, 20 Aug.1965, p.
12.

Montcalm co.
-UFO (CE-2)
1973, Oct.1
Ted Phillips, Physical Traces Associated with UFO Sightings (Evanston:
Center for UFO Studies, 1975), p.
110.

Montgomery
-UFO (?)
1971, April 14
"Northern Lights and ????" Skylook,
no.44 (July 1971):11, quoting Hillsdale Daily News (undated).

Moscow
-UFO (?)
1969, July 2/Ray Ostarmyer/E of town/
=blimp
Hillsdale Daily News, 3 July 1969.
"Michigan Silver Disc Identified,"
Skylook, no.22 (Sep.1969):8.

Mount Clemens
-Animal ESP
1961, March/Peggy Gambino
Peggy Gambino, "Thank God, My Dog
Was Psychic," Fate 27 (Nov.1974):
58-60.
-Erratic crocodilian
1958, Oct.

Detroit News, 18 Oct.1958.
-UFO (NL)
1951, Nov.24/Selfridge AFB
    U.S. Air Force, Projects Grudge and
    Blue Book Reports 1-12 (Washington:
    NICAP, 1968), pp.52-53.
1978, March 6/Maria Merino/Gratiot x
13 Mile Rd.
    Port Huron Times-Herald, 8 Mar.1978.
-UFO (R)
1950, March 9/Francis E. Parker/Self-
ridge AFB
    J. Allen Hynek, The Hynek UFO Report
    (N.Y.: Dell, 1977), pp.123-26,295-
    97.

Mount Pleasant
-UFO (CE-1)
1961, July/U.S.27
    Curtis Fuller, "The Boys Who 'Caught'
    a Flying Saucer," Fate 15 (Jan.
    1962):36-37.
-UFO (NL)
1961, July 12
    Curtis Fuller, "The Boys Who 'Caught'
    a Flying Saucer," Fate 15 (Jan.
    1962):36,38.

Munising
-Crisis apparition
n.d./Herm Manette/W. Superior St.
    Richard M. Dorson, Bloodstoppers and
    Bearwalkers (Cambridge: Harvard
    Univ., 1952), p.157.
-Healing
n.d./Dan Trumbauer
    Richard M. Dorson, Bloodstoppers and
    Bearwalkers (Cambridge: Harvard
    Univ., 1952), p.154.

Muskegon
-Disappearance
1967, Jan.14/William A. Sells
    Jay Gourley, The Great Lakes Triangle
    (Greenwich, Ct.: Fawcett, 1977),
    p.165.
-Fall of fish
1961, Sep.3/Arthur Tennant/North Shore
Garage
    Eugene Burr, "Birds Fall on the Em-
    pire State," Fate 24 (Apr.1971):75,
    80.
-Haunt
1950s-1960s/Lillian R. Pace
    Lillian R. Pace, "A Letter from Grand-
    ma," Fate 23 (May 1969):81-84.
-Lake monster
1892, July 15/Edward Maloney/"Cheney
Ames"/=hoax
    Muskegon Daily Chronicle, 15-16 July
    1892.
    Muskegon Morning News, 16 July 1892.
    Chicago (Ill.) Tribune, 24 July 1892.
-UFO (NL)
1958, Aug.11
    "Sighting Round-Up," UFO Inv. 1 (Aug.-
    Sep.1958):6.
1966, July 6
    John A. Keel, UFOs: Operation Trojan
    Horse (N.Y.: Putnam, 1970), p.155.

-UFO (NL) and mystery radio transmission
1972, March 8/Carl Van Dam
    Muskegon Chronicle, 9 Mar.1972.
    "UFO over Michigan," APRO Bull. 20
    (May-June 1972):4.

New Baltimore
-UFO (NL)
1978, March 6/I-94 x Hall Dr.
    Port Huron Times-Herald, 8 Mar.1978.

Newberry
-Haunt
1969, Feb.26-1970/William Nesbit
    Detroit Free Press, 4 Jan.1970.
    Jingo Vachon, "Dead GI's Ring Spells
    L-O-V-E," Fate 23 (June 1970):38-
    43. il.
    Edward & Nellie Cain, "More Messages
    from GI's Ring," Fate 23 (Dec.
    1970):84-89. il.

New Buffalo
-Humanoid
1973, fall
    John Green, Sasquatch: The Apes Among
    Us (Seattle: Hancock House, 1978),
    p.201.
-Phantom panther tracks
1977, Feb.
    David Fideler, "1977: Year of the
    Creature," Anomaly Rsch.Bull., no.
    8 (spring 1978):8,14.

Niles
-Aerial phantom
1883/G.H. Jerome/=mirage
    New York Times, 31 July 1883, p.3,
    quoting Chicago (Ill.) Tribune (un-
    dated).
-Phantom panther
1964/Samuel Johnson/=deer?
    (Editorial), Fate 17 (Dec.1964):27.
-UFO (CE-1)
1966, March 28
    "Typical Reports," UFO Inv. 3 (Mar.-
    Apr.1966):8.
-UFO (NL)
1897, April 11
    Lansing State Republican, 16 Apr.1897.
1974, April 15/Janice Washington/199
Briarcrest
    Niles Daily Star, 16 Apr.1974.

Norwood
-Cattle mutilation
1976, Oct.25
    (Editorial), Fate 30 (Feb.1977):39.

Novi
-UFO (NL)
1972, Aug./Florence MacDermid
    Glenn McWane & David Graham, The New
    UFO Sightings (N.Y.: Warner, 1974),
    pp.60-61, quoting Novi News (undat-
    ed).

Olivet
-UFO (NL)
1897, April 15

Lansing State Republican, 16 Apr.
1897.

Omer
-UFO (NL)
    1897, April 24
        Saginaw Courier-Herald, 27 Apr.1897.

Ontonagon
-Disappearance
    1970, May 31/Wayne Robertson/Cessna
    172
        Jay Gourley, The Great Lakes Triangle
        (Greenwich, Ct.: Fawcett, 1977), p.
        159.
-UFO (DD)
    1967, Aug.24-25
        Kansas City (Mo.) Times, 25 Aug.1967.

Orchard Lake
-UFO (DD)
    1947, July 7/Albert Weaver/country club
        Detroit News, 8 July 1947.
        Kenneth Arnold & Ray Palmer, The Com-
        ing of the Saucers (Boise: The Au-
        thors, 1952), p.176. il.
        Ted Bloecher, Report on the UFO Wave
        of 1947 (Washington: NICAP, 1967),
        p. IV-4. il.

Orleans
-UFO (CE-1)
    ca.1915/William J. Beaumont
        (Letter), Fate 24 (Jan.1971):144.

Oscoda
-Phantom helicopter
    1975, Oct.30-31/James Gowenlock/Wart-
    smith AFB
        "More Information on UFOs and the
        Government: c/o the Freedom of In-
        formation Act!" Int'l UFO Reporter
        3 (Apr.1978):Newsfront sec.
        Little Rock Arkansas Democrat, 19
        Jan.1979.
        Jackson Citizen Patriot, 22 Jan.1979.

Owosso
-Clairvoyance
    1928, Jan.16/Harold Lotridge
        Irene Turnbull, "Dreamer Traps a Mur-
        derer," Fate 16 (Sep.1963):74-75.
        Neville Stanley, "The Dream That
        Named a Murderer," Fate 17 (Mar.
        1964):73-81, quoting Owosso Argus-
        Press (undated).
-Humanoid
    ca.1957/Green Meadows
        Owosso Argus-Press, 21 Sep.1978.

Oxford
-UFO (CE-1)
    1973, Oct.24/Janet Fleischmann/1111 W.
    Seymore Lake
        "Michigan Woman Sees UFO," Skylook,
        no.74 (Jan.1974):6, quoting Oakland
        Press (undated).

Parma
-Crisis apparition

1905, Nov.27
    "A Collective Case," J.ASPR 2 (1908):
    365-73.

Paulding
-Ghost light
    1966-   /Dog Meadow
        Green Bay (Wisc.) Press-Gazette, 20
        Aug.1978; and 1 Oct.1978.

Pavilion
-UFO (NL)
    1897, April 11/George W. Sumers
        Chicago (Ill.) Times-Herald, 14 Apr.
        1897, p.2.

Paw Paw
-Fall of black snow
    1898
    1901, Feb.16
        "Colored Snow," Monthly Weather Rev.
        29 (Oct.1901):465.
-Pyrokinesis
    1882/A.W. Underwood
        New York Sun, 1 Dec.1882.
        "A Human Storage Battery," Sci.Am.
        48 (1883):264, quoting Michigan
        Med.News, 1882.

Pennfield twp.
-UFO (CE-2)
    1897, April 12/George Parks
        Detroit Evening News, 15 Apr.1897.

Pentwater
-Precognition
    1950s/Buell Mullen
        Danton Walker, Spooks Deluxe (N.Y.:
        Franklin Watts, 1956), pp.78-80.

Petoskey
-Lake monster
    ca.1892/=hoax?
        Chicago (Ill.) Tribune, 24 July 1892.
-UFO (?)
    1947, July 9
        Detroit Free Press, 10 July 1947.
-UFO (NL)
    1953, Jan.
        (Editorial), Fate 6 (June 1953):12.
    1978, Oct.9/George M. McInnis/Maxwell
    Rd.
        Petoskey News-Review, 13 Oct.1978.

Pinckney
-UFO (NL)
    1951, Aug.3/Wells Alan Webb/Camp Big
    Silver
        Wells Alan Webb, Mars: The New Fron-
        tier (San Francisco: Fearon, 1956).
        Richard Hall, ed.,The UFO Evidence
        (Washington: NICAP, 1964), p.50.

Pittsford
-UFO (NL)
    1897, April 16
        Adrian Evening Telegram, 17 Apr.1897.

Pontiac
-Animal ESP

1977/James Johnson
(Editorial), Fate 30 (Oct.1977):20-
21.
-Mystery shaking bed
1960, Feb.1/Mrs. Albert Kleino
(Editorial), Fate 13 (June 1960):24-
25.
-Spontaneous human combustion
1959, Dec.13/Billy Peterson
Detroit Free Press, 14 Dec.1959, p.1.
Paul Foght, "Guilty: The Mystery Ray
That Kills," Fate 14 (Mar.1961):31-
33.
"Boy Roasted in Mysterious Fire,"
APRO Bull. 12 (Mar.1964):5.
Allan W. Eckert, "The Baffling Burn-
ing Death," True, May 1964, pp.32,
104.
(Letter), Ted Lonergan, True, Aug.
1964, pp.4-5.
Larry E. Arnold, "Zounds, Holmes!
It's a Case of the Combustible
Corpse!" Pursuit 10 (summer 1977):
75-77.
Michael Harrison, Fire from Heaven
(N.Y.: Methuen, 1978), pp.75-79.
-UFO (CE-1)
1976, Aug.17/Beth Hamblin/=plane
Grand Rapids Press, 19 Aug.1976.
-UFO (NL)
1954, Dec.20/Earl Ball
"Case 43," CRIFO Newsl., 7 Jan.1955,
p.6.
1975, June 23/Metropolitan Stadium
Timothy Green Beckley, "Saucers over
Our Cities," Saga UFO Rept. 4 (Aug.
1977):24,74.

Portage
-UFO (CE-1)
1976, Aug.27
"UFOs of Limited Merit," Int'l UFO
Reporter 3 (Sep.1978):6,8.

Port Austin
-UFO (R-V)
1953, Feb.17
U.S. Air Force, Projects Grudge and
Blue Book Reports 1-12 (Washington:
NICAP, 1968), p.197.

Port Huron
-Haunt
1910/Mary J. Mace
(Letter), Fate 17 (Oct.1964):114-16.
-Humanoid
1969, April 23
Port Huron Times-Herald, 24 Apr.1969.
-Mystery plane crash
1950, March 31/K.E. Bjorkman/Fairchild
M62A-3
Jay Gourley, The Great Lakes Triangle
(Greenwich, Ct.: Fawcett, 1977),
pp.87-88.
-Religious apparition
1927, Feb.4-1930s/Otto Fetting
(Letter), Cecil D. Clayton, Fate 15
(Apr.1962):121.
-Telepathy
1974/Karam Sabagh

(Editorial), Fate 28 (Jan.1975):18-
20.
-UFO (?)
1957, Nov.6
Aimé Michel, Flying Saucers and the
Straight-Line Mystery (N.Y.: Criter-
ion, 1958), p.256.
-UFO (CE-1)
1963, Nov.12/Robert Baker
"UFO Sightings Centered in Western
U.S.," UFO Inv. 2 (Dec.1963-Jan.
1964):3.
"Close Saucer Sighting in Michigan,"
Saucer News 11 (Mar.1964):21-22.
-UFO (NL)
1947, July 4/Mrs. John R. Warner/SW of
town
Detroit News, 5 July 1947.
1969, March 12/Charles Karl
"Michigan Has Unidentified Objects
in March," Skylook, no.18 (May
1969):10, quoting Pontiac Press
(undated).
1975, Oct.7
"UFO Central," CUFOS News Bull., 1
Feb.1976, p.8.
-UFO (R-V)
1952, July 29/Ned Baker/ADC radar post
Donald E. Keyhoe, Flying Saucers from
Outer Space (N.Y.: Holt, 1953), pp.
105-107.
Edward J. Ruppelt, The Report on Un-
identified Flying Objects (Garden
City: Doubleday, 1956), pp.171-72.
Donald H. Menzel & Lyle G. Boyd, The
World of Flying Saucers (Garden
City: Doubleday, 1963), pp.160-61.
U.S. Air Force, Projects Grudge and
Blue Book Reports 1-12 (Washington:
NICAP, 1968), p.146.

Powers
-UFO (NL)
1978, June 4/Willie Charlier
Escanaba Daily Press, 5 June 1978.

Rapid River
-Humanoid myth
lutin
Richard M. Dorson, Bloodstoppers and
Bearwalkers (Cambridge: Harvard
Univ., 1952), pp.78-79.

Republic
-Norse ax
ca.1878
Hjalmar R. Holand, Westward from Vinland (N.Y.: Duell, Sloan & Pearce,
1940), pp.218-21. il.

Reynolds twp.
-UFO (CE-3)
1897, April 14/=hoax?
Saginaw Courier-Herald, 17 Apr.1897.
Lansing State Republican, 17 Apr.
1897.

Richmond
-UFO (CE-1)
1970, Nov./John Baker/Kroner Rd.

Richmond Review, 10 Dec.1970.

Rockwood
-UFO (CE-1)
  1978, May 3/Marie Schmidt/20954 Woodruff Rd.
    Monroe Evening News, 4 May 1978.

Romeo
-Disappearance
  1956, Nov.15/F-80
    "Case 254," CRIFO Orbit, 4 Jan.1957,
    p.1.

Romulus
-UFO (CE-1)
  1978, Feb.8
    Detroit News, 28 Feb.1978.
-UFO (NL)
  1958, Aug.9/nr. airport
    "Sighting Round-Up," UFO Inv. 1
    (Aug.-Sep.1958):6.

Roseville
-Mystery bird
  1975, Oct./Harry Easton/=hybrid duck?
    Grit, 12 Oct.1975.
-UFO (DD)
  1955, April 8/Dominic Sondy
    "Case 94," CRIFO Orbit, 1 July 1955,
    p.3.
-UFO (NL)
  1955, Aug.22/Frank Gallagher
    "Case 99," CRIFO Orbit, 2 Sep.1955,
    p.3.

Royal Oak
-UFO (DD)
  1947, July 2/Sidney L. Trezise
    Detroit Times, 6 July 1947.
-UFO (NL)
  1957, June 2/Theodore L. Walling/North-
  wood School
    (Letter), Fate 11 (Feb.1958):113-14.

Saginaw
-Humanoid
  1937/Saginaw R.
    John Green, Sasquatch: The Apes Among
    Us (Seattle: Hancock House, 1978),
    p.200.
-Inner development
  1930s/Spiritualist Mediums' Alliance/
  933 N. Charles St.
    Nandor Fodor, Encyclopaedia of Psy-
    chic Science (London: Arthurs,
    1933), p.367.
-UFO (NL)
  1897, April 16/Mr. Halsey
    Saginaw Evening News, 17 Apr.1897.
  1971, Oct.2/David Wazny/Hwy.81 x Hin-
  son St.
    "Michigan Sighting Reported," Skylook,
    no.61 (Dec.1972):6.

Saint Ignace
-Gravity anomaly
  Mystery Spot/5 mi.W
    (Letter), John W. Griffin, Fate 10
    (July 1957):124-26.

(Letter), R.E. Walters, Fate 10
  (Oct.1957):127-28.
-Hex and shape-shifting
  n.d.
    Richard M. Dorson, Bloodstoppers and
    Bearwalkers (Cambridge: Harvard
    Univ., 1952), pp.72-78.

Saint Joseph
-Rotating tombstone
  1970s/Scottsdale Spring Run Cemetery/
  =slippage on ice
    Emil Markwart, "Why Tombstone Ro-
    tates," Fate 26 (Jan.1973):104.
-UFO (NL)
  1897, April 13
    Detroit Free Press, 14 Apr.1897.
  1970, Dec.15/Oliver Harmon/U.S.33
    "Strange Glow in Michigan Sky," Sky-
    look, no.40 (Mar.1971):7.
  1978, July 27/Rocky Gap
    Muskegon Chronicle, 30 July 1978.

Salem
-Mystery plane crash
  1971, Oct.10/John W. Chadwick/PA-24
    Jay Gourley, The Great Lakes Triangle
    (Greenwich, Ct.: Fawcett, 1977),
    p.29.

Saline
-UFO (DD)
  1897, April 18
    Saginaw Evening News, 20 Apr.1897.
-UFO (NL)
  1967, Jan.16/Gerald Frank
    "Major Sighting Wave," UFO Inv. 3
    (Jan.-Feb.1967):1,4.

Sandusky
-UFO (NL)
  1953, Jan.
    (Editorial), Fate 6 (June 1953):12.

Sanford
-Mystery tracks
  1974, Dec./Naomi Whipple
    Naomi Ruth Whipple, "What Goes There?"
    Fate 32 (Jan.1979):51-52. il.

Sanilac co.
-Petroglyphs
    Mark Papworth, "The Sanilac County
    Rock Carvings," Michigan Arch. 3
    (1957):83-87.
    "The Sanilac Petroglyphs," Bull.Cran-
    brook Inst.Sci., no.36 (1958). il.
    "The Sanilac Petroglyphs," Michigan
    Arch. 15 (1969):93-99. il.
    Ira W. Butterfield, "The Sanilac Pet-
    roglyphs: An Archaeological Time
    Study," Michigan Arch. 17 (1971):41-
    44.

Sault Sainte Marie
-Humanoid
  1967
    John Green, Sasquatch: The Apes Among
    Us (Seattle: Hancock House, 1978),
    p.201.

-Precognition
  1764, May
    Alexander Henry, Travels and Adven-
    tures in Canada and the Indian Ter-
    ritories (N.Y.: I. Riley, 1809),
    pp.154-55,158-59.
-Psychokinesis
  1936, Feb.20/Jeffrey Derosier/War Memorial Hospital
    R. DeWitt Miller, Impossible: Yet It
    Happened! (N.Y.: Ace, 1947 ed.),
    pp.11-12, quoting Sault Ste. Marie
    Evening News (undated).
    Francois Ouitanon, "You Can't Pick
    Up the Mirror," Fate 3 (Nov.1950):
    81-82.
-Seance
  1764, June/Alexander Henry/shaking tent
    Alexander Henry, Travels and Adven-
    tures in Canada and the Indian Ter-
    ritories (N.Y.: I. Riley, 1809),
    pp.166-72.
-UFO (NL)
  1966, Aug.19/Algoma Steel Plant
    "Why Create a Mystery?" UFO Inv. 3
    (Aug.-Sep.1966):4.
  1969, Jan.13
    Sault Ste. Marie Evening News, 14
    Jan.1969.
-UFO (R)
  1967, Sep.11/Kincheloe AFB/=radar echo?
    Gordon D. Thayer, "Optical and Radar
    Analyses of Field Cases," in Edward
    U. Condon, ed., Scientific Study of
    Unidentified Flying Objects (N.Y.:
    Bantam, 1969 ed.), pp.115,164-66.
-UFO (R) and mystery plane crash
  1953, Nov.23/Felix Moncla, Jr./Kinross
  (Kincheloe) AFB
    Sault Ste. Marie Evening News, 23-
    24 Nov.1953.
    Donald E. Keyhoe, Flying Saucer Con-
    spiracy (N.Y.: Holt, 1955), pp.13-
    22.
    Donald H. Menzel & Lyle G. Boyd, The
    World of Flying Saucers (Garden
    City: Doubleday, 1963), pp.154-55.
    Richard Hall, ed., The UFO Evidence
    (Washington: NICAP, 1964), pp.114-15.
    Donald E. Keyhoe, Aliens from Space
    (Garden City: Doubleday, 1973), pp.
    201-203.
-UFO (R-V)
  1966, Sep.18/Kincheloe AFB
    Gordon D. Thayer, "Optical and Radar
    Analyses of Field Cases," in Edward
    U. Condon, ed., Scientific Study of
    Unidentified Flying Objects (N.Y.:
    Bantam, 1969 ed.), pp.115,130-31.

Scotts
-UFO (?)
  1897, April 11/2 mi.from town
    Chicago (Ill.) Times-Herald, 14 Apr.
    1897, p.2.

Seney
-UFO (CE-2)
  1968, Jan./Hwy.28
    Leonard H. Stringfield, Situation

Red: The UFO Siege (N.Y.: Fawcett
    Crest, 1977 ed.), pp.70-71.

Shelby
-UFO (NL)
  1897, April 15
    Lansing State Republican, 16 Apr.
    1897.

Sidnaw
-UFO (NL)
  1897, April 26
    Marquette Mining Journal, 1 May 1897.

Silver Creek twp.
-Humanoid
  1964, June/Patsy Clayton
    Columbus (O.) Dispatch, 7 Oct.1964,
    p.34B.
    Gene Caesar, "The Hellzapoppin' Hunt
    for the Michigan Monster," True,
    June 1966, pp.59,84.

Sister Lakes
-Humanoid
  1963/John Utrup
    Columbus (O.) Dispatch, 7 Oct.1964,
    p.34B.
  1964, May/Gordon Brown/Swisher Rd.
  1964, June 9/Mrs. John Utrup
    Nat'l Observer, 22 June 1964.
    Columbus (O.) Dispatch, 7 Oct.1964,
    p.34B.
    Gene Caesar, "The Hellzapoppin' Hunt
    for the Michigan Monster," True,
    June 1966, pp.59-60,84-85.
    Eric Norman [Brad Steiger], The Abom-
    inable Snowmen (N.Y.: Award, 1969),
    pp.131-34.
-Humanoid track
  1964, June/Howard Sheline
    (Editorial), Fate 17 (Oct.1964):22.

Six Lakes
-UFO (NL)
  1973, Sep.29/Cutler Rd.
    Greenville Daily News, 1 Oct.1973.

South Haven
-Mystery automobile crash
  1968, April 13/James Bell/109th St.
    Pauline Saltzman, Ghosts and Other
    Strangers (N.Y.: Lancer, 1968 ed.),
    pp.96-97, quoting AP release, 14
    Apr.1968.
-UFO (NL)
  1897, April
    South Haven Sentinel, 24 Apr.1897.
  1897, April 14/Elder Ketchum
    Chicago (Ill.) Tribune, 16 Apr.1897,
    p.4.

South Range
-Weather control
  1971, winter/Heikke Lunta
    "Snow Dancing," Fate 24 (June 1971):
    95.

Stambaugh
-Haunt

ca.1902/Aaron Kinney/Riverton Mine
Richard M. Dorson, Bloodstoppers and
Bearwalkers (Cambridge: Harvard
Univ., 1952), pp.259-61.

Suttons Bay
-UFO (NL)
1978, Nov.3/Mary Forten
Traverse City Record-Eagle, 18 Nov.
1978.

Temperance
-Humanoid
1965, Aug./Shirley Morrin
John A. Keel, Strange Creatures from
Time and Space (Greenwich, Ct.: Faw-
cett, 1970), p.109.

Three Rivers
-Mystery plane crash
1968, July 16/Charles N. Neblock/Cess-
na 150
Jay Gourley, The Great Lakes Triangle
(Greenwich, Ct.: Fawcett, 1970),
pp.130-31.
-UFO (NL)
1897, April 17
Port Huron Daily News, 20 Apr.1897.

Traverse City
-Talking dog
1959/D.O. Ball
(Editorial), Fate 12 (June 1959):22-
24.

Troy
-UFO (?)
1958, Feb.9/H.M. Stump/airport
Richard Hall, ed., The UFO Evidence
(Washington: NICAP, 1964), p.91.
-UFO (CE-2)
1976, June 3
"Sighting Reports," CUFOS News Bull.,
Sep.1976, p.5.

Utica
-UFO (NL)
1947, July 4/Warren M. Edwards/4 mi.E
Ted Bloecher, Report on the UFO Wave
of 1947 (Washington: NICAP, 1967),
Appendix, Case 274.
1969, March 12
Utica Daily Sentinel, 13 Mar.1969.
1977, Feb.16
"UFOs of Limited Merit," Int'l UFO
Reporter 2 (Apr.1977):5.

Vicksburg
-UFO (CE-2)
1966, March 31/Jeno Udvardy
"Close-Range Sightings Increase,"
UFO Inv. 3 (Mar.-Apr.1966):3.
Donald E. Keyhoe & Gordon I.R. Lore,
Jr., UFOs: A New Look (Washington:
NICAP, 1969), p.23.

Wakefield
-UFO (NL)
1897, April 18-19/Mr. Widosky
Jerome Clark & Lucius Farish, "The

1897 Story: Part 2," Flying Saucer
Rev. 14 (Nov.-Dec.1968):6,7.

Walker
-UFO (CE-1)
1971, Dec.2/Steve Loosenort/3360 Remem-
brance Rd. NW
Grand Rapids Press, 5 Dec.1971.

Walnut Lake
-UFO (NL)
1952, June 18
Edward J. Ruppelt, The Report on Un-
identified Flying Objects (Garden
City: Doubleday, 1956), p.146.

Warren
-Clairvoyance
1977, Nov.
(Editorial), Fate 31 (Oct.1978):30-
32.
-Fall of metallic object
1965, Dec.9
Jerome Clark, "The Greatest Flap Yet?
Part IV," Flying Saucer Rev. 12
(Nov.-Dec.1966):9,12.
-Precognition
1966, March/Lois Lyden
(Editorial), Fate 19 (July 1966):6.
-UFO (DD)
1958, Aug.17/Alex D. Chisholm
Thomas M. Olsen, ed., The Reference
for Outstanding UFO Sighting Reports
(Riderwood, Md.: UFO Information Re-
trieval Center, 1966), p.58.
-UFO (NL)
1966, March 28/Charles Spaulding
Columbus (O.) Citizen-Journal, 29
Mar.1966.

Washtenaw co.
-Dowsing
1950s/Murray J. Knowles
(Editorial), Fate 6 (July 1953):5.

Waterford
-UFO (NL)
1961, July 10/Duane Hart/Clintonville
Rd.
1961, July 12/Roger White
Curtis Fuller, "The Boys Who 'Caught'
a Flying Saucer," Fate 15 (Jan.
1962):36-38.

Westland
-Paranormal hypnosis research
1930s-1940s/Milton H. Erickson/Wayne
County Hospital
Milton H. Erickson, "An Experimental
Investigation of the Possible Anti-
Social Use of Hypnosis," Psychiatry
2 (1939):391-414.
Milton H. Erickson, "Hypnotic Inves-
tigation of Psychosomatic Phenomena:
Psychosomatic Interrelationships
Studied by Experimental Hypnosis,"
Psychosomatic Med. 5 (1943):51-58.
Milton H. Erickson & Lewis B. Hill,
"Unconscious Mental Activity in Hyp-
nosis: Psychoanalytic Implications,"

Psychoanalytic Quar. 13 (1944):60-78.

White Lake
-UFO (NL)
1978, Feb.5/John Kelly/Hwy.59 nr. Bogie Lake Rd.
Union Lake Spinal Column, 1 Mar.1978.

Whitmore Lake
-Ghost
1976, Sep./Helen Prescott
Helen Prescott, "The Ghost Who Wasn't Dead," Fate 31 (Dec.1978):52-53.

Willis
-UFO (NL)
1966, July 13/Jack Westbrook/Rawsonville Rd.
Ypsilanti Press, 15 July 1966.

Wolf Lake
-UFO (NL)
1969, March 1
Muskegon Chronicle, 3 Mar.1969.

Ypsilanti
-Haunt
1972/W of town
(Editorial), Fate 26 (Mar.1973):14-16, quoting Detroit News (undated).
-UFO (?)
1952, April 29
Ypsilanti Press, 30 Apr.1952.
-UFO (NL)
1967, Feb.17/Alfred Rogers/Eastern Michigan Univ.
Columbus (O.) Citizen-Journal, 17 Feb.1967.

Zeeland
-Anomalous artifacts
1897, March/Mr. Koats/Waverly Quarry, 4 mi.W/=flint implements in sandstone pocket
Beardstown (Ill.) Enterprise, 28 Mar. 1897, p.1.

B. Physical Features

Au Train L.
-Lake monster
1870s/Mr. Powell
Richard M. Dorson, Bloodstoppers and Bearwalkers (Cambridge: Harvard Univ., 1952), p.247.

Basswood L.
-Lake monster
n.d./Bill Powell
Richard M. Dorson, Bloodstoppers and Bearwalkers (Cambridge: Harvard Univ., 1952), p.247.

Black L.
-UFO (NL)
1897, April 11
Grand Rapids Evening Press, 12 Apr. 1897.

1965, July 25
Bill Adler, ed., Letters to the Air Force on UFOs (N.Y.: Dell, 1967), p.46.

Bois Blanc I.
-Archeological site
50-1400 A.D./Juntunen site
Alan McPherron, "The Juntunen Site and the Late Woodland Prehistory of the Upper Great Lakes," Anthro.Pap. Mus.Anthro.Univ.Michigan, no.30 (1967). il.

Caribou I.
-Haunt
n.d.
Charles M. Skinner, American Myths and Legends, 2 vols. (Philadelphia: Lippincott, 1903), 2:339-41.

Chief L.
-UFO (NL)
1955, June 17/M. Rhodes
(Letter), Fate 8 (Oct.1955):125-26.

Crystal L.
-Ancient inscriptions and coins
1894/=hoax?
"A 'Stamp' Tablet and Coin Found in a Michigan Mound," Am.Antiquarian 16 (1894):313.
"Frauds in Michigan," Am.Antiquarian 16 (1894):384.
Francis W. Kelsey, "A Persistent Forgery," Am.Antiquarian 33 (1911): 26-31.

Devil's L.
-Mystery plane crash
1970, July 27/James Charles Young/ Beech D-18
Jay Gourley, The Great Lakes Triangle (Greenwich, Ct.: Fawcett, 1977), pp.86-87.

Dowagiac Swamp
-Humanoid
1964, July 13
"Monsters Around the World," Saucer News 11 (Dec.1964):21-22.

DuVall Creek
-Humanoid tracks
1977, Oct.1/Thomas Rumhor
Alpena News, 3 Oct.1977.
Bay City Times, 4 Oct.1977.
Tawas City Herald, 5 Oct.1977.

Elizabeth L.
-Erratic crocodilian
1953
Detroit News, 7 July 1955.

Glen L.
-UFO (NL)
1954, July 15/Jerry Leimenstoll
"Photographic Evidence?" CRIFO Newsl., 4 Feb.1955, p.5.

Grand Sable Banks
-Phantom (myth)
    Charles M. Skinner, American Myths
    and Legends, 2 vols. (Philadelphia:
    Lippincott, 1903), 2:341-45.

Grand Traverse Bay
-Ancient inscription
    n.d.
        Charles Whittlesey, "Archaeological
        Frauds," Pub.Western Reserve & N.
        Ohio Hist.Soc'y, no.33 (Nov.1876),
        pp.2,8. il.

Green Point
-Archeological site
    Schultz site
        Henry T. Wright, "A Transitional Ar-
        chaic Campsite at Green Point (20
        SA 1)," Michigan Arch. 10 (1964):
        17-22.
        James E. Fitting, The Archeology of
        Michigan (Garden City: Natural His-
        tory Press, 1970), pp.91-95,116-28.
        James E. Fitting, ed., "The Schultz
        Site at Green Point," Mem.Mus.Anthro.
        Univ.Michigan, no.4 (1972).

Grosse Ile
-Ghost light
    ca.1785/William Macomb, Jr.
        Marie Caroline Watson Hamlin, Legends
        of Le Détroit (Detroit: Nourse,
        1884), pp.134-41.

Harris L.
-Erratic crocodilian
    1956, June
        Detroit News, 25 June 1956.

Holcombe Beach
-Archeological site
    ca.9000 B.C.
        James E. Fitting, Jerry DeVisscher &
        Edward J. Wahla, "The Paleo-Indian
        Occupation of the Holcombe Beach,"
        Anthro.Pap.Mus.Anthro.Univ.Michigan,
        no.27 (1966). il
        James E. Fitting, The Archeology of
        Michigan (Garden City: Natural His-
        tory Press, 1970), pp.45-57. il.
        Jerry DeVisscher & Edward J. Wahla,
        "Additional Paleo-Indian Campsites
        Adjacent to the Holcombe Site,"
        Michigan Arch. 16 (1970):1-24. il.

Huron, L.
-Mystery shipwreck
    1872, June 18/"Jamaica"
        John Brandt Mansfield, ed., History
        of the Great Lakes (Chicago: J.H.
        Beers, 1899), pp.723-24.
-Precognition
    ca.1910/Dave Beggs/"Aztec"
        Dwight Boyer, Strange Adventures of
        the Great Lakes (N.Y.: Dodd, Mead,
        1974), pp.225-27.
    1913, Nov.9/Milton Smith/"Charles Price"
        Dwight Boyer, True Tales of the Great
        Lakes (N.Y.: Dodd, Mead, 1971), pp.

266-302.
    Jay Gourley, The Great Lakes Triangle
    (Greenwich, Ct.: Fawcett, 1977),
    pp.153,174-75.

Huron R.
-Erratic crocodilian
    1938
        Detroit News, 7 July 1955.

Island L., Livingston co.
-UFO (CE-1)
    1978, Feb.8-9/Tom Beauchamp
        Brighton Argus, 15 Feb.1978.
        Howell Livingston County Press, 15
        Feb.1978.
        "Michigan Flap?" Int'l UFO Reporter
        3 (Apr.1978):Newsfront sec.

Island L., Oakland co.
-Erratic crocodilian
    1955, July 9
        Detroit News, 10 July 1955.

Isle Royale
-Ancient copper mines
    ca.4000 B.C.-recent
        James D. Baldwin, Ancient America in
        Notes on American Archaeology (N.Y.:
        Harper, 1872), pp.43-46.
        Henry Gillman, "The Mound-Builders
        and Platycnemism in Michigan," Ann.
        Rept.Smith.Inst., 1873, pp.364,384-
        90. il.
        A.C. Davis, "Antiquities of Isle
        Royale, Lake Superior," Ann.Rept.
        Smith.Inst., 1874, pp.369-70.
        T.H. Lewis, "Copper Mines Worked by
        the Mound Builders," Am.Antiquarian
        11 (1889):293-96.
        J.H. Lathrop, "Prehistoric Mines of
        Lake Superior," Am.Antiquarian 23
        (1901):248-58.
        George R. Fox, "The Ancient Copper
        Workings on Isle Royale," Wisconsin
        Arch. 10 (1911):73-100.
        Fred Dustin, "A Summary of the Arch-
        aeology of Isle Royale, Michigan,"
        Pap.Michigan Acad.Sci. 16 (1932):1-
        16. il.
        George I. Quimby & Albert C. Spauld-
        ing, "The Old Copper Culture and
        the Keweenaw Waterway," Fieldiana:
        Anthropology 36 (1957):189-201.
        Fred Dustin, "An Archeological Re-
        connaisance of Isle Royale," Mich-
        igan History 41 (1957):1-34.
        Roy Ward Drier & O.J. DuTemple, ed.,
        Prehistoric Copper Mining in the
        Lake Superior Region (Calumet, Mich.:
        The Authors, 1961).
        James B. Griffin, ed., "Lake Superior
        Copper and the Indians: Miscellane-
        ous Studies of Great Lakes Prehis-
        tory," Anthro.Pap.Mus.Anthro.Univ.
        Michigan, on.17 (1961).
        Minneapolis (Minn.) Tribune, 8 June
        1969.
        James E. Fitting, The Archeology of
        Michigan (Garden City: Natural His-

tory Press, 1970),pp.87-90. il.
Jack Parker, "The First Copper Miners
in Michigan," NEARA J. 10 (summer-
fall 1975):19-24.
Henriette Mertz, Atlantis: Dwelling
Place of the Gods (Chicago: The Au-
thor, 1976), pp.65-70.
-Ancient inscription
1874/S.W. Hill/L. Desor
Charles Whittlesey, "Archaeological
Frauds," Pub.Western Reserve & N.
Ohio Hist.Soc'y, no.33 (Nov.1876),
p.2.
-Disappearance
1927, Dec.5/Bill Brian/"Kamloops"
Dwight Boyer, Ghost Ships of the
Great Lakes (N.Y.: Dodd, Mead, 1968),
pp.126-43.

Kensington Metropolitan Park
-UFO (NL)
1978, Feb?/Mary Ratelle
Union Lake Spinal Column, 1 Mar.1978.

Keweenaw Point
-Ancient copper mines
ca.4000 B.C.-recent
T.H. Lewis, "Copper Mines Worked by
the Mound Builders," Am.Antiquarian
11 (1889):293-96.
(Editorial), Nature 45 (1891):39-40.
George I. Quimby & Albert C. Spauld-
ing, "The Old Copper Culture and
the Keweenaw Waterway," Fieldiana:
Anthropology 36 (1957):189-201.
Roy Ward Drier & O.J. DuTemple, ed.,
Prehistoric Copper Mining in the
Lake Superior Region (Calumet, Mich.:
The Authors, 1961).
Burton Straw, "Copper Mining Hammer-
stones from Upper Michigan," Wis-
consin Arch. 43 (1962):76. il.
Jack Parker, "The First Copper Miners
in Michigan," NEARA J. 10 (summer-
fall 1975):19-24.
-Disappearance
1952, Nov.28/F. Jake/Beech 35
Jay Gourley, The Great Lakes Triangle
(Greenwich, Ct.: Fawcett, 1977),
pp.24-25,159-60.
-Phantom ship
1930s?
Michigan Writers' Program, Michigan:
A Guide to the Wolverine State (N.Y.:
Oxford Univ., 1956), p.122.
-UFO (R)
1965, Aug.4/USAF radar base
Flint Journal, 5 Aug.1965.

Long L.
-UFO (NL)
1897, April
Grand Traverse Herald, 29 Apr.1897.

Lookout Pt.
-Fall of fish
1960, Sep./Mrs. Victor Mietens
(Editorial), Fate 14 (Feb.1961):6-8.

Lower Long L.
-Erratic crocodilian
1955, June-July
Detroit News, 7 July 1955.
1957, July 10
Detroit News, 10 July 1957.

Metropolitan Beach
-UFO (NL)
1978, March 6
Port Huron Times-Herald, 8 Mar.1978.

Michigan, L.
-Disappearance
1892, Oct.28/"W.H. Gilcher"
Chicago (Ill.) Tribune, 2 Nov.1892.
John Brandt Mansfield, ed., History
of the Great Lakes (Chicago: J.H.
Beers, 1899), p.763.
Dwight Boyer, Ghost Stories of the
Great Lakes (N.Y.: Dodd, Mead,
1966), pp.60-68.
-Meteor and electrical disturbance
1919, Nov.26
"A Celestial Short Circuit," Lit.
Digest 64 (28 Feb.1920):27-28, quot-
ing Electrical Experimenter (un-
dated).
-Mystery plane crash
1953, Aug.27/John William Wilson/F-86
Chicago (Ill.) Tribune, 28 Aug.1953.
1965, Aug.16/Melville W. Towle/Boeing
727
Jay Gourley, The Great Lakes Triangle
(Greenwich, Ct.: Fawcett, 1977),
pp.121-26.
-Phantom ship
n.d.
Michigan Writers' Program, Michigan:
A Guide to the Wolverine State
(N.Y.: Oxford Univ., 1956), pp.121-
22.

Munuscong L.
-Deer mutilation
1972, Nov.21/Walter Wegner
Detroit News, 23 Nov.1972.

Naomikong Point
-Archeological site
Donald R. Janzen, "The Naomikong
Point Site and the Dimensions of
Laurel in the Lake Superior Region,"
Anthro.Pap.Mus.Anthro.Univ.Michigan,
no.36 (1968). il.
James E. Fitting, The Archeology of
Michigan (Garden City: Natural His-
tory Press, 1970), pp.138-40,189-90.

Narrow L.
-Lake monster
1886, summer
New York Herald, 3 Sep.1886.

Paint R.
-River monster
1922/Mrs. Johnson
Ivan T. Sanderson, Things (N.Y.: Pyramid, 1967), pp.33-34.

Pictured Rocks
-Shape-shifting myth
    Charles M. Skinner, Myths and Legends
    of Our Own Land, 2 vols. (Philadel-
    phia: Lippincott, 1896), 2:128-29.

Pine L.
-Phantom panther
    1897, April
    Niles Weekly Mirror, 14 Apr.1897.
    Jerome Clark & Lucius Farish, "The
    1897 Story--1," Flying Saucer Rev.
    14 (Sep.-Oct.1968):13,14, quoting
    Saginaw Evening News (undated).
-UFO (CE-3)
    1897, April 15/William Megiveron/=hoax?
    Lansing State Republican, 17 Apr.
    1897.

Point aux Barques
-Mystery shipwreck
    1899, Aug.20/"Hunter Savidge"
    Chicago (Ill.) Tribune, 21 Aug.1899.
    Dwight Boyer, Strange Adventures of
    the Great Lakes (N.Y.: Dodd, Mead,
    1974), p.64.

Pond L.
-UFO (CE-1)
    1947, July 5/Willard Fisk
    Grand Rapids Herald, 7 July 1947.

Porcupine Mts.
-Skyquakes
    1840s
    New York Herald, 5 Oct.1845, p.1.

Rifle R.
-Archeological sites
    ca.1350-1450
    M.L. Leach, "Ancient Forts in Ogemaw
    County, Michigan," Ann.Rept.Smith.
    Inst., 1884, pp.849-51.
    W.B. Hinsdale, "The Missaukee Pre-
    serve and Rifle River Forts," Pap.
    Michigan Acad.Sci. 4 (1924):1-14.
    Fred Dustin, "Report on Indian Earth-
    works in Ogemaw County," Sci.Pub.
    Cranbrook Inst.Sci., no.1 (1932).
    Harold W. Moll, Norman G. Moll & El-
    don S. Cornelius, "Earthwork Enclo-
    sures in Ogemaw, Missaukee, and Al-
    cona Counties," Totem Pole, vol.41,
    no.3 (1958).
    James E. Fitting, The Archeology of
    Michigan (Garden City: Natural His-
    tory Press, 1970), pp.171-73.

Rouge R.
-Archeological site
    perforated skulls and humerus
    Henry Gillman, "Certain Characterist-
    ics Pertaining to Ancient Man in
    Michigan," Ann.Rept.Smith.Inst.,
    1875, pp.234-45. il.
    Henry Gillman, "Perforation of the
    Humerus Conjoined with Platycnemism,"
    Am.Naturalist 9 (1875):427-28.
    Bela Hubbard, Memorials of Half a
    Century (N.Y.: Putnam, 1887).

W.B. Hinsdale & Emerson F. Greenman,
    "Perforated Indian Crania in Mich-
    igan," Occ.Contrib.Mus.Anthro.Univ.
    Michigan, no.5 (1936). il.

Round I.
-Lake monster
    ca.1892/=hoax?
    Chicago (Ill.) Tribune, 24 July 1892.

Saint Clair, L.
-Mystery plane crash
    1959, Dec.16/Jack Stewart Murphy/Aero
    Design 560E
    Jay Gourley, The Great Lakes Triangle
    (Greenwich, Ct.: Fawcett, 1977),
    p.173.
-Phantom ship
    n.d.
    Marie Caroline Watson Hamlin, Legends
    of Le Détroit (Detroit: Nourse,
    1884), p.15.
-Skyquake
    1965, Dec.9/=meteor?
    Jerome Clark, "The Greatest Flap Yet?
    Part IV," Flying Saucer Rev. 12
    (Nov.-Dec.1966):9,11.
-UFO (?)
    1967, Jan.9/Grant Jaroslaw/38946 Lake
    Shore Dr./=hoax
    Detroit News, 10 Jan.1967; and 16
    Jan.1967. il.
    Detroit Free Press, 12 Jan.1967.
    New York Times, 17 Jan.1967, p.5. il.
    "Brothers Photograph Object," APRO
    Bull. 15 (Jan.-Feb.1967):6.
    Robert Loftin, Identified Flying Sau-
    cers (N.Y.: David McKay, 1968), pp.
    141-42.
    Herschel P. Fink, "A Tale of Two Sau-
    cers: or Which UFO Hangs on a
    String?" True, March 1968, pp.62-63,
    67-69. il.
    Philip J. Klass, UFOs Explained (N.Y.:
    Random House, 1974), pp.142-43.

Saint Clair R.
-Erratic shark
    1963, June 16/Harold Kiss/=monkfish
    (Editorial), Fate 16 (Oct.1963):6-8.

Saint Mary's R.
-Mystery stone
    1960, Oct./12 mi.W of Sault Ste. Marie
    (Editorial), Fate 14 (May 1961):23.

Silver Creek
-Humanoid tracks
    1978, June 25/Butch Knuppenburg
    Oscoda Press, 28 June 1978. il.
    Tawas City Herald, 28 June 1978. il.

Spring Creek
-Archeological site
    ca.1000 A.D.
    James E. Fitting, "The Spring Creek
    Site, 20 MU 3, Muskegon County,
    Michigan," Anthro.Pap.Mus.Anthro.
    Univ.Michigan, no.32 (1968):1-78. il.
    James E. Fitting, The Archeology of

Michigan (Garden City: Natural History Press, 1970), pp.173-77.

Summer I.
-Archeological site
  ca.250-1650
    Lewis R. Binford & George I. Quimby, "Indian Sites and Chipped Stone Materials in the Northern Lake Michigan Area," Fieldiana: Anthropology 36 (1963):277-307.
    David S. Brose, "The Archeology of Summer Island," Anthro.Pap.Mus.Anthro.Univ.Michigan, no.41 (1970).

Superior, L.
-Disappearance
  1908, Dec.1/"D.M. Clemson"
  1918, Nov.24/"Inkerman"
    Dwight Boyer, Ghost Stories of the Great Lakes (N.Y.: Dodd, Mead, 1966), pp.83-96,182-83.
-Lake monster myth
    Jay Gourley, The Great Lakes Triangle (Greenwich, Ct.: Fawcett, 1977), p.46.
-Mystery shipwreck
  1907, Oct.10/"Cyprus"
    Chicago (Ill.) Tribune, 13 Oct.1907.
    Dana Thomas Bowen, Shipwrecks of the Lakes (Cleveland: Freshwater, 1952), pp.229-33.
    William Ratigan, Great Lakes Shipwrecks and Survivals (N.Y.: Galahad, 1960), pp.255-56.
  1975, Nov.10/Ernest R. McSorley/"Edmund Fitzgerald"
    Jay Gourley, The Great Lakes Triangle (Greenwich, Ct.: Fawcett, 1977), pp.10-13.
-Mystery storm
  1913, summer/"Leafield"
  1913, summer/"James E. Davidson"
    Dwight Boyer, Ghost Stories of the Great Lakes (N.Y.: Dodd, Mead, 1966), pp.179-81.
-Phantom (myth)
    Charles M. Skinner, Myths and Legends of Our Own Land, 2 vols. (Philadelphia: Lippincott, 1896), 2:126-28.

Susan L.
-Erratic crocodilian
  1956, June
    Detroit News, 25 June 1956.
  1957, Aug.4
    Detroit News, 5 Aug.1957.

Swan L.
-Lake monster
  1946, Aug.15/=cow?
    "No Such Animal," Doubt, no.17 (1947):260.

Tawas L.
-Humanoid tracks
  1976, Nov.
    Oscoda Press, 28 June 1978.

Tittabawasee R.
-Humanoid
  1891, Oct./George W. Frost
    Colfax (Wash.) Commoner, 6 Nov.1891.

Trout Bay
-Lake monster
  ca.1926/Angus Steinhoff
    Richard M. Dorson, Bloodstoppers and Bearwalkers (Cambridge: Harvard Univ., 1952), pp.247-48.

Upper Scott L.
-Skyquake and anomalous hole in ice
  1970, Jan.1/James Eastep/YMCA Camp Sears
    Grand Rapids Press, 4 Jan.1970.
    Curt Sutherly, "The Inside Story of the New Hampshire UFO Crash," Saga UFO Rept. 4 (July 1977):22,63-64.

Waterloo State Recreation Area
-Human track in sandstone
    Wilbert Rusch, "Human Footprints in Rock," Creation Rsch.Soc'y Quar., Mar.1971, pp.204-205.

Whitefish Bay
-Flying humanoid
  1945, Oct./Paul E. Petosky (Letter), Fate 19 (Apr.1966):120.

Whitmore L.
-Mystery plane crash
  1971, June 12/Cessna 180
    Jay Gourley, The Great Lakes Triangle (Greenwich, Ct.: Fawcett, 1977), pp.77-78.

Williams L.
-UFO (CE-3)
  1976, May 15/Gerald Nestor
    Gray Barker, "UFO Creatures on the Prowl," Saga UFO Rept. 3 (Mar.1977):20-21.

Wilson L.
-UFO (NL)
  1978, Sep./Ray Czap
    Traverse City Record-Eagle, 30 Sep. 1978.

        C. Ethnic Groups

Ojibwa Indians
-Flood myth
    Richard M. Dorson, Bloodstoppers and Bearwalkers (Cambridge: Harvard Univ., 1952), pp.42-48.
-Humanoid myth
    Richard M. Dorson, Bloodstoppers and Bearwalkers (Cambridge: Harvard Univ., 1952), pp.54-55.

Ottawa Indians
-Hex
    M. Dejean, "Objections des Indiens non chrétiens contre la Religion catholique," Ann.de la Prop.de la

<u>Foi</u> 4 (1830):481-85.
-Mermaid myth
    James Athearn Jones, <u>Traditions of</u>
    <u>the North American Indians</u>, 3 vols.
    (London: Henry Colburn, 1830), 3:
    124-39.

        D. Unspecified Localities

-Giant wolf
    n.d./northern sector
      Ivan T. Sanderson, "The Dire Wolf,"
      <u>Pursuit</u> 7 (Oct.1974):91.

-Humanoid
    ca.1917/northern sector
      John Green, <u>Sasquatch: The Apes Among</u>
      <u>Us</u> (Seattle: Hancock House, 1978),
      p.200.

INDIANA

A. Populated Places

Abington
-Phantom panther
  1948, Aug.8-9/Art LeCamp
    Richmond Palladium-Item & Sun-Tele-
    gram, 9 Aug.1948, p.1; 10 Aug.1948,
    p.1; and 11 Aug.1948, p.1.
-UFO (CE-2)
  1978, Dec.16/Esther Drew/Old Creek Rd.
    Richmond Palladium-Item, 7 Jan.1979.

Allen co.
-Phantom panther
  1963, June
    (Editorial), Fate 16 (Oct.1963):9.

Anderson
-Archeological site
  300 B.C.-500 A.D./Mounds State Park
    (Editorial), Nature 45 (1891):20.
    James H. Kellar, "New Excavations at
    Mounds State Park," Outdoor Indiana
    34, no.7 (1969):4-9.
    James H. Kellar, Introduction to the
    Prehistory of Indiana (Indianapolis:
    Indiana Hist.Soc'y, 1973), pp.48-49.
    Franklin Folsom, America's Ancient
    Treasures (N.Y.: Rand McNally,
    1974), p.137.
    B.K. Schwartz, Jr., "Mounds State
    Park, Indiana," Central States Arch.
    J. 23 (1976):27-32. il.
-UFO (CE-2)
  1971, May 16/Gene Whitlock
    Ted Phillips, Physical Traces Associ-
    ated with UFO Sightings (Evanston:
    Center for UFO Studies, 1975), p.76.
-UFO (DD)
  1950s/Nina Ward Hughes
    (Letter), Fate 13 (Mar.1960):109-10.
  1951, Oct.
    Richard Hall, ed., The UFO Evidence
    (Washington: NICAP, 1964), pp.16,153.
-UFO (NL)
  1897, April 9/Mr. Fulton
    Cincinnati (O.) Enquirer, 15 Apr.1897.
  1897, April 11/I.J.O. Morrison
    New York Herald, 16 Apr.1897.
  1897, April 13
    Cincinnati (O.) Enquirer, 15 Apr.1897.
  1966, Sep.30/Dave Lehr/Madison Ave.
    "Police Sight UFO near Indiana Hos-
    pital," UFO Inv. 3 (Oct.-Nov.1966):5.

Angola
-UFO (NL)
  1897, April 12
    Angola Steuben Republican, 14 Apr.
    1897, p.4.
  1897, April 18/Byron Work
    Angola Steuben Republican, 21 Apr.
    1897, p.5.

Bedford
-UFO (?)
  1956, Jan.9
    "Jets Chase Saucers, Heralding in
    1956," CRIFO Orbit, 3 Feb.1956, p.1.
-UFO (CE-1)
  1956, Oct.16/John Michael
    "Case 267," CRIFO Orbit, 4 Jan.1957,
    p.3.
-UFO (CE-2)
  1955, Aug.3/ground markings only
    Ted Phillips, Physical Traces Associ-
    ated with UFO Sightings (Evanston:
    Center for UFO Studies, 1975), p.19.
  1955, Aug.25/Mrs. Lester Parsons/Hwy.5
    Indianapolis Star, 27 Aug.1957.
  1957, Nov.9/Watson Merry/Hwy.60
  1957, Nov.9/Pauline Baxter/Free Methodist Church
    Frank Edwards, "UFO Sightings and
    Alibis," Fate 11 (Mar.1958):27,32,
    quoting Bedford Times-Mail (undated).
-UFO (DD)
  1954, Nov.11
    "Louisville Stops Work to Watch Sau-
    cer," CRIFO Newsl., 3 Dec.1954, p.3.

Benton
-Haunt
  n.d./cemetery
    Jim Brandon, Weird America (N.Y.:
    Dutton, 1978), p.83.

Bentonville
-UFO (CE-2)
  1966, Oct./John Baker/=radar chaff?
    Don Worley, "The Incredible UFO Acti-
    vity under Wright-Patterson Air
    Force Base Radar," Official UFO 1
    (May 1976):35,59.

Beverly Shores
-UFO (NL)
  1947, July 7
    Chicago (Ill.) Sun, 8 July 1947.

Bicknell
-UFO (NL)
  1961, Oct.
    Bicknell Daily News, 16 Oct.1961.

Bloomington
-UFO (?)
  1954, June 23/Thad W. Culmer II/=meteor
    "Saucer Files Reviewed," CRIFO Newsl.,
    6 Aug.1954, p.4.
-UFO (CE-2)
  1956, July 9/quarry
    "Lull Is Broken...Saucers Are Back,"
    CRIFO Orbit, 3 Aug.1956, p.1.
    Frank Edwards, Flying Saucers: Serious
    Business (N.Y.: Bantam, 1966 ed.),
    pp.28-29.
-UFO (NL)

1877, Sep.7/John Graham
    Daniel Kirkwood, "Stationary Meteors,"
    Sci.Am. 37 (1877):193.
1959, June 3
    Richard Hall, ed., The UFO Evidence
    (Washington: NICAP, 1964), p.151.

Bluffton
-Fall of metallic object
1949, Dec./Max Lindsey/Hwy.124
    Lucius Farish, "The Mini-Saucers,"
    Fate 27 (Dec.1974):59,60.

Boonville
-Humanoid
1947, Dec.4
    "Run of the Mill," Doubt, no.20
    (1948):303,304.
-Precognition
1975-   /Lou Wright/Box 461
    Warren Smith, "Phenomenal Predictions
    for 1976," Saga, Jan.1976, pp.16,54.
    "Probe's 1977 Directory of the Psy-
    chic World," Probe the Unknown 5
    (spring 1977):32,65.

Brazil
-UFO (NL)
1966, March 24/Ronnie Thurston
    Columbus (O.) Dispatch, 26 Mar.1966,
    p.1.

Brewersville
-Giant human skeletons
1879/Mr. Robinson
    Indianapolis News, 10 Nov.1975.

Brook
-UFO (DD)
1958, Aug.24/Henry Hermansen
    "New Wave of UFO Sightings Cracks
    Censorship Wall," NICAP Spec.Bull.,
    Nov.1958, pp.1,2.

Brooksburg
-UFO (DD)
1968, Nov.26/7 mi.NE
    "Hoax Story Leads to Good Report,"
    APRO Bull. 17 (Nov.-Dec.1968):1,3.

Cambridge City
-UFO (NL)
1957, Nov.5
    Kokomo Tribune, 6 Nov.1957.

Cannelton
-UFO (CE-2)
1964, June/ground markings only
    "News Briefs," Saucer News 11 (Dec.
    1964):25.

Carmel
-Erratic kangaroo
1974, Nov.17/Amos Miller/Hwy.234 x Keystone
    David Fideler & Loren Coleman, "Kan-
    garoos from Nowhere," Fate 31 (Apr.
    1978):68,71.

Centerton
-Phantom panther and hog mutilations
1964, May/Jack Naugle
    Jerome Clark & Loren Coleman, "On
    the Trail of Pumas, Panthers and
    ULAs: Part 2," Fate 25 (July 1972):
    92,96.

Centerville
-Phantom panther
1947, fall/Louis Danels/SW of town
    Richmond Palladium-Item & Sun-Tele-
    gram, 30 July 1948, p.1.

Chester
-Phantom panther
1948, Aug.11
    Richmond Palladium-Item & Sun-Tele-
    gram, 12 Aug.1948, p.1.
-UFO (NL)
1947, July 5/Ralph Kramer
    Indianapolis Star, 6 July 1947.

Chesterfield
-Spirit mediums
1880s-   /Camp Chesterfield
    H. Dennis Bradley, And After (Lon-
    don: T. Werner Laurie, 1931), pp.
    256-76.
    Irving R. Gaertner, "The Actinic
    Power of Light," Psychic Rsch. 25
    (1931):3-4.
    Nandor Fodor, Encyclopaedia of Psy-
    chic Science (London: Arthurs,
    1933), pp.202,257.
    "Our Cover," Doubt, no.20 (1948):298.
    Marcus Bach, The Will to Believe
    (Englewood Cliffs, N.J.: Prentice-
    Hall, 1955).
    "Fraud Uncovered at Chesterfield
    Spiritualist Camp," Psychic Obser-
    ver, no.520 (10 July 1960):2-4. il.
    Andrija Puharich, "Dr. Andrija Puhar-
    ich Reports on the Frauds, Fakes
    and Fantasies of the Chesterfield
    Spiritualist Camp," Psychic Obser-
    ver, no.522 (10 Aug.1960):1-2. il.
    "Revelation at Camp Chesterfield,"
    Tomorrow 8 (autumn 1960):52.
    Long John Nebel, The Way Out World
    (N.Y.: Lancer, 1961 ed.), pp.153-54.
    James Crenshaw, "Fraud Is Where You
    Find It," Fate 15 (Apr.1962):51,
    55-56.
    Allen Spraggett, The Unexplained
    (N.Y.: Signet, 1968 ed.), pp.96-100.
    Don Worley, "23 Mediums...All in a
    Row," Fate 25 (May 1972):80-84. il.
    Betty Jean Johnson, "Artists Without
    Brushes," Fate 31 (May 1978):48-51.

Chesterton
-UFO (?)
1977, Aug.12/=slime mold
    Allan Hendry, "A Physical Trace Doth
    Not a CEII Make," Int'l UFO Report-
    er 2 (Sep.1977):4.
    "Case Wrap-Ups: The Galena & Chester-
    ton Fungus Rings," Int'l UFO Report-
    er 3 (Mar.1978):Newsfront sec.

-UFO (DD)
  1966, March 8
    Donald E. Keyhoe & Gordon I.R. Lore,
    Jr., UFOs: A New Look (Washington:
    NICAP, 1969), p.46.

Church
-UFO (CE-1)
  1909, Oct.
    Orvil R. Hartle, A Carbon Experiment?
    (LaPorte, Ind.: The Author, 1963).

Clear Creek
-Lightning anomaly
  1926, July 23/S of town
    B.M.V., "A Lightning Stroke Far from
    the Thunderstorm Cloud," Monthly
    Weather Rev. 54 (Aug.1926):344.
-Phantom panther
  1948, Aug.10/Herbert Turner
    Richmond Palladium-Item & Sun-Tele-
    gram, 10 Aug.1948, p.1.

Clifton
-Fall of worms
  1892, Feb.
    New Orleans (La.) Daily Picayune, 4
    Feb.1892.

Clinton
-Anomalous hole in ground
  1953, May 2/Charles Watts
    "Follow Up," Doubt, no.45 (1954):
    285,285.
-UFO (NL)
  1965, Nov.14/Joe Burton
    "Record Year for New UFO Evidence,"
    UFO Inv. 3 (Nov.-Dec.1965):2.

Columbus
-UFO (?)
  1959, July 8
    Richard Hall, ed., The UFO Evidence
    (Washington: NICAP, 1964), p.15.
-UFO (CE-1)
  1968, July 15
    Donald E. Keyhoe & Gordon I.R. Lore,
    Jr., UFOs: A New Look (Washington:
    NICAP, 1969), p.44.

Connorsville
-Phantom panther
  1948, Aug.15/Ernest Mace/Brookville Rd.
    Richmond Palladium-Item & Sun-Tele-
    gram, 17 Aug.1948, p.1.
-UFO (CE-1)
  1966, Oct.6/Jack Lewis
    "The 'UFO Circus' in Indiana," APRO
    Bull. 15 (Nov.-Dec.1966):4.
-UFO (CE-2)
  1966, Oct.5/John St.
    "UAO Landing in Indiana," APRO Bull.
    15 (Nov.-Dec.1966):1,3.
    Jim & Coral Lorenzen, UFOs over the
    Americas (N.Y.: Signet, 1968), pp.
    110-12.
-UFO (CE-3)
  1966, Aug.8?/Gale Johnson/2 mi.E
    Don Worley, "The Incredible UFO Acti-
    vity under Wright-Patterson Air

Force Base Radar," Official UFO 1
    (May 1976):34-35.
-UFO (DD)
  1973, Oct.15/Terry Eversole
    "1973 Reports Correlate," APRO Bull.
    24 (May 1976):1,3.
-UFO (NL)
  1966, Oct.4/John St.
    "UAO Landing in Indiana," APRO Bull.
    15 (Nov.-Dec.1966):1,3.
    Jim & Coral Lorenzen, UFOs over the
    Americas (N.Y.: Signet, 1968), p.
    110.
  1973, Oct.15/Bill Tremper/D & M Dish-
  washer plant
    Don Worley, "UFOs, Occupants and
    Artifacts in Eastern Indiana 1972-
    1973," Official UFO 1 (Jan.1976):
    16,18.
    "1973 Reports Correlate," APRO Bull.
    24 (May 1976):1,3.

Covington
-UFO (CE-2)
  1957, Oct.15/Robert Moudy
    Kevin Randle, "The Truth about the
    1957 UFO Flap," Official UFO 2
    (Mar.1977):24,25, quoting AP re-
    lease, 4 Nov.1957.

Crane
-Biorhythm research
  1975/Jacob M. Sanheim/Naval Ammunition
  Depot
    (Editorial), Fate 29 (Jan.1976):18-
    22.
-Phantom panther
  1948, Aug.10/Andrew Street/Naval Ammunition Depot
    Richmond Palladium-Item & Sun-Tele-
    gram, 12 Aug.1948, p.1.

Crawfordsville
-UFO (CE-1)
  1891, Sep.4-5/G.W. Switzer
    Brooklyn (N.Y.) Eagle, 10 Sep.1891.
    Vincent Gaddis, "Indiana's Sky Mon-
    ster," Doubt, no.14 (spring 1946):
    209-10.
    Vincent H. Gaddis, Mysterious Fires
    and Lights (N.Y.: Dell, 1968 ed.),
    pp.34-35.
-UFO (NL)
  1947, July 3/Kenneth Stanford
    Indianapolis Star, 8 July 1947.
  1961, Sep.13
    Richard Hall, ed., The UFO Evidence
    (Washington: NICAP, 1964), p.151.

Dale
-UFO (CE-2)
  1964, June 14/Charles Engelbrecht/2 mi.
  N
    "Physical Evidence Landing Reports,"
    UFO Inv. 2 (July-Aug.1964):4,6.
    "Saucer Landing in Indiana," Saucer
    News 2 (Dec.1964):23.

Danville
-Haunt

1850s-
  Vicki L. O'Dell, "The Haunted Bridge,"
  Indiana History Bull. 41 (1965):54.
-UFO (NL)
  1973, Oct.15
    Chicago (Ill.) Today, 16 Oct.1973.

Darlington
-UFO (?)
  1958, Aug.28
    Richard Hall, ed., The UFO Evidence
    (Washington: NICAP, 1964), p.15.

Decatur
-Fall of frogs
  1937, Sep.25
    "Falls of Frogs," Fortean Soc'y Mag.,
    no.3 (Jan.1940):7, quoting Indiana-
    polis Star, 26 Sep.1937, p.1.

DeKalb co.
-UFO (CE-2)
  1973, Oct.18
    Indianapolis Star, 23 Oct.1973.

Delphi
-UFO (NL)
  1952, July 12/Jack A. Green
    Donald E. Keyhoe, Flying Saucers from
    Outer Space (N.Y.: Holt, 1953), p.
    55.

Deputy
-Contactee
  1967-1975
    Don Worley, "Rachel Baker and Her
    Little Friends," Official UFO 1
    (Feb.1976):14-15,41-44.
-UFO (CE-2) and Men-in-black
  1966, Nov./Chicken Foot Rd.
  1967, Dec.8/Chicken Foot Rd.
    Don Worley, "Rachel Baker and Her
    Little Friends," Official UFO 1
    (Feb.1976):14-15,41-44.

Dogtown
-Humanoid
  1955, Aug.14/Mrs. Darwin Johnson/Ohio
  R.
    Evansville Press, 15 Aug.1955, p.1.
    Isabel Davis & Ted Bloecher, Close
    Encounter at Kelly and Others of
    1955 (Evanston: Center for UFO
    Studies, 1978), pp.181-82.

Dublin
-Haunt
  1937-   /Cry Woman Bridge
    Don Worley, "They Call It 'Cry Woman
    Bridge,'" Probe the Unknown 4 (Mar.
    1976):40-42. il.

Dugger
-UFO (?)
  1957, Nov.6
    Richard Hall, ed., The UFO Evidence
    (Washington: NICAP, 1964), p.98.

Eaton
-UFO (NL)
  1973, Oct.9

Thibodoux (La.) Daily Comet, 10 Oct.
    1973.

Elkhart
-UFO (CE-1)
  1974, Oct.20/County Rd.4
    George D. Fawcett, "The 'Unreported'
    UFO Wave of 1974," Saga UFO Rept.
    2 (spring 1975):50,76.
-UFO (NL)
  1897, April 11
    Chicago (Ill.) Times-Herald, 13 Apr.
    1897.

Elwood
-UFO (NL)
  1957, Aug.7
    "Flying Saucer Roundup," Fate 11
    (Feb.1958):29,32.

Etna Green
-UFO (CE-2)
  1973, Oct./Denny Baker
    Peter Guttilla, "Monster Menagerie,"
    Saga UFO Rept. 4 (Sep.1977):32,34.

Evansville
-Archeological site
  1400-1600/Angel Mounds
    Glenn A. Black, "Trait Complexes at
    the Angel Site," Proc.Indiana Acad.
    Sci. 51 (1942):34-43.
    Glenn A. Black, "Angel Site, Vander-
    burgh County, Indiana," Prehistoric
    Rsch.Ser., vol.2, no.5 (Dec.1944).
    il.
    Paul Squires, "The Angel Mounds of
    Southwestern Indiana," J.Illinois
    Arch.Soc'y 4, no.1 (1946):19-21. il.
    Hilda J. Curry, Negative Painted Pot-
    tery of Angel Mounds Site and Its
    Distribution in the New World (Bal-
    timore: Waverly, 1950). il.
    Glenn A. Black, Angel Site (Indiana-
    polis: Indiana Hist.Soc'y, 1967). il.
    James H. Kellar, An Introduction to
    the Prehistory of Indiana (Indiana-
    polis: Indiana Hist.Soc'y, 1973),
    pp.54-59.
    Franklin Folsom, America's Ancient
    Treasures (N.Y.: Rand McNally,
    1974), pp.136-37.
-Child prodigy
  1958/Billy McLimore
    (Editorial), Fate 12 (May 1959):20.
-Fall of pebbles
  1952, July 30-Aug.8/Louis Chaffin/U.S.
  41 x Old State Rd.
    "Rocks Fly," Doubt, no.38 (1952):162,
    163.
    Alson J. Smith, "The Rocks from No-
    where," Fate 5 (Dec.1952):42-51. il.
-Fall of unknown object
  1969, Oct.8/Marlin S. Adams/708 E. Virginia
    Evansville Press, 13 Oct.1969.
-Fire anomaly
  1961, Oct.19/Mrs. Jack Roll/1160 E.
  Riverside Dr.
    (Editorial), Fate 15 (Feb.1962):8.

-Phantom
  ca.1930/Mrs. Franklin Carter/5th x
  Court St.
    (Editorial), Fate 14 (July 1961):16,
    quoting Evansville Courier (undated).
  1960, Sep.
    Evansville Courier, 3 Oct.1960.
-Phantom airplane
  1956, July 26/Herman C. Wicker/Speaker
  Rd.
    Evansville Courier, 27 July 1956.
-Precognition
  1951, Aug.20/Mariechen Al-An'
    Mariechen Al-An', "Case of the Psy-
    chic Violins," Fate 5 (Apr.-May
    1952):22-24.
  1964, April/Dawson Holland
    Maxine Bell, "We Six Foresaw Our
    Father's Death," Fate 20 (Apr.1967)
    :94,96-97.
-UFO (?)
  1947, July 5?/Frank Hoffman
    Indianapolis Star, 6 July 1947.
-UFO (CE-1)
  1974, May 9/Oscar A. Jordan
    (Letter), Saga UFO Rept. 2 (fall
    1974):78.
  1976, Oct.28/Lee Golden/Emmett St.
    Francis Ridge, "New Close Encounter
    Case from Indiana," MUFON UFO J.,
    no.109 (Dec.1976):13,16.
-UFO (NL)
  1953
    George H. Gallup, Jr. & Tom Reinken,
    "Who Believes in UFOs?" Fate 27
    (Aug.1974):54,57.
  1961, Jan.24/Mariechen Al-An'
    (Letter), Fate 14 (June 1961):109-10.
  1962, Aug.2/Mariechen Al-An'
    (Letter), Fate 15 (Dec.1962):130-32.
  1970, Jan./Mariechen Al-An'/Fifth St.
    (Letter), Fate 24 (Jan.1971):142-43.

Fayette co.
-UFO (CE-1)
  1966, Oct.6
    Don Worley, "The Incredible UFO Acti-
    vity under Wright-Patterson Air
    Force Base Radar," Official UFO 1
    (May 1976):35,59.

Fish Lake
-Humanoid
  1839, summer/Fish L.
    Philadelphia (Pa.) Saturday Courier,
    28 Dec.1839, quoting Michigan City
    Gazette (undated).

Flat Rock
-Giant snake
  1946, July 19/Ray Rush
    "More Monsters," Doubt, no.16 (1946):
    236.

Fort Wayne
-Doubtful identity
  1962, Jan.28/Broadway x Taylor St.
    (Editorial), Fate 15 (Aug.1962):10-
    12.
-Fall of weblike substance

1954, Oct.19
  Leonard H. Stringfield, Inside Saucer Post...3-0 Blue (Cincinnati:
  CRIFO, 1957), p.49.
-Precognition
  1960s/Candy Bosselmann
    Hans Holzer, Ghosts I've Met (N.Y.:
    Ace, 1965 ed.), p.60.
-UFO (NL)
  1973, Oct./Glenbrook Shopping Center
    Don Worley, "UFOs, Occupants and
    Artifacts in Eastern Indiana 1972-
    1973," Official UFO 1 (Jan.1976):
    16,17.
  1975, Oct.5
    "Noteworthy UFO Sightings," Ufology
    2 (spring 1976):42.
-UFO (R)
  1973, Oct.15/Neal Rupert/Baer Field
    "Saucers in the News," Flying Sau-
    cers, winter 1974, pp.44,46.
-UFO (R-V)
  1965, Aug.2/Baer Field
    Columbus (O.) Dispatch, 3 Aug.1965,
    p.1.

Fountain City
-Phantom panther
  1947, fall
    Richmond Palladium-Item & Sun-Tele-
    gram, 12 Aug.1948, p.1.
-Phantom panther and hog killings
  1948, July/Dorten Moore/SE of town
    Richmond Palladium-Item & Sun-Tele-
    gram, 28 July 1948, p.1.

Frankfort
-UFO (DD)
  1957, July/Clarence Greeno
    Gray Barker, "Chasing the Flying Sau-
    cers," Flying Saucers, Feb.1958,
    pp.46,54.

Franklin
-Earthquake anomaly
  1897, April/George White
    Green Bay (Wisc.) Gazette, 3 May
    1897.
-UFO (NL)
  1952, July 28/Lee Sloan
    "Saucer Sightings by IFSB Members,"
    Space Rev. 1 (Oct.1952):10; 2 (Jan.
    1953):10.
    Albert K. Bender, Flying Saucers and
    the Three Men (N.Y.: Paperback Li-
    brary, 1968 ed.), pp.34-35.
  1954, July 23/Robert D. Wolfe
    Donald E. Keyhoe, Flying Saucer Con-
    spiracy (N.Y.: Holt, 1955), p.191.

Franklin co.
-Ancient inscription
    G.W. Homsher, "The Glidwell Mound,
    Franklin County, Indiana," Ann.Rept.
    Smith.Inst., 1882, pp.721-28,732.

Freetown
-UFO (CE-1)
  1967, Jan.17/Francis Bedel, Jr./5 mi.N
  on Hwy.135

Indianapolis News, 18 Jan.1967.
"UFO Caused Car Wreck?" APRO Bull.
15 (Jan.-Feb.1967):1.

Fremont
-UFO (CE-1)
  1966, July 22
    J. Allen Hynek, The UFO Experience
    (Chicago: Regnery, 1972), pp.95-96.

French Lick
-Humanoid
  1965, March/3 mi.S of airport
    Indianapolis News, 15 Mar.1965; and
    17 Mar.1965.

Friendship
-UFO (?)
  1957, Nov.6
    Aimé Michel, Flying Saucers and the
    Straight-Line Mystery (N.Y.: Criter-
    ion, 1958), p.256.

Galveston
-UFO (CE-3)
  1973, Oct./Jim Mays/The Pits
    Don Worley, "The UFO-Related Anthro-
    poids: An Important New Opportunity
    for Investigator-Researchers with
    Courage," in Proc.1976 CUFOS Con-
    ference (Evanston: Center for UFO
    Studies, 1976), pp.287,290-91.
    Don Worley, "The UFO Related Para-
    Anthropoids," Ufology 2 (fall 1976):
    10-12. il.
    Don Worley, "UFO Anthropoids in the
    U.S.A.," Argosy UFO, July 1977.
    Jerome Clark & Loren Coleman, Crea-
    tures of the Outer Edge (N.Y.:
    Warner, 1978), pp.82-84.

Garrett
-UFO (NL)
  1975, Oct.11
    "UFO Central," CUFOS News Bull., 1
    Feb.1976, p.8.

Gary
-Mystery bird deaths
  1974, Aug./Mrs. Pat Williams
    (Editorial), Fate 28 (Feb.1975):22.
-Mystery plane crash
  1970, April 4/Charles L. Upchurch
    Chicago (Ill.) Tribune, 6 Apr.1970.
    Jay Gourley, The Great Lakes Triangle
    (Greenwich, Ct.: Fawcett, 1977), p.
    77.
-UFO (CE-1)
  1972, June 16/Larry Alterwitz/Marquette
  Park
    Glenn McWane & David Graham, The New
    UFO Sightings (N.Y.: Warner, 1974),
    p.42.
-UFO (DD)
  1949, April 28/Leon Faber/E of town
    Kenneth Arnold & Ray Palmer, The Com-
    ing of the Saucers (Boise: The Au-
    thors, 1952), p.141.
-UFO (NL)
  1956, July 14/August Barnett

"Case 173," CRIFO Orbit, 7 Sep.1956,
p.1, quoting Gary Post-Tribune (undated).

Gas City
-UFO (CE-3)
  1897, April 14/John Roush/1 mi.E
    Chicago (Ill.) Chronicle, 15 Apr.
    1897.
    Cincinnati (O.) Enquirer, 15 Apr.
    1897.

Gaynorsville
-UFO (CE-2)
  1972, March 10-11/Donna Nelson/SE of
  town
    "Artifact Found--Disappears," APRO
    Bull. 21 (May-June 1973):1,3.
    Don Worley, "UFOs, Occupants and
    Artifacts in Eastern Indiana 1972-
    1973," Official UFO 1 (Jan.1976):
    16-17. il.

Goshen
-UFO (NL)
  1950, April 27/Robert Adickes
    Chicago (Ill.) Times, 29 Apr.1950.
    Curtis Fuller, "The Flying Saucers:
    Fact or Fiction?" Flying 47 (July
    1950):16-17,60.
    Donald E. Keyhoe, "Flight 117 and
    the Flying Saucer," True, Aug.1950,
    pp.24-25,75.
    Donald E. Keyhoe, Flying Saucers from
    Outer Space (N.Y.: Holt, 1953), pp.
    145-48.

Gosport
-Phantom panther and calf killing
  1948, Aug.10/William Sterwalt
    Jerome Clark & Loren Coleman, Crea-
    tures of the Outer Edge (N.Y.:
    Warner, 1978), p.133.

Greencastle
-UFO (CE-2)
  1957, June 25/George Bennett/Hwy.234
    Leonard H. Stringfield, Inside Sau-
    cer Post...3-0 Blue (Cincinnati:
    CRIFO, 1957), p.55.
    Gray Barker, "Chasing the Flying Sau-
    cers," Flying Saucers, Feb.1958, pp.
    46,52-53, quoting Putnam County
    Graphic (undated).

Greenfield
-UFO (CE-2)
  1978, Nov.8/Cindy Bridges/County Rd.
  525E
    Knightstown Farmweek, 23 Nov.1978.

Greensburg
-Spirit medium
  1854
    Emma Hardinge Britten, Modern Ameri-
    can Spiritualism (N.Y.: The Author,
    1870), p.399.
-UFO (NL)
  1897, April 14
    New York Herald, 15 Apr.1897, p.11.

Greens Fork
-Phantom panther and hog killings
  1948, Aug.25/John Hogatt
    Richmond Palladium-Item & Sun-Tele-
    gram, 26 Aug.1948, p.1.
  1948, Sep.12/Harry Rodenberg
    Richmond Palladium-Item & Sun-Tele-
    gram, 15 Sep.1948, p.1.
-UFO (NL)
  1957, Nov.5
    Kokomo Tribune, 6 Nov.1957.

Greenwood
-UFO (NL)
  1957, Aug.7
    "Flying Saucer Roundup," Fate 11
    (Feb.1958):29,32.

Hagerstown
-Phantom insect
  1899, July 10/William Bridget
    Chicago (Ill.) Tribune, 11 July 1899,
    p.3.

Hamilton
-UFO (NL)
  1975, Oct.30
    "UFO Central," CUFOS News Bull., 1
    Feb.1976, p.10.

Hammond
-Fall of fish
  1956, June 13/Julia Crowe
    "Falls," Doubt, no.53 (1956):417.
-UFO (CE-2)
  1957, Nov.10/Dennis Becky
    Hammond Times, 11 Nov.1957, p.1.
-UFO (NL)
  1975, July 22
    "UFO Central," CUFOS News Bull., 15
    Nov.1975, p.14.

Hartford City
-UFO (CE-3)
  1973, Oct.22/DeWayne Donathan/9 mi.E
  on Hwy.26
    Hartford City News-Times, 23 Oct.1973.
    "Occupants in Indiana," APRO Bull.
    22 (Sep.-Oct.1973):1,3.
    Don Worley, "UFOs, Occupants and Ar-
    tifacts in Eastern Indiana 1972-
    1973," Official UFO 1 (Jan.1976):16,
    45-46.
-UFO (NL)
  1957, Aug.7
    "Flying Saucer Roundup," Fate 11
    (Feb.1958):29,32.

Helmer
-UFO (CE-1)
  1903, March 17/Madge Brosius
    Coral & Jim Lorenzen, UFOs: The Whole
    Story (N.Y.: Signet, 1969), pp.14-
    16.
    Madge Brosius Allyn, "The Flying Cu-
    cumber of 1903," Fate 24 (Mar.1971):
    45-47.

Howard
-Humanoid

1972, Sep.20/Ruby Eastman
  (Editorial), Fate 26 (July 1973):28-
  30.

Huntingburg
-End-of-the-world prophecy
  1965, Jan./Juanita Coomer/Pentecostal
  Church
    Huntingburg Daily Enterprise, 29
    Jan.1965.

Huntington
-Fall of weblike substance
  1972, Oct.9/Francis D. Rittenhouse
    "Floating Strands over Indiana,"
    Skylook, no.60 (Nov.1972):10.
-Phantom panther and hog mutilations
  1962, June/Ed Moorman/Monument City
    Huntington Herald-Press, 27-29 June
    1962.
-River monster
  n.d./Wabash R.
    Charles M. Skinner, Myths and Legends
    of Our Own Land, 2 vols. (Philadel-
    phia: Lippincott, 1896), 2:298.
-UFO (?)
  1947, July 5?/Kenneth Johnson
    Indianapolis Star, 6 July 1947.
-UFO (CE-1)
  1973, Oct.15/Richard Pape
    Columbus (O.) Dispatch, 16 Oct.1973.
    Camden (Ark.) News, 16 Oct.1973, p.2.
  1976, April 4
    "Noteworthy UFO Sightings," Ufology
    2 (fall 1976):60.
-UFO (NL)
  1976, Feb.12
    "Noteworthy UFO Sightings," Ufology
    2 (summer 1976):62.

Indianapolis
-Acoustic anomaly
  1973-1976, winter/Michael J. Eskitch
    (Editorial), Fate 29 (June 1976):20-
    22, quoting Indianapolis Star (un-
    dated).
-Clairempathy
  1963, March 23/Mary Mack
    (Editorial), Fate 16 (Aug.1963):14.
-Clairvoyance
  1943/E.H. Elkins
    L.A. Dale, "Spontaneous Cases," J.
    ASPR 46 (1952):154,157-58.
-Contactee
  1957-
    (Letter), Anon., Saga UFO Rept. 3
    (Apr.1976):4.
-Crisis apparition
  1923, June 11/Gladys Watson
    L.A. Dale, "A Series of Spontaneous
    Cases in the Tradition of Phantasms
    of the Living," J.ASPR 45 (1951):
    85,92-93.
-Erratic crocodilian
  1959, Sep./Fall Creek
    Indianapolis Star, 10 Sep.1959, p.51.
-Mystery television transmission
  1954/Mrs. John Mackey
    (Editorial), Fate 8 (Feb.1955):14.
-Poltergeist

1962, March 11-26/Lina Gemmecke/2910
W. Delaware St.
  Indianapolis Star, 13 Mar.1962, p.1.
  Frank Edwards, "Two Midwest Polter-
  geists," Fate 15 (July 1962):25-32.
  il.
  William G. Roll, The Poltergeist
  (N.Y.: Signet, 1974), pp.51-63.
-Precognition
1960-1964/Clifford Steele
  Hans Holzer, Ghosts I've Met (N.Y.:
  Ace, 1965), pp.60-61.
1962, Aug.7/Mrs. Joseph Ammer
  (Editorial), Fate 15 (Dec.1962):18.
-Spirit medium
1957, Nov./Patricia Kord
  Frank Edwards, Stranger Than Science
  (N.Y.: Ace, 1959 ed.), pp.209-13.
-UFO (?)
1947/Charles Jones
  Janet Bord, "Are Psychic People More
  Likely to See UFOs?" Flying Saucer
  Rev. 18 (May-June 1972):20.
1948, July 29
  Jacques Vallee, Passport to Magonia
  (Chicago: Regnery, 1969), p.192.
1948, Aug.1/Leolin Troutman/=balloon
  Richmond Palladium-Item & Sun-Tele-
  gram, 2 Aug.1948, p.12; and 3 Aug.
  1948, p.2.
1957, Jan.24
  Richard Hall, ed., The UFO Evidence
  (Washington: NICAP, 1964), pp.15,36.
1977, March 10/Ricky Brandenburg/=hoax
  "Indiana Photo Case," APRO Bull. 25
  (Apr.1977):1,5. il.
  Hayden C. Hewes, "The Brandenburg
  UFO Photo--Famous Fake?" Saga UFO
  Rept. 5 (May 1978):36-39. il.
-UFO (CE-1)
1923/A.W. Crandall/U.S.40 x Hwy.100
  Gordon I.R. Lore, Jr. & Harold H. Den-
  eault, Jr., Mysteries of the Skies:
  UFOs in Perspective (Englewood
  Cliffs, N.J.: Prentice-Hall, 1968),
  p.106.
1968, July 16/Peter McNeall/W of town
  Peter McNeall, "Incident at Indiana-
  polis," MUFON UFO J., no.114 (May
  1977):13.
-UFO (CE-2)
1952, Oct.23/John Hobner
  George D. Fawcett, "The Dangers of
  Close UFO Encounters: UFOs Could Be
  Hazardous to Your Health," Official
  UFO 1 (Oct.1975):34,56.
1975, Jan.23
  "From the Center for UFO Studies,"
  Flying Saucer Rev. 21 (Aug.1975):
  32,33.
1978, March 29/I-70 E, nr. Hwy.465
  Charles L. Tucker, "Truckers Engulfed
  by 'UFO' Light," MUFON UFO J., no.
  126 (May 1978):3.
-UFO (DD)
1947, July 1/Kim McKinsey
  Indianapolis Star, 6 July 1947.
1947, July 7/nr. Indiana Girls School
  Indianapolis News, 7 July 1947.
1956, Oct.15/Evelyn Smith

"Case 265," CRIFO Orbit, 4 Jan.1957,
  p.3.
1975, Oct.11
  "UFO Central," CUFOS News Bull., p.3.
-UFO (NL)
1947, July 5/Harry Mossbaugh/Meridian
  x 38th St.
  Indianapolis Star, 6 July 1947.
1947, July 6/Susie Oliver/3725 Grace-
  land Ave.
  Indianapolis Star, 7 July 1947.
1947, July 11/Mrs. Charles Fleitz/2022
  Meridian Ave.
  Indianapolis Star, 12 July 1947.
1952, July 12/Richard Case
  Donald E. Keyhoe, Flying Saucers from
  Outer Space (N.Y.: Holt, 1953),
  pp.55-57.
1957, Sep.23/Edgar Ray
  (Letter), Fate 11 (May 1958):126.
1960, March 23/Earl I. Larsen
  Lloyd Mallan, "The Mysterious 12,"
  Sci.& Mech. 37 (Dec.1966):30,68.
1961, Oct.12/Frank Edwards/WTTV Studio
  "Frequent UFO Operations, Many at
  Night," UFO Inv. 2 (Jan.-Feb.1962):
  5.
  Frank Edwards, "My First UFO," Fate
  15 (Feb.1962):27-31.
1969, Feb.1/Charles Skelton/Guilford
  Ave.
  "Indiana Executive Reports UAO,"
  APRO Bull. 17 (Jan.-Feb.1969):8.

Jasper
-Giant snake
1926, summer
  "More Critters," Doubt, no.18
  (1947):273.

Jasper co.
-UFO (NL)
1915-1917
  Gordon I.R. Lore, Jr. & Harold H. Den-
  eault, Jr., Mysteries of the Skies:
  UFOs in Perspective (Englewood
  Cliffs, N.J.: Prentice-Hall, 1968),
  p.103.

Jeffersonville
-Medieval armor
1799
  Federal Writers' Program, Indiana: A
  Guide to the Hoosier State (N.Y.:
  Oxford Univ., 1941), pp.392-93.

Kent
-UFO (?)
1968, Nov./=hoax
  "Hoax Story Leads to Good Report,"
  APRO Bull. 17 (Nov.-Dec.1968):1,3.

Kentland
-Meteorite crater
1000 m.diam./certain
  Robert S. Dietz, "Meteorite Impact
  Suggested by Orientation of Shatter-
  cones at the Kentland, Indiana, Dis-
  turbance," Science 105 (1947):42-43.
  Ralph B. Baldwin, The Measure of the

Moon (Chicago: Univ. of Chicago, 1963), pp.96-98.
-UFO (NL)
  1975, Nov.15
    "Noteworthy UFO Sightings," Ufology 2 (spring 1976):42.

Kewanna
-UFO (?)
  1944, June 27/=meteor?
    Vincent H. Gaddis, "Visitors from the Void," Amazing Stories 21 (June 1947):159,161.

Kingsford Heights
-UFO (DD)
  1966, April 3/David Heath
    David Heath, "The Kingsford Heights, Indiana, Sighting," Flying Saucers, Oct.1966, pp.16-17. il.

Kirklin
-Precognition
  1956/Mrs. William H. Evans
    (Editorial), Fate 9 (Aug.1956):15.

Knox
-UFO (?)
  ca.1868/Ed W. French
    "More Notes of Charles Fort," Doubt, no.50 (1955):376,377.
-UFO (NL)
  1966, March 29/Harley Hanselman/SE of town
    Cincinnati (O.) Enquirer, 31 Mar. 1966, p.10.

Kokomo
-Fall of oil
  1943, May 25/=tornado
    "Rain of Oil," Fortean Soc'y Mag., no.10 (autumn 1944):143.
-Humanoid
  1973, April 25/Henry McDaniel
  1973, May 6/Henry McDaniel
    Baltimore (Md.) News-American, 7 May 1973.
-Precognition
  1975/Bette Egler/1728 Sussex-on-Berkeley Square
    Warren Smith, "Phenomenal Predictions for 1976," Saga, Jan.1976, pp.16,17.
-UFO (CE-1)
  1950, April 8/Earl Baker
    Kenneth Arnold & Ray Palmer, The Coming of the Saucers (Boise: The Author, 1952), pp.166-67.
    Jacques Vallee, Passport to Magonia (Chicago: Regnery, 1969), p.194.
-UFO (NL)
  1957, Nov.6
    Kokomo Tribune, 7 Nov.1957.
  1964, May 18/Joe Johns
    "Other Recent Sightings," UFO Inv. 2 (July-Aug.1964):7.
  1975, Oct.2
    "Noteworthy UFO Sightings," Ufology 2 (spring 1976):42.
-Windshield pitting
  1952, Sep.20-24/downtown area

Kokomo Tribune, 24 Sep.1952.
  Willard E. Moore, "The Kokomo Mystery," Fate 7 (June 1954):54-57. il.

Lafayette
-Haunt
  1837, spring/3 mi.W
    "More Notes of Charles Fort," Doubt, no.13 (winter 1945):197,199, quoting Religio-Philosophical J., 4 May 1872, p.15.
-UFO (CE-1)
  1961, Dec.21/Jerry Hislope/2 mi.N
    Indianapolis Indiana Journal, 28 Dec.1961.
-UFO (NL)
  1915-1917
    Gordon I.R. Lore, Jr. & Harold H. Deneault, Jr., Mysteries of the Skies: UFOs in Perspective (Englewood Cliffs, N.J.: Prentice-Hall, 1968), p.103.
  1954, Nov.11
    "Saucer's Erratic Behavior and Itinerary Rule Out Balloon," CRIFO Newsl., 3 Dec.1954, p.4.
  1956, Jan.1/Maurice Moody
    Marion Chronicle, 9 Jan.1956.
    "Jets Chase Saucers, Heralding in 1956," CRIFO Orbit, 3 Feb.1956, p.1.
  1958, Oct.26/T.C. Shafer
    Richard Hall, ed., The UFO Evidence (Washington: NICAP, 1964), p.50.

Lagrange
-UFO (CE-3)
  1897, April 11
    Cincinnati (O.) Enquirer, 13 Apr. 1897.

LaPorte
-UFO (?)
  1901, Nov.28/=aurora?
    Cleveland Abbe, "Auroral Light," Monthly Weather Rev. 29 (Nov.1901): 512.
-UFO (CE-1)
  1958, July/5 mi.N
  1958, July/Pine L.
    Orvil R. Hartle, A Carbon Experiment? (LaPorte: The Author, 1963), pp. 147,155.
-UFO (CE-2)
  1954, May
    Richard Hall, ed., The UFO Evidence (Washington: NICAP, 1964), p.74.
  1958, April
    Orvil R. Hartle, A Carbon Experiment? (LaPorte: The Author, 1963), p.148.
-UFO (NL)
  1909, Oct./Ruth Smith
  1952, July
  1961, Sep.30/Dennis Bealor/5 mi.S
    Orvil R. Hartle, A Carbon Experiment? (LaPorte: The Author, 1963), pp. 97,147-48,158.
  1966, March 19
    Fred V. Sacksteder, "Horned UFO Sighted at LaPorte," Flying Saucers, Oct.1966, p.15.

LaPorte co.
-Spirit medium
  1850s/Charles W. Cathcart
    Emma Hardinge Britten, <u>Modern Ameri-
    can Spiritualism</u> (N.Y.: The Author,
    1870), pp.333-45,387-88.

Laurel
-UFO (DD)
  1973, Oct.5
    Don Worley, "UFOs, Occupants and Art-
    ifacts in Eastern Indiana 1972-
    1973," <u>Official UFO</u> 1 (Jan.1976):
    16,17.
-UFO (NL)
  1966, Oct.6/Ray Cox/Hwy.121
    "The 'UFO Circus' in Indiana," <u>APRO
    Bull.</u> 15 (Nov.-Dec.1966):4.
  1973, Oct.11/Joel Burns
    Don Worley, "UFOs, Occupants and Art-
    ifacts in Eastern Indiana 1972-
    1973," <u>Official UFO</u> 1 (Jan.1976):
    16,18.
    "1973 Reports Correlate," <u>APRO Bull.</u>
    24 (May 1976):1.

Lawrence
-UFO (DD)
  1961, Sep.28/John R. Bernstein
    "Red Ball Flies Erratically in Indi-
    ana," <u>APRO Bull.</u> 10 (Mar.1962):6.

Lawrenceburg
-UFO (NL)
  1897, April 16
    <u>Columbus (O.) Evening Press</u>, 17 Apr.
    1897.

Lebanon
-Clairvoyance
  1963/Mrs. Norman Cain
    "Dream of Death," <u>Fate</u> 17 (May 1964):
    89.
-Phantom panther and cattle killings
  1946, Aug./Lulu Brownlee
    "More Monsters," <u>Doubt</u>, no.16 (1946):
    236.
  1946, Sep.4/Roy Graham
    "Land Beasties," <u>Doubt</u>, no.17 (1947):
    260.
-UFO (CE-2)
  1972, Aug.1
    <u>Lebanon Reporter</u>, 1 Aug.1972.
-UFO (NL)
  1956, Oct.18/Mrs. Ed Coupland
    "Case 268," <u>CRIFO Orbit</u>, 4 Jan.1957,
    p.4.

Lena
-Hex
  n.d./Paul Pickett
    Paul Pickett, "The Vindictive Truss,"
    <u>Fate</u> 5 (Jan.1952):22-24.

Lewisburg
-UFO (CE-2)
  1966, March 30/9 mi.N
    Jacques Vallee, <u>Passport to Magonia</u>
    (Chicago: Regnery, 1969), p.325.

Liberty
-Cattle mutilation
  1948, Aug.2
    <u>Richmond Palladium-Item & Sun-Tele-
    gram</u>, 5 Aug.1948, p.1.

Lilly Dale
-Phantom panther
  1961, May
    <u>Bloomington Daily Herald-Telephone</u>,
    31 May 1961.

Lincolnville
-UFO (NL)
  1957, Nov.6/Elizabeth Leach/Hwy.124
    <u>Wabash Plain Dealer</u>, 7 Nov.1957.

Linton
-UFO (NL)
  1973, Oct.15/Hwy.50
    "Saucers in the News," <u>Flying Sau-
    cers</u>, winter 1974, p.58.

Logansport
-UFO (DD)
  1947, July 6/Robert Miller
    <u>Indianapolis News</u>, 7 July 1947.

Lowell
-Phantom panther
  1946, Nov.2
    "Land Beasties," <u>Doubt</u>, no.17 (1947):
    260.
-UFO (NL)
  1978, July 16/Mr. Wheeler
  1978, Aug.3/Don Dowling
    <u>Charlotte (N.C.) Observer</u>, 15 Aug.
    1978.
    "UFOs of Limited Merit," <u>Int'l UFO
    Reporter</u> 3 (Sep.1978):6,8.

Madison co.
-Humanoid
  1977, Aug.10/Melinda Chestnut/County
    Rd.1100N
    <u>Anderson Herald</u>, 11 Aug.1977.

Marion
-Precognition
  1975/Bennie Garrison/Box 14827
    Warren Smith, "Phenomenal Predictions
    for 1975," <u>Saga</u>, Jan.1975, pp.20,23.
    Warren Smith, "Phenomenal Predictions
    for 1976," <u>Saga</u>, Jan.1976, pp.16,18.
-UFO (CE-3)
  1897, April 14
    <u>Cincinnati (O.) Enquirer</u>, 15 Apr.
    1897.
-UFO (NL)
  1957, Nov.6
    <u>Kokomo Tribune</u>, 7 Nov.1957.

Marion co.
-Phantom panther and calf killings
  1970, Feb./Glen McGown
    Jerome Clark & Loren Coleman, "On the
    Trail of Pumas, Panthers and ULAs:
    Part 2," <u>Fate</u> 25 (July 1972):92,100.

Markleville
-UFO (NL)
  1976, June 7
    "Noteworthy UFO Sightings," Ufology
    2 (fall 1976):60.

Martinsville
-UFO (CE-1)
  1957, Nov.10/Louise Wood
    Terre Haute Tribune, 12 Nov.1957.
-UFO (NL)
  1973, Oct.14/Shannon Buskirk
  1973, Oct.15/Robert Williams/NE of
  town
    "Saucers in the News," Flying Sau-
    cers, winter 1974, pp.44,58.

Mecca
-Paleoecology anomaly
    Rainer Zangerl & Eugene S. Richard-
    son, Jr., "The Paleoecological His-
    tory of Two Pennsylvanian Black
    Shales," Fieldiana: Geology Mem.,
    vol.4 (1963). il.
    David Techter, "The Mecca Project:
    Search into the Past," Fate 26
    (Apr.1973):59-70.

Merom
-UFO (CE-2)
  1957, Nov.6/René Gilham
    Sullivan Times, 11 Nov.1957.
    Terre Haute Tribune, 12 Nov.1957.
    Frank Edwards, Flying Saucers: Ser-
    ious Business (N.Y.: Bantam, 1966
    ed.), pp.32-33.

Metamora
-Phantom panther
  1948, Aug./Tom York
  1948, Aug.30/Herb Brewer
    Richmond Palladium-Item & Sun-Tele-
    gram, 1 Sep.1948, p.7.

Metz
-UFO (NL)
  1970, May 11/Ole B. Ritchey
    (Letter), Fate 24 (Feb.1971):159-60.

Michigan City
-Lake monster
  1867, Aug.6/Charles Sanger
    Chicago (Ill.) Tribune, 7 Aug.1867.
-Precognition
  n.d./William C. Eddy
    G.H. Irwin, "The Dream That Cheated
    Death," Fate 1 (fall 1948):22-25.

Middleboro
-Phantom panther
  1948, Aug.9/Robert Martin/1 mi.N
    Richmond Palladium-Item & Sun-Tele-
    gram, 10 Aug.1948, p.1.
  1948, Aug.11/Robert Martin/1 mi.N
    Richmond Palladium-Item & Sun-Tele-
    gram, 12 Aug.1948, p.1.
-Phantom panther tracks
  1948, Aug.12/Robert Martin
    Richmond Palladium-Item & Sun-Tele-
    gram, 13 Aug.1948, p.1.

Middlebury
-UFO (CE-2)
  1966, June 22/Perry Prough
    Goshen News, 24 June 1966. il.

Milan
-UFO (CE-1)
  1967, Jan.19/Reed Tompson
    "'Beanpot' Photo Taken in Indiana,"
    APRO Bull. 15 (Jan.-Feb.1967):1,3.
    il.

Monroe
-Humanoid
  1959, Jan.30/U.S.52
    Ron Schaffner, "Report on Ohio An-
    thropoids and Other Strange Crea-
    tures," in Bigfoot: Tales of Unex-
    plained Creatures (Rome, O.: Page
    Rsch. Library, 1978), pp.40,44.

Monterey
-UFO (NL)
  1952, Aug./John D. Moorman/Tippecanoe
  River
    Orvil R. Hartle, A Carbon Experiment?
    (LaPorte: The Author, 1963), p.151.

Monticello
-UFO (?)
  1953, Aug.2
    Harold T. Wilkins, Flying Saucers on
    the Attack (N.Y.: Ace, 1967 ed.),
    p.262.

Mooresville
-UFO (NL)
  1973, Oct.15
    Chicago (Ill.) Today, 16 Oct.1973.

Muncie
-Animal ESP
  1960s/Charles Johnson
    Rhea A. White, "The Investigation of
    Behavior Suggestive of ESP in Dogs,"
    J.ASPR 58 (1964):250,259.
-UFO (?)
  1897, April 17/=balloon
    Cincinnati (O.) Commercial Tribune,
    19 Apr.1897.
-UFO (CE-3)
  1897, April 21/George Haskell/=hoax?
    Chicago (Ill.) Inter Ocean, 26 Apr.
    1897.
-UFO (DD)
  1952, April 17
    Muncie Star, 18-19 Apr.1952; 21 Apr.
    1952; and 24 Apr.1952.
  1955, Sep./Charles Van Every
    (Letter), Fate 12 (Mar.1959):109.
-UFO (NL)
  1897, April 15/Herman Dalbey
    Danville (Ill.) Weekly Press, 21
    Apr.1897.
  1957, Aug.7
    "Flying Saucer Roundup," Fate 11
    (Feb.1958):29,32.

New Albany
-Phantom image

1891, Dec./Sophia Scharf/E. Fifth x
Spring St.
    Henry Winfred Splitter, "Nature's
    Strange Photographs," Fate 8 (Jan.
    1955):21,23-24.
-Phantom insects
1899, July 10/Martin Whiteman
    Chicago (Ill.) Tribune, 11 July 1899,
    p.3.
-UFO (DD)
1954, Nov.12/Robert E. Miller
    "Saucer's Erratic Behavior and Itin-
    erary Rule Out Balloon," CRIFO
    Newsl., 3 Dec.1954, p.4.
-UFO (NL)
1976, Nov.24
    "UFOs of Limited Merit," Int'l UFO
    Reporter 2 (Jan.1977):5.

New Carlisle
-UFO (NL)
1897, April 11
    Chicago (Ill.) Times-Herald, 13 Apr.
    1897, p.2.

New Castle
-UFO (CE-1)
1957, Nov.5/Mrs. Jasper Barlow/SE of
town
    Goshen News, 6 Nov.1957.
    New Castle News-Republican, 8 Nov.
    1957.

New Richmond
-UFO (CE-2)
1967, Jan.3
    Edward U. Condon, ed., Scientific
    Study of Unidentified Flying Objects
    (N.Y.: Bantam, 1969 ed.), pp.282-85.
    Donald H. Menzel & Ernest H. Taves,
    The UFO Enigma (Garden City: Double-
    day, 1977), p.101.

Noblesville
-Phantom panther
1951, Jan./David Simons/Stoney Creek
    Richmond Palladium-Item, 8 Jan.1951.
-UFO (CE-2)
1959, Aug.30/Nina Ward Hughes/Hwy.37 x
100
    (Letter), Fate 13 (Mar.1960):109-10.

Norristown
-Giant snake
1946, July/George Gearhart
    "More Monsters," Doubt, no,16 (1946):
    236.

North Manchester
-UFO (NL)
1897, April 12
    Cincinnati (O.) Enquirer, 14 Apr.1897.

North Vernon
-Fall of metallic object
1963, May 7/=military experiment?
    Gray Barker, Book of Saucers (Clarks-
    burg, W.V.: Saucerian, 1965), p.45.
-UFO (NL)
1959, July 8/James F. Baker/2 mi.N on

Road 7
    (Editorial), Fate 12 (Nov.1959):10-
    12, quoting Columbus Evening Repub-
    lican (undated).
1973, Sep.26/Duke Koenig/530 S. State
    North Vernon Sun, 29 Sep.1973.

Notre Dame
-Phantom
1975, Sep.18/Patrick Chestnutt/Wash-
ington Hall
    Brad Steiger, Gods of Aquarius (N.Y.:
    Harcourt Brace Jovanovich, 1976), p.
    187.
-Phantom insect
1899, July 11/Hannah Smith
    Chicago (Ill.) Tribune, 12 July
    1899, p.1.

Nyesville
-Anomalous coal
    G.K. Guennel & Richard C. Neavel,
    "Paper Coal in Indiana," Science
    129 (1959):1671-72.

Odon
-Fire anomaly
n.d./William Hackler
    (Advertisement), "This House Had 28
    Mysterious Fires in One Day!"
    Collier's, 19 Apr.1941.

Ogden Dunes
-UFO (NL)
1957, Aug.13/Elfa Levi
    Gary Post-Tribune, 14 Aug.1957.
    Gray Barker, "Chasing the Flying
    Saucers," Flying Saucers, Feb.1958,
    pp.46,54.

Oolitic
-UFO (NL)
1954, Nov.12/limestone quarry
    "Saucer's Erratic Behavior and Itin-
    erary Rule Out Balloon," CRIFO
    Newsl., 3 Dec.1954, p.4.

Osceola
-Poltergeist
1966, Oct.7-13/Walter Szlanfucht/Green-
lawn Ave.
    Chicago (Ill.) Sun-Times, 11 Oct.
    1966.
    Chicago (Ill.) Daily News, 11 Oct.
    1966; and 13-14 Oct.1966.
    Hartford Times, 13 Oct.1966.
    John Justin Smith, "The Messy Polter-
    geist of Osceola, Indiana," Fate 20
    (Mar.1967):43-48. il.

Otwell
-Giant snake
1946, Aug.4/Glennie Craig/2 mi.S
    "More Monsters," Doubt, no.16 (1946):
    236.

Owasco
-UFO (CE-1)
1958, Oct.3/Cecil Bridge
    Frank Edwards, "UFO Buzzes Train,"

Fate 12 (Feb.1959):25-30.

Owensville
-Precognition
ca.1939/public school
(Editorial), Fate 10 (Nov.1957):18.

Paradise
-Phantom panther
1958, Jan.23/Mrs. Walter Brink
Jerome Clark & Loren Coleman, "On the
Trail of Pumas, Panthers, and ULAs:
Part 2," Fate 25 (July 1972):92,94.

Parke co.
-Humanoid
1972, Sep.20
Crawfordville Journal & Review, 21
Sep.1972.

Pennville
-Phantom panther
1948, Aug.11/James Leo
Richmond Palladium-Item & Sun-Tele-
gram, 12 Aug.1948, p.1.

Peppertown
-Phantom panther
1948, Aug.28/Henry Ferguson, Jr.
Richmond Palladium-Item & Sun-Tele-
gram, 29 Aug.1948, p.1; 30 Aug.1948,
p.2; 31 Aug.1948, p.1; and 1 Sep.
1948, p.7.

Peru
-UFO (NL)
1975, Oct.6
"Noteworthy UFO Sightings," Ufology
2 (spring 1976):42.
-Windshield pitting
1952, Sep.24
Willard E. Moore, "The Kokomo Mystery," Fate 7 (June 1954):54,56.

Petersburg
-Giant snake
1913
"More Monsters," Doubt, no.16 (1946):
236.
ca.1921
Winslow Dispatch, 25 Nov.1921.
-UFO (DD)
1956, Nov.30/Charles Malott/S on Hwy.61
"Case 275," CRIFO Orbit, 1 Feb.1957,
p.3.

Plainfield
-UFO (NL)
1973, Oct.15
Chicago (Ill.) Today, 16 Oct.1973.

Plymouth
-UFO (NL)
1966, March 29/Dennis Dreibelbis
Cincinnati (O.) Enquirer, 31 Mar.1966,
p.10.
1975, Jan.16/Olive Carey/710 Mansfield
St.
(Letter), Flying Saucers, June 1975,
p.60.

Portage
-Clairaudience
1970, May 25/Romer Troxell
(Editorial), Fate 23 (Oct.1970):7-
14.

Portland
-UFO (NL)
1897, April 14
Cincinnati (O.) Enquirer, 16 Apr.
1897.
1957, Aug.7
"Flying Saucer Roundup," Fate 11
(Feb.1958):29,32.

Quakertown
-Phantom panther
1948, Aug.2/Clifford Fath/E of town
Richmond Palladium-Item & Sun-Tele-
gram, 3 Aug.1948, p.1; and 5 Aug.
1948, p.1.

Randolph co.
-Archeological site
E.G. Squier & E.H. Davis, Ancient
Monuments of the Mississippi Valley
(Washington: Smithsonian Institution,
Contrib.to Knowl., no.1, 1848), p.
94.

Rensselaer
-Erratic kangaroo
1974, Nov.12/Alfred Hentschel/Charles
St.
Rensselaer Republican, 12 Nov.1974.
1974, Nov.12/Charles James
1974, Nov.12/Bill Babcock, Sr.
Rensselaer Republican, 13 Nov.1974.
-UFO (DD)
1916, May?/8 mi.S
Gordon I.R. Lore, Jr. & Harold H. Den-
eault, Jr., Mysteries of the Skies:
UFOs in Perspective (Englewood
Cliffs, N.J.: Prentice-Hall, 1968),
pp.103-104.

Richmond
-Phantom panther
1948, July/J.R. Williams/Fouts Rd.
Richmond Palladium-Item & Sun-Tele-
gram, 29 July 1948, p.11.
1948, Aug.7/Arthur Turner/Backmeyer Rd.
Richmond Palladium-Item & Sun-Tele-
gram, 8 Aug.1948, p.1; and 10 Aug.
1948, p.1.
1948, Aug.9/Happy Hollow
Richmond Palladium-Item & Sun-Tele-
gram, 10 Aug.1948, p.1.
1948, Aug.10/Barbara Ann Perkins/3 mi.
S on Abington Pike
Richmond Palladium-Item & Sun-Tele-
gram, 11 Aug.1948, p.1.
1948, Aug.11-12/Russell Eggers/sewage
treatment plant
Richmond Palladium-Item & Sun-Tele-
gram, 12 Aug.1948, p.1; and 13 Aug.
1948, p.1.
1948, Aug.25/Martha Grant/1223 Ridge St.
Richmond Palladium-Item & Sun-Tele-
gram, 25 Aug.1948, p.2.

-UFO (?)
1954, May 24/Leo N. Brubaker/=reflection
    Frank Bowers, ed., The True Report on Flying Saucers (Greenwich, Ct.: Fawcett, 1967), pp.20-21. il.
1957, Nov.6
    Richard Hall, ed., The UFO Evidence (Washington: NICAP, 1964), p.166.
-UFO (NL)
1948, July 30/Thomas Bradfield/Chester Pike
    Richmond Palladium-Item & Sun-Telegram, 1 Aug.1948, p.12.
1975, June 19
    "From the Center for UFO Studies," Flying Saucer Rev. 21 (Apr.1976):24, 25.

Rising Sun
-Humanoid
1969, May 19/George Kaiser
    John A. Keel, Strange Creatures from Time and Space (Greenwich, Ct.: Fawcett, 1970), pp.94-95.
1977, April 12-13/Tom Courter
    Cincinnati (O.) Post, 15 Apr.1977.
-Phantom panther
1877, Dec./Mary Crane
    New York Times, 28 Dec.1877, p.2.
-UFO (CE-2)
1969, May 18/Lester Kaiser
    John A. Keel, Strange Creatures from Time and Space (Greenwich, Ct.: Fawcett, 1970), p.94.
-UFO (NL)
1969, May 20/Charles Rolfing
    John A. Keel, Strange Creatures from Time and Space (Greenwich, Ct.: Fawcett, 1970), p.95.

Roachdale
-Humanoid
1972, Aug./Lou Rogers
1972, Aug.14-24
1972, Aug.22/Carter Burdine/chicken killings
    Crawfordsville Journal & Review, 22-24 Aug.1972.
    Indianapolis News, 25 Aug.1972.
    Jerome Clark, "On the Trail of Unidentified Furry Objects," Fate 26 (Aug.1973):56-63.

Rolling Prairie
-UFO (CE-1)
1904, June/Tony Darby/5 mi.N
    Orvil R. Hartle, A Carbon Experiment? (LaPorte: The Author, 1963), p.164.
    Gordon I.R. Lore, Jr. & Harold H. Deneault, Jr., Mysteries of the Skies: UFOs in Perspective (Englewood Cliffs, N.J.: Prentice-Hall, 1968), pp.91-92.

Rush co.
-Fall of metal strips
1968, Oct.
    Don Worley, "The Incredible UFO Activity under Wright-Patterson Air Force Base Radar," Official UFO 1 (May 1976):34,59.

Rushville
-UFO (CE-1)
1966, Aug.1/Donna Glosser
    Jim & Coral Lorenzen, UFOs over the Americas (N.Y.: Signet, 1968), pp. 109-10.
-UFO (CE-2)
1966, Oct.5/4 mi.NE
    Don Worley, "The Incredible UFO Activity under Wright-Patterson Air Force Base Radar," Official UFO 1 (May 1976):35.
-UFO (NL)
1966, Oct.8/Ronnie Cameron/Hwy.44
    "The 'UFO Circus' in Indiana," APRO Bull. 15 (Nov.-Dec.1966):4.

Sailor
-Humanoid
1897, April 29/Adam Gardner
    Cleveland (O.) Plain Dealer, 1 May 1897.

Seymour
-Clairvoyance
1890, March-June/Jesse Streitt
    "Trance Phenomena of Jesse Streitt," J.ASPR 12 (1918):684-98.
-Fall of fish
1891, Aug.
    Philadelphia (Pa.) Public Ledger, 8 Aug.1891.
-UFO (CE-1)
1967, Jan.17/Phil Patton
    Indianapolis News, 18 Jan.1967.

Sharpsville
-Humanoid
1971, June-1972/Dale King
    Don Worley, "The UFO-Related Anthropoids: An Important New Opportunity for Investigator-Researchers with Courage," in Proc.1976 CUFOS Conference (Evanston: Center for UFO Studies, 1976), pp.287,289-90.
    Jerome Clark & Loren Coleman, Creatures of the Outer Edge (N.Y.: Warner, 1978), pp.76-81.

Shelby co.
-UFO (NL)
1952, July 28/Charles Longstreet
    Richard Hall, ed., The UFO Evidence (Washington: NICAP, 1964), pp.64, 161, quoting AP release, 28 July 1952.

Shelbyville
-UFO (CE-1)
1957, Aug?
    Gray Barker, "Chasing the Flying Saucers," Flying Saucers, Feb.1958, pp. 46,54-55.

Sheridan
-Erratic kangaroo
1974, Nov.25/Donald Johnson

Wall Street Journal, 11 Dec.1974, p. 1.
-UFO (CE-3)
 1965, Dec.11/Charles Jones
  Janet Bord, "Are Psychic People More
  Likely to See UFOs?" Flying Saucer
  Rev. 18 (May-June 1972):20-28. il.

Shoals
-UFO (?)
 1968, March 3/=rocket re-entry
  Philip J. Klass, UFOs Explained (N.Y.:
  Random House, 1974), pp.10-13.
-UFO (DD)
 1951, Nov.29/Walter E. McBride
  (Letter), Fate 5 (Apr.-May 1952):116.
  Harold T. Wilkins, Flying Saucers on
  the Attack (N.Y.: Ace, 1967 ed.),
  pp.241-42.

Solitude
-UFO (CE-1)
 1974, July 30/Gary McCarty/S on Hwy.69
  "Indiana Couple Reports Close Encounter in Auto," Skylook, no.83 (Oct.
  1974):9.

South Bend
-Clairvoyance
 1914/Mrs. Julius Brown
  Charles A. Streeter, "Murder in the
  First Degree," Fate 20 (May 1967):
  38-47.
-Disappearance
 1890? 1900?, Dec.24/Oliver Lerch/=hoax
  Harold T. Wilkins, "The Vanishing
  Boy of South Bend," in E. Haldeman-
  Julius, ed., Mysterious Disappear-
  ances of Men and Women in the U.S.A.,
  Britain and Europe (Girard, Kan.:
  Haldeman-Julius, 1948), pp.4-5.
  Joseph Rosenberger, "What Happened
  to Oliver Lerch?" Fate 3 (Sep.1950):
  28-31.
  Kevin Randle, "The Disappearance of
  Oliver Lerch," APRO Bull. 25 (Sep.
  1976):1,3-4.
-Fall of fish
 1937, July
  Los Angeles (Cal.) Times, 16 July
  1937.
-UFO (?)
 1947, July 7/Joseph J. Kuritz
  Indianapolis Star, 8 July 1947.
-UFO (NL)
 1912/Alice M. Johnson/2 mi.N
  (Letter), Fate 10 (Aug.1957):115-16.
 1952, July 23/Harold W. Kloth, Jr.
  Richard Hall, ed., The UFO Evidence
  (Washington: NICAP, 1964), pp.21,35,
  161, quoting UP release, 1 Aug.1952.

Stevenson
-Phantom panther
 1958, Jan.27
  Jerome Clark & Loren Coleman, "On the
  Trail of Pumas, Panthers and ULAs:
  Part 2," Fate 25 (July 1972):92,94.

Sullivan
-UFO (CE-4)
 1957, Aug./Peter Hawkins
  (Letter), Saga UFO Rept. 4 (Sep.
  1977):4.
-UFO (NL)
 1957, Nov.6
  Sullivan Times, 11 Nov.1957.

Switzerland co.
-Clairvoyance
 1845, Sep.15
  Robert Dale Owen, Footfalls on the
  Boundary of Another World (Philadelphia: Lippincott, 1860), pp.321-
  24.

Terre Haute
-Fall of lime
 1963, July 4, 14/Riley Parks/1827 S.
 Fourth St.
  (Editorial), Fate 16 (Nov.1963):9-10.
-UFO (CE-1)
 1950s/Irving P. King/E of town
  (Letter), Fate 9 (Aug.1956):118.
-UFO (DD)
 1951, Oct.9/R.L. Messmore/airport
  Terre Haute Star, 10 Oct.1951.
  Edward J. Ruppelt, The Report on Un-
  identified Flying Objects (Garden
  City: Doubleday, 1956), pp.112-13.
  U.S. Air Force, Projects Grudge and
  Blue Book Reports 1-12 (Washington:
  NICAP, 1968), pp.17,48.
  J. Allen Hynek, The Hynek UFO Report
  (N.Y.: Dell, 1977), pp.116-18.
-UFO (NL)
 1953, Feb.1
  Donald E. Keyhoe, Flying Saucers from
  Outer Space (N.Y.: Holt, 1953), p.
  240.

Thorntown
-Humanoid
 1949, July/Charles Jones/nr. Sugar
 Creek
  John Green, Sasquatch: The Apes Among
  Us (Seattle: Hancock House, 1978),
  p.204, quoting Richmond Palladium-
  Item (undated).

Tipton
-UFO (NL)
 1964, May 17/Stella Branham
  "Other Recent Sightings," UFO Inv. 2
  (July-Aug.1964):7.

Treaty
-Fall of toads
 1977, May 31/Martha Walker
  Martha Walker, "A Tale of Two Toad-
  falls," Fate 31 (May 1978):42.

Trevlac
-Fall of glass meteorite
 1940/Leonard Fishel
  Frank C. Cross, "Hypothetical Meteor-
  ites of Sedimentary Origin," Pop.
  Astron. 55 (1947):96-102.

Union Mills
-UFO (CE-1)
    1961, May 3?
        Richard Hall, ed., The UFO Evidence
        (Washington: NICAP, 1964), p.147.

Valparaiso
-UFO (?)
    1966, March 27/John Reschke/U.S.30/=
    balloon
    1966, March 28/Gary Whitledge/SW of
    town/=balloon
        Cincinnati (O.) Enquirer, 31 Mar.
        1966, p.10.
        Columbus (O.) Dispatch, 31 Mar.1966.
-UFO (CE-1)
    1957, Nov./Donald Dodge
        Frank Edwards, Flying Saucers: Ser-
        ious Business (N.Y.: Bantam, 1966
        ed.), p.16.
-UFO (NL)
    1897, April
        Chicago (Ill.) Times-Herald, 15 Apr.
        1897, p.7.

Versailles
-Spirit medium
    ca.1900-1909/Anna Stockinger
        Anna Stockinger, "My Spiritualistic
        Experiences to Date," J.ASPR 10
        (1916):285-308,334-66,400-24,455-83.

Vevay
-UFO (?)
    1869, Aug.7/Charles G. Boerner/=meteor?
        "Meteor Shower during the Eclipse,"
        J.Franklin Inst. 88 (1869):151.

Vincennes
-Erratic crocodilian
    1946, Dec.25/Mariah Creek
        Indianapolis Star, 31 Dec.1946, p.2.
-Fall of quartz
    1899, May 1?
        "Newspaper Fakes," Monthly Weather
        Rev. 27 (Apr.1899):155.
-UFO (NL)
    1897, April 16/M.P. Ghee
        Cincinnati (O.) Enquirer, 17 Apr.
        1897.

Wabash
-Ball lightning
    1891, May 22/L.L. Carpenter
        St. Louis (Mo.) Globe-Democrat, 23
        May 1891.
-Spontaneous human combustion
    1951, May 3/Carl C. Blocker
        Vincent H. Gaddis, Mysterious Fires
        and Lights (N.Y.: Dell, 1968 ed.),
        pp.193-94, quoting Elkhart Truth
        (undated).
-UFO (CE-1)
    1957, Nov.5/James Weesner/8 mi.NE
        Wabash Plain Dealer, 6 Nov.1957.
-UFO (NL)
    1897, April
        Peoria (Ill.) Journal, 15 Apr.1897,
        p.2.

Walkerton
-UFO (DD)
    1947, July 3/Mrs. Eugene Dixon
        Indianapolis Star, 6 July 1947.

Warsaw
-Humanoid tracks
    1977, March/Ron Wise/Hwy.15/=hoax?
        Warsaw Times-Union, 4 Mar.1977.
-UFO (NL)
    1897, April 11
        Moline (Ill.) Dispatch, 12 Apr.1897,
        p.5.

Washington
-UFO (NL)
    1897, April 16
        Columbus (O.) Evening Press, 17 Apr.
        1897.
    1956, July 10
        "Case 172," CRIFO Orbit, 7 Sep.1956,
        p.1, quoting Washington Daily Times
        (undated).

Washington co.
-UFO (CE-1)
    1978, Jan.15
        Leonard H. Stringfield, "The UFO
        Status Quo: Incidents in Kentucky,"
        MUFON UFO J., no.122 (Jan.1978):8-9.

Waterloo
-UFO (CE-3)
    1975, Aug.
        Don Worley, "The UFO-Related Anthro-
        poids: An Important New Opportunity
        for Investigator-Researchers with
        Courage," in Proc.1976 CUFOS Con-
        ference (Evanston: Center for UFO
        Studies, 1976), pp.287,291-92.
        Jerome Clark & Loren Coleman, Crea-
        tures of the Outer Edge (N.Y.:
        Warner, 1978), p.84.

Williamsport
-Phantom army
    n.d./12 mi.N
        Indiana Writers' Program, Indiana: A
        Guide to the Hoosier State (N.Y.:
        Oxford Univ., 1955), pp.121-22.

Willow Branch
-UFO (CE-2)
    1978, Nov.8/Cathy Wilfong/2 mi.S
        Indianapolis News, 15 Nov.1978.
        Indianapolis Star, 16 Nov.1978.
        Knightstown Farmweek, 23 Nov.1978.

Winamac
-UFO (?)
    1897, April 10/Pink Mink Marshes
        Parkersburg (W.V.) Daily State Jour-
        nal, 14 Apr.1897, p.5.

Winchester
-Fall of fish
    1876, March
        New York Times, 17 Mar.1876, p.4.

Windfall
-Fall of charred material
  1966, Sep./Carl Retherford
    St. Louis (Mo.) Post-Dispatch, 25
    Sep.1966.

Winslow
-Giant snake
  ca.1943/Edward Riley/Patoka R.
    "More Monsters," Doubt, no.16 (1946):
    236.
-Humanoid
  1970, Aug.13-14/McCord's Ford/SE of
  town
    Petersburg Press-Dispatch, 13 Aug.
    1970.
    Evansville Press, 15 Aug.1970.

Woodburn
-Animal ESP
  1927, Sep./Frederick W. Schlueter
    Frederick W. Schlueter, "My Grand-
    mother's Crow," Fate 19 (Dec.1966):
    96-100.

Yankeetown
-UFO (DD)
  1964, June 14
    "Saucer Landing in Indiana," Saucer
    News 11 (Dec.1964):23.

        B. Physical Features

Blue Clay Springs
-Humanoid
  1962, Aug./Jack Bowman, Jr.
    John A. Keel, Strange Creatures from
    Time and Space (Greenwich, Ct.:
    Fawcett, 1970), p.106.
    John Green, Sasquatch: The Apes Among
    Us (Seattle: Hancock House, 1978),
    pp.204-205.

Chapman L.
-Lake monster
  1934, Aug.16/H.W. Scott
    Jerome Clark & Loren Coleman, "Ameri-
    ca's Lake Monsters," Beyond Reality,
    no.14 (Mar.-Apr.1975):28,52, quoting
    Indianapolis News (undated).

Clifty Falls
-UFO (NL)
  1961, Jan.14
    "Odds and Ends," APRO Bull. 9 (Jan.
    1961):5.

Elkhorn Falls
-Phantom panther
  1948, Aug.5/Ivan Toney
    Richmond Palladium-Item & Sun-Tele-
    gram, 6 Aug.1948, p.1.

Hollow Block L.
-Lake monster
  1960, Aug./Carl Gearhart
    Cincinnati (O.) Enquirer, 7 Aug.1960.

Kankakee R.
-Archeological site
  Morrow site
    Charles H. Faulkner, "The Morrow
    Site: A Red Ocher Workshop Site in
    the Kankakee Valley, Indiana," Wis-
    consin Arch. 45 (1964):151-56.

Long L.
-Fall of toads
  ca.1927/Martha Walker
    Martha Walker, "A Tale of Two Toad-
    falls," Fate 31 (May 1978):42.

Manitou, L.
-Lake monster
  1838, July/=hoax?
    Logansport Telegraph, 21 July 1838;
    28 July 1838; 11 Aug.1838; 18 Aug.
    1838; 1 Sep.1838; and 15 Sep.1838.
    Logansport Herald, 9 Aug.1838; 16
    Aug.1838; and 30 Aug.1838.
    Albert S. Gatschet, "Water-Monsters
    of the American Aborigines," J.Am.
    Folklore 12 (1899):255-60.
    Donald Smalley, "The Logansport Tele-
    graph and the Monster of the Indi-
    ana Lakes," Indiana Mag.of History
    42 (1946):249-67.

Morse Reservoir
-UFO (NL)
  1973, Oct.18/Herschel Fueston
    "Object over Indiana Reservoir,"
    APRO Bull. 22 (Jan.-Feb.1974):10.

Nowlin Mound
-Archeological site
  Glenn A. Black, "Excavation of the
  Nowlin Mound," Indiana Hist.Bull.
  13 (1936):197-342. il.

Potato Creek
-Giant human skeletons
  1925, Oct./Mr. Vosburg
    Phyla Phillips, "Giants in Ancient
    America," Fate 1 (spring 1948):126-
    27, quoting South Bend Tribune (un-
    dated).

Sand Creek
-Haunts
    Robert W. Montgomery, "Ghost Stories
    from Decatur County," Midwest Folk-
    lore 11 (spring 1961):62-64.
-Phantom panther tracks and hog killing
  1948, Aug.22/Orris Tate
    Richmond Palladium-Item & Sun-Tele-
    gram, 24 Aug.1948, p.1.

Silver Creek
-Phantom panther tracks
  1948, Aug.3
    Richmond Palladium-Item & Sun-Tele-
    gram, 5 Aug.1948, p.1.

White R.
-Giant snake
  1943
    "More Monsters," Doubt, no.16 (1946):

236.

Wolf L.
-UFO (NL)
  1967, Oct.19/Hwy.109
    "UFOs--October--U.S.A.," _APRO Bull._
    16 (Nov.-Dec.1967):8.

Wyandotte Cave
-Archeological site
    H.C. Hovey, "Alabaster Quarries and
    Flint Works in Wyandot Cave, Indi-
    ana," _Am.Antiquarian_ 3 (1880):27-33.
    Franklin Folsom, _America's Ancient_
    Treasures (N.Y.: Rand McNally,
    1974), pp.137-39.

D. Unspecified Localities

-Ancient axes
    Warren K. Moorehead, _Stone Ornaments_
    Used by Indians in the United States
    and Canada (Andover, Mass.: Andover
    Press, 1917).

-Humanoid
  1837
    "More Notes of Charles Fort," _Doubt_,
    no.14 (1946):213,214.

OHIO

A. Populated Places

Academia
-UFO (?)
  1957, Nov.6
    Aimé Michel, <u>Flying Saucers and the
    Straight-Line Mystery</u> (N.Y.: Criter-
    ion, 1958), p.256.

Ada
-Phantom panther
  1977, June/Gary Braun
    Loren Coleman, "Phantom Panther on
    the Prowl," <u>Fate</u> 30 (Nov.1977):62,
    67.

Akron
-Haunt
  1940s/Anne Wolf
    Anne Wolf, "Our Ghost Story," <u>Fate</u> 4
    (Jan.1951):29-35.
  ca.1960/Edith O'Brien
    Hans Holzer, <u>Ghosts I've Met</u> (N.Y.:
    Ace, 1965 ed.), pp.61-62.
-Out-of-body experience
  1970s/Elaine Fortson
    <u>Columbus Dispatch</u>, 20 Jan.1977, p.B1.
-UFO (?)
  1962, March 27
    Frank Edwards, "Mystery Blast over
    Nevada," <u>Fate</u> 15 (Aug.1962):68,73.
-UFO (CE-1)
  1952/Marion Perretta
    (Letter), <u>Fate</u> 5 (Oct.1952):113-14.
  1971, Feb?/J. Earl D. Moore/Massillon
  Rd.
    (Letter), <u>FSR Case Histories</u>, no.15
    (June 1973):11-12.
-UFO (CE-2)
  1968, June 28
  1973, March 7
    Ted Phillips, <u>Physical Traces Associ-
    ated with UFO Sightings</u> (Evanston:
    Center for UFO Studies, 1975), pp.
    56,89.
-UFO (DD)
  1955, Oct.2/Donald J. Karaiskos/Cole
  Ave. x Hammel St.
  1961, July 13
    Richard Hall, ed., <u>The UFO Evidence</u>
    (Washington: NICAP, 1964), pp.70-71,
    95.
-UFO (NL)
  1897, April 15/John W. Hudson/476 E.
  Center St.
    <u>Akron Beacon & Republican</u>, 16 Apr.
    1897.
  1897, April 16/Mrs. Thomas Kyte/509 E.
  Thornton St.
    <u>Akron Beacon & Republican</u>, 17 Apr.
    1897; and 20 Apr.1897.
    <u>Akron Times-Democrat</u>, 21 Apr.1897.
  1897, April 19/Joan Hoagland/N. Howard
  x Lods St.

    <u>Akron Times-Democrat</u>, 21 Apr.1897.
  1925, July 14/Alfred M. Slagle
    Jerome Clark & Lucius Farish, "UFOs
    of the Roaring '20s," <u>Saga UFO Rept.</u>
    2 (fall 1975):48,60.
  1947, July 4/Forrest Shaver/824 Crest-
  view Ave.
    <u>Columbus Dispatch</u>, 5 July 1947.
  1955, Aug.22/George Popowitch
    "Case 99," <u>CRIFO Orbit</u>, 2 Sep.1955,
    p.3.
  1958, Sep.29/airport
    "The Night of September 29," <u>Fate</u>
    12 (Feb.1959):31,36-37.
  1959. Feb.24
    Richard Hall, ed., <u>The UFO Evidence</u>
    (Washington: NICAP, 1964), p.116.
  1961, July 4-5/Ernest Stadvec
    <u>Cleveland Plain Dealer</u>, 8 July 1961.
    "Ohio Pilot Sees Lights," <u>APRO Bull.</u>
    10 (July 1961):1,3.
  1969, May 16/A.E. Candusso
    "Ohio Editor Sees UFO," <u>Skylook</u>, no.
    21 (Aug.1969):3.
  1975, Nov.11
    "UFO Central," <u>CUFOS News Bull.</u>, 1
    Feb.1976, p.12.

Albany
-UFO (CE-3)
  1973, Oct.16/Mary Geddis
    George M. Eberhart, "The Little
    'Electric' Man," <u>Flying Saucer Rev.</u>
    20 (Mar.1975):10-12. il.

Alliance
-Fall of unknown object
  1971, Nov.4/Roger Cunningham/BBF Drive-
  In Restaurant
    <u>Alliance Review</u>, 5 Nov.1971; and 16
    Nov.1971.
    "A Fall and a Fire in Ohio," <u>INFO J.</u>,
    no.8 (winter-spring 1972):25-26.
-Humanoid
  1977, March/River Rd.
  1977, March 17/Atwater Ave.
    Mark W. Swift & Jum Rastetter, "A Re-
    port on Recent Bigfoot Type Crea-
    tures Seen in Northeastern Ohio," in
    <u>Bigfoot: Tales of Unexplained Crea-
    tures</u> (Rome, O.: Page Rsch.Library,
    1978), pp.24-25.
-UFO (?)
  1897, April 19
    <u>Canton Repository</u>, 20 Apr.1897.
-UFO (CE-1)
  1976, April 13
    "Noteworthy UFO Sightings," <u>Ufology</u>
    2 (fall 1976):60.
-UFO (CE-2)
  1966, April 22/Edward Vojtko/McCallum
  Ave.
    Donald E. Keyhoe & Gordon I.R. Lore,
    Jr., <u>UFOs: A New Look</u> (Washington:

NICAP, 1969), p.8.
-UFO (DD)
    1955, Oct.2/James Ansley, Jr./Harris-
    burg Rd.
        Richard Hall, ed., The UFO Evidence
        (Washington: NICAP, 1964), p.70.
-UFO (NL)
    1955, Oct.21/Walter N. Webb/S. Seneca
    Ave.
        (Letter), Fate 9 (Feb.1956):128-29.

Alma
-Derelict automobile
    1964, Aug.26/U.S.23
        (Editorial), Fate 18 (Jan.1965):12,
        quoting Chillicothe Gazette (undat-
        ed).

Amelia
-UFO (?)
    1977, March 20/=rocket re-entry
        Allan Hendry, "Multiple Witnesses,"
        Int'l UFO Reporter 2 (May 1977):8.

Amherst
-UFO (NL)
    1966, Feb.10/Joseph Wyatt, Jr.
        Otto O. Binder, "'Oddball' Saucers...
        That Fit No Pattern," Fate 21 (Feb.
        1968):54,55.

Arcadia
-Haunt
    1880s/Lake Erie & Western Railroad
        Huron Erie County Reporter, 23 Jan.
        1890.

Ashland
-Aerial phantom
    1890, March 12
        New York Sun, 16 March 1890.
-UFO (NL)
    1897, April 17
    1897, April 19/William McNabb/Orange St.
        Ashland Gazette, 20 Apr.1897.
    1897, April 21
        Ashland Gazette, 23 Apr.1897.

Ashtabula
-Disappearance
    1966, Dec.19/Anthony R. Farinacci/Cess-
    na 172
        Jay Gourley, The Great Lakes Triangle
        (Greenwich, Ct.: Fawcett, 1977), pp.
        30-31,160.
-Psychokinesis
    1948, summer/Barbara Martin
        Barbara Martin, "The Ghostly Dish-
        washer," Fate 4 (July 1951):14.
-Spirit medium
    1851
        Emma Hardinge Britten, Modern Ameri-
        can Spiritualism (N.Y.: The Author,
        1870), pp.392-99.
        Frank Podmore, Modern Spiritualism,
        2 vols. (London: Methuen, 1902),
        1:241-42.
-UFO (NL)
    1966, July 11/L. Erie
        John A. Keel, UFOs: Operation Trojan

Horse (N.Y.: Putnam, 1970), p.155.

Athens
-Archeological site
    1000 B.C.-400 A.D./Wolf Plains
        E.G. Squier & E.H. Davis, Ancient
        Monuments of the Mississippi Valley
        (Washington: Smithsonian Institution,
        Contrib.to Knowl., no.1, 1848), pp.
        64-65.
        E.F. Greenman, "Excavation of the
        Coon Mound and an Analysis of the
        Adena Culture," Ohio Arch.& Hist.
        Soc'y Quar. 41 (1932):369-523.
        James L. Murphy & Larry Picking,
        "Archaeology of The Plains Area,
        Athens County, Ohio," Ohio Arch. 6,
        no.2 (1966):48-57. il.
-Fall of rain from cloudless sky
    1892, Nov.
        H.E. Chapin, "Continuous Rain,"
        Science 21 (1893):94.
-UFO (?)
    1973, Oct.20/Hooper St./=balloon
        Athens Ohio University Post, 22 Oct.
        1973, p.8.
-UFO (CE-1)
    1967, April 3/Mrs. Johnny Clendenin/
    Madison Ave.
        Athens Messenger, 4 Apr.1967.
-UFO (NL)
    1965, July 12/J. Douglas Stewart
        Frank Bowers, ed., The True Report on
        Flying Saucers (Greenwich, Ct.:
        Fawcett, 1967), p.73. il.
    1966, March
        Columbus Dispatch, 3 Apr.1966, p.62A.
    1973, Oct.17-19/Boyd Sinclair
        Athens Ohio University Post, 22 Oct.
        1973, p.8.

Aurora
-Erratic baboon
    1966, Nov.
        Columbus Dispatch, 17 Nov.1966.

Austin
-Ancient iron furnace
    Overly farm
        Arlington H. Mallery, Lost America
        (Washington: Public Affairs, 1950),
        pp.202-203. il.
        William D. Connor, "Ohio's Ancient
        Iron Age," Fate 21 (Oct.1968):84-96.

Austinburg
-Spirit medium
    1850-1853
        Emma Hardinge Britten, Modern Ameri-
        can Spiritualism (N.Y.: The Author,
        1870), pp.392-99.

Avon
-Seance
    1962, Feb./Arthur Ford
        Jess Stearn, The Door to the Future
        (N.Y.: Macfadden, 1964), p.190.

Avon Lake
-UFO (CE-2)

1974, March 20-Oct.12/Jacqueline Booth
Allen Benz, "Did UFOs Effect a Mirac-
ulous Healing? The Avon Lake Inquiry," Official UFO 1 (July 1976):
43,64-66.

Ayersville
-Water anomaly
1975, July 5-10/Clyde Frederick
Nat'l Enquirer, 2 Sep.1975.

Bainbridge
-Archeological site
300 B.C.-500 A.D.
E.G. Squier & E.H. Davis, Ancient
Monuments of the Mississippi Valley
(Washington: Smithsonian Institution,
Contrib.to Knowl., no.1, 1848), pp.
92-93.
-Lake monster
1953/Joe Roush/Slaven's Pond
(Editorial), Fate 7 (Mar.1954):10-11,
quoting Columbus Citizen (undated).

Barberton
-Doubtful responsibility
1927/cat burglar
Bronx (N.Y.) Home News, 25 Sep.1927.
-UFO (?)
1956, Dec.18
Richard Hall, ed., The UFO Evidence
(Washington: NICAP, 1964), p.153.
-UFO (CE-1)
1970, March 20/Leslie Riddell/31st St.
A.E. Candusso, "Huge UFO Hovers,"
Skylook, no.31 (June 1970):4-5.
-UFO (CE-2)
1972, July/Edward Lunguy
Bradford (Pa.) Era, 25 Dec.1978.

Barnesville
-Petroglyph
James L. Swauger, "The Barnesville
Track Rocks Petroglyphs Site, 33 BL
2," Pennsylvania Arch. 44, no.4
(1974):29-41. il.
James Swauger, "The 'Lost' Petroglyph
Rock of the Barnesville Track Rocks
Petroglyph Site, 33 BL 2," Pennsyl-
vania Arch. 48 (1978):53-54.

Batavia
-UFO (DD)
1956, Sep.8/Mrs. Harold Thomas/Hwy.132
"Case 213," CRIFO Orbit, 5 Oct.1956,
p.4.
-UFO (NL)
1897, April 20
Cincinnati Commercial Tribune, 21
Apr.1897.

Bay Village
-Fall of crystalline rock
1964, July 11/Howard W. Morgan, Jr.
Columbus Dispatch, 13 July 1964.
-UFO (CE-1)
1975, July 20
"From the Center for UFO Studies,"
Flying Saucer Rev. 21 (Apr.1976):24.

Beachwood
-Fall of ice
1959, Oct.30
Coral E. Lorenzen, The Shadow of the
Unknown (N.Y.: Signet, 1970), p.120.
-UFO (?)
1958, Jan.5
Richard Hall, ed., The UFO Evidence
(Washington: NICAP, 1964), p.15.

Beallsville
-UFO (CE-2)
1968, March 19/Gregory L. Wells/2 mi.W
"Boy Burned by UAO in Ohio," APRO
Bull. 16 (Mar.-Apr.1968):1,3.
Leonard H. Stringfield, Situation
Red: The UFO Siege (N.Y.: Fawcett
Crest, 1977 ed.), pp.227-28.

Bedford
-Humanoid
1953, Sep./Ed Cashman/Bedford Park
(Editorial), Fate 7 (Jan.1954):11,
quoting Cleveland Press (undated).
-UFO (NL)
1957, July 13
Hayden C. Hewes & William H. Spaulding, "NASA Computer Analyses Prove
UFOs Exist!" Saga UFO Rept. 4 (June
1977):28,33. il.

Bellbrook
-UFO (CE-3)
1977, Sep.27
Ted Bloecher, "A Survey of CE3K Re-
ports for 1977," in 1978 MUFON UFO
Symposium Proc. (Seguin, Tex.:
MUFON, 1978), pp.14,36-37.

Bellefontaine
-UFO (?)
1897, May/=hoax
Bellefontaine Republican, 14 May
1897.
1947, July 9/Eva Mifflin
Columbus Citizen, 10 July 1947.
1948, Dec.3/William H. Reynolds/=flare
"You Asked for It," Doubt, no.24
(1949):363.
(Editorial), Fate 2 (May 1949):2,4-5.
-UFO (DD)
1952, Aug.1
"Busy Disc Views Dayton," CRIFO
Newsl., 7 May 1954, p.2.
U.S. Air Force, Projects Grudge and
Blue Book Reports 1-12 (Washington:
NICAP, 1968), p.32.

Belmont
-Haunt
ca.1900-1956/Woods School
"The Headless Horseman of Belmont,"
Fate 9 (June 1956):39.

Belpre
-UFO (CE-2)
1973, Oct.28
"Possible E-M Case in Ohio," APRO
Bull. 22 (Jan.-Feb.1974):1,4-5.
-UFO (CE-2) and poltergeist

1967
  John A. Keel, The Mothman Prophecies
  (N.Y.: Saturday Review, 1975), pp.
  177-78.

Berlin
-Ancient inscription
  1876, June 14/J.E. Sylvester/=Adena
  John P. MacLean, The Mound Builders
  (Cincinnati: Robert Clarke, 1904),
  pp.110-13. il.
  Franklin Folsom, America's Ancient
  Treasures (N.Y.: Rand McNally,
  1974), p.155. il.

Berlin Heights
-Spirit medium
  1850s-1910/Hudson Tuttle
  Hudson Tuttle, Arcana of Nature
  (Boston: Berry, Colby, 1860).
  Emma Hardinge Britten, Modern Ameri-
  can Spiritualism (N.Y.: The Author,
  1870), p.265.
  James H. Hyslop, "A Case Fifty Years
  Ago," J.ASPR 3 (1909):458-67.
  Hudson Tuttle, Stories from Beyond
  the Borderland (Berlin Heights: The
  Author, 1910).
  Nandor Fodor, Encyclopaedia of Psy-
  chic Science (London: Arthurs,
  1933), p.396.
-UFO (CE-2)
  1977, Aug./Steve Elmer
  Vera L. Perry, "UFO Responds to Torch
  Light," Awareness 6 (autumn 1977):21.

Bethlehem twp.
-Ghost dog
  n.d./Joseph Yerick/Woodside Pet Cemetery
  "Simply an Optical Illusion?" Probe
  the Unknown 3 (Sep.1975):47.
  Raymond Bayless, "Will Your Pet Survive Death?" Probe the Unknown 3
  (Nov.1975):41-42. il.

Bexley
-UFO (CE-1)
  1965, Oct.16
  Columbus Dispatch, 16 Oct.1965.

Blacklick
-UFO (?)
  1973, Oct.16
  Columbus Dispatch, 17 Oct.1973.

Bladensburg
-UFO (NL)
  1952, Sep.12/William Darling
  (Letter), Jack Montgomery, Fate 6
  (Feb.1953):108.

Blendon twp.
-Poltergeist
  1977, Jan.31-Feb./Charles W. Hunsinger/
  3670 Karikal Dr.
  Columbus Dispatch, 24-25 Feb.1977.

Bloomingdale
-Humanoid tracks

1978, Dec./Beverly Fletcher
  Bigfoot-Sasquatch Information Service 3 (Feb.1979):6-7, quoting
  Wheeling (W.V.) News-Republican
  (undated).

Blue Ash
-Poltergeist
  1892, Oct./Jerry Meyers/Hazelwood
  Chicago (Ill.) Tribune, 14 Oct.1892.
-UFO (DD)
  1956, Aug.15/Bill Jones
  "Case 189," CRIFO Orbit, 7 Sep.1956,
  p.4.

Bluffton
-Phantom panther and animal killings
  1977, March 22, 26/Elmer Nesbaum
  1977, April 25-26/Sherwood Burkholder/
  Rockport Rd.
  1977, April 28/Maria Henderson/Bentley
  Rd.
  1977, May 6/Lou Abial/Napoleon Rd.
  1977, May 9/Barbara Price/Hwy.81 x
  Swaney Dr.
  Toledo Blade, 29 Apr.1977; and 21
  May 1977.
  Lima News, 6 May 1977.
  Bluffton News, 5 May 1977; and 19
  May 1977.
  Loren Coleman, "Phantom Panther on
  the Prowl," Fate 30 (Nov.1977):62-
  67.
  "Anatomy of a Panther Wave," Anomaly
  Rsch.Bull., no.8 (spring 1978):14-
  15.
-UFO (NL)
  1897, April 14
  Bluffton News, 22 Apr.1897.

Boardman
-UFO (CE-3)
  1967, July 18/Anthony de Polo/Indian-
  ola Rd.
  Youngstown Vindicator, 20 July 1967.
  John A. Keel, "An Unusual Contact
  Claim from Ohio," Flying Saucer Rev.
  14 (Jan.-Feb.1968):25-26.
  (Letter), Virgil E. Tarlton, Flying
  Saucer Rev. 14 (May-June 1968):22.

Boston
-UFO (CE-2) and cattle killings
  1973, Oct.14/Petersburg Pike
  Fairborn Daily Herald, 15 Oct.1973.

Bowling Green
-Dowsing
  1955/Fred Zurcher
  (Editorial), Fate 8 (Oct.1955):11,
  quoting Toledo Blade (undated).
-Poltergeist
  1958, Oct.-1960/Doug Thornton/Univer-
  sity Apartments
  Harry Nix, "The Case of the Missing
  Macaroni," Fate 24 (Feb.1971):92-95.
-UFO (NL)
  1969, Jan.9/Eldon Nelson/E of town
  "Report from Ohio," APRO Bull. 17
  (Mar.-Apr.1969):8.

Braceville
-UFO (NL)
    1971, Aug.12/Hwy.82
    "Chop Chop," Skylook, no.47 (Oct.
    1971):4, quoting Fort Worth (Tex.)
    Cross Country News, 26 Aug.1971.

Braffetsville
-Phantom panther
    1948, Aug.15/James Waymar/NW of town
    Richmond (Ind.) Palladium-Item &
    Sun-Telegram, 18 Aug.1948, p.1; and
    19 Aug.1948, p.1.

Branch Hill
-Phantom panther
    1972, winter/Epworth Rd.
        Ron Schaffner, "A Report on Ohio An-
        thropoids and Other Strange Crea-
        tures," in Bigfoot: Tales of Unex-
        plained Creatures (Rome, O.: Page
        Rsch.Library, 1978), pp.40,49.
-UFO (CE-3)
    1955, May 25/Robert Hunnicutt/Madeira-
    Loveland Pike x Hopewell Rd.
        Leonard H. Stringfield, Inside Sau-
        cer Post...3-0 Blue (Cincinnati:
        CRIFO, 1957), pp.66-68. il.
        Ted Bloecher, "Occupant Case De-
        tailed," Skylook, no.84 (Nov.1974):
        4-8. il.
        Leonard H. Stringfield, Situation
        Red: The UFO Siege (N.Y.: Fawcett
        Crest, 1977 ed.), pp.111-16.
        Isabel Davis & Ted Bloecher, Close
        Encounter at Kelly and Others of
        1955 (Evanston: Center for UFO
        Studies, 1978), pp.138-48.

Brecksville
-UFO (DD)
    1978, Aug./Thomas J. McCoy/Brecksville
    Reservation
        Columbus Dispatch, 12 Aug.1978, p.A2.

Bridgetown
-UFO (NL)
    1955, Dec.15
        "Green Fireball Soars Low over Cin-
        cinnati," CRIFO Orbit, 6 Jan.1956,
        p.3.

Brimfield twp.
-UFO (NL)
    1977, Nov.13/Tallmadge Rd.
        Ravenna Record-Courier, 22 Nov.1977.

Bucyrus
-Ghost
    ca.1900/Frank Burbank
        James Reynolds, Ghosts in American
        Houses (N.Y.: Paperback Library,
        1967 ed.), pp.30-39.
-Precognition
    1959/Mike Hanzas
        (Editorial), Fate 13 (Sep.1960):22-
        23.
-UFO (?)
    1897, April 21/=kite
        Bucyrus Evening Telegraph, 22 Apr.

1897.

Burbank
-UFO (NL)
    1964, May 17
        "Other Recent Sightings," UFO Inv. 2
        (July-Aug.1964):7.

Butler
-Humanoid
    1978, July 8/Eugene Kline/Hwy.95
        Mansfield News-Journal, 11 July 1978.
    1978, July 12/Hwy.95
        Mansfield News-Journal, 13 July 1978.
-Humanoid tracks
    1978, July 9/Fred Horne
        Mansfield News-Journal, 11 July 1978.
-UFO (NL)
    1978, June 28/Franklin Church Rd.
        Mansfield News-Journal, 29 June 1978.

Butler co.
-Ancient inscription
    1874/inscribed ax/=hoax
        Charles Whittlesey, "Archaeological
        Frauds," Pub.Western Reserve & N.
        Ohio Hist.Soc'y, no.33 (Nov.1876):2.

Caldwell
-UFO (CE-2)
    1971, Sep./ground markings only
        Ted Phillips, Physical Traces Associ-
        ated with UFO Sightings (Evanston:
        Center for UFO Studies, 1975), p.78.

Calla
-UFO (NL)
    1897, April 23/Frank Rogers/6 mi.W
        Norwalk Daily Reflector, 26 Apr.1897.

Cambridge
-UFO (CE-2)
    1951, June/Thomas P. Weyer
        Lucius Farish & Dale Titler, "UFOs:
        Touching Is Believing," Saga UFO
        Rept. 1 (spring 1974):11,68.

Campbell
-Clairaudience
    1952, April-1965, spring/Virginia A.
    Santore/McCartney Rd.
        Virginia Santore, "My Personal Ban-
        shee," Fate 21 (Feb.1968):54,55.

Canal Fulton
-UFO (NL)
    1962, Sep.18/Dave Richey
        Richard Hall, ed., The UFO Evidence
        (Washington: NICAP, 1964), p.62.

Canfield
-UFO (NL)
    1954, May 4
        Donald E. Keyhoe, Flying Saucer Con-
        spiracy (N.Y.: Holt, 1955), p.144.

Canton
-Skyquake
    1927, Nov.10
        Canton Repository, 11 Nov.1927.

1928, Jan.16
   Canton Repository, 16 Jan.1928.
-UFO (CE-2)
   1971/Joan Hall
   (Letter), Fate 27 (July 1974):131-32.
-UFO (DD)
   1953, Jan.11
   Donald E. Keyhoe, Flying Saucers from
   Outer Space (N.Y.: Holt, 1953), p.
   218.
   1955, July 17
   Richard Hall, ed., The UFO Evidence
   (Washington: NICAP, 1964), p.150.
-UFO (NL)
   1973, March 14/Johannos Maas
   Canton Republic, 16 Mar.1973.

Cardington
-Spirit medium
   1850s/Mr. Vinson/=fraud
   Emma Hardinge Britten, Modern American Spiritualism (N.Y.: The Author,
   1870), pp.245-46.

Careytown
-Seance
   1959-1960/Georgia Mae Fields
   Georgia Mae Fields, "Table Up! or How
   to Tilt a Table," Fate 19 (Nov.
   1966):76-81.

Carlisle
-Phantom wolf
   1972, Oct./Ed Miller/NW of town
   Middletown Journal, 30 Oct.1972.
-UFO (NL)
   1960, Nov.23/=meteor?
   Curtis Fuller, "The Nov. 23 UFO,"
   Fate 14 (Mar.1961):46,50-51.

Carroll co.
-UFO (NL)
   1962, Sep.18/James Nelson/Hwy.80
   Richard Hall, ed., The UFO Evidence
   (Washington: NICAP, 1964), p.62.

Casstown
-UFO (CE-1)
   1897, April 14/James McKensie/1 mi.N
   Cincinnati Enquirer, 16 Apr.1897.

Cedarville
-Archeological site
   ca.500 B.C.-400 A.D./Williamson Mound
   E.G. Squier & E.H. Davis, Ancient
   Monuments of the Mississippi Valley
   (Washington: Smithsonian Institution,
   Contrib.to Knowl., no.1, 1848), pp.
   33-34.
   Xenia Daily Gazette, 12 June 1974,
   p.11. il.

Chardon
-Dowsing
   1966
   Dwight Boyer, "Dowser with a Ph.D,"
   Cleveland Plain Dealer Mag., 27 Nov.
   1966, pp.50-52. il.
-UFO (NL)
   1975, Sep.23/Eric Masshart

(Letter), Saga UFO Rept. 3 (June
   1976):6.

Cherry Grove
-UFO (CE-1)
   1975, Nov.20
   Leonard H. Stringfield, Situation
   Red: The UFO Siege (N.Y.: Fawcett
   Crest, 1977 ed.), pp.38-39.

Chesapeake
-Crisis apparition
   1905/Edward Giles
   Lonnie E. Legge, "I Never Heard the
   Train That Killed Me," Fate 12
   (Oct.1959):79-81.

Cheshire
-Flying humanoid
   1966, Nov.17/Hwy.7
   John A. Keel, The Mothman Prophecies
   (N.Y.: Saturday Review, 1975), p.
   64.
-UFO (CE-1)
   1966, Nov.17/Mrs. Roy Grose/Hwy.7
   "Objects Haunt Ohio Area," APRO Bull.
   15 (Nov.-Dec.1966):10.
   John A. Keel, The Mothman Prophecies
   (N.Y.: Saturday Review, 1975), p.
   64.
-UFO (CE-3)
   1966, Dec.8/Charles Hern
   John A. Keel, The Mothman Prophecies
   (N.Y.: Saturday Review, 1975), pp.
   83-84.

Chesterland
-UFO (CE-1)
   1975, Sep.2
   "From the Center for UFO Studies,"
   Flying Saucer Rev. 21 (Apr.1976):25.

Chillicothe
-Archeological sites
   300 B.C.-1500 A.D./Mound City and
   others
   Caleb Atwater, "Description of the
   Antiquities Discovered in the State
   of Ohio and Other Western States,"
   Trans.& Coll.Am.Antiquarian Soc'y 1
   (1820):105,145-51.
   E.G. Squier & E.H. Davis, Ancient
   Monuments of the Mississippi Valley
   (Washington: Smithsonian Institution,
   Contrib.to Knowl., no.1, 1848), pp.
   26-29,34-35,50-51,52-59,61-64,92,
   144-55,158-60,162-66.
   William Pidgeon, Traditions of De-
   coo-dah (N.Y.: Horace Thayer, 1858),
   pp.247-54.
   W.H. Holmes, "Notes upon Some Geo-
   metric Earthworks, with Contour
   Maps," Am.Anthro. 5 (1892):363-73.
   il.
   William C. Mills, "Excavations of the
   Adena Mound," Ohio State Arch.&
   Hist.Soc'y Quar. 10 (1902):452-79.
   William C. Mills, "Explorations of
   the Gartner Mound and Village Site,"
   Ohio State Arch.& Hist.Soc'y Quar.

13 (1904):129-89. il.
William C. Mills, "The Explorations of the Edwin Harness Mound," Ohio State Arch.& Hist.Quar. 16 (1907): 113-93. il.
Henry Clyde Shetrone, The Mound Builders (N.Y.: Appleton, 1930), pp.124-28,188,213-14,255-57.
William S. Webb & Charles E. Snow, The Adena People (Lexington: Univ. of Kentucky Pub.in Anthro.& Arch., no.6, 1945).
Olaf H. Prufer, "The Hopewell Cult," Sci.Am. 211 (Dec.1964):90-102. il.
Franklin Folsom, America's Ancient Treasures (N.Y.: Rand McNally, 1974), pp.152,153-54.
-Phantom panther
1897, May
Cincinnati Enquirer, 9 May 1897.
-UFO (CE-1)
1973, Oct.16/Shirley Johnson
(Editorial), Fate 27 (Feb.1974):30.
1975, Sep.27
"UFO Central," CUFOS News Bull., 15 Nov.1975, p.19.
-UFO (NL)
1966, April 1/Ted Scott
Columbus Dispatch, 2 Apr.1966.
1975, Nov.10
"UFO Central," CUFOS News Bull., 1 Feb.1976, p.12.

Cincinnati
-Ancient ax marks
ca.1800
Thomas Ashe, Travels in America in 1806 (London: William Sargent, 1808), pp.206-207.
Josiah Priest, American Antiquities and Discoveries in the West (Albany: Hoffman & White, 1834), p.125.
-Ancient inscription
1841, Nov./Erasmus Gest/5th x Mound St./ =Adena
E.G. Squier & E.H. Davis, Ancient Monuments of the Mississippi Valley (Washington: Smithsonian Institution, Contrib.to Knowl., no.1, 1848), pp. 274-76. il.
Henry A. & Kate B. Ford, History of Cincinnati, Ohio (Cleveland: L.A. Williams, 1881), pp.14-18.
"Supposed Discovery of the Calendar of the Mound Builders," Pop.Astron. 2 (1895):429.
John P. MacLean, The Mound Builders (Cincinnati: Robert Clarke, 1904), pp.105-10.
-Archeological site
Winthrop Sarjent, "A Drawing of Some Utensils, or Ornaments, Taken from an Old Indian Grave," Trans.Am.Phil. Soc'y 4 (1799):178-80. il.
Josiah Priest, American Antiquities and Discoveries in the West (Albany: Hoffman & White, 1834), pp.137-39.
Alexander Bradford, American Antiquities and Researches into the Origin and History of the Red Race (N.Y.:

Dayton & Saxton, 1841).
Cincinnati Commercial Gazette, 24 Apr.1876, p.3.
William C. Mills, Archaeological Atlas of Ohio (Columbus: F.J. Heer, 1914).
Henry Clyde Shetrone, The Mound-Builders (N.Y.: Appleton, 1930), p. 266.
Gerald Hawkins, Beyond Stonehenge (N.Y.: Harper & Row, 1973), pp.174-75.
-Fall of ice
1963, Dec.27/Earl McCosham
Coral E. Lorenzen, The Shadow of the Unknown (N.Y.: Signet, 1970), p.121.
-Fall of red liquid and men-in-black
1955, July 22/Ed Mootz/440 Boal St.
"The Case of the Deadly Red Rain," CRIFO Orbit, 2 Sep.1955, p.4.
(Editorial), Fate 9 (Jan.1956):10-11.
Leonard H. Stringfield, Inside Saucer Post...3-0 Blue (Cincinnati: CRIFO, 1957), pp.60-61.
Jim Kane, "UFO Kills Tree in Cincinnati," Fate 23 (Nov.1970):72-73. il.
Leonard H. Stringfield, Situation Red: The UFO Siege (N.Y.: Fawcett Crest, 1977 ed.), pp.204-206.
-Fall of weblike substance
1956, Sep.25/Dell Stringfield/=rayon pollutant
"Case 224," CRIFO Orbit, 2 Nov.1956, p.3.
"This Questionable Affair--Angel Hair," CRIFO Orbit, 7 Dec.1956, p.1.
Leonard H. Stringfield, Inside Saucer Post...3-0 Blue (Cincinnati: CRIFO, 1957), pp.51-52.
-Fire anomaly
1976, Nov.17/Preston Sandlin/2534 Liddell St.
Cincinnati Post, 17 Nov.1976, p.21.
-Ghost
1971, March/Virginia Cameron
Hans Holzer, The Witchcraft Report (N.Y.: Ace, 1973), pp.78-80.
-Humanoid
1959, Jan.30/Ohio R.
Cincinnati Post & Times Star, 30 Jan.-3 Feb.1959.
George Wagner, "Cincinnati's 'What-Was-It' Monster?" Beyond Reality, no.21 (July-Aug.1978):62.
1963/Mrs. Wallace Wright
John Green, The Sasquatch File (Agassiz, B.C.: Cheam, 1973), p.32.
1976, Feb.
Houston (Tex.) Chronicle, 2 Mar.1976.
-Inner development
1960s/James Guthrie
Hans Holzer, The New Pagans (Garden City: Doubleday, 1972), pp.70-72.
1968-1970/Bill Saffin
Hans Holzer, The Witchcraft Report (N.Y.: Ace, 1973), pp.76-78.
-Mystery beam of light
1975, Feb.
Leonard H. Stringfield, Situation Red: The UFO Siege (N.Y.: Fawcett

Crest, 1977 ed.), pp.57-60.
-Paranormal voice recordings and clair-
empathy
1975-1976/Janet Tubbs
Susy Smith, Voices of the Dead? (N.Y.:
Signet, 1977), p.87.
-Phantom
1974, Aug.30
Brad Steiger, Gods of Aquarius (N.Y.:
Harcourt Brace Jovanovich, 1976),
pp.85-86.
-Phantom image
1871, Jan.
New York Times, 18 Jan.1871, p.4.
-Poltergeist
1953, Nov.7-11/Dorothy Regner/1020 W.
8th St.
Guy Archette, "The Bewitched Apart-
ment in Cincinnati," Fate 7 (Sep.
1954):85-88.
-Precognition
1960s/Desiree Steiner
Desiree Steiner, "Precognition: Part
of My Life," Fate 24 (Aug.1971):85-
87.
1970, Jan.8/Mildred Barton
Herbert B. Greenhouse, Premonitions:
A Leap into the Future (N.Y.: War-
ner, 1973 ed.), p.159.
-Psychic photography
1876/Jay J. Hartman
Nandor Fodor, Encyclopaedia of Psychic Science (London: Arthurs,
1933), p.313.
-Psychokinesis
1964, Jan./Joan Strader
Hans Holzer, Ghosts I've Met (N.Y.:
Ace, 1965 ed.), pp.65-66.
-Skyquake
1916, Jan.12
New York Herald, 13 Jan.1916.
1972, Jan.28-31
Don Worley, "Things That Go Bump,"
Fate 25 (Nov.1972):101, quoting Cin-
cinnati Enquirer (undated).
-Spirit medium
1845-1846/Mr. Robinson
Emma Harding Britten, Modern Ameri-
can Spiritualism (N.Y.: The Author,
1870), pp.346-47.
1850s/Mrs. Bushnell
Eliab W. Capron, Modern Spiritualism:
Its Facts and Fanaticisms (Boston:
Bela Marsh, 1855), pp.288-308.
Emma Hardinge Britten, Modern Ameri-
can Spiritualism (N.Y.: The Author,
1870), pp.347-49.
1920s/Madam Bowerman/=trickery
Joseph Dunninger, Houdini's Spirit
World and Dunninger's Psychic Revelations (N.Y.: Tower, 1968 ed.),
pp.154-58.
1920s/Laura A. Pruden/Price Hill
Harry Price, Hereward Carrington &
J. Malcolm Bird, "The Slate-Writing
Mediumship of Mrs. Pruden," J.ASPR
20 (1926):137-44,213-20,352-64.
Charles R. Wild, "The Mediumship of
Mrs. Pruden," J.ASPR 21 (1927):369-
82.

Hereward Carrington, The Story of
Psychic Science (London: Rider,
1930).
Nandor Fodor, Encyclopaedia of Psy-
chic Science (London: Arthurs,
1933), pp.96,309-10.
-Spontaneous human combustion
1976, Nov.16/May Caplinger/1711 Harri-
son Ave.
Cincinnati Post, 17 Nov.1976, p.21.
-UFO (?)
1897, April 15/=hoax
Cincinnati Commercial Tribune, 16
Apr.1897.
1897, April 18/=hoax
Cincinnati Commercial Tribune, 18
Apr.1897.
1953, Oct.14/Joseph Hauck/Mt. Adams
1954, Jan.17/Leonard H. Stringfield
"Missile Pierces Metal Signboard,"
CRIFO Newsl., 7 May 1954, p.1.
1954, Aug.
"'Blue Dart' Phenomena," CRIFO Newsl.,
4 Feb.1955, p.3.
1955, Aug./Cumminsville/=hoax
Cincinnati Post, 27 Aug.1955, p.1.
Leonard H. Stringfield, Situation
Red: The UFO Siege (N.Y.: Fawcett
Crest, 1977 ed.), p.110.
1955, Aug.5/Leonard H. Stringfield/=
meteor
Cincinnati Enquirer, 6 Aug.1955.
Cincinnati Post, 6 Aug.1955.
"Case 97," CRIFO Orbit, 2 Sep.1955,
p.1.
1955, Aug.14/Walter Todd/Lunken Air-
port/=meteor
"Case 99," CRIFO Orbit, 2 Sep.1955,
p.2.
1956, March 20-22/=Venus
Cincinnati Enquirer, 22 Mar.1956.
"Much Ado About Venus," CRIFO Orbit,
6 Apr.1956, pp.3-4.
Leonard H. Stringfield, Inside Sau-
cer Post...3-0 Blue (Cincinnati:
CRIFO, 1957), pp.28-30.
1956, Nov.16/Mrs. Frank Simpson/=meteor?
"Case 252," CRIFO Orbit, 4 Jan.1957,
p.1.
1957, Feb.27
"Case 300," CRIFO Orbit, 1 Mar.1957,
p.4.
1962, May 3/=meteor?
"Green Flash over Cincinnati," APRO
Bull. 12 (July 1963):3, quoting Cincinnati Enquirer (undated).
1973, Oct.16
Leonard H. Stringfield, Situation
Red: The UFO Siege (N.Y.: Fawcett
Crest, 1977 ed.), p.157.
-UFO (CE-1)
1953, summer
"Four Mystery Photos of Hovering Object Reviewed by ATIC--Then Silence!"
CRIFO Newsl., 7 Apr.1954, p.2.
1955, Aug.21/Anderson Ferry
"Ohio's Aerial Tempest," CRIFO Orbit,
2 Sep.1955, p.2.
1955, Sep.3/Frank Flaig/Boomer Rd.
"Metallic Ball Lands in Yard--Departs

on Sound of Voice," CRIFO Orbit, 7 Oct.1955, p.2.

1956, Nov.30
"Case 276," CRIFO Orbit, 1 Feb.1957, pp.3-4.

1967, June 11/Price Hill
Cincinnati Enquirer, 12 June 1967.

1974, Nov.22/Hyde Park School
Len Stringfield, "Youths Report UFO Moving over School," Skylook, no.90 (May 1975):9-10.
Richard Hall, "Recapping and Commenting," Skylook, no.92 (July 1975):20.

-UFO (CE-2)
1954, Oct.23
"The Fort Wayne and Cincinnati Tie-in," CRIFO Newsl., 3 Dec.1954, p.5.

1955, Oct.9
"Case 112," CRIFO Orbit, 2 Dec.1955, p.3.

1956, Sep.27/Northern Hills
"Case 225," CRIFO Orbit, 2 Nov.1956, p.3.

1973, Oct.16/Northside

1975, Jan.4/June Putnam/ground markings only

1975, Nov.19/nr. Lunken Airport
Leonard H. Stringfield, Situation Red: The UFO Siege (N.Y.: Fawcett Crest, 1977 ed.), pp.38,61-62,156.

1976, June 7
"Sighting Reports," CUFOS News Bull., Sep.1976, p.5.

-UFO (CE-3)
1966, Oct.2

1973, Oct.21/Mrs. Heit
Leonard H. Stringfield, Situation Red: The UFO Siege (N.Y.: Fawcett Crest, 1977 ed.), pp.51-55,117-18.

-UFO (DD)
1947, July 3/Ault Park
Cincinnati Post, 3 July 1947.

1947, July 5/Elizabeth Taylor/Walnut Hills
Cincinnati Post, 5-6 July 1947.

1950, July
Richard Hall, ed., The UFO Evidence (Washington: NICAP, 1964), p.45.

1952, Aug.1/Henry Staley/General Electric plant
"G.E. Is Focal Point," CRIFO Newsl., 7 May 1954, p.2.

1955, Aug.29
"The Cincinnati Scene: Still UFO-Infested," CRIFO Orbit, 7 Oct.1955, p.1.

1956, Aug.31/Harry Baston
"Case 206," CRIFO Orbit, 5 Oct.1956, p.3.

1956, Sep.17/Frances Mueller/Young St.
"Case 220," CRIFO Orbit, 2 Nov.1956, p.2.

1960
"Air Guard Chase Reported," UFO Inv. 2 (Jan.-Feb.1963):4.

1974, March 28/Robert Schwier
Robert Schwier, "Official UFO Contest Winner No.2: The Robert Schwier Photo," Official UFO 1 (May 1976): 22-23,51-52. il.

1975, Oct.27
Len Stringfield, "Cincinnati Area Has Variety of Sightings," Skylook, no.98 (Jan.1976):5.

-UFO (NL)
1897, April 29/John Ringer/8th x Walnut St.
Toledo Blade, 30 Apr.1897.

1897, May 4/Louis Domhoff/112 Garfield Pl.
Cincinnati Enquirer, 5 May 1897.

1897, May 8/Mt. Auburn
Canton Repository, 9 May 1897.

1947, June 23/Thomas Nelson
Cincinnati Times-Star, 7 July 1947.

1947, July 1/Audrey Holbrook
Cincinnati Enquirer, 8 July 1947.

1947, July 2/Mike Zavisin/Cincinnati Milling Co.
Cincinnati Post, 7 July 1947.

1947, July 7/Everett Smith/May St.
Cincinnati Times-Star, 7 July 1947.

1954, March 9/John H. Stewart/Paddock Rd.
"Saucer Marginalia," CRIFO Newsl., 7 Apr.1954, p.4.
"Missile Pierces Metal Signboard," CRIFO Newsl., 7 May 1954, p.1.

1954, May 5/Herbert Clark/Strathmore Dr.

1954, May 5/Leonard H. Stringfield
"U.F.O. and Jet Activity over Cincinnati Area, May 5, 1954," CRIFO Newsl., 4 June 1954, p.5.

1954, June 23/David Platz
"C-7," CRIFO Newsl., 6 Aug.1954, p.5.

1954, Nov.12/Robert Ward
"Saucer's Erratic Behavior and Itinerary Rule Out Balloon," CRIFO Newsl., 3 Dec.1954, p.4.

1955, Jan.21/Carew Tower
Harold T. Wilkins, Flying Saucers Uncensored (N.Y.: Pyramid, 1967 ed.), p.262.

1955, May 24
"Saucer Sundries," CRIFO Newsl., 3 June 1955, p.6.

1955, July 29/Madison Place
"The Question of Interplanetary War," CRIFO Orbit, 2 Sep.1955, p.1.

1955, Aug.6
"Case 98," CRIFO Orbit, 2 Sep.1955, p.2.

1955, Aug.18/Dell Stringfield
"Ohio's Aerial Tempest," CRIFO Orbit, 2 Sep.1955, p.2.

1955, Sep.23/Mrs. Kenneth Martin/Mt. Washington
"The Cincinnati Scene: Still UFO-Infested," CRIFO Orbit, 7 Oct.1955, p.1.

1955, Oct./James Denning/Lunken Airport
Cincinnati Times-Star, 20 Oct.1955.

1956, Jan.2/Charles Deininger
"Jets Chase Saucers, Heralding in 1956," CRIFO Orbit, 3 Feb.1956, p.1.

1956, March
(Editorial), Fate 9 (July 1956):16-17.

1956, June 17/Ed Tasset
"Case 169," CRIFO Orbit, 3 Aug.1956,

p.2.
1956, Aug.30
"Case 205," CRIFO Orbit, 5 Oct.1956,
p.3.
1956, Sep.8
"Case 214," CRIFO Orbit, 5 Oct.1956,
p.4.
1956, Oct.14/Harry Baston
"Case 242," CRIFO Orbit, 7 Dec.1956,
p.3.
1957, Jan.24/Bob Pope/Spring Grove
"Case 298," CRIFO Orbit, 1 Mar.1957,
pp.3-4.
1957, Nov.3
Richard Hall, ed., The UFO Evidence
(Washington: NICAP, 1964), p.164.
1960, Nov.23/Escal Bennett/Abbe Observatory
Curtis Fuller, "The Nov.23 UFO,"
Fate 14 (Mar.1961):46,49-50.
1960, Dec.16/Dorothy Lefler
"Odds and Ends," APRO Bull. 9 (Jan.
1961):5,6.
1961, Aug.30
Curtis Fuller, "The Boys Who 'Caught'
a Flying Saucer," Fate 15 (Jan.1962)
:36,40.
1962, May 25/Mt. Washington
"Noises, Lights over Cincinnati,"
APRO Bull. 10 (May 1962):6.
1973, Oct.15
Cincinnati Post, 16 Oct.1973.
1975, Oct.6
"UFO Central," CUFOS News Bull., 1
Feb.1976, p.8.
1975, Oct.22
Len Stringfield, "Cincinnati Area
Has Variety of Flying Sightings," Sky-
look, no.98 (Jan.1976):5.
1975, Oct.27/Westwood
Leonard H. Stringfield, Situation
Red: The UFO Siege (N.Y.: Fawcett
Crest, 1977 ed.), p.37.
-UFO (R-V)
1955, Aug.23
"S.A.C. Jets 'Dogfight' Three UFO's
over Cincinnati," CRIFO Orbit, 2
Sep.1955, p.3.
-Windshield pitting
1954, spring
Harold T. Wilkins, Flying Saucers Un-
censored (N.Y.: Pyramid, 1967 ed.),
p.153.

Circleville
-Archeological site
Caleb Atwater, "Description of the
Antiquities Discovered in the State
of Ohio and Other Western States,"
Trans.& Coll.Am.Antiquarian Soc'y 1
(1820):105,141-45.
William Pidgeon, Traditions of De-
coo-dah (N.Y.: Horace Thayer, 1858),
pp.98-103,241-42.
F.W. Putnam, "Iron from the Ohio
Mounds," Proc.Am.Antiquarian Soc'y,
ser.2, 2 (1883):349-63.
Henry Clyde Shetrone, The Mound-
Builders (N.Y.: Appleton, 1930), pp.
251-53.

-Automatic writing
1850s/M.W. Potter
Emma Hardinge Britten, Modern American Spiritualism (N.Y.: The Author,
1870), p.402.
-UFO (?)
1947, July 4/Sherman Campbell/=balloon
Los Angeles (Cal.) Examiner, 5 July
1947.
Ted Bloecher, Report on the UFO Wave
of 1947 (Washington: NICAP, 1967),
p. I-10.
-UFO (DD)
1948, Feb.1/B. Stevenson
Jacques Vallee, Anatomy of a Phenomenon (N.Y.: Ace, 1965 ed.), p.188.

Clarkson
-UFO (NL)
1958, July 23/Mrs. Gerald Meek
(Editorial), Fate 11 (Dec.1958):21.

Cleveland
-Animal ESP
1959/Caroline Monks
Marjorie MacCreary, "Is Your Dog
Smarter Than You Are?" Fate 13
(Jan.1960):78-83.
Rhea A. White, "The Investigation of
Behavior Suggestive of ESP in Dogs,"
J.ASPR 58 (1964):250,260.
-Archeological site
E.G. Squier & E.H. Davis, Ancient
Monuments of the Mississippi Valley
(Washington: Smithsonian Institution,
Contrib.to Knowl., no.1, 1848), pp.
38-39,40.
-Astrology
1932-1950s/Ohio Astrological Ass'n
G.F. Utter, "The Stars Look Down,"
Fate 9 (Oct.1956):29-43.
-Autoscopy
1958, Dec.
Edward Podolsky, "Have You Seen Your
Double?" Fate 19 (Apr.1966):78-79.
-Clairempathy and healing
1960s-   /Herbert Beyer
W.G. Roll, "Free Verbal Response and
Identi-Kit Tests with a Medium," J.
ASPR 65 (1971):185-91.
-Clairvoyance
1958, May/Mary Ann Kestranek
"Dream That Foiled a Theft," Fate 11
(Dec.1958):56.
-Crisis apparition
ca.1887
"Incidents," J.ASPR 2 (1908):113-17.
-Fall of aluminum
1963, July 25/1734 Ivanhoe Rd.NE
(Editorial), Fate 16 (Nov.1963):12.
-Fall of cast iron
1963, March 6/Mrs. John Maxwell
"Fortean Items," Saucer News 10 (June
1963):23, quoting Cleveland news-
paper, 7 Mar.1963.
(Editorial), Fate 16 (July 1963):12.
-Fall of fish
1950, July 31/William Wallace
"Frogs and Fish," Doubt, no.30
(1950):34.

-Fall of ice
1894, May 17/Euclid Ave.
Francis H. Herrick, "Hailstones at
Cleveland, Ohio," Nature 50 (1894):
173.
-Fall of red rain
ca.1944, May
"Color Falls," Doubt, no.18 (1947):
267.
-Ghost
1919, March 7
"Apparition," J.ASPR 18 (1924):35-36.
-Haunt
1911/John Schell/1115 Leading Ave.
Stuart Palmer, "The Ghost That
Spoiled the Party," Fate 8 (May
1955):101-104.
1957, Nov.-1958, April/Thomas Todd/4207
Mason Ct. SE
(Editorial), Fate 11 (Aug.1958):6.
-Humanoid
1943-1968/Grace Lewis/Riverside Ceme-
tery
John A. Keel, Strange Creatures from
Time and Space (Greenwich, Ct.: Faw-
cett, 1970), p.114.
1968, April 22/William Schwark/Brook-
side Park
Cleveland Plain Dealer, 24 Apr.1968.
1972, Aug./Wayne E. Lewis
Cleveland Plain Dealer, 14 Aug.1972.
-Inner development
1970s/Biosophical Institute/Box 43091
Leslie Shepard, ed., Occultism Update, no.1 (1978):8.
-Lunar cycle and homicide
1958-1970
A.L. Lieber & C.R. Sherin, "Homicides
and the Lunar Cycle," Am.J.Psychia-
try 129 (1972):69-74.
-Mystery bird deaths
1958, Nov./Superior Ave.NE x E. 32d St.
(Editorial), Fate 12 (Feb.1959):10-
11, quoting Cleveland Plain Dealer
(undated).
-Mystery plane crash
1971, Oct.24/Edward S. Rambasek/Cessna
320
Jay Gourley, The Great Lakes Triangle
(Greenwich, Ct.: Fawcett, 1977), pp.
113-14.
-Out-of-body experience
1904/Bessie M. Fouts
Bessie M. Fouts, "My Other Body,"
Fate 8 (Mar.1955):86.
-Phantom
1954/Mildred J. Oates
(Letter), Fate 7 (Sep.1954):118-20.
-Phantom insect
1899, July 10/Mrs. Wealthy Derr
Chicago (Ill.) Tribune, 11 July 1899,
p.3.
-Precognition
1956, April/Julius Dittman/Huron Rd. x
Ontario St.
(Editorial), Fate 9 (Aug.1956):12-13.
-Seance
1920s/=hoax
Joseph Dunninger, Houdini's Spirit
World and Dunninger's Psychic Reve-

lations (N.Y.: Tower, 1968 ed.),
p.62.
1955/Arthur Ford
William H. Leach, "My Sitting with
Arthur Ford," Fate 9 (Jan.1956):37-
42.
-Spirit medium
n.d./Charles E. Watkins
Nandor Fodor, Encyclopaedia of Psychic Science (London: Arthurs,
1933), p.94.
1857/William Hume
Emma Hardinge Britten, Modern American Spiritualism (N.Y.: The Author,
1870), pp.303-306.
-Spontaneous human combustion
1930s
Larry E. Arnold, "Zounds, Holmes!
It's a Case of the Combustible
Corpse !" Pursuit 10 (summer 1977):
75,77-78.
-Telepathy
n.d.
"Telepathic Rescue," Fate 8 (Sep.
1955):31, quoting Cleveland News
(undated).
-UFO (?)
1897, May/Frank Kostering/=hoax
1897, May 5/Jud Wickham/=balloon
Cleveland Plain Dealer, 7 May 1897;
and 9 May 1897.
1952
Harold T. Wilkins, Flying Saucers on
the Attack (N.Y.: Ace, 1967 ed.),
p.144.
1958, April 9
Richard Hall, ed., The UFO Evidence
(Washington: NICAP, 1964), p.15.
1958, Oct.21/L. Erie/=meteor?
"The Night of September 29," Fate 12
(Feb.1959):31,35.
1965, Dec.9
Jerome Clark, "The Greatest Flap Yet?
Part IV," Flying Saucer Rev. 12
(Nov.-Dec.1966):9,11-12.
1969, Jan./L. Erie
John A. Keel, UFOs: Operation Trojan
Horse (N.Y.: Putnam, 1970), p.163.
1971, Nov.5/=satellite re-entry?
"Fireball Sighted in North Ohio,"
Skylook, no.50 (Jan.1972):20.
-UFO (CE-1)
1941, Nov./John Schroeder
"St. Louis Man Reports 1941 UFO,"
Skylook, no.29 (Apr.1970):3.
-UFO (CE-3)
1897, April 14/Joseph Singler/"Sea Wing"
Cincinnati Commercial Tribune, 16
Apr.1897.
Chicago (Ill.) Tribune, 16 Apr.1897,
p.4.
-UFO (DD)
1953, Sep.7/Don P. Hollister
1955, Nov.5/Kenneth R. Hoffman/Lee Rd.
x Shaker Blvd.
Richard Hall, ed., The UFO Evidence
(Washington: NICAP, 1964), pp.69-70.
1964, Sep.14, 17/Foundry Equipment Co./
Columbus Rd.
"UFO Sighting Wave Persists," UFO Inv.

2 (Sep.-Oct.1964):5,6.
-UFO (NL)
1897, April 25/Jud Wickham/Willson x
Euclid Ave.
Cleveland Plain Dealer, 29 Apr.1897.
1897, April 28
Cleveland Leader, 29 Apr.1897.
1897, May 4/L.M. Woolwine/Seneca x
Superior St.
Cleveland Plain Dealer, 5-6 May 1897.
1952/CAA tower
Richard Hall, ed., The UFO Evidence
(Washington: NICAP, 1964), p.45,
quoting AP release, 22 July 1952.
1952, April 13/airport/=planet?
Cleveland Press, 18 Apr.1952.
1953, Aug.13/George Popovic
Gray Barker, They Knew Too Much About
Flying Saucers (N.Y.: University,
1956), p.39.
1955, Oct.21/Nat'l Malleable Steel
Bldg.
Tom Comella, "UFO's: Problems in
Perception," Fate 12 (Jan.1959):92-
94.
1957, July 30
"Other 1957 Sightings by Air-Line
Pilots from Project Blue Book Files,"
CUFOS News Bull., summer 1977, p.10.
1958, Aug.12-13/Jason J. Nassau/Case
Tech
"Sighting Round-Up," UFO Inv. 1 (Aug.-
Sep.1958):6.
1959, Jan.27/Robert H. Jamison
"UFO Sightings Rapidly Increase,"
UFO Inv. 1 (Feb.-Mar.1959):5.
1973, Oct.1
Cleveland Plain Dealer, 1 Oct.1973.
-Windshield pitting
1954, April/Robert Cubbedge/Jalovec
Motors
(Editorial), Fate 7 (Aug.1954):8-9.

Cochransville
-UFO (NL)
1897, April 19
Cincinnati Commercial Tribune, 20
Apr.1897.

Columbia Station
-Phantom panther and animal killings
1959, May-June/Iva Witteman/Royalton
Rd.
(Editorial), Fate 12 (Oct.1959):6-8.

Columbus
-Animal ESP
1850s/John Rarey
Wil Hane, "The Man Who Talked to
Horses," Coronet 48 (June 1960):100-
104.
-Archeological sites
Charles Whittlesey, Descriptions of
Ancient Works in Ohio (Washington:
Smithsonian Institution, Contrib.to
Knowl., no.3, 1850), pp.10-11.
James Linn Rogers, "Ancient Earth-
works in Franklin County," in Alfred
E. Lee, History of the City of Co-
lumbus (N.Y.: Munsell, 1892), 1:44-61.

Franklin Folsom, America's Ancient
Treasures (N.Y.: Rand McNally,
1974), p.148.
-Clairempathy
1949, Dec.14/Alice Hill
L.A. Dale, "Spontaneous Cases," J.
ASPR 46 (1952):31,34-35.
-Contactee
1966-1975/Sally Seibert
Columbus Ohio State Lantern, 15 Apr.
1975, p.2.
-Crisis apparition
1921/Hettie Chesney
Hettie Chesney, "She Isn't Dead--We
Saw Her!" Fate 15 (June 1962):32-
35.
-Fall of gummy substance
1951, Sep./Hilltop
San Francisco (Cal.) Examiner, 23
Sep.1951.
-Fall of nuts and bolts
1963, Sep./Charles Morris
Philadelphia (Pa.) Evening Bulletin,
23 Sep.1963.
-Fall of rock
1971, May 2/Kazzie Jude/2495 Deming
Ave.
Columbus Citizen-Journal, 3 May 1971.
-Fall of unknown object
1897, April 24/S.W. Beebe/1096 Frank-
lin Ave.
Columbus Sunday Press, 25 Apr.1897.
-Inner development
1970s/Church of the Satanic Brother-
hood
Columbus Citizen-Journal, 18 Feb.
1974.
-Lunar cycle and insanity
1965/Upham Hall, Ohio State University
Roger Dean Osborn, "The Moon and the
Mental Hospital: An Investigation
of One Area of Folklore," J.Psych-
iatric Nursing & Mental Health Services 6 (1968):88-93.
-Mystery radio transmission
1956, June 22/John D. Kraus/Ohio State
University
John D. Kraus, "Impulsive Radio Signals from the Planet Venus," Nature
178 (1956):33.
John D. Kraus, "Radio Observations
of the Planet Venus at a Wave-length
of 11 m.," Nature 178 (1956):103-
104.
John D. Kraus, "Class II Radio Signals from Venus at a Wave-length of
11 Metres," Nature 178 (1956):159-
60.
Harlan J. Smith, "Non-Thermal Solar
System Sources Other Than Jupiter,"
Astron.J. 64 (1959):41-43.
John D. Kraus, "Apparent Radio Radiation at 11-m. Wave-length from Venus," Nature 186 (1960):462.
-Paranormal strength
1966, July/Carolyn Horn
(Editorial), Fate 20 (Jan.1967):30.
-Phantom panther
1938, April 29
"How to Prevent Panic," Fortean Soc'y

Mag., no.3 (Jan.1940):13.
-Phantom wolf
  1946, Sep.23
    "Land Beasties," _Doubt_, no.17 (1947)
    :260.
-Possession
  1972, Sep./Sherry Zerman
    Steve Erdmann, "Devils, Demons, and
    a Case of Possession," _Beyond Real-
    ity_, no.34 (Nov.-Dec.1978):20-22.
-Precognition
  1903-1907/Marie Shipley
    Marie F. Shipley, "A Record of Dreams
    and Other Coincidental Experiences,"
    Proc.ASPR 2 (1908):454-535.
    Harold Helfer, "The Dreams of Mrs.
    Shipley," _Fate_ 6 (Sep.1953):94-96.
-Seance
  ca.1860
    Emma Hardinge Britten, _Modern Ameri-
    can Spiritualism_ (N.Y.: The Author,
    1870), pp.294-95.
-Skyquake
  1947, Aug.14
    "Booms--No Clues," _Doubt_, no.21
    (1948):317.
  1956, Nov.27
    "Case 274," _CRIFO Orbit_, 1 Feb.1957,
    p.3, quoting _Columbus Dispatch_ (un-
    dated).
-Solar cycle and retardation
  1957/Columbus State School
    Hilda Knobloch & Benjamin Pasamanick,
    "Seasonal Variation in the Births
    of the Mentally Deficient," _Am.J.
    Public Health_ 48 (1958):1201-1208.
-Spirit medium
  1850s/George Walcutt
    Emma Hardinge Britten, _Modern Ameri-
    can Spiritualism_ (N.Y.: The Author,
    1870), pp.258-59,264-65.
  1904
    C.C. Carter, "Circle and Sitting with
    Mrs. R.," _J.ASPR_ 4 (1910):656-61.
  1913-1914/Susannah Harris
    Nandor Fodor, _Encyclopaedia of Psy-
    chic Science_ (London: Arthurs,
    1933), p.158, quoting _Light_ (undat-
    ed).
-Telepathy
  1864, Sep.1/J.P. Mitchell
    C.C. Carter, "Telepathic Experience
    of Mr. J.P. Mitchell," _J.ASPR_ 4
    (1910):674-76.
-UFO (?)
  1897, April 18/Thomas Morris
    Columbus Evening Press, 20 Apr.1897.
  1897, May 10/Ohio Penitentiary/=balloon
    Columbus Evening Press, 11 May 1897.
    Columbus Ohio State Journal, 11 May
    1897.
  1948, March 29
    "Disc Dirt," _Doubt_, no.21 (1948):314,
    316.
  1959, Jan.8/=meteor
    Donald H. Menzel & Lyle G. Boyd, _The
    World of Flying Saucers_ (Garden
    City: Doubleday, 1963), pp.113-14.
  1965, July 12/=balloon
    Columbus Dispatch, 13-14 July 1965.

  1965, Dec.9/=meteor
    Columbus Dispatch, 10 Dec.1965, p.1.
  1975, Feb.16-17
    Columbus Dispatch, 18 Feb.1975.
-UFO (CE-2)
  1973, Oct.14/Jesse Dunnigan/Hall Rd.
    Columbus Dispatch, 16 Oct.1973.
-UFO (DD)
  1947, July 7/Charles Williams/Ohio
  State University
    Columbus Dispatch, 8 July 1947.
  1948, Aug.
    Donald H. Menzel, _Flying Saucers_
    (Cambridge: Harvard Univ., 1953),
    pp.39-40.
  1949, July 31/David Boye
    Kenneth Arnold & Ray Palmer, _The Com-
    ing of the Saucers_ (Boise: The Au-
    thors, 1952), pp.143-44.
  1951, Dec.22
    U.S. Air Force, _Projects Grudge and
    Blue Book Reports 1-12_ (Washington:
    NICAP, 1968), pp.62,70-71.
  1952, March 12
    (Editorial), _Fate_ 5 (Sep.1952):7.
  1953, July 9/North American Aviation
  plant
  1953, Aug.23
  1953, Sep.24
    Richard Hall, ed., _The UFO Evidence_
    (Washington: NICAP, 1964), p.65.
  1956, Sep.28
    "Case 226," _CRIFO Orbit_, 2 Nov.1956,
    p.3, quoting _Columbus Dispatch_ (un-
    dated).
  1957, Aug.2/Fred Gage/Bethel x Postel-
  waite Rd.
    "Saucers in the News," _Flying Sau-
    cers_, Feb.1958, pp.70,72-73.
  1965, Sep.27
    Columbus Citizen-Journal, 28 Sep.
    1965.
  1973, Nov.3/Mervin Roland/nr. Appleton
  VOR
    Columbus Citizen-Journal, 6 Nov.1973.
-UFO (NL)
  1897, April 26/Samuel W. Six/227 W.
  Broad St.
    Columbus Evening Press, 27 Apr.1897.
  1947, July 2/E. Ascher/W on Hwy.79
  1947, July 4/William Pfeiffer/Franklin
  Park
    Columbus Citizen, 6 July 1947.
    Columbus Dispatch, 6 July 1947.
  1947, July 5/Edward Blackwell
    Columbus Citizen, 7 July 1947.
  1948, Jan.7/Jack Pickering/Lockbourne
  (Rickenbacker) AFB
    Donald H. Menzel, _Flying Saucers_
    (Cambridge: Harvard Univ., 1953),
    pp.20-21.
    "New Information on the Mantell Case,"
    APRO Bull. 25 (June 1977):8; (July
    1977):5-8.
  1953, Aug.14
    Columbus Ohio State Journal, 15 Aug.
    1953.
  1954, June 23/Harry L. Roe, Jr./W of
  town
    "C-6," _CRIFO Newsl._, 6 Aug.1954, p.5.

1955, Aug.5
"Case 97," CRIFO Orbit, 2 Sep.1955,
p.1.
1955, Aug.14
"Case 99," CRIFO Orbit, 2 Sep.1955,
p.2.
1958, April 2
Richard Hall, ed., The UFO Evidence
(Washington: NICAP, 1964), p.147.
1960, fall/Godown Rd.
Personal investigation.
1965, Aug.3/Charles Ridgeway/5595 Al-
kire Rd.
WTVN-TV news broadcast, 3 Aug.1965.
1966, March 20/Stelzer Rd.
1966, March 29/Edna Glass/373 Kelso Rd.
Columbus Dispatch, 30 Mar.1966.
1966, March 31/Virginia Clark/1702 Manchester Ave.
Columbus Dispatch, 1 Apr.1966, p.12.
1966, April 20/Michele Conrad/2970
Parkside Rd.
Columbus Citizen-Journal, 21 Apr.1966.
1966, Aug.3/Nathan Waller/1073 Franklin Ave.
Personal investigation.
1968, Jan.23
"New Close-Ups, Pacings," UFO Inv. 4
(Mar.1968):1,3.
1973, Oct.14-15/Scott Luzzak/2088 Lon-
don-Groveport Rd.
1973, Oct.15/Ken Chamberlain, Jr./Dem-
orest Rd. x Sullivant Ave.
Columbus Dispatch, 15-16 Oct.1973.
1973, Oct.19/Lillian Hatfield/Refugee
x Noe-Bixby Rd.
Columbus Dispatch, 20 Oct.1973, p.2.
1977, Aug.6/nr. Port Columbus
"UFOs of Limited Merit," Int'l UFO
Reporter 2 (Sep.1977):8.
-UFO (R-V)
1954, June 26/Fred Mowery
"C-9," CRIFO Newsl., 6 Aug.1954, p.5.
Donald E. Keyhoe, Flying Saucer Conspiracy (N.Y.: Holt, 1955), pp.168-
69.

Conneaut
-Archeological site and giant human skel-
etons
1000-1654
E.G. Squier & E.H. Davis, Ancient
Monuments of the Mississippi Valley
(Washington: Smithsonian Institution,
Contrib.to Knowl., no.1, 1848), p.
38.
William W. Williams, History of Ash-
tabula County, Ohio (Philadelphia:
Williams Bros., 1878), pp.154-55.
Curtis Dahl, "Mound-Builders, Mormons
and William Cullen Bryant," New Eng-
land Quar. 34 (1961):178-90.

Coolville
-UFO (NL)
1897, April 17
Athens Messenger & Herald, 22 Apr.
1897.

Copley
-UFO (NL)
1963, Sep.17/E.J. Diehl
"Late News Items," NICAP Spec.Rept.,
Nov.1963, p.2.

Cortland
-Inner development
1965-   /Light of the Universe
Maryona, The Light of the Universe I
(Tiffin: Light of the Universe,
1965).
J. Gordon Melton, Encyclopedia of
American Religions, 2 vols. (Wil-
mington, N.C.: Consortium, 1978),
2:120-21.

Coshocton
-Archeological site
Pygmy Cemetery
S.P. Hildreth, "Miscellaneous Observations Made during a Tour in May,
1835, to the Falls of the Cuyahoga,
near Lake Erie," Am.J.Sci., ser.1,
31 (1835):1,69.
William J. Bahmer, Centennial History of Coshocton County, Ohio, 2
vols. (Chicago: S.J. Clarke, 1909),
1:7-27.
Mabel V. Pollock, "Last of the Pyg-
mies," Columbus Dispatch Mag., 8
June 1975, p.37. il.
-UFO (?)
1954, June
Donald E. Keyhoe, Flying Saucer Conspiracy (N.Y.: Holt, 1955), p.164.

Covedale
-UFO (CE-3)
1973, Oct.21
Len Stringfield, "Creature Inside
Shield of Light," Skylook, no.87
(Feb.1975):3-6. il.

Covington
-Mystery television transmission
1961, July 25/Mrs. Fred Coghill/Russell
St.
(Editorial), Fate 14 (Nov.1961):23-
24.

Crestline
-UFO (NL)
1953, Aug.15
Richard Hall, ed., The UFO Evidence
(Washington: NICAP, 1964), p.65.
1972, July 7
Glenn McWane & David Graham, The New
UFO Sightings (N.Y.: Warner, 1974),
p.43, quoting Galion Inquirer (un-
dated).

Cromers
-UFO (CE-1) and Man-in-black
1973, Oct.
Personal investigation.

Crown City
-Phantom house
1953, spring/Luther Suthers

(Editorial), Fate 6 (June 1953):8-9,
quoting Columbus Citizen (undated).

Cutler
-UFO (NL)
1897, April 19/Ed Curtis
Marietta Daily Register, 20 Apr.1897.

Cuyahoga Falls
-UFO (?)
1897, May 5/William J. Rattle
Akron Beacon & Republican, 6 May
1897.
1957, July 17
Richard Hall, ed., The UFO Evidence
(Washington: NICAP, 1964), p.15.
-UFO (DD)
1954, Sep.20/Nick Bolanz
"Case 42," CRIFO Newsl., 7 Jan.1955,
p.6.
-UFO (NL)
1956, July 24/Paul Hanson
"Case 190," CRIFO Orbit, 5 Oct.1956,
p.1.

Darbydale
-UFO (NL)
1973, Oct.19/Ken Chamberlain, Jr./5626
Bellview Dr.
Columbus Dispatch, 20 Oct.1973, p.2.
il.

Darke co.
-UFO (CE-3)
1966/Mr. Miller
Don Worley, "The UFO Related Para-
Anthropoids," Ufology 2 (fall 1976):
10,12.

Dayton
-Archeological sites
E.G. Squier & E.H. Davis, Ancient
Monuments of the Mississippi Valley
(Washington: Smithsonian Institution,
Contrib.to Knowl., no.1, 1848), pp.
23-24,82-83.
Auguste F. Foerste, An Introduction
to the Geology of Dayton and Vicin-
ity (Indianapolis: Hollenbeck, 1915),
pp.37-41,135-48.
-Clairvoyance
1887, Feb.16
"A Dream Coincidence," J.ASPR 9
(1915):523-27.
"Dream Coinciding with External
Facts," J.ASPR 16 (1922):508-12.
1912/Edgar Monroe
Edgar Monroe, "Experiment with Clair-
voyance," Fate 9 (Mar.1956):80-83.
-Fall of green rain
1948, March 26
New York Times, 27 Mar.1948, p.15.
-Ghost
1920, June 20/Thomas Macquithey/354
Forrest Ave.
Raymond J. Ross, "Spirit Bride...Mor-
tal Groom," Fate 9 (Mar.1956):53-55.
-Inner development
1970s/Church of Satanic Brotherhood
Hans Holzer, The Witchcraft Report

(N.Y.: Ace, 1973), pp.157-68.
-Mystery plane crashes
1951
Harold T. Wilkins, Flying Saucers on
the Attack (N.Y.: Ace, 1967 ed.),
p.142.
-Skyquake
1946, Dec.28
"Explosions," Doubt, no.18 (1947):
271.
1950, April
Harold T. Wilkins, Flying Saucers on
the Attack (N.Y.: Ace, 1967 ed.),
pp.266-67.
-UFO (?)
1947, July 7/Ed Miller
Columbus Ohio State Journal, 8 July
1947.
1947, July 13
Richard Hall, ed., The UFO Evidence
(Washington: NICAP, 1964), p.158.
1947, Oct.20
Donald E. Keyhoe, Flying Saucers: Top
Secret (N.Y.: Putnam, 1960), p.89.
1952, Aug.23-24
Don Berliner, "The Ground Observers
Corps," Official UFO 1 (Aug.1976):
24,51.
1954/Richard T. Headrick
Richard Hall, ed., The UFO Evidence
(Washington: NICAP, 1964), p.25.
1957, Nov.20/=Venus
Jacques & Janine Vallee, Challenge
to Science (N.Y.: Ace, 1966 ed.),
p.132.
1968, March 3/=rocket re-entry
Philip J. Klass, UFOs Explained (N.Y.:
Random House, 1974), pp.11-13.
-UFO (CE-1)
1956, Sep.2/Dayton Country Club
Jacques Vallee, Anatomy of a Phenom-
enon (N.Y.: Ace, 1965 ed.), p.190.
-UFO (CE-2)
1975, May 6/E of Wright-Patterson AFB
Leonard H. Stringfield, Situation
Red: The UFO Siege (N.Y.: Fawcett
Crest, 1977 ed.), pp.173-74.
-UFO (DD)
1951, Feb.14/J.E. Cocker/Wright Field
"Wright Field Reports on 'Saucer,'"
Fate 4 (Aug.-Sep.1951):16.
1954, May 12/Mrs. Donald McDonald
"Incident 3: Disc Hovers over Dayton,
Ohio," CRIFO Newsl., 4 June 1954,
p.2.
1954, May 24
Edward J. Ruppelt, The Report on Un-
identified Flying Objects (Garden
City: Doubleday, 1956), pp.239-40.
1957, Sep.5/Mrs. Dewey Forrest/Hwy.55
(Letter), W.S. Mowery, Flying Saucers,
Feb.1958, p.65.
-UFO (NL)
1951, June 1
Richard Hall, ed., The UFO Evidence
(Washington: NICAP, 1964), p.23.
1954, June/Mrs. Donald McDonald
"C-8," CRIFO Newsl., 6 Aug.1954, p.5.
1954, July 9
Harold T. Wilkins, Flying Saucers Un-

censored (N.Y.: Pyramid, 1967 ed.),
pp.87-88.
1966, March 27/Richard Landversicht/
Wright-Patterson AFB
Columbus Dispatch, 13 Oct.1966.
1970, Jan.1/Ronn Sokol
"New Year Comes in with a Swish!"
Skylook, no.31 (June 1970):4.
1971, July 11/Leon Turner
Wendelle C. Stevens, "UFOs: Seeing
Is Believing," Saga UFO Rept. 2
(fall 1974):48,50. il.
1973, Oct.12/John Gedder
Columbus Dispatch, 13 Oct.1973.
1975, July 29
"UFO Central," CUFOS News Bull., 15
Nov.1975, p.15.
1975, Dec.10
"UFO Central," CUFOS News Bull., 1
Feb.1976, p.14.
-UFO (R-V)
1950, March 8/W.H. Kerr/airport
Edward J. Ruppelt, The Report on Un-
identified Flying Objects (Garden
City: Doubleday, 1956), pp.72-75.
Donald H. Menzel & Lyle G. Boyd, The
World of Flying Saucers (Garden
City: Doubleday, 1963), pp.70-72.
1952, Aug.1/James B. Smith/Wright-Pat-
terson AFB/=balloon?
Hartford (Ct.) Courant, 2 Aug.1952.
"Busy Disc Views Dayton," CRIFO
Newsl., 7 May 1954, p.2.
Edward J. Ruppelt, The Report on Un-
identified Flying Objects (Garden
City: Doubleday, 1956), pp.229-32.
Gordon D. Thayer, "Optical and Radar
Analyses of Field Cases," in Edward
U. Condon, ed., Scientific Study of
Unidentified Flying Objects (N.Y.:
Bantam, 1969 ed.), pp.115,161-63.
-UFOs (captured)
1952/Wright-Patterson AFB
1955/Wright-Patterson AFB
1957/Wright-Patterson AFB
1973/Wright-Patterson AFB
Leonard H. Stringfield, "Retrievals
of the Third Kind," in 1978 MUFON
UFO Symposium Proc. (Seguin, Tex.:
MUFON, 1978), pp.77,82-84,90-91,94-
95,98-100,101.
Leonard H. Stringfield, "Retrievals
of the Third Kind: Part 2," MUFON
UFO J., no.129 (Aug.1978):8,11,12-
14.

Defiance
-Humanoid
1972, July-Aug./Norfolk & Western RR/
=hoax?
Toledo Blade, 2 Aug.1972; and 9-10
Aug.1972.
(Editorial), Fate 26 (July 1973):30-
31.
-Men-in-black
1967, July 11-17/Robert Easley
"'Man in Black' Case in Ohio," Saucer
News 14 (fall 1967):12-13.
-UFO (CE-2)
ca.1963

Charles A. Maney, "Scientific Meas-
urement of UFO's," Fate 18 (June
1965):31,32-34.
-UFO (DD)
1964, Aug.11/John Dodson/nr. General
Motors plant
Jim & Coral Lorenzen, UFOs over the
Americas (N.Y.: Signet, 1968), pp.
103-104.
-UFO (NL)
1962, May 20/Charles A. Maney
Defiance Crescent-News, 21 May 1962;
and 2 June 1962.

Defiance co.
-Humanoid
1972, July
Columbus Dispatch, 9 Aug.1972, p.1.

Delaware
-UFO (DD)
1948, April 8
Frank Scully, Behind the Flying Saucers (N.Y.: Holt, 1950), p.193.
Harold T. Wilkins, Flying Saucers on
the Attack (N.Y.: Ace, 1967 ed.),
p.92.
-UFO (NL)
1947, July 4/Carl Thompson
Columbus Citizen, 5-6 July 1947.
1973, Oct.16/Dean Arnold/Curve Rd.
Columbus Dispatch, 17 Oct.1973.

Dellroy
-UFO (CE-2)
1965, June 28/Joseph Stavano/ground
markings only
Douglas M. Bloomfield, "A New O in
Ohio," Fate 19 (Oct.1966):102-104.
il.
Ted Phillips, Physical Traces Associ-
ated with UFO Sightings (Evanston:
Center for UFO Studies, 1975), p.36.

Dublin
-Ball lightning
1896, Aug./Newton J. Dominy/4 mi.SW
W.J. Humphreys, "Ball Lightning,"
Proc.Am.Phil.Soc'y 76 (1936):613-26.
-Humanoid
1973, Oct.
Ron Schaffner, "A Report on Ohio An-
thropoids and Other Strange Crea-
tures," in Bigfoot: Tales of Unex-
plained Creatures (Rome, O.: Page
Rsch.Library, 1978), pp.40,43.
-UFO (?)
1952, Aug.18
Don Berliner, "The Ground Observers
Corps," Official UFO 1 (Aug.1976):
24,51.

Duncan Falls
-UFO (CE-1)
1966, Oct./Leonard Elmore
John A. Keel, "From My Ohio Valley
Note Book," Flying Saucer Rev. 13
(May-June 1967):3.
John A. Keel, The Mothman Prophecies
(N.Y.: Saturday Review, 1975), pp.

148-49.

Dunkirk
-UFO (?)
1897, April 15/=star?
Kenton News-Republican, 16 Apr.1897.
-UFO (NL)
1897, April 15/Willis Mahon
Kenton News-Republican, 16 Apr.1897.

Dupont
-UFO (CE-2)
1897, April 24/airship message
Cincinnati Commercial Tribune, 25
Apr.1897.

East Liberty
-UFO (DD)
1947, July 9/James A. Rhoades
Columbus Citizen, 10 July 1947.

East Liverpool
-Fall of radium vial
1962, June
(Editorial), Fate 16 (Jan.1963):12.
-UFO (?)
1952, July 29/Paul C. Figley
(Letter), Fate 8 (Dec.1955):116.
-UFO (CE-2)
1966, Aug.19/Chris Ward
East Liverpool Review, 19 Aug.1966.
Youngstown Vindicator, 20 Aug.1966.

East Palestine
-UFO (NL)
1966, April 17/Wayne Huston
Columbus Dispatch, 18 Apr.1966, p.1.

Eaton
-Archeological site
6 mi.SE on Twin Creek
E.G. Squier & E.H. Davis, Ancient
Monuments of the Mississippi Valley
(Washington: Smithsonian Institution,
Contrib.to Knowl., no.1, 1848), p.
33.
H.Z. Williams, History of Preble
County, Ohio (Cleveland: W.W. Wil-
liams, 1881), pp.16-17.
Jon Douglas Singer, "Stone Forts of
the Midwest and the Appalachian Re-
gion: Are They Clues to the Enigma
of Mystery Hill?" NEARA J. 13 (win-
ter 1979):63-66.
-Humanoid
1977, May 18/Old Camden Pike
Eaton Register-Herald, 25 May 1977.
Ron Schaffner, "A Report on Ohio An-
thropoids and Other Strange Crea-
tures," in Bigfoot: Tales of Unexplained Creatures (Rome, O.: Page
Rsch.Library, 1978), pp.40,43-45.
il.
-UFO (CE-2)
1970, April 2/Verla Fonseca/Maple Grove
Rd.
"First the UFO, Then the Train Wreck,"
Skylook, no.37 (Dec.1970):7.
-UFO (NL)
1970, Oct.4/Verla Fonseca/Maple Grove

Rd.
"First the UFO, Then the Train Wreck,"
Skylook, no.37 (Dec.1970):7-8.

Elmore
-Haunt
1960s
Richard Gill, "The Headless Motor-
cyclist," J.Ohio Folklore Soc'y,
n.s., 1 (Dec.1972):46-48.
-UFO (NL)
1964, June 12/Richard Crawford/Hwy.51
x Nissen Rd.
Jacques & Janine Vallee, Challenge
to Science (N.Y.: Ace, 1966 ed.),
p.59.

Elyria
-UFO (?)
1965, Dec.9/=meteor
Columbus Dispatch, 10 Dec.1965, p.1.
Ivan T. Sanderson, "'Something' Landed in Pennsylvania," Fate 19 (Mar.
1966):33-35.
-UFO (NL)
1897, April 22/E.H. Hinman
Toledo Blade, 23 Apr.1897.
1958, April 8/L. Erie
Ivan T. Sanderson, Invisible Residents (N.Y.: World, 1970), pp.194-
95, quoting NICAP Bull., 9 July
1958.
1973, Oct.18/Bob Buckland/Third St.
Elyria Chronicle-Telegram, 19 Oct.
1973.

Enon
-Archeological site
Knob Prairie Mound
C.B. Palmer, "A Puzzle for Future
Archaeologists," Science 21 (1893):
246.
Henry Clyde Shetrone, The Mound-
Builders (N.Y.: Appleton, 1930), p.
267.
David R. Collins, "The Enon Mound,"
Ohio Arch. 3, no.3 (1953):10-12. il.
Franklin Folsom, America's Ancient
Treasures (N.Y.: Rand McNally
1974), p.150.
-UFO (NL)
1966, March 28/Howard E. Hill/2 mi.E
Columbus Dispatch, 29 Mar.1966, p.1.

Euclid
-UFO (NL)
1975, Dec.2
"UFO Central," CUFOS News Bull., 1
Feb.1976, p.14.

Fairborn
-UFO (NL)
1948, July 8
Donald E. Keyhoe, Flying Saucers: Top
Secret (N.Y.: Putnam, 1960), pp.89-
90.
1961, July 8
Jacques Vallee, Anatomy of a Phenomenon (N.Y.: Ace, 1965 ed.), p.219.

Fairfield
-Men-in-black
  1974/Geri Wilhelm
    Berthold Eric Schwarz, "The Man-in-
    Black Syndrome...1," Flying Saucer
    Rev. 23 (Jan.1978):9,13-14.
-UFO (CE-1)
  1975, Oct.23
    Leonard H. Stringfield, Situation
    Red: The UFO Siege (N.Y.: Fawcett
    Crest, 1977 ed.), p.36.
-UFO (CE-3)
  1974, Dec.22/Mrs. Page
    Geri Wilhelm & Leonard Stringfield,
    "UFO-Occupants Close Encounter,"
    Ohio Sky Watcher 2 (Mar.1976):10-11.
    Leonard H. Stringfield, Situation
    Red: The UFO Siege (N.Y.: Fawcett
    Crest, 1977 ed.), pp.120-21.

Fairfield co.
-UFO (CE-1)
  1897, April 15/Byron Rutter
    Lancaster Daily Eagle, 16 Apr.1897.

Fairview Lanes
-UFO (NL)
  1966, Aug.4/Fred Lanke/Ohio Soldiers &
    Sailors Home
    Cleveland Plain Dealer, 5 Aug.1966.

Felicity
-UFO (R-V)
  1966
    Leonard H. Stringfield, Situation
    Red: The UFO Siege (N.Y.: Fawcett
    Crest, 1977 ed.), p.164.

Findlay
-Contactee
  1897, April/Eleanor A. Woodruff/=delu-
    sion?
    Cincinnati Enquirer, 20 Apr.1897.
-Fire anomaly
  1889, Sep./Samuel Miller/6 mi.W
    St. Louis (Mo.) Globe-Democrat, 2
    Oct.1889.
-UFO (NL)
  1888, May 21
    New York Times, 23 May 1888, p.23.
  1969, Jan.9/Harold Lamb/I-75
    Bowling Green Daily Sentinel-Tribune,
    11 Jan.1969.
    "Report from Ohio," APRO Bull. 17
    (Mar.-Apr.1969):8.

Fitchville
-UFO (NL)
  1897, April 23
    Columbus Sunday Press, 25 Apr.1897.

Foraker
-Erratic crocodilian
  1897, March 31-April 2
    Kenton Daily Democrat, 3 Apr.1897.

Forestville
-UFO (NL)
  1955, Aug.17
    "Ohio's Aerial Tempest," CRIFO Orbit,

  2 Sep.1955, p.2.
  1955, Aug.23-24/Herbert Clark
    "S.A.C. Jets 'Dogfight' Three UFO's
    over Cincinnati," CRIFO Orbit, 2
    Sep.1955, p.3.

Fostoria
-Phantom wolf
  1884, Feb.
    Decatur (Ill.) Daily Republican, 6
    Feb.1884, p.4.

Fox
-Archeological site
  ca.500 A.D./Florence Mound
    Gerard Fowke, Archaeological History
    of Ohio (Columbus: F.J. Heer, 1902).
    Pete Fitzer, "Evidence for Horticul-
    ture during Early-Middle Woodland
    Times in the Eastern United States,"
    Pennsylvania Arch. 32, no.1 (1962):
    14-20.

Frankfort
-Archeological site
  300 B.C.-500 A.D.
    E.G. Squier & E.H. Davis, Ancient
    Monuments of the Mississippi Valley
    (Washington: Smithsonian Institution,
    Contrib.to Knowl., no.1, 1848), pp.
    60-61.
-Ancient iron furnace
  Allyn Mound
    Arlington H. Mallery, Lost America
    (Washington: Public Affairs, 1950),
    betw.pp.202-203.
    Clyde E. Keeler & Bennett E. Kelley,
    "Ancient Iron-Smelting Furnaces of
    Ohio," NEARA Newsl. 6 (June 1971):
    28-32.

Frazeysburg
-UFO (DD)
  1921, July
    (Letter), William Montgomery, Fate
    7 (Apr.1954):129.

Fremont
-UFO (NL)
  1947, July 6/Edward Jenck
    Columbus Citizen, 8 July 1947.

Gahanna
-UFO (NL)
  1966, March 30/Michael Davis/122 Green
    Meadows Dr.
    Columbus Dispatch, 1 Apr.1966.
  1973, Oct.19
    Columbus Dispatch, 20 Oct.1973, p.2.

Galion
-Poltergeist
  1958, Oct./Juanita Ramsey/937 Harding
    St.
    (Editorial), Fate 12 (Feb.1959):14.
-UFO (NL)
  1972, July 7
    Glenn McWane & David Graham, The New
    UFO Sightings (N.Y.: Warner, 1974),
    pp.43-44, quoting Galion Inquirer

(undated).

Gallia co.
-Humanoid
ca.1912
Ron Schaffner, "A Report on Ohio An-
thropoids and Other Strange Crea-
tures," in Bigfoot: Tales of Unex-
plained Creatures (Rome, O.: Page
Rsch.Library, 1978), p.40.
-UFO (DD)
ca.1918/J. Earl D. Moore
(Letter), FSR Case Histories, no.15
(June 1973):14.

Gallipolis
-Cattle mutilation
1967, Dec.
John A. Keel, Strange Creatures from
Time and Space (Greenwich, Ct.: Faw-
cett, 1970), p.171.
-Cattle mutilations and UFO (CE-3)
1963-1967
John A. Keel, Strange Creatures from
Time and Space (Greenwich, Ct.: Faw-
cett, 1970), pp.167-68.
John A. Keel, The Mothman Prophecies
(N.Y.: Saturday Review, 1975), pp.
138-39.
-Dog mutilation
1966, Nov./William Watson/Georges Creek
Rd.
Gallipolis Times-Sentinel, 20 Nov.
1966.
-Giant bird
1966, Dec.4/Everett Wedge/airport
John A. Keel, The Mothman Prophecies
(N.Y.: Saturday Review, 1975), p.77.
-Haunt
n.d./Henry Galbraith/Deluse farmhouse
Charles M. Skinner, Myths and Legends
of Our Own Land, 2 vols. (Philadel-
phia: Lippincott, 1896), 2:110-12.
Pauline Saltzman, Ghosts and Other
Strangers (N.Y.: Lancer, 1970 ed.),
pp.67-70.
-Phantom airplanes
ca.1966
John A. Keel, UFOs: Operation Trojan
Horse (N.Y.: Putnam, 1970), p.125.
-UFO (CE-1)
1966, Dec.9/Marilyn Taylor/Georges
Creek Rd.
John A. Keel, Strange Creatures from
Time and Space (Greenwich, Ct.: Faw-
cett, 1970), p.167.
-UFO (CE-2) and men-in-black
1967/N of town/ground markings only
John A. Keel, The Mothman Prophecies
(N.Y.: Saturday Review, 1975), pp.
152-55.
-UFO (CE-3)
1966, Nov.2
John A. Keel, The Mothman Prophecies
(N.Y.: Saturday Review, 1975), pp.
136-38.
-UFO (DD)
1966, summer/Mary Hyre
John A. Keel, The Mothman Prophecies
(N.Y.: Saturday Review, 1975), p.41.

Gates Mills
-UFO (NL)
1964, Aug.27/Dan Boras/Neill Green-
houses
"UFO Sighting Wave Persists," UFO
Inv. 2 (Sep.-Oct.1964):5.
Curtis Fuller, "Collected UFO Sight-
ings for August and September,"
Fate 18 (Jan.1965):35,37.

Geneva
-UFO (CE-1)
1964, May 15/Bill Mitchell/I-90
"UFO Landings in Ohio," Saucer News
11 (Sep.1964):10-11.

Germantown
-UFO (?)
1952, Aug.23
Don Berliner, "The Ground Observers
Corps," Official UFO 1 (Aug.1976):
24,51.

Glenford
-Archeological site
Fort Glenford
A.A. Graham, History of Fairfield
and Perry Counties, Ohio (Chicago:
W.H. Beers, 1883), pp.195-201.
Cyrus Thomas, "Report on the Mound
Explorations of the Bureau of Eth-
nology," Ann.Rept.Bur.Am.Ethn. 12
(1890-91):1,470-71.
Jon Douglas Singer, "Stone Forts of
the Midwest and the Appalachian
Region: Are They Clues to the Enigma
of Mystery Hill?" NEARA J. 13 (win-
ter 1979):63-66.

Glouster
-UFO (?)
1897, April 22/=hoax
Columbus Evening Press, 23 Apr.1897.
Columbus Ohio State Journal, 25 Apr.
1897.

Goshen
-UFO (CE-3)
1973, Oct.19
Leonard H. Stringfield, Situation
Red: The UFO Siege (N.Y.: Fawcett
Crest, 1977 ed.), pp.159-60.
Charles J. Wilhelm, "The Sam Case
1973," Ohio Sky Watcher, 1978 Double
Issue, p.1.
-UFO (NL)
1952, Aug.24
Don Berliner, "The Ground Observers
Corps," Official UFO 1 (Aug.1976):
24,51.

Grafton
-Ancient oil wells
J.S. Newberry, "Ancient Mining in
North America," Am.Antiquarian 11
(1889):164-67.

Granville
-Archeological sites
ca.300 B.C.-500 A.D.

E.G. Squier & E.H. Davis, Ancient
Monuments of the Mississippi Valley
(Washington: Smithsonian Institution,
Contrib.to Knowl., no.1, 1848), pp.
24-25,98-100.
-Haunt
1968, Dec.29-1969, Jan./Harry Nix
Harry Nix, "The Spirit That Dropped
in for New Year's," Fate 23 (Jan.
1970):59-65.
1970s/Orville Orr/Buxton Inn
Mary Bilderback Abel, "Ghostly Guests
Linger at an Inn in Granville," Co-
lumbus Dispatch Mag., 24 June 1979.

Greenfield
-UFO (CE-1)
1973, Oct./Mike Conklin
(Editorial), Fate 27 (Feb.1974):30-
31.

Greenhills
-UFO (?)
1955, Aug.25/Bill Wallace/=hoax
Cincinnati Enquirer, 28 Aug.1955.
"The Controversial Little Green Men
and the Tingling Facts," CRIFO Or-
bit, 2 Sep.1955, pp.3,4.
Isabel Davis & Ted Bloecher, Close
Encounter at Kelly and Others of
1955 (Evanston: Center for UFO
Studies, 1978), p.184.
-UFO (DD)
1947, July 3
Cincinnati Enquirer, 8 July 1947.
1954, Jan./Mr. Dinkelacker
"Disc Flies Beneath Thunderstorm in
Greenhills, Ohio," CRIFO Newsl., 7
May 1954, p.4.
-UFO (NL)
1952, July/Mr. Ostendorf/school
"Brilliant Object Hovers over Green-
hills Schoolhouse," CRIFO Newsl.,
7 May 1954, p.4.

Greensburg
-Fall of fishing line
1978, Sep./John Wright
St. Louis (Mo.) Post-Dispatch, 24
Sep.1978.

Greenville
-Phantom panther
1948, Aug.19/George Royer/Slagle gravel
pit
Richmond (Ind.) Palladium-Item & Sun-
Telegram, 22 Aug.1948, p.10.
-UFO (NL)
1975, Oct.3
"UFO Central," CUFOS News Bull., 1
Feb.1976, p.7.

Grove City
-Erratic kangaroo
1949, Jan./Louis Staub
Cincinnati Post, 10 Jan.1949.
-UFO (NL)
1973, Oct.17/Ken Chamberlain, Jr.
Columbus Dispatch, 18 Oct.1973; and
23 Oct.1973. il.

1973, Oct.18/Ronald Perrigo
Columbus Dispatch, 19 Oct.1973, p.4A.

Groveport
-UFO (NL)
1966, April 5/Mrs. Shelby Gordon
Columbus Dispatch, 8 Apr.1966.

Hamilton
-Archeological sites
ca.300 B.C.-1000 A.D.
E.G. Squier & E.H. Davis, Ancient
Monuments of the Mississippi Valley
(Washington: Smithsonian Institution,
Contrib.to Knowl., no.1, 1848), pp.
16-18,21-22,29,30-31,85-86,90-91.
John P. MacLean, The Mound Builders
(Cincinnati: Robert Clarke, 1909),
pp.171-227.
S. Frederick Starr, "The Archaeology
of Hamilton County, Ohio," J.Cincin-
nati Mus.Nat.Hist., vol.23, no.1
(June 1960). il.
-UFO (?)
1947/Bert Ruoff/Armco Steel plant/=
lens flares
(Editorial), Fate 6 (Feb.1953):9-10,
quoting Arm-co-operator (undated).
il.
"Saucer Jokes and UFO Hoaxes," in
Flying Saucers (New York: Look Mag.
special issue, 1967), p.44. il.
Colman S. Von Keviczsky, "A Re-Anal-
ysis," Can.UFO Rept., no.24 (summer
1976):19,21-22. il.
-UFO (NL)
1959, fall/John Roberts
1960, June 28/John Roberts
(Letter), Fate 14 (May 1961):109-10.
1960, Nov.23/Ben Fox
Curtis Fuller, "The Nov.23 UFO,"
Fate 14 (Mar.1961):46,50.
1962, May 20/Linda Baker
"UFO Seen by Prof. Maney, Others,"
APRO Bull. 10 (May 1962):3.

Hammondsville
-Ancient inscription
1868, fall/James Parsons
Los Angeles (Cal.) News, 17 Dec.1869,
quoting Cleveland Herald (undated).
Henry Winfred Splitter, "The Impossible Fossils," Fate 6 (Jan.1954):
65,67-68.

Hancock co.
-Aerial phantom
1857, Aug.
New York Sun, 5 Feb.1888, p.8.

Hardscrabble
-UFO (NL)
1958, Sep.29/Mike Kajowski/State Rd.
"The Night of September 29," Fate 12
(Feb.1959):31,37.

Harrison co.
-UFO (NL)
1973, Sep.3
New Philadelphia Times-Reporter, 4

Sep.1973.

Hilliard
-UFO (CE-3)
1967, Feb.5
"Startling Cases Investigated," UFO
Inv. 4 (May-June 1967):6.
-UFO (NL)
1966, March 29/Michael Richards
Columbus Dispatch, 29 Mar.1966, p.1.

Hillsboro
-UFO (NL)
1897, April 15
Cincinnati Commercial Tribune, 16
Apr.1897.

Hocking co.
-Haunts and phantoms
n.d.
C.C. Carter, "A Lesson in the Psych-
ology of Deception," J.ASPR 15
(1921):255-302,320-59.
-Livestock mutilations
1976, May 27-Aug.
Athens Messenger, 4 Aug.1976.
Ed Sanders, "On the Trail of the
Night Surgeons," Oui, May 1977, pp.
79,121-22.
-Phantom panther
1897, May
Akron Times-Democrat, 26 May 1897.

Holgate
-Humanoid
1964, winter/Dave Hohenburger/Maumee R.
Detroit (Mich.) Free Press, 20 Aug.
1965, p.12A.

Holland
-UFO (NL)
1952, July-1953, April 18/Louise An-
toine
John C. Ross, "Fate's Report on the
Flying Saucers," Fate 6 (Oct.1953):
6,7,11-12, quoting Columbus Dispatch
(undated).

Holmes co.
-UFO (CE-2)
1967, Dec.22
Jacques Vallee, Passport to Magonia
(Chicago: Regnery, 1969), p.356.

Hopetown
-Archeological site
100 B.C.-200 A.D./Hopeton Works
E.G. Squier & E.H. Davis, Ancient
Monuments of the Mississippi Valley
(Washington: Smithsonian Institution,
Contrib.to Knowl., no.1, 1848), pp.
51-52.
Cyrus Thomas, "Report on the Mound
Explorations of the Bureau of Eth-
nology," Ann.Rept.Bur.Am.Ethn. 12
(1890-91):1,472-74.
Henry Clyde Shetrone, The Mound-
Builders (N.Y.: Appleton, 1930), p.
254.
Kenneth Goodman, "A Hopewell Burial

Trait," Ohio Arch. 23, no.1 (winter
1973):24-25.

Hubbard
-UFO (NL)
1968, March 3/Joseph Tucciarone
"Observers' Notebook," Sky & Telescope 35 (May 1968):331.

Huber Heights
-Fall of fish
1975, June 14/Melissa John
Springfield News-Sun, 15 June 1975.

Hudson
-Out-of-body experience
n.d./Miriam Buckner Pond
William H. Leach, "The Apported Doc-
tor," Fate 9 (July 1956):33-35.
-Psychokinesis
1953, Aug./Eva Wilkinson
Cleveland Press, 25 Aug.1953.
-UFO (NL)
1962, Sep.18/Roger A. Stinard
Richard Hall, ed., The UFO Evidence
(Washington: NICAP, 1964), p.62.

Huntsville
-UFO (?)
1949, July 26
"If It's in the Sky It's a Saucer,"
Doubt, no.27 (1949):416.

Huron
-Humanoid
1970, Oct.23/S of Fox Rd.
John Green, Sasquatch: The Apes Among
Us (Seattle: Hancock House, 1978),
p.209.
-UFO (DD)
1967, June 6/John Ritter
Sandusky Register, 7 June 1967. il.

Independence
-Ancient inscription
1854/B. Wood
Charles Whittlesey, "Ancient Rock In-
scriptions in Ohio," Am.Naturalist
5 (1871):544-47.
W.R. Coates, History of Cuyahoga
County and the City of Cleveland, 2
vols. (Chicago: American Historical
Soc'y, 1924), 1:1-8. il.
Emerson F. Greenman, "The Upper Paleo-
lithic and the New World," Current
Anthro. 4 (Feb.1963):41-66. il.

Indian Hill
-UFO (NL)
1954, May 5/Donald Krueger/Demar Ave.
"U.F.O. and Jet Activity over Cin-
cinnati Area, May 5, 1954," CRIFO
Newsl., 4 June 1954, pp.5-6.

Ironton
-Airship inventor
1897, April
Bellefontaine Republican, 14 May
1897, quoting Ironton Register (undated).

-Humanoid
  1972, Nov.
    Cleveland Plain Dealer, 30 Nov.1972.
-Petroglyphs
    Daniel Wilson, Prehistoric Man (London: Macmillan, 1876).
    Don Rist, "Stone Carvings of Lawrence County, Ohio," Ohio Arch. 19, no. 2 (1969):55-56. il.

Jackson
-Humanoid tracks
  1977, Feb.
    Jackson Journal-Herald, 7 Feb.1977.
-Mystery radio transmission
  1963, May 22/A.E. Horsey
    Jackson Herald, 23 May 1963.
    G.D. Kaye, "The Number from Luna Earth," Fate 17 (Sep.1964):61-62.
    (Letter), Roger Lent, Fate 17 (Dec. 1964):128-30; 18 (June 1965):112.
-UFO (CE-1)
  1971, Jan.26/Jay Chase/Iron and Steel plant
    Columbus Dispatch, 27 Jan.1971.

Jacksontown
-Ancient inscription
  1867/David M. Johnson/=hoax
    Charles Whittlesey, "Archaeological Frauds," Pub.Western Reserve & N. Ohio Hist.Soc'y, no.33 (Nov.1876), p.2.

Jefferson co.
-Poltergeist
  1850s
    Emma Hardinge Britten, Modern American Spiritualism (N.Y.: The Author, 1870), pp.436-37.

Jerome
-UFO (CE-2)
  1954, Oct.22/Rodney Warrick/Jerome Elementary School
    Marysville Journal-Tribune, 25 Oct. 1954.
    "Web-Spinning Saucer Visits Marysville, Ohio," CRIFO Newsl., 3 Dec. 1954, p.5.
    Charles A. Maney & Richard Hall, The Challenge of Unidentified Flying Objects (Washington: The Authors, 1961), pp.40-42.
    Donald H. Menzel & Lyle G. Boyd, The World of Flying Saucers (Garden City: Doubleday, 1963), pp.222-23.
    Wendelle C. Stevens, "UFO Calling Card: Angel's Hair," Saga, Jan.1976, pp.24-25,60-61. il.

Kent
-Haunt
  1970/Van Campen Hall
    (Editorial), Fate 24 (Mar.1971):7, quoting Kent State University newspaper (undated).

Kenton
-Giant snake

1946, June 9/Orland Packer
    "More Monsters," Doubt, no.16 (1946):236.
-Lightning anomaly
  1946, May 20/Charles Brown
    "Not Books of Fort," Doubt, no.15 (summer 1946):228.
-UFO (NL)
  1897, April 14
    Kenton News-Republican, 15 Apr.1897.
  1897, May 2/Will Ries/railroad depot
    Kenton News-Republican, 3 May 1897.

Kingston
-UFO (CE-1)
  1957, Sep.30/Blanche F. Long
    (Letter), Flying Saucers, Feb.1958, p.66.
  1975, Aug.25
    "UFO Central," CUFOS News Bull., 15 Nov.1975, p.16.

Knox co.
-Humanoid
  1978, June/Hwy.95
    Mt. Vernon News, 18 July 1978.

Kunkle
-UFO (NL)
  1972, Oct.19/Kenneth Ray/Ohio Turnpike
    Toledo Blade, 20 Oct.1972.

Kyger
-UFO (CE-2)
  1959, March 19
    Gallipolis Daily Tribune, 20 Mar. 1959.

Lake co.
-UFO (NL)
  1957, Nov.6
    Jacques Vallee, Passport to Magonia (Chicago: Regnery, 1969), p.263.

Lake twp.
-UFO (CE-2)
  1973, Oct.17/John F. Clavitt
    George D. Fawcett, "What We Can Expect of UFOs in 1975," Official UFO 1 (Aug.1975):12,48.

Lake Milton
-UFO (NL)
  1970, Feb./Robert Hively
    Alliance Review, 23 Feb.1970.

Lamartine
-Phantom panther
  1895, May/Emanuel Hendrick, Jr.
    Cadiz Sentinel, 9 May 1895.

Lancaster
-Archeological sites
    E.G. Squier & E.H. Davis, Ancient Monuments of the Mississippi Valley (Washington: Smithsonian Institution, Contrib.to Knowl., no.1, 1848), p. 100.
    A.A. Graham, History of Fairfield and Perry Counties, Ohio (Chicago:

W.H. Beers, 1883), pp.17-21.
-Haunt
  1900s
    C.C. Carter, "The B--- House," J.
      ASPR 4 (1910):677-78.
-UFO (CE-2)
  1966, April 18/Paul Friend
    "Close Approaches Frighten Obser-
      vers," UFO Inv. 3 (May-June 1966):7.
-UFO (CE-3)
  1897, April/N of town
    Cincinnati Enquirer, 25 Apr.1897.
-UFO (NL)
  1955, Aug.5
    "Case 97," CRIFO Orbit, 2 Sep.1955,
      p.1.

Leavittsburg
-UFO (CE-1)
  1978, Aug.29/Dale Bungard/Denman Rubber
    Co.
    Warren Tribune-Chronicle, 31 Aug.
      1978.

Lebanon
-Hex
  1817/Richard McNemar/Union Village
    J.P. MacLean, A Sketch of the Life
      and Labors of Richard McNemar
      (Franklin, O.: The Chronicle, 1905).
-Poltergeist
  1880, Feb./John W. Lingo
    Charles Fort, The Books of Charles
      Fort (N.Y.: Holt, 1941), p.914,
      quoting Religio-Philosophical J.,
      6 Mar.1880.
-Spirit mediums, religious ecstasy, and
  out-of-body experiences
  1837-1847/Union Village
    J.P. MacLean, Shakers of Ohio (Co-
      lumbus: F.J. Heer, 1907), pp.392-
      415.
-UFO (?)
  1952, Aug.18
    Don Berliner, "The Ground Observers
      Corps," Official UFO 1 (Aug.1976):
      24,51.
  1953, Nov.14/Ethel Coleman
    "Infra Red Film with Red Filter Shows
      Disembodied Globe of Light," CRIFO
      Newsl., 7 May 1954, p.3.
-UFO (CE-2)
  1967, March 18/Robert W. Smith
    "UAO near WPAFB," APRO Bull. 15 (Mar.-
      Apr.1967):7.

Leo
-Petroglyphs
    Hubert C. Wachtel & Henry Peters,
      "The Jackson County Petroglyphs,"
      Ohio Arch. 6, no.2 (1956):60-62. il.

Leroy twp.
-UFO (CE-2)
  1965, May 20/Edward McDonald/Vrooman
    Rd.
    "Animals and Unidentified Flying Ob-
      jects," UFO Inv. 3 (June-July 1965):
      5.
    "Ohio Children Witness Near-Landing,"

Saucer News 12 (Dec.1965):17-18.

LeSourdsville
-Phantom airplane
  1971, Jan.18/B. Roman/trailer park
    Curt Sutherly & David Fideler, "The
      Phantom Starships," Saga UFO Rept.
      5 (May 1978):16-18, quoting Ohio
      UFO Reporter (undated).

Letart Falls
-Flying humanoid
  1967, March 12
    John A. Keel, The Mothman Prophecies
      (N.Y.: Saturday Review, 1975), pp.
      119-20.

Lima
-UFO (NL)
  1952, May 5/Lloyd S. Lora
    (Letter), Fate 5 (Dec.1952):110-11.
  1961, Jan.3/Paul D. Carroll
    "Ohio Sightings," APRO Bull. 10
      (Mar.1962):2.

Lloydsville
-UFO (NL)
  1973, Oct.5
    Martins Ferry Times-Leader, 6 Oct.
      1973.

Lockland
-Spontaneous human combustion
  1962, Aug.3/Mary Martin
    Cincinnati Enquirer, 3 Aug.1962.
-UFO (DD)
  1947, July 3
    Cincinnati Enquirer, 8 July 1947.

Lodi
-UFO (?)
  1951, Jan.
    Harold T. Wilkins, Flying Saucers on
      the Attack (N.Y.: Ace, 1967 ed.),
      p.138.

Logan
-UFO (CE-3)
  1897, April 16/Henry Rose/3 mi.S
    Columbus Sunday Press, 18 Apr.1897.

London
-UFO (CE-1)
  1973, Oct.14/Roger Spencer/Bureau of
    Criminal Investigation
    Columbus Dispatch, 15 Oct.1973, p.1.
  1973, Oct.16
    Madison Press, 17 Oct.1973.

Lorain
-Aerial phantom
  1924, June/Mrs. R.H. Nesbitt
    (Letter), Fate 12 (Nov.1959):122-24.
-Airship message
  1897, April 24
    Cleveland Plain Dealer, 25 Apr.1897.
-Humanoid
  1968, Nov.9/Mr. Cataldo
    Jerome Clark & Loren Coleman, Crea-
      tures of the Outer Edge (N.Y.: War-

ner, 1978), pp.112-13.
1973, Aug.
   "BHM in the NE USA," INFO J., no.11
   (summer 1973):26-27.
-UFO (CE-1)
1958, Sep.21/Mrs. Jack P. Stewart
   Robert J. Durant, The Fitzgerald Report (Akron: UFO Rsch.Committee,
   1958).
   "A Documented Case of Governmental
   Dishonesty," Pursuit 5 (Apr.1972):
   28-30.
-UFO (NL)
1966, Aug.4/Mrs. John Maracich
   Cleveland Plain Dealer, 5 Aug.1966.
1973, Oct.16/Mrs. Efrain Blanco/704 E.
   32d St.
   "Saucers in the News," Flying Saucers,
   winter 1974, pp.44,57.
-Windshield pitting
1956, July 17
   "First Prize," Doubt, no.53 (1956):
   412,413.

Loudonville
-Ghost light
1943-1956/Glen Zimmerman/Route 2
   (Editorial), Fate 9 (Oct.1956):14.

Loveland
-Humanoid
1972, March 3/Riverside Rd.
1972, March 17?/Riverside Rd.
   Richard Mackey, "Loveland, Ohio Crea-
   ture," Ohio Sky Watcher, June-Aug.
   1976, pp.1-2.
   Ron Schaffner, "A Report on Ohio An-
   thropoids and Other Strange Crea-
   tures," in Bigfoot: Tales of Unex-
   plained Creatures (Rome, O.: Page
   Rsch.Library, 1978), pp.40,46-48.
-UFO (CE-3)
1955, July
   Leonard H. Stringfield, Situation
   Red: The UFO Siege (N.Y.: Fawcett
   Crest, 1977 ed.), pp.111-14.
   Isabel Davis & Ted Bloecher, Close
   Encounter at Kelly and Others of
   1955 (Evanston: Center for UFO
   Studies, 1978), pp.126-37.
-UFO (NL)
1955, May 24
   Loveland Herald, 2 June 1955.
   Ted Bloecher, "Occupant Case De-
   tailed," Skylook, no.84 (Nov.1974):
   4,6-8.

Lowell
-Archeological site
   E.G. Squier & E.H. Davis, Ancient
   Monuments of the Mississippi Valley
   (Washington: Smithsonian Institution,
   Contrib.to Knowl., no.1, 1848), p.
   92.
-Fall of metallic object
1974, Sep.7/Keith Hammerman/=Cosmos
   satellite debris
   Theodore Spickler, "Another Mystery
   Sphere," APRO Bull. 23 (Sep.-Oct.
   1974):6-7. il.

Walt Andrus, "Ohio Steel Ball Re-
   turned to Foreign Nation," Skylook,
   no.85 (Dec.1974):15.
-Giant bird
1966, Nov.26/Marvin Shock
   Helen M. White, "Do Birds Come This
   Big?" Fate 20 (Aug.1967):74,76.
   John A. Keel, The Mothman Prophecies
   (N.Y.: Saturday Review, 1975), p.70.

Lumberton
-UFO (CE-3)
1977, March?/nr.I-71 x Hwy.68/crashed
   UFO
   Ted Bloecher, "A Survey of CE3K Re-
   ports for 1977," in 1978 MUFON UFO
   Symposium Proc. (Seguin, Tex.:
   MUFON, 1978), pp.14,25-26.
   Leonard H. Stringfield, "Retrievals
   of the Third Kind," in 1978 MUFON
   UFO Symposium Proc. (Seguin, Tex.:
   MUFON, 1978), pp.77,103-104.

Lynchburg
-Phantom helicopter
1974, Sep.27/Dan Richley
   Leonard H. Stringfield, Situation
   Red: The UFO Siege (N.Y.: Fawcett
   Crest, 1977 ed.), p.91.
-UFO (CE-2)
1973, Nov.12/Mrs. Long
   Leonard H. Stringfield, Situation
   Red: The UFO Siege (N.Y.: Fawcett
   Crest, 1977 ed.), p.152.
-UFO (NL)
1974, Sep.26/Dan Richley
   Leonard H. Stringfield, Situation
   Red: The UFO Siege (N.Y.: Fawcett
   Crest, 1977 ed.), pp.90-91.

Madeira
-UFO (NL)
1949, Sep.11/Donald R. Berger/St. Gertrude Church
   Leonard H. Stringfield, Inside Saucer Post...3-0 Blue (Cincinnati:
   CRIFO, 1957), p.73.

Madison
-UFO (CE-1)
1968, March 7-8/Jack Robbins
1968, March 11/Jack Robbins
1968, March 28/Jack Robbins
   "March Sighting Compared with 1897
   Flap," Skylook, no.12-13 (Aug.-Sep.
   1968):1,4.
-UFO (CE-2)
1957, Nov.10/Leita Kuhn
   Painesville Telegraph, 27 Nov.1957.
   Cleveland Plain Dealer, 1 Dec.1957.
   "The Case of the Radioactive U.F.O.,"
   Flying Saucers, Feb.1958, pp.30,33.
   Richard Hall, ed., The UFO Evidence
   (Washington: NICAP, 1964), p.98.

Madison co.
-Petroglyph
   B.E. Kelley, "The Stone Face," Ohio
   Arch. 17, no.1 (1967):42-43. il.

Manchester
-Petroglyphs
Ohio R.
Charles Rau, "Cups and Circles," Na-
ture 26 (1882):126-29.

Mansfield
-Clairvoyance
1913, June 25/G.W. Cupp
"Incidents," J.ASPR 8 (1914):365-66.
-Dowsing
1964/Ernest Black/Route 6
(Editorial), Fate 17 (Nov.1964):14,
quoting Cleveland Plain Dealer (un-
dated).
-Healing
1841-1844/Wright L. Coffinberry
Edmond P. Gibson, "Hypnotic Healings
of W.L. Coffinberry," Fate 13 (Dec.
1960):79-86.
-Humanoid
1963/C.W. Cox
"Fortean Items," Saucer News 10 (Dec.
1963):21.
1973, Aug.
John Green, Sasquatch: The Apes Among
Us (Seattle: Hancock House, 1978),
pp.209-10.
-UFO (CE-2)
1973, Oct.18/Lawrence J. Coyne/10 mi.E
Cleveland Plain Dealer, 20 Oct.1973.
Nat'l Enquirer, 28 June 1974.
Philip J. Klass, UFOs Explained (N.Y.:
Random House, 1974), pp.333-46.
J. Allen Hynek, "J. Allen Hynek An-
swers Phlip Klass on UFOs," Fate 28
(July 1975):51,58.
George W. Earley, "Phil Klass Debunks
UFOs: Part Two," Fate 28 (July 1975)
:60-66.
Jennie Zeidman, "UFO-Helicopter Close
Encounter over Ohio," Flying Saucer
Rev. 22 (Nov.1976):15-19.
(Letter), Omegus Comm'n, Saga UFO
Rept. 4 (May 1977):4-6.
(Letter), Philip J. Klass, Saga UFO
Rept. 4 (July 1977):4-6.
(Letter), Robert A. Goerman, Saga
UFO Rept. 4 (July 1977):6,79.
Jennie Zeidman, "Helicopter Case Up-
date," MUFON UFO J., no.120 (Nov.
1977):3.
Jennie Zeidman, "More on the Coyne
Helicopter Case," Flying Saucer Rev.
23 (Jan.1978):16-18.
Philip J. Klass, "The Other Side of
the Coyne Encounter," Fate 31 (Dec.
1978):72,74,76-82.
Jennie Zeidman, "Zeidman on Klass on
Coyne," Fate 31 (Dec.1978):73,75,
82-85.
(Letter), Edward J. Ramaley, Fate 32
(Mar.1979):113.
Jennie Zeidman, A Helicopter-UFO En-
counter over Ohio (Evanston: Center
for UFO Studies, 1979). il.
-UFO (CE-3)
1966, March 30/Ohio State Univ. branch
campus
Jacques Vallee, Passport to Magonia

(Chicago: Regnery, 1969), pp.325-26.
-UFO (CE-4)
1973, Oct./SW on I-71
David Webb, 1973: Year of the Human-
oids (Evanston: Center for UFO
Studies, 1976 ed.), p.11.
-UFO (DD)
1956, Sep.3/John Adamescu
"Case 239," CRIFO Orbit, 7 Dec.1956,
pp.2-3.

Mantua
-UFO (NL)
1966, April 17/Gerald Buchert
Columbus Dispatch, 19 Apr.1966, p.
23B.
Akron Beacon-Journal, 9 Oct.1966.

Maplewood
-UFO (CE-2)
1948, Aug.29
Jacques Vallee, Passport to Magonia
(Chicago: Regnery, 1969), p.193.

Mariemont
-UFO (CE-2)
1975, Jan.4
Ted Phillips, Physical Traces Associ-
ated with UFO Sightings (Evanston:
Center for UFO Studies, 1975), p.
106.
-UFO (CE-3)
1974, July 26/Kim Davis/Homewood St.
Ted Bloecher, "A Catalog of Humanoid
Reports for 1974," MUFON 1975 UFO
Symposium Proc. (Seguin, Tex.:
MUFON, 1975), pp.51,60.
Leonard H. Stringfield, Situation
Red: The UFO Siege (N.Y.: Fawcett
Crest, 1977 ed.), pp.121-22.

Marietta
-Archeological site
500 B.C.-300 A.D.
Thaddeus Mason Harris, Journal of a
Tour into the Territory Northwest
of the Allegheny Mountains (Boston:
Manning & Loring, 1805), pp.148-61.
Caleb Atwater, "Description of the
Antiquities Discovered in the State
of Ohio and Other Western States,"
Trans.& Coll.Am.Antiquarian Soc'y 1
(1820):105,133-40,168-76.
Josiah Priest, American Antiquities
and Discoveries in the West (Albany:
Hoffman & White, 1834), pp.39-43,
87-90,99.
Samuel P. Hildreth, Pioneer History
(Cincinnati: H.W. Derby, 1848).
E.G. Squier & E.H. Davis, Ancient
Monuments of the Mississippi Valley
(Washington: Smithsonian Institution,
Contrib.to Knowl., no.1, 1848), pp.
73-77.
William Pidgeon, Traditions of De-
coo-dah (N.Y.: Horace Thayer, 1858),
pp.271-74.
F.W. Putnam, "Iron from the Ohio
Mounds," Proc.Am.Antiquarian Soc'y,
ser.2, 2 (1883):349-63.

J.P. MacLean, "Ancient Works at Mari-
etta, Ohio," Ohio State Arch.& Hist.
Quar. 12 (1903):37-66.
Henry Clyde Shetrone, The Mound-
Builders (N.Y.: Appleton, 1930),
pp.9-13,261-63.
"Obsolete Theories about Mound Build-
ers," El Palacio 33 (1932):199-200.
-UFO (NL)
1897, April 19/Pat Highland/Ohio St./
=balloon?
Marietta Daily Register, 20 Apr.1897.

Marion
-Psychokinesis
1973, Aug.2/Harding Home and Museum
"Clock Marks Anniversary," Fate 28
(Feb.1975):68.
-Rotating tombstone
1905, July-1960s/Marion cemetery
Frank Edwards, Strange World (N.Y.:
Lyle Stuart, 1964), pp.128-29.
Jim Kane, "The Tombstone That Goes
Round and Round," Fate 23 (Dec.1970)
:90-91. il.
(Letter), Daniel Paduto, Fate 24
(Oct.1971):130-31.
(Letter), Benjamin Jacoby, Fate 25
(Mar.1972):144.
Jim Brandon, Weird America (N.Y.:
Dutton, 1978), pp.181-82.
-UFO (DD)
1952, July 25
Don Berliner, "The Ground Observers
Corps," Official UFO 1 (Aug.1976):
24,51.
-UFO (NL)
1897, April 16/H.R. Bolander
Marion Daily Star, 17 Apr.1897.

Marion co.
-Humanoid
1972, July
Columbus Dispatch, 9 Aug.1972, p.1.

Martinsburg
-UFO (NL)
1976, Nov.4
"UFOs of Limited Merit," Int'l UFO
Reporter 1 (Dec.1976):11.

Martinsville
-Fall of localized rain
1892, Oct.
Philadelphia (Pa.) Public Ledger, 19
Oct.1892.

Marysville
-UFO (NL)
1955, Aug.24
Marysville Journal-Tribune, 25 Aug.
1955.

Massillon
-Airship message
1897, April 21/Frank Reed
Toledo Blade, 22 Apr.1897.
-Humanoid
1973, Oct.
Akron Beacon-Journal, 27 Oct.1973.

-Spirit medium
1851/Abby Warner/St. Timothy's Church
Abel Underhill, The Arrest, Trial
and Acquittal of Abby Warner, for
Spirit Rapping (Cleveland: Gray &
Wood, 1852).
Emma Hardinge Britten, Modern American Spiritualism (N.Y.: The Author,
1870), pp.297-301.
Nandor Fodor, Encyclopaedia of Psychic Science (London: Arthurs,
1933), pp.322,404.
William Wingfield, "Jack London and
the Occult," Fate 28 (July 1975):
70,72.
-UFO (?)
1954, Nov./Fred Kirsch/=meteor?
"Ranging Fireball Explodes Soundless-
ly in Ohio," CRIFO Newsl., 6 May
1955, p.3.
-UFO (CE-2)
1964, May 17
Jacques Vallee, Passport to Magonia
(Chicago: Regnery, 1969), pp.298-
99.
-UFO (NL)
1897, April 20-21
Toledo Blade, 22 Apr.1897.

Maumee
-Poltergeist
1964, winter/William Simmons/=singing
mouse
(Editorial), Fate 17 (Aug.1964):6.
-UFO (NL)
1953, Aug.21
Richard Hall, ed., The UFO Evidence
(Washington: NICAP, 1964), p.65.

Mayfield Heights
-Human electrification
1967/Arthur C. Stephens
"An Electrifying Person," Fate 20
(Aug.1967):54, quoting Cleveland
Plain Dealer (undated).

Maynard
-UFO (NL)
1973, Oct.3/Mrs. George Ensign
Martins Ferry Times-Leader, 6 Oct.
1973.

Mecca
-Ancient oil wells
J.S. Newberry, "Ancient Mining in
North America," Am.Antiquarian 11
(1889):164-67.

Meigs co.
-UFO (CE-2)
1968/ground markings only
Ted Phillips, Physical Traces Associ-
ated with UFO Sightings (Evanston:
Center for UFO Studies, 1975), p.54.

Miamisburg
-Archeological site
John P. MacLean, The Mound Builders
(Cincinnati: Robert Clarke, 1904),
p.110.

Henry Clyde Shetrone, The Mound-Builders (N.Y.: Appleton, 1930), pp. 168,267. il.
Ernest L. Spoon, "The Miamisburg Mound," Bull.Ohio Indian Relic Collections Soc'y, no.25 (Sep.1950):11.
Robert N. Converse, "The Miamisburg Mound," Ohio Arch. 22, no.4 (1972): 16-17. il.
Robert Silverberg, The Mound Builders (N.Y.: Ballantine, 1974 ed.), pp. 4,75,119.
Franklin Folsom, America's Ancient Treasures (N.Y.: Rand McNally, 1974), p.152.
-UFO (CE-1)
1971, July 31/Ruth S. Madden
Ruth S. Madden, "The Silver UFO," Fate 27 (Mar.1974):58-60.

Middlefield
-Medical clairvoyance
1850s/Mr. Durkee
Emma Hardinge Britten, Modern American Spiritualism (N.Y.: The Author, 1870), pp.265-66.

Middleport
-Men-in-black
1967, Feb.22/Connie Gordon
John A. Keel, The Mothman Prophecies (N.Y.: Saturday Review, 1975), pp. 99-100.
-UFO (CE-1)
1967, April 17/Louis Ellis/Vanadium Corp.
"Startling Cases Investigated," UFO Inv. 4 (May-June 1967):6.

Middletown
-Horticultural anomaly
1950-1953/Dante S. Donisi/404 Baltimore St.
(Editorial), Fate 6 (July 1953):5.
-UFO (?)
1956/A.A. Hafen
(Editorial), Fate 9 (Dec.1956):12.
1969, Jan.
John A. Keel, UFOs: Operation Trojan Horse (N.Y.: Putnam, 1970), p.163.
-UFO (CE-2)
1941/John Bradshaw
Ted Phillips, Physical Traces Associated with UFO Sightings (Evanston: Center for UFO Studies, 1975), p.4, quoting Ohio UFO Reporter (undated).
-UFO (NL)
1965, Nov.4/Great Miami R.
Middletown Journal, 13 Nov.1965.
1973, Oct.
Don Worley, "UFOs, Occupants and Artifacts in Eastern Indiana 1972-1973," Official UFO 1 (Jan.1976): 16,17.

Milan
-Aerial phantom
1886, Dec.15
Huron Erie County Reporter, 23 Dec. 1886.

-Phantom image
1871/Mr. Horner
"Mysterious Photographs on Window Panes," Human Nature, June 1871, pp.328-29, quoting Chicago (Ill.) Times (undated).
-UFO (R)
1966, Aug.4/James Kanallay
Cleveland Plain Dealer, 5 Aug.1966.

Milford
-Archeological site
10,000 B.C.-1000 A.D./Gatch site
E.G. Squier & E.H. Davis, Ancient Monuments of the Mississippi Valley (Washington: Smithsonian Institution, Contrib.to Knowl., no.1, 1848), pp. 94-95.
J.L. Rockey, History of Clermont County, Ohio (Philadelphia: Louis H. Everts, 1880), pp.26-29.
-Humanoid
1964/Hwy.28
1976, April 4/Little Miami R.
Ron Schaffner, "A Report on Ohio Anthropoids and Other Strange Creatures," in Bigfoot: Tales of Unexplained Creatures (Rome, O.: Page Rsch.Library, 1978), pp.40,43.
-UFO (CE-2)
1967, Feb.11/Sharon Hildebrand
"Touch Landing in Ohio," APRO Bull. 15 (Jan.-Feb.1967):6.
Donald E. Keyhoe & Gordon I.R. Lore, Jr., UFOs: A New Look (Washington: NICAP, 1969), p.21.
-UFO (NL)
1949, Sep.17/Donald R. Berger
Leonard H. Stringfield, Inside Saucer Post...3-0 Blue (Cincinnati: CRIFO, 1957), p.73.

Millfield
-Spirit medium
1852-1858/Jonathan Koons
J. Everett, A Book for Skeptics: Being Communications from Angels (Columbus: Osgood & Blake, 1853).
Emma Hardinge Britten, Modern American Spiritualism (N.Y.: The Author, 1870), pp.307-33.
Nandor Fodor, Encyclopaedia of Psychic Science (London: Arthurs, 1933), pp.190,192,237,355.
Slater Brown, The Heyday of Spiritualism (N.Y.: Pocket Books, 1972 ed.), pp.190-97.

Minerva
-UFO (NL)
1962, Sep.18/David McCurry
Richard Hall, ed., The UFO Evidence (Washington: NICAP, 1964), p.62.

Mogadore
-UFO (CE-1)
1964, May 9/John Owens
"46 Days in 1964!" Flying Saucers, June 1965, pp.6,17.

Monroe
-Erratic kangaroo
  1968, May 24/Mike Severs/I-75 nr. Hwy.
  63
    Cincinnati Enquirer, 1 June 1968.
    "Kangarooiana," INFO J., no.5 (fall
    1969):14-15, quoting unidentified
    newspaper, 24 and 27 May 1968.

Montville
-UFO (CE-2)
  1957, Nov.6/Olden Moore/Hwy.86 x Hart
  Rd.
    Painesville Telegraph, 8 Nov.1957;
    3 Dec.1957; 12 Dec.1957; and 21
    Jan.1961.
    Cleveland Press, 8 Nov.1957.
    Cleveland Plain Dealer, 8 Nov.1957.
    Willoughby Lake County Republican-
    Herald, 12 Nov.1957.
    Chardon Geauga Record, 21 Nov.1957.
    C.W. Fitch, "The Olden Moore Story,"
    Saucer News 10 (June 1963):10-14.
    Donald H. Menzel & Lyle G. Boyd, The
    World of Flying Saucers (Garden
    City: Doubleday, 1963), pp.184-85.
    Richard Hall, ed., The UFO Evidence
    (Washington: NICAP, 1964), pp.114,
    169-70.

Morning Sun
-Phantom panther tracks
  1948, Sep.3/C.H. Roberts
    Richmond (Ind.) Palladium-Item & Sun-
    Telegram, 5 Sep.1948, p.1.

Mount Gilead
-UFO (NL)
  1897, April 17
    Mt. Gilead Union-Register, 12 May
    1897.

Mount Healthy
-UFO (CE-1)
  1974, Oct.
  1975, Oct.26, 29
    Leonard H. Stringfield, Situation
    Red: The UFO Siege (N.Y.: Fawcett
    Crest, 1977 ed.), pp.35,36-37.
-UFO (NL)
  1954, May 5
    "U.F.O. and Jet Activity over Cin-
    cinnati Area, May 5,1954," CRIFO
    Newsl., 4 June 1954, pp.5-6.
  1955, Aug.23/Walter Paner
    "S.A.C. Jets 'Dogfight' Three UFO's
    over Cincinnati," CRIFO Orbit, 2
    Sep.1955, p.3.
  1955, Sep.20/Charles Deininger
    "The Cincinnati Scene: Still UFO-In-
    fested," CRIFO Orbit, 7 Oct.1955,
    p.1.

Mount Repose
-UFO (CE-2)
  1973, Oct.16/Mrs. Raymond Belcher
    Leonard H. Stringfield, Situation
    Red: The UFO Siege (N.Y.: Fawcett
    Crest, 1977 ed.), pp.156-57.

Mount Sterling
-UFO (NL)
  1973, Oct.14/5 mi.N nr.Hwy.62
    Columbus Dispatch, 15 Oct.1973, p.1.

Mount Vernon
-Disease anomaly
  1932, Jan.-Feb./Stanley Paazig
    New York Sun, 3 Feb.1932.
-Fall of ice
  1961, May 18/William Wiley/212 Oak St.
    Frank Edwards, Strangest of All
    (N.Y.: Ace, 1962 ed.), p.148.
-UFO (?)
  1958, Oct.6
    Richard Hall, ed., The UFO Evidence
    (Washington: NICAP, 1964), p.15.
-UFO (CE-1)
  1975, Jan.5
    "From the Center for UFO Studies,"
    Flying Saucer Rev. 21 (Aug.1975):
    32,iii.
-UFO (DD)
  1953, July 24
    Richard Hall, ed., The UFO Evidence
    (Washington: NICAP, 1964), p.65.
-UFO (NL)
  1897, April 29/W.P. Bogardus
    Columbus Ohio State Journal, 1 May
    1897.
  1965, Sep.27
    Columbus Citizen-Journal, 28 Sep.
    1965.

Moxahala
-UFO (NL)
  1897, April 19-21
    Columbus Evening Press, 22 Apr.1897.

Moxahala Park
-Anomalous fossil
  1853/Jacob Richey/Jonathan's Creek/=
  human bones in solid rock/=exaggeration
    Zanesville Daily Courier, 22 July
    1853, p.2; 4 Aug.1853, p.2; 18 Aug.
    1853, p.2; 23 Aug.1853, p.2; 25
    Aug.1853, p.2; 29 Aug.1853, p.2;
    and 1 Sep.1853, p.2.

Munroe Falls
-UFO (CE-3)
  1967, March 28/David Morris/Munroe
  Falls Rd.
    "Youth's Car Strikes UAO Occupant,"
    APRO Bull. 15 (Mar.-Apr.1967):1,4.
    Jim & Coral Lorenzen, UFOs over the
    Americas (N.Y.: Signet, 1968), pp.
    36-38.
    Donald E. Keyhoe & Gordon I.R. Lore,
    Jr., UFOs: A New Look (Washington:
    NICAP, 1969), pp.30-31.
-UFO (NL)
  1897, April 29/C.N. Gaylord
    Akron Times-Democrat, 5 May 1897.

Neapolis
-UFO (DD)
  1947, July 5/J.L. Dobberteen
    Kansas City (Mo.) Star, 6 July 1947.

Nelson twp.
-Humanoid
  1977, March 8/Barbara Stone
    Ravenna Record-Courier, 10 Mar.1977.
    Columbus Dispatch, 12 Mar.1977.
    Mark W. Swift & Jim Rastetter, "A
    Report on Recent Bigfoot Type Crea-
    tures Seen in Northeastern Ohio,"
    in *Bigfoot: Tales of Unexplained
    Creatures* (Rome, O.: Page Rsch.Li-
    brary, 1978), pp.24-25.

Nelsonville
-Giant bird
  1966, Dec.7/Dixie Auflick/Johnny Apple-
    seed Roadside Park, U.S.33
    Helen M. White, "Do Birds Come This
    Big?" *Fate* 20 (Aug.1967):74,77.

New Albany
-UFO (NL)
  1973, Nov.9/Dublin-Granville Rd.
    Columbus Dispatch, 10 Nov.1973.

Newark
-Ancient inscriptions
  1860, June 28/David Wyrick/=hoax
    D. Francis Bacon, "The Ohio 'Holy
    Stone,'" *Harpers Weekly* 4 (1860):
    545-46.
    Charles Whittlesey, "Archaeological
    Frauds," *Pub.Western Reserve & N.
    Ohio Hist.Soc'y*, no.33 (Nov.1876),
    p.2.
    Garrick Mallery, "Pictographs of the
    North American Indians," *Ann.Rept.
    Bur.Am.Ethn.* 4 (1882-83):3,247-48.
    A. McBride, "Discoveries at Newark
    in 1875," in Timothy R. Jenkins,
    The Ten Tribes of Israel (Spring-
    field: Houck & Smith, 1883), pp.
    246-51.
    "Recent Proceedings of Scientific
    Societies," *Science* 3 (1884):334.
    "Notes and News," *Science* 3 (1884):
    464,467.
    John P. MacLean, *The Mound Builders*
    (Cincinnati: Robert Clarke, 1904),
    p.119.
    Ed W. Atkinson, "The 'Holy Stones'
    of Newark," *Ohio Arch.* 9, no.3
    (1959):96-97. il.
-Archeological site
  ca.650 B.C.
    Caleb Atwater, "A Description of the
    Antiquities Discovered in the State
    of Ohio and Other Western States,"
    Trans.& Coll.Am.Antiquarian Soc'y 1
    (1820):105,126-31.
    E.G. Squier & E.H. Davis, *Ancient
    Monuments of the Mississippi Valley*
    (Washington: Smithsonian Institution,
    Contrib.to Knowl., no.1, 1848), pp.
    67-72.
    Charles Whittlesey, *Descriptions of
    Ancient Works in Ohio* (Washington:
    Smithsonian Institution, Contrib.to
    Knowl., no.3, 1850), p.14.
    William Pidgeon, *Traditions of De-
    coo-dah* (N.Y.: Horace Thayer, 1858),

pp.254-58.
    J.W. Foster, *Prehistoric Races of
    the United States of America* (Chi-
    cago: S.C. Griggs, 1874).
    Cyrus Thomas, "Report on the Mound
    Explorations of the Bureau of Eth-
    nology," *Ann.Rept.Bur.Am.Ethn.* 12
    (1890-91):3,459-69.
    W.H. Holmes, "Notes upon Some Geo-
    metric Earthworks, with Contour
    Maps," *Am.Anthro.* 5 (1892):363-73.
    il.
    E.M.P. Brister, *Centennial History
    of the City of Newark and Licking
    County, Ohio*, 2 vols. (Chicago:
    S.J. Clarke, 1909), 1:111-46.
    Henry Clyde Shetrone, *The Mound-
    Builders* (N.Y.: Appleton, 1930),
    pp.52-53,263-65.
    Brandt G. Smythe, *Early Recollections
    of Newark* (Newark: Thomas E. Hite,
    1940). il.
    Franklin Folsom, *America's Ancient
    Treasures* (N.Y.: Rand McNally,
    1974), p.152.
-Fall of small particles
  1954, April/Mrs. Ralph McCort
    (Editorial), *Fate* 7 (Sep.1954):11-12.
-Human track in rock
  Licking R.
    W.A. Adams, "Foot-Marks and Other
    Artificial Impressions on Rocks,"
    Am.J.Sci., ser.1, 44 (1843):200-202.
-UFO (?)
  1955, Dec.
    "Jets Chase Saucers, Heralding in
    1956," *CRIFO Orbit*, 3 Feb.1956, p.1.
  1958, Oct.16/Mike Schultz
    Newark Advocate, 15 Nov.1958. il.
    Richard Hall, ed., *The UFO Evidence*
    (Washington: NICAP, 1964), p.92.
-UFO (NL)
  1897, April 16
    Caldwell Journal, 22 Apr.1897.
  1958, Oct.8/H.E. Sherburn
    "New Wave of UFO Sightings Cracks
    Censorship Wall," *NICAP Spec.Bull.*,
    Nov.1958, pp.1,2.
  1958, Oct.15/Glen Hyder
    "Hovering UFO Puzzles South African
    Officials," *UFO Inv.* 1 (Dec.1958):
    1,3.
  1961, May 29/Craig Seese
    Richard Hall, ed., *The UFO Evidence*
    (Washington: NICAP, 1964), p.95.
  1975, Dec.16
    "UFO Central," *CUFOS News Bull.*, 1
    Feb.1976, p.15.

New Baltimore
-Archeological site
  Great Miami R.
    E.G. Squier & E.H. Davis, *Ancient
    Monuments of the Mississippi Valley*
    (Washington: Smithsonian Institution,
    Contrib.to Knowl., no.1, 1848), pp.
    35-36.
-UFO (DD)
  1975, Oct.26
    Leonard H. Stringfield, *Situation*

Red: The UFO Siege (N.Y.: Fawcett
Crest, 1977 ed.), p.36.

New Bremen
-UFO (?)
1952, Aug.23
Don Berliner, "The Ground Observers
Corps," Official UFO 1 (Aug.1976):
24,51.

New Concord
-Ancient metal mask
1940s/Fred Wayble
Grit, 20 Nov.1977.
Rochester (Minn.) Post-Bulletin, 7
Dec.1977, quoting Zanesville Times-
Recorder (undated).

New Haven
-Men-in-black
1967, March 22/Connie Gordon
1967, Dec.22/Connie Gordon
John A. Keel, "West Virginia's Enig-
matic 'Bird,'" Flying Saucer Rev.
14 (July-Aug.1968):7,9-10.

New Lebanon
-UFO (CE-1)
1973, Oct.10/Robert E. Bales
Columbus Dispatch, 11 Oct.1973, p.13.
Cincinnati Enquirer, 12 Oct.1973.
Leonard H. Stringfield, Situation
Red: The UFO Siege (N.Y.: Fawcett
Crest, 1977 ed.), pp.153-55.
-UFO (NL)
1973, Oct.14/Richard Winkler
Leonard H. Stringfield, Situation
Red: The UFO Siege (N.Y.: Fawcett
Crest, 1977 ed.), pp.155-56.

New London
-Fall of fish
1897, May/George Yarker
Cleveland Plain Dealer, 16 May 1897.
-Phantom panther and livestock killings
1968, May-June/Ed Furman/New London Rd.
(Editorial), Fate 21 (Dec.1968):8-10.

New Madison
-Phantom panther
1948, Aug.18/Omah Stowe/W of town
1948, Aug.19/Daisy Mills
Richmond (Ind.) Palladium-Item & Sun-
Telegram, 19 Aug.1948, p.1.
-UFO (NL)
1962, Jan.3/Ernest J. Downing
Frank Edwards, "Mystery Blast over
Nevada," Fate 15 (Aug.1962):68,71-
72.

New Market
-Humanoid
1978, Sep.
Lynchburg News, 28 Sep.1978.

New Richmond
-Humanoid
1959, Jan.30/Ohio R.
George Wagner, "Cincinnati's 'What-
Was-It?' Monster," Beyond Reality,

no.21 (July-Aug.1976):62.

Newton Falls
-UFO (?)
1825, Nov.
Denison Olmsted, "Observations on
the Meteors of November 13th, 1833,"
Am.J.Sci., ser.1, 26 (1834):132,
133-34.

New Winchester
-UFO (DD)
1967, March 26
J. Allen Hynek, The UFO Experience
(Chicago: Regnery, 1972), pp.64-65.

Niles
-UFO (NL)
1966, Aug.4/Mrs. Martin Brutz/462
Bonnie Brae St.
Cleveland Plain Dealer, 5 Aug.1966.
1975, Oct.31
"UFO Central," CUFOS News Bull., 1
Feb.1976, p.10.

North Benton
-Archeological site
"Mound Builders' Temple, Ohio," Nature 146 (1940):455-56.
Willis H. Magrath, "The Temple of
the Effigy," Sci.Am. 163 (Aug.1940)
:76-78. il.
Norman D. Heestand, "The Temple Effigy Mound," Artifacts 3, no.1
(1973):18-120. il.

North Creek
-UFO (?)
1974
Ted Phillips, Physical Traces Associ-
ated with UFO Sightings (Evanston:
Center for UFO Studies, 1975), p.111.

North Georgetown
-UFO (DD)
1955, Oct.2/Wilma Faye Barker
Richard Hall, ed., The UFO Evidence
(Washington: NICAP, 1964), p.70.

North Kingsville
-Phantom cat (carcass)
1968, June/Mrs. Harry Anderson
(Editorial), Fate 21 (Dec.1968):10.

North Lawrence
-UFO (CE-2)
1964, May 17
"Other Recent Sightings," UFO Inv. 2
(July-Aug.1964):7.

North Olmsted
-Plant sensitivity
1966/Bonnie Howarth
"Plants Thrive on Love and Music,"
Fate 19 (Nov.1966):45.
-UFO (NL)
1973, Oct.16/Great Northern Blvd.
"Saucers in the News," Flying Saucers,
winter 1974, pp.44,57.

Norwalk
-Archeological site
    E.G. Squier & E.H. Davis, Ancient
    Monuments of the Mississippi Valley
    (Washington: Smithsonian Institution,
    Contrib.to Knowl., no.1, 1848), pp.
    37-38.
-UFO (DD)
    1952, July 25
    Don Berliner, "The Ground Observers
    Corps," Official UFO 1 (Aug.1976):
    24,51.
    1956, Oct.4/Muriel Gamble
    (Letter), Fate 17 (Apr.1964):114-16.
-UFO (NL)
    1897, May 9/Abe Parker
    Norwalk Daily Reflector, 11 May 1897.
    Cleveland Plain Dealer, 11 May 1897.
    1971, Jan.22
    "Press Reports," APRO Bull. 19 (Jan.-
    Feb.1971):6,7.

Norwood
-Archeological site
    Indian Mound Ave.
    Ohio Writers' Program, Cincinnati: A
    Guide to the Queen City and Its
    Neighbors (Cincinnati: Wiesen-Hart,
    1943), p.330.
-UFO (DD)
    1956, Sep.3/Eugene Kingman
    "Case 208," CRIFO Orbit, 5 Oct.1956,
    pp.3-4.
-UFO (NL)
    1947, June 30/Mrs. H.W. Stockwell/4000
    Floral Ave.
    Cincinnati Times-Star, 7 July 1947.
    1949, Aug.19/Donald R. Berger/St. Peter
    and Paul Church
    1949, Oct.23/Leo Davidson/St. Peter
    and Paul Church
    1949, Oct.24/Donald R. Berger/St. Peter
    and Paul Church
    1949, Nov.19/Donald R. Berger
    1949, Dec.20/Donald R. Berger
    1950, Jan.11/Donald R. Berger
    1950, March 10-11/Donald R. Berger
    Cincinnati Post, 20 Aug.1949; and
    6 Apr.1950.
    Leonard H. Stringfield, Inside Sau-
    cer Post...3-0 Blue (Cincinnati:
    CRIFO, 1957), pp.73-78. il.
    Leonard H. Stringfield, Situation
    Red: The UFO Siege (N.Y.: Fawcett
    Crest, 1977 ed.), pp.201-204.

Oberlin
-Clairvoyance
    1962/Oberlin College
    M. Rilling, J. Adams & C. Pettijohn,
    "A Summary of Some Clairvoyance Ex-
    periments Conducted in Classroom
    Situations," J.ASPR 56 (1962):125-
    30.
-Humanoid
    1973, Aug./Rudy Reinhold
    John Green, Sasquatch: The Apes Among
    Us (Seattle: Hancock House, 1978),
    p.210, quoting Cleveland Mag., Oct.
    1973.

-UFO (?)
    1965, Dec.9/=meteor?
    Columbus Dispatch, 10 Dec.1965, p.1.
-UFO (NL)
    1973, Oct.19/Park St.
    Elyria Chronicle-Telegram, 19 Oct.
    1973.

Ottawa
-UFO (CE-2)
    1975, June 6/ground markings only
    Ted Phillips, "Several Possible
    Traces Reported in 1975," Skylook,
    no.97 (Dec.1975):16.

Oxford
-UFO (NL)
    1977, April 29
    "UFOs of Limited Merit," Int'l UFO
    Reporter 2 (June 1977):3.

Oxford twp.
-Archeological site
    E.G. Squier & E.H. Davis, Ancient
    Monuments of the Mississippi Valley
    (Washington: Smithsonian Institution,
    Contrib.to Knowl., no.1, 1848), pp.
    29-30.
    R.W. McFarland, "Ancient Work near
    Oxford, Ohio," Ohio State Arch.&
    Hist.Quar. 1 (1887):265-71.

Padanaram
-Humanoid
    1954/Dean Averick/Dean's Boat Landing
    Homestead City (Fla.) News, 29 Aug.
    1977.

Painesville
-Fall of vegetable substance
    1973, June 4/Debbie Chapman/=slime mold
    Columbus Dispatch, 5 June 1973, p.4.
-Telepathy
    1958, fall/Fred Trusty/96 Riverside Dr.
    (Editorial), Fate 12 (Mar.1959):22-
    23.

Palestine
-Phantom panther
    1948, Aug.11/nr. Beach Grove Church
    Richmond (Ind.) Palladium-Item & Sun-
    Telegram, 12 Aug.1948, p.1.

Palmer twp.
-UFO (CE-2)
    1974, April 26/Roy Hiltner/County Rd.
    18A/ground markings only
    Dave Spencer, "Possible Landing Site
    Checked," Skylook, no.79 (June
    1974):6-7. il.

Paris twp.
-Humanoid
    1978, Aug.21/Herbert Cayton
    Cleveland Plain Dealer, 24 Aug.1978.
    1978, Aug.26/John Nutter
    Akron Beacon-Journal, 30 Aug.1978.

Parma
-Acoustic anomaly

1950, July-1952/Martin Lurtz
(Editorial), Fate 5 (July-Aug.1952):
9-10, quoting Akron Beacon-Journal
(undated).
-UFO (NL)
1975, Aug.20
"UFO Central," CUFOS News Bull., 15
Nov.1975, p.16.

Pemberville
-UFO (NL)
1964, June 13/Karen Fahle
"Other Recent Sightings," UFO Inv. 2
(July-Aug.1964):7,8.

Peninsula
-Giant snake
1944, June 8-Aug.1/Clarence Mitchell,
and others/Everett Swamp/=hoax?
Robert Bordner, "The Peninsula Py-
thon," Atlantic Monthly 176 (Nov.
1945):88-91.

Perry twp.
-Phantom panther and livestock killings
1895, May
Cadiz Sentinel, 9 May 1895.

Piketon
-Archeological sites
ca.300 B.C.-700 A.D.
E.G. Squier & E.H. Davis, Ancient
Monuments of the Mississippi Valley
(Washington: Smithsonian Institution,
Contrib.to Knowl., no.1, 1848), pp.
66-67,88-90,171-72.
Cyrus Thomas, "Report on the Mound
Explorations of the Bureau of Eth-
nology," Ann.Rept.Bur.Am.Ethn. 12
(1890-91):1,491-92.

Pioneer
-UFO (CE-3)
1958, Nov.5/L.M. Traxler/3 mi.N on
Buckeye Rd.
(Letter), Fate 21 (Nov.1968):128-29.

Piqua
-Archeological site
E.G. Squier & E.H. Davis, Ancient
Monuments of the Mississippi Valley
(Washington: Smithsonian Institution,
Contrib.to Knowl., no.1, 1848), p.
23.
W.H. Beers, The History of Miami
County, Ohio (Chicago: W.H. Beers,
1880), p.307.
John A. Rayner, The First Century of
Piqua, Ohio (Piqua: Magee Bros.,
1916), pp.5-14.
-Norse runestones
1870s/J.A. Raynor
C.T. Wiltheiss, "Inscribed Tablets
Found at Piqua, O.," Am.Antiquarian
2 (1879):70.
Warren K. Moorehead, The Stone Age
in North America, 2 vols. (Boston:
Houghton Mifflin, 1910), 1:350. il.
O.G. Landsverk, Runic Records of the
Norsemen in America (N.Y.: E.J.

Friis, 1974), pp.241-42. il.

Pleasantville
-Spontaneous human combustion
1956/Mrs. Cecil Rogers
Los Angeles (Cal.) Herald-Express,
14 Mar.1956.

Point Isabel
-Humanoid
1964, summer/Lew Lister/S on Hwy.222
1968, fall/Larry Abbott
Leonard H. Stringfield, Situation
Red: The UFO Siege (N.Y.: Fawcett
Crest, 1977 ed.), pp.86-89.
Ron Schaffner, "A Report on Ohio An-
thropoids and Other Strange Crea-
tures," in Bigfoot: Tales of Unex-
plained Creatures (Rome, O.: Page
Rsch.Library, 1978), pp.40,46.

Poland
-UFO (NL)
1833, Nov.13/Calvin Pease
Denison Olmsted, "Observations on
the Meteors of November 13th, 1833,"
Am.J.Sci., ser.1, 25 (1834):363,
391.
1962, Sep.18/Donald E. Corey
Richard Hall, ed., The UFO Evidence
(Washington: NICAP, 1964), p.62.

Port Clinton
-UFO (NL)
1953, July 31
Richard Hall, ed., The UFO Evidence
(Washington: NICAP, 1964), p.65.

Portsmouth
-Airship message
1897, April 27/Mr. Hughes
Portsmouth Blade, 28 Apr.1897.
-Archeological sites
ca.400 B.C.-1650 A.D.
Caleb Atwater, "A Description of the
Antiquities Discovered in the State
of Ohio and Other Western States,"
Trans.& Coll.Am.Antiquarian Soc'y 1
(1820):105,151-56.
E.G. Squier & E.H. Davis, Ancient
Monuments of the Mississippi Valley
(Washington: Smithsonian Institution,
Contrib.to Knowl., no.1, 1848), pp.
77-82,83-84.
Stephen D. Peet, "The Great Serpent
and Other Effigies," Am.Antiquarian
12 (1890):211-28.
-UFO (NL)
1897, April 23/Billy Barber
Portsmouth Blade, 24 Apr.1897.
1897, April 27/Market x 2d St.
Portsmouth Blade, 28 Apr.1897.

Preble co.
-Disappearance
1975, Aug.
Don Worley, "The UFO-Related Anthropoids: An Important New Opportunity
for Investigator-Researchers with
Courage," in Proc.1976 CUFOS Con-

ference (Evanston: Center for UFO
Studies, 1976), pp.287,291.
-Humanoid
   1975, July 10, 12/Tim Hurst
      Don Worley, "The UFO-Related Anthro-
      poids: An Important New Opportunity
      for Investigator-Researchers with
      Courage," in Proc.1976 CUFOS Con-
      ference (Evanston: Center for UFO
      Studies, 1976), pp.287,291.
      Don Worley, "The UFO Related Para-
      Anthropoids," Ufology 2 (fall 1976)
      :10,12.

Ravenna
-UFO (CE-1)
   1966, April 17/Dale Spaur/SE on U.S.
   224
      Ravenna Record-Courier, 18 Apr.1966.
      Columbus Dispatch, 18 Apr.1966, p.1;
      19 Apr.1966, p.23B; and 24 Apr.
      1966, p.4A.
      "Police Chase Low Flying UFO," UFO
      Inv. 3 (Mar.-Apr.1966):1.
      Akron Beacon-Journal, 9 Oct.1966.
      "The Ravenna Report," UFO Inv. 3
      (Oct.-Nov.1966):5.
      J. Allen Hynek, The UFO Experience
      (Chicago: Regnery, 1972), pp.100-
      108.
   1975, Nov.11/Mike Sauers/Hwy.59
      Akron Beacon-Journal, 13 Nov.1975.

Reading
-Ancient iron furnace
   Edwards farm
      F.W. Putnam, "Iron from the Ohio
      Mounds," Proc.Am.Antiquarian Soc'y,
      ser.2, 2 (1883):349-63.
-UFO (NL)
   1955, Aug.17
      "Ohio's Aerial Tempest," CRIFO Orbit,
      2 Sep.1955, p.2.

Reynoldsburg
-UFO (NL)
   1966, March 30/James Curtis/6962 Clymer Rd.
      Columbus Dispatch, 31 Mar.1966, p.1.
   1973, Oct.
      Columbus Dispatch, 17 Oct.1973.

Riceland
-UFO (?)
   1958/truck stop
      (Editorial), Fate 11 (July 1958):17.

Richmond Heights
-Fall of ice
   1972, July/Doris Klemencic/476 Jeanette
   Dr.
      (Editorial), Fate 26 (Jan.1976):38.

Ripley
-UFO (DD)
   1956, Oct.14/Harold Thomas/NW on U.S.
   52
      "Case 242," CRIFO Orbit, 7 Dec.1956,
      p.3.

Roseville
-UFO (?)
   1966, Nov.13/Ralph Ditter/=hoax
      "Saucer Photographed by Ohio Barber,"
      Saucer News 14 (summer 1967):20,
      28. il.
      "Ditter Photos Rejected," UFO Inv.
      4 (Oct.1967):5.
      Edward U. Condon, "Summary of the
      Study," in Scientific Study of Un-
      identified Flying Objects (N.Y.:
      Bantam, 1969 ed.), pp.7,36.
      (Letter), William E. Jones, Official
      UFO 2 (May 1977):8.
      Donald H. Menzel & Ernest H. Taves,
      The UFO Enigma (Garden City: Doub-
      leday, 1977), pp.215-16. il.

Ross
-UFO (CE-2)
   1975, Nov.4
      Leonard H. Stringfield, Situation
      Red: The UFO Siege (N.Y.: Fawcett
      Crest, 1977 ed.), p.38.
-UFO (NL)
   1973, Oct.11
      Cincinnati Enquirer, 12 Oct.1973.
   1975, Nov.10
      Leonard H. Stringfield, Situation
      Red: The UFO Siege (N.Y.: Fawcett
      Crest, 1977 ed.), p.38.

Rushville
-Norse runestone
      O.G. Landsverk, "Runic Inscriptions
      in the Western Hemisphere," NEARA
      J. 13 (summer 1978):15,16,18. il.

Saint Clairsville
-UFO (NL)
   1975, Oct.26
      "UFO Central," CUFOS News Bull., 1
      Feb.1976, p.10.

Saint Johns
-UFO (NL)
   1962, May 20/Quincy L. Dray, Jr.
      "UFO Seen by Prof. Maney, Others,"
      APRO Bull. 10 (May 1962):3.

Saint Mary's
-Photographic anomaly
   1897, July 29/L.E. Martindale
      "Peculiar Eclipse Pictures," Photo-
      graphy 10 (26 May 1898):355-56. il.

Salem
-Phantom airplane
   1968/Alice Allison
      (Letter), Can.UFO Rept., no.31 (sum-
      mer 1978):24-25.
-Phantom panther and humanoid
   1968, spring/Alice Allison
      Mark Swift, "The Strange Experiences
      of a Salem Family," Gray Barker's
      Newsl., Feb.1976.
-UFO (CE-3)
   1968, spring/Alice Allison
      Mark Swift, "The Strange Experiences
      of a Salem Family," Gray Barker's

Newsl., Feb.1976.
-UFO (NL)
1966, March 28
Columbus Dispatch, 29 Mar.1966, p.1.

Salem Heights
-Humanoid
1971
Mark Swift, "The Strange Experiences of a Salem Family," Gray Barker's Newsl., Feb.1976.

Sandusky
-Ancient inscriptions
1847/=discolorations
E. George Squier, "Hieroglyphical Mica Plates from the Mounds," Am.J. Sci., ser.2, 4 (1847):145.
-Animal ESP
1955, April-May/Vivian Alligood
"The Saga of Li-Ping," Fate 9 (May 1956):21.
-Mystery plane crash
1963, Sep.9/Cessna 195B
Jay Gourley, The Great Lakes Triangle (Greenwich, Ct.: Fawcett, 1977), p. 31.
-Phantom image
1871, Jan.
New York Times, 18 Jan.1871, p.4.
-Skyquake
1957, June
(Editorial), Fate 10 (Nov.1957):13.
-UFO (?)
1897, April 25-26/=signal kite
Sandusky Register, 28 Apr.1897.
-UFO (CE-2)
1967, Feb.10/Gary Butler/Plum Brook Station
"UFO over NASA Station," UFO Inv. 3 (Mar.-Apr.1967):6.
-UFO (DD)
1897, May 11/John E. Hopley
Bucyrus Evening Telegraph, 11 May 1897.
-UFO (NL)
1897, April 16/William McKean
Sandusky Register, 17 Apr.1897.
1967, Jan.30/Reinhardt N. Ausmus/Hwy. 99
"UFO over NASA Station," UFO Inv. 3 (Mar.-Apr.1967):6.

Sargents
-Archeological site
Gerard Fowke, Archaeological History of Ohio (Columbus: F.J. Heer, 1902).

Saybrook
-Phantom panther
1968, June/Georgia Lloyd
(Editorial), Fate 21 (Dec.1968):10.
-UFO (NL)
1975, Jan.2
Robert A. Goerman, "The UFO Modus Operandi: January 1975," Official UFO 1 (Aug.1976):46,47.

Scioto co.
-Ancient road

(Editorial), Fate 11 (Nov.1958):22. il.
-Anomalous fossil
=human bones in iron ore bed
"A Singular Iron Man Petrifaction," Sci.Am. 3 (1848):30, quoting Cincinnati Chronicle (undated).

Shaker Heights
-Fall of ice
1959, Oct.30/Highland Park golf course
Coral E. Lorenzen, The Shadow of the Unknown (N.Y.: Signet, 1970), pp. 119-20.
-UFO (DD)
1948, May 13/Tom Comella
1949, June 3/Tom Comella
(Letter), Fate 5 (July-Aug.1952): 124-28.
-UFO (NL)
1951, Nov.16/Tom Comella
1952, Jan.1/Tom Comella
(Letter), Fate 5 (July-Aug.1952): 124-28.

Sharonville
-Fall of burning substance
1955, April 3/Joseph Hauck/S of town
"Hot Coals and the Curious Hole from Nowhere," CRIFO Newsl., 6 May 1955, p.2.
-UFO (?)
1952, Aug.1
Richard Hall, ed., The UFO Evidence (Washington: NICAP, 1964), pp.98, 153.
-UFO (NL)
1960, Nov.23/B.J. Sharrock/=meteor?
Curtis Fuller, "The Nov.23 UFO," Fate 14 (Mar.1961):46,49.

Sheffield
-UFO (CE-2)
1978, July 27
"UFOs of Limited Merit," Int'l UFO Reporter 3 (Sep.1978):6,7.

Sheffield twp.
-Archeological sites
E.G. Squier & E.H. Davis, Ancient Monuments of the Mississippi Valley (Washington: Smithsonian Institution, Contrib.to Knowl., no.1, 1848), p. 39.

Sheffield Lake
-UFO (CE-1)
1958, Sep.21/Mrs. William H. Fitzgerald
Robert J. Durant, The Fitzgerald Report (Akron: UFO Rsch.Center, 1958).
"Akron Group Exposes AF Cover-Up," UFO Inv. 1 (Dec.1958):5.
Coral Lorenzen, "The Fitzgerald Investigation: What It Means," Flying Saucers, May 1959, pp.47-50.
Donald H. Menzel & Lyle G. Boyd, The World of Flying Saucers (Garden City: Doubleday, 1963), pp.279-88.
Richard Hall, ed., The UFO Evidence (Washington: NICAP, 1964), p.113.

"A Documented Case of Governmental
Dishonesty," Pursuit 5 (Apr.1972):
28-30.

Shelby
-UFO (CE-4)
1975, Nov.
Bill Jones, "New Ohio Abduction
Case," MUFON UFO J., no.115 (June
1977):9-10.

Shelby co.
-Medieval silver coin and steel chain
Timothy R. Jenkins, The Ten Tribes
of Israel! (Springfield: Houck &
Smith, 1883).

Shiloh, Montgomery co.
-UFO (DD)
1953/Wilgus A. Patton
Gray Barker, They Knew Too Much
About Flying Saucers (N.Y.: Univer-
sity, 1956), pp.38-39.

Shiloh, Richland co.
-UFO (CE-1)
1897, May 1/John S. Chamberlain
Ashland Press, 13 May 1897.

Sidney
-Phantom panther
n.d./Earl Barker/Miami R.
R.E. Buehler, "Looking Through the
Archives: The Big Cat," J.Ohio Folk-
lore Soc'y 1 (winter 1966):75.

Somerset
-Archeological site
Jon Douglas Singer, "Stone Forts of
the Midwest and the Appalachian Region: Are They Clues to the Enigma
of Mystery Hill?" NEARA J. 13 (winter 1979):63-66.
-Phantom image
1848-   /Otterbein Evangelical United
Brethren Church
"Mark of the Vengeful Spirit," Fate
10 (Feb.1957):21.
Robert Wunderlin, "Vengeance Rode a
Horse," Fate 26 (June 1973):46-49.
il.

Somerville
-Archeological site
E.G. Squier & E.H. Davis, Ancient
Monuments of the Mississippi Valley
(Washington: Smithsonian Institution,
Contrib.to Knowl., no.1, 1848), p.
90.

Springdale
-UFO (DD)
1956, Oct.9/Mrs. James Petrey
"Case 231," CRIFO Orbit, 2 Nov.1956,
p.4.

Springfield
-Spirit medium
1853
Jesse Babcock Ferguson, Spirit Com-

munion (Nashville: Union & American,
1854).
T.L. Nichols, Supramundane Facts in
the Life of the Rev. J.B. Ferguson
(London: F. Pitman, 1865).
Emma Hardinge Britten, Modern Ameri-
can Spiritualism (N.Y.: The Author,
1870), pp.408-11.
-UFO (?)
1952, Aug.18
Don Berliner, "The Ground Observers
Corps," Official UFO 1 (Aug.1976):
24,51.
-UFO (CE-1)
1950, Aug.
Harold T. Wilkins, Flying Saucers on
the Attack (N.Y.: Ace, 1967 ed.),
p.125.
-UFO (CE-2)
1957, Nov.5
Marietta Times, 6 Nov.1957.
1966, March 31/Charles Schneider/
ground markings only
Columbus Dispatch, 1 Apr.1966, p.1.
-UFO (CE-3)
1974, Jan.8/John E. Justice/Masonic
Home
Leonard H. Stringfield, Situation
Red: The UFO Siege (N.Y.: Fawcett
Crest, 1977 ed.), pp.118-20.
-UFO (DD)
1947, July 2/Donald Polen
Cincinnati Times-Star, 5 July 1947.
1977, Aug.1
"UFOs of Limited Merit," Int'l UFO
Reporter 2 (Sep.1977):8.

Stout
-Humanoid
1897, April 24
Cincinnati Enquirer, 27 Apr.1897.
Portsmouth Blade, 28 Apr.1897.
1897, May 26/Charles Lukins
Cleveland Plain Dealer, 27 May 1897.

Stow
-Deathbed apparition
1966/Mary Grohe
"Woman Who Lived to Tell of Death,"
Fate 20 (Mar.1967):48, quoting
Akron Beacon-Journal (undated).
-UFO (NL)
1956, Dec.4
"Case 279," CRIFO Orbit, 1 Feb.1957,
p.4.

Struthers
-Fall of chemicals
1946, Oct.3/=pollution?
"First Prize," Doubt, no.17 (1947):
250.

Sulphur Springs
-UFO (?)
1883, Nov.
"A Remarkable Phenomenon Seen at Sulphur Springs, Ohio," Sci.Am. 50
(1884):97.

Sunbury
-UFO (NL)
  1897, April 25/W.F. Whittier
    Dayton Daily Journal, 28 Apr.1897.

Tarlton
-Archeological site
  ca.300 B.C.-500 A.D.
    E.G. Squier & E.H. Davis, Ancient
    Monuments of the Mississippi Valley
    (Washington: Smithsonian Institution,
    Contrib.to Knowl., no.1, 1848), p.
    98.
    Harry R. McPherson, "The Cross Mound,"
    Bull.Ohio Indian Relic Collectors,
    no.25 (Sep.1950):38-40. il.
    Franklin Folsom, America's Ancient
    Treasures (N.Y.: Rand McNally,
    1974), p.154.

Terrace Park
-UFO (DD)
  1947, July 6/Mrs. A.C. Stollmaier/908
  Elm Ave.
    Cincinnati Enquirer, 7-8 July 1947.

Thompson
-Spirit medium
  1850s/Mr. Stockwell
    Emma Hardinge Britten, Modern Ameri-
    can Spiritualism (N.Y.: The Author,
    1870), p.105.
-UFO (NL)
  1957, Nov.7/Mrs. E.A. Markell
    Chardon Geauga Record, 21 Nov.1957.

Tiro
-UFO (CE-1)
  1957, Nov.23
    Richard Hall, ed., The UFO Evidence
    (Washington: NICAP, 1964), p.167.

Toledo
-Anomalous hole in ground
  1975-1976
    Toledo Blade, 28 Sep.1976.
-Archeological sites
  Maumee R.
    E.G. Squier & E.H. Davis, Ancient
    Monuments of the Mississippi Valley
    (Washington: Smithsonian Institution,
    Contrib.to Knowl., no.1, 1848), pp.
    40-42.
    S.S. Knabenshue, "Mound Builders'
    Fort within Toledo's Limits," Ohio
    State Arch.& Hist.Quar. 10 (1902):
    381-84.
    Albert Schulman, "The Toledo Mound:
    A Preliminary Report," Northwest
    Ohio Quar. 21 (1949):169-75.
-Ball lightning
  1923, summer/Mary Jiminez
    Eric Norman [Brad Steiger], Weird
    Unsolved Mysteries (N.Y.: Award,
    1969), pp.120-21, quoting Search,
    Mar.1968.
-Clairvoyance
  1928, June/Elizabeth E. Miller
    Elizabeth E. Miller, "A Vision Saved
    My Baby," Fate 9 (Jan.1956):51.

-Exploding broom
  1954, April/Dolly Kaminski/1602½
  Cherry St.
    (Editorial), Fate 7 (Nov.1954):14.
-Giant human skeletons
  1895, Oct./Henry T. Niles
    Chicago (Ill.) Record, 24 Oct.1895,
    p.1.
-Inner development
  1948-   /Our Lady of Endor Coven/Her-
  bert Arthur Sloane
    Hans Holzer, The New Pagans (Garden
    City: Doubleday, 1972), pp.72-84.
    Hans Holzer, The Witchcraft Report
    (N.Y.: Ace, 1973), pp.156-57.
    J. Gordon Melton, Encyclopedia of
    American Religions, 2 vols. (Wil-
    mington, N.C.: Consortium, 1978),
    2:301-302.
  1970s/Ass'n of Astrology, Metaphysics
  and Psychic Sciences/Box 6045 HD
    June & Nicholas Regush, Psi: The Oth-
    er World Catalogue (N.Y.: Putnam,
    1974), p.100.
-Mystery tracks
  1967, Feb./Mrs. Ralph McVickers
    Toledo Record, 13-14 Feb.1967.
-Phantom insect
  1899, July 11/Ptl. Freeman
    Chicago (Ill.) Tribune, 12 July 1899,
    p.1.
-Skyquake
  1958, Sep.29
    "The Night of September 29," Fate
    12 (Feb.1959):31,37.
-Spirit medium
  1900s-1920s/Ada Besinnet
    W. Usborne Moore, Glimpses of the
    Next State (London: Watts, 1911),
    pp.309-46.
    "Experiments with Trance Phenomena,"
    J.ASPR 4 (1910):53-62.
    W.H. Hamilton, J.S. Smyth & James H.
    Hyslop, "A Case of Hysteria," Proc.
    ASPR 5 (1911):1-670. il.
    James H. Hyslop, "The Burton Case
    of Hysteria and Other Phenomena,"
    J.ASPR 5 (1911):289-319.
    J.W. Coleman, "Notes in the Estima-
    tion of the Burton Case," J.ASPR 5
    (1911):665-77.
    George H. Johnson, "The Trance Phen-
    omena of Miss Ada Besinnet," J.ASPR
    17 (1923):49-62.
  1910s/J.B. Jonson/632 Orchard St.
    William Usborne Moore, Glimpses of
    the Next State (London: Watts,
    1911), pp.193-223.
    Walter F. Prince, "Experiments for
    Alleged Clairvoyance," J.ASPR 13
    (1919):451-91.
    John S. King, Dawn of the Awakened
    Mind (N.Y.: James A. McCann, 1920).
    Nandor Fodor, Encyclopaedia of Psy-
    chic Science (London: Arthurs,
    1933), p.187, quoting Psychic Sci.,
    Apr.1927.
-Telepathy
  1951, Feb.
    Cleveland Plain Dealer, 11 Feb.1951.

-Tornado anomaly
  1965, April 11/James Weyer
    B. Vonnegut & James Weyer, "Luminous
    Phenomena in Nocturnal Tornadoes,"
    Science 153 (1966):1213-20. il.
-UFO (?)
  1952, April 29/=vapor trails
    Ann Arbor (Mich.) News, 30 Apr.1952.
  1957, Nov.6
    Aimé Michel, Flying Saucers and the
    Straight-Line Mystery (N.Y.: Criter-
    ion, 1958), p.256.
  1966, March 25
    "Typical Reports," UFO Inv. 3 (Mar.-
    Apr.1966):8.
-UFO (CE-1)
  1964, June 13
    Jacques & Janine Vallee, Challenge
    to Science (N.Y.: Ace, 1966 ed.),
    p.60.
  1966, June 8/Sandusky Rd.
    Jacques Vallee, Passport to Magonia
    (Chicago: Regnery, 1969), p.331.
-UFO (DD)
  1977, Oct.14
    "This Month," Int'l UFO Reporter 2
    (Nov.1977):Newsfront sec.
-UFO (NL)
  1897, April 24/Howard Warn
    Cleveland Plain Dealer, 28 Apr.1897.
  1953, Aug.1
  1953, Nov.14
  1953, Dec.16
    Richard Hall, ed., The UFO Evidence
    (Washington: NICAP, 1964), p.65.
  1961, Nov.23/R.D. Osborn
    (Letter), Fate 15 (May 1962):106-108.
  1967, March 3/Joseph Czezur
    "Disc Seen over Expressway," APRO
    Bull. 15 (May-June 1967):10. il.
  1972, Feb.11/Kathy Senecal/4119 Parra-
    keet St.
    "Did You See This One?" Skylook, no.
    54 (May 1972):6.
    "Two Students Watch UFO--Planes Ap-
    parently Investigate," Skylook, no.
    55 (June 1972):6.
  1978, Jan.23
    "UFOs of Limited Merit," Int'l UFO
    Reporter 3 (Mar.1978):3.

Troy
UFO (NL)
  1952, Aug.24
    Don Berliner, "The Ground Observers
    Corps," Official UFO 1 (Aug.1976):
    24,51.
-UFO (NL) and skyquake
  1973, Oct.11-12/Early Thomas
    Columbus Dispatch, 12 Oct.1973, p.
    35A.

Uhrichsville
-UFO (CE-2)
  1955, Oct.2/Mrs. Albert Fanty
    Uhrichsville Evening Chronicle, 6
    Oct.1955.

Union
-UFO (NL)

1973, Oct.14/Fred Shaner
  Columbus Dispatch, 15 Oct.1973, p.1.
  Dayton Daily News, 15-16 Oct.1973.
  il.
  Leonard H. Stringfield, Situation
  Red: The UFO Siege (N.Y.: Fawcett
  Crest, 1977 ed.), p.155.

Unionville
-Lightning anomaly
  1903, Nov.18
    "Lightning Phenomenon," Monthly
    Weather Rev. 31 (Nov.1903):534.

Upper Sandusky
-Humanoid
  1972, Aug.9/N of town
    Columbus Dispatch, 9 Aug.1972, p.1.
-UFO (?)
  1966, March 25/Everett Will
    Columbus Dispatch, 26 Mar.1966, p.1.
-UFO (CE-1)
  1897, April 17/E.T. Kenan
    Cleveland Plain Dealer, 18 Apr.1897.

Urbana
-UFO (CE-1)
  1965, Aug.30/Michael Lilly/Powell Ave.
    Lloyd Mallan, "The Mysterious 12,"
    Sci.& Mech. 37 (Dec.1966):30,34-35,
    57.
    Lloyd Mallan, "Complete Directory of
    UFOs: Part 1," Sci.& Mech. 37 (Dec.
    1966):36,74-75.

Vandalia
-UFO (NL)
  1953, Sep.7
    "C-15," CRIFO Newsl., 3 Sep.1954, p.
    5.

Vermilion
-Erratic platypus
  1874, Oct.18
    Sandusky Register, 19 Oct.1874.
-UFO (?)
  1967, Sep.11/=meteor?
    Elyria Chronicle-Telegram, 11 Sep.
    1967.

Wadsworth
-UFO (NL)
  1948, June 24/Dan Rohn
    (Letter), Fate 1 (fall 1948):122.

Wapakoneta
-UFO (NL)
  1947, June 23/Richard L. Bitters
    Columbus Citizen, 7 July 1947.
  1975, March 30
    Wapakoneta Daily News, 1 Apr.1975.

Warren
-UFO (CE-1)
  1968, July 8/Richard Montgomery
    Donald E. Keyhoe & Gordon I.R. Lore,
    Jr., UFOs: A New Look (Washington:
    NICAP, 1969), p.5.
-UFO (CE-2)
  1953, Nov.14/Earl Pence/S of town

Keith Roberts, "Reconsidering the
Mysterious 'Little Men,'" Saucer
News 12 (Mar.1965):7,8.

Washington Court House
-Ancient iron furnace
  Waters site
    Clyde E. Keeler & Bennett E. Kelley,
    "Ancient Iron Smelting Furnaces of
    Ohio," NEARA Newsl. 6 (June 1971):
    28,30.
    Clyde E. Keeler & Bennett E. Kelley,
    "Early Iron and the Ohio Furnaces,"
    NEARA Newsl. 6 (Sep.1971):52-55. il.
-Mystery radio transmission
  1963, May/Mrs. Eugene Langen/702 Mc-
  Arthur Way
    G.D. Kaye, "The Number from Luna
    Earth," Fate 17 (Sep.1964):61-62.
-UFO (?)
  1897, April 14/=balloon
    Washington Court House Cyclone &
    Fayette Republican, 22 Apr.1897.
  1973, Oct.18/Highland Ave./=hoax
    Columbus Dispatch, 20 Oct.1973, p.2.

Waterloo
-Haunt
  1840-1950s/Columbian House
    Toledo Blade, 14 Aug.1960.
    Pauline Saltzman, Ghosts and Other
    Strangers (N.Y.: Lancer, 1970 ed.),
    pp.91-93.

Waverly
-Archeological site
    Gerard Fowke, Archaeological History
    of Ohio (Columbus: F.J. Heer, 1902).
    Miguel Covarrubias, The Eagle, the
    Jaguar, and the Serpent (N.Y.:
    Knopf, 1954). il.

Wayne co.
-Ancient iron ax
    G.U. Duer, "Iron Axe in a Mound," Am.
    Antiquarian 11 (1889):188.

Waynesville
-UFO (?)
  1961, June 12/Mrs. Howard Carnes
    "'Smoke Ring' in Ohio," APRO Bull.
    10 (July 1961):1.

Wellston
-Clairvoyance
  1921, fall
    Thomas E. Wade, "My Other Self,"
    Fate 9 (Dec.1956):72.

Westerville
-Airship message
  1897, April 23/Cyrus Riggle
    Columbus Sunday Press, 25 Apr.1897.
-Fall of marble cylinder
  1910/Daniel Lawyer
    "Small Meteor Startles Ohio Farmer,"
    Pop.Mechanics 14 (1910):801. il.
-Humanoid tracks
  1974, Sep.
    John Green, Sasquatch: The Apes Among

Us (Seattle: Hancock House, 1978),
p.210.
-UFO (NL)
  1897, April 22/John Haywood
    Columbus Evening Press, 23 Apr.1897.
    Columbus Ohio State Journal, 24 Apr.
    1897.
    Columbus Sunday Press, 25 Apr.1897.
  1975, June 27/Ron McClary/Westerville
  Rd.
    Columbus Dispatch, 27 June 1975.

West Jefferson
-Phantom bear
  1973, Oct.10
    Columbus Dispatch, 11 Oct.1973.
-UFO (NL)
  1973, Oct.14
    Columbus Dispatch, 15 Oct.1973, p.1.
  1978, Sep.6/Jim Chenault/Big Darby
  Creek
    London Madison Press, 8 Sep.1978.

West Union
-UFO (NL)
  1973, Oct.17
    West Union People's Defender, 18
    Oct.1973.

West Unity
-UFO (CE-2)
  1964/ground markings only
    Ted Phillips, Physical Traces Associ-
    ated with UFO Sightings (Evanston:
    Center for UFO Studies, 1975), p.29.

Whitehouse
-UFO (CE-2) and Men-in-black
  1967, July 13/Robert Richardson/NE of
  town
    "UAO Struck by Automobile in Ohio,"
    APRO Bull. 16 (July-Aug.1967):1,3.
-UFO (CE-3)
  1974, April 10
    Ted Bloecher, "A Catalog of Humanoid
    Reports for 1974," in MUFON 1975
    UFO Symposium Proc. (Seguin, Tex.:
    MUFON, 1975), pp.51,56.

Wickliffe
-Dowsing
  1959-1960/James J. Shumaker
    Gus Utter, "Quest for Natural Life
    Ray," Fate 13 (Dec.1960):67-71. il.

Willard
-Archeological site
  ca.7400 B.C.
    Cleveland Press, 30 Nov.1977.
-UFO (CE-1)
  1971, Jan.22/Richard Williams/Old
  River Rd.
    "Press Reports," APRO Bull. 19 (Jan.-
    Feb.1971):7.
    "Large UFO Reported near Willard,
    Ohio," Skylook, no.41 (Apr.1971):
    5-6.

Willoughby
-Crisis apparition

n.d./Mildred Eastman
Hans Holzer, Ghosts I've Met (N.Y.:
Ace, 1965 ed.), p.62.
-UFO (CE-1)
1955, Aug.1/W.M. Sheneman/Chardon x
Chillicothe Rd.
Donald E. Keyhoe, Flying Saucers: Top
Secret (N.Y.: Putnam, 1960), pp.
236-39.
Richard Hall, ed., The UFO Evidence
(Washington: NICAP, 1964), p.114.
Thomas M. Olsen, ed., The Reference
for Outstanding UFO Sighting Reports
(Riderwood, Md.: UFO Information
Retrieval Center, 1966), pp.40-41.

Willoughby Hills
-UFO (CE-3)
1955, Aug.30-Sep.1/David Ankenbrandt/
3 mi.E
Isabel Davis & Ted Bloecher, Close
Encounter at Kelly and Others of
1955 (Evanston: Center for UFO
Studies, 1978), pp.184-86.

Wilmington
-Ancient inscription
n.d./L.B. Welch/=hoax
John P. MacLean, The Mound Builders
(Cincinnati: Robert Clarke, 1904),
pp.116-19.
-Humanoid
1961, summer
Ron Schaffner, "A Report on Ohio An-
thropoids and Other Strange Crea-
tures," in Bigfoot: Tales of Unex-
plained Creatures (Rome, O.: Page
Rsch.Library, 1978), pp.40,42-43.
-UFO (NL)
1948, Jan.7/Clinton County AFB
Harold T. Wilkins, Flying Saucers on
the Attack (N.Y.: Ace, 1967 ed.),
p.86.
Brad Steiger, ed., Project Blue Book
(N.Y.: Ballantine, 1976), pp.51,58.

Woodlawn
-Humanoid
1976, Feb.
Leonard H. Stringfield, Situation
Red: The UFO Siege (N.Y.: Fawcett
Crest, 1977 ed.), p.89.
-UFO (NL)
1955, Aug.22/John Kluemper
Cincinnati Times-Star, 23 Aug.1955,
p.1.
"Case 99," CRIFO Orbit, 2 Sep.1955,
p.3.

Wooster
-Fall of metallic object
1935, Dec.25/Daniel L. Cayo
Los Angeles (Cal.) Examiner, 4 Mar.
1936.
"No Meteors," Fortean Soc'y Mag., no.
3 (Jan.1940):9.
-Precognition
1970s/Komar (Vernon Craig)/323 Ihrig
Warren Smith, "Phenomenal Predictions
for 1975," Saga, Jan.1975, pp.20,

48,50.
-UFO (NL)
1964, May 17/Donald Fry/NE of town
"Other Recent Sightings," UFO Inv.
2 (July-Aug.1964):7.
Jeffrey Liss, "UFO's That Look Like
Tops," Fate 17 (Nov.1964):66,67-68.

Worthington
-Archeological sites
ca.300 B.C.-500 A.D.
E.G. Squier & E.H. Davis, Ancient
Monuments of the Mississippi Valley
(Washington: Smithsonian Institution,
Contrib.to Knowl., no.1, 1848), pp.
36,84.
Opha Moore, History of Franklin
County, Ohio, 3 vols. (Topeka:
Historical Pub.Co., 1930), 1:73-84.
-UFO (?)
1833, Nov.13/John L. Riddell/=meteor
procession
Denison Olmsted, "Observations on
the Meteors of November 13, 1833,"
Am.J.Sci., ser.1, 25 (1834):363,
377-78.
1876, Dec.21/=meteor procession
James Glaisher, et al., "Observations
of Luminous Meteors during the Year
1876-77," Rept.Brit.Ass'n Adv.Sci.,
1877, pp.98,152.
Donald H. Menzel & Lyle G. Boyd, The
World of Flying Saucers (Garden
City: Doubleday, 1963), p.107.
-UFO (DD)
1957, Nov.12/James Lewis
"Silvery Saucer Seen by Ohio Police
Chief," Saucer News 5 (Feb.-Mar.
1958):22.
-UFO (NL)
1965, Aug.2
Columbus Dispatch, 3 Aug.1965, p.1.

Xenia
-Archeological sites
Massie's Creek
E.G. Squier & E.H. Davis, Ancient
Monuments of the Mississippi Valley
(Washington: Smithsonian Institution,
Contrib.to Knowl., no.1, 1848), pp.
95-96.
M.A. Broadstone, History of Greene
County, Ohio, 2 vols. (Indianapolis:
B.F. Bowen, 1918), 1:72-79.
-Out-of-body experience
1970s/Flo Thompson
Herbert B. Greenhouse, The Astral
Journey (N.Y.: Avon, 1969 ed.), pp.
212-17,335.
-Paranormal strength
1965, Nov.9/Dorothy Hawkins
(Editorial), Fate 19 (Sep.1966):18-
20.
-UFO (?)
1973, Oct.16/=hoax
Dayton Journal-Herald, 17 Oct.1973.
-UFO (DD)
1956/Douglas Jansen
(Letter), Fate 11 (Mar.1958):116.

Yellow Springs
-Archeological site
  Wolfgang Marschall, "Exploration of
  Glen Helen Mound," 40th Int'l Cong.
  Americanists (1972), 1:89-97. il.
-Phantom
  1963/Robert Anton Wilson
    Robert Anton Wilson, Cosmic Trigger:
    Final Secret of the Illuminati
    (Berkeley: And/Or, 1977), pp.24-25.
-Telepathy research
  1930s/Clarence Leuba/Antioch College
    Clarence Leuba, "An Experiment to
    Test the Role of Chance in ESP Re-
    search," J.Parapsych. 2 (1938):217-
    21.
-UFO (NL)
  1968, Aug.15
    Donald H. Menzel, "UFOs--The Modern
    Myth," in Carl Sagan & Thornton
    Page, eds., UFOs: A Scientific De-
    bate (Ithaca: Cornell Univ., 1972),
    pp.123,137-38.

Youngstown
-Dowsing
  1930s
    (Letter), Betty Bulvony, Fate 24
    (Dec.1971):127.
-Haunt
  1944/Virginia A. Santore
    Virginia A. Santore, "The House That
    Hated People," Fate 16 (Oct.1963):
    80-85.
  1950, July-Nov./Harry Wagner
    Virginia Santore, "The Vengeful Suc-
    cubus," Fate 30 (Sep.1977):43-46.
-Healing
  1910s-1920s/John D. Reese
    New York Herald-Tribune, 30 Nov.1931.
    New York Times, 30 Nov.1931, p.19.
-Hex
  1978, Jan.-June/Mike Gilboy
    Nat'l Enquirer, 15 Aug.1978.
-Mystery gas
  1967, July 4/Howard Moore/Market St.
    John A. Keel, "Mysterious Gas Attacks
    by Flying Saucers," Saga UFO Rept.
    2 (fall 1975):27.
-Psychokinesis
  1923-1957/Huldah Perkins Stevens
    Huldah Perkins Stevens & Virginia A.
    Santore, "Family 'Gestalt' Warns of
    Death," Fate 19 (Oct.1966):83-88.
-UFO (?)
  1954, Oct.21/Gladys I. Mikkelsen/=
  meteor?
    (Letter), Fate 8 (Apr.1955):117-18.
  1964, May 25
    Jeffrey Liss, "UFO's That Look Like
    Tops," Fate 17 (Nov.1964):66,69.
-UFO (DD)
  1967, March 22/Tom Downie
    Wendelle C. Stevens, "Fantastic UFO
    Photo Flap of 1967," Saga UFO Rept.
    3 (June 1976):25.
-UFO (NL)
  1958, Sep.29/John Simmerlink
    "The Night of September 29," Fate 12
    (Feb.1959):31,36-37.

1967, July 18
  John A. Keel, "An Unusual Contact
  Claim from Ohio," Flying Saucer Rev.
  14 (Jan.-Feb.1968):25,26.
1975, Aug.28
  "UFO Central," CUFOS News Bull., 15
  Nov.1975, p.16.

Zanesville
-Disappearance
  n.d./James Greer
    Gray Barker, Book of Saucers (Clarks-
    burg, W.V.: Saucerian, 1965), p.32,
    quoting Saucerian, Nov.1953.
-Human tracks in sandstone
  1839/Muskingum R./=incised
    W.A. Adams, "Foot-Marks and Other
    Artificial Impressions on Rocks,"
    Am.J.Sci., ser.1, 44 (1843):200-202.
-UFO (NL)
  1897, April 23/J.B. Rhodes
    Caldwell Journal, 29 Apr.1897.
  1947, July 5/Barry Peruzzo/airport
    Columbus Dispatch, 6 July 1947.

       B. Physical Features

Avon Point
-Disappearance
  1942, Dec.2/William H. Smith/"Clevco"
    Cleveland Plain Dealer, 3-4 Dec.
    1942; and 8 Dec.1942.
    Dana Thomas Bowen, Shipwrecks of the
    Lakes (Cleveland: Freshwater, 1952),
    pp.313-23.

Berlin L.
-UFO (CE-1)
  1970, July 20
    Lucius Farish, "The Mini-Saucers,"
    Fate 27 (Dec.1974):59,65, quoting
    Eyewitness (undated).

Brush Creek
-Ancient inscription
  1879/J.M. Baughman
    "A Slab of Sandstone Containing
    Hieroglyphics," Am.Antiquarian 3
    (1880):61-62.
    Daniel G. Brinton, "Remarks Relating
    to the Alleged Discovery of an In-
    scribed Tablet in a Mound in Brush
    Creek Township, Muskingum County,
    Ohio," Rept.Proc.Numismatic & Anti-
    quarian Soc'y, 1880, pp.17-18.
    J.F. Everhart, History of Muskingum
    County, Ohio (Columbus: The Author,
    1882), pp.21-24. il.

Charles Mill L.
-Humanoid
  1959, March/Michael Lane
    Mansfield News-Journal, 28 Mar.1959.
    Nat'l Observer, 22 June 1964.

Cowan Creek
-Archeological site
    "Cowan Creek Mound Exploration,"
    Museum Echoes 22 (July 1949):54-55.

Charles R. Wicke, "Pyramids and Temple Mounds: Mesoamerican Ceremonial Architecture in Eastern North America," Am.Antiquity 30 (1965):409-20. il.

Crystal L.
-Erratic jellyfish
1954, March
(Editorial), Fate 8 (Apr.1955):9.

Deer Creek
-Ancient iron furnace and artifacts
Arledge and Haskins Mounds/=colonial?
Arlington H. Mallery, Lost America (Washington: Public Affairs, 1950), pp.193-96,206-10. il.
William D. Connor, "Ohio's Ancient Iron Age," Fate 21 (Oct.1968):84-96.
Clyde E. Keeler & Bennett E. Kelley, "Ancient Iron-Smelting Furnaces of Ohio," NEARA Newsl. 6 (June 1971): 28-32.
Clyde E. Keeler & Bennett E. Kelley, "Early Iron and the Ohio Furnaces," NEARA Newsl. 6 (Sep.1971):52-55.
Clyde E. Keeler, "Burden of the Amateurs!" NEARA Newsl. 6 (Dec.1971): 62-66. il.
Clyde Keeler, "A Critique of 'Lost America,'" NEARA Newsl. 7 (Dec. 1972):64-67. il.
Clyde E. Keeler, "Professor Putnam's Ohio Iron Furnaces," NEARA Newsl. 8 (Mar.1973):14-19.
Alva McGraw, Bennett E. Kelley & Clyde Keeler, "Bog Iron in Pre-Columbian Graves?" NEARA Newsl. 8 (winter 1974):75-76.

Dover Reservoir
-Windshield pitting
1953, May/John A. Dahlheimer
(Editorial), Fate 6 (Nov.1953):8, quoting Canton Repository (undated).

Erie, L.
-Disappearance
1850s/"Kate Norton"
Dana Thomas Bowen, Memories of the Lakes (Cleveland: Freshwater, 1969), p.78.
1973, April 20/Robert Joy, Jr./Citabria landplane
Cleveland Plain Dealer, 22 Apr.1973.
Jay Gourley, The Great Lakes Triangle, (Greenwich, Ct.: Fawcett, 1977), pp.167-68.
-Electromagnetic anomaly
1951, Dec.20/B.E. Smelser/Curtis C-46E
Jay Gourley, The Great Lakes Triangle (Greenwich, Ct.: Fawcett, 1977), pp.82-85.
-Lake monster
1817, July 3
C.S. Rafinesque, "Dissertation on Water Snakes, Sea Snakes and Sea Serpents," Phil.Mag. 54 (1819):361, 365.
-Mystery plane crash

1962, July 20/Willard F. Bierema
1964, Feb.15/James M. Mixon/Aero Commander 560E
Jay Gourley, The Great Lakes Triangle (Greenwich, Ct.: Fawcett, 1977), pp.16-18,32-33.

Flint Ridge
-Archeological site
Charles M. Smith, "A Sketch of Flint Ridge, Licking County, Ohio," Ann. Rept.Smith.Inst., 1884, pp.851-73.
Jeff Carskadden, "An Adena Stone Mound, Flint Ridge, Ohio," Ohio Arch. 18, no.3 (July 1968):80-81.
Franklin Folsom, America's Ancient Treasures (N.Y.: Rand McNally, 1974), p.149.
Jon Douglas Singer, "Stone Forts of the Midwest and the Appalachian Region: Are They Clues to the Enigma of Mystery Hill?" NEARA J. 13 (winter 1979):63-66.

Fort Ancient State Memorial
-Archeological site
300 B.C.-600 A.D., 1000-1600 A.D.
E.G. Squier & E.H. Davis, Ancient Monuments of the Mississippi Valley (Washington: Smithsonian Institution, Contrib.to Knowl., no.1, 1848), pp. 18-21.
William Pidgeon, Traditions of De-coo-dah (N.Y.: Horace Thayer, 1858), pp.74-78,259-61.
Cyrus Thomas, "Fort Ancient, Warren County, Ohio," Science 8 (1886): 538-40.
Warren K. Moorehead, Fort Ancient (Cincinnati: Robert Clarke, 1890). il.
Stephen D. Peet, "Natural and Artificial Terraces," Am.Geologist 7 (1891):113-17.
Stephen D. Peet, "Defensive Works of the Mound-Builders," Am.Antiquarian 13 (1891):189,205-208.
Warren King Moorehead, "A Description of Fort Ancient," Ohio State Arch.& Hist.Quar. 4 (1895):362-77. il.
Albert Kern, "Fort Ancient, a Prehistoric Fortification," Ohio Mag. 2 (1907):209-14. il.
Henry Clyde Shetrone, The Mound-Builders (N.Y.: Appleton, 1930), pp.169-84. il.
James B. Griffin, The Fort Ancient Aspect (Ann Arbor: Univ. of Michigan, 1943).
Richard C. Morgan, Fort Ancient (Columbus: Ohio Hist.Soc'y, 1960). il.
Franklin Folsom, America's Ancient Treasures (N.Y.: Rand McNally, 1974), pp.149-50.

Fort Hill
-Archeological site
300 B.C.-600 A.D.
E.G. Squier & E.H. Davis, Ancient Monuments of the Mississippi Valley

(Washington: Smithsonian Institution,
Contrib.to Knowl., no.1, 1848), pp.
14-16.
William Pidgeon, Traditions of De-
coo-dah (N.Y.: Horace Thayer, 1858),
pp.274-78.
H.W. Overman, "Fort Hill," Ohio Arch.
& Hist.Soc'y Quar. 1 (1887):260-64.
Stephen D. Peet, "Defensive Works
of the Mound-Builders," Am.Anti-
quarian 13 (1891):189,205.
Henry Clyde Shetrone, The Mound-
Builders (N.Y.: Appleton, 1930),
pp.229-30.
Raymond S. Baby, "Archaeological Explorations at Fort Hill," Museum
Echoes 27, no.11 (1954):86-87. il.
Franklin Folsom, America's Ancient
Treasures (N.Y.: Rand McNally,
1974), p.150.
Jon Douglas Singer, "Stone Forts of
the Midwest and the Appalachian Region: Are They Clues to the Enigma
of Mystery Hill?" NEARA J. 13 (winter 1979):63-66.

Foster's Crossing
-Ancient iron furnace
=colonial?
E.G. Squier & E.H. Davis, Ancient
Monuments of the Mississippi Valley
(Washington: Smithsonian Institution,
Contrib.to Knowl., no.1, 1848), pp.
26-29.
F.W. Putnam, "Reports on Clarke's
Earthwork Mound (Foster's Cross-
ing)," Peabody Mus.Rept. 4 (1887-
1890):95-97.
Arlington H. Mallery, Lost America
(Washington: Public Affairs, 1950),
pp.205-206. il.
Clyde E. Keeler, "Professor Putnam's
Ohio Iron Furnaces," NEARA Newsl. 8
(Mar.1973):14-18.

Great Miami R.
-Archeological site
mouth
E.G. Squier & E.H. Davis, Ancient
Monuments of the Mississippi Valley
(Washington: Smithsonian Institution,
Contrib.to Knowl., no.1, 1848), pp.
25-26.

Greenbriar L.
-UFO (CE-1)
1968, Aug.16
Donald E. Keyhoe & Gordon I.R. Lore,
Jr., UFOs: A New Look (Washington:
NICAP, 1969), p.43.

Greenville Creek
-Ancient inscription
H.K. Landis, "Egyptian Glyphs in
Ohio," Pennsylvania Arch. 7, no.1
(1937):13-15. il.

Johnson's I.
-Ghost
ca.1900

"Ghost Army of Johnson's Island,"
Fate 11 (May 1958):92, quoting
Cleveland Plain Dealer Mag. (un-
dated).

Kelley's I.
-Petroglyph
1000-1650/Inscription Rock
N.E. Hills, A History of Kelley's
Island, Ohio (Toledo: The Author,
1925). il.
Franklin Folsom, America's Ancient
Treasures (N.Y.: Rand McNally,
1974), p.150.

Little Miami R.
-Ancient coin
ca.1800
Jedediah Morse, American Universal
Geography, 3 vols. (Boston: J.T.
Buckingham, 1805), 1:333.

Locust Point
-Lake monster
1887, May 12/Mr. Dusseau
New York Times, 14 May 1887, p.1.

Mad R.
-Erratic crocodilian
1935, June 29/Joe Steele/Huffman Pond
Xenia Evening Gazette, 3 July 1935.

Mill Creek
-Archeological site
E.G. Squier & E.H. Davis, Ancient
Monuments of the Mississippi Valley
(Washington: Smithsonian Institution,
Contrib.to Knowl., no.1, 1848), pp.
91-92.

Paint Creek
-Archeological sites
Hopewell Group and others
E.G. Squier & E.H. Davis, Ancient
Monuments of the Mississippi Valley
(Washington: Smithsonian Institution,
Contrib.to Knowl., no.1, 1848), pp.
57-58,87.
W.K. Moorehead, "The Hopewell Find,"
Am.Antiquarian 18 (1896):58-62.
Henry Clyde Shetrone, The Mound-
Builders (N.Y.: Appleton, 1930),
pp.200-13.
Jon Douglas Singer, "Stone Forts of
the Midwest and the Appalachian Re-
gion: Are They Clues to the Enigma
of Mystery Hill?" NEARA J. 13 (win-
ter 1979):63-66.

Pippin L.
-Archeological site
"Skeletons in an Ohio Mound," Science
76 (5 Aug.1932), supp., p.10.

Pleasant Hill L.
-Precognition
1959, June 7/Murray Kerr
(Editorial), Fate 12 (Oct.1959):12.

Seip Mound
-Archeological site and ancient coin
coin=19th c. merchant's token
 E.G. Squier & E.H. Davis, Ancient
 Monuments of the Mississippi Valley
 (Washington: Smithsonian Institution,
 Contrib.to Knowl., no.1, 1848), pp.
 4,58.
 William C. Mills, Explorations of
 the Seip Mound (Columbus: F.J. Heer,
 1909). il.
 Henry Clyde Shetrone, The Mound-
 Builders (N.Y.: Appleton, 1930),
 pp.40-43,49-51,102-103,211-20. il.
 Clyde E. Keeler, "the Seip Mound
 'Coin' Identified," NEARA Newsl. 7
 (June 1972):22-24. il.
 H.R. McPherson, "More About the Seip
 Mound and the 'Seip Mound Coin,'"
 NEARA Newsl. 8 (summer 1973):34-35.
 Robert Kozak, "Some Preliminary
 Thoughts on Seip Mound," Ohio Arch.
 23, no.3 (1973):32-33.
 Clyde Keeler, "Seip Mound 'Mystery'
 Coin Identified," Fate 26 (Oct.
 1973):88-92. il.
 Franklin Folsom, America's Ancient
 Treasures (N.Y.: Rand McNally,
 1974), p.153.
 Columbus Dispatch, 18 Aug.1974. il.
 Barry Fell, America B.C. (N.Y.: Quad-
 rangle, 1976), p.189.

Serpent Mound State Memorial
-Archeological site
ca.50 A.D.
 E.G. Squier & E.H. Davis, Ancient
 Monuments of the Mississippi Valley
 (Washington: Smithsonian Institution,
 Contrib.to Knowl., no.1, 1848), pp.
 96-98.
 William Henry Holmes, "A Sketch of
 the Great Serpent Mound," Science 8
 (1886):625-28.
 "The Serpent Mound Saved," Ohio Arch.
 & Hist.Soc'y Quar. 1 (1887):187-90.
 Stephen D. Peet, "The Great Serpent
 and Other Effigies," Am.Antiquarian
 12 (1890):211-28.
 F.W. Putnam, "The Serpent Mound of
 Ohio," Century Ill.Mag., n.s., 17
 (1890):871-88.
 "Ohio, the Site of the Garden of
 Eden," Ohio Arch.& Hist.Soc'y Quar.
 10 (1901):225-31.
 E.O. Randall, The Serpent Mound,
 Adams County, Ohio (Columbus: Ohio
 State Arch.& Hist.Soc'y, 1905). il.
 Charles C. Willoughby, "The Serpent
 Mound of Adams County, Ohio," Am.
 Anthro. 21 (1919):153-63. il.
 Henry Clyde Shetrone, The Mound-
 Builders (N.Y.: Appleton, 1930),
 pp.230-35. il.
 Emerson F. Greenman, Serpent Mound
 (Columbus: Ohio Hist.Soc'y, 1970).
 il.
 Richard R. Juday, "A Theory on the
 Possible Religious Symbolism of
 Serpent Mound," Artifacts 1, no.2

(1971):32-35. il.
 Franklin Folsom, America's Ancient
 Treasures (N.Y.: Rand McNally,
 1974), p.153.
 Thaddeus M. Cowan, "Effigy Mounds
 and Stellar Representation: A Com-
 parison of Old World and New World
 Alignment Schemes," in Anthony F.
 Aveni, ed., Archaeoastronomy in
 Precolumbian America (Austin: Univ.
 of Texas, 1975), pp.217-34.
 A. Eric Arctander, "Serpent Mound,
 Adams County, Ohio," Ohio Arch. 27,
 no.2 (1977):23-28. il.
-Meteorite crater
 6500 m.diam./certain
 Walter H. Bucher, "Über eine typ-
 ische kryptovulkanische Storung im
 südlichen Ohio," Geologische Rund-
 schau 23A (1933):65-80.
 Alvin J. Cohen, A.M. Reid & Ted E.
 Bunch, "Central Uplifts of Terres-
 trial and Lunar Craters," J.Geo-
 phys.Rsch. 67 (1962):1632-33.
-Psychokinesis
 1975, Nov.18/Robert W. Harner
 Robert W. Harner, "Dance of the
 Leaves," Fate 30 (June 1977):81-84.

South Bass I.
-UFO (NL)
 1978, Jan.3/Roger Higbee/Perry's Monument
 Elyria Chronicle-Telegram, 4 Jan.
 1978.

Spruce Hill
-Archeological sites, ancient iron fur-
naces and Norse runestone
300 B.C.-500 A.D.
 (Letter), James Foster, Am.Med.&
 Phil.Register 2 (1814):393-96.
 Caleb Atwater, "Description of the
 Antiquities Discovered in the State
 of Ohio and Other Western States,"
 Trans.& Coll.Am.Antiquarian Soc'y 1
 (1820):105,126-31.
 E.G. Squier & E.H. Davis, Ancient
 Monuments of the Mississippi Valley
 (Washington: Smithsonian Institution,
 Contrib.to Knowl., no.1, 1848), pp.
 11-13,86.
 Stephen D. Peet, "Defensive Works of
 the Mound-Builders," Am.Antiquarian
 13 (1891):189,196,215-16.
 William C. Mills, "Baum Prehistoric
 Village," Ohio Arch.& Hist.Soc'y
 Quar. 15 (1906):45-136. il.
 Arlington H. Mallery, Lost America
 (Washington: Public Affairs, 1950),
 pp.191-93,201-202,204. il.
 Tom Peter & Don McBeth, "An Addition-
 al Note on the Bourneville Mound,
 Ross County, Ohio," Ohio Arch. 10,
 no.4 (1960):112-15. il.
 William D. Connor, "Ohio's Ancient
 Iron Age," Fate 21 (Oct.1968):84-96.
 Clyde E. Keeler, "Burden of the Ama-
 teurs!" NEARA Newsl. 6 (Dec.1971):
 62-64.

Clyde E. Keeler, "Professor Putnam's
Ohio Iron Furnaces," NEARA Newsl.
8 (Mar.1973):14-19.
Clyde Keeler, "The Mystery Town at
the Foot of Spruce Hill, Ohio,"
NEARA Newsl. 9 (spring 1974):37-38.
Jon Douglas Singer, "Stone Forts of
the Midwest and the Appalachian Region: Are They Clues to the Enigma
of Mystery Hill?" NEARA J. 13 (winter 1979):63-66.

Tappan L.
-UFO (NL)
1966, May 30-Aug./Mrs. John S. Clark
Columbus Dispatch, 22 Aug.1966.

Toepfner Mound
-Archeological site
ca.700 B.C.
"The Toepfner Mound," Museum Echoes
26, no.12 (1953):95.
William S. Webb & Raymond S. Baby,
The Adena People No.2 (Columbus:
Ohio State Univ., 1957).

Turner Mounds
-Archeological site
F.W. Putnam, "Iron from the Ohio
Mounds," Proc.Am.Antiquarian Soc'y,
ser.2, 2 (1883):349-63.
Charles C. Willoughby, "The Turner
Group of Earthworks, Hamilton Coun-
ty, Ohio," Pap.Peabody Mus. 8, no.
3 (1911):65-67.
Henry Clyde Shetrone, The Mound-
Builders (N.Y.: Appleton, 1930),
pp.118-19,100,220-22.
Arlington H. Mallery, Lost America
(Washington: Public Affairs, 1950),
pp.201-203. il.
Clyde E. Keeler, "Professor Putnam's
Ohio Iron Furnaces," NEARA Newsl. 8
(Mar.1973):14-19. il.

Wayne National Forest
-Humanoid
1966
John Green, Sasquatch: The Apes Among
Us (Seattle: Hancock House, 1978),
p.209.

West Harbor
-UFO (NL)
1967, Aug./James A. Piatt/Hwy.357
"Former Air Force Member Reports
UFO," Skylook, no.24 (Nov.1969):12.

Wolf Creek
-Phantom panther
1897, May
Bluffton News, 6 May 1897.

C. Ethnic Groups

Mound Builder cultures
ca.1000 B.C.-300 A.D./Adena culture
ca.100 B.C.-750 A.D./Hopewell culture

Benjamin Barton, Observations on
Some Parts of Natural History (London: C. Dilly, 1787).
Caleb Atwater, "Description of the
Antiquities Discovered in the State
of Ohio and Other Western States,"
Trans.& Coll.Am.Antiquarian Soc'y 1
(1820):105-267.
Friedrich Assall, Nachrichten über
die Früheren Einwohner von Nord-
amerika und ihre Denkmäler (Heidel-
burg: A. Osswald, 1827).
William Henry Harrison, A Discourse
on the Aborigines of the Valley of
the Ohio (Cincinnati: The Express,
1838).
E.G. Squier & E.H. Davis, Ancient
Monuments of the Mississippi Valley
(Washington: Smithsonian Institution,
Contrib.to Knowl., no.1, 1848).
John D. Baldwin, Ancient America in
Notes on American Archaeology (N.Y.:
Harper, 1872).
Edward Fontaine, How the World Was
Peopled (N.Y.: Appleton, 1872).
J.W. Foster, Prehistoric Races of
the United States of America (Chi-
cago: S.C. Griggs, 1873).
John T. Short, North Americans of
Antiquity (N.Y.: Harper, 1880).
Ignatius Donnelly, Atlantis: The
Antediluvian World (N.Y.: Gramercy,
1949 ed.), pp.230-38.
Warren K. Moorehead, Primitive Man
in Ohio (N.Y.: Putnam, 1892).
Cyrus Thomas, "Report on the Mound
Explorations of the Bureau of Eth-
nology," Ann.Rept.Bur.Am.Ethn. 12
(1890-91):3-742. il.
John P. MacLean, The Mound Builders
(Cincinnati: Robert Clarke, 1904).
Lord Avebury, Prehistoric Times
(London: Williams & Norgate, 1913),
pp.250-79.
H.C. Shetrone, "The Culture Problem
in Ohio Archaeology," Am.Anthro. 22
(1920):144-72.
Henry Clyde Shetrone, The Mound-
Builders (N.Y.: Appleton, 1930).
William S. Webb & Raymond S. Baby,
The Adena People No.2 (Columbus:
Ohio Hist.Soc'y, 1957).
James B. Griffin, "Climatic Change:
A Contributory Cause of the Growth
and Decline of Northern Hopewellian
Culture," Wisconsin Arch. 41 (1960):
21-33.
Robert Myron, Shadow of the Hawk
(N.Y.: Putnam, 1964).
Joseph R. Caldwell & Robert L. Hall,
ed., Hopewellian Studies (Spring-
field: Illinois State Mus., Sci.Pap.
no.12, 1964).
Robert Silverberg, Mound Builders
of Ancient America (Greenwich, Ct.:
N.Y. Graphic Soc'y, 1968).
Clyde Keeler, "New Light on Ohio's
Ancient Iron Age," Fate 25 (Apr.
1972):88-93.
Robert Silverberg, The Mound Builders

(N.Y.: Ballantine, 1974 ed.).

Shawnee Indians
-Transatlantic crossing myth
    John Johnston, "Account of the Pres-
    ent State of the Indian Tribes In-
    habiting Ohio," Trans.& Coll.Am.
    Antiquarian Soc'y 1 (1820):269,273.

        D. Unspecified Localities

-Erratic boulders in coal seams
    Mark Stirrup, "On Foreign Boulders
    in Coal Seams," Rept.Brit.Ass'n Adv.
    Sci., 1887, pp.686-88.

-Humanoid
  1963-1973/nr. I-75
    Allen V. Noe, "...And Still the Re-
    ports Roll In," Pursuit 7 (Jan.
    1974):16,17.

-UFO (DD)
  1960, Nov.24
    "Scientist Reports Sightings," APRO
    Bull. 10 (May 1962):3.
    Richard Hall, ed., The UFO Evidence
    (Washington: NICAP, 1964), p.54.

WEST VIRGINIA

A. Populated Places

Albright
-Hex and shape-shifting myth
John Harrington Cox, "The Witch Bri-
dle," Southern Folklore Quar. 7
(Dec.1943):203-209.

Alderson
-Crisis apparition
1904/Fay Baker
Bob Lee Austin, "Little Boy on a
Ghost Horse," Fate 13 (Apr.1960):
82-84.

Barboursville
-UFO (NL)
1973, Oct./Stella Jordan
Wheeling News-Register, 22 Oct.1973.

Beckley
-UFO (CE-2)
ca.1956/H.H. Harvey
1961, Sep./H.H. Harvey/U.S.61
Gray Barker, Book of Saucers (Clarks-
burg, W.V.: Saucerian, 1965), pp.
20-22.
-UFO (NL)
1973, Oct.15/Howard Moneypenny/Raleigh
County Airport
Beckley Post-Herald, 16 Oct.1973.
Beckley Raleigh Register, 16 Oct.
1973.
Ted Spickler, "West Virginia 'Saucer'
Scare," APRO Bull. 22 (Sep.-Oct.
1973):9.

Big Chimney
-UFO (CE-2)
1975, June 12
"From the Center for UFO Studies,"
Flying Saucer Rev. 21 (Apr.1976):
24,25.

Bluefield
-Cat mutilations
1974, Feb.6/Marlene Hawthorne
Kansas City (Mo.) Star, 12 Feb.1974.
-UFO (NL)
1950, April/H. Charles Robertson/U.S.
219
(Letter), Fate 11 (Feb.1958):114-16.
1969, Jan.5-6/Pat Ross
"UFO over West Virginia," APRO Bull.
17 (Mar.-Apr.1969):5, quoting Bluefield Daily Telegraph (undated).

Braxton co.
-Corpse anomaly
1933, June/Rebecca Marlow
Lonnie E. Legge, "The Changeless
Corpse," Fate 11 (Feb.1958):19.

Bridgeport
-UFO (DD)
1968, spring/Benedum Airport
W.C. Stevens, "Bell-Shaped UFOs,"
Official UFO 1 (Nov.1975):34,35,
39. il.
-UFO (NL)
1963, June/nr. Benedum Airport
Gray Barker, Book of Saucers (Clarks-
burg, W.V.: Saucerian, 1965), p.22.

Brooks
-Haunt
n.d./Joe Blake
Ruth Ann Musick, The Telltale Lilac
Bush (Lexington: Univ. of Kentucky,
1965), pp.12-16.

Burnt House
-UFO (CE-1)
1976, Aug./Kenneth Britton/Hwy.47
Gray Barker, "Invading West Virginia's Saucer Lairs and Monster Hide-
outs," Saga UFO Rept. 3 (Dec.1976):
33,77.

Cascade
-Haunt
1938-1939/Ann Smith
Ann Smith, "The Little Casket That
Cried," Fate 23 (Oct.1970):90-93.

Cass
-Humanoid
1961/Willie Barkley/nr. Cole Run
(Editorial), Fate 14 (July 1961):18-
20, quoting Marlinton Pocahontas
Times (undated).

Ceredo
-Petroglyph
Ohio R.
Columbus (O.) Dispatch, 27 June 1975,
p.A14.

Charleston
-UFO (?)
1967, Dec.2/=balloon
Edward U. Condon, ed., Scientific
Study of Unidentified Flying Objects
(N.Y.: Bantam, 1969 ed.), pp.388-89.
-UFO (CE-2)
1975, May 12/Elmer Salisbury/Cameron
High School
Timothy Green Beckley, "Saucers over
Our Cities," Saga UFO Rept. 4 (Aug.
1977):24,74.
-UFO (NL)
1952, Sep.12/Alice Williams
Ivan T. Sanderson, Uninvited Visitors
(N.Y.: Cowles, 1967), p.50.
1967, March 29/Jackie Oberlinger
John A. Keel, The Mothman Prophecies
(N.Y.: Saturday Review, 1975), p.144.

1978, Oct.20/Tracy Gossard/Churchill
Dr.
    Charleston Gazette-Mail, 22 Oct.1978.
1978, Oct.21/R.B. Pritt
    Ted Spickler, "West Virginia Flap:
    Part 1," MUFON UFO J., no.132 (Nov.-
    Dec.1978):9-10.
    Wayne Laporte, "A Night to Remember:
    The UFO Siege over Charleston, West
    Virginia," Saga UFO Rept. 7 (Feb.
    1979):14,16, quoting Wheeling In-
    telligencer (undated).
-UFO (R-V)
 1966, May 4
    Gordon D. Thayer, "Optical and Radar
    Analyses of Field Cases," in Edward
    U. Condon, ed., Scientific Study of
    Unidentified Flying Objects (N.Y.:
    Bantam, 1969 ed.), pp.115,163.

Chesapeake
-UFO (R-V)
 1978, Oct.21/Bill Givens/Kanawha Airport
    Charleston Gazette-Mail, 22 Oct.1978.

Chestnut Ridge
-Snow anomaly
 1917, winter/W. Armstrong Price
    W. Armstrong Price, "Snow Doughnuts,"
    Science 50 (1919):591-92.

Clarksburg
-UFO (NL)
 1977, July 3
    "UFOs of Limited Merit," Int'l UFO
    Reporter 2 (Aug.1977):3.

Clendenin
-Flying humanoid
 1966, Nov.26/Kenneth Duncan/cemetery
    John A. Keel, "West Virginia's Enig-
    matic 'Bird,'" Flying Saucer Rev.
    14 (July-Aug.1968):7,13.

Cottageville
-Haunt
 1968, Dec./Charles Hannum/B & O railroad
    Ruth Ann Musick, Coffin Hollow (Lex-
    ington: Univ. of Kentucky, 1977),
    pp.29-30.

Davis
-Humanoid
 1960, summer
    John A. Keel, Strange Creatures from
    Time and Space (Greenwich, Ct.:
    Fawcett, 1970), pp.120-21.

Doddridge co.
-Haunt
 n.d.
    Ruth Ann Musick, Coffin Hollow (Lex-
    ington: Univ. of Kentucky, 1977),
    pp.70-71.

Dunbar
-UFO (CE-1) and Men-in-black
 1967, Jan.19, 26/Tad Jones/I-64

Charleston Gazette, 20 Jan.1967.
John A. Keel, "From My Ohio Valley
Notebook," Flying Saucer Rev. 13
(May-June 1967):3,4-5.
John A. Keel, The Mothman Prophecies
(N.Y.: Saturday Review, 1975), pp.
96-99.

Elkhorn
-UFO (NL)
 1973, Oct.13, 17/David Bodner
    Theodore Spickler, "Nocturnal UFO
    in West Virginia," MUFON UFO J.,
    no.115 (June 1977):3,7. il.

Elkins
-Precognition
 1963-   /Jeanne Gardner
    Bea Moore, A Grain of Mustard (N.Y.:
    Simon & Schuster, 1969).
    Herbert B. Greenhouse, Premonitions:
    A Leap into the Future (N.Y.: War-
    ner, 1973 ed.), pp.81,95-96,139-40,
    190,271-74.

Elmwood
-UFO (NL)
 1967, Nov.20/Albert Brown/Hwy.35
    John A. Keel, The Mothman Prophecies
    (N.Y.: Saturday Review, 1975), p.
    246.

Fairmont
-Phantom panther
 1929, July/nr. 93 Mine
    Ruth Ann Musick, The Telltale Lilac
    Bush (Lexington: Univ. of Kentucky,
    1965), p.148.
-UFO (?)
 1955, March 8
    Leonard H. Stringfield, Inside Sau-
    cer Post...3-0 Blue (Cincinnati:
    CRIFO, 1957), p.58.
-UFO (DD)
 1949, Sep.26
    "If It's in the Sky It's a Saucer,"
    Doubt, no.27 (1949):416,417.
 1978, Oct./Joyce Dehner
    Jacksonville (Ark.) News, 28 Oct.
    1978.

Falls Mill
-UFO (NL)
 1973, Oct.15-17/Louise Scott
    Wheeling News-Register, 22 Oct.1973.

Fayette co.
-Fall of ice and gravel
 1892/Lewis F. Forberg
    (Letter), Fate 11 (Aug.1958):116-18.

Fayetteville
-Disappearance
 1945, Dec.24/George Sodder
    "Puzzle of the Missing Five," Fate
    10 (Apr.1957):17.

Flatwoods
-UFO (CE-1)
 1907, June 18/John Hatfield/N of town

Gray Barker, "Invading West Virgin-
ia's Saucer Lairs and Monster Hide-
outs," Saga UFO Rept. 3 (Dec.1976):
33,78-80.
-UFO (CE-3)
1952, Sep.12/Kathleen May
Charleston Daily Mail, 14 Sep.1952,
p.2.
Charleston Gazette, 15 Sep.1952, p.1.
Sutton Braxton Democrat, 18 Sep.1952.
Gray Barker, "The Monster and the
Saucer," Fate 6 (Jan.1953):12-17.
"W.Va. 'Monster'--A Full Report,"
Saucerian 1, no.1 (Sep.1953):8-21.
Gray Barker, They Knew Too Much About
Flying Saucers (N.Y.: University,
1956), pp.12-35.
Ivan T. Sanderson, Uninvited Visitors
(N.Y.: Cowles, 1967), pp.39-52.
Gray Barker, "Invading West Virgin-
ia's Saucer Lairs and Monster Hide-
outs," Saga UFO Rept. 3 (Dec.1976):
33,36-37,74-75.

Follansbee
-UFO (CE-1)
1966, April 26
1967, March 9/Hwy.2
Jacques Vallee, Passport to Magonia
(Chicago: Regnery, 1969), pp.330,
341.

Fork
-UFO (NL)
1966, Oct.14/James Roberts
Jacques Vallee, Passport to Magonia
(Chicago: Regnery, 1969), p.337,
quoting NICAP Reporter, Jan.1967.

Frametown
-UFO (CE-3)
1952, Sep.13/George Snitowski
Jacques Vallee, Passport to Magonia
(Chicago: Regnery, 1969), pp.200-
201.

Gallipolis Ferry
-Erratic snowy owl
1966, Dec.
Huntington Herald-Dispatch, 28 Dec.
1966.
-UFO (CE-2)
1967, March 31-April 3/Harold Harmon
John A. Keel, The Mothman Prophecies
(N.Y.: Saturday Review, 1975), pp.
129-35.
-UFO (NL)
1931, Oct.10/Claude Carter
New York Times, 11 Oct.1931, p.28;
and 12 Oct.1931, p.21.
1967, April 6-7/John A. Keel/Five Mile
Creek Rd.
John A. Keel, The Mothman Prophecies
(N.Y.: Saturday Review, 1975), pp.
146-48.
1978, Oct.21/Frank Crump
Huntington Herald-Dispatch, 24 Oct.
1978.

Glenville
-Precognition
1900
Ruth Ann Musick, The Telltale Lilac
Bush (Lexington: Univ. of Kentucky,
1965), pp.49-50.

Grafton
-Erratic octopus
1954
"Displaced Critters," Doubt, no.48
(1955):341, quoting Pittsburgh
(Pa.) Press (undated).
-UFO (NL)
1968, July 31/Cecil Devers
Brad Steiger & Joan Whritenour, Flying Saucer Invasion: Target--Earth
(N.Y.: Award, 1969), p.99.
-Water anomaly
1953, April? Aug?/reservoir
Harold T. Wilkins, Flying Saucers on
the Attack (N.Y.: Ace, 1967 ed.),
pp.264-65.
Harold T. Wilkins, Flying Saucers Uncensored (N.Y.: Pyramid, 1967 ed.),
pp.176-77.

Grant Town
-Haunt
1946
Ruth Ann Musick, The Telltale Lilac
Bush (Lexington: Univ. of Kentucky,
1965), pp.78-79.
-UFO (CE-3) and Men-in-black
1965, April 23/Mrs. Ivan Frederick
1968, July/Jennings H. Frederick
Gray Barker, "Invading West Virginia's Saucer Lairs and Monster Hide-
outs," Saga UFO Rept. 3 (Dec.1976):
33-36.

Green Bank
-Extraterrestrial communication project
1958-1962/Project Ozma/Nat'l Radio
Astronomy Observatory
F.D. Drake, "How Can We Detect Radio
Transmissions from Distant Plane-
tary Systems?" Sky & Telescope 19
(Jan.1960):140-43.
Otto Struve, "Astronomers in Turmoil,"
Physics Today 13 (Sep.1960):18,22-
23.
F.D. Drake, "Project Ozma," Physics
Today 14 (Apr.1961):40-46.
New York Times, 8 Oct.1961, sec.12,
p.9.
Frank D. Drake, "Project Ozma," in
A.G.W. Cameron, ed., Interstellar
Communication (N.Y.: W.A. Benjamin,
1963), pp.176-77.
"PGANE News," IEE Trans.on Aerospace
& Navigational Electronics 9 (1962):
181,267; 10 (1963):78.
Edwin Diamond, The Rise and Fall of
the Space Age (Garden City: Double-
day, 1964), pp.125-34.
Walter Sullivan, We Are Not Alone
(N.Y.: Signet, 1966 ed.), pp.197-
206.

Greenbriar co.
-Phantom panther
  1765
    Harold T. Wilkins, Secret Cities of
    Old South America (N.Y.: Library
    Publishers, 1952), p.283.

Harrison co.
-Haunt
  n.d.
    Ruth Ann Musick, Coffin Hollow (Lex-
    ington: Univ. of Kentucky, 1977),
    pp.94-96.

Heaters
-UFO (NL)
  1952, Sep.12
    Ivan T. Sanderson, Uninvited Visitors
    (N.Y.: Cowles, 1967), p.50.

Holden
-UFO (NL)
  1978, Nov.27
    Williamson Daily News, 28 Nov.1978.

Holly
-UFO (CE-3)
  1957, Nov.8/Hank Mollohan
    Hank Mollohan & Gray Barker, "The
    Holly River Sighting," Flying Sau-
    cers, May 1958, pp.36-41.

Huntington
-Haunt
  ca.1900
    Ruth Ann Musick, Coffin Hollow (Lex-
    ington: Univ. of Kentucky, 1977),
    pp.25-28.
-Spirit medium
  1900s-1910s/Elizabeth Blake
    L.V. Guthrie, et al., "The Case of
    Mrs. Blake," Proc.ASPR 7 (1913):
    570-788.
    Nandor Fodor, Encyclopaedia of Psy-
    chic Science (London: Arthurs,
    1933), p.31.
-UFO (CE-1)
  1967, March 5/Beau Shertzer/Hwy.2
    John A. Keel, The Mothman Prophecies
    (N.Y.: Saturday Review, 1975), pp.
    117-18.
  1973, Oct.19
    Ted Spickler, "West Virginia 'Saucer'
    Scare," APRO Bull. 22 (Sep.-Oct.
    1973):9.
-UFO (NL)
  1909, Dec.31/Joseph Green
    New York Tribune, 1 Jan.1910, p.2.
  1916, July 19/Walter H. Eager
    Walter H. Eager, "An Unusual Aurora,"
    Sci.Am. 115 (1916):241.
    Elmer Harrold, "Another Explanation,"
    Sci.Am. 115 (1916):369.

Irona
-UFO (CE-2)
  1978, Feb.14/Larry Costilow
    Morgantown Dominion-Post, 19 Feb.
    1978.

Jolo
-Snake handling
  1961/Mrs. Robert Elkins/Church In
  Jesus
    M.E. Counselman, "I Saw Them Take
    Up Serpents," Fate 15 (Sep.1962):
    85,88.

Kanawha co.
-Fall of frogs
  1887, June/Lewis F. Forberg
    (Letter), Fate 11 (Aug.1958):116-18.

Knob Fork
-Haunt
  1850s
    Ruth Ann Musick, The Telltale Lilac
    Bush (Lexington: Univ. of Kentucky,
    1965), pp.72-75.

Lakin
-Ancient inscriptions
  1949
    "The Lakin Tablets," West Virginia
    Arch., no.2 (1950):1-3. il.
    Everette W. Schwartz, "Second Note
    on the Lakin Tablets," West Virgin-
    ia Arch., no.3 (1950):19-21. il.
    Everette W. Schwartz, "The Lakin
    Tablets," Ohio Arch. 14 (July 1964)
    :73-75. il.

Leon
-Flying humanoid
  1966, Dec.11/Kathryn Beaver/Hwy.35
    Helen M. White, "Do Birds Come This
    Big?" Fate 20 (Aug.1967):74,76.

Lewisburg
-Phantom army
  1863, Oct.1/Moses Dwyer
    Frank Moore, The Civil War in Song
    and Story (N.Y.: P.F. Collier,
    1889), p.373.
-Precognition
  1823, Aug.23/John Stuart
    Frank Ball, "To the Last, a Man of
    Precision," Fate 30 (Apr.1977):81.
-UFO (DD)
  1950
    Donald E. Keyhoe, Flying Saucers from
    Outer Space (N.Y.: Holt, 1953), p.
    145.

Lost Creek
-UFO (DD)
  1966, July 23/John Sheets
    "UFO Film Received at Saucer News
    Headquarters," Saucer News 13 (win-
    ter 1966-67):33.
    (Editorial), Saucer News 14 (spring
    1967):20. il.
    W.C. Stevens, "Bell-Shaped UFOs,"
    Official UFO 1 (Nov.1975):34,36,39.
    il.

Marlinton
-Humanoid
  1960, Oct./W.C. Priestley/3 mi.N
    Charleston Daily Mail, 5 Jan.1961.

Marmet
-UFO (NL)
　　1978, Oct.22/Harlan Burns
　　　Charleston Gazette-Mail, 26 Oct.1978.
　　　il.

Martinsburg
-UFO (?)
　　1976, Sep.7/Leon Senjanec/=hoax
　　　Midnight, 20 Dec.1976.
　　　Hagerstown (Md.) Morning Herald, 28
　　　Dec.1976.

Mason
-Phantom horse
　　n.d./George Miller
　　　Ruth Ann Musick, The Telltale Lilac
　　　Bush (Lexington: Univ. of Kentucky,
　　　1965), p.44.

Mason co.
-Humanoid
　　1966, Nov./Cecil Lucas
　　　John A. Keel, "West Virginia's Enig-
　　　matic 'Bird,'" Flying Saucer Rev.
　　　14 (July-Aug.1968):7,11.

Middleway
-Poltergeist
　　1791, Dec.-1797, Aug.21/Adam Living-
　　stone/Wizard's Clipp
　　　Peter Henry Lemcke, Life and Work
　　　of Prince Demetrius Agustine Gal-
　　　litzin (London: Longmans, Green,
　　　1940).
　　　Raphael Brown, The Mystery of Wizard's
　　　Clip (Richmond: Catholic Hist.Soc'y,
　　　1949).
　　　Philip Bartholomew, "Ghosts Who Named
　　　a Town," Fate 6 (Oct.1953):64-68.
　　　Ruth Ann Musick, "West Virginia Ghost
　　　Stories," Midwest Folklore 8
　　　(spring 1958):21,26-28.

Mill Creek
-Phantom
　　ca.1865
　　　Ruth Ann Musick, The Telltale Lilac
　　　Bush (Lexington: Univ. of Kentucky,
　　　1965), pp.46-47.

Milton
-Exploding grave
　　1969, summer/Warren Sovine
　　　R.M. Baker, "The Exploding Grave,"
　　　Fate 23 (Feb.1970):100.

Mineralwells
-Contactee
　　1966, Nov.2-1970s/Woodrow Derenberger
　　　Woodrow W. Derenberger & Harold W.
　　　Hubbard, Visitors from Lanulos
　　　(N.Y.: Vantage, 1971).
　　　Philip J. Klass, UFOs Explained (N.Y.:
　　　Random House, 1974), pp.249-50.
　　　John A. Keel, The Mothman Prophecies
　　　(N.Y.: Saturday Review, 1975), pp.
　　　48-52,54-55,63-64,76,84-85,111-14,
　　　151,156,248.

Monongah
-Ghost horses
　　1907-   /Number Six Mine
　　　Ruth Ann Musick, Coffin Hollow (Lex-
　　　ington: Univ. of Kentucky, 1977),
　　　pp.77-80.
-UFO (CE-1)
　　ca.1866/Mrs. Hess Bender/Booth's Creek
　　　Ruth Ann Musick, The Telltale Lilac
　　　Bush (Lexington: Univ. of Kentucky,
　　　1965), pp.71-72.

Montrose
-Fall of sandstone
　　1930s/Kathleen Auvil
　　　Frank C. Cross, "Hypothetical Meteor-
　　　ites of Sedimentary Origin," Pop.
　　　Astron. 55 (1947):96-102.

Monumental
-UFO (CE-1)
　　1919, Aug.12/Luella Freeland
　　　Ruth Ann Musick, Coffin Hollow (Lex-
　　　ington: Univ. of Kentucky, 1977),
　　　pp.135-37.

Morgantown
-UFO (DD)
　　1973, Oct.15/David Humphreys/Fort Hill
　　Elementary School
　　　Morgantown Gazette, 17 Oct.1973.
-UFO (NL)
　　1964, May 25/Mrs. Rik Harkness
　　　Jeffrey Liss, "UFO's That Look Like
　　　Tops," Fate 17 (Nov.1964):66,68-69.
　　1971, July 1/Beverly Cramer/Tyrone Rd.
　　　"Pink UFO Sighted at Morgantown, W.
　　　Va.," Kansas-Oklahoma Newsl., Feb.
　　　1972, p.3, quoting Morgantown Domin-
　　　ion-News (undated).
　　1973, Oct.16/VanVoorhis Rd.
　　　Morgantown Dominion-News, 17 Oct.
　　　1973.

Moundsville
-Archeological site and ancient inscrip-
tion
　　ca.500 B.C./Grave Creek Mound
　　　Thaddeus Harris, Journal of a Tour
　　　into the Territory Northwest of the
　　　Allegheny Mountains (Boston: Man-
　　　ning & Loring, 1805), pp.63-64.
　　　Caleb Atwater, "Description of the
　　　Antiquities Discovered in the State
　　　of Ohio and Other Western States,"
　　　Trans.& Coll.Am.Antiquarian Soc'y 1
　　　(1820):105,185-87.
　　　Cincinnati (O.) Chronicle, 2 Feb.
　　　1839.
　　　Samuel G. Morton, Crania Americana
　　　(Philadelphia: J. Dobson, 1839), pp.
　　　223-25.
　　　A.B. Tomlinson, "American Antiquities
　　　at Grave Creek," Am.Pioneer 2 (1843)
　　　:196-203.
　　　A.B. Tomlinson, "First Settlement of
　　　Grave Creek," Am.Pioneer 2 (1843):
　　　347-58.
　　　Henry R. Schoolcraft, Oneóta (N.Y.:
　　　Wiley & Putnam, 1845), p.69.

John D. Baldwin, Ancient America in
Notes on American Archaeology (N.Y.:
Harper, 1872).

Charles Whittlesey, "Archaeological
Frauds," Pub.Western Reserve & N.
Ohio Hist.Soc'y, no.33 (Nov.1876).
il.

Charles Whittlesey, "The Grave Creek
Inscribed Stone," Pub.Western Re-
serve & N.Ohio Hist.Soc'y, no.44
(Apr.1879). il.

M.C. Read, "Inscribed Stone of Grave
Creek Mound," Am.Antiquarian 1
(1879):139-49.

John P. MacLean, The Mound Builders
(Cincinnati: Robert Clarke, 1904),
pp.90-105. il.

Olaf Strandwold, Norse Inscriptions
on American Stones (Weehauken, N.J.:
Magnus Björndal, 1948), pp.7-8,38-
39. il.

Philip R. Hough, "My Part in the
Story of the Grave Creek Tablet,"
Tennessee Arch. 8 (1952):47-48. il.

Delf Norona, "Moundsville's Mammoth
Mound," West Virginia Arch., no.9
(Aug.1957):1-55. il.

Delf Norona, "The Dimensions of
Moundsville's Mammoth Mound," West
Virginia Arch., no.10 (Sep.1958):
13-19. il.

Delf Norona, "Comments on Townsend's
Account of the 1838 Excavation of
the Grave Creek Mound," West Virginia Arch., no.14 (Feb.1962):7-9.

Don W. Dragoo, Mounds for the Dead
(Pittsburgh: Carnegie Museum, 1963).

Barry Fell, America B.C. (N.Y.:
Quadrangle, 1976), pp.21,51,157-58,
163. il.

E. Thomas Hemmings, "The Core Drilling Project at Grave Creek Mound:
Preliminary Results and Radiocarbon
Date," West Virginia Arch., no.26
(1977):59-68. il.

Mountain Cove
-Spirit medium
 1851, Oct.-1852, Feb./James L. Scott/
 Apostolic Circle
   Eliab W. Capron, Modern Spiritualism:
   Its Facts and Fanaticisms (Boston:
   Bela Marsh, 1855), pp.119-31.
   John Humphrey Noyes, History of Amer-
   ican Socialisms (Philadelphia: Lip-
   pincott, 1870), pp.569-76.
   Emma Hardinge Britten, Modern Ameri-
   can Spiritualism (N.Y.: The Author,
   1870), pp.209-13.
   Nandor Fodor, Encyclopaedia of Psy-
   chic Science (London: Arthurs,
   1933), p.4.

Mount Carbon
-Archeological site
 1-1300 A.D./Buffalo Madonna
   Cyrus Thomas, "Report on the Mound
   Explorations of the Bureau of Ethnology," Ann.Rept.Bur.Am.Ethn. 12
   (1890-91):3,409-10.

J.P. Hale, Some Local Archaeology
(Charleston: Gazette Pub.Co., 1898),
pp.7-14.

Joseph Inghram, Sigfus Olafson & Edward V. McMichael, "The Mount Carbon Stone Walls: Description and
History," West Virginia Arch., no.
13 (July 1961):1-13. il.

James H. Kellar, "Excavations at
Mount Carbon, West Virginia," West
Virginia Arch., no.13 (July 1961):
14-18.

Edward V. McMichael, "Summary: The
Mount Carbon Walls So Far," West
Virginia Arch., no.13 (July 1961):
33-34.

Edward V. McMichael, "Preliminary
Report on Mount Carbon Village Excavations," West Virginia Arch.,
no.14 (Feb.1962):36-51. il.

John E. Guilday & Donald P. Tanner,
"Vertebrate Remains from the Mount
Carbon Site (46-Fa-7)," West Vir-
ginia Arch., no.18 (1965):1-14. il.

New Cumberland
-UFO (CE-1)
 1966, Oct.7/John Vujnovic/N on Hwy.66
   John A. Keel, The Mothman Prophecies
   (N.Y.: Saturday Review, 1975), p.
   47.

New Haven
-Acoustic anomaly
 1967, March 22/Connie Gordon
   John A. Keel, "West Virginia's Enig-
   matic 'Bird,'" Flying Saucer Rev.
   14 (July-Aug.1968):7,9.
-Flying humanoid
 1966, Nov.27/Connie Gordon/Mason County
 Golf Course
   Athens (O.) Messenger, 28 Nov.1966.
   John A. Keel, The Mothman Prophecies
   (N.Y.: Saturday Review, 1975), pp.
   16-17,78-79.
-Men-in-black
 1967, Dec.22/Connie Gordon
   John A. Keel, "West Virginia's Enig-
   matic 'Bird,'" Flying Saucer Rev.
   14 (July-Aug.1968):7,9-10.
   John A. Keel, The Mothman Prophecies
   (N.Y.: Saturday Review, 1975), pp.
   18-19.
-UFO (CE-1)
 1967, April 17/Lewis Summers
   "Startling Cases Investigated," UFO
   Inv. 4 (May-June 1967):6.

New Martinsville
-Ghost
 ca.1846/John Hindman
   Emma Hardinge Britten, Modern Ameri-
   can Spiritualism (N.Y.: The Author,
   1870), pp.522-23.
   Ruth Ann Musick, The Telltale Lilac
   Bush (Lexington: Univ. of Kentucky,
   1965), pp.84-86.
-UFO (?)
 1897, March 9/David Letsure/=meteor?
   New York Times, 11 Mar.1897.

Oceana
-Giant bird
  1978, Aug.
    Charleston Gazette, 15 Aug.1978.
-Humanoid
  1978, Aug.14/Bill Pruitt/Clear Fork R.
    Charleston Gazette, 15 Aug.1978.

Parkersburg
-Aerial phantom
  1878, July
    New York Times, 8 July 1878, p.2,
    quoting Cincinnati (O.) Commercial
    (undated).
-Contactee
  1966/Dr. Morgan
    John A. Keel, The Mothman Prophecies
    (N.Y.: Saturday Review, 1975), p.84.
-Human track in stone
  1870s/H.E. Huford/4 mi.N
    "Fossil Footprint," Am.Anthro. 9
    (1896):66.
-UFO (?)
  1897, April/=hoax
    Parkersburg Daily State Journal, 18
    Apr.1897.
  1954, May 29/Raymond Angier
    "Parkersburg, W.Va. Is Bee-Swarmed
    by Novel Dual-Flight Devices," CRIFO
    Newsl., 2 July 1954, p.2.
-UFO (CE-3)
  1966, Nov.2/Woodrow Derenberger/I-77
    Parkersburg Sentinel, 4 Nov.1966.
    "Sensational Saucer Landing in West
    Virginia," Saucer News 14 (spring
    1967):32-33.
    John A. Keel, The Mothman Prophecies
    (N.Y.: Saturday Review, 1975), pp.
    48-52.
-UFO (DD)
  1949, Sep.25/4 mi.SW
    Bruce S. Maccabee, "UFO Related In-
    formation from the FBI Files: Part
    5," MUFON UFO J., no.124 (Mar.1978):
    7,11,15.
-UFO (NL)
  1897, April 19
    Columbus (O.) Evening Press, 20 Apr,
    1897.
  1956, Aug.12
    "Case 187," CRIFO Orbit, 7 Sep.1956,
    p.3, quoting Parkersburg Sentinel
    (undated).
  1956, Nov.8/Raymond Angier/E of town
    "Case 245," CRIFO Orbit, 7 Dec.1956,
    p.4.
  1978, Oct.25
    Charleston Gazette-Mail, 26 Oct.1978.

Parsons
-Humanoid
  1960, summer
    John A. Keel, Strange Creatures from
    Time and Space (Greenwich, Ct.:
    Fawcett, 1970), p.121.

Pineville
-Flying cat
  1959, May/Doug Shelton
    (Editorial), Fate 12 (Oct.1959):10-11.

John A. Keel, Strange Creatures from
Time and Space (Greenwich, Ct.:
Fawcett, 1970), pp.37-40.

Point Pleasant
-Flying humanoid
  1966, Nov.1/Armory
    John A. Keel, The Mothman Prophecies
    (N.Y.: Saturday Review, 1975), p.54.
  1966, Nov.15/Roger Scarberry/TNT area
    Point Pleasant Register, 16 Nov.1966.
    John A. Keel, The Mothman Prophecies
    (N.Y.: Saturday Review, 1975), pp.
    59-61,68.
  1966, Nov.16/Raymond Wamsley
    Athens (O.) Messenger, 24 May 1967.
    John A. Keel, The Mothman Prophecies
    (N.Y.: Saturday Review, 1975), pp.
    62-63.
  1966, Nov.18/Paul Yoder/TNT area
  1966, Nov.24/TNT area
    John A. Keel, The Mothman Prophecies
    (N.Y.: Saturday Review, 1975), pp.
    64-65,68.
  1966, Nov.25/Thomas Ury/Hwy.62
    Point Pleasant Register, 26 Nov.1966.
    John A. Keel, The Mothman Prophecies
    (N.Y.: Saturday Review,1975), pp.
    68-69.
  1966, Dec.6/TNT area
    John A. Keel, "West Virginia's Enig-
    matic 'Bird,'" Flying Saucer Rev.
    14 (July-Aug.1968):7,13.
  1966, Dec.7-8/Connie Gordon/TNT area
    John A. Keel, The Mothman Prophecies
    (N.Y.: Saturday Review, 1975), pp.
    78-83.
  1966, Dec.11/TNT area
    John A. Keel, "West Virginia's Enig-
    matic 'Bird,'" Flying Saucer Rev.
    14 (July-Aug.1968):7,13.
  1967, Jan.11/Mabel McDaniel/Tony's
  Restaurant
    Point Pleasant Register, 14 Jan.1967.
    John A. Keel, The Mothman Prophecies
    (N.Y.: Saturday Review, 1975), p.94.
  1967, May 19/Hwy.62 nr. C.C. Lewis
  farm
    Athens (O.) Messenger, 24 May 1967.
-Humanoid
  1967, Nov.2/Virginia Thomas/TNT area
    John A. Keel, The Mothman Prophecies
    (N.Y.: Saturday Review, 1975), pp.
    244-45.
-Men-in-black
  1966, Dec./Marcella Bennett
    John A. Keel, The Mothman Prophecies
    (N.Y.: Saturday Review, 1975), p.87.
  1967, Jan.-Dec.22/Mary Hyre
    John A. Keel, "North America 1966,"
    Flying Saucer Rev. 13 (Mar.-Apr.
    1967):3,7.
    John A. Keel, The Mothman Prophecies
    (N.Y.: Saturday Review, 1975), pp.
    12-14,88-89,91,120,176,179,231.
  1967, March/Mabel McDaniel/Main St.
  1967, Sep.24/Linda Scarberry
  1967, Dec.23/Parke McDaniel
    John A. Keel, The Mothman Prophecies
    (N.Y.: Saturday Review, 1975), pp.

21-22,120-21,228-29.
-Phantom
  1967, March/Jackie Lilly
    John A. Keel, The Mothman Prophecies
    (N.Y.: Saturday Review, 1975), p.
    125.
-Phantom airplane
  1967, March/John A. Keel
    John A. Keel, The Mothman Prophecies
    (N.Y.: Saturday Review, 1975), pp.
    126-27.
-Phantom panther
  1978, Sep.17/Sam Tubaugh/Millstone Rd.
    Point Pleasant Register, 18-21 Sep.
    1978.
-Precognition
  1967, Nov./Mary Hyre
    John A. Keel, The Mothman Prophecies
    (N.Y.:Saturday Review, 1975), p.245.
-Telephone anomaly
  1967
    John A. Keel, The Mothman Prophecies
    (N.Y.: Saturday Review, 1975), pp.
    123-24.
-UFO (CE-1)
  1967, Jan.10/Wallie Barnett/Hwy.2
    John A. Keel, "From My Ohio Valley
    Notebook," Flying Saucer Rev. 13
    (May-June 1967):3-4.
  1967, March-April/Harold Harmon/TNT
  area
    Huntington Herald-Dispatch, 18 Apr.
    1967.
    John A. Keel, The Mothman Prophecies
    (N.Y.: Saturday Review, 1975), p.
    118.
  1967, May 19/Ohio River Jr. High School
    Athens (O.) Messenger, 24 Nov.1967.
-UFO (CE-2)
  1967, March-April/James Lilly/Camp
  Conley Rd.
    Athens (O.) Messenger, 13 Apr.1967.
    John A. Keel, The Mothman Prophecies
    (N.Y.: Saturday Review, 1975), pp.
    124-25,128-29,140-43.
  1967, April/Pat Siler/TNT area
    Point Pleasant Register, 13 Apr.1967.
-UFO (CE-3)
  1966, March/Point Pleasant School
    John A. Keel, The Mothman Prophecies
    (N.Y.: Saturday Review, 1975), pp.
    40-41.
-UFO (DD)
  1966, summer/Tony's Restaurant
    John A. Keel, The Mothman Prophecies
    (N.Y.: Saturday Review, 1975), p.41.
  1967, May/Ronald Plantz/35 Burdette
  Addition
    "UFO's Visit Point Pleasant, Ohio,"
    Skylook, no.27 (Feb.1970):10, quot-
    ing Athens (O.) Messenger (undated).
-UFO (NL)
  1966, Nov.16/TNT area
  1967, Nov.19/John A. Keel/TNT area
  1967, Dec.15/Gary Lilly/Camp Conley Rd.
    John A. Keel, The Mothman Prophecies
    (N.Y.: Saturday Review, 1975), pp.
    62,245-46,262-63.
  1968, March/Hwy.62

John A. Keel, UFOs: Operation Trojan
    Horse (N.Y.: Putnam, 1970), p.126.

Quick
-Religious apparition
  1964/Spencer Campbell
    (Editorial), Fate 17 (Oct.1964):20-
    22.

Ravenswood
-Haunt
  n.d./Thomas Schoffler/movie theater
    Ruth Ann Musick, Coffin Hollow (Lex-
    ington: Univ. of Kentucky, 1977),
    pp.30-33.
-Seance
  ca.1900/J.A. Daugherty
    Lee R. Gandee, "Dead Men Cry Gold,"
    Fate 3 (Aug.1950):77-80.
-UFO (CE-2)
  1967, spring/E of town
    John A. Keel, The Mothman Prophecies
    (N.Y.: Saturday Review,1975), pp.
    103-104.
-UFO (NL)
  1968, March 4
    John A. Keel, UFOs: Operation Trojan
    Horse (N.Y.: Putnam, 1970), p.158.

Ripley
-Haunt
  1926-   /Elaine Rowley/Ghost Ridge
    Elaine Rowley, "I Guess I Saw a
    Ghost," Fate 23 (Nov.1970):74-82.

Rivesville
-UFO (CE-3)
  1964, April 23/Ivah Frederick
    Jacques Vallee, Passport to Magonia
    (Chicago: Regnery, 1969), p.307.
    Ted Phillips, Physical Traces Associ-
    ated with UFO Sightings (Evanston:
    Center for UFO Studies, 1975), p.29.

Roane co.
-UFO (NL)
  1978, Oct.21
    Charleston Gazette-Mail, 24 Oct.1978.
    il.

Romney
-Archeological site
  cemetery
    Franklin Folsom, America's Ancient
    Treasures (N.Y.: Rand McNally,
    1974), p.154.
-Entombed bat
  1888, Nov.22/W.V. Herriott
    Baltimore (Md.) Sun, 27 Nov.1888.

Saint Albans
-Acoustic anomaly
  1967, Jan.20/Ralph Jarrett
    John A. Keel, The Mothman Prophecies
    (N.Y.: Saturday Review,1975), p.97.
-Archeological site
  7900-6200 B.C./Murad Mound
    Bettye J. Broyles, "Preliminary Re-
    port: The St. Albans Site (46 Ka 27),
    Kanawha County, West Virginia," West

Virginia Arch., no.19 (fall 1966):
1-43. il.
Sigfus Olafson, "Late Pleistocene
Climate and the St. Albans Site,"
West Virginia Arch., no.19 (fall
1966):44-47. il.
Edward V. McMichael, "Excavations
of the Murad Mound, Kanawha County,
West Virginia," Rept.Arch.Invest.
West Virginia Geol.& Econ.Survey,
no.1 (1969). il.
Bettye J. Broyes, "Second Prelimin-
ary Report: The St. Albans Site,"
Rept.Arch.Invest.West Virginia Geol.
& Econ.Survey, no.3 (1971). il.
-Flying humanoid
1966, Nov.26/Ruth Foster
1966, Nov.27/Sheila Cain
John A. Keel, The Mothman Prophecies
(N.Y.: Saturday Review, 1975), p.71.

Salem
-Haunt
n.d.
Ruth Ann Musick, "West Virginia
Ghost Stories," Midwest Folklore 8
(spring 1958):21,25-26.
-UFO (CE-2)
1966, Nov.14/Newell Partridge
Gallipolis (O.) Tribune, 18 Nov.1966.
John A. Keel, The Mothman Prophecies
(N.Y.: Saturday Review, 1975), pp.
56-57.

Sistersville
-UFO (CE-1)
1966, Nov./Joyce McGinnis/Ford Garage
John A. Keel, "More from My Ohio
Valley Note Book," Flying Saucer
Rev. 13 (July-Aug.1967):20.
-UFO (NL)
1897, April 18/W.E. Roe
Marietta (O.) Daily Register, 19
Apr.1897.
John A. Keel, "More from My Ohio
Valley Note Book," Flying Saucer
Rev. 13 (July-Aug.1967):20-21.
1966-1967/Robert Wright
John A. Keel, "More from My Ohio
Valley Note Book," Flying Saucer
Rev. 13 (July-Aug.1967):20-21.

Spencer
-UFO (NL)
1978, Oct.21/Gary Williams/Hwy.36
Charleston Gazette-Mail, 22 Oct.1978.

Sutton
-UFO (NL)
1952, Sep.12/airport
Ivan T. Sanderson, Uninvited Visitors
(N.Y.: Cowles, 1967), p.50.

Tattletown
-Phantom image
n.d./James K. Henry
Ruth Ann Musick, The Telltale Lilac
Bush (Lexington: Univ. of Kentucky,
1965), pp.2-3.

Terra Alta
-UFO (CE-3)
1973, Oct.26/Willard Zinn
Terra Alta Preston County News, 30
Oct.1973.
David Webb, 1973: Year of the Human-
oids (Evanston: Center for UFO
Studies, 1976 ed.), p.17.

Valley Bend
-Haunt
1933-1946/Ann Smith
Ann Smith, "My Grandmother...the
Ghost," Fate 24 (Mar.1970):92-96.
-Snow worms
1891, Jan?
"Snow Worms," Sci.Am. 64 (1891):116.

Vienna
-UFO (NL)
1967, April 12/WTAP TV tower
"Object over TV Towers in West Virginia," APRO Bull. 15 (May-June
1967):11.

West Liberty
-UFO (CE-1)
1975, Jan.7/Dorothy Sommerville/Hwy.88
Theodore Spickler, "Family Says UFO
Hovered over Home," Skylook, no.90,
(May 1975):18.

Weston
-Humanoid
1976, Aug.17/Ronald Stark
Gray Barker, "Invading West Virginia's Saucer Lairs and Monster Hide-
outs," Saga UFO Rept. 3 (Dec.1976):
33,77.
-Seance
1886, Jan./Henry Slade
Boston (Mass.) Herald, 2 Feb.1886.

Wetzel co.
-Ghost
n.d./Rock Camp
Ruth Ann Musick, "West Virginia
Ghost Stories," Midwest Folklore 8
(spring 1958):21,22-24.

Wheeling
-Giant rabbits
1952, Feb.
Pittsburgh (Pa.) Press, 28 Feb.1952.
-UFO (NL)
1973, Oct.17-18/Paul Carroll
Wheeling News-Register, 22 Oct.1973.
Colman Von Keviczky, "The 1973 UFO
Invasion: Part 1," Official UFO 1
(Aug.1975):16,19.

Williamson
-UFO (NL)
1958, May 20/David Hyden
(Letter), Ronald Hyden, Fate 11 (Oct.
1958):113-14.

Wrightsville
-Ghost light
1850s

Ruth Ann Musick, Coffin Hollow (Lexington: Univ. of Kentucky, 1977),
pp.86-87.

B. Physical Features

Blackwater R.
-Erratic octopus
  1946, Jan./Ted Peters
    "More Details Needed," Doubt, no.16
    (1946):242, quoting AP release, 14
    Jan.1946.

Campbells Creek
-Flying humanoid
  1966, Nov.20/Brenda Jones
    John A. Keel, The Mothman Prophecies
    (N.Y.: Saturday Review, 1975), p.65.

Cheat R.
-Phantom panther
  1765/George Wilson
    Harold T. Wilkins, Secret Cities of
    Old South America (N.Y.: Library
    Publishers, 1952), p.283.

Chief Cornstalk Park
-Flying humanoid
  ca.1961/Hwy.2
    John A. Keel, Strange Creatures from
    Time and Space (Greenwich, Ct.:
    Fawcett, 1970), p.210.
  1967, April/Hwy.2
    John A. Keel, The Mothman Prophecies
    (N.Y.: Saturday Review, 1975), pp.
    176-77.

Coal Mt.
-UFO (NL)
  1973, Oct.
    Wheeling News-Register, 22 Oct.1973.

Cole Mt.
-Ghost light
  1860s-
    Ruth Ann Musick, Coffin Hollow (Lex-
    ington: Univ. of Kentucky, 1977),
    pp.65-67.

Collins Fork
-UFO (DD)
  1978, Aug.17/Terry Daniel/Rowland Mine
    David White, "West Virginia Encoun-
    ter," Saga UFO Rept. 7 (Feb.1979):
    36-39,56-58.

Cresap Mound
-Archeological site
    Don W. Dragoo, "Preliminary Report on
    the Excavation of the Cresap Mound,
    Marshall County, West Virginia,"
    Bull.Eastern States Arch.Fed., no.
    18 (Oct.1959):14.
    Don W. Dragoo, Mounds for the Dead
    (Pittsburgh: Carnegie Museum, 1963),

Globe Hill
-Archeological site
  2170 B.C.

James L. Murphy, "Radiocarbon Date
from the Globe Hill Shell Heap 46
HK 34-1, Hancock County, West Virginia," Pennsylvania Arch. 47, no.
1 (1977):19-24. il.

Guyandot R.
-Petroglyphs
    E.G. Squier & E.H. Davis, Ancient
    Monuments of the Mississippi Valley
    (Washington: Smithsonian Institution,
    Contrib.to Knowl., no.1, 1848), pp.
    293-98. il.
    Sigfus Olafson, "Petroglyphs on the
    Guyandot River," West Virginia
    Arch., no.5 (1952):1-9. il.
    Delf Norona, "Discovery of the Guy-
    andot River Petroglyphs," West Vir-
    ginia Arch., no.5 (1952):10.

Hickory Flats
-Humanoid
  1960, Dec.30/Charles Stover
    Charleston Daily Mail, 31 Dec.1960.

Holts Run
-Cromniomancy
  19th c./Ann Kelly
    Clay Whiting, "She Knew Her Onions,"
    Fate 10 (Apr.1957):97-98.

Kanawha R.
-Phantom panther
  1790/Mr. Draper
    Harold T. Wilkins, Secret Cities of
    Old South America (N.Y.: Library
    Publishers, 1952), p.283.

Little Sewell Mt.
-Ghost
  1897, Feb.4-7/Mary Heaster/nr. Levisey's
  Mills
    "Incident from the Hodgson Collec-
    tion," J.ASPR 29 (1935):211-18.
    Edmond P. Gibson, "The Avenging Spir-
    it of Little Sewell Mountain," Fate
    4 (Jan.1951):57-62.
    Ruth Ann Musick, Coffin Hollow (Lex-
    ington: Univ. of Kentucky, 1977),
    pp.15-19.

Rich Mt.
-Haunt
  1867/Lewis Kittle
    Ruth Ann Musick, Coffin Hollow (Lex-
    ington: Univ. of Kentucky, 1977),
    pp.51-53.

Rowlesburg Reservoir
-Archeological sites
    Richard E. Jensen, "Archaeological
    Survey of the Rowlesburg Reservoir
    Area, West Virginia," Rept.Arch.In-
    vest.West Virginia Geol.& Econ.Sur-
    vey, no.2 (1970).

Triplett Creek
-Ancient inscription
  1931/Blaine Wilson
    Olaf Strandwold, Norse Inscriptions

on American Stones (Weehauken, N.J.:
Magnus Björndal, 1948), pp.36-37.
Frederick J. Pohl, Atlantic Crossings
Before Columbus (N.Y.: W.W. Norton,
1961), pp.202-204. il.
Clyde Keeler, "The Wilson-Braxton
Tablet," NEARA Newsl. 8 (fall 1973)
:56. il.
Barry Fell, America B.C. (N.Y.:
Quadrangle, 1976), p.158. il.
Julius Frasch Harmon, "Concerning
the Carvings on the Braxton and
Yarmouth Stones," West Virginia
History 37 (1976):133-39.

Twentymile Creek
-Archeological site
J.P. Hale, Some Local Archaeology
(Charleston: Gazette Pub.Co., 1898),
pp.1-6.

D. Unspecified Localities

-Sheep mutilation and humanoid
n.d.
Ruth Ann Musick, The Telltale Lilac
Bush (Lexington: Univ. of Kentucky,
1965), pp.147-48.

-UFO (CE-2)
n.d.
Gray Barker, "Invading West Virginia's Saucer Lairs and Monster Hide-
outs," Saga UFO Rept. 3 (Dec.1976):
33,78.

MARYLAND

A. Populated Places

Aberdeen
-UFO (NL)
1956, Nov.23
  Jacques Vallee, Anatomy of a Phenomenon (N.Y.: Ace, 1965 ed.), p.190.

Adamstown
-UFO (NL)
1971, Dec.2/Gerald Wait
  Frederick Post, 3 Dec.1971.

Adelphi
-Contactee
1967, Dec.10-1968/Tom Monteleone
  John A. Keel, The Mothman Prophecies
  (N.Y.: Saturday Review, 1975),
  pp.193-97.

Andrews
-Ghost light
1970s/Corbett Robbins
  "Marshlight," Skipjack, no.1 (winter
  1973):59-63.

Annapolis
-Fall of pebbles
1915, June 22/=encased in hail
  Oliver L. Fassig, "A Remarkable Fall
  of Hail in Maryland," Monthly Weather Rev. 43 (Sep.1915):446.
-Ghost
1850s
  Emma Hardinge Britten, Modern American Spiritualism (N.Y.: The Author,
  1870), pp.521-22.
-Haunt
n.d./Brice House/42 East St.
n.d./Chandler Mansion/Duke of Gloucester St.
  Charles M. Skinner, American Myths
  and Legends, 2 vols. (Philadelphia:
  Lippincott, 1903), 1:288-91.
-UFO (?)
ca.1936/Robert B. Maguire
  "Amazing Indifference," Doubt, no.
  33 (1951):83,84.
-Witch trial (hex)
1712, Oct.5/Virtue Violl
  Francis Neal Parke, Witchcraft in
  Maryland (Baltimore: Maryland Hist.
  Soc'y, 1937), pp.37-39.

Aquasco
-Ghost
1918, summer/William Brady
  Shirley Morgan, "The Bishop Remembers
  a Ghost," Fate 24 (Aug.1971):57-59.

Baltimore
-Erratic bear
1959, June 10/W. Lombard St.
  (Editorial), Fate 12 (Oct.1959):8.
-Erratic snake
1954, Sep.
  Garden City (N.Y.) Newsday, 10 Sep.
  1954.
  "Snakes Again," Doubt, no.47 (1955):
  318.
-Fall of brown rain
1955, March 12
  Philadelphia (Pa.) Evening Bulletin,
  12 Mar.1955.
-Fall of metallic object
1955, May/1500 block Russell St.
  Baltimore Sun, 10 May 1955.
-Ghost
1955, Sep.-   /Allen Ross Brougham/
"U.S.S. Constellation"/Pier 1, Perry
St./=hoax
  Baltimore Sun, 31 Dec.1955. il.
  Mary Margaret Fuller, "Ghost on the
  Constellation?" Fate 19 (Jan.1966):
  57-58. il.
  (Letter), John J. Maloney, Fate 19
  (July 1966):130-31.
  (Letter), Stephen E. Franklin, Fate
  19 (July 1966):131-33.
  Baltimore News-American, 26 Mar.1967.
  Hans Holzer, Window to the Past
  (Garden City: Doubleday, 1969).
  (Letter), Lee Belser, Fate 22 (Sep.
  1969):144-45.
-Haunt
ca.1865/Frank A. Boidie/Locust Point
  Dennis Bardens, Ghosts and Hauntings
  (N.Y.: Ace, 1965 ed.), pp.170-72.
1972, Dec.-1973, May/Henry Smith
  "Ghost Thwarts Efforts of Exorcist,"
  Probe the Unknown 1 (Oct.1973):64-
  65. il.
-Healing
1950s-   /Ambrose and Olga Worrall/
Mt. Washington Methodist Church
  Alson J. Smith, "Healing in Today's
  Churches," Fate 10 (Sep.1957):53-58.
  (Letter), Olga Worrall, Fate 11
  (Mar.1958):128.
  Curtis Fuller, "The Seership of Olga
  Worrall," Fate 16 (Sep.1963):26-34.
  (Letter), Fred H. Ohrenschall, Fate
  16 (Dec.1963):131-32.
  Olga N. Worrall, "Guardian Angel's
  Report," Fate 17 (Apr.1964):64-66.
  Ambrose A. & Olga N. Worrall, The
  Gift of Healing (N.Y.: Harper &
  Row, 1965).
  Ambrose & Olga Worrall, Explore Your
  Psychic World (N.Y.: Harper & Row,
  1970).
  Robert N. Miller, "The Positive Ef-
  fect of Prayer on Plants," Psychic
  3 (Apr.1972):24-25.
  Thelma Moss, The Probability of the
  Impossible (Los Angeles: J.P. Tar-
  cher, 1974), pp.62-64,79-83,89-90.
  Robert N. Miller, Philip B. Reinhart,

& Anita Kern, "Research Report: Er-
nest Holmes Research Foundation,"
Science of Mind, July 1974, pp.12-
16.
Edwina Cerutti, Olga Worrall: Mystic
with the Healing Hands (N.Y.: Harper & Row, 1975).
Edwina Cerutti, "Profile of a Psychic
Healer: Olga Worrall," Probe the
Unknown 3 (Sep.1975):50-53.
R.G. MacDonald, et al., "Preliminary
Physical Measurements of Psychophys-
ical Interactions with Three Psychic
Healers," in J.D. Morris, et al.,
eds., Research in Parapsychology
1976 (Metuchen, N.J.: Scarecrow,
1977).
Robert N. Miller, "Methods of Detect-
ing and Measuring Healing Energies,"
in John White & Stanley Krippner,
eds., Future Science (Garden City:
Anchor, 1977), pp.431-44.
1952/Ann Theresa O'Neill
(Editorial), Fate 16 (Aug.1963):21.
-Hex
1966, Nov.
London (Eng.) Times, 18 Nov.1966, p.
7.
-Inner development
1970-   /Aum Esoteric Study Center/
2405 Ruscombe Lane
June & Nicholas Regush, Psi: The Other World Catalogue (N.Y.: Putnam,
1974), p.156.
J. Gordon Melton, Encyclopedia of
American Religions, 2 vols. (Wilmington, N.C.: Consortium, 1978),
2:240-41.
1970s/Morgana
Hans Holzer, The Witchcraft Report
(N.Y.: Ace, 1973), p.54.
-Mystery bird deaths
1954, Sep.11/Friendship Airport
Donald E. Keyhoe, Flying Saucer Con-
spiracy (N.Y.: Holt, 1955), p.271.
-Phantom
n.d.
Brad Steiger, Revelation: The Divine
Fire (Englewood Cliffs, N.J.: Pren-
tice-Hall, 1973), pp.125-26.
-Poltergeist
1950, July
Los Angeles (Cal.) Herald-Examiner,
18 July 1950.
1960, Jan.14-Feb.8/Edgar J. Jones/1448
Meridene Dr.
Baltimore Sun, 14 Jan.1960; and 21
Jan.1960.
Michael Naver & Travis Kidd, "The
Baltimore Poltergeist," Tomorrow 8
(spring 1960):9-16.
Harlan Wilson, "The Pottery Went a-
Dancing," Fate 13 (June 1960):71-74.
Nandor Fodor, Between Two Worlds (W.
Nyack, N.Y.: Parker, 1964), pp.160-
69.
-Precipitating tree
1947, Oct./Sparrows Point
"Page J. Kilmer," Doubt, no.20
(1948):307.

-Precognition
n.d./City Hospital
J.C. Barker, Scared to Death (N.Y.:
Dell, 1969 ed.), p.72.
n.d.
(Editorial), Fate 24 (Jan.1971):34-
35.
1931, Oct.28/Walter Whyte Parker
Walter Whyte Parker, "An Interesting
Case-Record," J.ASPR 26 (1932):289-
94.
1972, Nov.22/Alan C. Ray
(Editorial), Fate 26 (May 1973):24-
26.
-Psychokinesis
1892, Nov./William E. Bartlett/St.
Anne's Church
New York Tribune, 30 Nov.1892.
"A Bewitched Doorbell," J.ASPR 18
(1924):478-79.
-Reincarnation
1969-1974/Kalvin Widener
Joseph J. Challmes, "The Countless
Lives of Kalvin Widener," Fate 27
(Apr.1974):50-55. il.
-Spirit medium
1850s/Mrs. Morrel
1850s-1860s/Mrs. Washington A. Danskin
Washington A. Danskin, How and Why I
Became a Spiritualist (Boston: Bela
Marsh, 1858).
Emma Hardinge Britten, Modern Ameri-
can Spiritualism (N.Y.: The Author,
1870), p.285.
Nandor Fodor, Encyclopaedia of Psy-
chic Science (London: Arthurs,
1933), p.231, quoting Banner of
Light, 11 Jan.1868.
-UFO (?)
1946, Aug.9-10, 14/East Brooklyn
1946, Nov.20
"Over Baltimore," Doubt, no.17
(1947):259.
1948-1950/Jack Engeman/St. Paul St. x
Mt. Vernon Pl.
"Saucers over Baltimore," Fate 3
(Dec.1950):67.
1952, Sep.12/=meteor?
Ivan T. Sanderson, Uninvited Visitors
(N.Y.: Cowles, 1967), p.41.
1956, Dec.3/Curvin Bush/Charles x
Centre St.
"Case 277," CRIFO Orbit, 1 Feb.1957,
p.4.
1957, Nov.4
"All About Sputs," Doubt, no.56
(1958):460,471.
1958, Sep.29/Hwy.40
"The Night of September 29," Fate
12 (Feb.1959):31,32, quoting Balti-
more Sun (undated).
1966, April 25/=meteor
John A. Keel, UFOs: Operation Trojan
Horse (N.Y.: Putnam, 1970), p.145.
-UFO (CE-2)
1957, June 25
Richard Hall, ed., The UFO Evidence
(Washington: NICAP, 1964), p.74.
1958, Oct.26/Philip Small
Richard Hall, ed., The UFO Evidence

(Washington: NICAP, 1964), pp.75,
99, quoting Baltimore newspaper, 27
Oct.1958.
-UFO (DD)
1952, Aug.5/James C. Bartlett, Jr.
"Two Huge UFOs Sighted by Baltimore
Astronomer," UFO Inv. 1 (Aug.-Sep.
1958):1,3.
1975, July 12
"UFO Central," CUFOS News Bull., 15
Nov.1975, p.13.
-UFO (NL)
1947, July 3/Gertrude Landry/2026
Ridgehill Ave.
Baltimore Sun, 6 July 1947.
1947, July 5/Kathleen Norris/Erdman
Ave.
1947, July 6/Larry Johnson
1947, July 7/Melvin Kearney
Baltimore News-Post, 7 July 1947.
1952, Feb.12
U.S. Air Force, Projects Grudge and
Blue Book Reports 1-12 (Washington:
NICAP, 1968), p.13.
1953, Sep./James C. Bartlett, Jr.
"Two Huge UFOs Sighted by Baltimore
Astronomer," UFO Inv. 1 (Aug.-Sep.
1958):1.
1954, March 24/Adolph Wagner
"Multiple Object Sightings by Credit-
able Observers Continue," CRIFO
Newsl., 2 July 1954, p.3.
1954, June 12, 14
Wilmington (Del.) Morning News, 9
July 1954.
1954, Sep.6/James C. Bartlett, Jr.
"Two Huge UFOs Sighted by Baltimore
Astronomer," UFO Inv. 1 (Aug.-Sep.
1958):1.
1955, April 10
"The 'Flying Alphabet' over Balti-
more," CRIFO Newsl., 6 May 1955, p.
6.
1964, Aug.22/Robert D. Briele
"UFO Sighting Wave Persists," UFO
Inv. 2 (Sep.-Oct.1964):5.
1966, Aug.1/Country Ridge
Baltimore News-American, 1 Aug.1966.
-Weeping icon
1960, March/Mary Ely
(Letter), Fate 13 (Aug.1960):122.

Bel Air
-Mystery plane crash
1955, Feb.8/B-57
Donald E. Keyhoe, Aliens from Space
(Garden City: Doubleday, 1973), p.
205.
-New energy source (inventor)
1977/Richard Kipp/=separation of hy-
drogen from water
(Editorial), Fate 30 (Sep.1977):24-
28, quoting Bel Air News (undated).
-UFO (NL)
1961, Aug.
Curtis Fuller, "The Boys Who 'Caught'
a Flying Saucer," Fate 15 (Jan.1962)
:36,40.

Bethesda
-UFO (CE-2)
1968, Oct.24
Ted Phillips, Physical Traces Associ-
ated with UFO Sightings (Evanston:
Center for UFO Studies, 1975), p.59.
-UFO (DD)
1947, July 5/Jack LaBous
Washington News, 7 July 1947.
1964, Dec.19/Anthony W. Schrecker/
Nat'l Institutes of Health
"New Sightings Put AF on Spot," UFO
Inv. 3 (Mar.-Apr.1965):1,4.
-UFO (NL)
1947, July 4/David Atamian
Washington Post, 6 July 1947.
1952, April 18
U.S. Air Force, Projects Grudge and
Blue Book Reports 1-12 (Washington:
NICAP, 1968), p.111.

Cambridge
-Fall of fish
1828, summer/Joseph E. Muse
Joseph E. Muse, "Notice on the Ap-
pearance of Fish and Lizards in
Extraordinary Circumstances," Am.
J.Sci., ser.1, 16 (1829):41-42.

Camp Springs
-UFO (?)
1948, Nov./=balloon
"What the Air Force Believes About
Flying Saucers," Fate 2 (Nov.1949):
69,71.

Caroline co.
-UFO (NL)
1966, Dec.1
Baltimore News-Journal, 2 Dec.1966.

Carroll co.
-Humanoid tracks
1944
Washington Post, 10 Oct.1976, maga-
zine sec.
-Spontaneous human combustion
1953, April/Bernard J. Hess/Baltimore
Pike
"Cremation Mystery in Baltimore,"
Fate 6 (Sep.1953):93.

Catonsville
-Haunt
n.d.
Dennis Bardens, Ghosts and Hauntings
(N.Y.: Ace, 1965 ed.), p.172.

Chestertown
-Psychokinesis research
1948
Carroll B. Nash, "An Exploratory An-
alysis for Displacement in PK," J.
ASPR 50 (1956):151-57.

Chevy Chase
-Ball lightning
1923, spring/G.W. Lewis
W.J. Humphreys, "Ball Lightning,"
Proc.Am.Phil.Soc'y 76 (1936):613-26.

Churchtown
-Humanoid
   1914/Hwy.155 x Glenville Rd.
      John Green, Sasquatch: The Apes Among
      Us (Seattle: Hancock House, 1978),
      p.227.

Clinton
-Haunt
   n.d./Surratt Tavern
      Hans Holzer, Haunted Houses (N.Y.:
      Crown, 1971), pp.41-44. il.

Colesville
-UFO (NL)
   1964, May 31/Nelson Rodeffer
      Washington Daily News, 6 June 1964.

College Park
-Clairvoyance
   1920, Feb.28/Richard L. Swain/Univ. of
   Maryland
      H.N. Gardiner, "Clairvoyant (?)
      Dreams," J.ASPR 14 (1920):594-604.
-UFO (NL)
   1966, Aug.1/John Rupprecht
      "New Reports by Space Experts Add to
      UFO Proof," UFO Inv. 3 (Aug.-Sep.
      1966):3,4.

Crisfield
-Ghost light
   n.d.
      George Carey, A Faraway Time and
      Place (Washington: Robert B. Luce,
      1971), p.203.
-Haunt
   n.d./Mr. Parks/nr. Asbury Church cemetery
   n.d./Horsey place
      George Carey, A Faraway Time and
      Place (Washington: Robert B. Luce,
      1971), pp.172-74.
-Hex
   n.d.
      George Carey, A Faraway Time and
      Place (Washington: Robert B. Luce,
      1971), pp.154,162-63.

Crofton
-Cave anomaly
      Washington Star-News, 25 July 1973;
      and 15 Aug.1973.

Crownsville
-Fall of metallic object
   1957, Nov.13/William A. Zick/State
   Hospital
      "Metal Object from Skies Rushed to
      ATIC for Analysis," UFO Inv. 1
      (Jan.1958):5-6.

Cumberland
-Mystery television transmission
   1952, July 20
      Richard Hall, ed., The UFO Evidence
      (Washington: NICAP, 1964), p.75,
      quoting AP release, 23 July 1952.

Darlington
-Humanoid tracks
   1975, May
      (Editorial), Fate 29 (Feb.1976):30,
      quoting Bel Air Aegis (undated).

Denton
-UFO (?)
   1958, Sep.29/M.I. Morgan/=meteor?
      "The Night of September 29," Fate
      12 (Feb.1959):31,32.

Derwood
-UFO (NL)
   1958, Sep.29/Jerome Scanlon/Nike base
      "The Nike UFO Case," NICAP Spec.
      Bull., Nov.1958, p.3.
      "The Night of September 29," Fate
      12 (Feb.1959):31-32.

Dorchester co.
-Ghost light
   n.d.
      George Carey, A Faraway Time and
      Place (Washington: Robert B. Luce,
      1971), p.203.

Dorsey
-UFO (NL)
   1973, Sep.11/Mike Elmore/Dorsey Rd.
      Glen Burnie Anne Arundel Times, 13
      Sep.1973.

Dundalk
-Fall of boulder
   1956, Jan.27
      Baltimore Sun, 27 Jan.1956.

Easton
-Fire immunity
   1871, Aug./Nathan Coker
      New York Herald, 7 Sep.1871, pp.4,7.
-UFO (NL)
   1971, Nov?/Burton Wheedleton/8 mi.S
      "Multiple Witness Case in Maryland,"
      APRO Bull. 20 (Nov.-Dec.1971):1,3.

Elkton
-Mystery plane crash
   1963, Dec.8/Boeing 707
      New York Times, 9 Dec.1963, p.1; 10
      Dec.1963, p.48; 11 Dec.1963, p.94;
      and 13 Dec.1963, p.69.
      Vincent Gaddis, Invisible Horizons
      (Philadelphia: Chilton, 1965), pp.
      190-91.
-UFO (CE-1)
   1971, Jan.21/Elvis Arnold/Oldfield
   Point Rd.
      "Two Objects Reported in Maryland,"
      APRO Bull. 19 (Mar.-Apr.1971):1,3.

Emmitsburg
-Haunt
   n.d./cemetery
      Sally M. Barach, Haunts of Adams and
      Other Counties (Indiana, Pa.: A.G.
      Halldin, 1972), pp.45-46.
-Phantom horse
   n.d./graveyard

Annie Weston Whitney & Caroline Canfield Bullock, "Folk-Lore from Maryland," Mem.Am.Folk-Lore Soc'y, vol.
18 (1925), p.185.
-UFO (NL)
 1959, Aug.24
  Richard Hall, ed., The UFO Evidence
  (Washington: NICAP, 1964), p.151.

Federalsburg
-UFO (CE-1)
 1978, June 30/Terri C. Butler/Hwy.313
 1978, July 1/Roy V.R. Grogan
  Federalsburg Times, 5 July 1978.

Fort Howard
-Haunt
 1975/Elmer H. Cook, Jr./Todd House/
 900 Old North Point Rd.
  "There Is Definitely Something Here,"
  Probe the Unknown 3 (May 1975):44.

Frederick co.
-Archeological sites
  Spencer O. Geasey, "Two Small Rock-
  Shelters in Frederick County, Mary-
  land," J.Arch.Soc'y Maryland 1, no.
  2 (1965):30-38. il.
  Spencer O. Geasey, "The Boyers Mill
  Rock-Shelter," J.Arch.Soc'y Mary-
  land 4, no.2 (1968):25-37. il.
  Spencer O. Geasey, "The Tuscarora
  Rock-Shelter," J.Arch.Soc'y Mary-
  land 7, no.1 (1971):1-16. il.
  Spencer O. Geasey, "The Stevens
  Rock-Shelter," J.Arch.Soc'y Mary-
  land 7, no.2 (1971):23-28. il.
  Spencer O. Geasey, "The Log Cabin
  Rock Shelter," J.Arch.Soc'y Mary-
  land 11, no.2 (1975):6-12. il.

Frankfort
-UFO (NL)
 1964, July/Mrs. Dwain Miller
 1964, Nov.30/Mrs.Dwain Miller
  (Letter), Fate 19 (Mar.1966):119-20.

Frostburg
-Phantom panther
 1971, Aug.
  Washington Post, 26 Aug.1971.
-UFO (DD)
 1947, July 20
  Bruce S. Maccabee, "UFO Related Information from the FBI Files: Part
  3," MUFON UFO J., no.121 (Dec.1977):
  10,13.

Galesville
-UFO (NL)
 1966, Oct.12/S.B. Wright
  "Capital Area Sightings," UFO Inv. 3
  (Oct.-Nov.1966):7.

Gapland
-Lightning anomaly
 1900, Aug.26/Mr. Heiskell
  "Notable Lightning," Monthly Weather
  Rev. 28 (July 1900):290-91.

Garrett Park
-Erratic galagos
 1969, Dec.
  Washington Star, 18 Dec.1969.

Glen Burnie
-UFO (CE-2)
 1952, March 29/Richey Hwy.
  J. Allen Hynek, The Hynek UFO Report (N.Y.: Dell, 1977), pp.196-98.
-UFO (DD)
 1966, Oct.16
  "Capital Area Sightings," UFO Inv.
  3 (Oct.-Nov.1966):7.

Golden Hill
-Haunt
 n.d./nr. Catholic Church
  George Carey, A Faraway Time and
  Place (Washington: Robert B. Luce,
  1971), p.172.

Graceham
-Plague of birds
 1973, fall-1974, spring/Edgar Emerich/
 Hwy.77
  (Editorial), Fate 27 (Aug.1974):32-
  36.

Great Mills
-UFO (CE-1)
 1978, Aug.11/Chancellors Run Rd.
  "UFOs of Limited Merit," Int'l UFO
  Reporter 3 (Sep.1978):6,9.

Greensboro
-UFO (CE-1)
 1966, Dec.2-4/Marie Wood
  Washington Post, 5 Dec.1966.

Hagerstown
-UFO (?)
 1947, July 6/Madelyn Ganoe/349 S. Can-
 non St./=aircraft?
  Hagerstown Morning Herald, 7-8 July
  1947.
 1952, Sep.12/=meteor?
  Ivan T. Sanderson, Uninvited Visitors
  (N.Y.: Cowles, 1967), p.41.
-UFO (DD)
 1977, Oct.29
  "UFOs of Limited Merit," Int'l UFO
  Reporter 2 (Dec.1977):3.

Harford co.
-Humanoid
 1976/Robert Chance
  Gettysburg (Pa.) Times, 24 July 1978,
  p.1.
 1976, March
 1977, July
  York (Pa.) Daily Record, 23 Feb.1978.
-UFO (NL)
 1977, March 22
  Bel Air Aegis, 24 Mar.1977.

Hebron
-UFO (NL)
 1952, July 16-17/Robert Burkehardt/1
 mi.W on Church St. Extension

Salisbury Times, 17-18 July 1952.
(Editorial), Fate 5 (Dec.1952):6-7.
H. Charles Robertson, "Maryland's
Ghost Light Road," Fate 11 (July
1958):92-96.

Hoopersville
-Haunt
  n.d.
    George Carey, A Faraway Time and
    Place (Washington: Robert B. Luce,
    1971), pp.173-74.

Howard co.
-UFO (CE-1)
  1977, July 3/Dorothy Moore/Annapolis
  Junction Rd.
    A.J. Graziano, "1977 CE I Case,"
    APRO Bull. 26 (May 1978):3-4.
-UFO (CE-2)
  1977, July 8/Raymond Coates
    A.J. Graziano, "1977 CE I Case,"
    APRO Bull. 26 (May 1978):3,4.

Hughesville
-UFO (NL)
  1978, Jan.13/Tracy King
    La Plata Maryland Independent, 1
    Feb.1978.

Indian Head
-Haunt
  1927, March-May 24/Albert M. Hinman
    Lieut. A.M.H., "An Apparition Iden-
    tified from a Photograph," Psychic
    Rsch. 25 (1931):53-57.
    Edmond P. Gibson, "This Ghost Blocked
    the Light," Fate 8 (Nov.1955):66-70.
-UFO (NL)
  1966, Oct.11
    "Capital Area Sightings," UFO Inv. 3
    (Oct.-Nov.1966):7.

Jefferson
-Archeological site
  ca.6000 B.C./Everhart Rockshelter
    Spencer O. Geasey, "Everhart Rock-
    shelter (Site 18FR4) Frederick
    County, Maryland," Pennsylvania
    Arch. 42 (1972):16-30. il.

Kensington
-UFO (DD)
  1966, Oct.16
    "Capital Area Sightings," UFO Inv. 3
    (Oct.-Nov.1966):7.

Lanham
-UFO (NL)
  1966, Aug.1/Frankie L. Dowling
    "New Reports by Space Experts Add to
    UFO Proof," UFO Inv. 3 (Aug.-Sep.
    1966):3,4.
  1975, Aug.29
    "UFO Central," CUFOS News Bull., 15
    Nov.1975, p.17.

Lansdowne
-Fall of rubberlike material
  1957, Aug.26/John Barton

Baltimore Sun, 26 Aug.1957.
-UFO (DD)
  1947, July 6/Anthony McDonald
    Baltimore News-Post, 7 July 1947.

Largo
-Paranormal voice recordings
  1970s/Thomas P. Bruck
    Susy Smith, Voices of the Dead?
    (N.Y.: Signet, 1977), pp.98-99.

Laurel
-UFO (?)
  1947, July/=hoax
    Bruce S. Maccabee, "UFO Related In-
    formation from the FBI Files: Part
    2," MUFON UFO J., no.120 (Nov.1977)
    :12.
-UFO (NL)
  1967, March 8
    Laurel Prince George's County News,
    16 Mar.1967.

LaVale
-Clairvoyance
  1970, April/R. Warren Hoover
    B.J. Baronitis, "Black Magic Murders
    Solved," Fate 31 (June 1978):50-
    56. il.

Laytonsville
-UFO (CE-1)
  1958, Oct.10/Allen Etzler
    "New Wave of UFO Sightings Cracks
    Censorship Wall," NICAP Spec.Bull.,
    Nov.1958, pp.1,2.

Leonardtown
-Mystery tracks
  n.d.
    Washington Post, 26 Aug.1978.

Lexington Park
-UFO (NL)
  1959, June 30/Patuxent River Naval
  Test Center
    Lloyd Mallan, "Complete Directory of
    UFOs: Part III," Sci.& Mech. 38
    (Feb.1967):56,58-59.
-UFO (R)
  1964, Dec.19/Bernard Sujka/Patuxent
  River Naval Test Center
    "New Sightings Put AF on Spot," UFO
    Inv. 3 (Mar.-Apr.1965):1,3.
    "Opposition Flap 1965," Flying Sau-
    cer Rev. 11 (May-June 1965):3,4.

Lonaconing
-Entombed frog
  1906, Dec.22/John Savage/Enterprise
  Mine
    New York Times, 24 Dec.1906, p.1.

Longwoods
-Bee attack
  1978, July/Dianne Schlotzhauer
    Washington Post, 26 July 1978.

Madonna
-Dog mutilation

1978, Feb.21
    York (Pa.) Daily Record, 23 Feb.1978.

Middletown
-Humanoid
    1934
        Washington Post, 10 Oct.1976, maga-
        zine sec.

Montgomery co.
-Archeological site
    Richard E. Stearns, "The Hughes
    Site," Proc.Nat.Hist.Soc'y Maryland,
    no.6 (1940). il.

Mount Airy
-UFO (CE-1)
    1965, March 8
        Jacques Vallee, Passport to Magonia
        (Chicago: Regnery, 1969), p.306.

Mount Ranier
-Out-of-body experience
    n.d./Francis M. Bell
        (Letter), Fate 7 (Aug.1954):109-10.
-Possession
    1949, Jan.15-May/Roland Doe
        "Report of a Poltergeist," Parapsych.
        Bull., no.15 (1949):2-3.
        D.R. Linson, "Washington's Haunted
        Boy," Fate 4 (Apr.1951):31-34.
        (Editorial), Fate 26 (Mar.1973):8-
        14, quoting Washington Star-News
        (undated).
        Steve Erdmann, "The Truth Behind
        'The Exorcist,'" Fate 28 (Jan.1975)
        :50-59.
-UFO (DD)
    1950s/Francis M. Bell
        (Letter), Fate 12 (Feb.1959):124-26.

New Windsor
-Phantom buggy
    1890s
        Hanover (Pa.) Herald, 3 July 1901.

Ocean City
-Sea monster
    1959, summer/Lee Hoffman
        (Editorial), Fate 12 (Oct.1959):8.

Oxford
-Precognition
    1750, July/Robert Morris/"Liverpool"
        Eleanor Young, Forgotten Patriot:
        Robert Morris (N.Y.: Macmillan,
        1950), pp.5-7.

Phelps Corner
-UFO (NL) and phantom helicopter
    1968, Aug.19/Gwen E. Donovan/racetrack
        Donald E. Keyhoe & Gordon I.R. Lore,
        Jr., UFOs: A New Look (Washington:
        NICAP, 1969), p.44.
        John A. Keel, UFOs: Operation Trojan
        Horse (N.Y.: Putnam, 1970), pp.140-
        41.

Pikesville
-UFO (?)

1966, April 25/=meteor
    John A. Keel, UFOs: Operation Trojan
    Horse (N.Y.: Putnam, 1970), p.145.
-UFO (CE-3)
    1973, Oct.17/Mrs. Jacob Bowers
        David Webb, 1973: Year of the Human-
        oids (Evanston: Center for UFO
        Studies, 1976 ed.), p.13.
        Gordon I.R. Lore, Jr., "UFO Pilots
        Key to Space Mystery," Saga UFO
        Rept. 3 (Mar.1977):26,60.

Piney Point
-Crisis apparition
    1840, May
        Robert Dale Owen, Footfalls on the
        Boundary of Another World (Phila-
        delphia: Lippincott, 1860), pp.327-
        29.

Pisgah
-UFO (?)
    1968, June 29/William E. Rison/=meteor
        "Some Recent Fireballs," Sky & Tele-
        scope 36 (Sep.1968):195.

Port Tobacco
-Phantom dog and lost treasure
    1850s-1860s/Rose Hill
        "Ghost of the Blue Dog," Fate 6
        (Nov.1953):34.

Potomac
-UFO (CE-2)
    1966, Oct.5
        "Capital Area Sightings," UFO Inv. 3
        (Oct.-Nov.1966):7.

Prince George's co.
-Erratic crocodilian
    1978, May 26/Capital Beltway
        Washington Star, 26 May 1978.
-UFO (CE-1)
    1966, Aug.1/Vasil Uzunoglu/Capital
    Beltway
        "New Reports by Space Experts Add to
        UFO Proof," UFO Inv. 3 (Aug.-Sep.
        1966):3,4.
        Donald E. Keyhoe & Gordon I.R. Lore,
        Jr., UFOs: A New Look (Washington:
        NICAP, 1969), p.12.

Queen Annes co.
-Ghost
    1791, March/William Briggs
        Authentic Account of the Appearance
        of a Ghost in Queen Ann's County,
        Maryland (Baltimore: Fryer & Rider,
        1807).
        F.D. Fleming, "The Spirit Return of
        Tom Harris," Fate 10 (Dec.1957):86-
        90.

Randallstown
-Humanoid tracks
    1971, winter
        "BHM in the NE USA," INFO J., no.11
        (summer 1973):26,27.
-UFO (NL)
    1975, Nov.6

"From the Center for UFO Studies,"
Flying Saucer Rev. 21 (Apr.1976):26.

Riverdale
-Erratic crocodilian
1933, Dec.4
Washington Times-Herald, 5 Dec.1933.

Rocks
-Humanoid
1975, April 28/Peter Hurenk
York (Pa.) Daily Record, 23 Feb.1978.
-Humanoid tracks
1978, Feb.
Bel Air Aegis, 9 Feb.1978.

Rocky Ridge
-Lightning anomaly
1890s/Mr. Heiskell
"Notable Lightning," Monthly Weather
Rev. 28 (July 1900):290-91.

Saint Mary's City
-Mystery bird deaths
1969, Jan.25
Washington Post, 26 Jan.1969.
-Witch trial (hex)
1674, Feb.17/John Cowman
1685, Oct./Rebecca Fowler
1686, April 27/Hannah Edwards
Francis Neal Parke, Witchcraft in
Maryland (Baltimore: Maryland Hist.
Soc'y, 1937), pp.9-10,32-37.

Saint Michaels
-UFO (NL)
1967, Jan.16
"Major Sighting Wave," UFO Inv. 3
(Jan.-Feb.1967):1,4.

Salisbury
-Witchcraft
n.d.
Annie Weston Whitney & Caroline Canfield Bullock, "Folk-Lore from Maryland," Mem.Am.Folk-Lore Soc'y, vol.
18 (1925), pp.200-201.

Seat Pleasant
-UFO (CE-3)
1952, Aug./Suzanne E. Knight
Donald E. Keyhoe & Gordon I.R. Lore,
Jr., UFOs: A New Look (Washington:
NICAP, 1969), pp.26-27.
-UFO (NL)
1975, July 23
"UFO Central," CUFOS News Bull., 15
Nov.1975, p.14.

Silver Spring
-Clairempathy
1970s/Sean (Lalsingh) Harribance/1142
Hornell Dr.
J.P. Stump, W.G. Roll & M. Roll,
"Some Exploratory Forced-Choice ESP
Experiments with Lalsingh Harri-
bance," J.ASPR 64 (1970):421-31.
Judith Klein, "Lalsingh Harribance,
Medium in Residence," Theta, no.31
(spring 1971).

Judith Klein, "A Comparison of Clair-
voyance and Telepathy," J.Parapsych.
35 (1971):335.
R.L. Morris, "Guessing Habits and
ESP," J.Parapsych. 35 (1971):335-
36.
W.G. Roll & J. Klein, "Further
Forced-Choice ESP Experiments with
Lalsingh Harribance," J.ASPR 66
(1972):103-12.
R.L. Morris, et al., "EEG Patterns
and ESP Results in Forced-Choice
Experiments with Lalsingh Harri-
bance," J.ASPR 66 (1972):253-68.
W.G. Roll, et al., "Free Verbal Re-
sponse Experiments with Lalsingh
Harribance," J.ASPR 67 (1973):197-
207.
Alan Vaughan, "Famous Western Sensi-
tives," in Edgar D. Mitchell, ed.,
Psychic Exploration (N.Y.: Putnam,
1974), pp.74,87.
Sean Harribance & N. Richard Neff,
This Man Knows You (San Antonio:
Naylor, 1976).
Washington Star, 25 Mar.1978.
-Fire anomaly
1953, March 28/Veronica Rae Klenke
(Editorial), Fate 6 (July 1953):5-6.
-Parapsychology research
1972-   /Mankind Research Unlimited/
1110 Spring St.
Washington Post Potomac Mag., 22
July 1973.
June & Nicholas Regush, Psi: The Oth-
er World Catalogue (N.Y.: Putnam,
1974), p.20.
Sheila Ostrander & Lynn Schroeder,
Handbook of Psi Discoveries (N.Y.:
Putnam, 1974), pp.80-81.
-Plant sensitivity
1970s/Eldon Byrd/Naval Ordnance Lab-
oratory
Peter Tompkins & Christopher Bird,
The Secret Life of Plants (N.Y.:
Harper & Row, 1973), pp.40-42.
-Poltergeist
1966-1967/Gene Shumate
Gene Shumate, "Our Peg-Legged Polter-
geist," Fate 31 (July 1978):82-84.
-UFO (?)
1965, Feb.26/Madelyn Rodeffer/=hoax
(Letter), Ronald W.J. Anstee, Flying
Saucer Rev. 12 (Jan.-Feb.1966):21-
22.
"Saucer Briefs," Saucer News 13
(Mar.1966):16,31. il.
(Letter), Robert E. Barrow, Flying
Saucer Rev. 12 (May-June 1966):18-
19.
-UFO (NL)
1966, March 23
"Nation-Wide Saucer Flap Continues,"
Saucer News 13 (June 1966):30,31.
1966, Oct.12/N. Smith
"Capital Area Sightings," UFO Inv. 3
(Oct.-Nov.1966):7.

Somerset co.
-Archeological site

Paul Cresthull, "Chance (18So5): A
Major Early Archaic Site," J.Arch.
Soc'y Maryland 7, no.2 (1971):31-
52. il.

Sykesville
-Humanoid
1973, May 29-July/Anthony Dorsey
Sykesville Herald, 31 May 1973.
John Green, Sasquatch: The Apes Among
Us (Seattle: Hancock House, 1978),
p.226.

Texas
-Fall of ferrochromium
1965, Aug.11/Peter Tuczinski
Baltimore News-American, 12 Aug.1965.
John A. Keel, UFOs: Operation Trojan
Horse (N.Y.: Putnam, 1970), p.175.

Thurmont
-Haunt
n.d./Auburn Mansion/5 mi.S
Sally M. Barach, Haunts of Adams and
Other Counties (Indiana, Pa.: A.G.
Halldin, 1972), pp.38-39.

Tilghman
-Fall of sulphuric acid
1949, Sep.3
"Run of the Mill," Doubt, no.29
(1950):27.

Towson
-Haunt
n.d./Hampton Nat'l Historic Site
Dennis Bardens, Ghosts and Hauntings
(N.Y.: Ace, 1965 ed.), pp.238-39.
-UFO (NL)
1977, April 21
"UFOs of Limited Merit," Int'l UFO
Reporter 2 (June 1977):3.

Tracys Landing
-Humanoid
1977, Aug.30/Ronald Jones/Hwy.258
Annapolis Evening Capital, 1 Sep.
1977.

Tyaskin
-Haunt
n.d.
George Carey, A Faraway Time and
Place (Washington: Robert B. Luce,
1971), pp.173-74.

Warfieldburg
-Phantom dog
ca.1887/Ore Mine Bridge
Annie Weston Whitney & Caroline Canfield Bullock, "Folk-Lore from Maryland," Mem.Am.Folk-Lore Soc'y, vol.
18 (1925), p.185.

Washington co.
-Haunts
n.d.
Annie Weston Whitney & Caroline Canfield Bullock, "Folk-Lore from Maryland," Mem.Am.Folk-Lore Soc'y, vol.

18 (1925), pp.188-89.

Washington D.C.
-Acoustic anomaly
1960-1961, June/Ed Koterba
United Press Int'l, "Ed Koterba's
'Harp of Angels,'" Fate 15 (Apr.
1962):32-36.
-Automatic writing
1861, Nov.18/Julia Ward Howe/Willard's
Hotel
Julia Ward Howe, Reminiscences 1819-
1899 (N.Y.: Negro Universities,
1969 ed.), pp.273-77.
1914-1923/James E. Padgett
James E. Padgett, Messages from
Jesus, 3 vols. (Washington: L.R.
Stone, 194-?-1969).
James E. Padgett, Book of Truths
(Washington: L.R. Stone, 1950).
-Ball lightning
1924, June 8/C.P. Thomas/Fairfax Rd.
W.J. Humphreys, "Ball Lightning,"
Proc.Am.Phil.Soc'y 76 (1936):613-
26.
1953, spring/Fred Blumenthal/Snows Ct.
Frank Edwards, Strange World (N.Y.:
Lyle Stuart, 1964), p.293.
-Biofeedback research
1974-   /Center for Preventive Therapy
and Rehabilitation/1640 Kalmia Rd.NW
June & Nicholas Regush, Psi: The Oth-
er World Catalogue (N.Y.: Putnam,
1974), p.206.
-Clairempathy
1970-1973/Don Cherry/police dep't
(Editorial), Fate 26 (May 1973):14-
18, quoting Washington Star-News
(undated).
-Clairvoyance
1840, winter/14th St. x New York Ave.
Robert Dale Owen, Footfalls on the
Boundary of Another World (Phila-
delphia: Lippincott, 1860), pp.
326-27.
-Contactee
1959, July 6/Naval commander
Robert Emenegger, UFOs: Past, Pres-
ent and Future (N.Y.: Ballantine,
1974), pp.55-62.
Jacques Vallee, The Invisible College
(N.Y.: Dutton, 1975), pp.72-76.
1968-   /Irmgard Lincoln/Cosmic Acad-
emy/Nat'l Press Bldg.
Washington Post, 20 Oct.1973.
Philip J. Klass, UFOs Explained (N.Y.:
Random House, 1974), p.291.
-Crisis apparition
1898, March 12
"Coincidental Raps," J.ASPR 8 (1914):
480-82.
-Disease anomaly
1975/U.S. Food & Drug Administration
offices
"Unexplainable Epidemic," Probe the
Unknown 3 (May 1975):44.
-Doubtful responsibility
1865, April 14/Edwin M. Stanton/Abra-
ham Lincoln assassination/=conspiracy?
Burke McCarthy, The Suppressed Truth

About the Assassination of Abraham
Lincoln (Roslyn, N.Y.: Chedney, n.
d.).
Otto Eisenschiml, Why Was Lincoln
Murdered? (Boston: Little, Brown,
1937).
Izola Forrester, This One Mad Act
(Boston: Hale, Cushman & Flint,
1937).
Otto Eisenschiml, In the Shadow of
Lincoln's Death (N.Y.: Funk, 1940).
Robert H. Fowler, "Was Stanton Be-
hind Lincoln's Murder?" Civil War
Times 3 (Aug.1961):4-23.
Vaughan Shelton, Mask for Treason
(Harrisburg: Stackpole, 1965).
Samuel Carter III, The Riddle of
Dr. Mudd (N.Y.: Putnam, 1974).
Dell Leonardi, The Reincarnation of
John Wilkes Booth (Old Greenwich,
Ct.: Devin-Adair, 1975).
Thomas R. Turner, "Public Opinion
and the Assassination of Abraham
Lincoln," Lincoln Herald 78 (1976):
17-24,66-76.
David W. Balsiger & Charles E. Sel-
lier, Jr., The Lincoln Conspiracy
(Los Angeles: Schick Sunn, 1977).
-Dowsing
1960s/George Maddox
Robert S. Plimpton, "We Dowsed for
Our Home on a Map," Fate 18 (May
1965):39,41-42.
1972-   /Soc'y for the Application of
Free Energy/1325½ Wisconsin Ave.
June & Nicholas Regush, Psi: The Oth-
er World Catalogue (N.Y.: Putnam,
1974), p.101.
-Erratic crocodilian
1962, Dec./Pennsylvania Ave.
Washington Post, 23 Dec.1962.
-Fall of fish
1951, Nov.
Buffalo (N.Y.) Evening News, 27 Nov.
1951.
1952, April
Roanoke (N.C.) Times, 1 June 1952.
1964, Jan./Thom Andrews/Bolling AFB
(Editorial), Fate 17 (Oct.1964):27.
-Fall of green chemical
1978, Sep./Jane Gillespie/Foggy Bottom
Washington Post, 11 Sep.1978; and 16
Sep.1978.
-Fall of ice
1968, Feb.5/Charles Morris/89 Elmira
Ave.
Ronald J. Willis, "Ice Falls," INFO
J., no.3 (spring 1968):12,17-19,22-
23. il.
-Fire anomaly
1802, March 19/Jonathan Dayton
"Spontaneous Decomposition of a Fab-
ric of Silk," Phil.Mag. 16 (1803):
92-93.
1954, May 4
Harold T. Wilkins, Flying Saucers Un-
censored (N.Y.: Pyramid, 1967 ed.),
p.116.
-Ghost
1850, March 3/John C. Calhoun

Daniel A. Buechner, "John C. Cal-
houn's Prophetic Dream," Fate 6
(Mar.1953):30-33.
-Haunt
1850s-   /Octagon/1799 New York Ave.
Marion Lowndes, Ghosts That Still
Walk (N.Y.: Knopf, 1941), pp.88-98.
William Oliver Stephens, Washington:
The Cinderella City (N.Y.: Dodd,
Mead, 1943), pp.171-75.
"Washington's Favorite Haunted House,"
Fate 17 (July 1964):56.
Hans Holzer, Ghosts I've Met (N.Y.:
Ace, 1965 ed.), pp.87-93.
Hans Holzer, Haunted Houses (N.Y.:
Crown, 1971), pp.34-36. il.
1900s-   /White House
Arthur Krock, "Ghosts in the White
House," Tomorrow 4 (summer 1956):
62-64.
New York Journal-American, 22 Mar.
1961.
Lillian Rogers Park, My Thirty Years
Backstairs at the White House (N.Y.:
Fleet, 1961), pp.67-71.
(Editorial), Fate 14 (Oct.1961):23-
24.
Susy Smith, Prominent American Ghosts
(N.Y.: Dell, 1969 ed.), pp.101-106.
1920s/Mary Roberts Rinehart
Mary Roberts Rinehart, My Story (N.Y.:
Farrar & Rinehart, 1931), pp.351-57.
Alice V. Hancock, "Mary Roberts Rine-
hart's True Mystery Story," in Mar-
tin Ebon, ed., True Experiences in
Communicating with the Dead (N.Y.:
Signet, 1968), pp.112-17.
1955/Pentagon
(Editorial), Fate 9 (Apr.1956):8.
(Letter), Fred Ide, Fate 9 (Sep.
1956):125-26.
1950s-1960s/Nick Roper/Halcyon House/
3400 Prospect St.
Washington Star, 9 Aug.1959.
Nick Roper, "I Lived in a Haunted
House," Boston (Mass.) Sunday Globe,
21 Apr.1963.
Hans Holzer, Ghosts I've Met (N.Y.:
Ace, 1965 ed.), pp.80-85.
1960s/Woodrow Wilson House/2340 S St.
Hans Holzer, The Ghosts That Walk in
Washington (Garden City: Doubleday,
1971).
1960, Aug.12-1961/Thomas H. Robbins/
Tingey House, Navy Yard
(Editorial), Fate 15 (Apr.1962):14-
16, quoting Washington Post (undated).
1962-1965/Robert Gray
(Editorial), Fate 18 (Oct.1965):18-
20.
1968-   /Ford's Theater
"Great Lincoln's Ghost!" Probe the
Unknown 4 (Nov.1976):58.
1970s/Capitol Bldg.
Anne Lear, "Capitol Ghosts," Mankind
5 (1976):31-33,48-50.
1972/Fort McNair
(Editorial), Fate 25 (Sep.1972):28.
1975, summer/Joan Coleman/William Petersen House/10th St.

"Great Lincoln's Ghost!" Probe the
Unknown 4 (Nov.1976):58.
1976, May/Albert Miller
Arlan Andrews, "Yes! The House Is
Haunted," Beyond Reality, no.32
(May-June 1978):34-35,58.
-Hex
1958-   /James G. Todd/Smithsonian
Institution
Joseph Goodavage, "The Curse of the
Hope Diamond," Fate 27 (Sep.1974):
34-43.
(Letter), David Taylor, Fate 28
(Mar.1975):113-14.
(Letter), Bim Schelderup, Fate 28
(July 1975):113-14.
-Inner development
1900s/Mr. Marsland/Order of the Ini-
tiates of Tibet
Washington Post, 31 Oct.1909.
1955-   /Church of Scientology/2125
S St.NW
L. Ron Hubbard, Dianetics (N.Y.: Her-
mitage, 1950).
L. Ron Hubbard, Scientology: The
Fundamentals of Thought (London:
Hubbard Ass'n of Scientologists
Int'l, 1956).
L. Ron Hubbard, Have You Lived Before
This Life? (N.Y.: Vantage, 1960).
L. Ron Hubbard, A New Slant on Life
(Edinburgh: Publications Organiza-
tion World Wide, 1965).
Richmond Edmond Saunders, "Scientol-
ogy and the FDA," Fate 19 (Oct.
1966):51-55.
Paulette Cooper, The Scandal of Sci-
entology (N.Y.: Tower, 1971).
John Godwin, Occult America (Garden
City: Doubleday, 1972), pp.76-99.
Richard E. Saunders, "Scientology
Wins in Court," Fate 25 (Mar.1972):
73-76.
Church of Scientology of California,
False Report Correction (Los Ange-
les: Church of Scientology, 1974).
Omar V. Garrison, The Hidden Scandal
of Scientology (Secaucus, N.J.:
Citadel, 1974).
J. Gordon Melton, Encyclopedia of
American Religions, 2 vols. (Wil-
mington, N.C.: Consortium, 1978),
2:221-23.
1958-   /Foundation Church of the New
Birth
John Paul Gibson, True Gospel Re-
vealed Anew (Washington: Church of
the New Birth, n.d.).
Brad Steiger, Revelation: The Divine
Fire (Englewood Cliffs, N.J.: Pren-
tice-Hall, 1973), pp.44-54.
J. Gordon Melton, Encyclopedia of
American Religions, 2 vols. (Wil-
mington, N.C.: Consortium, 1978),
2:127-28.
1960s-   /Benn Lewis/Washington Cosmic
Center/1327 Delafield Pl.NW
John Godwin, Occult America (Garden
City: Doubleday, 1972), pp.136-37.
-Mystery plane crash

1962, Nov.23/Viscount
"Thunderbirds Again--and Again,"
Pursuit 5 (Apr.1972):40-41, quoting
Saga, May 1963.
-Norse runestone
1867/=hoax
"Important Archaeological Discovery
--Perhaps," Sci.Am. 17 (1867):74.
John P. MacLean, The Mound Builders
(Cincinnati: Robert Clarke, 1904),
p.115.
-Out-of-body experience
n.d.
Richard Webb, Voices from Another
World (N.Y.: Manor, 1972 ed.),
pp.77-78.
-Paranormal voice recordings
ca.1918/Aaron Brylawski
Julius Weinberger, "On Apparatus
Communication with Discarnate Per-
sons," Int'l J.Parapsych. 3, no.1
(1961):56-76.
Susy Smith, Voices of the Dead?
(N.Y.: Signet, 1977), pp.115-18.
-Parapsychology research
1968-   /Gardner Murphy/George Wash-
ington University
"Interview: Gardner Murphy," Psychic
1 (Jan.-Feb.1970):4-7,32-39.
Gardner Murphy, "The Problem of Re-
peatability in Psychical Research,"
J.ASPR 65 (1971):3-16.
-Phantom image
1903
Henry Winfred Splitter, "Nature's
Strange Photographs," Fate 8 (Jan.
1955):21,29.
Frank Edwards, Stranger Than Science
(N.Y.: Ace, 1959 ed.), pp.185-86.
-Phantom insects
1899, June
Washington Post, 20 June 1899.
L.O. Howard, "Spider Bites and 'Kiss-
ing Bugs,'" Pop.Sci.Monthly 56
(1899):31-42.
William J. Fox, "Editorial," Ento-
mological News 10 (1899):205-206.
-Phantom panther
1948, Aug.7
"'Lower' Animals," Doubt, no.23
(1948):348.
1978, Jan.22/Nat'l Zoological Park
Washington Star, 23 Jan.1978.
-Poltergeist
1968, March-April/=exaggeration
William G. Roll, The Poltergeist
(N.Y.: Signet, 1974 ed.), pp.101-102.
-Precognition
1840, May/Senator Linn
Robert Dale Owen, Footfalls on the
Boundary of Another World (Phila-
delphia: Lippincott, 1860), pp.455-
59.
1865, March/Abraham Lincoln
Ward Hill Lamon, Recollections of
Abraham Lincoln (Chicago: A.S.
McClurg, 1895), pp.109-21.
Lloyd Lewis, Myths after Lincoln
(NY.: Readers Club, 1941), pp.289-
303.

1940s-   /Jeane Dixon/1312 19th St.
(Editorial), Fate 7 (Jan.1954):7-8.
"Washington's Incredible Crystal-
Gazer," Parade, 13 May 1956.
Jess Stearn, The Door to the Future
(N.Y.: Macfadden, 1964), pp.22-49.
John C. Ross, "Premonitions of Ken-
nedy's Death," Fate 17 (May 1964):
30,34-35.
Ruth Montgomery, A Gift of Prophecy
(N.Y.: William Morrow, 1965).
(Editorial), Fate 19 (May 1966):25-
30.
Allen Spraggett, The Unexplained
(N.Y.: Signet, 1967), pp.37-45,54-
55.
"Predictions for 1967," Fate 20
(June 1967):43-44.
C. Fritchey, "Gullibility in Wash-
ington," Harper's, June 1967, pp.
34-38.
(Editorial), Fate 21 (Oct.1968):20-
23, quoting Chicago (Ill.) Daily
News (undated).
Jeane Dixon, My Life and Prophecies
(N.Y.: William Morrow, 1969).
Ned Smith, Jeane Dixon: The Washing-
ton Prophetess (Springfield, Mo.:
Baptist Bible Tribune, 1969).
"Interview: Jeane Dixon," Psychic 1
(June-July 1969):5-7,34-39,43.
Mary Bringle, Jeane Dixon: Prophetess
or Fraud? (N.Y.: Tower, 1970).
Brad Steiger, "Scoring the Seers in
1969," Fate 23 (Jan.1970):66,68.
Walter J. McGraw, "Precognitive Pig
in a Palace," Fate 23 (Mar.1970):
70,74-76.
Kurt Saxon, Keeping Score on Our Mod-
ern Prophets (Eureka, Cal.: Atlan
Formularies, 1974).
David Wallechinsky & Irving Wallace,
The People's Almanac (Garden City:
Doubleday, 1975), pp.4-5.
Bob Schultz, "ESPecially Jeane
Dixon," Probe the Unknown 3 (Mar.
1975):42-43.
Denis Brian, Jeane Dixon: The Wit-
nesses (Garden City: Doubleday,
1976).
David Wallechinsky & Irving Wallace,
The People's Almanac #2 (N.Y.: Ban-
tam, 1978), pp.3-4.
1952, summer/Dorris C. Chambers
Laura A. Dale, Rhea White & Gardner
Murphy, "A Selection of Cases from
a Recent Survey of Spontaneous ESP
Phenomena," J.ASPR 56 (1962):3,20-
21.
-Psychic photography
1910s/Marguerite du Pont Lee
James H. Hyslop, "Some Unusual Phenomena in Photography," Proc.ASPR
8 (1914):395-464. il.
Walter Franklin Prince, "Supplementary Report on the Keeler-Lee Photographs," Proc.ASPR 13 (1919):529-
87. il.
-Seance
1864/Ira and William Davenport

P.B. Randolph, The Davenport Brothers (Boston: William White, 1869).
Slater Brown, The Heyday of Spiritualism (N.Y.: Pocket Books, 1972
ed.), pp.201-205.
1962/Arthur Ford
Herbert S. Greenhouse, Premonitions:
A Leap into the Future (N.Y.: Warner, 1973 ed.), p.81.
-Spirit medium
1850s/Mrs. C. Laurie
Eliab W. Capron, Modern Spiritualism: Its Facts and Fanaticisms
(Boston: Bela Marsh, 1855), pp.357-
59.
Emma Hardinge Britten, Modern American Spiritualism (N.Y.: The Author,
1870), pp.108,113-14.
1850s/A.P. Hascall
1850s/A.F. Cunningham
1854/Amelia J. Williams
Eliab W. Capron, Modern Spiritualism: Its Facts and Fanaticisms
(Boston: Bela Marsh, 1855), pp.335-
36,356-57,359.
1860s/H. Conkling
"President Lincoln's Manifesto for
the Abolition of Slavery," Psychic
Rsch. 24 (1930):115-16.
1862-1863/Nettie Colburn (Maynard) and
others
Chicago (Ill.) Tribune, 23 Apr.1863.
Thomas Richmond, God Dealing with
Slavery (Chicago: Religio-Philo-
sophical Pub.House, 1870).
Fayette Hall, The Secret and Polit-
ical History of the War of the Re-
bellion (New Haven: The Author,
1890).
Henrietta Sturdevant Maynard, Was
Abraham Lincoln a Spiritualist?
(Philadelphia: R.C. Hartranft, 1891).
J.J. Fitzgerrell, Lincoln Was a
Spiritualist (Los Angeles: Austin,
1924).
Nandor Fodor, Encyclopaedia of Psy-
chic Science (London: Arthurs,
1933), pp.50,203.
Jay Monaghan, "Was Abraham Lincoln
Really a Spiritualist?" J.Illinois
Hist.Soc'y 34 (1941):209-32.
G.H. Irwin, "Abraham Lincoln, Was He
a Mystic?" Fate 2 (Sep.1949):4-11.
James Logan Gordon, Was Abraham Lin-
coln a Spiritualist? (Washington:
The Author, n.d.).
"Spiritualism in the White House,"
Fate 5 (Dec.1952):11-14.
Ruth Painter Randall, Mary Lincoln:
Biography of a Marriage (Boston:
Little, Brown, 1953), pp.292-94.
Peggy Robbins, "The Lincolns and
Spiritualism," Civil War Times Ill.
15, no.5 (1976):4-10,46-47.
1880s-1900s/Pierre L.O.A. Keeler
Alfred Russell Wallace, My Life: A
Record of Events and Opinions, 2
vols. (N.Y.: Dodd, Mead, 1909), 2:
358-61.
W. Usborne Moore, Glimpses of the

Next State (London: Watts, 1911),
pp.347-54.
Walter Franklin Prince, "A Survey of
American Slate-Writing Mediumship,"
Proc.ASPR 15 (1921):315-592.
Joseph Dunninger, Houdini's Spirit
World and Dunninger's Psychic Rev-
elations (N.Y.: Tower, 1968 ed.),
pp.33-34.
1970s/Ruth S. Montgomery/2101 Connect-
icut Ave.NW
Ruth S. Montgomery, A World Beyond
(N.Y.: Coward, McCann & Geoghegan,
1971).
Ruth S. Montgomery, Companions Along
the Way (N.Y.: Coward, McCann &
Geoghegan, 1974).
Ruth S. Montgomery, The World Before
(N.Y.: Coward, McCann & Geoghegan,
1976).
-Telepathy
1853/Jesse Benton Fremont
Elizabeth Benton Fremont, Recollections (N.Y.: F.H. Hitchcock, 1912),
pp.69-72.
-UFO (?)
1947, Dec.13/=meteor
Washington Post, 14 Dec.1947.
1952, July 19/Capitol/=lens flare
"A 'Lens Flare' Classic and Other
Light Image Cases," Can.UFO Rept.,
no.24 (summer 1976):18-19.
Colman S. VonKevicsky, "A Re-Analy-
sis," Can.UFO Rept., no.24 (summer
1976):19-23. il.
1959, Feb.4/A.S. Frutin/Capitol/=air-
craft?
Frank Bowers, ed., The True Report
on Flying Saucers (Greenwich, Ct.:
Fawcett, 1967), pp.13,15. il.
Brad Steiger, Project Blue Book (N.Y.:
Ballantine, 1976), betw.pp.360-61.
il.
1967, Aug.23/=balloons
"FAA Warns Hoaxters," UFO Inv. 4
(Oct.1967):5.
1971, summer/=police helicopter
Philip J. Klass, UFOs Explained
(N.Y.: Random House, 1974), p.269.
1972, May-June/Curtis K. Sutherly/An-
drews AFB/=laser experiment?
(Letter), Fate 29 (Apr.1976):128-29.
(Letter), Yael Ruth Dragwyla, Fate
29 (Oct.1976):115-16.
(Letter), Jan Kauffman, Fate 29 (Oct.
1976):116-18.
(Letter), Curtis K. Sutherly, Fate
30 (Apr.1977):118-20.
-UFO (CE-1)
1967, July 9
Barry Greenwood, "UFO Notes," Sky-
look, no.61 (Dec.1972):15.
-UFO (CE-2)
1955, June 26/National Airport
Aime Michel, Flying Saucers and the
Straight-Line Mystery (N.Y.: Criter-
ion, 1958), p.236.
James M. McCampbell, "Further Evi-
dence of UFO Radiation," in 1977
MUFON UFO Symposium Proc. (Seguin,

Tex.: MUFON, 1977), pp.25,27.
-UFO (DD)
1897, April 23/Potomac R.
Pittsburgh (Pa.) Commercial Gazette,
24 Apr.1897.
1944, winter/Harry G. Barnes
Richard Hall, ed., The UFO Evidence
(Washington: NICAP, 1964), p.64.
1946, summer/William L. Witt/Patrick
Henry Dr.
Gordon I.R. Lore, Jr. & Harold H. Den-
eault, Jr., Mysteries of the Skies:
UFOs in Perspective (Englewood
Cliffs, N.J.: Prentice-Hall, 1968),
pp.147-48.
1947, July 3/Minnesota Ave.
Washington News, 5 July 1947.
1950, March 26/B.A. Totten
Washington Post, 27 Mar.1950.
1950, June 25
Bruce S. Maccabee, "UFO Related Information from the FBI Files: Part
7," MUFON UFO J., no.132 (Nov.-
Dec.1978):11.
1952, July 1/George Washington Univ.
Edward J. Ruppelt, The Report on Un-
identified Flying Objects (Garden
City: Doubleday, 1956), pp.151-52.
1952, Dec.13/S.L. Daw
Alan C. Rievman, "Saucer Sightings
by IFSB Members," Space Rev. 2
(Apr.1953):10.
1954, Aug.17/P. Wilson Redcay/Soldier's
Home
"C-16," CRIFO Newsl., 3 Sep.1954, p.
6.
1956, March 20
1956, July
Richard Hall, ed., The UFO Evidence
(Washington: NICAP, 1964), p.153.
1961, Dec.13/William John Meyer, Jr./
Virginia Ave. x E St.
Lloyd Mallan, "The Mysterious 12,"
Sci.& Mech. 37 (Dec.1966):30,63.
1964, March 28/Fred Steckling/11th x
F St.
Washington Daily News, 6 June 1964.
1965, Jan.11/Paul M. Dickey, Jr./Mu-
nitions Bldg.
Washington Star, 13 Jan.1965.
Richard Hall, "The CIA, UFOs and
Spacemen," Official UFO 1 (Oct.
1975):22-23.
-UFO (NL)
1897, April 15/Washington Monument
Topeka (Kan.) State Journal, 16 Apr.
1897, p.2.
1947, July 6/Hazen Kennedy/2615 4th St.
Washington Post, 7 July 1947.
1948, Nov.18/Henry G. Combs/Andrews AFB
Sidney Shallett, "What You Can Be-
lieve about Flying Saucers," Sat.
Eve.Post, 7 May 1949, pp.39,185.
Donald E. Keyhoe, Flying Saucers Are
Real (N.Y.: Fawcett, 1950), pp.95-
96.
Edward J. Ruppelt, The Report on Un-
identified Flying Objects (Garden
City: Doubleday, 1956), pp.67-68.
1952, July 18

1952, July 27/Maj. Turlin/Andrews AFB
Richard Hall, ed., The UFO Evidence
(Washington: NICAP, 1964), pp.160,
161.
1960, Aug.24/Georgetown Univ.
Harlan Wilson, "Strange Case of the
Mystery Satellite," Fate 14 (June
1961):25,26.
1968, April 12
"French General, Scientists, Report
UFOs," UFO Inv. 4 (May-June 1968):3.
1971, Oct.20/Curtis K. Sutherly/An-
drews AFB
Curtis K. Sutherly, "UFOs and the
Post-Blue Book Air Force," Caveat
Emptor, no.4 (summer 1972):16,17.
1973, Oct.17/=meteors?
Washington Star-News, 18 Oct.1973.
-UFO (R-V)
1952, July 19-20/Harry G. Barnes/
National Airport
1952, July 26/Jim Ritchey/National
Airport
Washington Post, 22 July 1952; 25
July 1952; and 27-30 July 1952.
New York Times, 22 July 1952, p.20;
28 July 1952, p.1; 29 July 1952,
p.20; and 30 July 1952, pp.1,10.
"Washington's Blips," Life, 4 Aug.
1952, p.40.
Chester Morrison, "Mirage or Not,
Radar Sees Those Saucers Too," Look,
9 Sep.1952, pp.98-99.
Donald E. Keyhoe, "What Radar Tells
about Flying Saucers," True, Dec.
1952, p.25.
R.C. Borden & T.K. Vickers, "A Pre-
liminary Study of Unidentified Tar-
gets Observed on Air Traffic Con-
trol Radars," CAA Tech.Development
Rept., no.180 (May 1953).
Donald E. Keyhoe, Flying Saucers from
Outer Space (N.Y.: Holt, 1953), pp.
62-70.
Washington Times-Herald, 26 Dec.1953.
"Radar Objects over Washington," Air
Weather Service Bull., Sep.1954, pp.
52-57.
Edward J. Ruppelt, The Report on Un-
identified Flying Objects (Garden
City: Doubleday, 1956), pp.158-71.
Aime Michel, The Truth About Flying
Saucers (N.Y.: Pyramid, 1967 ed.),
pp.86-92.
Donald H. Menzel & Lyle G. Boyd, The
World of Flying Saucers (Garden
City: Doubleday, 1963), pp.155-60.
Richard Hall, ed., The UFO Evidence
(Washington: NICAP, 1964), pp.45,
159-60.
"Secret Saucer Films Come to Light,"
Saucer News 12 (Dec.1965):18-19.
Gordon D. Thayer, "Optical and Radar
Analyses of Field Cases," in Edward
U. Condon, ed., Scientific Study of
Unidentified Flying Objects (N.Y.:
Bantam, 1969 ed.), pp.115,153-58,
862-67.
David Michael Jacobs, The UFO Con-
troversy in America (Bloomington:

Univ. of Indiana, 1975), pp.75-83.
Brad Steiger, ed., Project Blue Book
(N.Y.: Ballantine, 1976), pp.141-53.
Patrick A. Huyghe, "The 1952 UFO
'Raid' That Panicked Washington,
D.C.," Saga UFO Rept. 4 (Aug.1977):
38-41,62-63.
1952, July 20/Betty Ann Behl/Andrews
AFB
1952, July 29
Richard Hall, ed., The UFO Evidence
(Washington: NICAP, 1964), pp.21,
160,162.
1952, Nov.30/National Airport
U.S. Air Force, Projects Grudge and
Blue Book Reports 1-12 (Washington:
NICAP, 1968), p.173.
-Wireless inventor
1865/Mahlon Loomis
Mary Texanna Loomis, Radio Theory
and Operating (Washington: The
Author, 1925).
Charles Francis Jenkins, Vision by
Radio (Washington: National Capi-
tal, 1925).
George Wagner, "Radio Thirty Years
before Marconi," Fate 29 (Dec.1976)
:63-66.

Westminster
-Haunt
n.d./Leigh Master estate
Sally M. Barach, Haunts of Adams
and Other Counties (Indiana, Pa.:
A.G. Halldin, 1972), pp.37-38.
-Phantom horse
n.d./Maryland Hunt Cup Course
James Reynolds, Ghosts in American
Houses (N.Y.: Paperback Library,
1967 ed.), pp.75-77.

Wheaton
-UFO (?)
1974, Jan.22/Virginia Lott/Randolph
Hills Nursing Home/=balloon
Frank B. Salisbury, The Utah UFO Dis-
play (Greenwich, Ct.: Devin-Adair,
1974), pp.164-72.
-UFO (NL)
1957, Nov.15
Richard Hall, ed., The UFO Evidence
(Washington: NICAP, 1964), p.167.

White Marsh
-Healing
spring
Charles M. Skinner, Myths and Legends
of Our Own Land, 2 vols. (Philadelphia: Lippincott, 1896), 2:315.
-Humanoid
1976/Richard Stewart
John Green, Sasquatch: The Apes Among
Us (Seattle: Hancock House, 1978),
p.226

Woodlawn
-UFO (NL)
1947, July 6/Arthur Baer
Baltimore News-Post, 7 July 1947.

B. Physical Features

Calvert Cliffs
-Sea monster
1978, May/Bruce Hickman
Washington Post, 26 Aug.1978.

Church Creek
-Ghost mule
n.d.
Annie Weston Whitney & Caroline Canfield Bullock, "Folk-Lore from Maryland," Mem.Am.Folk-Lore Soc'y, vol.
18 (1925), pp.185-88.

Conowingo L.
-Humanoid
1973, July/John A. Lutz
"BHM in the NE USA," INFO J., no.11
(summer 1973):26,28.

Curtis Bay
-UFO (NL)
1957, Jan.24/Charles Ochlech/DuPont
plant
"Case 297," CRIFO Orbit, 1 Mar.1957,
p.3, quoting Baltimore News-Post
(undated).
-Windshield pitting
1954/Genevieva Cwalina/1005 Church St.
(Editorial), Fate 7 (Nov.1954):11.

Fresh Creek
-Norse discovery
1009/Thorfinn Karlsefni/=Hóp?
J.K. Tornöe, Norsemen Before Columbus
(London: Allen & Unwin, 1965), pp.
108-18.

Gambrill State Park
-Humanoid
1920s
"BHM in the NE USA," INFO J., no.11
(summer 1973):26,27, quoting Frederick newspaper (undated).

Gum Briar Swamp
-Haunt
n.d.
George Carey, A Faraway Time and
Place (Washington: Robert B. Luce,
1971), pp.165-66.

Herring Creek
-Erratic crocodilian
1942, Nov.18
Washington Post, 19 Nov.1942.

Langrells I.
-Ghost light
n.d.
George Carey, A Faraway Time and
Place (Washington: Robert B. Luce,
1971), p.173.

Liberty Reservoir
-Humanoid
1973, May 28
"BHM in the NE USA," INFO J., no.11
(summer 1973):26,28.

1978, June 17/Jack Kennedy/Oak Hill Dr.
Westminster Carroll County Times,
23 June 1978.

Loch Raven Dam
-UFO (CE-2)
1958, Oct.26/Alvin Cohen
Donald H. Menzel & Lyle G. Boyd, The
World of Flying Saucers (Garden
City: Doubleday, 1963), p.180.
Jacques & Janine Vallee, Challenge
to Science (N.Y.: Ace, 1966 ed.),
pp.212-16.
Thomas M. Olsen, The Reference for
Outstanding UFO Sightings (Rider-
wood, Md.: UFO Information Retrie-
val Center, 1966), pp.61-63.
J. Allen Hynek, The UFO Experience
(Chicago: Regnery, 1972), pp.121-
22.

Oyster Pt.
-Ghost
1836/Paddy Dabney
Charles M. Skinner, Myths and Legends
of Our Own Land, 2 vols. (Philadelphia: Lippincott, 1896), 2:272-73.

Patapsco State Park
-Humanoid
1973, June-July
John Green, Sasquatch: The Apes Among
Us (Seattle: Hancock House, 1978),
p.226.
-UFO (CE-3)
1978, March 22/Gary Oickle
Joe & Doris Graziano, "Object over
State Park," APRO Bull. 26 (Apr.
1978):1.

Potomac R.
-Erratic crocodilian
1926
"'Baby' Alligators Astray in Northern Rivers," Literary Digest 91
(11 Dec.1926):68-72, quoting Philadelphia (Pa.) Public Ledger (undated).

Smith I.
-Haunt
n.d.
George Carey, A Faraway Time and
Place (Washington: Robert B. Luce,
1971), pp.171,175-76.
-Phantom ship
n.d./Lacey Tyler/nr. Foggs Pt.
George Carey, A Faraway Time and
Place (Washington: Robert B. Luce,
1971), pp.165-66.

D. Unspecified Localities

-Aerial phantom
1886, July
Dorothy Donath, "Funeral in the Sky,"
Tomorrow 6 (summer 1958):79-81.

DELAWARE

A. Populated Places

Dover
-Haunt
  18th c./Inn of King George III
    Moritz Jagendorf, Upstate, Downstate
    (N.Y.: Vanguard, 1949), p.153.
-UFO (NL)
  1973, Oct.14/Dover AFB
    "UFO: Fact or Fiction?" Probe the
    Unknown 2 (spring 1974):8.

Georgetown
-Aerial phantom
  1881, Sep./William West
    "Visions in the Clouds," Sci.Am. 45
    (1881):291.

Greenwood
-UFO (?)
  1973, Oct./=balloon
    (Editorial), Fate 27 (Feb.1974):14.

Holly Oak
-Archeological site
    John C. Kraft & Ronald A. Thomas,
    "Early Man at Holly Oak, Delaware,"
    Science 192 (1976):756-61. il.
    Elizabeth Lockwood Coombs, "The
    Cresson Shell," Occ.Pub.Epigraphic
    Soc'y 6, no.136 (Jan.1979):192-94.
    il.

Laurel
-Aerial phantom
  1881, Sep.
    "Visions in the Clouds," Sci.Am. 45
    (1881):291.

Lewes
-Archeological site
  1550-1600/Townsend site
    H. Geiger Omwake, et al., "The Town-
    send Site near Lewes, Delaware,"
    Archeolog 15, no.1 (1963):1-72. il.
-Fall of oil
  1947, Sep.11/=pollution?
    "Run of the Mill," Doubt, no.20
    (1948):303.
-UFO (DD)
  1947, June 2/Forrest Wenyon
    Wilmington Journal Every Evening,
    8 July 1947.
    Ted Bloecher, Report on the UFO Wave
    of 1947 (Washington: NICAP, 1967),
    p. III-9.

Milford
-Medieval coin
  1851
    "Singular Old Coin," Sci.Am. 6 (1851)
    :250.

Newark
-Ghost dog
  1973, Nov.27/Gail P. Shevitz/Brookside
    Gail P. Shevitz, "Dog's Love Con-
    quers Death," Fate 28 (Apr.1975):
    64-67.
-Haunt
  1777, July/Iron Hill/=hoax
    Charles M. Skinner, Myths and Legends
    of Our Own Land, 2 vols. (Philadel-
    phia: Lippincott, 1896), 1:143.
-UFO (CE-1)
  1974, Jan.17/Delaware Ave. x Chapel
  St.
    "Woman, Son, See UFO at Busy Corner,"
    Skylook, no.101 (Apr.1976):10.

New Castle
-Precognition
  1970s/Judith Richardson/191 Christiana
  Rd., Suite 6
    Warren Smith, "Phenomenal Predictions
    for 1976," Saga, Jan.1976, pp.16,52.
-UFO (?)
  1949, April 11
    "If It's in the Sky It's a Saucer,"
    Doubt, no.27 (1949):416.
-UFO (R-V)
  1952, July 26
    Richard Hall, ed., The UFO Evidence
    (Washington: NICAP, 1964), p.161.

Odessa
-UFO (CE-1)
  1967, Feb.9/Donald Guseman/U.S.13
    Donald E. Keyhoe & Gordon I.R. Lore,
    Jr., UFOs: A New Look (Washington:
    NICAP, 1969), p.12.

Selbyville
-Humanoid
  n.d./2 mi.E of Cedar Swamp on U.S.113
    Report on file at SITU.

Wilmington
-Aerial phantom
  1881, Sep.
    "Visions in the Clouds," Sci.Am. 45
    (1881):291.
-Disintegrating clothes
  1964, Jan./Mrs. John J. Roseman
    (Editorial), Fate 17 (May 1964):6-8.
-Haunt
  1881/James Williamson/Riverview Cemetery, Brandywine
    Norfolk (Va.) Weekly Virginian, 22
    Sep.1881.
-Phantom image
  1957, Dec./Bertha Irene Ford/2410 La-
  mott St.
    Mabel Love, "Psychic Portrait of
    Jesus on a Handkerchief," Fate 13
    (Mar.1960):82-84. il.
    (Letter), Melvin L. Sutley, Fate 13

(Nov.1960):114-16.
(Letter), Mabel Love, _Fate_ 13 (Nov. 1960):116-17.
-Skyquake
  1956, Sep.12
    "Case 219," _CRIFO Orbit_, 2 Nov.1956, p.1, quoting _Wilmington Journal Every Evening_ (undated).
  1971, July 14-1972, Feb.10
    "Mystery Shocks in Delaware," _Earthquake Information Bull._ 4 (May-June 1972):22-23.
-UFO (?)
  1860, July 13/=meteor procession
    Wilmington Tribune, 20 July 1860.
  1897, Jan.
    Columbus (O.) Evening Press, 13 Apr.1897.
-UFO (DD)
  1953, April 18
    Wilmington Morning News, 9 July 1954.
-UFO (NL)
  1954, June 12
    Donald E. Keyhoe, _Flying Saucer Conspiracy_ (N.Y.: Holt, 1955), pp.161-62.
  1954, July 5/Robert O'Connor
    Wilmington Morning News, 9 July 1954.
  1957, Dec.
    "All About Sputs," _Doubt_, no.58 (1958):460,478.
  1966, March 28
    "Typical Reports," _UFO Inv._ 3 (Mar.-Apr.1966):8.
  1973, Oct./Thomas Little
    Little Rock _Arkansas Gazette_, 18 Oct.1973, p.10A.
-UFO (R-V)
  1952-1954
    Wilmington Morning News, 9 July 1954.

B. Physical Features

Brandywine Creek
-Haunt
  1830s-   /Gil Thoreau
    James Reynolds, _Ghosts in American Houses_ (N.Y.: Paperback Library, 1967 ed.), pp.120-25.

Henlopen, Cape
-Phantom lighthouse
  1655-1910
    James Reynolds, _Ghosts in American Houses_ (N.Y.: Paperback Library, 1967 ed.), pp.167-70.

Island Field
-Archeological site
  ca.1000 B.C.-1200 A.D.
    C.A. Weslager, _Delaware's Buried Past_ (New Brunswick, N.J.: Rutgers Univ., 1968 ed.), p.180.
    Franklin Folsom, _America's Ancient Treasures_ (N.Y.: Rand McNally, 1974), p.169.

C. Ethnic Groups

Delaware (Leni-Lenape) Indians
-Flood myth
    C.S. Rafinesque, _The American Nations_ (Philadelphia: The Author, 1836), pp.125-44.
    Daniel G. Brinton, _The Lenâpé and Their Legends_ (Philadelphia: The Author, 1885), pp.134,166-67.
    C.F. Voegelin, ed., _Walam Olum, or Red Score_ (Indianapolis: Indiana Hist.Soc'y, 1954).
    William W. Newcomb, Jr., "The Walam Olum of the Delaware Indians in Perspective," _Bull.Arch.Soc'y New Jersey_ 30 (1974):29-32.
-Healing and hex
    C.A. Weslager, _Magic Medicines of the Indians_ (Somerset, N.J.: Middle Atlantic, 1973).

D. Unspecified Localities

-Mermaid
  1880, Jan./Capt. Raymond
    Shreveport (La.) Times, 4 Feb.1880.

THE NORTHEAST

PENNSYLVANIA

A. Populated Places

Adamstown
-UFO (DD)
  1869, Aug.7
    Reading Eagle, 14 Aug.1869.

Allentown
-Cattle mutilation
  1967, Sep.
    David R. Saunders & R. Roger Harkins,
    UFOs? Yes! (N.Y.: Signet, 1968),
    p.157.
-Mystery bird deaths
  1954, Oct.9/airport
    Donald E. Keyhoe, Flying Saucer Con-
    spiracy (N.Y.: Holt, 1955), pp.271-
    272.
-UFO (CE-2)
  1966, July/E on I-78
    John A. Keel, Our Haunted Planet
    (Greenwich, Ct.: Fawcett, 1971), p.
    199.

Allison
-Humanoid
  n.d./Mario W. Pinardi
    John A. Keel, Strange Creatures from
    Time and Space (Greenwich, Ct.:
    Fawcett, 1970), p.116, quoting Real,
    Aug.1967.

Altoona
-Ghost
  1967, Jan./Rosella Rock
    (Editorial), Fate 20 (Sep.1967):8-9.
-Precognition
  1931-1949/Anna Maria Savino
    Lisa S. Emerson, "Three Dreams and
    You're Dead," Fate 29 (Oct.1976):
    66-71.
  1940s-1950s/Lillian Jackson Moyer
    Jess Stearn, The Door to the Future
    (N.Y.: Macfadden, 1964), pp.87-88.

Analomink
-UFO (CE-2)
  1950s/nr. Mt. Airy Lodge
    Berthold E. Schwarz, "Beauty of the
    Night," Flying Saucer Rev. 18 (July-
    Aug.1972):5,6-7.

Annville
-UFO (NL)
  1965, Sep.21/Ronald Young
    Curtis K. Sutherly, "Case History of
    a UFO Flap," Official UFO 1 (Dec.
    1976):40,60, quoting Lebanon Daily
    News (undated).
  1973, Nov.4/H.B. Kreider
    Curt K. Sutherly, "1973: Madness in
    the Keystone State," Official UFO
    1 (Apr.1976):20,52, quoting Lebanon
    Daily News (undated).

  1975, Oct.24
    "Noteworthy UFO Sightings," Ufology
    2 (spring 1976):43.

Arcadia
-Paranormal strength
  1949, July 15/Joe Sapp/Number One mine
    John K. McCarthy, "Superhuman Powers
    Saved My Life," Fate 16 (Apr.1963):
    44-46.

Archbald
-UFO (CE-1)
  1958
    Berthold E. Schwarz, "Beauty of the
    Night," Flying Saucer Rev. 18 (July-
    Aug.1972):5,7-9. il.

Ashland
-UFO (NL)
  1975, Jan.5/James Flanagan
    Robert A. Goerman, "The UFO Modus Op-
    erandi: January 1975," Official UFO
    1 (Aug.1976):46,64.

Aston twp.
-UFO (NL)
  1973, Oct.17
    Floyd Murray, "Over the Keystone
    State," Caveat Emptor, no.11 (Jan.-
    Feb.1974):35.

Avella
-Archeological site
  ca.17,000 B.C.-1700 A.D./Meadowcroft
  Rockshelter
    New York Times, 18 Aug.1974, sec.4,
    p.7; and 28 July 1977, sec.2, p.1.
    Patricia Plants, "Earliest Evidence
    of Human Habitation in Eastern U.S.,"
    Pop.Arch. 3 (Nov.-Dec.1974):48-53.
    il.
    J.M. Adovasio, et al., "Excavations
    at Meadowcroft Rockshelter, 1973-
    1974," Pennsylvania Arch. 44 (1975):
    1-30. il.
    J.M. Adovasio, et al., "Meadowcroft
    Rockshelter: Retrospect 1976," Penn-
    sylvania Arch. 47, no.2-3 (1977):
    1-93. il.
    "Tusk of Extinct Ice Age Mammal Ex-
    cavated at Pitt's," Pop.Arch. 6, no.
    4 (1977):4-5. il.
    J.M. Adovasio, et al., "Meadowcroft
    Rockshelter, 1977: An Overview,"
    Am.Antiquity 43 (1978):632-51. il.

Baden
-UFO (CE-2)
  1965, Aug.13/Leonard Chalupiak
    "Strange Effects from EM Waves," UFO
    Inv. 3 (Nov.-Dec.1965):5.
    Jacques Vallee, Passport to Magonia
    (Chicago: Regnery, 1969), p.313.

Bakers Summit
-UFO (?)
  1968, Nov.14
    "Around the Globe," APRO Bull. 17
    (Nov.-Dec.1968):6.

Barkeyville
-UFO (NL)
  1977, Oct.5/Richard Offutt/E of town
    Franklin News-Herald, 2 Nov.1978.

Barnesboro
-UFO (NL)
  1974, April 1/Howard Brown/Legion Hall
    Barnesboro Star, 4 Apr.1974.

Barto
-Contactee
  1943-1960s/Richard S. Shaver
    Richard S. Shaver, "I Remember Le-
    muria," Amazing Stories 19 (Mar.
    1945):12.
    Richard S. Shaver, "Thought Records
    of Lemuria," Amazing Stories 19
    (June 1945):16.
    "How to Use the Shaver Alphabet,"
    Amazing Stories 21 (June 1947):133-
    35.
    Richard S. Shaver, "Proofs," Amazing
    Stories 21 (June 1947):136-46.
    Robert K. Kidwell, "The Shaverian
    Hypothesis," Amazing Stories 22
    (Jan.1948):150.
    "The Proof of the Shaver Mystery,"
    Amazing Stories 22 (May 1948):7.
    Vincent H. Gaddis, "Shaverian Side-
    lights," Amazing Stories 23 (Jan.
    1949):130.
    Frank Patton, "The Shaver Mystery,"
    Fate 3 (May 1950):62-74.
    Winthrop Sargeant, "Through the In-
    terstellar Looking Glass," Life, 21
    May 1951, pp.127,134,137-38.
    Gray Barker, They Knew Too Much About
    Flying Saucers (N.Y.: University
    Books, 1956), pp.59-67.
    Ray Palmer, "The Man Who Started It
    All," Flying Saucers, June 1957, p.
    79.
    Richard S. Shaver, "Key to Mantong,
    the Ancient Language," Fantastic
    Sci.Fiction 32 (July 1958):111.
    Ray Palmer, ed., The Hidden World
    (Amherst, Wisc.: Palmer Pubs.,
    1961-62).
    Timothy Green Beckley, The Shaver
    Mystery and the Inner Earth (Clarks-
    burg, W.V.: Saucerian, 1967).
    Eric Norman, This Hollow Earth (N.Y.:
    Lancer, 1972), pp.145-66.

Bartville
-Skyquake
  1954, Sep.28
    "Case 51," CRIFO Newsl., 4 Feb.1955,
    p.4.

Beaver
-UFO (NL)
  1964, May

"More News Briefs," Saucer News 11
    (Sep.1964):23.

Beaver Falls
-Fall of black rain
  1956, Jan./=pollution?
    Beaver Falls News-Tribune, 12 Jan.
    1956.
-Giant bird
  1966, Nov./George Wolfe, Jr.
    John A. Keel, The Mothman Prophecies
    (N.Y.: Saturday Review, 1975), pp.
    69-70.
-UFO (NL)
  ca.1923/Beaver R.
    Jerome Clark & Lucius Farish, "UFOs
    of the Roaring 20's," Saga UFO Rept.
    2 (fall 1975):48,49.
  1976, April 30
    "Noteworthy UFO Sightings," Ufology
    2 (fall 1976):61.

Beaver Springs
-Clairaudience
  1945, summer/Paul F. Try/2 mi.W
    Paul F. Try, "My Guardian Voice,"
    Fate 23 (July 1970):71-72.

Beaver Valley
-Fall of mud
  1953, May 1
    "Falls," Doubt, no.41 (1953):221,222.

Bedford
-Fall of anomalous meteorite
  1957, Aug./Dean Koontz
    Pittsburgh Sun-Telegraph, 2 Aug.1957.

Bedford co.
-Giant human skeletons
    The History of Bedford, Somerset and
    Fulton Counties, Pennsylvania (Chi-
    cago: Waterman, Watkins, 1884).

Belfast
-UFO (NL)
  1973, March 23/Denis de Nardo
    Easton Express, 26 Mar.1973.

Bellefonte
-UFO (NL)
  1975, Oct.12
    "UFO Central," CUFOS News Bull., 1
    Feb.1976, p.9.
  1976, Feb.3, 17
    "Noteworthy UFO Sightings," Ufology
    2 (summer 1976):63.

Berks co.
-Ancient stone constructions
    Richard H. Shaner, "Irish Build 'Bee-
    hives' in Oley Hills," Am.Folklife
    3 (Oct.1974):6. il.
-Anomalous fossil
  =3-toed tracks in Silurian rock
    Reading Times, 15 Sep.1966.
    "Footprints--200 Million Years Out-
    of-Step?" INFO J., no.3 (spring
    1968):50-52. il.
    "A Three-Toed, Bipedal Worm!" Pur-

suit 4 (Jan.1971):14. il.

Bernville
-Fall of ice
    1957, July 30/Edward Groff
        Philadelphia Inquirer, 31 July 1957.
        (Editorial), Fate 10 (Dec.1957):6-8.
        Coral E. Lorenzen, The Shadow of the
        Unknown (N.Y.: Signet, 1970), pp.
        122-25.

Bethel Park
-UFO (NL)
    1967, Oct.21
        "UFOs--October--U.S.A.," APRO Bull.
        16 (Nov.-Dec.1967):8.
    1975, Jan.10
        Stan Gordon, "Pennsylvanians Report
        300 Sightings," Skylook, no.88
        (Mar.1975):13.

Bethlehem
-Fall of yellow snow
    1879, March 16/Lehigh University
        Waldo L. McAtee, "Showers of Organic
        Matter," Monthly Weather Rev. 45
        (May 1917):217,219.
-UFO (DD)
    1950s/William S. Eberman
        "The Search for Hidden Reports," UFO
        Inv. 4 (Mar.1968):7.
-UFO (NL)
    1962, May 25/John Holzinger
        (Editorial), Fate 15 (Oct.1962):9.

Birdsboro
-UFO (?)
    1969, Dec.22/Clark Painter/=aircraft?
        Reading Times, 23 Dec.1969.

Blawnox
-Divination
    1952, May 6/Peter Fitzpatrick/Allegheny
    R.
        W.E. Farbstein, "A Ritual That
        Worked," Fate 5 (Dec.1952):83-84.

Bloomsburg
-Fall of plastic pellets
    1965, Feb.19
        (Editorial), Fate 19 (Jan.1966):28-
        29.

Blue Ridge Summit
-Spirit medium
    1920s/M. Belle Cross
        Frederick Edwards, "Sitting with
        Miss M. Belle Cross," J.ASPR 17
        (1923):329-66.
        Frederick Edwards, "Second Sitting
        with Miss M. Belle Cross," J.ASPR
        17 (1923):489-519.
        Frederick Edwards, "Third Sitting
        with Miss M. Belle Cross," J.ASPR
        17 (1923):528-52.
-UFO (DD)
    1961, June 4/Mrs. James W. Annis
        Richard Hall, ed., The UFO Evidence
        (Washington: NICAP, 1964), p.71.

Boothwyn
-Bleeding icon
    1975, Sep.-Oct./Mrs. Russell Poore
        Kansas City (Mo.) Times, 26 Sep.
        1975; and 20 Oct.1975.
-UFO (NL)
    1973, Oct.17
        Floyd Murray, "Over the Keystone
        State," Caveat Emptor, no.11 (Jan.-
        Feb.1974):35,36.

Bowmansdale
-UFO (NL)
    1968, Jan.12/Richard Morris
        "New Close-ups, Pacings," UFO Inv. 4
        (Mar.1968):1.

Braddock
-Phantom
    1967, Feb.11/Edgar Thomson Works
        Pittsburgh Press, 21 Mar.1967.

Bradford
-Giant human skeletons
    n.d.
        Robert R. Lyman, Amazing Indeed!
        (Coudersport: Potter Enterprise,
        1973), p.9.
-UFO (NL)
    1947, July 8/Bert Bishop
        Philadelphia Bulletin, 9 July 1947.
    1952, April 23
        Bradford Era, 25 Apr.1952.
    1978, Nov.9/South Ave.
        Bradford Era, 10 Nov.1978; and 13
        Nov.1978.
    1978, Nov.16/Amm St.
        Bradford Era, 17 Nov.1978.

Bradford co.
-UFO (DD)
    1975, July 6
        Raymond E. Fowler, "Commercial Pilot
        Reports Daylight Disc," Skylook,
        no.98 (Jan.1976):16-18.

Brandon
-Petroglyph
    God Rock/Allegheny R.
        James L. Swauger, "The Indian God
        Rock Petroglyphs Site 36VE36," Penn-
        sylvania Arch. 47, no.1 (1977):1-
        13. il.

Bridgewater twp.
-Humanoid
    1837
        John Green, The Sasquatch File (Ag-
        assiz, B.C.: Cheam, 1973), p.7,
        quoting Dorchester County (Md.) Au-
        rora, 27 Aug.1838, and Montrose
        Spectator (undated).

Brighton twp.
-UFO (?)
    1965, Aug.8/James Lucci/=hoax?
        "New UFO Photos Prove Genuine," UFO
        Inv. 3 (Aug.-Sep.1965):1-2. il.
        John G. Fuller, Incident at Exeter
        (N.Y.: Berkley, 1967 ed.), pp.146-55.

Philip J. Klass, <u>UFOs--Identified</u>
(N.Y.: Random House, 1968), pp.
143-46.
Edward U. Condon, ed., <u>Scientific
Study of Unidentified Flying Objects</u>
(N.Y.: Bantam, 1969 ed.), pp.455-57.
il.
-UFO (CE-1)
1965, Aug.11/Donald de Turca
John G. Fuller, <u>Incident at Exeter</u>
(N.Y.: Berkley, 1967 ed.), pp.155-
56.

Bristol
-Flying humanoid
1909, Jan.17/John McOwen/Bath St.
1909, Jan.17/James Sackville/Buckley
St.
Jerome Clark & Loren Coleman, "The
Jersey Devil," <u>Beyond Reality</u>, no.4
(May 1973):35-36.
James F. McCloy & Ray Miller, Jr.,
<u>The Jersey Devil</u> (Wallingford, Pa.:
Middle Atlantic, 1976), pp.39-42.

Bristol twp.
-UFO (NL)
1973, Nov.10
Floyd Murray, "Over the Keystone
State," <u>Caveat Emptor</u>, no.11 (Jan.-
Feb.1974):35,36.

Brownsville
-Archeological site
Josiah Priest, <u>American Antiquities
and Discoveries in the West</u> (Albany:
Hoffman & White, 1834), p.84.
-Fall of ice
1958, July 11/O.B. Moore/Arch St.
"Falls," <u>Doubt</u>, no.59 (1959):37.
-Fall of localized rain
1892, Nov./Water St.
<u>St. Louis (Mo.) Globe-Democrat</u>, 19
Nov.1892.

Bryn Mawr
-Haunt
n.d.
Charles M. Skinner, <u>American Myths
and Legends</u>, 2 vols. (Philadelphia:
Lippincott, 1903), 1:260-64.

Bucks co.
-Witchcraft
17th c./Hexenkopf Mt.
Charles M. Skinner, <u>Myths and Legends
of Our Own Land</u>, 2 vols. (Philadel-
phia: Lippincott, 1896), 1:232-33.
Moritz Jagendorf, <u>Upstate Downstate</u>
(N.Y.: Vanguard, 1949), p.126.

Buffalo Mills
-Humanoid
1973, Aug.19
<u>Jeanette News-Dispatch</u>, 24 Aug.1973.

Bunker Hill
-UFO (CE-2) and Men-in-black
1965, July/Connie Wolferd
Curtis K. Sutherly, "Case History of

a UFO Flap," <u>Official UFO</u> 1 (Dec.
1976):40-41.

Burlington
-UFO (NL)
1975, Jan.2
Robert A. Goerman, "The UFO Modus Operandi: January 1975," <u>Official UFO</u>
1 (Aug.1976):46,47.

Burtville
-Haunt
1881
Coudersport <u>Potter County Journal</u>,
21 July 1881.

Bushkill twp.
-UFO (NL)
1973, March 21/Howard Kostenbader/Hwy.
512
<u>Stroudsburg Pocono Record</u>, 21 Mar.
1973, p.1.

Butler
-UFO (?)
1949, June 8
"If It's in the Sky It's a Saucer,"
<u>Doubt</u>, no.27 (1949):416.
-UFO (CE-1)
1975, July 27
Stan Gordon, "Pennsylvania Sightings
Continue," <u>Skylook</u>, no.97 (Dec.
1975):9.
-UFO (CE-3)
1967, March 20
Robert A. Schmidt, "Humanoids Seen
at Butler," <u>Flying Saucer Rev.</u> 14
(Sep.-Oct.1968):5-6.
-UFO (NL)
1971, April 3-Aug.12/John P. Bessor
(Letter), <u>Fate</u> 25 (Sep.1972):159.

Callery
-UFO (CE-3)
1971, April 14/Marion Lang/chemical
plant
Robert A. Schmidt, "Callery UFO and
Occupants," <u>Flying Saucer Rev.</u> 17
(July-Aug.1971):3-5.

Cambridge Springs
-Humanoid
1950s
John Green, <u>Sasquatch: The Apes Among
Us</u> (Seattle: Hancock House, 1978),
p.255.

Cannelton
-Ancient carving
=carved in 19th c.?
James L. Murphy, "The Cannelton 'Sun
God,' 36BV146 Beaver County, Pennsylvania," <u>Pennsylvania Arch.</u> 48,
no.3 (1978):16-19. il.

Carbondale
-Fall of localized rain
1922, June-July
<u>New York Tribune</u>, 3 July 1922.
-Fall of unknown object

1974, Nov.9/Bernard Gillott/silt pond
   New York Times, 12 Nov.1974, p.78.
Douglas K. Dains, "Object in Water
   Checked in Pennsylvania," Skylook,
   no.85 (Dec.1974):12.
Robert C. Warth, "The Carbondale
   (Pa.) UFO," Pursuit 8 (Jan.1975):5.
"Submerged UFO Really Identified?"
   APRO Bull. 23 (Jan.-Feb.1975):8-9.
Richard Hoffman, "Carbondale UFO:
   Hoax or Reality?" Ohio Sky Watcher
   2 (Mar.1976):3-6.
Curt Sutherly, "The Inside Story of
   the New Hampshire UFO Crash," Saga
   UFO Rept. 4 (July 1977):22,61-63.
-UFO (NL)
   1952, Oct./Arthur Gessler
      (Letter), Fate 10 (Nov.1957):113-14.

Cashtown
-Haunt
   1960s
      Sally M. Barach, Haunts of Adams and
      Other Counties (Indiana, Pa.: A.G.
      Halldin, 1972), p.14.

Center twp.
-UFO (?)
   1960, Nov.
      Beaver Beaver County Times, 29 Nov.
      1960.

Centerville
-Giant bird
   ca.1898
      Robert R. Lyman, Amazing Indeed!
      (Coudersport: Potter Enterprise,
      1973), p.95.

Centre co.
-Fall of gelatinous substance
   1970, Feb.
      Pat Morrison, "UFOs and Bigfoot Crea-
      tures: An Adventure into the Unex-
      plained," in Bigfoot: Tales of Un-
      explained Creatures (Rome, O.: Page
      Rsch.Library, 1978), pp.25,29.
-Humanoid
   1970, Jan.-Feb.
      Pat Morrison, "UFOs and Bigfoot Crea-
      tures: An Adventure into the Unex-
      plained," in Bigfoot: Tales of Un-
      explained Creatures (Rome, O.: Page
      Rsch.Library, 1978), pp.25,28-29.

Chambersburg
-Fall of pebbles
   1967, May 19/A.S. McCanns/N of town
      (Editorial), Fate 20 (Sep.1967):12-
      13.
-UFO (CE-1)
   1975, July 10
      Stan Gordon, "Pennsylvania Sightings
      Continue," Skylook, no.97 (Dec.1975)
      :9.

Cheltenham
-Haunt
   1970/Mrs. John Bockman/East Cheltenham
   Free Library/400 Myrtle Ave.

(Editorial), Fate 23 (July 1970):34-
   35, quoting Philadelphia Evening
   Bulletin (undated).
-UFO (NL)
   1947, July 8/Thomas Miller/Tookenay
   Park
      Philadelphia Inquirer, 9 July 1947.

Cherry Springs
-Ghost light
   1880s/Mrs. Jake Cannon/hotel
      Robert R. Lyman, Forbidden Land
      (Coudersport: Potter Enterprise,
      1971), p.16.

Cherryville
-UFO (CE-2)
   1933, summer
      "1933 Sighting Reported," APRO Bull.
      13 (July 1964):7-8.

Chester
-Dowsing
   1695/Robert Reman
      John F. Watson, Annals of Philadel-
      phia and Pennsylvania in the Olden
      Time, 2 vols. (Philadelphia: John
      Penington & Uriah Hunt, 1844), 1:
      266.
-Fall of ice
   1957, Sep.8/Jesse Demofonte
      Philadelphia Inquirer, 9 Sep.1957.
      Philadelphia Evening Bulletin, 9-10
      Sep.1957.
      (Editorial), Fate 11 (Jan.1958):6-9.
-Fall of molluscs
   1869, June 6/Y.S. Walter
      "Fall of Shell-Fish in a Rainstorm,"
      Am.Naturalist 3 (1870):556.
-Fall of sulphur
   1963, July 14/Buckman Village
      Philadelphia Daily News, 16 July
      1963.
-Humanoid
   1909, Jan.21
      James F. McCloy & Ray Miller, Jr.,
      The Jersey Devil (Wallingford, Pa.:
      Middle Atlantic, 1976), p.70.
-UFO (CE-1)
   1967, Aug.1/Village Green
      "Close Sighting in Chester, Pa.,"
      Saucer News 14 (fall 1967):33.
-UFO (NL)
   1969, June 28/Mrs. Louis Dallam/1018
   Engle St.
      "Strange Objects in Pennsylvania
      Sky," Skylook, no.32 (Sep.1969):9-
      10, quoting Chester Daily Times
      (undated).
   1969, July 14/Roxanne Peters/310 E.
   Ridge Rd.
   1969, July 15/William Focks/Caldwell x
   Ninth St.
      Chester Daily Times, 16 July 1969.

Chippewa twp.
-UFO (?)
   1965, Dec.9/Edward Bozic
      Jerome Clark, "The Greatest Flap Yet?
      Part IV," Flying Saucer Rev. 12

(Nov.-Dec.1966):9,12.

Claysville
-Humanoid
  1975, fall
    Ron Anjard, "A Pennsylvania Bigfoot,"
    Vestigia Newsl., no.3 (summer-fall
    1977):3-4.
    Ron Anjard, "Bigfoot in Western Penn-
    sylvania?" Fate 30 (Dec.1977):71.

Clearfield
-Plant sensitivity
  1952/James H. Stegner
    James H. Stegner, "ESP Revives 'Dead'
    Plant," Fate 25 (Jan.1972):92-95.
-UFO (DD)
  1975, Jan.5/Jeff Capatch
    Robert A. Goerman, "The UFO Modus Op-
    erandi: January 1975," Official UFO
    1 (Aug.1976):46,64.
-UFO (NL)
  1977, May 11
    "UFOs of Limited Merit," Int'l UFO
    Reporter 2 (June 1977):8.

Clearfield co.
-Humanoid
  1977, Feb.
    Uniontown Herald, 20 May 1977.

Clifton Heights
-Crisis apparition
  1953, Dec./Antoinette Terlingo
    Laura A. Dale, Rhea White & Gardner
    Murphy, "A Selection of Cases from
    a Recent Survey of Spontaneous ESP
    Phenomena," J.ASPR 56 (1962):3,9-12.

Coatesville
-Mystery gas
  1944, Feb.1
    "Gas in Coatesville," Doubt, no.11
    (winter 1944-45):156.
-Phantom panther
  1946, Feb.
    "More Monsters," Doubt, no.16 (1946):
    236.
-UFO (CE-3)
  1974, May 7/Margaret K. Roffe/Veterans
  Hospital
    George D. Fawcett, "The 'Unreported'
    UFO Wave of 1974," Saga UFO Rept. 2
    (spring 1975):50,52.

Cogan House twp.
-Phantom panther
  1954
    Bruce S. Wright, The Eastern Panther
    (Toronto: Clarke, Irwin, 1971), pp.
    108-109, quoting Mount Carmel Item
    (undated).

Colesburg
-UFO (CE-2)
  1966, summer
    Larry E. Arnold, "The Pennsylvania
    Triangle," Saga UFO Rept. 6 (Oct.
    1978):16,58.

Collingdale
-UFO (NL)
  1973, Oct.14/North St.
    Floyd Murray, "Over the Keystone
    State," Caveat Emptor, no.11 (Jan.-
    Feb.1974):35-36.

Columbia
-UFO (?)
  1978, Oct.6/Mrs. Andrew Sopko/15th St.
    Columbia News, 27 Oct.1978.
-UFO (NL)
  1973, Oct.18
    Lancaster Journal, 19 Oct.1973.

Concordville
-UFO (NL)
  1973, Oct.14
    Floyd Murray, "Over the Keystone
    State," Caveat Emptor, no.11 (Jan.-
    Feb.1974):35,36.

Confluence
-UFO (NL)
  1965, Nov.27
    Somerset Daily American, 29 Nov.1965.

Connellsville
-UFO (CE-2)
  1974, Oct.12/Eugene Loyal
    Stan Gordon, "Bright Object Damages
    Car," Skylook, no.86 (Jan.1975):15.

Conrad
-Disappearance
  1975, Aug.26
    Curt Sutherly, "If Oliver Lerch
    Didn't Vanish, Then Who Did?" Psy-
    chic World, May 1976, pp.48,50,86.

Coopersburg
-UFO (NL)
  1975, Nov.18
    "UFO Central," CUFOS News Bull., 1
    Feb.1976, p.13.

Corsica
-UFO (DD)
  1959, March 26
    Lloyd Mallan, "Complete Directory of
    UFOs: Part III," Sci.& Mech. 38
    (Feb.1967):56,59,92.

Costello
-Archeological site
    Coudersport Potter County Journal,
    8 July 1880, p.3.
    Robert R. Lyman, Amazing Indeed!
    (Coudersport: Potter Enterprise,
    1973), p.7.

Coudersport
-Clairvoyance
  1916, Aug./Miles O. Harris
    Robert R. Lyman, Amazing Indeed!
    (Coudersport: Potter Enterprise,
    1973), p.45.
-Giant bird
  ca.1940/Robert R. Lyman/2 mi.N on
  Sheldon Rd.

Robert R. Lyman, Amazing Indeed!
(Coudersport: Potter Enterprise,
1973), p.95.
-Poltergeist
1912-1928/Clara Porter Lawton/E. 2d St.
Robert R. Lyman, Amazing Indeed!
(Coudersport: Potter Enterprise,
1973), pp.52-53.
-Precognition
1911, spring/Nellie Carpenter
Robert R. Lyman, Amazing Indeed!
(Coudersport: Potter Enterprise,
1973), pp.39-40.
-Spontaneous human combustion
1966, Dec.5/John Irving Bentley/403 N.
Main St.
Coudersport Potter Enterprise, 7 Dec.
1966, p.1.
Larry E. Arnold, "The Flaming Fate
of Dr. John Irving Bentley," Pursuit
9 (fall 1976):75-82. il.
-Thermal anomaly
8 mi.NE at Camp Moxie/=perpetually cold
rocks
Larry E. Arnold, "The Pennsylvania
Triangle," Saga UFO Rept. 6 (Oct.
1978):16,17,19.
-UFO (CE-2)
1966, summer/Dutch Hill
Robert R. Lyman, Amazing Indeed!
(Coudersport: Potter Enterprise,
1973), p.82.

Crabtree
-UFO (NL)
1973, Jan.25
Stan Gordon, "Radar Failures Delay
Planes--UFOs Reported in Pennsylvania Sky," Skylook, no.64 (Mar.1973):
10,11.

Curwensville
-UFO (DD)
1975, Jan.2/James Loddo
Robert A. Goerman, "The UFO Modus Operandi: January 1975," Official UFO
1 (Aug.1976):46,47.

Darby twp.
-Fall of metallic object
1955, Jan.23/William C. Cunningham/Wil-
liams Ave. x Calcon Hook Rd.
"Case 45," CRIFO Newsl., 4 Feb.1955,
p.2.
(Editorial), Fate 8 (May 1955):14.

Dauphin
-Healing
1926/Mrs. Kennedy
C.P. Schultz, "The Kid's Powwow Healing," Fate 31 (Aug.1978):61-62.

Dauphin co.
-Mystery tracks
1978, March/Larry Arnold
Larry Arnold, "Has the Dover Devil
Visited South-Central Pennsylvania
in March 1978?" Pursuit 11 (summer
1978):121. il.
-Radionics

1952/Henry Gross/Farm Bureau Co-op
Poultry Farm
Edward Wriothesley Russell, Report
on Radionics (London: Spearman,
1973), pp.70,244.

Delaware co.
-Snow worms
1884-1885
E.W. Gudger, "Snow Worms," Natural
History 23 (1923):451-56.

Delmont
-UFO (CE-1)
1974, April 20
Stan Gordon, "Pennsylvania Sightings
Continue," Skylook, no.82 (Sep.
1974):15.

Delta
-Chicken mutilations
1978, Feb.13/Raymond Turner
York Record, 23 Feb.1978.
-Humanoid
1978, March 2/Norval Thomas/nr. Peach
Bottom Atomic Power Plant
York Record, 7 Mar.1978.
Harrisburg Patriot, 23 Mar.1978, p.1.
-Humanoid tracks
1978, Jan.28/Allen Hilsmeir/nr. Muddy
Creek
York Record, 23 Feb.1978. il.

Dents Run
-Giant bird
1892/Fred Murray
Robert R. Lyman, Amazing Indeed!
(Coudersport: Potter Enterprise,
1973), p.94.

Derry
-Humanoid
1973, Aug.21
B. Ann Slate & Alan Berry, Bigfoot
(N.Y.: Bantam, 1976), pp.122-23.
-Humanoid and Men-in-black
1973, Aug.24
Pat Morrison, "UFOs and Bigfoot Crea-
tures: An Adventure into the Unex-
plained," in Bigfoot: Tales of Un-
explained Creatures (Rome, O.: Page
Rsch.Library, 1978), pp.25,32-34.
-UFO (NL)
1972, April 24
Stan Gordon, "UFOs in Pennsylvania,"
Skylook, no.60 (Nov.1972):13.
1973, Jan.25
Stan Gordon, "Radar Failures Delay
Planes--UFOs Reported in Pennsylvan-
ia Sky," Skylook, no.64 (Mar.1973):
10,14.

Derry twp.
-UFO (NL)
1975, Oct.23-24/Scott Burns/landfill
Curt Sutherly, "OK, If It Wasn't the
Goodyear Blimp, What Was It?" Probe
the Unknown 4 (Mar.1976):49,50-51.

Downingtown
-Humanoid
   1932, Jan.21/John McCandless
      Curtis D. MacDougall, Hoaxes (N.Y.:
      Dover, 1958 ed.), p.34.

Doylestown
-Ancient inscription
   1872, spring/Bernard Hansell
      H.C. Mercer, The Lenape Stone (N.Y.:
      G.P. Putnam, 1885). il.
      George F. Carter, "That Elephant
      from Bucks County," Anthro.J.Canada
      4, no.3 (1966):2-6. il.
      Richard L. Greene, "The Lenape Stone,
      One Hundred Years Later," NEARA
      Newsl. 7 (Mar.1972):16-18. il.

Doylestown twp.
-UFO (CE-1)
   1975, Feb./Paul Cherubini
      Arthur J. Manaro, "1975 Pennsylvania
      Case," APRO Bull. 27 (Aug.1978):5-6.

Drexel Hill
-UFO (NL)
   1955, Nov.13/Harry Leisenring
      "Case 114," CRIFO Orbit, 2 Dec.1955,
      p.3.

DuBois
-UFO (?)
   1964, May 25
      Jeffrey Liss, "UFO's That Look Like
      Tops," Fate 17 (Nov.1964):66,69.

Duquesne
-Crisis apparition
   n.d./Mrs. H.J. Weidmann
      Hans Holzer, Ghosts I've Met (N.Y.:
      Ace, 1965 ed.), pp.62-63.
-UFO (DD)
   1977, Nov.3/Raymond Birmingham/Library
   St.
      McKeesport Daily News, 4 Nov.1977.

East Berlin
-Dowsing
   1940s/Birdes A. Jacobs
      Pennsylvania Dutchman, 15 May 1950.
      Alfred A. Shoemaker, "Water Witching,"
      Pennsylvania Folklife 12 (fall 1961)
      :25-26.
-UFO (NL)
   1978, July 6/Connie Spangler
      York Dispatch, 7 July 1978.

Easton
-UFO (?)
   1948, summer/Carl A. Mitchell
      Richard Hall, ed., The UFO Evidence
      (Washington: NICAP, 1964), p.49.
-UFO (CE-2)
   1953, Sep.29
      Richard Hall, ed., The UFO Evidence
      (Washington: NICAP, 1964), p.73.
-UFO (NL)
   1973, March 22/Ted Toulomelis/Hackett
   Park
      "Press Reports," APRO Bull. 20 (May-

June 1973):9, quoting Allentown
Morning Call (undated).

East Smithfield
-UFO (NL)
   1968, June 3
      "'Cigar' Sighted in Pa.," APRO Bull.
      17 (July-Aug.1968):5.

East Stroudsburg
-UFO (DD)
   1974, fall/W. Bush
      (Letter), Saga UFO Rept. 2 (summer
      1975):6.

Economy
-UFO (NL)
   1965, May 27
      Jacques & Janine Vallee, Challenge
      to Science (N.Y.: Ace, 1966 ed.),
      p.67.

Eddystone
-Bleeding icon
   1974-   /Chester Olszewski/St. Luke's
   Episcopal Church
      Nat'l Enquirer, 20 Jan.1976. il.
      "Bleeding Statue," Fortean Times,
      no.19 (Dec.1976):6-7.
      D. Scott Rogo, The Haunted Universe
      (N.Y.: Signet, 1977), pp.35-36.

Edinboro
-Humanoid
   1966, Aug.17/Edinboro L.
      Erie Times, 19 Aug.1966.
-UFO (CE-2)
   1952, Aug.24/Frank S. Holowach/Hwy.408
      (Editorial), Fate 6 (Feb.1953):11.

Eldred
-UFO (CE-2)
   1958, Aug.16
      Buffalo (N.Y.) Courier-Express, 16
      Aug.1958.

Elkins Park
-UFO (NL)
   1952, July 19
      J. Allen Hynek, The Hynek UFO Report
      (N.Y.: Dell, 1977), pp.76-77.

Ellisburg
-Giant bird legend
      Robert R. Lyman, Amazing Indeed!
      (Coudersport: Potter Enterprise,
      1973), p.94.
-Giant human skeleton
   1886, Dec./W.H. Scoville
      Robert R. Lyman, Forbidden Land
      (Coudersport: Potter Enterprise,
      1971), p.7.
      Robert R. Lyman, Amazing Indeed!
      (Coudersport: Potter Enterprise,
      1973), pp.7,9.

Ellwood City
-Precognition
   1952, Jan./W.H. Moore
      (Editorial), Fate 5 (June 1952):5.

-UFO (CE-2)
1958, March/Joseph Scala/Walnut Ridge
    Robert N. Webster, "Things That Fall
    from UFOs," Fate 11 (Oct.1958):25,
    29.

Elysburg
-UFO (CE-1)
1977, Dec.2/Phyllis Crowl/nr. Valley
    Gun Club
    Shamokin News-Item, 3 Dec.1977.
    Nat'l Enquirer, 24 Jan.1978, p.37.
1978, Jan.10/Philip Skeba
    Lewisburg Union County Journal, 6
    July 1978. il.
-UFO (NL)
1978, July 18/Judy Gappa
    Bloomsburg Morning Press, 22 July
    1978.
1978, Sep.28/Lindy Acres
    Shamokin News-Item, 29 Sep.1978.

Emporium
-Ghost
1942, Oct./Anthony Stephenson
    Robert R. Lyman, Amazing Indeed!
    (Coudersport: Potter Enterprise,
    1973), pp.61-62.
-UFO (NL)
1978, Nov.9
    Bradford Era, 10 Nov.1978.

Ephrata
-Seance
1945, Aug./Arthur Ford/Camp Silver Belle
    Jess Stearn, The Door to the Future
    (N.Y.: Macfadden, 1964), p.188.

Erie
-Ball lightning
1916, July/William Harrison
    (Letter), Fate 13 (June 1960):110-11.
-Men-in-black
1968
    Brad Steiger, Mysteries of Time and
    Space (N.Y.: Dell, 1976 ed.), p.200.
-UFO (?)
1965, Dec.9/=meteor?
    Ivan T. Sanderson, "'Something'
    Landed in Pennsylvania," Fate 19
    (Mar.1966):33-34.
-UFO (CE-3)
1966, Aug.3/Julie Helwig/W. Third St.
    John A. Keel, Strange Creatures from
    Time and Space (Greenwich, Ct.: Faw-
    cett, 1970), pp.161-62.
-UFO (DD)
1948, summer/Victor G. Didelot
    Richard Hall, ed., The UFO Evidence
    (Washington: NICAP, 1964), pp.55,56.
1953, Feb.22
    Donald E. Keyhoe, Flying Saucers from
    Outer Space (N.Y.: Holt, 1953), p.
    258.
1975, March 29/Gerald Law
    Mike Lindstrom, "The Lindstrom Photos,"
    Official UFO 1 (July 1976):28,30.
-UFO (NL)
1962, March 17/Kenneth N. Black/"Ojibwa"
    "Ice Cutter Encounters 'Lake Lights,'"

APRO Bull. 11 (July 1962):4.
1966, July 31/Abbas Lubbas
1966, Aug.1/Margaret Daniels/Cherry
    St.
    John A. Keel, "New Landing and Crea-
    ture Reports," Flying Saucer Rev.
    12 (Nov.-Dec.1966):5,8.
1966, Aug.3/William Rutledge
    John A. Keel, UFOs: Operation Trojan
    Horse (N.Y.: Putnam, 1970), p.28.

Fairfield
-Ghost light
n.d./Furnace Rd.
    Sally M. Barach, Haunts of Adams and
    Other Counties (Indiana, Pa.: A.G.
    Halldin, 1972), pp.9-10.
-Haunt
n.d./Bill Rombin/Rombin's Nest gift
    shop
n.d./Maria Furnace Rd.
    Sally M. Barach, Haunts of Adams and
    Other Counties (Indiana, Pa.: A.G.
    Halldin, 1972), pp.1-4,7-9.
-Phantom panther
n.d.
    Sally M. Barach, Haunts of Adams and
    Other Counties (Indiana, Pa.: A.G.
    Halldin, 1972), p.7.

Fairview
-UFO (NL)
1977, July 18
    "UFOs of Limited Merit," Int'l UFO
    Reporter 2 (Sep.1977):3.

Fawn Grove
-Humanoid
1978, Jan.10/nr. Kennard-Dale High
    School
    York Daily Record, 23 Feb.1978.
-UFO (CE-2)
1977, March 10/Mrs. Everett Miller
    (Editorial), Fate 30 (July 1977):14-
    15.

Fayette co.
-Petroglyphs
Francis Farm
    James L. Swauger, "The Francis Farm
    Petroglyphs Site, 36 FA 35," Penn-
    sylvania Arch. 34 (Sep.1964):53-61.
    il.
-UFO (CE-3)
1973, Oct.25
    Pat Morrison, "UFOs and Bigfoot Crea-
    tures: An Adventure into the Unex-
    plained," in Bigfoot: Tales of Un-
    explained Creatures (Rome, O.: Page
    Rsch.Library, 1978), pp.25-26.

Fishing Creek
-Skyquake
1954, Sep.28
    "Case 51," CRIFO Newsl., 4 Feb.1955,
    p.4.
-UFO (CE-1)
1967, April 1/Beatrice Turns
    "Objects Aim Light Beams, Drop 'Fire-
    balls,'" UFO Inv. 4 (May-June 1967):1.

Forks twp.
-UFO (NL)
1973, March 23/Floyd Stem
    Easton Express, 26 Mar.1973.

Forty Fort
-UFO (NL)
1973, Oct.17/Thomas Roccograndi
    Wilkes-Barre Times-Leader, 18 Oct.
    1973.

Fountain Hill
-Fall of ice
1958, Jan.6
    "Falls," Doubt, no.57 (1958):4,5.

Frackville
-UFO (?)
1978, July 23
    Shenandoah Evening Herald, 25 July
    1978.
-UFO (NL)
1977, Dec.10/Hwy.81
    Shamokin News-Item, 12 Dec.1977.

Fredericksburg
-UFO (CE-2)
1965, Sep.22/Dale E. Richard/Speedway
    Curtis K. Sutherly, "Case History of
    a UFO Flap," Official UFO 1 (Dec.
    1976):40,62.
-UFO (DD)
1966, Sep./Curtis K. Sutherly
    Curt Sutherly, "Profile of a Kid
    Ufologist," Anomaly Rsch.Bull., no.
    5 (Mar.1977):4,7-8; no.6 (June 1977)
    :3-4.
-UFO (NL)
1966, Dec./Curtis K. Sutherly
    Curt Sutherly, "Profile of a Kid
    Ufologist," Anomaly Rsch.Bull.,
    no.6 (June 1977):3,4-5.
1975, Oct.25/Bob Rumpf
1975, Oct.30/John Adams/Little Blue Mt.
    Curt Sutherly, "OK, If It Wasn't the
    Goodyear Blimp, What Was It?" Probe
    the Unknown 4 (Mar.1976):49,51.

Freemansburg
-Fall of ice
1958, Jan.18/Shirley Arawjo
    "Falls," Doubt, no.57 (1958):4,5.

Garrison
-Humanoid
1964, Sep./Glen Varner
    John Green, Sasquatch: The Apes Among
    Us (Seattle: Hancock House, 1978),
    p.255.

Gatchellville
-UFO (CE-2)
1977, March 8/Thelma Lowe
    "Case of High Merit," Int'l UFO Re-
    porter 2 (May 1977):6-7.
    (Letter), Charles L. Smith, Int'l
    UFO Reporter 2 (Oct.1977):2.
    "Close-Out on the Gatchellville, Pa.
    CE II," Int'l UFO Reporter 3 (Mar.
    1978):Newsfront sec.

Genesee twp.
-UFO (CE-1)
1966, April 25/Calvin C. Carpenter
    Robert R. Lyman, Amazing Indeed!
    (Coudersport: Potter Enterprise,
    1973), p.73.
    Larry E. Arnold, "The Pennsylvania
    Triangle," Saga UFO Rept. 6 (Oct.
    1978):16,58.

Georgetown
-UFO (NL)
1957, Oct.2
    "Flying Saucer Roundup," Fate 11
    (Feb.1958):29,35.

German twp.
-Humanoid
1977, May 15
    Uniontown Herald, 20 May 1977.

Gettysburg
-Archeological site
3½ mi.S/Heck Rockshelter
    W. Fred Kinsey, "An Early Woodland
    Rock Shelter in South Central Penn-
    sylvania," Pennsylvania Arch. 28
    (1958):1-4. il.
-Cloud anomaly
1917/R.A. Gillette/Camp Meade
    (Letter), Fate 9 (Feb.1956):116-18.
-Ghost
1833, Aug.13/John Swope
    Gettysburg Star & Sentinel, 15 Feb.
    1905.
-Haunt
1770s/tavern
n.d./Lutheran church
    Sally M. Barach, Haunts of Adams and
    Other Counties (Indiana, Pa.: A.G.
    Halldin, 1972), pp.14-16.
-Precognition
1863, July 2
    George C. Underwood, History of the
    Twenty-Sixth Regiment of the North
    Carolina Troops (Goldsboro, N.C.:
    Nash Bros., 1901).
    Mary A. Hancock, "Vision at Gettys-
    burg," Tomorrow 8 (summer 1960):20-
    24.
n.d./Black Mag
    Don Yoder, "Witch Tales from Adams
    County," Pennsylvania Folklife 12
    (summer 1962):29,33-34.
-Skyquake
1977, Dec.27-28
    "Even More Aerial Detonations," Res
    Bureaux Bull., no.30 (2 Mar.1978):
    1.
    "Aerial Detonations," Res Bureaux
    Bull., no.40 (9 Nov.1978):6.
-UFO (?)
1955, Nov?/nr. Eisenhower Farm
    "Saucers Stir the Pennsylvania
    Quiet," CRIFO Orbit, 2 Dec.1955, p.3.
-UFO (CE-2)
1974, July 8/ground markings only
    Harrisburg Patriot, 9 July 1974.
-UFO (DD)
1947, July 7/Frank Toms/nr. Pennsylvania

Monument
Philadelphia Inquirer, 8 July 1947.
-UFO (NL)
1961, March 20/Thomas F. Green
"UFOs Continue Earth Observation,"
UFO Inv. 1 (Apr.-May 1961):5.

Gibsonia
-Humanoids
1974, July/trailer court
Stan Gordon, "UFO, Creature Sightings Reported," Skylook, no.88 (Mar.
1975):12.
-UFO (CE-1)
1974, July
1974, Dec.30/Turnpike Bridge
Stan Gordon, "UFO, Creature Sightings Reported," Skylook, no.88 (Mar.
1975):12.
-UFO (CE-3)
1974, Sep.
Stan Gordon, "UFO, Creature Sightings Reported," Skylook, no.88 (Mar.
1975):12.

Glassport
-Humanoid hair sample
1973, Sep.3/=human hair
"Pennsylvania ABSMery," Pursuit 7
(Oct.1974):94-95.

Glenolden
-UFO (NL)
1973, Oct.8
Floyd Murray, "Over the Keystone
State," Caveat Emptor, no.11 (Jan.-
Feb.1974):35.

Glenshaw
-Fall of wire
1958, Sep.24/William Yost/208 Kleber
Rd.
"The Night of September 29," Fate 12
(Feb.1959):31,35-36.
-Humanoid
1977, June 14-15/John Tiskus
Pittsburgh North Hills News-Record,
18 June 1977.

Glenwood
-Haunt
n.d.
Charles M. Skinner, American Myths
and Legends, 2 vols. (Philadelphia:
Lippincott, 1903), 1:260-61.

Gowen City
-Fall of ice
1957, Aug.14/Rufus J. Boyer
"Ice, Hail and Tinsel," Doubt, no.55
(1957):449.
Coral E. Lorenzen, The Shadow of the
Unknown (N.Y.: Signet, 1970), pp.
125-29.

Grand Valley
-UFO (CE-2)
1964, Nov.26/Florence Rosenburgh
"High Radiation Follows UFO Sighting,"
Saucer News 12 (Mar.1965):16.

Greater Pittsburgh Airport
-UFO (CE-2)
1973, Jan.25
Jeannette News-Dispatch, 26 Jan.1973.

Greenacre
-UFO (NL)
1957, Nov.15
Hazleton Plain Speaker, 16 Nov.1957.

Greene co.
-Clairvoyance
1832, July/Martha McCready
"Such Stuff As Dreams Are Made of,"
Lippincott's Mag. 25 (Jan.1880):
120-22.
Portland (Me.) Transcript, 31 Jan.
1880.
Newton (N.C.) Enterprise, 14 Feb.
1880.
Clarence M. Fink, "Second Sight:
Great Grandma's Terrible Burden,"
Fate 21 (Oct.1968):74,79-83.
Adi-Kent Thomas Jeffrey, "Dream of
Murder: Martha McCready's Terrible
Burden," Fate 21 (Oct.1968):75-78.

Greensburg
-Dog mutilation
1972, July 13
"Dog Found Dead--All Hair Removed,"
Skylook, no.63 (Feb.1973):9.
-Humanoid
1972, summer/cemetery
John Green, Sasquatch: The Apes Among
Us (Seattle: Hancock House, 1978),
p.259.
1973, July
Pat Morrison, "UFOs and Bigfoot Crea-
tures: An Adventure into the Unex-
plained," in Bigfoot: Tales of Un-
explained Creatures (Rome, O.: Page
Rsch.Library, 1978), pp.25,29-31.
1973, July/Rhodabaugh Rd.
Stan Gordon, "UFOs in Relation to
Creature Sightings in Pennsylvania,"
in 1974 MUFON UFO Symposium (Seguin,
Tex.: MUFON, 1974), pp.133,135-36.
B. Ann Slate & Alan Berry, Bigfoot
(B.Y.: Bantam, 1976), pp.121-22.
1973, Aug.14/Greengate Mall
John Green, Sasquatch: The Apes Among
Us (Seattle: Hancock House, 1978),
p.260.
1973, Sep.9
Pat Morrison, "UFOs and Bigfoot Creatures: An Adventure into the Unex-
plained," in Bigfoot: Tales of Un-
explained Creatures (Rome, O.: Page
Rsch.Library, 1978), pp.25,26-28.
1973, Sep.21/St. Anne's Home
1973, Sep.24/St. Anne's Home
Allen V. Noe, "ABSMal Affairs in
Pennsylvania and Elsewhere," Pursuit
6 (Oct.1973):84,88.
"Pennsylvania ABSMery," Pursuit 7
(Oct.1974):94-95.
1975, May 19/Hwy.130
Stan Gordon, "UFO and Creature Observed in Same Area in Pennsylvania,"

<u>Skylook</u>, no.91 (June 1975):13.
-UFO (CE-1)
  1966, April 11
    Jacques Vallee, <u>Passport to Magonia</u>
    (Chicago: Regnery, 1969), p.328.
  1972, March 27?/Hannestown Rd.
    "UFO Reports from Pennsylvania," <u>Sky-look</u>, no.54 (May 1972):13.
  1972, April 16
    Stan Gordon, "UFOs in Pennsylvania,"
    <u>Skylook</u>, no.56 (July 1972):12.
  1972, June 9
    "Strange Report from Pennsylvania,"
    <u>Skylook</u>, no.58 (Sep.1972):15.
  1975, Oct.2
    Stan Gordon, "Strange Reports from
    Pennsylvania," <u>Skylook</u>, no.99 (Feb.
    1976):13.
-UFO (CE-2)
  1972, April 22
    <u>Latrobe New Edition</u>, 10 May 1972.
    Stan Gordon, "UFOs in Pennsylvania,"
    <u>Skylook</u>, no.56 (July 1972):12,13.
  1973, July
    Pat Morrison, "UFOs and Bigfoot Crea-
    tures: An Adventure into the Unex-
    plained," in <u>Bigfoot: Tales of Un-
    explained Creatures</u> (Rome, O.: Page
    Rsch.Library, 1978), pp.25,29.
  1974, Jan.26/Hwy.66
    Stan Gordon, "Pennsylvania Sightings
    Continue," <u>Skylook</u>, no.78 (May 1974)
    :12.
-UFO (DD)
  1975, Aug.
    Stan Gordon, "Pennsylvania Sightings
    Continue," <u>Skylook</u>, no.97 (Dec.1975)
    :9.
-UFO (NL)
  1972, April 2
    "UFO Reports from Pennsylvania," <u>Sky-look</u>, no.54 (May 1972):13.
  1972, April 17-21
    Stan Gordon, "UFOs in Pennsylvania,"
    no.56 (July 1972):12-13.
  1972, June 19
    Stan Gordon, "UFOs in Pennsylvania,"
    no.60 (Nov.1972):13.
  1975, May 18/Philip Arlotta/Gayville
    Stan Gordon, "UFO and Creature Ob-
    served in Same Area in Pennsylvania,"
    <u>Skylook</u>, no.91 (June 1975):13.

Greenville twp.
-Teleportation
  1883, March/Jesse Miller
    <u>New York World</u>, 25 Mar.1883.

Hamburg
-UFO (CE-1)
  1973, March 8/Sharyn Stemmel/Focht Lane
    <u>St. Mary's Daily Press</u>, 20 Mar.1973.
    Curt K. Sutherly, "1973: Madness in
    the Keystone State," <u>Official UFO</u> 1
    (Apr.1976):20.

Hammersley Fork
-Anomalous hole in ground
  1898, April/H.M. Cranmer
    Robert R. Lyman, <u>Forbidden Land</u>

(Coudersport: Potter Enterprise,
1971), p.51.
-Disappearance
  1897, Aug./Thomas Eggleton
    (Letter), H.M. Cranmer, <u>Fate</u> 9 (Nov.
    1956):122-24.
-Giant bird
  1922, April/H.M. Cranmer
  1957, March 28/H.M. Cranmer
  1957, April/H.M. Cranmer
    (Letter), <u>Fate</u> 16 (Sep.1963):116-17.
-Giant bird legend and disappearance
  ca.1860s/hotel
    (Letter), H.M. Cranmer, <u>Fate</u> 3 (Dec.
    1950):91-95.
    Robert R. Lyman, <u>Forbidden Land</u>
    (Coudersport: Potter Enterprise,
    1971), pp.42-43.
-Haunt
  17th c.-   /nr. Twin Sisters
    Robert R. Lyman, <u>Forbidden Land</u>
    (Coudersport: Potter Enterprise,
    1971), pp.8-10.
    Robert R. Lyman, <u>Amazing Indeed!</u>
    (Coudersport: Potter Enterprise,
    1973), pp.10-12.
-Skyquakes
  1901, Oct.-1921, Dec./H.M. Cranmer
    (Letter), <u>Fate</u> 10 (Sep.1957):120-24.
-UFO (?)
  1950, May 5
    (Letter), H.M. Cranmer, <u>Fate</u> 3 (Dec.
    1950):91,94.
  1951, Dec.9
  1952, Jan.9/post office
  1952, Jan.23/2 mi.E
  1952, Feb.1/Grange hall
    (Letter), H.M. Cranmer, <u>Fate</u> 6 (Feb.
    1953):108-11.
  1954, Oct.2/H.M. Cranmer
    Robert R. Lyman, <u>Amazing Indeed!</u>
    (Coudersport: Potter Enterprise,
    1973), p.82.
-UFO (DD)
  1899, summer/H.M. Cranmer
    (Letter), <u>Fate</u> 7 (Nov.1954):109-10.
  1940, July 6
    Leonard H. Stringfield, <u>Inside Sau-
    cer Post...3-0 Blue</u> (Cincinnati:
    CRIFO, 1957), p.86, quoting <u>Bluebook</u>,
    Nov.1955.
  1953, Oct.2/H.M. Cranmer
    (Letter), <u>Fate</u> 7 (Feb.1954):108.
  1954, April 13/H.M. Cranmer
    (Letter), <u>Fate</u> 7 (Nov.1954):109-10.
  1961, July 18
    Robert R. Lyman, <u>Amazing Indeed!</u>
    (Coudersport: Potter Enterprise,
    1973), p.82.

Hampton twp.
-Humanoid tracks
  1975, Dec./Harts Run Rd.
    Pittsburgh <u>North Hills News-Record</u>,
    18 June 1977.

Hanover
-Giant human skeletons
  1798, May 24/William A. Atlee
    <u>Hanover Sun</u>, 22 June 1963.

-Ghost
   1872, Feb.15/Pigeon Hills
      Hanover Herald, 21 Feb.1872, p.3.
-Healing
   n.d./Howard C. Resh
      Arthur Lewis, Hex (N.Y.: Trident,
      1969), pp.16,210-18.
-UFO (NL)
   1974, March 23
      Stan Gordon, "Pennsylvania Sightings
      Continue," Skylook, no.78 (May
      1974):12,13.

Harrisburg
-Fall of cloth
   1955, March/Harold Taylor/Front St.
      Harrisburg Patriot-News, 7 Mar.1955.
-Haunt
   1955-1960s/Brice Shade/Den Baron farm
      "Farm with a Built-In Ghost," Fate
      19 (June 1966):81, quoting Pennsyl-
      vania Farmer (undated).
   1956, Jan./Charles Damasko/State Capitol
      (Editorial), Fate 9 (June 1956):11-
      12, quoting Harrisburg Sunday Pa-
      triot-News (undated).
-Radionics
   1952-   /Homeotronic Foundation
      Edward Wriothesley Russell, Report
      on Radionics (London: Spearman,
      1973), pp.58-75.
      Peter Tompkins & Christopher Bird,
      The Secret Life of Plants (N.Y.:
      Harper & Row, 1973), pp.326-32.
-Reincarnation
   1941-1944/Eddie Carnarvon
      Pete Warner & Rayn Shawk, "Whatever
      Became of Eddie Carnarvon?" Fate 13
      (June 1960):64-70.
-Skyquake
   1973, Oct.25
      Curtis Sutherly, "What Was That?!?"
      Probe the Unknown 4 (Nov.1976):34,
      65.
-UFO (?)
   1957, Nov.15/=Venus
      Jacques & Janine Vallee, Challenge
      to Science (N.Y.: Ace, 1966 ed.),
      p.132.
   1967, July
      "Condon Committee Investigates East-
      ern UFO Reports," Saucer News 14
      (fall 1967):33-34.
      Edward U. Condon, ed., Scientific
      Study of Unidentified Flying Objects
      (N.Y.: Bantam, 1969 ed.), pp.332-34.
   1968, July 2/Jack Betz/=meteor
      Harrisburg Evening News, 3 July 1968.
-UFO (CE-1)
   1967, Aug.10
      "Sighting Evidence Grows," UFO Inv.
      4 (Nov.-Dec.1967):1.
   1968, Jan.12/Robert Willingham/North
   Mt.
      "New Close-Ups, Pacings," UFO Inv.
      4 (Mar.1968):1.
-UFO (CE-2)
   1967, June 15/Manor Hill
      Ted Phillips, Physical Traces Associ-

ated with UFO Sightings (Evanston:
Center for UFO Studies, 1975), p.49.
-UFO (NL)
   1968, Jan.20
      "New Close-Ups, Pacings," UFO Inv.
      4 (Mar.1968):1,3.
   1973, Jan./Gerald Summey
      Timothy Green Beckley, "Scientists'
      Changing Attitude Toward Flying
      Saucers," Saga UFO Rept. 1 (spring
      1974):14,46-48.

Harrison City
-UFO (DD)
   1972, Nov.7/nr. Penn Joint High School
      "Landing Case Report from Pennsyl-
      vania," Skylook, no.62 (Jan.1973):8.

Haycock twp.
-Ringing rocks
   Stony Garden
      Ivan T. Sanderson, Things (N.Y.:
      Pyramid, 1967), p.50.

Hazleton
-Ball lightning
   1948, June 27
      "Explosions, Etc.," Doubt, no.23
      (1948):349.
-UFO (CE-2)
   1957, Nov.14
      Hazleton Plain Speaker, 15 Nov.1957.
-UFO (NL)
   1957, Nov.12-15
      Hazleton Plain Speaker, 15 Nov.1957.

Hegins
-UFO (NL)
   1952, Sep./Mrs. Gable/nr. Hegins Mt.
      (Letter), James Gable, Saga UFO Rept.
      3 (June 1976):6.

Heilwood
-UFO (NL)
   1974, April 1/Mrs. John Tomasko/Hwy.422
      Barnesboro Star, 4 Apr.1974.

Hensel
-Skyquake
   1954, Sep.28
      "Case 51," CRIFO Newsl,, 4 Feb.1955,
      p.4.

Herminie
-Humanoid
   1973, Aug.24
      B. Ann Slate & Alan Berry, Bigfoot
      (N.Y.: Bantam, 1976), pp.123-24.

Hershey
-Fall of frogs
   ca.1938/David F. Gardner
      Letter to "Dear Abby" syndicated
      column, 29 Jan.1973.
-Radionics
   1950/H.H. Armstrong/Hershey Estates
      Edward Wriothesley Russell, Report
      on Radionics (London: Spearman,
      1973), pp.64-66,234-35,237-38.
-UFO (?)

1965, June 30/Lee Noll
"Saucer Photographed in Pennsylvania,"
Saucer News 12 (Dec.1965):16. il.

Highland Park
-Lightning anomaly
1892, July 19/Mr. Cassell
Henry F. Kretzer, Lightning Record
(St. Louis: The Author, 1895).

Hilltown
-UFO (CE-1)
1942, Nov./Margaret J. Rickert
(Letter), Fate 24 (June 1971):130.
1978, Jan.23/Mrs. Robert Grusheski/
Shirley Lane
Doylestown Daily Intelligencer, 24
Jan.1978.

Hooversville
-Humanoid
1978, July 30/Hwy.403
1978, Aug.1-2
Johnstown Tribune-Democrat, 5 Aug.
1978.

Huntingdon
-Ancient megalith
John Bakeless, Eyes of Discovery
(Philadelphia: Lippincott, 1950),
p.277.
Henriette Mertz, Atlantis: Dwelling
Place of the Gods (Chicago: The
Author, 1976), pp.50-52.
-UFO (?)
1954, July 11
Donald E. Keyhoe, Flying Saucer Con-
spiracy (N.Y.: Holt, 1955), p.190.

Indiana
-UFO (CE-3)
1969, Jan.24
Brad Steiger & Joan Whritenour, Fly-
ing Saucer Invasion: Target--Earth
(N.Y.: Award, 1969), p.96.
Brad Steiger, "Catching UFO Entities
Off Guard," Saga UFO Rept. 3 (Oct.
1976):30.
-UFO (NL)
1977, Oct.31
Indiana Evening Gazette, 1 Nov.1977.

Industry
-Clairvoyance
1973, Nov.29/Marianne Elko
(Editorial), Fate 27 (May 1974):36-
38, quoting Beaver Falls News-Tribune (undated).

Irvine
-Ancient stone chamber
Cyrus Thomas, "Report on the Mound
Explorations of the Bureau of Eth-
nology," Ann.Rept.Bur.Am.Ethn. 12
(1890-91):1,499-503.

Irwin
-UFO (CE-1)
1973, Jan.25
Stan Gordon, "Radar Failures Delay

Planes--UFOs Reported in Pennsylvania Sky," Skylook, no.64 (Mar.
1973):10-11.
-UFO (CE-2)
1973, July 29
Ted Phillips, Physical Traces Associated with UFO Sightings (Evanston:
Center for UFO Studies, 1975), p.91.
-UFO (NL)
1972, Nov.7
"Another Report from Pennsylvania,"
Skylook, no.62 (Jan.1973):8-9.
1973, Oct.14
Norwin Standard-Observer, 15 Oct.
1973.
1974, Jan.27/Pennsylvania Turnpike
Stan Gordon, "Pennsylvania Sightings
Continue," Skylook, no.78 (May
1974):12.

Jeannette
-Humanoid
1973, Aug.27/Beech Hills
Allen V. Noe, "ABSMal Affairs in
Pennsylvania and Elsewhere," Pur-
suit 6 (Oct.1973):84,86. il.
-Humanoid tracks
1977, June 29
Stan Gordon, "Bigfoot Sightings Con-
tinue," MUFON UFO J., no.117 (Aug.
1977):14-15.
-UFO (DD)
1973, July 18/David Baker
Wendelle C. Stevens, "UFOs: Seeing
Is Believing," Saga UFO Rept. 2
(fall 1974):48,50.
-UFO (NL)
1972, March 31/Hwy.130
"UFO Reports from Pennsylvania," Sky-
look, no.54 (May 1972):13.
1974, March 12
Stan Gordon, "Pennsylvania Sightings
Continue," Skylook, no.78 (May
1974):12-13.

Jefferson
-Fall of ice
1956, Jan./William Dolan
Pittsburgh Sun & Post-Gazette, 4
Jan.1956.
(Editorial), Fate 9 (June 1956):14.

Jenkintown
-Plant sensitivity
n.d./Randall Groves Hay
Peter Tompkins & Christopher Bird,
The Secret Life of Plants (N.Y.:
Harper & Row, 1973), p.180.

Jenner twp.
-Giant snake
19th c.
Annie Weston Whitney & Caroline Canfield Bullock, "Folk-Lore from Maryland," Mem.Am.Folk-Lore Soc'y, vol.
18 (1925), pp.192-93.

Jersey Shore
-Giant bird
1970, Oct.28/Judith Dingler/Hwy.220

1970, Nov.9/Clyde W. Mincer
1971, June 8/Linda L. Edwards/Cement
  Hollow Rd.
  Robert R. Lyman, Amazing Indeed!
  (Coudersport: Potter Enterprise,
  1973), pp.96-97.

Jim Thorpe
-Healing
  n.d./Helen Bechtel
  Arthur Lewis, Hex (N.Y.: Trident,
  1969), pp.226-31.

Johnstown
-Hex
  n.d./Zeda Mishler
  (Letter), Fate 23 (Oct.1970):141-42.
-Religious apparition
  1889, May 31
  Charles M. Skinner, Myths and Legends
  of Our Own Land, 2 vols. (Philadel-
  phia: Lippincott, 1896), 2:210.
-UFO (NL)
  1978, Oct.24
  Somerset American, 26 Oct.1978.
  Latrobe Bulletin, 27 Oct.1978.

Jonestown
-UFO (CE-2)
  1965, Sep.21/Giles Brown/Route One
  Curt K. Sutherly, "Case History of
  a UFO Flap," Official UFO 1 (Dec.
  1976):40-41,60-61. il.
  1967, April 5/John H. Demler/Hwy.72
  "Startling Cases Investigated," UFO
  Inv. 4 (May-June 1967):6.
-UFO (NL)
  1973, Nov.8/Ethel Reed/old Hwy.22
  Curt K. Sutherly, "1973: Madness in
  the Keystone State," Official UFO 1
  (Apr.1976):21,53.

Juniata Terrace
-UFO (CE-1)
  1956, Aug.27
  Thomas M. Olsen, The Reference for
  Outstanding UFO Sighting Reports
  (Riderwood, Md.: UFO Information
  Retrieval Center, 1966), p.48.

Karthaus
-Gasoline spring
  1940s-   /Leonard McGonigal/N of town
  (Editorial), Fate 17 (July 1964):20.
  1967/Hilda Rauch
  (Editorial), Fate 21 (Jan.1968):26-
  27.

Keating
-Petroglyph
  1858/nr. hotel
  D.S. Maynard, Historical View of
  Clinton County (Lock Haven, Pa.: The
  Enterprise, 1875).

Kecksburg
-UFO (?)
  1965, Dec.9/=meteorite?
  Ivan T. Sanderson, "'Something'
  Landed in Pennsylvania," Fate 19

(Mar.1966):33-35.
Jerome Clark, "The Greatest Flap Yet?
Part IV," Flying Saucer Rev. 12
(Nov.-Dec.1966):9,10.
-UFO (NL)
  1972, May 26
  Stan Gordon, "UFOs in Pennsylvania,"
  Skylook, no.60 (Nov.1972):13.

Kersey
-UFO (NL)
  1970, Aug.31/Thomas Herbstritt
  "Pennsylvania Residents See UFO,"
  Skylook, no.35 (Oct.1970):17.

Kirkwood
-UFO (CE-1)
  1966, July 11
  Jacques Vallee, Passport to Magonia
  (Chicago: Regnery, 1969), pp.332-
  33.

Koppel
-UFO (NL)
  1947, July 9/Rudi Petti/Third St.
  Beaver Falls News-Tribune, 10 July
  1947.

Kulpmont
-UFO (NL)
  1977, Nov.11/Hwy.61
  1977, Dec.1
  Shamokin News-Item, 29 Nov.1977; 3
  Dec.1977.
Kutztown
-Ball lightning
  n.d.
  (Letter), Howard Crane, Fate 19
  (Mar.1966):120-24.
-Hex
  n.d./Ruppert's Eck
  Richard H. Shaner, "Recollections
  of Witchcraft in the Oley Hills,"
  Pennsylvania Folklife (Folk Festi-
  val suppl., 1972):39-43.
-UFO (CE-1)
  1952, Aug.31/Herbert Long
  Harold T. Wilkins, Flying Saucers on
  the Attack (N.Y.: Ace, 1967 ed.),
  p.250.

Lackawaxen
-Ancient inscription
  1970, spring/Donald Ness
  "The Hawley Stone: Newest Discovery
  of a Possibly Pre-Columbian Inscription," NEARA Newsl. 5 (Dec.1970):
  88. il.
  R.P. Gravely, Jr., "Notes Concerning
  the Alleged Runestone from Hawley,
  Pennsylvania," Chesopean 9 (1971):
  33-34.
  Salvatore Michael Trento, The Search
  for Lost America (Chicago: Contemporary, 1978), pp.82-84.

Lafayette Hill
-UFO (NL)
  1975, Aug.5
  "UFO Central," CUFOS News Bull., 15

Nov.1975, p.15.

Lancaster
-Fall of metallic object
1971, Jan.26/Irvin Funk
"It Came Out of the Sky," Fate 24
(Dec.1971):73.
-Fall of nails
1957-1958/John S. Groff/625 E. Orange
St.
(Editorial), Fate 12 (Feb.1959):12-
13.
-Healing
1960s/Clair M. Frank/Willow St.
Arthur Lewis, Hex (N.Y.: Trident,
1969), pp.198-209.
-Out-of-body experience research
1840s/William B. Fahnestock
William Baker Fahnestock, Statuvolism
(Chicago: Religio-Philosophical
Pub.House, 1871).
Slater Brown, The Heyday of Spiri-
tualism (N.Y.: Pocket Books, 1972
ed.), pp.35-37.
-Snow worms
1892, March 2/Samuel Auxer
"Insects on the Surface of Snow,"
Insect Life 4 (June 1892):335-36.
-UFO (CE-2)
1969, March 10
"Light Beams with EM Effects Report-
ed," UFO Inv. 4 (May 1969):3.
-UFO (DD)
1957, Oct.5/Mrs. Robert Keely
"Flying Saucer Roundup," Fate 11
(Feb.1958):29,35.
1967, Feb./Kurt Kreitz
"Power Play," The New Report on Fly-
ing Saucers (Greenwich, Ct.: Fawcett,
1967), p.43.
-UFO (NL)
1952, April 11
Richmond (Va.) News-Leader, 12 Apr.
1952.
1955, Oct.9/Henry Howell
"Case 112," CRIFO Orbit, 2 Dec.1955,
p.3.
1957, Oct.13/George C. Jacobs/351 E.
Chestnut St.
"Flying Saucer Roundup," Fate 11
(Feb.1958):29,35-36.
1976, April 17
"Noteworthy UFO Sightings," Ufology
2 (fall 1976):60.

Lancaster co.
-Radionics
1952-1953
Edward Wriothesley Russell, Report
on Radionics (London: Spearman,
1973), pp.245-49.

Langhorne
-Mystery bloodstain
1967, March-Aug./Emmett P. LeCompte
"Enigma," Fate 21 (Apr.1968):75.

Lansdowne
-Fall of metallic object
1957, Dec.6/Mr. Lupfer

Philadelphia Bulletin, 12 Jan.1958.
-Haunt
1965/Jack Buffington/Lansdowne Ave.
Hans Holzer, Yankee Ghosts (N.Y.:
Ace, 1966), pp.77-90.
-UFO (NL)
1975, Oct.8
"UFO Central," CUFOS News Bull., 1
Feb.1976, p.8.

Lansford
-UFO (CE-1)
1957, Nov.7/Alice Beers/Weatherly
High School
"Children in Pennsylvania Town Make
Detailed Sighting," Saucer News 5
(Feb.-Mar.1958):21.
Aimé Michel, Flying Saucers and the
Straight-Line Mystery (N.Y.: Cri-
terion, 1958), p.264.

Latrobe
-Humanoid
1973, Sep.
Allen V. Noe, "ABSMal Affairs in
Pennsylvania and Elsewhere," Pur-
suit 6 (Oct.1973):84,87.
1973, Sep./tape recording of voice
Robert E. Jones, "Voice Print Anal-
ysis," Pursuit 7 (Jan.1974):14-16.
1974, Sep./Robert Jones/N of town
Robert E. Jones, "Pennsylvania
ABSMery: A Report," Pursuit 8 (Jan.
1975):19-21.
-Humanoid hair sample
1973, Aug.26/=cow hair
"Pennsylvania ABSMery," Pursuit 7
(Oct.1974):94-95.
-Phantom panther
1945, Sep.8/Wildcat Hollow
"More Animals," Doubt, no.14 (spring
1946):203,204.
-UFO (DD)
1975, July
Stan Gordon, "Pennsylvania Sightings
Continue," Skylook, no.97 (Dec.
1975):9.
-UFO (NL)
1978, Oct.25/Mark Withrow/Lee Valley Rd.
Latrobe Bulletin, 25 Oct.1978; and
27 Oct.1978.

Laurelville
-UFO (CE-1)
1974, Feb.7/Hwy.982
Stan Gordon, "Pennsylvania Sightings
Continue," Skylook, no.78 (May
1974):12.

Lebanon
-UFO (?)
1965, July 13
Curtis K. Sutherly, "Case History of
a UFO Flap," Official UFO 1 (Dec.
1976):40,41.
-UFO (NL)
1972, June 8/Tim Boltz/Horst Orchard,
4 mi.N
Curtis K. Sutherly, "The Horst Orchard Ghost Light," Caveat Emptor,

no.11 (Jan.-Feb.1974):5-7,20.
1975, Oct.23/John Lindermuth
Lebanon Daily News, 24 Oct.1975.
Curt Sutherly, "OK, If It Wasn't the
Goodyear Blimp, What Was It?" Probe
the Unknown 4 (Mar.1976):48.

Leechburg
-UFO (NL)
1955, summer/Joseph G. Sarene
(Letter), Fate 9 (Mar.1956):128-29.

Leiperville
-Humanoid
1909, Jan.20/Daniel Flynn/Chester Pike
James F. McCloy & Ray Miller, Jr.,
The Jersey Devil (Wallingford, Pa.:
Middle Atlantic, 1976), pp.59-60.

Level Green
-UFO (CE-2)
1976, March 28
Stan Gordon, "Low Level UFO Sightings
in Pennsylvania," MUFON UFO J., no.
103 (June 1976):18.

Levittown
-Haunt
1971, Nov./Bolton Mansion
Donald M. Gibson, Jr., "A Systematic
Investigation of an Allegedly Haunt-
ed House with Infrared Photographic
Documentation," J.Occult Studies 1
(winter-spring 1977-78):211-28. il.
-Reincarnation
1967
(Letter), Fate 20 (Aug.1967):123-24.
-UFO (CE-1)
1973, Oct.17/Blue Ridge section
Floyd Murray, "Over the Keystone
State," Caveat Emptor, no.11 (Jan.-
Feb.1974):35,36.
-UFO (NL)
1961, July 25/Joan H. Smith
(Letter), Fate 14 (Dec.1961):104-106.

Ligonier
-Humanoid
1964/Mellon Estate
Erie Times, 28 June 1977.
-UFO (CE-2)
1973, Oct.
Ted Phillips, Physical Traces Associ-
ated with UFO Sightings (Evanston:
Center for UFO Studies, 1975), p.92.
-UFO (NL)
1961, Oct.30/Carl H. Geary, Jr./U.S.30
"Frequent UFO Operations, Many at
Night," UFO Inv. 2 (Jan.-Feb.1962):6.
Richard Hall, ed., The UFO Evidence
(Washington: NICAP, 1964), p.2.

Liverpool
-Fall of sandstone
1889, Nov./Mrs. J.K. Blattenburg
New York Times, 2 Jan.1890, p.5.

Lloydsville
-UFO (DD)
1972, April 22/Donahue Rd.

Stan Gordon, "UFOs in Pennsylvania,"
Skylook, no.56 (July 1972):12,13.

Lock Haven
-Giant bird
1960s/Carrier Rd.
Robert R. Lyman, Amazing Indeed!
(Coudersport: Potter Enterprise,
1973), pp.95-96.
-UFO (R-V)
1959, Feb.24/A.D. Yates
Richard Hall, ed., The UFO Evidence
(Washington: NICAP, 1964), pp.43,
116.

Luthers Mills
-UFO (NL)
1975, Jan.2
Robert A. Goerman, "The UFO Modus Operandi: January 1975," Official UFO
1 (Aug.1976):46,47.

Luxor
-Humanoid
1973, Aug.26
Allen V. Noe, "ABSMal Affairs in
Pennsylvania and Elsewhere," Pur-
suit 6 (Oct.1973):84,86. il.

Lymansville
-UFO (CE-1)
ca.1923/Glenn M. Rees/S of town
Robert R. Lyman, Amazing Indeed!
(Coudersport: Potter Enterprise,
1973), p.66.

McKean co.
-Entombed frog
1880s/Eddie Marsh/coal mine
R.W. Shufeldt, "A Mummified Frog,"
Science 8 (1886):279-80. il.
-Giant bird
1937
(Letter), H.M. Cranmer, Fate 19 (Mar.
1966):131-32.
-Humanoid
1977, spring?
Uniontown Herald, 20 May 1977.

McKeesport
-Mystery bird deaths
1957, Feb.13
"Falls," Doubt, no.54 (1957):435,436,
quoting Pittsburgh Post-Gazette
(undated).
-New energy source (inventor)
1917/John Andrews/=gasoline substitute
Walter Scott Meriwether, "The Great-
est Invention?" Reader's Digest 26
(Apr.1935):35-38.
-UFO (DD)
1975, Jan.2
Stan Gordon, "Pennsylvanians Report
300 Sightings," Skylook, no.88
(Mar.1975):13.

Madison
-UFO (NL)
1973, Oct./Rosemary Smith
Jeannette News-Dispatch, 18 Oct.1973.

Mahaffey
-UFO (CE-1)
  1978, Oct.10/Kathy Moyer/Banner Ridge
    Clearfield Progress, 11 Oct.1978.

Mahoning
-Haunt
  1960s/G.A. Laughlin/1161 N. Liberty St.
    G.A. Laughlin & Virginia Santore,
    "Haunted House...Open for Business,"
    Fate 22 (Feb.1969):64-72. il.

Mahoning twp.
-UFO (DD)
  1978, Jan.17/Leo Goldberg/Mahoning Valley
    Allentown Morning Call, 18-19 Jan.
    1978. il.
    (Editorial), Can.UFO Rept., no.31
    (summer 1978):6. il.

Marshalls Creek
-UFO (NL)
  1973, March 27
    Stroudsburg Pocono Record, 28 Mar.
    1973.

Marshburg
-UFO (NL)
  1978, Nov.9
    Bradford Era, 13 Nov.1978.

Marysville
-UFO (NL)
  1975, Dec.3
    "UFO Central," CUFOS News Bull., 1
    Feb.1976, p.14.

Matamoras
-Ancient cavern
  Willehoosa
    Salvatore Michael Trento, The Search
    for Lost America (Chicago: Contem-
    porary, 1978), pp.91-92.

Meadville
-Automatic writing
  1898-   /Nella Stowell Wright
    Theon Wright, The Open Door (N.Y.:
    John Day, 1970). il.
-Clairvoyance
  1883, Feb./W.H. Hover
    "Incidents," J.ASPR 9 (1915):176-88.
-UFO (NL)
  1975, Nov.9
    "Noteworthy UFO Sightings," Ufology
    2 (spring 1976):43.

Mechanicsburg
-UFO (CE-1)
  1968, Jan.12-13/Gladys Lehman/Trindle
  Rd.
    "Saucer Chases Car," Skylook, no.6-7
    (Feb.-Mar.1968):1,5.

Media
-UFO (?)
  1947, Aug./W. Boyce
    Richard Hall, ed., The UFO Evidence
    (Washington: NICAP, 1964), p.33.

-UFO (NL)
  1973, Oct.4
    Wilmington (Del.) Evening Journal,
    5 Oct.1973.

Melrose Park
-Fall of rocks
  1963, May/Jack T. Siciliano/32 Dewey
  Rd.
    (Editorial), Fate 16 (Sep.1963):13-
    14.

Mercer
-Reincarnation
  1960s/Gail Habbyshaw
    Eugene Kinkead, "Is There Another
    Life After Death?" Look, 20 Oct.
    1970, pp.84,86-87.

Merion Station
-UFO (?)
  1949, Sep.29
    "If It's in the Sky It's a Saucer,"
    Doubt, no.27 (1949):416,417.

Meyersdale
-UFO (CE-1)
  1966, Jan.11
    J. Allen Hynek, The UFO Experience
    (Chicago: Regnery, 1972), pp.89-90.

Middletown
-UFO (NL)
  1973, Oct.4/Robert Bugjo/Pennsylvania
  State Univ.
    Philadelphia Inquirer, 6 Oct.1973.

Midland
-UFO (?)
  1965, Dec.9
    Ivan T. Sanderson, "'Something'
    Landed in Pennsylvania," Fate 19
    (Mar.1966):33.
-UFO (CE-2)
  1973, Nov.1-2
    Ted Phillips, Physical Traces Associ-
    ated with UFO Sightings (Evanston:
    Center for UFO Studies, 1975), p.96.

Milford
-UFO (CE-3)
  1956, Dec.17/Marie Carow/S of town at
  Conashaugh
    Milford Pike County Dispatch, 17
    Apr.1958.
    Berthold Eric Schwarz, "UFO Occupants:
    Fact or Fantasy?" Flying Saucer Rev.
    15 (Sep.-Oct.1969):14,16-18.
  1957, May/Frances Stichler
    Milford Pike County Dispatch, 19 Dec.
    1957.
    Berthold Eric Schwarz, "UFO Occupants:
    Fact or Fantasy?" Flying Saucer Rev.
    15 (Sep.-Oct.1969):14-16.

Millardsville
-UFO (CE-1)
  1973, Oct.21/Isabelle Brown/Hwy.422
    Lebanon News, 24 Oct.1973.

Millersville
-UFO (NL)
1975, Oct.30
"Noteworthy UFO Sightings," Ufology
2 (spring 1976):43.

Mill Run
-Cloud anomaly
1874, July 28
John P. Bessor, "The Battle of the
Clouds," Fate 6 (Mar.1953):92.

Millsboro
-Petroglyphs
James L. Swauger, "Petroglyphs Oppo-
site Millsboro, 36 FA 36," Pennsylvania Arch. 39 (Dec.1969):53-71. il.

Millvale
-Haunt
1930s/Croatian Catholic Church
Louis Adamic, "The Millvale Appari-
tion," Harper's Monthly Mag. 176
(Apr.1938):476-86.
"The Millvale Apparition," J.ASPR 32
(1938):253-56.
Hans Holzer, Ghosts I've Met (N.Y.:
Ace, 1965 ed.), pp.66-71.

Mina
-Haunt
ca.1875/Desira Sherwood
Robert R. Lyman, Forbidden Land
(Coudersport: Potter Enterprise,
1971), p.52.

Mohnton
-Healing
1974/Lawrence Althouse/Calvary Methodist Church
"Terminal Cancer Healed," Fate 28
(Apr.1975):85, quoting Nat'l Enquirer (undated).

Mohrsville
-UFO (NL)
1973, March 29/Curtis Lash/Rattlesnake
Hill Rd.
Reading Eagle, 30 Mar.1973.

Monaca
-UFO (CE-2)
1965, Oct.
Stan Gordon, "Possible Physical Evi-
dence Located," Skylook, no.84
(Nov.1974):12. il.

Monongahela
-Humanoid hair sample
1973, Aug.24/=human hair?
"Pennsylvania ABSMery," Pursuit 7
(Oct.1974):94-95.

Montour Park
-UFO (CE-1)
1978, April 5/Joanne Wasek/high school
J. Allen Smith, "Multiple UFOs in
Pennsylvania," APRO Bull. 27 (Aug.
1978):1-4.

Montoursville
-UFO (NL)
1969, Oct.17/Edward Hagerman
"Object Sighted in Pennsylvania,"
Skylook, no.26 (Jan.1970):10, quoting Williamsport Sun-Gazette (undated).

Morrisville
-Humanoid
1909, Jan.21/=hoax
James F. McCloy & Ray Miller, Jr.,
The Jersey Devil (Wallingford, Pa.:
Middle Atlantic, 1976), p.70.
-Telepathy
1958, Dec.24/Hazel Lambert
(Editorial), Fate 12 (Apr.1959):6-8,
quoting Philadelphia Inquirer (un-
dated).

Morton
-UFO (NL)
1976, April 9
"Noteworthy UFO Sightings," Ufology
2 (fall 1976):60.

Mount Carmel
-UFO (NL)
1977, Aug.
Shamokin News-Item, 1 Dec.1977.
1977, Nov.12, 17, 19
Shamokin News-Item, 29 Nov.1977.

Mount Gretna
-UFO (NL)
1975, Oct.23/Bill Sutcliffe/Hwy.117
Curt Sutherly, "OK, If It Wasn't the
Goodyear Blimp, What Was It?" Probe
the Unknown 4 (Mar.1976):49,50-51.

Mount Lebanon
-UFO (?)
1949, July 10
"If It's in the Sky It's a Saucer,"
Doubt, no.27 (1949):416.

Mount Morris
-UFO (NL)
1975, Jan.9/Charles Lemley
Robert A. Goerman, "The UFO Modus Operandi: January 1975," Official UFO
1 (Aug.1976):46,65.

Mount Pleasant
-UFO (NL)
1976, March 28
Stan Gordon, "Low Level UFO Sightings
in Pennsylvania," MUFON UFO J., no.
103 (June 1976):18.

Murrysville
-Giant bird
1954, July 26/Alvan Gillis
"Displaced Critters," Doubt, no.49
(1955):358.
-UFO (NL)
1957, Oct.2/Ralph Wright
"Saucers in the News," Flying Saucers,
Feb.1958, pp.70,76-77.

Narberth
-UFO (NL)
1956, Dec.21/Scott Cornelius
"Case 289," CRIFO Orbit, 1 Mar.1957,
p.2.

Nazareth
-UFO (CE-1)
1965, Dec.10
Allentown Sunday Call-Chronicle, 26
Dec.1965.
-UFO (NL)
1973, March 22/Todd Jones
"Press Reports," APRO Bull. 21 (May-
June 1973):9.

Nesquehoning
-Healing
n.d./Anne Fauzio
Arthur Lewis, Hex (N.Y.: Trident,
1969), pp.16,232-35.

Nether Providence twp.
-UFO (DD)
1973, Oct.10
Floyd Murray, "Over the Keystone
State," Caveat Emptor, no.11 (Jan.-
Feb.1974):35.

New Alexandria
-UFO (DD)
1973, Oct.
Jeannette News-Dispatch, 18 Oct.1973.

New Bloomfield
-Plant longevity
box huckleberry
"The Largest and Oldest Plant," Pur-
suit 3 (Apr.1970):46.
-UFO (NL)
1956, Oct.10/William Hand
Harrisburg Patriot-News, 14 Oct.1956.

New Castle
-Anomalous hole in ground
1954, April/6 mi.S on Hwy.18
"Mystery of the Sinking Road," Fate
8 (Nov.1955):75.
-UFO (?)
1966, Aug.1
New Castle News, 1 Aug.1966. il.
1967, June 28/ Gabriel Kozora
New Castle News, 28 June 1967. il.
Edward U. Condon, Scientific Study
of Unidentified Flying Objects
(N.Y.: Bantam, 1969 ed.), pp.326-29.
-UFO (NL)
1973, Nov.3/airport
New Castle News, 5 Nov.1973.
1975, July 21
"UFO Central," CUFOS News Bull., 15
Nov.1975, p.14.

New Freeport
-UFO (NL)
1964, Aug.15/Charles Bissett
"UFO Sighting Wave Persists," UFO
Inv. 2 (Sep.-Oct.1964):5.

New Kensington
-UFO (DD)
1969, March 30/Robert A. Goerman/600
block of Catalpa St.
"'Cigar-Shaped UFO's Reported All
Over the Globe," Skylook, no.20
(July 1969):9.
-UFO (NL)
1968, April 19/Victor Babinsack
"U.S. Reports," APRO Bull. 17 (Sep.-
Oct.1968):8.
1974, April 16
"Family Sees Egg-Shaped Object,"
Skylook, no.80 (July 1974):18.

New Oxford
-Haunt
1870s
Don Yoder, "Witch Tales from Adams
County," Pennsylvania Folklife 12
(summer 1962):29,34-35.

Newton
-Genetic anomaly
1953, Nov./Lamar Thompson
"First Prize," Doubt, no.44 (1954):
268,269, quoting Santa Monica (Cal.)
Evening Outlook, 6 Nov.1953.

Norristown
-Ancient inscription
1829, Nov.
J.B. Browne, "Singular Impression in
Marble," Am.J.Sci., ser.1, 19
(1831):361. il.
-Clairvoyance
1966, July/Pentecostal Church
(Editorial), Fate 20 (Mar.1967):20-
21.
-Hex
1973/Ottavio Perricone
(Editorial), Fate 27 (July 1974):32.
-UFO (NL)
1979, Jan.9/Walter Miller
Hatboro Today's Spirit, 10 Jan.1979.
King of Prussia Today's Post, 11
Jan.1979.

North East
-UFO (CE-2)
1954, Dec.5
North East Breeze, 5 Dec.1954.
-UFO (DD)
1977, Oct.29
"UFOs of Limited Merit," Int'l UFO
Reporter 2 (Dec.1977):3.
-UFO (NL)
1977, Oct.29
"UFOs of Limited Merit," Int'l UFO
Reporter 2 (Dec.1977):News sec.

North Lebanon twp.
-UFO (NL)
1975, Oct.23-24/trailer park
Lebanon Daily News, 31 Oct.1975.

Northumberland co.
-Shape-shifting
1890s/May Paul
Bernhardt J. Hurwood, Vampires, Were-

wolves, and Ghouls (N.Y.: Ace,
1968), pp.86-87.

Norwich twp.
-Fall of tektites
    ca.1916/Mrs. Harry S. Hull
        Robert R. Lyman, Amazing Indeed!
        (Coudersport: Potter Enterprise,
        1973), p.99.

Oakdale
-Phantom panther
    1978, Feb./Mary Harouse
        Texarkana (Tex.) Gazette-News, 4 Mar.
        1978.
-UFO (CE-2)
    1976, Feb.28
        Stan Gordon, "UFO/Creature Sightings
        Continue," Skylook, no.102 (May
        1976):10.

Ohiopyle
-UFO (CE-1)
    1967, March 17/Wilbur Daniels
        "Car Buzzing Incidents on Increase,"
        APRO Bull. 15 (May-June 1967):5.
-UFO (CE-3)
    1974, Feb.6
        Stan Gordon, "Pennyslvania Sightings
        Continue," Skylook, no.78 (May
        1974):12.

Oil City
-Fall of black snow
    1949, Nov.17
        "Black Snow," Doubt, no.28 (1950):3.
-UFO (?)
    1959, Feb.3
        Richard Hall, ed., The UFO Evidence
        (Washington: NICAP, 1964), p.99.
-UFO (NL)
    1975, Oct.26
        "Noteworthy UFO Sightings," Ufology
        2 (spring 1976):43.

Oleana
-Crisis apparition
    n.d.
        Robert R. Lyman, Forbidden Land
        (Coudersport: Potter Enterprise,
        1971), pp.36-37.
-Fire anomaly
    n.d./James Bassett/nr. Indian Run
        Robert R. Lyman, Forbidden Land
        (Coudersport: Potter Enterprise,
        1971), p.15.

Oley
-Precognition
    1748/John Kinsey
        John F. Watson, Annals of Philadel-
        phia and Pennsylvania in the Olden
        Time, 2 vols. (Philadelphia: John
        Penington & Uriah Hunt, 1844), 2:
        414-15.
        "John Ross of Oley Forge Writes 1748
        Letter on ESP," Am.Folklife 3 (Nov.
        1974):8.

Orrtanna
-UFO (?)
    1973, Nov.16
        Floyd Murray, "Over the Keystone
        State," Caveat Emptor, no.11 (Jan.-
        Feb.1974):35,36.

Palmerton
-UFO (NL)
    1964, May 26/Terry Balliet
        "Other Recent Sightings," UFO Inv.
        2 (July-Aug.1964):7-8.

Pavia
-Clairvoyance
    1856, April 24/Jacob Dibert
        E. Howard Blackburn & William H.
        Welfley, History of Bedford and
        Somerset Counties (N.Y.: Lewis,
        1906).
        Rhoda Bender, "The Lost Children of
        the Alleghenies," Fate 8 (Sep.
        1955):10-13.

Peach Bottom
-Humanoid
    1978, March 2/power plant
        Gettysburg Times, 24 July 1978, p.2.

Penn Hills
-Whirlwind anomaly
    1960, June 27/Vincent L. Varuolo/High-
    point Dr.
        (Editorial), Fate 13 (Nov.1960):6-8.

Pennsbury twp.
-Humanoid
    1901, July/Milton Brint/Stewart's
    Woods
        Jerome Clark & Loren Coleman, Crea-
        tures of the Outer Edge (N.Y.: War-
        ner, 1978), pp.63-65.

Penn Valley
-Fall of metal foil
    1957, Sep.
        Philadelphia Inquirer, 10 Sep.1957.

Philadelphia
-Astrology
    1700s/Christopher Witt/Germantown
        John F. Watson, Annals of Philadel-
        phia and Pennsylvania in the Olden
        Time, 2 vols. (Philadelphia: John
        Penington & Uriah Hunt, 1844), 1:
        267.
-Automatic writing
    1850s/Charles Linton
        Charles Linton, The Healing of the
        Nations (N.Y.: Soc'y for the Diffu-
        sion of Spiritual Knowledge, 1855).
        Nandor Fodor, Encyclopaedia of Psy-
        chic Science (London: Arthurs,
        1933), p.204.
        Slater Brown, The Heyday of Spirit-
        ualism (N.Y.: Pocket Books, 1972
        ed.), p.236.
-Autoscopy
    1961, Jan.
        Edward Podolsky, "Have You Seen Your

Double?" Fate 19 (Apr.1966):78,80.
-Ball lightning
1960/Louise Matthews/2546 Oakford St.
 (Editorial), Fate 13 (Nov.1960):16-
 18.
-Clairvoyance
1906-1913/Theodosia Prince
 Walter Franklin Prince, "The Doris
 Case of Multiple Personality," Proc.
 ASPR 9 (1915):1-700; 10 (1916):701-
 1332.
 James H. Hyslop & Walter F. Prince,
 "The Doris Fischer Case of Multiple
 Personality," J.ASPR 10 (1916):381-
 98,436-54,485-504,541-58,613-31,
 661-78.
 James H. Hyslop, "The Doris Fischer
 Case of Multiple Personality: Part
 III," Proc.ASPR 11 (1917):5-866.
 James H. Hyslop, "Experiments with
 the Doris Case," J.ASPR 11 (1917):
 153-77,213-37,266-91,324-43,385-
 406,459-92.
 Walter F. Prince, "Therapeutic Sug-
 gestions on the Doris Case," J.ASPR
 12 (1918):98-107.
 James H. Hyslop, "Doctor Schiller on
 the Doris Fischer Case," J.ASPR 12
 (1918):345-55.
 Walter F. Prince, The Psychic in the
 House (Boston: Boston SPR, 1926).
 Boston SPR, Walter Franklin Prince:
 A Tribute to His Memory (Boston: B.
 Humphries, 1935).
 Thomas R. Tietze, "Who Was the 'Real
 Doris'?" in Martin Ebon, ed., Exor-
 cism: Fact Not Fiction (N.Y.: Signet,
 1974), pp.177-85.
1912, April 15
 William Oliver Stevens, Psychics and
 Common Sense (N.Y.: Dutton, 1953),
 p.108.
-Cloud anomaly
1904, July/"Mohican"/Delaware R.
 Wailuku (Hawaii) Maui News, 13 Aug.
 1904.
-Contactee and Men-in-black
1964, fall-1965/Norman Schreibstein/
Rissler-Verstein Observatory
 Gray Barker, Book of Saucers (Clarksburg, W.V.: Saucerian, 1965), pp.
 66-70.
-Crisis apparition
1886, Aug.4/Mary Murnane/Montrose St.
 St. John D. Seymour & Harry L. Neli-
 gan, True Irish Ghost Stories (Dublin: Hodges, Figgis, 1914), pp.173-
 74.
1943, April 8/Mildred C. Harris
 "Cases," J.ASPR 37 (1943):143,144-47.
-Deathbed apparition
n.d.
 Martin C. Sampson, "When the Curtains
 of Death Parted," Reader's Digest
 74 (May 1959):48-51.
-Erratic crocodilian
1926
 "'Baby' Alligators Astray in Northern Rivers," Literary Digest 91 (11
 Dec.1926):68-72, quoting Philadel-

phia Public Ledger (undated).
-Eyeless vision
1970/Mary Donahue
 (Editorial), Fate 23 (Dec.1970):30-
 34, quoting Philadelphia Daily News
 (undated).
-Fall of burning substance
1813, Nov.13
 John F. Watson, Annals of Philadel-
 phia and Pennsylvania in the Olden
 Time, 2 vols. (Philadelphia: John
 Penington & Uriah Hunt, 1844), 2:
 369.
-Fall of gelatinous substance
1950, Sep.26/John Collins/Vare Blvd.
 x 26th St.
 "Sticky Purple Light," Fate 4 (Nov.-
 Dec.1951):35.
 Bruce S. Maccabee, "UFO Related In-
 formation from the FBI File: Part
 7," MUFON UFO J., no.132 (Nov.-
 Dec.1978):11,14-15.
-Fall of ice
1957, Sep.12
1957, Nov.7/Kensington
 "Falls," Doubt, no.57 (1958):4-5.
-Fall of money
1977, July 27/Jack Einhorn/Broad x
Vine St./=fell from armored car
 Philadelphia Inquirer, 28 July 1977.
-Fall of rocks
1941, July 25
 Philadelphia Evening Ledger, 26 July
 1941.
-Fall of sulphur
1748, May 4/Christopher Lehman
 John F. Watson, Annals of Philadel-
 phia and Pennsylvania in the Olden
 Time, 2 vols. (Philadelphia: John
 Penington & Uriah Hunt, 1844), 2:
 415.
-Fall of worms
1946, July 22/Howard Baer
 "Rain of Worms," Doubt, no.16 (1946)
 :240.
-Ghost
1890s/S. Weir Mitchell
 George K. Cherrie, Dark Trails: Ad-
 ventures of a Naturalist (N.Y.:
 Putnam, 1930).
-Haunt
n.d./Walnut x 5th St.
 John F. Watson, Annals of Philadel-
 phia and Pennsylvania in the Olden
 Time, 2 vols. (Philadelphia: John
 Penington & Uriah Hunt, 1844), 1:
 272-73.
n.d./Chalkley Hall
 Federal Writers' Project, Philadel-
 phia: A Guide to the Nation's Birth-
 place (Philadelphia: William Penn
 Ass'n, 1937).
1866/Samuel Durborow
 New York Times, 13 Feb.1866, p.3.
1880s/Louise Stockton
 "The Stockton 'Haunted House,'" J.
 ASPR 12 (1918):131-34.
1934/Jean Guthiel/Bouvier St.
 Jean Guthiel, "Bell-Ringing Door-
 Slamming Haunt," Fate 17 (Aug.1964):

74-77.
1963-1966/William Davy, Jr./North Philadelphia
  Hans Holzer, Gothic Ghosts (N.Y.:
  Pocket Books, 1972), pp.36-42.
1965-1969/Thomas J. Simmons/"The Sullivans"/Naval Base
  (Editorial), Fate 22 (Sep.1969):35.
1967, June-Aug.
  W.T. Joines, "Philadelphia Haunting,"
  Theta, no.23 (1968).
  D. Scott Rogo, An Experience of Phantoms (N.Y.: Dell, 1976 ed.), pp.155-56.
n.d./Harold Cameron
  Constance Westbie & Harold Cameron,
  Night Stalks the Mansion (Harrisburg: Stackpole, 1978).
1970s/Carpenter's Hall/310 Chestnut St.
  "Give Me Liberty or Give Me Death?"
  Probe the Unknown 2 (winter 1974):
  62-63.
-Healing
  n.d./Morris Bolber
  William Seabrook, Witchcraft: Its
  Power in the World Today (N.Y.: Lancer, 1968 ed.), p.23.
1958, March 28/Catherine Mack/Germantown Hospital
  W.E. Farbstein, "A Woman of Zion,"
  Fate 12 (Apr.1959):79-81. il.
-Hex
  n.d.
  E.S. Gifford, Jr., The Evil Eye:
  Studies in the Folklore of Vision
  (N.Y.: Macmillan, 1958), pp.101-103.
  Edward S. Gifford, Jr., "The Evil Eye
  in Philadelphia," Pennsylvania Folklife 20 (summer 1971):58-59.
1970s/Dolorez Amelia Gomez
  Jane C. Beck, "A Traditional Witch
  of the Twentieth Century," New York
  Folklore Quar. 30 (1974):101-16.
-Humanoid
  1909, Jan.20/J.H. White/1500 block Ellsworth St.
  1909, Jan.20/William Becker/Lime Kiln
  Pike
  1909, Jan.20/Martin Burns/Beach St. x
  Fairmount Ave.
  James F. McCloy & Ray Miller, Jr.,
  The Jersey Devil (Wallingford, Pa.:
  Middle Atlantic, 1976), pp.63-64.
-Inner development
  1970s/Pagan Way/Box 7712
  Hans Holzer, The Truth About Witchcraft (Garden City: Doubleday, 1969).
  Philadelphia Evening Bulletin, 11
  June 1971.
  Hans Holzer, The Witchcraft Report
  (N.Y.: Ace, 1973), pp.47-52.
  J. Gordon Melton, Encyclopedia of
  American Religions, 2 vols. (Wilmington, N.C.: Consortium, 1978),
  2:289-90.
-Invisibility experiment and teleportation
  1943, Oct./Carl M. Allen (Carlos Allende)/"U.S.S. Eldridge"/Navy Yards
  M.K. Jessup, The Case for the UFO

(Garland, Tex.: Varo, 1956 ed.).
Gray Barker, ed., The Strange Case
of Dr. M.K. Jessup (Clarksburg,
W.V.: Saucerian, 1963).
Ivan T. Sanderson, Uninvited Visitors (N.Y.: Cowles, 1967), pp.227-41.
Brad Steiger & Joan Whritenour, Allende Letters: New UFO Breakthrough
(N.Y.: Award, 1968), pp.56-77.
"Allende Letters a Hoax," APRO Bull.
18 (July-Aug.1969):1,3.
Alan Elliott, "Were the Allende Letters a College Prank?" Pursuit 9
(Apr.1976):43-44.
B.R. Strong, "The Allende Letters:
Fact or Fiction?" Official UFO 1
(Apr.1976):22-23,53-54. il.
William L. Moore & Charles Berlitz,
The Philadelphia Experiment: Project Invisibility (N.Y.: Grosset &
Dunlap, 1979).
-Lunar cycle and crime
  1960
  Darrell Huff, Cycles in Your Life
  (N.Y.: Norton, 1964).
-Midday darkness
  1823, Oct.5
  John F. Watson, Annals of Philadelphia and Pennsylvania in the Olden
  Time, 2 vols. (Philadelphia: John
  Penington & Uriah Hunt, 1844), 2:
  353.
-New energy source (inventor)
  1872-1898/John Worrall Keely
  New York Times, 4 Jan.1888, p.1; 18
  Mar.1888, p.1; 8 Apr.1888, p.2; 9
  Sep.1888, p.4; 26 Sep.1888, p.1; 12
  Nov.1888, p.4; 21 Nov.1888, p.4; 29
  Jan.1889, p.1; 28 Mar.1889, p.1; 18
  Dec.1889, p.1; 18 Dec.1890, p.1; 9
  Dec.1895, p.8; 29 Apr.1896, pp.4,14;
  3 May 1896, p.4; 5 May 1896, p.4;
  20 June 1897, p.5; 1 Dec.1897, p.6;
  26 Mar.1898, p.6; 19 Nov.1898, p.7;
  26 Nov.1898, p.6; 4 Jan.1899, p.2;
  20 Jan.1899, p.4; 26 Jan.1899, p.12;
  31 Jan.1899, p.7; and 7 May 1899,
  p.1.
  H.P. Blavatsky, The Secret Doctrine,
  2 vols. (London: Theosophical Soc'y,
  1888), 1:555-66.
  Clara Sophia Moore, Keely and His
  Discoveries: Aerial Navigation
  (London: Kegan Paul, Trench, Trübner, 1893).
  Charles Fort, The Books of Charles
  Fort (N.Y.: Holt, 1941), pp.1059-62.
  Gaston Burridge, "The Baffling Keely
  'Free Energy' Machines," Fate 10
  (July 1957):42-49. il.
  Arthur W.J.G. Ord-Hume, Perpetual
  Motion (London: Allen & Unwin, 1977).
-Out-of-body experience
  1750s
  Johann Heinrich Jung-Stilling, Theorie der Geisterkunde (Nürnberg: Raw,
  1808).
  Robert Dale Owen, Footfalls on the
  Boundary of Another World (Phila-

delphia: Lippincott, 1860), pp.317-
18.
-Parapsychology research
1884-1886/Seybert Commission
   Univ.of Pennsylvania, Seybert Commission for Investigating Modern Spiritualism, Preliminary Report of the
   Commission Appointed by the University of Pennsylvania to Investigate
   Modern Spiritualism (Philadelphia:
   Lippincott, 1887).
   A.B. Richmond, What I Saw at Cassadaga Lake (Boston: Colby & Rich,
   1888).
   A.B. Richmond, The Henry Seybert Be-
   quest, and What Has Become of It?
   (Boston: Banner of Light, 1896).
   Nandor Fodor, Encyclopaedia of Psy-
   chic Science (London: Arthurs,
   1933), pp.341-42.
1956-   /Parapsychology Lab, St. Jo-
seph's College/Carroll B. Nash
   Carroll B. & Catherine S. Nash,
   "Checking Success and the Relation-
   ship of Personality Traits to ESP,"
   J.ASPR 52 (1958):98-107.
   Carroll B. Nash, "Correlation between
   ESP and Religious Value," J.Para-
   psych. 22 (1958):204-209.
   C.B. Nash & M.G. Durkin, "Terminal
   Salience with Multiple Digit Tar-
   gets," J.Parapsych. 23 (1959):49-53.
   Carroll B. Nash, "Can Precognition
   Occur Diametrically?" J.Parapsych.
   24 (1960):26-32.
   Carroll B. Nash, "Two Exploratory
   Experiments in ESP: A Summary of
   Results," J.ASPR 54 (1960):136-37.
   Catherine S. & Carroll B. Nash, "An
   ESP Experiment with Targets That
   Differ in Degree of Similarity," J.
   ASPR 55 (1961):73-76.
   Carroll B. & Catherine S. Nash, "Neg-
   ative Correlation between the Scores
   of Subjects in Two Contemporaneous
   ESP Experiments," J.ASPR 56 (1962):
   80-83.
   Carroll B. Nash, "Retest of High
   Scoring Subjects in the Chesebrough-
   Pond's ESP Television Contest," J.
   ASPR 57 (1963):106-10.
   Carroll B. & Catherine B. Nash, "Ef-
   fect of Paranormally Conditioned
   Solution on Yeast Fermentation," J.
   Parapsych. 31 (1967):314.
   Carroll B. Nash, "Cutaneous Percep-
   tion of Color," J.ASPR 63 (1969):
   83-87.
   Carroll B. Nash, "Cutaneous Percep-
   tion of Color with a Head Box," J.
   ASPR 65 (1971):83-87.
   Rhea H. White, "Parapsychology Today,"
   in Edgar Mitchell, ed., Psychic Ex-
   ploration (N.Y.: Putnam, 1976 ed.),
   pp.195,200.
-Phantom sniper
1950, Nov.23-Dec.20
   "Philly Sniper Active," Doubt, no.32
   (1951):70.
-Plague of Japanese beetles

1978, July/Philadelphia Int'l Airport
   Wichita (Kan.) Eagle & Beacon, 8
   July 1978.
-Plague of slime
1957, March-1958/Edward Price/Mayfair
   (Editorial), Fate 11 (Oct.1958):6-8.
-Poltergeist
1866, Feb.1-4/S. Fifth St.
   Philadelphia Inquirer, 5 Feb.1866.
1930-1935
   Hereward Carrington & Nandor Fodor,
   Haunted People (N.Y.: Signet, 1968
   ed.), p.62.
-Precognition
1970s/Jack J. Gerber/1737 Chestnut St.,
Suite 1200
   Warren Smith, "Phenomenal Predictions
   for 1975," Saga, Jan.1975, pp.20,23.
-Reincarnation
1970s
   Ian Stevenson, Xenoglossy: A Review
   and Report of a Case (Charlottes-
   ville: Univ.of Virginia. 1974).
-Religious apparition and healing
1953, Sep.18/Fairmont Park
   (Editorial), Fate 7 (Mar.1954):12.
-Retrocognition
1893, March/Herman V. Hilprecht/Univ.
of Pennsylvania
   William Romaine Newbold, "Sub-con-
   scious Reasoning," Proc.SPR 12
   (Aug.1900):11,13-20.
   Walter Franklin Prince, ed., Noted
   Witnesses to Psychic Occurrences
   (Boston: Boston SPR, 1928), pp.25-
   30.
-Seance
1860s/Carl Schurz
   E. Sagerquist, "Abe Lincoln's Ghost,"
   Fate 1 (summer 1948):55.
1968, Aug.24/Olga Worrall
1968, Sep.17/Arthur Ford
   William V. Rauscher, "A Case of Cross
   Communication," Fate 23 (Oct.1970):
   84-88.
-Skyquake
1952, June 14
   "Bangs," Doubt, no.39 (1952):182.
1956, March 22/North Philadelphia Air-
port
   "Case 154," CRIFO Orbit, 4 May 1956,
   p.1.
-Spirit medium
1850s
   Anon., A History of the Recent Devel-
   opments in Spiritual Manifestations
   in the City of Philadelphia (Philadelphia: The Author, 1851).
   Eliab W. Capron, Modern Spiritualism:
   Its Facts and Fanaticisms (Boston:
   Bela Marsh, 1855), pp.251-69.
   Emma Hardinge Britten, Modern American Spiritualism (N.Y.: The Author,
   1870), pp.60,273-79.
1851-1880s/Henry Gordon
   Robert Hare, Experimental Investigation of the Spirit Manifestations
   (N.Y.:Partridge & Brittan, 1855).
   Emma Hardinge Britten, Modern American Spiritualism (N.Y.: The Author,

1870), pp.115-20.
Philadelphia Press, 19 Mar.1884.
Nandor Fodor, Encyclopaedia of Psychic Science (London: Arthurs,
1933), pp.153,195.
1860s/Augusta Currier
Emma Hardinge Britten, Modern American Spiritualism (N.Y.: The Author,
1870), p.277.
1870s/Nelson Holmes
Robert Dale Owen, "Touching Visitants
from a Higher Life," Atlantic Monthly 35 (1875):57-69.
Nandor Fodor, Encyclopaedia of Psychic Science (London: Arthurs,
1933), pp.171,191-92.
1870s/W.H. Powell
Nandor Fodor, Encyclopaedia of Psychic Science (London: Arthurs,
1933), p.295.
1950s-1971/Arthur Ford
Arthur Ford, Unknown But Known (N.Y.:
Harper & Row, 1968).
Allen Spraggett & William V. Rauscher,
Arthur Ford: The Man Who Talked
with the Dead (N.Y.: Signet, 1974).
-Spontaneous human combustion
1957, May 18/Anna Martin/5061 Reno St.
(Editorial), Fate 10 (Sep.1957):9-10.
"The Widow's Fiery Death," Fate 11
(June 1958):39.
-Telepathy research
1965/Jefferson Medical College
T.D. Duane & Thomas Behrendt, "Extra-
sensory Electroencephalographic In-
duction between Identical Twins,"
Science 150 (1965):367.
-Teleportation
1966, Aug./Chester Archey, Jr./North
Philadelphia
John A. Keel, Our Haunted Planet
(Greenwich, Ct.: Fawcett, 1972), p.
199.
-UFO (?)
1749, Dec.17
John F. Watson, Annals of Philadel-
phia and Pennsylvania in the Olden
Time, 2 vols. (Philadelphia: John
Penington & Uriah Hunt, 1844), 2:
369.
1953, Sep.28-Oct.1/Richard Regan/North
Philadelphia Airport/=meteor
Harlan Wilson, "There Are Meteors,
After All," Fate 7 (May 1954):40,
42-43.
1954, July
Donald E. Keyhoe, Flying Saucer Con-
spiracy (N.Y.: Holt, 1955), p.190.
-UFO (CE-1)
1947, July 5/Paul Moss
Philadelphia Inquirer, 6 July 1947.
1947, July 7/Henry Quin/Rising Sun x
Wyoming Ave.
Philadelphia Inquirer, 8 July 1947.
-UFO (CE-2)
1957, Oct.31/Stephen J. Brickner
(Letter), Fate 25 (Sep.1972):145-46.
1957, Nov.6
Philadelphia Inquirer, 7 Nov.1957.
1967, May 18/Ruth S. Smyth/Schuylkill

Expressway
"UAO Follows Moving Van," APRO Bull.
15 (May-June 1967):12.
-UFO (DD)
1947, July 4/M.K. Leisy/Market x 44th
St.
Philadelphia Inquirer, 5 July 1947.
1955, Nov.9/Charles W. James
"Case 113," CRIFO Orbit, 2 Dec.1955,
p.3.
1957, Oct.31/Stephen J. Brickner
(Letter), Fate 12 (Sep.1959):109-10.
1958, April/Stephen J. Brickner
(Letter), Fate 13 (Mar.1960):110-11.
1960, Oct.3/Stephen J. Brickner
(Letter), Fate 14 (Feb.1961):109-10.
1965, Nov.9/Walter Voelker
John G. Fuller, Incident at Exeter
(N.Y.: Berkley, 1967 ed.), pp.206-
207.
1967, Jan.5/Dolores Little
"Major Sighting Wave," UFO Inv. 3
(Jan.-Feb.1967):1,4.
1969, Nov.24/Laura E. Jackson/Twin
Bridges
(Letter), Fate 23 (Nov.1970):149-50.
-UFO (NL)
1947, July 5/Martin Forman/33d x Dauphin St.
Philadelphia Inquirer, 6 July 1947.
1947, July 8/Tom Morrell/Ridge x Midvale Ave.
Philadelphia Inquirer, 9 July 1947.
1947, Aug.6
Bruce S. Maccabee, "UFO Related Information from the FBI Files: Part
3," MUFON UFO J., no.121 (Dec.1977)
:10,14.
1949, July 10/George C. Wunsch/4101
Spruce St.
Kenneth Arnold & Ray Palmer, The Coming of the Saucers (Boise: The Authors, 1952), p.142.
1957, Aug.22/Donald E. Maring
(Letter), Fate 12 (Jan.1959):111-12.
1960, Aug./Stephen J. Brickner/Market
St. Post Office
(Letter), Fate 14 (June 1961):113-14.
1962, May 23/Zigmund Hill/4th x Ontario St.
"UAO over North Philly," APRO Bull.
10 (May 1962):2.
1963, Aug.26/Walter T. Jones, Jr.
"Another 'Mother' Ship," APRO Bull.
12 (July 1963):3.
n.d./Arthur Godfrey
"Arthur Godfrey Reveals UFO Encounter," UFO Inv. 3 (June-July 1965):1.
1966, April 26
(Letter), L.C., Fate 19 (Aug.1966):
126-28.
1967, spring/Stephen J. Brickner
(Letter), Fate 24 (Jan.1971):141-42.
1975, Oct.8/Michael Baldassaro
Timothy Green Beckley, "Saucers over
Our Cities," Saga UFO Rept. 4 (Aug.
1977):24,74.
-Windshield pitting
1952, March 27
"Ballisterics," Doubt, no.38 (1952):

163.
-Witch trial (hex)
  1683-1684/Margaret Mattson
    John F. Watson, Annals of Philadel-
    phia and Pennsylvania in the Olden
    Time, 2 vols. (Philadelphia: John
    Penington & Uriah Hunt, 1844), 1:
    265-66,274.
    George Smith, History of Delaware
    County, Pennsylvania (Philadelphia:
    H.B. Ashmead, 1862).
    William Renwick Riddell, "William
    Penn and Witchcraft," J.Am.Inst.
    Criminal Law & Criminology 18
    (1927):11-16.
    John F. Lewis, History of an Old
    Pennsylvania Land Title: 208 South
    Fourth Street (Philadelphia: Patter-
    son & White, 1934).
    George Lincoln Burr, Narratives of
    the Witchcraft Cases 1648-1706
    (N.Y.: Barnes & Noble, 1946), pp.
    85-87.

Phillipsburg
-UFO (?)
  1959, Jan.8/NW of town/=meteor?
    Donald H. Menzel & Lyle G. Boyd, The
    World of Flying Saucers (Garden
    City: Doubleday, 1963), p.113.

Phoenixville
-Ancient inscriptions
    Lawrence J. Mulligan, "New Findings
    in Pennsylvania: A Preliminary Re-
    port," NEARA J. 13 (winter 1979):
    59-62.
-UFO (CE-1)
  1973, Dec./Hwy.252
    King of Prussia Today's Post, 3 Dec.
    1973.
-UFO (NL)
  1972, Jan.14/Louelle Hynson/nr. high
  school
  1972, Jan.19/Albert Wissert, Jr.
    "Saucers Scan Skies Again," Caveat
    Emptor, no.4 (summer 1972):28-29.

Pike co.
-Humanoids
  1976, Jan.-Feb.
    Stan Gordon, "UFO/Creature Sightings
    Continue," Skylook, no.102 (May
    1976):10.

Pikes Creek
-UFO (?)
  1972, May 23
    "Press Reports," APRO Bull. 21 (July-
    Aug.1972):8.

Pine Grove
-UFO (CE-1)
  1973, Nov.4/Brian Hoffman/Hwy.501
    Curt K. Sutherly, "1973: Madness in
    the Keystone State," Official UFO 1
    (Apr.1976):20,21.

Pittsburgh
-Ancient inscription

ca.1820/Isaac Lea/Monongahela R.
  Isaac Lea, "Notice of a Singular Impression in Sand Stone," Am.J.Sci.,
  ser.1, 1 (1822):155. il.
-Animal ESP
  1945/Stanley C. Raye/340 North St.
    (Editorial), Fate 11 (June 1958):14.
-Crisis apparition
  n.d./Bertie Graham
    "Return of the General," Fate 7
    (Nov.1954):23.
-Fall of ice
  1850, Sep.27
    New York Herald, 4 Oct.1850, p.6.
-Fall of mud
  1953, May
    "Falls," Doubt, no.41 (1953):221,222.
-Fall of mussels, frogs and stones
  1834, Aug.9/Mr. Montgomery
    London (Eng.) Times, 30 Sep.1834, p.
    3, quoting Pittsburgh Gazette (un-
    dated).
-Ghost
  1947-1963/Jane Dempsey
  1963/KDKA-TV station
    Hans Holzer, Ghosts I've Met (N.Y.:
    Ace, 1965 ed.), pp.63-64,131-32.
-Glowing tombstone
  1953/St. Michael's Cemetery
    (Editorial), Fate 6 (Dec.1953):6-7.
-Haunt
  1900s/Henry Goetz/Tabernacle Church,
  Broad St.
    Henry Goetz & W.E. Farbstein, "Foot-
    steps in the Church," Fate 9 (Nov.
    1956):81-83.
  1954-1956/Harvey H. Mitchell/1724 Har-
  cor Dr.
    (Editorial), Fate 9 (Apr.1956):8-9,
    quoting Pittsburgh Press (undated).
  1963-1966/Sena Szurszewski/Hawthorne
  St.
    Sena Szurszewski, "Message from a
    Sobbing Ghost," Fate 21 (Apr.1968):
    67-72.
    (Letter), Ida Hunt, Fate 21 (Sep.
    1968):133.
    (Letter), Sena Szurszewski, Fate 21
    (Dec.1968):134,145.
    (Letter), Joan Finneran, Fate 22
    (Apr.1969):126-27.
    (Letter), D.M., Fate 22 (Apr.1969):
    128.
  1964-1966/Evelyn Kennedy/Mountview Pl.
    Hans Holzer, Gothic Ghosts (N.Y.:
    Pocket Books, 1972), pp.102-17.
-Healing
  1948-1976/Kathryn Kuhlman
    Kathryn Kuhlman, I Believe in Mira-
    cles (Englewood Cliffs, N.J.: Pren-
    tice-Hall, 1962).
    Allen Spraggett, The Unexplained
    (N.Y.: Signet, 1968 ed.), pp.156-78.
    (Letter), Fate 21 (June 1968):126-28.
    Allen Spraggett, Kathryn Kuhlman: The
    Woman Who Believes in Miracles (N.Y.:
    World, 1970).
    William A. Nolen, Healing: A Doctor
    in Search of a Miracle (N.Y.: Ran-
    dom House, 1975).

(Letter), Howard Hammitt, Jr., _Fate_ 28 (July 1975):115-16.

Antoinette May, "In Search of a Miracle: The Riddle of Kathryn Kuhlman," _Psychic_ 7 (Apr.1976):27-31. il.

Ruth Kramer Ziony, "How Kathryn Kuhlman Carried On," _Coast_ 17 (Aug. 1976):40-43.

-Mystery accident
ca.1945/Rudolph Bogovich/Westinghouse Co.
   "First Prize," _Doubt_, no.12 (spring-summer 1945):170, quoting _Denver (Colo.) Post_ (undated).

-Mystery animal
1963/Highland Park Zoo
   "Fortean Items," _Saucer News_ 10 (Sep.1963):17.

-New energy source (inventor)
1921-1928/Lester J. Hendershot
   New York Times, 25 Feb.1928, p.1; 26 Feb.1928, p.1; 27 Feb.1928, p.19; 28 Feb.1928, p.19; 1 Mar.1928, p. 16; 2 Mar.1928, p.2; 7 Mar.1928, p. 14; and 10 Mar.1928, p.1.
   F.D. Fleming, "The Hendershot Motor Mystery," _Fate_ 3 (Jan.1950):8-12.
   Harold T. Wilkins, _Flying Saucers Uncensored_ (N.Y.: Pyramid, 1967 ed.), pp.22-24.
   Gaston Burridge, "The Hendershot Motor Riddle," _Fate_ 10 (Feb.1957):41-48.
   (Letter), Arthur C. Aho, _Fate_ 15 (Feb.1962):130-31.

-Phantom dog
1908, July 26/Lt. Shields/Lincoln Ave.
   New York World, 29 July 1908.
   New York Tribune, 29 July 1908, p.7.

-Poltergeist
1971, summer-1972/Naomi Cramer
   Henry W. Pierce, "RSPK Phenomena Observed Independently by Two Families," _J.ASPR_ 67 (1973):86-101.

-Precognition
1940, Feb./Israel J. Weinstein/Penn Ave.
   Israel J. Weinstein & W.E. Farbstein, "The Day My Premonitions Came True," _Fate_ 13 (Oct.1960):46-48.
1955, Aug./Ray Hammerstrom/Jones & Laughlin Steel Co.
   Frank Edwards, _Strange World_ (N.Y.: Lyle Stuart, 1964), p.192.

-Psychokinesis
1948-1955/University of Pittsburgh
   R.A. McConnell, "Remote Night Tests for ESP," _J.ASPR_ 49 (1955):99-108.
   R.A. McDonnell, R.J. Snowdon & K.F. Powell, "Wishing with Dice," _J. Experimental Psychology_ 50 (1955): 269-75.

-Spontaneous human combustion
1907, Jan./Mrs. Albert Houck
   Toronto (Ont.) Globe, 28 Jan.1907.
n.d./Carl Brandt
   "Pyrotics," _Doubt_, no.29 (1950):26.

-UFO (?)
1897, April 19/=hoax

Pittsburgh Commercial Gazette, 20 Apr.1897.
1950, Dec.8
   "The Cloth Speaks," _Doubt_, no.32 (1951):67.
1953
   Harold T. Wilkins, _Flying Saucers on the Attack_ (N.Y.: Ace, 1967 ed.), p.146.
1957, Oct.22
   Richard Hall, ed., _The UFO Evidence_ (Washington: NICAP, 1964), p.15.
1969, Nov.2
   Pittsburgh Press, 2 Nov.1969.

-UFO (?) and Men-in-black
1968, June 7
   Brad Steiger & Joan Whritenour, _Flying Saucer Invasion: Target--Earth_ (N.Y.: Award, 1969), pp.124-25.

-UFO (DD)
1956, Aug.11/Florence Stauffer
   "Case 186," _CRIFO Orbit_, 7 Sep.1956, p.3, quoting _Pittsburgh Sun-Telegraph_ (undated).
1957, Nov.11
   Richard Hall, ed., _The UFO Evidence_ (Washington: NICAP, 1964), p.167.

-UFO (NL)
1939, July/J.M. Williams
   Gordon I.R. Lore, Jr. & Harold H. Deneault, Jr., _Mysteries of the Skies: UFOs in Perspective_ (Englewood Cliffs, N.J.: Prentice-Hall, 1968), p.138.
1958, Aug.22/Clark C. McClelland/Allegheny Observatory
   (Letter), _Fate_ 12 (Apr.1959):111-14.
1975, Jan.31
   Stan Gordon, "Pennsylvanians Report 300 Sightings," _Skylook_, no.88 (Mar.1975):13.
1978, March 1/Glenn A. Ricci/Highland Reservoir
   Pittsburgh Post-Gazette, 4 Mar.1978.
   J. Allen Smith, "Pennsylvania Report," _APRO Bull._ 27 (Nov.1978):4-5.

Pleasant Hills
-Bird attack
1977, Feb./Rick True
   Larry E. Arnold, "Birds on the Attack," _Fate_ 31 (Aug.1978):54,58.

Pleasant Mount
-Ancient inscription
1974, summer/James Knapp
   Honesdale _Wayne Independent_, 22 Mar. 1977, p.1.
   Salvatore Michael Trento, _The Search for Lost America_ (Chicago: Contemporary, 1978), pp.86-87. il.

Pleasureville
-Clairvoyance
1907, Nov.18/Susan Dellinger
   York Gazette, 29 Nov.1907.
   "An Apparently Clairvoyant Dream," _J.ASPR_ 3 (1909):290-302.

Plymouth
-UFO (NL)
1979, Jan.9/John Carsner
Hatboro Today's Spirit, 10 Jan.1979.

Pocopson twp.
-UFO (NL)
1973, Oct.16/Kathy E. McMaster/Pocop-
son Home
West Chester Daily Local News, 17
Oct.1973.

Polk twp.
-Moving rock
1867-   /Richard Slyhoff
"The Man Who Fled the Devil," Fate
13 (June 1960):81.

Poplar Grove
-UFO (CE-1)
1947, June 25/Mrs. G.E. Hart
Pittsburgh Post-Gazette, 8 July 1947.

Portage
-Fall of ice
1960, July 3/Dixie Lewis/608 Makin St.
(Editorial), Fate 13 (Oct.1960):11.

Port Allegany
-Ghost
n.d./John Roberson/Two Mile
Robert R. Lyman, Amazing Indeed!
(Coudersport: Potter Enterprise,
1973), pp.30-31.
-UFO (NL)
1978, Oct.25/Kenneth Howard
Bradford Era, 26 Oct.1978.
Port Allegany Reporter-Argus, 2 Nov.
1978.

Port Vue
-Fall of brown substance
1947, summer-Oct.
"Run of the Mill," Doubt, no.20
(1948):303.

Potter co.
-Acoustic anomaly
1863, July 3
Robert R. Lyman, Forbidden Land
(Coudersport: Potter Enterprise,
1971), pp.37-38.
-Ancient road
Boon Road/=built by French in 1756
Robert R. Lyman, Forbidden Land
(Coudersport: Potter Enterprise,
1971), pp.10-13.
Robert R. Lyman, Amazing Indeed!
(Coudersport: Potter Enterprise,
1973), pp.1-4.
-Radionics
1949-1950/H.H. Armstrong
Edward Wriothesley Russell, Report on
Radionics (London: Spearman, 1973),
pp.54,62-67,233-34.

Pottstown
-Phantom panther
1945, Nov./John Hipple/Sheep's Hill
Lebanon Daily News, 14 Nov.1945.

Curt Sutherly, "The 'Thing' of
Sheep's Hill," Pursuit 9 (Jan.1976)
:9-10.
1973, March 14-30
Curt K. Sutherly, "1973: Madness in
the Keystone State," Official UFO
1 (Apr.1976):20,21.
-Ringing rocks
Ivan T. Sanderson, Things (N.Y.:
Pyramid, 1967), p.50.
-Sheep mutilation
1968, Nov.21/Roland Hobson/7 mi.from
town
Lebanon Daily News, 22 Nov.1968.

Pottsville
-Fall of insects
1840, Dec.26
"More Notes of Charles Fort," Doubt,
no.16 (1946):245,246, quoting Niles
Nat'l Register (undated).
-Hex
1911, Sep.
Philadelphia Public Ledger, 24 Sep.
1911; 27 Sep.1911; 30 Sep.1911; and
1 Oct.1911.
-UFO (NL)
1973, Nov.19/R. Michael DeLong/S of
town
Shenandoah Evening Herald, 24 Nov.
1973.

Punxsutawney
-UFO (CE-2)
1975, Sep.20
Stan Gordon, "Strange Reports from
Pennsylvania," Skylook, no.99
(Feb.1976):13.

Quakertown
-Fall of snails
1946, Oct.14
"Fish and Snail Falls," Doubt, no.
17 (1947):253.
-Inner development
1868-   /Rosicrucian Fraternity/Bev-
erly Hall/Box 220
George Lippard, Paul Ardenheim, the
Monk of Wissahickon (Philadelphia:
T.B. Peterson, 1848).
F.B. Dowd, Temple of the Rosy Cross
(Philadelphia: J.R. Rue, Jr., 1882).
"The Propaganda for Reform," J.Am.
Medical Ass'n 81 (1923):2050-53.
Paschal Beverly Randolph, Soul (Qua-
kertown: Confederation of Initiates,
1932).
R. Swinburne Clymer, The Rosicrucian
Fraternity in America, 2 vols.
(Quakertown: Rosicrucian Fraternity,
1935).
Paschal Beverly Randolph, Ravalette:
The Rosicrucian's Story (Quakertown:
Philosophical Pub.Co., 1939).
Albert G. Mackey, Charles J. McClen-
achan & Reyes de Leon, "A History
of Rosicrucianism," Fate 14 (Apr.
1961):74,80-81.
J. Gordon Melton, Encyclopedia of
American Religions, 2 vols. (Wil-

mington, N.C.: Consortium, 1978),
2:179-80.

Quarryville
-Skyquake
  1954, Sep.28
  "Case 51," CRIFO Newsl., 4 Feb.1955,
    p.4.
-UFO (NL)
  1966, Nov.17
  Quarryville Sun & Christiana Ledger,
    14 Jan.1967.

Reading
-Healing
  1900s/Joseph B. Hageman
  Arthur Lewis, Hex (N.Y.: Trident,
    1969), pp.34-37, quoting North Amer-
    ican, 22 May 1900.
-UFO (NL)
  1972, Aug.20/S. 16th St.
  "Press Reports," APRO Bull. 21
    (Sep.-Oct.1972):11.

Red Lion
-UFO (CE-1)
  1978, April/Robert S. Hake/E. Market St.
  York Dispatch, 4 Apr.1978.
-UFO (NL)
  1978, Feb.9/Bruce Englar/Winterstown Rd.
  York Dispatch, 10 Feb.1978.

Renovo
-Anomalous artifact
  =iron chain in rock/=19th c. logger's
    chain
  "A Chain in Rock," Pursuit 3 (Apr.
    1970):45.
  Richard T. Grybos, "The Chain in the
    Rock," Pursuit 4 (July 1971):68-69.
-Clairvoyance
  1950, Jan./Dorcie Calhoun
  Philip Bartholomew, "Dream That Paid
    Off," Fate 4 (Nov.-Dec.1951):13.
-Giant bird
  1962, July 4/H.M. Cranmer/Hevner Run
    (Letter), Fate 16 (Sep.1963):116-17.
-UFO (DD)
  1953, Oct.2
    (Letter), H.M. Cranmer, Fate 7 (Feb.
    1954):108.
  1961, July 18
    (Letter), H.M. Cranmer, Fate 14 (Dec.
    1961):103-104.

Republic
-Humanoid
  1976
  Brownsville Telegraph, 21 May 1977.

Richlandtown
-Skyquake
  1978, Nov.19/Richlandtown Pike
  Quakertown Free Press, 20 Nov.1978.

Robesonia
-UFO (CE-3)
  1973, March 28/Clyde O. Donahower
  Easton Express, 29 Mar.1973.

Rockwood
-UFO (NL)
  1978, Jan./Helen Meyer
  Meyersdale Republican, 5 Jan.1978.

Roulette
-Ancient smelted iron
  n.d./Lanninger Creek
  Robert R. Lyman, Amazing Indeed!
    (Coudersport: Potter Enterprise,
    1973), pp.5-6.
-Clairvoyance
  1830s-1886/Laroy Lyman
  Robert R. Lyman, Forbidden Land
    (Coudersport: Potter Enterprise,
    1971), pp.65-71.
-UFO (CE-1)
  ca.1901/Hollis C. Lyman
  Robert R. Lyman, Amazing Indeed!
    (Coudersport: Potter Enterprise,
    1973), pp.34-35.

Safe Harbor
-Petroglyphs
  Donald A. Cadzow, Safe Harbor Re-
    ports, 2 vols. (Harrisburg: Pennsyl-
    vania Hist.& Museum Comm'n, 1934-
    35). il.

Saint Mary's
-UFO (CE-3)
  1950, March 15/Craig Hunter/S on Hwy.
  255
  St. Mary's Daily Press, 16-17 Mar.
    1950; and 21 Mar.1950.
  Clearfield Press, 31 Mar.1950.
  Kenneth Arnold & Ray Palmer, The Com-
    ing of the Saucers (Boise: The Au-
    thors, 1952), p.147.
  Isabel Davis & Ted Bloecher, Close
    Encounter at Kelly and Others of
    1955 (Evanston: Center for UFO
    Studies, 1978), pp. iv-v.
-UFO (NL)
  1969, June 28/Mark R. Herbstritt
  "The Reader Writes," Skylook, no.23
    (Oct.1969):21.

Saint Thomas
-UFO (NL)
  1975, Nov.19
  "UFO Central," CUFOS News Bull., 1
    Feb.1976, p.13.

Salladasburg
-Fall of unknown objects
  1972, Jan.24/Norma Flook/S on Hwy.287
  Robert R. Lyman, Amazing Indeed!
    (Coudersport: Potter Enterprise,
    1973), pp.99-100.

Sayre
-Giant human skeletons
  Tioga Point
  Robert R. Lyman, Forbidden Land
    (Coudersport: Potter Enter rise,
    1971), pp.6-7.

Scranton
-UFO (NL)

1970, March 21/Charles Reina
"Object over Scranton, Penna.," APRO
Bull. 18 (Mar.-Apr.1970):1,3.

Seneca
-Phantom wolf and calf killing
1977, Feb.8/Dale Fox
(Editorial), Fate 30 (July 1977):12-
14, quoting Tri-City Times-News
(undated).
-UFO (NL)
1977, Feb.7/William Franklin
(Editorial), Fate 30 (July 1977):10-
12, quoting Tri-City Times-News
(undated).

Seward
-UFO (NL)
1978, Oct.25
Latrobe Bulletin, 27 Oct.1978.

Sewickley
-UFO (NL)
1974, Jan.28
Stan Gordon, "Pennsylvania Sightings
Continue," Skylook, no.78 (May
1974):12.

Shamokin
-Phantom image
1977, April 7-   /Frank R. Knutti/Holy
Trinity Episcopal Church
Shamokin News-Item, 15 Apr.1977; 23
Apr.1977; 28 Apr.1977; and 5 May
1977.
Barrie E. Schlenker, "The Face on the
Altar Cloth," Fate 31 (Feb.1978):82-
86. il.
Harrisburg Sunday Patriot-News, 5
Mar.1978.
"The Shamokin Image," Fortean Times,
no.26 (summer 1978):33-36. il.
-UFO (CE-1)
1967, March 9/Forrest Kerstetter
"UFO Responds to Light," UFO Inv. 3
(Mar.-Apr.1967):8.
-UFO (NL)
1964, May 2/Melvin Kerstetter
"News Briefs," Saucer News 11 (Sep.
1964):18.
1967, Jan.18/James A. Krebs/Irish Val-
ley
1967, Jan.19/Belford Ensinger
Mt. Carmel Item, 19 Jan.1967.
"UFO Responds to Light," UFO Inv. 3
(Mar.-Apr.1967):8.
Donald E. Keyhoe & Gordon I.R. Lore,
Jr., UFOs: A New Look (Washington:
NICAP, 1969), p.43.

Sharon
-Fall of frogs
ca.1910/Pearl Potter
(Letter), Fate 13 (Sep.1960):114.
-Reincarnation research
1940s/Asa Roy Martin
Asa Roy Martin, Researches into Rein-
carnation and Beyond (Sharon: The
Author, 1942).
Margaret Gaddis, "We Remember Other

Lives," Fate 7 (Jan.1954):86,89-91.
-UFO (CE-3)
1897, April
Ceres Mail, 28 Apr.1897.
-UFO (NL)
1967, Sep.
Pittsburgh Post-Gazette, 9 Sep.1967.

Sharon Hill
-UFO (NL)
1975, Oct.8
"UFO Central," CUFOS News Bull., 1
Feb.1976, p.8.

Shenandoah
-Fall of blue ice
1969, Oct.13/Frank Kuzma/430 W. Centre
St.
Shenandoah Herald, 14 Oct.1969.

Sheppton
-Phantom
1963, Aug.13-27/David Fellin
Bill Schmeer, "The Entombed Miners'
Staircase to Heaven," Fate 18 (Mar.
1965):28-37.
Hans Holzer, Ghosts I've Met (N.Y.:
Ace, 1965 ed.), pp.71-75, quoting
AP release, 28 Aug.1963.

Shermans Dale
-UFO (CE-2)
1978, Jan.20/Pat Palakovic
New Bloomfield Perry County Times,
29 June 1978.

Shinglehouse
-Bird attack
1960, March/Carrie Gross
Larry E. Arnold, "Birds on the Attack," Fate 31 (Aug.1978):54,56.

Shirksville
-Sheep mutilation
1973, March
Curt K. Sutherly, "1973: Madness in
the Keystone State," Official UFO 1
(Apr.1976):20,21.

Shoemakersville
-UFO (NL)
1975, Nov.1
"From the Center for UFO Studies,"
Flying Saucer Rev. 21 (Apr.1976):
24,25-26.

Shrewsbury
-UFO (?)
1973, Oct.16/=bean picker
York Dispatch, 17 Oct.1973.

Siegersville
-Dowsing
1920s-1950s/Ralph E. Diefenderfer
Chester S. Geier, "Dowser Locates
Boy's Body," Fate 11 (Nov.1958):84-
86.

Silver Lake twp.
-Humanoid

1838
   John Green, The Sasquatch File (Ag-
      assiz, B.C.: Cheam, 1973), p.7, quo-
      ting Dorchester County (Md.) Aurora,
      and Montrose Spectator (undated).

Silver Spring
-UFO (NL)
   1972, March 25/Lamb's Gap
      Harrisburg Patriot-News, 26 Mar.1972.

Slatington
-UFO (CE-2)
   1975, Feb.26/Chris Newhard
      (Letter), Saga UFO Rept. 2 (winter
      1975):4.

Slippery Rock
-UFO (NL)
   1973/Robert L. Watson
      Butler Eagle, 3 Jan.1979.

Smock
-Humanoid
   1976
      Brownsville Telegraph, 21 May 1977.

Snow Shoe
-Archeological site and White Indian myth
   Baretown/S on Game Lands Rd.
      Henry W. Shoemaker, Pennsylvania
         Mountain Stories (Reading, Pa.:
         Reading Times, 1913).
      W. Mead Stapler, "Baretown: A Penn-
         sylvania Legend," NEARA Newsl. 7
         (Mar.1972):9-15. il.

Snydertown
-UFO (NL)
   1978, Sep.28
      Shamokin News-Item, 29 Sep.1978.

Somerset
-Haunt
   1966/Mr. Manner
      Hans Holzer, Gothic Ghosts (N.Y.:
         Pocket Books, 1972), pp.1-9.
-UFO (CE-1)
   1978, April 18/Harold Pyle
      Somerset American, 18 Apr.1978.

South Union twp.
-UFO (NL)
   1974, Feb.27
      Stan Gordon, "Pennsylvania Sightings
         Continue," Skylook, no.78 (May
         1974):12.

Spangler
-UFO (DD)
   1974, April 7
      Barnesboro Star, 11 Apr.1974.

Spencer
-Clairvoyance
   1975, Aug.3/Phil Jordan
      Phil Jordan, "Psychic's Search for a
         Missing Child," Fate 30 (Aug.1977):
         60-65.

Springfield
-UFO (CE-1)
   1962, April 24/Joseph A. Gasslein, Jr.
      Thomas M. Olsen, ed., The Reference
         for Outstanding UFO Sighting Reports
         (Riderwood, Md.: UFO Information
         Retrieval Center, 1966), pp.78-80.

Spring Grove
-Healing
   1960s/Leah Frank/Rohrbaugh Convales-
      cent Home
      Arthur Lewis, Hex (N.Y.: Trident,
         1969), pp.219-25.
-Humanoid
   1978, March/nr. P.H. Glatfelter Paper
      Co.
      York Dispatch, 9 Mar.1978.
-UFO (CE-1)
   1965, Oct.16/elementary school
      "Record Year for New UFO Evidence,"
         UFO Inv. 3 (Nov.-Dec.1965):2,3.

Spring Mills
-Whirlwind anomaly
   1966, April 17/Lee Dobson/3 mi.NE on
      Brush Mt.
      (Editorial), Fate 19 (Sep.1966):10-
         14.

Spring twp.
-UFO (NL)
   1976, Feb.3
      "Noteworthy UFO Sightings," Ufology
         2 (summer 1976):63.

Sterling Run
-Giant human skeleton
   1873
      Robert R. Lyman, Amazing Indeed!
         (Coudersport: Potter Enterprise,
         1973), p.9.

Stillwater
-UFO (NL)
   1972, May
      "Press Reports," APRO Bull. 21 (July-
         Aug.1972):8.

Strinestown
-UFO (CE-1)
   1978, April 2/Norma Smith/Old Susque-
      hanna Trail
      York Dispatch, 3 Apr.1978.
-UFO (NL)
   1978, March 30
      York Dispatch, 3 Apr.1978.

Stroudsburg
-Rock pillars
      Sharat K. Roy, "Columnar Structure
         in Limestone," Science 70 (1929):
         140-41.
-UFO (NL)
   1973, March 21/Richard Wolbert
      Stroudsburg Pocono Record, 21 Mar.
         1973, p.1.
   1973, March 27
      Stroudsburg Pocono Record, 28 Mar.
         1973.

-Weather control
1900, April 28/brewery
Pittsburgh Sun-Telegraph, 29 Apr.
1900.

Sullivan co.
-UFO (CE-2)
1964, April, May 8/ground markings only
"More News Briefs," Saucer News 11
(Sep.1964):23.

Summerdale
-UFO (NL)
1968, Jan.12/Gertrude Purdue
"New Close-Ups, Pacings," UFO Inv. 4
(Mar.1968):1.

Sweden Valley
-Fall of metallic object
1970, Aug.3/Philip Lehman
1970, Aug./Donald Kelsey
Bradford Era, 12 Aug.1970.
Coudersport Potter Enterprise, 19
Aug.1970.
"Introducing 'Fafrotskies,'" Pursuit
3 (Oct.1970):76-77.
Robert R. Lyman, Amazing Indeed!
(Coudersport: Potter Enterprise,
1973), p.99.
Larry E. Arnold, "The Pennsylvania
Triangle," Saga UFO Rept. 6 (Oct.
1978):16,62-64.

Tarentum
-UFO (?)
1957, Nov.6
Aimé Michel, Flying Saucers and the
Straight-Line Mystery (N.Y.: Criter-
ion, 1958), p.256.

Tidioute
-UFO (DD)
1965, Nov.9/Jerry Whitaker
"New Clues to UFO Electrical Interference," UFO Inv. 3 (Nov.-Dec.1965)
:3.

Titusville
-Fall of scoria
1947, June 21/Donald Bunce
Philadelphia Bulletin, 9 July 1947.
-Spirit medium
1867/Abram James
"The 'Spirit Guide' Struck Oil,"
Fate 13 (May 1960):34.

Tobyhanna
-UFO (DD)
1956, Oct.29/Harvey L.
Stroudsburg Daily Record, 14 Nov.
1956.

Towanda
-UFO (CE-1)
1947, July 6/Mrs. A.C. Smith
Harrisburg Patriot, 7 July 1947.
-UFO (CE-2)
1966, April 25/Robert W. Martz
Berthold Eric Schwarz, "UFOs: Delu-
sion or Dilemma?" in Beyond Condon

(Flying Saucer Rev. special issue,
no.2, June 1969), pp.46-47.
John A. Keel, UFOs: Operation Trojan
Horse (N.Y.: Putnam, 1970), p.145.
-UFO (NL)
1975, Jan.2
Robert A. Goerman, "The UFO Modus Op-
erandi: January 1975," Official UFO
1 (Aug.1976):46,47, quoting Towanda
Daily Review (undated).

Trees Mills
-UFO (CE-1)
1972, May 11
Stan Gordon, "UFOs in Pennsylvania,"
Skylook, no.60 (Nov.1972):13.

Tremont
-Healing
1950s/Sofia Bailer
Vincent R. Tortora, "Pennsylvania
Dutch 'Pow-wow' Healing," Fate 9
(Feb.1956):41-45.

Turtle Creek
-UFO (CE-2)
1962, June/Gregory Sciotti
John A. Keel, Strange Creatures from
Time and Space (Greenwich, Ct.:
Fawcett, 1970), p.169.

Ulysses
-Anomalous hole in ground
1874, April/Asa Raymond
Robert R. Lyman, Forbidden Land
(Coudersport: Potter Enterprise,
1971), pp.50-51.

Union Dale
-UFO (DD)
1958, Oct.27
Jacques Vallee, Passport to Magonia
(Chicago: Regnery, 1969), p.272.

Uniontown
-Humanoid
1973, Nov.
John Green, Sasquatch: The Apes Among
Us (Seattle: Hancock House, 1978),
p.263.
-UFO (?)
1951, Nov.26
Coral & Jim Lorenzen, UFOs: The Whole
Story (N.Y.: Signet, 1969), p.41.
-UFO (CE-3)
1973, Oct.25/George A. Kowalczyk, Jr.
Uniontown Evening Standard, 27 Oct.
1973.
"Witnesses Watch UFO Landing in Penn-
sylvania: Hairy Creatures Seen,"
Skylook, no.73 (Dec.1973):8.
"Are Creatures & UFO's Related?" Sky-
look, no.75 (Feb.1974):6-7.
Berthold Eric Schwarz, "Berserk: A
UFO-Creature Encounter," Flying Sau-
cer Rev. 20 (July 1974):3-11. il.
1974, Feb.6
Leonard H. Stringfield, Situation
Red: The UFO Siege (N.Y.: Fawcett
Crest, 1977 ed.), pp.85-86.

Upland
-Fall of anomalous meteorite
    1966, April 25/John Wesley Bloom/Sal-
    vation Army Camp
        John A. Keel, UFOs: Operation Trojan
        Horse (N.Y.: Putnam, 1970), pp.145-
        46.

Upper Black Eddy
-Ringing rocks
        Ossining (N.Y.) Citizen-Register, 24
        Apr.1956.
        Ivan T. Sanderson, Things (N.Y.: Pyr-
        amid, 1967), pp.50-58.
        "Ringing Rocks Again," Pursuit 1 (30
        Sep.1968):12-13.
        "Society News," Pursuit 2 (Jan.1969)
        :17.
        "Ringing Rocks," Pursuit 3 (Oct.
        1970):89.
        John Gibbons & Steven Schlossman,
        "Rock Music," Natural History 79
        (Dec.1970):36-41. il.
        "Why the Rocks Ring," Pursuit 4
        (Apr.1971):38-41.
        "Ringing Rocks," Pursuit 4 (Oct.
        1971):97.
        "The Ringing Rocks: Another Aspect,"
        Pursuit 5 (Jan.1972):6-7.

Upper Chichester twp.
-UFO (NL)
    1973, Oct.6
        Floyd Murray, "Over the Keystone
        State," Caveat Emptor, no.11 (Jan.-
        Feb.1974):35.

Venango co.
-Phantom wolf
    n.d./Cornplanter's Reserve
        Charles M. Skinner, American Myths
        and Legends, 2 vols. (Philadelphia:
        Lippincott, 1903), 1:254-56.

Verona
-Humanoid
    1973, Sep.22/Mr. Baird
        Allen V. Noe, "ABSMal Affairs in
        Pennsylvania and Elsewhere," Pursuit
        6 (Oct.1973):84,87-88. il.

Wallaceton
-UFO (NL)
    1973, Oct.18/John Gray
        DuBois Courier Express, 19 Oct.1973.

Walnutport
-Haunt
    1962, May
        (Editorial), Fate 15 (Sep.1962):14-
        15, quoting Allentown Morning Call
        (undated).
-UFO (DD)
    1966, Aug.23/Bonita Rodgers
        Otto O. Binder, "'Oddball' Saucers...
        That Fit No Pattern," Fate 21 (Feb.
        1968):54,55.

Waltz Mills
-UFO (CE-1)

1974, April 13/nuclear plant
    Stan Gordon, "Pennsylvania Sightings
    Continue," Skylook, no.82 (Sep.
    1974):15.
-UFO (NL)
    1974, April 14/I-70
        Stan Gordon, "Pennsylvania Sightings
        Continue," Skylook, no.82 (Sep.
        1974):15.

Warren
-UFO (?)
    1954, June
        Donald E. Keyhoe, Flying Saucer Con-
        spiracy (N.Y.: Holt, 1955), p.164.
-UFO (CE-1)
    1870s/Lewis M. Hazeltine/Kiantone Rd.
        (Letter), Kate R. Hazeltine, Fate
        17 (Oct.1964):117-18.
-UFO (NL)
    1947, July 3/Richard Betts
        Pittsburgh Post-Gazette, 8 July 1947.

Washington
-Fall of colored rain
    1957, Oct.25
        "All About Sputs," Doubt, no.56
        (1958):460,469.
-UFO (NL)
    1975, Jan.10/McClain Fram Rd.
        Robert A. Goerman, "The UFO Modus Op-
        erandi: January 1975," Official UFO
        1 (Aug.1976):46,65, quoting Wash-
        ington Observer-Reporter (undated).

Washington co.
-Humanoid
    1975, July 10
    1975, July 14/I-70
        Stan Gordon, "Creature Sightings Re-
        ported Again in Pennsylvania," Sky-
        look, no.93 (Aug.1975):19.

Washington Crossing
-Photographic anomaly
    1973, May 29/Stella Lansing
        Berthold Eric Schwarz, "Stella Lan-
        sing's Clocklike UFO Patterns,"
        Flying Saucer Rev. 20 (Jan.1975):3,
        4.
-UFO (NL)
    1978, April 26/Gene H. Epstein/Hwy.532
        Trenton (N.J.) Times, 29 Apr.1978.

Waterford
-UFO (CE-2)
    1972, April 21
        Stan Gordon, "UFOs in Pennsylvania,"
        Skylook, no.56 (July 1972):12,13.

Wattsburg
-UFO (CE-1)
    1932, June/Reuben D. Knight
        Gordon I.R. Lore, Jr. & Harold H. Den-
        eault, Jr., Mysteries of the Skies:
        UFOs in Perspective (Englewood
        Cliffs, N.J.: Prentice-Hall, 1968),
        pp.109-10.

Wayne
-UFO (DD)
1959, Aug.10
    Richard Hall, ed., The UFO Evidence
    (Washington: NICAP, 1964), p.156.

Waynesboro
-Clairvoyance
1977, Jan./Dorothy Allison
    (Editorial), Fate 30 (July 1977):33-
    34, quoting Waynesboro Record-Her-
    ald (undated).
-Haunt
n.d.
    Sally M. Barach, Haunts of Adams and
    Other Counties (Indiana, Pa.: A.G.
    Halldin, 1972), pp.24-25.

Wernersville
-Haunt and lost treasure
n.d.
    Charles M. Skinner, Myths and Legends
    of Our Own Land, 2 vols. (Philadel-
    phia: Lippincott, 1896), 2:288-89.

West Chester
-UFO (NL)
1975, July 23
    "UFO Central," CUFOS News Bull., 15
    Nov.1975, p.14.

West Decatur
-UFO (CE-1)
1977, March 29/Burton Woods/Hwy.970
    "UFOs of Limited Merit," Int'l UFO
    Reporter 2 (May 1977):5.
    T. Scott Crain, "Witness Runs Under-
    neath Object," MUFON UFO J., no.117
    (Aug.1977):16-18. il.

West Elizabeth
-Haunt
1960s/Helen Tosi
    Hans Holzer, Ghosts I've Met (N.Y.:
    Ace, 1965 ed.), p.64.

West Hickory
-Giant human skeleton
1869, Dec.28/William Thompson
    Oil City Times, 1 Jan.1870.

West Hill
-UFO (NL)
1968, Feb.24/Karl E. Will
    "French General, Scientists, Report
    UFOs," UFO Inv. 4 (May-June 1968):3.

West Mifflin
-UFO (NL)
1975, Nov./Frank Dorsey
    (Letter), Ufology 2 (spring 1976):49.

Westmoreland co.
-Humanoid
1973, Aug.25
    Pat Morrison, "UFOs and Bigfoot Crea-
    tures: An Adventure into the Unex-
    plained," in Bigfoot: Tales of Un-
    explained Creatures (Rome, O.: Page
    Rsch.Library, 1978), pp.25,34-36.

-Paranormal memory
1870s-1880s/Daniel McCartney
    J.H. Creighton, "A Prodigy of Mem-
    ory," Knowledge 11 (1888):274-75.

West Newton
-UFO (CE-2)
1974, March 13
    Stan Gordon, "Pennsylvania Sightings
    Continue," Skylook, no.78 (May
    1974):12,13.

West Point
-UFO (CE-1)
1966, June 3
    Jacques Vallee, Passport to Magonia
    (Chicago: Regnery, 1969), p.331.
-UFO (NL)
1973, Jan.25
    Stan Gordon, "Radar Failures Delay
    Planes--UFOs Reported in Pennsyl-
    vania Sky," Skylook, no.64 (Mar.
    1973):10.

Whitney
-Humanoid
1973, Sep.2/Chester Yothers
    Allen V. Noe, "ABSMal Affairs in
    Pennsylvania and Elsewhere," Pur-
    suit 6 (Oct.1973):84,87.

Wilcox
-UFO (NL)
1977, May 3
    "UFOs of Limited Merit," Int'l UFO
    Reporter 2 (June 1977):3.

Wilkes-Barre
-Hex
1931, April/Minnie Dilley
    William Seabrook, Witchcraft: Its
    Power in the World Today (N.Y.:
    Lancer, 1968 ed.), p.271.
-Mystery holes in clothing
1973/General Services Bldg.
    "Holey Terror," Fate 27 (July 1974):
    83.
-Skyquake
1954, Dec.14
    "Case 54," CRIFO Newsl., 4 Feb.1955,
    p.4.
-UFO (?)
1954, June
    Donald E. Keyhoe, Flying Saucer Con-
    spiracy (N.Y.: Holt, 1955), p.164.
-UFO (NL)
1952, July 8/Joseph J. Greiner
    Richard Hall, ed., The UFO Evidence
    (Washington: NICAP, 1964), p.45.
1965, Aug.11/Ray Hoffman/S of town
    "Pennsylvania Pilot Chases UFO," Sau-
    cer News 12 (Dec.1965):22-23.
    Jerome Clark, "The Greatest Flap Yet?
    Part 2," Flying Saucer Rev. 12 (Mar.-
    Apr.1966):8,10.
-Whirlwind anomaly
1891, March 16
    Brooklyn (N.Y.) Eagle, 17 Mar.1891.

Williams twp.
-UFO (NL)
1973, March 21
Stroudsburg Pocono Record, 21 Mar.
1973, p.1.

Williamsburg
-UFO (CE-2)
1974, July 22/George M. Frasher
George D. Fawcett, "The 'Unreported'
UFO Wave of 1974," Saga UFO Rept. 2
(spring 1975):50,53.

Williamsport
-Hex
1935, Feb./Dave Snyder
William Seabrook, Witchcraft: Its
Power in the World Today (N.Y.:
Lancer, 1968 ed.), p.271.
-Skyquake
1973, Oct.17
Floyd Murray, "Over the Keystone
State," Caveat Emptor, no.11 (Jan.-
Feb.1974):35,36.
-UFO (?)
1951, Nov.
San Francisco (Cal.) Chronicle, 4
Nov.1951.
1968, July 2/=meteor
Harrisburg News, 3 July 1968.
-UFO (DD)
1952, April 17
Williamsport Sun, 17 Apr.1952.
-UFO (NL)
1959, Feb.24/Peter W. Killian/13 mi.W
Detroit (Mich.) Times, 25 Feb.1959.
New York Herald-Tribune, 25 Feb.1959;
and 1 Mar.1959.
"AF Spokesman Ridicules UFO Witness-
es, Says Some Are Drunks," UFO Inv.
1 (Feb.-Mar.1959):1-3.
Long Island (N.Y.) Daily Press, 24
Mar.1959.
Curtis Fuller, "Saucers Trail Air-
liner," Fate 12 (Aug.1959):25-31.
Donald E. Keyhoe, Flying Saucers: Top
Secret (N.Y.: Putnam, 1960), pp.27-
36.
F.A. Kirsch, "Air Force Right on
Killian 'Saucer'?" Flying Saucers,
Aug.1960, p.17.
Donald H. Menzel & Lyle G. Boyd, The
World of Flying Saucers (Garden
City: Doubleday, 1963), pp.52-56.
Richard Hall, ed., The UFO Evidence
(Washington: NICAP, 1964), pp.42-43,
116-17.
1976, Jan.15
"Noteworthy UFO Sightings," Ufology
2 (summer 1976):62.
1976, May 26
"Noteworthy UFO Sightings," Ufology
2 (fall 1976):61.

Willow Grove
-UFO (CE-1)
1966, May 21/William C. Powell
Donald E. Keyhoe & Gordon I.R. Lore,
Jr., UFOs: A New Look (Washington:
NICAP, 1969), pp.6-7.

-UFO (NL)
1979, Jan.9/Walter Green/Pennsylvania
Turnpike
King of Prussia Today's Post, 11 Jan.
1979.

Windgap
-UFO (NL)
1973, March 21/Control Center
Stroudsburg Pocono Record, 21 Mar.
1973, p.1.

Winfield
-Ancient inscription
1921/Elwood D. Hummel/Susquehanna R.
(Editorial), Fate 9 (Sep.1956):13.

Wyalusing
-Electromagnetic anomaly
1962, April 27
(Letter), Charles D. Hastings, Fate
15 (Oct.1962):120.

Yeadon
-Fall of ice
1957, Sep.25/Elisha L. Parker
(Editorial), Fate 11 (Feb.1958):15.

York
-Animal ESP
1940, April/Gertrude I. Smith/1425 W.
King St.
York Gazette & Daily, 4 Apr.1940.
Gertrude Mack Mummert, "The Psychic
Hens Get the Telepathic Message,"
Fate 25 (May 1972):94-97.
-Ball lightning
1921, summer/John Henry Lehn
Vincent H. Gaddis, Mysterious Fires
and Lights (N.Y.: Dell, 1968 ed.),
pp.54-55, quoting Round Robin, Oct.
1958.
-Haunt
n.d./center square
Sally M. Barach, Haunts of Adams and
Other Counties (Indiana, Pa.: A.G.
Halldin, 1972), p.22.
-Healing
n.d./Erwin B. Emig
Arthur Lewis, Hex (N.Y.: Trident,
1969), pp.15-16,246-55.
-Hex
1920s/Andrew C. Lenhart/Linden St.
New York Times, 10 Dec.1928, p.10.
Arthur Lewis, Hex (N.Y.: Trident,
1969), pp.44-51.
1928, Nov.27/Nelson D. Rehmeyer
New York Times, 1 Dec.1928, p.3; 2
Dec.1928, p.2; 3 Dec.1928, p.29; 4
Dec.1928, p.14; and 10 Jan.1929, p.1.
A. Monroe Aurand, Jr., The "Pow-wow"
Book (Harrisburg: Aurand, 1929).
Philadelphia Inquirer, 6 Aug.1939.
C.N.W. Maxwell, "The Pennsylvania Hex
Murder," Fate 2 (May 1949):26-31.
Arthur Lewis, Hex (N.Y.: Trident,
1969).
-UFO (?)
1954, Feb.22
Donald E. Keyhoe, Flying Saucer Con-

spiracy (N.Y.: Holt, 1955), p.100.
1968, July 2/Gloria A. Jajich/=meteor
"Some Recent Fireballs," Sky & Tele-
scope 36 (Sep.1968):195.
1972, April/Curtis K. Sutherly/nr. L.
Redman
(Letter), Fate 29 (Apr.1976):128-29.
(Letter), Jan Kauffman, Fate 29
(Oct.1976):116-18.
(Letter), Fate 30 (Apr.1977):118-20.
-UFO (NL)
1966, June 12
York Gazette & Daily, 13 June 1966.
1975, Oct.23
"UFO Central," CUFOS News Bull., 1
Feb.1976, p.9.
1978, March 31/Keith Oberdick/Danskin
Co.
York Daily Record, 3 Apr.1978; and
5 Apr.1978.

York co.
-Ancient inscriptions
1940s/William W. Strong
Mechanicsburg News, 17 Apr.1948; 14
Oct.1960; and 18 Oct.1960.
Joseph C. Ayoob, Were the Phoenicians
the First to Discover America? (Ali-
quippa, Pa.: The Author, 1950).
Frederick J. Pohl, Atlantic Crossings
Before Columbus (N.Y.: W.W. Norton,
1961), pp.23-35. il.
Charles Micheal Boland, They All Dis-
covered America (N.Y.: Pocket Books,
1963 ed.), pp.40-47,399. il.
John Witthoft, "Alleged Phoenician
Inscriptions from York County, Penn-
sylvania," Pennsylvania Arch. 34,
no.2 (1964):93-94.
O.G. Landsverk, "The Symbols of Mech-
anicsburg," NEARA Newsl. 5 (June
1970):38-40. il.
Robert E. Stone, "Mechanicsburg
Stones: Two Distinct Types," NEARA
Newsl. 5 (Sep.1970):53.
Leon L. Morrill, Jr., "The Three Cat-
egories of the Mechanicsburg Stones,"
NEARA Newsl. 6 (Mar.1971):11.
Charles Milton, "The Mechanicsburg
Stones: A Geological Report," NEARA
Newsl. 6 (Sep.1971):56-57.
Barry Fell, "Epigraphy of the Susque-
hanna Steles," Occ.Pub.Epigraphic
Soc'y 2, no.45 (May 1975).
"The Celt-Iberian Culture of New Eng-
land, 1st Millenium B.C.," NEARA J.
10 (summer 1975):2,3-4.
Barry Fell, America B.C. (N.Y.: Quad-
rangle, 1976), pp.50-51,54,169,170.
il.
Salvatore Michael Trento, The Search
for Lost America (Chicago: Contem-
porary, 1978), pp.69-71.
-Radionics
1952-1953/Henry Gross
Edward Wriothesley Russell, Report on
Radionics (London: Spearman, 1973),
pp.69-72,242-47.

Youngstown
-Humanoid
1973, Sep.1/cemetery
Allen V. Noe, "ABSMal Affairs in
Pennsylvania and Elsewhere," Pur-
suit 6 (Oct.1974):84,87.
-UFO (CE-1)
1917, summer/John Boback/Mt. Braddock
Orvil R. Hartle, A Carbon Experiment?
(LaPorte, Ind.: The Author, 1963),
pp.156-57.
Gordon I.R. Lore, Jr. & Harold R. Den-
eault, Jr., Mysteries of the Skies:
UFOs in Perspective (Englewood
Cliffs, N.J.: Prentice-Hall, 1968),
pp.104-105.

Youngwood
-Humanoid
1975, July 2
Stan Gordon, "Creature Sightings Reported Again in Pennsylvania," Skylook, no.93 (Aug.1975):19.

B. Physical Features

Alvin R. Bush L.
-Giant bird
1969, summer/Albert Schoonover
Robert R. Lyman, Amazing Indeed!
(Coudersport: Potter Enterprise,
1973), p.95.

Big Valley
-Humanoid
1973
Allen V. Noe, "And Still the Reports
Roll In," Pursuit 7 (Jan.1974):16,
17.

Blue Mts.
-Haunt
1756, winter/mission house
Charles M. Skinner, American Myths
and Legends, 2 vols. (Philadelphia:
Lippincott, 1903), 1:248-51.

Brandywine Creek
-Precognition
1777, Sep./Lord Percy
Charles M. Skinner, Myths and Legends
of Our Own Land, 2 vols. (Philadelphia: Lippincott, 1896), 1:158-60.

Broad Mt.
-Animal ESP
1960s/Gus Malaska
(Editorial), Fate 17 (Nov.1964):10-
12.

Conewago Creek
-Haunt
n.d./bridge
n.d./Conewago Chapel
Sally M. Barach, Haunts of Adams and
Other Counties (Indiana, Pa.: A.G.
Halldin, 1972), pp.18,21-22.

Crooked Mt.
-UFO (CE-2)
1973, Oct.15/Edward Deutsch
Wilkes-Barre Times-Leader, 18 Oct.
1973.
"E-M Case in Pennsylvania," APRO
Bull. 22 (May-June 1974):1,3.
Timothy Green Beckley, "Strange Ef-
fects from Flying Saucers," Saga
UFO Rept. 2 (winter 1974):32,69-70.

Dark Hollow
-Phantom airplane
1955, Nov.18
"The 'Ghost Plane' Incident," CRIFO
Orbit, 6 Jan.1956, pp.2-3.

Depues Ferry
-UFO (CE-2)
1949, Nov.10
Leonard H. Stringfield, Inside Saucer Post...3-0 Blue (Cincinnati:
CRIFO, 1957), p.49, quoting Fantastic Universe (undated).

Devil's Race Course
-Ringing rocks
Ivan T. Sanderson, Things (N.Y.:
Pyramid, 1967), p.50.

East Mt.
-UFO (NL)
1974, Feb.24/Donald Decker
Scranton Tribune, 25 Feb.1974.

Fishing Creek
-Fall of snowballs
n.d./Robert R. Lyman
Robert R. Lyman, Amazing Indeed!
(Coudersport: Potter Enterprise,
1973), p.99.
-Haunt
1890s/Peter Church
Robert R. Lyman, Forbidden Land
(Coudersport: Potter Enterprise,
1971), pp.78-79.
-Phantom deer
1895/Zella Lyman Tauscher
Robert R. Lyman, Forbidden Land
(Coudersport: Potter Enterprise,
1971), p.80.

Huntingdon Creek
-UFO (?)
1968, July 28
Otto O. Binder, "The Mystery of Underground UFO Bases," Saga UFO Rept.
1 (spring 1974):22,44.

Ice Mt.
-Ice anomaly
Coudersport Ice Mine
Charles Arthur Vandermuelen, "An Ice
Mine That Freezes in Summer and
Melts in Winter," Sci.Am. 114 (1916)
:470,495. il.
Robert R. Lyman, Amazing Indeed!
(Coudersport: Potter Enterprise,
1973), pp.84-86.
Larry E. Arnold, "The Pennsylvania

Triangle," Saga UFO Rept. 6 (Oct.
1978):16,17-19.

Jordan's Valley
-Haunt
1917, fall-1971/Patricia Valley/rail-
road house
Patricia Valley, "Our Old Railroad
House: Depot for Ghosts," Fate 26
(Sep.1973):43-48.

Larry's Creek
-Giant bird
1971, Aug.7/Clair E. Koons
Robert R. Lyman, Amazing Indeed!
(Coudersport: Potter Enterprise,
1973), p.97.

Laurel Hill State Park
-UFO (CE-2)
1978, Jan./Larry Miller
Meyersdale Republican, 5 Jan.1978.

Little Pine Creek
-Giant bird
1968-1969/Mrs. John Boyle
Robert R. Lyman, Amazing Indeed!
(Coudersport: Potter Enterprise,
1973), p.97.

Muddy Creek
-Humanoid
1972/Robert Chance
Gettysburg Times, 24 July 1978, p.1.

Oil Creek
-Ancient oil wells
J.S. Newberry, "Ancient Mining in
North America," Am.Antiquarian 11
(1889):164-67.

Pine Creek
-Giant bird
1960s/nr. Tomb Run
Robert R. Lyman, Amazing Indeed!
(Coudersport: Potter Enterprise,
1973), p.96.

Presque Isle
-UFO (CE-3)
1966, July 31/Betty Jean Klem/Beach #6
Erie Daily Times, 1-2 Aug.1966.
Buffalo (N.Y.) Courier-Express, 3-4
Aug.1966.
"The Presque Isle Landing," APRO Bull.
15 (July-Aug.1966):3-4.
"The Creature (?) Returns," APRO Bull.
15 (Sep.-Oct.1966):5.
John A. Keel, "New Landing and Crea-
ture Reports," Flying Saucer Rev.
12 (Nov.-Dec.1966):5-8.
Lloyd Mallan, "UFO Hoaxes and Hallu-
cinations: Part II," Sci.& Mech. 38
(Apr.1967):44-47.
Berthold Eric Schwarz, "UFOs: Delu-
sion or Dilemma?" in Beyond Condon
(Flying Saucer Rev., special issue
no.2, June 1969), pp.46,49-51.
Brad Steiger, ed., Project Blue Book
(N.Y.: Ballantine, 1976), betw.pp.

56-57. il.
-UFO (NL)
1973, Oct.14/Marie Magee
Erie Daily Times, 15 Oct.1973.

Promised Land State Park
-Humanoid tracks
1976, Jan./Anthony Torriero, Jr.
West Chester Daily Local News, 24
Jan.1976.

Pymatuning L.
-UFO (CE-2)
1959, Jan.13/Robert Collins
Greenville Record-Argus, 31 Jan.1959.

Sartwell Creek
-UFO (DD)
1952, Oct.14
Robert R. Lyman, Amazing Indeed!
(Coudersport: Potter Enterprise,
1973), p.82.

Saylors L.
-UFO (NL)
1973, March 1/Mrs. Howard Pfeiffer
Stroudsburg Pocono Record, 2 Mar.
1973.
Easton Press, 2 Mar.1973.
Allentown Morning Call, 5 Mar.1973.
"'Flying Christmas Trees' over Penn-
sylvania," APRO Bull. 21 (Jan.-Feb.
1973):6.
Nat'l Enquirer, 13 May 1973.
1973, March 4/Carlo Uccio
Stroudsburg Pocono Record, 5 Mar.
1973.

Settler's Cabin Park
-Humanoid
1976, Feb.29
Stan Gordon, "UFO/Creature Sightings
Continue," Skylook, no.102 (May
1976):10.

Sheep Rock Shelter
-Archeological site
W. Fred Kinsey, "The Sheep Rock: A
Dry Shelter in Central Pennsylvan-
ia," Bull.Eastern States Arch.Fed.,
no.19 (1960):12.
E.J. Stackhouse & M.W. Corl, "The
Discovery of the Sheep Rock Shelter
(Site 36 Hu-1)," Pennsylvania Arch.
33, no.1 (1962):1-13. il.
Joseph W. Michels & Ira F. Smith,
eds., Archaeological Investigations
in the Sheep Rock Shelter, 2 vols.
(University Park: Pennsylvania
State Univ., 1967).

Shenango R.
-UFO (CE-2)
1967, Sep.7/Earl Holby
Brad Steiger & Joan Whritenour, Allen-
de Letters: New UFO Breakthrough
(N.Y.: Award, 1968), p.50.

Shoop site
-Archeological site

John Witthoft, "A Paleo-Indian Site
in Eastern Pennsylvania: An Early
Hunting Culture," Proc.Am.Phil.
Soc'y 96 (1952):464-95. il.

South Mt.
-Hex legends
Hexenshdedl
Charles M. Skinner, American Myths
and Legends, 2 vols. (Philadelphia:
Lippincott, 1903), 1:267-70.
-Ringing rocks
Ivan T. Sanderson, Things (N.Y.:
Pyramid, 1967), p.50.
-Shape-shifting
n.d.
Moritz Jagendorf, Upstate Downstate
(N.Y.: Vanguard, 1949), p.196.

Spring Mt.
-Ancient stone circle
Lawrence J. Mulligan, "New Findings
in Pennsylvania: A Preliminary Report," NEARA J. 13 (winter 1979):
59-60.

Tyler State Park
-Bird attacks
1978, April-May
Harrisburg Patriot, 26 May 1978, p.1.
"Birds and the Bees," Res Bureaux
Bull., no.38 (7 Sep.1978):3-4.

Valley Forge State Park
-Phantom
1778, winter/George Washington
George Lippard, The Legends of the
American Revolution (Philadelphia:
T.B. Peterson, 1847).
Ida Clarke, Men Who Wouldn't Stay
Dead (N.Y.: A. Ackerman, 1945).
Simon Mennick, "George Washington's
Psychic Vision of America's Future,"
Saga UFO Rept. 4 (Aug.1977):44-45,
60-62.

Wesuaking L.
-UFO (NL)
1975, Jan.2
Robert A. Goerman, "The UFO Modus Operandi: January 1975," Official UFO
1 (Aug.1976):46,47, quoting Towanda
Daily Review (undated).

Wolf Pond
-Lake monster
1887, Sep.
Charles M. Skinner, Myths and Legends
of Our Own Land, 2 vols. (Philadelphia: Lippincott, 1896), 2:299.

D. Unspecified Localities

-Dowsing
Alfred L. Shoemaker, "Water Witching," Pennsylvania Folklife 12
(fall 1961):25-27.

-Hex
John George Hohman, Pow-Wows: or,
Long Lost Friend (Westminster, Md.:
The Author, 1855 ed.).
W.J. Hoffman, "Folk Medicine of the
Pennsylvania Germans," Proc.Am.Phil.
Soc'y 26 (1889):329-53.
Julius F. Sachse, The German Pietists
of Provincial Pennsylvania (Phila-
delphia: The Author, 1895).
Emma G. White, "Folk Medicine Among
the Pennsylvania Germans," J.Am.
Folklore 10 (1897):78-80.
New York Evening World, 2 Jan.1929.
A. Monroe Aurand, Jr., The "Pow-Wow"
Book (Harrisburg: The Author, 1929).
Ann Hark, Hex Marks the Spot (Phila-
delphia: Lippincott, 1938).
Fredric Klees, The Pennsylvania
Dutch (N.Y.: Macmillan, 1950).
Paul Frazier, "Some Lore of Hexing
and Powwowing," Midwest Folklore 2
(1952):101-107.
Richard H. Shaner, "Living Occult
Practices in Dutch Pennsylvania,"
Pennsylvania Folklife 12 (fall 1961)
:62-63.
Don Yoder, "Witch Tales from Adams
County," Pennsylvania Folklife 12
(summer 1962):29-37.
Henry F. Hoffbower, "Hex Signs: Penn-
sylvania's Painted Prayers," Fate
18 (Oct.1965):46-52.
Arthur Lewis, Hex (N.Y.: Trident,
1969).
Marcia Westkott, "Powwowing in Berks
County," Pennsylvania Folklife 19
(winter 1970):2-9.
Richard H. Shaner, "Recollections of
Witchcraft in the Oley Hills," Penn-
sylvania Folklife 21 (Folk Festival
Supp., 1972):39-43.
Richard H. Shaner, "The Wizard of
the Oley Hills," Am.Folklife 3
(Jan.1975):5-7.
Lester P. Breininger, "Hohman's
Occult Tradition," Am.Folklife 3
(Feb.1975):4-5.

-Shape-shifting myth
Henry W. Shoemaker, "Neighbors: The
Werwolf in Pennsylvania," New York
Folklore Quar. 7 (1951):145-55.
Henry W. Shoemaker, "Another Werwolf,"
New York Folklore Quar. 7 (1951):
299.
Henry W. Shoemaker, "Werwolves in
the Pennsylvania Wilds, Once More,"
New York Folklore Quar. 8 (1952):
133-34.

-UFO (DD)
1914
Ray Palmer, "1914 UFO Photo Puzzles
Experts," Flying Saucers, Aug.1966,
pp.7-9. il.

NEW JERSEY

A. Populated Places

Andover
-Ghost
  18th c.
    Charles M. Skinner, Myths and Legends
    of Our Own Land, 2 vols. (Philadel-
    phia: Lippincott, 1896), 1:138-39.

Asbury Park
-Paranormal amnesia
  1967, Aug.22-Oct.24/Bruce Burkan
    John A. Keel, Our Haunted Planet
    (Greenwich, Ct.: Fawcett, 1971), pp.
    197-98.
-Skyquake
  1977, Dec.2
  1977, Dec.22
  1978, Jan.5
    U.S. Naval Rsch.Laboratory, NRL In-
    vestigations of East Coast Acoustics
    Events (Washington: Gov't Printing
    Office, 1978), pp.134,139.
-UFO (?)
  1966, April 25
    John A. Keel, UFOs: Operation Trojan
    Horse (N.Y.: Putnam, 1970), p.145.

Atlantic City
-Ball lightning
  1931, April/Reading Railroad station
    Charles Fitzhugh Talman, "Nature's
    Bag of Tricks," Reader's Digest 26
    (June 1935):89,91.
-Haunt
  1974-1976/Joseph Putnam/Fire Engine
  Co.3
    "Ghostly Gang Frustrates Firemen,"
    Probe the Unknown 4 (Jan.1976):10-
    11.
-Seance
  1922, June 17/Lady Doyle
    Sir Arthur Conan Doyle, The Edge of
    the Unknown (N.Y.: Berkley, 1968
    ed.), pp.28-31.
    Milbourne Christopher, Houdini: The
    Untold Story (N.Y.: Pocket Books,
    1970 ed.), pp.175-78.
-Skyquake
  1955, Nov.1
    "Bangs," Doubt, no.51 (1956):382.
-UFO (CE-1)
  1976, Jan.20/Frank Ingergiola
    Atlantic City Press, 21 Jan.1976.
-UFO (R-V)
  1967, Feb.24/Robert King/Garden State
  Parkway
    "FAA Confirms Radar Case," UFO Inv.
    3 (Mar.-Apr.1967):6.

Avalon twp.
-Plague of wildcats
  1977, July/Katherine Stickney/Avalon
  Manor

Dallas (Tex.) Times-Herald, 14 July
1977.
(Editorial), Fate 30 (Nov.1977):30-
34, quoting Philadelphia (Pa.) Inquirer (undated).

Batsto
-Flying humanoid
  1935/William Bozarth
    Alexander L. Crosby, ed., Matawan,
    1686-1936 (Newark: Newick Bros.,
    1936), pp.20-22.

Bayonne
-UFO (?)
  1962, Dec.15-16/Ronald Gounad
    Richard Hall, ed., The UFO Evidence
    (Washington: NICAP, 1964), p.96.
-UFO (DD)
  1966, Nov.19/Dave Millinger
    "Continuing Saucer Flap in Northern
    New Jersey," Saucer News 14 (spring
    1967):30,31.
-UFO (NL)
  1962, Nov.18/Bruce Fox
    Richard Hall, ed., The UFO Evidence
    (Washington: NICAP, 1964), p.96.

Bayville
-Fall of fiberglass
  1964, Nov.9/A. Kraig/Garden State Parkway
    "New 'Physical Evidence,'" Saucer
    News 12 (Mar.1965):17-18.
    "News Briefs," Saucer News 12 (June
    1965):22,23.
    (Letter), R.C. Stephen, Jr., Saucer
    News 12 (Sep.1965):7-8. il.

Beach Haven
-Roman coin
    Barbara Corcoran, "Ancient Coins
    Found Along the New Jersey Coast,"
    NEARA J. 10 (winter-spring 1976):49.
-UFO (CE-4)
  1974, July 7/Charles Book
    "Contactee," Ohio Sky Watcher 2 (Mar.
    1976):12-14.
-UFO (NL)
  1933, summer/Frank Van Keuren
    Coral & Jim Lorenzen, UFOs: The Whole
    Story (N.Y.: Signet, 1969), pp.19-20.

Bedminster
-Phantom automobile
  1957, spring/Sgt. Cramer
    Howard Menger, From Outer Space to
    You (Clarksburg, W.V.: Saucerian,
    1959).

Belmar
-Out-of-body experience
  1970s/Dorie Lawrence
    Herbert B. Greenhouse, The Astral

Journey (N.Y.: Avon, 1976 ed.), pp.
218-23.
-Skyquake
1977, Dec.2
U.S. Naval Rsch.Laboratory, NRL In-
vestigations of East Coast Acoustics
Events (Washington: Gov't Printing
Office, 1978), pp.135-36.

Belvidere
-UFO (CE-1)
1966, May 5
"Saucer Briefs," Saucer News 13
(fall 1966):26,28.

Bergen co.
-Haunt
1961
Hans Holzer, Ghost Hunter (N.Y.:
Ace, 1963 ed.), pp.76-82.

Bergenfield
-Precognition
1956, Nov./Mrs. G. Zabriskie
Laura A. Dale, Rhea White & Gardner
Murphy, "A Selection of Cases from
a Recent Survey of Spontaneous ESP
Phenomena," J.ASPR 56 (1962):3,17-
20.

Bernardsville
-Humanoid
1976, Aug.
Bernardsville News, 12 Aug.1976.

Bevans
-Ancient stone chamber
W of town
Edward J. Lenik, "The Sandyston Stone
Chamber in New Jersey," NEARA Newsl.
7 (Sep.1972):56-57. il.

Beverly
-Contactee
1920-1960s/Albert Coe
Albert Coe, The Shocking Truth (Beverly: Book Fund, 1969).

Blackwood
-UFO (NL)
1973, April 21/Alfred Egbert III
(Letter), Saga UFO Rept. 3 (Aug.
1976):4-6.

Blairstown
-UFO (NL)
1965, Sep.25/Ivan T. Sanderson/SW on
Blairstown-Delaware Rd.
Ivan T. Sanderson, Uninvited Visitors
(N.Y.: Cowles, 1967), pp.22-25.

Bloomfield
-UFO (?)
1966, Nov.
New York Post, 10 Nov.1966. il.
"Continuing Saucer Flap in Northern
New Jersey," Saucer News 14 (spring
1967):30,31. il.
-UFO (NL)
1958, Aug.19/Frank Sturm, Jr.

(Letter), Fate 12 (Jan.1959):112-13.

Bloomingdale
-UFO (?)
1963, Nov.15/Peter Valko
Jacques Vallee, Passport to Magonia
(Chicago: Regnery, 1969), pp.295-
96.

Boonton
-Phantom
1971, Nov./Lisa Terreri
Lisa Terreri, "The Demon That Comes
in the Night: My Mare," Fate 26
(Aug.1973):71-73.
-UFO (NL)
1978, March 31/Dixon Bros. yard
Denville Morris County Citizen, 12
Apr.1978.

Bordentown
-Flying humanoid
ca.1830s/Joseph Bonaparte
James F. McCloy & Ray Miller, Jr.,
The Jersey Devil (Wallingford, Pa.:
Middle Atlantic, 1976), p.31.

Brick twp.
-UFO (?)
1979, Jan.3/Joseph DeAngelo
New York News World, 5 Jan.1979.
New York Daily News, 5 Jan.1979.

Bridgeton
-Chicken mutilations
1909, Jan.21
Philadelphia (Pa.) Public Ledger, 22
Jan.1909.
James F. McCloy & Ray Miller, Jr.,
The Jersey Devil (Wallingford, Pa.:
Middle Atlantic, 1976), p.58.
-Fall of black rain
1965, June 10/Justin Case
(Letter), Saucer News 12 (Sep.1965):
6.
"'Fortean' Sample Is Difficult to
Analyze," Saucer News 12 (Dec.1965):
27.
-Flying humanoid
1873-1874, winter
James F. McCloy & Ray Miller, Jr.,
The Jersey Devil (Wallingford, Pa.:
Middle Atlantic, 1976), p.34.
-UFO (R)
1946, Jan.31
Philadelphia (Pa.) Inquirer, 1 Feb.
1946.

Bridgewater twp.
-UFO (NL)
1977, Aug.10
"UFOs of Limited Merit," Int'l UFO
Reporter 2 (Sep.1977):Newsfront sec.

Brookdale
-Ancient megalith
astronomical alignment
Elizabeth L. Coombs, "The Stone Pylon
of Brookdale, N.J.," NEARA J. 12
(spring 1978):69-70.

Brown's Mills
-Flying humanoid
  ca.1804/Stephen Decatur/Hanover Furnace
  1850s/Hannah Butler
    James F. McCloy & Ray Miller, Jr.,
    The Jersey Devil (Wallingford, Pa.:
    Middle Atlantic, 1976), pp.33-34.
-Flying humanoid (skeleton)
  1957, Oct.31/Wharton Tract/=hoax
    Jerome Clark & Loren Coleman, "The
    Jersey Devil," Beyond Reality, no.4
    (May 1973):35,50-52, quoting uniden-
    tified newspaper, 31 Oct.1957.
    James F. McCloy & Ray Miller, Jr.,
    The Jersey Devil (Wallingford, Pa.:
    Middle Atlantic, 1976), pp.94,97.

Burlington
-Flying humanoid
  1909, Jan.17/Joseph W. Lowden/High St.
  1909, Jan.20
  1909, Jan.21/Mrs. Michael Ryan/Penn x
  York St.
    Philadelphia (Pa.) Public Ledger, 22
    Jan.1909.
    James F. McCloy & Ray Miller, Jr.,
    The Jersey Devil (Wallingford, Pa.:
    Middle Atlantic, 1976), pp.42,50,
    58-59.
-Flying humanoid myth
  1735/Mother Leeds
    James F. McCloy & Ray Miller, Jr.,
    The Jersey Devil (Wallingford, Pa.:
    Middle Atlantic, 1976), pp.24-25.
-Humanoid tracks
  1909, Jan.17-18
    James F. McCloy & Ray Miller, Jr.,
    The Jersey Devil (Wallingford, Pa.:
    Middle Atlantic, 1976), pp.42-44.
-Skyquake
  1979, Feb.8
    Philadelphia (Pa.) Bulletin, 9 Feb.
    1979, p.9.
-Spirit medium
  1880-1888/Jonathan M. Roberts
    Jonathan M. Roberts, Antiquity Un-
    veiled (Philadelphia: Oriental,
    1892).

Burlington co.
-Humanoid tracks and animal disappearances
  1966, March-April/Alfred Potter
    Trenton Evening Times, 15 Apr.1966.

Burrs Mills
-Flying humanoid
  1899
    Charles M. Skinner, American Myths
    and Legends, 2 vols. (Philadelphia:
    Lippincott, 1903), 1:243.

Butler
-UFO (NL)
  1966, Aug.16
    John A. Keel, "The Night the Sky
    Turned On," Fate 20 (Sep.1967):30,36.

Caldwell
-Fall of fishing line

1970, Aug.2-31/A.P. Smith/85 Forest Ave.
    Caldwell Progress, 6 Aug.1970.
    "John Keel Writes," INFO J., no.7
    (fall 1970):11-12.
    "Sky-Lines," Pursuit 4 (Jan.1971):6.
    "More Sky-Lines," Pursuit 5 (July
    1972):53-54.

Camden
-Flying humanoid
  1909, Jan.19
  1909, Jan.21/Mr. Rouh/Black Hawk Social
  Club/Ferry Ave.
  1909, Jan.21/Mary Sorbinski/nr. Kaighn
  Hill
  1909, Jan.22/Mrs. Stenburg/Ferry Ave.
  x Vanhook St.
  1909, Jan.22/Louis Strehr/Third St.
    Philadelphia (Pa.) Public Ledger, 22
    Jan.1909.
    James F. McCloy & Ray Miller, Jr.,
    The Jersey Devil (Wallingford, Pa.:
    Middle Atlantic, 1976), pp.48,55,
    66-67,69.
-Haunt
  1967, July/Edna Martin/522 N. Fifth St.
    Hans Holzer, Gothic Ghosts (N.Y.:
    Pocket Books, 1972), pp.76-85.
-Humanoid tracks
  1909, Jan.19/Ms. Pine
  1909, Jan.19/Dialogue's Shipyard
    Philadelphia (Pa.) Public Ledger, 22
    Jan.1909.
    James F. McCloy & Ray Miller, Jr.,
    The Jersey Devil (Wallingford, Pa.:
    Middle Atlantic, 1976), p.47.
-UFO (?)
  1957, Aug.23/Ballassar Bottos/=balloon?
    "Saucers on the Hot Line," in Frank
    Bowers, ed., The True Report on Fly-
    ing Saucers (Greenwich, Ct.: Faw-
    cett, 1967), p.33. il.
-UFO (DD)
  1947, July 5/Ellen Desrocher/915 N.
  20th St.
    Philadelphia (Pa.) Inquirer, 7 July
    1947.
  1948, July 4/Edward E. Thompson/John-
  son Park
    (Letter), Fate 1 (winter 1949):93-94.
-Windshield pitting
  1927, Nov.-1928, winter
    New York Post, 26 Jan.1928.
    Charles Fort, The Books of Charles
    Fort (N.Y.: Holt, 1941), pp.701,
    893-94.

Cartaret
-Giant bird
  1977, Feb./=barn owl
    Gary Szelc, "On Tracking the 'Monkey
    Bird,'" Vestigia Newsl., no.3 (sum-
    mer-fall 1977):4.

Cedar Grove
-UFO (DD)
  1954, June 26/Hugh R. Long
    "C-18," CRIFO Newsl., 3 Sep.1954, p.
    6.

Cherry Hill
-Telephone anomaly
  1966, Dec./Gwendoline Martino
    John A. Keel, "The Cape May Incident,"
    in Beyond Condon (Flying Saucer Rev.
    special issue, no.2, June 1969), pp.
    57-62.
    John A. Keel, The Mothman Prophecies
    (N.Y.: Saturday Review, 1975), pp.
    73-74.
  1966, Dec.
    Cherry Hill News, 15 Dec.1966.
-UFO (CE-1)
  1966, Oct.30/Charles Paulus, Jr./RCA
  computer Plant/=radar antenna?
    "Huge UAO 'Lands' on RCA Building,"
    APRO Bull. 15 (May-June 1967):11-12.
    Otto O. Binder, "'Oddball' Saucers...
    That Fit No Pattern," Fate 21 (Feb.
    1968):54,61-62.
    (Letter), Edward Stanko, Fate 22
    (Apr.1969):125.
    (Letter), John A. Keel, Fate 22 (Nov.
    1969):148-50.
-UFO (NL)
  1966, Dec.
    Cherry Hill News, 22 Dec.1966.

Clayton
-Flying humanoid
  1909, Jan.21/William Wasso/=hoax?
    James F. McCloy & Ray Miller, Jr.,
    The Jersey Devil (Wallingford, Pa.:
    Middle Atlantic, 1976), pp.60-61.
-UFO (NL)
  1977, May 19
    "UFOs of Limited Merit," Int'l UFO
    Reporter 2 (July 1977):3.

Clifton
-Mystery explosion
  1958, Dec.8/Mrs. H.C. Mollen/=static
  electricity?
    "Exploding Doghouse," Fate 12 (Apr.
    1959):89.
-Photographic anomaly
  1973, Sep.19/Stella Lansing/Holy Face
  Monastery
    Berthold Eric Schwarz, "Stella Lan-
    sing's Clocklike UFO Patterns: Part
    4," Flying Saucer Rev. 21 (June
    1975):14-15. il.

Collingswood
-Humanoid tracks
  1909, Jan.20/Mr. Kirkwood
    James F. McCloy & Ray Miller, Jr.,
    The Jersey Devil (Wallingford, Pa.:
    Middle Atlantic, 1976), p.50.
-Windshield pitting
  1928, Feb./William T. Turnbull
    New York Herald-Tribune, 9 Feb.1928.

Colts Neck
-UFO (NL)
  1978, June 11/Michael E. Ford/Naval
  Weapons Station Earle
    "Case 3-7-130: Three UFOs over High
    Security Military Base?" Int'l UFO
    Reporter 3 (July 1978):4-5.

Columbia
-Architectural anomaly
  1929-   /Ivan T. Sanderson
    Ivan T. Sanderson, Investigating the
    Unexplained (Englewood Cliffs, N.J.:
    Prentice-Hall, 1972), pp.197-210.
-Dematerialization
  1973, June 15
    Sabina W. Sanderson, "Chipmunks and
    ITF," Pursuit 6 (July 1973):59.
-Dowsing research
  1960s/Ivan T. Sanderson
    "Mechanical Dowsing," Pursuit 1 (30
    Sep.1968):15-16; 3 (Apr.1970):45.
    Ivan T. Sanderson, More "Things"
    (N.Y.: Pyramid, 1969), pp.141-53.
-Entombed animal research
  1971/Sabina W. Sanderson
    "Entombed Toads, Other Amphibians,
    and Some Reptiles," Pursuit 4 (Oct.
    1971):97-98.
-Mechanical anomaly
  1973/Sabina W. Sanderson
    Sabina W. Sanderson, "The Mystery of
    the Continuous Roll," Pursuit 7
    (Jan.1974):10.
    Sabina W. Sanderson & Member #1205,
    "The Continuous Roll, Explained,"
    Pursuit 7 (Apr.1974):35. il.
-Men-in-black
  1967, fall
    John A. Keel, The Mothman Prophecies
    (N.Y.: Saturday Review, 1975), pp.
    233-35.
-Poltergeist
  n.d./Sabina W. Sanderson
    Walter J. McGraw, "On Hunting Polter-
    geists," Pursuit 4 (Oct.1971):81-82.
-UFO (NL)
  1966, July 31/Ivan T. Sanderson
    Ivan T. Sanderson, Uninvited Visitors
    (N.Y.: Cowles, 1967), pp.25-29.

Columbus
-Mystery tracks
  1909, Jan.18
    Philadelphia (Pa.) Public Ledger, 22
    Jan.1909.
    James F. McCloy & Ray Miller, Jr.,
    The Jersey Devil (Wallingford, Pa.:
    Middle Atlantic, 1976), p.44.

Cranbury
-Haunt
  19th c./Truxton House
    Charles M. Skinner, American Myths
    and Legends, 2 vols. (Philadelphia:
    Lippincott, 1903), 1:234-38.

Delran
-Inner development
  1975-   /Atlanteans/113 Swedes Run Dr.
    Marlyn Ervin Margulis, "The Atlante-
    ans Have Landed!" Psychic World,
    Sep.1976, pp.40-44. il.

Denville
-UFO (?)
  1959, March 18/Lee R. Munsic/=static
  electricity?

Jacques Vallee, "A New Look at Saucer Mysteries," in Frank Bowers, ed., The True Report on Flying Saucers (Greenwich, Ct.: Fawcett, 1967), pp. 16-17. il.

Dorothy
-Phantom panther
1960, Oct.
Jerome Clark & Loren Coleman, "The Jersey Devil," Beyond Reality, no.4 (May 1973):35,52.
James F. McCloy & Ray Miller, Jr., The Jersey Devil (Wallingford, Pa.: Middle Atlantic, 1976), p.97.

Dover
-Clairvoyance
1956, June 28/S.C. Vansant
Laura A. Dale, Rhea White & Gardner Murphy, "A Selection of Cases from a Recent Survey of Spontaneous ESP Phenomena," J.ASPR 56 (1962):3,43-46.
-Spontaneous human combustion
1916, Dec.23/Lillian Green/Lake Denmark Hotel
New York Herald, 27-28 Dec.1916.

Dover twp.
-Humanoid
1978, June
Sherman (Tex.) Democrat, 14 June 1978.

Dunellen
-UFO (NL)
1958, Dec.20/LeRoy A. Arboreen/Center St.
Richard Hall, ed., The UFO Evidence (Washington: NICAP, 1964), p.5.

East Orange
-Clairvoyance
1938, May 16/Mrs. Ernest Topp
"Premonition of Tragedy," Fate 8 (Jan.1955):98.
-Precognition
1920, Dec.6/Mary Grant Cramer/70 Lenox Ave.
New York Sun, 16 Dec.1920.
Walter F. Prince, "Peculiar Experiences Connected with Noted Persons," J.ASPR 15 (1921):109,123-25.
-UFO (NL)
1947, July 4/Lenora Woodruff/184 S. Arlington St.
Newark Star-Ledger, 6 July 1947.
1966, Aug.16/Louis Osborn
John A. Keel, "The Night the Sky Turned On," Fate 20 (Sep.1967):30,34.

East Paterson
-UFO (CE-1)
1945, Aug.10/Doris La Fountain/Market St.
Gordon I.R. Lore, Jr. & Harold H. Deneault, Jr., Mysteries of the Skies: UFOs in Perspective (Englewood Cliffs, N.J.: Prentice-Hall, 1968), p.145.

Eatontown
-Phantom panther
1958, May/William V. Garner
Bruce S. Wright, The Eastern Panther (Toronto: Clarke, Irwin, 1972), pp. 105-106.

Edgewater
-Clairempathy
1940s-1965/Florence Sternfels
Mary Ellen Frallie, "The Psychic Who Solves Crimes," Fate 5 (July-Aug. 1952):95-103.
Mabel Love, "The Woman Who Solves Crimes," Tomorrow 7 (spring 1959):9-18.
Hans Holzer, Ghost Hunter (N.Y.: Ace, 1963 ed.), p.22.
P.H. Hendrickson, "The Body in the House Next Door," Fate 18 (May 1965) :78-82.
Robert Fink & Virginia A. Santore, "The Disappearance of Carol Allen," Fate 18 (Sep.1965):52-57.
"Florence Sternfels Dies," Fate 18 (Nov.1965):53.
Hans Holzer, Psychic Photography (N.Y.: McGraw-Hill, 1969), pp.57-63.

Elizabeth
-Fall of salty hailstones
1874, June 9/James H. Hooley
"Soda Hailstones," Sci.Am. 31 (1874): 362.
-Men-in-black
1966, Oct./George Smyth
"Three Men Visit New Jersey Man," Saucer News 14 (winter 1967-68):28-29.
-Phantom
1966, Oct.11/James Yanchitis/4th x New Jersey St.
John A. Keel, Strange Creatures from Time and Space (Greenwich, Ct.: Fawcett, 1970), pp.176-78.
-Skyquake
1977, Dec.3, 21-22
U.S. Naval Rsch.Laboratory, NRL Investigations of East Coast Acoustics Events (Washington: Gov't Printing Office, 1978), pp.138-39.
-UFO (DD)
1947, July 6/Frederick Schlauch
Newark Star-Ledger, 7 July 1947.
-UFO (NL)
ca.1950/Madeline Moschenross
John G. Fuller, Incident at Exeter (N.Y.: Berkley, 1967 ed.), p.25.
1952, June/Mel Neff
Kevin D. Randle, "The UFO Pictures That Nobody Wanted," Official UFO 2 (Feb.1977):20,49. il.

Erial
-Flying humanoid
ca.1930/Howard Marcey
James F. McCloy & Ray Miller, Jr., The Jersey Devil (Wallingford, Pa.: Middle Atlantic, 1976), p.90.

Essex co.
-UFO (CE-2)
    1966, summer
        Stan Zebrowski, "Some Interesting
        Cases," Vestigia Newsl. 2 (summer
        1978):2-3.

Essex Fells
-UFO (NL)
    1947, July 4/Mrs. Harold Doner
        Newark Star-Ledger, 6 July 1947.

Estellville
-Flying humanoid myth
    1855/Mrs. Leeds
        Alexander L. Crosby, ed., Matawan,
        1686-1936 (Newark: Newick Bros.,
        1936), pp.20-22.
        James F. McCloy & Ray Miller, Jr.,
        The Jersey Devil (Wallingford, Pa.:
        Middle Atlantic, 1976), p.26.

Everittstown
-UFO (CE-3)
    1957, Nov.6/John Trasco
        Milford Delaware Valley News, 15 Nov.
        1957.
        Aimé Michel, Flying Saucers and the
        Straight-Line Mystery (N.Y.: Criter-
        ion, 1958), pp.273-74.

Fairview
-UFO (CE-1)
    1976, Jan.29
        Union City Hudson Dispatch, 27 Feb.
        1976.
        Ted Bloecher, "The 'Stonehenge' In-
        cidents of January 1975," Flying
        Saucer Rev. 22 (Oct.1976):3,6.

Farmingdale
-Skyquake
    1977, Dec.2, 20
        U.S. Naval Rsch.Laboratory, NRL In-
        vestigations of East Coast Acoustics
        Events (Washington: Gov't Printing
        Office, 1978), pp.137-38.

Flemington
-UFO (CE-1)
    1964, July 30/Jack Hall
        "UFO Sighting Wave Persists," UFO
        Inv. 2 (Sep.-Oct.1964):5, quoting
        Flemington Democrat (undated).
        "The Flemington, New Jersey Landing,"
        Saucer News 11 (Dec.1964):21.
-Weather control
    1960, Sep./Ethel Belmar/Hobby Horse
    Nursing School
        Fleimington Hunterdon County Democrat,
        15 Sep.1960.

Florham Park
-Mystery explosion
    1966, April 12/Helge Andersen/Andersen's
    Greenhouse
        (Editorial), Fate 19 (Sep.1966):10.

Fords
-UFO (NL)

1969, Feb.11-12/Hatco Chemical Co./
Meadow Rd.
    "U.S. Roundup," APRO Bull. 17 (Mar.-
    Apr.1969):6,7.

Fort Lee
-UFO (CE-1)
    1975, Oct.2
        "UFO Central," CUFOS News Bull., 1
        Feb.1976, p.7.

Fort Monmouth
-UFO (DD)
    1952, summer/Ed Asner
        Timothy Green Beckley, "Saucers and
        Celebrities," Saga UFO Rept. 3
        (Aug.1976):44.
-UFO (R-V)
    1951, Sep.10-11/=aircraft?
        Edward J. Ruppelt, The Report on Un-
        identified Flying Objects (Garden
        City: Doubleday, 1956), pp.91-92,
        111.
        U.S. Air Force, Projects Grudge and
        Blue Book Reports 1-12 (Washington:
        NICAP, 1968), pp.15,23-28.
        E.U. Condon, "UFOs: 1947-1968," in
        Scientific Study of Unidentified
        Flying Objects (N.Y.: Bantam, 1969
        ed.), pp.502,511-12.
        David Michael Jacobs, The UFO Con-
        troversy in America (Bloomington:
        Univ.of Indiana, 1975), pp.64-65,86.
    1952, July 1
        Edward J. Ruppelt, The Report on Un-
        identified Flying Objects (Garden
        City: Doubleday, 1956), p.151.
-UFO film (top secret military)
    1953, April
        Leonard H. Stringfield, "Retrievals
        of the Third Kind," in 1978 MUFON
        UFO Symposium Proc. (Seguin, Tex.:
        MUFON, 1978), pp.77,85-87.

Franklin
-UFO (CE-1)
    1966, April 3
        "Typical Reports," UFO Inv. 3 (Mar.-
        Apr.1966):8.

Fredon
-Haunt
    1922-1927/Frank Decker
        New York Herald-Tribune, 12 Sep.1927.

Freewood Acres
-Inner development
    1951-   /Mongolian Kalmuck lamasery
        Arturio F. Gonzalez, Jr., "New Jer-
        sey's Buddhist Shangri-La," Coronet,
        Apr.1959, pp.146-55.
        Geshe Wangyal, The Door of Liberation
        (N.Y.: Maurice Gerodias, 1973).
        Jim Brandon, Weird America (N.Y.:
        Dutton, 1978), p.140.

Garfield
-UFO (?)
    1971, Dec.1/Passaic St.
        "Boys Report UFOs--Police Laugh,"

Haddonfield
-Flying humanoid
    1894
        James F. McCloy & Ray Miller, Jr.,
        The Jersey Devil (Wallingford, Pa.:
        Middle Atlantic, 1976), p.34.
-Humanoid tracks
    1909, Jan.20/Dr. Glover
        Philadelphia (Pa.) Public Ledger, 22
        Jan.1909.
        James F. McCloy & Ray Miller, Jr.,
        The Jersey Devil (Wallingford, Pa.:
        Middle Atlantic, 1976), p.50.

Haddon Heights
-Flying humanoid
    1909, Jan.21/Lewis Boeger
        James F. McCloy & Ray Miller, Jr.,
        The Jersey Devil (Wallingford, Pa.:
        Middle Atlantic, 1976), pp.55-56.

Haledon
-Dowsing
    1955/Joe Richards
        (Editorial), Fate 6 (June 1953):8,
        quoting American Weekly (undated).
-Skyquake
    1977, Dec.2
        U.S. Naval Rsch.Laboratory, NRL In-
        vestigations of East Coast Acoustics
        Events (Washington: Gov't Printing
        Office, 1978), p.135.

Hamilton twp.
-UFO (NL)
    1955, Aug.19
        Trenton Trentonian, 3 Sep.1955.
    1978, Feb.3/Wilma Mihok/University
    Heights School
        Trenton Times, 4 Feb.1978.

Hammonton
-Phantom airplane
    1931, Dec.5/Elmer Craig/Folsom Swamp
        New York Times, 6 Dec.1931, p.31A;
        and 7 Dec.1931, p.4.
-Skyquake
    1977, Dec.2
        U.S. Naval Rsch.Laboratory, NRL In-
        vestigations of East Coast Acoustics
        Events (Washington: Gov't Printing
        Office, 1978), p.137.

Hampton Lakes
-UFO (CE-2)
    1965, June 28/ground markings only
        "Possible Saucer Landing in New Jer-
        sey," Saucer News 12 (Sep.1965):25.
        il.

Hardyston twp.
-UFO (CE-1)
    1966, April 1/Carol Vander Plate
        Berthold E. Schwarz, "UFOs in New
        Jersey," J.Med.Soc'y N.J. 66 (1969):
        460-64.
-UFO (DD)
    1967, Nov./Frank Scanlon/Rudeville Rd.
        Berthold E. Schwarz, "UFOs in New
        Jersey," J.Med.Soc'y N.J. 66 (1969):

460-64.

Haskell
-UFO (NL)
    1966, Jan.11/Anthony DeLano
        Edward J. Babcock & Timothy Green
        Beckley, "UFO Plagues N.J. Reser-
        voir," Fate 19 (Oct.1966):34,36,39.

Haworth
-Ancient inscription
    1966/Lee Dal Cero
        (Letter), Fate 24 (July 1971):144-47.

Hawthorne
-Precognition
    1965/Joseph Cuccinelli
        (Editorial), Fate 19 (Mar.1966):29.
-UFO (CE-1)
    1962, Sep.18
        Richard Hall, ed., The UFO Evidence
        (Washington: NICAP, 1964), p.140.
-UFO (DD)
    1962, Sep.23
        Richard Hall, ed., The UFO Evidence
        (Washington: NICAP, 1964), p.140.
-UFO (NL)
    1962, Sep.20-21/William Stocks/Braen's
    Quarry
        Passaic Herald, 21 Sep.1962.
        Berthold E. Schwarz, "Beauty of the
        Night," Flying Saucer Rev. 18 (July-
        Aug.1972):5,9.
    1962, Sep.24/George Della Penta
        "Disc Landing Reported in New Jersey,"
        UFO Inv. 2 (Oct.-Nov.1962):3.
        "Reports on Other UFO Films," UFO
        Inv. 2 (June-Sep.1963):5.
        Richard Hall, ed., The UFO Evidence
        (Washington: NICAP, 1964), pp.12,
        140.
        Berthold E. Schwarz, "Beauty of the
        Night," Flying Saucer Rev. 18 (July-
        Aug.1972):5,9.

Hazlet
-Fall of stones
    1978, June/George Tuschmann/Elm St.
        Kansas City (Mo.) Star, 29 June 1978.
        Shrewsbury Sunday Register, 9 July
        1978.
-Skyquake
    1977, Dec.2
        U.S. Naval Rsch.Laboratory, NRL In-
        vestigations of East Coast Acoustics
        Events (Washington: Gov't Printing
        Office, 1978), p.136.

Hedding
-Mystery tracks
    1909, Jan.18
        Philadelphia (Pa.) Public Ledger, 22
        Jan.1909.
        James F. McCloy & Ray Miller, Jr.,
        The Jersey Devil (Wallingford, Pa.:
        Middle Atlantic, 1976), p.44.

Heislerville
-UFO (CE-1)
    1976, Jan.19/Kay Peterson

Rick Barr, "Humanoids: Key to the
Puzzle," Official UFO 2 (Mar.1977):
31,51.

Helsinburg
-Ancient wells
1748
John F. Watson, Annals of Philadel-
phia and Pennsylvania in the Olden
Time, 2 vols. (Philadelphia: John
Penington & Uriah Hunt, 1844).

High Bridge
-Contactee
1932-1967/Howard Menger
(Editorial), Fate 10 (July 1957):12-
13.
Howard Menger, "Howard Menger's Own
Story," Flying Saucer Rev. 4 (Mar.-
Apr.1958):14-17.
Howard Menger, "The Howard Menger
Story," Flying Saucer Rev. 4 (July-
Aug.1958):10-12,iii.
Marla Baxter, My Saturnian Lover
(N.Y.: Vantage, 1958).
Howard Menger, From Outer Space to
You (Clarksburg, W.V.: Saucerian,
1959).
Long John Nebel, The Way Out World
(N.Y.: Lancer, 1962 ed.), pp.54-61.
Connie Menger, Song of Saturn (Clarks-
burg, W.V.: Saucerian, 1968).
John A. Keel, UFOs: Operation Trojan
Horse (N.Y.: Putnam, 1970), pp.203-
208.

Highland Lakes
-UFO (NL)
1966, fall/Estelle Conway
Berthold E. Schwarz, "UFOs in New
Jersey," J.Med.Soc'y N.J. 66 (1969):
460-64.

Highland Park
-UFO (NL)
1968, April 13/Marion Burdick/31 Lin-
coln Ave.
"UFO in New Jersey," Skylook, no.11
(July 1968):6.

Hillsdale
-Skyquake
1977, Dec.21
U.S. Naval Rsch.Laboratory, NRL In-
vestigations of East Coast Acoustics
Events (Washington: Gov't Printing
Office, 1978), p.139.
-UFO (CE-2)
1965, Nov.9
John J. Robinson, "Did UFO's Cause
the Great Northeastern Power Fail-
ure?" Saucer News 13 (Mar.1966):4,5.

Hillside
-UFO (NL)
1966, Jan.12/Michael Tulumello/Hwy.22
x Bloy St.
Edward J. Babcock & Timothy Green
Beckley, "UFO Plagues N.J. Reservoir," Fate 19 (Oct.1966):34,41.

Hoboken
-UFO (?)
1866, Oct.21/Ernest Turner
Ernest Turner, "A Green Meteor," Sci.
Am. 15 (1866):335.

Holland twp.
-UFO (NL)
1967, Aug./George Taylor/Gilbert Gen-
erating Station
Flemington Democrat, 21 Sep.1967.

Hope
-Haunt
1977/Betsy Zebrowski
Walter Puzia & Peter Jordan, "Strik-
ing Photographs on 'Experimental'
Film Purport to Show Spirit Enti-
ties," Vestigia Newsl. 2 (spring
1978):1-2. il.
Peter Jordan, Rita Allen & Rick Moran,
"The Haunting of Hope House," Saga
UFO Rept. 6 (Jan.1979):44-47,58-64.

Hopewell
-Clairvoyance
1932, March/Lindbergh home
Frank Edwards, Stranger Than Science
(N.Y.: Ace, 1962 ed.), pp.152-55.

Howell twp.
-Skyquake
1974, Sep.22, 25
Montreal (P.Q.) Star, 12 Oct.1974.
1977, Dec.2
U.S. Naval Rsch.Laboratory, NRL In-
vestigations of East Coast Acoustics
Events (Washington: Gov't Printing
Office, 1978), p.137.

Hunterdon co.
-UFO (CE-4)
1977, fall
Stan Zebrowski, "Some Interesting
Cases," Vestigia Newsl. 2 (summer
1978):2-3.

Ironia
-Anomalous hole in ground
1963, Nov./Albert W. Waldron
"Fortean Items," Saucer News 11 (Mar.
1964):20.

Irvington
-UFO (DD)
1956, Sep.3/Thomas Gann
"Case 207," CRIFO Orbit, 5 Oct.1956,
p.3, quoting Newark Star-Ledger (undated).
-UFO (NL)
1947, July 6/John E. Wludyka
Newark Star-Ledger, 7 July 1947.

Jackson
-UFO (CE-2)
1968, Jan.8/Robert LeChance
"French General, Scientists, Report
UFOs," UFO Inv. 4 (May-June 1968):3,
quoting Trenton Times (undated).

Jacksonville
-Mystery tracks
  1909, Jan.18
    James F. McCloy & Ray Miller, Jr.,
    The Jersey Devil (Wallingford, Pa.:
    Middle Atlantic, 1976), p.44.

Jefferson twp.
-UFO (CE-1)
  1966, March 31
    "Saucer Briefs," Saucer News 13
    (fall 1966):26,27.

Jersey City
-Derelict train
  1959, Nov.12/Joseph Hilinski/Jersey
    Central Railroad
    (Editorial), Fate 13 (Mar.1960):10-
    11.
-Ghost light
  1954, April-May/St. Joseph's Catholic
    Church
    (Editorial), Fate 7 (Sep.1954):10-11,
    quoting Jersey City Journal (un-
    dated).
    (Editorial), Fate 7 (Nov.1954):13-14.
-Haunt
  18th c./Wild Goose Tavern/Communipaw
    Charles M. Skinner, Myths and Legends
    of Our Own Land, 2 vols. (Philadel-
    phia: Lippincott, 1896), 1:118-21.
-UFO (?)
  1952, July 27/August C. Roberts/=lens
    flare?
    August C. Roberts, "Saucer Photo?"
    Saucers 1, no.2 (1953):1. il.
    Desmond Leslie & George Adamski, Fly-
    ing Saucers Have Landed (N.Y.: Brit-
    ish Book Centre, 1953), opp.p.176.
    il.
    Gray Barker, They Knew Too Much About
    Flying Saucers (N.Y.: University
    Books, 1956), pp.82-85.
    August C. Roberts, "The Skywatch
    Tower Case," Flying Saucers, Aug.
    1957, pp.8-15. il.
    Albert K. Bender, Flying Saucers and
    the Three Men (N.Y.: Paperback Li-
    brary, 1968 ed.), p.40.
    Colman S. VonKeviczky, "A Re-Analy-
    sis," Can.UFO Rept., no.24 (summer
    1976):19,21-22. il.
    Gray Barker, "Silenced: The Men in
    Black Are Back," Saga UFO Rept. 7
    (Feb.1979):49-52.
-UFO (NL)
  1879, April 12/Henry Harrison
    "A Curious Astronomical Phenomenon,"
    Sci.Am. 40 (1879):294.
    Henry Harrison, "The Curious Astro-
    nomical Phenomenon," Sci.Am.Supp.
    7 (1879):2884-85.
  1882, July 6/N.S. Drayton
    N.S. Drayton, "A Supposed Meteor,"
    Sci.Am. 47 (1882):53.
  1949, June/August C. Roberts
    Gray Barker, They Knew Too Much About
    Flying Saucers (N.Y.: University
    Books, 1956), pp.85-87.
  1975, Oct.4/Bergen

"Noteworthy UFO Sightings," Ufology
  2 (spring 1976):43.
  1979, Jan.3/Joseph Frank/Erie x 12th
    St.
    Jersey City Jersey Journal, 5 Jan.
    1979.

Keansburg
-Ghost
  1929, Jan./Thomas A. Kearney/St. Ann's
    Catholic Church
    New York Sun, 16 Jan.1929.

Kearny
-Ghost
  1886, Nov.19/Philip Fritz
    Kansas City (Mo.) Star, 24 Nov.1886,
    p.1.

Kingston
-Skyquake
  1977, Dec.12
    U.S. Naval Rsch.Laboratory, NRL In-
    vestigations of East Coast Acoustic
    Events (Washington: Gov't Printing
    Office, 1978), p.143.

Kingwood twp.
-Fall of fish
  1825, July 5/Nathaniel Atchley
    "Chronicle," Niles' Weekly Register
    28 (1825):416.

Kinkora
-Mystery tracks
  1909, Jan.18
    Philadelphia (Pa.) Public Ledger, 22
    Jan.1909.
    James F. McCloy & Ray Miller, Jr.,
    The Jersey Devil (Wallingford, Pa.:
    Middle Atlantic, 1976), p.44.

Kinnelon
-Ancient dolmen
  Smoke Rise
    Leon L. Morrill, Jr., "Possible Mega-
    lithic Astronomical Alignments in
    New England," NEARA Newsl. 6 (Mar.
    1971):15.
    Richard R. Szathmary, "A Closer Look
    at America B.C.," Fate 30 (Nov.1977)
    :38,42; (Dec.1977):79. il.
-Photographic anomaly
  1973, Sep.21/Stella Lansing
    Berthold Eric Schwarz, "Stella Lan-
    sing's Clocklike UFO Patterns: Part
    4," Flying Saucer Rev. 21 (June
    1975):14.
-Telepathy
  1961, winter/Mrs. Robert Magill
    (Editorial), Fate 14 (July 1961):12-
    13.

Lakehurst
-Fall of unknown object
  1935, July 31/Charles E. Rosendahl/Navy
    blimp ZMC-2
    "Do You Believe in Fairies?" Fortean
    Soc'y Mag., no.1 (Sep.1937):2.
    "More Bullets in the Air," Fortean

Soc'y Mag., no.2 (Oct.1937):8.

Lakewood
-Poltergeist
1959, July-Sep./Aaron Salomon/526 Toms
River Rd.
(Editorial), Fate 13 (Feb.1960):13-
16.
-UFO (CE-1)
1966, Dec.5
Lakewood Ocean County Citizen, 6
Dec.1966.

Lambertville
-Dowsing
1953, summer/Harvey Mathews
(Editorial), Fate 7 (Oct.1954):12.
-Photographic anomaly
1973, May 28-29/Stella Lansing
Berthold Eric Schwarz, "Stella Lan-
sing's Clocklike UFO Patterns," Fly-
ing Saucer Rev. 20 (Jan.1975):3,4.
-UFO (CE-3)
1967, Sep.
John A. Keel, "The Little Man of
Gaffney," Flying Saucer Rev. 14
(Mar.-Apr.1968):17,19.

Lavalette
-UFO (NL)
1952, July 20
J. Allen Hynek, The Hynek UFO Report
(N.Y.: Dell, 1977), pp.74-76.

Leeds Point
-Flying humanoid myth
1778
Henry Charlton Beck, Jersey Genesis:
The Story of the Mullica River (New
Brunswick: Rutgers Univ., 1945),
pp.240-44.
James F. McCloy & Ray Miller, Jr.,
The Jersey Devil (Wallingford, Pa.:
Middle Atlantic, 1976), pp.25-26.
-Flying humanoid
1930, Aug.
New York Times, 6 Aug.1930, p.4.
-Mystery tracks
1894-1895
Jerome Clark & Loren Coleman, "The
Jersey Devil," Beyond Reality, no.4
(May 1973):35,50.
James F. McCloy & Ray Miller, Jr.,
The Jersey Devil (Wallingford, Pa.:
Middle Atlantic, 1976), p.34.

Linden
-UFO (NL)
1978, Jan.4/Clark St.
Linden Leader, 5 Jan.1978.
1978, March 3/Dan Dalley
Linden Leader, 9 Mar.1978.

Livingston
-Skyquake
1979, Feb.8
New York Post, 9 Feb.1979.
-UFO (NL)
1978, Oct.25/Lee Schroeder/Riker Hill
Livingston West Essex Tribune, 26

Oct.1978.
1978, Nov.14/Andrew Licari/32 Cornell
Dr.
Livingston West Essex Tribune, 16
Nov.1978.

Lodi
-UFO (NL)
1963, Aug.13
"News Briefs," Saucer News 10 (Dec.
1963):22.

Long Branch
-Fall of ice
1967, Aug.5/Waverly Pl.
Long Branch Daily Record, 7 Aug.
1967. il.
-Mirage anomaly
1881, Sep.6
New York Times, 7 Sep.1881, p.5.
-Skyquake
1977, Dec.2
1978, Jan.18
U.S. Naval Rsch.Laboratory, NRL In-
vestigations of East Coast Acoustics
Events (Washington: Gov't Printing
Office, 1978), pp.134,140.
-Spirit medium
1960s/Reva Wood
Jess Stearn, The Door to the Future
(N.Y.: Macfadden, 1964), pp.184-86.
-UFO (CE-1)
1972, summer
(Letter), M.G., Saga UFO Rept. 2
(fall 1974):76.
-UFO (NL)
1971, July 22/Raymond Raupp
Bergen County Herald-News, 22 July
1971.

Longport
-Plague of clams
1940, March
Eric Frank Russell, "British Corres-
pondence," Fortean Soc'y Mag., no.5
(Oct.1941):4.

Long Valley
-Ghost light
1976, Nov.-   /High Bridge Railroad/
=piezoelectric effect?
C. Louis Wiedemann, "Report on Ves-
tigia's Experiments Concerning a New
Jersey Spooklight," Anomaly Rsch.
Bull., no.4 (Jan.1977):3-7.
C. Louis Wiedemann, "Results of the
N.J. 'Spook Light' Study," Vestigia
Newsl. 1 (spring 1977):1-5. il.
"Earth Science Team Report," Vestigia
Newsl. 2 (winter 1978):2,5-6.
Peter Jordan & Rita Allen, "Solving
the Spook Light Mystery," Saga UFO
Rept. 6 (Aug.1978):44-47,56-59,70.
il.
William Wagner, Ron Hulse & Jim Mc-
Grath, "Spook Lights: The Vestigia
Update," Vestigia Newsl. 2 (fall
1978):1,3-7.

Lower Bank
-Humanoid
  1966, fall
    John Green, Sasquatch: The Apes Among
    Us (Seattle: Hancock House, 1978),
    p.269.

Lyndhurst
-Mystery fog
  1957, June 25/Mrs. Frank Marvis/66 Ely-
  croft Parkway
    (Editorial), Fate 10 (Oct.1957):17.

Madison
-UFO (CE-1)
  1964, fall/Dorothy Angebauer
    Berthold Eric Schwarz, "Stella Lan-
    sing's Movies: Four Entities and a
    Possible UFO," in UFO Encounters
    (Flying Saucer Rev. special issue,
    no.5, Nov.1973), pp.2,6.

Madison twp.
-Fall of ice
  1958, fall/Raymond Dill, Jr./Esso Ser-
  vicenter
  1958, Dec.23/William Walls/Morristown
  Rd.
    (Editorial), Fate 12 (May 1959):16.

Mahwah
-UFO (DD)
  1967, Jan./James Bjornstad/Immaculate
  Conception Seminary
    (Letter), August C. Roberts, FSR Case
    Histories, no.12 (Dec.1972):14. il.

Manasquan
-Mystery metal sphere
  1971, Aug.22/"Zerda"/33 mi.SE
    Trenton Times, 23 Aug.1971.
-Norse ship
  1960, Sep./Albert Maraziti/=19th c.
  West Indian trader
    (Editorial), Fate 14 (Apr.1961):13-
    14.
    Charles Michael Boland, They All Dis-
    covered America (N.Y.: Pocket Books,
    1963 ed.), pp.300-302.
-UFO (NL)
  1954, Nov.26
    Richard Hall, ed., The UFO Evidence
    (Washington: NICAP, 1964), p.68.

Maple Shade
-Flying humanoid
  1909, Jan.20/John Smith/Mt. Carmel
  Cemetery
    Philadelphia (Pa.) Public Ledger, 21
    Jan.1909.
    James F. McCloy & Ray Miller, Jr.,
    The Jersey Devil (Wallingford, Pa.:
    Middle Atlantic, 1976), p.50.
-UFO (CE-1)
  1966, Oct.30/Charles Paulus, Jr./Hwy.
  38 x Coles Ave.
    Otto O. Binder, "'Oddball' Saucers...
    That Fit No Pattern," Fate 21 (Feb.
    1968):54,61.

Maplewood
-UFO (NL)
  1978, June 16/Robert Fiorentino/Valley
  St.
    Newark Star-Ledger, 18 June 1978.

Margate City
-UFO (NL)
  1973, Nov.5
    New York Times, 7 Nov.1973, p.99.

Mays Landing
-Erratic kangaroo
  1900/Amanda Sutts
    Jerome Clark & Loren Coleman, "The
    Jersey Devil," Beyond Reality, no.4
    (May 1973):35,50, quoting Trenton
    Evening Times, 1960.
-Flying humanoid
  1930, July 24/Mrs. William Sutton
    New York Times, 6 Aug.1930, p.4.
    Curtis D. MacDougall, Hoaxes (N.Y.:
    Dover, 1958 ed.), p.34, quoting
    Philadelphia (Pa.) Evening Ledger
    (undated).
-Skyquake
  1977, Dec.21
    U.S. Naval Rsch.Laboratory, NRL In-
    vestigations of East Coast Acoustics
    Events (Washington: Gov't Printing
    Office, 1978), p.139.

Mayville
-UFO (NL)
  1966, Nov.22/Edward Christiansen/Gar-
  den State Parkway
    John A. Keel, "The Cape May Incident,"
    in Beyond Condon (Flying Saucer Rev.
    special issue, no.2, June 1969), pp.
    57-58.
    John A. Keel, The Mothman Prophecies
    (N.Y.: Saturday Review, 1975), p.
    66.

Meadowbrook Village
-UFO (CE-1)
  1964, May 14/Douglas DeCicco
    "Very Close Sighting in New Jersey,"
    Saucer News 11 (Sep.1964):14.

Metuchen
-Haunt
  1960/Mr. Kane
    Hans Holzer, Ghost Hunter (N.Y.: Ace,
    1963 ed.), pp.31-40.
-UFO (?)
  1968, March 25/William Tarr/=balloon?
    St. Louis (Mo.) Post-Dispatch, 27
    Mar.1968.
    Little Rock Arkansas Gazette, 27 Mar.
    1968.
    Philip J. Klass, UFOs Explained (N.Y.:
    Random House, 1974), pp.25-26.

Mickleton
-Haunt
  1970, July/Christopher Costantino/Bodo
  Otto House
    (Editorial), Fate 24 (Aug.1971):32-
    34, quoting Woodbury Daily Times

(undated).

Middletown
-Humanoid
  1973, Oct.22
    Red Bank Daily Register, 23 Oct.1973.
    Robert C. Warth, "A UFO-ABSM Link?"
    Pursuit 8 (Apr.1975):31-32.
-Phantom image
  1965, June/Robert E. Lengler/Christ
  Episcopal Church
    Asbury Park Press, 19 June 1965.
-UFO (CE-1)
  1974, Dec.
  1975, Jan.7
    Robert C. Warth, "A UFO-ABSM Link?"
    Pursuit 8 (Apr.1975):31,32.
-UFO (NL)
  1973, Oct.21-22
    Asbury Park Press, 24 Oct.1973.

Millville
-UFO (DD)
  1973, Oct.24/Cedarville Rd.
    Millville Daily, 25 Oct.1973.
-UFO (NL)
  1954, Nov.26
    Richard Hall, ed., The UFO Evidence
    (Washington: NICAP, 1964), p.11.
  1961, spring
    J. Allen Hynek, The UFO Experience
    (Chicago: Regnery, 1972), p.39.
  1973, Oct.24/Cedarville Rd.
    Millville Daily, 25 Oct.1973.
  1978, Aug.22/Neida Berrios/Wade East
  Apts.
    Millville Daily, 23 Aug.1978.

Monmouth co.
-Skyquake
  1977, Dec.30
    "Aerial Detonations," Res Bureaux
    Bull., no.28 (19 Jan.1978):1,9.

Montclair
-Astrology
  1968-1971/Int'l Soc'y for Astrological
  Research/89 Clinton Ave.
    David Techter, "New Books," Fate 24
    (Feb.1971):121,124.
    Zipporah Dobyns, "Astrology in the
    United States Today," Fate 24 (Apr.
    1971):45,51.
-Deathbed apparition
  1913, May 20/Mrs. David H. Baldwin/24
  Christopher St.
    "Experience at a Deathbed," J.ASPR 18
    (1924):37-38.
-Haunt
  1945, summer/Audrey Meadows
    Dick Kleiner, "Audrey Meadows and the
    Rooming House Ghost," Fate 17 (Jan.
    1964):60-63.
-Psychokinesis
  1973, Jan.30/Ardis Schwarz
    Berthold Eric Schwarz, "Stella Lan-
    sing's Clocklike UFO Patterns: Part
    2," Flying Saucer Rev. 20 (Mar.1975)
    :20,23-24. il.
-UFO (NL)

1975, Oct.3
  "Noteworthy UFO Sightings," Ufology
  2 (spring 1976):43.

Montvale
-UFO (CE-1)
  1965, July 1/Mrs. G. Grannis
  (Letter), Saucer News 12 (Dec.1965):
  4.
-UFO (CE-3)
  1978, Jan.31/Montvale Memorial Elementary School
    Ted Bloecher, "CE-III Report from
    Montvale, N.J.: Preliminary Report,"
    MUFON UFO J., no.123 (Feb.1978):4-7.
    "A Possible Close Encounter of the
    Third Kind in New Jersey," Int'l
    UFO Reporter 3 (Apr.1978):3,7.

Montville
-Skyquake
  1979, Feb.10
    New York Times, 12 Feb.1979.
-UFO (CE-1)
  1975, Dec.5
    "UFO Central," CUFOS News Bull., 1
    Feb.1976, p.14.

Moorestown
-Clairaudience
  1921/Mrs. Russo
    Louis Whitsett, "The Dead Have
    Voices," Fate 12 (Oct.1959):52-54.

Morris co.
-Erratic crocodilian
  1973, summer
    Monster Times, Nov.1973, p.25.

Morris Plains
-UFO (NL)
  1978, Feb.28/Carol Kaftaniciyan/Hwy.10
    Morristown Daily Record, 2 Mar.1978.

Morristown
-Acoustic anomaly
  1964, Jan./County Prosecutor's Office
  (Editorial), Fate 17 (June 1964):20-
  21.
-Healing
  1960s-1970s/Ethel de Loach/Box 2071
    David St. Clair, Psychic Healers
    (Garden City: Doubleday, 1974), pp.
    118-45. il.
-Humanoid
  1965/Nat'l Historical Park
  1966, May 21/Raymond Todd/Nat'l Historical Park
    John A. Keel, Strange Creatures from
    Time and Space (Greenwich, Ct.: Faw-
    cett, 1970), pp.112-13.
-Lightning anomaly
  1907, Aug.5/Abbott Parker/Mt. Kemble
  Ave.
    New York World, 6 Aug.1907, p.1.
    James J. Flynn, "Abbott Parker's Pic-
    ture of the Crucifixion," N.Y.Folk-
    lore Quar. 17 (1961):138-48.
-Snow worms
  1884

E.W. Gudger, "Snow Worms," Natural
History 23 (1923):451-56.
-UFO (DD)
1947, July 10/John H. Janssen
Morristown Daily Record, 10 July 1947.
John H. Janssen, "My Encounter with
the Flying Disks," Fate 2 (Sep.
1949):12-16. il.

Mountain Lakes
-UFO (CE-2)
1975, July 4/Tom Cahill/Hwy.46
"Police Officers Continue to Sight
UFOs," UFO Inv., Aug.1975, pp.1,2.
Ted Bloecher, "Close Sighting Report-
ed by Couple," Skylook, no.94 (Sep.
1975):3-5.
"From the Center for UFO Studies,"
Flying Saucer Rev. 21 (Apr.1976):24,
25.

Mount Holly
-Fire anomaly
1962, Nov.-1963, Jan./E. James Jordan/
5 Woodpecker Lane
(Editorial), Fate 16 (May 1963):25.
-Flying humanoid
1909, Jan.21/William Cronk
Philadelphia (Pa.) Public Ledger, 22
Jan.1909.
James F. McCloy & Ray Miller, Jr.,
The Jersey Devil (Wallingford, Pa.:
Middle Atlantic, 1976), p.60.
-Haunt
1929, Jan./Walter Treichler/Fair Haven,
Rancacas Rd.
Stuart Palmer, "'Fair Haven' for
Ghosts," Fate 6 (Sep.1953):21-30.
-Skyquake
1977, Dec.2
U.S. Naval Rsch.Laboratory, NRL In-
vestigations of East Coast Acoustics
Events (Washington: Gov't Printing
Office, 1978), p.135.

Neptune
-Skyquake
1978, Jan.3
U.S. Naval Rsch.Laboratory, NRL In-
vestigations of East Coast Acoustics
Events (Washington: Gov't Printing
Office, 1978), p.139.

Neshanic Station
-UFO (NL)
1978, Sep.5/Richard Tippett/Wertsville
Rd.
1978, Sep.7, 10/Barbara Kulasinski/
Wertsville Rd.
New Brunswick Home News, 11 Sep.1978.

Newark
-Disappearance
1926, March 13/"Suduffco"
New York Times, 8 Apr.1926, p.2; 11
Apr.1926, p.3; 28 Apr.1926, p.27;
and 14 May 1926, p.17.
-Fall of gelatinous substance
1833, Nov.13
Denison Olmsted, "Observations on the

Meteors of November 13th, 1833," Am.
J.Sci., ser.1, 25 (1834):363,396,
quoting Newark newspaper (undated).
-Graphology
1960s/Dan Anthony
Wall Street Journal, 11 Sep.1967, p.
1.
-Hex
1939, July/John Baptistalk
Newark Ledger, 29 July 1939.
-Mystery gas
1947, April 1
"At the Same Time," Doubt, no.19
(1947):290,292.
-Mystery radio transmissions
1924, Aug.22/John R. Popelle/Station
WOR
New York Times, 24 Aug.1924, p.30.
St. Paul (Minn.) Pioneer Press, 13
May 1947.
Vincent H. Gaddis, "Radio's Strangest
Mystery," Fate 1 (spring 1948):49-
53.
"Well--Maybe," Doubt, no.20 (1948):
304.
-Parapsychology research
1962-   /E. Douglas Dean/Psi Communi-
cations Project/Newark College of En-
gineering
E. Douglas Dean, "The Plethysmograph
As an Indicator of ESP," J.ASPR 41,
no.4 (1962):351-53.
E. Douglas Dean, "Plethysmograph Re-
cordings as ESP Responses," Int'l
J.Parapsych. 2 (1966):439-46.
E. Douglas Dean & John Mihalasky,
Executive ESP (Englewood Cliffs,
N.J.: Prentice-Hall, 1974).
E. Douglas Dean, "The Effects of Heal-
ers on Biologically Significant
Molecules," New Horizons 1 (Jan.
1975):215-19.
Jeffrey Mishlove, The Roots of Con-
sciousness (N.Y.: Random House,
1975), pp.118,143-44,228,310.
-Phantom train
1870s
Elliott O'Donnell, The Midnight
Hearse and More Ghosts (N.Y.: Paper-
back Library, 1971 ed.), p.134.
-Poltergeist
1916-1917/Stanislaus Lysaj
New York Times, 29 Jan.1917, p.5.
1961, May 6-Dec./Maybelle Clark/Felix
Fuld Housing Project
Newark News, 11 May 1961.
Susy Smith, "Orbiting Crockery in
Newark, New Jersey," Fate 14 (Oct.
1961):34-41. il.
W.G. Roll, "The Newark Disturbances,"
J.ASPR 63 (1969):123-74.
William G. Roll, The Poltergeist
(N.Y.: Signet, 1974 ed.), pp.39-50.
-Telepathy research
1924/Station WOR
J. Malcolm Bird, "Telepathy and Radio,"
Sci.Am. 130 (1924):382,433-35.
-UFO (?)
1947, July 6/Dorothy Kingcade/218 Plane
St.

Newark Evening News, 7 July 1947.
-UFO (CE-1)
1947, July 6/Helene Berard/179 N. 12th
St.
Newark Evening News, 7 July 1947.
-UFO (DD)
1964, July 7
"Near-Landing in New Jersey," Saucer
News 11 (Sep.1964):22. il.
-UFO (NL)
1965, Nov.9
John G. Fuller, Incident at Exeter
(N.Y.: Berkley, 1967 ed.), p.207.
1966, March 29
Columbus (O.) Dispatch, 29 Mar.1966,
p.25.
1966, Oct.16/Joseph A. Montana
"UFO with Flashing Lights Seen over
Newark," UFO Inv. 3 (Oct.-Nov.1966):
7.
-Windshield pitting
1919, Sep.
New York Evening Telegram, 19 Sep.
1919.

New Brunswick
-Crisis apparition
ca.1949/Lois J. Myers/Spring Alley
(Letter), Fate 10 (Jan.1957):117-19.
-Haunt
1972-1973
Robert Rosenberg, "A Haunting in New
Jersey," Theta, no.39-40 (winter-
spring 1974):17-18.
-Out-of-body experience
1960s-1970s/Linda White
Herbert B. Greenhouse, The Astral
Journey (N.Y.: Avon, 1976), pp.187-
88,205-11.
-UFO (CE-3)
1962, Aug.15/Ray Bartkowech
Gray Barker, Book of Saucers (Clarks-
burg, W.V.: Saucerian, 1965), p.20.
-UFO (NL)
1957, Dec.
"All About Sputs," Doubt, no.56
(1958):460,478.

Newton
-Fall of metal pellets
1929, Feb.-March/County Prosecutor's
Office
Charles Fort, The Books of Charles
Fort (N.Y.: Holt, 1941), p.914,
quoting San Francisco (Cal.) Chron-
icle (undated).
-Petroglyph
Edward J. Lenik, "The Thom Petroglyph
in Newton, N.J.," NEARA Newsl. 8
(fall 1973):45-47. il.

North Bergen
-Inner development
1890s/Angel Dancers/Woodcliff
David Steven Cohen, "The 'Angel Dancers': The Folklore of Religious
Communitarianism," New Jersey History 95 (1977):5-20.
-UFO (CE-1)
1976, Jan.15/Bill Daliz/Stonehenge Apts.

Ted Bloecher, "The Stonehenge Inci-
dents: January 1975," in Proc.1976
CUFOS Conference (Evanston: Center
for UFO Studies, 1976), pp.25,27.
-UFO (CE-3)
1975, Jan.12/George O'Barski/North
Hudson Park
Village Voice, 1 Mar.1976.
Ted Bloecher, "Occupants Sighted in
New Jersey," Skylook, no.100 (Mar.
1976):3-7.
Ted Bloecher, "The Stonehenge Incidents: January 1975," in Proc.1976
CUFOS Conference (Evanston: Center
for UFO Studies, 1976), pp.25,32-
38.
1976, Feb.19-20/Teofilo Rodriguez/
Stonehenge Apts.
Ted Bloecher, "The Stonehenge Incidents: January 1975," in Proc.1976
CUFOS Conference (Evanston: Center
for UFO Studies, 1976), pp.25,27-28.
-UFO (DD)
1976, Feb.22/Eddy Obertubessing/Stone-
henge Apts.
Ted Bloecher, "The Stonehenge Incidents: January 1975," in Proc.1976
CUFOS Conference (Evanston: Center
for UFO Studies, 1976), pp.25,28.
-UFO (NL)
1972, Oct.14/Howard Averall/nr. North
Hudson Park
James D. White, "More New Jersey
UFOs," APRO Bull. 25 (July 1976):1,
3.
1975, Jan.6/Francisco Gonzalez/Stone-
henge Apts.
1976, Jan.29/Hudson R.
1976, Feb.28/Stonehenge Apts.
Ted Bloecher, "The Stonehenge Incidents: January 1975," in Proc.1976
CUFOS Conference (Evanston: Center
for UFO Studies, 1976), pp.25,27-30.

North Plainfield
-UFO (CE-3)
1977, Sep.18
Hackettstown Forum, 9 Nov.1977.

Nutley
-Clairvoyance
1976, May/Dorothy Allison
Chicago (Ill.) Tribune, 29 Mar.1978.
"Visions of the Dead," Newsweek, 17
Apr.1978. il.
-Fall of unknown object
1957, April 6/Vincent Guarino, Jr./82
Race St.
New York Times, 9 Apr.1957, p.36.
-UFO (DD)
1975, July 7
"UFO Central," CUFOS News Bull., 15
Nov.1975, p.13.

Oakland
-UFO (CE-1)
1957, spring/Janet Ahlers
Berthold E. Schwarz, "UFOs in New
Jersey," J.Med.Soc'y N.J. 66 (1969):
460-64.

Oak Ridge
-UFOs (?), precognition and haunt
n.d./Mrs. Merz
    Berthold E. Schwarz, "The Port Mon-
    mouth Landing," Flying Saucer Rev.
    17 (May-June 1971):21,26-27.
    Berthold E. Schwarz, "Woodstock UFO
    Festival, 1966--2," Flying Saucer
    Rev. 19 (Mar.-Apr.1973):18,19,22-23.
    il.

Ocean City
-UFO (NL)
1967, Nov.5/Herbert Chadwick/34th St.
x Asbury Ave.
    Jim & Coral Lorenzen, UFOs over the
    Americas (N.Y.: Signet, 1968), p.
    179.

Ocean co.
-UFOs (?) and skyquakes
1977, Dec.2-21
    Jon Douglas Singer, "Skyquakes: Things
    That Go Bump in the Night," Pursuit
    11 (spring 1978):45,47.

Ogdensburg
-UFO (NL)
1976, Jan.18
    "Noteworthy UFO Sightings," Ufology
    2 (summer 1976):62.

Old Bridge
-Fall of ice
1958, Sep.2/Dominic Bacigalupo/336
Greystone Rd.
    (Editorial), Fate 12 (Jan.1959):8-10.
-Skyquake
1977, Dec.2
    U.S. Naval Rsch.Laboratory, NRL In-
    vestigations of East Coast Acoustics
    Events (Washington: Gov't Printing
    Office, 1978), p.135.

Oradell
-UFO (NL)
1962, Sep.18
    Richard Hall, ed., The UFO Evidence
    (Washington: NICAP, 1964), p.140.

Orange
-Poltergeist
1901-1904/Sara C. Spottiswoode
    Hereward Carrington, The Problems of
    Psychical Research (N.Y.: W. Rickey,
    1914), pp.286-98.
-UFO (NL)
1947, July 4/Carol Bryla/Central Ave.
    Newark Star-Ledger, 6 July 1947.

Oyster Creek
-Skyquake
1977, Dec.2/nuclear power plant
    New York Times, 20 Dec.1977, p.31.

Park Ridge
-Passenger pigeon
1965/Stella Fenell/=mourning dove?
    (Letter), Fate 19 (Jan.1966):132.

Parsippany
-Petroglyph
ca.1400/Dale Rd.
    New York Times, 29 July 1973, p.54.
    il.
    Edward J. Lenik, "The Rock House
    Petroglyph in New Jersey," NEARA
    Newsl. 8 (fall 1973):47-48. il.
-UFO (NL)
1977, Sep.18/Hwy.46
    Hackettstown Forum, 9 Nov.1977.
1978, Jan.15/S. Beverwyck Rd.
    Passaic Herald-News, 16 Jan.1978.

Passaic
-Poltergeist
1955/Rose Deralczuk
    (Editorial), Fate 9 (Feb.1956):10.
-UFO (DD)
1952, July 28/George Stock
    "Saucers on the Hot Line," in Frank
    Bowers, ed., The True Report on
    Flying Saucers (Greenwich, Ct.: Faw-
    cett, 1967), p.34. il.
    Otto O. Binder, What We Really Know
    About Flying Saucers (Greenwich,
    Ct.: Fawcett, 1967), p.134. il.

Paterson
-Fall of ice
1972, June 16/James Mandel
    (Editorial), Fate 25 (Dec.1972):17,
    quoting Paterson News (undated). il.
-Haunt
1920s/MacGregor Bond
    Margaret Hudson, "The Shattered Se-
    cret," Fate 3 (Sep.1950):70-73.
1970s/Tim Lidner
    "Where Have All the Soldiers Gone?"
    Probe the Unknown 3 (Mar.1975):51.
-UFO (CE-1)
1965, Oct.15/Jack Peters
    Otto O. Binder, "'Oddball' Saucers...
    That Fit No Pattern," Fate 21 (Feb.
    1968):54,59-60.
1975, July 4
    "UFO Central," CUFOS News Bull., 15
    Nov.1975, p.12.
-UFO (CE-2)
1974, Dec.
    Timothy Green Beckley, "Saucers over
    Our Cities," Saga UFO Rept. 4 (Aug.
    1977):24,71.
-UFO (DD)
1947, July 6/Harold Baker/242 Sussex
St.
    Newark Evening News, 7 July 1947.
1972, Oct.9/Patrick D. Clossey/Garden
State Parkway
    "New Jersey Report," Skylook, no.61
    (Dec.1972):7.
-UFO (NL)
1946, Oct./Dolores Benante/Preakness
Mt.
    Gordon I.R. Lore, Jr. & Harold H. Den-
    eault, Jr., Mysteries of the Skies:
    UFOs in Perspective (Englewood
    Cliffs, N.J.: Prentice-Hall, 1968),
    pp.148-49.
1957, Nov./Ralph E. Nicholson

August C. Roberts, "The Nicholson
Photos," <u>Flying Saucers</u>, July-Aug.
1968, pp.84-85. il.
1964, May 18/Patricia Crabtree
"News Briefs," <u>Saucer News</u> 11 (Sep.
1964):19.

Pemberton
-Ancient inscription
1859
Thomas Ewbank, "Alleged Inscribed
Stone Axe," <u>Bull.Am.Ethn.Soc'y</u> 1
(1861):44-47.
Daniel Wilson, <u>Prehistoric Man</u> (London: Macmillan, 1862), p.412.
C.C. Abbott, "The Stone Age in New
Jersey," <u>Ann.Rept.Smith.Inst.</u>, 1875,
246,260-61.
Olaf Strandwold, <u>Norse Inscriptions
on American Stones</u> (Weehauken: Magnus Björndal, 1948), pp.42-43. il.
James P. Whittall II, "An Inscribed
Celt," <u>Bull.Early Sites Rsch.Soc'y</u>
5 (Feb.1977):9-12. il.
-Flying humanoid
1909, Jan.20/John Pursell
James F. McCloy & Ray Miller, Jr.,
<u>The Jersey Devil</u> (Wallingford, Pa.:
Middle Atlantic, 1976), p.50.
-UFO (CE-2)
1959, fall/Samuel Cowell, Jr.
Berthold Eric Schwarz, "Stella Lansing's Movies: Four Entities and a
Possible UFO," in <u>UFO Encounters</u>
(Flying Saucer Rev. special issue,
no.5, Nov.1973), pp.2,7.

Penns Grove
-UFO (NL)
1947, July 8
<u>Philadelphia (Pa.) Inquirer</u>, 9 July
1947.

Pequannock
-UFO (NL)
1965, July/John Cucci
Otto O. Binder, "'Oddball' Saucers...
That Fit No Pattern," <u>Fate</u> 21 (Feb.
1968):54,56.

Perth Amboy
-Out-of-body experience
1958-1970s/Agnes Adamczyk
Herbert B. Greenhouse, <u>The Astral
Journey</u> (N.Y.: Avon, 1976 ed.), pp.
223-27.
-Physiological anomaly
1976, Sep.8/John Papierowicz/Witco
Chemicals/=abrupt change in eye color
(Editorial), <u>Fate</u> 30 (Feb.1977):30.

Phillipsburg
-Fall of ice
1949, Oct.5
"If It's in the Sky It's a Saucer,"
<u>Doubt</u>, no.27 (1949):416,417.
-UFO (DD)
1947, July 7/Margaret Isarek
<u>Philadelphia (Pa.) Inquirer</u>, 8 July
1947.

Piscataway
-UFO (CE-1)
1976, Feb.3
"Sighting Reports," <u>CUFOS News Bull.</u>,
June 1976, p.4.

Pitman
-Humanoid
1909, Jan.20/Elmer Lacey
<u>Philadelphia (Pa.) Public Ledger</u>, 22
Jan.1909.
-Mystery tracks
1909, Jan.21
<u>Philadelphia (Pa.) Public Ledger</u> 22
Jan.1909.
James F. McCloy & Ray Miller, Jr.,
<u>The Jersey Devil</u> (Wallingford, Pa.:
Middle Atlantic, 1976), p.58.

Plainfield
-Clairvoyance
1918, June 25/Laura E. Osgood/17 Myrtle Ave.
"A Rare Type of Collective Visual
Hallucination," <u>J.ASPR</u> 16 (1922):
197-99.
-Haunt
1950s-1961/Dorothea Dix Lawrence
Wainwright Evans, "Living with Grandma's Ghost," <u>Fate</u> 14 (Sep.1961):62-
70.

Pleasantville
-Flying humanoid
1909, Jan.21/Theodore D. Hackett/Beaver
Pond
James F. McCloy & Ray Miller, Jr.,
<u>The Jersey Devil</u> (Wallingford, Pa.:
Middle Atlantic, 1976), pp.61-62,
quoting <u>Philadelphia (Pa.) Record</u>
(undated).
-Flying humanoid myth
n.d./500 block of S. Main St.
James F. McCloy & Ray Miller, Jr.,
<u>The Jersey Devil</u> (Wallingford, Pa.:
Middle Atlantic, 1976), p.28.

Point Pleasant
-Mystery flotsam
1959, Jan./Jack Baker/=Navy float light
(Editorial), <u>Fate</u> 12 (June 1959):17.
-Skyquake
1977, Dec.2
U.S. Naval Rsch.Laboratory, <u>NRL Investigations of East Coast Acoustics
Events</u> (Washington: Gov't Printing
Office, 1978), p.134.
-UFO (CE-2)
1957, Sep.19
Jacques Vallee, <u>Passport to Magonia</u>
(Chicago: Regnery, 1969), p.258.

Pompton Lakes
-Automatic writing
1942-1952/Anice Terhune/Sunnybank
Anice Terhune, <u>Across the Line</u> (N.Y.:
Dryden, 1945).
Irving Litvag, <u>The Master of Sunnybank</u> (N.Y.: Harper & Row, 1977), pp.
264-72.

-Ghost dog
  1917, summer/Appleton Grannis/Sunnybank
    Albert Payson Terhune, The Book of
    Sunnybank (N.Y.: Harper, 1934).
    Irving Litvag, The Master of Sunny-
    bank (N.Y.: Harper & Row, 1977), pp.
    262-63.
-UFO (NL)
  1966, Jan.11/Howard L. Ball, Jr./Ham-
  burg Turnpike x Colfax Ave.
    Lloyd Mallan, "What Happened at Wan-
    aque, N.J.?" Sci.& Mech. 38 (June
    1967):42,70-72.
  1966, Oct.11/Robert Gordon
    Lloyd Mallan, "What Happened at Wan-
    aque, N.J.?" Sci.& Mech. 38 (May
    1967):28-31.

Port Elizabeth
-UFO (CE-2)
  1972, Dec.7/Charles Willis/Weatherby
  Rd.
    Atlantic City Press, 13 Dec.1972.

Port Monmouth
-UFO (CE-2)
  1970, July 4, 11
    Middletown Courier, 18 July 1970.
    Berthold E. Schwarz, "The Port Mon-
    mouth Landing," Flying Saucer Rev.
    17 (May-June 1971):21-27. il.

Princeton
-Dowsing
  1964/water engineer
    (Editorial), Fate 17 (Apr.1964):6.

Rahway
-Fall of gelatinous substance
  1833, Nov.13
    Denison Olmsted, "Observations on the
    Meteors of November 13th, 1833," Am.
    J.Sci., ser.1, 25 (1834):363,396,
    quoting Rahway Advocate (undated).

Rancocas
-Mystery tracks
  1909, Jan.18
    Philadelphia (Pa.) Public Ledger, 22
    Jan.1909.
    James F. McCloy & Ray Miller, Jr.,
    The Jersey Devil (Wallingford, Pa.:
    Middle Atlantic, 1976), p.44.

Randolph
-UFO (NL)
  1978, March 1/Ken Roberts/Mt. Fern
    Morristown Daily Record, 2 Mar.1978.

Raritan
-Fall of nails
  1955, July/Daniel Franchino
    Sacramento (Cal.) Union, 29 July 1955.

Red Bank
-Erratic crocodilian
  1932, July 7/Wharf St.
    New York Sun, 8 July 1932.
-Skyquake
  1977, Dec.2

U.S. Naval Rsch.Laboratory, NRL In-
    vestigations of East Coast Acoustics
    Events (Washington: Gov't Printing
    Office, 1978), p.136.

Red Lion
-Phantom panther
  1966, Nov./William Ranck
    Columbus (O.) Dispatch, 17 Nov.1966.

Ridgefield Park
-Telepathy
  1940/George Barning
    New York Sun, 21 Mar.1940.

Ringwood
-UFO (NL)
  1966, Jan.11
    Edward J. Babcock & Timothy Green
    Beckley, "UFO Plagues N.J. Reser-
    voir," Fate 19 (Oct.1966):34-35.
  1966, March 10/Mt. St. Francis Convent
    Paterson Evening News, 11 Mar.1966.

River Edge
-UFO (NL)
  1952, July 18/Saul Pett
    Washington Star-News, 22 July 1952,
    p.A15.

Riverside
-Mystery tracks
  1909, Jan.20/Justice Ziegler
    James F. McCloy & Ray Miller, Jr.,
    The Jersey Devil (Wallingford, Pa.:
    Middle Atlantic, 1976), pp.52-53.

Rockaway
-Skyquake
  1978, Jan.12
    U.S. Naval Rsch.Laboratory, NRL In-
    vestigations of East Coast Acoustics
    Events (Washington: Gov't Printing
    Office, 1978), p.140.
-UFO (NL)
  1978, March 10/Mike Mahoney/Rockaway
  Townsquare Mall
    Morristown Morris County Daily Record,
    13 Mar.1978.

Roebling
-Mystery tracks
  1909, Jan.21
    James F. McCloy & Ray Miller, Jr.,
    The Jersey Devil (Wallingford, Pa.:
    Middle Atlantic, 1976), p.58.

Roxbury twp.
-UFO (CE-1)
  1973, Oct.28/Joe Kennedy/nr. Holland
  Manufacturing Co.
    Morristown Daily Record, 30 Oct.1973.

Rumson
-UFO (CE-1)
  1971, June 29/Shrewsbury R. bridge
    "Huge Disc over New Jersey," APRO
    Bull. 19 (May-June 1971):1,3.

Rutherford
-Fall of dust
  1957, June
    "Falls," Doubt, no.57 (1958):4,5.
-Humanoid
  1975, summer
    John Green, Sasquatch: The Apes Among
    Us (Seattle: Hancock House, 1978),
    p.268.

Saddle River
-Haunt
  1965/Mrs. Edward Tholl/Ringwood Manor
    Hans Holzer, Yankee Ghosts (N.Y.:
    Ace, 1966), pp.90-100.
    Hans Holzer, Haunted Houses (N.Y.:
    Crown, 1971), pp.50-52. il.
-UFO (NL)
  1969, Dec.19/Edward M. Judd
    "UFOs in New Jersey," Skylook, no.28
    (Mar.1970):8, quoting Ringwood Her-
    ald-News (undated).

Salem
-Doubtful responsibility
  1935, Aug.
    "Headstones Overturned," Fortean
    Soc'y Mag., no.2 (Oct.1937):6.
-Flying humanoid
  1909, Jan.22/Jacob Henderson
  1909, Feb.24/Leslie Garrison/nr.
  Schultz's store
    Salem Sunbeam, 22 Jan.1909; and 26
    Feb.1909.
    James F. McCloy & Ray Miller, Jr.,
    The Jersey Devil (Wallingford, Pa.:
    Middle Atlantic, 1976), pp.70-71.
-Humanoid
  ca.1927
    James F. McCloy & Ray Miller, Jr.,
    The Jersey Devil (Wallingford, Pa.:
    Middle Atlantic, 1976), pp.85-87.

Schooley's Mountain
-Haunt
  1788
    Charles M. Skinner, American Myths
    and Legends, 2 vols. (Philadelphia:
    Lippincott, 1903), 1:224-34.
-UFO (CE-3)
  1957, Dec.30/George Chowanski
    Jacques Vallee, Passport to Magonia
    (Chicago: Regnery, 1969), p.269,
    quoting Flying Saucers, Oct.1958.

Scotch Plains
-Haunt
  1970s/Vince Lindner
    Nat'l Examiner, 10 Oct.1977.
-UFO (CE-1)
  1975, June 21
    "From the Center for UFO Studies,"
    Flying Saucer Rev. 21 (Apr.1976):24.

Seaside Heights
-UFO (NL)
  1979, Jan.3/Joseph Petillo/Hooper Ave.
  x Fisher Blvd.
    Point Pleasant Beach Leader, 11 Jan.
    1979.

Secaucus
-UFO (NL)
  1979, Jan.22
    Secaucus Home News, 25 Jan.1979.

Ship Bottom
-Precognition
  1817, spring/Stephen Willets
    Edward Konstant, "The Captain's 'In-
    ner Voice,'" Fate 15 (Nov.1962):81.

Sidney
-Mystery tracks
  1978, Jan./Catherine Gansfuss/nr.
  Chicken Coop Tavern
    Whitehouse Station Hunterdon Review,
    1 Feb.1978.

Smithville
-Flying humanoid
  1894
    James F. McCloy & Ray Miller, Jr.,
    The Jersey Devil (Wallingford, Pa.:
    Middle Atlantic, 1976), p.34.

Somerville
-Fall of frogs
  1903, July/C.R. Richards
    (Letter), Fate 11 (Nov.1958):118.
-Humanoid
  1949
    Jerome Clark & Loren Coleman, "The
    Jersey Devil," Beyond Reality, no.4
    (May 1973):35,50.
-Mystery gas
  1968, Jan.9
    John A. Keel, "Mysterious Gas Attacks
    by Flying Saucers," Saga UFO Rept.
    2 (fall 1975):27,28.
-UFO (CE-1)
  1975, Jan.9
    "From the Center for UFO Studies,"
    Flying Saucer Rev. 21 (Aug.1975):
    iii.
-UFO (DD)
  1965, March 22/Ty Klock/Hamilton Rd.
    (Letter), Sci.& Mech. 38 (May 1967):
    72.

South Brunswick
-UFO (NL)
  1977, Aug.11
    "UFOs of Limited Merit," Int'l UFO
    Reporter 2 (Sep.1977):Newsfront sec.

South Plainfield
-Photographic anomaly
  1973, May 29/Stella Lansing
    Berthold Eric Schwarz, "Stella Lan-
    sing's Clocklike UFO Patterns," Fly-
    ing Saucer Rev. 20 (Jan.1975):3,4.

South River
-UFO (CE-3)
  1963, Oct.23/Old Bridge-South Amboy Rd.
    Ted Bloecher, "A Typical Humanoid
    Encounter," Skylook, no.93 (Aug.
    1975):5-7.

Spotswood
-Fall of ice
    1958, fall/Russell Kane
        (Editorial), Fate 12 (May 1959):16.

Spring Lake
-Sea monster
    1895, Sep.22/Willard P. Shaw
        "Another Sea Serpent," Sci.Am. 73
        (1895):211.

Springside
-Erratic kangaroo
    1909, Jan.20/Edward Davis
        James F. McCloy & Ray Miller, Jr.,
        The Jersey Devil (Wallingford, Pa.:
        Middle Atlantic, 1976), p.52.

Stanhope
-Phantom panther
    1977, June
    1978, Sep.
        Passaic Herald-News, 14 Jan.1979.
        Roberta Payne, "Black Panther Sight-
        ings," Vestigia Newsl. 3 (spring
        1979):5.

Stewartsville
-UFO (NL)
    1973, March 21
        Stroudsburg (Pa.) Pocono Record, 21
        Mar.1973.

Stone Harbor
-Skyquake
    1977, Dec.30
        U.S. Naval Rsch.Laboratory, NRL In-
        vestigations of East Coast Acoustics
        Events (Washington: Gov't Printing
        Office, 1978), p.139.

Sussex co.
-UFO (CE-1)
    1965, Nov.30/Helen Borsina
        (Letter), Fate 19 (May 1966):130.
-UFO (NL)
    1977, Oct.30
        Hackettstown Forum, 9 Nov.1977.

Swedesboro
-Flying humanoid
    1909, Jan.19
        Philadelphia (Pa.) Public Ledger, 22
        Jan.1909.
        James F. McCloy & Ray Miller, Jr.,
        The Jersey Devil (Wallingford, Pa.:
        Middle Atlantic, 1976), p.48.
    1929, Aug.
        New York Times, 6 Aug.1930, p.4.

Teterboro
-UFO (DD)
    1947, June 25/John J. Hassey/Hwy.6
        (Letter), Fate 1 (fall 1948):123.
-UFO (NL)
    1947, July/John J. Hassey/Hwy.6
        (Letter), Fate 1 (fall 1948):123.
    1963, Aug.13/airport
        "News Briefs," Saucer News 10 (Dec.
        1963):22.

Toms River
-Fall of ice
    1959, Dec./Clarence Webster/Cox Crow
    Rd.
        (Editorial), Fate 13 (May 1960):15.
-Skyquake
    1977, Dec.2, 21-22/Robert Levi
    1978, Jan.18
        Atlanta (Ga.) Constitution, 23 Dec.
        1977.
        Denver (Colo.) Post, 23 Dec.1977.
        Pittsburgh (Pa.) Press, 8 Jan.1978;
        and 29 Jan.1978.
        W.S. Wagner, R. Hulse & J. McGrath,
        "Vestigia's 'Airblast,'" Vestigia
        Newsl. 2 (fall 1978):7-8.
        U.S. Naval Rsch.Laboratory, NRL In-
        vestigations of East Coast Acoustics
        Events (Washington: Gov't Printing
        Office, 1978).

Totowa
-Aerial phantom
    1912, March/Thomas B. Chapman
        Thomas B. Chapman, "Ship in the Sky,"
        Fate 9 (May 1956):100.

Town Bank
-Humanoid tracks
    1968, summer
        Eric Norman [Brad Steiger], The Abom-
        inable Snowmen (N.Y.: Award, 1969),
        p.91.
-Skyquake
    1955, Sep.27
        "Bangs," Doubt, no.51 (1956):382.

Trenton
-Archeological sites
        Charles C. Abbott, "Are They Twist-
        ing Stones?" Am.Naturalist 7 (1873)
        :180-82.
        Charles C. Abbott, "Occurrence of Im-
        plements in the River Drift at Tren-
        ton, New Jersey," Am.Naturalist 7
        (1873):204-209.
        C.C. Abbott, "The Stone Age of New
        Jersey," Ann.Rept.Smith.Inst., 1875,
        pp.246-380.
        "The Antiquity of Man," Am.Naturalist
        19 (1885):211-12.
        W.H. Holmes, "Are There Traces of Man
        in the Trenton Gravels?" J.Geology
        1 (1893):15-37. il.
-Fall of frogs
    ca.1912/Alex Clark
    ca.1930/Elma Wittenborn/Stacey Park
        (Letter), Trenton Times, 10 Aug.1977.
-Fall of unknown object
    1966, fall/Mrs. Charles A. Green
        "Rogue Missiles," Pursuit 1 (30 Sep.
        1968):11-12.
-Fire anomaly
    1958, Nov.30-1959, Feb./Paul Suveg/18
    Roebling Ave.
        Emil Slaboda, "Trenton's Mysterious
        Blue Flames," Fate 12 (June 1959):
        75-79.
-Flying humanoid
    1909, Jan.21/William Cromley/driving

park
1909, Jan.21/E.P. Weedon
   James F. McCloy & Ray Miller, Jr.,
   The Jersey Devil (Wallingford, Pa.:
   Middle Atlantic, 1976), pp.56-57.
-Haunt
n.d.
   Louis C. Jones, Things That Go Bump
   in the Night (N.Y.: Hill & Wang,
   1959), pp.106-107.
-Humanoid tracks
1909, Jan.21/Mrs. William Batten/400
block of Center St.
   James F. McCloy & Ray Miller, Jr.,
   The Jersey Devil (Wallingford, Pa.:
   Middle Atlantic, 1976), pp.57-58.
-Phantom
1966, spring/nr. McGuire AFB
   John A. Keel, Strange Creatures from
   Time and Space (Greenwich, Ct.: Faw-
   cett, 1970), p.184.
-Skyquake
1957, April 2/State House
   (Editorial), Fate 10 (Aug.1957):8-10.
-UFO (CE-2)
1956, Oct.2/Harry Sturdevant/Delaware
R.
   Trenton Trentonian, 4 Oct.1956.
   Emil Slaboda, "He Collected on a Fly-
   ing Saucer," Fate 10 (June 1957):66-
   69.
-UFO (DD)
1959, Aug.19
   Jacques & Janine Vallee, Challenge to
   Science (N.Y.: Ace, 1966 ed.), pp.
   200-201.
-UFO (NL)
1947, July 8/S of town
   Philadelphia (Pa.) Inquirer, 9 July
   1947.
1957, summer/Tom Bevan
   (Letter), Fate 11 (Aug.1958):116.
1979, Feb.1/Labor St.
   Trenton Trentonian, 3 Feb.1979.
-UFO (R-V)
1957, May 22
   "World Roundup," Flying Saucer Rev.
   3 (July-Aug.1957):66-69.

Tuckerton
-Skyquake
1977, Dec.7, 21
   U.S. Naval Rsch.Laboratory, NRL In-
   vestigations of East Coast Acoustics
   Events (Washington: Gov't Printing
   Office, 1978), pp.138-39.

Upper Montclair
-Psychokinesis
1920, summer/James H. Hyslop
   Irwin Ross, "Death Can Stop Your
   Clock," Fate 27 (Nov.1974):95-97.
-Spirit medium
1962, Oct.-Nov.
   Gertrude Ogden Tubby, "My Strongest
   Evidence for Survival," Fate 17
   (Dec.1964):76-82.

Ventnor
-UFO (NL)

1976, Jan.19
   "Noteworthy UFO Sightings," Ufology
   2 (summer 1976):62.

Villas
-Skyquake
1955, Sep.27
   "Bangs," Doubt, no.51 (1956):382.
1977, Dec.21
1978, Jan.3-5
   U.S. Naval Rsch.Laboratory, NRL In-
   vestigations of East Coast Acoustics
   Events (Washington: Gov't Printing
   Office, 1978), pp.139-40.

Vincentown
-Flying humanoid
1899
   Charles M. Skinner, American Myths
   and Legends, 2 vols. (Philadelphia:
   Lippincott, 1903), 1:243.
   James F. McCloy & Ray Miller, Jr.,
   The Jersey Devil (Wallingford, Pa.:
   Middle Atlantic, 1976), p.34.
-Haunt
1890-   /Granite Castle
   James Reynolds, Ghosts in American
   Houses (N.Y.: Paperback Library,
   1967 ed.), pp.11-29.
-UFO (CE-1)
1965, June 24/Lorraine Moore
   "Possible Saucer Landing in New Jer-
   sey," Saucer News 12 (Sep.1965):25,
   quoting Mount Holly Burlington
   County Herald (undated).

Vineland
-Disappearance
1962, Dec.17
   "Mysterious Disappearance in New
   Jersey," Saucer News 10 (Sep.1963):
   15.
-Hex
1958/Juan Aponte
   Doreen Valiente, Where Witchcraft
   Lives (London: Aquarian, 1962).
-Humanoid
1972, July/Pasquale's Sandwich
   (Editorial), Fate 26 (July 1973):31.
   John Green, Sasquatch: The Apes Among
   Us (Seattle: Hancock House, 1978),
   p.265, quoting Vineland Times-Jour-
   nal (undated).
-UFO (CE-1)
1978, Feb.1/Donald Bennett/Sherman Ave.
x Hance Bridge Rd.
   Atlantic City Press, 3 Feb.1978.
-UFO (DD)
1978, Sep.24/Dina Freedman/Pear St. x
Sutliff Ave.
   Vineland Times-Journal, 25 Sep.1978.
-UFO (NL)
1978, Jan.27/Cheryl DeSantis/2410
Barry Dr.
   Vineland Times-Journal, 30 Jan.1978.
1978, Jan.31/Pat Martinelli/N. Maple Dr.
   Atlantic City Press, 3 Feb.1978.

Wall twp.
-Skyquake

1977, Dec.2
  U.S. Naval Rsch.Laboratory, <u>NRL Investigations of East Coast Acoustics</u>
  <u>Events</u> (Washington: Gov't Printing
  <u>Office</u>, 1978), p.135.
-UFO (DD)
  1966, March 30/Robert J. Salvo
  <u>Newark News</u>, 12 May 1966. il.

Wanaque
<u>-UFO (NL)</u>
  1966, Jan.11-12/Joseph Cisco
  1966, Jan.13/Tom Garrison/treatment
  plant
    Edward J. Babcock & Timothy Green
    Beckley, "UFO Plagues N.J. Reser-
    voir," <u>Fate</u> 19 (Oct.1966):34,36,39-
    42.

Wantage twp.
-Humanoid and rabbit mutilations
  1977, May 12-June/Barbara Sites/Wolf-
  pit Rd.
    <u>Newton Herald</u>, 17 May 1977.
    <u>Morristown Daily Record</u>, 5 June 1977;
    and 19 June 1977.
    Robert E. Jones, "The Report of a Re-
    cent Bigfoot Incident in Wantage
    Township, New Jersey, with Autopsy
    Report of Mutilated Rabbits," <u>Ves-
    tigia Newsl.</u>, no.3 (summer-fall
    1977):1-2.
    S.N. Mayne, "The Wantage Event," <u>Pur-
    suit</u> 10 (fall 1977):124-27.

Warren
-Skyquake
  1979, Feb.8-11
    <u>Stirling Echoes Sentinel</u>, 15 Feb.1979.
-UFO (NL)
  1979, Feb.11/Chanticler Restaurant
    <u>Stirling Echoes Sentinel</u>, 15 Feb.1979.

Warren co.
-Genetic anomaly
  1972
    "That Frog!" <u>Pursuit</u> 5 (Oct.1972):85-
    86. il.
-UFO (CE-1)
  1977, Oct.30
    <u>Hackettstown Forum</u>, 9 Nov.1977.
-UFO (CE-2)
  ca.1974
    (Letter), H.S., <u>Saga UFO Rept.</u> 2
    (spring 1975):4.

Washington twp.
<u>-UFO (NL)</u>
  1973, Oct.
    <u>Hackensack Record</u>, 10 Oct.1973.

Wayne
-Astrology
  1970s/Wanda Lawris Moore
    John Godwin, <u>Occult America</u> (Garden
    City: Doubleday, 1972), pp.18-20. il.
-Photographic anomaly
  1974, Dec.15/August C. Roberts/23 Barns-
  dale Rd.
    August C. Roberts, "Tele-Mystery,"

<u>Flying Saucer Rev.</u> 21 (Apr.1976):
    14-18.
    Berthold Eric Schwarz, "Commentary
    on the August Roberts Mystery,"
    <u>Flying Saucer Rev.</u> 21 (Apr.1976):
    18-19.
    (Letter), Geoffrey G. Doel, <u>Flying
    Saucer Rev.</u> 22 (Apr.1977):24.
-Poltergeist
  1970-1971/Leonard D'Aquino
    <u>Bergen Sunday Record-Call</u>, 20 June
    1971.
-Skyquake
  1978, Jan.6
    U.S. Naval Rsch.Laboratory, <u>NRL In-
    vestigations of East Coast Acoustics</u>
    <u>Events</u> (Washington: Gov't Printing
    <u>Office</u>, 1978), p.140.
-UFO (CE-3)
  1973, Oct.17/Hwy.23
    David Webb, <u>1973: Year of the Human-
    oids</u> (Evanston: Center for UFO
    Studies, 1976 ed.), p.14.
-UFO (DD)
  1965, Sep./Bruce Marcot
    Otto O. Binder, "'Oddball' Saucers...
    That Fit No Patterns," <u>Fate</u> 21 (Feb.
    1968):54,55.

Webster
-Fall of slag
  1957, April 7
    Leonard H. Stringfield, <u>Inside Sau-
    cer Post...3-0 Blue</u> (Cincinnati:
    CRIFO, 1957), p.59.

Weehauken
<u>-UFO (CE-1)</u>
  1971, Aug.23/Robert Aguilar/Penn Central Railroad
    "Close-Up Sighting in New Jersey,"
    <u>APRO Bull.</u> 20 (Jan.-Feb.1972):1,3,
    quoting <u>Jersey City Journal</u> (un-
    dated).

West Collingswood
-Flying humanoid
  1909, Jan.21/Charles Klos/Grant Ave.
    Alfred Heston, <u>Jersey Waggon Jaunts</u>
    (Pleasantville: Atlantic County
    Historical Soc'y, 1926).
    <u>Salem Standard & Jerseyman</u>, 29 Oct.
    1936, p.3.

Westfield
-Erratic crocodilian
  1942, Aug.16/Raymond Miller/L. Mindo-
  waskin
    <u>New York Times</u>, 17 Aug.1942, p.17.

West Milford
-Ancient inscription
  1962, fall/Robert Smith/Ridge Rd.
    Edward J. Lenik, "The West Milford
    Effigy Stones," <u>NEARA Newsl.</u> 8 (win-
    ter 1974):72-74. il.
-UFO (NL)
  1947, July 9/William T. Silverthorn/
  Union Valley Rd.
    <u>Morristown Daily Record</u>, 10 July 1947.

West New York
-UFO (?)
  1962, July 9
    Richard Hall, ed., The UFO Evidence
    (Washington: NICAP, 1964), p.154.
-UFO (CE-1)
  1975, Jan.11/Joseph Wamsley/67th St. x
  Blvd. E
    Ted Bloecher, "The Stonehenge Inci-
    dents: January 1975," in Proc.1976
    CUFOS Conference (Evanston: Center
    for UFO Studies, 1976), pp.25,30-31.
    James D. White, "More New Jersey
    UFOs," APRO Bull. 25 (July 1976):1,
    3.

West Orange
-Phantom panther
  1926, June
    Curtis D. MacDougall, Hoaxes (N.Y.:
    Dover, 1958 ed.), p.34, quoting AP
    release, 28 June 1926.
-Psychokinesis
  1931, Oct.18/Glenmont/Edison Nat'l Historic Site
    "Thomas A. Edison's Stopped Clock,"
    Fate 17 (Feb.1964):58, quoting Ford
    Times (undated).
    Berthold Eric Schwarz, "The Telepath-
    ic Hypothesis and Genius: A Note on
    Thomas Alva Edison," Corrective Psy-
    chiatry & J.of Social Therapy 13
    (1967):7-19.
-Telepathy and survival research
  1885-1931/Thomas Alva Edison/Edison
  Nat'l Historic Site
    Austin C. Lescarboura, "Edison's
    Views on Life and Death," Sci.Am.
    123 (1920):446,458-60.
    B.C. Forbes, "Edison Working on How
    to Communicate with the Next World,"
    American Mag. 90 (Oct.1920):10-11,
    82-85.
    Bascomb Jones, Jr., "The Man with
    the Gimlet Eyes," Fate 4 (Apr.1951):
    56-58.
    Wainwright Evans, "Scientists Research
    Machine to Contact the Dead," Fate
    16 (Apr.1963):38-43.
    Berthold Eric Schwarz, "The Telepath-
    ic Hypothesis and Genius: A Note on
    Thomas Alva Edison," Corrective Psy-
    chiatry & J.of Social Therapy 13
    (1967):7-19.
    Martin Ebon, They Knew the Unknown
    (N.Y.: World, 1971), pp.129-38.
    (Letter), John S. Poapst, Fate 25
    (July 1972):142-43.
    (Letter), Joseph R. Gitz, Fate 25
    (July 1972):143-44.
-UFO (DD)
  1965, Nov.9/Gerry Falk/Mt. Prospect Ave.
    John G. Fuller, Incident at Exeter
    (N.Y.: Berkley, 1967 ed.), p.206.

West Paterson
-Plant sensitivity
  1970s/Pierre Paul Sauvin
    Peter Tompkins & Christopher Bird,
    The Secret Life of Plants (N.Y.:

Harper & Row, 1973), pp.33-40,44-45.
-UFO (DD)
  1965, Nov.9/Jerry Marca
    Otto O. Binder, "'Oddball' Saucers...
    That Fit No Pattern," Fate 21 (Feb.
    1968):54,60.

West Trenton
-UFO (NL)
  1947, July 4/Marion Marshall/Reading
  Railroad station/=meteor?
    Ted Bloecher, Report on the UFO Wave
    of 1947 (Washington: NICAP, 1967),
    Appendix, Case 279.

Westville
-Fall of rocks
  1956, Oct.21-Nov./Naz Tomasetti/45
  Lehigh Ave.
    (Editorial), Fate 10 (Feb.1957):10-
    11.
-Flying humanoid
  1909, Jan.21
    James F. McCloy & Ray Miller, Jr.,
    The Jersey Devil (Wallingford, Pa.:
    Middle Atlantic, 1976), p.64.
-UFO (NL)
  1974, Dec.18/Alfred Egbert III
    (Letter), Saga UFO Rept. 3 (Aug.
    1976):4-6.

Westwood
-UFO (NL)
  1958, Aug.24/Richard Schulz
    Bergen Evening Record, 25 Aug.1958.
  1962, Sep.18
    Richard Hall, ed., The UFO Evidence
    (Washington: NICAP, 1964), p.140.

White Meadow Lake
-Acoustic anomaly
  1976, Aug.-Oct.
    C. Louis Wiedemann, "Mysteries Break-
    ing Out All Over," Fate 30 (Sep.
    1977):34,40.
-Cattle mutilation
  1976, Oct./Hwy.15
    C. Louis Wiedemann, "Mysteries Break-
    ing Out All Over," Fate 30 (Sep.
    1977):34,39-40.
-Humanoid
  1974, Nov./W on I-80
    C. Louis Wiedemann, "Difficulties of
    Tracking Down the Lizardman," Ves-
    tigia Newsl., no.3 (summer-fall
    1977):3.
    C. Louis Wiedemann, "Mysteries Break-
    ing Out All Over," Fate 30 (Sep.
    1977):34-35.
  1976, Aug.1
    Dover Advance, 3 Aug.1976.
    C. Louis Wiedemann, "Mysteries Break-
    ing Out All Over," Fate 30 (Sep.
    1977):34,38.
  1976, Sep.
    C. Louis Wiedemann, "Mysteries Break-
    ing Out All Over," Fate 30 (Sep.
    1977):34,36-37,40-41.
-Humanoid tracks
  1975, winter
    C. Louis Wiedemann, supra, pp.34,40.

-UFO (CE-1)
  1974, Sep.
    C. Louis Wiedemann, "Mysteries Break-
    ing Out All Over," Fate 30 (Sep.
    1977):34,35.
-UFO (NL)
  1976, Aug.-Sep.
    C. Louis Wiedemann, "Mysteries Break-
    ing Out All Over," Fate 30 (Sep.
    1977):34-42.

Whitesbog
-Humanoid tracks
  1952/F.A. Fralinger/=hoax
    James F. McCloy & Ray Miller, Jr.,
    The Jersey Devil (Wallingford, Pa.:
    Middle Atlantic, 1976), p.94.

Wildwood
-Skyquake
  1955, Sep.21
    "Bangs," Doubt, no.51 (1956):382.

Wildwood Crest
-Men-in-black
  1967, Jan.9/Edward Christiansen
    John A. Keel, "The Cape May Incident,"
    in Beyond Condon (Flying Saucer Rev.
    special issue, no.2, June 1969), pp.
    57-62.
    John A. Keel, The Mothman Prophecies
    (N.Y.: Saturday Review, 1975), pp.
    89-94.
-Phantom
  1967, Jan.13-15/Edward Christiansen
    John A. Keel, "The Cape May Incident,"
    in Beyond Condon (Flying Saucer Rev.
    special issue, no.2, June 1969), pp.
    57-62.
    John A. Keel, The Mothman Prophecies
    (N.Y.: Saturday Review, 1975), p.95.

Winfield
-Poltergeist
  1964, May/Theodore Borodynko/2-C Wave-
  crest Ave.
    (Editorial), Fate 17 (Sep.1964):20-
    21.

Woodbridge
-Mystery truck accidents
  1970, Feb.23/George Hermey/Garden State
  Parkway x Hwy.440
  1970, Feb.24/William R. Buchanan/Hwy.9
  x Bordentown Ave.
    Woodbridge News-Tribune, 24-25 Feb.
    1970.
-Poltergeist
  1834/Joseph Barron
    E.C. Rogers, Philosophy of Mysterious
    Agents (Cleveland: J.P. Jewett,
    1853), p.38.
    Eliab W. Capron, Modern Spiritualism:
    Its Facts and Fanaticisms (Boston:
    Bela Marsh, 1855), pp.26-29, quoting
    Newark Daily Advertiser (undated).
-UFO (NL)
  1975, Oct.4
    "UFO Central," CUFOS News Bull., 1
    Feb.1976, p.7.

-Witch trial (shape-shifting)
  1936, Oct.2/Terese Czinkota
    William Seabrook, Witchcraft: Its
    Power in the World Today (N.Y.:
    Lancer, 1968 ed.), pp.270-71.

Woodbury
-Fall of fish
  1875/William C. Biddle
    E.W. Gudger, "More Rains of Fishes,"
    Annals & Mag.of Natural History,
    ser.10, 3 (1929):1,21.
-Flying humanoid
  1909, Jan.17
  1909, Jan.22/Samuel Merchant
    Philadelphia (Pa.) Public Ledger, 22
    Jan.1909.
    James F. McCloy & Ray Miller, Jr.,
    The Jersey Devil (Wallingford, Pa.:
    Middle Atlantic, 1976), pp.39,70.
-UFO (NL)
  1962, July/Gwen Allen
    (Letter), Ufology 2 (spring 1976):
    48.

Woodcliff Lake
-UFO (NL)
  1974, June 4/Robert J. LeDonne
    J. Allen Hynek & Jacques Vallee, The
    Edge of Reality (Chicago: Regnery,
    1975), pp.280-88.

Woodstown
-Phantom wolf
  1935-1936/Philip Smith
    James F. McCloy & Ray Miller, Jr.,
    The Jersey Devil (Wallingford, Pa.:
    Middle Atlantic, 1976), p.90.

            B. Physical Features

Atsion L.
-Humanoid tracks
  1960/Berle Schwed
    John A. Keel, Strange Creatures from
    Time and Space (Greenwich, Ct.: Faw-
    cett, 1970), p.112.

Barnegat Bay
-Haunt
  n.d.
    James F. McCloy & Ray Miller, Jr.,
    The Jersey Devil (Wallingford, Pa.:
    Middle Atlantic, 1976), pp.31-32.

Bear Swamp
-Humanoid
  1975, Feb.-Oct.
    Robert E. Jones, "Bigfoot in New Jer-
    sey?" Pursuit 8 (July 1975):68-69.
    Robert B. Jones, "Bigfoot in New Jer-
    sey," Pursuit 8 (Oct.1975):101-102.
    Robert E. Jones, "Bigfoot Expedition,"
    Pursuit 9 (Jan.1976):5-7.
    John Green, Sasquatch: The Apes Among
    Us (Seattle: Hancock House, 1978),
    pp.9-10.

Brigantine Beach
-Flying humanoid
   1894
      James F. McCloy & Ray Miller, Jr.,
      The Jersey Devil (Wallingford, Pa.:
      Middle Atlantic, 1976), p.34.

Budd L.
-Erratic shark
   1965, June/Pamela Bird
      "Fishing--Unexplained," Pursuit 2
      (Jan.1969):10-11.

Canistear Reservoir
-UFO (CE-1)
   1958, July 8/John A. Collins
      Berthold E. Schwarz, "UFOs in New
      Jersey," J.Med.Soc'y N.J. 66 (1969)
      :460-64.

Delaware R.
-Anomalous artifact
      Charles C. Abbott, "On the Occurrence
      of a Stone Mask in New Jersey, U.S.A."
      Nature 12 (1875):49-50.

Delaware Water Gap
-Ancient inscriptions
      Edward J. Lenik, "Petroglyphs from
      the Upper Delaware Valley," Pennsyl-
      vania Arch. 47 (Apr.1977):14-18. il.
      Salvatore Michael Trento, The Search
      for Lost America (Chicago: Contem-
      porary, 1978), pp.75-77. il.
-UFO (DD)
   1958, Oct.2/Ivan T. Sanderson
      Richard Hall, ed., The UFO Evidence
      (Washington: NICAP, 1964), p.52.
      Ivan T. Sanderson, Uninvited Visitors
      (N.Y.: Cowles, 1967), pp.29-33.

East Creek
-Mystery tree stumps
   =evidence of cataclysm?
      Ivan T. Sanderson, Investigating the
      Unexplained (Englewood Cliffs, N.J.:
      Prentice-Hall, 1972), pp.101-14.

High Point State Park
-Humanoid
   1973, summer
      Allen V. Noe, "And Still the Reports
      Roll In," Pursuit 7 (Jan.1974):17-
      18.
   1975, spring
      (Editorial), Fate 29 (Feb.1976):28.
-Humanoid tracks
   1975, Feb.21
      John Green, Sasquatch: The Apes Among
      Us (Seattle: Hancock House, 1978),
      p.268.

Hopatcong L.
-UFO (CE-1)
   1966, Feb.27
      Berthold Eric Schwarz, "Beauty of the
      Night," Flying Saucer Rev. 18 (July-
      Aug.1972):5,8-9.

Kittatinny Mts.
-Ancient mines
      Salvatore Michael Trento, The Search
      for Lost America (Chicago: Contem-
      porary, 1978), pp.90-91.
-Cat mutilation
   1977, summer/Jean Christman
      C. Louis Wiedemann, "A Mutilated
      Kitten in New Jersey," Anomaly Rsch.
      Bull., no.7 (Sep.1977):10-11.
-Electromagnetic anomaly
   1967, June 5/Kittatinny Power Plant
      John A. Keel, "Is the 'EM' Effect a
      Myth?" Flying Saucer Rev. 14 (Nov.-
      Dec.1968):16,17.

Lions L.
-UFO (CE-2)
   1966, Aug.18
      John A. Keel, "Our Skies Are Filled
      with Junk," Fate 22 (Mar.1969):34,
      37.

Long Beach I.
-Flying humanoid
   1894
      James F. McCloy & Ray Miller, Jr.,
      The Jersey Devil (Wallingford, Pa.:
      Middle Atlantic, 1976), p.34.
-Skyquake
   1977, Dec.21
      "Aerial Detonations," Res Bureaux
      Bull., no.28 (19 Jan.1978):1,2.
-UFO (NL)
   1977, Dec.13/Robert Snyder
      Jon Douglas Singer, "Skyquakes: Things
      That Go Bump in the Night," Pursuit
      11 (spring 1978):45,47.

May, Cape
-Sea monster (carcass)
   1921, Nov./=baleen whale
      F.A, Mitchell Hedges, Battles with
      Giant Fish (London: Duckworth,
      1923), p.22.
-UFO (NL)
   1972, July 7/Frank Markley/Shunpike x
   Tabernacle Rd.
      Cape May County Gazette, 13 July
      1972. il.
-UFO (R)
   1951, Feb.
      "Astronomers and UFO's: A Survey,
      Part 2," Int'l UFO Reporter 2 (Apr.
      1977):3,4.

Minisink I.
-Petroglyph
      Herbert C. Kraft, "There Are Petro-
      glyphs in New Jersey," Bull.Arch.
      Soc'y N.J., Feb.1969, pp.13-16. il.

Mullica R.
-Dog and chicken mutilations
   1966, April/Steven Silkotch
      James F. McCloy & Ray Miller, Jr.,
      The Jersey Devil (Wallingford, Pa.:
      Middle Atlantic, 1976), pp.98-99.
-Flying humanoid myth
      n.d./Jane Leeds Johnson/Cale Cavileer's

Lane
James F. McCloy & Ray Miller, Jr.,
The Jersey Devil (Wallingford, Pa.:
Middle Atlantic, 1976), p.28.

North Shrewsbury R.
-River monster
1889, June/nr. Neptune Clubhouse
New York Times, 25 June 1889, p.1.

Oak Ridge Reservoir
-UFO (NL)
1966, April 1
Newark Evening News, 2 Apr.1966.

Oradell Reservoir
-UFO (CE-2)
1962, Sep.15-16/Steve Nagy
Hackensack Record, 17 Sep.1962.
Gray Barker, *Book of Saucers* (Clarks-
burg, W.V.: Saucerian, 1965), pp.
24-25.
-UFO (NL)
1962, Sep.24
Richard Hall, ed., *The UFO Evidence*
(Washington: NICAP, 1964), p.140.
Gray Barker, *Book of Saucers* (Clarks-
burg, W.V.: Saucerian, 1965), p.25.

Owassa L.
-Phantom airplane
1963, July/Lori Yesthal
N. Bradley King, "The Phantom Aircraft," *Fate* 29 (Nov.1976):77-80.

Pahaquarra site
-Archeological site
Herbert C. Kraft, "A Petroglyph
Knife," *Bull.Arch.Soc'y N.J.*,
spring-summer 1974, p.33. il.

Passaic R.
-Erratic crocodilian
1933, Sep.11
New York Times, 12 Sep.1933, p.3.

Pine Barrens
-Humanoid
1950s
John Green, *Sasquatch: The Apes Among
Us* (Seattle: Hancock House, 1978),
p.265.

Raritan Bay
-Sea monster (carcass)
1822, June/=basking shark
A.C. Oudemans, *The Great Sea-Serpent*
(Leiden: E.J. Brill, 1892), p.89,
quoting *New Yorker*, 15 June 1822.

Rockaway R.
-Humanoid
1939, fall
"The Berkshire Valley Bigfoot," *Vestigia Newsl.*, no.2 (spring 1977):
5-6.

Sandy Hook
-Auroral anomaly
1908, March 27/Wilmot E. Ellis

Wilmot E. Ellis, "A Study of the Remarkable Illumination of the Sky on
March 27, 1908," *Science* 28 (1908):
51-53.
-Sea monster
1879, Nov.28
New York Times, 29 Dec.1879, p.2.
1888/"Wisconsin"/30 mi. offshore
Bernard Heuvelmans, *In the Wake of
the Sea-Serpents* (N.Y.: Hill & Wang,
1968), p.293.
1963, Aug.19/Lionel A. Walford/"Chal-
lenger"
New York Times, 20 Aug.1963, p.35;
22 Aug.1963, p.21; and 26 Aug.1963,
p.29.
-UFO (CE-2)
1970, July 3
Berthold Eric Schwarz, "Possible
UFO-Induced Temporary Paralysis,"
Flying Saucer Rev. 17 (Mar.-Apr.
1971):4,6.
-UFO (DD)
1951, Sep.10/Edward Ballard
Edward J. Ruppelt, *The Report on Unidentified Flying Objects* (Garden
City: Doubleday, 1956), p.92.
Richard Hall, ed., *The UFO Evidence*
(Washington: NICAP, 1964), p.20,
quoting INS release, 12 Sep.1951.

Shark R.
-Haunt
n.d./Money Hill
Charles M. Skinner, *Myths and Legends
of Our Own Land*, 2 vols. (Philadelphia: Lippincott, 1896), 1:271-72.

Split Rock Reservoir
-UFO (CE-2)
1966, Oct.15/Jerry H. Simons
Berthold Eric Schwarz, "UFOs: Delu-
sion or Dilemma?" in *Beyond Condon*
(Flying Saucer Rev. special issue,
no.2, June 1969), pp.46,47-49.
Donald E. Keyhoe & Gordon I.R. Lore,
Jr., *UFOs: A New Look* (Washington:
NICAP, 1969), pp.9-10.

Wanaque Reservoir
-Phantom helicopters
1966, Oct.11/Ben Thompson
Lloyd Mallan, "What Happened at Wan-
aque, N.J.?" *Sci.& Mech.* 38 (June
1967):42,45-46.
-UFO (CE-2)
1966, Oct.11/Ben Thompson
"UFOs Return to Wanaque Reservoir,"
UFO Inv. 3 (Oct.-Nov.1966):6.
Lloyd Mallan, "What Happened at Wan-
aque, N.J.?" *Sci.& Mech.* 38 (May
1967):28-33,62-64; (June 1967):42-
47,70.
Ivan T. Sanderson, *Invisible Residents*
(N.Y.: World, 1970), pp.58-62.
-UFO (NL)
1940s
Ivan T. Sanderson, *Invisible Residents*
(N.Y.: World, 1970), pp.61-62.
1963, Jan./Jack Wardlaw/Cooper's Swamp

Fairfield Chronicle, 7 Feb.1979.
1966, Jan.11/Harry T. Wolfe
  Newark Evening News, 12 Jan.1966.
  Edward J. Babcock & Timothy Green
  Beckley, "UFO Plagues N.J. Reservoir," Fate 19 (Oct.1966):34,38.
  Lloyd Mallan, "What Happened at Wanaque, N.J.?" Sci.& Mech. 38 (June
  1967):42,71,73.
  Brad Steiger & August C. Roberts,
  Enemies from Outer Space: The Flying Saucer Menace (N.Y.: Award,
  1967), pp.22-26.
1966, Jan.11-12/Charles Theodora/pump-
ing station
  "National Press Spotlights UFOs,"
  UFO Inv. 3 (Jan.-Feb.1966):1,3.
  Dave Anderson, "The Saucer That Ter-
  rorized a Town," Saga, Aug.1966, pp.
  12-15,71-72.
  Edward J. Babcock & Timothy Green
  Beckley, "UFO Plagues N.J. Reservoir," Fate 19 (Oct.1966):34,36-41,
  43. il.

White City
-Mystery tracks
1909, Jan.17-18/Clarence B. Williams
  James F. McCloy & Ray Miller, Jr.,
  The Jersey Devil (Wallingford, Pa.:
  Middle Atlantic, 1976), p.42.

White Rock L.
-UFO (CE-1)
1966, March 31/Connie Bateman
  Dover Daily Advance, 1 Apr.1966, p.1.
  Berthold Eric Schwarz, "Stella Lan-
  sing's UFO Motion Pictures," Flying
  Saucer Rev. 18 (Jan.-Feb.1972):3,7.

      D. Unspecified Localities

-UFO (CE-1)
1960, July-Sep./Hans Ludwig
  "Floating Globes," APRO Bull. 10
  (Jan.1962):3-4.

-UFO (CE-2)
1975, June
  Howard Smukler, "The Diamond Mystery:
  Message from a UFO," Official UFO 2
  (May 1977):24,56. il.

NEW YORK

A. Populated Places

Adams
-Plague of birds
  1947, May 22/Glenn Potts
    "Run of the Mill," Doubt, no.20
    (1948):303.

Albany
-Ghost
  1941, March/Louis C. Jones
    Louis C. Jones, "The Ghost and I,"
    New York Folklore Quar. 10 (1954):
    123-26.
-Gravity anomaly
  1964, April 10/Teddy Bix/13 O'Connell
  St.
    (Editorial), Fate 17 (Aug.1964):14-
    18, quoting Albany Times-Union (un-
    dated).
-Haunt
  1965, Dec.-1968, Feb./Gloria Vittner
    Gloria Vittner, "Our Haunted Parson-
    age," Fate 26 (Dec.1973):84-87.
-Midday darkness
  1881, Sep.6
    "The Yellow Day in September 1881,"
    Weatherwise 25 (June 1972):118.
-Precognition
  1970s/Ann Fisher/75 Willett St.
    Warren Smith, "Phenomenal Predictions
    for 1976," Saga, Jan.1976, pp.16,18.
-Telephone anomaly and men-in-black
  1968, Feb./Jennifer Stevens
    Jennifer Stevens, "Mystery on the
    Mohawk," in Beyond Condon (Flying
    Saucer Rev. special issue, no.2,
    June 1969), pp.36-38.
    John A. Keel, The Mothman Prophecies
    (N.Y.: Saturday Review, 1975), pp.
    74-75.
-UFO (?)
  n.d.
    Albany Knickerbocker News, 30 Mar.
    1966, p.12A.
  1951, June 16-19/F.X. Gruber/=planets?
    (Letter), Fate 5 (Jan.1952):113.
    (Letter), W.P. Grant, Fate 5 (June
    1952):115-16.
-UFO (CE-1)
  1966, April 10/Patrick Olesko
    Albany Knickerbocker News, 28 Apr.
    1966, p.1A.
-UFO (DD)
  1950, May/Claire Oliver/C & S Bank Bldg.
    (Letter), Fate 10 (Oct.1957):116-19.
  1965, Aug.10/Hwy.9J
    "Saucer Flap Around Albany, New York,"
    Saucer News 12 (Dec.1965):23.
-UFO (NL)
  1966, April 10/John Albano/Hudson R.
    Albany Knickerbocker News, 11 Apr.
    1966, p.3B.
  1967, May 16/Frederic D. Weinstein/N

on Hwy.87
  "Sparks and Explosion," UFO Inv. 4
  (May-June 1967):3.

Alden
-Fall of ice
  1973, May 29/Esther Kochanowicz
    Syracuse Post-Standard, 30 May 1973.

Alder Creek
-Haunt
  n.d.
    Louis C. Jones, Things That Go Bump
    in the Night (N.Y.: Hill & Wang,
    1959), p.60.

Altamont
-Archeological site
  Knox Cave
    "Needs Investigating: An Interesting
    Trio," NEARA Newsl. 7 (June 1972):
    32-33.
-UFO (CE-3)
  1974, April 30/Ruth Currie
    "Investigation Reveals Unreported
    Sightings," UFO Inv., Nov.1974, p.1.

Amagansett
-UFO (?)
  1966, May 2/Mackay Radio Towers
  1967, Jan.20
    John A. Keel, "North America 1966:
    Development of a Great Wave," Fly-
    ing Saucer Rev. 13 (Mar.-Apr.1967):
    3,5-6.
-UFO (CE-2)
  1966, March 30/Bruce Field/Mackay Radio Towers
    East Hampton Star, 17 Apr.1966.
    "Close-Range Sightings Increase,"
    UFO Inv. 3 (Mar.-Apr.1966):3.
    Donald E. Keyhoe & Gordon I.R. Lore,
    Jr., UFOs: A New Look (Washington:
    NICAP, 1969), p.8.
  1966, April 14
    "Saucer Flap on Long Island," Saucer
    News 14 (spring 1967):34.

Amherst
-Fall of ice
  1959, Sep.11/George J. Trillizio/114
  Chestnut Ridge Rd.
    (Editorial), Fate 13 (Jan.1960):24.
-UFO (?)
  1966, May
    Amherst Bee, 26 May 1966. il.

Amityville
-Haunt
  1974, Dec.18-1975, Jan.15/George Lee
  Lutz/112 Ocean Ave./=hoax
    Jay Anson, The Amityville Horror (En-
    glewood Cliffs, N.J.: Prentice-Hall,
    1977).

Peter Jordan & Rick Moran, "The Amityville Horror: The Truth Behind
America's Most Infamous Haunted
House," Saga UFO Rept. 5 (June 1978)
:37-39,74-78. il.

Ancram
-Haunt
1961/Herbert Rockefeller
Hans Holzer, Ghosts I've Met (N.Y.:
Ace, 1965 ed.), pp.130-31.

Angola
-Precognition
1968, Oct.23/Jean Gallagher
Jean Gallagher, "Dreaming True: Blessing and Curse," Fate 23 (June 1970):
100,104-106.
-UFO (NL)
1966, fall/Norman Pease
"Chop Chop," Skylook, no.47 (Oct.
1971):4.

Apalachia
-UFO (CE-1)
1964, summer/Beverly Connelly
(Letter), Flying Saucer Rev. 19 (Jan.-
Feb.1975):32.

Arkwright twp.
-UFO (?)
1958, Aug.11
Richard Hall, ed., The UFO Evidence
(Washington: NICAP, 1964), p.99.

Atlantic Beach
-UFO (NL)
1975, Sep.3
"UFO Central," CUFOS News Bull., 15
Nov.1975, p.17.

Auburn
-Inner development
1850s/Apostolic Brotherhood
Emma Hardinge Britten, Modern Ameri-
can Spiritualism (N.Y.: The Author,
1870), pp.58-60,208-209.
-Possession
1849, spring-1850
Eliab W. Capron, Modern Spiritualism
(Boston: Bela Marsh, 1855), pp.106-
12.
-Roman coin
1929, Aug./Arthur C. Parker
New York Times, 19 Aug.1929, p.19.
-Seance
1850s/Kate Fox
Emma Hardinge Britten, Modern American Spiritualism (N.Y.: The Author,
1870), pp.55-57.
-Spirit medium
1848-1850s/Ann Benedict
Eliab W. Capron, Modern Spiritualism
(Boston: Bela Marsh, 1855), pp.111-
12,117-19.
Nandor Fodor, Encyclopaedia of Psychic Science (London: Arthurs,
1933), p.30.
1848-1850s/Sarah Tamlin
Eliab W. Capron, Modern Spiritualism

(Boston: Bela Marsh, 1855), pp.106-
18.

Au Sable Forks
-UFO (DD)
1957, Nov.8
"Did the Air Force Deceive the Pub-
lic About the November Sightings?"
UFO Inv. 1 (Jan.1958):1,8.

Babylon
-Acoustic anomaly
1967, Aug.3/Jaye P. Paro
John A. Keel, The Mothman Prophecies
(N.Y.: Saturday Review, 1975), p.
226.

Bainbridge
-UFO (DD)
1954, May 30/Mrs. Leo Ireland
(Letter), Fate 7 (Nov.1954):111.
Richard Hall, ed., The UFO Evidence
(Washington: NICAP, 1964), pp.146,
150.

Baldwin
-UFO (NL)
1952, April 16
Garden City Newsday, 17 Apr.1952.

Baldwinsville
-Lake monster
1871/mill pond/=hoax?
New York Times, 27 May 1871, p.4.
-UFO (CE-2)
1978, Sep.7/Seneca R.
Syracuse New Times, 19 Nov.1978.
-UFO (NL)
1978, April 5/Margaret Hargett
"Object Sighted, Confirmed by Radar,"
APRO Bull. 27 (Oct.1978):1,4.

Ballston Spa
-UFO (DD)
1969, Sep.22/George Volkins
Albany Knickerbocker News, 23 Sep.
1969, p.8C.

Barneveld
-Poltergeist
1884, June 16-17/George Sandford
New York Sun, 22 June 1884, p.1.

Barryville
-Ancient stone cairns
Salvatore Michael Trento, The Search
for Lost America (Chicago: Contemporary, 1978), pp.84-85.

Batavia
-Fall of frogs
1937, Oct.7
"Falls of Frogs," Fortean Soc'y Mag.,
no.3 (Jan.1940):7, quoting New York
World-Telegram (undated).
-Humanoid
1960/ Donald Palone/Tonawanda Creek
(Editorial), Fate 14 (Jan.1961):14-
15.

Bath
-UFO (NL)
  1975, July 3
    "UFO Central," CUFOS News Bull., 15
    Nov.1975, p.12.

Bay Shore
-Inner development
  1962-   /Ray Buckland/Museum of Witch-
  craft/6 First Ave.
    (Letter), Fate 22 (Aug.1969):127-28.
    New York Times, 31 Oct.1969.
    John Godwin, Occult America (Garden
    City: Doubleday, 1972), pp.71-72.
    Hans Holzer, The Witchcraft Report
    (N.Y.: Ace, 1973), pp.34-35.
    Raymond Buckland, Practical Candle-
    burning Rituals (St. Paul: Llewell-
    yn, 1976).
    J. Gordon Melton, Encyclopedia of
    American Religions, 2 vols. (Wil-
    mington, N.C.: Consortium, 1978),
    2:279-80.

Beacon
-Fall of brown snow
  1967, Nov.7/Shirley Dombroski/=pollu-
  tion?
    (Letter), Fate 21 (Apr.1968):130-31.

Bedford
-Haunt
  n.d.
    New York Writers' Program, New York:
    A Guide to the Empire State (N.Y.:
    Oxford Univ., 1956), p.113.

Bellmore
-Acoustic anomaly
  1950s/Mrs. C.W. Floyd
    (Letter), Fate 14 (July 1961):120-22.

Bellport
-Poltergeist
  1896, Feb./Mary Mack
    New York World, 17 Feb.1896; and 19
    Feb.1896.

Bellvale
-Ancient inscription
    Salvatore Michael Trento, The Search
    for Lost America (Chicago: Contem-
    porary, 1978), p.102. il.
-Phantom
  1903, winter
    Asa M. Russell, "Our Two-Angel Es-
    cort," Fate 11 (Oct.1958):32-33.

Bemis Heights
-Giant fossil human teeth
  n.d./Saratoga battlefield
    Benson J. Lossing, The Pictorial
    Field-Book of the Revolution, 2 vols.
    (N.Y.: Harper, 1855), 1:64n.

Berlin
-Deathbed apparition
  1848, Aug./Nancy Davis
    James L. Scott, Scenes Beyond the
    Grave (Dayton: Stephen Deuel, 1856).

Berne
-Haunt
  19th c./Simmons factory
    Louis C. Jones, Things That Go Bump
    in the Night (N.Y.: Hill & Wang,
    1959), pp.148-49.

Bethpage
-UFO (CE-2)
  1967, Sep.6/Edward W. Goldstein/Beth-
  page State Park
    Brad Steiger, Mysteries of Time and
    Space (N.Y.: Dell, 1976 ed.), pp.
    139-40.
-UFO (NL)
  1960, Aug.23-Sep.2
    London (Eng.) Daily Telegraph, 3
    Sep.1960.
    Richard Hall, ed., The UFO Evidence
    (Washington: NICAP, 1964), p.95.
    Orin Browning, "Mystery of the Alien
    Satellites," Saga UFO Rept. 2 (sum-
    mer 1975):34,36.
    Wendelle C. Stevens, "UFO Tracks in
    the Sky," Saga UFO Rept. 2 (fall
    1975):23.

Binghamton
-Ancient metal urn
  1973, summer
    Salvatore Michael Trento, The Search
    for Lost America (Chicago: Contem-
    porary, 1978), pp.71-73. il.
-Fall of metal pellets
  1954, spring
    (Editorial), Fate 7 (Nov.1954):11.
-Fall of metallic object
  1898, Jan./Park Ave.
    Harriman (Tenn.) Record, 8 Aug.1957.
-Ghost
  n.d.
    (Editorial), Fate 2 (May 1949):4.
-UFO (NL)
  1960, Nov.25/Marion T. Lee
    "Odds and Ends," APRO Bull. 9 (Jan.
    1961):5.
  1964, July 22-24/Edward Malone
    "New Flurries & Montana Flurries," UFO
    Inv. 2 (Sep.-Oct.1964):6, quoting
    Binghamton Press (undated).

Blasdell
-UFO (DD)
  1966, June 24/Richard Manning
    "Saucer Briefs," Saucer News 13
    (fall 1966):26,29.

Blue Point
-Mystery television transmission
  1953, Dec.9-11/Jerry Travers
    (Editorial), Fate 7 (Apr.1954):8-10.
    il.
    Vincent H. Gaddis, "When TV Tunes to
    Another Dimension," Probe the Un-
    known 3 (May 1975):32-33. il.

Boonville
-Poltergeist
  1951/Audrey F. Kahabka
    (Letter), Fate 4 (Oct.1951):115-16.

Boston
-UFO (?)
 1949, Sep.12
  "If It's in the Sky It's a Saucer,"
  Doubt, no.27 (1949):416,417.

Brentwood
-UFO (NL)
 1966, Oct.29/Leonard Victor
  (Editorial), Saucer News 14 (spring
  1967):19. il.

Brewerton
-Archeological site
 ca.3000-1700 B.C.
  William A. Ritchie, "Two Prehistoric
  Village Sites at Brewerton, New
  York," Rsch.Records Rochester Mus.
  Arts & Sci., no.5 (1940).
  William A. Ritchie, The Archaeology
  of New York State (Garden City:
  Natural History Press, 1969), pp.89-
  104. il.
-UFO (CE-2)
 1967, Oct./Joe Lamb
  T.M. Wright, "UFO's over Ithaca,"
  Fate 22 (Feb.1969):44,50-51.

Brewster
-Fall of carbonaceous substance
 1966, Oct.8/Gene Blaney/baseball field
  (Editorial), Fate 20 (May 1967):15-
  18.
-Psychic photography
 1931, July 4/Enid Beaupré
  Hereward Carrington, "A Case of
  'Spirit Photography,'" Psychic Rsch.
  26 (1932):20-22. il.

Briarcliff Manor
-Animal ESP
 1927-1932
  J. Malcolm Bird, "The Briarcliff
  Pony," Psychic Rsch. 23 (1929):26-
  31.
  Arthur Goadby, "Animal Metapsychics,"
  Psychic Rsch. 23 (1929):201-208.
  Arthur Goadby, "Conversing Animals,"
  Psychic Rsch. 25 (1931):151-63.
  Arthur Goadby, "Conversing Animals,"
  J.ASPR 26 (1932):22-30.
  Arthur Goadby, "Conversing Animals:
  The Spirit Hypothesis," J.ASPR 34
  (1940):194-204.
  Vincent & Margaret Gaddis, The Strange
  World of Animals and Pets (N.Y.:
  Pocket Books, 1971 ed.), pp.156-57,
  quoting Cosmopolitan, Aug.1928.

Brighton
-Precognition
 1940-1960/Lillian M. Corbett
  Lillian M. Corbett, "My ESP Diary,"
  Fate 25 (Feb.1972):73-75.

Broadalbin
-UFO (NL)
 1976, Dec.13
  "UFO Analysis," Int'l UFO Reporter 2
  (Jan.1977):Newsfront sec.

Brocton
-Inner development
 1867-1875/Thomas Lake Harris
  New York Sun, 30 Apr.1869.
  John Humphrey Noyes, History of Amer-
  ican Socialisms (Philadelphia: Lip-
  pincott, 1870), pp.577-94.
  Arthur A. Cuthbert, The Life and
  World-Work of Thomas Lake Harris
  (Glasgow: C.W. Pearce, 1908).
  Nandor Fodor, Encyclopaedia of Psy-
  chic Science (London: Arthurs,
  1933), p.159.

Brookfield
-Religious ecstasy
 n.d./John Crapsey
  Nandor Fodor, Encyclopaedia of Psychic Science (London: Arthurs,
  1933), p.329.

Brookhaven
-Hex
 1663, Dec.25/Ralph Hall
  Niles' Weekly Register, 11 Aug.1821.
  Edmund Bailey O'Callaghan, Document-
  ary History of the State of New
  York, 4 vols. (Albany: Charles Van
  Benthuysen, 1850), 4:133-36.
  George Lincoln Burr, ed., Narratives
  of the Witchcraft Cases 1648-1706
  (N.Y.: Barnes & Noble, 1946), pp.
  41-48.

Bucktown
-UFO (CE-1)
 1950, Feb.28/Harrison McGee
  Harrison McGee, "Fireball Omen,"
  Fate 26 (Feb.1973):74.

Buffalo
-Animal ESP
 1902-1906/Henry Brader/Smith x Howard
 St.
  (Letter), Fate 17 (June 1964):107-108.
 1953/Roy R. Salisbury
  "Psychic Canine," Fate 7 (Jan.1954):
  50.
-Clairvoyance and precognition
 1954, summer-   /Jean Gallagher
  Jean Gallagher, "Dreaming True: Bless-
  ing and Curse," Fate 23 (June 1970):
  100-106.
-Disappearance
 1902, Aug.
  New York Sun, 14 Aug.1902.
-Dowsing
 1955
  (Editorial), Fate 9 (May 1956):7.
-Fall of black rain
 1819, Nov.
  Hudson Northern Whig, 23 Nov.1819.
-Fall of fish
 1900, summer/Bailey Williams/Barthel x
 Genesee St.
  E.W. Gudger, "More Rains of Fishes,"
  Annals & Mag.of Natural History,
  ser.10, 3 (1929):1,22.
-Fall of metal pellets
 1955, April-June/South Buffalo

Buffalo News, 4 June 1955.
-Healing research
 1960s-   /Justa Smith/Rosary Hill
 College
    Justa Smith, "Paranormal Effects on
    Enzyme Activity," Proc.Parapsych.
    Ass'n 5 (1968):15-16.
    (Editorial), Fate 26 (May 1973):7-12.
    Andrija K. Puharich, "Psychic Re-
    search and the Healing Process," in
    Edgar Mitchell, ed., Psychic Explor-
    ation (N.Y.: Capricorn, 1976 ed.),
    pp.333,339-40.
-Hex
 1939, Aug.
    Buffalo Courier-Express, 13 Aug.1939.
-Inner development
 1967-   /Human Dimensions Institute/
 4380 Main St.
    June & Nicholas Regush, Psi: The Oth-
    er World Catalogue (N.Y.: Putnam,
    1974), p.8.
    Agatha J. Tutko, "Teaching the Blind
    to See," Fate 28 (May 1975):30-38.
    Rhea A. White, "Parapsychology Today,"
    in Edgar Mitchell, ed., Psychic Ex-
    ploration (N.Y.: Capricorn, 1976
    ed.), pp.195,211-12.
    Herbert B. Greenhouse, The Astral
    Journey (N.Y.: Avon, 1976), pp.314-
    15,336-37.
    Lawrence Cortesi, "Teaching the Blind
    to See Through ESP," Psychic World,
    Jan.1977, pp.46-50,83.
    (Editorial), Fate 32 (Mar.1979):8-12,
    quoting Buffalo Evening News (un-
    dated).
-Lunar cycle and suicide
 1964-1969
    David Lester, Gene W. Brockopp &
    Kitty Priebe, "Association Between
    a Full Moon and Completed Suicide,"
    Psych.Reports 25 (1969):598.
-Mystery plane crash
 1963, Dec.17/Beech C-45H
    Jay Gourley, The Great Lakes Triangle
    (Greenwich, Ct.: Fawcett, 1977),
    pp.85-86.
-Paranormal amnesia
 1967, Aug.15/Paul T. MacGregor
    John A. Keel, Our Haunted Planet
    (Greenwich, Ct.: Fawcett, 1971), p.
    198.
-Psychic photography
 1974/Wendy Sternberg/Buffalo State College
    Midnight Globe, 25 Apr.1978. il.
-Psychokinesis
 1852/Mr. Brooks
    Emma Hardinge Britten, Modern Ameri-
    can Spiritualism (N.Y.: The Author,
    1870), p.104.
-Seance
 1864, Jan.13, 23
    Emma Hardinge Britten, Modern Ameri-
    can Spiritualism (N.Y.: The Author,
    1870), pp.290-92.
-Skyquake
 1945, Nov.9
    "Noise and Jar," Doubt, no.16 (1946):

242.
-Spirit medium
 1850s/Charles Hammond
    Charles Hammond, Light from the
    Spirit World (Rochester: W. Heughes,
    1852).
    Slater Brown, The Heyday of Spirit-
    ualism (N.Y.: Pocket Books, 1972
    ed.), pp.181,227.
 1850s/George Redman
    Emma Hardinge Britten, Modern Ameri-
    can Spiritualism (N.Y.: The Author,
    1870), pp.251,257.
 1850s-1900/Marcia M. Swain
    Emma Hardinge Britten, Modern Ameri-
    can Spiritualism (N.Y.: The Author,
    1870), p.289.
    D.E. Bailey, Thoughts from the Inner
    Life (Boston: The Author, 1886).
    W. Usborne Moore, Glimpses of the
    Next State (London: Watts, 1911),
    pp.512-621.
    Carl A. Wickland, Thirty Years Among
    the Dead (Los Angeles: Nat'l Psych-
    ological Inst., 1924).
    Nandor Fodor, Encyclopaedia of Psy-
    chic Science (London: Arthurs,
    1933), p.373.
 1855-1870s/Ira and William Davenport
    T.L. Nichols, A Biography of the
    Brothers Davenport (London: Saunders,
    Otley, 1864).
    T.L. Nichols, ed., Supramundane Facts
    in the Life of Rev. Jesse Babcock
    Ferguson (London: Spiritual Lyceum,
    1865), pp.103-27.
    Robert Cooper, Spiritual Experiences
    (London: Heywood, 1867).
    Paschal B. Randolph, The Davenport
    Brothers (Boston: William White,
    1869).
    Arthur Conan Doyle, The Edge of the
    Unknown (N.Y.: Berkley, 1968 ed.),
    pp.32-37.
    Nandor Fodor, Encyclopaedia of Psy-
    chic Science (London: Arthurs,
    1933), pp.75-77,190.
    Joseph Dunninger, Houdini's Spirit
    World and Dunninger's Psychic Reve-
    lations (N.Y.: Tower, 1968 ed.),
    pp.64-71.
    Slater Brown, The Heyday of Spirit-
    ualism (N.Y.: Pocket Books, 1972
    ed.), pp.198-214.
 1857/James Sangster
 1863/Charles Reed
    Emma Hardinge Britten, Modern Ameri-
    can Spiritualism (N.Y.: The Author,
    1870), pp.286-90.
 1900s/Emily S. French
    Edward C. Randall, Frontiers of the
    After Life (N.Y.: Knopf, 1922).
    Nandor Fodor, Encyclopaedia of Psy-
    chic Science (London: Arthurs,
    1933), p.150.
 1930s-1963/Jack Kelly
    Marion Brader, "Jack Kelly: Medium,"
    Fate 30 (Jan.1977):76-80. il.
    (Letter), W.H., Fate 30 (July 1977):
    114-15.

(Letter), Daniel L. Zagora, Fate 30
(Dec.1977):116.
-UFO (?)
1957, Nov.6/=Venus
Jacques & Janine Vallee, Challenge
to Science (N.Y.: Ace, 1966 ed.),
p.132.
1960, Dec.26?
Brad Steiger, ed., Project Blue Book
(N.Y.: Ballantine, 1976), betw.pp.
56-57. il.
-UFO (CE-1)
1960, April 24/T.M. Arlington
(Letter), Fate 14 (Mar.1961):109-10.
-UFO (NL)
1947, July 7/North Buffalo
Albany Knickerbocker News, 7 July
1947.
-Windshield pitting
1954, spring
Harold T. Wilkins, Flying Saucers Uncensored (N.Y.: Ace, 1967 ed.), p.
153.

Camillus
-UFO (?)
1965, Nov.9/Mrs. Everett B. Jones/Cam-
illus Plaza
(Editorial), Fate 19 (Mar.1966):21,
quoting Syracuse Herald-American
(undated).

Canaan
-Glacial anomaly
Stephen Reed, "On Trains of Boulders,
and on the Transport of Boulders to
a Level Above That of Their Source,"
Am.J.Sci., ser.3, 5 (1873):218-19.

Canandaigua
-Seance
1937/Jack Kelly/Lily Dale
(Letter), W.H., Fate 30 (July 1977):
114-15.
-Spirit medium
1907-1908/Pierre L.O.A. Keeler/Lily
Dale
Hereward Carrington, "Lily Dale: A
Report of a Two-Weeks' Investigation
into Alleged Spiritualistic Phenom-
ena, Witnessed at Lily Dale, New
York," Proc.ASPR 2 (1908):7-117.
Hereward Carrington, "Experiences at
Lily Dale," J.ASPR 2 (1908):379-92.
James H. Hyslop, "Lily Dale As Seen
by Friendly Eyes," J.ASPR 2 (1908):
416-22.
1925/Lily Dale
Joseph Dunninger, Houdini's Spirit
World and Dunninger's Psychic Reve-
lations (N.Y.: Tower, 1968 ed.),
pp.53-55.
1929, 1960s/Arthur Ford/Lily Dale
George Lawton, The Drama of Life Af-
ter Death (N.Y.: Holt, 1932).
Allen Spraggett, The Unexplained
(N.Y.: Signet, 1968 ed.), pp.108-10.
1940s/Ann Taylor/Lily Dale
Danton Walker, Spooks Deluxe (N.Y.:
Franklin Watts, 1956), pp.116-17.

Cardiff
-Giant human skeleton
1869, Oct.16/George Hull/=sculpted
hoax
Arthur T. Vance, The Real David Har-
um (N.Y.: Baker & Taylor, 1900).
Harold W. Thompson, Body, Boots and
Britches (Philadelphia: Lippincott,
1940), pp.155-57.
Curtis D. MacDougall, Hoaxes (N.Y.:
Dover, 1958 ed.), pp.100-102. il.
Barbara Franco, "The Cardiff Giant:
A Hundred-Year-Old Hoax," New York
History 50 (1969):421-40.

Carlisle
-Fall of cast iron
1975, Jan.12/Mr. Tillapaugh
John L. Warren & Joseph Accetta,
"'Object From Sky' Analyzed," Sky-
look, no.97 (Dec.1975):14.

Carmel
-Haunt
1950s/Charles Lee
"Moved by a Ghost," Fate 14 (May
1961):71, quoting Weekend Mag., Nov.
1960.
C.B. Colby, Strangely Enough! (N.Y.:
Scholastic, 1963 ed.), pp.42-44.
-UFO (?)
1976, Aug.4/Robert Jankowski/=star
"UFO Sighting Puzzles Skeptics," UFO
Inv., Sep.1976, p.4.
"In Current Journals," Int'l UFO Re-
porter 1 (Dec.1976):10.

Castleton-On-Hudson
-UFO (?)
1965, Aug.10
"Saucer Flap Around Albany, New York,"
Saucer News 12 (Dec.1965):23.
-UFO (CE-1)
1966, April 5/Joseph Powers
Albany Times-Union, 6 Apr.1966.
Albany Knickerbocker News, 6 Apr.1966,
p.5B; and 11 Apr.1966, p.3B.

Catskill
-Precognition
1865, April/Maggie Plugh
Herbert B. Greenhouse, Premonitions:
A Leap into the Future (N.Y.: War-
ner, 1973 ed.), pp.84-85, quoting
The Progressive Thinker (undated).
-River monster
1886, summer/Charlie Spencer/Catskill
Pt.
New York Times, 20 Oct.1886, p.2.
-UFO (CE-1)
1976, Feb.12/Sandra Maldonaldo/N on
Vosenkill Rd.
Ted Bloecher, "Woman Drives Beneath
UFO," Skylook, no.100 (Mar.1976):
16-17.

Cedarhurst
-UFO (NL)
1954, Aug.10/Edward Heinhold
"C-14," CRIFO Newsl., 3 Sep.1954, p.5.

Centerport
-UFO (NL)
1973, Oct.21/Lee Gugliotto
J. Allen Hynek & Jacques Vallee, The
Edge of Reality (Chicago: Regnery,
1975), p.27.

Chautauqua
-Crisis apparition
1963, Nov.21
Marcus Bach, "The Case for Spirit
Communication: Part One," Fate 22
(Sep.1969):61,67.

Chenango Bridge
-Fall of unknown object
1969, spring
(Editorial), Fate 22 (Oct.1969):34.

Chenango co.
-Fire anomaly
1880s
G. Archie Stockwell, "Catacausis Eb-
riosus (Spontaneous Combustion),"
Therapeutic Gazette, ser.3, 5 (1889)
:168-74.

Cherry Creek
-UFO (CE-1)
1965, Aug.5
Jacques Vallee, Passport to Magonia
(Chicago: Regnery, 1969), pp.312-13.
-UFO (CE-2)
1965, Aug.19/Harold Butcher
"Landing Probed by NICAP, AF," UFO
Inv. 3 (Aug.-Sep.1965):7.
"The Cherry Creek Incident," APRO
Bull. 14 (Nov.-Dec.1965):7.
John G. Fuller, Incident at Exeter
(N.Y.: Berkley, 1967 ed.), pp.32-35.
Jim & Coral Lorenzen, UFOs over the
Americas (N.Y.: Signet, 1968), pp.
106-108.
J. Allen Hynek, The Hynek UFO Report
(N.Y.: Dell, 1977), pp.170-72.
-UFO (NL)
1965, Aug.20/Richard Ward
"Landing Probed by NICAP, AF," UFO
Inv. 3 (Aug.-Sep.1965):7.
1965, Aug.23/Harold Butcher
Jerome Clark, "The Greatest Flap Yet?
Part 2," Flying Saucer Rev. 12
(Mar.-Apr.1966):8,11.

Cherry Valley
-Haunt
n.d./Old Randall place
James Reynolds, Ghosts in American
Houses (N.Y.: Paperback Library,
1967 ed.), pp.99-108.
-Precognition
1778, Nov.10/Mrs. Samuel Clyde
Cherry Valley Glensfoot Herald, 26
July 1887.
James J. Flynn & Charles A. Huguenin,
"The Prophetic Dream of Mrs. Clyde,"
New York Folklore Quar. 14 (1958):
107-18.
-UFO (DD)
1954, Oct.11/Abraham B. Cox

Harold T. Wilkins, Flying Saucers Uncensored (N.Y.: Pyramid, 1967 ed.),
p.244.
Richard Hall, ed., The UFO Evidence
(Washington: NICAP, 1964), pp.3-4.

Churchville
-UFO (CE-3)
1967, July 31/Sidney Zipkin/Main St.
Rochester Democrat & Chronicle, 3
Aug.1967.

Cicero
-UFO (CE-1)
1965, May 20/Clifford Rockwell
(Letter), Fate 18 (Sep.1965):107-108.
1978, April?/Hwy.31
Syracuse News-Times, 19 Nov.1978.

Cincinnatus
-Haunt
n.d./Chenango Quarry
James Reynolds, Gallery of Ghosts
(N.Y.: Paperback Library, 1970 ed.),
pp.252-71.

Clarkstown twp.
-Witch trial (hex)
1816/Jane Kanniff
Frank Bertangue Green, History of
Rockland County (N.Y.: A.S. Barnes,
1886).
"The Witch of Clarkstown," York State
Tradition 28, no.2 (1974):28-30.

Clay
-UFO (NL)
1965, Nov.9/Weldon Ross
John G. Fuller, Incident at Exeter
(N.Y.: Berkley, 1967 ed.), pp.205-
206, quoting New York Journal-American (undated).

Clifton Park
-UFO (?)
1967, March 26
Albany Knickerbocker News, 3 Mar.
1969, p.5B.
-UFO (DD)
1968, Dec.11/Richard Snyder
Albany Knickerbocker News, 11 Dec.
1968, p.2B.

Clinton
-Seance
1920, Feb.22, July 3-4/Janet Schenck/
122 E. 82d St.
"Apparent Communication," J.ASPR 16
(1922):104-10.

Cobleskill
-Archeological site
ca.68,000 B.C.?
"New World Archaeology: A 70,000-Year-
Old Site," Science News, 26 May
1973, p.337. il.
A.H. Ashton, "Stone Age Artifacts
Found near Cobleskill, New York,"
Central States Arch.J. 20 (1973):
150-53.

"70,000-Year-Old N.Y. State Relics
Disputed," NEARA Newsl. 9 (spring
1974):18.
Leon J. Salter, "The Timlin 70,000-
Year Site in New York State," NEARA
Newsl. 9 (summer 1974):33.

Cohoes
-Spirit medium
1851
    Eliab W. Capron, Modern Spiritualism:
    Its Facts and Fanaticisms (Boston:
    Bela Marsh, 1855), pp.277-79.

Colonie
-UFO (NL)
1966, April 3/Jane Tucci
1966, April 7/Richard Doring
    Albany Knickerbocker News, 6 Apr.
    1966, p.5B; and 11 Apr.1966, p.3B.

Comstock
-UFO (NL)
1967, July 1
    Wido Hoville, "Comstock N.Y.," UFO-
    Québec, no.5 (1976):12.

Conewango Valley
-Human track in stone
1897
    (Letter), W.T. Fenton, Am.Archaeolo-
    gist 2 (Mar.1898):72. il.

Conklin
-UFO (CE-3)
1964, July 16/Edmund Travis
    Binghamton Press, 17 July 1964.

Cooperstown
-Ghosts and haunts
n.d./River St.
    James Fenimore Cooper, Legends and
    Traditions of a Northern County
    (N.Y.: Putnam, 1921 ed.), pp.41-60.

Cornwall-on-the-Hudson
-UFO (NL)
1973, Sep.21/Trudy Tynan
    Middletown Times Herald-Record, 22
    Sep.1973.

Cortland
-UFO (DD)
ca.1963
    Berthold Eric Schwarz, "New Berlin
    UFO Landing and Repair by Crew,"
    Flying Saucer Rev. 21 (Nov.1975):22,
    27.
-UFO (NL)
1956, Aug.14/Lynn Strauff
    "Case 188," CRIFO Orbit, 7 Sep.1956,
    pp.3-4.
1967, Oct.26/Sandy Cira/Hwy.4
    T.M. Wright, "UFO's over Ithaca,"
    Fate 22 (Feb.1969):44,48.

Coxsackie
-Anomalous fossil
3 mi.N
    New York Times, 12 Nov.1948, p.25.

Cross River
-Anomalous artifact
1973/=Central American pottery
    Edward J. Lenik, "An Unusual Pottery
    Find in New York," NEARA Newsl. 8
    (winter 1974):71. il.

Croton-On-Hudson
-Haunt
1950s/Mr. Kahn
    Hans Holzer, Ghost Hunter (N.Y.: Ace,
    1963 ed.), pp.22-31.
-Phantom carriage
n.d./Van Cortlandt Manor House
    "Miscellaneous Incidents," J.ASPR 4
    (1910):45,48-49.

Dannemora
-Electromagnetic anomaly
1920, Feb./Clinton Prison
    Mayne R. Coe, Jr., "Does Science Ex-
    plain Poltergeists?" Fate 12 (July
    1959):79,87-88, quoting Electrical
    Experimenter, June 1920, p.158.

Dansville
-UFO (NL)
1957, Nov.6
    Donald E. Keyhoe, Flying Saucers: Top
    Secret (N.Y.: Putnam, 1960), pp.124-
    25.

Deer Park
-Telepathy
1969, March 13-17/Rose Boccio/140
Wright Ave.
    (Editorial), Fate 22 (Aug.1969):28-
    32, quoting Garden City Newsday
    (undated).

Delaware co.
-Phantom
1968
    John A. Keel, Strange Creatures from
    Time and Space (Greenwich, Ct.: Faw-
    cett, 1970), pp.184-85.

Depew
-UFO (CE-3)
1958, Jan./Mrs. N.L. Collins/N.Y. State
Thruway
    Otto O. Binder, "'Oddball' Saucers...
    That Fit No Pattern," Fate 21 (Feb.
    1968):54,58-59.

De Ruyter
-UFO (NL)
1977, April 1
    "UFOs of Limited Merit," Int'l UFO
    Reporter 2 (May 1977):5.

DeWitt
-Skyquake
1971, Aug.7/Lyndon Park
    Syracuse Herald-Journal, 7 Aug.1971.

Dunkirk
-UFO (DD)
1910, Sep.22/Dennis Ready
    New York Tribune, 23 Sep.1910, p.1.

-UFO (NL)
  1963, Dec.2/L. Erie
    "Lake Searched for Objects," APRO
    Bull. 13 (Sep.1964):6.

Durhamville
-UFO (CE-1)
  1966, April 5
    Jacques Vallee, Passport to Magonia
    (Chicago: Regnery, 1969), p.327.

Dutchess co.
-Humanoid
  1971, Jan.
    John Green, Sasquatch: The Apes Among
    Us (Seattle: Hancock House, 1978),
    p.233.
-Precognition
  1833, summer/Joseph Hoag
    W. Franklin Prince, "The Vision of
    Joseph Hoag," J.ASPR 18 (1924):441-
    53.

East Berne
-UFO (CE-1)
  1971, Nov.8/Mrs. Harry M. Fries/Willsey
  Rd.
    Albany Times-Union, 14 Nov.1971.

Eastchester
-Ghost
  n.d.
    New York Writers' Program, New York:
    A Guide to the Empire State (N.Y.:
    Oxford Univ., 1956), p.114.

East Fishkill twp.
-Haunt
  18th c.
    Henry D.B. Bailey, Local Tales and
    Historical Sketches (Fishkill Land-
    ing: John W. Spaight, 1874), pp.119-
    32.

East Greenbush
-UFO (?)
  1965, Aug.27
    Albany Knickerbocker News, 30 Mar.
    1966, p.12A.

East Hampton
-Mystery radio transmissions
  1966, March/Bernice Letter
    John A. Keel, "Mysterious Voices from
    Outer Space," Saga UFO Rept. 2
    (winter 1975):36.
-UFO (CE-1)
  1966, May 11/Gary Hall/Indian Wells Hwy.
    East Hampton Star, 12 May 1966.
  1973, Aug.7/Trish McMenamin/Georgica
  Rd.
    Easthampton Summer Sun, 9 Aug.1973.
-UFO (NL)
  1973, Nov.20/Charles Pasamonte, Jr./
  Main Beach
    East Hampton Star, 3 Dec.1973.
-Water anomaly
  Jason's Rock/N of town
    (Editorial), Fate 19 (June 1966):14.
-Witch trial (hex)

1657-1658/Elizabeth Garlick
    Silas Wood, A Sketch of the First
    Settlement of the Several Towns in
    Long Island (Brooklyn: A. Spooner,
    1824), p.24.
    Benjamin F. Thompson, History of
    Long Island, 2 vols. (N.Y.: Gould,
    Banks, 1843), 1:302.
    J. Hammond Trumbull, ed., The Public
    Records of the Colony of Connecti-
    cut, 15 vols. (Hartford: Brown &
    Parsons, 1850), 1:572-73.
    David Gardiner, Chronicles of the
    Town of Easthampton (N.Y.: Bowne,
    1871).
    John M. Taylor, The Witchcraft Delu-
    sion in Colonial Connecticut (N.Y.:
    Grafton, 1908), pp.119-21.

East Hills
-UFO (?)
  1962, March 25/Victor Agne/Long Island
  Expressway/=meteor
    (Editorial), Fate 16 (July 1961):21-
    22.

East Northport
-Haunt
  1963-1968/Ralph Vignola/3 Purdy Ave.
    New York Long Island Press, 6 Feb.
    1968.

East Norwich
-UFO (NL)
  1973, Nov.6/Mary E.A. Bruschini/Mutton-
  town Bird Preserve
    Dick Ruhl, "Merging UFOs over Long
    Island," APRO Bull. 22 (Jan.-Feb.
    1974):1,4.

East Randolph
-Giant human skeleton
  n.d./Cowan's Corners
    Robert R. Lyman, Amazing Indeed!
    (Coudersport, Pa.: Potter Enterprise,
    1973), pp.9-10.

East Syracuse
-UFO (CE-3)
  1964, July/William C. Walker/nr. Hancock Field
    Otto O. Binder, "'Oddball' Saucers...
    That Fit No Pattern," Fate 21 (Feb.
    1968):54,56-57.

Eden
-Phantom panther
  1947, Jan.9
    "More Critters," Doubt, no.18 (1947):
    273,274.
-UFO (CE-3)
  1967, March 1/DeWitt Baldwin
    John A. Keel, Our Haunted Planet
    (Greenwich, Ct.: Fawcett, 1971), p.
    110.

Ellenville
-Ancient stone cairn
    Salvatore Michael Trento, The Search
    for Lost America (Chicago: Contem-

porary, 1978), p.92.

Elma
-Flying humanoid
  1974, Oct.31
    (Letter), Virginia Margaret Miller,
    Fate 29 (Mar.1976):127-29.

Elmira
-Fall of weblike substance
  1955, Feb.21
    "Bonny Quarter," Doubt, no.48 (1955):
    334.
-Phantom panther
  1977, July
    Elmira Star-Gazette, 28 July 1977.
-Spirit medium
  1963, Sep.9-   /Jane Roberts
    Jane Roberts, The Seth Material (En-
    glewood Cliffs, N.J.: Prentice-Hall,
    1970).
    Jane Roberts, The Education of Over-
    soul Seven (Englewood Cliffs, N.J.:
    Prentice-Hall, 1973).
    Jane Roberts, Adventures in Con-
    sciousness (Englewood Cliffs, N.J.:
    Prentice-Hall, 1974).
    Jane Roberts, The Nature of Personal
    Reality (Englewood Cliffs, N.J.:
    Prentice-Hall, 1974).
    Jane Roberts, Seth Speaks (N.Y.: Ban-
    tam, 1974).
    Jane Roberts, Dialogues of the Soul
    and Mortal Self in Time (Englewood
    Cliffs, N.J.: Prentice-Hall, 1975).
    Jane Roberts, The Coming of Seth
    ((N.Y.: Pocket Books, 1976).
-Telepathy
  1892, Jan.26/Adele Gleason
    Hornell Hart, The Enigma of Survival
    (London: Rider, 1959).
-UFO (?)
  1973, Nov./=balloon
    Philip J. Klass, UFOs Explained (N.Y.:
    Random House, 1974), pp.291-92.

Elmont
-Telepathy
  1963/Alva T. Stanforth Junior High
    Rhea A. White & Jean Angstadt, "A
    Second Classroom Experiment with
    Student-Agents Acting Simultaneous-
    ly," J.ASPR 57 (1963):227-32.

Endicott
-Skyquake
  1973, Oct.17
    "Bang!" INFO J., no.14 (Nov.1974):2,
    6, quoting New York Times, 19 Oct.
    1973.

Erie co.
-Norse runestone
  1950s/Eber Russell/Hubbard farm
    O.G. Landsverk, "Runic Inscriptions
    in the Western Hemisphere," NEARA J.
    13 (summer 1978):15,18-19. il.

Erieville
-Mystery stone sphere

Benjamin Silliman, Jr., "On the Origin of a Curious Spheroidal Structure," Proc.Am.Ass'n Adv.Sci. 4
(1850):10-12.

Farmingdale
-Disappearance
  1967, Aug./Agricultural College/hogs
    John A. Keel, Strange Creatures from
    Time and Space (Greenwich, Ct.:
    Fawcett, 1970), p.166.
-Skyquake
  1953
    Donald E. Keyhoe, Flying Saucer Con-
    spiracy (N.Y.: Holt, 1955), p.201.
-UFO (NL)
  1968, Feb.5
    John A. Keel, Strange Creatures from
    Time and Space (Greenwich, Ct.:
    Fawcett, 1970), p.166.

Fayetteville
-Skyquake
  1968, April 17
    Syracuse Post-Standard, 18 Apr.1968,
    p.11.
    "A Phantom Explosion," INFO J., no.
    4 (spring 1969):34.

Fishkill
-Humanoid
  ca.1900/Green Fly Swamp
    Augusta Knapp Osborne, "Counties
    (Dutchess): The Green Fly Monster,"
    New York Folklore Quar. 11 (1955):
    213-16.
-Phantom
  n.d.
    Arthur Goadby, "Conversing Animals,"
    J.ASPR 27 (1933):67,71-72.

Forestport
-Lake monster
  1893, June/McGuire's Pond/=hoax?
    Howard Thomas, Folklore from the Adi-
    rondack Foothills (Prospect, N.Y.:
    Prospect Books, 1958), pp.39-40.

Fort Johnson
-Haunt
  18th c.-
    Louis C. Jones, Things That Go Bump
    in the Night (N.Y.: Hill & Wang,
    1959), pp.132-34.

Fort Montgomery
-UFO (NL)
  1975, summer/Donna Reynolds
    Lee Walsh, "Lee Walsh Reports on the
    Strange and Unknown," Beyond Reality,
    no.18 (Jan.1976):10,56.

Fort Plain
-UFO (NL)
  1976, Feb.3/Deanna Smith/N on River St.
    (Letter), Saga UFO Rept. 3 (Aug.1976)
    :6.

Franklin
-UFO (NL)

1962, May 16/George Enneking/nr. O.H.
Hutchinson power station
"Railroad Men Spot Bullet-Shaped
UAO," APRO Bull. 10 (May 1962):2.

Franklin Springs
-UFO (NL)
1966, Sep.9
Jacques Vallee, Passport to Magonia
(Chicago: Regnery, 1969), p.336.

Fredonia
-UFO (NL)
1965, Sep.27/Addie Jones
Buffalo Evening News, 28 Sep.1965.

Freeport
-Fall of ice
1953, Feb.18/Benjamin Pinekowsky
"The Giant Ice Egg," Fate 6 (July
1953):43.
-UFO (CE-2)
1973, Nov.6/Gary Steinberg/Meadowbrook
Parkway
New York Long Island Press, 6 Nov.
1973.
Dick Ruhl, "Merging UFOs over Long
Island," APRO Bull. 22 (Jan.-Feb.
1974):1,3-4.
Dick Ruhl, "The UFOs of Long Island:
The Freeport Sighting," Official
UFO 1 (Oct.1975):24-26,48-49.

Fremont Center
-Anomalous hole in ground
1978, March 31/Mark Sherlock/Tilton Rd.
Syracuse Post-Standard, 10 Apr.1978.
il.

Gallupville
-UFO (CE-2)
1968, Aug.5
Ted Phillips, Physical Traces Associ-
ated with UFO Sightings (Evanston:
Center for UFO Studies, 1975), p.57.

Garden City
-UFO (?)
1951, Sep.10/Wilbert S. Rogers/Mitchel
AFB
(Editorial), Fate 5 (Jan.1952):7-8.
-UFO (DD)
1952, Jan.21/Mitchel AFB
Edward J. Ruppelt, The Report on Un-
identified Flying Objects (Garden
City: Doubleday, 1956), pp.121-23.
U.S. Air Force, Projects Grudge and
Blue Book Reports 1-12 (Washington:
NICAP, 1968), pp.63,72-76.
1959, Aug.19/6 mi.W of Mitchel AFB
Jacques & Janine Vallee, Challenge to
Science (N.Y.: Ace, 1966 ed.), p.
200.

Genesee twp.
-Anomalous quartz formation
Little Rock City
Charles Tooker, "Needs Investigating
No.2: A Further Report," NEARA Newsl.
6 (Mar.1971):13.

Geneseo
-Parapsychology research
1970s/State Univ. of New York
Lawrence Casler, "Hypnotic Maximiza-
tion of ESP Motivation," J.Para-
psych. 40 (1976):187-93.
Michael Venturino, "An Investigation
of the Relationship between EEG
Alpha Activity and ESP Performance,"
J.ASPR 72 (1978):141-52.

Geneva
-UFO (DD)
1947, July 8
Rochester Democrat-Chronicle, 9 July
1947.
1952, July 28
Richard Hall, ed., The UFO Evidence
(Washington: NICAP, 1964), p.161.

Glen Cove
-Haunt
1965/Morgan Hall
Hans Holzer, Gothic Ghosts (N.Y.:
Pocket Books, 1972), pp.85-94.
-Skyquake
1952, Oct.16, 18
"Bangs," Doubt, no.39 (1952):182.
"Sky Quakes," CRIFO Newsl., 4 Feb.
1955, p.3.
-Spontaneous human combustion
1963, Dec.4/Thomas Sweizerski
New York Long Island Press, 5 Dec.
1963.
-UFO (NL)
1954, Aug.17/Marion R. Kuczabinski
(Letter), Fate 8 (Apr.1955):115-16.

Glens Falls
-Precognition
1849, July 5/Charles Hill Willson
"A Case of Precognition," J.ASPR 1
(1907):165-68.
-UFO (CE-3)
n.d.
Albany Knickerbocker News, 3 Mar.1969.
Richard Bonenfant, "A Preliminary Report of UFO Coverage in the Knickerbocker News, Albany, New York, 1964-
1969," in Proc.1976 CUFOS Conference
(Evanston: Center for UFO Studies,
1976), pp.39,48.
-UFO (NL)
1947, June 25/Louis Stebbins
New York World-Telegram, 7 July 1947.

Granville
-Haunt
1955-1975/Phil Birmingham
Lawrence Cortesi, "Tormented Ghost
Speaks Up," Fate 29 (Oct.1976):44-
51. il.

Greece
-Poltergeist
1848, Oct./Deacon Hale
Eliab W. Capron, Modern Spiritualism:
Its Facts and Fanaticisms (Boston:
Bela Marsh, 1855), p.67.
-UFO (NL)

1977, June 26
"UFOs of Limited Merit," Int'l UFO
Reporter 2 (Aug.1977):3.

Greenburgh twp.
-Haunt
1870s
Elliott O'Donnell, The Screaming
Skulls and Other Ghosts (N.Y.: Pa-
perback Library, 1971), pp.26-33.

Greenlawn
-UFO (CE-1) and Men-in-black
1966, Oct./Joseph Henslik
"Another 'Man in Black' Case," Saucer
News 14 (fall 1967):14-15.

Greenport
-Jinx ship
1943-1958/John Pilles/"Correct"
"The Jinxed Fishing Boat," Fate 11
(June 1958):46.

Greenville
-UFO (?)
1965, Aug.11
Albany Knickerbocker News, 30 Mar.
1966, p.12A.

Greenwich
-Haunt
1968-1972/William R. Harris/St. Paul's
Episcopal Rectory
Brad Steiger, "1972: A Bumper Year
for Hauntings," Beyond Reality, no.
4 (May 1973):15,16-17, quoting Saratoga Springs Saratogian (undated).

Greenwood Lake
-Ancient stone circle
Salvatore Michael Trento, The Search
for Lost America (Chicago: Contemporary, 1978), pp.101-102. il.

Hamburg
-UFO (CE-1)
1966, June 23
Jacques Vallee, Passport to Magonia
(Chicago: Regnery, 1969), p.332.

Hamburg twp.
-Mystery explosion
1968, Sep.21/L. Erie, off Hamburg Town
Park
Buffalo Evening News, 21 Sep.1968.

Hampton Bays
-UFO (CE-2)
1953, June 24
Jacques Vallee, Passport to Magonia
(Chicago: Regnery, 1969), pp.202-203.

Harrison
-Archeological site
Hermit's Cave/Buckout Rd.
Charles A. Huguenin, "Another Look at
the 'Hermit's Cave' Site near White
Plains, N.Y.," NEARA Newsl. 3 (Sep.
1968):62-63. il.

Hastings-On-Hudson
-Ghost
1927, Sep.27/D.L. Dadirrian
J. Malcolm Bird, "Two Striking Cases
of Collective Apparition," Psychic
Rsch. 22 (1928):429-32.

Hauppauge
-Disease anomaly
1931, April/Valentine Minder
New York Times, 30 Apr.1931, p.25.
Charles Fort, The Books of Charles
Fort (N.Y.: Holt, 1941), pp.987-88.
-Skyquake
1953
Donald E. Keyhoe, Flying Saucer Con-
spiracy (N.Y.: Holt, 1955), p.201.

Haverstraw
-UFO (NL)
1976, Sep.
New York Times, 6 Sep.1976, p.17.

Hector
-UFO (?)
1966, April 25
John A. Keel, UFOs: Operation Trojan
Horse (N.Y.: Putnam, 1970), p.145.

Hempstead
-Disappearance
1913, Oct.13/Albert A. Jewel/Moisant
monoplane/Hempstead Plains airfield
New York Times, 14 Oct.1913, p.1.
-UFO (NL)
1952, Oct.29
Richard Hall, ed., The UFO Evidence
(Washington: NICAP, 1964), p.21.
Renato Vesco, Intercept UFO (N.Y.:
Zebra, 1974 ed.), pp.110-11.
1957, March 8/Raymond Castor/Elizabeth
Ave.
1957, Aug.5/Raymond Castor/Henry St.
(Letter), Flying Saucers, Feb.1958,
p.67.

Henderson
-UFO (NL)
1959, July 21
Jacques Vallee, Passport to Magonia
(Chicago: Regnery, 1969), pp.209-10.

Herkimer co.
-Snow worms
1891, winter
"Snow Worms," Sci.Am. 64 (1891):147.

Hewlett
-Fall of anomalous meteorite
1958, Sep.19/Marjorie Salomon/69 Harris
Ave.
Jerry Siegel, "Meteorites Attack Long
Island," Fate 12 (June 1959):48-50.

Highland
-Ancient inscription
Donal B. Buchanan, "Report of the
NEARA Inscription Co-Ordinating
Chairman," NEARA J. 13 (summer 1978)
:24.

Hogansburg
-Doubtful identity
  1800-1814/L.A. Muller/=Charles X?
    Curtis D. MacDougall, Hoaxes (N.Y.:
    Dover, 1958 ed.), p.108, quoting
    F. Reed Alvord, in Letters, 26 Oct.
    1936.
-UFO (CE-1)
  1951, Oct.2/Peter Phillips
    Robert N. Webster, "Let's Get Up to
    Date on the Flying Saucers," Fate
    5 (Jan.1952):4,8.

Hornell
-UFO (?)
  1897, April 14/=hoax
    Washington Court House (O.) Cyclone
    & Fayette Republican, 22 Apr.1897.

Horseheads
-Fall of metallic object
  1950, April 8/Ernest Ferris
    "Found on Ground," Doubt, no.42
    (1953):238,239.
-Fall of weblike substance
  1955, Feb.21/Charles L. Shull/=pollu-
  tion?
    Palo Alto (Cal.) Times, 23 Feb.1955.
    "A Bonny Quarter," Doubt, no.48
    (1955):334.
    Cliff R. Towner, "Cobwebs from the
    Sky," Fate 8 (Sep.1955):62-65. il.

Hudson
-Ancient stone circle
    John Finch, "On the Celtic Antiqui-
    ties of America," Am.J.Sci., ser.1,
    7 (1824):149-61.
-UFO (NL)
  1978, July 19
    "UFOs of Limited Merit," Int'l UFO
    Reporter 3 (Sep.1978):6.

Huntington
-Hex
  1939, July/Melinda Carman
    Riverhead Weekly News, 28 July 1939.
-Humanoid
  1931, July 19/Stockman Nursery
    New York Times, 20 July 1931, p.19.
    Charles Fort, The Books of Charles
    Fort (N.Y.: Holt, 1941), pp.903-904.
-Out-of-body experience
  n.d./Sheila Saperton
    Herbert B. Greenhouse, The Astral
    Journey (N.Y.: Avon, 1976 ed.), pp.
    116-17.
-Pink squirrel
  1963
    Gray Barker, Book of Saucers (Clarks-
    burg, W.V.: Saucerian, 1965), p.44.
-Precognition
  1962, Feb./Richard Parkinson, Sr.
    Jess Stearn, The Door to the Future
    (N.Y.: Macfadden, 1964), pp.159-60.
-Telepathy
  1960/Half Hollow Hills High School
    Rhea White & Jean Angstadt, "Student
    Preferences in a Two-Classroom GESP
    Experiment with Two Student Agents

Acting Simultaneously," J.ASPR 57
    (1963):32-42.
-UFO (NL)
  1967, Oct.4/John A. Keel
    John A. Keel, UFOs: Operation Trojan
    Horse (N.Y.: Putnam, 1970), pp.29-
    30.

Irondequoit
-UFO (DD)
  1959, July 25
    Lloyd Mallan, "Complete Directory of
    UFOs: Part III," Sci.& Mech. 38
    (Feb.1967):56,58.
-UFO (NL)
  1977, Oct.22
    "UFOs of Limited Merit," Int'l UFO
    Reporter 2 (Dec.1977):3.

Irvington
-Haunt
  1926/Dorothy Bonner/Ardsley-on-Hudson
    Dorothy Bonner, "The Room Where
    Death Lingered," Fate 10 (Sep.1957)
    :82-85.
  1946-1966/Carl Carmer
    New York Times, 2 Jan.1967, p.14. il.
-Precognition
  1898, Oct./Chauncey Depew/Ardsley-on-
  Hudson
    Philadelphia (Pa.) Press, 16 Oct.1898.
    "Premonitory Vision of Chauncey M.
    Depew," J.ASPR 12 (1918):172-77.
    V.N. Gebhardt, "A Glimpse into the
    Future," Fate 1 (fall 1948):21.
    Jess Stearn, The Door to the Future
    (N.Y.: Macfadden, 1964), p.161.

Island Park
-Weeping icon
  1960, March 16-April 18/Pagona Catsou-
  nis/41 Norfolk St.
    Mary Margaret Fuller, "Long Island's
    Crying Madonna," Fate 13 (July 1960)
    :68-71. il.
    (Editorial), Fate 13 (Aug.1960):12-
    14.
    (Editorial), Fate 13 (Sep.1960):11-
    12.
    T.F. James, "What Makes the Madonna
    Weep," Information, Oct.1960.
    Nandor Fodor, Between Two Worlds
    (W. Nyack: Parker, 1964), pp.264-65.

Ithaca
-Humanoid
  1967, fall
    John A. Keel, Strange Creatures from
    Time and Space (Greenwich, Ct.: Faw-
    cett, 1970), p.113.
-Mystery accident
  1967, fall
    John A. Keel, UFOs: Operation Trojan
    Horse (N.Y.: Putnam, 1970), p.245.
-Plant sensitivity
  1974/Kenneth A. Horowitz/New York State
  Veterinary College
    Kenneth A. Horowitz, Donald C. Lewis,
    & Edgar L. Gasteiger, "Plant 'Pri-
    mary Perception': Electrophysiolog-

Lafayette
-UFO (DD)
  1946, April?/Richard R. Hill/Lafayette
  Country Club Rd.
    "Case 84," CRIFO Newsl., 3 June 1955,
    p.4.

Lake Carmel
-UFO (NL)
  1966, March 24/Rose Placet
    "Nation-Wide Saucer Flap Continues,"
    Saucer News 13 (June 1966):30,31.

Lake George
-Clairempathy
  1940s-   /Millie Coutant
    "Psychic Leads Mother to Missing
    Daughters," Probe the Unknown 2
    (summer 1974):11.
    Lawrence Cortesi, "A Psychic Traps
    an Abductor," Fate 29 (Aug.1976):76-
    82. il.

Lancaster twp.
-Spontaneous human combustion
  1943, Feb.1/Arthur Baugard
    "3 Human Tinders," Fortean Soc'y Mag.,
    no.7 (June 1943):5.

Larchmont
-Haunt
  1969, June-1971, Sep./Pat Ramsdell
    Marilis Hornidge, "Lonely Little
    Ghost on the 3rd Floor Suite," Fate
    29 (Feb.1976):65-66.
-UFO (NL)
  1979, Jan.6/Vincent Wynds/Weaver St.
    Mamaroneck Daily Times, 7 Jan.1979.

Laurens
-UFO (NL)
  1966, Nov.19/John McBridge
    "Lights Baffle New York Area," APRO
    Bull. 16 (July-Aug.1967):8.

Leeds
-Haunt
  18th c.
    R. Lionel DeLisser, Picturesque Cat-
    skills (Northampton, Mass.: Pictur-
    esque, 1894).
    Mrs. J. Van V. Vedder, Historic Cat-
    skill (Catskill: The Author, 1922).
    Harold W. Thompson, Body, Boots and
    Britches (Philadelphia: Lippincott,
    1940), pp.120-21.
    Louis C. Jones, Things That Go Bump
    in the Night (N.Y.: Hill & Wang,
    1959), pp.135-38.

LeRoy
-UFO (DD)
  1952, Aug.28
    Richard Hall, ed., The UFO Evidence
    (Washington: NICAP, 1964), p.10.

Levittown
-UFO (?)
  1958, Dec.14/=lens reflection
    Frank Bowers, ed., The True Report

on Flying Saucers (Greenwich, Ct.:
    Fawcett, 1967), p.23. il.

Lindley
-UFO (CE-1)
  1977, Aug.17
    "The Lindley Episodes: CE III's in
    New York State," Int'l UFO Reporter
    2 (Sep.1977):5,7.
-UFO (CE-2)
  1977, Aug.14
    "The Lindley Episodes: CE III's in
    New York State," Int'l UFO Reporter
    2 (Sep.1977):5,7.
-UFO (CE-3)
  1977, July 23
  1977, July 25-26
  1977, Aug.1
    "The Lindley Episodes: CE III's in
    New York State," Int'l UFO Reporter
    2 (Sep.1977):5-7.
-UFO (NL)
  1977, July 28
    "The Lindley Episodes: CE III's in
    New York State," Int'l UFO Reporter
    2 (Sep.1977):5,7.

Little Falls
-UFO (NL)
  ca.1935/Harry Murphy
    Louis C. Jones, Things That Go Bump
    in the Night (N.Y.: Hill & Wang,
    1959), pp.48-49.

Liverpool
-UFO (NL)
  1968, Jan.26/Hwy.57
    T.M. Wright, "UFO's over Ithaca,"
    Fate 22 (Feb.1969):44,51, quoting
    Syracuse Herald-Journal (undated).

Livingston twp.
-Haunt
  19th c./Widow Mary's Place
    Eileen Thomas, "Ghosts in Widow Mary's
    Place," New York Folklore Quar. 5
    (1949):287-91.

Lockport
-Time anomaly
  1971, Oct.-1972/Bill Nelson
    Bill Nelson, "A Hop, Skip and a Jump
    in Time," Fate 30 (Mar.1977):61-64.
-UFO (NL)
  1967, Sep.15
    "State Troopers See UFO's," Skylook,
    no.29 (Apr.1970):21.

Long Beach
-UFO (?)
  1957, Nov.3/=Venus
    Jacques & Janine Vallee, Challenge
    to Science (N.Y.: Ace, 1966 ed.),
    p.131.

Loudonville
-UFO (NL)
  1974, Aug.20
    "New York Police See UFO," APRO Bull.
    23 (Ju y-Aug.1974):1.

Low Hampton
-End-of-world prophecy
  1831-1844/William Miller
    William Miller, Evidence from Script-
    ure and History of the Second Coming
    of Christ about the Year 1843 (Troy:
    Kemble & Hooper, 1836).
    Joshua V. Himes, Views of the Proph-
    ecies and Prophetic Chronology (Bos-
    ton: M.A. Dow, 1841).
    Francis D. Nichol, The Midnight Cry
    (Washington: Review & Herald, 1944).
    J. Gordon Melton, Encyclopedia of
    American Religions, 2 vols. (Wil-
    mington, N.C.: Consortium, 1978),
    1:459-62.

Lowville
-Fall of gelatinous substance
  1846, Nov.11
    "A Wonderful Meteor," Sci.Am. 2
    (1846):79, quoting New York Sun
    (undated).
-UFO (?)
  1968, July 2/Paul Repak/=meteor
    "Some Recent Fireballs," Sky & Tele-
    scope 36 (Sep.1968):195.

Ludlowville
-Witch trial (hex)
  ca.1810
    Ithaca Democrat, 5 May 1904.

Lycoming
-UFO (CE-1)
  1966, April 5
    Jacques Vallee, Passport to Magonia
    (Chicago: Regnery, 1969), p.327.

Lyons
-Ancient ax marks
  1830s
    Asahel Davis, The Discovery of New-
    England by the Northmen Five Hundred
    Years Before Columbus (Boston: Dut-
    ton & Wentworth, 1844).

Lyons Falls
-River monster
  1951/Wash Mellick/Black R.
    Ivan T. Sanderson, Things (N.Y.: Pyr-
    amid, 1967), p.29.

Lysander
-UFO (NL)
  1978, Sep.13
    Syracuse New Times, 19 Nov.1978.

Mahopac
-Ancient stone chambers
    Salvatore Michael Trento, The Search
    for Lost America (Chicago: Contem-
    porary, 1978), pp.56,121-29.

Malta
-UFO (NL)
  1974, Aug.20/Thomas Cole/Clifton Knolls
    "New York Police See UFO," APRO Bull.
    23 (July-Aug.1974):1,3.

Malverne
-Phantom panther
  1931, June 26/Mrs. E.H. Tandy/Star
  Cliff Dr.
    New York Herald-Tribune, 27 June
    1931.

Mamaroneck
-Haunt
  1932, June/Eleanor Small/Seven Oaks
    Hans Holzer, Ghost Hunter (N.Y.:
    Ace, 1963 ed.), pp.52-54.
  1950s/Henry Sweesy
    Henry Sweesy, "I Scared a Ghost,"
    Fate 15 (Sep.1962):30-35.
-Seance
  1927, spring/Virginia Shuflata
    Virginia Shuflata, "Ouija's 'Impos-
    sible' Answer," Fate 23 (June 1970):
    66-69.

Manhasset
-Haunt
  1952, March/Robert Schuler
    "Patrice Munsel's Ghost," Fate 7
    (July 1954):106.

Manlius
-UFO (?)
  1965, Nov.9/Tom Doxsee/27 Marie Dr.
    (Editorial), Fate 19 (Mar.1966):21,
    quoting Syracuse Herald-American
    (undated).

Manorville
-Precognition
  1957, May/Sam Woodson
    (Editorial), Fate 10 (Sep.1957):10-
    12.

Marbletown
-Gravity anomaly
  1815, Oct.
    "Unprecedented Phenomenon," Niles'
    Weekly Register 9 (1815):171-72.

Marcellus
-UFO (CE-2)
  1968, Nov.25/Elaine B. Peichy/Hwy.174
    "Four UFOs Pace Aircraft," UFO Inv.
    4 (Feb.-Mar.1969):3.

Mariaville
-UFO (CE-3)
  1957, Oct.10/Mabel Yeager/Duanesburg-
  Church Rd.
    "Space Ship Lands by Caravan," Flying
    Saucer Rev. 4 (May-June 1958):iii.
    Ted Phillips, Physical Traces Associ-
    ated with UFO Sightings (Evanston:
    Center for UFO Studies, 1975), p.21,
    quoting Saucerian Bull., 1 May 1958.

Marion
-UFO (NL)
  1961, June/John Dingfelder/Ball Rd.
    Rochester Democrat & Chronicle, 12
    June 1961.

Massena
-Clairvoyance
  1944, July/Jean Gallagher
    Jean Gallagher, "Dreaming True: Bless-
    ing and Curse," Fate 23 (June 1970):
    100-101.
-Precognition
  1946, Jan./Jean Gallagher
    Jean Gallagher, "Dreaming True: Bless -
    ing and Curse," Fate 23 (June 1970):
    100,101-102.

Mattydale
-UFO (CE-2)
  1954, winter/Bill Marsden/nr. Hancock
  Field/crashed UFO
    Raymond E. Fowler, "What About Crashed
    UFOs?" Official UFO 1 (Apr.1976):
    24,25,54-55.

Maybrook
-Humanoid
  n.d./Barren Rd.
    Lee Walsh, "Lee Walsh Reports on the
    Strange and Unknown," Beyond Reality,
    no.18 (Jan.1976):10,57.
-UFO (CE-1)
  1975, June 10/Ethel Kimbler
    Lee Walsh, "Lee Walsh Reports on the
    Strange and Unknown," Beyond Reality,
    no.18 (Jan.1976):10,56.
-UFO (NL)
  1975, May-July/Lee Walsh
  1975, May 30/Charles Reynolds
    Lee Walsh, "Lee Walsh Reports on the
    Strange and Unknown," Beyond Reality,
    no.18 (Jan.1976):10,56-57.

Mecklenburg
-Haunt
  1950s/Louis G. Wheeler
    (Letter), Fate 9 (June 1956):122-23.

Melville
-UFO (CE-1) and Men-in-black
  1967, spring
    John A. Keel, Our Haunted Planet
    (Greenwich, Ct.: Fawcett, 1971), p.
    109.
-UFO (CE-1) and telephone anomaly
  1967, Oct.3/Phillip Burkhardt/Round-
  tree Dr.
    John A. Keel, UFOs: Operation Trojan
    Horse (N.Y.: Putnam, 1970), pp.30-31.
-UFO (CE-2)
  n.d.
    John A. Keel, "Is the 'EM' Effect a
    Myth?" Flying Saucer Rev. 14 (Nov.-
    Dec.1968):16,17.

Menands
-Fire anomaly
  1971, June 24/V.A. Oberting/River Hill
  Rd.
    Columbus (O.) Dispatch, 25 June 1971,
    p.12B.
-UFO (DD)
  1965, Aug.11
    Albany Knickerbocker News, 30 Mar.
    1966, p.12A.

"Saucer Flap Around Albany, New York,"
  Saucer News 12 (Dec.1965):23-24.

Middleport
-Mystery plane crash
  1969, Oct.26/Cessna 140
    Jay Gourley, The Great Lakes Triangle
    (Greenwich, Ct.: Fawcett, 1978),
    p.133.

Middletown
-UFO (CE-1)
  1963, Aug./Jeanne Stevens
    Jeanne Stevens, "Twenty Minutes of
    Terror," Saucer News 11 (June 1964)
    :9.
-UFO (NL)
  1967/Frank Woznick
    Lee Walsh, "Lee Walsh Reports on the
    Strange and Unknown," Beyond Reality,
    no.18 (Jan.1976):10,56.

Millerton
-UFO (CE-2)
  1967, July 17/Emma Funk/N on Hwy.22
    Poughkeepsie Journal, 19 July 1967.
  1968, March/Mrs. D. Hoffman
    Ted Phillips, Physical Traces Associ-
    ated with UFO Sightings (Evanston:
    Center for UFO Studies, 1975), p.55.

Milton
-Astrology
  1971-   /Int'l Soc'y for Astrological
  Research
    (Letter), Zipporah Dobyns, Fate 24
    (Aug.1971):144.

Mineola
-Humanoid
  1931, June 20, 27/Lewis & Valentine's
  Nursery
  1931, June 29/George Ballis/Devon Ave.
  x I.U. Willets Rd.
    New York Times, 30 June 1931, p.2.

Mohawk
-Haunt
  1872-   /Jean Blair/Gelston Castle
    Kay Flansburg, "The Ghost of Gelston
    Castle," Fate 26 (Nov.1973):60.

Monkstown
-UFO (NL)
  1915, Feb.14
    New York Times, 15 Feb.1915, p.1.

Mooers
-Shape-shifting
  n.d./Joseph Hamelin
    Harold W. Thompson, Body, Boots and
    Britches (Philadelphia: Lippincott,
    1940), pp.116-17.
-UFO (?)
  n.d./Delphine Hamelin
    Harold W. Thompson, Body, Boots and
    Britches (Philadelphia: Lippincott,
    1940), pp.117-18.

Moravia
-Spirit medium
 1860s-1870s/Mary Andrews
   Thomas R. Hazard, Eleven Days in Moravia (Boston: Banner of Light, 1872).
   Eugene Crowell, The Identity of Primitive Christianity and Modern Spiritualism, 2 vols. (N.Y.: G.W. Carleton, 1874-75).
   Epes Sargent, The Proof Palpable of
   Immortality (Boston: Colby & Rich,
   1875).
   John W. Truesdell, The Bottom Facts
   Concerning the Science of Spiritualism (N.Y.: G.W. Dillingham, 1892).

Moriah Center
-UFO (CE-2)
 1957, April?
   Richard Hall, ed., The UFO Evidence
   (Washington: NICAP, 1964), p.74.
-UFO (DD)
 1956, Feb.1/Leon Brittell
   (Letter), Fate 11 (Mar.1958):116-18.

Morristown
-UFO (NL)
 1915, Feb.14
   New York Tribune, 15 Feb.1915.

Mount Marion
-UFO (NL)
 1973, Oct.
   Glenn McWane & David Graham, The New
   UFO Sightings (N.Y.: Warner, 1974),
   p.31.

Newark
-Poltergeist
 1848, March-May/Kate and Margaret Fox/
 2 mi.N at Hydesville
   A Report of the Mysterious Noises
   Heard in the House of Mr. John D.
   Fox, in Hydesville, Arcadia, Wayne
   County (Canandaigua, N.Y.: E.E.
   Lewis, 1848).
   Eliab W. Capron & Henry D. Barron,
   Explanation and History of the Mys-
   terious Communion with Spirits (Au-
   burn, N.Y.: Finn & Rockwell, 1850).
   D.M. Dewey, History of the Strange
   Sounds of Rappings, Heard in Roches-
   ter and Western New York (Rochester:
   Dewey, 1850).
   Eliab W. Capron, Modern Spiritualism:
   Its Facts and Fanaticisms (Boston:
   Bela Marsh, 1855), pp.33-56.
   Emma Hardinge Britten, Modern Ameri-
   can Spiritualism (N.Y.: The Author,
   1870), pp.27-38.
   A. Leah Underhill, The Missing Link
   in Modern Spiritualism (N.Y.: Thomas
   R. Knox, 1885), pp.5-36.
   Rochester Democrat & Chronicle, 23
   Nov.1904.
   Nandor Fodor, Encyclopaedia of Psy-
   chic Science (London: Arthurs,
   1933), pp.144-46.
   Mariam Buckner Pond, Time Is Kind:
   The Story of the Unfortunate Fox

   Family (N.Y.: Centennial, 1947).
   Charles A. Huguenin, "The Amazing
   Fox Sisters," New York Folklore
   Quar. 13 (1957):241-76.
   New York Times, 29 Mar.1970, sec.X,
   p.5.
   (Editorial), Fate 24 (Sep.1971):34-
   37.
   Herbert G. Jackson, Jr., The Spirit
   Rappers (Garden City: Doubleday,
   1972).
   R. Laurence Moore, "Spiritualism and
   Science: Reflections on the First
   Decade of the Spirit Rappings,"
   Am.Quar. 24 (1972):474-500.
-UFO (NL)
 1950, summer/Ronny Bearans/Jackson &
 Perkins Rose Gardens
   (Letter), Fate 4 (Nov.-Dec.1951):
   127-28.

Newark Valley
-UFO (CE-3)
 1964, April 24/Gary T. Wilcox/Wilson
 Creek Rd.
   Binghamton Sun-Bulletin, 1 May 1964.
   Binghamton Press, 9 May 1964.
   Olga M. Hotchkiss, "New York UFO and
   Its 'Little People,'" Fate 17 (Sep.
   1964):38-42.
   (Letter), Dulcie Brown, Fate 17
   (Dec.1964):123-24.
   (Letter), Olga M. Hotchkiss, Fate 18
   (Mar.1965):116-18.
   Berthold Eric Schwarz, "Gary Wilcox
   and the Ufonauts," in UFO Percipi-
   ents (Flying Saucer Rev. special
   issue, no.3, Sep.1969), pp.20-27.
   il.

New Berlin
-UFO (CE-3)
 1964, Nov.25/N on Old Hwy.80
   Ted Bloecher, "UFO Landing and Re-
   pair by Crew," Flying Saucer Rev.
   20 (Oct.1974):21-26; (Dec.1974):24-
   27.
   Ted Bloecher, "UFO Repair Reported,"
   Skylook, no.92 (July 1975):3-11.
   Everett Brazie, "Mother-in-Law Veri-
   fies Report," Skylook, no.92 (July
   1975):11-12.
   Berthold Eric Schwarz, "New Berlin
   UFO Landing and Repair by Crew,"
   Flying Saucer Rev. 21 (Nov.1975):22-
   28.

Newburgh
-Lightning anomaly
 1899, Aug.3/J.N. Weed
   "Lightning from a Cloudless Sky,"
   Monthly Weather Rev. 28 (July 1900):
   292-93.

Newfield
-UFO (CE-3)
 1967, Oct.24/Donald Chiszar/nr. White
 House Tavern
   Lloyd Mallan, "Ithaca's Terrifying
   Flying Saucer Epidemic: Part 2,"

Sci.& Mech. 39 (Aug.1968):51,52-53,
69-70.
Jim & Coral Lorenzen, UFOs over the
Americas (N.Y.: Signet, 1968), pp.
179-81.
Edward U. Condon, ed., Scientific
Study of Unidentified Flying Objects
(N.Y.: Bantam, 1969 ed.), pp.375-79.
T.M. Wright, "UFO's over Ithaca,"
Fate 22 (Feb.1969):44,46-47.
(Letter), Ronald S. Follett, Fate
22 (May 1969):130.
1968, Feb.12
Brad Steiger & Joan Whritenour, Fly-
ing Saucer Invasion: Target--Earth
(N.Y.: Award, 1969), p.96.

New Hackensack
-Poltergeist
1786, winter/Dr. Thorn
New York Packet, 10 Mar.1789.
Henry D.B. Bailey, Local Tales and
Historical Sketches (Fishkill Land-
ing: John W. Spaight, 1874), pp.
132-36.

New Hamburg
-Plague of flies
1880, Sep.4/"Martin"/Hudson R.
"Traveling Flies," Sci.Am. 43 (1880):
193.
"Remarkable Cloud of Flies," Nature
22 (1880):518.

New Lebanon
-Healing
1779-1784/Mother Ann Lee
Theodore Schroeder, Shaker Celibacy
and Salacity (N.Y.: A.R. Elliott,
1921).
Alson J. Smith, "Mother Ann's 'Work,'"
Fate 18 (Oct.1965):59-69.
J. Gordon Melton, Encyclopedia of
American Religions, 2 vols. (Wil-
mington, N.C.: Consortium, 1978),
2:36.
1780, July/Noah Wheaton
Alson J. Smith, "Mother Ann's 'Work,'"
Fate 18 (Oct.1965):59,63.
-Spirit medium
1840s/Philemon Stewart
Philemon Stewart, A Holy, Sacred and
Divine Roll and Book (Canterbury,
N.H.: United Soc'y, 1843).
Henry C. Blinn, The Manifestation of
Spiritualism Among the Shakers 1837-
1847 (E. Canterbury, N.H.: Shakers,
1899).

New Paltz
-UFO (CE-1)
1978, June 10/Hwy.299
"UFOs of Limited Merit," Int'l UFO
Reporter 3 (July 1978):3,4.

New Rochelle
-Ancient standing stone
E.G. Squier, Aboriginal Monuments of
the State of New York (Washington:
Smithsonian Institution, Contrib.to

Knowl., vol.2, 1849), p.164.
-Automatic writing
1906, April 28/Edith Traver Naylor
Hester N. & Kenneth R. Holcomb, "The
Typesetter's Warning," Fate 14
(July 1961):71-73.
-Erratic crocodilian
1938, Aug.15/Elvin L. Barr/Huguenot L.
New York Times, 16 Aug.1938, p.4;
and 20 Aug.1938, p.14.
-Giant bird
1960, March 15/Archie Flory
(Letter), Fate 13 (Dec.1960):120-21.
-Haunt
n.d.
Charles M. Skinner, Myths and Legends
of Our Own Land, 2 vols. (Philadel-
phia: Lippincott, 1896), 1:103-104.
-Possession
1922, May
Walter Franklin Prince, "The Cure of
Two Cases of Paranoia," Bull.Boston
SPR, vol.6 (Dec.1927).
-UFO (CE-1)
1975, Nov.29
"UFO Central," CUFOS News Bull., 1
Feb.1976, p.14.
-UFO (NL)
1959, Oct.28/Archie Flory
(Letter), Fate 13 (Apr.1960):111-14.
1978, March 25/William Ragone/Villas
Ave.
New Rochelle Standard-Star, 28 Mar.
1978.

New York City
-Airship inventor
1848/R. Porter & Co./Room 40, Sun Bldg.
Jerome Clark & Loren Coleman, "Mys-
tery Airships of the 1800's," Fate
26 (May 1973):84,85-88. il.
-Alchemy
1897-1900/Stephen H. Emmens
H. Carrington Bolton, "Recent Pro-
gress of Alchemy in America," Chem-
ical News 76 (1897):61-62.
(Letter), Stephen H. Emmens, Chemical
News 76 (1897):117-18.
Herbert C. Fyfe, "Changing Silver
into Gold," Pearson's Mag., Mar.
1898.
New York Herald, 5 Mar.1899.
Stephen H. Emmens, Argentaurana
(Bristol, Eng.: G. DuBoistel, 1899).
Rupert T. Gould, Enigmas (London:
Geoffrey Blas, 1929), pp.137-87.
-Ancient inscription
ca.1856/Oliver St./=colonial
"A Wonderful Relic," NEARA Newsl. 5
(June 1970):47.
Marjorie Kling, "Further Notes on a
'Wonderful Relic': The New York City
Tombstone," NEARA Newsl. 5 (Dec.
1970):78.
1894, fall/Alexander Chenoweth/Inwood
Cornelia Horsford, An Inscribed Stone
(Cambridge, Mass.: J. Wilson, 1895).
il.
Salvatore Michael Trento, The Search
for Lost America (Chicago: Contem-

porary, 1978), pp.97-98. il.
-Ancient wall
1751, April/Hudson R. at Wall St.
New York Gazette, 6 May 1751.
W. Mead Stapler, "A Pre-Colonial
Stone Wall in Manhattan?" NEARA
Newsl. 9 (summer 1974):40.
Salvatore Michael Trento, The Search
for Lost America (Chicago: Contem-
porary, 1978), pp.94-96.
-Animal ESP
1942, July/Green Parrot Restaurant/3d
Ave., Harlem
Edward D. Radin, Twelve Against the
Law (N.Y.: Duell, Sloan & Pearce,
1946), pp.3-19.
n.d./Guy Hedlund
Guy Hedlund, "How Did Tawney Get
Home?" Fate 9 (Aug.1956):80-82.
1972/Morris Schrem/1605 Ave. U
Brooklyn News, 6 Apr.1972.
-Archeological site
Greenpoint
"A Singular Discovery," Sci.Am. 5
(1850):42.
-Astrology
1899-1932/Evangeline Adams
Evangeline Adams, The Bowl of Heaven
(N.Y.: Dodd, Mead, 1926).
Evangeline Adams, Astrology: Your
Place in the Sun (N.Y.: Dodd, Mead,
1928).
Evangeline Adams, Astrology for Every-
one (N.Y.: Dodd, Mead, 1931).
New York Times, 11 Nov.1932, p.19.
Russell N. Case, "Evangeline Adams
Predicted the Windsor Hotel Disas-
ter," Fate 7 (Dec.1954):78-80.
Derek Parker, Astrology in the Modern
World (N.Y.: Taplinger, 1970), pp.
95,170.
1927-   /Astrologers' Guild of America
/223 W. 20th St.
John Godwin, Occult America (Garden
City: Doubleday, 1972), pp.17-18.
Leslie Shepard, ed., Occultism Update,
no.1 (1978):4.
1940s-   /John H. Nelson/RCA-Communi-
cations/Broad St.
Rex Pay, "Position of Planets Linked
to Solar Flare Prediction," Tech-
nology Week 20 (15 May 1967):35-38.
Carl Payne Tobey, "How Astrology
Helped Our Space Program," Fate 21
(Sep.1968):83-90.
TV Guide, 24 Oct.1969.
(Letter), Carl Payne Tobey, Fate 24
(Mar.1970):142-44.
Zipporah Dobyns, "Astrology in the
United States Today," Fate 24 (Apr.
1971):45,52.
1950s-   /Bruce King (Zolar)
Zolar, It's All in the Stars (N.Y.:
Fleet, 1962).
John Godwin, Occult America (Garden
City: Doubleday, 1972), pp.4-6.
1969-   /Nat'l Astrological Soc'y/127
Madison Ave.
June & Nicholas Regush, Psi: The Oth-
er World Catalogue (N.Y.: Putnam,

1974), pp.96-97.
Leslie Shepard, ed., Occultism Update,
no.1 (1978):30.
1970s/Congress of Astrological Organ-
izations/Box 75
Leslie Shepard, ed., Occultism Update,
no.1 (1978):11.
-Autoscopy
1959, April
Edward Podolsky, "Have You Seen Your
Double?" Fate 19 (Apr.1966):78,79.
-Ball lightning
1931/Jamaica
Charles Fitzhugh Talman, "Nature's
Bag of Tricks," Reader's Digest 26
(June 1935):89,91.
-Biofeedback research
1965-1970s/Neal E. Miller/Rockefeller
University
Neal E. Miller & Ali Banuazizi, "In-
strumental Learning by Curarized
Rats of a Specific Visceral Response,
Intestinal or Cardiac," J.Comp.&
Physiol.Psychology 65 (1968):1-7.
Neal Miller & Leo DiCara, "Instru-
mental Learning of Urine Formation
by Rats," Am.J.Physiology 215
(1968):677-83.
Leo V. DiCara & Neal E. Miller, "In-
strumental Learning of Vasomotor
Responses by Rats: Learning to Re-
spond Differentially in the Two
Ears," Science 159 (1968):1485-86.
Neal E. Miller, "Learning of Visceral
and Glandular Responses," Science
163 (1969):434-45.
Bruce A. Pappas, Leo V. DiCara & Neal
E. Miller, "Learning of Blood Pressure Responses in the Noncurarized
Rat," Physiol.Behavior 5 (1970):
1029-32.
Neal Miller, et al., "Learned Modi-
fications of Autonomic Functions,"
Circulation Rsch., Supp.1, 1970,
pp.26-27,1-3.
Inessa B. Koslovskaya, Robert P. Ver-
tes & Neal E. Miller, "Instrumental
Learning without Proprioceptive
Feedback," Physiol.Behavior 10
(1973):101-107.
1970s/Joseph Brudny/NYU Medical Center
Joseph Brudny, Bruce B. Grynbaum &
Julius Korein, "Spasmodic Torticol-
lis: Treatment by Feedback Display
of the EMG," Archives Phys.Med.&
Rehabilitation 55 (1974):403-408.
Joseph Brudny, et al., "Sensory Feedback Therapy As a Modality of Treatment in Central Nervous System Dis-
orders of Voluntary Movement," Neur-
ology 24 (1974):925-32.
-Clairempathy
1920s-1950s/Jacques Romano
W. Franklin Prince, "Rom-Romano Experiments in New York," J.ASPR 18
(1924):369-82.
Harold M. Sherman, "Jacques Romano,
96-Year-Old Psychic," Fate 13 (Sep.
1960):86-94.
Berthold Eric Schwarz, The Jacques

Romano Story (New Hyde Park, N.Y.:
University Books, 1968).
1923, Aug.14, Nov.20/Mrs. R.M. Bowden
Karl P. King, "Two Psychometric Ex-
periments with Mrs. Bowden," J.ASPR
19 (1925):134-58.
1950s/Stanley Jaks
George Groth, "He Writes with Your
Hand," Fate 5 (Oct.1952):39-43.
1970s/Shawn Robbins
Bryce Bond, "Shawn Robbins," Beyond
Reality, no.14 (Mar.-Apr.1975):24-
27,50-51.
David Wallechinsky & Irving Wallace,
The People's Almanac (Garden City:
Doubleday, 1975), p.10.
Lina Accurso, "The Proof of the Pre-
dictions," Fate 32 (Jan.1979):68,
71-72.
1970s/Irwyn Greif/2475 E. 11th
John Godwin, Occult America (Garden
City: Doubleday, 1972), pp.129-30.
-Clairvoyance
1866, Feb.3-1915, March/Mollie Fancher/
60 Steven Ct.
New York Times, 15 Dec.1878, p.5; 29
Dec.1878, p.12; 17 Aug.1881, p.5; 4
Feb.1915, p.7; 13 Nov.1915, p.11;
and 12 Feb.1916, p.11.
Abram H. Dailey, Mollie Fancher: The
Brooklyn Enigma (Brooklyn: Eagle,
1894).
Raymond J. Ross, "The Mystery of Mol-
lie Fancher," Fate 5 (July-Aug.1952)
:22-24.
ca.1900-1917
Walter F. Prince, "The Case of Mrs.
West," J.ASPR 16 (1922):249-68,292-
314,347-87.
1912, April 14
W.O. Stevens, The Mystery of Dreams
(N.Y.: Dodd, Mead, 1949).
1921, Aug.23/William W. Ayre/Brooklyn
(Letter), Fate 17 (May 1964):109-11.
n.d./May Pepper/Brooklyn
Nandor Fodor, Encyclopaedia of Psy-
chic Science (London: Arthurs,
1933), p.277.
n.d./Charles Fort/W. 42d St.
Charles Fort, The Books of Charles
Fort (N.Y.: Holt, 1941), pp.1036-37.
1942, Oct./Mary Camhi/Brooklyn
Mary Camhi, "Mind to Mind in World
War II," Fate 22 (Mar.1969):69-73.
1955, Nov.18/Mrs. Albert Harrison
(Editorial), Fate 9 (Apr.1956):13-14.
1959, Dec.31/Janet Falk/Jackson Hts.
Mercedes Colon, "A Child's Dream of
Death," Fate 26 (May 1973):58-60.
1960s-   /Maurice Woodruff
John Godwin, Occult America (Garden
City: Doubleday, 1972), pp.32-33.
-Clairvoyance and precognition
1860s/Teresa Sickles
James J. Flynn, "Teresa Sickles'
Dreams," New York Folklore Quar. 17
(1961):21-23.
-Contactee
1882-1891/John Ballou Newbrough
John Ballou Newbrough, Oahspe (N.Y.:

Oahspe, 1882).
Nandor Fodor, Encyclopaedia of Psychic Science (London: Arthurs,
1933), pp.24,263.
Jim Dennon, The Oahspe Story (King-
man, Ariz.: Faithist Journal, n.d.).
Jim Dennon, Dr. Newbrough and Oahspe
(Kingman, Ariz.: Faithist Journal,
n.d.).
J. Gordon Melton, Encyclopedia of
American Religions, 2 vols. (Wil-
mington, N.C.: Consortium, 1978),
2:115-16.
1950s-
Brad Steiger, "Space Intelligences
and Earth's New Species of Super-
Kids," Saga UFO Rept. 3 (Dec.1976):
26,28-29,56.
1960s
Roy Ald, The Man Who Took Trips
(N.Y.: Delacorte, 1971).
1962-   /Jackie Altisi/Star Light
Fellowship
J. Gordon Melton, Encyclopedia of
American Religions, 2 vols. (Wil-
mington, N.C,: Consortium, 1978),
2:204.
1963/Louise Livingston
"Saucer Briefs," Saucer News 10
(Sep.1963):16.
-Crisis apparition
1915, May 7/Big John Ryland/Empire
Theater, Broadway x 40th St.
n.d./David Belasco
Eugene Burr, "Broadway Bogies and
Other Phantoms," Fate 24 (Mar.1971):
78-83.
1920, Nov./Mathias Rivera/Brooklyn
Mathias Rivera, "The Man in the
Chair," Fate 5 (Jan.1952):84.
1922, March 31/George William Douglas
"An Apparitional Experience," J.ASPR
18 (1924):700-706.
1930, April/Church of St. Bartholomew
Chester Grady, "Case Record of Clair-
voyance," Psychic Rsch. 25 (1931):
181-82.
1944, July 27/Caroline Schneider/Brook-
lyn
New York Sunday News, 22 Mar.1966.
1945, Jan.25
William Oliver Stevens, Psychics and
Common Sense (N.Y.: Dutton, 1953),
pp.211-12.
1950, Nov.2-9/Gabriel Pascal
"Haunted by George Bernard Shaw,"
Fate 7 (Oct.1954):56.
n.d./Rose Margolies/Snyder Ave.
Hans Holzer, Ghosts I've Met (N.Y.:
Ace, 1965 ed.), pp.246-47.
1969
Herbert B. Greenhouse, The Astral
Journey (N.Y.: Avon, 1976 ed.), pp.
76-77.
-Deathbed apparition and out-of-body experience research
1957-   /Karlis Osis
Karlis Osis, Deathbed Observations
by Physicians and Nurses (N.Y.:
Parapsychology Foundation, 1961).

Karlis Osis, "Toward a Methodology for Experiments on Out-of-the-Body Experiences," in W.G. Roll, et al., eds., Research in Parapsychology 1972 (Metuchen, N.J.: Scarecrow, 1973), pp.78-79.

Karlis Osis, E. Bokert & M.L. Carlson, "Dimensions of the Meditative Experience," J.Transpersonal Psych. 5 (1973):109-35.

Karlis Osis, "Perspective for Out-of-Body Research," in W.G. Roll, et al., eds., Research in Parapsychology 1973 (Metuchen, N.J.: Scarecrow, 1974).

Karlis Osis, "Out-of-Body Research at the American Society for Psychical Research," Newsl.ASPR, no.22, summer 1974.

Herbert B. Greenhouse, The Astral Journal (N.Y.: Avon, 1976 ed.), pp. 278-92.

Karlis Osis, "Precognitive Remote Viewing," in J.D. Morris, et al., eds., Research in Parapsychology 1975 (Metuchen, N.J.: Scarecrow, 1976).

Martin Ebon, The Evidence for Life After Death (N.Y.: Signet, 1977), pp.64-76.

Karlis Osis & Erlendur Haraldsson, At the Hour of Death (N.Y.: Avon, 1977).

Norman Schreiber, "Life After Death," Saga UFO Rept. 5 (Nov.1977):41-43, 68-69.

-Disappearance
1910, Dec.12/Dorothy Arnold/Central Park
New York Times, 16 Jan.1911, p.1; 27 Jan.1911, p.1; 28 Jan.1911, p.1; 31 Jan.1911, p.1; 7 Feb.1911, p.7; 8 Feb.1911, p.4; 13 Feb.1911, p.1; 15 Feb.1911, p.1; 16 Feb.1911, p.1; 19 Feb.1911, p.1; 20 Feb.1911, p.1; 23 Feb.1911, p.1; 24 Feb.1911, p.1; 11 Mar.1911, p.1; 19 Mar.1911, p.1; 15 May 1911, p.1; 16 May 1911, p.22; 11 June 1911, p.1; 20 Aug.1911, pt. 3, p.1; 21 Feb.1912, p.1; 1 May 1912, p.10; 6 May 1912, p.9; 5 Dec. 1912, p.10; 13 June 1913, p.11; 16 Mar.1914, p.18; 10 Apr.1914, p.3; 11 Apr.1914, p.18; 18 Apr.1916, p. 6; 20 Apr.1916, p.16; and 23 Apr. 1916, p.12.
1930, Aug.6/Joseph Force Crater/W. 45th St.
New York Times, 4 Sep.1930, p.1; 5 Sep.1930, p.1; 6 Sep.1930, p.1; 7 Sep.1930, p.3; 8 Sep.1930, p.5; 9 Sep.1930, p.4; 10 Sep.1930, p.15; 12 Sep.1930, p.1; 13 Sep.1930, p.1; 14 Sep.1930, p.21; 16 Sep.1930, p. 1; 19 Sep.1930, p.1; 22 Sep.1930, p.1; 23 Sep.1930, p.1; 25 Sep.1930, p.20; 26 Sep.1930, p.14; 27 Sep. 1930, p.10; 2 Oct.1930, p.2; 3 Oct. 1930, p.20; 7 Oct.1930, p.5; 8 Oct. 1930, p.5; 11 Oct.1930, p.2; 15 Oct.

1930, p.2; 29 Oct.1930, p.2; 5 Nov. 1930, p.23; 8 Nov.1930, p.19; 20 Nov.1930, p.1; 21 Nov.1930, p.20; 22 Nov.1930, p.36; 10 Jan.1931, p. 34; 22 Jan.1931, p.1; 26 Jan.1931, p.4; 27 Jan.1931, p.25; 3 Feb.1931, p.6; 6 May 1931, p.11; 8 Aug.1931, p.14; 2 Oct.1931, sec.II, p.1; 2 May 1935, p.22; 6 Sep.1935, p.13; 28 Nov.1935, p.3; 26 Aug.1936, p. 8; 22 July 1937, p.1; 30 July 1937, p.38; 7 June 1939, p.16; and 11 Jan.1940, p.25.
G. Manning, "Most Tantalizing Disappearance of Our Time," Collier's Mag. 126 (29 July 1950):13-15. il.
Leland Lovelace, Lost Mines and Hidden Treasure (N.Y.: Ace, 1956), pp. 43-56.
Murray Teigh Bloom, "Is It Judge Crater's Body?" Harper's 219 (Nov. 1959):41-47.
J. Alexander, "What Happened to Judge Crater?" Sat.Eve.Post, 10 Sep.1960, pp.19-21.
Stella Crater, The Empty Robe (Garden City: Doubleday, 1961).
(Editorial), Fate 17 (Nov.1964):18.
ca.1955/George H. Wales/Brooklyn
Nat'l Enquirer, 4 May 1958.
Gordon Creighton, "More on Teleportations," Flying Saucer Rev. 18 (Sep.-Oct.1972):31, quoting Sentinel, no.38 (May 1971).
-Doubtful responsibility
1929, March 9/Isidor Fink/52 E. 132d St.
New York Times, 10 Mar.1929, p.24; and 11 Mar.1929, p.27.
Vincent H. Gaddis, "Fourth Dimensional Homicide," Fate 11 (May 1958):48-52.
(Letter), Ross L. Bralley, Fate 11 (Aug.1958):124-26.
(Letter), Conrad H.F. Creuz, Fate 11 (Aug.1958):126.
(Letter), Otto Meinecke, Fate 11 (Aug.1958):126-27.
(Letter), Conrad H.F. Creuz, Fate 11 (Nov.1958):120-22.
-Dowsing
1889/Mr. Heerdigen/Fulton x Nassau St.
"Professional Water Finding," Sci.Am. 62 (1890):179.
1890/T. Brown Alderson/Morrisania
New York Times, 12 Jan.1890, p.20.
1966/George J. Halasi-Kun/Columbia University
New York Times, 26 Sep.1966, p.43.
(Editorial), Fate 20 (Jan.1967):12-15.
-Electromagnetic anomaly
1977, Jan.15/Harlem
St. Louis (Mo.) Post-Dispatch, 20 Jan.1977.
-Erratic bear
1950, Jan./New York Int'l Airport
"Run of the Mill," Doubt, no.29 (1950):27.
1953/Brooklyn

"Follow Up," Doubt, no.45 (1954):
284,286.
-Erratic crocodilian
1932, June 28/Bronx R.
New York Times, 30 June 1932, p.25.
1935, Feb./E. 123d St. sewer
New York Times, 10 Feb.1935, p.29.
1937, June 1/Pier 9, East R.
New York Times, 1 June 1937, p.25.
1937, June 6/Brooklyn Museum subway
station
New York Times, 7 June 1937, p.21.
-Erratic swan
1910, Dec.12/Central Park
New York Sun, 13 Dec.1910.
-Eyeless vision
1960s-   /Biometrics Research/722 W.
168th St./="peeking"
(Letter), Joseph Zubin, Science 147
(1965):985.
-Fall of aluminum
1968, Jan.19/Corona
John A. Keel, "Our Skies Are Filled
with Junk," Fate 22 (Mar.1969):34.
(Letter), G.D., Fate 22 (July 1969):
130.
-Fall of anomalous meteorite
1886, May 12/Main x Temple St.
"Fall of Aerolites," Sci.Am. 68
(1893):325.
1887, July 17/Troy x Fulton Ave.
New York Times, 19 July 1887, p.8.
-Fall of ash
1953, April 29/Tiffany Thayer/3d Ave.
"Falls," Doubt, no.41 (1953):221,222.
-Fall of fish
1824
James E. De Kay, "Zoology of New
York," in N.Y.Geol.Survey, Natural
History of New York (Albany: The
Survey, 1842), pt.4, Fishes, pp.170-
72.
1946, Sep.23/Wormington's Restaurant
"Fish and Snail Falls," Doubt, no.
17 (1947):253.
-Fall of grain
1950, Aug.18/Empire State Bldg.
"Barley Rain," Doubt, no.30 (1950):
34.
"The Mystery of the Falling Grain,"
Fate 4 (Apr.1951):14.
-Fall of gray powder
1947, Oct.5/=pollution?
"Run of the Mill," Doubt, no.20
(1948):303.
-Fall of sand
1953, May 1/Times Square
New York Times, 2 May 1953, p.17. il.
-Fall of snakes
1897, May?/Richard E. White/129 W. 24th
St.
Canton (O.) Repository, 9 May 1897.
-Fall of unknown object
1891, March 16/Smith Morehouse/Vander-
bilt x Atlantic Ave.
New York Times, 17 Mar.1891, p.1.
1939, March 21/301 Fourth Ave./Brooklyn
"More Brooks," Fortean Soc'y Mag.,
no.10 (autumn 1944):141.
-Fasting and schizophrenia

1970s/Allan Cott/160 E.38th St.
Paul Martin, "Fasting for Mental,
Physical, Spiritual Health," Fate
29 (Oct.1976):36,39-40.
-Fire anomaly
1937, Aug.11/Charlotte Mullen/3905 Ave.
K
New York World-American, 11 Aug.1937.
1949, June 25/Will Whalen/Bronx
"Only Fortean Cleric a Pyrotic,"
Doubt, no.26 (1949):395.
1950, May 27/Annabell Culverwell/319
W. 100th St.
Annabell Culverwell, "The White Flame
Phenomenon," Fate 3 (Dec.1950):41-
43.
-Fire immunity
1938, Aug.2/Kuda Bux/Radio City
Vincent H. Gaddis, Mysterious Fires
and Lights (N.Y.: Dell, 1968 ed.),
pp.121-22.
-Flying humanoid
1877, Sep.18/William H. Smith/Brooklyn
New York Sun, 21 Sep.1877.
1880, Sep./Coney I.
New York Times, 12 Sep.1880, p.6.
-Ghost
1817, Jan.1/Ann Morris/Port Morris
Charles M. Skinner, Myths and Legends
of Our Own Land, 2 vols. (Philadel-
phia: Lippincott, 1896), 1:104-106.
James J. Flynn & Charles A. Huguenin,
"The Portrait That Came to Life,"
New York Folklore Quar. 15 (1959):
104-11.
1903, Feb.28/Ella Stainthorp/1096 La-
fayette Ave.
Isaac K. Funk, The Widow's Mite
(N.Y.: Funk & Wagnall, 1904), pp.
311-14.
1951, Nov.22/Bernard Ramsey/Roosevelt
Ave. Station
"Collision with a Ghost," Fate 5
(Apr.-May 1952):42.
ca.1952/Mrs. Roland/Riverside Museum
Hans Holzer, Ghost Hunter (N.Y.:
Ace, 1963 ed.), pp.40-43.
ca.1955/Metropolitan Opera
Danton Walker, Spooks Deluxe (N.Y.:
Franklin Watts, 1956), pp.135-36.
1955/Hans Holzer/Riverside Dr.
Hans Holzer, Ghosts I've Met (N.Y.:
Ace, 1965 ed.), p.26.
-Ghost and phantoms
1915-1917
Walter F. Prince, "Apparitional Ex-
periences of Mr. Marbeck," J.ASPR
12 (1918):426-39.
-Ghost dog
n.d./Mrs. Henry Wipperman/Howard Beach
Nandor Fodor, Between Two Worlds
(W. Nyack: Parker, 1964), p.230.
1955/Norma Kresgal
Nat'l Enquirer, 7 Jan.1973.
1972/G. Reeves/Brooklyn
The Star, 7 Jan.1973.
-Gravity anomaly
n.d./Brooklyn
Gray Barker, Book of Saucers (Clarks-
burg, W.V.: Saucerian, 1965), p.32,

quoting <u>Saucerian</u>, Nov.1953.
-Haunt
1660-   /Foreman Cole/St. Mark's-in-
the-Bouwerie Church/2d Ave. x E. 10th
St.
   Hans Holzer, <u>Ghost Hunter</u> (N.Y.: Ace,
   1963 ed.), pp.62-65.
   Hans Holzer, <u>Psychic Photography</u>
   (N.Y.: McGraw-Hill, 1969), p.98.
   Hans Holzer, <u>Haunted Houses</u> (N.Y.:
   Crown, 1971), pp.74-76. il.
1700s-   /Conference House/Hylan Blvd.,
Tottenville
   Hans Holzer, <u>Ghost Hunter</u> (N.Y.: Ace,
   1963 ed.), pp.68-71.
1780s-19th c./Bergen House/Brooklyn
   Charles A. Huguenin, "The Ghost in
   the Old Bergen House," <u>New York</u>
   <u>Folklore Quar.</u> 13 (1957):203-207.
19th c./Austen House/2 Hylan Blvd.
19th c./Tillary x Concord St.
   Charles M. Skinner, <u>Myths and Legends</u>
   <u>of Our Own Land</u>, 2 vols. (Philadelphia: Lippincott, 1896), 1:121-22,
   132-33.
1870-1871/Caroline B. LeRoss
   <u>New York Commercial Advertiser</u>, 15
   July 1884.
   "Physical and Other Phenomena," <u>J.</u>
   <u>ASPR</u> 12 (1918):334-41.
1880s/Central Park
   James Reynolds, <u>Ghosts in American</u>
   <u>Houses</u> (N.Y.: Paperback Library,
   1967 ed.), pp.55-64.
1890s-1900s/Benjamin Wood/Brooklyn
   Elizabeth Glidden Wood, "Experiences
   in a House," <u>Proc.ASPR</u> 14 (1920):
   360-418.
   Edmond P. Gibson, "The Insane Ghost,"
   <u>Fate</u> 3 (Jan.1950):38-43.
1900, May/Lilliace M. Mitchell/Bays-
water Rd.
   Lilliace M. Mitchell, "Haunted House
   at Far Rockaway," <u>Fate</u> 18 (Feb.
   1965):54-61. il.
1909-1912
   "A Case of Haunting in New York,"
   <u>Psychic Rsch.</u> 24 (1930):286-87.
1913/8th Ave.
   James H. Hyslop, "A Haunted House,"
   <u>J.ASPR</u> 8 (1914):542-47.
n.d./Shubert Alley
   Eugene Burr, "Broadway Bogies and
   Other Phantoms," <u>Fate</u> 24 (Mar.1971):
   78,82.
1930s-1960s/Old Merchant's House/29 E.
Fourth St.
   Hans Holzer, <u>Haunted Houses</u> (N.Y.:
   Crown, 1971), pp.72-73.
   Hans Holzer, <u>Gothic Ghosts</u> (N.Y.: Ace,
   1972), pp.51-65.
1937, April
   Hereward Carrington, <u>The Invisible</u>
   <u>World</u> (N.Y.: Beechhurst, 1946).
1939/Women's Detention Prison
   "Suicide Cell," <u>Fate</u> 27 (Dec.1974):
   52, quoting <u>Toledo (O.) Blade</u> (undated).
1939-1960/Jean Karsavina/27 Jane St.
   "Greenwich Village Ghost," <u>Fate</u> 10

(June 1957):61.
   Hans Holzer, <u>Ghost Hunter</u> (N.Y.: Ace,
   1963 ed.), pp.65-68.
1940s/Crawley House/Staten I.
   James Reynolds, <u>Ghosts in American</u>
   <u>Houses</u> (N.Y.: Paperback Library,
   1967 ed.), pp.55-64.
1940s/Dorothy Massey
1940s/William Sloane
   Danton Walker, <u>Spooks Deluxe</u> (N.Y.:
   Franklin Watts, 1956), pp.27-30,73-
   77.
1940s-1950s/Carleton Alsop/W. 57th St.
   Danton Walker, <u>Spooks Deluxe</u> (N.Y.:
   Franklin Watts, 1956), pp.19-26.
1943, May/W. 45th St.
   "Ghosts Active," <u>Fortean Soc'y Mag.</u>,
   no.10 (autumn 1944):142.
1944-1954/51 W. 10th St.
   Elizabeth Archer, "The Ghost of
   Tenth Street," <u>Tomorrow</u> 6 (spring
   1958):17-23.
   Hans Holzer, <u>Ghost Hunter</u> (N.Y.: Ace,
   1963 ed.), pp.43-51.
1944-1960/M. Daly Hopkins/471 Central
Park W.
   M. Daly Hopkins, "Ten Years with a
   Ghost," <u>Fate</u> 7 (July 1954):80-86.
   Hans Holzer, <u>Ghost Hunter</u> (N.Y.: Ace,
   1963 ed.), pp.54-62.
n.d./Da Vinci's/W. 56th St.
   Hans Holzer, <u>Ghosts I've Met</u> (N.Y.:
   Ace, 1965 ed.), pp.136-38.
n.d./Division Ave.
n.d./John Jay House
   Hans Holzer, <u>Yankee Ghosts</u> (N.Y.:
   Ace, 1966), pp.61-62,180-81.
1950s/Upper East Side
   Martin Ebon, "Ghost Against Ghost,"
   <u>Fate</u> 27 (Dec.1974):38-47.
1950s-1960s/Robert Cowan/1780 House,
Stamford Hill
   Hans Holzer, <u>Ghosts I've Met</u> (N.Y.:
   Ace, 1965 ed.), pp.38-54.
1953/Capt. Davis/226 W. Fifth Ave.
   Hans Holzer, <u>Ghost Hunter</u> (N.Y.: Ace,
   1963 ed.), pp.82-114, quoting <u>New</u>
   <u>York Times</u>, 13 July 1953.
   Hans Holzer, <u>Haunted Houses</u> (N.Y.:
   Crown, 1971), pp.60-62. il.
1956-1964/Mildred C. Hatt/21st St.
   Mildred C. Hatt, "My 8 Years in a
   Haunted House," <u>Fate</u> 27 (Mar.1974):
   54-57.
1957, Jan.-July/Harvey Slatin/11 Bank
St.
   Meyer Berger, "Greenwich Village
   Ghost," <u>Tomorrow</u> 6 (spring 1958):17-
   23.
   Hans Holzer, <u>Ghost Hunter</u> (N.Y.: Ace,
   1963 ed.), pp.15-21, quoting <u>New</u>
   <u>York Times</u>, 26 June 1957.
1957, July-Aug./Andrew J. Galet
   (Letter), <u>Fate</u> 11 (June 1958):120-24.
1959/Dave Garroway/63d St.
   <u>New York Post</u>, 20 Mar.1959.
1959-1960/Ruth Shaw/422½ W. 46th St.
   Wainwright Evans, "Ghost in Crino-
   line," <u>Tomorrow</u> 7 (spring 1959):93-
   100.

Hans Holzer, <u>Ghost Hunter</u> (N.Y.: Ace,
1963 ed.), pp.71-76.
Hans Holzer, <u>Ghosts I've Met</u> (N.Y.:
Ace, 1965 ed.), pp.10-11.
Hans Holzer, <u>Yankee Ghosts</u> (N.Y.:
Ace, 1966), pp.101-12.
Hans Holzer, <u>Haunted Houses</u> (N.Y.:
Crown, 1971), pp.57-59. il.
1960s/Edward Karalanian/Riverside Dr.
1960s/Joan Lowe/W. 12th St.
Hans Holzer, <u>Ghost Hunter</u> (N.Y.: Ace,
1963 ed.), pp.155-58.
1960s/Dakota Apts.
Susy Smith, <u>Ghosts Around the House</u>
(N.Y.: World, 1970).
1960s/Jan Bryant Bartell/10th St.
Hans Holzer, <u>Ghosts I've Met</u> (N.Y.:
Ace, 1965 ed.), pp.28-37.
Jan Bryant Bartell, <u>Spindrift: Spray</u>
<u>from a Psychic Sea</u> (N.Y.: Hawthorn,
1974).
1960s
Gertrude R. Schmiedler, "Quantitative
Investigation of a 'Haunted House,'"
<u>J.ASPR</u> 60 (1966):137-49.
1960, Jan.23-1963?/Renée Dubonnet/Park
Ave.
Susy Smith, "The Woman Who Bought a
Ghost," <u>Fate</u> 16 (Sep.1963):50-58.
1961, July 27/Renee Allmen/Cafe Bizarre
Hans Holzer, <u>Ghost Hunter</u> (N.Y.: Ace,
1963 ed.), pp.154-55.
Hans Holzer, <u>Haunted Houses</u> (N.Y.:
Ace, 1965 ed.), pp.54-56. il.
1961-1964/Bob Blackburn/34th St. x 3d
Ave.
Hans Holzer, <u>Ghosts I've Met</u> (N.Y.:
Ace, 1965 ed.), pp.108-14.
1963/Frank Paris/12 Gay St.
Hans Holzer, <u>Yankee Ghosts</u> (N.Y.:
Ace, 1966), pp.55-60.
Hans Holzer, <u>Haunted Houses</u> (N.Y.:
Crown, 1971), pp.63-64.
1964/Mrs. William De Geldern/W. 87th
St.
1964/Barrie Gaunt/Charles St.
Hans Holzer, <u>Ghosts I've Met</u> (N.Y.:
Ace, 1965 ed.), pp.245-52.
1964, Jan.19/Morris-Jumel Mansion/160th
St. x Edgecombe Ave.
Hans Holzer, <u>Ghosts I've Met</u> (N.Y.:
Ace, 1965 ed.), pp.232-45.
Margaret P. Gaddis, "Guardian of the
Mansion: Past and Present?" <u>Fate</u> 20
(Aug.1967):69-73.
(Letter), Lucy Musenshi, <u>Fate</u> 21
(Feb.1968):121-24. il.
Susy Smith, <u>Prominent American Ghosts</u>
(N.Y.: Dell, 1969 ed.), pp.107-19.
Hans Holzer, <u>Haunted Houses</u> (N.Y.:
Crown, 1971), pp.69-71. il.
1964-1965/June Havoc/44th St. x 9th
Ave.
(Editorial), <u>Fate</u> 18 (June 1965):26-
28.
Hans Holzer, <u>Yankee Ghosts</u> (N.Y.:
Ace, 1966), pp.34-47.
Hans Holzer, <u>Psychic Photography</u>
(N.Y.: McGraw-Hill, 1969), pp.98-
104. il.

Hans Holzer, <u>Haunted Houses</u> (N.Y.:
Crown, 1971), pp.65-68. il.
1965/Margaret Widdemer/Hotel des Ar-
tistes/1 W. 67th St.
1965/H.D. Settel/Riverside Dr.
Hans Holzer, <u>Yankee Ghosts</u> (N.Y.:
Ace, 1966), pp.170-73,181-90.
-Healing
1910s/John Moore Hickson/Trinity Chapel
James H. Hyslop, "Mr. Hickson's
Spiritual Healing," <u>J.ASPR</u> 14
(1920):266-72.
1931, July/Mr. Gaffney/Medical Center
Hospital
<u>New York World-Telegram</u>, 24 July
1931.
1935/hospital
William Oliver Stevens, <u>Psychics and</u>
<u>Common Sense</u> (N.Y.: Dutton, 1953),
pp.49-50.
1947, Dec.-1948, March/Joey Rizzuto/
115-56 203d St.
<u>New York Times</u>, 2 Apr.1948, p.25.
W.E. Farbstein, "Joey and the 'Magic
Medicine,'" <u>Fate</u> 11 (Nov.1958):62-
65.
1950s/Salamon Friedlander/2176 Grand
Concourse
Lesley Kuhn, "Miracle Rabbi: Salamon
Friedlander," <u>Fate</u> 10 (June 1957):
56-61.
1970s/Latin communities
Gloria Gastman, "Las Botanicas," <u>Be-</u>
<u>yond Reality</u>, no.14 (Mar.-Apr.1975):
46-49. il.
1970s/Dean Kraft/250 E. 63d St.
"Probe's 1977 Directory of the Psychic World," <u>Probe the Unknown</u> 5
(spring 1977):32,36-37.
1972, Oct.22/Emmanuel J. Scollo/Brook-
lyn
(Letter), <u>Fate</u> 26 (Oct.1973):128-29.
-Healing and exorcisms
1907-1940/Titus Bull
Titus Bull, <u>Analysis of Unusual Ex-</u>
<u>periences in Healing Relative to</u>
<u>Diseased Minds</u> (N.Y.: James H. Hys-
lop Foundation, 1932).
Nandor Fodor, <u>Encyclopaedia of Psy-</u>
<u>chic Science</u> (London: Arthurs,
1933), pp.40-41.
Titus Bull, <u>Man's Great Adventure</u>
(N.Y.: James H. Hyslop Foundation,
1934).
Titus Bull, <u>The Imperative Conquest</u>
(N.Y.: James H. Hyslop Foundation,
1936).
D. Scott Rogo, "Titus Bull, American
Exorcist," in Martin Ebon, ed., <u>Ex-</u>
<u>orcism: Fact Not Fiction</u> (N.Y.:
Signet, 1974), pp.167-76.
-Hex
1926, Jan.16/Joseph Musca/Park St.
<u>New York Times</u>, 16 Jan.1926, p.5.
1929, Feb./Mrs. Nathanial Conway
<u>Brooklyn Daily Eagle</u>, 25 Feb.1929.
1930s/Harlem
Claude McKay, <u>Harlem: Negro Metropo-</u>
<u>lis</u> (N.Y.: Dutton, 1940), pp.75-79.
1939, Dec./Salvatore Petruzzella/Coney

Island
  New York World-Telegram, 11 Dec.1939.
-Humanoid
  1974, Dec.7/Frank Pizzolato/nr. St.
  Andrew's Church, Richmond
  1975, Jan.21/Mrs. D. Daly/Richmond Rd.
    Staten Island Advance, 8 Dec.1974.
    Robert C. Warth, "A UFO-ABSM Link?"
      Pursuit 8 (Apr.1975):31-35.
-Inner development
  1875-1898/Helene Petrovna Blavatsky/
  Theosophical Society
    Charles J. Ryan, Madame Blavatsky
      and the Theosophical Movement (Point
      Loma, Cal.: Theosophical Soc'y,
      1937).
    Gertrude Marvin Williams, Madame Bla-
      vatsky: Priestess of the Occult
      (N.Y.: Knopf, 1946).
    Elsie Benjamin, "Theosophy in Ameri-
      ca," Fate 5 (Apr.-May 1952):65-68.
    J. Gordon Melton, Encyclopedia of
      American Religions, 2 vols. (Wil-
      mington, N.C.: Consortium, 1978),
      2:141-42.
  1880s-   /Societas Rosicruciana in
  America
    George Winslow Plummer, Principles
      and Practices of the Rosicrucians
      (N.Y.: Soc'y of Rosicrucians, 1947).
  1915-1927/Ancient and Mystical Order
  of the Rosae Crucis/321 W. 101st St.
    J. Gordon Melton, Encyclopedia of
      American Religions, 2 vols. (Wil-
      mington, N.C.: Consortium, 1978),
      2:182-83.
  1920s-   /Agni Yoga Society/319 W.
  107th St.
    Armand Biteaux, The New Conscious-
      ness (Willits, Cal.: Oliver, 1975),
      p.2.
    J. Gordon Melton, Encyclopedia of
      American Religions, 2 vols. (Wil-
      mington, N.C.: Consortium, 1978),
      2:175.
  1923-   /Alice Bailey/Arcane School/
  U.N. Plaza
    Alice Bailey, Thirty Years' Work
      (N.Y.: Lucis, 1952).
    J. Gordon Melton, Encyclopedia of
      American Religions, 2 vols. (Wil-
      mington, N.C.: Consortium, 1978),
      2:144-47.
  1960s-   /Leo Louis Martello/153 W.
  80th St., Suite 1B
    Leo Louis Martello, How to Prevent
      Psychic Blackmail (N.Y.: Hero, 1966).
    Leo Louis Martello, Weird Ways of
      Witchcraft (N.Y.: H.C. Publishers,
      1969).
    Charles B. Leland, Arcadia: The Gos-
      pel of the Witches (N.Y.: Hero,
      1971).
    John Godwin, Occult America (Garden
      City: Doubleday, 1972), pp.67-70.
    Hans Holzer, The New Pagans (Garden
      City: Doubleday, 1972), pp.36-39.
    Hans Holzer, The Witchcraft Report
      (N.Y.: Ace, 1973), pp.39-47.
    Leo Louis Martello, Witchcraft: The

  Old Religion (Secaucus, N.J.: Uni-
    versity Books, 1974).
  Warren Smith, "Phenomenal Predictions
    for 1975," Saga, Jan.1975, pp.20,50.
  J. Gordon Melton, Encyclopedia of
    American Religions, 2 vols. (Wil-
    mington, N.C.: Consortium, 1978),
    2:276-77.
1967-   /Awareness Center/685 West
End Ave.
  Armand Biteaux, The New Conscious-
    ness (Willets, Cal.: Oliver, 1975),
    p.11.
  Bernard Green, "Create Your Own Fu-
    ture," Fate 28 (May 1975):56-64.
1970s/Ed Buczynski/300 Henry St.
  Hans Holzer, The Witchcraft Report
    (N.Y.: Ace, 1973), pp.37-39.
1970-   /Arica Institute/24 W. 57th
St.
  New York Times, 8 Oct.1971.
  June & Nicholas Regush, Psi: The Oth-
    er World Catalogue (N.Y.: Putnam,
    1974), p.153.
  J. Gordon Melton, Encyclopedia of
    American Religions, 2 vols. (Wil-
    mington, N.C.: Consortium, 1978),
    2:239.
1970-   /Kundalini Research Foundation
/10 E. 39th St.
  Gopi Krishna, Higher Consciousness
    (N.Y.: Julian, 1973).
  Gene Kieffer, "Interview: Gopi Krish-
    na," Changes in the Arts, no.80
    (Mar.1973).
  Armand Biteaux, The New Conscious-
    ness (Willits, Cal.: Oliver, 1975),
    pp.87-88.
  John White & Stanley Krippner, eds.,
    Future Science (Garden City: An-
    chor, 1977), p.589.
-Intra-Mercurial planet
  1864, Feb.12/Samuel Beswick
    "Lescarbault's Planet(?)," Astronom-
      ical Register 2 (1864):161.
-Lightning anomaly
  1937, Aug.8/Robert Andrews/Rockaway Pt.
    New York Times, 9 Aug.1937, p.1.
    New York World-Telegram, 9 Aug.1937.
-Lunar cycle and births
  1948-1970s
    Walter & A. Menaker, "Lunar Period-
      icity in Human Reproduction," Am.J.
      Obstetrics & Gynecology 77 (1959):
      905-13.
    Walter Menaker, "Lunar Periodicity
      with Reference to Live Births," Am.
      J.Obstetrics & Gynecology 98 (1967):
      1002-1004.
    M. Osley, D. Summerville & L.B. Borst,
      "Natality and the Moon," Am.J.Obstet-
      rics & Gynecology 117 (1973):413-15.
-Men-in-black
  1967, spring/John A. Keel/42d St. x 3d
  Ave.
  1967, summer/Max's Kansas City/213
  Park Ave. S
    John A. Keel, The Mothman Prophecies
      (N.Y.: Saturday Review, 1975), pp.
      17-18,175-76.

-Musical sand
  H. Carrington Bolton & Alexis A. Ju-
  lien, "Musical Sand: Its Wide Dis-
  tribution and Properties," Proc.Am.
  Ass'n Adv.Sci. 33 (1884):408-13.
-Mystery bird deaths
  1937/Verdi Square
  Eric Frank Russell, "Invisible Death,"
  Fate 3 (Dec.1950):4,7.
  1948, Sep.2/Empire State Bldg.
  "Birds Crash," Doubt, no.23 (1948):
  350.
  1970, Sep.28/Empire State Bldg.
  Eugene Barr, "Birds Fall on the Em-
  pire State," Fate 24 (Apr.1971):
  75-76.
  (Letter), Mrs. L.H. Woodard, Fate 24
  (Oct.1971):145.
  (Letter), Charles A. Seibold, Fate
  25 (Sep.1972):141-42.
-Mystery death
  1891, July/Carl Gros/Maspeth
  Brooklyn Eagle, 8 July 1891.
-Mystery explosions
  1978, March 24/Bronx sewers
  New York Times, 19 Nov.1978.
-Mystery gas
  1942-1944/Flushing Ave. station/=pol-
  lution?
  "Brooklyn Smells Too," Doubt, no.11
  (winter 1944-45):156.
  1968, Jan.19
  John A. Keel, "Mysterious Gas Attacks
  by Flying Saucers," Saga UFO Rept.
  2 (fall 1975):27-28.
-Mystery plane crash
  1957, Feb.1/Alva Marsh/DC-6A/Riker's I.
  New York Times, 2 Feb.1957, p.1; 3
  Feb.1957, p.1; and 9 Feb.1957, p.34.
  "Case 282," CRIFO Orbit, 1 Mar.1957,
  p.1.
-Electromagnetic anomaly
  1965, Nov.9
  New York Times, 10 Nov.1965, pp.1,3;
  11 Nov.1965, p.36; 16 Nov.1965, pp.
  1,58; 17 Nov.1965, p.1; 20 Nov.1965,
  p.55; and 7 Dec.1965, p.1.
  "The Question of the Power Black-
  outs," APRO Bull. 14 (Nov.-Dec.
  1965):4-6.
  U.S. Federal Power Comm'n, Northeast
  Power Failure, Nov.9 and 10, 1965:
  Report to the President, Dec.1965.
  U.S. Congress, House, Interstate &
  Foreign Commerce Comm., Northeast
  Power Failure, Nov.9-10, Hearings
  before a special subcommittee to
  investigate power failures, 89th
  Cong., 1st & 2d sess., 1966.
  Gordon D. Friedlander, "The North-
  east Power Failure: A Blanket of
  Darkness," IEEE Spectrum 3 (Feb.
  1966):54-73.
  John G. Fuller, Incident at Exeter
  (N.Y.: Berkley, 1967 ed.), pp.203-
  209.
  R.J. Low, "Unexplained Electric Power
  Interruptions," in Edward U. Condon,
  ed., Scientific Study of Unidenti-
  fied Flying Objects (N.Y.: Bantam,

1969 ed.), pp.108,110-15.
-Numerology
  1960s/Marguerite Haymes
  Brad Steiger, "Find the Key to Your
  Life-Path," Fate 22 (Dec.1969):84-
  93.
-Orgone energy research
  1960s-   /American College of Orgon-
  omy/515 E. 88th St.
  John White & Stanley Krippner, eds.,
  Future Science (Garden City: An-
  chor, 1977), pp.582-83.
-Ornithomancy
  1958/Aida Acee/nr. Hotel New Yorker
  (Letter), Fate 25 (Sep.1972):145.
-Out-of-body experience
  1850s
  Isaac K. Funk, The Widow's Mite
  (N.Y.: Funk & Wagnalls, 1904), pp.
  380-82.
  1896/William McDonald/Second Ave.
  Raymond J. Ross, "Professor Wien's
  Astral Burglar," Fate 3 (Aug.1950):
  28-29.
  1920s/Margaret Linden
  Margaret Linden, "Don't Send Me
  Back!" Fate 7 (Jan.1954):101-102.
  1920, Jan./Harry M. Archer/East Side
  Frank B. Copley, "Two O'Clock in the
  Morning," Collier's 76 (8 Aug.1925):
  10.
  n.d./Hereward Carrington/Greenwich
  Village
  R. DeWitt Miller, Impossible--Yet It
  Happened! (N.Y.: Ace, 1947 ed.),
  pp.113-15.
  1938, Nov.13/Lawrence S. Aspey
  Hornell Hart, "ESP Projection: Spontaneous Cases and the Experimental
  Method," J.ASPR 48 (1954):121,127-
  28.
  n.d./Russell MacRobert/Lenox Hill Hos-
  pital
  Susy Smith, The Enigma of Out-of-
  Body Travel (N.Y.: Helix, 1965).
  n.d.
  Andrija Puharich, Beyond Telepathy
  (Garden City: Anchor, 1973), pp.
  60-72.
  1969/Sally Marsh
  1970s/Ed Corsino
  1971, Dec.15/Dorie Lawrence/Wickersham
  Hospital
  1972, Feb./Paul Lachlan Peck
  Herbert B. Greenhouse, The Astral
  Journey (N.Y.: Avon, 1976), pp.8-9,
  120,123-25,219-20,306-308.
  1972-   /Stuart Blue Harary
  Stuart Blue Harary & G. Solfvin, "A
  Study of Out-of-Body Experiences
  Using Auditory Targets," in J.D.
  Morris, et al., eds., Research in
  Parapsychology 1976 (Metuchen, N.J.:
  Scarecrow, 1977).
  D. Scott Rogo, ed., Mind Beyond the
  Body (N.Y.: Penguin, 1978), pp.97-
  99.
  Stuart Blue Harary, "A Personal Per-
  spective on Out-of-Body Experiences,"
  in D. Scott Rogo, ed., Mind Beyond

the Body (N.Y.: Penguin, 1978), pp.
260-69.
1977, Aug.15-22/D. Scott Rogo
  D. Scott Rogo, "The Ghost They See
  May Be Your Own," Fate 32 (Feb.1979)
  :45,48-52.
-Palmistry
1893-1909/Count Louis Hamon (Cheiro)/
Park Ave.
  New York World, 26 Nov.1893.
  New York Times, 10 June 1894, p.5;
  and 9 Oct.1936, p.25.
  Norman L. Beerman, "Mysterious Chei-
  ro," Fate 11 (Jan.1958):80,83-85.
  Irwin Ross, "The Incredible Cheiro,"
  Fate 20 (Oct.1967):80-84.
  Eleanor Touhey Smith, Psychic People
  (N.Y.: Morrow, 1968), pp.172-81.
-Paranormal strength
1920s/Betsy Anna Talks/149 14th Rd.,
Whitestone
  New York Herald-Tribune, 24 Jan.1932.
-Parapsychology research
1885-   /American Soc'y for Psychical
Research/5 W. 73d St.
  Nandor Fodor, Encyclopaedia of Psy-
  chic Science (London: Arthurs,
  1933), pp.2-3.
  Ernest Taves & L.A. Dale, "The Midas
  Touch in Psychical Research," J.ASPR
  37 (1943):57-83.
  Ernest Taves, L.A. Dale & Gardner
  Murphy, "A Further Report on the
  Midas Touch," J.ASPR 37 (1943):111-
  18.
  L.A. Dale, "The Psychokinetic Effect:
  The First A.S.P.R. Experiment," J.
  ASPR 40 (1946):123-51.
  L.A. Dale & J.L. Woodruff, "The Psy-
  chokinetic Effect: Further A.S.P.R.
  Experiments," J.ASPR 41 (1947):65-
  82.
  D.J. West, "The Parapsychology Labor-
  atory at Duke University and the
  American Society for Psychical Re-
  search: Some Impressions," J.SPR 35
  (1950):165,174-77.
  J.L. Woodruff & L.A. Dale, "Subject
  and Experimenter Attitudes in Rela-
  tion to ESP Scoring," J.ASPR 44
  (1950):87-112.
  J.L. Woodruff & L.A. Dale, "ESP Func-
  tion and the Psychogalvanic Response,"
  J.ASPR 46 (1952):62-65.
  J. Fraser Nicol & Betty M. Humphrey,
  "The Repeatability Problem in ESP-
  Personality Research," J.ASPR 49
  (1955):125-56.
  Rhea White & Jean Angstadt, "A Résumé
  of Research at the A.S.P.R. into
  Teacher-Pupil Attitudes and Clair-
  voyance Test Results, 1959-1960,"
  J.ASPR 55 (1961):142-47.
  Karlis Osis & Edwin Bokert, "ESP and
  Changed States of Consciousness In-
  duced by Meditation," J.ASPR 65
  (1971):17-65.
  Karlis Osis, Malcolm E. Turner, Jr.,
  & Mary Lou Carlson, "ESP over Dis-
  tance: Research on the ESP Channel,"
  J.ASPR 65 (1971):245-88.
  Karlis Osis & Mary Lou Carlson, "The
  ESP Channel: Open or Closed?" J.
  ASPR 66 (1972):310-20.
  June & Nicholas Regush, Psi: The Oth-
  er World Catalogue (N.Y.: Putnam,
  1974), pp.16-17.
1920-1930s/American Psychical Insti-
tute/20 W. 58th St.
  Nandor Fodor, Encyclopaedia of Psy-
  chic Science (London: Arthurs,
  1933), p.2.
1921-1952/Gardner Murphy/Columbia
University
  Gardner Murphy, "Field Theory and
  Survival," J.ASPR 39 (1945):181-209.
  Gardner Murphy, "An Approach to Precognition," J.ASPR 42 (1948):3-14.
  Gardner Murphy, "Psychical Research
  and Human Personality," Proc.SPR
  48 (1949):1-15.
  Gardner Murphy, "Autobiography of
  Gardner Murphy," J.Parapsych. 21
  (1957):165-78.
1940s-   /Gertrude R. Schmiedler/
City College of New York
  Gertrude Raffel Schmiedler, "Pre-
  dicting Good and Bad Scores in a
  Clairvoyance Experiment: A Prelim-
  inary Report," J.ASPR 37 (1943):
  103-10.
  Gertrude Raffel Schmiedler, "Pre-
  dicting Good and Bad Scores in a
  Clairvoyance Experiment: A Final
  Report," J.ASPR 37 (1943):210-21.
  Gertrude R. Schmiedler, "Comparison
  of ESP Scores with Rorschachs
  Scored by Different Workers," J.
  ASPR 43 (1949):94-97.
  L.Eilbert & Gertrude R. Schmiedler,
  "A Study of Certain Psychological
  Factors in Relation to ESP Perform-
  ance," J.Parapsych. 14 (1950):53-
  74.
  Gertrude R. Schmiedler, "Some Rela-
  tions between Picture-Frustration
  Ratings and ESP Scores," J.Person-
  ality 18 (1950):331-44.
  Gertrude R. Schmiedler, "Rorschachs
  and ESP Scores of Patients Suffer-
  ing from Cerebral Concussion," J.
  Parapsych. 16 (1952):80-89.
  Gertrude R. Schmiedler, "Picture-
  Frustration Ratings and ESP Scores
  for Subjects Who Showed Moderate
  Annoyance at the ESP Task," J.Para-
  psych. 18 (1954):137-52.
  R. Gerber & Gertrude R. Schmiedler,
  "An Investigation of Relaxation and
  of Acceptance of the Experimental
  Situation As Related to ESP Scores
  in Maternity Patients," J.Parapsych.
  21 (1957):47-57.
  Gertrude Schmiedler & R.A. McConnell,
  ESP and Personality Patterns (New
  Haven: Yale Univ., 1958).
  Gertrude Schmiedler, "Analysis and
  Evaluation of Proxy Sessions with
  Mrs. Caroline Chapman," J.Parapsych.
  22 (1958):137-55.

Gertrude R. Schmiedler, "Agent-Per-
cipient Relationships," J.ASPR 52
(1958):47-69.

Gertrude R. Schmiedler, "Evidence
for Two Kinds of Telepathy," Int'l
J.Parapsych. 3 (1961):5-48.

Gertrude R. Schmiedler, "ESP and
Tests of Perception," J.ASPR 56
(1962):48-51.

Frederick C. Dommeyer & Rhea White,
"Psychical Research in Colleges and
Universities," J.ASPR 57 (1963):3,
29-31.

Gertrude R. Schmiedler, "An Experiment in Precognitive Clairvoyance,"
J.Parapsych. 28 (1964):1-27,93-125.

Gertrude R. Schmiedler & Carol Lin-
demann, "ESP Calls Following an
'ESP' Test with Sensory Cues," J.
ASPR 60 (1966):357-62.

Gertrude Schmiedler, "ESP Breakthrough: Paranormal Effects in Real
Life," J.ASPR 61 (1967):506-25.

Gertrude R. Schmiedler, "A Search
for Feedback in ESP: Salience and
Stimulus Preference," J.ASPR 62
(1968):130-42.

Gertrude R. Schmiedler & Laurence
Lewis, "A Search for Feedback in
ESP: High ESP Scores After Two Suc-
cesses on Triple-Aspect Targets,"
J.ASPR 62 (1968):254-62.

Gertrude R. Schmiedler & Laurence
Lewis, "A Search for Feedback in
ESP: The Preferential Effect and
the Impatience Effect," J.ASPR 63
(1969):60-68.

Gertrude R. Schmiedler, "High ESP
Scores After a Swami's Brief In-
struction in Meditation and Breath-
ing," J.ASPR 64 (1970):100-103.

Gertrude R. Schmiedler & Lawrence
LeShan, "An Aspect of Body Image
Related to ESP Scores," J.ASPR 64
(1970):211-18.

John Hudesman & Gertrude R. Schmiedler, "ESP Scores Following Therapeutic Sessions," J.ASPR 65 (1971):
215-22.

Gertrude R. Schmiedler, "Mood and
Attitude in a Pretest As Predictors
of Retest ESP Performance," J.ASPR
65 (1971):324-25.

Larry Lewis & Gertrude R. Schmiedler,
"Alpha Relations with Non-Intention-
al and Purposeful ESP After Feedback," J.ASPR 65 (1971):455-67.

Gertrude R. Schmiedler & G. Craig,
"Moods and ESP Scores in Group Test-
ing," J.ASPR 66 (1972):280-87.

Gertrude R. Schmiedler, "PK Effects
upon Continuously Recorded Tempera-
tures," J.ASPR 67 (1973):325-40.

John Hudesman & Gertrude R. Schmiedler, "Changes in ESP Scores after
Therapy Sessions," J.ASPR 70 (1976):
371-80.

Gertrude R. Schmiedler, "Methods for
Controlled Research on ESP and PK,"
in Benjamin B. Wolman, ed., Handbook
of Parapsychology (N.Y.: Van Nostrand Reinhold, 1977), pp.131-59.

Michaeleen Maher & Gertrude R. Schmiedler, "Cerebral Lateralization Effects on ESP Processing," J.ASPR
71 (1977):26-71.

1951-   /Parapsychology Foundation/
19 W.57th St.

Jarl Fahler & Karlis Osis, "Checking
for Awareness of Hits in a Precognition Experiment with Hypnotized
Subjects," J.ASPR 60 (1966):340-46.

June & Nicholas Regush, Psi: The Other World Catalogue (N.Y.: Putnam,
1974), pp.8-9.

1962-   /Maimonides Medical Center/
4802 10th Ave., Brooklyn

Montague Ullman, "An Experimental
Approach to Dreams and Telepathy,"
Archives of General Psychiatry 14
(1966):605-13.

Stanley Krippner, "Experimentally-
Induced Telepathic Effects in Hyp-
nosis and Non-Hypnosis Groups," J.
ASPR 62 (1968):387-98.

Brad Steiger, "Dream Laboratory Ex-
plores Nature of Telepathy," Fate
21 (Sep.1968):44-54. il.

Stanley Krippner & Montague Ullman,
"Telepathic Perception in the Dream
State: Confirmatory Study Using EEG-
EOG Monitoring Techniques," Percep-
tual & Motor Skills 29 (1969):915-
18.

Brad Steiger, "The Importance of
Dreaming," Fate 22 (Aug.1969):80-
88.

Montague Ullman & Stanley Krippner,
Dream Studies and Telepathy (N.Y.:
Parapsychology Foundation, 1970).

Stanley Krippner, "Electrophysiologi-
cal Studies of ESP in Dreams: Sex
Differences in Seventy-Four Telepathy Sessions," J.ASPR 64 (1970):
277-85.

Montague Ullman, "The Experimentally-
Induced Telepathic Dream: Theoreti-
cal Implications," J.ASPR 64 (1970):
358-74.

Charles Honorton, "Effects of Feedback on Discrimination Between Correct and Incorrect ESP Responses,"
J.ASPR 64 (1970):404-10.

Montague Ullman & Stanley Krippner,
"An Experimental Approach to Dreams
and Telepathy," Am.J.Psychiatry 126
(1970):1282-89.

Stanley Krippner, Montague Ullman &
Charles Honorton, "A Precognitive
Dream Study with a Single Subject,"
J.ASPR 65 (1971):192-203.

Charles Honorton, Richard Davidson &
Paul Bindler, "Feedback-Augmented
EEG Alpha, Shifts in Subjective
State, and ESP Card-Guessing Per-
formance," J.ASPR 65 (1971):308-23.

Stanley Krippner, et al., "A Long
Distance 'Sensory Bombardment'
Study of ESP in Dreams," J.ASPR 65
(1971):468-75.

David Techter, "New Books," Fate 25 (Jan.1972):105-106.

Stanley Krippner, et al., Human Dimensions 1 (1972):14-19.

Charles Honorton, "Significant Factors in Hypnotically-Induced Clairvoyant Dreams," J.ASPR 66 (1972): 86-102.

Charles Honorton & Warren Barksdale, "PK Performance with Waking Suggestions for Muscle Tension Versus Relaxation," J.ASPR 66 (1972):208-14.

Charles Honorton, "Reported Frequency of Dream Recall and ESP," J.ASPR 66 (1972):369-74.

Montague Ullman & Stanley Krippner, Dream Telepathy (N.Y.: Macmillan, 1973).

Ellendale McCollam & Charles Honorton, "Effects of Feedback on Discrimination Between Correct and Incorrect ESP Responses," J.ASPR 67 (1973):77-85.

Charles Honorton, Sally A. Drucker & Harry C. Hermon, "Shifts in Subjective State and ESP under Conditions of Partial Sensory Deprivation," J.ASPR 67 (1973):191-96.

Geneva Steinberg, "The Caveat Emptor Interview: Inside an ESP Laboratory," Caveat Emptor, no.14 (July-Aug.1974) :7-10,22-23.

Stanley Krippner, Song of the Siren: A Parapsychological Odyssey (N.Y.: Harper & Row, 1975).

Charles Honorton, Margaret Ramsey & Carol Cabibbo, "Experimenter Effects in Extrasensory Perception," J.ASPR 69 (1975):135-139.

Stanley Krippner, "Dreams and Other Altered States," J.Communication 25 (1975):173-82.

Charles Honorton, "Psi and Mental Imagery: Keeping Score on the Betts Scale," J.ASPR 69 (1975):327-32.

Charles Honorton, "Objective Determination of Information Rate in Psi Tasks with Pictorial Stimuli," J. ASPR 69 (1975):353-59.

Charles Honorton, "Psi and Internal Attention States," in Benjamin B. Wolman, ed., Handbook of Parapsychology (N.Y.: Van Nostrand Reinhold, 1977), pp.435-72.

Sally A. Drucker, Athena A. Drewes, & Larry Rubin, "ESP in Relation to Cognitive Development and IQ in Young Children," J.ASPR 71 (1977): 289-98.

1970s/Foundation for Mind Research/ Robert E.L. Masters

R.E.L. Masters & Jean Houston, The Varieties of Psychedelic Experience (N.Y.: Holt, Rinehart & Winston, 1966).

New York Times, 16 Aug.1970, p.43.

"Mysticism in the Laboratory," Time, 5 Oct.1970, pp.72-74.

1970s/Foundation for Parasensory Investigation/1 W. 81st St.

June & Nicholas Regush, Psi: The Other World Catalogue (N.Y.: Putnam, 1974), p.9.

1973-   /Rex G. Stanford/St. John's University

Rex G. Stanford, "Extrasensory Effects upon Associative Processes in a Directed Free-Response Task," J.ASPR 67 (1973):147-90.

Rex G. Stanford, "An Experimentally Testable Model for Spontaneous Psi Events," J.ASPR 68 (1974):34-57, 321-56.

Rex G. Stanford & Brantz Mayer, "Relaxation As a Psi-Conducive State," J.ASPR 68 (1974):182-91.

Rex G. Stanford, et al., "Experiential Factors Related to Free-Response Clairvoyance Performance in a Sensory Uniformity Setting (Ganzfeld)," in J.D. Morris, et al., eds., Research in Parapsychology 1974 (Metuchen, N.J.: Scarecrow, 1975), pp.89-93.

Rex G. Stanford, et al., "Psychokinesis As Psi-Mediated Instrumental Response," J.ASPR 69 (1975):127-33.

Rex G. Stanford & John Palmer, "Free-Response ESP Performance and Occipital Alpha Rhythms," J.ASPR 69 (1975):235-44.

James C. Terry & Charles Honorton, "Psi Information Retrieval in the Ganzfeld: Two Confirmatory Studies," J.ASPR 70 (1976):207-17.

Mary Schmitt & Rex G. Stanford, "Free-Response ESP During Ganzfeld Stimulation: The Possible Influence of Menstrual Cycle Phase," J.ASPR 72 (1978):177-82.

-Phantom

n.d./Atlantic Bridge

Mark Feldman, "Strange and Unknown," Beyond Reality, no.14 (Mar.-Apr. 1975):10.

1969, spring/Peter Blair McDonald

Martha McDonald, "Something Wicked This Way Comes," Fate 31 (Aug.1978) :63-65.

1974-1976/David Barkow

(Letter), Fate 30 (Apr.1977):116-17.

-Phantom airplane

1910, Aug.30-31/Madison Square Tower

New York Tribune, 1 Sep.1910, p.1.

1933, Dec.26/C.V. Gedroyce/Central Park

New York Times, 27 Dec.1933, p.2.

1976, Jan.4/Raymond Simms/Patchogue Oil Terminal, Court St.

New York Times, 5 Jan.1976, p.32.

"Mystery Blast Rips Oil Tank," APRO Bull. 24 (Jan.1976):6.

-Phantom image

1931, April-May/Elizabeth Wallace Clark

Elizabeth Wallace Clark, "A Case-Report of a Psychic Healing," J.ASPR 28 (1934):48-54.

1932, Feb./Robert Norwood/St. Bartholomew's Church/Park Ave. x 50th St.

New York Times, 23 Feb.1932, p.19; and 24 Feb.1932, p.23.

1939, Jan./Charles Rauscher/Brooklyn
  "Spook Dog Etching," Fortean Soc'y
  Mag., no.3 (Jan.1940):13.
1971, Nov./Viola Mitchell/835 Trinity
Ave.
  New York Times, 19 Nov.1971, p.47.
  il.
-Phantom insects
1899, July 8
  New York Herald, 9 July 1899.
  Eugene Murray-Aaron, "The 'Kissing
  Bug' Scare," Sci.Am. 81 (1899):54.
-Phantom ship
1920, March/Victor Werner/Gravesend
Bay
  Victor Werner, "Ghost Ship of Grave-
  send Bay," Fate 25 (Nov.1972):88-
  90.
-Phrenology
1840s-1900s/Orson Fowler/Clinton Hall
  Madeleine B. Stern, Heads and Head-
  lines: The Phrenological Fowlers
  (Norman: Univ. of Oklahoma, 1971).
  il.
-Plant sensitivity
1970s/John C. Pierrakos/45 E. 78th St.
  John C. Pierrakos, The Energy Field
  in Man and Nature (N.Y.: Institute
  of Bioenergetic Analysis, 1971).
-Poltergeist
1882/Mrs. William Swift/52 Willoughby
St.
  Religio-Philosophical J., 15 July
  1882, quoting New York Sun (undated).
1883, Dec./Alexander Urquhart
  New York Sun, 22 Dec.1883.
1894, Nov.-Dec./J.L. Hope/Flushing
  New York Herald, 6 Jan.1895.
1965/Carol Packer/Henderson Ave.,
Staten I.
  Hans Holzer, Yankee Ghosts (N.Y.:
  Ace, 1966), pp.112-22.
1974, Feb.9-March/Bronx
  William Eisler, "The Bronx Polter-
  geist," in J.D. Morris, et al.,
  eds., Research in Parapsychology
  1974 (Metuchen, N.J.: Scarecrow,
  1975), pp.139-43.
-Possession
1905-1907/F.L. Thompson/Brooklyn
  J.H. Hyslop, "Observations on the
  Mediumistic Records in the Thompson
  Case," Proc.ASPR, vol.3 (1909).
  James H. Hyslop, Contact with the
  Other World (N.Y.: Century, 1919).
-Precognition
1795/Gilbert Stuart
  Raymond C. Otto, "I Painted Only
  What I Saw," Fate 24 (June 1971):95.
1850s/=fraudulent
  Q.K. Philander Doesticks [Mortimer
  Neal Thomson], The Witches of New
  York (N.Y.: Rudd & Carleton, 1859).
1883, Nov./Christopher C. Brooks/Brook-
lyn
  Baltimore (Md.) Sun, 8 Dec.1883.
  Mrs. Henry Sidgwick, "On the Evidence
  for Premonitions," Proc.SPR 5 (1888)
  :288,291-92.
n.d./Clara Morris/24th St.

Clara Morris, Life on the Stage
  (N.Y.: McClure, Phillips, 1901),
  pp.345-51.
Eugene Burr, "Broadway Bogies and
  Other Phantoms," Fate 24 (Mar.
  1971):78,83-84.
1898/Morgan Robertson/24th St.
  Morgan Robertson, Futility (N.Y.:
  M.F. Mansfield, 1898).
  Morgan Robertson, The Wreck of the
  Titan (N.Y.: McKinlay, Stone &
  Mackenzie, 1912).
  Merle Johnson, "American First Edi-
  tions: Morgan Robertson, 1861-1915,"
  Publishers Weekly 117 (1930):1591-
  92.
  Vincent H. Gaddis, "Man of Mystery:
  Morgan Robertson," Fate 2 (July
  1949):46-51.
  New York Herald-Tribune, 23 Nov.1958.
  Herbert B. Greenhouse, Premonitions:
  A Leap into the Future (N.Y.: War-
  ner, 1973 ed.), pp.32-48.
1899, March 16/Mrs. Adam Badeau/Wind-
sor Hotel
  Russell N. Case, "Evangeline Adams
  Predicted the Windsor Hotel Disas-
  ter," Fate 7 (Dec.1954):78-80.
  Heber V. Menner, "Hunch of a Holo-
  caust," Fate 9 (Feb.1956):38.
1909, Dec.19/Lester White/Central Park
  New York Tribune, 20 Dec.1909, p.3.
1909-1922/Edward M. Powers/Brooklyn
  Frederick Bligh Bond, "An American
  Nostradamus," Psychic Rsch. 25
  (1931):261-62.
1910-1950s/Ernest L. Batley
  Ernest L. Batley, "The Voice That
  Made Me Rock," Fate 9 (June 1956):
  76-79.
1917, Nov.27/Walter Franklin Prince/
Flushing
  W.F. Prince, "Four Particularly Characterized Dreams," J.ASPR 17 (1923):
  82,89-101.
1923, June 16/Fulton Oursler/1926
Broadway
  Fulton Oursler, "Some Apparently
  Prophetic Dreams," J.ASPR 19 (1925):
  11-14.
1930s/Mrs. Ebling
  Jocelyn Pierson, "War Prophecies,"
  J.ASPR 33 (1939):287-99.
1933, Oct.15
  "Apparition of a Hand (Premonitory
  of a Death)," J.ASPR 28 (1934):159-
  60.
1940s/Brooklyn Navy Yard
  (Editorial), Fate 13 (July 1960):10.
1944, April 27
  Jule Eisenbud, "Analysis of a Presump-
  tively Telepathic Dream," Psychiatric Quar. 22 (1948):1-33.
  Jule Eisenbud, "Behavioral Correspon-
  dences to Normally Unpredictable
  Events," Psychoanalytic Quar. 23
  (1954):205,215-33.
  Jess Stearn, The Door to the Future
  (N.Y.: Macfadden, 1964), pp.167-70.
1946, Feb./Mrs. Wernher

"First Prize," Doubt, no.15 (summer 1946):218.
1958, Sep.2/Aurea Cordero
New York Daily News, 3 Sep.1958.
Rudolph Boris, "A Glimpse of Paradise," Fate 12 (Apr.1959):82-85.
1960s/Adrienne Coulter
Herbert B. Greenhouse, Premonitions: A Leap into the Future (N.Y.: Paperback Library, 1973 ed.), pp.53,81, 133,137-39,271.
1960s/Jess Stearn
Walt Murray, "Jess Stearn: The Psychic-Aquarian Age in Perspective," Probe the Unknown 1 (Oct.1973):12, 15.
1960s-   /Bill Linn
David Wallechinsky & Irving Wallace, The People's Almanac (Garden City: Doubleday, 1975), p.7.
1960, Oct.16/Claire Blauvelt
Jess Stearn, The Door to the Future (N.Y.: Macfadden, 1964), pp.183-84.
1961, March 4/Patricia Ruffalo
(Editorial), Fate 14 (July 1961):12.
1965-   /Alan Vaughn/Williamsburg
John Godwin, Occult America (Garden City: Doubleday, 1972), pp.35-37.
Herbert B. Greenhouse, Premonitions: A Leap into the Future (N.Y.: Paperback Library, 1973 ed.), pp.28,75-77,93-94,97-98,135-37,205,237-38, 274.
1967/Marie Welt
Walt Murray, "Jess Stearn: The Psychic-Aquarian Age in Perspective," Probe the Unknown 1 (Oct.1973):12, 15.
1967-1971/John A. Keel/Manhattan
John A. Keel, The Mothman Prophecies (N.Y.: Saturday Review, 1975), pp. 181-82.
1970s/Kathleen Karter/66 W. 94th St.
Brad Steiger, Gods of Aquarius (N.Y.: Harcourt Brace Jovanovich, 1976), pp.226-27.
1970s/Allan Jones/Manhattan
Timothy Green Beckley, "Allan Jones Believes in Fate," Fate 27 (Dec. 1974):48-52. il.
-Precognition research
1968-   /Central Premonitions Registry /Times Square Station
(Letter), Robert D. Nelson, Fate 22 (Sep.1969):128.
Robert D. Nelson, "The Central Premonitions Registry," Psychic 1 (Apr.1970):26-30.
Herbert B. Greenhouse, Premonitions: A Leap into the Future (N.Y.: Paperback Library, 1973 ed.), pp.24-31.
Betsy Barley, "Dreamkeepers: A Clearinghouse for Premonitions," Probe the Unknown 2 (Feb.1974):52-55.
Kansas City (Mo.) Times, 21 July 1974, p.16.
-Psychic photography
1868-1884/William H. Mumler
New York Times, 13 Apr.1869, p.5; 21 Apr.1869, p.10; 22 Apr.1869, p.8;

24 Apr.1869, p.4; and 4 May 1869, p.1.
Elbridge T. Gerry, The Mumler "Spirit" Photograph Case (N.Y.: Baker, Voorhis, 1869).
William H. Mumler, The Personal Experiences of William H. Mumler in Spirit Photography (Boston: Colby & Rich, 1875).
James Coates, Photographing the Invisible (Chicago: Advanced Thought, 1911), pp.1-21. il.
Nandor Fodor, Encyclopaedia of Psychic Science (London: Arthurs, 1933), p.257.
Joseph Dunninger, Houdini's Spirit World and Dunninger's Psychic Revelations (N.Y.: Tower, 1968 ed.), pp.39-40.
1875/Mr. Evans
Nandor Fodor, Encyclopaedia of Psychic Science (London: Arthurs, 1933), p.312.
1900s-1959/John Myers
Nandor Fodor, Between Two Worlds (W. Nyack: Parker, 1964), pp.90-97.
Tom Patterson, 100 Years of Spirit Photography (London: Regency, 1969), pp.37-40. il.
Hans Holzer, Psychic Photography (N.Y.: McGraw-Hill, 1969), pp.9-20. il.
1931, Dec.-1932, Jan.
Frederick Bligh Bond, "A New Type of Metapsychic Phenomena," J.ASPR 26 (1932):241-50. il.
"Abnormal Markings on Plates," J.ASPR 27 (1933):363.
1953/Joseph Ruk
Hereward Carrington, "We Photographed Thoughts," Fate 6 (June 1953):64-72. il.
1970/Martha Seidler
Susy Smith, The Power of the Mind (Radnor, Pa.: Chilton, 1975), p. 131.
-Psychokinesis
1921/ASPR Laboratory
E.J. Dingwall, "More Experiments in 'Telekinesis,'" J.ASPR 16 (1922): 117-31.
1929, Oct.5/Charles Fort/Bronx
Charles Fort, The Books of Charles Fort (N.Y.: Holt, 1941), p.980.
1944, April/Cornelia Otis Skinner/Manhattan
(Editorial), Fate 11 (July 1958):10-12.
n.d./Dorothy Les Tina/Greenwich Village
Dorothy Les Tina, "Death's Sign of the Rose," Fate 10 (Sep.1957):59-61.
1974-   /Felicia Parise
Charles Honorton, et al., "Apparent Psychokinesis on Static Objects by a 'Gifted' Subject," in W.G. Roll, et al., eds., Research in Parapsychology 1973 (Metuchen, N.J.: Scarecrow, 1974), pp.128-34.
H.H.J. Keil, et al., "Directly Observable Voluntary PK Effects,"

Proc.SPR 56 (1976):197-235.
1975, May 21/Robert Skutch
J.G. Pratt & Ian Stevenson, "An In-
stance of Possible Metal-Bending
Indirectly Related to Uri Geller,"
J.ASPR 70 (1976):79-93.
-Psychokinesis, clairvoyance and out-of-
body experiences
1962-   /Ingo Swann
Larry Lewis & Gertrude R. Schmiedler,
"PK Effects upon Continually Record-
ed Temperature," J.ASPR 67 (1973):
326-40.
"Interview: Ingo Swann," Psychic 4
(Apr.1973):6-11,48-49. il.
Janet Mitchell, "Out of the Body
Vision," Psychic 4 (Apr.1973):44-47.
Harold Puthoff & Russell Targ, "PK
Experiments with Uri Geller and Ingo
Swann," in W.G. Roll, et al., eds.,
Research in Parapsychology 1973
(Metuchen, N.J.: Scarecrow, 1974),
pp.125-28.
Ingo Swann, To Kiss Earth Good-Bye
(N.Y.: Hawthorn, 1975).
Martin Ebon, "Ingo Swann: Parapsy-
chology's Most Popular 'Guinea Pig,'"
Probe the Unknown 3 (Nov.1975):49-
52,62-63.
B. Millar, "Thermistor PK," in J.D.
Morris, et al., eds., Research in
Parapsychology 1975 (Metuchen, N.J.:
Scarecrow, 1976), pp.71-73.
Edwin C. May & Charles Honorton, "A
Dynamic PK Experiment with Ingo
Swann," in J.D. Morris, et al., eds.,
Research in Parapsychology 1975
(Metuchen, N.J.: Scarecrow, 1976),
pp.88-89.
Harold Puthoff & Russell Targ, "Psy-
chic Research and Modern Physics,"
in Edgar D. Mitchell, ed., Psychic
Exploration (N.Y.: Capricorn, 1976
ed.), pp.524,535-38.
Adam Smith, Powers of Mind (N.Y.:
Dutton, 1976).
World Almanac Book of the Strange
(N.Y.: Signet, 1977), pp.308-16.
Martin Ebon, The Evidence for Life
After Death (N.Y.: Signet, 1977),
pp.127-38.
Russell Targ & Harold E. Puthoff,
Mind-Reach (N.Y.: Delacorte, 1977).
D. Scott Rogo, "The Psychic Warriors,"
Saga UFO Rept. 6 (Sep.1978):44-47,
72-73.
-Pyramid energy research
1976-   /Pyramid Research Group/56-37
Utopia Parkway
(Letter), David Fiedler, Fate 30
(Apr.1977):117-18.
-Religious apparition
1946/Joseph Vitolo, Jr./Bronx
"Bronx Miracle," Doubt, no.14 (spring
1946):203.
1968-   /Veronica Leuken/Bayside Hills
Kansas City (Mo.) Times, 23 May 1975.
"Our Lady of Bayside Hills," News-
week, 2 June 1975, p.46.
Philip Nobile, "Our Lady of Bayside,"

New York, 11 Dec.1978, pp.57-60. il.
Hartford (Ct.) Courant, 30 Dec.1978.
"Our Lady of Bayside, NY," Fortean
Times, no.28 (winter 1979):3-5.
-Sea monster
1883, Dec./Capt. Green/Long Branch
Life-Saving Station
New York Times, 8 Dec.1883, p.4.
1884, Feb.29/Elbert L. Poilon/Lower
Bay
New York Times, 1 Mar.1884, p.2.
1886, Nov.5/Bennie Vaughan/Flushing
Bay
New York Times, 7 Nov.1886, p.7.
1935/Silas King/"General Charles Hum-
phreys"/Governor's I./=python
Bernard Heuvelmans, In the Wake of
the Sea-Serpents (N.Y.: Hill &
Wang, 1968), p.464.
1969, March/City Island Bridge
(Editorial), Fate 22 (Aug.1969):32-
34, quoting Bronx Journal-News (undated).
-Seance
1850/Kate and Margaret Fox
New York Tribune, 8 June 1850, p.4.
Slater Brown, The Heyday of Spiritualism (N.Y.: Pocket Books, 1972
ed.), pp.130-35.
1871/Henry Ward Beecher/Plymouth Congregational Church
Eugene Crowell, The Identity of Primitive Christianity and Modern Spiritualism, 2 vols. (N.Y.: G.W. Carleton, 1874-75), 1:499.
1909-1911/Eusapia Palladino
Everard Feilding, W.W. Baggally &
Hereward Carrington, "Report on a
Series of Sittings with Eusapia
Palladino," Proc.SPR 23 (1909):306-
569.
W.S. Davis, "The New York Exposure
of Eusapia Palladino," J.ASPR 4
(1910):402-24.
Eusapia Palladino, "My Own Story,"
Cosmopolitan 48 (1910):292-300. il.
Hereward Carrington, The Story of
Psychic Science (London: Rider,
1930).
Nandor Fodor, Encyclopaedia of Psy-
chic Science (London: Arthurs,
1933), pp.274-75.
Joseph Dunninger, Houdini's Spirit
World and Dunninger's Psychic Reve-
lations (N.Y.: Tower, 1968 ed.),
pp.43-46.
Hereward Carrington, "Some Personal
Experiences with Eusapia Palladino,"
J.ASPR 33 (1939):238-49.
Hereward Carrington, The American
Seances with Eusapia Palladino (N.Y.:
Garrett, 1954).
R. DeWitt Miller, Stranger Than Life
(N.Y.: Ace, 1955 ed.), pp.79-81.
D.H. Rawcliffe, Illusions and Delu-
sions of the Supernatural and Oc-
cult (N.Y.: Dover, 1959), pp.331-32.
1919, April 24/Mr. Herrman/=fraudulent
Gertrude O. Tubby, "A Material Med-
ium," J.ASPR 14 (1920):577-82.

1923-1924/Nino Pecorara
New York Times, 11 Dec.1923, p.3; 15
Dec.1923, p.4; 19 Dec.1923, p.17;
22 Dec.1923, p.2; 21 Jan.1924, p.19;
and 24 Jan.1924, p.5.
Joseph Dunninger, Houdini's Spirit
World and Dunninger's Psychic Revelations (N.Y.: Tower, 1968 ed.),
pp.190-201. il.
1927, July 22/Naomi Anderson
Theron F. Pierce, "Communication from
One Not Known at the Time to Be
Dead," J.ASPR 21 (1927):582-84.
1928, March 6-Nov./Mrs. Ernest A. Bigelow
J. Malcolm Bird, "A Series of Psychical Experiments," Psychic Rsch.
22 (1929):209-32.
1936, Sep.13-15/Thomas Lacey
Hereward Carrington, "Preliminary Report on the Voice Phenomena of
Thomas Lacey," J.ASPR 33 (1939):
174-87.
n.d./Russell Patterson
Danton Walker, Spooks Deluxe (N.Y.:
Franklin Watts, 1956), pp.81-85.
1940s/Ann Marsters/Taft Hotel
Danton Walker, Spooks Deluxe (N.Y.:
Franklin Watts, 1956), pp.120-22.
1941/Mary Olson
Wainwright Evans, "Scientists Research Machine to Contact the Dead,"
Fate 16 (Apr.1963):38,40.
1942, March 1/Frank Decker/Hotel Wellington
W.D. Chesney, "Houdini's Message
from the Grave," Argosy, Sep.1971,
pp.52-55. il.
1960, Sep.7/Ethel Meyers/E. 46th St.
Hans Holzer, Ghosts I've Met (N.Y.:
Ace, 1965 ed.), pp.13-15.
1964, March 10/Vitold Mecevitch
Harold Sherman, "The Apported Sta-
tuette: A Gift from Nowhere," Fate
29 (Apr.1976):58-61. il.
1966, Oct.14/Elizabeth Nogales
Mercedes Colon, "Can the Dead Harm
the Living?" Fate 23 (July 1970):
92-97.
1967/Ethel Meyers/103d St.
Jack Appelbe, "Humphrey Bogart Warned
Californians," Fate 21 (Nov.1968):71.
-Skyquake
1939, Jan.9/Brooklyn
"Fortean Triumph," Fortean Soc'y Mag.,
no.3 (Jan.1940):9.
1946, Dec.29-30
"Explosions," Doubt, no.18 (1947):271.
-Spirit medium
1850s/Mrs. E.J. French
Benjamin Coleman, Spiritualism in
America (London: F. Pitman, 1861).
Nandor Fodor, Encyclopaedia of Psychic Science (London: Arthurs,
1933), pp.91,150.
1850s/Charles Partridge
1850s/Mr. Kellog
1850s/Thomas Lake Harris
1850s/J.V. Mansfield
Emma Hardinge Britten, Modern Ameri-

can Spiritualism (N.Y.: The Author,
1870), pp.72-76,103,197-98,213-17,
252.
1851-1880s/Cora L.V. Richmond
Cora L.V. Richmond, Discourses on
Religion, Morals, Philosophy and
Metaphysics (N.Y.: Hatch, 1858).
Cora L.V. Richmond, Discourses
Through the Mediumship of Mrs. Cora
L.V. Tappan (London: J. Burns, 1875).
Cora L.V. Richmond, The Nature of
Spiritual Existence (San Francisco:
Women's Co-Operative, 1884).
Cora L.V. Richmond, The Soul: Its
Nature, Relations and Expressions
in Human Embodiments (Chicago:
Spiritual Pub.Co., 1887).
Cora L.V. Richmond, Psychpathy (Rog-
ers Park, Ill.: W. Richmond, 1890).
Harrison D. Barrett, The Life Work
of Mrs. Cora L.V. Richmond (Chi-
cago: Hack & Anderson, 1895).
Cora L.V. Richmond, My Experiences
While Out of My Body and My Return
After Many Days (Boston: Christo-
pher, 1915).
Slater Brown, The Heyday of Spirit-
ualism (N.Y.: Pocket Books, 1972
ed.), pp.238-39,241.
1852/Edward Fowler
Emma Hardinge Britten, Modern Ameri-
can Spiritualism (N.Y.: The Author,
1870), pp.83-84,101-102.
1853-1860s/John Worth Edmonds
New York Courier, 1 Aug.1853.
New York Herald, 6 Aug.1853, p.2.
John Worth Edmonds, An Appeal to the
Public on Spiritualism (N.Y.: Par-
tridge & Brittan, 1853).
John Worth Edmonds & George T. Dexter, Spiritualism, 2 vols. (N.Y.:
Partridge & Brittan, 1853-55).
Eliab W. Capron, Modern Spiritualism:
Its Facts and Fanaticisms (Boston:
Bela Marsh, 1855), pp.195-97.
New York Tribune, 28 Mar.1859, p.5.
Nandor Fodor, Encyclopaedia of Psy-
chic Science (London: Arthurs,
1933), pp.117-18,411.
Slater Brown, The Heyday of Spirit-
ualism (N.Y.: Pocket Books, 1972
ed.), pp.228-35.
1855/Ada Hoyt Coan
1855-1870s/Emma Hardinge
Emma Hardinge Britten, Modern Ameri-
can Spiritualism (N.Y.: The Author,
1870), pp.135-40,249-51,253-55.
1860-1892/Kate Fox/W. 46th St.
Robert Dale Owen, The Debatable Land
(N.Y.: G.W. Carleton, 1872), pp.342-
68,374-90,482-99.
Isaac K. Funk, The Widow's Mite
(N.Y.: Funk & Wagnall, 1904), pp.
237-41.
W.G. Langworthy Taylor, Katie Fox:
Epochmaking Medium and the Making
of the Fox-Taylor Record (N.Y.:
Putnam, 1933).
Nandor Fodor, Encyclopaedia of Psychic Science (London: Arthurs,

1933), pp.147-48,208,225,253,400.
William H. Leach, "Materializations of Estelle Livermore," Fate 10 (Nov.1957):91-97.
1870s-1890/Mrs. Lindsley/1776 Lexington Ave.
"A Mediumistic Experience," J.ASPR 12 (1918):740-52.
1873-1878/Helene Petrovna Blavatsky
Henry S. Olcott, People from the Other World (Hartford, Ct.: American, 1875).
H.P. Blavatsky, Isis Unvelied, 2 vols. (N.Y.: J.W. Bouton, 1877).
Vsevolod Sergyeevich Solovyoff, A Modern Priestess of Isis (London: Longmans,Green, 1895).
Nandor Fodor, Encyclopaedia of Psychic Science (London: Arthurs, 1933), pp.31-33.
Gertrude Marvin Williams, Madame Blavatsky: Priestess of the Occult (N.Y.: Knopf, 1946).
J. Gordon Melton, Encyclopedia of American Religions, 2 vols. (Wilmington: Consortium, 1978), 2:135-44.
1880s/F.W. Monck
"Notes by the Way," Light 4 (4 Oct. 1884):405-406.
1890s/Carrie M. Sawyer
Nandor Fodor, Encyclopaedia of Psychic Science (London: Arthurs, 1933), p.334, quoting Annales des sciences psychiques, 1901.
Nandor Fodor, "Mind over Space: The Mystery of Teleportation," Fate 10 (Mar.1957):82,86-88, quoting Light, 16 Nov.1901.
1890s/Mrs. Mary A. Williams
Florence Marryat, There Is No Death (N.Y.: J.W. Lovell, 1891).
Nandor Fodor, Encyclopaedia of Psychic Science (London: Arthurs, 1933), p.406.
Joseph Dunninger, Houdini's Spirit World and Dunninger's Psychic Revelations (N.Y.: Tower, 1968 ed.), pp. 73-74.
1900s-1920s/Hugh Robert Moore/=fraudulent
E.J. Dingwall, "A Versatile Medium," J.ASPR 16 (1922):41-50.
1903, Feb./Brooklyn
Isaac K. Funk, The Widow's Mite (N.Y.: Funk & Wagnall, 1904), pp. 157-213.
1905-1906
Walter F. Prince, "A Sceptical Sitter," J.ASPR 12 (1918):356-74.
1919, summer/Violet Crockett
Albert Stevens Crockett, Revelations of Louise (N.Y.: Frederick A. Stokes, 1920).
Albert Stevens Crockett, "My Psychic Summer," Fate 17 (Apr.1964):82-88.
1919-1920s/Mrs. Hersey
Josephine Hall, "Nine Sittings with Mrs. Hersey," J.ASPR 17 (1923):184-208,242-55,282-98.

1920s
Marian W. Spencer, "Mediumistic Experiments with Mrs. Borden," J.ASPR 16 (1922):556-82,604-50.
Kate Bassett, "More Sittings with Mrs. Borden," J.ASPR 18 (1924): 585-616,639-72,726-57.
1920s/John Ticknor
"A Case of Spirit Identification," J.ASPR 21 (1927):566-70.
1920s-1930s/George Valiantine
J. Malcolm Bird, "Our First Test Seances," Sci.Am. 129 (1923):14,56, 64-65,69.
H. Dennis Bradley, Towards the Stars (London: T. Werner Laurie, 1924).
H. Dennis Bradley, The Wisdom of the Gods (London: T. Werner Laurie, 1925).
V.J. Woolley, "An Account of a Series of Sittings with Mr. George Valiantine," Proc.SPR 36 (1927):52-77.
Neville Whymant, "Some Valiantine Sittings and Oriental Voices," Psychic Rsch. 22 (1928):225-29.
Neville Whymant, Psychic Adventures in New York (London: Morley & Kennersley, 1931).
H. Dennis Bradley, And After (London: T. Werner Laurie, 1931), pp. 79-106,287-397. il.
Mrs. W.H. Salter, "The History of George Valiantine," Proc.SPR 40 (1932):389-410.
Lord Charles Hope, "Report on Some Sittings with Valiantine and Phoenix in 1927," Proc.SPR 40 (1932): 411-27.
Nandor Fodor, Encyclopaedia of Psychic Science (London: Arthurs, 1933), pp.69,288,397-99.
William Oliver Stevens, Psychics and Common Sense (N.Y.: Dutton, 1953), pp.76-77,195-97.
James Crenshaw, "The British Scholar Who Talked with Confucius," Fate 16 (Oct.1963):62-72; (Nov.1963):78-88.
1920s-1940s/Frank Decker/W. 73d St. x Amsterdam Ave.
John Goldstrom, "Flying Ghosts," Fate 8 (May 1955):19-28.
1921-1938, 1949-1971/Arthur Ford/205 W. 57th St.
New York Journal, 10 Feb.1928.
Francis R. Fast, The Houdini Messages: The Facts Concerning the Messages Received through the Mediumship of Arthur Ford (N.Y.: The Author, 1929).
Brooklyn Daily Eagle, 1 Apr.1931.
Joseph Dunninger, Houdini's Spirit World and Dunninger's Psychic Revelations (N.Y.: Tower, 1968 ed.), pp.177-78.
Lydia Emery, Houdini Unmasked (Lily Dale, N.Y.: Dale News, 1947).
Alan F. MacRobert, "Proxy Sittings," J.ASPR 48 (1954):71-73.
Arthur Ford & Marguerite Harmon Bro, Nothing So Strange (N.Y.: Harper & Row, 1958).

Siegfried Mandel, "His Man Fletcher," Saturday Rev., 12 July 1958, pp.18-19,32.

Edmond P. Gibson, "Is This Houdini's Telepathic Code?" Fate 14 (Apr. 1961):53-57.

S. Ralph Harlow, A Life After Death (Garden City: Doubleday, 1961).

Arthur Ford, Unknown But Known (N.Y.: Harper & Row, 1968).

Alan Vaughan, "Arthur Ford in Interview," Psychic 2 (Oct.1970):4-7,32-36.

Arthur Ford & Jerome Ellison, The Life Beyond Death (N.Y.: Dutton, 1971).

Joseph Dunninger, "Joseph Dunninger Discusses the Houdini-Ford Controversy," Fate 24 (Nov.1971):74-82.

Allen Spraggett & William V. Rauscher, Arthur Ford: The Man Who Talked with the Dead (N.Y.: Signet, 1974).

William V. Rauscher & Allen Spraggett, Spiritual Frontier (Garden City: Doubleday, 1975).

1927-1933/William Cartheuser
J. Malcolm Bird, "A Message from a Living Communicator," J.ASPR 21 (1927):166-69.

Jenny O'Hara Pincock, The Trails of Truth (Los Angeles: Austin, 1930).

J. Gay Stevens, "Spirits Speak for the Record," Fate 19 (Mar.1966):83-91.

Nandor Fodor, The Haunted Mind (N.Y.: Signet, 1968), pp.21-29.

D. Scott Rogo, "Tripping over the Ectoplasm," Fate 23 (Nov.1970):67, 68-69.

1930s/Chester Michael Grady
J. Gay Stevens, "The Girl with the Golden Hair," Fate 25 (Dec.1972): 40-51; 26 (Jan.1973):96-104.

1930s-1940s/E.A. Macbeth
Sherwood Eddy, You Will Survive After Death (N.Y.: Rinehart, 1950).

1930s-1970/Eileen J. Garrett
W.W. Carington, "The Quantitative Study of Trance Personalities," Proc. SPR 42 (1934):173-240; 43 (1935): 319-61.

K.M. Goldney & S.G. Soal, "Report on a Series of Sittings with Mrs. Eileen Garrett," Proc.SPR 45 (1938): 43-87.

Eileen J. Garrett, My Life As a Search for the Meaning of Mediumship (London: Rider, 1939).

William R. Birge & J.B. Rhine, "Unusual Types of Persons Tested for ESP," J.Parapsych. 6 (1942):85-94.

Eileen Garrett, Awareness (N.Y.: Creative Age, 1943).

Jan Ehrenwald, Telepathy and Medical Psychology (London: Allen & Unwin, 1947).

J.G. Pratt & William R. Birge, "Appraising Verbal Test Material in Parapsychology," J.Parapsych. 12 (1948):236-56.

Eileen J. Garrett, Adventures in the Supernormal (N.Y.: Creative Age, 1949).

C.C. Evans & E. Osborn, "An Experiment in the Electroencephalography of Mediumistic Trance," J.SPR 36 (1952):578-96.

J. Langdon Davies, "What Is the Agent's Role in ESP?" J.SPR 38 (1956):329-37.

Andrija Puharich, "Can Telepathy Penetrate the Iron Curtain?" Tomorrow 5 (winter 1957):7-16.

Ira Progoff, Image of an Oracle (N.Y.: Garrett, 1964).

Lawrence LeShan, "A 'Spontaneous' Psychometry Experiment with Mrs. Eileen Garrett," J.SPR 44 (1967): 14-19.

Eileen J. Garrett, Many Voices (N.Y.: Putnam, 1968).

Lawrence L. LeShan, "The Vanished Man: A Psychometry Experiment with Mrs. Eileen J. Garrett," J.ASPR 62 (1968):46-62.

Lawrence LeShan, Toward a General Theory of the Paranormal (N.Y.: Parapsych.Foundation, 1969).

"Interview: Eileen J. Garrett," Psychic 1 (June 1970):4-7,32-37.

Ian Stevenson, "Eileen Garrett: An Appreciation," J.ASPR 65 (1971): 336-43.

Andrija Puharich, Beyond Telepathy (Garden City: Anchor, 1973), pp.3-6,26-29,211-25.

Alan Angoff, Eileen Garrett and the World Beyond the Senses (N.Y.: Morrow, 1974).

1940s-1960s/Caroline Randolph Chapman
Sarah Parker White, "Elwood Worcester and the Case for Survival," J.ASPR 43 (1949):98-107.

Warren Weldon, A Happy Medium (Englewood Cliffs, N.J.: Prentice-Hall, 1970).

1950s-1960s/Betty Ritter
Hans Holzer, Ghosts I've Met (N.Y.: Ace, 1965 ed.), pp.15-20.

Hans Holzer, Psychic Photography (N.Y.: McGraw-Hill, 1969), pp.20-30. il.

1960s/Douglas Johnson
John G. Fuller, The Great Soul Trial (N.Y.: Macmillan, 1969).

1969-   /Alice McDermott
Hans Holzer, The New Pagans (Garden City: Doubleday, 1972), pp.151-98.

-Spontaneous human combustion
1959, July/Virginia Mottern/320 E. 57th St./=caused by cigarette?
New York Times, 5 July 1959, p.21.
(Letter), Anon., Fate 13 (July 1960): 120.

-Talking dog
1942/Arthur J. Devlin/Public School 48
Vincent & Margaret Gaddis, The Strange World of Animals and Pets (N.Y.: Pocket Books, 1971 ed.), pp.65-66, quoting New York Sun (undated).

-Telepathy
1865, fall/Henry Armitt Brown
Walter Franklin Prince, <u>Noted Wit-
nesses to Psychic Occurrences</u> (Boston: Boston SPR, 1928), pp.61-63.
1912, April 14/Mrs. Archibald Gracie
Herbert B. Greenhouse, <u>Premonitions:
A Leap into the Future</u> (N.Y.: Warner, 1973 ed.), pp.39-40.
1926
George H. Hyslop, "An Instance of
Apparent Spontaneous Telepathy,"
<u>J.ASPR</u> 42 (1948):56-60.
1937-1938/Harold Sherman
Harold T. Sherman, <u>Thoughts Through
Space</u> (N.Y.: Creative Age, 1942).
1939, April 12
Jan Ehrenwald, "Telepathy and the
Child-Parent Relationship," <u>J.ASPR</u>
48 (1954):43-45.
1945, Feb.-1946, July/Laura A. Dale
J. Hettinger, "Psychometric Tele-
pathy Across the Atlantic," <u>J.ASPR</u>
41 (1947):94-122.
1961, Dec.24/Ruth K. Weinstein/Brooklyn
Ruth K. Weinstein, "My Senseless
Urge 'Disturbed Death,'" <u>Fate</u> 24
(Nov.1971):91-93.
-Telephone anomaly
1967-1968/John A. Keel/Manhattan
John A. Keel, <u>The Mothman Prophecies</u>
(N.Y.: Saturday Review, 1975), pp.
232-43,250-53.
-Teleportation
1956, April/Thomas R. Kessell
<u>Lock Haven (Pa.) Express</u>, 7 June 1956.
-Time anomaly
1950, June 24/Rudolph Fentz/Times
Square
(Editorial), <u>Fate</u> 27 (Jan.1974):31-
34, quoting <u>Saga</u> (undated).
-UFO (?)
1950, March 20/Irving Underhill
Frank Bowers, ed., <u>The True Report
on Flying Saucers</u> (Greenwich, Ct.:
Fawcett, 1967), p.25. il.
1952, July 17/Staten I.
Richard Hall, ed., <u>The UFO Evidence</u>
(Washington: NICAP, 1964), p.14.
1956, March/Ozone Park
Isabel Davis & Ted Bloecher, <u>Close
Encounter at Kelly and Others of
1955</u> (Evanston: Center for UFO
Studies, 1978), p.178.
1957, Aug./Brooklyn
1960, June 8/Lee Ball
Richard Hall, ed., <u>The UFO Evidence</u>
(Washington: NICAP, 1964), pp.15,
50.
1963, June/United Nations Bldg.
Michael G. Mann, "Flying Saucers and
the United Nations," <u>Saucer News</u> 11
(June 1964):1,11-13. il.
"Spheres of Influence," in Frank
Bowers, ed., <u>The True Report on Fly-
ing Saucers</u> (Greenwich, Ct.: Faw-
cett, 1967), p.25. il.
1965, Nov.9/Arthur Rickerby
"The Disaster That Wasn't," <u>Time</u>, 19
Nov.1965, p.37. il.

1966, April 25/Mrs. Joseph Powlis/=
meteor
John A. Keel, <u>UFOs: Operation Trojan
Horse</u> (N.Y.: Putnam, 1970), p.145.
1977, May/Baker Field/=hoax
<u>Kansas City (Mo.) Star</u>, 16 May 1977.
1977, July/Ted Shaw/Kissena Park
(Letter), <u>Saga UFO Rept.</u> 5 (June
1978):8.
-UFO (CE-1)
1954, summer/Jan. P. Boshoff/"Groote
Beer"/80 mi.E
(Editorial), <u>Fate</u> 8 (Mar.1955):18.
n.d./Claudia Weill/Henry Hudson Park-
way
"Saucers and Celebrities," <u>Saga UFO
Rept.</u> 6 (Oct.1978):14.
1975, Jan./Claudia Montelione/Verra-
zano Narrows Bridge
Timothy Green Beckley, "Saucers over
Our Cities," <u>Saga UFO Rept.</u> 4 (Aug.
1977):24,27.
1975, Aug./Lloyd Kauffman/Plaza Hotel
Timothy Green Beckley, "Saucers over
Our Cities," <u>Saga UFO Rept.</u> 4 (Aug.
1977):24,72.
-UFO (CE-2)
1957, May 7
<u>Washington (D.C.) Star</u>, 8-9 May 1957.
1974, July 8/Brandon Blackman/Prospect
Park
Timothy Green Beckley, "The Strange
Effects of Flying Saucers," <u>Saga
UFO Rept.</u> 2 (winter 1974):32,72.
1975, Feb.11/Charles D'Amore/Barclay
Ave.
<u>Staten Island Advance</u>, 14 Feb.1975;
and 3 Mar.1975.
Robert C. Warth, "A UFO-ABSM Link?"
<u>Pursuit</u> 8 (Apr.1975):31,34-35.
Timothy Green Beckley, "Saucers over
Our Cities," <u>Saga UFO Rept.</u> 4 (Aug.
1977):24-26.
-UFO (CE-3)
1965, Nov.9/Stuart Whitman
Jerome Clark, "The Greatest Flap Yet?
Part IV," <u>Flying Saucer Rev.</u> 12
(Nov.-Dec.1966):9,10.
-UFO (DD)
1909, Dec.24/Fifth Ave. x 23d St./=
Venus?
<u>New York Tribune</u>, 25 Dec.1909, p.1.
1910, Sep.21/Manhattan
<u>New York Tribune</u>, 22 Sep.1910, p.1.
1937, July 18/8th Ave. x 39th St.
Ed Sparks, "Space Ships over Times
Square," <u>Saucer News</u> 11 (Mar.1964):
11-12.
1939, summer/George W. Dohmann/Van
Nest section, Brooklyn
(Letter), <u>Fate</u> 18 (Oct.1965):127-30.
1944, summer/Carl Goepper/Grand Central
Parkway
Gordon I.R. Lore, Jr. & Harold H. Den-
eault, Jr., <u>Mysteries of the Skies:
UFOs in Perspective</u> (Englewood
Cliffs, N.J.: Prentice-Hall, 1968),
pp.142-43.
1947, July 3/Nicholas Kronyak/Annadale
<u>New York World-Telegram</u>, 7 July 1947.

1947, July 8/Anna Scott/692 Evergreen St.
New York Journal-American, 8 July 1947.
1953, Dec.12/Robert A. Gahn/Brooklyn
"Multiple Object Sightings by Creditable Observers Continue," CRIFO Newsl., 2 July 1954, p.3.
1955, May 15/Warren Siegmond/Union Square
"Will You Be Lucky Enough to Get a Picture Like This?" Flying Saucer Rev. 2 (May-June 1956):5. il.
Paris Flammonde, The Age of Flying Saucers (N.Y.: Hawthorn, 1971), p. 17.
1956, Oct.7/Richard Winderman
"Case 230," CRIFO Orbit, 2 Nov.1956, p.4.
1957, Oct.5/Emil L. Vernei
Emil L. Varnei, "The Case of the Circling Jets," Flying Saucers, Feb. 1958, pp.22-29.
1964, May 30/World's Fair
Brad Steiger, Project Blue Book (N.Y.: Ballantine, 1976), betw.pp. 360-61. il.
1966, Nov.22/Donald R. McVay/750 Third Ave.
"Major Sighting Wave," UFO Inv. 3 (Jan.-Feb.1967):1,4.
1978, June 4/Daniel J. Noonan/NYU Medical School dormitory
New York Post, 5 June 1978. il.
Pete Mazzola, "UFO over New York," APRO Bull. 27 (Sep.1978):1-2. il.
1978, Nov.1/Columbus Circle
New York Post, 2 Nov.1978.
-UFO (NL)
1879, April 12/J. Spencer Devoe/Manhattan
New York Tribune, 26 Apr.1879, p.2.
1947, Aug./Arnold J. Lipman
Arnold J. Lipman, "Was It a Saucer?" Fate 3 (Dec.1950):87.
1952, Oct.14/Eli Kanew/JFK Airport
(Editorial), Fate 6 (Apr.1953):10.
1954, May 7/Mrs. I. Polk
(Letter), Fate 7 (Nov.1954):111-12.
1957, Aug.23/Chester Hagie/Annadale
(Letter), Clifford A. Marshall, Fate 11 (Mar.1958):113-14.
1957, Oct.19/Israel Demsky
New York Daily News, 25 Oct.1957.
1957, Nov.5/Van Cortland Park
Aimé Michel, Flying Saucers and the Straight-Line Mystery (N.Y.: Criterion, 1958), pp.241-42.
1963, Nov.3/Anthony Ingrassia/Corona
"UFO Sightings Centered in Western U.S.," UFO Inv. 2 (Dec.-Jan.1963-64):3.
1964, May 15/James Stroup/JFK Int'l Airport
"Other Recent Sightings," UFO Inv. 2 (July-Aug.1964):7.
1965, Oct.14/World's Fair
Bill Adler, ed., Letters to the Air Force on UFOs (N.Y.: Dell, 1967), p.79.

1965, Nov.9/Mrs. Sol Kaplan/Central Park West
John G. Fuller, Incident at Exeter (N.Y.: Berkley, 1967 ed.), p.206.
1966, March/Mark Roth/Queens
"A Well-Witnessed 'Invasion'--by Something," Life, 1 Apr.1966, pp. 24,26-27. il.
1966, Nov.21/Michael Glazer/Bronx (Letter), Sci.& Mech. 38 (May 1967): 34.
1966, Dec.28/Elsa Meinke/666 Fifth Ave.
Elsa Meinke, "UFO's over Manhattan," True Flying Saucers & UFOs Quar., no.1 (spring 1976):22-23.
1967, July/Nyle Rothenbach/Franklin Park
1967, Aug./Nyle Rothenbach
Nyle Rothenbach, "The Rothenbach Photo," Official UFO 1 (Oct.1975): 13,41.
1968, Jan.13/Jones Beach
John A. Keel, "Mysterious Gas Attacks by Flying Saucers," Saga UFO Rept. 2 (fall 1975):27,28.
1968, March 12/Throgs Neck Bridge
"U.S. Reports," APRO Bull. 17 (Sep.-Oct.1968):8.
1970, Dec.1/Muhammed Ali/Central Park
"Press Reports," APRO Bull. 19 (Nov.-Dec.1970):9.
"Saucers and Celebrities," Saga UFO Rept. 6 (July 1978):14.
1973, May 31
Timothy Green Beckley, "Scientists' Changing Attitude Toward Flying Saucers," Saga UFO Rept. 1 (spring 1974):14,48.
1973, June 28
Paris Flammonde, UFO Exist! (N.Y.: Putnam, 1976), p.314.
1975, Dec.6/Brooklyn
"Noteworthy UFO Sightings," Ufology 2 (spring 1976):43.
1976, Jan.29/Ann Carr/23d St. x 9th Ave.
James D. White, "More New Jersey UFOs," APRO Bull. 25 (July 1976): 1,3.
Ted Bloecher, "The 'Stonehenge' Incidents of January 1975," Flying Saucer Rev. 22 (Oct.1976):3,6.
1976, March 13/Manhattan
"Noteworthy UFO Sightings," Ufology 2 (summer 1976):62.
1976, June 13/Queens
"Noteworthy UFO Sightings," Ufology 2 (fall 1976):60.
1977, Nov.20/Staten I.
Tim Merwin, "The Furor over Close Encounters of the Third Kind," Saga UFO Rept. 5 (Mar.1978):41,43.
1978, June 4/Steve Horvatt/Ralph Ave.
New York Post, 5 June 1978.
-Unidentified submerged object
1960, July 15/"Alkaid"/East R.
New York Times, 16 July 1960, p.41; and 19 July 1960, p.58.
-Weather control
1965, June 30/Black Cloud/World's Fair

(Editorial), Fate 19 (Jan.1966):26-28.
-Weeping icon
1957, Feb./Jose Luis Incarnacion/201
Seigel St.
(Editorial), Fate 10 (June 1957):12.
-Weeping mounted deer's head
1955, Aug.15-18/Rose Adonelfi/2760
Stillwell Ave.
(Editorial), Fate 9 (Jan.1956):8-9.
-Windshield pitting
1954, July/Harry Scrivani/nr. New York
Journal-American offices
(Editorial), Fate 7 (Dec.1954):10.

Niagara Falls
-Haunt
1972, Feb.-1976/Bill Nelson
Bill Nelson, "The Exorcism That Al-
most Worked," Fate 29 (Dec.1976):
43-47.
-Mystery explosion
1958, Jan.
"Falls," Doubt, no.57 (1958):4,5-6.
-Mystery plane crash
1963, Feb.12/T.G. Stevens
Jay Gourley, The Great Lakes Triangle
(Greenwich, Ct.: Fawcett, 1977),
pp.18-19.
-Out-of-body experience
1956, March 28/John Otto
John Otto, "I Teleported Home," Fate
19 (Aug.1966):85-89.
-Skyquake
1953, March 23/Joseph Cloutier/north
Grand Island Bridge
"Mystery Explosion," Fate 6 (July
1953):34.
-UFO (CE-1)
1975, July 23
"UFO Central," CUFOS News Bull., 15
Nov.1975, p.14.
-UFO (DD)
1833, Nov.13/Horatio A. Parson
Denison Olmsted, "Observations on the
Meteors of November 13th, 1833," Am.
J.Sci., ser.1, 25 (1834):363,391.
-UFO (NL)
1960, July 26/Niagara R.
Buffalo Courier-Express, 27 July
1960.
1963, June 18/Bill Nelson
Niagara Falls Gazette, 19 June 1963.
"Recent Sightings Confirm Admissions,"
UFO Inv. 2 (June-Sep.1963):3,4.
-UFO (R-V)
1957, July 25/airport
Thomas M. Olsen, ed., The Reference
for Outstanding UFO Sighting Reports
(Riderwood, Md.: UFO Information
Retrieval Center, 1966), p.51.
Gordon D. Thayer, "Optical and Radar
Analyses of Field Cases," in Edward
U. Condon, ed., Scientific Study of
Unidentified Flying Objects (N.Y.:
Bantam, 1969 ed.), pp.115,145.

Niskayuna
-UFO (NL)
1966, April 4

Albany Knickerbocker News, 5 Apr.
1966, p.7C.

North Greenbush twp.
-Fall of mathematical papers
1973, July 24/Bob Hill/Lape Rd.
Albany Times-Union, 25 July 1973.

North Salem
-Ancient perched rock and stone chambers
John Finch, "On the Celtic Antiqui-
ties of America," Am.J.Sci., ser.1,
7 (1824):149-61.
Barry Fell, America B.C. (N.Y.:
Quadrangle, 1976), pp.130-31. il.
"Circular Soil Patterns in S.E. New
York State, near Stonework Sites,"
NEARA J. 12 (summer 1977):14. il.
Salvatore Michael Trento, The Search
for Lost America (Chicago: Contem-
porary, 1978), pp.121-37. il.

North Tonawanda
-Erratic deer
1978, May 23/Veronica Sikora
Ithaca Journal, 24 May 1978.
-UFO (CE-1)
1978, March 31/Roberts Dr.
Hugh Cochrane, "The Great Lakes UFO
Flap of 1978," Saga UFO Rept. 6
(Jan.1979):21,23,56.

Norwich
-UFO (NL)
1956, Sep.28/Mrs. Kenneth Leslie
"Case 227," CRIFO Orbit, 2 Nov.1956,
p.3.

Norwood
-UFO (?)
1884, July 3/L.C. Yale
"A Great Meteor," Ill.Sci.Monthly 2
(1884):136.

Nyack
-Haunt
n.d.
Danton Walker, Spooks Deluxe (N.Y.:
Franklin Watts, 1956), pp.162-63.
-Skyquake
1954, June 29
Donald E. Keyhoe, Flying Saucer Con-
spiracy (N.Y.: Holt, 1955), pp.201-
202.

Ocean Beach
-UFO (NL)
1967, July/Fredi Dundee
Timothy Green Beckley, "Saucers and
Celebrities," Saga UFO Rept. 3 (Mar.
1977):40-41.

Oceanside
-Weeping icon
1960, April-May/Antonia Koulis/41
Oceanside Park
T.F. James, "What Makes the Madonna
Weep," Information, Oct.1960.
Nandor Fodor, Between Two Worlds (W.
Nyack: Parker, 1964), p.265.

D. Scott Rogo, <u>The Haunted Universe</u>
(N.Y.: Signet, 1977), pp.37-38.

Ogdensburg
-Phantom airplane
1915, Feb.12
<u>New York Times</u>, 15 Feb.1915, p.1.

Old Westbury
-UFO (NL)
1958, Jan.3
J. Allen Hynek, <u>The Hynek UFO Report</u>
(N.Y.: Dell, 1977), pp.43-44.

Olean
-Gravity anomaly
1950s
(Letter), Ruth J. McConnell, <u>Fate</u> 6
(June 1953):124.
-Mystery radio transmission
1958, Aug.
<u>Buffalo Courier-Express</u>, 16 Aug.1958.

Oneida
-Spontaneous human combustion
1965, Dec./Katherine Elizabeth Chaires/
210 Liberty St.
Mary Margaret Fuller, "Three Cases
of Spontaneous Combustion," <u>Fate</u>
20 (June 1967):93,94.
-UFO (R-V)
1962, April 18
Frank Edwards, <u>Flying Saucers: Serious Business</u> (N.Y.: Bantam, 1966
ed.), p.151.

Oneida co.
-Snow worms
1891, winter
"Snow Worms," <u>Sci.Am.</u> 64 (1891):147.

Oneonta
-Haunt
1890s/Emelyn E. Gardner
Emelyn E. Gardner, "I Saw It," <u>New
York Folklore Quar.</u> 4 (1948):249-55.
-UFO (DD)
1954, Nov./Mrs. Leo Ireland
(Letter), <u>Fate</u> 8 (Apr.1955):118-19.
-UFO (NL)
1966, Nov.21/Frederic Fay Swift
"Lights Baffle New York Area," <u>APRO
Bull.</u> 16 (July-Aug.1967):8.

Onondaga
-Phantom (myth)
Ehn-kwa-si-yea/W of town
Harold T. Wilkins, "Pixie-Haunted
Moor," <u>Fate</u> 5 (July-Aug.1952):110,
115.
-UFO (NL)
1978, April 7/Paul Cunningham
<u>Syracuse Herald-American</u>, 9 Apr.1978,
il.

Orangeburg
-Haunt
n.d.
William Oliver Stevens, <u>Psychics and
Common Sense</u> (N.Y.: Dutton, 1953),

pp.143-44.
-Parapsychology research
1969-   /Center for the Study of Psychic Phenomena/Rockland State Hospital
"ESP: More Science, Less Mysticism,"
<u>Medical World News</u>, 21 Mar.1969,
pp.20-21.
Aristide H. Esser & Lawrence LeShan,
"A Transatlantic 'Chair Test,'"
<u>J.SPR</u> 45 (1969):167-70.
Rhea H. White, "Parapsychology Today," in Edgar Mitchell, ed., <u>Psy-
chic Exploration</u> (N.Y.: Capricorn,
1976 ed.), pp.195,197-98.

Orangetown twp.
-UFO (NL)
1976, Sep.
<u>New York Times</u>, 6 Sep.1976, p.17.

Orleans co.
-Ancient hearth
Daniel Tomlinson
O.T. Mason, "Archeological Enigmas,"
<u>Science</u> 8 (1886):528-29.
G.K. Gilbert, "Archeological Enig-
mas," <u>Science</u> 8 (1886):564-65.
"The Antiquity of Man in America,"
<u>Am.Antiquarian</u> 9 (1887):49-50.

Ossining
-Animal ESP
1929-1941/Sing Sing penitentiary
Vincent & Margaret Gaddis, <u>The Strange
World of Animals and Pets</u> (N.Y.:
Pocket Books, 1971 ed.), pp.19-21,
quoting <u>Coronet</u>, Mar.1945.
-Contactee
1974, March-   /Andrija Puharich
Brad Steiger, <u>Gods of Aquarius</u> (N.Y.:
Harcourt Brace Jovanovich, 1976),
pp.140-54.
Staurt Holroyd, <u>Prelude to the Land-
ing on Planet Earth</u> (London: W.H.
Allen, 1977).

Oswego
-Dog mutilation
1977, March
<u>Syracuse Herald-Journal</u>, 23 Mar.1977.
-Fall of ice
1889, June 9
<u>Turin Leader</u>, 12 June 1889.
"Winds," <u>Monthly Weather Rev.</u> 17
(June 1889):152.
-Haunt
19th c.-   /Fort Ontario
<u>Oswego Palladium-Times</u>, 28 Feb.1941.
Ethel Shepard, "Fort Ontario's
Ghost," <u>New York Folklore Quar.</u> 10
(1954):198-201.
Louis C. Jones, <u>Things That Go Bump
in the Night</u> (N.Y.: Hill & Wang,
1959), pp.130-32.
-UFO (CE-1)
1966, March 3
Jacques Vallee, <u>Passport to Magonia</u>
(Chicago: Regnery, 1969), p.323.

Otisville
-Erratic crocodilian
  1927, Sep.3/Kaufman Loomis
    New York Times, 4 Sep.1927, p.65.

Ouaquaga
-Fall of fish
  n.d./Ed Brady
    "Dear Abby" Syndicated column, 1
    Jan.1973.

Owasco
-Ancient urn
    Barry Fell, America B.C. (N.Y.: Quad-
    rangle, 1976), pp.150-51. il.

Owego
-UFO (CE-1)
  1973, Oct.22/Lincoln Howe
    Douglas Dains, "Close Encounter in
    New York," APRO Bull. 23 (Sep.-
    Oct.1974):1,3.

Oxbow
-Humanoid
  1976, fall
    John Green, Sasquatch: The Apes Among
    Us (Seattle: Hancock House, 1978),
    p.235.

Oyster Bay
-Witch trial (?)
  1660/Mary Wright
    George Bishop, New-England Judged
    (London: T. Sowle, 1703), pp.220,
    340,461.

Palmyra
-Religious apparition and ancient inscription
  1820-1827/Joseph Smith/Hill Cumorah
    Joseph Smith, The Book of Mormon
    (Palmyra: E.B. Grandin, 1830).
    Alexander Campbell, Delusions (Bos-
    ton: Benjamin H. Greene, 1832).
    E.D. Howe, Mormonism Unveiled
    (Painesville, O.: The Author, 1834).
    Joseph Smith, The Pearl of Great
    Price (Liverpool, Eng.: F.D. Rich-
    ards, 1851).
    Pomeroy Tucker, Origin, Rise and Pro-
    gress of Mormonism (N.Y.: Appleton,
    1867).
    Lu B. Cake, Peepstone Joe and the
    Peck Manuscript (N.Y.: The Author,
    1899).
    Walter Franklin Prince, "Psychologi-
    cal Tests for the Authorship of the
    Book of Mormon," Am.J.Psych. 28
    (1917):373-89.
    Francis W. Kirkham, A New Witness
    for Christ in America, 2 vols. (In-
    dependence, Mo.: Zion, 1942).
    Fawn M. Brodie, No Man Knows My His-
    tory (N.Y.: Knopf, 1945).
    Preston Nibley, The Witnesses of the
    Book of Mormon (Salt Lake City:
    Stevens & Wallis, 1946).
    Joseph Smith, et al., History of the
    Church of Jesus Christ of Latter-Day

Saints, 7 vols. (Salt Lake City:
Deseret, 1951-52).
Harold I. Velt, The Sacred Book of
Ancient America (Independence, Mo.:
Herald House, 1952).
Thomas F. O'Dea, The Mormons (Chi-
cago: Univ.of Chicago, 1957), pp.
2-6,22-40.
Riley L. Dixon, Just One Cumorah
(Salt Lake City: Bookcraft, 1958).
William Alexander Linn, The Story
of the Mormons (N.Y.: Russell &
Russell, 1963), pp.15-98.
Robert Mullen, The Latter-Day Saints
(Garden City: Doubleday, 1966).
James E. Talmage, A Study of the Ar-
ticles of Faith (Salt Lake City:
Church of Jesus Christ of Latter-
Day Saints, 1966), pp.255-93.
W.J. McK. McCormick, Occultism: The
True Origin of Mormonism (Belfast:
Raven, 1967).
Sidney B. Sperry, Answers to Book of
Mormon Questions (Salt Lake City:
Bookcraft, 1967).
Jerald & Sandra Tanner, The Case
Against Mormonism, 2 vols. (Salt
Lake City: Modern Microfilm, 1967).
Marcus Bach, "The Paranormal Basis
of Mormonism," Fate 22 (Feb.1969):
90-97.
(Letter), Helen A. Russell, Fate 22
(Aug.1969):133-34.
Richard Lloyd Anderson, "The Relia-
bility of the Early History of Lucy
and Joseph Smith," Dialogue 4
(summer 1969):12-28.
Colin Bord, "Angels and UFOs," Fly-
ing Saucer Rev. 18 (Sep.-Oct.1972):
17-19.
Ivan J. Barrett, Joseph Smith and
the Restoration (Provo: Brigham
Young Univ., 1973), pp.21-124.
Gary L. Bunker & Davis Britton,
"Mesmerism and Mormonism," Brigham
Young Univ.Studies 15 (1975):146-70.
David Techter, "Who Wrote the Book
of Mormon?" Fate 30 (Mar.1977):38-
46; (Apr.1977):73-77.
Donna Hill, Joseph Smith: The First
Mormon (Garden City: Doubleday,
1977).
(Editorial), Fate 31 (Apr.1978):10-
16, quoting Los Angeles (Cal.)
Times (undated).
(Letter), Walter A. Rumbarger III,
Fate 31 (Dec.1978):117-18.

Patchogue
-Haunt
  1860s-1885/Alvin Smith
    Brooklyn Eagle, 28 Feb.1895, p.7.
-UFO (NL)
  1966, Oct.21/James Mooney
    New York Times, 22 Oct.1966, p.20.
    "Saucer Flap on Long Island," Saucer
    News 14 (spring 1967):34. il.

Patterson
-Ancient stone chambers

Salvatore Michael Trento, <u>The Search</u>
<u>for Lost America</u> (Chicago: Contem-
porary, 1978), pp.121-29.

Peekskill
-Ancient megalith
    Jacob Green, "Notice of a Mineralized
    Tree--Rocking Stone, &c.," <u>Am.J.Sci.</u>,
    ser.1, 5 (1822):251,252-53.
-Archeological site
  Nelson's Hill/=historical
    Edward J. Lenik, "Fort Lookout, Peek-
    skill, N.Y.," <u>NEARA Newsl.</u> 8 (fall
    1973):49.
-Ghost
    18th c./Hans Anderson
    New York Writers' Program, <u>New York:</u>
    <u>A Guide to the Empire State</u> (N.Y.:
    Oxford Univ., 1956), p.113.
-Stigmata
    1922, July/Mary Reilly/Home of the Sis-
    ters of the Good Shepherd
    <u>London (Eng.) Daily Express</u>, 10 July
    1922.
-UFO (CE-3)
    1954, Feb./Mr. Forster
    Jacques Vallee, <u>Passport to Magonia</u>
    (Chicago: Regnery, 1969), p.205.

Pelham
-Haunt
    n.d.
    New York Writers' Program, <u>New York:</u>
    <u>A Guide to the Empire State</u> (N.Y.:
    Oxford Univ., 1956), pp.113-14.

Penfield
-UFO (NL)
    1971, Aug.17
    <u>Rochester Times-Union</u>, 18 Aug.1971.

Perry Center
-UFO (CE-2)
    1974, Oct.21/William Brown
    George D. Fawcett, "The 'Unreported'
    UFO Wave of 1974," <u>Saga UFO Rept.</u>
    2 (spring 1975):50,76.

Philadelphia
-Sheep mutilation
    1937, Jan.29
    "How to Prevent Panic," <u>Fortean Soc'y</u>
    <u>Mag.</u>, no.3 (Jan.1940):13.

Pine Plains
-Anomalous hole in ground
    n.d.
    George Wagner, "Lost Caves: Secret
    Saucer Bases?" <u>Saga UFO Rept.</u> 3
    (Oct.1976):34,58.
-UFO (DD)
    1944, Aug?
    Gordon I.R. Lore, Jr. & Harold H. Den-
    eault, Jr., <u>Mysteries of the Skies:</u>
    <u>UFOs in Perspective</u> (Englewood
    Cliffs, N.J.: Prentice-Hall, 1968),
    p.143.

Pittsford
-Cave anomaly

1890s
    George Wagner, "Lost Caves: Secret
    Saucer Bases?" <u>Saga UFO Rept.</u> 3
    (Oct.1976):34,56-58.
-Phantom insect
    1899, July 11/Mrs. William J. Agate
    <u>Chicago (Ill.) Tribune</u>, 12 July
    1899, p.1.

Plattekill
-Ancient wall
    Indian Dam/S of town
    Philip Smith, <u>Legends of the Shawan-</u>
    <u>gunk (Shon-Gum) and Its Environs</u>
    (Pawling, N.Y.: Smith, 1887), p.168.
    Salvatore Michael Trento, <u>The Search</u>
    <u>for Lost America</u> (Chicago: Contem-
    porary, 1978), pp.103-106.

Plattsburgh
-Musical sand
    L. Champlain
    H. Carrington Bolton & Alexis A. Ju-
    lien, "Musical Sand: Its Wide Dis-
    tribution and Properties," <u>Proc.Am.</u>
    <u>Ass'n Adv.Sci.</u> 33 (1884):408-13.
-UFO (CE-3)
    1955/Plattsburgh AFB
    "Latest Saucer Sightings," <u>Fate</u> 9
    (Apr.1956):43,46.
-UFO (DD)
    1957, Nov.8/Plattsburgh AFB
    "Did the Air Force Deceive the Pub-
    lic About the November Sightings?"
    <u>UFO Inv.</u> 1 (Jan.1958):1,8.

Pleasantville
-Erratic crocodilian
    1931, May 22/F.L. Adrian
    <u>New York Times</u>, 22 May 1931, p.30.

Plymouth
-Skyquake
    1977, Nov.23
    <u>Nat'l Enquirer</u>, 24 Jan.1978, p.37.

Point Au Rouche
-UFO (NL)
    1955/James F. Roddy
    "Latest Saucer Sightings," <u>Fate</u> 9
    (Apr.1956):43,44-45.

Pompey
-UFO (CE-1)
    1978, March 30/Joe LaBella/Pompey
    Center Rd.
    Robert Barrow, "Flying 'Boxcar' in
    New York," <u>APRO Bull.</u> 26 (June
    1978):5.

Poolville
-UFO (CE-2)
    1970, July 29/Douglas Dains/NE of town
    "APRO Members Sight UFOs," <u>APRO Bull.</u>
    19 (July-Aug.1970):8.

Port Byron
-Haunt
    n.d.
    Louis C. Jones, <u>Things That Go Bump</u>

in the Night (N.Y.: Hill & Wang,
1959), p.61.

Port Ewen
-Phantom panther
1977, June
Kingston Daily Freeman, 3 July 1977.

Port Jervis
-Erratic crocodilian
1929, July 2/Grant Baum/Matamoras
New York Times, 3 July 1929, p.8.

Portville
-Gravity anomaly
Promised Land Rd.
Robert R. Lyman, Amazing Indeed!
(Coudersport: Potter Enterprise,
1973), p.83.
-UFO (NL)
1960, July 24/Fred Porcello
Richard Hall, ed., The UFO Evidence
(Washington: NICAP, 1964), p.64.

Port Washington
-Haunt
1961/Carlton St.
Hans Holzer, Gothic Ghosts (N.Y.:
Pocket Books, 1971), pp.28-36.

Pottersville
-UFO (?)
1972
Ogden Blecher, "Saucer Bureau," Saga's
1973 UFO Special, p.4.

Poughkeepsie
-Ancient standing stone
Edward J. Lenik, "A Standing Stone
in Poughkeepsie, New York," NEARA
J. 11 (winter 1977):40.
Salvatore Michael Trento, The Search
for Lost America (Chicago: Contem-
porary, 1978), pp.106-108.
-Haunt
1947-1950/James Pike/Christ Church
rectory
Hans Holzer, Haunted Houses (N.Y.:
Crown, 1971), pp.77-79. il.
-Precognition
1895, June 20/L.O. Howard
"Premonitory Dreams," J.ASPR 9 (1915)
:474-82.
-Spirit medium
1843-1910/Andrew Jackson Davis
Andrew Jackson Davis, Lectures on
Clairmativeness (N.Y.: Searing &
Prall, 1845).
New York Tribune, 14 Nov.1846, p.2;
3 Aug.1847, p.1; and 6 Aug.1847, p.
1.
Andrew Jackson Davis, The Principles
of Nature (N.Y.: S.S. Lyon & W.
Fishbough, 1847).
Andrew Jackson Davis, The Great Har-
monia, 5 vols. (Boston: Bela Marsh,
1852-66).
Andrew Jackson Davis, The Penetralia
(Boston: Bela Marsh, 1856).
Andrew Jackson Davis, The Magic Staff

(N.Y.: J.S. Brown, 1857).
Emma Hardinge Britten, Modern American Spiritualism (N.Y.: The Author,
1870), pp.23-27.
Andrew Jackson Davis, Beyond the
Valley (Boston: Colby & Rich, 1891).
Frank Podmore, Mesmerism and Christian Science (London: Methuen, 1909),
pp.218-33.
Nandor Fodor, Encyclopaedia of Psychic Science (London: Arthurs,
1933), pp.16,77-79.
Amy Pearce Ver Nooy, "Dutchess County Men: Andrew Jackson Davis, the
Poughkeepsie Seer," Year Book Dutchess County Hist.Soc'y 32 (1947):
39-62.
Jan McCarthy, "Andrew Jackson Davis:
The Don Quixote of Spiritualism,"
Southern Speech J. 30 (1965):308-16.
Robert W. Delp, "Andrew Jackson Davis: Prophet of American Spiritualism," J.Am.History 54 (June 1967):
43-56.
Robert W. Delp, "Andrew Jackson Davis' Revelations, Harbinger of American Spiritualism," New York Hist.
Soc'y Quar. 55 (1971):211-34. il.
Slater Brown, The Heyday of Spiritualism (N.Y.: Pocket Books, 1972
ed.), pp.84-110.
Robert W. Delp, "American Spiritualism and Social Reform, 1847-1900,"
Northwest Ohio Quar. 44 (fall 1972):
85-99.
-UFO (NL)
1963, Dec.25
(Editorial), Fate 17 (Apr.1964):15.

Pound Ridge
-Archeological site
ca.8000 B.C.
New York Times, 7 May 1978.
-Hex
1929, summer/Leland Waterbury
New York Times, 1 Aug.1929, p.29;
and 8 Sep.1929, p.20.

Prospect
-Fall of sulphur
1860, June 18/James N. Walters
"Sulphur in Rain," Sci.Am. 3 (1860):
97.

Putnam co.
-Ancient stone chambers
Salvatore Michael Trento, The Search
for Lost America (Chicago: Contem-
porary, 1978), pp.55-56.
-Dowsing
1970s
Robert M. Goldenson, Mysteries of the
Mind (N.Y.: Harper & Row, 1974), pp.
84-85.

Putnam Valley
-Ancient stone constructions
William J. Blake, The History of Put-
nam County, New York (N.Y.: Baker
& Scribner, 1849), p.40.

Salvatore Michael Trento, The Search
for Lost America (Chicago: Contemporary, 1978), pp.116-29. il.

Quogue
-Ghost
1962/Gladys Topping
(Editorial), Fate 20 (Apr.1967):9-12.

Ramapo
-Ancient walls
Edward J. Lenik, "The Riddle of the
Prehistoric Walls of Ramapo, New
York," NEARA Newsl. 9 (fall 1974):
42-55. il.
Edward J. Lenik, "The Riddle of the
Prehistoric Walls, Ramapo, New
York," Bull.N.Y.State Arch.Ass'n,
no.63 (Mar.1975):1-14. il.
Richard R. Szathmary, "A Closer Look
at America B.C.," Fate 30 (Dec.
1977):79,80-81. il.
Salvatore Michael Trento, The Search
for Lost America (Chicago: Contem-
porary, 1978), pp.98-101. il.
-UFO (NL)
1976, Sep.
New York Times, 6 Sep.1976, p.17.

Red Hook
-Erratic crocodilian
1970, Aug.4
Kingston Daily Freeman, 5-6 Aug.1970.
Rhinebeck Gazette-Advertiser, 6 Aug.
1970.

Redwood
-Rock pillars
R.V. Dietrich, "Conical and Cylindri-
cal Structures in the Potsdam Sand-
stone, Redwood, New York," N.Y.
State Mus.Circular, no.34 (1953).

Rensselaer
-Fall of blue rain and pink snow
1954, Feb.28/=pollution?
"Colored Rain--Snow," Doubt, no.45
(1954):289.
-Haunt
1799/Forbes Manor
Harold W. Thompson, Body, Boots and
Britches (Philadelphia: Lippincott,
1940), pp.121-23.

Rensselaer co.
-Archeological site
Indian Chair
Pittstown Centinel, 25 Jan.1977.

Rexford
-UFO (NL)
1967, Aug.12
Albany Knickerbocker News, 14 Aug.
1967, p.1B.

Rhinebeck
-Healing
1930s
William Seabrook, Witchcraft: Its
Power in the World Today (N.Y.: Lan-

cer, 1968 ed.), p.255, quoting
Rhinebeck Gazette (undated).

Ripley
-Archeological site
Arthur C. Parker, "Excavations in
an Erie Indian Village and Burial
Site at Ripley, Chautauqua Co.,
New York," Bull.N.Y.State Mus., no.
117 (1907).

Riverhead
-Mystery radio transmissions
1957, Nov.7-8
Aimé Michel, Flying Saucers and the
Straight-Line Mystery (N.Y.: Cri-
terion, 1958), p.275.

Rochester
-Crisis apparition
1900s/Philip Block
William Dunseath Eaton, Spirit Life
(Chicago: Stanton & Van Vliet,
1920).
-Erratic snake
1947, May 9/Eastman Theater
"At the Same Time," Doubt, no.19
(1947):290,291-92.
-Fall of mud
1957, March 14
"Colored Rains," Doubt, no.54 (1957):
433, quoting New York Post (undated).
-Haunt
1905/Gene Saunders/Hawley St.
Alice S. Napier, "Haunted House on
Hawley Street," Fate 8 (July 1955):
88-92.
-Hex
1960s
David C. Tinling, "Voodoo, Root Work,
and Medicine," Psychosomatic Med.
29 (1967):483-90.
-Mystery plane crash
1972, March 3/Aero Commander 500B
Jay Gourley, The Great Lakes Triangle
(Greenwich, Ct.: Fawcett, 1977),
p.132.
-Spirit medium
1848-1849/A.H. Jarvis/4 West St.
Eliab W. Capron, Modern Spiritualism:
Its Facts and Fanaticisms (Boston:
Bela Marsh, 1855), pp.67-69.
1848, April-1860s/Kate and Margaret
Fox
Rochester Daily Magnet, 26 Feb.1850.
Buffalo Commercial Advertiser, 18-19
Feb.1851.
John Worth Edmonds, An Appeal to the
Public on Spiritualism (N.Y.: Par-
tridge & Brittan, 1853).
New York Courier, 1 Aug.1853.
Eliab W. Capron, Modern Spiritualism:
Its Facts and Fanaticisms (Boston:
Bela Marsh, 1855), pp.57-67,69-106,
172-95,270-73,309-34,337-55,383-438.
Emma Hardinge Britten, Modern Ameri-
can Spiritualism (N.Y.: The Author,
1870), pp.38-54,152-56.
A. Leah Underhill, The Missing Link
in Modern Spiritualism (N.Y.: Thomas

R. Knox, 1885).
Nandor Fodor, Encyclopaedia of Psy-
chic Science (London: Arthurs,
1933), pp.144-48.
Mariam Buckner Pond, Time Is Kind:
The Story of the Unfortunate Fox
Family (N.Y.: Centennial, 1947).
Philip Bartholomew, "The 'Confession'
of Margaretta Fox," Fate 4 (July
1951):52-53.
Earl Wesley Fornell, The Unhappy Me-
dium: Spiritualism and the Life of
Margaret Fox (Austin: Univ.of Texas,
1964).
John B. Wilson, "Emerson and the
Rochester Rappings," New England
Quar. 41 (1968):248-58.
Slater Brown, The Heyday of Spirit-
ualism (N.Y.: Pocket Books, 1972
ed.), pp.111-40.
George W. Corner, Doctor Kane of the
Arctic Seas (Philadelphia: Temple
Univ., 1972).
Herbert G. Jackson, Jr., The Spirit
Rappers (Garden City: Doubleday,
1972).
-UFO (?)
1883, Sep.11-13/Lewis Swift/Warner Ob-
servatory
"Discovery of Comet 1883c," Observa-
tory 6 (1883):308.
"Swift's New Comet," Observatory 6
(1883):345.
1971, Aug.16
Rochester Times-Union, 17 Aug.1971.
-UFO (CE-1)
1966, June 24/Paul Sterling/E.I. DuPont
de Nemours & Co.
Coral E. Lorenzen, Flying Saucers:
The Startling Evidence of the Inva-
sion from Outer Space (N.Y.: Signet,
1966 ed.), p.274.
1973, Oct.23/Frank Fusilli/52 Davy Dr.
Rochester Democrat & Chronicle, 24
Oct.1973.
-UFO (DD)
1958, Jan.12/Samuel John Ciurca, Jr./
Genesee Valley Park
(Letter), Fate 11 (June 1958):115-16.
-UFO (NL)
1947, July 6/Kenneth W. Ohley/96 Villa
St.
Rochester Democrat & Chronicle, 7
July 1947.
1959, Jan.3/William Neva
"UFO Sightings Rapidly Increase,"
UFO Inv. 1 (Feb.-Mar.1959):5.
1977, Oct.23
"UFOs of Limited Merit," Int'l UFO
Reporter 2 (Dec.1977):3.

Rome
-UFO (?)
1909, Dec.15/=Venus?
New York Sun, 16 Dec.1909.
1974, May 13/Barry Helm/Griffiss AFB
Ronald Draper, "The 'Radar UFOs' That
Haunt Griffiss Air Force Base," Saga
UFO Rept. 6 (July 1978):28,30.
-UFO (CE-2)

1968, April 2/Ernie R. Howard/Griffiss
AFB
Ronald Draper, "The 'Radar UFOs' That
Haunt Griffiss Air Force Base," Saga
UFO Rept. 6 (July 1978):28,29-30.
-UFO (DD)
1970, Nov.11/Stuart H. Tremble/Griffiss
AFB
Ronald Draper, "The 'Radar UFOs' That
Haunt Griffiss Air Force Base," Saga
UFO Rept. 6 (July 1978):28,30.
-UFO (R-V)
1975, April 29/Bill Myers/Griffiss AFB
Ronald Draper, "The 'Radar UFOs' That
Haunt Griffiss Air Force Base," Saga
UFO Rept. 6 (July 1978):28,30-31,56.

Rotterdam
-Electromagnetic anomaly
1961, Feb.-Nov./Eugene Binkowski
(Editorial), Fate 14 (July 1961):17-
18.
(Editorial), Fate 14 (Aug.1961):22-
23.
(Editorial), Fate 15 (Mar.1962):10-
12.
(Editorial), Fate 15 (June 1962):19.
il.
-Eyeless vision
1967/Mike Griesemer
(Editorial), Fate 20 (Dec.1967):10,
quoting Schenectady Union-Star (undated).
(Editorial), Fate 21 (Jan.1968):15.
il.
-UFO (DD)
1950, July 9/John Sokol/Coldbrook
Kenneth Arnold & Ray Palmer, The Coming of the Saucers (Boise: The Authors, 1952), pp.152-53.

Round Point
-Cave anomaly
1820s/Mr. Cronkite
George Wagner, "Lost Caves: Secret
Saucer Bases?" Saga UFO Rept. 3
(Oct.1976):34,58.

Rutland Center
-Archeological site
David S. Martin, "Ancient Works in
New York," Am.Naturalist 15 (1881):
489-90.

Rye
-Haunt
1957-1965/Molly Guion/Barberry Lane
Hans Holzer, Yankee Ghosts (N.Y.:
Ace, 1966), pp.10-28.
Hans Holzer, Haunted Houses (N.Y.:
Crown, 1971), pp.80-84. il.
-Parapsychology research
1941-   /Julius Weinberger
Julius Weinberger, "On Apparatus Com-
munication with Discarnate Persons,"
Int'l J.Parapsych. 3 (winter 1961):
56-76.
Julius Weinberger, "Apparatus Commun-
ication with Discarnate Persons,"
in John White & Stanley Krippner,

eds., Future Science (Garden City:
Anchor, 1977), pp.465-86.
Susy Smith, Voices of the Dead? (N.Y.:
Signet, 1977), pp.115-18.
-UFO (?)
1957, June 22/Long Island Sound
Port Chester Item, 22 June 1957.

Sackets Harbor
-Haunt
n.d./Samuel Guthrie home
Herbert A. Wisbey, Jr., "Dr. Guth-
rie's Ghost," New York Folklore
Quar. 13 (1957):193-95.

Sagetown
-Fall of metal foil
1956, Aug.27/Charles Reese/Pine City
Rd.
1956, Oct.3/Ernest S. Jacque/754 Mt.
Zoard St.
Cliff R. Towner, "Silver Chaff from
the Sky," Fate 10 (Mar.1957):94-98.
il.

Sag Harbor
-Haunt
n.d.
Louis C. Jones, Things That Go Bump
in the Night (N.Y.: Hill & Wang,
1959), p.71.
-Sea monster
1818, June 19
"American Sea-Serpent," Quar.J.Sci.
Lit.& Arts Royal Inst. 6 (1818):163.

Salamanca
-Humanoid myth
nearby cave
George Wagner, "Lost Caves: Secret
Saucer Bases?" Saga UFO Rept. 3
(Oct.1976):34,58.

Salem
-Haunt
n.d./schoolhouse
Louis C. Jones, Things That Go Bump
in the Night (N.Y.: Hill & Wang,
1959), pp.150-51.

Salina twp.
-UFO (DD)
1978, April 10/David Schell
Syracuse Post-Standard, 11 Apr.1978.

Sangerfield
-Snow worms
1850, Nov.18
"Worms on Snow," Sci.Am. 6 (1850):96.

Saranac Lake
-Humanoid
1975, June/Hwy.3
John Green, Sasquatch: The Apes Among
Us (Seattle: Hancock House, 1978),
p.234.

Saratoga co.
-Haunt
18th c.

New York Writers' Program, New York:
A Guide to the Empire State (N.Y.:
Oxford Univ., 1956), p.113.

Saratoga Springs
-Ancient megalith
Indian Watch Rocks site
"Needs Investigating: An Interesting
Trio," NEARA Newsl. 7 (June 1972):
32.
-Snow anomaly
1946, Jan.22
"Snowballs," Doubt, no.16 (1946):241.

Saugerties
-Bleeding icon
1954, June 29/St. Mary's cemetery
(Editorial), Fate 7 (Nov.1954):14.

Savannah
-Flying humanoid
1896, Nov.1/Hutch Newton/=balloon?
Sacramento (Cal.) Record-Union, 22
Nov.1896.

Schenectady
-Haunt
n.d.
Emelyn Elizabeth Gardner, Folklore
from the Schoharie Hills (Ann Arbor:
Univ.of Michigan, 1937), pp.96-97.
-Mystery tracks
1875, March/Mr. Veeder/37 Albany St.
Schenectady Union, 30 Mar.1875.
New York Times, 5 Apr.1875, p.5.
-Phantom image
n.d.
Charles M. Skinner, Myths and Legends
of Our Own Land, 2 vols. (Philadel-
phia: Lippincott, 1896), 1:76-77.
-UFO (?)
n.d./Vincent Schaefer/=piece of paper
Donald H. Menzel, Flying Saucers
(Cambridge, Mass.: Harvard Univ.,
1953), p.26.
1966, April 3
Albany Knickerbocker News, 6 Apr.
1966.
-UFO (NL)
1956, April 8/Raymond Ryan/=Venus?
Buffalo Evening News, 10 Apr.1956.
"Cover-Up Suspected in Reported Air-
UFO Chase," UFO Inv. 1 (Jan.1958):
10-12.
Donald E. Keyhoe, Flying Saucers: Top
Secret (N.Y.: Putnam, 1960), pp.
167-76.
Donald H. Menzel & Lyle G. Boyd, The
World of Flying Saucers (Garden
City: Doubleday, 1963), pp.68-70.
Richard Hall, ed., The UFO Evidence
(Washington: NICAP, 1964), pp.41-42.
1966, Aug.12/Charles Nelson/5 mi.W on
Hwy.7
(Letter), Sci.& Mech. 38 (May 1967):
35.
1967, Aug.12
Albany Knickerbocker News, 14 Aug.
1967.

Schoharie co.
-Hex
  n.d.
    Emelyn Elizabeth Gardner, Folklore
    from the Schoharie Hills, New York
    (Ann Arbor: Univ.of Michigan, 1937),
    pp.44-84.

Schroon Lake
-Fall of quartzite
  1880, fall
    "The Schroon Lake Meteor a Fraud,"
    Sci.Am. 43 (1880):272.

Scotia
-UFO (CE-1)
  1967, April
    Jennifer Stevens, "Mystery on the
    Mohawk," in Beyond Condon (Flying
    Saucer Rev. special issue, no.2,
    June 1969), pp.36-38.
-UFO (CE-3)
  1968, Feb.
    Jennifer Stevens, "Mystery on the
    Mohawk," in Beyond Condon (Flying
    Saucer Rev. special issue, no.2,
    June 1969), pp.36-38.
-UFO (NL)
  1967, Aug.12
    Albany Knickerbocker News, 14 Aug.
    1967, p.1B.

Sea Cliff
-Seance and weather control
  n.d./Harry Houdini
    Arthur Conan Doyle, The Edge of the
    Unknown (N.Y.: Berkley, 1968 ed.),
    pp.23-24.
    Milbourne Christopher, Houdini: The
    Untold Story (N.Y.: Pocket Books,
    1970 ed.), p.178.

Seaford
-Poltergeist
  1958, Feb.3-March 10/James M. Herrmann/
  1648 Redwood Path
    New York Times, 22 Feb.1958, p.10;
    24 Feb.1958, p.21; 27 Feb.1958, p.
    29; 4 Mar.1958, p.31; 5 Mar.1958,
    p.22; 7 Mar.1958, p.25; and 27 Mar.
    1958, p.35.
    Robert Wallace, "House of Flying Ob-
    jects," Life, 17 Mar.1958, pp.49-
    58. il.
    Jerry Siegel, "Seaford's Pop-Bottle
    Poltergeist," Fate 11 (June 1958):
    23-29.
    "Seaford Revisited: Post-Mortem on a
    Poltergeist," Tomorrow 6 (summer
    1958):9-19.
    Curtis Fuller, "Parapsychology Looks
    at Seaford," Fate 11 (Dec.1958):67-
    74.
    J.G. Pratt & W.G. Roll, "The Seaford
    Disturbances," J.Parapsych. 22 (1958)
    :79-124.
    J.L. Woodruff, "The Herrmann 'Polter-
    geist' Case," J.ASPR 52 (1958):108-
    13.
    William G. Roll, The Poltergeist (N.Y.:

Signet, 1974 ed.), pp.12-23.
-UFO (CE-1) and Men-in-black
  1967, Sep.26-30
    John A. Keel, The Mothman Prophecies
    (N.Y.: Saturday Review, 1975), pp.
    229-30,236.

Selden
-UFO (NL)
  1972, Oct.9
    "Flyover Reported from Long Island,"
    UFO Inv., Feb.1973, p.2.

Sharon
-Phantom horseman
  n.d.
    Harold W. Thompson, Body, Boots and
    Britches (Philadelphia: Lippincott,
    1940), p.119.

Shelter Island
-Haunt
  n.d.
    Louis C. Jones, Things That Go Bump
    in the Night (N.Y.: Hill & Wang,
    1959), p.71.

Sherburne
-UFO (CE-1)
  1964, July 27/Louis Daubert
    "New York & Montana Flurries," UFO
    Inv. 2 (Sep.-Oct.1964):6.
    Thomas M. Olsen, ed., The Reference
    for Outstanding UFO Sighting Reports
    (Riderwood, Md.: UFO Information
    Retrieval Center, 1966), p.101.

Sherman
-Humanoid
  ca.1965
    John A. Keel, Strange Creatures from
    Time and Space (Greenwich, Ct.: Faw-
    cett, 1970), p.113.

Sinclairville
-UFO (CE-2)
  1966, April/Robert Howard
    John A. Keel, UFOs: Operation Trojan
    Horse (N.Y.: Putnam, 1970), p.106.

Sloansville
-UFO (CE-1)
  1957, Nov.8
    Albany Times-Union, 9 Nov.1957.

Sloatsburg
-Skyquake
  1977, Dec.24
    U.S. Naval Rsch.Laboratory, NRL In-
    vestigations of East Coast Acoustics
    Events (Washington: Gov't Printing
    Office, 1978), p.139.
-UFO (NL)
  1960, Nov.4/Yolanda Pastore
    (Letter), Fate 14 (Mar.1961):110.

Southampton
-UFO (NL)
  1966, Oct.30
    Brad Steiger, ed., Project Blue Book

(N.Y.: Ballantine, 1976), betw.pp.
56-57. il.
-Witch trial (hex)
ca.1683/Mrs. Thomas Travally
George Rogers Howell, The Early History of Southampton, L.I., New York
(N.Y.: J.N. Hallock, 1866), p.98.

South Gilboa
-Haunt
n.d./Mr. Williams/Spook Woods
Harold W. Thompson, Body, Boots and
Britches (Philadelphia: Lippincott,
1940), p.109.

South Granville
-Fall of snake
1860, July 3/William Ruggles
William Ruggles, "Raining Snakes,"
Sci.Am. 3 (1860):112.

South Onondaga
-UFO (CE-1)
1978, April 7/Shirley Coyne/Cole Rd.
Syracuse New Times, 19 Nov.1978.

South Otselic
-Dowsing research
1965/Norman B. Evans/Central School
"Measuring the Force in Dowsing
Rods," Fate 18 (Oct.1965):69.

South Wales
-Precognition
1972, Sep.24/Elmer Jones
"Fire Foreseen," Fate 29 (May 1976):
81.

Southwood
-UFO (NL)
1978, April 7
Mark Bundy, "The Central New York
UFO Wave," Pursuit 13 (winter 1979):
35,36.

Spring Valley
-Flying humanoid
1899/George Saarosy/Lawrence St. Bridge
James F. McCloy & Ray Miller, Jr.,
The Jersey Devil (Wallingford, Pa.:
Middle Atlantic, 1976), pp.34-35,
quoting Suffern Rockland Independent
(undated).

Springwater
-Fall of hay
1971/Gary Robinson
(Editorial), Fate 25 (Feb.1972):24-
26.

Steuben co.
-Retrocognition
n.d.
Louis C. Jones, Things That Go Bump
in the Night (N.Y.: Hill & Wang,
1959), pp.75-76.

Stillwater
-UFO (DD)
1968, Dec.9/Richard Snyder

Albany Knickerbocker News, 11 Dec.
1968, p.2B.

Stony Brook
-Animal ESP
1973
Charles Walcott & Robert P. Green,
"Orientation of Homing Pigeons Al-
tered by a Change in the Direction
of an Applied Magnetic Field,"
Science 184 (1974):180-82.

Stony Point
-Haunt
1942-1952/Danton Walker
Danton Walker, Spooks Deluxe (N.Y.:
Franklin Watts, 1956), pp.172-78.
Hans Holzer, Ghost Hunter (N.Y.:
Ace, 1963 ed.), pp.136-55.
-UFO (NL)
1976, Aug.25/Bill Patrick
New York Times, 11 Oct.1976, p.31.
Nat'l Enquirer, 1 Feb.1977.
(Editorial), Fate 30 (Mar.1977):24-
25.

Suffern
-UFO (DD)
1976, Aug.30/Warren Berbit/Gov. Thomas
F. Dewey Thruway
New York Times, 6 Sep.1976, p.17;
and 11 Oct.1976, p.31.
Nat'l Enquirer, 1 Feb.1977.

Sullivan co.
-Hex
n.d./Old Meg
New York Writers' Program, New York:
A Guide to the Empire State (N.Y.:
Oxford Univ., 1956), pp.114-15.
-Snow worms
1884, Dec.26
New York Times, 27 Dec.1884.

Syracuse
-Fall of frozen hamburger
1957, Feb./Christine Cox
Los Angeles (Cal.) Times, 24 Feb.
1957.
-Fall of money
1951, July/E. Fayette x S. Warren St.
"Falls," Doubt, no.36 (1952):133,134.
-Fall of mud
1957, March 14
"Colored Rains," Doubt, no.54 (1957):
433, quoting New York Post (undated).
-Inner development
1960s-   /Atlantion Wicca
J. Gordon Melton, Encyclopedia of
American Religions, 2 vols. (Wil-
mington, N.C.: Consortium, 1978),
2:278.
-Poltergeist
1960, Nov.27-1961/Warren Bottrill
(Editorial), Fate 14 (Apr.1961):8.
-Precognition
1961, March 4
(Editorial), Fate 14 (July 1961):12.
-Terrestrial magnetism and insanity
1957-1961/Veteran's Administration Hos-

pital
"Magnetic Man," Newsweek, 13 May
1963, pp.90-91.
Howard Friedman, Robert O. Becker &
Charles H. Bachman, "Geomagnetic
Parameters and Psychiatric Hospital
Admissions," Nature 200 (1963):626-
28.
-UFO (?)
1962, Dec.2
Conneaut (O.) News-Herald, 3 Dec.1962.
1966, Oct.26
Brad Steiger, ed., Project Blue Book
(N.Y.: Ballantine, 1976), betw.pp.
56-57. il.
1968, March 8
"French General, Scientists, Report
UFOs," UFO Inv. 4 (May-June 1968):
3.
-UFO (CE-1)
1966, April 25/Thornden Park
Coral E. Lorenzen, Flying Saucers:
The Startling Evidence of the Inva-
sion from Outer Space (N.Y.: Sig-
net, 1966 ed.), pp.272-73.
1978, April 29/John Rudy/Hwy.690 x
Thompson Rd.
Mark Bundy, "The Central New York
UFO Wave," Pursuit 13 (winter 1979):
35,38-39.
-UFO (CE-2)
1968, March 4/Nicholas Sgouris
"French General, Scientists, Report
UFOs," UFO Inv. 4 (May-June 1968):3.
1978, May 9
Mark Bundy, "The Central New York
UFO Wave," Pursuit 13 (winter 1979):
35,39.
-UFO (CE-3)
1960, spring
Jacques Vallee, Passport to Magonia
(Chicago: Regnery, 1969), p.278.
-UFO (NL)
1965, Nov.9/William Stilwell
1965, Nov.9/Robert Walsh/S of Hancock
Field
Syracuse Herald-Journal, 16 Nov.1965,
p.1. il.
(Editorial), Fate 19 (Mar.1966):18-
20.
1968, March 13/Mrs. Robert Skinner
T.M. Wright, "UFOs over Ithaca,"
Fate 22 (Feb.1969):44,51.
1969, Sep.26/Upstate Medical Center
Peter Guttilla, "UFO's: The Future
of Civilization Is at Stake!" Saga,
July 1970, pp.34,79-80.
1974, Oct.24
1974, Oct.27/Daniel Wolnick
George D. Fawcett, "The 'Unreported'
UFO Wave of 1974," Saga UFO Rept. 2
(spring 1975):50,76.
1975, Oct.24
"Noteworthy UFO Sightings," Ufology
2 (spring 1976):43.
1977, Feb./Lyndon Golf Course
1978, March 29/Edgar Prue/Kramer St.
1978, April 7/S. Onondaga Hill
Mark Bundy, "The Central New York
UFO Wave," Pursuit 13 (winter 1979):

35-38.
-Weeping icon
1949, April 2-16/Shirley Anne Martin
Myron D. Lewis, Jr., "The Weeping
Statue of Syracuse," Fate 2 (Nov.
1949):60-64. il.

Taborton
-Shape-shifting
n.d./Dame Hohausen
Harold W. Thompson, Body, Boots and
Britches (Philadelphia: Lippincott,
1940), pp.110-11.

Tappan
-UFO (NL)
1976, Dec.18/Anthony Russo, Jr./18
Wayne Lane
Nyack Journal-News, 19 Dec.1976.

Tarrytown
-UFO (NL)
1956, Aug.9/Walter Kocher
"Case 183," CRIFO Orbit, 7 Sep.1956,
p.3.

Theresa
-Humanoid
1977, June 27-28
Watertown Daily Times, 2 Aug.1977.

Thompson
-Entombed toad
ca.1833
William A. Thompson, "On the Vitality
of Toads, &c. Enclosed in Firm Materials," Am.J.Sci., ser.1, 25
(1834):41,46-47.

Three Mile Bay
-UFO (CE-1)
1966, March 30/Dallas Spicer
East Hampton Star, 17 Apr.1966.

Ticonderoga
-Ghost
1758, July 8/Duncan Campbell/Fort Ti-
conderoga
Francis Parkman, Montcalm and Wolfe,
3 vols. (Boston: Little, Brown,
1903 ed.), 3:281-85.
F.B. Richards, The Black Watch at
Ticonderoga (Glen Falls, N.Y.: Ti-
conderoga Mus.Library, 1912).
Howard Drake Williams, "The Ghost of
Inverawe," Fate 4 (May-June 1951):
62-67.
Charles A. Huguenin, "The Ghost of
Ticonderoga," New York Folklore
Quar. 15 (1959):4-24.
-Haunt
n.d./Fort Ticonderoga
James Reynolds, Ghosts in American
Houses (N.Y.: Paperback Library,
1967 ed.), pp.87-91.
-UFO (CE-1)
n.d.
Albany Knickerbocker News, 30 Mar.
1966.

Tivoli
-River monster
  1886, Dec.30/Mr. Brown/Hudson R./=
  hoax?
    New York Times, 1 Jan.1887, p.4.

Tonawanda
-Fall of ice
  1963, May 6/Arthur Krolick
    "Fortean Items," Saucer News 10
    (Sep.1963):17.
-Out-of-body experience
  1954, Feb./Nicholas J. Laub
    (Letter), Fate 15 (May 1962):128-29.

Troy
-Jinxed ring
  1890s/Oliver Peterson/Lansingburgh
    T.C. Bridges, "Unlucky Possessions,"
    in Bernhardt J. Hurwood, ed., The
    First Occult Review Reader (N.Y.:
    Award, 1968), pp.37,40-41.
-Spirit medium
  1850s/Mr. Vosburgh
  1850s/Fanny Davis/Lansingburgh
  1850/Mr. Attwood
    Emma Hardinge Britten, Modern Ameri-
    can Spiritualism (N.Y.: The Author,
    1870), pp.61,77-79,113.
  1851/N.E. White
    Eliab W. Capron, Modern Spiritualism:
    Its Facts and Fanaticisms (Boston:
    Bela Marsh, 1855), pp.274-77.

Trumansburg
-UFO (?)
  1886, March 1/=meteor
    New York Herald, 2 Mar.1886, p.4.

Ulster co.
-UFO (CE-1)
  1977, March 10
    Kingston Daily Freeman, 23 Mar.1977.

Utica
-Fall of mud
  1957, March 14
    "Colored Rains," Doubt, no.54 (1957):
    433, quoting New York Post (undated).
-Snow worms
  1891, winter/George C. Hodges
    "Snow Worms," Sci.Am. 64 (1891):147.
-UFO (?)
  1966, April 25/Dana DeGeorge
    Columbus (O.) Dispatch, 26 Apr.1966,
    p.1. il.
-UFO (CE-1)
  1941, Dec.22/George Bogner/St. Agnes
  Ave. x Pleasant St.
    Gordon I.R. Lore, Jr. & Harold H. Den-
    eault, Jr., Mysteries of the Skies:
    UFOs in Perspective (Englewood
    Cliffs, N.J.: Prentice-Hall, 1968),
    p.141.
-UFO (DD)
  1954, July 2
    Donald E. Keyhoe, Flying Saucer Con-
    spiracy (N.Y.: Holt, 1955), p.175.
-UFO (R-V)
  1955, June 23/15 mi.E

Gordon D. Thayer, "Optical and Radar
Analyses of Field Cases," in Edward
U. Condon, ed., Scientific Study of
Unidentified Flying Objects (N.Y.:
Bantam, 1969 ed.), pp.115,143.

Valley Stream
-Fall of ice
  1957, March 2/Roy Kellett/Long Island
  Water Co.
    (Editorial), Fate 10 (July 1957):14,
    quoting Garden City Newsday (un-
    dated).
    "Ice," Doubt, no.54 (1957):432.
-Fall of rocks
  1968, June/Frank O'Bannon/151 Locust
  St.
    (Editorial), Fate 22 (Feb.1969):20-
    22, quoting New York Long Island
    Press (undated).
-UFO (NL)
  1947, July 6/John Heathcote
    New York World-Telegram, 7 July 1947.

Van Buren twp.
-UFO (NL)
  1978, April 7/Robert Waltz
    Mark Bundy, "The Central New York
    UFO Wave," Pursuit 13 (winter 1979):
    35,36.

Venice Center
-UFO (CE-2) and skyquake
  1966, Nov.12-1969, Nov.12/Howard Lacey/
  =ground markings only
    "Strange Crater in New York," APRO
    Bull. 17 (Nov.-Dec.1968):7.
    (Editorial), Fate 22 (Apr.1969):24-
    26.
    Buffalo Evening News, 21 Nov.1969.

Verdoy
-UFO (R-V)
  1974, Aug.20/Albany County Airport
    "New York Police See UFO," APRO Bull.
    23 (July-Aug.1974):1,3.

Verona
-UFO (NL)
  1978, Oct.23/Germany Rd.
    Syracuse New Times, 5 Nov.1978.

Walden
-UFO (NL)
  1975, April/Florence Thiele/23 Rifton
  Pl.
    Lee Walsh, "Lee Walsh Reports on the
    Strange and Unknown," Beyond Reality,
    no.18 (Jan.1976):10.

Walesville
-UFO (?)
  1954, July 2/William E. Atkins
    New York Times, 3 July 1954, p.1. il.
    "Jet 'Explodes' Chasing UFO near
    Utica, N.Y.," CRIFO Newsl., 1 Oct.
    1954, p.5.
    Donald E. Keyhoe, Flying Saucer Con-
    spiracy (N.Y.: Holt, 1955), pp.174-
    76.

Gordon D. Thayer, "Optical and Radar
Analyses of Field Cases," in Edward
U. Condon, ed., Scientific Study of
Unidentified Flying Objects (N.Y.:
Bantam, 1969 ed.), pp.115,161.
Donald E. Keyhoe, Aliens from Space
(Garden City: Doubleday, 1973), pp.
26-28.
J. Allen Hynek & Jacques Vallee, The
Edge of Reality (Chicago: Regnery,
1975), pp.161,164.

Warners
-UFO (R-V)
 1978, April 5/Dennis Kiteveles/E. Sor-
 rell Hill Rd.
  Syracuse Herald-Journal, 6 Apr.1978;
  and 9 Apr.1978.
  "Object Sighted, Confirmed by Radar,"
  APRO Bull. 27 (Oct.1978):1,4.
  Mark Bundy, "The Central New York
  UFO Wave," Pursuit 13 (winter 1979):
  35-36.

Warrensburg
-UFO (CE-1)
 1946, winter/Gertrude Fuller
 (Letter), Fate 11 (Apr.1958):116-18.

Waterford
-Haunt
 n.d./nr. St. Mary's Church
 ca.1900
  Louis C. Jones, Things That Go Bump
  in the Night (N.Y.: Hill & Wang,
  1959), pp.60,62-63.
-Spirit medium
 1853, March/John Prosser
  Eliab W. Capron, Modern Spiritualism:
  Its Facts and Fanaticisms (Boston:
  Bela Marsh, 1855), pp.284-87.

Waterloo
-Fall of clay meteorite
 n.d.
  C.F. Rammelsberg, "On Some North American Meteorites," Am.J.Sci., ser.2,
  34 (1862):297,298.

Watertown
-Humanoid
 1975, Jan./Steve Rich/State St.
  Watertown Daily Times, 2 Aug.1977.
 1976, Aug.10/Dennis Smith/Overlook Dr.
  Milton LaSalle, "Bigfoot Sighting,"
  Pursuit 10 (fall 1977):120-23.
-Inner development
 1970s/Gael Steele
 1970s/Amerisyche/141 Arsenal St.
  Hans Holzer, The Witchcraft Report
  (N.Y.: Ace, 1973), pp.59-73.
-UFO (CE-1)
 1959, Feb.4/Henry J. Fikes
  "UFO Sightings Rapidly Increase,"
  UFO Inv. 1 (Feb.-Mar.1959):5.
-UFO (NL)
 1969, Sep.19/Jane Daniels
  Peter Guttilla, "UFO's: The Future
  of Civilization Is at Stake!" Saga,
  July 1970, pp.35,80.

1976, June 20
 "Noteworthy UFO Sightings," Ufology
 2 (fall 1976):60.

Watervale
-Spanish inscription
 ca.1820/Philo Cleveland/=hoax
  Henry Rowe Schoolcraft, Notes on the
  Iroquois (Albany: E.H. Pease, 1842),
  pp.326-29.
  Henry A. Homes, The Pompey (N.Y.)
  Stone, with an Inscription and Date
  of A.D. 1520 (Utica: E.H. Roberts,
  1881). il.
  Syracuse Daily Journal, 9 June 1894;
  and 11 June 1894.
  Charles A. Huguenin, "The Pompey
  Stone," New York Folklore Quar. 14
  (1958):34-43.

Watervliet
-Religious ecstasy
 1837, summer-1840
  Frederick W. Evans, Shakers (N.Y.:
  Appleton, 1859).
  John Humphrey Noyes, History of Amer-
  ican Socialisms (Philadelphia: Lip-
  pincott, 1870), pp.595-613.
  New York Daily Graphic, 24 Nov.1874.
  Charles Nordhoff, The Communistic
  Societies of the United States
  (N.Y.: Harper, 1875).
  Henry S. Olcott, People from the Oth-
  er World (Hartford, Ct.: American,
  1875), pp.392-401.
  Henry C. Blinn, Spiritualism Among
  the Shakers (E. Canterbury, N.H.:
  Shakers, 1899).
  Marguerite F. Melcher, The Shaker
  Adventure (Princeton, N.J.: Prince-
  ton Univ., 1941).
  Edward Deming Andrews, The People
  Called Shakers (N.Y.: Oxford Univ.,
  1953).
  Alson J. Smith, "Mother Ann's 'Work,'
  or a History of the Shakers," Fate
  18 (Oct.1965):59-69.
  Henri Desroche, The American Shakers
  (Amherst: Univ.of Massachusetts,
  1971).

Watkins Glen
-Seance
 1908, April 26/Horace L. Cowper
  "Notes of a Sitting with a Planchette,"
  J.ASPR 2 (1908):627-40.

Wayne co.
-UFO (?)
 1958, Oct.13/L. Ontario
  Rochester Democrat & Chronicle, 13
  Oct.1958.

Webster
-Spirit medium
 1853/B.S. Hobbs
  Emma Hardinge Britten, Modern American Spiritualism (N.Y.: The Author,
  1870), pp.111-12.
-UFO (NL)

1961, June 5-11/Mrs. Frank Priestly/
805 DeWitt Rd.
  Curtis Fuller, "The Boys Who 'Caught'
  a Flying Saucer," Fate 15 (Jan.
  1962):36,41-42, quoting Rochester
  Democrat & Chronicle (undated).

Wellsville
-Haunt
  n.d./Pink House
  Louis C. Jones, Things That Go Bump
  in the Night (N.Y.: Hill & Wang,
  1959), pp.112-14.

Westchester co.
-Haunt
  1965/Paul Herring
  Hans Holzer, Yankee Ghosts (N.Y.:
  Ace, 1966), pp.63-64.
-Precognition
  1971-
  Lina Accurso, "The Proof of the Pre-
  dictions," Fate 32 (Jan.1979):68-
  74. il.
-Witch trial (hex)
  1670, July-Oct./Katherine Harrison
  Edmund Bailey O'Callaghan, Documen-
  tary History of the State of New
  York, 4 vols. (Albany: Charles van
  Benthuysen, 1850), 4:136-38.
  Samuel G. Drake, Annals of Witchcraft
  in New England (Boston: W.E. Wood-
  ward, 1869), pp.129-31.
  Victor Hugo Paltsits, ed., Minutes
  of the Executive Council of the
  Province of New York, 2 vols. (Al-
  bany: J.B. Lyon, 1910), 2:390-95.
  William Renwick Riddell, "Witchcraft
  in Old New York," J.Am.Inst.Criminal
  Law & Criminology 19 (1928):252-56.
  George Lincoln Burr, ed., Narratives
  of the Witchcraft Cases 1648-1706
  (N.Y.: Barnes & Noble, 1946), pp.
  41-43,48-52.

West Danby
-UFO (CE-2)
  1966, Nov./Hugh Barlow/ground markings
  only
  T.M. Wright, "UFO's over Ithaca,"
  Fate 22 (Feb.1969):44-46.

West Fulton
-Animal ESP
  19th c./Charley Shelmandine
  John Stuart Martin, "Why Did the
  Foxes Sing?" Pursuit 6 (July 1973):
  57-59.

Westhampton Beach
-UFO (DD)
  ca.1963, Aug./Arthur Treacher/Dune
  Deck Hotel
  "Teacher Reveals Sighting Details,"
  APRO Bull. 20 (Jan.-Feb.1972):4.

West Hempstead
-Inner development
  1939-1970s/Long Island Church of Aphrodite

"Church of Aphrodite," Newsweek, 27
Nov.1939, p.32.
J. Gordon Melton, Encyclopedia of
American Religions, 2 vols. (Wil-
mington, N.C.: Consortium, 1978),
2:286-87.

West Islip
-Haunt
  1948
  Hans Holzer, Ghost Hunter (N.Y.:
  Ace, 1963 ed.), pp.158-59.

West Nyack
-Haunt
  n.d.
  Danton Walker, Spooks Deluxe (N.Y.:
  Franklin Watts, 1956), p.162.
-UFO (DD)
  1962, Sep.15/J.J. McVicker
  Richard Hall, ed., The UFO Evidence
  (Washington: NICAP, 1964), p.140.

West Park
-Snow worms
  1892, Feb./John Burroughs
  "Insects on the Surface of Snow,"
  Insect Life 4 (1892):335-36.

West Point
-Fall of gelatinous substance
  1833, Nov.13
  Denison Olmsted, "On the Meteors of
  13th November," Am.J.Sci., ser.1,
  25 (1834):363,396.
-Haunt
  1972, Oct.21-Nov.12/Keith W. Bakken/
  Room 4714, Military Academy
  New York Times, 21 Nov.1972, p.45;
  22 Nov.1972, p.37; and 30 Nov.1972,
  p.45.
  Charles Lucas, "West Point's Ghostly
  Cavalryman: Mute Spook or Navy
  Hoax?" Probe the Unknown 1 (Oct.
  1973):50-54.
  David Edwards, "Ghost Watch at West
  Point," Fate 26 (Nov.1973):50-55.

West Seneca
-Retrocognition
  1966, Feb.22/Carolyn Becker/Sunbriar
  Dr.
  Carolyn Becker, "The Indians' Sacri-
  fice," Fate 20 (Aug.1967):101-102.

Whitehall
-Humanoid
  1976, Aug.24/Paul Gosselin
  Glen Falls Post-Star, 30 Aug.1976.

White Lake
-UFO (NL)
  1957, July
  New York Mirror, 26 July 1957.

White Plains
-Hex
  1974/Jose Lopez
  "The Devil Made Them Do It," Probe
  the Unknown 2 (summer 1974):11,62.

-UFO (R-V)
  1954, Aug?/James C. Beatty/USAF Filter
  Center
    Richard Hall, ed., The UFO Evidence
    (Washington: NICAP, 1964), pp.65-66.

Willsboro
-UFO (NL)
  1956, Aug.15/Mark Berman/Essex Ct.
    "Case 194," CRIFO Orbit, 5 Oct.1956,
    p.1.

Winfield twp.
-Ball lightning
  1894, Sep.9/Mary Fisher
    St. Louis (Mo.) Globe-Democrat, 10
    Sep.1894.

Wolcott
-Erratic crocodilian
  1929, Sep./Ralph Miles
    New York Sun, 23 Sep.1929.

Woodbury
-Acoustic anomaly
  1965, April 5-9/Mrs. John Buttel/40
  Harvard Dr.
    (Editorial), Fate 18 (Sep.1965):14-
    15, quoting Garden City Newsday,
    9 Apr.1965.

Woodstock
-Disappearance
  1974, winter/dogs
    John A. Keel, The Mothman Prophecies
    (N.Y.: Saturday Review, 1975), p.
    115.
-Haunts
    Anita M. Smith, Woodstock History and
    Hearsay (Saugerties, N.Y.: Catskill
    Mountain, 1957), pp.4-6.
-UFOs (CE-1), acoustic anomalies and poltergeist
  1966, spring-summer
    Berthold E. Schwarz, "Woodstock UFO
    Festival, 1966," Flying Saucer Rev.
    19 (Jan.-Feb.1973):3-6; (Mar.-Apr.
    1973):18-23.

Worcester
-Haunt
  n.d.
    Eileen Sonin, More Canadian Ghosts
    (Richmond Hill, Ont.: Pocket Books,
    1974 ed.), pp.20-21.

Yonkers
-Animal ESP
  1930, Nov.11/Ronald S. Rockwell/Brook
  Farm
    Danton Walker, Spooks Deluxe (N.Y.:
    Franklin Watts, 1956), pp.31-35.
-Clairvoyance
  1950, Nov.29/Mrs. William T. Russell
    New York Times, 27 Dec.1950.
-Crisis apparition
  1901, March 23/Katie Cain
    "Apparition," J.ASPR 8 (1914):584-92.
-Erratic crocodilian
  1932, July 1/Crestwood L.

New York Times, 2 July 1932, p.18.
1935, March 7/Joseph Domomico/Grassy
Sprain L.
  New York Times, 8 Mar.1935, p.23.
-Precognition
  1970s/Ingrid Sherman/102 Courter Ave.
    Warren Smith, "Phenomenal Predictions
    for 1976," Saga, Jan.1976, pp.16,52.
-UFO (NL)
  1897, April 30/Harry Folkersamb
    New York Herald, 1 May 1897.
  1954, July 30/Robert Frenhoff
    Harold T. Wilkins, Flying Saucers Un-
    censored (N.Y.: Pyramid, 1967 ed.),
    pp.49-50.
  1955, Aug.28-30/Leo E. Wiegers
    "The Saturnian Affair," CRIFO Orbit,
    6 Apr.1956, pp.1-2.
  1956, June 29-July 3/Leo E. Wiegers
    Yonkers Herald-Statesman, 5 July
    1956.
    "Case 166," CRIFO Orbit, 3 Aug.1956,
    p.1.

Youngstown
-UFO (NL)
  1955, summer/Roger Flint/Fort Niagara
    (Letter), Fate 9 (June 1956):111.

                B. Physical Features

Allegany State Park
-Anomalous quartz formations
    Thunder Rocks, Bear Cave
    Charles Tooker, "Needs Investigating,
    No.2: A Further Report," NEARA
    Newsl. 6 (Mar.1971):13.

Bear Creek
-UFO (?)
  1948, Oct.14
    Rochester Democrat & Chronicle, 14
    Oct.1948.

Bear Mountain State Park
-UFO (DD)
  1966, Dec.18/Vincent Perna/L. Tiorati
    Spring Valley Rockland Community
    News-Leader, 29 Dec.1966. il.
    "AF Rejects N.Y. Photos, NICAP Dis-
    sents," UFO Inv. 4 (May-June 1967):
    5. il.
    J. Allen Hynek, The Hynek UFO Report
    (N.Y.: Dell, 1977), pp.239-44. il.

Bearen I.
-River monster
  1886, Sep.2/Capt. Hitchcock
    New York Sun, 4 Sep.1886, p.4.
    New York Times, 4 Sep.1886, p.3.

Biddle Hollow
-Haunt
  n.d./Lucy Hawkins
    Vinnie Crandall Hicks, "The Ghosts
    of Biddle Hollow," Fate 3 (Nov.
    1950):76-80.

Black River Bay
-Archeological site
    David S. Marvin, "Ancient Works in
    New York," Am.Naturalist 15 (1881):
    489-90.

Catskill Mts.
-Phantom (myth)
    n.d.
        Charles M. Skinner, Myths and Legends
        of Our Own Land, 2 vols. (Philadel-
        phia: Lippincott, 1896), 1:21-22.
    1769, Sep./Rip Van Winkle
        Washington Irving, The Sketchbook of
        Geoffrey Crayon, Gent., Haskell
        Springer, ed. (Boston: Twayne,
        1978 ed.), pp.28-41.
        Charles M. Skinner, Myths and Legends
        of Our Own Land, 2 vols. (Philadel-
        phia: Lippincott, 1896), 1:17-21.
-UFO (CE-2)
    1968, Aug.
        Berthold Eric Schwarz, "Possible
        UFO-Induced Temporary Paralysis,"
        Flying Saucer Rev. 17 (Mar.-Apr.
        1971):4-9.
-UFO (DD)
    1975, summer/Neil Sedaka
        Timothy Green Beckley, "Saucers and
        Celebrities," Saga UFO Rept. 3
        (June 1976):40.

Chautauqua L.
-UFO (NL)
    1958, Aug.11/Fred C. Fair
        Richard Hall, ed., The UFO Evidence
        (Washington: NICAP, 1964), pp.58-59.

Dosoris I.
-Haunt
    18th c.-
        Charles M. Skinner, American Myths
        and Legends, 2 vols. (Philadelphia:
        Lippincott, 1903), 1:157-59.

Dunderberg
-Phantom (myth)
        Charles M. Skinner, Myths and Legends
        of Our Own Land, 2 vols. (Philadel-
        phia: Lippincott, 1896), 1:37-38.
        New York Writers' Program, New York:
        A Guide to the Empire State (N.Y.:
        Oxford Univ., 1956), pp.112-13.

Dutchess Quarry Cave
-Archeological site
        Robert E. Funk, George R. Walters &
        William F. Ehlers, Jr., "The Arch-
        aeology of Dutchess Quarry Cave,
        Orange County, New York," Pennsyl-
        vania Arch. 39 (1969):7-22.
        John E. Guilday, "A Possible Lawton-
        Paleo-Indian Association from Dutch-
        ess Quarry Cave, Orange County, New
        York," Bull.N.Y.State Arch.Ass'n,
        no.45 (1969):24-29.
        Robert E. Funk, George R. Walters &
        William F. Ehlers, Jr., "A Radiocar-
        bon Date for Early Man from the
        Dutchess Quarry cave," Bull.N.Y.

State Arch.Ass'n, no.46 (1969):19-
21.

Eagle Neck
-Ancient inscription
    ca.1888
        Daniel G. Brinton, "Long Island Tab-
        let," Archaeologist 1 (1893):201.
        il.
        Edmund Burke Delabarre, Dighton Rock
        (N.Y.: Walter Neale, 1928), pp.259-
        60. il.
        Barry Fell, America B.C. (N.Y.: Quad-
        rangle, 1976), pp.270-72. il.

Eastchester Bay
-Precognition
    1961, Jan.6/Eleanore Weissman
        Eleanore Weissman & Pauline Kappell-
        Prilucik, "Miracle of the Ice
        Cubes," Fate 14 (June 1961):71-74.

Eaton's Neck Point
-Sea monster
    1887, July/M.B. Smith
        New York Times, 28 July 1887, p.8.

Erie, L.
-Mystery shipwreck
    1950, Dec.18/"Sachem"
        Cleveland (O.) Plain Dealer, 19 Dec.
        1950.
        Jay Gourley, The Great Lakes Triangle
        (Greenwich, Ct.: Fawcett, 1977),
        pp.49-52.

Florence I.
-Fall of ice
    1901, Aug.8/H.S. Chandler
        "Hailstorm on the St. Lawrence,"
        Monthly Weather Rev. 29 (Nov.1901):
        506-507.

Gardiners I.
-UFO (?)
    1966, fall
        John A. Keel, "North America 1966:
        Development of a Great Wave," Fly-
        ing Saucer Rev. 13 (Mar.-Apr.1966):
        3,5.
-UFO (NL)
    1967, Jan.20
        John A. Keel, "North America 1966:
        Development of a Great Wave," Fly-
        ing Saucer Rev. 13 (Mar.-Apr.1966):
        3,6.

George, L.
-Lake monster
    1900s/=hoax
        Curtis D. MacDougall, Hoaxes (N.Y.:
        Dover, 1958 ed.), p.14.
-UFO (DD)
    1969
        Albany Knickerbocker News, 3 Mar.
        1969, p.5B.

Goodyear L.
-UFO (CE-1)
    1969, Jan.1/Debbie Monser

"U.S. Roundup," APRO Bull. 17 (Mar.-
Apr.1969):6.

Grand I.
-Sheep mutilations
   1943, April 10
   "Killer Dogs," Fortean Soc'y Mag.,
   no.9 (spring 1944):4.

Hampton Beach
-Sea monster
   1831
   Bernard Heuvelmans, In the Wake of
   the Sea-Serpents (N.Y.: Hill & Wang,
   1968), p.175.

Hawks Nest Mt.
-Ancient standing stones
   James M. Allerton, Hawks Nest, or
   the Last of the Cahoonshees (Port
   Jervis: Gazette Book & Job Print,
   1892), pp.5-6.
   Port Jervis Union-Gazette, 31 May
   1975, p.3.
   Salvatore Michael Trento, The Search
   for Lost America (Chicago: Contemporary, 1978), pp.77-82. il.

Heckscher State Park
-Precognition
   1962, Aug./Rosemarie Finger
   (Editorial), Fate 15 (Dec.1962):18-
   20.

Hither Hills State Park
-UFO (NL)
   1966, May 14/Curtis Tiedt
   East Hampton Star, 19 May 1966.

Hudson R.
-Giant bird
   1961, May
   "Thunderbirds Again--And Again," Pursuit 5 (Apr.1972):40-41, quoting
   Saga, May 1963.
-Norse discovery
   1009/Thorfinn Karlsefni/=Hóp?
   G.M. Gathorne-Hardy, The Norse Dis-
   coverers of America (Oxford: Clarendon, 1921), pp.275-81.
   1009/Thorfinn Karlsefni/=Straumfjord?
   Frederick J. Pohl, Atlantic Crossings
   Before Columbus (N.Y.: W.W. Norton,
   1961), pp.139-43.
   Charles Michael Boland, They All Discovered America (N.Y.: Pocket Books,
   1963 ed.), pp.256-57.
   Frederick J. Pohl, The Viking Settle-
   ments of North America (N.Y.: Clarkson N. Potter, 1972), pp.87-92,125-
   28.
-Phantom ship
   17th-19th c.
   Washington Irving, Bracebridge Hall
   (1822), "The Storm Ship" chapter.
   Charles M. Skinner, Myths and Legends
   of Our Own Land, 2 vols. (Philadelphia: Lippincott, 1896), 1:49-50.
-Weather control
   19th c.

Charles M. Skinner, Myths and Legends
of Our Own Land, 2 vols. (Philadelphia: Lippincott, 1896), 1:233.

Hyenga L.
-Flying humanoid
   1900s
   James F. McCloy & Ray Miller, Jr.,
   The Jersey Devil (Wallingford, Pa.:
   Middle Atlantic, 1976), p.35.

Indian Point
-Mystery steel object
   1965, Feb.5/nuclear power station
   "Mystery Object Jams Indian Point
   Control Rod," Nucleonics 23 (May
   1965):90. il.

Jones Beach State Park
-Sea monster
   1888, June 3/M.A. Russell
   New York Times, 9 June 1888, p.9.

Lake of the Woods
-Lake monster
   1929
   Ivan T. Sanderson, Things (N.Y.: Pyramid, 1966), pp.31-32.

Lamoka L.
-Archeological site
   ca.2500 B.C.
   William A. Ritchie, "The Lamoka Lake
   Site," Researches & Trans.N.Y.State
   Arch.Ass'n, vol.7, no.4 (1932).
   William A. Ritchie, The Archaeology
   of New York State (Garden City:
   Natural History Press, 1969), pp.36-
   83. il.

Letchworth State Park
-UFO (NL)
   1966, Aug.30/John A. Keel
   John A. Keel, "North America 1966:
   Development of a Great Wave," Flying Saucer Rev. 13 (Mar.-Apr.1966):
   3,9.

Long I.
-Contactee
   1967, June/Princess Moon Owl
   John A. Keel, The Mothman Prophecies
   (N.Y.: Saturday Review, 1975), pp.
   207-208,227.
-Expanding light bulb
   1973, Nov.-Dec.
   Garden City Newsday, 6 Dec.1973.
   "An Expanding Light Bulb," Pursuit
   7 (Jan.1974):9-10.
   "Department of Loose Ends," Pursuit
   7 (July 1974):75.
-Fall of mud
   1953, April 25
   "Falls," Doubt, no.41 (1953):221,222.
-Men-in-black
   1967, May
   John A. Keel, The Mothman Prophecies
   (N.Y.: Saturday Review, 1975), p.
   159.
-Mystery stench

1967, June/S shore
   John A. Keel, "Mysterious Gas Attacks
   by Flying Saucers," Saga UFO Rept.
   2 (fall 1975):27.
-Phantom
   1966, spring
      John A. Keel, UFOs: Operation Trojan
      Horse (N.Y.: Putnam, 1970), p.231.
-Phantom airplane
   1957
      John A. Keel, UFOs: Operation Trojan
      Horse (N.Y.: Putnam, 1970), p.124.
-Sea monster
   1819, Dec.17/"Sally"/=hoax?
      Bernard Heuvelmans, In the Wake of
      the Sea-Serpents (N.Y.: Hill & Wang,
      1968), p.170. il.
-Telephone anomaly
   ca.1962/Don Estrella
      John A. Keel, The Mothman Prophecies
      (N.Y.: Saturday Review, 1975), p.
      106.
-UFO (?)
   1909, Sep.8/William Leech
      John A. Keel, UFOs: Operation Trojan
      Horse (N.Y.: Putnam, 1970), p.112.
-UFO (CE-2)
   1966, March 30
      "Typical Reports," UFO Inv. 3 (Mar.-
      Apr.1966):8.
-UFO (CE-3)
   1967, spring
      John A. Keel, The Mothman Prophecies
      (N.Y.: Saturday Review, 1975), p.
      119.
-UFO (DD)
   1965, Aug.9
      J. Allen Hynek, The UFO Experience
      (Chicago: Regnery, 1972), pp.66-67.
-Water anomaly
   ca.1950
      "Polyponds," Pursuit 3 (Jan.1970):12-
      13.

Long Island Sound
-Norse discovery
   1009/Thorfinn Karlsefni/=Straumfjord?
      G.M. Gathorne-Hardy, The Norse Dis-
      coverers of America (Oxford: Clar-
      endon, 1921), pp.271-75.
-Sea monster
   1878, Sep.1/Mr. Kelly
      New York Times, 5 Sep.1878, p.5.

Long Sault I.
-Archeological site
   ca.300 B.C.
      William A. Ritchie, "Culture Influ-
      ences from Ohio in New York Archaeol-
      ogy," Am.Antiquity 2 (1937):182-94.
      William A. Ritchie & Don W. Dragoo,
      "The Eastern Dispersal of Adena,"
      Am.Antiquity 25 (1959):43-50.

Misery, Mt.
-Contactee
   1967, May-Dec.
      John A. Keel, The Mothman Prophecies
      (N.Y.: Saturday Review, 1975), pp.
      201-206,211,213-14,221-22,224,236.

-Humanoid
   1966-1969
   1969, Jan.12/Jaye P. Paro
      John A. Keel, Strange Creatures from
      Time and Space (Greenwich, Ct.:
      Fawcett, 1970), pp.96-97, quoting
      Beyond, July 1969.
-Men-in-black
   1967, April
   1967, June 21/Jaye P. Paro
   1967, Sep.30
      John A. Keel, The Mothman Prophecies
      (N.Y.: Saturday Review, 1975), pp.
      201,211,230.

Mohegan L.
-Humanoid
   1977, Dec.20/Joe Guisti
      New York Sunday News, 8 Jan.1978.
      Nat'l Star, 24 Jan.1978, p.24.

Muskeeta Cave
-Archeological site
      Bert Salwen, "Muskeeta Cave 2: A
      Stratified Woodland Site on Long
      Island," Am.Antiquity 33 (1968):
      322-40. il.

Nantucket Point
-UFO (NL)
   1963, Jan.5/Mr. Cherrington
      J. Allen Hynek, The Hynek UFO Report
      (N.Y.: Dell, 1977), pp.45-46.

Nine Cornered L.
-Haunt
   n.d.
      David J. Winslow, "The Ghosts of
      Nine Cornered Lake," New York Folk-
      lore Quar. 16 (1960):27-30.

Norwalk Islands
-Sea monster
   1877, Sep./=hoax
      New York Times, 14 Sep.1877, p.3.

Oneida L.
-Ghost light
   n.d.
      Charles M. Skinner, Myths and Legends
      of Our Own Land, 2 vols. (Philadel-
      phia: Lippincott, 1896), 2:288.

Onondaga L.
-Erratic sargassum fish
   1890s
      H.M. Smith, "Marine Animals in Inter-
      ior Waters," Science 17 (1903):114.
-Erratic seal
   1882, April 28/George F. Kennedy
      Syracuse Standard, 29 Apr.1882.
      New York Times, 2 May 1882, p.8.
-Erratic squid
   1902, Dec./Mr. Terry
      John M. Clarke, "The Squids from On-
      ondaga Lake, N.Y.," Science 16
      (1902):947.
      A.E. Ortmann, "Illex Illecebrosus
      (Lesueur), the 'Squid from Onondaga
      Lake, N.Y.," Science 17 (1903):30-31.

-Lake monster myth
  Mosqueto
    David Cusick, Sketches of Ancient
    History of the Six Nations (Lewis-
    ton, N.Y.: The Author, 1827).
-UFO legend
  Hiawatha
    Henry R. Schoolcraft, Information Re-
    specting the History, Condition and
    Prospects of the Indian Tribes of
    the United States, 6 vols. (Phila-
    delphia: Lippincott, Grambo, 1851-
    57), 3:315-17.

Ontario, L.
-Lake monster
  ca.1835
    "Miscellen," Notizen Gebiete Natur-
    und Heilkunde, Aug.1835.
-Lake monster myth
    David Cusick, Sketches of Ancient
    History of the Six Nations (Lewis-
    ton, N.Y.: The Author, 1827).

Pharaoh, Mt.
-Ancient cavern and lost treasure
  1840s/Peter Johnson
    Eric Norman, Buried Treasure Guide
    (N.Y.: Award, 1970), pp.45-49.

Placid, L.
-Midday darkness
  1881, Sep.6/=forest fire
    New York Times, 8 Sep.1881, p.3.

Pleasant, L.
-UFO (DD)
  1969, Sep.22/John O'Connell
    Albany Knickerbocker News, 23 Sep.
    1969, p.8C.

Port Mobil
-Archeological site
    Herbert C. Kraft, "The Paleo-Indian
    Sites at Port Mobil, Staten Island,"
    Researches & Trans.N.Y.State Arch.
    Ass'n 17 (1977):1-19. il.

Ramapo R.
-Phantom (myth)
  17th c.
    Charles M. Skinner, Myths and Legends
    of Our Own Land, 2 vols. (Philadel-
    phia: Lippincott, 1896), 1:53-56.

Rocky Point
-Sea monster
  1878, Aug./J.H. Merritt
    New York Times, 8 Aug.1878, p.8.
-Skyquake
  1952, Oct.3
    Garden City Newsday, 4 Oct.1952.

Rondout Creek
-Fall of ancient sword
  1883, April 17/T.O. Keator/=hoax
    New York Times, 17 June 1883, p.10.

Round I.
-River monster

1888, July 19/C.W. Sikes
    New York Times, 22 July 1888, p.1.

Rye Point
-Sea monster
  1817, Oct.3/James Guion
  1817, Oct.5/Thomas Herttell
    New York Columbian, 15 Oct.1817.
    Reports of a Committee of the Linn-
    aean Society of New England Rela-
    tive to a Large Marine Animal, Sup-
    posed to Be a Sea-Serpent Seen near
    Cape Ann, Massachusetts, in August
    1817 (Boston: The Society, 1817).

Saratoga L.
-UFO (DD)
  1969, Sep.22
    Albany Knickerbocker News, 23 Sep.
    1969, p.8C.

Seneca L.
-Skyquakes
  prehistory-
    "The 'Guns' of Lake Seneca, N.Y.,"
    Monthly Weather Rev. 31 (July 1903)
    :336.
    Kansas City (Mo.) Times, 24 Dec.
    1974, p.7A.
    William R. Corliss, ed., Strange
    Phenomena (Glen Arm, Md.: The Au-
    thor, 1974), vol.G1, pp.218-19.
-UFO (?)
  1952, Aug.26
    Buffalo Evening News, 26 Aug.1952.

Shark River Inlet
-Sea monster
  1885, July 15/Mr. Smith
    New York Times, 19 July 1885, p.3.

Shawangunk Mt.
-Ancient roads
    Philip Smith, Legends of the Shawan-
    gunk (Shon-Gum) and Its Environs
    (Pawling, N.Y.: Smith, 1887).
    Charles Gilbert Hine, The Old Mine
    Road (New Brunswick, N.J.: Rutgers
    Univ., 1963 ed.).
    Salvatore Michael Trento, The Search
    for Lost America (Chicago: Contem-
    porary, 1978), pp.87-89.
-Ancient stone cairns
    Salvatore Michael Trento, The Search
    for Lost America (Chicago: Contem-
    porary, 1978), pp.42,91-92.

Shinnecock Inlet
-Mystery plane crash
  1955, Aug.26/Paul Kane/Thunderflash
    "Case 109," CRIFO Orbit, 4 Nov.1955,
    p.3.

Silver L.
-Lake monster
  1855, July 13-Sep./=hoax
    Wyoming County Times, 18 July 1855;
    25 July 1855; and 1 Aug.1855.
    Frank D. Roberts, History of the
    Town of Perry, N.Y. (Perry, N.Y.:

C.G. Clarke, 1915).
Herbert J. Hawley, "The Sea Serpent of Silver Lake," New York Folklore Quar. 2 (1945):191-96.
Harry S. Douglas, "The Legend of the Serpent," New York Folklore Quar. 12 (1956):37-42.
John A. Keel, Strange Creatures from Time and Space (Greenwich, Ct.: Fawcett, 1970), pp.254-61.
Los Angeles (Cal.) Times, 5 Sep.1976.

Skaneateles L.
-Fall of stones
1973, Oct.27/John Cazzola
Syracuse Herald-Journal, 29 Oct.1973.
Syracuse Post-Standard,29 Oct.1973;
and 3 Nov.1973.
"The Skaneateles (New York) Stones," INFO J., no.14 (Nov.1974):24-26.
-UFO (DD)
1964, April 11/Warren B. Ochsner/S end
Thomas M. Olsen, ed., The Reference for Outstanding UFO Sighting Reports (Riderwood, Md.: UFO Information Retrieval Center, 1966), pp.89-92.

Sodus Bay
-Norse spearhead
1929
James Watson Curran, Here Was Vinland (Sault Sainte Marie, Ont.: Sault Daily Star, 1939), pp.294-98.
Rochester Democrat & Chronicle, 19 Apr.1970.
Charles A. Huguenin, "The Sodus Bay Spearhead," NEARA Newsl. 5 (Sep. 1970):65. il.

Storm King Mt.
-Ghost light
n.d.
James Reynolds, Ghosts in American Houses (N.Y.: Paperback Library, 1967 ed.), pp.94-95.

Tappan Zee
-Erratic swan
1944, Dec.19/George Cline
New York Times, 20 Dec.1944, p.25.
-Phantom ship
n.d.
Charles M. Skinner, Myths and Legends of Our Own Land, 2 vols. (Philadelphia: Lippincott, 1896), 1:50.
New York Writers' Program, New York: A Guide to the Empire State (N.Y.: Oxford Univ., 1956), p.112.
-UFO (NL)
1966, April/Gale Brownlee/Tappan Zee Bridge
Kingston Daily Freeman, 23 Apr.1966.

Thioughnioga R.
-Clairvoyance
1938, March/William Knapp
"Dream of a Drowning," Fate 7 (Dec. 1954):35.

Titicus Reservoir
-UFO (CE-1)
1955, Sep.17/Frank Bordes
Paul Gray, "The Mystery of Titicus Reservoir," Flying Saucer Rev. 1 (Nov.-Dec.1955):21.
(Editorial), Civilian Saucer Intelligence Pub., no.20 (25 July 1957): 21.

Trinity L.
-UFO (CE-2)
1975, Aug.1/Brad Condon
"UFO Submerged in N.Y. Lake," APRO Bull. 24 (May 1976):1,3.

Tug Hill
-Giant human skeleton
H.E. Krueger, "The Lesser Wilderness: Tug Hill," Conservationist 21 (Dec.-Jan.1966-67):12-16,38.
H.E. Krueger, "Tug Hill: A Place and a Legend," Conservationist 21 (Feb.-Mar.1967):18-22.
W. Mead Stapler, "A Mystery in History," North Jersey Highlander, spring 1973.

Van Hoevenberg, Mt.
-Haunt
n.d./Henry van Hoevenberg
George Wagner, "Lost Caves: Secret Saucer Bases?" Saga UFO Rept. 3 (Oct.1976):35,58.

Wading R.
-River monster
1936, July
Curtis D. MacDougall, Hoaxes (N.Y.: Dover, 1958 ed.), p.14.

Wappinger Creek
-Ancient inscription
1976, summer
Salvatore Michael Trento, The Search for Lost America (Chicago: Contempory, 1978), pp.108-109.

C. Ethnic Groups

Mohawk Indians
-Lake monster myth
Onyare
Albert S. Gatschet, "Water-Monsters of the American Aborigines," J.Am. Folklore 12 (1899):255-60.

Onondaga Indians
-Humanoid myth
Stone Giants
Buffalo Express, 2 Aug.1870.
Hartley Burr Alexander, North American Mythology (Boston: Marshall Jones, 1916), p.29.
Marvin A. Rapp, "Legend of the Stone Giants," New York Folklore Quar. 12 (1956):280-82.
-Phantom (myth)
Charles M. Skinner, American Myths

and Legends, 2 vols. (Philadelphia:
Lippincott, 1903), 1:195-97.

D. Unspecified Localities

-Haunt
  1964, Dec.-1967, April/Parker Keegan/
  Hwy.14
    Hans Holzer, Gothic Ghosts (N.Y.:
    Pocket Books, 1972), pp.9-18.

-Phantom
  1970s/New York State Thruway
    (Editorial), Fate 27 (Nov.1974):8-12.

-Precognition
  1944/Edward R. Dobson
    Sally Remaley, "Is Psychically Fore-
    warned Always Forearmed?" Fate 24
    (Sep.1971):81-83.
  1965-   /Daniel Logan
    Daniel Logan, The Reluctant Prophet
    (Garden City: Doubleday, 1968).
    John Godwin, Occult America (Garden
    City: Doubleday, 1972), pp.41-43.
    Daniel Logan, The Anatomy of Prophecy
    (Englewood Cliffs, N.J.: Prentice-
    Hall, 1975).

ONTARIO

A. Populated Places

Acton
-Entombed toad
  1893/Brown & Hall sawmill
    Henry Winfred Splitter, "The Impos-
    sible Fossils," Fate 7 (Jan.1954):
    65,71.

Ajax
-Haunt
  n.d.
    Eileen Sonin, More Canadian Ghosts
    (Richmond Hill, Ont.: Pocket Books,
    1974 ed.), pp.18,33-35.
-Mystery plane crash
  1954, Aug.23/CF-101 interceptor
    Jay Gourley, The Great Lakes Triangle
    (Greenwich, Ct.: Fawcett, 1977),
    p.31.
-UFO (CE-1)
  1978, March
    Hugh Cochrane, "The Great Lakes UFO
    Flap of 1978," Saga UFO Rept. 6
    (Jan.1979):21,23.

Alexandria
-UFO (NL)
  1974, July 15/John Van Nooten/Glen Robertson
    Alexandria Glengarry News, 18 July
    1974.

Alfred
-Flying cat
  1966, June 24/Jean J. Revers/wings=
  matted hair
    Alfred Le Carilon, 30 June 1966, p.
    1; and 8 Aug.1966. il.
    John A. Keel, Strange Creatures from
    Time and Space (Greenwich, Ct.: Faw-
    cett, 1970), pp.40-41.
    X, "Vampire Cats," Pursuit 9 (fall
    1976):93.
-UFO (CE-3)
  1973, July 29/Hwy.17
    Wido Hoville & Don Donderi, "Close
    Encounter near Ottawa," Can.UFO
    Rept., no.32 (fall 1978):7-8.
-UFO (NL)
  1952, May 1
    Ottawa Journal, 2 May 1952; and 10
    May 1952.

Alliston
-UFO (NL)
  1967, Nov.21/Paul Kendrick
    "On the Canadian Scene," APRO Bull.
    16 (Mar.-Apr.1968):4,5.

Ancaster
-UFO (NL)
  1973, Oct.21/Mary Marrin/Dundas Golf
  Club

Hamilton Spectator, 29 Oct.1973.

Arden
-UFO (NL)
  1969, May 7/Frank Harder
    "Around the Globe," APRO Bull. 18
    (July-Aug.1969):7,8.

Arnprior
-UFO (CE-1)
  1965, Oct.21/George McLean
    Jerome Clark, "The Greatest Flap Yet?
    Part IV," Flying Saucer Rev. 12
    (Nov.-Dec.1966):9.

Aurora
-UFO (CE-2)
  1978, July 2/high school/ground markings only
    "UFOs," Res Bureaux Bull., no.38 (7
    Sep.1978):2,3.
-UFO (DD)
  1977, April 17/Charles Wilkinson
    Aurora Banner, 20 Apr.1977; and 4
    May 1977.

Baldwin
-UFO (CE-2)
  1974, Oct.25/Pete Dmitrovic/ground
  markings only
    Uxbridge Times Journal, 30 Oct.1974.

Ballantrae
-UFO (CE-2)
  1964, June/Claus Slade/ground markings
  only
    "Another Canadian Circle," Skylook,
    no.26 (Jan.1970):14.
    Ted Phillips, Physical Traces Associ-
    ated with UFO Sightings (Evanston:
    Center for UFO Studies, 1975), p.29.

Balm Beach
-UFO (?)
  1966, Aug.
    Hamilton Spectator, 19 Oct.1973.

Bancroft
-Ghost
  n.d.
  1951, June
    Eileen Sonin, More Canadian Ghosts
    (Richmond Hill, Ont.: Pocket Books,
    1974 ed.), pp.88-91.

Barrie
-Archeological site
    Frank Ridley, "The Boys and Barrie
    Sites," Ontario Arch. 4 (1958):18-
    39. il.
-Disease anomaly
  1957
    John A. Keel, "Mysterious Gas Attacks
    by Flying Saucers," Saga UFO Rept. 2

(fall 1975):27,30.
-Haunt
  1968
    Eileen Sonin, More Canadian Ghosts
    (Richmond Hill, Ont.: Pocket Books,
    1974 ed.), pp.81-82.
-Mystery auto accidents
  1954/Marlene Holmes
    (Editorial), Fate 8 (Feb.1955):13-14.
-UFO (NL)
  1967, Nov.21/Ed Ziliotto/L. Simcoe
    "On the Canadian Scene," APRO Bull.
    16 (Jan.-Feb.1968):4,5.
  1979, Jan.5
    Barrie Examiner, 5 Jan.1979.

Barwick
-Clairvoyance
  1906/Herbert H. Wilkins
    (Letter), Fate 12 (Feb.1959):111-13.

Beachville
-UFO (NL)
  1973, Oct.21-23/Elizabeth Deadman
    Woodstock-Ingersoll Sentinel-Review,
    24 Oct.1973.

Beardmore
-Norse sword and ax
  1931, May 24/James Edward Dodd
    Winnipeg (Man.) Free Press, 27 Jan.
    1938.
    C.T. Currelly, "Viking Weapons Found
    near Beardmore, Ontario," Can.Hist.
    Rev. 20 (1939):4-7.
    O.C. Elliott, "The Case of the Beard-
    more Relics," Can.Hist.Rev. 22
    (1941):254-71, 275-79.
    C.T. Currelly, "Further Comments Re-
    garding the Beardmore Finds," Can.
    Hist.Rev. 22 (1941):271-75.
    Albert O. Hayes, "Reserving Judgment,"
    Bull.Arch.Soc'y New Jersey, no.7
    (1942):8-11.
    Johannes Brøndsted, "Norsemen in
    North America before Columbus," Ann.
    Rept.Smith.Inst. 103 (1953):367,
    377-82. il.
    Toronto Globe & Mail, 23 Nov.1956.
    A.D. Tushingham, The Beardmore Rel-
    ics: Hoax or History? (Toronto:
    Royal Ontario Mus., 1966). il.

Bedley
-UFO (NL)
  1974, Nov.11/Mrs. L. Lanchner
    Timothy Green Beckley, "Operation
    Contact," Saga UFO Rept. 3 (Apr.
    1976):39,62.

Belleville
-Haunt
  1960s/Mrs. John Palmer/16 mi.E on Ticonderoga Reserve
    (Editorial), Fate 17 (June 1964):21-
    22.
    Sheila Hervey, Some Canadian Ghosts
    (Richmond Hill, Ont.: Pocket Books,
    1973), pp.71-72.

Bells Corners
-UFO (CE-3)
  1958, Aug.18/Mrs. Couturier
    W.B. Smith & J.R. Buchanan, "The
    Bells Corner Mystery," Topside,
    June 1960, pp.3-4.
-UFO (NL)
  1952, July 17
    Marc Leduc, "Notes sur le projet
    'Magnet,'" UFO-Québec, no.4 (1975):
    12,15.

Bensfort Corners
-UFO (NL)
  1970, Aug.5/Griffin Pink/Otonabee R.
    Peterborough Examiner, 7 Aug.1970.

Blair
-Stratigraphic anomaly
    Douglas E. Cox, "Pillars, Polystrate
    Formations, and Potholes," Creation
    Rsch.Soc'y Quar. 14 (Dec.1977):149-
    55.

Bobcaygeon
-UFO (CE-2)
  1974, Dec.12/James Todd/Hwy.35
    Toronto Star, 12 Dec.1974.
    Timothy Green Beckley, "Operation
    Contact," Saga UFO Rept. 3 (Apr.
    1976):39,64.

Bolton
-Telepathy
  1953, July 15/Elmer Ferguson
    (Editorial), Fate 6 (Nov.1953):10.

Borden CFB
-UFO (NL)
  1978, May 1
    "Other UFOs," Res Bureaux Bull., no.
    35 (15 June 1978):3,4.

Boston Creek
-UFO (CE-2)
  1954, Aug.27/Bill Supa
    Harold T. Wilkins, Flying Saucers Un-
    censored (N.Y.: Pyramid, 1967 ed.),
    p.227, quoting Toronto newspaper
    (undated).

Bowmanville
-UFO (NL)
  1973, Nov.2/Fred Hirschfelds/Hwy.2 nr.
  Maple Grove
    Oshawa Times, 3 Nov.1973.

Bracebridge
-Psychokinesis
  n.d./Mrs. Matthews
    Eileen Sonin, More Canadian Ghosts
    (Richmond Hill, Ont.: Pocket Books,
    1974 ed.), pp.51-52.

Brampton
-Fall of ice
  1955, July 16
    Philadelphia (Pa.) Inquirer, 16 July
    1955.

Brantford
-Ancient bronze ax
 1907
    M.R. Harrington, "A Norse Bronze Im-
    plement from Canada," Indian Notes
    3 (1926):288-93. il.
    M.R. Harrington, "The Age of the
    Norse Bronze Implement from Canada,"
    Indian Notes 4 (1927):281-83.
-Fall of unknown substance
 1954, April 23
    "'Safety' Glass," Doubt, no.45
    (1954):293,294.
-Haunt
 1942/Margaret Baird/St. Luke's Angli-
 can Church
    Eileen Sonin, More Canadian Ghosts
    (Richmond Hill, Ont.: Pocket Books,
    1974 ed.), pp.113-14.
-Hex
 1977/Alma Greene
    Charles McArthur, "Heap Big Trouble
    for Totem Makers," Fate 30 (Oct.
    1977):79.
-Mystery oil spill
 1974
    Niagara Falls Review, 23 June 1978,
    p.3.
-UFO (CE-1)
 1976, Jan.12/Ed Morrison/Bell St.
    "Un homme rapporte avoir vu un OVNI,"
    UFO-Québec, no.6 (1976):6.
-UFO (CE-2)
 1966, Feb.15-17/David Brock
    Toronto Telegram, 29 Mar.1966, p.1.
    il.
 1975, July 6
    "UFO Central," CUFOS News Bull., 15
    Nov.1975, p.13.
-UFO (NL)
 1972, July 27
    "Press Reports," APRO Bull. 21 (July-
    Aug.1972):8.

Brechin
-Ghost light
 ca.1900-1952/L. Simcoe
    Toronto Globe & Mail, 5 Sep.1952.

Brent
-Meteorite crater
 4000 m.diam. x 455 m.deep/certain
    C.S. Beals, G.M. Ferguson & A. Landau,
    "The Holleford Crater in Ontario,"
    Sky & Telescope 15 (May 1956):296.
    C.S. Beals, "Fossil Meteorite Cra-
    ters," Sci.Am. 199 (July 1958):33-
    39.
    Peter M. Millman, et al., "The Brent
    Crater," Pub.Dominion Observatory,
    Ottawa, vol.24, no.1 (1960).
    J.B. Hartung, et al., "Potassium-
    Argon Dating of Shock Metamorphosed
    Rocks from the Brent Impact Crater,
    Ontario, Canada," J.Geophys.Rsch.
    76 (1971):5437-48.
    G.P. Lozej & F.W. Beales, "The Un-
    metamorphosed Sedimentary Fill of
    the Brent Meteorite Crater, South-
    eastern Ontario," Can.J.Earth Sci.

12 (1975):606-28.

Brighton
-UFO (DD)
 1954, Oct.7/A.H. Duncan
    (Letter), Fate 8 (May 1955):112-14.

Britt
-Precognition
 1956, Aug./Louise S. Lotz
    Laura A. Dale, Rhea White & Gardner
    Murphy, "A Selection of Cases from
    a Recent Survey of Spontaneous ESP
    Phenomena," J.ASPR 56 (1962):3,34-
    36.

Brockville
-Ghost
 1931/Mrs. A.G.M. Mainwaring/Alban's
 Point
    Sheila Hervey, Some Canadian Ghosts
    (Richmond Hill, Ont.: Pocket Books,
    1973), pp.124-27.
-Haunt
 1930s-
    Sheila Hervey, Some Canadian Ghosts
    (Richmond Hill, Ont.: Pocket Books,
    1973), pp.116-19, quoting Weekend
    Mag., 1972.
-Precognition
 1959, July 7/Madeleine Andress
    "A Glimpse of the Future," Fate 13
    (Apr.1960):94.
    Allen Spraggett, The Unexplained
    (N.Y.: Signet, 1968 ed.), pp.46-47.
-Skyquake
 1978, Nov.9/Long Beach
    Brockville Recorder & Times, 10 Nov.
    1978.
-UFO (NL)
 1915, Feb.14
    New York Times, 15 Feb.1915, p.1.

Brown Hill
-Mystery plane crash
 1960, June 5/Kenneth Charles McIntosh/
 Champion 7EC
    Jay Gourley, The Great Lakes Triangle
    (Greenwich, Ct.: Fawcett, 1977), p.
    73.

Burgessville
-Poltergeist
 1935, Jan./James Quinn
    R.S. Lambert, Exploring the Supernat-
    ural (Toronto: McClelland & Stewart,
    1955), pp.140-42, quoting Toronto
    Mail & Empire and Toronto Star (un-
    dated).

Burlington
-Skyquake
 1977-1978, March
    Hamilton Spectator, 7-8 Mar.1978.

Buttonville
-Haunt
 1969, Aug.-1972, April/Pamela Ball
    Sheila Hervey, Some Canadian Ghosts
    (Richmond Hill, Ont.: Pocket Books,

1973), pp.4-11.

Caledon East
-UFO (CE-1)
    1958, Oct.31
    Jacques Vallee, Passport to Magonia
    (Chicago: Regnery, 1969), pp.272-73.

Caledonia
-UFO (CE-3) and Men-in-black
    1967, June 13/Carmen Cuneo
    "June Sighting of Occupants in Can-
    ada," APRO Bull. 16 (Nov.-Dec.1967):
    4.
    Lawrence J. Fenwick, "Mysteries Fol-
    low Landing," Can.UFO Rept., no.27
    (spring 1977):8-12.

Cambridge
-Erratic crocodilian
    1929, June 17
    New York Times, 19 June 1929, p.24.
-Rock pillars
    Douglas E. Cox, "Pillars, Polystrate
    Formations, and Potholes," Creation
    Rsch.Soc'y Quar. 14 (Dec.1977):149-
    55.
-UFO (?)
    1979, Jan.19/=aircraft?
    "Recent UFO Reports," Res Bureaux
    Bull., no.44 (Feb.1979):4.
-UFO (CE-1)
    1957, Aug.14/Colleen Weller/King St.
    Galt Evening Reporter, 15 Aug.1957.
-UFO (CE-2)
    1957, July 30/Jack Stephens/Galt
    "'Monster' Theory Discarded in UFO
    Landing Case Witnessed in Galt, On-
    tario, Canada," UFO Inv. 1 (Aug.-
    Sep.1957):8.
    Gray Barker, "Chasing the Flying Sau-
    cers," Flying Saucers, Feb.1958, pp.
    46,48-49,61. il.
    Harlan Wilson, "The Saucer That Made
    Tracks," Fate 11 (Feb.1958):44-47.
    Ted Phillips, Physical Traces Associ-
    ated with UFO Sightings (Evanston:
    Center for UFO Studies, 1975), p.20,
    quoting Galt Reporter (undated).
-UFO (NL)
    1972, Aug./Galt
    Glenn McWane & David Graham, The New
    UFO Sightings (N.Y.: Warner, 1974),
    p.56.
    1976, Jan.1
    Cambridge Daily Reporter, 2 Jan.1976.
    1979, Jan.10/Preston
    1979, Jan.12
    "Recent UFO Reports," Res Bureaux
    Bull., no.44 (Feb.1979):4.

Campbellville
-Rock pillar
    Douglas E. Cox, "Pillars, Polystrate
    Formations, and Potholes," Creation
    Rsch.Soc'y Quar. 14 (Dec.1977):149-
    55.

Campden
-Humanoid

1965, Aug./Wayne Beach
    Beamsville Express, 25 Aug.1965; and
    28 Aug.1965.

Cannifton
-Fall of glass
    1968, Nov./Wesley Reid
    Belleville Intelligencer, 11 Nov.
    1968.

Carlisle
-UFO (CE-1)
    1967, Oct.28/Eddie Hewitson/Alderson
    Rd.
    "On the Canadian Scene," APRO Bull.
    16 (Jan.-Feb.1968):4.

Cedar Valley
-UFO (NL)
    1974, July 28/Marion Duncan
    Erin Advocate, 7 Aug.1974.

Chapleau.
-Fall of frogs
    1924-1929/Jean D. Byers
    (Letter), Fate 14 (Jan.1961):122,129.

Cherry Valley
-Haunt
    1930s/Wilfred Ashcroft
    Eileen Sonin, More Canadian Ghosts
    (Richmond Hill, Ont.: Pocket Books,
    1974 ed.), pp.57-58.

Chesterville
-UFO (CE-1)
    1965, July 20/Ronnie Servage
    "Record Year for New UFO Evidence,"
    UFO Inv. 3 (Nov.-Dec.1965):2.

Chippawa
-UFO (NL)
    1973, Nov.3/Sandra Burtch/Willoughby
    Dr.
    Welland-Port Colborne Tribune, 5
    Nov.1973.

Clarkson
-UFO (NL)
    1966, June 1/Richard H. Plewman/L. On-
    tario
    "New Reports by Space Experts Add to
    UFO Proof," UFO Inv. 3 (Aug.-Sep.
    1966):3,5.

Cobalt
-Humanoid
    1906, Sep./Violet Mine
    1923, July/J.A. MacAuley/NE of Wett-
    laufer Mine
    1946, April/nr. Gillies L.
    1970, Aug./Aimee Latreille/Cobalt Lode
    John Green, Sasquatch: The Apes Among
    Us (Seattle: Hancock House, 1978),
    pp.248-50, quoting North Bay Nugget
    (undated).
-UFO (CE-1)
    1954, Dec.27/Willis St. Jean/Agaunica
    Mine
    Morris Woodley, "The Gyrating UFO of

Cobalt," Fate 8 (Aug.1955):34-35.
-UFO (CE-2)
1957, Dec.3
North Bay Nugget, 4 Dec.1957.

Cobden
-UFO (NL)
1931, Jan.1/J. Stewart Childerhose/
Muskrat L.
Gordon I.R. Lore, Jr. & Harold H. Den-
eault, Jr., Mysteries of the Skies:
UFOs in Perspective (Englewood
Cliffs, N.J.: Prentice-Hall, 1968),
p.108.

Cobourg
-Cloud anomaly
1889, June 2
Toronto Globe, 3 June 1889.
-UFO (NL)
1979, Jan.2/Shelter Valley
Cobourg Daily Star, 3 Jan.1979.

Collingwood
-Precognition
1879, Nov.20/Mrs. W.D. Doupe
William Ratigan, Great Lakes Ship-
wrecks and Survivals (N.Y.: Galahad,
1960), pp.100-102.
Dwight Boyer, Ghost Ships of the
Great Lakes (N.Y.: Dodd, Mead, 1968),
pp.212-24.
1955, May/Allen Spraggett
Allen Spraggett, "Why I Believe in
Prayer," Fate 14 (Feb.1961):27-31.
-Telepathy
1954/Allen Spraggett
Allen Spraggett, The Unexplained
(N.Y.: Signet, 1968 ed.), pp.18-19.

Cooper
-UFO (CE-2)
1976, April/Reginald Trotter/ground
markings only
"Landing Traces in Canada?" Australian UFO Bull., Aug.1976, p.6.

Copper Cliff
-UFO (DD)
1953, Jan./Russel Howard
(Editorial), Fate 6 (June 1953):12,
quoting Sudbury Daily Star (undated).

Cornwall
-Skyquake
1977, Dec.12-1978, Jan.25
Cornwall Standard-Freeholder, 28 Dec.
1977, p.9; 6 Jan.1978, p.7; 10 Jan.
1978, p.1; 11 Jan.1978, p.13; 13
Jan.1978, p.1; 16 Jan.1978, p.1; and
19 Jan.1978, p.9.
Ottawa Citizen, 17 Jan.1978, p.41.
"More Aerial Detonations," Res Bureaux Bull., no.29 (9 Feb.1978):1-3.
-UFO (NL)
1973, Oct./Brian Sturgeon
Cornwall Standard-Freeholder, 1 Nov.
1973.

Corunna
-Archeological site
Douglas Leechman & Frederica de La-
guna, "The Parker Site," Bull.Nat'l
Mus.Canada, no.113 (1949):29-30.
Thomas E. Lee, "The Parker Earth-
work, Corunna, Ontario," Pennsylva-
nia Arch. 28 (1958):5-32. il.

Courtright
-Animal ESP
1927, Dec.1/Bill Brian/"Kamloops"
Dwight Boyer, Ghost Ships of the
Great Lakes (N.Y.: Dodd, Mead,
1968), pp.126-43.

Craigleith
-Gravity anomaly
1956, Sep./Frank Burnett
(Editorial), Fate 10 (Jan.1957):9-
10, quoting Toronto Star (undated).

Deep River
-UFO (CE-2)
1968, Feb./Mary McCarthy
"Spate of Sightings in Ontario, Canada," APRO Bull. 16 (Mar.-Apr.1968):
8.

Delhi
-UFO (NL)
1950, March 16/Paul Ripai
Kenneth Arnold & Ray Palmer, The Coming of the Saucers (Boise: The Authors, 1952), p.133.

Dixons Corners
-UFO (DD)
1957, June 6/Earle C. Shelley/Hwy.2
(Letter), Flying Saucers, Feb.1958,
pp.64-65.

Donaldson
-Archeological site
ca.700 B.C.-1000 A.D.
James V. Wright & James E. Anderson,
"The Donaldson Site," Bull.Nat'l
Mus.Canada, no.184 (1963). il.

Doon
-UFO (?)
1973, Oct./Dave MacDonald/Hwy.401/=air-
port beacon
Kitchener-Waterloo Record, 29 Oct.
1973.

Dundas
-Ghost
1940s, 1956/Mrs. Glasser
Eileen Sonin, More Canadian Ghosts
(Richmond Hill, Ont.: Pocket Books,
1974 ed.), pp.24-25.
-Precognition
n.d./Mrs. Glasser
Eileen Sonin, More Canadian Ghosts
(Richmond Hill, Ont.: Pocket Books,
1974 ed.), p.166.
-UFO (NL)
1978, Feb.4/Charles Purich
Hamilton Spectator, 6 Feb.1978.

Eganville
-Fall of metallic object
   n.d.
      Ivan T. Sanderson, Investigating the
      Unexplained (Englewood Cliffs, N.J.:
      Prentice-Hall, 1972), p.280, quot-
      ing Montreal (P.Q.) Star (ca.1964).
-UFO (CE-2)
   ca.1949/Allan Stuart
      Pembroke Observer, 19 June 1949.

Elk Lake
-Clairvoyance
   1956, Feb./Marion Spraggett
      Allen Spraggett, The Unexplained
      (N.Y.: Signet, 1968 ed.), pp.17-18.

Elliot Lake
-UFO (NL)
   1972, July 17/Marilyn Coulis
      Sudbury Star, 17 July 1972.

Elmvale
-Doubtful responsibility
   n.d./Earl Bonnell
      Joseph A. Murphy, "You Can't Stump
      the Experts," Fate 4 (Jan.1951):23,
      24-26.

Embrun
-UFO (CE-1)
   1973, Nov.8/Donna Bouchard/Hwy.417
      "Car Chase in Canada," APRO Bull. 22
      (Jan.-Feb.1974):1,4.
      Arthur Bray, "Car Chased Under
      Bridges," Can.UFO Rept., no.20
      (1975):11,13.

Erieau
-Fall of black rain
   1946, May 20
      "Black Rain," Doubt, no.15 (summer
      1946):223.

Erie Beach
-Fall of metallic object
   1976, Nov./Jack Carpenter/=satellite
   debris
      W. Ritchie Benedict, "Mystery Metal,"
      Fate 30 (Dec.1977):86.

Erin
-UFO (CE-1)
   1954, summer/Harry Winteler
      (Letter), Fate 9 (Aug.1956):124.

Etobicoke
-Phantom
   n.d./Mrs. Hutcheson/Mimico
      Eileen Sonin, More Canadian Ghosts
      (Richmond Hill, Ont.: Pocket Books,
      1974 ed.), p.32.
-Poltergeist
   1968, April 28-May 10/Roy Hawkins/
   Prince Edward Dr.
      Betty Lou White, "An Evil Poltergeist
      in Etobicoke," Fate 22 (Mar.1969):
      80-87. il.
      Sheila Hervey, Some Canadian Ghosts
      (Richmond Hill, Ont.: Pocket Books,

1973), pp.58-63.

Falconbridge
-UFO (R-V)
   1975, Nov.11/CFB Falconbridge
      Nat'l Enquirer, 3 Aug.1976.
      Robert Rickard, "UFOs: Fact or Fig-
      ment?" Can.UFO Rept., no.25 (fall
      1976):18.

Fenelon Falls
-UFO (?)
   1913, Feb.9/Walter H. Stevenson/=
   meteor procession
      C.A. Chant, "An Extraordinary Meteor
      Display," J.Roy.Astron.Soc'y Canada
      7 (1913):145,180-81.

Feversham
-Telepathy and healing
   1953/Allen Spraggett
      Allen Spraggett, "God Gets Around,"
      Fate 15 (Dec.1962):56,57-58.

Flamboro Centre
-UFO (DD)
   1975, March 18/Pat McCarthy
      Hamilton Spectator, 21 Mar.1975. il.
      Nicky Marchese, "Canadian UFO," Fate
      22 (Sep.1975):59. il.
      "Canadian Photo Case," APRO Bull. 24
      (Oct.1975):1,3. il.

Forest
-UFO (NL)
   1973, Oct.21/Fred DeWitt/Gallimere
   Beach
      Forest Standard, 24 Oct.1973.

Fort Erie
-Skyquake
   1946, Oct.12
      "Explosions, Etc.," Doubt, no.23
      (1948):350.
-UFO (NL)
   1973, Nov.3/Peter Bukator/Netherby Rd.
      Welland-Port Colborne Tribune, 5
      Nov.1973.

Fort Frances
-Skyquake
   1953
      Donald E. Keyhoe, Flying Saucer Con-
      spiracy (N.Y.: Holt, 1955), p.201.

Frankford
-UFO (CE-2)
   1965/ground markings only
      Ted Phillips, Physical Traces Associ-
      ated with UFO Sightings (Evanston:
      Center for UFO Studies, 1975), p.33.

Freelton
-UFO (NL)
   1975, March
      Timothy Green Beckley, "Operation
      Contact," Saga UFO Rept. 3 (Apr.
      1976):39,66.

Gananoque
-UFO (NL)
    1915, Feb.14
        New York Times, 15 Feb.1915, p.1.
    1975, Jan.22/Hwy.401
        Brockville Recorder & Times, 23 Jan.
        1975.

Garson
-UFO (CE-3)
    1954, July 2/Ennio La Sarza
        Sudbury Daily Star, 6 July 1954.
        (Editorial), Saucerian, Sep.1954,
        pp.22-23,31.
        Donald E. Keyhoe, Flying Saucer Con-
        spiracy (N.Y.: Holt, 1955), p.184.
        Paris Flammonde, The Age of Flying
        Saucers (N.Y.: Hawthorn, 1971), p.
        64.

Georgetown
-Ghost dog
    n.d./Hazel Langevin
        Eileen Sonin, More Canadian Ghosts
        (Richmond Hill, Ont.: Pocket Books,
        1974 ed.), pp.77-78.

Geraldton
-Humanoid
    1978, Oct.10/Randy Corcoran
        Montreal(P.Q.) Gazette, 23 Oct.1978;
        and 25 Oct.1978.
-Phantom
    n.d./Helen Lorusso
        Eileen Sonin, More Canadian Ghosts
        (Richmond Hill, Ont.: Pocket Books,
        1974 ed.), p.17.
-UFO (DD)
    1972, July 4
        Glenn McWane & David Graham, The New
        UFO Sightings (N.Y.: Warner, 1974),
        p.43, quoting Geraldton Times-Star
        (undated).

Glencairn
-UFO (NL)
    1972, July 25
        Glenn McWane & David Graham, The New
        UFO Sightings (N.Y.: Warner, 1974),
        pp.45-46, quoting Ottawa Journal
        (undated).

Glencoe
-UFO (CE-1)
    1957, Nov.29/Mrs. Gerald Alderman/2 mi.
        N on Hwy.80
        Lucius Farish, "The Mini-Saucers,"
        Fate 27 (Dec.1974):59,63, quoting
        London Free Press (undated).

Glenora
-UFO (?)
    1978, July 12/Jack Reed
        Kingston Whig-Standard, 12 July 1978.

Goodwood
-UFO (CE-1)
    1975, March 2
        "Reports from America," Australian
        UFO Bull., Feb.1976, p.7.

Gormley
-Haunt
    1968, April-1969, Aug./Pamela Ball
        Sheila Hervey, Some Canadian Ghosts
        (Richmond Hill, Ont.: Pocket Books,
        1973), pp.2-4.

Grand Bend
-UFO (?)
    1958, May 24/L. Huron
        Sarnia Observer, 24 May 1958.

Gravenhurst
-UFO (?)
    1978, March 3
        Timmins Press, 9 Mar.1978.

Guelph
-Erratic crocodilian
    1977, May 18
        Journal de Quebec, 20 May 1977.
-Haunt
    n.d./Mrs. James L. Beaton/Rexdale
        Eileen Sonin, More Canadian Ghosts
        (Richmond Hill, Ont.: Pocket Books,
        1974 ed.), pp.37-38.
-UFO (?)
    1972, Aug.
        Glenn McWane & David Graham, The New
        UFO Sightings (N.Y.: Warner, 1974),
        p.56.

Haliburton
-Phantom cat
    1966, winter
        Sheila Hervey, Some Canadian Ghosts
        (Richmond Hill, Ont.: Pocket Books,
        1973), pp.146-49.
-UFO (DD)
    1952, April 16/Mrs. Wesley Baker
        Toronto Daily Star, 17 Apr.1952.
-UFO (NL)
    1976, Jan.5/Mrs. Roger Vienot
        Hailburton County Echo, 14 Jan.1976.

Hamilton
-Clairvoyance
    1958, Oct./Madame Mojelski
        (Editorial), Fate 12 (Jan.1959):18-
        19.
-Ghost
    1929/ Lila M. Cameron
        Lila M. Cameron, "Willed from the
        Grave," Fate 25 (July 1972):88-91.
    n.d./Gertrude White
        Eileen Sonin, More Canadian Ghosts
        (Richmond Hill, Ont.: Pocket Books,
        1974 ed.), pp.69-70.
-Haunt
    1950s-1960s/Brucedale Ave.
        Sheila Hervey, Some Canadian Ghosts
        (Richmond Hill, Ont.; Pocket Books,
        1973), pp.99-101.
-Healing
    1964, Feb./Maria Buch
        (Editorial), Fate 17 (June 1964):20.
-Precognition
    1955, fall/Allen Spraggett
        Allen Spraggett, "God Gets Around,"
        Fate 15 (Dec.1962):56,59-60.

-Skyquake
  1948, Feb.1, 3, 19
    "Booms--No Clues," Doubt, no.21
    (1948):317.
-UFO (?)
  n.d.
    (Editorial), Fate 5 (Oct.1952):7.
-UFO (CE-1)
  1966, April 4
    Hamilton Spectator, 5 Apr.1966.
  1969, Aug.21/Bruce McAvella
    Brian C. Cannon, "UFO Alert in On-
    tario," Can.UFO Rept., no.6 (Nov.-
    Dec.1969):19,21.
-UFO (CE-2)
  1966, March 26/Charles Cozens/Upper
  Wellington St.
    Victoria (B.C.) Daily Colonist, 3
    Apr.1966.
    Hamilton Spectator, 4-5 Apr.1966.
-UFO (NL)
  1949, April 3
    "If It's in the Sky It's a Saucer,"
    Doubt, no.27 (1949):416.
  1952, April 16
    Hamilton Spectator, 17 Apr.1952.
  1957, July 9
    Richard Hall, ed., The UFO Evidence
    (Washington: NICAP, 1964), p.118.
  1966, March 27/Laverne Emery
    Hamilton Spectator, 4-5 Apr.1966.
  1971, Aug.11/R.G. Speck
    (Letter), Can.UFO Rept., no.11
    (1971):35.
  1973, Nov.2/Andy Dobie/Queen Elizabeth
  Way
    Hamilton Spectator, 2 Nov.1973.

Hammond
-UFO (CE-1)
  1969, April 22/Fussell Rd.
    "Light Beams with EM Effects Report-
    ed," UFO Inv. 4 (May 1969):4.
    "The Maritimes--Newest Playground
    for UFOs?" Flying Saucers, June
    1970, pp.12,15.

Hanmer
-UFO (NL)
  1972, July 27/Joan Laws
    Glenn McWane & David Graham, The New
    UFO Sightings (N.Y.: Warner, 1974),
    p.46, quoting Sudbury Star (undated).

Harriston
-UFO (NL)
  1975, Dec.22
    Guelph Daily Mercury, 22 Dec.1975.

Harrow
-UFO (CE-1)
  1966, March 17/Mr. Ward
    Jacques Vallee, Passport to Magonia
    (Chicago: Regnery, 1969), p.323,
    quoting Flying Saucers, Aug.1966.

Harrowsmith
-Phantom
  n.d./Judy Hubbard
    Eileen Sonin, More Canadian Ghosts

(Richmond Hill, Ont.: Pocket Books,
    1974 ed.), pp.85-86.

Hawkesbury
-UFO (DD)
  1952, April 18
    Toronto Daily Star, 18 Apr.1952.
-UFO (NL)
  1977, March 3
    (Editorial), Res Bureaux Bull., 21
    Apr.1977.
  1977, May 29
    Vankleeck Hill Review, 1 June 1977.

Holstein
-UFO (CE-2)
  1970, Oct.3/Mrs. Peter Dundys
    Ted Phillips, Physical Traces Associ-
    ated with UFO Sightings (Evanston:
    Center for UFO Studies, 1975), p.72.

Holyrood
-UFO (CE-2)
  1969, May 26/Raynard Ackert
    Brian C. Cannon, "UFO Alert in On-
    tario," Can.UFO Rept., no.6 (Nov.-
    Dec.1969):19,20.

Hymers
-UFO (NL)
  1947, Oct.25/Frank Sutch
    Kenneth Arnold & Ray Palmer, The Com-
    ing of the Saucers (Boise: The Au-
    thors, 1952), pp.131-32.

Indian River
-Ghost
  n.d./Ellen Shearer
    Eileen Sonin, More American Ghosts
    (Richmond Hill, Ont.: Pocket Books,
    1974 ed.), p.88.

Ingersoll
-Fall of ice
  1964, June/Edward Elliott
    (Editorial), Fate 17 (Oct.1964):10.
-UFO (?)
  1970, Dec./Herbert Dustin
    Regina (Sask.) Leader-Post, 28 Dec.
    1970.
-UFO (DD)
  1955, Dec.7?/Huron Clark
    "Latest Saucer Sightings," Fate 9
    (Apr.1956):43,47.

Inglewood
-Haunt
  1960s
    Eileen Sonin, More Canadian Ghosts
    (Richmond Hill, Ont.: Pocket Books,
    1974 ed.), pp.65-66.

Innerkip
-UFO (DD)
  1955, July 12
    Donald E. Keyhoe, Flying Saucer Con-
    spiracy (N.Y.: Holt, 1955), p.275,
    quoting London Free Press (undated).
-UFO (NL)
  1956, Aug.28/William Corbett/2 mi.S

(Editorial), Fate 9 (Dec.1956):11.

Inverhuron
-Archeological site
  ca.3000 B.C.-recent
    Walter A. Kenyon, "The Inverhuron
    Site," Occ.Pap.Roy.Ontario Mus.Art
    & Arch., no.1 (1957). il.

Iroquois
-Precognition
  n.d./Garnet Keeler
    Eileen Sonin, More Canadian Ghosts
    (Richmond Hill, Ont.: Pocket Books,
    1974 ed.), p.145.

Joyceville
-UFO (CE-3)
  1967, Aug.23/Stanley Moxon/nr. Glen
  Grove Rd.
    Toronto Telegram, 23 Aug.1967.
    Kingston Whig-Standard, 24 Aug.1967.
    Jim & Coral Lorenzen, UFOs over the
    Americas (N.Y.: Signet, 1968), pp.
    32-33,172-73.
    Toronto Sun, 8 Jan.1978.

Kapuskasing
-Animal ESP
  1956, Nov./Rheal Guindon
    (Editorial), Fate 10 (Apr.1957):10.

Kars
-UFO (NL)
  1952, May 24
    Marc Leduc, "Notes sur le projet
    'Magnet,'" UFO-Québec, no.4 (1975):
    12,15.

Kenora
-UFO (CE-1)
  1955, Aug.20
    J. Allen Hynek, The UFO Experience
    (Chicago: Regnery, 1972), pp.97-98.
-UFO (DD)
  n.d./Eleanor Jacobson
    "About Previous Cover Photo," Can.
    UFO Rept., no.10 (1971):35. il.
    "Straightening the Record," Can.UFO
    Rept., no.11 (1971):32. il.
-UFO (NL)
  1965, Feb.12
    Kenora Miner & News, 19 Feb.1965.

Kent co.
-UFO (?)
  1880, summer/David Muckle
    "A Curious Phenomenon," Sci.Am. 43
    (1880):24, quoting East Kent Plain-
    dealer (undated).

Keswick
-Poltergeist
  1963, May/Frederick Matthews
    Sheila Hervey, Some Canadian Ghosts
    (Richmond Hill, Ont.: Pocket Books,
    1973), pp.55-57.

Killaloe Station
-UFO (NL)

1968, Feb./Tom Ward/1 mi.E
  "Spate of Sightings in Ontario, Canada," APRO Bull. 16 (Mar.-Apr.1968):
  8.

Kilmarnock
-Precognition
  n.d./Mr. Crouch
    R.S. Lambert, Exploring the Super-
    natural (Toronto: McClelland & Stew-
    art, 1955), pp.162-63.

Kilworthy
-UFO (?)
  1978, March 3
    Timmins Press, 9 Mar.1978.

Kingsmere
-Ghost
  1954, June/Percy J. Philip
    Percy J. Philip, "I Talked with Mac-
    kenzie King's Ghost," Fate 8 (Oct.
    1955):82-87.

Kingston
-Ancient stone seat
    William B. Goodwin, The Ruins of
    Great Ireland in New England (Bos-
    ton: Meador, 1946), pp.405-407.
-Rock pillars
    J.E. Hawley & R.C. Hart, "Cylindri-
    cal Structures in Sandstone," Bull.
    Geol.Soc'y Am. 45 (1934):1017-34. il.
    Douglas E. Cox, "Pillars, Polystrate
    Formations, and Potholes," Creation
    Rsch.Soc'y Quar. 14 (Dec.1977):149-
    55. il.
-UFO (DD)
  1978, Jan.22/sewage plant
    "UFOs," Res Bureaux Bull., no.29
    (9 Feb.1978):4,5-6.
-UFO (NL)
  1975, Jan.18/12 mi.N
    Kingston Whig-Standard, 18 Jan.1975.

Kitchener
-Psychokinesis
  1951, March-May/Howard Santo
    "Still the Pallid Data March," Doubt,
    no.45 (1954):292.
-UFO (?)
  1978, Dec.10
    "Recent UFO Reports," Res Bureaux
    Bull., no.43 (Jan.1979):3,4.
-UFO (CE-2)
  1967, April 26/Brian Dorscht/nr. Nat'l
  Grocers Co.
    Kitchener-Waterloo Record, 27 Apr.
    1967.
-UFO (CE-4)
  n.d.
    Berthold Eric Schwarz, "Talks with
    Betty Hill: 2--The Things That Hap-
    pen Around Her," Flying Saucer Rev.
    23 (Oct.1977):11,12.
-UFO (DD)
  1979, Jan.18
    Kitchener-Waterloo Record, 18 Jan.
    1979.
-UFO (NL)

1969, Jan.4/Kurt Glemser
"Check Out," Skylook, no.16 (Mar.
1969):17.
1979, Jan.6, 10
Kitchener-Waterloo Record, 10 Jan.
1979.
"Recent UFO Reports," Res Bureaux
Bull., no.44 (Feb.1979):4.

Lambeth
-UFO (DD)
1953, Oct.31/Oscar Plewes
"Reports from Everywhere," Fate 7
(May 1954):23,28.

Leeds co.
-Spontaneous human combustion
1820s
"Last Notes," Res Bureaux Bull., no.
37 (17 Aug.1978):10,11.

Lindsay
-Haunt
1960s/Clothilde Lanklater/33 Cambridge
St.S
1960s
Eileen Sonin, More Canadian Ghosts
(Richmond Hill, Ont.: Pocket Books,
1974 ed.), pp.67-72.
-UFO (NL)
1974, Nov.23
Timothy Green Beckley, "Operation
Contact," Saga UFO Rept. 3 (Apr.
1976):39,62.

Lochlin
-UFO (NL)
1974, April/Mrs. Wallace Brown
Curt Sutherly, "The UFO Invasion of
Boshkung Lake," Fate 30 (Nov.1977):
55,58.

London
-Animal ESP
1957/Barbara Phipps
(Editorial), Fate 10 (Aug.1957):12-
13.
(Editorial), Fate 11 (Feb.1958):6-8,
quoting Toronto Telegram (undated).
Rhea A. White, "The Investigation of
Behavior Suggestive of ESP in Dogs,"
J.ASPR 58 (1964):250,262-65.
-Crisis apparition
ca.1844/Sarah Harris/Eldon House
W.T. Stead, Real Ghost Stories (Lon-
don: Review of Reviews, 1891).
R.S. Lambert, Exploring the Supernat-
ural (Toronto: McClelland & Stewart,
1955), pp.154-56.
-Fall of plastic
1961, Dec.7/Victor Neeb
"Who Put the Plastic in the Perth
Apple Tree?" APRO Bull. 10 (Mar.
1962):2.
-Fall of vegetable substance
1868, Feb.24/A.T. Machattie
A.T. Machattie, "On a Fall of Colour-
ed Hail and Snow in Western Canada,"
Chemical News 35 (1877):182.
-Haunt

1967, summer-1968, Feb./Colborne St.
London Free Press, 21 June 1969.
Sheila Hervey, Some Canadian Ghosts
(Richmond Hill, Ont.: Pocket Books,
1973), pp.49-55.
-Human electrification
1877-1878/Caroline Clare/No.25, 2d
Rodney Concession
Henry Winfred Splitter, "Electrical-
ly Charged People," Fate 8 (Mar.
1955):83-84.
-UFO (?)
1952/W. Gordon Graham
London Free Press, 1 May 1954.
1953, Sep.16/Mt. Pleasant Ave.
"Reports from Everywhere," Fate 7
(May 1954):23,28.
-UFO (DD)
1952, April 20
Toronto Globe & Mail, 21 Apr.1952.
1953, Nov.18/Billy McKibbin/Egerton
St. bridge
"Reports from Everywhere," Fate 7
(May 1954):23,28, quoting London
Free Press (undated).
-UFO (NL)
1875, Dec.29/J.J. Cornish/Thames R.
Harold I. Velt, The Sacred Book of
Ancient America (Independence, Mo.:
Herald House, 1952).
1957, Sep.18
"Flying Saucer Roundup," Fate 11
(Feb.1958):29,34.
1966, March 29/John Lewis/nr. Westmin-
ster Hospital
London Free Press, 30 Mar.1966.
1976, Aug.13
"Diary of a Mad Planet," Fortean
Times, no.18 (Oct.1976):8,19.
1977, April 15/Bruce Powell
John Brent Musgrave, "Red Lights &
Other UFOs over Canada," MUFON UFO
J., no.118 (Sep.1977):14.

Lyn
-UFO (NL)
1975, Jan.22
Brockville Recorder & Times, 23 Jan.
1975.

Madoc
-UFO (CE-2)
1975, Dec.12/Pauline Dudgeon/Hwy.12
Harry Tokarz, "Are UFOs Boon or Curse
to Medicine?" Can.UFO Rept., no.31
(summer 1978):8,9.

Meaford
-UFO (?)
1978, Dec.31/=balloon
Owen Sound Sun-Times, 8 Jan.1979.

Meath
-UFO (CE-2)
1969, June 2/Mrs. John McLaren/ground
markings only
Brian C. Cannon, "UFO Alert in Ontario," Can.UFO Rept., no.6 (Nov.-
Dec.1969):19,20.

Midland
-Psychokinesis
  1954, Sep.9/Margaret Stephens
    (Editorial), Fate 8 (Feb.1955):13.

Millbank
-Clairvoyance and precognition
  1920s-1970s/Vera McNichol
    Ernest Miles, "The Body in the Well,"
    Fate 27 (Nov.1974):70.

Milton
-Haunt
  1972, summer/Mike Spanpinato/Harland
  Rd.
    Brad Steiger, "1972: A Bumper Year
    for Hauntings," Beyond Reality, no.
    4 (May 1973):15,17,56.
-UFO (DD)
  1978, Sep.1
    Milton Champion, 6 Sep.1978.

Minden
-UFO (CE-1)
  1974, Nov.1/Ron Smith
    Timothy Green Beckley, "Operation
    Contact," Saga UFO Rept. 3 (Apr.
    1976):39,62.
-UFO (NL)
  1974, Aug.5/Shirley Newman
    Minden Progress, 15 Aug.1974.
  1974, Sep.20/Allan Rogers
    Minden Progress, 26 Sep.1974.
  1975, Feb.19/Tom Simmons
    Minden Progress, 20 Feb.1975.

Mississauga
-Deathbed apparition
  1975, May/Arthur Sanders
    W. Ritchie Benedict, "Back from the
    Dead," Fate 31 (July 1978):81.
-Erratic shark
  1977, June 25/Darryl Pepper/L. Ontario
    Toronto Sunday Sun, 26 June 1977, p.
    3.
-Ghost
  n.d./Mrs. James L. Beaton/Cooksville
    Eileen Sonin, More Canadian Ghosts
    (Richmond Hill, Ont.: Pocket Books,
    1974 ed.), pp.35-36.
-Haunt
  1972, spring
    Sheila Hervey, Some Canadian Ghosts
    (Richmond Hill, Ont.: Pocket Books,
    1973), pp.122-24.
-UFO (CE-1)
  1978, April 30
    Hugh Cochrane, "The Great Lakes UFO
    Flap of 1978," Saga UFO Rept. 6
    (Jan.1979):21,56.
-UFO (NL)
  1968, Aug.29/Toronto Int'l Airport
    "Around the World," APRO Bull. 17
    (Sep.-Oct.1968):5,6.
  1974, Aug.14/Dixie Rd.
    Mississauga Times, 14 Aug.1974.

Mono twp.
-UFO (NL)
  1978, Sep.13

Orangeville Weekend Banner, 15 Sep.
    1978.

Mountain
-UFO (NL)
  1977, May 16-17
    Hamilton Spectator, 17-18 May 1977;
    and 27 May 1977.

Mount Forest
-Crisis apparition
  n.d./Barbara Taylor
    Eileen Sonin, More Canadian Ghosts
    (Richmond Hill, Ont.: Pocket Books,
    1974 ed.), pp.31,164.

Mount Pleasant
-Acoustic anomaly
  1975, July 9/Joseph Borda
    Graham Conway, "Strange Voice Heard
    after UFO Landing," Can.UFO Rept.,
    no.24 (summer 1976):1-2.
-UFO (CE-2)
  1975, July 6/Joseph Borda
    Graham Conway, "Strange Voice Heard
    after UFO Landing," Can.UFO Rept.,
    no.24 (summer 1976):1-2. il.

Muskoka Beach
-UFO (NL)
  1974, July 22
    Gravenhurst News, 25 July 1974.

Napanee
-UFO (NL)
  1976, Nov./Howard Church/Deseronto Rd.
  1976, Nov.25/Mrs. Mike Church/Slash
  Rd.
    Napanee Beaver, 3 Dec.1976.
  1977, Jan./Lennox hydro station
    John Brent Musgrave, "Red Lights &
    Other UFOs over Canada," MUFON UFO
    J., no.118 (Sep.1977):14.

New Hamburg
-Land monster
  1950s/Clayton Ingold
    Ivan T. Sanderson, Things (N.Y.:
    Pyramid, 1967), pp.29-30.
-UFO (?)
  1976, Aug.16
    "Diary of a Mad Planet," Fortean
    Times, no.18 (Oct.1976):8,20.
-UFO (NL)
  1973, Oct./Mrs. Arthur Cook/Route 1
    Kitchener-Waterloo Record, 29 Oct.
    1973.

Niagara Falls
-Fire immunity and shamanism
  1720/Pierre F.X. de Charlevoix
    Pierre François Xavier de Charlevoix,
    Journal of a Voyage to North Ameri-
    ca, 2 vols., Louise Phelps Kellogg,
    ed. (Chicago: Caxton Club, 1923),
    2:153-68.
-Mystery plane crash
  1956, July 29/DeHavilland DHC1B2
    Jay Gourley, The Great Lakes Triangle
    (Greenwich, Ct.: Fawcett, 1977), p.

129.
-Mystery tracks
  1947, July 11
    "At the Same Time," Doubt, no.19
    (1947):290,292, quoting Toronto
    Daily Star (undated).
-Precognition
  1969, June 1/Janet Ecker
    Eileen Sonin, More Canadian Ghosts
    (Richmond Hill, Ont.: Pocket Books,
    1974 ed.), p.163.
-Seance
  1974, Oct.31/Anne Fisher
    (Editorial), Fate 29 (Mar.1976):14-
    16.
-UFO (NL)
  1968, April 3/Thomas Shumway/Sir Adam
  Back plant
    "Mysterious Lights Seen near Niagara
    Falls in 1968," Skylook, no.33
    (Aug.1970):12.

Niagara on the Lake
-UFO (NL)
  1977-1978/Harry Picken
    Hugh Cochrane, "The Great Lakes UFO
    Flap of 1978," Saga UFO Rept. 6
    (Jan.1979):20-22. il.

Nipissing
-Haunt
  1933-1937/Mrs. Russell Rousseau/Water-
  falls Lodge
    R.S. Lambert, Exploring the Supernat-
    ural (Toronto: McClelland & Stewart,
    1955), pp.143-44.

North Bay
-Archeological site
    Winnipeg (Man.) Free Press, 4 Apr.
    1975, p.20.
-Humanoid
  1937, March/Albert Caulman/Bankfield
  Mine
    R.S. Lambert, Exploring the Supernat-
    ural (Toronto: McClelland & Stewart,
    1955), pp.142-43, quoting North Bay
    Nugget (undated).
-UFO (?)
  1952, Sep.18
    (Editorial), APRO Bull., Nov.1952.
  1954, Aug.10/Wilbert B. Smith
    Coral & Jim Lorenzen, UFOs: The Whole
    Story (N.Y.: Signet, 1969), p.56.
  1976, June 24
    "Diary of a Mad Planet," Fortean
    Times, no.18 (Oct.1976):8,16.
-UFO (CE-1)
  1954, Aug.30/Sgt. Durdle/RCAF base
    Harold T. Wilkins, Flying Saucers Un-
    censored (N.Y.: Pyramid, 1967 ed.),
    pp.227-29.
  1976, Jan.5/Dave Stewart
    North Bay Nugget, 7 Jan.1976.
-UFO (DD)
  1952, April 16-17
    North Bay Nugget, 17-18 Apr.1952.
-UFO (NL)
  1952, Jan.1/RCAF base
    (Editorial), Fate 5 (Oct.1952):7.

Donald E. Keyhoe, Flying Saucers from
Outer Space (N.Y.: Holt, 1953),
pp.128-29.
  1952, April 12/RCAF base
    Montreal (P.Q.) Gazette, 16 Apr.1952.
    Ottawa Journal, 16 Apr.1952.
  1952, April 17
    North Bay Nugget, 18 Apr.1952.
  1953, Oct.
    John C. Ross, "Canada Hunts for Sau-
    cers," Fate 7 (May 1954):12,13.

North York
-Crisis apparition
  1967, Nov./Violet Clarkson
    Eileen Sonin, More Canadian Ghosts
    (Richmond Hill, Ont.: Pocket Books,
    1974 ed.), pp.25-26.
-Ghost
  1932, 1934/Florence Marion Trautman
    Eileen Sonin, More Canadian Ghosts
    (Richmond Hill, Ont.: Pocket Books,
    1974 ed.), pp.50-51.
-Haunt
  1972, April-1973/Pamela Ball
    Sheila Hervey, Some Canadian Ghosts
    (Richmond Hill, Ont.: Pocket Books,
    1973), pp.11-14.
-UFO (CE-2)
  1965, May/Willowdale
    Gene Duplantier, "The Mystery of the
    Burned Circles," in Brad Steiger &
    Joan Whritenour, Flying Saucer In-
    vasion: Target--Earth (N.Y.: Award,
    1969), pp.21-22.

Oakville
-Precognition
  1892, summer
    H. Addington Bruce, "Adventures in
    Precognition," Fate 7 (Oct.1954):
    86-88.
-UFO (CE-2)
  1976, July 7/Marsha Rasberry/Queen
  Elizabeth Thruway
    (Letter), Nicky Marchese, Fate 30
    (Jan.1977):118,127.
    (Letter), Lawrence J. Fenwick, Fate
    (June 1977):118.
-UFO (NL)
  1968, Aug.29
    "Around the World," APRO Bull. 17
    (Sep.-Oct.1968):5,6.
  1978, March/Derry Rd. nr. Hwy.25
    Hugh Cochrane, "The Great Lakes UFO
    Flap of 1978," Saga UFO Rept. 6
    (Jan.1979):21,56.

Orangeville
-UFO (CE-1)
  1956, Jan.17/Alfred N. Phillips
    Toronto Star, 19 July 1956.

Orillia
-Reincarnation
  1966/Joanne MacIver
    Jess Stearn, The Search for the Girl
    with the Blue Eyes (Garden City:
    Doubleday, 1968).
-UFO (?)

1978, March 3
Timmins Press, 9 Mar.1978.
-Weather control
1954, Sep.12/Rolf Alexander/Conchich-
ing Beach Park
John C. Ross, "Rolf Alexander: The
Man Who Smashes Clouds," Fate 8
(June 1955):42-45, quoting Orillia
Packet & Times (undated). il.
Rolf Alexander, "Psychokinesis,"
Flying Saucer Rev. 1 (Nov.-Dec.1955)
:8-10,30. il.
Rolf Alexander, The Power of the
Mind (London: Laurie, 1956).

Orr Lake
-Aerial phantom
1640
Paul Ragueneau, "Relation de ce qui
s'est passé en la Nouvelle France,"
in Reuben Gold Thwaites, ed., Jesuit
Relations and Allied Documents
(Cleveland: Burrows, 1898), 34:67,
162-65.

Oshawa
-UFO (CE-2)
1978, July 3/Jim Coren/Storie Park
Oshawa Times, 4 July 1978; and 7
July 1978.
-UFO (NL)
1958, Aug.8/Herbert Flintoff
"Sighting Round-Up," UFO Inv. 1
(Aug.-Sep.1958):6.
1975, April/Jim Wilkes
(Editorial), Can.UFO Rept., no.21
(1975):12, quoting Oshawa Times
(undated). il.
1976/Bernie Keating
(Letter), Can.UFO Rept., no.27
(spring 1977):23.
1979, Jan.7
Oshawa Times, 8 Jan.1979.
1979, Jan.31
Oshawa Times, 1 Feb.1979.

Ottawa
-Animal ESP
1954/Hugh Carson
"Paddy's 1,800-Mile Trip," Fate 8
(July 1955):82.
-Flying cat
1966, June
John A. Keel, Strange Creatures from
Time and Space (Greenwich, Ct.: Faw-
cett, 1970), p.40.
-Ghost
ca.1966/Pattigay Garlick
Eileen Sonin, More Canadian Ghosts
(Richmond Hill, Ont.: Pocket Books,
1974 ed.), pp.14-15.
-Mirage anomaly
1961/Herbert M. Katlein
(Editorial), Fate 15 (June 1962):22-
23.
-Plant sensitivity
1960s-   /Pearl Weinberger/Univ. of
Ottawa
Pearl Weinberger & Mary Measures,
"The Effect of Two Sound Frequencies

on the Germination and Growth of a
Spring and Winter Wheat," Can.J.
Botany 46 (1968):1151-58.
Pearl Weinberger & U. Graede, "The
Effect of Variable-Frequency Sounds
on Plant Growth," Can.J.Botany 51
(1973):1851-56.
Peter Tompkins & Christopher Bird,
The Secret Life of Plants (N.Y.:
Harper & Row, 1973), pp.151-52.
Mary Measures & Pearl Weinberger,
"The Effect of Four Audible Sound
Frequencies on the Growth of Marquis
Spring Wheat," Can.J.Botany 48
(1970):659-62.
Pearl Weinberger & G.Das, "The Ef-
fect of an Audible and Low Ultra-
sound Frequency on the Growth of
Synchronized Cultures of Scenedes-
mus obtusiusculus," Can.J.Botany
50 (1972):361-65.
-Psychokinesis research
1970s/James Penman Rae/Algonquin Col-
lege
James Penman Rae, The Algonquin Ex-
periments (Hazeldon, Ont.: Canadian
Inst.of Parapsychology, 1978).
-UFO (?)
1952, April 24
Toronto Daily Star, 25 Apr.1952.
1970, Nov.
"Press Reports," APRO Bull. 19 (Nov.-
Dec.1970):9.
1972, July 25
"Press Reports," APRO Bull. 21 (July-
Aug.1972):8.
-UFO (CE-1)
1965, Oct.21/Mrs. Mike Scissons
Jerome Clark, "The Greatest Flap Yet?
Part IV," Flying Saucer Rev. 12
(Nov.-Dec.1966):9.
-UFO (DD)
1952, July 25
Marc Leduc, "Notes sur le projet
'Magnet,'" UFO-Québec, no.4 (1975):
12,15.
-UFO (NL)
1947, July 4/Larry Laviolette/Billings
Bridge
Windsor Daily Star, 7 July 1947.
1952, May 1
Ottawa Journal, 2 May 1952; and 10
May 1952.
1952, June 20
1952, July 8, 20
Marc Leduc, "Notes sur le projet
'Magnet,'" UFO-Québec, no.4 (1975):
12,15.
1969, March 4/Government House
Hamilton Spectator, 19 Oct.1973.
1973, Nov.18
Claude MacDuff, "Le Observations du
18.11.73," UFO-Québec, no.3 (1975):
4-7.
-Windshield pitting
1954
Harold T. Wilkins, Flying Saucers Uncensored (N.Y.: Pyramid, 1967 ed.),
p.153.

Owen Sound
-UFO (NL)
  ca.1922/Joseph Kovacs
    (Letter), Can.UFO Rept., no.12
    (1972):30.

Paris
-UFO (NL)
  1972, July 27/D'al Illes/Nith R.
    Glenn McWane & David Graham, The New
    UFO Sightings (N.Y.: Warner, 1974),
    pp.47-48, quoting Brantford Expos-
    itor (undated).

Parry Sound
-UFO (NL)
  1968, April 18
    Brad Steiger & Joan Whritenour, Fly-
    ing Saucer Invasion: Target--Earth
    (N.Y.: Award, 1969), p.96.

Pembroke
-UFO (CE-1)
  1965, Oct.21/Barb Fraser
    Jerome Clark, "The Greatest Flap Yet?
    Part IV," Flying Saucer Rev. 12
    (Nov.-Dec.1966):9.
  1969, May/William R. McQuirter/S on
  Hwy.41
    Brian C. Cannon, "UFO Alert in On-
    tario," Can.UFO Rept., no.6 (Nov.-
    Dec.1969):19.

Perth
-UFO (NL)
  1978, Dec.28
    Perth Courier, 3 Jan.1979.

Petawawa
-UFO (CE-1)
  1969, July 13/Edgar Paquette/Black Bay
  Rd.
    "Around the Globe," APRO Bull. 18
    (July-Aug.1969):7,8.
    Brian C. Cannon, "UFO Alert in On-
    tario," Can.UFO Rept., no.6 (Nov.-
    Dec.1969):19,21.

Peterborough
-UFO (NL)
  1979, Jan.16
    "Recent UFO Reports," Res Bureaux
    Bull., no.44 (Feb.1979):4.

Peterborough co.
-Skyquake
  1977, Jan.13
    Cobourg Dail Star, 13 Jan.1977.
    Toronto Globe & Mail, 14 Jan.1977.
    Toronto Sun, 14 Jan.1977.

Pickering
-Dowsing
  n.d./Len Badowich
    Christopher Bird, "Applications of
    Dowsing: An Ancient Biopsychophysi-
    cal Art," in John White & Stanley
    Krippner, eds., Future Science (Gar-
    den City: Anchor, 1977), pp.346,352.
-UFO (NL)

1975, Jan.1, 31/Mike McKenna/nuclear
plant
1975, Feb.3/Mike McKenna/nuclear plant
  "A Travers le Canada," UFO-Québec,
  no.2 (1975):12, quoting Hydroscope,
  14 Feb.1975.
1977/nuclear plant
  Robert E. Jones, "A Light-Only Case,"
  Vestigia Newsl. 2 (summer 1978):5.
  il.

Picton
-Haunt
  n.d./Etha Reynolds/3 mi. from town
    Eileen Sonin, More Canadian Ghosts
    (Richmond Hill, Ont.: Pocket Books,
    1974 ed.), pp.46-47.
-Paranormal amnesia
  1960, July 30-Aug.4/Michael Helferty/
  Outlet Beach
    Brad Steiger, Strange Disappearances
    (N.Y.: Lancer, 1972), pp.151-52.
-Poltergeist
  1939, Aug./Mrs. James Ackerman/Queen
  St.
    Sheila Hervey, Some Canadian Ghosts
    (Richmond Hill, Ont.: Pocket Books,
    1973), pp.63-64, quoting Toronto
    Globe & Mail (undated).

Port Colborne
-Skyquake
  1964, Oct.10/L. Erie
    Toronto Daily Star, 10 Oct.1964.
-UFO (CE-1)
  1952, Aug.15/Joseph E. Suthren
    (Letter), Fate 7 (Nov.1954):110-11.

Port Credit
-UFO (NL)
  1952, April/William Beange
    (Letter), Fate 10 (July 1957):114-16.

Port Elgin
-UFO (NL)
  1967, Sep.11-18/Samuel Horton/hydro-
  electric plant/10 mi.S
    "UAO over Hydro Station near Port
    Elgin, Ontario," APRO Bull. 16
    (Sep.-Oct.1967):14.

Port Hope
-UFO (NL)
  1949, summer
    Harold T. Wilkins, Flying Saucers on
    the Attack (N.Y.: Ace, 1967 ed.),
    p.114.

Port Perry
-Mystery plane crash
  1971, May 23/DeHavilland DHC1B2
    Jay Gourley, The Great Lakes Triangle
    (Greenwich, Ct.; Fawcett, 1977),
    p.133.
-UFO (CE-2)
  1976, Sep.11/Paul Hood
    "Foreign Forum," Int'l UFO Reporter
    2 (Jan.1977):2.

Port Stanley
-UFO (CE-2)
 1975, Jan.10/Brad Jones/Bush Rd.
  St. Thomas Times-Journal, 13 Jan.
  1975.

Rainy River
-Archeological site
 ca.1000 A.D./Armstrong Mound
  Walter A. Kenyon, "The Armstrong
  Mound in Rainy River, Ontario," Can.
  Historic Sites 3 (1970):66-85.

Ramore
-Giant bird
 1951, April 17/Kelly Chamandy
  "Run on the Mill," Doubt, no.34
  (1951):108.
-UFO (CE-2)
 1954, Sep.20/Florian Giabowski
  Donald E. Keyhoe, Flying Saucer Con-
  spiracy (N.Y.: Holt, 1955), p.199.
  Harold T. Wilkins, Flying Saucers Un-
  censored (N.Y.: Pyramid, 1967 ed.),
  p.229.
-UFO (NL)
 1953, June 20
  U.S. Air Force, Projects Grudge and
  Blue Book Reports 1-12 (Washington:
  NICAP, 1968), p.221.

Red Rock
-UFO (NL)
 1978, Jan.19
  Thunder Bay Chronicle-Journal, 21
  Jan.1978.
  Sudbury Star, 25 Jan.1978.

Richmond
-Precognition
 n.d./Edna McBryde
  Eileen Sonin, More Canadian Ghosts
  (Richmond Hill, Ont.: Pocket Books,
  1974 ed.), pp.165-66.

Ridgeway
-UFO (CE-2)
 1954, June 21/Guy Baker
  George D. Fawcett, "Hostile Saucers:
  Postscript," Flying Saucers, Sep.
  1962, pp.32,34.
  (Letter), Valeria Baker, Can.UFO
  Rept., no.27 (spring 1977):22.

Ripley
-UFO (?)
 1947, July
  New York Times, 11 July 1947, p.7.

Ruthven
-Humanoid
 1977, June 4
  John Green, Sasquatch: The Apes Among
  Us (Seattle: Hancock House, 1978),
  p.251.

Saint Catherine's
-Fall of ash
 1976, July 14/Augustine Seles
  Hamilton Spectator, 17 July 1976.

-Fall of burning substance
 1954, April/Mrs. Gary May
  Toronto Globe & Mail, 26 Apr.1954.
  (Editorial), Fate 7 (Nov.1954):10-11.
-Poltergeist
 1970, Feb./Church St.
  Edmonton (Alb.) Journal, 16 Feb.1970.
  Sheila Hervey, Some Canadian Ghosts
  (Richmond Hill, Ont.: Pocket Books,
  1973), pp.97-99.
-UFO (?)
 1976, March 24/=hoax
  "Photo Sighting," Can.UFO Rept., no.
  25 (fall 1976):5-7. il.
  "St. Catherine's Photo," Can.UFO
  Rept., no.25 (fall 1976):23.
-UFO (NL)
 1967, April 26/Mary Ellen Roberts
  "Beam Spotlights Witness," UFO Inv.
  4 (May-June 1967):3.

Saint Thomas
-Haunt
 1920s-   /Alma College
  Eileen Sonin, More Canadian Ghosts
  (Richmond Hill, Ont.: Pocket Books,
  1974 ed.), pp.59-61.
-UFO (NL)
 1975, Jan.14/Wayne Roberts
  London Free Press, 15 Jan.1975.
  Montreal (P.Q.) Gazette, 16 Jan.1975.

Sarnia
-Fall of vegetable substance
 1868, Feb.24
  Toronto Globe, 3 Mar.1868, p.2.
  A.T. Machattie, "On a Fall of Coloured
  Hail and Snow in Western Canada,"
  Chemical News 35 (1877):182.
-Healing
 1965, April 25/Mrs. David Van Sickle
  (Editorial), Fate 16 (Aug.1963):18-
  20.
-UFO (DD)
 1960, Feb.22
  "Other Recent Sightings," UFO Inv. 1
  (Mar.1960):8.
-UFO (NL)
 1967, Nov.21/G.D. Nicholson/Cathcart
 Blvd.
  "On the Canadian Scene," APRO Bull.
  16 (Jan.-Feb.1968):4,5.

Sault Sainte Marie
-Ball lightning
 ca.1948, summer/E. Motluk
  Sault Sainte Marie Star, 13 July 1978.
-Fall of pike pole
 1979, Feb.7
  Toronto Globe & Mail, 9 Feb.1979, p.2.
-Mystery plane crash
 1973, Aug.26/Cessna 310F
  Jay Gourley, The Great Lakes Triangle
  (Greenwich, Ct.: Fawcett, 1977),
  pp.120-21.

Scarborough
-Haunt
 1970/Mark Carson/Lawrence Ave.E
  Sheila Hervey, Some Canadian Ghosts

(Richmond Hill, Ont.: Pocket Books, 1973), pp.101-104.

-UFO (?)
  1952, April 17
    Toronto Telegram, 17 Apr.1952.
    Toronto Daily Star, 18 Apr.1952.
  1968, June 17/Scarborough Bluff
    "Articles," UFO News (Tasmania), Nov.1968, p.2.
-UFO (CE-1)
  1974, Oct.22/Roy Fenton/Markham Rd.
    Scarborough Mirror, 23 Oct.1974.
-UFO (NL)
  1968, Sep.7/Shirley Shaw
    Coral & Jim Lorenzen, UFOs: The Whole Story (N.Y.: Signet, 1969), pp.296-97.
  1972, June 11
    "Press Reports," APRO Bull. 20 (May-June 1972):1,3, quoting Toronto Sun (undated).
  n.d.
    Hugh Cochrane, "The Great Lakes UFO Flap of 1978," Saga UFO Rept. 6 (Jan.1979):21,22.

Sesekinika
-UFO (NL)
  1973, March 16/Bert Harvey
    "Object Photographed in Canada," APRO Bull. 21 (May-June 1973):4. il.

Shallow Lake
-UFO (NL)
  1970, March 11/Donald Leonard
    Owen Sound Sun-Times, 12 Mar.1970.

Sharon
-UFO (CE-2)
  1975, July/ground markings only
    Ted Phillips, "Several Possible Traces Reported in 1975," Skylook, no.97 (Dec.1975):16-17.
-UFO (NL)
  1973, Sep.20/Beverley Hall/Maple Lane
  1973, Oct./Beverley Hall/Maple Lane
    Newmarket Aurora-Era, 31 Oct.1973.

Shebandowan
-UFO (CE-1)
  1969, March 11/Russell Barker/Hwy.11
    "The Maritimes--Newest Playground for UFOs?" Flying Saucers, June 1970, pp.13,15.

Sheguiandah
-Archeological site
  ca.28,000-4500 B.C.
    Thomas E. Lee, "A Preliminary Report on the Sheguiandah Site, Manitoulin Island," Bull.Can.Nat'l Mus., no. 128 (1953):58-67. il.
    Thomas E. Lee, "The First Sheguiandah Expedition, Manitoulin Island, Ontario," Am.Antiquity 20 (1954):101-11.
    Thomas E. Lee, "The Second Sheguiandah Expedition, Manitoulin Island, Ontario," Am.Antiquity 21 (1955):63-71.

Thomas E. Lee, "Position and Meaning of a Radiocarbon Sample from the Sheguiandah Site, Ontario," Am.Antiquity 22 (1956):79.
Thomas E. Lee, "The Antiquity of the Sheguiandah Site," Can.Field-Naturalist 71, no.3 (1957):118-37.
John T. Sanford, "Geologic Observations at the Sheguiandah Site," Can.Field-Naturalist 71, no.3 (1957):138-48.
George I. Quimby, "Lanceolate Points and Fossil Beaches in the Upper Great Lakes Region," Am.Antiquity 24 (1959):424-26.
Thomas E. Lee, "Sheguiandah: Workshop or Habitation?" Anthro.J.Canada 2, no.3 (1964):16-24.
John T. Sanford, "Sheguiandah Reviewed," Anthro.J.Canada 9, no.1 (1971):2-15. il.
Thomas E. Lee, "Sheguiandah in Retrospect," Anthro.J.Canada 10, no.1 (1972):28-30.
Thomas E. Lee, "Sheguiandah As Viewed in 1974," NEARA Newsl. 9 (summer 1974):34-37.
Franklin Folsom, America's Ancient Treasures (N.Y.: Rand McNally, 1974), p.184.

Simcoe
-Genetic anomaly
  1889, May/John H. Carter/=cow gives birth to lambs
    Toronto Globe, 25 May 1889.

Six Nations Reserve
-Haunt
  1880s-
    Hamilton Spectator, 22 Oct.1968.
-Shamanism
    C.A. Weslager, Magic Medicines of the Indians (N.Y.: Signet, 1974 ed.), pp.91,97,119,122,125,129.

Smithville
-Humanoid
  1965, Aug./Hwy.20
    Hamilton Spectator, 16-17 Aug.1965.

Southampton
-UFO (NL)
  1978, Jan.16
    Stratford Beacon-Times, 18 Jan.1978.

South Bay
-Ghost dog
  n.d./Mariners' Cemetery
    Eileen Sonin, More Canadian Ghosts (Richmond Hill, Ont.: Pocket Books, 1974 ed.), p.58.

Sowerby
-Horse mutilation
  1967, Nov.5/Lorne Wolgenuth
    Jacques Vallee, Passport to Magonia (Chicago: Regnery, 1969), p.48.
-UFO (CE-1)
  1967, Nov.5/Terry Goodmurphy/nr. Maple

Ridge Hill
    Jacques Vallee, <u>Passport to Magonia</u>
    (Chicago: Regnery, 1969), p.48.

Stirling
-UFO (?)
    1971, July-1972, May/traces=uric acid
    N. Miles & S.P. Mathur, "Seasonal In-
    cidence of Anhydrous Uric Acid
    Granules in the Collision Zone of
    Two Fairy Rings," <u>Can.J.Soil Sci.</u>
    52 (1972):515-17.

Straffordville
-UFO (CE-2)
    1978, Aug.28/Hwy.19
    <u>Tillsonburg News</u>, 8 Sep.1978.

Stratford
-Ghost
    1930s
    Eileen Sonin, <u>More Canadian Ghosts</u>
    (Richmond Hill, Ont.: Pocket Books,
    1974 ed.), pp.48-49.
-Ghost dog
    n.d./Jessie Tuthill
    Eileen Sonin, <u>More Canadian Ghosts</u>
    (Richmond Hill, Ont.: Pocket Books,
    1974 ed.), p.81.

Streetsville
-Haunt
    1970s/Mississauga Rd. x Steeles Ave.
    Sheila Hervey, <u>Some Canadian Ghosts</u>
    (Richmond Hill, Ont.: Pocket Books,
    1973), pp.119-21.

Sudbury
-Crisis apparition
    1910, Jan.21/Mary Travers
    "Return in the Night," <u>Fate</u> 10 (Oct.
    1957):89, quoting <u>Toronto Globe &</u>
    <u>Mail</u> (undated).
-Disappearance
    1940, Oct./Earl Kirk/Hwy.17/=accident
    "Mystery of the Missing Motorist,"
    <u>Fate</u> 8 (Feb.1955):73.
    (Letter), John King, <u>Fate</u> 9 (Mar.
    1956):119-20.
    Harold T. Wilkins, <u>Flying Saucers Un-</u>
    <u>censored</u> (N.Y.: Pyramid, 1967 ed.),
    p.224, quoting <u>Winnipeg (Man.) Trib-</u>
    <u>une</u> (undated).
-Humanoid tracks
    1974, July/Vince Lefebvre
    John Green, <u>Sasquatch: The Apes Among</u>
    <u>Us</u> (Seattle: Hancock House, 1978),
    pp.250-51.
-Meteorite crater
    100,000 m.diam./certain
    Robert S. Dietz, "Cryptoexplosion
    Structures: A Discussion," <u>Am.J.Sci.</u>
    261 (1963):650-64.
    Robert S. Dietz, "Sudbury Structure
    As an Astrobleme," <u>J.Geology</u> 72
    (1964):412-34. il.
    B.M. French, "Possible Relations be-
    tween Meteorite Impact and Igneous
    Petrogenesis," <u>Bull.Vulcanology</u> 34
    (1970):455-517.

-Reincarnation
    1973/Dorothy Rainville
    Morris & Dorothy Rainville, "Was I
    Madame Pompadour's Daughter?" <u>Fate</u>
    31 (Aug.1978):90-92.
-UFO (DD)
    1967, Nov.8/Ronald Berube
    "On the Canadian Scene," <u>APRO Bull.</u>
    16 (Jan.-Feb.1968):4-5.
    1974, July 15
    Wido Hoville, "Object Escorts Air-
    liner," <u>Can.UFO Rept.</u>, no.20
    (1975):7.
-UFO (NL)
    1972, July 27/Falconbridge Rd.
    Glenn McWane & David Graham, <u>The New</u>
    <u>UFO Sightings</u> (N.Y.: Warner, 1974),
    p.46, quoting <u>Sudbury Star</u> (undated).

Sunbury
-Mystery auto accident
    1969, Jan./Celina Legris
    <u>Brockville Recorder & Times</u>, 24 Jan.
    1969.

Swastika
-Poltergeist
    1952/Lucienne Desmarthais
    Sheila Hervey, <u>Some Canadian Ghosts</u>
    (Richmond Hill, Ont.: Pocket Books,
    1973), pp.72-73.
-UFO (CE-3)
    1948/Mr. Galbraith
    Jacques Vallee, <u>Passport to Magonia</u>
    (Chicago: Regnery, 1969), p.192.

Temagami
-Genetic anomaly
    1954, May/George B. Watterson/=bird
    with four wings
    (Editorial), <u>Fate</u> 7 (Sep.1954):10.
-UFO (NL)
    1949
    Ray Palmer, "Space Ships, Flying Sau-
    cers and Clean Noses," <u>Fate</u> 3 (May
    1950):36,44.

Thamesville
-UFO (?)
    1913, Feb.9/Catharine MacVicar Duncan/
    =meteor procession
    C.A. Chant, "An Extraordinary Meteor
    Display," <u>J.Roy.Astron.Soc'y Canada</u>
    7 (1913):145,200-201.

Thessalon
-Humanoid and livestock mutilations
    1950, July 12
    "Land Beasties," <u>Doubt</u>, no.30
    (1950):43.

Thornhill
-Haunt
    1973/John Sears/Annswell
    W. Ritchie Benedict, "Healer Haunts
    Her Old Home," <u>Fate</u> 27 (Oct.1974):48.

Thunder Bay
-Anomalous fossil
    =tracks in Precambrian rock

"More on the Devil's Hoofprints,"
Pursuit 4 (Jan.1971):4-5.
-Telepathy
  1941, March/Helen Moore Strickland
    Helen Moore Strickland, "Test of
    Telepathy," Fate 8 (Nov.1955):40.
-UFO (?)
  1949, Oct.24
    "If It's in the Sky It's a Saucer,"
    Doubt, no.27 (1949):416,417.
  1957, Nov.5/=Venus
    Jacques & Janine Vallee, Challenge to
    Science (N.Y.: Ace, 1966 ed.), p.131.
-UFO (CE-1)
  1959, Oct.25/Douglas Robinson/W on Hwy.
  1
    "World Round-up," Flying Saucer Rev.
    6 (Jan.-Feb.1960):14,17.
-Windshield pitting
  1954, April
    (Editorial), Fate 7 (Sep.1954):12.

Tillsonburg
-Humanoid
  1965, Sep.
    Kitchener-Waterloo Record, 4 Sep.
    1965.

Toronto
-Archeological site
  Black Creek
    Jeffrey Goodman, Psychic Archaeology
    (N.Y.: Berkley, 1978 ed.), p.159.
-Clairempathy
  1970s/J. Norman Emerson/University of
  Toronto
    J. Norman Emerson, "Intuitive Arch-
    aeology: A Psychic Approach," New
    Horizons 1, no.3 (Jan.1974):14-18.
    Jeffrey Goodman, Psychic Archaeology
    (N.Y.: Berkley, 1978 ed.), pp.157-
    71.
-Clairvoyance
  1944, Dec./Michael Savage/Deloraine
  Ave.
    Harry M. Savage, "Clairvoyance from
    a Two-Year-Old," Fate 22 (Jan.1969):
    82-84.
  1957, Aug.1/Frank Frabali
    (Editorial), Fate 10 (Dec.1957):11-
    12, quoting Toronto Daily Star (un-
    dated).
-Contactee
  1968-   /Joan Howard/3309½ Yonge St.
    Brad Steiger, Revelation: The Divine
    Fire (Englewood Cliffs, N.J.: Pren-
    tice-Hall, 1973), p.154.
    Glenn McWane & David Graham, The New
    UFO Sightings (N.Y.: Warner, 1974),
    pp.123-28.
-Dematerialization
  1954, March/Eberhardt Matuschka/Hungar-
  ian House
    Harold T. Wilkins, Flying Saucers Un-
    censored (N.Y.: Pyramid, 1967 ed.),
    p.85.
-Disappearance
  1919, Dec.2/Ambrose Small/Grand Opera
  House
    New York Times, 4 Jan.1920, p.14; 6

Jan.1920, p.21; 11 Jan.1920, p.18;
3 June 1920, p.17; 17 July 1920, p.
3; 14 Aug.1920, p.18; 24 Nov.1920,
p.5; 25 Dec.1920, p.4; 4 Jan.1921,
p.4; 25 Mar.1921, p.3; 16 Aug.1921,
p.11; 15 Mar.1922, p.21; 18 Mar.
1922, p.20; 21 Mar.1923, p.17; and
6 June 1923, p.24.
-Dowsing
  1956, July/Beatrice Sprowl
    (Editorial), Fate 9 (Nov.1956):6-8.
-Erratic crocodilian
  1929, June 18
    New York Times, 19 June 1929, p.24.
-Fall of burning substance
  1954, April/Marilyn Joblin
    Toronto Telegram, 26 Apr.1954.
-Fall of fish
  1939, March 21/Iola Martin/1122 E. D
  St.
    "Fall of Fish," Fortean Soc'y Mag.,
    no.3 (Jan.1940):7, quoting Los An-
    geles (Cal.) Herald-Examiner (un-
    dated).
  1954, March/John Murphy
    San Francisco (Cal.) Chronicle, 3
    Apr.1954.
    "The Day It Rained Frogs," Fate 11
    (May 1958):25,29.
-Fall of porous rock
  1978, Aug.20/Ruby Simpson
    Toronto Star, 21-22 Aug.1978.
-Ghost
  1934/Annie Beevor/Chisholm Ave.
  1944, fall/Urla Bayley/Sunnyside
  ca.1964/Ronald Secker/Walmer Rd.
  ca.1968/Margaret Marinoff/Bleeker St.
    Eileen Sonin, More Canadian Ghosts
    (Richmond Hill, Ont.: Pocket Books,
    1974 ed.), pp.19-20,54-56,63-64,
    107-10.
-Ghost dog
  n.d./Bud Hubbard/North Toronto
    Eileen Sonin, More Canadian Ghosts
    (Richmond Hill, Ont.: Pocket Books,
    1974 ed.), pp.83-84.
-Haunt
  1830s/James Kidd/Duke x Sherbourne St.
    Sheila Hervey, Some Canadian Ghosts
    (Richmond Hill, Ont.: Pocket Books,
    1973), pp.105-106.
  1860s-   /Alan Aylesworth/University
  College
    Eileen Sonin, More Canadian Ghosts
    (Richmond Hill, Ont.: Pocket Books,
    1974 ed.), pp.75-77.
  1930s/A.E. Cliffe/Humber R.
    R. DeWitt Miller, Stranger Than Life
    (N.Y.: Ace, 1955 ed.), pp.27-28.
  n.d./Kathie Lowe/Bay St.
  n.d./Shirley Kitchener/Dunfield St.
  n.d./Joy Chong/Jarvis St.
  n.d./Lillian Moore/Dundas St.
  n.d./Mrs. Matthews/College St.
  n.d./Evelyn Leonard/Bagot Court
  n.d./Kitty McCaulay/Queen St. W
    Eileen Sonin, More Canadian Ghosts
    (Richmond Hill, Ont.: Pocket Books,
    1974 ed.), pp.28-30,42-43,50,52-54,
    72-75,97-103.

1960-1966/Mackenzie House/82 Bond St.
Toronto Telegram, 27-28 June 1960.
Toronto Daily Star, 28 June 1960.
"The Haunted Home of William Lyon
Mackenzie," Fate 14 (Jan.1961):36-
43. il.
Susy Smith, Ghosts Around the House
(N.Y.: World, 1970).
Sheila Hervey, Some Canadian Ghosts
(Richmond Hill, Ont.: Pocket Books,
1973), pp.106-14.
1965/S. Tupper Bigelow/Old City Hall
Sheila Hervey, Some Canadian Ghosts
(Richmond Hill, Ont.: Pocket Books,
1973), pp.104-105.
1965-1968/Mynah Bird Club/Yorkville
Hans Holzer, Haunted Houses (N.Y.:
Crown, 1971), pp.98-100.
Hans Holzer, Gothic Ghosts (N.Y.:
Pocket Books, 1972), pp.158-67.
1967-1970/Elizabeth Ward/Wellesley St.
1968-1970/Peter Verboom/Sumach St.
Eileen Sonin, More Canadian Ghosts
(Richmond Hill, Ont.: Pocket Books,
1974 ed.), pp.111,115-16.
1969-1970/Herbert A. Graham/Colborne
Lodge
Herbert A. Graham, "Old Houses Remember," Fate 24 (Oct.1971):48-50.
il.
1970, July/Esme Nettleton
Eileen Sonin, More Canadian Ghosts
(Richmond Hill, Ont.: Pocket Books,
1974 ed.), pp.117-20.
1972/174 Avenue Rd.
Brad Steiger, "1972: A Bumper Year
for Hauntings," Beyond Reality, no.
4 (May 1973):15,17.
-Healing
1956, April 1/Paul Lesser
(Editorial), Fate 9 (Aug.1956):9.
1957-   /Alex Holmes
Allen Spraggett, The Unexplained
(N.Y.: Signet, 1968 ed.), pp.138-43.
-Inner development
1970s/Claremont Centre/85 Spadina Rd.
1970s/Evering Consultants, Ltd./43 Eg-
lington Ave. E, Suite 803
Armand Biteaux, The New Consciousness
(Willits, Cal.: Oliver, 1975), pp.
24,39.
-Lake monster
1882, Aug.21/L. Ontario
Toronto Mail, 22 Aug.1882.
New York Times, 25 Aug.1882, p.2.
1978, July 31/Danny Elliott/off Winder-
mere Ave.
Toronto Sun, 1 Aug.1978.
-Midday darkness
1881, Sep.5
Toronto Globe, 6 Sep.1881.
-Out-of-body experience
1961, Nov.19/Peter Urquhart/Rosedale
Robert Crookall, More Astral Projections (London, Eng.: Aquarian, 1964).
-Parapsychology research
1970s/Toronto Soc'y for Psychical Re-
search/10 N. Sherbourne St.
A.R.G. Owen, "Editorial," New Horizons 1, no.2 (summer 1973):65-68.

A.R.G. Owen, "The Shapes of Egyptian
Pyramids," New Horizons 1, no.2
(summer 1973):102-108.
1970s/Int'l Ass'n for Psychotronic Re-
search/43 Eglinton Ave. E
John White & Stanley Krippner, eds.,
Future Science (Garden City: Anchor,
1977), p.588.
-Phantom
1975, spring/Paul Mohamed
W. Ritchie Benedict, "The Mark of
the Cross," Fate 30 (July 1977):43.
-Poltergeist
1947, Jan./Mr. Sherman/Silverwood Ave.
R.S. Lambert, Exploring the Supernatural (Toronto: McClelland &
Stewart, 1955), p.146.
-Precognition
1900s-   /Jean Fraser
Alex Saunders, "Toronto's Fighting
Fortune Teller," Fate 15 (Aug.1962):
61-67.
1937/H. Addington Bruce
1941, Dec./H. Addington Bruce
H. Addington Bruce, "Adventures in
Precognition," Fate 7 (Oct.1954):
86,88-90.
n.d./Mrs. Pardoe
ca.1958/Doris Carr
Eileen Sonin, More Canadian Ghosts
(Richmond Hill, Ont.: Pocket Books,
1974 ed.), pp.149-50,154-55.
1962, Sep.13/James Wilkie
Allen Spraggett, The Unexplained
(N.Y.: Signet, 1968 ed.), pp.35-36.
-Seance
1967, Sep.3/Arthur Ford/Canadian Tele-
vision Network studio
New York Times, 27 Sep.1967, p.1; 28
Sep.1967, p.43; and 1 Oct.1967, sec.
IV, p.11.
Betty Lou White, "The Bishop Pike
Seance," Fate 21 (Feb.1968):34-47.
James A. Pike & Diane Kennedy, The
Other Side (Garden City: Doubleday,
1968).
Arthur Ford, Unknown But Known (N.Y.:
Harper & Row, 1968).
Allen Spraggett, The Bishop Pike
Story (N.Y.: Signet, 1970).
Merrill F. Unger, The Haunting of
Bishop Pike (Wheaton, Ill.: Tyndale,
1971).
William A. Rauscher & Allen Spraggett,
Arthur Ford: The Man Who Talked with
the Dead (N.Y.: Signet, 1974), pp.
244-68.
1972, Sep.-   /Iris Owen/Toronto SPR
Iris M. Owen & Margaret H. Sparrow,
"Generation of Paranormal Physical
Phenomena in Connection with an Im-
aginary 'Communicator,'" New Hor-
izons 1, no.3 (Jan.1974):6-13.
Iris M. Owen, "Philip's Story Con-
tinued," New Horizons 2, no.1
(1975):14-20.
Iris M. Owen, "Continuation of the
Philip Experiment," New Horizons 2,
no.2 (1976):3-6.
Iris M. Owen & Margaret Sparrow, Con-

juring Up Philip (N.Y.: Harper &
Row, 1976).
-Spirit medium
1850s/Mrs. Swain
Emma Hardinge Britten, Modern American Spiritualism (N.Y.: The Author,
1870), pp.463-64.
1918
J.W. Hayward, "Fortune Telling," J.
ASPR 15 (1921):185-205.
1930s/Ms. Wallace/200 Rosethorn Ave.
1940s-   /James Wilkie
Allen Spraggett, The Unexplained
(N.Y.: Signet, 1968 ed.), pp.57-72,
79-81,84-86,187.
-Spontaneous human combustion
1969, Dec.17/John Komar
Toronto Star, 17 Dec.1969.
-Telepathy
1924-   /Marion Smith
John C. Ross, "The Case of the Identical Twins," Fate 12 (May 1959):
66-67.
-UFO (?)
1968, Oct.26/Charles Luttor/=lens
flare
Colman S. VonKeviczky, "A Re-Analy-
sis," Can.UFO Rept., no.24 (summer
1976):19-21. il.
1978, March 8
Kitchener-Waterloo Record, 10 Mar.
1978.
-UFO (CE-1)
1957, Aug./Colleen Weiler/nr. Bank of
Montreal
Gray Barker, "Chasing the Flying Saucers," Flying Saucers, Feb.1958, pp.
46,49-50.
1967, April 28/Betty Cassar
"Beam Spotlights Witnesses," UFO Inv.
4 (May-June 1967):3.
-UFO (CE-2)
1957, Nov.4
Toronto Daily Star, 5 Nov.1957.
-UFO (DD)
1913, Feb.10/R.A. Adams/W. Wellington
St.
Toronto Daily Star, 10 Feb.1913.
1947, Sep.14/Raymond Johnson
Toronto Globe & Mail, 20 Sep.1947,
p.1. il.
1957, Nov.6
Richard Hall, ed., The UFO Evidence
(Washington: NICAP, 1964), p.165.
1978, April 9
"Foreign Forum," Int'l UFO Reporter
3 (Aug.1978):2.
-UFO (NL)
1950/L. Ontario
(Editorial), Fate 5 (Oct.1952):7-8.
1950, July 19
Bruce S. Maccabee, "UFO Related Information from the FBI Files: Part
7," MUFON UFO J., no.132 (Nov.-Dec.
1978):11,14.
1952, April 19
Toronto Globe & Mail, 20 Apr.1952.
1952, May 1
Desmond Leslie & George Adamski, Flying Saucers Have Landed (N.Y.: Brit-

ish Book Centre, 1953), p.64, quoting CKRN radio broadcast.
1954, April 23/Alex Saunders
(Letter), Fate 7 (Nov.1954):114-15.
1956, Dec.18/Alex Saunders
(Letter), Fate 10 (Apr.1957):114-16.
(Letter), Flying Saucers, Feb.1958,
p.62.
1957, Aug.1/Eric Aldwinckle
Richard Hall, ed., The UFO Evidence
(Washington: NICAP, 1964), p.71.
1957, Nov.6/S. Beaumont
Aimé Michel, Flying Saucers and the
Straight-Line Mystery (N.Y.: Criterion, 1958), p.249.
1966, Aug.7/Alan Clark
Toronto Star & Metro News, 8 Aug.1966.
1967, April 28/John J. Oosterdag/Downs-
view
"Objects Aim Light Beams, Drop 'Fireballs,'" UFO Inv. 4 (May-June 1967):
1,3.
ca.1968, summer/J.G. Holland
(Letter), Can.UFO Rept., no.20
(1975):22.
1968, April 8
"French General, Scientists, Report
UFOs," UFO Inv. 4 (May-June 1968):3.
1978, June/Cliff Crocker/Kimberley St.
Toronto Sun, 4 Feb.1979. il.
1979, Jan.7/Kathleen Balfour/Earl Bales
Park
Toronto Globe & Mail, 8 Jan.1979.
Toronto Sun, 8 Jan.1979.
-Windshield pitting
1954
Harold T. Wilkins, Flying Saucers Uncensored (N.Y.: Pyramid, 1967 ed.),
p.153.

Uptergrove
-Stigmata
1937-1950s/Mrs. Donald McIsaac
Frank Hamilton, "Is There a Miracle
at Uptergrove?" Maclean's Mag., 15
Sep.1950, pp.7-9,39-42. il.
Alex Saunders, "Canada's Unknown
Stigmatist," Fate 12 (Feb.1959):44-
51.

Utterson
-UFO (CE-3)
1975, Oct.7/Robert Suffern
Henry H. McKay, "UFO, Humanoid Re-
ported in Ontario," Skylook, no.95
(Oct.1975):3-4.
"Ontario Family Invaded by Media Fol-
lowing UFO, Humanoid Report," Sky-
look, no.95 (Oct.1975):4.
"Close Encounter in Canada," APRO
Bull. 24 (Jan.1976):6.
Harry Tokarz, "Hard Choice for Wit-
nesses," Can.UFO Rept., no.32 (fall
1978):9-10.

Vars
-UFO (CE-1)
1973, Nov./Ron Hamelin/Hwy.417
1973, Dec.1/Nora LaRocque/Hwy.417
Arthur Bray, "Car Chased under Bridge

Can.UFO Rept., no.20 (1975):11,13.

Wainfleet
-Mystery oil spill
  1978, June 9
    Niagara Falls Review, 23 June 1978,
    p.3.
    "Mystery Oil Spills on Lake Erie,"
    Res Bureaux Bull., no.37 (17 Aug.
    1978):4.
-Plant sensitivity
  1950s/Eugene Canby
    Peter Tompkins & Christopher Bird,
    The Secret Life of Plants (N.Y.:
    Harper & Row, 1973), p.148.

Walkerton
-UFO (CE-1)
  1960, summer
    J. Allen Hynek, The UFO Experience
    (Chicago: Regnery, 1972), pp.47-49.
-UFO (NL)
  1958, Nov.1/Edward Johnston
    "Hovering UFO Puzzles South African
    Officials," UFO Inv. 1 (Dec.1958):
    1,3.

Wallaceburg
-Archeological site
  ca.400 A.D.
    Houston (Tex.) Chronicle, 18 July
    1978.
-Poltergeist
  1829-1831, Jan./John McDonald/Baldoon
    Neil McDonald, The Belledoon Myster-
    ies: Weird and Startling Events
    (Wallaceburg: The Author, 1871).
    R.S. Lambert, Exploring the Supernat-
    ural (Toronto: McClelland & Stewart,
    1955), pp.63-88.
-UFO (NL)
  1947, July 1/Ray Stevens
  1947, July 5
    Windsor Daily Star, 7 July 1947.
  1978, Sep.15
    Chatham News, 18 Sep.1978.

Warsaw
-UFO (NL)
  1979, Feb.5
    "Recent UFO Reports," Res Bureaux
    Bull., no.44 (Feb.1979):4.

Warwick
-Aerial phantom
  1843, Oct.3/Charles Cooper
    Eli Curtis, A Wonderful Phenomenon
    (N.Y.: The Author, 1850).

Wasaga Beach
-Ghost
  n.d./Denise Tessier
    Eileen Sonin, More Canadian Ghosts
    (Richmond Hill, Ont.: Pocket Books,
    1974 ed.), pp.13-14.
-Lake monster
  1938, June
    R.S. Lambert, Exploring the Supernat-
    ural (Toronto: McClelland & Stewart,
    1955), p.198.

Waterdown
-UFO (CE-2)
  1967/ground markings only
    Ted Phillips, Physical Traces Associ-
    ated with UFO Sightings (Evanston:
    Center for UFO Studies, 1975), p.46.

Waterford
-UFO (NL)
  1974, Nov.26/Mrs. Andrew Ledwig
    Timothy Green Beckley, "Operation
    Contact," Saga UFO Rept. 3 (Apr.
    1976):39,62-64, quoting Simcoe Re-
    former (undated).

Waterloo
-UFO (?)
  1979, Jan.23
    "Recent UFO Reports," Res Bureaux
    Bull., no.44 (Feb.1979):4.
-UFO (CE-2)
  1974, Nov.1/Brent Smith
    Ted Phillips, Physical Traces Associ-
    ated with UFO Sightings (Evanston:
    Center for UFO Studies, 1975), p.105.
    (Letter), Homer Schaefer, Can.UFO
    Rept., no.20 (1975):22-23.

Welland
-Mystery plane crash
  1960, July 17/R. Wilson
    Jay Gourley, The Great Lakes Triangle
    (Greenwich, Ct.: Fawcett, 1977), pp.
    129-30.
-Skyquake
  1950, Feb.7
    "Bangs," Doubt, no.30 (1950):43.
-UFO (NL)
  1978, April 2/Teetsia Blokzyl
    Toronto Sun, 4 Apr.1978; and 6 Apr.
    1978.

Wellesley
-Poltergeist
  1880, July-Sep./Mr. Manser
    Toronto Globe, 9 Sep.1880.
    Halifax (N.S.) Citizen, 12 Sep.1880.

West Carleton
-UFO (NL)
  1978, Dec.11
    "Recent UFO Reports," Res Bureaux
    Bull., no.43 (Jan.1979):3,4.

West Flamboro
-UFO (NL)
  1973, summer
    Hamilton Spectator, 29 Oct.1973.

West Guilford
-Precognition
  1960s-   /Malva Dee/Enchanted Acres
    Brad Steiger & Warren Smith, "How the
    Seers Scored in 1968," Fate 22 (Jan.
    1969):72,77.
    Warren Smith, "Phenomenal Predictions
    for 1975," Saga, Jan.1975, pp.20,22.
    Warren Smith, "Phenomenal Predictions
    for 1976," Saga, Jan.1976, pp.16,17.
    "Probe's 1977 Directory of the Psy-

chic World," Probe the Unknown 5
(spring 1977):32,35. il.

Whitby
-UFO (NL)
    1978, March 25/Richard Davis
        Toronto Sunday Sun, 26 Mar.1978.

Wiarton
-Disappearance
    1881, Nov.25/"Jane Miller"/Colpoys Bay
        Dwight Boyer, Ghost Ships of the
        Great Lakes (N.Y.: Dodd, Mead, 1968),
        pp.238-45.
    1966, March 17/Ernest Eugene Nabors/
    Piper PA-30
    n.d./CF-101 interceptors
        Jay Gourley, The Great Lakes Triangle
        (Greenwich, Ct.: Fawcett, 1977),
        pp.169-70.
-Phantom panther
    1978, Oct./Art King/NW of town
        Kingston Whig-Standard, 20 Oct.1978,
        p.23.

Windsor
-Erratic crocodilian
    1970, Sep.20/Wyandotte St. W
        Windsor Star, 21 Sep.1970.
-Fall of soot
    1973, Aug.26/=pollution?
        Fort Wayne (Ind.) News-Sentinel, 28
        Aug.1973.
-Fire anomaly
    1941, Dec./Nicholas White/Dominion
    Golf and Country Club
        (Editorial), Fate 11 (June 1958):8-
        12, quoting Detroit (Mich.) Free
        Press (undated).
-UFO (?)
    1968-1973/sewage treatment plant
        Hamilton Spectator, 19 Oct.1973.
    1973, Oct.28?/Pat Whealen/=balloon
        Owen Sound Sun-Times, 6 Nov.1973.
-UFO (NL)
    1947, July 6/Walkerville
        Windsor Daily Star, 7 July 1947.
    1957, Dec.12/J.A. Miller/airport
        Windsor Daily Star, 13 Dec.1957.
    1978, March 6
        Windsor Daily Star, 7 Mar.1978.

Wingham
-UFO (?)
    1952, April 20
        Toronto Daily Star, 21 Apr.1952.

Wooler
-Poltergeist
    1968, July/Fred Coulthard
        Toronto Daily Star, 5 July 1968.
        "Poltergeists As Usual," Pursuit 2
        (Jan.1969):4-6.
        Mrs. W. Graystone, "Canada's UFO
        Poltergeist," in Beyond Condon (Fly-
        ing Saucer Rev. special issue, no.
        2, June 1969), pp.66-68,70.
        Joan Whritenour, "Invisible Beings
        Invade Canadian Home," in Brad Stei-
        ger & Joan Whritenour, eds., Flying

Saucer Invasion: Target--Earth
(N.Y.: Award, 1969), pp.60-63.
-UFO (CE-2)
    1962/ground markings only
        Ted Phillips, Physical Traces Associ-
        ated with UFO Sightings (Evanston:
        Center for UFO Studies, 1975), p.26.

B. Physical Features

Abitibi L.
-Clairvoyance
    1879, Feb.
        Ernest Thompson Seton, The Arctic
        Prairies (N.Y.: Scribner, 1911).

Algonquin Provincial Park
-Haunt
    n.d./nr. Canoe L.
        Toronto Globe & Mail, 23 May 1970.
        Sheila Hervey, Some Canadian Ghosts
        (Richmond Hill, Ont.: Pocket Books,
        1973), pp.46-49.

Askins Point
-Phantom ship
    n.d./Sebastian Lacelle
        Charles M. Skinner, Myths and Legends
        Beyond Our Border (Philadelphia:
        Lippincott, 1899), pp.149-52.

Ben Echo
-Deathbed apparition
    1919, Aug./Horace Traubel
        Raymond J. Ross, "Dying Vision of
        Horace Traubel," Fate 4 (May-June
        1951):37-38.

Berens L.
-Lake monster
    n.d./Leif Mannon
        R.S. Lambert, Exploring the Supernat-
        ural (Toronto: McClelland & Stewart,
        1955), p.198.

Black L.
-Poltergeist
    1935, Jan./Joseph Quinn
        Hereward Carrington & Nandor Fodor,
        Haunted People (N.Y.: Signet, 1968
        ed.), p.64.

Bonnechere R.
-Archeological site
        J. Norman Emerson, "Preliminary Re-
        port on the Excavations of the Kant
        Site, Renfrew County, Ontario,"
        Bull.Nat'l Mus.Canada, no.113 (1949):
        17-22.
        J. Norman Emerson, "The Kant Site:
        A Point Peninsula Manifestation in
        Renfrew County, Ontario," Trans.
        Roy.Can.Inst. 31 (1955):24-66. il.

Boshkung L.
-UFO (CE-1)
    1973, Nov.23/Earl Pitts/Hwy.25
        Curt Sutherly, "UFO Invasion of Bosh-
        kung Lake," Fate 30 (Nov.1977):55.

-UFO (CE-2)
  1974, Feb.26/Ashley Lunham
    Lindsay Post, 14 Mar.1974.
  1974, March 20
    George D. Fawcett, "The 'Unreported'
    UFO Wave of 1974," Saga UFO Rept. 2
    (spring 1975):50,51.
-UFO (NL)
  1973, Nov.12-1974, March/Ashley Lunham
    Minden Progress, 21 Feb.1974.
    Lindsay Post, 14 Mar.1974; and 20
    Mar.1974.
    "Ontario, Canada, Lake Scene of Re-
    ported Flap," Skylook, no.79 (June
    1974):19.
    Curt Sutherly, "UFO Invasion of Bosh-
    kung Lake," Fate 30 (Nov.1977):55-
    58.
  1974, March 10/Peter Courtney
    Minden Progress, 14 Mar.1974.

Brittania L.
-Precognition
  1945, summer
    Dorothy Carlos, "Premonition of a
    Fatal Fire," Fate 17 (June 1964):75-
    78.

Bruce Peninsula
-Disappearance
  1956, Aug.2/CF-100
    Jay Gourley, The Great Lakes Triangle
    (Greenwich, Ct.: Fawcett, 1977), p.
    58.

Cache Bay
-Pictographs
    Duane Depaepe, "Pictographs of Cache
    Bay, Ontario, Canada," Central States
    Arch.J. 7 (1960):36-37.

Cache L.
-Cloud anomaly
  1931, July/John Zeleny
    John Zeleny, "Rumbling Clouds and
    Luminous Clouds," Science 75 (1932):
    80-81.

Carlington Heights Reservoir
-UFO (CE-3)
  1965, Aug./Mr. Harris
    "Another Occupant Case," APRO Bull.
    21 (Sep.-Oct.1972):8.
    Coral & Jim Lorenzen, Encounters
    with UFO Occupants (N.Y.: Berkley,
    1976), pp.201-202.

Clearwater Bay
-UFO (DD)
  1958, July
    Brian C. Cannon, "Canadian Saw Saucer-
    Shaped Object in 1958," Skylook, no.
    31 (June 1970):12.

Coates Creek
-Archeological site
  ca.10,000 B.C.
    Peter J. Storch, "The Coates Creek
    Site: A Possible Late Paleo-Indian-
    Early Archaic Site in Simcoe County,

Ontario," Ontario Arch., no.30
(1978):25-46. il.

Crow R.
-UFO (CE-1)
  1947, Aug.16-17/Roy Simpson
    Kenneth Arnold, "Are Space Visitors
    Here?" Fate 1 (summer 1948):4,11-
    13. il.

Deer L.
-Norse runestone
  n.d./Oscar Lindokken
    Olaf Strandwold, Norse Inscriptions
    on American Stones (Weehauken, N.J.:
    Magnus Björndal, 1948), p.30. il.

Deschenes L.
-Lake monster
  1879-1880
    Ottawa Free Press, 7 July 1880; and
    29 July 1880.
    Toronto Globe, 8 July 1880.
    New York Times, 10 July 1880, p.3;
    and 1 Aug.1880, p.8.
    Ottawa Herald, 20 Aug.1880.
-UFO (DD)
  1947, June/H.S. Gauthier
    Windsor Daily Star, 2 July 1947.

Erie, L.
-Mystery plane crash
  1956, Dec.8/Aero Commander
    Jay Gourley, The Great Lakes Triangle
    (Greenwich, Ct.: Fawcett, 1977),
    p.76.

Etobicoke Creek
-Phantom ship
  1910, Aug./Rowley W. Murphy/mouth
    Rowley W. Murphy, "Ghosts of the
    Great Lakes," Inland Seas 17 (sum-
    mer 1961):94-96.

Falcon L.
-UFO (CE-2)
  1967, June 18
    J. Allen Hynek, The UFO Experience
    (Chicago: Regnery, 1972), pp.131-32.

French R.
-Hog mutilation
  1950, Nov./Joe Restoule
    Robert La Bour, "The Burning on the
    French," Fate 5 (Sep.1952):82-84.

Georgian Bay
-UFO (CE-3)
  1914, Aug./William J. Kiehl
    Paterson (N.J.) Evening News, 15 Aug.
    1966.
    Coral & Jim Lorenzen, Flying Saucer
    Occupants (N.Y.: Signet, 1967), pp.
    19-23.
    John Brent Musgrave, "The Behavior
    and Origins of Canadian UFO Occu-
    pants and Critters: Part Two," Can.
    UFO Rept., no.31 (summer 1978):20.

Glamor L.
-UFO (DD)
   1974, Aug.20/Mrs. George Bailey
   Minden Progress, 29 Aug.1974.

Holleford Crater
-Meteorite crater
   2340 m.diam. x 318 m.deep/certain
   C.S. Beals, G.M. Ferguson & A. Landau,
   "The Holleford Crater in Ontario,"
   Sky & Telescope 15 (May 1956):296.
   C.S. Beals, "Fossil Meteorite Crat-
   ers." Sci.Am. 199 (July 1958):33-39.
   C.S. Beals, "A Probable Meteorite
   Crater of Precolumbian Age at Holle-
   ford, Ontario," Pub.Dominion Obs.,
   Ottawa 24, no.6 (1960):117-42.
   Ted E. Bunch & Alvin J. Cohen, "Coes-
   ite and Shocked Quartz from Holle-
   ford Crater, Ontario, Canada," Sci-
   ence 142 (1963):379-81.

James Bay
-Seance
   1939/Regina Flannery/shaking tent
   Regina Flannery, "The Culture of
   Northeastern Indians," in Frederick
   Johnson, ed., Man in Northeastern
   North America (Andover, Mass.: Phil-
   lips Acad., Pap.Peabody Foundation,
   vol.3, 1946), pp.263-71.

Kettle Point
-UFO (NL)
   1966, March 27
   Victoria (B.C.) Daily Times, 28 Mar.
   1966.

Lake of Bays
-Animal ESP
   n.d./Marilyn Walker/Britannia Hotel
   Eileen Sonin, More Canadian Ghosts
   (Richmond Hill, Ont.: Pocket Books,
   1974 ed.), pp.17-18.
-Clairaudience
   1967/Jim Corey
   Eileen Sonin, More Canadian Ghosts
   (Richmond Hill, Ont.: Pocket Books,
   1974 ed.), p.107.
-Lake monster
   1946, Sep.8/Betsey Ewing/nr. Fairview I.
   Ivan T. Sanderson, "The Big Lake
   Monster Hunt," Fate 17 (Nov.1964):
   99,107-108.
   Ivan T. Sanderson, Things (N.Y.: Pyr-
   amid, 1967), p.33.

Lake of the Woods
-Petroglyphs
   A.C. Lawson, "Ancient Rock Inscrip-
   tions on the Lake of the Woods," Am.
   Naturalist 19 (1885):654-57. il.

La Prairie, L.
-UFO (NL)
   1973, Sep./Gerald St. Pierre
   Cornwall Standard-Freeholder, 1 Nov.
   1973.

Little Long L.
-Ghost light
   1937, March
   R.S. Lambert, Exploring the Supernatural (Toronto: McClelland & Stewart,
   1955), p.143, quoting North Bay
   Nugget (undated).

Manitoulin I.
-Haunt
   n.d.
   Charles M. Skinner, Myths and Legends
   Beyond Our Borders (Philadelphia:
   Lippincott, 1899), pp.154-55.

Marsh Point
-Ghost light
   1845, Sep.
   Richard S. Lambert, "Flying Saucers:
   Their Lurid Past," Saturday Night,
   17 May 1952, pp.9,18.

Maura L.
-UFO (DD)
   1951, July/J. Allan Smith
   Regina Graystone, "Immense UFO over
   Maura Lake," FSR Case Histories, no.
   3 (Feb.1971):14-15.

Mazinaw L.
-Lake monster
   San Antonio (Tex.) Express-News, 5
   June 1977.
   "Lake Monsters," Res Bureaux Bull.,
   no.20 (14 July 1977):4.
-Petroglyphs
   Hugh Cochrane, "Does the Great Lakes
   Region Hide a UFO Empire?" Probe
   the Unknown 3 (Nov.1975):34,67.

Meminisha, L.
-Lake monster
   1947, Aug./Albany R.
   Toronto Globe & Mail, 13 Aug.1947.
   "Run of the Mill," Doubt, no.20
   (1948):302.
   Peter Costello, In Search of Lake
   Monsters (N.Y.: Coward, McCann &
   Geoghegan, 1974), p.227.

Michipicoten I.
-UFO (?)
   1929, June 11/Frank Kushick/=meteor?
   New York Times, 19 June 1929, p.14.

Moose R.
-Phantom
   1936/Alfred Scadding
   (Editorial), Fate 9 (Sep.1956):8-9,
   quoting Toronto Daily Star (undated).

Muskrat L.
-Lake monster
   1968/Donald Humphries
   Philadelphia (Pa.) Evening Bulletin,
   8 July 1969.

Namakan L.
-UFO (CE-2)
   1971, winter/Allen Kielczewski

Minneapolis (Minn.) Star, 25 Jan. 1972.

Nipissing, L.
-Archeological site
  Frank Bay
    Frank Ridley, "The Frank Bay Site, Lake Nipissing, Ontario," *Am.Antiquity* 20 (1954):40-50. il.
-UFO (CE-1)
  1967, June 3
    "The Question of Submerging UFO's," *UFO Inv.* 4 (Mar.1968):4,5.
-UFO (DD)
  1951, fall
    John C. Ross, "Canada Hunts for Saucers," *Fate* 7 (May 1954):12,13.

Ontario, L.
-Aerial phantom
  1842, June 14/Charles Lyell
    Charles Lyell, *Travels in the United States of North America*, 2 vols. (N.Y.: Wiley & Putnam, 1845), 2:85.
-Disappearance
  1889/"Bavaria"/crew only
  1900/"Picton"
  1915, Nov./Capt. La Rush/"F.C. Barnes"
    Hugh F. Cochrane, "Lake Ontario's Mysterious Triangle of Death," *Saga UFO Rept.* 3 (Dec.1976):30-32.
  1960, Sep.27/CF-101 interceptor
    Jay Gourley, *The Great Lakes Triangle* (Greenwich, Ct.: Fawcett, 1977), pp. 170-71.
-Mystery plane crash
  1974, April 19/Bell 47J helicopter
    Jay Gourley, *The Great Lakes Triangle* (Greenwich, Ct.: Fawcett, 1977), pp.26-27.
-Mystery shipwreck
  1854/"Elenor Hamilton"
  1883/"Quinlan"
    Hugh F. Cochrane, "Lake Ontario's Mysterious Triangle of Death," *Saga UFO Rept.* 3 (Dec.1976):30,31.
-Water anomaly
  1872, June 13
    John Brandt Mansfield, ed., *History of the Great Lakes* (Chicago: J.H. Beers, 1899), p.723.

Ottawa R.
-River monster
  1874, Nov.13/R. Young/nr. mouth of Madewaska R.
    New York Times, 18 Nov.1874, p.3, quoting *Arnprior Review* (undated).

Owen Sound
-Mystery shipwreck
  1936, Nov.21/"Hibou"
    Cleveland (O.) Press, 21 Nov.1936.

Pelee I.
-UFO (DD)
  1947, July/R.C. Schramm/Scudder Bay (Letter), *Fate* 1 (fall 1948):126-27.

Pie I.
-Lake monster
  1782, May 3/Vincent St. Germain
    R.S. Lambert, *Exploring the Supernatural* (Toronto: McClelland & Stewart, 1955), pp.182-85, quoting *Canadian Mag.& Literary Repository*, May 1824.

Pigeon L.
-UFO (NL)
  1967, July 3/Doug Denniss
    "UFO Captured on Film," *Skylook*, no. 5 (Jan.1968):7.

Presqu'ile Point
-Disappearance
  1864/Capt. Paxton/"Speedy"
    Hugh F. Cochrane, "Lake Ontario's Mysterious Triangle of Death," *Saga UFO Rept.* 3 (Dec.1976):30,32,54.

Quinte, Bay of
-Lake monster
  19th c./E.J. Barker
    "Appearances in the Lakes," *Res Bureaux Bull.*, no.37 (17 Aug.1978):2,3.

Rice L.
-Archeological site
  7500 B.C.-1500 A.D./Serpent Mounds Provincial Park
    William R. Adams, "The Rice Lake Serpent Mound Group," *Bull.Roy.Ontario Mus.Arch.*, no.24 (1956):14-19. il.
    Richard B. Johnston, "The Findings After Two Years of Work at Serpent Mounds Site, Rice Lake, Ontario," *Proc.Indiana Acad.Sci.* 67 (1958): 96-97.
    Richard B. Johnston, "More Findings at the Serpent Mounds Site, Rice Lake, Ontario," *Proc.Indiana Acad. Sci.* 69 (1960):73-77. il.
    Richard B. Johnston, *The Archaeology of the Serpent Mounds Site* (Ottawa: Occ.Pap.Roy.Ontario Mus., no.10, 1968). il.
    Richard B. Johnston, "Archaeology of Rice Lake, Ontario," *Anthro.Pap. Nat'l Mus.Canada*, no.19 (1968). il.
    Robert J. Pearce, "Archaeological Investigations of the Pickering Phase in the Rice Lake Area," *Ontario Arch.*, no.29 (1978):17-24.

Rock L.
-Petroglyphs and archeological site
    Kenneth E. Kidd, "A Prehistoric Camp Site at Rock Lake, Algonquin Park, Ontario," *Southwestern J.Anthro.* 4 (1948):98-106. il.
    William Noble, "Vision Pits, Cairns and Petroglyphs at Rock Lake, Ontario," *Pub.Ontario Arch.Soc'y* 11 (1968):47-64. il.

Scorch L.
-UFO (NL)
  1975, Jan.19/Ken MacNair
    Toronto Sun, 20 Jan.1975.

Simcoe, L.
-Lake monster
  1881-   /Igopogo
    New York Times, 22 July 1881, p.2.
    Oakville Journal-Record, 27 July 1963.
    Sutton West Lake Simcoe Advocate, 6
    July 1977.
    Toronto Sun, 13 Mar.1978; and 31 July
    1978.
    Cannington Gleaner, 26 July 1978.
    Barrie Banner, 28 July 1978; and 11
    Aug.1978.
-Tasseography
  1940s
    Eileen Sonin, More Canadian Ghosts
    (Richmond Hill, Ont.: Pocket Books,
    1974 ed.), p.28.

Skeleton L.
-Meteorite crater
  3500 m.diam./possible
    J. Classen, "Catalogue of 230...Im-
    pact Structures," Meteoritics 12
    (1977):61,70.

Slate Is.
-Meteorite crater
  certain
    J. Classen, "Catalogue of 230...Im-
    pact Structures," Meteoritics 12
    (1977):61,69.

Steep Rock L.
-UFO (CE-3)
  1950, July 2/Clarence Harvey/=hoax?
    Port Arthur News-Chronicle, 18 Sep.
    1950.
    "Steep Rock Flying Saucer," Fate 5
    (Feb.-Mar.1952):68-72, quoting Steep
    Rock Echo, Sep.-Oct.1950.
    "1950 Steep Rock Lake, Ontario Case
    Possible Hoax," APRO Bull. 26 (Nov.
    1977):5.

Superior, L.
-Disappearance
  1902, Nov.21/"Bannockburn"
    Chicago (Ill.) Tribune, 28 Nov.1902.
    Dwight Boyer, Ghost Ships of the
    Great Lakes (N.Y.: Dodd, Mead, 1968),
    pp.14-27.
-Mystery plane crash
  1955, June 8/C.P. Day/Beech 35
    Jay Gourley, The Great Lakes Triangle
    (Greenwich, Ct.: Fawcett, 1977),
    p.31.
-Seance
  1820s/J.G. Kohl/shaking tent
    J.G. Kohl, Kitchi-Gami (London: Chap-
    man & Hall, 1860), pp.278-80.

Teggau L.
-Disappearance
  1959, May 21/Maurice J. Merickel/Piper
  PA-18
    Jay Gourley, The Great Lakes Triangle
    (Greenwich, Ct.: Fawcett, 1977), pp.
    171-72.

Thorah I.
-Poltergeist
  1891, Oct.25-31/Jennie L. Bramwell
    Toronto Globe, 9 Nov.1891.
    St. Louis (Mo.) Globe-Democrat, 19
    Dec.1891.
    R.S. Lambert, Exploring the Supernat-
    ural (Toronto: McClelland & Stewart,
    1955), pp.138-40.

Thunder Bay
-Archeological site
    Richard S. MacNeish, "A Possible
    Early Site in the Thunder Bay Dis-
    trict, Ontario," Bull.Nat'l Mus.
    Canada 126 (1952):23-47.

Travis, Point
-Mystery shipwreck
  1965/"Protostatis"
    Hugh F. Cochrane, "Lake Ontario's
    Mysterious Triangle of Death," Saga
    UFO Rept. 3 (Dec.1976):30,32.

Varwood, Point
-Hex
  1640/Père Brébeuf
    Paul LeJeune & Jerome Lalemant, "Re-
    lation de ce qui s'est passé en la
    Nouvelle France, en l'année 1640,"
    in Reuben Gold Thwaites, ed., The
    Jesuit Relations and Allied Docu-
    ments (Cleveland: Burrows, 1898),
    19:7,82-87.

Wanapitei L.
-Meteorite crater
  8500 m.diam./certain
    J. Classen, "Catalogue of 230...Im-
    pact Structures," Meteoritics 12
    (1977):61,70.

Wilcox L.
-UFO (DD)
  1952, April 26
    Toronto Daily Star, 26 Apr.1952.

            C. Ethnic Groups

Algonquin Indians (generally)
-Flood myth
    Daniel G. Brinton, The Myths of the
    New World (N.Y.: Holt, 1876), pp.
    216-17.
-Giant beaver legend
    Jane C. Beck, "The Giant Beaver: A
    Prehistoric Memory?" Ethnohistory 19
    (spring 1972):109-22.
-Giant bird legend
    A.F. Chamberlain, "The Thunder-Bird
    Amongst the Algonkins," Am.Anthro.
    3 (1890):51-54.
-Legend of Precolumbian Whites
  Lok
    Charles Leland, The Algonquin Legends
    of New England (Boston: Houghton,
    Mifflin, 1884).
    Hjalmar R. Holand, Explorations in

America Before Columbus (N.Y.:
Twayne, 1956), pp.246-47.
-Similarities to Western culture
Barry Fell, America B.C. (N.Y.: Quad-
rangle, 1976), pp.277-85.
Barry Fell, "Ancient Arabic Script
and Vocabulary of the Algonquian
Indians," Occ.Pub.Epigraphic Soc'y,
vol.3, no.54 (Sep.1976).

Cree Indians
-Humanoid
1907
R.S. Lambert, Exploring the Supernat-
ural (Toronto: McClelland & Stewart,
1955), p.175.
-Humanoid myth
John M. Cooper, "The Cree Witiko
Psychosis," Primitive Man 6 (1933):
20-24.
Regina Flannery, "The Culture of
Northeastern Indians," in Frederick
Johnson, ed., Man in Northeastern
North America (Andover, Mass.: Phil-
lips Acad., Pap.Peabody Foundation,
vol.3, 1946), pp.263,269.

Delaware Indians
-Shamanism
C.A. Weslager, Magic Medicines of
the Indians (N.Y.: Signet, 1974 ed.).

Huron Indians
-Humanoid myth
C.M. Barbeau, "Supernatural Beings of
the Huron and Wyandot," Am.Anthro.
16 (1914):288-313.
-Lake monster myth
onniont
Hierosme Lalemant, "Relation de ce
qui s'est passé...en la Nouvelle
France, és années 1647. & 1648," in
Reuben Gold Thwaites, ed., The Jes-
uit Relations and Allied Documents
(Cleveland: Burrows, 1899), 33:212-
15.
-Shamanism
Pere LeJeune, "Relation de ce qui
s'est passé dans le Pays des Hurons
en l'année 1636," in Reuben Gold
Thwaites, ed., Jesuit Relations and
Allied Documents (Cleveland: Burrows,
1897), 10:192-209.
Hierosme Lalemant, "Relation de ce
qui s'est passé...en la Nouvelle
France, és années 1647. & 1648," in
Reuben Gold Thwaites, ed., The Jes-
uit Relations and Allied Documents
(Cleveland: Burrows, 1899), 33:188-
227.

Ojibwa Indians
-Humanoid myth
windigo
J.G. Kohl, Kitchi-Gami (London: Chapman & Hall, 1860), pp.358-66.
Henry Y. Hind, Narrative of the Canadian Red River Exploring Expedition
of 1857 (London: Longman, Green,
Longman & Roberts, 1860).

Frank G. Speck, "Myths and Folklore
of the Timiskaming Algonquin and
Timagami Ojibwa," Anthro.Ser.Canada
Dep't of Mines, Geol.Survey, Mem.
71, no.9, 1915.
Morton I. Teicher, "Windigo Psycho-
sis," in Verne F. Ray, ed., Proc.
1960 Annual Spring Meeting, Am.
Ethn.Soc'y (Seattle: Am.Ethn.Soc'y,
1960).
Ruth Landes, The Ojibwa Woman (N.Y.:
AMS, 1969 ed.),
Ralph Christian Albertsen, "Windigo:
The Cannibal Demon," Fate 29 (Mar.
1976):38-45.
(Letter), J.M. Bradford, Fate 29
(Oct.1976):113-14.

Tuscarora Indians
-Land monster myth
quisquis
H.C. Mercer, The Lenape Stone: or,
The Indian and the Mammoth (N.Y.:
Putnam, 1885).

D. Unspecified Localities

-Lake monster
ca.1910/northern wilderness
Tim Dinsdale, The Leviathans (London:
Routledge & Kegan Paul, 1966), pp.
31-32.

QUEBEC

A. Populated Places

Acton Vale
-Poltergeist
  1969, Jan./M. Saint-Onges
    Owen Sound (Ont.) Sun-Times, 24 Jan.
    1969.
    Sheila Hervey, Some Canadian Ghosts
    (Richmond Hill, Ont.: Pocket Books,
    1973), pp.87-90.

Bagotville
-UFO (NL)
  1978, March 5/40 nautical mi. from CFB
  Bagotville
    "Other UFOs," Res Bureaux Bull., no.
    35 (15 June 1978):3,4.
-UFO (R-V)
  1978, April 27/CFB Bagotville
    "Other UFOs," Res Bureaux Bull., no.
    35 (15 June 1978):3-4.

Baie Comeau
-UFO (?)
  1979, Jan.18/=meteor
    Montréal La Presse, 20 Jan.1979.
-UFO (NL)
  1975, Sep.14
    Philippe Blaquière, "Les Observa-
    tions du 14.09.75," UFO-Québec, no.
    4 (1975):4.

Beauport
-Phantom image
  1977, March 8-1978/Adoring Missionary
  Dominican Sisters
    Sudbury (Ont.) Review, 22 July 1978.
    Woodstock-Ingersoll (Ont.) Sentinel-
    Review, 22 July 1978.

Beauvoir
-Ancient inscription
    Thomas E. Lee, "Hanno, Not Bjarni,
    Leif, or Christopher?" Anthro.J.
    Canada 13, no.2 (1975):2-5.

Beloeil
-UFO (DD)
  1977, July 24
    Philippe Blaquière, "Enquêtes au
    Québec," UFO-Québec, no.11 (1977):
    6-7.
-UFO (NL)
  1972, July 30
    Wido Hoville, "Reports from Quebec,"
    Can.UFO Rept., no.17 (1974):20.
  1975, May 5
    Philippe Blaquière, "Enquêtes re-
    centes," UFO-Québec, no.3 (1975):10.
  1976, Oct.17
    "Enquêtes recentes," UFO-Québec, no.
    9 (1977):4.
  1977, April 15
    John Brent Musgrave, "Red Lights &

Other UFOs over Canada," MUFON UFO
J., no.118 (Sep.1977):14.
  1977, Sep.11/Jean-Louis Blaquière
    Philippe Tournier, "Analyse d'un
    cas," UFO-Québec, no.14 (June 1978):
    16-18.

Berthierville
-UFO (NL)
  1973, Nov.18
    Claude MacDuff, "Les Observations du
    18.11.73," UFO-Québec, no.3 (1975):
    4-7.
  1973, Nov.30
    Monique Benoit, "La Lune tombe dans
    le bois!" UFO-Québec, no.3 (1975):
    7-8.
  1976, Jan.29
    Monique Benoit, "Berthierville,"
    UFO-Québec, no.5 (1976):6.
  1977, Feb.17/Hwy.40
    "Enquêtes au Québec," UFO-Quebec,
    no.9 (1977):4,5.

Betsiamites
-UFO (NL)
  1971, July 20
    Montréal Le Devoir, 23 July 1971.

Bic
-UFO (NL)
  1971, July 20
    Montréal Le Devoir, 23 July 1971.

Bristol
-Fall of frogs
  1864, July 11
    "Hail-Storm in Pontiac," Can.Natural-
    ist, ser.2, 1 (1864):308.

Bromptonville
-Ancient inscriptions
  ca.1910/Ludger Soucy
    Thomas E. Lee, "Hanno, Not Bjarni,
    Leif, or Christopher?" Anthro.J.
    Canada 13, no.2 (1975):2-5. il.
    James P. Whittall II, "The Inscribed
    Stones of Sherbrooke, Quebec," Bull.
    Early Sites Rsch.Soc'y 4 (May 1976):
    28-32. il.
    Barry Fell, "Decipherment of the Bi-
    facial Sherbrooke Stele," Bull.Early
    Sites Rsch.Soc'y 4 (May 1976):33-
    38. il.
    Thomas E. Lee, "The Sherbrooke In-
    scriptions," NEARA J. 11 (summer
    1976):6-7.
    Barry Fell, "Possible Libyan Petro-
    manteia in Quebec," Occ.Pub.Epigraph-
    ic Soc'y, vol.3, no.72 (Sep.1976).
    George Sotiroff, "Hiram, Hanta and
    Harvard," Anthro.J.Canada 15, no.2
    (1977):2-5.
    Thomas E. Lee, "If at First You Don't

Succeed..." Anthro.J.Canada 15, no.
3 (1977):11-14.
Thomas E. Lee, "The Ultimate in Sil-
liness," Anthro.J.Canada 16, no.1
(1978):40.
Salvatore Michael Trento, The Search
for Lost America (Chicago: Contemporary, 1978), pp.177-79. il.

Campbell's Bay
-UFO (CE-1)
1972, July 18-Aug.10/Donna Mercer
"Repeat Sightings in Canada," APRO
Bull. 21 (Sep.-Oct.1972):8.

Chapeau
-UFO (CE-2)
1969, May 11/Leo-Paul Chaput
Montréal Journal, 24 May 1969.
"Landing Report from Canada," APRO
Bull. 17 (May-June 1969):7.
Ted Phillips, "Physical Traces--Ma-
terial Evidence of UFO's?" Skylook,
no.54 (May 1972):11.
J. Allen Hynek, The UFO Experience
(Chicago: Regnery, 1972), pp.133-34.

Charlesbourg
-Haunt
18th c.-   /Château Bigot
Charles M. Skinner, Myths and Legends
Beyond Our Borders (Philadelphia:
Lippincott, 1899), pp.110-13.
Blodwen Davies, Romantic Quebec (N.Y.:
Dodd, Mead, 1932), pp.92-97.
-UFO (NL)
1975, Sep.9
Le Soleil, 26 Sep.1975.

Charlevoix co.
-UFO (DD)
1953, July 16/Jacques Simard
Jean Ferguson, "Enquêtes," UFO-Québec,
no.9 (1977):11-12.

Clarendon
-Poltergeist
1889, Sep.15-Nov.18/George Dagg
Brockville (Ont.) Daily Times, 13
Nov.1889.
(Editorial), Light, 28 Dec.1889.
(Editorial), Light, 22 Nov.1890, p.
567.
Herbert Thurston, Ghosts and Polter-
geists (Chicago: Regnery, 1954), pp.
288-303.
R.S. Lambert, Exploring the Supernat-
ural (Toronto: McClelland & Stewart,
1955), pp.106-21.

Coaticook
-UFO (CE-3)
1968, Sep.21
Ted Phillips, Physical Traces Associ-
ated with UFO Sightings (Evanston:
Center for UFO Studies, 1975), p.59.

Corbeil
-Precognition
1954, Aug.5/Mde. Ernest Dionne

James Brough, "We Were Five" (N.Y.:
Simon & Schuster, 1965).

Dalesville
-UFO (NL)
1940/Walter Gunn
Gordon I.R. Lore, Jr. & Harold H. Den-
eault, Jr., Mysteries of the Skies:
UFOs in Perspective (Englewood
Cliffs, N.J.: Prentice-Hall, 1968),
pp.138-40.

Daveluyville
-UFO (NL)
1974, July 14/Roger Coté
Jeff Holt, "Un UFO triangulaire est
aperçu à Daveluyville," UFO-Québec,
no.2 (1975):12.

Dorval
-UFO (NL)
1975, Aug.30/Robert Sapienza/Montréal
airport
Robert Sapienza, "UFO sur Dorval,"
UFO-Québec, no.5 (1976):5.

Douville
-UFO (NL)
1973, Nov.19
Claude MacDuff, "Les Observations du
18.11.73," UFO-Québec, no.3 (1975):
4-7.

Drummondville
-UFO (CE-3)
1974, June 25
Marc Leduc, "Un Atterrissage et des
humanoïdes à Drummondville," UFO-
Québec, no.1 (1975):10-12.
Marc Leduc, "Un Temoin sous hypnose,"
UFO-Québec, no.8 (1976):17-19.
-UFO (NL)
1974, July 14/Jean Roi
Marc Leduc, "Le Triangle du 14.7.74,"
UFO-Québec, no.2 (1975):9-11. il.

Ferme Neuve
-UFO (CE-3)
1929, June 12/Levis Brosseau
Jacques Vallee, Passport to Magonia
(Chicago: Regnery, 1969), p.189,
quoting GEPA Bull., Dec.1968.

Gaspé
-Phantom ship
18th c.-
Charles M. Skinner, Myths and Legends
Beyond Our Borders (Philadelphia:
Lippincott, 1899), pp.94-95.

Grandes-Bergeronnes
-UFO (NL)
1971, July 20
Montréal Le Devoir, 23 July 1971.

Hébertville
-UFO (NL)
1975, Sep.14
Philippe Blaquière, "Les Observations
du 14.09.75," UFO-Québec, no.5

(1976):4-5.

Hemmingford
-UFO (CE-3)
  1954, Aug.10/Gabriel Coupal
    Huntingdon Gleaner, 18 Aug.1954.
    (Editorial), Fate 8 (Mar.1955):19.
    Albany (N.Y.) Times-Union, 27 Nov.
    1955.
    Ted Bloecher, "UFO Landing and Re-
    pair by Crew: Part II," Flying Sau-
    cer Rev. 20 (Dec.1974):24,26.

Hudson
-Poltergeist
  1880, Sep.-Oct./Hudson Hotel
    Québec Daily Mercury, 6 Oct.1880.
    R.S. Lambert, Exploring the Supernat-
    ural (Toronto: McClelland & Stewart,
    1955), pp.135-36, quoting Toronto
    (Ont.) Globe (undated).

Hull
-Clairvoyance
  1965, April
    (Editorial), Fate 18 (Sep.1965):10-
    13, quoting Ottawa (Ont.) Citizen
    (undated).
-UFO (NL)
  1969, March 4
    Hamilton (Ont.) Spectator, 19 Oct.
    1973.

Ile Dupas
-Haunt
  n.d./church
    J. Castell Hopkins, French Canada and
    the Saint Lawrence (Philadelphia:
    John C. Winston, 1913), pp.311-12.

Joliette
-UFO (CE-3)
  1973, Nov.22
    "Possible Occupant Reported in Can-
    ada," Skylook, no.77 (Apr.1974):9.
    Wido Hoville, "Joliette 1973," UFO-
    Québec, no.2 (1975):7-9.
    Claude MacDuff, "The 1973 UFO-Inva-
    sion of Quebec," Ufology 2 (fall
    1976):14,19-20.
-UFO (NL)
  1968, July 2
    "Around the Globe," APRO Bull. 17
    (Nov.-Dec.1968):6.
  1973, Nov.18/Boulevard Industriel
  1973, Nov.21, 24
    Claude MacDuff, "The 1973 UFO-Inva-
    sion of Quebec," Ufology 2 (fall
    1976):14,19,21.

Kamouraska
-Humanoid
  1767, Oct.-Nov.
    La Gazette du Québec, 10 Dec.1767.

Kazabazua
-UFO (CE-1)
  1969, Oct.10/Ivan McConnell/Aylwin Rd.
    Lucius Farish & Dale M. Titler, "UFO
    Symbols: Message or Mystery," Offi-

cial UFO 1 (July 1976):16,40.

Labelle
-UFO (NL)
  1959, Oct.28/Joe Donovan/7 mi.W
    (Letter), Fate 13 (Aug.1960):110-12.

Lachenaie
-UFO (NL)
  1975, Sep.14
    Philippe Blaquière, "Les Observations
    du 14.09.75," UFO-Québec, no.4
    (1975):4.

Lachine
-Fall of anomalous meteorite
  1883, July 7/Mrs. John Popham
    Montréal Daily Star, 11 July 1883.
    E.W. Claypole, "The Lachine Aëro-
    lite," Nature 28 (1883):319.

Lachute
-Flying cat
  1966, June
    John A. Keel, Strange Creatures from
    Time and Space (Greenwich, Ct.: Faw-
    cett, 1970), p.40.

La Sarre
-UFO (CE-3)
  1972, Nov.28/Mario Mercier
    Jean Ferguson, "Enquêtes au Abitibi,"
    UFO-Québec, no.5 (1976):8,9-11.

La Tuque
-UFO (CE-1)
  1970, Oct.28
  1975, Nov.5
    Philippe Blaquière, "Les Observations
    de La Tuque," UFO-Québec, no.6
    (1976):4-5.
-UFO (CE-2)
  1971, May 30
    Ted Phillips, Physical Traces Associ-
    ated with UFO Sightings (Evanston:
    Center for UFO Studies, 1975), p.77.
-UFO (DD)
  1977, March 13/J.C. Grenon
    Philippe Blaquière, "Enquêtes au
    Québec," UFO-Québec, no.10 (1977):4.

Les Écureuils
-Fall of slag
  1960, June 12/St. Lawrence R./=foundry
  waste?
    "The Mysterious Chunk of Hardware at
    Ottawa," Topside, spring 1968, pp.
    1-4. il.
    Roy Craig, "Direct Physical Evidence,"
    in Edward U. Condon, ed., Scientific
    Study of Unidentified Flying Objects
    (N.Y.: Bantam, 1969 ed.), pp.86,90-
    92.
    "Ottawa's Mysterious Piece of Metal,"
    Can.UFO Rept., no.3 (May-June 1969):
    13-15. il.
    "More on Ottawa's Mysterious 'Chunk,'"
    Can.UFO Rept., no.6 (Nov.-Dec.1969):
    22-25.
    "Ottawa's 'Chunk' Again," Can.UFO

Rept., no.8 (fall 1970):14-15.
John Magor, Our UFO Visitors (Seattle:
Hancock House, 1977), pp.11-13.

Longueuil
-UFO (NL)
    1973, Nov.18
        Claude MacDuff, "Les Observations du
        18.11.73," UFO-Québec, no.3 (1975):
        4-7.

Maniwaki
-Clairvoyance
    1953, Aug./Lyse Thoreault
        (Editorial), Fate 6 (Dec.1953):7.

Marieville
-UFO (NL)
    1975, May 5
        Philippe Blaquière, "Enquêtes re-
        centes," UFO-Québec, no.3 (1975):10.

Montréal
-Archeological site
    1500s/Hochelaga
        John W. Dawson, Fossil Men and Their
        Modern Representatives (London:
        Hodder & Stoughton, 1880).
        John Bartlet Brebner, Explorers of
        North America (N.Y.: Macmillan,
        1933), pp.132-33.
        James F. Pendergast & Bruce G. Trig-
        ger, Cartier's Hochelaga and the
        Dawson Site (Montréal: McGill-
        Queen's Univ., 1972). il.
-Biofeedback research
    1970s/Fernand Poirier/Clinique d'Epi-
    lepsie
        Elmer & Alyce Green, Beyond Biofeed-
        back (N.Y.: Delta, 1978 ed.), pp.
        105-106.
-Clairvoyance
    1935-1950s/J. Raoul Desrosiers
        Roger Russell, "He 'Sees' Through
        Solid Earth," Fate 7 (Sep.1954):100-
        101.
-Disappearances
    1883, July
    1892, July-Aug.
        Charles Fort, The Books of Charles
        Fort (N.Y.: Holt, 1941), p.687.
-Earthquake luminescence
    1663, Feb.5
        Hierosme Lalemant, "Relation de ce
        qui s'est passé...en la Nouvelle
        France, és années 1662 & 1663," in
        Reuben Gold Thwaites, ed., The Jes-
        uit Relations and Allied Documents
        (Cleveland: Burrows, 1899), 48:23,
        40-51.
        François Ragueneau, "Relatio Terre-
        motus in Nova Francia, 1663," in
        Reuben Gold Thwaites, ed., The Jes-
        uit Relations and Allied Documents
        (Cleveland: Burrows, 1899), 48:
        196-99.
        Walter D. Edmonds, The Musket and the
        Cross (Boston: Little, Brown, 1968),
        pp.85-87.
-Erratic crocodilian

1973, July 28
    Toronto (Ont.) Star, 30 July 1973.
-Exorcisms
    1971-1974/Paul Sauvé/St. Augustine of
    Canterbury Church
        "Exorcist of Montreal," Fate 28
        (Apr.1975):56, quoting Nat'l En-
        quirer (undated).
-Fall of black rain
    1819, Nov.21-23
        "Black Rain," Edinburgh Phil.J. 2
        (1820):381-82.
        Frédéric Zurcher & Élie Margollé,
        Meteors, Aërolites, Storms, and At-
        mospheric Phenomena, trans. William
        Lackland (N.Y.: Charles Scribner,
        1871), p.238.
        New York Times, 23 Apr.1881, p.2.
        "The Dark Day in Canada," Sci.Am. 44
        (1881):329.
        "More Notes of Charles Fort," Fortean
        Soc'y Mag., no.6 (Jan.1942):14.
    1834, Oct.17
        W.B. Clarke, "On Certain Recent Me-
        teoric Phenomena...in Supposed Con-
        nection, with Volcanic Emanations,"
        Mag.Nat.History 8 (1835):129,137n.
-Fall of frogs
    1841, July 25/George Duncan Gibbs
        Carribber [George Duncan Gibbs], Odd
        Showers (London: Kirby, 1870).
-Fall of lizards
    1857, Dec.27
        Montréal Weekly Gazette, 28 Dec.1857.
-Fall of weblike substance
    1962, Oct.10/R.H. Pape
        Barrie Pottage, "Ring Clouds and An-
        gel Hair," Flying Saucer Rev. 10
        (May-June 1964):14,15-16.
-Ghost
    n.d./Pauline Houle/St. Sauvener
    1952/Ruth Brodie
    1961, Nov.18/Pierrette Champoux/Queen
    Elizabeth Hotel
        Eileen Sonin, More Canadian Ghosts
        (Richmond Hill, Ont.: Pocket Books,
        1974 ed.), pp.30,82-83,94-95.
-Ghost cat
    1960s/Brian Grey
        Sheila Hervey, Some Canadian Ghosts
        (Richmond Hill, Ont.: Pocket Books,
        1973), pp.82-85.
-Healing research
    1957-   /Bernard Grad/McGill Univer-
    sity
        Bernard Grad, R.J. Cadoret & G.I.
        Paul, "The Influence of an Unortho-
        dox Method of Treatment on Wound
        Healing in Mice," Int'l J.Parapsych.
        3 (1961):5-24.
        Bernard Grad, "A Telekinetic Effect
        on Plant Growth," Int'l J.Parapsych.
        5 (1963):117-33; 6 (1964):473-98.
        Bernard Grad, "Some Biological Ef-
        fects of the 'Laying on of Hands,'"
        J.ASPR 59 (1965):95-127.
        Berthold E. Schwarz, "Discussion of
        Dr. Grad's Paper," J.ASPR 59 (1965):
        127-29.
        Bernard Grad, "The 'Laying on of

Hands': Implications for Psychother-
apy, Gentling, and the Placebo Ef-
fect," J.ASPR 61 (1967):286-305.
Allen Spraggett, The Unexplained
(N.Y.: Signet, 1968 ed.), pp.133-37.
David Techter, "Experiments in Psy-
chic Healing," Fate 22 (Apr.1969):
73-78.
James Crenshaw, "ESP Comes of Age-II,"
Fate 23 (Jan.1970):78,81-84.
Bernard Grad, "Healing by the Laying
on of Hands: Review of Experiments
and Implications," Pastoral Psych.,
Sep.1970, pp.19-26.
Thelma Moss, The Probability of the
Impossible (Los Angles: J.P. Tar-
cher, 1974), pp.84-89.
A.R.G. Owen, Psychic Mysteries of
the North (N.Y.: Harper & Row, 1975),
pp.105-109,122.
-Humanoid
1968, July 2/Michel Michaud
"Around the Globe," APRO Bull. 17
(Nov.-Dec.1968):6, quoting Montréal
La Presse (undated).
-Inner development
1970s/Canadian Institute of Psychosyn-
thesis/3496, ave.Marlowe
June & Nicholas Regush, Psi: The Oth-
er World Catalogue (N.Y.: Putnam,
1974), pp.158-59.
Armand Biteaux, The New Conscious-
ness (Willits, Cal.: Oliver, 1975),
p.15.
-Lightning anomaly
1938, Aug.9/Ben Oliver
"Spook Dog Etching," Fortean Soc'y
Mag., no.3 (Jan.1940):13.
-Electromagnetic anomaly
1971, July 23
"Second Blackout Darkens Quebec--
Cause Unknown," Skylook, no.47
(Oct.1971):14.
-Phantom
1694, Nov.21/Hôtel-Dieu
Marie Morin, Annales de l'Hôtel-Dieu
de Montréal (Montréal: Soc.histor-
ique de Montréal, 1921), pp.183-84.
-Phantom image
1661, Aug.29/Père Le Maistre
J. Castell Hopkins, French Canada and
the St. Lawrence (Philadelphia: John
C. Winston, 1913), pp.301-302.
-Poltergeist
1929/Frances Smyth/Ste. Famille St.
Frances Smyth, "Knot-Tying Polter-
geist," Fate 16 (Nov.1963):36-39.
-Precognition
n.d./Dora Hewlitt/Esplanade
Eileen Sonin, More Canadian Ghosts
(Richmond Hill, Ont.: Pocket Books,
1974 ed.), p.142.
-Seance
1969, May/Pearl Freeman
Madeleine de La Rivière, "Messages
from Two Worlds," Fate 24 (Mar.1971)
:92-94.
-Skyquake
1952, Aug.2
"Bangs," Doubt, no.39 (1952):182.

-UFO (CE-1)
1975, Aug.31
Georges Ethier, "Enquêtes recentes,"
UFO-Québec, no.4 (1975):5.
1977, April 6/Claudine Richer/Parc
St.-Viateur
Wido Hoville, "Outremont," UFO-Qué-
bec, no.10 (1977):10.
-UFO (CE-2)
1977, April 6/Rue Cleroux
Wido Hoville, "Les Observations de
Ste. Dorothée," UFO-Québec, no.10
(1977):7-9.
-UFO (CE-3)
1962, May 31/Rue Ballechasse x St.-
Davis
Wido Hoville, "Les UFO's en Baril,"
UFO-Québec, no.6 (1976):12-15.
1977, Jan.6/Mrs. Malbouef/Rue Casgrain
x Beaubien
Montréal Sunday Express, 9 Jan.1977.
Toronto (Ont.) Star, 21 Feb.1977.
Marc Leduc & Wido Hoville, "Un UFO
sur une maison," UFO-Québec, no.9
(1977):6-10.
-UFO (DD)
1952, April 18
Montréal Gazette, 18 Apr.1952.
1973, Aug.5/Michel Imbeault
"Dossier photo," UFO-Québec, no.1
(1975):24. il.
"Cover Photo," Can.UFO Rept., no.30
(winter-spring 1978):13. il.
-UFO (NL)
1844, Oct.22/30 mi.S
Gordon I.R. Lore, Jr. & Harold H. Deneault, Jr., Mysteries of the Skies:
UFOs in Perspective (Englewood
Cliffs, N.J.: Prentice-Hall, 1968),
p.64, quoting W.J. Burrell, "A Phenomenon" (unattributed source).
1961, Oct.28/Frank J. DeKinder
(Editorial), Fate 15 (Jan.1962):25.
1973, Nov.21
1973, Nov.30/Metropolitan Blvd.
Claude MacDuff, "The 1973 UFO-Inva-
sion of Quebec," Ufology 2 (fall
1976):14,21-22.
1975, June 14/Ile Ste.-Hélène
Philippe Blaquière, "Enquêtes recentes," UFO-Québec, no.3 (1975):10.
1977, Jan.24
"Enquêtes au Québec," UFO-Québec, no.
9 (1977):4,5.
-Witch trial (scrying)
1742/Havard de Beaufort
R.S. Lambert, Exploring the Supernatural (Toronto: McClelland & Stewart,
1955), pp.57-59.

Montréal-Nord
-UFO (CE-1)
1977, May 2
Philippe Blaquière, "Enquêtes au Québec," UFO-Québec, no.11 (1977):4-5.

Montréal-Ouest
-UFO (?)
1978, June 28/=aircraft
Montréal Gazette, 30 June 1978.

-UFO (NL)
   1974, July 27/Notre-Dame-de-Grâces
   Don Donderi, "Montréal-Ouest," UFO-
   Québec, no.6 (1976):6.

Mont-Rolland
-Ghost
   n.d./Lucille Bruyère
      Eileen Sonin, More Canadian Ghosts
      (Richmond Hill, Ont.: Pocket Books,
      1974 ed.), pp.15-16.

Notre-Dame-du-Nord
-UFO (CE-3)
   1971, July 12/Gaétan Paquin
      Jean Ferguson, "Enquêtes," UFO-Qué-
      bec, no.9 (1977):11.

Oka
-UFO (CE-1)
   1967, Aug.29/Y. Guindon
      Québec Le Petit Journal, 1 Oct.1967.

Orsainville
-UFO (NL)
   1972, June/Pierre Leclerc
      Claude MacDuff, "Report from Canada,"
      Skylook, no.62 (Jan.1973):14.

Percé
-Haunt
   n.d.
      Charles M. Skinner, Myths and Legends
      Beyond Our Borders (Philadelphia:
      Lippincott, 1899), pp.61-62.

Pointe Noire
-UFO (NL)
   1979, Jan.16
      "Recent UFO Reports," Res Bureaux
      Bull., no.44 (Feb.1979):4.

Port Cartier
-UFO (NL)
   1979, Jan.20
      "Recent UFO Reports," Res Bureaux
      Bull., no.44 (Feb.1979):4.

Québec
-Crisis apparition
   1779/Augustin Fraser
      P.G. Roy, Les petites choses de
      notre histoire (Québec: Lévis, 1919).
-Ghost
   1967, Sep.18/Johanne Allison/Notre-
   Dame-de-Grâce
      Sheila Hervey, Some Canadian Ghosts
      (Richmond Hill, Ont.: Pocket Books,
      1973), pp.80-82, quoting Montréal
      Star (undated).
-Giant wolf
   1767/Saint-Rochs
      La Gazette de Québec, 14 July 1767;
      and 10 Dec.1767.
-Healing
   1700s-   /Ste. Anne de Beaupre
      "Canada's Healing Shrine," Fate 9
      (July 1956):77.
-Poltergeist
   1661-1667/Catherine de Saint-Augustin

Paul Ragueneau, La Vie de la Mère
   Catherine de Saint-Augustin (Paris:
   Chez Florentin Lambert, 1671).
Joyce Marshall, ed., Word from New
   France: The Selected Letters of
   Marie de l'Incarnation (Toronto:
   Oxford Univ., 1967), pp.264-65.
Robert-Lionel Seguin, La Sorcellerie
   au Québec du XVIIe au XIXe siècle
   (Ottawa: Lemeac, 1971), pp.17-43.
-Precognition
   1663, Feb.3
      Hierosme Lalemant, "Relation de ce
      qui s'est passé...en la Nouvelle
      France, és années 1662 & 1663," in
      Reuben Gold Thwaites, ed., The Jes-
      uit Relations and Allied Documents
      (Cleveland: Burrows, 1899), 48:23,
      50-57.
      François Ragueneau, "Relatio Terre-
      motus in Nova Francia, 1663," in
      Reuben Gold Thwaites, ed., The Jes-
      uit Relations and Allied Documents
      (Cleveland: Burrows, 1899), 48:186-
      91.
      Joyce Marshall, ed., Word from New
      France: The Selected Letters of
      Marie de l'Incarnation (Toronto:
      Oxford Univ., 1967), p.287.
   1701, March 10/Mère Minique/Castle of
   St. Louis
      Marie Caroline Watson Hamlin, Legends
      of Le Détroit (Detroit: Nourse,
      1884), pp.22-29.
   1908, July 29/Lord Roberts
      James Leigh, "Clairvoyance in Battle,"
      Fate 5 (Nov.1952):72-74.
-UFO (CE-3)
   1974, June 25
      George D. Fawcett, "The 'Unreported'
      UFO Wave of 1974," Saga UFO Rept. 2
      (spring 1975):50,53.
-UFO (DD)
   1952, July 19
      Richard Hall, ed., The UFO Evidence
      (Washington: NICAP, 1964), p.155.
-UFO (NL)
   1972, March 11
      Claude MacDuff, "Report from Canada,"
      Skylook, no.62 (Jan.1973):14.
-Witch trial (profanity)
   1661
      Paul Ragueneau, La Vie de la Mère
      Catherine de Saint-Augustin (Paris:
      Chez Florentin Lambert, 1671), pp.
      163-64.

Repentigny
-UFO (NL)
   1978, March 2
      Montréal Star, 3 Mar.1978.

Rimouski
-UFO (NL)
   1971, July 20
      Montréal Le Devoir, 23 July 1971.

Ristigouche
-Legend of Precolumbian Whites
   1676/Chrétien LeClerq

Chrétien LeClerq, <u>Nouvelle relation
de la Gaspésie</u> (Paris: A. Auroy,
1691).

Robertsonville
-UFO (NL)
1978, Jan.23
"UFOs," <u>Res Bureaux Bull.</u>, no.29
(9 Feb.1978):4,5.

Rougemont
-UFO (CE-1)
1971, July 20
Claude MacDuff, "Canadian Power Fail-
ures and UFO Sightings," <u>FSR Case
Histories</u>, no.17 (Dec.1973):2,4.
1972, Sep.20
Wido Hoville, "Reports from Quebec,"
<u>Can.UFO Rept.</u>, no.17 (1974):20-21.
Philippe Blaquière, "Le Cas de Rouge-
mont," <u>UFO-Québec</u>, no.1 (1975):4-6.

Routhierville
-Phantom
1952
"Handsome Dancer," <u>Time</u>, 24 Nov.1952,
p.45.

Rouyn
-UFO (NL)
1952, April 30
<u>Rouyn Norand Press</u>, 1 May 1952.

Saint-Alexandre-de-Kamouraska
-UFO (NL)
1975, Sep.9/Paul Martin/Hwy.20
<u>Le Soleil</u>, 26 Sep.1975.

Saint-Alexis-de-Montcalm
-UFO (CE-2)
1964, Nov.8/Nelson Lebel
"The Ten Landings," <u>UFO Inv.</u> 3 (June-
July 1965):2, quoting <u>Montréal Le
Nouveau Samedi</u>, 14 Nov.1964.

Saint-André-Avellin
-Flying humanoid
1977, May 21
<u>Montréal Star</u>, 27 May 1977.

Saint-Augustin
-Phantom horse
1690
J. Castell Hopkins, <u>French Canada and
the St. Lawrence</u> (Philadelphia: John
C. Winston, 1913), pp.312-13.

Saint-Barthélemy
-UFO (NL)
1977, Feb.17
John Brent Musgrave, "Red Lights &
Other UFOs over Canada," <u>MUFON UFO
J.</u>, no.118 (Sep.1977):14.

Saint-Basile
-Aerial phantom
1968, July 22
William F. Dawson, "So What's New
with Charles Fort?" <u>Fate</u> 23 (May
1969):76,79.

Saint-Bruno-de-Chambly
-Religious apparition
1968, July 22/Manon St. Jean
William F. Dawson, "So What's New
with Charles Fort?" <u>Fate</u> 23 (May
1969):76,79.
Sheila Hervey, <u>Some Canadian Ghosts</u>
(Richmond Hill, Ont.: Pocket Books,
1973), pp.85-87.

Saint-Cyrille-de-Wendover
-UFO (CE-3)
1974, June 25
Wido Hoville, "'Robot' Occupants Re-
ported," <u>Skylook</u>, no.84 (Nov.1974):
10-11.
"Robots in Quebec, Canada," <u>APRO
Bull.</u> 23 (Nov.-Dec.1974):1,3.
"Follow-up," <u>APRO Bull.</u> 24 (July
1975):2.

Sainte-Agathe-des-Monts
-UFO (NL)
1973, Oct.
<u>Hamilton (Ont.) Spectator</u>, 19 Oct.
1973.

Sainte-Dorothée
-UFO (NL)
1968, Dec.14/Guy Boisvert
1969, July 28/Guy Boisvert
1973, July/Mrs. Guy Boisvert
Pierre Favreau, "UFOs dans le Nord
québecois," <u>UFO-Québec</u>, no.3
(1975):8-9.

Sainte-Foy
-UFO (NL)
n.d./Aeodat Bouchard/St. Yves Church
(Editorial), <u>Fate</u> 8 (Aug.1955):15.

Saint-Esprit
-UFO (NL)
1978, Jan.16/Sylvie-Anne Turner
Philippe Blaquière, "UFO à St.-Es-
prit," <u>UFO-Québec</u>, no.14 (June 1978)
:4-6.

Saint-François-d'Orléans
-Weather control
1711, Aug.15-22/Jean Pierre Lavallée
Hovenden Walker, <u>A Journal</u> (London:
D. Browne, 1720), reprinted in Gerald S. Graham, ed., <u>The Walker Expedition to Quebec, 1711</u> (Toronto:
Champlain Soc'y, Pub.no.32), pp.44-
45,59-60.
Edward Farrer, "The Folk Lore of
Lower Canada," <u>Atlantic Monthly</u> 49
(1882):542,544-45.
"Les Sorciers de l'Ile Orléans,"
<u>Bull.des Recherches hist.</u> 10 (1904):
22-25.
R.S. Lambert, <u>Exploring the Supernat-
ural</u> (Toronto: McClelland & Stewart,
1955), pp.53-57,61-62.

Saint-Georges
-UFO (NL)
1975, Sep.14

Philippe Blaquière, "Les Observations
du 14.09.75," UFO-Québec, no.4
(1975):4.

Saint-Gérard-Magella
-UFO (NL)
1973, Nov.18
    Claude MacDuff, "Les Observations du
    18.11.73," UFO-Québec, no.3 (1975):
    4-7.

Saint-Hubert
-UFO (NL)
1959, April 12/CFB St.-Hubert
    Richard Hall, ed., The UFO Evidence
    (Washington: NICAP, 1964), p.118,
    quoting UPI release, 13 Apr.1959.
1973, Nov.21
    Claude MacDuff, "The 1973 UFO-Inva-
    sion of Quebec," Ufology 2 (fall
    1976):14,19,21.

Saint-Hyacinthe
-UFO (CE-2)
1971, July 20/Saint-Dominic Rd.
    Montréal Le Petit Journal, 24 Nov.
    1971.
    Claude MacDuff, "Canadian Power Fail-
    ures and UFO Sightings," FSR Case
    Histories, no.17 (Dec.1973):1,3-5.
    Claude MacDuff, "Reports from Que-
    bec," Can.UFO Rept., no.17 (1974):
    18,19-20.
-UFO (NL)
1972, Feb.25
1972, July 30
    Wido Hoville, "Reports from Quebec,"
    Can.UFO Rept., no.17 (1974):18,20.

Saint-Jean-d'Iberville
-UFO (CE-1)
1975, Oct.29/Real Boily
    Georges Ethier, "Enquêtes recentes,"
    UFO-Québec, no.4 (1975):5.

Saint-Laurent
-Dowsing
1940s-1970s/Romauld Morin
    A.R.G. Owen, Psychic Mysteries of
    the North (N.Y.: Harper & Row,
    1975), p.122.

Saint-Mathias-de-Chambly
-UFO (CE-3)
1973, Oct.6/Huron St.
    "Five Occupants, Two Landed Objects,"
    APRO Bull. 23 (Sep.-Oct.1974):1,3-4.
    Wido Hoville, "Un Atterrissage à
    Saint-Mathias-de-Chambly," UFO-Qué-
    bec, no.1 (1975):6-9.
    Claude MacDuff, "The 1973 UFO-Inva-
    sion of Quebec," Ufology 2 (fall
    1976):14-16.

Saint-Maurice
-Haunt
n.d./Vente-au-Diable
    J. Castell Hopkins, French Canada and
    the St. Lawrence (Philadelphia: John
    C. Winston, 1913), p.312.

Saint-Méthode
-Hex
1937/Achille Grondin/=murder
    R.S. Lambert, Exploring the Supernat-
    ural (Toronto: McClelland & Stewart,
    1955), pp.60-61.

Saint-Paul
-Fall of anomalous meteorite
1968, July 2/Paul-Emile Desbiens
    "Around the Globe," APRO Bull. 17
    (Nov.-Dec.1968):6.

Saint-Stanislaus-de-Kostka
-UFO (CE-3)
1968, July 28/Paul Sauvé
    Montréal La Presse, 7 Aug.1968.
    Gordon Creighton, "An Unprepossess-
    ing Creature Seen in Canada," Fly-
    ing Saucer Rev. 15 (May-June 1969):
    20-21.

Saint-Thérèse
-UFO (CE-2)
1971, Oct.28/Johane Warren
    Claude MacDuff, "Report from Canada,"
    Skylook, no.65 (Apr.1973):16.
-UFO (NL)
1979, Feb.10
    "Recent UFO Reports," Res Bureaux
    Bull., no.44 (Feb.1979):4.

Saint-Vincent-de-Paul
-Precognition
1955, May/Bluebell Stewart Phillips
    Bluebell Stewart Phillips, "Seen
    Across 3,000 Miles," Fate 9 (Dec.
    1956):41.

Shawbridge
-UFO (DD)
1957, Nov.6
    Aimé Michel, Flying Saucers and the
    Straight-Line Mystery (N.Y.: Criter-
    ion, 1958), p.265.

Shawville
-UFO (CE-2)
1969, summer/ground markings only
    Ted Phillips, Physical Traces Associ-
    ated with UFO Sightings (Evanston:
    Center for UFO Studies, 1975), p.67.

Sherbrooke
-Haunt
1920s/Polly Westman
    Eileen Sonin, More Canadian Ghosts
    (Richmond Hill, Ont.: Pocket Books,
    1974 ed.), pp.49-50.
-UFO (CE-2)
1953, Dec./Mrs. Orfei
    Jacques Vallee, Passport to Magonia
    (Chicago: Regnery, 1969), p.205.

Sorel
-UFO (NL)
1973, Nov.18
    Claude MacDuff, "The 1973 UFO-Inva-
    sion of Quebec," Ufology 2 (fall
    1976):14,19.

Tadoussac
-Archeological site
    G.R. Lowther, "Archaeology of the
    Tadoussac Area, Province of Quebec,"
    Anthropologica 7 (1965):27-37.
-Psychokinesis and precognition
    1782, April/Messire Compain
    Henri-Raymond Casgrain, Légendes can-
    adiennes (Montréal: A. Coté, 1876).
    J.C. Taché, Forestiers et voyageurs,
    moeurs et légendes canadiennes
    (Montreal: Librairie St.-Joseph,
    1884).
    Pauline Saltzman, Ghosts and Other
    Strangers (N.Y.: Lancer, 1970 ed.),
    pp.193-96.
    Robert-Lionel Séguin, La Sorcellerie
    au Québec du XVIIe au XIXe siècle
    (Ottawa: Lemeac, 1971), pp.30-33.

Temiscaming
-UFO (DD)
    1952, April 11
    North Bay (Ont.) Nugget, 19 Apr.1952.

Terrebonne
-Fire anomaly
    1948, Jan.12-28/Roland Cadieux
    R.S. Lambert, Exploring the Supernat-
    ural (Toronto: McClelland & Stewart,
    1955), pp.146-47.

Thetford Mines
-UFO (CE-2)
    1970, Aug.15/Adrien Bolduc
    "Landing Case in Quebec, Canada,"
    Skylook, no.38 (Jan.1971):17.

Tracy
-UFO (CE-3)
    1973, Nov.18
    Claude MacDuff, "Les Observations du
    18.11.73," UFO-Québec, no.3 (1975):
    4-7.

Trois Rivières
-UFO (CE-3)
    1969, Aug.
    Philippe Blaquière, "Les Humanoïdes
    de Trois-Rivières," UFO-Québec, no.
    2 (1975):4-5.
-UFO (DD)
    1977, Feb.17
    "Enquêtes au Québec," UFO-Québec, no.
    9 (1977):4,5.

Val d'Or
-UFO (CE-1)
    1974, Sep.3/Donat Lamontagne
    Jean Ferguson, "Enquêtes," UFO-Qué-
    bec, no.9 (1977):11,12.
-UFO (NL)
    1973, Sep.16/Sigma mine
    Jean Ferguson, "Enquêtes au Abitibi,"
    UFO-Québec, no.5 (1976):8-9.
    1974, April 24/Normand Michaud
    Jean Ferguson, "Enquêtes au Abitibi,"
    UFO-Québec, no.8 (1976):4-5.

Valleyfield
-UFO (CE-1)
    1976, Oct.30
    "Enquêtes au Québec," UFO-Québec,
    no.9 (1977):4-5.

Vandry
-UFO (CE-1)
    1944, July
    Marc Leduc, "Enquêtes en Abitibi,"
    UFO-Québec, no.11 (1977):9-10.

Verdun
-Crisis apparition
    n.d./Mrs. Turley
    Eileen Sonin, More Canadian Ghosts
    (Richmond Hill, Ont.: Pocket Books,
    1974 ed.), p.162.
-Ghost
    1960s/Mrs. F. Thornley
    Eileen Sonin, More Canadian Ghosts
    (Richmond Hill, Ont.: Pocket Books,
    1974 ed.), pp.31-32.
-UFO (DD)
    1951, Sep./A.V. Haslett
    (Letter), Fate 5 (Oct.1952):119.
    1953/E.J. Greenway
    Albert K. Bender, Flying Saucers and
    the Three Men (N.Y.: Paperback Li-
    brary, 1968 ed.), p.52.
-UFO (NL)
    1969, May 23/Jimmy Torres/500 St.-Fran-
    çois Rd.
    "The Maritimes--Newest Playground
    for UFOs?" Flying Saucers, June
    1970, pp.12,16.

Ville de Laval
-UFO (CE-2)
    1975, April 26
    Ted Phillips, Physical Traces Associ-
    ated with UFO Sightings (Evanston:
    Center for UFO Studies, 1975), p.
    106.

        B. Physical Features

Abitibi, L.
-Archeological site
    Thomas E. Lee, "A Small Prehistoric
    Quarry at Lake Abitibi, Quebec,"
    New World Antiquity 9 (1962):162-66.
    Thomas E. Lee, "A Patination Problem
    at Lake Abitibi, Canada," New World
    Antiquity 9 (1962):167-72.
    Thomas E. Lee, Archaeological Inves-
    tigations at Lake Abitibi, 1964
    (Québec: Univ. Laval, 1965). il.
    Frank Ridley, "Archaeology of Lake
    Abitibi, Ontario-Québec," Anthro.J.
    Canada 4, no.2 (1966):2-50. il.

Allumette I.
-UFO (CE-1)
    1969, Sep.3/Pauline Oulette
    "Press Reports," APRO Bull. 18 (Nov.-
    Dec.1969):8.

Baie Saint Paul
-Unidentified submerged object
  1965, March 10/Claude Laurin
    Toronto (Ont.) Globe & Mail, 11 Mar.
    1965.

Baskatong L.
-UFO (CE-2)
  1957, Nov.6/Jacques Jacobsen
    Aimé Michel, Flying Saucers and the
    Straight-Line Mystery (N.Y.: Criter-
    ion, 1958), pp.248-49, quoting APRO
    Bull., Jan.1958.
-UFO (NL)
  1978, March 11/Jacques Lavoie
    Montréal Star, 13 Mar.1978.
    Toronto (Ont.) Sun, 14 Mar.1978. il.

Bonaventure I.
-Humanoid myth
  gougou
    Sidney W. Dean & Marguerite Mooers
    Marshall, We Fell in Love with Que-
    bec (Philadelphia: Macrae Smith,
    1950).

Clearwater Lakes
-Meteorite crater
  32,000 m.diam. x 45 m.deep/probable
    C.S. Beals, G.M. Ferguson & A. Landau,
    "A Search for Analogies between Lu-
    nar and Terrestrial Topography on
    Photographs of the Canadian Shield,"
    J.Roy.Astron.Soc'y Canada 50 (1956)
    :203-22,250-61.
    C.S. Beals, M.J.S. Innes & J.A. Rot-
    tenberg, "The Search for Fossil Met-
    eorite Craters," Current Sci. 29
    (1960):205-18,249-62.
    S.H. Kranck & G.W. Sinclair, "Clear-
    water Lake, New Quebec," Bull.Geol.
    Survey Canada, no.100 (1963).
    R.W. Tanner, "Orbital Perturbation
    of a Very Large Twin Meteorite," J.
    Roy.Astron.Soc'y Canada 57 (1963):
    109-13.
    K.L. Currie & M.R. Dence, "On the
    Origin of Some 'Recent' Craters in
    the Canadian Shield," Meteoritics
    2 (1964):93-110.

Couture L.
-Meteorite crater
  15,000 m.diam./certain
    Ian Halliday & A.A. Griffin, "Appli-
    cation of the Scientific Method to
    Problems of Crater Recognition,"
    Meteoritics 2 (1964):79-84.

d'Espoir, Cap
-Phantom ship
  1711-
    Edward Farrer, "The Folk Lore of Low-
    er Canada," Atlantic Monthly 49
    (1882):542,546-47.
    Sidney W. Dean & Marguerite Mooers
    Marshall, We Fell in Love with Que-
    bec (Philadelphia: Macrae Smith,
    1950).
    R.S. Lambert, Exploring the Supernat-

ural (Toronto: McClelland & Stewart,
1955), p.57.

Gaspé Bay
-Legend of Precolumbian Whites
  1534, July 24/Jacques Cartier
    Charles de la Roncière, Jacques Car-
    tier et la découverte de la Nouvelle
    France (Paris: Librairie Plon,
    1931).

Gaspésian Provincial Park
-UFO (CE-3)
  1976, Aug.8/Freddy Chiasson
    Jean Ferguson, "Et en Gaspésie,"
    UFO-Québec, no.8 (1976):5-6,11.

Grand Lake Victoria
-Humanoid myth
  misabe
    D.S. Davidson, "Folktales from Grand
    Lake Victoria, Quebec," J.Am.Folk-
    lore 41 (1928):275-77.

Howard L.
-UFO (?)
  1973, June 10/J.F. Langevin/=hoax
    Wido Hoville, "UFO du Lac Howard,"
    UFO-Québec, no.9 (1977):16-19,21.
    il.
    Wido Hoville, "L'UFO du Lac Howard?
    Identifié," UFO-Québec, no.11
    (1977):19. il.

Ile-aux-Corneilles
-Ghost light
  n.d.
    J.C. Taché, Forestiers et voyageurs,
    moeurs et légendes canadiennes
    (Montréal: Librairie St.-Joseph,
    1884).

Ile-aux-Coudres
-Haunt
  n.d./Seal Rocks
    J. Castell Hopkins, French Canada and
    the Saint Lawrence (Philadelphia:
    John C. Hopkins, 1913), p.313.

Ile d'Orléans
-Haunt
  1763/Dubé
    Philippe de Gaspé, Les anciens Can-
    adiens (Québec: Desbarats, 1863).
    Charles M. Skinner, Myths and Legends
    Beyond Our Borders (Philadelphia:
    Lippincott, 1899), pp.122-26.

Ile Maligne
-Animal ESP
  1954, Jan.-March/H.D. Glendenning
    (Editorial), Fate 7 (Oct.1954):8-10.

Ile Saint-Ignace
-UFO (CE-1)
  1976, Oct.3
    "Enquêtes au Québec," UFO-Québec, no.
    9 (1977):4.

Kempt L.
-Archeological site
    Valerie Burger, "Indian Camp Sites
    on Kempt and Manowan Lakes in the
    Province of Quebec," Pennsylvania
    Arch. 23 (1953):32-45. il.

La Moinerie, L.
-Meteorite crater
    8000 m.diam./probable
    J. Classen, "Catalogue of 230...Im-
    pact Structures," Meteoritics 12
    (1977):61,70.

Macamic L.
-Meteorite crater
    1600 m.diam./doubtful
    C.S. Beals, G.M. Ferguson & A. Landau,
    "A Search for Analogies between Lu-
    nar and Terrestrial Topography on
    Photographs of the Canadian Shield,"
    J.Roy.Astron.Soc'y Canada 50 (1956)
    :203-22,250-61.

Malbaie L.
-Meteorite crater
    37,000 m.diam./certain
    P.B. Robertson, "Zones of Shock Meta-
    morphism at the Charlevoix Impact
    Structure, Québec," Bull.Geol.Soc'y
    Am. 86 (1975):1630-38.

Manicouagan L.
-Meteorite crater
    65,000 m.diam. x 300 m.deep/certain
    E.R. Rose, "Manicouagan Lake, Mush-
    alagan Lake Area, Quebec," Pap.Geol.
    Survey Canada, no.55-2 (1955).
    J. Berard, "Summary Geological In-
    vestigations in the Area Bordering
    Manicouagane and Mouchalagane Lakes,"
    Pap.Québec Dep't Nat.Resources, no.
    489 (1962).
    K.W. Currie, "Geology and Petrology
    of the Manicouagan Resurgent Cal-
    dera, Québec," Bull.Geol.Soc'y Can-
    ada, no.198 (1972).
    R. Floran & M.R. Dence, "Morphology
    of the Manicouagan Ring-Structure,
    Quebec, and Some Comparisons with
    Lunar Basins and Craters," Proc.
    Lunar Sci.Conference, 7th (1976),
    pp.2845-65.

Manicouagan Pt.
-UFO (NL)
    1971, July 23/hydroelectric station
    Claude MacDuff, "Canadian Power Fail-
    ures and UFO Sightings," FSR Case
    Histories, no.17 (Dec.1973):1,2.

Macatina Crater
-Meteorite crater
    3200 m.diam./doubtful
    C.S. Beals, G.M. Ferguson & A. Landau,
    "A Search for Analogies between Lu-
    nar and Terrestrial Topography on
    Photographs of the Canadian Shield,"
    J.Roy.Astron.Soc'y Canada 50 (1956)
    :203-22,250-61.

Mégantic, L.
-UFO (NL)
    1975, May 1
    L'Echo de Frontenac, 14 May 1975.
    Philippe Blaquière, "Enquêtes re-
    centes," UFO-Québec, no.3 (1975):
    10.

Mistassini, L.
-Archeological site
    Edward & Murray H. Rogers, "Archaeo-
    logical Reconnaissance of Lakes
    Mistassini and Albanel, Province of
    Quebec, 1947," Am.Antiquity 14
    (1948):81-90. il.
    Frederick Johnson, "The Rogers' Col-
    lection from Lakes Mistassini and
    Albanel, Province of Quebec," Am.
    Antiquity 14 (1948):91-98. il.
    Charles A. Martijn & Edward Rogers,
    Mistassini-Albanel: Contributions
    to the Prehistory of Quebec (Qué-
    bec: Univ. Laval, 1969). il.
-Meteorite crater
    1000 m.diam./certain
    J. Classen, "Catalogue of 230...Im-
    pact Structures," Meteoritics 12
    (1977):61,70.

Nastapoka Is.
-Meteorite crater
    440,000 m.diam. x 130 m.deep/doubtful
    C.S. Beals, M.J.S. Innes & J.A. Rot-
    tenberg, "The Search for Fossil
    Meteorite Craters," Current Sci. 29
    (1960):205-18,249-62.

New Quebec Crater
-Meteorite crater
    3200 m.diam. x 400 m.deep/certain
    N. Polunin, Arctic Unfolding (London:
    Hutchinson, 1949), p.198.
    Toronto (Ont.) Globe & Mail, 7-8 Aug.
    1950.
    V.B. Meen, "Chubb Crater, Ungava,
    Quebec," J.Roy.Astron.Soc'y Canada
    44 (1950):169-80. il.
    V.B. Meen, "The Canadian Meteor Cra-
    ter," Sci.Am. 184 (May 1951):64-69.
    il.
    Ben Meen, "Solving the Riddle of
    Chubb Crater," Nat'l Geogr.Mag. 101
    (Jan.1952):1-32. il.
    J.M. Harrison, "Ungava (Chubb) Crater
    and Glaciation," J.Roy.Astron.Soc'y
    Canada 48 (1954):16-20.
    Peter M. Milliman, "A Profile Study
    of the New Quebec Crater," Pub.Do-
    minion Observ.Ottawa 18, no.4
    (1956):61-82. il.
    E.M. Shoemaker, "Geological Recon-
    naissance of the New Quebec Crater,
    Canada," Semiann.Progress Rept., U.S.
    Geol.Survey, Astrogeol.Studies, 1961,
    pp.74-78.
    K.L. Currie & M.R. Dence, "On the
    Origin of Some 'Recent' Craters in
    the Canadian Shield," Meteoritics
    2 (1964):93-110.
    M.J.S. Innes, "Recent Advances in

Meteorite Crater Research at the
Dominion Observatory, Ottawa," Met-
eoritics 2 (1964):219,230-34. il.
K.L. Currie, "The Geology of the New
Quebec Crater," Can.J.Earth Sci. 2
(1965):141-60.

Pamiok I.
-Norse habitation site
ca.1100
    Thomas E. Lee, "The Norse in Ungava,"
    Anthro.J.Canada 4, no.2 (1966):51-
    54.
    Thomas E. Lee, "Archaeological In-
    vestigations, Deception Bay, Ungava
    Peninsula, 1965," Anthro.J.Canada 5,
    no.3 (1967):14-40. il.
    Thomas E. Lee, "Some Astonishing Dis-
    coveries in Ungava Bay, 1966,"
    Anthro.J.Canada 5, no.3 (1967):41-
    48. il.
    Stephen C. Jett, "A French Origin
    for the 'Beehive' Structures of Un-
    gava?" Anthro.J.Canada 7, no.2
    (1969):16-21. il.
    (Review), Birgitta L. Wallace, Am.
    Antiquity 34 (1969):185-87.
    Thomas E. Lee, "The Ungava Norse: A
    Reply to Birgitta Wallace," NEARA
    Newsl. 4 (Sep.1969):59-60.
    James Robert Enterline, Viking Amer-
    ica (Garden City: Doubleday, 1972),
    pp.70-71.
    Thomas E. Lee, Archaeological Inves-
    tigations of a Longhouse Ruin, Pam-
    iok Island, Ungava Bay, 1972 (Qué-
    bec: Centre d'Études Nordiques,
    Coll.Paléo-Québec, no.2, 1973). il.
    Thomas E. Lee, "Norse Investigations,
    Ungava Bay, 1972," Anthro.J.Canada
    11, no.2 (1973):20-23.
    Earl Syversen, "The Inhabitants of
    the Ungava Sites," Anthro.J.Canada
    13, no.1 (1975):31-32.
    Thomas E. Lee, "The Norse in Ungava,"
    NEARA J. 11 (summer 1976):5-6.

Payne L.
-Norse habitation site
ca.1100/Cartier site
    Thomas E. Lee, Fort Chimo and Payne
    Lake, Ungava, Archaeology, 1965
    (Québec: Centre d'Études Nordiques,
    1967).
    Thomas E. Lee, "A Summary of Norse
    Evidence at Payne Lake, Ungava,"
    NEARA Newsl. 4 (Sep.1969):55-57.
    Thomas E. Lee, "Preliminary Report
    on Cartier Site Investigations, Un-
    gava, 1974," NEARA J. 10 (spring
    1975):92-95.
    Thomas E. Lee, "The Cartier Site,
    Payne Lake, Ungava, in Its Norse
    Setting: Part 1," Anthro.J.Canada
    17, no.1 (1979):2-31. il.

Peribonka L.
-UFO (NL)
1972, Sep.19/Fernand Guay
    Danny Godin, "Observation au Lac Per-

ibonka," UFO-Québec, no.9 (1977):14.

Pohénégamook L.
-Lake monster
19th c.-   /ponik
    (Editorial), Fate 11 (Feb.1958):13-
    14.
    Michael Bradley, "The Pohenegamook
    Creature," Pursuit 9 (summer 1976):
    61-62.
    Toronto (Ont.) Sun, 2 May 1977.
    Edmonton (Alb.) Journal, 27 July
    1977.
    Montréal Gazette, 6 Aug.1977.
    Wall Street Journal, 17 Nov.1977,
    p.1.
    Lafayette (La.) Advertiser, 6 July
    1978.

Qikertaaluk I.
-Petroglyphs
    Fred Bruemmer, "Petroglyphs of Hud-
    son Strait," The Beaver, summer
    1973, pp.33-35. il.

Richmond Gulf
-Haunt
n.d.
    Charles M. Skinner, Myths and Legends
    Beyond Our Borders (Philadelphia:
    Lippincott, 1899), p.48.

Saguenay R.
-Phantom ship
n.d.
    Charles M. Skinner, Myths and Legends
    Beyond Our Borders (Philadelphia:
    Lippincott, 1899), p.60.

Saint-Jean, L.
-Archeological site
    Thomas E. Lee, "A Small Cache of
    Early Points, Lac St. John, Quebec,"
    Anthro.J.Canada 3, no.1 (1965):22-
    24.
-UFO (CE-3)
1966, summer/R.B. Leeming
    Wido Hoville, "Contact? L'étrange
    affaire 'Leeming,'" UFO-Québec, no.
    4 (1975):6-11.
-UFO (NL)
1971, June/James Richards
    (Letter), Can.UFO Rept., no.12
    (1972):32.

Saint Lawrence R.
-Fall of ashes
1814, July 3
    "The Notes of Charles Fort," Fortean
    Soc'y Mag., no.3 (Jan.1940):14, quot-
    ing Phil.Mag., ser.1, 44 (1815):91.

Saint-Louis, L.
-UFO (CE-1)
1972, July/R. Benoit
    Pierre Favreau, "Un Amerrissage sur
    le Lac St.-Louis?" UFO-Québec, no.2
    (1975):6.

Saint Maurice R.
-UFO (CE-2)
  1965, Oct.3
    <u>Shawinigan Falls Standard</u>, 3 Nov.
    1965.

Sorel Rapids
-Seance
  1609, July/Samuel de Champlain/shaking
    tent
      Samuel de Champlain, <u>Les Voyages</u>
      (1613), in H.P. Biggar ed. & John
      Squiar trans., <u>The Works of Samuel</u>
      <u>de Champlain</u>, 6 vols. (Toronto:
      Champlain Soc'y Pub., 1925), 2:86-
      89.

Taureau L.
-UFO (NL)
  1975, Aug.6?/Victor Audette
  1975, Aug.12/Victor Audette
    (Letter), <u>UFO-Québec</u>, no.6 (1976):7.

Val David
-UFO (NL)
  1976, Sep.2
    "Enquêtes au Québec," <u>UFO-Québec</u>, no.
    9 (1977):4.

          C. Ethnic Groups

Abnaki Indians
-Lake monster myth
  wiwilmeku
    Albert S. Gatschet, "Water-Monsters
    of the American Aborigines," <u>J.Am.</u>
    <u>Folklore</u> 12 (1899):255-60.

Micmac Indians
-Humanoid myth
    Silas T. Rand, "The Legends of the
    Micmacs," <u>Am.Antiquarian</u> 12 (1890):
    3,5-7.
    Stansbury Hagar, "Micmac Magic and
    Medicine," <u>J.Am.Folklore</u> 9 (1896):
    170-72.
    Elsie Clews Parsons, "Tales of the
    Micmac," <u>J.Am.Folklore</u> 38 (1925):
    55,56-59.
    Wilson D. & Ruth Sawtell Wallis, <u>The</u>
    <u>Micmac Indians of Eastern Canada</u>
    (Minneapolis: Univ.of Minnesota,
    1955), p.417.
-Legends of Precolumbian Whites
    Emelyn Partridge, <u>Glooscap, the Great</u>
    <u>Chief</u> (N.Y.: Sturgis & Walton, 1913).
-Use of Egyptian hieroglyphs
    Eugene Vetromile, <u>The Abnakis and</u>
    <u>Their History</u> (N.Y.: J.B. Kirker,
    1866), p.43. il.
    Barry Fell, <u>America B.C.</u> (N.Y.: Quad-
    rangle, 1976), pp.253-60,278,280-81.
    il.
    Barry Fell, "Medical Terminology of
    the Micmac and Abenaki Languages,"
    <u>Occ.Pub.Epigraphic Soc'y</u> 7, no.139
    (Apr.1979):7-20.

Montagnais Indians
-Humanoid myth
  mistabew, atchen
    Michael Bradley, "Quebec Sasquatches,
    a Brief Note," <u>Pursuit</u> 9 (summer
    1976):66.
-Seance and shamanism
  1630s/Paul le Jeune/shaking tent
    Paul le Jeune, "Relation de ce qui
    s'est passé en la Nouvelle France,
    en l'année 1634," in Reuben Gold
    Thwaites ed., <u>The Jesuit Relations</u>
    <u>and Allied Documents</u> (Cleveland:
    Burrows, 1897), 6:91,156-227.
    Paul le Jeune, "Relation de ce qui
    s'est passé en la Nouvelle France,
    en l'année 1637," in Reuben Gold
    Thwaites ed., <u>The Jesuit Relations</u>
    <u>and Allied Documents</u> (Cleveland:
    Burrows, 1898), 12:6-23.
    R.S. Lambert, <u>Exploring the Supernat-</u>
    <u>ural</u> (Toronto: McClelland & Stewart,
    1955), pp.14-24.

Tête-de-Boule Indians
-Humanoid myth
    D.S. Davidson, "Some Tete-de-Boule
    Tales," <u>J.Am.Folklore</u> 41 (1928):
    262,267.
    Joseph E. Guinard, "Witiko Among the
    Tete-de-Boule," <u>Primitive Man</u> 3
    (1930):69-71.

          D. Unspecified Localities

-Doubtful geography
  Saguenay
    Joseph E. King, "The Glorious King-
    dom of Saguenay," <u>Can.Hist.Rev.</u> 31
    (1950):390-400.
    <u>Boston (Mass.) Sunday Globe</u>, 27 July
    1969.
    Samuel Eliot Morison, <u>The European</u>
    <u>Discovery of America: The Northern</u>
    <u>Voyages</u> (N.Y.: Oxford Univ., 1971),
    pp.430-63.
    Astri A. Stromsted, <u>Ancient Pioneers</u>
    (N.Y.: E.J. Friis, 1974).

-Humanoid
  n.d.
    Ivan T. Sanderson, <u>Abominable Snow-</u>
    <u>men: Legend Come to Life</u> (Philadel-
    phia: Chilton, 1961), pp.43-44.
  1920s
    Michael Bradley, "Quebec Sasquatches,
    a Brief Note," <u>Pursuit</u> 9 (summer
    1976):66.
  1972, Oct.
    B. Ann Slate & Alan Berry, <u>Bigfoot</u>
    (N.Y.: Bantam, 1976), pp.83-85.

CONNECTICUT

A. Populated Places

Ansonia
-UFO (NL)
  1978, Jan.11
    Ansonia Evening Sentinel, 17 Jan.
    1978.

Berlin
-UFO (DD)
  1965, Oct.11/Roger Labas
    "News Briefs," Saucer News 13 (Mar.
    1966):26.

Bethel
-UFO (CE-2)
  1956, fall/Danti Vaghi/Federal Rd. C/
  ground markings only
    Bethel Home News, 25 Nov.1969.
  1967, June/Deborah Rondeau/Sunset Hill
    Ted Phillips, Physical Traces Associ-
    ated with UFO Sightings (Evanston:
    Center for UFO Studies, 1975), p.49,
    quoting New Times, 15 July 1969.

Bethlehem
-Fall of stones
  1951-1952/Michael D. Healey
    (Editorial), Fate 6 (Mar.1953):4-5,
    quoting Waterbury Republican (un-
    dated).

Branford
-Phantom panther
  1967, fall/Lucy T. Hammer
    (Editorial), Fate 21 (July 1968):30-
    31.
-Possession
  1650s
    Cotton Mather, Remarkable Providences
    (Boston: Joseph Brunning, 1689), in
    George Lincoln Burr, ed., Narratives
    of the Witchcraft Cases 1648-1706
    (N.Y.: Barnes & Noble, 1946), pp.93,
    136.
-UFO (NL)
  1955, Dec.12
    Richard Hall, ed., The UFO Evidence
    (Washington: NICAP, 1964), p.155.

Bridgeport
-Crisis apparition
  1944, Feb.14/Mrs. John Cullen
  1944, Dec.20/Mrs. Stephen Utz
    "Cases," J.ASPR 40 (1946):163-72.
-Contactee and Men-in-black
  1953, March 15-1961/Albert K. Bender
    Gray Barker, They Knew Too Much About
    Flying Saucers (N.Y.: University,
    1956), pp.109-47.
    E.R. Lee, "Was This What Bender Found
    Out?" Flying Saucer Rev. 4 (Mar.-
    Apr.1958):10-13.
    Albert K. Bender, Flying Saucers and
    the Three Men (N.Y.: Paperback Li-
    brary, 1968 ed.), pp.69-157.
    Jerome Clark, "The Bender Mystery:
    A Re-Examination," Flying Saucers,
    Dec.1975, pp.46-59.
-Doubtful responsibility
  1872, June/Capt. Colvocoresses/=pre-
  meditated murder
    Bridgeport Standard, 4 June 1872, p.
    3.
    New York Times, 1 July 1872, p.4;
    and 8 July 1872, p.2.
  1925, Feb.20-1928, June 1/phantom
  stabber
    New York Times, 15 Aug.1926, p.12;
    and 28 Aug.1927, p.12.
    New York Herald-Tribune, 27 Aug.
    1927.
    Charles Fort, The Books of Charles
    Fort (N.Y.: Holt, 1941), pp.896-97.
-Out-of-body experience
  1862/Mrs. Wilmot
    Herbert B. Greenhouse, The Astral
    Journey (N.Y.: Avon, 1976 ed.), pp.
    106-107.
-Phantom
  1953, Jan./Albert K. Bender
    Albert K. Bender, Flying Saucers and
    the Three Men (N.Y.: Paperback Li-
    brary, 1968 ed.), p.49.
-Poltergeist
  1974, Nov.-Dec./Marcia Goodin/Lindley
  St.
    Kansas City (Mo.) Star, 27 Nov.1974.
    Kansas City (Mo.) Times, 13 Dec.
    1974.
-Precognition
  1945, Aug.16/Barbara Wolfe
    "Cases," J.ASPR 40 (1946):163,172-75.
  1970, Aug.17
    Herbert B. Greenhouse, Premonitions:
    A Leap into the Future (N.Y.: War-
    ner, 1973 ed.), p.28.
-Sea monster
  1878, Sep.3/John Murphy/1 mi.SW of
  Black Rock Light House
    Bridgeport Standard, 5 Sep.1878.
    New York Times, 8 Sep.1878, p.10.
-Seance
  1851
    Emma Hardinge Britten, Modern Ameri-
    can Spiritualism (N.Y.: The Author,
    1870), p.81.
-Skyquake
  1953, Feb.7-8
    Albert K. Bender, Flying Saucers and
    the Three Men (N.Y.: Paperback Li-
    brary, 1968 ed.), pp.52-53.
-UFO (?)
  1952, summer/Seaside Park
    Albert K. Bender, Flying Saucers and
    the Three Men (N.Y.: Paperback Li-
    brary, 1968 ed.), p.19.
-UFO (CE-1)

1967, Feb.20/Gerald W. Lombard/City
Hall
  Bridgeport Post, 21 Feb.1967.
-UFO (DD)
  1952, July 28/Barbara Knorr
    "Saucer Sightings by IFSB Members,"
    Space Rev. 1 (Oct.1952):10.
  1956, Aug.23/Elwin Cramer/nr. Sikorsky
  Stratford plant
    (Letter), Fate 10 (Oct.1957):113-16.
-UFO (NL)
  1978, April 9/Michael Jacabacci/Thorme
  St.
    Bridgeport Telegram, 10 Apr.1978.

Bristol
-Precognition
  1976/Frank Mola, Jr.
    (Editorial), Fate 30 (July 1977):34-
    35.
-UFO (?)
  1908, summer
    New York Sun, 1 Nov.1908.

Canton
-Phantom horseman
  n.d.
    Connecticut Writers' Program, Con-
    necticut: A Guide to Its Roads, Lore
    and People (Boston: Houghton Miff-
    lin, 1938), p.427.

Cheshire
-UFO (CE-1)
  1966, May 10/Sterling Jewett
    "Big Saucer Flap in Connecticut and
    Massachusetts," Saucer News 14 (sum-
    mer 1967):18,19-20.

Colchester
-Fall of ice
  1965, Aug.14/Arthur W. Curtis
    (Editorial), Fate 18 (Dec.1965):24.

Colebrook
-Humanoid
  1895, Aug.17/Riley W. Smith
    Hartford Courant, 21 Aug.1895.
-Lightning anomaly
  1822, Aug./Martin Rockwell
    Ralph Emerson, "Cure of Asthma by a
    Stroke of Lightning," Am.J.Sci.,
    ser.1, 6 (1823):329-30.

Cornwall Bridge
-Haunt
  1747-   /Dudleytown, 2 mi.SW
    Jim Brandon, Weird America (N.Y.:
    Dutton, 1978), p.53.

Coventry
-UFO (CE-2)
  1967, July 5/Mary Ahern/Hwy.31 nr Depot Rd.
    Hartford Courant, 12 July 1967.
    "'Nests' in Connecticut," APRO Bull.
    16 (July-Aug.1967):7.
    Edward U. Condon, ed., Scientific
    Study of Unidentified Flying Objects
    (N.Y.: Bantam, 1968 ed.), pp.329-31.

Elise Vider, "Strangers in the Sky,"
    Connecticut 42 (Aug.1979):43,44.

Cromwell
-River monster
  1886, Sep.8/Col. Stocking/Connecticut
  R.
    New York Times, 9 Sep.1886, p.1.
-UFO (CE-1)
  1967, Jan.24/Nicholas J. Rinaldi
    "Big Saucer Flap in Connecticut and
    Massachusetts," Saucer News 14
    (summer 1967):18-19.

Danbury
-Ancient stone chambers and inscriptions
    Barry Fell, America B.C. (N.Y.: Quad-
    rangle, 1976), pp.131,137,299. il.
    Salvatore Michael Trento, The Search
    for Lost America (Chicago: Contem-
    porary, 1978), pp.121-29,134-35.
-UFO (CE-1)
  1961, Sep./nr. Merritt Parkway
    Philip J. Klass, UFOs--Identified
    (N.Y.: Random House, 1968), pp.45-
    51.
-UFO (CE-2)
  1967, July 9/Ronald E. Januzzi/ground
  markings only
    "'Nests' in Connecticut," APRO Bull.
    16 (July-Aug.1967):7.
    Ted Phillips, Physical Traces Associ-
    ated with UFO Sightings (Evanston:
    Center for UFO Studies, 1975), p.49,
    quoting New Times, 15 July 1967.
-UFO (NL)
  1976, Aug.30/Peter Winter
    Elise Vider, "Strangers in the Sky,"
    Connecticut 42 (Aug.1979):43,46.

Danielson
-Healing
  1974-   /Benjamin O. Bibb/260 N. Main
  St.
    Joseph J. Weed, "'Anyone Can Heal,'
    Says the Amazing Ben Bibb," Fate
    29 (May 1976):54-61. il.
    Benjamin O. Bibb & Joseph J. Weed,
    The Amazing Secrets of Psychic Heal-
    ing (Englewood Cliffs, N.J.: Pren-
    tice-Hall, 1976).
    (Letter), Julia Whitten, Fate 30
    (Mar.1977):113.

Darien
-Erratic crocodilian
  1929, Oct.2/Collender's Point
    New York Times, 3 Oct.1929, p.38.

East Hartford
-Haunt
  18th c./Hockanum Causeway
    Joseph O. Goodwin, East Hartford: Its
    History and Traditions (Hartford:
    Case, Lockwood & Brainard, 1879),
    p.240.
-UFO (CE-1)
  1979, March/Barbara Kimball/Hockanum
  School
    Elise Vider, "Strangers in the Sky,"

Connecticut 42 (Aug.1979):43,44-45.
-UFO (NL)
  1956, Aug.8/Mary Calaci
    "Case 181," CRIFO Orbit, 7 Sep.1956,
    p.3.
  1975, Nov.2
    "UFO Central," CUFOS News Bull., 1
    Feb.1976, p.11.

East Hartland
-UFO (DD)
  1963, Oct.4/L.B. Martin
    "UFO Sightings Centered in Western
    U.S.," UFO Inv. 2 (Dec.-Jan.1963-
    64):3.

East Haven
-Hex and shape-shifting
  1690s
    John Warner Barber, Connecticut His-
    torical Collections (New Haven:
    Durrie & Peck, 1838), p.208.
-UFO (NL)
  1977, Jan.29
    "UFOs of Limited Merit," Int'l UFO
    Reporter 2 (Mar.1977):5.

East Killingly
-Skyquake
  1774, fall
  1778
    John Warner Barber, Connecticut His-
    torical Collections (New Haven:
    Durrie & Peck, 1838), pp.428-29.

East Lyme
-Ancient inscription
  McCook's Point
    Hartford Courant, 13 Mar.1978.

Enfield
-UFO (CE-1)
  1975, Feb.24/Paul Rogers
  1975, March 4/John Foy
    "Police Officers Continue to Sight
    UFOs," UFO Inv., Aug.1975, p.1.

Essex
-UFO (NL)
  1967, Jan.8
    "Big Saucer Flap in Connecticut and
    Massachusetts," Saucer News 14
    (summer 1967):18.

Fairfield
-UFO (NL)
  1949, May 21
    "If It's in the Sky It's a Saucer,"
    Doubt, no.27 (1949):416.
-Witch trial (?)
  1653, May/Mrs. Knapp
    Samuel G. Drake, Annals of Witchcraft
    in New England (Boston: W.E. Wood-
    ward, 1869), pp.75-86.
    John M. Taylor, The Witchcraft Delu-
    sion in Colonial Connecticut (N.Y.:
    Grafton, 1908), pp.122-41.

Fairfield co.
-Entombed toad

1854, July
  Nat'l Anti-Slavery Standard, 5 Aug.
  1854, quoting Boston (Mass.) Courier (undated).
-Witch trial (hex)
  1692, Sep./Mercy Disborough
    Sylvester Judd, History of Hadley
    (Northampton: Metcalf, 1863), pp.
    233-34.
    Gershom Bulkeley, "Will and Doom,"
    in Connecticut Hist.Soc'y Coll. 3
    (1895):69,233-35.
    John M. Taylor, The Witchcraft Delu-
    sion in Colonial Connecticut (N.Y.:
    Grafton, 1908), pp.62-78.

Farmington
-Spirit medium
  1914/Mrs. E.W. Friend
    E.W. Friend, "A Series of Recent
    'Non-Evidential' Scripts," J.ASPR
    9 (1915):7-22,98-131.
-UFO (NL)
  1978, July 26/Brian Mark/I-84 nr.Exit
  39
    Hartford Courant, 27 July 1978.

Glastonbury
-Dog mutilations
  ca.1938
    "How to Prevent Panic," Fortean
    Soc'y Mag., no.3 (Jan.1940):13.

Green Manorville
-UFO (CE-1)
  1978, April 13
    Manchester Journal Inquirer, 15 Apr.
    1978.

Greenwich
-Animal ESP
  1955/H.S. Gatchell
    "Dog with a Vocabulary," Fate 8
    (June 1955):101.

Groton
-Ancient stone constructions
    Leon L. Morrill, Jr., "Possible Mega-
    lithic Astronomical Alignments in
    New England," NEARA Newsl. 6 (Mar.
    1971):15.
    Barry Fell, America B.C. (N.Y.: Quad-
    rangle, 1976), p.201. il.
    James P. Whittall II, "The Gungywamp
    Complex, Groton, Connecticut," Bull.
    Early Sites Rsch.Soc'y 4 (May 1976):
    15-27. il.
    Salvatore Michael Trento, The Search
    for Lost America (Chicago: Contem-
    porary, 1978), pp.153-56.
-Fall of frogs
  1930/Mrs. C.H. Holden
    (Letter), Fate 8 (Aug.1955):120.
-Precognition
  1963/William H. Van Slot/Hwy.1
    (Editorial), Fate 16 (June 1963):23-
    24.
-UFO (NL)
  1975, Jan.13
    Donald R. Todd, "Rhode Island Sight-

ings," APRO Bull. 24 (Sep.1975):4,5.

Groton Long Point
-Haunt
  1940s/Danton Walker
    Danton Walker, Spooks Deluxe (N.Y.:
    Franklin Watts, 1956), pp.169-72.

Guilford
-Ancient inscription
  Stony Creek
    Johannes Brøndsted, "Norsemen in
    North America Before Columbus," Ann.
    Rept.Smith.Inst. 103 (1953):367,398.
    Charles Michael Boland, They All Dis-
    covered America (N.Y.: Pocket Books,
    1963 ed.), p.38.
-Skyquake
  1953, Jan.1
    Donald E. Keyhoe, Flying Saucer Con-
    spiracy (N.Y.: Holt, 1955), p.201.

Haddam
-Witchcraft
  17th c.
    Charles M. Skinner, Myths and Legends
    of Our Own Land, 2 vols. (Philadel-
    phia: Lippincott, 1896), 2:46-48.

Hadlyme
-Animal ESP
  n.d./Guy Hedlund
    Guy Hedlund, "Mentally Calling
    Tawny," Fate 10 (Sep.1957):67-70.

Hamden
-UFO (NL)
  1975, July 1
    "From the Center for UFO Studies,"
    Flying Saucer Rev. 21 (Apr.1976):24.

Hartford
-Fall of snails
  1883, Nov.11/L.W. Gray
    New York Times, 29 Nov.1883, p.3.
-Healing
  1850s/Samantha Mettler
    Emma Hardinge Britten, Modern Ameri-
    can Spiritualism (N.Y.: The Author,
    1870), pp.202-203.
-Lightning anomaly
  1942, Aug.16/Joseph H. Sargent
    (Letter), Fate 16 (Sep.1963):129.
-Medical clairvoyance
  1850s-   /Griswold Drugstore
    Hartford Courant, 6 Dec.1964.
-Midday darkness
  1780, May 19
    John Warner Barber, Connecticut His-
    torical Collections (New Haven:
    Durrie & Peck, 1838), p.403.
  1881, Sep.6
    New York Times, 7 Sep.1881, p.5.
-Poltergeist
  1683/Nicholas Desborough
    Increase Mather, Remarkable Provi-
    dences (Boston: Joseph Browning,
    1684), reprinted in George Lincoln
    Burr, ed., Narratives of the Witch-
    craft Cases 1684-1706 (N.Y.: Barnes

& Noble, 1946), pp.8,33-34.
-Precognition
  1953, July
    D.H.B., "Dream of Murder Becomes
    Reality," Fate 11 (June 1955):94-96.
-Seance
  1853, March/Daniel Dunglas Home
    Hartford Times, 18 Mar.1853.
-UFO (DD)
  1978, April 10
    Hartford Courant, 11 Apr.1978.
-UFO (NL)
  1837, Jan.25
    Hartford Watchman, 28 Jan.1837.
  1954/William Call
    Donald E. Keyhoe, Aliens from Space
    (Garden City: Doubleday, 1973), pp.
    53-54.
  1956, Aug.8
    Richard Hall, ed., The UFO Evidence
    (Washington: NICAP, 1964), p.135.
  1978, April 10
    Manchester Journal Inquirer, 15 Apr.
    1978.
-Witch trial (hex)
  1665, March/Elizabeth Seager
    Sylvester Judd, History of Hadley
    (Northampton: Metcalf, 1863), p.233.
    John M. Taylor, The Witchcraft Delu-
    sion in Colonial Connecticut (N.Y.:
    Grafton, 1908), pp.79-85.
-Witch trial (invocation)
  1646-1648/Mary Johnson
    Cotton Mather, Memorable Providences
    (Boston: Joseph Brunning, 1689), re-
    printed in George Lincoln Burr, ed.,
    Narratives of the Witchcraft Cases
    1648-1706 (N.Y.: Barnes & Noble,
    1946), pp.93,135-36.
    Samuel G. Drake, Annals of Witchcraft
    in New England (Boston: W.E. Wood-
    ward, 1869), pp.62-63.
    John M. Taylor, The Witchcraft Delu-
    sion in Colonial Connecticut (N.Y.:
    Grafton, 1908), pp.143-45.
    William K. Holdworth, "Adultery or
    Witchcraft? A New Note on an Old
    Case in Connecticut," New England
    Quar. 48 (1975):394-409.
-Witch trial (pact)
  1662, Dec./Nathaniel Greensmith
    John M. Taylor, The Witchcraft Delu-
    sion in Colonial Connecticut (N.Y.:
    Grafton, 1908), pp.96-100.
-Witch trial (possession)
  1662/Anne Cole
    Letter from John Whiting to Increase
    Mather, 1682, in Massachusetts Hist.
    Soc'y Coll., ser.4, 8 (1868):466-69.
    Increase Mather, Remarkable Providen-
    ces (Boston: Joseph Browning, 1684),
    reprinted in George Lincoln Burr,
    ed., Narratives of the Witchcraft
    Cases 1648-1706 (N.Y.: Barnes &
    Noble, 1946), pp.8,18-21.
    Thomas Hutchinson, The History of the
    Province of Massachusetts Bay, 3
    vols. (Boston: Thomas & John Fleet,
    1828), 2:18.
    Samuel G. Drake, Annals of Witchcraft

in New England (Boston: W.E. Woodward, 1869), pp.119-25.
C.J. Hoadly, "A Case of Witchcraft
in Hartford," Connecticut Mag. 5
(1899):557-60.

Hebron
-Entombed frog
  1770/Samuel Peters
    Sabina W. Sanderson, "Entombed
    Toads," Pursuit 6 (July 1973):60,
    61-62, quoting letter from Samuel
    Peters to Samuel Harrison, 10 Jan.
    1806.

Jewett City
-Lightning anomaly
  1891, May/George Rood
    St. Louis (Mo.) Globe-Democrat, 24
    May 1891.

Kensington
-Mystery fog
  1758, April 3
    "Chronicle," Annual Register 1
    (1758):90-91.

Kent
-Ancient inscription
  1789, Nov./Ezra Stiles/Housatonic R./
  Molly Fisher Rock
    Edmund B. Delabarre, Dighton Rock
    (N.Y.: Walter Neale, 1928), pp.
    260-64. il.
    Edward J. Lenik, "Ancient Inscrip-
    tions in Western Connecticut," NEARA
    J. 11 (winter 1977):34-38. il.
    Salvatore Michael Trento, The Search
    for Lost America (Chicago: Contem-
    porary, 1978), pp.142-43.
-UFO (DD)
  1957, summer/Robert Klein
    Timothy Green Beckley, "Saucers and
    Celebrities," Saga UFO Rept. 2
    (fall 1975):38-39.

Lakeville
-UFO (NL)
  1967, Jan.12-24/Richard Gipstein
  Hartford Courant, 23 Jan.1967.
    "Glowing Object Is Photographed in
    Connecticut," APRO Bull. 15 (Jan.-
    Feb.1967):4. il.
    "Big Saucer Flap in Connecticut and
    Massachusetts," Saucer News 14
    (summer 1967):18,28. il.
    Edward U. Condon, ed., Scientific
    Study of Unidentified Flying Objects
    (N.Y.: Bantam, 1969 ed.), pp.478-
    80. il.

Madison
-Phantom airplane
  1947, April 16
    "At the Same Time," Doubt, no.19
    (1947):290,291.
-UFO (CE-1)
  1975, July 3
    "From the Center for UFO Studies,"
    Flying Saucer Rev. 21 (Apr.1976):24.

Manchester
-Seance
  1852, Aug.8/Daniel Dunglas Home/levi-
  tation
    Henry Spicer, Sights and Sounds (Lon-
    don: Thomas Bosworth, 1853), pp.
    125-32.
    S.B. Brittan & B.W. Richmond, A Dis-
    cussion of the Facts and Philosophy
    of Ancient and Modern Spiritualism
    (N.Y.: Partridge & Brittan, 1853),
    p.248.
    Slater Brown, The Heyday of Spirit-
    ualism (N.Y.: Pocket Books, 1972
    ed.), pp.262-63, quoting Hartford
    Times (undated).

Mansfield Center
-Ancient stone wall
  =historical?
    Jewell Friedman, "A Passion for
    Stones," Yankee 37 (Nov.1973):120-
    23,158-63. il.
    (Letter), Robert E. Smart, Yankee 38
    (Feb.1974).

Massapeag
-UFO (NL)
  1975, Jan.13
    Donald R. Todd, "Rhode Island Sight-
    ings," APRO Bull. 24 (Sep.1975):4,5.

Meriden
-Fall of unknown object
  1948, April 4/Broad St.
    "Disc Dirt," Doubt, no.21 (1948):314,
    316.
-UFO (CE-1)
  1978, April 18/Gary Boehringer/Old
  Colony Rd.
    Meriden Record, 20 Apr.1978.
-UFO (NL)
  1947, July 22/Dorothy Treiber/Colony
  St.
    Meriden Record, 23 July 1947.
-Witchcraft
  n.d./Mrs. Bentham
    C. Bancroft Gillespie & George M.
    Curtis, A Century of Meriden: "The
    Silver City" (Meriden: Journal Pub.
    Co., 1906), pt.1, pp.257-58.

Middletown
-UFO (NL)
  1976, May 7
    "Noteworthy UFO Sightings," Ufology
    2 (fall 1976):60.

Milford
-Ancient tunnel
  Edgemont Rd./=colonial?
    Bridgeport Post, 30 Sep.1972.
-Electromagnetic anomaly
  1965, Oct.24/Alfred Stanford/"Vision 4"
    (Editorial), Fate 19 (Mar.1966):9-10.
-UFO (DD)
  1952, summer
    Albert K. Bender, Flying Saucers and
    the Three Men (N.Y.: Paperback Li-
    brary, 1968 ed.), p.19.

Montville
-UFO (CE-2)
    1978, April 6/Gladys Johnston/Hidden
    Acres Rd.
        New London Day, 11 Apr.1978.
-UFO (NL)
    1978, May 20
        Norwich Bulletin, 21 May 1978.

Moodus
-Acoustic anomaly
    1700-   /Moodus noises
        New London Connecticut Gazette, 20
        Aug.1790.
        Benjamin Trumbull, A Complete History
        of Connecticut (Hartford: Hudson &
        Goodwin, 1797).
        John Warner Barber, Connecticut His-
        torical Collections (New Haven:
        Durrie & Peck, 1838), pp.526-28.
        "Earthquake in Connecticut, &c.," Am.
        J.Sci., ser.1, 39 (1840):335-42.
        Charles M. Skinner, Myths and Legends
        of Our Own Land, 2 vols. (Philadel-
        phia: Lippincott, 1896), 2:43-45.
        Clifton Johnson, Highways and Byways
        of New England (N.Y.: Macmillan,
        1915).
        Buffalo (N.Y.) Evening News, 2 Mar.
        1940.
        Harrison V. Brooke, "Thunder of the
        Mackimoodus," Fate 28 (Oct.1975):
        70-79.

Naugatuck
-Clairempathy and precognition
    1970s/Edward Snedeker/411 Donovan Rd.
        Charlie Leerhsen, "The Psychic with
        Horse Sense," Psychic World, May
        1977, pp.61-64,91. il.

New Britain
-UFO (DD)
    1955, Dec.29
        Richard Hall, ed., The UFO Evidence
        (Washington: NICAP, 1964), p.150.
-UFO (NL)
    1966, Jan.18/Robert E. Schomburg/Fafnir
    Bearing Co.
        "National Press Spotlights UFOs," UFO
        Inv. 3 (Jan.-Feb.1966):1,3.

New Canaan
-Medieval Latin inscription
    1964/=Henry III of England?
        (Editorial), Fate 17 (Nov.1964):24-
        25, quoting Boston (Mass.) Sunday
        Globe (undated).
-Skyquake
    1977, Dec.20
        Dallas (Tex.) Times-Herald, 24 Dec.
        1977.

New Hartford
-Entombed toad
    1873/Moses Gains
        A.W. Arnold, "A Toad in the Solid
        Rock," Sci.Am. 29 (1873):212.

New Haven
-Acoustic anomaly
    1877, Sep./Church x Chapel St.
        New Haven Palladium, 10 Sep.1877.
        New York Times, 11 Sep.1877, p.3.
-Aerial phantom
    1646, June
        John Winthrop, Winthrop's Journal,
        ed. James Kendall Hosmer, 2 vols.
        (N.Y.: Barnes & Noble, 1946 ed.),
        2:346.
        Cotton Mather, Magnalia Christi Amer-
        icana (London: Thomas Parkhurst,
        1702), Bk. I, ch.6.
        John Warner Barber, Connecticut His-
        torical Collections (New Haven:
        Durrie & Peck, 1838), p.161.
        Edward E. Atwater, History of the
        Colony of New Haven (New Haven: The
        Author, 1881).
        Marguerite Steedman, "The Bewitched
        Ship," Fate 6 (Nov.1953):71-73.
        William Rutledge III, "New Haven's
        Phantom Shippe of 1646," Fate 19
        (Nov.1966):82-85. il.
-Dowsing
    1960s
        (Editorial), Fate 17 (Apr.1964):6.
-Fall of anomalous meteorite
    1953, Aug.19/Middletown Ave. x Front
    St.
        Bridgeport Herald, 20 Aug.1953.
        "The Fireball Incident in New Haven,
        Conn.," Space Rev. 2 (Oct.1953):1.
        "Missile Pierces Metal Signboard,"
        CRIFO Newsl., p.1.
-Paraphysics and biorhythm research
    1930s-1960s/Harold Saxton Burr/Yale
    University
        H.S. Burr & F.S.C. Northrop, "The
        Electro-dynamic Theory of Life,"
        Quar.Rev.Biology 10 (1935):322-33.
        H.S. Burr, M. Taffel & S.C. Harvey,
        "An Electrometric Study of the Heal-
        ing Wound in Man," Yale J.Biology &
        Med. 10 (1940):483-85.
        H.S. Burr & L. Langman, "Electromet-
        ric Timing of Human Ovulation," Am.
        J.Obstetrics & Gynec. 44 (1942):223-
        25.
        H.S. Burr, "Moon-Madness," Yale J.
        Biology & Med. 16 (1943):249-56.
        H.S. Burr, "Electrometrics of Atypi-
        cal Growth," Yale J.Biology & Med.
        25 (1952):67-75.
        Leonard J. Ravitz, "History, Measure-
        ment and Applicability of Periodic
        Changes in the Electromagnetic Field
        in Health and Disease," Annals N.Y.
        Acad.Sci. 98 (1962):1144-1201.
        Edward W. Russell, Design for Living
        (London: Spearman, 1971).
        Harold S. Burr, Blueprint for Immor-
        tality (London: Spearman, 1972).
        Harold Saxton Burr, The Fields of
        Life (N.Y.: Ballantine, 1973).
        Edward W. Russell, "The Fields of
        Life," in John White & Stanley Krip-
        pner, eds., Future Science (Garden
        City: Anchor, 1977), pp.59-72.

-Parapsychology research
  1970s/Psychic Research Institute
    Kathy O. Tarree, Earthseeds (Meriden: Earthseeds, 1975).
-Phantom panther
  1967, fall/Valley St.
    (Editorial), Fate 21 (July 1968):30.
-Poltergeist
  1690s
    Charles M. Skinner, Myths and Legends of Our Own Land, 2 vols. (Philadelphia: Lippincott, 1896), 1:236-37.
  1883, March/33 Church St.
    New York Times, 12 Mar.1883, p.5.
    Charles Fort, The Books of Charles Fort (N.Y.: Holt, 1941), p.937, quoting Religio-Philosophical J., 31 Mar.1883.
-Psychokinesis research
  1950s/Yale University
    "A PK Experiment at Yale Starts a Controversy," J.ASPR 46 (1952):111-17.
-Spirit medium
  1976-
    Sandra Gibson, Beyond the Body (N.Y.: Belmont Tower, 1979).
-UFO (?)
  1813, March 20/S.E. Dwight/=meteor
    "Meteor," Niles' Weekly Register 5 (1813):64.
    S.E. Dwight, "Notice of a Meteoric Fire Ball," Am.J.Sci., ser.1, 13 (1828):35-37.
  1927-1929/Vincent Anyzeski/=meteor?
    Vincent Anyzeski, "Some Notes on a Possible Meteoric Phenomenon," Pop. Astron. 54 (1946):203-204.
  1947, July 7/John Maffey
    New Haven Journal-Courier, 8 July 1947.
-UFO (DD)
  1909, Dec.25/George S. Barrows
    Bangor (Me.) Daily News, 28 Dec.1909.
  1947, July 7/George Johnston
    New Haven Journal-Courier, 8 July 1947.
  1952, summer
    Albert K. Bender, Flying Saucers and the Three Men (N.Y.: Paperback Library, 1968 ed.), p.19.
  1966, Oct.1/Pasquale Riccitelli
    (Editorial), Saucer News 14 (spring 1967):19. il.
-UFO (NL)
  1947, July 7/Peter Santos/Long Island Sound
    New Haven Journal-Courier, 8 July 1947.
  1950, Oct.20
    Bruce S. Maccabee, "UFO Related Information from the FBI Files: Part 7," MUFON UFO J., no.132 (Nov.-Dec. 1978):11,15.
-Witch trial (hex and precognition)
  1653-1655/Elizabeth Godman
    Records of the Colony and Plantation of New Haven, 2 vols. (Hartford: Case, Tiffany, 1857), 1:29,151.
    Samuel G. Drake, Annals of Witchcraft in New England (Boston: W.E. Woodward, 1869), pp.88-97.
    John M. Taylor, The Witchcraft Delusion in Colonial Connecticut (N.Y.: Grafton, 1908), pp.85-96.

Newington
-UFO (NL)
  1956, Aug.19/Marguerite Wermann/79 Willard Ave.
    Hartford Times, 2 Jan.1957.

New London
-Haunt
  n.d.
    James Reynolds, Ghosts in American Houses (N.Y.: Paperback Library, 1967 ed.), pp.140-44.
-Moving rock
  1736, Aug.
    Boston (Mass.) New England Weekly Journal, 31 Aug.1736.
    Joshua Hempstead, Diary of Joshua Hempstead of New London, Connecticut (New London: County Hist.Soc'y, 1901).
-Sea monster
  1769, April/=hoax
    Salem Essex Gazette, 9-16 May 1769.
-Skyquake
  1883, Feb.27
    "Earthquakes," Monthly Weather Rev., Feb.1883, p.50.
-UFO (NL)
  1813, Dec.2
    "The Notes of Charles Fort," Fortean Soc'y Mag., no.2 (Oct.1937):14,16.

New Milford
-UFO (?)
  1949, April 19
    "If It's in the Sky It's a Saucer," Doubt, no.27 (1949):416.

New Preston
-Ancient inscription
  1789, Oct./Ezra Stiles/Cobble Hill
    Ezra Stiles, Extracts from the Itineraries and Other Miscellanies of Ezra Stiles, 1755-1794 (New Haven: Yale Univ., 1916).
    Edward J. Lenik, "Ancient Inscriptions in Western Connecticut," NEARA J. 11 (winter 1977):34-38. il.
    Salvatore Michael Trento, The Search for Lost America (Chicago: Contemporary, 1978), pp.138-42.

Newtown
-UFO (NL)
  1948, summer/Billy Rose
    Kenneth Arnold & Ray Palmer, The Coming of the Saucers (Boise: The Authors, 1952), pp.139-40.

Niantic
-Petroglyph
  cup-marks
    Charles Rau, "Cups and Circles," Nature 26 (1882):126-29.

North Granby
-UFO (NL)
  1967, Jan.15/Helen Godard/Hwy.189
    Edward U. Condon, ed., Scientific
    Study of Unidentified Flying Objects
    (N.Y.: Bantam, 1969 ed.), pp.285-86.
    Donald E. Keyhoe & Gordon I.R. Lore,
    Jr., UFOs: A New Look (Washington:
    NICAP, 1969), p.45.
    Donald H. Menzel & Ernest H. Taves,
    The UFO Enigma (Garden City: Double-
    day, 1977), pp.101-102.
    Elise Vider, "Strangers in the Sky,"
    Connecticut 42 (Aug.1979):43,47.

North Haven
-Fall of gelatinous substance
  1780s/Samuel Mix
    Franklin Bowditch Dexter, ed., The
    Literary Diary of Ezra Stiles, 3
    vols. (N.Y.: Scribner, 1901), 3:335.
-Inner development
  1970s/New England Coven of Welsh Traditional Witches
    J. Gordon Melton, Encyclopedia of
    American Religions, 2 vols. (Wil-
    mington, N.C.: Consortium, 1978),
    2:272-73.

North Woodstock
-Haunt
  1951-1961/Florence Viner/Brickyard Rd.
    Hans Holzer, Gothic Ghosts (N.Y.:
    Pocket Books, 1972), pp.167-75.
-UFO (CE-2)
  1967, Feb.10/William Rowe
    Raymond E. Fowler, UFOs: Interplan-
    etary Visitors (Jericho, N.Y.: Ex-
    position, 1974), p.344.
    Elise Vider, "Strangers in the Sky,"
    Connecticut 42 (Aug.1979):43,46.

Norwalk
-Sea monster
  1886, Oct.13/nr. Seymour's Rock
    New York Times, 16 Oct.1886, p.5.
-UFO (CE-1)
  1966, April 8/Mike Dorsey/Redcoat Rd.
    Norwalk Hour, 9 Apr.1966.
    Jim & Coral Lorenzen, UFOs over the
    Americas (N.Y.: Signet, 1968), pp.
    108-109.
  1977, May 30/Joseph Patchen
    (Letter), INFO J., no.25 (Sep.-Oct.
    1977), betw.pp.8-9.

Norwich
-Ancient stone cairn
  Shetucket R./Greenville
    Salvatore Michael Trento, The Search
    for Lost America (Chicago: Contem-
    porary, 1978), p.157.
-Haunt
  1967, June-1968, summer/David M. Mannes
    David M. Mannes, "The Spirit of Spite
    House," Fate 29 (May 1976):62-64.
-UFO (CE-1)
  1974, June
    (Letter), Anon., Saga UFO Rept. 2
    (winter 1975):78.

-UFO (NL)
  1965, Sep.28/Ken Skinner
    "News Briefs," Saucer News 12 (Dec.
    1965):25, quoting Norwich Bulletin
    (undated). il.
  1978, May 20
    Norwich Bulletin, 21 May 1978.

Old Lyme
-Archeological site
  ca.2000 B.C.
    Boston (Mass.) Sunday Globe, 21 Sep.
    1975.

Old Mystic
-UFO (NL)
  1975, Jan.13/Mr. Gannon
    Donald R. Todd, "Rhode Island Sight-
    ings," APRO Bull. 24 (Sep.1975):4,5.

Old Saybrook
-Ancient stone constructions
    Salvatore Michael Trento, The Search
    for Lost America (Chicago: Contem-
    porary, 1978), pp.148-49.
-UFO (CE-3)
  1957, Dec.16/Mary M. Starr
    Mary M. Starr, "My First UFO," Fate
    13 (Mar.1960):61-62.
    Mary M. Starr, "My Visitor from Out-
    er Space," Flying Saucer Rev. 6
    (May-June 1960):7-8.
    Donald E. Keyhoe & Gordon I.R. Lore,
    Jr., UFOs: A New Look (Washington:
    NICAP, 1969), pp.27-28.

Plainfield
-UFO (CE-1)
  1974, Oct.28/S on Hwy.49
    Donald R. Todd, "Huge UFOs in Eastern
    U.S.A.," APRO Bull. 23 (Jan.-Feb.
    1975):1,4.

Plantsville
-Paranormal amnesia
  1897, April 15/Thomas Carson Hanna
    Boris Sidis, The Psychology of Sug-
    gestion (N.Y.: Appleton, 1898), pp.
    216-17.

Pomfret Center
-UFO (CE-1)
  1974, fall/Margaret Grey
    (Letter), Saga UFO Rept. 2 (spring
    1975):4-6.

Putnam
-UFO (NL)
  1976, Nov.10
    "UFOs of Limited Merit," Int'l UFO
    Reporter 1 (Dec.1976):11.

Redding
-UFO (CE-1)
  1957, Feb./Ina Salter/Hwy.53
    "Connecticut Landing, 1957," APRO
    Bull. 10 (Mar.1962):1.

Ridgefield
-Haunt

1925, April/Alice Cary Williams
Alice Cary Williams, "The Ghost with
the Wooden Leg," Fate 24 (May 1971):
96-97.

Riverside
-Ancient inscription
1975/Mrs. Paul Phenix
B.W. Powell, "Possible Aboriginal
Glyphs from Southern Connecticut,"
Pennsylvania Arch. 48 (1978):44-47.
il.
Salvatore Michael Trento, The Search
for Lost America (Chicago: Contem-
porary, 1978), pp.113-14. il.

Salisbury
-Moving rocks
1820s
Petrus [Charles A. Lee], "On Certain
Rocks Supposed to Move Without Any
Apparent Cause," Am.J.Sci., ser.1,
5 (1822):34-37.
J. Adams, "Remarks...Relating to
Some Phenomena of Moving Rocks," Am.
J.Sci., ser.1, 9 (1825):136-44.
Charles A. Lee, "Remarks on the Mov-
ing Rocks of Salisbury," Am.J.Sci.,
ser.1, 9 (1825):239-41.
-Poltergeist
1802, Nov./Ezekiel Landon
John Warner Barber, Connecticut His-
torical Collections (New Haven:
Durrie & Peck, 1838), pp.489-90.

Sandy Hook
-UFO (NL)
1978, Dec.
Newtown Bee, 15 Dec.1978.

Sharon
-Haunt
1754-
Charles M. Skinner, Myths and Legends
of Our Own Land, 2 vols. (Philadelphia: Lippincott, 1896), 2:309.

Shelton
-UFO (NL)
1959, Aug.19
Jacques & Janine Vallee, Challenge
to Science (N.Y.: Ace, 1966 ed.),
p.201.
1975, Sep.4
"UFO Central," CUFOS News Bull., 15
Nov.1975, p.17.
1978, Jan.11/Nancy Stillwell/Nells
Rock Rd.
Ansonia Evening Sentinel, 13 Jan.
1978; and 17 Jan.1978.

Somers
-Precognition
1920s/Charles C. Hayes
(Letter), Fate 15 (Dec.1962):128-30.

Southington
-UFO (CE-1)
1965, Oct.2-4/Ronald Rubenstein
"Saucer Landing in Connecticut," Sau-

cer News 12 (Dec.1965):27.

South Kent
-Ancient inscription
1976, winter/Edward J. Lenik
Edward J. Lenik, "Ancient Inscrip-
tions in Western Connecticut," NEARA
J. 11 (winter 1977):34-38.

Southport
-UFO (?)
1952, Feb.23
Albert K. Bender, Flying Saucers and
the Three Men (N.Y.: Paperback Li-
brary, 1968 ed.), p.53.
-UFO (CE-1)
1966, March 14
"Close-Range Sightings Increase,"
UFO Inv. 3 (Mar.-Apr.1966):3.

Stamford
-Fall of granite
1823, Aug./Brimstone Hill
Robert Mair, "Sulphur in Granite,"
Am.J.Sci., ser.1, 7 (1824):56-57.
-UFO (CE-1)
1976, March 6
"Noteworthy UFO Sightings," Ufology
2 (summer 1976):62.
-Whirlwind anomaly
1957, March 6/Mrs. Edward Waronecki/
109 Prudence Dr.
(Editorial), Fate 10 (July 1957):13-
14.
1965, June 25/Long Ridge Swim Club
(Editorial), Fate 18 (Nov.1965):22-
24.
-Witch trial (hex)
1692, Sep./Elizabeth Clawson
John M. Taylor, The Witchcraft Delu-
sion in Colonial Connecticut (N.Y.:
Grafton, 1908), pp.101-16.

Sterling
-Fall of frogs
1921, July 31/Anton Wagner
New York Evening World, 1 Aug.1921.

Stratford
-Poltergeist
1850, March 10-1851, Dec./Eliakim
Phelps
New Haven Journal & Courier, 19 Apr.
1850.
New York Sun, 29 Apr.1850.
(Editorial), New Jerusalem Mag. 23
(1850):225-26.
Andrew Jackson Davis, The Philosophy
of Spiritual Intercourse (N.Y.:
Fowler & Wells, 1851), pp.46-70.
Charles Wyllys Elliott, Mysteries
(N.Y.: Harper, 1852), pp.171-211.
Eliab W. Capron, Modern Spiritualism:
Its Facts and Fanaticisms (Boston:
Bela Marsh, 1855), pp.132-77.
Emma Hardinge Britten, Modern Ameri-
can Spiritualism (N.Y.: The Author,
1870), p.60.
Charles Beecher, Spiritual Manifesta-
tions (Boston: Lee & Shepard, 1879),

pp.18-24.
Nandor Fodor, Encyclopaedia of Psychic Science (London: Arthurs,
1933), pp.281-82.
Slater Brown, The Heyday of Spiritualism (N.Y.: Pocket Books, 1972
ed.), pp.141-57.
-Sea monster
1896, Sep./=hoax
Bernard Heuvelmans, In the Wake of
the Sea-Serpents (N.Y.: Hill & Wang,
1968), p.357, quoting Amsterdam
(Neth.) Telegraph, Sep.1896.
-UFO (DD)
1970, Aug.7/Harvey B. Courtney
"APRO Members Sight UFOs," APRO Bull.
19 (July-Aug.1970):8.
-UFO (NL)
1947, July 6/Elmer Holloway
Windsor Daily Star, 7 July 1947.
-Witch trial (?)
1651, May/Mrs. Bassett
Samuel G. Drake, Annals of Witchcraft
in New England (Boston: W.E. Woodward, 1869), pp.72-74.
John M. Taylor, The Witchcraft Delu-
sion in Colonial Connecticut (N.Y.:
Grafton, 1908), pp.148-49.
-Witch trial (hex)
1693, May/Hugh Crohsaw
John M. Taylor, The Witchcraft Delu-
sion in Colonial Connecticut (N.Y.:
Grafton, 1908), pp.117-19.

Terryville
-UFO (CE-2)
1964, Nov.30
"Increased Landings Hint New UFO
Phase," UFO Inv. 3 (June-July 1965):
1,2.

Thompson
-Ancient stone constructions
Salvatore Michael Trento, The Search
for Lost America (Chicago: Contemporary, 1978), pp.156-59.
Andrew Rothovius, "Editor's Comments
on Mr. Devine's Article," NEARA J.
13 (fall 1978):35.

Thompsonville
-UFO (DD)
1952, Sep.6/George McCracken/Osborn
Prison Farm
(Editorial), Fate 6 (Feb.1953):10-11,
quoting Thompsonville Northern Connecticut News (undated).

Torrington
-UFO (DD)
1955, April 18/Edward Lake
(Letter), Fate 9 (Sep.1956):113.
-UFO (NL)
1957, Dec.5/Edward Lake/Charlotte Hun-
gerford Hospital
(Letter), Fate 11 (June 1958):114-15.
1967, Oct.
Hartford Courant, 21 Oct.1967.

Trumbull
-Humanoid
ca.1970
John Green, Sasquatch: The Apes Among
Us (Seattle: Hancock House, 1978),
p.231.

Vernon
-UFO (NL)
1967, Jan.15/Mrs. Peter Merson
"Glowing Object Is Photographed in
Connecticut," APRO Bull. 15 (Jan.-
Feb.1967):4.
1968, March 21/Rockville
"U.S. Reports," APRO Bull. 17 (Sep.-
Oct.1968):8.

Voluntown
-Disappearance
1973, Dec.-1974, Jan./dogs
John A. Keel, The Mothman Prophecies
(N.Y.: Saturday Review, 1975), p.
115.

Washington
-Ancient standing stones
Salvatore Michael Trento, The Search
for Lost America (Chicago: Contemporary, 1978), pp.137-38.

Waterbury
-UFO (?)
1947, July 5
Boston (Mass.) Globe, 6 July 1947.

Westbrook
-Poltergeist
1950s-1960s/John Bergner
Hans Holzer, Yankee Ghosts (N.Y.:
Ace, 1966), pp.68-71.

West Granby
-UFO (NL)
1977, Nov.16/Mark Charette
Hartford Courant, 18 Nov.1977.

West Hartford
-Phantom
n.d./Reginald Gresley/reservoir
R. DeWitt Miller, Stranger Than Life
(N.Y.: Ace, 1955 ed.), p.33.
-Precognition
1967, Dec.-1969, Nov./Joe Morris
(Editorial), Fate 22 (Apr.1969):34-
35, quoting Hartford Courant (un-
dated).
Herbert B. Greenhouse, Premonitions:
A Leap into the Future (N.Y.: War-
ren, 1973 ed.), p.53.
-UFO (DD)
1947, July 6/John Rose/84 Whiting Lane
Hartford Times, 7 July 1947.
-UFO (NL)
1956, Aug.14
"Case 188," CRIFO Orbit, 7 Sep.1956,
p.4, quoting Hartford Times (undat-
ed).
1967, Sep.2/Ronald Sheldon
"Connecticut Policemen Sight 'Sound-

less' Object," Saucer News 14 (winter 1967-68):20.

Weston
-Photographic anomaly
1966/John Van Zwienen
Brad Steiger, Gods of Aquarius (N.Y.:
Harcourt Brace Jovanovich, 1976),
p.19. il.
-Skyquake
1807, Dec.14/=meteor
Profs. Silliman & Kingsley, "An Account of the Meteor Which Burst
over Weston in Connecticut, in December, 1807, and of the Falling of
Stones on That Occasion," Am.J.Sci.,
ser.2, 47 (1869):1-8.

Westport
-Corpse anomaly
1958, Sep./Henry Kalabany/Greens Farms
Congregational Church Cemetery
(Editorial), Fate 12 (Aug.1959):11-
12.
-Mystery fish
1957
(Editorial), Fate 10 (July 1957):16.
-UFO (?)
1966, March 9-23/=balloon
Lloyd Mallan, "UFO Hoaxes and Hallu-
cinations: Part II," Sci.& Mech. 38
(Apr.1967):44,82-83, quoting West-
port Town Crier (undated).
-UFO (CE-1)
1966, June 11
Jacques Vallee, Passport to Magonia
(Chicago: Regnery, 1969), p.331.
-Weather control
1959-1966/Charles R. Kelley/neo-Reich-
ian method
Charles R. Kelley, A New Method of
Weather Control (Stanford: Inter-
science Research Inst., 1961).
Charles R. Kelley, Primal Scream and
Genital Character (Santa Monica,
Cal.: Interscience Workshop, 1971).

West Redding
-UFO (?)
1956, Aug.11
Richard Hall, ed., The UFO Evidence
(Washington: NICAP, 1964), p.135.

Wethersfield
-Witch trial (?)
1651, Feb./John Carrington
John M. Taylor, The Witchcraft Delu-
sion in Colonial Connecticut (N.Y.:
Grafton, 1908), p.147.
-Witch trial (hex and shape-shifting)
1669, May/Katherine Harrison
Public Records of the Colony of Con-
necticut, 15 vols. (Hartford: Case,
Lockwood & Brainard, 1850-90), 2:132.
Sylvester Judd, History of Hadley
(Northampton: Metcalf, 1863), p.233.
John M. Taylor, The Witchcraft Delu-
sion in Colonial Connecticut (N.Y.:
Grafton, 1908), pp.47-61.

Willimantic
-Seance
1850s
Adin Ballou, Spirit Manifestations
(Boston: The Author, 1852).
-UFO (DD)
1976, Dec.10/Philip E. Sikes
(Letter), Fate 30 (Apr.1977):113-14.
-UFO (NL)
1909, Dec.23
New York Sun, 24 Dec.1909.
New York Tribune, 24 Dec.1909, p.1.

Wilton
-Horse mutilation
1972, Sep.
New York Sunday News, 10 Sep.1972.

Winchester Center
-UFO (NL)
1967, Sep.9
Edward U. Condon, ed., Scientific
Study of Unidentified Flying Objects
(N.Y.: Bantam, 1969 ed.), pp.342-44.
Donald H. Menzel & Ernest H. Taves,
The UFO Enigma (Garden City: Double-
day, 1977), p.105.

Windsor
-Witch trial (?)
1647, May/Alse Young
John M. Taylor, The Witchcraft Delu-
sion in Colonial Connecticut (N.Y.:
Grafton, 1908), pp.145-47.

Winsted
-UFO (CE-1)
1976, June 28/Ira Leifer/Camp Delaware
"Daylight CE I Seen by 4 Witnesses
in Connecticut," Int'l UFO Reporter
1 (Nov.1976):6-7.
-UFO (CE-2)
1967, Sep.20/Mrs. Charles Pasko
"September Landing in Conn.," APRO
Bull. 16 (Nov.-Dec.1967):4.
-UFO (CE-3)
1967, Sep.15/Carol Luke/Wallens Hill
Rd.
Jim & Coral Lorenzen, UFOs over the
Americas (N.Y.: Signet, 1968), pp.
167-68.
Edward U. Condon, ed., Scientific
Study of Unidentified Flying Objects
(N.Y.: Bantam, 1969 ed.), pp.347-51.
Donald H. Menzel & Ernest H. Taves,
The UFO Enigma (Garden City: Double-
day, 1977), pp.105-106.

Woodbury
-Ball lightning
1966, May
"Saucer Briefs," Saucer News 13
(fall 1966):26,28, quoting Waterbury
Republic (undated).
-Hex
n.d./Moll Cramer
William Cothren, History of Ancient
Woodbury, Connecticut, 3 vols.
(Waterbury: Bronson Bros.,1854), 1:
160.

B. Physical Features

Basile L.
-Lake monster
  1949
    Report on file at SITU.

Cockaponsett State Forest
-Ancient sculptures
    Frederick J. Pohl, "Cockaponsett Car-
    vings," Occ.Pub.Epigraphic Soc'y 6,
    no.134 (Jan.1979):181-88. il.
    John Gallagher, "Inscriptions and
    Other Features at Cockaponsett,"
    Occ.Pub.Epigraphic Soc'y 6, no.137
    (Jan.1979):195-99.

Connecticut R.
-Mystery stone spheres
    H.B.W., "The Concretions of the Con-
    necticut Valley," Nature 63 (1901):
    566.
-Norse discovery
  1005/Thorvald Eriksson/=camp?
    Charles Michael Boland, They All Dis-
    covered America (N.Y.: Pocket Books,
    1963 ed.), pp.230-31.

Great Captain I.
-Sea monster
  1879, Jan.2/Capt. Dalton/"Jane Elize"
    New Haven Palladium, 22 Jan.1879.
    New York Times, 26 Jan.1879, p.8.

Pilot Pt.
-Ancient stone cairns
    Frank Glynn, "Excavation of the Pilot
    Point Stone Heaps," Bull.Arch.Soc'y
    Connecticut, no.38 (Aug.1973):77-89.

Riga, Mt.
-Haunt
  1802-
    Connecticut Writers' Program, Connect-
    icut: A Guide to Its Roads, Lore and
    People (Boston: Houghton Mifflin,
    1938), p.421.
    Hans Holzer, Ghosts I've Met (N.Y.:
    Ace, 1965 ed.), p.27.

Shepaug R.
-Archeological site
  ca.10,000 B.C.
    Michael Knight, "Paleo-Artifacts Are
    Found in Connecticut," Pop.Arch. 6,
    no.5-6 (1977):8-9.
    Houston (Tex.) Chronicle, 3 Sep.1977.

Talcott Mts.
-Phantom
  1967, Sep./Hwy.44
    Brad Steiger & Joan Whritenour, Allen-
    de Letters: New UFO Breakthrough
    (N.Y.: Award, 1968), p.90.

West Peak
-Phantom wolf
  1890-1893/W.H.C. Pynchon
    Connecticut Writers' Program, Connect-
    icut: A Guide to Its Roads, Lore and

People (Boston: Houghton Mifflin,
1938), p.400.
Phillip M. Perry, "Death Follows the
Black Dog of the Hanging Hills,"
Fate 27 (Feb.1974):43-48, quoting
Connecticut Quar., 1898.

D. Unspecified Localities

-Clairolfaction
  1921, Nov.-1922, May
    Pamela A. Salton, "An Apparent Case
    of Psychic Odor," J.ASPR 19 (1925):
    528-34.
    (Letter), Edward L. Morris, J.ASPR
    19 (1925):660-61.

RHODE ISLAND

A. Populated Places

Alton
-UFO (NL)
 1973, April 7
  Donald Todd, "Flap over Rhode Island," APRO Bull. 21 (May-June 1973)
  :8,9.

Ashaway
-UFO (NL)
 1975, Jan.15
  Donald R. Todd, "Rhode Island Sightings," APRO Bull. 24 (Sep.1975):4,5.

Barrington
-Haunt
 1970s/James Baron
  Craig Smith & Francine Jackson, "A
  Journalistic Presentation of the
  Baron Farm Phenomena," J.Occult
  Studies 1 (Aug.1977):121-27.
  Steffan Aletti, "Analysis of the
  Baron Photograph," J.Occult Studies
  1 (Aug.1977):127-34. il.
  Howard Smukler, "Analysis of the
  Baron Photograph," J.Occult Studies
  1 (Aug.1977):135-40. il.

Central Falls
-UFO (NL)
 1971, June-1972, Feb.
  (Letter), A.C., Saga UFO Rept. 6
  (Oct.1978):6-8.

Charlestown
-Portuguese cannon
 Ft. Ninigret/=pre-Colonial?
  Manuel Luciano da Silva, Portuguese
  Pilgrims and Dighton Rock (Bristol,
  R.I.: The Author, 1971), pp.79-81.
  "Portuguese Contacts with Pre-1620
  New England," NEARA Newsl. 6 (Dec.
  1971):70-71.

Coventry
-Ancient stone cairns
 George Parker Woodland
  Ken Weber, Twenty-Five Walks in Rhode
  Island (Somersworth, N.H.: New Hamp-
  shire Pub.Co., 1978), p.78.
  Charles M. Devine, "The Hill of
  Cairns--Coventry, R.I.," NEARA J. 13
  (fall 1978):29-35.
  Andrew Rothovius, "Editor's Comments
  on Mr. Devine's Article," NEARA J.
  13 (fall 1978):35.
-UFO (?)
 n.d./=balloon
  Donald H. Menzel, Flying Saucers (Cam-
  bridge: Harvard Univ., 1953), p.262.
-UFO (NL)
 1975, Jan.15
  Donald R. Todd, "Rhode Island Sight-

ings," APRO Bull. 24 (Sep.1975):4,5.

Cranston
-Haunt
 n.d./Howard
  Dennis Bardens, Ghosts and Hauntings
  (N.Y.: Ace, 1965 ed.), pp.180-81.

Cumberland
-UFO (DD)
 1967, July 3/Joseph L. Ferriere
  August C. Roberts, "The Cumberland,
  Rhode Island, Incident," Flying
  Saucer Rev. 19 (May-June 1973):27-
  28. il.

Dennison
-Ancient inscription
  Edmund Burke Delabarre, Dighton Rock
  (N.Y.: Walter Neale, 1928), pp.260-
  61.

East Greenwich
-Animal ESP
 1955-1962/George H. Wood, Jr.
  John Edward Malloy, "Chris: The Mathematical Dog," Fate 8 (Nov.1955):
  35-39. il.
  G.H. Wood & R.J. Cadoret, "Tests of
  Clairvoyance in a Man-Dog Relationship," J.Parapsych. 22 (1958):29-39.
  (Editorial), Fate 15 (Dec.1962):22-
  24, quoting Nat'l Enquirer (undated).
  J.G. Pratt, Parapsychology: An In-
  sider's View of ESP (N.Y.: Dutton,
  1966).
-UFO (DD)
 1973, April 2/Patrick Casey/Our Lady
 of Mercy School
  "Students Watch UFO in Rhode Island,"
  APRO Bull. 21 (Mar.-Apr.1973):4.

East Providence
-Precognition
 1957, Feb.25/Mary Tourtellot/Rumford
  Laura A. Dale, Rhea White & Gardner
  Murphy, "A Selection of Cases from
  a Recent Survey of Spontaneous ESP
  Phenomena," J.ASPR 56 (1962):3,15-
  16.
-UFO (NL)
 1947, July 6/Mrs. Herbert Fuller/3286
 Pawtucket Ave.
  Providence Journal, 7 July 1947.

Exeter
-Shape-shifting
 n.d.
  Rhode Island Writers' Program, Rhode
  Island: A Guide to the Smallest
  State (Boston: Houghton Mifflin,
  1937), p.109.
-UFO (NL)
 1973, March 28/Stony Lane

Donald Todd, "Flap over Rhode Island," APRO Bull. 21 (May-June 1973)
:8,9.

Foster
-Haunt
1855/Ramtail Factory
J. Earl Clauson, These Plantations
(Providence: E.A. Johnson, 1937),
pp.95-98.

Glocester twp.
-UFO (NL)
1973, March 23/Anthony Calouri/Snake
Hill Rd.
Donald Todd, "Flap over Rhode Island," APRO Bull. 21 (May-June 1973)
:8.

Hope Valley
-UFO (NL)
1973, March 6
Donald Todd, "Flap over Rhode Island," 21 APRO Bull. (May-June 1973)
:8.

Johnston
-Poltergeist
1960, Aug.24-Sep./Anna Perez/40 Pocasset St.
(Editorial), Fate 14 (Feb.1961):10-
14, quoting Providence Evening Bulletin (undated).

Kent co.
-UFO (CE-1)
1973, March 27/I-95
Donald Todd, "Flap over Rhode Island," APRO Bull. 21 (May-June 1973)
:8,9.

Kenyon
-UFO (CE-2)
1977, Dec.17/Marguerite Camp/Biscuit
City Rd.
Don Todd, "Large Object Stalls Autos,"
APRO Bull. 27 (July 1978):4-5.

Kingston
-UFO (NL)
1973, March 13/Ladd School
1973, March 21/Donald R. Todd/Hwy.138
Donald Todd, "Flap over Rhode Island," APRO Bull. 21 (May-June 1973)
:8-9.

Middletown
-Ancient inscription
Edmund Burke Delabarre, Dighton Rock
(N.Y.: Walter Neale, 1928), pp.221-
25. il.

Narragansett
-Automatic writing
1908/Will Hannegan
Helen Lambert, "A Record of Experi-
ments," Proc.ASPR 2 (1908):304-78.
Helen Lambert, "A Further Record of
Experiments," Proc.ASPR 2 (1908):
379-453.

-Haunt
19th c./Wedderburn House
James Reynolds, Ghosts in American
Houses (N.Y.: Paperback Library,
1967 ed.), pp.132-35.
-Hex
n.d./Tuggie Bannocks
Charles M. Skinner, American Myths
and Legends, 2 vols. (Philadelphia:
Lippincott, 1903), 1:122-25.
-Musical sand
H. Carrington Bolton & Alexis A. Julien, "Musical Sand: Its Wide Dis-
tribution and Properties," Proc.Am.
Ass'n Adv.Sci. 33 (1884):408-13.
-UFO (CE-1)
1973, April 12/Curtis Sherman/Pt. Judith Rd.
Donald Todd, "Flap over Rhode Island," APRO Bull. 21 (May-June 1973)
:8,9.

Newport
-Disappearance
1750/"Seabird"/Easton's Beach/crew
only
Sarah S. Canoone, Visit to Grand-
Papa (N.Y.: Taylor & Dodd, 1840),
pp.69-74.
Edgar Mayhew Bacon, Narragansett Bay:
Its Historic and Romantic Associa-
tions (N.Y.: Putnam, 1904), pp.294-
95.
Rhode Island Writers' Program, Rhode
Island: A Guide to the Smallest
State (Boston: Houghton Mifflin,
1937), pp.108-109.
Barnet Hyams, "The Ghost Ship 'Sea-
bird,'" Fate 6 (Apr.1953):24-26.
Vincent Gaddis, Invisible Horizons
(Philadelphia: Chilton, 1965), pp.
116-17, quoting Coronet, Dec.1952.
-Norse or Celtic tower and inscription
Touro Park
T.H. Webb, "Account of an Ancient
Structure in Newport, Rhode-Island,"
in Charles Christian Rafn, Supple-
ment to the Antiquitates Americanae
(Copenhagen: Roy.Soc'y of Northern
Antiquaries, 1841).
Charles Timothy Brooks, The Contro-
versy Touching the Old Stone Mill
(Newport: C.E. Hammett, Jr., 1851).
R.G. Hatfield, "The 'Old Mill' at
Newport: A New Study of an Old Prob-
lem," Scribner's Monthly 17 (1879):
632-41.
George C. Mason, "The Old Stone Mill
at Newport," Mag.of Am.History 3
(1879):541-49.
Barthinius L. Wick, Did the Norsemen
Erect the Newport Round Tower? (Ce-
dar Rapids, Ia.: Torch, 1911).
F.H. Shelton, "More Light on the Old
Mill," Bull.Newport Hist.Soc'y, Jan.
1917, pp.7-12.
F.J. Allen, "The Ruined Mill, or
Round Church of the Norsemen, of
Newport, Rhode Island, U.S.A., Com-
pared with the Round Church at Cam-

bridge and Others in Europe," Communications Cambridge Antiquarian Soc'y 22 (1921):90-107.

Edmund Burke Delabarre, Dighton Rock (N.Y.: Walter Neale, 1928), pp.220-21. il.

Philip Ainsworth Means, The Newport Tower (N.Y.: Holt, 1942). il.

Frederick J. Pohl, "Was the Newport Tower Standing in 1632?" New England Quar. 13 (1945):501-506.

Hjalmar R. Holand, America 1355-1364 (N.Y.: Duell, Sloan & Pearce, 1946).

Kenneth J. Conant, "Newport Tower or Mill," Rhode Island History 7 (Jan. 1948):2-7.

Olaf Strandwold, Norse Inscriptions on American Stones (Weehauken, N.J.: Magnus Björndal, 1948), pp.7,31. il.

Kathleen Merrick O'Loughlin, Newport Tower (St. Catherine's, Ont.: The Author, 1948).

Herbert Olin Brigham, The Old Stone Mill (Newport: Franklin, 1948).

Hjalmar R. Holand, "The Origin of the Newport Tower," Rhode Island History 7 (July 1948):65-73.

Frederick J. Pohl, "A Key to the Problem of the Newport Tower," Rhode Island History 7 (July 1948):75-83.

William S. Godfrey, Jr., "The Newport Puzzle," Archaeology 2 (autumn 1949):146-49. il.

William S. Godfrey, Jr., "The Newport Tower II," Archaeology 3 (summer 1950):82-86. il.

Frederick J. Pohl, "The Newport Tower: An Answer to Mr. Godfrey," Archaeology 3 (autumn 1950):183-84.

Arlington H. Mallery, Lost America (Washington: Public Affairs, 1950).

William S. Godfrey, Jr., "The Newport Tower: A Reply to Mr. Pohl," Archaeology 4 (spring 1951):54-55.

Hjalmar R. Holand, "The Age of the Newport Tower," Archaeology 4 (autumn 1951):155-58. il.

William S. Godfrey, "The Archaeology of the Old Stone Mill in Newport," Am.Antiquity 17 (1951):120-29.

Frederick J. Pohl, The Lost Discovery (N.Y.: W.W. Norton, 1952), pp.174-94. il.

Johannes Brøndsted, "Norsemen in North America Before Columbus," Ann. Rept.Smith.Inst. 103 (1953):367,382-91. il.

Arlington H. Mallery, et al., Newport Tower: A Special Interim Report Made to the Council of the City of Newport (Newport: The Authors, 1955).

Edmond P. Gibson, "Did Ancient Celts Build Newport Tower?" Fate 9 (Feb. 1956):68-72.

Edward Adams Richardson, "The Builder of the Newport (Rhode Island) Tower," J.Surveying & Mapping Div., Proc. Am.Soc'y Civil Engineers 86 (Feb. 1960):73-95. il.

Frederick J. Pohl, Atlantic Crossings Before Columbus (N.Y.: W.W. Norton, 1961), pp.176-90.

Charles Michael Boland, They All Discovered America (N.Y.: Pocket Books, 1963 ed.), pp.277-95. il.

Alf Mongé & O.G. Landsverk, Norse Medieval Cryptography in Runic Carvings (Glendale, Cal.: Norseman, 1967), pp.154-57. il.

Manuel Luciano da Silva, Portuguese Pilgrims and Dighton Rock (Bristol, R.I.: The Author, 1971), pp.74-78. il.

Horace F. Silliman, "The Newport Tower and the Chesterton Windmill," NEARA Newsl. 6 (June 1971):34-36.

Clarence W. Kinsman, "Date on the Newport Tower," NEARA Newsl. 7 (Sep. 1972):58-59.

Earl Syversen, "The Newport Tower," Am.-Scandinavian Rev. 61 (Mar.1973): 4-15. il.

O.G. Landsverk, Runic Records of the Norsemen in America (N.Y.: E.J. Friis, 1974), pp.158-61.

Clyde Keeler, "A Latin Inscription on the Newport Tower," NEARA J. 9 (winter 1974-75):79-80. il.

Clyde E. Keeler, "Mystery Tower of Newport," Fate 30 (June 1977):46-52. il.

(Letter), Clyde E. Keeler, Fate 30 (Sep.1977):113.

-UFO (DD)
1961, April 29/John P. Gallagher/Bailey's Beach
"'Head' Floats--Flies," APRO Bull. 10 (July 1961):4.
ca.1974/Nyle Rothenbach/Newport Tower
Bernard O'Connor, "Official UFO Contest Winner No.1: The Rothenbach Photo," Official UFO 1 (Oct.1975): 12-13,41-42. il.

-UFO (NL)
1973, April 11
Donald Todd, "Flap over Rhode Island," APRO Bull. 21 (May-June 1973) :8,9.

North Kingstown
-Haunt
n.d./Swamptown
George W. Gardiner, Facts and Fancies Concerning North Kingstown, Rhode Island (N. Kingstown: The Author, 1941), pp.66-72.

North Smithfield twp.
-Erratic armadillo
1945, Nov.28
"More Animals," Doubt, no.14 (spring 1946):203.

Pawtucket
-Medical clairvoyance
1836/Cynthia Gleason
Charles Poyen, Progress of Animal Magnetism in New England (Boston: Weeks, Jordan, 1837).

-UFO (NL)

1909, Dec.21/Mrs. William S. Forsythe/
85 Evergreen St.
New York Tribune, 22 Dec.1909, p.7.

Portsmouth
-Ancient inscription
1767/Ezra Stiles
Edmund Burke Delabarre, Dighton Rock
(N.Y.: Walter Neale, 1928), pp.205-
15. il.

Providence
-Clairaudience
ca.1937/W. Frederick Williams, Jr.
Ethel Traphagen Leigh, "The Disembod-
ied Voice," Fate 14 (Dec.1961):61.
-Clairvoyance
1978, Feb.-Mar.
Howard Smukler, "A Remote Viewing
Experiment: California to Rhode
Island," Metascience Quar. 1 (spring
1979):25-32.
-Fall of frogs and fishes
1920s/Mrs. C.H. Holden
(Letter), Fate 8 (Aug.1955):120.
-Fall of white substance
1903/Mrs. C.H. Holden
(Letter), Fate 8 (Aug.1955):120.
-Healing
1952-1957/O.P. Stites
O.P. Stites, "Multiple Sclerosis--
Healed by the Holy Spirit," Fate 25
(Apr.1972):84-87.
-Mesmerism
1836/Charles Poyen
Charles Poyen, Progress of Animal
Magnetism in New England (Boston:
Weeks, Jordan, 1837).
Slater Brown, The Heyday of Spirit-
ualism (N.Y.: Pocket Books, 1972
ed.), pp.16-17.
1840s/LaRoy Sunderland
LaRoy Sunderland, Pathetism (N.Y.:
P.P. Good, 1843).
LaRoy Sunderland, "Confessions of a
Magnetiser" Exposed! (Boston: Red-
ding, 1845).
Slater Brown, The Heyday of Spirit-
ualism (N.Y.: Pocket Books, 1972
ed.), pp.21-24.
-Midday darkness
1881, Sep.6
Providence Journal, 7 Sep.1881.
New York Times, 7 Sep.1881, p.5.
-Phantom carriage
n.d./Peter Rugg's gig
Amy Lowell, Legends (Boston: Hough-
ton Mifflin, 1921), pp.238-52.
Pauline Saltzman, Ghosts and Other
Strangers (N.Y.: Lancer, 1970 ed.),
pp.81-84.
-Psychic photography
1970s
Donald Durand, "An Experiment in Pho-
tographing the Human Aura with Infra
Red, Recorder, High Speed and Normal
B/W Film," Metascience Quar. 1
(spring 1979):57-60.
-Skyquake
1956, March 3

Providence Bulletin, 6 Mar.1956.
-Spirit medium
1850s/Anna A. Wilbur
1850s/Mrs. Johnson
1850s/Ms. Thorp
1850s/Mrs. James D. Simmons
Eliab W. Capron, Modern Spiritualism:
Its Facts and Fanaticisms (Boston:
Bela Marsh, 1855), pp.226-31,244-50.
New York Tribune, 11 Jan.1851, p.4.
Emma Hardinge Britten, Modern American Spiritualism (N.Y.: The Author,
1870), pp.106-107.
n.d./Almira Beazeley/=fraudulent
Vergilious Ferm, A Brief Dictionary
of American Superstitions (N.Y.:
Philosophical Library, 1959), p.185.
-UFO (?)
1970, Dec.5/=satellite re-entry?
Little Rock Arkansas Gazette, 6 Dec.
1970.
-UFO (NL)
1909, Dec.23
Providence Journal, 24 Dec.1909.
1973, April 8/Brookfield Hills
Donald Todd, "Flap over Rhode Island," APRO Bull. 21 (May-June 1973)
:8,9.

Saunderstown
-Norse ax
1889
Frederick J. Pohl, The Lost Discovery
(N.Y.: W.W. Norton, 1952), p.291.

Shannock
-UFO (DD)
1973, March 5/Ann Gardner/fire tower
Donald Todd, "Flap over Rhode Island," APRO Bull. 21 (May-June 1973)
:8.
-UFO (NL)
1973, March 5/Ann Gardner
1973, March 20-21/Ann Gardner
1973, April 5-6/Ann Gardner/fire tower
Donald Todd, "Flap over Rhode Island," APRO Bull. 21 (May-June 1973)
:8-9.

Tiverton
-Ancient inscription
1768/Ezra Stiles
Edmund Burke Delabarre, Dighton Rock
(N.Y.: Walter Neale, 1928), pp.226-
36. il.

Wakefield
-UFO (CE-1)
1975, March 26/W on U.S.1
1975, March 27/Mrs. Warner Sweet/W on
U.S.1
Donald R. Todd, "Rhode Island Car
Paced by UFO," APRO Bull. 24 (Feb.
1976):5-6.
-UFO (DD)
1975, Jan.5/Tower Hill Rd.
Donald R. Todd, "Huge UFOs in Eastern
U.S.A.," APRO Bull. 23 (Jan.-Feb.
1975):1,5.
-UFO (NL)

1973, April 12-13/Warner Sweet
   Donald Todd, "Flap over Rhode Island," APRO Bull. 21 (May-June 1973)
   :8,9.
1975, March 28
   Donald R. Todd, "Rhode Island Car
   Paced by UFO," APRO Bull. 24 (Feb.
   1976):5,6.
1978, June 15/Donald R. Todd
   Donald R. Todd, "F.I. Paced by
   U.F.O.," APRO Bull. 26 (June 1978):
   4-5.

Warren
-Ancient inscription
   Edmund B. Delabarre, "A Unique In-
   dian Implement from Warren," Rhode
   Island Hist.Coll. 12 (1919):96-100.
   Edmund Burke Delabarre, Dighton Rock
   (N.Y.: Walter Neale, 1928), pp.255-
   58. il.
-Clairvoyance
   1910s/Beulah Miller
   James H. Hyslop, "The Case of Beulah
   Miller," J.ASPR 8 (1914):28-46.

Warwick
-Ancient inscription
   1770/Ezra Stiles
   Edmund Burke Delabarre, Dighton Rock
   (N.Y.: Walter Neale, 1928), pp.237-
   54. il.
-UFO (NL)
   1975, Jan.15/Hwy.95
   Donald R. Todd, "Rhode Island Sight-
   ings," APRO Bull. 24 (Sep.1975):4,5.

Washington co.
-UFO (CE-1)
   1973, April 10/Mrs. Joseph De Blasi/
   U.S.1
   Donald Todd, "Flap over Rhode Island," APRO Bull. 21 (May-June 1973)
   :8,9.

Watch Hill
-Dowsing
   1966, May/Jim Kidd/Misquamicut Club
   Robert S. Plimpton, "The Millionaires
   and the Dowser," Fate 20 (July 1967)
   :32-41. il.

Westerly
-Dowsing
   1962, spring/Roger Savaria/Watch Hill
   x Avondale Rd.
   Robert S. Plimpton, "We Dowsed for
   Our Home on a Map," Fate 18 (May
   1965):39-45. il.
-UFO (NL)
   1960, Nov.7/Harold Shea, Jr.
   (Letter), Fate 14 (Apr.1961):109-10.

Wood River Junction
-UFO (CE-1)
   1973, April 9/post office
   Donald Todd, "Flap over Rhode Island," APRO Bull. 21 (May-June 1973)
   :8,9.
-UFO (NL)

1973, March 24/Ann Gardner/United Nuclear Plant
1973, March 27/Ann Gardner/United Nuclear Plant
   Donald Todd, "Flap over Rhode Island," APRO Bull. 21 (May-June 1973)
   :8-9.

Woonsocket
-Stigmata
   1916, March 17-1936/Rose Ferron/86
   Asylum St.
   New York Herald Tribune, 25 Mar.
   1928.
   John E. Malloy, "Miracle Girl of
   Woonsocket," Fate 9 (May 1956):95-
   100.
-UFO (?)
   1965, Nov.9
   John G. Fuller, Incident at Exeter
   (N.Y.: Berkley, 1967 ed.), p.207.
-UFO (DD)
   1966, July 24/Harold A. Trudel/nr.
   Elder Ballou Meeting House Rd.
   Woonsocket Call, 22 Aug.1966.
   Joseph L. Ferriere, "We Photographed
   UFOs," Fate 20 (Mar.1967):52-55. il.
   1967, June 16/Harold A. Trudel
   "UFO Photos," Beyond Reality, no.18
   (Jan.1976):20,23. il.

B. Physical Features

Arnold's Point
-Petroglyph
   1910
   Edmund Burke Delabarre, Dighton Rock
   (N.Y.: Walter Neale, 1928), pp.216-
   20. il.

Block I.
-Haunt
   1876
   Samuel T. Livermore, A History of
   Block Island (Hartford: Case, Lock-
   wood & Brainard, 1877).
-Phantom ship
   1738-   /"Palatine" light
   W.P. Sheffield, An Historical Sketch
   of Block Island (Newport: J.P. San-
   born, 1876), pp.38-46.
   Samuel T. Livermore, A History of
   Block Island (Hartford: Case, Lock-
   wood & Brainard, 1877), pp.89-118.
   Newport Mercury, 23 Mar.1878.
   Thomas R. Hazard, Recollections of
   Olden Times (Newport: J.P. Sanborn,
   1879), pp.127-29.
   Edward E. Pettee, Block Island Illustrated (Boston: Deland & Barta,
   1884), pp.96-106.
   New York Times, 19 Oct.1884, p.4.
   Edgar Mayhew Bacon, Narragansett Bay:
   Its Historic and Romantic Associa-
   tions (N.Y.: Putnam, 1904), pp.356-
   62.
   Depositions of Officers of the Palatine Ship "Princess Augusta" (Prov-
   idence: General Court of the Soc'y

of Colonial Wars in the State of
Rhode Island, 1939).
John Kobler, "The Mystery of the
Palatine Light," Sat.Eve.Post, 11
June 1960, pp.44-45,55-58.
Vincent Gaddis, Invisible Horizons
(Philadelphia: Chilton, 1965), pp.
87-92.
Raymond Lamont Brown, Phantoms of
the Sea (N.Y.: Taplinger, 1973),
pp.177-79.
Frank Smyth, Ghosts and Poltergeists
(Greenwich, Ct.: Danbury, 1976),
pp.66-67.
Larry E. Arnold, "Ahoy, Mate! Which
Flamin' Phantom Ship Sails Thar?"
Pursuit 11 (summer 1978):109,111-13.
-UFO (NL)
1973, March 18/nr. Shelter Harbor
Donald Todd, "Flap over Rhode Is-
land," APRO Bull. 21 (May-June 1973)
:8.

Brenton Point
-Underwater ruins
(Editorial), Fate 13 (May 1960):16-
18.
(Editorial), Fate 13 (Sep.1960):20-
22.
Charles Berlitz, Mysteries from For-
gotten Worlds (Garden City: Doubleday, 1972), pp.96-97.

Fogland Ferry
-Ancient inscription
1788/Ezra Stiles
Edmund Burke Delabarre, Dighton Rock
(N.Y.: Walter Neale, 1928), pp.215-
16.

Gardner's Point
-Ancient inscription
Edmund Burke Delabarre, Dighton Rock
(N.Y.: Walter Neale, 1928), p.255.

Great Swamp Wildlife Management Area
-UFO (NL)
1975, March 2
"Object Emits Small Spheres," APRO
Bull. 24 (Aug.1975):4.

Hopkins Hill
-Haunt
n.d./Witch Rock
Charles M. Skinner, Myths and Legends
of Our Own Land, 2 vols. (Philadelphia: Lippincott, 1896), 2:32-33.

Judith Point
-Norse discovery
1005/Thorvald Eriksson/=Kiálnarnes?
Charles Michael Boland, They All Discovered America (N.Y.: Pocket Books,
1963 ed.), p.233.
-Sea monster
1888, Aug.4/Capt. Delory/"Mary Lane"/
2 mi.SW
New York Times, 7 Aug.1888, p.5.

Mount Hope Bay
-Ancient inscription
1780/Ezra Stiles
Edmund Burke Delabarre, Dighton Rock
(N.Y.: Walter Neale, 1928), pp.187-
203. il.
Olaf Strandwold, Norse Inscriptions
on American Stones (Weehauken, N.J.:
Magnus Björndal, 1948), p.39. il.
Barry Fell, America B.C. (N.Y.: Quad-
rangle, 1976), pp.98-100,122. il.

Quonset Point
-Skyquake
1956, Feb.16
1956, March 3
"Skyquakes--The Ageless Enigma,"
CRIFO Orbit, 4 May 1956, p.1.

Tom, Mt.
-Haunt
n.d./Moaning Bones
Rhode Island Writers' Program, Rhode
Island: A Guide to the Smallest
State (Boston: Houghton Mifflin,
1937), pp.109-10.

Tower Hill
-UFO (NL)
1975, Jan.15
Donald R. Todd, "Rhode Island Sightings," APRO Bull. 24 (Sep.1975):4,5.

MASSACHUSETTS

A. Populated Places

Abington
-Phantom wolf and horse killing
  1976, April 30/Philip Kane
    Boston Globe, 8 May 1976.
    (Editorial), Fate 29 (Sep.1976):10-
    12.
-UFO (NL)
  1966, April 17
    Raymond E. Fowler, UFOs: Interplane-
    tary Visitors (Jericho, N.Y.: Expo-
    sition, 1974), p.338.

Acton
-Disappearance
  1943/Fook Shung Jung
    "Mystery of the Chinese Farmers,"
    Fate 18 (Feb.1965):61, quoting Bos-
    ton Globe (undated).

Agawam
-Humanoid tracks
  1976, Dec.27/Angela Rossi/Westfield R./
  =hoax
    Springfield Morning Union, 30-31 Dec.
    1976.
    Boston Globe, 1-2 Jan.1977.
    (Editorial), INFO J., no.26 (Nov.-
    Dec.1977); inside front cover. il.
-Phantom helicopter
  1975, Dec./Marianne Cascio
    Berthold Eric Schwarz, "Talks with
    Betty Hill:2--The Things That Happen
    Around Her," Flying Saucer Rev. 23
    (Oct.1977):11.
-UFO (NL)
  1975, Dec.7/Marianne Cascio
    Berthold Eric Schwarz, "Talks with
    Betty Hill:2--The Things That Happen
    Around Her," Flying Saucer Rev. 23
    (Oct.1977):11.

Amesbury
-Fall of sulphur
  1860, June 18
    "Notes and Queries," Sci.Am. 3
    (1860):46.
    "Sulphur in Rain," Sci.Am. 3 (1860):
    97.
-Haunt
  n.d./Barrow Hill
  n.d./Mrs. Whitcher
    Charles M. Skinner, Myths and Legends
    of Our Own Land, 2 vols. (Philadel-
    phia: Lippincott, 1896), 1:231-32.
-UFO (CE-1)
  n.d./Diane Drew/Hunt Rd.
    John G. Fuller, Incident at Exeter
    (N.Y.: Berkley, 1967 ed.), pp.48-49,
    quoting Boston Globe (undated).
-UFO (CE-3)
  1973, Oct.13
    David Webb, 1973: Year of the Human-

oids (Evanston: Center for UFO
Studies, 1976 ed.), p.10.

Amherst
-Fall of gelatinous substance
  1819, Aug.13/Erastus Dewey/=nostoc or
  slime mold?
    Rufus Graves, "Account of a Gelatin-
    ous Meteor," Am.J.Sci., ser.1, 2
    (1820):335-37.
    Edward Hitchcock, "On the Meteors of
    Nov.13, 1833," Am.J.Sci., ser.1, 25
    (1834):354,362.
    Edward F. Free, "Pwdre Ser," Nature
    85 (1910):6.
-UFO (?)
  1965, Nov.9
    John G. Fuller, Incident at Exeter
    (N.Y.: Berkley, 1967 ed.), p.207.
-UFO (DD)
  1967, Sep.23
    Raymond E. Fowler, UFOs: Interplane-
    tary Visitors (Jericho, N.Y.: Expo-
    sition, 1974), p.349.
-UFO (NL)
  1810s/Noah Webster
    Noah Webster, "Luminous Appearance
    in the Atmosphere," Am.J.Sci., ser.
    1, 12 (1827):380.
  1967, Feb.16
  1967, March 7
    Raymond E. Fowler, UFOs: Interplane-
    tary Visitors (Jericho, N.Y.: Expo-
    sition, 1974), pp.344-45.

Andover
-Ancient pavement
    Arthur M. Hoffman, "A Stone Pavement
    at Andover, Massachusetts," Bull.
    Mass.Arch.Soc'y 3 (1942):25-26. il.
-Ancient stone cairn
  Turtle Effigy
    William B. Goodwin, The Ruins of
    Great Ireland in New England (Bos-
    ton: Meador, 1946), pp.100-108. il.
    Frank Glynn, "'The Effigy Mound': A
    Covered Cairn Burial Site," NEARA
    Newsl. 4 (Dec.1969):75-79. il.
    Salvatore Michael Trento, The Search
    for Lost America (Chicago: Contem-
    porary, 1978), pp.178-82. il.
-UFO (CE-1)
  1967, Feb.17/I-93 x I-495
    "V-Shaped Craft Hovers over Car,"
    UFO Inv. 3 (Mar.-Apr.1967):6.
    Raymond E. Fowler, UFOs: Interplane-
    tary Visitors (Jericho, N.Y.: Expo-
    sition, 1974), p.344.
  1975, Feb.20/Nancy Rose/Phillips Academy
    John Giambrone, "Students Report
    Close Approach," Skylook, no.89
    (Apr.1975):8-9.
-UFO (NL)

1965, Sep.27
1967, March 9/country club
  Raymond E. Fowler, UFOs: Interplanetary Visitors (Jericho, N.Y.: Exposition, 1974), pp.334,345.

Ashby
-Phantom
  1975/Jane Frances T. Woodruff
  (Letter), Fate 31 (Mar.1978):128.
-UFO (CE-1)
  1966, April 24
  Jacques Vallee, Passport to Magonia
  (Chicago: Regnery, 1969), p.330.
  1977, Nov.3/Mrs. Robert Loughlin/Rich-
  ardson Rd.
  Fitchburg Sentinel & Enterprise, 17
  Dec.1977.

Ashfield
-UFO (DD)
  1955, Dec.6
  "Case 123," CRIFO Orbit, 6 Jan.1956,
  p.4.

Ashland
-UFO (NL)
  1909, Dec.23
  Providence (R.I.) Journal, 24 Dec.
  1909.

Athol
-Seance
  1852, March/Daniel Dunglas Home
  Herman Snow, Spirit-Intercourse (Bos-
  ton: Crosby, Nichols, 1853).
-UFO (?)
  1947, July 7
  Boston Globe, 8 July 1947.

Attleboro
-UFO (DD)
  1957, March 1/Patrick J. Crisileo
  (Letter), Fate 10 (Sep.1957):113.
-UFO (NL)
  1967, June/Ethel Rogers
  "Massachusetts Reader Sees Three
  UFO's," Skylook, no.30 (May 1970):7.
  1968, Nov.1/Phillips St.
  Attleboro Sun, 4 Nov.1968.

Avon
-UFO (DD)
  1957, Dec.24/Edward Waite
  (Letter), Fate 11 (June 1958):115.
-UFO (NL)
  1957, July 1
  Richard Hall, ed., The UFO Evidence
  (Washington: NICAP, 1964), p.146.

Ayer
-Spontaneous human combustion
  1890, May 12
  Charles Fort, The Books of Charles
  Fort (N.Y.: Holt, 1941), pp.661-62.
-UFO (NL)
  1957, Sep.17/Fort Devens
  Richard Hall, ed., The UFO Evidence
  (Washington: NICAP, 1964), p.29.

Barre
-Fire anomaly
  1960, July 16/Rose Howe/New Braintree
  Rd.
  (Editorial), Fate 13 (Nov.1960):19.

Bedford
-UFO (NL)
  1952, July 1
  Edward J. Ruppelt, The Report on Unidentified Flying Objects (Garden
  City: Doubleday, 1956), pp.150-51.
  1954, June 13/Ernest Taillacq/20 mi.W
  of airport
  (Letter), Roy Baltozen, Fate 8 (Mar.
  1958):113-14.
  1961, Feb.5
  "'Flaming, Blinking Lights' at Bedford, Mass.," APRO Bull. 9 (Jan.
  1961):6.

Bellingham
-UFO (CE-1)
  1966, April 19/Rock Hill Veterans Home
  Jacques Vallee, Passport to Magonia
  (Chicago: Regnery, 1969), p.329.
  Raymond E. Fowler, UFOs: Interplane-
  tary Visitors (Jericho, N.Y.: Expo-
  sition, 1974), p.339.

Belmont
-UFO (NL)
  1967, Dec.24
  J. Allen Hynek, The UFO Experience
  (Chicago: Regnery, 1972), pp.39-42.

Bernardston
-UFO (?)
  1955, Nov.
  "Case 123," CRIFO Orbit, 6 Jan.1956,
  p.4.
-UFO (DD)
  1946, March/Fred J. Stange
  "Saucers of Yesteryear: The Link to
  Credulity," CRIFO Newsl., 3 June
  1955, pp.3-4.

Beverly
-Ancient inscriptions
  1871/Nathan Patch
  1885/Nathan Patch
  Beverly Citizen, 14 Sep.1889; and 21
  Sep.1889. il.
  Edmund Burke Delabarre, Dighton Rock
  (N.Y.: Walter Neale, 1928), pp.281-
  82. il.
-Fall of unknown substance
  1977, Jan.24/beach
  P.J. Willis, "Old McCarthy Had a
  Pond," INFO J., no.22 (Mar.1977):14.
-Precognition
  1898, July 4/Harriett L. White
  Edna White Chandler, "The Lucky Day
  We Missed the Boat," Fate 27 (Feb.
  1974):60-63.
  (Letter), W. Karl Lations, Fate 27
  (June 1974):142-43.
-UFO (?)
  1967, Aug.2/Chester M. Ladd/airport/=
  flares

"Worldwide Sightings Showing In-
crease," UFO Inv. 4 (Oct.1967):1,4.
"Cape Ann Sightings Reevaluated," UFO
Inv. 4 (Nov.-Dec.1967):3.
Edward U. Condon, Scientific Study
of Unidentified Flying Objects (N.Y.:
Bantam, 1969 ed.), pp.339-41.
-UFO (CE-2)
1966, April 22/Nancy Modugno/Beverly
High School
Edward U. Condon, ed., Scientific
Study of Unidentified Flying Objects
(N.Y.: Bantam, 1969 ed.), pp.266-70.
J. Allen Hynek, The UFO Experience
(Chicago: Regnery, 1972), pp.93-95.
Raymond E. Fowler, UFOs: Interplane-
tary Visitors (Jericho, N.Y.: Expo-
sition, 1974), pp.130-36.
Donald H. Menzel & Ernest H. Taves,
The UFO Enigma (Garden City: Double-
day, 1977), pp.96-98.
-UFO (DD)
1968, spring/Centerville School
1970, Sep.20/golf course
1972, Aug.31/Hwy.128
Raymond E. Fowler, UFOs: Interplanetary Visitors (Jericho, N.Y.: Exposition, 1974), pp.351,356,358.
-UFO (NL)
1966, Nov.15/nr. Beverly Farms
1968, April 14/New England Power Plant
Raymond E. Fowler, UFOs: Interplanetary Visitors (Jericho, N.Y.: Exposition, 1974), pp.342,352.

Blackstone
-Clairaudience
1941, Sep./Sally Stryk
Sally Stryk, "Kindly Think of Me?"
Fate 24 (Sep.1971):89-90.
-Seance
1851, Oct./Harvey Chase
Slater Brown, The Heyday of Spirit-
ualism (N.Y.: Pocket Books, 1972
ed.), p.166.
-UFO (DD)
1967, July 17/Harold A. Trudel
Woonsocket (R.I.) Call, 26 July 1967.
Wendelle C. Stevens, "Fantastic UFO
Photo Flap of 1967: Part II," Saga
UFO Rept. 3 (Aug.1976):24,26-27. il.

Blandford
-UFO (NL)
1962, May 26
Lloyd Mallan, "Complete Directory of
UFOs: Part 1," Sci.& Mech. 37 (Dec.
1966):36,71-72.

Boston
-Alchemy
1650s/George Starkey
Harold Jantz, "America's First Cosmopolitan," Proc.Mass.Hist.Soc'y 84
(1972):3-25.
-Animal ESP
1963, Aug./Arthur Perkins/20 American
Legion Hwy.
(Editorial), Fate 16 (Dec.1963):22-
24.

-Anomalous artifact
1851/Meeting House Hill/=metallic ves-
sel
"A Relic of a By-Gone Age," Sci.Am.
7 (1852):298, quoting Boston Tran-
script (undated).
1964, March/Frank McNamara, Jr./149
M St./=sculpted stone head
(Editorial), Fate 17 (Nov.1964):22-
24.
-Autoscopy
1962
Edward Podolsky, "Have You Seen
Your Double?" Fate 19 (Apr.1966):
78,81.
-Clairempathy
1964/Peter Hurkos
Paul Mandel, "Now a Seer Stalks the
Boston Strangler," Life, 6 Mar.
1964, pp.49-50. il.
Walter McGraw,"Peter Hurkos and the
Boston Strangler," Fate 20 (May
1967):48-58.
Norma L. Browning, Peter Hurkos: I
Have Many Lives (Garden City: Doub-
leday, 1976).
-Clairvoyance
1858, July/Ms. Munson/13 Lagrange Pl.
Richard H. Dillon, "The Clairvoyant
and the Castaways," Fate 10 (Feb.
1957):94-98.
1883, Aug.28/Byron Somes/=hoax
Boston Globe, 28 Aug.1883.
Florence Finch Kelly, Flowing Stream
(N.Y.: Dutton, 1939).
Jess Stearn, The Door to the Future
(N.Y.: Macfadden, 1964), pp.136-39.
1958, July/Mrs. March/147 Ashmont St.
Alson J. Smith, "Do We Have the Right
Time?" Fate 12 (Mar.1959):57-58.
-Crisis apparition
1687, May 2/Joseph Beacon
Cotton Mather, Magnalia Christi Amer-
icana (Boston: Thomas Parkhurst,
1702), Bk.VI.
Samuel P. Fowler, Salem Witchcraft
(Boston: W. Veazie, 1865).
1909, Feb.14/Olive N. Dalke
"Death Coincidence," J.ASPR 8 (1914):
536-42.
1941, Dec.6/Albert Hagner
"Cases," J.ASPR 38 (1944):48-52.
-Deathbed weight research
1906/Duncan MacDougall/Massachusetts
General Hospital
Duncan MacDougall, "Hypothesis Con-
cerning Soul Substance, Together
with Experimental Evidence of Such
Substance," J.ASPR 1 (1907):237-44.
"Correspondence," J.ASPR 1 (1907):
263-75.
Hereward Carrington, "On Dr. MacDoug-
all's Experiments," J.ASPR 1 (1907):
276-83.
Duncan MacDougall, "Mr. Carrington's
Criticisms," J.ASPR 1 (1907):343-46.
-Disappearance
1969, March 2/William Boisvert/Logan
Airport/Beechcraft 18-S
Ronald Drucker, "Space Intruders Are

Zeroing In on New England," Saga
UFO Rept. 3 (Aug.1976):40,66.
-Disease anomaly
1932, Jan./Harvard Medical School
New York Herald Tribune, 30 Jan.1932.
-Doubtful responsibility
1930, Nov.-1931, Feb./phantom sniper
Charles Fort, The Books of Charles
Fort (N.Y.: Holt, 1941), p.894.
-Erratic shark
1977, Dec.9
Boston Globe, 10 Dec.1977.
-Fall of caterpillars
1646, July
John Winthrop, Winthrop's Journal,
ed. James Kendall Hosmer, 2 vols.
(N.Y.: Barnes & Noble, 1946 ed.),
2:277.
-Fall of fish
1841, June 30
David P. Thomson, Introduction to
Meteorology (Edinburgh: W. Black-
wood, 1849), p.163.
1963/New England Telephone Co. bldg./
Dorchester
(Editorial), Fate 17 (Apr.1964):21.
-Fall of red snow
1688, winter
Cotton Mather, The Way to Prosperity
(Boston: Brunning, Gill & Woode,
1690).
-Fall of soot
1960, May 13/South Boston/=pollution?
(Editorial), Fate 13 (Sep.1960):24.
-Haunt
n.d./Boston Harbor
Hans Holzer, Yankee Ghosts (N.Y.:
Ace, 1966), p.50.
1912, fall-1913, Jan.19/Gerald Varick/
1 Garnett St.
Edmond P. Gibson, "House with the
Padded Carpets," Fate 9 (July 1956):
88-99.
1956-1960s
New York Journal-American, 27 Oct.
1963, magazine sec.
-Healing
1880s/R.C. Flower
"Notes by the Way," Light 4 (1884):
134, quoting Boston Sunday Globe
(undated).
1920s/Elwood Worcester/186 Marlboro St.
William Oliver Stevens, Psychics and
Common Sense (N.Y.: Dutton, 1953),
pp.51-52,110-11,208-10.
-Hex
n.d./Tom Walker/Brighton/=based on
German folklore
Washington Irving, "The Devil and
Tom Walker," in Tales of a Traveller
(1824).
Charles G. Zug III, "The Construction
of 'The Devil and Tom Walker,': A
Study of Irving's Later Use of Folk-
lore," N.Y.Folklore Quar. 24 (1968):
243-60.
-Mesmerism
1836/Charles Poyen
Charles Poyen, Progress of Animal
Magnetism in New England (Boston:

Weeks, Jordan, 1837).
Slater Brown, The Heyday of Spiritualism (N.Y.: Pocket Books, 1972
ed.), pp.15-16.
1850s/LaRoy Sunderland
LaRoy Sunderland, Book of Psychology
(N.Y.: Stearns, 1853).
LaRoy Sunderland, Theory of Nutri-
tion (Boston: Bela Marsh, 1855).
Slater Brown, The Heyday of Spirit-
ualism (N.Y.: Pocket Books, 1972
ed.), pp.21-24,159,164-65.
-Midday darkness
1881, Sep.6
New York Times, 7 Sep.1881, p.5; and
9 Sep.1881, p.3.
-Mystery bird deaths
1953, Oct.5
"Fish, Birds Fall," Doubt, no.45
(1954):294.
-Mystery shipwreck
1925, April/"Raifuku Maru"/ocean to E/
=caused by storm
Charles Hocking, Dictionary of Dis-
asters at Sea During the Age of
Steam (London: Lloyd's Register of
Shipping, 1969), p.577.
Richard Winer, The Devil's Triangle
(N.Y.: Bantam, 1974), pp.75-78.
-Paranormal hypnosis
1952, Dec.10-1953/Alwyn Stevenson
Alwyn Stevenson, "The Dead Can Come
Back--My Way," Fate 12 (Oct.1959):
89-94.
-Parapsychology research
1882-1884/American Psychical Soc'y
1925-1930s/Boston Soc'y for Psychical
Research/346 Beacon St.
Nandor Fodor, Encyclopaedia of Psy-
chic Science (London: Arthurs,
1933), pp.2,35-36.
-Phrenology
1832/Johann Gaspar Spurzheim
J.G. Spurzheim, Phrenology (Boston:
Marsh, Capen & Lyon, 1833).
Shelly Lowenkopf, "Science and Fad
of Phrenology," in Strange Stranger
Strangest (N.Y.: Paperback Library,
1966 ed.), pp.110-18.
-Possession
1692, summer-1693, March 16/Mercy Short
Cotton Mather, A Brand Pluck'd Out
of the Burning (1693), reprinted in
George Lincoln Burr, ed., Narratives
of the Witchcraft Cases 1648-1706
(N.Y.: Barnes & Noble, 1946 ed.),
pp.259-87.
William F. Poole, "Witchcraft in Bos-
ton," in Justin Winsor, ed., The
Memorial History of Boston, 4 vols.
(Boston: James R. Osgood, 1881), 2:
131,146-52.
1693, Sep./Margaret Rule
Robert Calef, More Wonders of the In-
visible World (London: Nathaniel
Hillar, 1700), reprinted in George
Lincoln Burr, ed., Narratives of the
Witchcraft Cases 1648-1706 (N.Y.:
Barnes & Noble, 1946 ed.), pp.296,
308-41.

William F. Poole, "Witchcraft in Boston," in Justin Winsor, ed., The Memorial History of Boston, 4 vols. (Boston: James R. Osgood, 1881), 2: 131,156-57.

Cotton Mather, "Diary," in Coll.Mass. Hist.Soc'y, ser.7, 7 (1911):171-79.

1898/Sally Beauchamp

Morton Prince, "The Development and Genealogy of the Misses Beauchamp: A Preliminary Report of a Case of Multiple Personality," Proc.SPR 15 (1901):466-83.

Morton Prince, The Dissociation of a Personality (N.Y.: Longmans, Green, 1905).

W. M'Dougall, "The Case of Sally Beauchamp," Proc.SPR 19 (1907):410-31.

Alson J. Smith, "The Three Sally Beauchamps," Fate 6 (Mar.1953):18-26.

-Precognition

1783, April/James Otis
"Premonition or Coincidence," J.ASPR 12 (1918):170-72.

19th c./Josiah Quincy
Edward Everett Hale, James Russell Lowell and His Friends (Boston: Houghton Mifflin, 1901), p.18.

1876/E.C. Coolidge
E.C. Coolidge, "Predictive Vision of a Living Man," J.ASPR 18 (1924):192.

1884, March 24/Lizzie E. Bickford/ M.I.T.
"Premonitory Dream," J.ASPR 9 (1915): 640-62.

1888, Dec./Sheridan Paul Wait
Sheridan Paul Wait, "Premonitory Vision of the Funeral of a Sister," J.ASPR 18 (1924):190-92.

n.d./Reuben Beyfus
Cheiro, "Warning on the Mirror," Fate 13 (Aug.1960):42-47.

-Psychic photography

1861-1868/William H. Mumler
William H. Mumler, The Personal Experiences of William H. Mumler in Spirit Photography (Boston: Colby & Rich, 1875).

Nandor Fodor, Encyclopaedia of Psychic Science (London: Arthurs, 1933), pp.257,312.

-Psychokinesis

1917-1918/James H. Hyslop
James H. Hyslop, "Experiments in Telekinesis," J.ASPR 14 (1920):534-55.

1949, July 10/Michael J. Hogan/186 Marlborough St.
"An Extraordinary Incident: Attested by Five Witnesses," J.ASPR 44 (1950):118-21.

-Pyramid energy research

1970s/Garland Junior College
William Schramm, "The Pyramid Dehydration Effect: Inhibition of the Natural Hygroscopicity of Sodium Hydroxide Pellets," Metascience Quar. 1 (spring 1979):33-36.

-Scrying

n.d./Isador H. Coriat
H. Addington Bruce, "Have You Tried Scrying?" Fate 10 (Apr.1957):75,76-77.

-Seance

1855, Dec.7

1857, June 25-27/Kate Fox/Albion Bldg.
Emma Hardinge Britten, Modern American Spiritualism (N.Y.: The Author, 1870), pp.185-94,267-70.

1908/Victor Severy/Emerson College
Enid S. Smith, "How I Found My Brother," Fate 8 (May 1955):86-88.

1923, April 24, June 3/Mrs. J.M. Grant/ 144 Huntington Ave.
Frederick Edwards, "Sitting with Mrs. J.M. Grant," J.ASPR 17 (1923):393-422,687-709.

-Skyquake

1647, May 30
John Winthrop, Winthrop's Journal, ed. James Kendall Hosmer, 2 vols. (N.Y.: Barnes & Noble, 1946 ed.), 2:323.

-Spirit medium

1850s/Mrs. W.R. Hayden
[Robert Chambers], "The Spirits Come to Town," Chambers Edinburgh J. 19 (1853):321-24.

Sophia Elizabeth de Morgan, From Matter to Spirit (London: Longmans, Green, 1863).

Sophia Elizabeth de Morgan, Memoir of Augustus de Morgan (London: Longmans, Green, 1882).

Frank Podmore, Modern Spiritualism, 2 vols. (London: Methuen, 1902), 2:4-8.

Nandor Fodor, Encyclopaedia of Psychic Science (London: Arthurs, 1933), p.166.

1850s/Ms. Feilding
Slater Brown, The Heyday of Spiritualism (N.Y.: Pocket Books, 1972 ed.), pp.170-77.

1850s/Margaretta S. Cooper
Emma Hardinge Britten, Modern American Spiritualism (N.Y.: The Author, 1870), pp.60,164-66.

1853/Allen Putnam

1855-1857/Frederick Willis

1858-1875/Mrs. J.H. Conant
Emma Hardinge Britten, Modern American Spiritualism (N.Y.: The Author, 1870), pp.166-68,173-85.

Allen Putnam, Flashes of Light from the Spirit-Land (Boston: W. White, 1872).

1870s/Mrs. M.B. Thayer

1870s/Mary Hardy
Nandor Fodor, Encyclopaedia of Psychic Science (London: Arthurs, 1933), pp.157-58,289,380.

1870s-1880s/Mrs. H.B. Fay
Florence Marryat, There Is No Death (N.Y.: J.W. Lovell, 1891).

Frank Podmore, Modern Spiritualism, 2 vols. (London: Methuen, 1902), 2: 84-85,157-59.

Nandor Fodor, Encyclopaedia of Psychic Science (London: Arthurs, 1933), p.137.

1880s/Mrs. Ross
Alfred Russell Wallace, My Life: A Record of Events and Opinions, 2 vols. (N.Y.: Dodd, Mead, 1905), 2: 354-58.

1884-1927/Leonora Piper
Frederic W.H. Myers, et al., "A Record of Observations of Certain Phenomena of Trance," Proc.SPR 6 (1890):436-659.
Richard Hodgson, "A Record of Observations of Certain Phenomena of Trance," Proc.SPR 8 (1892):1-167.
William Romaine Newbold, "A Further Record of Observations of Certain Phenomena of Trance," Proc.SPR 14 (1898):6-49.
Frank Podmore, "Discussion of the Trance-Phenomena of Mrs. Piper," Proc.SPR 14 (1898):50-78.
Richard Hodgson, "A Further Record of Observations of Certain Phenomena of Trance," Proc.SPR 13 (1898): 284-582.
Mrs. Henry Sidgwick & Andrew Lang, "Discussions of the Trance-Phenomena of Mrs. Piper," Proc.SPR 15 (1900):16-52.
James H. Hyslop, "A Further Record of Observations of Certain Trance Phenomena," Proc.SPR 16 (1901):1-649.
New York Herald, 20 Oct.1901; and 26 Oct.1901.
Boston Advertiser, 25 Oct.1901.
Minot J. Savage, Can Telepathy Explain? (N.Y.: Putnam, 1902), pp. 73-78.
Hereward Carrington, "Discussion of the Trance Phenomena of Mrs. Piper," Proc.SPR 17 (1903):337-59.
J.H. Hyslop, "Remarks on Mr. Carrington's Paper," Proc.SPR 17 (1903): 360-73.
Frank Podmore, "On Professor Hyslop's Report on His Sittings with Mrs. Piper," Proc.SPR 17 (1903):374-88.
James H. Hyslop, "Reply to Mr. Podmore's Criticism," Proc.SPR 18 (1903):78-101.
M. Sage, Mrs. Piper and the Society for Psychical Research (N.Y.: Scott-Thaw, 1904).
James Hervey Hyslop, "Experiments with Mrs. Piper Since Dr. Richard Hodgson's Death," J.ASPR 1 (1907): 93-107.
James Hervey Hyslop, "Further Experiments Relating to Dr. Hodgson Since His Death," J.ASPR 1 (1907):125-48.
James Hervey Hyslop, "Conclusion of Experiments Relative to Dr. Hodgson's Theories," J.ASPR 1 (1907): 183-228.
J.G. Piddington, "A Series of Concordant Automatisms," Proc.SPR 22 (1908):19-416.

Mrs. Henry Sidgwick, "An Incident in Mrs. Piper's Trance," Proc.SPR 22 (1908):417-40.
William James, "Report on Mrs. Piper's Hodgson-Control," Proc.SPR 23 (1909):2-121.
Mrs. H. Sidgwick & J.G. Piddington, "Notes on Mrs. Piper's Hodgson-Control in England in 1906-7," Proc.SPR 23 (1909):122-26.
Oliver Lodge, "Report on Some Trance Communications Received Chiefly through Mrs. Piper," Proc.SPR 23 (1909):127-285.
William James, "Report on Mrs. Piper's Hodgson-Control," Proc.ASPR 3 (1909):470-592.
James H. Hyslop, "Mr. Piddington's Report," J.ASPR 3 (1909):505-32.
James H. Hyslop, "A Record and Discussion of Mediumistic Experiments," Proc.ASPR 4 (1910):1-787.
Mrs. Henry Sidgwick, Mrs. A.W. Verrall & J.G. Piddington, "Further Experiments with Mrs. Piper in 1908," Proc.SPR 24 (1910):31-200.
Helen de G. Verrall, "Report on the Junot Sittings with Mrs. Piper," Proc.SPR 24 (1910):351-664.
James H. Hyslop, "The Junot Sittings with Mrs. Piper," J.ASPR 5 (1911): 329-35.
Anna Hude, "The Latin Message Experiment," Proc.SPR 26 (1912):147-73.
Mrs. Henry Sidgwick, "A Contribution to the Study of the Psychology of Mrs. Piper's Trance Phenomena," Proc.SPR 28 (1915):1-652.
James H. Hyslop, "An Experiment in Automatic Writing," J.ASPR 10 (1916):275-84.
James H. Hyslop, "Mrs. Sidgwick's Report on the Piper Trance," J.ASPR 11 (1917):1-71,73-123.
M.A. Rayner, "The Last Word on Mrs. Piper," J.ASPR 11 (1917):133-52.
James H. Hyslop, "Chance Coincidence and Guessing in a Mediumistic Experiment," Proc.ASPR 13 (1919):5-88.
Anne Manning Robbins, Past and Present with Mrs. Piper (N.Y.: Holt, 1921).
A.W. Trethewy, "Mrs. Piper and the Imperator Band of Controls," Proc. SPR 35 (1925):445-65.
Alta L. Piper, The Life and Work of Mrs. Piper (London: Kegan, Paul, Trench, Trubner, 1929).
Nandor Fodor, Encyclopaedia of Psychic Science (London: Arthurs, 1933), pp.22,52-55,57-58,83,276, 282,283-87,378,389.
Alexander T. Baird, Richard Hodgson (London: Psychic Press, 1949).
Lydia W. Allison, "In Memory of Mrs. Leonora Piper," J.ASPR 45 (1951):37-39.
Hereward Carrington, "Mediumship of Mrs. Piper," Fate 9 (July 1956):

70-77. il.

Alson J. Smith, "Leonore Piper: Prof. William James' 'One White Crow,'" Fate 15 (July 1962):78-86.

Robert Somerlott, "The Medium Had the Message: Mrs. Piper and the Professors," Am.Heritage 22, no.2 (1971):33-37,94-95.

1900s-1910s/Minnie Soule

James H. Hyslop, "A Case of Veridical Hallucinations," Proc.ASPR 3 (1909):1-469.

James H. Hyslop, "A Mediumistic Experiment," J.ASPR 3 (1909):468-90; 4 (1910):69-102,138-60,186-209.

James H. Hyslop, "A Mediumistic Performance," J.ASPR 5 (1911):418-41.

James H. Hyslop, "A Record of Experiments," Proc.ASPR 6 (1912):1-939.

James H. Hyslop, "Tests of a Professional Medium," J.ASPR 6 (1912):107-14.

James H. Hyslop, "A Complicated Group of Experiences and Experiments," J.ASPR 6 (1912):181-265.

Robert Hyslop, "Experiments Continued," J.ASPR 6 (1912):536-58,609-33, 680-702,717-42.

James H. Hyslop, "Experiments Continued," J.ASPR 7 (1913):90,112,170-97.

James H. Hyslop, "An Important Experiment," J.ASPR 7 (1913):698-706.

James H. Hyslop, "A Diagnosis," J. ASPR 8 (1914):76-86.

James H. Hyslop, "Another Diagnosis," J.ASPR 8 (1914):87-94.

James H. Hyslop, "Some Secondary Evidences," J.ASPR 8 (1914):225-52.

James H. Hyslop, "Experiments with a Supposed Case of Dissociation or Secondary Personality," J.ASPR 9 (1915):209-22.

James H. Hyslop, "Another Case of Spirit Influence," J.ASPR 9 (1915): 223-29.

James H. Hyslop, "A Group of Important Incidents," J.ASPR 9 (1915):322-29.

James H. Hyslop, "Some Mediumistic Experiments," J.ASPR 9 (1915):355-91,395-424,434-68,494-511.

James H. Hyslop, "Incipient Mediumship," J.ASPR 9 (1915):425-28.

James H. Hyslop, "Important Experiments," J.ASPR 9 (1915):558-71.

James H. Hyslop, "Communications from Mr. Friend, Who Was Lost in the Lusitania," J.ASPR 10 (1916):148-72.

James H. Hyslop, "A Mediumistic Experiment," J.ASPR 10 (1916):224-50.

James H. Hyslop, "Experiments with the Doris Case," J.ASPR 11 (1917): 153-77,213-37,266-91,324-43,385-406, 459-92.

James H. Hyslop, "The Return of Professor Muensterburg," J.ASPR 11 (1917):564-615.

James H. Hyslop, "Incidents of an Illness," J.ASPR 12 (1918):328-34.

James H. Hyslop, "Recent Experiments in Communication," J.ASPR 13 (1919): 10-30,94-127,153-71,518-47,623-47.

James H. Hyslop, "Mrs. Chenoweth's Reading," J.ASPR 13 (1919):57-58.

James H. Hyslop, "Cross Reference Experiments for Mark Twain," Proc. ASPR 14 (1920):1-225.

Gertrude Ogden Tubby, "Three Evidential Chenoweth Sittings," J.ASPR 14 (1920):9-40.

James H. Hyslop, "Recent Experiments Continued," J.ASPR 14 (1920):163-95.

James H. Hyslop, "War Predictions Through Mrs. Chenoweth," J.ASPR 14 (1920):320-52.

James Hervey Hyslop, "The Chenoweth and Drew Automatic Scripts," Proc. ASPR 15 (1921):1-188.

James H. Hyslop, "Dr. Hodgson As Communicator," J.ASPR 15 (1921):1-15.

William Bruce, "Experiences, Chiefly with Mrs. Chenoweth," J.ASPR 15 (1921):520-36.

William Bruce, "Further on 'Experiences, Chiefly with Mrs. Chenoweth,'" J.ASPR 16 (1922):200-12.

John F. Thomas, Case Studies Bearing upon Survival (Boston: Boston SPR, 1929).

L.W. Allison, Leonard and Soule Experiments (Boston: Boston SPR, 1929).

John F. Thomas, Beyond Normal Cognition (Boston: Boston SPR, 1937).

Gertrude O. Tubby, "Mrs. Chenoweth (In Memoriam)," J.ASPR 35 (1941): 31-39.

1900s-1910s/Mrs. Willis M. Cleaveland

James H. Hyslop, "Preliminary Report on the Trance Phenomena of Mrs. Smead," Proc.ASPR 1 (1907):525-722.

James H. Hyslop, "A Case of Veridical Hallucinations," Proc.ASPR 3 (1909):1-469.

James H. Hyslop, "A Record of Experiments," Proc.ASPR 6 (1912):1-939.

Robert Hyslop, "Experiments Continued," J.ASPR 6 (1912):536-58,609-33, 680-702,717-42.

James H. Hyslop, "Experiments Continued," J.ASPR 7 (1913):90-112, 170-97.

James H. Hyslop, "The Smead Case," Proc.ASPR 12 (1918):1-735. il.

1909-1910/Mrs. M.E. Keeler

Prescott F. Hall, "Some Account of Sittings with Mrs. M.E. Keeler," J. ASPR 5 (1911):225-40.

1920s

Anita M. Mühl, "Automatic Writing As an Indicator of the Fundamental Factors Underlying the Personality," J.Abnormal Psych. 17 (1922):162-83.

1920s/Madame Vesta/=fraudulent

Joseph Dunninger, Houdini's Spirit World and Dunninger's Psychic Revelations (N.Y.: Tower, 1968 ed.), pp. 116-20.

1923, May-1941/Mina Crandon/10 Lime St.
Harry Houdini, Houdini Exposes the
Tricks Used by the Boston Medium
"Margery" (N.Y.: Adams, 1924).
E.E. Free, "Our Psychic Investiga-
tion," Sci.Am. 130 (1924):304.
J. Malcolm Bird, "Margery" the Medium
(Boston: Small, Maynard, 1925).
Mark W. Richardson, et al., Margery,
Harvard, Veritas: A Study in Psych-
ics (Boston: Blanchard, 1925).
L.R.G. Crandon, et al., "The Margery
Case," J.ASPR 19 (1925):113-34.
J. Malcolm Bird, "Dr. McDougall and
the Margery Mediumship," J.ASPR 19
(1925):190-227.
William McDougall, "Further Observa-
tions on the 'Margery' Case," J.ASPR
19 (1925):297-309.
J. Malcolm Bird, "Mr. Dingwall and
Margery," J.ASPR 19 (1925):309-14.
L.R.G. Crandon, "Dr. McDougall and
the Margery Mediumship," J.ASPR 19
(1925):361-69.
E.J. Dingwall, "Professor McDougall,
'Margery,' and Mr. Bird," J.ASPR 19
(1925):455-58.
Mark Wyman Richardson, "The Margery
Mediumship," J.ASPR 19 (1925):673-
80.
J. Malcolm Bird, "Dr. Richardson's
Voice-Control Machine," J.ASPR 19
(1925):680-69.
J. Malcolm Bird, "The Latest Margery
'Exposure,'" J.ASPR 19 (1925):717-
29.
Hudson Hoagland, "Science and the
Medium," Atlantic Monthly 136 (1925)
:666-81.
E.J. Dingwall, "A Report on a Series
of Sittings with the Medium Mar-
gery," Proc.SPR 36 (1926):79-158.
L.R.G. Crandon, "The Margery Medium-
ship," J.ASPR 20 (1926):321-33.
J. Malcolm Bird, "The Margery Med-
iumship," J.ASPR 20 (1926):385-406.
J. Malcolm Bird, "Mr. Dingwall Re-
ports on Margery," J.ASPR 20 (1926):
480-93.
J. Malcolm Bird, ed., "The Margery
Mediumship: An Experiment in Fraud-
Proof Control of a New Type," J.
ASPR 20 (1926):674-82.
R.J. Tillyard, "Some Recent Personal
Experiences with Margery," J.ASPR
20 (1926):705-17.
Mark W. Richardson, "The Margery Med-
iumship," J.ASPR 21 (1927):129-36.
"Normal and Supernormal Phenomena,"
Nature 122 (1928):229-31.
R.J. Tillyard, "Evidence of Survival
of a Human Personality," Nature 122
(1928):243-46,606-607.
J. Malcolm Bird, "Teleplasmic Thumb-
prints," Psychic Rsch. 22 (1928):7-
15,563-71.
Mark W. Richardson, Josephine L. Rich-
ardson & E.E. Dudley, "Teleplasmic
Thumbprints-II," Psychic Rsch. 22
(1928):99-113.

E.E. Dudley & J. Malcolm Bird, "Tele-
plasmic Thumbprints," Psychic Rsch.
22 (1928):191-218,453-69,684-707;
23 (1929):573-87,637-66.
Mark Wyman Richardson, "Experiments
in Thought Transference," Psychic
Rsch. 22 (1928):255-69,354-61,414-
20,496-514.
R.J. Tillyard, "The Normal Produc-
tion of Psychic Gloves," Psychic
Rsch. 22 (1928):402-408.
Neville Whymant, "The Chinese Scripts
by Margery," Psychic Rsch. 22
(1928):571-74.
L.R.G. Crandon, "Feda and Walter,"
Psychic Rsch. 23 (1929):295-313.
"Margery's Chinese Scripts," Psychic
Rsch. 23 (1929):428-38.
Hamlin Garland, "Two Test Sittings
with 'Margery,'" Psychic Rsch. 24
(1930):71-76.
Frederick Bligh Bond, "The Boston-
Venice Cross-Correspondence," Psy-
chic Rsch. 24 (1930):206-14.
L.R.G. Crandon, "The Margery Medium-
ship," Psychic Rsch. 24 (1930):255-
64; J.ASPR 29 (1935):36-51. il.
Charles S. Hill, "The Margery Medium-
ship," Psychic Rsch. 24 (1930):445-
46.
Frederick Bligh Bond, "Varieties of
Cross Correspondence," Psychic Rsch.
24 (1930):498-513.
Arthur Conan Doyle, The Edge of the
Unknown (N.Y.: Berkley, 1968 ed.),
pp.9-13.
R.J. Tillyard, "The Margery Medium-
ship," Psychic Rsch. 25 (1931):137-
45.
William H. Button, "The Margery Med-
iumship," Psychic Rsch. 25 (1931):
146-50; 26 (1932):298-319,335-38.
il.
Walter B. Gibson, Houdini's Magic
(N.Y.: Harcourt, Brace, 1932).
Mark W. Richardson, "The Judge's
Sign-Manual," J.ASPR 26 (1932):48-
60. il.
Brackett K. Thorogood, "The Sir Oli-
ver Lodge Finger Impressions," J.
ASPR 26 (1932):97-132. il.
William H. Button, "Walter Helps to
Perfect the Control," J.ASPR 26
(1932):133-41. il.
Brackett K. Thorogood, "The Margery
Mediumship," J.ASPR 26 (1932):266-
71; 28 (1934):324-33. il.
"The Margery Mediumship," J.ASPR 26
(1932):403-406.
Mark W. Richardson, "The Margery
Mediumship: Apports and Reports,"
J.ASPR 26 (1932):434-37.
Nandor Fodor, Encyclopaedia of Psy-
chic Science (London: Arthurs,
1933), pp.67-68,69,72,209,228,256,
288,338-39,386,404,406.
William H. Button, "Mr. Thorogood's
Report on Fingerprint Phenomena in
the Margery Mediumship," J.ASPR 28
(1934):9-13.

H.F. Prevost Battersby, "The Real
Enigma of the 'Margery' Mediumship,"
J.ASPR 28 (1934):104-106.
Stanley de Brath, "The 'Walter' Fing-
er-Print Report," J.ASPR 28 (1934):
106-109.
W.T. Hutchinson, et al., "The Margery
Mediumship: What Happened to Hutch-
inson's Wax?" J.ASPR 28 (1934):201-
19.
Hamlin Garland, Afternoon Neighbors
(N.Y.: Macmillan, 1934).
"Mr. Bond and the 'Margery' Medium-
ship," J.ASPR 29 (1935):159-62.
William H. Button, "The Margery Med-
iumship: Cross-Correspondences,"
J.ASPR 29 (1935):293-309.
T.H. Pierson, "The Transmission of
Mental Concepts," J.ASPR 30 (1936):
44-50.
Helen T. Bigelow, "A Psychic Cure by
'Walter,'" J.ASPR 30 (1936):220-24.
William H. Button, "The Margery Med-
iumship," J.ASPR 32 (1938):1-4,40-
47,97-104,129-31,165-70,225,257-59,
292-95,323-28,357-62.
Oliver Lodge, "The Margery Medium-
ship," J.ASPR 32 (1938):193-215.
Alson J. Smith, "Margery Was a Fraud!"
Fate 13 (Mar.1960):65-77.
W.D. Chesney, "Margery Was 'The
Greatest!" Fate 13 (Apr.1960):88-
94. il.
Brackett K. Thorogood, "My Evidence
for Margery," Fate 16 (June 1963):
74-81. il.
Brackett K. Thorogood, "Margery's
Psychic Phonograph," Fate 17 (Mar.
1964):54-55.
Brackett K. Thorogood, "Mystery of
the Linked Rings," Fate 17 (Sep.
1964):50-54.
Walter McGraw, "Was This Margery?"
Fate 18 (Aug.1965):79-89.
Milbourne Christopher, Houdini: The
Untold Story (N.Y.: Pocket Books,
1970 ed.), pp.197-220,247-50.
Thomas R. Tietze, Margery (N.Y.:
Harper & Row, 1973).
R. Laurence Moore, In Search of White
Crows (N.Y.: Oxford Univ., 1977),
pp.177-81.
-Spontaneous human combustion
1956, Dec./Catherine Cahill/Roxbury
Boston Sunday Globe, 9 Dec.1956.
-Telephone anomaly
1959
(Editorial), Fate 13 (Mar.1960):18.
-UFO (?)
1644, Aug.26/nr. Pullen Pt./=meteor?
John Winthrop, Winthrop's Journal,
ed. James Kendall Hosmer, 2 vols.
(N.Y.: Barnes & Noble, 1946 ed.),
2:193.
1689, Oct.1
Cotton Mather, The Way to Prosperity
(Boston: Brunning, Gill & Woode,
1690).
1760, May 10/Roxbury/=meteor?
John Winthrop, "An Account of a Met-

eor Seen in New England and of a
Whirlwind Felt in That Country,"
Philosophical Trans.Roy.Soc'y 52
(1761):6-16.
1765, Aug.14/Fort Hill/=hoax
Boston Gazette & Country Journal,
19 Aug.1765.
1965, Oct.2
"Bulletin," UFO Inv. 3 (Aug.-Sep.
1965):1.
(Editorial), UFO Inv. 3 (Nov.-Dec.
1965):6.
-UFO (CE-1)
1947, Jan./George Massinger/Brighton x
Harvard Ave.
(Letter), Fate 12 (June 1959):110-12.
1965, April 1/Elizabeth Chorney
"News Briefs," Saucer News 12 (June
1965):22.
1967, Feb.17/Dorchester
Raymond E. Fowler, UFOs: Interplane-
tary Visitors (Jericho, N.Y.: Exposition, 1974), p.344.
1972, July 22/Dorchester
Barry Greenwood, "UFO Notes," Skylook, no.61 (Dec.1972):15.
-UFO (CE-2)
1966, April 12/Pearl Moses/24 Thane
St.
Boston Record-American, 13 Apr.1966.
1966, April 24/Jeanne Kalnicki/Dor-
chester
Boston Record-American, 25 Apr.1966.
-UFO (DD)
ca.1936/Dick Kellar/Narragansett x
North Ave.
J. Allen Hynek, The Hynek UFO Report
(N.Y.: Dell, 1977), pp.118-20.
1946/George Dalton/nr. Faneuil Hall
Gordon I.R. Lore, Jr. & Harold H. Deneault, Jr., Mysteries of the Skies:
UFOs in Perspective (Englewood
Cliffs, N.J.: Prentice-Hall, 1968),
pp.145-46.
1947, July 7/John Stewart/Dorchester
Boston Globe, 8 July 1947.
1947, Aug.4
Bruce S. Maccabee, "UFO Related Information from the FBI Files: Part
3," MUFON UFO J., no.121 (Dec.1977):
10,14.
n.d./Joseph E. Panek
Ray Palmer, "Space Ships, Flying Saucers and Clean Noses," Fate 3 (May
1950):36,43.
1954, June 1/Charles Kratovil/10 mi.N
Richard Hall, ed., The UFO Evidence
(Washington: NICAP, 1964), p.40,
quoting UP release, 1 June 1954.
-UFO (NL)
1641, Sep.11
1644, Jan.18
1644, Jan.25?/Nottles I.
John Winthrop, Winthrop's Journal,
ed. James Kendall Hosmer, 2 vols.
(N.Y.: Barnes & Noble, 1946 ed.),
2:42,155-56.
1909, Dec.20/Mr. Hoe
New York Tribune, 21 Dec.1909, p.3.
1909, Dec.23/Alexander Rambell/Boston

Common
  New York Sun, 24 Dec.1909.
  New York Tribune, 24 Dec.1909, p.1.
  Providence (R.I.) Journal, 24 Dec.
    1909.
1947, July 1/Mrs. Edward Williams/Wash-
  ington Park
  Boston Globe, 6 July 1947.
1950, April 7/Logan Airport
  J. Allen Hynek, The Hynek UFO Report
    (N.Y.: Dell, 1977), pp.65-68.
1962, July 7/Dorchester
  Richard Hall, ed., The UFO Evidence
    (Washington: NICAP, 1964), p.156.
1972, Aug./Dorchester High School
  Barry Greenwood, "UFO Notes," Sky-
    look, no.61 (Dec.1972):15.
-Witch trial (?)
  ca.1648/Mrs. H. Lake/Dorchester
  John Hale, A Modest Enquiry into the
    Nature of Witchcraft (Boston: B.
    Green & J. Allen, 1702), reprinted
    in George Lincoln Burr, ed., Narra-
    tives of the Witchcraft Cases 1648-
    1706 (N.Y.: Barnes & Noble, 1946
    ed.), pp.399,408-409.
  1655/Anne Hibbins
  Samuel Gardner Drake, The History
    and Antiquities of Boston (Boston:
    L. Stevens, 1856), p.346.
  William F. Poole, "Witchcraft in
    Boston," in Justin Winsor, ed., The
    Memorial History of Boston, 4 vols.
    (Boston: James R. Osgood, 1881), 2:
    131,138-41.
-Witch trial (herbalism)
  1648, June/Margaret Jones
  John Winthrop, Winthrop's Journal,
    ed. James Kendall Hosmer, 2 vols.
    (N.Y.: Barnes & Noble, 1946 ed.),
    2:344-45.
  Samuel G. Drake, Annals of Witchcraft
    in New England (Boston: W.E. Wood-
    ward, 1869), pp.58-61.
  William F. Poole, "Witchcraft in Bos-
    ton," in Justin Winsor, ed., The
    Memorial History of Boston, 4 vols.
    (Boston: James R. Osgood, 1881), 2:
    131,133-37.
-Witch trial (hex)
  1688, summer/Mrs. Glover
  Cotton Mather, Memorable Providences
    (Boston: Joseph Brunning, 1689),
    reprinted in George Lincoln Burr,
    ed., Narratives of the Witchcraft
    Cases 1648-1706 (N.Y.: Barnes &
    Noble, 1946 ed.), pp.93,99-131.
  Cotton Mather, Pietas in Patriam:
    The Life of His Excellency Sir Wil-
    liam Phips (London: Nath. Hiller,
    1697).
  Thomas Hutchinson, The History of
    the Province of Massachusetts Bay,
    3 vols. (Boston: Thomas & John
    Fleet, 1828), 2:16.
  Letter of Joshua Moody to Increase
    Mather, in Mass.Hist.Soc'y Coll.,
    ser.4, 8 (1868):365-68.
  William F. Poole, "Witchcraft in Bos-
    ton," in Justin Winsor, ed., The

  Memorial History of Boston, 4 vols.
    (Boston: James R. Osgood, 1881), 2:
    131,142-46.
  David Levin, ed., What Happened in
    Salem? (N.Y.: Harcourt, Brace &
    World, 1960), pp.96-106.

Bourne
-Ancient inscription
  n.d./Aptuxcet Trading Post
  Olaf Strandwold, Norse Inscriptions
    on American Stones (Weehauken, N.J.:
    Magnus Björndal, 1948), p.25. il.
  Hartford (Conn.) Courant, 17 Apr.
    1975.
  James P. Whittall, Jr., "The In-
    scribed Stone from Comassakumkanit,"
    Occ.Pub.Epigraphic Soc'y, vol.2,
    no.44, pt.1 (May 1975).
  Barry Fell, "An Iberian Punic Stele
    of Hanno," Occ.Pub.Epigraphic Soc'y,
    vol.2, no.44, pt.2 (May 1975).
  Barry Fell, America B.C. (N.Y.: Quad-
    rangle, 1976), pp.51,95,160. il.

Braintree
-UFO (NL)
  1970, Dec.25
  Raymond E. Fowler, UFOs: Interplane-
    tary Visitors (Jericho, N.Y.: Expo-
    sition, 1974), p.357.
-UFO (R-V)
  1952, July 23
  Donald E. Keyhoe, Flying Saucers from
    Outer Space (N.Y.: Holt, 1953),
    p.97.
  Edward J. Ruppelt, The Report on Un-
    identified Flying Objects (Garden
    City: Doubleday, 1956), p.163.

Bridgewater
-Fall of slag
  1837, May 5
  Boston Daily Advertiser, 10 June
    1837.
  "Meteorite," Am.J.Sci., ser.1, 32
    (1837):395.
  Charles U. Shepard, "East Bridge-
    water Meteorite," Am.J.Sci., ser.1,
    50 (1847):322.
-Humanoid
  1969, Dec.-1970, April/nr. Correction-
    al Institution
  Boston Herald Traveler, 9 Apr.1970.
-Skyquake
  1760, May 10
  John Winthrop, "An Account of a Met-
    eor Seen in New England, and of a
    Whirlwind Felt in That Country,"
    Philosophical Trans.Roy.Soc'y 52
    (1761):6-16.
-UFO (NL)
  1908, Oct.31
  New York Sun, 1 Nov.1908.
  1976, March 28
  "Noteworthy UFO Sightings," Ufology
    2 (summer 1976):62.

Brockton
-UFO (?)

1952, April 26
  Desmond Leslie & George Adamski, Flying Saucers Have Landed (N.Y.: British Book Centre, 1953), p.62.
-UFO (DD)
  1964, Oct.11/David Hanson
  "Disc Chases Jets," UFO Inv. 3 (May-
  June 1966):4.
  Raymond E. Fowler, UFOs: Interplanetary Visitors (Jericho, N.Y.: Exposition, 1974), pp.26-28.
-UFO (NL)
  1966, April 12
  Raymond E. Fowler, UFOs: Interplanetary Visitors (Jericho, N.Y.: Exposition, 1974), p.337.

Brookline
-Biofeedback research
  1970s/Institute for Psychoenergetics/
  126 Harvard
  Buryl Payne, Getting There without
  Drugs (N.Y.: Viking, 1973).
  June & Nicholas Regush, Psi: The Oth-
  er World Catalogue (N.Y.: Putnam,
  1974), p.138.
-Child prodigy
  1899-1944/William Sidis
  Boris Sidis, Philistine and Genius
  (N.Y.: Moffat & Yard, 1911).
  Frank Folupa [William Sidis], Notes
  on the Collection of Transfers
  (Philadelphia: Dorrance, 1926).
  Jared L. Manley, "Where Are They
  Now? April Fool!" New Yorker, 14
  Aug.1937, pp.22-26.
  Robert M. Goldenson, Mysteries of
  the Mind (N.Y.: Harper & Row, 1974),
  pp.109-19.
-UFO (CE-2)
  1639/James Everell
  John Winthrop, Winthrop's Journal,
  ed. James Kendall Hosmer, 2 vols.
  (N.Y.: Barnes & Noble, 1946 ed.),
  1:294.

Burlington
-UFO (DD)
  1962, May 15
  Brad Steiger, ed., Project Blue Book
  (N.Y.: Ballantine, 1976), betw.pp.
  360-61.
-UFO (NL)
  1963, June 19
  Richard Hall, ed., The UFO Evidence
  (Washington: NICAP, 1964), p.140.

Buzzards Bay
-Giant human skeleton
  1891, July/Joseph Hefferson/=hoax?
  New York Times, 5 July 1891, p.13.
-UFO (CE-2)
  1953, June/Capt. Suggs/Otis AFB
  "Was UFO Responsible?" Skylook, no.
  35 (Oct.1970):7.
  Clarence O. Dargie, "Retired Air
  Force Man Relates Remarkable Ac-
  count of Disappearing Jet," Sky-
  look, no.63 (Feb.1973):4-5.
  Raymond E. Fowler, "UFO Watergate,"

Official UFO 1 (May 1976):18,20-21.

Byfield
-Norse runestones
  1930-1948/Lawrence M. Rogers
  Olaf Strandwold, Norse Inscriptions
  on American Stones (Weehauken, N.J.:
  Magnus Björndal, 1948), pp.19-24,
  26,35-36. il.
  Alf Mongé & Ole G. Landsverk, Norse
  Medieval Cryptography in Runic Carv-
  ings (Glendale, Cal.: Norseman,
  1967), pp.123-27. il.
  O.G. Landsverk, Ancient Norse Mess-
  ages on American Stones (Rushford,
  Minn.: Norseman, 1969).
  O.G. Landsverk, Runic Records of the
  Norsemen in America (N.Y.: E.J.
  Friis, 1974), pp.117-21,156-58,161-
  64. il.
-UFO (NL)
  1967, July 26/Paul Munier
  Raymond E. Fowler, UFOs: Interplane-
  tary Visitors (Jericho, N.Y.: Expo-
  sition, 1974), p.152.

Cambridge
-Acoustic anomaly
  1968, May 27-28
  Coral E. Lorenzen, The Shadow of the
  Unknown (N.Y.: Signet, 1970), p.81.
-Haunt
  1950s/Mrs. Putnam/Riedesel mansion
  H. Addington Bruce, "Why I Believe
  in Survival," Tomorrow 5 (autumn
  1956):58,60-61.
-Midday darkness
  1881, Sep.6
  "The Yellow Day in September 1881,"
  Weatherwise 25 (June 1972):118.
-Out-of-body experience
  ca.1883
  William James, "A Possible Case of
  Projections of the Double," J.ASPR
  3 (1909):253-54.
-Parapsychology research
  1950s/Harvard University
  S. David Kahn, "Studies in Extrasen-
  sory Perception: Experiments Util-
  izing an Electronic Scoring Device,"
  Proc.ASPR 25 (1952):1-48.
  R.A. McConnell, "Some Comments on
  the Recent Harvard Research in
  ESP," J.ASPR 47 (1953):80-83.
  J.G. Pratt, "A Review of Kahn's
  'Studies in Extrasensory Percep-
  tion,'" J.Parapsych. 17 (1953):215-
  22.
  Frederick C. Dommeyer & Rhea White,
  "Psychical Research in Colleges and
  Universities," J.ASPR 57 (1963):3,
  9-16.
-Precognition
  1775, July 8/Moll Pitcher
  Madeleine Field, "Molly Pitcher:
  Revolutionary Seer," Fate 19 (June
  1966):73,76-77.
  1960, June/Clinton H. Elliott
  (Editorial), Fate 13 (Nov.1960):20-
  22.

1962/Stanley Krippner
Herbert B. Greenhouse, Premonitions:
A Leap into the Future (N.Y.: Pap-
erback Library, 1973 ed.), pp.82-84.
-Spirit medium
1930s/Mrs. Carl H. Litzelmann
William H. Button, "The Mediumship
of Mrs. Litzelmann," J.ASPR 32
(1938):65-68.
-Telepathy research
1920s/G.H. Estabrooks/Harvard Univ.
G.H. Estabrooks, "A Contribution to
Experimental Telepathy," Bull.Bos-
ton SPR 5 (1927):1-30.
-UFO (DD)
1947, July 8/Silas Flashman/Harvard
Bridge
Boston Globe, 8 July 1947.
1964, May 26/Sears & Roebuck store
Thomas M. Olsen, ed., The Reference
for Outstanding UFO Sighting Reports
(Riderwood, Md.: UFO Information
Retrieval Center, 1966), pp.96-98.
1969/Fresh Pond
Barry Greenwood, "UFO Notes," Skylook, no.61 (Dec.1972):15.
1971, Nov.17
Raymond E. Fowler, UFOs: Interplanetary Visitors (Jericho, N.Y.: Exposition, 1974), p.358.
-UFO (NL)
1947, July 7
Boston Traveller, 7 July 1947.
1965, Feb.24
1967, Oct.3
1968, Aug.16
Raymond E. Fowler, UFOs: Interplanetary Visitors (Jericho, N.Y.: Exposition, 1974), pp.331,350,354.
-Witch trial (hex)
ca.1650/Mrs. Kendal
John Hale, A Modest Enquiry into the
Nature of Witchcraft (Boston: B.
Green & J. Allen, 1702), reprinted
in George Lincoln Burr, ed., Narratives of the Witchcraft Cases 1648-
1706 (N.Y.: Barnes & Noble, 1946
ed.), pp.397,409-10.

Canton
-UFO (NL)
1976, Nov.29/Warren Martin/Knollwood
Cemetery
Stoughton Chronicle, 9 Dec.1976.

Charlemont
-UFO (CE-1)
1965, Oct.1
"Bulletin," UFO Inv. 3 (Aug.-Sep.
1965):1.

Charlton
-Haunt
1960s/Massachusetts Turnpike Information Center
(Editorial), Fate 23 (May 1970):34-
36, quoting Boston Herald-Traveller
(undated).

Chicopee
-UFO (DD)
1967, Jan.13/William E. Varner/West-
over AFB
Wendelle C. Stevens, "Fantastic UFO
Photo Flap of 1967," Saga UFO Rept.
3 (June 1976):24,27. il.

Chilmark
-Ancient dolmen
Quista Knoll
Edgartown Vineyard Gazette, 7 May
1943.
James P. Whittall, Jr., "The Quista
Dolmen," NEARA Newsl. 6 (Mar.1971):
16. il.

Cohasset
-Ancient vault
Cedar St.
Sinclair Bowman, "A Massachusetts
Analogue to the Newport Tower
Arches," NEARA Newsl. 3 (Sep.1968):
59.
-Haunt
1964/Mrs. E. Stoddard Marsh/Ship's
Chandlery
Hans Holzer, Yankee Ghosts (N.Y.:
Ace, 1966), pp.71-77.
-UFO (NL)
1966, April 18
Raymond E. Fowler, UFOs: Interplane-
tary Visitors (Jericho, N.Y.: Expo-
sition, 1974), p.339.

Concord
-Dowsing research
1970s/Rexford Daniels/Interference
Consultants Co.
Peter Tompkins & Chrsitopher Bird,
The Secret Life of Plants (N.Y.:
Harper & Row, 1973), pp.298-99.

Conway
-UFO (NL)
1956, July 2/Jack Pease
"Case 165," CRIFO Orbit, 3 Aug.1956,
p.1, quoting Greenfield Recorder-
Gazette (undated).

Dalton
-Fall of ice
1960, March 27/Mrs. Larry Roche
"Icy Missile," Fate 14 (Feb.1961):
54.

Danvers
-UFO (DD)
1964, Oct.1/Richard Fowler/Endicott St.
1966, April 17
Raymond E. Fowler, UFOs: Interplanetary Visitors (Jericho, N.Y.: Exposition, 1974), pp.22-23,337.
-UFO (NL)
1967, Nov.28
Raymond E. Fowler, UFOs: Interplanetary Visitors (Jericho, N.Y.: Exposition, 1974), p.350.

-Witch trials (hex)
  1692, Feb.-1693, May/Bridget Bishop
  and others
    Deodat Lawson, A Brief and True Nar-
    rative of Witchcraft at Salem Vil-
    lage (Boston: Benjamin Harris,
    1692), reprinted in George Lincoln
    Burr, ed., Narratives of the Witch-
    craft Cases 1648-1706 (N.Y.: Barnes
    & Noble, 1946 ed.), pp.152-64.
    Cotton Mather, Wonders of the Invis-
    ible World (Boston: Benjamin Har-
    ris, 1693), reprinted in George
    Lincoln Burr, ed., Narrative of the
    Witchcraft Cases 1648-1706 (N.Y.:
    Barnes & Noble, 1946 ed.), pp.209-
    51.
    Thomas Maule, Truth Held Forth and
    Maintained (N.Y.: William Bradford,
    1695).
    Robert Calef, More Wonders of the
    Invisible World (London: Nathaniel
    Hillar, 1700), reprinted in George
    Lincoln Burr, ed., Narratives of
    the Witchcraft Cases 1648-1706
    (N.Y.: Barnes & Noble, 1946 ed.),
    pp.296-307,341-93.
    John Hale, A Modest Enquiry into the
    Nature of Witchcraft (Boston: B.
    Green & J. Allen, 1702), reprinted
    in George Lincoln Burr, ed., Narra-
    tives of the Witchcraft Cases 1648-
    1706 (N.Y.: Barnes & Noble, 1946
    ed.), pp.399-432.
    W. Eliot Woodward, ed., Records of
    Salem Witchcraft, 2 vols. (Roxbury:
    W.E. Woodward, 1864).
    Samuel G. Drake, The Witchcraft De-
    lusion in New England, 3 vols.
    (Roxbury: W.E. Woodward, 1866).
    Charles W. Upham, Salem Witchcraft,
    2 vols. (Boston: Wiggin & Lunt,
    1867).
    Samuel Sewall, Diary, 3 vols., in
    Coll.Mass.Hist.Soc'y, ser.5, 5
    (1878):358-59,362-68.
    George H. Moore, "Notes on the His-
    tory of Witchcraft in Massachu-
    setts," Proc.Am.Antiquarian Soc'y,
    ser.2, 2 (1882):162-92.
    George H. Moore, Final Notes on
    Witchcraft in Massachusetts (N.Y.:
    The Author, 1885).
    Winfield S. Nevins, Witchcraft in
    Salem Village in 1692 (Salem: North
    Shore, 1892).
    Cotton Mather, Diary, in Coll.Mass.
    Hist.Soc'y, ser.7, vol.7-8 (1911).
    Charles Sutherland Tapley, Rebecca
    Nurse (Boston: Marshall Jones,
    1930).
    Marion Starkey, The Devil in Massa-
    chusetts (N.Y.: Knopf, 1949).
    Rossell Hope Robbins, Encyclopedia
    of Witchcraft and Demonology (N.Y.:
    Crown, 1959), pp.61-63,109-11,116,
    260,341-43,401-403,429-48.
    David Levin, ed., What Happened in
    Salem? (N.Y.: Harcourt, Brace &
    World, 1960).
    Montague Summers, Geography of Witch-
    craft (Secaucus, N.J.: Citadel,
    1965 ed.), pp.288-348.
    Sanford J. Fox, Science and Justice:
    The Massachusetts Witchcraft Trials
    (Baltimore: Johns Hopkins, 1968).
    Chadwick Hansen, Witchcraft at Salem
    (N.Y.: George Braziller, 1969).
    Eleanor Early, "Salem Is Still Hung
    Up on Witches," Fate 22 (Aug.1969):
    36-41. il.
    Joyce Bednarski, "The Salem Witch-
    Scare Viewed Sociologically," in
    Max Markwick, ed., Witchcraft and
    Sorcery (Baltimore: Penguin, 1970),
    pp.151-63.
    Marion Starkey, The Visionary Gods
    (Boston: Little, Brown, 1973).
    Paul Boyer & Stephen Nissenbaum,
    ed., Salem Possessed: The Social
    Origins of Witchcraft (Cambridge:
    Harvard, 1974).
    Chadwick Hansen, "The Metamorphosis
    of Tituba, or Why American Intel-
    lectuals Can't Tell an Indian
    Witch from a Negro," New England
    Quar. 47 (1974):3-12.
    Esther I. Wik, "The Jailkeeper at
    Salem in 1692," Hist.Coll.Essex
    Inst. 111 (1975):221-27.
    Robert Detweiler, "Shifting Per-
    spectives on the Salem Witches,"
    History Teacher 8 (1975):596-610.
    Linda R. Caporael, "Ergotism: The
    Satan Loosed in Salem?" Science
    192 (1976):21-26.
    Nicholas P. Spanos & Jack Gottlieb,
    "Ergotism and the Salem Village
    Witch Trials," Science 194 (1976):
    1390-94.
    Paul Boyer & Stephen Nissembaum, ed.,
    The Salem Witchcraft Papers, 3 vols.
    (N.Y.: DaCapo, 1977).

Deerfield
-Archeological site
  10,000 B.C.
    Greenfield Recorder, 5 July 1978; 12
    July 1978; 14 July 1978; and 11
    Aug.1978.

Dennis
-UFO (CE-2)
  1971, Jan.7/John Brogan, Jr./Scarge L.
    Raymond E. Fowler, UFOs: Interplane-
    tary Visitors (Jericho, N.Y.: Expo-
    sition, 1974), p.357.
    Ted Phillips, Physical Traces Associ-
    ated with UFO Sightings (Evanston:
    Center for UFO Studies, 1975), p.74.
-UFO (NL)
  1968, Nov.25
    Raymond E. Fowler, UFOs: Interplane-
    tary Visitors (Jericho, N.Y.: Expo-
    sition, 1974), p.355.

Dighton
-Ancient inscription
    Edmund Burke Delabarre, Dighton Rock
    (N.Y.: Walter Neale, 1928), pp.258-

59. il.
-Haunt
n.d./Col. Richmond House
D. Hamilton Hurd, <u>A History of Bristol County, Massachusetts</u> (Philadelphia: J.W. Lewis, 1883), pp.223-
24.
-Portuguese inscription
Dighton Rock State Park
(Letter), Cotton Mather, <u>Philosoph-
ical Trans.Roy.Soc'y</u> 29 (1714):70-
71. il.
James Winthrop, "Account of an Inscribed Rock," <u>Mem.Am.Acad.</u> 2, pt.
2 (1804):126-29. il.
John Davis, "An Attempt to Explain
the Inscription on the Dighton
Rock," <u>Mem.Am.Acad.</u> 3, pt.1 (1809):
197-205. il.
Carl Christian Rafn, <u>Antiquitates
Americanae</u> (Copenhagen: Schultz,
1837), pp.355-96.
John Warner Barber, <u>Historical Collections of Every Town in Massachu-
setts</u> (Worcester: Door, Howland,
1841), pp.117-19.
Charles Rau, "Observations on the
Dighton Rock Inscription," <u>Am.Anti-
quarian</u> 1 (1878):38-41.
D.I. Bushnell, "An Early Account of
Dighton Rock," <u>Am.Anthro.</u> 10 (1908)
:251-54. il.
Edward B. Delabarre, "Early Interest
in Dighton Rock," <u>Pub.Colonial Soc'y
Mass.</u> 18 (1917):235-99,417.
Edward B. Delabarre, "Middle Period
of Dighton Rock History," <u>Pub.Colo-
nial Soc'y Mass.</u> 19 (1918):46-149.
J.F. Collins, "Report on Marine
Growths on Rock," <u>Pub.Colonial Soc'y
Mass.</u> 20 (1919):396.
Edward B. Delabarre, "Recent History
of Dighton Rock," <u>Pub.Colonial Soc'y
Mass.</u> 21 (1920):438-62.
Edmund Burke Delabarre, <u>Dighton Rock</u>
(N.Y.: Walter Neale, 1928). il.
Olaf Strandwold, <u>Norse Inscriptions
on American Stones</u> (Weehauken, N.J.:
Magnus Björndal, 1948), pp.34-35.
il.
Charles Michael Boland, <u>They All Dis-
covered America</u> (N.Y.: Pocket Books,
1963 ed.), pp.172-77.
George F.W. Young, <u>Miguel Corte-Real
and the Dighton Writing-Rock</u> (Taun-
ton, R.I.: Old Colony Hist.Soc'y,
1970).
Manuel Luciano da Silva, <u>Portuguese
Pilgrims and Dighton Rock</u> (Bristol,
R.I.: The Author, 1971). il.
Manuel L. da Silva, "Dighton Rock,"
<u>Américas</u> 25, no.6-7 (1973):30-35.

Dover
-Humanoid
1977, April 21-23/Bill Bartlett/Farm
St.
<u>Dover-Sherborn Suburban Press</u>, 19
May 1977, p.1.
Jerome Clark, "The Dover Humanoid,"

<u>Fate</u> 31 (Mar.1978):50-55.
-UFO (?)
1969, June/Mr. Acheson
Jerome Clark & Loren Coleman, <u>Crea-
tures of the Outer Edge</u> (N.Y.: Warner, 1978), p.218.

Dracut
-Spirit medium
1909-1912/Amy H. Harrison
Prescott F. Hall, "The Harrison
Case," <u>Proc.ASPR</u> 13 (1920):285-477.
R.H. Goodhue, "Further Communica-
tions Through Mrs. Harrison," <u>J.
ASPR</u> 14 (1920):242-51.

Duxbury
-UFO (CE-3)
1974, Sep.3
Ted Bloecher, "A Catalog of Humanoid
Reports for 1974," in <u>MUFON 1975
Symposium Proc.</u> (Seguin, Tex.:
MUFON, 1975), pp.50,60-61.

East Orleans
-Norse ax
1914/Albert H. Moulton
Frederick J. Pohl, <u>The Lost Discov-
ery</u> (N.Y.: W.W. Norton, 1952), pp.
290-91.

Essex
-UFO (CE-1)
1976, April 4/Jean Lerra/Essex Rd.
Ray Fowler, "UFO Buzzes Air Force
Base," <u>Official UFO</u> 1 (Oct.1976):
18-19,46.
-UFO (NL)
1976, April 11
Raymond E. Fowler, "MUFON Quarterly
UFO Activity Report," <u>MUFON UFO J.</u>,
no.104 (July 1976):3.

Everett
-UFO (DD)
1947, July 9/Joseph Mulledy
<u>Boston Globe</u>, 9 July 1947.

Exeter
-Hex
1892, April/Edwin A. Brown
Rossell Hope Robbins, <u>Encyclopedia
of Witchcraft and Demonology</u> (N.Y.:
Crown, 1959), p.473.

Fairhaven
-UFO (NL)
1956, Aug.27/Mrs. F.W. Bence
"Case 202," <u>CRIFO Orbit</u>, 5 Oct.1956,
p.3.

Fall River
-Erratic shark
1957, Nov.
<u>Pittsburgh (Pa.) Press</u>, 1 Dec.1957.
-Midday darkness
1881, Sep.6
<u>Fall River News</u>, 6 Sep.1881.
-Norse skeleton in armor
1831/5th x Hartley St./=Amerindian with

Elizabethan copper plates
  Carl Christian Rafn, Antiquitates
  Americanae (Copenhagen: Schultz,
  1837).
  John Warner Barber, Historical Col-
  lections of Every Town in Massachu-
  setts (Worcester: Door, Howland,
  1841), pp.123-25, quoting American
  Mag., 1837.
  E.G. Squier, Aboriginal Monuments of
  the State of New York (Washington:
  Smithsonian Institution, Contrib.to
  Knowl., vol.2, 1849), pp.183-84.
  O.T. Mason, "The Skeleton in Armor,"
  Am.Anthro. 1 (1888):189-90.
  F.W. Putnam, "Skeleton in Armor," Am.
  Anthro., n.s., 3 (1901):388-89.
  Philip Ainsworth Means, The Newport
  Tower (N.Y.: Holt, 1942).
  Charles Michael Boland, They All Dis-
  covered America (N.Y.: Pocket Books,
  1963 ed.), pp.236-42.
  Horace F. Silliman, "Further Notes
  on the Copper Breastplates of the
  New England Indians," NEARA Newsl.
  5 (Mar.1970):14-17.

Falmouth
-UFO (NL)
  1947, June 30/Edward H. Murphy
  Boston Traveller, 7 July 1947.

Fitchburg
-Automatic writing
  1850/Edward Hooper
  Emma Hardinge Britten, Modern Ameri-
  can Spiritualism (N.Y.: The Author,
  1870), p.81.
-Phantom image
  1977, Oct.30/St. Anthony's Catholic
  Church
  Worcester Telegram, 31 Oct.1977.
-Poltergeist
  1868, July 3-Aug.27/Mary Carrick
  H.A. Willis, "A Remarkable Case of
  'Physical Phenomena,'" Atlantic
  Monthly 22 (Aug.1868):129-35.
  "New Light on an Old Poltergeist,"
  J.ASPR 29 (1935):225-38.
-UFO (CE-1)
  1973, Oct.18/Anne Lawler/Hwy.2
  Worcester Telegram, 19 Oct.1973.
-UFO (NL)
  1957, Nov.12
  Richard Hall, ed., The UFO Evidence
  (Washington: NICAP, 1964), p.167.

Framingham
-UFO (CE-1)
  1965, July 29
  Raymond E. Fowler, UFOs: Interplane-
  tary Visitors (Jericho, N.Y.: Expo-
  sition, 1974), p.68.
-UFO (NL)
  1973, Oct.22/Clayton Sawin/Hemenway
  School
  Framingham South Middlesex Daily
  News, 22 Oct.1973.
  1976, Dec.22/Indian Head Rd.
  Framingham South Middlesex Daily

News, 23 Dec.1976.
  1976, Dec.23/Peter Van Gel/Hwy.30
  Framingham South Middlesex Daily
  News, 24 Dec.1976.

Gardner
-UFO (DD)
  1947, July 13/Warren Baker Eames/Hwy.2
  Richard Hall, ed., The UFO Evidence
  (Washington: NICAP, 1964), p.66.
  Ted Bloecher, Report on the UFO Wave
  of 1947 (Washington: NICAP, 1967),
  p.III-1.

Gill twp.
-Ancient coin
  1842/Joseph D. Comming/Connecticut R.
  "Ancient Coin," Am.Pioneer 2 (1843):
  169-70. il.

Gloucester
-Dowsing
  1973, Jan./George Riley/Johnson Rd.
  "Divining in Massachusetts," Fate
  27 (Aug.1974):74, quoting Gloucester
  Daily Times (undated).
-Phantom army
  1692, July/Ebenezer Babson
  Cotton Mather, Magnalia Christi
  Americana (London: Thomas Park-
  hurst, 1702), Bk.VII.
  Charles M. Skinner, Myths and Legends
  of Our Own Land, 2 vols. (Philadel-
  phia: Lippincott, 1896), 1:238-41.
-Sea monster
  1817, Aug.10-23/Amos Story, and others/
  Gloucester Harbor
  Boston Weekly Messenger, 28 Aug.1817.
  Linnaean Soc'y of New England, Re-
  port of a Committee of the Linnaean
  Society of New England, Relative to
  a Large Marine Animal, Supposed to
  be a Sea-Serpent (Boston: Cumming &
  Hilliard, 1817).
  "The Sea-Serpent," Lit.Gazette, no.
  47 (1817):376.
  "American Sea-Serpent," Quar.J.Sci.
  Lit.& Arts Roy.Inst. 4 (1818):378-
  81.
  "On the History of the Great Sea-
  Serpent," Blackwood's Mag. 3 (Apr.
  1818):33-42.
  A.C. Oudemans, The Great Sea-Serpent
  (Leiden: E.J. Brill, 1892), pp.159-
  85.
  Bernard Heuvelmans, In the Wake of
  the Sea-Serpents (N.Y.: Hill & Wang,
  1968), pp.149-54.
  1818, July 22-30/William Sargent/Glou-
  cester Harbor
  Boston Weekly Messenger, 30 July
  1818, p.665; 6 Aug.1818, p.675; and
  13 Aug.1818, p.693.
  1819, Aug.26/Cheever Felch/"Science"/
  nr. Ten Pound I.
  Jacob Bigelow, "Documents and Remarks
  Respecting the Sea Serpent," Am.J.
  Sci., ser.1, 2 (1820):147,157-59.
  Boston Daily Advertiser, 25 Nov.
  1848.

1877, July 15/George S. Wasson/"Gul-
nare"
  J.G. Wood, "The Trail of the Sea-
  Serpent," Atlantic Monthly 53 (1884)
  :799,810-11.
1886, Aug.22/George W. Scott
  New York Times, 23 Aug.1886, p.1.
1960, July/Harry Heath
  (Editorial), Fate 13 (Nov.1960):12.
  "Amazing Denizens of the Sea," Fate
  15 (May 1962):48.
1975, April 29/John Randazza/"Debbie
Rose"/15 mi.SE/=whale
  Gloucester Daily Times, 30 Apr.1975;
  and 31 May 1975.
  Gary S. Mangiacopra, "The Randazza
  (Not a) Sea Serpent Sighting," Pur-
  suit 11 (summer 1978):82-83.
-Shape-shifting
  1745, June 16/Margaret Wesson
  Samuel A. Drake, A Book of New Eng-
  land Legends and Folk Lore (Boston:
  Roberts Bros., 1888).
  James R. Pringle, History of the
  Town and City of Gloucester, Massa-
  chusetts (Gloucester: The Author,
  1892), p.62.
-UFO (?)
  1967, Aug.2/Carol Chisolm/=flare
  "Worldwide Sightings Showing In-
  crease," UFO Inv. 4 (Oct.1967):1,3.
  "Cape Ann Sightings Reevaluated,"
  UFO Inv. 4 (Nov.-Dec.1967):3.
  David R. Saunders & R. Roger Harkins,
  UFOs? Yes! (N.Y.: Signet, 1968),
  pp.122-23.
  Edward U. Condon, ed., Scientific
  Study of Unidentified Flying Objects
  (N.Y.: Bantam, 1969 ed.), pp.338-41.
  Raymond E. Fowler, UFOs: Interplane-
  tary Visitors (Jericho, N.Y.: Expo-
  sition, 1974), pp.155-61.
  1974, June 8/=planet?
  Dave Webb & John Oswald, "New Hamp-
  shire Report May Be a Hoax," Sky-
  look, no.93 (Aug.1975):14.
-UFO (NL)
  1968, Aug.12
  Raymond E. Fowler, UFOs: Interplane-
  tary Visitors (Jericho, N.Y.: Exposition, 1974), p.354.
  1976, Jan.9/Joseph Aiello/Cherry St.
  "Teacher, Student Report Massachusetts Sighting," Skylook, no.101
  (Apr.1976):9.
  Raymond Fowler, "UFOs over Essex
  County," MUFON UFO J., no.117 (Aug.
  1977):8-9.

Goshen
-Ancient tunnel
  cemetery
  Leland H. Godfrey, "The Goshen Stone
  Mystery," Yankee 35 (Nov.1971):218-
  23.
  Salvatore Michael Trento, The Search
  for Lost America (Chicago: Contemporary, 1978), pp.150-53.

Grafton
-UFO (NL)
  1909, Dec.23
  Providence (R.I.) Journal, 24 Dec.
  1909.

Greenfield
-Spirit medium
  1860s
  Emma Hardinge Britten, Modern American Spiritualism (N.Y.: The Author,
  1870), pp.270-71.
-UFO (?)
  1947, June 22/=meteor?
  Ted Bloecher, Report on the UFO Wave
  of 1947 (Washington: NICAP, 1967),
  Appendix, Case 22.
  Bruce S. Maccabee, "UFO Related In-
  formation rfom the FBI Files: Part
  3," MUFON UFO J., no.121 (Dec.
  1977):10,12.
-UFO (CE-2)
  1954, June 10/Mrs. Fred Zappy/70 Congress St.
  R. DeWitt Miller, Stranger Than Life
  (N.Y.: Ace, 1955 ed.), pp.100-101.
-UFO (DD)
  1952, Feb.20/Albert H. Baller
  (Letter), Fate 5 (Oct.1952):119-20.
  "Reverend Baller...Saucers and Greenfield, Mass.," CRIFO Newsl., 2 July
  1954, p.4.
  Richard Hall, ed., The UFO Evidence
  (Washington: NICAP, 1964), p.69.
  1952, March 30
  Boston Traveller, 5 May 1952.
  1953, June 11/Albert H. Baller
  1953, June 12/George Kendrick/10 mi.S
  "Reverend Baller...Saucers and Greenfield, Mass.," CRIFO Newsl., 2 July
  1954, p.4.
  1955, Dec.6/Lillian Steiner
  "Case 123," CRIFO Orbit, 6 Jan.1956,
  p.4.
  1958, Oct.18
  "Hovering UFO Puzzles South African
  Officials," UFO Inv. 1 (Dec.1958):1,
  3.
-UFO (NL)
  1955, Dec.15/Leo Bousquet, Jr.
  "Case 124," CRIFO Orbit, 6 Jan.1956,
  p.4, quoting Greenfield Recorder-
  Gazette (undated).
  1956, Aug.1/George Kendrick
  "Case 180," CRIFO Orbit, 7 Sep.1956,
  pp.2-3.

Groton
-Crisis apparition
  1912, April 14/Henrietta M. Chase
  "An Apparently Coincidental Vision,"
  J.ASPR 13 (1919):31-36.
-Possession
  1671, Oct.30-1672, Feb./Elizabeth
  Knapp/=hysteria
  Samuel Willard, Useful Instructions
  for a Professing People in Times of
  Great Security and Degeneracy (Cam-
  bridge: Samuel Green, 1673).
  Increase Mather, Remarkable Provi-

dences (Boston: Joseph Browning,
1684), reprinted in George Lincoln
Burr, ed., Narratives of the Witch-
craft Cases 1648-1706 (N.Y.: Barnes
& Noble, 1946 ed.), pp.8,21-23.
Cotton Mather, Pietas in Patriam: The
Life of His Excellency Sir William
Phips (London: Nath. Hillar, 1697).
"Samuel Willard's Account of the
Strange Case of Elizabeth Knapp of
Groton," Coll.Mass.Hist.Soc'y, ser.
4, 8 (1868):555-70.
Samuel Abbott Green, Groton in the
Witchcraft Times (Cambridge: J.
Wilson, 1883), pp.7-21.

Groton twp.
-Phantom panther tracks
1960, Feb.13/Roland G. Gaudette
Bruce S. Wright, The Eastern Panther
(Toronto: Clarke, Irwin, 1972), p.
104, quoting Outdoor Maine, June
1960, p.17.

Groveland
-UFO (CE-1)
1965, Feb.16/Gary Smythe
Raymond E. Fowler, UFOs: Interplanetary Visitors (Jericho, N.Y.: Exposition, 1974), pp.62-63.

Hadley
-Doubtful responsibility
1675, Sep.1/Phineas Cooke
Sylvester Judd, History of Hadley
(Northampton: Metcalf, 1863).
Ezra Stiles, Extracts from the Itin-
eraries and Other Miscellanies of
Ezra Stiles, 1755-1794 (New Haven:
Yale Univ., 1916).
Phillip M. Perry, "The Mysterious
Savior of Hadley," Fate 27 (Sep.
1974):62-64.
-Haunt
1770s-   /James Lincoln Huntington/
Porter-Phelps-Huntington House/130
River Dr.
"The Purposeful Phantom," Fate 10
(Dec.1957):57.
Louis C. Jones, Things That Go Bump
in the Night (N.Y.: Hill & Wang,
1959), pp.81-83.
Susy Smith, Prominent American Ghosts
(N.Y.: Dell, 1969 ed.), pp.63-71.
19th c./Elm Valley
"Miscellaneous Incidents," J.ASPR 4
(1910):45,49.
-Witch trial (hex)
1683-1685/Mary Webster
Samuel G. Drake, Annals of Witchcraft
in New England (Boston: W.E. Wood-
ward, 1869), pp.168-71.

Halifax
-Haunt
1950s-1960s/David A. Davis
Curtis B. Norris, "A Ghost with Yankee Habits," Fate 21 (Mar.1968):
96-100. il.

Hardwick
-Ancient marker stones
Thresher Rd. nr.Hwy.32A
Worcester Evening Gazette, 9 June
1972.
"The Mystery of the Thirty-Two
Stones of Hardwick, Mass.," NEARA
Newsl. 7 (June 1972):40.

Harvard
-Ancient stone chamber
William B. Goodwin, The Ruins of
Great Ireland in New England (Bos-
ton: Meador, 1946), pp.156,388-89,
413. il.
-Haunt
1960-1963/Peter Hofmann
Hans Holzer, Yankee Ghosts (N.Y.:
Ace, 1966), pp.49-50.

Harwich Port
-Sea monster
1957, summer/Bud McKenny/"Wanderer"/
=hoax?
(Editorial), Fate 10 (Dec.1957):20-
21, quoting Boston Globe (undated).

Haverhill
-Ancient carving
Barry Fell, America B.C. (N.Y.: Quadrangle, 1976), p.152.
-Shape-shifting
n.d./Mrs. Morse
Charles M. Skinner, Myths and Legends
of Our Own Land, 2 vols. (Philadelphia: Lippincott, 1896), 1:231-32.
-UFO (CE-1)
1964, Oct.6/Robert Soucy/Broadway
Raymond E. Fowler, UFOs: Interplanetary Visitors (Jericho, N.Y.: Exposition, 1974), pp.23-24.
-UFO (CE-3)
1967, spring/airport
Raymond E. Fowler, UFOs: Interplanetary Visitors (Jericho, N.Y.: Exposition, 1974), p.348.
-UFO (DD)
1957, Nov.5/Kenneth Chadwick
Haverhill Gazette, 6 Nov.1957.
1965, Aug.20/Hwy.110
Raymond E. Fowler, UFOs: Interplanetary Visitors (Jericho, N.Y.: Exposition, 1974), p.70.
-UFO (NL)
1966, March 29/Russell Conway
Raymond E. Fowler, UFOs: Interplanetary Visitors (Jericho, N.Y.: Exposition, 1974), pp.115-16.
-Witchcraft
n.d./Susie Martin
Charles M. Skinner, Myths and Legends
of Our Own Land, 2 vols. (Philadelphia: Lippincott, 1896), 1:232.

Hawthorne
-Fall of snakes
n.d./Margaret McDonald
Charles Fort, The Books of Charles
Fort (N.Y.: Holt, 1941), p.593.

Hingham
-Patterned ground
　　Oliver H. Howe, "The Hingham Red
　　Felsite Boulder Train," Science 84
　　(1936):394-96.

Holbrook
-Ghost
　1926, June/Jules Wolfe
　　Jules Wolfe & B. Ann Slate, "The
　　Graverobbers and the Ghost," Fate
　　25 (Mar.1972):54-58.

Holland
-UFO (CE-3)
　1976, Dec.15
　　"UFOs of Limited Merit," Int'l UFO
　　Reporter 2 (Feb.1977):5.

Holliston
-Erratic armadillo
　1978, Dec.23
　　Framingham South Middlesex Daily
　　News, 24 Dec.1978, p.1.

Holyoke
-Ghost
　n.d.
　　Clifton Johnson, What They Say in
　　New England (Boston: Lee & Shepard,
　　1897), pp.249-52.
-UFO (?)
　1952, July
　　Edward J. Ruppelt, The Report on Un-
　　identified Flying Objects (Garden
　　City: Doubleday, 1956), p.163.
　1965, Nov.9
　　John G. Fuller, Incident at Exeter
　　(N.Y.: Berkley, 1967 ed.), p.207.

Hopedale
-Inner development
　1841-1856/Adin Ballou/Hopedale Commun-
　ity
　　Adin Ballou, Spirit Manifestations
　　(Boston: The Author, 1852).
　　Adin Ballou, Autobiography 1803-1890
　　(Lowell, Mass.: Vox Populi, 1896).
　　Adin Ballou, History of the Hopedale
　　Community (Lowell, Mass.: Thompson
　　& Hill, 1897).
　　Nandor Fodor, Encyclopaedia of Psy-
　　chic Science (London: Arthurs,
　　1933), pp.176,331.
-UFO (NL)
　1909, Dec.23
　　Providence (R.I.) Journal, 24 Dec.
　　1909.

Hopkinton
-Ancient stone chamber
　　William B, Goodwin, The Ruins of
　　Great Ireland in New England (Bos-
　　ton: Meador, 1946), pp.44-45,52-56.
　　il.
-Haunt
　1968, fall
　　Raymond A. LaJoie, "Ted Rabouin: New
　　England Warlock," Fate 24 (Mar.
　　1970):38,42.

Hubbardston
-UFO (NL)
　1978, Feb.3
　　Worcester Telegram, 4 Feb.1978.

Hyannis
-Disappearance
　1944, Oct.16/two Navy planes
　　(Letter), Am.Legion Mag., June 1962.

Ipswich
-Ghost
　1729, Nov.
　　Joseph B. Felt, History of Ipswich,
　　Essex, and Hamilton (Cambridge: C.
　　Folsom, 1834), pp.208-209, quoting
　　New England J. (undated).
-Hex
　1692, June/Elizabeth How
　　Cotton Mather, Wonders of the Invis-
　　ible World (Boston: Benjamin Har-
　　ris, 1693), reprinted in George
　　Lincoln Burr, ed., Narratives of
　　the Witchcraft Cases 1648-1706
　　(N.Y.: Barnes & Noble, 1946 ed.),
　　pp.209,237-40.
　1878/Daniel Spofford
　　Sibyl Wilbur, The Life of Mary Baker
　　Eddy (N.Y.: Concord, 1908).
-Phantom
　1740/George Whitefield/Congregational
　Church
　　Charles M. Skinner, Myths and Legends
　　of Our Own Land, 2 vols. (Philadel-
　　phia: Lippincott, 1896), 1:242.
-UFO (?)
　1967, Aug.2/Winthrop Ashworth/=flare
　　"Worldwide Sightings Showing In-
　　crease," UFO Inv. 4 (Oct.1967):1,4.
　　"Cape Ann Sightings Reevaluated,"
　　UFO Inv. 4 (Nov.-Dec.1967):3.
　　Edward U. Condon, ed., Scientific
　　Study of Unidentified Flying Objects
　　(N.Y.: Bantam, 1969 ed.), pp.339-41.
　　Raymond E. Fowler, UFOs: Interplane-
　　tary Visitors (Jericho, N.Y.: Expo-
　　sition, 1974), pp.155-61.
-UFO (CE-1)
　1968, Jan.17
　　Raymond E. Fowler, UFOs: Interplane-
　　tary Visitors (Jericho, N.Y.: Expo-
　　sition, 1974), p.351.
　1976, April 4/Donald Robichaud/South
　Parish Green
　　Ray Fowler, "UFO Buzzes Air Force
　　Base," Official UFO 1 (Oct.1976):
　　18,46-47.
-UFO (CE-2)
　1965, Sep.3/Dennis Winters/Candlewood
　Golf Course
　　Raymond E. Fowler, UFOs: Interplane-
　　tary Visitors (Jericho, N.Y.: Expo-
　　sition, 1974), pp.92-93.
-UFO (DD)
　1968, Jan.17
　　Raymond E. Fowler, UFOs: Interplane-
　　tary Visitors (Jericho, N.Y.: Expo-
　　sition, 1974), p.350.
-UFO (NL)
　1966, Sep.17

1967, Oct.2
1968, April 10
1968, April 19
1968, April 30
   Raymond E. Fowler, UFOs: Interplanetary Visitors (Jericho, N.Y.: Exposition, 1974), pp.341,350-53.
1976, April 4/Nancy Feener/Town Farm
Rd.
   Raymond E. Fowler, "MUFON Quarterly
   UFO Activity Report," MUFON UFO J.,
   no.104 (July 1976):3.
   Ray Fowler, "UFO Buzzes Air Force
   Base," Official UFO 1 (Oct.1976):
   18,47.
-Witch trial (?)
1652/John Bradstreet
1680/Margaret Read
   Rossell Hope Robbins, Encyclopedia
   of Witchcraft and Demonology (N.Y.:
   Crown, 1959), p.520.

Jefferson
-UFO (NL)
1975, Aug.10
   "UFO Central," CUFOS News Bull., 15
   Nov.1975, p.15.

Lakeville
-UFO (CE-2)
1961, Feb.28/Clarence Blackwood
   "Low-Flying UFO Puts Out Lights,"
   UFO Inv. 2 (July-Aug.1961):5.

Lawrence
-Ancient sculpture
n.d./Merrimack R.
   Barry Fell, America B.C. (N.Y.: Quad-
   rangle, 1976), p.152. il.
-Fall of unknown object
1955, Aug.11/Rei Bernard
   "Flaming Object Bashes Hole in Side
   of House," CRIFO Orbit, 3 Feb.1956,
   p.3, quoting Lawrence Evening Trib-
   une (undated).
-Phantom image
1870, Aug.
   Charles Fort, The Books of Charles
   Fort (N.Y.: Holt, 1941), p.960,
   quoting New York Herald, 20 Aug.
   1870.
-Poltergeist
1963, Nov./Francis Martin/26 Florence
St.
   (Editorial), Fate 17 (Mar.1964):18-
   20.
   Raymond Bayless, The Enigma of the
   Poltergeist (N.Y.: Ace, 1967 ed.),
   pp.98-107.
-UFO (CE-2)
1965, May 14/Mt. Vernon ballfield
   "Saucer Landing in Massachusetts(?)"
   Saucer News 12 (June 1965):24.
-UFO (NL)
1964, May 18/Robert L. Smith, Jr./air-
port
   "Pilot Observes Maneuvering UFO,"
   UFO Inv. 3 (May-June 1966):4.
1966, Oct.28
   Raymond E. Fowler, UFOs: Interplane-

tary Visitors (Jericho, N.Y.: Exposition, 1974), p.342.

Lee
-Disappearance
1919, May 29/Mansell R. James/biplane
   New York Times, 2 June 1919, p.1;
   and 7 June 1919, p.8.

Leicester
-Fall of frogs
1953, Sep.7/Paxton Ave.
   (Editorial), Fate 7 (Jan.1954):5-6.
   "Falls and Balls," Doubt, no.43
   (1954):256.

Leominster
-Ancient dolmen
North Monoosock Hill
   "Field Notes of the 1973 Season,"
   NEARA Newsl. 8 (fall 1973):59-60.
   il.
-Ancient inscription
   William B. Goodwin, The Ruins of
   Great Ireland in New England (Bos-
   ton: Meador, 1946), pp.109-14. il.
-Gravity anomaly
1939, July 13/Lowe Street Hill
   "Two 'Magnetic' Hills," Fortean
   Soc'y Mag., no.3 (Jan.1940):13.
-UFO (CE-2)
1967, March 8/William Wallace/St. Leo's
Cemetery
   "Driver Shocked, Paralyzed," UFO
   Inv. 3 (Mar.-Apr.1967):7.
   J. Allen Hynek, The UFO Experience
   (Chicago: Regnery, 1972), pp.120-
   21.
   Raymond E. Fowler, UFOs: Interplane-
   tary Visitors (Jericho, N.Y.: Expo-
   sition, 1974), pp.143-48.
-UFO (NL)
1967-1970/Clem Bisceglia
   Leominster Enterprise, 10 Jan.1970.

Lexington
-Clairvoyance
1874, Jan.26
   "Premonition," J.ASPR 9 (1915):230-
   40.
-Phantom
1974, spring/Jane Frances T. Woodruff
   (Letter), Fate 31 (Mar.1978):128.
-UFO (DD)
1952, April 23/R.C. Munroe
   Richard Hall, ed., The UFO Evidence
   (Washington: NICAP, 1964), p.57.
-UFO (NL)
1969, Jan.22
   Raymond E. Fowler, UFOs: Interplane-
   tary Visitors (Jericho, N.Y.: Expo-
   sition, 1974), p.355.

Littleton
-Ancient habitation site
   Robert E. Stone, "Mystery Hill and
   NEARA Research Progress Report--
   1975," NEARA J. 10 (summer-fall
   1975):7,11.
-Skyquakes

n.d./Nashoba Hill
  Charles M. Skinner, Myths and Legends
  of Our Own Land, 2 vols. (Philadelphia: Lippincott, 1896), 2:45.
-UFO (CE-1)
  1964, Aug.25/Norman Sheldrick/nr. Porter Field
    "Close-Range Sightings near Boston,"
    UFO Inv. 2 (Sep.-Oct.1964):6.
    Raymond E. Fowler, UFOs: Interplane-
    tary Visitors (Jericho, N.Y.: Expo-
    sition, 1974), pp.15-17.
-UFO (NL)
  1964, Aug.28/Paul Ellis/Harwood Ave. x
  Hwy.495
    Raymond E. Fowler, UFOs: Interplane-
    tary Visitors (Jericho, N.Y.: Expo-
    sition, 1974), pp.15-17.
-Witch trial (hex)
  1720
    Thomas Hutchinson, The History of the
    Province of Massachusetts Bay, 3
    vols. (Boston: Thomas & John Fleet,
    1828), 2:20-21.

Longmeadow
-Weather control
  n.d.
    Clifton Johnson, What They Say in
    New England (Boston: Lee & Shepard,
    1897), pp.238-39.

Lowell
-Fall of gelatinous substance
  ca.1905/Joel Powers/Lawrence St.
    Frank Schlesinger, "Pwdre Ser," Na-
    ture 84 (1910):105-106.

Lynn
-Clairaudience
  1878, fall/Augustine Jones
    Walter F. Prince, "Experiences of
    Augustine Jones," J.ASPR 12 (1918):
    718-25.
-Midday darkness
  1717, Oct.21
  1780, May 19
    Alonzo Lewis, The History of Lynn
    (Boston: J.H. Eastburn, 1829).
-Precognition
  1775-1813/Moll Pitcher/High Rock
    Bathsheba H. Crane, Life, Letters
    and Wayside Gleanings for the Folks
    (Boston: J.H. Earle, 1880).
    Richard M. Dorson, Jonathan Draws
    the Long Bow (Cambridge: Harvard
    Univ., 1947), pp.42-44, quoting
    Granite Monthly, June 1879.
    Madeleine Field, "Moll Pitcher: Rev-
    olutionary Seer," Fate 19 (June
    1966):73-81.
-Psychokinesis
  1886/Ellen F. Wetherell
    "A Case of Telekinesis," J.ASPR 4
    (1910):384-89.
-Sea monster
  1947, Sep.4/John Ruhl/off Lynn Beach
    "Run of the Mill," Doubt, no.20
    (1948):302.
-Spirit medium

1851-1887/John Murray Spear/High Rock
  S.C. Hewitt, Messages from the Superior State (Boston: Bela Marsh,
  1852).
  Eliab W. Capron, Modern Spiritualism:
  Its Facts and Fanaticisms (Boston:
  Bela Marsh, 1855), pp.218-25.
  A.E. Newton, ed., The Educator (Bos-
  ton: Office of Practical Spiritual-
  ists, 1857), pp.9-39,238-57.
  Emma Hardinge Britten, Modern Ameri-
  can Spiritualism (N.Y.: The Author,
  1870), pp.217-29.
  Frank Podmore, Modern Spiritualism,
  2 vols. (London: Methuen, 1902),
  1:214-16,274-76,298-99.
  Slater Brown, The Heyday of Spirit-
  ualism (N.Y.: Pocket Books, 1972
  ed.), pp.178-89.
  Neil Lehman, The Life of John Murray
  Spear (PhD. dissertation, Ohio
  State University, 1973).
-UFO (?)
  1972, Aug.30
    Glenn McWane & David Graham, The
    New UFO Sightings (N.Y.: Warner,
    1974), p.62, quoting Boston Globe
    (undated).
-UFO (CE-1)
  1964, Aug.3/William Angelos/Washington
  St.
    "Close-Range Sightings near Boston,"
    UFO Inv. 2 (Sep.-Oct.1964):6.
-UFO (CE-2)
  1964, June 15/William Angelos
    "Other Recent Sightings," UFO Inv.
    2 (July-Aug.1964):7,8.
    Donald E. Keyhoe & Gordon I.R. Lore,
    Jr., UFOs: A New Look (Washington:
    NICAP, 1969), p.14.
    Raymond E. Fowler, UFOs: Interplane-
    tary Visitors (Jericho, N.Y.: Expo-
    sition, 1974), pp.13-14.
-UFO (DD)
  1947, July 7/General Electric plant
    Boston Globe, 8 July 1947.
  1952, July 1
    Edward J. Ruppelt, The Report on Un-
    identified Flying Objects (Garden
    City: Doubleday, 1956), p.150.
  1965, Aug.13
  1970, July 21
    Raymond E. Fowler, UFOs: Interplane-
    tary Visitors (Jericho, N.Y.: Expo-
    sition, 1974), pp.333,356.
-UFO (NL)
  1909, Dec.23
    New York Sun, 24 Dec.1909.
    New York Tribune, 24 Dec.1909, p.1.
  1964, Aug.25/Richard J. Pratt/Lenox
  Hill
    "Close-Range Sightings near Boston,"
    UFO Inv. 2 (Sep.-Oct.1964):6.
    Raymond E. Fowler, UFOs: Interplane-
    tary Visitors (Jericho, N.Y.: Expo-
    sition, 1974), pp.17-19.
  1975, Oct.22
    "UFO Central," CUFOS News Bull., 1
    Feb.1976, p.9.

Malden
-Haunt
  n.d./cemetery
    Charles M. Skinner, American Myths
    and Legends, 2 vols. (Philadelphia:
    Lippincott, 1903), 1:101-104.
-UFO (NL)
  1968, April 19
    Raymond E. Fowler, UFOs: Interplane-
    tary Visitors (Jericho, N.Y.: Expo-
    sition, 1974), p.353.

Manchester
-Musical sand
    H. Carrington Bolton & Alexis A. Ju-
    lien, "The Singing Beach of Man-
    chester, Mass.," Proc.Am.Ass'n Adv.
    Sci. 32 (1883):251-52.
    H. Carrington Bolton & Alexis A. Ju-
    lien, "Musical Sand: Its Wide Dis-
    tribution and Properties," Proc.Am.
    Ass'n Adv.Sci. 33 (1884):408-13.

Manomet
-Ancient sculpture
  1959, May 14/Joseph Notini
    Charles Michael Boland, They All Dis-
    covered America (N.Y.: Pocket Books,
    1963 ed.), pp.219-20. il.
-Sea monster
  1840s/Daniel Webster
    Henry David Thoreau, Summer: from
    the Journal of Henry D. Thoreau
    (Boston: Houghton Mifflin, 1884),
    pp.137-38.

Marblehead
-Clairvoyance
  18th c./John Dimond
    Samuel Roads, The History and Trad-
    itions of Marblehead (Boston:
    Houghton, Osgood, 1880), pp.42-43.
    D. Hamilton Hurd, ed., History of
    Essex County, Massachusetts, 2
    vols. (Philadelphia: J.W. Lewis,
    1888), 2:1069.
-Fall of pig iron
  1857
    A.A. Hayes, "On the Supposed Meteor-
    ite from Marblehead," Am.J.Sci.,
    ser.2, 25 (1858):135.
-Ghost
  n.d./Oakum Bay
    Samuel Roads, The History and Trad-
    itions of Marblehead (Boston:
    Houghton, Osgood, 1880), pp.37-38.
-Haunt
  1972, summer/Nancy Boyle
    Nancy Boyle & Celestine L. Sager,
    "The Burial Stone That Was 'Live,'"
    Fate 28 (July 1975):83-86.
-Hex
  n.d./Mammy Red
    Samuel Roads, The History and Trad-
    itions of Marblehead (Boston:
    Houghton, Osgood, 1880), p.33.

Marlborough
-UFO (NL)
  1909, Dec.14-23

New York Tribune, 23 Dec.1909, p.1;
    and 24 Dec.1909, p.1.
    New York Sun, 24 Dec.1909.
  1967, Feb.26
    Raymond E. Fowler, UFOs: Interplane-
    tary Visitors (Jericho, N.Y.: Expo-
    sition, 1974), p.345.

Marshfield
-Haunt
  n.d.
    Ira Dember, "The Ghost of Marshfield:
    Fact or Legend?" New England Galaxy
    15 (fall 1973):26-32.
-Possession
  1681/Mary Ross
    Charles Chauncy, The Wonderful Nar-
    rative (Boston: Rogers & Fowle,
    1742), pp.84-86.
    Samuel G. Drake, Annals of Witchcraft
    in New England (Boston: W.E. Wood-
    ward, 1869), pp.158-59.
-UFO (DD)
  1972, July 3/Paul Kamp/Dog Lane Rd.
    "UFO Seen in Massachusetts," Sky-
    look, no.58 (Sep.1972):12, quoting
    Boston Globe (undated).

Medford
-Erratic eels
  1972, June/975 Fellsway Dr.
    Boston Globe, 16 June 1972.
    "Eels Out of Faucets," Pursuit 5
    (Oct.1972):85.
-Haunt
  n.d./Rock Hill Estate
    Charles M. Skinner, Myths and Legends
    of Our Own Land, 2 vols. (Philadel-
    phia: Lippincott, 1896), 2:271.
-UFO (NL)
  1964, Sep.6/Tom Brooks/Upper Mystic L.
  1966, Oct.10/Hwy.93
    Raymond E. Fowler, UFOs: Interplane-
    tary Visitors (Jericho, N.Y.: Expo-
    sition, 1974), pp.21-22,341.

Medway
-Haunt
  n.d./Dinglehole
    E.O. Jameson, The History of Medway,
    Mass. (Providence: J.A. & R.A. Reid,
    1886), pp.13-14.
-UFO (DD)
  1978, June 25/Samuel Torrey/62 Main St.
    Milford Daily News, 26 June 1978.
    Richard Hall, "Wobbling UFO in New
    England," MUFON UFO J., no.132
    (Nov.-Dec.1978):16.

Mendon
-Ancient stone construction
    William B. Goodwin, The Ruins of
    Great Ireland in New England (Bos-
    ton: Meador, 1946), pp.182-85.

Merrimacport
-Ancient bronze dagger
  n.d./C.A. Kershaw/Indian Flats
    Warren King Moorehead, The Merrimack
    Archaeological Society: A Prelim-

inary Survey (Salem, Mass.: Peabody
Museum, 1931), p.13. il.
Charles C. Willoughby, Antiquities
of the New England Indians (Cam-
bridge: Peabody Museum, 1935), pp.
114-15. il.
Frederick J. Pohl, Atlantic Cross-
ings Before Columbus (N.Y.: W.W.
Norton, 1961), pp.15-16.
James P. Whittall, Jr., "An Unique
Dagger," NEARA Newsl. 5 (Dec.1970):
77. il.
Barry Fell, America B.C. (N.Y.: Quad-
rangle, 1976), pp.127-28. il.

Methuen
-Clairvoyance
1940/Fred Rother
"Dream Fortune," Fate 5 (July-Aug.
1952):33.
-Poltergeist
1963, Oct.29-Nov.1/Francis Martin/1
Linton Ave.
(Editorial), Fate 17 (Mar.1964):15-
18.
Raymond Bayless, The Enigma of the
Poltergeist (N.Y.: Ace, 1967 ed.),
pp.98-107.
-UFO (CE-2)
1967, Jan.20/Kimberly Lodge/Washington
St.
"Major Sighting Wave," UFO Inv. 3
(Jan.-Feb.1967):1,3-4.
J. Allen Hynek, The UFO Experience
(Chicago: Regnery, 1972), pp.118-20.
Raymond E. Fowler, UFOs: Interplane-
tary Visitors (Jericho, N.Y.: Expo-
sition, 1974), pp.138-43.
-UFO (NL)
1957, July/Gregory C. Melvin
(Letter), Fate 11 (Apr.1958):113-14.

Middleboro
-Plant sensitivity
1950s/John C. Brown
John Edward Malloy, "Farmer Brown's
Health Germ," Fate 9 (Mar.1956):69-
74.
-UFO (CE-1)
1966, Dec.1
Raymond E. Fowler, UFOs: Interplanetary Visitors (Jericho, N.Y.: Exposition, 1974), p.342.

Milford
-UFO (NL)
1909, Dec.23
Providence (R.I.) Journal, 24 Dec.
1909.

Milton
-Haunt
n.d./Milton Hill
Charles Fort, The Books of Charles
Fort (N.Y.: Holt, 1941), p.696.

Monson
-Acoustic anomaly
n.d./gneiss quarries
C.F. Marvin, "Report on the Earth-

quake of October 31, 1895," Monthly
Weather Rev. 23 (Oct.1895):374-75.
-Photographic anomaly
1973, April 15, 20/Stella Lansing
Berthold Eric Schwarz, "Stella Lan-
sing's Clocklike UFO Patterns,"
Flying Saucer Rev. 20 (Jan.1975):
3,4.

Monterey
-Clairempathy
1920s
Nellie M. Smith, "The Charleburg
Record," Proc.ASPR, vol.17 (1923).
Margaret P. Gaddis, "The Joan Dale
Psychometry Experiment," Fate 22
(July 1969):86-96.

Nahant
-Sea monster
1819, Aug.12-13/James Prince
Boston Daily Advertiser, 19 Aug.
1819; 26 Aug.1819; and 25 Nov.1848.
Jacob Bigelow, "Documents and Remarks Respecting the Sea-Serpent,"
Am.J.Sci., ser.1, 2 (1820):147,
154-57.
J.B. Holder, "The Great Unknown,"
Century Mag., n.s., 22 (1892):247,
252-53.
A.C. Oudemans, The Great Sea-Serpent
(Leiden: E.J. Brill, 1892), pp.206-
13.
1820, Aug./T.H. Perkins
"The Great Sea-Serpent," Zoologist
7 (1849):2359,2362.
1821, summer/T.H. Perkins/"Ann Marie"
Boston Daily Advertiser, 25 Nov.
1848.
1822, summer
1823, July 12/Francis Johnson, Jr.
Bernard Heuvelmans, In the Wake of
the Sea-Serpents (N.Y.: Hill & Wang,
1968), p.171.
1833, July
Robert Hamilton, The Natural History
of the Amphibious Carnivora, in
William Jardine, The Naturalist's
Library: Mammalia , 14 vols. (Edinburgh: W.H. Lizars, 1839), 8:320.
1839, Aug./Thomas Grattan
Thomas Grattan, Civilized America
(London: Bradbury & Evans, 1859),
p.39.
Bernard Heuvelmans, In the Wake of
the Sea-Serpents (N.Y.: Hill & Wang,
1968), p.178, quoting Neue Notizen,
Oct.1839.
1887, July 29/Relay House
New York Times, 31 July 1887, p.9.
-UFO (NL)
1952, July 23
Richard Hall, ed., The UFO Evidence
(Washington: NICAP, 1964), p.160.

Nantucket
-Sea monster
1821, Sep.25/Francis Joy, Jr.
"Miscellen," Notizbl.Gebiete Natur-
und Heilkunde, no.19 (Jan.1822):294-

95.
1846, Aug.
Bénédict-Henry Révoil, Pêches dans
l'Amérique du Nord (Paris: Hachette,
1863).
1964, May 12/Alf H. Wilhelmsen/"Blue
Sea"/30 mi.S of Round Shoal Buoy
New Bedford Standard Times, 14 May
1964.
1964, May/Thomas Keeping/"Friendship"/
40 mi.ESE of Round Shoal Buoy
New Bedford Standard Times, 22 May
1964.
-UFO (CE-1)
1975, Sep.15
(Letter), Dorothy Hawkes, Ufology 2
(spring 1976):48.
-UFO (DD)
1977, spring
Kal Korf, "Prize Selections from a
Researcher's Collection," Saga UFO
Rept. 6 (Nov.1978):38,42. il.

Natick
-Haunt
1963/Anne Valukis
Hans Holzer, Yankee Ghosts (N.Y.:
Ace, 1966), p.51.
-UFO (NL)
1909, Dec.23
Providence (R.I.) Journal, 24 Dec.
1909.

Needham
-UFO (DD)
1964, Dec.14
Donald B. Hanlon, "Virginia 1965
Flap," Flying Saucer Rev. 12 (Mar.-
Apr.1966):14.
-UFO (NL)
1968, Sep.29
Raymond E. Fowler, UFOs: Interplane-
tary Visitors (Jericho, N.Y.: Expo-
sition, 1974), p.354.

New Bedford
-Biofeedback research
1960s/Veterans Administration hospital
Thomas Mulholland & S. Runnals, "Evaluation of Attention and Alertness
with a Stimulus-Brain Feedback
Loop," Electroencephalography &
Clinical Neurophysiology 14 (1962):
847-52.
Thomas Mulholland & C.R. Evans, "Ocu-
lomotor Function and the Alpha Act-
ivarion Cycle," Nature 211 (1966):
1278-79.
-Derelict ship
1887, Sep.7/George Lyman Howland/"Canton"
Henry Galus, "Was God the Skipper?"
Fate 5 (Apr.-May 1952):61-64.
-Fall of frogs
1948, July 26
"Green Rain Again," Doubt, no.23
(1948):350.
-Haunt
1974, Oct.-1975, Jan.
Fred W. Mathews & Gerald F. Solfvin,

"A Case of RSPK in Massachusetts,"
in J.D. Morris, et al., eds., Research in Parapsychology 1976 (Metuchen, N.J.: Scarecrow, 1977), pp.
223-27.
-Poltergeist
1975, Feb.
Fred W. Mathews & Gerald F. Solfvin,
"A Case of RSPK in Massachusetts,"
in J.D. Morris, et al., eds., Research in Parapsychology 1976 (Metuchen, N.J.: Scarecrow, 1977), pp.
219-23.
-UFO (DD)
1974, Nov.4/I-195 nr. Reed Rd.
Donald R. Todd, "Huge UFOs in Eastern U.S.A.," APRO Bull. 23 (Jan.-
Feb.1975):1,4.
-UFO (R-V)
1960, Aug.26/Nat'l Space Surveillance
Control Center
Harlan Wilson, "Strange Case of the
Mystery Satellite," Fate 14 (June
1961):25,26-27.

Newbury
-Poltergeist
1679, Nov.27-1680, Feb./William Morse
Increase Mather, Remarkable Providences (Boston: Joseph Browning,
1684), reprinted in George Lincoln
Burr, ed., Narratives of the Witchcraft Cases 1648-1706 (N.Y.: Barnes
& Noble,1946 ed.), pp.8,23-32.
Joshua Coffin, A Sketch of the History of Newbury, Newburyport, and
West Newbury (Boston: S.G. Drake,
1845), pp.122-35.
Mrs. E. Vale Smith, History of Newburyport (Newburyport: Damrell &
Moore, 1854), pp.28-33.
Samuel G. Drake, Annals of Witchcraft
in New England (Boston: W.E. Woodward, 1869), pp.141-50,258-96.

Newburyport
-Ancient cellar
Watts Cellar/Market Square
"An Archeological Dig for Watts'
Cellar?" NEARA Newsl. 7 (Sep.1972):
60.
-Haunt
1700s/Jeremy Probart
James Reynolds, Ghosts in American
Houses (N.Y.: Paperback Library,
1967 ed.), pp.171-78.
-Phantom carriage
n.d./Peter Rugg's gig
Pauline Saltzman, Ghosts and Other
Strangers (N.Y.: Lancer, 1972 ed.),
pp.81-84.
-Poltergeist
1870, Oct.-1875/Lucy Perkins/32 Charles
St.
H.R. Davis, Exposé of Newburyport
Eccentricities, Witches and Witch-
craft (Newburyport: The Author,
1873).
"Newburyport's Haunted Schoolhouse,"
Yankee, Sep.1964.

Pauline Saltzman, Ghosts and Other
Strangers (N.Y.: Lancer, 1972 ed.),
pp.74-80.
-UFO (?)
1954, June
Donald E. Keyhoe, Flying Saucer Conspiracy (N.Y.: Holt, 1955), p.164.
-UFO (DD)
1954, April 26/Russell M. Peirce/high
school
Richard Hall, ed., The UFO Evidence
(Washington: NICAP, 1964), pp.66-67.
-Witchcraft
n.d./Mrs. Morse/Market x High St.
Charles M. Skinner, Myths and Legends
of Our Own Land, 2 vols. (Philadelphia: Lippincott, 1896), 1:232.

Newton
-Mystery gas
1928, May/William M. Duncan
New York Sun, 22 May 1928.

Norfolk co.
-UFO (DD)
1957, Oct.8/Joseph L. Flynn
New York World Telegram & Sun, 8
Oct.1957.
New York Daily Mirror, 9 Oct.1957.

North Adams
-Snow worms
1892, Feb./S.F. Clark/Blackinton
"Insects on the Surface of Snow,"
Insect Life 4 (1892):335-36.
-UFO (CE-1)
1968, Nov./Mrs. Gigliotti
"More U.S.A. November Reports," APRO
Bull. 16 (Jan.-Feb.1968):6-7.
1975, Nov.17
"UFO Central," CUFOS News Bull., 1
Feb.1976, p.13.

Northampton
-Fall of anomalous hailstones
1870, June 20
Horace C. Hovey, "The Hail-storm of
June 20th, 1870," Am.J.Sci., ser.2,
50 (1870):403-404.
William Ferrel, A Popular Treatise
on the Winds (N.Y.: John Wiley,
1911), p.425.
-Photographic anomaly
1972, Sep.24/Stella Lansing
Berthold Eric Schwarz, "Stella Lan-
sing's Clocklike UFO Patterns," Fly-
ing Saucer Rev. 20 (Jan.1975):3,4-
5. il.
-UFO (NL)
1961, Sep./Stella Lansing
Berthold Eric Schwarz, "Stella Lan-
sing's Movies: Four Entities and a
Possible UFO," in UFO Encounters
(Flying Saucer Rev. special issue,
no.5, Nov.1973), p.2.
-Witch trial (hex)
1674, July/Mary Parsons
Sylvester Judd, History of Hadley
(Northampton: Metcalf, 1863), p.233.
Samuel G. Drake, Annals of Witchcraft

in New England (Boston: W.E. Woodward, 1869), pp.134-36.
1679, March/Mrs. John Stebbins
Samuel G. Drake, Annals of Witchcraft
in New England (Boston: W.E. Woodward, 1869), pp.140-41.

Northboro
-UFO (NL)
1909, Dec.23
Providence (R.I.) Journal, 24 Dec.
1909.

Northfield
-Ancient stone constructions
King Philip's Hill
Greenfield Recorder, 24 Mar.1977.
Andrew Rothovius, "The Berkshires
Sites," NEARA J. 12 (spring 1978):
71.

North Grafton
-UFO (NL)
1909, Dec.23
Providence (R.I.) Journal, 24 Dec.
1909.

North Reading
-UFO (CE-1)
1976, April 19
Raymond E. Fowler, "MUFON Quarterly
UFO Activity Report," MUFON UFO J.,
no.104 (July 1976):3.

North Scituate
-UFO (?)
1960, Sep.10
Richard Hall, ed., The UFO Evidence
(Washington: NICAP, 1964), p.17.

Norton
-Hex
n.d.
George F. Clark, A History of the
Town of Norton, Bristol County,
Massachusetts (Boston: Crosby,
Nichols, 1859), pp.532-33.
-UFO (?)
1976, Dec.17
P.J. Willis, "Old McCarthy Had a
Pond," INFO J., no.22 (Mar.1977):14.
-UFO (DD)
1967, July/Ethel Rogers
"Massachusetts Reader Sees Three
UFO's," Skylook, no.30 (May 1970):7.
-UFO (NL)
1968, May/Ethel Rogers/Hwy.123
"Massachusetts Reader Sees Three
UFO's," Skylook, no.30 (May 1970):7.

Oak Bluffs
-Ancient inscription
19th c.
Frederick J. Pohl, Atlantic Cross-
ings Before Columbus (N.Y.: W.W.
Norton, 1961), pp.199-200.

Onset
-Spirit mediums
1880s-1890s/Etta Roberts

"Camp Meetings in America," Light 4
(1884):335.
(Letter), Susan E. Gay, Light 4
(1884):355.
Nandor Fodor, Encyclopaedia of Psychic Science (London: Arthurs,
1933), p.331, quoting Light, 19
Dec.1891.

Orange
-Spirit medium
1908/Fred E. Foskett
Prescott F. Hall, "Report of Five
Test Experiments," J.ASPR 3 (1909):
36-53.

Orleans
-Skyquake
1948, July-Sep.25
"Explosions, Etc.," Doubt, no.23
(1948):349.

Oxford
-UFO (?)
1967, Feb./=hoax
Philip J. Klass, UFOs--Identified
(N.Y.: Random House, 1968), pp.140-
41, quoting Worcester Evening Gazette (undated).

Palmer
-Contactee, UFOs, and photographic anomalies
1965-   /Stella Lansing
Berthold Eric Schwarz, "Stella Lan-
sing's UFO Motion Pictures," Flying
Saucer Rev. 18 (Jan.-Feb.1972):3-
12,19. il.
Berthold Eric Schwarz, "Stella Lan-
sing's Movies: Four Entities and a
Possible UFO," in UFO Encounters
(Flying Saucer Rev. special issue,
no.5, Nov.1973), pp.2-10. il.
Berthold Eric Schwarz, "Stella Lan-
sing's Clocklike UFO Patterns," Fly-
ing Saucer Rev. 20 (Jan.1975):3-9;
(Mar.1975):20-27; (Apr.1975):18-22;
21 (June 1975):14-17. il.
(Letter), David K. Bowman, Flying
Saucer Rev. 21 (June 1975):29-30.
I. Grattan-Guinness, "A Note on the
Significance of Stella Lansing,"
Flying Saucer Rev. 21 (Aug.1975):23.
Berthold Eric Schwarz, "Commentary
on the August Roberts Mystery," Fly-
ing Saucer Rev. 21 (Apr.1976):18-19.
Berthold Eric Schwarz, "UFO Con-
tactee Stella Lansing: Possible
Medical Implications of Her Motion
Picture Experiment," J.Am.Soc'y
Psychosomatic Med.& Dentistry 23,
no.2 (1976):60-68.
Brad Steiger, Gods of Aquarius (N.Y.:
Harcourt Brace Jovanovich, 1976),
pp.189-95. il.

Peabody
-UFO (CE-1)
1966, April 19/Hwy.114
Jacques Vallee, Passport to Magonia

(Chicago: Regnery, 1969), p.329.
Raymond E. Fowler, UFOs: Interplanetary Visitors (Jericho, N.Y.: Exposition, 1974), p.339.
-UFO (NL)
1966, April 18
Raymond E. Fowler, UFOs: Interplanetary Visitors (Jericho, N.Y.: Exposition, 1974), p.338.

Pelham
-Ancient underground structure
Packardville Rd.
Jim Brandon, Weird America (N.Y.:
Dutton, 1978), pp.110-11.

Pepperell
-UFO (NL)
1979, Jan.1/Paula Clapp/Oakland Rd.
East Pepperell Times-Free Press, 3
Jan.1979.

Phillipston
-UFO (NL)
1967, March 10
1967, April 21/Duck Pond
Raymond E. Fowler, UFOs: Interplanetary Visitors (Jericho, N.Y.: Exposition, 1974), pp.346,348.
1976, Dec.20/Gordon Tallman
Orange Enterprise & Journal, 22 Dec.
1976.

Pigeon Cove
-Sea monster
1886, Aug.12/Granville B. Putnam
New York Sun, 14 Aug.1886, p.1; and
20 Aug.1886, p.1.
New York Times, 14 Aug.1886, p.1.

Pinehurst
-Eyeless vision
1964/Linda Anderson/Albion Rd.
(Editorial), Fate 18 (Jan.1965):8-9.

Pittsfield
-Anomalous artifact
1815/=Jewish phylactery
Ethan Smith, View of the Hebrews
(Poultney, Vt.: Smith & Shute,
1825).
-Phantom train
1958, Feb.-March/John Quirk/nr. North
St. Bridge
"The Pittsfield Ghost Train," Fate
11 (Sep.1958):75.
-Retrocognition
1946-1966/Francis J. Sibolski
Francis J. Sibolski, "The Phantom
Fighters," Fate 20 (Jan.1967):101-
106.
-UFO (NL)
1908, summer
New York Sun, 1 Nov.1908.

Plymouth
-Ancient standing stones
John Finch, "On the Celtic Antiquities of America," Am.J.Sci., ser.1,
7 (1824):149-61.

-Fall of frogs
  1926, summer/Priscilla Alden Draffone
    (Letter), Fate 13 (Aug.1960):114-16.
-Retrocognition
  1955, summer/Erin Murphy
    Frank Reeds, "A Summer of Theatre's
    Phantom Players," Fate 10 (Apr.
    1957):82-85.
-Sea monster
  1875, July 17/Joseph Garton/"Norman"
    Decatur (Ill.) Republican, 1 Sep.
    1875, p.1.
    J.G. Wood, "The Trail of the Sea-
    Serpent," Atlantic Monthly 53 (1884)
    :799,810.
-UFO (NL)
  1956, July 26
    "Case 192," CRIFO Orbit, 5 Oct.1956,
    p.1, quoting Concord Monitor (un-
    dated).
-Witchcraft
  n.d./Deborah Burden
    William Root Bliss, The Old Colony
    Town, and Other Sketches (Boston:
    Houghton Mifflin, 1893), pp.108-11.

Pocasset
-Norse ship
  1958/Albert Wheeler
    Charles Michael Boland, They All Dis-
    covered America (N.Y.: Pocket Books,
    1963 ed.), pp.402-403. il.

Provincetown
-Acoustic anomaly
  1929, Jan./"Bruin"
    Vincent H. Gaddis, "Cape Cod's
    Strangest Mystery," Fate 3 (Mar.
    1950):43-46.
-Ancient wall
  Cottage x Tremont St.
    Edward J. Lenik, "The 'Norse Wall'
    Stone at Provincetown, Mass.," NEARA
    Newsl. 8 (summer 1973):37.
-Phantoms and UFO (CE-1)
  1966, fall
    John A. Keel, "North America 1966:
    Development of a Great Wave," Fly-
    ing Saucer Rev. 13 (Mar.-Apr.1967):
    3,5.
-Sea monster
  ca.1886/George Washington Ready/Pas-
  ture Pond
    Herman A. Jennings, Provincetown
    (Yarmouthport: F. Hallett, 1890),
    pp.172-75.
    Charles M. Skinner, Myths and Legends
    of Our Own Land, 2 vols. (Philadel-
    phia: Lippincott, 1896), 2:280-81.
-Sea monster (carcass)
  1939/Herring Cove Beach
    Bernard Heuvelmans, In the Wake of
    the Sea-Serpents (N.Y.: Hill & Wang,
    1968), p.464.
-UFO (R-V)
  1950, Sep.21
    J. Allen Hynek, The Hynek UFO Report
    (N.Y.: Dell, 1977), pp.139-41.
  1978, Aug.27/Arthur Silva/10 mi.NNW
    Raymond E. Fowler, "Pilot/Radar

Sighting," MUFON UFO J., no.129
  (Aug.1978):5-7.

Quincy
-Fall of pebbles
  1963, July 21/Isabel Urick/Wonder Bowl
    (Editorial), Fate 16 (Nov.1963):8-9,
    quoting Boston Record-American (un-
    dated).
-Land monster
  1964, Nov.13-15/Toni Ruggiano/St.
  Mary's Cemetery
    (Editorial), Fate 18 (Mar.1965):21-
    22, quoting Boston Traveller (un-
    dated).
-Spirit medium
  1850s/Joseph D. Siles
    Josiah Brigham, Twelve Messages from
    the Spirit of John Quincy Adams
    (Boston: Bela Marsh, 1859).
    Slater Brown, The Heyday of Spirit-
    ualism (N.Y.: Pocket Books, 1972
    ed.), pp.236-37.
-UFO (DD)
  1947, July 7/Eugene P. Irwin/Squantum
    Boston Globe, 8 July 1947.
-UFO (NL)
  1963, July 25/Richard Pothier
    "Newsman Reports Filming UFOs," UFO
    Inv. 2 (June-Sep.1963):5, quoting
    Quincy Patriot-Ledger (undated).
    "News Briefs," Saucer News 10 (Dec.
    1963):22.
  1966, April 19
  1968, Oct.19/West Quincy
    Raymond E. Fowler, UFOs: Interplane-
    tary Visitors (Jericho, N.Y.: Expo-
    sition, 1974), pp.339,354.
  1975, Sep.11
    "UFO Central," CUFOS News Bull., 15
    Nov.1975, p.18.
  1975, Otc.3
    "UFO Central," CUFOS News Bull., 1
    Feb.1976, p.7.

Rehoboth
-Haunt
  1940s-1964/Doris Armfield
    Hans Holzer, Yankee Ghosts (N.Y.:
    Ace, 1966), pp.173-76.
-UFO (CE-1)
  1966, March 30/Joseph Moitoza
    Gordon I.R. Lore, Jr. & Harold H. Den-
    eault, Jr., Mysteries of the Skies:
    UFOs in Perspective (Englewood
    Cliffs, N.J.: Prentice-Hall, 1968),
    pp.178-79.
    Raymond E. Fowler, UFOs: Interplane-
    tary Visitors (Jericho, N.Y.: Expo-
    sition, 1974), pp.125-27.
-UFO (NL)
  1910, Dec./Florence M. Varley/Hwy.118
    Gordon I.R. Lore, Jr. & Harold H. Den-
    eault, Jr., Mysteries of the Skies:
    UFOs in Perspective (Englewood
    Cliffs, N.J.: Prentice-Hall, 1968),
    p.101.

Revere
-Phantom panther

1972, Jan.
Washington (D.C.) Post, 13 Jan.1972.
-UFO (?)
1968, June 21/=ball lightning?
Raymond E. Fowler, UFOs: Interplanetary Visitors (Jericho, N.Y.: Exposition, 1974), p.353.

Rockland
-UFO (NL)
1963, June 26
Richard Hall, ed., The UFO Evidence
(Washington: NICAP, 1964), p.140.

Rockport
-UFO (?)
1967, Aug.2/Henry L. Witham, Jr./=
flare
"Worldwide Sightings Showing
Increase," UFO Inv. 4 (Oct.1967):
1,3.
"Cape Ann Sightings Reevaluated,"
UFO Inv. 4 (Nov.-Dec.1967):3.
Edward U. Condon, ed., Scientific
Study of Unidentified Flying Objects
(N.Y.: Bantam, 1969 ed.), pp.339-
41.
-UFO (NL)
1967, Nov.28
Raymond E. Fowler, UFOs: Interplane-
tary Visitors (Jericho, N.Y.: Expo-
sition, 1974), p.350.
-Witchcraft
n.d./Tammy Younger
1740s/Margaret Wesson
George Willis Solley, Alluring Rock-
port (Rockport: G. Butman, 1925).

Rowe
-Ancient stone construction
Andrew Rothovius, "The Berkshires
Sites," NEARA J. 12 (spring 1978):
71.

Rowley
-UFO (CE-1)
1966, Dec.13
Raymond E. Fowler, UFOs: Interplane-
tary Visitors (Jericho, N.Y.: Expo-
sition, 1974), p.343.
1969, Aug.
David Webb & Ted Bloecher, "MUFON's
Humanoid Study Group Very Active,"
Skylook, no.93 (Aug.1975):9,10.
-UFO (NL)
1967, July 26/Rosemarie Ricker
Haverhill Gazette, 1 Aug.1967.
Raymond E. Fowler, UFOs: Interplane-
tary Visitors (Jericho, N.Y.: Expo-
sition, 1974), pp.151-52.
-Witch trial (?)
1652, Sep./John Bradstreet
Joseph B. Felt, History of Ipswich,
Essex, and Hamilton (Cambridge: C.
Folsom, 1834).
Charles W. Upham, Salem Witchcraft,
2 vols. (Boston: Wiggin & Lunt,
1867).

Rutland
-Ancient inscription
ca.1800/W. White
Jedediah Morse, American Universal
Geography, 3 vols. (Boston: J.T.
Buckingham, 1805), 1:394.
Edmund Burke Delabarre, Dighton Rock
(N.Y.: Walter Neale, 1928), p.279.

Salem
-Alchemy
1720/North x Essex St.
Charles M. Skinner, Myths and Legends
of Our Own Land, 2 vols. (Philadelphia: Lippincott, 1896), 1:296-98.
-Midday darkness
1780, May 19
1825, Oct.8
Joseph B. Felt, Annals of Salem
(Boston: James Munroe, 1849), p.143.
-Psychic photography
ca.1940/Joseph Dunninger/Rebecca Nurse
house
Berthold Eric Schwarz, "Stella Lansing's Clocklike UFO Patterns: Part
3," Flying Saucer Rev. 20 (Apr.
1975):18,19.
-Sea monster
1818, Aug.1
Bernard Heuvelmans, In the Wake of
the Sea Serpents (N.Y.: Hill & Wang,
1968), p.166.
-Spirit medium
1850s-1880s/Charles H. Foster
Thomas P. Barkas, Outlines of Ten
Years Investigations into the Phenomena of Modern Spiritualism (Lon-
don: F. Pitman, 1862).
John Ashburner, Notes and Studies in
the Philosophy of Animal Magnetism
and Spiritualism (London: H. Bal-
lière, 1867).
Epes Sargent, Planchette: or, The
Despair of Science (Boston: Roberts
Bros., 1869).
Emma Hardinge Britten, Modern Ameri-
can Spiritualism (N.Y.: The Author,
1870), p.196.
John W. Truesdell, Bottom Facts Concerning the Science of Spiritualism
(N.Y.: G.W. Carleton, 1883).
George C. Bartlett, The Salem Seer
(N.Y.: Lovell, Gestefeld, 1891).
Adin Ballou, Autobiography 1803-1890
(Lowell, Mass.: Vox Populi, 1896).
Nandor Fodor, Encyclopaedia of Psy-
chic Science (London: Arthurs,
1933), p.143.
Slater Brown, The Heyday of Spirit-
ualism (N.Y.: Pocket Books, 1972
ed.), pp.215-23.
-UFO (?)
1950, fall
E. Macer-Story, "Contactee: The Mon-
roe Example," Ufology 2 (fall 1976):
29.
1952, July 16/Shell Alpert/Coast Guard
Air Station/=reflection?
Donald H. Menzel & Lyle G. Boyd, The
World of Flying Saucers (Garden

City, 1963), p.122. il.
Richard Hall, ed., The UFO Evidence
(Washington: NICAP, 1964), p.88.
Coral E. Lorenzen, Flying Saucers:
The Startling Evidence of the Inva-
sion from Outer Space (N.Y.: Signet,
1966 ed.), p.40.
Raymond E. Fowler, UFOs: Interplane-
tary Visitors (Jericho, N.Y.: Expo-
sion, 1974), p.94.
Brad Steiger, ed., Project Blue Book
(N.Y.: Ballantine, 1976), betw.pp.
360-61. il.
J. Allen Hynek, The Hynek UFO Report
(N.Y.: Dell, 1977), pp.231-34. il.
-UFO (CE-1)
1965, Aug.15
Raymond E. Fowler, UFOs: Interplanetary Visitors (Jericho, N.Y.: Exposition, 1974), p.333.
-UFO (NL)
1965, Oct.2/James Centorino/New England Power Station
1965, Nov./Francis Burnham/Dearborn St.
Raymond E. Fowler, UFOs: Interplanetary Visitors (Jericho, N.Y.: Exposition, 1974), pp.94-96.

Salisbury
-Witch trial (?)
1669-1674/Susannah Martin
Samuel G. Drake, Annals of Witchcraft
in New England (Boston: W.E. Woodward, 1869), pp.128-29.

Scituate
-Photographic anomaly
1973, April 30/Stella Lansing/flea
market
Berthold Eric Schwarz, "Stella Lan-
sing's Clocklike UFO Patterns,"
Flying Saucer Rev. 20 (Jan.1975):3,
4.
-Sea monster (carcass)
1970, Nov.15/=basking shark
"We're Sorry, But It Was a Shark,"
Pursuit 4 (Jan.1971):10-11.
-UFO (NL)
1972, April 20
Raymond E. Fowler, UFOs: Interplane-
tary Visitors (Jericho, N.Y.: Expo-
sition, 1974), p.358.
-Witch trial (shape-shifting)
1660/Mrs. William Holmes
Samuel Deane, History of Scituate,
Massachusetts (Boston: J. Loring,
1831), p.152.

Sharon
-UFO (NL)
1965, Oct.
1966, April 19/Bernard Coffee/7 Holly
Lane
1967, March 1
Donald E. Keyhoe & Gordon I.R. Lore,
Jr., UFOs: A New Look (Washington:
NICAP, 1969), p.13.
Raymond E. Fowler, UFOs: Interplane-
tary Visitors (Jericho, N.Y.: Expo-
sition, 1974), pp.128-30,335,345.

1970, June 25/Joy Barish
(Letter), Fate 24 (Feb.1971):160-61.
Raymond E. Fowler, UFOs: Interplanetary Visitors (Jericho, N.Y.: Exposition, 1974), p.356.

Shrewsbury
-Disappearance
1961, Sep./Alice Dorton/5 days only
(Editorial), Fate 15 (May 1962):22.

Shutesbury
-Ancient stone chamber
Great Altar Shrine
William B. Goodwin, The Ruins of
Great Ireland in New England (Bos-
ton: Meador, 1946), p.409.
Andrew Rothovius, "The Berkshires
Sites," NEARA J. 12 (spring 1978):
71-72. il.

Somerville
-Haunt
n.d.
Charles M. Skinner, Myths and Legends
of Our Own Land, 2 vols. (Philadel-
phia: Lippincott, 1896), 1:249-51.
Edward A. Samuels & Henry A. Kimball,
Somerville Past and Present (Bos-
ton: The Authors, 1897), p.42.
1886, Feb./T.H. Mayo/Linwood x Wash-
ington St.
New York Herald, 2 Mar.1886, p.4.
1964-1965/Marsha Campano/Washington St.
Hans Holzer, Yankee Ghosts (N.Y.:
Ace, 1966), pp.162-70.
-UFO (CE-3)
1938, summer/Malcolm B. Perry
Gordon I.R. Lore, Jr. & Harold H. Den-
eault, Jr., Mysteries of the Skies:
UFOs in Perspective (Englewood
Cliffs, N.J.: Prentice-Hall, 1968),
pp.136-37.

Southampton
-Precognition
1840s-1850s/Josiah A. Gridley
Josiah A. Gridley, Astounding Facts
from the Spirit World (Southampton:
The Author, 1854).

South Ashburnham
-UFO (CE-4)
1967, Jan.25/Betty Ann Andreasson
Raymond E. Fowler, The Andreasson
Affair (Englewood Cliffs, N.J.:
Prentice-Hall, 1979). il.

Southbridge
-UFO (CE-1)
1975, Oct.26
"UFO Central," CUFOS News Bull., 1
Feb.1976, p.10.
-UFO (NL)
1975, Oct.29
"UFO Central," CUFOS News Bull., 1
Feb.1976, p.10.

South Dartmouth
-UFO (DD)

1955, Oct.23/Kenneth S. Pickering
(Letter), Fate 10 (July 1957):113.
-UFO (NL)
1954, July 1
Donald E. Keyhoe, Flying Saucer Con-
spiracy (N.Y.: Holt, 1955), p.179.

South Hadley
-Anomalous artifact
1930s/Oxbow Flats/=Acheulean hand axe
"What Is This Acheulean Hand Axe Do-
ing in a New World Context?" NEARA
J. 12 (spring 1978):73. il.

South Lee
-UFO (CE-2)
1957, Oct.24/Beverly Potter
Ted Phillips, Physical Traces Associ-
ated with UFO Sightings (Evanston:
Center for UFO Studies, 1975), p.21.

South Royalston
-Phantom panther
1953/New Boston Rd.
Bruce S. Wright, The Eastern Panther
(Toronto: Clarke, Irwin, 1972), p.
104.

Springfield
-Ball lightning
1898, summer/Leonard B. Loeb
W.J. Humphreys, "Ball Lightning,"
Proc.Am.Phil.Soc'y 76 (1936):613-26.
-Ghost
1869, May/hotel
Springfield Republican, 14 May 1869.
-Midday darkness
1881, Sep.6
Springfield Republican, 6 Sep.1881.
-Poltergeist
1959, Jan.4-16/Clayton Papineau/7 But-
ler St.
John C. Parker, "The Exploding Win-
dows of Springfield, Mass.," Fate
12 (May 1959):61-65.
(Editorial), Fate 12 (June 1959):27.
-Possession
ca.1645
Montague Summers, The Geography of
Witchcraft (Secaucus, N.J.: Citadel,
1965 ed.), p.257.
-Spirit medium
1850s
Emma Hardinge Britten, Modern Ameri-
can Spiritualism (N.Y.: The Author,
1870), pp.169-70.
1852-1855/Daniel Dunglas Home
D.D. Home, Incidents of My Life, 2
vols. (N.Y.: Carleton, 1863-72).
Mde. Dunglas Home, D.D. Home: His
Life and Mission (London: Trübner,
1888).
Mde. Dunglas Home, The Gift of D.D.
Home (London: Kegan Paul, Trench &
Trübner, 1890).
Jean Burton, Heyday of a Wizard
(N.Y.: Knopf, 1944).
-Spontaneous human combustion
1954, Feb./Catherine Sutton/2132 Main
St.

(Editorial), Fate 7 (Nov.1954):10.
-UFO (?)
1958, Sep.26/=meteor
"The Night of September 29," Fate
12 (Feb.1959):31,37-38.
-UFO (CE-2)
1975, Nov.3
Stan Gordon, "UFO/Creature Sightings
Continue," Skylook, no.102 (May
1976):10.
-UFO (NL)
1956, July 23/Virginia Maratea
1956, July 25/Virginia Maratea
"Case 236," CRIFO Orbit, 7 Dec.1956,
pp.1-2.
"Case 237," CRIFO Orbit, 7 Dec.1956,
p.2.
1961, July 4/Patricia Biczynski
"Cigar near Springfield, Mass.,"
APRO Bull. 10 (July 1961):4.
-Windshield pitting
1961, March 5
1961, Aug.20
(Editorial), Fate 15 (Jan.1962):20-
22.
-Witch trial (?)
1691, Sep.29/Mary Randall
Samuel G. Drake, Annals of Witchcraft
in New England (Boston: W.E. Wood-
ward, 1869), pp.185-86.
-Witch trial (hex)
1650-1651/Hugh Parsons
Edward Johnson, Wonder-Working Prov-
idence (1654), reprinted in J.
Franklin Jameson, ed., Johnson's
Wonder-Working Providence 1628-1651
(N.Y.: Scribner, 1910), p.237.
Sylvester Judd, History of Hadley
(Northampton: Metcalf, 1863).
Samuel G. Drake, Annals of Witchcraft
in New England (Boston: W.E. Wood-
ward, 1869), pp.66-72,219-58.

Sturbridge
-UFO (CE-1)
1979, Jan.2/W on Massachusetts Turnpike
Worcester Telegram, 3 Jan.1979.

Sudbury
-Fire anomaly
1965, April 28/Robert Bowen
(Editorial), Fate 18 (Sep.1965):28-
29.
-UFO (CE-1)
1974, June 18
Dave Webb & John Oswald, "New Hampshire Report May Be a Hoax," Skylook, no.93 (Aug.1975):14.
-UFO (CE-2)
1965, Sep./Ronald Schofield/Wayside
Inn Rd.
Raymond E. Fowler, UFOs: Interplanetary Visitors (Jericho, N.Y.: Exposition, 1974), p.93.
1973, Oct.22/June Margolin
Raymond E. Fowler, "'Angel Hair':
Spider's Web or UFO's Wisp?" Ufology
2 (fall 1976):25-26. il.

Swampscott
-Dowsing
  1963, June 13/Paul A. Polisson
    Frederick H. Goddard, "Where the
    Twig Bends the Water Lies," Fate
    16 (Dec.1963):88-92.
-Precognition and clairvoyance
  1940s-1950s/Harry Ingalls
    Raymond J. Ross, "Harry Ingalls: The
    Yankee Seer," Fate 10 (May 1957):
    77-79. il.
-Sea monster
  1820, Aug.10/Andrew Reynolds/Phillip's
    Beach
    J.G. Wood, "The Trail of the Sea-
    Serpent," Atlantic Monthly 53 (1884)
    :799,806.
  1875, July 30/Arthur Lawrence/"Prin-
    cess"
    New York Times, 5 Aug.1875, p.3.
    J.G. Wood, "The Trail of the Sea-
    Serpent," Atlantic Monthly 53 (1884)
    :799,807-808.

Topsfield
-UFO (CE-1)
  1976, April 29
    Raymond E. Fowler, "MUFON Quarterly
    UFO Activity Report," MUFON UFO J.,
    no.104 (July 1976):3.
    Ray Fowler, "UFO Buzzes Air Force
    Base," Official UFO 1 (Oct.1976):
    18,48.

Truro
-Doubtful responsibility
  1844, Oct.15/"Commerce"
    Juliette Laine, "Another Unaccount-
    able Sea Tragedy," Fate 21 (Jan.
    1968):43.
-Hex
  n.d.
    Shebnah Rich, Truro--Cape Cod (Bos-
    ton: D. Lothrop, 1883), p.101.

Upton
-Ancient stone chamber
    Milford Journal, 26 Apr.1893.
    William B. Goodwin, The Ruins of
    Great Ireland in New England (Bos-
    ton: Meador, 1946), pp.41-56. il.
    James P. Whittall III, "A Report on
    the Pearson Stone-Chamber, Upton,
    Mass.," Bull.Early Sites Rsch.Soc'y
    1, no.1 (1973):12-22. il.
    Barry Fell, America B.C. (N.Y.: Quad-
    rangle, 1976), p.88. il.
-UFO (NL)
  1909, Dec.23
    Providence (R.I.) Journal, 24 Dec.
    1909.

Wakefield
-Healing
  1958, Feb./Newton Dillaway
    Lucile M. McCurtain, "Healing a Sick
    Mind," Fate 24 (Nov.1971):105-106.

Waltham
-UFO (CE-1)

1975, Sep.16
    "From the Center for UFO Studies,"
    Flying Saucer Rev. 21 (Apr.1976):
    24,26.
-UFO (DD)
  1964, Oct.7/Richard Forristall
    Raymond E. Fowler, UFOs: Interplane-
    tary Visitors (Jericho, N.Y.: Expo-
    sition, 1974), pp.24-26.
-UFO (NL)
  1968, April 19
  1971, March 27
  1972, Dec.4
    Raymond E. Fowler, UFOs: Interplane-
    tary Visitors (Jericho, N.Y.: Expo-
    sition, 1974), pp.352,357,359.

Ware
-Erratic crocodilian
  1922/Stephen Fabirkiewicz/Dismal Swamp
    Curtis D. MacDougall, Hoaxes (N.Y.:
    Dover, 1958 ed.), pp.31-32, quoting
    Ware River News (undated).
-UFO (NL)
  1908, Oct.
    New York Sun, 1 Nov.1908.

Wareham
-UFO (NL)
  1967, May 11
    Raymond E. Fowler, UFOs: Interplane-
    tary Visitors (Jericho, N.Y.: Expo-
    sition, 1974), p.348.

Warren
-Haunt
  n.d./Waternomee Falls
    Charles M. Skinner, Myths and Legends
    of Our Own Land, 2 vols. (Philadel-
    phia: Lippincott, 1896), 1:219.

Washington
-Ancient stone cairn
    Mystery Monument
      Springfield Union, 17 July 1969, p.
      31.
      Salvatore Michael Trento, The Search
      for Lost America (Chicago: Contem-
      porary, 1978), pp.143-45.

Watertown
-Electromagnetic anomaly
  1961/Andrea Whalen
    (Editorial), Fate 14 (June 1961):13.
-Erratic killer whale
  1978, April 23/Watertown High School
    Boston Globe, 24 Apr.1978.
-Haunt
  1900s/Daniel Chase
    Eva A. Speare, New Hampshire Folk
    Tales (Plymouth, N.H.: The Author,
    1964), pp.178-80.
-Norse discovery
  ca.1000/=Norumbega?
    Eben Norton Horsford, The Discovery
    of America by Northmen (Boston:
    Houghton Mifflin, 1888).
    Eben Norton Horsford, The Discovery
    of the Ancient City of Norumbega
    (Boston: Houghton Mifflin, 1890).

Eben Norton Horsford, The Defenses
of Norumbega (Boston: Houghton Mifflin, 1891).
Eben Norton Horsford, The Landfall
of Leif Erikson, A.D.1000 (Boston:
Damrell & Upham, 1892).
-UFO (DD)
1965, July 19/Sally Ann McPherson
Boston Globe, 21 July 1965.
Raymond E. Fowler, UFOs: Interplanetary Visitors (Jericho, N.Y.: Exposition, 1974), pp.67-68.
-UFO (NL)
1966, May 1/arsenal
Raymond E. Fowler, UFOs: Interplanetary Visitors (Jericho, N.Y.: Exposition, 1974), p.341.

Webster
-Ancient stone chamber
William B. Goodwin, The Ruins of
Great Ireland in New England (Bos-
ton: Meador, 1946), pp.393-95. il.
-UFO (CE-3)
1947, June 19
Worcester Daily Telegram, 7 July
1947, p.1.

Wellesley
-Contactee and clairempathy
1845-1873/William Denton
William & Elizabeth M.F. Denton, The
Soul of Things (Boston: Walker,
Wise, 1863).
William Denton, Christianity No Fi-
nality (Boston: The Author, 1870).
William Denton, Who Killed Mary Stan-
nard? (Wellesley: The Author, 1880).
Mitch Martin, "Space Travellers in
1870?" Fate 11 (Sep.1958):44-50.
-Phantom
ca.1966/Billy Squier/golf course
Timothy Green Beckley, "Saucers
and Celebrities," Saga UFO Rept. 4
(Aug.1977):18.
-Precognition
1974, Jan.
M. Dewey Bogart, "Dream Recovery,"
Fate 29 (Sep.1976):45.
-UFO (DD)
1960, Dec.11/Wellesley Hills
"Bright Objects at Norwell, Massa-
chusetts," APRO Bull. 9 (Jan.1961):
3.

Wendell
-Ancient underground structure
Mt. Mineral
Jim Brandon, Weird America (N.Y.:
Dutton, 1978), p.111.

Wendell Depot
-Spirit medium
1927-   /Elwood Babbitt
Charles H. Hapgood, Voices of Spirit
(N.Y.: Leisure Books, 1975).
Herbert B. Greenhouse, The Astral
Journey (N.Y.: Avon, 1976), pp.165,
228-36.

Wenham
-Ball lightning
1673, May 18/Richard Goldsmith
Increase Mather, Remarkable Providences (Boston: Samuel Green,
1683), ch.3.
-UFO (NL)
1947, July 5
1947, July 6/A.H. Pembroke
Boston Traveller, 7 July 1947.
1966, April 22/Vivian Russell/Gordon
College
Raymond E. Fowler, UFOs: Interplanetary Visitors (Jericho, N.Y.: Exposition, 1974), p.136.

West Barnstable
-Witchcraft
n.d./Liza Tower Hill
Amos Otis, Genealogical Notes of
Barnstable Families (Barnstable:
F.B. & F.P. Goss, 1888-90), p.101.

Westboro
-Precognition and clairvoyance
1960s/Ted Rabouin/Bowman St.
Raymond A. LaJoie, "Ted Rabouin:
New England Warlock," Fate 24 (Mar.
1970):38-46. il.

Westfield
-Poltergeist
1972, Nov.-1973, Dec./James Fanion
(Editorial), Fate 27 (July 1974):34,
quoting Springfield Union, Dec.
1973.
-UFO (?)
1787, Aug.23/=meteor?
(Editorial), APRO Bull., May 1957,
quoting Noah Atwater's Diary.
-UFO (CE-2)
1955
Timothy Green Beckley, "Saucers and
Celebrities," Saga UFO Rept. 3
(Oct.1976):40,41.
-UFO (CE-3)
1955/Dotty Buckowski
Timothy Green Beckley, "Saucers and
Celebrities," Saga UFO Rept. 3
(Oct.1976):40,41.
-UFO (NL)
1962, May 26/Hwy.23 nr. Hwy.20
Jacques Vallee, Anatomy of a Phenom-
enon (N.Y.: Ace, 1965 ed.), p.212.

Westford
-Ancient inscription
"New England Stone Puzzles Recently
Brought to NEARA's Attention,"
NEARA Newsl. 9 (spring 1974):19. il.
-Medieval inscription
Depot St.
Frank Glynn, "A Unique Punched Por-
trait in Massachusetts," Bull.East-
ern States Arch.Federation, no.16
(Jan.1957).
Lawrence F. Willard, "Westford's
Mysterious Knight," Yankee 22
(1958):60-61,84-89.
Roland Wells Robbins & Evan Jones,

Hidden America (N.Y.: Knopf, 1959),
pp.145-47. il.
William S. Fowler, "The Westford In-
dian Rock," Bull.Mass.Arch.Soc'y 21
(Jan.1960):21-22.
Charles Michael Boland, They All Dis-
covered America (N.Y.: Pocket Books,
1963 ed.), pp.376-77. il.
Andrew E. Rothovius, "The Scotsman
Who Discovered America," Fate 16
(Aug.1963):26-31. il.
Iain Moncrieffe, The Highland Clans
(N.Y.: Clarkson N. Potter, 1967),
pp.160-68. il.
Frank Glynn, "A Second Medieval Mark-
er at Westford, Mass.," Bull.East-
ern States Arch.Federation, no.26
(1967):14.
Frederick J. Pohl, Prince Henry Sin-
clair (N.Y.: Clarkson N. Potter,
1974), pp.155-67.
-UFO (CE-2)
1964
"Astronomers and UFO's: A Survey,
Part 2," Int'l UFO Reporter 2 (Apr.
1977):3,4.

West Newbury
-Ancient inscription
Hanging Rock
G.L. Pool, "An Antiquity Discovered
in the Valley of the Merrimack,"
New England Hist.& Geneal.Register
8 (1854):185. il.
Edmund Burke Delabarre, Dighton Rock
(N.Y.: Walter Neale, 1928), pp.279-
80.
Olaf Strandwold, Norse Inscriptions
on American Stones (Weehauken, N.J.:
Magnus Björndal, 1948), pp.27-29.
il.
Laurie D. Williams, "Rediscovery of
the 'Whittier Runestone' in Massa-
chusetts," NEARA J. 6 (fall 1976):
22-24. il.
-Ancient stone chamber
James P. Whittall II & Laurie Will-
iams, "A Report on the Emergy Stone
Chamber, West Newbury, Mass.," Bull.
Early Sites Rsch.Soc'y 1, no.1
(1973):409. il.
-Shape-shifting
1790s/Mrs. Sloper
Charles M. Skinner, Myths and Legends
of Our Own Land, 2 vols. (Philadelphia: Lippincott, 1896), 1:232.

Weston
-Healing
1976, Nov./Walter M. Abbott
(Editorial), Fate 30 (June 1977):24-
28.
-Norse runestone
Cornelia Horsford, An Inscribed Stone
(Cambridge: J. Wilson, 1895). il.
Salvatore Michael Trento, The Search
for Lost America (Chicago: Contem-
porary, 1978), pp.160-62.
-UFO (NL)
1966, Jan.14

J. Allen Hynek, The UFO Experience
(Chicago: Regnery, 1972), pp.37-38,
45-47.
1966, April 16
Raymond E. Fowler, UFOs: Interplanetary Visitors (Jericho, N.Y.: Exposition, 1974), p.337.

Westport
-Ancient standing stones
Daniel Ricketson, The History of
New Bedford (New Bedford: The Auth-
or, 1858).
James P. Whittall, Jr., "The Hassa-
neghk Dolmen," NEARA Newsl. 4
(June 1969):38-39, il.
Barry Fell, America B.C. (N.Y.: Quad-
rangle, 1976), pp.131-32. il.
-UFO (CE-1)
1966, June 11/Ronald Petit/Hwy.88
Boston Traveller, 13 June 1966.

West Springfield
-UFO (?)
1947, July 7
Boston Globe, 8 July 1947.

West Stockbridge
-Elastic marble
C. Dewey, "Notice of the Flexible
or Elastic Marble of Berkshire
County," Am.J.Sci., ser.1, 9
(1825):241-42.

Westwood
-Telepathy
1955, June 4/Thomas Whittaker/Wash-
ington St.
"Saved by a Premonition," Fate 8
(Oct.1955):67.
Betty & Fraser Nicol, "Buried Alive:
Saved by Telepathy," Tomorrow 5
(spring 1957):9-13.
J. Fraser & Betty Nicol, "Investiga-
tion of a Curious 'Hunch,'" J.ASPR
52 (1958):24-34.

West Wrentham
-Ancient inscription
Harris H. Wilder, "A Petroglyph from
Eastern Massachusetts," Am.Anthro.
13 (1911):65.
Edmund Burke Delabarre, Dighton Rock
(N.Y.: Walter Neale, 1928), p.259.

Weymouth
-UFO (CE-1)
1963, June 26/Enrico Gilberti/North
Weymouth
Raymond E. Fowler, UFOs: Interplanetary Visitors (Jericho, N.Y.: Exposition, 1974), pp.3-7.
-UFO (NL)
1965, July 31/Edwin Finley/North Weymouth
1969, Jan.20
Raymond E. Fowler, UFOs: Interplanetary Visitors (Jericho, N.Y.: Exposition, 1974), pp.69,355.

Whately
-Telephone anomaly
  1927, March/=practical joke
    E.W. Rogers II, "The Haunted Tele-
    phone," Fate 30 (Jan.1977):68.
    (Letter), J.S. Lankowski, Fate 30
    (June 1977):113.
-UFO (NL)
  1971, Jan.6/Joseph Korpiewski
    "Press Reports," APRO Bull. 19 (Jan.-
    Feb.1971):6-7.

Whitinsville
-Healing
  1950s/Agnes Sanford
    Alson J. Smith, "Healing in Today's
    Churches," Fate 10 (Sep.1957):53,54.

Whitman
-Haunt
  1972-1973/David English
    "Who's Been Sleeping in My Bed?"
    Probe the Unknown 1 (Dec.1973):64.
    "A Haunted Bed," Fate 27 (Aug.1974):
    53, quoting Brockton Daily Enter-
    prise (undated).
-Precognition
  n.d./Mrs. James Dorey
    (Editorial), Fate 9 (Apr.1956):14.

Williamstown
-Clairvoyance
  1880, June
    "Coincidental Dream," J.ASPR 8 (1914)
    :483-500.
-Entombed bugs
  1806-1814/P.S. Putnam
    John Warner Barber, Historical Col-
    lections of Every Town in Massachu-
    setts (Worcester: Door, Howland,
    1841), pp.108-109, quoting Middle-
    bury (Vt.) Repository, 1816.

Winthrop
-Ancient lamp
  1954/James Polansky
    "Found on Beaches," Doubt, no.46
    (1954):310.

Woburn
-Ghost light
  1870/Boston & Lowell Railroad
    Burlington Daily Free Press, 12
    Feb.1870.
-Haunt
  n.d./John Flagg/Black House
  n.d./Central House
  n.d./Horn Pond
  n.d./Dunham's Pond
  n.d./Wright's Pond
    Parker L. Converse, Legends of Woburn,
    2 vols. (Woburn: The Author, 1892-
    96).
    Charles M. Skinner, American Myths
    and Legends, 2 vols. (Philadelphia:
    Lippincott, 1903), 1:73-77.
-Phantom
  n.d./First Baptist Church
    Parker L. Converse, Legends of Woburn,
    2 vols. (Woburn: The Author, 1892-

96).
-UFO (DD)
  1962, May 25/F. DiMambro
    Richard Hall, ed., The UFO Evidence
    (Washington: NICAP, 1964), p.96.

Woods Hole
-Disappearance
  1960, Aug.15-16/Kathy Cramer/1 Park
  St./8 hours only
    (Editorial), Fate 13 (Dec.1960):18-
    19.
-Snow worms
  1893, winter
    E.W. Gudger, "Snow Worms," Natural
    History 23 (1923):451-56.

Worcester
-Airplane inventor
  1909, Dec./Wallace E. Tillinghast
    New York Tribune, 24 Dec.1909, p.1.
    New York Times, 25 Dec.1909, p.3.
    John E. Keel, UFOs: Operation Trojan
    Horse (N.Y.: Putnam, 1970), pp.111-
    19.
-Exploding bottles
  1959, fall/Violet M. Reilly/12 Berk-
  mans St.
    (Editorial), Fate 13 (Mar.1960):8-10.
-Exploding refrigerator
  1955, Nov.-1959, Oct./Roland J. Bibeau/
  89 Endicott St.
    (Editorial), Fate 13 (Feb.1960):16-
    18, quoting Worcester Evening Ga-
    zette (undated).
    (Editorial), Fate 13 (Mar.1960):10.
    (Editorial), Fate 13 (July 1960):20.
-Midday darkness
  1881, Sep.6
    New York Times, 7 Sep.1881, p.5.
-Spirit medium
  1858/Mr. Paine/=fraud
    Emma Hardinge Britten, Modern Ameri-
    can Spiritualism (N.Y.: The Author,
    1870), pp.241-42.
-UFO (NL)
  1909, Dec.22
    New York Times, 23 Dec.1909, p.1.
    New York Tribune, 23 Dec.1909, p.1.

Woronoco
-Phantom panther
  1960, Nov.15/Harry N. Donaldson/Massa-
  chusetts Turnpike
    Bruce S. Wright, The Eastern Panther
    (Toronto: Clarke, Irwin, 1972), pp.
    104-105.

Worthington
-Acoustic anomaly
  1972/Jerri Bunce
    (Editorial), Fate 25 (Sep.1972):30-
    32.

Wrentham
-Medical clairvoyance
  1840s
    Emma Hardinge Britten, Modern Ameri-
    can Spiritualism (N.Y.: The Author,
    1870), pp.157-63.

Nandor Fodor, Encyclopaedia of Psychic Science (London: Arthurs,
1933), pp.11,46,390,408.
-Precognition
1734, April 19/John Day
Boston News-Letter, 2 May 1734; and
9 May 1734.

Yarmouth
-UFO (NL)
1975, Nov.1
"UFO Central," CUFOS News Bull., 1
Feb.1976, p.11.

B. Physical Features

Ann, Cape
-Phantom panther
17th c.
William Wood, New England's Prospect
(London: Thomas Cotes, 1634), ch.
vi.
-Sea monster
ca.1639
John Josselyn, An Account of Two Voyages to New England (London: Giles
Widdows, 1674), p.23.
1641
Fred A. Wilson, Some Annals of Nahant, Massachusetts (Boston: Old
Corner Book Store, 1928), p.161,
quoting Journal of Obadiah Turner,
5 Sep.1641.
1817, Aug.6
1817, Aug.28/Sewell Toppan/"Laura"/2
mi.E
1817, Aug.30?
Linnaean Soc'y of New England, Report
of a Committee of the Linnaean Society of New England, Relative to
a Large Marine Animal, Supposed to
be a Sea-Serpent (Boston: Cumming &
Hilliard, 1817).
Boston Daily Advertiser, 25 Nov.1848.
A.C. Oudemans, The Great Sea-Serpent
(Leiden: E.J. Brill, 1892), pp.163,
185-88.
1818, June 21/Shubael West/"Delia"/=
hoax?
Boston Weekly Messenger, 2 July 1818,
pp.598-99.
1879, June 20/Capt. Wells/"Aeronaut"
New York Times, 1 Aug.1879, p.4.
-UFO (?)
1645, Aug.20/Capt. Wall
John Winthrop, Winthrop's Journal,
ed. James Kendall Hosmer, 2 vols.
(N.Y.: Barnes & Noble, 1946 ed.),
2:246.

Annisquam Bay
-Sea monster
1818, Aug.12/Timothy Hodgkins
Boston Weekly Messenger, 28 Aug.1818.
1818, Aug.19/Richard Rich
1818, Sep.3/Richard Rich/=bluefin tuna
Boston Daily Advertiser, 4 Sep.1818.
Boston Weekly Messenger, 10 Sep.1818,
pp.756,758.

Jacob Bigelow, "Documents and Remarks Respecting the Sea Serpent,"
Am.J.Sci., ser.1, 2 (1820):147-49.
T.H. Perkins, "The Great Sea-Serpent," Zoologist 7 (1849):2359,
2362.
Bernard Heuvelmans, In the Wake of
the Sea-Serpents (N.Y.: Hill & Wang,
1968), pp.166-67.

Apple I.
-Ghost
1900
Edward Rowe Snow, The Islands of
Boston Harbor 1630-1971 (N.Y.: Dodd,
Mead, 1971), pp.146-47.

Assawompsett Pond
-Ancient carving
1957
Charles Michael Boland, They All Discovered America (N.Y.: Pocket Books,
1963 ed.), p.38. il.
Boston Herald, 7 Mar.1971.

Assonet Neck
-Norse discovery
1005/Thorvald Eriksson/=landing?
Charles Michael Boland, They All Discovered America (N.Y.: Pocket Books,
1963 ed.), pp.233-36.

Bass R.
-Norse discovery
1001/Leif Eriksson/=Vinland?
Abner Morse, Further Traces of the
Ancient Northmen in America (Bos-
ton: H.W. Dutton, 1861).
Frederick J. Pohl, The Lost Discovery
(N.Y.: W.W. Norton, 1952), pp.60-
68,75-77.
J.K. Tornöe, Norsemen Before Columbus
(London: George Allen & Unwin,
1965), pp.49-75.

Berkshire Hills
-Ancient standing stones
"New Information on an Interesting
Berkshires Site," NEARA Newsl. 5
(Mar.1970):7. il.
"A Remarkable Standing-Stones Site
Located," NEARA Newsl. 6 (June
1971):40.
Columbus (O.) Dispatch, 4 Aug.1971.
"The Standing-Stones Site on a West-
ern Massachusetts Mountaintop,"
NEARA Newsl. 6 (Sep.1971):60. il.
"Sites Adjacent to the Western Mass-
achusetts Standing Stones Grouping,"
NEARA Newsl. 8 (Mar.1973):20. il.
John B. Jones, Jr., "The Fall Equin-
ox at the Berkshires Standing Stones
Site," NEARA J. 12 (winter 1978):
48-50. il.
Andrew Rothovius, "The Berkshires
Sites," NEARA J. 12 (spring 1978):
71-72. il.
Marjorie R. Kling, "Statement of
NEARA Policy Regarding the 'Stand-
ing Stones Site,'" NEARA J. 12

(spring 1978):73.
Marjorie R. Kling, "The May, 1977
NEARA Finds at the Berkshires Stand-
ing Stones Sites," NEARA J. 13
(summer 1978):11-15. il.
-Out-of-body experience
1960s/Kevin Lampro
Herbert B. Greenhouse, The Astral
Journey (N.Y.: Avon, 1976 ed.), pp.
191-96.

Buffumville Reservoir
-UFO (CE-1)
1971, May 29/Warren MacCarthy
Spencer Leader, 3 June 1971.
Raymond E. Fowler, UFOs: Interplanetary Visitors (Jericho, N.Y.: Exposition, 1974), pp.178-80.

Bull Brook
-Archeological site
7500-6500 B.C.
William Eldridge & Joseph Vacaro,
"The Bull Brook Site, Ipswich, Mass-
achusetts," Bull.Mass.Arch.Soc'y 13
(1952)::39-43. il.
Douglas S. Byers, "Bull Brook: A
Fluted Point Site in Ipswich, Mass-
achusetts," Am.Antiquity 19 (1954):
343-51.
Douglas S. Byers, "Additional Infor-
mation on the Bull Brook Site, Mass-
achusetts," Am.Antiquity 20 (1955):
274-76.
Douglas S. Byers, "Ipswich B.C.,"
Bull.Mass.Arch.Soc'y 18 (1957):49-
55. il.
Douglas S. Byers, "Radiocarbon Dates
from Bull Brook," Bull.Mass.Arch.
Soc'y 20 (1959):33.
William S. Fowler, "Bull Brook: A
Paleo Complex Site," Bull.Mass.Arch.
Soc'y 34, no.1-2 (1973):1-6.

Burnt Mt.
-Ancient dolmen
Barry Fell, America B.C. (N.Y.: Quad-
rangle, 1976), pp.134,154.

Buzzards Bay
-Hex
n.d.
William Root Bliss, The Old Colony
Town, and Other Sketches (Boston:
Houghton Mifflin, 1893), pp.106-107.

Captain's Hill
-Norse discovery
1005/Thorvald Eriksson/=landfall?
J.K. Tornöe, Norsemen Before Columbus
(London: George Allen & Unwin,
1965), pp.76-84.

Clark's I.
-Haunt
n.d.
Clifton Johnson, New England: A Human
Interest Geographical Reader (N.Y.:
Macmillan, 1922), p.129.

Cod, Cape
-Fall of bituminous substance
1681, July 24/Edward Ladd/"Albemarle"
Increase Mather, Remarkable Provi-
dences (Boston: Samuel Green,
1684), ch.III.
M. Arago, "On Thunder and Lightning,"
Edinburgh New Philosophical J. 26
(1838):81,86.
-Haunt
1930s
Harlan Jacobs, "Four Months in a
Haunted House," Harper's 169 (1934)
:733-41.
-Norse discovery
986/Bjarni Herjolfsson/=landfall?
Frederick J. Pohl, The Lost Discovery
(N.Y.: W.W. Norton, 1952), pp.23-30.
1001/Leif Eriksson/=Vinland?
A.S. Packard, "Who First Saw the
Labrador Coast?" J.Am.Geogr.Soc'y
20 (1888):197-207.
William Hovgaard, The Voyages of the
Norsemen to America (N.Y.: Ameri-
can-Scandinavian Foundation, 1914).
G.M. Gathorne-Hardy, The Norse Dis-
coverers of America (Oxford: Clar-
endon, 1921), pp.251-60.
-Phantom ship
n.d.
James Reynolds, Ghosts in American
Houses (N.Y.: Paperback Library,
1967 ed.), pp.145-46.
-Sea monster
1719, Sep.17
Boston News-Letter, 21-28 Sep.1719.
1826, June 18
William J. Hooker, "Additional Tes-
timony Respecting the Sea-Serpent
of the American Seas," Edinburgh
J.Sci. 6 (1827):126.
-UFO (NL)
1963, Sep.12/Patrick Loreno/Texas
Tower II
Jim & Coral Lorenzen, UFOs over the
Americas (N.Y.: Signet, 1968), p.
53.

Crane's Beach
-UFO (DD)
1945, summer/Helen Allen
Gordon I.R. Lore, Jr. & Harold H. Den-
eault, Jr., Mysteries of the Skies:
UFOs in Perspective (Englewood
Cliffs, N.J.: Prentice-Hall, 1968),
p.148.
-UFO (NL)
1966, Sep.17/Ronald MacGilvary
"'Satellite' UFO Landing Case in
Massachusetts," UFO Inv. 3 (Oct.-
Nov.1966):4.

East Chop
-UFO (NL)
1958, April/Anne Lesnikowski
Robert N. Webster, "Things That Fall
from UFO's," Fate 11 (Oct.1958):25,
30.

Follins Pond
-Norse discovery and mooring stones
 1001/Leif Eriksson/=Vinland?
  Frederick J. Pohl, The Lost Discovery
  (N.Y.: W.W. Norton, 1952), pp.71-86,
  89-94,292-95.
  Benjamin L. Smith, "A Report on the
  Follins Pond Investigation," Bull.
  Mass.Arch.Soc'y 14 (1953):82-88.
  Frederick J. Pohl, "Comments on the
  Follins Pond Investigation," Bull.
  Mass.Arch.Soc'y 14 (1953):105-109.
  Frederick J. Pohl, "Can the Ship's
  Shoring at Follins Pond be Radio-
  carbon Dated?" Bull.Mass.Arch.Soc'y
  17 (1956):49-50.
  Frederick J. Pohl, "Further Proof of
  Vikings at Follins Pond, Cape Cod,"
  Bull.Mass.Arch.Soc'y 21 (1960):
  48-49.
  Frederick J. Pohl, Atlantic Crossings
  Before Columbus (N.Y.: W.W. Norton,
  1961), pp.93-101,103-26.
  Charles Michael Boland, They All Dis-
  covered America (N.Y.: Pocket Books,
  1963 ed.), pp.201-202,212-16.
  J.K. Tornöe, Norsemen Before Columbus
  (London: George Allen & Unwin,
  1965), pp.49-75.
  Frederick J. Pohl, The Viking Settle-
  ments of North America (N.Y.: Clarkson N. Potter, 1972), pp.31,74-76,
  184-215,222-33,253-55.

Foxboro Forest
-Ancient stone table
  William B. Goodwin, The Ruins of
  Great Ireland in New England (Bos-
  ton: Meador, 1946), pp.216,410-12.
  il.

Georges Bank
-Mystery knife embedded in codfish
 1885, Sep.15/John Q. Getchell/"Vinnie
 M. Getchell"
  E.W. Gudger, "Foreign Bodies Embedded
  in the Tissue of Fishes," Natural
  History 22 (1922):452-57. il.
-Sea monster
 1888, June 19/Ofc. Muir/"Venetian"
  New York Times, 21 June 1888, p.5.

Georges I.
-Haunt
 1860s/Fort Warren
  Edward Rowe Snow, The Islands of Bos-
  ton Harbor 1630-1971 (N.Y.: Dodd,
  Mead, 1971), p.36.

Great Point
-Norse discovery
 1001/Leif Eriksson/=Leif's island?
  Frederick J. Pohl, The Lost Discovery
  (N.Y.: W.W. Norton, 1952), pp.53-56.
  Frederick J. Pohl, The Viking Settle-
  ments of North America (N.Y.: Clark-
  son N. Potter, 1972), pp.178-83.

Gurnet Point
-Sea monster

1823, July/Mr. Weston
  Bernard Heuvelmans, In the Wake of
  the Sea-Serpents (N.Y.: Hill & Wang,
  1968), p.171.

Hingham Bay
-Sea monster
 1879, June 17
  "The Sea Serpent of 1879," Fate 16
  (Nov.1963):66-67, quoting St. Louis
  (Mo.) Post-Dispatch, Jan.1880.

Howe Pond
-UFO (DD)
 1971, May 30/Ted Fiske
  Spencer Leader, 3 June 1971.

Jeffrey's Ledge
-Sea monster
 1818, July/Capt. Spark/"Mary"/=hoax
  Boston Weekly Messenger, 23 July
  1818, p.651.

Loblolly Cove
-Sea monster (carcass)
 1817, Sep./=deformed black snake
  Linnaean Soc'y of New England, Re-
  port of a Committee of the Linnaean
  Society of New England, Relative to
  a Large Marine Animal, Supposed to
  Be a Sea-Serpent (Boston: Cumming &
  Hilliard, 1817).
  "On the History of the Great Sea-
  Serpent," Blackwood's Mag. 3 (Apr.
  1818):33-42.
  Henri-Marie Ducrotay de Blainville,
  "Sur un nouveau genre de Serpent,
  Scoliophis, et le Serpent-de-mer vu
  en Amérique en 1817," J.de phys.
  chim.et hist.nat. 86 (1818):297-304.
  Charles Alexandre Lesueur, "Sur le
  serpent nommé Scoliophis," J.de
  phys.chim.et hist.nat. 86 (1818):
  466-69.
  Bernard Heuvelmans, In the Wake of
  the Sea-Serpents (N.Y.: Hill & Wang,
  1968), pp.154-55.

Martha's Vineyard
-Ancient stone construction
  Frederick Johnson, "The Dolmen on
  Martha's Vineyard," Bull.Mass.Arch.
  Soc'y 6 (1945):29-32. il.
  William B. Goodwin, The Ruins of
  Great Ireland in New England (Bos-
  ton: Meador, 1946), p.390. il.
  Johannes Brøndsted, "Norsemen in
  North America Before Columbus," Ann.
  Rept.Smith.Inst. 103 (1953):367,398.
-Anomalous artifact
 =Polynesian adze
  Howard R. Sargent, "A Polynesian
  Adze from Martha's Vineyard," Bull.
  Mass.Arch.Soc'y 12 (1951):27-28. il.
-Sea monster
 1700
 1930
  Joseph C. Allen, Tales and Trails of
  Martha's Vineyard (Boston: Little,
  Brown, 1938), pp.229-30.

Massachusetts Bay
-Phantom ship
 n.d.
    Charles M. Skinner, American Myths
    and Legends, 2 vols. (Philadelphia:
    Lippincott, 1903), 2:218-19.
-Sea monster
 1819, Sep.
    C.S. Rafinesque, "Dissertation on
    Water Snakes, Sea Snakes and Sea
    Serpents," Phil.Mag. 54 (1819):
    361,366-67.
    A.C. Oudemans, The Great Sea-Serpent
    (Leiden: E.J. Brill, 1892), pp.219-
    20.

Mill Pond
-Norse mooring stone
    Frederick J. Pohl, The Lost Discovery
    (N.Y.: W.W. Norton, 1952), pp.79-82.
    Frederick J. Pohl, Atlantic Crossings
    Before Columbus (N.Y.: W.W. Norton,
    1961), pp.158-70.
    Frederick J. Pohl, The Viking Settle-
    ments of North America (N.Y.: Clark-
    son N. Potter, 1972), pp.249-53.

Mill R.
-Ancient inscription
    James P. Whittall II, "The Mill River
    Inscription," Bull.Early Sites Rsch.
    Soc'y 4 (May 1976):8-10. il.
    Barry Fell, America B.C. (N.Y.: Quad-
    rangle, 1976), p.89. il.

Mumford R.
-Erratic crocodilian
 1927, Nov.
    New York Times, 13 Nov.1927, sec.III,
    p.4.

Nantucket Channel
-UFO (DD)
 1958, Oct.7/Joseph Gwooz/"Nantucket"
    Richard Hall, ed., The UFO Evidence
    (Washington: NICAP, 1964), p.71.

Nantucket I.
-Sea monster
 1827/Capt. Coleman/"Levant"
    Bernard Heuvelmans, In the Wake of
    the Sea-Serpents (N.Y.: Hill & Wang,
    1968), p.172.

No Man's Land
-Clairvoyance
 1870s
    Joseph C. Allen, Tales and Trails of
    Martha's Vineyard (Boston: Little,
    Brown, 1938), pp.192-94.
-Norse discovery
 1001/Leif Eriksson/=Vinland?
    Edward F. Gray, Leif Erickson, Dis-
    coverer of America (N.Y.: Oxford
    Univ., 1930).
-Norse runestone
 1926/Joshua Crane
    Edward F. Gray, Leif Erickson, Dis-
    coverer of America (N.Y.: Oxford
    Univ., 1930). il.

Edmund B. Delabarre, "The Runic Rock
    on No Man's Land, Massachusetts,"
    New England Quar. 8 (1935):365-77.
    il.
    Olaf Strandwold, Norse Inscriptions
    on American Stones (Weehauken, N.J.:
    Magnus Björndal, 1948), pp.40-42.
    il.

Notown Reservoir
-Ancient wall
    William B. Goodwin, The Ruins of
    Great Ireland in New England (Bos-
    ton: Meador, 1946), p.109.

Plum I.
-Ghost
 n.d.
    Samuel Adams Drake, A Book of New
    England Legends and Folklore (Bos-
    ton: Roberts Bros., 1884).
-Sea monster
 1824, Aug.11/Mr. Ruggles
    A.C. Oudemans, The Great Sea-Serpent
    (Leiden: E.J. Brill, 1892), p.232,
    quoting Newburyport Journal (un-
    dated).

Poge, Cape
-Sea monster
 ca.1939/Joe Patrick
    Tim Dinsdale, Monster Hunt (Washing-
    ton: Acropolis, 1972), pp.238-41.

Quannapowette, L.
-Ghost
 1957/Aimee Violante
    Hans Holzer, Yankee Ghosts (N.Y.:
    Ace, 1966), p.48.

Race Point
-Sea monster
 1819, June 6/Hawkins Wheeler/"Concord"
    /15 mi.NW
    Jacob Bigelow, "Documents and Re-
    marks Respecting the Sea-Serpent,"
    Am.J.Sci., ser.1, 2 (1820):147,
    161-62.
 1835, spring/Capt. Shibbles/"Manhegan"
    "A Sea Serpent," Am.J.Sci., ser.1,
    28 (1835):372,373.
 1878, Aug.29/Robert Platt/"Drift"
    B.A. Colonna, "The Sea-Serpent,"
    Science 8 (1886):258.

Rocky Nook Point
-Archeological site and Norse ax
 pre-1638/Joseph Howland site
    James Deetz, "Excavations at the
    Joseph Howland Site, Rocky Nook,
    Kingston, Mass., 1959," Howland
    Quar., vol.24, no.2-3 (Jan.-Apr.
    1960).
    James Deetz, "The Howlands at Rocky
    Nook," Howland Quar., vol.24, no.4
    (July 1960).
    Charles Michael Boland, They All Dis-
    covered America (N.Y.: Pocket Books,
    1963 ed.), pp.216-21.
-Norse discovery

1001/Leif Eriksson/=Vinland?
  Charles Michael Boland, They All Discovered America (N.Y.: Pocket Books,
  1963 ed.), pp.212-14,266-76.

Simpson Hollow
-Witchcraft
  n.d./Granny Bates
  Clifton Johnson, What They Say in
  New England (Boston: Lee & Shepard,
  1897), pp.242-44.

Skaket Beach
-Sea monster (carcass)
  1964, Dec./Elmer Costa/=basking shark
  Orleans Cape Codder, 24 Dec.1964.

Smith's Point
-Sea monster
  1937/Edward Crocker/=hoax?
  Bernard Heuvelmans, In the Wake of
  the Sea-Serpent (N.Y.: Hill & Wang,
  1968), p.464.

Three Mile R.
-Ancient inscription
  1917/=hoax
  Boston Sunday Post, 26 June 1921.
  Edmund Burke Delabarre, Dighton Rock
  (N.Y.: Walter Neale, 1928), pp.275-
  79. il.

Vineyard Sound
-Sea monster
  1934/Thomas Ratcliffe
  Bernard Heuvelmans, In the Wake of
  the Sea-Serpents (N.Y.: Hill & Wang,
  1968), p.464.

Wampanoag L.
-UFO (NL)
  1976, June/Walford G. Erickson
  1978, Dec.30/Craig Pultorak/Camp Collier
  Worcester Telegram, 5 Jan.1979.

Warren's Cove
-Sea monster
  1815, June 20-21/Elkanah Finney
  Linnaean Soc'y of New England, Re-
  port of a Committee of the Linnaean
  Society of New England, Relative to
  a Large Marine Animal, Supposed to
  Be a Sea-Serpent (Boston: Cumming &
  Hilliard, 1817).
  A.C. Oudemans, The Great Sea-Serpent
  (Leiden: E.J. Brill, 1892), pp.
  153-57.

Washington Mt.
-UFO (CE-1)
  1953, June 15/Robert Lambert
  Pittsfield Berkshire Evening Eagle,
  29 June 1953.

            C. Ethnic Groups

Wampanoag Indians
-Flood myth

Elizabeth Reynard, The Narrow Land
  (Boston: Houghton Mifflin, 1968),
  pp.21-23.
-Humanoid myth
  pukwudgees
  Elizabeth Reynard, The Narrow Land
  (Boston: Houghton Mifflin, 1968),
  pp.27-29.
-Similarity to Norse
  Astri Stromsted, Ancient Pioneers
  (N.Y.: E.J. Friis, 1974).
-Similarity to Portuguese
  Manuel Luciano da Silva, Portuguese
  Pilgrims and Dighton Rock (Bristol,
  R.I.: The Author, 1971), pp.66-73.

        D. Unspecified Localities

-Contactee
  1953-   /Marianne Ferrarini
  Brad Steiger, Gods of Aquarius (N.Y.:
  Harcourt Brace Jovanovich, 1976),
  pp.132-36.

-Sea monster
  ca.1787/Capt. Lillis
  Linnaean Soc'y of New England, Re-
  port of a Committee of the Linnaean
  Society of New England, Relative to
  a Large Marine Animal, Supposed to
  Be a Sea-Serpent (Boston: Cumming &
  Hilliard, 1817).

VERMONT

A. Populated Places

Barnet
-Clairaudience
    1802/Elizabeth McCullom
    St. Johnsbury Caledonian, 2 Feb.1865.

Bellows Falls
-Ancient inscription
    Edmund Burke Delabarre, The Dighton
    Rock (N.Y.: Water Neale, 1928), pp.
    264-66. il.
    William B. Goodwin, The Ruins of
    Great Ireland in New England (Bos-
    ton: Meador, 1946), p.396. il.

Bennington
-Fall of anomalous hailstones
    1950, June 27
    "Metal-Colored Hail," Doubt, no.30
    (1950):36.

Bethel
-UFO (NL)
    1965, Jan.4/Richard S. Woodruff/Hwy..12
    John G. Fuller, Incident at Exeter
    (N.Y.: Berkley, 1967 ed.), pp.51-52.
    Raymond E. Fowler, UFOs: Interplane-
    tary Visitors (Jericho, N.Y.: Expo-
    sition, 1974), pp.57-60.

Brattleboro
-Automatic writing
    1872, Dec.25-1873, July/Thomas P. James
    Boston (Mass.) Post, 11 Sep.1873.
    Charles Dickens, The Mystery of Edwin
    Drood, Complete (Brattleboro: T.P.
    James, 1873 ed.).
    Theodore Flournoy, Spiritism and Psy-
    chology (N.Y.: Harper, 1911).
    Arthur Conan Doyle, "The Alleged
    Posthumous Writing of Great Auth-
    ors," Fortnightly Rev. 128 (1927):
    721-27.
    Arthur Conan Doyle, The Edge of the
    Unknown (N.Y.: Berkley, 1968 ed.),
    pp.96-99.
    Jerome E. Kelly, "Mystery of Dickens'
    Unfinished Mystery," Fate 11 (Feb.
    1958):81-83.
-UFO (CE-2)
    1965, Sep.10/Sandy Daszuta
    "News Briefs," Saucer News 12 (Dec.
    1965):25.

Burlington
-Entombed toads
    1786, summer/Samuel Lane
    Samuel Williams, History of Vermont
    (Walpole, N.H.: I. Thomas & D. Car-
    lisle, 1794), p.126.
    Jedediah Morse, American Universal
    Geography, 3 vols. (Boston: J.T.
    Buckingham, 1805), 1:333.

-UFO (CE-1)
    1907, July 2/John S. Michaud/Church x
    College St.
    William H. Alexander, "A Possible
    Case of Ball Lightning," Monthly
    Weather Rev. 35 (July 1907):310.

Cabot
-Mathematical prodigy
    1810-1840/Zerah Colburn
    Zerah Colburn, A Memoir of Zerah
    Colburn (Springfield, Mass.: G. &
    C. Merriam, 1833).
    E.W. Scripture, "Arithmetical Prod-
    igies," Am.J.Psych. 4 (1891):1-59.

Calais
-Medical clairvoyance
    1833-1901/Lucy Ainsworth (Cooke)
    Iris Barry, "The Story of Sleeping
    Lucy," Fate 8 (Dec.1955):100-104.
    il.

Cavendish
-Autoscopy
    n.d./Sam Connor
    "Sam Connor's Ghost," Scribbler,
    vol.1, nos.14-15 (summer 1901).

Chittenden
-Spirit medium
    1870s/Horatio and William Eddy
    Henry S. Olcott, People from the
    Other World (Hartford, Ct.: Ameri-
    can, 1875).
    Mary Dana Shindler, A Southerner
    Among the Spirits (Memphis: South-
    ern Baptist, 1877).
    D.D. Home, Lights and Shadows of
    Spiritualism (N.Y.: G.W. Carleton,
    1877), pp.260-64.
    Nandor Fodor, Encyclopaedia of Psy-
    chic Science (London: Arthurs,
    1933), pp.117,222,231,268, quoting
    Light, 15 Mar.1902.
    W.D. Chesney, "The Wonderful Eddy
    Children," Fate 5 (Feb.-Mar.1952):
    9-14.

Corinth
-Haunt
    1873
    Barre Daily Times, 8 Nov.1935.

Danville
-Dowsing research
    1958-   /American Society of Dowsers
    Raymond C. Willey, "Why We Must
    Study Dowsing," Fate 19 (Dec.1966):
    85-91.
    Raymond C. Willey, "Controversy on
    Dowsing," Fate 23 (Aug.1970):57-62.
    June & Nicholas Regush, Psi: The Oth-
    er World Catalogue (N.Y.: Putnam,

1974), pp.102-105.
"In Vermont: Is Dowsing Going to the Dogs?" Time, 9 Oct.1978, pp.11-12.

Essex Junction
-Ghost lights
    1901
        (Letter), Lois F. Clark, Fate 9 (Nov. 1956):128-29.
-UFO (NL)
    1976, May 16/Jean Cater
        (Letter), Saga UFO Rept. 3 (Oct.1976) :6,75-76.

Fairfield
-UFO (NL)
    1977, Oct.11
        "UFO Analysis," Int'l UFO Reporter 2 (Nov.1977):Newsfront sec.

Grand Isle
-Skyquake
    1953
        Donald E. Keyhoe, Flying Saucer Conspiracy (N.Y.: Holt, 1955), p.201.

Hammondsville
-Poltergeist
    1861, April
        (Editorial), Religio-Philosophical J., 19 Apr.1873, p.2.

Hardwick
-Skyquake
    1977, Nov.26
        U.S. Naval Rsch.Laboratory, NRL Investigations of East Coast Acoustics Events (Washington: Gov't Printing Office, 1978), p.134.

Mendon
-UFO (NL)
    1947, July 3/Clara Spieski
        Rutland Herald, 9 July 1947.

Middlebury
-Out-of-body experience
    1920s/Caroline D. Larsen
        Caroline D. Larsen, My Travels in the Spirit World (Burlington: Lane, 1927).
        Herbert B. Greenhouse, The Astral Journey (N.Y.: Avon, 1976 ed.), pp. 31-33.

Montpelier
-Ghost
    1966/Lyse Savard
        "Sues over 'Seeing the Dead,'" Fate 20 (May 1967):85.
-Human hibernation
    n.d.
        Rutland Herald, 24 May 1939.
        Charles Edward Crane, Winter in Vermont (N.Y.: Knopf, 1941).

Mount Snow
-UFO (CE-2)
    1969, spring-summer
        Berthold Eric Schwarz, "Stella Lan-

sing's UFO Motion Pictures," Flying Saucer Rev. 18 (Jan.-Feb.1972): 3,9.

Plainfield
-UFO (CE-1)
    1968, Oct.31/Paul Montague/Goddard College
        (Letter), Can.UFO Rept., no.30 (winter-spring 1978):23.

Pownal
-Precognition
    1976, Sep.11/Thomas Arroyo
        (Editorial), Fate 30 (Feb.1977):38.

Putney
-UFO (CE-2)
    1956, Oct.29/Virginia Maratea
        "Case 244," CRIFO Orbit, 7 Dec. 1956, p.3.

Reading
-Ancient standing stone
        Barry Fell, America B.C. (N.Y.: Quadrangle, 1976), pp.67-68,147. il.

Rockingham
-UFO (CE-1)
    1966, Nov.25
        Louisville (Ky.) Courier-Journal, 11 Dec.1966.

Rutland
-Humanoid
    1974, July
        John Green, Sasquatch: The Apes Among Us (Seattle: Hancock House, 1978), p.231.
-UFO (NL)
    1947, June 27/Mrs. W.F. Dunning
    1947, July 2/Rose LePan
        Rutland Herald, 9 July 1947.
    1947, July 7/Mrs. Albert Steele/13 Forest St.
        Rutland Herald, 8 July 1947.

Saint Albans
-UFO (NL)
    1953, Nov.24/Edward Lake/Hwy.7
        (Letter), Fate 9 (Sep.1956):113.
    1973, Oct.6/French Hill
        Burlington Sunday News, 7 Oct.1973.

Saint Johnsbury
-UFO (?)
    1954, June 24/Roy Bonnette
        "C-5," CRIFO Newsl., 6 Aug.1954, p.4.

Shaftsbury
-Dowsing
    1970s/Herbert Douglas
        Bennington Banner, 17 Dec.1973, p.5.

South Pomfret
-Ancient inscription
        Barry Fell, America B.C. (N.Y.: Quadrangle, 1976), pp.226-28,244-45. il.

South Royalton
-Ancient stone constructions and inscrip-
tions
　Eye of Bel
　　William B. Goodwin, The Ruins of
　　Great Ireland in New England (Bos-
　　ton: Meador, 1946), pp.397-98. il.
　　Byron E. Dix, "An Early Calendar
　　Site in Central Vermont," Occ.Pub.
　　Epigraphic Soc'y, vol.3, no.51 (Aug.
　　1975).
　　Barry Fell, America B.C. (N.Y.: Quad-
　　rangle, 1976), pp.54-55,70-71,135,
　　142-43,152-53,196,199,202,207. il.
　　Byron E. Dix, "A Possible Plinth
　　Monument in Central Vermont," Occ.
　　Pub.Epigraphic Soc'y, vol.3, no.60
　　(Sep.1976).
　　Salvatore Michael Trento, The Search
　　for Lost America (Chicago: Contem-
　　porary,1978), pp.168-70. il.

South Woodstock
-Ancient stone constructions
　　Barry Fell & John Williams, "Inscribed
　　Sarsen Stones in Vermont," Occ.Pub.
　　Epigraphic Soc'y, vol.3, no.53 (Aug.
　　1975).
　　Byron E. Dix, "An Early Calendar
　　Site (II) in Central Vermont," NEARA
　　J. 10 (winter-spring 1976):34.
　　Barry Fell, America B.C. (N.Y.: Quad-
　　rangle, 1976), pp.54-57,129,134-36,
　　138-39,141,144,198,203-205,208-209,
　　214,216,219-25,228,237,240-45. il.
　　Byron E. Dix, "A Second Early Calen-
　　dar Site in Central Vermont," Occ.
　　Pub.Epigraphic Soc'y, vol.3, no.61
　　(Sep.1976).
　　Byron E. Dix, "Possible Evidence of
　　the Megalithic Yard at Calendar
　　Site II, Vermont," NEARA J. 6 (fall
　　1976):25-28.
　　Salvatore Michael Trento, The Search
　　for Lost America (Chicago: Contem-
　　porary, 1978), pp.168-74. il.

Stamford
-UFO (?)
　1967, Nov./=meteor?
　　"More U.S.A. November Reports," APRO
　　Bull. 16 (Jan.-Feb.1968):6-7.

Townshend
-UFO (CE-2)
　1974, Dec.19/ground markings only
　　Ted Phillips, Physical Traces Associ-
　　ated with UFO Sightings (Evanston:
　　Center for UFO Studies, 1975), p.
　　106.

Waterbury
-UFO (CE-1)
　1978, July 11/3 mi.S on Hwy.100
　　"UFOs of Limited Merit," Int'l UFO
　　Reporter 3 (Aug.1978):3,4.

Waterford twp.
-Haunt
　n.d./Washburn barn

James Reynolds, Ghosts in American
Houses (N.Y.: Paperback Library,
1967 ed.), pp.46-54.
1880s
　James Reynolds, Gallery of Ghosts
　(N.Y.: Paperback Library, 1970 ed.),
　pp.237-43.

West Arlington
-UFO (NL)
　1978, April 26
　1978, May 3/Peter Johnson
　　Concord (N.H.) Monitor, 11 May 1978.

White River Junction
-Ancient underground structure
　　Barry Fell, America B.C. (N.Y.: Quad-
　　rangle, 1976), pp.6,152-53,297,299.
　　il.
-UFO (NL)
　1908, summer
　　New York Sun, 1 Nov.1908.

Williamstown
-Humanoid
　1879, Oct.10/S of town
　　New York Times, 18 Oct.1879, p.1.
-UFO (?)
　1950, Oct.9
　　Richard Hall, ed., The UFO Evidence
　　(Washington: NICAP, 1964), p.154.

Windham co.
-Ancient stone chamber
　　James P. Whittall II, "Stone Cham-
　　ber: Windham County, Vt.," Work
　　Rept., Early Sites Rsch.Soc'y, vol.
　　3, no.31 (1977). il.

Windsor
-Water anomaly
　1955, Sep./William Waterman
　　"The Water from Nowhere," Fate 9
　　(July 1956):42.

Winooski
-UFO (NL)
　1970, May 28
　　"Report from Vermont," APRO Bull. 18
　　(May-June 1970):1.

Woodstock
-Fire anomaly
　1947, April/Wendall Walker
　　"Miscellany," Time, 7 Apr.1947, p.18.
-Precognition
　1840s/Hiram Powers
　　Woodstock Standard, July 1873.

　　　　　　B. Physical Features

Champlain, L.
-Lake monster
　1609, July-　　/champ
　　H.P. Biggar, ed., The Works of Sam-
　　uel de Champlain, 6 vols. (Toronto:
　　Champlain Soc'y, 1925), 2:91.
　　Whitehall (N.Y.) Times, 26 Sep.1873.
　　Burlington Free Press, 7 Nov.1879.

Swanton Courier, 31 July 1880.
Plattsburgh (N.Y.) Republican, 4 Aug.
  1883.
Plattsburgh (N.Y.) Sentinel, 27 May
  1887.
New York Times, 11 July 1887, p.1.
Keeseville Essex County (N.Y.) Re-
  publican, 27 Sep.1894.
Marjorie L. Porter, "The Champlain
  Monster," Vermont Life, summer 1970,
  pp.47-50.
Washington (D.C.) Post, 29 Aug.1970.
Los Angeles (Cal.) Times, 10 Jan.
  1971; and 18 Jan.1976.
Nat'l Enquirer, 2 May 1971.
Baltimore (Md.) Sun, 9 Dec.1971.
(Editorial), Fate 25 (Mar.1972):28-
  31.
Jerome Clark & Loren Coleman, "Amer-
  ica's Lake Monsters," Beyond Reality,
  no.14 (Mar.-Apr.1975):28,30.
Joseph W. Zarzynski, "Courtship with
  a Lake Monster," INFO J., no.28
  (Mar.-Apr.1978):2-4.
"Monster Watch," INFO J., no.29
  (May-June 1978):11.
Joseph W. Zarzynski, "The Lake Cham-
  plain Monsters: A 1978 Update,"
  Vestigia Newsl. 3 (spring 1979):4-5.

Connecticut R.
-River monster
  1968, summer/Douglas Gove
  "A Miniature Whatsis," Fate 22 (Feb.
    1969):52.

Dead Creek
-River monster
  1909, May/=hoax
  Swanton Courier, 3 June 1909.

Elephant Valley
-Ancient stone constructions
  William B. Goodwin, The Ruins of
    Great Ireland in New England (Bos-
    ton: Meador, 1946), pp.400-401. il.
  Roland Wells Robbins & Evan Jones,
    Hidden America (N.Y.: Knopf, 1959),
    pp.141-43. il.
  Barry Fell, America B.C. (N.Y.: Quad-
    rangle, 1976), pp.202,209. il.

Glastenbury Mt.
-Disappearances
  1945, Nov.-1950, Nov.6/Paula Jean Wel-
    den
    R.D. Stock & John Zeller, "The Strange
    Disappearances at Mt. Glastenbury,"
    Fate 10 (July 1957):50-54.

Isle La Motte
-Archeological site
  1800-1200 B.C.
    Franklin Folsom, America's Ancient
    Treasures (N.Y.: Rand McNally,
    1974), p.188.

Memphremagog, L.
-Haunt
  n.d.

James Reynolds, Ghosts in American
  Houses (N.Y.: Paperback Library,
  1967 ed.), pp.92-93.
-Lake monster
  n.d.
    John Ross Dix, A Hand Book for Lake
    Memphremagog (Boston: Evans, 1860),
    p.48.

Reagen site
-Archeological site
  ca.4000 B.C.
    William A. Ritchie, "A Probable Pa-
    leo-Indian Site in Vermont," Am.
    Antiquity 18 (1953):249-58.
    William A. Ritchie, "Traces of Early
    Man in the Northeast," N.Y.State
    Mus.Sci.Serv.Bull., no.358 (1957).
    il.

West R.
-Petroglyph
  mouth
    Benjamin H. Hall, History of Eastern
    Vermont (N.Y.: Appleton, 1858), pp.
    587-92. il.
    Mary R. Cabot, Annals of Brattleboro,
    2 vols. (Brattleboro: E.L. Hildreth,
    1921), 1:4.
    Edmund Burke Delabarre, Dighton Rock
    (N.Y.: Walter Neale, 1928), pp.264-
    66. il.

Winooski R.
-River monster
  1952, July/nr. mouth
    Jerome Clark & Loren Coleman, "Amer-
    ica's Lake Monsters," Beyond Reality,
    no.14 (Mar.-Apr.1975):28,30.

D. Unspecified Localities

-Climatic anomaly
  1816, summer
    T.D. Seymour Bassett, "The Cold Sum-
    mer of 1816 in Vermont: Fact and
    Folklore," New England Galaxy 15,
    no.1 (1973):15-19.

-Fall of fish
  ca.1858
    (Letter), O.P. Hubbard, Proc.Boston
    Soc'y Nat.Hist., vol.6 (1859).

-UFO (CE-2)
  1969, July 17
    "Possible E-M Effects in Vermont
    Sighting," APRO Bull. 18 (Sep.-Oct.
    1969):6-7.

NEW HAMPSHIRE

A. Populated Places

Acworth
-Ancient stone chamber
  William B. Goodwin, The Ruins of
  Great Ireland in New England (Bos-
  ton: Meador, 1946), pp.158-66. il.
  Jonathan Hall & Eric Woodman, "The
  Purpose of the Bee-Hive Shaped Stone
  Structures in Southwestern New Hamp-
  shire," NEARA Newsl. 8 (Mar.1973):
  2-6. il.

Alstead
-Lightning anomaly
  1961, July 23/Mabel Metcalf
  (Editorial), Fate 14 (Nov.1961):12-
  13, quoting Manchester Union-Leader
  (undated).

Alton
-UFO (DD)
  1947, July 8/Thomas F. Dale
  Manchester Morning Union, 9 July
  1947.

Atkinson
-Ancient stone construction
  "The Atkinson, New Hampshire Stone
  Structure," NEARA Newsl. 6 (Sep.
  1971):59. il.

Bartlett
-Ancient dolmen
  Barry Fell, America B.C. (N.Y.: Quad-
  rangle, 1976), pp.131,133. il.

Benton
-Haunt
  ca.1840s/Hazen Whitcher
  Exeter News-Letter, 26 July 1842.

Berlin
-UFO (?)
  1962, June 14
  Paris Flammonde, The Age of Flying
  Saucers (N.Y.: Hawthorne, 1971),
  p.159.

Bethlehem
-UFO (CE-2)
  1958, fall
  Walter N. Webb, "UFO & Paralysis,"
  Official UFO 1 (Feb.1975):34,48.

Boscawen
-Ancient stone construction
  Robert E. Stone, "Arrows Carved in
  Bedrock, near a Stone Structure:
  Boscawen, N.H.," NEARA Newsl. 9
  (spring 1974):11.

Bradford
-UFO (CE-1)

  1967, Jan.16/Robert B. Fuller
  "'Purring' UFO Hovers Low," UFO Inv.
  3 (Mar.-Apr.1967):5.
-UFO (NL)
  1978, Aug.14/Jeff Thurston/I-91
  Woodsville Journal-Opinion, 17 Aug.
  1978.

Brentwood
-Human tracks in basalt
  Gertrude B. Johnson, "The Brentwood
  Prints," NEARA Newsl. 5 (Mar.1970):
  24. il.

Campton
-UFO (CE-1)
  1978, Oct.20/Kate Chmurney/Hwy.49
  Laconia Lakes Region Trader, 1 Nov.
  1978.
-UFO (NL)
  1957, Nov.21
  Richard Hall, The UFO Evidence (Washington: NICAP, 1964), p.167.

Canterbury
-UFO (CE-1)
  1972, May 13/Holly Hill
  Ray Fowler, "Several Witnesses See
  Low Flying UFO over New Hampshire,"
  Skylook, no.59 (Oct.1972):5-7.

Center Harbor
-UFO (NL)
  1973, March 28/Bruce Wingate/Belknap
  College
  "Students Observe UFO in New Hampshire," APRO Bull. 21 (May-June
  1973):5-6.

Center Sandwich
-Humanoid
  1942, summer
  John Green, Sasquatch: The Apes Among
  Us (Seattle: Hancock House, 1978),
  p.230.
-Humanoid tracks
  1977, Feb.
  John Green, Sasquatch: The Apes Among
  Us (Seattle: Hancock House, 1978),
  p.230.

Chester
-Ancient stone seat
  William B. Goodwin, The Ruins of
  Great Ireland in New England (Bos-
  ton: Meador, 1946), p.387. il.

Claremont
-UFO (CE-1)
  1968, July 30/Robert's Hill
  "Structured Object Reports Continue,"
  UFO Inv. 4 (June-July 1969):2.
  Donald E. Keyhoe & Gordon I.R. Lore,
  Jr., UFOs: A New Look (Washington:

NICAP, 1969), p.21.

Concord
-Clairvoyance
1885, Aug.14/Mollie S. Leonard
"Second Prize for Men," J.ASPR 8
(1914):210-11.
-Phantom
1873/Franklin B. Evans
Nandor Fodor, Encyclopaedia of Psy-
chic Science (London: Arthurs,
1933), p.266.
-UFO (NL)
1974, Aug.12/James McGonigle, Jr.
Timothy Green Beckley, "Saucers over
Our Cities," Saga UFO Rept. 4 (Aug.
1977):24,76.
1975, July 26
"UFO Central," CUFOS News Bull., 15
Nov.1975, p.14.

Conway
-UFO (CE-2)
1966, April 18/Herman Banfill
"Saucer Briefs," Saucer News 13
(fall 1966):26,28, quoting UPI re-
lease, 19 Apr.1966.
-UFO (NL)
1958, Nov.5
Richard Hall, ed., The UFO Evidence
(Washington: NICAP, 1964), p.151.

Danville
-Ancient stone construction
William B. Goodwin, The Ruins of
Great Ireland in New England (Bos-
ton: Meador, 1946), pp.369,371-72.
il.

Derry
-Ancient sculptures
Charles J, Lemay, "The Two Stone
Faces of Derry, N.H.," NEARA Newsl.
7 (Sep.1972):42-46. il.
Barry Fell, America B.C. (N.Y.: Quad-
rangle, 1976), p.244.
-UFO (CE-3)
1974, Aug.20
Ted Bloecher, "A Catalog of Humanoid
Reports for 1974," in MUFON 1975
UFO Symposium Proc. (Seguin, Tex.:
MUFON, 1975), pp.51,60.

Dover
-Auroral anomaly
1833, Nov.13
Denison Olmsted, "Observations on
the Meteors of November 13th, 1833,"
Am.J.Sci., ser.1, 25 (1834):363,397-
98.
-Fall of fish
1954, June/Hwy.16
New York Times, 9 June 1954.
-Midday darkness
1780, May 19
Jeremy Belknap, The History of New-
Hampshire, 3 vols. (Boston: Brad-
ford & Read, 1813), 3:22-23.
-UFO (?)
1972, Oct.9

Barry Greenwood, "UFO Notes," Skylook, no.61 (Dec.1972):15.

Durham
-Ancient standing stone
John Finch, "On the Celtic Antiqui-
ties of America," Am.J.Sci., ser.1,
7 (1824):149-61.
-UFO (CE-3)
1973, Sep.18
David Webb, 1973: Year of the Human-
oids (Evanston: Center for UFO
Studies, 1976 ed.), p.9.
-UFO (DD)
1932, April?
Richard Hall, ed., The UFO Evidence
(Washington: NICAP, 1964), p.145.

East Derry
-Phantom helicopters
1965, Aug.28/Dorothy Doone
Raymond E. Fowler, UFOs: Interplanetary Visitors (Jericho, N.Y.: Exposition, 1974), pp.71-74.
-UFO (NL)
1973, Oct.2/John Hanson/Rainbow L.
Boston (Mass.) Morning Globe, 4 Oct.
1973.

East Kingston
-Ancient sculpture
Arlene W. St. Laurent, "Stone
'Whale' Discovered in East Kingston,
N.H.," NEARA Newsl. 6 (June 1971):
25. il.

East Madison
-UFO (NL)
1960, Feb.4
Richard Hall, ed., The UFO Evidence
(Washington: NICAP, 1964), p.71.

Enfield
-Spirit mediums
1830s-1840s
Hervey Elkins, Fifteen Years in the
Senior Order of Shakers (Hanover,
N.H.: Dartmouth, 1853).
Slater Brown, The Heyday of Spirit-
ualism (N.Y.: Pocket Books, 1972
ed.), pp.80-81.

Exeter
-Skyquake
1810, Nov.9/Samuel Tenney
William T. Brigham, "Volcanic Manifestations in New England," Mem.
Boston Soc'y Nat.Hist. 2 (1871):1,
16.
-Spirit medium
1880s-1890s/Sarah E.A. Browne
Walter F. Prince, "Mrs. Browne, Private Medium," J.ASPR 13 (1919):648.
-UFO (CE-1)
1965, July 29/Lillian Pearce/Hwy.88
1965, Sep./Ron Smith/Shaw Hill
1965, Sep./Joseph Mazalewski/2 McKinley St.
1965, Sep.21/Mrs. Parker Blodgett/Shaw
Hill

1965, Sep.27/Mrs. Harlow Spinney
1965, Oct.20/Lillian Pearce
John G. Fuller, Incident at Exeter
(N.Y.: Berkley, 1967 ed.), pp.59,
63-66,72,74,85-86,88-90,99-107,185-
87,199-201.
1966, March 21/Gene Bertrand
Raymond E. Fowler, UFOs: Interplanetary Visitors (Jericho, N.Y.: Exposition, 1974), pp.112-15.
-UFO (CE-3)
1973, Aug.
J. Allen Hynek, "The Embarrassment
of Riches," in MUFON UFO Symposium
Proc. 1973 (Quincy, Ill.: MUFON,
1973), p.62.
-UFO (NL)
1965, Sep./Lora Davis/Country Club Rd.
1965, Sep.17/Lillian Pearce
1965, Oct.21/John G. Fuller/Hwy.88
John G. Fuller, Incident at Exeter
(N.Y.: Berkley, 1967 ed.), pp.86-88,
105,109-11,173-74.
1975, July 15
"UFO Central," CUFOS News Bull., 15
Nov.1975, p.13.
1976, April 28
1976, May 26
"Noteworthy UFO Sightings," Ufology
2 (fall 1976):60.

Fitzwilliam
-Ball lightning
1937, Aug.10/Mary Ethel Hunneman
Vincent H. Gaddis, Mysterious Fires
and Lights (N.Y.: Dell, 1968 ed.),
pp.50-51, quoting Science, 10 Sep.
1937.
-UFO (NL)
1977, Dec.28/Robin Brow
Keene Sentinel, 29 Dec.1977.

Francestown
-UFO (?)
1968
Ted Phillips, Physical Traces Associ-
ated with UFO Sightings (Evanston:
Center for UFO Studies, 1975), p.109.

Franconia
-Precognition
1780s/Henry Houghton
Lawrence E. Webber, "The Dream of a
Mortal Wound," Fate 24 (Jan.1971):
79.

Fremont
-UFO (CE-1)
1965, Oct.19/Bessie Healey
John G. Fuller, Incident at Exeter
(N.Y.: Berkley, 1967 ed.), pp.124-26.
-UFO (NL)
1965, Sep.-Nov./Mr. Heselton/Hwy.107
John G. Fuller, Incident at Exeter
(N.Y.: Berkley, 1967 ed.), pp.118-
24,126-35,190.

Goffstown
-UFO (CE-3)
1973, Nov.1/Florence Dow/Parker Station

1973, Nov.2/Lyndia Morel/Hwy.114
1973, Nov.4/Rex Snow/Chip St.
"UFO Terrifies Woman," Skylook, no.
74 (Jan.1974):5-6, quoting Manchester Union-Leader (undated).
"Occupant Encounter in New Hampshire," APRO Bull. 22 (Jan.-Feb.
1974):5-7.
Raymond E. Fowler, UFOs: Interplanetary Visitors (Jericho, N.Y.: Exposition, 1974), pp.322-26.
Raymond E. Fowler, "The Goffstown
Creatures," Official UFO 1 (Aug.
1975):37,56-57.

Gorham
-UFO (CE-3)
1977, April 4/Mrs. Fortier
Ted Bloecher, "A Survey of CE3K Re-
ports for 1977," in 1978 MUFON UFO
Symposium Proc. (Seguin, Tex.:
MUFON, 1978), pp.14,22-24,32-33.

Greenfield
-Fall of localized rain
1966, Aug.2/Robert H. Stanley/Pine
Ridge Rd.
R.E. Lautzenheiser, et al., "Remark-
able Point Rainfall at Greenfield,
N.H., Evening of August 2, 1966,"
Monthly Weather Rev. 98 (Feb.1970):
164-68.

Greenland
-UFO (NL)
1974, April 28
Dave Webb & John Oswald, "New Hampshire Report May Be a Hoax," Skylook, no.93 (Aug.1975):14.

Groveton
-UFO (NL)
1978, Nov.16/Bob Hart
Berlin Reporter, 29 Nov.1978.

Hampton
-Ancient inscription
Edmund Burke Delabarre, Dighton Rock
(N.Y.: Walter Neale, 1928), pp.281-
82. il.
Andrew E. Rothovius, "The Hampton,
N.H. Runestone," NEARA Newsl. 9
(spring 1974):13.
-Phantom
1769/Jonathan Moulton
Exeter News-Letter, 3 July 1843.
Samuel Adams Drake, The Heart of the
White Mountains (N.Y.: Harper, 1882),
pp.11-14.
Samuel Adams Drake, A Book of New
England Legends and Folk Lore (Bos-
ton: Roberts Bros., 1884), pp.322-
28.
Warren Brown, History of the Town of
Hampton Falls, N.H., 2 vols. (Con-
cord: Rumford, 1900-18), 1:540.
Mrs. Moody P. Gore & Mrs. Guy E.
Speare, New Hampshire Folk Tales
(Plymouth: N.H. Federation of Wom-
en's Clubs, 1932), pp.184-90.

Susy Smith, Prominent American Ghosts
(N.Y.: Dell, 1969 ed.), pp.92-96.
-UFO (CE-1)
1965, Sep.3
John G. Fuller, Incident at Exeter
(N.Y.: Berkley, 1967 ed.), p.71.
1966, March 29/Rodney Grimsley
Raymond E. Fowler, UFOs: Interplanetary Visitors (Jericho, N.Y.: Exposition, 1974), p.117.
-UFO (NL)
1965, Oct./Virginia Hale
1965, Oct.31
John G. Fuller, Incident at Exeter
(N.Y.: Berkley, 1967 ed.), pp.71,
117.
-Witch trial (?)
1656-1673/Eunice Cole
Samuel G. Drake, Annals of Witchcraft
in New England (Boston: W.E. Woodward, 1869), pp.99-103.
-Witch trial (hex)
1680/Rachel Fuller
Samuel G. Drake, Annals of Witchcraft
in New England (Boston: W.E. Woodward, 1869), pp.150-57.

Hampton Beach
-UFO (CE-1)
1965, Aug.2/Walter Shipman
John G. Fuller, Incident at Exeter
(N.Y.: Berkley, 1967 ed.), pp.80-
81,177,183-84.
-UFO (CE-3)
1974, May 20/=hoax?
David F. Webb, "Occupant Sighting Reported," Skylook, no.82 (Sep.1974):
10-11.
Dave Webb & John Oswald, "New Hampshire Report May Be a Hoax," Skylook, no.93 (Aug.1975):14.

Hampton Falls
-UFO (CE-2)
1966, March 29
Raymond E. Fowler, UFOs: Interplanetary Visitors (Jericho, N.Y.: Exposition, 1974), pp.117-24.

Hancock
-Fall of colored snow
1948, March 2
"Pied Snow," Doubt, no.21 (1948):319,
quoting Boston (Mass.) Globe (undated).

Hanover
-UFO (NL)
1979, Jan.3-6/William Barnum
Lebanon Valley News, 12 Jan.1979.

Hemlock Center
-UFO (NL)
1957, Nov.9/Lillian Stickney
Bellows Falls (Vt.) Times, 14 Nov.
1957.

Henniker
-Haunt
1814-   /Ocean Born Mary House

Leander W. Cogswell, The History of
the Town of Henniker, Merrimack
County, New Hampshire (Concord: Re-
publican Press Ass'n, 1880).
Carl Carmer, The Hurricane's Chil-
dren (N.Y.: Farrar & Rinehart,
1937), pp.29-37.
Louis M.A. Roy & Pauline Saltzman,
"The House That Haunts a Ghost,"
Tomorrow 6 (winter 1958):51-57.
Eva A. Speare, New Hampshire Folk
Tales (Plymouth, N.H.: The Author,
1964), pp.201-203.
Hans Holzer, Yankee Ghosts (N.Y.:
Ace, 1966), pp.122-48.
Susy Smith, Prominent American Ghosts
(N.Y.: Dell, 1969 ed.), pp.120-28.
(Letter), John P. Bessor, Fate 23
(Jan.1970):133-34.
Hans Holzer, Haunted Houses (N.Y.:
Crown, 1971), pp.46-48. il.

Hillsboro
-Ancient stone construction
Franklin Pierce Barbecue Oven
"Needs Investigating: An Interesting
Trio," NEARA Newsl. 7 (June 1972):
32. il.

Hinsdale
-Reincarnation
1965/George Field
Loring G. Williams, "Reincarnation
of a Civil War Victim," Fate 19
(Dec.1966):44-58.
-UFO (CE-2)
1973, July/ground markings only
Ted Phillips, Physical Traces Associ-
ated with UFO Sightings (Evanston:
Center for UFO Studies, 1975), p.90.
-UFO (DD)
1946/George Kendrick
"Case 83," CRIFO Newsl., 3 June 1955,
pp.3,4.

Hollis
-Humanoid
1977, May 7/Gerald St. Louis
Boston (Mass.) Herald-American, 16-
17 May 1977.

Hooksett
-UFO (CE-1)
1965, Oct.22/Merrimack St.
Manchester Union-Leader, 23 Oct.1965.
-UFO (DD)
1947, June 28/Mrs. Henry Price
Manchester Union-Leader, 8 July 1947.
1965, Oct.22/Oscar J. Angar/Pleasant
St.
Manchester Union-Leader, 23 Oct.1965.

Hopkinton
-UFO (CE-1)
ca.1820
C.C. Lord, Life and Times in Hopkin-
ton, N.H. (Concord: Republican Press
Ass'n, 1890).
-Witchcraft
n.d./Moody Gore/Dimond Hill

Mrs. Moody P. Gore & Mrs. Guy A. Speare, New Hampshire Folk Tales (Plymouth: N.H. Federation of Women's Clubs, 1932).

Hudson
-UFO (NL)
  1975, July 25
    "UFO Central," CUFOS News Bull., 15 Nov.1975, p.14.

Intervale
-UFO (DD)
  1958, Nov.4/James E. McLoughlin
    "Hovering UFO Puzzles South African Officials," UFO Inv. 1 (Dec.1958): 1,3.
-UFO (NL)
  1960, Feb.3/William M. Kendrick
    Richard Hall, ed., The UFO Evidence (Washington: NICAP, 1964), p.71.

Jackson
-Petroglyph
    "Another Stone Fish in New Hampshire," NEARA Newsl. 6 (Dec.1971):71. il.

Jaffrey
-UFO (CE-2)
  1965/ground markings only
    Ted Phillips, Physical Traces Associated with UFO Sightings (Evanston: Center for UFO Studies, 1975), p.33, quoting Monadnock Ledger (undated).

Keene
-Ancient stone construction
  West Hill
    Andrew E. Rothovius, "The Purpose of the Bee-Hive Shaped Stone Structures in Southwestern New Hampshire," NEARA Newsl. 8 (Mar.1973):2,4-6.
-UFO (?)
  1968, March 27/=meteor?
    Little Rock Arkansas Gazette, 29 Mar.1968.
-UFO (DD)
  1974, Aug.12/Hwy.101
    David Webb, "Daylight UFO Sighting," Skylook, no.84 (Nov.1974):9,20.
-Weather control
  1960s/Charles H. Hapgood
    Ivan T. Sanderson, Investigating the Unexplained (Englewood Cliffs, N.J.: Prentice-Hall, 1972), p.227.
    Charles H. Hapgood, Voices of Spirit (N.Y.: Leisure, 1975), pp.39-40.

Kensington
-Lightning anomaly
  1856
    "A Lightning Well Borer," Sci.Am. 11 (1856):344.
-UFO (CE-1)
  1965, Sep.3/Norman J. Muscarello/Hwy. 150
    "UFOs Panic Police, Motorists," UFO Inv. 3 (Aug.-Sep.1965):1,3.
    Haverhill (Mass.) Gazette, 27 Oct. 1965.

"Further Information on the Exeter, New Hampshire Sightings," Saucer News 13 (Mar.1966):21-22.
U.S., Congress, House, Comm.on Armed Services, Unidentified Flying Objects, 89th Cong., 2d sess., 1966.
John G. Fuller, "Trade Winds," Saturday Rev., 16 Apr.1966, pp.10-12, 77.
John G. Fuller, Incident at Exeter (N.Y.: Berkley, 1967 ed.), pp.9-15, 19-22,44-47,57-63,69-72,111-14,140-43,178-80,187-89,211-20.
Jean Fuller, "The Exeter Incidents," Flying Saucer Rev. 13 (Sep.-Oct. 1967):25-27.
Philip J. Klass, UFOs--Identified (N.Y.: Random House, 1968), pp.12-25,40-42.
Raymond E. Fowler, UFOs: Interplanetary Visitors (Jericho, N.Y.: Exposition, 1974), pp.76-91.
J. Allen Hynek, The Hynek UFO Report (N.Y.: Dell, 1977), pp.154-65.

Kingston
-Ancient stone construction
    Charles Michael Boland, They All Discovered America (N.Y.: Pocket Books, 1963 ed.), p.39.
-Precognition and haunts
  n.d.
    Berthold Eric Schwarz, "Talks with Betty Hill: 2--The Things That Happen Around Her," Flying Saucer Rev. 23 (Oct.1977):11,13-14.
-UFO (CE-1)
  1967, April 27/Mrs. Alan J. Keiran
    "Worldwide Sightings Showing Increase," UFO Inv. 4 (Oct.1967):1,3.
  1974, May 20
    Dave Webb & John Oswald, "New Hampshire Report May Be a Hoax," Skylook, no.93 (Aug.1975):14.
-UFO (NL)
  1975, Dec.7/Betty Hill
    Berthold Eric Schwarz, "Talks with Betty Hill: 2--The Things That Happen Around Her," Flying Saucer Rev. 23 (Oct.1977):11.

Laconia
-Inner development
  1973-   /Seax-Wicca/Weirs Beach
    J. Gordon Melton, Encyclopedia of American Religions, 2 vols. (Wilmington, N.C.: Consortium, 1978), 2:284.
-UFO (CE-1)
  1974, Aug.14
    George D. Fawcett, "The 'Unreported' UFO Wave of 1974," Saga UFO Rept. 2 (spring 1975):50,74.
-UFO (NL)
  1978, Aug.30/Danny Wylie/Wingate Apts.
    Laconia Evening Citizen, 1 Sep.1978.

Lancaster
-Poltergeist
  1818/Farrar House
    Eva A. Speare, Folk Tales of New

Hampshire (Plymouth, N.H.: The Author, 1964), pp.180-83.

Lebanon
-Clairvoyance
  1898, Nov.2/Nellie Titus
    Lebanon Granite State Free Press, 11
    Nov.1898.
    William James, "A Case of Clairvoy-
    ance," Proc.ASPR 1 (1907):221-36.
    Susy Smith, "Clairvoyant Finds Mis-
    sing Girl," Fate 15 (Sep.1962):55-
    59.
-Spirit medium
  1930/Elsa Barr
    Frederick Bligh Bond, "The 'Tad' Epi-
    sode," Psychic Rsch. 24 (1930):437-
    39. il.
-UFO (NL)
  1975, July 6
    "UFO Central," CUFOS News Bull., 15
    Nov.1975, p.13.

Lincoln
-UFO (CE-4)
  1961, Sep.19/Betty and Barney Hill/U.S.
  3
    John G. Fuller, The Interrupted Jour-
    ney (N.Y.: Dial, 1966). il.
    Philip J. Klass, UFOs--Identified
    (N.Y.: Random House, 1968), pp.226-
    48.
    "USAF Report on Hill Case," APRO
    Bull. 20 (Jan.-Feb.1972):6.
    (Letter), Betty Hill, UFO Inv., July
    1973, p.4.
    Philip J. Klass, UFOs Explained (N.Y.:
    Random House, 1974), pp.250-54.
    Marjorie E. Fish, "Validation of the
    Betty Hill Map," Pursuit 7 (Jan.
    1974):4-8.
    Marjorie E. Fish, "Journey into the
    Hill Star Map," in 1974 MUFON UFO
    Symposium Proc. (Quincy, Ill.:
    MUFON, 1974), pp.70-80.
    Walter N. Webb, "An Analysis of the
    Fish Model," APRO Bull. 23 (Sep.-
    Oct.1974):8-9; (Nov.-Dec.1974):3-7.
    Terence Dickinson, "The Zeta-Reticuli
    Incident," Astronomy 2 (Dec.1974):
    4-18. il.
    J. Allen Hynek & Jacques Vallee, The
    Edge of Reality (Chicago: Regnery,
    1975), pp.89-101,108-109.
    "More on Star Map," APRO Bull. 24
    (June 1976):1,3.
    Robert Sheaffer, "The New Hampshire
    Abduction Explained," Official UFO
    1 (Aug.1976):14-16,32,40-43.
    (Letter), Charles Amacker, Official
    UFO 1 (Dec.1976):8.
    (Letter), Robert Sheaffer, Official
    UFO 1 (Dec.1976):8,14.
    Donald H. Menzel & Ernest H. Taves,
    The UFO Enigma (Garden City: Double-
    day, 1977), pp.239-49.

Lockmere
-Spirit medium
  1920s/Mrs. A.L. Sinclair

May C. Walker, "A Versatile Medium,"
J.ASPR 21 (1927):51-54.

Londonderry
-Ancient stone construction
    Robert E. Stone, "Mystery Hill and
    NEARA Research Progress Report--
    1975," NEARA J. 10 (summer-fall
    1975):7,10-11.
-Healing
  n.d.
    Charles M. Skinner, Myths and Legends
    of Our Own Land, 2 vols. (Philadel-
    phia: Lippincott, 1896), 2:315.
-UFO (DD)
  1947, July 6/Harold Healy
    Manchester Morning Union, 7 July
    1947.

Manchester
-Ancient pottery
    Amoskeag
    Barry Fell, America B.C. (N.Y.: Quad-
    rangle, 1976), pp.150-51,166-67,
    248.
-Archeological site
    Harlan A. Marshall, "Some Ancient
    Indian Village Sites Adjacent to
    Manchester, New Hampshire," Am.
    Antiquity 7 (1942):359-63. il.
-Spontaneous human combustion
  1949, Dec.14/Ellen King Coutres
    "Pyrotic," Doubt, no.28 (1950):3,
    quoting AP release, 15 Dec.1949.
-UFO (?)
  1957, Nov.6
    Aimé Michel, Flying Saucers and the
    Straight-Line Mystery (N.Y.: Cri-
    terion, 1958), p.256.
-UFO (NL)
  1947, July 7/Roger Plaisant
    Manchester Morning Union, 8 July
    1947.
  1947, July 9/Mrs. Earl O. Anderson/79
  Kennard Rd.
    Manchester Morning Union, 10 July
    1947.

Meredith
-Anomalous artifact
  1872/Seneca A. Ladd
    D.J. Tapley, "A Remarkable Indian
    Relic," Am.Naturalist 6 (1872):696-
    701.

Mount Sunapee
-Ancient dolmen
    Leon L. Morrill, Jr., "Possible Mega-
    lithic Astronomical Alignments in
    New England," NEARA Newsl. 6 (Mar.
    1971):15.
-UFO (CE-1)
  1966, June 16/Mrs. Gordon M. Avery
    "Unpublicized Sightings Continue,"
    UFO Inv. 3 (Oct.-Nov.1966):4.

Nashua
-UFO (DD)
  1947, July 9/Omer J. Levesque/Lund Rd.
    Manchester Morning Union, 10 July

1947.
-UFO (NL)
  1974, May 19
    Dave Webb & John Oswald, "New Hamp-
    shire Report May Be a Hoax," Sky-
    look, no.93 (Aug.1975):14.

New Castle
-Poltergeist
  1682, June-Aug./George Walton
    Increase Mather, Remarkable Provi-
    dences (Boston: Joseph Browning,
    1684), reprinted in George Lincoln
    Burr, ed., Narratives of the Witch-
    craft Cases 1648-1706 (N.Y.: Barnes
    & Noble, 1946 ed.), pp.8,34-36.
    Richard Chamberlain, Lithobolia (Lon-
    don: E. Whitlook, 1698), reprinted
    in George Lincoln Burr, ed., Narra-
    tives of the Witchcraft Cases 1648-
    1706 (N.Y.: Barnes & Noble, 1946
    ed.), pp.58-77.
    John Albee, New Castle: Historic and
    Picturesque (Boston: Rand Avery,
    1884), pp.43-47.
    Mary R.P. Hatch, "The Stone-Throwing
    Devil of New Castle," New England
    Mag. 32 (Mar.1905):57-65.

New Ipswich
-Ancient stone construction
  =colonial
    "New Ipswich, N.H. Stone Structure,"
    NEARA Newsl. 4 (Dec.1969):73.
-Haunt
  1954-1963/Dixie-Lee Danforth
    Hans Holzer, Yankee Ghosts (N.Y.:
    Ace, 1966), pp.28-34.

Newton
-Ancient stone construction
    (Editorial), NEARA Newsl. 4 (Mar.
    1969):10-11.
    "Discovery of Two Additional Struc-
    tures in the Newton Area Complex,
    New Hampshire," NEARA Newsl. 5
    (Dec.1970):78.
    "The Newton, N.H. Stone Structure
    #3," NEARA Newsl. 6 (Dec.1971):80.
    il.
-UFO (NL)
  1967, July 27/Gary M. Storey
    Raymond E. Fowler, UFOs: Interplane-
    tary Visitors (Jericho, N.Y.: Expo-
    sition, 1974), pp.151-54.
    Raymond E. Fowler, "Telepathy and a
    UFO: Coincidence or Contact?" Offi-
    cial UFO 1 (Jan.1976):14-15,43-44.

North Hampton
-Ball lightning
  1664, April 28/Henry Condliff
    Increase Mather, Remarkable Provi-
    dences (Boston: Joseph Browning,
    1684), ch.3.

North Salem
-Ancient stone constructions
  ca.1000 B.C./Mystery Hill
    Edgar Gilbert, History of Salem, N.H.

(Concord, N.H.: Rumford, 1907).
Wesley S. Griswold, "Stone Village
  Mystery," Hartford (Ct.) Courant,
  19 June 1938, magazine sec.
Hugh Hencken, "The 'Irish Monastery'
  at North Salem, New Hampshire," New
  England Quar. 12 (1939):428-42.
William B. Goodwin, The Ruins of
  Great Ireland in New England (Bos-
  ton: Meador, 1946), pp.58-99,420-
  21. il.
Frederick J. Pohl, The Lost Discovery
  (N.Y.: W.W. Norton, 1952), pp.262-
  74.
Gary S. Vescelius, "Excavations at
  Pattee's Caves," Bull.Eastern States
  Arch.Fed., no.15 (1956):13-14.
Raymond P. Holden, "The North Salem
  Mystery," Historical New Hampshire
  14 (Dec.1958):1-15. il.
Frank Glynn, Report on Excavations
  at North Salem (Harrisburg, Pa.:
  Eastern States Arch.Fed., 1959).
Charles Michael Boland, They All Dis-
  covered America (N.Y.: Pocket Books,
  1963 ed.), pp.23-24,31,33-39,138-
  48,165. il.
Andrew E. Rothovius, "Mysterious
  Stone Village in North Salem, N.H.,"
  Fate 15 (Sep.1962):60-66. il.
Andrew E. Rothovius, "The Strange
  Stone Structures of North Salem,
  New Hampshire," Anthro.J.Canada 1,
  no.3 (1963):19-24.
Robert F. Meader, "Mystery Hill
  Caves, North Salem, New Hampshire,"
  New World Antiquity 10, no.5-6
  (1963):57-61.
Andrew E. Rothovius, "A Possible
  Megalithic Settlement Complex at
  North Salem, N.H.," Bull.N.Y.State
  Arch.Ass'n, no.27 (1963):2-12. il.
Andrew E. Rothovius, "Pattee's
  Caves: Possibly Related Sites Else-
  where in New England," Bull.N.Y.
  State Arch.Ass'n, no.28 (1963):17-
  18.
Gertrude P. Johnson, "Notes on Tri-
  angular Stone Found in the Ruined
  Chamber, Mystery Hill, May 17,
  1969," NEARA Newsl. 4 (June 1969):
  27-28. il.
James P. Whittall, Jr., "Clay Pipes
  at Mystery Hill," NEARA Newsl. 4
  (June 1969):29.
James P. Whittall, Jr., "2995 B.P.
  ±180," NEARA Newsl. 4 (Sep.1969):
  50-54. il.
James P. Whittall, Jr., "Mystery
  Hill Excavations 1969," NEARA Newsl.
  4 (Dec.1969):80-81. il.
Robert E. Stone, "A Strange Well at
  Mystery Hill, N. Salem, N.H.,"
  NEARA Newsl. 5 (Mar.1970):8-11. il.
Robert E. Stone, "A Guide Map to
  Mystery Hill," NEARA Newsl. 5 (Sep.
  1970):58-59. il.
Warren R. Martel, Jr., "Astronomical
  Alignments Research at Mystery
  Hill," NEARA Newsl. 6 (June 1971):

22-23.
"New Radiocarbon Dating Indicates an
Even Greater Antiquity for North
Salem Megalithic Site," NEARA Newsl.
6 (June 1971):40.
Edward J. Lenik, "Excavations at
Mystery Hill's Upper Processional
Path," NEARA Newsl. 7 (Dec.1972):
62-63. il.
Arthur Goldsmith, "New Hampshire's
Incredible 'Mystery Hill,'" Argosy,
Jan.1973, pp.48-49,60,86. il.
"The Grape Vines at the North Salem
Site: Native American After All,"
NEARA Newsl. 8 (Mar.1973):12-13.
Osborn Stone, "Summary of 1973 Re-
search at the North Salem, N.H.
(Mystery Hill) Megalithic Site,"
NEARA Newsl. 8 (winter 1974):62.
R.E. Stone, "Quartz Finds at Mystery
Hill, N. Salem, N.H.," NEARA Newsl.
9 (fall 1974):55-56.
Robert E. Stone, "1974 Progress Re-
port on the North Salem, N.H. Mega-
lithic Site," NEARA J. 10 (spring
1975):95-99.
Barry Fell, "Celtic Iberian Inscrip-
tions of New England," Occ.Pub.Epi-
graphic Soc'y, vol.3, no.50 (Aug.
1975).
James P. Whittall II, "Precolumbian
Parallels between Mediterranean and
New England Archeology," Occ.Pub.
Epigraphic Soc'y, vol.3, no.52
(Aug.1975).
Robert E. Stone, "Mystery Hill and
NEARA Research Progress Report--
1975," NEARA J. 10 (summer-fall
1975):7-13.
Barry Fell, "The Romano-Celtic Phase
at Mystery Hill, New Hampshire, in
New England," Occ.Pub.Epigraphic
Soc'y, vol.3, no.67 (Sep.1975).
Barry Fell, America B.C. (N.Y.: Quad-
rangle, 1976), pp.51,54-55,83-92,
122,144-45,197,200-201,204-206,209-
15. il.
Frank Glynn, "Field Report 1957:
North Salem, N.H.," Work Rept.Early
Sites Rsch.Soc'y, vol.1, no.10
(1976).
Frank Glynn, "Field Report 1958-59:
North Salem, N.H.," Work Rept.Early
Sites Rsch.Soc'y, vol.2, no.19
(1976).
Mark Feldman, "Mystery Hill," Amateur
Arch. 1, no.1 (1976):22-26. il.
Robert E. Stone, "Mystery Hill: New
Information on the Status of Its
Structures in 1938," NEARA J. 11
(fall 1976):18-21.
Andrew Rothovius, "Mystery Hill: An
American Stonehenge," East-West J.,
Oct.1976.
Mark Feldman, The Mystery Hill Story
(Derry, N.H.: Mystery Hill Press,
1977). il.
James P. Whittall, Jr., "Structure
XIB: North Salem, N.H.," Bull.Early
Sites Rsch.Soc'y 5 (Feb.1977):22-

28. il.
James P. Whittall, Jr., "Excavation
Report: Oracle Chamber Drain," Bull.
Early Sites Rsch.Soc'y 5 (Feb.1977)
:18-21. il.
Marjorie R. Kling, "The Enigma of
the North Salem, N.H., 'Little
Stone,'" NEARA J. 11 (spring 1977):
50-55. il.
Junius Bird, "Excavation Report:
North Salem, New Hampshire (1945),"
Work Rept.Early Sites Rsch.Soc'y,
vol.3, no.27 (1977). il.
Charles R. Pettis III, "Underground
Energy Patterns Marked by Megalith-
ic Sites: Mystery Hill Revealed,"
NEARA J. 12 (fall 1977):30-32. il.
Richard R. Szathmary, "A Closer Look
at America B.C.," Fate 30 (Nov.
1977):38-41; (Dec.1977):79-86. il.
Salvatore Michael Trento, The Search
for Lost America (Chicago: Contem-
porary, 1978), pp.182-89. il.
Alexandru V. Manaila, "Mystery Hill:
A Local Historical Development or
Part of a World-Wide Culture?"
NEARA J. 12 (spring 1978):62-66; 13
(summer 1978):2-10; (fall 1978):26-
29; (winter 1979):50-53.
Osborn Stone, "Standing Stones and
Stone Circles," NEARA J. 12 (summer
1978):22.
Wesley Gordeuk, "The Megalithic Geom-
eters of Mystery Hill: Was π Known
to Them?" NEARA J. 13 (winter
1979):56-59.
Jon Douglas Singer, "The Quest for
Norumbega: Ancient Civilizations in
New England?" Pursuit 13 (winter
1979):13-19.

Orford
-Human electrification
  1837, Jan.25-Feb.28
    Willard Hosford, "Extraordinary Case
    of Electrical Excitement," Am.J.Sci.,
    ser.1, 33 (1838):394-98.

Pelham
-Archeological site
  ca.2100 B.C.
    Salem Observer, 27 Apr.1977.
-Fall of meteoritic dust
  1884/Dr. Batchelder
    "Meteoric Dust," Sci.Am. 52 (1885):
    83.

Peterborough
-UFO (NL)
  1978, Dec.14/Windy Row
    Peterborough Transcript, 4 Jan.1979.

Pittsfield
-Poltergeist
  1971, Jan.-March/Frank Ehrhardt
    Lebanon Valley News, 16 Jan.1971.
    Minneapolis (Minn.) Star, 11 Mar.
    1971.

Plaistow
-UFO (NL)
  ca.1953/Hwy.125
    John G. Fuller, The Interrupted Jour-
    ney (N.Y.: Dell, 1967 ed.), p.55.

Plymouth
-UFO (NL)
  1960, April 25/Arnold W. Spencer
    "Recent UFO Sightings," NICAP Spec.
    Bull., May 1960, p.4.
    Richard Hall, ed., The UFO Evidence
    (Washington: NICAP, 1964), p.68.

Portsmouth
-Chicken mutilation
  1976, Sep.19/Betty Hill
    (Letter), Phenomena Rsch.Spec.Rept.,
    no.3 (Oct.1977):10.
-Electromagnetic anomaly, telephone anomaly, Men-in-black, etc.
  1969-   /Betty Hill
    Berthold Eric Schwarz, "Talks with
    Betty Hill: 1--Aftermath of Encoun-
    ter," Flying Saucer Rev. 23 (Aug.
    1977):16-19.
    Berthold Eric Schwarz, "Talks with
    Betty Hill: 2--The Things That Hap-
    pen Around Her," Flying Saucer Rev.
    23 (Oct.1977):11-14,31.
    Berthold Eric Schwarz, "Talks with
    Betty Hill: 3--Experiments and Con-
    clusions," Flying Saucer Rev. 23
    (Jan.1978):28-31.
-Haunt
  n.d.
    Charles W. Brewster, Rambles About
    Portsmouth, 2 vols. (Portsmouth:
    C.W. Brewster, 1859-69), pp.212-13.
-Hex
  1770s/Molly Bridget
    Thomas Bailey Aldrich, An Old Town by
    the Sea (Boston: Houghton Mifflin,
    1893), pp.72-73.
-Phantom dog
  n.d.
    James Reynolds, Ghosts in American
    Houses (N.Y.: Paperback Library,
    1967 ed.), pp.126-31.
-Sea monster
  1821, Aug.2/Samuel Duncan
    Bernard Heuvelmans, In the Wake of
    the Sea-Serpents (N.Y.: Hill & Wang,
    1968), p.171.
-UFO (DD)
  1954, summer/K. Dorn
    Brinsley Le Poer Trench, The Flying
    Saucer Story (N.Y.: Ace, 1966 ed.),
    pp.98-99.
-UFO (NL)
  1975, March
    Ronald Drucker, "Space Intruders Are
    Zeroing In on New England," Saga
    UFO Rept. 3 (Aug.1976):40,43.
  1978, April 15/Rye Beach
    Portsmouth Herald, 19 Apr.1978.
-UFO (R)
  1961, Sep.20/Pease AFB
    "USAF Report on Hill Case," APRO
    Bull. 20 (Jan.-Feb.1972):6.

-UFO (R-V)
  n.d./Pease AFB
    John G. Fuller, Incident at Exeter
    (N.Y.: Berkley, 1967 ed.), pp.181-
    82.
-Unidentified submerged object
  1959, Oct.5/Hyman Rickover/"Sea Drag-
  on" (submarine)
    New York Times, 7 Oct.1959, p.84.
    (Editorial), Fate 13 (Feb.1960):8-
    10.
-Witch trial (hex, shape-shifting)
  1656, March/Jane Walford
    Nathaniel Adams, Annals of Ports-
    mouth (Portsmouth: The Author,
    1825), pp.38-49.
    Samuel G. Drake, Annals of Witchcraft
    in New England (Boston: W.E. Wood-
    ward, 1869), pp.103-106.

Raymond
-Ancient stone constructions
  Long Hill
    William B. Goodwin, The Ruins of
    Great Ireland in New England (Bos-
    ton: Meador, 1946), pp.115-55,414-
    15. il.
    Carolyn C. Robbins, "Thoughts on the
    Raymond, N.H. Stone Circles," NEARA
    Newsl. 4 (June 1969):40-41.
    Robert E. Stone, "Further Notes on
    the Stone Rings at Raymond, N.H.,"
    NEARA Newsl. 4 (Dec.1969):88-89.
    Leon L. Morrill, Jr., "Possible Mega-
    lithic Astronomical Alignments in
    New England," NEARA Newsl. 6 (Mar.
    1971):15.
    Salem Observer, 22 Oct.1975. il.
    Barry Fell, America B.C. (N.Y.: Quad-
    rangle, 1976), pp.56-57,72-73,166-
    67. il.

Rindge
-Dowsing research
  1976/William Jack
    (Editorial), Fate 30 (May 1977):36-
    37.
    (Editorial), Fate 30 (July 1977):22-
    23.

Rumney
-UFO (CE-2)
  1957, Nov.12
    Plymouth Record, 14 Nov.1957.
-UFO (NL)
  1960, Aug.24/Kenneth Elliott
    "UFO Sighting Increase Worries Air
    Force," NICAP Spec.Bull., Oct.1960,
    p.3.
    Richard Hall, ed., The UFO Evidence
    (Washington: NICAP, 1964), p.147.

Salem
-UFO (NL)
  1967, April 27/Dora Lowe
    "Worldwide Sightings Showing In-
    crease," UFO Inv. 4 (Oct.1967):1,3.

Sanbornton
-UFO (CE-1)

1974, Aug.11/Mark Paine
"UFO Flap Reported in New Hampshire,"
Skylook, no.82 (Sep.1974):13.

Seabrook
-UFO (NL)
1965, Oct./Albert Doughty
John G. Fuller, Incident at Exeter
(N.Y.: Berkley, 1967 ed.), pp.176-
77.

South Hampton
-UFO (CE-1)
1974, June 6/Vivian Stevens/Exeter Rd.
Christian Science Monitor, 2 Aug.
1974.
"Close Look at UFO in New Hampshire,"
Skylook, no.82 (Sep.1974):11-12,
quoting Amesbury (Mass.) News (undated).

South Kingston
-UFO (CE-1)
1966, Feb.22
Donald E. Keyhoe & Gordon I.R. Lore,
Jr., UFOs: A New Look (Washington:
NICAP, 1969), p.44.

Stratham
-UFO (CE-1)
1976, Feb.24/Jane Smith/Hwy.101 by-
pass
Raymond E. Fowler & John P. Oswald,
"New Hampshire Close Encounter,"
MUFON UFO J., no.115 (June 1977):
14-18.

Suncook
-UFO (NL)
1965, Oct.22/Oscar J. Augur/Pleasant
St.
Manchester Union-Leader, 23 Oct.1965.

Surry
-Ancient stone construction
Andrew E. Rothovius, "The Purpose of
the Bee-Hive Shaped Stone Structures
in Southwestern New Hampshire,"
NEARA Newsl. 8 (Mar.1973):2,4.

Swanzey Center
-Ancient stone construction
Andrew E. Rothovius, "The Purpose of
the Bee-Hive Shaped Stone Structures
in Southwestern New Hampshire,"
NEARA Newsl. 8 (Mar.1973):2,4.

Troy
-Haunt
n.d.
Melvin T. Stone, Historical Sketch
of the Town of Troy, New Hampshire
(Keene: Sentinel, 1897), pp.235-38.

Wakefield
-Anomalous hole in ice
1977, Jan.10/William McCarthy
Boston (Mass.) Herald-American, 14
Jan.1977. il.
Allen Hendry, "The Wakefield Inci-

dent: Telling a UFO from a Hole in
the Ground," Int'l UFO Reporter 2
(Feb.1977):8.
"Wakefield Wrap-Up," Int'l UFO Re-
porter 2 (Feb.1977):Newsfront sec.
Curt Sutherly, "The Inside Story of
the New Hampshire UFO Crash," Saga
UFO Rept. 4 (July 1977):22,60-64.

Walpole
-Anomalous fossil
1965/Peter D. Kosor/=animal track in
Devonian rock
"New England Stone Puzzles Recently
Brought to NEARA's Attention,"
NEARA Newsl. 9 (spring 1974):19.
-UFO (CE-2)
1971, May/ground markings only
Ted Phillips, Physical Traces Associ-
ated with UFO Sightings (Evanston:
Center for UFO Studies, 1975), p.76.

Warner
-Hex
n.d./Mrs. Davis
Walter Harriman, The History of War-
ner, N.H. (Concord: Republican
Press Ass'n, 1879), p.548.

Warren
-Precognition
1783, June/Mr. Heath
C.B. Colby, Strangely Enough! (N.Y.:
Scholastic, 1963 ed.), pp.73-74.

Waterville Valley
-Phantom
n.d./=hoax
Arthur Conan Doyle, The Coming of
the Fairies (London: Hodder &
Stoughton, 1922), pp.160-61. il.

Weare
-Phantom
1973, Nov.
David Webb, 1973: Year of the Human-
oids (Evanston: Center for UFO
Studies, 1976 ed.), p.19.

Wentworth
-Witchcraft
n.d./Simeon Smith
George F. Plummer, History of Went-
worth, New Hampshire (Concord:
Rumford, 1930), p.344.

West Plymouth
-UFO (DD)
1964, May 19/Mrs. Henry Kelley
"Other Recent Sightings," UFO Inv.
2 (July-Aug.1964):7.

West Rumney
-UFO (DD)
1964, May 18/Samuel Abbott
"Other Recent Sightings," UFO Inv.
2 (July-Aug.1964):7.

West Thornton
-UFO (?)

1960, April 28
(Editorial), NICAP Spec.Bull., May
1960, p.4.

Whitefield
-Haunt
1955-1964/Erlend Jacobsen
Hans Holzer, Yankee Ghosts (N.Y.:
Ace, 1966), pp.149-62.

Wilmot
-UFO (CE-2)
1965, Jan.15/Charles Knee, Jr.
Lebanon Valley News, 18 Jan.1965.

Windham
-Ancient bronze shield
Charles Michael Boland, They All Discovered America (N.Y.: Pocket Books,
1963 ed.), p.39.

Wolfeboro
-UFO (NL)
1974, Aug.
George D. Fawcett, "The 'Unreported'
UFO Wave of 1974," Saga UFO Rept.
2 (spring 1975):50,74.

B. Physical Features

Appledore I.
-Ghost
1826/Babb's Cove
Celia Thaxter, Among the Isles of
Shoals (Boston: James R. Osgood,
1873), pp.173-83.

Franconia Notch
-UFO (CE-2)
1978, Oct.23/Paul Sitchin/U.S.3
(Letter), Saga UFO Rept. 7 (Feb.
1979):4.

Goose Pond
-UFO (NL)
1978, July 13/Robert P. Tobin
Lebanon Valley News, 15 July 1978.

Isles of Shoals
-Haunt
n.d.
Horace P. Beck, The Folklore of
Maine (Philadelphia: Lippincott,
1957), pp.148-52.
-Phantom ship
n.d.
Horace P. Beck, The Folklore of
Maine (Philadelphia: Lippincott,
1957), p.150.

Kearsage Mt.
-Ancient stone construction
"Needs Investigating: No.4," NEARA
Newsl. 6 (Sep.1971):46. il.

Moore L.
-Unidentified submerged object
1968, May 20/Richard Hansen
Richard Wolkomir, "The Glowing 'Thing'

in Moore Lake," Fate 21 (Nov.1968):
32-36.

Prescott Hill
-UFO (NL)
1974, Aug./Kathy Lagiuex
"UFO Flap Reported in New Hampshire,"
Skylook, no.82 (Sep.1974):13.

Red Hill
-UFO (CE-2)
1967, March 3/Charles Fellows/Hwy.113
"Object Startles Couple," UFO Inv.
3 (Mar.-Apr.1967):6.

Shaw, Mt.
-Ancient sculpture
Charles Michael Boland, They All Discovered America (N.Y.: Pocket Books,
1963 ed.), p.31.

Washington, Mt.
-Ancient inscribed brass plate
ca.1802
John H. Spaulding, Historical Relics
of the White Mountains (Boston:
N. Noyes, 1855), p.48.

White I.
-Haunt
n.d.
Henry J. Finn, Whimwhams (Boston:
S.G. Goodrich, 1828), pp.135-50.
(Editorial), Granite Monthly 58
(Mar.1925):100-102.

White Mts.
-Ghost horse
n.d./Angus McDougall
Angus McDougall, "Sounds of a Ghost
Horse," Tomorrow 8 (spring 1960):
74-76.

Winnepesaukee L.
-Ancient standing stone
Ragged I.
Leon L. Morrill, Jr., "Possible Mega-
lithic Astronomical Alignments in
New England," NEARA Newsl. 6 (Mar.
1971):15.
-Ancient stone ax
William B. Goodwin, The Ruins of
Great Ireland in New England (Bos-
ton: Meador, 1946), pp.390-91.

D. Unspecified Localities

-Whirlwind anomaly
1782, June 22
Jeremy Belknap, The History of New-
Hampshire, 3 vols. (Boston: Bradford & Read, 1813), 3:20.

MAINE

A. Populated Places

Alfred
-Haunt
  1827, Oct.-1837/owl tree
    Charles M. Skinner, Myths and Legends
    of Our Own Land, 2 vols. (Philadel-
    phia: Lippincott, 1896), 1:205-207.

Auburn
-UFO (NL)
  1969, Oct.15
    "Bright Rocket-Like Light Seen in
    Maine," Skylook, no.24 (Nov.1969):
    17, quoting Lewiston Daily Star
    (undated).

Augusta
-Fall of fish
  1829, May 24/Capitol Hill
    "Domestic Items," Niles' Weekly Reg-
    ister 36 (1829):232, quoting Maine
    Patriot (undated).
-Spirit medium and clairvoyance
  1857
    Emma Hardinge Britten, Modern Ameri-
    can Spiritualism (N.Y.: The Author,
    1870), p.205.
-UFO (?)
  1948, Dec.7
    "You Asked for It," Doubt, no.24
    (1949):363.
  1956, Dec.21/=meteor?
    "Case 288," CRIFO Orbit, 1 Mar.1957,
    p.2, quoting Augusta Daily Kennebec
    Journal (undated).
-UFO (DD)
  1947, July 5/Dan Kelly
    Augusta Daily Kennebec Journal, 7
    July 1947.

Bangor
-Midday darkness
  1881, Sep.6
    Bangor Commercial, 6 Sep.1881.
-Spirit medium
  1923/Lottie Folsom Kent
    Frederick Edwards, "Sitting with Mrs.
    Lottie Folsom Kent," J.ASPR 18
    (1924):43-68.
-Talking dog
  1928, Feb./Mabel Robinson
    New York Herald Tribune, 21 Feb.1928.
    Charles Fort, The Books of Charles
    Fort (N.Y.: Holt, 1941), pp.864-65.
-UFO (?)
  1959, Dec.7/airport
    Portland Press-Herald, 8 Dec.1959.
-UFO (CE-2)
  1966, March 23/John T. King
    "Close-Range Sightings Increase,"
    UFO Inv. 3 (Mar.-Apr.1966):3.
  1973, March 11/Lannon Stanley/nr. air-
    port

Ronald Drucker, "Space Intruders Are
    Zeroing In on New England," Saga
    UFO Rept. 3 (Aug.1976):40,66.
-UFO (NL)
  1970, May 14
    J. Allen Hynek, The UFO Experience
    (Chicago: Regnery, 1972), pp.42-43.

Bath
-Radiesthesia
  1975, April/Bob Ater
    Bob Ater & Frances Sullivan, "Dowser
    Finds White Mountain Hikers," Fate
    30 (July 1977):52-55.

Belfast
-Fall of unknown object
  1963, May 10/Rene Gagne/Maplewood
    Poultry Co.
    Waterville Morning Sentinel, 11 May
    1963.
-Haunt
  n.d.
    James Reynolds, Ghosts in American
    Houses (N.Y.: Paperback Library,
    1967 ed.), pp.136-39.
-UFO (CE-2)
  1945, March/George P. Miller
    Jacques Vallee, Passport to Magonia
    (Chicago: Regnery, 1969), p.190,
    quoting Flying Saucers, May 1959.

Bernard
-Phantom image
  1867-   /Elias Rich/cemetery
    "Captain Rich's Tombstone," Fate 28
    (Jan.1975):59, quoting Bangor Daily
    News (undated).

Berwick
-Poltergeist
  1682, June/Mary Hortado
    Increase Mather, Remarkable Provi-
    dences (Boston: Joseph Browning,
    1684), reprinted in George Lincoln
    Burr, ed., Narratives of the Witch-
    craft Cases 1648-1706 (N.Y.: Barnes
    & Noble, 1946 ed.), pp.8,37-38.
    Samuel G. Drake, Annals of Witchcraft
    in New England (Boston: W.E. Wood-
    ward, 1869), pp.159-65.

Biddeford
-Dowsing
  1930s-   /Henry Gross
    Kenneth Roberts, "The Mystery of the
    Forked Twig," Country Gentleman,
    Sep.1944.
    L.A. Dale, et al., "Dowsing: A Field
    Experiment in Water Divining," J.
    ASPR 45 (1951):3-16.
    Kenneth Roberts, Henry Gross and His
    Divining Rod (Garden City: Double-
    day, 1951).

Kenneth Roberts, The Seventh Sense (Garden City: Doubleday, 1953).
Kenneth Roberts, Water Unlimited (Garden City: Doubleday, 1957).
Allen Angoff, "The Kenneth Roberts Crusade," Tomorrow 7 (summer 1959): 108-18.
Berthold Eric Schwarz, "Physiological Aspects of Henry Gross's Dowsing," Parapsychology 4, no.2 (1962):71-86.
Berthold Eric Schwarz, Psychic Dynamics (N.Y.: Pageant, 1965).
-Healing
n.d./Biddeford Pool
Charles M. Skinner, Myths and Legends of Our Own Land, 2 vols. (Philadelphia: Lippincott, 1896), 2:315.
-Sea monster (carcass)
1967, Aug.
Boston (Mass.) Herald-Traveler, 9 Aug.1967.

Bingham
-UFO (CE-3)
1966, April 23/Kimberley Baker/nr. Kennebec Mill
Waterville Morning Sentinel, 6 May 1966, p.20.
Richard Bonenfant, "The Baker Sighting: A Retrospective Investigation," Flying Saucer Rev. 22 (July 1976): 2-6.

Boothbay Harbor
-Sea monster
ca.1773/Paul Reed
Jacob Bigelow, "Documents and Remarks Respecting the Sea Serpent," Am.J. Sci., ser.1, 2 (1820):147,151.
1831/Capt. Walden/"Detector"
Bernard Heuvelmans, In the Wake of the Sea-Serpents (N.Y.: Hill & Wang, 1968), pp.174-75.

Brooklin
-Haunt
1974, Oct.-1977/Beatrice E. Cooper
Beatrice E. Cooper, "The House That Ruined Our Lives," Fate 30 (Dec. 1977):67-71.

Brunswick
-UFO (NL)
1961, Feb.
Portland Press-Herald, 9 Feb.1961.
1966, Feb.16/Naval Air Station
Jacques Vallee, Passport to Magonia (Chicago: Regnery, 1969), p.322.

Buckfield
-UFO (NL)
1975, Nov.18/Eldon Bartlett/Hwy.140
Robert S. Niss, "The Stephens Abduction in Oxford, Maine," Official UFO 1 (July 1976):20,47-48.

Bucksport
-Phantom image
1762-   /Jonathan Buck
James O. Whittemore, "The Witch's

Curse," New England Mag. 27 (1902): 111-13. il.
A. Hyatt Verrill, Romantic and Historic Maine (N.Y.: Dodd, Mead, 1938).
Belle M. Drake, "The Foot on Colonel Buck's Grave," Fate 3 (Sep.1950):38.
Adelaide Weese, "The Witch's Revenge," Fate 27 (Feb.1974):91-92. il.
(Letter), Arthur L. Robertson, Fate 27 (May 1974):142-44. il.
(Letter), Elizabeth Webb, Fate 27 (May 1974):144-45.
(Letter), Kurt Peterson, Fate 27 (May 1974):145-46.
(Letter), Adelaide Weese, Fate 27 (May 1974):146.

Burnham
-UFO (NL)
1966, March 16/Daniel Estes
Waterville Morning Sentinel, 17 Mar. 1966.

Cape Elizabeth
-Ball lightning
1771, Aug.12
Boston Massachusetts Spy, 5 Sep.1771.
-Ghost light
n.d./Pond Cove
Charles M. Skinner, Myths and Legends of Our Own Land, 2 vols.(Philadelphia: Lippincott, 1896), 1:192-93.
-UFO (NL)
1978, Sep.14/Greg Tinsman
Portland Press-Herald, 15 Sep.1978.

Cape Neddick
-UFO (?)
1968, April 12
"French General, Scientists, Report UFOs," UFO Inv. 4 (May-June 1968):3.
Donald E. Keyhoe & Gordon I.R. Lore, Jr., UFOs: A New Look (Washington: NICAP, 1969), p.44.

Castine
-Ancient pottery
1971, summer/Norman Bakeman
Atlanta (Ga.) Journal & Constitution, 2 Jan.1977.
Barry Fell, "Amphorettas from Maine and Iberia," Occ.Pub.Epigraphic Soc'y 4, no.96 (Jan.1977):1-3.
James P. Whittall II, "Anforetas Recovered in Maine," Bull.Early Sites Rsch.Soc'y 5 (Feb.1977):1-5. il.
Salvatore Michael Trento, The Search for Lost America (Chicago: Contemporary, 1978), pp.193-94.
-Sea monster
1834, July
Bernard Heuvelmans, In the Wake of the Sea-Serpents (N.Y.: Hill & Wang, 1968), p.176.

Chapman
-Mystery plane crash
1956, Nov.30
"Case 283," CRIFO Orbit, 1 Mar.1957,

p.1.

Cumberland co.
-Mystery bird deaths
  1974, May
    Washington (D.C.) Star-News, 28 May
    1974.

Cushing
-Ancient stone construction
  McCobb's Narrows
    Cyrus Eaton, History of Thomaston,
    Rockland and South Thomaston, Maine
    (Hallowell: Masters, Smith, 1865),
    p.376.
    Cyrus Eaton, Annals of the Town of
    Warren, in Knox County, Maine (Hal-
    lowell: Masters & Livermore, 1877),
    p.32.

Darkharbor
-Haunt
  n.d.
    James Reynolds, Gallery of Ghosts
    (N.Y.: Paperback Library, 1970 ed.),
    pp.243-52.

Deer Isle
-Spontaneous human combustion
  1943, Jan.13/Allen M. Small/Eggemoggin
  Reach Rd.
    Ellsworth American, 14 Jan.1943.

Denmark
-Possession
  ca.1889/Susie Smith
    Roy M. Frisen, "Can Spirits Possess
    the Dead?" Fate 7 (Nov.1954):68-70.

Dennysville
-UFO (NL)
  1966, June 19/Druscilla Clemens
    (Letter), Sci.& Mech. 38 (May 1967):
    71-72.

Dexter
-Clairvoyance
  1860s
    Walter Franklin Prince, They Saw Be-
    yond (N.Y.: Olympia, 1972 ed.), pp.
    24-26.

Douglas Hill
-Ghost
  ca.1958/Dorothy L. Pierce
    (Letter), Fate 17 (May 1964):108-109.

Dover-Foxcroft
-UFO (DD)
  1970, Dec.28/Mary C. Kimball
    "Maine Reader Observes Square UFO,"
    Skylook, no.40 (Mar.1971):16.
-UFO (NL)
  1962, Jan.23/Mary C. Kimball
    "Maneuvering 'Star,'" APRO Bull. 10
    (Mar.1962):2.

Dry Mills
-Ancient stone chamber
    William B. Goodwin, The Ruins of

Great Ireland in New England (Boston: Meador, 1946), p.169.

Durham
-Humanoid
  1973, July 25/Neota Hutchinson
    Brunswick Times-Record, 27 July 1973.
    Portland Press-Herald, 28 July 1973.
    Lewiston Daily Sun, 28 July 1973.

East Corinth
-Deathbed apparition
  1952, summer/Thurston Wiggin
    Robert E. Allten, "Why the Christian
    Church Must Study Survival," Fate
    14 (Dec.1961):54-56.

Edgecomb
-Roman coin
  1967, June 27/Pauline Mukhalian
    Lesley E. Hall, "A Roman Find at
    Edgecomb, Maine?" NEARA Newsl. 2
    (Sep.1967):47.

Eliot
-Contactee
  1959/Mrs. Swan
    Robert Emenegger, UFOs: Past, Pres-
    ent and Future (N.Y.: Ballantine,
    1974), pp.55-62.
-Phantom wolf
  1966, April
    Jerome Clark & Loren Coleman, Crea-
    tures of the Outer Edge (N.Y.:
    Warner, 1978), pp.158-59.
-UFO (CE-1)
  n.d.
    Dan Clements, "Saucer Safari," Of-
    ficial UFO 1 (Nov.1976):35.
-UFO (DD)
  1966, March 29
    "Close-Range Sightings Increase,"
    UFO Inv. 3 (Mar.-Apr.1966):3.
-UFO (NL)
  1966, March 16
    "Close-Range Sightings Increase,"
    UFO Inv. 3 (Mar.-Apr.1966):3.

Ellsworth
-Ancient inscription
    Charles C. Willoughby, "Prehistoric
    Burial Places in Maine," Pap.Pea-
    body Mus. 1, no.6 (1898):11-12. il.
    Olaf Strandwold, Norse Inscriptions
    on American Stones (Weehauken, N.J.:
    Magnus Björndal, 1948), pp.43-44.
    il.
-Archeological site
  ca.2500-1400 B.C.
    Douglas Byers, "The Eastern Archaic:
    Some Problems and Hypotheses," Am.
    Antiquity 24 (1959):233-56. il.

Falmouth
-UFO (?)
  1949, Sep.8
    "If It's in the Sky It's a Saucer,"
    Doubt, no.27 (1949):416,417.

Farmington
-Entombed toad
  1868
    Henry Winfred Splitter, "The Impos-
    sible Fossils," Fate 7 (Jan.1954):
    65,70.

Fayette
-Haunt
  1750s/Jolly Hollow
    Paul Coffin, "Memoir and Journals of
    Rev. Paul Coffin," Coll.Maine Hist.
    Soc'y, ser.1, 4 (1856):235-407.
    Augusta Daily Kennebec Journal, 30
    Oct.1976.
-Spirit medium
  1900s-1910s/Katie B. Adams
    Oscar E. Young, et al., "Experiences
    Centering in the Young Family,"
    Proc.ASPR 14 (1920):287-359.

Fort Kent
-UFO (DD)
  1963, Aug.18
    Madawasha St. John Valley Times, 29
    Aug.1963.

Freeport
-Phantom ship
  1812
    Florence G. Thurston & Harmon S.
    Cross, Three Centuries of Freeport,
    Maine (Freeport: Southworth-Anthoen-
    sen, 1940), pp.63-64.

Glen Cove
-Clairempathy
  1956/Peter Hurkos
    Jess Stearn, The Door to the Future
    (N.Y.: Macfadden, 1964), pp.213-15.
    Andrija Puharich, Beyond Telepathy
    (Garden City: Anchor, 1973 ed.),
    pp.29-59.
-Telepathy research
  1950s/Andrija Puharich
    Andrija Puharich, Beyond Telepathy
    (Garden City: Anchor, 1973 ed.).
-UFO (CE-2)
  1956/Peter Hurkos
    B. Ann Slate, "The Amazing UFO Dis-
    coveries of Peter Hurkos," Saga,
    Nov.1974, pp.28,76.

Great Pond
-Skyquake
  1945, Aug.1/Raymond Stickney
    "Sky Blast," Doubt, no.14 (spring
    1946):204.
-UFO (NL)
  1947, July 7/Orrin Williams
    Augusta Daily Kennebec Journal, 8
    July 1947.

Greenacre
-Clairempathy
  1898, Sep.1/Elizabeth T. Stansell
    Walter F. Prince, "A 'Psychometric'
    Experiment," J.ASPR 14 (1920):196-
    214.

Greenville
-Dowsing
  1960s/Eileen Farrell
    (Editorial), Fate 20 (Jan.1967):15.

Hallowell
-Phantom ship
  n.d.
    Lewiston Journal, 6 Jan.1938.
-Witchcraft
  ca.1890/Haunted Valley
    Portland Express, 3 July 1940.

Harborside
-UFO (DD)
  1947, July 3/John F. Cole
    Ted Bloecher, Report on the UFO Wave
    of 1947 (Washington: NICAP, 1967),
    p. III-18.

Harmony
-Ancient inscription
  Devil's Head/=recent
    Edward J. Lenik, "Riddles on Rock:
    Non-Aboriginal Petroglyphs in
    Maine," NEARA J. 12 (spring 1978):
    76,77-78. il.

Harpswell Center
-Phantom ship
  n.d.
    Charles M. Skinner, Myths and Legends
    of Our Own Land, 2 vols. (Philadel-
    phia: Lippincott, 1896), 1:190-91.

Hollis Center
-Haunt
  n.d./John Livingston/sawmill
    Bangor Journal, 10 Apr.1931; and 9
    Jan.1937.

Jonesboro
-Ancient pottery
    James P. Whittall II, "Anforetas
    Recovered in Maine," Bull.Early
    Sites Rsch.Soc'y 5 (1977):1-5.
-Haunt
  ca.1812-   /Hilton's Neck
    Charles M. Skinner, American Myths
    and Legends, 2 vols. (Philadelphia:
    Lippincott, 1903), 1:20-22.
-Precognition
  1746-1775/Nell Hilton
    Charles M. Skinner, American Myths
    and Legends, 2 vols. (Philadelphia:
    Lippincott, 1903), 1:20-22.

Jonesport
-UFO (?)
  1955, May 9
    Leonard H. Stringfield, Inside Sau-
    cer Post...3-0 Blue (Cincinnati:
    CRIFO, 1957), p.58.

Kennebec
-Sea monster
  1830/Mr. Gooch
  1839/Capt. Smith
    Bernard Heuvelmans, In the Wake of
    the Sea-Serpents (N.Y.: Hill & Wang,

1968), pp.174,178.

Kennebunkport
-Haunt
    1964-1968/Jane Morgan
        (Editorial), Fate 18 (June 1965):28-
        29, quoting New York World-Telegram
        & Sun (undated).
        (Letter), Bertram W. Hanscom, Fate
        18 (Nov.1965):124-27.
        Hans Holzer, Yankee Ghosts (N.Y.:
        Ace, 1966), pp.178-80.
        (Editorial), Fate 21 (Mar.1968):32-
        33, quoting Long Island Star-Journal
        (undated).
        Susy Smith, Prominent American Ghosts
        (N.Y.: Dell, 1969 ed.), pp.46-52.
-UFO (NL)
    1961, Feb.7/H. David Walley
        Richard Hall, ed., The UFO Evidence
        (Washington: NICAP, 1964), p.68.

Kittery
-Hex
    1725-1726/Sarah Keene
        Neal W. Allen, Jr., "A Maine Witch,"
        Old-Time New England 61, no.3
        (1971):75-81.
-UFO (NL)
    1966, April 5
        Jacques Vallee, Passport to Magonia
        (Chicago: Regnery, 1969), p.327.

Lewiston
-Clairvoyance
    1870, June 12/Sarah Burton
        Boston (Mass.) Journal, 17 Oct.1873.
        C. Maldram Wilds, "Dream Witness to
        Murder," Fate 14 (June 1961):59-61.

Limestone
-UFO (?)
    1975, Nov./Loring AFB
        Little Rock Arkansas Democrat, 19
        Jan.1979.

Long Sands
-UFO (NL)
    1978, April 23/Robert Lassones
        Manchester (N.H.) Union-Leader, 25
        Apr.1978.

Manchester
-Humanoid
    1975, Sep.22/Camp Rd.
    1975, Nov.
        John Green, Sasquatch: The Apes Among
        Us (Seattle: Hancock House, 1978),
        p.229.
-Human track in stone
    Meeting House cemetery
        Jim Brandon, Weird America (N.Y.:
        Dutton, 1978), p.99.
-UFO (NL)
    1947, July 7/Charles Crockett/nr. Four
    Corners
        Augusta Daily Kennebec Journal, 8
        July 1947.

Matinicus
-Sea monster
    1875, Aug.22/Frederick York/"Emily
    Holden"/10 mi.SSW
        New York Times, 30 Aug.1875, p.8.

Medomak
-Norse carving
    1920s/=blasted from quarry
        "The Medomak 'Viking Sail' Stone:
        Hardly Half a Century Old!" NEARA
        Newsl. 7 (Dec.1972):78. il.

Mexico
-UFO (NL)
    1975, Dec.7
        "UFO Central," CUFOS News Bull., 1
        Feb.1976, p.14.

Millinocket
-UFO (CE-2)
    1964, May 24/Millinocket Lake Rd.
        Jacques Vallee, Passport to Magonia
        (Chicago: Regnery, 1969), p.299.

Minot
-Hex
    1800s/Aunt Woodward
        Charles M. Skinner, Myths and Legends
        of Our Own Land, 2 vols. (Philadel-
        phia: Lippincott, 1896), 1:237-38.

Monson
-Disappearance
    1924, June/Harry Davis/Sprague's Barn
        "The Barn That Vanished," Fate 19
        (July 1966):80, quoting Bangor
        Daily News (undated).

Newcastle
-Ancient stone constructions
        Cyrus Eaton, Annals of the Town of
        Warren, in Knox County, Maine (Hal-
        lowell: Masters & Livermore, 1877),
        p.20.

Newfield
-Haunt
    1958-1960s/Darrell McLaughlin/Old
    Straw Place
        Susy Smith, Prominent American Ghosts
        (N.Y.: Dell, 1969 ed.), pp.154-59.

New Harbor
-Sea monster
    1880, summer/S.W. Hanna/=shark?
        Bernard Heuvelmans, In the Wake of
        the Sea-Serpents (N.Y.: Hill & Wang,
        1968), pp.138-39, quoting Sea-Side
        Press, Aug.1880.

Nobleboro
-Cloud anomaly
    1823, Aug.7
        Prof. Cleaveland, "Notice of the
        Late Meteor in Maine," Am.J.Sci.,
        ser.1, 7 (1824):171-72.
        "Aerolite of Maine," Am.J.Sci., ser.
        1, 9 (1825):400.

North Berwick
-UFO (CE-1)
1978, May 23/Joyce Smith/Somersworth
Rd.
    Biddeford Journal-Tribune, 25 May
    1978.

Northeast Harbor
-Deathbed apparition
1926, Aug.21/Charles W. Eliot
    William H. Gysan, "An Exception to
    the Rule," Fate 24 (July 1971):72.

North Haven
-UFO (NL)
1978, Sep.19/June Hopkins
    Rockland Courier-Gazette, 21 Sep.
    1978.

North Windham
-UFO (DD)
1956, Aug.14/Hyman Jacobson/Little
Sebago L.
    "Case 193," CRIFO Orbit, 5 Oct.1956,
    p.1, quoting Hartford (Conn.) Times
    (undated).

Oakland
-UFO (NL)
1968, July 29
    Brent Raynes, "Flying Saucer Landings
    and UFO Kidnapping Reports," Flying
    Saucers, June 1970, p.32.

Old Orchard Beach
-Haunt
ca.1974/Herbert Hopkins
    Berthold Eric Schwarz, "The Man-In-
    Black Syndrome: 2," Flying Saucer
    Rev. 23 (Feb.1978):22,24-25.
-Men-in-black
1976, Sep.11/Herbert Hopkins
1976, Sep.24/John Hopkins
    Berthold Eric Schwarz, "The Man-In-
    Black Syndrome: 1," Flying Saucer
    Rev. 23 (Jan.1978):9-15.
    Alex Evans, "The Stephens UFO Kid-
    napping: The Men in Black Return,"
    Saga UFO Rept. 6 (Sep.1978):20-23,
    56-61.
-Precognition
1957/Herbert Hopkins
    Berthold Eric Schwarz, "The Man-In-
    Black Syndrome: 2," Flying Saucer
    Rev. 23 (Feb.1978):22,23-24.
-UFO (NL)
1978, May 20
    Biddeford Journal-Tribune, 24 May
    1978.
1978, Sep.14
    Portland Press-Herald, 15 Sep.1978.

Orono
-Snow anomaly
1919, March 3
    Leon Elmer Woodman, "A Snow Effect,"
    Science 50 (1919):210-11.

Orrington
-Petroglyph

Center Dr.
    "A Grouping of Possible Ancient Corn
    Grinding Holes Discovered in Maine,"
    NEARA Newsl. 9 (spring 1974):19.

Palermo
-UFO (CE-1)
1968, spring/Merton Haskel
    Brent Raynes, "Flying Saucers and
    UFO Kidnapping Reports," Flying
    Saucers, June 1970, p.32.
-UFO (CE-2)
1965, Nov.10
    Brent Raynes, "Flying Saucers and
    UFO Kidnapping Reports," Flying
    Saucers, June 1970, p.32.
1967/ground markings only
    Ted Phillips, Physical Traces Associ-
    ated with UFO Sightings (Evanston:
    Center for UFO Studies, 1975), p.45.
-UFO (DD)
1968, June
    Brent Raynes, "Flying Saucer Land-
    ings and UFO Kidnapping Reports,"
    Flying Saucers, June 1970, p.32.

Paris
-Healing
1809, winter/Molly Ockett
    Charles Eugene Hamlin, The Life and
    Times of Hannibal Hamlin (Cambridge:
    Riverside Press, 1899), p.18.
    Bangor Daily News, 28 July 1965.
    Frank Ball, "Molly Ockett, For and
    Against," Fate 27 (Aug.1974):90.

Parker Head
-Ancient tower
=Colonial?
    Edward J. Lenik, "Archeological Sur-
    vey of Spirit Pond, Campbell Island,
    Atkins Bay, and Parker Head," NEARA
    Newsl. 8 (winter 1974):68-70.

Pemaquid
-Ancient stone construction
    J. Henry Cartland, Twenty Years at
    Pemaquid (Boothbay Harbor: L.A.
    Moore, 1914).

Popham Beach
-Sea monster
1887, July/Fort Popham
    London (Eng.) Globe & Traveller, 15
    Aug.1887.

Portland
-Clairempathy
ca.1890/Mrs. Chapman
    Walter F. Prince, "Experiments in
    Psychometry," J.ASPR 14 (1920):100-
    105.
-Fall of pebbles
1873, Aug.8/Capt. Winchester/"New York"
/33 mi.E
    Decatur (Ill.) Republican, 14 Aug.
    1873, p.3.
-Healing
1859-1866/Phineas Parkhurst Quimby
    Horatio W. Dresser, ed., The Quimby

Manuscripts (N.Y.: T.Y. Crowell, 1921).
Nandor Fodor, Encyclopaedia of Psychic Science (London: Arthurs, 1933), p.243.
Phineas P. Quimby, The Science of Health and Hygiene (N.Y.: The Author, 1939 ed.).
Virginia Stumbough, "Quimby: Father of Mental Healing," Fate 10 (Oct. 1957):78-82.
(Letter), Will B. Davis, Fate 11 (Apr.1958):127-28.
Lee R. Gandee, "Dr. Quimby: Pioneer Parapsychologist," Fate 13 (Apr. 1960):53-60.
-Midday darkness
1881, Sep.6
Portland Press, 7 Sep.1881.
-Out-of-body experience and clairvoyance
1960s-   /Alex Tanous
Herbert B. Greenhouse, The Astral Journey (N.Y.: Avon, 1976 ed.), pp. 237-50,283-84,290-91,334-35.
Alex Tanous & Harvey Ardman, Beyond Coincidence (Garden City: Doubleday, 1976).
-Sea monster
1818, June 27
Boston (Mass.) Weekly Messenger, 9 July 1818, p.620.
1818, July 12
Boston (Mass.) Weekly Messenger, 23 July 1818, p.651.
1875, Sep.15/John Trefethen/Brown's Wharf
New York Times, 19 Sep.1875, p.10.
ca.1912/Mrs. F.W. Saunderson
Bernard Heuvelmans, In the Wake of the Sea-Serpents (N.Y.: Hill & Wang, 1968), p.359.
-UFO (NL)
1952, May 1
Portland Evening Express, 2 May 1952.
1961, Feb.5-7
Portland Press-Herald, 9 Feb.1961.
-Unidentified submerged object
1963, Aug.9/John Larson/"Resolute"
Boston (Mass.) Globe, 10 Aug.1963.

Presque Isle
-UFO (?)
1952, Oct.10/Presque Isle AFB/=Jupiter
Donald E. Menzel & Lyle G. Boyd, The World of Flying Saucers (Garden City: Doubleday, 1963), pp.139-42.
-UFO (DD)
n.d.
Ronald Drucker, "Space Intruders Are Zeroing In on New England," Saga UFO Rept. 3 (Aug.1976):40,43.
1953, Jan.29
Richard Hall, ed., The UFO Evidence (Washington: NICAP, 1964), p.21.
J. Allen Hynek, The Hynek UFO Report (N.Y.: Dell, 1977), p.58.

Rangeley
-Orgone energy research, weather control, and UFOs

1946-1957/Wilhelm Reich/Orgonon
Wilhelm Reich, The Discovery of the Orgone (N.Y.: Orgone Institute Press, 1942).
Wilhelm Reich, The Function of the Orgasm (N.Y.: Orgone Institute Press, 1942).
Wilhelm Reich, "Orgonotic Pulsation," Int'l J.Sex-Economy & Orgone-Rsch. 3 (Oct.1944):97-150.
Wilhelm Reich, The Cancer Biopathy (N.Y.: Orgone Institute Press, 1948).
Wilhelm Reich, The Oranur Experiment (N.Y.: Orgone Energy Press, 1951).
Wilhelm Reich, Cosmic Superimposition (Rangeley: Wilhelm Reich Foundation, 1951).
Wilhelm Reich, The Einstein Affair (Rangeley: Orgone Institute Press, 1953).
Wilhelm Reich, Contact with Space (Rangeley: Core Pilot, 1957).
Walter Edwards, "Healing Energy Called 'Orgone,'" Fate 14 (June 1961):75-80.
Ilse Ollendorff Reich, Wilhelm Reich (N.Y.: St. Martin's, 1969).
Ola Raknes, Wilhelm Reich and Orgonomy (N.Y.: St. Martin's, 1970).
Jerome Eden, Orgone Energy: The Answer to Atomic Suicide (Hicksville, N.Y.: Exposition, 1972).
Jerome Eden, Planet in Trouble: The UFO Assault on Earth (Hicksville, N.Y.: Exposition, 1973).
W. Edward Mann, Orgone, Reich and Eros (N.Y.: Simon & Schuster, 1973).
David Boadella, Wilhelm Reich: The Evolution of His Work (London: Vision, 1973).
Jerome Greenfield, Wilhelm Reich vs. the U.S.A. (N.Y.: W.W. Norton, 1974).
Jerome Eden, "The Scientist Who Disabled UFOs," Official UFO 1 (Oct. 1975):20-21,42-45.
Jerome Eden, "The Propulsive Power of UFOs," Official UFO 1 (Jan.1976) :32-33,54-58.
Jerome Eden, "The Interplanetary Valley Forge," Official UFO 1 (Apr. 1976):26-28,38,45-46.
Trevor James Constable, The Cosmic Pulse of Life (Santa Ana, Cal.: Merlin, 1976), pp.293-347.
K.L. Woodward, "Reassessing Reich," Newsweek, 13 Dec.1976, pp.63-64.

Richmond
-UFO (CE-2)
1949, fall
Brent Raynes, "Flying Saucer Landings and UFO Kidnapping Reports," Flying Saucers, June 1970, p.32.

Rockland
-UFO (NL)
1970, Aug.12/Marilin Turner
"Two Watch UFO at Rockland, Maine,"

Skylook, no.35 (Oct.1970):8.

Round Pond
-Sea monster
1751, May/Joseph Kent/"Intrepid"/Broad
Bay
1780, May/George Little/"Boston"/Broad
Bay
    Jacob Bigelow, "Documents and Re-
    marks Respecting the Sea Serpent,"
    Am.J.Sci., ser.1, 2 (1820):147,
    152-53.

Sanford
-Haunt
n.d.
    Sanford Tribune, 28 Jan.1932.

Sebago Lake
-UFO (?)
1957, Aug.2
    Richard Hall, ed., _The UFO Evidence_
    (Washington: NICAP, 1964), p.98.

Sebasco Estates
-Norse runestone
1968/John Dabney, Jr./Sebasco Rd./=
scrapings by plow
    "Sebasco Inscriptions Apparently Not
    Runic," _NEARA Newsl._ 8 (summer
    1973):35.
    John Dabney, Jr., "Runic Inscriptions
    at Sebasco, Maine," _NEARA Newsl._ 9
    (spring 1974):12-13.

Sebec
-Ancient inscription
n.d./Charles Chatfield
    Olaf Strandwold, _Norse Inscriptions_
    on American Stones (Weehauken, N.J.:
    Magnus Björndal, 1948), p.45. il.

Sheepscott
-Ancient stone constructions
    Samuel Johnson, "Account of an An-
    cient Settlement on Sheepscot River,"
    Coll.Maine Hist.Soc'y, ser.1, 2
    (1847):229-37.
    David Cushman, "Ancient Settlement
    of Sheepscot," _Coll.Maine Hist.Soc'y_,
    ser.1, 4 (1856):207-33.
    Johannes Brøndsted, "Norsemen in
    North America Before Columbus," _Ann._
    Rept.Smith.Inst. 103 (1953):367.

Skowhegan
-Retrocognition
1931/Francis J. Sibolski/Mud Pond
    Francis J. Sibolski, "The Specter of
    Mud Pond," _Fate_ 24 (Jan.1971):45.
-UFO (R-V)
1966, Feb.11/Robert E. Barnes
    Bangor Daily News, 14 Feb.1966.
    "National Press Spotlights UFOs," _UFO_
    Inv. 3 (Jan.-Feb.1966):1-2.

Snow Falls
-Hex
1809, winter/Molly Ockett
    Frank Ball, "Molly Ockett, For and

Against," _Fate_ 27 (Aug.1974):90.

Solon
-Petroglyph
    Elisa H. Burleigh, _Maine Indians in_
    History and Legend (Portland: Sev-
    ern-Wylie-Jewett, 1953).
    Lesley E. Hall, "Maine's Greatest
    Indian Rock Carving," _NEARA Newsl._
    4 (Sep.1969):66-68. il.

South Berwick
-Ancient stone chamber
    William B. Goodwin, _The Ruins of_
    Great Ireland in New England (Bos-
    ton: Meador, 1946), p.157.

South Portland
-Dowsing
1970s/Gordon MacLean
    Peter Tompkins & Christopher Bird,
    The Secret Life of Plants (N.Y.:
    Harper & Row, 1973), p.298.
    "In Vermont: Is Dowsing Going to the
    Dogs?" _Time_, 9 Oct.1978, p.11.
-UFO (NL)
1975, Sep.23
    "UFO Central," _CUFOS News Bull._, 15
    Nov.1975, p.19.

South Windham
-Ancient stairway
    William B. Goodwin, _The Ruins of_
    Great Ireland in New England (Bos-
    ton: Meador, 1946), pp.168-70. il.

Sullivan
-Ghost
1799, Aug.9-1800, Aug./Lydia Blaisdell
    Abraham Cummings, _Immortality Proved_
    by the Testimony of Sense (Bath:
    J.G. Torrey, 1826).
    William Oliver Stevens, _Unbidden_
    Guests (London: Allen & Unwin,
    1949).
    John P. Bessor, "The Return of Nelly
    Butler," _Fate_ 6 (Dec.1953):36-41.
    Susy Smith, _Prominent American Ghosts_
    (N.Y.: Dell, 1969 ed.), pp.14-26.
    Muriel Roll, "A Nineteenth-Century
    Matchmaking Apparition," _J.ASPR_ 63
    (1969):396-408.

Surry
-UFO (NL)
1977, Dec.28
    Ellsworth American, 12 Jan.1978.

Timberlake
-UFO (DD)
1958, July 7
    Hayden C. Hewes & William H. Spauld-
    ing, "NASA Computer Analyses Prove
    UFOs Exist!" _Saga UFO Rept._ 4 (June
    1977):28,30-33. il.

Topsfield
-Humanoid
n.d.
    John Green, _Sasquatch: The Apes Among_

Us (Seattle: Hancock House, 1978),
p.228.

Turner
-Plague of beetles
  1978, July
    Wichita (Kan.) Eagle & Beacon, 8
    July 1978.
-UFO (NL)
  1959, summer/Emily Deneault
    John G. Fuller, Incident at Exeter
    (N.Y.: Berkley, 1967 ed.), pp.53-54.

Waldo
-UFO (CE-2)
  1969, July 20/Randy Whitcomb/Birches Rd.
    Portland Press-Herald, 23 July 1969.

Warren
-Anomalous artifacts
  Indian cemetery/=copper objects
    Cyrus Eaton, Annals of the Town of
    Warren, in Knox County, Maine (Hal-
    lowell: Masters & Livermore, 1877),
    pp.17-18.

Washburn
-UFO (NL)
  1955, Dec.21/Roberta Vesta Jacobs
    Thomas M. Olsen, ed., The Reference
    for Outstanding UFO Sighting Reports
    (Riderwood, Md.: UFO Information
    Retrieval Center, 1966), pp.43-44.

Waterville
-Psychic photography and paranormal
voice recordings
  1967, Aug.1-   /Richard Veilleux
    Jeanne P. Rindge, William Cook &
    A.R.G. Owen, "An Investigation of
    Psychic Photography with the Veil-
    leux Family," New Horizons 1 (sum-
    mer 1972):28-32. il.
    Susy Smith, "Psychic Photography in
    Maine," Psychic 5 (Oct.1974):12-18.
    il.
    Jule Eisenbud, "The Merveilleux Veil-
    leux: Their Psychic Photography,"
    Fate 28 (Nov.1975):46-54; (Dec.1975)
    :72-81. il.
    (Letter), Henry J. Hoffman, Fate 29
    (Apr.1976):118,127.
    Susy Smith, Voices of the Dead? (N.Y.:
    Signet, 1977), pp.76-81.
-Skyquake
  1947, Dec.8
    "Booms--No Clues," Doubt, no.21
    (1948):317.
-UFO (DD)
  1965, Dec.10/Marjorie Fernald/Fairfield
  Junior High School
    Waterville Morning Sentinel, 11 Dec.
    1965.
-UFO (NL)
  1945, fall/airport
    Brent Raynes, "Flying Saucer Landings
    and UFO Kidnaping Reports," Flying
    Saucers, June 1970, p.32.
  1947, July 7/Perry Mosher
    Augusta Daily Kennebec Journal, 8

July 1947.

Welchville
-UFO (CE-2)
  1975, Nov.5/David Stephens
    Robert S. Niss, "The Stephens Abduc-
    tion in Oxford, Maine," Official
    UFO 1 (July 1976):20,47.

Weld
-Skyquake
  1854, July 18/Stillman Masterman
    Stillman Masterman, "Observations on
    Thunder and Lightning," Ann.Rept.
    Smith.Inst., 1855, pp.265,282.

Wells
-Haunt
  n.d./Haunted Valley
    Sanford Tribune, 28 Jan.1932.

Wells Beach
-Ancient inscription
  1952/August L. Guest/=recent
    Edward J. Lenik, "Riddles on Rock:
    Non-Aboriginal Petroglyphs in
    Maine," NEARA J. 12 (spring 1978):
    76,77-78. il.

Wesley
-UFO (CE-1)
  1977, Nov?
    Framingham (Mass.) South Middlesex
    Sunday News, 20 Nov.1977.

Westbrook
-Ghost
  n.d./The Ledges, Saccarappa
    Portland Telegram, 13 Jan.1935.

West Buxton
-Precognition
  1960s/Shirley Harrison
    Herbert B. Greenhouse, Premonitions:
    A Leap into the Future (N.Y.: War-
    ner, 1973 ed.), pp.53,73.

Westfield
-UFO (NL)
  1959, July 23
    Richard Hall, ed., The UFO Evidence
    (Washington: NICAP, 1964), p.160.

West Paris
-UFO (NL)
  1977, Sep.
    Biddeford Journal-Tribune, 24 Jan.
    1978.

Winthrop
-UFO (NL)
  1947, July 7
    Augusta Daily Kennebec Journal, 8
    July 1947.

Wiscasset
-Haunt
  19th c.-   /Lee Payson Smith House
    Marion Lowndes, Ghosts That Still
    Walk (N.Y.: Knopf, 1941), pp.79-87.

Susy Smith, Prominent American Ghosts
(N.Y.: Dell, 1969 ed.), pp.81-86.
-Precognition
n.d./Molly Molasses
Fannie S. Chase, Wiscasset in Pownal-
borough (Wiscasset: Southworth-An-
thoensen, 1941), pp.24-25.

Yarmouth
-Animal ESP
1962, July 21/William Miles
Barbara Landry, "Maine's Telepathic
Cat," Fate 16 (Mar.1963):32-35.

York
-Haunt
1820s
George Alexander Emery, The Ancient
City of Georgeana and Modern Town
of York, Maine (Boston: The Author,
1873), pp.176-78.
-Witchcraft
1740s/Mary Nasson
Edward C. Moody, Handbook History of
the Town of York (Augusta: York,
1914), pp.183-84.
Laurance E. Webber, "Witch's Grave,"
Fate 22 (June 1969):64.

York Beach
-Ancient inscription
Freeman St.
Edward J. Lenik, "Riddles on Rock:
Non-Aboriginal Petroglyphs in Maine,"
NEARA J. 12 (spring 1978):76,78. il.

B. Physical Features

Agrys Point
-Ancient chimneys and archeological site
Joseph Williamson, "The Northmen in
Maine," Historical Mag., ser.2, 5
(1869):30-31.
Edward J. Lenik, "A Preliminary Sur-
vey of Agry's Point, Pittston,
Maine," NEARA Newsl. 9 (winter 1974-
75):62-66.

Annabesacook L.
-Ancient inscription
1976
Edward J. Lenik, "Riddles on Rock:
Non-Aboriginal Petroglyphs in Maine,"
NEARA J. 12 (spring 1978):76.

Arrowsic I.
-Ancient inscription
1974/=recent
Edward J. Lenik, "The Arrowsic Island
Petroglyph," NEARA Newsl. 9 (winter
1974-75):67-68. il.

Auburn L.
-UFO (CE-1)
1975, Oct.23/Joseph H. Fourse
Ronald Drucker, "Space Intruders Are
Zeroing In on New England," Saga
UFO Rept. 3 (Aug.1976):40-41.

Bagaduce Point
-Sea monster
1782
Linnaean Soc'y of New England, Report
of a Committee of the Linnaean Society of New England, Relative to
a Large Marine Animal, Supposed to
be a Sea-Serpent (Boston: Cumming &
Hilliard, 1817).

Boon I.
-UFO (NL)
1951, winter
Horace P. Beck, The Folklore of
Maine (Philadelphia: Lippincott,
1957), pp.152-53.

Boyden L.
-Lake monster myth
Albert S. Gatschet, "Water-Monsters
of the American Aborigines," J.Am.
Folklore 12 (1899):255-60.

Brewer Pond
-Clairvoyance
1906, June 12/Eva Jordan
H.N. Gardiner, "Investigation of
Clairvoyance in a Drowning Accident
at Brewer, Maine," J.ASPR 4 (1910):
447-64.

Carver's I.
-Ancient chimneys
Cyrus Eaton, Annals of the Town of
Warren, in Knox County, Maine (Hal-
lowell: Masters & Livermore, 1877),
p.20.

Chain Lakes
-Lake monster
Charles M. Skinner, American Myths
and Legends, 2 vols. (Philadelphia:
Lippincott, 1903), 2:277-79.

Cochnewagan Pond
-Phantom
1838, May/Asenath White
"Maine Goes to the Devil," Fate 27
(May 1974):64.

Damariscotta R.
-Archeological site
P.A. Chadbourne, "Oyster Shell Depos-
it in Damariscotta," Coll.Maine
Hist.Soc'y 6 (1859):345-51.
W.H. Bradley, "Radiocarbon Age of
the Damariscotta Shell Heaps," Am.
Antiquity 22 (1957):296.
Franklin Folsom, America's Ancient
Treasures (N.Y.: Rand McNally,
1974), p.170.

Deer Point
-Haunt
19th c./Peabody Ghost House
Lewiston Journal, 13 Feb.1937.

Estes L.
-UFO (CE-1)
1978, Jan.19/Richard Wakefield

Biddeford Journal-Tribune, 24 Jan.
1978.

Fox I.
-Sea monster
  ca.1777/Eleazar Crabtree
  ca.1794
  ca.1799
    Jacob Bigelow, "Documents and Re-
    marks Respecting the Sea Serpent,"
    Am.J.Sci., ser.1, 2 (1820):147,152,
    153-54.

Georges R.
-Ancient stone depressions
  mouth
    William B. Goodwin, The Ruins of
    Great Ireland in New England (Bos-
    ton: Meador, 1946), p.171.

Great Pond
-UFO (NL)
  1978, Sep./Howard Hill
    Augusta Daily Kennebec Journal, 2
    Jan.1979.

Harrow L.
-UFO (NL)
  1978, Sep.2/Wilmot S. Dow
    Portland Press-Herald, 27 Sep.1978.

Johnson's Bay
-Haunt
  n.d./Pirate's Creek
    Bangor Daily News, 13 July 1937.

Katahdin, Mt.
-Phantom panther legend
    Charles M. Skinner, American Myths
    and Legends, 2 vols. (Philadelphia:
    Lippincott, 1903), 1:38-39.

Machias Bay
-Petroglyph
    Garrick Mallery, "Picture-Writing of
    the American Indians," Ann.Rept.Bur.
    Am.Ethn. 10 (1888):1,81-83. il.
    Edward Burke Delabarre, Dighton Rock
    (N.Y.: Walter Neale, 1928), pp.267-
    70. il.
    Eric Lahti, "The Machias Petroglyphs,"
    Bull.Maine Arch.Soc'y 16, no.2
    (1976):3-6. il.

Machias L.
-Lake monster
  1881/E. Hall
    Aledo (Ill.) Democrat, 9 Dec.1881,
    p.2, quoting Bangor Commercial (un-
    dated).

Malden I.
-UFO (NL)
  1972, Aug.20/Robert Yeo
    Glenn McWane & David Graham, The New
    UFO Sightings (N.Y.: Warner, 1974),
    pp.59-60.

Manana I.
-Norse runestone or ancient inscription

1808? 1850s?/Augustus C. Hamlin
    Edmund Burke Delabarre, Dighton Rock
    (N.Y.: Walter Neale, 1928), pp.284-
    85. il.
    Olaf Strandwold, Norse Inscriptions
    on American Stones (Weehauken, N.J.:
    Magnus Bjőrndal, 1948), pp.33-34.
    il.
    Frederick J. Pohl, Atlantic Cross-
    ings Before Columbus (N.Y.: W.W.
    Norton, 1961), pp.196-99. il.
    Geoffrey Ashe, The Quest for America
    (N.Y.: Praeger, 1971), p.161.
    Donal P. Buchanan, "The Spirit Pond
    Stones: Hoax or History?" Pop.Arch.
    4 (May-June 1975):22. il.
    Barry Fell, America B.C. (N.Y.: Quad-
    rangle, 1976), pp.58,100-101,122.
    il.
    James P. Whittall, Jr., "The Monhe-
    gan Inscriptions," Bull.Early Sites
    Rsch.Soc'y 4 (May 1976):1-7. il.
    James P. Whittall, Jr., "Copper/Tin
    Projectile, Monhegan, Maine," Bull.
    Early Sites Rsch.Soc'y 5 (Feb.1977)
    :7-9. il.
    Salvatore Michael Trento, The Search
    for Lost America (Chicago: Contem-
    porary, 1978), pp.190-93. il.

Matinicus Rock
-Haunt
  n.d./light house
    Horace P. Beck, The Folklore of
    Maine (Philadelphia: Lippincott,
    1957), pp.158-59.

Meduncook R.
-Sea monster
  ca.1778
    James Bigelow, "Documents and Re-
    marks Respecting the Sea Serpent,"
    Am.J.Sci., ser.1, 2 (1820):147,151.

Milinickert Rips
-Phantom panther
  1823
    Charles M. Skinner, American Myths
    and Legends, 2 vols. (Philadelphia:
    Lippincott, 1903), 1:39-40.

Molasses Pond
-UFO (NL)
  1963, Aug.13
    Richard Hall, ed., The UFO Evidence
    (Washington: NICAP, 1964), p.141.

Monhegan I.
-Out-of-body experience
  1920s/Harrison Smith
    William Seabrook, Witchcraft: Its
    Power in the World Today (N.Y.: Lan-
    cer, 1968 ed.), pp.169-77.
-Sea monster
  1880, June 5/M.D. Ingalls/"Chalcedony"/
  =whale?
    Portland Argus, 8 June 1880.
    New York Times, 10 June 1880, p.5.

Moosehead L.
-Disease anomaly
1870s
    "The 'Jumpers' of Maine," Sci.Am. 44
    (1881):117.

Mount Desert I.
-Sea monster
ca.1815
ca.1827/David Thurlo, Jr./"Lydia"/=
hoax
    Bernard Heuvelmans, In the Wake of
    the Sea-Serpents (N.Y.: Hill & Wang,
    1968), pp.146,172.
-Skyquakes
n.d./Capt. Bishop/"Susie Prescott"
    "'Barisal Guns' and 'Mist Pouffers,'"
    Sci.Am. 74 (1896):403.

Muscongus I.
-Sea monster
ca.1777
    Jacob Bigelow, "Documents and Re-
    marks Respecting the Sea Serpent,"
    Am.J.Sci., ser.1, 2 (1820):147,153.

North Haven I.
-Archeological site
ca.3300-1600 B.C.
    Kansas City (Mo.) Times, 27 Feb.1975.

Penobscot Bay
-Sea monster
ca.1779/Stephan Tuckey
ca.1780/=hoax
ca.1784/Mr. Crocket
ca.1810/Mr. Miller
    William D. Peck, "Some Observations
    on the Sea-Serpent," Mem.Am.Acad.
    Arts & Sci. 4 (1818):86-91.
    Jacob Bigelow, "Documents and Re-
    marks Respecting the Sea-Serpent,"
    Am.J.Sci., ser.1, 2 (1820):147,152.
1818, May 20/Joseph Woodward/"Adamant"
    "American Sea Serpent," Quar.J.Sci.
    Lit.& Arts Roy.Soc'y 6 (1818):163.
    "The Great Sea-Serpent," Zoologist
    6 (1848):2028.

Penobscot R.
-Phantom
n.d.
    Ernest E. Bisbee, The State o'Maine
    Scrap Book (Lancaster: Bisbee, 1940).

Pickering I.
-Haunt
n.d.
    Lewiston Journal, 17 Oct.1936.
    Bangor News, 14 Jan.1939.

Popham Beach State Park
-Norse runestone
1945
    Olaf Strandwold, Norse Inscriptions
    on American Stones (Weehauken, N.J.:
    Magnus Björndal, 1948), p.32. il.
    O.G. Landsverk, Runic Records of the
    Norsemen in America (N.Y.: Erik J.
    Friis, 1974), pp.161-64.

Pushaw Stream
-Archeological site
ca.5000-100 B.C.
    New York Long Island Press, 21 Sep.
    1975.

Quoddy Head
-Norse discovery
1001/Leif Eriksson/=Vinland?
    Edward Reman, The Norse Discoveries
    and Explorations in America (Berke-
    ley: Univ. of California, 1949),
    pp.76-101.

Rams I.
-UFO (NL)
1978, Sep.8/Gregory Clark/light house
    Portland Press-Herald, 15 Sep.1978.

Rosoi, Cape
-Sea monster
1802, July/Abraham Cummings
    Jacob Bigelow, "Documents and Re-
    marks Respecting the Sea Serpent,"
    Am.J.Sci., ser.1, 2 (1820):140,150-
    52.

Rum Brook
-UFO (DD)
1969, July 6/Edward Vickery
    "UFO in Maine," Skylook, no.23
    (Oct.1969):14.

Russell Pond
-UFO (NL)
1978, Sep.2/Gene Letourneau
    Portland Press-Herald, 13 Sep.1978;
    and 27 Sep.1978.

Somes Sound
-Norse discovery
1005/Thorvald Eriksson
    Frederick J. Pohl. The Lost Discovery
    (N.Y.: W.W. Norton, 1952), pp.127-
    40.
    Frederick J. Pohl, The Viking Settle-
    ments of North America (N.Y.: Clark-
    son N. Potter, 1972), pp.47-55.

Spirit Pond
-Norse runestones and archeological site
1971, June 3/Walter L. Elliott
    James P. Whittall, Jr., "The Spirit
    Pond Runestones," NEARA Newsl. 6
    (Sep.1971):42-46. il.
    Ivan T. Sanderson, "A Rather 'Dis-
    gusting' Case," Pursuit 5 (Apr.
    1972):42-43.
    Einar Haugen, "The Rune Stones of
    Spirit Pond, Maine," Man in the
    Northeast 4 (1972):62-80. il.
    New England Antiquities Research
    Ass'n, The Spirit Pond Runestones
    (Milford, N.H.: NEARA, 1972). il.
    (Letter), Sander Svensson, Fate 26
    (Feb.1973):140-41.
    "The Excavations at Spirit Pond,
    Maine, August-November, 1972,"
    NEARA Newsl. 8 (Mar.1973):8-9.
    O.G. Landsverk, "Cryptograms on the

Spirit Pond Runestones," NEARA Newsl. 8 (Mar.1973):9-12.

James P. Whittall, Jr., "Observations at Spirit Pond," NEARA Newsl. 8 (Mar.1973):21-26. il.

O.G. Landsverk, "The Spirit Pond Cryptography," Man in the Northeast 6 (1973):67-75.

Earl Syversen, "The Spirit Pond Runestones," NEARA Newsl. 8 (summer 1973):38-40.

Donal P. Buchanan, "Further Thoughts on the Spirit Pond Runes," NEARA Newsl. 8 (fall 1973):57.

(Letter), C.G. Forrester, Fate 26 (Oct.1973):143-44.

Robert J. French, "Spirit Pond Surface Archaeology," NEARA Newsl. 8 (winter 1974):63-68.

Cyrus H. Gordon, Riddles in History (N.Y.: Crown, 1974), pp.36-44,119-44. il.

O.G. Landsverk, Runic Records of the Norsemen in America (N.Y.: Erik J. Friis, 1974), pp.166-220. il.

Earl Syversen, "Comments on Dr. Haugen's Rejection of the Spirit Pond Runes," NEARA Newsl. 9 (spring 1974):14-15.

Edward J. Lenik, "Excavations at Spirit Pond," Man in the Northeast 9 (1975):54-60.

Donal S. Buchanan, "Abstract of a Translation of the Spirit Pond Runestones," Bull.Eastern States Arch. Fed. 34 (1975):13.

Donal S. Buchanan, "The Spirit Pond Rune Stones: Hoax or History?" Pop. Arch. 4 (May-June 1975):23-29. il.

Edward J. Lenik, "Report on the Spirit Pond Shellheap Excavations," NEARA J. 12 (summer 1977):2-5.

Sysladobsis L.
-Lake monster
    Charles M. Skinner, Myths and Legends of Our Own Land, 2 vols. (Philadelphia: Lippincott, 1896), 2:299.

Thompson L.
-UFO (CE-4)
    1975, Oct.27/David Stephens
        Beverly (Mass.) Newsline Times, 3 Mar.1976, p.18.

    Brent M. Raynes, "The Twilight Side of a UFO Encounter," Flying Saucer Rev. 22 (July 1976):11-14.

    Shirley C. Fickett, "The Maine UFO Encounter: Investigation under Hypnosis," Flying Saucer Rev. 22 (July 1976):14-17.

    Berthold Eric Schwarz, "Comments on the Psychiatric-Paranormal Aspects of the Maine Case," Flying Saucer Rev. 22 (July 1976):18-22.

    Robert S. Niss, "The Stephens Abduction in Oxford, Maine," Official UFO 1 (July 1976):20-21,46-48.

    (Letter), Shirley C. Fickett, Fate 31 (June 1978):122-23.

Alex Evans, "The Stephens UFO Kidnapping: The Men in Black Return," Saga UFO Rept. 6 (Sep.1978):20-23, 56-61.

Wood I.
-Sea monster
    1903
    1905, Aug.5/H.C. Merriam
        R. DeWitt Miller, Impossible: Yet It Happened! (N.Y.: Ace, 1947 ed.), pp.32-34.

C. Ethnic Groups

Penobscot Indians
-Humanoid myth
    kiwakwe
        Frank G. Speck, "Penobscot Tales and Religious Beliefs," J.Am.Folklore 48 (1935):1,81-82.

Wabanaki Indians
-Use of Egyptian hieroglyphs
    Eugene Vetromile, The Abnakis and Their History (N.Y.: J.B. Kirker, 1866).

    Barry Fell, America B.C. (N.Y.: Quadrangle, 1976), pp.259-60.

    Barry Fell, "Medical Terminology of the Micmac and Abenaki Languages," Occ.Pub.Epigraphic Soc'y 7, no.139 (Apr.1979):7-20. il.

D. Unspecified Localities

-Doubtful geography
    16th c./Norumbega
        Benjamin F. DeCosta, Ancient Norombega (Albany: J. Munsell, 1890).

        Peter de Roo, History of America Before Columbus, 2 vols. (Philadelphia: Lippincott, 1900), 2:301.

        Herbert Sylvester, Maine Coast Romance, 4 vols. (Boston: Stanhope, 1904-1908).

        Samual Purchas, Hakluytus Posthumus, or Purchas His Pilgrimes (Glasgow: James MacLehose, 1905), 18:243-44.

        Sigmund Diamond, "Norumbega: New England Xanadu," Am.Neptune 11 (1951):95-107.

        Hjalmar H. Holand, Explorations in America Before Columbus (N.Y.: Twayne, 1956), pp.252-56.

        R.A. Skelton, Explorer's Maps (London: Routledge & Kegan Paul, 1958), pp.82,92.

        Ellsworth American, 27 Sep.1967.

        Raymond H. Ramsey, No Longer on the Map (N.Y.: Ballantine, 1973 ed.), pp.143-56.

        Astri A. Stromsted, Ancient Pioneers (N.Y.: E.J. Friis, 1974).

        Jon Douglas Singer, "The Quest for Norumbega: Ancient Civilizations in New England?" Pursuit 12 (winter 1979):13-19; (spring 1979):

-Precognition
  1945, Aug.2/Madelon Rice
    Sally Remaley, "Is Psychically Fore-
    warned Always Forearmed?" Fate 24
    (Sep.1971):81,85-86.

-Sea monster
  1779, June/Edward Preble/"Protector"
    James Fenimore Cooper, Lives of Dis-
    tinguished American Naval Officers,
    2 vols. (Philadelphia: Carey & Hart,
    1846), 1:180-82.

-UFOs and Men-in-black
  1966-1974, May
    Don Worley, "UFO Occupants: The Heart
    of the Enigma," Official UFO 1 (Nov.
    1976):15,47-48.

NEW BRUNSWICK

A. Populated Places

Alma
-Psychokinesis
  1940s/logging camp
    Sheila Hervey, Some Canadian Ghosts
    (Richmond Hill, Ont.: Pocket Books,
    1973), pp.163-64.

Bathurst
-Haunt
  1889/"Squando"
    Edward Rowe Snow, Mysteries and Ad-
    ventures along the Atlantic Coast
    (N.Y.: Dodd, Mead, 1948), pp.159-61.
-UFO (CE-1)
  1967, Oct./Ronald Rauigne
    (Letter), Can.UFO Rept., no.3 (May-
    June 1969):2.

Belledune
-UFO (NL)
  1969, Feb.22/Mrs. Blair Wright
    "Maritime Sighting," Can.UFO Rept.,
    no.3 (May-June 1969):12, quoting
    Bathurst Northern Light (undated).

Boiestown
-UFO (CE-2)
  1962, April 4/Hubert Howe
    "Strange 'Jelly' Fires Truck," APRO
    Bull. 10 (Mar.1962):6.

Caraquet
-UFO (CE-2)
  1978, June 26
    "UFOs," Res Bureaux Bull., no.38
    (7 Sep.1978):2,3.

Charlotte co.
-Skyquake
  1890s/coast
    "'Barisal Guns' and 'Mist Pouffers,'"
    Sci.Am. 74 (1896):403.
    Samuel W. Kain, "Seismic and Oceanic
    Noises," Monthly Weather Rev. 26
    (Apr.1898):153.

Chatham
-Mystery plane crash
  1955, Feb.8/two RCAF Sabre jets
    Donald E. Keyhoe, Aliens from Space
    (Garden City: Doubleday, 1973), p.
    205.
-UFO (NL)
  1978, June 29/RCAF base
    "UFOs," Res Bureaux Bull., no.38
    (7 Sep.1978):2,3.
  1978, Oct.30/RCAF base
    "UFOs," Res Bureaux Bull., no.41
    (30 Nov.1978):1,3.

Clarendon
-Whirlwind anomaly

1900, May 24/Keith A. Barber/6 mi.
from town
    Samuel W. Kain, "Notes on Local
    Whirlwinds in New Brunswick,"
    Monthly Weather Rev. 28 (Nov.1900):
    488.

Dawson
-Dowsing
  1949-1956/Carl Windrum
    (Editorial), Fate 9 (Nov.1956):8.

East Saint John
-UFO (NL)
  1947, July 4/Paul Falkjar
    Montreal (P.Q.) Star, 5 July 1947.

Fredericton
-UFO (CE-1)
  1969, Feb./Wallace Cail
    "The Maritimes: Newest Playground
    for UFOs?" Flying Saucers, June
    1970, pp.12,13.
-UFO (CE-2)
  1965, April 14/John Lint/McLeod Hill
    Gregory M. Kanon, "UFOs over the
    Maritimes," Can.UFO Rept., no.24
    (summer 1976):15.

Grand Bay
-Fall of fish
  1955/Walter Hudson
    "Falls," Doubt, no.50 (1955):368.

Grand Falls
-Ghost light
  n.d.
    Charles M. Skinner, Myths and Legends
    Beyond Our Borders (Philadelphia:
    Lippincott, 1899), p.48.

Lorneville
-Haunt
  Ghost Rock
    Staurt Trueman, An Intimate History
    of New Brunswick (Toronto: McClel-
    land & Stewart, 1970), pp.31-32.

Miramichi
-UFO (?)
  1950, Aug./=meteor
    Harold T. Wilkins, Flying Saucers on
    the Attack (N.Y.: Ace, 1967 ed.),
    p.125.

Moncton
-Gravity anomaly
  1933, June-   /Magnetic Hill
    Lowell Thomas & Rex Barton, In New
    Brunswick We'll Find It (N.Y.:
    Appleton-Century, 1939). il.
    (Editorial), Fate 5 (Dec.1952):7.
    (Editorial), Fate 22 (Feb.1969):18.
    Stuart Trueman, An Intimate History

of New Brunswick (Toronto: McClelland & Stewart, 1970), pp.111-14.
-Haunt
  1919/Reinsborough Place/3½ mi. off
  Moncton Hwy.
  1960s/Fisher Place
    Sheila Hervey, Some Canadian Ghosts
    (Richmond Hill, Ont.: Pocket Books,
    1973), pp.172,174.
-Humanoid
  1890s/A. Fulton Johnson
    John Green, The Sasquatch File (Ag-
    assix, B.C.: Cheam, 1973), p.6.
-UFO (NL)
  1968, Dec.4/Lutes Mt.
  1969, April 2/Sunny Brae
    "The Maritimes: Newest Playground
    for UFOs?" Flying Saucers, June
    1970, pp.12,13-14.
  1973, Nov.11-12
    Moncton Times, 13 Nov.1973.
-UFO (R-V)
  1978, April 27
    "Other UFOs," Res Bureaux Bull., no.
    35 (15 June 1978):3-4.

Queen's co.
-Phantom panther
  1951, Nov.22/Herman Belyea/The Narrows
    Bruce S. Wright, The Eastern Panther
    (Toronto: Clarke, Irwin, 1972), p.
    74.

Richibucto
-Phantom ship
  Northumberland Strait
    Roland H. Sherwood, Story Parade
    (Sackville, N.B.: Tribune, n.d.),
    p.19.
    Edward D. Ives, "The Burning Ship of
    Northumberland Strait: Some Notes
    on That Apparition," Midwest Folk-
    lore 8 (1958):199-203.

Sackville
-UFO (NL)
  1973, Nov.5
    W. Ritchie Benedict, "Canadian Sol-
    diers Report UFO," Fate 29 (Jan.
    1976):63.

Saint Hilaire
-Poltergeist
  1957, fall/Armand F. Albert/=gas in
  pipe
    (Editorial), Fate 11 (Mar.1958):12-
    13, quoting St. John Telegraph-
    Journal (undated).

Saint John
-Automobile inventor
  1851, Jan./T. Turnbull
    New Brunswick Courier, 1 Feb.1851.
-Ghost
  1892/J.E.B. McCready
    (Letter), J.ASPR 1 (1907):486-89.
-UFO (DD)
  1967/20 mi.NE
    Wendelle C. Stevens, "Fantastic UFO
    Photo Flap of 1967, Part II," Saga

UFO Rept. 3 (Aug.1976):26. il.

Saint Martin's
-Phantom ship
  1963, fall/Bay of Fundy
    Sheila Hervey, Some Canadian Ghosts
    (Richmond Hill, Ont.: Pocket Books,
    1973), pp.175-76.

Salmon Beach
-Phantom ship
  1958/Bay of Chaleur
    (Editorial), Fate 17 (Aug.1964):10.

Shediac
-UFO (?)
  1968
    Hamilton (Ont.) Spectator, 19 Oct.
    1973.

Smith's Creek
-Crisis apparition
  1958, winter/Elizabeth McEwen
    Eileen Sonin, More Canadian Ghosts
    (Richmond Hill, Ont.: Pocket Books,
    1974 ed.), pp.144-45.

Stonehaven
-Phantom ship
  1964, March 22-23/Frank Hornibrook/Bay
  of Chaleur
    (Editorial), Fate 17 (Aug.1964):10.
  1969, Sep.9/Bert Wood/Bay of Chaleur
    Sheila Hervey, Some Canadian Ghosts
    (Richmond Hill, Ont.: Pocket Books,
    1973), pp.166-68.

Woodstock
-Fire anomaly
  1887, Aug.6-7/Reginald C. Hoyt/Vic-
  toria St.
    New York World, 8 Aug.1887.
    R.S. Lambert, Exploring the Supernat-
    ural (Toronto: McClelland & Stewart,
    1955), pp.136-38, quoting Carleton
    Sentinel and Boston (Mass.) Herald
    (undated).

        B. Physical Features

Chaleur Bay
-Phantom ship
  19th c.-
    Edward Farrer, "The Folk Lore of
    Lower Canada," Atlantic Monthly 49
    (1882):542-50.
    Charles M. Skinner, Myths and Legends
    Beyond Our Borders (Philadelphia:
    Lippincott, 1899), p.88.
    Eliza B. Chase, In Quest of the
    Quaint (Philadelphia: Ferris &
    Leach, 1902), p.53.
    W.F. Ganong, "The Fact Basis of the
    Fire (or Phantom) Ship of Bay Cha-
    leur," Bull.Nat.Hist.Soc'y New
    Brunswick 5 (1906):419-23.
    Helen Champion, Over on the Island
    (Toronto: Ryerson, 1939).
    "Ghost Ship of Bay Chaleur," Fate

11 (June 1958):29.
(Letter), Maude Elizabeth Weinschenk,
Fate 17 (Feb.1964):114-15.
(Editorial), Fate 17 (Aug.1964):10-
12.

Grand Manan I.
-Skyquake
1890s
Samuel W. Kain, "Seismic and Oceanic
Noises," Monthly Weather Rev. 26
(Apr.1898):152-54.
-UFO (NL)
1968, May/Marguerite Green/Ingalls Head
Winnipeg (Man.) Free Press, 8 May
1968.

Holt's Point
-Petroglyphs
William S. Fowler, "Cache of Engraved
Pebbles from New Brunswick," Bull.
Mass.Arch.Soc'y 28, no.1 (Oct.1966):
15-17. il.

Kennebecasis Bay
-Skyquake
1890s
W.F. Ganong, "Upon Remarkable Sounds,
Like Gun Reports, Heard upon Our
Southern Coast," Bull.Nat.Hist.Soc'y
New Brunswick 3 (1896):40-42.
Samuel W. Kain, "Seismic and Oceanic
Noises," Monthly Weather Rev. 26
(Apr.1898):152-54.

Mirimachi R.
-Haunt
n.d./logging camp
Sheila Hervey, Some Canadian Ghosts
(Richmond Hill, Ont.: Pocket Books,
1973), pp.168-70.

Miscou I.
-Humanoid myth
1590s/gougou
Samuel de Champlain, Des sauvages
(1603), in H.P. Biggar, ed., The
Works of Samuel de Champlain (Toronto: Champlain Soc'y, 1922), 1:186.
R.S. Lambert, Exploring the Supernatural (Toronto: McClelland & Stewart,
1955), p.181.

Passamaquoddy Bay
-Skyquake
1890s/Edward Jack
Samuel W. Kain, "Seismic and Oceanic
Noises," Monthly Weather Rev. 26
(Apr.1898):152,153.

Portland Point
-Archeological site
1631-1850
J. Russell Harper, "Portland Point,
Crossroads of New Brunswick History,"
Hist.Studies New Brunswick Mus. 9
(1956):1-20.

Restigouche R.
-Phantom dog

18th c.
Charles M. Skinner, Myths and Legends
Beyond Our Borders (Philadelphia:
Lippincott, 1899), p.35.

Saint John R.
-Haunt
1860s/Paddy Hollow Camp
Stuart Trueman, An Intimate History
of New Brunswick (Toronto: McClelland & Stewart, 1970), p.31.

Shippegan I.
-Phantom ship
n.d.
Larry E. Arnold, "Ahoy, Mate! Which
Flamin' Phantom Ship Sails Thar?"
Pursuit 11 (summer 1978):109,113-14.

Skiff L.
-Lake monster
19th c.
New York Times, 1 Aug.1887, p.4.
Charles M. Skinner, Myths and Legends
Beyond Our Borders (Philadelphia:
Lippincott, 1899), p.44.

Trout Brook L.
-UFO (CE-1)
1967/Barry A. Nason
"French General, Scientists, Report
UFOs," UFO Inv. 4 (May-June 1968):3.

Utopia L.
-Lake monster
1870s
Stuart Trueman, An Intimate History
of New Brunswick (Toronto: McClelland & Stewart, 1970), pp.27-28.
Jerome Clark & Loren Coleman, "America's Lake Monsters," Beyond Reality,
no.14 (Mar.-Apr.1975):31. il.
1951, spring/Mrs. Fred McKillop
Stuart Trueman, An Intimate History
of New Brunswick (Toronto: McClelland & Stewart, 1970), pp.27-28.

C. Ethnic Groups

Passamaquoddy Indians
-Legend of Precolumbian Whites
Caansoo
Staurt Trueman, An Intimate History
of New Brunswick (Toronto: McClel-
land & Stewart, 1970), pp.139-40.
-Sea monster myth
weewillmekq
Charles Leland, Algonquin Legends of
New England (Boston: Houghton Mif-
flin, 1884), pp.324-29.

NOVA SCOTIA

A. Populated Places

Amherst
-Poltergeist
  1878, Sep.-1879, July/Esther Cox/Prin-
  cess x Church St.
    "Notes by the Way," Light 4 (1884):
    123-24.
    Walter Hubbell, The Great Amherst
    Mystery (N.Y.: Brentano's, 1916).
    Walter F. Prince, "A Critical Study
    of The Great Amherst Mystery," Proc.
    ASPR 13 (1919):89-103.
    Sacheverell Sitwell, Poltergeists
    (London: Faber & Faber, 1940).
    J. Lewis Toole, "The Possession of
    Esther Cox," Fate 5 (Jan.1952):77-
    84.
    R.S. Lambert, Exploring the Supernat-
    ural (Toronto: McClelland & Stewart,
    1955), pp.89-105.

Arisaig
-Sea monster
  1844, Oct./Mr. Barry
    Charles Lyell, A Second Visit to the
    United States of North America, 2
    vols. (London: John Murray, 1849),
    1:133.

Baddeck
-Anomalous hole in ground
  1959, May/Martin Murphy
    "When the Earth Opened," Fate 13
    (Feb.1960):92.
-UFO (?)
  1891, Sep.11/Alexander Graham Bell/
  Beinn Bhreagh/=aurora?
    "A Rare Phenomenon," Nature 45 (1891)
    :79.

Barrington
-Skyquakes
  1977-1978, Oct./Hattie Perry
    Yarmouth Vanguard, 25 Jan.1978; and
    18 Oct.1978.
    Halifax Mail-Star, 27 Jan.1978, p.2.
    Hamilton (Ont.) Spectator, 6 Mar.
    1978; and 8 Mar.1978.

Berwick
-Humanoid
  1969, April
    John A. Keel, Strange Creatures from
    Space and Time (Greenwich, Conn.:
    Fawcett, 1970), pp.10-11.

Broad Cove
-Precognition
  n.d.
    Helen Creighton, Bluenose Ghosts
    (Toronto: Ryerson, 1957).

Caledonia Mills
-Poltergeist
  1921, spring-1922/Alexander McDonald
    New York Times, 26 Feb.1922, p.20;
    and 16 Mar.1922, p.1.
    Walter F. Prince, "An Investigation
    of Poltergeist and Other Phenomena
    near Antigonish," J.ASPR 16 (1922):
    422-41.
    R.S. Lambert, Exploring the Supernat-
    ural (Toronto: McClelland & Stewart,
    1955), pp.122-31.

Chezzetcook
-Fall of toads
  n.d./Grace Weir
    Grace Weir, "Caught in a Toadstorm,"
    Fate 7 (Oct.1954):72.
-UFO (NL)
  1968, May/Mrs. L.O. Gaetz
    Winnipeg (Man.) Free Press, 8 May
    1968.

Cole Harbour
-Norse ax
  1880
    Olaf Strandwold, Norse Inscriptions
    on American Stones (Weehauken, N.J.:
    Magnus Björndal, 1948), pp.46-47.
    il.
    Hjalmar R. Holand, Explorations in
    America Before Columbus (N.Y.:
    Twayne, 1956), pp.93-94.

Cornwallis
-UFO (CE-2)
  1965, Nov.29/Ian Kinsey
    "National Press Spotlights UFOs,"
    UFO Inv. 3 (Jan.-Feb.1966):1,4.

Country Harbour Cross Roads
-Clairvoyance
  1960s
    Sheila Hervey, Some Canadian Ghosts
    (Richmond Hill, Ont.: Pocket Books,
    1973), pp.153-54.

Dartmouth
-UFO (NL)
  1967, Oct.4
    William F. Dawson, "UFO Down off
    Shag Harbor," Fate 21 (Feb.1968):
    48,49.

Debert
-Archeological site
  8000 B.C.
    D.S. Byers, "The Debert Archaeologi-
    cal Project," Quaternaria 8 (1966):
    33-47.
    G.F. MacDonald, "The Technology and
    Settlement Pattern of a Paleo-Indian
    Site at Debert, Nova Scotia," Qua-
    ternaria 8 (1966):33-47.

R. Stuckenrath, "The Debert Archaeological Project: Radiocarbon Dating,"
Quaternaria 8 (1966):75-80.
George F. MacDonald, "Debert: A Paleo-Indian Site in Central Nova Scotia," Anthro.Pap.Nat'l Mus.Canada,
no.16 (1968). il.

Doucetteville
-UFO (CE-2)
1977, Feb.10/Tom Thibault
Digby Courier, 24 Feb.1977.

East Chezzetcook
-Plague of flying ants
1968, July
William F. Dawson, "So What's New
with Charles Fort?" Fate 23 (May
1969):76,78.
-UFO (NL)
1968, May
Winnipeg (Man.) Free Press, 8 May
1968.

Eastern Passage
-Haunt
1950s?/Mrs. Edmund Henneberry/Devil's
I.
"The Flames That Didn't Burn," Fate
10 (Feb.1957):73, quoting Toronto
Daily Star (undated).
-Poltergeist
1943, Dec.24-1944, Jan.9/Louis Hilchie
R.S. Lambert, Exploring the Supernat-
ural (Toronto: McClelland & Stewart,
1955), pp.144-46.
Halifax Star-Mail, 19 Aug.1960.

Fourchu
-UFO (CE-2)
1888, May
Halifax Herald, 19 May 1888.
New York Times, 23 May 1888, p.23.

Framboise
-Sea monster (carcass)
1976, July/=basking shark
St. Catherines Standard, 17 July
1976.

Gabarus
-Sea monster
1976, Aug.17/Jim Flinn
Sydney Cape Breton Post, 20 Aug.1976.
-UFO (NL)
1977, Dec.27
Sydney Cape Breton Post, 28 Dec.1977.

Glace Bay
-Fire anomaly
1963, April-May/Douglas MacDonald/Gil-
day St.
James Hayes, "Canadian House of
Fires," Fate 17 (July 1964):84-88.
-UFO (NL)
1972, Aug.9
Glenn McWane & David Graham, The New
UFO Sightings (N.Y.: Warner, 1974),
p.57, quoting Sydney Post (undated).

Glenholme
-UFO (NL)
1973, Nov.12/Leo MacCallum/Hwy.104
Truro Daily News, 14 Nov.1973.

Greenwood
-UFO (?)
1968, Nov.
"The Maritimes: Newest Playground
for UFOs?" Flying Saucers, June
1970, p.12.

Guysborough
-Medieval Celtic discovery
ca.1398/Henry Sinclair/=Trin Harbor?
Frederick J. Pohl, The Lost Discovery
(N.Y.: W.W. Norton, 1952), pp.220-
24.
Frederick J. Pohl, Prince Henry Sin-
clair (N.Y.: Clarkson N. Potter,
1974), pp.124-31.
-Plague of flies
1880, Sep.5
Halifax Citizen, 7 Sep.1830.
Brooklyn (N.Y.) Eagle, 7 Sep.1880.

Halifax
-Fall of soot
1968, July 6/Central Common
William F. Dawson, "So What's New
with Charles Fort?" Fate 23 (May
1969):76-78.
-Ghost
n.d./Citadel Hill
n.d./Mr. Donovan
Helen Creighton, Bluenose Ghosts
(Toronto: Ryerson, 1957).
1947, June
Sheila Hervey, Some Canadian Ghosts
(Richmond Hill, Ont.: Pocket Books,
1973), pp.44-45.
-Precognition
1881, Sep.11/James Cox
Mrs. Henry Sidgwick, "On the Evidence
for Premonitions," Proc.SPR 5
(1888):288,330-31.
1917/Robert Elwood Martins
Chris Vanderventer, "I Walk with the
Dead," Fate 8 (Dec.1955):95,98-99.
-Sea monster
1825, July 15/William Barry
Bernard Heuvelmans, In the Wake of
the Sea-Serpents (N.Y.: Hill & Wang,
1968), pp.171-72.
1853, Aug.2/Peter McNab, Jr.
Halifax Nova-Scotian, 3 Aug.1853,
p.252.
-Skyquakes
1978, Oct.-1979, Jan.
Cape Breton Post, 9 Jan.1979.
-Telepathy
n.d./Helen Creighton
Helen Creighton, Bluenose Ghosts
(Toronto: Ryerson, 1957).
-UFO (?)
n.d./Gerald Bishop
Kenneth Arnold, "Are Space Visitors
Here?" Fate 1 (summer 1948):4,12,
quoting Halifax Mail (undated).
-UFO (CE-1)

1968, Nov.30/Eric Horne/N of town
"The Maritimes: Newest Playground
for UFOs?" Flying Saucers, June
1970, p.12.
-UFO (DD)
1952, June 15
Marc Leduc, "Notes sur le projet
'Magnet,'" UFO-Québec, no.4 (1975):
12,15.
Gregory M. Kanon, "UFOs over the Maritimes," Can.UFO Rept., no.24 (summer
1976):15.
1960, Nov.23
"More on November 23, 1960 Sightings,"
APRO Bull. 9 (May 1961):5.
1963, Sep.10/Norland
Harold T. Wilkins, Flying Saucers on
the Attack (N.Y.: Ace, 1967 ed.),
p.315.
1973, Oct.
Hamilton (Ont.) Spectator, 19 Oct.
1973.
-UFO (NL)
1952, May 26
1952, July 18
Marc Leduc, "Notes sur le projet
'Magnet,'" UFO-Québec, no.4 (1975):
12,15.
1967, Sep.28/Armdale Rotary
William F. Dawson, "UFO Down off
Shag Harbor," Fate 21 (Feb.1968):48.
1968, Dec.2/Frank R. Stapley/Prospect
Hwy.
1969, March 13
"The Maritimes: Newest Playground
for UFOs?" Flying Saucers, June
1970, pp.12-13.

Harrietsfield
-UFO (DD)
1979, Jan.12
"Recent UFO Reports," Res Bureaux
Bull., no.44 (Feb.1979):4.

Leonardville
-Tide anomaly
1954, Dec.8
Harold T. Wilkins, Flying Saucers Uncensored (N.Y.: Pyramid, 1967 ed.),
p.256.

Lismore
-Plague of flies
1880, Aug.21
Halifax Citizen, 21 Aug.1880.

Liverpool
-Sea monster
ca.1854, July
John Braddock, "Monsters of the Maritimes," Atlantic Advocate 58 (Jan.
1968):12,13.

Lunenburg co.
-UFO (CE-1)
1978, June 24
"UFOs," Res Bureaux Bull., no.38 (7
Sep.1978):2,3.

Merigomish
-Sea monster
1845, Aug.
Charles Lyell, A Second Visit to the
United States of North America, 2
vols. (London: John Murray, 1849),
1:132.
1880, Aug.
New York Times, 2 Sep.1880, p.1.

Mineville
-Haunt
1960s/Ed Mercel
Eileen Sonin, More Canadian Ghosts
(Richmond Hill, Ont.: Pocket Books,
1974 ed.), pp.111-13.

New Glasgow
-UFO (?)
1977, Aug.9/=meteor?
Halifax Chronicle-Herald, 10 Aug.
1977.

New Minas
-Aerial phantom
1796, Oct.
Simeon Perkins, The Diary of Simeon
Perkins 1790-1796 (Toronto: Champlain Soc'y, Pub.no.39, 1961), p.
430.

North Sydney
-Hex
1957/Mary Johnston
"The Hexed Railroad," Fate 11 (June
1958):93.

Overton
-UFO (NL)
1968, May
Winnipeg (Man.) Free Press, 8 May
1968.

Parrsboro
-UFO (NL)
1968, Nov.30/Eldon George
1968, Dec.10/Eldon George
"The Maritimes: Newest Playground
for UFOs?" Flying Saucers, June
1970, p.12.

Pictou
-Fall of yellow substance
1841, June/harbor/=pollen?
"Yellow Showers of Pollen," Am.J.Sci.,
ser.1, 42 (1842):196-97.
-Plague of flies
1880, Aug.21
New York Times, 6 Sep.1880, p.8; 7
Sep.1880, p.1; and 8 Sep.1880, p.5.

Pinehurst
-UFO (R-V)
1967, Aug.23/Pierre Guy Charbonneau/
ocean to S
"Worldwide Sightings Showing Increase," UFO Inv. 4 (Oct.1967):1.

Pleasant Valley
-UFO (NL)

1976, Dec.23/W.H. MacLeod
New Glasgow News, 26 Dec.1976.

Plymouth
-Ancient inscription
1966/Percy Wyman
Andrew E. Rothovius, "The Inscribed
Stones of Southwestern Nova Scotia,"
NEARA Newsl. 7 (Dec.1972):67,69. il.

Port Hastings
-Fall of fish
1955, Nov./Canso Causeway
"Falls," Doubt, no.52 (1956):402,
quoting New York Times, 29 Nov.1955.

Port Hawkesbury
-UFO (CE-1)
n.d.
Mary L. Fraser, Folklore of Nova
Scotia (Toronto: Catholic Truth
Soc'y of Canada, 1931).

Prince William
-UFO (?)
1969, March 12
"The Maritimes: Newest Playground
for UFOs?" Flying Saucers, June
1970, pp.12,13.

Quinan
-UFO (CE-1)
1967, Nov.29/Percy McBride
"Landing near Yarmouth, N.S.," APRO
Bull. 16 (Jan.-Feb.1968):3-4.

River John
-Sea monster (carcass)
1968, Nov./=sea turtle?
Vancouver (B.C.) Sun, 21 Nov.1968.

Rockingham
-Fall of toads
ca.1903/W. West
(Letter), Fate 12 (June 1959):114.

Saint Ann's
-UFO (NL)
1974, Sep.8
Cape Breton Post, 24 Sep.1974.

Sandford
-UFO (NL)
1969, Jan.22/Allison Williams
"The Maritimes: Newest Playground
for UFOs?" Flying Saucers, June
1970, pp.12,13.

Shag Harbour
-UFO (CE-2)
1967, Oct.4/Laurie Wiggins
Halifax Chronicle-Herald, 6 Oct.1967.
Yarmouth Light Herald, 12 Oct.1967.
William F. Dawson, "UFO Down off Shag
Harbor," Fate 21 (Feb.1968):48-53.
Jim & Coral Lorenzen, UFOs over the
Americas (N.Y.: Signet, 1968), pp.
56-57.
Edward U. Condon, ed., Scientific
Study of Unidentified Flying Objects

(N.Y.: Bantam, 1969 ed.), pp.351-
53.
Donald H. Menzel & Ernest H. Taves,
The UFO Enigma (Garden City: Doubleday, 1977), pp.106-107.

Sheet Harbour
-Sea monster
1901, summer
Halifax Evening Mail, 4 Sep.1901, p.
8.

South Bar
-UFO (CE-2)
1974, Sep.9/Karen Vernon
Sydney Post, 8 Nov.1974.
Gregory M. Kanon, "UFOs over the
Maritimes," Can.UFO Rept., no.24
(summer 1976):15-16.

South Ohio
-UFO (NL)
1968, April
Yarmouth Light Herald, 2 May 1968.

Springhill
-Phantom
1965, Dec.15/Ken Sterling
(Letter), Carl Wilson, Fate 19 (June
1966):121-24.
-UFO (CE-2)
1965, Nov.29/Kevin Davis/Copper Creek
mining area
"National Press Spotlights UFOs,"
UFO Inv. 3 (Jan.-Feb.1966):1,4.

Stellarton
-Medieval Celtic discovery
ca.1398/Henry Sinclair/bituminous coal
seams/=smoking hill?
Frederick J. Pohl, The Lost Discovery
(N.Y.: W.W. Norton, 1952), pp.219-
22.
Frederick J. Pohl, Prince Henry Sinclair (N.Y.: Clarkson N. Potter,
1974), pp.116-31.

Sydney
-Crisis apparition
1785, Oct.15/John Coape Sherbrooke
Philip Henry, 5th Earl Stanhope,
Notes of Conversations with the Duke
of Wellington (London: J. Murray,
1888).
A. Patchett Martin, Life and Letters
of the Right Honourable Robert Lowe
Viscount Sherbrooke, 2 vols. (London: Longmans, Green, 1893), 2:594-
95.
Jonathan G. MacKinnon, Old Sydney
(Sydney: D. MacKinnon, 1918).
"An Apparition," J.ASPR 13 (1919):
377-82.
-Sea monster
ca.1939/Charles Ballard
Bernard Heuvelmans, In the Wake of
the Sea-Serpents (N.Y.: Hill & Wang,
1968), pp.464-65.
-UFO (?)
1968/=meteor

Hamilton (Ont.) Spectator, 19 Oct.
1973.
-UFO (NL)
1978, Jan.13/Lingan Rd.
"UFOs," Res Bureaux Bull., no.29 (9
Feb.1978):4,5-6.
1978, Sep.21/10 mi.NNW
"UFOs," Res Bureaux Bull., no.41 (30
Nov.1978):1,3.

Trenton
-Fall of frogs
ca.1917/W. West
(Letter), Fate 12 (June 1959):114.

Truro
-Skyquake
1873, Dec.3
Truro Colchester Sun, 3 Dec.1873, p.
2.
-UFO (?)
1977, Aug.9/=meteor?
Halifax Chronicle-Herald, 10 Aug.1977.
-UFO (CE-2)
1974, Jan.2
George D. Fawcett, "The 'Unreported'
UFO Wave of 1974," Saga UFO Rept.
2 (spring 1975):50.
-UFO (DD)
1970, Oct.5/Paul Scott
Toronto (Ont.) Daily Star, 6 Oct.1970.
"World Round-Up," Flying Saucer Rev.
16 (Nov.-Dec.1970):29.
-UFO (NL)
1974, Sep.25/Robert Hagell
Gregory M. Kanon, "UFOs over the
Maritimes," Can.UFO Rept., no.24
(summer 1976):15.

Westphal
-UFO (NL)
1968, May/John Van Noord
Winnipeg (Man.) Free Press, 8 May
1968.

Windsor
-Poltergeist
1906-1907/=hoax
James H. Hyslop & Hereward Carrington, "A Case of the Alleged Movement of Physical Objects without
Contact," Proc.ASPR 1 (1907):431-
519.

Wolfville
-UFO (CE-1)
1969, Oct./Patricia Spencer
(Letter), Can.UFO Rept., no.24 (summer 1976):23-24.

Woods Harbour
-UFO (NL)
1967, Oct./Lockland Cameron
Halifax Chronicle-Herald, 12 Oct.1967.

Yarmouth
-Norse runestone
1812/Richard Fletcher
Henry Phillips, Jr., "On a Supposed
Runic Inscription at Yarmouth, N.S.,"

Rept.Numismatic & Antiquarian Soc'y
of Philadelphia, 5 Feb.1880.
Henry Phillips, Jr., "On the Supposed
Runic Inscription at Yarmouth, Nova
Scotia," Proc.Am.Phil.Soc'y 21
(1884):491.
Beckles Willson, Nova Scotia: The
Province That Has Been Passed By
(London: Constable, 1912), p.102.
M.H. Nickerson, "A Short Note on the
Yarmouth 'Runic Stone,'" Coll.Nova
Scotia Hist.Soc'y 17 (1913):51-52.
H. Piers, "Remarks on the Fletcher
and Related Stones of Yarmouth,
N.S.," Coll.Nova Scotia Hist.Soc'y
17 (1913):53-56.
Olaf Strandwold, The Yarmouth Stone
(Prosser, Wash.: Prosser, 1934).
Charles Michael Boland, They All Dis-
covered America (N.Y.: Pocket Books,
1963 ed.), pp.261-62. il.
Andrew E. Rothovius, "The Inscribed
Stones of Southwestern Nova Scotia,"
NEARA Newsl. 7 (Dec.1972):67-68. il.
Julius Frasch Harmon, "Concerning
the Carvings on the Braxton and Yar-
mouth Stones," West Virginia History
37 (1976):133-39.
-UFO (NL)
1968, May
Winnipeg (Man.) Free Press, 8 May
1968.

B. Physical Features

Annapolis R.
-Norse discovery
1009/Thorfinn Karlsefni/=anchorage?
Frederick J. Pohl, The Viking Settle-
ments of North America (N.Y.:
Clarkson N. Potter, 1974), pp.120-
24.

Apple R.
-Norse discovery
1009/Thorfinn Karlsefni/=anchorage?
Frederick J. Pohl, The Viking Settle-
ments of North America (N.Y.:
Clarkson N. Potter, 1974), pp.120-
24.

Breton, Cape
-Ghost light
n.d.
Malcolm Campbell, "Donald John Mac-
Mullin," Cape Breton's Mag., no.10
(Apr.1975):29-32.
-Sea monster
1800s/W. Lee
C.S. Rafinesque, "Dissertation on
Water Snakes, Sea Snakes and Sea
Serpents," Phil.Mag. 54 (1819):361,
365-66.

Canso, Strait of
-Sea monster
1656/Pierre Rouleau
Nicolas Denys, Description and Natural History of the Coasts of North

America (Toronto: Champlain Soc'y,
Pub.no.2, 1908), pp.80-81.

Cape Sable I.
-Sea monster
1976, July/Eisner Penney
Vancouver (B.C.) Sun, 30 July 1976.

Chignecto Bay
-Anomalous fossils
Charles Lyell, "On the Upright Fossil
Trees Found at Different Levels in
the Coal Strata," Am.J.Sci., ser.1,
45 (1843):353-56.

Cobequid Bay
-UFO (?)
1947, July/Mabel Berry
Windsor (Ont.) Daily Star, 7 July
1947.

Cornwallis R.
-UFO (DD)
1968, Sep.15/David Taylor/dike
Halifax Chronicle-Herald, 18 Sep.
1968.
"Boys Report UFO in River," APRO Bull.
17 (Sep.-Oct.1968):4.

d'Or, Cape
-Medieval Celtic discovery
ca.1398/Henry Sinclair
Frederick J. Pohl, Prince Henry Sinclair (N.Y.: Clarkson N. Potter,
1974), pp.143-53.

Fundy, Bay of
-Phantom ship
n.d.
Larry E. Arnold, "Ahoy, Mate! Which
Flamin' Phantom Ship Sails Thar?"
Pursuit 11 (summer 1978):109,113.

Laidlaw's Hill
-Anomalous quartz formation
Benjamin Silliman, Jr., "On the So-
Called 'Barrel-Quartz,' of Nova
Scotia," Am.J.Sci., ser.2, 38
(1864):104-106.

Mahone Bay
-Phantom ship
19th c.-
Roland H. Sherwood, The Phantom Ship
of Northumberland Strait (Windsor,
N.S.: Lancelot, 1975), pp.35-36.
Larry E. Arnold, "Ahoy, Mate! Which
Flamin' Phantom Ship Sails Thar?"
Pursuit 11 (summer 1978):109,110-11.
-Sea monster
1833, May 15/W. Sullivan
"The Sea-Serpent," Zoologist 5
(1847):1714-15.

Miller's I.
-Sea monster
1872, Aug.
John Braddock, "Monsters of the Maritimes," Atlantic Advocate 58 (Jan.
1968):12,13.

Mule R.
-UFO (CE-1)
ca.1888
Mary L. Fraser, Folklore of Nova
Scotia (Toronto: Catholic Truth
Soc'y of Canada, 1931).

Northumberland Strait
-Phantom ship
19th c.-
L.M. Rich, "The Phantom Ship of Nova
Scotia," Fate 2 (Nov.1949):28-31.
(Editorial), Fate 7 (Apr.1954):4.
(Letter), Roy Grant, Fate 7 (May
1954):107.
Edward D. Ives, "The Burning Ship of
Northumberland Strait: Some Notes
on That Apparition," Midwest Folk-
lore 8 (1958):199-203.
Vincent Gaddis, Invisible Horizons
(Philadelphia: Chilton, 1965), pp.
94-95, quoting AP release, 8 Dec.
1953.
Roland H. Sherwood, The Phantom Ship
of Northumberland Strait (Windsor,
N.S.: Lancelot, 1975).
Larry E. Arnold, "Ahoy, Mate! Which
Flamin' Phantom Ship Sails Thar?"
Pursuit 11 (summer 1978):109,116;
(fall 1978):144-50.
New Glasgow News, 11 Jan.1979.
-Skyquakes
n.d.
Sterling Ramsay, Folklore: Prince
Edward Island (Charlottetown, P.E.I.:
Square Deal, 1973).

Oak I.
-Lost treasure and doubtful responsibility
ca.1795
H.L. Bowdoin, "Solving the Mystery
of Oak Island," Colliers Mag., 19
Aug.1911, pp.19-20.
Parker Morell, "The Money Pit," Sat.
Eve.Post, 14 Oct.1939, pp.6-10,111-
20. il.
Harold T. Wilkins, "Mystery of the
Pirate's Chart," Fate 3 (Dec.1950):
28-33. il.
Thomas P. Leary, The Oak Island Enig-
ma (Omaha: The Author, 1953).
R.V. Harris, The Oak Island Mystery
(Toronto: Ryerson, 1958).
Jack Sivley, "Tragedy Stalks a Tan-
talizing Treasure," True, Jan.1967,
pp.33-35,84-87. il.
"Hidden Treasure?" Newsweek, 8 Nov.
1971, pp.71-72.
Rupert Furneaux, The Money Pit Mys-
tery (N.Y.: Dodd, Mead, 1972). il.
Ron Rosenbaum, "The Mystery of Oak
Island," Esquire 79 (Feb.1973):77-
85,154-60.
Garnet Basque, Canadian Treasure
Trove (Vancouver: Garnet, 1973), pp.
76-101. il.
Columbus (O.) Dispatch, 28 Nov.1974,
p.F-11.
Steve Schwartz, "Update on the Money
Pit," Yankee 40 (Mar.1976):72-79,

114-18. il.

Peggy's Cove
-Sea monster
    1940, Feb.3/Richard Crooks/=whale
    Halifax Herald, 4 Feb.1940, p.4; and
    9 Feb.1940, p.3.
    "The Sea Monsters of Canada," Res
    Bureaux Bull., no.39 (28 Sep.1978):
    4,5.

Pictou I.
-Sea monster
    1879, July/Capt. Samson/"Louisa Mont-
    gomery"/10 mi.E
    New York Times, 30 July 1879, p.5.

Sable, Cape
-Ancient inscription
    1975/Locke Smith
        Donal B. Buchanan, "The Cape Sable
        and Seal Island, Nova Scotia, In-
        scriptions: An Attempt at Transla-
        tion," NEARA J. 13 (winter 1979):
        54-55.
-Giant squid
    1870, Feb./J.M. Jones
        A.E. Verrill, "The Cephalopods of
        the North-Eastern Coast of North
        America," Trans.Conn.Acad.Arts &
        Sci. 5 (1879):177,193-94.
        Elizabeth MacAlaster, Cephalopods in
        the Nova Scotia Museum Collection
        (Halifax: Nova Scotia Mus., n.d.).

Sable I.
-Haunts
    18th c.-
        Charles M. Skinner, Myths and Legends
        Beyond Our Borders (Philadelphia:
        Lippincott, 1899), pp.77-80.
        Edgar Rowe Snow, Mysteries and Adven-
        tures Along the Atlantic Coast (N.Y.:
        Dodd, Mead, 1948), pp.25-26.

Saint Margaret's Bay
-Sea monster
    1846, summer/James Wilson/western shore
    ca.1846/George Dauphiney/Hackett's Cove
    1860s/William Crooks
        John Ambrose, "Some Account of the
        Petrel--the Sea-Serpent--and the
        Albicore as Observed at St. Margar-
        et's Bay," Trans.Nova Scotian Inst.
        Nat.Sci. 1 (1864):37-40.

Scatari I.
-Norse discovery
    1001/Leif Eriksson/=first landing?
        J. Kr. Tornøe, Norsemen Before Colum-
        bus (London: Allen & Unwin, 1965),
        pp.60-62.

Seal I.
-Ancient inscription
        Andrew E. Rothovius, "The Inscribed
        Stones of Southwestern Nova Scotia,"
        NEARA Newsl. 7 (Dec.1972):67,68.
        Donal B. Buchanan, "The Cape Sable
        and Seal Island, Nova Scotia, In-

scriptions: An Attempt at Translation," NEARA J. 13 (winter 1979):
54-55. il.
-UFO (CE-2)
    1968, May 4/Woodrow Atwood/"Which Way
    In"/ocean to S
        "Object Heats Up Boat in N.S.,"
        APRO Bull. 17 (July-Aug.1968):4.

South West I.
-Sea monster
    1849, summer/Joseph Holland
        John Ambrose, "Some Account of the
        Petrel--the Sea-Serpent--and the
        Albicore as Observed at St. Margar-
        et's Bay," Trans.Nova Scotian Inst.
        Nat.Sci. 1 (1864):37-40.

Tantramar Basin
-Ghost light
    n.d.
        Larry E. Arnold, "Ahoy, Mate! Which
        Flamin' Phantom Ship Sails Thar?"
        Pursuit 11 (summer 1978):109,111.

Tor Bay
-Norse ax
    n.d.
        Frederick J. Pohl, Atlantic Cross-
        ings Before Columbus (N.Y.: W.W.
        Norton, 1961), p.207.

Tusket R.
-Norse runestone and cellars
        Henry Phillips, Jr., "On the Supposed
        Runic Inscription at Yarmouth, Nova
        Scotia," Proc.Am.Phil.Soc'y 21
        (1884):491.
        Andrew E. Rothovius, "The Inscribed
        Stones of Southwestern Nova Scotia,"
        NEARA Newsl. 7 (Dec.1972):67,68.

White Head I.
-Haunt
    1926, fall/lighthouse
        Harold T. Wilkins, "The Noises in
        the Light Tower," Fate 5 (Feb.-Mar.
        1952):98-101.

Yarmouth Bay
-Ancient inscription
    n.d./J.G. Farish
        Charles Whittlesey, "Archaeological
        Frauds," Pub.W.Reserve & N.Ohio
        Hist.Soc'y, no.33 (Nov.1876):1-2.

                C. Ethnic Groups

Souriké Indians
-Similarity to Norse
        Peter de Roo, History of America Be-
        fore Columbus, 2 vols. (Philadel-
        phia: Lippincott, 1900), 2:318-19.

            D. Unspecified Localities

-Clairaudience
    1890s

Mary L. Fraser, <u>Folklore of Nova Scotia</u> (Toronto: Catholic Truth Soc'y of Canada, 1931).

-Moving rocks
 1878, fall
    Earl of Dunraven, "Moose-Hunting in Canada," <u>Nineteenth Century</u> 6 (1879):45,64-65.

PRINCE EDWARD ISLAND

A. Populated Places

Augustine Cove
-UFO (DD)
  1947, July 3/Brenton Clark
    Windsor (Ont.) Daily Star, 5 July
    1947.

Burton
-UFO (NL)
  1968, Sep.21/Ivan Collicut
    "Near-Landing Observed by RCAF," UFO
    Inv. 3 (Oct.-Nov.1966):4, quoting
    Summerside Journal-Pioneer (undated).

Charlottetown
-Ghost
  1710
    J. Castell Hopkins, French Canada
    and the St. Lawrence (Philadelphia:
    John C. Winston, 1913), pp.315-16.
-Haunt
  1857, Feb.-1877/Mrs. Pennée/Binstead
    F.W.H. Myers, "On Recognised Appari-
    tions Occurring More Than a Year
    after Death," Proc.SPR 6 (1889):13,
    60-63.

Johnstons River
-UFO (NL)
  1957, July 7/Robert Brazil
    (Letter), Sci.& Mech. 38 (May 1967):
    72.

New Haven
-UFO (NL)
  1968, Dec.30/Rick MacPhee
    "The Maritimes: Newest Playground
    for UFOs?" Flying Saucers, June
    1970, pp.12,13.

New London
-Sea monster
  1880, Oct./Duncan Adams/=hoax?
    New York Times, 21 Oct.1880, p.5.
    New York Tribune, 21 Oct.1880, p.1.

North Bedeque
-UFO (DD)
  1947, July 1/C.K. Gunn
    Montreal (P.Q.) Star, 3 July 1947.

Sherbrooke
-UFO (DD)
  1947, July 3/James Harris
    Windsor (Ont.) Daily Star, 5 July
    1947.

Summerside
-UFO (DD)
  1968, Sep.21
    "Near-Landing Observed by RCAF," UFO
    Inv. 3 (Oct.-Nov.1966):4, quoting
    Summerside Journal-Pioneer (undated).

Village Green
-UFO (DD)
  1947, July 3/Ewen McNeill
    Windsor (Ont.) Daily Star, 7 July
    1947.

West Peters
-UFO (NL)
  1977, Jan.21
    John Brent Musgrave, "Red Lights &
    Other UFOs over Canada," MUFON UFO
    J., no.118 (Sep.1977):14.

West Point
-Sea monster
  1902, May
  ca.1938/Leslie MacLean
  ca.1956/Raeford MacLean
    Sterling Ramsay, Folklore: Prince
    Edward Island (Charlottetown:
    Square Deal, 1973), pp.84-85.

B. Physical Features

Holland Cove
-Ghost
  1765, July 14
    Charles M. Skinner, Myths and Legends
    Beyond Our Borders (Philadelphia:
    Lippincott, 1899), pp.81-82.

D. Unspecified Localities

-Sea monster
  1845, summer/off E coast
    Charles Lyell, A Second Visit to the
    United States of North America, 2
    vols. (London: John Murray, 1849),
    1:133.

-UFO (DD)
  1975, July-Aug.
    Kal Korf, "Prize Selections from a
    Researcher's Photo Collection,"
    Saga UFO Rept. 6 (Nov.1978):38,42.
    il.

NEWFOUNDLAND

A. Populated Places

Benton
-UFO (CE-1)
  1978, Dec.20
    "Recent UFO Sightings," Res Bureaux
    Bull., no.43 (Jan.1979):3,4.

Bishop's Falls
-UFO (DD)
  1968, Nov.26
    "The Maritimes: Newest Playground
    for UFOs?" Flying Saucers, June
    1970, pp.12,14.

Bonavista
-UFO (NL)
  1979, Jan.17
    "Recent UFO Sightings," Res Bureaux
    Bull., no.44 (Feb.1979):4.

Brigus
-Giant squid
  1879, Oct.
    A.E. Verrill, "The Cephalopods of the
    North-Eastern Coast of North Ameri-
    ca," Trans.Conn.Acad.Arts & Sci. 5
    (1879):177,194.

Catalina
-Giant squid
  1877, Sep.24
    A.E. Verrill, "Occurrence of Another
    Gigantic Cephalopod on the Coast of
    Newfoundland," Am.J.Sci., ser.3, 14
    (1877):425-26.

Clarenville
-UFO (NL)
  1978, Oct.12
    "UFOs," Res Bureaux Bull., no.41 (30
    Nov.1978):1,2.
  1978, Oct.26/James Blackwood
    Toronto (Ont.) Sunday Sun, 29 Oct.
    1978.
    Toronto (Ont.) Globe & Mail, 31 Oct.
    1978.
    "UFOs," Res Bureaux Bull., no.41 (30
    Nov.1978):1,2-3.

Codroy
-UFO (NL)
  1947, July 10-11
    J. Allen Hynek, The Hynek UFO Report
    (N.Y.: Dell, 1977), p.15.
    Bruce S. Maccabee, "UFO Related In-
    formation from the FBI Files: Part
    2," MUFON UFO J., no.121 (Dec.1977)
    :10,13.

Conche
-Ghost
  1873, March/John Dower
    Joseph Robert Smallwood, ed., The

Book of Newfoundland, 2 vols. (St.
John's: Newfoundland, 1937).
Lee R. Gandee, "The Woman of Conche,"
Fate 4 (May-June 1951):8-11.

Corner Brook
-UFO (?)
  1969/=Venus?
    Hamilton (Ont.) Spectator, 19 Oct.
    1973.
-UFO (NL)
  1952, April 18
    Quebec Chronicle-Telegraph, 19 Apr.
    1952.
  1968, Dec.30/Blomidon Country Club
    "The Maritimes: Newest Playground
    for UFOs?" Flying Saucers, June
    1970, pp.12,14.

Dildo
-Giant squid
  1933, Dec.
    Nancy Frost, "Notes on a Giant Squid
    (Architeuthis sp.) Captured at Dil-
    do, Newfoundland, in December,
    1933," Rept.Newfoundland Fisheries
    Comm'n, 1933, pp.104-13.

Flat Rock
-Fire anomaly
  1954, Nov./Mike Parsons
    (Editorial), Fate 8 (May 1955):13-14.
    R.S. Lambert, Exploring the Supernat-
    ural (Toronto: McClelland & Stewart,
    1955), p.149.

Gander
-UFO (CE-1)
  1951, Feb.10/Navy R5D transport/50 mi.E
    Donald E. Keyhoe, Flying Saucers: Top
    Secret (N.Y.: Putnam, 1960), pp.16-
    20.
    "Casebook," UFO Inv., Sep.1970, p.3;
    and Oct.1970, p.3.
    Philip J. Klass, UFOs Explained
    (N.Y.: Random House, 1974), pp.52-
    58.
-UFO (NL)
  1974, Oct.10/John Breen
    Gregory M. Kanon, "Something's Up
    Here with Us!" Can.UFO Rept., no.
    30 (winter-spring 1978):3-4.
  1978, Nov.1/E of town
  1978, Nov.2/airport
  1978, Nov.18
    "UFOs," Res Bureaux Bull., no.41 (30
    Nov.1978):1,2-3,5.

Glenwood
-UFO (NL)
  1978, Nov.4/nr. Salmon Pond
    "UFOs," Res Bureaux Bull., no.41 (30
    Nov.1978):1,3.

Grand Falls
-UFO (NL)
  1947, July 9
    Bruce S. Maccabee, "UFO Related In-
    formation from the FBI Files: Part
    3," MUFON UFO J., no.121 (Dec.1977)
    :10,13.

Hampden
-Giant squid
  ca.1929
    Bruce S. Wright, "How to Catch a
    Giant Squid--Maybe!" Atlantic Advo-
    cate, Aug.1961, p.19.

Harbour Grace
-Giant squid
  1875, winter
    A.E. Verrill, "The Gigantic Cephalo-
    pods of the North Atlantic," Am.J.
    Sci., ser.3, 9 (1875):177,180.
-Out-of-body experience
  1860/Cromwell Varley
    Paul Joire, Psychical and Supernor-
    mal Phenomena (London: W. Rider,
    1916).

Inglewood
-Giant squid
  1900, Nov.11
    Bruce S. Wright, "How to Catch a
    Giant Squid--Maybe!" Atlantic Advo-
    cate, Aug.1961, p.17.

Lamaline
-Giant squid
  1871, winter/M. Gabriel
    Alexander Murray, "Capture of a Gi-
    gantic Squid at Newfoundland," Am.
    Naturalist 8 (1874):120-23.

Lethbridge
-UFO (NL)
  1978, Nov.1
    "UFOs," Res Bureaux Bull., no.41 (30
    Nov.1978):1,3.

Marystown
-UFO (NL)
  1978, April 11
    "Other UFOs," Res Bureaux Bull., no.
    35 (15 June 1978):3,4.

O'Donnells
-UFO (NL)
  1978, April 11
    "Other UFOs," Res Bureaux Bull., no.
    35 (15 June 1978):3,4.

Saint Anthony
-UFO (DD)
  1974, Oct.
    Gregory M. Kanon, "Something's Up
    There with Us!" Can.UFO Rept., no.
    30 (winter-spring 1978):3,4.
-UFO (NL)
  1978, Nov.14
    "UFOs," Res Bureaux Bull., no.41 (30
    Nov.1978):1,5.

Saint Brides
-Phantom deer
  1804/Thomas Conway
    Joseph Robert Smallwood, ed., The
    Book of Newfoundland, 2 vols. (St.
    John's: Newfoundland, 1937), 2:234.

Saint Jacques
-UFO (NL)
  1978, April 11
    "Other UFOs," Res Bureaux Bull., no.
    35 (15 June 1978):3,4.

Saint John's
-Aerial phantom
  1949, Aug./Blackmarsh Rd.
    St. John's Sunday Herald, 3 Aug.1949.
-Clairvoyance
  1956, Dec./Keith Gilbert
    Aaron H. Downes, "Terrifying Dream
    Comes True," Fate 10 (Sep.1957):94.
-Sea monster
  1610/Richard H. Whitbourne/"Maremaid"
    Richard Whitbourne, Westward Hoe for
    Avalon in the New-Found-Land (Lon-
    don: Sampson Low, Son, & Marston,
    1870 ed.), pp.46-47.
  1888, Aug./=hoax
    St. John's Evening Telegram, 25 Aug.
    1888.
-UFO (NL)
  1947, July 10
    Bruce S. Maccabee, "UFO Related In-
    formation from the FBI Files: Part
    3," MUFON UFO J., no.121 (Dec.1977)
    :10,13.
  1950, Feb.1/Pat Walsh
    Kenneth Arnold & Ray Palmer, The Com-
    ing of the Saucers (Boise: The Au-
    thors, 1952), p.132.

Saint Lunaire
-UFO (CE-1)
  1978, Nov.10
    "UFOs," Res Bureaux Bull., no.41 (30
    Nov.1978):1,4.

Stephenville
-Fire anomaly
  1957, Aug./Lawrence Maden
    (Editorial), Fate 10 (Dec.1957):13.
-UFO (?)
  1947, July 20/Ernest Harmon AFB
    Donald E. Keyhoe, Flying Saucers Are
    Real (N.Y.: Fawcett, 1950), pp.8,
    30-31.
    Ted Bloecher, Report on the UFO Wave
    of 1947 (Washington: NICAP, 1967),
    p. 1-14.
    Bruce S. Maccabee, "UFO Related In-
    formation from the FBI Files: Part
    3," MUFON UFO J., no.121 (Dec.1977)
    :10,13.
-UFO (CE-2)
  1953, summer
    Leonard H. Stringfield, Situation
    Red: The UFO Siege (N.Y.: Fawcett
    Crest, 1977 ed.), pp.169-70.
-UFO (NL)
  1953, Jan.22/Ernest Harmon AFB

U.S.Air Force, Projects Grudge and
Blue Book Reports 1-12 (Washington:
NICAP, 1968), p.191.

Trepassey
-UFO (NL)
1978, Nov.10/Hickeys Hill
"UFOs," Res Bureaux Bull., no.41 (30
Nov.1978):1,4.

B. Physical Features

Bonavista Bay
-Giant squid
1872, Dec./Moses Harvey
M. Harvey, "How I Discovered the
Great Devil-Fish," Wide World Mag.
2 (1899):732-40.
1874/A. Munn
A.E. Verrill, "Occurrence of Gigantic Cuttle-fishes on the Coast of
Newfoundland," Am.J.Sci., ser.3, 7
(1874):158-61.
1879, Nov.1/James's Cove
A.E. Verrill, "The Cephalopods of
the North-Eastern Coast of America,"
Trans.Conn.Acad.Arts & Sci. 5 (1879)
:177-446.
St. John's Morning Chronicle, 9 Dec.
1879.

Chance Cove
-Whirlwind anomaly
1875, Aug./John Moran/"Mary"
London (Eng.) Times, 24 Sep.1875, p.
7.

Conception Bay
-Unidentified submerged object
1977, Jan.16
(Letter), Graham Conway, Can.UFO
Rept., no.27 (spring 1977):23-24,
quoting CP release, 18 Jan.1977.

Coomb's Cove
-Giant squid
1872, winter/T.R. Bennett
A.E. Verrill, "The Gigantic Cephalo-
pods of the North Atlantic," Am.J.
Sci., ser.3, 9 (1875):177,179.

Epaves Bay
-Norse discovery
1009/Thorfinn Karlsefni/=Straumfjord?
Farley Mowat, Westviking (Totowa,
N.J.: Minerva, 1968 ed.), pp.212-25.
-Norse habitation site
ca.1010/L'Anse au Meadows
Helge Ingstad, "Vinland Ruins Prove
Vikings Found the New World," Nat'l
Geographic 126 (Nov.1964):708-34.
il.
William D. Connor, "Arlington Mal-
lery's Norsemen in America," Fate
20 (Nov.1967):40-50.
Farley Mowat, Westviking (Totowa,
N.J.: Minerva, 1968 ed.), pp.212-
25,450-57.
Helge & Anne Stine Ingstad, "The

Norseman's Discovery of America,"
Trans.37th Int'l Cong.Americanists,
1968, 4:89-125.
Helge Ingstad, Westward to Vinland
(N.Y.: St. Martin's, 1969). il.
Anne Stine Ingstad, The Discovery of
a Norse Settlement in America, 2
vols. (Oslo: Universitets-forlaget,
1977). il.

Flat Rock Cove
-Norse discovery
1001/Leif Eriksson/=Helluland?
Hjalmar R. Holand, Explorations in
America before Columbus (N.Y.:
Twayne, 1956), p.40.

Fortune Bay
-Giant squid
1874, Dec./George Simms
A.E. Verrill, "Notice of the Occur-
rence of Another Gigantic Cephalo-
pod (Architeuthis) on the Coast of
Newfoundland, in December, 1874,"
Am.J.Sci., ser.3, 10 (1875):213-14.

Grand Banks
-Giant squid
1871, Oct.20/Capt. Campbell/"B.D. Haskins"
A.S. Packard, Jr., "Colossal Cuttle-
fishes," Am.Naturalist 7 (1873):
87-94.
1875, Oct./J.W. Collins/"Howard"
A.E. Verrill, "Report on the Cephalopods of the Northeastern Coast
of America," Rept.U.S.Fish Comm'n,
1879, p.211.
-Sea monster
1879, Nov.6/F.G. Rowell/"Anchoria"
New York Times, 11 Nov.1879, p.8.
1883
Wellington New Zealand Times, 12
Dec.1883.
1886, Oct.11/"Hattie F. Walker"/=
hoax
St. John's Evening Mercury, 12 Sep.
1887.
1893, Dec.2/"American"
New York Tribune, 7 Dec.1893, p.3.
1913, Aug.30/G. Batchelor/"Corinthian"
London (Eng.) Daily Sketch, 25 Sep.
1913, p.6.
Bernard Heuvelmans, In the Wake of
the Sea Serpents (N.Y.: Hill & Wang,
1968), pp.392-94.

Great Bell I.
-Giant squid
1873, Oct.25/Theophilus Picot
New York Times, 28 Sep.1874, p.5.
M. Harvey, "Gigantic Cuttlefishes in
Newfoundland," Annals & Mag.of Nat.
Hist., ser.4, 13 (1874):67-69.
Alexander Murray, "Capture of a Gi-
gantic Squid at Newfoundland," Am.
Naturalist 8 (1874):120-23.

Hampden Bay
-Norse discovery

1009/Thorfinn Karlsefni/=Hóp?
Farley Mowat, Westviking (Totowa,
N.J.: Minerva, 1968 ed.), pp.273-77.

Harbour Main
-Giant squid
1935, Nov.12/Joe Ezekiel
Nancy Frost, "A Further Species of
Giant Squid (Architeuthis sp.) from
Newfoundland Waters," Rept.Newfound-
land Fisheries Comm'n, 1935, pp.89-
95.

Heart's Delight Harbour
-Giant squid
1902, Nov.
Bruce S. Wright, "How to Catch a
Giant Squid--Maybe!" Atlantic Advo-
cate, Aug.1961, p.17.

Indian Tickle
-Giant squid
1901, July/William Parr
Bruce S. Wright, "How to Catch a
Giant Squid--Maybe!" Atlantic Advo-
cate, Aug.1961, p.17.

Lance Cove
-Fall of unknown object
1978, April 2/Jim Bickford
St. John's Evening Telegram, 3 Apr.
1978; 6 Apr.1978; 10 Apr.1978; and
12 Apr.1978.
Toronto (Ont.) Globe & Mail, 3 Apr.
1978, p.1.
Ottawa (Ont.) Journal, 4 Apr.1978,
p.5.
"Menace from the Sky," Res Bureaux
Bull., no.32 (13 Apr.1978):4.
"More on the Lance Cove Menace," Res
Bureaux Bull., no.35 (15 June 1978)
:4-6.
-Giant squid
1877, Nov.21
A.E. Verrill, "The Cephalopods of
the North-Eastern Coast of America,"
Trans.Conn.Acad.Arts & Sci. 5 (1879)
:177,190.

Little Barrisway
-Giant squid
1902, Jan.9
Bruce S. Wright, "How to Catch a
Giant Squid--Maybe!" Atlantic Advo-
cate, Aug.1961, p.17.

Logia Bay
-Giant squid
1873, Nov.
Alexander Murray, "Capture of a Gi-
gantic Squid at Newfoundland," Am.
Naturalist 8 (1874):120-23.
A.E. Verrill, "The Cephalopods of
the North-Eastern Coast of America,"
Trans.Conn.Acad.Arts & Sci. 5 (1879)
:177,184-86.

Manuels R.
-Archeological site
David R. Hughes, "Human Remains from

near Manuels River, Conception Bay,
Newfoundland," Bull.Nat'l Mus.Can-
ada, no.224 (1969):195-207.

Notre Dame Bay
-Giant squid
1876, Nov.20/Hammer Cove
A.E. Verrill, "The Cephalopods of
the North-Eastern Coast of America," Trans.Conn.Acad.Arts & Sci. 5
(1879):177,190.

Pistolet Bay
-Norse discovery
1001/Leif Eriksson/=Vinland?
Arlington Mallery, Lost America
(Washington: Public Affairs, 1950).

Port au Choix
-Archeological site
ca.4500 B.C.-850 A.D.
Elmer Harp, Jr. & David R. Hughes,
"Five Prehistoric Burials from
Port-aux-Choix, Newfoundland,"
Polar Notes 8 (June 1968):1-47.
James Tuck, "An Archaic Indian Ceme-
tery in Newfoundland," Sci.Am. 222
(June 1970):112-21. il.
James A. Tuck, "An Archaic Cemetery
at Port au Choix, Newfoundland,"
Am.Antiquity 36 (1971):343-58. il.
James A. Tuck, Ancient People of
Port au Choix (St. John's: Inst.of
Social & Economic Rsch., 1976). il.
-Ghost
1883, Dec.15/James Shenicks
"Notes," Light 4 (1884):233, quoting
Church Times, 16 May 1884.

Race, Cape
-UFO (NL)
1887, Nov.12/Capt. Moore/"Siberian"
"La foudre globulaire," L'Astronomie
7 (1888):76.
T.C. Mendenhall, "On Globular Lightning," Am.Meteorological J. 6
(1890):437,443.

Saint Paul's Bay
-Norse discovery
1009/Thorfinn Karlsefni/=Hóp?
Farley Mowat, Westviking (Totowa,
N.J.: Minerva, 1968 ed.), pp.238-42.

Salmon Cove
-Giant squid
1911, Dec.4
Bruce S. Wright, "How to Catch a
Giant Squid--Maybe!" Atlantic Advo-
cate, Aug.1961, p.17.

Sculpin I.
-Norse habitation site
David Putnam, David Goes to Baffin
Land (N.Y.: Putnam, 1927).
William B. Goodwin, The Ruins of
Great Ireland in New England (Bos-
ton: Meador, 1946), p.418. il.
Arlington Mallery, Lost America
(Washington: Public Affairs, 1950).

Sops Arm
-Giant squid
   1927
      Bruce S. Wright, "How to Catch a
      Giant Squid--Maybe!" Atlantic Advo-
      cate, Aug.1961, p.17.

Sops I.
-Norse habitation site
      Arlington Mallery, Lost America
      (Washington: Public Affairs, 1950).
      Arlington H. Mallery, "The Pre-Colum-
      bian Discovery of America: A Reply
      to W.S. Godfrey," Am.Anthro. 60
      (1958):141-52.

Thimble Tickle
-Giant squid
   1878, Nov.2/Stephen Sherring
      Boston Traveller, 30 Jan.1879.
      A.E. Verrill, "The Cephalopods of
      the North-Eastern Coast of America,"
      Trans.Conn.Acad.Arts & Sci. 5 (1879)
      :177,190.

Three Arms
-Giant squid
   1878, Dec.2/William Budgell
      Boston Traveller, 30 Jan.1879.
      A.E. Verrill, "The Cephalopods of
      the North-Eastern Coast of America,"
      Trans.Conn.Acad.Arts & Sci. 5 (1879)
      :177,192-93.

Tickle Cove Bay
-Norse discovery
   1001/Leif Eriksson/=Vinland?
      Farley Mowat, Westviking (Totowa,
      N.J.: Minerva, 1968 ed.), pp.120-
      31,430-38.

            C. Ethnic Groups

Beothuk Indians
-Similarity to Norse
      Stuart S. Seaman, "Who Came Before
      Columbus?" Creation Rsch.Soc'y Quar.
      13 (Dec.1976):150,153-54.

LABRADOR

A. Populated Places

Black Tickle
-UFO (DD)
  1978, Nov.13
    "UFOs," Res Bureaux Bull., no.41 (30
    Nov.1978):1,5.

Goose Bay
-UFO (?)
  1952, Nov.26
    Donald E. Keyhoe, Flying Saucers from
    Outer Space (N.Y.: Holt, 1953), p.
    149.
-UFO (CE-1)
  1978, Nov.6/Happy Valley
    "UFOs," Res Bureaux Bull., no.41 (30
    Nov.1978):1,4.
-UFO (DD)
  1954, June 30/James Howard
    John Carnell, "BOAC's Flying Jelly-
    fish," Fate 7 (Nov.1954):16-23.
    Leonard Cramp, "Mystery over Labra-
    dor," Flying Saucer Rev. 1 (spring
    1955):6-8.
    Richard Hall, ed., The UFO Evidence
    (Washington: NICAP, 1964), p.126.
    Gordon D. Thayer, "Optical and Radar
    Analyses of Field Cases," in Edward
    U. Condon, ed., Scientific Study of
    Unidentified Flying Objects (N.Y.:
    Bantam, 1969 ed.), pp.115,139-40.
-UFO (NL)
  1952/USAF base
    Edward J. Ruppelt, The Report on Un-
    identified Flying Objects (Garden
    City: Doubleday, 1956), pp.146-49.
  1959, Aug.10/RCAF base
    Lloyd Mallan, "Complete Directory of
    UFOs: Part III," Sci.& Mech, 38
    (Feb.1967):56,59.
-UFO (R)
  1948, summer/Edwin A. Jerome/RCAF base
    Richard Hall, ed., The UFO Evidence
    (Washington: NICAP, 1964), pp.83-
    84.
  1948, Nov.1/RCAF base
    Donald E. Keyhoe, Flying Saucers from
    Outer Space (N.Y.: Holt, 1953), p.
    33.
-UFO (R-V)
  1948, Oct.29, 31/RCAF base
    Donald E. Keyhoe, Flying Saucers Are
    Real (N.Y.: Fawcett, 1950), p.162.
  1952, June 19/USAF base
    Donald E. Keyhoe, Flying Saucers from
    Outer Space (N.Y.: Holt, 1953), p.
    52.
    Edward J. Ruppelt, The Report on Un-
    identified Flying Objects (Garden
    City: Doubleday, 1956), p.146.
  1952, Dec.15
    Gordon D. Thayer, "Optical and Radar
    Analyses of Field Cases," in Edward

U. Condon, ed., Scientific Study of
Unidentified Flying Objects (N.Y.:
Bantam, 1969 ed.), pp.115,126-27.

Hebron
-Meteorite crater
  195 m.diam. x 48 m.deep/=possible
  V.B. Meen, "Merewether Crater: A
  Possible Meteor Crater," Proc.Geol.
  Ass'n Canada 9 (1957):49-67. il.

Hopedale
-Archeological site
  Junius Bird, "Archaeology of the
  Hopedale Area, Labrador," Anthro.
  Pap.Am.Mus.Nat.Hist., no.39 (1945).
  il.

Labrador City
-UFO (?)
  ca.1970
    "The Maritimes: Newest Playground
    for UFOs?" Flying Saucers, June
    1970, pp.12,14.

L'Anse Amour
-Archeological site
  ca.5000 B.C.
    James A. Tuck & Robert McGhee, "Ar-
    chaic Cultures in the Strait of
    Belle Isle Region, Labrador," Arc-
    tic Anthro. 12 (1975):76-91.
    James A. Tuck & Robert J. McGhee,
    "An Archaic Indian Burial Mound in
    Labrador," Sci.Am. 235 (Nov.1976):
    122-29. il.

Mistastin
-Meteorite crater
  28,000 m.diam.
    J. Classen, "Catalogue of 230...Im-
    pact Structures," Meteoritics 12
    (1977):61,70.

West Saint Modeste
-Giant squid
  1875
    A.E. Verrill, "The Gigantic Cephalo-
    pods of the North Atlantic," Am.J.
    Sci., ser.3, 9 (1875):177,180.

B. Physical Features

Chibongamon L.
-Humanoid myth
  Wi'tigo'
    Julius E. Lips, The Savage Hits
    Back (New Haven: Yale Univ., 1937).
    R.S. Lambert, Exploring the Supernat-
    ural (Toronto: McClelland & Stewart,
    1955), p.173.

Chidley, Cape
-UFO (CE-1)
   1972, Dec.24/"Moldoveanu"
     Ion Hobana & Julien Weverbergh, UFOs
     from Behind the Iron Curtain (N.Y.:
     Bantam, 1975 ed.), p.279.

Forteau Bay
-Archeological site
   ca.4000 B.C.
     Elmer Harp, "Evidence of Boreal Ar-
     chaic Culture in Southern Labrador
     and Newfoundland," Bull.Nat'l Mus.
     Canada, no.193 (1964):184,191-94.
     Salvatore Michael Trento, The Search
     for Lost America (Chicago: Contem-
     porary, 1978), pp.36-37.

Leopold I.
-Norse discovery
   986/Bjarni Herjolfsson/=Bear Island?
     Farley Mowat, Westviking (Totowa,
     N.J.: Minerva, 1968 ed.), pp.194-96.

Melville L.
-Norse discovery
   1005/Thorvald Eriksson/=anchorage?
     Farley Mowat, Westviking (Totowa,
     N.J.: Minerva, 1968 ed.), pp.265-
     68,444-47.

Porcupine, Cape
-Norse discovery
   1001/Leif Eriksson/=Markland?
   1009/Thorfinn Karlsefni/=Kialarness?
     Farley Mowat, Westviking (Totowa,
     N.J.: Minerva, 1968 ed.), pp.202-
     203,422.

Rattler's Bight
-Archeological site
   2000 B.C.
     "Were the First Norsemen Here 4000
     Years Ago?" NEARA Newsl. 7 (Dec.
     1972):80.

Sandwich Bay
-Norse discovery
   1009/Thorfinn Karlsefni/=landfall?
     Farley Mowat, Westviking (Totowa,
     N.J.: Minerva, 1968 ed.), pp.205-
     207.

Tabor I.
-Mineralogical anomaly
     "How Big Can a Crystal Be?" Pursuit
     4 (Oct.1971):87-88.

Traverspine R.
-Humanoid
   ca.1913/Mrs. Michelin
     Elliott Merrick, True North (N.Y.:
     Charles Scribner, 1933).
     Bruce Wright, Wildlife Sketches Near
     and Far (Fredericton, N.B.: Univ.
     of New Brunswick, 1962).

C. Ethnic Groups

Naskapi Indians
-Divination
     Alika Podolinsky, "Divination Rites,"
     The Beaver, summer 1964, pp.40-41.

GREENLAND

A. Populated Places

Godthåb
-Fall of steel meteorite
  n.d./A. Heilprin
    E. Goldsmith, "A Tempered Steel Met-
    eorite," Proc.Acad.Nat.Sci.Philadel-
    phia, 1893, pp.373-76.
    "A Tempered Steel Meteorite," Nature
    49 (1894):372.
-Sea monster
  1734, July 6/Hans Egede
    Hans Egede, Det gamle Grønlands nye
    Perlustration (Copenhagen: J.C.
    Groth, 1741).
    Poul Egede, Continuation af Relation-
    erne betreffende den Grønlandske
    Missions Tilstand og Beskaffenhed
    (Copenhagen: J.C. Groth, 1741).
    Hans Egede, A Description of Green-
    land (London: C. Hatch, 1745), pp.
    85-89.
    Poul Egede, Efterretninger om Grøn-
    land (Copenhagen: H.C. Schrøder,
    1788).
    Henry Lee, Sea Monsters Unmasked
    (London: W. Clowes, 1883).
    A.C. Oudemans, The Great Sea-Serpent
    (Leiden: E.J. Brill, 1892), pp.112-
    20.

Herjolfsnes
-Archeological site
  ca.1000-1480
    Poul Nørlund, "Buried Norsemen at
    Herjolfsnes," Meddelelser om Grøn-
    land, vol.67 (1924). il.

Kangamiut
-Archeological site
  1350-1500
    Therkel Mathiassen, "Ancient Eskimo
    Settlements in the Kangamiut Area,"
    Meddelelser om Grønland, vol.91,
    no.1 (1931).
-Fall of red snow
  1954, March 13
    "Colored Rain--Snow," Doubt, no.45
    (1954):289.

Niaqornarssuk
-UFO (DD)
  1957, Aug.13
  1957, Sep.25/Qapak Jeremiassen
    Jacques & Janine Vallee, Challenge
    to Science (N.Y.: Ace, 1966 ed.),
    pp.35-37.

Sarqaq
-Archeological site
  ca.800-200 B.C.
    Jørgen Meldgaard, "A Paleo-Eskimo
    Culture in West Greenland," Am.An-
    tiquity 17 (1952):22-30.

Hans-Georg Bandi, Eskimo Prehistory
    (College: Univ.of Alaska, 1969),
    pp.162-65.

Sermermiut
-Archeological site
  ca.1000 B.C.-1400 A.D.
    Therkel Mathiassen, "The Sermermiut
    Excavations, 1955," Meddelelser om
    Grønland, vol.161, no.3 (1958). il.

Thule
-UFO (CE-1)
  1975, June
    Rufus Drake, "UFO Crisis over Green-
    land," Saga, Oct.1976, pp.36,54,60.
-UFO (NL)
  1942, Dec./James B. Nilreck
    Rufus Drake, "UFO Crisis over Green-
    land," Saga, Oct.1976, pp.36,54.
  1953, Feb.
    "Saucer Sundries," CRIFO Newsl., 3
    Dec.1954, p.6.
-UFO (R)
  1960, Oct.5/BMEWS Station
    Manchester (Eng.) Guardian, 30 Nov.
    1960.
    New York Times, 8 Dec,1960, p.71;
    and 23 Dec.1960, p.6.
    John A. Keel, UFOs:Operation Trojan
    Horse (N.Y.: Putnam, 1970), pp.13-
    14.

B. Physical Features

Disko Bugt
-Archeological sites
    Helge Larsen & Jørgen Meldgaard,
    "Paleo-Eskimo Cultures in Disko
    Bugt," Meddelelser om Grønland, vol.
    161, no.2 (1958). il.
-Unidentified submerged object
  1972, Dec.7-9
    New York Times, 13 Dec.1972, p.13;
    and 14 Dec.1972, p.9.
    Washington (D.C.) Post, 15 Dec.1972.

Hagens Fjord
-Meteorite craters
  =doubtful
    K. Ellitsgaard-Rasmussen, "Meteorit-
    ic Shower in North-East Greenland?"
    Meddelelser Dansk.Geol.Foren. 12
    (1954):433=35.

Independence Fjord
-Archeological site
  ca.2600-600 B.C.
    Eigil Knuth, "An Outline of the Arch-
    aeology of Pearyland," Arctic 5
    (1952):17-33.
    Eigil Knuth, "Pearyland's Arkaeolo-
    gi," Naturens Verden, 1965, pp.170-

84,2-6-79.
Hans-Georg Bandi, Eskimo Prehistory
(College: Univ.of Alaska, 1969), pp.
157-62.

Inlandsis
-Fall of unknown objects
  1912, Oct./Ejnar Mikkelson
    Ejnar Mikkelson, Lost in the Arctic
    (N.Y.: G.H. Doran, 1913).
-Skyquake
  1931, winter/Augustine Courtauld
    New York Times, 29 May 1931, p.1.
-UFO (CE-1)
  1974, May 2/Martin L. Carey
    Rufus Drake, "UFO Crisis over Green-
    land," Saga, Oct.1976, pp.36-38.
-UFO (NL)
  ca.1973
    Rufus Drake, "UFO Crisis over Green-
    land," Saga, Oct.1976, pp.36,38.

Inugsuk I.
-Archeological site
  ca.1300
    Therkel Mathiassen, "Preliminary Re-
    port of the Fifth Thule Expedition,"
    21st Int'l Congress of Americanists,
    1925, pp.202-15.
    Therkel Mathiassen, "Inugsuk, a Me-
    dieval Eskimo Settlement in Uper-
    nivik District, West Greenland,"
    Meddelelser om Grønland, vol.77, no.
    4 (1930). il.

Jesup, Kap
-UFO (DD)
  1956/Valentin Akkuratov
    Feliz Ziegel, "Unidentified Flying
    Objects," Soviet Life, Feb.1968,
    pp.27,28-29.
    Joe Brill, "UFO's Behind the Iron
    Curtain," Skylook, no.92 (July
    1975):18.

Kingigtorssuak I.
-Norse runestone
  1824/Willem Graah
    Magnus Olsen, "Kingigtorssuak-stenen
    og sproget: de Grønlandske runeind-
    skrifter," Norsk Tidsskrift for
    Sprogvidenskab 5 (1932):189-257. il.
    Alf Mongé & O.G. Landsverk, Norse
    Medieval Cryptography in Runic Car-
    vings (Glendale, Cal.: Norseman,
    1967), pp.98-102. il.
    Alf Mongé, "The 13th Century Kingig-
    torssuak Runic Concealment Cipher,"
    NEARA J. 10 (spring 1975):82-90.

Lincoln Sea
-Doubtful geography
  1871/Charles Francis Hall/Grant's Land/
  =ice island?
    Chauncey C. Loomis, Weird and Tragic
    Shores (N.Y.: Knopf, 1971), p.276.

Marshall Bay
-Archeological site
  ca.800-1300

Erik Holtved, "Archaeological Investigations in the Thule District,"
Meddelelser om Grønland 141, no.1
(1944):298-302.

Nûgssuaq
-Archeological site
  ca.1100/Bjørnefaelden
    Jørgen Meldgaard, Nordboerne i
    Groenland (Copenhangen: Munksgaard,
    1965), pp.83-84.

Onfak
-Giant meteorite
  "Huge Meteorites from Greenland,"
  Sci.Am.Suppl. 2 (1876):510.

Smith Sound
-Archeological sites
  Clark Wissler, "Archaeology of the
  Polar Eskimo," Anthro.Pap.Am.Mus.
  Nat.Hist., vol.22, pt.3 (1918).

York, Kap
-Giant meteorite
  n.d./Robert E. Peary
    Robert E. Peary, Northward over the
    Great Ice, 2 vols. (N.Y.: Freder-
    ick A. Stokes, 1898), 2:127-29,
    145-48,553-618. il.
    Frederick C. Leonard, "The Total
    Known Weight of the Cape York,
    Greenland, Siderite Fall," Pop.
    Astron. 59 (1951):377-79.

C. Ethnic Groups

Eskimo
-Humanoid myth
  tornit
    Franz Boas, "The Central Eskimo,"
    Ann.Rept.Bur.Am.Eth. 6 (1885):643-
    48.
    Alfred L. Kroeber, "Tales of the
    Smith Sound Eskimo," J.Am.Folklore
    12 (1899):166-68.
-Shamanism
  Henry Rink, Danish Greenland (Lon-
  don: Henry S. King, 1877), pp.199-
  206.
  Peter Freuchen, Book of the Eskimos
  (Cleveland: Worls, 1961 ed.), pp.
  187-283.

D. Unspecified Localities

-Aerial phantom
  1820, July 18/William Scoresby/"Baffin"
    David Brewster, Letters on Natural
    Magic (London: J. Murray, 1832).

-Cartographic anomalies
  1441-19th c.
    Justin Winsor, ed., Narrative and
    Critical History of America, 8 vols.
    (Boston: Houghton Mifflin, 1884-89),
    1:117-32.

Fridtjof Nansen, In Northern Mists, 2 vols. (N.Y.: Frederick A. Stokes, 1911).

Axel Anthon Bjørnbo, "Cartographia Groenlandica," Meddelelser om Grønland, vol.48 (1912). il.

William Herbert Hobbs, "Zeno and the Cartography of Greenland," Imago Mundi 6 (1949):15-19.

R.A. Skelton, Thomas E. Marston & George D. Painter, The Vinland Map and the Tartar Relation (New Haven: Yale Univ., 1965). il.

G.R. Crone, "The Vinland Map Cartographically Considered," Geographical J. 132 (Mar.1966):75-80.

Ib Rønne Kejlbo, "Claudius Clavus and the Vinland Map," Am.-Scandinavian Rev. 54 (June 1966):126-31.

Einar Haugen, "The Sources of the Vinland Map," Arctic 19 (1966):287-95.

Alf Mongé & O.G. Landsverk, Norse Medieval Cryptography in Runic Carvings (Glendale, Cal.: Norseman, 1967), pp.118-22.

Stanislaw Bernatt, "Zweite Deutsche Nordpolar-Expedition 1869/70 ein Beweis gegen die Echtheit der 'Yale' Vinlandkarte vom Jahre 1441," Polarforschung, Bd.6, Jgd.38 (1968):223-24.

Rolf Lindemann, "Die Vinlandkarte und die Zweite Deutsche Nordpol-Expedition," Polarforschung, Bd.6, Jgd.39 (1969-70):264-69.

Leon Koczy, "Die Vinlandkarte als ein Polarforschungsproblem," Polarforschung, Bd.6, Jgd.38 (1968):250-53.

Vsevolod Slessarev & Pirie Sublett, "The Vinland Caption Reexamined," Terrae Incognitae 1 (1969):23-24.

Wilcomb E. Washburn, ed., Proceedings of the Vinland Map Conference (Chicago: Univ.of Chicago, 1971).

Leon Koczy, "Die 'Inventio Fortunata' und die Entdeckung des Nordpols," Polarforschung, Bd.7, Jgd.41 (1971): 149-52.

Ib Rønne Kejlbo, "Hans Egede and the Frobisher Strait," Geografisk Tidsskrift 70 (1971):59-139. il.

L.A. Vigneras, "Greenland, Vinland, and the Yale Map," Terrae Incognitae 4 (1972):53-93.

"Ink Study Suggests Vinland Map Fraud," Chemical & Engineering News, 11 Feb.1974, p.21.

Walter B. & Lucy McCrone, "The Vinland Map Ink," Geographical J. 140 (June 1974):212-14.

O.G. Landsverk, "The Vinland Map Is Authentic!" NEARA Newsl. 9 (fall 1974):58-60.

Astri A. Stromsted, Ancient Pioneers (N.Y.: E.J. Friis, 1974).

Walter C. McCrone, "Authenticity of Medieval Document Tested by Small Particle Analysis," Analytical Chemistry 48 (1976):676-78. il.

George M. Eberhart, The Mapping of Greenland (M.A. thesis, Univ.of Chicago, 1976). il.

George M. Eberhart, "Climatic Variation and the Exploration of Greenland," Pursuit 11 (fall 1978):136-42. il.

-Disease anomaly
  arctic hysteria
    A.A. Brill, "Pibloktoq or Hysteria among Peary's Eskimos," J.Nervous & Mental Disease 40 (1913):514-20.

    N.N. Sengupta, "Mind in Different Physical Settings," Indian J. Psych. 17 (1942):49-57.

    David F. Aberle, "'Arctic Hysteria' and Latah in Mongolia," Trans.N.Y. Acad.Sci. 14 (1952):291-97.

    Edward F. Foulks, "Arctic Hysteria: A Research Problem," Pennsylvania Psychiatric Quar. 8 (1968):50-55.

    Joseph D. Bloom & Richard D. Gelardin, "Eskimo Sleep Paralysis," Arctic 29 (1976):20-26.

-Pre-Norse discovery
    Strabo, Geography 2.4.1.
    Pliny, Historia naturalis 4.30.
    Cleomedes, De motu circulari 1.17.
    Plutarch, De facie quae in orbe lunae apparet 26.
    Dicuil, Liber de mensura orbis terrae, Gustavo Parthey, ed. (Berlin: F. Nicolai, 1870), p.42.

    William H. Tillinghast, "The Geographical Knowledge of the Ancients Considered in Relation to the Discovery of America," in Justin Winsor, ed., Narrative and Critical History of America, 8 vols. (Boston: Houghton Mifflin, 1884-89), 1:1-58.

    Clements R. Markham, "Pytheas, the Discoverer of Britain," Geographical J. 1 (1893):504-24.

    Gaston E. Broche, Pythéas le Massaliote (Paris: Soc.française d'imprim.et de libr., 1935).

    Vilhjalmar Stefansson, Ultima Thule (N.Y.: Macmillan, 1940).

    Rhys Carpenter, Beyond the Pillars of Heracles (N.Y.: Delacorte, 1966).

    E.D. Phillips, "Κρόνιον πέλαγος: Notions of the Arctic Ocean in Ancient Geography," Evphrosyne, n.s., 2 (1969):193-97.

    George M. Eberhart, "Climatic Variation and the Exploration of Greenland," Pursuit 11 (fall 1978):136-42.

-UFO (?)
  1948/north coast
    Rufus Drake, "UFO Crisis over Greenland," Saga, Oct.1976, pp.36,54.
-UFO (DD)
  1932/Peter Grunnert/east coast
  1971
    Rufus Drake, "UFO Crisis over Greenland," Saga, Oct.1976, pp.36,54,60.

n.d./Mr. Laing
 "Psychic Sightings," Can.UFO Rept.,
  no.10 (1971):2,4.
-Unidentified submerged object
 1940s
  John A. Keel, "Mystery of the Alien
  Submarines," Saga UFO Rept. 2 (fall
  1974):28.

ADDENDA

ALASKA

Middleton I.
-UFO (R-V)
   1977, April 23/Richard Drzal/Northwest
   Orient Flight 27/50 mi.E
   "Radar/Visual in Alaska," Int'l UFO
   Reporter 2 (July 1977):4.

WASHINGTON

Ocean Shores
-Fall of fish
   1972, Jan.10/Tom James
   "Animals," INFO J., no.9 (fall 1972):
   12,16-17.

WYOMING

Teton Village
-UFO (NL)
   1975, Oct.2
   "Noteworthy UFO Sightings," Ufology
   2 (spring 1976):43.

NEBRASKA

Hartington
-Phantom helicopter
   1974/Gordon Gruber
   Washington (D.C.) Post, 8 Sep.1974.
   Tommy Roy Blann, "The Mysterious
   Link between UFOs and Animal Muti-
   lations," Saga UFO Rept. 3 (Apr.
   1976):18,69-70.

KANSAS

Pittsburg
-UFO (CE-2)
   1974, spring/Richard Rethurst/airport
   (Letter), Saga UFO Rept. 2 (fall
   1975):4.

TEXAS

Bells
-UFO (NL)
   1965, Aug.2/Bob Campbell
   Wichita (Kan.) Beacon, 4 Aug.1965,
   p.5A. il.
   Jacques & Janine Vallee, Challenge
   to Science (N.Y.: Ace, 1966 ed.),
   pp.66-67.
   J. Allen Hynek, The UFO Experience
   (Chicago: Regnery,1972), betw.pp.
   52-53. il.

LOUISIANA

Unspecified locality
-Fall of fish

1883
   Decatur (Ill.) Daily Republican, 4
   Jan.1884, p.2.

VIRGINIA

Fairfax co.
-UFO (NL)
   1952, Sep.22/Douglas Dunn
   Washington (D.C.) Times-Herald, 22
   Sep.1952.

ILLINOIS

Galesburg
-UFO (NL)
   1897, April 10/O.C. Lanphear
   Chicago Tribune, 11 Apr.1897, p.4.
   Galesburg Evening Mail, 12 Apr.1897,
   p.1.
   1897, April 12/Ray Norton
   Galesburg Evening Mail, 13 Apr.1897,
   p.1.
   1897, April 14
   Galesburg Evening Mail, 15 Apr.1897,
   p.1.
   1897, April 19
   Galesburg Evening Mail, 20 Apr.1897,
   p.4.
   1957, Nov.5
   Richard Hall, ed., The UFO Evidence
   (Washington: NICAP, 1964), p.165.
   1967, March 6,8/Frank Courson
   Chicago Daily News, 9 Mar.1967.

INDIANA

Butler
-UFO (CE-1)
   1972, Sep.11/Jane Kempf/County Rd.34
   Auburn Evening News, 14 Sep.1972.
   "City Editor Present When Woman Reports UFO to Police," Skylook, no.
   60 (Nov.1972):5.

Porter co.
-Ghost
   1965
   Deborah Koss, "A Collection of Interviews about a Porter County Ghost
   Hunt," Indiana Folklore 8, no.1-2
   (1975):99-125.

Wheatfield
-Contactee
   1960s/Walter A. Kooistra
   (Letter), Fate 23 (Sep.1970):134,145.

OHIO

Columbus
-Precognition
   1963, Nov.20/Ricky E. McDowell/Doctor's
   Hospital

Columbus Dispatch, 29 Dec.1963, p.27B.

MARYLAND

Frederick
-Healing
  1960s-   /L. Richard Batzler
    Martin Ebon, The Evidence for Life
    after Death (N.Y.: Signet, 1977),
    pp.139-45.
-UFO (?)
  1952, Sep.12/=meteor?
    Ivan T. Sanderson, Uninvited Visitors
    (N.Y.: Cowles, 1967), p.41.

Severna Park
-UFO (CE-1)
  1967, Feb.23/Mr. Rice/Severn R. at
  Linstead
    Baltimore News-American, 25 Feb.1967.

NEW YORK

New York City
-Plant sensitivity
  1966-   /Cleve Backster/165 W. 46th
  St., Suite 404
    Cleve Backster, "Evidence of a Pri-
    mary Perception in Plant Life,"
    Int'l J.Parapsych. 10 (1968):329-48.
    F.L. Kunz, "Feeling in Plants," Main
    Currents in Modern Thought 25 (1969)
    :143.
    "ESP: More Science, Less Mysticism,"
    Medical World News, 21 Mar.1969,
    pp.20-21.
    Walter McGraw, "Plants Are Only Hu-
    man," Argosy, June 1969, pp.24-27.
    Ivan T. Sanderson, "The Backster
    Effect: Commentary," Argosy, June
    1969, p.26.
    Walter McGraw, "Please Don't Hurt
    the Daisies," Fate 22 (Oct.1969):
    61-71.
    L. George Lawrence, "Electronics
    Proves Plants Can Feel," Fate 23
    (Nov.1970):38-44.
    (Editorial), Fate 24 (Sep.1971):7-20.
    Wall Street Journal, 2 Feb.1972, p.1.
    John W. White, "Plants, Polygraphs
    and Paraphysics," Psychic 4 (Dec.
    1972):12-17,24.
    Peter Tompkins & Christopher Bird,
    The Secret Life of Plants (N.Y.:
    Harper & Row, 1973), pp.3-16.
    Ingo Swann, To Kiss Earth Good-Bye
    (N.Y.: Hawthorn, 1975), pp.33-36.
    Marcel Vogel, "Man-Plant Communica-
    tion," in Edgar D. Mitchell, ed.,
    Psychic Exploration (N.Y.: Capri-
    corn, 1976 ed.), pp.289-92.
-Poltergeist
  1895, Jan.4-5/Adam Colwell/84 Guernsey
  St.
    New York Herald, 6 Jan.1895.
-Possession
  1961, Feb./Teri Goldenberg
    Lesley Kuhn, "Exorcising a Demon in

the Bronx," Fate 16 (Apr.1963):26-
30.

ONTARIO

Kirkland Lake
-UFO (NL)
  1973, Oct.16
    Wido Hoville, "Observation et photo-
    graphie d'un UFO en forme de ci-
    gare," UFO-Québec, no.14 (June 1978)
    :8-10. il.

CONNECTICUT

Bridgeport
-Poltergeist
  1974, Nov.24-   /Laura Goodin
    Lawrence Cortesi, "Noisy Ghost That
    Turned a Town Upside Down," Psychic
    World, Nov.1976, pp.29-32,86-88. il.

Greenwich
-Haunt
  1968, fall-1971/William Harris/St.Paul's
  Episcopal Church rectory
    Lawrence Cortesi, "The Minister Who
    Came Eye-to-Eye with a Spirit," Psy-
    chic World, Sep.1976, pp.58-61,82-
    83. il.

Hartford
-Crisis apparition
  1956, July 27/H. Addington Bruce
    H. Addington Bruce, "Why I Believe in
    Survival," Tomorrow 5 (autumn 1956):
    58,64.

VERMONT

Fairlee
-UFO (NL)
  1978, July 13/Wendy Baade
    West Lebanon (N.H.) Valley News, 18
    July 1978.

Mystery animal, 353,452,456,787
Mystery auto accidents, 82,314,659,823, 887,902
Mystery balls of fiber, 34
Mystery beam of light, 127,691
Mystery bird, 658
Mystery bird deaths, 25,69,95,146,154, 274,310,320,322-23,345,368,380,383, 388,435,456-57,468,562,575,582,601, 672,695,742,748,761,777,853,947,999
Mystery deaths, 8,112,149,158,573,853; see also Doubtful responsibility
Mystery elk and caribou deaths, 4,249
Mystery escape, 646
Mystery explosion, 108,276,400-401,450, 488,505,509,803,805,838,853,865; see also Exploding objects
Mystery fish, 149,936
Mystery flotsam, 110,151,179-80,653,816
Mystery fog, 415,524,532,580,811,930
Mystery gas, 52,118,353,381,544,576,724, 766,813,818,853,967
Mystery glass etchings, 398
Mystery ground markings, 467
Mystery haze, 11,263
Mystery holes in clothing, 414,794; see also Disintegrating clothes
Mystery horse deaths, 199,248
Mystery knife embedded in codfish, 979
Mystery metal sphere, 7,430,811
Mystery metallic object, 444,881
Mystery oil spill, 888,906
Mystery plane crash, (Pacific) 55,124, 126,133,139,142,157; (Southwest) 192, 207,228; (Great Plains) 261,340,344; (Southeast) 390,411,414,418,421,439, 480,496,501; (North Central) 528,534, 539,544,604,609,626,629,631,636,639, 641-43,646,649,651-53,657-61,663-65, 672,695,699,718,725,743-44,751; (North-east) 831,843,853,865,870,883,886,888, 896,899-900,906,908,910-11,998,1011
Mystery radio transmissions, 28,67,71,80, 142,210,241,303,314,344,429,463,541, 556,591,655,696,706,722,813,835,866, 870
Mystery radioactive disc, 251
Mystery rock markings, 200
Mystery shaking bed, 657
Mystery sheep deaths, 200
Mystery shipwreck, 161,350,418,430,472, 662,664-65,880,910-11,947
Mystery stain, 416,776
Mystery stench, 142,564,580,881
Mystery stone, 664
Mystery stone spheres, 110,273,292,294, 321,494,525,637,836,937
Mystery storm, 665
Mystery television transmission, 71,310, 353,538,546,629,673,698,744,829
Mystery tracks, 56,169,235,379,454,658, 720,746,767,803,806-807,809-10,816-18, 826,872,897; see also Humanoid tracks and Phantom panther tracks
Mystery train accident, 376
Mystery tree stumps, 824
Mystery vault, 488
Mystery vibrations, 493
Mystery voices, 573

Neanderthaloid skulls, 619
New energy source (inventor), 71,118,491, 743,777,783,787; see also Magnetic ion motor (inventor)
Norse altar, 619
Norse axes and hatchets, 596,604,607,609, 612,616,618-19,634,657,887,941,957,980, 1014,1020
Norse boats and ships, 618,811,969
Norse boathook, 604,618
Norse carvings, 12,1001
Norse cellars, 1020
Norse discovery, 13,290,470,488,755,881-82,937,943,973,977-80,1008,1018,1020, 1025-27,1029
Norse drinking horn, 556
Norse firesteel, 605,618
Norse fish-hook, 605
Norse habitation site, 601,616-17,924, 1025-27
Norse halberd, 299,604
Norse harpoon, 293
Norse mooring stone, 286,528,600,605,608, 618-19,633,979-80
Norse runestone, 292,294,296,298,331,335-37,605,609,636,716-17,727,751,836,908, 939,954,975,980,1004,1007-1008,1018, 1020,1031
Norse skeleton in armor, 957
Norse spearhead, 604-605,619,639,884
Norse sword, 605,608,617,887
Norse tower, 939
Numerology, 145,853

Oceanographic anomaly, 147,181,423,431
Orgone energy research, 853,1003
Oriented lakes, 9
Ornithomancy, 92,853
Out-of-body experience, (Pacific) 25,45, 55,80,82,118,129,139,152,155,170,174, 179; (Southwest) 214,226,236,243; (Great Plains) 277,323,340,348; (South-east) 428,432,476-77,514; (North Cen-tral) 528,550,580,611,623,685,695,705, 707,723,747,751; (Northeast) 783,800, 814,816,839,853,859,865,875,904,926, 954,978,983,1003,1007,1024
Out-of-body experience death, 641
Out-of-body experience legend, 219,368
Out-of-body experience research, 776,847
Ovomancy, 384

Paleoastronomy, 218,234,312,339
Paleoecology anomaly, 677
Palmistry, 108,143,145,346,386,854
Paranormal amnesia, 189,197,800,831,899, 933
Paranormal flotation, 414
Paranormal hypnosis, 422,947
Paranormal hypnosis research, 660
Paranormal longevity, 550
Paranormal memory, 794
Paranormal somnambulism, 648
Paranormal strength, 158,204,269,425,450, 580,696,723,761,854
Paranormal voice recordings, 88,102,108, 157,692,746,751,1005
Paraphysics research, 93,103,122,125,136,

OBSERVER INDEX

SHIP INDEX

ETHNIC GROUP INDEX

ABOUT THE COMPILER

George M. Eberhart is Serials/Reader Services Librarian at the University of Kansas Law Library in Lawrence. His articles have appeared in *Pursuit* and *Wilson Library Bulletin.*